To Grannie Ork

Thanks for all of your help, love and patience,

Lots of love

Grace xxxx

Alison xxx

Keith X.

CHAMBERS

CHAMBERS

Family SCRABBLE Dictionary

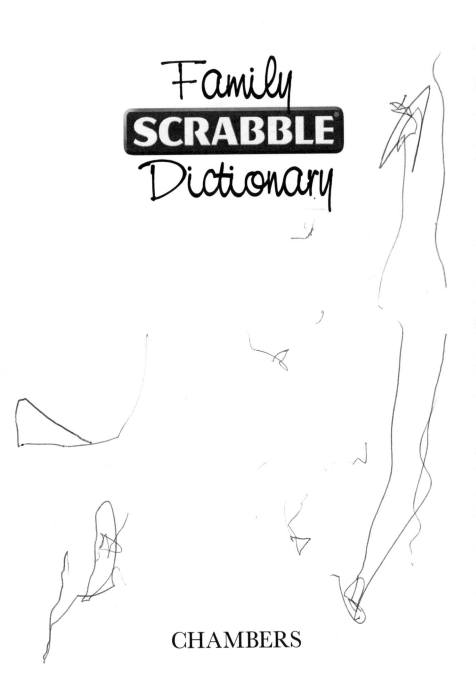

CHAMBERS

SCRABBLE® is a registered trademark of J W Spear & Sons Ltd,
Maidenhead SL6 4UB, England, a Mattel Company, and is used
under licence from Mattel Europa BV.

CHAMBERS
An imprint of Chambers Harrap Publishers Ltd
7 Hopetoun Crescent
Edinburgh
EH7 4AY

www.chambers.co.uk

First published by Chambers 2001
Copyright © Chambers Harrap Publishers Ltd 2001

Reprinted 2002

A CIP catalogue record for this book is available from the British Library.

We have made every effort to mark as such all words which we
believe to be trademarks. We should also like to make it clear
that the presence of a word in this book, whether marked or unmarked,
in no way affects its legal status as a trademark.

ISBN 0-550-12011-4

Designed and typeset by Chambers Harrap Publishers Ltd
Printed in Italy by Rotolito Lombarda SpA

Contents

Contributors

Project Manager
Una McGovern

Consultant Editor
Catherine Schwarz

Editor
Elaine Higgleton

Contributors
Kay Cullen
Hazel Norris
Megan Thomson

Prepress
Marina Karapanovic

Preface

Chambers Family Scrabble® Dictionary is a major new Scrabble title which answers a frequently-expressed need for a word-book specially designed for family and recreational players. Here are all the words they are likely to play — or hope to play — in their Scrabble games.

This dictionary includes main words (headwords) up to nine letters long and their inflected forms, for example plurals and verb endings (this means that there are many words that are longer than nine letters in the dictionary). Each headword has a definition, to help with learning, and also remembering, words.

As this book is intended for family use, many words included in *Official Scrabble®* Words, the word source for tournament Scrabble, have been omitted: there are no offensive or vulgar terms, and only very few archaic or obsolete terms. Although all the words in *OSW* are not included in this book, all the words listed here *are* in *OSW,* so this book can also be seen as a stepping-stone for players who may want to go on to play Scrabble at club or tournament level.

Chambers Family Scrabble® Dictionary includes many of the unusual 2- and 3-letter words from the full Scrabble word source as these are particularly useful for playing words parallel to or alongside existing words on the board. These small but valuable words have been included in their alphabetical position in panels throughout the text, so they can be easily spotted and memorized. Some of these panels also include handy hints on Scrabble, highlighting the particularly valuable 2- and 3-letter words, especially those that include Z or Q.

Panels are shown too for many 4- and 5-letter words which use the high-scoring 'power' tiles J, Q, X and Z. Again, these can be easily spotted in the text.

The dictionary also contains a useful section on the basics of Scrabble play, with some hints on aspects of Scrabble strategy. This section will be of particular interest to new or younger players, but everyone is sure to find something helpful in it.

It is important to remember that, as *Chambers Family Scrabble®* Dictionary is primarily an aid to Scrabble playing, it does not set out to give full information about the words included in it (for example, not all possible parts of speech are given, nor are all definitions and usages). For these, *The Chambers Dictionary* is recommended.

Introduction

Definitions

Chambers Family Scrabble® Dictionary gives a succinct definition for each headword. These are given as an example, and an aid to vocabulary learning, rather than to show exhaustive information about the words included. For full definitions the user is referred to *The Chambers Dictionary.*

Word length

Chambers Family Scrabble® Dictionary includes words up to nine letters in length and their inflections. This 9-letter word length covers most of the words easily or most commonly played. Longer words need to be made up from words (rather than the odd letter) on the board.

As the relevant inflections of these 9-letter words are included (namely plurals, verb forms, comparatives and superlatives) the result is that words up to 13 letters long appear in *Chambers Family Scrabble® Dictionary.*

Here are some examples:

the 9-letter noun SADDLEBAG gives rise to the 10-letter plural SADDLEBAGS;

the 9-letter noun ALLOTROPY gives rise to the 11-letter plural ALLOTROPIES;

the 9-letter verb CALCULATE gives rise to these verb inflections: CALCULATES, CALCULATING, and CALCULATED, having 10 or 11 letters;

the 8-letter verb SQUIRREL gives rise to SQUIRRELS, SQUIRRELLING, and SQUIRRELLED, having 9, 12, or 11 letters

If any inflected form of a 9-letter word is also a singular noun in its own right, then a headword is given for that noun, and its plural is also shown.

For example:

the 9-letter verb CATERWAUL gives rise to these verb inflections: CATERWAULS, CATERWAULING, CATERWAULED; but since CATERWAULING is also a noun it is shown as a headword with the plural CATERWAULINGS

Accents

Accents are shown in this dictionary, although there are no accented letters in English-language Scrabble sets. Where a word is shown with accented characters in the dictionary, the accents can be ignored when playing the word in Scrabble.

Basics of the game

The hardware

A Scrabble set contains letter tiles, a Scrabble board, 4 racks, a bag, scoring pads, and a full set of rules for playing and scoring. The rules are explained later; first we have a look at the tiles and the board, with a glance at the racks and bag.

Tiles

There are 100 tiles in each (English-language) Scrabble set, the values of which range from 0 to 10. Basically, the high-value tiles, **Q** and **Z**, then **J** and **X**, are more difficult to use; but the low-value tiles can be made to work very well for you. The point values and distribution of the tiles are shown on page xiv.

The Scrabble board

The Scrabble board has 225 squares, 61 of which are premium squares. Premium squares increase the points value of the tiles played on them. There are four kinds of such squares, two applying to the whole word played (triple and double word squares), and two applying to individual tiles (triple and double letter squares).

It is interesting to note that the premium squares are symmetrically placed on the board.

In this book, the premium squares are shown in dark red (triple word), light red (double word), dark grey (triple letter) and light grey (double letter). Ordinary squares are shown in white. On an actual Scrabble board dark red is used for triple word squares, light red for double word squares, dark blue for triple letter squares and light blue for double letter squares; ordinary squares are green.

In the centre of the board there is a starred square, on to which the first word of a game must be played. This is in effect a double word square. The horizontal numbers and vertical letters round the board can be useful for reference and description. For example, the starred centre square could be referred to as H8.

The racks and bag

When playing, players should keep their tiles on their racks. This enables them to look at them, and shuffle them around (which often results in a good play coming to light), without the tiles being visible to the other players.

The bag should be used as a container for the unpicked tiles, from which they can be drawn as the game progresses.

The Scrabble board

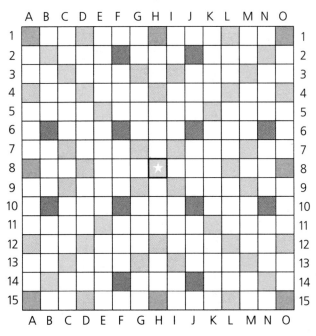

	triple word score		double word score		triple letter score		double letter score

Letter values and distribution

Letter	Value	Distribution
A	1	9
B	3	2
C	3	2
D	2	4
E	1	12
F	4	2
G	2	3
H	4	2
I	1	9
J	8	1
K	5	1
L	1	4
M	3	2
N	1	6
O	1	8
P	3	2
Q	10	1
R	1	6
S	1	4
T	1	6
U	1	4
V	4	2
W	4	2
X	8	1
Y	4	2
Z	10	1
blank	0	2

Playing

Your Scrabble set comes with a full set of rules, but it is worth running through them here.

- Scrabble is a game for two to four players.

- To begin: place all the letters face down at the side of the board, or in the bag provided, and shuffle them. Draw for first play. The player drawing the letter nearest the beginning of the alphabet plays first. The exposed letters are replaced in the pool or bag and reshuffled. The players then draw seven tiles each, placing them on their individual racks.

- The first player uses two or more letters to form a word, placing them on the board, either across or down, with one letter on the centre square. Having then counted and announced the score for the turn, the player draws as many new letters as have been played, thus always keeping seven on the rack.

- Play passes to the left. Each player in turn adds one or more letters to those already played so as to form new words. All letters played in one turn must be placed in one row, across or down, and if they touch any other letters in adjacent rows, they must form complete words, crossword-fashion, with all such letters. The player scores for all words formed or modified in each turn.

- New words may be formed by:
    (a) adding one or more letters to a word already on the board (Turn 2 below);
    (b) placing a word at right angles to a word already on the board (Turns 3, 4 and 7 below);
    (c) placing a complete word parallel to a word already played, so that adjoining letters also form complete words (Turns 5 and 6 below).

- No letter may be moved after it has been played.

- A blank tile may be used as any letter. A player playing a blank must say what letter it represents, after which it cannot be changed during the game.

- A player may use their turn to change any or all of the letters on their rack. To do this, place the unwanted letters face down to one side, draw the same number of new letters, then mix the discarded letters into the pool or bag. Changing can only be done instead of, not as well as, placing letters on the board for that turn, and earns a score of zero.

- Any player may challenge a word played by an opponent before the next player starts the next turn. If the word cannot be found in *The Chambers Dictionary* or *Official Scrabble®* Words, the player must take back the tiles and loses the turn.

- Play continues until all tiles have been drawn and all the tiles on one player's rack have been used, or all possible plays have been made.

Scoring

- Keep a running total of each player's score. The value of each letter is shown by a number at the bottom of the tile. The value of a blank is zero.

- The score for each turn is the sum of the values of all the letters in each word formed or modified in that turn, along with any extra points gained for the use of the premium squares.

- Premium Letter Squares: a light blue square doubles the score of a letter placed on it; a dark blue square trebles the score.

- Premium Word Squares: the score for the entire word is doubled when one of its letters is placed on a square; it is trebled when a letter is placed on a square. Include any premiums for double or triple letter scores before doubling or trebling the word score.

If a word covers two double word squares, its score is doubled then redoubled (multiplied by four); if it covers two triple word squares, its score is trebled then retrebled (multiplied by nine). Note the centre square is light red, and therefore doubles the score for the first word played.

- The above letter and word premiums only apply in the turn in which they are first played. In subsequent turns, letters count at face value.

- If a blank tile falls on a light red or dark red square, the sum of the letters in the word is doubled or trebled even though the blank itself scores zero.

- If two or more words are formed in one turn, each is scored. The common letter is counted (with full premium value, if any) in the score for each word in which it appears (Turns 4, 5 and 6 below).

- A player playing all seven tiles in a single turn scores an extra 50 points in addition to the regular score for that turn. This is called a bonus, or in the US, a bingo.

- At the end of the game, each player's score is reduced by the sum of their unplayed letters. The score of any player whose letters have all been used is increased by the sum of the unplayed letters of all the other players.

The opening of a game

Here is a possible opening of a game, showing seven successive turns and the scoring for each turn. The **I** of **RING** has been placed on the centre square.

- Turn 1: **RING**. Scores 5 doubled=10.

- Turn 2: **CRINGED**. Scores 13. The **D** is doubled but not the whole word.

- Turn 3: **MINE**. Scores 6.

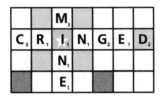

- Turn 4: **BLISTER** and **MINES**. Scores 9×4=36 for **BLISTER** +7 for **MINES** +50 for using all seven tiles. Total 93.

- Turn 5: **BOY, BE** and **OR**. Scores 9+1+4=14 for **BOY**, 9+1=10 for **BE**, and 2 (not doubled) for **OR**. Total 26.

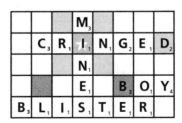

				M_3						
	C_3	R_1	I_1	N_1	G_2	E_1	D_2			
			N_1				R_1	O_1	O_1	F_4
			E_1		B_3	O_1	Y_4			
B_3	L_1	I_1	S_1	T_1	E_1	R_1				

• Turn 7: **OFFER**. Scores 12×3=36. Note the **R** is doubled before the whole word is trebled.

				M_3						
	C_3	R_1	I_1	N_1	G_2	E_1	D_2			O_1
			N_1				R_1	O_1	O_1	F_4
			E_1		B_3	O_1	Y_4			F_4
B_3	L_1	I_1	S_1	T_1	E_1	R_1				E_1
										R_1

How to make new words

As we saw in the previous section there are several different ways to play new words on the Scrabble board; in some cases it is possible to make more than one word in the same go and experienced players usually aim to do this. Making more than one word in one go will allow you to score more points.

Making one new word

The easiest way to make a word in Scrabble is by joining a new word on to one letter in a word that is already on the board.

• You can play a new word by extending an existing word. You do this by playing a new word on to the end of an existing word, on to the beginning of an existing word, or on to both ends of an existing word:

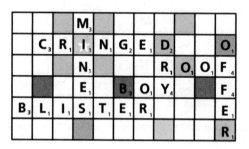

and

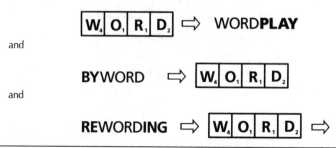

and

- You can play a new word down from one of the letters of the existing word:

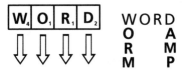

```
WORD
O      A
R      M
M      P
```

- And you can play a new word through an existing word:

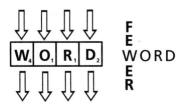

```
F
E
WORD
E
R
```

Hooking

Hooking is a way of making two new words in one go. You play a new word on to one end of an existing word, changing that existing word into another word at the same time. It is a very useful way of playing the word on your rack on to an existing word on the board, and it allows you to score points for two words in the same go.

- You can hook a new word down on to an existing word:

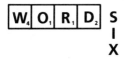

```
        G
        R
        E
WORDY
```

- You can hook down from an existing word:

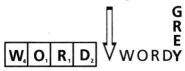

```
WORD S
     I
     X
```

- And you can hook through an existing word:

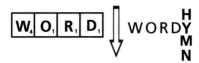

```
            H
WORDY
            M
            N
```

• Avoid leaving a premium square at the beginning or end of a word. Your opponent could hook on to this to score more points. For example:

You have just played ATE and EXIT, but your opponent can now play FEZ down from FATE and use the DOUBLE WORD square for both FATE and FEZ to score 44 points.

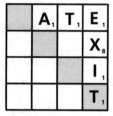

• Any letter that can be placed at the beginning or end of a word to form another word is a hook. Obviously, the letter **S** is the commonest hooking letter, but there are some others that are also useful. Many verbs ending in **E** have a **D** hook, and, also for words ending in **E**, the **R** is very useful.

• Here are some useful front-hooks — hooks where the letter goes at the front of the word.

ABROAD	**B**ROADSIDE	**C**HIPPY	**D**ZHO
ELAND	**F**UNFAIR	**G**LADDER	**H**OVER
ISLANDER	**J**OTTER	**K**HAT	**L**ADDER
MUTTERED	**N**EVERMORE	**O**ROTUND	**P**LUMBER
QAT	**R**EVOKING	**S**KIPPER	**T**RUSTY
UPRISE	**V**ROOM	**W**HOSE	**X**IS
YAWN	**Z**INCITE		

• Here are some useful end-hooks — hooks where the letter goes at the end of the word.

PAST**A**	SUPER**B**	AMNESIA**C**	HOAR**D**
BARGE**E**	FIE**F**	ASPIRIN**G**	BRAS**H**
COAT**I**	HAD**J**	CHIC**K**	TRIVIA**L**
MINI**M**	BROKE**N**	FLAMING**O**	MANTRA**P**
TALA**Q**	CASTE**R**	PRINCES**S**	COMPLETES**T**
QUIP**U**	GO**V**	HALLO**W**	GATEAU**X**
FLATTER**Y**	QUART**Z**		

Tagging

Tagging is another way to make more than word in a single go, and in some cases players can tag words to make three, four or even five words in a single go. Players tag when they play a new word parallel to an existing word, to create words in both directions at the same time.

• You can tag to create two new words in one go. For example:

- You can tag to create three new words in one go, for example:

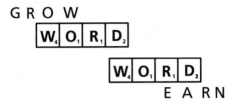

- Here are two examples of tagging to make four words in one go:

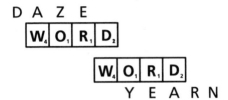

- And here are examples of tagging to make five new words in one go:

- You can of course tag vertically as well as horizontally:

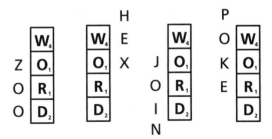

• Tagging is important for two main reasons. Firstly, as we have already seen, if you can tag words then you can make more than one word in a single go and so score more points. Secondly, and perhaps more importantly, knowing how to tag words can help you find places to play good 7-letter words hiding on your rack. For example, your opponent has just played:

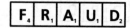

You have the letters **AGILLOR** on your rack, and spot that these spell **GORILLA**. But where do you play it? You could play it down on to the **R** in **FRAUD** like this:

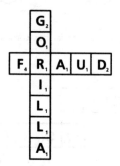

This would use six of the letters on your rack and would score eight points (assuming that you have not played any letters on premium squares).

You could also play it down on to the **A** in **FRAUD**, and, assuming no premium squares again, this would also score eight points and use up six of your letters.

But if you know your 2-letter words, you would know that you could tag **GORILLA** on to **FRAUD** like this:

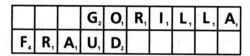

or like this:

This would allow you to use all seven letters on your rack, and, again assuming that you haven't used any premium squares, these plays would each score 64 points, 14 points for the tiles played, plus 50 bonus points for playing all seven tiles in a single go. Much better than eight points!

• You will see from this that the clue to successful tagging is knowing the list of 2-letter words allowed for Scrabble. Some of these words are unusual and rare, but they are in *The Chambers Dictionary* and they are all valid for Scrabble. Knowing some of these words, and being able to use them to tag words, can help improve your game.

Remembering and learning words

One of the most important aspects of playing Scrabble is the ability to remember a wide variety of strange and unusual words that you probably won't use except for Scrabble. Inexperienced players should probably aim to learn only a few of the key words for Scrabble, and to build up gradually from there.

Experienced Scrabble players have several different techniques to help them remember words, and we're going to look at some of them here.

Mnemonics

A mnemonic is a way of remembering something by means of a mental trick or short cut. A common mnemonic is the one for remembering the colours of the rainbow:

Richard Of York Gave Battle In Vain

The initial letters of each word in this mnemonic match the initial letter of the colours of the rainbow; so *red, orange, yellow, green, etc.*

Another mnemonic, used by mathematicians, is that for the value of pi:

May I have a large container of coffee?

This time it is the number of the letters in each word which is important. The number of letters in these eight words gives the first eight figures for pi: 3.1415926.

Some Scrabble players use mnemonics a lot. Others ignore them, finding it easier just to remember the words rather than the mnemonics. Here are a few ideas on making mnemonics to help you recall words.

- Many players find the hardest 3-letter words to remember are the little exclamations and interjections. Is it **OOH** you can have or **AAH**? Are **OHO, AHA** and **UHU** all allowed? Which of **BOH, HOH, WOH, LOH, FOH** and **YOH** are OK?

- Here's how you can make a mnemonic to help you remember some of these words.

1. Use the dictionary to find out which letters can go before **OH** to make a 3-letter word. These are: **B D F H N O P S**

2. Next, make up a sentence, Richard of York style, where the initial letter of each word will give you the letters you need. There are lots of possibilities, such as:

Please Don't Holler So, Be Nice For Once

3. This should remind you that the following words are all allowable for Scrabble:

BOH	a cry of 'bo', used for calling attention to or to startle
DOH	in sol-fa notation: the first note of the major scale
FOH	an expression of disgust or contempt
HOH	an obsolete word meaning to stop
NOH	a traditional style of Japanese drama
OOH	an expression of pleasure, surprise, excitement or pain
POH	an exclamation expressing impatient contempt
SOH	in sol-fa notation: the fifth note of a major or minor scale

• Here's another example of a mnemonic. This time, it's for the letters that can be put before **AE** to form 3-letter words:

Not Many Down-trodden Headmasters Know Greek, Something
That's Very Worrying

This tells you that the following are all allowable for Scrabble:

DAE	Scots form of 'do'
GAE	Scots word for 'go'
HAE	Scots form of 'have'
KAE	an obsolete word meaning 'to serve'
MAE	Scots word for 'more'
NAE	Scots form of 'no'
SAE	Scots form of 'so'
TAE	Scots form of 'toe'
VAE	a bay or creek in Orkney or Shetland
WAE	Scots word for 'woe'

• The trick with mnemonics is to come up with a good phrase that will give you the letters that you need, and that you will be able to remember easily. You might find phrases that relate to your life, family and friends easier to remember.

Anagrams

Anagrams are a popular form of word-play. They appear frequently in crosswords, and can be amusing and easy to remember. Did you know, for example, that **SCHOOLMASTER** is an anagram of **THE CLASSROOM**? Or that **ALTERATION** is an anagram of **NEAT TAILOR**? Or that **CONIFER** is an anagram of **FIR CONE**?

• Scrabble players need to know how the same letters can be arranged in different orders to form words because this helps them play words on the board. For example, you might have the word **SHORE** on your rack, but may not be able to play it. Knowing that the same letters can be rearranged to spell **HORSE** means that you might have more opportunities to play these tiles.

• So anagrams play a huge part in Scrabble and regular players often have their own favourites, especially for bonus-winning 7- and 8-letter words.

• Anagrams can sometimes be memorable because, quite by coincidence, their meanings are connected. Here are a few examples:

SEAHORSE and **SEASHORE**
AVARICE and **CAVIARE**
PARENTAL, **PATERNAL** and **PRENATAL**

• And some anagrams may be spelt almost exactly the same as each other, but have very different meanings, for example:

MISFIELD and **MISFILED**
REINFORM and **RENIFORM**
SUNTRAP and **UNSTRAP**
INFIDEL and **INFIELD**

- Sometimes you might be able to remember an obscure word because it is an anagram of a well-known word. Finding the well-known word can trigger your memory into recalling the lesser-known anagram. For example:

> Finding **BAPTISM** reminds you of **BITMAPS**.
> Finding **ICKIEST** reminds you of **EKISTIC**.
> Finding **TOILETS** reminds you of **LITOTES**.
> Finding **TOURISTY** reminds you of **YTTRIOUS**.

- It would be much harder to remember **BITMAPS**, **EKISTIC**, **LITOTES** and **YTTRIOUS** if they did not have their more familiar anagrams to guide us towards them.

- Another way of using anagrams to help you remember words is to notice that some words are anagrams of brand names. You might find that the letters on your rack could be turned into one of these trade names:

CORTINA   FORMICA   RENAULT   TOSHIBA

None of these words are allowed for Scrabble as, being trade names, they are spelt with a capital letter. But if you find them on your rack they might lead you to a 7-letter word that will earn you that 50-point bonus:

CAROTIN   ACIFORM   NEUTRAL   ISOBATH

- So the trick is developing a 'familiar word to remember unfamiliar anagram' technique, so that you have more words at your fingertips when you play Scrabble.

Flashcards

Another popular way of learning new words is to use flashcards. This involves getting some small index cards, writing a 'clue' or 'question' on one side, and the answer on the reverse.

- For example, you could make a flashcard to help you remember the 13 2-letter words beginning with **A**, which would look like this:

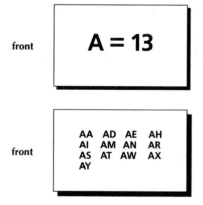

front

A = 13

front

AA AD AE AH
AI AM AN AR
AS AT AW AX
AY

- You could use flashcards to help you learn all sorts of words. You could, for example, put all of the letters that can be placed before **OH** on a flashcard to help you remember these 3-letter words. Or you could use flashcards to help you learn words that contain the high-scoring letters **Q, J, X** and **Z**.

- You could test yourself by quickly flicking through your flashcards whenever you get a spare minute, or get someone to test you.

Number plates

You could also practise with car number plates. There are a number of games that you can play (if you are not the driver!).

- Find the shortest word containing the three letters of the number plate (ignoring the letter denoting the year).

- Look for 7-letter words by converting the numerals to letters thus: 1 = **I**, 2 = **Z**, 3 = **E**, 4 = **A**, 5 = **S**, 6 = **G**, 7 = **T**, 8 = **B**, 9 = **G**, 0 = **O** Following this system, DGF 105H makes DOGFISH!

- Look for 7-letter words by taking the four letters on the number plate and adding the letters **A**, **E** and **I**, **E**, **I** and **S** or similar, to give a good 'rack'.

Remembering words with J, Q, X and Z

If you have trouble remembering words using the high-scoring tiles **Q, J, X** and **Z**, then try the following solo game.

- Take the **Q, J, X, Z** and one **U** out of the bag and put to one side. Next, pick six letters from the bag and place them on your rack. Now give yourself a couple of minutes to see how many different words you can make using the six letters on your rack and each of the high-scoring tiles in turn. Use the **U** that you have taken from the bag when you come to looking for words with **Q**. Check which of your words, formed with each of the high-scoring tiles, has the highest score. Check the number of words that you have found against either the words in this dictionary or the fuller wordlists in *Chambers Official Scrabble® Words*.

Some other aspects of Scrabble strategy

The first move

The player who opens the game plays the first word on to or from the starred square in the centre of the board. The starred square is a DOUBLE WORD score square, and doubles the points for the first word.

- If you are first to play then take the advantage and put yourself ahead immediately with a good DW score.

• Try and play a 5-letter word with a high value letter at the beginning or end reaching one of the DL squares

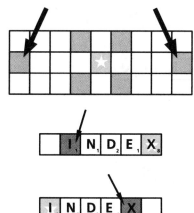

not . . .

I N₁ D₂ E₁ X₈

but . . .

I₁ N₁ D₂ E₁ X₈

4-letter words

Very few of the top players are actually familiar with all of the 4-letter words allowable for Scrabble. Experienced players tend to concentrate on the following:

• Those that are formed from 3-letter words.

• Those that contain the higher-scoring tiles, especially **J, Q, X** and **Z**.

• Those that are useful for sorting out vowel problems, for example, if you have too many vowels on your rack, or too many of one particular vowel.

Tile tracking

It is acceptable in tournament Scrabble to keep a note of the number of letters in the set and mark it as letters are played.

• This will tell you which tiles may be left in the bag or on your opponent's rack, and will help you decide what to do with any difficult letters on your rack. For example, if you have a blank tile, and know that the **Q** might still be in the bag, then you could decide to hang on to your blank just in case you pick up the **Q** later on.

• Experienced players will use the information about tiles played to judge whether it is worth keeping letters in the chance of playing a bonus word.

• Tile tracking will help you learn how many of each of the letters are found in the Scrabble set.

• If you don't want to keep a note of all the tiles as they are played, it is a good idea to keep a note of the vowels, the **S**, the blank tiles and **J, Q, X** and **Z**.

Rack balance

Try and keep a balanced rack, that is, two or three vowels and four or five consonants. Here are some rack examples, with suggestions of what you should do with them.

- **Rack 1**

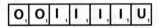

Unbalanced; too many vowels.
Exchange the lot.

- **Rack 2**

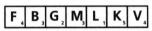

Unbalanced; too many consonants.
Exchange the lot.

- **Rack 3**

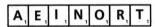

All the most frequent letters; too many vowels but at least they are all different.

Look for good combinations to produce 8-letter bonus words hooking on to available letters on the board

AERATION	**ANTERIOR**
CREATION	**NOTARIES**
OBTAINER	**BARITONE**
ORIENTAL	**ORDINATE**

plus the 7-letter word **OTARINE** (which means 'like a sea lion').

- **Rack 4**

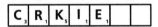

Two blanks; rest balanced.
With the combinations **CK** and **ER** there are several bonus words here:

> **BRICKED, CLINKER, COCKIER, CRICKET, FLICKER**
> **LUCKIER, PRICKLE, QUICKER, TRICKED, TRICKLE** etc

Changing tiles

You can use a go to change any of the tiles on your rack (unless there are fewer than seven tiles left in the bag), and it can be a good idea to change some or all of your tiles. Here are some suggestions for when you might want to consider changing tiles.

- Is your rack unbalanced? You should consider changing if you have a lot of vowels or consonants and cannot score very many points with any of the words that you could play, or would leave a premium square open for your opponent to use.

• Do you have a **Q** but no **U**? It might be worth changing this tile if you cannot play any of the U-less words that you know, cannot use a **U** in the board, do not have a blank tile, and are not confident of being able to use your **Q** later on. It might be worth keeping your **Q** if there are still I's left to use (and so you might be able to play **QI** later on), and if you can score well with your other tiles.

• Do you have a promising 6-letter combination that would combine with several other letters to form 7-letter words, but not with the seventh letter on your rack? In this case it might be good to change just the letter which doesn't combine with the remaining six to try to find a bonus word. The time to make a change like this is when you are behind and desperately need the bonus score to catch up.

Using premium squares

Premium squares are very useful, but you do need to take care to try not to leave premium squares open for your opponent to use.

• Avoid playing a 3- or 4-letter word that can be hooked on the DOUBLE WORD lines. For example:

Your opponent could hook words beginning with: **B, F, L, M, P, R, S, T, V** or **W.**

• Avoid playing a 3-letter word with vowels next to the four DL squares; they could be tagged with high-scoring letters. For example:

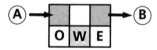

Your opponent could tag words at A ending in . . .

B, D, G, H, J, K, L, M, N, P, S, T, W, Y, Z

or at **B** beginning with . . .

A, B, E, H, M, N, O, R, T, W, Y

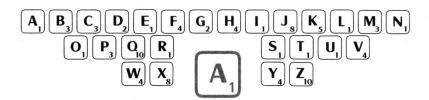

AA *noun* **AAS** a type of lava
(i) This word is useful for using up **A**s, eg at the end of a game.

AARDVARK *noun* **AARDVARKS** a nocturnal African burrowing mammal with a thick set body, large snout and donkey-like ears

ABA *noun* **ABAS** an outer garment worn by some Arab women

ABACA *noun* **ABACAS** the fibre from a plant grown in the Philippine Islands

ABACK *adverb* surprised or shocked, especially by something unpleasant or unexpected

ABACUS *noun* **ABACUSES, ABACI** an arithmetical calculating device, known to the Greeks, Romans and other ancient peoples, consisting of several rows of beads strung on horizontal wires or rods mounted in a frame

ABAFT *adverb* in or towards the stern of a ship □ *prep* behind

ABALONE *noun* **ABALONES** a marine gastropod mollusc which has a single flattened oval shell lined with bluish mother-of-pearl

ABANDON *verb* **ABANDONS, ABANDONING, ABANDONED** to give something up completely □ *noun* **ABANDONS** uncontrolled or uninhibited behaviour

ABANDONED *adj* deserted; behaving as if one had no sense of shame or morality

ABANDONEE *noun* **ABANDONEES** an insurer to whom a wreck has been abandoned

ABASE *verb* **ABASES, ABASING, ABASED** to humiliate or degrade (someone else or oneself)

ABASEMENT *noun* **ABASEMENTS** humiliation

ABASHED *adj* embarrassed or disconcerted, especially because of shyness

ABATE *verb* **ABATES, ABATING, ABATED** to become or make less strong or severe

ABATEMENT *noun* **ABATEMENTS** the ending or lessening of something

ABATTOIR *noun* **ABATTOIRS** a slaughterhouse

ABB *noun* **ABBS** a textile yarn

ABBACY *noun* **ABBACIES** the office or authority of an abbot or abbess

ABBESS *noun* **ABBESSES** a woman in charge of a group of nuns living in an abbey

ABBEY *noun* **ABBEYS** a group of nuns or monks living as a community under an abbot or abbess

ABBOT *noun* **ABBOTS** the man in charge of a group of monks living in an abbey

ABDABS *plural noun* habdabs

ABDICATE *verb* **ABDICATES, ABDICATING, ABDICATED** to give up one's right to (the throne)

ABDOMEN *noun* **ABDOMENS** in vertebrates: the lower part of the main body cavity, containing the digestive, excretory and reproductive organs

ABDOMINAL *adj* relating to or concerning the abdomen

ABDUCT *verb* **ABDUCTS, ABDUCTING, ABDUCTED** to take someone away illegally by force or deception

ABDUCTION *noun* **ABDUCTIONS** the illegal taking away of someone by force or deception

ABDUCTOR *noun* **ABDUCTORS** a person who abducts someone

ABEAM *adverb* in a line at right angles to the length of a ship or aircraft

ABERRANCE *noun* **ABERRANCES** a departure from what is normal

ABERRANCY *noun* **ABERRANCIES** an aberrance

ABERRANT *adj* differing or departing from what is normal or accepted as standard

ABET *verb* **ABETS, ABETTING, ABETTED** to help or encourage someone to do something wrong, especially to commit an offence

ABETTER *noun* **ABETTERS** a person who abets someone

ABETTOR *noun* **ABETTORS** an abetter

ABEYANCE *noun* **ABEYANCES** said of laws, customs, etc: the condition of not being used or followed, usually only temporarily

ABHOR *verb* **ABHORS, ABHORRING, ABHORRED** to hate or dislike (usually something one considers morally wrong) very much

ABHORRENT *adj* hated or disliked

ABIDE *verb* **ABIDES, ABIDING, ABODE, ABIDED** to put up with or tolerate someone or something

ABIDING *adj* permanent, lasting or continuing for a long time

ABIDINGLY *adverb* in an abiding way

ABILITY *noun* **ABILITIES** the power, skill or knowledge to do something

ABJECT *adj* said of living conditions, etc: extremely sad, miserable or poor; wretched

ABJECTLY *adverb* in an abject way

ABJURE *verb* **ABJURES, ABJURING, ABJURED** to promise solemnly, especially under oath, to stop believing or doing something

ABLATE *verb* **ABLATES, ABLATING, ABLATED** to remove or decrease something by the process of ablation

ABLATION *noun* **ABLATIONS** the removal of an organ, body tissue, tumour, etc, especially by surgical means

ABLATIVAL *adj* relating to the ablative case

ABLATIVE *noun* **ABLATIVES** in eg Latin: the form of a noun, pronoun or adjective which expresses the place, means, manner or instrument of an action

ABLAUT *noun* **ABLAUTS** a variation in the vowel in the different inflections or tenses of a word, eg *song*, *sing*, *sang*, *sung*

ABLAZE *adj* burning, especially strongly

ABLE *adj* **ABLER, ABLEST** having the necessary knowledge, power, time, opportunity, etc to do something

ABLUTION *noun* **ABLUTIONS** the washing of the body, the hands or the ritual vessels as part of a religious ceremony

ABLY *adverb* in an efficient or competent way

ABNORMAL *adj* not normal; different from what is expected or usual

ABOARD *prep* on, on to, in or into (a ship, train, aircraft, etc)

ABODE [1] *noun* **ABODES** the house or place where one lives; a dwelling

ABODE [2] a past form of **abide**

ABOLISH *verb* **ABOLISHES, ABOLISHING, ABOLISHED** to stop or put an end to (customs, laws, etc)

ABOLITION *noun* **ABOLITIONS** the act of abolishing something; the state of being abolished

ABOMASUM *noun* **ABOMASA** the fourth or true stomach of a ruminant animal

ABOMINATE *verb* **ABOMINATES, ABOMINATING, ABOMINATED** to dislike or hate something greatly; to find it loathsome

ABORIGINE *noun* **ABORIGINES** a member of any people who were first to live in a country or region, especially as compared to later arrivals

ABORT *verb* **ABORTS, ABORTING, ABORTED** to miscarry

ABORTION *noun* **ABORTIONS** the removal of an embryo or fetus from the uterus before it is sufficiently developed to survive independently

ABORTIVE *adj* unsuccessful

ABOULIA *noun* **ABOULIAS** abulia

ABOUND *verb* **ABOUNDS, ABOUNDING, ABOUNDED** to exist in large numbers

ABOUNDING *adj* abundant

ABOUT *prep* concerning or relating to someone or something; on the subject of them or it ◻ *adverb* nearly or just over; approximately

ABOVE *prep* higher than or over something ◻ *adverb* at, in or to a higher position, place, rank, etc ◻ *adj* appearing or mentioned in an earlier or preceding passage of written or printed text ◻ *noun* something already mentioned

ABRADE *verb* **ABRADES, ABRADING, ABRADED** to scrape or wear something away, especially by rubbing

ABRASION *noun* **ABRASIONS** a damaged area of skin, rock, etc which has been worn away by scraping or rubbing

ABRASIVE *adj* said of a material: capable of wearing away the surface of skin, wood, etc by rubbing and scraping ◻ *noun*

ABRASIVES any hard material, such as sandpaper, pumice or emery, that is used to wear away the surface of other materials, usually in order to smooth or shape them

ABREAST *adverb* side by side and facing in the same direction

ABRIDGE *verb* **ABRIDGES, ABRIDGING, ABRIDGED** to make (a book, etc) shorter

ABROAD *adverb* in or to a foreign country or countries

ABROGATE *verb* **ABROGATES, ABROGATING, ABROGATED** to cancel (a law, agreement, etc) formally or officially

ABRUPT *adj* **ABRUPTER, ABRUPTEST** sudden and unexpected; very quick

ABRUPTLY *adverb* in an abrupt way

ABSCESS *noun* **ABSCESSES** a localized collection of pus in a cavity surrounded by inflamed tissue, usually caused by bacterial infection

ABSCISSA *noun* **ABSCISSAS, ABSCISSAE** in coordinate geometry: the first of a pair of numbers x and y, known as the x-coordinate, which specifies the distance of a point from the vertical or y-axis

ABSCOND *verb* **ABSCONDS, ABSCONDING, ABSCONDED** to depart or leave quickly and usually secretly, especially in order to avoid punishment or arrest

ABSCONDER *noun* **ABSCONDERS** a person who absconds

ABSEIL *verb* **ABSEILS, ABSEILING, ABSEILED** to go down a rock face, etc using a double rope wound round the body and fixed to a point higher up ◻ *noun* **ABSEILS** an act of abseiling

ABSEILING *noun* **ABSEILINGS** the act of going down a rock face, etc using a double rope wound round the body and fixed to a point higher up

ABSENCE *noun* **ABSENCES** the state of being away, eg from work

ABSENT *adj* not in its or one's expected place; not present ◻ *verb* **ABSENTS, ABSENTING, ABSENTED** to stay away from a meeting, gathering, etc

ABSENTEE *noun* **ABSENTEES** someone who is not present at a particular or required time, or in a particular place

ABSENTLY *adverb* in a way which shows one is not paying attention or concentrating

ABSINTH *noun* **ABSINTHS** a strong green alcoholic drink flavoured with substances from certain plants, such as aniseed and wormwood

ABSINTHE *noun* **ABSINTHES** absinth

ABSOLUTE *adj* complete; total; perfect ◻ *noun* **ABSOLUTES** a rule, standard, etc which is thought to be true or right in all situations

ABSOLVE *verb* **ABSOLVES, ABSOLVING, ABSOLVED** to release someone or pronounce them free from a promise, duty, blame, etc

ABSORB *verb* **ABSORBS, ABSORBING, ABSORBED** to take in or suck up (knowledge, etc)

ABSORBED *adj* engrossed; intently interested

ABSORBENT *noun* **ABSORBENTS** something that absorbs liquids, etc

ABSORBING *adj* engrossing; fascinating

ABSTAIN *verb* **ABSTAINS, ABSTAINING, ABSTAINED** to choose not to take, have, do or undertake something

ABSTAINER *noun* **ABSTAINERS** a person who abstains

ABSTINENT *adj* abstaining; temperate or self-restrained in one's appetites

ABSTRACT *adj* **ABSTRACTER, ABSTRACTEST** referring to something which exists only as an idea or quality ◻ *noun* **ABSTRACTS** a brief statement of the main points (of a book, speech, etc) ◻ *verb* **ABSTRACTS, ABSTRACTING, ABSTRACTED** to take out or remove something

ABSTRACTED *adj* said of a person: thinking about something so much that they do not notice what is happening around them

ABSTRUSE *adj* **ABSTRUSER, ABSTRUSEST** hard to understand

ABSURD *adj* **ABSURDER,**

ABSURDEST not at all suitable or appropriate

ABSURDITY *noun* **ABSURDITIES** being absurd; something that is absurd

ABSURDLY *adverb* in an absurd way

ABULIA *noun* **ABULIAS** a reduction in or absence of willpower, a common symptom of schizophrenia

ABUNDANCE *noun* **ABUNDANCES** a large amount, sometimes more than is needed

ABUNDANT *adj* existing in large amounts

ABUSE *noun* **ABUSES** wrong use of one's position, power, etc ❑ *verb* **ABUSES, ABUSING, ABUSED** to use (one's position, power, etc) wrongly

ABUSIVE *adj* insulting or rude; using insulting or rude language

ABUSIVELY *adverb* in an abusive way

ABUT *verb* **ABUTS, ABUTTING, ABUTTED** said of countries, areas of land, buildings, etc: to join, touch or lean against another

ABUTMENT *noun* **ABUTMENTS** the support at the end of an arch, eg in a bridge or similar structure

ABUZZ *adj* in a state of noisy activity or excitement

ABY *verb* **ABYES, ABYING, ABOUGHT** an archaic word meaning to pay (as) a penalty

ABYSMAL *adj* extremely bad

ABYSMALLY *adverb* in an abysmal way

ABYSS *noun* **ABYSSES** a very large and deep chasm

ACACIA *noun* **ACACIAS** any of various trees and shrubs found mainly in Australia, Africa and S America, most of which bear large spines and clusters of small yellow flowers

ACADEME *noun* **ACADEMES** the world of scholars

ACADEMIA *noun* **ACADEMIAS** the scholarly world or life

ACADEMIC *adj* to do with learning, study, education or teaching ❑ *noun* **ACADEMICS** a member of the teaching or research staff at a university or college

ACADEMY *noun* **ACADEMIES** a school or college that gives training in a particular subject or skill

ACANTHUS *noun* **ACANTHUSES** any of various perennial plants with spiny leaves and bracts, including ornamental species cultivated for their white, pink or purple flowers and attractive foliage

ACCEDE *verb* **ACCEDES, ACCEDING, ACCEDED** to take office, especially to become king or queen

ACCENT *noun* **ACCENTS** the particular way words are pronounced by people who live in a particular place, belong to a particular social group, etc ❑ *verb* **ACCENTS, ACCENTING, ACCENTED** to pronounce something with an accent

ACCEPT *verb* **ACCEPTS, ACCEPTING, ACCEPTED** to agree or be willing to take or receive (something offered)

ACCEPTOR *noun* **ACCEPTORS** an organization or individual that accepts a bill of exchange

ACCESS *noun* **ACCESSES** a means of approaching or entering a place ❑ *verb* **ACCESSES, ACCESSING, ACCESSED** to locate or retrieve (information stored in the memory of a computer)

ACCESSARY *noun* **ACCESSARIES** someone who helps a criminal do something wrong

ACCESSION *noun* **ACCESSIONS** the act or process of taking up a new office or responsibility, or of becoming a king or queen

ACCESSORY *noun* **ACCESSORIES** something additional to, but less important than, something else

ACCIDENCE *noun* **ACCIDENCES** the part of grammar that deals with the inflections of words, eg to indicate the plural or past tense

ACCIDENT *noun* **ACCIDENTS** an unexpected event which causes damage or harm

ACCIDIE *noun* **ACCIDIES** sloth; torpor

ACCLAIM *verb* **ACCLAIMS, ACCLAIMING, ACCLAIMED** to declare someone to be a specified thing, with noisy enthusiasm ❑ *noun* **ACCLAIMS** approval or agreement

ACCLIVITY *noun* **ACCLIVITIES** an upward slope

ACCOLADE *noun* **ACCOLADES** a sign or expression of great praise or approval

ACCOMPANY *verb* **ACCOMPANIES, ACCOMPANYING, ACCOMPANIED** to come or go with someone

ACCORD *verb* **ACCORDS, ACCORDING, ACCORDED** to give someone (a welcome, etc) or grant them (permission, a request, etc) ❑ *noun* **ACCORDS** agreement or consent; harmony

ACCORDING *adverb* as said or told by someone

ACCORDION *noun* **ACCORDIONS** a portable musical instrument consisting of two box-like parts joined by a folding bellows-like middle section

ACCOST *verb* **ACCOSTS, ACCOSTING, ACCOSTED** to approach someone and speak to them, especially boldly or in a threatening way

ACCOUNT *noun* **ACCOUNTS** a description or report ❑ *verb* **ACCOUNTS, ACCOUNTING, ACCOUNTED** to consider someone or something to be as specified

ACCOUNTING *noun* **ACCOUNTINGS** the skill or practice of preparing or keeping the financial records of a company, etc

ACCREDIT *verb* **ACCREDITS, ACCREDITING, ACCREDITED** to state officially that something is of a satisfactory standard

ACCREDITED *adj* officially recognized

ACCRETE *verb* **ACCRETES, ACCRETING, ACCRETED** to form or grow together

ACCRETION *noun* **ACCRETIONS** an extra layer of material which has formed on something else

ACCRETIVE *adj* of or relating to accretion

ACCRUAL *noun* **ACCRUALS** an addition; an accumulation

ACCRUE *verb* **ACCRUES, ACCRUING, ACCRUED** to come in addition, as a product, result or development

ACCURACY *noun* **ACCURACIES** exactness; the state of being absolutely correct and making no mistakes, especially through careful effort

ACCURATE *adj* absolutely correct; making no mistakes

ACCURSED *adj* disliked or hated

ACCUSE *verb* **ACCUSES, ACCUSING, ACCUSED** to charge someone with (an offence)

ACCUSER *noun* **ACCUSERS** a person who accuses or blames

ACCUSING *adj* of a tone of voice or an expression: indicating a belief in someone's guilt

ACCUSTOM *verb* **ACCUSTOMS, ACCUSTOMING, ACCUSTOMED** to make someone or oneself familiar with something

ACCUSTOMED *adj* usual; customary

ACE *noun* **ACES** the card in each of the four suits with a single symbol on it, having either the highest value or the value one ▫ *adj* excellent

ACERBIC *adj* bitter and sour in taste

ACERBITY *noun* **ACERBITIES** applied to taste: sourness; bitterness

ACETATE *noun* **ACETATES** a salt or ester of acetic acid

ACETIC *adj* consisting of or like vinegar

ACETONE *noun* **ACETONES** a colourless flammable volatile liquid with a characteristic pungent odour, widely used as a solvent for paints and varnishes, and as a raw material in the manufacture of plastics

ACETYL *noun* **ACETYLS** the radical of acetic acid

ACETYLENE *noun* **ACETYLENES** a colourless highly flammable gas with a sweet odour, used in lighting, oxyacetylene welding, and the manufacture of organic compounds

ACH *exclamation* Scots or Irish, expressing impatience or regret

ACHE *verb* **ACHES, ACHING, ACHED** to feel a dull continuous pain ▫ *noun* **ACHES** a dull continuous pain

ACHIEVE *verb* **ACHIEVES, ACHIEVING, ACHIEVED** to reach, realize or attain (a goal, ambition, etc), especially through hard work

ACHIEVER *noun* **ACHIEVERS** a person who achieves or accomplishes something

ACHING *adj* giving continuous pain

ACHROMAT *noun* **ACHROMATS** a lens designed to minimize distortion

ACHY *adj* **ACHIER, ACHIEST** giving continuous pain

ACID *noun* **ACIDS** any of a group of compounds that have a sour or sharp taste, turn blue litmus paper red, and react with bases to form salts ▫ *adj* **ACIDER, ACIDEST** sour to taste

ACIDIC *adj* like, or containing, acid

ACIDIFY *verb* **ACIDIFIES, ACIDIFYING, ACIDIFIED** to make or become acid

ACIDITY *noun* **ACIDITIES** the quality of being acid or sour

ACIDLY *adverb* in an acid way

ACIDOSIS *noun* **ACIDOSES** a condition in which there is excessive acid in the blood, eg as in diabetes or in kidney disease

ACIDULATE *verb* **ACIDULATES, ACIDULATING, ACIDULATED** to make something slightly acid or sour

ACIDULATED *adj* slightly sour

ACIFORM *adj* needle-shaped

ACIDULOUS *adj* slightly sour

ACINUS *noun* **ACINI** one of the small fruits that make up a composite fruit like the raspberry

ACME *noun* **ACMES** the highest point of achievement, success, excellence, etc

ACNE *noun* **ACNES** a skin disorder, common in adolescence, caused by overactivity of the sebaceous glands, especially on the face, chest and back

ACOLYTE *noun* **ACOLYTES** someone who assists a priest in certain religious ceremonies

ACONITE *noun* **ACONITES** any of various herbaceous plants, usually with hooded bluish-purple flowers, and roots containing a toxic alkaloid compound formerly used to poison wolves

ACORN *noun* **ACORNS** the nut-like fruit of the oak tree, which has a cup-shaped outer case

ACOUSTIC *adj* relating to, producing or operated by sound

ACOUSTICS *singular noun* the scientific study of the production and properties of sound waves

ACQUAINT *verb* **ACQUAINTS, ACQUAINTING, ACQUAINTED** to let know; to inform

ACQUIESCE *verb* **ACQUIESCES, ACQUIESCING, ACQUIESCED** to accept something or agree to it without objection

ACQUIRE *verb* **ACQUIRES, ACQUIRING, ACQUIRED** to get, gain or develop something, especially through skill or effort

ACQUIT *verb* **ACQUITS, ACQUITTING, ACQUITTED** said of a court or jury, etc: to declare a person accused of a crime to be innocent

ACQUITTAL *noun* **ACQUITTALS** a declaration in a court of law that someone is not guilty of the crime, etc of which they have been accused

ACRE *noun* **ACRES** in the imperial system: a measure of land area equal to 4840 square yards (4047 sq m)

ACREAGE *noun* **ACREAGES** the number of acres in a piece of land

ACRID *adj* **ACRIDER, ACRIDEST** having a very bitter and pungent smell or taste

ACRIDITY *noun* **ACRIDITIES** bitterness of taste or in manner

ACRIMONY *noun* **ACRIMONIES** bitterness in feeling, temper or speech

ACROBAT *noun* **ACROBATS** an entertainer, eg in a circus, who performs skilful balancing acts and other athletic tricks

ACROBATIC *adj* agile; able to perform gymnastic tricks

ACROBATICS *plural noun* acrobatic movements

ACRONYM *noun* **ACRONYMS** a word made from the first letters or syllables of other words, and usually pronounced as a word in its own right, eg *NATO*

ACRONYMIC *adj* of or relating to acronyms

ACROPOLIS *noun* **ACROPOLISES** the upper fortified part or citadel of an ancient Greek city, now especially Athens

ACROSS *prep* to, at or on the other side of something ▫ *adverb* to, at or on the other side

ACROSTIC *noun* **ACROSTICS** a poem or puzzle in which the first, last or middle letters in each line, or a combination of these, form a word or proverb

ACRYLIC *noun* **ACRYLICS** any of various synthetic products derived from acrylic acid, especially acrylic paint or acrylic resin ▫ *adj* relating to, containing or derived from acrylic acid

ACT *noun* **ACTS** a thing done; a deed ▫ *verb* **ACTS, ACTING, ACTED** to behave or function in a specified way

ACTABLE *adj* capable of being acted (on stage)

ACTING *noun* **ACTINGS** the profession or art of performing in a play or film ◻ *adj* temporarily doing someone else's job or duties

ACTINIDE *noun* **ACTINIDES** any of a series of radioactive elements, from atomic number 89 upwards

ACTINIUM *noun* **ACTINIUMS** a silvery-white radioactive metal found in uranium ores

ACTION *noun* **ACTIONS** the process of doing something

ACTIVATE *verb* **ACTIVATES, ACTIVATING, ACTIVATED** to make something start working or go into operation

ACTIVATOR *noun* **ACTIVATORS** a person, thing or substance that activates

ACTIVE *adj* said of a person, etc: moving, working and doing things; full of energy; in grammar: denoting or relating to a verbal construction in which the subject performs the action or has the state described by the verb ◻ *noun* **ACTIVES** the form or forms that an active verb takes

ACTIVELY *adverb* in an active way

ACTIVISM *noun* **ACTIVISMS** a policy of direct, vigorous and sometimes militant action

ACTIVIST *noun* **ACTIVISTS** someone who is very active, especially as a member of a political group

ACTIVITY *noun* **ACTIVITIES** the state of being active or busy

ACTOR *noun* **ACTORS** a man or woman who performs in plays or films, especially as their profession

ACTRESS *noun* **ACTRESSES** a female actor

ACTUAL *adj* existing as fact; real

ACTUALITY *noun* **ACTUALITIES** fact; reality

ACTUALLY *adverb* really; in fact

ACTUARIAL *adj* relating to actuaries or their work

ACTUARY *noun* **ACTUARIES** someone who calculates insurance risks, and gives advice to insurance companies, etc on what premiums to set

ACTUATE *verb* **ACTUATES, ACTUATING, ACTUATED** to make (a mechanism, etc) go into action

ACTUATION *noun* **ACTUATIONS** the process of making (a mechanism, etc) go into action

ACUITY *noun* **ACUITIES** sharpness or acuteness, eg of the mind or senses

ACUMEN *noun* **ACUMENS** the ability to judge quickly and well; keen insight

ACUTE *adj* **ACUTER, ACUTEST** said of the senses: keen, good or sharp; penetrating ◻ *noun* **ACUTES** a sign placed above a vowel in some languages, either to indicate a particular pronunciation of the vowel, as with *é* in French, or, as in Spanish, to indicate that the vowel is to be stressed

ACUTELY *adverb* extremely, painfully

ACUTENESS *noun* **ACUTENESSES** the quality of being acute, used especially of mental perception

ACYL *noun* **ACYLS** a carboxylic acid

AD *noun* **ADS** an advertisement

ADAGE *noun* **ADAGES** a proverb or maxim

ADAGIO *adverb* slowly ◻ *adj* slow ◻ *noun* **ADAGIOS** a piece of music to be played slowly; a slow movement

ADAMANT *adj* completely determined; not likely to change one's mind or opinion

ADAMANTLY *adverb* determinedly

ADAPT *verb* **ADAPTS, ADAPTING, ADAPTED** to change something, oneself, etc so as to fit new circumstances, etc; to make something suitable for a new purpose

ADAPTABLE *adj* said of a person: good at fitting into new circumstances, situations, etc

ADAPTER *noun* **ADAPTERS** a device designed to connect two parts of different sizes

ADAPTIVE *adj* characterized by adaptation

ADAPTOR *noun* **ADAPTORS** a device designed to connect two parts of different sizes

ADD *verb* **ADDS, ADDING, ADDED** to put together or combine (two or more things)

ADDED *adj* additional; extra

ADDENDUM *noun* **ADDENDA** an addition

ADDER *noun* **ADDERS** the common European viper, a brown, olive or greyish snake with a dark zigzag line running down its back

ADDICT *noun* **ADDICTS** someone who is physically or psychologically dependent on the habitual intake of a drug such as alcohol, nicotine, heroin, etc

ADDICTED *adj* dependent on something (especially a drug)

ADDICTION *noun* **ADDICTIONS** the state of being addicted

ADDICTIVE *adj* relating to or tending to cause addiction; habit-forming

ADDITION *noun* **ADDITIONS** the act or operation of adding

ADDITIVE *noun* **ADDITIVES** any chemical substance that is deliberately added to another substance, usually in small quantities, for a specific purpose, eg a food flavouring or colouring

ADDLE *verb* **ADDLES, ADDLING, ADDLED** to confuse or muddle

ADDLED *adj* confused or muddled

ADDRESS *noun* **ADDRESSES** the number or name of the house or building, and the name of the street and town, where a person lives or works ◻ *verb* **ADDRESSES, ADDRESSING, ADDRESSED** to put the name and address on (an envelope, etc)

ADDRESSEE *noun* **ADDRESSEES** the person to whom a letter, etc is addressed

ADDUCE *verb* **ADDUCES, ADDUCING, ADDUCED** to mention (a fact) as a supporting reason, piece of evidence, etc

ADDUCIBLE *adj* able to be cited as evidence

ADENINE *noun* **ADENINES** a base, derived from purine, which is one of the four bases found in nucleic acid

ADENOIDAL *adj* relating to the adenoids

ADENOIDS *plural noun* a pair of lymph glands located in the upper part of the throat at the back of the nasal cavity

ADEPT *adj* **ADEPTER, ADEPTEST** skilful at doing (something); proficient ◻ *noun* **ADEPTS** an expert at something

ADEPTLY *adverb* skilfully or proficiently

ADEPTNESS *noun* **ADEPTNESSES** the quality of being adept

ADEQUACY *noun* **ADEQUACIES** being adequate; sufficiency

ADEQUATE *adj* enough; sufficient

ADHERE *verb* **ADHERES, ADHERING, ADHERED** to stick or remain fixed to something

ADHERENCE *noun* **ADHERENCES** the act of sticking or adhering

ADHERENT *noun* **ADHERENTS** a follower; a supporter ◻ *adj* sticking or adhering

ADHESION *noun* **ADHESIONS** the process of sticking or adhering

ADHESIVE *adj* sticky; able to make

things stick together ▫ *noun*

ADHESIVES any substance that is used to bond two surfaces together

ADIEU *noun* **ADIEUS** a goodbye

ADIPOSE *adj* relating to, containing or consisting of fat; fatty

ADJACENCY *noun* **ADJACENCIES** the state of lying beside or next to something

ADJACENT *adj* lying beside or next to something

ADJECTIVE *noun* **ADJECTIVES** a word that describes or modifies a noun or pronoun, as *dark* describes *hair* in *She has dark hair*, and *sad* describes *him* in *The story made him sad*

ADJOIN *verb* **ADJOINS, ADJOINING, ADJOINED** to be next to and joined to something

ADJOINING *adj* next to and joined to something

ADJOURN *verb* **ADJOURNS, ADJOURNING, ADJOURNED** to put off (a meeting, etc) to another time

ADJUDGE *verb* **ADJUDGES, ADJUDGING, ADJUDGED** to declare or judge officially

ADJUNCT *noun* **ADJUNCTS** something attached or added to something else but not an essential part of it

ADJURE *verb* **ADJURES, ADJURING, ADJURED** to request, beg or command someone formally or solemnly

ADJUST *verb* **ADJUSTS, ADJUSTING, ADJUSTED** to change something or oneself, etc slightly so as to be more suitable for a situation, etc

ADJUSTER *noun* **ADJUSTERS** a person or thing that adjusts

ADJUTANCY *noun* **ADJUTANCIES** the office of an adjutant

ADJUTANT *noun* **ADJUTANTS** an army officer who does administrative work

ADMAN *noun* **ADMEN** a person whose job is to produce or write advertisements

ADMIN *noun* **ADMINS** administration

ADMIRABLE *adj* worthy of being admired

ADMIRABLY *adverb* in an admirable way

ADMIRAL *noun* **ADMIRALS** a high-ranking officer in the navy

ADMIRE *verb* **ADMIRES, ADMIRING, ADMIRED** to regard with respect or approval

ADMIRER *noun* **ADMIRERS** someone who admires a particular person or thing

ADMIRING *adj* full of admiration

ADMISSION *noun* **ADMISSIONS** the act of allowing someone or something in or of being allowed in

ADMIT *verb* **ADMITS, ADMITTING, ADMITTED** to agree to the truth of something, especially unwillingly

ADMIXTURE *noun* **ADMIXTURES** anything that is added to the main ingredient of a mixture

ADMONISH *verb* **ADMONISHES, ADMONISHING, ADMONISHED** to warn

ADO *noun* **ADOS** difficulty or trouble; fuss or bustle

ADOBE *noun* **ADOBES** a kind of building material made of clay and straw, and dried in the sun

ADOPT *verb* **ADOPTS, ADOPTING, ADOPTED** to take (a child of other parents) into one's own family, becoming its legal parent

ADOPTED *adj* taken by adoption

ADOPTION *noun* **ADOPTIONS** the action of adopting or being adopted

ADOPTIVE *adj* that adopts or is adopted

ADORABLE *adj* worthy of being adored

ADORABLY *adverb* in an adorable way

ADORATION *noun* **ADORATIONS** worship; great love

ADORE *verb* **ADORES, ADORING, ADORED** to love someone deeply

ADORER *noun* **ADORERS** a person who adores

ADORING *adj* showing great love or worship

ADORINGLY *adverb* in an adoring way

ADORN *verb* **ADORNS, ADORNING, ADORNED** to decorate

ADORNMENT *noun* **ADORNMENTS** an ornament decoration

ADRENAL *adj* referring or relating to the kidneys

ADRENALIN *noun* **ADRENALINS** a hormone secreted by the adrenal glands in response to fear, excitement or anger, which causes an increase in heartbeat and blood pressure and diverts blood towards the muscles

ADRIFT *adj* said of a boat: not tied up; floating about without being steered ▫ *adverb* said of a boat: not tied up; floating about without being steered

ADROIT *adj* **ADROITER, ADROITEST** quick and clever in action or thought

ADROITLY *adverb* quickly and cleverly

ADSORB *verb* **ADSORBS, ADSORBING, ADSORBED** said of a solid, eg charcoal, or more rarely a liquid: to accumulate a thin layer of atoms or molecules of (a solid, liquid, or gas) on its surface

ADSORBENT *adj* able to adsorb substances ▫ *noun* **ADSORBENTS** a substance on whose surface adsorption takes place

ADULATE *verb* **ADULATES, ADULATING, ADULATED** to praise or flatter someone far too much

ADULATION *noun* **ADULATIONS** great flattery

ADULATOR *noun* **ADULATORS** a person who praises excessively

ADULATORY *adj* showing excessive praise or flattery

ADULT *adj* fully grown; mature ▫ *noun* **ADULTS** a fully grown person, animal, bird or plant

ADULTERER *noun* **ADULTERERS** a man who commits adultery

ADULTERY *noun* **ADULTERIES** sexual relations willingly undertaken between a married person and a person who is not their spouse

ADULTHOOD *noun* **ADULTHOODS** the time of being an adult

ADUMBRATE *verb* **ADUMBRATES, ADUMBRATING, ADUMBRATED** to indicate or describe in a general way

ADVANCE *verb* **ADVANCES, ADVANCING, ADVANCED** to put, move or go forward, sometimes in a threatening way ▫ *noun* **ADVANCES** progress; a move forward ▫ *adj* done, made or given beforehand

ADVANCED *adj* having progressed or developed well or far

ADVANTAGE *noun* **ADVANTAGES** a favourable circumstance; benefit or usefulness ▫ *verb* **ADVANTAGES, ADVANTAGING, ADVANTAGED** to benefit someone or improve their position

ADVANTAGED *adj* having a good social or financial situation

ADVENT *noun* **ADVENTS** coming

or arrival; first appearance

ADVENTURE noun **ADVENTURES** an exciting and often dangerous experience

ADVERB noun **ADVERBS** a word which describes or adds to the meaning of a verb, adjective or another adverb, such as *very* and *quietly* in *They were talking very quietly*

ADVERBIAL adj of or like an adverb

ADVERSARY noun **ADVERSARIES** an opponent in a competition, etc

ADVERSE adj **ADVERSER, ADVERSEST** unfavourable to one's interests

ADVERSELY adverb unfavourably

ADVERSITY noun **ADVERSITIES** circumstances that cause trouble or sorrow

ADVERT[1] noun **ADVERTS** an advertisement, a public notice, picture, etc that announces something

ADVERT[2] verb **ADVERTS, ADVERTING, ADVERTED** to turn one's attention (to)

ADVERTISE verb **ADVERTISES, ADVERTISING, ADVERTISED** to draw attention to or describe (goods for sale, services offered, etc) in newspapers, on TV, etc, to encourage people to buy or use them

ADVERTISING noun **ADVERTISINGS** the business or profession of producing advertisements for goods

ADVERTIZE verb **ADVERTIZES, ADVERTIZING, ADVERTIZED** to advertise

ADVICE noun **ADVICES** suggestions or opinions given to someone about what they should do in a particular situation

ADVISABLE adj said of action to be taken, etc: to be recommended; wise

ADVISABLY adverb in an advisable way

ADVISE verb **ADVISES, ADVISING, ADVISED** to give advice to someone

ADVISED adj considered; judged

ADVISEDLY adverb after careful thought; on purpose

ADVISER noun **ADVISERS** someone who advises

ADVISOR noun **ADVISORS** an adviser

ADVISORY adj appointed in order to give advice

ADVOCAAT noun **ADVOCAATS** a liqueur made from raw eggs, sugar and brandy

ADVOCACY noun **ADVOCACIES** recommendation or active support of an idea, etc

ADVOCATE noun **ADVOCATES** especially in Scotland: a lawyer who speaks for the defence or prosecution in a trial □ verb **ADVOCATES, ADVOCATING, ADVOCATED** to recommend or support (an idea, proposal, etc), especially in public

ADZ noun **ADZES** an adze

ADZE noun **ADZES** a tool with an arched blade set at right angles to its handle, used for cutting and shaping wood

AE adj a Scots word for *one*

AEGIS noun **AEGISES** protection or patronage

AEGROTAT noun **AEGROTATS** in some universities: a medical certificate, or a degree or credit awarded, when illness has prevented someone from taking examinations, etc

AEON noun **AEONS** a long period of time; an endless or immeasurable period of time

AERATE verb **AERATES, AERATING, AERATED** to expose something to or mix it with air or oxygen

AERATED adj of a liquid: charged with carbon dioxide or some other gas

AERATION noun **AERATIONS** exposure to the action of air

AERIAL noun **AERIALS** a wire, rod or other device, especially on a radio or television receiver □ adj relating to or found in the air

AERIE noun **AERIES** an eyrie

AEROBE noun **AEROBES** any organism that requires oxygen in order to obtain energy from the breakdown of carbohydrates or other foodstuffs by the process of respiration

AEROBIC adj said of an organism: requiring oxygen in order to obtain energy from the breakdown of carbohydrates or other foodstuffs by the process of respiration

AEROBICS singular noun a system of physical exercise consisting of rapidly repeated, energetic movements, which increases the supply of oxygen in the blood and strengthens the heart and lungs □ plural noun energetic exercises

AERODROME noun **AERODROMES** an area of land and its associated buildings, smaller than an airport, used for the take-off and landing of private and military aircraft

AEROFOIL noun **AEROFOILS** any body or part shaped so as to provide lift or thrust when it is moving through the air, eg the wings, tail fins and propeller blades of an aeroplane

AEROGRAM noun **AEROGRAMS** a thin piece of paper on which to write letters for sending by air, designed so that it can be folded and sealed without being put into an envelope

AEROPLANE noun **AEROPLANES** a powered machine used for travelling in the air, that is heavier than air and supported in its flight by fixed wings

AEROSOL noun **AEROSOLS** a suspension of fine particles of a solid or liquid suspended in a gas

AEROSPACE noun **AEROSPACES** the Earth's atmosphere and the space beyond it, considered as a zone available for the flight of aircraft and spacecraft

AESTHETE noun **AESTHETES** someone who has or claims to have a special appreciation of art and beauty

AESTHETIC adj able to appreciate beauty

AESTHETICS singular noun the branch of philosophy concerned with the study of the principles of beauty, especially in art

AESTIVAL adj referring or relating to summer

AESTIVATE verb **AESTIVATES, AESTIVATING, AESTIVATED** said of certain animals: to survive the hot summer months in a dormant or torpid state

AETHER noun **AETHERS** the clear upper air or a clear sky

AETIOLOGY noun **AETIOLOGIES** the science or philosophy of causes

AFAR adverb at a distance; far away

AFFABLE adj pleasant and friendly in manner; easy to talk to

AFFABLY adverb pleasantly

AFFAIR noun **AFFAIRS** a concern, matter or thing to be done

AFFECT verb **AFFECTS, AFFECTING, AFFECTED** to have an effect on someone or something □ noun **AFFECTS** the emotion linked with a particular idea or mental image

AFFECTED *adj* not genuine; false or pretended

AFFECTING *adj* causing people to feel strong emotion, especially sadness, pity, sympathy, joy, etc

AFFECTION *noun* **AFFECTIONS** a feeling of love or strong liking

AFFECTIVE *adj* relating to, arising from, or influencing emotion

AFFERENT *adj* said especially of a nerve or blood vessel: leading inwards or towards a central part

AFFIANCE *verb* **AFFIANCES, AFFIANCING, AFFIANCED** to be or become engaged to be married to someone

AFFIDAVIT *noun* **AFFIDAVITS** a written statement, sworn to be true by the person who makes it, for use as evidence in a court of law

AFFILIATE *verb* **AFFILIATES, AFFILIATING, AFFILIATED** to connect or associate a person or organization with a group or a larger organization ◻ *noun* **AFFILIATES** a person or organization, etc that has an association with a group or larger body

AFFINITY *noun* **AFFINITIES** a strong natural liking for or feeling of attraction or closeness towards someone or something

AFFIRM *verb* **AFFIRMS, AFFIRMING, AFFIRMED** to state something positively and firmly; to state something as a fact

AFFIX *verb* **AFFIXES, AFFIXING, AFFIXED** to attach or fasten ◻ *noun* **AFFIXES** a word-forming element of one or more syllables which can be added to a word to form another, related, word, eg *un-* in *unhappy* or *-ness* in *sadness*; a prefix, suffix or infix

AFFLICT *verb* **AFFLICTS, AFFLICTING, AFFLICTED** to cause someone physical or mental suffering

AFFLUENCE *noun* **AFFLUENCES** wealth

AFFLUENT *adj* having more than enough money; rich

AFFORD *verb* **AFFORDS, AFFORDING, AFFORDED** to have enough money, time, etc to spend on something

AFFOREST *verb* **AFFORESTS, AFFORESTING, AFFORESTED** to carry out the process of afforestation on (a piece of land)

AFFRAY *noun* **AFFRAYS** a fight in a public place; a breach of the peace by fighting

AFFRICATE *noun* **AFFRICATES** a consonant sound that begins as a plosive and becomes a fricative, such as *ch* in *church*

AFFRONT *noun* **AFFRONTS** an insult, especially one delivered in public ◻ *verb* **AFFRONTS, AFFRONTING, AFFRONTED** to insult someone, especially in public

AFGHAN *noun* **AFGHANS** a heavy knitted or crocheted woollen blanket or shawl

AFIELD *adverb* to or at a distance

AFIRE *adj* on fire; burning ◻ *adverb* on fire; burning

AFLAJ plural of **falaj**

AFLAME *adj* in flames; burning

AFLATOXIN *noun* **AFLATOXINS** a toxic substance, produced by a fungus, which contaminates stored corn, soya beans, peanuts, etc in warm humid regions, and causes cancer in some animals

AFLOAT *adj* floating ◻ *adverb* floating

AFOOT *adj* being prepared or already in progress or operation ◻ *adverb* being prepared or already in progress or operation

AFORE *adverb* before ◻ *prep* before

AFORESAID *adj* said or mentioned already

AFRAID *adj* feeling fear; frightened of someone or something

AFRESH *adverb* again, especially from the beginning; with a fresh start

AFRO *noun* **AFROS** a hairstyle consisting of thick bushy curls standing out from the head

AFT *adj* at or towards the stern, rear or tail ◻ *adverb* at or towards the stern, rear or tail

AFTER *prep* coming later in time than something ◻ *adverb* later in time ◻ *conj* after the time when ◻ *adj* later; following an earlier event

AFTERCARE *noun* **AFTERCARES** care and support given to someone after a period of treatment, a surgical operation, a prison sentence, etc

AFTERGLOW *noun* **AFTERGLOWS** a glow remaining in the sky after the Sun has set

AFTERMATH *noun* **AFTERMATHS** circumstances that follow and are a result of something, especially a great and terrible event

AFTERNOON *noun* **AFTERNOONS** the period of the day between noon and the evening

AFTERS *plural noun* dessert; pudding

AFTERWARD *adverb* later; following an earlier event

AFTERWARDS *adverb* later; following an earlier event

AGA *noun* **AGAS** a Turkish commander or chief officer

AGAIN *adverb* once more; another time

AGAINST *prep* close to or leaning on something; in contact with it

AGAPE [1] *adj* said of the mouth: gaping; open wide

AGAPE [2] *noun* **AGAPAE** Christian brotherly love, as distinct from erotic love

AGAR *noun* **AGARS** a gelatinous substance extracted from certain red seaweeds, used as a food stabilizer and thickening agent

AGARIC *noun* **AGARICS** any of various fungi that produce an umbrella-shaped spore-bearing structure with a central vertical stem supporting a circular cap, eg field mushroom, death cap

AGATE *noun* **AGATES** a fine-grained variety of chalcedony consisting of concentrically arranged bands of two or more colours, used as a semiprecious stone in jewellery and ornaments

AGAVE *noun* **AGAVES** any of various evergreen perennial plants, native to Central and S America, with fleshy sword-shaped, leaves and tall flower stalks

AGE *noun* **AGES** the period of time during which a person, animal, plant or phenomenon has lived or existed ◻ *verb* **AGES, AGEING, AGED** to show signs of growing old

AGED *adj* having a specified age

AGEING *adj* growing old; elderly ◻ *noun* **AGEINGS** the process of growing old

AGEISM *noun* **AGEISMS** the practice of treating people differently, and usually unfairly, on the grounds of age only, especially because they are too old

AGEIST *noun* **AGEISTS** a person who discriminates on grounds of age

AGELESS *adj* never growing old or fading; never looking older

AGENCY *noun* **AGENCIES** an office or business that provides a particular service, eg matching workers with employers in specific areas

AGENDA *singular noun* **AGENDAS** a list of things to be done or discussed

AGENT *noun* **AGENTS** someone who represents an organization and acts on its behalf

AGGRAVATE *verb* **AGGRAVATES, AGGRAVATING, AGGRAVATED** to make (a bad situation, an illness, etc) worse

AGGRAVATED *adj* said of an offence: made more serious, eg by violence

AGGRAVATING *adj* persistently annoying

AGGREGATE *noun* **AGGREGATES** a collection of separate units brought together; a total ▫ *adj* formed of separate units combined together ▫ *verb* **AGGREGATES, AGGREGATING, AGGREGATED** to combine or be combined into a single unit or whole

AGGRESSOR *noun* **AGGRESSORS** in a fight, war, etc: the person, group or country that attacks first, especially if the attack is unprovoked

AGGRIEVED *adj* angry, hurt or upset because one feels that one has been badly or unfairly treated

AGGRO *noun* **AGGROS** fighting; violent or threatening behaviour

AGHAST *adj* filled with fear or horror

AGILE *adj* **AGILER, AGILEST** able to move, change direction, etc quickly and easily; nimble; active

AGILELY *adverb* in an agile way

AGILITY *noun* **AGILITIES** nimbleness; swiftness and suppleness

AGING *adj* growing old; elderly ▫ *noun* **AGINGS** the process of growing old

AGIST *noun* **AGISTS** an ageist

AGITATE *verb* **AGITATES, AGITATING, AGITATED** to excite or trouble (a person, their feelings, nerves, etc)

AGITATED *adj* excited or troubled

AGITATION *noun* **AGITATIONS** public discussion for or against something

AGITATO *adverb* in an agitated

restless manner ▫ *adj* agitated; restless and wild

AGITATOR *noun* **AGITATORS** someone who tries continually to stir up public feeling, especially over serious political or social issues

AGITPROP *noun* **AGITPROPS** the spreading of political propaganda, especially by communists

AGLET *noun* **AGLETS** the metal tag on the end of a lace

AGLITTER *adj* glittering; sparkling

AGLOW *adj* shining with colour or warmth; glowing

AGNAIL *noun* **AGNAILS** a hangnail

AGNATE *adj* in genealogy, etc: related on one's father's side or through a male ancestor ▫ *noun* **AGNATES** a person related to another on their father's side or through a male ancestor

AGNOSTIC *noun* **AGNOSTICS** someone who believes that one can know only about material things and so believes that nothing can be known about the existence of God ▫ *adj* relating to this view

AGO *adverb* in the past; earlier

AGOG *adj* very interested and excited; eager to know more ▫ *adverb* eagerly; expectantly

AGONISE *verb* **AGONISES, AGONISING, AGONISED** to agonize

AGONISED *adj* agonized

AGONISING *adj* agonizing

AGONIZE *verb* **AGONIZES, AGONIZING, AGONIZED** to worry intensely or suffer great anxiety about something

AGONIZED *adj* suffering or showing great anxiety, worry or agony

AGONIZING *adj* causing great bodily or mental suffering

AGONY *noun* **AGONIES** severe bodily or mental pain

AGRARIAN *adj* relating to land or its management

AGREE *verb* **AGREES, AGREEING, AGREED** to be of the same opinion as someone about something

AGREEABLE *adj* pleasant; friendly

AGREEABLY *adverb* pleasantly

AGREEMENT *noun* **AGREEMENTS** a contract or promise

AGRIMONY *noun* **AGRIMONIES** an erect perennial plant which has pairs of small leaflets alternating with large ones, and small yellow flowers in long terminal spikes

AGRONOMY *noun* **AGRONOMIES** the scientific study of the cultivation of field crops and soil management

AGROUND *adj* said of ships: stuck on the bottom of the sea or rocks, usually in shallow water

AGUE *noun* **AGUES** a fit of shivering

AH *exclamation* expressing joy, surprise etc ▫ *verb* **AHS, AHING, AHED** to make the exclamation *ah*

AHA *exclamation* expressing pleasure, satisfaction, triumph or surprise, according to the intonation of the speaker's voice

AHEAD *adverb* at or in the front; forwards

AHEM *exclamation* a sound made in the back of the throat, used to gain people's attention or to express doubt or disapproval

AHIMSA *noun* **AHIMSAS** in Hinduism, Buddhism and especially Jainism: the principle of respect for all life and the practice of non-injury to living things

AHOY *exclamation* a shout to greet or attract the attention of another ship

AI *noun* **AIS** the three-toed sloth

AIA *noun* **AIAS** an Indian or South African nurse

AID *noun* **AIDS** help ▫ *verb* **AIDS, AIDING, AIDED** to help or support someone

AIDE *noun* **AIDES** a confidential assistant or adviser, especially to the head of a government

AIGUILLE *noun* **AIGUILLES** a sharp, needle-like pinnacle of rock

AIKIDO *noun* **AIKIDOS** a Japanese form of self-defence, based on a system of locks and holds and the movements of the attacker or opponent

AIL *verb* **AILS, AILING, AILED** to be ill and weak

AILERON *noun* **AILERONS** one of a pair of hinged flaps situated at the rear edge of each wing of an aircraft, used to control roll about the craft's longitudinal axis

AILING *adj* ill; in poor health

AILMENT *noun* **AILMENTS** an illness, especially a minor one

AIM *verb* **AIMS, AIMING, AIMED** to point or direct a weapon, attack, remark, etc at someone or something □ *noun* **AIMS** what a person, etc intends to do; the achievement aimed at

AIMLESS *adj* without any purpose

AIMLESSLY *adverb* in an aimless way

AIN *adj* a Scots word for *own*

AIOLI *noun* **AIOLIS** a garlic-flavoured mayonnaise

AIR *noun* **AIRS** the invisible odourless tasteless mixture of gases that forms the atmosphere surrounding the Earth, essential for the survival of all living organisms that depend on oxygen for respiration □ *verb* **AIRS, AIRING, AIRED** to hang (laundry) in a warm dry place to make it completely dry or to remove unpleasant smells

AIRBORNE *adj* said of aircraft, etc: flying in the air, having just taken off

AIRCRAFT *singular or plural noun* any structure, machine or vehicle that is designed for travelling through air supported by its own buoyancy or by the action of air on its surfaces, eg an aeroplane or helicopter

AIRER *noun* **AIRERS** a frame on which clothes are dried

AIRFIELD *noun* **AIRFIELDS** an open expanse that is used by aircraft for landing and take-off

AIRFRAME *noun* **AIRFRAMES** the body of an aircraft as opposed to its engines

AIRHEAD *noun* **AIRHEADS** an idiot

AIRHOLE *noun* **AIRHOLES** a hole for the passage of air, usually for ventilation

AIRIER see under **airy**

AIRIEST see under **airy**

AIRILY *adverb* flippantly; nonchalantly

AIRINESS *noun* **AIRINESSES** the state of having plenty of cool fresh air

AIRING *noun* **AIRINGS** the act of airing (laundry, a room, the sheets, etc on a bed, etc) or fact of being aired

AIRLESS *adj* said of the weather: unpleasantly warm, with no wind

AIRLIFT *noun* **AIRLIFTS** the transporting of large numbers of people or large amounts of goods in aircraft when other routes are blocked □ *verb* **AIRLIFTS,**

AIRLIFTING, AIRLIFTED to transport (people, goods, etc) in this way

AIRLINE *noun* **AIRLINES** a company or organization which provides a regular transport service for passengers or cargo by aircraft

AIRLINER *noun* **AIRLINERS** a large passenger aircraft

AIRLOCK *noun* **AIRLOCKS** a bubble of air or gas that obstructs or blocks the flow of liquid through a pipe

AIRMAIL *noun* **AIRMAILS** the system of carrying mail by air □ *verb* **AIRMAILS, AIRMAILING, AIRMAILED** to send something by airmail

AIRMAN *noun* **AIRMEN** a pilot or member of the crew of an aeroplane, especially in an air force

AIRPLANE *noun* **AIRPLANES** an aeroplane

AIRPORT *noun* **AIRPORTS** a place where civil aircraft arrive and depart, with facilities for passengers and cargo, etc

AIRSHIP *noun* **AIRSHIPS** a power-driven steerable aircraft that consists of a streamlined envelope or hull containing helium gas, with an engine and a gondola suspended from it

AIRSICK *adj* affected by nausea due to the motion of an aircraft

AIRSIDE *noun* **AIRSIDES** in aviation: the area of an airport with direct access to the aircraft, entry to which is controlled

AIRSPACE *noun* **AIRSPACES** the part of the atmosphere directly above a country, considered as part of that country

AIRSPEED *noun* **AIRSPEEDS** the speed of an aircraft, missile, etc in relation to the air through which it is moving

AIRSTRIP *noun* **AIRSTRIPS** a strip of ground where aircraft can land and take off but which has no facilities

AIRTIGHT *adj* said of a container, etc: which air cannot get into, out of, or through

AIRTIME *noun* **AIRTIMES** on TV or radio: the length of time given to a particular item, programme or topic

AIRWAVES *plural noun* the radio waves used for radio and television broadcasting

AIRWAY *noun* **AIRWAYS** a passage for air, especially for ventilation

AIRWOMAN *noun* **AIRWOMEN** a pilot or member of the crew of an aeroplane, especially in an air force

AIRWORTHY *adj* said of aircraft: in a condition to fly safely

AIRY *adj* **AIRIER, AIRIEST** with plenty of fresh cool air

AISLE *noun* **AISLES** a passage between rows of seats, eg in an aircraft, theatre, or church

AIT *noun* **AITS** a small island

AITCH *noun* **AITCHES** the letter 'H' or 'h'

AITCHBONE *noun* **AITCHBONES** the rump bone in cattle

AJAR *adj* partly open □ *adverb* partly open

AKE *verb* **AKES, AKING, AKED** an old spelling of *ache*

AKIMBO *adj* with hands on hips and elbows bent outward □ *adverb* with hands on hips and elbows bent outward

AKIN *adj* similar; being of the same kind

ALA *noun* **ALAE** an outgrowth on a fruit

ALABASTER *noun* **ALABASTERS** a type of white stone used for ornaments, etc □ *adj* made of or like alabaster

ALACRITY *noun* **ALACRITIES** quick and cheerful enthusiasm

ALARM *noun* **ALARMS** sudden fear produced by awareness of danger □ *verb* **ALARMS, ALARMING, ALARMED** to frighten

ALARMING *adj* disturbing or frightening

ALARMISM *noun* **ALARMISMS** scaremongering

ALARMIST *noun* **ALARMISTS** someone who spreads unnecessary alarm □ *adj* causing unnecessary alarm

ALAS *exclamation* expressing grief or misfortune

ALB *noun* **ALBS** a long white garment reaching to the feet, worn by some Christian priests

ALBATROSS *noun* **ALBATROSSES** a large seabird, with a powerful hooked beak, a stout body, long narrow wings, and white plumage with black patches

ALBEIT *conj* even if; although

ALBINISM *noun* **ALBINISMS** in a living organism: the inherited lack of pigmentation, which in vertebrates is caused by a lack of the enzyme responsible for the production of the dark pigment melanin

ALBINO *noun* **ALBINOS** in an animal or human: an abnormal lack of pigmentation in the hair, skin and eyes

ALBUM *noun* **ALBUMS** a book with blank pages for holding photographs, stamps, etc

ALBUMEN *noun* **ALBUMENS** the white of an egg

ALBUMIN *noun* **ALBUMINS** any of various water-soluble globular proteins that coagulate when heated, found in egg white, milk, blood serum, etc

ALCHEMIST *noun* **ALCHEMISTS** a person who practised alchemy

ALCHEMY *noun* **ALCHEMIES** the forerunner of modern chemistry, which centred around attempts to convert ordinary metals into gold, and to discover a universal remedy for illness, known as the elixir of life

ALCOHOL *noun* **ALCOHOLS** any of numerous organic chemical compounds containing one or more hydroxyl groups, used as solvents for dyes, resins, varnishes, perfume oils, etc, and as fuels

ALCOHOLIC *adj* relating to, containing or having the properties of alcohol □ *noun* **ALCOHOLICS** a person who is dependent on alcohol

ALCOVE *noun* **ALCOVES** a recess in the wall of a room or garden

ALDEHYDE *noun* **ALDEHYDES** any of numerous organic chemical compounds formed by the oxidation of alcohols, including aromatic compounds which are used as flavourings and perfumes

ALDER *noun* **ALDERS** any of various deciduous trees and shrubs with dark fissured bark, oval or rounded leaves, and male and female flowers in catkins on separate plants

ALDERMAN *noun* **ALDERMEN** in England and Wales until 1974: a member of a town, county or borough council elected by fellow councillors, below the rank of mayor

ALDRIN *noun* **ALDRINS** a chlorinated hydrocarbon used as a contact insecticide

ALE *noun* **ALES** a light-coloured beer, higher in alcohol content than lager and with a fuller body, flavoured with hops

ALEATORIC *adj* depending on chance

ALEATORY *adj* aleatoric

ALEE *adverb* on or towards the lee side

ALEPH *noun* **ALEPHS** the first letter of the Phoenician and Hebrew alphabets

ALERT *adj* **ALERTER, ALERTEST** thinking and acting quickly □ *noun* **ALERTS** a warning of danger □ *verb* **ALERTS, ALERTING, ALERTED** to warn someone of (a danger); to make them aware of (a fact or circumstance)

ALERTLY *adverb* in an alert way

ALERTNESS *noun* **ALERTNESSES** the state of being alert

ALEWIFE *noun* **ALEWIVES** a fish related to the herring, common off the NE coast of America

ALEXIA *noun* **ALEXIAS** loss of the ability to read, caused by brain disease

ALFALFA *noun* **ALFALFAS** a perennial plant of the pulse family with purple flowers and spirally twisted pods, widely cultivated as a forage crop, especially in the USA

ALFRESCO *adverb* in the open air □ *adj* open-air

ALGAE *plural noun* a large and very diverse group of mainly aquatic organisms, ranging from single-celled members of the plant plankton to large multicellular seaweeds

ALGEBRA *noun* **ALGEBRAS** the branch of mathematics that uses letters and symbols to represent variable quantities and numbers, and to express generalizations about them

ALGEBRAIC *adj* relating to or involving algebra

ALGINATE *noun* **ALGINATES** a salt of alginic acid, found in seaweeds, and used in food manufacturing as a thickening agent

ALGORITHM *noun* **ALGORITHMS** any procedure involving a series of steps that is used to find the solution to a specific problem, eg to solve a mathematical equation

ALIAS *noun* **ALIASES** a false or assumed name □ *adverb* also known as

ALIASING *noun* **ALIASINGS** in image technology: image imperfections arising from insufficiently detailed input to a raster display and resulting eg in a diagonal line appearing stepped

ALIBI *noun* **ALIBIS** a plea of being somewhere else when a crime was committed

ALICYCLIC *adj* said of organic compounds: having the properties of aliphatic compounds but containing a ring of carbon atoms instead of an open chain

ALIEN *noun* **ALIENS** a foreign-born resident of a country who has not adopted that country's nationality □ *adj* foreign

ALIENABLE *adj* said of property: able to be transferred to another owner

ALIENATE *verb* **ALIENATES, ALIENATING, ALIENATED** to make someone become unfriendly or estranged

ALIGHT [1] *adj* on fire

ALIGHT [2] *verb* **ALIGHTS, ALIGHTING, ALIGHTED, ALIT** to get down from or out of (a vehicle)

ALIGN *verb* **ALIGNS, ALIGNING, ALIGNED** to put something in a straight line or bring it into line

ALIGNMENT *noun* **ALIGNMENTS** setting in a line or lines

ALIKE *adj* like one another; similar □ *adverb* in a similar manner

ALIMENT *noun* **ALIMENTS** nourishment; food

ALIMONY *noun* **ALIMONIES** money for support paid by a man to his wife or by a woman to her husband, when they are legally separated or divorced

ALIPHATIC *adj* said of an organic compound: having carbon atoms arranged in chains rather than in rings

ALIQUOT *adj* said of a number or quantity: into which a given number or quantity can be exactly divided without any remainder

ALIT a past form of **alight** [2]

ALIVE *adj* living; having life; in existence

ALKALI *noun* **ALKALIS, ALKALIES** a hydroxide of any of various metallic elements, eg sodium or potassium, that dissolves in water to produce an alkaline solution, and neutralizes acids to form salts

ALKALINE *adj* relating to or having the properties of an alkali

ALKALOID *noun* **ALKALOIDS** any of numerous nitrogen-containing organic compounds with toxic or medicinal properties that occur naturally in certain plants, eg caffeine, nicotine

ALKANE *noun* **ALKANES** the general name for a hydrocarbon of the methane series

ALKENE *noun* **ALKENES** any of the unsaturated hydrocarbons of the ethylene series

ALL *adj* the whole amount, number or extent of something; every □ *noun* **ALLS** every one of the people or things concerned; the whole of something □ *adverb* entirely; quite

ALLANTOIC *adj* relating to the allantois

ALLANTOIS *noun* **ALLANTOISES** a membranous sac-like appendage for effecting oxygenation in the embryos of mammals, birds and reptiles

ALLAY *verb* **ALLAYS, ALLAYING, ALLAYED** to make (pain, fear, suspicion, etc) less intense

ALLEGE *verb* **ALLEGES, ALLEGING, ALLEGED** to claim or declare something to be the case, usually without proof

ALLEGED *adj* presumed and claimed, but not proved, to be as stated

ALLEGEDLY *adverb* seemingly; supposedly

ALLEGORY *noun* **ALLEGORIES** a story, play, poem, picture, etc in which the characters represent moral or spiritual ideas or messages

ALLEGRO *adverb* in a quick lively manner □ *adj* quick and lively □ *noun* **ALLEGROS** a piece of music to be played in this way

ALLELE *noun* **ALLELES** any of the possible alternative forms of the same gene, of which every individual inherits two (one from each parent), different combinations of which produce different characteristics

ALLELUIA *exclamation* expressing praise to God □ *noun* **ALLELUIAS** the exclamation of 'hallelujah'

ALLERGEN *noun* **ALLERGENS** any foreign substance, usually a protein, that induces an allergic reaction in the body of a person who is hypersensitive to it, eg pollen

ALLERGIC *adj* having an allergy caused by abnormal sensitivity to something

ALLERGY *noun* **ALLERGIES** a hypersensitive reaction of the body

to certain foreign substances known as allergens, which may be caused by specific foods, inhalation of dust or pollen, contact with the hair of dogs, cats, etc, and certain drugs

ALLEVIATE *verb* **ALLEVIATES, ALLEVIATING, ALLEVIATED** to make (pain, a problem, suffering, etc) less severe

ALLEY *noun* **ALLEYS** a narrow passage behind or between buildings

ALLIANCE *noun* **ALLIANCES** the state of being allied

ALLIED *adj* joined by political agreement or treaty

ALLIES plural of **ally**

ALLIGATOR *noun* **ALLIGATORS** either of two species of a large reptile similar to a crocodile but with a broader head and blunter snout, and teeth that do not protrude over its jaws

ALLOCABLE *adj* said of financial resources: able to be assigned or allocated

ALLOCATE *verb* **ALLOCATES, ALLOCATING, ALLOCATED** to give, set apart or assign something to someone or for some particular purpose

ALLOT *verb* **ALLOTS, ALLOTTING, ALLOTTED** to give (a share of or place in something) to each member of a group

ALLOTMENT *noun* **ALLOTMENTS** one of the subdivisions of a larger piece of public ground rented to individuals to grow vegetables, etc

ALLOTROPE *noun* **ALLOTROPES** any of the two or more structural forms in which some elements can exist, often due to differences in crystal structure, eg graphite and diamond (allotropes of carbon)

ALLOTROPY *noun* **ALLOTROPIES** the existence of an element in allotropes

ALLOW *verb* **ALLOWS, ALLOWING, ALLOWED** to permit (someone to do something, something to happen, etc)

ALLOWABLE *adj* able to be admitted or accepted

ALLOWABLY *adverb* in an allowable way

ALLOWANCE *noun* **ALLOWANCES** a fixed sum of money, amount of something, etc given regularly

ALLOY *noun* **ALLOYS** a material consisting of a mixture of two or more metals, or a metal and a non-

metal, eg steel, bronze, brass □ *verb* **ALLOYS, ALLOYING, ALLOYED** to mix (one metal with another)

ALLSPICE *noun* **ALLSPICES** an aromatic spice prepared from the dried unripe berries of a small tropical evergreen tree, used to flavour foods, especially meat

ALLUDE *verb* **ALLUDES, ALLUDING, ALLUDED** to mention something indirectly or speak about it in passing

ALLURE *noun* **ALLURES** attractiveness, appeal or charm □ *verb* **ALLURES, ALLURING, ALLURED** to attract, charm or fascinate

ALLURING *adj* enticing; seductive; attractive

ALLUSION *noun* **ALLUSIONS** any indirect reference to something else

ALLUSIVE *adj* referring indirectly to something

ALLUVIAL *adj* of or derived from alluvium

ALLUVIUM *noun* **ALLUVIA** fine particles of silt, clay, mud and sand that are carried and deposited by rivers

ALLY *noun* **ALLIES** a country, state, sovereign, etc that has formally agreed to help and support another, especially in times of war □ *verb* **ALLIES, ALLYING, ALLIED** said of a country, state, sovereign, etc: to join or become joined politically or militarily with another, especially with a formal agreement

ALMANAC *noun* **ALMANACS** a book, published yearly, with a calendar, information about the phases of the Moon and stars, dates of religious festivals, public holidays, etc

ALMIGHTY *adj* having complete power □ *adverb* extremely

ALMOND *noun* **ALMONDS** a kind of small tree related to the peach; the nut-like seed from the fruit of this tree

ALMONER *noun* **ALMONERS** a medical social worker

ALMOST *adverb* nearly but not quite

ALMS *plural noun* charity donations of money, food, etc to the poor

ALOE *noun* **ALOES** any of various succulent African plants with tall trunk-like stems, long sword-shaped fleshy leaves with spiny edges, and bell-shaped or tubular yellow to red flowers

ALOFT *adverb* in the air; overhead

ALOHA *exclamation* in Hawaii and the S Pacific: an exclamation made when meeting or parting from someone

ALONE *adj* by oneself □ *adverb* by oneself

ALONG *adverb* in some direction □ *prep* by the side of something or near something

ALONGSIDE *prep* close to the side of something □ *adverb* to or at the side

ALOOF *adj* unfriendly and distant □ *adverb* away; apart; distant

ALOOFLY *adverb* in an aloof way

ALOOFNESS *noun* **ALOOFNESSES** the state of being aloof

ALOPECIA *noun* **ALOPECIAS** baldness, either of the hereditary type, such as the normal gradual loss of head hair in men, or of the type caused by disease or old age

ALOUD *adverb* loud enough to be able to be heard; not silently

ALP *noun* **ALPS** a high mountain

ALPACA *noun* **ALPACAS** a herbivorous hoofed S American mammal, closely related to the llama, reared mainly for its long straight fleece

ALPENHORN *noun* **ALPENHORNS** a long straight or slightly curved horn, made of wood and bark with an upturned bell and used in the Alps for calling cattle home from the hillside or as a musical instrument

ALPHA *noun* **ALPHAS** the first letter of the Greek alphabet

ALPHABET *noun* **ALPHABETS** a set of letters, characters, symbols, etc, usually arranged in a fixed order that, by convention, are used to represent the spoken form of a language in writing and printing

ALPHORN *noun* **ALPHORNS** an alpenhorn

ALPINE *adj* belonging or relating to alps or high mountains □ *noun* **ALPINES** a plant that grows in high mountain areas

ALREADY *adverb* before the present time or the time in question

ALRIGHT *adj* unhurt; safe; feeling fine

ALS *adverb* an obsolete form of *also* or *as*

ALSO *adverb* in addition; as well as

ALT *noun* **ALTS** a high tone in a voice or instrument

ALTAR *noun* **ALTARS** a table, raised structure, etc where sacrifices are made to a god; a communion table

ALTER *verb* **ALTERS, ALTERING, ALTERED** to change; to become, or make something or someone become, different

ALTERABLE *adj* able to be changed

ALTERCATE *verb* **ALTERCATES, ALTERCATING, ALTERCATED** to argue or dispute, especially angrily, heatedly, etc

ALTERNATE *adj* said of two feelings, states, conditions, etc: arranged or coming one after the other in turn □ *verb* **ALTERNATES, ALTERNATING, ALTERNATED** said of two things: to succeed or make them succeed each other by turns □ *noun* **ALTERNATES** a substitute, especially a person who covers in someone's absence

ALTHAEA *noun* **ALTHAEAS** a plant such as the hollyhock and marshmallow that has bright, usually pink, flowers

ALTHEA *noun* **ALTHEA** althaea

ALTHORN *noun* **ALTHORNS** a brass instrument of the saxhorn family

ALTHOUGH *conj* in spite of the fact that; apart from the fact that; though

ALTIMETER *noun* **ALTIMETERS** a device used in aircraft for measuring height above sea or ground level

ALTITUDE *noun* **ALTITUDES** height, especially above sea level, of a mountain, aircraft, etc

ALTO *noun* **ALTOS** the lowest female singing voice □ *adj* said of a musical instrument, etc: having a high pitch

ALTRICIAL *adj* said of a bird: that produces chicks that hatch at a relatively immature stage, without feathers and blind, and so needing a great deal of parental care

ALTRUISM *noun* **ALTRUISMS** an unselfish concern for the welfare of others

ALTRUIST *noun* **ALTRUISTS** someone who shows altruism

ALULA *noun* **ALULAE** a group of feathers, usually three to six in number, that grows from the first digit in some birds

ALUM *noun* **ALUMS** aluminium potassium sulphate, a white

crystalline compound used in dyeing and tanning, and as a medical astringent to stop bleeding

ALUMINA *noun* **ALUMINAS** a white crystalline compound that is the main ingredient of bauxite and that also occurs in the form of the mineral

ALUMINISE *verb* **ALUMINISES, ALUMINISING, ALUMINISED** to aluminize

ALUMINIUM *noun* **ALUMINIUMS** a silvery-white light metallic element that forms strong alloys which are used in the construction of aircraft and other vehicles, door and window frames, household utensils, drink cans, etc

ALUMINIZE *verb* **ALUMINIZES, ALUMINIZING, ALUMINIZED** to coat (a mirror or other surface) with aluminium

ALUMINOUS *adj* consisting of, containing or resembling alum, alumina or aluminium

ALUMINUM *noun* **ALUMINUMS** aluminium

ALUMNA *noun* **ALUMNAE** a female alumnus

ALUMNUS *noun* **ALUMNI** a former pupil or student of a school, college or university

ALVEOLAR *adj* referring or relating to the sockets in the upper jaw where the teeth are held in place

ALVEOLUS *noun* **ALVEOLI** in the lungs: any of the millions of tiny thin-walled air sacs in which oxygen from inhaled air is exchanged for carbon dioxide from the bloodstream

ALWAYS *adverb* on every occasion

ALYSSUM *noun* **ALYSSUMS** any of various low-growing bushy plants with narrow leaves and white, yellow or purple cross-shaped flowers, widely cultivated as an ornamental plant

AM a form of **be**

AMADAVAT *noun* **AMADAVATS** a small Indian songbird related to the weaverbirds

AMALGAM *noun* **AMALGAMS** a mixture or blend

AMANITA *noun* **AMANITAS** any of various fungi some of which, eg fly agaric, are poisonous

AMARANTH *noun* **AMARANTHS** any of various species of plant that produce spikes of small brightly coloured flowers

AMARETTO *noun* **AMARETTOS** an

almond-flavoured liqueur from Italy

AMARYLLIS noun **AMARYLLISES** any of various plants, especially a S African species with strap-shaped leaves and large pink or white trumpet-shaped scented flowers

AMASS verb **AMASSES, AMASSING, AMASSED** to gather or collect (money, possessions, knowledge, points, etc), especially in great quantity

AMATEUR noun **AMATEURS** someone who takes part in a sport, pastime, etc as a hobby and without being paid for it

AMATORIAL adj of or relating to a lover or sexual love

AMATORY adj belonging or relating to, or showing, sexual love or desire

AMAUROSIS noun **AMAUROSES** an eye condition that affects the optic nerve and which results in partial or total blindness, often without any external signs of damage to the eye

AMAZE verb **AMAZES, AMAZING, AMAZED** to surprise someone greatly; to astonish them

AMAZED adj surprised; astonished

AMAZEDLY adverb in an amazed way

AMAZEMENT noun **AMAZEMENTS** astonishment mingled with wonder

AMAZING adj astonishing; wonderful

AMAZINGLY adverb extremely; astonishingly

AMAZON noun **AMAZONS** a female soldier

AMAZONIAN adj relating to or like an amazon

AMBER noun **AMBERS** a transparent yellow or reddish fossilized resin that was exuded by coniferous trees, often carved and polished and used to make jewellery, ornaments, etc, and which sometimes contains insects, etc trapped within it

AMBERGRIS noun **AMBERGRISES** a pale-grey waxy substance with a strong smell, produced in the intestines of sperm whales, and widely used until recently in the perfume industry

AMBERJACK noun **AMBERJACKS** any of several varieties of tropical and subtropical fish that live in the Atlantic

AMBEROID noun **AMBEROIDS** amberoid

AMBIANCE noun **AMBIANCES** ambience

AMBIENCE noun **AMBIENCES** the surroundings or atmosphere of a place

AMBIENT adj said of air, temperature, etc: surrounding

AMBIGUITY noun **AMBIGUITIES** uncertainty of meaning

AMBIGUOUS adj having more than one possible meaning; not clear

AMBIT noun **AMBITS** range or extent

AMBITION noun **AMBITIONS** a strong desire for success, fame or power

AMBITIOUS adj having a strong desire for success, etc

AMBLE verb **AMBLES, AMBLING, AMBLED** to walk without hurrying; to stroll □ noun **AMBLES** a leisurely walk

AMBLYOPIA noun **AMBLYOPIAS** a form of vision impairment, especially one that is caused by damage to the retina or optic nerve by noxious substances

AMBROID noun **AMBROIDS** amber that has been moulded or pressed and combined with other substances

AMBROSIA noun **AMBROSIAS** in Greek mythology: the food of the gods, believed to give them eternal youth and beauty

AMBROSIAL adj fragrant; delicious

AMBROSIAN adj ambrosial

AMBULANCE noun **AMBULANCES** a specially equipped vehicle for carrying sick or injured people to hospital

AMBULANT adj said especially of someone who is sick or injured: walking or able to walk

AMBUSCADE verb **AMBUSCADES, AMBUSCADING, AMBUSCADED** to ambush □ noun **AMBUSCADES** an ambush

AMBUSH noun **AMBUSHES** the act of lying in wait to attack someone by surprise □ verb **AMBUSHES, AMBUSHING, AMBUSHED** to lie in wait for someone or attack them by surprise

AMEBA noun **AMEBAS, AMEBAE** an amoeba

AMEBIC adj amoebic

AMEER noun **AMEERS** amir

AMEN exclamation usually said at the end of a prayer, hymn, etc: so be it

AMENABLE adj ready to accept (someone else's idea, proposal, advice, guidance, etc)

AMENABLY adverb in an amenable way

AMEND verb **AMENDS, AMENDING, AMENDED** to correct, improve or make minor changes to (especially a book, document, etc)

AMENDABLE adj able to be amended

AMENDMENT noun **AMENDMENTS** an addition or alteration, especially to a motion, official document, etc

AMENITY noun **AMENITIES** a valued public facility

AMERICIUM noun **AMERICIUMS** a silvery-white radioactive metallic element that occurs naturally in trace amounts and is produced artificially by bombarding plutonium with neutrons

AMETHYST noun **AMETHYSTS** a pale- to deep-purple transparent or translucent variety of the mineral quartz used as a gemstone

AMI noun **AMIS** French word for *friend*

AMIABLE adj friendly, pleasant and good-tempered

AMIABLY adverb in an amiable way

AMIANTHUS noun **AMIANTHUSES** a variety of silky asbestos

AMIANTUS noun **AMIANTUSES** amianthus

AMICABLE adj friendly

AMICABLY adverb in an amicable way

AMID prep in the middle of something; among

AMIDE noun **AMIDES** any member of a class of organic compounds that contain the $CONH_2$ group, formed when one or more of the hydrogen atoms of ammonia is replaced by an acyl group

AMIDSHIPS adverb in, into or near the middle of a ship

AMIDST prep amid

AMIGO noun **AMIGOS** especially in Spanish-speaking areas: a term used to address a friend or comrade

AMINE noun **AMINES** any member of a class of organic compounds, produced by decomposing organic matter, in which one or more of the hydrogen atoms of ammonia has been replaced by an organic group

AMIR noun **AMIRS** the title borne by certain Muslim princes

AMISS adj wrong; out of order ▫ adverb wrongly

AMITOSIS noun **AMITOSES** a simple form of cell division in which normal chromosome formation and separation do not occur

AMITOTIC adj of or relating to amitosis

AMITY noun **AMITIES** friendship; friendliness

AMMETER noun **AMMETERS** a device used for measuring electric current in a circuit, usually in amperes

AMMO noun **AMMOS** short form of ammunition

AMMONIA noun **AMMONIAS** a colourless pungent gas formed naturally by the bacterial decomposition of proteins, etc, and also manufactured industrially, used in liquefied form as a refrigerant, and in the form of its compounds in fertilizers and explosives

AMMONITE noun **AMMONITES** an extinct marine cephalopod mollusc with a flat, tightly coiled shell, widespread during the Mesozoic era

AMMONIUM noun **AMMONIUMS** a positively charged ion formed by the reaction of ammonia with acid, found in many salts

AMNESIA noun **AMNESIAS** the loss or impairment of memory, caused by physical injury, disease, drugs or emotional trauma

AMNESIAC noun **AMNESIACS** someone suffering from amnesia

AMNESIC adj relating to amnesia

AMNESTY noun **AMNESTIES** a general pardon, especially for people convicted or accused of political crimes

AMNIO noun **AMNIOS** short form of amniocentesis

AMNION noun **AMNIA** the innermost membrane that surrounds the embryo of mammals, birds and reptiles

AMOEBA noun **AMOEBAS**, **AMOEBAE** any of numerous microscopic protozoan animals, including some disease-causing parasites, that inhabit water or damp soil and have no fixed shape,

but move by continually pushing out bulging parts in different directions

AMOEBIC adj of or concerning amoebae

AMOK adverb violently and out of control

AMONG prep used of more than two things, people, etc: in the middle of them

AMONGST prep among

AMORAL adj having no moral standards or principles

AMORIST noun **AMORISTS** a lover

AMOROSO noun **AMOROSOS** a deep-coloured sweet sherry

AMOROUS adj showing, feeling or relating to love, especially sexual love

AMOROUSLY adverb in an amorous way

AMORPHOUS adj without definite shape or structure

AMORTISE verb **AMORTISES**, **AMORTISING**, **AMORTISED** to amortize

AMORTIZE verb **AMORTIZES**, **AMORTIZING**, **AMORTIZED** to gradually pay off (a debt) by regular payments of money

AMOUNT noun **AMOUNTS** a quantity; a total or extent ▫ verb **AMOUNTS**, **AMOUNTING**, **AMOUNTED** to be equal to something or add up to it in size, number, significance, etc

AMOUR noun **AMOURS** a love affair, especially one that is kept secret

AMP noun **AMPS** an ampere; an amplifier

AMPERAGE noun **AMPERAGES** the magnitude or strength of an electric current expressed in amperes

AMPERE noun **AMPERES** the SI unit of electric current

AMPERSAND noun **AMPERSANDS** the symbol & which means 'and'

AMPHIBIAN noun **AMPHIBIANS** any of numerous cold-blooded vertebrates belonging to the class amphibia, eg frogs, toads and newts, the adults of which live partly or entirely on land but return to water to lay their eggs; a vehicle that can operate both on land or in water ▫ adj referring or relating to animals or vehicles which can live or operate both on land and in water

AMPHIBOLE noun **AMPHIBOLES** any of various complex silicate

minerals that are widely distributed in igneous and metamorphic rocks, eg hornblende

AMPHIBOLY noun **AMPHIBOLIES** a piece of language whose grammatical construction makes the meaning ambiguous, as in *She could see the girl with her binoculars*

AMPHIPOD noun **AMPHIPODS** any of numerous species belonging to an order of crustaceans with different pairs of legs adapted for swimming, walking or jumping, eg sandhoppers, freshwater shrimps

AMPHORA noun **AMPHORAE** a large narrow-necked Greek or Roman jar with a handle on either side, used for storing liquids such as wine or oil

AMPHORIC adj sounding like the noise of someone blowing into a bottle

AMPLE adj **AMPLER**, **AMPLEST** more than enough; plenty

AMPLIFIER noun **AMPLIFIERS** an electronic device that amplifies the strength of an electrical or radio signal without appreciably altering its characteristics, used in audio equipment, radio and television sets, etc

AMPLIFY verb **AMPLIFIES**, **AMPLIFYING**, **AMPLIFIED** to increase the strength of (an electrical or radio signal) by transferring power from an external energy source

AMPLITUDE noun **AMPLITUDES** spaciousness, wide range or extent

AMPLY adverb widely or extensively

AMPOULE noun **AMPOULES** a small sealed container, usually of glass or plastic, containing one sterile dose of a drug for injection

AMPULE noun **AMPULES** an ampoule

AMPULLA noun **AMPULLAE** the dilated end of a duct or canal

AMPUTATE verb **AMPUTATES**, **AMPUTATING**, **AMPUTATED** to remove (all or part of a limb), usually in cases of severe injury, or following death or decay of the tissue caused by gangrene or frostbite

AMPUTEE noun **AMPUTEES** someone who has had a limb surgically removed

AMRITA noun **AMRITAS** an ambrosial drink of the gods

believed to bestow immortality

AMULET noun **AMULETS** a small object, charm or jewel worn to protect the wearer from witchcraft, evil, disease, etc

AMUSE verb **AMUSES, AMUSING, AMUSED** to make someone laugh

AMUSED adj made to laugh

AMUSEDLY adverb in an amused way

AMUSEMENT noun **AMUSEMENTS** the state of being amused

AMUSING adj mildly funny, diverting or entertaining

AMUSINGLY adverb in an amusing way

AMYGDALA noun **AMYGDALAS** an almond-shaped body part, such as a lobe of the cerebellum or one of the palatal tonsils

AMYGDALE noun **AMYGDALES** a cavity formed by escaping gas in a lava flow which then becomes filled with a mineral such as quartz

AMYGDULE noun **AMYGDULES** an amygdale

AMYLASE noun **AMYLASES** any of various enzymes present in digestive juices, which play a part in the breakdown of starch and glycogen

AMYTAL noun **AMYTALS** a white crystalline powder used as a sedative

AN indefinite article used before a vowel or vowel sound: used chiefly with a singular noun, usually where the thing referred to has not been mentioned before, or where it is not a specific example known to the speaker or listener

ANA noun **ANAS** a collection of anecdotes, literary gossip, special possessions, etc, especially one that belongs or relates to an author

ANABAS noun **ANABASES** an E Indian fish that sometimes leaves the water and has even been known to climb trees in search of prey

ANABLEPS noun **ANABLEPSES** any of several varieties of bony fish with open air-bladders and projecting eyes that are divided in two, each part being specialized for seeing either in the water or out of it

ANABOLIC adj relating to anabolism

ANABOLISM noun **ANABOLISMS** in the cells of living organisms: the process whereby complex molecules such as proteins, fats and carbohydrates are

manufactured from smaller molecules

ANACONDA noun **ANACONDAS** the largest snake, a non-venomous constrictor of the boa family, native to tropical S America, which has an olive green body covered with large round black spots

ANAEMIA noun **ANAEMIAS** an abnormal reduction in the amount of the oxygen-carrying pigment haemoglobin in the red blood cells, characterized by pallid skin, fatigue and breathlessness, and caused by blood loss, iron deficiency, etc

ANAEMIC adj suffering from anaemia

ANAEROBE noun **ANAEROBES** any organism that does not require oxygen in order to obtain energy from the breakdown of carbohydrates or other foodstuffs, or that cannot survive in the presence of oxygen

ANAEROBIC adj denoting an organism, especially a bacterium, that does not require oxygen in order to obtain energy from the breakdown of carbohydrates or other foodstuffs by the process of respiration, or that cannot survive in the presence of oxygen

ANAGLYPH noun **ANAGLYPHS** an ornament, such as a cameo, in low relief

ANAGRAM noun **ANAGRAMS** a word, phrase or sentence that is formed by changing the order of the letters of another word, phrase or sentence

ANAL adj relating to or in the region of the anus

ANALGESIA noun **ANALGESIAS** a reduction in or loss of the ability to feel pain, without loss of consciousness or deadening of sensation, either deliberately induced by pain-killing drugs, eg aspirin, or a symptom of diseased or damaged nerves

ANALGESIC noun **ANALGESICS** any drug or other agent that relieves pain, eg paracetamol, morphine

ANALLY adverb by way of the anus

ANALOG adj analogue ◻ noun **ANALOGS** an analogue

ANALOGISE verb **ANALOGISES, ANALOGISING, ANALOGISED** to analogize

ANALOGIZE verb **ANALOGIZES, ANALOGIZING, ANALOGIZED** to

use analogy, especially in order to clarify a point or for rhetorical effect

ANALOGOUS adj similar or alike in some way

ANALOGUE noun **ANALOGUES** something regarded in terms of its similarity or parallelism to something else ◻ adj said of a device or physical quantity: changing continuously rather than in a series of discrete steps, and therefore capable of being represented by an electric voltage

ANALOGY noun **ANALOGIES** a likeness or similarity in some ways

ANALYSAND noun **ANALYSANDS** someone who is being psychoanalyzed

ANALYSE verb **ANALYSES, ANALYSING, ANALYSED** to examine the structure or content of something in detail, eg to examine data in order to discover the general principles underlying a particular phenomenon

ANALYSIS noun **ANALYSES** a detailed examination of the structure and content of something

ANALYST noun **ANALYSTS** someone who is skilled in analysis, especially chemical, political or economic

ANALYTIC adj concerning or involving analysis

ANALYZE verb **ANALYZES, ANALYZING, ANALYZED** to analyse

ANAMNESIS noun **ANAMNESES** the ability to remember past events; recollection

ANAPAEST noun **ANAPAESTS** in verse: a metrical foot that consists of two short or unstressed syllables followed by a long or stressed one

ANAPHASE noun **ANAPHASES** the stage of mitosis during which the chromosomes move to opposite ends of the cell

ANAPHORA noun **ANAPHORAS** the repetition of a word or group of words at the start of a sequence of clauses, sentences, lines of poetry, etc

ANAPHORIC adj referring to a preceding word or group of words

ANARCHIC adj refusing to obey any rules

ANARCHISM noun **ANARCHISMS** the teaching of the anarchists

ANARCHIST noun **ANARCHISTS** someone who believes that governments and laws are unnecessary and should be abolished

ANARCHY noun **ANARCHIES** confusion and lack of order

ANATHEMA noun **ANATHEMAS** someone or something that is detested or abhorred

ANATOMIST noun **ANATOMISTS** a scientist who specializes in anatomy

ANATOMY noun **ANATOMIES** the scientific study of the structure of living organisms, including humans, especially as determined by dissection and microscopic examination

ANATTO noun **ANATTOS** an American tree that produces pulpy seeds from which a yellowish-red dye is obtained

ANCESTOR noun **ANCESTORS** someone, usually more distant than a grandparent, from whom a person is directly descended

ANCESTRAL adj belonging to or inherited from one's ancestors

ANCESTRY noun **ANCESTRIES** lineage or family descent, especially when it can be traced back over many generations

ANCHOR noun **ANCHORS** a heavy piece of metal attached by a cable to a ship and put overboard so that the barbs catch in the seabed or riverbed to restrict the ship's movement ◻ verb **ANCHORS, ANCHORING, ANCHORED** to fasten (a ship) using an anchor

ANCHORAGE noun **ANCHORAGES** a place where a ship may anchor

ANCHORITE noun **ANCHORITES** someone who lives alone or separate from other people, usually for religious reasons

ANCHOVY noun **ANCHOVIES** any of numerous species of small fish related to the herring, with a pungent flavour, widely used as a flavouring for fish pastes and other foods

ANCIENT adj dating from very long ago ◻ noun **ANCIENTS** someone who lived in ancient times, especially applied to the Greeks, Romans and Hebrews

ANCIENTLY adverb in or from ancient times

ANCILLARY adj helping or giving support to something else, eg medical services ◻ noun **ANCILLARIES** someone or something used as support or back-up

AND conj used to show addition ◻ noun **ANDS** an unspecified problem or matter

ANDANTE adj played, etc in a slow, steady manner ◻ adverb in a slow, steady manner ◻ noun **ANDANTES** a piece of music to be played in this way

ANDIRON noun **ANDIRONS** a decorated iron bar, usually one of a pair, for supporting logs and coal in a big fireplace

ANDROGEN noun **ANDROGENS** any of a group of steroid hormones, produced mainly by the testes, that control the growth and functioning of the male sex organs and the appearance of male secondary sexual characteristics

ANDROID noun **ANDROIDS** a robot that resembles a human being in form or features ◻ adj relating to or resembling a human being

ANDROLOGY noun **ANDROLOGIES** the branch of medicine concerned with the diagnosis and treatment of diseases and disorders that affect the reproductive organs of the male body

ANE noun **ANES** a Scots word for one

ANECDOTAL adj consisting of or in the nature of anecdotes

ANECDOTE noun **ANECDOTES** a short entertaining account of an incident

ANECHOIC adj denoting a room, chamber, etc, in which there is little or no reflection of sound, and hence no echoes

ANEMIA noun **ANEMIAS** anaemia

ANEMONE noun **ANEMONES** any of several plants of the buttercup family, especially a cultivated species with red, purple, blue or white cup-shaped flowers on tall slender stems

ANEROID noun **ANEROIDS** a type of barometer used to measure atmospheric pressure and to estimate altitude

ANEURISM noun **ANEURISMS** a balloon-like swelling in the wall of an artery, caused by a congenital defect in the muscular wall, or by a disorder such as arteriosclerosis

ANEURYSM noun **ANEURYSMS** an aneurism

ANEW adverb once more, again

ANGEL noun **ANGELS** a messenger or attendant of God

ANGELIC adj said of someone's face, expression, temperament, behaviour, etc: like that of an angel, especially in being pure, innocent, beautiful, etc

ANGELICA noun **ANGELICAS** any of various tall perennial plants with leaves divided into oval leaflets, and clusters of white or greenish flowers

ANGELUS noun **ANGELUSES** a Roman Catholic prayer said in the morning, at noon and at sunset, in honour of the Incarnation

ANGER noun **ANGERS** a feeling of great displeasure or annoyance, usually brought on by some real or perceived injustice, injury, etc ◻ verb **ANGERS, ANGERING, ANGERED** to cause a feeling of anger in someone; to displease

ANGINA noun **ANGINAS** severe pain behind the chest-bone, often spreading to the left shoulder and arm, usually induced by insufficient blood supply to the heart muscle during exertion, which is commonly caused by thickening of the artery walls

ANGIOGRAM noun **ANGIOGRAMS** a type of x-ray photograph that is achieved by angiography (the examination and recording of the condition of blood vessels)

ANGIOMA noun **ANGIOMAS, ANGIOMATA** a benign tumour composed of a mass of blood or lymphatic vessels

ANGLE[1] noun **ANGLES** a measure of the rotation of a line about a point, usually measured in degrees, radians or revolutions

ANGLE[2] verb **ANGLES, ANGLING, ANGLED** to use a rod and line for catching fish

ANGLER noun **ANGLERS** someone who fishes with a rod and line

ANGLICISE verb **ANGLICISES, ANGLICISING, ANGLICISED** to anglicize

ANGLICISM noun **ANGLICISMS** an English word, phrase or idiom, especially one that slips into a sentence in another language

ANGLICIZE verb **ANGLICIZES, ANGLICIZING, ANGLICIZED** to make something English in form or character

ANGLING noun **ANGLINGS** the action or sport of catching fish with rod, line and hook

ANGORA noun **ANGORAS** the wool or cloth made from the soft silky wool of the angora goat ◻ *adj* denoting a breed of domestic goat that is bred for its soft silky wool, known as mohair

ANGRILY *adverb* in an angry way

ANGRY *adj* **ANGRIER, ANGRIEST** feeling or showing annoyance, resentment, wrath, disapproval, etc

ANGST *noun* **ANGSTS** a feeling of apprehension, anxiety or foreboding

ANGSTROM *noun* **ANGSTROMS** a unit of length, formerly used to measure wavelengths of electromagnetic radiation and the sizes of molecules and atoms

ANGUISH *noun* **ANGUISHES** severe mental distress or torture ◻ *verb* **ANGUISHES, ANGUISHING, ANGUISHED** to suffer or cause to suffer severe mental distress or torture

ANGULAR *adj* said of someone or part of someone's body, etc: thin and bony

ANHYDRIDE *noun* **ANHYDRIDES** any chemical compound formed by the removal of water from another compound, especially an acid

ANHYDROUS *adj* denoting a chemical compound that contains no water, especially one that lacks water of crystallization

> **ANI** *noun* **ANIS** a tropical American bird

ANICONIC *adj* said of imagery of gods, etc: not in recognizable animal or human form

ANICONISM *noun* **ANICONISMS** worship or veneration of an object that represents a deity without being an image

ANICONIST *noun* **ANICONISTS** a person who practises aniconism

ANIL *noun* **ANILS** a leguminous W Indian plant from which indigo is obtained

ANILINE *noun* **ANILINES** a colourless oily highly toxic liquid organic compound, used in the manufacture of rubber, plastics, drugs, dyes and photographic chemicals

ANIMA *noun* **ANIMAS** a Jungian term for the 'inner' personality as opposed to the personality presented in public

ANIMAL *noun* **ANIMALS** any member of the kingdom of organisms that are capable of voluntary movement, have

specialized sense organs that allow rapid response to stimuli, and lack chlorophyll and cell walls ◻ *adj* belonging or relating to, from or like, an animal

ANIMALISE *verb* **ANIMALISES, ANIMALISING, ANIMALISED** to animalize

ANIMALISM *noun* **ANIMALISMS** a display of or obsession with anything that is physical as opposed to the spiritual or intellectual

ANIMALIST *noun* **ANIMALISTS** a person who practises or believes in animalism

ANIMALITY *noun* **ANIMALITIES** someone's animal nature or behaviour

ANIMALIZE *verb* **ANIMALIZES, ANIMALIZING, ANIMALIZED** to make someone brutal or sensual

ANIMATE *verb* **ANIMATES, ANIMATING, ANIMATED** to give life to someone or something ◻ *adj* alive

ANIMATED *adj* lively; spirited; moving as if alive

ANIMATION *noun* **ANIMATIONS** liveliness; vivacity

ANIMATOR *noun* **ANIMATORS** someone who makes the original drawings that will be put together to produce an animated film or cartoon

ANIMISM *noun* **ANIMISMS** the belief that plants and natural phenomena such as rivers, mountains, etc have souls

ANIMIST *noun* **ANIMISTS** someone who believes in animism

ANIMISTIC *adj* of or relating to animism

ANIMOSITY *noun* **ANIMOSITIES** a strong dislike or hatred

ANIMUS *noun* **ANIMUSES** a feeling of strong dislike or hatred

ANION *noun* **ANIONS** any negatively charged ion, which moves towards the anode

ANIONIC *adj* of or relating to anions

ANISE *noun* **ANISES** an annual plant with small umbelliferous flowers and small greyish-brown aromatic fruits containing liquorice-flavoured seeds

ANISEED *noun* **ANISEEDS** the liquorice-flavoured seeds of the anise plant, used as a food flavouring in cakes and other baked products, sweets, liqueurs and other beverages

ANKH *noun* **ANKHS** the ancient Egyptian symbol of life in the form of a T-shaped cross with a loop above the horizontal bar

ANKLE *noun* **ANKLES** the joint that connects the leg and the foot

ANKLET *noun* **ANKLETS** a chain or ring worn around the ankle

ANKYLOSIS *noun* **ANKYLOSES** a disorder characterized by immobility or stiffening of a joint, the bones of which often become fixed in an abnormal position, as a result of injury, disease, surgery, etc

ANLAGE *noun* **ANLAGES** a group of cells that can be identified as a future body part

> **ANN** *noun* **ANNS** an old Scots word for a payment to a parish minister's widow

ANNALIST *noun* **ANNALISTS** a writer of annals

ANNALS *plural noun* yearly historical records of events

ANNATES *plural noun* a special payment made by newly-appointed bishops, etc to the pope

ANNATTO *noun* **ANNATTOS** an American tree that produces pulpy seeds from which a yellowish-red dye is obtained

ANNEAL *verb* **ANNEALS, ANNEALING, ANNEALED** to heat (a material such as metal or glass) and then slowly cool it in order to make it softer, less brittle and easier to work

ANNEALING *noun* **ANNEALINGS** the process of heating a substance and then slowly cooling it in order to make it softer, less brittle and easier to work

ANNELID *noun* **ANNELIDS** any member of a phylum of invertebrate animals that characteristically have long soft cylindrical bodies composed of many similar ring-shaped segments, eg the earthworm or the leech

ANNEX *verb* **ANNEXES, ANNEXING, ANNEXED** to take possession of land or territory, especially by conquest or occupation ◻ *noun* **ANNEXES** an annexe

ANNEXE *noun* **ANNEXES** an additional room, building, area, etc that provides supplementary space

ANNOTATE verb **ANNOTATES, ANNOTATING, ANNOTATED** to add notes and explanations to (a book, article, etc)

ANNOTATED adj said of a book, etc: augmented with explanatory or critical notes about the text, the author, etc

ANNOTATOR noun **ANNOTATORS** a person who annotates something

ANNOUNCE verb **ANNOUNCES, ANNOUNCING, ANNOUNCED** to make something known publicly

ANNOUNCER noun **ANNOUNCERS** someone who introduces programmes or reads the news on radio or TV

ANNOY verb **ANNOYS, ANNOYING, ANNOYED** to anger or distress

ANNOYANCE noun **ANNOYANCES** something that annoys

ANNOYED adj angry; irritated

ANNOYING adj irritating

ANNUAL noun **ANNUALS** a plant that germinates, flowers, produces seed, and dies within a period of one year, eg marigold ▫ adj done or happening once a year or every year

ANNUALISE verb **ANNUALISES, ANNUALISING, ANNUALISED** to annualize

ANNUALIZE verb **ANNUALIZES, ANNUALIZING, ANNUALIZED** to calculate (rates of interest, inflation, etc) for a year based on the figures for only part of it

ANNUALLY adverb every year

ANNUITY noun **ANNUITIES** a yearly grant or allowance

ANNUL verb **ANNULS, ANNULLING, ANNULLED** to declare publicly that a marriage, legal contract, etc is no longer valid

ANNULAR adj referring or relating to a ring or rings; ring-shaped

ANNULATE adj formed from or marked with rings

ANNULET noun **ANNULETS** a small ring

ANNULMENT noun **ANNULMENTS** the act of annulling

ANNULUS noun **ANNULI** the figure formed by two concentric circles on a plane surface, ie a disc with a central hole

ANODAL adj of an anode

ANODE noun **ANODES** in an electrolytic cell: the positive electrode, towards which negatively charged ions, usually in solution, are attracted

ANODIC adj of an anode

ANODISE verb **ANODISES, ANODISING, ANODISED** to anodize

ANODIZE verb **ANODIZES, ANODIZING, ANODIZED** to coat (an object made of metal, especially aluminium) with a thin protective oxide film by making that object the anode in a cell to which an electric current is applied

ANODYNE noun **ANODYNES** a medicine or drug that relieves or alleviates pain ▫ adj able to relieve physical pain or mental distress

ANOINT verb **ANOINTS, ANOINTING, ANOINTED** to put oil or ointment on (someone's head, feet, etc), usually as part of a religious ceremony, eg baptism

ANOINTED adj smeared with oil or ointment, usually as part of a religious ceremony

ANOINTER noun **ANOINTERS** a person who anoints someone

ANOMALOUS adj different from the usual; irregular; peculiar

ANOMALY noun **ANOMALIES** something that is unusual or different from what is expected

ANOMIE noun **ANOMIES** a lack of regard for the generally accepted social or moral standards either in an individual or in a social group

ANOMY noun **ANOMIES** anomie

ANON adverb some time soon

ANONYMITY noun **ANONYMITIES** the state of being anonymous

ANONYMOUS adj having no name

ANOPHELES noun **ANOPHELES** any of various kinds of mosquito many of which are germ-carrying, including the mosquito that transmits malaria

ANORAK noun **ANORAKS** a hooded waterproof jacket

ANOREXIA noun **ANOREXIAS** loss of appetite

ANOREXIC noun **ANOREXICS** someone who suffers from anorexia or anorexia nervosa

ANOSMIA noun **ANOSMIAS** loss of the sense of smell

ANOTHER pronoun one more

ANOXIA noun **ANOXIAS** a complete lack of oxygen in the tissues

ANOXIC adj causing anoxia

ANSATE adj fitted with a handle or handles or with something that will serve as a handle

ANSERINE adj referring to or like a goose

ANSWER noun **ANSWERS** something said or done in response to a question, request, letter, particular situation, etc ▫ verb **ANSWERS, ANSWERING, ANSWERED** to make a spoken or written reply to something or someone

ANT noun **ANTS** any of numerous social insects belonging to the same order as bees and wasps, characterized by the possession of elbowed antennae and a narrow waist, often equipped with a protective sting, and usually lacking wings

ANTACID noun **ANTACIDS** an alkaline substance that neutralizes excess acidity in the digestive juices of the stomach, and is used to relieve pain and discomfort caused by indigestion, peptic ulcer, etc ▫ adj said of a substance, especially a medicine: able to neutralize excess acid in the stomach

ANTBIRD noun **ANTBIRDS** a forest-dwelling bird, native to the New World tropics, so called because it follows ant armies, feeding on the insects, spiders, lizards, etc that they disturb

ANTE noun **ANTES** a stake put up by a player, usually in poker, but also in other card games, before receiving any cards ▫ verb **ANTES, ANTEING, ANTED** to put up as a stake

ANTEATER noun **ANTEATERS** any of various Central and S American mammals, related to armadillos and sloths, with a long cylindrical snout and an untidily bushy tail

ANTEDATE verb **ANTEDATES, ANTEDATING, ANTEDATED** to belong to an earlier period than (some other date)

ANTEFIX noun **ANTEFIXES** an ornamental tile, etc used, especially in ancient buildings, to cover up the place at the eaves and cornices where the ordinary roof tiles end

ANTELOPE noun **ANTELOPES** any of various species of hoofed mammal with a smooth brown or grey coat and usually with paired horns, found mainly in Africa, eg gazelle, springbok, gnu

ANTENATAL adj formed or occurring before birth

ANTENNA noun **ANTENNAE, ANTENNAS** in certain invertebrate animals, especially insects and crustaceans: one of a pair of long slender jointed structures on the head which act as feelers but are also concerned with the sense of smell

ANTERIOR *adj* earlier in time

ANTEROOM *noun* **ANTEROOMS** a small room which opens into another, more important, room

ANTHELION *noun* **ANTHELIA** a luminous white spot that occasionally appears in the sky directly opposite the Sun

ANTHEM *noun* **ANTHEMS** a song of praise or celebration, especially a national anthem

ANTHER *noun* **ANTHERS** in flowering plants: the two-lobed structure at the tip of the stamen which contains the pollen sacs within which the pollen grains are produced

ANTHESIS *noun* **ANTHESES** the opening of a flower-bud

ANTHOLOGY *noun* **ANTHOLOGIES** a collection of poems, usually by different authors but with some kind of thematic link

ANTHRAX *noun* **ANTHRAXES** an acute infectious disease, mainly affecting sheep and cattle, which can be transmitted to humans by contact with infected meat, hides, excrement, etc, and is often fatal if left untreated

ANTHURIUM *noun* **ANTHURIUMS** a plant that is highly valued as a house plant because of its flamboyantly stripey leaves and its unusual spike of flowers at the end of a long slender stalk which are surrounded by a large white or red conical bract

ANTI *adj* opposed to (a particular policy, party, ideology, etc) □ *noun* **ANTIS** someone who is opposed to something, especially a particular policy, party, ideology, etc

ANTIBODY *noun* **ANTIBODIES** a protein that is produced by certain white blood cells in response to the presence in the body of an antigen, and forms an important part of the body's immune response

ANTIC *noun* **ANTICS** a playful caper or trick

ANTICLINE *noun* **ANTICLINES** a geological fold in the form of an arch, formed as a result of compressional forces acting in a horizontal plane on rock strata

ANTIDOTE *noun* **ANTIDOTES** any agent, eg a drug, that counteracts or prevents the action of a poison

ANTIGAY *adj* opposed or hostile to homosexuals or gay rights movements, activities, etc

ANTIGEN *noun* **ANTIGENS** any foreign substance (usually a protein), eg a bacterium or virus, that stimulates the body's immune system to produce antibodies

ANTIKNOCK *noun* **ANTIKNOCKS** any substance that is added to petrol in order to reduce knocking sounds in the engines of motor vehicles

ANTIMONY *noun* **ANTIMONIES** a brittle bluish-white metallic element used to increase the hardness of lead alloys, and also used in storage batteries, semiconductors, flameproofing, paints, ceramics and enamels

ANTINODE *noun* **ANTINODES** a point halfway between the nodes in a standing wave, that indicates a position of maximum displacement or intensity

ANTINOISE *adj* said of a device, product, etc: preventing noise

ANTINOMY *noun* **ANTINOMIES** a contradiction between two laws or beliefs that are reasonable in themselves

ANTIPAPAL *adj* opposed to the pope or the papal system

ANTIPASTO *noun* **ANTIPASTOS** any of a variety of cold food such as marinated vegetables and fish, pork sausage, mushroom salad, etc served either as a cocktail snack or at the beginning of a meal to sharpen the appetite

ANTIPATHY *noun* **ANTIPATHIES** a feeling of strong dislike or hostility

ANTIPHON *noun* **ANTIPHONS** a hymn or psalm sung alternately by two groups of singers

ANTIPHONY *noun* **ANTIPHONIES** the rendition of a musical piece as an antiphon

ANTIPODAL *adj* of or relating to the antipodes

ANTIPODES *plural noun* two points on the Earth's surface that are diametrically opposite each other, especially Australia and New Zealand as being opposite Europe

ANTIPOPE *noun* **ANTIPOPES** a pope elected in opposition to one already canonically chosen

ANTIQUARY *noun* **ANTIQUARIES** someone who collects, studies or

deals in antiques or antiquities

ANTIQUATED *adj* old and out of date; old-fashioned

ANTIQUE *noun* **ANTIQUES** a piece of furniture, china, etc which is old and often valuable, and is sought after by collectors □ *adj* old and often valuable

ANTIQUITY *noun* **ANTIQUITIES** ancient times, especially before the end of the Roman Empire in AD 476

ANTIRUST *adj* said of a product, etc: preventing rust

ANTISERUM *noun* **ANTISERUMS, ANTISERA** a blood serum containing antibodies that are specific for, and neutralize the effects of, a particular antigen, used in vaccines

ANTITANK *adj* said of weapons: designed to destroy or immobilize military tanks

ANTITHEFT *adj* said of a device, product, etc: preventing theft

ANTITOXIN *noun* **ANTITOXINS** a type of antibody, produced by the body or deliberately introduced into it by vaccination, which neutralizes a toxin that has been released by invading bacteria, viruses, etc

ANTITRADES *plural noun* winds that blow above and in the opposite direction to trade winds

ANTITYPE *noun* **ANTITYPES** a contrary type

ANTIVENIN *noun* **ANTIVENINS** an antidote to a venom, especially that of a snake

ANTIWAR *adj* opposed to war

ANTLER *noun* **ANTLERS** either of a pair of solid bony outgrowths, which may or may not be branched, on the head of an animal belonging to the deer family

ANTLERED *adj* having antlers

ANTONYM *noun* **ANTONYMS** a word that in certain contexts is the opposite in meaning to another word, eg *straight* has many antonyms, eg *curved, unconventional, gay, indirect*

ANTRORSE *adj* turning or pointing forward or upwards

ANTRUM *noun* **ANTRUMS** a cavity or sinus, especially in a bone

ANURIA *noun* **ANURIAS** failure or inability of the kidneys to produce urine

ANUS *noun* **ANUSES** the opening at the end of the alimentary canal, through which the faeces are expelled from the body

ANVIL noun **ANVILS** a heavy iron block on which metal objects can be hammered into shape

ANXIETY noun **ANXIETIES** a strong feeling of fear or distress which occurs as a normal response to a dangerous or stressful situation, symptoms of which may include trembling, sweating, rapid pulse rate, dry mouth, nausea, etc

ANXIOUS adj worried, nervous or fearful

ANXIOUSLY adverb in an anxious way

ANY adj one, no matter which ▫ pronoun any one or any amount ▫ adverb in any way whatever

ANYBODY pronoun any person, no matter which

ANYHOW adverb in spite of what has been said, done, etc; anyway

ANYONE pronoun anybody

ANYTHING pronoun a thing of any kind; a thing, no matter which ▫ adverb in any way; to any extent

ANYWAY conj used as a sentence connector or when resuming an interrupted piece of dialogue: and so ▫ adverb nevertheless; in spite of what has been said, done, etc

ANYWHERE adverb in, at or to any place ▫ pronoun any place

AORIST noun **AORISTS** a tense of a verb in some inflected languages, especially Greek, that expresses action in simple past time with no implications of completion, duration or repetition

AORISTIC adj of or relating to the aorist tense

AORTA noun **AORTAS** in mammals: the main artery in the body, which carries oxygenated blood from the heart to the smaller arteries that in turn supply the rest of the body

AORTIC adj of or relating to the aorta

APACE adverb quickly

APACHE noun **APACHES** a lawless ruffian or hooligan

APANAGE noun **APANAGES** appanage

APART adverb in or into pieces

APARTHEID noun **APARTHEIDS** an official state policy, especially that operating in South Africa until 1992, of keeping different races segregated in such areas as housing, education, sport, etc,

together with the privileging of one race, in the case of South Africa the White minority, over any others

APARTMENT noun **APARTMENTS** a single room in a house or flat

APATETIC adj said of the coloration or markings of an animal, etc: closely resembling those of another creature or species, or closely resembling its surroundings

APATHETIC adj feeling or showing little or no emotion; indifferent

APATHY noun **APATHIES** lack of interest or enthusiasm

APATITE noun **APATITES** a common phosphate mineral, widely distributed in small amounts in many igneous and metamorphic rocks

APE noun **APES** any of several species of primate that differ from most monkeys, and resemble humans, in that they have a highly developed brain, lack a tail and are capable of walking upright ▫ verb **APES, APING, APED** to imitate (someone's behaviour, speech, habits, etc)

APEMAN noun **APEMEN** any of various extinct primates thought to have been intermediate in development between humans and the higher apes

APERIENT adj having a mild laxative effect ▫ noun **APERIENTS** a drug or other remedy that has this effect

APERITIF noun **APERITIFS** an alcoholic drink taken before a meal to stimulate the appetite

APERTURE noun **APERTURES** a small hole or opening

APERY noun **APERIES** the conduct of someone who apes; any ape-like action

APEX noun **APEXES, APICES** the highest point or tip

APHAGIA noun **APHAGIAS** inability or unwillingness to eat

APHASIA noun **APHASIAS** loss or impairment of the ability to speak or write, or to understand the meaning of spoken or written language, which in right-handed people is caused by damage to the left side of the brain

APHELION noun **APHELIA** the point in a planet's orbit when it is farthest from the Sun

APHERESIS noun **APHERESES** the omission of a sound or syllable

(or sometimes more than one) at the beginning of a word, eg *telephone* becomes *phone*, where the missing element is sometimes suggested by an apostrophe as in *'gator* for *alligator*

APHESIS noun **APHESES** the gradual weakening and disappearance of an unstressed vowel at the beginning of a word, eg *alone* becomes *lone*

APHETIC adj resulting from aphesis

APHID noun **APHIDS** any of numerous small bugs, including serious plant pests, which have a soft pear-shaped body, a small head and slender beak-like mouthparts that are used to pierce plant tissues and suck the sap, eg greenfly, blackfly

APHIS noun **APHIDS, APHIDES** an aphid

APHONIA noun **APHONIAS** inability to speak, which may be caused by hysteria, laryngitis or some other disorder of the larynx, or by brain damage

APHORISM noun **APHORISMS** a short and often clever or humorous saying expressing some well-known truth, eg *A little knowledge is a dangerous thing*

APHORIST noun **APHORISTS** a person who creates aphorisms

APHOTIC adj said of a plant: able to grow in the absence of sunlight

APHTHA noun **APHTHAE** the small white ulcers that appear on mucus membranes in conditions such as thrush

APHYLLOUS adj said of some plants: naturally leafless

APHYLLY noun **APHYLLIES** the state of being leafless

APIAN adj referring or relating to bees

APIARIAN adj relating to bee-keeping

APIARIST noun **APIARISTS** a bee-keeper

APIARY noun **APIARIES** a place where honey bees are kept, usually for the purpose of breeding and honey production, but sometimes to aid the pollination of seed and fruit crops

APICAL adj belonging to, at or forming an apex

APIECE adverb to, for, by or from each one

APISH adj like an ape

APLASTIC adj characterized by the congenital absence or malformation of an organ or other body part

APLENTY adverb in great numbers or abundance

APLOMB noun **APLOMBS** calm self-assurance and poise

APNEA noun **APNEAS** apnoea

APNOEA noun **APNOEAS** a temporary cessation of breathing, which occurs in some adults during sleep, and in some newborn babies

APOCOPE noun **APOCOPES** the loss of pronunciation of the final sound or sounds of a word, either because they are weakly stressed, eg the gradual disappearance of the inflected endings in English, or for reasons of economy in colloquial speech, eg *television* becomes *telly*

APOCRINE adj denoting any of various sweat glands located in hairy regions of the body

APOCRYPHA plural noun those books of the Bible included in the ancient Greek and Latin versions of the Old Testament but not in the Hebrew version, and which are excluded from modern Protestant Bibles but included in Roman Catholic and Orthodox Bibles

APODAL adj said of snakes, eels, etc: lacking feet; lacking limbs, especially hind ones

APODICTIC adj proved to be true by demonstration

APODOSIS noun **APODOSES** the consequent clause in a conditional sentence or propositon, eg in *If Winter comes, can Spring be far behind?* the part following the comma is the 'apodosis'

APODOUS adj apodal

APOGAMOUS adj characterized by apogamy

APOGAMY noun **APOGAMIES** the absence of sexual reproduction as found in some species of fern where new plants can develop without the fusion of gametes

APOGEE noun **APOGEES** the point in the orbit of the Moon or an artifical satellite around the Earth when it is at its greatest distance from the Earth

APOLLO noun **APOLLOS** a stunningly handsome young man

APOLOGIA noun **APOLOGIAS** a formal statement in defence of a

belief, cause, someone's behaviour, etc

APOLOGISE verb **APOLOGISES, APOLOGISING, APOLOGISED** to apologize

APOLOGIST noun **APOLOGISTS** someone who formally defends a belief or cause

APOLOGIZE verb **APOLOGIZES, APOLOGIZING, APOLOGIZED** to acknowledge a mistake or offence and express regret for it

APOLOGY noun **APOLOGIES** an expression of regret for a mistake or offence

APOPHYGE noun **APOPHYGES** the outward curve of a column where it rises from its base or merges into its capital

APOPHYSIS noun **APOPHYSES** any naturally occurring knobbly outgrowth such as on bones, especially vertebrae, pine cone scales, moss stalks, etc

APOPLEXY noun **APOPLEXIES** the former name for a stroke caused by a cerebral haemorrhage

APORT adj on or towards the port side □ adverb on or towards the port side

APOSTASY noun **APOSTASIES** the relinquishment or rejection of one's religion or principles or of one's affiliation to a specified political party, etc

APOSTATE noun **APOSTATES** someone who rejects a religion, belief, political affiliation, etc that they previously held □ adj relating to apostasy

APOSTLE noun **APOSTLES** in Christianity: someone sent out to preach about Christ in the early church, especially one of the twelve original disciples

APOSTOLIC adj relating to the apostles in the early Christian Church, or to their teaching

APOTHEGM noun **APOTHEGMS** a short saying expressing some general truth, usually one that is snappier than an aphorism

APOTHEM noun **APOTHEMS** the perpendicular from the centre of a regular polygon to any of its sides

APPAL verb **APPALS, APPALLING, APPALLED** to shock, dismay or horrify

APPALLING adj causing feelings of shock or horror

APPANAGE noun **APPANAGES** the provision made for the maintenance of younger children,

especially the younger sons of a king

APPARATUS noun **APPARATUSES** the equipment needed for a specified purpose, especially in a science laboratory, gym, military campaign, etc

APPAREL noun **APPARELS** clothing

APPARENT adj easy to see or understand; obvious

APPEAL noun **APPEALS** an urgent or formal request for help, money, medical aid, food, etc □ verb **APPEALS, APPEALING, APPEALED** to make an urgent or formal request

APPEALING adj attractive

APPEAR verb **APPEARS, APPEARING, APPEARED** to become visible or come into sight

APPEASE verb **APPEASES, APPEASING, APPEASED** to calm, quieten, pacify, etc, especially by making some kind of concession

APPEASER noun **APPEASERS** someone who appeases

APPEASING adj pacifying; calming

APPELLANT noun **APPELLANTS** someone who makes an appeal to a higher court to review the decision of a lower one □ adj belonging, relating or referring to an appeal or appellant

APPELLATE adj concerned with appeals

APPEND verb **APPENDS, APPENDING, APPENDED** to add or attach something to a document, especially as a supplement, footnote, etc

APPENDAGE noun **APPENDAGES** anything added or attached to a larger or more important part

APPENDIX noun **APPENDIXES, APPENDICES** a section containing extra information, notes, etc at the end of a book or document

APPERTAIN verb **APPERTAINS, APPERTAINING, APPERTAINED** to belong or relate to

APPETENCE noun **APPETENCES** a craving or desire

APPETENCY noun **APPETENCIES** appetence

APPETENT adj showing an eager natural craving

APPETISE verb **APPETISES, APPETISING, APPETISED** to appetize

APPETISER noun **APPETISERS** an appetizer

APPETISING adj appetizing

APPETITE noun **APPETITES** a natural physical desire, especially for food

APPETIZE verb **APPETIZES, APPETIZING, APPETIZED** to create or whet the appetite in

APPETIZER noun **APPETIZERS** a small amount of food or drink taken before a meal to stimulate the appetite

APPETIZING adj stimulating the appetite, especially by looking or smelling delicious; tasty

APPLAUD verb **APPLAUDS, APPLAUDING, APPLAUDED** to show approval by clapping

APPLAUSE noun **APPLAUSES** approval or appreciation shown by clapping

APPLE noun **APPLES** any of numerous varieties of a small deciduous tree with pink or white flowers and edible fruit; the fruit of such a tree

APPLIANCE noun **APPLIANCES** any electrical device, usually a tool or machine, that is used to perform a specific task, especially in the home, eg a washing machine, iron or toaster

APPLICANT noun **APPLICANTS** someone who has applied for a job, a university place, a grant, etc

APPLIED adj said of a skill, theory, etc: put to practical use

APPLIQUÉ noun **APPLIQUÉS** a decorative technique whereby pieces of differently textured and coloured fabrics are cut into various shapes and stitched onto each other

APPLY verb **APPLIES, APPLYING, APPLIED** to make a formal request, proposal or submission, eg for a job

APPOINT verb **APPOINTS, APPOINTING, APPOINTED** to give someone a job or position

APPOINTED adj said of an arranged time, place, etc: fixed upon; settled in advance

APPOINTEE noun **APPOINTEES** a person appointed to a job, position or office

APPORTION verb **APPORTIONS, APPORTIONING, APPORTIONED** to share out fairly or equally

APPOSITE adj suitable; well chosen; appropriate

APPRAISAL noun **APPRAISALS** evaluation; estimation of quality

APPRAISE verb **APPRAISES, APPRAISING, APPRAISED** to decide the value or quality of (someone's skills, ability, etc)

APPRAISER noun **APPRAISERS** a person who values property

APPREHEND verb **APPREHENDS, APPREHENDING, APPREHENDED** to arrest

APPRISE verb **APPRISES, APPRISING, APPRISED** to give notice to; to inform

APPROACH verb **APPROACHES, APPROACHING, APPROACHED** to come near or nearer in space, time, quality, character, state, etc ▫ noun **APPROACHES** the act of coming near

APPROVAL noun **APPROVALS** a favourable opinion; esteem

APPROVE verb **APPROVES, APPROVING, APPROVED** to agree to or permit

APPROVING adj showing approval

APRAXIA noun **APRAXIAS** an inability to make deliberate movements with accuracy, usually as a result of brain disease

APRICOT noun **APRICOTS** a small deciduous tree with oval toothed leaves and white or pale pink flowers; the edible fruit of this tree

APRON noun **APRONS** a piece of cloth, plastic, etc tied around the waist and worn over the front of clothes to protect them

APROPOS adj said of remarks: suitable or to the point ▫ adverb by the way; appropriately

APSE noun **APSES** a semicircular recess, especially when arched and domed and at the east end of a church

APSIS noun **APSIDES** either of two points in the orbit of a planet, satellite, etc, that lie furthest from or closest to the body about which it is orbiting

APT adj **APTER, APTEST** suitable

APTEROUS adj without wings

APTERYX noun **APTERYXES** any flightless bird belonging to the kiwi family, found in New Zealand

APTITUDE noun **APTITUDES** a natural skill or talent

APTLY adverb suitably; appropriately

APTNESS noun **APTNESSES** suitability

AQUA noun **AQUAE, AQUAS** water

AQUALUNG noun **AQUALUNGS** a device that enables a diver to breathe under water, consisting of a mouth tube connected to one or more cylinders of compressed air strapped to the diver's back

AQUAPLANE noun **AQUAPLANES** a board similar to a water ski but shorter and wider so that the rider puts both feet on it while being towed along at high speed by a motor boat ▫ verb **AQUAPLANES, AQUAPLANING, AQUAPLANED** to ride on an aquaplane

AQUAPLANING noun **AQUAPLANINGS** the sport of riding aquaplanes

AQUARELLE noun **AQUARELLES** a method of painting using very transparent watercolours

AQUARIAN adj of or relating to an aquarium

AQUARIUM noun **AQUARIUMS, AQUARIA** a glass tank that fish, other water animals and water plants are kept in so that they can be observed or displayed

AQUATIC adj denoting any organism that lives or grows in, on or near water ▫ noun **AQUATICS** an aquatic animal or plant

AQUATINT noun **AQUATINTS** a method of intaglio etching that gives a transparent granular effect similar to that of watercolour ▫ verb **AQUATINTS, AQUATINTING, AQUATINTED** to etch using this technique

AQUAVIT noun **AQUAVITS** a Scandinavian spirit made from potatoes and other starch-rich plants such as grains and flavoured with caraway seeds, traditionally drunk like schnapps without being diluted

AQUEDUCT noun **AQUEDUCTS** a channel or canal that carries water, especially one that is in the form of a tall bridge across a valley, river, etc

AQUEOUS adj relating to water

AQUIFER noun **AQUIFERS** any body of water-bearing rock that is highly porous and permeable to water and can be tapped directly by sinking wells or pumping the water into a reservoir

AQUILEGIA noun **AQUILEGIAS** a columbine

AQUILINE adj relating or referring to, or like, an eagle

AQUIVER adverb in a trembling or excited state

AR noun **ARS** the letter 'R'

ARABESQUE *noun* **ARABESQUES** a position in which the dancer stands with one leg stretched out backwards and the body bent forwards from the hips

ARABICA *noun* **ARABICAS** a variety of coffee that is grown in S America, especially Brazil

ARABLE *adj* said of land: suitable or used for ploughing and growing crops

ARACHNID *noun* **ARACHNIDS** any invertebrate animal belonging to the class which includes spiders, scorpions, mites, ticks, and harvestmen

ARACHNOID *adj* relating to or resembling an arachnid □ *noun* **ARACHNOIDS** the middle of the three membranes that cover the brain and spinal cord, so called because it resembles a cobweb in texture

ARAGONITE *noun* **ARAGONITES** a mineral form of calcium carbonate that occurs in some alpine metamorphic rocks, sedimentary rocks and the shells of certain molluscs

ARAK *noun* **ARAKS** arrack

ARALIA *noun* **ARALIAS** a plant of the ivy family that is often cultivated as a decorative house plant

ARB *noun* **ARBS** a person who profits by judicious dealing in stocks and shares

ARBITER *noun* **ARBITERS** someone who has the authority or influence to settle arguments or disputes between other people

ARBITRARY *adj* capricious; whimsical

ARBITRATE *verb* **ARBITRATES, ARBITRATING, ARBITRATED** to help the parties involved in a dispute or disagreement find grounds for agreement

ARBITRESS *noun* **ARBITRESSES** a woman who arbitrates

ARBOR *noun* **ARBORS** a tree-like structure

ARBOREAL *adj* relating to or resembling a tree

ARBOREOUS *adj* densely wooded

ARBORETUM *noun* **ARBORETA** a botanical garden where trees and shrubs are grown and displayed for scientific, educational and recreational purposes

ARBOUR *noun* **ARBOURS** a shady area in a garden formed by trees or

climbing plants, usually with a seat

ARC *noun* **ARCS** a continuous section of a circle or other curve □ *verb* **ARCS, ARCKING, ARCING, ARCKED, ARCED** to form an arc

ARCADE *noun* **ARCADES** a covered walk or passage, usually lined with shops

ARCANE *adj* mysterious, secret or obscure; understood only by a few; difficult to understand

ARCANELY *adverb* in an arcane way

ARCH *adj* **ARCHER, ARCHEST** chief, principal □ *noun* **ARCHES** a curved structure forming an opening, and consisting of wedge-shaped stones or other pieces supporting each other by mutual pressure, used to sustain an overlying weight such as a roof or bridge, or for ornament □ *verb* **ARCHES, ARCHING, ARCHED** to form an arch

ARCHAIC *adj* ancient; relating or referring to, or from, a much earlier period

ARCHAISE *verb* **ARCHAISES, ARCHAISING, ARCHAISED** to archaize

ARCHAISM *noun* **ARCHAISMS** an archaic word, expression or style

ARCHAIZE *verb* **ARCHAIZES, ARCHAIZING, ARCHAIZED** to make something archaic in appearance or style

ARCHANGEL *noun* **ARCHANGELS** an angel of the highest rank

ARCHDUCHY *noun* **ARCHDUCHIES** the area ruled by an archduke

ARCHDUKE *noun* **ARCHDUKES** the title of some princes, especially formerly the son of the Emperor of Austria

ARCHED *adj* having an arch or arches

ARCHER *noun* **ARCHERS** someone who uses a bow and arrow

ARCHERY *noun* **ARCHERIES** the art or sport of shooting with a bow and arrow

ARCHETYPE *noun* **ARCHETYPES** an original model; a prototype

ARCHIL *noun* **ARCHILS** orchil

ARCHITECT *noun* **ARCHITECTS** someone who is professionally qualified to design buildings and other large structures and supervise their construction

ARCHIVAL *adj* of or relating to archives

ARCHIVE *noun* **ARCHIVES** a collection of old public

documents, records, etc □ *verb* **ARCHIVES, ARCHIVING, ARCHIVED** to store (documents, data, etc) in an archive

ARCHIVIST *noun* **ARCHIVISTS** someone who collects, keeps, catalogues, records, etc archives

ARCHIVOLT *noun* **ARCHIVOLTS** the underside curve of an arch or the decorative moulding around it

ARCHLY *adverb* cleverly; slyly; in a self-consciously playful manner

ARCHNESS *noun* **ARCHNESSES** the quality of being clever and cunning

ARCHWAY *noun* **ARCHWAYS** a passage or entrance under an arch or arches

ARCO *adverb* a direction to the player of a stringed instrument to resume using the bow after a pizzicato passage

ARCTIC *adj* belonging or relating to the Arctic, north pole or the north

ARCTOID *adj* relating to or resembling a bear

ARD *noun* **ARDS** a primitive type of plough

ARDENT *adj* enthusiastic; eager

ARDENTLY *adverb* in an ardent way

ARDOUR *noun* **ARDOURS** a great enthusiasm or passion

ARDUOUS *adj* difficult; needing a lot of work, effort or energy

ARDUOUSLY *adverb* in an arduous way; laboriously

ARE[1] a form of **be**

ARE[2] *noun* **ARES** a unit of land measure equal to 100m

AREA *noun* **AREAS** a measure of the size of any surface, measured in square units, eg m^2

ARECA *noun* **ARECAS** a tall palm tree found in SE Asia which produces the betel nut

ARENA *noun* **ARENAS** an area surrounded by seats, for public shows, sports contests, etc

AREOLA *noun* **AREOLAE** the ring of brownish or pink pigmented tissue surrounding a nipple

ARÊTE *noun* **ARÊTES** a sharp ridge or rocky ledge on the side of a mountain

ARGALI *noun* **ARGALIS** a wild sheep found in the arid mountainous regions of central Asia, the males of which have huge curly horns

ARGIL *noun* **ARGILS** white clay, especially the kind used in pottery

ARGININE *noun* **ARGININES** one of the essential amino acids found in plant and animal proteins

ARGOL *noun* **ARGOLS** the harmless crystalline potassium deposit that is left on the sides of wine vats during fermentation

ARGON *noun* a colourless odourless inert gas, one of the noble gases, used to provide inert atmospheres in light bulbs, discharge tubes, and in arc welding

ARGOT *noun* **ARGOTS** slang that is only used and understood by a particular group of people

ARGUABLE *adj* capable of being argued or disputed

ARGUABLY *adverb* in certain people's opinion (although this opinion could be disagreed with)

ARGUE *verb* **ARGUES, ARGUING, ARGUED** to put forward one's case, especially in a clear and well-ordered manner

ARGUER *noun* **ARGUERS** someone who argues

ARGUMENT *noun* **ARGUMENTS** a quarrel or unfriendly discussion

ARGYLE *noun* **ARGYLES** a diamond pattern on knitwear, etc

ARIA *noun* **ARIAS** a long accompanied song for one voice, especially in an opera or oratorio

ARID *adj* **ARIDER, ARIDEST** denoting a region or climate characterized by very low rainfall, often supporting only desert vegetation

ARIDLY *adverb* dully; uninterestingly

ARIEL *noun* **ARIELS** a type of gazelle found in W Asia and Africa

ARIETTA *noun* **ARIETTAS** a light short air, usually with no second part

ARIGHT *adverb* correctly

ARIOSO *adverb* in a melodious manner ◻ *adj* melodious ◻ *noun* **ARIOSOS, ARIOSI** a piece of music to be played in this way

ARISE *verb* **ARISES, ARISING, AROSE, ARISEN** to come into being

ARISTA *noun* **ARISTAS, ARISTAE** a bristly part found on the ears of some cereals and grasses

ARISTO *noun* **ARISTOS** short form of aristocrat

ARK *noun* **ARKS** in the Bible: the vessel built by Noah in which his family and animals survived the Flood

ARKOSE *noun* **ARKOSES** a type of sandstone that is rich in feldspar

ARM[1] *noun* **ARMS** in humans: either of the two upper limbs of the body, from the shoulders to the hands

ARM[2] *verb* **ARMS, ARMING, ARMED** to equip (with weapons)

ARMADA *noun* **ARMADAS** a fleet of ships

ARMADILLO *noun* **ARMADILLOS** a small nocturnal burrowing American mammal, the head and body of which are covered with horny plates

ARMAMENT *noun* **ARMAMENTS** weapons or military equipment

ARMATURE *noun* **ARMATURES** the moving part of an electromagnetic device in which a voltage is induced by a magnetic field, eg the rotating wire-wound coil of an electric motor or generator

ARMBAND *noun* **ARMBANDS** a strip of cloth worn round the arm, usually to indicate an official position, such as being captain of a team, or as a sign of mourning

ARMCHAIR *noun* **ARMCHAIRS** a comfortable chair with arms at each side

ARMED *adj* supplied with weapons

ARMFUL *noun* **ARMFULS** an amount that can be held in someone's arms

ARMHOLE *noun* **ARMHOLES** the opening at the shoulder of a garment where the arm goes through

ARMIGER *noun* **ARMIGERS** someone who is entitled to bear heraldic arms

ARMISTICE *noun* **ARMISTICES** an agreement between warring factions to suspend all fighting so that they can discuss peace terms; a truce

ARMLESS *adj* without arms

ARMLET *noun* **ARMLETS** a band or bracelet worn round the arm

ARMOR *noun* **ARMORS** armour

ARMORIAL *adj* relating to heraldry or coats of arms ◻ *noun* **ARMORIALS** a book that catalogues coats of arms

ARMOUR *noun* **ARMOURS** a metal or chainmail, etc suit or covering worn by men or horses to protect them against injury in battle

ARMOURED *adj* protected by armour, armour plate, etc

ARMOURER *noun* **ARMOURERS** someone whose job is to make or repair suits of armour, weapons, etc

ARMOURY *noun* **ARMOURIES** a place where weapons are kept

ARMPIT *noun* **ARMPITS** the hollow under the arm at the shoulder

ARMY *noun* **ARMIES** a large number of people armed and organized for fighting on land

ARNICA *noun* **ARNICAS** a composite plant with yellow flowers, found in N temperate and arctic zones and valued for its medicinal properties

AROMA *noun* **AROMAS** a distinctive, usually pleasant, smell that a substance has or gives off

AROMATIC *adj* having a strong, but sweet or pleasant smell ◻ *noun* **AROMATICS** anything, such as a herb, plant, drug, etc, that gives off a strong fragrant smell

AROMATISE *verb* **AROMATISES, AROMATISING, AROMATISED** to aromatize

AROMATIZE *verb* **AROMATIZES, AROMATIZING, AROMATIZED** to introduce a flavour or smell to (a product)

AROSE past form of **arise**

AROUND *adverb* on every side; in every direction ◻ *prep* on all sides of something

AROUSAL *noun* **AROUSALS** awakening (of feelings)

AROUSE *verb* **AROUSES, AROUSING, AROUSED** to cause or produce (an emotion, reaction, sexual desire or response, etc)

ARPEGGIO *noun* **ARPEGGIOS** a chord whose notes are played one at a time in rapid succession rather than simultaneously

ARQUEBUS *noun* **ARQUEBUSES** an early type of portable gun

ARRACK *noun* **ARRACKS** an alcoholic drink made in Eastern and Middle Eastern countries from grain or rice and sugar and sometimes coconut juice

ARRAIGN *verb* **ARRAIGNS, ARRAIGNING, ARRAIGNED** to bring someone (usually someone who is already in custody) to a court of law to answer a criminal charge or charges

ARRAIGNER *noun* **ARRAIGNERS** someone who arraigns

ARRANGE *verb* **ARRANGES, ARRANGING, ARRANGED** to put into the proper or desired order

ARRANGED *adj* in order, settled

ARRANT *adj* out-and-out; notorious

ARRAS *noun* **ARRASES** a colourful woven tapestry, often depicting figures and animals in outdoor scenes, especially hunting ones, used as a wall hanging or for concealing an alcove or door

ARRAY *noun* **ARRAYS** a large and impressive number, display or collection ▫ *verb* **ARRAYS, ARRAYING, ARRAYED** to put in order; to display

ARREARS *plural noun* an amount or quantity which still needs to be done or paid back

ARREST *verb* **ARRESTS, ARRESTING, ARRESTED** to take someone into custody, especially by legal authority ▫ *noun* **ARRESTS** the act of taking, or state of being taken, into custody, especially by the police

ARRESTER *noun* **ARRESTERS** a person who, or thing which, arrests

ARRESTING *adj* strikingly individual or attractive

ARRIS *noun* **ARRISES** a sharp edge on stone, metal or wood where two surfaces meet

ARRIVAL *noun* **ARRIVALS** the act of coming to a destination

ARRIVE *verb* **ARRIVES, ARRIVING, ARRIVED** to reach a place during a journey or come to a destination at the end of a journey

ARROGANCE *noun* **ARROGANCES** undue assumption of importance; conceit, self-importance

ARROGANT *adj* said of someone or their behaviour: aggressively and offensively self-assertive; having or showing too high an opinion of one's own abilities or importance; impudently over-presumptive

ARROGATE *verb* **ARROGATES, ARROGATING, ARROGATED** to claim a responsibility, power, etc without having any legal right to do so

ARROW *noun* **ARROWS** a thin straight stick with a sharp point at one end and feathers at the other, which is fired from a bow either at a scoring target as in archery, or at prey or an enemy

ARROWROOT *noun* **ARROWROOTS** a perennial plant cultivated in tropical regions for its swollen underground tubers, which produce a highly digestible form of starch

ARROWWOOD *noun* **ARROWWOODS** a N American tree with particularly straight stems which are very suitable for making arrows

ARSENAL *noun* **ARSENALS** a store for weapons, explosives, etc

ARSENIC *noun* **ARSENICS** a metalloid chemical element that occurs in three different forms, the commonest and most stable of which is a highly toxic grey shiny solid

ARSENICAL *adj* composed of or containing arsenic ▫ *noun* **ARSENICALS** a substance containing arsenic

ARSENIDE *noun* **ARSENIDES** a compound of arsenic with another element, such as hydrogen or a metal, or with an organic radical

ARSENIOUS *adj* composed of or containing arsenic

ARSENITE *noun* **ARSENITES** a salt of arsenious acid

ARSINE *noun* **ARSINES** a poisonous colourless gas used by the military

ARSON *noun* **ARSONS** the crime under English law of deliberately setting fire to a building, etc and which in Scots law is termed fire-raising

ARSONIST *noun* **ARSONISTS** someone who commits arson, especially habitually

ART[1] *noun* **ARTS** the creation of works of beauty, especially visual ones

ART[2] used with *thou*: a form of **be**

ARTEFACT *noun* **ARTEFACTS** a handcrafted object, eg a tool, a cave painting, etc, especially one that is historically or archaeologically interesting

ARTEMISIA *noun* **ARTEMISIAS** any of various aromatic herbs and shrubs with silvery hair-covered leaves and small yellow flowers, including several species with medicinal properties

ARTERIAL *adj* affecting, relating to or like an artery or arteries

ARTERIOLE *noun* **ARTERIOLES** a small artery

ARTERY *noun* **ARTERIES** a blood vessel that carries oxygenated blood from the heart to the body tissues, the only exception being the pulmonary artery, which conveys deoxygenated blood from the heart to the lungs

ARTFUL *adj* cunning, especially in being able to achieve what one wants, often by underhand means

ARTFULLY *adverb* in an artful way

ARTHRITIC *noun* **ARTHRITICS** someone who is suffering from arthritis ▫ *adj* relating to or typical of arthritis

ARTHRITIS *noun* **ARTHRITISES** inflammation of one or more joints, associated with swelling, pain, redness, local heat, and often restricted movement of the affected part

ARTHROPOD *noun* **ARTHROPODS** any invertebrate animal of the Arthropoda, the largest phylum in the animal kingdom, that includes insects, crustaceans, arachnids, and myriapods

ARTICHOKE *noun* **ARTICHOKES** a thistlelike perennial plant whose grey-green flower-head is eaten as a vegetable

ARTICLE *noun* **ARTICLES** a thing or object, especially one that has been mentioned previously ▫ *verb* **ARTICLES, ARTICLING, ARTICLED** to bind (a trainee or apprentice, especially in the legal profession) for a set number of years, at the end of which the trainee or apprentice is qualified

ARTICLED *adj* said of a trainee lawyer, accountant, etc: bound by a legal contract while working in an office to learn the job

ARTICULAR *adj* relating to or associated with a joint of the body

ARTIFACT *noun* **ARTIFACTS** an artefact

ARTIFICE *noun* **ARTIFICES** a clever trick; a crafty plan or ploy

ARTIFICER *noun* **ARTIFICERS** a skilled craftsman

ARTILLERY *noun* **ARTILLERIES** large guns for use on land

ARTISAN *noun* **ARTISANS** someone who does skilled work with their hands

ARTIST *noun* **ARTISTS** someone who produces works of art, especially paintings

ARTISTE *noun* **ARTISTES** a professional performer, especially a singer or dancer, in a theatre, circus, etc

ARTISTIC *adj* relating to or characteristic of art or artists

ARTISTRY *noun* **ARTISTRIES** artistic skill and imagination

ARTLESS *adj* simple and natural in manner

ARTLESSLY adverb in an artless way

ARTWORK noun **ARTWORKS** any original material in the form of illustrations, drawings, design, etc, produced by an artist, illustrator or designer for reproduction in a book, magazine or other printed medium

ARTY adj **ARTIER, ARTIEST** affectedly or ostentatiously artistic

ARUM noun **ARUMS** any of various perennial plants with a characteristic flower-head consisting of numerous tiny flowers around the base of a club-shaped spadix which is enclosed by a leaf-like spathe, eg cuckoo pint

ARVO noun **ARVOS** afternoon

ARY adj a dialect word for *any*

ARYL adj in an organic chemical compound: referring or relating to the group produced by removal of a hydrogen atom from an aromatic hydrocarbon

ARYTENOID noun **ARYTENOIDS** one of the cartilages in the larynx that are involved in controlling the vibrations of the vocal cords

AS conj when; while; during □ prep in the role of something □ adverb in whatever degree, proportion or manner

ASANA noun **ASANAS** any of the various positions in yoga

ASBESTOS noun **ASBESTOSES** any of a group of fibrous silicate minerals that are highly resistant to heat and chemically inert, formerly used in fireproof curtains, protective clothing, felt, plaster, roofing materials, etc, but now known to cause asbestosis and lung cancer

ASCARID noun **ASCARIDS** a parasitic nematode worm, such as the roundworm, that infests the gut of humans and pigs, causing diarrhoea, vomiting and attendant weight loss

ASCEND verb **ASCENDS, ASCENDING, ASCENDED** to climb, go or rise up

ASCENDANT adj having more influence or power □ noun **ASCENDANTS** supremacy; increasing influence or power

ASCENDENT adj ascendant □ noun **ASCENDENTS** ascendant

ASCENDER noun **ASCENDERS** someone or something that goes or climbs up

ASCENDING adj rising; moving upwards

ASCENSION noun **ASCENSIONS** an act of climbing or moving upwards

ASCENT noun **ASCENTS** the act of climbing, ascending or rising

ASCERTAIN verb **ASCERTAINS, ASCERTAINING, ASCERTAINED** to find out; to discover (the truth, etc)

ASCESIS noun **ASCESES** the custom, observance or practice of self-discipline

ASCETIC noun **ASCETICS** someone who shuns or abstains from all physical comfort and pleasure, especially someone who does so in solitude and for religious reasons □ adj characterized by the shunning of or abstinence from physical pleasure and comfort

ASCOSPORE noun **ASCOSPORES** a spore, usually one of eight, produced in the ascus of certain fungi

ASCRIBE verb **ASCRIBES, ASCRIBING, ASCRIBED** to attribute; assign

ASCUS noun **ASCI** in certain fungi: a small elongated sac-like reproductive structure that contains (usually eight) ascospores

ASEISMIC adj said of a particular geographical area: not liable to earthquakes

ASEPALOUS adj said of a plant or flower: without sepals

ASEPSIS noun **ASEPSES** the condition of being free from germs or other infection-causing micro-organisms

ASEPTIC adj not liable to, or preventing, decay or putrefaction □ noun **ASEPTICS** an aseptic substance

ASEXUAL adj denoting reproduction that does not involve sexual processes, and in which genetically identical offspring are produced from a single parent, eg budding of yeasts or vegetative propagation in plants

ASEXUALLY adverb in an asexual way

ASH noun **ASHES** the dusty residue that remains after something has been burnt

ASHAMED adj troubled by feelings of guilt, embarrassment, humiliation, etc

ASHAMEDLY adverb in an ashamed way

ASHEN adj said of a face: grey or very pale, usually from shock, illness, etc

ASHET noun **ASHETS** a large oval plate or dish, usually used for serving meat

ASHLAR noun **ASHLARS** a large square-cut stone that is used for building or facing walls

ASHLER noun **ASHLERS** an ashlar

ASHORE adverb to, towards or onto the shore or land

ASHRAM noun **ASHRAMS** a place of retreat, especially in India, for a holy-man or for a religious community, where members lead lives of austere self-discipline

ASHY adj **ASHIER, ASHIEST** consisting of ashes

ASIDE adverb on, to, towards or over to one side □ noun **ASIDES** words said by a character in a play which the audience can hear, but which the other characters cannot

ASININE adj relating to or resembling an ass

ASK verb **ASKS, ASKING, ASKED** to question someone about something

ASKANCE adverb sideways

ASKEW adj squint; not properly straight or level; awry □ adverb squint; not properly straight or level; awry

ASLEEP adj in a sleeping state □ adverb into a sleeping state

ASOCIAL adj not social; antisocial; not gregarious

ASP noun **ASPS** any of various small venomous S European snakes, often with dark slanting markings on the back of the body, and an upturned snout

ASPARAGUS noun **ASPARAGUSES** any of several species of plant with cylindrical green shoots or 'spears' that can be cooked and eaten as a vegetable

ASPARTAME noun **ASPARTAMES** an artificial sweetener, 200 times sweeter than sugar but without the bitter aftertaste of saccharin, widely used in the food industry and by diabetics and dieters

ASPECT noun **ASPECTS** a particular or distinct part or element of a problem, subject, etc

ASPECTUAL adj of or relating to aspect

ASPEN noun **ASPENS** a deciduous tree of the poplar family, widespread in Europe, with smooth greyish-brown bark and round or oval greyish-green leaves that tremble in the slightest breeze

ASPERITY *noun* **ASPERITIES** roughness, bitterness or harshness, especially of temper

ASPERSION *noun* **ASPERSIONS** calumny; slander

ASPHALT *noun* **ASPHALTS** a brown or black semi-solid bituminous material that occurs in natural deposits and is also prepared synthetically by distillation from petroleum ▫ *verb* **ASPHALTS, ASPHALTING, ASPHALTED** to cover with asphalt

ASPHALTIC *adj* containing asphalt

ASPHODEL *noun* **ASPHODELS** any of various perennial plants of the lily family, native to S Europe, with long narrow leaves and yellow or white star-shaped flowers, including many species that grow in damp habitats

ASPHYXIA *noun* **ASPHYXIAS** suffocation caused by any factor that interferes with respiration and prevents oxygen from reaching the body tissues, such as choking, drowning or inhaling poisonous gases

ASPIC *noun* **ASPICS** a savoury jelly made from meat or fish stock and sometimes flavoured with port, Madeira or sherry, and used as a glaze or to make a mould for terrines, fish, eggs, etc

ASPIRANT *noun* **ASPIRANTS** someone who works hard to achieve something, especially a position of great status ▫ *adj* trying to achieve a higher position

ASPIRATE *noun* **ASPIRATES** the sound represented in English and several other languages by the letter *h* ▫ *verb* **ASPIRATES, ASPIRATING, ASPIRATED** to pronounce a word with an *h* sound as opposed to 'dropping' it, eg to give the word *hedgehog* its full phonetic value, rather than saying *'edge'og*, as in some varieties of English

ASPIRATOR *noun* **ASPIRATORS** a device used to withdraw liquid, gas or solid debris from a cavity of the body, eg during dental treatment

ASPIRE *verb* **ASPIRES, ASPIRING, ASPIRED** to have a strong desire to achieve or reach (an objective or ambition)

ASPIRIN *noun* **ASPIRINS** an analgesic drug that is widely used to relieve mild to moderate pain and to reduce inflammation and fever, and is sometimes also used in daily doses to prevent coronary thrombosis and stroke in susceptible individuals

ASPIRING *adj* ambitious; hopeful of becoming something specified

ASS *noun* **ASSES** any of various species of hoofed mammal resembling, but smaller than, a horse, with longer ears, a grey or brownish coat, a short erect mane, and a characteristic bray

ASSAGAI *noun* **ASSAGAIS** an assegai

ASSAIL *verb* **ASSAILS, ASSAILING, ASSAILED** to make a strong physical attack

ASSAILANT *noun* **ASSAILANTS** someone who attacks something or someone, either verbally or physically

ASSAILER *noun* **ASSAILERS** someone who assails; an assailant

ASSASSIN *noun* **ASSASSINS** someone who kills someone else, especially for political or religious reasons

ASSAULT *noun* **ASSAULTS** a violent physical or verbal attack ▫ *verb* **ASSAULTS, ASSAULTING, ASSAULTED** to make an assault on someone or something

ASSAY *noun* **ASSAYS** the analysis and assessment of the composition and purity of a metal in an ore or mineral, or of a chemical compound in a mixture of compounds ▫ *verb* **ASSAYS, ASSAYING, ASSAYED** to perform such an analysis on, or to determine the commercial value of (an ore or mineral) on the basis of such an analysis

ASSEGAI *noun* **ASSEGAIS** a thin light iron-tipped wooden spear used in southern Africa

ASSEMBLE *verb* **ASSEMBLES, ASSEMBLING, ASSEMBLED** to gather or collect together

ASSEMBLER *noun* **ASSEMBLERS** a computer program designed to convert a program written in assembly language into one written in machine code

ASSEMBLY *noun* **ASSEMBLIES** a group of people gathered together, especially for a meeting

ASSENT *noun* **ASSENTS** consent or approval, especially official ▫ *verb* **ASSENTS, ASSENTING, ASSENTED** to express agreement

ASSERT *verb* **ASSERTS, ASSERTING, ASSERTED** to state firmly

ASSERTION *noun* **ASSERTIONS** a positive or strong statement or claim

ASSERTIVE *adj* said of someone or their attitude: inclined to expressing wishes and opinions in a firm and confident manner; pushy

ASSESS *verb* **ASSESSES, ASSESSING, ASSESSED** to judge the quality or importance of something

ASSESSOR *noun* **ASSESSORS** someone who assesses the importance or quality of something, eg the performance of pupils, students, workers, etc

ASSET *noun* **ASSETS** anything that is considered valuable or useful, such as a skill, quality, person, etc

ASSETS *plural noun* the total value of the property and possessions of a person or company, especially when thought of in terms of whether or not it is enough to cover any debts

ASSIDUITY *noun* **ASSIDUITIES** constant care and attention that is shown towards someone, or to what one is doing

ASSIDUOUS *adj* hard-working

ASSIGN *verb* **ASSIGNS, ASSIGNING, ASSIGNED** to give (a task, etc) to someone

ASSIGNEE *noun* **ASSIGNEES** someone to whom property, interest, etc is given by contract

ASSIGNOR *noun* **ASSIGNORS** someone who gives property, interest, etc by contract

ASSIST *verb* **ASSISTS, ASSISTING, ASSISTED** to help

ASSISTANT *noun* **ASSISTANTS** a person whose job is to help someone of higher rank, position, etc

ASSIZES *plural noun* in England and Wales: court sittings which used to be held at regular intervals in each county and which were presided over by itinerant judges, but whose criminal jurisdiction was transferred to the Crown Court under the Courts Act of 1971

ASSOCIATE *verb* **ASSOCIATES, ASSOCIATING, ASSOCIATED** to connect in the mind ▫ *noun* **ASSOCIATES** a business partner or

colleague □ *adj* joined with another, especially in a business

ASSOCIATED *adj* used in the name of a company to show that it has been formed from several smaller companies

ASSONANCE *noun* **ASSONANCES** a correspondence or resemblance in the sounds of words or syllables, either between their vowels, eg in *meet* and *bean*, or between their consonants, eg in *keep* and *cape*

ASSORTED *adj* mixed; consisting of or containing various different kinds

ASSUAGE *verb* **ASSUAGES, ASSUAGING, ASSUAGED** to make (a pain, sorrow, hunger, etc) less severe

ASSUMABLE *adj* that can be assumed or taken for granted

ASSUMABLY *adverb* as can be taken for granted

ASSUME *verb* **ASSUMES, ASSUMING, ASSUMED** to accept something without proof; to take for granted

ASSUMED *adj* false; not genuine

ASSUMEDLY *adverb* as can be taken for granted

ASSUMING *adj* said of someone or their attitude: arrogant; presumptuous □ *conj* if it is taken as a fact

ASSURABLE *adj* that can be assured

ASSURANCE *noun* **ASSURANCES** a promise, guarantee or statement that something is true

ASSURE *verb* **ASSURES, ASSURING, ASSURED** to state positively and confidently; to guarantee

ASSURED *adj* said of someone or their attitude, behaviour, etc: confident and poised

ASSUREDLY *adverb* certainly, in truth, undoubtedly

ASSURER *noun* **ASSURERS** a person who gives assurance

ASSURGENT *adj* said of stems, leaves, etc: curving or growing upwards

ASTATIC *adj* lacking the tendency to remain in a fixed position; unstable

ASTATINE *noun* **ASTATINES** a radioactive chemical element, the heaviest of the halogens, that occurs naturally in trace amounts and is produced artificially by bombarding bismuth with alpha particles

ASTER *noun* **ASTERS** any of numerous mainly perennial plants with daisy-like flower-heads consisting of a central yellow disc of true flowers surrounded by blue, purple, pink or white rays, eg Michaelmas daisy

ASTERISK *noun* **ASTERISKS** a star-shaped symbol (*) used in printing and writing: to mark a cross-reference to a footnote, an omission etc □ *verb* **ASTERISKS, ASTERISKING, ASTERISKED** to mark with an asterisk

ASTERN *adverb* in or towards the stern □ *adj* in or towards the stern

ASTEROID *noun* **ASTEROIDS** any of thousands of small rocky objects, 1km to 1000km in diameter, that orbit around the Sun, mainly between the orbits of Mars and Jupiter □ *adj* star-shaped

ASTHENIA *noun* **ASTHENIAS** a condition characterized by an abnormal lack of energy or strength; weakness

ASTHENIC *adj* characterized by or relating to asthenia □ *noun* **ASTHENICS** someone who suffers from asthenia

ASTHMA *noun* **ASTHMAS** a respiratory disorder in which breathlessness and wheezing occur, caused by excessive contraction of muscles in the walls of the air passages, most commonly associated with allergic reactions, but sometimes precipitated by infections, physical exertion, stress, etc

ASTHMATIC *adj* relating to or suffering from asthma □ *noun* **ASTHMATICS** someone who suffers from asthma

ASTIR *adj* awake and out of bed □ *adverb* awake and out of bed

ASTONISH *verb* **ASTONISHES, ASTONISHING, ASTONISHED** to surprise greatly

ASTONISHED *adj* greatly surprised

ASTONISHING *adj* wonderful or surprising; extraordinary

ASTOUND *verb* **ASTOUNDS, ASTOUNDING, ASTOUNDED** to amaze or shock

ASTOUNDED *adj* amazed or shocked

ASTOUNDING *adj* amazing or shocking

ASTRAGAL *noun* **ASTRAGALS** a small circular moulding, often round a column

ASTRAKHAN *noun* **ASTRAKHANS** a kind of fur made from the dark tightly-curled wool and skin of very young or stillborn lambs, which is used to line and trim coats, make hats, etc

ASTRAL *adj* belonging or relating to, consisting of, or like, the stars; starry

ASTRAY *adj* out of the right or expected way □ *adverb* out of the right or expected way

ASTRIDE *adverb* with a leg on each side □ *prep* with a leg on each side of something

ASTRODOME *noun* **ASTRODOMES** a transparent covering over the fuselage of an aircraft that allows astronomical observations to be made

ASTROLABE *noun* **ASTROLABES** a navigational instrument used to observe the positions of the Sun and bright stars, and to estimate the local time by determining the altitude of the Sun or specific stars above the horizon

ASTROLOGY *noun* **ASTROLOGIES** the study of the movements of the stars and planets and the interpretation of these movements in terms of how they are thought to exert influences on people's lives, character traits, etc

ASTRONAUT *noun* **ASTRONAUTS** someone who is trained to travel in a space vehicle

ASTRONOMY *noun* **ASTRONOMIES** the scientific study of celestial bodies, including the planets, stars and galaxies, as well as interstellar and intergalactic space, and the universe as a whole

ASTUTE *adj* **ASTUTER, ASTUTEST** said of someone or their ideas, attitude, etc: having or showing the ability to judge and act intelligently and decisively; mentally perceptive; shrewd

ASTUTELY *adverb* in an astute way

ASUNDER *adverb* apart or into pieces

ASYLUM *noun* **ASYLUMS** a place of safety or protection

ASYMMETRY *noun* **ASYMMETRIES** a lack of symmetry

ASYMPTOTE *noun* **ASYMPTOTES** a line, usually a straight one, which is continually approached by a curve that never actually meets the line

ASYNDETIC adj not connected by conjunctions

ASYNDETON noun **ASYNDETONS** the omission of a conjunction in a grammatical construction

ASYNERGIA noun **ASYNERGIAS** asynergy

ASYNERGY noun **ASYNERGIES** lack of co-ordination between muscles or other body parts which usually work together

ASYSTOLE noun **ASYSTOLES** absence or cessation of heartbeat

AT prep used to indicate position or place: in, within, on, near, etc

ATABRIN noun **ATABRINS** a proprietary name for the artificial anti-malarial drug mepacrine

ATAMAN noun **ATAMANS** an elected Cossack leader of a village or military division

ATARACTIC adj calm

ATARAXIA noun **ATARAXIAS** calmness

ATARAXIC adj calm

ATARAXY noun **ATARAXIES** calmness

ATAVISM noun **ATAVISMS** a resemblance to ancestors rather than immediate parents

ATAVISTIC adj relating to or resembling ancestors

ATAXIA noun **ATAXIAS** inability of the brain to co-ordinate voluntary movements of the limbs, resulting in jerky movements and a staggering gait, and caused by a disorder of the sensory nerves or by disease of the cerebellum

ATAXY noun **ATAXIES** ataxia

ATE past form of **eat**

ATEBRIN noun **ATEBRINS** a proprietary name for the artificial anti-malarial drug mepacrine

ATELIER noun **ATELIERS** a workshop or artist's studio

ATHEISM noun **ATHEISMS** the belief that there is no god

ATHEIST noun **ATHEISTS** someone who believes that there is no god

ATHEISTIC adj relating to atheism

ATHEMATIC adj in music: not composed of tunes

ATHEROMA noun **ATHEROMAS** in atherosclerosis: a fatty deposit that develops on the inner surface of an artery wall

ATHLETE noun **ATHLETES** someone who trains for and competes in field and track events such as running events, the high jump, long jump, pole vault, etc

ATHLETIC adj said of someone or their build: physically fit and strong

ATHLETICS singular noun competitive track and field sports such as running, jumping, throwing and walking events

ATHWART adverb transversely □ prep across, from side to side of

ATISHOO exclamation the sound of a sneeze □ noun **ATISHOOS** a sneeze

ATLAS noun **ATLASES** a book of maps and geographical charts

ATMAN noun **ATMANS** in Hinduism: the human soul or essential self, which, in the teachings of the Upanishads, is seen as being one with the Absolute, and is identified with Brahman

ATMOLYSIS noun **ATMOLYSES** a method of separating or partially separating mixed gases or vapours that relies on the fact that they will pass through a porous substance at different rates

ATMOMETER noun **ATMOMETERS** an instrument for measuring the amount or rate of evaporation of water from a moist surface into the atmosphere

ATOLL noun **ATOLLS** a continuous or broken circle of coral reef that surrounds a lagoon, and is itself surrounded by open sea

ATOM noun **ATOMS** the smallest unit of a chemical element that can display the properties of that element, and which is capable of combining with other atoms to form molecules

ATOMIC adj relating to atoms

ATOMICITY noun **ATOMICITIES** the number of atoms in a molecule of a chemical element

ATOMISE verb **ATOMISES, ATOMISING, ATOMISED** to atomize

ATOMISER noun **ATOMISERS** an atomizer

ATOMISM noun **ATOMISMS** a philosophical tradition that dates back to c.500 BC which maintains that everything that exists is made up of minute indivisible particles, and that all phenomena must be explained in terms of such 'fundamental particles' and their interactions

ATOMIZE verb **ATOMIZES, ATOMIZING, ATOMIZED** to reduce to atoms or small particles

ATOMIZER noun **ATOMIZERS** a container that releases liquid, containing eg perfume, medicine, etc, as a fine spray

ATONAL adj lacking tonality; not written in a particular key

ATONALISM noun **ATONALISMS** the writing of atonal music

ATONALITY noun **ATONALITIES** lack of tonality

ATONE verb **ATONES, ATONING, ATONED** to make amends for (a wrongdoing, crime, sin, etc)

ATONEMENT noun **ATONEMENTS** an act of making amends for, making up for, or paying for a wrongdoing, crime, sin, etc

ATONY noun **ATONIES** lack of normal muscle tone

ATOP adverb on top; at the top □ prep on top of, or at the top of, something

ATRIAL adj of or belonging to an atrium

ATRIUM noun **ATRIA, ATRIUMS** a central court or entrance hall in an ancient Roman house

ATROCIOUS adj very bad

ATROCITY noun **ATROCITIES** wicked or cruel behaviour

ATROPHY verb **ATROPHIES, ATROPHYING, ATROPHIED** to make or become weak and thin through lack of use or nourishment □ noun **ATROPHIES** the process of atrophying

ATROPIN noun **ATROPINS** atropine

ATROPINE noun **ATROPINES** a poisonous alkaloid drug, obtained from deadly nightshade, which is used as a premedication before general anaesthesia, as a treatment for peptic ulcers, and for dilating the pupil during eye examinations

ATTACH verb **ATTACHES, ATTACHING, ATTACHED** to fasten or join

ATTACHÉ noun **ATTACHÉS** a junior official in an embassy

ATTACHED adj joined; connected

ATTACK verb **ATTACKS, ATTACKING, ATTACKED** to make a sudden violent attempt to hurt, damage or capture; to take the initiative in a game, contest, etc to attempt to score a goal, points, etc □ noun **ATTACKS** an act or the action of attacking

ATTACKER noun **ATTACKERS** someone who makes a physical, verbal, sporting, etc attack

ATTACKING adj said of a team:

ready and willing to seize goal- or point-scoring opportunities

ATTAIN *verb* **ATTAINS, ATTAINING, ATTAINED** to complete successfully; to accomplish; to achieve

ATTAINDER *noun* **ATTAINDERS** the loss of someone's civil rights following their conviction for felony or for an act of treason

ATTAR *noun* **ATTARS** a fragrant essential oil that is distilled from rose petals, especially those of the damask rose

ATTEMPT *verb* **ATTEMPTS, ATTEMPTING, ATTEMPTED** to try □ *noun* **ATTEMPTS** an effort; an endeavour

ATTEND *verb* **ATTENDS, ATTENDING, ATTENDED** to be present at something

ATTENDANT *noun* **ATTENDANTS** someone whose job is to help, guide or give some other service, especially to the public □ *adj* being in or giving attendance

ATTENDER *noun* **ATTENDERS** a person who pays attention or is attentive

ATTENTION *noun* **ATTENTIONS** the act of concentrating or directing the mind

ATTENTIVE *adj* said of someone or their attitude: characterized by showing close concentration; alert and watchful

ATTENUATE *verb* **ATTENUATES, ATTENUATING, ATTENUATED** to make or become thin and weak

ATTENUATED *adj* thin

ATTEST *verb* **ATTESTS, ATTESTING, ATTESTED** to affirm or be proof of the truth or validity of something

ATTESTED *adj* said of a fact, statement, etc: supported by evidence or proof

ATTIC *noun* **ATTICS** a space or room at the top of a house under the roof

ATTIRE *noun* **ATTIRES** clothes, especially formal or elegant ones □ *verb* **ATTIRES, ATTIRING, ATTIRED** to dress or adorn or be dressed or adorned

ATTITUDE *noun* **ATTITUDES** a way of thinking or behaving

ATTORNEY *noun* **ATTORNEYS** someone able to act for another in legal or business matters

ATTRACT *verb* **ATTRACTS, ATTRACTING, ATTRACTED** to cause (attention, notice, a crowd,

interest, etc) to be directed towards oneself, itself, etc

ATTRIBUTE *noun* **ATTRIBUTES** a quality, characteristic, feature, etc, usually one that has positive or favourable connotations □ *verb* **ATTRIBUTES, ATTRIBUTING, ATTRIBUTED** to think of something as being written, made, said, or caused by someone or something

ATTRITION *noun* **ATTRITIONS** a rubbing together; friction

ATTUNE *verb* **ATTUNES, ATTUNING, ATTUNED** to adjust to or prepare for (a situation, etc)

ATYPICAL *adj* not typical, representative, usual, etc

AUBERGINE *noun* **AUBERGINES** the large cylindrical or egg-shaped edible fruit of the aubergine plant, with a smooth skin that is deep purple in colour □ *adj* deep purple in colour

AUBRIETIA *noun* **AUBRIETIAS** any of numerous varieties of dwarf perennial plant with greyish leaves and purple, lilac, blue or pink cross-shaped flowers, widely cultivated as an ornamental plant in rock gardens

AUBURN *adj* especially said of hair: reddish-brown

AUCTION *noun* **AUCTIONS** a public sale in which each item is sold to the person who offers the most money □ *verb* **AUCTIONS, AUCTIONING, AUCTIONED** to sell something in an auction

AUDACIOUS *adj* bold and daring

AUDACITY *noun* **AUDACITIES** boldness

AUDIBLE *adj* loud enough to be heard

AUDIBLY *adverb* in an audible way; aloud

AUDIENCE *noun* **AUDIENCES** a group of people watching a performance, eg of a play, concert, film, etc

AUDIO *noun* **AUDIOS** reproduction of recorded or broadcast sound □ *adj* relating to hearing or sound

AUDIOGRAM *noun* **AUDIOGRAMS** a record of a person's hearing ability, in the form of a graph, as measured by an audiometer

AUDIT *noun* **AUDITS** an official inspection of an organization's accounts by an accountant □ *verb* **AUDITS, AUDITING, AUDITED** to examine (accounts) officially

AUDITION *noun* **AUDITIONS** a test of the suitability of an actor, singer,

musician, etc for a particular part or role, which involves them giving a short performance □ *verb* **AUDITIONS, AUDITIONING, AUDITIONED** to test or be tested by means of an audition

AUDITOR *noun* **AUDITORS** a person who is professionally qualified to audit accounts

AUDITORY *adj* belonging, relating or referring to hearing or the organs involved in hearing

AUF *noun* **AUFS** an obsolete word for an elf's child

AUGER *noun* **AUGERS** a hand-tool with a corkscrew-like point for boring holes in wood

AUGHT *pronoun* an archaic or literary word for *anything*

AUGMENT *verb* **AUGMENTS, AUGMENTING, AUGMENTED** to make or become greater in size, number, strength, amount, etc

AUGMENTED *adj* having become or been made greater in size, etc

AUGMENTOR *noun* **AUGMENTORS** a nerve that increases the rate of activity of an organ

AUGUR *verb* **AUGURS, AUGURING, AUGURED** to be a good or bad sign for the future

AUGURY *noun* **AUGURIES** a sign or omen

AUGUST *adj* **AUGUSTER, AUGUSTEST** noble; imposing

AUGUSTLY *adverb* in an august way

AUK *noun* **AUKS** any of various species of small diving seabirds with a heavy body, black and white plumage, and short wings, found in cool northern seas

AULD *adj* **AULDER, AULDEST** old

AUNT *noun* **AUNTS** the sister of one's father or mother

AUNTIE *noun* **AUNTIES** an aunt

AUNTY *noun* **AUNTIES** an aunt

AURA *noun* **AURAS, AURAE** a distinctive character or quality around a person or in a place

AURAL *adj* relating to the sense of hearing or to the ears

AURALLY *adverb* by means of hearing

AUREATE *adj* made of or covered in gold; gilded

AUREOLA *noun* **AUREOLAS** aureole

AUREOLE *noun* **AUREOLES** a bright disc of light that surrounds the head or, less usually, the whole body of a holy figure, eg a saint, Christ, the Virgin Mary, etc, in Christian painting and iconography

AURICLE *noun* **AURICLES** the outer part of the ear

AURICULAR *adj* belonging or relating to the ear or sense of hearing

AUROCHS *noun* **AUROCHSES** an extinct wild ox, considered to be the ancestor of domestic cattle, and depicted in numerous Stone Age cave paintings

AURORA *noun* **AURORAS, AURORAE** the appearance of diffuse bands of coloured lights in the night sky, most often observed from the Arctic and Antarctic regions, caused by a burst of charged particles from the Sun which collide with oxygen and nitrogen atoms in the upper atmosphere to produce electrical discharges

AUROUS *adj* said of compounds: containing gold, especially in the monovalent state

AUSPICE *noun* **AUSPICES** protection; patronage

AUSTERE *adj* **AUSTERER, AUSTEREST** severely simple and plain; stern

AUSTERELY *adverb* in an austere way

AUSTERITY *noun* **AUSTERITIES** the state of being austere; strictness or harshness

AUSTRAL *adj* southern

AUTACOID *noun* **AUTACOIDS** any naturally occurring internal secretion such as adrenaline, thyroxine, insulin, etc that either stimulates or inhibits reactions in the body

AUTARCHIC *adj* absolute; despotic

AUTARCHY *noun* **AUTARCHIES** government of a country by a ruler who has absolute power

AUTARKIC *adj* of or relating to autarky; self-sufficient

AUTARKIST *noun* **AUTARKISTS** a person who practises or advocates autarky

AUTARKY *noun* **AUTARKIES** a system or policy of economic self-sufficiency in a country, state, etc where tariffs and other trade barriers are erected so that international trade is hindered or prevented altogether

AUTEUR *noun* **AUTEURS** a film director, especially one whose

work is regarded as having some distinctively personal quality about it

AUTHENTIC *adj* genuine

AUTHOR *noun* **AUTHORS** the writer of a book, article, play, etc □ *verb* **AUTHORS, AUTHORING, AUTHORED** to be the author of (a book, article, play, etc)

AUTHORESS *noun* **AUTHORESSES** a woman writer

AUTHORIAL *adj* of or relating to an author

AUTHORISE *verb* **AUTHORISES, AUTHORISING, AUTHORISED** to authorize

AUTHORITY *noun* **AUTHORITIES** the power or right to control or judge others, or to have the final say in something

AUTHORIZE *verb* **AUTHORIZES, AUTHORIZING, AUTHORIZED** to give someone the power or right to do something

AUTISM *noun* **AUTISMS** a mental disorder that develops in early childhood and is characterized by learning difficulties, inability to relate to other people and the outside world, and repetitive body movements

AUTISTIC *adj* affected by autism

AUTO *noun* **AUTOS** a motor car

AUTOBAHN *noun* **AUTOBAHNS** a motorway in Austria, Switzerland or Germany

AUTOCLAVE *noun* **AUTOCLAVES** a strong steel container that can be made airtight and filled with pressurized steam in order to sterilize equipment, eg surgical instruments

AUTOCRACY *noun* **AUTOCRACIES** absolute government by one person; dictatorship

AUTOCRAT *noun* **AUTOCRATS** a ruler with absolute power

AUTOCROSS *noun* **AUTOCROSSES** a motor-racing sport for cars of varying classes that takes place against the clock over a rough grass track of between 500 and 800yd (c.455–730m)

AUTOCUE *noun* **AUTOCUES** in broadcasting: a screen hidden from the camera which slowly displays a script line by line, so that the newscaster or speaker can read the script but appears to be speaking without a prompt

AUTODYNE *adj* said of an electronic circuit: configured so that the same elements and valves

are used both as oscillator and detector

AUTOGAMIC *adj* self-fertilizing

AUTOGAMY *noun* **AUTOGAMIES** in flowering plants: self-fertilization

AUTOGIRO *noun* **AUTOGIROS** a type of aircraft that differs from a helicopter in that its rotor blades are not mechanically powered, but produce lift because they are turned by the air (rather like the sails of a windmill) when the aircraft is moving forwards

AUTOGRAPH *noun* **AUTOGRAPHS** someone's signature, especially a famous person's, that is kept as a souvenir □ *verb* **AUTOGRAPHS, AUTOGRAPHING, AUTOGRAPHED** to sign (a photograph, book, poster, etc)

AUTOGYRO *noun* **AUTOGYROS** an autogiro

AUTOHARP *noun* **AUTOHARPS** a stringed musical instrument similar to a zither, plucked either with the fingers or with a plectrum, which has a set of dampers that allow chords to be played, and which is commonly used in country-and-western music

AUTOLYSIS *noun* **AUTOLYSES** the breakdown of cells or tissues by enzymes produced within them, which occurs either as a symptom of certain diseases and disorders, or after the death of those cells or tissues

AUTOMAT *noun* **AUTOMATS** a fast-food outlet where hot and cold food may be bought from automatic vending machines

AUTOMATE *verb* **AUTOMATES, AUTOMATING, AUTOMATED** to apply automation to (a technical process)

AUTOMATED *adj* said of a factory, production process, etc: mechanized and automatic, and often under the control of a computer

AUTOMATIC *adj* said of a machine or device: capable of operating on its own by means of a self-regulating mechanism, and requiring little human control once it has been activated □ *noun* **AUTOMATICS** an automatic firearm

AUTOMATON *noun* **AUTOMATONS, AUTOMATA** a machine or robot that has been programmed to perform specific actions in a manner imitative of a human or animal, especially such a device used as a toy, amusement or decoration

AUTONOMIC adj self-governing

AUTONOMY noun **AUTONOMIES** the power or right of self-government, administering one's own affairs, etc

AUTOPILOT noun **AUTOPILOTS** an electronic control device that automatically steers a vehicle, especially an aircraft, space vehicle or ship

AUTOPISTA noun **AUTOPISTAS** in Spain: a motorway

AUTOPSY noun **AUTOPSIES** any dissection and analysis

AUTOROUTE noun **AUTOROUTES** in France and other French-speaking countries: a motorway

AUTOSOMAL adj of or belonging to an autosome

AUTOSOME noun **AUTOSOMES** a chromosome other than a sex chromosome

AUTOTIMER noun **AUTOTIMERS** a facility on a cooker that allows the oven to come on and go off at preset times

AUTOTOMY noun **AUTOTOMIES** a reflex reaction in certain animals in which part of the body drops off, especially in order to allow them to escape when being attacked, eg some lizards shed their tails in this way

AUTOTYPE noun **AUTOTYPES** a technique of photographic reproduction in monochrome that uses a carbon pigment to give a print that is less susceptible to fading of the image

AUTUMN noun **AUTUMNS** the season of the year, between summer and winter, when leaves change colour and fall and harvests ripen

AUTUNITE noun **AUTUNITES** a common yellow or green fluorescent mineral that occurs in uranium deposits

AUXESIS noun **AUXESES** growth in plant or animal tissue that results from an increase in cell size as opposed to an increase in cell number

AUXILIARY adj helping or supporting ◻ noun **AUXILIARIES** a helper

AUXIN noun **AUXINS** any of numerous plant hormones that promote growth of plant tissues by

an increase in the size of existing cells, rather than an increase in cell number, and are used commercially as rooting powders and weedkillers

AVA adverb a Scots word meaning at all

AVADAVAT noun **AVADAVATS** a small Indian songbird related to the weaverbirds

AVAIL verb **AVAILS, AVAILING, AVAILED** to help or be of use ◻ noun **AVAILS** use; advantage

AVAILABLE adj able or ready to be obtained or used

AVAILABLY adverb so as to be capable of being obtained or used

AVALANCHE noun **AVALANCHES** the rapid movement of a large mass of snow or ice down a mountain slope under the force of gravity ◻ verb **AVALANCHES, AVALANCHING, AVALANCHED** to come down like an avalanche

AVARICE noun **AVARICES** excessive desire for money, possessions, etc; greed

AVATAR noun **AVATARS** in Hinduism: the appearance of a god, especially Vishnu, in human or animal form

AVE noun **AVES** a prayer to the Virgin Mary

AVENGE verb **AVENGES, AVENGING, AVENGED** to carry out some form of retribution for (some previous wrong-doing)

AVENGER noun **AVENGERS** a person who avenges

AVENUE noun **AVENUES** a broad road or street, often with trees along the sides

AVER verb **AVERS, AVERRING, AVERRED** to state firmly and positively

AVERAGE noun **AVERAGES** the usual or typical amount, extent, quality, number, etc ◻ adj usual or ordinary ◻ verb **AVERAGES, AVERAGING, AVERAGED** to obtain the numerical average of (several numbers)

AVERSE adj reluctant about or opposed to

AVERSELY adverb reluctantly

AVERSION noun **AVERSIONS** a strong dislike

AVERT verb **AVERTS, AVERTING, AVERTED** to turn away

AVIAN adj belonging, relating or referring to birds

AVIARIST noun **AVIARISTS** a person who keeps an aviary

AVIARY noun **AVIARIES** a large enclosed area where birds are kept

AVIATION noun **AVIATIONS** the science or practice of mechanical flight through the air, especially by powered aircraft

AVIATOR noun **AVIATORS** an aircraft pilot

AVID adj **AVIDER, AVIDEST** very enthusiastic

AVIDIN noun **AVIDINS** a protein found in egg-white, which combines with biotin in such a way that it prevents the biotin from being absorbed

AVIDLY adverb enthusiastically

AVIFAUNA noun **AVIFAUNAS, AVIFAUNAE** the bird-life of a specific area

AVIONICS singular noun the scientific study of the development and use of electronic and electrical devices for aircraft and spacecraft ◻ plural noun the electrical and electronic equipment that is on board an aircraft or spacecraft or that is used in connection with controlling its flight

AVOCADO noun **AVOCADOS** a tropical evergreen tree of the laurel family, with large oval leaves, small yellowish flowers and a pear-shaped fruit

AVOCATION noun **AVOCATIONS** a diversion or distraction from one's main occupation; a hobby

AVOCET noun **AVOCETS** any of various large wading birds with black and white plumage, long legs and a long slender upward curving bill

AVOID verb **AVOIDS, AVOIDING, AVOIDED** to keep away from (a place, person, action, etc)

AVOIDABLE adj capable of being avoided

AVOIDANCE noun **AVOIDANCES** the act of avoiding or shunning someone or something

AVOW verb **AVOWS, AVOWING, AVOWED** to state openly; to declare or admit

AVOWABLE adj capable of being avowed

AVOWAL noun **AVOWALS** a declaration, acknowledgement or confession

AVOWED adj openly stated and determinedly sought after

AVOWEDLY adverb in an avowed way

AVOWER noun **AVOWERS** someone who avows

AVUNCULAR adj relating to or like an uncle, especially in being kind and caring

AW exclamation used to express disappointment sympathy, etc

AWA adverb a Scots word for *away*

AWAIT verb **AWAITS, AWAITING, AWAITED** to wait for something

AWAKE verb **AWAKES, AWOKE, AWAKED, AWOKEN** to stop sleeping or cause to stop sleeping □ adj not sleeping

AWAKEN verb **AWAKENS, AWAKENING, AWAKENED** to wake up

AWARD verb **AWARDS, AWARDING, AWARDED** to present or grant someone something, especially in recognition of some achievement □ noun **AWARDS** a payment, prize, etc given in this way

AWARE adj **AWARER, AWAREST** acquainted with or mindful of something or someone

AWARENESS noun **AWARENESSES** the fact or state of being aware, or conscious, especially of matters that are particularly relevant or topical

AWASH adj covered or flooded with water □ adverb covered or flooded with water

AWAY adverb from one place, position, person or time towards another; off □ adj not present; not at home □ noun **AWAYS** a match played or won by a team playing on their opponent's ground

AWE noun **AWES** admiration, fear and wonder □ verb **AWES, AWING, AWED** to fill with awe

AWEIGH adverb said of an anchor: in the process of being raised from the bottom of the sea

AWESOME adj causing awe; dreaded

AWESTRUCK adj filled with awe

AWFUL adj **AWFULLER, AWFULLEST** very bad □ adverb very

AWFULLY adverb very; very badly

AWFULNESS noun **AWFULNESSES** terribleness, dreadfulness

AWHILE adverb for a short time

AWKWARD adj **AWKWARDER, AWKWARDEST** clumsy and ungraceful

AWKWARDLY adverb in an awkward way

AWL noun **AWLS** a pointed tool used for boring small holes, especially in leather

AWN noun **AWNS** in some grasses, eg barley: a small stiff bristle projecting from the glumes

AWNED adj having an awn

AWNING noun **AWNINGS** a soft, often striped, plastic or canvas covering over the entrance or window of a shop, hotel, caravan, etc, that can be extended to give shelter from the sun or rain

AWNLESS adj without awns

AWRY adj twisted to one side □ adverb twisted to one side

AX noun **AXES** an axe □ verb **AXES, AXING, AXED** to axe

AXE noun **AXES** a hand-tool with a long handle and a heavy metal blade, used for cutting down trees, chopping wood, etc □ verb **AXES, AXING, AXED** to get rid of, dismiss or put a stop to something

AXEL noun **AXELS** a jump in figure skating in which the skater starts from the forward outside edge of one skate, makes a turn and a half in the air, and comes down on the backward outside edge of the other skate

AXEMAN noun **AXEMEN** someone who wields an axe

AXES plural of **axis**

AXIAL adj relating to, forming or placed along an axis

AXIALITY noun **AXIALITIES** the quality of being axial

AXIALLY adverb in the direction of the axis

AXIL noun **AXILS** the angle between the upper surface of a leaf or stem and the stem or branch from which it grows

AXILE adj coinciding with an axis

AXILLAR adj relating to the axil

AXIOLOGY noun **AXIOLOGIES** the theory of moral and aesthetic values

AXIOM noun **AXIOMS** a proposition, fact, principle, etc which, because it is long-established, is generally accepted as true

AXIOMATIC adj obvious; self-evident

AXIS noun **AXES** an imaginary straight line around which an object, eg a planet, rotates

AXLE noun **AXLES** a fixed or rotating rod designed to carry a wheel or one or more pairs of wheels which may be attached to it, driven by it, or rotate freely on it

AXOLOTL noun **AXOLOTLS** a rare salamander, found in certain Mexican lakes, that is unusual in that it generally lays eggs while still in its aquatic larval stage, and only rarely leaves the water and develops into an adult

AXON noun **AXONS** the long extension of a neurone which carries nerve impulses outward away from the cell body

AY noun **AYS** a vote in favour of something, especially in the House of Commons

AYAH noun **AYAHS** formerly in India and other parts of the British Empire: a governess, lady's maid or children's nurse, especially one of Asian origin

AYATOLLAH noun **AYATOLLAHS** in the hierarchy of Shi'ite religious leaders in Iran: someone who can demonstrate a highly advanced knowledge of the Islamic religion and laws

AYE adverb always; still; continually □ noun **AYES** a vote in favour of something, especially in the House of Commons

AYU noun **AYUS** a small edible Japanese fruit

AYURVEDA noun **AYURVEDAS** an ancient system of Hindu medicine, still widely practised in India, involving numerous forms of treatment, eg herbal remedies, fasting, bathing, special diets, enemas, massage, prayers and yoga

AYURVEDIC adj of or relating to the ayurveda

AZALEA noun **AZALEAS** any of various deciduous shrubs closely related to the evergreen rhododendron, especially hybrid varieties with large clusters of funnel-shaped pink, orange, red, yellow, white or purple flowers

AZAN noun **AZANS** any of the five calls to Muslim public prayer that are chanted daily by the muezzin from the minaret of a mosque

AZEOTROPE noun **AZEOTROPES** a mixture of liquids which boils at a constant temperature and whose constituents do not change on distillation

AZIDE *noun* **AZIDES** any member of a large class of compounds that are synthesized from hydrazoic acid

AZIMUTH *noun* **AZIMUTHS** in astronomy and surveying: the bearing of an object, eg a planet or star, measured in degrees as the angle around the observer's horizon clockwise from north, which is the zero point

AZIMUTHAL *adj* of or relating to the azimuth

AZINE *noun* **AZINES** an organic chemical compound consisting of a six-membered ring composed of carbon and nitrogen atoms, eg pyridine

AZOIC *adj* showing no trace of life

AZONAL *adj* not confined to, or arranged in, zones or regions

AZURE *adj* deep sky-blue in colour ❏ *noun* **AZURES** a deep sky-blue colour

AZYGOUS *adj* said of body parts, organs, etc: occurring or developing singly; without a counterpart

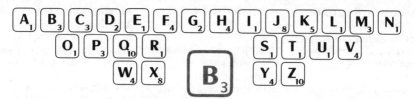

BA *noun* **BAS** in ancient Egyptian religion: the soul

BAA *noun* **BAAS** the cry of a sheep or lamb □ *verb* **BAAS, BAAING, BAAED** to make this cry; to bleat

BABA *noun* **BABAS** a type of small sponge cake soaked in a rum-flavoured syrup

BABBLE *verb* **BABBLES, BABBLING, BABBLED** to talk or say something quickly, especially in a way that is hard to understand

BABBLING *adj* said eg of gently flowing water: making a murmuring sound

BABE *noun* **BABES** (often used as a term of affection) a girl or young woman

BABEL *noun* **BABELS** a confused sound of voices

BABOON *noun* **BABOONS** any of various large ground-dwelling mainly African monkeys, which have a long dog-like muzzle, large teeth and a long tail

BABUSHKA *noun* **BABUSHKAS** an old Russian woman

BABY *noun* **BABIES** a newborn or very young child or animal □ *verb* **BABIES, BABYING, BABIED** to treat someone as a baby

BABYHOOD *noun* **BABYHOODS** the period of being a baby

BABYISH *adj* childish; immature

BAC *noun* **BACS** a baccalaureate, a degree or diploma

BACCARAT *noun* **BACCARATS** a card game in which players bet money against the banker

BACCHANAL *noun* **BACCHANALS** a noisy and drunken party

BACCY *noun* **BACCIES** tobacco

BACHELOR *noun* **BACHELORS** an unmarried man

BACILLUS *noun* **BACILLI** any of a large group of rod-shaped bacteria that are widely distributed in soil and air, including many species that cause food spoilage and serious diseases such as tuberculosis and tetanus

BACK *noun* **BACKS** the rear part of the human body from the neck to the base of the spine □ *adj* located or situated behind or at the back □ *adverb* to or towards the rear; away from the front □ *verb* **BACKS, BACKING, BACKED** to help or support someone or something, usually with money

BACKACHE *noun* **BACKACHES** a pain in the back

BACKBEAT *noun* **BACKBEATS** a breakbeat

BACKBITE *verb* **BACKBITES, BACKBITING, BACKBIT** to speak unkindly about someone who is absent

BACKBITING *noun* **BACKBITINGS** unkind remarks about someone who is absent

BACKBONE *noun* **BACKBONES** the spine

BACKCHAT *noun* **BACKCHATS** impertinent or rude replies, especially to a superior

BACKCOURT *noun* **BACKCOURTS** in tennis: the part of the court behind the service line

BACKDROP *noun* **BACKDROPS** the painted cloth at the back of a stage, forming part of the scenery

BACKER *noun* **BACKERS** a person who gives financial backing to a project, etc

BACKFILL *verb* **BACKFILLS, BACKFILLING, BACKFILLED** to refill (eg foundations or an excavation) with earth or other material □ *noun* **BACKFILLS** the material used for backfilling

BACKFIRE *verb* **BACKFIRES, BACKFIRING, BACKFIRED** said of an engine or vehicle: to make a loud bang as the result of an explosion of accumulated unburnt or partially burned gases in the exhaust or inlet system

BACKHAND *noun* **BACKHANDS** in tennis, squash etc: a stroke made with the back of the hand turned towards the ball

BACKING *noun* **BACKINGS** support, especially financial support

BACKLASH *noun* **BACKLASHES** a sudden violent reaction to an action or situation, etc

BACKLIST *noun* **BACKLISTS** a publisher's list of previously issued titles that are still in print

BACKLOG *noun* **BACKLOGS** a pile or amount of uncompleted work

BACKPACK *noun* **BACKPACKS** a rucksack □ *verb* **BACKPACKS, BACKPACKING, BACKPACKED** to go hiking with a pack on one's back

BACKPACKING *noun* **BACKPACKINGS** hiking with a pack on one's back

BACKSIDE *noun* **BACKSIDES** the buttocks

BACKSLIDE *verb* **BACKSLIDES, BACKSLIDING, BACKSLID** to relapse into former bad behaviour, habits, etc

BACKSLIDING *noun* **BACKSLIDINGS** relapsing into former bad behaviour, habits, etc

BACKSPACE *verb* **BACKSPACES, BACKSPACING, BACKSPACED** to move the carriage of a typewriter, or a computer cursor, back one or more spaces □ *noun* **BACKSPACES** the key on a typewriter or computer keyboard to backspace

BACKSPIN *noun* **BACKSPINS** the spinning of a ball in the opposite direction to the way it is travelling, which reduces the speed of the ball when it hits a surface

BACKSTAGE *adverb* behind a theatre stage □ *adj* not seen by the public

BACKSTOP *noun* **BACKSTOPS** a wall or screen which acts as a barrier in various sports

BACKSWING *noun* **BACKSWINGS** the first stage in the swing of a club or racket, etc, when it is swung back and away from the ball

BACKTRACK *verb* **BACKTRACKS, BACKTRACKING, BACKTRACKED** to return the way one came

BACKWARD *adj* directed behind or towards the back □ *adverb* towards the back or rear

BACKWARDS *adverb* towards the back or rear

For longer words, see *The Chambers Dictionary*

BACKWASH noun **BACKWASHES** waves washed backwards by the movement of a ship or oars, etc through the water

BACKWATER noun **BACKWATERS** a pool of stagnant water connected to a river

BACKWOODS plural noun remote uncleared forest

BACKYARD noun **BACKYARDS** a yard at the back of a house

BACLAVA noun **BACLAVAS** a baklava

BACON noun **BACONS** meat from the back and sides of a pig, usually salted or smoked

BACTERIA plural noun an extremely diverse group of microscopic and usually single-celled organisms that occur in soil, water and air, including many parasitic species that cause numerous infectious diseases

BACTERIAL adj of, relating to, or caused by bacteria

BAD adj **WORSE, WORST** not good □ adverb badly; greatly; hard □ noun **BADS** evil; badness

BADDY noun **BADDIES** a criminal or villain, especially one in a film or book, etc

BADE past form of **bid** [2]

BADGE noun **BADGES** a small emblem or mark worn to show rank, membership of a society, etc

BADGER [1] noun **BADGERS** a small stocky burrowing mammal with a short tail and short powerful legs, especially a European species with white fur on its head and two broad black stripes running from behind its ears to the tip of its muzzle

BADGER [2] verb **BADGERS, BADGERING, BADGERED** to pester or worry someone

BADINAGE noun **BADINAGES** playful bantering talk

BADLY adverb **WORSE, WORST** poorly; inefficiently

BADMINTON noun **BADMINTONS** a game for two or four players played with rackets and a shuttlecock which is hit across a high net

BADMOUTH verb **BADMOUTHS, BADMOUTHING, BADMOUTHED** to criticize or malign someone or something

BADNESS noun **BADNESSES** being bad

BAFFLE verb **BAFFLES, BAFFLING, BAFFLED** to confuse or puzzle □ noun **BAFFLES** a device

for controlling the flow of gas, liquid or sound through an opening

BAFFLING adj confusing or puzzling

BAG noun **BAGS** a container made of a soft material with an opening at the top, for carrying things □ verb **BAGS, BAGGING, BAGGED** to put something into a bag

BAGATELLE noun **BAGATELLES** a game played on a board with holes into which balls are rolled

BAGEL noun **BAGELS** a hard ring-shaped bread roll

BAGFUL noun **BAGFULS** the amount a bag can hold

BAGGAGE noun **BAGGAGES** a traveller's luggage

BAGGILY adverb in a baggy way

BAGGINESS noun **BAGGINESSES** the state or condition of being baggy

BAGGY adj **BAGGIER, BAGGIEST** hanging loose or bulging

BAGPIPER noun **BAGPIPERS** a player of the bagpipes

BAGPIPES plural noun a musical instrument consisting of a bag into which air is blown and a fingered reed pipe (the chanter) by means of which the melody is created

BAGUETTE noun **BAGUETTES** a long narrow French loaf

BAH exclamation expressing displeasure, scorn or disgust

BAIL [1] noun **BAILS** in cricket: one of the cross-pieces laid on top of the stumps

BAIL [2] verb **BAILS, BAILING, BAILED** to remove (water) from a boat with a bucket or scoop

BAILEY noun **BAILEYS** the outer wall of a castle

BAILIFF noun **BAILIFFS** an officer of a lawcourt, especially one with the power to seize the property of a person who has not paid money owed to the court

BAILIWICK noun **BAILIWICKS** one's area of jurisdiction

BAIRN noun **BAIRNS** a child

BAIT noun **BAITS** food put on a hook or in a trap to attract fish or animals □ verb **BAITS, BAITING, BAITED** to put food on or in (a hook or trap)

BAITING noun **BAITINGS** the action of setting dogs on an animal which is chained to a stake or put in a pit

BAIZE noun **BAIZES** a woollen cloth, usually green and used as a

covering on snooker and card tables, etc

BAJU noun **BAJUS** a short jacket worn in Malaya

BAKE verb **BAKES, BAKING, BAKED** to cook (cakes, bread, vegetables, etc) using dry heat in an oven

BAKEHOUSE noun **BAKEHOUSES** a bakery

BAKER noun **BAKERS** a person who bakes and sells bread and cakes, etc, especially as their profession

BAKERY noun **BAKERIES** a place where bread, cakes, etc are made or sold

BAKING adj extremely hot, especially from the sun □ noun **BAKINGS** the process by which bread and cakes, etc are baked

BAKLAVA noun **BAKLAVAS** a rich cake of Middle-Eastern origin made of layers of filo pastry, with a filling of honey, nuts and spices

BAKSHEESH noun **BAKSHEESHES** in some Eastern countries: money given as a tip or present

BALACLAVA noun **BALACLAVAS** a warm knitted hat that covers the head and neck, with an opening for the face

BALALAIKA noun **BALALAIKAS** a Russian stringed musical instrument with a triangular body, a neck like a guitar, and normally three strings

BALANCE noun **BALANCES** a state of physical stability in which the weight of a body is evenly distributed □ verb **BALANCES, BALANCING, BALANCED** a device which regulates the speed of a clock or watch

BALANCED adj in a state of balance

BALCONY noun **BALCONIES** a platform surrounded by a wall or railing, projecting from the wall of a building

BALD adj **BALDER, BALDEST** said of a person: having little or no hair on their head

BALDACHIN noun **BALDACHINS** a baldaquin

BALDAQUIN noun **BALDAQUINS** a canopy, especially one supported at each corner by a pole and carried over a sacred object in a religious procession, or placed over a throne, altar or pulpit

BALDING adj becoming bald
BALDLY adverb in a plain and often hurtful way
BALDNESS noun **BALDNESSES** the partial or total loss of hair from parts of the body where it normally grows, especially the head
BALDRIC noun **BALDRICS** a broad leather belt or silk sash, worn around the waist or over the right shoulder to support a sword or bugle, etc
BALDRICK noun **BALDRICKS** a baldric
BALE noun **BALES** a large tied bundle of a commodity such as hay or cloth □ verb **BALES, BALING, BALED** to make (hay, etc) into bales
BALEEN noun **BALEENS** whalebone
BALEFUL adj evil; harmful
BALEFULLY adverb with menace; threateningly
BALER noun **BALERS** a machine for making bales of hay, etc
BALK verb **BALKS, BALKING, BALKED** to hesitate, or refuse to go on, because of some obstacle □ noun **BALKS** in eg snooker: the part of the table behind a line near one end, from within which the start and restarts are made
BALKANISE verb **BALKANISES, BALKANISING, BALKANISED** to balkanize
BALKANIZE verb **BALKANIZES, BALKANIZING, BALKANIZED** to break up (a country or area) into mutually hostile areas
BALL noun **BALLS** a round or roundish object used in some sports; anything round or nearly round in shape □ verb **BALLS, BALLING, BALLED** to form or gather into a ball
BALLAD noun **BALLADS** a slow, usually romantic song
BALLADE noun **BALLADES** a poem consisting of verses grouped in threes
BALLAST noun **BALLASTS** heavy material used to keep a ship steady when it is carrying little or no cargo, or to weigh down and stabilize a hot-air balloon
BALLCOCK noun **BALLCOCKS** a floating ball that rises and falls with the water level in a tank or cistern and, by means of a hinged rod to which it is attached, operates a valve controlling the inflow of water

BALLERINA noun **BALLERINAS** a female ballet-dancer, especially one who takes leading roles
BALLET noun **BALLETS** a classical style of dancing and mime, using set steps and body movements
BALLETIC adj of the art of ballet; in or similar to the style of ballet
BALLISTIC adj referring or relating to projectiles
BALLISTICS singular noun the scientific study of the movement, behaviour and effects of projectiles, such as bullets, rockets and guided missiles
BALLOON noun **BALLOONS** a small, usually brightly-coloured, rubber pouch with a neck, that can be inflated with air or gas and used as a toy or decoration, etc □ verb **BALLOONS, BALLOONING, BALLOONED** to swell out like a balloon
BALLOONING noun **BALLOONINGS** travelling by hot-air balloon
BALLOT noun **BALLOTS** a method or system of voting, usually in secret, by putting a marked paper into a box or other container □ verb **BALLOTS, BALLOTING, BALLOTED** to take the vote or ballot of (a group of people)
BALLPOINT noun **BALLPOINTS** a pen which has a tiny ball as the writing point, around which the ink flows as it is moved across the paper
BALLROOM noun **BALLROOMS** a large room with a spacious dance floor, in which large-scale dances are held
BALLYHOO noun **BALLYHOOS** a noisy confused situation □ verb **BALLYHOOS, BALLYHOOING, BALLYHOOED** to create loud publicity or sensationalism over something or someone
BALM noun **BALMS** an oil obtained from certain types of trees, having a pleasant smell and used in healing or reducing pain
BALMILY adverb in a balmy way
BALMINESS noun **BALMINESSES** warmness and softness (of the air)
BALMORAL noun **BALMORALS** a round flat bonnet with a pompom on the top, worn by certain Scottish regiments
BALMY adj **BALMIER, BALMIEST** said of the air: warm and soft
BALONEY noun **BALONEYS** nonsense

BALSA noun **BALSAS** a tropical American tree
BALSAM noun **BALSAMS** a pleasant-smelling thick sticky substance obtained from some trees and plants, used to make medicines and perfumes
BALSAMIC adj producing balsam
BALUSTER noun **BALUSTERS** any one of a series of posts or pillars supporting a rail

BAM verb **BAMS, BAMMING, BAMMED** to hoax or cheat

BAMBOO noun **BAMBOOS** a tall grass that rarely flowers found mainly in tropical regions, with jointed hollow woody stems and deciduous leaves
BAMBOOZLE verb **BAMBOOZLES, BAMBOOZLING, BAMBOOZLED** to trick or cheat someone
BAN noun **BANS** an official order stating that something is not allowed □ verb **BANS, BANNING, BANNED** to forbid something
BANAL adj **BANALER, BANALEST** boring or trivial; not saying, doing or providing, etc anything interesting or original
BANALITY noun **BANALITIES** cliché, triviality, triteness
BANALLY adverb in a banal way
BANANA noun **BANANAS** a large perennial SE Asian plant, superficially resembling a tree, that is cultivated throughout the tropics as a staple food crop
BAND noun **BANDS** a group of people with a common purpose or interest □ verb **BANDS, BANDING, BANDED** to act as a group, or to organize (people) to act as a group or to work for a common purpose
BANDAGE noun **BANDAGES** a strip of cloth for winding round a wound or a broken limb □ verb **BANDAGES, BANDAGING, BANDAGED** to wrap (especially a wound or a broken limb) in a bandage
BANDANA noun **BANDANAS** a large brightly-coloured cotton or silk square, folded and worn around the neck or head
BANDANNA noun **BANDANNAS** a bandana
BANDEAU noun **BANDEAUX** a narrow band of soft material worn around the head
BANDED adj marked with a stripe or stripes of a different colour
BANDEROLE noun **BANDEROLES**

a long narrow flag, usually with a forked end

BANDICOOT noun **BANDICOOTS** a nocturnal marsupial, found in Australia and Papua New Guinea, with elongated hindlegs and a long flexible snout □ verb **BANDICOOTS, BANDICOOTING, BANDICOOTED** to remove (potatoes) from the ground without disturbing the tops of the plants

BANDIER see under **bandy** [1]

BANDIEST see under **bandy** [1]

BANDING noun **BANDINGS** the division of children in the final year of primary school into three groups according to ability, in order to obtain an even spread in the mixed-ability classes usual in comprehensive schools

BANDIT noun **BANDITS** an armed robber, especially a member of a gang that attacks travellers or isolated homes and villages

BANDOG noun **BANDOGS** a dog bred for exceptional ferocity, usually a cross between an American pit bull terrier and a mastiff, rottweiler or Rhodesian ridgeback

BANDOLEER noun **BANDOLEERS** a leather shoulder belt, especially one for carrying bullets

BANDOLIER noun **BANDOLIERS** a bandoleer

BANDSMAN noun **BANDSMEN** a member of a musical band, especially a brass band

BANDSTAND noun **BANDSTANDS** a platform with a roof, often in a park, where bands play music

BANDWAGON noun **BANDWAGONS** a fashionable movement, a trend enjoying current success

BANDWIDTH noun **BANDWIDTHS** the width or spread of the range of frequencies used for the transmission of radio or TV signals

BANDY [1] adj **BANDIER, BANDIEST** said of a person's or animal's legs: curved or bending wide apart at the knees

BANDY [2] verb **BANDIES, BANDYING, BANDIED** to pass (a story, information, etc) from one person to another

BANE noun **BANES** the cause of trouble or evil

BANEFUL adj evil; causing harm

BANG noun **BANGS** a sudden loud explosive noise □ verb **BANGS,**

BANGING, BANGED to make, or cause something to make, a loud noise by hitting, dropping or closing it violently, etc □ adverb suddenly

BANGER noun **BANGERS** a sausage

BANGLE noun **BANGLES** a piece of jewellery in the form of a solid band, worn round the arm or leg

BANIAN noun **BANIANS** a banyan

BANISH verb **BANISHES, BANISHING, BANISHED** to send someone away from a place, usually from the country they were born in

BANISTER noun **BANISTERS** a row of posts and the hand-rail they support, running up the side of a staircase

BANJAX verb **BANJAXES, BANJAXING, BANJAXED** to ruin, stymie or destroy

BANJO noun **BANJOS, BANJOES** a stringed musical instrument with a long neck and a round body, played like a guitar

BANJOIST noun **BANJOISTS** a player of the banjo

BANK noun **BANKS** a financial organization which keeps money in accounts for its clients, lends money, exchanges currency, etc □ verb **BANKS, BANKING, BANKED** to put (money) into a bank

BANKABLE adj in the film industry: likely to ensure profitability

BANKER noun **BANKERS** a person who owns or manages a bank

BANKING noun **BANKINGS** the business done by a bank or banker

BANKROLL noun **BANKROLLS** money resources; funds □ verb **BANKROLLS, BANKROLLING, BANKROLLED** to finance; to provide the capital for something

BANKRUPT noun **BANKRUPTS** someone who is legally recognized, by a court adjudication order, as not being able to pay their debts □ adj not having money to pay one's debts; insolvent □ verb **BANKRUPTS, BANKRUPTING, BANKRUPTED** to make someone bankrupt

BANKSIA noun **BANKSIAS** an Australian shrub or small tree with small sharply-toothed leathery leaves and cream, orange, red or purplish flowers

BANNER noun **BANNERS** a large

piece of cloth or cardboard, with a design or slogan, etc, carried or displayed at public meetings and parades

BANNISTER noun **BANNISTERS** a banister

BANNOCK noun **BANNOCKS** a small flat round cake, usually made from oatmeal

BANNS plural noun a public announcement in church of two people's intention to marry

BANQUET noun **BANQUETS** a sumptuous formal dinner □ verb **BANQUETS, BANQUETING, BANQUETED** to eat or take part in a banquet

BANQUETTE noun **BANQUETTES** a built-in wall-sofa used instead of individual seats, eg in a restaurant

BANSHEE noun **BANSHEES** a female spirit whose sad wailing outside a house warns that a member of the family will die in the near future

BANTAM noun **BANTAMS** a small breed of farm chicken

BANTER noun **BANTERS** light-hearted friendly talk □ verb **BANTERS, BANTERING, BANTERED** to tease someone or joke

BANTERING noun **BANTERINGS** teasing or joking

BANTU noun **BANTUS** a group of languages spoken in southern and central Africa □ adj belonging or relating to the bantu languages or bantu-speaking people

BANYAN noun **BANYANS** an Indian fruit tree with branches from which shoots grow down into the ground and take root

BANZAI exclamation a Japanese battle-cry and salute to the emperor

BAOBAB noun **BAOBABS** a large deciduous African tree with a massive soft trunk which serves as a water store, and a relatively small crown

BAP noun **BAPS** a large flat elliptical breakfast roll

BAPTISE verb **BAPTISES, BAPTISING, BAPTISED** to baptize

BAPTISM noun **BAPTISMS** the religious ceremony of baptizing a person by immersion in, or sprinkling with, water

BAPTISMAL adj of or relating to baptism

BAPTIST noun **BAPTISTS** a person who baptizes or baptized

BAPTISTRY *noun* **BAPTISTRIES** the part of a church where baptisms are carried out, whether a separate building or part of the church

BAPTIZE *verb* **BAPTIZES, BAPTIZING, BAPTIZED** to dip or immerse someone in, or sprinkle them with, water as a sign of them having become a member of the Christian Church (in the case of babies, this is usually accompanied by name-giving)

BAR *noun* **BARS** a block of some solid substance □ *verb* **BARS, BARRING, BARRED** to fasten something with a bar

BARB *noun* **BARBS** a point on a hook facing in the opposite direction to the main point, which makes it difficult to pull the hook out □ *verb* **BARBS, BARBING, BARBED** to fit or provide something with barbs or a barb

BARBARIAN *noun* **BARBARIANS** someone who is cruel and wild in behaviour □ *adj* cruel and wild; uncivilized

BARBARIC *adj* cruel and brutal; excessively harsh or vicious

BARBARISM *noun* **BARBARISMS** the state of being uncivilized, coarse, etc

BARBARITY *noun* **BARBARITIES** barbarism

BARBAROUS *adj* uncultured and uncivilized

BARBECUE *noun* **BARBECUES** a frame on which food is grilled over an open fire, especially a charcoal fire □ *verb* **BARBECUES, BARBECUING, BARBECUED** to cook (food) on a barbecue, often coating it with a highly-seasoned sauce

BARBED *adj* having a barb or barbs

BARBEL *noun* **BARBELS** a large freshwater fish of the carp family, widespread in European rivers, which has a slender body and four long sensory feelers around its mouth

BARBER *noun* **BARBERS** someone who cuts and styles men's hair and shaves their beards

BARBERRY *noun* **BARBERRIES** a bushy plant or shrub with thorns, yellow flowers and red berries

BARBET *noun* **BARBETS** a plump brightly-coloured tropical bird that has a beardlike growth of feathers at the base of its large bill

BARBICAN *noun* **BARBICANS** a tower over the outer gate of a castle or town, for the purpose of defending the gate

BARBIE *noun* **BARBIES** a barbecue

BARBULE *noun* **BARBULES** any of numerous parallel hairlike filaments on a feather

BARCAROLE *noun* **BARCAROLES** a gondolier's song, or a piece of music with a similar rhythm

BARD *noun* **BARDS** a poet

BARDIC *adj* of or relating to bards

BARE *adj* **BARER, BAREST** not covered by clothes; naked □ *verb* **BARES, BARING, BARED** to uncover

BAREBACK *adj* on a horse without a saddle □ *adverb* on a horse without a saddle

BAREFACED *adj* having no shame or regret; impudent

BAREFOOT *adj* not wearing shoes or socks □ *adverb* not wearing shoes or socks

BARELY *adverb* scarcely or only just

BARENESS *noun* **BARENESSES** nakedness; lack of cover

BARF *verb* **BARFS, BARFING, BARFED** to vomit

BARGAIN *noun* **BARGAINS** an agreement made between people buying and selling things, offering and accepting services, etc □ *verb* **BARGAINS, BARGAINING, BARGAINED** to discuss the terms for buying or selling, etc

BARGAINER *noun* **BARGAINERS** a person who bargains

BARGE *noun* **BARGES** a long flat-bottomed boat used on rivers and canals □ *verb* **BARGES, BARGING, BARGED** to move in a clumsy ungraceful way

BARGEE *noun* **BARGEES** a person in charge of a barge

BARGEPOLE *noun* **BARGEPOLES** a long pole used to move or guide a barge

BARITE *noun* **BARITES** barytes

BARITONE *noun* **BARITONES** the second lowest male singing voice, between bass and tenor □ *adj* referring to the pitch and compass of a baritone

BARIUM *noun* **BARIUMS** a soft silvery-white metallic element, soluble compounds of which burn with a green flame and are used in fireworks and flares

BARK *noun* **BARKS** the short sharp cry of a dog or fox, etc □ *verb*

BARKS, BARKING, BARKED to make this sound

BARKER *noun* **BARKERS** a person outside a circus or show, etc who shouts to attract customers

BARLEY *noun* **BARLEYS** a cereal of the grass family which bears a dense head of grains with long slender awns, and is an important crop in north temperate regions

BARM *noun* **BARMS** the froth formed on fermenting liquor

BARMAID *noun* **BARMAIDS** a woman who serves drinks in a bar or public house

BARMAN *noun* **BARMEN** a man who serves drinks in a bar or public house

BARMY *adj* **BARMIER, BARMIEST** crazy; mentally unsound

BARN *noun* **BARNS** a building in which grain or hay, etc is stored, or for housing cattle, etc

BARNACLE *noun* **BARNACLES** a marine crustacean with a shell consisting of several plates, which cements itself firmly by means of its head to rocks, hulls of boats, and other underwater objects

BARNEY *noun* **BARNEYS** a rough noisy quarrel

BARNSTORM *verb* **BARNSTORMS, BARNSTORMING, BARNSTORMED** to tour a country, stopping briefly in each town to give theatrical performances or political speeches

BARNYARD *noun* **BARNYARDS** the area around or adjoining a barn

BAROGRAPH *noun* **BAROGRAPHS** a type of barometer that produces a continuous printed chart which records fluctuations in atmospheric pressure over a period of time

BAROMETER *noun* **BAROMETERS** an instrument which measures atmospheric pressure, especially in order to predict changes in the weather or to estimate height above sea level

BARON *noun* **BARONS** a man holding the lowest rank of the British nobility

BARONESS *noun* **BARONESSES** a baron's wife

BARONET *noun* **BARONETS** a British hereditary title ranking below baron, not part of the peerage

BARONETCY *noun* **BARONETCIES** the rank or title of a baronet

BARONIAL *adj* relating to or suitable for a baron or barons

BARONY *noun* **BARONIES** the rank of baron

BAROQUE *noun* **BAROQUES** a bold complex decorative style of architecture, art, decoration and music, popular in Europe from the late 16c to the early 18c

BARPERSON *noun* **BARPERSONS** a woman or man who serves drinks in a bar or public house

BARQUE *noun* **BARQUES** a small sailing ship with three masts

BARRACK *noun* **BARRACKS** a building or group of buildings for housing soldiers □ *verb* **BARRACKS, BARRACKING, BARRACKED** to house (soldiers) in barracks

BARRACKING *noun* **BARRACKINGS** a hostile demonstration (at a sports event, etc)

BARRACUDA *noun* **BARRACUDAS** a large tropical sea fish which feeds on other fish and sometimes attacks people

BARRAGE *noun* **BARRAGES** a long burst of gunfire which keeps an enemy back while soldiers move forward

BARRE *noun* **BARRES** a rail fixed to a wall at waist level, which dancers use to balance themselves while exercising

BARRED *adj* having, marked or fitted with bars

BARREL *noun* **BARRELS** a large round container with a flat top and bottom and curving out in the middle, usually made of planks of wood held together with metal bands □ *verb* **BARRELS, BARRELLING, BARRELLED** to put something in barrels

BARRELFUL *noun* **BARRELFULS** the amount a barrel can hold

BARREN *adj* said of a woman: not able to bear children

BARRICADE *noun* **BARRICADES** a barrier, especially an improvised one made of anything which can be piled up quickly, eg to block a street □ *verb* **BARRICADES, BARRICADING, BARRICADED** to block or defend something with a barricade

BARRIER *noun* **BARRIERS** a fence, gate or bar, etc put up to defend, block, protect, separate, etc

BARRISTER *noun* **BARRISTERS** in England and Wales: a lawyer qualified to act for someone in the higher law courts

BARROW *noun* **BARROWS** a small one-wheeled cart used to carry tools, earth, etc

BARTENDER *noun* **BARTENDERS** someone who serves drinks in a bar; a barperson

BARTER *verb* **BARTERS, BARTERING, BARTERED** to trade or exchange (goods or services) without using money □ *noun* **BARTERS** trade by exchanging goods rather than by selling them for money

BARTERER *noun* **BARTERERS** someone who barters

BARYON *noun* **BARYONS** a heavy subatomic particle involved in strong interactions with other subatomic particles and composed of three quarks bound together by gluon

BARYTES *noun* **BARYTES** the mineral form of barium sulphate, the chief ore of barium

BAS plural of **ba**

BASAL *adj* at, referring to or forming a base

BASALT *noun* **BASALTS** a fine-grained dark volcanic rock, formed by the solidification of thin layers of molten lava that spread out following a volcanic eruption

BASALTIC *adj* of, like, or consisting of basalt

BASCULE *noun* **BASCULES** an apparatus one end of which rises as the other sinks

BASE [1] *noun* **BASES** the lowest part or bottom; the part which supports something or on which something stands □ *verb* **BASES, BASING, BASED** to make or form a base for something or someone

BASE [2] *adj* **BASER, BASEST** lacking morals; wicked

BASEBALL *noun* **BASEBALLS** a game played by two teams of nine people using a truncheon-shaped bat and a ball, in which the person batting attempts to run as far as possible round a diamond-shaped pitch formed by four bases, aiming to get back to the home plate to score a run

BASELESS *adj* having no cause or foundation

BASELY *adverb* in a base way

BASEMENT *noun* **BASEMENTS** the lowest floor of a building, usually below ground level

BASENESS *noun* **BASENESSES** immorality; wickedness

BASES plural of **base** [1], **basis**

BASH *verb* **BASHES, BASHING, BASHED** to strike or smash something bluntly; to beat or batter □ *noun* **BASHES** a heavy blow or knock

BASHER *noun* **BASHERS** someone or something that bashes a specified thing

BASHFUL *adj* lacking confidence; shy; self-conscious

BASHFULLY *adverb* in a bashful way

BASHING *noun* **BASHINGS** an instance of severe physical or verbal assault

BASHO *noun* **BASHO** in sumo: a tournament

BASIC *adj* referring to or forming the base or basis of something

BASICS *plural noun* the essential parts or facts; the simplest principles

BASICALLY *adverb* fundamentally, essentially

BASIDIUM *noun* **BASIDIA** in fungi: a terminal club-shaped reproductive structure which contains spores

BASIL *noun* **BASILS** a bushy aromatic annual plant with purplish-green oval leaves and white or purplish flowers, widely cultivated as a culinary herb

BASILAR *adj* relating to, situated at or growing from the base

BASILICA *noun* **BASILICAS** an ancient Roman public hall, with a rounded wall at one end and a row of stone pillars along each side, used as a lawcourt, for public assemblies or for commerce

BASILISK *noun* **BASILISKS** in mythology: a snake which can kill people by breathing on them or looking at them

BASIN *noun* **BASINS** a wide open dish, especially one for holding water

BASINFUL *noun* **BASINFULS** the amount a basin can hold

BASIS *noun* **BASES** a principle on which an idea or theory, etc is based

BASK *verb* **BASKS, BASKING, BASKED** to lie in comfort, especially in warmth or sunshine

BASKET *noun* **BASKETS** a container made of plaited or interwoven twigs, rushes, canes or similar flexible material, often with a handle across the top

BASKETFUL noun **BASKETFULS** the amount a basket can hold

BASKETRY noun **BASKETRIES** the art or business of making baskets and similar articles of basketwork

BASQUE noun **BASQUES** a tight-fitting bodice for women, often with a continuation below the waist to the hips, worn either as an undergarment or as a lightweight top

BASS noun **BASSES** the lowest male singing voice □ adj **BASSER, BASSEST** said of a musical instrument, voice or sound: low in pitch and range

BASSET noun **BASSETS** a breed of dog with a long body, smooth hair, short legs and long drooping ears

BASSINET noun **BASSINETS** a baby's basket-like bed or pram, usually covered at one end with a hood

BASSIST noun **BASSISTS** a person who plays a bass guitar or double-bass

BASSOON noun **BASSOONS** a large woodwind instrument which produces a very low sound, formed of a long jointed wooden pipe doubled back on itself, fitted with metal keys and a curved crook with a double reed

BAST noun **BASTS** the conductive material in a plant; phloem

BASTE verb **BASTES, BASTING, BASTED** to pour hot fat, butter or juices over something (especially roasting meat), during cooking

BASTINADO noun **BASTINADOES** beating of the soles of the feet with a stick as a form of torture or punishment □ verb **BASTINADOES, BASTINADOING, BASTINADOED** to beat someone on the soles of the feet with a stick

BASTING noun **BASTINGS** a thrashing

BASTION noun **BASTIONS** a kind of tower which sticks out at an angle from a castle wall

BAT noun **BATS** a shaped piece of wood, with a flat or curved surface, for hitting a ball in cricket, baseball, tennis etc □ verb **BATS, BATTING, BATTED** to take a turn at hitting a ball with a bat; to have an innings

BATCH noun **BATCHES** a number of things or people dealt with at the same time □ verb **BATCHES, BATCHING, BATCHED** to arrange or treat something in batches

BATE noun **BATES** a rage

BATED adj diminished; restrained

BATH noun **BATHS** a large open container for water, in which to wash the whole body while sitting in it □ verb **BATHS, BATHING, BATHED** to wash someone or something in a bath

BATHCUBE noun **BATHCUBES** a small block of bath salts

BATHE verb **BATHES, BATHING, BATHED** to swim in the sea, etc for pleasure □ noun **BATHES** an act of swimming in the sea, etc; a swim or dip

BATHER noun **BATHERS** a person who bathes or is bathing

BATHETIC adj said of speech or writing: characterized by bathos

BATHOLITH noun **BATHOLITHS** a large igneous rock mass, typically granite, that has intruded while molten into the surrounding rock

BATHOS noun **BATHOSES** in speech or writing: a sudden descent from very important, serious or beautiful ideas to very ordinary or trivial ones

BATHROBE noun **BATHROBES** a loose towelling coat used especially before and after taking a bath

BATHROOM noun **BATHROOMS** a room containing a bath and now usually other washing facilities, a lavatory, etc

BATHTUB noun **BATHTUBS** a bath

BATIK noun **BATIKS** a technique of printing coloured patterns on cloth, in which those parts not to be coloured or dyed are covered with wax

BATMAN noun **BATMEN** an officer's personal servant in the armed forces

BATON noun **BATONS** a light thin stick used by the conductor of an orchestra or choir, etc to direct them

BATS adj crazy; batty

BATSMAN noun **BATSMEN** a man who bats or is batting

BATTALION noun **BATTALIONS** an army unit made up of several smaller companies, and forming part of a larger brigade

BATTEN noun **BATTENS** a long flat piece of wood used for keeping other pieces in place □ verb **BATTENS, BATTENING, BATTENED** to fasten, strengthen or shut (eg a door) with battens

BATTER noun **BATTERS** a mixture of eggs, flour and either milk or water, beaten together and used in cooking, eg to coat fish or to make pancakes □ verb **BATTERS, BATTERING, BATTERED** to strike or hit something or someone hard and often, or continuously

BATTERED adj said of fish or other food: coated in batter and deep-fried

BATTERING noun **BATTERINGS** a beating

BATTERY noun **BATTERIES** a device that converts chemical energy into electrical energy in the form of direct current, eg a car battery, or a dry battery used as a portable energy source in a torch, etc

BATTING noun **BATTINGS** in ball games such as cricket: using, managing, playing or hitting with a bat

BATTLE noun **BATTLES** a fight between opposing armies, naval or air forces, etc or people □ verb **BATTLES, BATTLING, BATTLED** to fight

BATTLER noun **BATTLERS** someone who battles

BATTY adj **BATTIER, BATTIEST** crazy; eccentric

BAUBLE noun **BAUBLES** a small cheap ornament or piece of jewellery; a trinket

BAUD noun **BAUDS** in a computer system: the number of bits or other signalling elements that can be transmitted between computers per second

BAULK noun **BAULKS** balk □ verb **BAULKS, BAULKING, BAULKED** to balk

BAUXITE noun **BAUXITES** a white, yellow, red or brown clay-like substance, which is the main ore of aluminium and is formed by weathering of igneous rocks in tropical regions

BAWDILY adverb in a bawdy way

BAWDINESS noun **BAWDINESSES** lewdness of language or writing

BAWDY adj **BAWDIER, BAWDIEST** said of language or writing, etc: containing coarsely humorous references to sex; lewd

BAWL verb **BAWLS, BAWLING, BAWLED** to cry or shout loudly

BAY[1] adj said of a horse: reddish-brown in colour, usually with black mane and tail

BAY[2] noun **BAYS** a body of water

that forms a wide-mouthed indentation in the coastline

BAY[3] *verb* **BAYS, BAYING, BAYED** said especially of large dogs: to make a deep howling bark or cry, especially when hunting

BAYBERRY *noun* **BAYBERRIES** a shrub that bears small waxy berries

BAYONET *noun* **BAYONETS** a steel knife that fixes to the muzzle of a soldier's rifle □ *verb* **BAYONETS, BAYONETING, BAYONETED** to stab someone or something with a bayonet

BAYOU *noun* **BAYOUS** in the US: a marshy offshoot of a lake or river

BAZAAR *noun* **BAZAARS** a sale of goods, etc usually in order to raise money for a particular organization or purpose

BAZOOKA *noun* **BAZOOKAS** a portable anti-tank gun which fires small rockets

BAZOUKI *noun* **BAZOUKIS** a bouzouki

BE *verb* **AM, IS, ARE, BEING, WAS, WERE, BEEN** to exist or live

BEACH *noun* **BEACHES** the sandy or stony shore of a sea or lake □ *verb* **BEACHES, BEACHING, BEACHED** to push, pull or drive (especially a boat) on to a beach

BEACHHEAD *noun* **BEACHHEADS** an area of shore captured from the enemy, on which an army can land men and equipment

BEACON *noun* **BEACONS** a warning or guiding device for aircraft or ships, eg a lighthouse or a radio transmitter that broadcasts signals

BEAD *noun* **BEADS** a small and usually round ball made of glass or stone, etc strung with others, eg in a necklace □ *verb* **BEADS, BEADING, BEADED** to decorate something with beads or beading

BEADED *adj* having beads or a bead

BEADING *noun* **BEADINGS** thin strips of patterned wood used to decorate the edges of furniture or walls, etc

BEADLE *noun* **BEADLES** a person who leads formal processions in church or in some old universities and institutions

BEADY *adj* **BEADIER, BEADIEST** said of a person's eyes: small, round and bright

BEAGLE *noun* **BEAGLES** a breed of small hunting-dog with a short

coat □ *verb* **BEAGLES, BEAGLING, BEAGLED** to hunt with beagles

BEAGLER *noun* **BEAGLERS** someone who hunts with beagles

BEAGLING *noun* **BEAGLINGS** hunting with beagles

BEAK *noun* **BEAKS** the horny projecting jaws of a bird

BEAKED *adj* having a beak

BEAKER *noun* **BEAKERS** a large drinking-glass, or a large cup (often a plastic one) without a handle

BEAKY *adj* **BEAKIER, BEAKIEST** resembling a beak

BEAM *noun* **BEAMS** a long straight thick piece of wood, used eg as a main structural component in a building □ *verb* **BEAMS, BEAMING, BEAMED** to smile broadly with pleasure

BEAMING *adj* radiant or shining □ *noun* **BEAMINGS** radiation or emission

BEAN *noun* **BEANS** a general name applied to the edible kidney-shaped seeds of plants belonging to the pea family, especially those of the runner bean □ *verb* **BEANS, BEANING, BEANED** to hit someone on the head with something

BEANFEAST *noun* **BEANFEASTS** a party or celebration

BEANO *noun* **BEANOS** a beanfeast or jollification

BEANPOLE *noun* **BEANPOLES** a tall supporting pole for a bean plant to climb up as it grows

BEANSTALK *noun* **BEANSTALKS** the stem of a bean plant

BEAR[1] *noun* **BEARS** any of various large carnivorous animals with a heavily built body covered with thick fur, short powerful limbs, small eyes and ears, strong claws and a short tail

BEAR[2] *verb* **BEARS, BEARING, BORE, BORNE** to support or sustain (a weight or load)

BEARABLE *adj* able to be suffered or tolerated

BEARABLY *adverb* in a bearable way

BEARD[1] *verb* **BEARDS, BEARDING, BEARDED** to face, defy or oppose someone openly, boldly or resolutely

BEARD[2] *noun* **BEARDS** the hair that grows on a man's chin and neck

BEARDED *adj* having a beard

BEARDLESS *adj* having no beard

BEARER *noun* **BEARERS** a person or thing that bears, carries or brings something

BEARING *noun* **BEARINGS** the way a person stands, walks, behaves, etc

BEARISH *adj* said of a person: bad-tempered and rough

BÉARNAISE *noun* **BÉARNAISES** in cookery: a sauce made from egg yolks, butter, shallots, herbs and wine vinegar

BEARSKIN *noun* **BEARSKINS** the skin of a bear, used eg as a rug or cloak

BEAST *noun* **BEASTS** any large wild animal, especially a four-footed one

BEASTIE *noun* **BEASTIES** a small animal, especially an insect or spider, etc

BEASTLY *adj* **BEASTLIER, BEASTLIEST** unpleasant; horrid; disagreeable □ *adverb* extremely and unpleasantly

BEAT *noun* **BEATS** a regular recurrent stroke, or its sound □ *verb* **BEATS, BEATING, BEAT, BEATEN** to hit (a person, animal, etc) violently and repeatedly, especially to harm or punish them □ *adj* worn out; exhausted

BEATABLE *adj* capable of being defeated

BEATEN *adj* defeated or outmanoeuvred

BEATER *noun* **BEATERS** a person or thing that beats

BEATIFIC *adj* expressing or revealing supreme peaceful happiness

BEATIFY *verb* **BEATIFIES, BEATIFYING, BEATIFIED** to declare the blessed status of someone who has died, conferring the title 'Blessed' upon them, usually as the first step towards full canonization

BEATING *noun* **BEATINGS** a physical assault or punishment

BEATITUDE *noun* **BEATITUDES** the group of statements made by Christ during the Sermon on the Mount (in Matthew 5.3–11) about the kinds of people who receive God's blessing

BEATNIK *noun* **BEATNIKS** a young person with scruffy or unconventional clothes, long hair, unusual lifestyle, etc

BEAU *noun* **BEAUX** a boyfriend or male lover

BEAUT *adj* excellent; fine □ *noun*

BEAUTS someone or something exceptionally beautiful, pleasing or remarkable; a beauty

BEAUTEOUS *adj* beautiful

BEAUTIFUL *adj* having an appearance or qualities which please the senses or give rise to admiration in the mind

BEAUTIFY *verb* **BEAUTIFIES, BEAUTIFYING, BEAUTIFIED** to make something or someone beautiful, often by decorating it or them; to adorn or grace

BEAUTY *noun* **BEAUTIES** a quality pleasing to the senses, especially to the eye or ear, or giving aesthetic pleasure generally ▫ *exclamation* enthusiastically expressing approval; great!

BEAVER [1] *noun* **BEAVERS** either of two species of a large semi-aquatic squirrel-like rodent with soft dark-brown fur, large incisor teeth, webbed hind feet and a broad flat scaly tail

BEAVER [2] *verb* **BEAVERS, BEAVERING, BEAVERED** to work very hard and persistently at something

BEBOP *noun* **BEBOPS** a variety of jazz music which added new harmonies, melodic patterns and highly syncopated rhythms to accepted jazz style

BECALMED *adj* said of a sailing ship: motionless and unable to move because of lack of wind

BECAUSE *conj* for the reason that

BÉCHAMEL *noun* **BÉCHAMELS** in cookery: a white sauce flavoured with onion and herbs

BECK *noun* **BECKS** a stream or brook

BECKON *verb* **BECKONS, BECKONING, BECKONED** to summon someone towards oneself, especially by making a sign or repeated gesture with the hand

BECOME *verb* **BECOMES, BECOMING, BECAME, BECOME** to come or grow to be something; to develop into something

BECOMING *adj* said of behaviour, etc: suitable or proper

BECQUEREL *noun* **BECQUERELS** in the SI system: the unit of radioactivity, equivalent to one disintegration of a radioactive source per second

BED *noun* **BEDS** a piece of furniture for sleeping on, generally a wooden and/or metal frame with a mattress and coverings, etc on it ▫ *verb* **BEDS, BEDDING, BEDDED** to go to bed, or put someone in bed or in a place to sleep

BEDAZZLE *verb* **BEDAZZLES, BEDAZZLING, BEDAZZLED** to dazzle or impress someone greatly

BEDAZZLED *adj* dazzled or greatly impressed

BEDBUG *noun* **BEDBUGS** the common name for any of various species of household pest that infest bedding and feed on human blood

BEDCOVER *noun* **BEDCOVERS** a top cover for a bed

BEDDABLE *adj* sexually attractive

BEDDING *noun* **BEDDINGS** bedclothes, and sometimes also mattress and pillows, etc

BEDECK *verb* **BEDECKS, BEDECKING, BEDECKED** to cover something or someone with decorations; to adorn

BEDEVIL *verb* **BEDEVILS, BEDEVILING, BEDEVILED** to cause continual difficulties or trouble to someone or something

BEDFELLOW *noun* **BEDFELLOWS** a partner or associate

BEDLAM *noun* **BEDLAMS** a very noisy confused place or situation; a madhouse

BEDOUIN *noun* **BEDOUINS** a member of a nomadic tent-dwelling Arab tribe that lives in the deserts of the Middle East

BEDPAN *noun* **BEDPANS** a wide shallow pan used as a toilet by people who are unable to get out of bed

BEDPOST *noun* **BEDPOSTS** the corner support of a bedstead

BEDRIDDEN *adj* not able to get out of bed, especially because of old age or sickness

BEDROCK *noun* **BEDROCKS** the solid rock forming the lowest layer under soil and rock fragments

BEDROOM *noun* **BEDROOMS** a room for sleeping in

BEDSIDE *noun* **BEDSIDES** the place or position next to a bed, especially that of a sick person

BEDSORE *noun* **BEDSORES** an ulcer on a person's skin, caused by lying in bed for long periods

BEDSPREAD *noun* **BEDSPREADS** a top cover for a bed

BEDSTEAD *noun* **BEDSTEADS** the frame of a bed

BEDSTRAW *noun* **BEDSTRAWS** a small plant with a fragile stem, narrow leaves arranged in whorls and tiny white, yellow or greenish flowers in open clusters

BEDTIME *noun* **BEDTIMES** the time for going to bed

BEDUIN *noun* **BEDUINS** a bedouin

BEE *noun* **BEES** any of numerous four-winged insects, the female of which almost always bears a sting, and some species of which live in colonies and are often kept for their honey

BEECH *noun* **BEECHES** a deciduous tree or shrub with smooth grey bark, pale-green glossy leaves, and triangular edible fruits

BEEF *noun* **BEEVES** a steer or cow, especially one fattened for butchering ▫ *verb* **BEEFS, BEEFING, BEEFED** to complain or grumble, especially vigorously or at length

BEEFALO *noun* **BEEFALOS, BEEFALOES** a cross between a domestic cow and a N American buffalo, bred for its high-protein, low-fat meat

BEEFCAKE *noun* **BEEFCAKES** a muscular man or men, especially when displayed in photographs, etc

BEEFEATER *noun* **BEEFEATERS** a Yeoman of the Guard, or a Yeoman Warder at the Tower of London, both of whom wear the same Tudor-style ceremonial uniform

BEEFSTEAK *noun* **BEEFSTEAKS** a thick slice of beef for grilling or frying

BEEFY *adj* **BEEFIER, BEEFIEST** made of or like beef

BEEHIVE *noun* **BEEHIVES** a box or hut in which bees are kept, and where they store their honey

BEEKEEPER *noun* **BEEKEEPERS** a person who keeps bees for their honey, as a hobby, etc

BEELINE *noun* **BEELINES** a straight line between two places

BEEN a past form of **be**

BEEP *noun* **BEEPS** a short high-pitched sound, like that made by a car horn or by some electronic machines ▫ *verb* **BEEPS, BEEPING, BEEPED** to produce a beep on or with something

BEEPER *noun* **BEEPERS** a device that makes a beep, eg to attract someone's attention

BEER *noun* **BEERS** an alcoholic drink brewed by the slow fermentation of malted cereal

For longer words, see *The Chambers Dictionary*

grains, usually barley, flavoured with hops, eg ale, lager and stout

BEERY adj **BEERIER, BEERIEST** made of or like beer

BEESWAX noun **BEESWAXES** a solid yellowish substance produced by bees for making the cells in which they live

BEET noun **BEETS** any of several types of plant with large round or carrot-shaped roots which are cooked and used as food, or for making beet sugar

BEETLE noun **BEETLES** any of numerous species of insect with thickened forewings that are not used for flight but modified to form rigid horny cases which cover and protect the delicate membranous hindwings □ verb **BEETLES, BEETLING, BEETLED** to move quickly or as if in a hurry to get away; to scurry

BEETLING adj of cliffs, etc: overhanging

BEETROOT noun **BEETROOTS** a type of plant with a round dark-red root which is cooked and used as a vegetable □ adj said of someone's complexion: deep or rosy red, especially as a result of embarrassment or exertion

BEFALL verb **BEFALLS, BEFALLING, BEFELL, BEFALLEN** to happen

BEFIT verb **BEFITS, BEFITTING, BEFITTED** to be suitable or right for something or someone

BEFITTING adj suitable or right

BEFORE prep earlier than something □ conj earlier than the time when something occurs □ adverb previously; in the past

BEFOUL verb **BEFOULS, BEFOULING, BEFOULED** to make something or someone foul or dirty; to soil

BEFRIEND verb **BEFRIENDS, BEFRIENDING, BEFRIENDED** to become the friend of, or start a friendship with, someone

BEFUDDLE verb **BEFUDDLES, BEFUDDLING, BEFUDDLED** to confuse someone, eg with the effects of alcohol

BEFUDDLED adj confused, eg with the effects of alcohol

BEG verb **BEGS, BEGGING, BEGGED** to ask for (money or food, etc)

BEGET verb **BEGETS, BEGETTING, BEGOT, BEGOTTEN** to cause; to give rise to something

BEGGAR noun **BEGGARS** a person who lives by begging

BEGGARLY adj extremely small or poor; paltry

BEGGARY noun **BEGGARIES** extreme poverty; the state of being a beggar

BEGIN verb **BEGINS, BEGINNING, BEGAN, BEGUN** to start

BEGINNER noun **BEGINNERS** someone who is just starting to learn, or is still learning, how to do something

BEGINNING noun **BEGINNINGS** the point or occasion at which something begins

BEGONE exclamation go away; be off with you!

BEGONIA noun **BEGONIAS** a kind of tropical plant with brightly coloured waxy flowers and unevenly shaped leaves

BEGOT a past form of **beget**

BEGOTTEN a past form of **beget**

BEGRUDGE verb **BEGRUDGES, BEGRUDGING, BEGRUDGED** to do, give or allow something unwillingly or with regret

BEGUILE verb **BEGUILES, BEGUILING, BEGUILED** to charm or captivate

BEGUILING adj deceptively charming or amusing

BEGUINE noun **BEGUINES** a dance of French W Indian origin, in bolero rhythm

BEGUM noun **BEGUMS** a Muslim woman of high rank

BEGUN a past form of **begin**

BEHALF noun **BEHALVES** interest, benefit

BEHAVE verb **BEHAVES, BEHAVING, BEHAVED** to act in a specified way

BEHAVIOR noun **BEHAVIORS** behaviour

BEHAVIOUR noun **BEHAVIOURS** way of behaving; manners

BEHEAD verb **BEHEADS, BEHEADING, BEHEADED** to cut off the head of someone, usually as a form of capital punishment

BEHEADING noun **BEHEADINGS** the cutting off of someone's head

BEHEMOTH noun **BEHEMOTHS** something huge or monstrous

BEHEST noun **BEHESTS** a command or request

BEHIND prep at or towards the back or the far side of something or someone □ adverb in or to the back or far side of something or

someone □ adj not up to date; late □ noun **BEHINDS** the part of the body a person sits on; the buttocks

BEHOLD verb **BEHOLDS, BEHOLDING, BEHELD** to see; to look at something or someone

BEHOLDEN adj bound in gratitude (to)

BEHOLDER noun **BEHOLDERS** an observer or onlooker

BEHOOVE verb **BEHOOVES, BEHOOVING, BEHOOVED** to behove

BEHOVE verb **BEHOVES, BEHOVING, BEHOVED** of a person: to be necessary or fitting on their part

BEIGE noun **BEIGES** a very pale pinkish-brown or yellowish-brown colour □ adj having, referring to, made in, etc this colour

BEIGEL noun **BEIGELS** a bagel

BEING noun **BEINGS** existence; life

BEL noun **BELS** a unit used to represent the ratio of two different power levels, eg of sound, equal to 10 decibels

BELABOR verb **BELABORS, BELABORING, BELABORED** to belabour

BELABOUR verb **BELABOURS, BELABOURING, BELABOURED** to argue about or discuss something at excessive length

BELATED adj happening or coming late, or too late

BELATEDLY adverb in a belated way

BELAY verb **BELAYS, BELAYING, BELAYED** to make (a climber) safe by tying their rope to a rock or a wooden or metal belaying pin □ noun **BELAYS** an act of belaying

BELCH verb **BELCHES, BELCHING, BELCHED** to give out air noisily from the stomach through the mouth; to burp □ noun **BELCHES** an act of belching

BELEAGUER verb **BELEAGUERS, BELEAGUERING, BELEAGUERED** to cause someone bother or worry; to beset

BELEAGUERED adj besieged; beset

BELFRY noun **BELFRIES** the upper part of a tower or steeple, where the bells are hung

BELIE verb **BELIES, BELYING, BELIED** to show something to be untrue or false

BELIEF noun **BELIEFS** a principle or idea, etc accepted as true, especially without proof

BELIEVE verb **BELIEVES,**

BELIEVING, BELIEVED to accept what is said by someone as true **BELIEVER** noun **BELIEVERS** a person who believes, especially someone who believes in God

BELITTLE verb **BELITTLES, BELITTLING, BELITTLED** to treat something or someone as unimportant, or of little or no significance; to speak or write disparagingly about it or them

BELITTLING adj having the effect of making something or someone out to be insignificant

BELL noun **BELLS** a deep hollow object, usually one made of metal, rounded at one end and wide and open at the other, which makes a ringing sound when struck by the small hammer or clapper fixed inside it ◻ verb **BELLS, BELLING, BELLED** to attach or fit a bell to something

BELLE noun **BELLES** a beautiful woman

BELLHOP noun **BELLHOPS** a man or boy who works in a hotel, carrying guests' bags and delivering messages, etc, who may be summoned by ringing a bell provided

BELLICOSE adj likely to, or seeking to, cause an argument or war; aggressive; warlike

BELLOW verb **BELLOWS, BELLOWING, BELLOWED** to make a loud deep cry like that of a bull ◻ noun **BELLOWS** the loud roar of a bull

BELLOWS singular or plural noun a device having a bag-like part with folds in it, which is squeezed to create a current of air, used eg to fan a fire

BELLY noun **BELLIES** the part of the human body below the chest, containing the organs used for digesting food ◻ verb **BELLIES, BELLYING, BELLIED** to bulge out, or make something bulge or swell out

BELLYFUL noun **BELLYFULS** enough to eat

BELONG verb **BELONGS, BELONGING, BELONGED** to have a proper place, or have the right qualities to fit (especially with or in something or someone); to go along or together with it or them

BELONGING noun fitting in or acceptability within a group

BELONGINGS plural noun personal possessions

BELOVED adj much loved; very dear ◻ noun **BELOVEDS** a person who is much loved

BELOW prep lower in position, rank, amount, degree, number or status, etc than a specified thing ◻ adverb at, to or in a lower place, point or level

BELT noun **BELTS** a long narrow piece of leather or cloth worn around the waist to keep clothing in place, or for decoration, etc ◻ verb **BELTS, BELTING, BELTED** to put a belt around someone or something

BELTED adj having or wearing a belt

BELTER noun **BELTERS** something or someone that stands out from the others as strikingly admirable, enjoyable, thrilling, etc

BELTMAN noun **BELTMEN** the member of a life-saving team responsible for bringing the lifeline, attached to his belt, when he swims out to help someone in trouble

BELTWAY noun **BELTWAYS** a road that goes around the outskirts of a town or an inner city area

BELUGA noun **BELUGAS** a kind of large sturgeon

BELVEDERE noun **BELVEDERES** a turret, lantern or room built on the top of a house, with open or glazed sides to provide a view or to let in light and air

BEMOAN verb **BEMOANS, BEMOANING, BEMOANED** to express great sadness or regret about something

BEMUSE verb **BEMUSES, BEMUSING, BEMUSED** to puzzle or confuse someone

BEMUSED adj puzzled or confused

BEN noun **BENS** especially in place names: a mountain or mountain peak

BENCH noun **BENCHES** a long wooden or stone seat for seating several people ◻ verb **BENCHES, BENCHING, BENCHED** to provide or furnish something with benches

BENCHER noun **BENCHERS** a senior member of an Inn of Court

BENCHMARK noun **BENCHMARKS** anything taken or used as a standard or point of reference

BEND verb **BENDS, BENDING, BENT, BENDED** to make or become angled or curved ◻ noun **BENDS** a curve or bent part

BENDER noun **BENDERS** a drunken spree; a spell of uncontrolled drinking

BENDY adj **BENDIER, BENDIEST** having many bends or curves

BENEATH prep under; below; in a lower position, so as to be covered or hidden by something or someone ◻ adverb below; underneath

BENEFICE noun **BENEFICES** a position as a priest or minister, or other church office, and the income from land or buildings, etc which goes with it

BENEFICED adj holding a benefice

BENEFIT noun **BENEFITS** something good gained or received ◻ verb **BENEFITS, BENEFITING, BENEFITED** to gain an advantage or receive something good from something or as a result of something

BENIGHTED adj said of eg a people, a land or a race: lacking intelligence or a sense of morality

BENIGN adj kind; gentle

BENIGNANT adj said of a disease or growth, etc: not fatal; benign

BENIGNITY noun **BENIGNITIES** kindness; benevolence

BENIGNLY adverb in a benign way

BENNY noun **BENNIES** an amphetamine tablet

BENT adj not straight; curved or having a bend ◻ noun **BENTS** a natural inclination, liking or aptitude

BENTHIC adj of or relating to the living organisms found at the bottom of a sea or lake

BENTHOS noun **BENTHOSES** the living organisms that are found at the bottom of a sea or lake

BENTONITE noun **BENTONITES** a pale soft porous rock, capable of absorbing large quantities of water, and used in papermaking and as a bleaching and decolourizing agent

BENTWOOD noun **BENTWOODS** wood artificially curved for making furniture, etc

BENUMB verb **BENUMBS, BENUMBING, BENUMBED** to make someone or something numb

BENZENE noun **BENZENES** an inflammable colourless liquid hydrocarbon, mainly obtained from petroleum, that has an aromatic odour and is widely used as a solvent and in the manufacture of plastics, dyes, drugs and other organic chemicals

For longer words, see The Chambers Dictionary

BENZINE noun **BENZINES** a volatile mixture of hydrocarbons distilled from petroleum, used as a motor fuel and solvent, etc

BENZOIN noun **BENZOINS** the aromatic resinous sap of a tree native to Java and Sumatra, used in perfumery, incense, etc and as an expectorant, respiratory inhalant and antiseptic

BEQUEATH verb **BEQUEATHS, BEQUEATHING, BEQUEATHED** to leave (personal property) in a will

BEQUEST noun **BEQUESTS** an act of leaving personal property in a will

BERATE verb **BERATES, BERATING, BERATED** to scold someone severely

BEREAVE verb **BEREAVES, BEREAVING, BEREAVED, BEREFT** to widow, orphan or deprive someone of a close relative or friend by death

BEREAVED adj said of a person: having recently suffered the death of a close relative or friend

BEREFT adj deprived of something; having had something precious taken away (especially, in a formal context, some immaterial possession)

BERET noun **BERETS** a round flat cap made of wool or other soft material

BERG noun **BERGS** a mountain, especially in S Africa

BERGAMOT noun **BERGAMOTS** a small citrus tree that produces acidic pear-shaped fruits

BERIBERI noun **BERIBERIS** a deficiency disease, most widespread in the tropics, caused by lack of thiamine, which results in inflammation of the nerves, paralysis of the limbs, oedema and heart failure

BERK noun **BERKS** a fool or twit

BERKELIUM noun **BERKELIUMS** a radioactive metallic element manufactured artificially by bombarding americium-241 with alpha particles

BERLEY noun **BERLEYS** humbug; rubbish

BERM noun **BERMS** a narrow ledge or path beside an embankment, road or canal, etc

BERRY noun **BERRIES** an indehiscent fleshy fruit that contains anything from several to many seeds which are not surrounded by a stony protective layer, eg grape, cucumber, tomato, citrus fruits

BERSERK adj violently angry; wild and destructive

BERSERKER noun **BERSERKERS** a Norse warrior

BERTH noun **BERTHS** a sleeping-place in a ship or train, etc □ verb **BERTHS, BERTHING, BERTHED** to tie up (a ship) in its berth

BERYL noun **BERYLS** a hard mineral, used as a source of beryllium and as a gemstone, the most valuable varieties being aquamarine and emerald

BERYLLIUM noun **BERYLLIUMS** a silvery-grey metal, obtained from the mineral beryl, used to make windows in X-ray tubes, and also used together with copper to make strong alloys

BESEECH verb **BESEECHES, BESEECHING, BESOUGHT** to ask someone earnestly; to beg

BESEECHING adj appealing or entreating □ noun **BESEECHINGS** earnest appealing

BESET verb **BESETS, BESETTING, BESET** to worry or harass someone, or to hamper or complicate something (with problems, temptations, obstacles, etc)

BESIDE prep next to, by the side of or near something or someone

BESIDES prep in addition to, as well as or apart from something or someone □ adverb also; as well

BESIEGE verb **BESIEGES, BESIEGING, BESIEGED** to surround (a town or stronghold) with an army in order to force it to surrender

BESMEAR verb **BESMEARS, BESMEARING, BESMEARED** to smear or daub someone or something with something greasy, sticky or dirty, etc

BESMIRCH verb **BESMIRCHES, BESMIRCHING, BESMIRCHED** to spoil or stain (the reputation, character, name, etc of someone)

BESOM noun **BESOMS** a large brush made from sticks tied to a long wooden handle

BESOTTED adj foolishly infatuated

BESOUGHT past form of **beseech**

BESPANGLE verb **BESPANGLES, BESPANGLING, BESPANGLED** to decorate something with objects which shine or sparkle

BESPATTER verb **BESPATTERS, BESPATTERING, BESPATTERED** to cover something or someone with spots, splashes or large drops (especially of a dirty liquid)

BESPEAK verb **BESPEAKS, BESPEAKING, BESPOKE, BESPOKEN** to claim, engage or order something in advance

BESPOKE adj said of clothes: made to fit a particular person, or made according to a particular person's requirements

BEST adj most excellent, suitable or desirable □ adverb most successfully or skilfully, etc □ noun **BESTS** the most excellent or suitable person or thing; the most desirable quality or result, etc □ verb **BESTS, BESTING, BESTED** to beat or defeat someone

BESTIAL adj cruel; savage; brutish

BESTIARY noun **BESTIARIES** a kind of book popular in Europe in the Middle Ages, containing pictures and descriptions of animals, often used for moral instruction

BESTIR verb **BESTIRS, BESTIRRING, BESTIRRED** to make an effort to become active

BESTOW verb **BESTOWS, BESTOWING, BESTOWED** to give or present (a title, award, quality, etc) to someone

BESTOWAL noun **BESTOWALS** an act of bestowing

BESTREWN adj said of a surface, eg the ground, a floor, or table-top: littered or covered loosely, usually with things which have been thrown casually or scattered randomly

BESTRIDE verb **BESTRIDES, BESTRIDING, BESTRODE, BESTRIDDEN** to sit or stand across something (eg a horse) with one leg on each side

BET verb **BETS, BETTING, BET, BETTED** to risk (a sum of money or other asset) on predicting the outcome or result of a future event, especially a race or other sporting event, in such a way that the better wins money if the outcome is as predicted, and loses the stake if it is not □ noun **BETS** an act of betting

BETA noun **BETAS** the second letter of the Greek alphabet

BETAKE verb **BETAKES, BETAKING, BETOOK, BETAKEN** to go; to take oneself to a specified place

BETATRON noun **BETATRONS** a

type of particle accelerator which continuously increases the magnetic flux within the orbit of a charged particle

BETEL *noun* **BETELS** a palm, native to Asia, the fruit of which is mixed with lime and chewed as a mild stimulant

BETIDE *verb* **BETIDES, BETIDING, BETID, BETIDED** to befall; to happen to

BETOKEN *verb* **BETOKENS, BETOKENING, BETOKENED** to be evidence, or a sign or omen of something; to signify

BETOOK a past form of **betake** ¹

BETRAY *verb* **BETRAYS, BETRAYING, BETRAYED** to hand over or expose (a friend or one's country, etc) to an enemy

BETRAYAL *noun* **BETRAYALS** the or an act of betraying

BETRAYER *noun* **BETRAYERS** a traitor

BETROTHAL *noun* **BETROTHALS** engagement to be married

BETROTHED *adj* said of a person: engaged to marry someone □ *noun* **BETROTHEDS** a person to whom someone is betrothed

BETTER *adj* more excellent, suitable or desirable, etc □ *adverb* more excellently, successfully or fully, etc □ *noun* **BETTERS** a person superior in quality or status, etc □ *verb* **BETTERS, BETTERING, BETTERED** to beat or improve on something

BETTING *noun* **BETTINGS** gambling by predicting the outcome of some future event, especially a race or other sporting event

BETTOR *noun* **BETTORS** a person who bets

BETWEEN *prep* in, to, through or across the space dividing (two people, places, times, etc) □ *adverb* in or into the middle of (two points in space or time, etc)

BETWIXT *adverb* between □ *adj* undecided; in a middle position

BEVATRON *noun* **BEVATRONS** a type of proton accelerator that produces particles with an energy content of the order of billions of electron-volts

BEVEL *noun* **BEVELS** a sloping edge to a surface, meeting another surface at an angle between the horizontal and the vertical □ *verb* **BEVELS, BEVELLING, BEVELLED** to give a bevel or slant to (eg a piece of wood)

BEVELLED *adj* cut to an oblique angle, sloped off

BEVERAGE *noun* **BEVERAGES** a prepared drink, especially a hot drink (eg tea or coffee) or an alcoholic drink (eg beer)

BEVVY *noun* **BEVVIES** alcoholic drink, or an individual alcoholic drink

BEVY *noun* **BEVIES** a group, especially and originally a group of women or girls

BEWAIL *verb* **BEWAILS, BEWAILING, BEWAILED** to express great sorrow about something, or to lament over it

BEWARE *verb* **BEWARES, BEWARING, BEWARED** to take heed; to be on one's guard

BEWILDER *verb* **BEWILDERS, BEWILDERING, BEWILDERED** to confuse, disorientate or puzzle thoroughly, often by numerous things happening or moving at the same time or in rapid succession

BEWILDERED *adj* confused, disorientated or puzzled

BEWILDERING *adj* confusing, disorientating or puzzling

BEWITCH *verb* **BEWITCHES, BEWITCHING, BEWITCHED** to charm, fascinate or enchant

BEWITCHING *adj* alluring; charming

BEY *noun* **BEYS** a Turkish governor

BEYOND *prep* on the far side of something □ *adverb* farther away; to or on the far side of something □ *noun* **BEYONDS** the unknown, especially life after death

BEZ *noun* **BEZES** the second tine of a deer's horn
ⓘ This word scores 14 points and is a useful word for using up both a **B** and a **Z**, especially on a tight board offering few good scoring opportunities.

BEZEL *noun* **BEZELS** the sloped surface of a cutting tool

BEZIQUE *noun* **BEZIQUES** a card game for two, three or four players, using two packs of cards from which all cards of a value below seven have been removed

BHAGEE *noun* **BHAGEES** an Indian appetizer consisting of vegetables in a batter of flour and spices, formed into a ball and deep-fried

BHAKTI *noun* **BHAKTIS** loving devotion and surrender to God, recommended as the most effective path to salvation in most popular Hindu texts

BHANG *noun* **BHANGS** the leaves and shoots of the cannabis plant, used as a narcotic and intoxicant

BHANGRA *noun* **BHANGRAS** a style of pop music created from a mix of traditional Punjabi and Western pop which originated among the British Asian community in the late 1970s

BHINDI *noun* **BHINDIS** in Indian cookery: okra

BI *noun* **BIS** a bisexual person

BIANNUAL *adj* occurring or produced, etc twice a year

BIAS *noun* **BIASES** an inclination to favour or disfavour one side against another in a dispute, competition, etc; a prejudice □ *verb* **BIASES, BIASING, BIASED, BIASSES, BIASSING, BIASSED** to influence or prejudice, especially unfairly or without objective grounds

BIASED *adj* predisposed to favour one side, group, person, etc rather than another

BIASSED *adj* biased

BIATHLON *noun* **BIATHLONS** an outdoor sporting event in which competitors cross a 20km (12.43ml) course on skis, stopping at intervals to shoot at targets with rifles

BIAXIAL *adj* said especially of a crystal: having two axes

BIB *noun* **BIBS** a piece of cloth or plastic fastened under a baby's or child's chin to protect its clothes while eating or drinking

BIBLE *noun* **BIBLES** the sacred writings of the Christian Church, consisting of the Old and New Testaments

BIBULOUS *adj* liking alcohol too much, or drinking too much of it

BICAMERAL *adj* said of a legislative body: made up of two parts or chambers, such as the House of Commons and the House of Lords in the British parliament

BICEPS *noun* **BICEPSES** any muscle that has two points of origin, especially the muscle at the front of the upper arm, which is used to flex the forearm

BICKER *verb* **BICKERS, BICKERING, BICKERED** to argue

or quarrel in a petty way, especially about or over something trivial

BICKERING noun **BICKERINGS** tedious petty quarrelling

BICONCAVE adj said of a structure, especially a lens: concave on both sides

BICONVEX adj said of a structure, especially a lens: convex on both sides

BICUSPID adj said especially of a tooth: having two cusps or points ▫ noun **BICUSPIDS** a premolar tooth

BICYCLE noun **BICYCLES** a vehicle consisting of a metal frame with two wheels one behind the other, and a saddle between and above them, which is driven by turning pedals with the feet and steered by handlebars attached to the front wheel ▫ verb **BICYCLES, BICYCLING, BICYCLED** to ride a bicycle

BICYCLIST noun **BICYCLISTS** a cyclist

BID [1] verb **BIDS, BIDDING, BID** to offer (an amount of money) when trying to buy something, especially at an auction ▫ noun **BIDS** an offer of an amount of money in payment for something, especially at an auction

BID [2] verb **BIDS, BIDDING, BIDDEN, BADE** to express (a wish or greeting, etc)

BIDDABLE adj compliant; obedient; docile

BIDDER noun **BIDDERS** someone who makes an offer for something, especially at an auction

BIDDING noun **BIDDINGS** a command, request or invitation

BIDDY noun **BIDDIES** a woman, especially an old, doddery, fussy or cantankerous one

BIDE verb **BIDES, BIDING, BIDED, BODE** to wait or stay

BIDET noun **BIDETS** a small low basin with taps, on which a person sits to wash their genital and anal areas

BIENNIAL adj said of an event: occurring once in every two years ▫ noun **BIENNIALS** a plant which takes two years to complete its life cycle, germinating and accumulating food reserves in the first year, and flowering, producing seed and dying during the second year, eg carrot

BIER noun **BIERS** a movable stand for a coffin

BIFF verb **BIFFS, BIFFING, BIFFED** to hit someone or something very hard, usually with the fist ▫ noun **BIFFS** a hard sharp blow, usually with the fist; a punch

BIFID adj divided into two parts by a deep split; forked

BIFOCAL adj having two different focal lengths

BIFOCALS plural noun a pair of glasses with bifocal lenses, which allow the wearer to look at distant objects through the upper part of the lens, and to read or look at close objects through the lower part

BIFURCATE verb **BIFURCATES, BIFURCATING, BIFURCATED** said of roads, etc: to divide into two parts or branches; to fork ▫ adj forked or branched into two parts

BIG adj **BIGGER, BIGGEST** large or largest in size, amount, weight, number, power, etc ▫ adverb in a boastful, extravagant or ambitious way

BIGAMIST noun **BIGAMISTS** a person who has committed bigamy

BIGAMOUS adj involving bigamy

BIGAMY noun **BIGAMIES** the crime of being married to two wives or husbands at the same time

BIGFOOT noun **BIGFEET** in the folklore of N America: a large hairy primate reputed to inhabit wilderness areas

BIGGIE noun **BIGGIES** a biggy

BIGGISH adj fairly big

BIGGY noun **BIGGIES** a large or important thing or person, especially as seen in comparison with others of a similar kind

BIGHEADED adj conceited or arrogant

BIGHORN noun **BIGHORNS** either of two species of wild sheep (the N American and Siberian) that inhabit mountains, especially cliffs

BIGHT noun **BIGHTS** a stretch of gently curving coastline

BIGMOUTH noun **BIGMOUTHS** a boastful, or tactless, talkative person

BIGNESS noun **BIGNESSES** bulk, size

BIGOT noun **BIGOTS** someone who is persistently prejudiced, especially about religion or politics, and refuses to tolerate the opinions of others

BIGOTED adj having the qualities of a bigot

BIGOTRY noun **BIGOTRIES** blind or excessive zeal, especially in religious or political matters

BIGWIG noun **BIGWIGS** an important or powerful person

BIJOU noun **BIJOUX** a small delicate jewel or trinket ▫ adj small and elegant

BIKE noun **BIKES** a bicycle ▫ verb **BIKES, BIKING, BIKED** to ride a bicycle or motorcycle

BIKER noun **BIKERS** a member of a gang of motorcycle riders

BIKEWAY noun **BIKEWAYS** a lane or road, etc specially designed or set aside for the use of pedal cycles

BIKING noun **BIKINGS** the sport or pastime of cycling or riding a motorcycle

BIKINI noun **BIKINIS** a small two-piece swimming costume for women

BILABIAL adj said of a consonant: made with both lips touching or almost touching each other, as with the letters b and w ▫ noun **BILABIALS** a bilabial consonant

BILATERAL adj said of a treaty, agreement, conference, talks, etc: involving the participation of, affecting, or signed or agreed by, two countries, parties or groups, etc

BILBERRY noun **BILBERRIES** a small deciduous shrub, native to heaths and moorland of Europe and N Asia, which has bright green oval leaves and pink globular flowers

BILE noun **BILES** a thick yellowish-green alkaline liquid produced by the liver, stored by the gall bladder and secreted into the duodenum, where it plays a major role in the digestion of fats

BILGE noun **BILGES** the broadest part of a ship's bottom

BILHARZIA noun **BILHARZIAS** another name for the parasitic disease schistosomiasis

BILIARY adj concerned with, relating or belonging to bile, the bile ducts or the gall bladder

BILINGUAL adj written or spoken in two languages ▫ noun **BILINGUALS** a person who speaks two languages

BILIOUS adj affected by or sick with a disorder relating to the secretion, especially excessive secretion, of bile; bad-tempered

BILIOUSLY adverb in a bilious way

BILIRUBIN noun **BILIRUBINS** a

yellowish-orange pigment found in bile and formed from biliverdin, excess of which in the blood causes jaundice

BILK verb **BILKS, BILKING, BILKED** to avoid paying someone money one owes them

BILKER noun **BILKERS** a person who avoids paying money they owe

BILL noun **BILLS** a printed or written statement of the amount of money owed for goods or services received; an invoice ◻ verb **BILLS, BILLING, BILLED** to send or give a bill to someone, requesting payment for goods, etc; to charge

BILLABONG noun **BILLABONGS** a pool of water left when most of a river or stream has become dry

BILLBOARD noun **BILLBOARDS** a large board, eg by a roadside or railway platform, on which advertising posters are displayed

BILLET noun **BILLETS** a house, often a private home, where soldiers are given board and lodging temporarily ◻ verb **BILLETS, BILLETING, BILLETED** to give or assign lodging to, or to accommodate (soldiers, etc)

BILLFOLD noun **BILLFOLDS** a soft case, pocketbook or wallet for holding banknotes, and often credit cards and documents, etc

BILLHOOK noun **BILLHOOKS** a wooden-handled cutting tool used for pruning, lopping off stems, etc, having a long curved blade with a sharp inner edge, and often a hooked tip

BILLIARD adj for, belonging or referring to the game of billiards

BILLIARDS singular noun an indoor game played with a cue and coloured balls on a cloth-covered table with high cushioned edges, which has pockets at the sides and corners into which the balls can be struck to score points

BILLING noun **BILLINGS** the importance of a performer in a play or concert, especially as shown by the position of the name on the poster advertising the performance

BILLION noun **BILLIONS** a thousand million

BILLIONTH noun **BILLIONTHS** a thousand millionth

BILLOW verb **BILLOWS, BILLOWING, BILLOWED** said eg of smoke: to move in large waves or clouds ◻ noun **BILLOWS** a rolling upward-moving mass of smoke or mist, etc

BILLOWING adj said eg of smoke: moving in large waves or clouds

BILLOWY adj **BILLOWIER, BILLOWIEST** giving the impression of billowing

BILLY noun **BILLIES** a metal container with a lid and wire handle, used for carrying and boiling water in, especially when camping

BILOBATE adj having or made up of two lobes

BILOBED adj bilobate

BIMANUAL adj using or performed with two hands

BIMBO noun **BIMBOS** a young woman who is physically attractive, but empty-headed

BIMONTHLY adj occurring or produced, etc once every two months ◻ adverb every two months

BIN noun **BINS** a container for depositing or storing rubbish ◻ verb **BINS, BINNING, BINNED** to put (eg rubbish) into a bin

BINARY adj consisting of or containing two parts or elements ◻ noun **BINARIES** a thing made up of two parts

BINAURAL adj having, using or relating to two ears

BIND verb **BINDS, BINDING, BOUND** to tie or fasten tightly ◻ noun **BINDS** a difficult, tedious or annoying situation

BINDER noun **BINDERS** a hard book-like cover in which loose pieces of paper can be kept in order

BINDERY noun **BINDERIES** a place where books are bound

BINDING noun **BINDINGS** the part of a book cover on to which the pages are stuck ◻ adj formally or legally obliging or constraining someone to do something

BINDWEED noun **BINDWEEDS** any of numerous perennial plants with funnel-shaped flowers consisting of five fused petals, including many climbing species which twine around the stems of other plants

BINGE noun **BINGES** a bout of over-indulgence, usually in eating and drinking ◻ verb **BINGES, BINGING, BINGED** to indulge in a binge

BINGLE noun **BINGLES** a car-crash; a smash

BINGO noun **BINGOS** a game of chance in which each player has a card with a set of numbers on it, and may cover a number if it is called out at random, the winner being the first player with a card on which all or a certain sequence of the numbers have been called

BINMAN noun **BINMEN** a refuse-collector

BINNACLE noun **BINNACLES** a case for a ship's compass

BINOCULAR adj relating to the use of both eyes simultaneously

BINOCULARS plural noun an optical instrument designed for viewing distant objects, consisting of two small telescopes arranged side by side so that the observer is able to use both eyes at once

BINOMIAL noun **BINOMIALS** an algebraic expression that contains two variables, eg $6x - 3y$

BINTURONG noun **BINTURONGS** a SE Asian carnivorous mammal of the civet family, with thick black fur and a prehensile tail

BIO noun **BIOS** a biography

BIOASSAY noun **BIOASSAYS** the assessment of the concentration of a chemical substance by testing its effect on a living organism, eg its effect on plant or bacterial growth

BIOGAS noun **BIOGASES** domestic or commercial gas (especially methane and carbon dioxide) produced by bacterial fermentation of naturally occurring materials such as animal manure and other organic waste

BIOGRAPHY noun **BIOGRAPHIES** an account of a person's life, usually written by someone else and published or intended for publication

BIOLOGIST noun **BIOLOGISTS** someone who studies biology

BIOLOGY noun **BIOLOGIES** the scientific study of living organisms

BIOMASS noun **BIOMASSES** the total mass of living organisms in an ecosystem, population or designated area at a given time

BIOME noun **BIOMES** a major ecological community of living organisms, usually defined by the plant habitat with which they are associated, eg grassland, rainforest

BIOMETRIC adj of or relating to biometry

BIOMETRICS *singular noun* biometry

BIOMETRY *noun* **BIOMETRIES** the branch of biology concerned with the applications of statistical methods of analysis to biological systems

BIONIC *adj* using, or belonging or relating to, bionics

BIONICS *singular noun* the study of how living organisms function, and the application of the principles observed to develop computers and other machines which work in similar ways

BIONOMIC *adj* of or relating to bionomics

BIONOMICS *singular noun* the study of the relationships between living organisms and their environment

BIOPIC *noun* **BIOPICS** a film telling the life-story of a famous person, frequently in an uncritically admiring or superficial way

BIOPSY *noun* **BIOPSIES** the removal and examination of a small piece of living tissue from an organ or part of the body in order to determine the nature of any suspected disease

BIOSCOPE *noun* **BIOSCOPES** a cinema

BIOSPHERE *noun* **BIOSPHERES** that part of the earth's surface and its atmosphere in which living organisms are known to exist

BIOTA *noun* **BIOTAS** the living organisms present in a particular area

BIOTIC *adj* belonging or relating to life or living organisms

BIOTIN *noun* **BIOTINS** a member of the vitamin B complex, produced by the bacteria that inhabit the gut of animals, and also found in yeast, liver, egg yolk, cereals and milk

BIPARTITE *adj* consisting of or divided into two parts

BIPED *noun* **BIPEDS** an animal with two feet, eg man □ *adj* said of an animal: having two feet; walking on two feet

BIPLANE *noun* **BIPLANES** an early type of aeroplane with two sets of wings, one above the other

BIPOLAR *adj* having two poles or extremes

BIRCH *noun* **BIRCHES** a slender deciduous tree or shrub of N temperate and Arctic regions, with smooth silvery-white bark that often peels off in long papery strips □ *adj* made of birch wood □ *verb* **BIRCHES, BIRCHING, BIRCHED** to flog someone with a birch rod; to whip them

BIRD *noun* **BIRDS** any member of a class of warm-blooded vertebrate animals characterized by the possession of feathers, front limbs modified to form wings, and projecting jaws modified to form a horny beak

BIRDBATH *noun* **BIRDBATHS** a basin, usually one on a pedestal, set up outside for birds to bathe in

BIRDCAGE *noun* **BIRDCAGES** a cage, usually made of wire or wicker, for keeping a bird in

BIRDCALL *noun* **BIRDCALLS** a bird's song

BIRDER *noun* **BIRDERS** a birdwatcher, someone who studies birds as a hobby

BIRDIE *noun* **BIRDIES** in golf: a score of one stroke under par for a particular hole on a course □ *verb* **BIRDIES, BIRDIEING, BIRDIED** in golf: to complete (a hole) with a birdie score

BIRDING *noun* **BIRDINGS** the scientific observation of birds in their natural habitat

BIRDSEED *noun* **BIRDSEEDS** seed used for feeding cagebirds, etc, eg a mixture of small seeds such as hemp

BIRDSHOT *noun* **BIRDSHOTS** small pellets suitable for shooting birds

BIRETTA *noun* **BIRETTAS** a stiff square cap with three flat upright projections on top, worn by Roman Catholic clergy

BIRTH *noun* **BIRTHS** the act or process of bearing children

BIRTHDAY *noun* **BIRTHDAYS** the anniversary of the day on which a person was born

BIRTHMARK *noun* **BIRTHMARKS** a blemish or mark that is present on the skin at birth and may be temporary or permanent

BIRYANI *noun* **BIRYANIS** a type of spicy Indian dish consisting mainly of rice, with meat or fish and vegetables, etc

BIS *adverb* twice

BISCUIT *noun* **BISCUITS** a small thin sweet crisp cake, in any of numerous varieties or flavours, etc □ *adj* pale golden brown or pale tan in colour

BISCUITY *adj* like a biscuit in flavour, texture or colour

BISECT *verb* **BISECTS, BISECTING, BISECTED** to divide something into two equal parts

BISECTION *noun* **BISECTIONS** division into two parts

BISECTOR *noun* **BISECTORS** a line that divides an angle, etc into two equal parts

BISEXUAL *adj* sexually attracted to both males and females □ *noun* **BISEXUALS** a bisexual person or organism, etc

BISHOP *noun* **BISHOPS** a senior priest or minister in the Roman Catholic, Anglican and Orthodox Churches, in charge of a group of churches in an area, or of a diocese

BISHOPRIC *noun* **BISHOPRICS** the post or position of bishop

BISMUTH *noun* **BISMUTHS** a hard silvery-white metallic element with a pinkish tinge, used to make lead alloys for use in fire-detection devices, electrical fuses, etc, the insoluble compounds of which are used to treat stomach upsets, skin disorders, etc

BISON *noun* **BISONS** either of two species of large hoofed mammal with a dark-brown coat, broad humped shoulders, short upward-curving horns and long shaggy hair on its head, neck, shoulders and forelegs

BISQUE *noun* **BISQUES** a thick rich soup, usually made from shellfish, cream and wine

BISTABLE *adj* said of a valve or transistor circuit: having two stable states □ *noun* **BISTABLES** an electronic circuit that stays in one of two stable states until it receives a suitable electric pulse, which causes it to switch to the other state

BISTORT *noun* **BISTORTS** any of various plants found mainly in northern temperate regions, with lance-shaped or oblong leaves and small white, pink or red flowers with terminal spikes

BISTRO *noun* **BISTROS** a small bar or informal restaurant

BIT *noun* **BITS** a small piece, part or amount of something

BITCH *noun* **BITCHES** a female of the dog family □ *verb* **BITCHES, BITCHING, BITCHED** to complain or talk bitchily

BITCHILY *adverb* in a bitchy way

BITCHY *adj* **BITCHIER, BITCHIEST**

spiteful; petulantly bad-tempered or malicious

BITE verb **BITES, BITING, BIT, BITTEN** to grasp, seize or tear with the teeth □ noun **BITES** an act or an instance of biting

BITER noun **BITERS** a person or thing that bites

BITESIZE adj referring to a morsel of food which is small enough to be put into the mouth and eaten in one

BITING adj bitterly and painfully cold □ noun **BITINGS** the action of grasping, seizing or tearing with the teeth

BITMAP noun **BITMAPS** in computing: a method of organizing the screen display whereby each pixel is assigned to one or more binary digits in memory

BITONAL adj said of a composition, etc: using two keys simultaneously

BITTEN a past form of **bite**

BITTER adj **BITTERER, BITTEREST** having a sharp, acid and often unpleasant taste □ noun **BITTERS** a type of beer with a slightly bitter taste, strongly flavoured with hops

BITTERLY adverb in a bitter way

BITTERN noun **BITTERNS** a long-legged European bird that lives on or near water and makes a very loud deep sound

BITTERS plural noun a liquid made from bitter herbs or roots, used to help digestion or to flavour certain alcoholic drinks

BITTS noun **BITTS** a pair of posts or bollards for fastening the anchoring cables, etc around on the deck of a ship

BITTY adj **BITTIER, BITTIEST** consisting of small unrelated bits or parts, especially when put together awkwardly or untidily; scrappy; disjointed

BITUMEN noun **BITUMENS** any of various black solid or tarry flammable substances composed of an impure mixture of hydrocarbons, either occurring naturally or obtained by the distillation of petroleum, and which is used for surfacing roads and pavements, etc

BIVALENCY noun **BIVALENCIES** the quality of being bivalent

BIVALENT adj said of an atom: able to combine with two atoms of hydrogen or the equivalent

BIVALVE adj said of a mollusc: having a shell composed of two valves hinged together by a ligament □ noun **BIVALVES** any of numerous mainly marine species of mollusc with a shell composed of two valves hinged together by a tough horny ligament, eg clam, cockle, mussel and scallop

BIVARIATE adj involving two variables

BIVOUAC noun **BIVOUACS** a temporary camp or camping place without tents, especially one used by soldiers and mountaineers □ verb **BIVOUACS, BIVOUACKING, BIVOUACKED** to camp out temporarily at night without a tent

BIZ noun **BIZZES** a slang word for *business*
ⓘ This word scores 14 points and is useful for getting rid of both a **B** and a **Z**.

BIZARRE adj weirdly odd or strange

BLAB verb **BLABS, BLABBING, BLABBED** to tell or divulge (a secret, etc)

BLABBER verb **BLABBERS, BLABBERING, BLABBERED** to talk nonsense, especially without stopping or without being understood; to babble □ noun **BLABBERS** a person who talks foolishly and indiscreetly

BLABBING noun **BLABBINGS** indiscreet talking □ adj that tells or divulges (a secret, etc)

BLACK adj **BLACKER, BLACKEST** having the darkest colour, the same colour as coal; reflecting no light □ noun **BLACKS** the colour of coal, etc, the darkest colour, or absence of colour □ verb **BLACKS, BLACKING, BLACKED** to make something black

BLACKBALL verb **BLACKBALLS, BLACKBALLING, BLACKBALLED** to vote against (a candidate for membership of something), originally by putting a black ball in the ballot box

BLACKBALLING noun **BLACKBALLINGS** voting against (a candidate for membership of something)

BLACKBIRD noun **BLACKBIRDS** a small European bird, the male of which is black with a yellow beak

BLACKCAP noun **BLACKCAPS** a small songbird, the male of which has a black-topped head

BLACKCOCK noun **BLACKCOCKS** the male of the black grouse

BLACKEN verb **BLACKENS, BLACKENING, BLACKENED** to make or become black or very dark in colour

BLACKHEAD noun **BLACKHEADS** a small black spot on the skin caused by sweat blocking one of the skin's tiny pores or hair follicles

BLACKING noun **BLACKINGS** black polish, especially for shining shoes or fireplaces, etc

BLACKJACK noun **BLACKJACKS** pontoon or a similar game; a cosh □ verb **BLACKJACKS, BLACKJACKING, BLACKJACKED** to hit someone with a cosh

BLACKLEG noun **BLACKLEGS** a person who refuses to take part in a strike, or who works in a striker's place during a strike □ verb **BLACKLEGS, BLACKLEGGING, BLACKLEGGED** to refuse to take part in a strike; to work as a blackleg

BLACKLIST noun **BLACKLISTS** a list of people convicted or suspected of something, or not approved of, to be boycotted or excluded, etc □ verb **BLACKLISTS, BLACKLISTING, BLACKLISTED** to put someone on such a list

BLACKLY adverb in an angry or threatening way

BLACKMAIL verb **BLACKMAILS, BLACKMAILING, BLACKMAILED** to extort money, etc illegally from someone by threatening to reveal harmful information about them □ noun **BLACKMAILS** an act of blackmailing someone

BLACKNESS noun **BLACKNESSES** the quality or state of being black

BLACKOUT noun **BLACKOUTS** an enforced period during which all the lights in an area are turned out, eg during World War II as a precaution during an air raid at night

BLACKTOP noun **BLACKTOPS** bituminous material used for surfacing roads, etc

BLADDER noun **BLADDERS** in all mammals, and some fish, amphibians and reptiles: a hollow sac-shaped organ with a thin muscular wall, in which urine produced by the kidneys is stored before it is discharged from the body

BLADE *noun* **BLADES** the cutting part of a knife or sword, etc

BLAG *verb* **BLAGS, BLAGGING, BLAGGED** to rob or steal something □ *noun* **BLAGS** a theft or robbery; a scrounge

BLAGGER *noun* **BLAGGERS** someone who robs or steals

BLAH *noun* **BLAHS** bunkum; pretentious nonsense □ *verb* **BLAHS, BLAHING, BLAHED** to talk stupidly or insipidly

BLAIN *noun* **BLAINS** a boil or blister

BLAMABLE *adj* capable of being blamed

BLAME *verb* **BLAMES, BLAMING, BLAMED** to consider someone as responsible for (something bad, wrong or undesirable) □ *noun* **BLAMES** responsibility for something bad, wrong or undesirable

BLAMEABLE *adj* blamable

BLAMELESS *adj* free from blame; innocent

BLANCH *verb* **BLANCHES, BLANCHING, BLANCHED** to make something white by removing the colour

BLAND *adj* **BLANDER, BLANDEST** said of food: having a very mild taste; tasteless; insipid

BLANDISH *verb* **BLANDISHES, BLANDISHING, BLANDISHED** to persuade by gentle flattery; to coax or cajole

BLANDLY *adverb* in a bland way

BLANDNESS *noun*
BLANDNESSES the quality or state of being bland

BLANK *adj* **BLANKER, BLANKEST** said of paper: not written or printed on □ *noun* **BLANKS** an empty space; a void □ *verb* **BLANKS, BLANKING, BLANKED** to hide something or form a screen in front of it

BLANKET *noun* **BLANKETS** a thick covering of wool or other material, used to cover beds or for wrapping a person in for warmth □ *adj* general; applying to or covering all cases, people, etc □ *verb*
BLANKETS, BLANKETING, BLANKETED to cover something with, or as if with, a blanket

BLANKLY *adverb* in a blank way; expressionlessly

BLANKNESS *noun*
BLANKNESSES the quality or state of being blank

BLARE *verb* **BLARES, BLARING,**

BLARED to make a sound like a trumpet or a loud harsh sound □ *noun* **BLARES** a loud harsh sound

BLARNEY *noun* **BLARNEYS** flattering words used to persuade, deceive or cajole □ *verb*
BLARNEYS, BLARNEYING, BLARNEYED to persuade using flattery; to cajole or charm

BLASÉ *adj* lacking enthusiasm or interest, especially as a result of over-familiarity

BLASPHEME *verb* **BLASPHEMES, BLASPHEMING, BLASPHEMED** to speak disrespectfully or rudely about God, a divine being or sacred matters

BLASPHEMY *noun* **BLASPHEMIES** speaking about God or sacred matters in a disrespectful or rude way

BLAST *noun* **BLASTS** an explosion, or the strong shock waves spreading out from it □ *verb*
BLASTS, BLASTING, BLASTED to blow up (a tunnel or rock, etc) with explosives □ *exclamation* expressing annoyance or exasperation, etc

BLASTED *adj* (often used as an intensifier) annoying; damned; stupid; infuriating □ *adverb* (used as an intensifier) extremely

BLASTER *noun* **BLASTERS** a person or thing that blasts

BLASTING *noun* **BLASTINGS** blowing up with explosives

BLASTULA *noun* **BLASTULAS, BLASTULAE** a hollow sphere of cells, one cell thick, formed during the division process early in the development of a multicellular embryo

BLATANT *adj* very obvious and without shame

BLATANTLY *adverb* in a blatant way

BLATHER *verb* **BLATHERS, BLATHERING, BLATHERED** to blether □ *noun* **BLATHERS** blether

BLAZE *noun* **BLAZES** a bright strong fire or flame □ *verb*
BLAZES, BLAZING, BLAZED to burn or shine brightly

BLAZER *noun* **BLAZERS** a light jacket, often in the colours of a school or club and sometimes worn as part of a uniform

BLAZERED *adj* wearing a blazer

BLAZES *plural noun* the fires of hell

BLAZING *adj* burning brightly

BLAZON *noun* **BLAZONS** a shield or coat of arms □ *verb* **BLAZONS,**

BLAZONING, BLAZONED to describe (a coat of arms) in technical terms

BLAZONRY *noun* **BLAZONRIES** a coat of arms, or heraldic arms collectively

BLEACH *verb* **BLEACHES, BLEACHING, BLEACHED** to whiten or remove colour from (a substance) by exposure to sunlight or certain chemicals □ *noun*
BLEACHES a liquid chemical used to bleach clothes, etc

BLEACHER *noun* **BLEACHERS** any liquid chemical eg hydrogen peroxide, used to whiten or remove colour from cloth, paper, hair, etc

BLEACHERS *plural noun* at a sports ground, etc: cheap open-air seats for spectators, usually tiered benches

BLEACHING *noun* **BLEACHINGS** the process of whitening or removing colour □ *adj* that whitens or removes colour

BLEAK *adj* **BLEAKER, BLEAKEST** exposed and desolate

BLEAKLY *adverb* in a bleak way

BLEAKNESS *noun* **BLEAKNESSES** the quality of being bleak

BLEARILY *adverb* in a bleary way

BLEARY *adj* **BLEARIER, BLEARIEST** said of a person's eyes: red and dim, usually from tiredness or through crying

BLEAT *verb* **BLEATS, BLEATING, BLEATED** to cry like a sheep, goat or calf

BLEATING *noun* **BLEATINGS** the crying of a sheep, goat or calf □ *adj* that cries like a sheep, goat or calf

BLEED *verb* **BLEEDS, BLEEDING, BLED** to lose or let out blood

BLEEDER *noun* **BLEEDERS** a person who bleeds

BLEEDING *adj* (used as an intensifier) expressing anger or disgust; bloody □ *adverb* (used as an intensifier) expressing anger or disgust; bloody

BLEEP *noun* **BLEEPS** a short high-pitched burst of sound, usually made by an electronic machine □ *verb* **BLEEPS, BLEEPING, BLEEPED** said of an electronic machine, etc: to give out a short high-pitched sound

BLEEPER *noun* **BLEEPERS** a portable radio receiver that emits a single short bleeping sound when it picks up a signal, used especially to call a doctor or police officer carrying such a device

BLEMISH noun **BLEMISHES** a stain, mark or fault ◻ verb **BLEMISHES, BLEMISHING, BLEMISHED** to stain or spoil the beauty of something

BLENCH verb **BLENCHES, BLENCHING, BLENCHED** to start back or move away, especially in fear

BLEND verb **BLENDS, BLENDING, BLENDED** to mix (different sorts or varieties) into one ◻ noun **BLENDS** a mixture or combination

BLENDE noun **BLENDES** any naturally occurring metal sulphide, eg zinc blende

BLENDER noun **BLENDERS** a machine for mixing food or especially for making it into a liquid or purée

BLENNY noun **BLENNIES** the common name for any of various small fishes which have a long tapering slimy body, no scales, long pelvic fins, and jaws with many small teeth

BLESBOK noun **BLESBOKS** a type of S African antelope with a large white blaze on its forehead

BLESS verb **BLESSES, BLESSING, BLESSED** to ask for divine favour or protection for someone or something

BLESSED adj holy

BLESSEDLY adverb in a blessed way

BLESSING noun **BLESSINGS** a wish or prayer for happiness or success

BLETHER verb **BLETHERS, BLETHERING, BLETHERED** to talk foolishly and long-windedly ◻ noun **BLETHERS** long-winded nonsense

BLETHERING noun **BLETHERINGS** foolish talking ◻ adj talking foolishly and long-windedly

BLEW a past form of **blow**

BLIGHT noun **BLIGHTS** a fungal disease of plants that usually attacks an entire crop, or one specific crop throughout a particular region ◻ verb **BLIGHTS, BLIGHTING, BLIGHTED** to affect with blight

BLIGHTED adj affected with blight

BLIGHTER noun **BLIGHTERS** a scoundrel or contemptible person, usually a man

BLIMEY exclamation expressing surprise or amazement

BLIMP noun **BLIMPS** a type of large balloon or airship, used for publicity, observation or defence

BLIMPISH adj conservative, old-fashioned and reactionary

BLIND adj **BLINDER, BLINDEST** not able to see ◻ adverb blindly; without being able to see ◻ noun **BLINDS** a screen to stop light coming through a window, eg one which rolls up (a roller blind) or folds up (a Venetian blind) when not in use ◻ verb **BLINDS, BLINDING, BLINDED** to make someone blind

BLINDER noun **BLINDERS** a heavy drinking session, especially over many hours or several days

BLINDFOLD noun **BLINDFOLDS** a piece of cloth (often a handkerchief or scarf) used to cover the eyes to prevent a person from seeing ◻ verb **BLINDFOLDS, BLINDFOLDING, BLINDFOLDED** to cover the eyes of someone to prevent them from seeing

BLINDING noun **BLINDINGS** the act of making someone blind, especially violently ◻ adj said of a light, etc: intensely strong and bright, causing temporary lack of vision

BLINDLY adverb in a blind manner

BLINDNESS noun **BLINDNESSES** serious or total loss of vision in one or both eyes, caused by disease, injury or the normal ageing process

BLINDWORM noun **BLINDWORMS** a slowworm

BLINK verb **BLINKS, BLINKING, BLINKED** to shut and open the eyes again quickly, especially involuntarily ◻ noun **BLINKS** an act of blinking

BLINKER noun **BLINKERS** one of two small flat pieces of leather attached to a horse's bridle to prevent it from seeing sideways ◻ verb **BLINKERS, BLINKERING, BLINKERED** to put blinkers on (a horse)

BLINKERED adj said of a horse: wearing blinkers

BLINKING adj used to express mild annoyance, frustration or disapproval, or as a general intensifier ◻ adverb used to express mild annoyance, frustration or disapproval, or as a general intensifier

BLIP noun **BLIPS** a sudden sharp sound produced by a machine such as a monitor or radar screen ◻ verb **BLIPS, BLIPPING, BLIPPED** to make a blip

BLISS noun **BLISSES** very great happiness

BLISSFUL adj completely happy; utterly joyful

BLISTER noun **BLISTERS** a small swelling on or just beneath the surface of the skin, containing watery fluid and occasionally blood or pus, usually caused by friction or a burn ◻ verb **BLISTERS, BLISTERING, BLISTERED** to make a blister or blisters occur on something

BLISTERED adj affected with blisters

BLISTERING adj said of weather or conditions, etc: very hot; burning

BLISTERY adj **BLISTERIER, BLISTERIEST** affected with blisters

BLITHE adj **BLITHER, BLITHEST** happy; without worries or cares

BLITHELY adverb in a blithe way

BLITZ noun **BLITZES** a sudden strong attack, or period of such attacks, especially from the air ◻ verb **BLITZES, BLITZING, BLITZED** to attack, damage or destroy something as if by an air raid

BLITZED adj thoroughly drunk or very high on drugs

BLIZZARD noun **BLIZZARDS** a severe snowstorm characterized by low temperatures and strong winds

BLOAT verb **BLOATS, BLOATING, BLOATED** to swell or make something swell or puff out with air, pride, food, etc, especially unpleasantly or uncomfortably

BLOATED adj swollen

BLOATER noun **BLOATERS** a herring that has been salted in brine and partially smoked

BLOB noun **BLOBS** a small soft round mass of something

BLOC noun **BLOCS** a group of countries or people, etc that have a common interest, purpose or policy

BLOCK noun **BLOCKS** a mass of solid wood, stone, ice or other hard material, usually with flat sides ◻ verb **BLOCKS, BLOCKING, BLOCKED** to obstruct or impede; to put an obstacle in the way of someone or something

BLOCKADE noun **BLOCKADES** the closing off of a port or region, etc by surrounding it with troops, ships and/or air-power, in order to prevent people or goods, etc from passing in and out, or to obtain a particular political aim or force a surrender □ *verb* **BLOCKADES, BLOCKADING, BLOCKADED** to impose a blockade on (a port or country, etc)

BLOCKAGE *noun* **BLOCKAGES** anything that causes a pipe or roadway, etc to be blocked

BLOCKED *adj* closed or obstructed with obstacles

BLOCKER *noun* **BLOCKERS** a person or thing that blocks

BLOCKHEAD *noun* **BLOCKHEADS** a stupid person

BLOKE *noun* **BLOKES** a man or chap

BLOKEDOM *noun* **BLOKEDOMS** the world or lifestyle of blokes

BLOKEISH *adj* typical of, suited to or like, one of the blokes, ie an ordinary chap

BLOKEY *adj* **BLOKIER, BLOKIEST** matey, hearty, like one of the blokes

BLOND *adj* **BLONDER, BLONDEST** said of a person or people: having light-coloured hair, between pale yellowish-gold and very light chestnut □ *noun* **BLONDS** a person with this colour of hair

BLONDE *adj* **BLONDER, BLONDEST** feminine form of *blond* □ *noun* **BLONDES** feminine form of *blond*

BLOOD *noun* **BLOODS** a fluid tissue that circulates in the arteries, veins, and capillaries of the body as a result of muscular contractions of the heart □ *verb* **BLOODS, BLOODING, BLOODED** to give (a young hound) its first taste of a freshly killed animal

BLOODED *adj* said of a person or animal: having blood or temperament of a specified kind

BLOODILY *adverb* with bloodshed

BLOODLESS *adj* without violence or anybody being killed

BLOODLUST *noun* **BLOODLUSTS** an appetite or desire for bloodshed

BLOODSHED *noun* **BLOODSHEDS** the shedding of blood or killing of people; slaughter

BLOODSHOT *adj* said of the eyes: having small streaks of red across the white of the eye due to inflamed blood vessels in the conjunctiva; red and irritated or swollen

BLOODY *adj* **BLOODIER, BLOODIEST** stained or covered with blood □ *adverb* (used as an intensifier) expressing annoyance, etc □ *verb* **BLOODIES,**

BLOODYING, BLOODIED to stain or cover something with blood

BLOOM *noun* **BLOOMS** a flower, especially one on a plant valued for its flowers □ *verb* **BLOOMS, BLOOMING, BLOOMED** said of a plant: to be in or come into flower

BLOOMER *noun* **BLOOMERS** an idiotic and embarrassing mistake

BLOOMERS *plural noun* women's underpants or knickers, especially large or baggy ones

BLOOMING *adj* said of a plant: flowering

BLOOP *noun* **BLOOPS** a howling sound on a soundtrack or made by a radio □ *verb* **BLOOPS, BLOOPING, BLOOPED** said of a radio, etc: to make such a sound

BLOOPER *noun* **BLOOPERS** a stupid and embarrassing mistake; a bloomer

BLOSSOM *noun* **BLOSSOMS** a flower or mass of flowers, especially on a fruit tree □ *verb* **BLOSSOMS, BLOSSOMING, BLOSSOMED** said of a plant, especially a fruit tree or bush: to produce blossom or flowers

BLOSSOMING *adj* that produces blossom or flowers

BLOSSOMY *adj* covered with flowers, flowery

BLOT *noun* **BLOTS** a spot or stain, especially of ink □ *verb* **BLOTS, BLOTTING, BLOTTED** to make a spot or stain on something, especially with ink

BLOTCH *noun* **BLOTCHES** a large irregular-shaped coloured patch or mark on the skin, etc □ *verb* **BLOTCHES, BLOTCHING, BLOTCHED** to cover or mark with blotches

BLOTCHY *adj* **BLOTCHIER, BLOTCHIEST** covered in blotches; discoloured in patches

BLOTTER *noun* **BLOTTERS** a large sheet or pad of blotting paper with a hard backing

BLOTTO *adj* helplessly drunk

BLOUSE *noun* **BLOUSES** a woman's garment very similar to a shirt □ *verb* **BLOUSES, BLOUSING, BLOUSED** to arrange (a garment or drapery, etc) in loose folds

BLOUSON *noun* **BLOUSONS** a loose jacket or top gathered in tightly at the waist

BLOW ¹ *verb* **BLOWS, BLOWING, BLEW, BLOWN** said of a current of air or wind etc: to be moving, especially rapidly □ *verb* **BLOWS,**

BLOWING, BLEW, BLOWED used in mild curses, expressions of astonishment etc: to damn, curse or blast

BLOW ² *noun* **BLOWS** a forceful stroke or knock with the hand or with a weapon

BLOWER *noun* **BLOWERS** a device or machine that blows out a current of air

BLOWFLY *noun* **BLOWFLIES** any of various species of fly whose eggs are laid in rotting flesh or excrement on which the hatched larvae subsequently feed, eg bluebottle

BLOWHARD *noun* **BLOWHARDS** a boastful or loudmouthed person

BLOWHOLE *noun* **BLOWHOLES** a hole in an area of surface ice, where marine mammals, eg seals, can go to breathe

BLOWLAMP *noun* **BLOWLAMPS** a small portable burner, usually fuelled with liquid gas, that produces an intense hot flame, used for paint-stripping, melting soft metal, etc

BLOWN a past form of **blow**

BLOWPIPE *noun* **BLOWPIPES** in glass-blowing: a long narrow iron tube on which a mass of molten glass is gathered before air is forced down the tube to form a bubble of air within the glass, which can then be shaped as it cools

BLOWSY *adj* **BLOWSIER, BLOWSIEST** blowzy

BLOWTORCH *noun* **BLOWTORCHES** a blowlamp

BLOWY *adj* **BLOWIER, BLOWIEST** blustery; windy

BLOWZY *adj* **BLOWZIER, BLOWZIEST** said of a woman: red-faced or flushed; slovenly

BLUB *verb* **BLUBS, BLUBBING, BLUBBED** to weep or sob

BLUBBER *noun* **BLUBBERS** the fat of sea animals such as the whale □ *verb* **BLUBBERS, BLUBBERING, BLUBBERED** to weep, especially noisily or unrestrainedly

BLUDGE *verb* **BLUDGES, BLUDGING, BLUDGED** to scrounge; to impose on or sponge off someone □ *noun* **BLUDGES** an easy job that requires no effort; a spell of loafing about

BLUDGEON *noun* **BLUDGEONS** a stick or club with a heavy end □ *verb* **BLUDGEONS, BLUDGEONING, BLUDGEONED** to hit someone or something with or as if with a bludgeon

BLUDGER noun **BLUDGERS** a scrounger or loafer; a person who bludges

BLUE adj **BLUER, BLUEST** with the colour of a clear cloudless sky; having any of the shades of this colour, which falls between green and violet on the spectrum ◻ noun **BLUES** the colour of a clear cloudless sky; any blue shade or hue ◻ verb **BLUES, BLUEING, BLUED** to make something blue

BLUEBELL noun **BLUEBELLS** a bulbous spring-flowering perennial plant with narrow shiny leaves and erect stems with one-sided clusters of bell-shaped flowers that are usually blue

BLUEBERRY noun **BLUEBERRIES** any of various species of deciduous shrub, native to N America, with white or pinkish bell-shaped flowers and edible berries

BLUEBIRD noun **BLUEBIRDS** any of various birds of the thrush family, native to N and Central America, and so called because the male has bright blue plumage on its back

BLUEGRASS noun **BLUEGRASSES** a simple style of country music originating in Kentucky and popular in southern states of America, played on unamplified stringed instruments, especially banjo, fiddle and guitar

BLUENESS noun **BLUENESSES** the quality or state of being blue

BLUEPRINT noun **BLUEPRINTS** a pattern, model or prototype ◻ verb **BLUEPRINTS, BLUEPRINTING, BLUEPRINTED** to make a blueprint of (a plan or project, etc)

BLUER adj more blue

BLUES singular or plural noun a feeling of sadness or depression

BLUESY adj **BLUESIER, BLUESIEST** like the blues

BLUEY adj **BLUIER, BLUIEST** tending towards blue in colour ◻ noun **BLUEYS** a bundle or swag, often wrapped in a blue blanket or cloth

BLUFF [1] adj **BLUFFER, BLUFFEST** said of a person, character, manner, etc: rough, cheerful and honest; outspoken and hearty

BLUFF [2] verb **BLUFFS, BLUFFING, BLUFFED** to deceive or try to deceive someone by pretending to be stronger, cleverer or more

determined, etc than one really is ◻ noun **BLUFFS** an act of bluffing

BLUFFNESS noun **BLUFFNESSES** roughness, cheerfulness and honesty

BLUISH adj rather blue

BLUNDER noun **BLUNDERS** a foolish or thoughtless, and usually serious, mistake ◻ verb **BLUNDERS, BLUNDERING, BLUNDERED** to make a blunder

BLUNDERER noun **BLUNDERERS** someone who makes a blunder or blunders

BLUNDERING adj that makes serious mistakes

BLUNT adj **BLUNTER, BLUNTEST** said of a pencil, knife or blade, etc: having no point or sharp edge ◻ verb **BLUNTS, BLUNTING, BLUNTED** to make blunt or less sharp

BLUNTLY adverb honestly; directly

BLUNTNESS noun **BLUNTNESSES** abruptness of manner

BLUR noun **BLURS** a thing not clearly seen or heard, or happening too fast or too distantly, etc to be clearly seen, comprehended or recognized ◻ verb **BLURS, BLURRING, BLURRED** to make or become less clear or distinct

BLURB noun **BLURBS** a brief description of a book, usually printed on the jacket in order to promote it

BLURRED adj smudged; indistinct

BLURT verb **BLURTS, BLURTING, BLURTED** to say something suddenly or without thinking of the effect or result

BLUSH verb **BLUSHES, BLUSHING, BLUSHED** to become red or pink in the face because of shame, embarrassment, excitement, joy, etc ◻ noun **BLUSHES** a red or pink glow on the skin of the face, caused by shame, embarrassment, excitement, joy, etc

BLUSHER noun **BLUSHERS** a cosmetic cream or powder, usually in a pinkish shade, used to give colour to the cheeks

BLUSHING adj that blushes

BLUSTER verb **BLUSTERS, BLUSTERING, BLUSTERED** to speak in a boasting, angry or threatening way, often to hide fear ◻ noun **BLUSTERS** speech that is ostentatiously boasting, angry or threatening

BLUSTERER noun **BLUSTERERS** a person that blusters

BLUSTERING adj boasting, angry or threatening

BLUSTERY adj **BLUSTERIER, BLUSTERIEST** said of the weather: rough and windy

BO exclamation **BOS** a sound made when trying to startle someone

BOA noun **BOAS** a boa constrictor, or any similar snake of the mainly S American type that kill by winding themselves round their prey and crushing it

BOAR noun **BOARS** a wild ancestor of the domestic pig, native to Europe, Africa and Asia, which has thick dark hair, and the male of which has tusks

BOARD noun **BOARDS** a long flat strip of wood ◻ verb **BOARDS, BOARDING, BOARDED** to enter or get on to (a ship, aeroplane, bus, etc)

BOARDING noun **BOARDINGS** a structure or collection of wooden boards laid side by side

BOARDROOM noun **BOARDROOMS** a room in which the directors of a company meet

BOARDWALK noun **BOARDWALKS** a footpath made of boards, especially on the seafront

BOAST verb **BOASTS, BOASTING, BOASTED** to talk with excessive pride about one's own abilities or achievements, etc ◻ noun **BOASTS** an act of boasting; a brag

BOASTER noun **BOASTERS** a person who boasts

BOASTFUL adj given to boasting about oneself

BOASTING noun **BOASTINGS** ostentatious talking ◻ adj that brags or boasts

BOAT noun **BOATS** a small vessel for travelling over water ◻ verb **BOATS, BOATING, BOATED** to sail or travel in a boat, especially for pleasure

BOATER noun **BOATERS** a straw hat with a flat top and a brim

BOATHOUSE noun **BOATHOUSES** a building in which boats are stored, especially by a lake or river

BOATIE noun **BOATIES** a person who enjoys boating as a regular pastime or passion

BOATING noun **BOATINGS** the sailing or rowing, etc of boats for pleasure

BOATMAN *noun* **BOATMEN** a man who is in charge of, or hires out, etc a small passenger-carrying boat or boats

BOATSWAIN *noun* **BOATSWAINS** a warrant officer in the navy, or the foreman of a crew, who is in charge of a ship's lifeboats, rigging, sails, etc and its maintenance

BOB *verb* **BOBS, BOBBING, BOBBED** to move up and down quickly □ *noun* **BOBS** a quick up-and-down bouncing movement

BOBBIN *noun* **BOBBINS** a small cylindrical object on which thread or yarn, etc is wound, used in sewing and weaving machines

BOBBLE *noun* **BOBBLES** a bobbing motion, especially one that is rapid or repeated □ *verb* **BOBBLES, BOBBLING, BOBBLED** to bob rapidly or continuously

BOBBLY *adj* **BOBBLIER, BOBBLIEST** of cloth: pilled

BOBBY *noun* **BOBBIES** a policeman

BOBCAT *noun* **BOBCATS** a solitary nocturnal member of the cat family, native to mountains and deserts of N America, which has a brown coat with dark spots, white underparts and tufted ears

BOBSLED *noun* **BOBSLEDS** a bobsleigh

BOBSLEIGH *noun* **BOBSLEIGHS** a sleigh with metal runners, used on snow and ice, made up of two short sledges coupled together

BOBSTAYS *plural noun* ropes used on a ship to hold the bowsprit down to the stem, and counteract the strain of the foremast-stays

BOBTAIL *noun* **BOBTAILS** a short or cropped tail

BOBTAILED *adj* with the tail cut short

BOD *noun* **BODS** a person or chap

BODE *verb* **BODES, BODING, BODED** to be a sign of something; to portend

BODEGA *noun* **BODEGAS** especially in Spain and other Spanish-speaking countries: a wine-shop

BODGE *verb* **BODGES, BODGING, BODGED** to make a mess of something; to do it badly or carelessly □ *noun* **BODGES** a piece of poor or clumsy workmanship

BODHRAN *noun* **BODHRANS** a shallow one-sided drum often played in Scottish and Irish folk-music

BODICE *noun* **BODICES** the close-fitting upper part of a woman's dress, from shoulder to waist

BODIED *adj* having a body of the type specified

BODILY *adj* belonging or relating to, or performed by, the body □ *adverb* as a whole; taking the whole body

BODKIN *noun* **BODKINS** a large blunt needle

BODY *noun* **BODIES** the whole physical structure of a person or animal □ *verb* **BODIES, BODYING, BODIED** to give something body or form

BODYGUARD *noun* **BODYGUARDS** a person or group of people whose job is to accompany and give physical protection to an important person, etc

BODYLINE *noun* **BODYLINES** in cricket: the policy of bowling the ball straight at the batsman so that it will strike the body

BODYSUIT *noun* **BODYSUITS** a legless tight-fitting one-piece garment for women, fastening at the crotch

BODYWORK *noun* **BODYWORKS** the metal outer shell of a motor vehicle

BOFFIN *noun* **BOFFINS** a scientist engaged in research, especially for the armed forces or the government

BOG *noun* **BOGS** a flat or domed area of wet spongy poorly-drained ground, composed of acid peat and slowly decaying plant material, and dominated by sphagnum moss, sedges, rushes, etc □ *verb* **BOGS, BOGGING, BOGGED** to sink

BOGEY[1] *noun* **BOGIES, BOGEYS** an evil or mischievous spirit

BOGEY[2] *verb* **BOGEYS, BOGEYING, BOGEYED** in golf: to complete (a specified hole) in one over par

BOGGINESS *noun* **BOGGINESSES** the state or condition of being boggy

BOGGLE *verb* **BOGGLES, BOGGLING, BOGGLED** to be amazed or unable to understand or imagine

BOGGY *adj* **BOGGIER, BOGGIEST** like a bog; swampy

BOGIE *noun* **BOGIES** a frame with four or six wheels used as part of a pivoting undercarriage, supporting part of a long vehicle such as a railway carriage

BOGUS *adj* false; not genuine

BOGY *noun* **BOGIES** a bogey

> **BOH** *noun* **BOHS** a cry of 'bo', used for calling attention or to startle

BOIL *verb* **BOILS, BOILING, BOILED** said of a liquid: to reach boiling point □ *noun* **BOILS** the act or point of boiling

BOILER *noun* **BOILERS** any closed vessel that is used to convert water into steam, especially by burning coal, oil or some other fuel, in order to drive a steam turbine, steamship, steam locomotive, etc

> **BOK** *noun* **BOKS** a S African word for a goat or an antelope

BOLAS *singular or plural noun* a S American hunting missile made of two or more balls or stones strung together on a cord, used by swinging them around and then hurling them so as to entangle the animal's legs

BOLD *adj* **BOLDER, BOLDEST** daring or brave; confident and courageous

BOLDLY *adverb* in a bold way

BOLDNESS *noun* **BOLDNESSES** daring or courage

BOLE *noun* **BOLES** the trunk of a tree

BOLERO *noun* **BOLEROS** a traditional Spanish dance, generally danced by a couple

BOLIVAR *noun* **BOLIVARS** the standard monetary unit of Venezuela

BOLIVIANO *noun* **BOLIVIANOS** the standard monetary unit of Bolivia; the Bolivian dollar

BOLL *noun* **BOLLS** a rounded capsule containing seeds, especially of a cotton or flax plant

BOLLARD *noun* **BOLLARDS** a small post used to mark a traffic island or to keep traffic away from a certain area

BOLONEY *noun* **BOLONEYS** nonsense

BOLSHEVIK *noun* **BOLSHEVIKS** a member of the radical faction of the Russian socialist party, which became the Communist Party in 1918

BOLSHIE *adj* **BOLSHIER, BOLSHIEST** bad-tempered and unco-operative; difficult or rebellious □ *noun* **BOLSHIES** a bolshevik

BOLSHY adj BOLSHIER, BOLSHIEST bolshie ◻ noun BOLSHIES a bolshevik

BOLSTER noun BOLSTERS a long narrow, sometimes cylindrical, pillow ◻ verb BOLSTERS, BOLSTERING, BOLSTERED to support something; to hold up

BOLT noun BOLTS a bar or rod that slides into a hole or socket to fasten a door or gate, etc ◻ verb BOLTS, BOLTING, BOLTED to fasten (a door or window, etc) with a bolt

BOLTHOLE noun BOLTHOLES a refuge from danger; a secluded private place to hide away in

BOLUS noun BOLUSES a soft rounded mass, especially of chewed food

BOMB noun BOMBS a hollow case or other device containing a substance capable of causing an explosion, fire or smoke, etc ◻ verb BOMBS, BOMBING, BOMBED to attack or damage, etc with a bomb or bombs

BOMBARD verb BOMBARDS, BOMBARDING, BOMBARDED to attack (a place, target, etc) with large, heavy guns or bombs

BOMBAST noun BOMBASTS pretentious, boastful or insincere words having little real force or meaning

BOMBASTIC adj said of language, etc: sounding impressive but insincere or meaningless

BOMBE noun BOMBES a dessert, usually ice cream, frozen in a round or melon-shaped mould

BOMBED adj very drunk or high on drugs; stoned

BOMBER noun BOMBERS an aeroplane designed for carrying and dropping bombs

BOMBING noun BOMBINGS the action of dropping bombs

BOMBORA noun BOMBORAS a submerged reef

BOMBSHELL noun BOMBSHELLS a piece of surprising and usually disappointing or devastating news

BOMBSITE noun BOMBSITES an area where buildings, etc have been destroyed by a bomb or an air-raid

BON adj French word for *good*

BONANZA noun BONANZAS an unexpected and sudden source of good luck or wealth

BONBON noun BONBONS a sweet, especially a fancy chocolate- or sugar-coated piece of confectionery

BONCE noun BONCES the head

BOND noun BONDS something used for tying, binding or holding ◻ verb BONDS, BONDING, BONDED to join, secure or tie together

BONDAGE noun BONDAGES slavery ◻ adj said of clothes and accessories, usually made of black leather: having chains, metal studs, buckles or similar aggressive-looking features

BONDING noun BONDINGS the forming of a close emotional attachment, especially between a mother and her newborn child

BONE noun BONES the hard dense tissue that forms the skeleton of vertebrates, providing structural support for the body and serving as an attachment for muscles ◻ verb BONES, BONING, BONED to take bone out of (meat, etc)

BONED adj having bones; having the bones removed

BONEHEAD noun BONEHEADS a stupid person; a blockhead

BONELESS adj lacking bones; having the bones removed

BONER noun BONERS a blunder or howler

BONFIRE noun BONFIRES a large outdoor fire, for burning garden refuse, etc, or burned as a signal or as part of a celebration

BONG noun BONGS a long deep hollow or ringing sound ◻ verb BONGS, BONGING, BONGED to make such a sound

BONGO noun BONGOS each of a pair of small, usually connected, drums held between the knees and played with the hands

BONHOMIE noun BONHOMIES easy good nature; cheerful friendliness

BONINESS noun the state of being bony

BONK noun BONKS the act of banging; a blow or thump ◻ verb BONKS, BONKING, BONKED to bang or hit something

BONKERS adj mad or crazy

BONNET noun BONNETS a type of hat fastened under the chin with ribbon, formerly worn by women but now worn especially by babies

BONNILY adverb attractively; prettily

BONNY adj BONNIER, BONNIEST attractive; pretty

BONSAI noun BONSAIS the ancient Japanese art of cultivating

artificially miniaturized trees in small containers

BONTEBOK noun BONTEBOKS a S African antelope, very similar to the blesbok, its coat having several shades of brown with white blaze, legs, rump and belly

BONUS noun BONUSES an extra sum of money given on top of what is due as wages, interest or dividend, etc

BONY adj BONIER, BONIEST consisting of, made of or like bone

BOO exclamation a sound expressing disapproval, or made when trying to frighten or surprise someone ◻ noun BOOS a sound expressing disapproval, or made when trying to frighten or surprise someone ◻ verb BOOS, BOOING, BOOED to shout 'boo' to express disapproval

BOOB noun BOOBS a stupid or foolish mistake; a blunder ◻ verb BOOBS, BOOBING, BOOBED to make a stupid or foolish mistake

BOOBY noun BOOBIES any of various large tropical seabirds of the gannet family which have white plumage with dark markings, long powerful wings, a large head and a colourful conical bill

BOODLE noun BOODLES money, especially money gained dishonestly or as a bribe, or counterfeit

BOOGIE verb BOOGIES, BOOGIEING, BOOGIED to dance to pop, rock or jazz music ◻ noun BOOGIES a dance, or dancing, to pop, rock or jazz music

BOOK noun BOOKS a number of printed pages bound together along one edge and protected by covers ◻ verb BOOKS, BOOKING, BOOKED to reserve (a ticket, seat, etc), or engage (a person's services) in advance

BOOKABLE adj said of seats for a performance, etc: able to be booked or reserved in advance

BOOKCASE noun BOOKCASES a piece of furniture with shelves for books

BOOKIE noun BOOKIES a bookmaker

BOOKING noun BOOKINGS a reservation of a theatre seat, hotel room, seat on a plane or train, etc

BOOKISH adj extremely fond of reading and books

BOOKLET noun BOOKLETS a

small book or pamphlet with a paper cover

BOOKMAKER *noun*
BOOKMAKERS a person whose job is to take bets on horse races, etc and pay out winnings

BOOKMARK *noun* **BOOKMARKS** a strip of leather, card, etc put in a book to mark a particular page, especially the reader's current place in the book

BOOKPLATE *noun* **BOOKPLATES** a piece of decorated paper stuck into the front of a book and bearing the owner's name, etc

BOOKSHELF *noun*
BOOKSHELVES a shelf for standing books on

BOOKSHOP *noun* **BOOKSHOPS** a shop where books are sold

BOOKSTALL *noun* **BOOKSTALLS** a small shop in a station, etc where books, newspapers, magazines, etc are sold

BOOKSTAND *noun* **BOOKSTANDS** a bookstall

BOOKSTORE *noun* **BOOKSTORES** a bookshop

BOOKWORM *noun* **BOOKWORMS** a person who is extremely fond of reading

BOOM *noun* **BOOMS** a deep resounding sound, like that made by a large drum or gun □ *verb* **BOOMS, BOOMING, BOOMED** to make a deep resounding sound

BOOMERANG *noun*
BOOMERANGS a piece of flat curved wood used by Australian Aborigines for hunting, often so balanced that, when thrown to a distance, it returns towards the person who threw it □ *verb* **BOOMERANGS, BOOMERANGING, BOOMERANGED** said of an act or statement, etc: to go wrong and harm the perpetrator rather than the intended victim; to recoil or rebound

BOON[1] *adj* close, convivial, intimate or favourite

BOON[2] *noun* **BOONS** an advantage, benefit or blessing; something to be thankful for

BOONDOCKS *plural noun* wild or remote country

BOOR *noun* **BOORS** a coarse person with bad manners

BOORISH *adj* said of a person, or a person's manner: coarse, rough or rude

BOORISHLY *adverb* in a boorish way

BOOST *verb* **BOOSTS, BOOSTING, BOOSTED** to improve or encourage something or someone □ *noun* **BOOSTS** a piece of help or encouragement, etc

BOOSTER *noun* **BOOSTERS** a person or thing that boosts

BOOT *noun* **BOOTS** an outer covering, made of leather or rubber, etc, for the foot and lower part of the leg □ *verb* **BOOTS, BOOTING, BOOTED** to kick

BOOTABLE *adj* of a computer: able to be started by loading the programs which control its basic functions

BOOTEE *noun* **BOOTEES** a soft knitted boot for a baby

BOOTH *noun* **BOOTHS** a small temporary roofed structure or tent, especially a covered stall at a fair or market

BOOTLACE *noun* **BOOTLACES** a piece of cord, string or ribbon, etc used to tie up a boot

BOOTLEG *verb* **BOOTLEGS, BOOTLEGGING, BOOTLEGGED** to make, sell or transport (alcoholic drink) illegally, especially in a time of prohibition □ *noun* **BOOTLEGS** illegally produced, sold or transported goods, especially alcoholic drink or recorded material

BOOTLEGGING *noun*
BOOTLEGGINGS making, selling or transporting (alcoholic drink) illegally, especially in a time of prohibition

BOOTLESS *adj* useless; vain; unprofitable

BOOTS *noun* **BOOTS** a male employee at a hotel who carries guests' luggage, cleans their shoes, runs messages, etc

BOOTSTRAP *noun* **BOOTSTRAPS** a short program used to boot up a computer by transferring the disk-operating system's program from storage on disk into a computer's working memory □ *verb* **BOOTSTRAPS, BOOTSTRAPPING, BOOTSTRAPPED** to boot up or start (a computer) by activating the bootstrap program

BOOTY *noun* **BOOTIES** valuable goods taken in wartime or by force; plunder

BOOZE *noun* **BOOZES** alcoholic drink □ *verb* **BOOZES, BOOZING, BOOZED** to drink a lot of alcohol, or too much of it

BOOZER *noun* **BOOZERS** a public house or bar

BOOZILY *adverb* in a boozy way; drunkenly

BOOZY *adj* **BOOZIER, BOOZIEST** said of an occasion, etc: including or entailing a lot of boozing; drunken

BOP *noun* **BOPS** a dance to popular music □ *verb* **BOPS, BOPPING, BOPPED** to dance to popular music

BOPPER *noun* **BOPPERS** a person who dances to popular music

BOR *noun* **BORS** an East Anglian form of address meaning *neighbour*

BORACIC *adj* boric

BORAGE *noun* **BORAGES** an annual European plant with oval hairy leaves and small bright-blue star-shaped flowers

BORAK *noun* **BORAKS** nonsense or banter

BORATE *noun* **BORATES** a salt or ester of boric acid

BORAX *noun* **BORAXES** a colourless crystalline salt, found in saline lake deposits, used in the manufacture of glass, and as a mild antiseptic and source of boric acid

BORDELLO *noun* **BORDELLOS** a brothel

BORDER *noun* **BORDERS** a band or margin along the edge of something □ *adj* belonging or referring to the border, or on the border □ *verb* **BORDERS, BORDERING, BORDERED** to be a border to, adjacent to, or on the border of something

BORDERED *adj* having a border; edged

BORDERER *noun* **BORDERERS** a person who lives in or comes from the border area of a country

BORE[1] *noun* **BORES** a dull, uninteresting or tedious person or thing □ *verb* **BORES, BORING, BORED** to make someone feel tired and uninterested, by being dull, tedious, uninteresting, etc

BORE[2] *verb* **BORES, BORING, BORED** to make a hole in something by drilling

BORE[3] a past from of **bear**[2]

BORED *adj* tired and uninterested from being unoccupied or under-occupied

BOREDOM *noun* **BOREDOMS** the state of being bored

For longer words, see *The Chambers Dictionary*

BOREHOLE *noun* **BOREHOLES** a deep narrow hole made by drilling, especially one made in the ground to find oil or water, etc

BORER *noun* **BORERS** a machine or tool for drilling holes

BORIC *adj* relating to or containing boron

BORING [1] *adj* tedious and uninteresting

BORING [2] *noun* **BORINGS** the act of making a hole in anything

BORINGLY *adverb* in a boring way

BORN *adj* brought into being by birth

BORNE a past form of bear □ *adj* carried by a specified thing

BORON *noun* **BORONS** a non-metallic element consisting of a dark brown powder or black crystals, found only in compounds, eg borax and boric acid

BOROUGH *noun* **BOROUGHS** in England: a town or urban area represented by at least one member of Parliament

BORROW *verb* **BORROWS, BORROWING, BORROWED** to take something temporarily, usually with permission and with the intention of returning it

BORROWER *noun* **BORROWERS** a person who borrows something, eg money from a bank

BORROWING *noun* **BORROWINGS** something borrowed, especially a word taken from one language into another

BORSCHT *noun* **BORSCHTS** a Russian and Polish beetroot soup, often served with sour cream

BORSTAL *noun* **BORSTALS** an institution which was both a prison and a school, to which young criminals were sent, replaced in 1983 by detention centres and youth custody centres

BORTSCH *noun* **BORTSCHES** borscht

BORZOI *noun* **BORZOIS** a large breed of dog with a tall slender body, a long thin muzzle, a long tail and a long soft coat, formerly used to hunt wolves

BOS plural of **bo**

BOSH *noun* **BOSHES** nonsense; foolish talk

BOSOM *noun* **BOSOMS** a person's chest or breast, now especially that of a woman

BOSOMY *adj* **BOSOMIER, BOSOMIEST** said of a woman: having large breasts

BOSON *noun* **BOSONS** a category of subatomic particle

BOSS *noun* **BOSSES** a person who employs others, or who is in charge of others; a leader, master or manager □ *verb* **BOSSES, BOSSING, BOSSED** to give orders in a domineering way □ *adj* **BOSSER, BOSSEST** excellent; great

BOSSED *adj* embossed, or ornamented with bosses, round raised knobs or studs

BOSSILY *adverb* in a bossy way

BOSSINESS *noun* **BOSSINESSES** the quality of being disagreeably domineering

BOSSY *adj* **BOSSIER, BOSSIEST** inclined (especially over-inclined) to give orders like a boss; disagreeably domineering

BOSUN *noun* **BOSUNS** a warrant officer in the navy, or the foreman of a crew, who is in charge of a ship's lifeboats, rigging, sails, etc and its maintenance

BOT [1] *noun* **BOTS** the maggot of a botfly, which lives as a parasite under the skin of the horse, sheep and other animals

BOT [2] *verb* **BOTS, BOTTING, BOTTED** to cadge

BOTANIC *adj* relating to botany or plants

BOTANICAL *adj* botanic

BOTANIST *noun* **BOTANISTS** a person who specializes in, or has a detailed knowledge of, botany

BOTANY *noun* **BOTANIES** the branch of biology concerned with the scientific study of plants, including their structure, function, ecology, evolution and classification

BOTCH *verb* **BOTCHES, BOTCHING, BOTCHED** to do something badly and unskilfully; to make a mess or bad job of something □ *noun* **BOTCHES** a badly or carelessly done piece of work, repair, etc

BOTCHED *adj* badly or carelessly done or repaired, etc

BOTCHER *noun* **BOTCHERS** a person who does things badly and unskilfully

BOTCHY *adj* **BOTCHIER, BOTCHIEST** said of work, etc: done carelessly or badly

BOTFLY *noun* **BOTFLIES** any of various two-winged insects, the larvae of which are parasitic on mammals, especially horses and sheep

BOTH *adj* the two; the one and the other □ *pronoun* the two; the one and the other □ *adverb* as well

BOTHER *verb* **BOTHERS, BOTHERING, BOTHERED** to annoy, worry or trouble someone □ *noun* **BOTHERS** a minor trouble or worry □ *exclamation* expressing slight annoyance or impatience

BOTHY *noun* **BOTHIES** a simple rough cottage or hut used as temporary accommodation or shelter

BOTT *noun* **BOTTS** a bot

BOTTLE *noun* **BOTTLES** a hollow glass or plastic container with a narrow neck, for holding liquids □ *verb* **BOTTLES, BOTTLING, BOTTLED** to put something into, enclose or store it in bottles

BOTTLEFUL *noun* **BOTTLEFULS** the amount a bottle can hold

BOTTLER *noun* **BOTTLERS** a person or machine that bottles

BOTTOM *adj* lowest or last □ *noun* **BOTTOMS** the lowest position or part; the base on which something stands or rests □ *verb* **BOTTOMS, BOTTOMING, BOTTOMED** to put a bottom on (a seat or container, etc)

BOTULISM *noun* **BOTULISMS** a severe form of food poisoning, caused by swallowing a bacterial toxin that is most commonly found in canned raw meat, and is destroyed by cooking

BOUCLÉ *noun* **BOUCLÉS** a type of wool with curled or looped threads □ *adj* made of or referring to bouclé wool or material

BOUDOIR *noun* **BOUDOIRS** a woman's private sitting-room or bedroom

BOUFFANT *adj* said of a hairstyle, or a skirt, sleeve, dress, etc: very full and puffed out

BOUGH *noun* **BOUGHS** a branch of a tree

BOUGHT past form of **buy**

BOUGIE *noun* **BOUGIES** an instrument which can be inserted into body passages, eg to deliver medication

BOUILLON *noun* **BOUILLONS** a thin clear soup or stock made by boiling meat and vegetables in water, often used as a basis for thicker soups

BOULDER *noun* **BOULDERS** a large piece of rock that has been rounded and worn smooth by weathering and abrasion during transport

BOULES *singular noun* a form of bowls popular in France, played on rough ground, in which the players try to hit a small metal ball (the jack) with larger balls rolled along the ground

BOULEVARD *noun* **BOULEVARDS** a broad street in a town or city, especially one lined with trees

BOULT *verb* **BOULTS, BOULTING, BOULTED** to pass (flour, etc) through a sieve

BOUNCE *verb* **BOUNCES, BOUNCING, BOUNCED** said of a ball, etc: to spring or jump back from a solid surface ▫ *noun* **BOUNCES** the ability to spring back or bounce well; springiness

BOUNCER *noun* **BOUNCERS** a person employed by a club or restaurant, etc to stop unwanted guests such as drunks from entering, and to throw out people who cause trouble

BOUNCILY *adverb* in a bouncy way

BOUNCING *adj* said especially of a baby: strong, healthy, and lively

BOUNCY *adj* **BOUNCIER, BOUNCIEST** able to bounce well, or tending to bounce

BOUND [1] *adj* tied with or as if with a rope or other binding

BOUND [2] *noun* **BOUNDS** a jump or leap upwards ▫ *verb* **BOUNDS, BOUNDING, BOUNDED** to spring or leap in the specified direction; to move energetically

BOUNDARY *noun* **BOUNDARIES** a line or border marking the farthest limit of an area, etc

BOUNDEN *adj* which must be done; obligatory

BOUNDER *noun* **BOUNDERS** a badly-behaved person; a cad

BOUNDLESS *adj* having no limit; extensive or vast

BOUNTEOUS *adj* generous; beneficent

BOUNTIFUL *adj* said of a person, etc: bounteous; generous

BOUNTY *noun* **BOUNTIES** a reward or premium given, especially by a government, as encouragement eg to kill or capture dangerous animals, criminals, etc

BOUQUET *noun* **BOUQUETS** a bunch of flowers arranged in an artistic way, given eg as a gift on a special occasion, or carried by a bride, etc

BOURBON *noun* **BOURBONS** a type of whisky made from maize and rye, popular in the US

BOURDON *noun* **BOURDONS** a bass stop in an organ or harmonium

BOURGEOIS *adj* characteristic of the middle class; conventional or humdrum; conservative; materialistic ▫ *noun*

BOURGEOISES a member of the middle class, especially someone regarded as politically conservative and socially self-interested

BOURN *noun* **BOURNS** a limit or boundary

BOURNE *noun* **BOURNES** a limit or bound

BOURSE *noun* **BOURSES** a European stock exchange, especially that in Paris

BOUT *noun* **BOUTS** a period or turn of some activity; a spell or stint

BOUTIQUE *noun* **BOUTIQUES** a small shop, especially one selling fashionable clothes and accessories

BOUZOUKI *noun* **BOUZOUKIS** a Greek musical instrument with a long neck and metal strings, related to the mandolin

BOVINE *adj* belonging or relating to, or characteristic of, cattle

BOVINELY *adverb* dully or stupidly

BOW [1] *noun* **BOWS** a weapon made of a thin piece of flexible wood bent by a string stretched between its two ends, for shooting arrows

BOW [2] *noun* **BOWS** a long, thin piece of wood with horsehair stretched along its length, for playing the violin or cello etc

BOW [3] *verb* **BOWS, BOWING, BOWED** to bend (the head or the upper part of the body) forwards and downwards ▫ *noun* **BOWS** an act of bowing

BOWEL *noun* **BOWELS** an intestine, especially the large intestine in humans

BOWER *noun* **BOWERS** a place in a garden, etc which is enclosed and shaded from the sun by plants and trees

BOWING *noun* **BOWINGS** the technique of using the bow when playing a stringed instrument

BOWL [1] *noun* **BOWLS** a round deep dish for mixing or serving food, or for holding liquids or flowers, etc

BOWL [2] *noun* **BOWLS** a heavy ball for rolling, especially one for use in the game of bowls ▫ *verb* **BOWLS, BOWLING, BOWLED** to roll (a ball or hoop, etc) smoothly along the ground; in cricket: to throw (the ball) towards the person batting at the wicket

BOWLER *noun* **BOWLERS** a person who bowls the ball in cricket, etc

BOWLFUL *noun* **BOWLFULS** the amount a bowl can hold

BOWLINE *noun* **BOWLINES** a rope used to keep a sail taut against the wind

BOWLING *noun* **BOWLINGS** the game of bowls

BOWLS *singular noun* a game played on smooth grass with bowls, the object being to roll these as close as possible to a smaller ball called the jack

BOWMAN *noun* **BOWMEN** an archer

BOWSER *noun* **BOWSERS** a light tanker used for refuelling aircraft on an airfield

BOWSHOT *noun* **BOWSHOTS** the distance to which an arrow can be shot from a bow

BOWSPRIT *noun* **BOWSPRITS** a strong spar projecting from the front of a ship, often with ropes from the sails fastened to it

BOWSTRING *noun* **BOWSTRINGS** the string on a bow, which is drawn back and then released to project the arrow

BOX [1] *noun* **BOXES** a container made from wood, cardboard or plastic, etc, usually square or rectangular and with a lid

BOX [2] *verb* **BOXES, BOXING, BOXED** to fight with the hands formed into fists and protected by thick leather gloves, especially as a sport

BOXCAR *noun* **BOXCARS** a closed railway goods-wagon

BOXED *adj* contained in or provided with a box

BOXER *noun* **BOXERS** a person who boxes, especially as a sport

BOXERCISE *noun* **BOXERCISES** a workout involving a mixture of aerobics and movements simulating boxing blows

BOXFUL *noun* **BOXFULS** the amount a box can hold

BOXINESS noun **BOXINESSES** the state of being like a box

BOXING noun **BOXINGS** the sport or practice of fighting with the fists, especially wearing boxing gloves

BOXROOM noun **BOXROOMS** a small room, usually without a window, used to store bags and boxes, etc or as an extra bedroom

BOXY adj **BOXIER, BOXIEST** shaped like a box

BOY noun **BOYS** a male child □ exclamation expressing excitement, surprise or pleasure

BOYCOTT verb **BOYCOTTS, BOYCOTTING, BOYCOTTED** to refuse to have any business or social dealings with (a company or a country, etc), or to attend or take part in (negotiations, or a meeting, etc) □ noun **BOYCOTTS** an act or instance of boycotting, usually as a form of disapproval or coercion

BOYFRIEND noun **BOYFRIENDS** a regular male friend and companion, especially as a partner in a romantic or sexual relationship

BOYHOOD noun **BOYHOODS** the period of a man's life in which he is a boy

BOYISH adj like a boy in appearance or behaviour

BOYISHLY adverb in a boyish way

BOYO noun **BOYOS** a boy or young man

BOZO noun **BOZOS** a dim-witted fellow; a dope or wally

BRA noun **BRAS** an undergarment worn by a woman to support and cover the breasts

BRACE noun **BRACES** a device, usually made from metal, which supports, strengthens or holds two things together □ verb **BRACES, BRACING, BRACED** to make something tight or stronger, usually by supporting it in some way

BRACELET noun **BRACELETS** a band or chain worn as a piece of jewellery round the arm or wrist

BRACER noun **BRACERS** something that clamps, binds, etc

BRACHIAL adj belonging or relating to the arm

BRACHIATE adj having opposite widely spreading branches

BRACING adj said of the wind, air, climate, etc: stimulatingly cold and fresh

BRACKEN noun **BRACKENS** the commonest species of fern in the UK, which has tall fronds, spreads rapidly by means of its underground rhizomes and is poisonous to livestock

BRACKET noun **BRACKETS** either member of several pairs of symbols, < > , { }, ( ), [ ], used to group together or enclose words, figures, etc □ verb **BRACKETS, BRACKETING, BRACKETED** to enclose or group together (words, etc) in brackets

BRACKISH adj said of water: slightly salty; somewhat salt rather than fresh

BRACT noun **BRACTS** a modified leaf, usually smaller than a true leaf and green in colour, in whose axil an inflorescence develops

BRACTEAL adj relating to bracts

BRAD noun **BRADS** a thin flattish nail, tapering in width, with the head either flush with the sides or slightly projecting on one side

BRADAWL noun **BRADAWLS** a small chisel-edged handtool for making holes in wood or leather, etc

BRAE noun **BRAES** a slope on a hill

BRAG verb **BRAGS, BRAGGING, BRAGGED** to talk boastfully or too proudly about oneself, or what one has done, etc □ noun **BRAGS** a boastful statement or boastful talk

BRAGGART noun **BRAGGARTS** someone who brags a lot □ adj boastful

BRAID noun **BRAIDS** a band or tape, often made from threads of gold and silver twisted together, used as a decoration on uniforms, etc □ verb **BRAIDS, BRAIDING, BRAIDED** to twist (several lengths of thread or hair, etc) together, placing one over the other in a regular sequence

BRAIDED adj plaited; trimmed with braid

BRAIDING noun **BRAIDINGS** braid decoration; work in braid

BRAILLER noun **BRAILLERS** a machine for writing in Braille, a system of printing for the blind

BRAIN noun **BRAINS** the highly developed mass of nervous tissue that co-ordinates and controls the activities of the central nervous system of animals □ verb **BRAINS, BRAINING, BRAINED** to hit someone hard on the head

BRAINED adj having a brain or brains of a specified type

BRAINLESS adj without brains or understanding; silly

BRAINWASH verb **BRAINWASHES, BRAINWASHING, BRAINWASHED** to force someone to change their beliefs or ideas, etc by applying continual and prolonged mental pressure

BRAINWASHING noun **BRAINWASHINGS** the process of subjecting someone to such mental pressure or systematic indoctrination, so as to change their beliefs, etc

BRAINY adj **BRAINIER, BRAINIEST** clever; intelligent

BRAISE verb **BRAISES, BRAISING, BRAISED** to cook (meat, vegetables, etc) slowly with a small amount of liquid in a closed dish, usually after browning in a little fat

BRAISED adj said of food, especially meat: cooked by braising

BRAKE noun **BRAKES** a device used to slow down or stop a moving vehicle or machine, or to prevent the movement of a parked vehicle □ verb **BRAKES, BRAKING, BRAKED** to apply or use a brake

BRAKEMAN noun **BRAKEMEN** a man who is responsible for operating the brake of a railway train

BRALESS adj said of a woman: not wearing a bra

BRAMBLE noun **BRAMBLES** a blackberry bush

BRAMBLING noun **BRAMBLINGS** a small bird of the finch family with an orange breast and shoulder patch, a white rump and a black tail

BRAMBLY adj **BRAMBLIER, BRAMBLIEST** full of brambles

BRAN noun **BRANS** the outer covering of cereal grain, removed during the preparation of white flour, and often added to foods because it is an important source of vitamin B and dietary fibre

BRANCH noun **BRANCHES** an offshoot arising from the trunk of a tree or the main stem of a shrub □ verb **BRANCHES, BRANCHING, BRANCHED** to divide from the main part

BRANCHED adj having branches

BRANCHING adj that grows branches □ noun **BRANCHINGS** the action of growing branches

BRANCHY adj **BRANCHIER, BRANCHIEST** growing branches

BRAND noun **BRANDS** a distinctive maker's name or trademark, symbol or design, etc used to identify a product or group of products □ verb **BRANDS, BRANDING, BRANDED** to mark (cattle, etc) with a hot iron

BRANDIED adj heartened or strengthened with brandy

BRANDISH verb **BRANDISHES, BRANDISHING, BRANDISHED** to flourish or wave (a weapon, etc) as a threat or display □ noun **BRANDISHES** a flourish or wave (of a weapon, etc)

BRANDY noun **BRANDIES** a strong alcoholic drink distilled from grape wine

BRASH adj **BRASHER, BRASHEST** very loud, flashy or showy

BRASS noun **BRASSES** an alloy of copper and zinc, which is strong and ductile, resistant to corrosion, and suitable for casting □ singular or plural noun wind instruments made of brass, such as the trumpet and horn □ adj made of brass

BRASSERIE noun **BRASSERIES** a bar serving food

BRASSICA noun **BRASSICAS** any member of a genus of plants that includes several commercially important crop vegetables, eg cabbage, cauliflower, broccoli, brussels sprout, turnip, swede

BRASSIÈRE noun **BRASSIÈRES** the full name for bra

BRASSILY adverb insolently

BRASSY adj **BRASSIER, BRASSIEST** said especially of colour: like brass in appearance

BRAT noun **BRATS** a child, especially a rude or badly-behaved one

BRATTISH adj of or like a brat

BRATTY adj **BRATTIER, BRATTIEST** spoiled and badly behaved

BRATWURST noun **BRATWURSTS** a type of German pork sausage

BRAVA exclamation addressed to a woman: well done! excellent!

BRAVADO noun **BRAVADOS, BRAVADOES** a display of confidence or daring, often a boastful and insincere one

BRAVE adj **BRAVER, BRAVEST** said of a person, or their character, actions, etc: having or showing courage in facing danger or pain, etc; daring or fearless □ noun **BRAVES** a warrior, especially one from a Native American tribe □ verb **BRAVES, BRAVING, BRAVED** to meet or face up to (danger, pain, etc) boldly or resolutely; to defy

BRAVELY adverb with bravery; boldly

BRAVERY noun **BRAVERIES** a brave quality; being brave or courageous

BRAVI exclamation addressed to a number of people: well done! excellent!

BRAVO exclamation well done! excellent! □ noun **BRAVOS, BRAVOES** a cry of 'bravo'

BRAVURA noun **BRAVURAS** a display of great spirit, dash or daring

BRAW adj **BRAWER, BRAWEST** fine or splendid

BRAWL noun **BRAWLS** a noisy quarrel or fight, especially in public; a punch-up □ verb **BRAWLS, BRAWLING, BRAWLED** to quarrel or fight noisily

BRAWLER noun **BRAWLERS** a person given to brawling

BRAWLING noun **BRAWLINGS** noisy quarrelling or fighting

BRAWN noun **BRAWNS** muscle; muscular or physical strength

BRAWNY adj **BRAWNIER, BRAWNIEST** muscular; strong

> **BRAXY** noun **BRAXIES** a disease of sheep

BRAY verb **BRAYS, BRAYING, BRAYED** said of an ass or donkey: to make its characteristic loud harsh cry □ noun **BRAYS** the loud harsh braying sound made by an ass or donkey

BRAZE verb **BRAZES, BRAZING, BRAZED** to join (two pieces of metal) by melting an alloy with a lower melting point than either of the metals to be joined, and applying it to the joint

BRAZEN adj bold; impudent; shameless □ verb **BRAZENS, BRAZENING, BRAZENED** to face (out) impudently

BRAZENLY adverb in a brazen way

BRAZIER noun **BRAZIERS** a metal frame or container for holding burning coal or charcoal, used especially by people who have to work outside in cold weather

BRAZIL noun **BRAZILS** an edible type of long white oily nut with a hard three-sided shell, obtained from a tropical American tree

BREACH noun **BREACHES** an act of breaking, especially breaking of a law or promise, etc, or a failure to fulfil or carry out a duty, promise, etc □ verb **BREACHES, BREACHING, BREACHED** to break (a promise, etc) or fail to carry out (a duty or commitment, etc)

BREAD noun **BREADS** one of the oldest and most important staple foods known to man, usually prepared from wheat or rye flour mixed with water or milk, kneaded into a dough with a leavening agent, eg yeast, and baked □ verb **BREADS, BREADING, BREADED** to cover (a piece of food) with breadcrumbs before cooking

BREADED adj covered with breadcrumbs before cooking

BREADLINE noun **BREADLINES** a queue of poor or down-and-out people waiting for handouts of bread or other food, from charity or government sources

BREADTH noun **BREADTHS** the measurement from one side of something to the other; width or broadness

BREAK verb **BREAKS, BREAKING, BROKE, BROKEN** to divide or become divided into two or more parts as a result of stress or a blow □ noun **BREAKS** an act or result of breaking

BREAKABLE adj able to be broken □ noun **BREAKABLES** a breakable object

BREAKAGE noun **BREAKAGES** the act of breaking

BREAKAWAY noun **BREAKAWAYS** an act of breaking away or escaping □ adj that has broken away; separate

BREAKBEAT noun **BREAKBEATS** a short sample of rhythm (eg of drum beats) that is looped to create a new rhythm, often taken from old soul or jazz records and used in house music, hip-hop and drum-and-bass music

BREAKDOWN noun **BREAKDOWNS** a failure in a machine or device

BREAKER noun **BREAKERS** a large wave which breaks on rocks or on the beach

BREAKFAST noun **BREAKFASTS** the first meal of the day, normally taken soon after getting up in the morning □ verb **BREAKFASTS, BREAKFASTING, BREAKFASTED** to have breakfast

BREAKNECK *adj* said of speed: extremely fast, and usually dangerously fast

BREAKTIME *noun* **BREAKTIMES** a short interval in work or lessons, etc

BREAM *noun* **BREAMS** any of various freshwater fish of the carp family which have a deep body covered with silvery scales, and mouthparts which can be pushed out to form a tube for feeding

BREAST *noun* **BREASTS** in women: each of the two mammary glands, which form soft protuberances on the chest □ *verb* **BREASTS, BREASTING, BREASTED** to face, confront or fight against something

BREASTED *adj* having a breast or breasts of the specified type

BREATH *noun* **BREATHS** the air drawn into, and then expelled from, the lungs

BREATHE *verb* **BREATHES, BREATHING, BREATHED** to respire by alternately drawing air into and expelling it from the lungs

BREATHER *noun* **BREATHERS** a short rest or break from work or exercise

BREATHILY *adverb* in a breathy way

BREATHING *noun* **BREATHINGS** in terrestrial animals: the process whereby air is alternately drawn into the lungs and then expelled from them, as a result of which oxygen is taken into the body and carbon dioxide is released from it

BREATHY *adj* **BREATHIER, BREATHIEST** said of a speaking voice: accompanied by a sound of unvocalized breathing

BRECCIA *noun* **BRECCIAS** coarse sedimentary rock, composed of a mixture of angular rock cemented together by finer-grained material, and usually formed by processes such as landslides and geological faulting

BREECH *noun* **BREECHES** the back part of a gun barrel, where it is loaded

BREECHES *plural noun* short trousers fastened usually just below the knee

BREECHING *noun* **BREECHINGS** in a horse's harness: a strap attached to the saddle, and passing around the horse's rump

BREED *verb* **BREEDS, BREEDING, BRED** said of animals and plants: to reproduce sexually □ *noun*

BREED an artificially maintained subdivision within an animal species, especially farm livestock or pet animals, produced by domestication and selective breeding, eg Friesian cattle

BREEDER *noun* **BREEDERS** a person or thing that breeds

BREEDING *noun* **BREEDINGS** controlling the manner in which plants or animals reproduce in such a way that certain characteristics are selected for and passed on to the next generation

BREEZE *noun* **BREEZES** a gentle wind □ *verb* **BREEZES, BREEZING, BREEZED** to move briskly, in a cheery and confident manner

BREEZILY *adverb* confidently and casually

BREEZY *adj* **BREEZIER, BREEZIEST** rather windy

BRETHREN plural of **brother**

BREVE *noun* **BREVES** a note twice as long as a semibreve

BREVIARY *noun* **BREVIARIES** a book containing the hymns, prayers and psalms which form the daily service

BREVITY *noun* **BREVITIES** using few words; conciseness

BREW *verb* **BREWS, BREWING, BREWED** to make (eg beer) by mixing, boiling and fermenting □ *noun* **BREWS** a drink produced by brewing, especially beer

BREWER *noun* **BREWERS** a person or company that brews and sells beer

BREWERY *noun* **BREWERIES** a place where beer and ale are brewed

BREWING *noun* **BREWINGS** the act or an instance of making liquor from malt

BRIAR *noun* **BRIARS** any of various prickly shrubs, especially a wild rose bush

BRIBE *noun* **BRIBES** a gift, usually of money, offered to someone to persuade them to do something illegal or improper □ *verb* **BRIBES, BRIBING, BRIBED** to offer or promise a bribe, etc to someone

BRIBER *noun* **BRIBERS** a person who offers or gives a bribe

BRIBERY *noun* **BRIBERIES** the act or practice of offering or taking bribes

BRICK *noun* **BRICKS** a rectangular block of baked clay used for building □ *adj* made of brick or of

bricks □ *verb* **BRICKS, BRICKING, BRICKED** to close, cover, fill in or wall up (eg a window) with bricks

BRICKBAT *noun* **BRICKBATS** an insult or criticism

BRICKWORK *noun* **BRICKWORKS** the part of a building, etc that is constructed of brick, eg the walls

BRICKWORKS *singular noun* a factory producing bricks

BRICKYARD *noun* **BRICKYARDS** a place where bricks are made

BRIDAL *adj* belonging or relating to a bride or a wedding

BRIDE *noun* **BRIDES** a woman who has just been married, or is about to be married

BRIDGE *noun* **BRIDGES** a structure that spans a river, road, railway, valley, ravine or other obstacle, providing a continuous route across it for pedestrians, motor vehicles or trains □ *verb* **BRIDGES, BRIDGING, BRIDGED** to form or build a bridge over (eg a river or railway)

BRIDLE *noun* **BRIDLES** the leather straps put on a horse's head which help the rider to control the horse □ *verb* **BRIDLES, BRIDLING, BRIDLED** to put a bridle on (a horse)

BRIEF *adj* **BRIEFER, BRIEFEST** lasting only a short time □ *noun* **BRIEFS** in law: a summary of the facts and legal points of a case, prepared for the barrister who will be dealing with the case in court □ *verb* **BRIEFS, BRIEFING, BRIEFED** to prepare someone by giving them instructions in advance

BRIEFCASE *noun* **BRIEFCASES** a light, usually flat, case for carrying papers, etc

BRIEFING *noun* **BRIEFINGS** a meeting at which instructions and information are given, or any instance of making or giving a brief

BRIEFLESS *adj* said of a barrister: holding no brief; without a client

BRIEFLY *adverb* using few words; for a short time

BRIEFNESS *noun* **BRIEFNESSES** being brief, especially using few words; brevity

BRIEFS *plural noun* a woman's or man's close-fitting underpants without legs

BRIER *noun* **BRIERS** a briar

BRIG *noun* **BRIGS** a type of sailing ship with two masts and square sails

For longer words, see *The Chambers Dictionary*

BRIGADE noun **BRIGADES** one of the subdivisions in the army, consisting eg of a group of regiments, usually commanded by a brigadier

BRIGADIER noun **BRIGADIERS** an officer commanding a brigade

BRIGAND noun **BRIGANDS** a member of a band of robbers, especially one operating in a remote mountain area

BRIGANDRY noun **BRIGANDRIES** the behaviour or actions of brigands

BRIGHT adj **BRIGHTER, BRIGHTEST** giving out or shining with much light □ adverb brightly

BRIGHTEN verb **BRIGHTENS, BRIGHTENING, BRIGHTENED** to become, or make something or someone, bright or brighter

BRIGHTLY adverb in a bright way

BRILL ¹ adj **BRILLER, BRILLEST** excellent

BRILL ² noun **BRILLS** a large flatfish, found mainly in shallow European coastal waters, which has a freckled sandy brown body and is valued as a food fish

BRILLIANT adj very bright and sparkling □ noun **BRILLIANTS** a diamond or other gem

BRIM noun **BRIMS** the top edge or lip of a cup, glass, bowl, etc □ verb **BRIMS, BRIMMING, BRIMMED** to be, or become, full to the brim

BRIMFUL adj full to the brim

BRIMLESS adj said especially of a hat: not having a brim

BRIMSTONE noun **BRIMSTONES** sulphur

BRINDLED adj said of animals: brown or grey, and marked with streaks or patches of a darker colour

BRINE noun **BRINES** very salty water, used for preserving food

BRING verb **BRINGS, BRINGING, BROUGHT** to carry or take something or someone to a stated or implied place or person

BRINGER noun **BRINGERS** a person who brings something

BRINISH adj like brine

BRINJAL noun **BRINJALS** especially in Indian cookery: the aubergine

BRINK noun **BRINKS** the edge or border of a steep dangerous place or of a river

BRINY adj **BRINIER, BRINIEST** said of water: very salty □ noun the sea

BRIOCHE noun **BRIOCHES** a type of light soft cake-like bread or roll, made with a yeast dough, eggs and butter

BRIQUET noun **BRIQUETS** a briquette

BRIQUETTE noun **BRIQUETTES** a brick-shaped block made of compressed coal-dust or charcoal, etc, used for fuel

BRISK adj **BRISKER, BRISKEST** lively, active or quick

BRISKET noun **BRISKETS** meat from next to the ribs of a bull or cow

BRISKLY adverb in a brisk way

BRISKNESS noun **BRISKNESSES** liveliness, activity or quickness

BRISLING noun **BRISLINGS** a small marine fish of the herring family, fished in Norwegian fjords, and usually processed and canned in oil

BRISTLE noun **BRISTLES** a short stiff hair on an animal or plant □ verb **BRISTLES, BRISTLING, BRISTLED** said of an animal's or a person's hair: to stand upright and stiff

BRISTLED adj having or fitted with bristles

BRISTLING adj said of a beard or eyebrows, etc: thick and rough

BRISTLY adj **BRISTLIER, BRISTLIEST** having bristles; rough or prickly

BRISTOLS plural noun female breasts

BRITCHES plural noun short trousers fastened usually just below the knee

BRITTLE adj **BRITTLER, BRITTLEST** said of a substance: hard but easily broken or likely to break □ noun **BRITTLES** a type of hard crunchy toffee made from caramelized sugar and nuts

BRITTLELY adverb in a brittle way

BRITTLY adverb brittlely

BRO noun **BROS** a place for which one feels a strong affinity

BROACH verb **BROACHES, BROACHING, BROACHED** to raise (a subject, especially one likely to cause arguments or problems) for discussion □ noun **BROACHES** a long tapering pointed tool for making and rounding out holes

BROAD adj **BROADER, BROADEST** large in extent from one side to the other □ noun

BROADS a series of low-lying shallow lakes connected by rivers in E Anglia

BROADBAND adj across, involving or designed to operate across a wide range of frequencies

BROADCAST verb **BROADCASTS, BROADCASTING, BROADCAST** to transmit (a radio or TV programme, speech, etc) for reception by the public □ noun **BROADCASTS** a radio or TV programme □ adj communicated or sent out by radio or TV □ adverb in all directions; widely

BROADCASTING noun **BROADCASTINGS** the action of transmitting (a radio or TV programme, etc) for reception by the public

BROADEN verb **BROADENS, BROADENING, BROADENED** to become or make something broad or broader

BROADLOOM adj said especially of a carpet: woven on a wide loom to give broad widths

BROADLY adverb widely; generally

BROADNESS noun **BROADNESSES** the state or quality of being broad

BROADSIDE noun **BROADSIDES** a strongly critical verbal attack

BROCADE noun **BROCADES** a heavy silk fabric with a raised design on it, often one using gold or silver threads

BROCADED adj woven or worked in the manner of brocade

BROCCOLI noun **BROCCOLIS** a type of cultivated cabbage grown for its green leafy stalks and branched heads of flower buds

BROCH noun **BROCHS** a circular tower built of dry stone, dating from the late Iron Age, with galleries in the thickness of the wall and an open central area

BROCHETTE noun **BROCHETTES** a small metal or wooden skewer for holding food together or steady while it is being cooked

BROCHURE noun **BROCHURES** a booklet or pamphlet, especially one giving information or publicity about holidays, products, etc

BROGUE noun **BROGUES** a strong but gentle accent, especially the type of English spoken by an Irish person

BROIL verb **BROILS, BROILING, BROILED** to grill (food)

BROILER *noun* **BROILERS** a quickly-reared young chicken sold ready for broiling

BROKE *adj* having no money; bankrupt

BROKEN *adj* smashed; fractured

BROKENLY *adverb* in a broken way

BROKER *noun* **BROKERS** a person employed to buy and sell stocks and shares; a stockbroker

BROKERAGE *noun* **BROKERAGES** the profit taken by, or fee charged by, a broker for transacting business for other people; commission

BROKING *noun* **BROKINGS** the trade or business of a broker

BROLGA *noun* **BROLGAS** a large grey Australian crane

BROLLY *noun* **BROLLIES** an umbrella

BROMELIAD *noun* **BROMELIADS** any of numerous plants, most of which are epiphytes found in the canopy of tropical rainforests that typically have large strap-shaped fleshy leaves forming a rosette around a central cup in which water accumulates

BROMIDE *noun* **BROMIDES** any chemical compound that is a salt of hydrobromic acid, including various compounds used medicinally as sedatives, and silver bromide, which is used to coat photographic film

BROMINE *noun* **BROMINES** a non-metallic element consisting of a dark-red highly-corrosive liquid with a pungent smell, compounds of which are used in photographic film, water purification, anti-knock petrol additives, and in the manufacture of plastics and organic chemicals

BRONCHIAL *adj* relating to either of the two main airways to the lungs, known as the bronchi

BRONCHUS *noun* **BRONCHI** either of the two main airways to the lungs that branch off the lower end of the trachea

BRONCO *noun* **BRONCOS** a wild or half-tamed horse from the western US

BRONZE *noun* **BRONZES** an alloy of copper and tin that is harder than pure copper, resistant to corrosion, and suitable for casting □ *adj* made of bronze □ *verb* **BRONZES, BRONZING, BRONZED** to give a bronze colour, surface or appearance to something

BRONZED *adj* having a bronze colour; suntanned

BRONZING *noun* **BRONZINGS** the process of giving or acquiring a bronze-like colour or surface

BRONZY *adj* **BRONZIER, BRONZIEST** resembling bronze

BROOCH *noun* **BROOCHES** a decoration or piece of jewellery with a hinged pin at the back for fastening it to clothes

BROOD *noun* **BROODS** a number of young animals, especially birds, that are produced or hatched at the same time □ *verb* **BROODS, BROODING, BROODED** said of a bird: to sit on eggs in order to hatch them

BROODER *noun* **BROODERS** a person or animal that broods

BROODING *adj* said of a person: thinking anxiously or resentfully about something

BROODY *adj* **BROODIER, BROODIEST** said of a bird: ready and wanting to brood

BROOK [1] *noun* **BROOKS** a small stream

BROOK [2] *verb* **BROOKS, BROOKING, BROOKED** to tolerate, endure or accept

BROOM *noun* **BROOMS** a long-handled sweeping brush, formerly made from the stems of the broom plant, but now usually made from straw or synthetic material

BROOMRAPE *noun* **BROOMRAPES** an annual or perennial plant that lacks chlorophyll, produces dense spikes of brownish flowers, has leaves reduced to scales and is parasitic on broom, ivy and members of the daisy family

BROTH *noun* **BROTHS** a thin clear soup made by boiling meat, fish or vegetables, etc in water

BROTHEL *noun* **BROTHELS** a house where men can go to have sexual intercourse with prostitutes for money (currently illegal in the UK and most of the US)

BROTHER *noun* **BROTHERS, BRETHREN** a boy or man with the same natural parents as another person or people

BROTHERLY *adj* like a brother; kind, affectionate

BROUGHAM *noun* **BROUGHAMS** a type of light, closed carriage pulled by four horses, with a raised open seat for the driver

BROUGHT past form of **bring**

BROUHAHA *noun* **BROUHAHAS** noisy, excited and confused activity; a commotion or uproar

BROW *noun* **BROWS** short form of eyebrow

BROWBEAT *verb* **BROWBEATS, BROWBEATING, BROWBEATEN** to frighten or intimidate someone by speaking angrily or sternly, or by looking fierce; to bully

BROWBEATEN *adj* frightened or intimidated; bullied

BROWN *adj* **BROWNER, BROWNEST** having the colour of dark soil or wood, or any of various shades of this colour tending towards red or yellow □ *noun* **BROWNS** any of various dark earthy colours, like those of bark, tanned skin or coffee, etc □ *verb* **BROWNS, BROWNING, BROWNED** to make or become brown by cooking, tanning in the sun, etc

BROWNIE *noun* **BROWNIES** a friendly goblin or fairy, traditionally said to help with domestic chores

BROWNING *noun* **BROWNINGS** a substance used to turn gravy a rich brown colour

BROWNISH *adj* somewhat brown in colour

BROWNNESS *noun* **BROWNNESSES** the quality or state of being brown

BROWNY *adj* **BROWNIER, BROWNIEST** brownish

BROWSE *verb* **BROWSES, BROWSING, BROWSED** to look through a book, etc, or look around a shop, etc in a casual, relaxed or haphazard way □ *noun* **BROWSES** an act of browsing

BROWSER *noun* **BROWSERS** a person, animal or thing that browses

BRUISE *noun* **BRUISES** an area of skin discoloration and swelling caused by the leakage of blood from damaged blood vessels following injury; a similar injury to a fruit or plant □ *verb* **BRUISES, BRUISING, BRUISED** to mark and discolour (the surface of the skin or of a fruit, etc) in this way

BRUISED *adj* marked by a bruise or bruises

BRUISER *noun* **BRUISERS** a big strong person, especially one who likes fighting or who looks aggressive

BRUISING *noun* **BRUISINGS**

dark-coloured marks which show on bruised skin □ *adj* said eg of experience: hurting in an emotional or mental way

BRUIT *verb* **BRUITS, BRUITING, BRUITED** to spread or report (news or rumours, etc) □ *noun* **BRUITS** something widely rumoured

BRÛLÉ *adj* in cookery: with a coating of caramelized brown sugar on top

BRUMMAGEM *noun* **BRUMMAGEMS** something, especially imitation jewellery, that is showy, cheap and tawdry □ *adj* showy; sham; tawdry; worthless

BRUNCH *noun* **BRUNCHES** a meal that combines breakfast and lunch, eaten around midday or late in the morning

BRUNET *noun* **BRUNETS** a brunette

BRUNETTE *noun* **BRUNETTES** a woman or girl with brown or dark hair

BRUNT *noun* **BRUNTS** the main force or shock of (a blow or attack, etc); the most damaging, burdensome or painful part of something

BRUSH *noun* **BRUSHES** a tool with lengths of stiff nylon, wire, hair, bristles or something similar set into it, used for tidying the hair, cleaning, painting, etc □ *verb* **BRUSHES, BRUSHING, BRUSHED** to sweep, groom or clean, etc with a brush; to pass a brush over (eg the floor) or through (eg the hair)

BRUSHED *adj* smoothed, rubbed, straightened, etc with a brush

BRUSHER *noun* **BRUSHERS** a person who brushes, or uses a brush

BRUSHING *noun* **BRUSHINGS** sweeping with a brush

BRUSHWOOD *noun* **BRUSHWOODS** dead, broken or lopped-off branches and twigs, etc from trees and bushes

BRUSHWORK *noun* **BRUSHWORKS** a particular technique or manner a painter uses to apply the paint to a canvas, etc

BRUSQUE *adj* **BRUSQUER, BRUSQUEST** said of a person or their manner, etc: blunt and often impolite; curt

BRUSQUELY *adverb* in a brusque way

BRUT *adj* said of wines, especially champagne: very dry

BRUTAL *adj* savagely cruel or violent

BRUTALISE *verb* **BRUTALISES, BRUTALISING, BRUTALISED** to brutalize

BRUTALISM *noun* **BRUTALISMS** applied to art, architecture and literature, etc: deliberate crudeness or harshness of style

BRUTALITY *noun* **BRUTALITIES** savage cruelty or violence

BRUTALIZE *verb* **BRUTALIZES, BRUTALIZING, BRUTALIZED** to make someone brutal

BRUTALLY *adverb* in a brutal way

BRUTE *noun* **BRUTES** a cruel, brutal or violent person □ *adj* irrational or stupid; instinctive, not involving rational thought

BRUTISH *adj* like, or belonging or relating to, a brute; cruel or coarse

BRUTISHLY *adverb* in a brutish way

BRYONY *noun* **BRYONIES** a perennial climbing plant, related to the yam, which has heart-shaped or three-lobed glossy green leaves, and tiny yellowish-green flowers followed by bright-red highly poisonous berries

BRYOPHYTE *noun* **BRYOPHYTES** any member of the division (Bryophyta) of the plant kingdom that includes mosses, liverworts and hornworts

BUB *noun* **BUBS** an old word for a strong drink

BUBBLE *noun* **BUBBLES** a thin film of liquid forming a hollow sphere filled with air or gas, especially one which floats in liquid □ *verb* **BUBBLES, BUBBLING, BUBBLED** to form or give off bubbles, or to rise in bubbles

BUBBLY *adj* **BUBBLIER, BUBBLIEST** having bubbles, or being like bubbles □ *noun* **BUBBLIES** champagne

BUBO *noun* **BUBOES** a swollen tender lymph node, especially in the armpit or groin, commonly developing as a symptom of bubonic plague, syphilis or gonorrhoea

BUBONIC *adj* relating to or characterized by buboes

BUCCAL *adj* relating to the mouth or the inside of the cheek

BUCCANEER *noun* **BUCCANEERS** a pirate, especially an adventurer who attacked and plundered

Spanish ships in the Caribbean during the 17c

BUCCANEERING *adj* said of a person: living or acting as a buccaneer □ *noun*

BUCCANEERINGS piracy; unscrupulous adventuring

BUCK *noun* **BUCKS** a male animal, especially a male deer, goat, antelope, rabbit, hare or kangaroo □ *verb* **BUCKS, BUCKING, BUCKED** said of a horse, etc: to make a series of rapid jumps into the air, with the back arched and legs held stiff, especially in an attempt to throw off a rider

BUCKED *adj* pleased and encouraged

BUCKER *noun* **BUCKERS** an animal that bucks

BUCKET *noun* **BUCKETS** a round open-topped container for holding or carrying liquids and solids such as sand, etc □ *verb* **BUCKETS, BUCKETING, BUCKETED** said of rain: to pour down heavily

BUCKETFUL *noun* **BUCKETFULS** the amount a bucket can hold

BUCKHORN *noun* **BUCKHORNS** horn from a buck, used for making handles for knives, etc

BUCKLE *noun* **BUCKLES** a flat piece of metal or plastic, etc usually attached to one end of a strap or belt, with a pin in the middle which goes through a hole in the other end of the strap or belt to fasten it □ *verb* **BUCKLES, BUCKLING, BUCKLED** to fasten or be fastened with a buckle

BUCKLED *adj* bent or warped

BUCKLER *noun* **BUCKLERS** a small round shield, usually with a raised centre

BUCKRAM *noun* **BUCKRAMS** stiffened cotton or linen used to line clothes or cover books, etc

BUCKSHEE *adj* free of charge; gratis

BUCKSHOT *noun* **BUCKSHOTS** a large type of lead shot used in hunting

BUCKSKIN *noun* **BUCKSKINS** the skin of a deer

BUCKTHORN *noun* **BUCKTHORNS** any of various northern temperate shrubs or small trees, especially a thorny deciduous shrub with bright-green oval toothed leaves and small yellowish-green sweetly-scented flowers followed by black berries

BUCKTOOTH *noun* **BUCKTEETH** a large front tooth which sticks out

BUCKWHEAT noun **BUCKWHEATS** an erect fast-growing annual plant, native to Central Asia, with leathery spear-shaped leaves and terminal clusters of tiny pink or white flowers

BUCKYBALL noun **BUCKYBALLS** common name for the molecule buckminsterfullerene

BUCOLIC adj concerned with the countryside or people living there; pastoral; rustic □ noun **BUCOLICS** a poem about the countryside or pastoral life

BUD noun **BUDS** in a plant: an immature knob-like shoot, often enclosed by protective scales, that will eventually develop into a leaf or flower □ verb **BUDS, BUDDING, BUDDED** said of a plant, etc: to put out or develop buds

BUDDING noun **BUDDINGS** the formation of buds on a plant shoot □ adj said of a person: developing; beginning to show talent in a specified area

BUDDLEIA noun **BUDDLEIAS** any of various deciduous shrubs or small trees, native to China, with spear-shaped leaves and long pointed purple, lilac, orange-yellow or white fragrant flower-heads

BUDDY noun **BUDDIES** a friend or companion □ verb **BUDDIES, BUDDYING, BUDDIED** to become friendly

BUDGE verb **BUDGES, BUDGING, BUDGED** to move, or to make something or someone move

BUDGET noun **BUDGETS** a plan, especially one covering a particular period of time, specifying how money coming in, eg to a household or a business project, will be spent and allocated □ verb **BUDGETS, BUDGETING, BUDGETED** to calculate how much money one is earning and spending, so that one does not spend more than one has; to draw up a budget

BUDGETARY adj relating to or connected with a budget or financial planning

BUDGIE noun **BUDGIES** a budgerigar

BUFF noun **BUFFS** a dull-yellowish colour □ adj dull yellow in colour □ verb **BUFFS, BUFFING, BUFFED** to polish something with a piece of soft material

BUFFALO noun **BUFFALOES** a member of the cattle family, which has a heavy black or brown body, thick horns curving upwards at their tips, and large drooping ears

BUFFER noun **BUFFERS** an apparatus designed to take the shock when an object such as a railway carriage or a ship hits something, especially a device using springs, on a railway carriage, etc, or a cushion of rope on a ship □ verb **BUFFERS, BUFFERING, BUFFERED** to add a buffer to something

BUFFERED adj equipped with a buffer or buffers

BUFFET [1] noun **BUFFETS** a meal set out on tables from which people help themselves

BUFFET [2] verb **BUFFETS, BUFFETING, BUFFETED** to strike or knock someone or something with the hand or fist

BUFFETING noun **BUFFETINGS** repeated knocks or blows

BUFFOON noun **BUFFOONS** a person who sets out to amuse people with jokes and foolish or comic behaviour, etc; a clown

BUG noun **BUGS** the common name for any of thousands of insects with a flattened oval body and mouthparts modified to form a beak for piercing and sucking, eg aphids □ verb **BUGS, BUGGING, BUGGED** to hide a microphone in (a room, telephone, etc) so as to be able to listen in to any conversations carried on there

BUGABOO noun **BUGABOOS** an imaginary thing which causes fear or anxiety

BUGBEAR noun **BUGBEARS** an object of fear, dislike or annoyance, especially when that fear, etc is irrational or needless

BUGGY noun **BUGGIES** a light open carriage pulled by one horse

BUGLE noun **BUGLES** a brass or copper instrument similar to a small trumpet but normally without any valves, used mainly for sounding military calls or fanfares, etc □ verb **BUGLES, BUGLING, BUGLED** to sound a bugle

BUGLER noun **BUGLERS** a person who plays the bugle

BUGLOSS noun **BUGLOSSES** any of several plants of the borage family

BUILD verb **BUILDS, BUILDING, BUILT** to make or construct something from parts □ noun **BUILDS** physical form, especially that of the human body; style of construction

BUILDER noun **BUILDERS** a person who builds, or organizes and supervises the building of, houses, etc

BUILDING noun **BUILDINGS** the business, process, art or occupation of constructing houses, etc

BULB noun **BULBS** in certain plants, eg tulip and onion: a swollen underground organ that functions as a food store and consists of a modified shoot, with overlapping layers of fleshy leaf bases or scales, and roots growing from its lower surface

BULBOUS adj like a bulb in shape; fat, bulging or swollen

BULBOUSLY adverb in a bulbous way

BULGE noun **BULGES** a swelling, especially where one would expect to see something flat □ verb **BULGES, BULGING, BULGED** to swell outwards

BULGHUR noun **BULGHURS** bulgur

BULGING adj swelling out; overfull

BULGUR noun **BULGURS** wheat that has been boiled, dried, lightly milled and cracked

BULGY adj **BULGIER, BULGIEST** swollen

BULIMIA noun **BULIMIAS** compulsive overeating, caused either by psychological factors or by damage to the hypothalamus of the brain

BULIMIC noun **BULIMICS** a person suffering from bulimia nervosa

BULK noun **BULKS** size, especially when large and awkward □ verb **BULKS, BULKING, BULKED** to swell, fill out or increase in bulk, or to make something do so

BULKHEAD noun **BULKHEADS** a wall in a ship or aircraft, etc which separates one section from another, so that if one section is damaged, the rest is not affected

BULKILY adverb in a bulky way

BULKINESS noun **BULKINESSES** the quality of being large in size

BULKY adj **BULKIER, BULKIEST** large in size, filling a lot of space and awkward to carry or move

BULL noun **BULLS** the uncastrated male of animals in the cattle family

BULLDOG noun **BULLDOGS** a

breed of dog with a heavy body, a short brown or brown and white coat, a large square head with a flat upturned muzzle, short bowed legs and a short tail

BULLDOZE verb **BULLDOZES, BULLDOZING, BULLDOZED** to use a bulldozer to move, flatten or demolish something

BULLDOZER noun **BULLDOZERS** a large, powerful, heavy tractor with a vertical blade at the front, for pushing heavy objects, clearing the ground or making it level

BULLET noun **BULLETS** a small metal cylinder with a pointed or rounded end, for firing from a small gun or rifle

BULLETIN noun **BULLETINS** a short official statement of news issued as soon as the news is known

BULLFIGHT noun **BULLFIGHTS** a public show, especially in Spain and Portugal, etc in which people on horseback and on foot bait, and usually ultimately kill, a bull

BULLFINCH noun **BULLFINCHES** a small bird of the finch family, native to Europe and Asia, the male of which has a short black bill, and a conspicuous red breast

BULLFROG noun **BULLFROGS** any of various large frogs with a loud call

BULLHEAD noun **BULLHEADS** a small bottom-dwelling freshwater fish, native to N Europe, which has a stout body and a broad flattened head

BULLION noun **BULLIONS** gold or silver that has not been coined, especially in large bars, or in mass

BULLISH adj like a bull, especially in temper; aggressive

BULLISHLY adverb in a bullish way

BULLOCK noun **BULLOCKS** a young male ox

BULLY noun **BULLIES** a person who hurts, frightens or torments weaker or smaller people □ verb **BULLIES, BULLYING, BULLIED** to act like a bully towards someone; to threaten or persecute them

BULRUSH noun **BULRUSHES** a tall waterside plant with long narrow greyish leaves and one or two thick spikes of tightly packed dark-brown flowers

BULWARK noun **BULWARKS** a wall built as a defence, often one made of earth; a rampart □ verb **BULWARKS, BULWARKING,**

BULWARKED to defend or fortify something

BUM[1] noun **BUMS** the buttocks

BUM[2] verb **BUMS, BUMMING, BUMMED** to get something by begging, borrowing or cadging

BUMBLE verb **BUMBLES, BUMBLING, BUMBLED** to move or do something in an awkward or clumsy way

BUMBLER noun **BUMBLERS** a bungler

BUMBLING adj inept; blundering

BUMF noun **BUMFS** miscellaneous useless leaflets, official papers and documents, etc

BUMMER noun **BUMMERS** a difficult or unpleasant thing

BUMP verb **BUMPS, BUMPING, BUMPED** to knock or hit someone or something, especially heavily or with a jolt □ noun **BUMPS** a knock, jolt or collision

BUMPER noun **BUMPERS** a bar on the front or back of a motor vehicle which lessens the shock or damage if it hits anything □ adj exceptionally good or large

BUMPH noun **BUMPHS** bumf

BUMPILY adverb in a bumpy way

BUMPINESS noun **BUMPINESSES** the state of being bumpy

BUMPKIN noun **BUMPKINS** an awkward, simple or stupid person, especially a simple fellow who lives in the country

BUMPTIOUS adj offensively or irritatingly conceited or self-important

BUMPY adj **BUMPIER, BUMPIEST** having a lot of bumps

BUN noun **BUNS** a small, round, usually sweetened, roll, often containing currants, etc

BUNCH noun **BUNCHES** a number of things fastened or growing together □ verb **BUNCHES, BUNCHING, BUNCHED** to group together in, or to form, a bunch or bunches

BUNCHING noun **BUNCHINGS** gathering together in bunches

BUNCHY adj **BUNCHIER, BUNCHIEST** resembling, growing in, or in the form of, a bunch or bunches

BUNCO noun **BUNCOS** a confidence trick in which the victim is swindled or taken somewhere and robbed

BUNCOMBE noun **BUNCOMBES** bunkum

BUNDLE noun **BUNDLES** a number of things loosely fastened or tied together □ verb **BUNDLES, BUNDLING, BUNDLED** to make something into a bundle or bundles

BUNG noun **BUNGS** a small round piece of wood, rubber or cork, etc used to close a hole eg in the bottom of a barrel or small boat, or in the top of a jar or other container □ verb **BUNGS, BUNGING, BUNGED** to block (a hole) with a bung

BUNGALOW noun **BUNGALOWS** a single-storey house

BUNGHOLE noun **BUNGHOLES** a hole by which a barrel, etc is emptied or filled and into which a bung is fitted

BUNGLE verb **BUNGLES, BUNGLING, BUNGLED** to do something carelessly or badly; to spoil or mismanage (a job or procedure) □ noun **BUNGLES** carelessly or badly done work; a mistake or foul-up

BUNGLED adj carelessly or badly done

BUNGLER noun **BUNGLERS** a careless unskilful worker

BUNGLING noun **BUNGLINGS** careless or unskilful work □ adj clumsy, awkward

BUNION noun **BUNIONS** a painful swelling on the first joint of the big toe

BUNK noun **BUNKS** a narrow bed attached to the wall in a cabin in a ship, caravan, etc □ verb **BUNKS, BUNKING, BUNKED** to lie down and go to sleep, especially in some improvised place

BUNKER noun **BUNKERS** an obstacle on a golf course consisting of a hollow area containing sand □ verb **BUNKERS, BUNKERING, BUNKERED** in golf: to play (the ball) into a bunker

BUNKHOUSE noun **BUNKHOUSES** a building containing sleeping accommodation for workers, especially ranch workers

BUNKO noun **BUNKOS** a bunco

BUNKUM noun **BUNKUMS** nonsense; foolish talk; claptrap

BUNNY noun **BUNNIES** a pet name or child's word for a rabbit

BUNT noun **BUNTS** in baseball: an act or instance of pushing or blocking (the ball) with the bat, rather than swinging at it □ verb **BUNTS, BUNTING, BUNTED** to push or block (the ball) with the bat, rather than swinging at it

BUNTING noun **BUNTINGS** any of various small finch-like birds with a short stout bill and a sturdy body, usually with streaked brown plumage

BUNYIP noun **BUNYIPS** in folklore: a frightening monster that lives in water-holes, lakes, swamps, etc

BUOY noun **BUOYS** a brightly-coloured floating object fastened to the bottom of the sea by an anchor, to warn ships of rocks, etc or to mark channels, etc □ verb **BUOYS, BUOYING, BUOYED** to mark (eg an obstruction or a channel) with a buoy or buoys

BUOYANCY noun **BUOYANCIES** the quality or capacity of being buoyant

BUOYANT adj said of an object: able to float in or on the surface of a liquid

BUR noun **BURS** any seed or fruit with numerous hooks or prickles which are caught in the fur or feathers of passing mammals and birds, and so dispersed over considerable distances

BURBLE verb **BURBLES, BURBLING, BURBLED** to speak at length but with little meaning or purpose □ noun **BURBLES** a bubbling murmuring sound

BURBOT noun **BURBOTS** a large fish, the only freshwater species in the cod family, and an important food fish in the former Soviet Union

BURDEN noun **BURDENS** something to be carried; a load □ verb **BURDENS, BURDENING, BURDENED** to weigh someone down with a burden, difficulty, problem, etc

BURDOCK noun **BURDOCKS** any of various perennial plants, native to Europe and Asia, with heart-shaped lower leaves and oval heads of tiny purple flowers, followed by spiny fruits or burs

BUREAU noun **BUREAUS, BUREAUX** a desk for writing at, with drawers and usually a front flap which opens downwards to provide the writing surface

BURETTE noun **BURETTES** a long vertical glass tube marked with a scale and having a tap at the bottom, used to deliver controlled volumes of liquid, eg during chemical titrations

BURGEON verb **BURGEONS, BURGEONING, BURGEONED** to grow or develop quickly; to flourish

BURGEONING adj growing or developing quickly; flourishing

BURGER noun **BURGERS** a hamburger

BURGESS noun **BURGESSES** an inhabitant or citizen of a borough or burgh

BURGH noun **BURGHS** in Scotland until 1975: an incorporated town or borough, with a certain amount of self-government under a town council

BURGHER noun **BURGHERS** a citizen of a town, especially a town on the Continent, or of a borough

BURGLAR noun **BURGLARS** a person who commits the crime of burglary

BURGLARY noun **BURGLARIES** the crime of entering a building or other permanent structure illegally in order to steal, or to commit grievous bodily harm or rape

BURGLE verb **BURGLES, BURGLING, BURGLED** to enter (a building, etc) illegally and steal from it; to steal from someone or something

BURGUNDY noun **BURGUNDIES** a French wine made in the Burgundy region, especially a red wine

BURIAL noun **BURIALS** the burying of a dead body in a grave

BURIN noun **BURINS** a tempered steel tool for engraving copper or wood, etc

BURK noun **BURKS** a berk

BURL noun **BURLS** a small knot or lump in wool or thread □ verb **BURLS, BURLING, BURLED** to remove the burls from (a fabric)

BURLAP noun **BURLAPS** a coarse canvas made from jute or hemp, used for sacks or wrappings

BURLESQUE noun **BURLESQUES** a piece of literature, acting or some other presentation which exaggerates, demeans or mocks a serious subject or art form □ adj belonging to or like a burlesque □ verb **BURLESQUES, BURLESQUING, BURLESQUED** to make fun of something using burlesque; to make a burlesque of it

BURLEY noun **BURLEYS** humbug; rubbish

BURLINESS noun **BURLINESSES** the state of being burly

BURLY adj **BURLIER, BURLIEST** said of a person: strong and heavy in build; big and sturdy

BURN verb **BURNS, BURNING, BURNT, BURNED** to be on fire or set something on fire □ noun **BURNS** an injury or mark caused by fire, heat, acid, friction, etc

BURNER noun **BURNERS** the part of a gas lamp or stove, etc which produces the flame

BURNING adj on fire

BURNISH verb **BURNISHES, BURNISHING, BURNISHED** to make (metal) bright and shiny by polishing □ noun **BURNISHES** polish; lustre

BURNISHED adj made bright by polishing

BURNISHING noun **BURNISHINGS** the action of brightening (metal) by polishing

BURNOUS noun **BURNOUSES** a long cloak with a hood, worn by Arabs

BURNT a past form of **burn**

BURP verb **BURPS, BURPING, BURPED** to let air escape noisily from one's stomach through one's mouth □ noun **BURPS** a belch

BURQA noun **BURQAS** a long loose garment, with veiled eyeholes, worn in public by Muslim women

BURR noun **BURRS** a continual humming sound made eg by a machine □ verb **BURRS, BURRING, BURRED** to make a humming sound

BURRITO noun **BURRITOS** a Mexican dish consisting of a tortilla folded around a filling of meat, cheese, refried beans, etc

BURROW noun **BURROWS** a hole in the ground, especially one dug by a rabbit or other small animal for shelter or defence □ verb **BURROWS, BURROWING, BURROWED** to make a hole or tunnel

BURSA noun **BURSAE** a sac or pouch of liquid occurring at a point of friction between two structures, especially between a tendon and a bone

BURSAR noun **BURSARS** a treasurer in a school, college or university

BURSARY noun **BURSARIES**

especially in Scotland and New Zealand: an award or grant of money made to a student; a scholarship

BURSITIS noun **BURSITISES** inflammation of a bursa

BURST verb **BURSTS, BURSTING, BURST** to break or fly open or into pieces, usually suddenly and violently ◻ noun **BURSTS** an instance of bursting or breaking open

BURSTING adj very eager to do something

BURTHEN noun **BURTHENS** the amount of cargo a ship can carry; its capacity

BURTON noun **BURTONS** a drink

BURY verb **BURIES, BURYING, BURIED** to place (a dead body) in a grave, the sea, etc

BUS noun **BUSES** a road vehicle, usually a large one, which carries passengers to and from established stopping points along a fixed route for payment ◻ verb **BUSES, BUSSES, BUSING, BUSSING, BUSED, BUSSED** to go by bus

BUSBY noun **BUSBIES** a tall fur hat with a bag hanging on its right side, worn as part of some military uniforms, especially that of the hussar

BUSH noun **BUSHES** a low woody perennial plant, especially one having many separate branches originating at or near ground level; wild uncultivated land covered with shrubs or small trees, especially in semi-arid regions of Africa, Australia or New Zealand ◻ verb **BUSHES, BUSHING, BUSHED** to grow thick or bushy

BUSHED adj extremely tired

BUSHEL noun **BUSHELS** in the imperial system: a unit for measuring dry or liquid goods (especially grains, potatoes or fruit) by volume, equal to 8 gallons or 36.4 litres in the UK (35.2 litres in the USA)

BUSHFIRE noun **BUSHFIRES** a fire in forest or scrub

BUSHINESS noun **BUSHINESSES** the state or condition of being bushy

BUSHMAN noun **BUSHMEN** someone who lives or travels in the bush

BUSHVELD noun **BUSHVELDS** veld made up largely of woodland

BUSHWALK verb **BUSHWALKS, BUSHWALKING, BUSHWALKED**

to walk or hike through the bush as a leisure activity ◻ noun **BUSHWALKS** a walk through the bush

BUSHWALKING noun **BUSHWALKINGS** walking or hiking through the bush as a leisure activity

BUSHWHACK verb **BUSHWHACKS, BUSHWHACKING, BUSHWHACKED** to travel through woods or bush, especially by clearing a way through it

BUSHWHACKING noun **BUSHWHACKINGS** travelling in this way

BUSHY adj **BUSHIER, BUSHIEST** full of or like bushes; thick and spreading

BUSIED past form of **busy**

BUSIER see under **busy**

BUSIES a form of **busy**

BUSIEST see under **busy**

BUSILY adverb in a busy way

BUSINESS noun **BUSINESSES** the buying and selling of goods and services

BUSK verb **BUSKS, BUSKING, BUSKED** to sing, play music, etc in the street for money

BUSKER noun **BUSKERS** someone who performs in the street for money

BUSKING noun **BUSKINGS** singing, playing music, etc in the street for money

BUST ¹ noun **BUSTS** the upper, front part of a woman's body; breasts or bosom

BUST ² verb **BUSTS, BUSTING, BUSTED** to break or burst ◻ adj broken or burst

BUSTARD noun **BUSTARDS** any one of various species of large ground-dwelling bird with speckled grey or brown plumage and long powerful legs

BUSTER noun **BUSTERS** a form of address (often used aggressively) for a man or boy

BUSTIER noun **BUSTIERS** a short tight-fitting strapless bodice for women, worn as a bra and top combined

BUSTLE verb **BUSTLES, BUSTLING, BUSTLED** to busy oneself in a brisk, energetic and/or noisy manner ◻ noun **BUSTLES** hurried, noisy and excited activity

BUSTLER noun **BUSTLERS** a person who bustles or works with ostentatious haste

BUSTLING adj lively and busy

BUSTY adj **BUSTIER, BUSTIEST** said of a woman: having large breasts

BUSY adj **BUSIER, BUSIEST** fully occupied; having much work to do ◻ verb **BUSIES, BUSYING, BUSIED** to occupy; to make busy

BUSYBODY noun **BUSYBODIES** someone who is always interfering in other people's affairs

BUSYNESS noun **BUSYNESSES** the state or condition of being busy

BUT conj contrary to expectation ◻ noun **BUTS** an objection or doubt

BUTANE noun **BUTANES** a colourless highly flammable gas belonging to the alkane series of hydrocarbon compounds, and used in the manufacture of synthetic rubber, and in liquid form as a fuel supply for portable stoves, etc

BUTCH adj **BUTCHER, BUTCHEST** said of a person: tough and strong-looking; aggressively masculine in manner or looks, etc

BUTCHER noun **BUTCHERS** a person or shop that sells meat ◻ verb **BUTCHERS, BUTCHERING, BUTCHERED** to kill and prepare (an animal) for sale as food

BUTCHERY noun **BUTCHERIES** the preparing of meat for sale as food; the trade of a butcher

BUTLER noun **BUTLERS** the chief male servant in a house

BUTLERY noun **BUTLERIES** the pantry in which the glassware, dinner service and silverware, etc is kept

BUTT verb **BUTTS, BUTTING, BUTTED** to push or hit hard or roughly with the head, in the way a ram or goat might ◻ noun **BUTTS** a blow with the head or horns

BUTTE noun **BUTTES** an isolated flat-topped residual hill with steep sides, formed by erosion of a mesa when a remnant of hard rock protects the softer rock underneath

BUTTER noun **BUTTERS** a solid yellowish food, made from the fats in milk by churning, and used for spreading on bread, and in cooking ◻ verb **BUTTERS, BUTTERING, BUTTERED** to put butter on or in something

BUTTERCUP noun **BUTTERCUPS** any of various perennial plants, often found on damp soils, which have erect branched stems, lobed leaves and cup-shaped flowers, usually with five glossy yellow petals

BUTTERED *adj* spread with butter

BUTTERFLY *noun* **BUTTERFLIES** the common name for any of thousands of species of insect which have four broad, often brightly coloured wings covered with tiny overlapping scales, and a long proboscis for sucking nectar from flowers

BUTTERY *adj* **BUTTERIER, BUTTERIEST** like butter; smeared with butter or the like □ *noun* **BUTTERIES** a room, especially in a college or university, where food is kept and supplied to students

BUTTOCK *noun* **BUTTOCKS** each of the fleshy parts of the body between the base of the back and the top of the legs, on which a person sits

BUTTON *noun* **BUTTONS** a small round piece of metal or plastic, etc sewn on to a piece of clothing, which fastens it by being passed through a buttonhole □ *verb* **BUTTONS, BUTTONING, BUTTONED** to fasten or close something using a button or buttons

BUTTRESS *noun* **BUTTRESSES** a projecting support made of brick or masonry, etc built on to the outside of a wall □ *verb* **BUTTRESSES, BUTTRESSING, BUTTRESSED** to support (a wall, etc) with buttresses

BUTTY *noun* **BUTTIES** a sandwich; a piece of bread and butter, as a snack

BUXOM *adj* **BUXOMER, BUXOMEST** said of a woman: attractively plump, lively and healthy-looking

BUY *verb* **BUYS, BUYING, BOUGHT** to obtain something by paying a sum of money for it □ *noun* **BUYS** a thing bought

BUYER *noun* **BUYERS** a person who buys; a customer

BUZZ *verb* **BUZZES, BUZZING, BUZZED** to make a continuous, humming or rapidly vibrating sound, like that made by the wings of an insect such as the bee □ *noun* **BUZZES** a humming or rapidly vibrating sound, such as that made by a bee

BUZZARD *noun* **BUZZARDS** any of several large hawks that resemble eagles in their effortless gliding flight, rising on warm air currents for long periods

BUZZER *noun* **BUZZERS** an electrical device which makes a buzzing sound, used as a signal or for summoning someone, eg in a doctor's surgery or an office, etc

BWANA *noun* **BWANAS** often used as a form of address or respect: master; sir

BWAZI *noun* **BWAZIS** an African shrub

BY *prep* next to, beside or near □ *adverb* aside; away; in reserve □ *noun* **BYS** a bye

BYE ¹ *exclamation* goodbye

BYE ² *noun* **BYES** a pass into the next round of a competition, given to a competitor or team that has not been given an opponent in the current round

BYGONE *noun* **BYGONES** events, troubles or arguments which occurred in the past

BYLINE *noun* **BYLINES** a line under the title of a newspaper or magazine article which gives the name of the author

BYNAME *noun* **BYNAMES** another name, or an additional name, by which a person is known

BYPASS *noun* **BYPASSES** a major road which carries traffic on a route that avoids a city centre, town or congested area □ *verb* **BYPASSES, BYPASSING, BYPASSED** to avoid (a congested or blocked place) by taking a route which goes round or beyond it

BYPATH *noun* **BYPATHS** an out-of-the-way, little-used or indirect path

BYRE *noun* **BYRES** a cowshed

BYROAD *noun* **BYROADS** a minor, secondary or secluded road

BYSTANDER *noun* **BYSTANDERS** a person who happens to be standing by, who sees but does not take part in what is happening; an onlooker

BYTE *noun* **BYTES** in computing: a group of adjacent binary digits that are handled as a single unit, especially a group of eight bits representing one alphanumerical character or two decimal digits

BYWAY *noun* **BYWAYS** a byroad

BYWORD *noun* **BYWORDS** a person or thing that is well known as an example of something

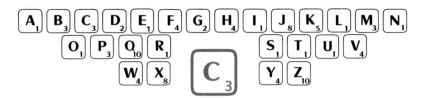

CAB *noun* **CABS** a taxi

CABAL *noun* **CABALS** a small group formed within a larger body, for secret, especially political, discussion, planning, etc □ *verb* **CABALS, CABALLING, CABALLED** to form a cabal; to plot

CABALA *noun* **CABALAS** the cabbala

CABARET *noun* **CABARETS** entertainment with songs, dancing, etc at a restaurant or nightclub

CABBAGE *noun* **CABBAGES** any of several varieties of a leafy biennial plant, grown for its compact head of green, white or red edible leaves

CABBALA *noun* **CABBALAS** a secret traditional lore of Jewish rabbis, who can interpret hidden meanings in the Old Testament

CABBALISM *noun* **CABBALISMS** the science of the cabbala

CABBALIST *noun* **CABBALISTS** someone versed in the cabbala

CABBIE *noun* **CABBIES** a cabby

CABBY *noun* **CABBIES** a taxi-driver

CABER *noun* **CABERS** a heavy wooden pole of c.3–4m in length, that must be carried upright and then tipped end over end, during a contest called tossing the caber

CABIN *noun* **CABINS** a small house, especially one made of wood □ *verb* **CABINS, CABINING, CABINED** to shut up in a confined space

CABINET *noun* **CABINETS** a piece of furniture with shelves and doors, for storing or displaying items

CABLE *noun* **CABLES** a strong wire cord or rope used for supporting loads, lifting, hauling, towing, etc □ *verb* **CABLES, CABLING, CABLED** to tie up or provide with a cable or cables

CABOCHON *noun* **CABOCHONS** a precious stone that is polished but uncut

CABOODLE *noun* **CABOODLES** the whole lot; everything

CABOOSE *noun* **CABOOSES** a guard's van on a railway train

CABRIOLE *noun* **CABRIOLES** a furniture leg ornamentally curved to resemble an animal's leg

CABRIOLET *noun* **CABRIOLETS** a light two-wheeled carriage drawn by one horse

CACAO *noun* **CACAOS** a small evergreen tree, native to S and Central America, but widely cultivated in other tropical regions for its seeds

CACHE *noun* **CACHES** a hiding-place, eg for weapons □ *verb* **CACHES, CACHING, CACHED** to put or collect in a cache

CACHET *noun* **CACHETS** something which brings one respect or admiration; a distinction

CACHEXIA *noun* **CACHEXIAS** a condition characterized by physical weakness, abnormally low body weight and general ill health, usually associated with a chronic disease such as cancer or tuberculosis

CACKLE *noun* **CACKLES** a raucous laugh □ *verb* **CACKLES, CACKLING, CACKLED** to laugh raucously

CACOPHONY *noun* **CACOPHONIES** often said of music: a disagreeable combination of loud noises

CACTUS *noun* **CACTI, CACTUSES** any of numerous mostly spiny plants, found mainly in the arid deserts of N and Central America, which usually store water in swollen, often barrel-like stems

CAD *noun* **CADS** a man who behaves discourteously or dishonourably, especially towards a woman

CADAVER *noun* **CADAVERS** a human corpse, especially one used for dissection

CADDIE *noun* **CADDIES** someone whose job is to carry the golf clubs around the course for a golf-player □ *verb* **CADDIES, CADDYING, CADDIED** to act as a caddie

CADDIS *noun* **CADDISES** the larva of the caddis fly, found in ponds

and streams, which builds a protective cylindrical case around itself consisting of sand grains, fragments of shell, small pieces of twig and leaf fragments

CADDISH *adj* like a cad

CADDY *noun* **CADDIES** a caddie □ *verb* **CADDIES, CADDYING, CADDIED** to caddie

CADENCE *noun* **CADENCES** a fall of pitch in the voice

CADENTIAL *adj* pertaining to cadence

CADENZA *noun* **CADENZAS** an elaborate virtuoso passage given by a solo performer towards the end of a movement

CADET *noun* **CADETS** a student undergoing preliminary training for the armed forces or police

CADGE *verb* **CADGES, CADGING, CADGED** to get something (especially money or food) by scrounging or begging

CADGER *noun* **CADGERS** a sponger

CADI *noun* **CADIS** in Muslim countries: a judge or magistrate

CADMIUM *noun* **CADMIUMS** a soft bluish-white metallic element used in alloys, corrosion-resistant plating, control rods in nuclear reactors and nickel-cadmium batteries

CADRE *noun* **CADRES** in the military: a permanent core unit which can be expanded when required, eg by conscription

CAECAL *adj* relating to the caecum

CAECILIAN *noun* **CAECILIANS** a tropical amphibian with a worm-like body and no legs, which burrows into forest floors or river beds

CAECUM *noun* **CAECA** a blind-ended pouch, to the lower end of which the appendix is attached, at the junction of the small and large intestines

CAESIUM *noun* **CAESIUMS** a soft silvery-white metallic element formed by the fission of uranium, and used in photoelectric cells and certain optical instruments

For longer words, see *The Chambers Dictionary*

CAESURA noun **CAESURAE, CAESURAS** a pause near the middle of a line of verse

CAFÉ noun **CAFÉS** a restaurant (usually a small one) that serves light meals or snacks

CAFETERIA noun **CAFETERIAS** a self-service restaurant

CAFETIÈRE noun **CAFETIÈRES** a coffee-pot with a plunger for separating the grounds from the liquid by pushing them to the bottom

CAFFEINE noun **CAFFEINES** a bitter-tasting alkaloid, found in coffee beans, tea leaves and cola nuts, a stimulant of the central nervous system

CAFTAN noun **CAFTANS** originally in Middle Eastern countries: a long loose-fitting robe, often tied at the waist, worn by men

CAGE noun **CAGES** an enclosure, sometimes portable and usually with bars, in which captive birds and animals are kept □ verb **CAGES, CAGING, CAGED** to put in a cage; to imprison or confine

CAGEBIRD noun **CAGEBIRDS** a bird, such as a canary, suitable for keeping in a cage

CAGED adj confined

CAGEY adj **CAGIER, CAGIEST** secretive and cautious; not forthcoming

CAGILY adverb in a cagey way

CAGINESS noun the state or quality of being cagey

CAGOULE noun **CAGOULES** a lightweight waterproof hooded anorak, pulled on over the head and often reaching down to the knees

CAGY adj **CAGIER, CAGIEST** cagey

CAHOOTS plural noun company or partnership

CAIMAN noun **CAIMANS** a cayman

CAIQUE noun **CAIQUES** a light narrow boat propelled by one or more oars, used in Turkish waters, particularly on the Bosporus

CAIRN noun **CAIRNS** a heap of stones piled up to mark something, especially a grave or pathway

CAIRNGORM noun **CAIRNGORMS** a yellow or smoky-brown variety of the mineral quartz, often used as a gemstone

CAISSON noun **CAISSONS** a watertight rectangular or cylindrical chamber used to protect construction workers during the building of underwater foundations, bridges, piers, etc

CAJOLE verb **CAJOLES, CAJOLING, CAJOLED** to persuade (into) using flattery, promises, etc; to coax

CAJOLER noun **CAJOLERS** a person who cajoles

CAJOLERY noun **CAJOLERIES** persuasion using flattery, promises, etc

CAKE noun **CAKES** a solid food made by baking a mixture of flour, fat, eggs, sugar, etc □ verb **CAKES, CAKING, CAKED** to dry as a thick hard crust

CAKEWALK noun **CAKEWALKS** a prancing march with intricate improvised steps originally performed by Black Americans as part of a competition □ verb **CAKEWALKS, CAKEWALKING, CAKEWALKED** to perform a cakewalk

CALABASH noun **CALABASHES** an evergreen tree, native to tropical S America, which has clusters of lance-shaped leaves, bell-shaped flowers, and flask-shaped woody fruits

CALABOOSE noun **CALABOOSES** a small local prison

CALABRESE noun **CALABRESES** a type of green sprouting broccoli, eaten as a vegetable

CALAMARI plural noun in Mediterranean cookery: squid

CALAMINE noun **CALAMINES** a fine pink powder containing zinc oxide and small amounts of ferric oxide, used in the form of a lotion or ointment to soothe insect bites and stings, and to treat sunburn, eczema and other skin complaints

CALAMITY noun **CALAMITIES** a catastrophe, disaster or serious misfortune causing great loss or damage

CALCES plural of **calx**

CALCICOLE noun **CALCICOLES** a plant that requires soil with a high lime or chalk content

CALCIFUGE noun **CALCIFUGES** a plant that grows best in acid soil with a low lime or chalk content

CALCIFY verb **CALCIFIES, CALCIFYING, CALCIFIED** to harden as a result of the deposit of calcium salts

CALCITE noun **CALCITES** a white or colourless mineral, composed of crystalline calcium carbonate, that is the main constituent of limestone and marble rocks

CALCIUM noun **CALCIUMS** a soft, silvery-white metallic element which occurs mainly in the form of calcium carbonate minerals such as chalk, limestone and marble, and which is an important constituent of bones, teeth, milk and plant cell walls

CALCULATE verb **CALCULATES, CALCULATING, CALCULATED** to work out, find out or estimate, especially by mathematical means

CALCULATED adj intentional; deliberate

CALCULATING adj deliberately shrewd and selfish, especially in terms of how one can use other people and situations to benefit oneself

CALCULUS noun **CALCULI, CALCULUSES** the branch of mathematics concerned with the differentiation and integration of functions

CALDERA noun **CALDERAS** a large crater formed by the collapse of the central part of a volcano after an eruption

CALDRON noun **CALDRONS** a very large metal pot, often with handles, for boiling or heating liquids

CALENDAR noun **CALENDARS** an almanac or table of months, says, seasons, or of facts about specific days etc □ verb **CALENDARS, CALENDARING, CALENDARED** to place or record in a calendar

CALENDER noun **CALENDERS** a machine consisting of a vertical arrangement of heated rollers through which paper or cloth is passed in order to give it a smooth shiny finish □ verb **CALENDERS, CALENDERING, CALENDERED** to give a smooth finish to (paper or cloth) by passing it through such a machine

CALENDS plural noun in the ancient Roman calendar: the first day of each month

CALF noun **CALVES** the young of any bovine animal, especially domestic cattle

CALFSKIN noun **CALFSKINS** leather made from the skin of a calf

CALIBRATE verb **CALIBRATES, CALIBRATING, CALIBRATED** to mark a scale on (a measuring instrument) so that it can be used to take readings in suitable units

CALIBRE noun **CALIBRES** the

internal diameter of a gun barrel or tube

CALICO noun **CALICOS, CALICOES** a kind of cotton cloth, usually plain white or in its natural unbleached state

CALIF noun **CALIFS** a caliph

CALIPASH noun **CALIPASHES** the part of a turtle which is closest to the upper shell, composed of a greenish, gelatinous substance

CALIPEE noun **CALIPEES** the part of a turtle which is closest to the lower shell, composed of a yellowish gelatinous substance

CALIPER noun **CALIPERS** a calliper

CALIPH noun **CALIPHS** the chief Muslim civil and religious leader

CALIPHATE noun **CALIPHATES** the office, rank or government of, or area ruled by, a caliph

CALL verb **CALLS, CALLING, CALLED** to shout or speak loudly in order to attract attention or in announcing something ▫ noun **CALLS** a shout or cry

CALLER noun **CALLERS** a person or thing that calls

CALLING noun **CALLINGS** a trade or profession

CALLIOPE noun **CALLIOPES** a keyboard musical instrument similar to an organ, with a set of whistles operated by steam or compressed air

CALLIPER noun **CALLIPERS** a measuring device, consisting of two hinged prongs attached to a scale, which is used to measure the linear distance between the prongs, eg in order to determine the diameters of pipes

CALLOSITY noun **CALLOSITIES** a callus

CALLOUS adj unconcerned for the feelings of others; coldly and deliberately cruel

CALLOUSLY adverb unfeelingly; cruelly

CALLOW adj **CALLOWER, CALLOWEST** young and inexperienced

CALLUS noun **CALLUSES** a thickened hardened pad of skin which develops on parts of the body that are subjected to constant friction or pressure, such as the palms of the hands and soles of the feet

CALM adj **CALMER, CALMEST** relaxed and in control; not anxious, upset, angry, etc ▫ noun

CALMS peace, quiet and tranquillity ▫ verb **CALMS, CALMING, CALMED** to become calmer

CALMLY adverb in a calm way

CALMNESS noun **CALMNESSES** the state or quality of being calm

CALORIE noun **CALORIES** a metric unit denoting the amount of heat required to raise the temperature of one gram of water by $1\,°C$ (1K) at one atmospheric pressure, now replaced by the SI unit joule

CALORIFIC adj referring or relating to, or generating, heat

CALQUE noun **CALQUES** a compound word or phrase, adopted into a language, whose parts are a literal translation of the corresponding parts of the phrase in the language it has been borrowed from, eg in English, *superman* is a calque of German *Übermensch*

CALUMET noun **CALUMETS** a tobacco-pipe, smoked as a token of peace by Native Americans

CALUMNY noun **CALUMNIES** an untrue and malicious spoken statement about a person

CALVE verb **CALVES, CALVING, CALVED** to give birth to (a calf)

CALVES plural of **calf**

CALX noun **CALXES, CALCES** the powdery metal oxide that remains after an ore has been roasted in air

CALYPSO noun **CALYPSOS** a type of popular song originating in the West Indies, usually dealing with current happenings in an amusing way, and often improvised by the singer

CALYX noun **CALYXES, CALYCES** the outermost whorl of a flower, consisting of the sepals

CALZONE noun **CALZONES** a folded round of pizza dough stuffed with a savoury filling

CAM noun **CAMS** an irregular projection on a wheel or rotating shaft, shaped so as to transmit regular movement to another part in contact with it

CAMBER noun **CAMBERS** a slight convexity on the upper surface of a road, ship's deck, wing section of an aeroplane, etc, designed to promote drainage of water ▫ verb **CAMBERS, CAMBERING, CAMBERED** to form (a slight convexity) on the upper surface of a structure or to give (a slight convexity) to such a surface

CAMBIUM noun **CAMBIUMS** in the roots and stems of woody plants: a layer of actively dividing cells between the xylem and the phloem, which produces an increase in lateral growth or girth

CAMBRIC noun **CAMBRICS** a fine white cotton or linen fabric

CAMCORDER noun **CAMCORDERS** a portable video camera that is used to record images and sound as electronic signals on a small cassette of video tape, which can then be played back through a standard television receiver using a videocassette recorder incorporated within the camera

CAME past form of **come**

CAMEL noun **CAMELS** a large herbivorous mammal with a long neck and legs, coarse hair, a tufted tail and one or two humps on its back, which contain fat and act as a food reserve

CAMELEER noun **CAMELEERS** someone who drives or rides a camel

CAMELLIA noun **CAMELLIAS** an evergreen shrub, native to SE Asia, widely cultivated for its conspicuous white, pink or crimson flowers and glossy dark green leaves

CAMEO noun **CAMEOS** a smooth rounded gemstone with a raised design of a head in profile carved on it, especially one where the design is a different colour from the gemstone

CAMERA noun **CAMERAS** an optical device that focuses light from an object through a lens on to light-sensitive film, in order to record the image as a photograph

CAMERAMAN noun **CAMERAMEN** in TV or film-making: someone who operates a camera

CAMISOLE noun **CAMISOLES** a woman's loose undergarment, with narrow shoulder straps for the top half of the body

CAMOMILE noun **CAMOMILES** a strongly scented perennial plant, native to Europe and SW Asia, which has finely divided leaves, and daisy-like flower-heads consisting of outer white ray florets and inner yellow disc florets

CAMP[1] noun **CAMPS** a piece of ground on which tents have been erected ▫ verb **CAMPS, CAMPING, CAMPED** to stay in a tent or tents, cooking meals in the open air, etc

CAMP² *adj* **CAMPER, CAMPEST** said of a man or his behaviour: using mannerisms that are typically associated with women, especially in a deliberate, exaggerated or theatrical way

CAMPAIGN *noun* **CAMPAIGNS** an organized series of actions intended to gain support for or build up opposition to a particular practice, group, etc □ *verb* **CAMPAIGNS, CAMPAIGNING, CAMPAIGNED** to organize or take part in a campaign

CAMPANILE *noun* **CAMPANILES** especially in Italy: a free-standing bell tower, ie not attached to a church, etc

CAMPANULA *noun* **CAMPANULAS** any of numerous north temperate plants with bell-shaped flowers, usually blue, borne either singly or in long flower-heads

CAMPER *noun* **CAMPERS** someone who camps

CAMPHOR *noun* **CAMPHORS** a white or colourless crystalline compound with a strong aromatic odour, used as a plasticizer in the manufacture of celluloid, as a medicinal liniment and inhalant, and as an insect repellent

CAMPHORIC *adj* of or relating to camphor

CAMPION *noun* **CAMPIONS** any of various annual or perennial north temperate plants, especially the red campion and white campion, which have bright pink and white flowers, respectively, and a tubular calyx

CAMPSITE *noun* **CAMPSITES** a piece of land on which people are allowed to camp

CAMPUS *noun* **CAMPUSES** the grounds of a college or university

CAMSHAFT *noun* **CAMSHAFTS** a shaft to which one or more cams are attached

CAN¹ *verb* **COULD** to be able to

CAN² *noun* **CANS** a sealed container, usually of tin plate or aluminium, used to preserve food and protect it from bacterial contamination, or to retain the carbon dioxide in fizzy drinks □ *verb* **CANS, CANNING, CANNED** to seal (food or drink) in metal containers in order to preserve it

CANAKIN *noun* **CANAKINS** a cannikin

CANAL *noun* **CANALS** an artificial channel or waterway, usually constructed for navigation or irrigation

CANALISE *verb* **CANALISES, CANALISING, CANALISED** to canalize

CANALIZE *verb* **CANALIZES, CANALIZING, CANALIZED** to make or convert into a canal or a system of canals

CANAPÉ *noun* **CANAPÉS** a small piece of bread or toast spread or topped with something savoury

CANARD *noun* **CANARDS** a false report or piece of news; a rumour, hoax, etc

CANARY *noun* **CANARIES** a small finch, with bright yellow plumage, very popular as a caged bird □ *adj* canary coloured

CANASTA *noun* **CANASTAS** a card game similar to rummy played with two packs of cards, in which the aim is to collect sets of cards of the same value

CANCAN *noun* **CANCANS** a lively dance which is usually performed by dancing girls, who execute high kicks, raising their skirts to reveal their petticoats

CANCEL *verb* **CANCELS, CANCELLING, CANCELLED** to stop (something already arranged) from taking place, by an official announcement, etc; to call off

CANCER *noun* **CANCERS** any form of malignant tumour that develops when the cells of a tissue or organ multiply in an uncontrolled manner

CANCEROUS *adj* of, like or affected with cancer

CANDELA *noun* **CANDELAS** the SI unit of luminous intensity

CANDID *adj* **CANDIDER, CANDIDEST** honest and open about what one thinks; outspoken

CANDIDACY *noun* **CANDIDACIES** the status of a candidate

CANDIDATE *noun* **CANDIDATES** someone who is competing with others for a job, prize, parliamentary seat, etc

CANDIDLY *adverb* in a candid way

CANDIED *adj* preserved or encrusted with sugar; crystallized

CANDLE *noun* **CANDLES** a piece of wax or (especially formerly) tallow, formed around a wick, which is burnt to provide light □ *verb* **CANDLES, CANDLING, CANDLED** to test (eggs, etc) by examining against a bright light

CANDOUR *noun* **CANDOURS** the quality of being candid; frankness and honesty

CANDY *noun* **CANDIES** a sweet □ *verb* **CANDIES, CANDYING, CANDIED** to reduce (sugar) to a crystalline form by boiling and evaporating slowly

CANDYTUFT *noun* **CANDYTUFTS** an annual or perennial evergreen plant, native to Europe and Asia, which has narrow leaves and flattened heads of small white or mauve flowers

CANE *noun* **CANES** the long jointed hollow or pithy stem of certain plants, especially various small palms (eg rattan) and larger grasses (eg bamboo and sugar cane) □ *verb* **CANES, CANING, CANED** to beat someone with a cane as a punishment

CANFUL *noun* **CANFULS** the amount a can will hold

CANIKIN *noun* **CANIKINS** a small can, often used as a drinking vessel

CANINE *adj* relating to or resembling a dog □ *noun* **CANINES** any animal belonging to the dog family

CANING *noun* **CANINGS** a beating with a cane

CANISTER *noun* **CANISTERS** a metal or plastic container for storing tea or other dry foods

CANKER *noun* **CANKERS** a fungal, bacterial or viral disease of trees and woody shrubs, eg fruit trees, in which hardened tissue forms over sunken or cracked dead areas on the bark or near a wound

CANKEROUS *adj* corroding like a canker

CANNABIS *noun* **CANNABISES** a narcotic drug, prepared from the leaves and flowers of the hemp plant, the use of which is prohibited in many countries

CANNED *adj* contained or preserved in cans

CANNERY *noun* **CANNERIES** a factory where goods are canned

CANNIBAL *noun* **CANNIBALS** someone who eats human flesh

CANNIER see under **canny**

CANNIEST see under **canny**

CANNIKIN *noun* **CANNIKINS** a small can, often used as a drinking vessel

CANNILY *adverb* in a canny way

CANNINESS *noun* **CANNINESSES** the quality or state of being canny

CANNON *noun* **CANNONS** a large gun mounted on wheels; a shot in billiards, pool etc in which the cue ball strikes one object ball and then strikes another □ *verb* **CANNONS, CANNONING, CANNONED** in billiards, pool and snooker: to play a cannon shot

CANNONADE *noun* **CANNONADES** a continuous bombardment by heavy guns □ *verb* **CANNONADES, CANNONADING, CANNONADED** to attack with or as if with a cannon

CANNOT *verb* can not

CANNULA *noun* **CANNULAS, CANNULAE** a thin hollow tube used to introduce fluid to, or remove it from, body cavities

CANNY *adj* **CANNIER, CANNIEST** wise, clever and alert; shrewd

CANOE *noun* **CANOES** a light narrow boat propelled manually by one or more single- or double-bladed paddles □ *verb* **CANOES, CANOEING, CANOED** to travel by canoe

CANOEING *noun* **CANOEINGS** the sport or activity of paddling a canoe

CANOEIST *noun* **CANOEISTS** someone who paddles a canoe

CANON *noun* **CANONS** a basic law, rule or principle; an officially accepted collection of writing

CANONICAL *adj* according to, of the nature of or included in a canon

CANONISE *verb* **CANONISES, CANONISING, CANONISED** to canonize

CANONIZE *verb* **CANONIZES, CANONIZING, CANONIZED** to officially declare someone to be a saint

CANOODLE *verb* **CANOODLES, CANOODLING, CANOODLED** to hug and kiss; to cuddle

CANOPIED *adj* covered with a canopy

CANOPY *noun* **CANOPIES** an ornamental covering hung over a bed, throne, etc

CANST used with *thou*: a form of **can**

CANT *noun* **CANTS** a slope □ *verb* **CANTS, CANTING, CANTED** to tilt, slope or tip up

CANTABILE *adverb* in a flowing and melodious manner □ *adj* flowing and melodious □ *noun* **CANTABILES** a piece of music to be played this way

CANTALOUP *noun* **CANTALOUPS** a type of large melon with a thick ridged skin and orange-coloured flesh

CANTATA *noun* **CANTATAS** a musical work, especially on a religious theme, which is sung, with parts for chorus and soloists

CANTEEN *noun* **CANTEENS** a restaurant, especially a cafeteria, attached to a factory, office, etc for the use of employees

CANTER *noun* **CANTERS** a horse-riding pace between trotting and galloping □ *verb* **CANTERS, CANTERING, CANTERED** to move or cause to move at this pace

CANTICLE *noun* **CANTICLES** a non-metrical hymn or chant with a text taken from the Bible

CANTING *adj* sloping or slanting

CANTO *noun* **CANTOS** a section of a long poem

CANTON *noun* **CANTONS** a division of a country, especially one of the separately governed regions of Switzerland □ *verb* **CANTONS, CANTONING, CANTONED** to divide into cantons

CANTOR *noun* **CANTORS** in a synagogue service: a man who chants the liturgy and leads the congregation in prayer

CANVAS *noun* **CANVASES** a thick heavy coarse cloth, made from hemp or flax, used to make sails, tents, etc and for painting pictures on

CANVASS *verb* **CANVASSES, CANVASSING, CANVASSED** to ask for votes or support from someone □ *noun* **CANVASSES** a solicitation of information, votes, opinions, etc

CANVASSER *noun* **CANVASSERS** a person who canvasses

CANYON *noun* **CANYONS** a deep gorge or ravine with steep sides, usually cut into the bedrock of arid or semi-arid regions by the action of a stream or river

CAP *noun* **CAPS** any of various types of hat, eg with a flat or rounded crown and a peak □ *verb* **CAPS, CAPPING, CAPPED** to put a cap on or cover the top or end of something, with a cap

CAPABLE *adj* **CAPABLER, CAPABLEST** clever; able; efficient

CAPABLY *adverb* in a capable way

CAPACIOUS *adj* having plenty of room for holding things; roomy

CAPACITOR *noun* **CAPACITORS** a device consisting of two conducting surfaces separated by a dielectric material, eg waxed paper, that can store energy in the form of electric charge

CAPACITY *noun* **CAPACITIES** the amount that something can hold

CAPARISON *noun* **CAPARISONS** a decorative covering, harness, etc for a horse □ *verb* **CAPARISONS, CAPARISONING, CAPARISONED** to put a caparison on (especially a horse)

CAPE *noun* **CAPES** a short cloak

CAPER *verb* **CAPERS, CAPERING, CAPERED** to jump or dance about playfully □ *noun* **CAPERS** a playful jump

CAPILLARY *noun* **CAPILLARIES** a tube, usually made of glass, which has a very small diameter □ *adj* said of a tube: having a very small diameter

CAPITAL *noun* **CAPITALS** the chief city of a country, usually where the government is based □ *adj* principal; chief

CAPITALLY *adverb* in an excellent way

CAPIZ *noun* **CAPIZES** the translucent shell of a bivalve mollusc

CAPON *noun* **CAPONS** a castrated male chicken fattened for eating

CAPRICCIO *noun* **CAPRICCIOS, CAPRICCI** a piece of music played in a free and lively style

CAPRICE *noun* **CAPRICES** a sudden change of mind for no good or obvious reason

CAPRINE *adj* belonging or relating to, or characteristic of, a goat

CAPSICUM *noun* **CAPSICUMS** the red, green or yellow fruit of a tropical shrub of the potato family, which has a hollow seedy interior, and is eaten raw in salads or cooked as a vegetable

CAPSIZE *verb* **CAPSIZES, CAPSIZING, CAPSIZED** usually said of a boat: to tip over completely; to overturn

CAPSTAN *noun* **CAPSTANS** a cylinder-shaped apparatus that is turned to wind a heavy rope or cable, eg that of a ship's anchor

CAPSULAR *adj* in the form of, or resembling, a capsule

CAPSULE *noun* **CAPSULES** a hard or soft soluble case, usually made of gelatine, containing a single dose of a powdered drug to be taken orally

CAPSULISE *verb* **CAPSULISES, CAPSULISING, CAPSULISED** to capsulize

CAPSULIZE verb **CAPSULIZES, CAPSULIZING, CAPSULIZED** to present (information) in a concise form

CAPTAIN noun **CAPTAINS** a leader or chief □ verb **CAPTAINS, CAPTAINING, CAPTAINED** to be captain of something

CAPTAINCY noun **CAPTAINCIES** the rank or commission of a captain

CAPTION noun **CAPTIONS** the words that accompany a photograph, cartoon, etc to explain it □ verb **CAPTIONS, CAPTIONING, CAPTIONED** to provide a caption or captions for something

CAPTIOUS adj inclined to criticize and find fault

CAPTIVATE verb **CAPTIVATES, CAPTIVATING, CAPTIVATED** to delight, charm or fascinate

CAPTIVATING adj delightful, charming or fascinating

CAPTIVE noun **CAPTIVES** a person or animal that has been caught or taken prisoner □ adj kept prisoner

CAPTIVITY noun **CAPTIVITIES** the condition or period of being captive or imprisoned

CAPTOR noun **CAPTORS** someone who takes a person or animal captive

CAPTURE verb **CAPTURES, CAPTURING, CAPTURED** to catch; to take prisoner; to gain control of someone or something □ noun **CAPTURES** the capturing of someone or something

CAPTURER noun **CAPTURERS** a captor

CAPUCHIN noun **CAPUCHINS** an acrobatic intelligent New World monkey with a prehensile tail, formerly a popular pet for street musicians

CAPYBARA noun **CAPYBARAS** the largest living rodent, native to Central and S America, which has a deep square snout, partially webbed toes and no tail

CAR noun **CARS** a self-propelled four-wheeled road vehicle designed to carry passengers and powered by an internal combustion engine

CARACUL noun **CARACULS** karakul

CARAFE noun **CARAFES** a wide-necked bottle or flask for wine, etc, for use on the table

CARAMBOLA noun **CARAMBOLAS** a SE Asian tree

CARAMEL noun **CARAMELS** a brown substance with a characteristic flavour produced by heating sugar solution until it darkens, used as a food colouring and flavouring □ adj caramel-coloured

CARAPACE noun **CARAPACES** the hard thick shell, resembling a shield, that covers the upper part of the body of some tortoises, turtles and crustaceans

CARAT noun **CARATS** a unit of mass, equal to 0.2g, used to measure the mass of gemstones, especially diamonds

CARAVAN noun **CARAVANS** a large vehicle fitted for living in, designed for towing by a motor vehicle □ verb **CARAVANS, CARAVANING, CARAVANNING, CARAVANED, CARAVANNED** to go travelling with or stay in a caravan

CARAVEL noun **CARAVELS** a light sailing vessel, usually with three masts, used for trade in the Mediterranean in the 14c–17c

CARAWAY noun **CARAWAYS** an annual plant, native to Europe and Asia, which has finely divided leaves and clusters of small white flowers with deeply notched petals

CARBIDE noun **CARBIDES** any chemical compound consisting of carbon and another element (except for hydrogen), usually a metallic one

CARBINE noun **CARBINES** a short light rifle

CARBON noun **CARBONS** a non-metallic element that occurs in all organic compounds, and as two crystalline allotropes, namely diamond and graphite

CARBONATE noun **CARBONATES** any salt of carbonic acid □ adj relating to any salt of carbonic acid □ verb **CARBONATES, CARBONATING, CARBONATED** to combine or treat (eg a liquid) with carbon dioxide, to make it fizzy

CARBONATED adj said of a drink: made fizzy by being filled with carbon dioxide

CARBONIC adj said of a compound: containing carbon, especially carbon with a valency of four

CARBONISE verb **CARBONISES, CARBONISING, CARBONISED** to carbonize

CARBONIZE verb **CARBONIZES, CARBONIZING, CARBONIZED** to convert or reduce (a substance containing carbon) into carbon, either by heating or by natural methods such as fossilization

CARBOY noun **CARBOYS** a large glass or plastic bottle, usually protected by a basketwork casing, used for storing or transporting corrosive liquids

CARBUNCLE noun **CARBUNCLES** a cluster of boils on the skin, usually caused by bacterial infection

CARCASE noun **CARCASES** a carcass

CARCASS noun **CARCASSES** the dead body of an animal

CARCINOMA noun **CARCINOMAS, CARCINOMATA** any cancer that occurs in the skin or in the tissue that lines the internal organs of the body, and may spread via the bloodstream

CARD[1] noun **CARDS** a kind of thick, stiff paper or thin cardboard

CARD[2] verb **CARDS, CARDING, CARDED** to comb (wool etc) before spinning

CARDAMOM noun **CARDAMOMS** the dried aromatic seeds of a tropical shrub, which are used as a spice

CARDAMON noun **CARDAMONS** cardamom

CARDAMUM noun **CARDAMUMS** cardamom

CARDBOARD noun **CARDBOARDS** a stiff material manufactured from pulped waste paper, used for making boxes, card, etc □ adj not realistic or life-like

CARDIAC adj relating to or affecting the heart □ noun **CARDIACS** someone suffering from heart disease

CARDIGAN noun **CARDIGANS** a long-sleeved knitted jacket that fastens down the front

CARDINAL noun **CARDINALS** one of a group of leading clergy, who elect and advise the pope □ adj highly important; principal

CARDPHONE noun **CARDPHONES** a payphone operated with a phonecard

CARE noun **CARES** attention and thoroughness □ verb **CARES, CARING, CARED** to mind or be upset by something, or the possibility of something

CAREEN verb **CAREENS, CAREENING, CAREENED** to turn

(a boat) over on its side for cleaning, etc

CAREER *noun* **CAREERS** one's professional life; one's progress in one's job □ *verb* **CAREERS, CAREERING, CAREERED** to rush in an uncontrolled or headlong way

CAREERISM *noun* **CAREERISMS** concern with the advancement of one's career

CAREERIST *noun* **CAREERISTS** someone who is chiefly interested in the advancement or promotion of their career

CAREFREE *adj* having few worries; cheerful

CAREFUL *adj* giving or showing care and attention; thorough

CAREFULLY *adverb* in a careful way

CARELESS *adj* not careful or thorough enough; inattentive

CARER *noun* **CARERS** the person who has the responsibility for looking after an ill, disabled or otherwise dependent person

CARESS *verb* **CARESSES, CARESSING, CARESSED** to touch or stroke gently and lovingly □ *noun* **CARESSES** a gentle loving touch; a gentle embrace

CARET *noun* **CARETS** a mark (∧) made on written or printed material to show where a missing word, letter, etc should be inserted

CARETAKER *noun* **CARETAKERS** a person whose job is to look after a house or a public building, eg a school, especially at times when the building would otherwise be unoccupied

CAREWORN *adj* worn out with or marked by worry and anxiety

CARFUFFLE *noun* **CARFUFFLES** a commotion; agitation

CARGO *noun* **CARGOES** the goods carried by a ship, aircraft or other vehicle

CARIBOU *noun* **CARIBOUS** a large deer belonging to the same species as the reindeer, found in N America and Siberia

CARIES *noun* **CARIES** the progressive decomposition and decay of a tooth or bone, accompanied by softening and discoloration

CARILLON *noun* **CARILLONS** a set of bells hung usually in a tower and played mechanically or by means of a keyboard

CARING *adj* showing concern for others; sympathetic and helpful

CARMINE *noun* **CARMINES** a deep red colour; crimson □ *adj* carmine-coloured

CARNAGE *noun* **CARNAGES** great slaughter

CARNAL *adj* belonging to the body or the flesh, as opposed to the spirit or intellect

CARNALITY *noun* **CARNALITIES** the state of being carnal

CARNALLY *adverb* in a carnal way

CARNATION *noun* **CARNATIONS** a plant with tufted leaves and strongly scented pink, white, red, yellow, orange or multicoloured flowers

CARNAUBA *noun* **CARNAUBAS** a Brazilian palm tree

CARNELIAN *noun* **CARNELIANS** a red and white form of agate, used as a semi-precious stone and for making seals

CARNIVAL *noun* **CARNIVALS** a period of public festivity with eg street processions, colourful costumes, singing and dancing

CARNIVORE *noun* **CARNIVORES** an animal that feeds mainly on the flesh of other animals

CAROB *noun* **CAROBS** an evergreen tree, native to the Mediterranean region, which produces large reddish-brown seedpods rich in sugars and gums

CAROL *noun* **CAROLS** a religious song, especially one sung at Christmas □ *verb* **CAROLS, CAROLLING, CAROLLED** to sing carols

CAROM *noun* **CAROMS** a form of billiards popular in Europe, played on a table without pockets with the object of making cannons

CAROTENE *noun* **CAROTENES** any of a number of reddish-yellow pigments, widely distributed in plants, that are converted to vitamin A in the body

CAROTID *noun* **CAROTIDS** either of the two major arteries that supply blood to the head and neck □ *adj* relating to either of these arteries

CAROTIN *noun* **CAROTINS** carotene

CAROUSAL *noun* **CAROUSALS** a drinking bout or party; a noisy revel

CAROUSE *verb* **CAROUSES, CAROUSING, CAROUSED** to take

part in a noisy drinking party □ *noun* **CAROUSES** a carousal

CAROUSEL *noun* **CAROUSELS** a revolving belt in an airport, etc onto which luggage is unloaded so that passengers can collect it as it passes by

CARP [1] *noun* **CARPS** a deep-bodied freshwater fish

CARP [2] *verb* **CARPS, CARPING, CARPED** to complain, find fault or criticize, especially unnecessarily

CARPAL *adj* relating to the carpus

CARPEL *noun* **CARPELS** the female reproductive part of a flowering plant

CARPENTER *noun* **CARPENTERS** someone skilled in working with wood, eg in building houses, etc or in making and repairing fine furniture □ *verb* **CARPENTERS, CARPENTERING, CARPENTERED** to do the work of a carpenter

CARPENTRY *noun* **CARPENTRIES** the art or skill of a carpenter

CARPER *noun* **CARPERS** a person who carps

CARPET *noun* **CARPETS** a covering for floors and stairs, made of heavy, usually woven and tufted, fabric □ *verb* **CARPETS, CARPETING, CARPETED** to cover something with or as if with a carpet

CARPETING *noun* **CARPETINGS** fabric used to make carpets

CARPING *noun* **CARPINGS** cavilling; fault-finding

CARPINGLY *adverb* in a cavilling or fault-finding way

CARPORT *noun* **CARPORTS** a roofed shelter for a car, usually attached to the side of a house

CARPUS *noun* **CARPI** in terrestrial vertebrates: the set of small bones that forms the wrist or corresponding part of the forelimb

CARRAGEEN *noun* **CARRAGEENS** a type of purplish-red, edible seaweed found in the N Atlantic

CARREL *noun* **CARRELS** a small individual compartment or desk in a library, for private study

CARRELL *noun* **CARRELLS** a carrel

CARRIAGE *noun* **CARRIAGES** a four-wheeled horse-drawn passenger vehicle

CARRIER *noun* **CARRIERS** a person or thing that carries

CARRION *noun* **CARRIONS** dead and rotting animal flesh

CARROT *noun* **CARROTS** a plant with divided leaves, small white, pink, or yellow flowers, and an edible orange root

CARROTY adj **CARROTIER**, **CARROTIEST** said of hair: having a strong reddish colour

CARRY verb **CARRIES**, **CARRYING**, **CARRIED** to hold something in one's hands, have it in a pocket, bag etc, or support its weight on one's body, while moving from one place to another ◻ noun **CARRIES** an act of carrying

CARRYCOT noun **CARRYCOTS** a light box-like cot with handles, for carrying a baby

CARRYING adj said of a voice: easily heard at a distance

CART noun **CARTS** a two- or four-wheeled, horse-drawn vehicle for carrying goods or passengers ◻ verb **CARTS**, **CARTING**, **CARTED** to carry in a cart

CARTE noun **CARTES** quarte

CARTEL noun **CARTELS** a group of firms that agree, especially illegally, on similar fixed prices for their products, so as to reduce competition and keep profits high

CARTILAGE noun **CARTILAGES** in humans: a tough flexible material that forms the skeleton of the embryo, but is converted into bone before adulthood, persisting in the adults in structures such as the larynx and trachea

CARTON noun **CARTONS** a plastic or cardboard container in which food or drink of various types is packaged for sale

CARTOON noun **CARTOONS** a humorous drawing in a newspaper, etc, often ridiculing someone or something

CARTOUCHE noun **CARTOUCHES** a paper case containing the explosive charge for a gun, etc; a cartridge

CARTRIDGE noun **CARTRIDGES** a metal case containing the propellant charge for a gun

CARTWHEEL noun **CARTWHEELS** an acrobatic movement in which one throws one's body sideways with the turning action of a wheel, supporting one's body weight on each hand and foot in turn ◻ verb **CARTWHEELS**, **CARTWHEELING**, **CARTWHEELED** to perform a cartwheel

CARVE verb **CARVES**, **CARVING**, **CARVED** to cut (wood, stone, etc) into a shape; to cut (meat) into slices

CARVEL noun **CARVELS** a caravel

CARVER noun **CARVERS** someone who carves

CARVERY noun **CARVERIES** a restaurant where meat is carved from a joint for customers on request

CARVING noun **CARVINGS** a figure or pattern, etc produced by carving wood, stone, etc

CARYATID noun **CARYATIDS**, **CARYATIDES** a carved female figure used as a support for a roof, etc, instead of a column or pillar

CASBAH noun **CASBAHS** a kasbah

CASCADE noun **CASCADES** a waterfall or series of waterfalls ◻ verb **CASCADES**, **CASCADING**, **CASCADED** to fall like a waterfall

CASE[1] noun **CASES** a box, container or cover, used for storage, transportation, etc ◻ verb **CASES**, **CASING**, **CASED** to put something in a case

CASE[2] noun **CASES** someone receiving some sort of treatment or care; a matter requiring investigation

CASEBOOK noun **CASEBOOKS** a written record of cases dealt with by a doctor, lawyer, etc

CASEIN noun **CASEINS** a milk protein that is the main constituent of cheese

CASEMENT noun **CASEMENTS** a window with vertical hinges that opens outwards like a door

CASEWORK noun **CASEWORKS** social work concerned with the close study of the background and environment of individuals and families

CASH noun **CASHES** coins or paper money, as distinct from cheques, credit cards, etc ◻ verb **CASHES**, **CASHING**, **CASHED** to obtain or give cash in return for (a cheque, traveller's cheque, postal order, etc)

CASHEW noun **CASHEWS** a curved edible nut, rich in oil and protein; the small evergreen tree, of Central and S America, which bears these nuts

CASHIER[1] noun **CASHIERS** in a business firm, bank, etc: any person who receives, pays out and generally deals with the cash

CASHIER[2] verb **CASHIERS**, **CASHIERING**, **CASHIERED** to dismiss (an officer) from the armed forces in disgrace

CASHLESS adj said of a

transaction, etc: paid by credit card, debit card or other electronic transfer of money, rather than by cash or cheque

CASHMERE noun **CASHMERES** a type of very fine soft wool from a long-haired Asian goat

CASING noun **CASINGS** a protective covering, eg of plastic for electric cables

CASINO noun **CASINOS** a public building or room for gambling

CASK noun **CASKS** a barrel for holding liquids, especially alcoholic liquids ◻ verb **CASKS**, **CASKING**, **CASKED** to put in a cask

CASKET noun **CASKETS** a small case for holding jewels, etc

CASQUE noun **CASQUES** a cover for the head

CASSAVA noun **CASSAVAS** a shrubby plant cultivated throughout the tropics for its fleshy tuberous edible roots

CASSEROLE noun **CASSEROLES** an ovenproof dish with a lid, in which meat, vegetables, etc can be cooked and served ◻ verb **CASSEROLES**, **CASSEROLING**, **CASSEROLED** to cook in a casserole

CASSETTE noun **CASSETTES** a small, usually plastic, case, containing a long narrow ribbon of magnetic tape wound around two reels, that can be inserted into a suitable audio or video tape recorder for recording or playback

CASSIS noun **CASSISES** a syrupy blackcurrant drink or flavouring

CASSOCK noun **CASSOCKS** a long black or red garment worn in church by clergymen and male members of a church choir

CASSOWARY noun **CASSOWARIES** a large flightless bird, native to New Guinea and N Australia, which has a bony crest on its head, bright blue or red naked skin on its neck and head, and long black feathers on its body

CAST verb **CASTS**, **CASTING**, **CAST** to throw ◻ noun **CASTS** a throw; an act of throwing (eg dice, a fishing-line)

CASTANETS plural noun a musical instrument consisting of two hollow pieces of wood or plastic attached to each other by string, which are held in the palm and struck together rhythmically, using the middle finger

CASTAWAY noun **CASTAWAYS** someone who has been shipwrecked ◻ adj cast adrift; shipwrecked

CASTE noun **CASTES** any of the four hereditary social classes into which Hindu society is divided

CASTER noun **CASTERS** someone or something that casts

CASTIGATE verb **CASTIGATES, CASTIGATING, CASTIGATED** to criticize or punish severely

CASTING noun **CASTINGS** the process of forming a solid object with a fixed shape by pouring molten material, eg metal, alloy, glass or plastic, into a mould and allowing it to cool and solidify

CASTLE noun **CASTLES** a large, fortified, especially medieval, building with battlements and towers ◻ verb **CASTLES, CASTLING, CASTLED** in chess: to make a move allowed once to each player in a game, in which the king is moved two squares along its rank towards either castle, and the castle is placed on the square the king has passed over

CASTOR noun **CASTORS** a small swivelling wheel fitted to the legs or underside of a piece of furniture so that it can be moved easily

CASTRATE verb **CASTRATES, CASTRATING, CASTRATED** to remove the testicles of a male person or animal

CASTRATED adj gelded; rendered ineffective

CASTRATO noun **CASTRATI** in 17c and 18c opera: a male singer castrated before puberty in order to preserve his soprano or contralto voice

CASUAL adj happening by chance ◻ noun **CASUALS** an occasional worker

CASUALLY adverb carelessly

CASUALTY noun **CASUALTIES** someone killed or hurt in an accident or war

CASUIST noun **CASUISTS** someone who uses cleverly misleading arguments, especially to make things that are morally wrong seem acceptable

CASUISTIC adj relating to casuists or casuistry

CASUISTRY noun **CASUISTRIES** the application of ethical principles to cases concerned with moral conscience

CAT noun **CATS** any of a wide range of carnivorous mammals, including large cats such as the lion, tiger, jaguar, leopard and cheetah, as well as the domestic cat

CATACLYSM noun **CATACLYSMS** an event, especially a political or social one, causing tremendous change or upheaval

CATACOMB noun **CATACOMBS** an underground burial place, especially one consisting of a system of tunnels with recesses dug out for the tombs

CATALEPSY noun **CATALEPSIES** a trance-like state characterized by the abnormal maintenance of rigid body postures, and an apparent loss of sensation, most commonly associated with catatonia

CATALOGUE noun **CATALOGUES** a list of items arranged in a systematic order, especially alphabetically ◻ verb **CATALOGUES, CATALOGUING, CATALOGUED** to make a catalogue of (a library, books, etc)

CATALYSE verb **CATALYSES, CATALYSING, CATALYSED** said of a catalyst: to alter the rate of (a chemical reaction), usually by increasing it, without itself undergoing any permanent chemical change

CATALYSIS noun **CATALYSES** the process effected by a catalyst

CATALYST noun **CATALYSTS** any substance that catalyses a chemical reaction

CATALYTIC adj of or relating to catalysis

CATALYZE verb **CATALYZES, CATALYZING, CATALYZED** to catalyse

CATAMARAN noun **CATAMARANS** a sailing-boat with two hulls lying parallel to each other, joined across the top by the deck

CATAPLEXY noun **CATAPLEXIES** a sudden attack of muscular weakness, caused by strong emotion, eg laughter or anger, which affects the whole body and causes collapse without loss of consciousness

CATAPULT noun **CATAPULTS** a Y-shaped stick with an elastic or rubber band fitted between its prongs, used especially by children for firing stones, etc ◻ verb **CATAPULTS, CATAPULTING, CATAPULTED** to fire or send flying with, or as if with, a catapult

CATARACT noun **CATARACTS** an opaque area within the lens of the eye that produces blurring of vision

CATARRH noun **CATARRHS** inflammation of the mucuous membranes lining the nose and throat, causing an excessive discharge of thick mucus

CATARRHAL adj of or relating to catarrh

CATATONIA noun **CATATONIAS** an abnormal mental state characterized either by stupor, mutism and immobility, or by excessive excitement and violent or unco-ordinated activity

CATATONIC adj characterized by catatonia ◻ noun **CATATONICS** a person affected by catatonia

CATCALL noun **CATCALLS** a long shrill whistle expressing disagreement or disapproval ◻ verb **CATCALLS, CATCALLING, CATCALLED** to whistle at someone in this way

CATCH verb **CATCHES, CATCHING, CAUGHT** to stop (a moving object) and hold it; to manage to get hold of ◻ noun **CATCHES** an act of catching

CATCHABLE adj capable of being caught

CATCHER noun **CATCHERS** someone who catches

CATCHING adj infectious

CATCHMENT noun **CATCHMENTS** the area of land that is drained by a particular river system or lake

CATCHUP noun **CATCHUPS** any of various sauces containing vinegar and the juices of vegetables, nuts, etc

CATCHWORD noun **CATCHWORDS** a much-repeated well-known word or phrase

CATCHY adj **CATCHIER, CATCHIEST** said of a song, etc: tuneful and easily remembered

CATECHISE verb **CATECHISES, CATECHISING, CATECHISED** to catechize

CATECHISM noun **CATECHISMS** a series of questions and answers about the Christian religion, or a book containing this, used for instruction

CATECHIST noun **CATECHISTS** a person who catechizes

CATECHIZE verb **CATECHIZES, CATECHIZING, CATECHIZED** to instruct someone in the ways of the Christian faith, especially by means of a catechism

CATEGORIC *adj* said of a statement, refusal, denial, etc: absolute or definite; making no exceptions and giving no room for doubt or argument

CATEGORY *noun* **CATEGORIES** a group of things, people or concepts classed together because of some quality or qualities they have in common

CATENARY *noun* **CATENARIES** the curve formed by a flexible chain or cable supported at both ends and hanging freely, acted on by no force other than gravity

CATER *verb* **CATERS, CATERING, CATERED** to supply food, accommodation or entertainment

CATERER *noun* **CATERERS** a person whose professional occupation is to provide food, etc for social occasions

CATERING *noun* **CATERINGS** the provision of food, etc

CATERWAUL *verb* **CATERWAULS, CATERWAULING, CATERWAULED** said of a cat: to make a loud high wailing noise ▫ *noun*
CATERWAULS a loud high wail
CATERWAULING *noun*
CATERWAULINGS the loud high wailing noise of a cat or cats

CATFISH *noun* **CATFISHES** any of several hundred mainly freshwater species of fish, all of which have long whisker-like sensory barbels around the mouth

CATGUT *noun* **CATGUTS** a strong cord made from the dried intestines of sheep and other animals (and formerly from those of cats), used in surgery for making stitches and ligatures, and also used for stringing violins, etc

CATHARSIS *noun* **CATHARSES** the emotional relief that results either from allowing repressed thoughts and feelings to surface, as in psychoanalysis, or from an intensely dramatic experience

CATHARTIC *adj* resulting in catharsis ▫ *noun* **CATHARTICS** a purgative drug or medicine

CATHEDRAL *noun* **CATHEDRALS** the principal church of a diocese, in which the bishop has his throne

CATHETER *noun* **CATHETERS** a hollow slender flexible tube that can be introduced into a narrow opening or body cavity, usually in order to drain a liquid, especially urine

CATHEXIS *noun* **CATHEXES** a

charge of mental energy directed towards a particular idea or object

CATHODE *noun* **CATHODES** in an electrolytic cell: the negative electrode, towards which positively charged ions, usually in solution, are attracted

CATHOLIC *adj* said of a person's interests and tastes: broad; wide-ranging

CATION *noun* **CATIONS** any positively charged ion, which moves towards the cathode during electrolysis

CATKIN *noun* **CATKINS** in certain tree species, eg birch, hazel: a flowering shoot that bears many small unisexual flowers, adapted for wind pollination

CATMINT *noun* **CATMINTS** a square-stemmed perennial plant native to Europe and Asia, with oval toothed leaves and spikes of white two-lipped flowers spotted with purple

CATNAP *noun* **CATNAPS** a short sleep ▫ *verb* **CATNAPS, CATNAPPING, CATNAPPED** to doze; to sleep briefly, especially without lying down

CATNIP *noun* **CATNIPS** catmint

CATSUIT *noun* **CATSUITS** a close-fitting one-piece garment, combining trousers and top, usually worn by women

CATSUP *noun* **CATSUPS** catchup

CATTERY *noun* **CATTERIES** a place where cats are bred or looked after in their owner's absence

CATTILY *adverb* in a catty way

CATTINESS *noun* **CATTINESSES** the quality of being catty

CATTLE *plural noun* any of various large heavily built grass-eating mammals, including wild species, which are all horned, and domestic varieties

CATTLEYA *noun* **CATTLEYAS** a highly popular cultivated orchid, native to SE Asia and S America, which has swollen green bulb-like stems for storing water, and spikes of large yellow, pink or violet flowers

CATTY *adj* **CATTIER, CATTIEST** malicious; spiteful

CAUCUS *noun* **CAUCUSES** a small dominant group of people taking independent decisions within a larger organization

CAUDAL *adj* relating to, resembling, or in the position of a tail

CAUDATE *adj* having a tail or a tail-like appendage

CAUDATED *adj* caudate

CAUGHT past form of **catch**

CAUL *noun* **CAULS** a membrane that sometimes surrounds an infant's head at birth, and consists of part of the amnion

CAULDRON *noun* **CAULDRONS** a very large metal pot, often with handles, for boiling or heating liquids

CAULK *verb* **CAULKS, CAULKING, CAULKED** to fill up (the seams or joints of a boat) with oakum

CAUSAL *adj* relating to or being a cause

CAUSALITY *noun* **CAUSALITIES** the relationship between cause and effect

CAUSALLY *adverb* by way of cause and effect

CAUSATION *noun* **CAUSATIONS** the relationship of cause and effect; causality

CAUSATIVE *adj* making something happen; producing an effect ▫ *noun* **CAUSATIVES** a causative verb

CAUSE *noun* **CAUSES** something which produces an effect; the person or thing through which something happens ▫ *verb* **CAUSES, CAUSING, CAUSED** to produce as an effect; to bring about something

CAUSEWAY *noun* **CAUSEWAYS** a raised roadway crossing low-lying marshy ground or shallow water

CAUSTIC *adj* said of a chemical substance, eg sodium hydroxide: strongly alkaline and corrosive to living tissue ▫ *noun* **CAUSTICS** the curve produced when parallel rays of light are reflected in a large concave mirror, or refracted by a convex lens

CAUTERISE *verb* **CAUTERISES, CAUTERISING, CAUTERISED** to cauterize

CAUTERIZE *verb* **CAUTERIZES, CAUTERIZING, CAUTERIZED** to destroy (living tissue) by the direct application of a heated instrument, an electric current, a laser beam, or a caustic chemical

CAUTION *verb* **CAUTIONS, CAUTIONING, CAUTIONED** to warn or admonish someone

CAUTIOUS *adj* having or showing caution; careful; wary

CAVALCADE *noun* **CAVALCADES** a

ceremonial procession of cars, horseback riders, etc

CAVALIER *noun* **CAVALIERS** a horseman or knight □ *adj* said of a person's behaviour, attitude, etc: thoughtless, offhand, casual or disrespectful

CAVALRY *noun* **CAVALRIES** the part of an army consisting of soldiers on horseback

CAVE *noun* **CAVES** a large natural hollow chamber either underground, usually with an opening to the surface, or in the side of a mountain, hillside or cliff □ *verb* **CAVES, CAVING, CAVED** to hollow something out

CAVEAT *noun* **CAVEATS** a warning

CAVEMAN *noun* **CAVEMEN** a person of prehistoric times, who lived in caves, etc

CAVER *noun* **CAVERS** someone whose pastime is exploring caves

CAVERN *noun* **CAVERNS** a large cave or an underground chamber □ *verb* **CAVERNS, CAVERNING, CAVERNED** to enclose something in a cavern

CAVERNOUS *adj* said of a hole or space: deep and vast

CAVETTO *noun* **CAVETTI** a hollowed moulding with a curvature of a quarter of a circle, used chiefly in cornices, eg on ancient Egyptian buildings

CAVIAR *noun* **CAVIARS** the salted hard roe of the sturgeon, used as food and considered a delicacy

CAVIARE *noun* **CAVIARES** caviar

CAVIL *verb* **CAVILS, CAVILLING, CAVILLED** to make trivial objections to something □ *noun* **CAVILS** a trivial objection

CAVILLER *noun* **CAVILLERS** a person who cavils

CAVING *noun* **CAVINGS** the sport of exploring caves

CAVITY *noun* **CAVITIES** a hollow or hole

CAVORT *verb* **CAVORTS, CAVORTING, CAVORTED** to jump or caper about

CAVY *noun* **CAVIES** any of various rodents native to S America, including guinea pigs

CAW *noun* **CAWS** the loud harsh cry of a crow or rook □ *verb* **CAWS, CAWING, CAWED** to make such a cry

CAY *noun* **CAYS** a small low island or reef formed of sand, coral, rock or mud, especially one off the coast of Florida

CAYENNE *noun* **CAYENNES** a hot spice made from the seeds of various types of capsicum

CAYMAN *noun* **CAYMANS** a reptile closely related to the alligator, native to tropical regions of Central and S America, which often has bony plates embedded in the skin of its belly

CEASE *verb* **CEASES, CEASING, CEASED** to bring or come to an end

CEASELESS *adj* continuous; going on without a pause or break

CEBADILLA *noun* **CEBADILLAS** a sabadilla

CECAL *adj* caecal

CECUM *noun* **CECA** a caecum

CEDAR *noun* **CEDARS** any of various tall coniferous trees belonging to the pine family, with a flat crown, widely spreading branches, needle-like leaves and reddish-brown bark □ *adj* made of cedar

CEDE *verb* **CEDES, CEDING, CEDED** to hand over or give up something formally

CEDILLA *noun* **CEDILLAS** in French and Portuguese: a diacritic put under *c* in some words, eg *façade*, to show that it is to be pronounced like *s*, not like *k*

CEE *noun* **CEES** the letter 'C'

CEILIDH *noun* **CEILIDHS** in Scotland and Ireland: an informal social gathering, with songs, story-telling, music and dancing

CEILING *noun* **CEILINGS** the inner roof of a room, etc

CEL *noun* **CELS** celluloid

CELANDINE *noun* **CELANDINES** a low-growing perennial plant, native to Europe and W Asia, which has heart-shaped dark-green leaves, and flowers with glossy golden-yellow petals that gradually fade to white

CELEBRANT *noun* **CELEBRANTS** someone who performs a religious ceremony

CELEBRATE *verb* **CELEBRATES, CELEBRATING, CELEBRATED** to mark (an occasion, especially a birthday or anniversary) with festivities

CELEBRATED *adj* famous; renowned

CELEBRITY *noun* **CELEBRITIES** a famous person

CELERIAC *noun* **CELERIACS** a variety of celery, widely cultivated for the swollen edible base of its stem

CELERITY *noun* **CELERITIES** quickness; rapidity of motion or thought

CELERY *noun* **CELERIES** a plant with deeply grooved swollen leaf stalks which can be eaten raw or cooked as a vegetable

CELESTA *noun* **CELESTAS** a keyboard instrument, resembling a small upright piano, from which soft bell-like sounds are produced by hammers striking steel plates suspended over wooden resonators

CELESTIAL *adj* belonging or relating to the sky

CELIAC *adj* coeliac □ *noun* **CELIACS** coeliac

CELIBACY *noun* **CELIBACIES** the unmarried state, especially as adhered to under a religious vow

CELIBATE *adj* unmarried, especially in obedience to a religious vow □ *noun* **CELIBATES** someone who is unmarried, especially because of a religious vow

CELL *noun* **CELLS** a small room occupied by an inmate in a prison or monastery

CELLAR *noun* **CELLARS** a room, usually underground, for storage, eg of wine □ *verb* **CELLARS, CELLARING, CELLARED** to store in a cellar

CELLARAGE *noun* **CELLARAGES** the volume of cellar space in a building

CELLIST *noun* **CELLISTS** someone who plays the cello

CELLO *noun* **CELLOS** a large stringed musical instrument of the violin family, which is played sitting, with the neck of the instrument resting against the player's shoulder

CELLPHONE *noun* **CELLPHONES** a portable telephone for use in a cellular radio system

CELLULAR *adj* composed of cells or divided into cell-like compartments

CELLULE *noun* **CELLULES** a small cell

CELLULITE *noun* **CELLULITES** deposits of fat cells said to be resistant to changes in diet or exercise regime, and which give the skin a dimpled, pitted appearance

CELLULOSE *noun* **CELLULOSES** a

complex carbohydrate that is the main constituent of plant cell walls, and is used in the manufacture of paper, rope, textiles, (eg cotton and linen) and plastics (eg Cellophane)

CELOM noun **CELOMS** the coelum

CELT noun **CELTS** a prehistoric axe-like took

CEMENT noun **CEMENTS** a fine powder, composed of a mixture of clay and limestone, that hardens when mixed with water, and is used to make mortar and concrete ▫ verb **CEMENTS, CEMENTING, CEMENTED** to stick together with cement

CEMENTUM noun **CEMENTA** the thin layer of hard bony tissue that anchors the roots of the teeth to the jaws

CEMETERY noun **CEMETERIES** a burial ground for the dead, especially one that is not attached to a church

CENOTAPH noun **CENOTAPHS** a tomb-like monument in honour of a person or persons buried elsewhere, especially soldiers killed in war

CENSER noun **CENSERS** a container in which incense is burnt, used eg in some churches

CENSOR noun **CENSORS** an official who examines books, films, newspaper articles, etc, with the power to cut out any parts thought politically sensitive or offensive, and to forbid publication or showing altogether ▫ verb **CENSORS, CENSORING, CENSORED** to alter or cut out parts of something, or forbid its publication, showing or delivery

CENSORIAL adj relating to a censor, or to the correction of public morals

CENSURE noun **CENSURES** severe criticism or disapproval ▫ verb **CENSURES, CENSURING, CENSURED** to criticize severely or express strong disapproval of someone or something

CENSUS noun **CENSUSES** an official count of a population, carried out at periodic intervals, which covers information such as sex, age, job, etc

CENT noun **CENTS** a currency unit of several countries, worth one hundredth of the standard unit, eg of the US dollar

CENTAUR noun **CENTAURS** in mythology: a creature with a man's head, arms and trunk, joined to the four-legged body of a horse

CENTAVO noun **CENTAVOS** a currency unit of several countries, worth one hundredth of the standard unit, eg of the Columbian peso

CENTENARY noun **CENTENARIES** the one-hundredth anniversary of some event, or the celebration of it ▫ adj occurring every 100 years

CENTER noun **CENTERS** centre ▫ adj centre ▫ verb **CENTERS, CENTERING, CENTERED** to centre

CENTIGRAM noun **CENTIGRAMS** the one-hundredth part of a gram

CENTIME noun **CENTIMES** a currency unit of several countries, worth one hundredth of the standard unit, eg of the French franc

CENTIPEDE noun **CENTIPEDES** any of numerous species of terrestrial arthropod which have a long segmented body and a pair of legs for each body segment

CENTRAL adj at or forming the centre of something

CENTRALLY adverb in a central position

CENTRE noun **CENTRES** a part at the middle of something ▫ adj at the centre; central ▫ verb **CENTRES, CENTRING, CENTRED** to place in or at the centre; to position centrally or symmetrically

CENTRIOLE noun **CENTRIOLES** in animal cells: a tiny cylindrical structure that plays an important role in cell division

CENTRISM noun **CENTRISMS** the practice of sticking to the middle ground in politics

CENTRIST adj having moderate, non-extreme political opinions ▫ noun **CENTRISTS** someone holding such opinions

CENTURION noun **CENTURIONS** in the army of ancient Rome: an officer in charge of a company of (originally) 100 foot soldiers

CENTURY noun **CENTURIES** any 100-year period counted forwards or backwards from an important event, especially the birth of Christ

CEP noun **CEPS** a kind of edible mushroom

CEPHALIC adj relating to the head or the head region

CERAMIC noun **CERAMICS** any of a number of hard brittle materials, eg enamels, porcelain and brick, produced by moulding or shaping and then baking or firing clays at high temperatures ▫ adj relating to or made of such a material

CERAMICS singular noun the art and technique of making pottery

CERE noun **CERES** the bare wax-like patch at the base of the upper part of a bird's beak, containing the nostrils

CEREAL noun **CEREALS** a member of the grass family that is cultivated as a food crop for its nutritious edible seeds, ie grains, eg barley, wheat, rice, etc ▫ adj relating to edible grains

CEREBRAL adj relating to or in the region of the brain

CEREBRATE verb **CEREBRATES, CEREBRATING, CEREBRATED** to think; to use one's brain

CEREBRUM noun **CEREBRUMS, CEREBRA** in higher vertebrates: the front part of the brain, consisting of two cerebral hemispheres linked by the corpus callosum, which initiates and co-ordinates all voluntary activity

CEREMONY noun **CEREMONIES** a ritual performed to mark a particular, especially public or religious, occasion

CERISE noun **CERISES** a bright cherry-red colour ▫ adj cerise-coloured

CERIUM noun **CERIUMS** a soft silvery-grey metallic element belonging to the lanthanide series, used in catalytic converters, alloys for cigarette-lighter flints, etc

CERMET noun **CERMETS** a hard strong composite material, resistant to corrosion and wear, made from a ceramic and a metal, and used to make cutting tools and brake linings

CERT noun **CERTS** a certainty, especially a horse that is bound to win a race

CERTAIN adj proved or known beyond doubt

CERTAINLY adverb without any doubt

CERTAINTY noun **CERTAINTIES** something that cannot be doubted or is bound to happen

CERTIFIED adj possessing a certificate

CERTIFIER *noun* **CERTIFIERS** a person who certifies

CERTIFY *verb* **CERTIFIES, CERTIFYING, CERTIFIED** to declare or confirm officially

CERTITUDE *noun* **CERTITUDES** a feeling of certainty

CERUMEN *noun* **CERUMENS** earwax

CERVICAL *adj* relating to or in the region of the cervix

CERVINE *adj* relating to or resembling a deer

CERVIX *noun* **CERVIXES, CERVICES** the neck of the uterus, consisting of a narrow passage leading to the inner end of the vagina

CESIUM *noun* **CESIUMS** a soft silvery-white metallic element formed by the fission of uranium, and used in photoelectric cells and certain optical instruments

CESSATION *noun* **CESSATIONS** a stopping or ceasing; a pause

CESSION *noun* **CESSIONS** the giving up or yielding of territories, rights, etc to someone else

CESSPIT *noun* **CESSPITS** a pit for the collection and storage of sewage

CESSPOOL *noun* **CESSPOOLS** a tank, well, etc for the collection and storage of sewage and waste water

CESURA *noun* **CESURAE, CESURAS** a caesura

CETACEAN *noun* **CETACEANS** in the animal kingdom: any animal belonging to the order which includes dolphins, porpoises and whales □ *adj* relating or belonging to the cetaceans

CETANE *noun* **CETANES** a colourless liquid hydrocarbon found in petroleum, used as a solvent and in the determination of the ignition quality of diesel fuel

CEVADILLA *noun* **CEVADILLAS** a sabadilla

CH *pronoun* an obsolete dialect word meaning *I*
ⓘ This is a useful word for using up C and/or H without using any vowels.

CHA *noun* **CHAS** tea

CHACONNE *noun* **CHACONNES** an old slow Spanish dance

CHADAR *noun* **CHADARS** a chador

CHADOR *noun* **CHADORS** a thick veil worn by Muslim women that covers the head and body

CHAFE *verb* **CHAFES, CHAFING, CHAFED** to make or become sore or worn by rubbing □ *noun* **CHAFES** an irritation caused by rubbing

CHAFER *noun* **CHAFERS** any of various species of large nocturnal beetle, found mainly in the tropics, and including several pests

CHAFF *noun* **CHAFFS** light-hearted joking or teasing □ *verb* **CHAFFS, CHAFFING, CHAFFED** to tease or make fun of someone in a good-natured way

CHAFFINCH *noun* **CHAFFINCHES** either of two birds of the finch family, especially a species with a blue crown, brown body, stout bill, conspicuous white wing bars and a greenish rump

CHAGRIN *noun* **CHAGRINS** acute annoyance or disappointment □ *verb* **CHAGRINS, CHAGRINING, CHAGRINED** to annoy or embarrass someone

CHAIN *noun* **CHAINS** a series of interconnecting links or rings, especially of metal, used for fastening, binding, holding, supporting, transmitting motion or, eg in jewellery, for ornament □ *verb* **CHAINS, CHAINING, CHAINED** to fasten, bind or restrict with, or as if with, chains

CHAINSAW *noun* **CHAINSAWS** a portable power-driven saw with cutting teeth linked together in a continuous chain, used mainly for cutting timber

CHAIR *noun* **CHAIRS** a seat for one person, with a back-support and usually four legs □ *verb* **CHAIRS, CHAIRING, CHAIRED** to control or conduct (a meeting) as chairman or chairwoman

CHAIRLIFT *noun* **CHAIRLIFTS** a series of seats suspended from a moving cable, for carrying skiers, etc up a mountain

CHAIRMAN *noun* **CHAIRMEN** someone who conducts or controls a meeting or debate

CHAISE *noun* **CHAISES** a light open two-wheeled horse-drawn carriage, for one or more persons

CHAKRA *noun* **CHAKRAS** in yoga: one of a number of centres of spiritual power in the body

CHALAZA *noun* **CHALAZAS** in a bird's egg: one of a pair of twisted strands of albumen that hold the yolk sac in position

CHALET *noun* **CHALETS** a style of house typical of snowy Alpine regions, built of wood, with window-shutters and a heavy sloping wide-eaved roof

CHALICE *noun* **CHALICES** a wine cup; a goblet

CHALK *noun* **CHALKS** a soft fine-grained porous rock, composed of calcium carbonate; a material similar to this used for writing and drawing, especially on a blackboard □ *verb* **CHALKS, CHALKING, CHALKED** to write or mark in chalk

CHALKY *adj* **CHALKIER, CHALKIEST** like or consisting of chalk

CHALLENGE *verb* **CHALLENGES, CHALLENGING, CHALLENGED** to call on someone to settle a matter by any sort of contest □ *noun* **CHALLENGES** an invitation to a contest

CHALLENGED *adj* a supposedly neutral term, denoting some kind of handicap, impairment or disability

CHALLENGING *adj* of a task, etc: stimulating effort and interest

CHALUMEAU *noun* **CHALUMEAUX** an early reed-pipe which evolved into the clarinet at the beginning of the 18c

CHAMBER *noun* **CHAMBERS** a room, especially a bedroom

CHAMBRAY *noun* **CHAMBRAYS** a fine cotton or linen fabric, with interwoven white and coloured threads

CHAMBRÉ *adj* said of wine: at room temperature

CHAMELEON *noun* **CHAMELEONS** a slow-moving lizard, found mainly in Africa, whose granular skin changes colour rapidly in response to changes in its environment, acting as camouflage and as a means of communication with rivals

CHAMFER *verb* **CHAMFERS, CHAMFERING, CHAMFERED** to give a smooth rounded shape to (an edge or corner) □ *noun* **CHAMFERS** a rounded or bevelled edge

CHAMOIS *noun* **CHAMOIS** an agile hoofed mammal, native to S Europe, Asia Minor and the Caucasus region, which has short vertical horns with backward-pointing tips, and a long reddish-brown, brown or black coat

CHAMOMILE *noun* **CHAMOMILES** camomile

CHAMP *verb* **CHAMPS, CHAMPING, CHAMPED** to munch noisily □ *noun* **CHAMPS** the sound of munching

CHAMPAGNE *noun* **CHAMPAGNES** a sparkling white wine made in the Champagne district of France, which is traditionally drunk at celebrations □ *adj* champagne-coloured

CHAMPERS *singular noun* champagne

CHAMPERTY *noun* **CHAMPERTIES** an illegal bargain between a party to litigation and an uninvolved third party, whereby the third party provides financial assistance in return for a share in the proceeds

CHAMPION *noun* **CHAMPIONS** in games, competitions, etc: a competitor that has defeated all others □ *verb* **CHAMPIONS, CHAMPIONING, CHAMPIONED** to strongly support or defend (a person or cause) □ *adj* excellent □ *adverb* excellently

CHAMPLEVÉ *noun* **CHAMPLEVÉS** a technique of enamelling on metal

CHANCE *noun* **CHANCES** the way that things happen; unplanned and unforeseen □ *verb* **CHANCES, CHANCING, CHANCED** to risk something

CHANCEFUL *adj* full of risk or danger

CHANCEL *noun* **CHANCELS** the eastern part of a church containing the altar, usually separated from the nave by a screen or steps

CHANCER *noun* **CHANCERS** someone inclined to take any opportunity to profit, whether honestly or dishonestly

CHANCERY *noun* **CHANCERIES** a division of the High Court of Justice

CHANCRE *noun* **CHANCRES** a small hard growth that develops in the primary stages of syphilis and certain other diseases

CHANCROUS *adj* of or relating to a chancre

CHANCY *adj* **CHANCIER, CHANCIEST** risky; uncertain

CHANDLER *noun* **CHANDLERS** a dealer in ship's supplies and equipment

CHANDLERY *noun* **CHANDLERIES** the business of, premises of, or goods sold by a chandler

CHANGE *verb* **CHANGES, CHANGING, CHANGED** to make or become different □ *noun* **CHANGES** the process of changing or an instance of it

CHANGEFUL *adj* full of change; changeable

CHANGER *noun* **CHANGERS** someone who changes something

CHANNEL *noun* **CHANNELS** any natural or artificially constructed water course, eg the bed of a stream or an irrigation channel □ *verb* **CHANNELS, CHANNELLING, CHANNELLED** to make a channel or channels in something

CHANT *verb* **CHANTS, CHANTING, CHANTED** to recite in a singing voice □ *noun* **CHANTS** a type of singing used in religious services for passages in prose, with a simple melody and several words sung on one note

CHANTER *noun* **CHANTERS** on a set of bagpipes: the pipe on which the melody is played

CHANTING *adj* that chants

CHANTRY *noun* **CHANTRIES** an endowment provided for the chanting of masses

CHANTY *noun* **CHANTIES** a rhythmical song formerly sung by sailors

CHAOS *noun* **CHAOSES** complete confusion or disorder

CHAOTIC *adj* confused

CHAP [1] *noun* **CHAPS** a man or boy; a fellow

CHAP [2] *verb* **CHAPS, CHAPPING, CHAPPED** said of the skin: to make or become cracked, roughened and red as a result of rubbing or exposure to cold

CHAPARRAL *noun* **CHAPARRALS** in the southwestern USA: a dense growth of low evergreen thorny shrubs and trees, often forming tangled thickets

CHAPATI *noun* **CHAPATIS** in Indian cooking: a thin flat portion of unleavened bread

CHAPATTI *noun* **CHAPATTIS** a chapati

CHAPEL *noun* **CHAPELS** a recess within a church or cathedral, with its own altar

CHAPERON *noun* **CHAPERONS** chaperone □ *verb* **CHAPERONS, CHAPERONING, CHAPERONED** to chaperone

CHAPERONE *noun* **CHAPERONES** an older woman accompanying a younger unmarried one on social occasions, for respectability's sake □ *verb* **CHAPERONES, CHAPERONING, CHAPERONED** to act as chaperone to someone

CHAPLAIN *noun* **CHAPLAINS** a member of the clergy attached to a school, hospital or other institution, sometimes having a chapel, or to the armed forces

CHAPLET *noun* **CHAPLETS** a wreath of flowers or a band of gold, etc worn on the head

CHAPMAN *noun* **CHAPMEN** a travelling dealer; a pedlar

CHAPPED *adj* said of the skin and lips: dry and cracked

CHAPPIE *noun* **CHAPPIES** a chap

CHAPS *plural noun* a cowboy's protective leather riding leggings, worn over the trousers

CHAPTER *noun* **CHAPTERS** one of the numbered or titled sections into which a book is divided □ *verb* **CHAPTERS, CHAPTERING, CHAPTERED** to divide into chapters

CHAR [1] *verb* **CHARS, CHARRING, CHARRED** to blacken or be blackened by burning; to scorch

CHAR [2] *noun* **CHARS** tea

CHARABANC *noun* **CHARABANCS** a single-decker coach for tours, sightseeing, etc

CHARACTER *noun* **CHARACTERS** the combination of qualities that makes up a person's nature or personality

CHARADE *noun* **CHARADES** a ridiculous pretence; a farce

CHARCOAL *noun* **CHARCOALS** a black porous form of carbon produced by heating organic material, especially wood, in the absence of air, and which is used for adsorbing gases and clarifying liquids, as a fuel, and as an artist's material □ *adj* charcoal-coloured

CHARGE *verb* **CHARGES, CHARGING, CHARGED** to ask for an amount as the price of something □ *noun* **CHARGES** an amount charged; a price, fee, or cost

CHARGED *adj* filled with excitement or other strong emotion

CHARGER *noun* **CHARGERS** a strong horse used by a knight in battle, etc

CHARILY *adverb* in a chary way

CHARINESS *noun* **CHARINESSES**

the state or condition of being chary

CHARIOT noun **CHARIOTS** a two-wheeled vehicle pulled by horses, used in ancient times for warfare or racing

CHARISMA noun **CHARISMAS** a strong ability to attract people, and inspire loyalty and admiration

CHARITY noun **CHARITIES** assistance given to those in need

CHARLADY noun **CHARLADIES** a woman employed to clean a house, office, etc

CHARLATAN noun **CHARLATANS** someone posing as an expert in some profession, especially medicine

CHARLIE noun **CHARLIES** a fool

CHARLOCK noun **CHARLOCKS** a rough hairy annual plant, related to mustard, with toothed and lobed leaves and yellow cross-shaped flowers

CHARM noun **CHARMS** the power of delighting, attracting or fascinating □ verb **CHARMS, CHARMING, CHARMED** to delight, attract or fascinate someone

CHARMED adj seemingly protected by magic

CHARMER noun **CHARMERS** someone with an attractive winning manner

CHARMING adj delightful; pleasing; attractive; enchanting

CHARMLESS adj devoid of charm

CHARR noun **CHARRS** a fish related to and resembling the salmon

CHART noun **CHARTS** a map, especially one designed as an aid to navigation by sea or air, or one on which weather developments are shown □ verb **CHARTS, CHARTING, CHARTED** to make a chart of something, eg part of the sea

CHARTER noun **CHARTERS** a formal deed guaranteeing the rights and privileges of subjects, issued by a sovereign or government □ verb **CHARTERS, CHARTERING, CHARTERED** to grant a charter to someone

CHARTERED adj qualified according to the rules of a professional body that has a royal charter

CHARTERER noun **CHARTERERS** the holder of a charter; a freeholder

CHARTISM noun **CHARTISMS** the

use of charts to forecast future trends

CHARTIST noun **CHARTISTS** a person who makes and/or studies charts of past performances, especially of stocks and shares, with a view to forecasting future trends

CHARWOMAN noun **CHARWOMEN** a woman employed to clean a house, office, etc

CHARY adj **CHARIER, CHARIEST** cautious or wary

CHASE noun **CHASES** a pursuit □ verb **CHASES, CHASING, CHASED** to pursue; to hunt

CHASER noun **CHASERS** a drink taken after one of a different kind, eg beer after spirits

CHASING noun **CHASINGS** the art of engraving on the outside of raised metalwork

CHASM noun **CHASMS** a deep crack or opening in the ground or in the floor of a cave

CHASSÉ noun **CHASSÉS** a gliding step used in ballroom dancing □ verb **CHASSÉS, CHASSÉING, CHASSÉED** to perform this step

CHASSEUR adj applied to a sauce or food cooked in a sauce containing mushrooms, shallots, white wine, etc

CHASSIS noun **CHASSIS** the structural framework of a motor vehicle, to which the body and movable working parts eg wheels are attached

CHASTE adj **CHASTER, CHASTEST** sexually virtuous or pure; refraining from sexual relations either outside marriage or altogether

CHASTELY adverb in a chaste way

CHASTEN verb **CHASTENS, CHASTENING, CHASTENED** to free someone from faults by punishing them

CHASTISE verb **CHASTISES, CHASTISING, CHASTISED** to punish someone severely, especially by beating

CHASTITY noun **CHASTITIES** the state of being chaste

CHASUBLE noun **CHASUBLES** a long sleeveless garment worn by a priest when celebrating Mass or Communion

CHAT verb **CHATS, CHATTING, CHATTED** to talk or converse in a friendly informal way □ noun **CHATS** informal familiar talk; a friendly conversation

CHÂTEAU noun **CHÂTEAUX** a French castle or country seat

CHATTEL noun **CHATTELS** any kind of moveable property

CHATTER verb **CHATTERS, CHATTERING, CHATTERED** to talk rapidly and unceasingly, usually about trivial matters □ noun **CHATTERS** idle talk or gossip

CHATTERER noun **CHATTERERS** someone who or something that chatters

CHATTY adj **CHATTIER, CHATTIEST** given to amiable chatting

CHAUFFEUR noun **CHAUFFEURS** someone employed to drive a car for someone else □ verb **CHAUFFEURS, CHAUFFERING, CHAUFFEURED, CHAUFFERED** to act as a driver for someone

CHE pronoun a dialect form of *I*

CHEAP adj **CHEAPER, CHEAPEST** low in price; inexpensive □ adverb cheaply

CHEAPEN verb **CHEAPENS, CHEAPENING, CHEAPENED** to cause to appear cheap or not very respectable

CHEAPLY adverb at a low price

CHEAPNESS noun **CHEAPNESSES** the quality of being cheap

CHEAT verb **CHEATS, CHEATING, CHEATED** to trick, deceive or swindle □ noun **CHEATS** someone who cheats

CHEATER noun **CHEATERS** a person who cheats

CHECK verb **CHECKS, CHECKING, CHECKED** to establish that something is correct or satisfactory, especially by investigation or enquiry; to verify □ noun **CHECKS** an inspection or investigation made to find out about something or to ensure that something is as it should be

CHECKED adj having a squared pattern

CHECKER noun **CHECKERS** a chequer □ verb **CHECKERS, CHECKERING, CHECKERED** to chequer

CHECKERS singular noun chequers

CHECKLIST noun **CHECKLISTS** a list of things to be done or systematically checked

CHECKMATE noun **CHECKMATES** in chess: a winning position, putting one's opponent's king under inescapable attack □ verb

For longer words, see *The Chambers Dictionary*

CHECKMATES, CHECKMATING, CHECKMATED in chess: to put the (opposing king) into checkmate

CHECKOUT noun **CHECKOUTS** the pay desk in a supermarket

CHEEK noun **CHEEKS** either side of the face below the eye; the fleshy wall of the mouth

CHEEKBONE noun **CHEEKBONES** either of a pair of bones that lie beneath the prominent part of the cheeks

CHEEKILY adverb in a cheeky way

CHEEKY adj **CHEEKIER, CHEEKIEST** impudent or disrespectful in speech or manner

CHEEP verb **CHEEPS, CHEEPING, CHEEPED** said especially of young birds: to make high-pitched noises; to chirp ▫ noun **CHEEPS** a sound of this sort

CHEER noun **CHEERS** a shout of approval or encouragement ▫ verb **CHEERS, CHEERING, CHEERED** to show approval or encouragement of someone or something by shouting

CHEERFUL adj **CHEERFULLER, CHEERFULLEST** happy; optimistic

CHEERILY adverb in a cheery way

CHEERING adj bringing comfort; making one feel glad or happier

CHEERIO exclamation goodbye ▫ noun **CHEERIOS** an act or instance of saying goodbye

CHEERLESS adj dismal, depressing, dreary or dull

CHEERS exclamation used as a toast before drinking

CHEERY adj **CHEERIER, CHEERIEST** cheerful; lively; jovial

CHEESE noun **CHEESES** a solid or soft creamy food that is prepared from the curds of milk

CHEESY adj **CHEESIER, CHEESIEST** like cheese eg in smell, flavour, etc

CHEETAH noun **CHEETAHS** a large member of the cat family and the fastest land mammal, found in Africa and SW Asia, which has a tawny coat with black spots, a small head, and very long legs

CHEF noun **CHEFS** a cook in a restaurant etc, especially the principal one, and usually a man

CHELATE noun **CHELATES** any organic chemical compound, eg haemoglobin, in which a central metal ion is attached to one or more rings of atoms

CHELOID noun **CHELOIDS** keloid

CHEMICAL adj relating to or used in the science of chemistry ▫ noun **CHEMICALS** a substance that has a specific molecular composition, and takes part in or is formed by reactions in which atoms or molecules undergo changes

CHEMISE noun **CHEMISES** a woman's shirt or loose-fitting dress

CHEMIST noun **CHEMISTS** a scientist who specializes in chemistry

CHEMISTRY noun **CHEMISTRIES** the scientific study of the composition, properties, and reactions of chemical elements and their compounds

CHENILLE noun **CHENILLES** a soft shiny velvety fabric

CHEQUE noun **CHEQUES** a printed form on which to fill in instructions to one's bank to pay a specified sum of money from one's account to another account

CHEQUER noun **CHEQUERS** a pattern of squares alternating in colour as on a chessboard ▫ verb **CHEQUERS, CHEQUERING, CHEQUERED** to mark in squares of different colours

CHEQUERED adj patterned with squares or patches of alternating colour

CHEQUERS singular noun the game of draughts

CHERISH verb **CHERISHES, CHERISHING, CHERISHED** to care for lovingly

CHERNOZEM noun **CHERNOZEMS** a dark, highly fertile soil, rich in humus and soluble calcium salts, found in cool regions with low humidity, especially semi-arid grasslands

CHEROOT noun **CHEROOTS** a cigar that is cut square at both ends

CHERRY noun **CHERRIES** a small round red, purplish or yellow fruit containing a small smooth stone surrounded by pulpy flesh

CHERT noun **CHERTS** flint

CHERUB noun **CHERUBS** an angel, represented in painting and sculpture as a winged child

CHERUBIC adj angelic

CHERVIL noun **CHERVILS** an annual plant, native to Europe and Asia, with small white flowers borne in flat-topped clusters, and smooth oblong fruits

CHESS noun **CHESSES** a game of skill played on a chequered board by two people, each with 16 playing-pieces, the object of which is to trap the opponent's king

CHESSMAN noun **CHESSMEN** one of the 32 figures used as playing-pieces in chess

CHEST noun **CHESTS** the front part of the body between the neck and the waist; the non-technical name for the thorax

CHESTNUT noun **CHESTNUTS** a deciduous tree which has simple toothed glossy leaves and prickly globular fruits containing large edible nuts

CHESTY adj **CHESTIER, CHESTIEST** liable to, suffering from or caused by illness affecting the lungs

CHEVALIER noun **CHEVALIERS** in France: a member of a modern order such as the Legion of Honour, or of one of the historical knighthood orders

CHEVRON noun **CHEVRONS** a V-shaped mark or symbol, especially one worn on a uniform sleeve to indicate non-commissioned rank

CHEW verb **CHEWS, CHEWING, CHEWED** to use the teeth to break up (food) inside the mouth before swallowing ▫ noun **CHEWS** an act of chewing

CHEWY adj **CHEWIER, CHEWIEST** requiring a lot of chewing

CHI noun **CHIS** the life force that is believed to flow along a network of meridians in a person's body and which is vital to their physical and spiritual health

CHIASMA noun **CHIASMAS** the point where the optic nerves cross each other in the brain

CHIC adj **CHICER, CHICEST** said of clothes, people, etc: appealingly elegant or fashionable ▫ noun **CHICS** stylishness; elegance

CHICANE noun **CHICANES** on a motor-racing circuit: a series of sharp bends ▫ verb **CHICANES, CHICANING, CHICANED** to use trickery or chicanery

CHICANERY noun **CHICANERIES** clever talk intended to mislead

CHICK noun **CHICKS** the young of a bird, especially a domestic fowl

CHICKEN noun **CHICKENS** the domestic fowl, bred virtually worldwide for its meat and eggs ▫ adj cowardly

CHICKPEA noun **CHICKPEAS** a leafy branching annual plant with white or bluish flowers, cultivated for its wrinkled yellow pea-like edible seeds

CHICKWEED noun **CHICKWEEDS** a low-growing sprawling annual plant, native to Europe, which has oval pointed leaves and tiny white flowers with deeply lobed petals

CHICLY adverb in a chic way

CHICORY noun **CHICORIES** a plant with stalked lower leaves, stalkless upper leaves, bright blue flower-heads and a long stout tap root

CHIDE verb **CHIDES, CHIDING, CHID, CHIDED, CHIDDEN** to scold or rebuke

CHIDING noun **CHIDINGS** a scolding or a rebuke

CHIEF adj **CHIEFER, CHIEFEST** used in titles, etc: first in rank; leading ◻ noun **CHIEFS** the head of a tribe, clan, etc

CHIEFLY adverb mainly

CHIEFTAIN noun **CHIEFTAINS** the head of a tribe or clan

CHIFFON noun **CHIFFONS** a very fine transparent silk or nylon fabric

CHIGGER noun **CHIGGERS** the bright red larval stage of a mite, which feeds by sucking the blood of small mammals and humans

CHIGNON noun **CHIGNONS** a soft bun or coil of hair worn at the back of the neck

CHIGOE noun **CHIGOES** a chigger

CHIHUAHUA noun **CHIHUAHUAS** the smallest domestic breed of dog, which has a tiny body and a disproportionately large head

CHILBLAIN noun **CHILBLAINS** a painful red itchy swelling of the skin, especially on the fingers, toes or ears, caused by abnormal constriction of the blood vessels of the skin on exposure to cold

CHILD noun **CHILDREN** a boy or girl between birth and physical maturity

CHILDHOOD noun **CHILDHOODS** the state or time of being a child

CHILDISH adj silly; immature

CHILDLESS adj without children

CHILDLIKE adj like a child; innocent

CHILI noun **CHILIS** chilli

CHILL noun **CHILLS** a feeling of coldness ◻ verb **CHILLS, CHILLING, CHILLED** to make or become cold

CHILLED adj made cold

CHILLI noun **CHILLIS** the fruit or 'pod' of one of the varieties of capsicum, which has a hot spicy flavour and is used in cooking, often in powdered form

CHILLING adj frightening

CHILLY adj **CHILLIER, CHILLIEST** rather cold

CHIMAERA noun **CHIMAERAS** a wild or impossible idea

CHIME noun **CHIMES** an individual bell or a set of tuned bells ◻ verb **CHIMES, CHIMING, CHIMED** said of bells: to ring

CHIMERA noun **CHIMERAS** a chimaera

CHIMERIC adj relating to, or of the nature of, a chimaera

CHIMNEY noun **CHIMNEYS** a vertical structure made of brick, stone or steel, that carries smoke, steam, fumes or heated air away from a fireplace, stove, furnace or engine

CHIMP noun **CHIMPS** a chimpanzee

CHIN noun **CHINS** the front protruding part of the lower jaw

CHINA singular noun articles made from a fine translucent earthenware, originally from China ◻ adj made of china

CHINE noun **CHINES** the backbone ◻ verb **CHINES, CHINING, CHINED** to cut (the carcass of an animal) along the backbone

CHINK noun **CHINKS** a faint short ringing noise ◻ verb **CHINKS, CHINKING, CHINKED** to make or cause to make a faint ringing noise

CHINLESS adj having a small weak, backwards-sloping chin

CHINOS plural noun trousers made from a strong khaki-like twilled cotton

CHINSTRAP noun **CHINSTRAPS** a helmet strap which fastens under the chin

CHINTZ noun **CHINTZES** a cotton fabric printed generally in bright colours on a light background, especially used for soft furnishings

CHINTZY adj **CHINTZIER, CHINTZIEST** sentimentally or quaintly showy

CHINWAG noun **CHINWAGS** a chat

CHIP verb **CHIPS, CHIPPING, CHIPPED** to knock or strike small pieces off (a hard object or material) ◻ noun **CHIPS** a small piece chipped off

CHIPBOARD noun **CHIPBOARDS** thin solid board made from compressed wood chips

CHIPMUNK noun **CHIPMUNKS** any of several small ground squirrels, found in N America and N Asia, with reddish-brown fur

CHIPOLATA noun **CHIPOLATAS** a small sausage

CHIPPED adj damaged by chips

CHIPPER adj said of a person: cheerful and lively

CHIPPY noun **CHIPPIES** a chip shop

CHIROPODY noun **CHIROPODIES** the diagnosis, treatment and prevention of foot disorders

CHIRP verb **CHIRPS, CHIRPING, CHIRPED** said of birds, grasshoppers, etc: to produce a short high-pitched sound ◻ noun **CHIRPS** a chirping sound

CHIRPILY adverb in a chirpy way

CHIRPY adj **CHIRPIER, CHIRPIEST** lively and merry

CHIRRUP verb **CHIRRUPS, CHIRRUPING, CHIRRUPED** said of some birds and insects: to chirp, especially in little bursts ◻ noun **CHIRRUPS** a burst of chirping

CHIRRUPY adj cheerful

CHISEL noun **CHISELS** a hand tool which has a strong metal blade with a cutting edge at the tip, used for cutting and shaping wood or stone ◻ verb **CHISELS, CHISELLING, CHISELLED** to cut or shape (wood or stone) with a chisel

CHIT noun **CHITS** a short note or voucher recording money owed or paid

CHITCHAT noun **CHITCHATS** chatter; gossip ◻ verb **CHITCHATS, CHITCHATTING, CHITCHATTED** to gossip idly

CHITIN noun **CHITINS** a complex carbohydrate substance that serves to strengthen the tough outer covering or cuticle of insects and crustaceans

CHITINOUS adj of, or consisting of, chitin

CHITLINGS singular or plural noun the intestines of a pig or another edible animal prepared as food

CHIVALRY noun **CHIVALRIES** courtesy and protectiveness especially as shown towards women or the weak

CHIVE noun **CHIVES** a plant of the onion family with purple flowers and long thin hollow leaves used as a flavouring or garnish

CHIVVY verb **CHIVVIES, CHIVVYING, CHIVVIED** to harass or pester someone, especially to hurry or to get some task done

CHIVY *verb* **CHIVIES, CHIVYING, CHIVIED** to chivvy

CHLAMYDIA *noun* **CHLAMYDIAS** a virus-like bacterium that is parasitic in humans and animals, causing diseases such as trachoma, psittacosis and urinogenital infections

CHLORAL *noun* **CHLORALS** an oily colourless toxic liquid with a pungent odour used in the manufacture of DDT

CHLORATE *noun* **CHLORATES** any salt of chloric acid, including several compounds that are used in defoliant weedkillers

CHLORIC *adj* relating to, containing or obtained from chlorine

CHLORIDE *noun* **CHLORIDES** a compound of chlorine with another element or radical

CHLORINE *noun* **CHLORINES** a greenish-yellow poisonous gas with a pungent smell, widely used as a disinfectant and bleach, and in the chemical industry

CHOC *noun* **CHOCS** chocolate or a chocolate

CHOCK *noun* **CHOCKS** a heavy block or wedge used to prevent movement of a wheel, etc ▫ *verb* **CHOCKS, CHOCKING, CHOCKED** to wedge or immobilize something with chocks

CHOCOLATE *noun* **CHOCOLATES** a food product, made from cacao beans, that may be eaten on its own or used as a coating or flavouring ▫ *adj* made from or coated with chocolate

CHOCOLATY *adj* **CHOCOLATIER, CHOCOLATIEST** made with or as if with chocolate

CHOICE *adj* **CHOICER, CHOICEST** select; worthy of being chosen ▫ *noun* **CHOICES** the act or process of choosing

CHOIR *noun* **CHOIRS** an organized group of trained singers, especially one that performs in church

CHOIRBOY *noun* **CHOIRBOYS** a young boy who sings in a church choir

CHOIRGIRL *noun* **CHOIRGIRLS** a young girl who sings in a church choir

CHOKE *verb* **CHOKES, CHOKING, CHOKED** to prevent or be prevented from breathing by an obstruction in the throat, fumes, emotion, etc ▫ *noun* **CHOKES** the sound or act of choking

CHOKER *noun* **CHOKERS** a close-fitting necklace or broad band of velvet, etc worn round the neck

CHOLER *noun* **CHOLERS** anger or irritability

CHOLERA *noun* **CHOLERAS** an acute and potentially fatal bacterial infection of the small intestine, characterized by severe vomiting and diarrhoea

CHOLERAIC *adj* of or relating to cholera

CHOLERIC *adj* irritable or bad-tempered

CHOLINE *noun* **CHOLINES** an organic compound that is a component of the neurotransmitter acetylcholine, and is also involved in the transport of fats in the body

CHOMP *verb* **CHOMPS, CHOMPING, CHOMPED** to munch noisily ▫ *noun* **CHOMPS** an act or sound of chomping

CHOOSE *verb* **CHOOSES, CHOOSING, CHOSE, CHOSEN** to take or select (one or more things or persons) from a larger number, according to one's own preference or judgement

CHOOSY *adj* **CHOOSIER, CHOOSIEST** difficult to please; fussy

CHOP *verb* **CHOPS, CHOPPING, CHOPPED** to cut with a vigorous downward or sideways slicing action, with an axe, knife, etc ▫ *noun* **CHOPS** a slice of pork, lamb or mutton containing a bone, especially a rib

CHOPHOUSE *noun* **CHOPHOUSES** a restaurant specializing in steak and chops

CHOPPER *noun* **CHOPPERS** a helicopter

CHOPPY *adj* **CHOPPIER, CHOPPIEST** said of the sea, weather etc: rather rough

CHOPS *plural noun* the jaws or mouth, especially of an animal

CHORAL *adj* relating to, or to be sung by, a choir or chorus ▫ *noun* **CHORALS** a chorale

CHORALE *noun* **CHORALES** a hymn tune with a slow dignified rhythm and strong harmonization

CHORALLY *adverb* in the manner of a chorus; suitable for a choir

CHORD *noun* **CHORDS** a combination of musical notes played together

CHORDATE *noun* **CHORDATES** any animal which belongs to the type

that possesses a notochord at some stage in their development

CHORE *noun* **CHORES** a domestic task

CHOREA *noun* **CHOREAS** either of two disorders of the nervous system that cause rapid involuntary movements of the limbs and sometimes of the face

CHORION *noun* **CHORIA** the outer membrane which surrounds a fetus

CHORISTER *noun* **CHORISTERS** a singer in a choir, especially a church or cathedral choir

CHOROID *adj* resembling or relating to the chorion ▫ *noun* **CHOROIDS** in the eye of terrestrial vertebrates: the layer of pigmented cells, rich in blood vessels, which lies between the retina and the sclerotic

CHORTLE *verb* **CHORTLES, CHORTLING, CHORTLED** to laugh joyfully ▫ *noun* **CHORTLES** a joyful laugh

CHORUS *noun* **CHORUSES** a set of lines in a song, sung as a refrain after each verse ▫ *verb* **CHORUSES, CHORUSING, CHORUSED** to say, sing or utter simultaneously

CHOSE a past form of **choose**

CHOSEN a past form of **choose**

CHOUGH *noun* **CHOUGHS** a red-legged black bird of the crow family

CHOW *noun* **CHOWS** a breed of dog originally from China, with thick fur, a curled tail and a blue tongue

CHOWDER *noun* **CHOWDERS** a thick soup or stew made from clams or fish with vegetables

CHRISM *noun* **CHRISMS** holy oil used for anointing in the Roman Catholic and Greek Orthodox Churches

CHRISMAL *adj* relating to chrism

CHRISOM *noun* **CHRISOMS** chrism

CHRISTEN *verb* **CHRISTENS, CHRISTENING, CHRISTENED** to give a person, especially a baby, a name as part of the religious ceremony of receiving them into the Christian Church

CHRISTENING *noun* **CHRISTENINGS** the ceremony of baptism

CHROMATIC *adj* relating to colours; coloured

CHROMATID *noun* **CHROMATIDS** one of the two thread-like structures formed by the longitudinal division of a chromosome

CHROMATIN noun **CHROMATINS** in a cell nucleus: the loose network of thread-like material, composed of DNA, RNA and proteins, which becomes organized into visible chromosomes at the time of cell division

CHROME noun **CHROMES** chromium, especially when used as a silvery plating for other metals □ verb **CHROMES, CHROMING, CHROMED** in dyeing: to treat with a chromium solution

CHROMITE noun **CHROMITES** a mineral, composed of chromium and iron oxides, that occurs as compact masses of black crystals with a metallic lustre and is the main source of chromium

CHROMIUM noun **CHROMIUMS** a hard silvery metallic element that is resistant to corrosion, which is used in electroplating and in alloys with iron and nickel to make stainless steel

CHRONIC adj said of a disease or symptoms: long-lasting, usually of gradual onset and often difficult to treat

CHRONICLE noun **CHRONICLES** a record of historical events year by year in the order in which they occurred □ verb **CHRONICLES, CHRONICLING, CHRONICLED** to record (an event) in a chronicle

CHRYSALID noun **CHRYSALIDS** a chrysalis

CHRYSALIS noun **CHRYSALISES** the pupa of insects that undergo metamorphosis, eg butterflies, moths

CHUB noun **CHUBS** a small fat river-fish of the carp family

CHUBBY adj **CHUBBIER, CHUBBIEST** plump, especially in a childishly attractive way

CHUCK verb **CHUCKS, CHUCKING, CHUCKED** to throw or fling □ noun **CHUCKS** a toss, fling or throw

CHUCKLE verb **CHUCKLES, CHUCKLING, CHUCKLED** to laugh quietly, especially in a half-suppressed private way □ noun **CHUCKLES** an amused little laugh

CHUDDAR noun **CHUDDARS** a chador

CHUFF verb **CHUFFS, CHUFFING, CHUFFED** said of a steam train: to progress with regular puffing noises

CHUFFED adj very pleased

CHUG verb **CHUGS, CHUGGING, CHUGGED** said of a motor boat, motor car, etc: to progress while making a quiet thudding noise □ noun **CHUGS** a short dull thudding noise, typical of an engine

CHUKKA noun **CHUKKAS** a chukker

CHUKKER noun **CHUKKERS** any of the six periods of play in polo each of which normally lasts for seven and a half minutes

CHUM noun **CHUMS** a close friend □ verb **CHUMS, CHUMMING, CHUMMED** to make friends with someone

CHUMMY adj **CHUMMIER, CHUMMIEST** friendly

CHUMP noun **CHUMPS** an idiot; a fool

CHUNDER verb **CHUNDERS, CHUNDERING, CHUNDERED** to vomit; to be sick □ noun **CHUNDERS** vomit

CHUNK noun **CHUNKS** a thick, especially irregularly shaped, piece

CHUNKY adj **CHUNKIER, CHUNKIEST** thick-set; stockily or strongly built

CHUNNEL noun **CHUNNELS** the tunnel underneath the English Channel, connecting England and France

CHURCH noun **CHURCHES** a building for public Christian worship

CHURCHMAN noun **CHURCHMEN** a member of the clergy or of a church

CHURL noun **CHURLS** an ill-bred surly person

CHURLISH adj ill-mannered or rude

CHURN noun **CHURNS** a machine in which milk is vigorously shaken to make butter □ verb **CHURNS, CHURNING, CHURNED** to make (butter) in a churn

CHUTE noun **CHUTES** a sloping channel down which to send water, rubbish, etc

CHUTNEY noun **CHUTNEYS** a type of pickle, originally from India, made with fruit, vinegar, spices, sugar, etc

CHUTZPAH noun **CHUTZPAHS** self-assurance bordering on impudence; audacity; effrontery

CHYLE noun **CHYLES** a milky fluid, consisting of lymph containing fats that have been

absorbed from the small intestine during digestion

CHYME noun **CHYMES** the partially digested food that passes into the duodenum and small intestine from the stomach

CIABATTA noun **CIABATTAS, CIABATTE** Italian bread with a sponge-like texture, made with olive oil

CIAO exclamation an informal Italian greeting used on meeting and parting, which has now become fashionable in English

CICADA noun **CICADAS** a large predominantly tree-dwelling hemipterous insect of mainly tropical regions, the male of which is noted for its high-pitched warbling whistle, produced by vibrating tambourine-like membranes on either side of the body

CICALA noun **CICALAS** a cicada

CICATRICE noun **CICATRICES** the scar tissue that lies over a healed wound

CICATRISE verb **CICATRISES, CICATRISING, CICATRISED** to cicatrize

CICATRIX noun **CICATRIXES** cicatrice

CICATRIZE verb **CICATRIZES, CICATRIZING, CICATRIZED** said of a wound: to heal by generating a scar

CICELY noun **CICELIES** any of various umbelliferous plants related to chervil, especially sweet cicely

CID noun CIDS a chief, captain or hero

CIDER noun **CIDERS** an alcoholic drink made from apples

CIG noun **CIGS** a cigarette

CIGAR noun **CIGARS** a long slender roll of tobacco leaves for smoking

CIGARETTE noun **CIGARETTES** a tube of finely cut tobacco rolled in thin paper, for smoking

CIGARILLO noun **CIGARILLOS** a small cigar

CIGGY noun **CIGGIES** short for cigarette

CILIATE noun **CILIATES** any of numerous microscopic single-celled organisms that typically possess cilia and which are found free-living in all kinds of aquatic and terrestrial habitats, and as parasites

CILIUM *noun* **CILIA** any of the short hair-like appendages that project from the surface of certain cells, and whose rhythmic movement aids cell locomotion, or causes movement of the water surrounding some single-celled aquatic organisms

CIMBALOM *noun* **CIMBALOMS** a form of dulcimer used in Hungary and other E European countries

CIMEX *noun* **CIMICES** an insect such as the bed bug

CINCH *noun* **CINCHES** an easily accomplished task ◻ *verb* **CINCHES, CINCHING, CINCHED** to make certain of something

CINCHONA *noun* **CINCHONAS** any tree of the type yielding bark from which quinine and related by-products are obtained

CINCTURE *noun* **CINCTURES** a belt or girdle

CINDER *noun* **CINDERS** a piece of burnt coal or wood

CINDERY *adj* consisting of cinders

CINEAST *noun* **CINEASTS** a cineaste

CINEASTE *noun* **CINEASTES** someone who is interested in, or who makes, cinema films

CINEMA *noun* **CINEMAS** a theatre in which motion pictures are shown

CINEMATIC *adj* relating to, suitable for, or characteristic of, the cinema

CINERARIA *noun* **CINERARIAS** a dwarf shrub native to Africa and Madagascar, which has rounded lobed leaves, the undersurfaces densely covered with white hairs, and numerous red, deep blue, violet, or variegated daisy-like flowerheads

CINERARY *adj* relating to ashes

CINNABAR *noun* **CINNABARS** a bright red mineral form of mercury sulphide, the principal source of mercury and also used as a pigment

CINNAMON *noun* **CINNAMONS** a spice obtained from the cured dried bark of a SE Asian tree ◻ *adj* of the brownish-orange colour of cinnamon

CIPHER *noun* **CIPHERS** a secret code ◻ *verb* **CIPHERS, CIPHERING, CIPHERED** to write (a message, etc) in code

CIRCA *prep* used especially with dates: about; approximately

CIRCADIAN *adj* relating to a biological rhythm that is more or less synchronized to a 24-hour cycle, eg the pattern of sleeping and waking in adult humans

CIRCLE *noun* **CIRCLES** a perfectly round two-dimensional figure that is bordered by the circumference, every point of which is an equal distance from a fixed point within the figure called the centre ◻ *verb* **CIRCLES, CIRCLING, CIRCLED** to move in a circle

CIRCLER *noun* **CIRCLERS** someone or something that moves in a circle or surrounds

CIRCLET *noun* **CIRCLETS** a simple band or hoop of gold, silver, etc worn on the head

CIRCUIT *noun* **CIRCUITS** a complete course, journey or route round something ◻ *verb* **CIRCUITS, CIRCUITING, CIRCUITED** to go round

CIRCUITRY *noun* **CIRCUITRIES** a plan or system of electric circuits used in a particular electronic or electrical device

CIRCULAR *adj* having the form of a circle ◻ *noun* **CIRCULARS** a letter or notice which is addressed and copied to a number of people

CIRCULATE *verb* **CIRCULATES, CIRCULATING, CIRCULATED** to move or cause to move round freely, especially in a fixed route

CIRCUS *noun* **CIRCUSES** a travelling company of performers including acrobats, clowns and often trained animals, etc

CIRCUSSY *adj* resembling a circus

CIRQUE *noun* **CIRQUES** a deep semicircular hollow with steep side and back walls, located high on a mountain slope and formed as a result of glacial erosion

CIRRHOSIS *noun* **CIRRHOSES** a progressive disease of the liver, especially alcohol related, which results in a wasting away of normal tissue, and an overgrowth of abnormal lumpy tissue

CIRRIPED *noun* **CIRRIPEDS** any of the class of sea creatures that includes barnacles

CIRRIPEDE *noun* **CIRRIPEDES** a cirriped

CIRRUS *noun* **CIRRI** a common type of high cloud composed of ice crystals, with a wispy fibrous or feathery appearance and which indicates fair weather

CISSY *noun* **CISSIES** a sissy ◻ *adj* **CISSIER, CISSIEST** sissy

CIST *noun* **CISTS** a chest-shaped tomb, lined and covered with slabs of stone

CISTERN *noun* **CISTERNS** a tank storing water, usually in the roof-space of a house, or connected to a flushing toilet

CISTRON *noun* **CISTRONS** that part of a chain of DNA that is functionally equivalent to a gene

CIT *noun* **CITS** a contemptuous term for someone who is not a gentleman

CITABLE *adj* that can be cited

CITADEL *noun* **CITADELS** a fortress built close to or within a city, for its protection and as a place of refuge

CITATION *noun* **CITATIONS** the quoting or citing of something as example or proof

CITE *verb* **CITES, CITING, CITED** to quote (a book, its author or a passage from it) as an example or proof

CITHER *noun* **CITHERS** a cittern

CITHERN *noun* **CITHERNS** a cittern

CITIZEN *noun* **CITIZENS** an inhabitant of a city or town

CITIZENRY *noun* **CITIZENRIES** the citizens of a town, country, etc

CITRATE *noun* **CITRATES** a salt or ester of citric acid

CITRIC *adj* derived from citric acid

CITRON *noun* **CITRONS** a fruit like a large lemon, with a thick sweet-smelling yellow rind

CITRUS *noun* **CITRUSES** any of a group of edible fruits with a tough outer peel enclosing juicy flesh rich in vitamin C, citric acid and water

CITTERN *noun* **CITTERNS** a plucked stringed instrument which resembles the lute and was popular in the 16c and 17c

CITY *noun* **CITIES** any large town

CITYSCAPE *noun* **CITYSCAPES** a view or picture of a city

CIVET *noun* **CIVETS** a small spotted and striped carnivorous mammal found in Asia and Africa

CIVIC *adj* relating to a city, citizen or citizenship

CIVICALLY *adverb* in a civic way

CIVICS *singular noun* the study of local government and of the rights and duties of citizenship

CIVIL *adj* relating to the community

CIVILIAN *noun* **CIVILIANS** anyone

who is not a member of the armed forces or the police force

CIVILISE verb **CIVILISES, CIVILISING, CIVILISED** to civilize

CIVILISED adj civilized

CIVILITY noun **CIVILITIES** politeness

CIVILIZE verb **CIVILIZES, CIVILIZING, CIVILIZED** to lead out of a state of barbarity to a more advanced stage of social development

CIVILIZED adj socially, politically and technologically advanced

CIVILLY adverb politely

CIVVY noun **CIVVIES** a civilian

CLACK noun **CLACKS** a sharp noise made by one hard object striking another ▫ verb **CLACKS, CLACKING, CLACKED** to make or cause something to make this kind of noise

CLAD adj clothed; covered ▫ verb **CLADS, CLADDING, CLADDED** to cover one material with another, eg brick or stonework with a different material, especially to form a protective layer

CLADDING noun **CLADDINGS** a thin covering applied to the external surface of a building in order to improve its appearance or to give it extra protection

CLAIM noun **CLAIMS** a statement of something as a truth ▫ verb **CLAIMS, CLAIMING, CLAIMED** to state something firmly, insisting on its truth

CLAIMABLE adj that can be claimed

CLAIMANT noun **CLAIMANTS** a person who makes a claim

CLAM noun **CLAMS** any of various bivalve shellfish ▫ verb **CLAMS, CLAMMING, CLAMMED** to gather clams

CLAMANT adj noisy

CLAMBER verb **CLAMBERS, CLAMBERING, CLAMBERED** to climb using one's hands as well as one's feet ▫ noun **CLAMBERS** an act of clambering

CLAMMILY adverb in a clammy way

CLAMMY adj **CLAMMIER, CLAMMIEST** moist or damp, especially unpleasantly so

CLAMOROUS adj noisy, boisterous

CLAMOUR noun **CLAMOURS** a noise of shouting or loud talking ▫ verb **CLAMOURS, CLAMOURING, CLAMOURED** to make a loud continuous outcry

CLAMP noun **CLAMPS** a tool with adjustable jaws for gripping things firmly or pressing parts together ▫ verb **CLAMPS, CLAMPING, CLAMPED** to fasten together or hold with a clamp

CLAMPDOWN noun **CLAMPDOWNS** a suppressive measure

CLAN noun **CLANS** in Scotland or among people of Scots origin: a group of families, generally with the same surname, and (especially formerly) led by a chief

CLANG verb **CLANGS, CLANGING, CLANGED** to ring or make something ring loudly and deeply ▫ noun **CLANGS** this ringing sound

CLANGER noun **CLANGERS** a tactless, embarrassing and all-too-obvious blunder

CLANGOUR noun **CLANGOURS** a loud resounding noise

CLANK noun **CLANKS** a sharp metallic sound like pieces of metal striking together ▫ verb **CLANKS, CLANKING, CLANKED** to make or cause something to make such a sound

CLANNISH adj said of a group of people: closely united, with little interest or trust in people not belonging to the group

CLANSMAN noun **CLANSMEN** a member of a clan

CLAP verb **CLAPS, CLAPPING, CLAPPED** to strike the palms of (one's hands) together with a loud noise, in order to mark (a rhythm), gain attention, etc ▫ noun **CLAPS** an act of clapping

CLAPPER noun **CLAPPERS** the dangling piece of metal inside a bell that strikes against the sides to make it ring

CLAPTRAP noun **CLAPTRAPS** meaningless, insincere or pompous talk

CLAQUE noun **CLAQUES** a group of people paid to applaud a speaker at a meeting or performer in a theatre, etc

CLARET noun **CLARETS** a French red wine, especially from the Bordeaux area in SW France

CLARIFIER noun **CLARIFIERS** a person or thing that clarifies

CLARIFY verb **CLARIFIES, CLARIFYING, CLARIFIED** to make or become clearer or easier to understand

CLARINET noun **CLARINETS** a woodwind instrument with a cylindrical tube and a single reed

CLARION noun **CLARIONS** an old kind of trumpet with a shrill sound, used to call men to arms, etc

CLARITY noun **CLARITIES** the quality of being clear and pure

CLARSACH noun **CLARSACHS** in Scotland and Ireland: a small harp strung with wire

CLASH noun **CLASHES** a loud noise, like that of metal objects striking each other ▫ verb **CLASHES, CLASHING, CLASHED** said of metal objects, etc: to strike against each other noisily

CLASP noun **CLASPS** a fastening on jewellery, a bag, etc made of two parts that link together ▫ verb **CLASPS, CLASPING, CLASPED** to hold or take hold of someone or something firmly

CLASS noun **CLASSES** a lesson or lecture ▫ verb **CLASSES, CLASSING, CLASSED** to regard someone or something as belonging to a certain class or category

CLASSIC adj made of or belonging to the highest quality; established as the best ▫ noun **CLASSICS** an established work of literature

CLASSICAL adj said of literature, art, etc: from ancient Greece and Rome

CLASSICS singular noun the study of Latin and Greek

CLASSIFIED adj arranged in groups or classes

CLASSIFY verb **CLASSIFIES, CLASSIFYING, CLASSIFIED** to put into a particular group or category

CLASSLESS adj said of a community, society etc: not divided into social classes

CLASSMATE noun **CLASSMATES** a fellow pupil or student in one's class at school or college

CLASSROOM noun **CLASSROOMS** a room in a school or college where classes are taught

CLASSY adj **CLASSIER, CLASSIEST** stylish; superior

CLASTIC adj said of sedimentary rock: composed of fragments, or clasts, of older rock

CLATTER noun **CLATTERS** a loud noise made by hard objects striking each other, or falling onto a hard surface ▫ verb **CLATTERS, CLATTERING, CLATTERED** to make or cause to make a loud rattling noise

CLAUSAL adj of or relating to a clause or clauses

For longer words, see *The Chambers Dictionary*

CLAUSE noun **CLAUSES** a group of words that includes a subject and its related finite verb, and which may or may not constitute a sentence (eg *if time permits* and *we will come tomorrow*)

CLAVICLE noun **CLAVICLES** in vertebrates: either of two short slender bones linking the shoulder-blades with the top of the breastbone

CLAW noun **CLAWS** a hard curved pointed nail on the end of each digit of the foot in birds, most reptiles and many mammals ❑ verb **CLAWS, CLAWING, CLAWED** to tear or scratch something with claws, nails or fingers

CLAWBACK noun **CLAWBACKS** recovery of expenditure by taxation

CLAY noun **CLAYS** a poorly draining soil consisting mainly of aluminium silicates, which is pliable when wet and is used to make pottery, bricks, ceramics, etc

CLAYEY adj **CLAYIER, CLAYIEST** made, covered with, or like, clay

CLAYMORE noun **CLAYMORES** a two-edged broadsword used by Scottish highlanders

CLEAN adj **CLEANER, CLEANEST** free from dirt or contamination ❑ adverb straight or directly; encountering no obstruction ❑ verb **CLEANS, CLEANING, CLEANED** to make or become free from dirt ❑ noun an act of cleaning

CLEANER noun **CLEANERS** someone employed to clean inside buildings, offices, etc

CLEANLY adj **CLEANLIER, CLEANLIEST** hygienic in one's personal habits ❑ adverb in a clean way

CLEANNESS noun the quality or state of being clean

CLEANSE verb **CLEANSES, CLEANSING, CLEANSED** to clean or get rid of dirt from someone or something

CLEANSER noun **CLEANSERS** a substance that cleans, eg a cream or liquid for cleaning the face

CLEAR adj **CLEARER, CLEAREST** transparent; easy to see through ❑ adverb in a clear manner ❑ verb **CLEARS, CLEARING, CLEARED** to make or become clear, free of obstruction, etc

CLEARANCE noun **CLEARANCES** the act of clearing

CLEARING noun **CLEARINGS** an area in a forest, etc that has been cleared of trees, etc

CLEARLY adverb in a clear manner

CLEARNESS noun **CLEARNESSES** the quality or state of being clear

CLEARWAY noun **CLEARWAYS** a stretch of road on which cars may not stop except in an emergency

CLEAT noun **CLEATS** a wedge ❑ verb **CLEATS, CLEATING, CLEATED** to strengthen something with a cleat

CLEAVABLE adj capable of being cleft

CLEAVAGE noun **CLEAVAGES** a series of cell divisions of an ovum immediately after it has been fertilized

CLEAVE ¹ verb **CLEAVES, CLEAVING, CLOVE, CLEFT, CLOVEN** to split or divide

CLEAVE ² verb **CLEAVES, CLEAVING, CLEAVED** to cling or stick

CLEAVER noun **CLEAVERS** a knife with a large square blade, used especially by butchers for chopping meat

CLEF noun **CLEFS** in music: a symbol placed on a stave to indicate the pitch of the notes written on it

CLEFT noun **CLEFTS** a past form of **cleave** ¹ ❑ a split, fissure, wide crack or deep indentation

CLEG noun **CLEGS** a horsefly

CLEMATIS noun **CLEMATISES** a garden climbing with purple, yellow or white flowers

CLEMENCY noun **CLEMENCIES** the quality of being clement

CLEMENT adj said of the weather: mild; not harsh or severe

CLEMENTLY adverb mildly; mercifully

CLENCH verb **CLENCHES, CLENCHING, CLENCHED** to close one's teeth or one's fists tightly, especially in anger ❑ noun **CLENCHES** the action of clenching

CLERGY singular or plural noun **CLERGIES** the ordained ministers of the Christian church, or the priests of any religion

CLERGYMAN noun **CLERGYMEN** a member of the clergy

CLERIC noun **CLERICS** a clergyman

CLERICAL adj relating to clerks, office workers or office work

CLERIHEW noun **CLERIHEWS** a humorous poem about a famous person, consisting of two short couplets

CLERK noun **CLERKS** in an office or bank: someone who deals with letters, accounts, records, files, etc

CLERKESS noun **CLERKESSES** a female clerk

CLERKISH adj like a clerk

CLERKSHIP noun **CLERKSHIPS** the office or position of a clerk

CLEVER adj **CLEVERER, CLEVEREST** good or quick at learning and understanding

CLEVERLY adverb in a clever way

CLEW noun **CLEWS** the corner of a ship's sail ❑ verb **CLEWS, CLEWING, CLEWED** to coil up into a ball

CLICHÉ noun **CLICHÉS** a once striking and effective phrase which has become stale and hackneyed through overuse

CLICHÉED adj filled with clichés

CLICK noun **CLICKS** a short sharp sound like that made by two parts of a mechanism locking into place ❑ verb **CLICKS, CLICKING, CLICKED** to make or cause to make a click

CLIENT noun **CLIENTS** someone using the services of a professional institution eg a bank, a law firm, an estate agent, etc

CLIENTELE noun **CLIENTELES** the clients of a professional person, customers of a shopkeeper, etc

CLIFF noun **CLIFFS** a high steep rock face, especially on the coast or the side of a mountain

CLIMACTIC adj relating to a climax

CLIMATE noun **CLIMATES** the average weather conditions of a particular region of the world over a long period of time, with regard to temperature, rainfall, air pressure, etc

CLIMATIC adj relating to climate

CLIMAX noun **CLIMAXES** the high point or culmination of a series of events or of an experience ❑ verb **CLIMAXES, CLIMAXING, CLIMAXED** to come or bring to a climax

CLIMB verb **CLIMBS, CLIMBING, CLIMBED** to mount or ascend (a hill, ladder, etc), often using hands and feet ❑ noun **CLIMBS** an act of climbing

CLIMBABLE adj that can be climbed

CLIMBER noun **CLIMBERS** a mountaineer

CLIMBING noun **CLIMBINGS** the sport of climbing rock faces

CLIME noun **CLIMES** a region of the world

CLINCH verb **CLINCHES, CLINCHING, CLINCHED** to settle something finally and decisively, eg an argument, deal, etc □ noun **CLINCHES** an act of clinching

CLINCHER noun **CLINCHERS** a point, argument or circumstance that finally settles or decides a matter

CLINE noun **CLINES** a gradual change in the form of an animal or plant species across different parts of its geographical or environmental range

CLING verb **CLINGS, CLINGING, CLUNG** to hold firmly or tightly; to stick

CLINGER noun **CLINGERS** a person or thing that clings

CLINGFILM noun **CLINGFILMS** a thin clear plastic material that adheres to itself, used for wrapping food, covering containers, etc

CLINGY adj **CLINGIER, CLINGIEST** liable or tending to cling

CLINIC noun **CLINICS** a private hospital or nursing home that specializes in the treatment and care of patients with particular diseases or disorders

CLINICAL adj relating to, or like, a clinic or hospital

CLINICIAN noun **CLINICIANS** a doctor who works directly with patients, in a clinic, etc, as opposed to conducting experimental or theoretical work

CLINK noun **CLINKS** a short sharp ringing sound □ verb **CLINKS, CLINKING, CLINKED** to make or cause to make such a sound

CLINKER noun **CLINKERS** a mass of fused ash or slag left unburnt in a furnace

CLINT noun **CLINTS** one of a series of limestone blocks or ridges divided by fissures

CLIP noun **CLIPS** any of various devices, usually small ones, for holding things together or in position □ verb **CLIPS, CLIPPING, CLIPPED** to fasten something with a clip

CLIPBOARD noun **CLIPBOARDS** a firm board with a clip at the top for holding paper, forms, etc which can be used as a portable writing surface

CLIPPED adj said of the form of a word: shortened, eg deli from delicatessen

CLIPPER noun **CLIPPERS** a fast sailing ship with large sails

CLIPPERS plural noun a clipping device

CLIPPING noun **CLIPPINGS** a piece clipped off

CLIQUE noun **CLIQUES** a group of friends, professional colleagues, etc who stick together and are hostile towards outsiders

CLIQUEY adj **CLIQUIER, CLIQUIEST** characteristic of a clique; socially exclusive

CLIQUISH adj cliquey

CLITORAL adj of or relating to the clitoris

CLITORIS noun **CLITORISES** in female mammals: a small highly sensitive organ located in front of the opening of the vagina, which like the penis in males becomes erect when sexually stimulated

CLOACA noun **CLOACAE** in most vertebrates apart from mammals: the terminal region of the gut, into which the alimentary canal and the urinary and reproductive systems all open and discharge their contents

CLOACAL adj of or relating to a cloaca or sewer

CLOAK noun **CLOAKS** a loose outdoor garment, usually sleeveless, fastened at the neck so as to hang from the shoulders □ verb **CLOAKS, CLOAKING, CLOAKED** to cover up or conceal something

CLOAKROOM noun **CLOAKROOMS** especially in a public building: a room where coats, hats, etc may be left

CLOBBER [1] verb **CLOBBERS, CLOBBERING, CLOBBERED** to beat or hit someone very hard

CLOBBER [2] noun **CLOBBERS** clothing

CLOCHE noun **CLOCHES** a transparent glass or, now usually, plastic covering, bell-shaped or tunnel shaped, for protecting young plants from frost, etc

CLOCK noun **CLOCKS** a device for measuring and indicating time, usually by means of a digital display or pointers on a dial □ verb **CLOCKS, CLOCKING, CLOCKED** to measure or record (time) using such a device

CLOCKWISE adj moving, etc in the same direction as that in which the hands of a clock move □ adverb moving, etc in the same direction as that in which the hands of a clock move

CLOCKWORK noun **CLOCKWORKS** a mechanism like that of some clocks, working by means of gears and a spring that must be wound periodically □ adj operated by clockwork

CLOD noun **CLODS** a lump of earth, clay, etc

CLODDISH adj like a clod or clods

CLOG noun **CLOGS** a shoe carved entirely from wood, or having a thick wooden sole □ verb **CLOGS, CLOGGING, CLOGGED** to obstruct or become obstructed so that movement is difficult or impossible

CLOGGED adj choked up; blocked

CLOISONNÉ noun **CLOISONNÉS** a form of decoration with the pattern being formed in wire and filled in using coloured enamel □ adj decorated in this way

CLOISTER noun **CLOISTERS** a covered walkway built around a garden or quadrangle, which has an open colonnade on one side and a solid outer wall on the other □ verb **CLOISTERS, CLOISTERING, CLOISTERED** to keep someone away from the problems of normal life in the world

CLOISTERED adj secluded

CLOISTRAL adj relating or confined to a cloister; secluded

CLONAL adj having the characteristics of a clone

CLONE noun **CLONES** any of a group of genetically identical cells or organisms derived from a single parent cell or organism by asexual reproduction □ verb **CLONES, CLONING, CLONED** to produce a set of identical cells or organisms from (a single parent cell or organism)

CLONK noun **CLONKS** a noise of a heavy, especially metal, object striking something □ verb **CLONKS, CLONKING, CLONKED** to make or cause to make a clonking noise

CLOP noun **CLOPS** the hollow sound of a horse's hooves on hard ground □ verb **CLOPS, CLOPPING, CLOPPED** said of a horse: to walk along making this noise

CLOQUÉ noun **CLOQUÉS** an embossed fabric

CLOSE [1] adj **CLOSER, CLOSEST**

near in space or time; at a short distance ▫ *adverb* in a close manner; closely
CLOSE [2] *verb* **CLOSES, CLOSING, CLOSED** to shut ▫ *noun* **CLOSES** an end or conclusion
CLOSED *adj* shut; blocked
CLOSELY *adverb* in a close way; with close attention
CLOSENESS *noun* **CLOSENESSES** nearness in space or time
CLOSET *noun* **CLOSETS** a cupboard ▫ *verb* **CLOSETS, CLOSETING, CLOSETED** to shut up or away in private, eg for confidential discussion
CLOSURE *noun* **CLOSURES** the act of closing something, eg a business or a transport route; a parliamentary procedure for cutting short a debate ▫ *verb* **CLOSURES, CLOSURING, CLOSURED** to use this procedure for ending a debate, etc
CLOT *noun* **CLOTS** a soft semi-solid mass, especially one formed during the coagulation of blood ▫ *verb* **CLOTS, CLOTTING, CLOTTED** to form into clots
CLOTH *noun* **CLOTHS** woven, knitted or felted material
CLOTHE *verb* **CLOTHES, CLOTHING, CLOTHED, CLAD** to cover or provide someone with clothes
CLOTHES *plural noun* articles of dress for covering the body, for warmth, decoration, etc
CLOTHING *noun* **CLOTHINGS** clothes collectively
CLOUD *noun* **CLOUDS** a visible floating mass of small water droplets or ice crystals suspended in the atmosphere above the Earth's surface ▫ *verb* **CLOUDS, CLOUDING, CLOUDED** to make or become misty or cloudy
CLOUDILY *adverb* in a cloudy way; dimly
CLOUDLESS *adj* said especially of the sky: having no clouds
CLOUDY *adj* **CLOUDIER, CLOUDIEST** full of clouds; overcast
CLOUT *noun* **CLOUTS** a blow or cuff ▫ *verb* **CLOUTS, CLOUTING, CLOUTED** to hit or cuff
CLOVE [1] *noun* **CLOVES** one of the sections into which a compound bulb, especially of garlic, naturally splits
CLOVE [2] a past form of **cleave** [1]
CLOVEN [1] a past form of **cleave** [1] ▫ *adj* split; divided

CLOVER *noun* **CLOVERS** a small herbaceous plant that grows wild in temperate regions and which has leaves divided into three leaflets and small dense red or white flowers
CLOWN *noun* **CLOWNS** in a circus or pantomime, etc: a comic performer, usually wearing ridiculous clothes and make-up ▫ *verb* **CLOWNS, CLOWNING, CLOWNED** to play the clown
CLOWNERY *noun* **CLOWNERIES** a clown's performance
CLOWNISH *adj* of or like a clown
CLOY *verb* **CLOYS, CLOYING, CLOYED** to become distasteful through excess, especially of sweetness
CLOYING *adj* that cloys, especially through being excessively sweet
CLUB *noun* **CLUBS** a stick, usually thicker at one end, used as a weapon; a society or association ▫ *verb* **CLUBS, CLUBBING, CLUBBED** to beat or strike (a person, animal, etc) with a club
CLUBBABLE *adj* friendly; able to mix well socially
CLUBBED *adj* said of the fingers and toes: thickened at the tips
CLUBBER *noun* **CLUBBERS** a person who frequents nightclubs
CLUBBING *noun* **CLUBBINGS** a thickening of the tips of the fingers and toes
CLUBHOUSE *noun* **CLUBHOUSES** a building where a club meets, especially the premises of a sports club
CLUBMAN *noun* **CLUBMEN** a man who is a member of a lot of clubs
CLUBROOT *noun* **CLUBROOTS** a fungal disease of plants of the cabbage family, characterized by gall-like swellings of the roots and discoloration of the leaves
CLUBWOMAN *noun* **CLUBWOMEN** a woman who is a member of a lot of clubs
CLUCK *noun* **CLUCKS** the sound made by a hen ▫ *verb* **CLUCKS, CLUCKING, CLUCKED** said of a hen: to make such a sound
CLUE *noun* **CLUES** a fact or circumstance which helps towards the solution of a crime or a mystery ▫ *verb* **CLUES, CLUEING, CLUED** to direct or indicate by giving a clue
CLUELESS *adj* stupid, incompetent or ignorant
CLUMP *noun* **CLUMPS** a group or

cluster of something, eg trees, plants or people standing close together ▫ *verb* **CLUMPS, CLUMPING, CLUMPED** to form into clumps
CLUMPY *adj* **CLUMPIER, CLUMPIEST** like a clump
CLUMSILY *adverb* in a clumsy way
CLUMSY *adj* **CLUMSIER, CLUMSIEST** unskilful with the hands or awkward and ungainly in movement
CLUNG past form of **cling**
CLUNK *noun* **CLUNKS** the sound of a heavy object, especially a metal one, striking something ▫ *verb* **CLUNKS, CLUNKING, CLUNKED** to make or cause to make a clunking sound
CLUNKY *adj* **CLUNKIER, CLUNKIEST** making a clunking noise
CLUSTER *noun* **CLUSTERS** a small group or gathering ▫ *verb* **CLUSTERS, CLUSTERING, CLUSTERED** to form into a cluster or clusters
CLUSTERED *adj* grouped
CLUSTERY *adj* growing in clusters
CLUTCH [1] *noun* **CLUTCHES** a number of eggs laid in a single nest or at the same time
CLUTCH [2] *verb* **CLUTCHES, CLUTCHING, CLUTCHED** to grasp something tightly
CLUTTER *noun* **CLUTTERS** an untidy accumulation of objects, or the confused overcrowded state caused by it ▫ *verb* **CLUTTERS, CLUTTERING, CLUTTERED** to overcrowd something or make it untidy with accumulated objects
CLUTTERED *adj* made untidy with accumulated objects

CLY *verb* **CLIES, CLYING, CLIED** an old word meaning to seize or steal

COACH *noun* **COACHES** a bus designed for long-distance travel; a horse-drawn carriage ▫ *verb* **COACHES, COACHING, COACHED** to travel by coach
COACHING *noun* **COACHINGS** tutoring; instruction
COACHMAN *noun* **COACHMEN** the driver of a horse-drawn coach
COACHWORK *noun* **COACHWORKS** the painted outer bodywork of a motor or rail vehicle
COAGULANT *noun* **COAGULANTS**

a substance which causes or facilitates coagulation

COAGULATE verb COAGULATES, COAGULATING, COAGULATED to cause (blood or a liquid) to clot, curdle, or form a soft semi-solid mass

COAGULUM noun COAGULA a mass of coagulated matter

COAL noun COALS a hard brittle carbonaceous rock, usually black or brown in colour, formed by the compaction of partially decomposed plant material and used as a fuel □ verb COALS, COALING, COALED to take in or provide with coal

COALESCE verb COALESCES, COALESCING, COALESCED to come together so as to form a single mass

COALFACE noun COALFACES in a coal mine: the exposed surface from which coal is being cut

COALFIELD noun COALFIELDS an area where there is coal underground

COALFISH noun COALFISHES a coley

COALITION noun COALITIONS a combination or temporary alliance, especially between political parties

COAMING noun COAMINGS the raised edging round the hatches on a ship, to keep out water

COARSE adj COARSER, COARSEST rough or open in texture

COARSELY adverb in a coarse way

COARSEN verb COARSENS, COARSENING, COARSENED to make or become coarse

COAST noun COASTS the zone of land that borders the sea □ verb COASTS, COASTING, COASTED to travel downhill, eg on a bicycle or in a motor vehicle, relying on gravity or momentum rather than power

COASTAL adj of or relating to the coast

COASTER noun COASTERS a vessel that sails along the coast taking goods to coastal ports

COASTLINE noun COASTLINES the shape of the coast, especially as seen on a map, or from the sea or air

COAT noun COATS an outer garment with long sleeves, typically reaching to the knees □ verb COATS, COATING, COATED to cover with a layer of something

COATI noun COATIS a raccoon-like mammal, which has reddish-brown fur, a long narrow muzzle with an overhanging tip, and a long banded tail, and which lives in N and S America

COATING noun COATINGS a covering or outer layer

COAX verb COAXES, COAXING, COAXED to persuade someone, using flattery, promises, kind words, etc

COAXER noun COAXERS a person who coaxes

COAXIAL adj having or mounted on a common axis

COAXINGLY adverb in a coaxing way

COB noun COBS a short-legged sturdy horse used for riding

COBALT noun COBALTS an element commonly used in alloys to produce cutting tools and magnets

COBALTIC adj of or relating to cobalt

COBBER noun COBBERS used as a form of address: a pal or mate

COBBLE [1] noun COBBLES a rounded stone used especially formerly to surface streets

COBBLE [2] verb COBBLES, COBBLING, COBBLED to mend (shoes)

COBBLED adj paved with cobblestones

COBBLER noun COBBLERS someone who makes or mends shoes

COBBLERS plural noun nonsense

COBRA noun COBRAS any of various species of venomous snake found in Africa and Asia which, when threatened, rear up and spread the skin behind the head to form a flattened hood

COBWEB noun COBWEBS a web of fine sticky threads spun by a spider

COBWEBBY adj COBWEBBIER, COBWEBBIEST covered with cobwebs

COBZA noun COBZAS a Romanian folk instrument

COCA noun COCAS either of two S American shrubs whose leaves contain cocaine

COCAINE noun COCAINES an addictive narcotic drug, obtained from the leaves of the coca plant, which is sometimes used medicinally as a local anaesthetic

but more commonly used as an illegal stimulant

COCCUS noun COCCI a spherical bacterium

COCCYX noun COCCYGES in humans and certain apes: a small triangular tail-like bone at the base of the spine

COCHINEAL noun COCHINEALS a bright red pigment widely used as a food colouring, eg in alcoholic drinks

COCHLEA noun COCHLEAS in the inner ear of vertebrates: a hollow spirally coiled structure which converts the vibrations of sound waves into nerve impulses, which are then interpreted by the brain as sound

COCHLEAR adj relating to the cochlea of the ear; spoon-shaped

COCK noun COCKS a male bird, especially an adult male chicken □ verb COCKS, COCKING, COCKED to lift; to stick up

COCKADE noun COCKADES a feather or a rosette of ribbon worn on the hat as a badge

COCKATEEL noun COCKATEELS a cockatiel

COCKATIEL noun COCKATIELS a small crested Australian parrot of the cockatoo family

COCKATOO noun COCKATOOS any of 16 species of the parrot family found in woodland areas in Australasia, which are light-coloured with a brightly coloured erectile crest on their heads

COCKER noun COCKERS a small long-haired breed of spaniel with silky ears

COCKEREL noun COCKERELS a young cock

COCKFIGHT noun COCKFIGHTS a fight between cocks wearing sharp metal spurs

COCKILY adverb in a cocky way

COCKINESS noun COCKINESSES cheeky self-confidence

COCKLE noun COCKLES any of about 200 species of edible bivalve shellfish with a rounded and ribbed shell

COCKNEY noun COCKNEYS a native of London, especially of the East End □ adj relating to Cockneys or their dialect

COCKPIT noun COCKPITS in an aircraft: the compartment for the pilot and crew

COCKROACH noun COCKROACHES a large insect

with a flattened body, long slender antennae and biting mouthparts, which feeds mainly nocturnally on decaying animal and vegetable matter

COCKSCOMB *noun* **COCKSCOMBS** the fleshy red crest on a cock's head

COCKSURE *adj* foolishly over-confident

COCKSWAIN *noun* **COCKSWAINS** a coxswain

COCKTAIL *noun* **COCKTAILS** a mixed drink of spirits and other liquors

COCKY *adj* **COCKIER, COCKIEST** cheekily self-confident

COCO *noun* **COCOS** a coconut tree

COCOA *noun* **COCOAS** the seed of the cacao tree

COCONUT *noun* **COCONUTS** a tropical palm tree cultivated for its edible fruit

COCOON *noun* **COCOONS** the protective silky covering that many animals, eg spiders and earthworms, spin around their eggs ◻ *verb* **COCOONS, COCOONING, COCOONED** to wrap someone or something up as if in a cocoon

COCOONING *noun* the practice of choosing to spend one's spare time with a partner or one's family, rather than taking part in more social activities

COCOTTE *noun* **COCOTTES** a small lidded pot for oven and table use, usually intended for an individual portion

COD [1] *noun* **COD** a large soft-finned fish, found mainly in the N Atlantic Ocean, which is popular in western countries as a food fish

COD [2] *verb* **CODS, CODDING, CODDED** to hoax someone

CODA *noun* **CODAS** a passage added to the end of a movement or piece, to bring it to a satisfying conclusion

CODDLE *verb* **CODDLES, CODDLING, CODDLED** to cook something (especially eggs) gently in hot, rather than boiling, water

CODE *noun* **CODES** a system of words, letters or symbols, used in place of those really intended, for secrecy's or brevity's sake ◻ *verb* **CODES, CODING, CODED** to put something into a code

CODEINE *noun* **CODEINES** a morphine derivative that relieves

mild to moderate pain, has a sedative effect and suppresses the coughing reflex

CODEX *noun* **CODICES** an ancient manuscript volume, bound in book form

CODFISH *noun* **CODFISHES** a cod

CODGER *noun* **CODGERS** a man, especially an old and strange one

CODICIL *noun* **CODICILS** a supplement to a will, which makes extra provisions or revokes some part of the original draft

CODIFIER *noun* **CODIFIERS** a person who codifies

CODIFY *verb* **CODIFIES, CODIFYING, CODIFIED** to arrange something into a systematic code, eg laws, etc

CODLING *noun* **CODLINGS** a young cod

CODON *noun* **CODONS** in a molecule of DNA or messenger RNA: a set of three bases that is specific for one particular amino acid

CODPIECE *noun* **CODPIECES** a pouch attached to the front of a man's breeches, covering his genitals

COELIAC *adj* relating to the abdomen ◻ *noun* **COELIACS** someone suffering from a condition in which the lining of the small intestine is abnormally sensitive to gluten

COELOM *noun* **COELOMS** in multicellular animals: the main body cavity which typically forms the cavity around the gut in eg annelids and vertebrates

COENOBITE *noun* **COENOBITES** a member of a monastic community

COERCE *verb* **COERCES, COERCING, COERCED** to force or compel someone to do something, using threats, etc

COERCIBLE *adj* capable of being coerced

COERCION *noun* **COERCIONS** restraint; government by force

COERCIVE *adj* having power to coerce; compelling

COEVAL *adj* belonging to the same age or period of time ◻ *noun* **COEVALS** someone or something from the same age or period of time

COFFEE *noun* **COFFEES** a popular drink, usually containing caffeine, made from the roasted and ground beans of the coffee plant

COFFER *noun* **COFFERS** a large chest for holding valuables

COFFERDAM *noun* **COFFERDAMS** a watertight chamber allowing construction workers to carry out building work underwater

COFFIN *noun* **COFFINS** a box into which a corpse is put for cremation or burial ◻ *verb* **COFFINS, COFFINING, COFFINED** to place in a coffin

COG *noun* **COGS** one of a series of teeth on the edge of a wheel or bar which engage with another series of teeth to bring about motion

COGENCY *noun* **COGENCIES** convincing or persuasive force

COGENT *adj* said of arguments, reasons, etc: strong; persuasive; convincing

COGENTLY *adverb* in a cogent way

COGITATE *verb* **COGITATES, COGITATING, COGITATED** to think deeply; to ponder

COGNATE *adj* descended from or related to a common ancestor ◻ *noun* **COGNATES** something that is related to something else

COGNATION *noun* **COGNATIONS** relationship

COGNISANT *adj* cognizant

COGNITION *noun* **COGNITIONS** the mental processes, such as perception, reasoning, problem-solving, etc, which enable humans to experience and process knowledge and information

COGNITIVE *adj* relating to cognition

COGNIZANT *adj* aware of something or having knowledge of something

COGNOMEN *noun* **COGNOMENS** a Roman's third name, often in origin an epithet or nickname, which became their family name

COGWHEEL *noun* **COGWHEELS** a toothed wheel

COHABIT *verb* **COHABITS, COHABITING, COHABITED** to live together as husband and wife, usually without being married

COHABITEE *noun* **COHABITEES** a person who cohabits with someone, usually without being married to them

COHERE *verb* **COHERES, COHERING, COHERED** to stick together

COHERENCE *noun* **COHERENCES** a sticking together; consistency

COHERENT *adj* said of a description or argument: logically and clearly developed; consistent

COHESION *noun* **COHESIONS** the

process or state of sticking together

COHESIVE *adj* having the power of cohering

COHORT *noun* **COHORTS** in the ancient Roman army: one of the ten divisions of a legion

COIF *noun* **COIFS** a hairstyle □ *verb* **COIFS, COIFING, COIFED** to dress (hair); to dress someone's hair

COIFFEUR *noun* **COIFFEURS** a male hairdresser

COIFFEUSE *noun* **COIFFEUSES** a female hairdresser

COIFFURE *noun* **COIFFURES** a hairstyle □ *verb* **COIFFURES, COIFFURING, COIFFURED** to dress (hair); to dress someone's hair

COIL *verb* **COILS, COILING, COILED** to wind round and round in loops to form rings or a spiral □ *noun* **COILS** something looped into rings or a spiral

COIN *noun* **COINS** a small metal disc stamped for use as currency □ *verb* **COINS, COINING, COINED** to manufacture (coins) from metal

COINAGE *noun* **COINAGES** the process of coining

COINCIDE *verb* **COINCIDES, COINCIDING, COINCIDED** to happen at the same time

COIR *noun* **COIRS** fibre from coconut shells, used for making ropes, matting, etc

COITAL *adj* relating to sexual intercourse

COITION *noun* **COITIONS** sexual intercourse

COITUS *noun* **COITUSES** coition

COKE *noun* **COKES** a brittle greyish-black porous solid consisting of the residue of carbon and ash after destructive distillation, most commonly used as a smokeless fuel for domestic heating □ *verb* **COKES, COKING, COKED** to convert (coal) into coke

COL *noun* **COLS** in a mountain range: a pass between two adjacent peaks, or the lowest point in a ridge, often used for lines of communication, eg roads

COLA *noun* **COLAS** an evergreen tree, native to Africa but cultivated in other tropical regions for its seeds called cola nuts

COLANDER *noun* **COLANDERS** a perforated bowl made from metal or plastic used to drain the water from cooked vegetables, etc

COLD *adj* **COLDER, COLDEST** low in temperature; not hot or warm

□ *adverb* without preparation or rehearsal □ *noun* **COLDS** lack of heat or warmth; cold weather

COLDLY *adverb* with an unfriendly manner

COLDNESS *noun* **COLDNESSES** the condition of being cold

COLE *noun* **COLES** any of various vegetables belonging to the cabbage family

COLECTOMY *noun* **COLECTOMIES** the surgical removal of the colon (part of the large intestine)

COLESLAW *noun* **COLESLAWS** a salad made with finely-cut raw cabbage, onion and carrots, etc, bound together, usually with mayonnaise

COLEUS *noun* **COLEUSES** a perennial plant, native to Java, which is widely grown as a house plant for its ornamental and variegated leaves

COLEY *noun* **COLEYS** a large edible fish belonging to the cod family with white or grey flesh, found in the inshore waters of the N Atlantic

COLIC *noun* **COLICS** severe spasmodic abdominal pain, usually caused in adults by constipation or partial or complete obstruction of the intestine

COLICKY *adj* **COLICKIER, COLICKIEST** like, suffering from or causing colic

COLISEUM *noun* **COLISEUMS** a large stadium or amphitheatre for sports and other entertainment

COLITIS *noun* **COLITISES** inflammation of the colon (part of the large intestine)

COLLAGE *noun* **COLLAGES** a design or picture made up of pieces of paper, cloth, photographs, etc glued onto a background surface

COLLAGEN *noun* **COLLAGENS** a tough fibrous protein of connective tissue found in skin, bones, teeth, cartilage, ligaments, etc

COLLAGIST *noun* **COLLAGISTS** a person who makes collages

COLLAPSE *verb* **COLLAPSES, COLLAPSING, COLLAPSED** said of buildings, etc: to fall, give way or cave in □ *noun* **COLLAPSES** a process or act of collapsing

COLLAR *noun* **COLLARS** a band or flap of any of various shapes, folded over or standing up round the neck of a garment □ *verb* **COLLARS,**

COLLARING, COLLARED to seize something by the collar

COLLARED *adj* having a collar

COLLATE *verb* **COLLATES, COLLATING, COLLATED** to study and compare (texts, evidence, etc)

COLLATION *noun* **COLLATIONS** the act of collating

COLLATOR *noun* **COLLATORS** a person or device which collates

COLLEAGUE *noun* **COLLEAGUES** a fellow-worker, especially in a profession

COLLECT[1] *verb* **COLLECTS, COLLECTING, COLLECTED** to bring or be brought together; to gather □ *adj* said of a telephone call: paid for by the person receiving it □ *adverb* reversing the charges

COLLECT[2] *noun* **COLLECTS** a short form of prayer used in the Anglican and Roman Catholic Churches

COLLECTED *adj* said of a writer's works: all published together in a single volume or a uniform set of volumes

COLLECTOR *noun* **COLLECTORS** someone who collects, as a job or hobby

COLLEEN *noun* **COLLEENS** a girl

COLLEGE *noun* **COLLEGES** an institution, either self-contained or part of a university, which provides higher education, further education or professional training

COLLIDE *verb* **COLLIDES, COLLIDING, COLLIDED** to crash together or crash into someone or something

COLLIE *noun* **COLLIES** any of several medium-sized highly intelligent long-haired breeds of dog, usually black and white or brown and white, originally used for herding sheep

COLLIER *noun* **COLLIERS** a coal-miner

COLLIERY *noun* **COLLIERIES** a coalmine with its surrounding buildings

COLLIMATE *verb* **COLLIMATES, COLLIMATING, COLLIMATED** to make parallel

COLLINEAR *adj* lying on the same straight line

COLLISION *noun* **COLLISIONS** a violent meeting of objects; a crash

COLLOCATE *verb* **COLLOCATES, COLLOCATING, COLLOCATED** to arrange or group together in some kind of order

COLLOID noun **COLLOIDS** an intermediate state between a suspension and a true solution, in which fine particles of one substance are spread evenly throughout another

COLLOIDAL adj of or relating to a colloid

COLLOQUY noun **COLLOQUIES** a conversation; talk

COLLUDE verb **COLLUDES, COLLUDING, COLLUDED** to plot secretly with someone, especially with a view to committing fraud

COLLUSION noun **COLLUSIONS** secret and illegal co-operation for the purpose of fraud or other criminal activity, etc

COLLUSIVE adj relating to a collusion; conspiratorial

COLOGNE noun **COLOGNES** a mild type of perfume, originally made in Cologne in Germany in 1709

COLON noun **COLONS** a punctuation mark (:), properly used to introduce a list, an example or an explanation

COLONEL noun **COLONELS** a senior army officer, in charge of a regiment

COLONELCY noun **COLONELCIES** the rank or office of colonel

COLONIAL adj relating to, belonging to or living in a colony or colonies ▫ noun **COLONIALS** an inhabitant of a colony

COLONIC adj of or relating to the colon (part of the large intestine)

COLONISE verb **COLONISES, COLONISING, COLONISED** to colonize

COLONIST noun **COLONISTS** someone who settles in a colony

COLONIZE verb **COLONIZES, COLONIZING, COLONIZED** to establish a colony in (an area or country)

COLONNADE noun **COLONNADES** a row of columns placed at regular intervals

COLONY noun **COLONIES** a settlement abroad established and controlled by the founding country

COLOPHON noun **COLOPHONS** an inscription at the end of a printed book or manuscript giving the name of the writer, printer, etc and place and date of production

COLOR noun **COLORS** colour ▫ verb **COLORS, COLORING, COLORED** to colour

COLORANT noun **COLORANTS** a substance used for colouring

COLOSSAL adj huge; vast

COLOSSEUM noun **COLOSSEUMS** a large stadium or amphitheatre for sports and other entertainment

COLOSSUS noun **COLOSSUSES** a gigantic statue

COLOSTOMY noun **COLOSTOMIES** an operation in which part of the colon is brought to the surface of the body through an incision in the abdomen, forming an artificial anus through which the colon can be emptied

COLOSTRUM noun **COLOSTRUMS** in mammals: the yellowish milky fluid secreted by the mammary glands immediately before and after giving birth, which is followed by the secretion of the true milk

COLOUR noun **COLOURS** the visual sensation produced when light of different wavelengths is absorbed by the cones of the retina and relayed, in the form of nerve impulses, to the brain ▫ verb **COLOURS, COLOURING, COLOURED** to put colour on to something

COLOURANT noun **COLOURANTS** a colorant

COLOURED adj having colour, or a specified colour

COLOUREDS plural noun coloured items of clothing for washing

COLOURFUL adj full of especially bright colour

COLOURING noun **COLOURINGS** a substance used to give colour, eg to food

COLOURISE verb **COLOURISES, COLOURISING, COLOURISED** to colourize

COLOURIST noun **COLOURISTS** someone skilled in the use of colour, especially an artist

COLOURIZE verb **COLOURIZES, COLOURIZING, COLOURIZED** to add colour to (a film made in black and white), with the aid of a computer

COLOURS plural noun the flag of a nation, regiment or ship

COLOURWAY noun **COLOURWAYS** a combination of colours in patterned material, etc

COLT noun **COLTS** a male horse or pony less than four years old

COLTISH adj youthfully awkward in movement or behaviour

COLTSFOOT noun **COLTSFOOTS** a perennial wild plant with bright yellow flowers and large soft heart-shaped leaves

COLUGO noun **COLUGOS** a nocturnal mammal, native to SE Asia, with a large membrane between its fore and hind limbs extending to the tail, which it uses to glide through the air

COLUMBINE noun **COLUMBINES** a perennial wild flower related to the buttercup

COLUMBIUM noun **COLUMBIUMS** former name for niobium

COLUMN noun **COLUMNS** a vertical pillar, usually cylindrical, with a base and a capital (the slab of stone that forms the top section)

COLUMNAR adj relating to columns; like a column

COLUMNED adj having columns

COLUMNIST noun **COLUMNISTS** someone who writes a regular section of a newspaper

COMA noun **COMAS** a prolonged state of deep unconsciousness from which a person cannot be awakened, caused by head injury, brain damage, stroke, etc

COMATOSE adj in a coma

COMB noun **COMBS** a rigid toothed device for tidying and arranging the hair ▫ verb **COMBS, COMBING, COMBED** to arrange, smooth or clean something with a comb

COMBAT noun **COMBATS** fighting; a struggle or contest ▫ verb **COMBATS, COMBATING, COMBATED** to fight against someone or something; to oppose something

COMBATANT adj involved in or ready for a fight ▫ noun **COMBATANTS** someone involved in or ready for a fight

COMBATIVE adj inclined to fight or argue

COMBE noun **COMBES** a coomb

COMBINE verb **COMBINES, COMBINING, COMBINED** to join together; to unite ▫ noun **COMBINES** a group of people or businesses associated for a common purpose

COMBO noun **COMBOS** a small jazz dance band

COME verb **COMES, COMING, CAME** to move in the direction of the speaker or hearer; to reach a place; to arrive

COMEBACK noun **COMEBACKS** a return to former success, or to the stage, etc after a period of retirement or obscurity

COMEDIAN noun **COMEDIANS** an

entertainer who tells jokes, performs comic sketches, etc

COMEDO *noun* **COMEDOS** a mass of fatty material forming a plug blocking one of the sebaceous ducts in the skin

COMEDOWN *noun* **COMEDOWNS** a decline in social status

COMEDY *noun* **COMEDIES** a light amusing play or film

COMELY *adj* **COMELIER, COMELIEST** said of a person: attractive in a wholesome way

COMER *noun* **COMERS** someone who comes at the specified time

COMET *noun* **COMETS** in the solar system: a small body which follows an elliptical orbit around the Sun, leaving a trail

COMFIT *noun* **COMFITS** a type of sweet, containing a sugar-coated nut, liquorice, etc

COMFORT *noun* **COMFORTS** a state of contentedness or wellbeing *verb* **COMFORTS, COMFORTING, COMFORTED** to relieve from suffering; to console or soothe

COMFORTER *noun* **COMFORTERS** someone who comforts

COMFREY *noun* **COMFREYS** a bristly, robust, perennial plant belonging to the borage family, with tubular white, pink or purple flowers, traditionally used medicinally

COMFY *adj* **COMFIER, COMFIEST** comfortable

COMIC *adj* characterized by or relating to comedy; intended to amuse *noun* **COMICS** a comedian

COMICAL *adj* funny; amusing; humorous; ludicrous

COMICALLY *adverb* in a comical way

COMING *noun* **COMINGS** an arrival or approach

COMITY *noun* **COMITIES** civility; politeness; courtesy

COMMA *noun* **COMMAS** a punctuation mark (,) indicating a slight pause or break made for the sake of clarity, to separate items in a list, etc

COMMAND *verb* **COMMANDS, COMMANDING, COMMANDED** to order formally *noun* **COMMANDS** an order

COMMANDER *noun* **COMMANDERS** someone who commands

COMMANDING *adj* powerful; leading; controlling

COMMANDO *noun* **COMMANDOS** a unit of soldiers specially trained to carry out dangerous and difficult attacks or raids

COMMENCE *verb* **COMMENCES, COMMENCING, COMMENCED** to begin

COMMEND *verb* **COMMENDS, COMMENDING, COMMENDED** to praise someone

COMMENSAL *adj* said of two organisms of different species: living in close association with each other, with one gaining from the relationship, while the other remains unaffected by it *noun* **COMMENSALS** the organism in a commensal relationship which benefits from it

COMMENT *noun* **COMMENTS** a remark or observation, especially a critical one *verb* **COMMENTS, COMMENTING, COMMENTED** to make observations, remarks, etc

COMMERCE *noun* **COMMERCES** the buying and selling of commodities and services

COMMIE *noun* **COMMIES** short form of communist *adj* short form of communist

COMMINUTE *verb* **COMMINUTES, COMMINUTING, COMMINUTED** to crush (a solid) into tiny pieces

COMMIS *noun* **COMMIS** an assistant or trainee waiter or chef

COMMISSAR *noun* **COMMISSARS** in the former Soviet Union: the head of a government department

COMMIT *verb* **COMMITS, COMMITTING, COMMITTED** to carry out or perpetrate (a crime, offence, error, etc); to have someone put in a prison or mental institution

COMMITTAL *noun* **COMMITTALS** the action of committing someone to a prison or mental institution

COMMITTEE *noun* **COMMITTEES** a group of people selected by and from a larger body, eg a club, to undertake certain duties on its behalf

COMMODE *noun* **COMMODES** a chair with a hinged seat, designed to conceal a chamber pot

COMMODITY *noun* **COMMODITIES** something that is bought and sold, especially a manufactured product or raw material

COMMODORE *noun* **COMMODORES** in the navy: an officer just below a rear admiral in rank

COMMON *adj* **COMMONER, COMMONEST** often met with; frequent; familiar *noun*

COMMONS a piece of land that is publicly owned or available for public use

COMMONER *noun* **COMMONERS** someone who is not a member of the nobility

COMMONS *plural noun* the ordinary people

COMMOTION *noun* **COMMOTIONS** a disturbance; an upheaval

COMMUNAL *adj* relating or belonging to a community

COMMUNE [1] *noun* **COMMUNES** a number of unrelated families and individuals living together as a mutually supportive community, with shared accommodation, supplies, responsibilities, etc

COMMUNE [2] *verb* **COMMUNES, COMMUNING, COMMUNED** to communicate intimately or confidentially

COMMUNION *noun*

COMMUNIONS the sharing of thoughts, beliefs or feelings

COMMUNISM *noun*

COMMUNISMS a political ideology advocating a classless society, the abolition of private ownership and all sources of wealth and production being collectively owned and controlled by the people

COMMUNIST *noun* **COMMUNISTS** a supporter of or believer in communism *adj* relating to communism

COMMUNITY *noun* **COMMUNITIES** the group of people living in a particular place

COMMUTATE *verb* **COMMUTATES, COMMUTATING, COMMUTATED** to change an alternating current into a direct one and vice versa

COMMUTE *verb* **COMMUTES, COMMUTING, COMMUTED** to travel regularly between two places which are a significant distance apart, especially between home and work in a city, etc

COMMUTER *noun* **COMMUTERS** someone who regularly travels a significant distance between home and work

COMPACT *adj* **COMPACTER, COMPACTEST** firm and dense in form or texture *verb* **COMPACTS, COMPACTING, COMPACTED** to compress *noun* **COMPACTS** a small case for women's face powder, usually including a mirror

COMPACTLY *adverb* in a compact way

COMPANION *noun* **COMPANIONS** a friend, comrade or frequent associate

COMPANY *noun* **COMPANIES** the presence of another person or other people; companionship

COMPARE *verb* **COMPARES, COMPARING, COMPARED** to examine (items, etc) to see what differences or similarities they have

COMPASS *noun* **COMPASSES** any device for finding direction, especially one consisting of a magnetized needle that swings freely on a pivot and points to magnetic north, from which true north can be calculated □ *verb* **COMPASSES, COMPASSING, COMPASSED** to pass or go round

COMPEER *noun* **COMPEERS** an equal; a companion or comrade

COMPEL *verb* **COMPELS, COMPELLING, COMPELLED** to force; to drive

COMPELLING *adj* powerful; forcing one to agree, etc

COMPERE *noun* **COMPERES** someone who hosts a radio or television show, introduces performers, etc □ *verb* **COMPERES, COMPERING, COMPERED** to act as compere for (a show)

COMPETE *verb* **COMPETES, COMPETING, COMPETED** to take part in a contest

COMPETENT *adj* efficient

COMPILE *verb* **COMPILES, COMPILING, COMPILED** to collect and organize (information, etc) from different sources

COMPILER *noun* **COMPILERS** someone who compiles information, etc

COMPLAIN *verb* **COMPLAINS, COMPLAINING, COMPLAINED** to express dissatisfaction or displeasure

COMPLAINING *adj* that complains

COMPLAINT *noun* **COMPLAINTS** the act of complaining

COMPLETE *adj* **COMPLETER, COMPLETEST** whole; finished; with nothing missing □ *verb* **COMPLETES, COMPLETING, COMPLETED** to finish

COMPLEX *adj* composed of many interrelated parts □ *noun*

COMPLEXES something made of interrelating parts, eg a multi-purpose building

COMPLIANT *adj* inclined to comply with or yield to the wishes of others; obedient; submissive

COMPLIN *noun* **COMPLINS** compline

COMPLINE *noun* **COMPLINES** the seventh of the canonical hours, completing the set hours for prayer

COMPLY *verb* **COMPLIES, COMPLYING, COMPLIED** to act in obedience to an order, command, request, etc; to agree

COMPONENT *noun* **COMPONENTS** any of the parts or elements that make up a machine, engine, instrument, etc □ *adj* functioning as one of the parts of something; constituent

COMPORT *verb* **COMPORTS, COMPORTING, COMPORTED** to behave in a specified way

COMPOSE *verb* **COMPOSES, COMPOSING, COMPOSED** to create (music)

COMPOSED *adj* said of a person: calm; controlled

COMPOSER *noun* **COMPOSERS** someone who composes, especially music

COMPOSITE *adj* made up of different parts, materials or styles □ *noun* **COMPOSITES** a member of the largest family of flowering plants (Compositae) with a flower head consisting of a crowd of tiny florets often surrounded by a circle of bracts, eg daisy □ *verb* **COMPOSITES, COMPOSITING, COMPOSITED** to pool and combine proposals from local branches eg of a political party, etc, so as to produce a satisfactory list for discussion at a national level

COMPOST *noun* **COMPOSTS** a mixture of decomposed organic substances such as rotting vegetable matter, etc, which is used to enrich soil and nourish plants □ *verb* **COMPOSTS, COMPOSTING, COMPOSTED** to treat with compost

COMPOSURE *noun* **COMPOSURES** mental and emotional calmness; self-control

COMPOUND *noun* **COMPOUNDS** a substance composed of two or more elements combined in fixed proportions and held together by chemical bonds □ *adj* composed of a number of parts or ingredients

□ *verb* **COMPOUNDS, COMPOUNDING, COMPOUNDED** to make (especially something bad) much worse

COMPRESS *verb* **COMPRESSES, COMPRESSING, COMPRESSED** to press, squeeze or squash together □ *noun* **COMPRESSES** a cloth or pad soaked in water and pressed against a part of the body to reduce swelling, stop bleeding, etc

COMPRISE *verb* **COMPRISES, COMPRISING, COMPRISED** to contain, include or consist of something specified

COMPUTE *verb* **COMPUTES, COMPUTING, COMPUTED** to calculate, estimate or reckon, especially with the aid of a computer

COMPUTER *noun* **COMPUTERS** an electronic device which processes data at great speed according to a program stored within the device

COMRADE *noun* **COMRADES** a friend or companion

COMRADELY *adj* like a comrade

CON *noun* **CONS** a confidence trick □ *verb* **CONS, CONNING, CONNED** to swindle or trick someone, especially after winning their trust

CONCAVE *adj* said of a surface or shape: inward-curving, like the inside of a bowl □ *verb* **CONCAVES, CONCAVING, CONCAVED** to make or become concave

CONCAVITY *noun* **CONCAVITIES** the quality of being concave; a hollow

CONCEAL *verb* **CONCEALS, CONCEALING, CONCEALED** to hide; to place out of sight

CONCEALER *noun* **CONCEALERS** a person or thing that conceals

CONCEDE *verb* **CONCEDES, CONCEDING, CONCEDED** to admit to be true or correct

CONCEDER *noun* **CONCEDERS** a person who concedes

CONCEIT *noun* **CONCEITS** an inflated opinion of oneself

CONCEITED *adj* having too good an opinion of oneself

CONCEIVE *verb* **CONCEIVES, CONCEIVING, CONCEIVED** to become pregnant

CONCENTRE *verb* **CONCENTRES, CONCENTRING, CONCENTRED** to meet or cause to meet in a common centre

CONCEPT *noun* **CONCEPTS** a notion; an abstract or general idea

CONCERN *verb* **CONCERNS, CONCERNING, CONCERNED** to have to do with someone or something; to be about someone or something □ *noun* **CONCERNS** worry or a cause of worry

CONCERNED *adj* worried

CONCERT *noun* **CONCERTS** a musical performance given before an audience by singers or players □ *verb* **CONCERTS, CONCERTING, CONCERTED** to endeavour or plan by arrangement

CONCERTED *adj* planned and carried out jointly

CONCERTO *noun* **CONCERTOS, CONCERTI** a composition for an orchestra and one or more solo performers

CONCH *noun* **CONCHS, CONCHES** any of a family of large marine snails, native to warm shallow tropical waters, which have large colourful shells with a long narrow opening and an outer lip which is generally expanded to form a broad plate

CONCIERGE *noun* **CONCIERGES** a warden or caretaker of a block of flats, especially one who lives on the premises

CONCISE *adj* **CONCISER, CONCISEST** brief but comprehensive

CONCISELY *adverb* in a concise way

CONCISION *noun* **CONCISIONS** the quality of being concise

CONCLAVE *noun* **CONCLAVES** a private or secret meeting

CONCLUDE *verb* **CONCLUDES, CONCLUDING, CONCLUDED** to come or bring to an end

CONCOCT *verb* **CONCOCTS, CONCOCTING, CONCOCTED** to make something, especially ingeniously from a variety of ingredients

CONCOCTER *noun* **CONCOCTERS** a person who concocts

CONCOCTOR *noun* **CONCOCTORS** a concocter

CONCORD *noun* **CONCORDS** agreement; peace or harmony

CONCORDAT *noun* **CONCORDATS** an agreement between church and state, especially the Roman Catholic church and a secular government

CONCOURSE *noun* **CONCOURSES** in a railway station, airport, etc: a large open area where people can gather

CONCRETE *noun* **CONCRETES** a building material consisting of a mixture of cement, sand, gravel and water, which forms a hard rock-like mass when dry □ *adj* relating to items which can be felt, touched, seen, etc □ *verb* **CONCRETES, CONCRETING, CONCRETED** to cover with or embed in concrete

CONCUBINE *noun* **CONCUBINES** a woman who lives with a man and has sexual intercourse with him, without being married to him

CONCUR *verb* **CONCURS, CONCURRING, CONCURRED** to agree

CONCUSS *verb* **CONCUSSES, CONCUSSING, CONCUSSED** to cause injury to someone's brain often with temporary loss of consciousness, eg by a blow or fall

CONDEMN *verb* **CONDEMNS, CONDEMNING, CONDEMNED** to declare something to be wrong or evil

CONDENSE *verb* **CONDENSES, CONDENSING, CONDENSED** to decrease the volume, size or density of (a substance)

CONDENSER *noun* **CONDENSERS** an apparatus for changing a vapour into a liquid by cooling it and allowing it to condense

CONDIGN *adj* usually said of punishment: well-deserved; fitting

CONDIGNLY *adverb* in a condign way

CONDIMENT *noun* **CONDIMENTS** any seasoning or sauce, eg salt, pepper, mustard, etc, added to food at the table, to give extra flavour

CONDITION *noun* **CONDITIONS** a particular state of existence □ *verb* **CONDITIONS, CONDITIONING, CONDITIONED** to accustom or train someone or something to behave or react in a particular way; to influence them or it

CONDOLE *verb* **CONDOLES, CONDOLING, CONDOLED** to express sympathy

CONDOM *noun* **CONDOMS** a thin rubber sheath worn on the penis during sexual intercourse, to prevent conception and the spread of sexually transmitted diseases

CONDONE *verb* **CONDONES, CONDONING, CONDONED** to pardon or overlook (an offence or wrong)

CONDOR *noun* **CONDORS** either of two species of large American vulture, with a wingspan of up to 3m

CONDUCE *verb* **CONDUCES, CONDUCING, CONDUCED** to help or contribute (to a result, especially a desirable one)

CONDUCIVE *adj* likely to achieve a desirable result; encouraging

CONDUCT *verb* **CONDUCTS, CONDUCTING, CONDUCTED** to lead or guide □ *noun* **CONDUCTS** behaviour

CONDUCTOR *noun* **CONDUCTORS** the person who conducts a choir or orchestra

CONDUIT *noun* **CONDUITS** a channel, pipe, tube or duct through which a fluid, a liquid or a gas, may pass

CONE *noun* **CONES** a solid, three-dimensional figure with a flat base in the shape of a circle or ellipse, and a curved upper surface that tapers to a fixed point □ *verb* **CONES, CONING, CONED** to shape like a cone

CONEY *noun* **CONEYS** a rabbit

CONFAB *noun* **CONFABS** a conversation □ *verb* **CONFABS, CONFABBING, CONFABBED** to chat

CONFER *verb* **CONFERS, CONFERRING, CONFERRED** to consult or discuss together

CONFESS *verb* **CONFESSES, CONFESSING, CONFESSED** to own up to (a fault, wrongdoing, etc)

CONFESSED *adj* admitted

CONFESSOR *noun* **CONFESSORS** a priest who hears confessions and gives spiritual advice

CONFETTI *noun* **CONFETTI** at a wedding: tiny pieces of coloured paper traditionally thrown over the bride and groom by the wedding guests

CONFIDANT *noun* **CONFIDANTS** a close male friend with whom one discusses personal matters, especially concerning love affairs

CONFIDE *verb* **CONFIDES, CONFIDING, CONFIDED** to tell (a secret, etc)

CONFIDENT *adj* certain; sure

CONFIDING *adj* trusting; unsuspicious

CONFINE *verb* **CONFINES, CONFINING, CONFINED** to restrict or limit

For longer words, see *The Chambers Dictionary*

CONFINED *adj* narrow; restricted

CONFIRM *verb* **CONFIRMS, CONFIRMING, CONFIRMED** to provide support for the truth or validity of something

CONFIRMED *adj* so firmly settled into a state, habit, etc as to be unlikely to change

CONFLATE *verb* **CONFLATES, CONFLATING, CONFLATED** to blend or combine (two things, especially two different versions of a text, story, etc) into a single whole

CONFLICT *noun* **CONFLICTS** disagreement; fierce argument; a quarrel □ *verb* **CONFLICTS, CONFLICTING, CONFLICTED** to be incompatible or in opposition

CONFLICTING *adj* clashing; competing; contradictory

CONFLUENT *adj* flowing together; running into one; uniting

CONFLUX *noun* **CONFLUXES** the meeting and flowing together of two or more rivers, streams, glaciers, etc

CONFORM *verb* **CONFORMS, CONFORMING, CONFORMED** to behave, dress, etc in obedience to some standard considered normal by the majority

CONFORMER *noun* **CONFORMERS** a person who complies with social, etc norms

CONFOUND *verb* **CONFOUNDS, CONFOUNDING, CONFOUNDED** to puzzle; to baffle

CONFOUNDED *adj* confused

CONFRÈRE *noun* **CONFRÈRES** a fellow of one's profession, etc; a colleague

CONFRONT *verb* **CONFRONTS, CONFRONTING, CONFRONTED** to face someone, especially defiantly or accusingly

CONFUSE *verb* **CONFUSES, CONFUSING, CONFUSED** to put into a muddle or mess

CONFUSED *adj* perplexed; disordered

CONFUSING *adj* that confuses or perplexes

CONFUSION *noun* **CONFUSIONS** the act of confusing or state of being confused

CONFUTE *verb* **CONFUTES, CONFUTING, CONFUTED** to prove (a person, theory, etc) wrong or false

CONGA *noun* **CONGAS** an originally Cuban dance of three steps followed by a kick, performed by people moving in single file □ *verb* **CONGAS, CONGAING, CONGAED** to dance the conga

CONGÉ *noun* **CONGÉS** permission to depart

CONGEAL *verb* **CONGEALS, CONGEALING, CONGEALED** said of a liquid, especially blood: to thicken, coagulate or solidify, especially through cooling

CONGENER *noun* **CONGENERS** a plant or animal of the same genus as another plant or animal

CONGENIAL *adj* said of people: compatible; having similar interests

CONGER *noun* **CONGERS** a large marine eel, which can grow to lengths of 2.75m

CONGERIES *singular or plural noun* **CONGERIES** a miscellaneous accumulation; a confused heap

CONGEST *verb* **CONGESTS, CONGESTING, CONGESTED** to excessively crowd or become excessively crowded

CONGESTED *adj* overcrowded

CONGRATS *plural noun* often as an exclamation: a short form of congratulations

CONGRESS *noun* **CONGRESSES** a large, especially international, assembly of delegates, gathered for discussion

CONGRUENT *adj* said of two or more figures: identical in size and shape

CONGRUITY *noun* **CONGRUITIES** agreement between things; consistency; suitability

CONGRUOUS *adj* corresponding

CONIC *adj* relating to or resembling a cone

CONICAL *adj* conic

CONIFER *noun* **CONIFERS** any of various, mostly evergreen, trees and shrubs with narrow needle-like leaves, which produce their pollen and seeds in cones, eg pine, spruce, cedar, yew, etc

CONJOIN *verb* **CONJOINS, CONJOINING, CONJOINED** to join together, combine or unite

CONJOINED *adj* united; in conjunction

CONJOINT *adj* joint; associated; united

CONJUGAL *adj* relating to marriage, or to the relationship between husband and wife

CONJUGATE *verb* **CONJUGATES, CONJUGATING, CONJUGATED** to give the inflected parts of (a verb), indicating number, person, tense, mood and voice □ *adj* joined, connected or coupled □ *noun* **CONJUGATES** a conjugate word or thing

CONJURE *verb* **CONJURES, CONJURING, CONJURED** to perform magic tricks, especially ones which deceive the eye or seem to defy nature

CONJURER *noun* **CONJURERS** someone who performs magic tricks, etc, especially for the entertainment of others

CONJURING *noun* **CONJURINGS** the performing of magic tricks

CONJUROR *noun* **CONJURORS** a conjurer

CONK *noun* **CONKS** the nose □ *verb* **CONKS, CONKING, CONKED** to hit someone on the nose or head

CONKER *noun* **CONKERS** the brown shiny seed of the horse chestnut tree

CONN *verb* **CONNS, CONNING, CONNED** to direct the steering of (a ship)

CONNECT *verb* **CONNECTS, CONNECTING, CONNECTED** to join; to link

CONNECTER *noun* **CONNECTERS** a connector

CONNECTOR *noun* **CONNECTORS** a person or thing that connects

CONNEXION *noun* **CONNEXIONS** the act of connecting or state of being connected

CONNIVE *verb* **CONNIVES, CONNIVING, CONNIVED** to conspire or plot

CONNIVER *noun* **CONNIVERS** a person who connives

CONNOTE *verb* **CONNOTES, CONNOTING, CONNOTED** said of a word: to suggest, in addition to its literal meaning

CONNUBIAL *adj* pertaining to marriage or to relations between a husband and wife

CONQUER *verb* **CONQUERS, CONQUERING, CONQUERED** to gain possession or dominion over (territory) by force

CONQUERING *adj* victorious

CONQUEROR *noun* **CONQUERORS** a person who conquers; a victor

CONQUEST *noun* **CONQUESTS** the act of conquering

CONSCIOUS *adj* awake, alert and aware of one's thoughts and one's surroundings □ *noun*

CONSCIOUSES the part of the human mind which is responsible for such awareness, and is concerned with perceiving and reacting to external objects and events

CONSCRIPT verb **CONSCRIPTS, CONSCRIPTING, CONSCRIPTED** to enlist for compulsory military service ◻ noun **CONSCRIPTS** someone who has been conscripted

CONSENSUS noun **CONSENSUSES** general feeling or agreement; the majority view

CONSENT verb **CONSENTS, CONSENTING, CONSENTED** to give one's permission; to agree ◻ noun **CONSENTS** agreement; assent; permission

CONSERVE verb **CONSERVES, CONSERVING, CONSERVED** to keep safe from damage, deterioration, loss or undesirable change ◻ noun **CONSERVES** a type of jam, especially one containing chunks of fresh fruit

CONSIDER verb **CONSIDERS, CONSIDERING, CONSIDERED** to go over something in one's mind

CONSIDERED adj carefully thought about

CONSIDERING adverb taking the circumstances into account ◻ conj taking into account ◻ prep in view of; when one considers

CONSIGN verb **CONSIGNS, CONSIGNING, CONSIGNED** to hand over; to entrust

CONSIGNEE noun **CONSIGNEES** someone to whom something is consigned

CONSIGNER noun **CONSIGNERS** someone who consigns

CONSIGNOR noun **CONSIGNORS** a consigner

CONSIST verb **CONSISTS, CONSISTING, CONSISTED** to be composed or made up of several elements or ingredients

CONSOLE [1] verb **CONSOLES, CONSOLING, CONSOLED** to comfort in distress, grief or disappointment

CONSOLE [2] noun **CONSOLES** the part of an organ with the keys, pedals and panels of stops

CONSOLER noun **CONSOLERS** someone who consoles

CONSOLS plural noun irredeemable government securities

CONSOMMÉ noun **CONSOMMÉS** a type of thin clear soup

CONSONANT noun **CONSONANTS** any speech-sound produced by obstructing the passage of the breath ◻ adj in harmony or suitable with something

CONSORT noun **CONSORTS** a wife or husband, especially of a reigning sovereign

CONSPIRE verb **CONSPIRES, CONSPIRING, CONSPIRED** to plot secretly together, especially for an unlawful purpose

CONSTABLE noun **CONSTABLES** a police officer of the most junior rank

CONSTANCY noun **CONSTANCIES** fixedness; unchangeableness; steadfastness

CONSTANT adj never stopping ◻ noun **CONSTANTS** a symbol representing an unspecified number, which remains unchanged, unlike a variable

CONSTRAIN verb **CONSTRAINS, CONSTRAINING, CONSTRAINED** to force; to compel

CONSTRAINED adj awkward; embarrassed; forced

CONSTRICT verb **CONSTRICTS, CONSTRICTING, CONSTRICTED** to squeeze or compress

CONSTRUCT verb **CONSTRUCTS, CONSTRUCTING, CONSTRUCTED** to build; to form or put together ◻ noun **CONSTRUCTS** something constructed, especially in the mind

CONSTRUE verb **CONSTRUES, CONSTRUING, CONSTRUED** to interpret or explain

CONSUL noun **CONSULS** an official representative of a state, stationed in a foreign country to look after its commercial interests there, the interests of its citizens living there, etc

CONSULAR adj relating to a consul

CONSULATE noun **CONSULATES** the post or official residence of a consul

CONSULT verb **CONSULTS, CONSULTING, CONSULTED** to ask the advice of

CONSULTING adj acting as an adviser

CONSUME verb **CONSUMES, CONSUMING, CONSUMED** to eat or drink

CONSUMER noun **CONSUMERS** someone who buys goods and services for personal use or need

CONSUMING adj overwhelming

CONTACT noun **CONTACTS** the condition of touching physically ◻ verb **CONTACTS, CONTACTING,**

CONTACTED to get in touch with someone; to communicate with someone

CONTAGION noun **CONTAGIONS** the transmission of a disease by direct physical contact with an infected person

CONTAIN verb **CONTAINS, CONTAINING, CONTAINED** to hold or be able to hold

CONTAINER noun **CONTAINERS** an object designed for holding or storing, such as a box, tin, carton, etc

CONTEMN verb **CONTEMNS, CONTEMNING, CONTEMNED** to despise, disdain or scorn

CONTEMPT noun **CONTEMPTS** scorn

CONTEND verb **CONTENDS, CONTENDING, CONTENDED** to struggle, strive, fight or compete

CONTENDER noun **CONTENDERS** a person who contends

CONTENT adj satisfied; happy; uncomplaining ◻ verb **CONTENTS, CONTENTING, CONTENTED** to satisfy or make (oneself or another) satisfied ◻ noun **CONTENTS** peaceful satisfaction

CONTENTED adj peacefully happy or satisfied

CONTEST noun **CONTESTS** a competition ◻ verb **CONTESTS, CONTESTING, CONTESTED** to enter the competition or struggle for something

CONTESTED adj disputed; contended for

CONTESTER noun **CONTESTERS** a person who contests

CONTEXT noun **CONTEXTS** the pieces of writing in a passage which surround a particular word, phrase, etc and which contribute to the full meaning of the word, phrase, etc in question

CONTINENT [1] adj able to control one's bowels and bladder

CONTINENT [2] noun **CONTINENTS** any of the seven main land masses of the world, namely Europe, Asia, N America, S America, Africa, Australia and Antarctica

CONTINUAL adj constantly happening or done; frequent

CONTINUE verb **CONTINUES, CONTINUING, CONTINUED** to go on without stopping

CONTINUO noun **CONTINUOS** a bass part for a keyboard or stringed instrument

For longer words, see *The Chambers Dictionary*

CONTINUUM noun **CONTINUA** a continuous sequence; an unbroken progression

CONTORT verb **CONTORTS, CONTORTING, CONTORTED** to twist violently out of shape

CONTORTED adj twisted

CONTOUR noun **CONTOURS** the distinctive outline of something □ verb **CONTOURS, CONTOURING, CONTOURED** to shape the contour of, or shape so as to fit a contour

CONTRA noun **CONTRAS** a member of a right-wing guerilla group in Central America, who attempted to overthrow the government in Nicaragua

CONTRACT noun **CONTRACTS** an agreement, especially a legally binding one □ verb **CONTRACTS, CONTRACTING, CONTRACTED** to make or become smaller

CONTRALTO noun **CONTRALTOS** the female singing voice that is lowest in pitch

CONTRARY adj opposite; quite different; opposed □ noun **CONTRARIES** an extreme opposite

CONTRAST noun **CONTRASTS** difference or dissimilarity between things or people that are being compared □ verb **CONTRASTS, CONTRASTING, CONTRASTED** to compare so as to reveal differences

CONTRITE adj sorry for something one has done

CONTRIVE verb **CONTRIVES, CONTRIVING, CONTRIVED** to manage or succeed

CONTRIVED adj forced or artificial

CONTROL noun **CONTROLS** authority or charge; power to influence or guide □ verb **CONTROLS, CONTROLLING, CONTROLLED** to have or exercise power over someone or something

CONTUMACY noun **CONTUMACIES** obstinate refusal to obey; resistance to authority

CONTUMELY noun **CONTUMELIES** scornful or insulting treatment or words

CONTUSE verb **CONTUSES, CONTUSING, CONTUSED** to bruise

CONTUSION noun **CONTUSIONS** the act of bruising or the state of being bruised

CONUNDRUM noun **CONUNDRUMS** a confusing problem

CONVECTOR noun **CONVECTORS** an electrical device used to heat the surrounding air in rooms, etc, by convection

CONVENE verb **CONVENES, CONVENING, CONVENED** to assemble or summon to assemble

CONVENER noun **CONVENERS** someone who convenes or chairs a meeting

CONVENOR noun **CONVENORS** a convener

CONVENT noun **CONVENTS** a community of nuns

CONVERGE verb **CONVERGES, CONVERGING, CONVERGED** to move towards or meet at one point

CONVERSE [1] verb **CONVERSES, CONVERSING, CONVERSED** to hold a conversation; to talk

CONVERSE [2] adj reverse; opposite □ noun **CONVERSES** opposite

CONVERT verb **CONVERTS, CONVERTING, CONVERTED** to win over, or be won over, to another religion, opinion etc □ noun **CONVERTS** someone who has been converted to a new religion, practice, etc

CONVERTER noun **CONVERTERS** a person or thing that converts

CONVERTOR noun **CONVERTORS** a converter

CONVEX adj said of a surface or shape: outward-curving, like the surface of the eye

CONVEXITY noun **CONVEXITIES** roundness of form on the outside

CONVEY verb **CONVEYS, CONVEYING, CONVEYED** to carry; to transport

CONVICT verb **CONVICTS, CONVICTING, CONVICTED** to prove or declare someone guilty (of a crime) □ noun **CONVICTS** someone serving a prison sentence

CONVINCE verb **CONVINCES, CONVINCING, CONVINCED** to persuade someone of something; to make or cause to make them believe it

CONVINCED adj firm in one's belief

CONVINCING adj believable

CONVIVIAL adj lively, jovial, sociable and cheerful

CONVOKE verb **CONVOKES, CONVOKING, CONVOKED** to call together; to assemble

CONVOY noun **CONVOYS** a group of vehicles or merchant ships travelling together, or under escort □ verb **CONVOYS, CONVOYING, CONVOYED** to accompany for protection

CONVULSE verb **CONVULSES, CONVULSING, CONVULSED** to jerk or distort violently by or as if by a powerful spasm

CONY noun **CONIES** a rabbit

COO noun **COOS** the soft murmuring call of a dove □ verb **COOS, COOING, COOED** to make a sound like a dove

COOEE exclamation a usually high-pitched call used to attract attention □ verb **COOEES, COOEEING, COOEED** to make a high-pitched call in order to attract attention

COOK verb **COOKS, COOKING, COOKED** to prepare (food) or be prepared by heating □ noun **COOKS** someone who cooks or prepares food

COOKBOOK noun **COOKBOOKS** a book of recipes

COOKER noun **COOKERS** an apparatus for cooking food; a stove

COOKERY noun **COOKERIES** the art or practice of cooking food

COOKIE noun **COOKIES** a biscuit

COOL adj **COOLER, COOLEST** between cold and warm; fairly cold □ noun **COOLS** a cool part or period; coolness □ verb **COOLS, COOLING, COOLED** to become cool

COOLANT noun **COOLANTS** a liquid or gas used as a cooling agent, especially to absorb and remove heat from its source in a system such as a car radiator, nuclear reactor, etc

COOLER noun **COOLERS** a container or device for cooling things

COOLLY adverb with composure; indifferently

COOLNESS noun **COOLNESSES** moderate cold

COOMB noun **COOMBS** in S England: a short deep valley

COOMBE noun **COOMBES** a coomb

COOP noun **COOPS** a cage for hens □ verb **COOPS, COOPING, COOPED** to confine in a small space

COOPER noun **COOPERS** someone who makes or repairs barrels

COOT noun **COOTS** any of 10 species of aquatic bird belonging to the rail family, native to Europe and Asia, with dark plumage, a characteristic white shield above the bill and large feet with lobed toes

For longer words, see *The Chambers Dictionary*

COP noun **COPS** a policeman □ verb **COPS, COPPING, COPPED** to catch

COPE [1] verb **COPES, COPING, COPED** to manage; to get by

COPE [2] noun **COPES** a long sleeveless cape worn by clergy on ceremonial occasions

COPIER noun **COPIERS** a person or machine which makes copies

COPING noun **COPINGS** a capping along the top row of stones in a wall, designed to protect it from the weather

COPIOUS adj plentiful

COPIOUSLY adverb plentifully

COPPER noun **COPPERS** a soft-reddish brown metallic element which is an excellent conductor of heat and electricity □ adj made from copper □ verb **COPPERS, COPPERING, COPPERED** to cover with copper

COPPERY adj like copper

COPPICE noun **COPPICES** an area of woodland in which trees are regularly cut back to ground level to encourage the growth of side shoots, which are then periodically harvested for firewood, fencing, etc □ verb **COPPICES, COPPICING, COPPICED** to cut back (trees, bushes, etc) to form a coppice

COPRA noun **COPRAS** the dried kernel of the coconut, rich in coconut oil

COPSE noun **COPSES** a coppice

COPULA noun **COPULAS** a verb that links the subject and complement of a sentence

COPULATE verb **COPULATES, COPULATING, COPULATED** to have sexual intercourse

COPY noun **COPIES** an imitation or reproduction □ verb **COPIES, COPYING, COPIED** to imitate

COPYBOOK noun **COPYBOOKS** a book of handwriting examples for copying □ adj unoriginal

COPYCAT noun **COPYCATS** an imitator or person who copies the work of another

COPYIST noun **COPYISTS** someone who copies (documents, etc) in writing, especially as an occupation

COPYRIGHT noun **COPYRIGHTS** the sole right, granted by law, to print, publish, translate, perform, film or record an original literary, dramatic, musical or artistic work for a certain number of years □ adj protected by copyright □ verb **COPYRIGHTS, COPYRIGHTING, COPYRIGHTED** to secure the copyright of something

COQUETRY noun **COQUETRIES** the act of coquetting

COQUETTE noun **COQUETTES** a flirtatious woman □ verb **COQUETTES, COQUETTING, COQUETTED** to flirt

COR exclamation expressing surprise or pleasure

CORACLE noun **CORACLES** a small oval rowing-boat made of wickerwork covered with hides or other waterproof material

CORAL adj pinkish-orange in colour □ noun **CORALS** a pinkish-orange colour

CORALLINE adj consisting of, containing or like coral □ noun **CORALLINES** a common seaweed of a delicate pinkish or purplish colour

CORBEL noun **CORBELS** a projecting piece of stone or timber, coming out from a wall and taking the weight of (eg a parapet, arch or bracket) □ verb **CORBELS, CORBELLING, CORBELLED** to project or cause to project on corbels

CORBELLED adj having corbels

CORBELLING noun **CORBELLINGS** stone or brickwork made into corbels

CORBIE noun **CORBIES** a crow or raven

CORD noun **CORDS** a thin rope or string consisting of several separate strands twisted together □ verb **CORDS, CORDING, CORDED** to bind with a cord

CORDATE adj heart-shaped

CORDED adj fastened with cords

CORDIAL adj warm and affectionate □ noun **CORDIALS** a concentrated fruit-flavoured drink, which is usually diluted before being drunk

CORDIALLY adverb in a cordial way

CORDITE noun **CORDITES** any of various smokeless explosive materials containing a mixture of cellulose nitrate and nitroglycerine, used as a propellant for guns, etc

CORDLESS adj said of an electrical appliance: operating without a flex connecting it to the mains, powered instead by an internal battery

CORDON noun **CORDONS** a line of police or soldiers, or a system of road blocks, encircling an area so as to prevent or control passage into or out of it □ verb **CORDONS, CORDONING, CORDONED** to close off (an area) with a cordon

CORDUROY noun **CORDUROYS** a thick ribbed cotton fabric □ adj made from corduroy

CORE noun **CORES** the fibrous case at the centre of some fruits, eg apples and pears, containing the seeds □ verb **CORES, CORING, CORED** to remove the core of (an apple, etc)

CORED adj with the core removed

CORER noun **CORERS** a knife with a hollow cylindrical blade for coring fruit

CORGI noun **CORGIS** a sturdy short-legged breed of dog with a thick coat and fox-like head

CORIANDER noun **CORIANDERS** an annual plant, native to Europe and Asia, with narrowly lobed leaves, flat-topped clusters of small white, pink or lilac flowers, and globular aromatic fruits

CORIUM noun **CORIUMS** the dermis

CORK noun **CORKS** a layer of tissue that forms below the epidermis in the stems and roots of woody plants, eg trees, which is often cultivated for commercial use □ verb **CORKS, CORKING, CORKED** to stop up (a bottle, etc) with a cork

CORKAGE noun **CORKAGES** the fee charged by a restaurant for serving customers wine, etc that they have bought off the premises

CORKED adj said of wine: spoiled as a result of having a faulty cork, which has affected the taste of the wine

CORKER noun **CORKERS** someone or something marvellous

CORKINESS noun **CORKINESSES** the state or condition of being corky

CORKSCREW noun **CORKSCREWS** a tool with a spiral spike for screwing into bottle corks to remove them □ verb **CORKSCREWS, CORKSCREWING, CORKSCREWED** to move spirally

CORKY adj **CORKIER, CORKIEST** of or resembling cork

CORM noun **CORMS** in certain plants, eg crocus: a swollen underground stem, which functions primarily as a food store between one growing season and the next, and is also involved in the production of new plants

CORMORANT *noun* **CORMORANTS** any of over 30 species of seabird with an upright stance, dark brown or black plumage, webbed feet, a long neck and a slender bill

CORN *noun* **CORNS** in the UK: the most important cereal crop of a particular region, especially wheat in England, and oats in Scotland and Ireland □ *verb* **CORNS, CORNING, CORNED** to preserve with salt or brine

CORNCRAKE *noun* **CORNCRAKES** a bird belonging to the rail family, native to Europe and W Asia, which has light brown streaky plumage, chestnut wings and a barred tail

CORNEA *noun* **CORNEAS** in vertebrates: the convex transparent membrane that covers the front of the eyeball

CORNEAL *adj* of or relating to the cornea

CORNED *adj* preserved in salt or brine

CORNELIAN *noun* **CORNELIANS** a red and white form of agate, used as a semi-precious stone and for making seals

CORNER *noun* **CORNERS** a point or place where lines or surface-edges meet □ *verb* **CORNERS, CORNERING, CORNERED** to force into a place or position from which escape is difficult

CORNET *noun* **CORNETS** a brass musical instrument similar to the trumpet

CORNETIST *noun* **CORNETISTS** someone who plays the cornet

CORNFLOUR *noun* **CORNFLOURS** a finely ground flour, usually made from maize, which is used for thickening sauces, etc

CORNICE *noun* **CORNICES** a decorative border of moulded plaster round a ceiling

CORNY *adj* **CORNIER, CORNIEST** said of a joke: old and stale

COROLLA *noun* **COROLLAS** the collective name for the petals of a flower

COROLLARY *noun* **COROLLARIES** something that directly follows from another thing that has been proved

CORONA *noun* **CORONAS,**

CORONAE the outer atmosphere of the Sun, consisting of a halo of hot luminous gases that boil from its surface, visible during a total solar eclipse

CORONARY *adj* denoting vessels, nerves, etc which encircle a part or organ, especially the arteries which supply blood to the heart muscle □ *noun* **CORONARIES** the formation of a blood clot in one of the two coronary arteries, which blocks the flow of blood to the heart and usually gives rise to a heart attack

CORONER *noun* **CORONERS** a public official whose chief responsibility is the investigation of sudden, suspicious or accidental deaths

CORONET *noun* **CORONETS** a small crown

CORPORAL[1] *noun* **CORPORALS** a non-commissioned officer in the army or air force

CORPORAL[2] *adj* relating or belonging to the body

CORPORATE *adj* shared by members of a group; joint

CORPOREAL *adj* relating to the body as distinct from the soul; physical

CORPS *noun* **CORPS** a military body or division forming a tactical unit

CORPSE *noun* **CORPSES** the dead body of a human being □ *verb* **CORPSES, CORPSING, CORPSED** said of an actor on stage: to laugh or to forget one's lines

CORPULENT *adj* fat; fleshy; obese

CORPUS *noun* **CORPORA** a body of writings, eg by a particular author, on a particular topic, etc

CORPUSCLE *noun* **CORPUSCLES** any small particle or cell within a tissue or organ, especially a red or white blood cell

CORRAL *noun* **CORRALS** an enclosure for driving horses or cattle into □ *verb* **CORRALS, CORRALLING, CORRALLED** to herd or pen into a corral

CORRECT *verb* **CORRECTS, CORRECTING, CORRECTED** to set or put right; to remove errors from something □ *adj* free from error; accurate

CORRECTLY *adverb* without error; accurately

CORRECTOR *noun* **CORRECTORS** a person or thing that corrects

CORRELATE *verb* **CORRELATES, CORRELATING, CORRELATED** said of two or more things: to have a connection or correspondence; to relate one to another □ *noun* **CORRELATES** either of two things which are related to each other

CORRIDOR *noun* **CORRIDORS** a passageway connecting parts of a building or off which rooms open

CORRIE *noun* **CORRIES** in the Scottish Highlands: a semicircular hollow on a hillside

CORRODE *verb* **CORRODES, CORRODING, CORRODED** said of a material or object: to eat or be eaten away, especially by rust or chemicals

CORROSION *noun* **CORROSIONS** the gradual wearing away and eventual destruction of a metal or alloy as a result of its oxidation by air, water or chemicals, eg the rusting of iron

CORROSIVE *adj* capable of eating away □ *noun* **CORROSIVES** a corrosive thing or substance

CORRUGATE *verb* **CORRUGATES, CORRUGATING, CORRUGATED** to fold into parallel ridges, so as to make stronger

CORRUGATED *adj* ridged

CORRUPT *verb* **CORRUPTS, CORRUPTING, CORRUPTED** to change for the worse, especially morally □ *adj* **CORRUPTER, CORRUPTEST** morally evil

CORRUPTER *noun* **CORRUPTERS** a person or thing that corrupts

CORRUPTLY *adverb* in a corrupt way

CORSAGE *noun* **CORSAGES** a small spray of flowers for pinning to the bodice of a dress

CORSAIR *noun* **CORSAIRS** a pirate or pirate ship

CORSELET *noun* **CORSELETS** a protective garment or piece of armour for the upper part of the body

CORSET *noun* **CORSETS** a tightly fitting undergarment, usually worn by women, which has been stiffened by strips of bone or plastic, and is used for shaping or controlling the figure □ *verb* **CORSETS, CORSETING, CORSETED** to put on a corset

CORSETIER *noun* **CORSETIERS** a maker or seller of corsets

CORSETRY *noun* **CORSETRIES** corsets; the making or selling of corsets

For longer words, see *The Chambers Dictionary*

CORSLET *noun* **CORSLETS** a corselet

CORTÈGE *noun* **CORTÈGES** a procession, especially at a funeral

CORTEX *noun* **CORTEXES, CORTICES** the outer layer of an organ or tissue, when this differs in structure or function from the inner region, eg the cerebral cortex

CORTICAL *adj* relating to the cortex; external

CORTICOID *noun* **CORTICOIDS** any steroid hormone, eg cortisone, manufactured by the adrenal cortex

CORTISONE *noun* **CORTISONES** a naturally occurring steroid hormone which, in synthetic form, is used to treat rheumatoid arthritis, certain eye and skin disorders, etc

CORUNDUM *noun* **CORUNDUMS** a hard aluminium oxide mineral, used as an abrasive and as a constituent of emery, with its coloured crystalline forms including the gemstones ruby and sapphire

CORUSCANT *adj* flashing

CORUSCATE *verb* **CORUSCATES, CORUSCATING, CORUSCATED** to sparkle; to give off flashes of light

CORUSCATING *adj* flashing

CORVETTE *noun* **CORVETTES** a small warship for escorting larger vessels

CORVINE *adj* pertaining to or resembling a crow

COS *noun* **COSES** a type of lettuce with crisp slim leaves

COSECANT *noun* **COSECANTS** for a given angle in a right-angled triangle: a function that is the ratio of the length of the hypotenuse to the length of the side opposite the angle under consideration; the reciprocal of the sine of an angle

COSH *noun* **COSHES** a club, especially a rubber one filled with metal, used as a weapon □ *verb* **COSHES, COSHING, COSHED** to hit with a cosh or something heavy

COSILY *adverb* in a cosy way

COSINE *noun* **COSINES** in a right-angled triangle: a function that is the ratio of the length of the side adjacent to the angle to the length of the hypotenuse

COSINESS *noun* **COSINESSES** the quality or state of being cosy

COSMETIC *adj* used to beautify the face, body or hair □ *noun* **COSMETICS** any application

intended to improve the appearance of the body, especially the face

COSMIC *adj* relating to the Universe; universal

COSMOGONY *noun* **COSMOGONIES** the study of the origin and development of the Universe as a whole, or of specific celestial objects or systems, especially the Solar System

COSMOLOGY *noun* **COSMOLOGIES** the scientific study of the origin, nature, structure and evolution of the Universe

COSMONAUT *noun* **COSMONAUTS** a Russian astronaut

COSMOS *noun* **COSMOSES** the Universe seen as an ordered system

COSSET *verb* **COSSETS, COSSETING, COSSETED** to treat too kindly; to pamper □ *noun* **COSSETS** a hand-reared animal, especially a lamb

COST *verb* **COSTS, COSTING, COST** to be obtainable at a certain price □ *verb* **COSTS, COSTING, COSTED** to estimate or decide the cost of something □ *noun* **COSTS** what something costs; the price paid or required to be paid

COSTA *noun* **COSTAE** the technical name for the rib

COSTAL *adj* of or near the ribs

COSTIVE *adj* constipated

COSTLY *adj* **COSTLIER, COSTLIEST** expensive

COSTUME *noun* **COSTUMES** a set of clothing of a special kind, especially of a particular historical period or particular country □ *verb* **COSTUMES, COSTUMING, COSTUMED** to arrange or design the clothes for (a play, film, etc)

COSTUMIER *noun* **COSTUMIERS** someone who makes or supplies costumes

COSY *adj* **COSIER, COSIEST** warm and comfortable □ *noun* **COSIES** a cover to keep something warm, especially a teapot or boiled egg

COT *noun* **COTS** a small bed with high, barred sides for a child

COTANGENT *noun* **COTANGENTS** for a given angle in a right-angled triangle: a function that is the ratio of the length of the side adjacent to the angle under consideration, to the length of the side opposite it; the reciprocal of the tangent of an angle

COTE *noun* **COTES** a small shelter for birds or animals

COTERIE *noun* **COTERIES** a small exclusive group of people who have the same interests

COTINGA *noun* **COTINGAS** a bird, with a broad, hooked bill, native to the New World tropics

COTTAGE *noun* **COTTAGES** a small house, especially an old stone one, in a village or the countryside

COTTAGER *noun* **COTTAGERS** someone who lives in a cottage

COTTAGING *noun* **COTTAGINGS** the practice of using a public lavatory for anonymous sex between men

COTTAR *noun* **COTTARS** a farm labourer occupying a cottage rent-free, in return working on the farm

COTTER *noun* **COTTERS** a cottar

COTTON *noun* **COTTONS** the soft white fibre of the cotton plant woven into cloth or yarn □ *adj* made from cotton □ *verb* **COTTONS, COTTONING, COTTONED** to begin to understand something

COTTONY *adj* like cotton; soft; downy

COTYLEDON *noun* **COTYLEDONS** in flowering plants: one of the leaves produced by the embryo, providing the initial food source for the plant

COUCH *noun* **COUCHES** a sofa or settee □ *verb* **COUCHES, COUCHING, COUCHED** to lie down or cause to lie down

COUCHETTE *noun* **COUCHETTES** on a ship or train: a sleeping-berth, converted from ordinary seating

COUCHING *noun* **COUCHINGS** an operation to remove a cataract

COUGAR *noun* **COUGARS** a puma

COUGH *verb* **COUGHS, COUGHING, COUGHED** to expel air, mucus, etc from the throat or lungs with a rough sharp noise □ *noun* **COUGHS** an act or sound of coughing

COULD past form of **can** [1]

COULIS *noun* **COULIS** a purée of fruit, vegetables, etc often served as a sauce surrounding a meal

COULOMB *noun* **COULOMBS** the SI unit of electric charge, equal to the amount of charge transported by a current of one ampere in one second

COUNCIL *noun* **COUNCILS** a body of people whose function is to advise, administer, organize, discuss or legislate

COUNSEL noun **COUNSELS** advice □ verb **COUNSELS, COUNSELLING, COUNSELLED** to advise

COUNSELOR noun **COUNSELORS** an adviser

COUNT [1] verb **COUNTS, COUNTING, COUNTED** to recite numbers in ascending order

COUNT [2] noun **COUNTS** a European nobleman, equal in rank to a British earl

COUNTABLE adj able to be counted

COUNTER verb **COUNTERS, COUNTERING, COUNTERED** to oppose, act against or hit back □ adverb in the opposite direction to something; in contradiction of something □ adj contrary; opposing □ noun **COUNTERS** a return blow; an opposing move

COUNTESS noun **COUNTESSES** the wife or widow of an earl or count

COUNTLESS adj numerous; so many as to be impossible to count

COUNTRY noun **COUNTRIES** an area of land distinguished from other areas by its culture, climate, inhabitants, political boundary, etc

COUNTY noun **COUNTIES** any of the geographical divisions within England, Wales and Ireland that form the larger units of local government □ adj upper class; pertaining to the landed gentry

COUP noun **COUPS** a successful move; a masterstroke

COUPE noun **COUPES** a dessert made with fruit and ice cream

COUPÉ noun **COUPÉS** a car with four seats, two doors and a sloping rear

COUPLE noun **COUPLES** a pair of people attached in some way, often romantically, eg a wife and husband, a man and woman, two women or two men, etc □ verb **COUPLES, COUPLING, COUPLED** to associate; to link

COUPLET noun **COUPLETS** a pair of consecutive lines of verse, especially ones which rhyme and have the same metre

COUPLING noun **COUPLINGS** a link for joining things together

COUPON noun **COUPONS** a slip of paper entitling one to something, eg a discount

COURAGE noun **COURAGES** bravery

COURANTE noun **COURANTES** a lively dance in triple time

COURGETTE noun **COURGETTES** a variety of small marrow

COURIER noun **COURIERS** a guide who travels with, and looks after, parties of tourists

COURSE noun **COURSES** the path in which anyone or anything moves □ verb **COURSES, COURSING, COURSED** to move or flow

COURSER noun **COURSERS** someone who goes hare coursing

COURSING noun **COURSINGS** the hunting of hares using dogs

COURT noun **COURTS** the judge, law officials and members of the jury gathered to hear and decide on a legal case □ verb **COURTS, COURTING, COURTED** to try to win the love of someone

COURTEOUS adj polite; considerate; respectful

COURTESAN noun **COURTESANS** a prostitute with wealthy or noble clients

COURTESY noun **COURTESIES** courteous behaviour; politeness

COURTIER noun **COURTIERS** someone in attendance at a royal court

COURTLY adj **COURTLIER, COURTLIEST** having fine manners

COURTROOM noun **COURTROOMS** a room in which a lawcourt is held

COURTSHIP noun **COURTSHIPS** the courting or wooing of an intended spouse

COURTYARD noun **COURTYARDS** an open space surrounded by buildings or walls

COUSCOUS noun **COUSCOUSES** a N African dish of crushed semolina, which is steamed and served with eg vegetables, chicken, fish, etc

COUSIN noun **COUSINS** a son or daughter of one's uncle or aunt

COUTURE noun **COUTURES** the designing, making and selling of fashionable clothes

COUTURIER noun **COUTURIERS** a fashion designer

COVE noun **COVES** a small and usually sheltered bay or inlet on a rocky coast

COVEN noun **COVENS** a gathering of witches

COVENANT noun **COVENANTS** a formal sealed agreement to do something, eg pay a sum of money

regularly to a charity □ verb **COVENANTS, COVENANTING, COVENANTED** to agree by covenant to do something

COVER verb **COVERS, COVERING, COVERED** to form a layer over someone or something □ noun **COVERS** something that covers

COVERAGE noun **COVERAGES** an amount covered

COVERALL noun **COVERALLS** a one-piece protective garment worn over normal clothes □ adj covering or including everything

COVERING noun **COVERINGS** something that covers, eg a blanket, protective casing, etc

COVERLET noun **COVERLETS** a thin top cover for a bed; a bedspread

COVERT adj secret; concealed □ noun **COVERTS** a thicket or woodland providing cover for game

COVERTLY adverb in a covert way

COVET verb **COVETS, COVETING, COVETED** to long to possess something (especially something belonging to someone else)

COVETABLE adj greatly desirable

COVETOUS adj envious; greedy

COVEY noun **COVEYS** a small flock of game birds of one type, especially partridge or grouse

COW [1] noun **COWS** the mature female of any bovine animal, especially domesticated cattle

COW [2] verb **COWS, COWING, COWED** to frighten something into submission

COWARD noun **COWARDS** someone easily frightened, or lacking courage to face danger or difficulty

COWARDICE noun **COWARDICES** lack or courage; timidity

COWARDLY adj having the character of a coward

COWBELL noun **COWBELLS** a bell hanging from a cow's neck, which sounds when the cow moves

COWBERRY noun **COWBERRIES** a small evergreen shrub, native to northern temperate regions, with drooping bell-shaped pinkish-white flowers and edible red berries

COWBOY noun **COWBOYS** in the western USA: a man who tends cattle, usually on horseback

COWER verb **COWERS, COWERING, COWERED** to shrink away in fear

COWHAND noun **COWHANDS** a cowman

COWHERD noun **COWHERDS** a cowman

COWHIDE noun **COWHIDES** the leather made from the hide of a cow

COWHOUSE noun **COWHOUSES** a cowshed

COWL noun **COWLS** a monk's large loose hood or hooded habit

COWLICK noun **COWLICKS** a tuft of hair standing up stiffly from the forehead

COWLING noun **COWLINGS** the streamlined metal casing, usually having hinged or removable panels, that houses the engine of an aircraft or other vehicle

COWMAN noun **COWMEN** someone assisting with cattle or having charge of them

COWPAT noun **COWPATS** a flat deposit of cow dung

COWPEA noun **COWPEAS** the black-eye bean

COWPOX noun **COWPOXES** a viral infection of the udders of cows that can be transmitted to humans by direct contact, causing mild symptoms similar to smallpox, against which it is used as a vaccine

COWRIE noun **COWRIES** any of about 150 species of marine snail, found mainly in tropical waters

COWRY noun **COWRIES** a cowrie

COWSHED noun **COWSHEDS** a building for housing cattle; a byre

COWSLIP noun **COWSLIPS** a perennial plant native to Europe and Asia with a cluster of yellow sweet-smelling flowers

COX noun **COXES** short for coxswain □ verb **COXES, COXING, COXED** to act as cox of (a boat)

COXCOMB noun **COXCOMBS** a cockscomb

COXSWAIN noun **COXSWAINS** someone who steers a small boat

COY adj **COYER, COYEST** shy; modest; affectedly bashful □ verb **COYS, COYING, COYED** a Shakespearean word meaning to caress or to disdain

COYLY adverb in a coy way

COYNESS noun **COYNESSES** the quality of being coy

COYOTE noun **COYOTES** a small N American wolf with a pointed face, tawny fur and a black-tipped bushy tail, which was originally found mainly in deserts, prairies and open woodland, but is becoming increasingly known as an urban scavenger

COYPU noun **COYPUS** a large rat-like aquatic rodent, native to S America and introduced elsewhere as a result of escape from captivity, which has a broad blunt muzzle and webbed hind feet

---

COZ noun **COZES** a cousin
ⓘ This word is worth 14 points, and is useful for using up both a C and a Z.

CRAB noun **CRABS** any of a species of mostly marine crustaceans, with a hard flattened shell and five pairs of jointed legs, the front pair being developed into pincers

CRABBED adj bad-tempered; grouchy

CRABBEDLY adverb in a crabbed way

CRABBY adj **CRABBIER, CRABBIEST** bad-tempered

CRABWISE adverb moving sideways

CRACK verb **CRACKS, CRACKING, CRACKED** to fracture or cause to fracture partially without falling to pieces □ noun **CRACKS** a sudden sharp sound □ adj expert

CRACKDOWN noun **CRACKDOWNS** a firm action taken against someone or something

CRACKED adj crazy; mad

CRACKER noun **CRACKERS** a thin crisp unsweetened biscuit

CRACKERS adj mad

CRACKING adj very good □ adverb very fast

CRACKLE verb **CRACKLES, CRACKLING, CRACKLED** to make a faint continuous cracking or popping sound □ noun **CRACKLES** a faint continuous cracking or popping sound

CRACKLING noun **CRACKLINGS** the crisp skin of roast pork

CRACKLY adj **CRACKLIER, CRACKLIEST** producing a crackling or rustling noise

CRACKNEL noun **CRACKNELS** a light brittle biscuit

CRACKPOT adj crazy □ noun **CRACKPOTS** a crazy person

CRADLE noun **CRADLES** a cot for a small baby, especially one that can be rocked □ verb **CRADLES,**

CRADLING, CRADLED to rock or hold gently

CRAFT noun **CRAFTS** a skill, trade or occupation, especially one requiring the use of the hands □ verb **CRAFTS, CRAFTING, CRAFTED** to make something skilfully

CRAFTILY adverb in a crafty way

CRAFTSMAN noun **CRAFTSMEN** someone skilled at a craft

CRAFTY adj **CRAFTIER, CRAFTIEST** clever, shrewd, cunning or sly

CRAG noun **CRAGS** a rocky peak or jagged outcrop of rock

CRAGGY adj **CRAGGIER, CRAGGIEST** full of crags

CRAM verb **CRAMS, CRAMMING, CRAMMED** to stuff full □ noun **CRAMS** a crush

CRAMMER noun **CRAMMERS** a person or school that prepares pupils for examinations by rapid study

CRAMP noun **CRAMPS** a painful involuntary prolonged contraction of a muscle or group of muscles □ verb **CRAMPS, CRAMPING, CRAMPED** to restrict

CRAMPED adj overcrowded; closed in

CRAMPON noun **CRAMPONS** a spiked iron attachment for climbing boots, to improve grip on ice or rock

CRANBERRY noun **CRANBERRIES** a dwarf evergreen shrub with oval pointed leaves, pink flowers and red berries

CRANE noun **CRANES** a machine with a long pivoted arm from which lifting gear is suspended, allowing heavy weights to be moved both horizontally and vertically □ verb **CRANES, CRANING, CRANED** to stretch (one's neck), or lean forward, in order to see better

CRANEFLY noun **CRANEFLIES** a long-legged, two-winged insect

CRANIAL adj relating to or in the region of the skull

CRANIUM noun **CRANIA, CRANIUMS** the dome-shaped part of the skull, consisting of several fused bones, that encloses and protects the brain

CRANK noun **CRANKS** a device consisting of an arm connected to and projecting at right angles from the shaft of an engine or motor, used to communicate motion to or from the shaft, or to convert reciprocating motion into rotary motion or vice versa

CRANKILY adverb in a cranky way

CRANKY adj **CRANKIER, CRANKIEST** eccentric or faddy

CRANNIED adj having crannies or fissures

CRANNY noun **CRANNIES** a narrow opening; a cleft or crevice

CRAP noun **CRAPS** a gambling game on which the player rolls two dice

CRAPE noun **CRAPES** crêpe

CRAPULENT adj suffering from sickness caused by overdrinking

CRAPULOUS adj crapulent

CRASH verb **CRASHES, CRASHING, CRASHED** to fall or strike with a banging or smashing noise ◻ noun **CRASHES** a violent impact or breakage, or the sound of it

CRASHING adj utter; extreme

CRASS adj **CRASSER, CRASSEST** gross; vulgar

CRASSLY adverb in a crass way

CRASSNESS noun the quality of being crass

CRATE noun **CRATES** a strong wooden, plastic or metal case with partitions, for storing or carrying breakable or perishable goods ◻ verb **CRATES, CRATING, CRATED** to pack in a crate

CRATER noun **CRATERS** the bowl-shaped mouth of a volcano or geyser ◻ verb **CRATERS, CRATERING, CRATERED** to form craters in (a road, a surface, etc)

CRATERED adj having craters

CRATEROUS adj like a crater

CRATON noun **CRATONS** a relatively rigid and immobile part of the Earth's crust that has been stable for at least 1500 million years

CRAVAT noun **CRAVATS** a formal style of neckerchief worn chiefly by men instead of a tie

CRAVE verb **CRAVES, CRAVING, CRAVED** to long for something; to desire it overwhelmingly

CRAVEN adj cowardly; cringing ◻ noun **CRAVENS** a coward

CRAVENLY adv in a craven way

CRAVING noun **CRAVINGS** a longing or great desire

CRAW noun **CRAWS** the thin-walled pouch in the gullet of birds where food is stored before it is digested

CRAWFISH noun **CRAWFISHES** a crayfish

CRAWL verb **CRAWLS, CRAWLING, CRAWLED** said of insects, worms, etc: to move along the ground slowly ◻ noun **CRAWLS** a crawling motion

CRAWLER noun **CRAWLERS** an abject, obsequious or sycophantic person

CRAYFISH noun **CRAYFISHES** an edible, freshwater crustacean, similar to a small lobster

CRAYON noun **CRAYONS** a small pencil or stick made from coloured wax, chalk, charcoal or clay and used for drawing ◻ verb **CRAYONS, CRAYONING, CRAYONED** to draw or colour with a crayon

CRAZE noun **CRAZES** an intense but passing enthusiasm or fashion ◻ verb **CRAZES, CRAZING, CRAZED** to make crazy

CRAZILY adverb in a crazy way

CRAZINESS noun **CRAZINESSES** the quality of being crazy

CRAZY adj **CRAZIER, CRAZIEST** mad; insane

CREAK noun **CREAKS** a sharp grating or squeaking noise made typically by an unoiled hinge or loose floorboard ◻ verb **CREAKS, CREAKING, CREAKED** to make or seem to make a sharp grating or squeaking noise

CREAKILY adverb in a creaky way

CREAKY adj **CREAKIER, CREAKIEST** squeaky; tending to creak

CREAM noun **CREAMS** the yellowish fatty substance that rises to the surface of milk, and yields butter when churned ◻ verb **CREAMS, CREAMING, CREAMED** to beat (eg butter and sugar) till creamy

CREAMER noun **CREAMERS** a powdered milk substitute, used in coffee

CREAMERY noun **CREAMERIES** a place where dairy products are made or sold

CREAMWARE noun **CREAMWARES** a hard durable type of earthenware, usually with a cream-coloured glaze, which was first produced in Staffordshire in the 18c

CREAMY adj **CREAMIER, CREAMIEST** full of cream

CREASE noun **CREASES** a line made by folding, pressing or crushing ◻ verb **CREASES,**

CREASING, CREASED to make a crease or creases in (paper, fabric, etc); to develop creases

CREASER noun **CREASERS** a person or thing that creases

CREASY adj **CREASIER, CREASIEST** full of creases; liable or tending to crease

CREATE verb **CREATES, CREATING, CREATED** to form or produce from nothing

CREATIN noun **CREATINS** an organic compound, found in muscle, whose phosphate serves as an important source of energy for muscle contraction

CREATINE noun **CREATINES** creatin

CREATION noun **CREATIONS** the act of creating

CREATIVE adj having or showing the ability to create

CREATOR noun **CREATORS** someone who creates

CREATURE noun **CREATURES** a bird, beast or fish

CRÈCHE noun **CRÈCHES** a nursery where babies and young children can be left and cared for while their parents are at work, shopping, etc

CRED noun **CREDS** credibility

CREDAL adj relating to a creed

CREDENCE noun **CREDENCES** faith or belief placed in something

CREDIBLE adj capable of being believed

CREDIBLY adverb in a credible way

CREDIT noun **CREDITS** faith placed in something ◻ verb **CREDITS, CREDITING, CREDITED** to believe; to place faith in someone or something

CREDITOR noun **CREDITORS** a person or company to whom one owes money

CREDO noun **CREDOS** a belief or set of beliefs

CREDULITY noun **CREDULITIES** a tendency to believe something without proper proof

CREDULOUS adj apt to be too ready to believe something, without sufficient evidence

CREED noun **CREEDS** a statement of the main points of Christian belief

CREEDAL adj of or relating to a creed

CREEK noun **CREEKS** a small narrow inlet or bay in the shore of a lake, river, or sea

CREEL noun **CREELS** a large wicker basket for carrying fish

CREEP verb **CREEPS, CREEPING, CREPT** to move slowly, with stealth or caution □ noun **CREEPS** an act of creeping

CREEPER noun **CREEPERS** a plant which grows along the ground, up a wall, etc

CREEPERS plural noun shoes with thick quiet soles

CREEPING adj that creeps

CREEPY adj **CREEPIER, CREEPIEST** slightly scary; spooky; eerie

CREMATE verb **CREMATES, CREMATING, CREMATED** to burn something, especially a corpse, to ashes

CREMATION noun **CREMATIONS** the act or process of cremating a corpse, as an alternative to burial

CREMATORY noun **CREMATORIES** a crematorium (a place where corpses are cremated)

CRÈME noun **CRÈMES** cream, or a creamy food

CRENEL noun **CRENELS** an indentation in a parapet

CRENELLE noun **CRENELLES** a crenel

CREOLE noun **CREOLES** a pidgin language that has become the accepted language of a community or region

CREOSOTE noun **CREOSOTES** a thick dark oily liquid with a penetrating odour, obtained by distilling coal tar, used as a wood preservative □ verb **CREOSOTES, CREOSOTING, CREOSOTED** to treat (wood) with creosote

CRÊPE noun **CREPES** a thin finely-wrinkled silk fabric, dyed black for mourning wear

CRÊPEY adj **CRÊPIER, CRÊPIEST** crêpy

CREPITANT adj crackling

CREPITATE verb **CREPITATES, CREPITATING, CREPITATED** to rattle; to crackle

CREPITUS noun **CREPITUSES** a harsh grating noise produced when the ends of a fractured bone rub together or by bone rubbing on roughened cartilage, usually occurring in the movement of arthritic joints

CREPT past form of **creep**

CRÊPY adj **CRÊPIER, CRÊPIEST** like crêpe

CRESCENDO noun **CRESCENDOS** a gradual increase in loudness □ verb **CRESCENDOS, CRESCENDOING, CRESCENDOED** to increase gradually in loudness □ adverb played with increasing loudness

CRESCENT noun **CRESCENTS** the curved shape of the Moon during its first or last quarter, when it appears less than half illuminated

CRESS noun **CRESSES** any of various plants of the cabbage family, especially a species cultivated for its edible seed leaves which are eaten raw with mustard leaves in salads, sandwiches, etc

CREST noun **CRESTS** a comb or a tuft of feathers or fur on top of the head of certain birds and mammals; the topmost part of something □ verb **CRESTS, CRESTING, CRESTED** to reach the top of (a hill, mountain, etc)

CRESTED adj having a crest

CRETIN noun **CRETINS** someone suffering from cretinism

CRETINISM noun **CRETINISMS** a chronic condition caused by a congenital deficiency of thyroid hormone resulting in dwarfism and mental retardation

CRETINOUS adj of or relating to a cretin

CRETONNE noun **CRETONNES** a strong cotton material, usually with a printed design, used for curtains, chair-covers, etc

CREVASSE verb **CREVASSES, CREVASSING, CREVASSED** to make a fissure in (a wall, a dyke, etc) □ noun **CREVASSES** a deep vertical crack in a glacier, formed by stresses that build up as different parts of the glacier move at different rates

CREVICE noun **CREVICES** a narrow crack or fissure, especially in a rock

CREW [1] noun **CREWS** the team of people manning a ship, aircraft, train, bus, etc □ verb **CREWS, CREWING, CREWED** to serve as a crew member on a yacht, etc

CREW [2] past form of **crow**

CREWEL noun **CREWELS** thin loosely twisted yarn for tapestry or embroidery

CRIB noun **CRIBS** a baby's cot or cradle □ verb **CRIBS, CRIBBING, CRIBBED** to copy or plagiarize

CRIBBAGE noun **CRIBBAGES** a card game for two to four players, who each try to be first to score a certain number of points

CRICK noun **CRICKS** a painful spasm or stiffness of the muscles, especially in the neck □ verb **CRICKS, CRICKING, CRICKED** to wrench (eg one's neck or back)

CRICKET [1] noun **CRICKETS** an outdoor game played using a ball, bats and wickets, between two sides of eleven players, the object of which is for one team to score more runs than the other by the end of play

CRICKET [2] noun **CRICKETS** a species of mainly nocturnal insect related to the grasshopper, which has long slender antennae and whose males can produce a distinctive chirping sound by rubbing their forewings together

CRICKETER noun **CRICKETERS** a person who plays cricket

CRICOID adj ring-shaped or resembling a ring

CRIED past form of **cry**

CRIER noun **CRIERS** an official who announces news by shouting it out in public

CRIES a form of **cry**

CRIKEY exclamation an expression of astonishment

CRIME noun **CRIMES** an illegal act; an act punishable by law

CRIMINAL noun **CRIMINALS** someone guilty of a crime or crimes □ adj against the law

CRIMP verb **CRIMPS, CRIMPING, CRIMPED** to press into small regular ridges; to wave or curl hair with crimping-irons □ noun **CRIMPS** a curl or wave in the hair

CRIMPED adj pressed into small regular ridges; corrugated

CRIMPER noun **CRIMPERS** a person or device that crimps or corrugates

CRIMPERS plural noun a tong-like device with two metal plates with waves cut into them, which can be heated; hair can then be placed between the plates so as to give it a crimped appearance

CRIMSON noun **CRIMSONS** a deep purplish red colour □ verb **CRIMSONS, CRIMSONING, CRIMSONED** to dye crimson

CRINGE noun **CRINGES** an act of cringing □ verb **CRINGES, CRINGING, CRINGED** to cower away in fear

CRINGER noun **CRINGERS** a person who cringes

CRINKLE verb **CRINKLES, CRINKLING, CRINKLED** to wrinkle or crease □ noun **CRINKLES** a wrinkle or crease; a wave

CRINKLY *adj* **CRINKLIER, CRINKLIEST** wrinkly ◻ *noun* **CRINKLIES** an elderly person

CRINOID *noun* **CRINOIDS** a primitive echinoderm with a cup-shaped body and branching arms

CRINOIDAL *adj* shaped like a lily

CRINOLINE *noun* **CRINOLINES** a stiff fabric made from horsehair and cotton

CRIPPLE *verb* **CRIPPLES, CRIPPLING, CRIPPLED** to make lame; to disable ◻ *noun* **CRIPPLES** someone who is lame or badly disabled

CRISIS *noun* **CRISES** a crucial or decisive moment

CRISP *adj* **CRISPER, CRISPEST** dry and brittle ◻ *noun* **CRISPS** thin deep-fried slices of potato, usually flavoured and sold in packets as a snack ◻ *verb* **CRISPS, CRISPING, CRISPED** to make or become crisp

CRISPLY *adverb* in a crisp way

CRISPNESS *noun* **CRISPNESSES** the state or quality of being crisp

CRISPY *adj* **CRISPIER, CRISPIEST** crisp

CRITERION *noun* **CRITERIA** a standard or principle on which to base a judgement

CRITIC *noun* **CRITICS** a professional reviewer of literature, art, drama, music, etc

CRITICAL *adj* fault-finding; disapproving

CRITICISE *verb* **CRITICISES, CRITICISING, CRITICISED** to criticize

CRITICISM *noun* **CRITICISMS** fault-finding

CRITICIZE *verb* **CRITICIZES, CRITICIZING, CRITICIZED** to find fault; to express disapproval of someone or something

CRITIQUE *noun* **CRITIQUES** a critical analysis

CROAK *noun* **CROAKS** the harsh throaty noise typically made by a frog or crow ◻ *verb* **CROAKS, CROAKING, CROAKED** to make a harsh throaty sound

CROCHET *noun* **CROCHETS** decorative work consisting of intertwined loops, made with wool or thread and a hooked needle ◻ *verb* **CROCHETS, CROCHETING, CROCHETED** to work in crochet

CROCK *noun* **CROCKS** an earthenware pot

CROCKERY *noun* **CROCKERIES** earthenware or china dishes collectively, especially domestic pottery, ie plates, cups, etc

CROCKET *noun* **CROCKETS** in Gothic architecture: a carved decoration in the shape of a stylized leaf or flower, often used as an ornamental capital on columns, and on the sloping sides of pinnacles, spires and canopies

CROCODILE *noun* **CROCODILES** a large aquatic reptile found in tropical regions with a bulky body, short legs, powerful jaws that narrow to form a long snout and a thick scaly skin

CROCUS *noun* **CROCUSES** a small perennial plant belonging to the iris family, with yellow, purple or white flowers and an underground corm

CROFT *noun* **CROFTS** especially in the Scottish Highlands: a small piece of enclosed farmland attached to a house

CROFTER *noun* **CROFTERS** someone who runs or farms a croft

CROFTING *noun* **CROFTINGS** the practice of farming a croft

CROISSANT *noun* **CROISSANTS** a flaky crescent-shaped bread roll, made from puff pastry or leavened dough

CROMLECH *noun* **CROMLECHS** a prehistoric stone circle

CRONE *noun* **CRONES** an old woman

CRONY *noun* **CRONIES** a close friend

CROOK *noun* **CROOKS** a bend or curve ◻ *adj* ill ◻ *verb* **CROOKS, CROOKING, CROOKED** to bend or curve

CROOKED *adj* **CROOKEDER, CROOKEDEST** bent, curved, angled or twisted

CROOKEDLY *adverb* in a crooked way

CROON *verb* **CROONS, CROONING, CROONED** to sing in a subdued tone and reflective or sentimental style ◻ *noun* **CROONS** this style of singing

CROONER *noun* **CROONERS** a person who croons

CROP *noun* **CROPS** a plant that is cultivated to produce food for man, fodder for animals or raw materials, eg cereals, clover, barley, etc ◻ *verb* **CROPS, CROPPING, CROPPED** to trim; to cut short

CROPPER *noun* **CROPPERS** a person or thing which crops

CROQUET *noun* **CROQUETS** a game played on a lawn, in which the players use mallets to drive wooden balls through a sequence of hoops in a particular order, to try to be first to reach and hit a central peg ◻ *verb* **CROQUETS, CROQUETING, CROQUETED** to drive away a ball by placing it in contact with one's own and striking both with the mallet

CROQUETTE *noun* **CROQUETTES** a ball or round cake made from eg minced meat, fish, potato, etc which is coated in breadcrumbs and fried

CROSIER *noun* **CROSIERS** a bishop's hooked staff, carried as a symbol of office

CROSS *noun* **CROSSES** a mark, structure or symbol composed of two lines, one crossing the other in the form + or × ◻ *verb* **CROSSES, CROSSING, CROSSED** to move, pass or get across (a road, a path, etc) ◻ *adj* **CROSSER, CROSSEST** angry; in a bad temper

CROSSBAR *noun* **CROSSBARS** a horizontal bar, especially between two upright posts

CROSSBEAM *noun* **CROSSBEAMS** a beam which stretches across from one support to another

CROSSBILL *noun* **CROSSBILLS** any of various types of finch with a beak in which the points cross instead of meeting

CROSSBOW *noun* **CROSSBOWS** a bow placed crosswise on a stock, with a crank to pull back the bow and a trigger to release arrows

CROSSE *noun* **CROSSES** a long stick with a netted pocket at one end, used in playing lacrosse

CROSSFIRE *noun* **CROSSFIRES** gunfire coming from different directions

CROSSING *noun* **CROSSINGS** the place where two or more things cross each other

CROSSWAYS *adj* crosswise ◻ *adverb* crosswise

CROSSWIND *noun* **CROSSWINDS** a wind blowing across the path of a vehicle or aircraft

CROSSWISE *adj* lying or moving across, or so as to cross ◻ *adverb* lying or moving across, or so as to cross

CROSSWORD *noun* **CROSSWORDS** a puzzle in which numbered clues are solved and their answers in words inserted into their correct places in a grid of squares that cross vertically and horizontally

For longer words, see The Chambers Dictionary

CROTCH noun **CROTCHES** the place where the body or a pair of trousers forks into the two legs

CROTCHET noun **CROTCHETS** in music: a note equal to two quavers or half a minim in length

CROTCHETY adj **CROTCHETIER, CROTCHETIEST** irritable; peevish

CROUCH verb **CROUCHES, CROUCHING, CROUCHED** to bend low or squat with one's knees and thighs against one's chest and often also with one's hands on the ground □ noun **CROUCHES** a crouching position or action

CROUP noun **CROUPS** a condition in young children characterized by inflammation of the larynx, resulting in a hoarse cough, difficulty in breathing and fever

CROUPIER noun **CROUPIERS** in a casino: someone who presides over a gaming-table, collecting the stakes, dealing the cards, paying the winners, etc

CROUPY adj **CROUPIER, CROUPIEST** of or resembling croup

CROÛTON noun **CROÛTONS** a small cube of fried or toasted bread, served in soup, etc

CROW noun **CROWS** any of about 100 species of large black bird, including the carrion crow, rook, raven, etc, usually with a powerful black beak and shiny feathers □ verb **CROWS, CROWING, CROWED, CREW, CROWED** said of a cock: to cry shrilly

CROWBAR noun **CROWBARS** a heavy iron bar with a bent flattened end, used as a lever

CROWD noun **CROWDS** a large number of people gathered together □ verb **CROWDS, CROWDING, CROWDED** to gather or move in a large, usually tightly-packed, group

CROWDED adj full of people

CROWN noun **CROWNS** the circular, usually jewelled, gold headdress of a sovereign □ verb **CROWNS, CROWNING, CROWNED** to place a crown ceremonially on the head of someone, thus making them a monarch

CROWNING adj highest; greatest □ noun **CROWNINGS** the stage of labour when the top part of the baby's head is just passing through the vaginal opening

CROZIER noun **CROZIERS** a crosier

CRU noun **CRUS** a French word meaning *vineyard* or *vintage*

CRUCES a plural of **crux**

CRUCIAL adj decisive; critical

CRUCIBLE noun **CRUCIBLES** an earthenware pot in which to heat metals or other substances

CRUCIFIX noun **CRUCIFIXES** a representation, especially a model, of Christ on the cross

CRUCIFORM adj cross-shaped

CRUCIFY verb **CRUCIFIES, CRUCIFYING, CRUCIFIED** to put to death by fastening or nailing to a cross by the hands and feet

CRUD noun **CRUDS** dirt or filth, especially if sticky

CRUDDY adj **CRUDDIER, CRUDDIEST** dirty, unpleasant, worthless

CRUDE adj **CRUDER, CRUDEST** in its natural unrefined state; vulgar; tasteless □ noun **CRUDES** short for crude oil

CRUDELY adverb vulgarly; tastelessly

CRUDENESS noun **CRUDENESSES** the state or quality of being crude

CRUDITY noun **CRUDITIES** crudeness; a crude action

CRUEL adj **CRUELLER, CRUELLEST** deliberately and pitilessly causing pain or suffering

CRUELLY adverb in a cruel way

CRUELTY noun **CRUELTIES** the quality of being cruel

CRUET noun **CRUETS** a small container which holds salt, pepper, mustard, vinegar, etc, for use at table

CRUISE verb **CRUISES, CRUISING, CRUISED** to sail about for pleasure, calling at a succession of places □ noun **CRUISES** an instance of cruising, especially an ocean voyage undertaken for pleasure

CRUISER noun **CRUISERS** a large fast warship

CRUMB noun **CRUMBS** a particle of dry food, especially bread □ verb **CRUMBS, CRUMBING, CRUMBED** to coat in breadcrumbs

CRUMBLE verb **CRUMBLES, CRUMBLING, CRUMBLED** to break into crumbs or powdery fragments □ noun **CRUMBLES** a baked dessert of stewed fruit covered with a crumbled mixture of sugar, butter and flour

CRUMBLY adj **CRUMBLIER, CRUMBLIEST** having a tendency to crumble

CRUMBS exclamation an expression of mild surprise, dismay, etc

CRUMBY adj **CRUMBIER, CRUMBIEST** full of or in crumbs

CRUMHORN noun **CRUMHORNS** a krummhorn

CRUMMY adj **CRUMMIER, CRUMMIEST** shoddy, dingy, dirty or generally inferior

CRUMPET noun **CRUMPETS** a thick round cake made of soft light dough, eaten toasted and buttered

CRUMPLE verb **CRUMPLES, CRUMPLING, CRUMPLED** to make or become creased or crushed

CRUNCH verb **CRUNCHES, CRUNCHING, CRUNCHED** to crush or grind noisily between the teeth or under the foot □ noun **CRUNCHES** a crunching action or sound □ adj crucial or decisive

CRUNCHY adj **CRUNCHIER, CRUNCHIEST** able to be crunched; crisp

CRUSADE noun **CRUSADES** a strenuous campaign in aid of a cause □ verb **CRUSADES, CRUSADING, CRUSADED** to engage in a crusade; to campaign

CRUSADER noun **CRUSADERS** someone engaged in a crusade

CRUSH verb **CRUSHES, CRUSHING, CRUSHED** to break, damage, bruise, injure or distort by compressing violently □ noun **CRUSHES** violent compression

CRUSHABLE adj capable of being crushed

CRUSHED adj broken, damaged, injured, etc by being compressed violently

CRUSHER noun **CRUSHERS** someone or something that crushes or subdues

CRUSHING adj that crushes; overwhelming

CRUST noun **CRUSTS** the hard-baked outer surface of a loaf of bread □ verb **CRUSTS, CRUSTING, CRUSTED** to cover with or form a crust

CRUSTILY adverb cantankerously

CRUSTY [1] adj **CRUSTIER, CRUSTIEST** having a crisp crust

CRUSTY [2] noun **CRUSTIES** a New-Age traveller or someone with a similar outlook on life

CRUTCH noun **CRUTCHES** a stick, usually one of a pair, used as a support by a lame person, with a bar fitting under the armpit or a grip for the elbow □ *verb* **CRUTCHES, CRUTCHING, CRUTCHED** to support with a crutch or crutches

CRUX *noun* **CRUXES, CRUCES** a decisive, essential or crucial point

CRY *verb* **CRIES, CRYING, CRIED** to shed tears; to weep □ *noun* **CRIES** a shout or shriek

CRYBABY *noun* **CRYBABIES** a person, especially a child, who weeps at the slightest upset

CRYING *adj* demanding urgent attention

CRYOLITE *noun* **CRYOLITES** a pale grey mineral, composed of sodium, aluminium and fluorine, used in the smelting of aluminium ores

CRYONICS *singular noun* the preservation by freezing of living cells eg blood, human eggs, sperm, etc, especially the practice of freezing human corpses, with the idea that advances in science will enable them to be revived at a later date

CRYPT *noun* **CRYPTS** an underground chamber or vault, especially one beneath a church, often used for burials

CRYPTIC *adj* puzzling, mysterious, obscure or enigmatic

CRYPTOGAM *noun* **CRYPTOGAMS** a general term for a plant that reproduces by means of spores, such as a seaweed, moss or fern

CRYSTAL *noun* **CRYSTALS** colourless transparent quartz □ *adj* belonging or relating to, or made of, crystal

CUB *noun* **CUBS** the young of certain carnivorous mammals, such as the fox, wolf, lion and bear □ *verb* **CUBS, CUBBING, CUBBED** to give birth to cubs

CUBE *noun* **CUBES** a solid figure having six square faces of equal area, in which the angle between any two adjacent sides is a right angle □ *verb* **CUBES, CUBING, CUBED** to raise (a number or quantity) to the third power

CUBIC *adj* relating to or resembling a cube

CUBICAL *adj* cubic

CUBICLE *noun* **CUBICLES** a small compartment for sleeping or undressing in, screened for privacy

CUBISM *noun* **CUBISMS** an early-

20c movement in painting, initiated by Pablo Picasso and Georges Braque, which represented natural objects as geometrical shapes

CUBIST *noun* **CUBISTS** an artist who works in the cubist style

CUBIT *noun* **CUBITS** an old unit of measurement equal to the length of the forearm from the elbow to the tip of the middle finger

CUBOID *adj* resembling a cube in shape □ *noun* **CUBOIDS** a cube-shaped bone in the foot

CUCKOLD *noun* **CUCKOLDS** a man whose wife is unfaithful □ *verb* **CUCKOLDS, CUCKOLDING, CUCKOLDED** to make a cuckold of (a man)

CUCKOLDRY *noun* **CUCKOLDRIES** the act of making a cuckold

CUCKOO *noun* **CUCKOOS** any of about 130 species of insectivorous birds, the common variety of which is found in Europe, Asia and America, and lays its eggs in the nests of other birds □ *adj* insane; crazy

CUCUMBER *noun* **CUCUMBERS** a creeping plant cultivated for its edible fruit

CUD *noun* **CUDS** in ruminant animals, eg cattle: the partially digested food that is regurgitated from the first stomach into the mouth to be chewed again

CUDDLE *verb* **CUDDLES, CUDDLING, CUDDLED** to hug or embrace affectionately □ *noun* **CUDDLES** an affectionate hug

CUDDLY *adj* **CUDDLIER, CUDDLIEST** pleasant to cuddle; attractively soft and plump

CUDGEL *noun* **CUDGELS** a heavy stick or club used as a weapon □ *verb* **CUDGELS, CUDGELLING, CUDGELLED** to beat with a cudgel

CUE *noun* **CUES** in billiards, snooker and pool: a stick tapering almost to a point, used to strike the ball □ *verb* **CUES, CUEING, CUING, CUED** to strike (a ball) with the cue

CUFF [1] *noun* **CUFFS** a band or folded-back part at the lower end of a sleeve, usually at the wrist

CUFF [2] *verb* **CUFFS, CUFFING, CUFFED** to hit with an open hand

CUIRASS *noun* **CUIRASSES** a piece of armour consisting of a breastplate with a back plate attached to it

CUISINE *noun* **CUISINES** a style of cooking

CULINARY *adj* relating to cookery or the kitchen

CULL *verb* **CULLS, CULLING, CULLED** to select and kill (weak or surplus animals) from a group in order to keep the population under control □ *noun* **CULLS** an act of culling

CULM *noun* **CULMS** the jointed hollow stem of a grass □ *verb* **CULMS, CULMING, CULMED** to form a culm

CULMINATE *verb* **CULMINATES, CULMINATING, CULMINATED** to reach the highest point or climax

CULOTTES *plural noun* flared trousers for women, intended to look like a skirt

CULPABLE *adj* deserving blame

CULPABLY *adverb* in a culpable way

CULPRIT *noun* **CULPRITS** someone guilty of a misdeed or offence

CULT *noun* **CULTS** a system of religious belief

CULTIC *adj* relating to or characteristic of a cult

CULTISH *adj* of, relating to or like a cult

CULTISM *noun* **CULTISMS** adherence to a cult

CULTIST *noun* **CULTISTS** a person who practises cultism

CULTIVAR *noun* **CULTIVARS** a variety of a plant that does not occur naturally in the wild, but has been developed and maintained by cultivation using horticultural or agricultural techniques

CULTIVATE *verb* **CULTIVATES, CULTIVATING, CULTIVATED** to prepare and use (land or soil) for growing crops

CULTIVATED *adj* well bred and knowledgeable

CULTURAL *adj* relating to a culture

CULTURE *noun* **CULTURES** the customs, ideas, values, etc of a particular civilization, society or social group, especially at a particular time □ *verb* **CULTURES, CULTURING, CULTURED** to grow (micro-organisms, cells, tissues, etc) in a culture medium for study

CULTURED *adj* well-educated; having refined tastes and manners

CULVERT *noun* **CULVERTS** a covered drain or channel carrying water or electric cables underground, eg under a road or railway

CUM *prep* combined with; with the addition of

CUMIN *noun* **CUMINS** an umbelliferous plant of the Mediterranean region
CUMMIN *noun* **CUMMINS** cumin
CUMQUAT *noun* **CUMQUATS** a kumquat
CUMULATE *verb* **CUMULATES, CUMULATING, CUMULATED** to heap together; to accumulate □ *adj* heaped together
CUMULUS *noun* **CUMULI** a fluffy heaped cloud with a rounded white upper surface and a flat horizontal base, which is composed of water droplets and usually develops over a heat source, eg a volcano or hot land surface
CUNEIFORM *adj* relating to any of several ancient Middle-Eastern scripts with impressed wedge-shaped characters □ *noun* **CUNEIFORMS** cuneiform writing
CUNNING *adj* **CUNNINGER, CUNNINGEST** clever, sly or crafty □ *noun* **CUNNINGS** slyness; craftiness
CUNNINGLY *adverb* in a cunning way
CUP *noun* **CUPS** a small, round, open container, usually with a handle, used to drink from □ *verb* **CUPS, CUPPING, CUPPED** to form (one's hands) into a cup shape
CUPBOARD *noun* **CUPBOARDS** a piece of furniture or a recess, fitted with doors, shelves, etc, for storing provisions or personal effects
CUPFUL *noun* **CUPFULS** the amount a cup will hold
CUPID *noun* **CUPIDS** a figure of Cupid, the Roman god of love, represented in art or sculpture
CUPIDITY *noun* **CUPIDITIES** greed for wealth and possessions
CUPOLA *noun* **CUPOLAS** a small dome or turret on a roof
CUPPA *noun* **CUPPAS** a cup of tea
CUPPING *noun* **CUPPINGS** the former practice of applying heated cups to the skin, which was thought to promote healing by drawing 'harmful' blood away from diseased organs to the surface of the skin
CUPRIC *adj* denoting any compound of copper in which the element has a valency of two, eg cupric chloride
CUPRITE *noun* **CUPRITES** a red oxide mineral that is an important source of copper
CUPROUS *adj* denoting any compound of copper in which the element has a valency of one, eg cuprous chloride
CUR *noun* **CURS** a surly mongrel dog
CURABLE *adj* capable of being cured
CURACY *noun* **CURACIES** the office or benefice of a curate
CURARE *noun* **CURARES** a black resin obtained from certain tropical plants in South America, which is used as a paralysing poison smeared on arrow-tips by S American Indian hunters, and which also has medicinal uses as a muscle relaxant
CURATE *noun* **CURATES** a clergyman who acts as assistant to a vicar or rector
CURATIVE *adj* able or tending to cure □ *noun* **CURATIVES** a substance that cures
CURATOR *noun* **CURATORS** the custodian of a museum or other collection
CURB *noun* **CURBS** something that restrains or controls □ *verb* **CURBS, CURBING, CURBED** to restrain or control
CURD *noun* **CURDS** the clotted protein substance, as opposed to the liquid component, formed when fresh milk is curdled, and used to make cheese, etc □ *verb* **CURDS, CURDING, CURDED** to make or turn into curd
CURDLE *verb* **CURDLES, CURDLING, CURDLED** to turn into curd; to coagulate
CURE *verb* **CURES, CURING, CURED** to restore someone to health or normality; to heal them □ *noun* **CURES** something that cures or remedies
CURETTAGE *noun* **CURETTAGES** the process of using a curette
CURETTE *noun* **CURETTES** a spoon-shaped device used to scrape tissue from the inner surface of an organ or body cavity for diagnostic purposes, or to remove diseased tissue from such a cavity □ *verb* **CURETTES, CURETTING, CURETTED** to scrape with a curette
CURFEW *noun* **CURFEWS** an official order restricting people's movements, especially after a certain hour at night
CURIE *noun* **CURIES** the former unit of radioactivity which has now been replaced by the becquerel in SI units
CURIO *noun* **CURIOS** an article valued for its rarity or unusualness
CURIOSITY *noun* **CURIOSITIES** eagerness to know; inquisitiveness
CURIOUS *adj* **CURIOUSER** strange; odd
CURIOUSLY *adverb* in a curious way
CURIUM *noun* **CURIUMS** a radioactive element formed by bombarding plutonium-239 with alpha particles
CURL *verb* **CURLS, CURLING, CURLED** to twist, roll or wind (hair) into coils or ringlets □ *noun* **CURLS** a small coil or ringlet of hair
CURLER *noun* **CURLERS** a type of roller for curling the hair
CURLEW *noun* **CURLEWS** a large wading bird, with a slender down-curved bill, long legs and a two-syllable fluting call, found on open plains, moors and marshes across Europe and Asia
CURLICUE *noun* **CURLICUES** a fancy twist or curl
CURLINESS *noun* **CURLINESSES** the state or quality of being curly
CURLING *noun* **CURLINGS** a team game played on ice with smooth heavy stones with handles, that are slid towards a circular target marked on the ice
CURLY *adj* **CURLIER, CURLIEST** having curls; full of curls
CURRAJONG *noun* **CURRAJONGS** a kurrajong
CURRANT *noun* **CURRANTS** a small dried seedless grape
CURRAWONG *noun* **CURRAWONGS** any of several Australian songbirds, with black, grey and white feathers
CURRENCY *noun* **CURRENCIES** the system of money, or the coins and notes, in use in a country
CURRENT *adj* belonging to the present □ *noun* **CURRENTS** the continuous steady flow of a body of water, air, heat, etc, in a particular direction
CURRENTLY *adverb* at the present time
CURRY [1] *noun* **CURRIES** a dish, originally Indian, of meat, fish, or vegetables usually cooked with hot spices
CURRY [2] *verb* **CURRIES, CURRYING, CURRIED** to groom (a horse)
CURSE *noun* **CURSES** a blasphemous or obscene

expression, usually of anger; an oath ◻ verb **CURSES, CURSING, CURSED** to utter a curse against; to revile with curses

CURSED adj under a curse

CURSIVE adj said of handwriting: flowing; having letters which are joined up rather than printed separately ◻ noun cursive writing

CURSIVELY adverb in a cursive way

CURSOR noun **CURSORS** on the screen of a visual display unit: any of various types of special symbol or character, usually an underline character or a rectangular box, that flashes on and off and serves to indicate where the next character to be entered on the keyboard will appear

CURSORY adj hasty; superficial; not thorough

CURT adj **CURTER, CURTEST** rudely brief; dismissive; abrupt

CURTAIL verb **CURTAILS, CURTAILING, CURTAILED** to reduce; to cut short

CURTAIN noun **CURTAINS** a hanging cloth over a window, round a bed, etc for privacy or to exclude light ◻ verb **CURTAINS, CURTAINING, CURTAINED** to surround or enclose something with a curtain

CURTLY adverb in a curt way

CURTNESS noun **CURTNESSES** the quality of being curt

CURTSEY noun **CURTSEYS** a curtsy ◻ verb **CURTSEYS, CURTSEYING, CURTSEYED** to curtsy

CURTSY noun **CURTSIES** a slight bend of the knees with one leg behind the other, performed as a formal gesture of respect by women ◻ verb **CURTSIES, CURTSYING, CURTSIED** to perform a curtsy

CURVATURE noun **CURVATURES** an act of curving or bending

CURVE noun **CURVES** a line no part of which is straight, or a surface no part of which is flat, eg part of a circle or sphere ◻ verb **CURVES, CURVING, CURVED** to form or form into a curve; to move in a curve

CURVY adj **CURVIER, CURVIEST** having many curves, or curved in shape

CUSHION noun **CUSHIONS** a fabric case stuffed with soft material, used for making a seat comfortable, for kneeling on, etc

◻ verb **CUSHIONS, CUSHIONING, CUSHIONED** to reduce the unpleasant or violent effect of something

CUSHY adj **CUSHIER, CUSHIEST** comfortable; easy; undemanding

CUSP noun **CUSPS** a point formed by the meeting of two curves, corresponding to the point where the two tangents coincide

CUSPATE adj shaped like a cusp

CUSS noun **CUSSES** a curse ◻ verb **CUSSES, CUSSING, CUSSED** to curse or swear

CUSSED adj obstinate, stubborn, awkward or perverse

CUSTARD noun **CUSTARDS** a sauce made with sugar, milk and cornflour

CUSTODIAL adj relating to custody; involving custody

CUSTODIAN noun **CUSTODIANS** someone who has care of something, eg a public building or ancient monument; a guardian or curator

CUSTODY noun **CUSTODIES** protective care, especially the guardianship of a child, awarded to someone by a court of law

CUSTOM noun **CUSTOMS** a traditional activity or practice ◻ adj made to order

CUSTOMARY adj usual; traditional; according to custom

CUSTOMER noun **CUSTOMERS** someone who purchases goods from a shop, uses the services of a business, etc

CUT verb **CUTS, CUTTING, CUT** to slit, pierce, slice or sever (a person or thing) using a sharp instrument ◻ noun **CUTS** an act of cutting; a cutting movement or stroke

CUTAWAY adj said of a diagram, etc: having outer parts omitted so as to show the interior ◻ noun **CUTAWAYS** in film-making: a move away from the main action of the scene

CUTBACK noun **CUTBACKS** a reduction in spending, use of resources, etc

CUTE adj **CUTER, CUTEST** attractive; pretty

CUTELY adverb in a cute way

CUTENESS noun **CUTENESSES** the quality of being cute

CUTICLE noun **CUTICLES** especially the outer layer of cells in hair, and the dead hardened skin at the base of fingernails and toenails

CUTICULAR adj of or relating to a cuticle

CUTIS noun **CUTISES** the anatomical name for the skin

CUTLASS noun **CUTLASSES** a short, broad, slightly curved sword with one cutting edge

CUTLER noun **CUTLERS** someone who manufactures and sells cutlery

CUTLERY noun **CUTLERIES** knives, forks and spoons used to eat food

CUTLET noun **CUTLETS** a small piece of meat with a bone attached, usually cut from a rib or the neck

CUTTER noun **CUTTERS** a small single-masted sailing ship

CUTTING noun **CUTTINGS** an extract, article or picture cut from a newspaper, etc ◻ adj hurtful; sarcastic

---

CUZ noun **CUZZES** a cousin
ⓘ This word may be obsolete, but it uses up both a **C** and a **Z**, and scores 14 points.

CWM noun **CWMS** in Wales: a valley
ⓘ This is an extremely valuable word as it does not contain any vowels, and uses up several of the higher-scoring consonants. Playing **CWM** scores 10 points.

CYAN noun **CYANS** a greenish blue colour ◻ adj cyan-coloured

CYANIDE noun **CYANIDES** any of the poisonous salts of hydrocyanic acid, which smell of bitter almonds, and which are extremely toxic and rapidly cause death

CYANITE noun **CYANITES** kyanite

CYANOGEN noun **CYANOGENS** a compound of carbon and nitrogen, consisting of a colourless inflammable poisonous gas with a smell of bitter almonds

CYANOSED adj said of the skin: showing symptoms typical of cyanosis

CYANOSIS noun **CYANOSES** a bluish discoloration of the skin usually caused by lack of oxygen in the blood

CYANOTIC adj affected with cyanosis

CYBERPUNK noun **CYBERPUNKS** a genre of science fiction depicting a society rigidly controlled by computer networks and the actions of hackers who rebel against it

CYCAD noun **CYCADS** a tropical or subtropical gymnosperm, more closely resembling a palm than a conifer, with an unbranched trunk covered with the remains of old leaf bases and a crown of tough leathery leaves

CYCLAMATE noun **CYCLAMATES** any of a number of sweet chemical compounds formerly used as sweetening agents

CYCLAMEN noun **CYCLAMENS** a dark reddish-purple colour, characteristic of the flowers of the cyclamen plant ▫ adj cyclamen-coloured

CYCLE noun **CYCLES** a constantly repeating series of events or processes; short for bicycle ▫ verb **CYCLES, CYCLING, CYCLED** to ride a bicycle

CYCLEWAY noun **CYCLEWAYS** a lane or road, etc specially designed or set aside for the use of pedal cycles

CYCLIC adj relating to, containing, or moving in a cycle

CYCLICAL adj cyclic

CYCLIST noun **CYCLISTS** the rider of a bicycle, motorcycle, etc

CYCLOID noun **CYCLOIDS** the curve traced by a point on the circumference of a circle as the circle rolls along a straight line ▫ adj resembling a circle

CYCLOIDAL adj of or relating to a cycloid

CYCLONE noun **CYCLONES** an area of low atmospheric pressure, often associated with stormy weather, in which winds spiral inward towards a central low

CYCLONIC adj of or relating to a cyclone

CYCLORAMA noun **CYCLORAMAS** a large picture painted on to a cylindrical wall which is designed so that people viewing it from the middle of the room see it in its natural perspective

CYCLOTRON noun **CYCLOTRONS** a circular type of particle accelerator

CYDER noun **CYDERS** cider

CYGNET noun **CYGNETS** a young swan

CYLINDER noun **CYLINDERS** a solid figure of uniform circular cross-section, in which the curved surface is at right angles to the base

CYLINDRIC adj shaped like a cylinder

CYMA noun **CYMAS** in classical orders of architecture: an ogee moulding of the cornice

CYMATIUM noun **CYMATIA** a cyma

CYMBAL noun **CYMBALS** a thin plate-like brass percussion instrument, either beaten with a drumstick, or used as one of a pair that are struck together to produce a ringing clash

CYMBALIST noun **CYMBALISTS** a cymbal-player

CYMBIDIUM noun **CYMBIDIUMS, CYMBIDIA** an orchid native to tropical forests which is widely cultivated for its large showy flowers

CYME noun **CYMES** an inflorescence in which the main stem and each of its branches ends in a flower, and all subsequent flowers develop from lateral buds arising below the apical flowers

CYMOSE adj bearing cymes

CYNIC noun **CYNICS** someone who takes a pessimistic view of human goodness or sincerity

CYNICAL adj disinclined to believe in the goodness or sincerity of others

CYNICALLY adverb in a cynical way

CYNICISM noun **CYNICISMS** the attitude, beliefs or behaviour of a cynic

CYNOSURE noun **CYNOSURES** the focus of attention; the centre of attraction

CYPHER noun **CYPHERS** a cipher ▫ verb **CYPHERS, CYPHERING, CYPHERED** to cipher

CYPRESS noun **CYPRESSES** a slim, dark-green coniferous tree, sometimes associated with death and mourning

CYST noun **CYSTS** an abnormal sac that contains fluid, semi-solid material or gas

CYSTEINE noun **CYSTEINES** an amino acid found in many proteins

CYSTIC adj relating to or like a cyst

CYSTINE noun **CYSTINES** an amino acid that is found in proteins, especially keratin

CYSTITIS noun **CYSTITISES** inflammation of the urinary bladder which is usually caused by bacterial infection and is characterized by a desire to pass urine frequently, and pain or a burning sensation when passing urine

CYTOKININ noun **CYTOKININS** kinin

CYTOLOGY noun **CYTOLOGIES** the scientific study of the structure and function of individual cells, especially as revealed by examination with a microscope

CYTOPLASM noun **CYTOPLASMS** the part of a living cell, excluding the nucleus, that is enclosed by the cell membrane and which contains a range of organelles

CYTOSINE noun **CYTOSINES** one of the four bases found in nucleic acid

CYTOTOXIC adj describing any agent, especially a drug, that destroys or prevents the division of cells, and is used in chemotherapy to treat various forms of cancer

CYTOTOXIN noun **CYTOTOXINS** any substance that has a destructive effect on living cells

CZAR noun **CZARS** a tsar

CZAREVNA noun **CZAREVNAS** a tsarevna

CZARINA noun **CZARINAS** a tsarina

DA *noun* **DAS** dad

DAB *verb* **DABS, DABBING, DABBED** to touch something lightly and usually repeatedly with a cloth, etc □ *noun* **DABS** a small amount of something creamy or liquid

DABBLE *verb* **DABBLES, DABBLING, DABBLED** to do something or study something without serious effort □ *noun* **DABBLES** an act of dabbling

DABBLER *noun* **DABBLERS** someone who dabbles in some activity

DABBLING *noun* **DABBLINGS** an instance of doing or studying something without serious effort

DABCHICK *noun* **DABCHICKS** the little grebe

DACE *noun* **DACES** a small European river fish

DACHA *noun* **DACHAS** a country house or cottage in various parts of the former Soviet Union, especially one provided for the use of a person of importance

DACHSHUND *noun* **DACHSHUNDS** a small breed of dog with a long body and very short legs

DACOIT *noun* **DACOITS** a member of a gang of armed robbers or bandits in India or Burma, especially in the 18c and 19c

DACOITY *noun* **DACOITIES** violent robbery by dacoits

DACTYL *noun* **DACTYLS** a metrical foot consisting of one long or stressed syllable followed by two short or unstressed ones

DACTYLIC *adj* of or relating to a dactyl

DAD *noun* **DADS** a father

DADDY *noun* **DADDIES** a father

DADO *noun* **DADOS, DADOES** the lower part of the wall of a room when decorated differently from the upper part, often consisting of panelling

DAE *verb* **DAES, DAEING, DID, DONE** Scots form of *do*

DAEMON *noun* **DAEMONS** a spirit regarded as halfway between gods and men

DAEMONIC *adj* supernatural

DAFF *noun* **DAFFS** a daffodil

DAFFODIL *noun* **DAFFODILS** a yellow narcissus, occurring naturally in many parts of Europe, now much cultivated in many varieties varying widely in colour and shape □ *adj* yellow

DAFFY [1] *noun* **DAFFIES** a daffodil

DAFFY [2] *adj* **DAFFIER, DAFFIEST** daft; crazy

DAFT *adj* **DAFTER, DAFTEST** silly or foolish

DAFTIE *noun* **DAFTIES** a daft person; an imbecile

DAFTLY *adverb* in a daft way

DAFTNESS *noun* **DAFTNESSES** the quality of being daft

DAG *noun* **DAGS** a dirt- or dung-clotted tuft of wool on a sheep □ *verb* **DAGS, DAGGING, DAGGED** to cut away the dags from (a sheep)

DAGGA *noun* **DAGGAS** Indian hemp, or other forms of hemp, smoked as a narcotic

DAGGER *noun* **DAGGERS** a knife or short sword with a pointed end, used for stabbing

DAGGY *adj* **DAGGIER, DAGGIEST** scruffy; dishevelled

DAGLOCK *noun* **DAGLOCKS** a dag

DAH *noun* **DAHS** a word representing the dash in the spoken form of Morse code

DAHL *noun* **DAHLS** dal

DAHLIA *noun* **DAHLIAS** a garden plant with large brightly coloured flowers, some varieties having ball-like heads with many petals

DAILY *adj* happening, appearing, etc every day, or every day except Sunday, or now often every day except Saturday and Sunday □ *adverb* every day; every weekday □ *noun* **DAILIES** a newspaper published every day except Sunday

DAIMON *noun* **DAIMONS** a daemon

DAIMONIC *adj* daemonic

DAINTILY *adverb* in a dainty way

DAINTY *adj* **DAINTIER, DAINTIEST** small and pretty, and, usually, delicate □ *noun* **DAINTIES** something small and nice to eat, especially a small cake or sweet

DAIQUIRI *noun* **DAIQUIRIS** a drink made with rum, lime juice and sugar

DAIRY *noun* **DAIRIES** the building on a farm where milk is cooled and temporarily stored

DAIRYING *noun* **DAIRYINGS** keeping a dairy farm

DAIRYMAID *noun* **DAIRYMAIDS** a milkmaid

DAIRYMAN *noun* **DAIRYMEN** someone who looks after the dairy cows on a farm

DAIS *noun* **DAISES** a raised platform in a hall, eg for speakers at a meeting

DAISY *noun* **DAISIES** any of various common wild and cultivated flowering plants belonging to the sunflower family

DAK *noun* **DAKS** in India: the mail or post; a letter

DAKOIT *noun* **DAKOITS** a dacoit

DAL *noun* **DALS** any of various edible dried split pea-like seeds

DALE *noun* **DALES** a valley, especially one in the North of England

DALESMAN *noun* **DALESMEN** a man belonging to the dales of the north of England, especially Yorkshire

DALLIANCE *noun* **DALLIANCES** idle wasting of time

DALLY *verb* **DALLIES, DALLYING, DALLIED** to waste time idly or frivolously

DALMATIC *noun* **DALMATICS** a loose-fitting, wide-sleeved, ecclesiastical vestment, worn especially by deacons of the RC church

DALTON *noun* **DALTONS** the atomic mass unit

DALTONISM *noun* **DALTONISMS** colour-blindness, especially confusion between red and green

DAM *noun* **DAMS** a barrier built to contain water and prevent flooding □ *verb* **DAMS, DAMMING, DAMMED** to hold back (water, etc) with a dam

DAMAGE *noun* **DAMAGES** harm or injury, or loss caused by injury □ *verb* **DAMAGES, DAMAGING, DAMAGED** to cause harm, injury or loss to someone or something

DAMAGED *adj* harmed; injured; broken

DAMAGING *adj* having a bad effect on a person's reputation

DAMASCENE *noun* **DAMASCENES** inlay of metal, especially gold, or of other materials, on steel, etc □ *verb* **DAMASCENES, DAMASCENING, DAMASCENED** to decorate (especially steel) by inlaying or encrusting

DAMASK *noun* **DAMASKS** a type of cloth, originally silk, now usually linen, with a pattern woven into it, often used for tablecloths, curtains, etc □ *adj* greyish-pink or greyish-red

DAME *noun* **DAMES** a woman who has been honoured by the Queen or the Government for services or merit

DAMFOOL *adj* stupid; ridiculous

DAMMED past form of **dam**

DAMMING a form of **dam**

DAMMIT *exclamation* damn it!

DAMN *verb* **DAMNS, DAMNING, DAMNED** to sentence someone to never-ending punishment in hell □ *adj* used for emphasis: annoying; hateful

DAMNABLE *adj* hateful; awful; deserving to be condemned

DAMNABLY *adverb* annoyingly; very

DAMNATION *noun* **DAMNATIONS** never-ending punishment in hell □ *exclamation* expressing annoyance or disappointment

DAMNATORY *adj* bringing or incurring damnation

DAMNED *adj* **DAMNEDER, DAMNEDEST** sentenced to damnation □ *adverb* extremely; very

DAMNIFY *verb* **DAMNIFIES, DAMNIFYING, DAMNIFIED** to cause loss or damage to someone

DAMNING *adj* proving or suggesting guilt

DAMP *adj* **DAMPER, DAMPEST** slightly wet □ *noun* **DAMPS** slight wetness, eg in walls or the air, especially if cold and unpleasant

□ *verb* **DAMPS, DAMPING, DAMPED** to make something slightly wet

DAMPEN *verb* **DAMPENS, DAMPENING, DAMPENED** to make something slightly wet

DAMPER *noun* **DAMPERS** something which lessens enthusiasm, interest, etc

DAMPISH *adj* slightly damp

DAMPLY *adverb* in a damp way

DAMPNESS *noun* **DAMPNESSES** the condition or quality of being damp

DAMSEL *noun* **DAMSELS** a girl or young woman

DAMSELFLY *noun* **DAMSELFLIES** a large predatory insect with a long body and two pairs of slender wings which are typically held together over the abdomen when at rest

DAMSON *noun* **DAMSONS** a small purple plum

DAN *noun* **DANS** any of the ten grades of black belt awarded for particular levels of skill in judo, karate, etc

DANCE *verb* **DANCES, DANCING, DANCED** to make a usually repeated series of rhythmic steps or movements (usually in time to music) □ *noun* **DANCES** a series of fixed steps, usually made in time to music

DANCEABLE *adj* suitable for dancing with

DANCER *noun* **DANCERS** someone who dances, especially professionally

DANCING *noun* **DANCINGS** the action of making a usually repeated series of rhythmic steps or movements (usually in time to music)

DANDELION *noun* **DANDELIONS** a perennial plant, widespread in most temperate regions, producing single yellow flowerheads on hollow stems containing white latex sap and having a rosette of deeply notched leaves

DANDER *noun* **DANDERS** anger; passion

DANDIFY *verb* **DANDIFIES, DANDIFYING, DANDIFIED** to dress someone up like a dandy

DANDILY *adverb* in a dandy way

DANDLE *verb* **DANDLES, DANDLING, DANDLED** to bounce or dance (usually a small child) on one's knee

DANDRUFF *noun* **DANDRUFFS** thin whitish flakes of dead skin shed from the scalp

DANDY *noun* **DANDIES** a man who pays a lot of attention to his appearance, dressing very fashionably or elegantly □ *adj* **DANDIER, DANDIEST** good; fine

DANDYISH *adj* like a dandy

DANDYISM *noun* **DANDYISMS** the manners or style of a dandy

DANELAW *noun* **DANELAW** the Danish law that prevailed in that part of England occupied by the Danes during the 9c–11c

DANGER *noun* **DANGERS** a situation or state in which someone or something may suffer harm, an injury or a loss

DANGEROUS *adj* likely or able to cause harm or injury

DANGLE *verb* **DANGLES, DANGLING, DANGLED** to hang loosely, sometimes swinging or swaying

DANK *adj* **DANKER, DANKEST** usually said of a place: unpleasantly wet and cold

DANKISH *adj* slightly dank

DANKNESS *noun* **DANKNESSES** the state of being dank

DANSEUR *noun* **DANSEURS** a male dancer

DANSEUSE *noun* **DANSEUSES** a female dancer; a ballerina

DAP *verb* **DAPS, DAPPING, DAPPED** to fish with a fly bounced gently on the surface of the water □ *noun* **DAPS** a bounce

DAPHNE *noun* **DAPHNES** any of various evergreen shrubs that bear clusters of small flowers

DAPPER *adj* **DAPPERER, DAPPEREST** usually said of men: neat and smart in appearance and lively in movement

DAPPERLY *adverb* in a dapper way

DAPPLED *adj* marked with spots or rounded patches of a different, usually darker, colour

DARE *verb* **DARES, DARING, DARED, DURST** to be brave enough to do something frightening, difficult or dangerous □ *noun* **DARES** a challenge to do something dangerous, etc

DARING *adj* bold, courageous or adventurous □ *noun* boldness, courage

DARINGLY *adverb* in a daring way

DARIOLE *noun* **DARIOLES** a shell of pastry, etc, or a small round mould

DARK *adj* **DARKER, DARKEST** without light ◻ *noun* **DARKS** the absence of light

DARKEN *verb* **DARKENS, DARKENING, DARKENED** to make or become dark or darker

DARKENED *adj* made dark or darker

DARKISH *adj* slightly dark

DARKLY *adverb* in a mysterious, gloomy, sinister or threatening way or tone of voice

DARKNESS *noun* **DARKNESSES** the absence of light

DARKROOM *noun* **DARKROOMS** a room into which no ordinary light is allowed, used for developing photographs

DARLING *noun* **DARLINGS** often used as a term of affection: a dearly loved person ◻ *adj* well loved

DARN *verb* **DARNS, DARNING, DARNED** to mend (a hole, a garment, etc) by sewing with rows of stitches which cross each other ◻ *noun* **DARNS** a place in a garment where a hole has been darned

DARNED *adj* **DARNEDER, DARNEDEST** irritating; disliked

DARNEL *noun* **DARNELS** a species of rye grass which grows as a weed in cornfields of Asia and Europe

DARNER *noun* **DARNERS** a person who darns

DARNING *noun* **DARNINGS** the action of mending a hole, a garment, etc by sewing with rows of stitches which cross each other

DARSHAN *noun* **DARSHANS** in Hinduism: a blessing conferred by seeing or touching a great or holy person

DART *noun* **DARTS** a narrow pointed weapon that can be thrown or fired ◻ *verb* **DARTS, DARTING, DARTED** to move suddenly and quickly

DARTBOARD *noun* **DARTBOARDS** a circular target in the game of darts which is divided into numbered sections, with points being scored according to the section each dart hits

DARTER *noun* **DARTERS** a person or thing which darts

DARTS *noun* **DARTS** a game in which darts are thrown at a dartboard

DASH *verb* **DASHES, DASHING, DASHED** to run quickly; to rush ◻ *noun* **DASHES** a quick run or sudden rush

DASHBOARD *noun* **DASHBOARDS** a panel with dials, switches and instruments, etc in front of the driver's seat in a motor vehicle, boat, etc

DASHEEN *noun* **DASHEENS** the taro plant

DASHEKI *noun* **DASHEKIS** a dashiki

DASHIKI *noun* **DASHIKIS** a type of long, loose, brightly coloured shirt worn chiefly by Blacks in Africa, the Caribbean and the US

DASHING *adj* smart; stylish

DASHINGLY *adverb* in a dashing way

DASSIE *noun* **DASSIES** the hyrax

DASTARDLY *adj* cowardly, mean and cruel

DATA *singular or plural noun* **DATA** one or more pieces of information or facts, especially those obtained by scientific observation or experiment

DATABANK *noun* **DATABANKS** a collection of databases

DATABASE *noun* **DATABASES** a collection of computer data

DATABLE *adj* dateable

DATAGLOVE *noun* **DATAGLOVES** an electronically wired glove which transmits the wearer's movements to a virtual-reality monitor

DATE *noun* **DATES** the day of the month and/or the year, recorded by a number or series of numbers ◻ *verb* **DATES, DATING, DATED** to put a date on something

DATEABLE *adj* capable of being given a date

DATED *adj* old-fashioned

DATELESS *adj* without a date or fixed limits

DATIVE *noun* **DATIVES** in certain languages, eg Latin, Greek and German: the form or case of a noun, pronoun or adjective which is used chiefly to show that the word is the indirect object of a verb

DATUM *noun* **DATA** a piece of information

DATURA *noun* **DATURAS** any plant of a group of plants including the thorn apple, which have strong narcotic or toxic properties

DAUB *verb* **DAUBS, DAUBING, DAUBED** to spread something roughly or unevenly onto or over a surface ◻ *noun* **DAUBS** soft, sticky material such as clay, often used as a covering for walls

DAUBE *noun* **DAUBES** a meat stew

DAUBER *noun* **DAUBERS** a person who daubs

DAUGHTER *noun* **DAUGHTERS** a female child considered in relation to her parents ◻ *adj* derived by some process from, and thought of as being like a daughter of, something

DAUNT *verb* **DAUNTS, DAUNTING, DAUNTED** to frighten, worry or discourage someone

DAUNTING *adj* intimidating; discouraging

DAUNTLESS *adj* fearless; not easily discouraged

DAVENPORT *noun* **DAVENPORTS** a type of desk

DAVIT *noun* **DAVITS** either of a pair of crane-like devices on a ship on which a lifeboat is hung

DAW *verb* **DAWS, DAWING, DAWED** a Scots word meaning to dawn

DAWDLE *verb* **DAWDLES, DAWDLING, DAWDLED** to walk more slowly than necessary or desirable

DAWDLER *noun* **DAWDLERS** a person who dawdles

DAWN *noun* **DAWNS** the time of day when light first appears as the sun rises ◻ *verb* **DAWNS, DAWNING, DAWNED** said of the day: to begin; to become light

DAY *noun* **DAYS** a period of 24 hours, especially a day from midnight to midnight

DAYBREAK *noun* **DAYBREAKS** the time in the morning when light first appears in the sky; dawn

DAYDREAM *noun* **DAYDREAMS** pleasant thoughts which take one's attention away from what one is, or should be, doing ◻ *verb* **DAYDREAMS, DAYDREAMING, DAYDREAMED** to be engrossed in daydreams

DAYGLO *adj* coloured luminously brilliant green, yellow, pink or orange

DAYLIGHT *noun* **DAYLIGHTS** the light given by the Sun

DAYLONG *adj* during the whole day

DAYTIME *noun* **DAYTIMES** the time when there is normally daylight, between sunrise and sunset

DAZE *verb* **DAZES, DAZING, DAZED** to make someone feel confused or unable to think clearly (eg by a blow or shock) ◻ *noun* **DAZES** a confused, forgetful or inattentive state of mind

DAZED *adj* affected by a blow or shock; mentally confused

DAZEDLY *adverb* in a dazed way

DAZZLE *verb* **DAZZLES, DAZZLING, DAZZLED** to make someone unable to see properly, with or because of a strong light

DAZZLER *noun* **DAZZLERS** a person who impresses greatly by their beauty, charm, skill, etc

DAZZLING *adj* temporarily blinding

DEACON *noun* **DEACONS** a member of the lowest rank of clergy in the Roman Catholic and Anglican churches

DEACONESS *noun* **DEACONESSES** in some churches: a woman who has similar duties to those of a deacon

DEAD *adj* **DEADER, DEADEST** no longer living □ *adverb* absolutely; quite; exactly; very

DEADEN *verb* **DEADENS, DEADENING, DEADENED** to lessen, weaken or make less sharp, strong, etc

DEADENER *noun* **DEADENERS** a person or thing that deadens

DEADENING *adj* that deadens

DEADHEAD *verb* **DEADHEADS, DEADHEADING, DEADHEADED** to remove withered or dead flowers from (plants)

DEADLINE *noun* **DEADLINES** a time by which something must be done

DEADLOCK *noun* **DEADLOCKS** a situation in which no further progress towards an agreement is possible □ *verb* **DEADLOCKS, DEADLOCKING, DEADLOCKED** to make or come to a situation of deadlock

DEADLY *adj* **DEADLIER, DEADLIEST** causing or likely to cause death □ *adverb* very; absolutely

DEADNESS *noun* **DEADNESSES** lack of sensation or feeling

DEADPAN *adj* said of someone's expression, etc: showing no emotion or feeling, especially when joking but pretending to be serious

DEAF *adj* **DEAFER, DEAFEST** unable to hear at all or unable to hear well

DEAFEN *verb* **DEAFENS, DEAFENING, DEAFENED** to make someone deaf or temporarily unable to hear

DEAFENING *adj* that deafens

DEAFLY *adverb* without hearing

DEAFNESS *noun* **DEAFNESSES** partial or total loss of hearing in one or both ears

DEAL *noun* **DEALS** a bargain, agreement or arrangement, especially in business or politics □ *verb* **DEALS, DEALING, DEALT** to divide the cards among the players in a card game

DEALER *noun* **DEALERS** a person or firm dealing in retail goods; a trader; the player who deals in a card game

DEALINGS *plural noun* one's manner of acting towards others

DEAN *noun* **DEANS** a senior clergyman in an Anglican cathedral

DEANERY *noun* **DEANERIES** the position or office of a dean

DEAR *adj* **DEARER, DEAREST** lovable; high in price □ *noun* **DEARS** a charming or lovable person

DEARLY *adverb* affectionately; earnestly; at great cost

DEARNESS *noun* **DEARNESSES** the quality of being dear

DEARTH *noun* **DEARTHS** a scarceness or lack of something

DEASIL *adverb* in the direction of the sun

DEATH *noun* **DEATHS** the time, act or manner of dying, or the state of being dead

DEATHLESS *adj* immortal; unforgettable

DEATHLIKE *adj* deadly; like death

DEATHLY *adj* **DEATHLIER, DEATHLIEST** deadly; deathlike

DEB *noun* **DEBS** a debutante

DEBACLE *noun* **DEBACLES** total disorder, defeat, collapse of organization, etc

DEBAG *verb* **DEBAGS, DEBAGGING, DEBAGGED** to remove the trousers from someone as a prank or punishment

DEBAR *verb* **DEBARS, DEBARRING, DEBARRED** to stop someone from joining, taking part in, doing, etc something

DEBARK *verb* **DEBARKS, DEBARKING, DEBARKED** to disembark

DEBARMENT *noun* **DEBARMENTS** the act of debarring

DEBASE *verb* **DEBASES, DEBASING, DEBASED** to lower the value, quality, or status of something

DEBASED *adj* lowered in value or status; spoiled

DEBASER *noun* **DEBASERS** a person who debases

DEBASING *adj* that debases

DEBATABLE *adj* doubtful; able to be argued about; uncertain

DEBATE *noun* **DEBATES** a formal discussion, often in front of an audience, in which two or more people put forward opposing views on a particular subject □ *verb* **DEBATES, DEBATING, DEBATED** to hold or take part in such a discussion

DEBATER *noun* **DEBATERS** someone who takes part in a debate

DEBATING *noun* formal discussion of a question

DEBAUCH *verb* **DEBAUCHES, DEBAUCHING, DEBAUCHED** to corrupt someone; to cause or persuade someone to take part in immoral, especially sexual, activities or excessive drinking □ *noun* **DEBAUCHES** a period of debauched behaviour

DEBAUCHED *adj* corrupted; immoral

DEBAUCHEE *noun* **DEBAUCHEES** someone who likes sensual indulgence

DEBBY *adj* **DEBBIER, DEBBIEST** belonging to, suitable for or like a debutante or debutantes

DEBENTURE *noun* **DEBENTURES** a type of loan to a company or government agency which is usually made for a set period of time and carries a fixed rate of interest

DEBILITY *noun* **DEBILITIES** weakness and languor

DEBIT *noun* **DEBITS** an entry in an account recording what is owed or has been spent □ *verb* **DEBITS, DEBITING, DEBITED** to take from (an account, etc)

DEBONAIR *adj* said especially of a man: cheerful, charming and of elegant appearance and good manners

DEBOUCH *verb* **DEBOUCHES, DEBOUCHING, DEBOUCHED** said of troops or a river, etc: to come out of a narrow place or opening into a wider or more open place

DEBRIEF *verb* **DEBRIEFS, DEBRIEFING, DEBRIEFED** to gather information from (a diplomat, astronaut, soldier, etc) after a battle, event, mission, etc

DEBRIEFING *noun* **DEBRIEFINGS** interrogation after a completed mission, etc

DEBRIS *noun* **DEBRIS** what remains of something crushed, smashed, destroyed, etc

DEBT *noun* **DEBTS** something which is owed

DEBTOR *noun* **DEBTORS** someone owing money

DEBUG *verb* **DEBUGS, DEBUGGING, DEBUGGED** to remove secret microphones from (a room, etc)

DEBUNK *verb* **DEBUNKS, DEBUNKING, DEBUNKED** to show (a person's claims, good reputation, etc) to be false or unjustified

DEBUS *verb* **DEBUSSES, DEBUSSING, DEBUSSED** to unload from, or get out of, a bus or other vehicle

DEBUT *noun* **DEBUTS** the first public appearance of a performer

DEBUTANTE *noun* **DEBUTANTES** a young woman making her first formal appearance as an adult in upper-class society, usually at a ball

DECADE *noun* **DECADES** a period of 10 years

DECADENCE *noun* **DECADENCES** a falling from high to low standards in morals, art, etc

DECADENT *adj* having low moral standards

DECAFF *adj* without caffeine □ *noun* **DECAFFS** coffee without caffeine

DECAGON *noun* **DECAGONS** a polygon with 10 sides and 10 angles

DECAGONAL *adj* having 10 sides and 10 angles

DECAL *noun* **DECALS** a picture or design prepared for permanent transfer to glass, china, plastic, etc

DECALCIFY *verb* **DECALCIFIES, DECALCIFYING, DECALCIFIED** to remove calcium from (bones), or deprive (bones) of calcium

DECALITRE *noun* **DECALITRES** a measure of volume equal to 10 litres

DECAMETRE *noun* **DECAMETRES** a measure of length equal to 10 metres

DECAMP *verb* **DECAMPS, DECAMPING, DECAMPED** to go away suddenly, especially secretly

DECANAL *adj* belonging or relating to a dean or deanery

DECANT *verb* **DECANTS,**

DECANTING, DECANTED to pour (wine, etc) from one bottle or container to another, leaving any sediment behind

DECANTER *noun* **DECANTERS** an ornamental bottle with a stopper, used for decanted wine, sherry, whisky, etc

DECAPOD *noun* **DECAPODS** any of various crustaceans which have 10 limbs, including pincers, eg crabs, lobsters, prawns

DECATHLON *noun* **DECATHLONS** an athletic competition (usually for men) in which competitors take part in the following 10 events over two days: 100m, long jump, shot put, high jump, 400m, 110m hurdles, discus, pole vault, javelin and 1500m

DECAY *verb* **DECAYS, DECAYING, DECAYED** to make or become rotten, ruined, weaker in health or power, etc □ *noun* **DECAYS** the natural breakdown of dead organic matter

DECAYED *adj* rotten

DECEASE *noun* **DECEASES** death

DECEASED *adj* dead, especially recently dead

DECEDENT *noun* **DECEDENTS** a deceased person

DECEIT *noun* **DECEITS** an act of deceiving or misleading

DECEITFUL *adj* disposed or tending to deceive; insincere

DECEIVE *verb* **DECEIVES, DECEIVING, DECEIVED** to mislead or lie to someone

DECEIVER *noun* **DECEIVERS** a person who deceives

DECENCY *noun* **DECENCIES** decent behaviour or character

DECENNIAL *adj* happening every 10 years

DECENT *adj* **DECENTER, DECENTEST** respectable; suitable; modest, not vulgar or immoral

DECENTLY *adverb* in a decent way

DECEPTION *noun* **DECEPTIONS** an act of deceiving or the state of being deceived

DECEPTIVE *adj* deceiving; misleading

DECIBEL *noun* **DECIBELS** a unit equal to $\frac{1}{10}$ of a bel, used for comparing levels of power, especially sound, on a logarithmic scale

DECIDE *verb* **DECIDES, DECIDING, DECIDED** to settle something; to make the final result of something certain

DECIDED *adj* clear and definite; unmistakeable

DECIDEDLY *adverb* undoubtedly; definitely

DECIDER *noun* **DECIDERS** someone or something that decides

DECIDUOUS *adj* denoting plants which shed all their leaves at a certain time of year, usually the autumn in temperate regions

DECILITRE *noun* **DECILITRES** one tenth of a litre

DECILLION *noun* **DECILLIONS** a million raised to the tenth power

DECIMAL *adj* based on the number 10; relating to powers of 10 or the base 10 □ *noun* **DECIMALS** a decimal fraction

DECIMATE *verb* **DECIMATES, DECIMATING, DECIMATED** to reduce greatly in number; to destroy a large part or number of something

DECIMATOR *noun* **DECIMATORS** a person or thing that decimates

DECIMETRE *noun* **DECIMETRES** one tenth of a metre

DECIPHER *verb* **DECIPHERS, DECIPHERING, DECIPHERED** to translate (a message or text in code or in an unfamiliar or strange form of writing) into ordinary understandable language

DECISION *noun* **DECISIONS** the act of deciding

DECISIVE *adj* putting an end to doubt or dispute

DECK [1] *noun* **DECKS** a platform extending from one side of a ship to the other, and forming a floor or covering

DECK [2] *verb* **DECKS, DECKING, DECKED** to decorate or embellish something

DECKED *adj* adorned, decorated

DECKING *noun* **DECKINGS** the act of adorning; adornment

DECKLE *noun* **DECKLES** in paper-making: a device for fixing the width of a sheet

DECKO *noun* **DECKOS** a look

DECLAIM *verb* **DECLAIMS, DECLAIMING, DECLAIMED** to make (a speech) in an impressive and dramatic manner

DECLAIMER *noun* **DECLAIMERS** a person who declaims

DECLARE *verb* **DECLARES, DECLARING, DECLARED** to announce something publicly or formally

DECLARER noun **DECLARERS** a person who declares
DECLINE verb **DECLINES, DECLINING, DECLINED** to become less strong or healthy; to refuse (an invitation, etc), especially politely □ noun **DECLINES** a lessening of strength, health, quality, quantity, etc
DECLIVITY noun **DECLIVITIES** a downward slope
DECLUTCH verb **DECLUTCHES, DECLUTCHING, DECLUTCHED** to release the clutch of (a motor vehicle)
DECOCT verb **DECOCTS, DECOCTING, DECOCTED** to extract the essence, etc of (a substance) by boiling
DECOCTION noun **DECOCTIONS** a liquid obtained by boiling something in water, eg to extract its flavour
DECODE verb **DECODES, DECODING, DECODED** to translate (a coded message) into ordinary language
DECODER noun **DECODERS** a person or device that decodes
DECOKE verb **DECOKES, DECOKING, DECOKED** to remove carbon from (an internal-combustion engine)
DECOLLATE verb **DECOLLATES, DECOLLATING, DECOLLATED** to separate (continuous stationery) into separate sheets or forms
DÉCOLLETÉ adj said of a woman's dress, etc: having the neckline cut low at the front
DECOLOR verb **DECOLORS, DECOLORING, DECOLORED** to decolour
DECOLOUR verb **DECOLOURS, DECOLOURING, DECOLOURED** to deprive something of colour
DECOMPOSE verb **DECOMPOSES, DECOMPOSING, DECOMPOSED** said of a dead organism: to rot, usually as a result of the activity of fungi and bacteria
DECONTROL verb **DECONTROLS, DECONTROLLING, DECONTROLLED** to remove control, especially official controls or restrictions, from something □ noun **DECONTROLS** removal of control
DÉCOR noun **DÉCORS** the style of decoration, furnishings, etc in a room or house
DECORATE verb **DECORATES, DECORATING, DECORATED** to put paint or wallpaper on (a wall, etc)

DECORATOR noun **DECORATORS** someone who decorates buildings professionally
DECOROUS adj said of behaviour or appearance: correct or socially acceptable; showing proper respect
DECORUM noun **DECORUMS** correct or socially acceptable behaviour
DECOUPAGE noun **DECOUPAGES** the craft of applying decorative paper cut-outs to eg wood surfaces, practised since the 18c
DECOY verb **DECOYS, DECOYING, DECOYED** to lead or lure into a trap □ noun **DECOYS** someone or something used to lead or lure (a person or animal) into a trap
DECREASE verb **DECREASES, DECREASING, DECREASED** to make or become less □ noun **DECREASES** a lessening or loss
DECREE noun **DECREES** a formal order or ruling made by someone in high authority (eg a monarch) and which becomes law □ verb **DECREES, DECREEING, DECREED** to order or decide something formally or officially
DECREMENT noun **DECREMENTS** decreasing; decrease
DECREPIT adj weak or worn out because of old age
DECRETAL noun **DECRETALS** a papal decree □ adj belonging or relating to a decree
DECRIAL noun **DECRIALS** the act of decrying
DECRIER noun **DECRIERS** a person who decries
DECRY verb **DECRIES, DECRYING, DECRIED** to express disapproval of someone or something; to criticize someone or something as worthless or unsuitable
DECRYPT verb **DECRYPTS, DECRYPTING, DECRYPTED** to decode something
DECUMBENT adj lying down
DEDICATE verb **DEDICATES, DEDICATING, DEDICATED** to give or devote (oneself or one's time, money, etc) wholly or chiefly to some purpose, cause, etc
DEDICATED adj working very hard at or spending a great deal of one's time and energy on something
DEDICATEE noun **DEDICATEES** a person to whom something is dedicated
DEDICATOR noun **DEDICATORS** someone who makes a dedication

DEDUCE verb **DEDUCES, DEDUCING, DEDUCED** to think out or judge on the basis of what one knows or assumes to be fact
DEDUCIBLE adj capable of being deduced
DEDUCT verb **DEDUCTS, DEDUCTING, DEDUCTED** to take away (a number, amount, etc)
DEDUCTION noun **DEDUCTIONS** the act or process of deducting
DEDUCTIVE adj said of a logical process of thought: deducing or involving deduction of particular facts from general truths

DEE verb **DEES, DEEING, DEED** to damn

DEED noun **DEEDS** something someone has done
DEEJAY noun **DEEJAYS** a disc jockey
DEEM verb **DEEMS, DEEMING, DEEMED** to judge, think or consider
DEEP adj **DEEPER, DEEPEST** far down from the top or surface; with a relatively great distance from the top or surface to the bottom □ adverb deeply □ noun **DEEPS** the ocean
DEEPEN verb **DEEPENS, DEEPENING, DEEPENED** to make or become deeper, greater, more intense, etc
DEEPLY adverb very greatly
DEEPNESS noun **DEEPNESSES** depth
DEER noun **DEER** any of numerous ruminant mammals, found throughout Europe, Asia and N and S America, and distinguished by the presence of antlers in the male
DEERSKIN noun **DEERSKINS** the skin of deer or leather made from it

DEF adj **DEFFER, DEFFEST** excellent, brilliant

DEFACE verb **DEFACES, DEFACING, DEFACED** to deliberately spoil the appearance of something (eg by marking or cutting)
DEFACER noun **DEFACERS** a person or thing that defaces
DEFALCATE verb **DEFALCATES, DEFALCATING, DEFALCATED** to embezzle or misuse money held in trust
DEFAME verb **DEFAMES, DEFAMING, DEFAMED** to attack

the good reputation of someone by saying something unfavourable about them

DEFAT verb **DEFATS, DEFATTING, DEFATTED** to remove fat or fats from something

DEFAULT verb **DEFAULTS, DEFAULTING, DEFAULTED** to fail to do what one should do, especially to fail to pay what is due □ noun **DEFAULTS** a failure to do or pay what one should

DEFAULTER noun **DEFAULTERS** a person who defaults, especially in paying a debt

DEFEAT verb **DEFEATS, DEFEATING, DEFEATED** to beat or win a victory over someone, eg in a war, competition, game or argument □ noun **DEFEATS** the act of defeating or state of being defeated

DEFEATISM noun **DEFEATISMS** a state of mind in which one too readily expects or accepts defeat or failure

DEFEATIST adj readily expecting or accepting defeat or failure □ noun **DEFEATISTS** someone who readily expects or accepts defeat or failure

DEFECATE verb **DEFECATES, DEFECATING, DEFECATED** to empty the bowels of waste matter

DEFECT noun **DEFECTS** a flaw, fault or imperfection □ verb **DEFECTS, DEFECTING, DEFECTED** to leave one's country, political party or group, especially to support or join an opposing one

DEFECTION noun **DEFECTIONS** (an act of) desertion

DEFECTIVE adj imperfect; having a defect or defects

DEFECTOR noun **DEFECTORS** a person who deserts or betrays their country, etc

DEFENCE noun **DEFENCES** the act of defending against attack

DEFEND verb **DEFENDS, DEFENDING, DEFENDED** to guard or protect someone or something against attack or when attacked

DEFENDANT noun **DEFENDANTS** someone against whom a charge is brought in a law-court

DEFENDER noun **DEFENDERS** someone who defends against attack, especially in military and sporting contexts

DEFENSE noun **DEFENSES** a defence

DEFENSIVE adj defending or ready to defend

DEFER verb **DEFERS, DEFERRING, DEFERRED** to put off something or leave it until a later time

DEFERABLE adj capable of being deferred

DEFERENCE noun **DEFERENCES** willingness to consider or respect the wishes, etc of others

DEFERMENT noun **DEFERMENTS** a delay or postponement

DEFERRAL noun **DEFERRALS** a delay or postponement

DEFERRED past form of **defer**

DEFERRER noun **DEFERRERS** a procrastinator

DEFERRING a form of **defer**

DEFIANCE noun **DEFIANCES** an act of defying or of open disobedience; challenging or opposition, especially in a way that shows lack of respect

DEFIANT adj openly disobedient or challenging

DEFIANTLY adverb in a defiant way

DEFICIENT adj not good enough; not having all that is needed

DEFICIT noun **DEFICITS** the amount by which some quantity, especially a sum of money, is less than what is required, eg the amount by which expenditure is greater than income

DEFIED past form of **defy**

DEFIER noun **DEFIERS** a person who defies

DEFIES a form of **defy**

DEFILE ¹ verb **DEFILES, DEFILING, DEFILED** to make something dirty or polluted

DEFILE ² noun **DEFILES** a narrow valley or passage between mountains

DEFILER noun **DEFILERS** a person who defiles

DEFINABLE adj capable of being defined or described precisely

DEFINABLY adverb in a definable way

DEFINE verb **DEFINES, DEFINING, DEFINED** to fix or state the exact meaning of (a word, etc)

DEFINER noun **DEFINERS** a person or thing that defines

DEFINITE adj fixed or firm; not liable to change

DEFLATE verb **DEFLATES, DEFLATING, DEFLATED** to collapse or grow smaller by letting out gas

DEFLATED adj having the air or gas removed

DEFLATER noun **DEFLATERS** a person or thing that deflates

DEFLATION noun **DEFLATIONS** the act of deflating or the process of being deflated

DEFLATOR noun **DEFLATORS** a deflater

DEFLECT verb **DEFLECTS, DEFLECTING, DEFLECTED** to turn aside from the correct or intended course or direction

DEFLECTOR noun **DEFLECTORS** a device for deflecting a flame, electric arc, etc

DEFLOWER verb **DEFLOWERS, DEFLOWERING, DEFLOWERED** to deprive someone (especially a woman) of their virginity

DEFOLIANT noun **DEFOLIANTS** a type of herbicide that causes the leaves to fall off plants

DEFOLIATE verb **DEFOLIATES, DEFOLIATING, DEFOLIATED** to make leaves fall off (plants, trees, etc)

DEFOREST verb **DEFORESTS, DEFORESTING, DEFORESTED** to cut down forest trees for commercial use, or to clear land for agriculture, without replacing them

DEFORM verb **DEFORMS, DEFORMING, DEFORMED** to change the shape of something without breaking it, so that it looks ugly, unpleasant, unnatural or spoiled

DEFORMED adj misshapen, disfigured

DEFORMITY noun **DEFORMITIES** being deformed or misshapen

DEFRAUD verb **DEFRAUDS, DEFRAUDING, DEFRAUDED** to dishonestly prevent someone getting or keeping something which belongs to them or to which they have a right

DEFRAUDER noun **DEFRAUDERS** a person who defrauds

DEFRAY verb **DEFRAYS, DEFRAYING, DEFRAYED** to provide the money to pay (someone's costs or expenses)

DEFRAYAL noun **DEFRAYALS** the action of defraying

DEFRAYER noun **DEFRAYERS** a person who defrays

DEFREEZE verb **DEFREEZES, DEFREEZING, DEFROZE, DEFROZEN** to thaw something out; to defrost (especially frozen food)

DEFROCK verb **DEFROCKS, DEFROCKING, DEFROCKED** to

DEFROST verb **DEFROSTS, DEFROSTING, DEFROSTED** to remove ice from something or have the ice removed from something; to unfreeze

DEFROSTER noun **DEFROSTERS** a device for defrosting (especially a windscreen)

DEFT adj **DEFTER, DEFTEST** skilful, quick and neat

DEFTLY adverb in a deft way

DEFTNESS noun **DEFTNESSES** the quality of being deft

DEFUNCT adj no longer living, existing, active, usable or in use

DEFUSE verb **DEFUSES, DEFUSING, DEFUSED** to remove the fuse from (a bomb, etc)

DEFY verb **DEFIES, DEFYING, DEFIED** to resist or disobey someone boldly and openly

DEGAS verb **DEGASSES, DEGASSING, DEGASSED** to remove gas from something

DEGRADE verb **DEGRADES, DEGRADING, DEGRADED** to disgrace or humiliate someone

DEGRADING adj humiliating; debasing

DEGREASE verb **DEGREASES, DEGREASING, DEGREASED** to strip or cleanse something of grease

DEGREE noun **DEGREES** an amount or extent

DEHISCENT adj denoting a fruit, or the anther of a stamen, that bursts open spontaneously at maturity to release the seeds or pollen

DEHORN verb **DEHORNS, DEHORNING, DEHORNED** to remove the horns from (an animal, etc)

DEHORNER noun **DEHORNERS** a person or tool that dehorns animals

DEHYDRATE verb **DEHYDRATES, DEHYDRATING, DEHYDRATED** to remove water from (a substance or organism)

DEHYDRATED adj having lost too much water

DEI a plural of **deus**

DEIFIC adj making something or someone godlike or divine, or treating it or them as if they were godlike or divine

DEIFICAL adj deific

DEIFY verb **DEIFIES, DEIFYING,**

DEIFIED to regard or worship someone or something as a god

DEIGN verb **DEIGNS, DEIGNING, DEIGNED** to do something reluctantly and in a way that shows that one considers the matter hardly important or beneath one's dignity

DEISM noun **DEISMS** belief in the existence of God without acceptance of any religion or message revealed by God to man

DEIST noun **DEISTS** a person who believes in the existence of God, but not in a divinely revealed religion

DEISTIC adj of or relating to deists or deism

DEITY noun **DEITIES** a god or goddess

DEJECTED adj sad; miserable

DEJECTION noun **DEJECTIONS** being dejected or sad

DEKKO noun **DEKKOS** a look

DEL noun **DELS** another word for *nabla*

DELAY verb **DELAYS, DELAYING, DELAYED** to slow someone or something down or make them late □ noun **DELAYS** the act of delaying or state of being delayed

DELAYER noun **DELAYERS** a person or thing that delays

DELE noun **DELES** a direction, usually found in the margin of a manuscript or other text, to remove a letter or word, indicated by δ

DELEGABLE adj capable of being delegated

DELEGACY noun **DELEGACIES** a system or the process of delegating

DELEGATE verb **DELEGATES, DELEGATING, DELEGATED** to give (part of one's work, power, etc) to someone else □ noun **DELEGATES** someone chosen to be the representative for another person or group of people eg at a conference or meeting

DELETE verb **DELETES, DELETING, DELETED** to rub out, score out or remove something, especially from something written or printed

DELETION noun **DELETIONS** the action of deleting; something deleted

DELF noun **DELFS** a type of earthenware originally made at Delft in the Netherlands, typically with a blue design on a white background

DELFT noun **DELFTS** delf

DELI noun **DELIS** a delicatessen (a shop or counter selling eg cooked meats, cheeses etc)

DELICACY noun **DELICACIES** the state or quality of being delicate

DELICATE adj easily damaged or broken

DELICIOUS adj with a very pleasing taste or smell

DELIGHT verb **DELIGHTS, DELIGHTING, DELIGHTED** to please greatly □ noun **DELIGHTS** great pleasure

DELIGHTED adj highly pleased; thrilled

DELIMIT verb **DELIMITS, DELIMITING, DELIMITED** to mark or fix the limits or boundaries of (powers, etc)

DELINEATE verb **DELINEATES, DELINEATING, DELINEATED** to show something by drawing or by describing in words

DELIRIOUS adj affected by delirium, usually as a result of fever or other illness

DELIRIUM noun **DELIRIUMS, DELIRIA** a state of madness or mental confusion and excitement, often caused by fever or other illness, drugs, etc

DELIVER verb **DELIVERS, DELIVERING, DELIVERED** to carry (goods, letters, etc) to a person or place

DELIVERER noun **DELIVERERS** someone who delivers, especially goods, letters, etc

DELIVERY noun **DELIVERIES** the carrying of (goods, letters, etc) to a person or place

DELL noun **DELLS** a small valley or hollow, usually wooded

DELOUSE verb **DELOUSES, DELOUSING, DELOUSED** to free someone or something of lice

DELPH noun **DELPHS** delf

DELTA noun **DELTAS** the fourth letter of the Greek alphabet; an area of silt, sand, gravel or clay, often roughly triangular, formed at the mouth of some rivers

DELTAIC adj relating to a delta

DELTOID adj triangular; having the shape of the Greek capital letter delta □ noun **DELTOIDS** a deltoid muscle (the large triangular muscle of the shoulder)

DELUDABLE adj capable of being deluded

DELUDE verb **DELUDES, DELUDING, DELUDED** to deceive or mislead

DELUDER *noun* **DELUDERS** a person who deludes

DELUGE *noun* **DELUGES** a flood □ *verb* **DELUGES, DELUGING, DELUGED** to flood; to cover in water

DELUSION *noun* **DELUSIONS** the act of deluding or the state of being deluded

DELUSIVE *adj* deluding or likely to delude; deceptive

DELUSORY *adj* delusive

DELVE *verb* **DELVES, DELVING, DELVED** to search or rummage deep

DEMAGOGIC *adj* of or relating to a demagogue

DEMAGOGUE *noun* **DEMAGOGUES** someone who tries to win political power or support by appealing to people's emotions and prejudices

DEMAGOGY *noun* **DEMAGOGIES** the behaviour or actions of a demagogue

DEMAND *verb* **DEMANDS, DEMANDING, DEMANDED** to ask or ask for firmly, forcefully or urgently □ *noun* **DEMANDS** a forceful request or order

DEMANDER *noun* **DEMANDERS** a person who demands

DEMANDING *adj* requiring a lot of effort, ability, etc

DEMANNING *noun* **DEMANNINGS** the deliberate reduction of the number of employees in a particular industry, etc

DEMARCATE *verb* **DEMARCATES, DEMARCATING, DEMARCATED** to mark out the limits or boundaries of something

DÉMARCHE *noun* **DÉMARCHES** a step, measure or initiative, especially in diplomatic affairs

DEME *noun* **DEMES** a group of plants or animals that are closely related and live in a single distinct locality

DEMEAN *verb* **DEMEANS, DEMEANING, DEMEANED** to lower the dignity of or lessen respect for someone, especially oneself

DEMEANING *adj* that demeans

DEMEANOR *noun* **DEMEANORS** demeanour

DEMEANOUR *noun* **DEMEANOURS** manner of behaving

DEMENTED *adj* mad; out of one's mind

DEMENTIA *noun* **DEMENTIAS** a loss or severe lessening of normal mental ability and functioning, occurring especially in the elderly

DEMERARA *noun* **DEMERARAS** a form of crystallized brown sugar

DEMERGE *verb* **DEMERGES, DEMERGING, DEMERGED** said of companies, etc: to undergo a reversal of a merger; to become separate again

DEMERGER *noun* **DEMERGERS** the reversal of a merger

DEMERIT *noun* **DEMERITS** a fault or failing

DEMERSAL *adj* living underwater; found on or near the bottom of the sea, a lake etc

DEMIGOD *noun* **DEMIGODS** someone who is part human and part god, especially someone believed to be the offspring of a human and a god

DEMIJOHN *noun* **DEMIJOHNS** a large bottle with a short narrow neck and one or two small handles, used for storing eg wine

DEMISE *noun* **DEMISES** death

DEMIST *verb* **DEMISTS, DEMISTING, DEMISTED** to free (a vehicle's windscreen, etc) from condensation by blowing warm air over it

DEMISTER *noun* **DEMISTERS** a mechanical device which frees a vehicle's windscreen, etc from condensation by blowing warm air over it

DEMITASSE *noun* **DEMITASSES** a small cup of coffee, especially black coffee

DEMO *noun* **DEMOS** a demonstration, a public display of opinion

DEMOB *noun* **DEMOBS** release from service in the armed forces

DEMOCRACY *noun* **DEMOCRACIES** a form of government in which the people govern themselves or elect representatives to govern them

DEMOCRAT *noun* **DEMOCRATS** someone who believes in democracy as a principle

DÉMODÉ *adj* out of fashion

DEMODED *adj* no longer in fashion

DEMOLISH *verb* **DEMOLISHES, DEMOLISHING, DEMOLISHED** to pull or tear down (a building, etc)

DEMON *noun* **DEMONS** an evil spirit

DEMONIAC *adj* characteristic of, belonging to or like a demon or demons

DEMONIC *adj* characteristic of, belonging to or like a demon or demons

DEMONISM *noun* **DEMONISMS** a belief in or worship of demons

DEMOTE *verb* **DEMOTES, DEMOTING, DEMOTED** to reduce someone to a lower rank or grade

DEMOTIC *adj* said especially of a language: used in everyday affairs; popular

DEMOTION *noun* **DEMOTIONS** the act of demoting; reduction in rank or grade

DEMULCENT *adj* soothing □ *noun* **DEMULCENTS** a drug, etc, that soothes irritation

DEMUR *verb* **DEMURS, DEMURRING, DEMURRED** to object

DEMURE *adj* **DEMURER, DEMUREST** said of a person: quiet, modest and well-behaved

DEMURELY *adverb* in a demure way

DEMURRAL *noun* **DEMURRALS** an act of demurring, objection

DEMYSTIFY *verb* **DEMYSTIFIES, DEMYSTIFYING, DEMYSTIFIED** to remove the mystery from something

DEN *noun* **DENS** a wild animal's home □ *verb* **DENS, DENNING, DENNED** to retire to a den

DENARIUS *noun* **DENARII** an ancient Roman silver coin

DENARY *adj* containing or having the number 10 as a basis

DENATURE *verb* **DENATURES, DENATURING, DENATURED** to change the structure or composition of (something)

DENAZIFY *verb* **DENAZIFIES, DENAZIFYING, DENAZIFIED** to free someone or something from Nazi ideology and influence

DENDRITE *noun* **DENDRITES** any of a number of cytoplasmic projections that radiate outwards from the star-shaped cell body of a neurone

DENDRITIC *adj* tree-like

DENDROID *adj* tree-like; having branches

DENDRON *noun* **DENDRONS** a dendrite

DENGUE *noun* **DENGUES** an acute tropical viral fever, seldom fatal, transmitted by mosquitos

DENIABLE *adj* able to be denied

DENIABLY *adverb* disputably

DENIAL *noun* **DENIALS** an act of

denying or declaring something not to be true

DENIED past form of **deny**

DENIER noun **DENIERS** the unit of weight of silk, rayon or nylon thread, usually used as a measure of the fineness of stockings or tights

DENIES a form of **deny**

DENIGRATE verb **DENIGRATES, DENIGRATING, DENIGRATED** to scorn or criticize someone; to attack or belittle the reputation, character or worth of someone

DENIM noun **DENIMS** a kind of hard-wearing, usually blue, twilled cotton cloth used for making jeans, overalls, etc □ adj made of denim

DENIZEN noun **DENIZENS** an inhabitant, either human or animal

DENOTE verb **DENOTES, DENOTING, DENOTED** to mean; to be the name of or sign for something

DENOUNCE verb **DENOUNCES, DENOUNCING, DENOUNCED** to inform against or accuse someone publicly

DENSE adj **DENSER, DENSEST** closely packed or crowded together

DENSELY adverb in a dense way

DENSENESS noun **DENSENESSES** the quality of being dense

DENSITY noun **DENSITIES** the state of being dense or the degree of denseness

DENT noun **DENTS** a hollow in the surface of something, especially something hard, made by pressure or a blow □ verb **DENTS, DENTING, DENTED** to make a dent in something

DENTAL adj concerned with or for the teeth or dentistry □ noun **DENTALS** a dental sound, made by putting the tongue to the teeth, eg th in the word the

DENTATE adj with a tooth-like notched pattern round the edge

DENTIL noun **DENTILS** each of a series of small square or rectangular blocks or projections, especially those set beneath the cornice in classical orders

DENTIN noun **DENTINS** dentine

DENTINE noun **DENTINES** the hard material that forms the bulk of a tooth

DENTIST noun **DENTISTS** someone who is professionally trained and qualified to practise dentistry

DENTISTRY noun **DENTISTRIES**

the branch of medicine concerned with the diagnosis, treatment and prevention of diseases of the oral cavity and teeth

DENTITION noun **DENTITIONS** the number, arrangement and type of teeth in a human or animal

DENTURE noun **DENTURES** a false tooth or set of false teeth

›**DENUDE** verb **DENUDES, DENUDING, DENUDED** to make someone or something completely bare

DENY verb **DENIES, DENYING, DENIED** to declare something not to be true

DEODAR noun **DEODARS** a cedar tree belonging to the Himalayas

DEODORANT noun **DEODORANTS** a substance that prevents or conceals unpleasant smells, especially the smell of stale sweat on the human body

DEODORISE verb **DEODORISES, DEODORISING, DEODORISED** to deodorize

DEODORIZE verb **DEODORIZES, DEODORIZING, DEODORIZED** to remove, conceal or absorb the unpleasant smell of something

DEONTIC noun **DEONTICS** the study of duty and obligations □ adj concerning duty and obligation

DEOXIDATE verb **DEOXIDATES, DEOXIDATING, DEOXIDATED** to deoxidize

DEOXIDISE verb **DEOXIDISES, DEOXIDISING, DEOXIDISED** to deoxidize

DEOXIDIZE verb **DEOXIDIZES, DEOXIDIZING, DEOXIDIZED** to remove oxygen from something or to chemically reduce it

DEPART verb **DEPARTS, DEPARTING, DEPARTED** to leave

DEPARTED adj that has gone away

DEPARTURE noun **DEPARTURES** an act of going away or leaving

DEPEND verb **DEPENDS, DEPENDING, DEPENDED** to rely on someone or something; to be able to trust them or it

DEPENDANT noun **DEPENDANTS** a person who is kept or supported financially by another

DEPENDENT adj relying on something or someone for financial or other support

DEPICT verb **DEPICTS, DEPICTING, DEPICTED** to paint or draw something

DEPICTER noun **DEPICTERS** a person who depicts

DEPICTION noun **DEPICTIONS** the action of depicting; a painting or drawing

DEPICTIVE adj having the quality of depicting

DEPICTOR noun **DEPICTORS** a depicter

DEPILATE verb **DEPILATES, DEPILATING, DEPILATED** to remove hair from (a part of the body)

DEPLANE verb **DEPLANES, DEPLANING, DEPLANED** to disembark from an aeroplane

DEPLETE verb **DEPLETES, DEPLETING, DEPLETED** to reduce greatly in number, quantity, etc; to use up (supplies, money, energy, resources, etc)

DEPLETION noun **DEPLETIONS** the act of emptying or exhausting

DEPLORE verb **DEPLORES, DEPLORING, DEPLORED** to feel or express great disapproval of or regret for something

DEPLOY verb **DEPLOYS, DEPLOYING, DEPLOYED** to spread out and position (troops) ready for battle

DEPONENT noun **DEPONENTS** someone whose written testimony (deposition) is used as evidence in a court

DEPORT verb **DEPORTS, DEPORTING, DEPORTED** to legally remove or expel (a person) from a country

DEPORTEE noun **DEPORTEES** someone who has been or is about to be expelled from a country

DEPOSABLE adj capable of being deposed

DEPOSE verb **DEPOSES, DEPOSING, DEPOSED** to remove someone from a high office or powerful position

DEPOSER noun **DEPOSERS** a person who removes someone from a high office or powerful position

DEPOSIT verb **DEPOSITS, DEPOSITING, DEPOSITED** to put down or leave something; to put (money, etc) in a bank, etc □ noun **DEPOSITS** a sum of money, etc, deposited in a bank, etc

DEPOSITOR noun **DEPOSITORS** someone who deposits money in a bank or building society, especially in a deposit account

DEPOT noun **DEPOTS** a storehouse or warehouse

DEPRAVE verb **DEPRAVES,**

DEPRAVING, DEPRAVED to make someone evil or morally corrupt

DEPRAVED *adj* morally corrupted

DEPRAVITY *noun* **DEPRAVITIES** a vitiated or corrupt state of moral character

DEPRECATE *verb* **DEPRECATES, DEPRECATING, DEPRECATED** to express disapproval of something; to deplore something

DEPRECATING *adj* expressing contempt, disapproval, disparagement

DEPRESS *verb* **DEPRESSES, DEPRESSING, DEPRESSED** to make someone sad and gloomy

DEPRESSED *adj* sad and gloomy

DEPRESSING *adj* causing low spirits

DEPRESSOR *noun* **DEPRESSORS** something or someone that depresses

DEPRIVE *verb* **DEPRIVES, DEPRIVING, DEPRIVED** to take or keep something from someone; to prevent them from using or enjoying it

DEPRIVED *adj* said of a person: suffering from hardship through lack of money, reasonable living conditions, etc

DEPTH *noun* **DEPTHS** deepness; the distance from the top downwards, from the front to the back or from the surface inwards

DEPUTE *verb* **DEPUTES, DEPUTING, DEPUTED** to formally appoint someone to do something □ *adj* in Scotland: appointed deputy □ *noun* **DEPUTES** in Scotland: a deputy

DEPUTISE *verb* **DEPUTISES, DEPUTISING, DEPUTISED** to deputize

DEPUTIZE *verb* **DEPUTIZES, DEPUTIZING, DEPUTIZED** to act as deputy

DEPUTY *noun* **DEPUTIES** a person appointed to act on behalf of, or as an assistant to, someone else □ *adj* in some organizations: next in rank to the head and having the authority to act on their behalf

DERAIL *verb* **DERAILS, DERAILING, DERAILED** to leave or make (a train, etc) leave the rails

DERANGE *verb* **DERANGES, DERANGING, DERANGED** to make someone insane

DERANGED *adj* insane

DERBY *noun* **DERBIES** a horse race held annually at Epsom Downs, England

DERELICT *adj* abandoned □ *noun* **DERELICTS** a tramp; someone with no home or money

DERIDE *verb* **DERIDES, DERIDING, DERIDED** to laugh at or make fun of someone

DERIDER *noun* **DERIDERS** a person who derides

DERISION *noun* **DERISIONS** the act of deriding; scornful laughter

DERISIVE *adj* scornful; mocking

DERISORY *adj* ridiculous and insulting, especially ridiculously small

DERIVABLE *adj* obtainable

DERIVE *verb* **DERIVES, DERIVING, DERIVED** to descend, issue or originate

DERMAL *adj* belonging or relating to skin, especially the dermis

DERMIC *adj* dermal

DERMIS *noun* **DERMISES** the thick lower layer of the skin that lies beneath the epidermis, containing blood capillaries, nerve endings, hair follicles, sweat glands, lymph vessels and some muscle fibres

DEROGATE *verb* **DEROGATES, DEROGATING, DEROGATED** to lessen by taking away; to detract

DERRICK *noun* **DERRICKS** a type of crane with a movable arm

DERRIÈRE *noun* **DERRIÈRES** the behind; the buttocks

DERRINGER *noun* **DERRINGERS** a short American pistol

DERRIS *noun* **DERRISES** a tropical climbing plant related to peas and beans

DERV *noun* **DERVS** diesel oil used as a fuel for road vehicles

DERVISH *noun* **DERVISHES** a member of any of various Muslim religious groups who have taken vows of poverty, some of whom perform spinning dances as part of their religious ritual

DESCALE *verb* **DESCALES, DESCALING, DESCALED** to remove scales from (especially fish)

DESCANT *noun* **DESCANTS** a melody played or harmony sung above the main tune □ *adj* said of a musical instrument: having a higher pitch and register than others of the same type

DESCEND *verb* **DESCENDS, DESCENDING, DESCENDED** to go or move down from a higher to a lower place or position

DESCENDER *noun* **DESCENDERS**

someone or something that descends

DESCENDING *adj* moving or coming down or downwards

DESCENT *noun* **DESCENTS** the act or process of coming or going down

DESCHOOL *verb* **DESCHOOLS, DESCHOOLING, DESCHOOLED** to free (children) from the restrictions of traditional classroom learning and a set curriculum, and educate them in a less formal way, especially at home

DESCHOOLING *noun* **DESCHOOLINGS** educating children in a less formal way, especially at home

DESCRIBE *verb* **DESCRIBES, DESCRIBING, DESCRIBED** to say what someone or something is like

DESCRIBER *noun* **DESCRIBERS** a person who describes

DESCRY *verb* **DESCRIES, DESCRYING, DESCRIED** to see or catch sight of something

DESECRATE *verb* **DESECRATES, DESECRATING, DESECRATED** to treat or use (a sacred object) or behave in (a holy place) in a way that shows a lack of respect or causes damage

DESELECT *verb* **DESELECTS, DESELECTING, DESELECTED** said of a branch of a political party: to reject (the existing Member of Parliament or local councillor) as a candidate for the next election

DESERT[1] *verb* **DESERTS, DESERTING, DESERTED** to leave or abandon (a place or person), intending not to return

DESERT[2] *noun* **DESERTS** an arid area of land where rainfall is less than potential evaporation, vegetation is scarce or non-existent, and which is characterized by extremely high or low temperatures

DESERTED *adj* said of a building, etc: empty or abandoned

DESERTER *noun* **DESERTERS** someone who leaves military service without permission

DESERTION *noun* **DESERTIONS** an act of deserting; the state of being deserted

DESERTS *plural noun* what one deserves, usually something unfavourable

DESERVE *verb* **DESERVES, DESERVING, DESERVED** to have earned, be entitled to or be worthy of (a reward or punishment, etc)

DESERVING *adj* worthy of being given support, a reward, etc

DESEX *verb* **DESEXES, DESEXING, DESEXED** to deprive someone or something of sexual character or quality

DESICCANT *noun* **DESICCANTS** a substance that absorbs water and so can be used as a drying agent to remove water from, or prevent absorption of water by, other substances ▫ *adj* drying; having the power of drying

DESICCATE *verb* **DESICCATES, DESICCATING, DESICCATED** to dry or remove the moisture from something, especially from food in order to preserve it

DESICCATED *adj* of food: dried for preservation

DESIGN *verb* **DESIGNS, DESIGNING, DESIGNED** to develop or prepare a plan, drawing or model of something before it is built or made ▫ *noun* **DESIGNS** a plan, drawing or model showing how something is to be made

DESIGNATE *verb* **DESIGNATES, DESIGNATING, DESIGNATED** to name, choose or specify someone or something for a particular purpose or duty ▫ *adj* having been appointed to some official position but not yet holding it

DESIGNER *noun* **DESIGNERS** someone who makes designs, plans, patterns, drawings, etc, especially as a profession ▫ *adj* designed by and bearing the name of a famous fashion designer

DESIGNING *adj* using cunning and deceit to achieve a purpose

DESIRABLE *adj* pleasing; worth having

DESIRABLY *adverb* in a desirable way

DESIRE *noun* **DESIRES** a longing or wish ▫ *verb* **DESIRES, DESIRING, DESIRED** to want

DESIROUS *adj* wanting something keenly

DESIST *verb* **DESISTS, DESISTING, DESISTED** to stop

DESK *noun* **DESKS** a sloping or flat table, often with drawers, for sitting at while writing, reading, etc

DESKILL *verb* **DESKILLS, DESKILLING, DESKILLED** to remove the element of human skill from a job, operation, process, etc, through automation, computerization, etc

DESKTOP *adj* small enough to fit on the top of a desk ▫ *noun*

DESKTOPS a computer small enough to use at a desk

DESOLATE *adj* said of a place: deserted, barren and lonely ▫ *verb* **DESOLATES, DESOLATING, DESOLATED** to overwhelm someone with sadness or grief

DESOLATED *adj* made desolate

DESPAIR *verb* **DESPAIRS, DESPAIRING, DESPAIRED** to lose or lack hope ▫ *noun* **DESPAIRS** the state of having lost hope

DESPAIRING *adj* giving up hope; involving or indicating a loss of hope

DESPATCH *noun* **DESPATCHES** a dispatch ▫ *verb* **DESPATCHES, DESPATCHING, DESPATCHED** to dispatch

DESPERADO *noun* **DESPERADOS, DESPERADOES** especially in 19c western USA: a bandit or outlaw

DESPERATE *adj* extremely anxious, fearful or despairing

DESPISE *verb* **DESPISES, DESPISING, DESPISED** to look down on someone or something with scorn and contempt

DESPITE *prep* in spite of

DESPOIL *verb* **DESPOILS, DESPOILING, DESPOILED** to rob or steal everything valuable from (a place)

DESPOILER *noun* **DESPOILERS** a person who despoils

DESPOT *noun* **DESPOTS** someone who has very great or total power, especially if they use such power in a cruel or oppressive way

DESPOTIC *adj* having absolute power; tyrannical

DESPOTISM *noun* **DESPOTISMS** complete or absolute power

DESSERT *noun* **DESSERTS** a sweet food served after the main course of a meal

DESTINE *verb* **DESTINES, DESTINING, DESTINED** (often by fate) to ordain or appoint to a certain use or state

DESTINY *noun* **DESTINIES** the purpose or future as arranged by fate or God

DESTITUTE *adj* lacking money, food, shelter, etc; extremely poor

DESTROY *verb* **DESTROYS, DESTROYING, DESTROYED** to knock down, break into pieces, completely ruin, etc

DESTROYER *noun* **DESTROYERS** someone or something that destroys or causes destruction

DESTRUCT *verb* **DESTRUCTS, DESTRUCTING, DESTRUCTED** said of equipment, especially a missile in flight: to destroy or be destroyed, especially for safety reasons

DESUETUDE *noun* **DESUETUDES** disuse; discontinuance

DESULTORY *adj* jumping from one thing to another with no plan, purpose or logical connection

DETACH *verb* **DETACHES, DETACHING, DETACHED** to unfasten or separate

DETACHED *adj* said of a building: not joined to another on either side

DETAIL *noun* **DETAILS** a small feature, fact or item ▫ *verb* **DETAILS, DETAILING, DETAILED** to describe or list fully

DETAILED *adj* giving full particulars; exhaustive

DETAIN *verb* **DETAINS, DETAINING, DETAINED** to stop, hold back, keep waiting or delay someone or something

DETAINEE *noun* **DETAINEES** a person held under guard eg by the police, especially for political reasons

DETECT *verb* **DETECTS, DETECTING, DETECTED** to see or notice

DETECTION *noun* **DETECTIONS** the act or process of detecting or state of being detected

DETECTIVE *noun* **DETECTIVES** a police officer whose job is to solve crime by observation and gathering evidence

DETECTOR *noun* **DETECTORS** an instrument or device used for detecting the presence of something

DETENTION *noun* **DETENTIONS** the act of detaining or the state of being detained, especially in prison or police custody

DETER *verb* **DETERS, DETERRING, DETERRED** to discourage or prevent someone or something from doing something because of fear of unpleasant consequences

DETERGE *verb* **DETERGES, DETERGING, DETERGED** to cleanse (a wound, etc)

DETERGENT *noun* **DETERGENTS** a surface-active cleansing agent which, unlike soaps, does not produce a scum in hard water ▫ *adj* having the power to clean

DETERMENT *noun* **DETERMENTS** the action of deterring

DETERMINE *verb* **DETERMINES, DETERMINING, DETERMINED** to fix or settle the exact limits or nature of something

DETERMINED *adj* firm in purpose; resolute

DETERRED past form of **deter**

DETERRENT *noun* **DETERRENTS** something which deters, especially a weapon intended to deter attack □ *adj* capable of deterring

DETERRING a form of **deter**

DETEST *verb* **DETESTS, DETESTING, DETESTED** to dislike something intensely; to hate

DETHRONE *verb* **DETHRONES, DETHRONING, DETHRONED** to remove (a monarch) from the throne

DETONATE *verb* **DETONATES, DETONATING, DETONATED** to explode or make something explode

DETONATOR *noun* **DETONATORS** an explosive substance or a device used to make a bomb, etc explode

DETOUR *noun* **DETOURS** a route away from and longer than a planned or more direct route □ *verb* **DETOURS, DETOURING, DETOURED** to make a detour

DETOX *noun* **DETOXES** detoxification □ *verb* **DETOXES, DETOXING, DETOXED** to detoxify

DETOXIFY *verb* **DETOXIFIES, DETOXIFYING, DETOXIFIED** to make (a toxic substance) harmless

DETRACT *verb* **DETRACTS, DETRACTING, DETRACTED** to take away from something or lessen it

DETRACTOR *noun* **DETRACTORS** a belittler or disparager

DETRAIN *verb* **DETRAINS, DETRAINING, DETRAINED** to set down or get down out of a railway train

DETRIMENT *noun* **DETRIMENTS** harm or loss

DETRITAL *adj* of or relating to detritus

DETRITION *noun* **DETRITIONS** the wearing away of rock etc by wind, water or glaciers

DETRITUS *noun* **DETRITUS** the loosened fragments of rock produced by detrition

DEUCE *noun* **DEUCES** in tennis: a score of forty points each in a game or five games each in a match

DEUS *noun* **DEI, DI** a Latin word for *god*

DEUTERIUM *noun* **DEUTERIUMS**
one of the three isotopes of hydrogen

DEUTERON *noun* **DEUTERONS** the nucleus of an atom of deuterium, composed of a proton and a neutron

DEVALUATE *verb* **DEVALUATES, DEVALUATING, DEVALUATED** to devalue

DEVALUE *verb* **DEVALUES, DEVALUING, DEVALUED** to reduce the value of (a currency) in relation to the values of other currencies

DEVASTATE *verb* **DEVASTATES, DEVASTATING, DEVASTATED** to cause great destruction in or to something

DEVASTATED *adj* said of a person: overwhelmed with shock or grief

DEVASTATING *adj* completely destructive

DEVELOP *verb* **DEVELOPS, DEVELOPING, DEVELOPED** to make or become more mature, more advanced, more complete, more detailed, etc

DEVELOPER *noun* **DEVELOPERS** a chemical used to process photographic film

DEVIANCE *noun* **DEVIANCES** departure from normal standards or methods

DEVIANCY *noun* **DEVIANCIES** deviance

DEVIANT *adj* not following the normal patterns, accepted standards, etc □ *noun* **DEVIANTS** someone who does not behave in what is considered to be a normal or acceptable fashion, especially sexually

DEVIATE *verb* **DEVIATES, DEVIATING, DEVIATED** to turn aside or move away from what is considered a correct or normal course, standard of behaviour, way of thinking, etc □ *noun* **DEVIATES** a deviant

DEVIATION *noun* **DEVIATIONS** the act of deviating

DEVICE *noun* **DEVICES** something made for a special purpose, eg a tool or instrument

DEVIL *noun* **DEVILS** the most powerful evil spirit; Satan □ *verb* **DEVILS, DEVILLING, DEVILLED** to prepare or cook (meat, etc) with a spicy seasoning

DEVILISH *adj* characteristic of or like a devil; as if from, produced by, etc a devil □ *adverb* very

DEVILMENT *noun* **DEVILMENTS** mischievous fun

DEVILRY *noun* **DEVILRIES** mischievous fun

DEVIOUS *adj* not totally open or honest; deceitful

DEVIOUSLY *adverb* in a devious way

DEVISE *verb* **DEVISES, DEVISING, DEVISED** to invent, make up or put together (a plan, etc) in one's mind

DEVISER *noun* **DEVISERS** someone who devises plans, etc

DEVISOR *noun* **DEVISORS** someone who bequeaths property by will

DEVOID *adj* **DEVOIDER, DEVOIDEST** destitute, free; empty

DEVOLVE *verb* **DEVOLVES, DEVOLVING, DEVOLVED** said of duties, power, etc: to be transferred to someone else

DEVOTE *verb* **DEVOTES, DEVOTING, DEVOTED** to use or give up (a resource such as time or money) wholly to some purpose

DEVOTED *adj* loving and loyal (to)

DEVOTEDLY *adverb* in a devoted way

DEVOTEE *noun* **DEVOTEES** a keen follower or enthusiastic supporter

DEVOTION *noun* **DEVOTIONS** great love or loyalty; enthusiasm for or willingness to do what is required by someone

DEVOUR *verb* **DEVOURS, DEVOURING, DEVOURED** to eat up something greedily

DEVOURER *noun* **DEVOURERS** a person who eats greedily

DEVOUT *adj* **DEVOUTER, DEVOUTEST** sincerely religious in thought and behaviour

DEVOUTLY *adverb* in a devout way

DEW *verb* **DEWS, DEWING, DEWED** to moisten (as) with dew □ *noun* **DEWS** tiny droplets of water that are deposited on eg leaves close to the ground on cool clear nights

DEWAR *noun* **DEWARS** an insulated vessel with double walls, the inner space surrounded by a vacuum and silvered so that heat losses by convection and radiation are reduced to a minimum

DEWILY *adverb* in the manner of dew

DEWINESS *noun* **DEWINESSES** the state of being dewy

DEWLAP *noun* **DEWLAPS** a flap of loose skin hanging down from the throat of certain cattle, dogs and other animals

For longer words, see *The Chambers Dictionary*

DEWY *adj* **DEWIER, DEWIEST** covered in dew

DEXTER *adj* on the right-hand side

DEXTERITY *noun* **DEXTERITIES** skill in using one's hands

DEXTEROUS *adj* having, showing or done with dexterity; skilful

DEXTRAL *adj* associated with, or located on, the right side, especially the right side of the body

DEXTRALLY *adverb* to the right-hand side

DEXTRAN *noun* **DEXTRANS** a carbohydrate formed in sugar solutions, used as a substitute for blood plasma in transfusions

DEXTRIN *noun* **DEXTRINS** any of a group of short-chain polysaccharides produced during the breakdown of starch or glycogen by enzymes, used as a thickener in foods and adhesives

DEXTRINE *noun* **DEXTRINES** dextrin

DEXTRORSE *adj* rising spirally and turning anticlockwise

DEXTROSE *noun* **DEXTROSES** a type of glucose

DEXTROUS *adj* dexterous

DEY *noun* **DEYS** formerly, the pasha of Algiers

DHAL *noun* **DHALS** dal

DHARMA *noun* **DHARMAS** truth

DHOBI *noun* **DHOBIS** in India, Malaya, etc: a man who does washing

DHOOTI *noun* **DHOOTIS** a dhoti

DHOTI *noun* **DHOTIS** a garment worn by some Hindu men, consisting of a long strip of cloth wrapped around the waist and between the legs

DHOW *noun* **DHOWS** a type of lateen ship with one or more sails, used in countries around the Indian Ocean

DI a plural of **deus**

DIABETES *noun* **DIABETES** any of various disorders, especially diabetes mellitus, that are characterized by thirst and excessive production of urine

DIABETIC *noun* **DIABETICS** someone suffering from diabetes □ *adj* relating to or suffering from diabetes

DIABLERIE *noun* **DIABLERIES** magic, especially black magic or witchcraft

DIABOLIC *adj* characteristic of,

like or belonging to a devil; devilish

DIABOLISM *noun* **DIABOLISMS** the worship of the Devil or devils; witchcraft; black magic

DIABOLIST *noun* **DIABOLISTS** a person who participates in or studies diabolism

DIABOLO *noun* **DIABOLOS** a game in which a two-headed top is spun, tossed and caught on a string attached to two sticks held one in each hand

DIACID *adj* having two replaceable hydrogen atoms

DIACONAL *adj* belonging to or relating to a deacon

DIACONATE *noun* **DIACONATES** the position of deacon

DIACRITIC *noun* **DIACRITICS** a mark written or printed over, under or through a letter to show that that letter has a particular sound, as in *é, è, ç, ñ* □ *adj* functioning as a diacritic; distinguishing

DIADEM *noun* **DIADEMS** a crown or jewelled headband, worn by a royal person

DIAERESIS *noun* **DIAERESES** a mark (¨) placed over a vowel to show that it is to be pronounced separately from the vowel before it, as in naïve

DIAGNOSE *verb* **DIAGNOSES, DIAGNOSING, DIAGNOSED** to identify (an illness) from a consideration of its symptoms

DIAGNOSIS *noun* **DIAGNOSES** the process whereby a disease or disorder is provisionally identified on the basis of its symptoms and the patient's medical history

DIAGONAL *adj* said of a straight line: joining any two non-adjacent corners of a polygon or any two vertices not on the same face in a polyhedron □ *noun* **DIAGONALS** a diagonal line

DIAGRAM *noun* **DIAGRAMS** a line drawing, often labelled with text, that shows something's structure or the way in which it functions

DIAL *noun* **DIALS** a disc or plate on a clock, radio, meter, etc with numbers or symbols on it and a movable indicator, used to indicate eg measurements or selected settings □ *verb* **DIALS, DIALLING, DIALLED** to use a telephone dial or keypad to call (a number)

DIALECT *noun* **DIALECTS** a form of a language spoken in a particular

region or by a certain social group, differing from other forms in grammar, vocabulary, and in some cases pronunciation

DIALECTAL *adj* belonging to a dialect

DIALECTIC *noun* **DIALECTICS** the art or practice of establishing truth by discussion

DIALLER *noun* **DIALLERS** a person who surveys by dial (a miner's compass with sights for surveying)

DIALOG *noun* **DIALOGS** a dialogue

DIALOGUE *noun* **DIALOGUES** a conversation, especially a formal one

DIALYSE *verb* **DIALYSES, DIALYSING, DIALYSED** to separate something by dialysis

DIALYSER *noun* **DIALYSERS** a machine which carries out dialysis

DIALYSIS *noun* **DIALYSES** the separation of particles in a solution by diffusion through a semi-permeable membrane

DIALYZE *verb* **DIALYZES, DIALYZING, DIALYZED** to dialyse

DIAMAGNET *noun* **DIAMAGNETS** a substance which, when suspended between the poles of a magnet, arranges itself across the lines of force

DIAMETER *noun* **DIAMETERS** the length of a straight line drawn from one side of a circle to the other, and passing through its centre, equal to twice the radius of the circle

DIAMETRIC *adj* belonging or relating to a diameter

DIAMOND *noun* **DIAMONDS** a crystalline allotrope of carbon, colourless when pure and the hardest known mineral, highly prized as a gemstone □ *adj* resembling, made of or marked with diamonds

DIAMONDED *adj* covered with, decorated with or wearing diamonds

DIANTHUS *noun* **DIANTHUSES** any plant of the herbaceous family of flowers to which carnations and pinks belong

DIAPASON *noun* **DIAPASONS** the whole range or compass of tones

DIAPAUSE *noun* **DIAPAUSES** in the life cycle of an insect: a period during which growth and development are arrested, often until environmental conditions become more favourable

DIAPER *noun* **DIAPERS** a type of

linen or cotton cloth with a pattern of small diamond or square shapes

DIAPHRAGM *noun* **DIAPHRAGMS** in mammals: the sheet of muscle that separates the thorax from the abdomen

DIARCHY *noun* **DIARCHIES** a form of government in which two people, states or bodies are jointly vested with supreme power

DIARIST *noun* **DIARISTS** a person who writes a diary, especially one which is published

DIARRHEA *noun* **DIARRHEAS** diarrhoea

DIARRHOEA *noun* **DIARRHOEAS** a condition in which the bowels are emptied more frequently and urgently than usual and the faeces are very soft or liquid

DIARY *noun* **DIARIES** a written record of daily events in a person's life

DIASTASE *noun* **DIASTASES** the component of malt containing β-amylase, an enzyme that converts starch into sugar, produced in germinating seeds and in pancreatic juice and used in the brewing industry

DIASTASIC *adj* of or relating to diastase

DIASTATIC *adj* diastasic

DIASTOLE *noun* **DIASTOLES** the rhythmic expansion of the chambers of the heart during which they fill with blood

DIASTOLIC *adj* of or relating to diastole

DIATHERMY *noun* **DIATHERMIES** the treating of internal organs with heat by passing electric currents through them

DIATHESIS *noun* **DIATHESES** a particular condition or habit of the body, especially one predisposing someone to certain diseases

DIATHETIC *adj* of or relating to diathesis

DIATOM *noun* **DIATOMS** a microscopic one-celled alga

DIATOMIC *adj* denoting a molecule that consists of two identical atoms

DIATOMITE *noun* **DIATOMITES** in geology: a soft whitish powdery deposit containing silica and composed mainly of the remains of cell walls of diatoms

DIATONIC *adj* of music: relating to, or using notes from, the diatonic scale

DIATRIBE *noun* **DIATRIBES** a bitter or abusive critical attack in speech or writing

DIAZEPAM *noun* **DIAZEPAMS** a tranquillizing drug which relieves anxiety and acts as a muscle relaxant, but whose long-term use causes addiction

DIAZO *noun* **DIAZOS, DIAZOES** a photocopy made using a diazo compound decomposed by exposure to light

DIB *verb* **DIBS, DIBBING, DIBBED** to fish by dapping

DIBASIC *adj* denoting an acid that contains two replaceable hydrogen atoms, eg sulphuric acid (H_2SO_4), allowing formation of two series of salts, the normal and acid salt

DIBBLE *noun* **DIBBLES** a short pointed hand-tool used for making holes in the ground, etc for seeds, young plants, etc □ *verb* **DIBBLES, DIBBLING, DIBBLED** to plant (seeds, etc) with a dibble

DIBS *plural noun* money

DICE *noun* **DICE** a small cube with a different number of spots, from 1 to 6, on each of its sides or faces, used in certain games of chance □ *verb* **DICES, DICING, DICED** to cut (vegetables, etc) into small cubes

DICEY *adj* **DICIER, DICIEST** risky

DICHOTOMY *noun* **DICHOTOMIES** a division or separation into two groups or parts, especially when these are sharply opposed or contrasted

DICHROIC *adj* having two colours

DICHROISM *noun* **DICHROISMS** a property of some crystals, that reflect certain colours when viewed from one angle, and different colours when viewed from another angle

DICKENS *noun* **DICKENS** the devil, used especially for emphasis

DICKER *verb* **DICKERS, DICKERING, DICKERED** to argue about the price or cost of something □ *noun* **DICKERS** haggling or bargaining; barter

DICKEY *noun* **DICKEYS** a dicky

DICKIE *noun* **DICKIES** a dicky

DICKY [1] *noun* **DICKIES** a false shirt front, especially when worn with evening dress

DICKY [2] *adj* **DICKIER, DICKIEST** shaky; unsteady

DICTA *plural of* **dictum**

DICTATE *verb* **DICTATES, DICTATING, DICTATED** to say or

read out something for someone else to write down □ *noun* **DICTATES** an order or instruction

DICTATION *noun* **DICTATIONS** something read or spoken for another person to write down

DICTATOR *noun* **DICTATORS** a ruler with complete and unrestricted power

DICTATORY *adj* characteristic of, like or suggesting a dictator

DICTION *noun* **DICTIONS** the way in which one speaks

DICTUM *noun* **DICTA** a formal or authoritative statement of opinion

DID a past form of **do**

DIDACTIC *adj* intended to teach or instruct

DIDACTICS *singular noun* the art or science of teaching

DIDDICOY *noun* **DIDDICOYS** a didicoy

DIDDLE *verb* **DIDDLES, DIDDLING, DIDDLED** to cheat or swindle

DIDDLER *noun* **DIDDLERS** a cheat or swindler

DIDDY *adj* **DIDDIER, DIDDIEST** small; tiny

DIDICOI *noun* **DIDICOIS** a didicoy

DIDICOY *noun* **DIDICOYS** an itinerant tinker or scrap dealer, not a true gypsy

DIDO *noun* **DIDOS, DIDOES** an antic or caper; an act of mischief

DIDST an archaic past form of **do**

DIDYMOUS *adj* twin; twinned; growing in pairs

DIE [1] *verb* **DIES, DYING, DIED** to stop living; to cease to be alive

DIE [2] *noun* **DIES** a metal tool or stamp for cutting or shaping metal or making designs on coins, etc

DIEBACK *noun* **DIEBACKS** the death of young shoots of trees and shrubs, often followed by the death of larger branches and stems, due to damage, disease, or lack of water, minerals, light, etc

DIELDRIN *noun* **DIELDRINS** a crystalline compound used as a contact insecticide

DIENE *noun* **DIENES** an alkene containing two double bonds between carbon atoms

DIERESIS *noun* **DIERESES** a diaeresis

DIESEL *noun* **DIESELS** a train, etc driven by a diesel engine

DIESIS *noun* **DIESES** in music: the difference between a major and a minor semitone

DIET *noun* **DIETS** the food and

drink habitually consumed by a person or animal ◻ verb **DIETS, DIETING, DIETED** to restrict the quantity or type of food that one eats, especially in order to lose weight

DIETARY adj belonging to or concerning a diet

DIETER noun **DIETERS** someone who is on a diet

DIETETIC adj concerning or belonging to diet

DIETETICS singular noun the scientific study of diet and its relation to health

DIETHYL adj having two ethyl groups

DIETICIAN noun **DIETICIANS** someone who is trained in dietetics

DIETITIAN noun **DIETITIANS** a dietician

DIFFER verb **DIFFERS, DIFFERING, DIFFERED** said of two or more people or things: to be different or unlike each other in some way

DIFFERENT adj not the same; unlike

DIFFICULT adj requiring great skill, intelligence or effort

DIFFIDENT adj lacking in confidence; too modest or shy

DIFFRACT verb **DIFFRACTS, DIFFRACTING, DIFFRACTED** to cause diffraction in (light, etc)

DIFFUSE verb **DIFFUSES, DIFFUSING, DIFFUSED** to spread or send out in all directions ◻ adj widely spread; not concentrated

DIFFUSED adj widely spread; dispersed

DIFFUSELY adverb in a diffuse way

DIFFUSER noun **DIFFUSERS** someone or something that diffuses

DIFFUSION noun **DIFFUSIONS** the act of diffusing or state of being diffused

DIFFUSIVE adj characterized by diffusion

DIG verb **DIGS, DIGGING, DUG** to turn up or move (earth, etc) especially with a spade ◻ noun **DIGS** a remark intended to irritate, criticize or make fun of someone

DIGEST [1] verb **DIGESTS, DIGESTING, DIGESTED** to break down (food) in the stomach, intestine, etc into a form which the body can use

DIGEST [2] noun **DIGESTS** a collection of summaries or shortened versions of news stories

or current literature, etc, usually regularly published

DIGESTER noun **DIGESTERS** a closed vessel in which strong extracts are produced from animal and vegetable substances by means of heat and pressure

DIGESTION noun **DIGESTIONS** the process whereby food is broken down by enzymes in the alimentary canal

DIGESTIVE adj concerned with or for digestion ◻ noun **DIGESTIVES** a type of plain slightly sweetened biscuit made from wholemeal flour

DIGGABLE adj able to be dug

DIGGER noun **DIGGERS** a machine used for digging and excavating

DIGGING a form of **dig**

DIGGINGS plural noun a place where people dig, especially for gold or precious stones

DIGIT noun **DIGITS** any of the ten figures 0 to 9

DIGITAL adj showing numerical information in the form of a set of digits, rather than by means of a pointer on a dial, eg as on a digital watch

DIGITALIN noun **DIGITALINS** a glucoside or mixture of glucosides obtained from digitalis leaves, used as a heart stimulant

DIGITALIS noun **DIGITALISES** any plant of the genus that includes the foxglove

DIGITATE adj said of leaves: consisting of several finger-like sections

DIGITATED adj digitate

DIGITISE verb **DIGITISES, DIGITISING, DIGITISED** to digitize

DIGITISER noun **DIGITISERS** a digitizer

DIGITIZE verb **DIGITIZES, DIGITIZING, DIGITIZED** to convert (data) into binary form

DIGITIZER noun **DIGITIZERS** a device which converts analogue signals to digital codes

DIGNIFIED adj marked or consistent with dignity

DIGNIFY verb **DIGNIFIES, DIGNIFYING, DIGNIFIED** to make something impressive or dignified

DIGNITARY noun **DIGNITARIES** someone of high rank or position, especially in public life or the Church

DIGNITY noun **DIGNITIES** stateliness, seriousness and formality of manner and appearance

DIGRAPH noun **DIGRAPHS** a pair of letters that represent a single sound, eg the ph of digraph

DIGRESS verb **DIGRESSES, DIGRESSING, DIGRESSED** to wander from the point, or from the main subject in speaking or writing

DIGS plural noun lodgings

DIHEDRAL adj formed or bounded by two planes ◻ noun **DIHEDRALS** the figure made by two intersecting planes

DIKE noun **DIKES** a dyke ◻ verb **DIKES, DIKING, DIKED** to dyke

DIKTAT noun **DIKTATS** a forceful, sometimes unreasonable, order which must be obeyed

DILATE verb **DILATES, DILATING, DILATED** said especially of an opening in the body, the pupil of the eye, etc: to make or become larger, wider or further open

DILATION noun **DILATIONS** dilating; becoming or making larger

DILATORY adj slow in doing things; inclined to or causing delay

DILEMMA noun **DILEMMAS** a situation in which one must choose between two or more courses of action, both (or all) equally undesirable

DILIGENCE noun **DILIGENCES** careful and hard-working effort

DILIGENT adj hard-working and careful

DILL noun **DILLS** a European herb, the fruit of which is used in flavouring, especially pickles, and to relieve wind

DILLY [1] noun **DILLIES** an excellent or very pleasing person or thing

DILLY [2] adj **DILLIER, DILLIEST** foolish; silly

DILUENT noun **DILUENTS** any solvent that is used to dilute a solution

DILUTABLE adj capable of being diluted

DILUTE verb **DILUTES, DILUTING, DILUTED** to decrease the concentration of a solute in a solution by adding more solvent, especially water ◻ adj said of a solution: containing a relatively small amount of solute compared to the amount of solvent present

DILUTION noun **DILUTIONS** the process of making a liquid thinner or weaker

DILUVIAL adj concerning or pertaining to a flood, especially the Flood mentioned in the Book of Genesis in the Bible

DILUVIAN adj diluvial

DIM adj **DIMMER, DIMMEST** not bright or distinct �‖ verb **DIMS, DIMMING, DIMMED** to make or become dim

DIME noun **DIMES** a coin of the US and Canada worth ten cents or one tenth of a dollar

DIMENSION noun **DIMENSIONS** a measurement of length, width or height

DIMER noun **DIMERS** a chemical compound composed of two monomers

DIMERIC adj of or relating to a dimer

DIMINISH verb **DIMINISHES, DIMINISHING, DIMINISHED** to become or make something less or smaller

DIMINISHED adj made less or smaller

DIMITY noun **DIMITIES** a stout cotton fabric, woven with raised stripes or other pattern

DIMLY adverb in a dim way; faintly or indistinctly

DIMMED past form of **dim**

DIMMER noun **DIMMERS** a control used to modify the brightness of a light

DIMMEST see under **dim**

DIMMING a form of **dim**

DIMMISH adj somewhat dim

DIMNESS noun **DIMNESSES** being dim or faint

DIMORPHIC adj showing dimorphism, ie occurring in two distinct forms within a species of living organism

DIMPLE noun **DIMPLES** a small hollow, especially in the skin of the cheeks, chin or, especially in babies, at the knees and elbows �‖ verb **DIMPLES, DIMPLING, DIMPLED** to show or form into dimples

DIMPLED adj having dimples or slight hollows on the surface

DIMWIT noun **DIMWITS** a stupid person

DIN noun **DINS** a loud, continuous and unpleasant noise �‖ verb **DINS, DINNING, DINNED** to assail (the ears) with noise

DINAR noun **DINARS** the standard unit of currency in Bosnia-Herzegovina, Macedonia, Yugoslavia and several Arab countries

DINE verb **DINES, DINING, DINED** to eat dinner

DINER noun **DINERS** someone who dines

DINETTE noun **DINETTES** an alcove or other small area of a room, etc, set apart for meals

DING noun **DINGS** a ringing sound �‖ verb **DINGS, DINGING, DANG, DUNG, DINGED** to make a ding

DINGBAT noun **DINGBATS** something whose name one has forgotten or wishes to avoid using; thingummy

DINGBATS adj daft; crazy

DINGES noun **DINGESES** a dingbat

DINGHY noun **DINGHIES** a small open boat propelled by oars, sails or an outboard motor

DINGINESS noun **DINGINESSES** the quality or condition of being dingy

DINGLE noun **DINGLES** a deep wooded hollow; a dell

DINGO noun **DINGOES** a species of wild dog found in Australia

DINGY adj **DINGIER, DINGIEST** faded and dirty-looking

DINKUM adj real; genuine; honest

DINKY [1] noun **DINKIES** *d*ouble *i*ncome *no k*ids, an acronym applied to a member of a young, childless (usually married) couple both earning a good salary, who thus enjoy an affluent lifestyle

DINKY [2] adj **DINKIER, DINKIEST** neat; dainty

DINNED a past form of **din**

DINNER noun **DINNERS** the main meal of the day, eaten in the middle of the day or in the evening

DINNING a form of **din**

DINOSAUR noun **DINOSAURS** any member of a large group of prehistoric reptiles that dominated life on land during the Mesozoic era, becoming extinct at the end of the Cretaceous period

DINT noun **DINTS** a hollow made by a blow; a dent

DIOCESAN adj relating to a diocese

DIOCESE noun **DIOCESES** the district over which a bishop has authority

DIODE noun **DIODES** an electronic device containing two electrodes, an anode and a cathode, that allows current to flow in one direction only

DIOECIOUS adj said of a plant: having male and female flowers on different plants

DIOPTER noun **DIOPTERS** dioptre

DIOPTRE noun **DIOPTRES** a unit that is used to express the power of a lens

DIOPTRICS singular noun the branch of optics that deals with refraction

DIOXIDE noun **DIOXIDES** a compound formed by combining two atoms of oxygen with one atom of another element

DIOXIN noun **DIOXINS** an aromatic halogenated hydrocarbon that is highly toxic

DIP verb **DIPS, DIPPING, DIPPED** to put something into a liquid for a short time �‖ noun **DIPS** an act of dipping

DIPEPTIDE noun **DIPEPTIDES** a peptide formed by the combination of two amino acids

DIPHENYL noun **DIPHENYLS** a hydrocarbon consisting of two phenyl groups, used eg in dye manufacture and as a fungicide

DIPHTHONG noun **DIPHTHONGS** two vowel sounds pronounced as one syllable, such as the sound represented by the *ou* in *sounds*

DIPLOID adj describing an organism, cell or nucleus in which there are two sets of chromosomes, one set being derived from each of the parents

DIPLOMA noun **DIPLOMAS** a document certifying that one has passed a certain examination or completed a course of study

DIPLOMACY noun **DIPLOMACIES** the art or profession of making agreements, treaties, etc between countries, or of representing and looking after the affairs and interests of one's own country in a foreign country

DIPLOMAT noun **DIPLOMATS** a government official or representative engaged in diplomacy

DIPLOMATE noun **DIPLOMATES** someone who holds a diploma

DIPOLAR adj having two poles

DIPOLE noun **DIPOLES** a separation of electric charge, in which two equal and opposite charges are separated from each other by a small distance

DIPPED past form of **dip**

DIPPER noun **DIPPERS** something that dips, especially a type of ladle

DIPPING a form of **dip**

DIPPY adj **DIPPIER, DIPPIEST** crazy; mad

For longer words, see *The Chambers Dictionary*

DIPSO *noun* **DIPSOS** a dipsomaniac

DIPSTICK *noun* **DIPSTICKS** a stick used to measure the level of a liquid in a container, especially the oil in a car engine

DIPTERA *noun* **DIPTERAS** any one of many two-winged insects or flies

DIPTERAL *adj* two-winged

DIPTEROUS *adj* two-winged

DIPTYCH *noun* **DIPTYCHS** a work of art, especially on a church altar, consisting of a pair of pictures painted on hinged wooden panels which can be folded together like a book

DIRE *adj* **DIRER, DIREST** dreadful; terrible

DIRECT *adj* **DIRECTER, DIRECTEST** straight; following the quickest and shortest path from beginning to end or to a destination □ *verb* **DIRECTS, DIRECTING, DIRECTED** to point, aim or turn something in a particular direction □ *adverb* directly; by the quickest or shortest path

DIRECTION *noun* **DIRECTIONS** the place or point towards which one is moving or facing

DIRECTIVE *noun* **DIRECTIVES** an official instruction issued by a higher authority, eg by the EC to the governments of member states □ *adj* having the power or tendency to direct

DIRECTLY *adverb* in a direct manner

DIRECTOR *noun* **DIRECTORS** any of the most senior managers of a business firm

DIRECTORY *noun* **DIRECTORIES** a book with a (usually alphabetical) list of names and addresses of people or organizations

DIRECTRIX *noun* **DIRECTRIXES, DIRECTRICES** a straight line from which the distance to any point on a conic section is in a constant ratio to the distance between that point and a fixed point

DIREFUL *adj* dreadful; terrible

DIREFULLY *adverb* in a direful way

DIRGE *noun* **DIRGES** a funeral song or hymn

DIRHAM *noun* **DIRHAMS** a unit of currency in various N African and Middle Eastern countries, eg the standard unit in Morocco and the United Arab Emirates

DIRIGIBLE *noun* **DIRIGIBLES** an airship

DIRIGISME *noun* **DIRIGISMES** control by the State in economic and social spheres

DIRIGISTE *adj* relating to or involving dirigisme

DIRK *noun* **DIRKS** a small knife or dagger

DIRNDL *noun* **DIRNDLS** a traditional alpine peasant-woman's dress, with a tight-fitting bodice and a very full skirt

DIRT *noun* **DIRTS** any unclean substance, eg mud or dust

DIRTILY *adverb* in a dirty way

DIRTINESS *noun* **DIRTINESSES** the quality or state of being dirty

DIRTY *adj* **DIRTIER, DIRTIEST** marked with dirt; soiled □ *verb* **DIRTIES, DIRTYING, DIRTIED** to make dirty □ *adverb* dirtily; very

DISABLE *verb* **DISABLES, DISABLING, DISABLED** to deprive someone of a physical or mental ability

DISABLED *adj* said of a person: having a physical or mental handicap

DISABUSE *verb* **DISABUSES, DISABUSING, DISABUSED** to undeceive or set right

DISAFFECT *verb* **DISAFFECTS, DISAFFECTING, DISAFFECTED** to make dissatisfied

DISAFFECTED *adj* dissatisfied and no longer loyal or committed

DISAGREE *verb* **DISAGREES, DISAGREEING, DISAGREED** said of two or more people: to have conflicting opinions

DISALLOW *verb* **DISALLOWS, DISALLOWING, DISALLOWED** to formally refuse to allow or accept something

DISAPPEAR *verb* **DISAPPEARS, DISAPPEARING, DISAPPEARED** to go out of sight; to vanish

DISARM *verb* **DISARMS, DISARMING, DISARMED** to take weapons away from someone

DISARMING *adj* taking away anger or suspicion; quickly winning confidence or affection

DISARRAY *noun* **DISARRAYS** a state of disorder or confusion □ *verb* **DISARRAYS, DISARRAYING, DISARRAYED** to throw something into disorder

DISASTER *noun* **DISASTERS** an event causing great damage, injury or loss of life

DISAVOW *verb* **DISAVOWS, DISAVOWING, DISAVOWED** to deny knowledge of, a connection with, or responsibility for something or someone

DISAVOWAL *noun* **DISAVOWALS** the action of disavowing

DISBAND *verb* **DISBANDS, DISBANDING, DISBANDED** to stop operating as a group; to break up

DISBAR *noun* **DISBARS** to expel someone from the Bar (the profession of barristers)

DISBELIEF *noun* **DISBELIEFS** inability or refusal to believe something

DISBUD *verb* **DISBUDS, DISBUDDING, DISBUDDED** to remove buds from (a plant, etc)

DISBURSE *verb* **DISBURSES, DISBURSING, DISBURSED** to pay out (a sum of money), especially from a fund

DISC *noun* **DISCS** a flat thin circular object

DISCARD *verb* **DISCARDS, DISCARDING, DISCARDED** to get rid of something as useless or unwanted □ *noun* **DISCARDS** something or someone that has been discarded

DISCERN *verb* **DISCERNS, DISCERNING, DISCERNED** to perceive, notice or make out something; to judge

DISCERNING *adj* having or showing good judgement

DISCHARGE *verb* **DISCHARGES, DISCHARGING, DISCHARGED** to allow someone to leave; to dismiss or send away (a person), especially from employment □ *noun* **DISCHARGES** the act of discharging

DISCIPLE *noun* **DISCIPLES** someone who believes in, and follows, the teachings of another

DISCLAIM *verb* **DISCLAIMS, DISCLAIMING, DISCLAIMED** to deny (eg involvement with or knowledge of something)

DISCLOSE *verb* **DISCLOSES, DISCLOSING, DISCLOSED** to make something known; to show something or make it visible

DISCO *noun* **DISCOS** a party with dancing to recorded music □ *adj* suitable for, or designed for, discos

DISCOID *adj* disc-shaped

DISCOIDAL *adj* disc-shaped

DISCOLOR *verb* **DISCOLORS, DISCOLORING, DISCOLORED** to discolour

DISCOLOUR *verb* **DISCOLOURS, DISCOLOURING, DISCOLOURED** to stain or dirty something; to change in colour

DISCOMFIT *verb* **DISCOMFITS, DISCOMFITING, DISCOMFITED** to make someone feel embarrassed or uneasy; to perplex them
DISCORD *noun* **DISCORDS** disagreement; conflict; failure to get on
DISCOUNT *noun* **DISCOUNTS** an amount deducted from the normal price, eg for prompt payment ▫ *verb* **DISCOUNTS, DISCOUNTING, DISCOUNTED** to make a deduction from (a price)
DISCOURSE *noun* **DISCOURSES** a formal speech or essay on a particular subject ▫ *verb* **DISCOURSES, DISCOURSING, DISCOURSED** to speak or write at length, formally or with authority
DISCOVER *verb* **DISCOVERS, DISCOVERING, DISCOVERED** to be the first person to find something or someone
DISCOVERY *noun* **DISCOVERIES** the act of discovering
DISCREDIT *noun* **DISCREDITS** loss of good reputation, or the cause of it ▫ *verb* **DISCREDITS, DISCREDITING, DISCREDITED** to make someone or something be disbelieved or regarded with doubt or suspicion
DISCREET *adj* **DISCREETER, DISCREETEST** careful to prevent suspicion or embarrassment, especially by keeping a secret
DISCRETE *adj* **DISCRETER, DISCRETEST** separate; distinct
DISCUS *noun* **DISCUSES** a heavy disc, thicker at the centre than the edge, thrown in athletic competitions
DISCUSS *verb* **DISCUSSES, DISCUSSING, DISCUSSED** to examine or consider something in speech or writing
DISDAIN *noun* **DISDAINS** dislike due to a feeling that something is not worthy of attention; contempt; scorn ▫ *verb* **DISDAINS, DISDAINING, DISDAINED** to refuse or reject someone or something out of disdain
DISEASE *noun* **DISEASES** a lack of health, a disorder or illness caused by infection rather than by an accident
DISEASED *adj* affected by or suffering from disease
DISEMBARK *verb* **DISEMBARKS, DISEMBARKING, DISEMBARKED** to take or go from a ship on to land
DISEMBODIED *adj* said eg of a spirit or soul: separated from the body; having no physical existence
DISEMBODY *verb* **DISEMBODIES, DISEMBODYING, DISEMBODIED** to remove or free (a spirit or soul) from the body
DISENGAGE *verb* **DISENGAGES, DISENGAGING, DISENGAGED** to release or detach someone or something from a connection
DISENGAGED *adj* free from engagement; at leisure
DISESTEEM *verb* **DISESTEEMS, DISESTEEMING, DISESTEEMED** to disapprove of or dislike someone or something ▫ *noun* **DISESTEEMS** lack of esteem; disregard
DISFAVOR *noun* **DISFAVORS** disfavour
DISFAVOUR *noun* **DISFAVOURS** a state of being disliked, unpopular or disapproved of
DISFIGURE *verb* **DISFIGURES, DISFIGURING, DISFIGURED** to spoil the beauty or general appearance of something
DISFOREST *verb* **DISFORESTS, DISFORESTING, DISFORESTED** to clear (land) of forest
DISGORGE *verb* **DISGORGES, DISGORGING, DISGORGED** to vomit
DISGRACE *noun* **DISGRACES** shame or loss of favour or respect ▫ *verb* **DISGRACES, DISGRACING, DISGRACED** to bring shame upon someone
DISGUISE *verb* **DISGUISES, DISGUISING, DISGUISED** to hide the identity of someone or something by a change of appearance ▫ *noun* **DISGUISES** a disguised state
DISGUST *verb* **DISGUSTS, DISGUSTING, DISGUSTED** to sicken; to provoke intense dislike or disapproval in someone ▫ *noun* **DISGUSTS** intense dislike; loathing
DISGUSTED *adj* feeling disgust; sickened
DISGUSTING *adj* that disgusts; sickening
DISH *noun* **DISHES** a shallow container in which food is served or cooked ▫ *verb* **DISHES, DISHING, DISHED** to put (food) into a dish for serving at table
DISHED *adj* shaped like a dish; concave
DISHEVEL *verb* **DISHEVELS, DISHEVELLING, DISHEVELLED** to make (hair or clothing) messy or untidy
DISHEVELLED *adj* said of clothes or hair: untidy; in a mess
DISHIER see under **dishy**
DISHIEST see under **dishy**
DISHONEST *adj* not honest; likely to deceive or cheat; insincere
DISHONOR *noun* **DISHONORS** dishonour ▫ *verb* **DISHONORS, DISHONORING, DISHONORED** to dishonour
DISHONOUR *noun* **DISHONOURS** shame or loss of honour ▫ *verb* **DISHONOURS, DISHONOURING, DISHONOURED** to bring dishonour on someone or something
DISHTOWEL *noun* **DISHTOWELS** a cloth for drying dishes
DISHWATER *noun* **DISHWATERS** water in which dirty dishes have been washed
DISHY *adj* **DISHIER, DISHIEST** sexually attractive
DISINFECT *verb* **DISINFECTS, DISINFECTING, DISINFECTED** to clean with a substance that kills germs
DISINTER *verb* **DISINTERS, DISINTERRING, DISINTERRED** to dig up (especially a body from a grave)
DISINVEST *verb* **DISINVESTS, DISINVESTING, DISINVESTED** to remove financial investment
DISK *noun* **DISKS** a flat circular sheet of material used to store programs and computer-generated data
DISKETTE *noun* **DISKETTES** in computing: formerly used to refer to a 5.25in floppy disk
DISLIKE *verb* **DISLIKES, DISLIKING, DISLIKED** to consider someone or something unpleasant or unlikeable ▫ *noun* **DISLIKES** mild hostility; aversion
DISLOCATE *verb* **DISLOCATES, DISLOCATING, DISLOCATED** to dislodge (a bone) from its normal position in a joint
DISLODGE *verb* **DISLODGES, DISLODGING, DISLODGED** to force something out of a fixed or established position
DISLOYAL *adj* not loyal or faithful
DISMAL *adj* **DISMALLER, DISMALLEST** not cheerful; causing or suggesting sadness
DISMALLY *adverb* in a dismal way
DISMANTLE *verb* **DISMANTLES, DISMANTLING, DISMANTLED** to

take something to pieces; to demolish it

DISMAST *verb* **DISMASTS, DISMASTING, DISMASTED** to topple or remove the mast or masts of (a sailing vessel)

DISMAY *noun* **DISMAYS** a feeling of sadness arising from deep disappointment or discouragement □ *verb* **DISMAYS, DISMAYING, DISMAYED** to make someone discouraged, sad or alarmed

DISMEMBER *verb* **DISMEMBERS, DISMEMBERING, DISMEMBERED** to tear or cut the limbs from (the body)

DISMISS *verb* **DISMISSES, DISMISSING, DISMISSED** to refuse to consider or accept (an idea, claim, etc); to put someone out of one's employment

DISMISSAL *noun* **DISMISSALS** an act of dismissing, especially of a person from employment

DISMOUNT *verb* **DISMOUNTS, DISMOUNTING, DISMOUNTED** to get off a horse, bicycle, etc

DISOBEY *verb* **DISOBEYS, DISOBEYING, DISOBEYED** to act contrary to the orders of someone; to refuse to obey (a person, a law, etc)

DISORDER *noun* **DISORDERS** lack of order; confusion or disturbance

DISORDERED *adj* confused, deranged

DISORIENT *verb* **DISORIENTS, DISORIENTING, DISORIENTED** to make someone lose all sense of position, direction or time

DISOWN *verb* **DISOWNS, DISOWNING, DISOWNED** to deny having any relationship to, or connection with, someone or something

DISPARAGE *verb* **DISPARAGES, DISPARAGING, DISPARAGED** to speak of someone or something with contempt

DISPARAGING *adj* contemptuous; showing disapproval

DISPARATE *adj* completely different; too different to be compared

DISPARITY *noun* **DISPARITIES** great or fundamental difference; inequality

DISPATCH *verb* **DISPATCHES, DISPATCHING, DISPATCHED** to send (mail, a person, etc) to a place for a particular reason □ *noun* **DISPATCHES** an official

(especially military or diplomatic) report

DISPEL *verb* **DISPELS, DISPELLING, DISPELLED** to drive away or banish (thoughts or feelings)

DISPENSE *verb* **DISPENSES, DISPENSING, DISPENSED** to give out (eg advice)

DISPENSER *noun* **DISPENSERS** someone who dispenses, eg a pharmacist who makes up and gives out medicines

DISPERSAL *noun* **DISPERSALS** distribution; the spread of a species to a new area

DISPERSE *verb* **DISPERSES, DISPERSING, DISPERSED** to spread out over a wide area

DISPIRIT *verb* **DISPIRITS, DISPIRITING, DISPIRITED** to dishearten or discourage someone

DISPIRITED *adj* dejected, discouraged

DISPLACE *verb* **DISPLACES, DISPLACING, DISPLACED** to put or take something or someone out of the usual place

DISPLAY *verb* **DISPLAYS, DISPLAYING, DISPLAYED** to put someone or something on view □ *noun* **DISPLAYS** the act of displaying

DISPLEASE *verb* **DISPLEASES, DISPLEASING, DISPLEASED** to annoy or offend someone

DISPORT *verb* **DISPORTS, DISPORTING, DISPORTED** to indulge (oneself) in lively amusement

DISPOSAL *noun* **DISPOSALS** getting rid of something

DISPOSE *verb* **DISPOSES, DISPOSING, DISPOSED** to place something in an arrangement or order

DISPROOF *noun* **DISPROOFS** the act of disproving

DISPROVE *verb* **DISPROVES, DISPROVING, DISPROVED** to prove something to be false or wrong

DISPUTE *verb* **DISPUTES, DISPUTING, DISPUTED** to question or deny the accuracy or validity of (a statement, etc) □ *noun* **DISPUTES** an argument

DISQUIET *noun* **DISQUIETS** a feeling of anxiety or uneasiness □ *verb* **DISQUIETS, DISQUIETING, DISQUIETED** to make someone feel anxious, uneasy, etc

DISQUIETING *adj* that causes anxiety, uneasiness, etc

DISREGARD *verb* **DISREGARDS, DISREGARDING, DISREGARDED** to pay no attention to someone or something □ *noun* **DISREGARDS** dismissive lack of attention or concern

DISREPAIR *noun* **DISREPAIRS** bad condition or working order owing to a need for repair and maintenance

DISREPUTE *noun* **DISREPUTES** the state of having a bad reputation

DISROBE *verb* **DISROBES, DISROBING, DISROBED** to undress

DISRUPT *verb* **DISRUPTS, DISRUPTING, DISRUPTED** to disturb the order or peaceful progress of (an activity, process, etc)

DISS *verb* **DISSES, DISSING, DISSED** to reject or dismiss someone with contempt; to bad mouth them

DISSECT *verb* **DISSECTS, DISSECTING, DISSECTED** to cut open (a plant or dead body) for scientific or medical examination

DISSECTED *adj* deeply cut into narrow segments

DISSEMBLE *verb* **DISSEMBLES, DISSEMBLING, DISSEMBLED** to conceal or disguise (true feelings or motives)

DISSENT *noun* **DISSENTS** disagreement, especially open or hostile □ *verb* **DISSENTS, DISSENTING, DISSENTED** to differ in opinion from or to disagree with someone

DISSENTER *noun* **DISSENTERS** someone who disagrees

DISSENTING *adj* disagreeing

DISSIDENT *noun* **DISSIDENTS** someone who disagrees publicly, especially with a government □ *adj* disagreeing; dissenting

DISSIPATE *verb* **DISSIPATES, DISSIPATING, DISSIPATED** to separate and scatter

DISSIPATED *adj* over-indulging in pleasure and enjoyment; debauched

DISSOLUTE *adj* indulging in pleasures considered immoral; debauched

DISSOLVE *verb* **DISSOLVES, DISSOLVING, DISSOLVED** to break up and merge with a liquid

DISSONANT *adj* lacking in harmony; harsh-sounding

DISSUADE *verb* **DISSUADES, DISSUADING, DISSUADED** to

DISTAFF *noun* **DISTAFFS** the rod on which a bunch of wool, flax, etc is held ready for spinning by hand

DISTAL *adj* in anatomy: farthest from the point of attachment

DISTANCE *noun* **DISTANCES** the measured length between two points in space □ *adj* said of races: over a long distance □ *verb* **DISTANCES, DISTANCING, DISTANCED** to put someone or something at a distance

DISTANT *adj* far away or far apart in space or time

DISTANTLY *adverb* coldly or aloofly

DISTASTE *noun* **DISTASTES** dislike; aversion

DISTEMPER *noun* **DISTEMPERS** any water-based paint, especially when mixed with glue or size and used eg for poster-painting or murals □ *verb* **DISTEMPERS, DISTEMPERING, DISTEMPERED** to paint with distemper

DISTEND *verb* **DISTENDS, DISTENDING, DISTENDED** to make or become swollen, inflated or stretched

DISTIL *verb* **DISTILS, DISTILLING, DISTILLED** to purify a liquid by the process of distillation

DISTILLER *noun* **DISTILLERS** a person or company that makes alcoholic spirits

DISTINCT *adj* **DISTINCTER, DISTINCTEST** easily seen, heard or recognized; clear or obvious

DISTORT *verb* **DISTORTS, DISTORTING, DISTORTED** to twist something out of shape

DISTRACT *verb* **DISTRACTS, DISTRACTING, DISTRACTED** to divert someone's attention from something

DISTRACTED *adj* confused, bewildered

DISTRACTING *adj* that distracts; bewildering

DISTRAIN *verb* **DISTRAINS, DISTRAINING, DISTRAINED** to seize (eg property) as, or in order to force, payment of a debt

DISTRAINT *noun* **DISTRAINTS** seizure of property or goods in order to meet a debt or obligation

DISTRAIT *adj* thinking of other things

DISTRESS *noun* **DISTRESSES** mental or emotional pain □ *verb* **DISTRESSES, DISTRESSING,**

DISTRESSED to cause distress to someone; to upset someone

DISTRESSED *adj* suffering mentally or physically

DISTRESSING *adj* causing distress

DISTRICT *noun* **DISTRICTS** an area or region, especially one forming an administrative or geographical unit

DISTRUST *verb* **DISTRUSTS, DISTRUSTING, DISTRUSTED** to have no trust in someone or something; to doubt them or it □ *noun* **DISTRUSTS** suspicion; lack of trust

DISTURB *verb* **DISTURBS, DISTURBING, DISTURBED** to interrupt someone

DISTURBED *adj* emotionally upset or confused; maladjusted

DISTURBING *adj* that causes emotional upset or confusion

DISUNITE *verb* **DISUNITES, DISUNITING, DISUNITED** to drive (people, etc) apart; to cause disagreement or conflict between (people) or within (a group)

DISUNITY *noun* **DISUNITIES** lack of unity, dissension

DISUSE *noun* **DISUSES** the state of no longer being used, practised or observed; neglect

DISUSED *adj* no longer in use

DIT *verb* **DITS, DITTING, DITTED, DITTIT** a Scots word meaning to block

DITCH *noun* **DITCHES** a narrow channel dug in the ground for drainage or irrigation or as a boundary □ *verb* **DITCHES, DITCHING, DITCHED** to get rid of someone or something; to abandon them

DITHER *verb* **DITHERS, DITHERING, DITHERED** to act in a nervously uncertain manner; to waver □ *noun* **DITHERS** a state of nervous indecision

DITHERER *noun* **DITHERERS** a person who dithers

DITHERY *adj* **DITHERIER, DITHERIEST** inclined to dither

DITSY *adj* **DITSIER, DITSIEST** scatterbrained; flighty

DITTO *noun* **DITTOS** the same thing; the above; that which has just been said □ *adverb* likewise; the same

DITTY *noun* **DITTIES** a short simple song or poem

DITZY *adj* **DITZIER, DITZIEST** ditsy

DIURETIC *noun* **DIURETICS** a drug or other substance that increases the volume of urine produced and excreted □ *adj* said of a substance: increasing the production and excretion of urine

DIURNAL *adj* daily

DIURNALLY *adverb* daily

DIV *noun* **DIVS** an evil spirit in Persian mythology

DIVA *noun* **DIVAS** a great female singer, especially in opera

DIVALENT *adj* said of an atom: able to combine with two atoms of hydrogen or the equivalent

DIVAN *noun* **DIVANS** a sofa with no back or sides

DIVE *verb* **DIVES, DIVING, DOVE, DIVED** to throw oneself into water, usually headfirst, or plunge down through water □ *noun* **DIVES** an act of diving

DIVER *noun* **DIVERS** someone who dives

DIVERGE *verb* **DIVERGES, DIVERGING, DIVERGED** to separate and go in different directions

DIVERGENT *adj* diverging

DIVERS *adj* various; many different

DIVERSE *adj* various; assorted

DIVERSELY *adverb* in a different way; differently

DIVERSIFY *verb* **DIVERSIFIES, DIVERSIFYING, DIVERSIFIED** to become or make something diverse

DIVERSION *noun* **DIVERSIONS** the act of diverting; the state of being diverted

DIVERSITY *noun* **DIVERSITIES** variety in kind; being varied or different

DIVERT *verb* **DIVERTS, DIVERTING, DIVERTED** to make someone or something change direction

DIVERTING *adj* amusing, entertaining

DIVEST *verb* **DIVESTS, DIVESTING, DIVESTED** to take away or get rid of something

DIVI *noun* **DIVIS** a dividend or share

DIVIDE *verb* **DIVIDES, DIVIDING, DIVIDED** to split up or separate into parts □ *noun* **DIVIDES** a disagreement; a gap or split

DIVIDEND *noun* **DIVIDENDS** a portion of a company's profits paid to a shareholder

DIVIDERS *plural noun* a V-shaped device with movable arms ending in points, used in geometry, etc for measuring

DIVINE *adj* **DIVINER, DIVINEST** belonging or relating to, or coming from God or a god □ *verb* **DIVINES, DIVINING, DIVINED** to foretell something □ *noun* **DIVINES** a member of the clergy who is expert in theology

DIVINELY *adverb* in a divine way

DIVINER *noun* **DIVINERS** a person who divines

DIVING *noun* **DIVINGS** the activity or sport of plunging into water

DIVINITY *noun* **DIVINITIES** theology

DIVISIBLE *adj* able to be divided

DIVISION *noun* **DIVISIONS** the act of dividing; the state of being divided

DIVISIVE *adj* tending to cause disagreement or conflict

DIVISOR *noun* **DIVISORS** a number by which another number, the dividend, is divided

DIVORCE *noun* **DIVORCES** the legal ending of a marriage □ *verb* **DIVORCES, DIVORCING, DIVORCED** to legally end marriage to someone

DIVORCED *adj* having had one's marriage legally ended

DIVORCEE *noun* **DIVORCEES** someone who has been divorced

DIVOT *noun* **DIVOTS** a clump of grass and earth removed, especially by the blade of a golf club

DIVULGE *verb* **DIVULGES, DIVULGING, DIVULGED** to make something known; to reveal (a secret, etc)

DIVVY *noun* **DIVVIES** a dividend or share □ *verb* **DIVVIES, DIVVYING, DIVVIED** to divide or share (something)

DIXIE *noun* **DIXIES** a metal cooking-pot or kettle

DIZYGOTIC *adj* developed from two zygotes or fertilized eggs

DIZZILY *adverb* in a dizzy way

DIZZINESS *noun* **DIZZINESSES** the state of being dizzy

DIZZY *adj* **DIZZIER, DIZZIEST** experiencing or causing a spinning sensation resulting in loss of balance □ *verb* **DIZZIES, DIZZYING, DIZZIED** to make someone dizzy

DJINN *noun* **DJINN** a jinni

DJINNI *noun* **DJINN** a jinni

DO *verb* **DOES, DOING, DID, DONE** to carry out, perform or commit something □ *noun* **DOS** a party or other gathering

DOABLE *adj* able to be done

DOB *verb* **DOBS, DOBBING, DOBBED** to inform on or betray someone

DOBBER *noun* **DOBBERS** a person who informs on or betrays someone

DOC *noun* **DOCS** a doctor

DOCILE *adj* **DOCILER, DOCILEST** easy to manage or control; submissive

DOCILITY *noun* **DOCILITIES** a docile manner

DOCK *noun* **DOCKS** a harbour where ships are loaded, unloaded, and repaired □ *verb* **DOCKS, DOCKING, DOCKED** to bring or come into a dock

DOCKER *noun* **DOCKERS** a labourer who loads and unloads ships

DOCKET *noun* **DOCKETS** any label or note accompanying a parcel or package, eg detailing contents or recording receipt □ *verb* **DOCKETS, DOCKETING, DOCKETED** to fix a label to something; to record the contents or delivery of something

DOCKLAND *noun* **DOCKLANDS** the district round about the docks

DOCKYARD *noun* **DOCKYARDS** a shipyard, especially a naval one

DOCTOR *noun* **DOCTORS** someone trained and qualified to practise medicine □ *verb* **DOCTORS, DOCTORING, DOCTORED** to falsify (eg information)

DOCTORAL *adj* relating to a doctorate

DOCTORATE *noun* **DOCTORATES** a high academic degree, awarded especially for research

DOCTRINAL *adj* of or relating to doctrine

DOCTRINE *noun* **DOCTRINES** a thing or things taught, especially any one of a set of religious or political beliefs, or such a set of beliefs

DOCUDRAMA *noun* **DOCUDRAMAS** a play or film based on real events and characters

DOCUMENT *noun* **DOCUMENTS** any piece of writing of an official nature, eg a certificate □ *verb*

DOCUMENTS, DOCUMENTING, DOCUMENTED to record something, especially in written form

DOD *verb* **DODS, DODDING, DODDED** a dialect word meaning to cut the hair

DODDER *verb* **DODDERS, DODDERING, DODDERED** to move in an unsteady trembling fashion, usually as a result of old age

DODDERER *noun* **DODDERERS** a person who dodders

DODDERING *adj* failing in body and mind; senile

DODDERY *adj* **DODDERIER, DODDERIEST** unsteady with age

DODDLE *noun* **DODDLES** something easily done or achieved

DODECAGON *noun* **DODECAGONS** a flat geometric figure with 12 sides and angles

DODGE *verb* **DODGES, DODGING, DODGED** to avoid (a blow, a person, etc) by moving quickly away, especially sideways □ *noun* **DODGES** a sudden movement aside

DODGEMS *plural noun* a fairground amusement consisting of a rink in which drivers of small electric cars try to bump each other

DODGER *noun* **DODGERS** a shirker; a trickster

DODGY *adj* **DODGIER, DODGIEST** difficult or risky

DODO *noun* **DODOS, DODOES** a large flightless bird that became extinct around the middle of the 17c

DOE *noun* **DOES** an adult female rabbit, hare or small deer, eg the fallow deer

DOER *noun* **DOERS** a person who does something

DOES a form of **do**

DOFF *verb* **DOFFS, DOFFING, DOFFED** to lift (one's hat) in greeting

DOG *noun* **DOGS** any carnivorous mammal belonging to the family which includes the wolves, jackals and foxes □ *verb* **DOGS, DOGGING, DOGGED** to follow very closely; to track someone

DOGCART *noun* **DOGCARTS** a two-wheeled horse-drawn passenger carriage with seats back-to-back

DOGE *noun* **DOGES** the chief

magistrate in the former republics of Venice and Genoa

DOGFIGHT *noun* **DOGFIGHTS** a battle at close quarters between two fighter aircraft

DOGFISH *noun* **DOGFISHES** any of various kinds of small shark

DOGGED [1] *adj* **DOGGEDER**, **DOGGEDEST** determined; resolute

DOGGED [2] past form of **dog**

DOGGEDLY *adverb* determinedly; resolutely

DOGGEREL *noun* **DOGGERELS** badly written poetry □ *adj* of poor quality

DOGGIER see under **doggy**

DOGGIES plural of **doggy**

DOGGIEST see under **doggy**

DOGGING a form of **dog**

DOGGISH *adj* like or characteristic of a dog

DOGGO *adverb* quiet and hidden

DOGGONE *exclamation* indicating annoyance □ *adj* damned □ *adverb* damned

DOGGY *adj* **DOGGIER**, **DOGGIEST** belonging to, like or relating to dogs □ *noun* **DOGGIES** a child's word for a dog

DOGMA *noun* **DOGMAS** a belief or principle laid down by an authority as unquestionably true

DOGMATIC *adj* said of an opinion: forcefully and arrogantly stated as if unquestionable

DOGMATISE *verb* **DOGMATISES**, **DOGMATISING**, **DOGMATISED** to dogmatize

DOGMATISM *noun* **DOGMATISMS** the quality of being, or the tendency to be, dogmatic

DOGMATIST *noun* **DOGMATISTS** a person who makes positive assertions

DOGMATIZE *verb* **DOGMATIZES**, **DOGMATIZING**, **DOGMATIZED** to state one's opinions dogmatically

DOGS *plural noun* greyhound racing

DOGSBODY *noun* **DOGSBODIES** someone who does menial tasks for someone else

DOGTROT *noun* **DOGTROTS** a gentle trotting pace

DOGWOOD *noun* **DOGWOODS** a European shrub with small white flowers and purple berries

DOH *noun* **DOHS** in sol-fa notation: the first note of the major scale

DOILY *noun* **DOILIES** a small decorative napkin of lace or lace-like paper laid on plates under sandwiches, cakes, etc

DOINGS *plural noun* activities; behaviour □ *singular noun* something whose name cannot be remembered or is left unsaid

DOJO *noun* **DOJOS** a place where judo or karate, etc are taught or practised

DOLCE *adj* to be sung or played gently or sweetly □ *adverb* gently or sweetly (especially of music)

DOLE *noun* **DOLES** unemployment benefit □ *verb* **DOLES**, **DOLING**, **DOLED** to hand something out or give it out

DOLEFUL *adj* sad; expressing or suggesting sadness; mournful

DOLEFULLY *adverb* in a doleful way

DOLL *noun* **DOLLS** a toy in the form of a model of a human being, especially a baby □ *verb* **DOLLS**, **DOLLING**, **DOLLED** to dress smartly or showily

DOLLAR *noun* **DOLLARS** (symbol $) the standard unit of currency in the US, Canada, Australia and numerous other countries, divided into 100 cents

DOLLOP *noun* **DOLLOPS** a small shapeless mass of any semi-solid substance, especially food

DOLLY *noun* **DOLLIES** a child's name for a doll

DOLMA *noun* **DOLMAS** a vine or cabbage leaf with a savoury stuffing

DOLMEN *noun* **DOLMENS** a simple prehistoric monument consisting of a large flat stone supported by several vertical stones

DOLOMITE *noun* **DOLOMITES** a mineral composed of calcium magnesium carbonate, formed by the replacement of limestone

DOLOR *noun* **DOLORS** dolour

DOLOROSO *adj* sorrowful (especially of music) □ *adverb* sorrowfully (especially of music)

DOLOROUS *adj* causing, involving, or suggesting sorrow or grief

DOLOUR *noun* **DOLOURS** sorrow or grief

DOLPHIN *noun* **DOLPHINS** a small toothed whale found in seas almost worldwide, both in deep water and near to coasts

DOLT *noun* **DOLTS** a stupid person

DOLTISH *adj* dull; stupid

DOMAIN *noun* **DOMAINS** the scope of any subject or area of interest

DOME *noun* **DOMES** a roof in the shape of a hemisphere

DOMED *adj* said of a building, etc: having a dome or domes

DOMESTIC *adj* belonging or relating to the home, the family or private life □ *noun* **DOMESTICS** a row, usually in the home, between members of a household unit

DOMICILE *noun* **DOMICILES** a house □ *verb* **DOMICILES**, **DOMICILING**, **DOMICILED** to establish or be settled in a fixed residence

DOMINANCE *noun* **DOMINANCES** command or influence over others

DOMINANT *adj* most important, evident or active; foremost □ *noun* **DOMINANTS** the fifth note on a musical scale

DOMINATE *verb* **DOMINATES**, **DOMINATING**, **DOMINATED** to have command or influence over someone

DOMINATING *adj* that dominates

DOMINEER *verb* **DOMINEERS**, **DOMINEERING**, **DOMINEERED** to behave in an arrogantly dominant way

DOMINEERING *adj* overbearing; behaving arrogantly towards others

DOMINION *noun* **DOMINIONS** rule; power; influence

DOMINO *noun* **DOMINOES**, **DOMINOS** any of a set of small rectangular tiles marked, in two halves, with varying numbers of spots, used in the game of dominoes

DON [1] *noun* **DONS** a university lecturer, especially at Oxford or Cambridge

DON [2] *verb* **DONS**, **DONNING**, **DONNED** to put on (clothing)

DOÑA *noun* **DOÑAS** a Spanish form of address, similar to Madam, which is used to indicate respect

DONATE *verb* **DONATES**, **DONATING**, **DONATED** to give, especially to charity

DONATION *noun* **DONATIONS** a formal gift, usually of money; an amount given as a gift

DONDER *verb* **DONDERS**, **DONDERING**, **DONDERED** to beat up or thrash someone □ *noun* **DONDERS** a scoundrel; a rogue

DONE [1] *adj* finished; completed

DONE [2] a past form of **do**

DONG *noun* **DONGS** a deep ringing sound □ *verb* **DONGS, DONGING, DONGED** to make a deep ringing sound

DONGA *noun* **DONGAS** a gully made by soil erosion

DONING *noun* **DONINGS** the act of donating (especially blood)

DONJON *noun* **DONJONS** a heavily fortified central tower in a medieval castle

DONKEY *noun* **DONKEYS** the domestic ass, a hoofed herbivorous mammal with a large head and long ears, related to but smaller than the horse

DONNED past form of **don**

DONNING a form of **don**

DONNISH *adj* relating to or acting like a college don

DONOR *noun* **DONORS** someone who donates something, especially money

DONUT *noun* **DONUTS** a doughnut

DOO *noun* **DOOS** a Scots word for *dove*

DOODAD *noun* **DOODADS** a doodah

DOODAH *noun* **DOODAHS** a thing whose name one does not know or cannot remember

DOODLE *verb* **DOODLES, DOODLING, DOODLED** to scrawl or scribble aimlessly and meaninglessly □ *noun* **DOODLES** a meaningless scribble

DOODLEBUG *noun* **DOODLEBUGS** the larva of an ant-lion or other insect

DOODLER *noun* **DOODLERS** a person who doodles

DOOLALLY *adj* mentally unbalanced; crazy

DOOM *noun* **DOOMS** inescapable death, ruin or other unpleasant fate □ *verb* **DOOMS, DOOMING, DOOMED** to condemn someone to death or some other dire fate

DOOMSDAY *noun* **DOOMSDAYS** the last day of the world, which in Christianity is the day on which God will judge the human race

DOOMWATCH *noun*

DOOMWATCHES pessimism about the contemporary situation and the future, especially of the environment

DOONA *noun* **DOONAS** a duvet

DOOR *noun* **DOORS** a movable barrier opening and closing an entrance, eg to a room, cupboard or vehicle

DOORBELL *noun* **DOORBELLS** a bell on or at a door, rung by visitors at the door as a sign of arrival

DOORMAT *noun* **DOORMATS** a mat for wiping shoes on before entering

DOORPOST *noun* **DOORPOSTS** one of the two vertical side pieces of a door frame

DOORSTEP *noun* **DOORSTEPS** a step positioned immediately in front of a door □ *verb* **DOORSTEPS, DOORSTEPPING, DOORSTEPPED** said especially of politicians, their agents, etc: to go from door to door canvassing (people or an area)

DOORSTOP *noun* **DOORSTOPS** a device, especially a wedge, for holding a door open

DOORWAY *noun* **DOORWAYS** an entrance to a building or room

DOP *verb* **DOPS, DOPPING, DOPPED** an obsolete word meaning to dip

DOPA *noun* **DOPAS** an amino acid derivative that plays an important role in the production of adrenalin and noradrenalin, and of the neurotransmitter dopamine

DOPAMINE *noun* **DOPAMINES** an important chemical compound that functions as a neurotransmitter and is also an intermediate in the manufacture of adrenalin and noradrenalin

DOPE *noun* **DOPES** a drug taken for pleasure, especially cannabis □ *verb* **DOPES, DOPING, DOPED** to give or apply drugs to (a person or animal), especially dishonestly or furtively

DOPEY *adj* **DOPIER, DOPIEST** sleepy or inactive, as if drugged

DOPINESS *noun* the state of being dopey

DOPING *noun* **DOPINGS** the addition of very small amounts of impurities (eg antimony, arsenic) to a crystal of silicon, germanium, etc, in order to convert it into a semiconductor

DOPY *adj* **DOPIER, DOPIEST** dopey

DOR *verb* **DORS, DORRING, DORRED** an obsolete word meaning to mock

DORM *noun* **DORMS** a dormitory

DORMANCY *noun* **DORMANCIES** the state of being dormant

DORMANT *adj* temporarily quiet, inactive or out of use

DORMER *noun* **DORMERS** a window fitted vertically into an extension built out from a sloping roof

DORMIE *adj* in golf: as many holes up or ahead of one's opponent as there are yet to play

DORMITORY *noun* **DORMITORIES** a large bedroom for several people

DORMOUSE *noun* **DORMICE** a small nocturnal rodent with rounded ears, large eyes, velvety fur, and a bushy tail

DORMY *adj* dormie

DORP *noun* **DORPS** a small town or village

DORSAL *adj* belonging or relating to the back

DORY *noun* **DORIES** a golden-yellow fish of the mackerel family

DOSAGE *noun* **DOSAGES** the prescribed amount of a dose of a medicine or drug

DOSE *noun* **DOSES** the measured quantity of medicine, etc that is prescribed by a doctor to be administered to a patient □ *verb* **DOSES, DOSING, DOSED** to give someone medicine, especially in large quantities

DOSH *noun* **DOSHES** money

DOSIMETER *noun* **DOSIMETERS** an instrument for measuring the absorbed dose of radiation

DOSS *verb* **DOSSES, DOSSING, DOSSED** to settle down to sleep, especially on an improvised bed

DOSSER *noun* **DOSSERS** a homeless person sleeping on the street or in a doss-house

DOSSIER *noun* **DOSSIERS** a file of papers containing information on a person or subject

DOST used with *thou*: a form of **do**

DOT *noun* **DOTS** a small round mark; a spot; a point □ *verb* **DOTS, DOTTING, DOTTED** to put a dot on something

DOTAGE *noun* **DOTAGES** a state of feeble-mindedness owing to old age; senility

DOTARD *noun* **DOTARDS** someone in their dotage

DOTE *verb* **DOTES, DOTING, DOTED** to be foolish or weak-minded especially because of old age

DOTH *verb* do (old-fashioned form)

DOTING *adj* foolishly or excessively fond of someone

DOTTED past form of **dot**

DOTTINESS *noun* **DOTTINESSES** silly behaviour; an instance of this

DOTTING a form of **dot**

DOTTY *adj* **DOTTIER, DOTTIEST** silly; crazy

DOUBLE *adj* made up of two similar parts; paired; in pairs □ *adverb* twice □ *noun* **DOUBLES** a double quantity □ *verb* **DOUBLES, DOUBLING, DOUBLED** to make or become twice as large in size, number, etc

DOUBLES *singular noun* a competition in tennis, etc between two teams of two players each

DOUBLET *noun* **DOUBLETS** a close-fitting man's jacket, with or without sleeves, popular from the 14c to the l7c

DOUBLOON *noun* **DOUBLOONS** a gold coin formerly used in Spain and S America

DOUBLY *adverb* to twice the extent; very much more

DOUBT *verb* **DOUBTS, DOUBTING, DOUBTED** to feel uncertain about something; to be suspicious or show mistrust of it □ *noun* **DOUBTS** a feeling of uncertainty, suspicion or mistrust

DOUBTER *noun* **DOUBTERS** someone who feels doubt or uncertainty

DOUBTFUL *adj* feeling doubt

DOUBTLESS *adverb* probably; certainly

DOUCHE *noun* **DOUCHES** a powerful jet of water that is used to clean a body orifice, especially the vagina □ *verb* **DOUCHES, DOUCHING, DOUCHED** to apply or make use of a douche

DOUGH *noun* **DOUGHS** a mixture of flour, liquid (water or milk) and yeast, used in the preparation of bread, pastry, etc

DOUGHNUT *noun* **DOUGHNUTS** a portion of sweetened dough fried in deep fat, sometimes made with a hole in the middle, often filled eg with cream or jam

DOUGHTILY *adverb* in a doughty way

DOUGHTY *adj* **DOUGHTIER, DOUGHTIEST** brave; stout-hearted

DOUGHY *adj* **DOUGHIER, DOUGHIEST** like dough, or having the consistency of dough

DOUR *adj* **DOURER, DOUREST** stern; sullen

DOURLY *adverb* in a dour way

DOURNESS *noun* **DOURNESSES** the state of being dour

DOUSE *verb* **DOUSES, DOUSING, DOUSED** to throw water over something; to plunge something into water

DOVE [1] a past form of **dive**

DOVE [2] *noun* **DOVES** any of several members of the pigeon family, especially the smaller species

DOVECOT *noun* **DOVECOTS** a building or shed in which domestic pigeons are kept

DOVETAIL *noun* **DOVETAILS** a corner joint, especially in wood, made by fitting v-shaped pegs into corresponding slots □ *verb* **DOVETAILS, DOVETAILING, DOVETAILED** to fit using one or more dovetails

DOW *verb* **DOWS, DOWING, DOCHT, DOUGHT, DOWED** an obsolete and Scots word meaning to be able

DOWAGER *noun* **DOWAGERS** a title given to a nobleman's widow, to distinguish her from the wife of her husband's heir

DOWDILY *adverb* in a dowdy way

DOWDINESS *noun* **DOWDINESSES** the quality of being dowdy

DOWDY *adj* **DOWDIER, DOWDIEST** said especially of a woman or her clothing: dull, plain and unfashionable

DOWEL *noun* **DOWELS** a thin cylindrical (especially wooden) peg, especially used to join two pieces by fitting into corresponding holes in each

DOWER *noun* **DOWERS** a widow's share, for life, in her deceased husband's property

DOWN [1] *adverb* towards or in a low or lower position, level or state; on or to the ground; in a crossword: in the vertical direction □ *prep* in a lower position on something □ *adj* sad; in low spirits □ *verb* **DOWNS, DOWNING, DOWNED** to drink something quickly, especially in one gulp

DOWN [2] *noun* soft fine feathers or hair

DOWNBEAT *adj* pessimistic; cheerless □ *noun* **DOWNBEATS** the first beat of a bar or the movement

of the conductor's baton indicating this

DOWNCAST *adj* glum; dispirited

DOWNER *noun* **DOWNERS** a state of depression

DOWNFALL *noun* **DOWNFALLS** failure or ruin, or its cause

DOWNGRADE *verb* **DOWNGRADES, DOWNGRADING, DOWNGRADED** to reduce to a lower grade

DOWNHILL *adverb* downwards □ *adj* downwardly sloping □ *noun* **DOWNHILLS** a ski race down a hillside

DOWNLOAD *verb* **DOWNLOADS, DOWNLOADING, DOWNLOADED** to transfer (data) from one computer to another

DOWNPOUR *noun* **DOWNPOURS** a very heavy fall of rain

DOWNRIGHT *adj* plainspoken; blunt □ *adverb* utterly

DOWNSIDE *noun* **DOWNSIDES** the lower or under side

DOWNSIZE *verb* **DOWNSIZES, DOWNSIZING, DOWNSIZED** to reduce the size of a workforce, especially by redundancies

DOWNSTAGE *adj* at or towards the front of a theatre stage □ *adverb* at or towards the front of a theatre stage

DOWNSWING *noun* **DOWNSWINGS** a decline in economic activity, etc

DOWNTIME *noun* **DOWNTIMES** time during which work ceases because a machine, especially a computer, is not working

DOWNTURN *noun* **DOWNTURNS** a decline in economic activity

DOWNWARD *adj* leading or moving down; descending; declining □ *adverb* to or towards a lower position or level

DOWNWARDS *adverb* to or towards a lower position or level

DOWNWIND *adverb* in or towards the direction in which the wind is blowing; with the wind blowing from behind □ *adj* moving with, or sheltered from, the wind

DOWNY *adj* **DOWNIER, DOWNIEST** covered with or made of down; soft like down

DOWRY *noun* **DOWRIES** an amount of wealth handed over by a woman's family to her husband on marriage

DOWSE *verb* **DOWSES, DOWSING, DOWSED** to search for underground water with a divining-rod

DOWSER noun **DOWSERS** a person who searches for underground water with a divining-rod

DOXOLOGY noun **DOXOLOGIES** a Christian hymn, verse or fixed expression praising God

DOYEN noun **DOYENS** the most senior and most respected member of a group or profession

DOYENNE noun **DOYENNES** a female doyen

DOYLEY noun **DOYLEYS** a small decorative napkin of lace or lace-like paper laid on plates under sandwiches, cakes, etc

DOZE verb **DOZES, DOZING, DOZED** to sleep lightly ▫ noun **DOZES** a brief period of light sleep

DOZEN noun **DOZENS** a set of twelve

DOZENTH adj twelfth

DOZINESS noun **DOZINESSES** the state of being dozy

DOZY adj **DOZIER, DOZIEST** sleepy

DRAB adj **DRABBER, DRABBEST** dull; dreary

DRABLY adverb in a drab way

DRABNESS noun **DRABNESSES** the state of being drab

DRACHM noun **DRACHMS** a measure equal to $\frac{1}{8}$ of an ounce or fluid ounce, formerly used by pharmacists

DRACHMA noun **DRACHMAS, DRACHMAE** the standard unit of currency in Greece

DRACONIAN adj said of a law, etc: harsh; severe

DRACONIC adj draconian

DRAFT noun **DRAFTS** a written plan; a preliminary sketch ▫ verb **DRAFTS, DRAFTING, DRAFTED** to set something out in preliminary sketchy form

DRAFTY adj **DRAFTIER, DRAFTIEST** draughty

DRAG verb **DRAGS, DRAGGING, DRAGGED** to pull someone or something roughly or violently; to pull them or it along slowly and with force ▫ noun **DRAGS** an act of dragging; a dragging effect

DRAGGLE verb **DRAGGLES, DRAGGLING, DRAGGLED** to make or become wet and dirty through trailing along the ground or as if doing so

DRAGNET noun **DRAGNETS** a heavy net pulled along the bottom of a river, lake, etc in a search for something

DRAGON noun **DRAGONS** a large, mythical, fire-breathing, reptile-like creature with wings and a long tail

DRAGONFLY noun **DRAGONFLIES** an insect with a fairly long slender brightly coloured body often metallic in appearance, and gauzy translucent wings that cannot be closed

DRAGOON noun **DRAGOONS** still used in titles of certain British regiments: a heavily armed mounted soldier ▫ verb **DRAGOONS, DRAGOONING, DRAGOONED** to force or bully someone into doing something

DRAGSTER noun **DRAGSTERS** a car designed or adapted to be used in a drag race (a contest in acceleration over a short distance)

DRAIN verb **DRAINS, DRAINING, DRAINED** to empty (a container) by causing or allowing liquid to escape ▫ noun **DRAINS** a device, especially a pipe, for carrying away liquid

DRAINAGE noun **DRAINAGES** the process or a method or system of draining

DRAINER noun **DRAINERS** a device on which articles can be left to drain, or a draining board

DRAINPIPE noun **DRAINPIPES** a pipe carrying waste water or rainwater, especially water from a roof into a drain below ground

DRAKE noun **DRAKES** a male duck

DRAM noun **DRAMS** a small amount of alcoholic spirit, especially whisky

DRAMA noun **DRAMAS** a play; any work performed by actors

DRAMATIC adj belonging or relating to plays, the theatre or acting in general

DRAMATICS plural noun exaggeratedly emotional behaviour

DRAMATISE verb **DRAMATISES, DRAMATISING, DRAMATISED** to dramatize

DRAMATIST noun **DRAMATISTS** a writer of plays

DRAMATIZE verb **DRAMATIZES, DRAMATIZING, DRAMATIZED** to make something into a work for public performance

DRANK a past form of **drink**

DRAPE verb **DRAPES, DRAPING, DRAPED** to hang cloth loosely over something ▫ noun **DRAPES** a curtain or hanging

DRAPER noun **DRAPERS** someone who sells fabric, and often haberdashery

DRAPERY noun **DRAPERIES** fabric; textiles

DRASTIC adj extreme; severe

DRAT exclamation expressing anger or annoyance

DRATTED adj damned

DRAUGHT noun **DRAUGHTS** a current of air, especially indoors ▫ adj said of beer: pumped direct from the cask to the glass

DRAUGHTS singular noun a game for two people played with 24 discs on a chequered board

DRAUGHTY adj **DRAUGHTIER, DRAUGHTIEST** prone to or suffering draughts of air

DRAW verb **DRAWS, DRAWING, DREW, DRAWN** to make a picture of something or someone, especially with a pencil ▫ noun **DRAWS** a result in which neither side is the winner; a tie

DRAWBACK noun **DRAWBACKS** a disadvantage

DRAWER noun **DRAWERS** a sliding lidless storage box fitted as part of a desk or other piece of furniture

DRAWING noun **DRAWINGS** any picture made up of lines, especially one drawn in pencil

DRAWL verb **DRAWLS, DRAWLING, DRAWLED** to speak or say in a slow lazy manner, especially with prolonged vowel sounds

DRAWN adj showing signs of mental strain or tiredness

DRAY noun **DRAYS** a low horse-drawn cart used for heavy loads

DREAD noun **DREADS** great fear or apprehension ▫ verb **DREADS, DREADING, DREADED** to look ahead to something with dread ▫ adj inspiring awe or great fear

DREADED adj greatly feared

DREADFUL adj inspiring great fear; terrible

DREAM noun **DREAMS** a series of unconscious thoughts and mental images that are experienced during sleep ▫ verb **DREAMS, DREAMING, DREAMT, DREAMED** to have thoughts and visions during sleep

DREAMBOAT noun **DREAMBOATS** an ideal romantic partner

DREAMER noun **DREAMERS** a person who dreams

DREAMILY adverb in a dreamy way

DREAMLESS *adj* free from dreams

DREAMY *adj* **DREAMIER, DREAMIEST** unreal, as if in a dream

DREARILY *adverb* in a dreary way

DREARY *adj* **DREARIER, DREARIEST** dull and depressing

DREDGE *verb* **DREDGES, DREDGING, DREDGED** to clear the bottom of or deepen (the sea or a river) by bringing up mud and waste □ *noun* **DREDGES** a machine for dredging, with a scooping or sucking action

DREDGER *noun* **DREDGERS** a barge or ship fitted with a dredge

DREGS *plural noun* solid particles in a liquid that settle at the bottom

DRENCH *verb* **DRENCHES, DRENCHING, DRENCHED** to make something or someone soaking wet □ *noun* **DRENCHES** a dose of liquid medicine for an animal

DRESS *verb* **DRESSES, DRESSING, DRESSED** to put clothes on; to wear, or make someone wear, clothes (of a certain kind) □ *noun* **DRESSES** a woman's garment with top and skirt in one piece □ *adj* formal; for wear in the evenings

DRESSAGE *noun* **DRESSAGES** the training of a horse in, or performance of, set manoeuvres signalled by the rider

DRESSER *noun* **DRESSERS** a free-standing kitchen cupboard with shelves above, for storing and displaying dishes, etc

DRESSING *noun* **DRESSINGS** any sauce added to food, especially salad

DRESSMAKE *verb* **DRESSMAKES, DRESSMAKING, DRESSMADE** to make clothes

DRESSMAKING *noun* **DRESSMAKINGS** the craft or business of making especially women's clothes

DRESSY *adj* **DRESSIER, DRESSIEST** dressed or dressing stylishly

DREW a past form of **draw**

DREY *noun* **DREYS** a squirrel's nest

DRIBBLE *verb* **DRIBBLES, DRIBBLING, DRIBBLED** to fall or flow in drops □ *noun* **DRIBBLES** a small quantity of liquid, especially saliva

DRIBLET *noun* **DRIBLETS** a very small amount, especially of liquid

DRIED past form of **dry**

DRIER *noun* **DRIERS** a device or substance that dries clothing, hair, paint, etc

DRIES a form of **dry**

DRIFT *noun* **DRIFTS** superficial deposits of rock material that have been carried from their place of origin by glaciers □ *verb* **DRIFTS, DRIFTING, DRIFTED** to float or be blown along or into heaps

DRIFTER *noun* **DRIFTERS** a fishing-boat that uses large nets which drift with the tide

DRIFTWOOD *noun* **DRIFTWOODS** wood floating near, or washed up on, a shore

DRILL *noun* **DRILLS** a tool for boring holes □ *verb* **DRILLS, DRILLING, DRILLED** to make (a hole) with a drill; to make a hole in something with a drill

DRILY *adverb* in a dry manner

DRINK *verb* **DRINKS, DRINKING, DRANK, DRUNK** to swallow (a liquid); to consume (a liquid) by swallowing □ *noun* **DRINKS** an act of drinking

DRINKABLE *adj* fit to be drunk

DRINKER *noun* **DRINKERS** someone who drinks, especially alcohol, and especially too much

DRINKING *noun* **DRINKINGS** the act or habit of drinking □ *adj* fit for or intended for drinking

DRIP *verb* **DRIPS, DRIPPING, DRIPPED** to release or fall in drops □ *noun* **DRIPS** the action or noise of dripping

DRIPPING *noun* **DRIPPINGS** fat from roasted meat, especially when solidified

DRIVABLE *adj* driveable

DRIVE *verb* **DRIVES, DRIVING, DROVE, DRIVEN** to control the movement of (a vehicle) □ *noun* **DRIVES** a trip in a vehicle; travel by road

DRIVEABLE *adj* capable of being driven

DRIVEL *noun* **DRIVELS** nonsense □ *verb* **DRIVELS, DRIVELLING, DRIVELLED** to talk nonsense

DRIVER *noun* **DRIVERS** someone who drives a vehicle

DRIVEWAY *noun* **DRIVEWAYS** a path for vehicles leading from a private residence to the road outside

DRIVING *noun* **DRIVINGS** the act, practice or way of driving vehicles □ *adj* producing or transmitting operating power

DRIZZLE *noun* **DRIZZLES** fine light rain □ *verb* **DRIZZLES,**

DRIZZLING, DRIZZLED to rain lightly

DRIZZLY *adj* **DRIZZLIER, DRIZZLIEST** resembling drizzle

DROGUE *noun* **DROGUES** a conical canvas sleeve open at both ends, used as one form of sea-anchor, to check the way of an aircraft, etc

DROLL *adj* **DROLLER, DROLLEST** oddly amusing or comical

DROLLERY *noun* **DROLLERIES** drollness; a comic show, picture or story

DROLLY *adverb* in a droll way

DROMEDARY *noun* **DROMEDARIES** a breed of single-humped camel, capable of moving at speed across the desert, and much used as a means of transport in N Africa, the Middle East and India

DRONE *verb* **DRONES, DRONING, DRONED** to make a low humming noise □ *noun* **DRONES** a deep humming sound

DRONGO *noun* **DRONGOS, DRONGOES** an idiot; a no-hoper

DROOL *verb* **DROOLS, DROOLING, DROOLED** to dribble or slaver

DROOP *verb* **DROOPS, DROOPING, DROOPED** to hang loosely; to sag □ *noun* **DROOPS** a drooping state

DROOPILY *adverb* in a droopy way

DROOPY *adj* **DROOPIER, DROOPIEST** hanging loosely; drooping

DROP *verb* **DROPS, DROPPING, DROPPED** to fall or allow to fall □ *noun* **DROPS** a small round or pear-shaped mass of liquid, especially when falling; a small amount (of liquid)

DROPLET *noun* **DROPLETS** a tiny drop

DROPOUT *noun* **DROPOUTS** a student who quits before completing a course of study

DROPPER *noun* **DROPPERS** a short narrow glass tube with a rubber bulb on one end, for applying liquid in drops

DROPPINGS *plural noun* animal or bird faeces

DROPSICAL *adj* affected with dropsy

DROPSY *noun* **DROPSIES** the former name for oedema

DROSS *noun* waste coal

DROSSY *adj* **DROSSIER, DROSSIEST** like dross; impure; worthless

For longer words, see *The Chambers Dictionary*

DROUGHT noun **DROUGHTS** a prolonged lack of rainfall

DROVE [1] a past form of **drive**

DROVE [2] noun **DROVES** a moving herd of animals, especially cattle

DROVER noun **DROVERS** someone employed to drive farm animals to and from market

DROWN verb **DROWNS, DROWNING, DROWNED** to die by suffocation as a result of inhaling liquid, especially water, into the lungs

DROWSE verb **DROWSES, DROWSING, DROWSED** to sleep lightly for a short while; to be in a pleasantly sleepy state

DROWSILY adverb in a drowsy way

DROWSY adj **DROWSIER, DROWSIEST** sleepy; causing sleepiness

DRUB verb **DRUBS, DRUBBING, DRUBBED** to defeat severely

DRUBBING noun **DRUBBINGS** a thorough defeat

DRUDGE verb **DRUDGES, DRUDGING, DRUDGED** to do hard, tedious or menial work ◻ noun **DRUDGES** a servant; a labourer

DRUDGERY noun **DRUDGERIES** hard or humble labour

DRUG noun **DRUGS** any chemical substance which, when taken into the body or applied externally, has a specific effect on its functioning ◻ verb **DRUGS, DRUGGING, DRUGGED** to administer a drug to (a person or animal)

DRUGGET noun **DRUGGETS** thick coarse woollen fabric

DRUGGIST noun **DRUGGISTS** a pharmacist

DRUGGY noun **DRUGGIES** a drug addict

DRUID noun **DRUIDS** a member of a Celtic order of priests in N Europe in pre-Christian times

DRUIDIC adj of or relating to the druids

DRUIDICAL adj druidic

DRUIDISM noun **DRUIDISMS** the doctrines which the druids taught; the ceremonies they practised

DRUM noun **DRUMS** a percussion instrument consisting of a hollow frame with a skin or other membrane stretched tightly across its opening, sounding when struck ◻ verb **DRUMS, DRUMMING, DRUMMED** to beat a drum

DRUMBEAT noun **DRUMBEATS** the sound made when a drum is hit

DRUMHEAD noun **DRUMHEADS** the part of a drum that is struck; the skin

DRUMLIN noun **DRUMLINS** a small elongated oval hill produced by the pressure of ice moving over glacial deposits, often found in groups

DRUMMER noun **DRUMMERS** someone who plays drums

DRUMSTICK noun **DRUMSTICKS** a stick used for beating a drum

DRUNK a past form of **drink** ◻ adj **DRUNKER, DRUNKEST** lacking control in movement, speech, etc through having consumed an excess of alcohol ◻ noun **DRUNKS** a drunk person, especially one regularly so

DRUNKARD noun **DRUNKARDS** someone who is often drunk

DRUNKEN adj drunk

DRUNKENLY adverb in a drunken way

DRUPE noun **DRUPES** a fleshy fruit containing one or more seeds that are surrounded by the endocarp, eg plum, cherry, peach, holly

DRUPELET noun **DRUPELETS** a small drupe, forming part of a fruit, as in the raspberry

DRUSE noun **DRUSES** a rock cavity lined with crystals

DRUXY adj **DRUXIER, DRUXIEST** said of timber: having decayed spots concealed by healthy wood

DRY adj **DRIER, DRIEST** free from or lacking moisture or wetness ◻ verb **DRIES, DRYING, DRIED** to make or become dry

DRYAD noun **DRYADS** a woodland nymph or fairy, often with demigod status

DRYER noun **DRYERS** a device or substance that dries clothing, hair, paint, etc

DRYLY adverb drily

DRYNESS noun **DRYNESSES** absence or lack of moisture

DSO noun **DSOS** a zo

DUAL adj consisting of or representing two separate parts ◻ verb **DUALS, DUALLING, DUALLED** to upgrade (a road) by making it into a dual carriageway

DUALISM noun **DUALISMS** the belief that reality is made up of two separate parts, one spiritual and one physical, or influenced by two separate forces, one good and one bad

DUALISTIC adj consisting of two; relating to dualism

DUALITY noun **DUALITIES** the state of being double

DUB verb **DUBS, DUBBING, DUBBED** to add a new soundtrack to (eg a film), especially one in a different language ◻ noun **DUBS** a type of reggae music in which bass, drums and the artistic arrangement are given prominence over voice and other instruments

DUBBIN noun **DUBBINS** a wax-like mixture of oil and tallow for softening and waterproofing leather

DUBIETY noun **DUBIETIES** dubiousness; doubt

DUBIOUS adj feeling doubt; unsure; uncertain

DUBIOUSLY adverb in a dubious way

DUCAL adj belonging or relating to a duke

DUCAT noun **DUCATS** a former European gold or silver coin of varying value

DUCHESS noun **DUCHESSES** the wife or widow of a duke

DUCHY noun **DUCHIES** the territory owned or ruled by a duke or duchess

DUCK [1] noun **DUCKS** a water bird with short legs, webbed feet, and a large flattened beak

DUCK [2] verb **DUCKS, DUCKING, DUCKED** to lower the head or body suddenly, especially to avoid notice or a blow

DUCKING noun **DUCKINGS** immersion of a person or animal in water

DUCKLING noun **DUCKLINGS** a young duck

DUCKWEED noun **DUCKWEEDS** any of a family of plants whose broad flat leaves grow on the surface of water

DUCKY noun **DUCKIES** a term of endearment ◻ adj **DUCKIER, DUCKIEST** excellent; attractive or pleasing

DUCT noun **DUCTS** any tube in the body, especially one for carrying glandular secretions away from a gland

DUCTILE adj denoting certain metals, eg copper, that can be drawn out into a thin wire or thread without breaking

DUCTILITY *noun* **DUCTILITIES** the capacity of metal to be stretched or pressed into shape

DUD *noun* **DUDS** a counterfeit article ▫ *adj* useless

DUDE *noun* **DUDES** a man; a guy

DUDGEON *noun* **DUDGEONS** resentment; offended indignation

DUE *adj* owed; payable ▫ *noun* **DUES** what is owed; that which can be rightfully claimed or expected ▫ *adverb* directly

DUEL *noun* **DUELS** a pre-arranged fight between two people to settle a matter of honour ▫ *verb* **DUELS, DUELLING, DUELLED** to fight a duel

DUELLER *noun* **DUELLERS** a duellist

DUELLIST *noun* **DUELLISTS** someone who fights duels

DUENNA *noun* **DUENNAS** an older woman acting as a chaperone to a girl or young woman

DUET *noun* **DUETS** a piece of music for two singers or players

DUETTIST *noun* **DUETTISTS** someone who takes part in a duet

DUFF [1] *noun* **DUFFS** a heavy boiled or steamed pudding, especially one containing fruit

DUFF [2] *adj* **DUFFER, DUFFEST** useless; broken

DUFF [3] *verb* **DUFFS, DUFFING, DUFFED** to bungle something

DUFFEL *noun* **DUFFELS** a thick coarse woollen fabric

DUFFER *noun* **DUFFERS** a clumsy or incompetent person

DUFFLE *noun* **DUFFLES** duffel

DUG [1] past form of **dig**

DUG [2] *noun* **DUGS** an animal's udder or nipple

DUGONG *noun* **DUGONGS** a seal-like plant-eating tropical sea mammal

DUGOUT *noun* **DUGOUTS** a canoe made from a hollowed-out log

DUKE *noun* **DUKES** a nobleman of the highest rank outside the royal family

DUKEDOM *noun* **DUKEDOMS** the title or property of a duke

DULCET *adj* said of sounds: sweet and pleasing to the ear

DULCIMER *noun* **DULCIMERS** a percussion instrument consisting of a flattish box with tuned strings stretched across, struck with small hammers

DULL *adj* **DULLER, DULLEST** said of colour or light: lacking brightness or clearness ▫ *verb* **DULLS, DULLING, DULLED** to make or become dull

DULLNESS *noun* **DULLNESSES** a dull or uninteresting state

DULLY *adverb* in a dull way

DULSE *noun* **DULSES** an edible red seaweed

DULY *adverb* in the proper way; at the proper time

DUMB *adj* **DUMBER, DUMBEST** not having the power of speech

DUMBFOUND *verb* **DUMBFOUNDS, DUMBFOUNDING, DUMBFOUNDED** to astonish or confound, originally so as to leave speechless

DUMBLY *adverb* in silence; mutely

DUMBNESS *noun* **DUMBNESSES** inability to speak; muteness

DUMBO *noun* **DUMBOS** a stupid person

DUMDUM *noun* **DUMDUMS** a bullet that expands on impact, causing severe injury

DUMFOUND *verb* **DUMFOUNDS, DUMFOUNDING, DUMFOUNDED** to dumbfound

DUMMY *noun* **DUMMIES** a life-size model of the human body, eg used for displaying clothes ▫ *adj* **DUMMIER, DUMMIEST** false; sham; counterfeit ▫ *verb* **DUMMIES, DUMMYING, DUMMIED** to make as if to move one way before sharply moving the other, in order to deceive (an opponent)

DUMP *verb* **DUMPS, DUMPING, DUMPED** to put something down heavily or carelessly ▫ *noun* **DUMPS** a place where rubbish may be dumped

DUMPBIN *noun* **DUMPBINS** in a shop etc: a display stand or a container for especially bargain items

DUMPER *noun* **DUMPERS** something or someone that dumps

DUMPLING *noun* **DUMPLINGS** a baked or boiled ball of dough served with meat

DUMPS *plural noun* dullness or gloominess of mind, ill-humour, low spirits

DUMPY *adj* **DUMPIER, DUMPIEST** short and plump

DUN [1] *adj* **DUNNER, DUNNEST** having a greyish-brown dusky colour ▫ *noun* **DUNS** a dun colour

DUN [2] *verb* **DUNS, DUNNING, DUNNED** to press someone persistently for payment

DUNCE *noun* **DUNCES** a stupid person; a slow learner

DUNE *noun* **DUNES** a ridge or hill formed by the accumulation of windblown sand, usually on a seashore or in a hot desert

DUNG *noun* **DUNGS** animal excrement

DUNGAREES *plural noun* loose trousers with a bib and shoulder straps attached, worn as casual wear or overalls

DUNGEON *noun* **DUNGEONS** a prison cell, especially underground

DUNK *verb* **DUNKS, DUNKING, DUNKED** to dip (eg a biscuit) into tea or a similar beverage

DUNLIN *noun* **DUNLINS** a small brown wading bird with a slender probing bill

DUNNED past form of **dun** [2]

DUNNER see under **dun** [1]

DUNNEST see under **dun** [1]

DUNNING a form of **dun** [2]

DUNNOCK *noun* **DUNNOCKS** the hedge sparrow

DUO *noun* **DUOS** a pair of musicians or other performers

DUODENAL *adj* relating to or affecting the duodenum

DUODENUM *noun* **DUODENA** the first part of the small intestine, into which food passes after leaving the stomach

DUOLOGUE *noun* **DUOLOGUES** a dialogue between two actors

DUOPOLY *noun* **DUOPOLIES** a situation in which two companies, etc monopolize trading in a particular commodity

DUP *verb* **DUPS, DUPPING, DUPPED** a Shakespearean word meaning to undo

DUPABLE *adj* capable of being duped

DUPE *verb* **DUPES, DUPING, DUPED** to trick or deceive ▫ *noun* **DUPES** a person who is deceived

DUPLE *adj* double; twofold

DUPLEX *noun* **DUPLEXES** a flat on two floors ▫ *adj* double; twofold

DUPLICATE *adj* identical to another ▫ *noun* **DUPLICATES** said especially of documents: an exact copy ▫ *verb* **DUPLICATES, DUPLICATING, DUPLICATED** to make or be an exact copy or copies of something

DUPLICITY *noun* **DUPLICITIES**

deception; trickery; double-dealing

DURABLE *adj* lasting a long time without breaking; sturdy ▫ *noun* **DURABLES** a durable item, especially one not frequently replaced

DURABLY *adverb* in a durable way; lastingly

DURATION *noun* **DURATIONS** the length of time that something lasts

DURESS *noun* **DURESSES** the influence of force or threats; coercion

DURING *prep* throughout the time of something

DURUM *noun* **DURUMS** a kind of spring wheat whose flour is popular for making pasta

DUSK *noun* **DUSKS** twilight; the period of semi-darkness before night

DUSKILY *adverb* in a dusky way; dimly

DUSKINESS *noun* **DUSKINESSES** dimness

DUSKY *adj* **DUSKIER, DUSKIEST** dark; shadowy

DUST *noun* **DUSTS** earth, sand or household dirt in the form of a fine powder ▫ *verb* **DUSTS, DUSTING, DUSTED** to remove dust from (furniture, etc)

DUSTBIN *noun* **DUSTBINS** a large, usually cylindrical, lidded container for household rubbish, especially one kept outside

DUSTCART *noun* **DUSTCARTS** a vehicle in which household rubbish is collected

DUSTER *noun* **DUSTERS** a cloth for removing household dust

DUSTILY *adverb* curtly; rudely

DUSTINESS *noun* **DUSTINESSES** the state of being dusty

DUSTMAN *noun* **DUSTMEN** someone employed to collect household rubbish

DUSTY *adj* **DUSTIER, DUSTIEST** covered with or containing dust

DUTEOUS *adj* dutiful

DUTIABLE *adj* said of goods: on which duty is payable

DUTIFUL *adj* attentive to duty; respectful

DUTIFULLY *adverb* in a dutiful way

DUTY *noun* **DUTIES** something one is or feels obliged to do; a moral or legal responsibility, or the awareness of it

DUVET *noun* **DUVETS** a thick quilt filled with feathers or man-made fibres, for use on a bed instead of a sheet and blankets

DUX *noun* **DUXES** the top academic prize-winner in a school or class

DWARF *noun* **DWARFS, DWARVES** an abnormally small person ▫ *verb* **DWARFS, DWARFING, DWARFED** to make something seem small or unimportant

DWARFISH *adj* like a dwarf; very small

DWARFISM *noun* **DWARFISMS** the condition of being a dwarf

DWEEB *noun* **DWEEBS** an idiot; a nerd

DWELL *verb* **DWELLS, DWELLING, DWELT, DWELLED** to reside

DWELLER *noun* **DWELLERS** someone who lives in a particular place or area

DWELLING *noun* **DWELLINGS** a place of residence; a house

DWINDLE *verb* **DWINDLES, DWINDLING, DWINDLED** to shrink in size, number or intensity

DYABLE *adj* dyeable

DYBBUK *noun* **DYBBUKS** in folklore: an evil spirit or the soul of a dead person, which enters the body of a living person and controls their behaviour until exorcized by a religious rite

DYE *verb* **DYES, DYEING, DYED** to colour or stain something, or undergo colouring or staining, often permanently ▫ *noun* **DYES** a coloured substance, either natural or synthetic, that is used in solution to impart colour to another material

DYEABLE *adj* capable of being dyed

DYER *noun* **DYERS** someone who dyes cloth, etc, especially as a business

DYESTUFF *noun* **DYESTUFFS** a substance which can be used as a dye or from which a dye can be produced

DYING a form of **die** [1] ▫ *adj* expressed or occurring immediately before death

DYKE *noun* **DYKES** a wall or embankment built to prevent flooding ▫ *verb* **DYKES, DYKING, DYKED** to protect or drain with a dyke

DYNAMIC *adj* full of energy, enthusiasm and new ideas

DYNAMICS *singular noun* the branch of mechanics that deals with the motion of objects and the forces that act to produce such motion

DYNAMISM *noun* **DYNAMISMS** limitless energy and enthusiasm

DYNAMITE *noun* **DYNAMITES** any of a group of powerful blasting explosives ▫ *verb* **DYNAMITES, DYNAMITING, DYNAMITED** to explode something with dynamite

DYNAMO *noun* **DYNAMOS** an electric generator that converts mechanical energy into electrical energy, usually in the form of direct current

DYNASTIC *adj* relating to or associated with a dynasty

DYNASTY *noun* **DYNASTIES** a succession of rulers from the same family

DYNE *noun* **DYNES** a unit of force, producing an acceleration of one centimetre per second every second on a mass of one gram

DYSENTERY *noun* **DYSENTERIES** severe infection and inflammation of the intestines caused by bacteria, protozoa or parasitic worms

DYSLEXIA *noun* **DYSLEXIAS** a disorder characterized by difficulty in reading and writing, and in spelling correctly

DYSLEXIC *adj* affected by dyslexia ▫ *noun* **DYSLEXICS** someone affected by dyslexia

DYSPEPSIA *noun* **DYSPEPSIAS** indigestion

DYSPEPTIC *adj* suffering from dyspepsia

DYSPHASIA *noun* **DYSPHASIAS** difficulty in expressing or understanding thought in spoken or written words, caused by brain damage

DYSPLASIA *noun* **DYSPLASIAS** abnormal development of tissue, eg skin or bone, sometimes associated with cancer

DYSPNEA *noun* **DYSPNEAS** dyspnoea

DYSPNOEA *noun* **DYSPNOEAS** difficulty in breathing, often associated with serious disease of the heart or lungs

DYSTROPHY *noun* **DYSTROPHIES** any of various unrelated disorders of organs or tissues, especially muscle, arising from an inadequate supply of nutrients

DZHO *noun* **DZHOS** a zo

DZO *noun* **DZOS** a zo
ⓘ This is a useful word for using up both **D** and **Z**, and is worth 13 points.

EA *noun* **EAS** a dialect word meaning *river*

EACH *adj* applied to every one of two or more people or items considered separately □ *pronoun* every single one of two or more people, animals or things □ *adverb* to, for or from each one

EAGER *adj* **EAGERER, EAGEREST** feeling or showing great desire or enthusiasm; keen to do or get something

EAGERLY *adverb* in an eager way

EAGERNESS *noun* **EAGERNESSES** the state or quality of being eager

EAGLE *noun* **EAGLES** any of various kinds of large birds of prey

EAGLET *noun* **EAGLETS** a young eagle

EAGRE *noun* **EAGRES** a sudden tidal flood in a river

EAN *verb* **EANS, EANING, EANED** a Shakespearean word meaning to give birth to

EAR *noun* **EARS** the sense organ that is concerned with hearing

EARACHE *noun* **EARACHES** pain or an ache in the inner part of the ear

EARBASH *verb* **EARBASHES, EARBASHING, EARBASHED** to pester someone with non-stop talking

EARCON *noun* **EARCONS** an audio signal given by a computer, as opposed to an icon

EARDROPS *plural noun* medicinal drops for the ear

EARDRUM *noun* **EARDRUMS** the small thin membrane inside the ear, which transmits vibrations made by sound waves to the inner ear

EARED *adj* having ears

EARFLAP *noun* **EARFLAPS** one of two coverings for the ears, attached to a cap, to protect them from cold or injury

EARFUL *noun* **EARFULS** a long complaint or telling-off; a rough scolding

EARL *noun* **EARLS** a male member of the British nobility ranking below a marquess and above a viscount

EARLDOM *noun* **EARLDOMS** the status or position of an earl

EARLESS *adj* without ears

EARLINESS *noun* **EARLINESSES** the state or condition of being early

EARLOBE *noun* **EARLOBES** the soft, loosely hanging piece of flesh which forms the lower part of the ear

EARLY *adj* **EARLIER, EARLIEST** characteristic of or near the beginning of (a period of time, period of development, etc) □ *adverb* characteristic of or near the beginning of (a period of time, period of development, etc)

EARMARK *verb* **EARMARKS, EARMARKING, EARMARKED** to set aside or intend something or someone for a particular purpose □ *noun* **EARMARKS** an owner's mark on an animal's ear

EARMUFFS *plural noun* coverings worn over the ears to protect them from cold or noise

EARN *verb* **EARNS, EARNING, EARNED** to gain (money, wages, one's living, etc) by working

EARNER *noun* **EARNERS** a person who earns

EARNEST[1] *adj* serious or over-serious

EARNEST[2] *noun* **EARNESTS** a part payment made in advance, especially (in law) one made to confirm an agreement

EARNESTLY *adverb* in an earnest way

EARNINGS *plural noun* money earned

EARPHONES *plural noun* a device consisting of two small sound receivers, either held over the ears by a metal strap passed over the head, or inserted into the ear, for listening to a radio, CD player, personal stereo, etc

EARPIECE *noun* **EARPIECES** the part of a telephone or hearing-aid which is placed at or in the ear

EARPLUG *noun* **EARPLUGS** a piece of wax or rubber, etc placed in the ear as a protection against noise, cold or water

EARRING *noun* **EARRINGS** a piece of jewellery worn attached to the ear

EARSHOT *noun* **EARSHOTS** the distance at which sound can be heard

EARTH *noun* **EARTHS** the planet on which we live, the third planet in order of distance from the Sun □ *verb* **EARTHS, EARTHING, EARTHED** to connect to the ground

EARTHEN *adj* said of a floor, etc: made of earth

EARTHIER see under **earthy**

EARTHIEST see under **earthy**

EARTHLING *noun* **EARTHLINGS** in science fiction: a native of the Earth

EARTHLY *adj* **EARTHLIER, EARTHLIEST** referring, relating or belonging to this world; not spiritual

EARTHMAN *noun* **EARTHMEN** especially in science fiction: a male native of the Earth

EARTHWARD *adverb* towards Earth □ *adj* moving toward Earth; Earth-directed

EARTHWORK *noun* **EARTHWORKS** excavation and embanking, eg as one process in road-building

EARTHWORM *noun* **EARTHWORMS** any of several types of worm which live in and burrow through the soil

EARTHY *adj* **EARTHIER, EARTHIEST** consisting of, relating to, or like earth or soil

EARWAX *noun* **EARWAXES** a waxy substance secreted by the glands of the ear

EARWIG *noun* **EARWIGS** an insect with pincers at the end of its body □ *verb* **EARWIGS, EARWIGGING, EARWIGGED** to scold

EAS plural of **ea**

EASE noun **EASES** freedom from pain or anxiety ▫ verb **EASES, EASING, EASED** to free someone from pain, trouble or anxiety

EASEFUL adj relaxing; quiet; restful

EASEL noun **EASELS** a stand for supporting a blackboard or an artist's canvas, etc

EASEMENT noun **EASEMENTS** the right to use something, especially land, that is not one's own, or to prevent its owner making an inconvenient use of it

EASIER see under **easy**

EASIEST see under **easy**

EASILY adverb without difficulty

EASINESS noun **EASINESSES** the quality of not being difficult

EAST noun **EASTS** the direction from which the sun rises at the equinox ▫ adj in the east; on the side which is on or nearest the east ▫ adverb in, to or towards the east

EASTBOUND adj going or leading towards the east

EASTERLY adj said of a wind, etc: coming from the east ▫ adverb to or towards the east ▫ noun **EASTERLIES** an easterly wind

EASTERN adj situated in, directed towards or belonging to the east or the East

EASTERNER noun **EASTERNERS** a person who lives in or comes from the east, especially the eastern US

EASTING noun **EASTINGS** the total distance travelled towards the east by a ship, etc

EASTWARD adverb towards the east ▫ adj toward the east

EASY adj **EASIER, EASIEST** not difficult ▫ adverb in a slow, calm or relaxed way

EAT verb **EATS, EATING, ATE, EATEN** to bite, chew and swallow (food)

EATABLE adj fit to be eaten ▫ noun **EATABLES** an item of food

EATER noun **EATERS** a person who eats in a specified way

EATERY noun **EATERIES** a small restaurant

EATS plural noun food

EAU noun **EAUS, EAUX** the French word for *water*
ⓘ This is a good word for using up vowels from a vowel-heavy rack. The plural **eaux** is a good word for using up **X**.

EAVES plural noun the part of a roof that sticks out beyond the wall, or the underside of it

EAVESDROP verb **EAVESDROPS, EAVESDROPPING, EAVESDROPPED** to listen secretly to a private conversation

EBB verb **EBBS, EBBING, EBBED** said of the tide: to move back from the land ▫ noun **EBBS** the movement of the tide away from the land

EBBTIDE noun **EBBTIDES** the ebbing tide

EBONISE verb **EBONISES, EBONISING, EBONISED** to ebonize

EBONITE noun **EBONITES** hard black vulcanized rubber

EBONIZE verb **EBONIZES, EBONIZING, EBONIZED** to make or become like ebony

EBONY noun **EBONIES** a type of extremely hard, heavy and almost black wood ▫ adj made from this wood

EBULLIENT adj very high-spirited; full of cheerfulness or enthusiasm

EBURNEAN adj made of or like ivory

ECAD noun **ECADS** a plant form which is assumed to have adapted to its environment

ÉCARTÉ noun **ÉCARTÉS** in ballet: a position in which the arm and leg are extended to the side

ECCENTRIC adj said of a person or behaviour, etc: odd; unusual or unconventional ▫ noun **ECCENTRICS** an eccentric person

ECCRINE adj said of a gland, especially a sweat gland: secreting externally

ECDYSIAST noun **ECDYSIASTS** a striptease performer

ECDYSIS noun **ECDYSES** in animals with a rigid exoskeleton, such as insects and crustaceans: the act of shedding the exoskeleton so that growth can occur

ECH verb **ECHES, ECHING, ECHED** a Shakespearean word meaning to eke out

ÉCHAPPÉ noun **ÉCHAPPÉS** in ballet: a double leap from two feet, starting in fifth position, landing in second or fourth, and finishing in fifth

ECHELON noun **ECHELONS** a level or rank in an organization, etc

ECHIDNA noun **ECHIDNAS** the spiny anteater, an egg-laying mammal of Australia and New Guinea, with a long snout and long claws

ECHINOID noun **ECHINOIDS** a sea urchin ▫ adj like a sea urchin

ECHINUS noun **ECHINUSES** a type of sea urchin, eg the edible sea urchin from the Mediterranean

ECHO noun **ECHOES** the repeating of a sound caused by the sound waves striking a surface and coming back ▫ verb **ECHOES, ECHOING, ECHOED** to send back an echo of something

ECHOIC adj said of a sound: referring to or like an echo

ECHOLALIA noun **ECHOLALIAS** senseless or compulsive repetition of words heard

ECHOLESS adj giving no echo

ECHT adj genuine; authentic

ÉCLAIR noun **ÉCLAIRS** a long cake of choux pastry with a cream filling and chocolate icing

ECLAMPSIA noun **ECLAMPSIAS** a toxic condition which may develop during the last three months of pregnancy

ÉCLAT noun **ÉCLATS** striking effect; showy splendour

ECLECTIC adj said of a style of writing or art, or a set of beliefs: selecting material or ideas from a wide range of sources or authorities ▫ noun **ECLECTICS** a person who adopts eclectic methods

ECLIPSE noun **ECLIPSES** the total or partial obscuring of one planet or heavenly body by another, eg of the Sun when the Moon comes between it and the Earth (a solar eclipse) or of the Moon when the Earth's shadow falls across it (a lunar eclipse) ▫ verb **ECLIPSES, ECLIPSING, ECLIPSED** to cause an eclipse of (a heavenly body)

ECLIPTIC noun **ECLIPTICS** the course which the Sun seems to follow in relation to the stars

ECLOGUE noun **ECLOGUES** a pastoral poem, often in the form of a dialogue

ECLOSION noun **ECLOSIONS** emergence, especially that of an insect larva from its egg, or an adult insect from its pupal case

ECOCIDE noun **ECOCIDES** destruction of the aspects of the environment which enable it to support life

ECOLOGIC *adj* relating to, or concerned with, ecology

ECOLOGIST *noun* **ECOLOGISTS** an expert in ecology

ECOLOGY *noun* **ECOLOGIES** the relationship between living things and their surroundings

ECONOMIC *adj* relating to or concerned with economy or economics

ECONOMICS *singular noun* the study of the production, distribution and consumption of money, goods and services

ECONOMISE *verb* **ECONOMISES, ECONOMISING, ECONOMISED** to economize

ECONOMIST *noun* **ECONOMISTS** an expert in economics

ECONOMIZE *verb* **ECONOMIZES, ECONOMIZING, ECONOMIZED** to cut down on spending or waste

ECONOMY *noun* **ECONOMIES** the organization of money and resources within a nation or community, etc, especially in terms of the production, distribution and consumption of goods and services

ECOSPHERE *noun* **ECOSPHERES** the parts of the universe, especially of the Earth, in which living things can exist

ÉCOSSAISE *noun* **ÉCOSSAISES** a lively country dance or music for it in 2/4 time

ECOSYSTEM *noun* **ECOSYSTEMS** a community of living things and their relationships to their surroundings

ECOTOXIC *adj* poisonous to plants or animals; harmful to the environment

ECOTYPE *noun* **ECOTYPES** a group of organisms which have adapted to a particular environment and so have become different from other groups within the species

ECRU *noun* **ECRUS** an off-white or greyish-yellow colour; fawn □ *adj* off-white or greyish-yellow; fawn

ECSTASY *noun* **ECSTASIES** a feeling of immense joy; rapture

ECSTATIC *adj* relating to, showing or causing ecstasy

ECTOBLAST *noun* **ECTOBLASTS** the outer cell-layer of a gastrula

ECTODERM *noun* **ECTODERMS** in a multicellular animal that has two or more layers of body tissue: the external germinal layer of epiblast of the embryo

ECTOMORPH *noun* **ECTOMORPHS** a person of thin light body build

ECTOPIC *adj* in an abnormal position

ECTOPLASM *noun* **ECTOPLASMS** the outer layer of a cell's protoplasm, the material which makes up the living part

ECU *noun* **ECUS** a trading currency whose value is based on the combined values of several European currencies

ECUMENIC *adj* bringing together different branches of the Christian church

ECUMENICS *singular noun* the study of ecumenical awareness and the ecumenical movement in the Christian church

ECUMENISM *noun* the principles or practice of Christian unity

ECZEMA *noun* **ECZEMAS** a skin disorder in which red blisters form on the skin, usually causing an itching or burning sensation

EDAPHIC *adj* belonging or relating to the soil

EDDY *noun* **EDDIES** a current of water running back against the main stream or current, forming a small whirlpool □ *verb* **EDDIES, EDDYING, EDDIED** to move or make something move round and round

EDELWEISS *noun* **EDELWEISSES** a small European mountain plant of the same family as the daisy and the dandelion, with white woolly leaves around the flower-heads

EDEMA *noun* **EDEMAS** oedema

EDENTATE *adj* having few or no teeth □ *noun* **EDENTATES** an animal belonging to a group of mammals which have few or no teeth, such as the anteater, armadillo and sloth

EDGE *noun* **EDGES** the part farthest from the middle of something; a border or boundary; the rim □ *verb* **EDGES, EDGING, EDGED** to form or make a border to something, edged with flowers

EDGED *adj* having an edge of a specified kind

EDGER *noun* **EDGERS** a garden tool for trimming the edge of a lawn

EDGEWAYS *adverb* sideways

EDGEWISE *adverb* sideways

EDGINESS *noun* **EDGINESSES** the state of being edgy

EDGING *noun* **EDGINGS** a border around something or to be applied to something, especially a decorative one

EDGY *adj* **EDGIER, EDGIEST** easily annoyed; anxious, nervous or tense

EDH *noun* **EDHS** eth

EDIBILITY *noun* **EDIBILITIES** fitness for being eaten

EDIBLE *adj* fit to be eaten; suitable to eat

EDIBLES *plural noun* food; things that are fit to be eaten

EDICT *noun* **EDICTS** an order issued by a monarch or government

EDICTAL *adj* of or relating to an edict or edicts

EDIFICE *noun* **EDIFICES** a building, especially a large impressive one

EDIFY *verb* **EDIFIES, EDIFYING, EDIFIED** to improve the mind or morals of someone

EDIFYING *adj* intellectually or morally stimulating

EDIT *verb* **EDITS, EDITING, EDITED** to prepare (a book, newspaper, programme, film, etc) for publication or broadcasting, especially by making corrections or alterations □ *noun* **EDITS** a period or instance of editing

EDITED *adj* of a book, newspaper, film etc: prepared for publication or broadcasting, especially by having had corrections or alterations made

EDITION *noun* **EDITIONS** the total number of copies of a book, etc printed at one time, or at different times without alteration

EDITOR *noun* **EDITORS** a person who edits books, etc

EDITORIAL *adj* referring or relating to editors or editing □ *noun* **EDITORIALS** an article written by or on behalf of the editor of a newspaper or magazine, usually one offering an opinion on a current topic

EDUCABLE *adj* capable of being educated

EDUCATE *verb* **EDUCATES, EDUCATING, EDUCATED** to train and teach

EDUCATED *adj* having received an education, especially to a level higher than average

EDUCATION *noun* **EDUCATIONS** the process of teaching

EDUCATIVE *adj* educating; characteristic of or relating to education

EDUCATOR *noun* **EDUCATORS** a person who educates
EDUCATORY *adj* having an educating influence
EDUCE *verb* **EDUCES, EDUCING, EDUCED** to bring out or develop
EDUCIBLE *adj* capable of being educed
EDUCTION *noun* **EDUCTIONS** the act of educing; the exhaust of an engine

EE *noun* **EEN** a Scots word for *eye*

EEK *exclamation* used in comics, etc: representing a scream, etc
EEL *noun* **EELS** any of several kinds of fish with a long smooth snake-like body and very small fins
EELGRASS *noun* **EELGRASSES** a grasslike flowering plant of the pondweed family, which grows in seawater
EELPOUT *noun* **EELPOUTS** a freshwater edible fish
EELWORM *noun* **EELWORMS** any of various nematode worms
EELWRACK *noun* **EELWRACKS** eelgrass

EEN plural of **ee**

EERIE *adj* **EERIER, EERIEST** strange and disturbing or frightening
EERILY *adverb* in an eerie way
EERINESS *noun* **EERINESSES** the quality of being eerie

EF *noun* **EFS** the letter 'F'

EFFACE *verb* **EFFACES, EFFACING, EFFACED** to rub or wipe out something
EFFECT *noun* **EFFECTS** a result ▫ *verb* **EFFECTS, EFFECTING, EFFECTED** to do something; to make something happen, or to bring it about
EFFECTIVE *adj* having the power to produce, or producing, a desired result ▫ *noun* **EFFECTIVES** a serviceman or body of servicemen equipped and prepared for action
EFFECTOR *adj* causing a response to stimulus ▫ *noun* **EFFECTORS** an organ or substance which produces a response to stimulus
EFFECTUAL *adj* producing the intended result
EFFENDI *noun* **EFFENDIS** in Turkey: the oral form of address equivalent to *Mr*

EFFERENT *adj* said of a nerve: carrying impulses out from the brain
EFFETE *adj* said of an institution or organization, etc: lacking its original power or authority
EFFETELY *adverb* in an effete way
EFFICACY *noun* **EFFICACIES** the power of producing an effect; effectiveness
EFFICIENT *adj* producing satisfactory results with an economy of effort and a minimum of waste
EFFIGY *noun* **EFFIGIES** a crude doll or model representing a person, on which hatred of, or contempt for, the person can be expressed, eg by burning it
EFFLUENCE *noun* **EFFLUENCES** the act or process of flowing out
EFFLUENT *noun* **EFFLUENTS** liquid industrial waste or sewage released into a river or the sea, etc ▫ *adj* flowing out
EFFLUVIUM *noun* **EFFLUVIA** an unpleasant smell or vapour given off by something, eg decaying matter
EFFLUX *noun* **EFFLUXES** the act or process of flowing out
EFFORT *noun* **EFFORTS** hard mental or physical work, or something that requires it
EFFULGENT *adj* shining brightly; brilliant
EFFUSE *verb* **EFFUSES, EFFUSING, EFFUSED** to pour out ▫ *adj* loosely spreading
EFFUSION *noun* **EFFUSIONS** the act or process of pouring or flowing out
EFFUSIVE *adj* expressing feelings, especially happiness or enthusiasm, in an excessive or very showy way

EFS plural of **ef**

EGG¹ *noun* **EGGS** the reproductive cell produced by a female animal, bird, etc, from which the young one develops
EGG² *verb* **EGGS, EGGING, EGGED** to urge or encourage
EGGAR *noun* **EGGARS** an egger
EGGCUP *noun* **EGGCUPS** a small cup-shaped container for holding a boiled egg in its shell while it is being eaten
EGGER *noun* **EGGERS** any of various large brown European moths, which develop out of egg-shaped cocoons
EGGHEAD *noun* **EGGHEADS** a very clever person; an intellectual
EGGNOG *noun* **EGGNOGS** a drink made from raw eggs, milk, sugar and an alcoholic spirit, especially rum or brandy
EGGSHELL *noun* **EGGSHELLS** the hard thin porous calcareous covering of an egg ▫ *adj* said of paint or varnish: having a slightly glossy finish
EGGWASH *noun* **EGGWASHES** a thin mixture of egg and milk or egg and water, used for glazing pastry
EGGY *adj* **EGGIER, EGGIEST** tasting and/or smelling of egg
EGLANTINE *noun* **EGLANTINES** a fragrant species of wild rose, the sweet-brier
EGO *noun* **EGOS** personal pride
EGOISM *noun* **EGOISMS** the principle that self-interest is the basis of morality
EGOIST *noun* **EGOISTS** a person who believes in self-interest as a moral principle
EGOISTIC *adj* relating to or displaying egoism
EGOMANIA *noun* **EGOMANIAS** extreme self-interest which prevents one from allowing other people to come between oneself and the achievement of one's desires
EGOMANIAC *noun* **EGOMANIACS** a person who is governed by extreme self-interest
EGOS plural of **ego**
EGOTISM *noun* **EGOTISMS** the habit of speaking too much about oneself
EGOTIST *noun* **EGOTISTS** a self-centred person
EGOTISTIC *adj* showing egotism; self-important; conceited
EGREGIOUS *adj* outrageous; shockingly bad
EGRESS *noun* **EGRESSES** the act of leaving a building or other enclosed place
EGRESSION *noun* **EGRESSIONS** the act of going out; departure
EGRET *noun* **EGRETS** any of various white long-legged wading birds similar to herons
EH *exclamation* used to request that a question or remark, etc be repeated
EIDER *noun* **EIDERS** a large sea duck from northern countries

EIDERDOWN *noun* **EIDERDOWNS** the down or soft feathers of the eider

EIDETIC *adj* said of a mental image: extraordinarily clear and vivid, as though actually visible □ *noun* **EIDETICS** a person who is able to reproduce a vividly clear visual image of what has been previously seen

EIGENTONE *noun* **EIGENTONES** a tone characteristic of a particular vibrating system

EIGHT *noun* **EIGHTS** the cardinal number 8 □ *adj* totalling eight

EIGHTEEN *noun* **EIGHTEENS** the cardinal number 18 □ *adj* totalling eighteen

EIGHTFOLD *adj* equal to eight times as much □ *adverb* by eight times as much

EIGHTH *adj* in counting: next after seventh □ *noun* **EIGHTHS** one of eight equal parts □ *adverb* eighthly

EIGHTHLY *adverb* used to introduce the eighth point in a list

EIGHTIES *plural noun* the period of time between one's eightieth and ninetieth birthdays

EIGHTIETH *adj* in counting: next after seventy-ninth □ *noun* **EIGHTIETHS** one of eighty equal parts

EIGHTSOME *noun* **EIGHTSOMES** a set or group of eight people

EIGHTY *noun* **EIGHTIES** the cardinal number 80 □ *adj* totalling eighty

EIK *verb* **EIKS, EIKING, EIKED** a Scots word meaning *eke*

EITHER *adj* any one of two □ *pronoun* any one of two things or people, etc □ *adverb* also; as well

EJACULATE *verb* **EJACULATES, EJACULATING, EJACULATED** said of a man or male animal: to discharge (semen) □ *noun* **EJACULATES** semen

EJECT *verb* **EJECTS, EJECTING, EJECTED** to throw out someone or something with force

EJECTION *noun* **EJECTIONS** discharge; expulsion

EJECTIVE *adj* having the power to eject

EJECTOR *noun* **EJECTORS** a person or device that ejects something or someone

EKE *verb* **EKES, EKING, EKED** to add to or increase; to lengthen

EKISTIC *adj* of or relating to ekistics

EKISTICS *singular noun* the science or study of human settlements

EL *noun* **ELS** the letter 'L'

ELABORATE *adj* complicated in design; complex □ *verb* **ELABORATES, ELABORATING, ELABORATED** to add detail to

ÉLAN *noun* **ÉLANS** impressive and energetic style

ELAND *noun* **ELANDS** a large African antelope with spiral horns

ELAPSE *verb* **ELAPSES, ELAPSING, ELAPSED** said of time: to pass

ELASTASE *noun* **ELASTASES** an enzyme found in the pancreatic juice that decomposes elastin

ELASTIC *adj* said of a material or substance: able to return to its original shape or size after being pulled or pressed out of shape □ *noun* **ELASTICS** stretchable cord or fabric woven with strips of rubber

ELASTIN *noun* **ELASTINS** a protein which is the chief constituent of elastic tissue

ELASTOMER *noun* **ELASTOMERS** any rubberlike substance

ELATE *verb* **ELATES, ELATING, ELATED** to make someone intensely happy

ELATED *adj* intensely happy

ELATEDLY *adverb* in an elated way

ELATION *noun* **ELATIONS** an elated state; euphoria

ELBOW *noun* **ELBOWS** the joint where the human arm bends □ *verb* **ELBOWS, ELBOWING, ELBOWED** to push or strike something with the elbow

ELD *noun* **ELDS** an old word meaning age or old age

ELDER *adj* older □ *noun* **ELDERS** a person who is older

ELDERLY *adj* rather old

ELDEST *adj* oldest □ *noun* someone who is the oldest of three or more

ELDRITCH *adj* weird; uncanny

ELECT *verb* **ELECTS, ELECTING, ELECTED** to choose someone to be an official or representative by voting □ *adj* elected to a position, but not yet formally occupying it

ELECTABLE *adj* capable of being elected, especially to political office

ELECTED *adj* chosen by voting

ELECTION *noun* **ELECTIONS** the process or act of choosing people for office, especially political office, by taking a vote

ELECTIVE *adj* said of a position or office, etc: to which someone is appointed by election □ *noun* **ELECTIVES** an optional placement or course of study chosen by a student

ELECTOR *noun* **ELECTORS** someone who has the right to vote at an election

ELECTORAL *adj* concerning or relating to elections or electors

ELECTRET *noun* **ELECTRETS** a permanently polarized dielectric material, or a piece of this

ELECTRIC *adj* relating to, produced by, worked by or generating electricity

ELECTRICS *plural noun* electrical appliances

ELECTRIFY *verb* **ELECTRIFIES, ELECTRIFYING, ELECTRIFIED** to give an electric charge to something

ELECTRIFYING *adj* extremely exciting

ELECTRO *noun* **ELECTROS** an electroplate; electrotype

ELECTRODE *noun* **ELECTRODES** either of the two conducting points by which electric current enters or leaves a battery or other electrical apparatus

ELECTRON *noun* **ELECTRONS** a particle, present in all atoms, which has a negative electric charge and is responsible for carrying electricity in solids

ELECTUARY *noun* **ELECTUARIES** a medicine mixed with honey or syrup

ELEGANCE *noun* **ELEGANCES** the state or quality of being elegant

ELEGANCY *noun* **ELEGANCIES** the state or quality of being elegant

ELEGANT *adj* having or showing good taste in dress or style, combined with dignity and gracefulness

ELEGANTLY *adverb* in an elegant way

ELEGIAC *adj* mournful or thoughtful

ELEGIACAL *adj* mournful or thoughtful

ELEGIACS *plural noun* elegiac verse

ELEGISE *verb* **ELEGISES, ELEGISING, ELEGISED** to elegize

ELEGIST *noun* **ELEGISTS** a person who writes elegies

ELEGIZE *verb* **ELEGIZES, ELEGIZING, ELEGIZED** to write an elegy about someone or something
ELEGY *noun* **ELEGIES** a mournful or thoughtful song or poem, especially one whose subject is death or loss
ELEMENT *noun* **ELEMENTS** a part of anything; a component or feature
ELEMENTAL *adj* basic or primitive
ELEMI *noun* **ELEMIS** a fragrant resinous substance obtained from various tropical trees, used especially in varnishes and inks
ELEPHANT *noun* **ELEPHANTS** the largest living land animal, with thick greyish skin, a nose in the form of a long hanging trunk, and two curved tusks
ELEVATE *verb* **ELEVATES, ELEVATING, ELEVATED** to raise or lift
ELEVATED *adj* said of a rank or position, etc: very high; important □ *noun* **ELEVATEDS** an elevated railroad
ELEVATING *adj* improving the mind; morally uplifting
ELEVATION *noun* **ELEVATIONS** the act of elevating or state of being elevated
ELEVATOR *noun* **ELEVATORS** a lift
ELEVATORY *adj* able or tending to raise
ELEVEN *noun* **ELEVENS** the cardinal number 11 □ *adj* totalling eleven
ELEVENSES *plural noun* a snack, usually consisting of coffee, tea, biscuits, etc, taken at about eleven o'clock in the morning
ELEVENTH *adj* in counting: next after tenth □ *noun* **ELEVENTHS** one of eleven equal parts
ELF *noun* **ELVES** in folklore: a tiny supernatural being with a human form, with a tendency to play tricks
ELFIN *adj* said of physical features, etc: small and delicate
ELFISH *adj* elf-like or mischievous
ELICIT *verb* **ELICITS, ELICITING, ELICITED** to cause something to happen; to bring something out into the open
ELIDE *verb* **ELIDES, ELIDING, ELIDED** to omit (a vowel or syllable) at the beginning or end of a word
ELIGIBLE *adj* suitable, or deserving to be chosen (for a job, as a husband, etc)

ELIGIBLY *adverb* in an eligible way
ELIMINATE *verb* **ELIMINATES, ELIMINATING, ELIMINATED** to get rid of or exclude
ELISION *noun* **ELISIONS** the omission of a vowel or syllable, as in *I'm* and *we're*
ELITE *noun* **ELITES** the best, most important or most powerful people within society □ *adj* best, most important or most powerful
ELITISM *noun* **ELITISMS** the belief in the need for a powerful social elite
ELITIST *noun* **ELITISTS** a supporter of elitism □ *adj* favouring or creating an elite
ELIXIR *noun* **ELIXIRS** in medieval times: a liquid chemical preparation believed to have the power to give people everlasting life or to turn base metals into gold
ELK *noun* **ELKS** in Europe and Asia: the moose

ELL *noun* **ELLS** a measure of length

ELLIPSE *noun* **ELLIPSES** a regular oval, as formed by a diagonal cut through a cone above the base
ELLIPSIS *noun* **ELLIPSES** a figure of speech in which a word or words needed for the sense or grammar are omitted but understood
ELLIPSOID *noun* **ELLIPSOIDS** a surface or solid object of which every plane section is an ellipse or a circle
ELLIPTIC *adj* relating to, or having the shape of, an ellipse
ELM *noun* **ELMS** any of various tall deciduous trees with broad serrated leaves and clusters of small flowers which develop into winged fruits □ *adj* made of elm
ELOCUTION *noun* **ELOCUTIONS** the art of speaking clearly and effectively
ELONGATE *verb* **ELONGATES, ELONGATING, ELONGATED** to lengthen or stretch something out
ELONGATED *adj* long and narrow
ELOPE *verb* **ELOPES, ELOPING, ELOPED** to run away secretly, especially with a lover in order to get married
ELOPEMENT *noun* **ELOPEMENTS** the action of eloping
ELOPER *noun* **ELOPERS** a person who elopes
ELOQUENCE *noun* **ELOQUENCES** the art or power of using speech to impress, move or persuade

ELOQUENT *adj* having or showing eloquence

ELS plural of **el**

ELSE *adverb* different from or in addition to something or someone known or already mentioned □ *adj* different from or in addition to something or someone known or already mentioned
ELSEWHERE *adverb* somewhere else

ELT *noun* **ELTS** a dialect word meaning a young sow

ELUANT *noun* **ELUANTS** a liquid used for elution
ELUATE *noun* **ELUATES** a liquid obtained by eluting
ELUCIDATE *verb* **ELUCIDATES, ELUCIDATING, ELUCIDATED** to make clear or explain; to shed light on something
ELUDE *verb* **ELUDES, ELUDING, ELUDED** to escape or avoid something by quickness or cleverness
ELUENT *noun* **ELUENTS** an eluant
ELUSIVE *adj* difficult to find or catch
ELUSIVELY *adverb* in an elusive way
ELUTE *verb* **ELUTES, ELUTING, ELUTED** to wash out (a substance) by using a solvent
ELUTION *noun* **ELUTIONS** purification or separation by washing
ELUTRIATE *verb* **ELUTRIATES, ELUTRIATING, ELUTRIATED** to separate something by washing it into coarser and finer portions
ELVER *noun* **ELVERS** a young eel
ELVES plural of **elf**
ELVISH *adj* elf-like or mischievous
ELYTRON *noun* **ELYTRONS** a beetle's forewing modified to form a case for the hindwing
ELYTRUM *noun* **ELYTRA** an elytron
EM *noun* **EMS** in printing: the unit of measurement, based on the 12-point lower-case 'm', used in spacing material, and in estimating dimensions of pages
EMACIATE *verb* **EMACIATES, EMACIATING, EMACIATED** to make (a person or animal) extremely thin, especially through illness or starvation, etc
EMACIATED *adj* extremely thin, especially through illness or starvation, etc

For longer words, see The Chambers Dictionary

EMAIL *noun* **EMAILS** a message sent electronically from one computer to another, eg over the Internet □ *verb* **EMAILS, EMAILING, EMAILED** to send someone an electronic message
EMANATE *verb* **EMANATES, EMANATING, EMANATED** said of an idea, etc: to emerge or originate
EMANATION *noun* **EMANATIONS** the process of emanating or originating from something else
EMBALM *verb* **EMBALMS, EMBALMING, EMBALMED** to preserve (a dead body) from decay, originally with oils and spices, but now by treatment with chemicals or drugs
EMBALMER *noun* **EMBALMERS** a person whose occupation is to embalm dead bodies
EMBARGO *noun* **EMBARGOES** an official order forbidding something, especially trade with another country □ *verb* **EMBARGOES, EMBARGOING, EMBARGOED** to place something under an embargo
EMBARK *verb* **EMBARKS, EMBARKING, EMBARKED** to go or put on board ship or an aircraft
EMBARRASS *verb* **EMBARRASSES, EMBARRASSING, EMBARRASSED** to make someone feel, or become anxious, self-conscious or ashamed
EMBARRASSED *adj* perplexed; disconcerted
EMBARRASSING *adj* said of an incident or remark, etc: causing awkwardness or self-consciousness
EMBASSY *noun* **EMBASSIES** the official residence of an ambassador
EMBATTLED *adj* troubled by problems or difficulties; engaged in a struggle
EMBED *verb* **EMBEDS, EMBEDDING, EMBEDDED** to set or fix something firmly and deeply
EMBELLISH *verb* **EMBELLISHES, EMBELLISHING, EMBELLISHED** to make (a story, etc) more interesting by adding details which may not be true
EMBELLISHED *adj* made beautiful with ornaments; decorated
EMBER *noun* **EMBERS** a piece of glowing or smouldering coal or wood
EMBEZZLE *verb* **EMBEZZLES,**

EMBEZZLING, EMBEZZLED to take or use dishonestly (money or property with which one has been entrusted)
EMBEZZLER *noun* **EMBEZZLERS** a person who embezzles
EMBITTER *verb* **EMBITTERS, EMBITTERING, EMBITTERED** to make someone feel bitter
EMBITTERED *adj* soured; having been made cynical or disappointed
EMBLAZON *verb* **EMBLAZONS, EMBLAZONING, EMBLAZONED** to decorate with a coat of arms or some other bright design
EMBLEM *noun* **EMBLEMS** an object chosen to represent an idea, a quality, a country, etc
EMBODY *verb* **EMBODIES, EMBODYING, EMBODIED** to be an expression or a representation of something in words, actions or form; to typify or personify
EMBOLDEN *verb* **EMBOLDENS, EMBOLDENING, EMBOLDENED** to make someone bold; to encourage
EMBOLISM *noun* **EMBOLISMS** the blocking of a blood vessel by an air bubble, a blood clot or a fragment of tissue, etc, which has travelled through the bloodstream
EMBOLUS *noun* **EMBOLUSES, EMBOLI** any obstruction in a blood vessel, especially a blood clot
EMBOSS *verb* **EMBOSSES, EMBOSSING, EMBOSSED** to carve or mould a raised design on (a surface)
EMBOSSED *adj* carved or moulded with a raised design
EMBRACE *verb* **EMBRACES, EMBRACING, EMBRACED** to hold someone closely in the arms, affectionately or as a greeting □ *noun* **EMBRACES** an act of embracing
EMBRASURE *noun* **EMBRASURES** an opening in the wall of a castle, etc for shooting through
EMBROIDER *verb* **EMBROIDERS, EMBROIDERING, EMBROIDERED** to decorate (cloth) with sewn designs
EMBROIL *verb* **EMBROILS, EMBROILING, EMBROILED** to involve in a dispute or argument
EMBRYO *noun* **EMBRYOS** in animals: the developing young organism until hatching or birth
EMBRYONIC *adj* in an early stage of development; rudimentary
EMBUS *verb* **EMBUSSES,**

EMBUSSING, EMBUSSED to put (troops) on to a bus
EMCEE *noun* **EMCEES** a master of ceremonies □ *verb* **EMCEES, EMCEEING, EMCEED** to act as master of ceremonies at (an event)

EME *noun* **EMES** an obsolete word for *uncle*

EMEND *verb* **EMENDS, EMENDING, EMENDED** to edit (a text), removing errors and making improvements
EMERALD *noun* **EMERALDS** a deep green variety of beryl, highly valued as a gemstone
EMERGE *verb* **EMERGES, EMERGING, EMERGED** to come out from hiding or into view
EMERGENCE *noun* **EMERGENCES** emerging; first appearance
EMERGENCY *noun* **EMERGENCIES** an unexpected and serious happening which calls for immediate and determined action
EMERGENT *adj* emerging; developing
EMERITUS *adj* retired or honourably discharged from office, but retaining a former title as an honour
EMERSION *noun* **EMERSIONS** the reappearance of a celestial body after an eclipse or occultation
EMERY *noun* **EMERIES** a very hard mineral, a variety of corundum, usually used in powder form, for polishing or abrading
EMETIC *adj* making one vomit □ *noun* **EMETICS** an emetic medicine
EMIGRANT *noun* **EMIGRANTS** someone who emigrates or who has emigrated □ *adj* belonging or relating to emigrants
EMIGRATE *verb* **EMIGRATES, EMIGRATING, EMIGRATED** to leave one's native country and settle in another
ÉMIGRÉ *noun* **ÉMIGRÉS** a person who has emigrated, usually for political reasons
EMINENCE *noun* **EMINENCES** honour, distinction or prestige
EMINENT *adj* famous and admired
EMINENTLY *adverb* very; obviously
EMIR *noun* **EMIRS** a title given to various Muslim rulers, especially in the Middle East or W Africa
EMIRATE *noun* **EMIRATES** the

position or authority of, or the territory ruled by, an emir

EMISSARY *noun* **EMISSARIES** a person sent on a mission, especially on behalf of a government

EMISSION *noun* **EMISSIONS** the act of emitting

EMISSIVE *adj* emitting or sending out

EMIT *verb* **EMITS, EMITTING, EMITTED** to give out (light, heat, a sound or smell, etc)

EMOLLIENT *adj* softening or soothing the skin ◻ *noun* **EMOLLIENTS** a substance which softens or soothes the skin

EMOLUMENT *noun* **EMOLUMENTS** any money earned or otherwise gained through a job or position, eg salary or fees

EMOTE *verb* **EMOTES, EMOTING, EMOTED** to display exaggerated or insincere emotion

EMOTION *noun* **EMOTIONS** a strong feeling

EMOTIONAL *adj* referring or relating to the emotions

EMOTIVE *adj* tending or designed to excite emotion

EMPANEL *verb* **EMPANELS, EMPANELLING, EMPANELLED** to enter (the names of prospective jurors) on a list

EMPATHIC *adj* able to share others' feelings

EMPATHISE *verb* **EMPATHISES, EMPATHISING, EMPATHISED** to empathize

EMPATHIZE *verb* **EMPATHIZES, EMPATHIZING, EMPATHIZED** to feel empathy

EMPATHY *noun* **EMPATHIES** the ability to share, understand and feel another person's feelings

EMPENNAGE *noun* **EMPENNAGES** an aeroplane's tail unit, including elevator, rudder and fin

EMPEROR *noun* **EMPERORS** the male ruler of an empire or of a country which was once the centre of an empire

EMPHASIS *noun* **EMPHASES** special importance or attention given to something

EMPHASISE *verb* **EMPHASISES, EMPHASISING, EMPHASISED** to emphasize

EMPHASIZE *verb* **EMPHASIZES, EMPHASIZING, EMPHASIZED** to put emphasis on something

EMPHATIC *adj* expressed with or expressing emphasis

EMPHYSEMA *noun* **EMPHYSEMAS** the presence of air in the body tissues

EMPIRE *noun* **EMPIRES** a group of nations or states under the control of a single ruler or ruling power, especially an emperor or empress ◻ *adj* referring especially to dress or furniture: relating to, or in the style of, the first French Empire (1804–14)

EMPIRIC *adj* empirical

EMPIRICAL *adj* based on experiment, observation or experience, rather than on theory

EMPLACE *verb* **EMPLACES, EMPLACING, EMPLACED** to put something in place

EMPLOY *verb* **EMPLOYS, EMPLOYING, EMPLOYED** to give work, usually paid work, to someone

EMPLOYED *adj* having a job; working

EMPLOYEE *noun* **EMPLOYEES** a person who works for another in return for payment

EMPLOYER *noun* **EMPLOYERS** a person or company that employs workers

EMPORIUM *noun* **EMPORIUMS, EMPORIA** a shop, especially a large one that sells a wide variety of goods

EMPOWER *verb* **EMPOWERS, EMPOWERING, EMPOWERED** to give someone authority or official permission to do something

EMPRESS *noun* **EMPRESSES** the female ruler of an empire or of a country which was once the centre of an empire

EMPTILY *adverb* in an empty way

EMPTINESS *noun* **EMPTINESSES** the state of being empty; lack of substance

EMPTY *adj* **EMPTIER, EMPTIEST** having nothing inside ◻ *verb* **EMPTIES, EMPTYING, EMPTIED** to make or become empty ◻ *noun* **EMPTIES** an empty container, especially a bottle

EMPYEMA *noun* **EMPYEMAS** a collection of pus in any cavity, especially the pleura

EMPYREAL *adj* formed of pure fire or light; of or relating to the highest and purest region of heaven; sublime

EMPYREAN *noun* **EMPYREANS** the heavens; the sky

EMU *noun* **EMUS** a large flightless but swift-running bird, almost 2m

(6ft 6in) tall with coarse brown plumage, found in deserts, plains and forests in Australia

EMULATE *verb* **EMULATES, EMULATING, EMULATED** to try hard to equal or be better than someone or something

EMULATION *noun* **EMULATIONS** the act of emulating or attempting to equal or excel

EMULOUS *adj* keen to achieve the same success or excellence as someone

EMULOUSLY *adverb* in an emulous way

EMULSIFY *verb* **EMULSIFIES, EMULSIFYING, EMULSIFIED** to make or become an emulsion

EMULSION *noun* **EMULSIONS** a colloid consisting of a stable mixture of two immiscible liquids (such as oil and water), in which small droplets of one liquid are dispersed uniformly throughout the other, eg salad cream and low-fat spreads; a water-based paint

EN *noun* **ENS** in printing: half of an em

ENABLE *verb* **ENABLES, ENABLING, ENABLED** to make someone able; to give them the necessary means, power or authority (to do something)

ENABLER *noun* **ENABLERS** a person who enables

ENACT *verb* **ENACTS, ENACTING, ENACTED** to act or perform something on stage or in real life

ENACTMENT *noun* **ENACTMENTS** the act of passing, or the passing of, a parliamentary bill into law

ENAMEL *noun* **ENAMELS** a hardened coloured glass-like substance applied as a decorative or protective covering to metal or glass ◻ *verb* **ENAMELS, ENAMELLING, ENAMELLED** to cover or decorate something with enamel

ENAMORED *adj* enamoured

ENAMOURED *adj* in love

ENCAMP *verb* **ENCAMPS, ENCAMPING, ENCAMPED** to settle in a camp

ENCASE *verb* **ENCASES, ENCASING, ENCASED** to enclose something in, or as if in, a case

ENCASH *verb* **ENCASHES, ENCASHING, ENCASHED** to convert something into cash; to cash

ENCAUSTIC *adj* said of ceramics: decorated by any process that burns in colours, especially using pigments melted in wax and burnt into the clay ▫ noun **ENCAUSTICS** an ancient method of painting in melted wax

ENCHAIN verb **ENCHAINS, ENCHAINING, ENCHAINED** to put in chains

ENCHANT verb **ENCHANTS, ENCHANTING, ENCHANTED** to charm or delight

ENCHANTED adj under the power of enchantment; beguiled or captivated

ENCHANTER noun **ENCHANTERS** a person who enchants

ENCHANTING adj charming; delightful

ENCHASE verb **ENCHASES, ENCHASING, ENCHASED** to set (gold, silver, etc) with jewels

ENCHILADA noun **ENCHILADAS** a Mexican dish consisting of a flour tortilla with a meat filling, served with a chilli-flavoured sauce

ENCIPHER verb **ENCIPHERS, ENCIPHERING, ENCIPHERED** to put something into cipher or code

ENCIRCLE verb **ENCIRCLES, ENCIRCLING, ENCIRCLED** to surround or form a circle round something

ENCLAVE noun **ENCLAVES** a small country or state entirely surrounded by foreign territory

ENCLITIC adj said of a word or especially a particle: without stress; treated as if part of the previous word ▫ noun **ENCLITICS** a word or particle which always follows another word, and is enclitic to it

ENCLOSE verb **ENCLOSES, ENCLOSING, ENCLOSED** to put something inside a letter or in its envelope

ENCLOSED adj placed inside something, especially an envelope

ENCLOSURE noun **ENCLOSURES** the process of enclosing or being enclosed, especially with reference to common land

ENCODE verb **ENCODES, ENCODING, ENCODED** to express something in, or convert it into, code

ENCOMIUM noun **ENCOMIUMS, ENCOMIA** a formal speech or piece of writing praising someone

ENCOMPASS verb **ENCOMPASSES, ENCOMPASSING, ENCOMPASSED** to include or

contain something, especially to contain a wide range or coverage of something

ENCORE noun **ENCORES** a repetition of a performance, or an additional performed item, after the end of a concert, etc ▫ exclamation an enthusiastic call from the audience for such a performance ▫ verb **ENCORES, ENCORING, ENCORED** to call for an extra performance of something

ENCOUNTER verb **ENCOUNTERS, ENCOUNTERING, ENCOUNTERED** to meet someone or something, especially unexpectedly ▫ noun **ENCOUNTERS** a chance meeting

ENCOURAGE verb **ENCOURAGES, ENCOURAGING, ENCOURAGED** to give support, confidence or hope to someone

ENCOURAGING adj that gives support, confidence or hope to someone

ENCROACH verb **ENCROACHES, ENCROACHING, ENCROACHED** to intrude or extend gradually or stealthily (on someone else's land, etc)

ENCRUST verb **ENCRUSTS, ENCRUSTING, ENCRUSTED** to cover something with a thick hard coating, eg of jewels or ice

ENCRYPT verb **ENCRYPTS, ENCRYPTING, ENCRYPTED** to put information (eg computer data or TV signals) into a coded form

ENCUMBER verb **ENCUMBERS, ENCUMBERING, ENCUMBERED** to prevent the free and easy movement of someone or something; to hamper or impede

ENCYST verb **ENCYSTS, ENCYSTING, ENCYSTED** to enclose or become enclosed in a cyst or vesicle

ENCYSTED adj enclosed in a cyst or vesicle

END noun **ENDS** the point or part farthest from the beginning, or either of the points or parts farthest from the middle, where something stops ▫ verb **ENDS, ENDING, ENDED** to finish or cause something to finish

ENDANGER verb **ENDANGERS, ENDANGERING, ENDANGERED** to put someone or something in danger

ENDEAR verb **ENDEARS, ENDEARING, ENDEARED** to make beloved or liked

ENDEARING adj arousing feelings of affection

ENDEAVOR verb **ENDEAVORS, ENDEAVORING, ENDEAVORED** to endeavour ▫ noun **ENDEAVORS** an endeavour

ENDEAVOUR verb **ENDEAVOURS, ENDEAVOURING, ENDEAVOURED** to try to do something, especially seriously and with effort ▫ noun **ENDEAVOURS** a determined attempt or effort

ENDED adj brought to an end

ENDEMIC adj said of a disease, etc: regularly occurring in a particular area or among a particular group of people

ENDERMIC adj said of a medicine, etc: that acts through, or is applied directly to, the skin

ENDGAME noun **ENDGAMES** the final stage in a game of chess, or certain other games

ENDING noun **ENDINGS** the end, especially of a story or poem, etc

ENDIVE noun **ENDIVES** a plant, related to chicory, whose crisp curly or broad leaves are used in salads

ENDLESS adj having no end, or seeming to have no end

ENDLESSLY adverb in an endless way; for ever

ENDMOST adj farthest; nearest the end

ENDOCARP noun **ENDOCARPS** the inner layer of the pericarp of a fruit, usually hard, eg a plum stone

ENDOCRINE adj relating to internal secretions, or to a pathway or structure that secretes internally ▫ noun **ENDOCRINES** an endocrine gland

ENDODERM noun **ENDODERMS** in humans: the innermost layer of cells of the embryo, which develops into the digestive system of the adult

ENDOGAMY noun **ENDOGAMIES** the practice or rule of marrying only within one's own group

ENDOMORPH noun **ENDOMORPHS** a person of rounded or plump build, sometimes said to be associated with a calm easy-going personality

ENDOPHYTE noun **ENDOPHYTES** a plant living within another, whether parasitically or not

ENDOPLASM noun **ENDOPLASMS** the central portion of the cytoplasm of a cell

ENDORPHIN noun **ENDORPHINS**

any of a group of chemical compounds that occur naturally in the brain and have similar pain-relieving properties to morphine

ENDORSE *verb* **ENDORSES, ENDORSING, ENDORSED** to write one's signature on the back of (a document), especially on the back of (a cheque) to specify oneself or another person as payee

ENDORSEE *noun* **ENDORSEES** the person to whom a bill, etc is assigned by endorsement

ENDORSER *noun* **ENDORSERS** a person who endorses

ENDOSCOPE *noun* **ENDOSCOPES** a long thin flexible instrument containing bundles of optical fibres and having a light at one end, used for viewing internal body cavities and organs

ENDOSCOPY *noun* **ENDOSCOPIES** examination of the internal organs by means of an endoscope

ENDOSPERM *noun* **ENDOSPERMS** nutritive tissue within the seed of some plants

ENDOW *verb* **ENDOWS, ENDOWING, ENDOWED** to provide a source of income for (a hospital or place of learning, etc), often by a bequest

ENDOWMENT *noun* **ENDOWMENTS** the act of endowing

ENDUE *verb* **ENDUES, ENDUING, ENDUED** to supply or provide with

ENDURABLE *adj* capable of being endured

ENDURABLY *adverb* in an endurable way

ENDURANCE *noun* **ENDURANCES** the capacity for, or the state of, patient toleration

ENDURE *verb* **ENDURES, ENDURING, ENDURED** to bear something patiently; to put up with it

ENDURING *adj* lasting

ENDWAYS *adverb* with the end forward or upward

ENDWISE *adverb* endways

ENE *noun* **ENES** an obsolete, dialect or poetic word for *evening*

ENEMA *noun* **ENEMAS, ENEMATA** the injection of a liquid into the rectum, eg to clean it out or to introduce medication

ENEMY *noun* **ENEMIES** a person

who is actively opposed to someone else □ *adj* hostile; belonging to a hostile nation or force

ENERGETIC *adj* having or displaying energy; forceful or vigorous

ENERGISE *verb* **ENERGISES, ENERGISING, ENERGISED** to energize

ENERGISER *noun* **ENERGISERS** an energizer

ENERGIZE *verb* **ENERGIZES, ENERGIZING, ENERGIZED** to stimulate, invigorate or enliven

ENERGIZER *noun* **ENERGIZERS** a person or thing that energizes

ENERGY *noun* **ENERGIES** the capacity for vigorous activity; liveliness or vitality

ENERVATE *verb* **ENERVATES, ENERVATING, ENERVATED** to take energy or strength from something

ENERVATING *adj* that enervates

ENFEEBLE *verb* **ENFEEBLES, ENFEEBLING, ENFEEBLED** to make someone weak

ENFEEBLED *adj* made weak

ENFILADE *noun* **ENFILADES** a continuous burst of gunfire sweeping from end to end across a line of enemy soldiers □ *verb* **ENFILADES, ENFILADING, ENFILADED** to direct an enfilade at someone or something

ENFOLD *verb* **ENFOLDS, ENFOLDING, ENFOLDED** to wrap up or enclose

ENFORCE *verb* **ENFORCES, ENFORCING, ENFORCED** to cause (a law or decision) to be carried out

ENFORCED *adj* not voluntary or optional

ENG *noun* **ENGS** a phonetic symbol

ENGAGE *verb* **ENGAGES, ENGAGING, ENGAGED** to take someone on as a worker

ENGAGED *adj* bound by a promise to marry someone

ENGAGING *adj* charming; attractive

ENGENDER *verb* **ENGENDERS, ENGENDERING, ENGENDERED** to produce or cause (especially feelings or emotions)

ENGINE *noun* **ENGINES** a machine that is used to convert some form of energy into mechanical energy that can be used to perform useful work

ENGINEER *noun* **ENGINEERS** someone who designs, makes, or works with machinery, including electrical equipment □ *verb* **ENGINEERS, ENGINEERING, ENGINEERED** to arrange or bring something about by skill or deviousness

ENGINEERING *noun* **ENGINEERINGS** the application of scientific knowledge to the practical problems of design, construction, operation and maintenance of devices encountered in everyday life

ENGORGED *adj* crammed full

ENGRAFT *verb* **ENGRAFTS, ENGRAFTING, ENGRAFTED** to graft (a shoot, etc) on to a stock

ENGRAIN *verb* **ENGRAINS, ENGRAINING, ENGRAINED** to ingrain

ENGRAINED *adj* ingrained

ENGRAVE *verb* **ENGRAVES, ENGRAVING, ENGRAVED** to carve (letters or designs) on stone, wood or metal, etc

ENGRAVER *noun* **ENGRAVERS** a person who engraves letters or designs, especially as their profession

ENGRAVING *noun* **ENGRAVINGS** the art or process of carving or incising designs on wood or metal, etc, especially for the purpose of printing impressions from them

ENGROSS *verb* **ENGROSSES, ENGROSSING, ENGROSSED** to take up someone's attention and interest completely

ENGROSSED *adj* with one's attention and interest completely engaged

ENGROSSING *adj* engaging one's full attention; highly interesting

ENGULF *verb* **ENGULFS, ENGULFING, ENGULFED** to swallow something up completely

ENHANCE *verb* **ENHANCES, ENHANCING, ENHANCED** to improve or increase the value, quality or intensity of something (especially something already good)

ENIGMA *noun* **ENIGMAS** a puzzle or riddle

ENIGMATIC *adj* obscure, ambiguous or puzzling

ENJOIN *verb* **ENJOINS, ENJOINING, ENJOINED** to order or command someone to do something

ENJOY *verb* **ENJOYS, ENJOYING,**

ENJOYED to find pleasure in something

ENJOYABLE *adj* capable of being enjoyed; offering pleasure

ENJOYABLY *adverb* in an enjoyable way

ENJOYMENT *noun* **ENJOYMENTS** enjoying; deriving pleasure

ENLACE *verb* **ENLACES, ENLACING, ENLACED** to encircle something with, or as if with, laces; to bind

ENLARGE *verb* **ENLARGES, ENLARGING, ENLARGED** to make or become larger

ENLARGER *noun* **ENLARGERS** an apparatus with a lens, used for enlarging photographs

ENLIGHTEN *verb* **ENLIGHTENS, ENLIGHTENING, ENLIGHTENED** to give more information to someone

ENLIGHTENED *adj* well-informed

ENLIGHTENING *adj* that enlightens

ENLIST *verb* **ENLISTS, ENLISTING, ENLISTED** to join one of the armed forces

ENLIVEN *verb* **ENLIVENS, ENLIVENING, ENLIVENED** to make active or more active, lively or cheerful

ENLIVENER *noun* **ENLIVENERS** a person or thing that enlivens

ENMESH *verb* **ENMESHES, ENMESHING, ENMESHED** to catch or trap something in a net, or as if in a net; to entangle

ENMITY *noun* **ENMITIES** the state or quality of being an enemy

ENNOBLE *verb* **ENNOBLES, ENNOBLING, ENNOBLED** to make something noble or dignified

ENNUI *noun* **ENNUIS** boredom or discontent caused by a lack of activity or excitement

ENORMITY *noun* **ENORMITIES** outrageousness or wickedness

ENORMOUS *adj* extremely large; huge

ENOUGH *adj* in the number or quantity needed; sufficient □ *adverb* to the necessary degree or extent □ *pronoun* the amount needed

ENPRINT *noun* **ENPRINTS** a standard size of photographic print produced from a negative, usually approximately 12.7cm × 9cm

ENQUIRE *verb* **ENQUIRES, ENQUIRING, ENQUIRED** to inquire

ENQUIRY *noun* **ENQUIRIES** an inquiry

ENRAGE *verb* **ENRAGES, ENRAGING, ENRAGED** to make someone extremely angry

ENRAGED *adj* very angry; furious

ENRAPT *adj* intensely pleased or delighted

ENRAPTURE *verb* **ENRAPTURES, ENRAPTURING, ENRAPTURED** to give intense pleasure or joy to someone

ENRAPTURED *adj* intensely pleased or delighted

ENRICH *verb* **ENRICHES, ENRICHING, ENRICHED** to make something rich or richer, especially better or stronger in quality, value or flavour, etc

ENRICHED *adj* made rich or richer, especially better or stronger in quality, value or flavour, etc

ENROL *verb* **ENROLS, ENROLLING, ENROLLED** to add the name of (a person) to a list or roll, eg of members or pupils

ENROLL *verb* **ENROLLS, ENROLLING, ENROLLED** to enrol

ENROLMENT *noun* **ENROLMENTS** the act of enrolling

ENSCONCE *verb* **ENSCONCES, ENSCONCING, ENSCONCED** to settle comfortably or safely

ENSEMBLE *noun* **ENSEMBLES** a small group of (usually classical) musicians who regularly perform together

ENSHRINE *verb* **ENSHRINES, ENSHRINING, ENSHRINED** to enter and protect (a right or idea, etc) in the laws or constitution of a state, constitution of an organization, etc

ENSHROUD *verb* **ENSHROUDS, ENSHROUDING, ENSHROUDED** to cover something completely; to hide something by covering it up

ENSIGN *noun* **ENSIGNS** the flag of a nation or regiment

ENSILAGE *noun* **ENSILAGES** the process of making silage

ENSILE *verb* **ENSILES, ENSILING, ENSILED** to turn (fodder) into silage

ENSLAVE *verb* **ENSLAVES, ENSLAVING, ENSLAVED** to make someone into a slave

ENSNARE *verb* **ENSNARES, ENSNARING, ENSNARED** to catch something or someone in, or as if in, a trap; to trick or lead them dishonestly (into doing something)

ENSUE *verb* **ENSUES, ENSUING, ENSUED** to follow something; to happen after it

ENSUING *adj* that follows; resulting

ENSURE *verb* **ENSURES, ENSURING, ENSURED** to make something certain; to assure or guarantee it

ENTAIL *verb* **ENTAILS, ENTAILING, ENTAILED** to have something as a necessary result or requirement; to bequeath (property) to one's descendants, not allowing them the option to sell it □ *noun* **ENTAILS** the practice of entailing (property)

ENTANGLE *verb* **ENTANGLES, ENTANGLING, ENTANGLED** to cause something to get caught in some obstacle, eg a net

ENTASIS *noun* **ENTASES** the slightly bulging outline of a column or similar structure

ENTENTE *noun* **ENTENTES** a friendly agreement or relationship between nations or states

ENTER *verb* **ENTERS, ENTERING, ENTERED** to go or come in or into (eg a room)

ENTERABLE *adj* capable of being entered

ENTERER *noun* **ENTERERS** a person who enters

ENTERIC *adj* intestinal □ *noun* **ENTERICS** typhoid fever

ENTERITIS *noun* **ENTERITISES** inflammation of the intestines, especially the small intestine

ENTERTAIN *verb* **ENTERTAINS, ENTERTAINING, ENTERTAINED** to provide amusement or recreation for someone

ENTERTAINING *adj* interesting and amusing; giving entertainment □ *noun* **ENTERTAININGS** provision of entertainment

ENTHALPY *noun* **ENTHALPIES** the amount of heat energy possessed by a substance, expressed per unit mass

ENTHRAL *verb* **ENTHRALS, ENTHRALLING, ENTHRALLED** to fascinate; to hold the attention or grip the imagination of someone

ENTHRALL *verb* **ENTHRALLS, ENTHRALLING, ENTHRALLED** to enthral

ENTHRALLED *adj* fascinated

ENTHRALLING *adj* fascinating

ENTHRONE *verb* **ENTHRONES, ENTHRONING, ENTHRONED** to place someone on a throne

ENTHUSE *verb* **ENTHUSES, ENTHUSING, ENTHUSED** to be

enthusiastic, or make someone enthusiastic

ENTICE *verb* **ENTICES, ENTICING, ENTICED** to tempt or persuade, by arousing hopes or desires or by promising a reward

ENTICER *noun* **ENTICERS** a person or thing that entices

ENTICING *adj* alluring; fascinating

ENTIRE *adj* whole or complete ▫ *noun* **ENTIRES** a stallion

ENTIRELY *adverb* fully or absolutely

ENTIRETY *noun* **ENTIRETIES** completeness; wholeness; the whole

ENTITLE *verb* **ENTITLES, ENTITLING, ENTITLED** to give a title or name to (a book, etc)

ENTITY *noun* **ENTITIES** something that has a physical existence, as opposed to a quality or mood

ENTOMB *verb* **ENTOMBS, ENTOMBING, ENTOMBED** to put (a body) in a tomb

ENTOURAGE *noun* **ENTOURAGES** a group of followers or assistants, especially one accompanying a famous or important person

ENTRAILS *plural noun* the internal organs of a person or animal

ENTRAIN *verb* **ENTRAINS, ENTRAINING, ENTRAINED** to board or put someone on board a train

ENTRANCE [1] *noun* **ENTRANCES** a way in, eg a door

ENTRANCE [2] *verb* **ENTRANCES, ENTRANCING, ENTRANCED** to grip or captivate someone's attention and imagination

ENTRANCING *adj* gripping the imagination; fascinating; delightful

ENTRANT *noun* **ENTRANTS** someone who enters something, especially an examination, a competition or a profession

ENTRAP *verb* **ENTRAPS, ENTRAPPING, ENTRAPPED** to catch something in a trap

ENTRAPPER *noun* **ENTRAPPERS** a person who entraps

ENTREAT *verb* **ENTREATS, ENTREATING, ENTREATED** to ask passionately or desperately; to beg

ENTREATY *noun* **ENTREATIES** a passionate or desperate request

ENTRECHAT *noun* **ENTRECHATS** in ballet: a leap in which the dancer crosses their feet and beats their heels together

ENTRECÔTE *noun* **ENTRECÔTES** in cookery: a boneless steak cut from between two ribs

ENTRÉE *noun* **ÉNTREES** a small dish served after the fish course and before the main course at a formal dinner

ENTRENCH *verb* **ENTRENCHES, ENTRENCHING, ENTRENCHED** to fix or establish something firmly, often too firmly

ENTREPOT *noun* **ENTREPOTS** a port through which goods are imported and exported, especially one from which goods are re-exported without duty being paid on them

ENTROPIC *adj* of or relating to entropy

ENTROPY *noun* **ENTROPIES** a measure of the amount of disorder in a system, or of the unavailability of energy for doing work

ENTRUST *verb* **ENTRUSTS, ENTRUSTING, ENTRUSTED** to give in trust; to give responsibility to trustingly

ENTRY *noun* **ENTRIES** the act of coming or going in

ENTRYISM *noun* **ENTRYISMS** the practice of joining a political party in large enough numbers to gain power and change the party's policies

ENTRYIST *noun* **ENTRYISTS** someone who engages in political entryism

ENTWINE *verb* **ENTWINES, ENTWINING, ENTWINED** to wind or twist (two or more things) together

ENUMERATE *verb* **ENUMERATES, ENUMERATING, ENUMERATED** to list one by one

ENUNCIATE *verb* **ENUNCIATES, ENUNCIATING, ENUNCIATED** to pronounce words clearly

ENURE *verb* **ENURES, ENURING, ENURED** to inure

ENURESIS *noun* **ENURESES** involuntary urination, especially during sleep

ENURETIC *adj* of or relating to enuresis

ENVELOP *verb* **ENVELOPS, ENVELOPING, ENVELOPED** to cover or wrap something or someone completely

ENVELOPE *noun* **ENVELOPES** a thin flat sealable paper packet or cover, especially for a letter

ENVIABLE *adj* likely to cause envy; highly desirable

ENVIABLY *adverb* in an enviable way

ENVIOUS *adj* feeling or showing envy

ENVIOUSLY *adverb* in an envious way

ENVIRON *verb* **ENVIRONS, ENVIRONING, ENVIRONED** to surround or encircle

ENVIRONS *plural noun* surrounding areas, especially the outskirts of a town or city

ENVISAGE *verb* **ENVISAGES, ENVISAGING, ENVISAGED** to picture something in the mind

ENVOI *noun* **ENVOIS** the concluding part of a poem or book, eg the short concluding verse at the end of a ballad

ENVOY *noun* **ENVOYS** a diplomat ranking next below an ambassador

ENVY *noun* **ENVIES** a feeling of resentment or regretful desire for another person's qualities, better fortune or success ▫ *verb* **ENVIES, ENVYING, ENVIED** to feel envy towards someone

ENZOOTIC *adj* said of a disease: prevalent in a particular district or at a particular season ▫ *noun* **ENZOOTICS** an enzootic disease

ENZYMATIC *adj* of or relating to enzymes

ENZYME *noun* **ENZYMES** a specialized protein molecule that acts as a catalyst for the biochemical reactions that occur in living cells

ENZYMIC *adj* of or relating to enzymes

EOLITHIC *adj* belonging to the early part of the Stone Age, when crude stone implements were first used by man

EON *noun* **EONS** a long period of time; an endless or immeasurable period of time

EONISM *noun* **EONISMS** the practice of transvestism

EOSIN *noun* **EOSINS** a red acidic dye

EPACT *noun* **EPACTS** the Moon's age at the beginning of the calendar year

EPARCH *noun* **EPARCHS** a bishop or metropolitan in the Orthodox Church

EPAULET *noun* **EPAULETS** an epaulette

EPAULETTE *noun* **EPAULETTES** a decoration on the shoulder of a coat or jacket, especially of a military uniform

For longer words, see *The Chambers Dictionary*

ÉPÉE *noun* ÉPÉES a sword with a narrow flexible blade

EPHEDRINE *noun* EPHEDRINES an alkaloid drug, with similar effects to adrenaline, now mainly used as a nasal decongestant

EPHEMERA *noun* EPHEMERAS, EPHEMERAE a mayfly

EPHEMERAL *adj* lasting a short time ◻ *noun* EPHEMERALS a plant or animal that completes its life cycle within weeks, days or even hours

EPHEMERIS *noun* EPHEMERIDES a table that shows the predicted future positions of celestial bodies such as the Sun, Moon, planets, certain stars and comets

EPHEMERON *noun* EPHEMERA an insect which lives for one day only

EPIBLAST *noun* EPIBLASTS the outer germinal layer of an embryo

EPIC *noun* EPICS a long narrative poem telling of heroic acts, the birth and death of nations, etc ◻ *adj* referring to or like an epic, especially in being large-scale and imposing

EPICALYX *noun* EPICALYXES, EPICALYCES an apparent accessory calyx outside the true calyx

EPICARP *noun* EPICARPS the outermost layer of the pericarp of fruit; the skin

EPICENE *adj* having characteristics of both sexes, or of neither sex

EPICENTER *noun* EPICENTERS the epicentre

EPICENTRE *noun* EPICENTRES the point on the Earth's surface which is directly above the focus of an earthquake, or directly above or below a nuclear explosion

EPICURE *noun* EPICURES someone who has refined taste, especially one who enjoys good food and drink

EPICUREAN *noun* EPICUREANS someone who likes pleasure and good living; an epicure ◻ *adj* given to luxury or to the tastes of an epicure

EPICURISM *noun* EPICURISMS the pursuit of pleasure, especially as found in good food and drink

EPICYCLE *noun* EPICYCLES a circle whose centre rolls around the circumference of another fixed circle

EPICYCLIC *adj* of or relating to epicycles

EPIDEMIC *noun* EPIDEMICS a sudden outbreak of infectious disease which spreads rapidly and affects a large number of people, animals or plants in a particular area for a limited period of time ◻ *adj* referring to or like an epidemic

EPIDERMAL *adj* of or relating to the epidermis

EPIDERMIS *noun* EPIDERMISES the outermost layer of a plant or animal, which serves to protect the underlying tissues from infection, injury and water loss

EPIDURAL *adj* situated on, or administered into, the dura mater ◻ *noun* EPIDURALS the epidural injection of an anaesthetic to remove all sensation below the waist, used especially during childbirth

EPIGENE *adj* acting, formed or taking place at the Earth's surface

EPIGRAM *noun* EPIGRAMS a witty or sarcastic saying

EPIGRAPH *noun* EPIGRAPHS a quotation or motto at the beginning of a book or chapter

EPIGRAPHY *noun* EPIGRAPHIES the study of inscriptions, especially those left by earlier civilizations

EPILATE *verb* EPILATES, EPILATING, EPILATED to remove (hair) by any method

EPILATION *noun* EPILATIONS the action of removing hair by the roots

EPILATOR *noun* EPILATORS a device that removes hair by the roots

EPILEPSY *noun* EPILEPSIES any of a group of disorders of the nervous system characterized by recurring attacks that involve impairment, or sudden loss, of consciousness

EPILEPTIC *adj* referring or relating to, or like epilepsy ◻ *noun* EPILEPTICS someone who suffers from epilepsy

EPILOG *noun* EPILOGS an epilogue

EPILOGUE *noun* EPILOGUES the closing section of a book or programme, etc

EPINASTY *noun* EPINASTIES an active growth on the upper side of an organ of a plant, causing a downward bend

EPIPHYSIS *noun* EPIPHYSES the growing end of a long bone

EPIPHYTE *noun* EPIPHYTES a plant that grows on another plant for support, but which is not a parasite

EPISCOPAL *adj* belonging or relating to bishops

EPISODE *noun* EPISODES one of several events or distinct periods making up a longer sequence

EPISODIC *adj* consisting of several distinct periods

EPISTLE *noun* EPISTLES a letter, especially a long one, dealing with important matters

EPISTYLE *noun* EPISTYLES a beam that forms the bottom part of an entablature and which rests across the top of a row of columns

EPITAPH *noun* EPITAPHS an inscription on a gravestone

EPITAXIAL *adj* resulting from epitaxy

EPITAXY *noun* EPITAXIES the growth of a thin layer of crystals on another crystal, so that they have the same structure

EPITHET *noun* EPITHETS an adjective or short descriptive phrase which captures the particular quality of the person or thing it describes

EPITHETIC *adj* relating to an epithet; having or using many epithets

EPITOME *noun* EPITOMES a miniature representation of a larger or wider idea, issue, etc

EPITOMISE *verb* EPITOMISES, EPITOMISING, EPITOMISED to epitomize

EPITOMIST *noun* EPITOMISTS someone who abridges something

EPITOMIZE *verb* EPITOMIZES, EPITOMIZING, EPITOMIZED to typify or personify

EPIZOAN *adj* of or relating to epizoons ◻ *noun* EPIZOANS an epizoon

EPIZOIC *adj* living on an animal

EPIZOON *noun* EPIZOA an animal that lives on the surface of another animal, either parasitically or commensally

EPIZOOTIC *adj* affecting animals as an epidemic affects humans ◻ *noun* EPIZOOTICS an epizootic disease

EPIZOOTICS *singular noun* the study of epidemic animal diseases

EPOCH *noun* EPOCHS a major division or period of history, or of a person's life, etc, usually marked by some important event

EPOCHAL *adj* relating to, or lasting for, an epoch

EPONYM *noun* **EPONYMS** the name of a person after whom something is named, especially the main character in a play or novel, etc whose name provides its title

EPONYMOUS *adj* said of a character in a story, etc: having the name which is used as the title

EPOXY *adj* consisting of an oxygen atom bonded to two carbon atoms □ *noun* **EPOXIES** any of a group of synthetic thermosetting resins, that are tough, resistant to abrasion and chemical attack, and form strong adhesive bonds

EPSILON *noun* **EPSILONS** the fifth letter of the Greek alphabet

EQUABLE *adj* said of a climate: never showing very great variations or extremes

EQUABLY *adverb* in an equable way

EQUAL *adj* the same in size, amount or value, etc □ *noun* **EQUALS** a person or thing of the same age, rank, ability or worth, etc □ *verb* **EQUALS, EQUALLING, EQUALLED** to be the same in amount, value or size, etc as someone or something

EQUALISE *verb* **EQUALISES, EQUALISING, EQUALISED** to equalize

EQUALISER *noun* **EQUALISERS** an equalizer

EQUALITY *noun* **EQUALITIES** the condition of being equal; sameness; evenness

EQUALIZE *verb* **EQUALIZES, EQUALIZING, EQUALIZED** to make or become equal

EQUALIZER *noun* **EQUALIZERS** a person or thing that equalizes, especially a goal or point scored which makes one equal to one's opponent

EQUALLY *adverb* to an equal degree or extent

EQUATE *verb* **EQUATES, EQUATING, EQUATED** to be or be regarded, treated, etc as equal

EQUATION *noun* **EQUATIONS** a mathematical statement of the equality between two expressions involving constants and/or variables

EQUATOR *noun* **EQUATORS** the imaginary great circle that passes around the Earth at latitude 0 at an equal distance from the North and South Poles, and divides the Earth's surface into the northern and southern hemispheres

EQUERRY *noun* **EQUERRIES** an official who serves as a personal attendant to a member of a royal family

EQUID *noun* **EQUIDS** a member of the family Equidae (a family of hoofed mammals)

EQUINE *adj* belonging or relating to, or like, a horse or horses

EQUINOX *noun* **EQUINOXES** either of the two occasions on which the Sun crosses the equator, making night and day equal in length

EQUIP *verb* **EQUIPS, EQUIPPING, EQUIPPED** to fit out or provide someone or something with the necessary tools, supplies, abilities, etc

EQUIPAGE *noun* **EQUIPAGES** a horse-drawn carriage with its footmen

ÉQUIPE *noun* **ÉQUIPES** a sports team, especially a motor-racing team

EQUIPMENT *noun* **EQUIPMENTS** the clothes, machines, tools or instruments, etc necessary for a particular kind of work or activity

EQUIPOISE *noun* **EQUIPOISES** a state of balance □ *verb* **EQUIPOISES, EQUIPOISING, EQUIPOISED** to balance; to counterpoise

EQUITABLE *adj* fair and just

EQUITABLY *adverb* in an equitable way

EQUITY *noun* **EQUITIES** fair or just conditions or treatment

EQUIVOCAL *adj* ambiguous; of doubtful meaning

ER *exclamation* expressing hesitation

ERA *noun* **ERAS** a distinct period in history marked by or beginning at an important event

ERADICATE *verb* **ERADICATES, ERADICATING, ERADICATED** to get rid of something completely

ERASABLE *adj* capable of being erased

ERASE *verb* **ERASES, ERASING, ERASED** to rub out (pencil marks, etc)

ERASER *noun* **ERASERS** something that erases, especially a rubber for removing pencil or ink marks

ERASURE *noun* **ERASURES** a place where something written has been erased

ERBIUM *noun* **ERBIUMS** a soft silvery metallic element, that absorbs neutrons and has a high electrical resistivity

ERE *prep* before □ *conj* before

ERECT *adj* upright; not bent or leaning □ *verb* **ERECTS, ERECTING, ERECTED** to put up or to build something

ERECTER *noun* **ERECTERS** a person or thing that erects or raises

ERECTILE *adj* said of an organ, etc: capable of becoming erect

ERECTION *noun* **ERECTIONS** the act of erecting or the state of being erected

ERECTLY *adverb* in an erect way

ERECTNESS *noun* **ERECTNESSES** the quality or condition of being erect

ERECTOR *noun* **ERECTORS** an erecter

EREPSIN *noun* **EREPSINS** an enzyme in the small intestine

ERF *noun* **ERVEN** a garden plot or small piece of ground

ERG *noun* **ERGS** in the cgs system: a unit of work or energy

ERGO *adverb* therefore

ERGONOMIC *adj* of or relating to ergonomics

ERGONOMICS *singular noun* the study of the relationship between people and their working environment, including machinery, computer sytems, etc

ERGOT *noun* **ERGOTS** a disease of rye and other cereals caused by a fungus

ERGOTISM *noun* **ERGOTISMS** poisoning caused by the consumption of bread made from rye infected with ergot

ERICA *noun* **ERICAS** any plant of the heath genus

ERK *noun* **ERKS** a slang word for *aircraftsman*

ERMINE *noun* **ERMINES** the stoat in its winter phase, when its fur has turned white except for the tip of the tail, which remains dark

ERN *verb* **ERNS, ERNING, ERNED** an old spelling of *earn*

ERODE *verb* **ERODES, ERODING, ERODED** to wear away, destroy or be destroyed gradually

For longer words, see *The Chambers Dictionary*

ERODIBLE *adj* able to be eroded

EROGENIC *adj* erogenous

EROGENOUS *adj* said of areas of the body: sensitive to sexual stimulation

EROSION *noun* **EROSIONS** the loosening, fragmentation and transport from one place to another of rock material by water, wind, ice, gravity or living organisms

EROSIVE *adj* causing erosion

EROTIC *adj* arousing; referring or relating to sexual desire, or giving sexual pleasure

EROTICA *plural noun* erotic literature or pictures, etc

EROTICISM *noun* **EROTICISMS** the erotic quality of a piece of writing or a picture, etc

ERR *verb* **ERRS, ERRING, ERRED** to make a mistake, be wrong, or do wrong

ERRAND *noun* **ERRANDS** a short journey made in order to get or do something, especially for someone else

ERRANT *adj* doing wrong; erring

ERRANTRY *noun* **ERRANTRIES** an errant or wandering state

ERRATIC *adj* irregular; having no fixed pattern or course □ *noun* **ERRATICS** a mass of rock transported by ice and deposited at a distance

ERRATUM *noun* **ERRATA** an error in writing or printing

ERRED past form of **err**

ERRING a form of **err**

ERRONEOUS *adj* wrong or mistaken

ERROR *noun* **ERRORS** a mistake, inaccuracy or misapprehension

ERSATZ *adj* substitute; imitation □ *noun* **ERSATZES** a cheaper substitute, often used because the genuine article is unavailable

ERSTWHILE *adj* former; previous

ERUDITE *adj* showing or having a great deal of knowledge; learned

ERUDITELY *adverb* in an erudite or learned manner

ERUDITION *noun* **ERUDITIONS** the state of being learned

ERUPT *verb* **ERUPTS, ERUPTING, ERUPTED** said of a volcano: to throw out lava, ash and gases

ERUPTION *noun* **ERUPTIONS** the process of erupting, especially by a volcano

ERUPTIVE *adj* attended by or producing eruption; produced by eruption

ERVEN plural of **erf**

ERYTHEMA *noun* **ERYTHEMAS** redness of the skin, caused by dilation of the blood capillaries

---

ES *noun* **ESSES** the letter 'S'

ESCALATE *verb* **ESCALATES, ESCALATING, ESCALATED** to increase or be increased rapidly in scale or degree, etc

ESCALATOR *noun* **ESCALATORS** a type of conveyor belt which forms a continuous moving staircase

ESCALLOP *noun* **ESCALLOPS** a scallop

ESCALOPE *noun* **ESCALOPES** a thin slice of boneless meat, especially veal

ESCAPABLE *adj* that can be escaped

ESCAPADE *noun* **ESCAPADES** a daring, adventurous or unlawful act

ESCAPE *verb* **ESCAPES, ESCAPING, ESCAPED** to gain freedom □ *noun* **ESCAPES** an act of escaping

ESCAPEE *noun* **ESCAPEES** someone who has escaped, especially from prison

ESCAPER *noun* **ESCAPERS** someone who escapes

ESCAPISM *noun* **ESCAPISMS** the means of escaping, or the tendency to escape, from unpleasant reality into day-dreams or fantasy

ESCAPIST *adj* characterized by escapism □ *noun* **ESCAPISTS** someone who indulges in escapism

ESCARGOT *noun* **ESCARGOTS** an edible snail

ESCHEAT *noun* **ESCHEATS** the handing over of property to the state or a feudal lord in the absence of a legal heir □ *verb* **ESCHEATS, ESCHEATING, ESCHEATED** said of property: to fall to the state or a feudal lord

ESCHEW *verb* **ESCHEWS, ESCHEWING, ESCHEWED** to avoid, keep away from, or abstain from something

ESCHEWAL *noun* **ESCHEWALS** the act of avoiding, keeping away from, or abstaining from something

ESCORT *noun* **ESCORTS** one or more people or vehicles, etc accompanying another or others for protection, guidance, or as a mark of honour □ *verb* **ESCORTS, ESCORTING, ESCORTED** to

accompany someone or something as an escort

ESCUDO *noun* **ESCUDOS** the standard unit of currency of Portugal

ESCULENT *adj* edible □ *noun* **ESCULENTS** any edible substance

ESKER *noun* **ESKERS** a long narrow hill of gravel and sand which may wind for long distances along a valley floor

ESOTERIC *adj* understood only by those few people who have the necessary special knowledge; secret or mysterious

ESPALIER *noun* **ESPALIERS** a trellis or arrangement of wires against which a shrub or fruit tree is trained to grow flat, eg against a wall

ESPARTO *noun* **ESPARTOS** a tough coarse grass native to Spain and N Africa, used to make rope, etc

ESPECIAL *adj* special

ESPIED past form of **espy**

ESPIES a form of **espy**

ESPIONAGE *noun* **ESPIONAGES** the activity of spying, or the use of spies to gather information

ESPLANADE *noun* **ESPLANADES** a long wide pavement next to a beach

ESPOUSAL *noun* **ESPOUSALS** the act of espousing (a cause, etc)

ESPOUSE *verb* **ESPOUSES, ESPOUSING, ESPOUSED** to adopt or give one's support to (a cause, etc)

ESPRESSO *noun* **ESPRESSOS** coffee made by forcing steam or boiling water through ground coffee beans

ESPRIT *noun* **ESPRITS** liveliness or wit

ESPY *verb* **ESPIES, ESPYING, ESPIED** to catch sight of someone or something; to observe

ESQUIRE *noun* **ESQUIRES** a title used after a man's name when no other form of address is used, especially when addressing letters

ESSAY *noun* **ESSAYS** a short formal piece of writing, usually one dealing with a single subject; an attempt □ *verb* **ESSAYS, ESSAYING, ESSAYED** to attempt

ESSAYIST *noun* **ESSAYISTS** a writer of literary essays

ESSENCE *noun* **ESSENCES** the basic distinctive part or quality of something, which determines its nature or character

---

For longer words, see *The Chambers Dictionary*

ESSENTIAL *adj* absolutely necessary □ *noun* **ESSENTIALS** something necessary

ESSES plural of **es**

EST *noun* **ESTS** a programme designed to develop human potential

ESTABLISH *verb* **ESTABLISHES, ESTABLISHING, ESTABLISHED** to settle someone firmly in a position, place or job, etc

ESTABLISHED *adj* settled or accepted

ESTATE *noun* **ESTATES** a large piece of land owned by a person or group of people

ESTEEM *verb* **ESTEEMS, ESTEEMING, ESTEEMED** to value, respect or think highly of someone or something □ *noun* **ESTEEMS** high regard or respect

ESTEEMED *adj* respected

ESTER *noun* **ESTERS** an organic chemical compound formed by the reaction of an alcohol with an organic acid, with the loss of a water molecule

ESTERIFY *verb* **ESTERIFIES, ESTERIFYING, ESTERIFIED** to make something into an ester

ESTHETE *noun* **ESTHETES** someone who has or claims to have a special appreciation of art and beauty

ESTIMABLE *adj* highly respected; worthy of respect

ESTIMABLY *adverb* in an estimable way

ESTIMATE *verb* **ESTIMATES, ESTIMATING, ESTIMATED** to judge or calculate (size, amount or value, etc) roughly or without measuring □ *noun* **ESTIMATES** a rough assessment (of size, etc)

ESTIMATOR *noun* **ESTIMATORS** someone who estimates

ESTIVAL *adj* aestival

ESTIVATE *verb* **ESTIVATES, ESTIVATING, ESTIVATED** to aestivate

ESTRADIOL *noun* **ESTRADIOLS** the most important female sex hormone

ESTRANGE *verb* **ESTRANGES, ESTRANGING, ESTRANGED** to cause someone to break away from a previously friendly state or relationship

ESTRANGED *adj* no longer friendly or supportive; alienated

ESTROGEN *noun* **ESTROGENS** oestrogen

ESTRUS *noun* **ESTRUSES** oestrus

ESTUARIAL *adj* of or relating to an estuary

ESTUARINE *adj* of or belonging to an estuary

ESTUARY *noun* **ESTUARIES** the broad mouth of a river that flows into the sea, where fresh water mixes with tidal sea water

ETA *noun* **ETAS** the seventh letter of the Greek alphabet

ETALON *noun* **ETALONS** an interferometer used to measure wavelengths

ETCETERAS *plural noun* additional things or people; extras

ETCH *verb* **ETCHES, ETCHING, ETCHED** to make designs on (metal or glass, etc) using an acid to eat out the lines

ETCHER *noun* **ETCHERS** a person who etches, especially as their profession

ETCHING *noun* **ETCHINGS** the act or art of making etched designs

ETERNAL *adj* without beginning or end; everlasting

ETERNALLY *adverb* for ever; without end or constantly

ETERNITY *noun* **ETERNITIES** time regarded as having no end

ETESIAN *adj* said especially of NW winds in the E Mediterranean in the summer: recurring annually

ETH *noun* **ETHS** a letter used in Old English

ETHANE *noun* **ETHANES** a colourless odourless flammable gas belonging to the alkane series of hydrocarbons, and found in natural gas

ETHANOL *noun* **ETHANOLS** a colourless volatile flammable alcohol that is produced by fermentation of the sugar in fruit or cereals, and is used as an intoxicant in alcoholic beverages, and as a fuel

ETHENE *noun* **ETHENES** ethylene

ETHER *noun* **ETHERS** any of a group of organic chemical compounds formed by the dehydration of alcohols, that are volatile and highly flammable, and contain two hydrocarbon groups linked by an oxygen atom

ETHEREAL *adj* having an unreal lightness or delicateness; fairy-like

ETHIC *noun* **ETHICS** the moral

system or set of principles particular to a certain person, community or group, etc

ETHICAL *adj* relating to or concerning morals, justice or duty

ETHICALLY *adverb* from an ethical point of view

ETHICS *singular noun* the study or the science of morals □ *plural noun* rules or principles of behaviour

ETHNIC *adj* relating to or having a common race or cultural tradition □ *noun* **ETHNICS** a member of a particular racial group or cult, especially a minority one

ETHNICITY *noun* **ETHNICITIES** racial status or distinctiveness

ETHNOLOGY *noun* **ETHNOLOGIES** the scientific study of different races and cultural traditions, and their relations with each other

ETHOLOGY *noun* **ETHOLOGIES** the study of animal behaviour

ETHOS *noun* **ETHOSES** the typical spirit, character or attitudes (of a group or community, etc)

ETHYL *noun* **ETHYLS** in organic chemical compounds: the (C_2H_5-) group, as for example in ethylamine ($C_2H_5NH_2$)

ETHYLENE *noun* **ETHYLENES** a colourless flammable gas with a sweet smell, belonging to the alkene series of hydrocarbons

ETHYNE *noun* **ETHYNES** acetylene

ETIOLATED *adj* said of a plant: having foliage that has become yellow through lack of sunlight

ETIOLOGY *noun* **ETIOLOGIES** the science or philosophy of causes

ETIQUETTE *noun* **ETIQUETTES** conventions of correct or polite social behaviour

ÉTUDE *noun* **ÉTUDES** a short piece of music written for a single instrument, intended as an exercise or a means of showing talent

ETYMOLOGY *noun* **ETYMOLOGIES** the study of the origin and development of words and their meanings

ETYMON *noun* **ETYMONS, ETYMA** the earliest recorded form, or reconstructed earliest form, of a word

EUCARYOTE *noun* **EUCARYOTES** eukaryote

EUCHRE *noun* **EUCHRES** a N American card-game for two, three or four players, played with 32 cards □ *verb* **EUCHRES, EUCHRING, EUCHRED** to prevent (a player) from winning three tricks

EUGENIC *adj* relating to genetic improvement of a race by judicious mating and helping the better stock to prevail

EUGENICS *singular noun* the science concerned with the detection and elimination of human hereditary diseases and disorders by genetic counselling of parents who may be carriers of such conditions

EUK *verb* **EUKS, EUKING, EUKED** a dialect word meaning to itch

EUKARYOTE *noun* **EUKARYOTES** an organism in which the cells have a distinct nucleus containing the genetic material and separated from the cytoplasm by a nuclear membrane

EULOGISE *verb* **EULOGISES, EULOGISING, EULOGISED** to eulogize

EULOGIZE *verb* **EULOGIZES, EULOGIZING, EULOGIZED** to praise highly

EULOGY *noun* **EULOGIES** a speech or piece of writing in praise of someone or something

EUNUCH *noun* **EUNUCHS** a man who has been castrated

EUPEPSIA *noun* **EUPEPSIAS** good digestion

EUPEPSY *noun* **EUPEPSIES** eupepsia

EUPEPTIC *adj* relating to good digestion; cheerful

EUPHEMISM *noun* **EUPHEMISMS** a mild or inoffensive term used in place of one considered offensive or unpleasantly direct

EUPHENICS *singular noun* the science concerned with the physical improvement of human beings by modifying their development after birth

EUPHONIC *adj* pleasing to the ear

EUPHONIUM *noun* **EUPHONIUMS** a four-valved brass instrument of the tuba family usually found in brass and military bands

EUPHONY *noun* **EUPHONIES** a pleasing sound, especially in speech

EUPHORIA *noun* **EUPHORIAS** a feeling of wild happiness and well-being

EUPHORIC *adj* characterized by a feeling of wild happiness and well-being

EUPHRASY *noun* **EUPHRASIES** any plant of the figwort family, especially eyebright

EUPHUISM *noun* **EUPHUISMS** a pompous and affected style of writing

EUREKA *exclamation* expressing triumph at finding something or solving a problem, etc

EURHYTHMY *noun* **EURHYTHMIES** harmony of proportion

EURO *noun* **EUROS** a common unit of currency used by several members of the European Union

EUROPIUM *noun* **EUROPIUMS** a soft silvery metallic element belonging to the lanthanide series

EURYTHMY *noun* **EURYTHMIES** harmony of proportion

EUSTASY *noun* **EUSTASIES** worldwide change in sea-level caused by advancing or receding polar ice caps

EUSTATIC *adj* of, relating to, or caused by eustasy

EUTROPHIC *adj* said of a body of water: suffering from eutrophication (a process whereby the water becomes over-enriched with nutrients)

EVACUATE *verb* **EVACUATES, EVACUATING, EVACUATED** to leave (a place), especially because of danger

EVACUEE *noun* **EVACUEES** an evacuated person

EVADE *verb* **EVADES, EVADING, EVADED** to escape or avoid something or someone by trickery or skill

EVAGINATE *verb* **EVAGINATES, EVAGINATING, EVAGINATED** to turn an organ inside out

EVALUATE *verb* **EVALUATES, EVALUATING, EVALUATED** to form an idea or judgement about the worth of something

EVANESCE *verb* **EVANESCES, EVANESCING, EVANESCED** said of smoke or mist, etc: to disappear gradually; to fade from sight

EVAPORATE *verb* **EVAPORATES, EVAPORATING, EVAPORATED** to change or cause something to change from a liquid into a vapour at a temperature below the boiling point of the liquid

EVAPORITE *noun* **EVAPORITES** a mineral deposit formed as a result of the evaporation of all or most of the water from a saline solution such as sea water

EVASION *noun* **EVASIONS** the act of evading, especially evading a commitment or responsibility

EVASIVE *adj* intending or intended to evade something, especially trouble or danger

EVASIVELY *adverb* in an evasive way

EVE *noun* **EVES** the evening or day before some notable event

EVEN *adj* **EVENER, EVENEST** smooth and flat □ *adverb* used with a comparative to emphasize a comparison with something else as in *He's good, but she's even better* □ *verb* **EVENS, EVENING, EVENED** to make even or smooth; to put on an equal basis □ *noun* **EVENS** an even number, or something designated by one

EVENING *noun* **EVENINGS** the last part of the day, usually from late afternoon until bedtime □ *adj* referring to or during the evening

EVENINGS *adverb* in the evening; in the evening on a number of occasions

EVENLY *adverb* in an even way; uniformly

EVENNESS *noun* **EVENNESSES** the quality or state of being smooth and flat

EVENSONG *noun* **EVENSONGS** the service of evening prayer

EVENT *noun* **EVENTS** something that occurs or happens; an incident, especially a significant one

EVENTER *noun* **EVENTERS** a person or horse that takes part in eventing

EVENTFUL *adj* full of important or significant events

EVENTIDE *noun* **EVENTIDES** evening

EVENTING *noun* **EVENTINGS** the practice of taking part in horse-riding events, especially the three-day event

EVENTUAL *adj* happening after or at the end of a period of time or a process, etc

EVENTUATE *verb* **EVENTUATES, EVENTUATING, EVENTUATED** to result; to turn out

EVER *adverb* at any time

EVERGLADE *noun* **EVERGLADES** a large shallow lake or marsh

EVERGREEN *adj* denoting plants that bear leaves all the year round, eg pines or firs □ *noun* **EVERGREENS** a tree or shrub that bears leaves all the year round

EVERMORE *adverb* for all time to come; eternally

EVERSIBLE adj able to be turned outwards or inside out

EVERSION noun **EVERSIONS** the act of turning (an eyelid or other organ) outwards or inside out

EVERT verb **EVERTS, EVERTING, EVERTED** to turn (an eyelid or other organ) outwards or inside out

EVERY adj each one or single of a number or collection; omitting none □ adverb at, in, or at the end of, each stated period of time or distance, etc

EVERYBODY pronoun every person

EVERYDAY adj happening, done or used, etc daily, or on ordinary days, rather than on special occasions

EVERYMAN noun **EVERYMEN** the ordinary or common person; anybody; mankind

EVERYONE pronoun every person

EVICT verb **EVICTS, EVICTING, EVICTED** to put someone out of a house, etc or off land by force of law

EVICTION noun **EVICTIONS** the process of evicting people, especially from a building

EVIDENCE noun **EVIDENCES** information, etc that gives grounds for belief; that which points to, reveals or suggests something □ verb **EVIDENCES, EVIDENCING, EVIDENCED** to be evidence of something; to prove

EVIDENT adj clear to see or understand; obvious or apparent

EVIDENTLY adverb obviously; apparently

EVIL adj **EVILLER, EVILLEST** morally bad or offensive □ noun **EVILS** wickedness or moral offensiveness, or the source of it

EVILLY adverb in an evil way

EVILNESS noun **EVILNESSES** the state of being evil; an evil act

EVINCE verb **EVINCES, EVINCING, EVINCED** to show or display something (usually a personal quality) clearly

EVINCIBLE adj that may be evinced

EVOCATION noun **EVOCATIONS** the act of causing or producing (a response or reaction, etc)

EVOCATIVE adj bringing a feeling vividly to mind

EVOKE verb **EVOKES, EVOKING, EVOKED** to cause or produce (a response or reaction, etc)

EVOLUTE noun **EVOLUTES** in geometry: the original curve from which the involute is described

EVOLUTION noun **EVOLUTIONS** the process of evolving

EVOLVE verb **EVOLVES, EVOLVING, EVOLVED** to develop or produce gradually

EWE noun **EWES** a female sheep

EWER noun **EWERS** a large water-jug with a wide mouth

EWK verb **EWKS, EWKING, EWKED** to euk

EWT noun **EWTS** an old form of newt

EX noun **EXES** a person who is no longer what he or she was, especially a former husband, wife or lover

EXACT adj absolutely accurate or correct □ verb **EXACTS, EXACTING, EXACTED** to demand (payment, etc) from

EXACTING adj making difficult or excessive demands

EXACTION noun **EXACTIONS** the act of demanding payment, or the payment demanded

EXACTLY adverb just; quite, precisely or absolutely

EXACTNESS noun **EXACTNESSES** the quality of being exact or precise; accuracy

EXALT verb **EXALTS, EXALTING, EXALTED** to praise (eg God) highly

EXALTED adj noble; very moral

EXALTEDLY adverb in an exalted way

EXAM noun **EXAMS** an examination

EXAMINE verb **EXAMINES, EXAMINING, EXAMINED** to inspect, consider or look into something closely

EXAMINEE noun **EXAMINEES** a candidate in an examination

EXAMINER noun **EXAMINERS** someone who sets an examination

EXAMPLE noun **EXAMPLES** someone or something that is a typical specimen

EXANTHEMA noun **EXANTHEMATA** a rash or other skin eruption

EXCAVATE verb **EXCAVATES, EXCAVATING, EXCAVATED** to dig up or uncover something (especially historical remains)

EXCAVATOR noun **EXCAVATORS** someone who excavates or digs up ground

EXCEED verb **EXCEEDS, EXCEEDING, EXCEEDED** to be greater than someone or something

EXCEL verb **EXCELS, EXCELLING, EXCELLED** to have good qualities in large measure; to perform exceptional actions

EXCELLENT adj of very high quality; extremely good

EXCENTRIC adj said of circles: not concentric; not having the same centre □ noun **EXCENTRICS** a circle not having the same centre as another

EXCEPT prep leaving out; not including □ verb **EXCEPTS, EXCEPTING, EXCEPTED** to leave out or exclude

EXCEPTING prep leaving out; not including or counting

EXCEPTION noun **EXCEPTIONS** someone or something not included

EXCERPT noun **EXCERPTS** a short passage or part taken from a book, film or musical work, etc □ verb **EXCERPTS, EXCERPTING, EXCERPTED** to select extracts from (a book, etc)

EXCERPTOR noun **EXCERPTORS** a person who selects extracts from a book, etc

EXCESS noun **EXCESSES** the act of going, or the state of being, beyond normal or suitable limits □ adj greater than is usual, necessary or permitted

EXCESSIVE adj too great; beyond what is usual, right or appropriate

EXCHANGE noun **EXCHANGES** the giving and taking of one thing for another □ verb **EXCHANGES, EXCHANGING, EXCHANGED** to give, or give up, something, in return for something else

EXCHANGER noun **EXCHANGERS** a person who exchanges money or goods, etc, especially as a profession

EXCHEQUER noun **EXCHEQUERS** the government department in charge of the financial affairs of a nation

EXCISABLE adj liable to excise duty

EXCISE noun **EXCISES** the tax or duty payable on goods, etc produced and sold within a country, and on certain trading licences □ verb **EXCISES, EXCISING, EXCISED** to charge excise on (goods, etc)

EXCISEMAN noun **EXCISEMEN** an officer whose job was to collect excise duty and prevent smuggling

EXCISION noun **EXCISIONS** a cutting out or off of any kind

EXCITABLE adj easily made excited, flustered, frantic, etc

EXCITANCY noun **EXCITANCIES** the property of being excitant

EXCITANT noun **EXCITANTS** something which stimulates the vital activity of the body; a stimulant □ adj exciting or stimulating

EXCITE verb **EXCITES, EXCITING, EXCITED** to make someone feel lively expectation or a pleasant tension and thrill

EXCITED adj emotionally aroused; thrilled

EXCITEDLY adverb in an excited way

EXCITER noun **EXCITERS** a person or thing that excites

EXCITING adj arousing a lively expectation or a pleasant tension and thrill

EXCITON noun **EXCITONS** in physics: a bound pair comprising an electron and a hole

EXCITOR noun **EXCITORS** an exciter

EXCLAIM verb **EXCLAIMS, EXCLAIMING, EXCLAIMED** to call or cry out suddenly and loudly, eg in surprise or anger

EXCLAVE noun **EXCLAVES** a part of a country or province etc, separated from the main part and enclosed in foreign territory

EXCLUDE verb **EXCLUDES, EXCLUDING, EXCLUDED** to prevent someone from sharing or taking part

EXCLUSION noun **EXCLUSIONS** the act of excluding, or the state of being excluded

EXCLUSIVE adj involving the rejection or denial of something else or everything else □ noun **EXCLUSIVES** a report or story published in only one newspaper or magazine

EXCORIATE verb **EXCORIATES, EXCORIATING, EXCORIATED** to strip the skin from (a person or animal)

EXCREMENT noun **EXCREMENTS** waste matter passed out of the body, especially faeces

EXCRETA plural noun excreted matter; faeces or urine

EXCRETE verb **EXCRETES,**

EXCRETING, EXCRETED said of a plant or animal: to eliminate (waste products)

EXCRETION noun **EXCRETIONS** in plants and animals: the removal of excess waste, or harmful material produced by the organism

EXCRETIVE adj able to excrete; concerned with excretion

EXCRETORY adj of or relating to the excretion of waste matter

EXCULPATE verb **EXCULPATES, EXCULPATING, EXCULPATED** to free someone from guilt or blame; to absolve or vindicate

EXCURSION noun **EXCURSIONS** a short trip, usually one made for pleasure

EXCURSIVE adj tending to wander from the main point

EXCUSABLE adj that may be excused

EXCUSABLY adverb so as to deserve being excused

EXCUSE verb **EXCUSES, EXCUSING, EXCUSED** to pardon or forgive someone □ noun **EXCUSES** an explanation for a wrongdoing, offered as an apology or justification

EXEAT noun **EXEATS** formal leave of absence from a college or boarding school, etc eg for a weekend

EXECRABLE adj detestable

EXECRABLY adverb in an execrable way

EXECRATE verb **EXECRATES, EXECRATING, EXECRATED** to feel or express hatred or loathing of something

EXECUTANT noun **EXECUTANTS** someone who carries out or performs something, especially a technically accomplished musician

EXECUTE verb **EXECUTES, EXECUTING, EXECUTED** to perform or carry out something; to put someone to death by order of the law

EXECUTER noun **EXECUTERS** someone who carries out (a plan, etc) or puts (a law, etc) into effect

EXECUTION noun **EXECUTIONS** the act, or an instance, of putting someone to death by law

EXECUTIVE adj in a business organization, etc: concerned with management or administration □ noun **EXECUTIVES** someone in an organization, etc who has power to direct or manage

EXECUTOR noun **EXECUTORS** a male or female person appointed to carry out instructions stated in a will

EXECUTORY adj relating to the carrying out of laws or orders

EXECUTRIX noun **EXECUTRIXES, EXECUTRICES** a female executor

EXEGESIS noun **EXEGESES** a critical explanation of a text, especially of the Bible

EXEGETIC adj critically explaining a text

EXEMPLAR noun **EXEMPLARS** a person or thing worth copying; a model

EXEMPLARY adj worth following as an example

EXEMPLIFY verb **EXEMPLIFIES, EXEMPLIFYING, EXEMPLIFIED** to be an example of something

EXEMPT verb **EXEMPTS, EXEMPTING, EXEMPTED** to free someone from a duty or obligation that applies to others □ adj free from some obligation; not liable

EXEMPTION noun **EXEMPTIONS** the act of exempting; the state of being exempt

EXEQUIAL adj of or relating to a funeral

EXEQUIES plural noun funeral rites

EXERCISE noun **EXERCISES** physical training or exertion for health or pleasure □ verb **EXERCISES, EXERCISING, EXERCISED** to give exercise to (oneself, or someone or something else)

EXERCISER noun **EXERCISERS** a person or thing that exercises

EXERT verb **EXERTS, EXERTING, EXERTED** to bring something into use or action forcefully

EXERTION noun **EXERTIONS** strenuous activity

EXES plural noun expenses

EXEUNT verb as a stage direction: leave the stage; they leave the stage

EXFOLIATE verb **EXFOLIATES, EXFOLIATING, EXFOLIATED** said of bark, rocks or skin, etc: to shed or peel off in flakes or layers

EXHALE verb **EXHALES, EXHALING, EXHALED** to breathe out

EXHAUST verb **EXHAUSTS, EXHAUSTING, EXHAUSTED** to make (a person or animal) very tired □ noun **EXHAUSTS** the escape of waste gases from an engine, etc

EXHAUSTED adj tired out

EXHAUSTING *adj* that causes extreme tiredness

EXHIBIT *noun* **EXHIBITS** an object displayed publicly, eg in a museum □ *verb* **EXHIBITS, EXHIBITING, EXHIBITED** to present or display something for public appreciation

EXHIBITOR *noun* **EXHIBITORS** a person who provides an exhibit for a public display

EXHORT *verb* **EXHORTS, EXHORTING, EXHORTED** to urge or advise someone strongly and sincerely

EXHUME *verb* **EXHUMES, EXHUMING, EXHUMED** to dig up (a body) from a grave

EXIGENCY *noun* **EXIGENCIES** urgent need

EXIGENT *adj* pressing; urgent

EXIGUITY *noun* **EXIGUITIES** scarceness or meagreness; insufficiency

EXIGUOUS *adj* scarce or meagre; insufficient

EXILE *noun* **EXILES** enforced or regretted absence from one's country or town, especially for a long time and often as a punishment □ *verb* **EXILES, EXILING, EXILED** to send someone into exile

EXIST *verb* **EXISTS, EXISTING, EXISTED** to be, especially to be present in the real world or universe rather than in story or imagination

EXISTENCE *noun* **EXISTENCES** the state of existing

EXISTENT *adj* having an actual being; existing

EXIT *noun* **EXITS** a way out of a building, etc □ *verb* **EXITS, EXITING, EXITED** to go out, leave or depart

EXOCARP *noun* **EXOCARPS** the outer layer of the epicarp

EXOCRINE *adj* relating to external secretions, or to a pathway or structure that secretes externally □ *noun* **EXOCRINES** an exocrine gland

EXODERM *noun* **EXODERMS** in a multicellular animal that has two or more layers of body tissue: the external germinal layer of epiblast of the embryo

EXODUS *noun* **EXODUSES** a mass departure of people

EXOGAMIC *adj* relating to exogamy

EXOGAMOUS *adj* marrying outside of one's own group

EXOGAMY *noun* **EXOGAMIES** the practice of marrying only outside of one's own group

EXOGENOUS *adj* originating outside a cell, organ or organism

EXON *noun* **EXONS** any segment of DNA in a gene that is transcribed into messenger RNA and then into protein

EXONERATE *verb* **EXONERATES, EXONERATING, EXONERATED** to free someone from blame, or acquit them of a criminal charge

EXORCISE *verb* **EXORCISES, EXORCISING, EXORCISED** to exorcize

EXORCISM *noun* **EXORCISMS** the act of exorcizing or expelling evil spirits by certain ceremonies

EXORCIST *noun* **EXORCISTS** a person who exorcizes or pretends to expel evil spirits by command

EXORCIZE *verb* **EXORCIZES, EXORCIZING, EXORCIZED** in some beliefs: to drive away (an evil spirit or influence) with prayer or holy words

EXOSPHERE *noun* **EXOSPHERES** the outermost layer of the Earth's atmosphere, which starts at an altitude of about 500km

EXOTIC *adj* introduced from a foreign country, especially a distant and tropical country □ *noun* **EXOTICS** an exotic person or thing

EXOTICA *plural noun* strange or rare objects

EXOTICISM *noun* **EXOTICISMS** a tendency to accept or adopt that which is foreign or exotic

EXPAND *verb* **EXPANDS, EXPANDING, EXPANDED** to make or become greater in size, extent or importance

EXPANDED *adj* said of plastic: combined with a gas during manufacture to produce a lightweight insulating or packaging material

EXPANDER *noun* **EXPANDERS** a device used for exercising and developing muscles

EXPANSE *noun* **EXPANSES** a wide area or space

EXPANSION *noun* **EXPANSIONS** the act or state of expanding

EXPANSIVE *adj* ready or eager to talk; open or effusive

EXPAT *noun* **EXPATS** a person living or working abroad

EXPATIATE *verb* **EXPATIATES,**

EXPATIATING, EXPATIATED to talk or write at length or in detail

EXPECT *verb* **EXPECTS, EXPECTING, EXPECTED** to think of something as likely to happen or come

EXPECTANT *adj* eagerly waiting; hopeful

EXPEDIENT *adj* suitable or appropriate □ *noun* **EXPEDIENTS** a suitable method or solution, especially one quickly thought of to meet an urgent need

EXPEDITE *verb* **EXPEDITES, EXPEDITING, EXPEDITED** to speed up, or assist the progress of something

EXPEL *verb* **EXPELS, EXPELLING, EXPELLED** to dismiss from or deprive someone of membership of (a club or school, etc), usually permanently as punishment for misconduct

EXPELLEE *noun* **EXPELLEES** a person who is expelled

EXPEND *verb* **EXPENDS, EXPENDING, EXPENDED** to use or spend (time, supplies or effort, etc)

EXPENSE *noun* **EXPENSES** the act of spending money, or the amount of money spent

EXPENSIVE *adj* involving much expense; costing a great deal

EXPERT *noun* **EXPERTS** someone with great skill in, or extensive knowledge of, a particular subject □ *adj* highly skilled or extremely knowledgeable

EXPERTISE *noun* **EXPERTISES** special skill or knowledge

EXPERTLY *adverb* in an expert way

EXPIABLE *adj* capable of being atoned for or done away with

EXPIATE *verb* **EXPIATES, EXPIATING, EXPIATED** to make amends for (a wrong)

EXPIATION *noun* **EXPIATIONS** the act of expiating; the means by which atonement is made

EXPIATOR *noun* **EXPIATORS** someone who expiates

EXPIATORY *adj* that expiates

EXPIRE *verb* **EXPIRES, EXPIRING, EXPIRED** to come to an end or cease to be valid

EXPIRY *noun* **EXPIRIES** the ending of the duration or validity of something

EXPLAIN *verb* **EXPLAINS, EXPLAINING, EXPLAINED** to make something clear or easy to understand

EXPLETIVE *noun* **EXPLETIVES** a

swear-word or curse □ *adj* being, or like, a swear-word or curse

EXPLICATE *verb* **EXPLICATES, EXPLICATING, EXPLICATED** to explain (especially a literary work) in depth, with close analysis of particular points

EXPLICIT *adj* stated or shown fully and clearly

EXPLODE *verb* **EXPLODES, EXPLODING, EXPLODED** said of a substance: to undergo an explosion

EXPLODED *adj* blown up

EXPLOIT *noun* **EXPLOITS** an act or feat, especially a bold or daring one □ *verb* **EXPLOITS, EXPLOITING, EXPLOITED** to take unfair advantage of something or someone so as to achieve one's own aims

EXPLOITER *noun* **EXPLOITERS** a person who exploits

EXPLORE *verb* **EXPLORES, EXPLORING, EXPLORED** to search or travel through (a place) for the purpose of discovery

EXPLORER *noun* **EXPLORERS** a person who explores unfamiliar territory, especially as a profession or habitually

EXPLOSION *noun* **EXPLOSIONS** a sudden and violent increase in pressure, which generates large amounts of heat and destructive shock waves that travel outward from the point of explosion and are heard as a loud bang

EXPLOSIVE *adj* likely, tending or able to explode □ *noun* **EXPLOSIVES** any substance that is capable of producing an explosion, especially one created to do so

EXPO *noun* **EXPOS** a large public exhibition

EXPONENT *noun* **EXPONENTS** someone able to perform some art or activity, especially skilfully

EXPORT *verb* **EXPORTS, EXPORTING, EXPORTED** to send or take (goods, etc) to another country, especially for sale □ *noun* **EXPORTS** the act or business of exporting

EXPORTER *noun* **EXPORTERS** a person or business that exports goods commercially

EXPOSAL *noun* **EXPOSALS** exposure; exposition

EXPOSE *verb* **EXPOSES, EXPOSING, EXPOSED** to remove cover, protection or shelter from

something, or to allow this to be the case

EXPOSÉ *noun* **EXPOSÉS** an article or programme which exposes a public scandal or crime, etc

EXPOSURE *noun* **EXPOSURES** the act of exposing or the state of being exposed

EXPOUND *verb* **EXPOUNDS, EXPOUNDING, EXPOUNDED** to explain something in depth

EXPOUNDER *noun* **EXPOUNDERS** someone who expounds

EXPRESS *verb* **EXPRESSES, EXPRESSING, EXPRESSED** to put something into words □ *adj* said of a train, etc: travelling especially fast, with few stops □ *noun* **EXPRESSES** an express train □ *adverb* by express delivery service

EXPRESSLY *adverb* clearly and definitely

EXPRESSO *noun* **EXPRESSOS** espresso

EXPULSION *noun* **EXPULSIONS** the act of expelling from school or a club, etc

EXPULSIVE *adj* having the power to expel or drive out

EXPUNGE *verb* **EXPUNGES, EXPUNGING, EXPUNGED** to cross out or delete something (eg a passage from a book)

EXPUNGER *noun* **EXPUNGERS** someone who expunges

EXPURGATE *verb* **EXPURGATES, EXPURGATING, EXPURGATED** to revise (a book) by removing objectionable or offensive words or passages

EXQUISITE *adj* extremely beautiful or skilfully produced

EXTANT *adj* still existing; surviving

EXTEMPORE *adj* without planning or preparation; off the cuff □ *adverb* without planning or preparation; off the cuff

EXTEND *verb* **EXTENDS, EXTENDING, EXTENDED** to make something longer or larger

EXTENSION *noun* **EXTENSIONS** the process of extending something, or the state of being extended

EXTENSIVE *adj* large in area, amount, range or effect

EXTENSOR *noun* **EXTENSORS** any of various muscles that straighten out parts of the body

EXTENT *noun* **EXTENTS** the area over which something extends

EXTENUATE *verb* **EXTENUATES, EXTENUATING, EXTENUATED** to

reduce the seriousness of (an offence) by giving an explanation that partly excuses it

EXTENUATING *adj* said especially of a circumstance: reducing the seriousness of an offence by partially excusing it

EXTERIOR *adj* on, from, or for use on the outside □ *noun* **EXTERIORS** an outside part or surface

EXTERNAL *adj* belonging to, for, from or on the outside □ *noun* **EXTERNALS** an outward appearance or feature, especially when superficial or insignificant

EXTINCT *adj* said of a species of animal, etc: no longer in existence

EXTIRPATE *verb* **EXTIRPATES, EXTIRPATING, EXTIRPATED** to destroy completely

EXTOL *verb* **EXTOLS, EXTOLLING, EXTOLLED** to praise enthusiastically

EXTOLLER *noun* **EXTOLLERS** someone who extols

EXTOLMENT *noun* **EXTOLMENTS** the act of extolling; the state of being extolled

EXTORT *verb* **EXTORTS, EXTORTING, EXTORTED** to obtain (money or information, etc) by threats or violence

EXTORTION *noun* **EXTORTIONS** illegal securing of money by compulsion or violence

EXTRA *adj* additional; more than is usual, necessary or expected □ *noun* **EXTRAS** an additional or unexpected thing □ *adverb* unusually or exceptionally

EXTRACT *verb* **EXTRACTS, EXTRACTING, EXTRACTED** to pull or draw something out, especially by force or with effort □ *noun* **EXTRACTS** a passage selected from a book, etc

EXTRACTOR *noun* **EXTRACTORS** a person or thing that extracts

EXTRADITE *verb* **EXTRADITES, EXTRADITING, EXTRADITED** to return (a person accused of a crime) for trial in the country where the crime was committed

EXTRADOS *noun* **EXTRADOSES** the outer or upper curve of an arch

EXTRAVERT *noun* **EXTRAVERTS** an extrovert □ *adj* extrovert

EXTREME *adj* **EXTREMER, EXTREMEST** very high, or highest, in degree or intensity □ *noun* **EXTREMES** either of two people or things as far, or as different, as possible from each other

EXTREMELY *adverb* to an extreme degree

EXTREMISM *noun* **EXTREMISMS** a tendency to favour extreme measures

EXTREMIST *adj* relating to, or favouring, extreme measures

EXTREMITY *noun* **EXTREMITIES** the furthest point

EXTRICATE *verb* **EXTRICATES, EXTRICATING, EXTRICATED** to free someone or something from difficulties; to disentangle

EXTRINSIC *adj* external

EXTROVERT *noun* **EXTROVERTS** someone who is more concerned with the outside world and social relationships than with their inner thoughts and feelings ▫ *adj* having the temperament of an extrovert; sociable or outgoing

EXTROVERTED *adj* concerned with the outside world and social relationships rather than with inner thoughts and feelings

EXTRUDE *verb* **EXTRUDES, EXTRUDING, EXTRUDED** to squeeze something or force it out

EXTRUDER *noun* **EXTRUDERS** a machine that extrudes

EXTRUSION *noun* **EXTRUSIONS** the act or process of extruding

EXUBERANT *adj* in very high spirits

EXUDATE *noun* **EXUDATES** any substance released from an organ or cell of a plant or animal to the exterior through a gland, pore, or membrane, eg resin and sweat

EXUDATION *noun* **EXUDATIONS** the act of exuding or discharging through pores

EXUDE *verb* **EXUDES, EXUDING, EXUDED** to give off or give out (an odour or sweat)

EXUL *noun* **EXULS** a Spenserian word meaning an exile

EXULT *verb* **EXULTS, EXULTING, EXULTED** to rejoice exceedingly

EXULTANT *adj* joyfully or triumphantly elated

EXURB *noun* **EXURBS** a prosperous residential area outside the suburbs of a town

EXURBAN *adj* belonging or relating to or situated in an exurb

EXURBIA *noun* **EXURBIAS** exurbs collectively

EXUVIAE *plural noun* cast-off skins, shells, or other coverings of animals

EXUVIAL *adj* relating to exuviae

EYE *noun* **EYES** the organ of vision, usually one of a pair ▫ *verb* **EYES, EYEING, EYED** to look at something carefully

EYEBALL *noun* **EYEBALLS** the nearly spherical body of the eye ▫ *verb* **EYEBALLS, EYEBALLING, EYEBALLED** to face someone; to confront them

EYEBOLT *noun* **EYEBOLTS** a bolt with an eye instead of the normal head, used for lifting or fastening

EYEBRIGHT *noun* **EYEBRIGHTS** a small annual plant with white flowers marked with purple, used in herbal medicine to treat sore eyes

EYEBROW *noun* **EYEBROWS** the arch of hair on the bony ridge above each eye

EYED *adj* having eyes of a specified kind

EYEFUL *noun* **EYEFULS** an interesting or beautiful sight

EYEGLASS *noun* **EYEGLASSES** a single lens in a frame, to assist weak sight

EYELASH *noun* **EYELASHES** any of the short protective hairs that grow from the edge of the upper and lower eyelids

EYELESS *adj* without eyes or sight

EYELET *noun* **EYELETS** a small hole in fabric, etc through which a lace, etc is passed

EYELID *noun* **EYELIDS** in many animals, including humans: a protective fold of skin and muscle, lined with a membrane, that can be moved to cover or uncover the front of the eyeball

EYELINER *noun* **EYELINERS** a cosmetic used to outline the eye

EYESHADE *noun* **EYESHADES** a visor

EYESHADOW *noun* **EYESHADOWS** a coloured cosmetic for the eyelids

EYESIGHT *noun* **EYESIGHTS** the ability to see; power of vision

EYESORE *noun* **EYESORES** an ugly thing, especially a building

EYESTRAIN *noun* **EYESTRAINS** tiredness or irritation of the eyes

EYRIE *noun* **EYRIES** the nest of an eagle or other bird of prey, built in a high inaccessible place

FA noun **FAS** fah

FAB adj **FABBER, FABBEST** fabulous

FABLE noun **FABLES** a story with a moral, usually with animals as characters □ verb **FABLES, FABLING, FABLED** to tell fictitious tales

FABLED adj made famous by legend

FABLER noun **FABLERS** someone who writes fables

FABRIC noun **FABRICS** woven, knitted or felted cloth

FABRICATE verb **FABRICATES, FABRICATING, FABRICATED** to invent or make up (a story, evidence, etc)

FABULIST noun **FABULISTS** someone who invents fables

FABULOUS adj marvellous; wonderful; excellent

FAÇADE noun **FAÇADES** the front of a building

FACE noun **FACES** the front part of the head, from forehead to chin □ verb **FACES, FACING, FACED** to be opposite to something or someone; to turn to look at or look in some direction

FACED adj having a face

FACELESS adj without a face

FACER noun **FACERS** a tool for smoothing or adding a facing to a surface

FACET noun **FACETS** any of the faces of a cut jewel □ verb **FACETS, FACETING, FACETED** to cut a facet on (a jewel)

FACETIOUS adj said of a person or remark, etc: intending or intended to be amusing or witty, especially unsuitably so

FACIA noun **FACIAS** a fascia

FACIAL adj belonging or relating to the face □ noun **FACIALS** a beauty treatment for the face

FACIALLY adverb as regards the face

FACIES noun **FACIES** the general form and appearance, especially of plant, animal or geological species or formations

FACILE adj **FACILER, FACILEST** said of success, etc: too easily achieved

FACILELY adverb in a facile way

FACILITY noun **FACILITIES** skill, talent or ability

FACING noun **FACINGS** an outer layer, eg of stone covering a brick wall

FACSIMILE noun **FACSIMILES** an exact copy made, eg of a manuscript, picture, etc □ verb **FACSIMILES, FACSIMILEING, FACSIMILED** to make an exact copy of something

FACT noun **FACTS** a thing known to be true, to exist or to have happened

FACTION noun **FACTIONS** an active or trouble-making group within a larger organization

FACTIONAL adj of or belonging to a faction or factions

FACTIOUS adj turbulent; quarrelsome

FACTITIVE adj in grammar: denoting a verb which can take both a direct object and a complement, eg the verb *made* in *made him president*

FACTOID noun **FACTOIDS** a statement which is not (or may not be) true but has achieved acceptance by its appearance or frequent repetition in print

FACTOR noun **FACTORS** a circumstance that contributes to a result; the manager of an estate □ verb **FACTORS, FACTORING, FACTORED** to act as a factor (on someone's behalf)

FACTORIAL noun **FACTORIALS** the number resulting when a whole number and all whole numbers below it are multiplied together □ adj relating to a factorial

FACTORISE verb **FACTORISES, FACTORISING, FACTORISED** to factorize

FACTORIZE verb **FACTORIZES, FACTORIZING, FACTORIZED** to find the factors of (a number)

FACTORY noun **FACTORIES** a building or buildings with

equipment for the large-scale manufacture of goods

FACTOTUM noun **FACTOTUMS** a person employed to do a large number of different jobs

FACTUAL adj concerned with, or based on, facts

FACULTY noun **FACULTIES** any of the range of mental or physical powers

FAD noun **FADS** a shortlived fashion; a craze

FADDINESS noun **FADDINESSES** the quality of having many (often unusual) likes and dislikes where food is concerned

FADDISH adj fussy, especially with regard to food

FADDY adj **FADDIER, FADDIEST** having many (often unusual) likes and dislikes where food is concerned

FADE verb **FADES, FADING, FADED** to lose or cause to lose strength, freshness or colour

FAECAL adj of or relating to faeces

FAECES plural noun the solid waste matter discharged from the body through the anus

FAFF verb **FAFFS, FAFFING, FAFFED** to act in a fussy, uncertain way, not achieving very much; to dither

FAG noun **FAGS** a cigarette □ verb **FAGS, FAGGING, FAGGED** to tire someone out; to exhaust someone

FAGGOT noun **FAGGOTS** a ball or roll of chopped pork and liver mixed with breadcrumbs and herbs, and eaten fried or baked

FAGOT noun **FAGOTS** a faggot

FAH noun **FAHS** in sol-fa notation: the fourth note of the major scale

FAIENCE noun **FAIENCES** glazed decorated pottery

FAIL verb **FAILS, FAILING, FAILED** not to succeed; to be unsuccessful in (an undertaking) □ noun **FAILS** a failure, especially in an exam

FAILING noun **FAILINGS** a fault; a weakness □ adj referring to something that is in the process of failing □ prep if … is impossible or does not happen

FAILURE noun **FAILURES** the act of failing; lack of success

FAIN adj **FAINER, FAINEST** glad or joyful ▫ adverb gladly; willingly

FAINT adj **FAINTER, FAINTEST** pale; dim; indistinct; slight ▫ verb **FAINTS, FAINTING, FAINTED** to lose consciousness; to collapse ▫ noun **FAINTS** a sudden loss of consciousness

FAINTLY adverb in a faint way

FAINTNESS noun **FAINTNESSES** lack of strength; feebleness of colour, light, etc

FAIR [1] adj **FAIRER, FAIREST** just; not using dishonest methods or discrimination ▫ adverb in a fair way

FAIR [2] noun **FAIRS** a collection of sideshows and amusements, often set up temporarily on open ground and travelling from place to place

FAIRING noun **FAIRINGS** an external structure fitted to an aircraft, vessel or other vehicle to improve streamlining and reduce drag

FAIRLY adverb justly; honestly; quite, rather

FAIRNESS noun **FAIRNESSES** the quality or condition of being fair

FAIRWAY noun **FAIRWAYS** in golf: a broad strip of short grass extending from the tee to the green, distinguished from the uncut rough, and from hazards

FAIRY noun **FAIRIES** any of various supernatural beings with magical powers, generally of diminutive and graceful human form, common in folklore ▫ adj like a fairy; fanciful or whimsical; delicate

FAIRYLAND noun **FAIRYLANDS** the home of fairies

FAIRYLIKE adj like fairies or like something in fairyland ▫ adverb like fairies or like something in fairyland

FAITH noun **FAITHS** trust or confidence

FAITHFUL adj having or showing faith ▫ plural noun the believers in a particular religion, especially Islam

FAITHLESS adj disloyal; treacherous

FAKE noun **FAKES** someone or something, or an act that is not genuine ▫ adj not genuine; false; counterfeit ▫ verb **FAKES, FAKING, FAKED** to alter something dishonestly; to falsify something or make something up

FAKERY noun **FAKERIES** the act of faking

FAKIR noun **FAKIRS** a wandering Hindu or Muslim holy man depending on begging for survival

FALAFEL noun **FALAFELS** a felafel

FALAJ noun **AFLAJ** a water channel in the ancient irrigation system of Oman

FALCATE adj shaped like a sickle

FALCIFORM adj falcate

FALCON noun **FALCONS** a type of long-winged bird of prey that can be trained to hunt for sport

FALCONER noun **FALCONERS** someone who sports with, or breeds and trains, falcons or hawks for hunting small birds and animals

FALCONRY noun **FALCONRIES** the art or practice of breeding and training falcons for hunting

FALDERAL noun **FALDERALS** a meaningless refrain in songs

FALDSTOOL noun **FALDSTOOLS** a bishop's armless seat, used when officiating at their own church away from their throne, or at another church

FALL verb **FALLS, FALLING, FELL, FALLEN** to descend or drop freely and involuntarily, especially accidentally, by force of gravity ▫ noun **FALLS** an act or way of falling

FALLACY noun **FALLACIES** a mistaken notion

FALLEN adj having lost one's virtue, honour or reputation

FALLIBLE adj capable of making mistakes

FALLIBLY adverb in a fallible way

FALLOUT noun **FALLOUTS** a cloud of radioactive dust caused by a nuclear explosion

FALLOW adj **FALLOWER, FALLOWEST** said of land: left unplanted after ploughing, to recover its natural fertility ▫ noun **FALLOWS** land that has been left for a year or more unsown after having been ploughed ▫ verb **FALLOWS, FALLOWING, FALLOWED** to plough land without seeding

FALSE adj **FALSER, FALSEST** untrue; mistaken; insincere ▫ adverb in a false manner; incorrectly; dishonestly

FALSEHOOD noun **FALSEHOODS** dishonesty

FALSELY adj in a false way

FALSENESS noun **FALSENESSES** the quality of being false

FALSETTO noun **FALSETTOS** an artificially high voice, especially produced by a tenor above his normal range

FALSIES plural noun pads of rubber or other material inserted into a bra to exaggerate the size of the breasts

FALSIFIER noun **FALSIFIERS** someone who falsifies

FALSIFY verb **FALSIFIES, FALSIFYING, FALSIFIED** to alter something dishonestly or make something up, in order to deceive or mislead

FALSITY noun **FALSITIES** the quality of being false; a false assertion

FALTER verb **FALTERS, FALTERING, FALTERED** to move unsteadily; to stumble

FAME noun **FAMES** the condition of being famous; celebrity

FAMED adj famous; renowned

FAMILIAL adj belonging to, typical of, or occurring in, a family

FAMILIAR adj well known or recognizable ▫ noun **FAMILIARS** a close friend

FAMILY noun **FAMILIES** a group consisting of a set of parents and children

FAMINE noun **FAMINES** a severe general shortage of food, usually caused by a population explosion or failure of food crops

FAMISHED adj very hungry; starving

FAMOUS adj well known; celebrated; renowned

FAMOUSLY adverb in a famous or celebrated way

FAN noun **FANS** a hand-held device made of paper, silk, etc, usually semicircular and folding flat when not in use, for creating a current of air to cool the face ▫ verb **FANS, FANNING, FANNED** to cool something or someone by blowing a current of air onto it or them, with or as if with a fan

FANATIC noun **FANATICS** someone with an extreme or excessive enthusiasm for something, especially a religion, or religious issues ▫ adj fanatical

FANATICAL adj excessively enthusiastic about something

FANCIABLE adj of a person: sexually attractive

FANCIER noun **FANCIERS** someone with a special interest in something, especially a breeder of a certain kind of bird or animal, or a grower of a certain kind of plant

FANCIFUL adj indulging in fancies; imaginative or over-imaginative

FANCY noun **FANCIES** the imagination ◻ adj **FANCIER, FANCIEST** elaborate ◻ verb **FANCIES, FANCYING, FANCIED** to think or believe something ◻ exclamation expressing surprise

FANCYWORK noun **FANCYWORKS** fine decorative needlework

FANDANGLE noun **FANDANGLES** elaborate ornament; nonsense

FANDANGO noun **FANDANGOS** an energetic Spanish dance

FANFARE noun **FANFARES** a short piece of music played on trumpets to announce an important event or arrival

FANFOLD adj said of paper: scored or perforated so as to fall flat in sections, one sheet on top of the other, used for computer print-outs

FANG noun **FANGS** the pointed canine tooth of a carnivorous animal

FANGED adj having fangs or anything resembling them

FANGLESS adj without fangs

FANLIGHT noun **FANLIGHTS** a semicircular window over a door or window, usually found in Georgian and Regency buildings

FANNINGS plural noun the tiny pieces of tea leaves which are sifted out of tea

FANTAIL noun **FANTAILS** a tail shaped like a fan

FANTASIA noun **FANTASIAS** a musical composition that is free and unconventional in form

FANTASISE verb **FANTASISES, FANTASISING, FANTASISED** to fantasize

FANTASIST noun **FANTASISTS** a person who creates or indulges in fantasies

FANTASIZE verb **FANTASIZES, FANTASIZING, FANTASIZED** to indulge in pleasurable fantasies or daydreams

FANTASTIC adj splendid; excellent

FANTASY noun **FANTASIES** a pleasant daydream; something longed-for but unlikely to happen

FANZINE noun **FANZINES** a magazine written, published and distributed by and for supporters of football, or amateur enthusiasts of science fiction, pop music, etc

FAP adj a Shakespearean word meaning *fuddled* or *drunk*

FAR adverb at, to or from a great distance ◻ adj distant; remote

FARAD noun **FARADS** the SI unit of electrical capacitance, defined as the capacitance of a capacitor in which a charge of one coulomb produces a potential difference of one volt between its terminals

FARADAY noun **FARADAYS** a unit of electrical charge

FARADIC adj referring or relating to the laws or theories of Michael Faraday

FARANDOLE noun **FARANDOLES** a Provençal folk dance, usually in 6/8 time

FARAWAY adj distant

FARCE noun **FARCES** a comedy involving a series of ridiculously unlikely turns of events

FARCEUR noun **FARCEURS** a male joker

FARCEUSE noun **FARCEUSES** a female joker

FARCICAL adj resembling a farce; ludicrous

FARE noun **FARES** the price paid by a passenger to travel on a bus, train, etc ◻ verb **FARES, FARING, FARED** to get on (in a specified way)

FAREWELL exclamation goodbye! ◻ noun **FAREWELLS** an act of saying goodbye; an act of departure ◻ adj parting; valedictory; final

FARINA noun **FARINAS** flour; meal

FARM noun **FARMS** a piece of land with its buildings, used for growing crops or breeding and keeping livestock ◻ verb **FARMS, FARMING, FARMED** to prepare and use (land) for crop-growing, animal-rearing, etc; to be a farmer

FARMER noun **FARMERS** someone who earns a living by managing or operating a farm, either as owner or tenant

FARMHOUSE noun **FARMHOUSES** the farmer's house on a farm

FARMING noun **FARMINGS** the business of running a farm by growing crops and/or raising livestock for sale

FARMOST adj most distant or most remote

FARMSTEAD noun **FARMSTEADS** a farmhouse and the buildings round it

FARMYARD noun **FARMYARDS** the central yard at a farm, surrounded by farm buildings

FARNESS noun **FARNESSES** the state or condition of being far away

FARO noun **FAROS** a game of chance played by betting on the order of appearance of certain cards taken singly from the top of the pack

FAROUCHE adj shy

FARRAGO noun **FARRAGOES** a confused mixture; a hotchpotch

FARRIER noun **FARRIERS** a person who shoes horses

FARRIERY noun **FARRIERIES** the art or work of a farrier

FARROW noun **FARROWS** a sow's litter of piglets ◻ verb **FARROWS, FARROWING, FARROWED** said of a sow: to give birth to (piglets)

FARTHER adj further (with reference to physical distance) ◻ adverb further (with reference to physical distance)

FARTHEST adj furthest (with reference to physical distance) ◻ adverb furthest (with reference to physical distance)

FARTHING noun **FARTHINGS** one quarter of an old British penny

FARTLEK noun **FARTLEKS** alternate fast and slow running, done as training for marathons and other long-distance races

FASCES plural noun a bundle of rods with an axe in the middle, carried before magistrates as a symbol of authority

FASCIA noun **FASCIAS** the board above a shop entrance, bearing the shop name and logo, etc

FASCIAL adj relating to the connective tissue sheathing a muscle or organ

FASCICLE noun **FASCICLES** a fascicule

FASCICULE noun **FASCICULES** one part of a book published in separate parts

FASCINATE verb **FASCINATES, FASCINATING, FASCINATED** to interest strongly; to intrigue

FASCINATING adj intriguing; deeply interesting

FASCINE noun **FASCINES** a bundle of brushwood, used to fill ditches or trenches, protect a shore, etc, in order to hold back an attack

FASCISM noun **FASCISMS** a

political movement or system characterized mainly by a belief in the supremacy of the chosen national group over all others, and in which there is, typically, state control of all aspects of society, a supreme dictator, suppression of democratic bodies such as trade unions and emphasis on nationalism and militarism

FASCIST noun **FASCISTS** an exponent or supporter of Fascism or (loosely) anyone with extreme right-wing nationalistic, etc views □ adj belonging or relating to Fascism

FASCISTIC adj belonging or relating to Fascism

FASHION noun **FASHIONS** style, especially the latest style, in clothes, music, lifestyle, etc, particularly that which prevails among those whose lead is accepted □ verb **FASHIONS, FASHIONING, FASHIONED** to form or make something into a particular shape, especially with the hands

FASHIONER noun **FASHIONERS** a maker or creator

FAST¹ adj **FASTER, FASTEST** moving, or able to move, quickly □ adverb quickly; rapidly

FAST² verb **FASTS, FASTING, FASTED** to go without food, or restrict one's diet, especially as a religious discipline □ noun **FASTS** a period of fasting

FASTBACK noun **FASTBACKS** a type of car whose roof slopes smoothly down towards the rear, giving a streamlined effect

FASTBALL noun **FASTBALLS** in baseball: a high-speed, rising delivery of the ball from the pitcher

FASTEN verb **FASTENS, FASTENING, FASTENED** to make something firmly closed or fixed

FASTENER noun **FASTENERS** a device that fastens something; a clasp or catch

FASTENING noun **FASTENINGS** a device that fastens something; a clasp or catch

FASTER noun **FASTERS** a person who fasts

FASTING noun **FASTINGS** religious abstinence from food

FASTISH adj somewhat fast

FASTNESS noun **FASTNESSES** the quality of being firmly fixed or, with reference to fabric colours, not liable to run or fade

FAT noun **FATS** any of a group of organic compounds that occur naturally in animals and plants, are solid at room temperature, and are insoluble in water □ adj **FATTER, FATTEST** having too much fat on the body; plump; overweight □ verb **FATS, FATTING, FATTED** to fatten something

FATAL adj causing death; deadly

FATALISM noun **FATALISMS** the philosophical doctrine that all events are controlled by fate, and happen by unavoidable necessity, so that humans cannot control them

FATALIST noun **FATALISTS** a person who believes in fatalism

FATALITY noun **FATALITIES** an accidental or violent death

FATALLY adverb with death as the result

FATE noun **FATES** the apparent power that determines the course of events, over which humans have no control

FATED adj destined or intended by fate

FATEFUL adj said of a remark, etc: prophetic

FATEFULLY adverb in a fateful way

FATHER noun **FATHERS** a male parent □ verb **FATHERS, FATHERING, FATHERED** to be the father of (a child); to beget (offspring); to procreate

FATHERLY adj benevolent, protective and encouraging, as a father ideally is to a child

FATHOM noun **FATHOMS** in the imperial system: a unit of measurement of the depth of water, equal to 6ft (1.8m) □ verb **FATHOMS, FATHOMING, FATHOMED** to work out a problem; to get to the bottom of a mystery

FATIGABLE adj capable of being fatigued; easily fatigued

FATIGUE noun **FATIGUES** tiredness after work or effort, either mental or physical; exhaustion □ verb **FATIGUES, FATIGUING, FATIGUED** to exhaust or become exhausted

FATLY adverb grossly; lumberingly

FATNESS noun **FATNESSES** the quality or state of being fat

FATSIA noun **FATSIAS** an evergreen spreading shrub of the ivy family, with leathery leaves and clusters of white flowers in the form of umbels

FATTEN verb **FATTENS, FATTENING, FATTENED** to make or become fat

FATTENER noun **FATTENERS** something that makes fat

FATTENING adj that makes fat □ noun **FATTENINGS** growing fat

FATTINESS noun **FATINESSES** the state or condition of containing a lot of fat

FATTISH adj somewhat fat

FATTY adj **FATTIER, FATTIEST** containing fat □ noun **FATTIES** a fat person

FATUITOUS adj showing fatuity

FATUITY noun **FATUITIES** foolishness; stupidity

FATUOUS adj foolish, especially in a self-satisfied way; empty-headed; inane

FATWA noun **FATWAS** a formal legal opinion or decree issued by a Muslim authority

FATWAH noun **FATWAHS** a fatwa

FAUBOURG noun **FAUBOURGS** a suburb just beyond the city walls, or a district recently included within a city

FAUCES noun **FAUCES** the upper part of the throat between the back of the mouth and the pharynx

FAUCET noun **FAUCETS** a tap fitted to a barrel

FAULT noun **FAULTS** a weakness or failing; a flaw or defect; a misdeed or slight offence □ verb **FAULTS, FAULTING, FAULTED** to commit a fault

FAULTILY adverb in a faulty way

FAULTLESS adj perfect; without fault or defect

FAULTY adj **FAULTIER, FAULTIEST** having a fault or faults

FAUN noun **FAUNS** a mythical creature with a man's head and body and a goat's horns, hind legs and tail

FAUNA noun **FAUNAS, FAUNAE** the wild animals of a particular region, country, or time period

FAUNAL adj of or relating to fauna

FAUTEUIL noun **FAUTEUILS** an armchair

FAVELA noun **FAVELAS** especially in Brazil: a shanty town

FAVOR noun **FAVORS** a favour □ verb **FAVORS, FAVORING, FAVORED** to favour

FAVORABLE adj showing or giving agreement or consent

FAVORED adj favoured

FAVORITE adj favourite □ noun **FAVORITES** a favourite

FAVOUR noun **FAVOURS** a kind or helpful action performed out of goodwill □ *verb* **FAVOURS, FAVOURING, FAVOURED** to regard someone or something with goodwill

FAVOURED *adj* enjoying favour or preferential treatment

FAVOURER *noun* **FAVOURERS** someone who supports or promotes a project, opinion, etc

FAVOURITE *adj* best-liked; preferred □ *noun* **FAVOURITES** a favourite person or thing

FAW *noun* **FAWS** a gypsy

FAWN *noun* **FAWNS** a young deer of either sex □ *adj* having the colour of a fawn; beige □ *verb* **FAWNS, FAWNING, FAWNED** said of deer: to give birth to young

FAWNER *noun* **FAWNERS** a person who flatters to gain favour

FAWNING *noun* **FAWNINGS** servile flattery □ *adj* showing servile flattery

FAWNINGLY *adverb* in a fawning way

FAX *noun* **FAXES** a machine that scans documents electronically and transmits a photographic image of the contents to a receiving machine by telephone line □ *verb* **FAXES, FAXING, FAXED** to transmit a photographic image of (a document) using a fax machine

FAY *noun* **FAYS** a fairy

FAYRE *noun* **FAYRES** a fair

FAZE *verb* **FAZES, FAZING, FAZED** to disturb, worry or fluster

FAZENDA *noun* **FAZENDAS** especially in Brazil: a large estate, plantation or cattle ranch

FEALTY *noun* **FEALTIES** the loyalty sworn by a vassal or tenant to his feudal lord

FEAR *noun* **FEARS** anxiety and distress caused by the awareness of danger or expectation of pain □ *verb* **FEARS, FEARING, FEARED** to be afraid of someone or something

FEARFUL *adj* afraid

FEARFULLY *adj* in a fearful way

FEARLESS *adj* without fear; brave

FEARSOME *adj* causing fear

FEASIBLE *adj* capable of being done or achieved; possible

FEASIBLY *adverb* in a feasible way

FEAST *noun* **FEASTS** a large rich meal, eg to celebrate some occasion □ *verb* **FEASTS, FEASTING, FEASTED** to take part in a feast, ie to eat and drink a lot

FEASTER *noun* **FEASTERS** a guest at a feast

FEASTING *noun* **FEASTINGS** the act of taking part in a feast

FEAT *noun* **FEATS** a deed or achievement, especially a remarkable one requiring extraordinary strength, skill or courage

FEATHER *noun* **FEATHERS** any of the light growths that form the soft covering of a bird □ *verb* **FEATHERS, FEATHERING, FEATHERED** to provide, cover or line with feathers

FEATHERED *adj* covered or fitted with feathers or something featherlike

FEATHERING *noun* **FEATHERINGS** plumage

FEATHERY *adj* **FEATHERIER, FEATHERIEST** relating to, resembling, or covered with feathers or an appearance of feathers

FEATURE *noun* **FEATURES** any of the parts of the face, eg eyes, nose, mouth, etc; a characteristic □ *verb* **FEATURES, FEATURING, FEATURED** to have as a feature or make a feature of something

FEATURED *adj* said of an actor, etc: prominent in a particular film, etc

FEBRIFUGE *noun* **FEBRIFUGES** a medicine, treatment, etc that reduces fever

FEBRILE *adj* relating to fever; feverish

FECAL *adj* faecal

FECES *plural noun* faeces

FECKLESS *adj* helpless; clueless

FECULENCE *noun* **FECULENCES** foulness

FECULENT *adj* containing or consisting of faeces or sediment; foul; turbid

FECUND *adj* fruitful; fertile; richly productive

FECUNDATE *verb* **FECUNDATES, FECUNDATING, FECUNDATED** to make something fruitful or fertile; to impregnate

FECUNDITY *noun* **FECUNDITIES** fruitfulness, fertility

FED [1] *noun* **FEDS** US slang for a Federal Agent

FED [2] past form of **feed** [1]

FEDAYEE *noun* **FEDAYEEN** an Arab commando or guerilla fighter, especially one involved in the conflict against Israel

FEDERAL *adj* belonging or relating to a country consisting of a group of states independent in local matters but united under a central government for other purposes, eg defence, foreign policy

FEDERATE *verb* **FEDERATES, FEDERATING, FEDERATED** to unite to form a federation □ *adj* united by a federal union; federated

FEDORA *noun* **FEDORAS** a brimmed felt hat, dented lengthways

FEE *noun* **FEES** a charge made for professional services, eg by a doctor or lawyer □ *verb* **FEES, FEEING, FEED** to pay a fee to someone

FEEBLE *adj* **FEEBLER, FEEBLEST** lacking strength; weak

FEEBLY *adverb* in a feeble way

FEED [1] *verb* **FEEDS, FEEDING, FED** to give or supply food to (animals, etc) □ *noun* **FEEDS** an act or session of feeding

FEED [2] past form of **fee**

FEEDBACK *noun* **FEEDBACKS** responses and reactions to an inquiry or report, etc that provide guidelines for adjustment and development

FEEDER *noun* **FEEDERS** a person, especially a baby or animal, with particular eating habits

FEEDING *noun* **FEEDINGS** the act of giving food

FEEDSTOCK *noun* **FEEDSTOCKS** raw material used in an industrial process or machine

FEEL *verb* **FEELS, FEELING, FELT** to become aware of something through the sense of touch □ *noun* **FEELS** a sensation or impression produced by touching

FEELER *noun* **FEELERS** a tentacle

FEELGOOD *adj* reinforcing or associated with pleasant feelings of comfort, security, etc

FEELING *noun* **FEELINGS** the sense of touch, a sensation or emotion □ *adj* sensitive; sympathetic

FEELINGLY *adverb* with sincerity resulting from experience

FEET plural of **foot**

FEIGN *verb* **FEIGNS, FEIGNING, FEIGNED** to pretend to have (eg an illness) or feel (an emotion, etc); to invent

FEIGNED *adj* pretended

FEIGNING *noun* **FEIGNINGS** an instance of pretending

FEINT [1] *noun* **FEINTS** said in

boxing, fencing or other sports: a mock attack; a movement intended to deceive or distract one's opponent □ verb **FEINTS, FEINTING, FEINTED** to make a feint, eg a mock attack

FEINT ² adj said of paper: ruled with pale, fine horizontal lines to guide writing

FEISTY adj **FEISTIER, FEISTIEST** spirited; lively

FELAFEL noun **FELAFELS** a deep-fried ball of ground chick-peas, with onions, peppers, etc and spices, usually served in a roll or a round of pitta bread

FELDSPAR noun **FELDSPARS** any of a large group of rock-forming minerals, mainly aluminium silicates, found in most igneous and many metamorphic rocks, eg orthoclase, plagioclase

FELICIA noun **FELICIAS** any member of a S African genus of the daisy family, with blue or lilac flowers

FELICITY noun **FELICITIES** happiness

FELINE adj relating to the cat or cat family, eg cats, lions, leopards, cheetahs □ noun **FELINES** any animal of the cat family; a cat

FELL ¹ verb **FELLS, FELLING, FELLED** to cut down (a tree) □ noun **FELLS** a quantity of timber felled at one time

FELL ² adj **FELLER, FELLEST** destructive; deadly

FELL ³ past form of **fall**

FELLABLE adj that may be felled

FELLAH noun **FELLAHS, FELLAHIN** a peasant in Arabic-speaking countries, especially in Egypt

FELLER noun **FELLERS** a fellow

FELLOW noun **FELLOWS** a companion or equal

FELON noun **FELONS** a person guilty of felony

FELONIOUS adj involving or constituting felony

FELONY noun **FELONIES** a serious crime

FELSPAR noun **FELSPARS** feldspar

FELT ¹ noun **FELTS** a fabric formed by matting or pressing together wool fibres, rather than by weaving, using the natural tendency of the fibres to cling together □ verb **FELTS, FELTING, FELTED** to make into felt; to mat

FELT ² past form of **feel**

FELTING noun **FELTINGS** the art or process of making felt or matting fibres together

FEMALE adj belonging or relating to the sex that gives birth to young, produces eggs, etc □ noun **FEMALES** a woman or girl

FEMININE adj typically belonging or relating to, or characteristic of, a woman □ noun **FEMININES** the feminine gender

FEMINISE verb **FEMINISES, FEMINISING, FEMINISED** to feminize

FEMINISM noun **FEMINISMS** a belief or movement advocating the cause of women's rights and opportunities, particularly equal rights with men, by challenging inequalities between the sexes in society

FEMINIST noun **FEMINISTS** a person who adheres to the tenets of feminism □ adj relating to feminism

FEMINIZE verb **FEMINIZES, FEMINIZING, FEMINIZED** to make or become feminine

FEMME noun **FEMMES** someone who is dressed up in a particularly feminine way □ adj said especially of lesbians: dressed in a particularly feminine way

FEMORAL adj belonging or relating to, or in the region of, the femur or the thigh

FEMUR noun **FEMURS** the longest and largest bone of the human skeleton, the upper end of which articulates with the hip joint, and the lower end with the knee joint

FEN noun **FENS** a waterlogged area of lowland dominated by grasses, sedges and rushes, having an alkaline soil

FENCE noun **FENCES** a barrier eg of wood or wire, for enclosing or protecting land □ verb **FENCES, FENCING, FENCED** to enclose with a fence, or as if with a fence

FENCELESS adj without a fence or enclosure, open

FENCER noun **FENCERS** someone who builds fences

FENCIBLE noun **FENCIBLES** a volunteer enlisted to defend their country

FENCING noun **FENCINGS** the art, act or sport of attack and defence with a foil, épée or sabre

FEND verb **FENDS, FENDING, FENDED** to defend oneself from (blows, questions, etc)

FENDER noun **FENDERS** a low guard fitted round a fireplace to keep ash, coals, etc within the hearth

FENESTRA noun **FENESTRAS** a window or other wall opening

FENESTRAL adj of or like a window

FENI noun **FENIS** an alcoholic spirit produced in Goa from coconuts or cashew nuts

FENKS plural noun the fibrous parts of the blubber of a whale, forming the refuse when the oil has been melted out

FENLAND noun **FENLANDS** a fen

FENMAN noun **FENMEN** someone who lives in fen country

FENNEC noun **FENNECS** a little African fox with large ears

FENNEL noun **FENNELS** a strong-smelling, yellow-flowered, umbelliferous plant, whose seeds and leaves are used in cooking

FENNY adj **FENNIER, FENNIEST** marshy; boggy

FENUGREEK noun **FENUGREEKS** a white-flowered leguminous plant with strong-smelling seeds, native to SW Asia and the Mediterranean region and widely cultivated in India, grown as animal fodder and also used in curries and salads

FEOFF verb **FEOFFS, FEOFFING, FEOFFED** to grant possession (of a fief or property) in land

FEOFFEE noun **FEOFFEES** the person invested with the fief

FEOFFER noun **FEOFFERS** the person who grants the fief

FEOFFMENT noun **FEOFFMENTS** the gift of a fief

FEOFFOR noun **FEOFFORS** a feoffer

FERAL adj said of animals normally found in a domestic situation or in captivity: wild; fending for itself

FERETORY noun **FERETORIES** a shrine for relics of saints, often carried in processions

FERIAL adj relating to any day of the week which is neither a fast nor a festival

FERMATA noun **FERMATAS** a pause

FERMENT noun **FERMENTS** a substance that causes something to ferment, such as a bacterium, yeast or mould □ verb **FERMENTS, FERMENTING, FERMENTED** to undergo or make something undergo fermentation, a biochemical process in which micro-organisms break down an organic compound, usually a carbohydrate, in the absence of oxygen, eg the conversion of sugar into alcohol

FERMENTED *adj* having undergone fermentation

FERMI *noun* **FERMIS** a unit of length equal to 10^{-5} angstrom, or 10^{-15} metres

FERMION *noun* **FERMIONS** one of a group of subatomic particles

FERMIUM *noun* **FERMIUMS** an artificially produced metallic radioactive element

FERN *noun* **FERNS** a flowerless feathery-leaved plant that reproduces by spores rather than seeds

FERNBIRD *noun* **FERNBIRDS** a small brown and white New Zealand bird with fern-like tail feathers

FERNY *adj* **FERNIER, FERNIEST** belonging or relating to, or resembling, a fern

FEROCIOUS *adj* savagely fierce; cruel; savage

FEROCITY *noun* **FEROCITIES** a fierce or cruel temperament

FERRATE *noun* **FERRATES** a salt of ferric acid

FERREL *noun* **FERRELS** a ferrule

FERRET *noun* **FERRETS** a small, half-tame, albino type of polecat, used for driving rabbits and rats from their holes ◻ *verb* **FERRETS, FERRETING, FERRETED** to hunt (rabbits, etc) with a ferret

FERRETER *noun* **FERRETERS** someone who ferrets

FERRETY *adj* like a ferret

FERRIAGE *noun* **FERRIAGES** transportation by ferry

FERRIC *adj* referring or relating to iron

FERRIES plural of **ferry**

FERRITE *noun* **FERRITES** any of a class of ceramic materials composed of oxides of iron and some other metal, eg copper, nickel, etc, that have magnetic properties and a low electrical conductivity, and are used in loudspeaker magnets, tape-recorder heads, etc

FERROUS *adj* belonging or relating to iron

FERRULE *noun* **FERRULES** a metal ring or cap for protecting the tip of a walking-stick or umbrella

FERRY *noun* **FERRIES** a boat that carries passengers and often cars across a river or strip of water, especially as a regular service ◻ *verb* **FERRIES, FERRYING, FERRIED** to transport or go by ferry

FERRYMAN *noun* **FERRYMEN** someone who conveys passengers by ferry

FERTILE *adj* **FERTILER, FERTILEST** said of land, soil, etc: containing the nutrients required to support an abundant growth of crops, plants, etc

FERTILELY *adverb* in a fertile way

FERTILISE *verb* **FERTILISES, FERTILISING, FERTILISED** to fertilize

FERTILITY *noun* **FERTILITIES** fruitfulness; richness; abundance

FERTILIZE *verb* **FERTILIZES, FERTILIZING, FERTILIZED** said of a male gamete, especially a sperm cell: to fuse with (a female gamete, especially an egg cell) to form a zygote

FERULE *noun* **FERULES** a cane or rod formerly used for punishment

FERVENCY *noun* **FERVENCIES** heat; eagerness; emotional warmth

FERVENT *adj* **FERVENTER, FERVENTEST** enthusiastic; earnest or ardent

FERVENTLY *adverb* in a fervent way

FERVID *adj* **FERVIDER, FERVIDEST** fervent; full of fiery passion or zeal

FERVIDITY *noun* **FERVIDITIES** intense heat; passion or zeal

FERVIDLY *adverb* in a fervid way

FERVOUR *noun* **FERVOURS** passionate enthusiasm; intense eagerness or sincerity

FESCUE *noun* **FESCUES** a tufted grass with inrolled bristle-like leaves, which forms much of the turf on chalk downs

FESS [1] *verb* **FESSES, FESSING, FESSED** to confess to having committed a crime

FESS [2] *noun* **FESSES** a fesse

FESSE *noun* **FESSES** one of the simple heraldic forms consisting of a band between two horizontal lines over the middle of an escutcheon, usually covering one third of it

FEST *noun* **FESTS** a party, gathering or festival for a specified activity

FESTER *verb* **FESTERS, FESTERING, FESTERED** said of a wound: to form or discharge pus ◻ *noun* **FESTERS** a small sore discharging pus

FESTIVAL *noun* **FESTIVALS** a day or period of celebration, especially one kept traditionally

FESTIVE *adj* relating to a festival or holiday

FESTIVELY *adverb* in a festive way

FESTIVITY *noun* **FESTIVITIES** a lighthearted event; celebration, merrymaking

FESTOON *noun* **FESTOONS** a decorative chain of flowers, ribbons, etc looped between two points ◻ *verb* **FESTOONS, FESTOONING, FESTOONED** to hang or decorate with festoons

---

FET *verb* **FETS, FETTING, FETTED** an obsolete form of *fetch*

FETA *noun* a crumbly salty white low-fat cheese originating in Greece and the Middle East, traditionally made from goat's or ewe's milk, and now sometimes from cow's milk

FETAL *adj* belonging or relating to, or resembling, a fetus

FETCH *verb* **FETCHES, FETCHING, FETCHED** to go and get something, and bring it back ◻ *noun* **FETCHES** an act of bringing

FETCHING *adj* said of appearance: attractive, charming

FÊTE *noun* **FÊTES** an outdoor event with entertainment, competitions, stalls, etc, usually to raise money for a charity ◻ *verb* **FÊTES, FÊTING, FÊTED** to entertain or honour someone lavishly

FETID *adj* **FETIDER, FETIDEST** having a strong disgusting smell

FETIDNESS *noun* **FETIDNESSES** the quality or state of being fetid

FETISH *noun* **FETISHES** in primitive societies: an object worshipped for its perceived magical powers

FETISHISE *verb* **FETISHISES, FETISHISING, FETISHISED** to fetishize

FETISHISM *noun* **FETISHISMS** the worship of a fetish

FETISHIST *noun* **FETISHISTS** someone who takes part in fetishism

FETISHIZE *verb* **FETISHIZES,**

FETISHIZING, FETISHIZED to make a fetish of someone or something
FETLOCK *noun* **FETLOCKS** the thick projection at the back of a horse's leg just above the hoof
FETOSCOPY *noun* **FETOSCOPIES** a procedure for viewing the fetus directly, within the uterus, or for taking a sample of fetal blood from the placenta, by inserting a hollow needle through the abdomen into the uterus, in order to determine if there are any disorders
FETTA *noun* **FETTAS** feta
FETTER *noun* **FETTERS** a chain or shackle fastened to a prisoner's ankle ❑ *verb* **FETTERS, FETTERING, FETTERED** to put someone in fetters
FETTLE *verb* **FETTLES, FETTLING, FETTLED** to get ready or put in order; prepare something or oneself ❑ *noun* **FETTLES** spirits; condition; state of health
FETTLER *noun* **FETTLERS** a person who fettles, especially a maintenance worker on Australian railways
FETTUCINE *noun* **FETTUCINES** fettucini
FETTUCINI *noun* **FETTUCINIS** pasta made in long ribbons
FETUS *noun* **FETUSES** the embryo of a viviparous mammal during the later stages of development in the uterus, when it has started to resemble the fully-formed animal
FETWA *noun* **FETWAS** a fatwa
FEU *noun* **FEUS** a tenure of land where the vassal makes a return in grain or in money, in place of military service ❑ *verb* **FEUS, FEUING, FEUED** to grant (land, etc) on such terms
FEUD *noun* **FEUDS** a long-drawn-out bitter quarrel between families, individuals or clans ❑ *verb* **FEUDS, FEUDING, FEUDED** to carry on a feud with someone
FEUDAL *adj* relating to feudalism
FEUDALISE *verb* **FEUDALISES, FEUDALISING, FEUDALISED** to feudalize
FEUDALISM *noun* **FEUDALISMS** a system of social and political organization prevalent in W Europe in the Middle Ages, in which powerful land-owning lords granted degrees of privilege and protection to lesser subjects holding a range of positions within a rigid social hierarchy
FEUDALIST *noun* **FEUDALISTS** a representative or supporter of the feudal system
FEUDALIZE *verb* **FEUDALIZES, FEUDALIZING, FEUDALIZED** to create a feudal system
FEUDING *adj* carrying on a feud ❑ *noun* **FEUDINGS** long-drawn-out bitter quarrelling between families, individuals or clans
FEUDIST *noun* **FEUDISTS** a writer on feuds
FEUILLETÉ *noun* **FEUILLETÉS** puff-pastry
FEVER *noun* **FEVERS** in humans: any rise in body temperature above the normal level (37°C or 98.6°F), usually accompanied by shivering, thirst and headache ❑ *verb* **FEVERS, FEVERING, FEVERED** to put into a fever
FEVERED *adj* affected with fever
FEVERFEW *noun* **FEVERFEWS** a perennial plant of the daisy family, closely related to camomile, reputed to relieve the symptoms of migraine
FEVERISH *adj* suffering from, or showing symptoms of, fever
FEVEROUS *adj* feverish
FEW *adj* **FEWER, FEWEST** not many; a small number; hardly any ❑ *pronoun* (used as a plural) hardly any things, people, etc
FEY *adj* **FEYER, FEYEST** strangely fanciful; whimsical
FEZ *noun* **FEZES, FEZZES** a hat shaped like a flat-topped cone, with a tassel, worn by some Muslim men
FIACRE *noun* **FIACRES** a hackney coach; a cab
FIANCÉ *noun* **FIANCÉS** a man to whom one is engaged to be married
FIANCÉE *noun* **FIANCÉES** a woman to whom one is engaged to be married
FIAR *noun* **FIARS** the owner of the fee simple (ie the right to unconditional inheritance) of a property (contrasted with a life-renter of a property)
FIASCO *noun* **FIASCOS, FIASCOES** originally referring to a musical performance: a ludicrous or humiliating failure
FIAT *noun* **FIATS** an official command; a decree
FIB *noun* **FIBS** a trivial lie ❑ *verb* **FIBS, FIBBING, FIBBED** to tell fibs
FIBBER *noun* **FIBBERS** someone who fibs
FIBER *noun* **FIBERS** a fibre
FIBRE *noun* **FIBRES** a fine thread or thread-like cell of a natural or artificial substance, eg cellulose, nylon
FIBRED *adj* having fibre
FIBRELESS *adj* without fibre, strength or nerve
FIBRIL *noun* **FIBRILS** a small fibre or part of a fibre
FIBRILLAR *adj* relating to, of the nature of, or having fibrils or a fibrous structure
FIBRIN *noun* **FIBRINS** an insoluble protein produced from fibrinogen during the blood-clotting process
FIBRO *noun* **FIBROS** a board for lining walls made from a compressed asbestos and cement mixture
FIBROID *adj* fibrous ❑ *noun* **FIBROIDS** a benign tumour consisting of fibrous tissue, one or more of which may develop in the muscular walls of the uterus
FIBROSIS *noun* **FIBROSES** the formation of an abnormal amount of fibrous connective tissue over the surface of or in place of normal tissue of body part, usually as a result of inflammation or injury
FIBROUS *adj* consisting of, containing or like fibre
FIBULA *noun* **FIBULAS** in the human skeleton: the outer and narrower of the two bones in the lower leg, between the knee and the ankle
FIBULAR *adj* of or relating to the fibula
FICHE *noun* **FICHES** short form of microfiche
FICKLE *adj* **FICKLER, FICKLEST** inconstant or changeable in affections, loyalties or intentions
FICTILE *adj* capable of being moulded, especially in clay
FICTION *noun* **FICTIONS** literature concerning imaginary characters or events, eg a novel or story
FICTIONAL *adj* occurring in or created for fiction
FID *noun* **FIDS** a conical pin of hard wood used to open the strands of rope in splicing
FIDDLE *noun* **FIDDLES** a violin, especially when used to play folk music or jazz ❑ *verb* **FIDDLES, FIDDLING, FIDDLED** to trifle or idle; to handle things aimlessly
FIDDLER *noun* **FIDDLERS** a person who plays the fiddle
FIDDLING *adj* unimportant; trifling

FIDDLY adj **FIDDLIER, FIDDLIEST** awkward to handle or do, especially if the task requires delicate finger movements

FIDELITY noun **FIDELITIES** faithfulness; loyalty or devotion (often to a sexual partner)

FIDGET verb **FIDGETS, FIDGETING, FIDGETED** to move about restlessly and aimlessly □ noun **FIDGETS** a person who fidgets

FIDGETY adj **FIDGETIER, FIDGETIEST** restless; uneasy

FIDUCIAL adj applied to a point or line: serving as a standard basis of measuring

FIDUCIARY adj held or given in trust □ noun **FIDUCIARIES** someone who holds anything in trust; a trustee

FIE exclamation expressing disapproval or disgust, real or feigned

FIEF noun **FIEFS** land granted to a vassal by his lord in return for military service, or on other conditions

FIEFDOM noun **FIEFDOMS** a piece of land held as a fief

FIELD noun **FIELDS** a piece of land enclosed for crop-growing or pasturing animals □ verb **FIELDS, FIELDING, FIELDED** said of a team: to be the team whose turn it is to retrieve balls hit by the batting team

FIELDER noun **FIELDERS** in sport: a player in the field; a member of the fielding side, as distinct from the batting side

FIELDFARE noun **FIELDFARES** a species of thrush, having a reddish-yellow throat and breast spotted with black

FIELDSMAN noun **FIELDSMEN** a fielder

FIELDWORK noun **FIELDWORKS** practical work or research done at a site away from the laboratory or place of study

FIEND noun **FIENDS** a devil; an evil spirit

FIENDISH adj like a fiend

FIERCE adj **FIERCER, FIERCEST** violent and aggressive

FIERCELY adverb in a fierce way

FIERILY adverb passionately; spiritedly

FIERINESS noun **FIERINESSES** quickness of temper

FIERY adj **FIERIER, FIERIEST** consisting of fire; like fire

FIESTA noun **FIESTAS** especially in Spain and Latin America: a religious festival with dancing, singing, etc

FIFE noun **FIFES** a small type of flute played in military bands □ verb **FIFES, FIFING, FIFED** to play on the fife

FIFER noun **FIFERS** a fife player

FIFTEEN noun **FIFTEENS** the cardinal number 15 □ adj totalling fifteen

FIFTEENTH adj in counting: next after fourteenth □ noun **FIFTEENTHS** one of fifteen equal parts

FIFTH adj in counting: next after fourth □ noun **FIFTHS** one of five equal parts □ adverb fifthly

FIFTHLY adverb used to introduce the fifth point in a list

FIFTIES plural noun the period of time between one's fiftieth and sixtieth birthdays

FIFTIETH adj in counting: next after forty-ninth □ noun **FIFTIETHS** one of fifty equal parts

FIFTY noun **FIFTIES** the cardinal number 50 □ adj totalling fifty

FIFTYISH adj about fifty years old

FIG noun **FIGS** any of a group of tropical and sub-tropical trees and shrubs of the mulberry family bearing a soft pear-shaped fruit full of tiny seeds

FIGHT verb **FIGHTS, FIGHTING, FOUGHT** to attack or engage (an enemy, army, etc) in combat □ noun **FIGHTS** a battle; a physically violent struggle

FIGHTER noun **FIGHTERS** a person who fights, especially a professional boxer

FIGHTING adj engaged in, or eager or fit for, war or combat □ noun **FIGHTINGS** the act of fighting or contending

FIGMENT noun **FIGMENTS** something imagined or invented

FIGURANT noun **FIGURANTS** a ballet dancer or actor who is one of a group forming background for the solo dancers

FIGURE noun **FIGURES** the form of anything in outline □ verb **FIGURES, FIGURING, FIGURED** to think; to reckon

FIGURED adj marked or decorated with figures

FIGURINE noun **FIGURINES** a small carved or moulded figure, usually representing a human form

FIL noun **FILS** a Shakespearean word for the shaft of a vehicle

FILAGREE noun **FILAGREES** filigree

FILAMENT noun **FILAMENTS** a fine thread or fibre

FILAR adj having threads or wires

FILARIA noun **FILARIAS** any worm of the genus Filaria of nematode worms, introduced into the blood of vertebrates by mosquitoes

FILARIAL adj of or relating to the genus Filaria of nematode worms

FILBERT noun **FILBERTS** the nut of the cultivated hazel

FILCH verb **FILCHES, FILCHING, FILCHED** to steal something small or trivial

FILE noun **FILES** a steel hand tool with a rough surface consisting of fine parallel grooves with sharp cutting edges, used to smooth or rub away wood, metal, etc □ verb **FILES, FILING, FILED** to smooth or shape (a surface) using a file

FILED adj smoothed or shaped by means of a file

FILENAME noun **FILENAMES** any name or reference used to specify a collection of data stored in a computer

FILER noun **FILERS** a person or thing that files

FILET noun **FILETS** the French word for fillet

FILIAL adj belonging or relating to, or resembling, a son or daughter

FILIBEG noun **FILIBEGS** a kilt

FILICIDE noun **FILICIDES** someone who murders their own child

FILIGREE noun **FILIGREES** delicate work in gold or silver wire, twisted into convoluted forms and soldered together, used in jewellery, etc

FILINGS plural noun particles or shavings rubbed off with a file

FILL verb **FILLS, FILLING, FILLED** to make full □ noun **FILLS** anything used to fill something

FILLER noun **FILLERS** a person or thing that fills

FILLET noun **FILLETS** a piece of meat or fish without bone □ verb **FILLETS, FILLETING, FILLETED** to cut fillets from (meat or fish)

FILLING noun **FILLINGS** a specially prepared substance, such as amalgam, gold or composite resin, that is inserted into a cavity that has been drilled in a decaying tooth ◻ *adj* said of food, a meal, etc: substantial and satisfying

FILLIP *noun* **FILLIPS** something that has a stimulating or brightening effect; a boost ◻ *verb* **FILLIPS, FILLIPING, FILLIPED** to excite or stimulate

FILLY *noun* **FILLIES** a young female horse or pony

FILM *noun* **FILMS** a strip of thin flexible plastic or other substance, coated so as to be light-sensitive and exposed inside a camera to produce still or moving pictures ◻ *verb* **FILMS, FILMING, FILMED** to record any series of images, usually moving objects, using a TV camera, cine camera, video camera, camcorder, etc

FILMABLE *adj* particularly suited to being made into a film

FILMGOER *noun* **FILMGOERS** a person who regularly attends the cinema and is usually particularly knowledgeable about it

FILMIC *adj* referring or relating to the cinema, film or cinematography

FILMSET *verb* **FILMSETS, FILMSETTING, FILMSET** to set (text, etc) by filmsetting

FILMSETTING *noun* **FILMSETTINGS** typesetting by exposing text on to film which is then transferred to printing plates

FILMY *adj* **FILMIER, FILMIEST** said of a fabric: thin, light and transparent

FILO *noun* **FILOS** a type of Greek flaky pastry made in thin sheets

FILTER *noun* **FILTERS** a porous substance that allows liquid, gas, smoke, etc through, but traps solid matter, impurities, etc ◻ *verb* **FILTERS, FILTERING, FILTERED** to pass something through a filter, often to remove impurities, particles, etc

FILTH *noun* repulsive dirt; any foul matter

FILTHILY *adverb* in a filthy way

FILTHY *adj* **FILTHIER, FILTHIEST** extremely dirty

FILTRABLE *adj* able to pass through a filter; capable of being filtered

FILTRATE *noun* **FILTRATES** the clear liquid obtained after filtration ◻ *verb* **FILTRATES, FILTRATING, FILTRATED** to filter

FIN *noun* **FINS** a thin wing-like projection on a fish's body

consisting of a thin fold of skin supported by bone or cartilage, used for propelling the fish through the water, balancing, steering, display and in some cases protection

FINABLE *adj* liable to a fine

FINAGLE *verb* **FINAGLES, FINAGLING, FINAGLED** to obtain by guile or swindling, to wangle

FINAL *adj* occurring at the end; last in a series, after all the others ◻ *noun* **FINALS** the last part of a competition at which the winner is decided

FINALE *noun* **FINALES** the grand conclusion to a show, etc

FINALISE *verb* **FINALISES, FINALISING, FINALISED** to finalize

FINALIST *noun* **FINALISTS** someone who reaches the final round in a competition

FINALITY *noun* **FINALITIES** the state of being final or concluded

FINALIZE *verb* **FINALIZES, FINALIZING, FINALIZED** to sign (especially a commercial agreement), taking into account the concluding stages of discussion and negotiation

FINALLY *adverb* at last; in the end; eventually

FINANCE *noun* **FINANCES** money affairs and the management of them ◻ *verb* **FINANCES, FINANCING, FINANCED** to provide funds for something

FINANCIAL *adj* relating to finance or finances

FINANCIER *noun* **FINANCIERS** someone engaged in large financial transactions

FINBACK *noun* **FINBACKS** a rorqual

FINCH *noun* **FINCHES** any of several small songbirds with short stout conical beaks adapted for cracking seeds, eg sparrow, canary, chaffinch, goldfinch

FIND *verb* **FINDS, FINDING, FOUND** to discover through search, enquiry, mental effort or chance ◻ *noun* **FINDS** something or someone that is found; an important discovery

FINDER *noun* **FINDERS** someone who finds something

FINDING *noun* **FINDINGS** a thing that is found or discovered

FINE [1] *adj* **FINER, FINEST** of high quality; excellent; splendid ◻ *adverb* satisfactorily

FINE [2] *noun* **FINES** an amount of

money to be paid as a penalty, constituting a punishment for breaking a regulation or law ◻ *verb* **FINES, FINING, FINED** to impose a fine on someone

FINELY *adverb* splendidly; admirably

FINENESS *noun* **FINENESSES** the state, fact or degree of being fine

FINERY *noun* **FINERIES** splendour; very ornate and showy clothes, jewellery, etc

FINESSE *noun* skilful elegance or expertise ◻ *noun* **FINESSES** in cards: an attempt by a player holding a high card to win a trick with a lower one ◻ *verb* **FINESSES, FINESSING, FINESSED** in cards: to attempt to win a trick by finesse

FINGER *noun* **FINGERS** one of the five jointed extremities of the hand ◻ *verb* **FINGERS, FINGERING, FINGERED** to touch or feel something with the fingers, often affectionately or lovingly; to caress

FINGERED *adj* soiled or dirtied by a lot of touching

FINGERING *noun* **FINGERINGS** the correct positioning of the fingers for playing a particular musical instrument or piece of music

FINGERTIP *noun* **FINGERTIPS** the end or tip of one's finger

FINICKETY *adj* **FINICKETIER, FINICKETIEST** finicky

FINICKY *adj* **FINICKIER, FINICKIEST** too concerned with detail

FINISH *verb* **FINISHES, FINISHING, FINISHED** to bring something to an end, or come to an end; to reach a natural conclusion ◻ *noun* **FINISHES** the last stage; the end

FINISHED *adj* no longer useful, productive, creative, wanted or popular

FINISHER *noun* **FINISHERS** a person who finishes

FINITE *adj* having an end or limit

FINITELY *adverb* in a finite way

FINITUDE *noun* **FINITUDES** the state of being finite

FINLESS *adj* without fins

FINNAN *noun* **FINNANS** haddock cured in the smoke from peat, turf or green wood

FINNED *adj* having fins

FINNY *adj* **FINNIER, FINNIEST** finned

FINOCCHIO *noun* **FINOCCHIOS** a dwarf variety of fennel

FIORD noun **FIORDS** a fjord

FIORITURA noun **FIORITURE** a florid embellishment to a piece of music, especially by the performer

FIPPLE noun **FIPPLES** the piece of wood, etc that plugs the mouthpiece of a recorder or other similar wind instrument, with a narrow slit through which the player blows

FIR noun **FIRS** any of various coniferous evergreen trees native to north temperate regions and Central America, and usually having silvery or bluish foliage, with leathery needle-like leaves

FIRE noun **FIRES** flames coming from something that is burning □ verb **FIRES, FIRING, FIRED** to discharge (a gun); to send off (a bullet or other missile) from a gun, catapult, bow, etc □ exclamation a cry, warning others of a fire

FIREARM noun **FIREARMS** a gun, pistol, revolver or rifle, carried and used by an individual

FIREBALL noun **FIREBALLS** ball lightning

FIREBRAND noun **FIREBRANDS** a piece of burning wood

FIREBRICK noun **FIREBRICKS** a heat-resistant brick made from fire clay used to line furnaces, fireplaces, etc

FIREBUG noun **FIREBUGS** an arsonist

FIRED adj referring to ceramics which have been baked in a kiln

FIREDAMP noun **FIREDAMPS** an explosive mixture of methane gas and air, formed in coalmines by the decomposition of coal

FIREDOG noun **FIREDOGS** an andiron

FIREFLY noun **FIREFLIES** any of a number of species of small winged nocturnal beetles, found mainly in tropical regions, that emit light in a series of brief flashes

FIREGUARD noun **FIREGUARDS** a metal or wire-mesh screen for putting round an open fire to protect against sparks or falling coal, logs, etc

FIRELESS adj having no fire

FIREMAN noun **FIREMEN** a male member of a fire brigade, officially called a firefighter

FIREPLACE noun **FIREPLACES** mainly in homes: the recess of an open fire in a room and its surrounding area which has an opening to a chimney above it

FIREPROOF adj resistant to fire and fierce heat □ verb **FIREPROOFS, FIREPROOFING, FIREPROOFED** to make something resistant to fire

FIRER noun **FIRERS** a person who fires (a gun, etc)

FIRESHIP noun **FIRESHIPS** a ship which carries firefighters and firefighting equipment, for putting out fires on ships, oil rigs, etc

FIRESIDE noun **FIRESIDES** the area round a fireplace, especially as a symbol of home □ adj domestic; familiar

FIRETHORN noun **FIRETHORNS** pyracantha, a thorny evergreen shrub with bright red, yellow or orange berries

FIREWEED noun **FIREWEEDS** rose-bay willow-herb, often the first vegetation to spring up on burned ground

FIREWOOD noun **FIREWOODS** wood for burning as fuel

FIREWORK noun **FIREWORKS** a device containing combustible chemicals, designed to produce spectacular coloured sparks, flares, etc, often with accompanying loud bangs, when ignited

FIRING noun **FIRINGS** a discharge of guns, etc

FIRKIN noun **FIRKINS** a measure equal to 9 gallons (c. 40 l)

FIRM [1] adj **FIRMER, FIRMEST** strong; compact; steady □ adverb in a determined and unyielding manner; with resolution □ verb **FIRMS, FIRMING, FIRMED** to make something firm or secure

FIRM [2] noun **FIRMS** any organization or individual engaged in economic activity with the aim of producing goods or services for sale to others; a business or company

FIRMAMENT noun **FIRMAMENTS** the sky; heaven

FIRMLY adverb in a firm way; earnestly, sincerely

FIRMNESS noun **FIRMNESSES** the state or quality of being firm

FIRMWARE noun **FIRMWARES** a software program which cannot be altered and is held in a computer's read-only memory, eg the operating system

FIRST adj in counting: before all others; before the second and following ones □ adverb before anything or anyone else □ noun

FIRSTS a person or thing coming first, eg in a race or exam

FIRSTLY adverb used to introduce a list of things: before all others; in the first place; to begin with

FIRTH noun **FIRTHS** especially in Scotland: a river estuary or an inlet

FISCAL adj belonging or relating to government finances or revenue □ noun **FISCALS** a procurator fiscal (a public official in Scotland)

FISCALLY adverb from a fiscal point of view

FISH noun **FISH, FISHES** any cold-blooded aquatic vertebrate that has no legs, and typically possesses paired fins, breathes by means of gills, and has a bony or cartilaginous skeleton and a body covered with scales □ verb **FISHES, FISHING, FISHED** to catch or try to catch fish

FISHER noun **FISHERS** any animal that catches fish for food

FISHERMAN noun **FISHERMEN** a person who fishes as a job or hobby

FISHERY noun **FISHERIES** an area of water where fishing takes place, particularly sea waters; a fishing ground

FISHGIG noun **FISHGIGS** a harpoon

FISHINESS noun **FISHINESSES** the state of being fishy

FISHING noun **FISHINGS** the sport or business of catching fish

FISHWIFE noun **FISHWIVES** a loud-voiced, coarse-mannered woman

FISHY adj **FISHIER, FISHIEST** relating to fish; like a fish

FISSILE adj said of certain rocks, eg shale: tending to split or capable of being split

FISSION noun **FISSIONS** a splitting or division into pieces

FISSIVE adj relating to fission

FISSURE noun **FISSURES** a long narrow crack or fracture especially in a body of rock, the Earth's surface or a volcano □ verb **FISSURES, FISSURING, FISSURED** to crack, split or divide

FIST noun **FISTS** a tightly closed or clenched hand with the fingers and thumb doubled back into the palm □ verb **FISTS, FISTING, FISTED** to strike or hit with the fist

FISTFUL noun **FISTFULS** an amount that can be held in a closed hand; a handful

FISTULA noun **FISTULAS,**

FISTULAE an abnormal connection between two internal organs or body cavities, or between an internal organ or body cavity and the surface of the skin, usually caused by infection or injury

FISTULAR adj relating to a fistula

FIT ¹ verb **FITS, FITTING, FIT, FITTED** to be the right shape or size for something or someone □ adj **FITTER, FITTEST** healthy; feeling good

FIT ² noun **FITS** a sudden attack of one or more symptoms, usually of an involuntary and relatively violent nature, eg convulsions in grand mal epilepsy, eg *epileptic fit*, or paroxysms of coughing, eg *coughing fit*

FITCH noun **FITCHES** a polecat

FITFUL adj irregular, spasmodic or intermittent; not continuous

FITFULLY adverb in a fitful way

FITLY adverb appropriately; suitably

FITMENT noun **FITMENTS** a piece of equipment or furniture which is fixed to a wall, floor, etc

FITNESS noun **FITNESSES** the state of being suitable or (especially referring to health) fit

FITTED adj made to fit closely

FITTER noun **FITTERS** a person who installs, adjusts or repairs machinery, equipment, etc

FITTING adj suitable; appropriate □ noun **FITTINGS** an accessory or part

FITTINGLY adverb in a fitting way

FIVE noun **FIVES** the cardinal number 5 □ adj totalling five

FIVEFOLD adj equal to five times as much or many □ adverb by five times as much

FIVEPINS singular noun a bowling game using five skittles, similar to ninepins and tenpins

FIVER noun **FIVERS** a five-pound note

FIVES singular noun a game like squash played in a walled court, in which a gloved hand or a bat is used to hit the ball

FIX verb **FIXES, FIXING, FIXED** to attach or place something firmly □ noun **FIXES** a situation which is difficult to escape from; a predicament

FIXATE verb **FIXATES, FIXATING, FIXATED** to become or make something (eg the eyes) become fixed on something

FIXATED adj affected by or engaged in fixation

FIXATION noun **FIXATIONS** an (often abnormal) attachment, preoccupation or obsession

FIXATIVE noun **FIXATIVES** a liquid sprayed on a drawing, painting or photograph to preserve and protect it

FIXED adj fastened; immovable

FIXEDLY adverb steadily; intently

FIXEDNESS noun **FIXEDNESSES** the state of being fixed

FIXER noun **FIXERS** a chemical solution that fixes photographic images

FIXITY noun **FIXITIES** the quality of being fixed, steady, unchanging, unmoving or immovable

FIXTURE noun **FIXTURES** a permanently fixed piece of furniture or equipment

---

FIZ verb **FIZZES, FIZZING, FIZZED** to make a hissing or spluttering sound
ⓘ This word is worth 15 points, and is valuable for using up both **F** and **Z**.

FIZGIG noun **FIZGIGS** a giddy or flirtatious girl

FIZZ verb **FIZZES, FIZZING, FIZZED** said of a liquid: to give off bubbles of carbon dioxide with a hissing sound □ noun **FIZZES** a hiss or spluttering sound; fizziness

FIZZER noun **FIZZERS** something which fizzes; a very fast ball in cricket

FIZZLE verb **FIZZLES, FIZZLING, FIZZLED** to make a faint hiss □ noun **FIZZLES** a faint hissing sound

FIZZY adj **FIZZIER, FIZZIEST** giving off bubbles of carbon dioxide with a hissing sound; effervescent

FJORD noun **FJORDS** a long narrow steep-sided inlet of the sea in a mountainous coast, eg in Norway, Greenland or New Zealand, formed by the flooding of a previously glaciated valley

FLAB noun **FLABS** excess flesh or fat on the body

FLABBILY adverb in a flabby way

FLABBY adj **FLABBIER, FLABBIEST** said of flesh: sagging, not firm

FLACCID adj **FLACCIDER, FLACCIDEST** limp and soft; not firm

FLACCIDLY adverb in a flaccid way

FLACON noun **FLACONS** a small bottle with a stopper, especially for perfume

FLAG ¹ noun **FLAGS** a piece of cloth, usually rectangular in shape, with a distinctive design, flown from a pole to represent a country, political party, etc, or used for signalling

FLAG ² verb **FLAGS, FLAGGING, FLAGGED** to grow weak or tired after a period of intense work or activity

FLAGELLUM noun **FLAGELLA** the long whip-like structure that projects from the cell surface of sperm, and certain bacteria, unicellular algae and protozoans, used to propel the cell through a liquid medium

FLAGEOLET noun **FLAGEOLETS** a small pale green bean which is a type of kidney bean

FLAGON noun **FLAGONS** a large bottle or jug with a narrow neck, usually with a spout and handle

FLAGPOLE noun **FLAGPOLES** a pole from which a flag is flown

FLAGRANCY noun **FLAGRANCIES** the quality of being flagrant

FLAGRANT adj said of something bad: undisguised; blatant; outrageous; brazen or barefaced

FLAGSHIP noun **FLAGSHIPS** the ship that carries and flies the flag of the fleet commander

FLAGSTAFF noun **FLAGSTAFFS** a flagpole

FLAGSTONE noun **FLAGSTONES** a large flat stone for paving

FLAIL noun **FLAILS** a threshing tool consisting of a long handle with a free-swinging wooden or metal bar attached to the end □ verb **FLAILS, FLAILING, FLAILED** to beat with or as if with a flail

FLAIR noun **FLAIRS** a natural ability or talent for something

FLAK noun **FLAKS** anti-aircraft fire

FLAKE noun **FLAKES** a small flat particle which has broken away or is breaking away from a larger object □ verb **FLAKES, FLAKING, FLAKED** to come off in flakes

FLAKINESS noun **FLAKINESSES** the state of being flaky

FLAKY adj **FLAKIER, FLAKIEST** made of flakes or tending to form flakes

FLAMBÉ adj said of food: soaked in spirit, usually brandy, and set alight before serving

FLAMBÉED *adj* flambé

FLAMBEAU *noun* **FLAMBEAUX, FLAMBEAUS** a pole dipped in wax and set alight as a flaming torch, used in processions at festivals, etc

FLAME *noun* **FLAMES** a hot, luminous and flickering tongue shape of burning gases coming from something that is on fire □ *verb* **FLAMES, FLAMING, FLAMED** to burn with flames; to blaze

FLAMENCO *noun* **FLAMENCOS** a rhythmical, emotionally stirring type of Spanish gypsy music, usually played on the guitar, originally from the S Spanish region of Andalusia

FLAMING *adj* blazing

FLAMINGO *noun* **FLAMINGOS, FLAMINGOES** any of several large wading birds, found in flocks of many thousands on lakes and lagoons in tropical regions, with white or pinkish plumage, a long neck and long legs, webbed feet, and a broad down-curving bill

FLAMMABLE *adj* liable to catch fire; inflammable

FLAN *noun* **FLANS** an open pastry or sponge case with a savoury or fruit filling, usually round in shape

FLANGE *noun* **FLANGES** a broad flat projecting rim, eg round a wheel, added for strength or for connecting with another object or part □ *verb* **FLANGES, FLANGING, FLANGED** to put a flange on something

FLANGED *adj* fitted with a flange

FLANK *noun* **FLANKS** the side of an animal, between the ribs and hip □ *verb* **FLANKS, FLANKING, FLANKED** to be on the edge of (an object, a body of things, etc)

FLANKER *noun* **FLANKERS** one of a detachment of soldiers responsible for guarding the flanks of an army

FLANNEL *noun* **FLANNELS** flattery or meaningless talk □ *verb* **FLANNELS, FLANNELLING, FLANNELLED** to flatter or persuade by flattery, or to talk flannel

FLAP *verb* **FLAPS, FLAPPING, FLAPPED** to wave something up and down, or backwards and forwards □ *noun* **FLAPS** a broad piece or part of something attached along one edge and hanging loosely, usually as a cover to an opening

FLAPJACK *noun* **FLAPJACKS** a thick biscuit made with oats and syrup

FLAPPABLE *adj* easily perturbed, agitated, irritated, flustered, etc

FLAPPER *noun* **FLAPPERS** a fashionable and frivolous young woman of the 1920s

FLAPPY *adj* **FLAPPIER, FLAPPIEST** in a state of nervousness or panic; in a fluster

FLARE *verb* **FLARES, FLARING, FLARED** to burn with sudden brightness □ *noun* **FLARES** a sudden blaze of bright light

FLARES *plural noun* trousers with legs which are very tight around the thigh and widen greatly below the knee, popular in the late 1960s and early 1970s, and revived as fashion items in the late 1980s

FLASH *noun* **FLASHES** a sudden brief blaze of light □ *verb* **FLASHES, FLASHING, FLASHED** to shine briefly or intermittently □ *adj* **FLASHER, FLASHEST** sudden and severe; smart and expensive

FLASHBACK *noun* **FLASHBACKS** especially in a film, novel, etc: a scene depicting events which happened before the current ones □ *verb* **FLASHBACKS, FLASHBACKING, FLASHBACKED** to shift to a scene which happened before the current one

FLASHBULB *noun* **FLASHBULBS** a small light bulb used to produce a brief bright light in photography

FLASHER *noun* **FLASHERS** a light that flashes

FLASHGUN *noun* **FLASHGUNS** a device with an electronic flash or a flashbulb that produces a momentary bright illumination for indoor or night photography

FLASHILY *adverb* in a flashy way

FLASHY *adj* **FLASHIER, FLASHIEST** ostentatiously smart and showy, often in a superficial way

FLASK *noun* **FLASKS** a small flat pocket bottle for alcoholic spirits

FLAT [1] *adj* **FLATTER, FLATTEST** level; horizontal; even □ *adverb* stretched out rather than curled up, crumpled, etc

FLAT [2] *noun* **FLATS** a set of rooms for living in as a self-contained unit, in a building or tenement with a number of such units

FLATBACK *noun* **FLATBACKS** a pottery figure with a flat surface at the back of it, designed to stand on a mantelpiece, hang on a wall, etc

FLATFISH *noun* **FLATFISHES** any of about 500 species of fish with a body that is flat horizontally rather than vertically, with both eyes on the upper surface of the body, eg sole, plaice, halibut, flounder, etc

FLATIRON *noun* **FLATIRONS** a clothes-pressing iron heated on the fire or stove

FLATLET *noun* **FLATLETS** a small flat

FLATLY *adverb* emphatically

FLATMATE *noun* **FLATMATES** someone one shares a flat with

FLATNESS *noun* **FLATNESSES** the quality or condition of being flat

FLATTEN *verb* **FLATTENS, FLATTENING, FLATTENED** to make or become flat or flatter

FLATTER *verb* **FLATTERS, FLATTERING, FLATTERED** to compliment someone excessively or insincerely, especially in order to win a favour from them

FLATTERER *noun* **FLATTERERS** a person who flatters others, especially in order to win a favour from them

FLATTERING *adj* that enhances the appearance

FLATTERY *noun* **FLATTERIES** the act of flattering

FLATTISH *adj* somewhat flat

FLATULENT *adj* suffering from or caused by flatulence (excessive gas in the stomach and intestines)

FLATUS *noun* **FLATUSES** gas generated in the stomach or intestines

FLATWORM *noun* **FLATWORMS** a type of worm (distinct from eg roundworms) with a flattened body, a definite head but no true body cavity, eg the tapeworm

FLAUNT *verb* **FLAUNTS, FLAUNTING, FLAUNTED** to display or parade oneself or something, especially one's clothes, in an ostentatious way, in the hope of being admired

FLAUNTER *noun* **FLAUNTERS** a person who flaunts

FLAUNTING *adj* that flaunts

FLAUNTY *adj* **FLAUNTIER, FLAUNTIEST** gaudy or showy

FLAUTIST *noun* **FLAUTISTS** someone skilled in playing the flute

FLAVOR *noun* **FLAVORS** a flavour □ *verb* **FLAVORS, FLAVORING, FLAVORED** to flavour

FLAVORING noun **FLAVORINGS** flavouring

FLAVOUR noun **FLAVOURS** a sensation perceived when eating or drinking which is a combination of taste and smell ◻ verb **FLAVOURS, FLAVOURING, FLAVOURED** to add something (usually to food) to give it a particular flavour or quality

FLAVOURING noun **FLAVOURINGS** any substance added to food, etc to give it a particular taste

FLAW noun **FLAWS** a fault, defect, imperfection or blemish

FLAWED adj having flaws; imperfect

FLAWLESS adj without flaws

FLAX noun **FLAXES** a slender herbaceous plant that usually has blue flowers and is cultivated in many parts of the world for the fibre of its stem and for its seeds (flaxseeds)

FLAXEN adj said of hair: very fair

FLAY verb **FLAYS, FLAYING, FLAYED** to strip the skin from (an animal or a person)

FLAYER noun **FLAYERS** a person who flays

FLEA noun **FLEAS** any of about 1800 species of wingless, blood-sucking, jumping insects, that live as parasites on mammals (including humans) and some birds

FLEAWORT noun **FLEAWORTS** any of several biennial or perennial European plants with clusters of small daisy-like flower heads

FLÈCHE noun **FLÈCHES** a small slender spire rising from the ridge of a church roof in some large churches, usually from the intersection of the nave and transepts

FLÉCHETTE noun **FLÉCHETTES** a steel dart dropped or thrown from an aeroplane during World War I

FLECK noun **FLECKS** a spot or marking ◻ verb **FLECKS, FLECKING, FLECKED** to spot or speckle

FLECKED adj spotted; dappled

FLEDGED adj said of a young bird: able to fly because the feathers are fully developed

FLEDGLING noun **FLEDGLINGS** a young bird that has just grown its feathers and is still unable to fly

FLEE verb **FLEES, FLEEING, FLED** to run away quickly

FLEECE noun **FLEECES** a sheep's woolly coat ◻ verb **FLEECES, FLEECING, FLEECED** to cut wool from (sheep); to shear (sheep)

FLEECER noun **FLEECERS** a person who strips, plunders or charges exorbitantly

FLEECY adj **FLEECIER, FLEECIEST** woolly, like a fleece

FLEER noun **FLEERS** someone who is fleeing

FLEET[1] noun **FLEETS** a number of ships under one command and organized as a tactical unit

FLEET[2] verb **FLEETS, FLEETING, FLEETED** to flit or pass swiftly ◻ adj **FLEETER, FLEETEST** swift; rapid

FLEETING adj passing swiftly; brief; short-lived

FLEETNESS noun **FLEETNESSES** the state of being fleet

FLENCH verb **FLENCHES, FLENCHING, FLENCHED** to cut the blubber from (a whale, seal, etc) and slice it up

FLENSE verb **FLENSES, FLENSING, FLENSED** to flench

FLESH noun **FLESHES** in animals: the soft tissues covering the bones, consisting chiefly of muscle ◻ verb **FLESHES, FLESHING, FLESHED** to train (eg dogs) for hunting by giving them raw meat

FLESHINGS plural noun flesh-coloured tights

FLESHLESS adj without flesh; lean

FLESHLY adj relating to the body as distinct from the soul; worldly

FLESHY adj **FLESHIER, FLESHIEST** plump

FLETCHER noun **FLETCHERS** a person whose job is to make arrows

FLEW a past form of **fly**[1]

FLEWS plural noun the pendulous upper lips of a bloodhound or similar dog

FLEX[1] verb **FLEXES, FLEXING, FLEXED** to bend (a limb or joint)

FLEX[2] noun **FLEXES** flexible insulated electrical cable

FLEXIBLE adj bending easily; pliable

FLEXIBLY adverb in a flexible way

FLEXILE adj flexible

FLEXION noun **FLEXIONS** the bending of a limb or joint, especially a flexor muscle

FLEXITIME noun **FLEXITIMES** a system of flexible working hours operated in some organizations

whereby employees may choose their time of arrival and departure, provided they work the agreed number of hours, usually including certain hours each day when everyone must be at work

FLEXOR noun **FLEXORS** any muscle that causes bending of a limb or other body part

FLEXUOUS adj full of bends or curves

FLEXURAL adj of or relating to flexure

FLEXURE noun **FLEXURES** a bend or turning

FLIC noun **FLICS** a French policeman

FLICK verb **FLICKS, FLICKING, FLICKED** to move or touch something with a quick light movement ◻ noun **FLICKS** a flicking action

FLICKER verb **FLICKERS, FLICKERING, FLICKERED** to burn or shine unsteadily by alternately flashing bright and dying away again ◻ noun **FLICKERS** a brief or unsteady light

FLIER[1] noun **FLIERS** a leaflet used to advertise a product, promote an organization, etc, usually distributed on street corners or as an insert in a newspaper, etc

FLIER[2] see under **fly**[3]

FLIES a form of **fly**[1], plural of **fly**[2]

FLIEST see under **fly**[3]

FLIGHT[1] noun **FLIGHTS** the act of fleeing; escape

FLIGHT[2] verb **FLIGHTS, FLIGHTING, FLIGHTED** to impart a deceptive trajectory or a deceptively slow speed to (eg, a cricket ball)

FLIGHTILY adverb in a flighty way

FLIGHTY adj **FLIGHTIER, FLIGHTIEST** irresponsible; frivolous; flirtatious

FLIMSILY adverb in a flimsy way

FLIMSY adj **FLIMSIER, FLIMSIEST** said of clothing, etc: light and thin

FLINCH verb **FLINCHES, FLINCHING, FLINCHED** to start or jump in pain, fright, surprise, etc

FLINCHER noun **FLINCHERS** someone who flinches

FLING verb **FLINGS, FLINGING, FLUNG** to throw something, especially violently or vigorously ◻ noun **FLINGS** the act of flinging

FLINT noun **FLINTS** a crystalline form of quartz, found in chalk and limestone, consisting of hard dark-grey or black nodules encrusted with white, and used as an abrasive

For longer words, see The Chambers Dictionary

FLINTILY adverb harshly or cruelly

FLINTLOCK noun **FLINTLOCKS** a gun in which the powder was lit by a spark from a flint

FLINTY adj **FLINTIER, FLINTIEST** made of or containing flint

FLIP verb **FLIPS, FLIPPING, FLIPPED** to toss (eg a coin) so that it turns over in mid-air □ noun **FLIPS** a flipping action □ adj flippant; over-smart

FLIPPANCY noun **FLIPPANCIES** impertinence; levity

FLIPPANT adj not serious enough about grave matters; disrespectful; irreverent; frivolous

FLIPPER noun **FLIPPERS** a limb adapted for swimming, eg in the whale, seal, penguin, etc

FLIPPING adj used to express annoyance □ adverb used to express annoyance

FLIRT verb **FLIRTS, FLIRTING, FLIRTED** to behave in a playful sexual manner towards someone □ noun **FLIRTS** someone who flirts

FLIRTY adj **FLIRTIER, FLIRTIEST** flirting, flirtatious

FLIT verb **FLITS, FLITTING, FLITTED** to move about lightly and quickly from place to place □ noun **FLITS** an act of flitting

FLITCH noun **FLITCHES** a salted and cured side of pork

FLITTER verb **FLITTERS, FLITTERING, FLITTERED** to flutter

FLIX noun **FLIXES** fur or beaver-down

FLOAT verb **FLOATS, FLOATING, FLOATED** to rest or move, or make something rest or move, on the surface of a liquid □ noun **FLOATS** something that floats or is designed to keep something afloat

FLOATABLE adj able to float

FLOATAGE noun **FLOATAGES** flotage

FLOATEL noun **FLOATELS** a flotel

FLOATER noun **FLOATERS** someone or something that floats

FLOATING adj not fixed; moving about

FLOATS plural noun floodlights

FLOATY adj **FLOATIER, FLOATIEST** able to float

FLOCCOSE adj said of plant structures: covered in small hairs giving a downlike appearance

FLOCCULUS noun **FLOCCULI** a light or dark cloudy patch on the sun's surface caused by calcium or hydrogen vapour and usually appearing near sun spots

FLOCCUS noun **FLOCCI** a tuft of woolly hair

FLOCK noun **FLOCKS** a group of creatures, especially birds or sheep □ verb **FLOCKS, FLOCKING, FLOCKED** to gather or move in a group or a crowd

FLOE noun **FLOES** a sheet of ice other than the edge of an ice shelf or glacier, floating in the sea

FLOG verb **FLOGS, FLOGGING, FLOGGED** to beat; to whip repeatedly, particularly as a form of punishment

FLOKATI noun **FLOKATIS** a hand-woven Greek rug with a thick shaggy wool pile

FLONG noun **FLONGS** in printing: papier-mâché for making moulds

FLOOD noun **FLOODS** an overflow of water from rivers, lakes or the sea on to dry land □ verb **FLOODS, FLOODING, FLOODED** to overflow or submerge (land) with water

FLOODGATE noun **FLOODGATES** a gate for controlling the flow of a large amount of water

FLOODTIDE noun **FLOODTIDES** the rising tide

FLOODWALL noun **FLOODWALLS** a wall built as protection against floods from the sea, a river, etc

FLOODWAY noun **FLOODWAYS** an artificial passage to direct floodwater away from an endangered area, eg an overflowing dam, a town, etc

FLOOR noun **FLOORS** the lower interior surface of a room or vehicle □ verb **FLOORS, FLOORING, FLOORED** to construct the floor of (a room, etc)

FLOORED adj said of lofts, attics, etc: having flat floor-covering rather than exposed beams, etc

FLOORING noun **FLOORINGS** material for constructing floors

FLOOSIE noun **FLOOSIES** a woman or girl, especially a disreputable or immodestly dressed one

FLOOZIE noun **FLOOZIES** a floosie

FLOOZY noun **FLOOZIES** a floosie

FLOP verb **FLOPS, FLOPPING, FLOPPED** to fall, drop, move or sit limply and heavily □ noun **FLOPS** a flopping movement or sound □ adverb with a flop

FLOPPILY adverb in a floppy way

FLOPPY adj **FLOPPIER, FLOPPIEST** tending to flop; loose and insecure □ noun **FLOPPIES** a floppy disk

FLOR noun **FLORS** a yeasty growth which is allowed to form on the surface of sherries after fermentation and which gives them a nutty taste

FLORA noun **FLORAS, FLORAE** the wild plants of a particular region, country or time period

FLORAL adj consisting of or relating to flowers

FLORALLY adverb like a flower

FLOREATED adj floriated

FLORET noun **FLORETS** a small flower; one of the single flowers in the head of a composite flower, such as a daisy or sunflower

FLORIATED adj decorated with floral ornament

FLORID adj **FLORIDER, FLORIDEST** over-elaborate

FLORIDITY noun **FLORIDITIES** the quality or condition of being florid

FLORIDLY adverb in a florid way

FLORIFORM adj flower-shaped

FLORIN noun **FLORINS** a name for the coin worth two shillings or 24 old British pence, minted from 1849 and worth 10 new pence when currency was decimalized in 1971

FLORIST noun **FLORISTS** someone who sells or arranges flowers; sometimes someone who also grows flowers

FLORISTIC adj of or relating to the study of plants and their distribution

FLORISTRY noun **FLORISTRIES** the profession of selling flowers

FLORUIT noun **FLORUITS** a period during which someone was most active, produced most works, etc, used especially when exact birth and death dates are unknown

FLOSS noun **FLOSSES** loose strands of fine silk which are not twisted together, used in embroidery, for tooth-cleaning (dental floss), etc □ verb **FLOSSES, FLOSSING, FLOSSED** to clean the teeth with dental floss

FLOSSY adj **FLOSSIER, FLOSSIEST** made of or like floss

FLOTAGE noun **FLOTAGES** buoyancy; the capacity for floating

FLOTATION noun **FLOTATIONS** the launching of a commercial company with a sale of shares to raise money

FLOTEL noun **FLOTELS** a rig or boat containing the sleeping accommodation and eating, leisure, etc facilities for workers on oil-rigs

FLOTILLA noun **FLOTILLAS** a small fleet, or a fleet of small ships

FLOTSAM noun **FLOTSAMS** goods lost by shipwreck and found floating on the sea

FLOUNCE [1] verb **FLOUNCES, FLOUNCING, FLOUNCED** to move in a way expressive of impatience or indignation

FLOUNCE [2] noun **FLOUNCES** a deep frill on a dress, etc

FLOUNCING noun **FLOUNCINGS** material for flounces

FLOUNCY adj **FLOUNCIER, FLOUNCIEST** decorated with flounces

FLOUNDER [1] verb **FLOUNDERS, FLOUNDERING, FLOUNDERED** to thrash about helplessly, as when caught in a bog

FLOUNDER [2] noun **FLOUNDERS** a type of European flatfish with greyish-brown mottled skin with orange spots, used as food

FLOUR noun **FLOURS** the finely ground meal of wheat or any other cereal grain ◻ verb **FLOURS, FLOURING, FLOURED** to cover or sprinkle something with flour

FLOURISH verb **FLOURISHES, FLOURISHING, FLOURISHED** to be strong and healthy; to grow well ◻ noun **FLOURISHES** a decorative twirl in handwriting

FLOURISHED adj decorated with flourishes

FLOURISHING adj thriving; prosperous

FLOURY adj **FLOURIER, FLOURIEST** covered with flour; like flour

FLOUT verb **FLOUTS, FLOUTING, FLOUTED** to defy (an order, convention, etc) openly; to disrespect (authority, etc)

FLOW verb **FLOWS, FLOWING, FLOWED** to move along like water ◻ noun **FLOWS** the action of flowing

FLOWER noun **FLOWERS** in a flowering plant: the structure that bears the reproductive organs, which consists of a leafy shoot in which the leaves are modified to form sepals, petals, etc ◻ verb **FLOWERS, FLOWERING, FLOWERED** to produce flowers; to bloom

FLOWERER noun **FLOWERERS** a plant that flowers

FLOWERING noun **FLOWERINGS** the putting forth of flowers ◻ adj that bears flowers

FLOWERPOT noun **FLOWERPOTS** a clay or plastic container for growing plants in

FLOWERY adj **FLOWERIER, FLOWERIEST** decorated or patterned with flowers

FLOWING adj moving as a fluid

FLOWINGLY adverb in a flowing way

FLOWN a past form of **fly** [1]

FLU noun **FLUS** influenza

FLUB noun **FLUBS** a gaffe; a mistake ◻ verb **FLUBS, FLUBBING, FLUBBED** to make a mess of something; to botch it

FLUCTUANT adj that moves like water

FLUCTUATE verb **FLUCTUATES, FLUCTUATING, FLUCTUATED** to vary in amount, value, level, etc; to rise and fall

FLUE noun **FLUES** an outlet for smoke or gas, eg through a chimney

FLUENCY noun **FLUENCIES** smoothness or ease of speech, writing or movement

FLUENT adj having full command of a foreign language

FLUENTLY adverb in a fluent way

FLUFF noun **FLUFFS** small bits of soft woolly or downy material ◻ verb **FLUFFS, FLUFFING, FLUFFED** to shake or arrange something into a soft mass

FLUFFY adj **FLUFFIER, FLUFFIEST** consisting of or resembling fluff

FLUID noun **FLUIDS** a substance, such as a liquid or gas, which can move about with freedom and has no fixed shape ◻ adj able to flow like a liquid; unsolidified

FLUIDIC adj of or relating to fluidics

FLUIDICS singular noun the study and use of systems based on the movement of jets of fluid in pipes, used as an alternative to electronic devices to control instruments, industrial processes, etc

FLUIDISE verb **FLUIDISES, FLUIDISING, FLUIDISED** to fluidize

FLUIDITY noun **FLUIDITIES** the quality or condition of being fluid

FLUIDIZE verb **FLUIDIZES, FLUIDIZING, FLUIDIZED** to make something fluid

FLUIDNESS noun **FLUIDNESSES** the state of being fluid

FLUKE noun **FLUKES** a success achieved by accident or chance ◻ verb **FLUKES, FLUKING, FLUKED** to make, score or achieve something by a fluke

FLUKEY adj **FLUKIER, FLUKIEST** achieved by accident or chance rather than by skill

FLUKY adj **FLUKIER, FLUKIEST** flukey

FLUME noun **FLUMES** a descending chute with flowing water at a swimming pool, used for riding or sliding down; a water-slide

FLUMMERY noun **FLUMMERIES** a jelly made with oatmeal, milk, egg and honey

FLUMMOX verb **FLUMMOXES, FLUMMOXING, FLUMMOXED** to confuse someone; to bewilder someone

FLUMP verb **FLUMPS, FLUMPING, FLUMPED** to throw something down heavily ◻ noun **FLUMPS** the dull sound produced by this action

FLUNG past form of **fling**

FLUNK verb **FLUNKS, FLUNKING, FLUNKED** to fail (a test, examination, etc)

FLUNKEY noun **FLUNKEYS** a uniformed manservant, eg a footman

FLUNKY noun **FLUNKIES** a flunkey

FLUOR noun **FLUORS** a material that absorbs electrons or radiation, especially ultraviolet light, and converts these into radiation of a different wavelength, usually visible light, which it then emits

FLUORESCE verb **FLUORESCES, FLUORESCING, FLUORESCED** to demonstrate fluorescence (the emission of light and other radiation by an object after it has absorbed electrons or radiation of a different wavelength)

FLUORIDE noun **FLUORIDES** any chemical compound consisting of fluorine and another element, especially sodium fluoride, which is added to drinking water supplies and toothpaste to prevent tooth decay in children

FLUORINE noun **FLUORINES** a highly corrosive poisonous yellow gas (one of the halogens) that is the most electronegative and reactive chemical element

FLUORITE noun **FLUORITES** fluorspar

FLUORSPAR noun **FLUORSPARS**

calcium fluoride, a mineral that is transparent when pure, but commonly occurs as blue or purple crystals

FLURRY *noun* **FLURRIES** a sudden commotion; a sudden bustle or rush ▫ *verb* **FLURRIES, FLURRYING, FLURRIED** to agitate, confuse or bewilder someone

FLUSH [1] *noun* **FLUSHES** a redness or rosiness, especially of the cheeks or face; a blush

FLUSH [2] *adj* level or even with an adjacent surface ▫ *adverb* so as to be level with an adjacent surface

FLUSH [3] *verb* **FLUSHES, FLUSHING, FLUSHED** to startle (game birds) so that they rise from the ground

FLUSHED *adj* suffused with a rosy colour; excited or elated

FLUSTER *verb* **FLUSTERS, FLUSTERING, FLUSTERED** to agitate, confuse or upset someone; to make them hot and flurried ▫ *noun* **FLUSTERS** a state of confused agitation

FLUSTERY *adj* confused and agitated

FLUTE *noun* **FLUTES** a wind instrument consisting of a wooden or metal tube with holes stopped by the fingertips or by keys, which is held horizontally and played by directing the breath across the mouthpiece ▫ *verb* **FLUTES, FLUTING, FLUTED** to produce or utter (sounds) like the high shrill tones of a flute

FLUTED *adj* in architecture: ornamented with grooves and furrows

FLUTING *noun* **FLUTINGS** a series of parallel grooves cut into wood or stone

FLUTIST *noun* **FLUTISTS** a flautist

FLUTTER *verb* **FLUTTERS, FLUTTERING, FLUTTERED** said of a bird, etc: to flap (its wings) lightly and rapidly; to fly with a rapid wing movement ▫ *noun* **FLUTTERS** a quick flapping or vibrating motion

FLUTY *adj* **FLUTIER, FLUTIEST** like a flute in tone

FLUVIAL *adj* relating to or found in rivers

FLUX *noun* **FLUXES** any substance added to another in order to aid the process of melting ▫ *verb* **FLUXES, FLUXING, FLUXED** to apply flux to (a metal, etc) when soldering

FLY [1] *verb* **FLIES, FLYING, FLEW, FLOWN** said of birds, bats, insects and certain other animals: to move through the air using wings or structures resembling wings

FLY [2] *noun* **FLIES** a two-winged insect, especially the common housefly

FLY [3] *adj* **FLIER, FLYER, FLIEST, FLYEST** cunning; smart

FLYBOAT *noun* **FLYBOATS** a long narrow boat used on canals which is relatively fast compared with a conventional canal boat

FLYBOOK *noun* **FLYBOOKS** a small case or wallet used by anglers for holding fishing-flies

FLYER *noun* **FLYERS** a leaflet used to advertise a product, promote an organization, etc, usually distributed on street corners or as an insert in a newspaper, etc

FLYING *adj* hasty; brief ▫ *noun* **FLYINGS** flight

FLYLEAF *noun* **FLYLEAVES** a blank page at the beginning or end of a book

FLYOVER *noun* **FLYOVERS** a bridge that takes a road or railway over another

FLYPAPER *noun* **FLYPAPERS** a strip of paper with a sticky poisonous coating that attracts, traps and kills flies

FLYPITCH *noun* **FLYPITCHES** a market stall for which the operator does not have a licence

FLYTRAP *noun* **FLYTRAPS** a device for catching flies

FLYWAY *noun* **FLYWAYS** a migration route of birds

FLYWEIGHT *noun* **FLYWEIGHTS** a class of boxers, wrestlers and weight-lifters of not more than a specified weight (51kg or 112 lb in professional boxing, similar weights in the other sports)

FLYWHEEL *noun* **FLYWHEELS** a heavy wheel on a revolving shaft that stores kinetic energy and regulates the action of a machine by maintaining a constant speed of rotation over the whole cycle

FOAL *noun* **FOALS** the young of a horse or of a related animal ▫ *verb* **FOALS, FOALING, FOALED** to give birth to a foal

FOAM *noun* **FOAMS** a mass of tiny bubbles forming on the surface of liquids ▫ *verb* **FOAMS, FOAMING, FOAMED** to produce or make something produce foam

FOAMINESS *noun* **FOAMINESSES** the state of being foamy

FOAMING *noun* **FOAMINGS** the production of foam

FOAMLESS *adj* without foam

FOAMY *adj* **FOAMIER, FOAMIEST** said of a liquid: covered with foam; with foam floating on the top of it

FOB [1] *verb* **FOBS, FOBBING, FOBBED** to cheat; to give as genuine

FOB [2] *noun* **FOBS** a chain attached to a watch

FOCACCIA *noun* **FOCACCIAS** a flat round of Italian bread topped with olive oil and herbs or spices

FOCAL *adj* relating to, or at, a focus

FOCALISE *verb* **FOCALISES, FOCALISING, FOCALISED** to focalize

FOCALIZE *verb* **FOCALIZES, FOCALIZING, FOCALIZED** to focus something

FOCIMETER *noun* **FOCIMETERS** an instrument for measuring the focal length of a lens

FOCUS *noun* **FOCUSES, FOCI** the point at which rays of light or sound waves converge or appear to diverge ▫ *verb* **FOCUSES, FOCUSING, FOCUSED** to bring or be brought into focus; to meet or make something meet or converge at a focus

FODDER *noun* **FODDERS** any bulk feed, especially hay and straw, for cattle and other animal livestock ▫ *verb* **FODDERS, FODDERING, FODDERED** to supply (livestock) with fodder

FOE *noun* **FOES** an enemy

FOEHN *noun* **FOEHNS** a föhn

FOETAL *adj* fetal

FOETID *adj* **FOETIDER, FOETIDEST** fetid

FOETUS *noun* **FOETUSES** a fetus

FOG *noun* **FOGS** a suspension of tiny water droplets or ice crystals forming a cloud close to the ground surface and reducing visibility to less than 1 km; thick mist ▫ *verb* **FOGS, FOGGING, FOGGED** to obscure or become obscured with, or as if with, fog or condensation

FOGBOUND *adj* usually said eg of an airport: brought to a standstill by fog

FOGEY *noun* **FOGEYS** someone with boring, old-fashioned and usually conservative ideas and attitudes

FOGEYISH *adj* boring and old-fashioned

FOGGAGE *noun* **FOGGAGES** the grass that grows after the hay is cut

FOGGINESS *noun* **FOGGINESSES** the condition of being foggy

FOGGY *adj* **FOGGIER, FOGGIEST** covered with or thick with fog; misty, damp

FOGHORN *noun* **FOGHORNS** a horn that sounds at regular intervals to ships in fog as a warning of some danger or obstruction, eg land, other vessels, etc

FOGLESS *adj* without fog, clear

FOGY *noun* **FOGIES** a fogey

FOH *exclamation* an expression of disgust or contempt

FÖHN *noun* **FÖHNS** a hot dry wind which blows to the lee of a mountain range, especially down the valleys to the north side of the Alps

FOIBLE *noun* **FOIBLES** a slight personal weakness or eccentricity in someone

FOIL ¹ *verb* **FOILS, FOILING, FOILED** to prevent, thwart or frustrate someone or something

FOIL ² *noun* **FOILS** metal beaten or rolled out into thin sheets

FOIST *verb* **FOISTS, FOISTING, FOISTED** to inflict or impose something unwanted on someone

FOLATE *adj* relating to folic acid □ *noun* **FOLATES** a salt of folic acid

FOLD *verb* **FOLDS, FOLDING, FOLDED** to double something over so that one part lies on top of another □ *noun* **FOLDS** a doubling of one layer over another

FOLDABLE *adj* able to be folded

FOLDAWAY *adj* referring to something that can be folded and put away

FOLDER *noun* **FOLDERS** a cardboard or plastic cover in which to keep loose papers

FOLDEROL *noun* **FOLDEROLS** falderal

FOLDING *adj* referring to something that can be folded away so that it takes up less space, particularly for storage □ *noun* **FOLDINGS** a fold or plait

FOLIAGE *noun* **FOLIAGES** the green leaves on a tree or plant

FOLIATE *adj* leaflike or having leaves □ *verb* **FOLIATES, FOLIATING, FOLIATED** to cover with leaf-metal or foils

FOLIO *noun* **FOLIOS** a leaf of a manuscript, etc, numbered on one side

FOLIOLE *noun* **FOLIOLES** a leaflet of a compound leaf

FOLK *singular or plural noun* **FOLKS** people in general □ *adj* traditional among, or originating from, a particular group of people or nation

FOLKIE *noun* **FOLKIES** someone who enjoys listening to folk music

FOLKLORE *noun* **FOLKLORES** the customs, beliefs, stories, traditions, etc of a particular group of people, usually passed down through the oral tradition

FOLKLORIC *adj* of or relating to folklore

FOLKSY *adj* **FOLKSIER, FOLKSIEST** simple and homely, especially in an over-sweet or twee way

FOLLICLE *noun* **FOLLICLES** a small cavity or sac within a tissue or organ, eg the pit surrounding the root of a hair

FOLLOW *verb* **FOLLOWS, FOLLOWING, FOLLOWED** to go or come after someone, either immediately or shortly afterwards

FOLLOWER *noun* **FOLLOWERS** someone or something that follows or comes after others

FOLLOWING *noun* **FOLLOWINGS** a body of supporters, devotees, etc □ *adj* coming after; next □ *prep* after

FOLLY *noun* **FOLLIES** foolishness; a foolish act

FOMENT *verb* **FOMENTS, FOMENTING, FOMENTED** to encourage or foster (ill-feeling, etc)

FOMENTER *noun* **FOMENTERS** a person or thing that foments

FON *verb* **FONS, FONNING, FONNED** to play the fool

FOND *adj* **FONDER, FONDEST** loving; tender

FONDANT *noun* **FONDANTS** a soft sweet or paste made with sugar and water, often flavoured and used for the fillings of chocolates, or as icing

FONDLE *verb* **FONDLES, FONDLING, FONDLED** to touch, stroke or caress someone or something lovingly, affectionately or lustfully

FONDLER *noun* **FONDLERS** someone who fondles

FONDLING *noun* **FONDLINGS** touching, stroking or caressing someone or something lovingly, affectionately or lustfully

FONDLY *adverb* affectionately or lovingly

FONDNESS *noun* **FONDNESSES** affection

FONDUE *noun* **FONDUES** a dish, originally Swiss, consisting of hot cheese sauce into which bits of bread are dipped

FONT *noun* **FONTS** the basin in a church that holds water for baptisms

FONTAL *adj* relating to a font or origin

FONTANEL *noun* **FONTANELS** a soft membrane-covered gap between the immature bones of the skull of a fetus or young infant, or of a young animal

FOOD *noun* **FOODS** a substance taken in by a living organism that provides it with energy and materials for growth, maintenance and repair of tissues

FOODIE *noun* **FOODIES** a person who is greatly or excessively interested in the preparation and eating of food, especially wholefoods and additive-free foods

FOODISM *noun* **FOODISMS** great interest in, or concern over, food

FOODSTUFF *noun* **FOODSTUFFS** a substance used as food

FOOL *noun* **FOOLS** someone who lacks common sense or intelligence □ *verb* **FOOLS, FOOLING, FOOLED** to deceive someone so that they appear foolish or ridiculous

FOOLERY *noun* **FOOLERIES** stupid or ridiculous behaviour

FOOLHARDY *adj* **FOOLHARDIER, FOOLHARDIEST** taking foolish risks; rash; reckless

FOOLISH *adj* **FOOLISHER, FOOLISHEST** unwise; senseless

FOOLISHLY *adverb* in a foolish way

FOOLPROOF *adj* said of a plan, etc: designed so that it is easy to follow and very unlikely to go wrong; unable to go wrong

FOOLSCAP *noun* **FOOLSCAPS** a large size of printing- or writing-paper, measuring $17\frac{1}{2} \times 13\frac{1}{2}$in ($432\frac{1}{2} \times 343$mm)

FOOT *noun* **FEET** the part of the leg on which a human being or animal stands or walks; a unit of length equal to 12in (30.48cm)

FOOTAGE *noun* **FOOTAGES** measurement or payment by the foot

FOOTBALL *noun* **FOOTBALLS** any of several team games played with a large ball that players try to kick or head into the opposing team's goal or carry across their opponents' goal line

FOOTED *adj* provided with a foot or feet

FOOTER *noun* **FOOTERS** football

FOOTFALL *noun* **FOOTFALLS** the sound of a footstep

FOOTFAULT *noun* **FOOTFAULTS** in tennis: a fault that makes the stroke invalid, caused by stepping over the baseline when serving

FOOTHILL *noun* **FOOTHILLS** a lower hill on the approach to a high mountain or mountain range

FOOTHOLD *noun* **FOOTHOLDS** a place to put one's foot when climbing

FOOTIE *noun* **FOOTIES** football

FOOTING *noun* **FOOTINGS** the stability of one's feet on the ground

FOOTLE *verb* **FOOTLES, FOOTLING, FOOTLED** to waste time, potter, wander aimlessly □ *noun* **FOOTLES** silly nonsense

FOOTLESS *adj* having no feet

FOOTLIGHT *noun* **FOOTLIGHTS** one of a row of lights set along the front edge of a theatre stage

FOOTLING *adj* trivial

FOOTLOOSE *adj* free to go where, or do as, one likes; not hampered by any ties

FOOTMAN *noun* **FOOTMEN** a uniformed male attendant

FOOTMARK *noun* **FOOTMARKS** a footprint

FOOTNOTE *noun* **FOOTNOTES** a comment at the bottom of a page, often preceded by a numbered mark or asterisk, etc which relates the comment to a particular part of the main text

FOOTPATH *noun* **FOOTPATHS** a path or track for walkers, usually in the countryside, eg alongside fields, through a wood, etc

FOOTPLATE *noun* **FOOTPLATES** in a steam train: a platform for the driver and fireman, who are known as the footplatemen

FOOTPRINT *noun* **FOOTPRINTS** the mark or impression of a foot or shoe left eg in sand, in soft ground, etc

FOOTREST *noun* **FOOTRESTS** a support for the feet, such as a stool or rail, used when sitting down

FOOTS *plural noun* footlights

FOOTSLOG *verb* **FOOTSLOGS, FOOTSLOGGING, FOOTSLOGGED** to go on foot; to trudge

FOOTSORE *adj* having sore and tired feet from prolonged walking

FOOTSTALK *noun* **FOOTSTALKS** the stalk or petiole of a leaf

FOOTSTEP *noun* **FOOTSTEPS** the sound of a step in walking

FOOTSTOOL *noun* **FOOTSTOOLS** a low stool for supporting the feet while sitting

FOOTWAY *noun* **FOOTWAYS** a passage for pedestrians

FOOTWEAR *singular noun* shoes, boots, socks, etc

FOOTWORK *noun* **FOOTWORKS** the agile use of the feet in dancing or sport

FOOTY *noun* **FOOTIES** football

FOP *noun* **FOPS** a man who is very consciously elegant in his dress and manners; a dandy

FOPPERY *noun* **FOPPERIES** vanity in dress or manners; affectation

FOPPISH *adj* vain and showy in dress; affectedly refined in manners

FOR *prep* intended to be given or sent to someone □ *conj* because; as

FORA a plural of **forum**

FORAGE *noun* **FORAGES** a crop grown for consumption by livestock, eg grass, kale, swede, which may be either grazed directly or harvested and stored for later use □ *verb* **FORAGES, FORAGING, FORAGED** to search around, especially for food

FORAGER *noun* **FORAGERS** a person or thing that forages

FORAMEN *noun* **FORAMINA** a naturally occurring small opening, particularly in the bone

FORAMINAL *adj* of or relating to a foramen

FORAY *noun* **FORAYS** a raid or attack □ *verb* **FORAYS, FORAYING, FORAYED** to raid; to pillage; to forage

FORAYER *noun* **FORAYERS** someone who forays

FORBEAR [1] *verb* **FORBEARS, FORBEARING, FORBORE, FORBORNE** to tolerate something

FORBEAR [2] *noun* **FORBEARS** a forebear

FORBEARING *adj* long-suffering; patient and tolerant

FORBID *verb* **FORBIDS, FORBIDDING, FORBAD, FORBADE, FORBIDDEN** to order someone not to do something

FORBIDDEN *adj* prohibited; not allowed; not permitted, eg access to somewhere

FORBIDDING *adj* threatening; grim

FORBORE a past form of **forbear** [1]

FORBORNE a past form of **forbear** [1]

FORCE *noun* **FORCES** strength; power; impact or impetus □ *verb* **FORCES, FORCING, FORCED** to make or compel someone to do something

FORCED *adj* said of a smile, laugh, etc: unnatural; unspontaneous

FORCEDLY *adverb* in a forced way

FORCEFUL *adj* powerful; effective; influential

FORCELESS *adj* weak

FORCEMEAT *noun* **FORCEMEATS** a mixture of chopped or minced ingredients, eg vegetables, or sausage meat, herbs, etc, used as stuffing

FORCEPS *noun* **FORCEPSES, FORCIPES** an instrument like pincers, for gripping firmly, used especially in surgery and dentistry

FORCER *noun* **FORCERS** a person or thing that forces, especially the piston of a force-pump

FORCIBLE *adj* done by or involving force

FORCIBLY *adverb* in a forcible way

FORD *noun* **FORDS** a crossing-place in a river, where a road or track crosses by passing through shallow water □ *verb* **FORDS, FORDING, FORDED** to ride, drive or wade across (a stream, river, etc) by passing through shallow water

FORDABLE *adj* able to be forded

FORE [1] *adj* towards the front □ *noun* **FORES** the front part

FORE [2] *exclamation* in golf: ball coming!; a warning shout to anybody who may be in the ball's path

FOREARM *noun* **FOREARMS** the lower part of the arm between wrist and elbow □ *verb* **FOREARMS, FOREARMING, FOREARMED** to prepare someone or arm someone beforehand

FOREBEAR *noun* **FOREBEARS** an ancestor, usually more remote than grandfather or grandmother

FOREBODE *verb* **FOREBODES, FOREBODING, FOREBODED** to foretell; to prophesy

FOREBODING noun **FOREBODINGS** a feeling of approaching trouble

FOREBRAIN noun **FOREBRAINS** the largest part of the brain in vertebrates, consisting of the left and right cerebral hemispheres, the thalamus and the hypothalamus

FORECAST verb **FORECASTS, FORECASTING, FORECASTED, FORECAST** to give warning of something; to predict something ◻ noun **FORECASTS** a warning, prediction or advance estimate

FORECLOSE verb **FORECLOSES, FORECLOSING, FORECLOSED** said of a mortgager, bank, etc: to repossess a property because of failure on the part of the mortgagee to repay agreed amounts of the loan

FORECOURT noun **FORECOURTS** a courtyard or paved area in front of a building, eg a filling-station

FOREDATE verb **FOREDATES, FOREDATING, FOREDATED** to mark something with a date that is prior to the current date

FOREFOOT noun **FOREFEET** either of the two front feet of a four-legged animal

FOREFRONT noun **FOREFRONTS** the very front

FOREGO verb **FOREGOES, FOREGOING, FOREWENT, FOREGONE** to precede, either in position or time

FOREGOING adj just mentioned ◻ noun **FOREGOINGS** the thing or person just mentioned

FOREHAND adj said of a tennis, etc stroke: with the palm in front, as opposed to backhand ◻ noun **FOREHANDS** a stroke made with the palm facing forward ◻ adverb with the hand in forehand position

FOREHEAD noun **FOREHEADS** the part of the face between the eyebrows and hairline; the brow

FOREIGN adj belonging or relating to, or coming from another country

FOREIGNER noun **FOREIGNERS** a person from another country

FOREJUDGE verb **FOREJUDGES, FOREJUDGING, FOREJUDGED** to pass judgement before hearing the facts and proof

FOREKNOW verb **FOREKNOWS, FOREKNOWING, FOREKNEW, FOREKNOWN** to know something before it happens; to foresee something

FORELAND noun **FORELANDS** a point of land running forward into the sea; a headland

FORELEG noun **FORELEGS** either of the two front legs of a four-legged animal

FORELOCK noun **FORELOCKS** a lock of hair growing or falling over the brow

FOREMAN noun **FOREMEN** someone in charge of a department or group of workers, who usually also has a role as worker as well as carrying out a supervisory role

FOREMAST noun **FOREMASTS** the mast that is nearest to the bow of a ship

FOREMOST adj leading; best ◻ adverb leading; coming first

FORENAME noun **FORENAMES** used on official forms, etc: one's personal name as distinct from one's family name or surname

FORENAMED adj mentioned before

FORENOON adj referring to morning ◻ noun **FORENOONS** the morning

FORENSIC adj belonging or relating to courts of law, or to the work of a lawyer in court

FOREPART noun **FOREPARTS** the front; the early part

FOREPLAY noun **FOREPLAYS** sexual stimulation, often leading up to sexual intercourse

FORESAID adj already mentioned

FORESEE verb **FORESEES, FORESEEING, FORESAW, FORESEEN** to see that something will happen in advance, or know in advance, often by circumstantial evidence

FORESHORE noun **FORESHORES** the area on the shore between the positions that the high and low tides reach, regularly covered and uncovered by the tide

FORESIGHT noun **FORESIGHTS** the ability to foresee

FORESKIN noun **FORESKINS** the retractable fold of skin that covers the end of the penis

FOREST noun **FORESTS** a plant community extending over a large area and dominated by trees, the crowns of which form an unbroken covering layer or canopy ◻ adj relating to or consisting of a forest ◻ verb **FORESTS, FORESTING, FORESTED** to cover (an area) with trees; to cover (an area) thickly with tall, upright objects

FORESTALL verb **FORESTALLS, FORESTALLING, FORESTALLED** to prevent something by acting in advance

FORESTALLING noun **FORESTALLINGS** the prevention of something by acting in advance

FORESTED adj covered with trees

FORESTER noun **FORESTERS** a person whose job is to manage a forest; someone trained in forestry

FORESTRY noun **FORESTRIES** the management of forest and woodland for the commercial production of timber, including the growing and maintenance of trees, the felling of mature trees, etc

FORETASTE noun **FORETASTES** a brief experience of what is to come

FORETELL verb **FORETELLS, FORETELLING, FORETOLD** to tell about something beforehand; to predict or prophesy something

FORETHINK verb **FORETHINKS, FORETHINKING, FORETHOUGHT** to anticipate in the mind

FORETHOUGHT noun **FORETHOUGHTS** consideration taken or provision made for the future

FORETOP noun **FORETOPS** the platform at the top or head of the foremast

FOREVER adverb always; eternally; for all time ◻ noun an endless or indefinite length of time

FOREWARN verb **FOREWARNS, FOREWARNING, FOREWARNED** to warn beforehand; to give previous notice

FOREWENT a past form of **forego**

FOREWOMAN noun **FOREWOMEN** a woman in charge of a department or group of workers, who usually also has a role as worker as well as carrying out a supervisory role

FOREWORD noun **FOREWORDS** an introduction to a book, often by a writer other than the author; preface

FORFEIT noun **FORFEITS** something that one must surrender as a penalty ◻ adj surrendered or liable to be surrendered as a penalty ◻ verb **FORFEITS, FORFEITING, FORFEITED** to hand over as a penalty

FORGATHER verb **FORGATHERS, FORGATHERING, FORGATHERED** to meet together; to assemble

FORGAVE past form of **forgive**

FORGE *noun* **FORGES** a special furnace for heating metal, especially iron, prior to shaping it □ *verb* **FORGES, FORGING, FORGED** to shape metal by heating and hammering, or by heating and applying pressure more gradually

FORGEABLE *adj* that may be forged

FORGER *noun* **FORGERS** a person who commits forgery, especially illegally

FORGERY *noun* **FORGERIES** imitating pictures, documents, signatures, etc for a fraudulent purpose

FORGET *verb* **FORGETS, FORGETTING, FORGOT, FORGOTTEN** to fail to remember something or be unable to remember something

FORGETFUL *adj* inclined to forget

FORGIVE *verb* **FORGIVES, FORGIVING, FORGAVE, FORGIVEN** to stop being angry with (someone who has done something wrong) or about (an offence)

FORGIVING *adj* ready to forgive; patient and tolerant

FORGO *verb* **FORGOES, FORGOING, FORWENT, FORGONE** to do without something; to sacrifice something or give it up

FORGOT a past form of **forget**

FORGOTTEN a past form of **forget**

FORINT *noun* **FORINTS** the standard unit of currency of Hungary since 1946

FORJUDGE *verb* **FORJUDGES, FORJUDGING, FORJUDGED** to deprive someone of a right, etc, by a judgement

FORK *noun* **FORKS** an eating or cooking implement with prongs (usually three), for spearing and lifting food □ *verb* **FORKS, FORKING, FORKED** said of a road, etc: to divide into two branches

FORKED *adj* dividing into two branches or parts; shaped like a fork

FORKER *noun* **FORKERS** someone who lifts or moves something with a fork

FORKFUL *noun* **FORKFULS** the amount which can be held on a fork

FORLORN *adj* **FORLORNER, FORLORNEST** exceedingly unhappy; miserable

FORLORNLY *adverb* in a forlorn way

FORM *noun* **FORMS** shape □ *verb*

FORMS, FORMING, FORMED to organize or set something up

FORMABLE *adj* that can be formed

FORMAL *adj* relating to or involving etiquette, ceremony or conventional procedure generally

FORMALIN *noun* **FORMALINS** a clear solution of formaldehyde in water used as a preservative, antiseptic and disinfectant

FORMALISE *verb* **FORMALISES, FORMALISING, FORMALISED** to formalize

FORMALISM *noun* **FORMALISMS** concern, especially excessive concern, with outward form, to the exclusion of content

FORMALIST *noun* **FORMALISTS** a person having exaggerated regard to rules or established usages

FORMALITY *noun* **FORMALITIES** a procedure gone through as a requirement of etiquette, ceremony, the law, etc

FORMALIZE *verb* **FORMALIZES, FORMALIZING, FORMALIZED** to make something precise; to give a clear statement of something

FORMALLY *adverb* in a formal way

FORMANT *noun* **FORMANTS** the dominant component or components which determine the particular sound quality of all vowels and some consonants

FORMAT *noun* **FORMATS** the size and shape of something, especially a book or magazine □ *verb* **FORMATS, FORMATTING, FORMATTED** to design, shape or organize in a particular way

FORMATION *noun* **FORMATIONS** the process of forming, making, developing or establishing something

FORMATIVE *adj* relating to development or growth

FORMATTER *noun* **FORMATTERS** a program for formatting a disk, tape, etc

FORME *noun* **FORMES** in printing: the type and blocks assembled in a frame, ready for printing

FORMER *adj* belonging to an earlier time

FORMERLY *adverb* previously; in the past; before this time

FORMIC *adj* relating to or derived from ants

FORMING *noun* **FORMINGS** the process of being formed

FORMLESS *adj* lacking a clear shape or structure

FORMULA *noun* **FORMULAS,**

FORMULAE the combination of ingredients used in a product, etc

FORMULAIC *adj* containing a set form of words

FORMULARY *noun* **FORMULARIES** a book or collection of set wordings, especially legal or religious ones

FORMULATE *verb* **FORMULATES, FORMULATING, FORMULATED** to express something in systematic terms

FORNICATE *verb* **FORNICATES, FORNICATING, FORNICATED** to have sexual intercourse outside marriage

FORSAKE *verb* **FORSAKES, FORSAKING, FORSOOK, FORSAKEN** to desert; to abandon

FORSAKEN *adj* completely abandoned; forlorn

FORSWEAR *verb* **FORSWEARS, FORSWEARING, FORSWORE, FORSWORN** to give up or renounce (one's foolish ways, etc)

FORSYTHIA *noun* **FORSYTHIAS** a deciduous shrub cultivated for its bright yellow flowers that appear before the leaves

FORT *noun* **FORTS** a fortified military building, enclosure or position

FORTE [1] *noun* **FORTES** something one is good at; a strong point

FORTE [2] *adj* loud

FORTH *adverb* into existence or view; forwards

FORTHWITH *adverb* immediately; at once

FORTIES *plural noun* the period of time between one's fortieth and fiftieth birthdays

FORTIETH *adj* in counting: next after thirty-ninth □ *noun* **FORTIETHS** one of forty equal parts

FORTIFIER *noun* **FORTIFIERS** a person or thing that fortifies

FORTIFY *verb* **FORTIFIES, FORTIFYING, FORTIFIED** to strengthen (a building, city, etc) in preparation for an attack

FORTIS *adj* articulated with considerable muscular effort and pressure of breath □ *noun* **FORTES** a consonant that is produced in this way

FORTITUDE *noun* **FORTITUDES** uncomplaining courage in pain or misfortune

FORTNIGHT *noun* **FORTNIGHTS** a period of 14 days; two weeks

FORTRESS *noun* **FORTRESSES** a

fortified town, or large fort or castle

FORTUITY noun **FORTUITIES** chance, accident

FORTUNATE adj lucky; favoured by fate

FORTUNE noun **FORTUNES** chance as a force in human affairs; fate

FORTY noun **FORTIES** the cardinal number 40 □ adj totalling forty

FORTYISH adj about forty years old

FORUM noun **FORUMS, FORA** a public square or market place, especially that in ancient Rome where public business was conducted and law courts held

FORWARD adverb in the direction in front or ahead of one □ adj **FORWARDER, FORWARDEST** in the direction in front or ahead; presumptuous, bold □ noun **FORWARDS** a player whose task is to attack rather than defend □ verb **FORWARDS, FORWARDING, FORWARDED** to send (mail) on to another address from the one to which it arrived

FORWARDLY adverb presumptuously or boldly

FORWENT a past form of **forgo**

FOSS noun **FOSSES** a fosse

FOSSA noun **FOSSAS** a Madagascan civet

FOSSE noun **FOSSES** a ditch, moat, trench or canal

FOSSIL noun **FOSSILS** the petrified remains, impression or cast of an animal or plant preserved within a rock

FOSSILISE verb **FOSSILISES, FOSSILISING, FOSSILISED** to fossilize

FOSSILIZE verb **FOSSILIZES, FOSSILIZING, FOSSILIZED** to change or be changed into a fossil

FOSSORIAL adj adapted for digging

FOSTER verb **FOSTERS, FOSTERING, FOSTERED** to bring up (a child that is not one's own)

FOSTERER noun **FOSTERERS** someone who brings up a child that is not their own

FOSTERING noun **FOSTERINGS** bringing up a child that is not one's own

FOU adj a Scots word meaning *drunk*

FOUETTÉ noun **FOUETTÉS** in ballet: a step in which the foot

makes a sideways whiplike movement

FOUGHT past form of **fight**

FOUL adj **FOULER, FOULEST** soiled; filthy □ noun **FOULS** a breach of the rules □ verb **FOULS, FOULING, FOULED** to commit an act against (an opponent) which breaches the rules □ adverb in a foul manner; unfairly

FOULARD noun **FOULARDS** a soft untwilled silk fabric

FOULLY adverb in a foul manner

FOULNESS noun **FOULNESSES** a foul condition

FOUND [1] verb **FOUNDS, FOUNDING, FOUNDED** to start or establish (an organization, institution, city, etc), often with a provision for future funding

FOUND [2] past form of **find**

FOUNDER [1] noun **FOUNDERS** someone who founds or endows an institution, etc

FOUNDER [2] verb **FOUNDERS, FOUNDERING, FOUNDERED** said of a ship: to sink

FOUNDING noun **FOUNDINGS** the casting of metal or glass by melting and pouring it into a mould

FOUNDLING noun **FOUNDLINGS** an abandoned child of unknown parents

FOUNDRY noun **FOUNDRIES** a place where metal or glass is melted and cast

FOUNT noun **FOUNTS** a spring or fountain

FOUNTAIN noun **FOUNTAINS** a jet or jets of water for ornamental effect

FOUR noun **FOURS** the cardinal number 4 □ adj totalling four

FOURFOLD adj equal to four times as much □ adverb by four times as much

FOURSCORE adj eighty □ noun **FOURSCORES** eighty

FOURSOME noun **FOURSOMES** a set or group of four people

FOURTEEN noun **FOURTEENS** the cardinal number 14 □ adj totalling fourteen

FOURTH adj in counting: next after third □ noun **FOURTHS** one of four equal parts □ adverb fourthly

FOURTHLY adverb used to introduce the fourth point in a list

FOUSTY adj **FOUSTIER, FOUSTIEST** mouldy or damp

FOVEA noun **FOVEAE** a shallow depression in the retina at the back

of the eye in birds, lizards and primates where vision is sharpest

FOVEAL adj of or like a fovea

FOVEATE adj pitted

FOWL noun **FOWLS** a farmyard bird, eg a chicken or turkey □ verb **FOWLS, FOWLING, FOWLED** to hunt or trap wild birds

FOWLER noun **FOWLERS** a person who fowls

FOWLING noun **FOWLINGS** hunting or trapping wild birds

FOX noun **FOXES** any of various carnivorous mammals belonging to the dog family, found in most parts of the world, with a pointed muzzle, large pointed ears and a long bushy tail □ verb **FOXES, FOXING, FOXED** to puzzle, confuse or baffle someone

FOXED adj baffled; bamboozled

FOXGLOVE noun **FOXGLOVES** a biennial or perennial plant, that produces tall spikes with many thimble-shaped purple or white flowers, and whose leaves are a source of digitalis

FOXHOLE noun **FOXHOLES** a hole in the ground from which a soldier may shoot while protected from the enemy's guns

FOXHOUND noun **FOXHOUNDS** a breed of dog bred and trained to chase foxes

FOXINESS noun **FOXINESSES** the quality of being foxy

FOXING noun **FOXINGS** discoloration in the form of brownish marks on paper that has been allowed to become damp

FOXTROT noun **FOXTROTS** a ballroom dance with gliding steps, alternating between quick and slow □ verb **FOXTROTS, FOXTROTTING, FOXTROTTED** to perform this dance

FOXY adj **FOXIER, FOXIEST** referring to foxes; foxlike

FOY noun **FOYS** a Shakespearean word meaning *loyalty*

FOYER noun **FOYERS** the entrance hall of a theatre, hotel, etc

FOZY adj **FOZIER, FOZIEST** spongy

FRA noun **FRAS** an Italian word meaning brother or friar

FRABJOUS adj joyous; wonderful

FRACAS noun **FRACAS** a noisy quarrel; a fight or brawl

FRACTAL noun **FRACTALS** an

irregular curve or surface produced by repeated subdivision, eg a *snowflake curve* (resembling a snowflake in outline), produced by repeatedly dividing the sides of an equilateral triangle into three segments and adding another triangle to the middle section

FRACTION noun **FRACTIONS** an expression that indicates one or more equal parts of a whole, usually represented by a pair of numbers separated by a horizontal or diagonal line, where the upper number (the numerator) represents the number of parts selected and the lower number (the denominator) the total number of parts

FRACTIOUS adj cross and quarrelsome; inclined to quarrel and complain

FRACTURE noun **FRACTURES** the breaking or cracking of anything hard, especially bone, rock or mineral □ verb **FRACTURES, FRACTURING, FRACTURED** to break or crack something, especially a bone

FRAENUM noun **FRAENA** a frenum

FRAGILE adj **FRAGILER, FRAGILEST** easily broken; liable to break

FRAGILELY adverb in a fragile way

FRAGMENT noun **FRAGMENTS** a piece broken off; a small piece of something that has broken □ verb **FRAGMENTS, FRAGMENTING, FRAGMENTED** to break into pieces

FRAGMENTED adj consisting of small pieces, not usually amounting to a complete whole; in fragments

FRAGRANCE noun **FRAGRANCES** sweetness of smell

FRAGRANCY noun **FRAGRANCIES** sweetness of smell

FRAGRANT adj sweet-scented

FRAIL adj **FRAILER, FRAILEST** easily broken or destroyed; delicate; fragile

FRAILLY adverb in a frail way

FRAILNESS noun **FRAILNESSES** weakness; infirmity

FRAILTY noun **FRAILTIES** weakness; infirmity

FRAME noun **FRAMES** a hard main structure or basis to something, round which something is built or to which other parts are added □ verb **FRAMES, FRAMING, FRAMED** to put a frame round something

FRAMER noun **FRAMERS** a person who makes frames for pictures, etc

FRAMEWORK noun **FRAMEWORKS** a basic supporting structure

FRAMING noun **FRAMINGS** the act of constructing; a frame or setting

FRANC noun **FRANCS** the standard unit of currency of various countries, including France, Belgium, Switzerland, and several other French-speaking countries

FRANCHISE noun **FRANCHISES** the right to vote, especially in a parliamentary election □ verb **FRANCHISES, FRANCHISING, FRANCHISED** to grant a franchise to (a person)

FRANCIUM noun **FRANCIUMS** a radioactive metallic element, the heaviest of the alkali metals, obtained by bombarding thorium with protons

FRANCOLIN noun **FRANCOLINS** a partridge native to Africa and S Asia

FRANK adj **FRANKER, FRANKEST** open and honest in speech or manner; candid □ verb **FRANKS, FRANKING, FRANKED** to mark (a letter), either cancelling the stamp or, in place of a stamp, to show that postage has been paid □ noun **FRANKS** a franking mark on a letter

FRANKLY adverb to be frank; in a frank manner

FRANKNESS noun **FRANKNESSES** the quality of being frank

FRANTIC adj desperate, eg with fear or anxiety

FRAPPÉ adj iced; artificially cooled □ noun **FRAPPÉS** an iced drink

FRASCATI noun **FRASCATIS** an Italian wine, usually white

FRATERNAL adj concerning a brother; brotherly

FRAU noun **FRAUS** usually said of a German woman: a woman or wife, usually used as a title equivalent to *Mrs* or *Ms*

FRAUD noun **FRAUDS** an act of deliberate deception, with the intention of gaining some benefit

FRAUDSTER noun **FRAUDSTERS** a cheat; a swindler

FRAUGHT adj **FRAUGHTER, FRAUGHTEST** causing or feeling anxiety or worry

FRÄULEIN noun **FRÄULEINS** an unmarried woman

FRAY[1] verb **FRAYS, FRAYING, FRAYED** said of cloth or rope: to wear away along an edge or at a point of friction, so that individual threads come loose

FRAY[2] noun **FRAYS** a fight, quarrel or argument

FRAZIL noun **FRAZILS** ice formed in small spikes and plates in rapidly-moving streams

FRAZZLE noun **FRAZZLES** a state of nervous and physical exhaustion □ verb **FRAZZLES, FRAZZLING, FRAZZLED** to tire out physically and emotionally

FREAK noun **FREAKS** a person, animal or plant of abnormal shape or form □ verb **FREAKS, FREAKING, FREAKED** to become or make someone mentally or emotionally over-excited

FREAKISH adj very unusual; odd

FREAKY adj **FREAKIER, FREAKIEST** odd; strange; unusual; eccentric; way-out

FRECKLE noun **FRECKLES** a small yellowish-brown benign mark on the skin, especially of fair-skinned people, which sometimes appears in large numbers, usually becoming darker and more prominent with exposure to the sun □ verb **FRECKLES, FRECKLING, FRECKLED** to mark, or become marked, with freckles

FRECKLED adj covered in freckles

FRECKLY adj **FRECKLIER, FRECKLIEST** covered in freckles

FREE adj **FREER, FREEST** allowed to move as one pleases; not shut in □ adverb without payment □ verb **FREES, FREEING, FREED** to allow someone to move without restriction after a period in captivity, prison, etc; to set or make someone free; to liberate someone

FREEBASE noun **FREEBASES** cocaine refined for smoking by being heated with ether □ verb **FREEBASES, FREEBASING, FREEBASED** to purify cocaine by heating with ether

FREEBEE noun **FREEBEES** a freebie

FREEBIE noun **FREEBIES** something given or provided without charge, particularly as a sales promotion

FREEBORN adj born as a free citizen, not a slave

FREED past form of **free**

FREEDMAN noun **FREEDMEN** a man who has been a slave and has been emancipated

FREEDOM noun **FREEDOMS** the condition of being free to act, move, etc without restriction

FREEHAND adj said of a drawing, etc: done without the help of a ruler, compass, etc ◻ adverb said of a drawing, etc: done without the help of a ruler, compass, etc

FREEHOLD adj said of land, property, etc: belonging to the owner for life and without limitations ◻ noun **FREEHOLDS** ownership of such land, property, etc

FREELANCE noun **FREELANCES** a self-employed person offering their services where needed, not under contract to any single employer ◻ adverb as a freelance ◻ verb **FREELANCES, FREELANCING, FREELANCED** to work as a freelance

FREELOAD verb **FREELOADS, FREELOADING, FREELOADED** to eat, live, enjoy oneself, etc at someone else's expense

FREELY adverb in a free way

FREEMAN noun **FREEMEN** a man who is free or enjoys liberty

FREEMASON noun **FREEMASONS** a member of an international secret male society, organized into lodges, having among its purposes mutual help and brotherly fellowship

FREENESS noun **FREENESSES** the state of being free

FREEPHONE noun **FREEPHONES** a telephone service whereby calls made to a business or organization are charged to that organization rather than to the caller

FREER noun **FREERS** a liberator

FREESHEET noun **FREESHEETS** a newspaper, available or distributed without charge, financed by its advertisements

FREESIA noun **FREESIAS** a plant of southern Africa belonging to the iris family, which has an underground bulb and is widely cultivated for its fragrant trumpet-shaped white, yellow, purple or crimson flowers

FREESTONE noun **FREESTONES** any fine-grained stone, eg sandstone or limestone, that can be shaped easily for building without a tendency to split in layers ◻ adj said of certain types of eg peaches and nectarines: having a stone from which the flesh comes away easily when ripe

FREESTYLE adj applied to a competition or race in which competitors are allowed to choose their own style or programme ◻ noun **FREESTYLES** a freestyle competition or race

FREEWARE noun **FREEWARES** software which is in the public domain, allowing it to be copied legally and at no charge, but not resold commercially

FREEWAY noun **FREEWAYS** a toll-free highway

FREEWHEEL noun **FREEWHEELS** the mechanism on a bicycle by which the back wheel can run free from the gear mechanism with the pedals stationary ◻ verb **FREEWHEELS, FREEWHEELING, FREEWHEELED** to travel, usually downhill, on a bicycle, in a car, etc without using mechanical power

FREEWOMAN noun **FREEWOMEN** a woman who is free or enjoys liberty

FREEZABLE adj that can be frozen

FREEZE verb **FREEZES, FREEZING, FROZE, FROZEN** to change (a liquid) into a solid by cooling it to below its freezing point, eg to change water into ice ◻ noun **FREEZES** a period of very cold weather with temperatures below freezing-point ◻ exclamation a command to stop instantly or risk being shot

FREEZER noun **FREEZERS** a refrigerated cabinet or compartment in which to preserve food at a temperature below freezing-point

FREIGHT noun **FREIGHTS** transport of goods by rail, road, sea or air ◻ verb **FREIGHTS, FREIGHTING, FREIGHTED** to transport (goods) by rail, road, sea or air

FREIGHTER noun **FREIGHTERS** a ship or aircraft that carries cargo rather than passengers

FRENETIC adj frantic, distracted, hectic or wildly energetic

FRENUM noun **FRENA** a ligament restraining the motion of a part of the body, such as the ligament under the tongue

FRENZIED adj characterized by frenzy

FRENZY noun **FRENZIES** wild agitation or excitement

FREON noun **FREONS** any of the family of chemicals containing fluorine, used as refrigerants, etc

FREQUENCY noun **FREQUENCIES** the condition of happening often

FREQUENT adj **FREQUENTER, FREQUENTEST** recurring at short intervals ◻ verb **FREQUENTS, FREQUENTING, FREQUENTED** to visit or attend (a place, an event, etc) often

FREQUENTER noun **FREQUENTERS** someone who visits or attends a place, etc often

FRESCO noun **FRESCOS, FRESCOES** a picture painted on a wall, usually while the plaster is still damp

FRESCOED adj painted in fresco

FRESCOER noun **FRESCOERS** someone who paints in fresco

FRESCOIST noun **FRESCOISTS** a frescoer

FRESH adj **FRESHER, FRESHEST** newly made, gathered, etc ◻ adverb in a fresh way

FRESHEN verb **FRESHENS, FRESHENING, FRESHENED** to make something fresh or fresher

FRESHER noun **FRESHERS** a student in their first year at university or college

FRESHET noun **FRESHETS** a stream of fresh water flowing into the sea

FRESHLY adverb with freshness; newly; anew

FRESHMAN noun **FRESHMEN** a fresher

FRESHNESS noun **FRESHNESSES** the quality or condition of being fresh

FRET[1] verb **FRETS, FRETTING, FRETTED** to worry, especially unnecessarily; to show or express anxiety

FRET[2] noun **FRETS** any of the narrow metal ridges across the neck of a guitar or similar musical instrument, onto which the strings are pressed in producing the various notes

FRETFUL adj anxious and unhappy; tending to fret; peevish

FRETFULLY adverb in a fretful way

FRETSAW noun **FRETSAWS** a narrow-bladed saw for cutting designs in wood or metal

FRETWORK noun **FRETWORKS** decorative carved openwork in wood or metal

FRIABLE adj easily broken; easily reduced to powder

FRIAR noun **FRIARS** a member of any of various religious orders of the Roman Catholic Church who, especially formerly, worked as teachers of the Christian religion and lived by begging, often named according to the order they belong to, such as the Franciscans, Dominicans, Carmelites, Augustinians, etc

FRIARBIRD noun **FRIARBIRDS** an Australian honey-eating bird with a featherless head

FRIARY noun **FRIARIES** a building inhabited by a community of friars

FRICADEL noun **FRICADELS** a frikkadel

FRICASSEE noun **FRICASSEES** a cooked dish, usually of pieces of meat or chicken served in a sauce ▫ verb **FRICASSEES, FRICASSEEING, FRICASSEED** to prepare meat as a fricassee

FRICATIVE adj said of a sound: produced partly by friction, the breath being forced through a narrowed opening ▫ noun **FRICATIVES** a fricative consonant, eg sh, f and th

FRICTION noun **FRICTIONS** the rubbing of one thing against another

FRIDGE noun **FRIDGES** a refrigerator, especially a household refrigerator

FRIED past form of **fry** [1]

FRIEND noun **FRIENDS** someone whom one knows and likes, and to whom one shows loyalty and affection; a close or intimate acquaintance

FRIENDLY adj **FRIENDLIER, FRIENDLIEST** kind; behaving as a friend ▫ noun **FRIENDLIES** in sport: a friendly match

FRIER noun **FRIERS** a frying pan

FRIES [1] plural noun long thin strips of potato deep-fried in oil, usually longer and thinner than chips

FRIES [2] a form of **fry** [1]

FRIEZE noun **FRIEZES** a decorative strip running along a wall

FRIGATE noun **FRIGATES** a naval escort vessel, smaller than a destroyer

FRIGHT noun **FRIGHTS** sudden fear; a shock

FRIGHTEN verb **FRIGHTENS, FRIGHTENING, FRIGHTENED** to make someone afraid; to alarm them

FRIGHTENED adj afraid; alarmed

FRIGHTENING adj that frightens

FRIGHTFUL adj ghastly; frightening

FRIGID adj **FRIGIDER, FRIGIDEST** cold and unfriendly; without spirit or feeling

FRIGIDITY noun **FRIGIDITIES** coldness; sexual unresponsiveness

FRIGIDLY adverb in a frigid way

FRIJOL noun **FRIJOLES** the kidney bean

FRIKKADEL noun **FRIKKADELS** a fried ball of minced meat

FRILL noun **FRILLS** a gathered or pleated strip of cloth attached along one edge to a garment, etc as a trimming

FRILLIES plural noun women's underwear with lacey frills

FRILLY adj **FRILLIER, FRILLIEST** with frills

FRINGE noun **FRINGES** a border of loose threads on a carpet, tablecloth, garment, etc ▫ verb **FRINGES, FRINGING, FRINGED** to decorate something with a fringe

FRIPPERY noun **FRIPPERIES** showy and unnecessary finery or adornment

FRISK verb **FRISKS, FRISKING, FRISKED** to jump or run about happily and playfully ▫ noun **FRISKS** a frolic; spell of prancing or jumping about

FRISKER noun **FRISKERS** someone who searches a person or place for concealed weapons, drugs, etc

FRISKILY adverb in a frisky way

FRISKY adj **FRISKIER, FRISKIEST** lively; playful; high-spirited; frolicsome

FRISSON noun **FRISSONS** a shiver of fear or excitement

FRIT noun **FRITS** the mixed materials for making glass, glazes for ceramics, etc ▫ verb **FRITS, FRITTING, FRITTED** to fuse (substances) partially in the process of making frit

FRITTER [1] noun **FRITTERS** a piece of meat, fruit, etc coated in batter and fried

FRITTER [2] verb **FRITTERS, FRITTERING, FRITTERED** to waste (time, money, energy, etc) on unimportant things; to squander something

FRITTERER noun **FRITTERERS** a person who wastes time

FRIVOLITY noun **FRIVOLITIES** frivolous behaviour; being frivolous

FRIVOLOUS adj silly; not sufficiently serious

FRIZZ noun **FRIZZES** said mainly of hair: a mass of tight curls ▫ verb **FRIZZES, FRIZZING, FRIZZED** to form or make something form a frizz

FRIZZANTE adj said of wine: sparkling

FRIZZLE [1] verb **FRIZZLES, FRIZZLING, FRIZZLED** said of food: to fry till scorched and brittle

FRIZZLE [2] noun **FRIZZLES** a curl

FRIZZY adj **FRIZZIER, FRIZZIEST** tightly curled

FRO prep an obsolete word for *from*

FROCK noun **FROCKS** a woman's or girl's dress

FROG noun **FROGS** a tailless amphibian, found worldwide except in Arctic and Antarctic regions, with a moist smooth skin, protruding eyes, powerful hind legs for swimming and leaping, and webbed feet

FROGGING noun **FROGGINGS** a set of attachments to a belt for carrying weapons, especially on a military uniform

FROGGY adj **FROGGIER, FROGGIEST** froglike; having or abounding in frogs

FROGMAN noun **FROGMEN** an underwater swimmer wearing a protective rubber suit and using breathing equipment

FROGMARCH verb **FROGMARCHES, FROGMARCHING, FROGMARCHED** to force someone forward, holding them firmly by the arms ▫ noun **FROGMARCHES** the act or process of frogmarching

FROLIC verb **FROLICS, FROLICKING, FROLICKED** to frisk or run about playfully; to gambol about ▫ noun **FROLICS** a spell of happy playing or frisking; a gambol

FROM prep a starting-point in place or time

FROND noun **FRONDS** a large compound leaf, especially of a fern or palm

FRONT noun **FRONTS** the side or part of anything that is furthest forward or nearest to the viewer; the most important side or part, eg the side of a building where the main door is ▫ verb **FRONTS, FRONTING, FRONTED** said of a building: to have its front facing or beside something specified □ adj relating to, or situated at or in the front

FRONTAGE noun **FRONTAGES** the front of a building, especially in relation to the street, etc along which it extends

FRONTAGER noun **FRONTAGERS** someone who owns or occupies property along a road, river, shore, etc

FRONTAL adj relating to the front □ noun **FRONTALS** the façade of a building

FRONTED adj formed with a front

FRONTIER noun **FRONTIERS** the part of a country bordering onto another country

FRONTLESS adj lacking a front

FRONTLET noun **FRONTLETS** something worn on the forehead

FRONTON noun **FRONTONS** a pediment crowning a window or other small opening

FRONTWARD adverb towards the front

FRONTWARDS adverb frontward

FROST noun **FROSTS** a white feathery or powdery deposit of ice crystals formed when water vapour comes into contact with a surface whose temperature is below the freezing point of water □ verb **FROSTS, FROSTING, FROSTED** to cover or become covered with frost

FROSTBITE noun **FROSTBITES** damage to the body tissues, usually of the extremities, especially fingers or toes, caused by exposure to very low temperatures, with the affected parts becoming pale and numb as a result of lack of oxygen □ verb **FROSTBITES, FROSTBITING, FROSTBIT, FROSTBITTEN** to affect with frost or frostbite

FROSTBITTEN adj suffering from frostbite; affected by frost

FROSTED adj covered by frost

FROSTILY adverb in a cold and unfriendly manner

FROSTING noun **FROSTINGS** cake icing

FROSTLESS adj free from frost

FROSTLIKE adj resembling frost

FROSTWORK noun **FROSTWORKS** tracery made by frost, eg on windows

FROSTY adj **FROSTIER, FROSTIEST** covered with frost

FROTH noun **FROTHS** a mass of tiny bubbles forming eg on the surface of a liquid, or round the mouth in certain diseases □ verb **FROTHS, FROTHING, FROTHED** to produce or make something produce froth

FROTHILY adverb in a frothy way

FROTHLESS adj lacking froth

FROTHY adj **FROTHIER, FROTHIEST** full of or like froth

FROTTAGE noun **FROTTAGES** a technique, analogous to brass-rubbing, in which paper is placed over a textured surface such as wood or fabric and rubbed with a soft pencil or crayon to produce an impression

FROWN verb **FROWNS, FROWNING, FROWNED** to wrinkle one's forehead and draw one's eyebrows together in worry, disapproval, deep thought, etc □ noun **FROWNS** the act of frowning

FROWST noun **FROWSTS** hot stuffy fustiness

FROWSTY adj **FROWSTIER, FROWSTIEST** stuffy; stale-smelling

FROWSY adj **FROWSIER, FROWSIEST** said of someone's appearance: untidy, dishevelled or slovenly

FROWZY adj **FROWZIER, FROWZIEST** frowsy

FROZE past form of **freeze**

FROZEN adj preserved by keeping at a temperature below freezing point

FRUCTOSE noun **FRUCTOSES** a six-carbon sugar found in fruit, honey and combined with glucose in sucrose, whose derivatives, in the form of fructose phosphates, play an important role in the chemical reactions that take place in living cells

FRUGAL adj thrifty; economical; not generous; careful, particularly in financial matters

FRUGALITY noun **FRUGALITIES** economy; thrift

FRUGALLY adverb in a frugal way

FRUIT noun **FRUITS** the fully ripened ovary of a flowering plant, containing one or more seeds that have developed from fertilized ovules, and sometimes including associated structures such as the receptacle □ verb **FRUITS, FRUITING, FRUITED** to produce fruit

FRUITCAKE noun **FRUITCAKES** a cake containing dried fruit, nuts, etc

FRUITER noun **FRUITERS** a tree, etc that bears fruit

FRUITERER noun **FRUITERERS** a person whose job is to sell fruit

FRUITFUL adj producing good or useful results; productive; worthwhile

FRUITION noun **FRUITIONS** the achievement of something that has been aimed at and worked for

FRUITLESS adj useless; unsuccessful; done in vain

FRUITY adj **FRUITIER, FRUITIEST** full of fruit; having the taste or appearance of fruit

FRUMP noun **FRUMPS** a woman who dresses in a dowdy, old-fashioned way

FRUMPISH adj dressed in a dowdy unattractive way

FRUMPY adj **FRUMPIER, FRUMPIEST** frumpish

FRUSTRATE verb **FRUSTRATES, FRUSTRATING, FRUSTRATED** to prevent someone from doing or getting something; to thwart or foil (a plan, attempt, etc)

FRUSTRATED adj a feeling of agitation and helplessness at not being able to do something

FRUSTRATING adj that frustrates

FRUSTUM noun **FRUSTUMS, FRUSTA** a slice of a solid body

FRY[1] verb **FRIES, FRYING, FRIED** to cook (food) in hot oil or fat, either in a frying-pan, or by deep-frying □ noun **FRIES** a dish of anything fried, eg the offal of a pig or lamb

FRY[2] plural noun young or newly spawned fish

FRYER noun **FRYERS** a frying pan

FUB verb **FUBS, FUBBING, FUBBED** an old word meaning to put off

FUCHSIA noun **FUCHSIAS** a shrub with purple, red or white hanging flowers

FUCHSINE noun **FUCHSINES** dark-green crystals which, when dissolved in water, form a purplish-red solution, used as a disinfectant, a clothes dye, etc

FUD noun **FUDS** a Scots word for a rabbit's or hare's tail

FUDDLE verb **FUDDLES, FUDDLING, FUDDLED** to muddle

the wits of; to confuse or stupefy ◻ *noun* **FUDDLES** a state of confusion or intoxication

FUDGE [1] *noun* **FUDGES** a soft toffee made from butter, sugar and milk ◻ *exclamation* expressing annoyance or frustration: damn

FUDGE [2] *verb* **FUDGES, FUDGING, FUDGED** to invent or concoct (an excuse, etc)

FUEL *noun* **FUELS** any material that releases energy when it is burned, which can be used as a source of heat or power ◻ *verb* **FUELS, FUELLING, FUELLED** to fill or feed with fuel

FUELLER *noun* **FUELLERS** a person or thing that supplies fuel

FUG *noun* **FUGS** a stale-smelling stuffy atmosphere, often very hot, close and airless

FUGAL *adj* of or relating to fugues

FUGALLY *adverb* in a fugal way

FUGATO *adj* in the manner of a fugue, without strictly being a fugue ◻ *adverb* in the manner of a fugue, without strictly being a fugue

FUGGY *adj* **FUGGIER, FUGGIEST** stale-smelling and stuffy

FUGITIVE *noun* **FUGITIVES** a person who is fleeing someone or something, usually some kind of authority, such as the law, an army, a political system, etc ◻ *adj* fleeing away

FUGUE *noun* **FUGUES** a style of composition in which a theme is introduced in one part and developed as successive parts take it up

FULCRUM *noun* **FULCRUMS, FULCRA** the point on which a lever turns, balances or is supported

FULFIL *verb* **FULFILS, FULFILLING, FULFILLED** to carry out or perform (a task, promise, etc)

FULFILL *verb* **FULFILLS, FULFILLING, FULFILLED** to fulfil

FULGENCY *noun* **FULGENCIES** brightness

FULGENT *adj* shining; bright

FULL *adj* **FULLER, FULLEST** holding, containing or having as much as possible, or a large quantity ◻ *adverb* completely; at maximum capacity ◻ *verb* **FULLS, FULLING, FULLED** to make something with gathers or puckers

FULLBACK *noun* **FULLBACKS** a defence player positioned towards the back of the field to protect the goal

FULLER *noun* **FULLERS** someone who shrinks and beats cloth to thicken it

FULLNESS *noun* **FULLNESSES** the condition of being full or complete

FULLY *adverb* to the greatest possible extent

FULMAR *noun* **FULMARS** a gull-like sea bird found in Arctic and sub-Arctic regions

FULMINANT *adj* developing suddenly or rapidly

FULMINATE *verb* **FULMINATES, FULMINATING, FULMINATED** to utter angry criticism or condemnation

FULNESS *noun* **FULNESSES** fullness

FULSOME *adj* **FULSOMER, FULSOMEST** said of praise, compliments, etc: so overdone as to be distasteful

FULSOMELY *adverb* in a fulsome way

FULVOUS *adj* dull yellow; yellowish-brown; tawny

> **FUM** *noun* **FUMS** a fabulous Chinese bird

FUMAROLE *noun* **FUMAROLES** a hole from which gases issue in a volcano or volcanic region

FUMBLE *verb* **FUMBLES, FUMBLING, FUMBLED** to handle something, or grope, clumsily ◻ *noun* **FUMBLES** an act of fumbling

FUMBLER *noun* **FUMBLERS** a person who fumbles

FUME *noun* **FUMES** smoke, gases or vapour, especially if strong-smelling or toxic, emanating from heated materials, operating engines or machinery, etc ◻ *verb* **FUMES, FUMING, FUMED** to be furious; to fret angrily

FUMED *adj* said of wood, especially oak: darkened by ammonia fumes

FUMIGANT *noun* **FUMIGANTS** a gaseous form of a chemical compound that is used to fumigate a place

FUMIGATE *verb* **FUMIGATES, FUMIGATING, FUMIGATED** to disinfect (a room, a building, etc) with fumes, in order to destroy pests, especially insects and their larvae

FUMIGATOR *noun* **FUMIGATORS** an apparatus used to fumigate a place

FUMITORY *noun* **FUMITORIES** an annual plant with slender stems, bluish-green leaves and flowers with four pink petals with blackish-purple tips, found as a common weed on cultivated ground

FUMOUS *adj* giving off fumes

FUN *noun* **FUNS** enjoyment; merriment ◻ *adj* intended for amusement, enjoyment, etc

FUNCTION *noun* **FUNCTIONS** the special purpose or task of a machine, person, bodily part, etc ◻ *verb* **FUNCTIONS, FUNCTIONING, FUNCTIONED** to work; to operate

FUND *noun* **FUNDS** a sum of money on which some enterprise is founded or on which the expenses of a project are supported ◻ *verb* **FUNDS, FUNDING, FUNDED** to provide money for a particular purpose

FUNDAMENT *noun* **FUNDAMENTS** the buttocks or anus

FUNDED *adj* invested in public funds

FUNDER *noun* **FUNDERS** a financial backer

FUNDI *noun* **FUNDIS** an expert

FUNDING *noun* **FUNDINGS** financial backing; funds ◻ *adj* providing funds; relating to funding

FUNDUS *noun* **FUNDI** in anatomy: the rounded bottom of a hollow organ

FUNERAL *noun* **FUNERALS** the ceremonial burial or cremation of a dead person ◻ *adj* relating to funerals

FUNERARY *adj* belonging to or used for funerals

FUNEREAL *adj* associated with or suitable for funerals

FUNFAIR *noun* **FUNFAIRS** a collection of sideshows, amusements, rides, etc, often set up temporarily on open ground and moving from town to town

FUNGAL *adj* relating to, caused by, or resembling fungus

FUNGIBLES *plural noun* perishable goods which may be estimated by weight, number and measure and which are consumed in use

FUNGICIDE *noun* **FUNGICIDES** a chemical that kills or limits the growth of fungi

FUNGOID *adj* resembling a fungus

For longer words, see The Chambers Dictionary

in nature or consistency; fungus-like

FUNGOUS adj of or like fungus; soft; spongy

FUNGUS noun **FUNGUSES, FUNGI** any organism that superficially resembles a plant, but does not have leaves and roots, and lacks chlorophyll, so that it must obtain its nutrients from other organisms, by living either as a parasite on living organisms, or by feeding on dead organic matter

FUNICULAR adj said of a mountain railway: operating by a machine-driven cable, with two cars, one of which descends while the other ascends □ noun **FUNICULARS** a funicular railway

FUNK noun **FUNKS** a state of fear or panic □ verb **FUNKS, FUNKING, FUNKED** to avoid doing something from panic; to balk at something or shirk from fear

FUNKHOLE noun **FUNKHOLES** a place of refuge; a dug-out

FUNKY adj **FUNKIER, FUNKIEST** said of jazz or rock music: strongly rhythmical and emotionally stirring

FUNNEL noun **FUNNELS** a tube with a cone-shaped opening through which liquid, etc can be poured into a narrow-necked container □ verb **FUNNELS, FUNNELLING, FUNNELLED** to rush through a narrow space

FUNNELLED adj with a funnel; funnel-shaped

FUNNILY adverb in a funny way

FUNNINESS noun the quality of being funny

FUNNY adj **FUNNIER, FUNNIEST** amusing; causing laughter □ noun **FUNNIES** a joke

FUR noun **FURS** the thick fine soft coat of a hairy animal □ verb **FURS, FURRING, FURRED** to coat or become coated with a fur-like deposit

FURBELOW noun **FURBELOWS** a dress trimming in the form of a ruched or pleated strip, ruffle or flounce

FURBISH verb **FURBISHES, FURBISHING, FURBISHED** to restore, decorate or clean something

FURBISHER noun **FURBISHERS** someone who restores, decorates or cleans something

FURCATE adj forked

FURCATION noun **FURCATIONS** a forking; a fork-like division

FURCULA noun **FURCULAE** the united clavicles of a bird; the wishbone

FURFUR noun **FURFURS** dandruff; scurf

FURIOSO adverb in a vigorous manner □ adj vigorous

FURIOUS adj violently or intensely angry

FURIOUSLY adverb in a furious way

FURL verb **FURLS, FURLING, FURLED** said of flags, sails or umbrellas: to roll up

FURLONG noun **FURLONGS** a measure of distance now used mainly in horse-racing, equal to one eighth of a mile, or 220 yards (201.2m)

FURLOUGH noun **FURLOUGHS** leave of absence, especially from military duty abroad

FURNACE noun **FURNACES** an enclosed chamber in which heat is produced, eg for smelting metal, heating water or burning rubbish

FURNISH verb **FURNISHES, FURNISHING, FURNISHED** to provide (a house, etc) with furniture

FURNISHED adj usually said of a house, flat, etc: stocked with furniture

FURNISHINGS plural noun articles of furniture, fittings, carpets, curtains, etc

FURNITURE noun **FURNITURES** movable household equipment such as tables, chairs, beds, etc

FUROR noun **FURORS** a furore

FURORE noun **FURORES** a general outburst of exitement or indignation in reaction to something

FURRIER noun **FURRIERS** someone whose job is to make or sell furs

FURRINESS noun **FURRINESSES** the state or condition of being furry

FURRING noun **FURRINGS** fur trimmings

FURROW noun **FURROWS** a groove or trench cut into the earth by a plough; a rut □ verb **FURROWS, FURROWING, FURROWED** to plough (land) into furrows

FURRY adj **FURRIER, FURRIEST** covered with fur

FURTHER adj more distant or remote (than something else) □ adverb at or to a greater distance

or more distant point □ verb **FURTHERS, FURTHERING, FURTHERED** to help the progress of something

FURTHEST adj most distant or remote □ adverb at or to the greatest distance or most distant point

FURTIVE adj secretive; stealthy; sly

FURTIVELY adverb in a furtive way

FURUNCLE noun **FURUNCLES** a boil

FURY noun **FURIES** violent or frenzied anger; an outburst of this

FURZE noun **FURZES** gorse

FUSE [1] noun **FUSES** a cord or cable containing combustible material, used for detonating a bomb or explosive charge

FUSE [2] verb **FUSES, FUSING, FUSED** to melt as a result of the application of heat

FUSELAGE noun **FUSELAGES** the main body of an aircraft, which carries crew and passengers, and to which the wings and tail unit are attached

FUSIBLE adj able to be fused; easily fused

FUSIFORM adj spindle-shaped; tapering from the middle towards each end

FUSIL noun **FUSILS** a light musket

FUSILIER noun **FUSILIERS** an infantryman armed with a fusil

FUSILLADE noun **FUSILLADES** a simultaneous or continuous discharge of firearms

FUSILLI singular or plural noun **FUSILLI** pasta shaped into short thick spirals

FUSION noun **FUSIONS** the process of melting, whereby a substance changes from a solid to a liquid

FUSS noun **FUSSES** agitation and excitement, especially over something trivial □ verb **FUSSES, FUSSING, FUSSED** to worry needlessly

FUSSER noun **FUSSERS** someone who fusses

FUSSILY adverb in a fussy way

FUSSINESS noun **FUSSINESSES** the quality of being fussy

FUSSY adj **FUSSIER, FUSSIEST** choosy; discriminating

FUSTIAN noun **FUSTIANS** a kind of coarse twilled cotton fabric with a nap, including moleskin, velveteen, corduroy, etc □ adj made of fustian

FUSTIC *noun* **FUSTICS** the wood of a tropical American tree

FUSTILY *adverb* in a fusty way

FUSTINESS *noun* **FUSTINESSES** a fusty condition

FUSTY *adj* **FUSTIER, FUSTIEST** stale-smelling; old and musty

FUTHARK *noun* **FUTHARKS** the runic alphabet

FUTHORK *noun* **FUTHORKS** futhark

FUTILE *adj* **FUTILER, FUTILEST** unproductive, unavailing, foolish, vain or pointless

FUTILELY *adverb* in a futile way

FUTILITY *noun* **FUTILITIES** uselessness

FUTON *noun* **FUTONS** a thin cloth-filled mattress designed to be used on the floor, and meant to be rolled up when not in use

FUTTOCK *noun* **FUTTOCKS** one of the crooked timbers of a wooden ship

FUTURE *adj* yet to come or happen □ *noun* **FUTURES** the time to come; events that are still to occur

FUTURISM *noun* **FUTURISMS** a movement founded in Italy in 1909 by the poet Marinetti, concerned with expressing the motion of machines in all art forms

FUTURIST *noun* **FUTURISTS** a person whose chief interests are in what is to come; a believer in futurism

FUTURITY *noun* **FUTURITIES** the future

FUZE *noun* **FUZES** fuse □ *verb* **FUZES, FUZING, FUZED** to fuse

FUZEE *noun* **FUZEES** the spindle in a watch or clock on which the chain is wound

FUZZ *noun* **FUZZES** a mass of fine fibres or hair, usually curly □ *verb* **FUZZES, FUZZING, FUZZED** to make or become fuzzy

FUZZILY *adverb* in a fuzzy way

FUZZINESS *noun* **FUZZINESSES** the quality or state of being fuzzy

FUZZY *adj* **FUZZIER, FUZZIEST** indistinct; blurred

FY *exclamation* expressing disapproval

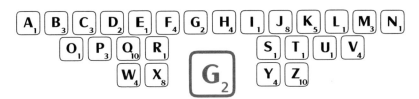

GAB *noun* **GABS** idle talk; chat □ *verb* **GABS, GABBING, GABBED** to talk idly, especially at length

GABARDINE *noun* **GABARDINES** gaberdine

GABBLE *verb* **GABBLES, GABBLING, GABBLED** to talk or say something quickly and unclearly □ *noun* **GABBLES** fast indistinct talk

GABBLING *noun* **GABBLINGS** the act of talking quickly and unclearly

GABBRO *noun* **GABBROS** a coarse-grained crystalline igneous rock with a low silica content

GABBY *adj* **GABBIER, GABBIEST** garrulous; gossipy

GABERDINE *noun* **GABERDINES** a closely woven twill fabric, especially one made of wool or cotton

GABFEST *noun* **GABFESTS** a gathering characterized by gossipy conversation

GABLE *noun* **GABLES** the triangular upper part of a side wall between the sloping parts of a roof

GABLED *adj* having a gable or gables

GAD *verb* **GADS, GADDING, GADDED** to go from place to place busily, especially in the hope of finding amusement or pleasure

GADABOUT *noun* **GADABOUTS** a person who gads about

GADFLY *noun* **GADFLIES** any of various large flies that suck the blood of cattle and other animal livestock, inflicting painful bites

GADGET *noun* **GADGETS** any small device or appliance, especially one more ingenious than necessary

GADGETRY *noun* **GADGETRIES** gadgets

GADI *noun* **GADIS** an Indian throne

GADOID *noun* **GADOIDS** any fish (including cod and hake) that belongs to the family Gadidae of marine fishes, with small scales, and pectoral and pelvic fins situated close together □ *adj* said of a fish: belonging to this order

GADROON *noun* **GADROONS** an embossed, cable-like decoration used as an edging on silverware, etc

GADROONED *adj* decorated with gadroons

GADWALL *noun* **GADWALLS** a dabbling duck related to the mallard, native to northern inland waters

GAE *verb* **GAES, GAUN, GAED, GANE** a Scots word meaning to go

GAFF *noun* **GAFFS** a long pole with a hook, for landing large fish □ *verb* **GAFFS, GAFFING, GAFFED** to catch (a fish) with a gaff

GAFFE *noun* **GAFFES** a socially embarrassing action or remark

GAFFER *noun* **GAFFERS** a boss or foreman

GAG *verb* **GAGS, GAGGING, GAGGED** to silence someone by putting something in or over their mouth □ *noun* **GAGS** something put into or over a person's mouth to prevent them from making any sound

GAGA *adj* weak-minded through old age; senile

GAGE *verb* **GAGES, GAGING, GAGED** to gauge □ *noun* **GAGES** a gauge

GAGGLE *noun* **GAGGLES** a flock of geese □ *verb* **GAGGLES, GAGGLING, GAGGLED** said of geese: to cackle

GAIETY *noun* **GAIETIES** the state of being merry or bright

GAILY *adverb* in a light-hearted, merry way

GAIN *verb* **GAINS, GAINING, GAINED** to get, obtain or earn (something desirable) □ *noun* **GAINS** something gained, eg profit

GAINFUL *adj* profitable

GAINFULLY *adverb* in a gainful way

GAINSAY *verb* **GAINSAYS, GAINSAYING, GAINSAID** to deny or contradict

GAINSAYER *noun* **GAINSAYERS** an opposer

GAIT *noun* **GAITS** a way of walking

GAITED *adj* having a specified gait

GAITER *noun* **GAITERS** a leather or cloth covering for the lower leg and ankle, often with a strap fitting under the shoe

GAL *noun* **GALS** a unit of gravitational acceleration, equal to one centimetre per second per second, used in geological surveying

GALA *noun* **GALAS** an occasion of special entertainment or a public festivity of some kind, eg a carnival

GALACTIC *adj* relating to a galaxy or the Galaxy

GALACTOSE *noun* **GALACTOSES** a sugar obtained by hydrolysis from lactose

GALAH *noun* **GALAHS** an Australian cockatoo with grey wings and back and pink underparts

GALANTINE *noun* **GALANTINES** boneless cooked white meat or fish served cold in aspic

GALAXY *noun* **GALAXIES** a huge collection of stars, dust and gas held together by mutual gravitational attraction

GALE *noun* **GALES** any very strong wind

GALENA *noun* **GALENAS** the most important ore of lead which occurs as compact masses of very dense dark grey crystals consisting mainly of lead sulphide

GALETTE *noun* **GALETTES** a round flat sweet or savoury cake, pastry or pancake

GALL *noun* **GALLS** a sore or painful swelling on the skin, especially of horses, caused by chafing □ *verb* **GALLS, GALLING, GALLED** to annoy

GALLANT *adj* **GALLANTER, GALLANTEST** brave □ *noun* **GALLANTS** a woman's lover

GALLANTLY *adverb* in a gallant way

GALLANTRY *noun* **GALLANTRIES** bravery

GALLEON *noun* **GALLEONS** a large Spanish ship, usually with three

For longer words, see *The Chambers Dictionary*

masts, used for war or trade from 15c to 18c

GALLERIA noun **GALLERIAS** a collection of small shops under one roof

GALLERIED adj having a gallery

GALLERY noun **GALLERIES** a room or building used to display works of art; a balcony along an inside upper wall

GALLEY noun **GALLEYS** a long single-deck ship propelled by sails and oars

GALLFLY noun **GALLFLIES** any of various small insects, the larva of which often produces small abnormal growths in plant tissues

GALLIARD noun **GALLIARDS** a lively dance for couples, in triple time, popular in 16c and 17c

GALLICISE verb **GALLICISES, GALLICISING, GALLICISED** to gallicize

GALLICISM noun **GALLICISMS** a French word or idiom used in another language

GALLICIZE verb **GALLICIZES, GALLICIZING, GALLICIZED** to assimilate or conform to French attitudes, habits, etc

GALLING adj irritating

GALLINGLY adverb in a galling way

GALLIUM noun **GALLIUMS** a soft silvery metallic element found in zinc blende, bauxite and kaolin, used in alloys with low melting points and in luminous paints

GALLIVANT verb **GALLIVANTS, GALLIVANTING, GALLIVANTED** to go out looking for entertainment or amusement

GALLNUT noun **GALLNUTS** any round nutlike abnormal growth on the stem or leaf of a plant

GALLON noun **GALLONS** in the imperial system: a unit of liquid measurement equal to four quarts or eight pints, equivalent to 4.546 litres in the UK, and 3.785 litres in the USA

GALLONAGE noun **GALLONAGES** an amount in gallons

GALLOP noun **GALLOPS** the fastest pace at which a horse or similar animal moves, during which all four legs are off the ground together □ verb **GALLOPS, GALLOPING, GALLOPED** said of a horse or similar animal: to move at a gallop

GALLOPER noun **GALLOPERS** a person or thing that gallops

GALLOPING adj proceeding at a gallop; advancing rapidly

GALLOWS noun **GALLOWSES** a wooden frame on which criminals are put to death by hanging

GALLSTONE noun **GALLSTONES** a small hard mass, usually consisting of cholesterol crystals, bile pigments, and calcium salts, that is formed in the gall bladder or one of its ducts

GALOOT noun **GALOOTS** a clumsy person

GALOP noun **GALOPS** a lively 19c dance for couples

GALORE adverb (placed after the noun) in large amounts or numbers

GALOSH noun **GALOSHES** a waterproof overshoe

GALUMPH verb **GALUMPHS, GALUMPHING, GALUMPHED** to stride along triumphantly

GALVANIC adj relating to or producing an electric current, especially a direct current, by chemical means

GALVANISE verb **GALVANISES, GALVANISING, GALVANISED** to galvanize

GALVANISED adj galvanized

GALVANISM noun **GALVANISMS** any form of medical treatment involving the application of pulses of electric current to body tissues

GALVANIZE verb **GALVANIZES, GALVANIZING, GALVANIZED** to coat (a metallic surface, usually iron or steel) with a thin layer of zinc, in order to protect it from corrosion

GALVANIZED adj said of a metallic surface, usually iron or steel: coated with a thin layer of zinc

GAM noun **GAMS** a school of whales □ verb **GAMS, GAMMING, GAMMED** to join up in a gam

GAMBIER noun **GAMBIERS** an astringent substance prepared from the leaves of a climbing shrub of SE Asia, used in tanning and dyeing

GAMBIR noun **GAMBIRS** gambier

GAMBIT noun **GAMBITS** a chess move made early in a game, in which a pawn or other piece is sacrificed in order to gain an overall advantage

GAMBLE verb **GAMBLES, GAMBLING, GAMBLED** to bet (usually money) on the result of a card game, horse race, etc □ noun **GAMBLES** an act of gambling; a bet

GAMBLER noun **GAMBLERS** someone who gambles

GAMBLING noun **GAMBLINGS** making a bet

GAMBOGE noun **GAMBOGES** a gum resin obtained from various tropical Asian trees, used as a source of a yellow pigment or as a laxative

GAMBOL verb **GAMBOLS, GAMBOLLING, GAMBOLLED** to jump around playfully □ noun **GAMBOLS** jumping around playfully; a frolic

GAMBREL noun **GAMBRELS** the hock of a horse

GAMBROON noun **GAMBROONS** a twilled cloth of worsted and cotton, or linen

GAME noun **GAMES** an amusement or pastime □ adj **GAMER, GAMEST** ready and willing to undertake something □ verb **GAMES, GAMING, GAMED** to gamble

GAMECOCK noun **GAMECOCKS** a cock that is bred and trained for cock-fighting

GAMELY adverb bravely, sportingly

GAMENESS noun **GAMENESSES** the state of being game

GAMESTER noun **GAMESTERS** a gambler

GAMETE noun **GAMETES** in sexually reproducing organisms: a specialized sex cell, especially an ovum or sperm, which fuses with another gamete of the opposite type during fertilization

GAMETIC adj of or relating to gametes

GAMEY adj **GAMIER, GAMIEST** gamy

GAMIER see under **gamy**

GAMIEST see under **gamy**

GAMIN noun **GAMINS** a cheeky and mischievous little boy □ adj said of a little boy: precocious, impish and mischievous

GAMINE noun **GAMINES** a girl or young woman with a mischievous, boyish appearance □ adj said of a girl or young woman: boyish and mischievous in appearance

GAMINESS noun **GAMINESSES** the state of being gamy

GAMING noun **GAMINGS** gambling

GAMMA noun **GAMMAS** the third letter of the Greek alphabet

GAMMADION noun **GAMMADIA** a figure composed of Greek capital gammas, especially a swastika

GAMMON [1] noun **GAMMONS** cured meat from the upper leg and hindquarters of a pig, usually cut into thick slices

GAMMON [2] verb **GAMMONS, GAMMONING, GAMMONED** to defeat your opponent in backgammon by removing all your men before your opponent removes any

GAMMY adj **GAMMIER, GAMMIEST** lame with a permanent injury

GAMP noun **GAMPS** an umbrella

GAMUT noun **GAMUTS** the whole range of anything, eg a person's emotions

GAMY adj **GAMIER, GAMIEST** said of meat: having the strong taste or smell of meat which has been kept for a long time

GANDER noun **GANDERS** a male goose

GANG [1] noun **GANGS** a group, especially one of criminals or troublemakers

GANG [2] verb **GANGS, GANGING, GANGED** to arrange (tools) for simultaneous use

GANGER noun **GANGERS** the foreman of a group of workers

GANGLAND noun **GANGLANDS** the world of organized crime

GANGLIAR adj relating to a ganglion

GANGLING adj tall and thin, and usually awkward in movement

GANGLION noun **GANGLIONS, GANGLIA** in the central nervous system: a group of nerve cell bodies, usually enclosed by a sheath or capsule

GANGLY adj **GANGLIER, GANGLIEST** gangling

GANGPLANK noun **GANGPLANKS** a movable plank, usually with projecting crosspieces fixed to it, serving as a gangway for a ship

GANGRENE noun **GANGRENES** the death and subsequent decay of part of the body due to some failure of the blood supply to that region as a result of disease, injury, frostbite, etc

GANGSTA noun **GANGSTAS** a style of rap music with violent, and often misogynistic, lyrics or subject matter

GANGSTER noun **GANGSTERS** a member of a gang of violent criminals

GANGUE noun **GANGUES** any of the mainly non-metallic minerals associated with an ore deposit that are not considered to be economically valuable

GANGWAY noun **GANGWAYS** a small movable bridge used for getting on and off a ship ▫ exclamation make way!

GANISTER noun **GANISTERS** a hard sedimentary rock containing silica, found beneath coal seams

GANJA noun **GANJAS** marijuana

GANNET noun **GANNETS** any of several large seabirds which have a heavy body, white plumage with dark wing tips, a long straight conical bill and webbed feet

GANNETRY noun **GANNETRIES** a breeding-place for gannets

GANNISTER noun **GANNISTERS** ganister

GANOID adj said of the scales of certain primitive fish: rhomboid-shaped with a hard shiny enamel-like outer layer

GANSEY noun **GANSEYS** a woollen sweater

GANTRY noun **GANTRIES** a large metal supporting framework, eg serving as a bridge for a travelling crane, overhead for railway signals, or used at the side of a rocket's launch pad

GAOL noun **GAOLS** jail ▫ verb **GAOLS, GAOLING, GAOLED** to jail

GAOLER noun **GAOLERS** a jailer

GAP noun **GAPS** a break or open space, eg in a fence, etc

GAPE verb **GAPES, GAPING, GAPED** to stare with the mouth open, especially in surprise or wonder ▫ noun **GAPES** a wide opening

GAPER noun **GAPERS** in cricket: an easy catch

GAPING adj wide open

GAPINGLY adverb in a gaping way

GAPPY adj **GAPPIER, GAPPIEST** full of gaps

GAR noun **GARS** a garfish

GARAGE noun **GARAGES** a building in which motor vehicles are kept ▫ verb **GARAGES, GARAGING, GARAGED** to put or keep (a car, etc) in a garage

GARAGING noun **GARAGINGS** accommodation for vehicles

GARB noun **GARBS** clothing, especially as worn by people in a particular job or position ▫ verb **GARBS, GARBING, GARBED** to dress or clothe

GARBAGE noun **GARBAGES** domestic waste; refuse

GARBANZO noun **GARBANZOS** a chickpea

GARBLE verb **GARBLES, GARBLING, GARBLED** to mix up the details of something unintentionally

GARBLED adj said of a report or account: muddled

GARBO noun **GARBOS** a dustman or refuse collector

GARBOLOGY noun **GARBOLOGIES** the investigation of the refuse discarded by a society as part of the study of that society

GARÇON noun **GARÇONS** a waiter, especially a French one, in a restaurant or cafe ▫ exclamation a call to attract a waiter's attention

GARDA noun **GARDAI** a member of the Police Force in the Irish Republic

GARDEN noun **GARDENS** an area of land, usually one adjoining a house, where grass, trees, ornamental plants, fruit, vegetables, etc, are grown ▫ adj said of a plant: cultivated, not wild ▫ verb **GARDENS, GARDENING, GARDENED** to cultivate, work in or take care of a garden, especially as a hobby

GARDENER noun **GARDENERS** someone who gardens; someone skilled in gardening

GARDENIA noun **GARDENIAS** an evergreen shrub or small tree, native to tropical and subtropical regions, with glossy leaves and flattened rosettes of large, usually white, fragrant flowers

GARDENING noun **GARDENINGS** the laying out and cultivation of gardens

GARFISH noun **GARFISHES** any of various slim fast-swimming fishes with a long beak-like mouth containing many sharp teeth

GARGLE verb **GARGLES, GARGLING, GARGLED** to cleanse, treat or freshen the mouth and throat by breathing out through (a medicinal liquid) that is held there for a while before spitting it out ▫ noun **GARGLES** an act of gargling or the sound produced while gargling

GARGOYLE noun **GARGOYLES** a grotesque carved open-mouthed head or figure acting as a rainwater spout from a roof-gutter, especially on a church

GARIAL noun **GARIALS** a gharial

GARIBALDI noun **GARIBALDIS** a kind of flat, oblong biscuit containing currants

GARISH adj unpleasantly bright or colourful; very gaudy

GARISHLY adverb in a garish way

GARLAND noun **GARLANDS** a circular arrangement of flowers or leaves worn round the head or neck, or hung up as a decoration ▫ verb **GARLANDS, GARLANDING, GARLANDED** to decorate something or someone with a garland

GARLIC noun **GARLICS** a perennial plant of the onion family, widely cultivated for its underground bulb, which is divided into segments known as cloves

GARLICKY adj **GARLICKIER, GARLICKIEST** smelling or tasting of garlic

GARMENT noun **GARMENTS** an article of clothing

GARNER verb **GARNERS, GARNERING, GARNERED** to collect and usually store (information, knowledge, etc)

GARNET noun **GARNETS** any of various silicate minerals found mainly in metamorphic rocks, especially a deep red variety used as a semi-precious stone

GARNI adj with a garnish

GARNISH noun **GARNISHES** a decoration, especially one added to food ▫ verb **GARNISHES, GARNISHING, GARNISHED** to decorate (especially food to be served)

GARNITURE noun **GARNITURES** decorations, embellishments or accessories

GAROTTE noun **GAROTTES** a garrotte ▫ verb **GAROTTES, GAROTTING, GAROTTED** to garrotte

GARPIKE noun **GARPIKES** a garfish

GARRAN noun **GARRANS** a garron

GARRET noun **GARRETS** an attic room, often a dingy one

GARRISON noun **GARRISONS** a body of soldiers stationed in a town or fortress in order to defend it

GARRON noun **GARRONS** a small horse, used especially in Ireland and Scotland

GARROTE noun **GARROTES** a garrotte ▫ verb **GARROTES,**

GARROTING, GARROTED to garrotte

GARROTTE noun **GARROTTES** a wire loop or metal collar that can be tightened around the neck to cause strangulation ▫ verb **GARROTTES, GARROTTING, GARROTTED** to execute or kill someone with a garrotte

GARROTTER noun **GARROTTERS** a person who garrottes someone

GARROTTING noun **GARROTTINGS** killing by means of a garrotte

GARRULITY noun **GARRULITIES** loquacity

GARRULOUS adj said of a person: tending to talk a lot, especially about trivial things

GARRYOWEN noun **GARRYOWENS** in rugby: a high kick forward that the kicker follows up with a rush towards the landing-place of the ball

GARTER noun **GARTERS** a band of tight material, usually elastic, worn on the leg to hold up a stocking or sock

GAS noun **GASES** a form of matter that has no fixed shape, is easily compressed, and which will expand to occupy all the space available because its molecules are in constant rapid motion and can move about freely and independently of each other ▫ verb **GASES, GASSES, GASSING, GASSED** to kill (people or animals) with poisonous gas

GASBAG noun **GASBAGS** someone who talks a lot or too much

GASEOUS adj in the form of, or like, gas

GASFIELD noun **GASFIELDS** a region that is rich in economically valuable natural gas

GASH noun **GASHES** a deep open cut or wound ▫ verb **GASHES, GASHING, GASHED** to make a gash in something

GASIFY verb **GASIFIES, GASIFYING, GASIFIED** to convert something into gas, especially to convert coal into a gaseous hydrocarbon fuel

GASKET noun **GASKETS** a compressible ring or sheet made of rubber, paper or asbestos that fits tightly in the join between two metal surfaces to form an airtight seal

GASLIGHT noun **GASLIGHTS** a lamp powered by gas

GASOHOL noun **GASOHOLS** a mixture of petrol and a small amount of alcohol, used as fuel

GASOLINE noun **GASOLINES** petrol

GASOMETER noun **GASOMETERS** a large metal tank, the top section of which can move freely up and down, used for storing coal gas or natural gas before it is distributed to customers

GASP verb **GASPS, GASPING, GASPED** to take a sharp breath in, through surprise, sudden pain, etc ▫ noun **GASPS** a sharp intake of breath

GASPER noun **GASPERS** a cheap cigarette

GASSED past form of **gas**

GASSES a form of **gas**

GASSINESS noun **GASSINESSES** the state of being gassy

GASSING a form of **gas**

GASSY adj **GASSIER, GASSIEST** like gas; full of gas

GASTRIC adj relating to or affecting the stomach

GASTRITIS noun **GASTRITISES** inflammation of the lining of the stomach

GASTROPOD noun **GASTROPODS** any member of a class of invertebrate animals which typically possess a large flattened muscular foot and often have a single spirally coiled shell, eg snail, slug, whelk, winkle

GAT noun **GATS** in Indian music: the second and usually final section of a raga

GATE noun **GATES** a door or barrier, usually a hinged one, which is moved in order to open or close an entrance in a wall, fence, etc leading eg into a garden, field or city ▫ verb **GATES, GATING, GATED** to confine (pupils) to school after hours

GATEAU noun **GATEAUS, GATEAUX** a large rich cake, especially one filled with cream and decorated with fruit, nuts, etc

GATECRASH verb **GATECRASHES, GATECRASHING, GATECRASHED** to join or attend (a party, meeting, etc) uninvited or without paying

GATED adj having a gate or gates

GATEFOLD noun **GATEFOLDS** a large page, eg containing a diagram or illustration, which is folded to fit into a book, and is unfolded when used

GATEHOUSE *noun* **GATEHOUSES** a building at or above the gateway to a city, castle, etc, often occupied by the person who guards it

GATEPOST *noun* **GATEPOSTS** either of the posts on each side of a gate

GATEWAY *noun* **GATEWAYS** an entrance, especially to a city, park, etc, with a gate across it

GATHER *verb* **GATHERS, GATHERING, GATHERED** to bring or come together in one place ❑ *noun* **GATHERS** a small fold in material, often stitched

GATHERING *noun* **GATHERINGS** a meeting or assembly

GATING *noun* **GATINGS** confinement of pupils to school after hours

GAU *noun* **GAUS** under the Nazi regime, a German political district

GAUCHE *adj* **GAUCHER, GAUCHEST** ill-at-ease, awkward in social situations

GAUCHERIE *noun* **GAUCHERIES** an instance of social awkwardness

GAUCHO *noun* **GAUCHOS** a modern cowboy of the S American plains

GAUD *noun* **GAUDS** a showy ornament

GAUDILY *adverb* in a gaudy way

GAUDINESS *noun* **GAUDINESSES** the quality of being gaudy

GAUDY [1] *adj* **GAUDIER, GAUDIEST** coarsely and brightly coloured or decorated

GAUDY [2] *noun* **GAUDIES** in some schools and colleges: an entertainment or feast

GAUGE *verb* **GAUGES, GAUGING, GAUGED** to measure something accurately ❑ *noun* **GAUGES** any of various instruments that are used to measure a quantity such as weight, volume, pressure, etc

GAUGEABLE *adj* that can be gauged

GAULEITER *noun* **GAULEITERS** under the Nazi regime: a chief official of a district

GAUNT *adj* **GAUNTER, GAUNTEST** thin or thin-faced; lean, haggard

GAUNTLET *noun* **GAUNTLETS** a metal or metal-plated glove worn by medieval soldiers

GAUNTLY *adverb* in a gaunt way

GAUNTNESS *noun* **GAUNTNESSES** the condition of being gaunt

GAUSS *noun* **GAUSSES** the cgs unit of magnetic flux density, which in the SI system has been replaced by the tesla

GAUZE *noun* **GAUZES** thin transparent fabric, especially cotton muslin as used to dress wounds

GAUZINESS *noun* **GAUZINESSES** the state of being gauzy

GAUZY *adj* **GAUZIER, GAUZIEST** resembling gauze

GAVE a past form of **give**

GAVEL *noun* **GAVELS** a small hammer used by a judge, auctioneer, etc to call attention

GAVIAL *noun* **GAVIALS** a gharial

GAVOTTE *noun* **GAVOTTES** a lively French country dance that was popular during the 18c

GAWK *verb* **GAWKS, GAWKING, GAWKED** to stare blankly or stupidly; to gawp ❑ *noun* **GAWKS** an awkward, clumsy or stupid person

GAWKINESS *noun* **GAWKINESSES** the quality of being gawky

GAWKY *adj* **GAWKIER, GAWKIEST** awkward-looking, ungainly, and usually tall and thin

GAWP *verb* **GAWPS, GAWPING, GAWPED** to stare stupidly, especially open-mouthed; to gape

GAY *adj* **GAYER, GAYEST** homosexual; relating to, frequented by, or intended for, homosexuals ❑ *noun* **GAYS** a homosexual

GAYNESS *noun* **GAYNESSES** the state of being homosexual

GAZAR *noun* **GAZARS** a silk fabric of loose construction with a stiff finish

GAZE *verb* **GAZES, GAZING, GAZED** to stare fixedly, usually for a long time ❑ *noun* **GAZES** a fixed stare

GAZEBO *noun* **GAZEBOS, GAZEBOES** a small summerhouse or open hut, especially in a garden, and usually situated in a place that offers pleasant views

GAZELLE *noun* **GAZELLES** a fawn-coloured antelope with a white rump and belly, and black-and-white face markings, found in arid plains of Africa and Asia

GAZETTE *noun* **GAZETTES** an official newspaper giving lists of government, military and legal notices ❑ *verb* **GAZETTES, GAZETTING, GAZETTED** to announce or publish something in an official gazette

GAZETTEER *noun* **GAZETTEERS** a book or part of a book which lists place names and describes the places

GAZOO *noun* **GAZOOS** a kazoo

GAZPACHO *noun* **GAZPACHOS** a spicy Spanish vegetable soup, served cold

GAZUMP *verb* **GAZUMPS, GAZUMPING, GAZUMPED** said of someone selling a property: to raise the price that has already been verbally agreed with (a prospective buyer), usually because someone else has offered a higher price

GAZUMPING *noun* **GAZUMPINGS** the act of raising the price that has already been verbally agreed on a property, usually because someone else has offered a higher price

GAZUNDER *verb* **GAZUNDERS, GAZUNDERING, GAZUNDERED** said of a buyer: to lower the sum offered to (a seller of property) just before contracts are due to be signed

GAZY *adj* **GAZIER, GAZIEST** affording a wide prospect

GEAN *noun* **GEANS** the European wild cherry

GEAR *noun* **GEARS** a toothed wheel or disc that engages with another wheel or disc having a different number of teeth, and turns it, so transmitting motion from one rotating shaft to another ❑ *verb* **GEARS, GEARING, GEARED** to supply something with, or connect it by, gears

GEARBOX *noun* **GEARBOXES** especially in a motor vehicle: the set or system of gears that transmits power from the engine to the road wheels, allowing the road speed to be varied while maintaining the engine speed at a constant high level

GEARING *noun* **GEARINGS** a set of gears as a means of transmission of motion

GEARSHIFT *noun* **GEARSHIFTS** a lever or similar device for engaging and disengaging gears, especially in a motor vehicle, by moving the gears in relation to each other

GEARWHEEL *noun*
GEARWHEELS a gear

GECKO *noun* **GECKOS, GECKOES** any of numerous mainly nocturnal lizards found in warm countries, known for the ease with which some species can climb smooth vertical surfaces

GED *noun* **GEDS** a dialect word for the fish *pike*

GEE ¹ *exclamation* expressing surprise, admiration or enthusiasm

GEE ² *verb* **GEES, GEEING, GEED** to encourage (a horse, etc) to move or move faster

GEEK *noun* **GEEKS** a strange or eccentric person

GEEKY *adj* **GEEKIER, GEEKIEST** weird

GEEP *noun* **GEEPS** a creature produced by artificially combining DNA from a goat and a sheep

GEESE plural of **goose**

GEEZER *noun* **GEEZERS** a man, especially an old man, often one who is odd in some way

GEISHA *noun* **GEISHAS** a Japanese girl or woman who is trained to entertain men with music, dancing and the art of conversation

GEIST *noun* **GEISTS** spirit, any inspiring or dominating principle

GEL *noun* **GELS** a colloid consisting of a solid and a liquid that are dispersed evenly throughout a material and have set to form a jellylike mass, feg gelatine □ *verb* **GELS, GELLING, GELLED** to jell

GELATIN *noun* **GELATINS** gelatine

GELATINE *noun* **GELATINES** a clear tasteless protein extracted from animal bones and hides that forms a stiff jelly when dissolved in water

GELATION *noun* **GELATIONS** a solidification by cooling

GELD *verb* **GELDS, GELDING, GELDED** to castrate (a male animal, especially a horse) by removing its testicles

GELDING *noun* **GELDINGS** a castrated male animal, especially a horse

GELID *adj* **GELIDER, GELIDEST** icy cold; frosty

GELIGNITE *noun* **GELIGNITES** a powerful explosive, used especially in mining, made from a mixture of nitroglycerine, cellulose nitrate, sodium nitrate and wood pulp

GELLY *noun* **GELLIES** gelignite

GEM *noun* **GEMS** a precious or semi-precious stone or crystal, especially one that has been cut and polished for use in jewellery or other ornaments, eg a diamond or ruby

GEMEL *noun* **GEMELS** in heraldry: a pair of bars placed close together

GEMINATE *adj* doubled □ *verb* **GEMINATES, GEMINATING, GEMINATED** to double

GEMINATED *adj* doubled or arranged in pairs

GEMMA *noun* **GEMMAE** a leaf bud

GEMMATION *noun* **GEMMATIONS** the formation of gemmae

GEMSBOK *noun* **GEMSBOKS** a large S African antelope of the oryx family with long straight horns and distinctive markings on its face and underparts

GEMSTONE *noun* **GEMSTONES** a gem

GEMÜTLICH *adj* amiable; kindly

GEN *noun* the required or relevant information

GENDARME *noun* **GENDARMES** a member of an armed police force in France and other French-speaking countries

GENDER *noun* **GENDERS** the condition of being male or female; one's sex

GENE *noun* **GENES** the basic unit of inheritance, consisting of a sequence of DNA that occupies a specific position on a chromosome

GENEALOGY *noun* **GENEALOGIES** a person's direct line of descent from an ancestor

GENERA a plural of **genus**

GENERAL *adj* relating to, involving or applying to all or most parts, people or things; widespread, not specific, limited, or localized □ *noun* **GENERALS** an officer in the army

GENERALLY *adverb* usually

GENERATE *verb* **GENERATES, GENERATING, GENERATED** to produce or create something

GENERATOR *noun* **GENERATORS** a machine that converts mechanical energy into electrical energy, eg a dynamo

GENERIC *adj* said especially of a drug: not protected by a trademark and sold as a specific brand; non-proprietary □ *noun* **GENERICS** a generic drug

GENEROUS *adj* giving or willing to give or help unselfishly

GENESIS *noun* **GENESES** a beginning or origin

GENET *noun* **GENETS** a carnivore related to the civet

GENETIC *adj* referring or relating to genes or genetics; inherited

GENETICAL *adj* referring or relating to genes or genetics; inherited

GENETICS *singular noun* the scientific study of heredity and of the mechanisms by which characteristics are transmitted from one generation to the next □ *plural noun* the genetic makeup of an organism or group

GENETTE *noun* **GENETTES** a genet

GENIAL *adj* cheerful; friendly; sociable

GENIALITY *noun* **GENIALITIES** cheerfulness; friendliness

GENIALLY *adverb* in a genial way

GENIC *adj* relating to a gene

GENIE *noun* **GENIES** in folk or fairy stories: a spirit with the power to grant wishes

GENII a plural of **genius**

GENISTA *noun* **GENISTAS** the plant broom

GENITAL *adj* relating to or affecting the genitals

GENITALIA *plural noun* the genitals

GENITALS *plural noun* the external sexual organs

GENITIVAL *adj* belonging to the genitive case

GENITIVE *noun* **GENITIVES** in certain languages, eg Latin, Greek and German: the form or case of a noun, pronoun or adjective which shows possession or association □ *adj* belonging to or in the genitive case

GENIUS *noun* **GENIUSES, GENII** someone who has outstanding creative or intellectual ability

GENOA *noun* **GENOAS** a large jib sail

GENOCIDAL *adj* of or relating to genocide

GENOCIDE *noun* **GENOCIDES** the deliberate killing of a whole nation or people

GENOME *noun* **GENOMES** the complete set of genetic material in the cell of a living organism

GENOTYPE *noun* **GENOTYPES** the particular set of genes possessed by an organism, which interacts with environmental factors to determine the organism's phenotype

GENOTYPIC adj relating to a genotype

GENRE noun **GENRES** a particular type or kind of literature, music or other artistic work

GENT noun **GENTS** a gentleman

GENTEEL adj **GENTEELER**, **GENTEELEST** polite or refined in an artificial, affected way approaching snobbishness

GENTEELLY adverb in a genteel way

GENTIAN noun **GENTIANS** any of numerous mostly low-growing perennial plants with opposite leaves and erect funnel-shaped or bell-shaped flowers, often deep blue in colour

GENTILE noun **GENTILES** used especially by Jews: a person who is not Jewish □ adj used especially by Jews: not Jewish

GENTILITY noun **GENTILITIES** good manners and respectability

GENTLE adj **GENTLER**, **GENTLEST** mild-mannered, not stern, coarse or violent □ noun **GENTLES** a soft maggot used as bait by anglers

GENTLEMAN noun **GENTLEMEN** (especially as a term of reference or address) a polite name for a man

GENTLY adverb in a gentle way

GENTOO noun **GENTOOS** a species of long-tailed penguin that is common in the Falkland Islands

GENTRIFY verb **GENTRIFIES**, **GENTRIFYING**, **GENTRIFIED** to convert or renovate (housing) to conform to middle-class taste

GENTRY noun **GENTRIES** people belonging to the class directly below the nobility

GENTS singular noun a men's public toilet

GENU noun **GENUS** in anatomy: the knee, a knee-like bend or structure

GENUFLECT verb **GENUFLECTS**, **GENUFLECTING**, **GENUFLECTED** to bend one's knee in worship or as a sign of respect

GENUINE adj authentic, not artificial or fake

GENUINELY adverb in a genuine way

GENUS noun **GENUSES**, **GENERA** in taxonomy: any of the groups, eg Canis (the dogs), into which a family is divided and which in turn is subdivided into one or more species

GEO noun **GEOS** a gully or creek

GEODE noun **GEODES** a hollow rock cavity that is lined with crystals which point inward towards its centre

GEODESIC adj relating to or determined by geodesy □ noun **GEODESICS** a line on a plane or curved surface that represents the shortest distance between two points

GEODESY noun **GEODESIES** the scientific study of the Earth's surface by surveying (especially by satellite) and mapping in order to determine its exact shape and size, and to measure its gravitational field

GEODETIC adj geodesic □ noun **GEODETICS** a geodesic

GEOGRAPHY noun **GEOGRAPHIES** the scientific study of the Earth's surface, especially its physical features, climate, resources, population, etc

GEOID noun **GEOIDS** the shape of the Earth, ie a slightly flattened sphere, taken as the reference for geodesic measurement

GEOLOGISE verb **GEOLOGISES**, **GEOLOGISING**, **GEOLOGISED** to geologize

GEOLOGIST noun **GEOLOGISTS** an expert in geology

GEOLOGIZE verb **GEOLOGIZES**, **GEOLOGIZING**, **GEOLOGIZED** to study the geology of (a specified area, etc)

GEOLOGY noun **GEOLOGIES** the scientific study of the origins and structure, composition, etc of the Earth, especially its rocks

GEOMETER noun **GEOMETERS** a person skilled in geometry

GEOMETRIC adj relating to or using the principles of geometry

GEOMETRID noun **GEOMETRIDS** a type of moth

GEOMETRY noun **GEOMETRIES** the branch of mathematics dealing with lines, angles, shapes, etc and their relationships

GEORGETTE noun **GEORGETTES** a kind of thin silk material

GEOSPHERE noun **GEOSPHERES** the non-living part of the Earth, including the lithosphere, hydrosphere and atmosphere

GEOTROPIC adj of or relating to geotropism (the growth of the roots or shoots of plants in response to gravity)

GERANIUM noun **GERANIUMS** any of several plants of the

pelargonium family widely cultivated as houseplants

GERBERA noun **GERBERAS** a plant belonging to the Gerbera genus of composite plants of S Africa, etc

GERBIL noun **GERBILS** any of numerous small burrowing rodents with long hind legs and a long furry tail

GERFALCON noun **GERFALCONS** a gyrfalcon

GERIATRIC adj for or dealing with old people; relating to geriatrics □ noun **GERIATRICS** an old person

GERIATRICS singular noun the branch of medicine concerned with the care of the elderly, and with the diagnosis and treatment of diseases and disorders associated with ageing

GERM noun **GERMS** an imprecise term for any micro-organism, especially a bacterium or virus that causes disease

GERMAN adj characterized by having both parents the same

GERMANE adj said of ideas, remarks, etc: relevant; closely related (to the topic under discussion)

GERMANELY adverb in a germane manner

GERMANIUM noun **GERMANIUMS** a hard greyish-white metalloid element, widely used as a semiconductor in electronic devices

GERMICIDE noun **GERMICIDES** any agent that destroys disease-causing micro-organisms such as bacteria and viruses

GERMINAL adj relating to or similar to a germ or germs

GERMINATE verb **GERMINATES**, **GERMINATING**, **GERMINATED** said of a seed or spore: to show the first signs of development into a new individual

GERUND noun **GERUNDS** a noun that is formed from a verb and which describes an action. In English it ends in -ing, eg 'the *baking* of bread' and '*Smoking* damages your health'

GERUNDIAL adj relating to a gerund

GERUNDIVE noun **GERUNDIVES** an adjectival form of a verb, used to indicate that something deserves or requires to be done, as in *agenda* 'requiring to be done'

GESSO noun **GESSOES** plaster for sculpting with or painting on

GESTALT noun **GESTALTS** a whole pattern or structure perceived as something greater than simply the sum of its separate parts

GESTAPO noun **GESTAPOS** any secret police organization, especially one associated with harsh and unscrupulous methods

GESTATE verb **GESTATES, GESTATING, GESTATED** said of a mammal that bears live young: to carry (young) or be carried in the uterus, and to undergo physical development, during the period between fertilization and birth

GESTATION noun **GESTATIONS** in mammals that bear live young: the period between fertilization of the egg and birth, during which the embryo develops in the uterus of the mother

GESTURAL adj relating to gesture

GESTURE noun **GESTURES** a movement of a part of the body as an expression of meaning, especially when speaking □ verb **GESTURES, GESTURING, GESTURED** to make gestures

GET verb **GETS, GETTING, GOT, GOTTEN** to receive or obtain

GETA noun **GETAS** a Japanese wooden sandal with a thong between the big toe and the other toes

GETAWAY noun **GETAWAYS** an escape, especially after committing a crime

GETTER noun **GETTERS** any of various substances used for removing the residual gas from the vacuum in valves

GEUM noun **GEUMS** a perennial plant with lobed leaves and brilliant yellow, orange or scarlet flowers, often grown in rock gardens

GEWGAW noun **GEWGAWS** a flashy trinket

GEY adverb a Scots word meaning *fairly*

GEYSER noun **GEYSERS** in an area of volcanic activity: a type of hot spring that intermittently spouts hot water and steam into the air, used as a source of geothermal energy in some parts of the world

GHARIAL noun **GHARIALS** a large narrow-snouted Indian crocodile

GHASTLY adj **GHASTLIER, GHASTLIEST** extremely frightening, hideous or horrific □ adverb extremely; unhealthily

GHAT noun **GHATS** a mountain pass

GHEE noun **GHEES** in Indian cookery: clarified butter made from cow's or buffalo's milk and used as a cooking oil

GHERKIN noun **GHERKINS** a variety of cucumber that bears very small fruits

GHETTO noun **GHETTOS, GHETTOES** a poor area densely populated by people from a deprived social group, especially a racial minority

GHETTOISE verb **GHETTOISES, GHETTOISING, GHETTOISED** to ghettoize

GHETTOIZE verb **GHETTOIZES, GHETTOIZING, GHETTOIZED** to think of (a group of people or things) as being confined to a specific restricted function or area of activity; to pigeonhole

GHI noun **GHIS** ghee

GHILLIE noun **GHILLIES** a gillie

GHOST noun **GHOSTS** the spirit of a dead person when it is visible in some form to a living person □ verb **GHOSTS, GHOSTING, GHOSTED** to be a ghost writer (someone who writes books, speeches etc on behalf of another person) for a person or of (some written work)

GHOSTLY adj **GHOSTLIER, GHOSTLIEST** belonging to or like a ghost or ghosts

GHOUL noun **GHOULS** someone who is interested in morbid or disgusting things

GHOULISH adj like or typical of a ghoul

GHYLL noun **GHYLLS** a deep wooded ravine

GI noun **GIS** a judo or karate costume

GIANT noun **GIANTS** in stories: a huge, extremely strong, often cruel creature of human form □ adj belonging to a particularly large species, in implied contrast to smaller ones

GIANTESS noun **GIANTESSES** a female giant

GIB noun **GIBS** a small metal or wooden wedge used for keeping a machine part in place □ verb **GIBS, GIBBING, GIBBED** to secure with a gib

GIBBER verb **GIBBERS, GIBBERING, GIBBERED** to talk so fast that one cannot be understood

GIBBERING adj that gibbers

GIBBERISH noun **GIBBERISHES** speech that is meaningless or difficult to understand

GIBBET noun **GIBBETS** a gallows-like frame on which the bodies of executed criminals were hung as a public warning □ verb **GIBBETS, GIBBETING, GIBBETED** formerly, to hang someone on a gibbet

GIBBON noun **GIBBONS** the smallest of the apes, with very long arms, and the only ape to walk upright habitually, found in SE Asia

GIBBOSITY noun **GIBBOSITIES** the state of being gibbous

GIBBOUS adj said of the moon or a planet: not fully illuminated but more than half illuminated

GIBE verb **GIBES, GIBING, GIBED** to mock, scoff or jeer □ noun **GIBES** a jeer

GIBER noun **GIBERS** someone who gibes

GIBING adj mocking or jeering

GIBINGLY adverb in a gibing way

GIBLETS plural noun the heart, liver and other edible internal organs of a chicken or other fowl

GID noun **GIDS** a sheep disease

GIDDILY adverb in a giddy way

GIDDINESS noun **GIDDINESSES** the condition of being giddy

GIDDY adj **GIDDIER, GIDDIEST** suffering an unbalancing spinning sensation

GIE verb **GIES, GIEING, GIED, GAE, GIEN** a Scots word for *give*

GIFT noun **GIFTS** something given; a present □ verb **GIFTS, GIFTING, GIFTED** to give something as a present to someone

GIFTED adj having a great natural ability

GIG noun **GIGS** a pop, jazz or folk concert □ verb **GIGS, GIGGING, GIGGED** to play a gig or gigs

GIGA noun **GIGAS** a gigue

GIGANTIC adj huge; enormous

GIGANTISM noun **GIGANTISMS** excessive overgrowth of the whole human body, usually owing to overactivity of the pituitary gland

GIGGLE verb **GIGGLES, GIGGLING, GIGGLED** to laugh quietly in short bursts or in a nervous or silly way □ noun **GIGGLES** such a laugh

GIGGLER noun **GIGGLERS** someone who giggles

GIGGLING noun **GIGGLINGS** the

action of laughing quietly in short bursts or in a nervous or silly way ◻ *adj* that giggles

GIGGLY *adj* **GIGGLIER, GIGGLIEST** giggling or likely to giggle

GIGOLO *noun* **GIGOLOS** a young, and usually attractive, man who is paid by an older woman to be her companion, escort and, sometimes, lover

GIGOT *noun* **GIGOTS** a leg of lamb or mutton

GIGUE *noun* **GIGUES** the music for a lively dance, usually in 6/8 time, in two repeated sections

GILA *noun* **GILAS** a venomous lizard with dark colouring and yellow mottling, bead-like scales, a blunt head and a thick tail, found in the SW states of the US

GILD *verb* **GILDS, GILDING, GILT, GILDED** to cover something with a thin coating of gold or something similar

GILDER *noun* **GILDERS** a guilder

GILET *noun* **GILETS** a garment like a waistcoat

GILL *noun* **GILLS** in all fishes and many other aquatic animals: a respiratory organ that extracts dissolved oxygen from the surrounding water

GILLIE *noun* **GILLIES** a guide or assistant to a game-hunter or fisherman, especially in Scotland

GILT 1 *adj* covered with a thin coating of gold or apparently so covered; gilded

GILT 2 *noun* **GILTS** a young female pig, especially one that has not produced a litter

GIMBALS *plural noun* a device that allows a navigation instrument mounted on it to rotate freely about two perpendicular axes, and so to remain in a horizontal position at sea or in the air

GIMCRACK *adj* cheap, showy and badly made ◻ *noun* **GIMCRACKS** a cheap and showy article

GIMLET *noun* **GIMLETS** a T-shaped hand-tool for boring holes in wood

GIMME *noun* **GIMMES** in golf: a short putt that a player is willing to accept as successfully played by their opponent without it actually being played

GIMMICK *noun* **GIMMICKS** a scheme or object used to attract attention or publicity, especially to bring in customers

GIMMICKRY *noun* **GIMMICKRIES** gimmicks, or the use of gimmicks

GIMMICKY *adj* **GIMMICKIER, GIMMICKIEST** designed to catch attention

GIMP *noun* **GIMPS** a strip of silk or other fabric with a core of wire or cord, used as a decoration in dressmaking, etc

GIN 1 *noun* **GINS** an alcoholic spirit made from barley, rye or maize and flavoured with juniper berries

GIN 2 *verb* **GINS, GINNING, GINNED** to snare or trap (game) in a gin (a wire noose)

GINGER *noun* **GINGERS** an aromatic spicy swollen root or rhizome, often dried and ground to a yellow powder and widely used as a flavouring in biscuits, cakes, curries, etc or preserved in syrup ◻ *adj* flavoured with ginger ◻ *verb* **GINGERS, GINGERING, GINGERED** to urge, persuade or force someone or something to become more lively, active, interesting or efficient

GINGERLY *adj* very cautious or wary ◻ *adverb* with delicate caution

GINGERY *adj* tasting of, flavoured with, coloured like, etc ginger

GINGHAM *noun* **GINGHAMS** striped or checked cotton cloth

GINGILI *noun* **GINGILIS** the plant sesame

GINGIVAL *adj* relating to the gums

GINGKO *noun* **GINGKOES** a ginkgo

GINGLYMUS *noun* **GINGLYMI** a joint, such as the knee or elbow, that permits movement in one plane only; a hinge joint

GINK *noun* **GINKS** someone, especially a man, who is considered a bit odd

GINKGO *noun* **GINKGOES** a deciduous cone-bearing tree, native to China and Japan, which has fan-shaped leaves similar to those of the maidenhair fern

GINORMOUS *adj* exceptionally huge

GINSENG *noun* **GINSENGS** a plant cultivated in China for its roots

GIO *noun* **GIOS** a geo

GIOCOSO *adverb* in a lively or humorous manner ◻ *adj* lively or humorous

GIP *noun* **GIPS** a college servant at Cambridge and Durham

GIPSY *noun* **GIPSIES** a gypsy

GIRAFFE *noun* **GIRAFFES** a very

tall African mammal with an extremely long neck and legs, a small head, large eyes and a pale buff coat boldly marked with irregular chestnut or dark brown blotches

GIRANDOLE *noun* **GIRANDOLES** a branched wall-bracket for candles

GIRASOL *noun* **GIRASOLS** an opal that seems to send a fire-like glow from within in certain lights

GIRASOLE *noun* **GIRASOLE** a girasol

GIRD *verb* **GIRDS, GIRDING, GIRT, GIRDED** to encircle or fasten something (especially part of the body) with a belt or something similar

GIRDER *noun* **GIRDERS** a large beam of wood, iron or steel used to support a floor, wall, road or bridge

GIRDLE *noun* **GIRDLES** a woman's close-fitting elasticated undergarment that covers the area from waist to thigh ◻ *verb* **GIRDLES, GIRDLING, GIRDLED** to put a girdle on someone or something

GIRL *noun* **GIRLS** a female child

GIRLHOOD *noun* **GIRLHOODS** the state or time of being a girl

GIRLIE *adj* said of a magazine, picture, etc: featuring naked or nearly naked young women in erotic poses ◻ *noun* **GIRLIES** a girl, especially used as an endearment

GIRLISH *adj* like a girl

GIRLISHLY *adverb* in a girlish way

GIRLY *noun* **GIRLIES** a girl

GIRNER *noun* **GIRNERS** someone who makes grotesque faces as an entertainment at country fairs, etc

GIRO *noun* **GIROS** a banking system by which money can be transferred from one account directly to another

GIRT a past form of **gird**

GIRTH *noun* **GIRTHS** the strap round a horse's belly that holds a saddle in place ◻ *verb* **GIRTHS, GIRTHING, GIRTHED** to put a girth on (a horse)

GISM *noun* **GISMS** energy; force

GISMO *noun* **GISMOS** a gadget, a thingummyjig

GISMOLOGY *noun* **GISMOLOGIES** gadgetry; technology involving gadgetry, especially strange or baffling examples of it

GIST *noun* **GISTS** the general meaning or main point of something said or written

GIT *noun* **GITS** a stupid or contemptible person

GITE *noun* **GITES** in France: a self-catering holiday cottage

GIVE *verb* **GIVES, GIVING, GAVE, GIVEN** to transfer ownership of something; to transfer possession of something temporarily □ *noun* **GIVES** capacity to yield; flexibility

GIVEAWAY *noun* **GIVEAWAYS** an act of accidentally revealing secrets, etc □ *adj* extremely cheap

GIVEN *adj* stated or specified □ *conj* accepting (a specified thing) as a basis for discussion; assuming □ *prep* accepting (a specified thing) as a basis for discussion; assuming

GIVING *adj* generous; liberal

GIZMO *noun* **GIZMOS** a gismo

GIZMOLOGY *noun* **GIZMOLOGIES** gismology

GIZZ *noun* **GIZZES** a Scots word for a wig

GIZZARD *noun* **GIZZARDS** in birds, earthworms and certain other animals: a muscular chamber specialized for grinding up indigestible food

GJU *noun* **GJUS** a gue

GLABELLA *noun* **GLABELLAE** the part of the forehead between the eyebrows and just above

GLABRATE *adj* glabrous

GLABROUS *adj* smooth; hairless

GLACÉ *adj* coated with a sugary glaze; candied □ *verb* **GLACÉS, GLACÉING, GLACÉED** to crystallize (fruit, etc)

GLACIAL *adj* relating to or resembling a glacier □ *noun* **GLACIALS** a glacial period; an ice age

GLACIATE *verb* **GLACIATES, GLACIATING, GLACIATED** said of land, etc: to become covered with glaciers or ice sheets

GLACIER *noun* **GLACIERS** a large body of ice, formed by the compaction of snow, that slowly moves either down a gradient or outward in all directions until it reaches a point where it melts or breaks up into icebergs

GLAD *adj* **GLADDER, GLADDEST** happy or pleased

GLADDEN *verb* **GLADDENS, GLADDENING, GLADDENED** to make someone (or their heart, etc) happy or pleased

GLADE *noun* **GLADES** an open space in a wood or forest

GLADIATOR *noun* **GLADIATORS** in ancient Rome: a man trained to fight against other men or animals in an arena

GLADIOLUS *noun* **GLADIOLI** a perennial plant with upright sword-shaped leaves borne in flat fans and one-sided spikes of brightly coloured funnel-shaped flowers

GLADLY *adverb* with gladness; willingly

GLADNESS *noun* **GLADNESSES** the state of being glad

GLAIR *noun* **GLAIRS** egg-white, or a similar substance, used as a glaze or an adhesive □ *verb* **GLAIRS, GLAIRING, GLAIRED** to apply glair to something

GLAM *adj* glamorous □ *noun* **GLAMS** glamour

GLAMORISE *verb* **GLAMORISES, GLAMORISING, GLAMORISED** to glamorize

GLAMORIZE *verb* **GLAMORIZES, GLAMORIZING, GLAMORIZED** to make someone or something glamorous

GLAMOROUS *adj* full of glamour

GLAMOUR *noun* **GLAMOURS** the quality of being fascinatingly, if perhaps falsely, attractive

GLANCE *verb* **GLANCES, GLANCING, GLANCED** to look quickly or indirectly at someone or something □ *noun* **GLANCES** a brief (and often indirect) look

GLANCING *adj* flying off obliquely on striking □ *noun* **GLANCINGS** the action of looking quickly or indirectly at something or someone

GLAND *noun* **GLANDS** in humans and animals: an organ that produces a specific chemical substance (eg a hormone) for use inside the body

GLANDERS *singular noun* a highly infectious bacterial disease of horses, donkeys and mules

GLANDULAR *adj* relating to, containing or affecting a gland or glands

GLANS *noun* **GLANDES** an acorn-shaped part of the body, especially the end of the penis

GLARE *verb* **GLARES, GLARING, GLARED** to stare angrily □ *noun* **GLARES** an angry stare

GLARING *adj* unpleasantly bright

GLARINGLY *adverb* in a glaring way

GLASNOST *noun* **GLASNOSTS** a policy of openness and willingness to provide information on the part of governments, especially the Soviet government under Mikhail Gorbachev (President 1988–91)

GLASS *noun* **GLASSES** a hard brittle non-crystalline material that is usually transparent or translucent, used to make windows, bottles and other containers, cooking utensils, lenses, etc □ *verb* **GLASSES, GLASSING, GLASSED** to supply or cover something with glass

GLASSFUL *noun* **GLASSFULS** the amount held by a drinking glass

GLASSINE *noun* **GLASSINES** a glossy, translucent, greaseproof paper

GLASSWARE *noun* **GLASSWARES** articles made of glass

GLASSWORT *noun* **GLASSWORTS** a marsh plant that yields soda, formerly used in making glass

GLASSY *adj* **GLASSIER, GLASSIEST** like glass

GLAUCOMA *noun* **GLAUCOMAS** any of various eye diseases in which increased pressure within the eyeball causes impaired vision and which, if left untreated, can lead to blindness

GLAUCOUS *adj* having a dull green or blue colour

GLAZE *verb* **GLAZES, GLAZING, GLAZED** to fit glass panes into (a window, door, etc) □ *noun* **GLAZES** a hard glassy coating on pottery or the material for this coating before it is applied or fired

GLAZED *adj* fitted or covered with glass

GLAZIER *noun* **GLAZIERS** someone whose job is to fit glass in windows, doors, etc

GLAZING *noun* **GLAZINGS** the act or art of setting glass; the art of covering with a vitreous substance

GLEAM *noun* **GLEAMS** a gentle glow □ *verb* **GLEAMS, GLEAMING, GLEAMED** to glow gently

GLEAMING *adj* glowing gently

GLEAN *verb* **GLEANS, GLEANING, GLEANED** to collect (information, etc) bit by bit, often with difficulty

GLEANER *noun* **GLEANERS** a person who gleans (eg information)

GLEANINGS *plural noun* things which have been or may be gleaned, especially bits of information

GLEBE *noun* **GLEBES** a piece of church-owned land providing income in rent, etc for the resident minister

GLEE *noun* **GLEES** great delight; joy

GLEEFUL *adj* joyful; merry

GLEI *noun* **GLEIS** gley

GLEN *noun* **GLENS** especially in Scotland: a long narrow valley

GLENGARRY *noun* **GLENGARRIES** a narrow brimless cap creased in the middle from front to back and usually with two ribbons hanging at the back, worn eg by some Scottish regiments

GLEY *noun* **GLEYS** a bluish-grey sticky clay found under some types of very damp soil □ *verb* **GLEYS, GLEYING, GLEYED** to form into a gley

GLIA *noun* **GLIAS** the supporting tissue of the brain and spinal cord

GLIAL *adj* of or relating to glia

GLIB *adj* **GLIBBER, GLIBBEST** speaking or spoken readily and persuasively, but neither sincere nor reliable

GLIBLY *adverb* in a glib manner

GLIBNESS *noun* **GLIBNESSES** the quality of being glib

GLIDE *verb* **GLIDES, GLIDING, GLIDED** to move smoothly and often without any visible effort □ *noun* **GLIDES** a gliding movement

GLIDER *noun* **GLIDERS** a fixed-wing aircraft that is designed to glide and soar in air currents without using any form of engine power

GLIDING[1] *adj* moving smoothly and easily

GLIDING[2] *noun* **GLIDINGS** the sport of flying in a glider

GLIDINGLY *adverb* in a gliding way

GLIMMER *verb* **GLIMMERS, GLIMMERING, GLIMMERED** to glow faintly □ *noun* **GLIMMERS** a faint glow; a twinkle

GLIMMERING *adj* glowing faintly □ *noun* **GLIMMERINGS** a glimmer; an inkling

GLIMPSE *noun* **GLIMPSES** a very brief look □ *verb* **GLIMPSES, GLIMPSING, GLIMPSED** to see something or someone momentarily

GLINT *verb* **GLINTS, GLINTING, GLINTED** to give off tiny flashes of

bright light □ *noun* **GLINTS** a brief flash of light

GLIOMA *noun* **GLIOMAS, GLIOMATA** a tumour of glial cells

GLIOSIS *noun* **GLIOSES** excessive growth of fibrous tissue in the glia

GLISSADE *noun* **GLISSADES** a sliding ballet step □ *verb* **GLISSADES, GLISSADING, GLISSADED** to perform a glissade

GLISSANDO *noun* **GLISSANDOS** the effect produced by sliding the finger along a keyboard or a string

GLISTEN *verb* **GLISTENS, GLISTENING, GLISTENED** often said of something wet or icy: to shine or sparkle

GLISTENING *adj* shining or sparkling

GLISTER *verb* **GLISTERS, GLISTERING, GLISTERED** to glitter

GLITCH *noun* **GLITCHES** a sudden brief irregularity or failure to function, especially in electronic equipment

GLITTER *verb* **GLITTERS, GLITTERING, GLITTERED** to shine with bright flashes of light; to sparkle □ *noun* **GLITTERS** sparkle

GLITTERING *adj* brightly shining

GLITTERY *adj* **GLITTERIER, GLITTERIEST** sparkly

GLITZ *noun* showiness; garishness

GLITZY *adj* **GLITZIER, GLITZIEST** extravagantly showy; flashy

GLOAMING *noun* **GLOAMINGS** dusk; twilight

GLOAT *verb* **GLOATS, GLOATING, GLOATED** to feel or show smug or vindictive satisfaction, especially in one's success or in another's misfortune □ *noun* **GLOATS** an act of gloating

GLOB *noun* **GLOBS** a small amount of thick liquid; a blob or dollop

GLOBBY *adj* of or like a glob

GLOBAL *adj* affecting the whole world

GLOBALLY *adverb* in a global way

GLOBE *noun* **GLOBES** the Earth

GLOBIN *noun* **GLOBINS** in animals: any of a group of soluble proteins that are present in the iron-containing pigments haemoglobin (in red blood cells) and myoglobin (in muscle cells)

GLOBULAR *adj* shaped like a globe or globule

GLOBULE *noun* **GLOBULES** a small drop, especially of liquid

GLOGG *noun* **GLOGGS** a Swedish hot spiced drink, of wine, a spirit and fruit, often served at Christmas

GLOMERATE *adj* clustered into a head or heads

GLOOM *noun* **GLOOMS** near-darkness □ *verb* **GLOOMS, GLOOMING, GLOOMED** said of the sky: to be dark and threatening

GLOOMILY *adverb* in a gloomy way

GLOOMY *adj* **GLOOMIER, GLOOMIEST** dark; dimly lit

GLOP *noun* **GLOPS** a mushy mess of something, especially of unappetizing food

GLORIA *noun* **GLORIAS** a doxology beginning with the word 'gloria'

GLORIFIED *adj* given a fancy name or appearance

GLORIFY *verb* **GLORIFIES, GLORIFYING, GLORIFIED** to exaggerate the beauty, importance, etc of something or someone

GLORIOUS *adj* having or bringing glory

GLORY *noun* **GLORIES** great honour and prestige □ *verb* **GLORIES, GLORYING, GLORIED** to exult proudly; to rejoice

GLOSS *noun* **GLOSSES** shiny brightness on a surface □ *verb* **GLOSSES, GLOSSING, GLOSSED** to give a shiny finish to something

GLOSSARY *noun* **GLOSSARIES** a list of explanations of obscure or unusual words, often at the end of a book

GLOSSILY *adverb* in a glossy way

GLOSSY *adj* **GLOSSIER, GLOSSIEST** smooth and shiny □ *noun* **GLOSSIES** a magazine that is printed on glossy paper

GLOTTAL *adj* relating to or produced by the glottis

GLOTTIS *noun* **GLOTTISES, GLOTTIDES** the opening through which air passes from the pharynx to the trachea, including the space between the vocal cords

GLOVE *noun* **GLOVES** a covering for the hand which usually has individual casings for each finger □ *verb* **GLOVES, GLOVING, GLOVED** to cover something with a glove or gloves

GLOVER *noun* **GLOVERS** a glove-maker

GLOW *verb* **GLOWS, GLOWING, GLOWED** to give out a steady heat or light without flames □ *noun* **GLOWS** a steady flameless heat or light

GLOWER *verb* **GLOWERS,**

GLOWERING, GLOWERED to stare angrily □ noun **GLOWERS** an angry stare; a scowl

GLOWING adj commendatory; full of praise

GLOWINGLY adverb in a glowing way

GLOXINIA noun **GLOXINIAS** any of various plants, native to Brazil, with large velvety funnel-shaped white, pink, red or purple flowers

GLUCAGON noun **GLUCAGONS** a hormone secreted by the pancreas, which accelerates glycogen breakdown in the liver, so increasing blood sugar levels

GLUCOSE noun **GLUCOSES** the most common six-carbon monosaccharide in living cells, and in animals the main form in which energy derived from carbohydrates is transported around the bloodstream

GLUCOSIDE noun **GLUCOSIDES** any of various derivatives of glucose in which the first hydroxyl group is replaced by another group, and which yields glucose when treated with enzymes or acids

GLUE noun **GLUES** any adhesive obtained by extracting natural substances, especially from bone, in boiling water □ verb **GLUES, GLUING, GLUED** to use such an adhesive to stick (two materials or parts) together

GLUEY adj **GLUIER, GLUIEST** containing glue; like glue; sticky

GLUEYNESS noun **GLUEYNESSES** the state of being gluey

GLUG noun **GLUGS** the sound of liquid being poured, eg from a bottle or down someone's throat □ verb **GLUGS, GLUGGING, GLUGGED** to make such a sound

GLÜHWEIN noun **GLÜHWEINS** mulled wine, especially as prepared in Germany, Austria, etc

GLUM adj **GLUMMER, GLUMMEST** in low spirits; sullen

GLUME noun **GLUMES** in grasses and sedges: an outer sterile bract which, alone or with others, encloses the spikelet

GLUMLY adverb in a glum way

GLUMNESS noun **GLUMNESSES** the condition of being glum

GLUON noun **GLUONS** a hypothetical particle with no mass, the carrier of the force that is believed to hold quarks together

GLUT noun **GLUTS** an excessive supply of goods, etc □ verb **GLUTS, GLUTTING, GLUTTED** to feed or supply something to excess

GLUTAMATE noun **GLUTAMATES** a salt of glutamic acid

GLUTEAL adj of or relating to the glutei

GLUTEN noun **GLUTENS** a mixture of two plant storage proteins occurring in wheat flour that gives bread dough elastic properties and is responsible for the condition known as coeliac disease in people who are abnormally sensitive to it

GLUTENOUS adj consisting of or containing gluten

GLUTEUS noun **GLUTEI** any of the three large muscles in the human buttock

GLUTINOUS adj like glue; sticky

GLUTTON noun **GLUTTONS** someone who eats too much

GLUTTONY noun **GLUTTONIES** the habit or practice of eating too much

GLYCERIDE noun **GLYCERIDES** an ester of glycerol

GLYCERIN noun **GLYCERINS** glycerol

GLYCERINE noun **GLYCERINES** glycerol

GLYCEROL noun **GLYCEROLS** a colourless viscous sweet-tasting liquid that is soluble in water and alcohol

GLYCOGEN noun **GLYCOGENS** a highly branched chain of glucose molecules, the main form in which carbohydrate is stored (especially in the liver and muscles) in vertebrates

GLYCOL noun **GLYCOLS** any of a class of compounds with two hydroxyl groups on adjacent carbon atoms, and so intermediate between *glyc*erine and alcoh*ol*

GLYCOSIDE noun **GLYCOSIDES** any of a group of compounds derived from simple sugars by replacing the hydroxyl group with another group

GLYPH noun **GLYPHS** in architecture: an ornamental channel or fluting, usually vertical

GLYPTIC adj relating to carving or engraving, especially gem-carving

GNARLED adj said of tree trunks, branches, human hands, etc: twisted, with knotty swellings, usually as a result of age

GNARLY adj **GNARLIER, GNARLIEST** gnarled

GNASH verb **GNASHES,**

GNASHING, GNASHED to grind (the teeth) together, especially in anger or pain

GNASHERS plural noun teeth, especially false ones

GNAT noun **GNATS** any of various small fragile biting flies

GNATHAL adj gnathic

GNATHIC adj relating to the jaw

GNAW verb **GNAWS, GNAWING, GNAWED** to bite with a scraping or nibbling movement; to wear away

GNAWING adj that gnaws

GNEISS noun **GNEISSES** a coarse-grained metamorphic rock that contains bands of quartz and feldspar alternating with bands of mica

GNEISSOSE adj having the structure of gneiss

GNOCCHI noun **GNOCCHIS** a dish of small dumplings made from flour, semolina or potato and served in a sauce

GNOME noun **GNOMES, GNOMAE** a pithy aphorism, usually in verse, that embodies some moral sentiment or precept

GNOMIC adj said of speech or writing: expressed in gnomes; moralizing

GNOMISH adj like a gnome (a fairy-tale creature, usually in the form of a small misshapen old man)

GNOMON noun **GNOMONS** on a sundial: the raised arm that casts the shadow which points to the hour

GNOSTIC adj relating to knowledge, especially mystical or religious knowledge

GNU noun **GNUS** either of two species of large African antelope with a stocky body, a large bull-like head, horns in both sexes, a long mane and tufts of hair growing from the muzzle, throat and chest

GO[1] verb **GOES, GOING, WENT, GONE** to walk, move or travel in the direction specified □ noun **GOES** a turn or spell

GO[2] noun **GOS** a Japanese board game

GOA noun **GOAS** a grey-brown Tibetan gazelle, with backward-curving horns

GOAD verb **GOADS, GOADING, GOADED** to urge or provoke someone to action □ noun **GOADS**

a sharp-pointed stick used for driving cattle, etc

GOAL noun **GOALS** in various sports, especially football: a set of posts with a crossbar, through which the ball is struck to score points

GOALIE noun **GOALIES** a goalkeeper

GOALLESS adj with no goals scored; unambitious

GOALMOUTH noun **GOALMOUTHS** in various sports: the area around the goal

GOALPOST noun **GOALPOSTS** in various sports: each of two upright posts forming the goal

GOAT noun **GOATS** any of numerous species of herbivorous mammal, noted for its physical agility and sure-footedness

GOATEE noun **GOATEES** a pointed beard growing on the front of the chin only

GOATHERD noun **GOATHERDS** someone who looks after goats out in the pastures

GOATISH adj like a goat

GOB noun **GOBS** a soft wet lump

GOBBET noun **GOBBETS** a lump or chunk

GOBBLE verb **GOBBLES, GOBBLING, GOBBLED** said of a male turkey: to make a loud gurgling sound in the throat □ noun **GOBBLES** the loud gurgling sound made by a male turkey

GOBBLER noun **GOBBLERS** a male turkey

GOBLET noun **GOBLETS** a drinking-cup with a base and stem but no handles, often made from metal or glass

GOBLIN noun **GOBLINS** in folk-tales: an evil or mischievous spirit in the form of a small man

GOBY noun **GOBIES** any of numerous small, usually colourful, marine fishes with large eyes, fleshy lips, and the pelvic fins fused together to form a disc-shaped sucker

GOD noun **GODS** a superhuman male being with power over nature and humanity; a male object of worship □ verb **GODS, GODDING, GODDED** to deify

GODCHILD noun **GODCHILDREN** a child that a godparent is responsible for

GODDAM adj damned, accursed

GODDESS noun **GODDESSES** a

superhuman female being who has power over nature and humanity; a female object of worship

GODETIA noun **GODETIAS** a highly-prized garden plant valued for its showy red or purplish-red flowers and closely related to the evening primrose

GODFATHER noun **GODFATHERS** a male godparent

GODHEAD noun **GODHEADS** the state of being a god

GODLESS adj not religious; not believing in God

GODLIKE adj like God or a god; divine

GODLINESS noun **GODLINESSES** the quality of being godly

GODLY adj **GODLIER, GODLIEST** religious; pious

GODMOTHER noun **GODMOTHERS** a female godparent

GODOWN noun **GODOWNS** in Eastern countries: a warehouse or storeroom

GODPARENT noun **GODPARENTS** someone who takes on the responsibility of the religious education of another, especially a child and who, in the case of a child, agrees to supervise its upbringing in the event of the death of its parents

GODROON noun **GODROONS** a gadroon

GODSEND noun **GODSENDS** someone or something whose arrival is unexpected but very welcome

GODSON noun **GODSONS** a male godchild

GODSPEED exclamation expressing good wishes for a person's safety on a journey

GODWIT noun **GODWITS** any of various wading birds which have a long straight or slightly upcurved bill, long legs and greyish-brown plumage in winter with bright chestnut markings in summer

GOE noun **GOES** an old form of geo

GOER noun **GOERS** someone who makes visits, especially regular ones, to a specified place

GOFER noun **GOFERS** in an office or on a film set: a junior employee who runs errands

GOFFER verb **GOFFERS, GOFFERING, GOFFERED** to crimp (paper, etc) or make it wavy

GOGGLE verb **GOGGLES, GOGGLING, GOGGLED** to look with wide staring eyes □ noun **GOGGLES** a wide-eyed stare

GOGGLES plural noun protective spectacles with edges that fit closely against the face

GOING noun **GOINGS** leaving; a departure □ adj flourishing, successful

GOITER noun **GOITERS** a goitre

GOITRE noun **GOITRES** an abnormal enlargement of the thyroid gland which often results in a large visible swelling in the neck

GOLD noun **GOLDS** a soft yellow precious metallic element used for making jewellery, coins, etc □ adj **GOLDER, GOLDEST** made of gold

GOLDCREST noun **GOLDCRESTS** a small European and Asian woodland bird with a yellow or orange crest on its head

GOLDEN adj gold-coloured

GOLDENROD noun **GOLDENRODS** a late-flowering perennial garden plant with long pointed lance-shaped leaves and numerous spikes of tiny golden-yellow flowers, originally native to N America

GOLDFIELD noun **GOLDFIELDS** an area where gold is mined

GOLDFINCH noun **GOLDFINCHES** any of numerous species of European and Asian finch that are distinguished by having a broad yellow bar across each wing

GOLDFISH noun **GOLDFISHES** any of numerous yellow, orange or golden-red varieties of a freshwater fish belonging to the carp family, which are often kept as pets or used to stock aquariums and artificial ponds

GOLDSMITH noun **GOLDSMITHS** someone who makes articles out of gold

GOLF noun **GOLFS** a game played on a golf course, the object being to hit a small ball into each of a series of nine or eighteen holes using a set of long-handled clubs, taking as few strokes as possible □ verb **GOLFS, GOLFING, GOLFED** to play this game

GOLFER noun **GOLFERS** someone who plays golf

GOLFIANA noun **GOLFIANAS** a collector's or dealer's term for items of golfing interest

GOLLIWOG noun **GOLLIWOGS**

formerly, a child's cloth or knitted doll with a black face, bristling hair and bright clothes

GOLLOP verb **GOLLOPS, GOLLOPING, GOLLOPED** to gulp greedily or hastily

GOLLY [1] exclamation expressing surprise or admiration

GOLLY [2] noun **GOLLIES** a golliwog

GOLLYWOG noun **GOLLYWOGS** a golliwog

GOLOSH noun **GOLOSHES** a galosh

GON noun **GONS** a geometrical grade

GONAD noun **GONADS** an organ in which eggs or sperm are produced, especially the ovary or testis

GONDOLA noun **GONDOLAS** a long narrow flat-bottomed boat with pointed upturned ends, used to transport passengers on the canals of Venice

GONDOLIER noun **GONDOLIERS** someone who propels a gondola in Venice

GONE a past form of **go** [1] □ adj departed

GONER noun **GONERS** someone or something that is considered beyond hope of recovery

GONFALON noun **GONFALONS** a banner hung from a horizontal bar, especially one used in some medieval Italian republics

GONG noun **GONGS** a hanging metal plate that makes a resonant sound when struck

GONNA contraction going to

GONORRHEA noun **GONORRHEAS** a sexually transmitted disease which, if left untreated, may cause sterility, arthritis and inflammation of the heart

GONZO adj applied especially to eccentric subjective journalism: bizarre; weird

GOO noun **GOOS** any sticky substance

GOOD adj **BETTER, BEST** having desirable or necessary (positive) qualities; admirable □ noun **GOODS** moral correctness; virtue □ exclamation expressing approval or satisfaction □ adverb very well

GOODIES plural noun things considered pleasant or desirable

GOODLY adj **GOODLIER, GOODLIEST** quite large

GOODNESS exclamation expressing surprise or relief □ noun **GOODNESSES** the state or quality of being good; generosity; kindness; moral correctness

GOODS plural noun articles for sale; merchandise

GOODWILL noun **GOODWILLS** a feeling of kindness towards others

GOODY noun **GOODIES** a hero in a film, book, etc

GOOEY adj **GOOIER, GOOIEST** sticky

GOOF noun **GOOFS** a silly or foolish person □ verb **GOOFS, GOOFING, GOOFED** to make a stupid mistake

GOOFY adj **GOOFIER, GOOFIEST** silly; crazy

GOOGLY noun **GOOGLIES** in cricket: a ball bowled so that it changes direction unexpectedly after bouncing

GOOGOL noun **GOOGOLS** a fanciful term for ten to the power of 100

GOON noun **GOONS** a silly person

GOOP noun **GOOPS** a rude, ill-mannered person

GOOSANDER noun **GOOSANDERS** a large duck with a large dark head bearing a stiff double crest, and a long slender pointed red bill, native to Europe and N America

GOOSE noun **GEESE** any of numerous large wild or domesticated waterfowl, related to ducks and swans, with a stout body, long neck and broad flat bill □ verb **GOOSES, GOOSING, GOOSED** to poke or pinch someone on the buttocks

GOOSEFOOT noun **GOOSEFOOTS** a plant of various species in the beet family, with a leaf shaped like a goose's foot

GOOSEGOG noun **GOOSEGOGS** a gooseberry

GOPAK noun **GOPAKS** a high-leaping Ukrainian folk-dance for men

GOPHER noun **GOPHERS** a small burrowing N American rodent with a stocky body, short legs, large chisel-like incisor teeth and two large external fur-lined cheek pouches □ verb **GOPHERS, GOPHERING, GOPHERED** to carry on small-scale mining

GORBLIMEY exclamation expressing surprise □ adj vulgar

GORBLIMY exclamation gorblimey

GORE [1] noun **GORES** blood from a wound, especially when clotted

GORE [2] verb **GORES, GORING, GORED** to pierce something or someone with horn or tusk

GORED adj made with gores (triangular pieces of material)

GORGE noun **GORGES** a deep narrow valley, usually containing a river □ verb **GORGES, GORGING, GORGED** to eat or swallow greedily

GORGEOUS adj extremely beautiful or attractive; magnificent

GORGET noun **GORGETS** a piece of armour for the throat

GORGIO noun **GORGIOS** a gypsy word for a non-gypsy

GORGON noun **GORGONS** in mythology: any of the three female monsters which had live snakes for hair and were capable of turning people to stone

GORILLA noun **GORILLAS** the largest of the apes, native to African rainforests, which has a heavily built body, broad chest, strong hands and feet and jet black skin covered with dense fur

GORILY adverb in a gory way

GORINESS noun **GORINESSES** the state of being gory

GORMLESS adj stupid; dim

GORSE noun **GORSES** a highly branched evergreen shrub with leaves reduced to very sharp deeply furrowed spines and bright yellow flowers

GORSY adj **GORSIER, GORSIEST** resembling or covered with gorse

GORY adj **GORIER, GORIEST** causing or involving bloodshed

GOS plural of **go** [2]

GOSH exclamation expressing mild surprise

GOSHAWK noun **GOSHAWKS** a large hawk with bluish-grey plumage with paler underparts, short rounded wings and a long tail

GOSLING noun **GOSLINGS** a young goose

GOSPEL noun **GOSPELS** the life and teachings of Christ

GOSSAMER noun **GOSSAMERS** fine filmy spider-woven threads seen on hedges or floating in the air

GOSSAMERY adj like gossamer; flimsy

GOSSIP noun **GOSSIPS** talk or

writing about the private affairs of others, often spiteful and untrue □ *verb* **GOSSIPS, GOSSIPING, GOSSIPED** to engage in, or pass on, malicious gossip

GOSSIPING *noun* **GOSSIPINGS** the act of telling idle or malicious tales □ *adj* that gossips

GOSSIPY *adj* inclined to gossip

GOT a past form of **get**

GOTHIC *adj* relating to 18c mystery novels with gloomy sinister backgrounds

GOTTA *contraction* got to; must

GOTTEN a past form of **get**

GOUACHE *noun* **GOUACHES** a painting technique using a blend of watercolour and a glue-like substance, giving an opaque matt surface

GOUGE *noun* **GOUGES** a chisel with a rounded hollow blade, used for cutting grooves or holes in wood □ *verb* **GOUGES, GOUGING, GOUGED** to cut something out with or as if with a gouge

GOUGÈRE *noun* **GOUGÈRES** a kind of choux pastry that has grated cheese added to it before baking

GOUJONS *plural noun* strips of fish or meat coated in flour, batter or breadcrumbs and deep-fried

GOULASH *noun* **GOULASHES** a thick meat stew heavily seasoned with paprika, originally from Hungary

GOURD *noun* **GOURDS** any of various mostly climbing plants related to the cucumber, that produce a large fruit with a hard woody outer shell

GOURMAND *noun* **GOURMANDS** a greedy eater; a glutton

GOURMET *noun* **GOURMETS** someone who has expert knowledge of, and a passion for, good food and wine

GOUT *noun* **GOUTS** a disease in which excess uric acid accumulates in the bloodstream and is deposited as crystals in the joints, causing acute arthritis, especially of the big toe

GOUTINESS *noun* the state of being gouty

GOUTY *adj* **GOUTIER, GOUTIEST** afflicted with gout

GOV *noun* **GOVS** short form of *governor*

GOVERN *verb* **GOVERNS,**

GOVERNING, GOVERNED to control and direct the affairs of (a country, state, or organization)

GOVERNESS *noun* **GOVERNESSES** a woman employed to teach, and perhaps look after, children, usually while living in their home

GOVERNING *adj* having control

GOVERNOR *noun* **GOVERNORS** the elected head of a US state

GOWN *noun* **GOWNS** a woman's long formal dress

GRAB *verb* **GRABS, GRABBING, GRABBED** to seize suddenly and often with violence □ *noun* **GRABS** an act or an instance of grabbing something

GRACE *noun* **GRACES** elegance and beauty of form or movement □ *verb* **GRACES, GRACING, GRACED** to honour (an occasion, person, etc), eg with one's presence

GRACEFUL *adj* having or showing elegance and beauty of form or movement

GRACELESS *adj* awkward in form or movement

GRACIOUS *adj* kind and polite □ *exclamation* expressing surprise

GRADATE *verb* **GRADATES, GRADATING, GRADATED** to shade off; to change imperceptibly

GRADATION *noun* **GRADATIONS** a series of gradual and successive stages or degrees

GRADE *noun* **GRADES** a stage or level on a scale of quality, rank, size, etc □ *verb* **GRADES, GRADING, GRADED** to arrange (things or people) in different grades

GRADER *noun* **GRADERS** a machine that makes a smooth surface for road-building

GRADIENT *noun* **GRADIENTS** the steepness of a slope

GRADUAL *adj* developing or happening slowly, by degrees □ *noun* **GRADUALS** in the Roman Catholic church: an antiphon sung between the epistle and the gospel

GRADUALLY *adverb* in a gradual way

GRADUAND *noun* **GRADUANDS** someone who is about to be awarded a higher-education degree

GRADUATE *verb* **GRADUATES, GRADUATING, GRADUATED** to receive an academic degree from a higher-education institution □ *noun* **GRADUATES** someone who

has a higher-education degree or (in N America) a high-school diploma

GRAFFITI *noun* **GRAFFITIS** words or drawings, usually humorous, political or rude, scratched, sprayed or painted on walls, etc in public places

GRAFFITO *noun* **GRAFFITI** sgraffito

GRAFT *noun* **GRAFTS** a piece of plant tissue that is inserted into a cut in the outer stem of another plant, resulting in fusion of the tissues and growth of a single plant □ *verb* **GRAFTS, GRAFTING, GRAFTED** to attach something as a graft

GRAFTER *noun* **GRAFTERS** a hard worker

GRAIL *noun* **GRAILS** in medieval legend: the platter or cup used by Christ at the Last Supper, in which Joseph of Arimathea caught his blood at the Crucifixion and which became the object of quests by medieval knights

GRAIN *noun* **GRAINS** the small hard fruit of a cereal plant; the arrangement, size and direction of the fibres or layers in wood, leather etc □ *verb* **GRAINS, GRAINING, GRAINED** to paint or stain something with a pattern like the grain of wood or leather

GRAINED *adj* granulated; having a grain

GRAINING *noun* **GRAININGS** painting to imitate the grain of wood

GRAINY *adj* **GRAINIER, GRAINIEST** said of a photograph: having larger individual particles (grains) which go to compose the picture

GRAM *noun* **GRAMS** in the metric system: the basic unit of mass, equal to one thousandth of a kilogram (0.035oz)

GRAMMAR *noun* **GRAMMARS** the accepted rules by which words are formed and combined into sentences

GRAMME *noun* **GRAMMES** a gram

GRAMPUS *noun* **GRAMPUSES** a large grey dolphin with a bulbous forehead, no beak, an extensively scarred body, relatively short flippers and a tall fin

GRAN *noun* **GRANS** short form of granny

GRANARY *noun* **GRANARIES** a building where grain is stored □ *adj*

said of bread: containing whole grains of wheat

GRAND *adj* **GRANDER, GRANDEST** large or impressive in size, appearance or style ❑ *noun* **GRANDS** a thousand dollars or pounds

GRANDAD *noun* **GRANDADS** the father of one's father or mother

GRANDADDY *noun* **GRANDADDIES** a grandad

GRANDDAD *noun* **GRANDDADS** a grandad

GRANDEE *noun* **GRANDEES** a Spanish or Portuguese nobleman of the highest rank

GRANDEUR *noun* **GRANDEURS** greatness of character, especially dignity or nobility

GRANDIOSE *adj* exaggeratedly impressive or imposing, especially on a ridiculously large scale

GRANDLY *adverb* in a grand way

GRANDMA *noun* **GRANDMAS** the mother of one's father or mother

GRANDNESS *noun* **GRANDNESSES** magnificence; splendour

GRANDPA *noun* **GRANDPAS** a grandad

GRANDPAPA *noun* **GRANDPAPAS** a grandad

GRANDSON *noun* **GRANDSONS** a son of one's son or daughter

GRANGE *noun* **GRANGES** a country house with attached farm buildings

GRANITE *noun* **GRANITES** a hard coarse-grained igneous rock, consisting mainly of quartz, feldspar and mica, widely used in the construction of buildings and roads

GRANITIC *adj* relating to, consisting of, or like granite

GRANNIE *noun* **GRANNIES** a grandma

GRANNY *noun* **GRANNIES** a grandma

GRANOLA *noun* **GRANOLAS** a mixture of oats, dried fruit, nuts and brown sugar, usually eaten with milk for breakfast

GRANT *verb* **GRANTS, GRANTING, GRANTED** to give, allow or fulfil ❑ *noun* **GRANTS** something granted, especially an amount of money from a public fund for a specific purpose

GRANTED *conj* though it is admitted that ❑ *prep* though (a specified thing) is admitted

GRANTEE *noun* **GRANTEES** the person to whom a grant is made

GRANTOR *noun* **GRANTORS** the person who makes a grant

GRANULAR *adj* made of or containing tiny particles or granules

GRANULATE *verb* **GRANULATES, GRANULATING, GRANULATED** to break down into small particles or granules

GRANULE *noun* **GRANULES** a small particle or grain

GRANULOMA *noun* **GRANULOMAS** a small localized tumour composed of growing connective tissue and caused by infection or invasion by a foreign body

GRAPE *noun* **GRAPES** a pale green or purplish-black juicy edible berry which may be eaten fresh, pressed to make wine or dried to form currants, raisins, etc

GRAPESHOT *noun* **GRAPESHOTS** ammunition in the form of small iron balls which scatter when fired in clusters from a cannon

GRAPEVINE *noun* **GRAPEVINES** a vine on which grapes grow

GRAPEY *adj* **GRAPIER, GRAPIEST** made of or like grapes

GRAPH *noun* **GRAPHS** a diagram that illustrates the way in which one quantity varies in relation to another, usually consisting of horizontal and vertical axes which cross each other at a point called the origin ❑ *verb* **GRAPHS, GRAPHING, GRAPHED** to represent something with or as a graph

GRAPHEME *noun* **GRAPHEMES** all the letters or combinations of letters that may be used to represent a single phoneme

GRAPHEMIC *adj* of or relating to graphemes

GRAPHIC *adj* described or shown vividly and in detail

GRAPHICAL *adj* graphic

GRAPHICS *plural noun* the photographs and illustrations used in a magazine ❑ *singular noun* the art or science of drawing according to mathematical principles, especially the drawing of three-dimensional objects on a two-dimensional surface

GRAPHITE *noun* **GRAPHITES** a soft black allotrope of carbon that is used as a lubricant and electrical contact, and is mixed with clay to form the 'lead' in pencils

GRAPHITIC *adj* of or relating to graphite

GRAPNEL *noun* **GRAPNELS** a large multi-pointed hook on one end of a rope, used for securing a heavy object on the other end

GRAPPA *noun* **GRAPPAS** a brandy (originally from Italy) distilled from what is left after the grapes have been pressed for wine-making

GRAPPLE *verb* **GRAPPLES, GRAPPLING, GRAPPLED** struggle and fight, especially at close quarters, eg in hand-to-hand combat ❑ *noun* **GRAPPLES** a hook or other device for securing

GRASP *verb* **GRASPS, GRASPING, GRASPED** to take a firm hold of something or someone; to clutch ❑ *noun* **GRASPS** a grip or hold

GRASPING *adj* greedy, especially for wealth

GRASS *noun* **GRASSES** any of a family of flowering plants (eg cereals, bamboos, etc) that typically have long narrow leaves with parallel veins, a jointed upright hollow stem and flowers (with no petals) borne alternately on both sides of an axis ❑ *verb* **GRASSES, GRASSING, GRASSED** to plant something with grass or turf

GRASSLAND *noun* **GRASSLANDS** permanent pasture

GRASSY *adj* **GRASSIER, GRASSIEST** covered with, or like, grass

GRAT a past form of **greet** [2]

GRATE [1] *verb* **GRATES, GRATING, GRATED** to cut (eg vegetables or cheese) into shreds by rubbing them against a rough or perforated surface

GRATE [2] *noun* **GRATES** a framework of iron bars for holding coal, etc in a fireplace or furnace

GRATEFUL *adj* feeling thankful

GRATER *noun* **GRATERS** a device with a rough surface, and usually with sharpened perforations, for grating food

GRATICULE *noun* **GRATICULES** a ruled grid for the identification of points on a map or the field of a telescope, etc

GRATIFY *verb* **GRATIFIES, GRATIFYING, GRATIFIED** to please someone

GRATIFYING *adj* that gratifies or satisfies

GRATIN adj said of a dish: covered with breadcrumbs, or grated cheese, or a combination of both, cooked in the oven and/or browned under the grill, so that a crisp, golden topping is formed

GRATINÉ adj cooked and served gratin

GRATINÉE adj gratiné

GRATING adj said of sounds, etc: harsh ◻ noun **GRATINGS** a grating sound

GRATIS adj free; without charge ◻ adverb free; without charge

GRATITUDE noun **GRATITUDES** the state or feeling of being grateful; thankfulness

GRATUITY noun **GRATUITIES** a sum of money given as a reward for good service; a tip

GRAVADLAX noun **GRAVADLAXES** gravlax

GRAVAMEN noun **GRAVAMINA** the principal ground of a complaint or accusation

GRAVE[1] adj **GRAVER, GRAVEST** giving cause for great concern; very dangerous

GRAVE[2] adverb in a solemn manner

GRAVE[3] noun **GRAVES** a deep trench dug in the ground for burying a dead body

GRAVEL noun **GRAVELS** a mixture of small loose rock fragments and pebbles, coarser than sand, found on beaches and in the beds of rivers, streams and lakes ◻ verb **GRAVELS, GRAVELLING, GRAVELLED** to cover (eg a path) with gravel

GRAVELLY adj full of, or containing, small stones

GRAVELY adverb in a grave way

GRAVEN adj carved or engraved

GRAVENESS noun **GRAVENESSES** solemnity

GRAVER noun **GRAVERS** an engraving tool, eg a burin

GRAVEYARD noun **GRAVEYARDS** a burial place; a cemetery

GRAVID adj pregnant

GRAVIES plural of **gravy**

GRAVITAS noun **GRAVITASES** seriousness of manner; solemnity, authoritativeness; weight

GRAVITATE verb **GRAVITATES, GRAVITATING, GRAVITATED** to fall or be drawn under the force of gravity

GRAVITY noun **GRAVITIES** the observed effect of the force of

attraction that exists between two massive bodies

GRAVLAX noun **GRAVLAXES** a dish originating in Scandinavia, of salmon dry-cured with spice, sugar, salt and pepper

GRAVURE noun **GRAVURES** any process of making an intaglio printing plate, a technique in printmaking in which a design is incised into a metal plate, ink is forced into the cut lines and wiped off the rest of the surface, damp paper is laid on top and both plate and paper are rolled through a press

GRAVY noun **GRAVIES** the juices released by meat as it is cooking

GRAY adj **GRAYER, GRAYEST** grey ◻ noun **GRAYS** grey ◻ verb **GRAYS, GRAYING, GRAYED** to make or become grey

GRAYLING noun **GRAYLINGS** any of various freshwater fishes, related to the salmon, that have silvery scales with a greenish-gold sheen, dark zigzag lines along the length of the body and a large purplish spiny dorsal fin

GRAZE[1] verb **GRAZES, GRAZING, GRAZED** said of animals: to eat grass

GRAZE[2] verb **GRAZES, GRAZING, GRAZED** to suffer a break in (the skin of eg a limb), through scraping against a hard rough surface ◻ noun **GRAZES** an area of grazed skin

GRAZER noun **GRAZERS** an animal that grazes

GRAZING noun **GRAZINGS** the act or practice of grazing

GREASE noun **GREASES** animal fat softened by melting or cooking; any thick oily substance ◻ verb **GREASES, GREASING, GREASED** to lubricate or dirty something with grease

GREASER noun **GREASERS** someone whose job is to grease machinery

GREASILY adverb in a greasy way

GREASY adj **GREASIER, GREASIEST** containing, or covered in, grease

GREAT adj **GREATER, GREATEST** outstandingly talented and much admired and respected; very large in size, quantity, intensity or extent ◻ adverb very well ◻ noun **GREATS** a person who has achieved lasting fame, deservedly or not

GREATCOAT noun **GREATCOATS** a heavy overcoat

GREATLY adverb to a great extent; highly; exceedingly

GREATNESS noun **GREATNESSES** the quality of being great in size, extent or degree

GREAVE noun **GREAVES** armour for the legs below the knee

GREBE noun **GREBES** any of various waterfowl with short wings, a pointed bill, almost no tail and, in most species, colourful plumes on the head

GREED noun **GREEDS** an excessive desire for, or consumption of, food

GREEDILY adverb in a greedy way

GREEDY adj **GREEDIER, GREEDIEST** filled with greed

GREEGREE noun **GREEGREES** a grisgris

GREEN adj **GREENER, GREENEST** like the colour of the leaves of most plants ◻ noun **GREENS** the colour of the leaves of most plants ◻ verb **GREENS, GREENING, GREENED** to make or become green

GREENBACK noun **GREENBACKS** a US currency note, a dollar bill

GREENERY noun **GREENERIES** green plants or their leaves, either when growing or when cut for decorative use

GREENFLY noun **GREENFLIES** any of various species of aphid

GREENGAGE noun **GREENGAGES** any of several cultivated varieties of tree, sometimes regarded as a subspecies of the plum

GREENHORN noun **GREENHORNS** an inexperienced person; a novice

GREENING noun **GREENINGS** becoming or making green

GREENISH adj somewhat green

GREENMAIL noun **GREENMAILS** a form of business blackmail in which a company buys a strategically significant block of shares in another company, sufficient to threaten takeover, and thus forces the company to buy back its shares at an inflated price

GREENNESS noun **GREENNESSES** the condition of being green

GREENROOM noun **GREENROOMS** a backstage room in a theatre, etc where actors, musicians, etc can relax and receive visitors

GREENY adj **GREENIER, GREENIEST** somewhat green

GREET[1] verb **GREETS,**

GREETING, GREETED to address or welcome someone, especially in a friendly way

GREET[2] *verb* **GREETS, GREETING, GRAT, GRUTTEN** to weep or cry

GREETING *noun* **GREETINGS** a friendly expression or gesture used on meeting or welcoming someone

GREMIAL *noun* **GREMIALS** a cloth laid on a bishop's knees to keep the vestments clean during Mass or ordination

GREMLIN *noun* **GREMLINS** an imaginary mischievous creature blamed for faults in machinery or electronic equipment

GRENADE *noun* **GRENADES** a small bomb thrown by hand or fired from a rifle

GRENADIER *noun* **GRENADIERS** a member of a regiment of soldiers formerly trained in the use of grenades

GRENADINE *noun* **GRENADINES** a syrup made from pomegranate juice, used to flavour drinks, especially alcoholic ones

GREW a past form of **grow**

GREY *adj* **GREYER, GREYEST** of a colour between black and white, the colour of ash and slate □ *noun* **GREYS** a colour between black and white □ *verb* **GREYS, GREYING, GREYED** to make or become grey

GREYBEARD *noun* **GREYBEARDS** an old man

GREYHOUND *noun* **GREYHOUNDS** a tall dog with a slender body, short coat, arched back, long powerful legs and a long tail, renowned for its speed and raced for sport

GREYISH *adj* somewhat grey

GREYLY *adverb* with a hint of grey

GREYNESS *noun* **GREYNESSES** the condition of being grey

GRID *noun* **GRIDS** a network of evenly spaced horizontal and vertical lines that can be superimposed on a map, chart, etc, especially in order to locate specific points

GRIDDLE *noun* **GRIDDLES** a flat iron plate that is heated for baking or frying, either set into the top of a stove or separate, and which looks like a flat pan with a handle

GRIDIRON *noun* **GRIDIRONS** a frame of iron bars used for grilling food over a fire

GRIDLOCK *noun* **GRIDLOCKS** a severe traffic jam in which no vehicles are able to move

GRIEF *noun* **GRIEFS** great sorrow and unhappiness, especially at someone's death

GRIEVANCE *noun* **GRIEVANCES** a real or perceived cause for complaint, especially unfair treatment at work

GRIEVE *verb* **GRIEVES, GRIEVING, GRIEVED** to feel grief, especially at a death

GRIEVOUS *adj* very severe or painful

GRIFFIN *noun* **GRIFFINS** a winged monster with an eagle's head and a lion's body

GRIFFON *noun* **GRIFFONS** any of various small dogs with a square body, a rounded head, a short muzzle and a coarse wiry blackish or black and tan coat

GRILL *noun* **GRILLS** a device on a cooker which radiates heat downwards □ *verb* **GRILLS, GRILLING, GRILLED** to cook under a grill

GRILLE *noun* **GRILLES** a protective framework of metal bars or wires, eg over a window or a car radiator

GRILLING *noun* **GRILLINGS** the action of interrogating someone at length

GRILSE *noun* **GRILSES** a young salmon returning from the sea to fresh water for the first time

GRIM *adj* **GRIMMER, GRIMMEST** stern and unsmiling

GRIMACE *noun* **GRIMACES** an ugly twisting of the face that expresses pain or disgust, or that is pulled for amusement □ *verb* **GRIMACES, GRIMACING, GRIMACED** to make a grimace

GRIME *noun* **GRIMES** thick ingrained dirt or soot □ *verb* **GRIMES, GRIMING, GRIMED** to soil something heavily; to make something filthy

GRIMILY *adverb* in a grimy way

GRIMINESS *noun* **GRIMINESSES** the condition of being grimy

GRIMLY *adverb* in a grim way

GRIMNESS *noun* **GRIMNESSES** the quality or condition of being grim

GRIMY *adj* **GRIMIER, GRIMIEST** covered with grime; dirty

GRIN *verb* **GRINS, GRINNING, GRINNED** to smile broadly, showing the teeth □ *noun* **GRINS** a broad smile, showing the teeth

GRIND *verb* **GRINDS, GRINDING,** **GROUND** to crush something into small particles or powder between two hard surfaces □ *noun* **GRINDS** the act or sound of grinding

GRINDER *noun* **GRINDERS** a person or machine that grinds

GRINDING *adj* crushing; oppressive

GRINNING *adj* that grins

GRIP *verb* **GRIPS, GRIPPING, GRIPPED** to take or keep a firm hold of something □ *noun* **GRIPS** a firm hold; the action of taking a firm hold

GRIPE *verb* **GRIPES, GRIPING, GRIPED** to complain persistently □ *noun* **GRIPES** a complaint

GRIPPER *noun* **GRIPPERS** a person or thing that grips

GRIPPING *adj* holding the attention; exciting

GRISAILLE *noun* **GRISAILLES** a style of painting in greyish tints in imitation of bas-relief, eg on ceilings or on pottery

GRISETTE *noun* **GRISETTES** a young French working girl

GRISGRIS *noun* **GRISGRIS** an African charm or fetish

GRISLY *adj* **GRISLIER, GRISLIEST** horrible; ghastly; gruesome

GRIST *noun* **GRISTS** grain that is to be, or that has been, ground into flour

GRISTLE *noun* **GRISTLES** cartilage, especially in meat

GRISTLY *adj* **GRISTLIER, GRISTLIEST** full of gristle

GRIT *noun* **GRITS** small particles of a hard material, especially of stone or sand □ *verb* **GRITS, GRITTING, GRITTED** to spread grit on (icy roads, etc)

GRITS *plural noun* coarsely ground grain, especially oats, with the husks removed □ *singular noun* a dish of this, boiled and eaten for breakfast in the southern US

GRITTER *noun* **GRITTERS** a vehicle for spreading grit (on icy roads, etc)

GRITTY *adj* **GRITTIER, GRITTIEST** full of or covered with grit

GRIZZLE *verb* **GRIZZLES, GRIZZLING, GRIZZLED** said especially of a young child: to cry fretfully

GRIZZLED *adj* said of the hair or a beard: grey or greying

GRIZZLY *adj* **GRIZZLIER, GRIZZLIEST** grey or greying; grizzled □ *noun* **GRIZZLIES** a grizzly bear

For longer words, see The Chambers Dictionary

GROAN verb **GROANS, GROANING, GROANED** to make a long deep sound in the back of the throat, expressing pain, distress, disapproval, etc ◻ noun **GROANS** an act, or the sound, of groaning

GROANER noun **GROANERS** someone who groans

GROANING noun **GROANINGS** the action of making a long deep sound in the back of the throat, expressing pain, distress, disapproval, etc ◻ adj that groans

GROAT noun **GROATS** an obsolete British silver coin worth four old pennies

GROATS plural noun crushed grain, especially oats, with the husks removed

GROCER noun **GROCERS** someone whose job is selling food and general household goods

GROCERY noun **GROCERIES** the trade or premises of a grocer

GROCKLE noun **GROCKLES** a tourist or holidaymaker, especially in SW England

GROG noun **GROGS** a mixture of alcoholic spirit (especially rum) and water, as formerly drunk by sailors

GROGGY adj **GROGGIER, GROGGIEST** weak, dizzy and unsteady on the feet, eg from the effects of illness or alcohol

GROGRAM noun **GROGRAMS** a coarse fabric made from a mix of silk and wool or mohair

GROIN noun **GROINS** the part of the body where the lower abdomen joins the upper thigh; the edge formed by the joining of two vaults in a roof or the rib covering the intersection ◻ verb **GROINS, GROINING, GROINED** to build (a vault, etc) with groins

GROINED adj formed into groins; built in groins

GROINING noun **GROININGS** the action of building (a vault, etc) with groins

GROMMET noun **GROMMETS** a rubber or plastic ring around a hole in metal, to protect a tube or insulate a wire passing through

GROOM noun **GROOMS** someone who looks after horses and cleans stables ◻ verb **GROOMS, GROOMING, GROOMED** to clean, brush and generally smarten (animals, especially horses)

GROOMSMAN noun **GROOMSMEN** an attendant on a

bridegroom, either alone (as best man) or one of a group

GROOVE noun **GROOVES** a long narrow channel ◻ verb **GROOVES, GROOVING, GROOVED** to cut a groove in something

GROOVY adj **GROOVIER, GROOVIEST** excellent, attractive or fashionable

GROPE verb **GROPES, GROPING, GROPED** to search by feeling about with the hands, eg in the dark

GROPER noun **GROPERS** a grouper

GROPING adj searching about with the hands, eg in the dark

GROPINGLY adverb in a groping way

GROSBEAK noun **GROSBEAKS** any of various finches with a stout conical beak, found mainly in N America

GROSCHEN noun **GROSCHENS** an Austrian coin, a 100th part of a schilling

GROSGRAIN noun **GROSGRAINS** a heavy corded silk used especially for ribbons and hat bands

GROSS adj **GROSSER, GROSSEST** total, with no deductions ◻ noun **GROSSES** twelve dozen, 144 ◻ verb **GROSSES, GROSSING, GROSSED** to earn (a specified sum) as a gross income or profit, before tax is deducted

GROSSLY adverb excessively; flagrantly; glaringly

GROSSNESS noun **GROSSNESSES** vulgarity; coarseness

GROT noun **GROTS** rubbish ◻ adj dirty; worthless

GROTESQUE adj **GROTESQUER, GROTESQUEST** very unnatural or strange-looking, so as to cause fear or laughter ◻ noun **GROTESQUES** a 16c style in art which features animals, plants and people mixed together in a strange or fantastic manner

GROTTO noun **GROTTOS, GROTTOES** a cave, especially a small and picturesque one

GROTTY adj **GROTTIER, GROTTIEST** unpleasantly dirty or shabby

GROUCH verb **GROUCHES, GROUCHING, GROUCHED** to grumble or complain ◻ noun **GROUCHES** a complaining person

GROUCHILY adverb in a grouchy way

GROUCHY adj **GROUCHIER, GROUCHIEST** bad-tempered; tending to grumble

GROUND [1] noun **GROUNDS** the solid surface of the Earth, or any part of it; soil; land ◻ verb **GROUNDS, GROUNDING, GROUNDED** to hit or cause (a ship) to hit the seabed or shore and remain stuck ◻ adj on or relating to the ground

GROUND [2] past form of **grind**

GROUNDHOG noun **GROUNDHOGS** a N American marmot

GROUNDING noun **GROUNDINGS** a foundation of basic knowledge or instruction

GROUNDNUT noun **GROUNDNUTS** any of various N American climbing plants of the pulse family that produce small edible underground tubers, seed pods, etc, eg the peanut plant

GROUNDSEL noun **GROUNDSELS** an annual plant and common weed with irregularly toothed oblong leaves and numerous small cylindrical flower-heads consisting of clusters of yellow florets

GROUP noun **GROUPS** a number of people or things gathered, placed or classed together ◻ verb **GROUPS, GROUPING, GROUPED** to form (things or people) into a group

GROUPER noun **GROUPERS** a name given to various fishes, especially ones resembling bass

GROUPIE noun **GROUPIES** an ardent follower of a touring pop star or group

GROUPWARE noun **GROUPWARES** software that is designed for use on several computers, workstations, etc at the same time

GROUSE verb **GROUSES, GROUSING, GROUSED** to complain ◻ noun **GROUSES** a complaint or spell of complaining

GROUSER noun **GROUSERS** someone who grouses

GROUT noun **GROUTS** thin mortar applied to the joints between bricks or especially ceramic tiles, as a decorative finish ◻ verb **GROUTS, GROUTING, GROUTED** to apply grout to the joints of something

GROUTING noun **GROUTINGS** filling up or finishing with grout

GROVE noun **GROVES** a small group of trees, often planted for shade or ornament

GROVEL verb **GROVELS, GROVELLING, GROVELING, GROVELLED, GROVELED** to act with exaggerated (and usually insincere) respect or humility, especially to gain the favour of a superior

GROVELER noun **GROVELERS** a groveller

GROVELING adj grovelling

GROVELLER noun **GROVELLERS** someone who grovels

GROVELLING adj abject, cringing, servile

GROW verb **GROWS, GROWING, GREW, GROWN** said of a living thing: to develop into a larger more mature form

GROWL verb **GROWLS, GROWLING, GROWLED** said of animals: to make a deep rough sound in the throat, showing hostility ◻ noun **GROWLS** an act or the sound of growling

GROWLER noun **GROWLERS** someone or something that growls

GROWLING noun **GROWLINGS** the act of make a deep rough sound in the throat ◻ adj that growls

GROWLY adj **GROWLIER, GROWLIEST** resembling a growl

GROWN adj developed to a specified degree

GROWTH noun **GROWTHS** the process or rate of growing

GROYNE noun **GROYNES** a breakwater built to check land erosion

GRUB noun **GRUBS** the worm-like larva of an insect, especially a beetle ◻ verb **GRUBS, GRUBBING, GRUBBED** to dig or search in the soil

GRUBBY adj **GRUBBIER, GRUBBIEST** dirty

GRUBSTAKE noun **GRUBSTAKES** supplies or money given to a prospector in return for a share in any finds ◻ verb **GRUBSTAKES, GRUBSTAKING, GRUBSTAKED** to provide someone with such supplies

GRUDGE noun **GRUDGES** a long-standing feeling of resentment ◻ verb **GRUDGES, GRUDGING, GRUDGED** to envy (a person something); to give or allow (something to a person) unwillingly

GRUDGING adj resentful

GRUEL noun **GRUELS** thin porridge

GRUELING adj gruelling

GRUELLING adj exhausting; punishing

GRUESOME adj **GRUESOMER, GRUESOMEST** inspiring horror or disgust; sickening; macabre

GRUFF adj **GRUFFER, GRUFFEST** said of a voice: deep and rough

GRUFFLY adverb in a gruff way

GRUFFNESS noun **GRUFFNESSES** the quality or condition of being gruff

GRUMBLE verb **GRUMBLES, GRUMBLING, GRUMBLED** to complain in a bad-tempered way ◻ noun **GRUMBLES** a complaint

GRUMBLER noun **GRUMBLERS** someone who grumbles

GRUMBLING noun **GRUMBLINGS** the action of complaining in a bad-tempered way ◻ adj that grumbles

GRUMBLY adj **GRUMBLIER, GRUMBLIEST** inclined to grumble

GRUMMET noun **GRUMMETS** a grommet

GRUMP noun **GRUMPS** a grumpy person

GRUMPILY adverb in a grumpy way

GRUMPY adj **GRUMPIER, GRUMPIEST** bad-tempered; surly

GRUNGE noun **GRUNGES** dirt; rubbish; trash

GRUNGY adj **GRUNGIER, GRUNGIEST** dirty; messy

GRUNT verb **GRUNTS, GRUNTING, GRUNTED** said of animals, especially pigs: to make a low rough sound in the back of the throat ◻ noun **GRUNTS** an act or the sound of grunting

GRUNTER noun **GRUNTERS** a person or animal that grunts

GRUNTING noun **GRUNTINGS** the action of making a low rough sound in the back of the throat ◻ adj that grunts

GRUTTEN a past form of **greet** [2]

GRYPHON noun **GRYPHONS** a griffin

GU noun **GUS** a kind of violin formerly used in Shetland

GUACAMOLE noun **GUACAMOLES** a traditional Mexican dish of mashed avocado mixed with spicy seasoning, tomatoes and onions, eaten cold, eg as a dip

GUANINE noun **GUANINES** a base, derived from purine, which is one of the four bases found in nucleic acid

GUANO noun **GUANOS** the accumulated droppings of large colonies of bats, fish-eating seabirds or seals

GUARANTEE noun **GUARANTEES** a formal agreement, usually in writing, that a product, service, etc will conform to specified standards for a particular period of time ◻ verb **GUARANTEES, GUARANTEEING, GUARANTEED** to provide (eg a product, service, etc) with a guarantee

GUARANTEED adj of a product, service, etc: provided with a guarantee

GUARANTOR noun **GUARANTORS** someone who gives a guarantee

GUARANTY noun **GUARANTIES** an agreement, usually backed up by some kind of collateral, under which one person becomes liable for the debt or default of another

GUARD verb **GUARDS, GUARDING, GUARDED** to protect someone or something from danger or attack ◻ noun **GUARDS** a person or group whose job is to provide protection, eg from danger or attack, or to prevent escape

GUARDED adj cautious

GUARDEDLY adverb in a guarded way

GUARDIAN noun **GUARDIANS** someone who is legally responsible for the care of another, especially an orphaned child

GUARDRAIL noun **GUARDRAILS** a rail, eg on a ship or train, which acts as a safety barrier

GUARDROOM noun **GUARDROOMS** a building or room for guards on duty, especially at the gate of a military camp, often also housing prisoners

GUARDSMAN noun **GUARDSMEN** a member of a regiment of Guards

GUAVA noun **GUAVAS** any of various small tropical trees cultivated for their edible fruits, especially a species native to Central America

GUBBINS noun **GUBBINSES** a worthless object

GUDGEON noun **GUDGEONS** a small freshwater fish related to the carp, which has a blackish or greenish back with dark spots, a silvery underside and a pair of sensory feelers or barbels at the corners of its mouth

GUE noun **GUES** a gu

GUENON noun **GUENONS** any of several species of long-tailed African monkeys

GUERILLA noun **GUERILLAS** a guerrilla

GUERNSEY noun **GUERNSEYS** a hand-knitted woollen pullover, originally one worn by sailors

GUERRILLA noun **GUERRILLAS** a member of a small, independent, often politically motivated armed force making surprise attacks, eg against government troops

GUESS verb **GUESSES, GUESSING, GUESSED** to make an estimate or form an opinion about something, based on little or no information ◻ noun **GUESSES** an estimate based on guessing

GUESSABLE adj that can be guessed

GUESSER noun **GUESSERS** someone who guesses

GUESSING noun **GUESSINGS** the action of making an estimate or forming an opinion about something, based on little or no information ◻ adj that guesses

GUESSWORK noun **GUESSWORKS** the process or result of guessing

GUEST noun **GUESTS** someone who receives hospitality in the home of, or at the expense of, another; a person specially invited to take part ◻ verb **GUESTS, GUESTING, GUESTED** to appear as a guest, eg on a television show

GUFF noun **GUFFS** nonsense

GUFFAW noun **GUFFAWS** a loud coarse laugh ◻ verb **GUFFAWS, GUFFAWING, GUFFAWED** to laugh in this way

GUIDANCE noun **GUIDANCES** help, advice or counselling; the act or process of guiding

GUIDE verb **GUIDES, GUIDING, GUIDED** to lead, direct or show the way to someone ◻ noun **GUIDES** someone who leads the way for eg tourists or mountaineers

GUIDEBOOK noun **GUIDEBOOKS** a book containing information about a particular place or instructions for a practical activity

GUIDELINE noun **GUIDELINES** an indication of what future action is required or recommended

GUILD noun **GUILDS** a medieval association of merchants or craftsmen for maintaining

standards and providing mutual support

GUILDER noun **GUILDERS** the standard unit of currency of the Netherlands

GUILDHALL noun **GUILDHALLS** a hall where members of a guild or other association meet

GUILE noun **GUILES** the ability to deceive or trick

GUILEFUL adj crafty; deceitful

GUILELESS adj without deceit; artless

GUILLEMOT noun **GUILLEMOTS** any of various seabirds of the auk family, with black and white plumage, a long narrow bill and short narrow wings

GUILT noun **GUILTS** a feeling of shame or remorse resulting from a sense of having done wrong

GUILTILY adverb in a guilty way

GUILTLESS adj innocent

GUILTY adj **GUILTIER, GUILTIEST** responsible for a crime or wrongdoing, or judged to be so

GUINEA noun **GUINEAS** an obsolete British gold coin worth 21 shillings (£1.05)

GUIPURE noun **GUIPURES** heavy lace which has a large open pattern with no background

GUISE noun **GUISES** assumed appearance; pretence

GUISER noun **GUISERS** someone, especially a child, who goes from house to house in disguise, especially at Hallowe'en, entertaining with songs, etc and receiving small gifts in return

GUITAR noun **GUITARS** a musical instrument with a body generally shaped like a figure eight, a long fretted neck and usually six strings that are plucked or strummed

GUITARIST noun **GUITARISTS** someone who plays the guitar

GULAG noun **GULAGS** a network of political prisons or labour camps that formerly existed in the Soviet Union

GULCH noun **GULCHES** a narrow rocky ravine with a fast-flowing stream running through it

GULDEN noun **GULDENS** same as guilder

GULES noun **GULES** in heraldry: red

GULF noun **GULFS** a very large inlet of the sea extending far into the land, much more deeply indented and more enclosed than a bay

GULL [1] noun **GULLS** any of various omnivorous seabirds with a stout body, predominantly white or greyish plumage, a hooked bill, long pointed wings and webbed feet

GULL [2] verb **GULLS, GULLING, GULLED** to cheat or deceive

GULLERY noun **GULLERIES** a place where gulls breed

GULLET noun **GULLETS** the oesophagus or throat

GULLEY noun **GULLEYS** a gully

GULLIBLE adj easily tricked or fooled

GULLY noun **GULLIES** a small channel or cutting with steep sides formed by running water especially during heavy rainstorms in tropical and semi-arid regions

GULP verb **GULPS, GULPING, GULPED** to swallow (food, drink, etc) eagerly or in large mouthfuls ◻ noun **GULPS** a swallowing motion

GUM noun **GUMS** a substance found in certain trees that produces a sticky solution when added to water and is used as glue ◻ verb **GUMS, GUMMING, GUMMED** to smear, glue or unite something with gum

GUMBO noun **GUMBOS** a thick soup or stew made from meat or fish and thickened with okra

GUMBOIL noun **GUMBOILS** a small abscess on the flesh surrounding the teeth

GUMBOOT noun **GUMBOOTS** a wellington boot

GUMDROP noun **GUMDROPS** a sweet made from transparent hard jelly

GUMMINESS noun **GUMMINESSES** the state of being gummy

GUMMY adj **GUMMIER, GUMMIEST** sticky

GUMPTION noun **GUMPTIONS** common sense; initiative

GUMSHIELD noun **GUMSHIELDS** a flexible pad worn in the mouth to protect the teeth

GUMSHOE noun **GUMSHOES** a rubber overshoe; a galosh

GUN noun **GUNS** any weapon which fires bullets or shells from a metal tube ◻ verb **GUNS, GUNNING, GUNNED** to rev up (a car engine) noisily

GUNBOAT noun **GUNBOATS** a small warship with large mounted guns

GUNFIGHT noun **GUNFIGHTS** a

fight involving two or more people with guns, especially formerly in the American West

GUNFIRE *noun* **GUNFIRES** the act of firing guns

GUNGE *noun* **GUNGES** any messy, slimy or sticky substance □ *verb* **GUNGES, GUNGING, GUNGED** to be covered or blocked with gunge

GUNGY *adj* **GUNGIER, GUNGIEST** of the consistency of gunge; slimy and sticky

GUNK *noun* **GUNKS** any slimy or oily semi-solid substance

GUNLOCK *noun* **GUNLOCKS** the mechanism in some guns that causes the charge to explode

GUNMAN *noun* **GUNMEN** an armed criminal

GUNMETAL *noun* **GUNMETALS** any of several dark-grey alloys, composed mainly of copper with small amounts of tin and zinc, formerly used to make cannons □ *adj* dark-grey

GUNNEL *noun* **GUNNELS** a small eel-like coastal fish of the blenny family

GUNNER *noun* **GUNNERS** any member of an armed force who operates a heavy gun

GUNNERY *noun* **GUNNERIES** the use of guns

GUNNY *noun* **GUNNIES** thick coarse jute cloth, used especially for sacking

GUNPLAY *noun* **GUNPLAYS** the use of guns, especially in a fight or display of skill

GUNPOINT *noun* **GUNPOINTS** the muzzle, or directed aim, of a gun

GUNPOWDER *noun* **GUNPOWDERS** the oldest known explosive, consisting of a mixture of potassium nitrate, sulphur and charcoal, still used in fireworks and for quarry blasting

GUNROOM *noun* **GUNROOMS** a room where guns are kept

GUNRUNNER *noun* **GUNRUNNERS** someone who smuggles weapons into a country, often to help terrorists, etc

GUNSHOT *noun* **GUNSHOTS** bullets fired from a gun

GUNSMITH *noun* **GUNSMITHS** someone whose job is to make and/or repair firearms

GUNWALE *noun* **GUNWALES** the upper edge of a ship's side

GUNYAH *noun* **GUNYAHS** a temporary or improvised shelter, originally an Aboriginal hut

GUP *noun* **GUPS** a slang word for *gossip* or *prattle*

GUPPY *noun* **GUPPIES** a small brightly coloured freshwater fish that varies widely in form and colour, breeds prolifically, and is a popular aquarium fish

GUR *noun* **GURS** an unrefined cane sugar

GURDWARA *noun* **GURDWARAS** a Sikh place of worship

GURGLE *verb* **GURGLES, GURGLING, GURGLED** said of water: to make a bubbling noise when flowing □ *noun* **GURGLES** the sound of gurgling

GURU *noun* **GURUS** a Hindu or Sikh spiritual leader or teacher

GUS plural of **gu**

GUSH *verb* **GUSHES, GUSHING, GUSHED** said of a liquid: to flood out or make it flood out suddenly and violently □ *noun* **GUSHES** a sudden violent flooding-out

GUSHER *noun* **GUSHERS** an oil well that oil flows from without the use of pumps

GUSHING *adj* flowing violently or copiously

GUSHINGLY *adverb* in a gushing way

GUSHY *adj* **GUSHIER, GUSHIEST** effusively sentimental

GUSSET *noun* **GUSSETS** a piece of material sewn into a garment for added strength or to allow for freedom of movement, eg at the crotch

GUST *noun* **GUSTS** a sudden blast or rush, eg of wind or smoke □ *verb* **GUSTS, GUSTING, GUSTED** said of the wind: to blow in gusts

GUSTINESS *noun* **GUSTINESSES** the state of being gusty

GUSTO *noun* **GUSTOS** enthusiastic enjoyment; zest

GUSTY *adj* **GUSTIER, GUSTIEST** blowing in gusts; stormy

GUT *noun* **GUTS** the alimentary canal or part of it □ *verb* **GUTS, GUTTING, GUTTED** to take the guts out of (an animal, especially fish) □ *adj* based on instinct and emotion, not reason

GUTLESS *adj* cowardly; lacking determination

GUTROT *noun* **GUTROTS** a stomach upset

GUTSINESS *noun* **GUTSINESSES** the state of being gutsy

GUTSY *adj* **GUTSIER, GUTSIEST** courageous and determined

GUTTED past form of **gut** □ *adj* extremely shocked or disappointed

GUTTER *noun* **GUTTERS** a channel for carrying away rainwater, fixed to the edge of a roof or built between a pavement and a road □ *verb* **GUTTERS, GUTTERING, GUTTERED** said of a candle: to have its melted wax, etc suddenly pour down a channel which forms on its side

GUTTERING *noun* **GUTTERINGS** gutters collectively

GUTTING a form of **gut**

GUTTURAL *adj* said of sounds: produced in the throat or the back of the mouth □ *noun* **GUTTURALS** a sound produced in the throat or the back of the mouth

GUV *noun* **GUVS** gov

GUY *noun* **GUYS** a rope or wire used to hold something, especially a tent, firm or steady □ *verb* **GUYS, GUYING, GUYED** to secure something with guys

GUZZLE *verb* **GUZZLES, GUZZLING, GUZZLED** to eat or drink greedily

GUZZLER *noun* **GUZZLERS** someone who guzzles

GYBE *verb* **GYBES, GYBING, GYBED** said of a sail: to swing, or make it swing, over from one side of a boat to the other □ *noun* **GYBES** an act of gybing

GYM *noun* **GYMS** gymnastics; gymnasium

GYMKHANA *noun* **GYMKHANAS** a local public event consisting of competitions in various sports, especially horse-riding

GYMNASIUM *noun* **GYMNASIUMS, GYMNASIA** a building or room with equipment for physical exercise

GYMNAST *noun* **GYMNASTS** someone who is skilled in gymnastics

GYMNASTIC *adj* relating to gymnastics

GYMNASTICS *singular noun* physical training designed to strengthen the body and improve agility, usually using special equipment □ *plural noun* feats of agility

GYNAECIUM *noun* **GYNAECIA** the female reproductive parts of a flower

GYNOECIUM *noun* **GYNOECIA** gynaecium

GYP *verb* **GYPS, GYPPING, GYPPED** to cheat or swindle someone ◻ *noun* **GYPS** someone who cheats

GYPSUM *noun* **GYPSUMS** a soft mineral composed of calcium sulphate, used to make plaster of Paris, cement, rubber and paper

GYPSY *noun* **GYPSIES** a member of a dark-skinned travelling people, originally from NW India, now scattered throughout Europe and N America

GYRATE *verb* **GYRATES, GYRATING, GYRATED** to move with a circular or spiralling motion

GYRATION *noun* **GYRATIONS** a whirling motion

GYRE *noun* **GYRES** a vortex ◻ *verb* **GYRES, GYRING, GYRED** to whirl

GYRFALCON *noun* **GYRFALCONS** the largest of all the falcons, with plumage ranging from dark greyish-brown to almost white

GYROSCOPE *noun* **GYROSCOPES** a device consisting of a small flywheel with a heavy rim, mounted so that once in motion it resists any changes in the direction of motion, used in ship steering systems of aircraft, missiles, etc

GYRUS *noun* **GYRI** a convoluted fold, eg of the brain

HA *exclamation* expressing surprise, happiness, triumph, etc

HÁČEK *noun* **HÁČEKS** a diacritic (˘) placed over a consonant in some Slavonic languages, eg Czech, to modify the sound

HAAR *noun* **HAARS** a cold mist or fog off the North Sea

HABANERA *noun* **HABANERAS** a slow Cuban dance in 2-4 time

HABDABS *plural noun* a state of extreme nervousness

HABIT *noun* **HABITS** a tendency to behave or act in a specific way ◻ *verb* **HABITS, HABITING, HABITED** to clothe

HABITABLE *adj* suitable for living in

HABITABLY *adverb* in a habitable manner

HABITAT *noun* **HABITATS** the natural home of an animal or plant

HABITUAL *adj* seen, done, etc regularly and repeatedly

HABITUATE *verb* **HABITUATES, HABITUATING, HABITUATED** to make someone accustomed or used to something

HABITUÉ *noun* **HABITUÉS** a regular or frequent visitor to a place, eg a restaurant

HACHURE *noun* **HACHURES** a system of parallel lines on a map to show the contours of hills, in which the closeness of the lines indicates steepness ◻ *verb* **HACHURES, HACHURING, HACHURED** to shade with hachures

HACIENDA *noun* **HACIENDAS** in Spain and Spanish-speaking countries: a ranch or large estate with a main dwelling-house on it

HACK *noun* **HACKS** a horse kept for general riding, especially one for hire ◻ *verb* **HACKS, HACKING, HACKED** to ride a horse at a leisurely pace ◻ *adj* mediocre, banal or commonplace

HACKAMORE *noun* **HACKAMORES** a halter used in breaking in foals

HACKBERRY *noun* **HACKBERRIES** a hagberry

HACKER *noun* **HACKERS** someone or something that hacks; someone skilled in using computers, particularly in programming them

HACKERY *noun* **HACKERIES** an ox-drawn cart used in India for transporting goods

HACKETTE *noun* **HACKETTES** a woman journalist

HACKING [1] *adj* said of a cough: rough and dry

HACKING [2] *noun* **HACKINGS** the act or practice of gaining unauthorized access to computer files

HACKLE *noun* **HACKLES** any of the long shining feathers on the neck of certain birds, eg cocks; a comb for flax or hemp ◻ *verb* **HACKLES, HACKLING, HACKLED** to comb flax or hemp with a hackle

HACKLER *noun* **HACKLERS** someone who hackles (flax or hemp)

HACKLES *plural noun* the hairs or feathers on the back of the neck of some animals and birds, which are raised when they are angry

HACKLY *adj* **HACKLIER, HACKLIEST** rough, broken or jagged

HACKNEY *noun* **HACKNEYS** a horse with a high-stepping trot, bred to draw light carriages

HACKNEYED *adj* said of a word, phrase, etc: meaningless and trite through too much use

HAD [1] *verb* **HADS, HADDING, HADDEN** a Scots form of *hold*

HAD [2] past form of **have**

HADDOCK *noun* **HADDOCKS** a commercially important N Atlantic sea-fish similar to but smaller than the cod

HADE *noun* **HADES** in geology: the angle between the plane of a fault, etc and a vertical plane ◻ *verb* **HADES, HADING, HADED** to incline from the vertical

HADJ *noun* **HADJES** hajj

HADJI *noun* **HADJIS** a hajji

HADRON *noun* **HADRONS** one of a class of subatomic particles, comprising baryons and mesons, that interact strongly with other subatomic particles

HADRONIC *adj* of or relating to hadrons

HADST used with *thou*: a form of **have**

HAE *verb* **HAEING** Scots form of *have*

HAEM *noun* **HAEMS** the iron compound which combines with the protein globin to form the respiratory pigment haemoglobin, and which gives the red blood cells their colour

HAEMAL *adj* relating to the blood or blood-vessels

HAEMATIC *adj* referring or relating to blood

HAEMATIN *noun* **HAEMATINS** a bluish or brownish derivative of haemoglobin after removal of the protein and oxidation of the haem

HAEMATITE *noun* **HAEMATITES** a dense and relatively hard mineral containing ferric oxide, the most important ore of iron, used as a pigment (red ochre) and as a polishing agent

HAEMATOMA *noun* **HAEMATOMAS** a swelling resulting from bleeding into tissues

HAEMIC *adj* haematic

HAEMOCYTE *noun* **HAEMOCYTES** a blood cell, especially an erythrocyte

HAEMOSTAT *noun* **HAEMOSTATS** a chemical substance or surgical device that stops bleeding

HAEREMAI *exclamation* welcome!

HAFNIUM *noun* **HAFNIUMS** a metallic element found mainly in zirconium minerals and used in electrodes

HAFT *noun* **HAFTS** a handle of a knife, sword, axe, etc ◻ *verb* **HAFTS, HAFTING, HAFTED** to fit with a haft

HAG [1] *noun* **HAGS** an ugly old woman

HAG² *verb* **HAGS, HAGGING, HAGGED** a Scots word meaning to cut or hew

HAGBERRY *noun* **HAGBERRIES** an American tree related to the elm

HAGFISH *noun* **HAGFISHES** an eel-like marine vertebrate related to the lamprey, which feeds on the tissues of other animals and on dead organic material

HAGGARD *adj* looking very tired and thin-faced, because of pain, worry, etc □ *noun* **HAGGARDS** an untamed hawk, or one caught when adult, especially a female

HAGGARDLY *adverb* in a haggard way

HAGGIS *noun* **HAGGISES** a Scottish dish made from sheep's or calf's offal mixed with suet, oatmeal and seasonings and then boiled in a bag traditionally made from the animal's stomach

HAGGISH *adj* old and ugly like a hag

HAGGISHLY *adverb* in a haggish way

HAGGLE *verb* **HAGGLES, HAGGLING, HAGGLED** to bargain over or argue about (a price, etc)

HAGGLER *noun* **HAGGLERS** someone who haggles

HAGIOLOGY *noun* **HAGIOLOGIES** literature about the lives and legends of saints

HAH *exclamation* ha

HAHNIUM *noun* **HAHNIUMS** a name proposed for the radioactive elements of atomic number 105 and 108

HAIK *noun* **HAIKS** an oblong cloth which Arabs wrap round the head and body as an outer garment

HAIKU *noun* **HAIKU** a Japanese poem which consists of three lines of five, seven and five syllables, usually comical or epigrammatic, and often incorporates a word or phrase that symbolizes one of the seasons

HAIL *noun* **HAILS** grains of ice which fall from the clouds when there are strong rising air currents □ *verb* **HAILS, HAILING, HAILED** said of hail: to fall from the clouds

HAILSTONE *noun* **HAILSTONES** a single grain of hail

HAIQUE *noun* **HAIQUES** a haik

HAIR *noun* **HAIRS** each of many long thread-like structures that grow from follicles beneath the skin of animals

HAIRBRUSH *noun* **HAIRBRUSHES** a brush for smoothing and arranging one's hair

HAIRCLOTH *noun* **HAIRCLOTHS** a coarse cloth made from woven horsehair, once used in upholstery

HAIRCUT *noun* **HAIRCUTS** the cutting of someone's hair

HAIRDO *noun* **HAIRDOS** a woman's haircut, especially after styling and setting

HAIRDRIER *noun* **HAIRDRIERS** a hairdryer

HAIRDRYER *noun* **HAIRDRYERS** a piece of electrical equipment which dries hair by blowing hot air over it

HAIRED *adj* having a specified kind of hair

HAIRGRIP *noun* **HAIRGRIPS** a small wire clasp for holding the hair in place

HAIRIER see under **hairy**

HAIRIEST see under **hairy**

HAIRINESS *noun* **HAIRINESSES** the state or condition of being hairy

HAIRLESS *adj* having no hair

HAIRLIKE *adj* resembling hair

HAIRLINE *noun* **HAIRLINES** the line along the forehead where the hair begins to grow

HAIRNET *noun* **HAIRNETS** any kind of netting, usually worn by women, to keep the hair in place

HAIRPIECE *noun* **HAIRPIECES** a wig or piece of false hair worn over a bald area on the head

HAIRPIN *noun* **HAIRPINS** a thin flat U-shaped piece of wire for keeping the hair in place

HAIRSPRAY *noun* **HAIRSPRAYS** lacquer sprayed from a can or bottle onto the hair to hold it in place

HAIRSTYLE *noun* **HAIRSTYLES** the way in which someone's hair is cut or shaped

HAIRY *adj* **HAIRIER, HAIRIEST** covered in hair

HAJ *noun* **HAJES** hajj

HAJI *noun* **HAJIS** a hajji

HAJJ *noun* **HAJJES** the pilgrimage to Mecca that every Muslim is supposed to make at least once in their lifetime

HAJJI *noun* **HAJJIS** a Muslim who has been on pilgrimage to Mecca

HAKA *noun* **HAKAS** a Maori war-dance accompanied by chanting

HAKE *noun* **HAKES** a sea-fish that resembles cod, used for food

HAKIM *noun* **HAKIMS** a Muslim physician

HALAL *noun* **HALALS** meat from an animal which has been killed according to Muslim holy law □ *verb* **HALALS, HALALLING, HALALLED** to slaughter (an animal) according to Muslim holy law

HALATION *noun* **HALATIONS** blurring in a photograph, usually seen as a bright ring surrounding a source of light

HALBERD *noun* **HALBERDS** a long spear with an axe-blade and a pick at one end

HALBERT *noun* **HALBERTS** a halberd

HALCYON *adj* peaceful, calm and happy □ *noun* **HALCYONS** in Greek mythology: a bird which charmed the sea at the time of the winter solstice, usually identified with the kingfisher

HALE *adj* **HALER, HALEST** strong and healthy

HALENESS *noun* **HALENESSES** the state of being hale

HALF *noun* **HALVES** one of two equal parts which together form a whole □ *adj* forming or equal to half of something □ *adverb* to the extent or amount of one half

HALFPENNY *noun* **HALFPENNIES** a small British coin worth half a new penny, withdrawn from circulation in 1985 □ *adj* valued at a halfpenny

HALFWAY *adverb* at, to or referring to a point equally far from two others

HALFWIT *noun* **HALFWITS** a foolish or stupid person

HALIBUT *noun* **HALIBUTS** either of two species of very large commercially important flatfish found in the N Atlantic and N Pacific

HALIDE *noun* **HALIDES** a binary compound (eg sodium chloride) formed by a halogen and a metal or radical

HALITE *noun* **HALITES** a mineral which consists of sodium chloride in cubic crystalline form and occurs in sedimentary beds and dried salt lakes, a major source of table salt

HALITOSIS *noun* **HALITOSES** unpleasant-smelling breath

HALL *noun* **HALLS** a room or

passage just inside the entrance to a house, which usually allows access to other rooms and the stairs

HALLIARD *noun* **HALLIARDS** a halyard

HALLMARK *noun* **HALLMARKS** an official series of marks stamped on gold, silver and platinum articles to guarantee their authenticity □ *verb* **HALLMARKS, HALLMARKING, HALLMARKED** to stamp with a hallmark

HALLO *exclamation* used as a greeting □ *verb* **HALLOS, HALLOING, HALLOED** to greet someone by saying 'hallo'

HALLOA *verb* **HALLOAS, HALLOAING, HALLOAED** to halloo

HALLOO *verb* **HALLOOS, HALLOOING, HALLOOED** to urge on hunting dogs with shouts

HALLOUMI *noun* **HALLOUMIS** a Greek dish of fried goat's cheese, eaten as a starter

HALLOW *verb* **HALLOWS, HALLOWING, HALLOWED** to make or regard as holy

HALLOWED *adj* holy, revered

HALLUX *noun* **HALLUCES** the innermost digit of the hind foot of a bird, mammal, reptile or amphibian

HALLWAY *noun* **HALLWAYS** an entrance hall or corridor

HALM *noun* **HALMS** haulm

HALMA *noun* **HALMAS** a board game in which players try to reach their opponents' bases

HALO *noun* **HALOS, HALOES** in paintings etc: a ring of light around the head of a saint, angel, etc □ *verb* **HALOS, HALOES, HALOING, HALOED** to put a halo round someone or something

HALOGEN *noun* **HALOGENS** any of the non-metallic elements fluorine, chlorine, bromine, iodine and astatine which form salts when in union with metals

HALOID *adj* having the composition of a halide

HALON *noun* **HALONS** any of a class of organic chemical compounds containing bromine combined with other halogens (eg bromotrifluoromethane) used in fire extinguishers, being very potent destroyers of the ozone layer

HALOPHILE *noun* **HALOPHILES** an organism that thrives in or can tolerate very salty conditions

HALT *noun* **HALTS** an interruption or stop to movement, progression or growth □ *verb* **HALTS, HALTING, HALTED** to come or bring to a halt □ *exclamation* a command to halt, especially one given as an order when marching

HALTER *noun* **HALTERS** a rope or strap for holding and leading a horse by its head □ *verb* **HALTERS, HALTERING, HALTERED** to put a halter on (a horse, etc)

HALTERES *plural noun* the pair of modified hindwings of flies that are used to maintain balance during flight

HALTING *adj* pausing frequently; hesitant

HALTINGLY *adverb* in a halting way

HALVA *noun* **HALVAS** an Eastern delicacy which contains sesame seeds, nuts, honey and saffron

HALVE *verb* **HALVES, HALVING, HALVED** to divide into two equal parts or halves

HALVES *plural of* **half**

HALYARD *noun* **HALYARDS** a rope for raising or lowering a sail or flag on a ship

HAM [1] *noun* **HAMS** the top part of the back leg of a pig

HAM [2] *verb* **HAMS, HAMMING, HAMMED** to overact or exaggerate

HAMADRYAD *noun* **HAMADRYADS** a nymph who lives in a tree and dies when it dies

HAMBURGER *noun* **HAMBURGERS** a flat round cake of finely chopped beef, usually fried and served in a soft bread roll

HAME *noun* **HAMES** either of the two curved bars attached to the collar of a draught animal

HAMLET *noun* **HAMLETS** a small village, especially and originally one without a church

HAMMER *noun* **HAMMERS** a tool with a heavy metal head on the end of a handle, used for driving nails into wood, breaking hard substances, etc □ *verb* **HAMMERS, HAMMERING, HAMMERED** to strike or hit with or as if with a hammer

HAMMERING *noun* **HAMMERINGS** a severe beating

HAMMOCK *noun* **HAMMOCKS** a piece of canvas or net hung by the corners and used as a bed

HAMMY *adj* **HAMMIER, HAMMIEST** said of an actor: inclined to overact

HAMPER [1] *verb* **HAMPERS, HAMPERING, HAMPERED** to hinder the progress or movement of someone or something

HAMPER [2] *noun* **HAMPERS** a large basket with a lid, used especially for carrying food

HAMSTER *noun* **HAMSTERS** a small nocturnal Eurasian rodent with a short tail and pouches in its mouth for storing food, often kept as a pet

HAMSTRING *noun* **HAMSTRINGS** in humans: one of the tendons at the back of the knee that are attached to muscles in the thigh □ *verb* **HAMSTRINGS, HAMSTRINGING, HAMSTRINGED** to make powerless or hinder

HAMULUS *noun* **HAMULI** the hook or hook-shaped apparatus between the fore and hind wings of a bee

HAN a Spenserian form of *have*

HAND *noun* **HANDS** in humans: the extremity of the arm below the wrist, consisting of a thumb, four fingers and a palm □ *verb* **HANDS, HANDING, HANDED** to deliver or give something using the hand or hands

HANDBAG *noun* **HANDBAGS** a woman's small bag, often with a strap, for carrying personal articles

HANDBALL *noun* **HANDBALLS** a game in which two or four players hit a small ball against a wall with their hands

HANDBELL *noun* **HANDBELLS** a small bell with a handle, rung by hand

HANDBILL *noun* **HANDBILLS** a small printed notice or advertisement distributed by hand

HANDBOOK *noun* **HANDBOOKS** a manual that gives guidelines on maintenance or repair, eg of a car

HANDBRAKE *noun* **HANDBRAKES** a brake on a motor vehicle, operated by a lever

HANDCART *noun* **HANDCARTS** a small light cart which can be pushed or pulled by hand

HANDCLAP *noun* **HANDCLAPS** a clap of the hands

HANDCRAFT *noun* **HANDCRAFTS** an activity which requires skilful use of the hands, eg pottery

HANDCUFF *verb* **HANDCUFFS, HANDCUFFING, HANDCUFFED** to put handcuffs on someone

HANDCUFFS *plural noun* a pair of

steel rings, joined by a short chain, for locking round the wrists eg of prisoners, etc

HANDED *adj* using one hand in preference to the other

HANDFUL *noun* **HANDFULS** the amount or number that can be held in one hand

HANDGUN *noun* **HANDGUNS** a firearm that can be held and fired in one hand, eg a revolver

HANDICAP *noun* **HANDICAPS** a physical or mental disability that results in partial or total inability to perform social, occupational or other normal everyday activities □ *verb* **HANDICAPS, HANDICAPPING, HANDICAPPED** to impede or hamper someone

HANDICAPPED *adj* physically or mentally disabled

HANDIER see under **handy**

HANDIEST see under **handy**

HANDILY *adverb* in a handy way

HANDINESS *noun* **HANDINESSES** the quality of being handy

HANDIWORK *noun* **HANDIWORKS** work, especially skilful work, produced by hand

HANDLE *noun* **HANDLES** the part of a utensil, door, etc by which it is held so that it may be used, moved or picked up □ *verb* **HANDLES, HANDLING, HANDLED** to touch, hold, move or operate with the hands

HANDLEBAR *noun* **HANDLEBARS** the steering-bar of a cycle, or one half of it

HANDLED *adj* having handles of a specified type or number

HANDLER *noun* **HANDLERS** someone who trains and controls an animal, especially a police dog

HANDLESS *adj* without hands

HANDLING *noun* **HANDLINGS** the action of touching, holding, moving or operating with the hands

HANDMADE *adj* made by a person's hands or with tools held in the hands, not by machine

HANDMAID *noun* **HANDMAIDS** a female servant

HANDOUT *noun* **HANDOUTS** money, food, etc given to people who need it

HANDOVER *noun* **HANDOVERS** the transfer of power from one person or group of people to another

HANDRAIL *noun* **HANDRAILS** a narrow rail running alongside a stairway, etc for support

HANDSEL *noun* **HANDSELS** a good-luck present given at the start of a new year, new undertaking, etc □ *verb* **HANDSELS, HANDSELLING, HANDSELLED** to give a handsel to someone

HANDSET *noun* **HANDSETS** a telephone mouthpiece and earpiece together in a single unit

HANDSHAKE *noun* **HANDSHAKES** the act of holding or shaking a person's hand, especially as a greeting or when concluding a deal

HANDSOME *adj* **HANDSOMER, HANDSOMEST** said of a man: good-looking

HANDSTAND *noun* **HANDSTANDS** the act of balancing one's body on one's hands with one's legs in the air

HANDY *adj* **HANDIER, HANDIEST** ready to use and conveniently placed

HANDYMAN *noun* **HANDYMEN** a man skilled at, or employed to do, odd jobs around the house

HANEPOOT *noun* **HANEPOOTS** a kind of grape for eating and wine-making

HANG *verb* **HANGS, HANGING, HUNG** to fasten or be fastened from above, especially with the lower part free □ *verb* **HANGS, HANGING, HANGED** to suspend or be suspended by a rope or something similar round the neck until dead □ *noun* **HANGS** the way something hangs, falls or droops

HANGAR *noun* **HANGARS** a large shed or building in which aircraft are kept

HANGDOG *adj* said of someone's appearance or manner: ashamed, guilty or downcast

HANGER *noun* **HANGERS** a metal, wooden or plastic frame on which jackets, dresses, etc are hung up to keep their shape

HANGING *noun* **HANGINGS** the execution of someone by suspending their body by the neck □ *adj* suspended; not fixed below; overhanging

HANGMAN *noun* **HANGMEN** an official who carries out executions by hanging

HANGNAIL *noun* **HANGNAILS** a piece of loose skin that has been partly torn away from the base or side of a fingernail

HANGOVER *noun* **HANGOVERS** a collection of unpleasant physical

symptoms that may follow a period of heavy drinking

HANK *noun* **HANKS** a coil, loop or skein of wool, string, rope, etc

HANKER *verb* **HANKERS, HANKERING, HANKERED** to have a longing or craving for something

HANKERING *noun* **HANKERINGS** a longing or craving

HANKIE *noun* **HANKIES** a handkerchief

HANKY *noun* **HANKIES** a handkerchief

HANSOM *noun* **HANSOMS** a small two-wheeled horse-drawn carriage with a fixed roof and the driver's seat high up at the back, used as a taxi

HAP *noun* **HAPS** luck; chance □ *verb* **HAPS, HAPPING, HAPPED** to happen

HAPHAZARD *adj* careless □ *adverb* at random

HAPLESS *adj* unlucky; unfortunate

HAPLESSLY *adverb* in a hapless way

HAPLOID *adj* said of a cell nucleus: having a single set of unpaired chromosomes □ *noun* **HAPLOIDS** a haploid cell or organism

HAPLOIDY *noun* **HAPLOIDIES** the condition of being haploid

HAPLOLOGY *noun* **HAPLOLOGIES** the omission of a recurring sound or syllable in fluent speech, as in pronouncing *deteriorate* as *deteriate*

HAPPED past form of **hap**

HAPPEN *verb* **HAPPENS, HAPPENING, HAPPENED** to take place or occur □ *adverb* perhaps

HAPPENING *noun* **HAPPENINGS** an event □ *adj* fashionable and up to the minute

HAPPILY *adverb* in a happy way

HAPPINESS *noun* **HAPPINESSES** the quality or condition of being happy

HAPPING a form of **hap**

HAPPY *adj* **HAPPIER, HAPPIEST** feeling or showing pleasure or contentment

HAPTIC *adj* relating to or based on the sense of touch

HAPTICS *singular noun* the study of data obtained by means of touch

HARAMBEE *noun* **HARAMBEES** a rallying-cry used in Kenya

HARANGUE *noun* **HARANGUES** a loud forceful speech either to attack people or to try to persuade them to do something ◻ *verb* **HARANGUES, HARANGUING, HARANGUED** to address such a speech to someone or to a crowd of people

HARASS *verb* **HARASSES, HARASSING, HARASSED** to pester, torment or trouble someone by continually questioning or attacking them

HARASSED *adj* pestered, tormented or troubled by being continually questioned or attacked

HARBINGER *noun* **HARBINGERS** a person or thing that announces or predicts something to come; a forerunner ◻ *verb* **HARBINGERS, HARBINGERING, HARBINGERED** to announce the approach or arrival of something

HARBOR *noun* **HARBORS** a harbour ◻ *verb* **HARBORS, HARBORING, HARBORED** to harbour

HARBORAGE *noun* **HARBORAGES** shelter or refuge, as for a ship

HARBOUR *noun* **HARBOURS** a place of shelter for ships ◻ *verb* **HARBOURS, HARBOURING, HARBOURED** to give shelter or protection to someone, especially to a criminal

HARD *adj* **HARDER, HARDEST** said of a substance: resistant to scratching or indentation; firm; solid ◻ *adverb* with great effort or energy

HARDBACK *noun* **HARDBACKS** a book with a hard cover

HARDBALL *noun* **HARDBALLS** no-nonsense tough tactics, used especially for political gain

HARDBOARD *noun* **HARDBOARDS** light strong board made by compressing wood pulp

HARDEN *verb* **HARDENS, HARDENING, HARDENED** to make or become hard or harder

HARDENED *adj* made hard or harder

HARDENER *noun* **HARDENERS** a person whose job is to harden metals

HARDIER see under **hardy**

HARDIEST see under **hardy**

HARDIHOOD *noun* **HARDIHOODS** courage or daring

HARDILY *adverb* in a hardy way

HARDINESS *noun* **HARDINESSES** the quality or condition of being hardy

HARDLINER *noun* **HARDLINERS** someone who adopts an uncompromising attitude or policy

HARDLY *adverb* barely; scarcely

HARDNESS *noun* **HARDNESSES** the quality or condition of being hard

HARDSHIP *noun* **HARDSHIPS** living conditions that are difficult to endure

HARDTACK *noun* **HARDTACKS** a kind of hard biscuit, formerly given to sailors as food on long journeys

HARDWARE *noun* **HARDWARES** metal goods such as pots, cutlery, tools, etc

HARDWOOD *noun* **HARDWOODS** the wood of a slow-growing deciduous tree, such as the oak, mahogany or teak

HARDY *adj* **HARDIER, HARDIEST** tough; strong; able to bear difficult conditions

HARE *noun* **HARES** a herbivorous mammal like a rabbit but slightly larger and with longer legs and ears ◻ *verb* **HARES, HARING, HARED** to run very fast or wildly

HAREBELL *noun* **HAREBELLS** a wild plant with violet-blue bell-shaped flowers

HAREEM *noun* **HAREEMS** a harem

HAREM *noun* **HAREMS** a separate part of a traditional Muslim house in which wives, concubines, etc live

HARICOT *noun* **HARICOTS** a small white dried bean, used as food

HARK *verb* **HARKS, HARKING, HARKED** to listen to something or to someone attentively

HARKEN *verb* **HARKENS, HARKENING, HARKENED** to listen or pay attention to something or someone

HARL *noun* **HARLS** roughcast ◻ *verb* **HARLS, HARLING, HARLED** to roughcast (eg a wall)

HARLEQUIN *noun* **HARLEQUINS** a humorous character from traditional Italian plays who wears a black mask and a brightly coloured, diamond-patterned costume ◻ *adj* in varied bright colours

HARLING *noun* **HARLINGS** the action of roughcasting anything

HARLOT *noun* **HARLOTS** a prostitute

HARLOTRY *noun* **HARLOTRIES** prostitution

HARM *noun* **HARMS** physical, mental or moral injury or damage ◻ *verb* **HARMS, HARMING,**

HARMED to injure physically, mentally or morally

HARMFUL *adj* causing or tending to cause harm

HARMFULLY *adverb* in a harmful way

HARMLESS *adj* not able or likely to cause harm

HARMONIC *adj* relating or referring to, or producing, harmony; harmonious ◻ *noun* **HARMONICS** an overtone of a fundamental note, produced on a stringed instrument by touching one of the strings lightly at one of the points which divide the string into exact fractions

HARMONICA *noun* **HARMONICAS** a small rectangular wind instrument with metal reeds along one side, played by being held against the mouth, blown or sucked, and moved from side to side to change the notes

HARMONICS *singular noun* the science of musical sounds and their acoustic properties

HARMONISE *verb* **HARMONISES, HARMONISING, HARMONISED** to harmonize

HARMONIST *noun* **HARMONISTS** someone skilled in the theory or composition of harmony

HARMONIUM *noun* **HARMONIUMS** a musical instrument with a keyboard, in which air from bellows pumped by the feet makes the reeds vibrate to produce sound

HARMONIZE *verb* **HARMONIZES, HARMONIZING, HARMONIZED** to be in or bring into musical harmony

HARMONY *noun* **HARMONIES** a pleasing combination of notes or sounds produced simultaneously

HARNESS *noun* **HARNESSES** a set of leather straps used to attach a cart to a horse, and to control the horse's movements ◻ *verb* **HARNESSES, HARNESSING, HARNESSED** to put a harness on (a horse)

HARP *noun* **HARPS** a large three-sided musical instrument with a series of strings stretched vertically across it, played by plucking the strings with the fingers ◻ *verb* **HARPS, HARPING, HARPED** to play the harp

HARPER *noun* **HARPERS** a harpist

HARPIST *noun* **HARPISTS** someone who plays the harp

HARPOON *noun* **HARPOONS** a barbed spear fastened to a rope, used for catching whales □ *verb* **HARPOONS, HARPOONING, HARPOONED** to strike (a whale, etc) with a harpoon

HARPOONER *noun* **HARPOONERS** someone who throws or fires a harpoon

HARPY *noun* **HARPIES** an evil creature with the head and body of a woman and the wings and feet of a bird

HARQUEBUS *noun* **HARQUEBUSES** an arquebus

HARRIDAN *noun* **HARRIDANS** a bad-tempered, scolding old woman; a nag

HARRIER *noun* **HARRIERS** a diurnal bird of prey with broad wings and long legs

HARROW *noun* **HARROWS** a heavy metal framed farm implement with spikes or teeth, used to break up clods of soil and cover seed □ *verb* **HARROWS, HARROWING, HARROWED** to pull a harrow over (land)

HARROWING *adj* acutely distressing

HARRY *verb* **HARRIES, HARRYING, HARRIED** to ravage or destroy (a town, etc), especially in war

HARSH *adj* **HARSHER, HARSHEST** rough; grating; unpleasant to the senses

HARSHLY *adverb* in a harsh way

HARSHNESS *noun* **HARSHNESSES** the quality of being harsh

HART *noun* **HARTS** a male deer, especially one over five years old, when the antlers begin to appear

HARTAL *noun* **HARTALS** in India: a stoppage of work in protest or boycott

HARTSHORN *noun* **HARTSHORNS** sal volatile, a former name for ammonium carbonate, especially in a solution used as smelling salts

HARUSPEX *noun* **HARUSPICES** in ancient Rome: someone who foretold events, especially by examining the entrails of animals

HARUSPICY *noun* **HARUSPICIES** foretelling events by examining the entrails of animals

HARVEST *noun* **HARVESTS** the gathering in of ripened crops, usually in late summer or early autumn □ *verb* **HARVESTS, HARVESTING, HARVESTED** to

gather (a ripened crop) from the place where it has grown

HARVESTER *noun* **HARVESTERS** someone who harvests

HARVESTING *noun* **HARVESTINGS** the action of gathering in ripened crops

HAS a form of **have**

HASH *noun* **HASHES** a dish of cooked meat and vegetables chopped up together and recooked □ *verb* **HASHES, HASHING, HASHED** to chop up into small pieces

HASHEESH *noun* **HASHEESHES** cannabis

HASHISH *noun* **HASHISHES** cannabis

HASLET *noun* **HASLETS** a loaf of cooked minced pig's offal, eaten cold

HASP *noun* **HASPS** a metal fastening for a door, box, etc consisting of a flat metal strip with a narrow slit in it, which fits over a small curved metal bar and is secured by a pin or padlock □ *verb* **HASPS, HASPING, HASPED** to secure (a door, window, etc) with a hasp

HASSLE *noun* **HASSLES** trouble, annoyance or inconvenience, or a cause of this □ *verb* **HASSLES, HASSLING, HASSLED** to annoy or bother someone, especially repeatedly; to harass

HASSOCK *noun* **HASSOCKS** a firm cushion for kneeling on, especially in church

HAST *verb* the form of the present tense of the verb *have* used with *thou*

HASTATE *adj* said of a leaf: with a pointed tip and two outward-pointing lobes at the base

HASTE *noun* **HASTES** speed, especially speed in an action □ *verb* **HASTES, HASTING, HASTED** to hasten

HASTEN *verb* **HASTENS, HASTENING, HASTENED** to hurry or cause to hurry

HASTILY *adverb* in a hasty way

HASTINESS *noun* **HASTINESSES** the hurry; rashness

HASTY *adj* **HASTIER, HASTIEST** hurried; swift; quick

HAT *noun* **HATS** a covering for the head, usually worn out of doors □ *verb* **HATS, HATTING, HATTED** to provide someone with a hat or put a hat on someone

HATABLE *adj* deserving to be hated

HATBAND *noun* **HATBANDS** a band of cloth or ribbon around a hat just above the brim

HATBOX *noun* **HATBOXES** a large rounded box or case for storing or carrying hats

HATCH *verb* **HATCHES, HATCHING, HATCHED** said of an animal or bird: to break out of an egg □ *noun* **HATCHES** the act or process of hatching

HATCHBACK *noun* **HATCHBACKS** a sloping rear end of a car with a single door which opens upwards, allowing access to the compartment inside

HATCHERY *noun* **HATCHERIES** a place where eggs, especially fish eggs, are hatched under artificial conditions

HATCHET *noun* **HATCHETS** a small axe held in one hand

HATCHING *noun* **HATCHINGS** shading in fine lines

HATCHMENT *noun* **HATCHMENTS** a diamond-shaped tablet displaying the coat of arms of a dead person, fixed to the front of their former home

HATCHWAY *noun* **HATCHWAYS** an opening in a ship's deck for loading cargo through

HATE *verb* **HATES, HATING, HATED** to dislike intensely □ *noun* **HATES** an intense dislike

HATEABLE *adj* hatable

HATEFUL *adj* causing or deserving great dislike; loathsome; detestable

HATEFULLY *adverb* in a hateful way

HATH *verb* the form of the present tense of *have*, used where we would now use *has*

HATLESS *adj* without a hat

HATPIN *noun* **HATPINS** a long metal pin, often decorated, pushed through a woman's hat and hair to keep the hat in place

HATRED *noun* **HATREDS** intense dislike; enmity; ill-will

HATSTAND *noun* **HATSTANDS** a piece of furniture with pegs for hanging hats, coats, umbrellas, etc on

HATTER *noun* **HATTERS** someone who makes or sells hats

HAUBERK *noun* **HAUBERKS** a long coat of chain-mail

HAUGHTILY *adverb* in a haughty way

HAUGHTY *adj* **HAUGHTIER, HAUGHTIEST** very proud; arrogant or contemptuous

HAUL verb **HAULS, HAULING, HAULED** to pull with great effort or difficulty ▫ noun **HAULS** the distance to be travelled

HAULAGE noun **HAULAGES** the act or labour of hauling

HAULER noun **HAULERS** a person or thing that hauls

HAULIER noun **HAULIERS** a person or company that transports goods by road, especially in lorries

HAULM noun **HAULMS** the stalks or stems of potatoes, peas, beans or grasses, collectively

HAUNCH noun **HAUNCHES** the fleshy part of the buttock or thigh

HAUNT verb **HAUNTS, HAUNTING, HAUNTED** said of a ghost or spirit: to be present in (a place) or visit (a person or place) regularly ▫ noun **HAUNTS** a place visited frequently

HAUNTED adj frequented or visited by ghosts or spirits

HAUNTING adj said of a place, memory, piece of music, etc: making a very strong and moving impression; poignant

HAUSFRAU noun **HAUSFRAUS** a German housewife, especially one exclusively interested in domestic matters

HAUTBOY noun **HAUTBOYS** an oboe

HAUTEUR noun **HAUTEURS** haughtiness; arrogance

HAVE verb **HAS, HAVING, HAD** to possess or own ▫ noun **HAVES** people who have wealth and the security it brings

HAVELOCK noun **HAVELOCKS** a white cover for a military cap with a flap hanging over the back of the neck to protect the head and neck from the sun

HAVEN noun **HAVENS** a place of safety or rest

HAVER verb **HAVERS, HAVERING, HAVERED** to babble; to talk nonsense ▫ noun **HAVERS** foolish talk; nonsense

HAVERSACK noun **HAVERSACKS** a canvas bag carried over one shoulder or on the back

HAVERSINE noun **HAVERSINES** half the value of the versed sine

HAVILDAR noun **HAVILDARS** a non-commissioned officer in the Indian army, equivalent in rank to sergeant

HAVING a form of **have**

HAVOC noun **HAVOCS** great destruction or damage

HAW¹ noun **HAWS** a hawthorn berry

HAW² verb **HAWS, HAWING, HAWED** to make indecisive noises

HAWFINCH noun **HAWFINCHES** a type of European finch with a stout beak

HAWK noun **HAWKS** a relatively small diurnal bird of prey with short rounded wings and very good eyesight which hunts by pouncing on small birds and mammals ▫ verb **HAWKS, HAWKING, HAWKED** to hunt with a hawk

HAWKER noun **HAWKERS** someone who hunts with a hawk

HAWKING noun **HAWKINGS** hunting with a hawk

HAWKLIKE adj resembling a hawk

HAWKSBILL noun **HAWKSBILLS** a small tropical turtle with a hook-like mouth, from which tortoiseshell is derived

HAWKWEED noun **HAWKWEEDS** a perennial plant which has leaves arranged spirally around the stem, or forming a rosette at the base, and yellow flower heads that may be solitary or in loose clusters

HAWSE noun **HAWSES** the part of a vessel's bow in which the hawseholes are cut

HAWSEHOLE noun **HAWSEHOLES** a hole in the bow or stem of a vessel through which an anchor cable passes

HAWSEPIPE noun **HAWSEPIPES** a strong metal pipe fitted into a hawsehole through which an anchor cable passes

HAWSER noun **HAWSERS** a thick rope or steel cable for tying ships to the quayside

HAWTHORN noun **HAWTHORNS** a thorny tree or shrub with pink or white flowers and red berries

HAY noun **HAYS** grass, clover, etc that has been cut and allowed to dry in the field before being baled and stored for use as winter fodder for animal livestock ▫ verb **HAYS, HAYING, HAYED** to cut, dry and store (grass, clover, etc) as fodder

HAYBOX noun **HAYBOXES** an airtight box full of hay used to continue the cooking of preheated food by placing it within the hay which acts as a heat insulator

HAYCOCK noun **HAYCOCKS** a small cone-shaped pile of hay in a field

HAYFORK noun **HAYFORKS** a long-handled, long-pronged fork for tossing and lifting hay

HAYMAKER noun **HAYMAKERS** a person employed in making hay, especially one who lifts, tosses and spreads the hay after it is cut

HAYMAKING noun **HAYMAKINGS** the action of making hay ▫ adj that makes hay

HAYMOW noun **HAYMOWS** the part of a barn where hay is stored

HAYRICK noun **HAYRICKS** a haystack

HAYSTACK noun **HAYSTACKS** a large firm stack of hay built in an open field and protected by plastic sheets or thatching

HAYWIRE adj said of things: out of order; not working properly

HAZAN noun **HAZANS** a cantor in a synagogue

HAZARD noun **HAZARDS** a risk of harm or danger ▫ verb **HAZARDS, HAZARDING, HAZARDED** to put forward (a guess, suggestion, etc)

HAZARDOUS adj very risky; dangerous

HAZE noun **HAZES** a thin mist, vapour or shimmer in the atmosphere which obscures visibility ▫ verb **HAZES, HAZING, HAZED** to make or become hazy

HAZEL noun **HAZELS** a small deciduous shrub or tree with edible nuts that is widespread in Europe ▫ adj greenish-brown in colour

HAZELNUT noun **HAZELNUTS** the edible nut of the hazel tree, with a smooth hard shiny shell

HAZER noun **HAZERS** someone who subjects fellow students to abuse or bullying

HAZILY adverb in a hazy way

HAZINESS noun **HAZINESSES** the quality of being hazy

HAZING noun **HAZINGS** the action of subjecting fellow students to abuse or bullying

HAZY adj **HAZIER, HAZIEST** vague; not clear

HE pronoun a male person or animal already referred to ▫ noun **HES** a male person or animal

HEAD noun **HEADS** the uppermost or foremost part of an animal's body, containing the brain and the organs of sight, smell, hearing and taste ▫ verb **HEADS, HEADING, HEADED** to be at the front of or top of something

HEADACHE noun **HEADACHES** any continuous pain felt deep inside the head

HEADACHY adj **HEADACHIER, HEADACHIEST** suffering from a headache

HEADBAND noun **HEADBANDS** a band worn round the head, especially for decoration

HEADBOARD noun **HEADBOARDS** a board at the top end of a bed

HEADDRESS noun **HEADDRESSES** a covering for the head, especially one which is highly decorative and is used in ceremonies

HEADED adj having a heading

HEADER noun **HEADERS** a fall or dive forwards

HEADGEAR noun **HEADGEARS** anything worn on the head

HEADHUNT verb **HEADHUNTS, HEADHUNTING, HEADHUNTED** to practise headhunting

HEADHUNTING noun **HEADHUNTINGS** the practice in certain societies of taking the heads of one's dead enemies as trophies

HEADIER see under **heady**

HEADIEST see under **heady**

HEADILY adverb in a heady way

HEADINESS noun **HEADINESSES** the quality of being heady

HEADING noun **HEADINGS** a title at the top of a page, letter, section of a report, etc

HEADLAMP noun **HEADLAMPS** a headlight

HEADLAND noun **HEADLANDS** a strip of land which sticks out into a sea or other expanse of water

HEADLESS adj lacking a head

HEADLIGHT noun **HEADLIGHTS** a powerful light on the front of a vehicle

HEADLINE noun **HEADLINES** the title or heading of a newspaper article, written above the article in large letters ◻ verb **HEADLINES, HEADLINING, HEADLINED** to provide (an article or page) with a headline

HEADLONG adj moving especially quickly with one's head in front or bent forward ◻ adverb moving especially quickly with one's head in front or bent forward

HEADMAN noun **HEADMEN** a tribal chief or leader

HEADRACE noun **HEADRACES** the channel leading to a waterwheel, turbine, etc

HEADREST noun **HEADRESTS** a cushion which supports the head, fitted to the top of a car seat, etc

HEADROOM noun **HEADROOMS** the space between the top of a vehicle and the underside of a bridge

HEADSCARF noun **HEADSCARVES** a scarf worn over the head and tied under the chin

HEADSET noun **HEADSETS** a pair of headphones, often with a microphone attached

HEADSHIP noun **HEADSHIPS** the position of, or time of being, head or leader of an organization, especially a school

HEADSMAN noun **HEADSMEN** an executioner who beheaded condemned persons

HEADSTALL noun **HEADSTALLS** the part of a bridle which fits round a horse's head

HEADSTOCK noun **HEADSTOCKS** a device for supporting the end or head of a part of a machine

HEADSTONE noun **HEADSTONES** a keystone

HEADWAY noun **HEADWAYS** a ship's movement forwards

HEADWORD noun **HEADWORDS** a word forming a heading, especially for a dictionary or an encyclopedia entry

HEADWORK noun **HEADWORKS** mental work

HEADY adj **HEADIER, HEADIEST** said of alcoholic drinks: tending to make one drunk quickly

HEAL verb **HEALS, HEALING, HEALED** to cause (a person, wound, etc) to become healthy again

HEALER noun **HEALERS** someone who heals a person, wound, etc

HEALING noun **HEALINGS** the action of causing a person, wound, etc to become healthy again ◻ adj that heals

HEALTH noun **HEALTHS** a state of physical, mental and social well-being accompanied by freedom from illness or pain

HEALTHFUL adj causing or bringing good health

HEALTHILY adverb in a healthy way

HEALTHY adj **HEALTHIER, HEALTHIEST** having or showing good health

HEAP noun **HEAPS** a collection of things in an untidy pile or mass ◻ verb **HEAPS, HEAPING, HEAPED** to collect or be collected together in a heap

HEAPED adj denoting a spoonful that forms a rounded heap on the spoon

HEAPS adverb very much

HEAR verb **HEARS, HEARING, HEARD** to perceive (sounds) with the ear

HEARER noun **HEARERS** someone who hears; a listener

HEARING noun **HEARINGS** the sense that involves the perception of sound

HEARKEN verb **HEARKENS, HEARKENING, HEARKENED** to hear attentively; to listen

HEARSAY noun **HEARSAYS** rumour; gossip

HEARSE noun **HEARSES** a vehicle used for carrying a coffin at a funeral

HEART noun **HEARTS** in vertebrates: the hollow muscular organ that contracts and pumps blood through the blood vessels of the body ◻ verb **HEARTS, HEARTING, HEARTED** said of vegetables: to form a compact head or inner mass

HEARTACHE noun **HEARTACHES** great sadness or mental suffering

HEARTBEAT noun **HEARTBEATS** the pulsation of the heart, produced by the alternate contraction and relaxation of the heart muscle as it pumps blood around the body

HEARTBURN noun **HEARTBURNS** a feeling of burning in the chest caused by indigestion

HEARTED adj having a heart or character as specified, as in *warm-hearted*

HEARTEN verb **HEARTENS, HEARTENING, HEARTENED** to make or become happier, more cheerful or encouraged

HEARTENING adj that heartens

HEARTFELT adj sincerely and deeply felt

HEARTH noun **HEARTHS** the floor of a fireplace, or the area surrounding it

HEARTIER see under **hearty**

HEARTIEST see under **hearty**

HEARTILY adverb in a hearty way

HEARTLAND noun **HEARTLANDS** a central or vitally important area or region

HEARTLESS *adj* cruel; very unkind

HEARTS *singular noun* a card game in which the aim is to avoid winning tricks containing hearts or the queen of spades

HEARTWOOD *noun* **HEARTWOODS** the dark, hard wood at the centre of a tree trunk or branch, consisting of dead cells containing oils, gums and resins

HEARTY *adj* **HEARTIER, HEARTIEST** very friendly and warm in manner □ *noun* **HEARTIES** a hearty person, especially one who is very keen on sports

HEAT *noun* **HEATS** a form of energy that is stored as the energy of vibration or motion (kinetic energy) of the atoms or molecules of a material □ *verb* **HEATS, HEATING, HEATED** to make or become hot or warm

HEATED *adj* having been made hot or warm

HEATER *noun* **HEATERS** an apparatus for heating a room, building, water in a tank, etc

HEATH *noun* **HEATHS** an area of open land, usually with dry sandy acidic soil, dominated by low-growing evergreen shrubs, especially heathers

HEATHEN *noun* **HEATHENS** someone who is not a Christian, Jew or Muslim, but who follows another religion, especially one with many gods; a pagan □ *adj* having no religion; pagan

HEATHER *noun* **HEATHERS** a low evergreen shrub with many side shoots with small scale-like leaves and small pink or purple bell-shaped flowers □ *adj* having a heather colour

HEATHY *adj* **HEATHIER, HEATHIEST** abounding with heath

HEATING *noun* **HEATINGS** any of various systems for maintaining the temperature inside a room or building at a level higher than that of the surroundings

HEAVE *verb* **HEAVES, HEAVING, HOVE, HEAVED** to lift or pull with great effort □ *noun* **HEAVES** an act of heaving

HEAVEN *noun* **HEAVENS** the place believed to be the abode of God, angels and the righteous after death

HEAVENLY *adj* **HEAVENLIER, HEAVENLIEST** very pleasant; beautiful

HEAVENS *exclamation* expressing surprise, anger, dismay, etc

HEAVER *noun* **HEAVERS** a person or thing that heaves

HEAVES *singular and plural noun* a chronic respiratory disease of horses

HEAVILY *adverb* in a heavy way; with or as if with weight

HEAVINESS *noun* **HEAVINESSES** the state or quality of being heavy

HEAVY *adj* **HEAVIER, HEAVIEST** having great weight □ *noun* **HEAVIES** a large, violent and usually not very intelligent man □ *adverb* with a heavy burden

HEBETATE *adj* blunt or soft-pointed; dull □ *verb* **HEBETATES, HEBETATING, HEBETATED** to make or become dull or blunt

HECATOMB *noun* **HECATOMBS** a great public sacrifice, originally of oxen

HECK *exclamation* mildly expressing anger, annoyance, surprise, etc

HECKLE *verb* **HECKLES, HECKLING, HECKLED** to interrupt (a speaker) with critical or abusive shouts and jeers, especially at a public meeting

HECKLER *noun* **HECKLERS** someone who heckles

HECTARE *noun* **HECTARES** in the metric system: a metric unit of land measurement, equivalent to 100 ares, or 10 000 square metres (2.471 acres)

HECTIC *adj* agitated; very excited, flustered or rushed

HECTOGRAM *noun* **HECTOGRAMS** one hundred grams

HECTOR *verb* **HECTORS, HECTORING, HECTORED** to bully, intimidate or threaten □ *noun* **HECTORS** a bully or tormentor

HEDDLE *noun* **HEDDLES** a series of vertical cords or wires, each with a loop in the middle to receive the warp thread

HEDGE *noun* **HEDGES** a boundary formed by bushes and shrubs planted close together, especially between fields □ *verb* **HEDGES, HEDGING, HEDGED** to enclose or surround (an area of land) with a hedge

HEDGED *adj* enclosed with a hedge

HEDGEHOG *noun* **HEDGEHOGS** a small, prickly-backed insectivorous mammal with a short tail and a hoglike snout, that lives in bushes and hedges

HEDGER *noun* **HEDGERS** someone who avoids making a decision or giving a clear answer

HEDGEROW *noun* **HEDGEROWS** a row of bushes, hedges or trees forming a boundary

HEDONIC *adj* of or relating to hedonics

HEDONICS *singular noun* the part of ethics or psychology that deals with pleasure

HEDONISM *noun* **HEDONISMS** the belief that pleasure is the most important achievement or the highest good in life

HEDONIST *noun* **HEDONISTS** someone who believes in or practises hedonism

HEED *verb* **HEEDS, HEEDING, HEEDED** to pay attention to or take notice of something, especially advice or a warning, etc □ *noun* **HEEDS** careful attention; notice

HEEDFUL *adj* attentive or cautious

HEEDFULLY *adverb* in a heedful way

HEEDLESS *adj* taking no care; careless

HEEL *noun* **HEELS** the rounded back part of the foot below the ankle □ *verb* **HEELS, HEELING, HEELED** to execute or perform with the heel

HEELED *adj* having a heel or heels

HEFTILY *adverb* in a hefty way

HEFTINESS *noun* **HEFTINESSES** the state of being hefty

HEFTY *adj* **HEFTIER, HEFTIEST** said of a person: strong, robust or muscular

HEGEMONY *noun* **HEGEMONIES** authority or control, especially of one state over another within a confederation

HEGIRA *noun* **HEGIRAS** the flight of the Prophet Muhammad from Mecca to Yathrib (Medina) in AD 622, marking the beginning of the Muslim era

HEIFER *noun* **HEIFERS** a female cow over one year old that has either not calved, or has calved only once

HEIGH *exclamation* expressing enquiry, encouragement or exultation

HEIGHT *noun* **HEIGHTS** the condition of being high, or the distance from the base of something to the top

HEIGHTEN *verb* **HEIGHTENS, HEIGHTENING, HEIGHTENED** to make higher, greater, stronger, etc

HEINOUS *adj* extremely wicked or evil; odious

HEINOUSLY *adverb* in a heinous way

HEIR *noun* **HEIRS** someone who by law receives or is entitled to receive wealth, a title, etc when the previous owner or holder dies

HEIRESS *noun* **HEIRESSES** a female heir

HEIRLESS *adj* without an heir

HEIRLOOM *noun* **HEIRLOOMS** a personal article or piece of property which descends to the legal heir by means of a will or special custom

HEIST *noun* **HEISTS** a robbery □ *verb* **HEISTS, HEISTING, HEISTED** to steal or rob in a heist

HEISTER *noun* **HEISTERS** a robber

HEJAB *noun* **HEJABS** a covering for a Muslim woman's face and head, sometimes reaching to the ground

HEJIRA *noun* **HEJIRAS** hegira

HELD past form of **hold**

HELIACAL *adj* solar or relating to the Sun, especially to the rising and setting of stars which coincide with those of the Sun

HELICAL *adj* relating to or like a helix; coiled

HELIDECK *noun* **HELIDECKS** a landing deck for helicopters on a ship

HELIOSTAT *noun* **HELIOSTATS** a device where a mirror is used to reflect a beam of sunlight in a fixed direction either for studying the Sun or for signalling purposes

HELIOTYPE *noun* **HELIOTYPES** photography by heliotypy

HELIOTYPY *noun* **HELIOTYPIES** the photo-mechanical process where the imprint is taken from the gelatine relief itself

HELIPAD *noun* **HELIPADS** a landing place for a helicopter, usually a square marked with a large H

HELIPORT *noun* **HELIPORTS** a place where helicopters take off and land, usually for commercial purposes

HELIUM *noun* **HELIUMS** a colourless odourless inert gas found in natural gas deposits, also formed in stars by nuclear fusion

HELIX *noun* **HELIXES, HELICES** a spiral or coiled structure, eg the thread of a screw

HELL *noun* **HELLS** the place or state of infinite punishment for the wicked after death □ *exclamation* expressing annoyance or exasperation

HELLEBORE *noun* **HELLEBORES** any plant of the buttercup or lily family, with white, greenish-white or purplish flowers

HELLENISE *verb* **HELLENISES, HELLENISING, HELLENISED** to hellenize

HELLENIZE *verb* **HELLENIZES, HELLENIZING, HELLENIZED** to make Greek

HELLFIRE *noun* **HELLFIRES** the fire of hell

HELLHOUND *noun* **HELLHOUNDS** a hound or agent of hell

HELLION *noun* **HELLIONS** a troublesome or mischievous child or person

HELLISH *adj* relating to or resembling hell

HELLISHLY *adverb* in a hellish way

HELLO *exclamation* used as a greeting □ *verb* **HELLOS, HELLOING, HELLOED** to greet someone by saying 'hello'

HELLOVA *adj* one hell of a; great, very

HELLUVA *adj* hellova

HELM *noun* **HELMS** the steering apparatus of a boat or ship, such as a wheel or tiller

HELMET *noun* **HELMETS** an armoured and protective covering for the head, worn by police officers, firefighters, soldiers, motorcyclists, bicyclists, etc

HELMETED *adj* wearing a helmet

HELMINTH *noun* **HELMINTHS** a worm

HELMSMAN *noun* **HELMSMEN** someone who steers a boat or ship

HELOT *noun* **HELOTS** a member of the serf class, especially in ancient Sparta, who was bound to the state

HELP *verb* **HELPS, HELPING, HELPED** to contribute towards the success of something; to assist or aid □ *noun* **HELPS** an act of helping □ *adj* giving help, aid or support

HELPABLE *adj* that can be helped

HELPER *noun* **HELPERS** someone who helps; an assistant

HELPFUL *adj* giving help or aid; being useful

HELPING *noun* **HELPINGS** a single portion of food served at a meal

HELPLESS *adj* unable or unfit to do anything for oneself

HELPLINE *noun* **HELPLINES** a telephone line which may be used (often free of charge) by people with specific problems in order to contact advisers and counsellors who are specifically qualified to deal with them

HELPMATE *noun* **HELPMATES** a friend or partner, especially a husband or wife

HELVE *noun* **HELVES** the handle of an axe or other similar tool □ *verb* **HELVES, HELVING, HELVED** to provide with a handle

HEM *noun* **HEMS** a bottom edge or border of a piece of cloth that is folded over and sewn down □ *verb* **HEMS, HEMMING, HEMMED** to form a border or edge on a piece of cloth

HEMAL *adj* haemal

HEME *noun* **HEMES** haem

HEMLOCK *noun* **HEMLOCKS** a poisonous umbelliferous plant with small white flowers and a spotted stem

HEMP *noun* **HEMPS** a tall annual plant which is native to Asia and grown commercially for its stem fibres, a drug and an oil

HEMPEN *adj* made of hemp

HEN *noun* **HENS** a female bird of any kind, especially the domestic fowl □ *verb* **HENS, HENNING, HENNED** to challenge to a daring act

HENBANE *noun* **HENBANES** a poisonous wild plant of the nightshade family, with hairy leaves, light-green flowers, and an unpleasant smell

HENCE *adverb* for this reason or cause

HENCHMAN *noun* **HENCHMEN** a faithful supporter or right-hand man, especially one who obeys and assists without question

HENDIADYS *noun* **HENDIADYSES** a rhetorical figure in which a notion, normally expressible by an adjective and a noun, is instead expressed by two nouns linked by a conjunction, as in *clad in cloth and green*

HENEQUEN *noun* **HENEQUENS** a Mexican agave

HENEQUIN *noun* **HENEQUINS** henequen

HENGE *noun* **HENGES** a circular or oval area surrounded by a bank and ditch, often containing burial chambers

HENIQUIN *noun* **HENIQUINS** henequen

HENNA *noun* **HENNAS** reddish-brown dye obtained from the leaves of the henna plant ◻ *verb* **HENNAS, HENNAING, HENNAED** to dye or stain using henna

HENPECKED *adj* usually said of a man: constantly harassed, criticized and dominated by a woman, especially a wife, girlfriend, etc

HENRY *noun* **HENRYS, HENRIES** in the SI system: the unit of electrical inductance, defined as the inductance that produces an electromotive force of one volt when the electric current in a closed circuit changes at the rate of one ampere per second

HEP [1] *adj* **HEPPER, HEPPEST** an old-fashioned variant of hip, used especially in relation to jazz

HEP [2] *noun* **HEPS** a rosehip

HEPARIN *noun* **HEPARINS** a chemical substance formed in most tissues of the body (eg liver, lung, etc) that prevents the clotting of the blood

HEPATIC *adj* relating or referring to the liver ◻ *noun* **HEPATICS** a liverwort

HEPATITIS *noun* **HEPATITISES** inflammation of the liver, caused either by a viral infection, or as a reaction to toxic substances such as alcohol or drugs, the symptoms of which include jaundice, fever and nausea

HEPTAD *noun* **HEPTADS** a group of seven

HEPTAGON *noun* **HEPTAGONS** a plane figure with seven angles and sides

HEPTANE *noun* **HEPTANES** a hydrocarbon which is seventh of the methane series

HEPTARCH *noun* **HEPTARCHS** the ruler of a heptarchy

HEPTARCHY *noun* **HEPTARCHIES** government by a group of seven leaders, or a country ruled in this way

HER *pronoun* the form of *she* used as the object of a verb or preposition ◻ *adj* referring to a female person or animal, or something personified or thought of as female, eg a ship

HERALD *noun* **HERALDS** in ancient and medieval societies: a person who announces important news, or an officer whose task it is to make public proclamations and arrange ceremonies ◻ *verb*

HERALDS, HERALDING, HERALDED to be a sign of the approach of something; to proclaim or usher it in

HERALDIC *adj* of or relating to heralds or heraldry

HERALDRY *noun* **HERALDRIES** the art of recording genealogies, and blazoning coats of arms

HERB *noun* **HERBS** a flowering plant which, unlike a shrub or tree, has no woody stem above the ground

HERBAGE *noun* **HERBAGES** herbs collectively; herbaceous vegetation covering a large area, especially for use as pasture

HERBAL *adj* composed of or relating to herbs ◻ *noun* **HERBALS** a book describing the use of plants, or substances extracted from them, for medicinal purposes

HERBALISM *noun* **HERBALISMS** herbal medicine, the use of (extracts of) roots, seeds, etc for medicinal purposes

HERBALIST *noun* **HERBALISTS** a person who practises herbalism

HERBARIUM *noun* **HERBARIUMS, HERBARIA** a classified collection of preserved plants (in a room or building, etc)

HERBICIDE *noun* **HERBICIDES** a substance used to kill weeds, etc, especially when used as a selective weedkiller

HERBIST *noun* **HERBISTS** a person who researches, collects and sells herbs and plants

HERBIVORE *noun* **HERBIVORES** an animal, especially an ungulate that feeds on grass, herbage or other vegetation

HERBIVORY *noun* **HERBIVORIES** living on herbage or other vegetation

HERCULEAN *adj* extremely difficult or dangerous

HERD *noun* **HERDS** a company of animals, especially large ones, that habitually remain together ◻ *verb* **HERDS, HERDING, HERDED** to associate as if in a herd; to gather together in a crowd like an animal in a herd

HERDSMAN *noun* **HERDSMEN** the keeper of a herd of animals

HERE *adverb* at, in or to this place ◻ *noun* this place or location ◻ *exclamation* calling for attention

HEREABOUT *adverb* hereabouts

HEREABOUTS *adverb* around or near this place; within this area

HEREAFTER *adverb* after this time; in a future time, life or state

HEREAT *adverb* because of or by reason of this

HEREBY *adverb* not far off

HEREDITY *noun* **HEREDITIES** the transmission of recognizable and genetically based characteristics from one generation to the next

HEREIN *adverb* in this case or respect

HEREOF *adverb* relating to or concerning this

HEREON *adverb* on, upon or to this point

HERESY *noun* **HERESIES** an opinion or belief contrary to the authorized teaching of the religious community to which one ostensibly belongs

HERETIC *noun* **HERETICS** someone who believes in and endorses heresy

HERETICAL *adj* of or relating to heresy or heretics

HERETO *adverb* to this place or document

HEREUNDER *adverb* in a document: below; following

HEREUNTO *adverb* to this point in time; to this place or matter

HEREUPON *adverb* on this

HEREWITH *adverb* with this; enclosed or together with this letter, etc

HERITABLE *adj* said of property: able to be inherited or passed down

HERITABLY *adverb* in a heritable way

HERITAGE *noun* **HERITAGES** something that is inherited

HERITOR *noun* **HERITORS** a person who inherits, either legally or by tradition

HERL *noun* **HERLS** a harl

HERMETIC *adj* perfectly closed or sealed so as to be airtight

HERMETICS *singular noun* esoteric or obscure science; alchemy

HERMIT *noun* **HERMITS** an ascetic who leads an isolated life for religious reasons

HERMITAGE *noun* **HERMITAGES** the dwelling-place of a hermit

HERNIA *noun* **HERNIAS** the protrusion of an organ (especially part of the viscera) through an opening or weak spot in the wall of its surroundings

HERNIAL *adj* of or relating to a hernia

HERNIATED adj affected with a hernia

HERO noun **HEROES** a man of distinguished bravery and strength; any illustrious person

HEROIC adj supremely courageous and brave

HEROICS noun **HEROICS** over-dramatic or extravagant speech

HEROIN noun **HEROINS** a powerful drug produced from morphine, used medicinally to lessen pain, and illegally for pleasure, but with continued use likely to lead to dependence and addiction

HEROINE noun **HEROINES** a woman with heroic characteristics

HEROISM noun **HEROISMS** the qualities of a hero; courage, boldness and strength

HERON noun **HERONS** a large wading bird with a long neck and legs, and commonly grey or white in colour

HERONRY noun **HERONRIES** a place where herons breed

HERPES noun **HERPESES** any of various contagious skin diseases caused by a virus which gives rise to watery blisters

HERPETIC adj relating to or resembling herpes

HERRING noun **HERRINGS** a small silvery sea-fish of considerable commercial value, found in large shoals in northern waters, and eaten either fresh or cured

HERS pronoun the one or ones belonging to her

HERSELF pronoun the reflexive form of her and she

HERTZ noun **HERTZ** in the SI system: the unit of frequency, equal to one cycle per second

HESITANCE noun **HESITANCES** wavering, doubt, delay, etc

HESITANCY noun **HESITANCIES** hesitance

HESITANT adj uncertain; holding back; doubtful

HESITATE verb **HESITATES, HESITATING, HESITATED** to falter or delay in speaking, acting or making a decision; to be in doubt

HESSIAN noun **HESSIANS** a coarse cloth made from jute, similar to sacking

HET a dialect past form of heated

HETAERA noun **HETAERAE** in ancient Greece: a prostitute, especially a courtesan

HETAIRA noun **HETAIRAI, HETAIRAS** a hetaera

HETERO noun **HETEROS** a heterosexual

HETERODOX adj holding an opinion other than or different from the one generally received, especially in theology; heretical

HETERONYM noun **HETERONYMS** a word which has the same spelling as another, but has a different pronunciation and meaning, such as lead

HETEROSIS noun **HETEROSES** in biology: the increased size and vigour of a hybrid relative to its parents

HETMAN noun **HETMANS** a Polish or Cossack military commander

HEURISTIC adj serving or leading to discover or find out

HEURISTICS plural noun the principles used to make decisions when all possibilities cannot be explored

HEW verb **HEWS, HEWING, HEWED, HEWN, HEWED** to cut, fell or sever something using a cutting instrument, eg axe, sword, etc

HEX noun **HEXES** a witch, wizard or wicked spell □ verb **HEXES, HEXING, HEXED** to bring misfortune; to bewitch

HEXACHORD noun **HEXACHORDS** a diatonic series of six notes, with a semitone between the third and fourth notes

HEXAD noun **HEXADS** a series of six items

HEXAGON noun **HEXAGONS** a plane figure with six sides and angles

HEXAGONAL adj of the form of a hexagon

HEXAGRAM noun **HEXAGRAMS** a star-shaped figure created by extending the lines of a uniform hexagon until they meet at six points

HEXAMETER noun **HEXAMETERS** a line or verse with six measures or feet

HEXANE noun **HEXANES** a hydrocarbon that is a toxic flammable liquid, and the sixth member of the methane series

HEXAPOD noun **HEXAPODS** an animal with six legs, ie an insect

HEXASTYLE adj said of a temple or façade of a building: having six columns

HEXOSE noun **HEXOSES** a monosaccharide carbohydrate with six carbon atoms in each molecule

HEY noun **HEYS** a winding country-dance □ verb **HEYS, HEYING, HEYED** to dance this dance

HEYDAY noun **HEYDAYS** the period or climax of the most success, power, prosperity, popularity, etc

HI exclamation a casual form of greeting

HIATUS noun **HIATUSES** an opening or gap; a break in something which should be continuous

HIBERNAL adj referring or belonging to the winter; wintry

HIBERNATE verb **HIBERNATES, HIBERNATING, HIBERNATED** said of certain animals: to pass the winter in a dormant state; to be completely inactive

HIBISCUS noun **HIBISCUSES** a tree or shrub, usually from tropical climes, with large brightly coloured flowers

HIC exclamation representing a hiccup

HICCOUGH noun **HICCOUGHS** a hiccup □ verb **HICCOUGHS, HICCOUGHING, HICCOUGHED** to hiccup

HICCUP noun **HICCUPS** an involuntary inhalation of air caused by a spasm in the diaphragm □ verb **HICCUPS, HICCUPING, HICCUPED** to produce a hiccup or hiccups

HICK noun **HICKS** someone from the country

HICKEY noun **HICKEYS** a love bite

HICKORY noun **HICKORIES** a N American tree of the walnut family, with edible nuts and heavy strong wood

HIDDEN adj concealed; kept secret; unknown

HIDE verb **HIDES, HIDING, HID, HIDDEN** to conceal someone or something from sight; to keep something secret □ noun **HIDES** a concealed shelter used for observing birds and wild animals

HIDEOUS adj said of a person or thing: dreadful; revolting; extremely ugly

HIDEOUSLY adverb in a hideous way

HIDEOUT noun **HIDEOUTS** a refuge or retreat; concealment

HIDING noun **HIDINGS** a severe beating

HIE verb **HIES, HIEING, HYING, HIED** to hasten or hurry

HIERARCH noun **HIERARCHS** a holy ruler; a chief priest

HIERARCHY noun **HIERARCHIES** an organization or body that classifies people or things in order of rank or importance

HIGH adj **HIGHER, HIGHEST** elevated; tall; towering ◻ adverb at or to a height; in or into an elevated position ◻ noun **HIGHS** a high point or level

HIGHBALL noun **HIGHBALLS** an alcoholic drink of spirits and soda served with ice in a long glass

HIGHBROW adj said of art, literature, etc: intellectual; cultured ◻ noun **HIGHBROWS** an intellectual or learned person

HIGHJACK verb **HIGHJACKS, HIGHJACKING, HIGHJACKED** to hijack

HIGHLAND noun **HIGHLANDS** a mountainous area of land

HIGHLIGHT noun **HIGHLIGHTS** the most memorable or outstanding feature, event, experience, etc ◻ verb **HIGHLIGHTS, HIGHLIGHTING, HIGHLIGHTED** to draw attention to or emphasize something

HIGHLY adverb very; extremely

HIGHNESS noun **HIGHNESSES** an address used for royalty

HIGHTAIL verb **HIGHTAILS, HIGHTAILING, HIGHTAILED** to hurry away

HIGHWAY noun **HIGHWAYS** a public road that everyone has the right to use

HIJAB noun **HIJABS** a hejab

HIJACK verb **HIJACKS, HIJACKING, HIJACKED** to take control of a vehicle, especially an aircraft, and force it to go to an unscheduled destination, often taking any passengers present as hostages

HIJACKER noun **HIJACKERS** a person who hijacks

HIKE noun **HIKES** a long walk, usually in the country ◻ verb **HIKES, HIKING, HIKED** to go on or for a hike

HIKER noun **HIKERS** someone who hikes

HILARIOUS adj extravagantly funny or humorous; merry

HILARITY noun **HILARITIES** merriment; laughter; elation

HILL noun **HILLS** a raised area of land or mound, smaller than a mountain

HILLINESS noun **HILLINESSES** the state of being hilly

HILLOCK noun **HILLOCKS** a small hill

HILLOCKY adj having hillocks

HILLSIDE noun **HILLSIDES** the sloping side of a hill

HILLTOP noun **HILLTOPS** the summit of a hill

HILLY adj **HILLIER, HILLIEST** full of hills

HILT noun **HILTS** the handle, especially of a sword, dagger, knife, etc

HILUM noun **HILA** a scar on the seed of a plant indicating where it was attached to its stalk

HIM pronoun a male person or animal, the object form of *he*

HIMSELF pronoun the reflexive form of *him* and *he*

HIN noun **HINS** a Hebrew liquid measure

HIND adj at the back; referring to the area behind ◻ noun **HINDS** a female red deer, usually older than three years of age

HINDBRAIN noun **HINDBRAINS** the lowest part of the brain containing the cerebellum and the medulla oblongata

HINDER verb **HINDERS, HINDERING, HINDERED** to delay or hold back; to prevent the progress of something

HINDERER noun **HINDERERS** a person or thing that hinders

HINDMOST adj the furthest behind

HINDRANCE noun **HINDRANCES** someone or something that hinders; an obstacle or prevention

HINDSIGHT noun **HINDSIGHTS** wisdom or knowledge after an event

HINGE noun **HINGES** the movable hook or joint by which a door is fastened to a door-frame or a lid is fastened to a box, etc and also on which they turn when opened or closed ◻ verb **HINGES, HINGING, HINGED** to provide a hinge or hinges for something

HINNY noun **HINNIES** the offspring of a stallion and a female donkey or ass

HINT noun **HINTS** a distant or

indirect indication or allusion; an insinuation or implication ◻ verb **HINTS, HINTING, HINTED** to indicate something indirectly

HIP 1 noun **HIPS** the haunch or upper fleshy part of the thigh just below the waist ◻ verb **HIPS, HIPPING, HIPPED** to carry on the hip

HIP 2 adj **HIPPER, HIPPEST** informed about, knowledgeable of, or following, current fashions in music, fashion, etc

HIPPED adj possessing a hip or hips

HIPPIE noun **HIPPIES** especially in the 1960s: someone, typically young, with long hair and wearing brightly-coloured clothes, stressing the importance of self-expression and love, and rebelling against the more conservative standards and values of society

HIPPO noun **HIPPOS** short for hippopotamus

HIPPY adj **HIPPIER, HIPPIEST** having large hips ◻ noun **HIPPIES** a hippie

HIPSTERS plural noun trousers which hang from the hips rather than the waist

HIRABLE adj that can be hired

HIRE verb **HIRES, HIRING, HIRED** to procure the temporary use of something belonging to someone else in exchange for payment ◻ noun **HIRES** payment for the use or hire of something

HIREABLE adj hirable

HIRELING noun **HIRELINGS** a hired servant

HIRSUTE adj hairy; shaggy

HIS adj referring or belonging to a male person or animal ◻ pronoun the one or ones belonging to him

HISPID adj covered with strong hairs and bristles

HISPIDITY noun **HISPIDITIES** the state of being hispid

HISS noun **HISSES** a sharp sibilant sound like a sustained *s* ◻ verb **HISSES, HISSING, HISSED** said of an animal, such as a snake or goose, or a person: to make such a sound, especially as a sign of disapproval or anger

HIST exclamation a demand for silence and attention

HISTAMINE noun **HISTAMINES** a chemical compound released by body tissues during allergic reactions, causing discomfort

HISTIDINE noun **HISTIDINES** an amino acid obtained from proteins

HISTOGENY noun **HISTOGENIES** the development and differentiation of tissues

HISTOGRAM noun **HISTOGRAMS** a statistical graph in which vertical rectangles of differing heights are used to represent a frequency distribution

HISTOLOGY noun **HISTOLOGIES** the study of the microscopic structure of cells and tissues of living organisms

HISTORIAN noun **HISTORIANS** a person who studies or writes about history, often an expert or specialist

HISTORIC adj famous, important or significant in history

HISTORY noun **HISTORIES** an account of past events and developments

HIT verb **HITS, HITTING, HIT** to strike someone or something ▫ noun **HITS** a stroke or blow

HITCH verb **HITCHES, HITCHING, HITCHED** to move something jerkily ▫ noun **HITCHES** a small temporary setback or difficulty

HITCHER noun **HITCHERS** someone who travels, especially long distances, by obtaining free lifts from passing vehicles

HITHER adverb to this place ▫ adj nearer of usually two things

HITHERTO adverb up to this or that time

HIVE noun **HIVES** a box or basket for housing bees ▫ verb **HIVES, HIVING, HIVED** to gather or collect into a hive

HIVES plural noun urticaria, an allergic skin reaction with raised red or white itchy patches

HIYA exclamation a familiar greeting

HIZZ verb **HIZZES, HIZZING, HIZZED** a Shakespearean spelling of *hiss*

HO exclamation a call or shout to attract attention or indicate direction or destination

HOA noun **HOAS** cessation ▫ verb **HOAS, HOAING, HOAED** an obsolete word meaning to stop

HOACTZIN noun **HOACTZINS** a hoatzin

HOAR adj white or greyish-white, especially with age or frost

HOARD noun **HOARDS** a store of money, food or treasure, usually one hidden away for use in the future ▫ verb **HOARDS, HOARDING, HOARDED** to store or gather (food, money or treasure), often secretly, and especially for use in the future

HOARDER noun **HOARDERS** someone who hoards

HOARDING noun **HOARDINGS** a screen of light boards, especially round a building site

HOARINESS noun **HOARINESSES** the state of being hoary

HOARSE adj **HOARSER, HOARSEST** said of the voice: rough and husky, especially because of a sore throat or excessive shouting

HOARSELY adverb in a hoarse way

HOARSEN verb **HOARSENS, HOARSENING, HOARSENED** to make or become hoarse

HOARY adj **HOARIER, HOARIEST** white or grey with age

HOATZIN noun **HOATZINS** a S American bird with a large crop and, while young, a temporary claw used for climbing trees and swimming

HOAX noun **HOAXES** a deceptive trick played either humorously or maliciously ▫ verb **HOAXES, HOAXING, HOAXED** to trick or deceive with a hoax

HOB noun **HOBS** the flat surface on which pots are heated, either on top of a cooker or as a separate piece of equipment

HOBBIT noun **HOBBITS** one of an imaginary race of people, half the size of humans and hairy-footed, living below the ground

HOBBLE verb **HOBBLES, HOBBLING, HOBBLED** to walk awkwardly and unsteadily by taking short unsteady steps ▫ noun **HOBBLES** an awkward and irregular gait

HOBBY noun **HOBBIES** an activity carried out in one's spare time for amusement or relaxation

HOBGOBLIN noun **HOBGOBLINS** a mischievous or evil spirit; a frightful apparition

HOBNAIL noun **HOBNAILS** a short nail with a large strong head for protecting the soles of boots, shoes and horseshoes

HOBNAILED adj furnished with hobnails

HOBNOB verb **HOBNOBS, HOBNOBBING, HOBNOBBED** to associate or spend time with someone socially; to talk informally with someone

HOBO noun **HOBOES, HOBOS** a tramp

HOC adj Latin word for *this* ▫ pronoun Latin word for *this*

HOCK [1] noun **HOCKS** the joint on the hindleg of horses and other hoofed mammals, corresponding to the ankle-joint on a human leg

HOCK [2] verb **HOCKS, HOCKING, HOCKED** to pawn

HOCKEY noun **HOCKEYS** a ball game played by two teams of eleven players with long clubs curved at one end, each team attempting to score goals

HOD [1] noun **HODS** an open V-shaped box on a pole, used for carrying bricks on one's shoulder

HOD [2] verb **HODS, HODDING, HODDED** a Scots word meaning to bob or jog

HODOGRAPH noun **HODOGRAPHS** a curve whose radius vector represents the velocity of a moving point

HODOMETER noun **HODOMETERS** a device for measuring and displaying the distance travelled by a wheeled vehicle or a person, eg the milometer incorporated in the speedometer of a car

HOE noun **HOES** a long-handled tool with a narrow blade at one end, used for loosening soil, digging out and controlling weeds, etc ▫ verb **HOES, HOEING, HOED** to dig, loosen, clean or weed (the ground, etc) using a hoe

HOEDOWN noun **HOEDOWNS** a country dance, especially a square dance

HOG noun **HOGS** a general name for pig ▫ verb **HOGS, HOGGING, HOGGED** to take, use or occupy something selfishly

HOGBACK noun **HOGBACKS** an object, eg a hill-ridge, shaped like a hog's back, by having sides with a sharp crest but gentle end slopes

HOGGET noun **HOGGETS** a yearling sheep or colt

HOGGISH adj characteristic of a hog or pig

HOGGISHLY *adverb* in a hoggish way

HOGSHEAD *noun* **HOGSHEADS** a large cask for liquids

HOGTIE *verb* **HOGTIES, HOGTYING, HOGTIED** to tie someone up so that they are unable to move their arms and legs

HOGWASH *noun* **HOGWASHES** the refuse from a kitchen, brewery, etc given to pigs; pigswill

HOGWEED *noun* **HOGWEEDS** a robust perennial plant with ribbed hairy stems, large coarse leaves, and white or pinkish flowers; the cow-parsnip

HOH *verb* **HOHS, HOHING, HOHED** hoa □ *noun* **HOHS** hoa

HOI *exclamation* a word used to attract attention

HOICK *verb* **HOICKS, HOICKING, HOICKED** to lift up sharply; to heave up

HOIK *verb* **HOIKS, HOIKING, HOIKED** to hoick

HOIST *verb* **HOISTS, HOISTING, HOISTED** to lift or heave something up (especially something heavy) □ *noun* **HOISTS** the act of hoisting

HOISTER *noun* **HOISTERS** someone or something that lifts

HOKKU *noun* **HOKKU** a haiku

HOKUM *noun* **HOKUMS** an action done for the sake of pleasing an audience

HOLD *verb* **HOLDS, HOLDING, HELD** to have or keep something in one's hand or hands; to grasp □ *noun* **HOLDS** the act of holding; a grasp

HOLDER *noun* **HOLDERS** someone or something that holds or grips

HOLDFAST *noun* **HOLDFASTS** something that holds fast or firmly

HOLDING *noun* **HOLDINGS** land held by lease

HOLDOVER *noun* **HOLDOVERS** something or someone held over from a previous era; a relic

HOLE *noun* **HOLES** a hollow area or cavity in something solid □ *verb* **HOLES, HOLING, HOLED** to make a hole in something

HOLEY *adj* **HOLIER, HOLIEST** full of holes

HOLIDAY *noun* **HOLIDAYS** a period of recreational time spent away from work, study or general routine □ *verb* **HOLIDAYS, HOLIDAYING, HOLIDAYED** to

spend or go away for a holiday in a specified place or at a specified time

HOLIER see under **holey, holy**

HOLIEST see under **holey, holy**

HOLILY *adverb* in a holy way

HOLINESS *noun* **HOLINESSES** the state of being holy; sanctity

HOLING a form of **hole**

HOLISM *noun* **HOLISMS** the theory stating that a complex entity or system is more than merely the sum of its parts or elements

HOLIST *noun* **HOLISTS** a believer in holism

HOLISTIC *adj* of or relating to holism

HOLLA *noun* **HOLLAS** a hollo

HOLLAND *noun* **HOLLANDS** a smooth, hard-wearing linen fabric, either unbleached or dyed brown, often used for covering furniture, etc

HOLLER *verb* **HOLLERS, HOLLERING, HOLLERED** to shout or yell □ *noun* **HOLLERS** a shout or yell

HOLLO *noun* **HOLLOS, HOLLOES** an encouraging shout or a call for attention □ *verb* **HOLLOS, HOLLOES, HOLLOING, HOLLOED** to shout

HOLLOW *adj* **HOLLOWER, HOLLOWEST** containing an empty space within or below; not solid □ *noun* **HOLLOWS** a hole or cavity in something □ *verb* **HOLLOWS, HOLLOWING, HOLLOWED** to make a hollow in something; to form something by making a hollow

HOLLOWLY *adverb* in a hollow way

HOLLY *noun* **HOLLIES** an evergreen tree or shrub with dark shiny prickly leaves and red berries, usually used for Christmas decorations

HOLLYHOCK *noun* **HOLLYHOCKS** a tall garden plant of the mallow family, with thick hairy stalks and colourful flowers, brought into Europe from the Holy Land

HOLM *noun* **HOLMS** in placenames: a small island, especially in a river

HOLMIUM *noun* **HOLMIUMS** a soft silver-white metallic element with no apparent uses, though its compounds are highly magnetic

HOLOCAUST *noun* **HOLOCAUSTS** a large-scale slaughter or destruction of life, often by fire

HOLOGRAM *noun* **HOLOGRAMS** a

photograph produced without a lens, by the interference between two split laser beams which, when suitably illuminated, shows a three-dimensional image

HOLOGRAPH *adj* said of a document: completely in the handwriting of the author □ *noun* **HOLOGRAPHS** a holograph document □ *verb* **HOLOGRAPHS, HOLOGRAPHING, HOLOGRAPHED** to make a hologram of something

HOLOPHYTE *noun* **HOLOPHYTES** an organism that is able to obtain its nutrients by generating them from inorganic matter, eg by photosynthesis

HOLS *plural noun* short form of holidays

HOLSTER *noun* **HOLSTERS** a leather pistol-case, usually hung on a saddle or on a belt round a person's hips

HOLT *noun* **HOLTS** an animal's den, especially that of an otter

HOLY *adj* **HOLIER, HOLIEST** associated with God or gods; religious or sacred

HOMAGE *noun* **HOMAGES** a display of great respect towards someone or something; an acknowledgement of their superiority

HOME *noun* **HOMES** the place where one lives, often with one's family □ *adj* being at or belonging to one's home, country, family, sports ground, etc □ *adverb* to or at one's home □ *verb* **HOMES, HOMING, HOMED** to go or find the way home

HOMEBUYER *noun* **HOMEBUYERS** someone in the process of arranging to buy their own home

HOMELAND *noun* **HOMELANDS** one's native country; the country of one's ancestors

HOMELESS *adj* referring to people without a home, who therefore live and sleep in public places or squats

HOMELY *adj* **HOMELIER, HOMELIEST** relating to home; familiar

HOMEOPATH *noun* **HOMEOPATHS** someone who believes in or practises homeopathy

HOMER *noun* **HOMERS** a breed of pigeon that can be trained to return home from a distance

HOMESICK *adj* pining for one's home and family when away from them, with resulting sadness and depression

HOMESPUN *adj* said of character, advice, thinking, etc: artless, simple and straightforward ◻ *noun* **HOMESPUNS** a cloth produced at home

HOMESTEAD *noun* **HOMESTEADS** a dwelling-house and its surrounding land and buildings

HOMEWARD *adj* going home ◻ *adverb* towards home

HOMEWARDS *adverb* towards home

HOMEWORK *noun* **HOMEWORKS** work or study done at home, especially for school

HOMEY *adj* **HOMIER, HOMIEST** homelike; homely

HOMICIDAL *adj* referring or pertaining to homicide

HOMICIDE *noun* **HOMICIDES** the murder or manslaughter of one person by another

HOMILETIC *adj* relating to or involving a homily or sermon

HOMILETICS *singular noun* the art of preaching

HOMILY *noun* **HOMILIES** a sermon, based more on practical than religious teachings

HOMING *adj* said of animals, especially pigeons: trained to return home, usually from a distance

HOMINID *noun* **HOMINIDS** a primate belonging to the family which includes modern man and his fossil ancestors

HOMINOID *adj* resembling man; manlike ◻ *noun* **HOMINOIDS** any member of the primate family, comprising man, the modern apes and their fossil ancestors

HOMINY *noun* **HOMINIES** coarsely ground maize boiled with milk or water to make a porridge

HOMO *noun* **HOMOS** the generic name for modern man and his ancestors

HOMOGAMY *noun* **HOMOGAMIES** a condition in which all the flowers on the same axis or of an inflorescence are sexually alike

HOMOGENY *noun* **HOMOGENIES** a similarity owing to common descent or origin

HOMOGRAPH *noun* **HOMOGRAPHS** a word with the same spelling as another, but with a different meaning, origin, and sometimes a different pronunciation, eg *like* (similar)

and *like* (be fond of), and *entrance* (a way in) and *entrance* (to charm or delight)

HOMOLOG *noun* **HOMOLOGS** a homologue

HOMOLOGUE *noun* **HOMOLOGUES** anything which has a related function or position to something else, such as a human arm and a bird's wing

HOMOLOGY *noun* **HOMOLOGIES** the state of having a related function or position (to something else)

HOMOMORPH *noun* **HOMOMORPHS** something that has the same form as something else

HOMONYM *noun* **HOMONYMS** a word with the same sound and spelling as another, but with a different meaning, eg *kind* (helpful) and *kind* (sort)

HOMOPHOBE *noun* **HOMOPHOBES** a person with a strong aversion to or hatred of homosexuals

HOMOPHONE *noun* **HOMOPHONES** a word which sounds the same as another word but is different in spelling and/or meaning, eg *bear* and *bare*

HOMOPHONY *noun* **HOMOPHONIES** a style of composition in which one part or voice carries the melody, and other parts or voices add texture with simple accompaniment

HOMUNCULE *noun* **HOMUNCULES** a small man; a dwarf

HON *noun* **HONS** short for *honey*, as a term of endearment

HONCHO *noun* **HONCHOS** an important person, especially someone in charge; a big shot

HONE *noun* **HONES** a smooth stone used for sharpening tools ◻ *verb* **HONES, HONING, HONED** to sharpen with or as if with a hone

HONEST *adj* **HONESTER, HONESTEST** not inclined to steal, cheat or lie; truthful and trustworthy ◻ *adverb* honestly

HONESTLY *adverb* in an honest way ◻ *exclamation* expressing annoyance

HONESTY *noun* **HONESTIES** the state of being honest and truthful

HONEY *noun* **HONEYS** a sweet viscous fluid made by bees from the nectar of flowers, and stored in honeycombs, used as a food and

sweetener ◻ *verb* **HONEYS, HONEYING, HONEYED** to sweeten

HONEYCOMB *noun* **HONEYCOMBS** the structure made up of rows of hexagonal wax cells in which bees store their eggs and honey ◻ *verb* **HONEYCOMBS, HONEYCOMBING, HONEYCOMBED** to form like a honeycomb

HONEYED *adj* said of a voice, words, etc: sweet, flattering or soothing

HONEYMOON *noun* **HONEYMOONS** the first weeks after marriage, often spent on holiday, before settling down to the normal routine of life ◻ *verb* **HONEYMOONS, HONEYMOONING, HONEYMOONED** to spend time on a honeymoon

HONIED *adj* honeyed

HONING a form of **hone**

HONK *noun* **HONKS** the cry of a wild goose ◻ *verb* **HONKS, HONKING, HONKED** to make or cause something to make a honking noise

HONOR *noun* **HONORS** honour ◻ *verb* **HONORS, HONORING, HONORED** to honour

HONORAND *noun* **HONORANDS** someone who receives an award, especially an honorary degree

HONORARY *adj* conferring or bestowing honour

HONORIFIC *adj* showing or giving honour or respect ◻ *noun* **HONORIFICS** a form of title, address or mention

HONOUR *noun* **HONOURS** the esteem or respect earned by or paid to a worthy person ◻ *verb* **HONOURS, HONOURING, HONOURED** to respect or venerate; to hold in high esteem

HONOURS *plural noun* said of a university degree: a higher grade of distinction for specialized or advanced work

HOO *exclamation* a Shakespearean exclamation expressing boisterous emotion

HOOCH *noun* **HOOCHS, HOOCHES** any strong alcoholic drink, such as whisky, especially when distilled or obtained illegally

HOOD *noun* **HOODS** a flexible covering for the whole head and back of the neck, often attached to a coat at the collar ◻ *verb* **HOODS,**

HOODING, HOODED to cover with a hood; to blind

HOODED *adj* having, covered with, or shaped like a hood

HOODLUM *noun* **HOODLUMS** a small-time criminal

HOODOO *noun* **HOODOOS** voodoo ▫ *verb* **HOODOOS, HOODOOING, HOODOOED** to bring bad luck to someone

HOODWINK *verb* **HOODWINKS, HOODWINKING, HOODWINKED** to trick or deceive someone into doing something

HOOEY *noun* **HOOEYS** nonsense

HOOF *noun* **HOOFS, HOOVES** the horny structure that grows beneath and covers the ends of the digits in the feet of certain mammals, eg horses ▫ *verb* **HOOFS, HOOFING, HOOFED** to kick or strike with a hoof

HOOFER *noun* **HOOFERS** a professional dancer

HOOK *noun* **HOOKS** a curved piece of metal or similar material, used for catching or holding things ▫ *verb* **HOOKS, HOOKING, HOOKED** to catch, fasten or hold with or as if with a hook

HOOKA *noun* **HOOKAS** a hookah

HOOKAH *noun* **HOOKAHS** a tobacco-pipe used by Turks, Arabs, etc consisting of a tube which passes through water, used to cool the smoke before it is inhaled

HOOKED *adj* curved like a hook

HOOKER *noun* **HOOKERS** someone or something that hooks

HOOKEY *noun* **HOOKEYS** truant (in the phrase *play hookey*)

HOOKY *noun* **HOOKIES** hookey

HOOLIGAN *noun* **HOOLIGANS** a violent, destructive or badly-behaved youth

HOOP *noun* **HOOPS** a thin ring of metal, wood, etc, especially those used round casks ▫ *verb* **HOOPS, HOOPING, HOOPED** to bind or surround with a hoop or hoops

HOOPOE *noun* **HOOPOES** a crested bird with salmon-coloured feathers and black-and-white striped wings

HOORAH *exclamation* a shout of joy, enthusiasm or victory ▫ *verb* **HOORAHS, HOORAHING, HOORAHED** to shout 'hoorah'

HOORAY *exclamation* a shout of joy, enthusiasm or victory ▫ *verb* **HOORAYS, HOORAYING, HOORAYED** to shout 'hooray'

HOOSEGOW *noun* **HOOSEGOWS** a prison or jail

HOOSGOW *noun* **HOOSGOWS** a hoosegow

HOOT *noun* **HOOTS** the call of an owl, or a similar sound ▫ *verb* **HOOTS, HOOTING, HOOTED** said of an owl: to make a hoot

HOOTCH *noun* **HOOTCHES** hooch

HOOTER *noun* **HOOTERS** a person or thing that makes a hooting sound

HOOTNANNY *noun* **HOOTNANNIES** an informal concert of folk music

HOOVER *noun* **HOOVERS** a vacuum cleaner ▫ *verb* **HOOVERS, HOOVERING, HOOVERED** to clean (a carpet, etc) with or as if with a vacuum cleaner

HOOVES a plural of **hoof**

HOP *verb* **HOPS, HOPPING, HOPPED** said of a person: to jump up and down on one leg, especially forwards as a form of movement ▫ *noun* **HOPS** an act of hopping; a jump on one leg

HOPE *noun* **HOPES** a desire for something, with some confidence or expectation of success ▫ *verb* **HOPES, HOPING, HOPED** to wish or desire that something may happen, especially with some reason to believe or expect that it will

HOPEFUL *adj* feeling, or full of, hope ▫ *noun* **HOPEFULS** a person, especially a young one, who is ambitious or expected to succeed

HOPEFULLY *adverb* in a hopeful way

HOPELESS *adj* without hope

HOPPER *noun* **HOPPERS** a person, animal or insect that hops

HOPPING *noun* **HOPPINGS** the time of the hop harvest

HOPPY *adj* **HOPPIER, HOPPIEST** smelling or tasting of hops

HOPSACK *noun* **HOPSACKS** a coarse fabric made from hemp and jute, used to make sacking for hops

HOPSCOTCH *noun* **HOPSCOTCHES** a children's game in which players take turns at throwing a stone into one of a series of squares marked on the ground, and hopping in the others around it in order to fetch it

HORDE *noun* **HORDES** a huge crowd or multitude, especially a noisy one ▫ *verb* **HORDES, HORDING, HORDED** to come together to form a horde

HORIZON *noun* **HORIZONS** the line at which the Earth and the sky seem to meet

HORMONAL *adj* relating to or involving hormones

HORMONE *noun* **HORMONES** a substance secreted by an endocrine gland, and carried in the bloodstream to organs and tissues located elsewhere in the body, where it performs a specific physiological action

HORN *noun* **HORNS** one of a pair of hard hollow outgrowths, usually pointed, on the heads of many ruminant animals, such as cattle, sheep, etc ▫ *verb* **HORNS, HORNING, HORNED** to fit with a horn or horns ▫ *adj* made of horn

HORNBEAM *noun* **HORNBEAMS** a tree similar to a beech, with hard tough wood

HORNBILL *noun* **HORNBILLS** a tropical bird with a horn-like growth on its beak

HORNBOOK *noun* **HORNBOOKS** a first book for children, consisting of a single page of basic information, such as the alphabet and numbers, and covered with a thin plate of semitransparent horn for protection

HORNED *adj* having a horn or horns, or something shaped like a horn

HORNET *noun* **HORNETS** any of several large social wasps, with a brown and yellow striped body, and a more painful sting

HORNFELS *noun* **HORNFELS** any of various hard fine-grained rocks that are formed from sedimentary rocks under heat and/or pressure

HORNPIPE *noun* **HORNPIPES** an old Welsh musical instrument, often with a mouthpiece or bell made from horn; a lively solo jig

HORNY *adj* **HORNIER, HORNIEST** relating to or resembling horn, especially in hardness

HOROLOGER *noun* **HOROLOGERS** an expert in horology

HOROLOGIC *adj* relating or referring to horology

HOROLOGY *noun* **HOROLOGIES** the art of measuring time or of making clocks and watches

HOROSCOPE *noun* **HOROSCOPES** an astrologer's prediction of someone's future based on the position of the stars and planets at the time of their birth

HOROSCOPY *noun* **HOROSCOPIES** the art of predicting someone's future from their horoscope

HORRIBLE *adj* causing horror, dread or fear

HORRIBLY *adverb* in a horrible way

HORRID *adj* **HORRIDER, HORRIDEST** revolting; detestable or nasty

HORRIDLY *adverb* in a horrid way

HORRIFIC *adj* causing horror; terrible or frightful

HORRIFIED *adj* greatly shocked; moved to horror

HORRIFY *verb* **HORRIFIES, HORRIFYING, HORRIFIED** to shock greatly; to cause a reaction of horror

HORRIFYING *adj* causing horror

HORROR *noun* **HORRORS** intense fear, loathing or disgust

HORSE *noun* **HORSES** a large hoofed mammal, with a slender head, a long neck, a mane and long legs, used in many countries for pulling and carrying loads, and for riding ▫ *verb* **HORSES, HORSING, HORSED** to mount or put someone on, or as if on, a horse

HORSEBACK *noun* **HORSEBACKS** the back of a horse

HORSEFLY *noun* **HORSEFLIES** any of several large flies that bite horses and cattle

HORSEHAIR *noun* **HORSEHAIRS** a hair or mass of hairs taken from a horse's mane or tail ▫ *adj* made of or filled with horsehair

HORSEMAN *noun* **HORSEMEN** a horse rider

HORSEPLAY *noun* **HORSEPLAYS** rough boisterous play

HORSESHOE *noun* **HORSESHOES** a piece of curved iron nailed to the bottom of a horse's hoof to protect the foot

HORSETAIL *noun* **HORSETAILS** the tail of a horse

HORSEWHIP *noun* **HORSEWHIPS** a long whip, used for driving or managing horses ▫ *verb* **HORSEWHIPS, HORSEWHIPPING, HORSEWHIPPED** to beat, especially severely, with a horsewhip

HORSEY *adj* **HORSIER, HORSIEST** referring or relating to horses; very interested in horses

HORSINESS *noun* **HORSINESSES** the state of being horsey

HORST *noun* **HORSTS** a block of the Earth's crust that has remained in position while the ground around it has subsided, due to one or more faults in the surrounding area

HORSY *adj* **HORSIER, HORSIEST** horsey

HORTATION *noun* **HORTATIONS** the action of giving advice or encouragement

HORTATIVE *adj* giving advice or encouragement

HORTATORY *adj* hortative

HOSANNA *exclamation* a shout of adoration and praise to God

HOSE 1 *noun* **HOSES** a flexible tube for conveying water, eg for watering plants ▫ *verb* **HOSES, HOSING, HOSED** to direct water at something or clean something with a hose

HOSE 2 *noun* **HOSE, HOSEN** a covering for the legs and feet, such as stockings, socks and tights

HOSIER *noun* **HOSIERS** a person who makes or deals in hosiery

HOSIERY *noun* **HOSIERIES** stockings, socks and tights collectively

HOSPICE *noun* **HOSPICES** a home or institution that specializes in the care of the terminally ill, and provides support for their families

HOSPITAL *noun* **HOSPITALS** an institution, staffed by doctors and nurses, for the treatment and care of people who are sick or injured

HOST *noun* **HOSTS** someone who entertains guests or strangers in his or her own home ▫ *verb* **HOSTS, HOSTING, HOSTED** to be the host of (an event, programme, show, etc)

HOSTA *noun* **HOSTAS** a perennial plant native to China and Japan, grown for its decorative ribbed leaves and spikes of tubular white or violet flowers

HOSTAGE *noun* **HOSTAGES** someone who is held prisoner as a guarantee or security that the captor's demands and conditions are carried out and fulfilled

HOSTEL *noun* **HOSTELS** a residence providing shelter for the homeless, especially one run for charitable rather than for profitable purposes

HOSTELER *noun* **HOSTELERS** a hosteller

HOSTELLER *noun* **HOSTELLERS** someone who lives in or regularly uses a hostel, especially a youth hostel

HOSTELRY *noun* **HOSTELRIES** an inn or public house

HOSTESS *noun* **HOSTESSES** a female host

HOSTILE *adj* expressing enmity, aggression or angry opposition

HOSTILELY *adverb* in a hostile way

HOSTILITY *noun* **HOSTILITIES** enmity, aggression or angry opposition

HOT *adj* **HOTTER, HOTTEST** having or producing a great deal of heat; having a high temperature ▫ *adverb* in a hot way ▫ *verb* **HOTS, HOTTING, HOTTED** to heat something

HOTBED *noun* **HOTBEDS** a glass-covered bed of earth heated by a layer of fermenting manure, to encourage rapid plant growth

HOTEL *noun* **HOTELS** a commercial building providing accommodation, meals and other services to visitors for payment

HOTELIER *noun* **HOTELIERS** a person who owns or manages a hotel

HOTFOOT *adverb* in haste; as fast as possible ▫ *verb* **HOTFOOTS, HOTFOOTING, HOTFOOTED** to rush or hasten

HOTHEAD *noun* **HOTHEADS** an easily angered or agitated person

HOTHEADED *adj* impetuous and headstrong

HOTHOUSE *noun* **HOTHOUSES** a greenhouse which is kept warm for growing tender or tropical plants

HOTLY *adverb* with great heat; excitedly or passionately

HOTNESS *noun* **HOTNESSES** the state of being hot

HOTPOT *noun* **HOTPOTS** chopped meat and vegetables, seasoned and covered with sliced potatoes, and cooked slowly in a sealed pot

HOTSHOT *noun* **HOTSHOTS** a person who is, often boastfully or pretentiously, successful or skilful

HOTTED past form of **hot**

HOTTER see under **hot**

HOTTEST see under **hot**

HOTTING *noun* **HOTTINGS** the performing of stunts and skilful manoeuvres at high speed in a stolen car

HOUDAH *noun* **HOUDAHS** a howdah

HOUMMOS *noun* **HOUMMOSES** hummus

HOUMUS *noun* **HOUMUSES** hummus

HOUND noun **HOUNDS** a dog ❑ verb **HOUNDS, HOUNDING, HOUNDED** to chase or bother relentlessly

HOUR noun **HOURS** sixty minutes, or the twenty-fourth part of a day

HOURI noun **HOURIS** a nymph in the Muslim Paradise

HOURLY adj happening or done every hour ❑ adverb every hour

HOUSE noun **HOUSES** a building in which people, especially a single family, live ❑ verb **HOUSES, HOUSING, HOUSED** to provide with a house or similar shelter

HOUSEBOAT noun **HOUSEBOATS** a barge or boat, usually stationary, with a deck-cabin designed and built for living in

HOUSECOAT noun **HOUSECOATS** a woman's long loose garment similar to a dressing-gown, worn in the home

HOUSEFLY noun **HOUSEFLIES** a common fly often found in houses

HOUSEHOLD noun **HOUSEHOLDS** the people who live together in a house, making up a family ❑ adj relating to the house or family living there; domestic

HOUSEMAID noun **HOUSEMAIDS** a maid employed to keep a house clean and tidy

HOUSEMAN noun **HOUSEMEN** a recently qualified doctor holding a junior resident post in a hospital to complete their training

HOUSEROOM noun **HOUSEROOMS** room in one's house for accommodating someone or something

HOUSETOP noun **HOUSETOPS** the roof of a house, especially seen in a row against the skyline

HOUSEWIFE noun **HOUSEWIVES** a woman who looks after the house, her husband or partner, and the family, and who often does not have a paid job outside the home

HOUSEWORK noun **HOUSEWORKS** the work involved in keeping a house clean and tidy

HOUSING noun **HOUSINGS** an ornamental covering or saddle-cloth for a horse

HOVE a past form of **heave**

HOVEL noun **HOVELS** a small, dirty and dismal dwelling

HOVER verb **HOVERS, HOVERING, HOVERED** said of a bird, helicopter, etc: to remain in the air without moving in any direction ❑ noun **HOVERS** an act or state of hovering

HOVERPORT noun **HOVERPORTS** a port for hovercraft, a vehicle able to move over land or water, supported by down-driven air

HOW adverb in what way; by what means ❑ conj in which manner or condition ❑ noun **HOWS** a manner or means of doing something

HOWBEIT conj be it how it may; however

HOWDAH noun **HOWDAHS** a seat, usually one with a sun-shade, used for riding on an elephant's back

HOWDY exclamation hello

HOWEVER adverb in spite of that; nevertheless ❑ conj in spite of that; nevertheless

HOWITZER noun **HOWITZERS** a short heavy gun which fires shells high in the air and at a steep angle, especially used in trench warfare

HOWL noun **HOWLS** a long mournful cry of a wolf or dog ❑ verb **HOWLS, HOWLING, HOWLED** to make a long, mournful cry or similar wailing noise

HOWLER noun **HOWLERS** someone or something that howls

HOWLING adj very great; tremendous

HOWSOEVER adverb in whatever way; to whatever extent

HOWZAT exclamation in cricket: an appeal to the umpire to give the batsman out

---

HOX verb **HOXES, HOXING, HOXED** Shakespearean word meaning to hock or hamstring

---

HOY noun **HOYS** a large one-decked boat, usually rigged as a sloop

HOYDEN noun **HOYDENS** a wild lively girl; a tomboy

HOYDENISH adj boisterous

HOYDENISM noun **HOYDENISMS** the character of a hoyden

HUB noun **HUBS** the centre of a wheel; a nave

HUBBUB noun **HUBBUBS** a confused noise of many sounds, especially voices

HUBBY noun **HUBBIES** an affectionate contraction of husband

HUBRIS noun **HUBRISES** arrogance or over-confidence, especially when likely to result in disaster or ruin

HUBRISTIC adj contemptuous

HUCKABACK noun **HUCKABACKS** a coarse linen or cotton fabric with alternately woven threads forming a raised surface, used for towels, etc

HUCKSTER noun **HUCKSTERS** a street trader; a hawker or pedlar ❑ verb **HUCKSTERS, HUCKSTERING, HUCKSTERED** to hawk or peddle (goods, etc)

HUDDLE verb **HUDDLES, HUDDLING, HUDDLED** to heap or crowd together closely, eg because of cold ❑ noun **HUDDLES** a confused mass or crowd

HUDDLED adj crouching or curled up

HUE noun **HUES** a colour, tint or shade

HUED adj having a hue of a specified kind

HUELESS adj lacking colour

HUFF noun **HUFFS** a fit of anger, annoyance or offended dignity ❑ verb **HUFFS, HUFFING, HUFFED** to blow or puff loudly

HUFFILY adverb in a huffy way

HUFFINESS noun **HUFFINESSES** the state of being huffy

HUFFISH adj offended

HUFFY adj **HUFFIER, HUFFIEST** offended

HUG verb **HUGS, HUGGING, HUGGED** to hold tightly in one's arms, especially to show love ❑ noun **HUGS** a tight grasp with the arms; a close embrace

HUGE adj **HUGER, HUGEST** very large or enormous

HUGELY adj very; very much

HUGENESS noun **HUGENESSES** the quality or condition of being huge

HUGGABLE adj pleasant to hug

HUH exclamation expressing disgust, disbelief or inquiry

HUI noun **HUI, HUIS** a Maori gathering; a social gathering

HULA noun **HULAS** a Hawaiian dance in which the dancer, usually a woman, sways their hips and moves their arms gracefully

HULK noun **HULKS** the dismantled body of an old ship

HULKING adj big and clumsy

HULL noun **HULLS** the frame or body of a ship or airship ❑ verb **HULLS, HULLING, HULLED** to pierce the hull of (a ship, etc)

HULLO exclamation used as a greeting ❑ verb **HULLOS, HULLOING, HULLOED** to greet someone by saying 'hullo'

HUM *verb* **HUMS, HUMMING, HUMMED** to make a low, steady murmuring sound similar to that made by a bee ▫ *noun* **HUMS** a humming sound ▫ *exclamation* expressing embarrassment or hesitation

HUMAN *adj* referring or belonging to people ▫ *noun* **HUMANS** a human being

HUMANE *adj* **HUMANER, HUMANEST** kind and sympathetic

HUMANELY *adverb* in a humane way

HUMANISE *verb* **HUMANISES, HUMANISING, HUMANISED** to humanize

HUMANISM *noun* **HUMANISMS** a system of thought which rejects the supernatural, any belief in a god, etc, but holds that human interests and the human mind are paramount, that humans are capable of solving the problems of the world and deciding what is or is not correct moral behaviour

HUMANIST *noun* **HUMANISTS** a follower of humanism

HUMANITY *noun* **HUMANITIES** the human race; mankind

HUMANIZE *verb* **HUMANIZES, HUMANIZING, HUMANIZED** to render, make or become human

HUMANKIND *noun* **HUMANKINDS** the human species

HUMANLY *adverb* in a human or humane way

HUMANNESS *noun* **HUMANNESSES** the state of being human

HUMANOID *noun* **HUMANOIDS** any of the ancestors from which modern humankind is descended and to which they are immediately related, more closely than to anthropoids

HUMBLE *adj* **HUMBLER, HUMBLEST** having a low opinion of oneself and one's abilities, etc ▫ *verb* **HUMBLES, HUMBLING, HUMBLED** to make humble or modest

HUMBLING *adj* that makes humble or modest

HUMBLY *adverb* in a humble way

HUMBUG *noun* **HUMBUGS** a trick or deception ▫ *verb* **HUMBUGS, HUMBUGGING, HUMBUGGED** to deceive or hoax ▫ *exclamation* expressing annoyance or irritation

HUMDINGER *noun* **HUMDINGERS** an exceptionally good person or thing

HUMDRUM *adj* dull or monotonous; ordinary ▫ *noun* **HUMDRUMS** a dull or stupid person

HUMECTANT *adj* moistening; dampening ▫ *noun* **HUMECTANTS** a substance used to retain moisture or prevent moisture loss in another substance

HUMERAL *adj* relating to or in the region of the humerus or shoulders

HUMERUS *noun* **HUMERI** the bone in the upper arm

HUMIC *adj* of or relating to humus

HUMID *adj* **HUMIDER, HUMIDEST** damp; moist

HUMIDIFY *verb* **HUMIDIFIES, HUMIDIFYING, HUMIDIFIED** to make something damp or humid (eg the air or atmosphere)

HUMIDITY *noun* **HUMIDITIES** the amount of water vapour in the atmosphere, usually expressed as a percentage

HUMIDLY *adverb* in a humid way

HUMIDNESS *noun* **HUMIDNESSES** humidity

HUMIDOR *noun* **HUMIDORS** a box or room for keeping cigars or tobacco moist

HUMIFY *verb* **HUMIFIES, HUMIFYING, HUMIFIED** to make or turn into humus

HUMILIATE *verb* **HUMILIATES, HUMILIATING, HUMILIATED** to injure someone's pride, or make them feel ashamed or look foolish, especially in the presence of others

HUMILIATING *adj* that injures someone's pride, or makes them feel ashamed or look foolish, especially in the presence of others

HUMILITY *noun* **HUMILITIES** the quality or state of being humble

HUMMABLE *adj* capable of being hummed

HUMMOCK *noun* **HUMMOCKS** a low hill; a hillock

HUMMOCKY *adj* **HUMMOCKIER, HUMMOCKIEST** characterized by hummocks

HUMMUS *noun* **HUMMUSES** a Middle-Eastern hors d'oeuvre or dip containing puréed cooked chickpeas and tahini, flavoured with lemon juice and garlic

HUMONGOUS *adj* huge or enormous

HUMOR *noun* **HUMORS** humour ▫ *verb* **HUMORS, HUMORING, HUMORED** to humour

HUMORAL *adj* referring or relating to body fluid

HUMORIST *noun* **HUMORISTS** someone with a talent for talking, behaving or writing humorously

HUMOROUS *adj* containing humour; funny or amusing

HUMOUR *noun* **HUMOURS** the quality of being amusing ▫ *verb* **HUMOURS, HUMOURING, HUMOURED** to please or gratify someone by doing what they wish

HUMOUS *adj* of or relating to humus

HUMP *noun* **HUMPS** a large rounded lump of fat on the back of a camel that serves as an energy store when food is scarce ▫ *verb* **HUMPS, HUMPING, HUMPED** to hunch or bend in a hump

HUMPBACK *noun* **HUMPBACKS** a back with a hump or hunch

HUMPH *exclamation* expressing doubt, displeasure or hesitation

HUMPY *adj* **HUMPIER, HUMPIEST** having a hump or humps

HUMUNGOUS *adj* humongous

HUMUS *noun* **HUMUSES** dark-brown organic material produced in the topmost layer of soil due to the decomposition of plant and animal matter

HUNCH *noun* **HUNCHES** an idea, guess or belief based on feelings, suspicions or intuition rather than on actual evidence ▫ *verb* **HUNCHES, HUNCHING, HUNCHED** to bend or arch; to hump

HUNCHBACK *noun* **HUNCHBACKS** someone with a large rounded lump on their back, due to spinal deformity

HUNDRED *noun* **HUNDREDS** the number which is ten times ten ▫ *adj* totalling or to the number of 100

HUNDREDTH *adj* the last of 100 people or things ▫ *noun* **HUNDREDTHS** one of 100 equal parts

HUNG *adj* said of a parliament or jury: with neither side having a majority

HUNGER *noun* **HUNGERS** the desire or need for food ▫ *verb* **HUNGERS, HUNGERING, HUNGERED** to crave or long for food

HUNGRILY *adverb* in a hungry way

HUNGRY *adj* **HUNGRIER, HUNGRIEST** having a need or craving for food

HUNK *noun* **HUNKS** a lump or piece, sometimes broken or cut off from a larger piece

HUNKY *adj* **HUNKIER, HUNKIEST** said of a man: strong, muscular and sexually attractive

HUNT *verb* **HUNTS, HUNTING, HUNTED** to chase and kill (animals) for food or sport □ *noun* **HUNTS** the act of hunting

HUNTER *noun* **HUNTERS** someone who hunts

HUNTING *noun* **HUNTINGS** the activity or sport of pursuing, capturing or killing wild animals

HUNTRESS *noun* **HUNTRESSES** a female hunter, especially applied to the goddess Diana

HUNTSMAN *noun* **HUNTSMEN** someone who hunts

HUP *verb* **HUPS, HUPPING, HUPPED** to turn (a horse) to the right □ *noun* **HUPS** a cry requesting such a turn

HURDLE *noun* **HURDLES** one of a series of portable frames, hedges or barriers to be jumped in a race □ *verb* **HURDLES, HURDLING, HURDLED** to jump over (a hurdle in a race, an obstacle, etc)

HURDLER *noun* **HURDLERS** a person or horse that runs hurdle races

HURDLING *noun* **HURDLINGS** racing over hurdles

HURL *verb* **HURLS, HURLING, HURLED** to fling violently □ *noun* **HURLS** an act of hurling

HURLEY *noun* **HURLEYS** hurling

HURLING *noun* **HURLINGS** a traditional Irish game resembling hockey, played by two teams of 15, with curved broad-bladed sticks and a hide-covered cork ball

HURRAH *exclamation* a shout of joy, enthusiasm or victory □ *verb* **HURRAHS, HURRAHING, HURRAHED** to shout or cheer 'hurrah'

HURRICANE *noun* **HURRICANES** an intense, often devastating, cyclonic tropical storm with average wind speeds exceeding 118kph, or force 12 on the Beaufort scale

HURRIED *adj* carried out or forced to act quickly, especially too quickly

HURRIEDLY *adverb* in a hurried way

HURRY *verb* **HURRIES, HURRYING, HURRIED** to urge forward or hasten; to make someone or something move or act quickly □ *noun* **HURRIES** great haste or speed; a driving forward

HURT *verb* **HURTS, HURTING, HURT** to injure or cause physical pain to someone □ *noun* **HURTS** an injury or wound □ *adj* aggrieved; upset

HURTFUL *adj* causing mental pain; emotionally harmful

HURTFULLY *adverb* in a hurtful way

HURTLE *verb* **HURTLES, HURTLING, HURTLED** to move or throw very quickly or noisily

HUSBAND *noun* **HUSBANDS** a man to whom a woman is married □ *verb* **HUSBANDS, HUSBANDING, HUSBANDED** to manage (money, resources, etc) wisely and economically

HUSBANDRY *noun* **HUSBANDRIES** the farming business

HUSH *exclamation* silence!; be still! □ *noun* **HUSHES** silence or calm, especially after noise □ *verb* **HUSHES, HUSHING, HUSHED** to make or become silent, calm or still

HUSHABY *noun* **HUSHABIES** a lullaby used to soothe or lull babies to sleep □ *verb* **HUSHABIES, HUSHABYING, HUSHABIED** to soothe or lull to sleep

HUSHED *adj* silent; very quiet or calm

HUSK *noun* **HUSKS** the thin dry covering of certain fruits and seeds □ *verb* **HUSKS, HUSKING, HUSKED** to remove the husk of (a fruit, etc)

HUSKILY *adverb* in a husky way

HUSKINESS *noun* **HUSKINESSES** the quality or condition of being husky

HUSKY *adj* **HUSKIER, HUSKIEST** said of a voice: rough and dry in sound □ *noun* **HUSKIES** an Inuit dog with a thick coat and curled tail, used as a sledge-dog in the Arctic

HUSSAR *noun* **HUSSARS** a soldier in a cavalry regiment who carries only light weapons

HUSSY *noun* **HUSSIES** an immoral or promiscuous girl or woman

HUSTINGS *singular or plural noun* **HUSTINGS** the platform, etc from which speeches are given by candidates during a political election campaign

HUSTLE *verb* **HUSTLES, HUSTLING, HUSTLED** to push or shove quickly and roughly; to jostle □ *noun* **HUSTLES** lively or frenzied activity

HUSTLER *noun* **HUSTLERS** a lively or energetic person

HUT *noun* **HUTS** a small and crudely built house, usually made of wood □ *verb* **HUTS, HUTTING, HUTTED** to quarter (troops) in a hut or huts

HUTCH *noun* **HUTCHES** a box, usually made of wood and with a wire-netting front, in which small animals, eg rabbits, are kept

HUTMENT *noun* **HUTMENTS** an encampment of huts

HYACINTH *noun* **HYACINTHS** a plant of the lily family, which grows from a bulb, and has sweet-smelling clusters of purple, pink or white flowers

HYAENA *noun* **HYAENAS** a hyena

HYALINE *adj* referring to or like glass; clear or transparent

HYALINISE *verb* **HYALINISES, HYALINISING, HYALINISED** to hyalinize

HYALINIZE *verb* **HYALINIZES, HYALINIZING, HYALINIZED** said of tissue: to change into a firm, glassy consistency

HYALITE *noun* **HYALITES** a transparent colourless opal

HYALOID *adj* clear and transparent; hyaline

HYBRID *noun* **HYBRIDS** an animal or plant produced by crossing two different species, varieties, races or breeds; a mongrel □ *adj* being produced by combining elements from different sources; mongrel

HYBRIDISE *verb* **HYBRIDISES, HYBRIDISING, HYBRIDISED** to hybridize

HYBRIDISM *noun* **HYBRIDISMS** the state of being hybrid

HYBRIDITY *noun* **HYBRIDITIES** the state of being hybrid

HYBRIDIZE *verb* **HYBRIDIZES, HYBRIDIZING, HYBRIDIZED** to cause different species, etc to breed together or interbreed

HYBRIDOMA *noun* **HYBRIDOMAS** a hybrid cell formed by combining a cancer cell with an antibody-producing cell

HYDATID *noun* **HYDATIDS** a watery cyst or vesicle formed in the body of an animal, especially one containing a tapeworm larva □ *adj* containing or resembling a hydatid

HYDRA *noun* **HYDRAS** a freshwater polyp with a tube-like body and tentacles round the mouth, remarkable for its ability to multiply when cut or divided

HYDRANGEA *noun* **HYDRANGEAS** a garden shrub, native to China and Japan, that has large clusters of white, pink or blue flowers

HYDRANT *noun* **HYDRANTS** a pipe connected to the main water supply, especially in a street, with a nozzle for attaching a hose when fighting fires

HYDRATE *noun* **HYDRATES** a compound containing water which is chemically combined, and which may be expelled without affecting the composition of the other substance ▫ *verb* **HYDRATES, HYDRATING, HYDRATED** to form (such a compound) by combining with water

HYDRATION *noun* **HYDRATIONS** the process whereby water molecules become attached to the constituent ions of a solute as it is being dissolved in water

HYDRAULIC *adj* relating to hydraulics

HYDRAULICS *singular noun* the science of hydrodynamics, or the mechanical properties of fluids, especially water, at rest or in motion, and their practical applications, eg to water pipes

HYDRIC *adj* relating to or containing hydrogen

HYDRIDE *noun* **HYDRIDES** a chemical compound of hydrogen with another element or radical

HYDRO *noun* **HYDROS** a hotel or clinic, often situated near a spa, providing hydropathic treatment

HYDROCELE *noun* **HYDROCELES** a swelling containing serous fluid, often in the scrotum

HYDROFOIL *noun* **HYDROFOILS** a device on a boat which raises it out of the water as it accelerates

HYDROGEN *noun* **HYDROGENS** a flammable colourless odourless gas which is the lightest of all known substances and by far the most abundant element in the universe

HYDROID *adj* belonging, referring or similar to a hydra; polypoid ▫ *noun* **HYDROIDS** a type of coelenterate which reproduces asexually; a polyp

HYDROLOGY *noun* **HYDROLOGIES** the scientific study of the

occurrence, movement and properties of water on the Earth's surface, and in the atmosphere

HYDROLYSE *verb* **HYDROLYSES, HYDROLYSING, HYDROLYSED** to subject to or occur by hydrolysis

HYDROLYTE *noun* **HYDROLYTES** a body subjected to hydrolysis

HYDROLYZE *verb* **HYDROLYZES, HYDROLYZING, HYDROLYZED** to hydrolyse

HYDROMEL *noun* **HYDROMELS** mead

HYDROUS *adj* said of a substance: containing water

HYDROXIDE *noun* **HYDROXIDES** a chemical compound containing one or more hydroxyl groups

HYDROXYL *noun* **HYDROXYLS** a compound radical containing one oxygen atom and one hydrogen atom

HYDROZOAN *noun* **HYDROZOANS** a coelenterate of the mainly marine class Hydrozoa, in which alternation of generations typically occurs, eg the zoophytes ▫ *adj* of or belonging to the class Hydrozoa

HYE *verb* **HYES, HYEING, HYED** an obsolete form of *hie* or *high*

HYENA *noun* **HYENAS** any of various kinds of carrion-feeding doglike mammals native to Africa and Asia, which have a long thick neck, coarse mane, and a sloping body, and known for their howls which resemble hysterical laughter

HYGIENE *noun* **HYGIENES** the practice or study of preserving one's health and preventing the spread of disease, especially by keeping oneself and one's surroundings clean

HYGIENIC *adj* promoting and preserving health; sanitary

HYGIENICS *singular noun* the principles of hygiene

HYGIENIST *noun* **HYGIENISTS** a person skilled in the practice of hygiene

HYGROLOGY *noun* **HYGROLOGIES** the study of humidity in gases, especially the atmosphere

HYING a form of **hie**

HYMEN *noun* **HYMENS** a thin membrane that covers the opening of the vagina, and may be broken the first time a woman has sexual intercourse, but is usually at least partially ruptured before puberty

HYMENAL *adj* relating to the hymen

HYMN *noun* **HYMNS** a song of praise, especially to God, but also to a nation, etc ▫ *verb* **HYMNS, HYMNING, HYMNED** to celebrate in song or worship by hymns

HYMNAL *noun* **HYMNALS** a book containing hymns ▫ *adj* referring or relating to hymns

HYMNARY *noun* **HYMNARIES** a hymnal

HYMNIC *adj* hymnal

HYMNIST *noun* **HYMNISTS** someone who composes hymns

HYMNODIST *noun* **HYMNODISTS** someone who composes hymns

HYMNODY *noun* **HYMNODIES** the writing or singing of hymns

HYMNOLOGY *noun* **HYMNOLOGIES** the study or composition of hymns

HYOID *adj* referring to the hyoid bone, a curved bone at the base of the tongue

HYOSCINE *noun* **HYOSCINES** an alkaloid drug obtained from certain plants, eg henbane, with actions on the intestines and nervous system, given for travel sickness, used as a truth drug, etc

HYP *verb* **HYPS, HYPPING, HYPPED** to offend

HYPALLAGE *noun* **HYPALLAGES** a figure of speech where the standard relations of words are mutually interchanged

HYPE *noun* **HYPES** intensive, exaggerated or artificially induced excitement about, or enthusiasm for, something or someone ▫ *verb* **HYPES, HYPING, HYPED** to promote or advertise something intensively

HYPER *adj* said of a person: over-excited; over-stimulated

HYPERBOLA *noun* **HYPERBOLAS** the curve produced when a plane cuts through a cone so that the angle between the base of the cone and the plane is greater than the angle between the base and the sloping side of the cone

HYPERBOLE *noun* **HYPERBOLES** the use of an overstatement or exaggeration for effect

HYPEREMIA *noun* **HYPEREMIAS** an excess or congestion of blood in any part or organ of the body

HYPERLINK *noun* **HYPERLINKS** a link between pieces of information in various media (hypermedia), such as text, graphics, video clips, etc

HYPERON noun **HYPERONS** any of a class of elementary particles with masses greater than that of a neutron

HYPERTEXT noun **HYPERTEXTS** computer-readable text in which cross-reference links (hyperlinks) have been inserted, enabling the user to call up relevant data from other files, or parts of the same file, by clicking on a coded word or symbol, etc

HYPHA noun **HYPHAE** in multicellular fungi: any of many thread-like filaments that form the mycelium

HYPHAL adj of or relating to the hyphae of a fungus

HYPHEN noun **HYPHENS** a punctuation mark (-) used to join two words to form a compound (eg, *booby-trap, double-barrelled*) or, in texts, to split a word between the end of one line and the beginning of the next □ verb **HYPHENS, HYPHENING, HYPHENED** to hyphenate

HYPHENATE verb **HYPHENATES, HYPHENATING, HYPHENATED** to join or separate two words or parts of words with a hyphen

HYPHENATED adj containing a hyphen

HYPNOID adj in a state like or similar to sleep or hypnosis

HYPNOIDAL adj hypnoid

HYPNOLOGY noun **HYPNOLOGIES** the scientific study of sleep and hypnosis

HYPNOSIS noun **HYPNOSES** an induced sleeplike state in which a person is deeply relaxed, and in which the mind responds to external suggestion and can recover memories of events thought to have been forgotten

HYPNOTIC adj relating to, causing or caused by, hypnosis □ noun **HYPNOTICS** a drug that produces sleep

HYPNOTISE verb **HYPNOTISES, HYPNOTISING, HYPNOTISED** to hypnotize

HYPNOTISM noun **HYPNOTISMS** the science or practice of hypnosis

HYPNOTIST noun **HYPNOTISTS** a person who practises or is skilled in hypnotism

HYPNOTIZE verb **HYPNOTIZES, HYPNOTIZING, HYPNOTIZED** to put someone in a state of hypnosis

HYPO noun **HYPOS** a hypodermic syringe or injection

HYPOBLAST noun **HYPOBLASTS** the inner layer of the gastrula

HYPOCAUST noun **HYPOCAUSTS** in ancient Rome: a form of heating system in which hot air was passed through a hollow space between the walls and under the floor

HYPOCRISY noun **HYPOCRISIES** the act of pretending to have feelings, beliefs or principles which one does not actually have

HYPOCRITE noun **HYPOCRITES** a person who practises hypocrisy

HYPODERMA noun **HYPODERMAS** the tissue beneath the epidermis or surface

HYPOGEAL adj existing or growing underground

HYPOGEAN adj hypogeal

HYPOGENE adj formed beneath the Earth's surface; plutonic

HYPOGEUM noun **HYPOGEA** an underground or subterranean chamber, especially for use as a tomb

HYPOID adj a type of bevel gear in which the axes of the driving and driven shafts are at right angles but not in the same plane

HYPONASTY noun **HYPONASTIES** an increased growth on the lower side of an organ of a plant, causing an upward bend

HYPONYM noun **HYPONYMS** any of a group of specific terms whose meanings are included in a more

general term, eg *oak* and *cedar* are hyponyms of *tree* and also of *wood*, and *spaniel* and *terrier* are hyponyms of *dog*

HYPONYMY noun **HYPONYMIES** the relation between hyponyms

HYPOSTYLE adj having the roof supported by pillars □ noun **HYPOSTYLES** a hypostyle construction

HYPOTHEC noun **HYPOTHECS** a lien or security, rather than possession, over goods or property in respect of a debt due by the owner of the goods or property

HYPOTONIA noun **HYPOTONIAS** a hypotonic condition

HYPOTONIC adj said of muscles: lacking normal tone

HYPOXIA noun **HYPOXIAS** a deficiency of oxygen reaching the body tissues

HYPOXIC adj of or relating to hypoxia

HYRAX noun **HYRAXES, HYRACES** any of a group of mammals, native to Africa and Arabia, related to the elephant, which superficially resemble a large guinea pig, with a pointed muzzle, round ears, and short legs and tail

HYSSOP noun **HYSSOPS** a small shrubby aromatic plant, native to S Europe and W Asia, with narrow leaves and clusters of long blue flowers, formerly cultivated as a medicinal herb

HYSTERIA noun **HYSTERIAS** a psychoneurosis characterized by mental and physical symptoms such as hallucinations, convulsions, amnesia or paralysis

HYSTERIC noun **HYSTERICS** someone suffering from hysteria

HYSTERICS plural noun a fit of hysteria

IAMB *noun* **IAMBS** an iambus

IAMBIC *adj* in verse: relating to, or using, iambuses □ *noun* **IAMBICS** an iambus

IAMBUS *noun* **IAMBUSES, IAMBI** in verse: a metrical foot containing one short or unstressed syllable followed by one long or stressed one, the most common measure in English verse

IBEX *noun* **IBEXES, IBICES** any of various species of wild mountain goat with large ridged backward-curving horns, found in precipitous mountain regions of Europe, N Africa and Asia

IBIDEM *adverb* in the same book, article, passage, etc as was previously mentioned or cited

IBIS *noun* **IBISES** any of various large wading birds with a long slender downward-curving beak, found in warm temperate and tropical regions

IBUPROFEN *noun* **IBUPROFENS** a non-steroidal anti-inflammatory drug used to relieve rheumatic and arthritic pain, headache, etc

ICE *noun* **ICES** water in its solid frozen state □ *verb* **ICES, ICING, ICED** to cover (a cake) with icing

ICEBERG *noun* **ICEBERGS** a huge mass of ice broken off from a glacier or polar ice sheet and floating in the sea, with only a small part of it projecting above the surface of the sea

ICEBLINK *noun* **ICEBLINKS** a glare reflected in the sky from the distant masses of ice

ICEBOUND *adj* said of a ship, etc: covered, surrounded or immobilized by ice

ICEBOX *noun* **ICEBOXES** a refrigerator compartment where food is kept frozen and ice is made and stored

ICECAP *noun* **ICECAPS** a thick permanent covering of ice, eg on top of a mountain or at the North or South Pole

ICED *adj* covered or cooled with, or affected by, ice

ICH *verb* **ICHES, ICHING, ICHED** a Shakespearean word meaning to eke or augment

ICHNEUMON *noun* **ICHNEUMONS** any of thousands of species of small winged insects which lay their larvae in or on the larvae of other insects

ICHTHYOID *adj* belonging or relating to a fish; fishlike □ *noun* **ICHTHYOIDS** a fishlike vertebrate

ICICLE *noun* **ICICLES** a long hanging spike of ice, formed by water freezing as it drips

ICILY *adverb* in an icy way

ICINESS *noun* **ICINESSES** the quality of being icy

ICING *noun* **ICINGS** any of various sugar-based coatings for cakes, etc

ICKY *adj* **ICKIER, ICKIEST** sickly; cloying or sticky

ICON *noun* **ICONS** especially in the Orthodox Church: an image of Christ, the Virgin Mary or a saint, usually painted on wood or done as a mosaic

ICONIC *adj* of or relating to an icon

ICONOLOGY *noun* **ICONOLOGIES** a development of iconography, involving the historical study of the social, political and religious meanings of works of art

ICTUS *noun* **ICTUSES** in verse: rhythmic or metrical stress

ICY *adj* **ICIER, ICIEST** very cold

ID *noun* **IDS** in Freudian theory: the part of the unconscious mind that is regarded as the source of primitive biological instincts and urges for survival and reproduction

IDE *noun* **IDES** a type of fish

IDEA *noun* **IDEAS** a thought, image, notion or concept formed by the mind

IDEAL *adj* perfect; highest and best possible or conceivable □ *noun* **IDEALS** the highest standard of behaviour, perfection, beauty, etc

IDEALISE *verb* **IDEALISES, IDEALISING, IDEALISED** to idealize

IDEALISER *noun* **IDEALISERS** an idealizer

IDEALISM *noun* **IDEALISMS** a tendency to show or present things in an ideal or idealized form rather than as they really are

IDEALIST *noun* **IDEALISTS** someone who lives or tries to live according to ideals

IDEALIZE *verb* **IDEALIZES, IDEALIZING, IDEALIZED** to regard or treat someone or something as perfect or ideal

IDEALIZER *noun* **IDEALIZERS** someone who idealizes

IDEALLY *adverb* in an ideal way; in ideal circumstances

IDEM *adverb* in the same place as previously mentioned

IDENTICAL *adj* said of two different items: exactly similar in every respect

IDENTIFY *verb* **IDENTIFIES, IDENTIFYING, IDENTIFIED** to recognize someone or something as being a particular person or thing; to establish their or its identity

IDENTIKIT *noun* **IDENTIKITS** a series of transparent strips, each one showing a different typical facial feature, from which it is possible to put together an impression or rough picture of a criminal or suspect from witnesses' descriptions

IDENTITY *noun* **IDENTITIES** the state or quality of being a specified person or thing; who or what a person or thing is

IDEOGRAM *noun* **IDEOGRAMS** on a sign or label, etc: a written symbol designed to convey an abstract concept, or one which stands for a real object without being a direct representation of it

IDEOGRAPH *noun* **IDEOGRAPHS** an ideogram

IDEOLOGUE *noun* **IDEOLOGUES** someone who supports a particular ideology very rigidly, often when it is not appropriate or practical

IDEOLOGY *noun* **IDEOLOGIES** the

body of ideas and beliefs which form the basis for a social, economic or political system

IDES *singular or plural noun* **IDES** in the ancient Roman calendar: the fifteenth day of March, May, July and October, and the thirteenth day of the other months

IDIOCY *noun* **IDIOCIES** a foolish action or foolish behaviour

IDIOLECT *noun* **IDIOLECTS** the individual and distinctive way a particular person has of speaking

IDIOM *noun* **IDIOMS** an expression with a meaning which cannot be guessed at or derived from the meanings of the individual words which form it

IDIOMATIC *adj* characteristic of a particular language

IDIOT *noun* **IDIOTS** a foolish or stupid person

IDIOTIC *adj* relating to or like an idiot; foolish

IDLE *adj* **IDLER, IDLEST** not in use; not being used; unoccupied □ *verb* **IDLES, IDLING, IDLED** to spend time doing nothing or being idle

IDLENESS *noun* **IDLENESSES** the state or condition of being idle

IDLER *noun* **IDLERS** a person who wastes time or is reluctant to work

IDLY *adverb* in an idle way

IDOL *noun* **IDOLS** an image or symbol, especially an image of a god, used as an object of worship

IDOLATER *noun* **IDOLATERS** someone who worships idols

IDOLATRY *noun* **IDOLATRIES** the worship of idols

IDOLISE *verb* **IDOLISES, IDOLISING, IDOLISED** to idolize

IDOLISER *noun* **IDOLISERS** an idolizer

IDOLIZE *verb* **IDOLIZES, IDOLIZING, IDOLIZED** to love, honour, admire, etc someone or something too much

IDOLIZER *noun* **IDOLIZERS** someone who idolizes

IDYL *noun* **IDYLS** an idyll

IDYLL *noun* **IDYLLS** a short poem or prose work describing a simple, pleasant, usually rural or pastoral scene

IDYLLIC *adj* relating to or typical of an idyll

IF *conj* in the event that; on condition that; supposing that □ *noun* **IFS** a condition or supposition

IFF *conj* used in logic to express 'if and only if'

IFFY *adj* uncertain; doubtful; dubious

IGLOO *noun* **IGLOOS** a dome-shaped Inuit house built with blocks of snow and ice

IGNEOUS *adj* belonging or relating to, or like, fire

IGNITABLE *adj* capable of being ignited

IGNITE *verb* **IGNITES, IGNITING, IGNITED** to set fire to something

IGNITER *noun* **IGNITERS** someone or something that ignites, eg an apparatus for firing an explosive or explosive mixture

IGNITIBLE *adj* capable of being ignited

IGNITION *noun* **IGNITIONS** the point at which combustion of a chemical substance begins

IGNOBLE *adj* **IGNOBLER, IGNOBLEST** said of an action, etc: causing shame; dishonourable; mean

IGNOBLY *adverb* in an ignoble way

IGNOMINY *noun* **IGNOMINIES** public shame or dishonour

IGNORAMUS *noun* **IGNORAMUSES** an ignorant or uneducated person

IGNORANCE *noun* **IGNORANCES** lack of knowledge or awareness

IGNORANT *adj* knowing very little; uneducated

IGNORE *verb* **IGNORES, IGNORING, IGNORED** to deliberately take no notice of someone or something

IGNORER *noun* **IGNORERS** someone who ignores

IGUANA *noun* **IGUANAS** any member of a family of large insectivorous lizards with a crest of spines along their back

IGUANODON *noun* **IGUANODONS** a large bipedal herbivorous dinosaur of the Jurassic and Cretaceous periods, with teeth like those of the iguana

IKAT *noun* **IKATS** a technique of tie-dyeing yarn before weaving it, resulting in a fabric with a geometric pattern of colours

IKEBANA *noun* **IKEBANAS** the Japanese art of flower-arranging, in which blooms (or a single bloom), leaves and other materials are arranged in a formal and carefully balanced way

IKON *noun* **IKONS** especially in the Orthodox Church: an image of Christ, the Virgin Mary or a saint, usually painted on wood or done as a mosaic

ILEAC *adj* of or relating to the ileum

ILEOSTOMY *noun* **ILEOSTOMIES** an operation in which the ileum is brought through a permanent artificial opening in the abdominal wall, so that its contents can be discharged directly to the outside of the body, bypassing the colon

ILEUM *noun* **ILEA** in mammals: the lowest part of the small intestine, lying between the jejunum and the caecum, whose main function is the digestion and absorption of food

ILEX *noun* **ILEXES, ILICES** a shrub or tree of the genus that includes holly

ILIAC *adj* of or relating to the ilium

ILIUM *noun* **ILIA** the largest of the three bones that form the upper part of each side of the pelvis

ILK *noun* **ILKS** type; kind; class □ *adj* same

ILL *adj* not in good health; sick or unwell □ *adverb* badly; wrongly □ *noun* **ILLS** evil; harm; trouble

ILLEGAL *adj* against the law; not legal

ILLEGALLY *adverb* in an illegal way

ILLEGIBLE *adj* difficult or impossible to read

ILLEGIBLY *adverb* in an illegible way

ILLIBERAL *adj* having strict opinions about morality, behaviour, etc; narrow-minded; prejudiced

ILLICIT *adj* not permitted by law, rule or social custom

ILLICITLY *adverb* in an illicit way

ILLNESS *noun* **ILLNESSES** a disease

ILLOGICAL *adj* not based on careful thinking or reason

ILLUMINE *verb* **ILLUMINES, ILLUMINING, ILLUMINED** to illuminate

ILLUSION *noun* **ILLUSIONS** a deceptive or misleading appearance

ILLUSIVE *adj* seeming to be, or having the characteristics of, an illusion

ILLUSORY *adj* illusive

ILMENITE *noun* **ILMENITES** a black

or dark-brown mineral composed of iron, titanium and oxygen, found in igneous rocks, and in metamorphic rocks such as gneiss and schist

IMAGE *noun* **IMAGES** a likeness of a person or thing, especially in the form of a portrait or statue □ *verb* **IMAGES, IMAGING, IMAGED** to form a likeness or image of something or someone

IMAGERY *noun* **IMAGERIES** figures of speech in writing, literature, etc that produce a specified effect

IMAGINARY *adj* existing only in the mind or imagination; not real

IMAGINE *verb* **IMAGINES, IMAGINING, IMAGINED** to form a mental picture of something

IMAGINER *noun* **IMAGINERS** someone who imagines

IMAGING *noun* **IMAGINGS** image formation

IMAGININGS *plural noun* things seen or heard which do not exist; fancies or fantasies

IMAGO *noun* **IMAGOES, IMAGOS** the final stage in the life cycle of an insect, when it is a sexually mature adult

IMAM *noun* **IMAMS** a leader of prayers in a mosque

IMAMATE *noun* **IMAMATES** the territory governed by an imam

IMARI *noun* **IMARIS** a type of Japanese porcelain, richly decorated in red, green and blue

IMBALANCE *noun* **IMBALANCES** a lack of balance or proportion; inequality

IMBECILE *noun* **IMBECILES** someone of very low intelligence, especially someone who is capable of keeping out of danger and of performing simple tasks only if someone else is supervising □ *adj* mentally weak; stupid; foolish

IMBED *verb* **IMBEDS, IMBEDDING, IMBEDDED** to set or fix something firmly and deeply

IMBIBE *verb* **IMBIBES, IMBIBING, IMBIBED** to drink, especially alcoholic drinks

IMBIBER *noun* **IMBIBERS** someone who imbibes

IMBRICATE *adj* said of fish scales, leaves, layers of tissue, teeth, etc: overlapping like roof tiles □ *verb* **IMBRICATES, IMBRICATING, IMBRICATED** to overlap or be overlapping like roof tiles

IMBROGLIO *noun* **IMBROGLIOS** a

confused and complicated situation

IMBUE *verb* **IMBUES, IMBUING, IMBUED** to fill or inspire, especially with ideals or principles

IMITABLE *adj* capable of being imitated

IMITATE *verb* **IMITATES, IMITATING, IMITATED** to copy the behaviour, manners, appearance, etc of someone; to use them as a model

IMITATION *noun* **IMITATIONS** an act of imitating

IMITATIVE *adj* imitating, copying or mimicking

IMITATOR *noun* **IMITATORS** someone who imitates

IMMANENCE *noun* **IMMANENCES** the concept of an immanent Supreme Being

IMMANENCY *noun* **IMMANENCIES** immanence

IMMANENT *adj* existing or remaining within something; inherent

IMMATURE *adj* not fully grown or developed; not mature or ripe

IMMEDIACY *noun* **IMMEDIACIES** the quality of being immediate or appealing directly to the emotions, understanding, etc

IMMEDIATE *adj* happening or done at once and without delay

IMMENSE *adj* **IMMENSER, IMMENSEST** very or unusually large or great

IMMENSELY *adverb* vastly, hugely, greatly

IMMENSITY *noun* **IMMENSITIES** the quality or condition of being immense

IMMERSE *verb* **IMMERSES, IMMERSING, IMMERSED** to dip something or someone into or under the surface of a liquid completely

IMMERSION *noun* **IMMERSIONS** immersing or being immersed

IMMIGRANT *noun* **IMMIGRANTS** someone who immigrates or has immigrated □ *adj* belonging or relating to immigrants

IMMIGRATE *verb* **IMMIGRATES, IMMIGRATING, IMMIGRATED** to come to a foreign country with the intention of settling in it

IMMINENCE *noun* **IMMINENCES** the fact of being imminent

IMMINENT *adj* likely to happen in the near future; looming or impending

IMMOBILE *adj* not able to move or be moved

IMMODEST *adj* shameful; indecent; improper

IMMODESTY *noun* **IMMODESTIES** shamefulness; indecency; impropriety

IMMOLATE *verb* **IMMOLATES, IMMOLATING, IMMOLATED** to kill or offer as a sacrifice

IMMOLATOR *noun* **IMMOLATORS** someone who immolates

IMMORAL *adj* morally wrong or bad; evil

IMMORALLY *adverb* in an immoral way

IMMORTAL *adj* living forever and never dying □ *noun* **IMMORTALS** someone who will live forever, or who will always be remembered

IMMOVABLE *adj* impossible to move; not meant to be moved

IMMOVABLY *adverb* in an immovable way

IMMUNE *adj* having a natural resistance to or protected by inoculation from (a particular disease)

IMMUNISE *verb* **IMMUNISES, IMMUNISING, IMMUNISED** to immunize

IMMUNITY *noun* **IMMUNITIES** the condition of being immune

IMMUNIZE *verb* **IMMUNIZES, IMMUNIZING, IMMUNIZED** to produce artificial immunity to a disease in someone by injecting them with an antiserum or a treated antigen

IMMURE *verb* **IMMURES, IMMURING, IMMURED** to enclose or imprison within, or as if within, walls

IMMUTABLE *adj* unable to be changed

IMMUTABLY *adverb* in an immutable way

IMP ¹ *noun* **IMPS** a small mischievous or evil spirit

IMP ² *verb* **IMPS, IMPING, IMPED** to engraft (a hawk) with new feathers

IMPACT *noun* **IMPACTS** the act of an object hitting or colliding with another object; a collision □ *verb* **IMPACTS, IMPACTING, IMPACTED** to press (two objects) together with force

IMPACTED *adj* said of a tooth, especially a wisdom tooth: unable to erupt through the gum into a normal position because it is firmly wedged between the jawbone and another tooth

IMPACTION noun **IMPACTIONS** the act of pressing together, or of fixing a substance tightly in a body cavity; the condition so produced

IMPAIR verb **IMPAIRS, IMPAIRING, IMPAIRED** to damage or weaken something, especially in terms of its quality or strength

IMPALA noun **IMPALAS** an antelope of S and E Africa, distinguished by the long high elegant leaps it takes when running

IMPALE verb **IMPALES, IMPALING, IMPALED** to pierce with, or as if with, a long, pointed object or weapon

IMPANEL verb **IMPANELS, IMPANELLED, IMPANELLING** to empanel

IMPART verb **IMPARTS, IMPARTING, IMPARTED** to make (information, knowledge, etc) known; to communicate (news, etc)

IMPARTIAL adj not favouring one person, etc more than another; fair and unbiased

IMPASSE noun **IMPASSES** a situation in which progress is impossible and from which there is no way out; a deadlock

IMPASSION verb **IMPASSIONS, IMPASSIONING, IMPASSIONED** to fill with passion; to rouse emotionally

IMPASSIONED adj fervent, zealous or animated

IMPASSIVE adj incapable of feeling and expressing emotion

IMPASTO noun **IMPASTOS** in painting and pottery: the technique of laying paint or pigment on thickly

IMPASTOED adj having had paint applied thickly, with clearly visible brushwork

IMPATIENS noun **IMPATIENS** any of numerous annual or perennial plants with translucent stems, oval-toothed leaves and flowers that hang from a slender stalk

IMPATIENT adj unwilling or lacking the patience to wait or delay

IMPEACH verb **IMPEACHES, IMPEACHING, IMPEACHED** to charge someone with a serious crime, especially a crime against the state or treason

IMPEDANCE noun **IMPEDANCES** the effective resistance of an electric circuit or circuit component to the passage of an electric current

IMPEDE verb **IMPEDES, IMPEDING, IMPEDED** to prevent or delay the start or progress of (an activity, etc); to obstruct or hinder something or someone

IMPEDING adj that impedes, obstructs or hinders

IMPEL verb **IMPELS, IMPELLING, IMPELLED** to push, drive or urge something forward; to propel

IMPELLENT adj impelling or driving on

IMPELLER noun **IMPELLERS** someone or something that impels

IMPEND verb **IMPENDS, IMPENDING, IMPENDED** to be about to happen

IMPENDING adj that is about to happen; imminent

IMPERFECT adj having faults; spoilt ▫ noun **IMPERFECTS** in grammar: the imperfect tense

IMPERIAL adj belonging to or suitable for an empire, emperor or empress ▫ noun **IMPERIALS** a traditional paper size, in Britain 22 × 30in (559 × 762mm) or in USA 23 × 33in (584 × 838mm)

IMPERIL verb **IMPERILS, IMPERILLING, IMPERILLED** to put in peril or danger; to endanger

IMPERIOUS adj arrogant, haughty and domineering

IMPETIGO noun **IMPETIGOS** a highly contagious skin disease, most common in babies and young children, characterized by the development of pustules and yellow crusty sores

IMPETUOUS adj acting or done hurriedly and without thinking; rash

IMPETUS noun **IMPETUSES** the force or energy with which something moves; momentum

IMPIETY noun **IMPIETIES** lack of piety or devotion

IMPINGE verb **IMPINGES, IMPINGING, IMPINGED** to interfere with or encroach on something or someone

IMPIOUS adj lacking respect or proper reverence, especially for a divine being

IMPIOUSLY adverb in an impious way

IMPISH adj like an imp; mischievous

IMPISHLY adverb in an impish way

IMPLANT verb **IMPLANTS,**

IMPLANTING, IMPLANTED to fix or plant something securely; to embed ▫ noun **IMPLANTS** any object, tissue, substance, etc implanted in the body, eg silicone breast implants, hormones, etc

IMPLEMENT noun **IMPLEMENTS** a tool or utensil ▫ verb **IMPLEMENTS, IMPLEMENTING, IMPLEMENTED** to carry out, fulfil or perform

IMPLICATE verb **IMPLICATES, IMPLICATING, IMPLICATED** to show or suggest that someone is involved or took part in something, especially in a crime

IMPLICIT adj implied or meant, although not stated directly

IMPLIED adj suggested or expressed indirectly

IMPLODE verb **IMPLODES, IMPLODING, IMPLODED** to collapse or make something collapse inwards, especially suddenly or violently

IMPLORE verb **IMPLORES, IMPLORING, IMPLORED** to entreat or beg someone

IMPLORING adj that entreats or begs

IMPLOSION noun **IMPLOSIONS** a violent collapse or bursting inward, eg when the seal of a vacuum-filled glass vessel is broken or when material capable of nuclear fission is compressed by ordinary explosives in a nuclear weapon

IMPLOSIVE adj likely, tending or able to implode

IMPLY verb **IMPLIES, IMPLYING, IMPLIED** to suggest or express something indirectly; to hint at it

IMPOLITE adj **IMPOLITER, IMPOLITEST** rude, disrespectful

IMPOLITIC adj unwise; not to be advised

IMPORT verb **IMPORTS, IMPORTING, IMPORTED** to bring (goods, etc) in to a country from another country ▫ noun **IMPORTS** a commodity, article, etc that has been imported

IMPORTANT adj having great value, influence, significance or effect

IMPORTER noun **IMPORTERS** someone who brings goods, etc in to a country from another country

IMPORTUNE verb **IMPORTUNES, IMPORTUNING, IMPORTUNED** to make persistent and usually annoying requests of someone

IMPOSE *verb* **IMPOSES, IMPOSING, IMPOSED** to make payment of (a tax, fine, etc) or performance of (a duty) compulsory; to enforce it

IMPOSING *adj* impressive, especially in size, dignity, handsome appearance, etc

IMPOST *noun* **IMPOSTS** a tax, especially one on imports

IMPOSTER *noun* **IMPOSTERS** an impostor

IMPOSTOR *noun* **IMPOSTORS** someone who pretends to be someone else in order to deceive others

IMPOSTURE *noun* **IMPOSTURES** an act, instance or the process of deceiving, especially by pretending to be someone else

IMPOTENCE *noun* **IMPOTENCES** powerlessness; helplessness

IMPOTENT *adj* powerless; lacking the necessary strength

IMPOUND *verb* **IMPOUNDS, IMPOUNDING, IMPOUNDED** to shut (eg an animal) up in, or as if in, a pound; to confine

IMPOUNDER *noun* **IMPOUNDERS** someone who impounds something

IMPRECATE *verb* **IMPRECATES, IMPRECATING, IMPRECATED** to call (eg an evil curse) down

IMPRECISE *adj* inaccurate

IMPRESS *verb* **IMPRESSES, IMPRESSING, IMPRESSED** to produce a strong, lasting, and usually favourable impression on someone □ *noun* **IMPRESSES** the act or process of impressing

IMPREST *noun* **IMPRESTS** a loan or advance of money, especially one from government funds for some public purpose

IMPRINT *noun* **IMPRINTS** a mark or impression made by pressure □ *verb* **IMPRINTS, IMPRINTING, IMPRINTED** to mark or print an impression of something on (eg a surface)

IMPRINTING *noun* **IMPRINTINGS** the process by which animals rapidly learn the appearance, sound or smell of significant individual members of their own species (eg parents, offspring, suitable mates)

IMPRISON *verb* **IMPRISONS, IMPRISONING, IMPRISONED** to put in prison

IMPROBITY *noun* **IMPROBITIES** dishonesty; wickedness

IMPROMPTU *adj* made or done without preparation or rehearsal; improvised; spontaneous □ *adverb* without preparation; spontaneously □ *noun* **IMPROMPTUS** something that is impromptu, eg a spontaneous speech or composition

IMPROPER *adj* not conforming to accepted standards of modesty and moral behaviour; unseemly; indecent

IMPROVE *verb* **IMPROVES, IMPROVING, IMPROVED** to make or become better or of higher quality or value; to make or cause something to make progress

IMPROVER *noun* **IMPROVERS** a person or thing that improves

IMPROVING *adj* tending to cause improvement

IMPROVISE *verb* **IMPROVISES, IMPROVISING, IMPROVISED** to compose, recite or perform (music, verse, etc) without preparing it in advance

IMPRUDENT *adj* said of a person, act, etc: lacking in good sense or caution; rash; heedless

IMPUDENCE *noun* **IMPUDENCES** rudeness, insolence or impertinence

IMPUDENT *adj* rude, insolent or impertinent

IMPUGN *verb* **IMPUGNS, IMPUGNING, IMPUGNED** to call into question or raise doubts about (the honesty, integrity, etc of someone or something); to criticize or challenge

IMPULSE *noun* **IMPULSES** a sudden push forwards; a force producing sudden movement forwards; a thrust

IMPULSION *noun* **IMPULSIONS** an act of urging, forcing or pushing forwards, into motion or into action, or the state of being so urged

IMPULSIVE *adj* said of a person: tending or likely to act suddenly and without considering the consequences

IMPUNITY *noun* **IMPUNITIES** freedom or exemption from punishment, injury, loss or other bad consequences

IMPURE *adj* **IMPURER, IMPUREST** mixed with something else; adulterated or tainted

IMPURELY *adverb* in an impure way

IMPURITY *noun* **IMPURITIES** the state of being impure

IMPUTABLE *adj* capable of being imputed or charged; open to accusation

IMPUTE *verb* **IMPUTES, IMPUTING, IMPUTED** to ascribe (usually something evil, dishonest, etc)

IN *prep* used to express the position of someone or something with regard to what encloses, surrounds or includes them or it; within □ *adverb* to or towards the inside; indoors □ *adj* inside; internal; inwards

INABILITY *noun* **INABILITIES** the lack of sufficient power, means or ability

INACTION *noun* **INACTIONS** lack of action; sluggishness; inactivity

INACTIVE *adj* taking little or no exercise; idle or sluggish

INAMORATA *noun* **INAMORATAS** a woman who is in love or who is beloved; a girlfriend

INAMORATO *noun* **INAMORATOS** a man who is in love or who is beloved; a male lover or sweetheart

INANE *adj* **INANER, INANEST** without meaning or point

INANELY *adverb* in an inane way

INANIMATE *adj* without life; not living

INANITION *noun* **INANITIONS** emptiness or exhaustion, especially of a physical kind, due to lack of nutrients in the blood resulting from starvation or some intestinal disease

INANITY *noun* **INANITIES** an inane remark or action, etc

INAPT *adj* not apt or appropriate

INAPTLY *adverb* in an inapt way

INAPTNESS *noun* **INAPTNESSES** the state of being inapt

INAUDIBLE *adj* not audible; not loud enough to be heard

INAUDIBLY *adverb* in an inaudible way

INAUGURAL *adj* relating to or describing a ceremony that officially marks the beginning of something □ *noun* **INAUGURALS** an inaugural speech or lecture

INBOARD *adj* said especially of a boat's motor or engine: situated inside the hull □ *adverb* said especially of a boat's motor or engine: situated inside the hull

INBORN *adj* said of a human attribute or characteristic:

possessed or apparently possessed from birth; innate or hereditary

INBOUND *adj* said of a vehicle, flight, carriageway, etc: coming towards its destination; arriving

INBRED *adj* said of a plant or animal: produced by inbreeding

INBREED *verb* **INBREEDS, INBREEDING, INBRED** to allow reproduction between closely related individuals of a species, especially over several generations

INBREEDING *noun* **INBREEDINGS** breeding within a closely-related group, which eventually results in an increased frequency of abnormalities, eg certain mental defects in humans

INCAPABLE *adj* lacking the necessary ability, power, character, etc to do something; not capable

INCAPABLY *adverb* in an incapable or incompetent way

INCARNATE *adj* in bodily, especially human, form □ *verb* **INCARNATES, INCARNATING, INCARNATED** to give bodily, especially human, form to (a spirit or god)

INCENSE *noun* **INCENSES** a spice or other substance which gives off a pleasant smell when burned, used especially during religious services □ *verb* **INCENSES, INCENSING, INCENSED** to make very angry; to enrage

INCENTIVE *noun* **INCENTIVES** something that motivates or encourages an action, work, etc, such as extra money paid to workers to increase output

INCEPTION *noun* **INCEPTIONS** beginning; outset

INCEPTIVE *adj* beginning or marking the beginning

INCESSANT *adj* going on without stopping; continual

INCEST *noun* sexual intercourse between people who are too closely related to be allowed to marry, eg between brother and sister

INCH *noun* **INCHES** in the imperial system: a unit of length equal to 2.54cm or one twelfth of a foot □ *verb* **INCHES, INCHING, INCHED** to move or be moved slowly, carefully and by small degrees

INCHOATE *adj* at the earliest stage of development; just beginning □ *verb* **INCHOATES, INCHOATING, INCHOATED** to begin

INCIDENCE *noun* **INCIDENCES** the

frequency with which something happens or the extent of its influence

INCIDENT *noun* **INCIDENTS** an event or occurrence □ *adj* belonging naturally to something or being a natural consequence of something

INCIPIENT *adj* beginning to exist; in an early stage

INCISE *verb* **INCISES, INCISING, INCISED** to cut into, especially precisely and with a specialized sharp tool

INCISION *noun* **INCISIONS** a cut, especially one made by a surgeon

INCISIVE *adj* clear and sharp; to the point; acute

INCISOR *noun* **INCISORS** in mammals: a sharp chisel-edged tooth in the front of the mouth, used for biting and nibbling

INCITE *verb* **INCITES, INCITING, INCITED** to stir up or provoke to action, etc

INCITER *noun* **INCITERS** a person or thing that incites

INCLEMENT *adj* said of weather: stormy or severe; harsh

INCLINE *verb* **INCLINES, INCLINING, INCLINED** to lean or make someone lean towards (a particular opinion or conduct); to be, or make someone, disposed towards it □ *noun* **INCLINES** a slope; an inclined plane

INCLINED *adj* sloping or bent

INCLOSE *verb* **INCLOSES, INCLOSING, INCLOSED** to put something inside a letter or in its envelope

INCLOSURE *noun* **INCLOSURES** the process of enclosing or being enclosed, especially with reference to common land

INCLUDE *verb* **INCLUDES, INCLUDING, INCLUDED** to take in or consider something or someone along with other things or people, as part of a group

INCLUSION *noun* **INCLUSIONS** the act or process of including; the state of being included

INCLUSIVE *adj* incorporating something; taking it in

INCOGNITO *adj* keeping one's identity a secret, eg by using a disguise and a false name □ *noun* **INCOGNITOS** the disguise and false name of a person who wishes to keep their identity secret

INCOME *noun* **INCOMES** money received over a period of time as

payment for work, etc or as interest or profit from shares or investment

INCOMER *noun* **INCOMERS** someone who comes to live in a place, not having been born there

INCOMING *adj* coming in; approaching

INCOMMODE *verb* **INCOMMODES, INCOMMODING, INCOMMODED** to cause bother, trouble or inconvenience to someone

INCORRECT *adj* not accurate; containing errors or faults

INCREASE *verb* **INCREASES, INCREASING, INCREASED** to make or become greater in size, intensity or number □ *noun* **INCREASES** the act or process of increasing or becoming increased; growth

INCREASING *adj* growing in size, number, or frequency, etc □ *noun* **INCREASINGS** growing in size, number, or frequency, etc

INCREMENT *noun* **INCREMENTS** an increase, especially of one point or level on a fixed scale, eg a regular increase in salary

INCRUST *verb* **INCRUSTS, INCRUSTING, INCRUSTED** to cover something with a thick hard coating, eg of jewels or ice

INCUBATE *verb* **INCUBATES, INCUBATING, INCUBATED** said of birds: to hatch (eggs) by sitting on them to keep them warm

INCUBATOR *noun* **INCUBATORS** a transparent boxlike container in which a prematurely born baby can be nurtured under controlled conditions and protected from infection

INCUBUS *noun* **INCUBUSES, INCUBI** an evil male spirit which is supposed to have sexual intercourse with sleeping women

INCUDES plural of **incus**

INCULCATE *verb* **INCULCATES, INCULCATING, INCULCATED** to teach or fix (ideas, habits, a warning, etc) firmly in someone's mind by constant repetition

INCULPATE *verb* **INCULPATES, INCULPATING, INCULPATED** to blame someone or show them to be guilty of a crime; to incriminate

INCUMBENT *adj* imposed as a duty or heavy responsibility on someone □ *noun* **INCUMBENTS** a holder of an office, especially a church office or benefice

INCUR *verb* **INCURS, INCURRING,**

INCURRED to bring (something unpleasant) upon oneself

INCURABLE *adj* said eg of a condition or disease: unable to be corrected or put right by treatment; not curable □ *noun* **INCURABLES** an incurable person or thing

INCURABLY *adverb* in an incurable way

INCURIOUS *adj* showing no interest; lacking a normal curiosity; indifferent

INCURSION *noun* **INCURSIONS** a brief or sudden attack made into enemy territory

INCURSIVE *adj* making incursions; aggressive; invasive

INCUS *noun* **INCUDES** a small, anvil-shaped bone in the middle ear which, together with two other bones, the malleus and stapes, transmits sound waves from the eardrum to the inner ear

INDABA *noun* **INDABAS** an important conference or discussion between members of different tribes

INDEBTED *adj* having reason to be grateful or obliged to someone

INDECENCY *noun* **INDECENCIES** the quality of being indecent

INDECENT *adj* **INDECENTER, INDECENTEST** offensive to accepted standards of morality or sexual behaviour; revolting or shocking

INDECORUM *noun* **INDECORUMS** improper or unseemly behaviour; lack of decorum

INDEED *adverb* without any question; in truth □ *exclamation* expressing irony, surprise, disbelief, disapproval, etc, or simple acknowledgement of a previous remark

INDELIBLE *adj* said eg of a mark or writing, or of a memory, etc: unable to be removed or rubbed out

INDELIBLY *adverb* in an indelible way

INDEMNIFY *verb* **INDEMNIFIES, INDEMNIFYING, INDEMNIFIED** to provide someone with security or protection against (loss or misfortune)

INDEMNITY *noun* **INDEMNITIES** compensation for loss or damage

INDENT *verb* **INDENTS, INDENTING, INDENTED** to form a dent in something or mark it with dents □ *noun* **INDENTS** a hollow, depression or dent

INDENTION *noun* **INDENTIONS** the indenting of a line or paragraph

INDENTURE *noun* **INDENTURES** a contract binding an apprentice to a master □ *verb* **INDENTURES, INDENTURING, INDENTURED** to bind (eg an apprentice) by indentures

INDEX *noun* **INDEXES, INDICES** an alphabetical list of names, subjects, etc dealt with in a book, usually given at the end of that book, and with the page numbers on which each item appears; a scale of numbers which shows changes in price, wages, rates of interest, etc □ *verb* **INDEXES, INDEXING, INDEXED** to provide (a book, etc) with an index

INDEXAL *adj* of or relating to an index

INDEXER *noun* **INDEXERS** someone who compiles an index, or whose job is to compile indexes

INDEXING *noun* **INDEXINGS** the linking of prices, wages, rates of interest, etc to changes in an index

INDICATE *verb* **INDICATES, INDICATING, INDICATED** to point out or show

INDICATOR *noun* **INDICATORS** an instrument or gauge that shows the level of temperature, fuel, pressure, etc

INDICES a plural of **index**

INDICT *verb* **INDICTS, INDICTING, INDICTED** to accuse someone of, or charge them formally with, a crime, especially in writing

INDICTEE *noun* **INDICTEES** someone who is indicted

INDIE *noun* **INDIES** a small independent and usually non-commercial record or film company

INDIGENCE *noun* **INDIGENCES** poverty

INDIGENT *adj* very poor; needy

INDIGNANT *adj* feeling or showing anger or a sense of having been treated unjustly or wrongly

INDIGNITY *noun* **INDIGNITIES** any act or treatment which causes someone to feel shame or humiliation; disgrace or dishonour

INDIGO *noun* **INDIGOS, INDIGOES** a violet-blue dye either obtained naturally from a plant or made synthetically □ *adj* violet-blue

INDIRECT *adj* said of a route, course, line, etc: not direct or straight

INDISPOSE *verb* **INDISPOSES, INDISPOSING, INDISPOSED** to render indisposed

INDISPOSED *adj* slightly ill; averse, unwilling

INDIUM *noun* **INDIUMS** a soft, silvery-white metallic element used in the manufacture of mirrors, semiconductor devices, metal bearings and certain alloys

INDOLENCE *noun* **INDOLENCES** laziness; idleness

INDOLENT *adj* said of a person: lazy; disliking and avoiding work and exercise

INDOOR *adj* used, belonging, done, happening, etc inside a building

INDOORS *adverb* in or into a building

INDORSE *verb* **INDORSES, INDORSING, INDORSED** to endorse

INDRAFT *noun* **INDRAFTS** an indraught

INDRAUGHT *noun* **INDRAUGHTS** an inward flow (eg of air) or current (eg of water)

INDRAWN *adj* said especially of the breath: drawn or pulled in

INDRI *noun* **INDRIS** a rare type of lemur that lives in tree tops feeding on leaves, and has a dark coat with white legs and hindquarters, fluffy round ears, a very short tail and a loud far-reaching cry

INDRIS *noun* **INDRISES** an indri

INDUCE *verb* **INDUCES, INDUCING, INDUCED** to persuade, influence or cause someone to do something

INDUCIBLE *adj* capable of being induced

INDUCT *verb* **INDUCTS, INDUCTING, INDUCTED** to place (eg a priest) formally and often ceremonially in an official position; to install

INDUCTION *noun* **INDUCTIONS** the act or process of inducting or being inducted, especially into office; installation, initiation or enrolment

INDUCTIVE *adj* relating to or using induction

INDUCTOR *noun* **INDUCTORS** a component of an electrical circuit that shows the property of inductance

INDUE *verb* **INDUES, INDUING, INDUED** to provide someone or something with (a specified quality)

INDULGE verb **INDULGES, INDULGING, INDULGED** to allow oneself or someone else pleasure or the pleasure of (a specified thing)

INDULGENT adj quick or too quick to overlook or forgive faults or gratify the wishes of others; too tolerant or generous

INDUSTRY noun **INDUSTRIES** the business of producing goods; all branches of manufacturing and trade

INEBRIATE verb **INEBRIATES, INEBRIATING, INEBRIATED** to make someone drunk; to intoxicate □ noun **INEBRIATES** someone who is drunk, especially on a regular basis

INEBRIETY noun **INEBRIETIES** the state of being drunk

INEDIBLE adj said of food: not fit or suitable to be eaten, eg because it is poisonous or indigestible, or it has gone off

INEFFABLE adj unable to be described or expressed in words, especially because of size, magnificence, etc

INEFFABLY adverb in an ineffable way

INELEGANT adj lacking grace or refinement

INEPT adj **INEPTER, INEPTEST** awkward; done without, or not having, skill

INEPTLY adverb in an inept way

INEPTNESS noun **INEPTNESSES** the state of being inept

INEQUABLE adj not fair or just

INEQUITY noun **INEQUITIES** an unjust action

INERT adj **INERTER, INERTEST** tending to remain in a state of rest or uniform motion in a straight line unless acted upon by an external force

INERTIA noun **INERTIAS** the tendency of an object to remain at rest, or to continue to move in the same direction at constant speed, unless it is acted on by an external force

INERTIAL adj of or relating to inertia

INERTLY adverb in an inert way

INERTNESS noun **INERTNESSES** the state of being inert

INEXACT adj not quite correct or true

INEXACTLY adverb in an inexact way

INEXPERT adj unskilled

INFAMOUS adj having a very bad reputation; notoriously bad

INFAMY noun **INFAMIES** bad reputation; notoriety; shame

INFANCY noun **INFANCIES** the state or time of being an infant

INFANT noun **INFANTS** a very young child in the first period of life; a baby □ adj at an early stage of development

INFANTA noun **INFANTAS** a daughter of the reigning monarch of Spain or Portugal who is not heir to the throne, especially the eldest daughter

INFANTE noun **INFANTES** a son of the king of Spain or Portugal who is not heir to the throne, especially the second son

INFANTILE adj belonging or relating to infants or infancy

INFANTRY noun **INFANTRIES** a body of soldiers trained and equipped to fight on foot

INFATUATE verb **INFATUATES, INFATUATING, INFATUATED** to inspire someone with, or make them feel, passionate, foolish, intense, etc love or admiration

INFATUATED adj filled with passion for someone or something; besotted with them or it

INFECT verb **INFECTS, INFECTING, INFECTED** to contaminate (a living organism) with a pathogen, such as a bacterium, virus or fungus, and thereby cause disease

INFECTION noun **INFECTIONS** the process of infecting or state of being infected

INFECTIVE adj said of a disease: caused by bacteria, viruses or other micro-organisms, and therefore capable of being transmitted through air, water, etc

INFER verb **INFERS, INFERRING, INFERRED** to conclude or judge from facts, observation and deduction

INFERABLE adj that may be inferred or deduced

INFERENCE noun **INFERENCES** an act of inferring, especially of reaching a conclusion from facts, observation and careful thought

INFERIOR adj poor or poorer in quality □ noun **INFERIORS** someone or something which is inferior

INFERNAL adj belonging or relating to the underworld

INFERNO noun **INFERNOS** hell

INFERTILE adj said of soil, etc: lacking the nutrients required to support an abundant growth of crops or other plants; barren

INFEST verb **INFESTS, INFESTING, INFESTED** said of parasites such as fleas, lice and certain fungi: to invade and occupy another animal or plant

INFIDEL noun **INFIDELS** someone who rejects a particular religion, especially Christianity or Islam □ adj relating to unbelievers; unbelieving

INFIELD noun **INFIELDS** the area of the field close to the wicket

INFIELDER noun **INFIELDERS** a player who stands in the infield

INFILL noun **INFILLS** the act of filling or closing gaps, holes, etc □ verb **INFILLS, INFILLING, INFILLED** to fill in (a gap, hole, etc)

INFINITE adj having no boundaries or limits in size, extent, time or space □ noun **INFINITES** anything which has no limits, boundaries, etc

INFINITY noun **INFINITIES** space, time, distance or quantity that is without limit or boundaries

INFIRM adj **INFIRMER, INFIRMEST** weak or ill, especially from old age

INFIRMARY noun **INFIRMARIES** a hospital

INFIRMITY noun **INFIRMITIES** the state or quality of being sick, weak or infirm

INFIX verb **INFIXES, INFIXING, INFIXED** to fix something firmly in (eg the mind) □ noun **INFIXES** an affix inserted into the middle of a word

INFLAME verb **INFLAMES, INFLAMING, INFLAMED** to arouse strong or violent emotion in someone or something

INFLAMED adj experiencing strong or violent emotion

INFLATE verb **INFLATES, INFLATING, INFLATED** to swell or cause something to swell or expand with air or gas

INFLATED adj blown up or filled with air or gas; distended

INFLATION noun **INFLATIONS** a general increase in the level of prices accompanied by a fall in the purchasing power of money, caused by an increase in the amount of money in circulation and credit available

INFLECT verb **INFLECTS,**

INFLECTING, INFLECTED to change the form of (a word) to show eg tense, number, gender or grammatical case

INFLEXION noun **INFLEXIONS** the change in the form of a word which shows tense, number, gender, grammatical case, etc

INFLICT verb **INFLICTS, INFLICTING, INFLICTED** to impose (something unpleasant, eg a blow, defeat or pain)

INFLICTER noun **INFLICTERS** someone who inflicts something on someone else

INFLICTOR noun **INFLICTORS** an inflicter

INFLOW noun **INFLOWS** the act or process of flowing in

INFLOWING noun **INFLOWINGS** the action of flowing in; influx

INFLUENCE noun **INFLUENCES** the power that one person or thing has to affect another ▫ verb **INFLUENCES, INFLUENCING, INFLUENCED** to have an effect, especially an indirect or unnoticed one, on (a person or their work, or events, etc)

INFLUENZA noun **INFLUENZAS** a highly infectious viral infection, with symptoms including headache, fever, a sore throat and muscular aches and pains

INFLUX noun **INFLUXES** a continual stream or arrival of large numbers of people or things

INFO noun **INFOS** information

INFOBAHN noun **INFOBAHNS** the Internet

INFOLD verb **INFOLDS, INFOLDING, INFOLDED** to wrap up or enclose

INFORM verb **INFORMS, INFORMING, INFORMED** to give someone knowledge or information about something; to tell them about it

INFORMAL adj without ceremony or formality; relaxed and friendly

INFORMANT noun **INFORMANTS** someone who informs, eg against another person, or who gives information

INFORMED adj said especially of a person: having or showing knowledge, especially in being educated and intelligent

INFORMER noun **INFORMERS** someone who informs against another, especially to the police and usually for money or some other reward

INFRA adverb in books, texts, etc: below; lower down on the page or further on in the book

INFRARED adj said of electromagnetic radiation: with a wavelength between the red end of the visible spectrum and microwaves and radio waves ▫ noun **INFRAREDS** infrared radiation

INFRINGE verb **INFRINGES, INFRINGING, INFRINGED** to break or violate (eg a law or oath)

INFURIATE verb **INFURIATES, INFURIATING, INFURIATED** to make someone very angry

INFURIATING adj maddening; causing great anger or annoyance

INFUSE verb **INFUSES, INFUSING, INFUSED** to soak, or cause (an organic substance, eg herbs or tea) to be soaked, in hot water to release flavour or other qualities

INFUSIBLE adj capable of being infused

INFUSION noun **INFUSIONS** an act or the process of infusing something

INFUSIVE adj having the power of infusion, or of being infused

INGENIOUS adj marked by, showing or having skill, originality and inventive cleverness

INGÉNUE noun **INGÉNUES** a naïve and unsophisticated young woman

INGENUITY noun **INGENUITIES** inventive cleverness, skill or originality; ingeniousness

INGENUOUS adj innocent and childlike, especially in being frank, honest and incapable of deception

INGEST verb **INGESTS, INGESTING, INGESTED** to take (eg food or liquid) into the body

INGESTION noun **INGESTIONS** the action of ingesting; the taking in of food

INGLENOOK noun **INGLENOOKS** a corner or alcove in a large open fireplace

INGOING adj going in; entering

INGOT noun **INGOTS** a brick-shaped block of metal, especially one of gold or silver

INGRAFT verb **INGRAFTS, INGRAFTING, INGRAFTED** to graft (a shoot, etc) on to a stock

INGRAIN verb **INGRAINS, INGRAINING, INGRAINED** to dye something in a lasting colour

INGRAINED adj difficult to remove or wipe off or out

INGRATE noun **INGRATES** an ungrateful person ▫ adj ungrateful

INGRESS noun **INGRESSES** the act of going in or entering

INGROWING adj growing inwards, in or into something

INGROWN adj having grown inwards, in or into something

INGUINAL adj belonging or relating to, or situated in the area of, the groin

INHABIT verb **INHABITS, INHABITING, INHABITED** to live in or occupy (a place)

INHALANT noun **INHALANTS** a medicinal preparation, especially a drug in the form of a gas, vapour or aerosol, inhaled via the nose for its therapeutic effect, especially in the treatment of respiratory disorders ▫ adj inhaling; drawing in

INHALE verb **INHALES, INHALING, INHALED** to draw (air or other substances, eg tobacco smoke) into the lungs; to breathe in

INHALER noun **INHALERS** a small, portable device used for inhaling certain medicinal preparations, eg in the treatment of asthma

INHERE verb **INHERES, INHERING, INHERED** said of character, a quality, etc: to be an essential or permanent part of it or them

INHERENT adj said of a quality, etc: existing as an essential, natural or permanent part

INHERIT verb **INHERITS, INHERITING, INHERITED** to receive (money, property, a title, position, etc) after someone's death or through legal descent from a predecessor; to succeed to something

INHERITOR noun **INHERITORS** someone who inherits or may inherit; an heir

INHIBIT verb **INHIBITS, INHIBITING, INHIBITED** to make someone feel nervous or frightened about acting freely or spontaneously, eg by causing them to doubt their abilities

INHIBITED adj said of a person or their disposition, actions, thinking, etc: restrained; held in check

INHIBITER noun **INHIBITERS** an inhibitor

INHIBITOR noun **INHIBITORS** a substance that interferes with a chemical or biological process

INHUMAN *adj* without human feeling; cruel and unfeeling; brutal

INHUMANE *adj* showing no kindness, sympathy or compassion; cruel; unfeeling

INHUMANLY *adverb* in an inhuman way

INIMICAL *adj* tending to discourage; unfavourable

INIQUITY *noun* **INIQUITIES** an unfair, unjust, wicked or sinful act

INITIAL *adj* belonging or relating to, or at, the beginning ◻ *noun* **INITIALS** the first letter of a word, especially the first letter of a personal or proper name ◻ *verb* **INITIALS, INITIALLING, INITIALLED** to mark or sign something with the initials of one's name, especially as a sign of approval

INITIALLY *adverb* at first

INITIATE *verb* **INITIATES, INITIATING, INITIATED** to make something begin (eg a relationship, project, conversation, etc); to accept a new member into a society etc ◻ *noun* **INITIATES** someone who has recently been or is soon to be initiated ◻ *adj* having been recently initiated or soon to be initiated

INITIATOR *noun* **INITIATORS** someone who initiates

INJECT *verb* **INJECTS, INJECTING, INJECTED** to introduce (a liquid, eg medicine) into the body of a person or animal using a hypodermic syringe

INJECTION *noun* **INJECTIONS** the act or process of introducing a liquid, eg medicine into the body with a hypodermic syringe

INJURE *verb* **INJURES, INJURING, INJURED** to do physical harm or damage to someone

INJURIOUS *adj* causing injury or damage; harmful

INJURY *noun* **INJURIES** physical harm or damage

INJUSTICE *noun* **INJUSTICES** unfairness or lack of justice

INK *noun* **INKS** a liquid, or sometimes a paste or powder, consisting of a pigment or a dye, used for writing, drawing or printing on paper and other materials ◻ *verb* **INKS, INKING, INKED** to mark something with ink

INKIER see under **inky**

INKIEST see under **inky**

INKINESS *noun* **INKINESSES** the state of being inky

INKLING *noun* **INKLINGS** a hint; a vague or slight idea or suspicion

INKSTAND *noun* **INKSTANDS** a small rack for ink bottles and pens on a desk

INKWELL *noun* **INKWELLS** a small container for ink, especially one which fits into a hole in a desk

INKY *adj* **INKIER, INKIEST** covered with ink

INLAID *adj* said of a design, etc: set into a surface

INLAND *adj* belonging or relating to, or in, that part of a country which is not beside the sea ◻ *noun* **INLANDS** that part of a country that is not beside the sea ◻ *adverb* in or towards the inner regions of a country away from the sea

INLAY *verb* **INLAYS, INLAYING, INLAID** to set or embed (eg pieces of wood, metal, etc) in another material in such a way that the surfaces are flat ◻ *noun* **INLAYS** a decoration or design made by inlaying

INLAYING *noun* **INLAYINGS** a method of decorating furniture and other wooden objects by cutting away part of the surface of the solid material and replacing it with a thin sheet of wood in another colour or texture, or occasionally a sliver of ivory, bone, shell, etc

INLET *noun* **INLETS** a narrow arm of water running inland from a sea coast or lake shore, or forming a passage between two islands

INMATE *noun* **INMATES** any of the people living in or confined to an institution, especially a prison or a hospital

INMOST *adj* furthest within; closest to the centre

INN *noun* **INNS** a public house or small hotel providing food and accommodation ◻ *verb* **INNS, INNING, INNED** an old word meaning to lodge

INNARDS *plural noun* the inner organs of a person or animal, especially the stomach and intestines

INNATE *adj* belonging to or existing from birth; inherent

INNATELY *adverb* in an innate way

INNER *adj* further in; situated inside, close or closer to the centre

INNERMOST *adj* furthest within; closest to the centre

INNING *noun* **INNINGS** in a baseball or softball game: any one of the nine divisions per game in which each team has an opportunity to bat

INNINGS *noun* **INNINGS** a team's or a player's turn at batting

INNKEEPER *noun* **INNKEEPERS** someone who owns or manages an inn

INNOCENCE *noun* **INNOCENCES** harmlessness; blamelessness; guilelessness

INNOCENT *adj* free from sin; pure ◻ *noun* **INNOCENTS** an innocent person, especially a young child or simple and trusting adult

INNOCUOUS *adj* harmless; inoffensive

INNOVATE *verb* **INNOVATES, INNOVATING, INNOVATED** to make changes; to introduce new ideas, methods, etc

INNOVATOR *noun* **INNOVATORS** someone who innovates

INNUENDO *noun* **INNUENDOS, INNUENDOES** a remark that indirectly conveys some unpleasant, critical or spiteful meaning, etc, especially about someone's reputation or character

INOCULATE *verb* **INOCULATES, INOCULATING, INOCULATED** to produce a mild form of a particular infectious disease in (a person or animal), and thereby create immunity by injecting a harmless form of an antigen which stimulates the body to produce its own antibodies

INORGANIC *adj* not composed of material that has or formerly had the structure and characteristics of living organisms

INPUT *noun* **INPUTS** the data that is transferred from a disk, tape or input device into the main memory of a computer ◻ *verb* **INPUTS, INPUTTING, INPUTTED** to transfer (data) from a disk, tape or input device into the main memory of a computer

INPUTTER *noun* **INPUTTERS** someone who supplies data, a program, etc

INQUEST *noun* **INQUESTS** an official investigation into an incident, especially an inquiry into a sudden and unexpected death, held in a coroner's court before a jury

INQUIRE *verb* **INQUIRES, INQUIRING, INQUIRED** to seek or ask for information

INQUIRER *noun* **INQUIRERS**

someone who inquires; an investigator or questioner

INQUIRING *adj* eager to discover or learn things

INQUIRY *noun* **INQUIRIES** an act or the process of asking for information

INQUORATE *adj* said of a meeting, etc: not making up a quorum

INRO *noun* **INRO** a small set of decorative, usually lacquer, nested containers for pills, ink, seals, etc, once hung from the obi by a silk cord, as part of traditional Japanese dress

INROAD *noun* **INROADS** a large or significant using up or consumption

INRUSH *noun* **INRUSHES** a sudden crowding or rushing in; an influx

INRUSHING *adj* rushing in; entering with great speed □ *noun* **INRUSHINGS** a rushing in

INSANE *adj* **INSANER, INSANEST** said of a person: not of sound mind; mentally ill

INSANELY *adverb* in an insane way

INSANITY *noun* **INSANITIES** the state of being insane

INSATIETY *noun* **INSATIETIES** the state of not being satisfied, or of being incapable of being so

INSCRIBE *verb* **INSCRIBES, INSCRIBING, INSCRIBED** to write, print or engrave (words) on (paper, metal, stone, etc), often as a lasting record

INSCRIBER *noun* **INSCRIBERS** a person who inscribes

INSECT *noun* **INSECTS** an invertebrate animal, such as the fly, beetle, ant and bee, belonging to the class Insecta, typically having a segmented body and two pairs of wings

INSECURE *adj* not firmly fixed; unstable

INSELBERG *noun* **INSELBERGE** a steep-sided hill rising from a plain, often found in semi-arid regions of tropical countries

INSENSATE *adj* not able to perceive physical sensations or experience consciousness; inanimate

INSERT *verb* **INSERTS, INSERTING, INSERTED** to put or fit something inside something else □ *noun* **INSERTS** something inserted, especially a loose sheet in a book or magazine, or piece of material in a garment

INSERTER *noun* **INSERTERS**

someone who puts or fits something inside something else

INSERTION *noun* **INSERTIONS** an act of inserting

INSET *noun* **INSETS** something set in or inserted, eg a piece of lace or cloth set into a garment, or a page or pages set into a book □ *verb* **INSETS, INSETTING, INSET** to put in, add or insert something

INSHALLAH *exclamation* if Allah wills

INSHORE *adverb* in or on the water, but near or towards the shore □ *adj* in or on the water, but near or towards the shore

INSIDE *noun* **INSIDES** the inner side, surface or part of something □ *adj* being on, near, towards or from the inside □ *adverb* to, in or on the inside or interior □ *prep* to or on the interior or inner side of something; within

INSIDER *noun* **INSIDERS** a recognized or accepted member of an organization or group who has access to confidential or exclusive information about it

INSIDIOUS *adj* developing gradually without being noticed but causing very great harm

INSIGHT *noun* **INSIGHTS** the ability to gain a relatively rapid, clear and deep understanding of the real, often hidden and usually complex nature of a situation, problem, etc

INSIGNIA *singular or plural noun* **INSIGNIAS** badges or emblems of office, honour or membership

INSINCERE *adj* not genuine; false; hypocritical

INSINUATE *verb* **INSINUATES, INSINUATING, INSINUATED** to suggest or hint (something unpleasant) in an indirect way

INSINUATING *adj* said of a person: wheedling, or acting in a subtle, cunning or devious way

INSIPID *adj* having little or no interest or liveliness; boring

INSIPIDLY *adverb* in an insipid way

INSIST *verb* **INSISTS, INSISTING, INSISTED** to maintain, state or assert something firmly

INSISTENT *adj* making continual forceful demands; insisting

INSOLE *noun* **INSOLES** a loose inner sole which can be put in a shoe or boot for extra warmth or to make it slightly smaller

INSOLENCE *noun* **INSOLENCES** rudeness; impudence

INSOLENT *adj* rude or insulting; showing a lack of respect

INSOLUBLE *adj* said of a substance: not able to be dissolved in a particular solvent (especially water) to form a solution

INSOLUBLY *adverb* in an insoluble way

INSOLVENT *adj* not having enough money to pay debts, creditors, etc □ *noun* **INSOLVENTS** an insolvent person

INSOMNIA *noun* **INSOMNIAS** the chronic and habitual inability to fall asleep or remain asleep for an adequate length of time

INSOMNIAC *noun* **INSOMNIACS** someone who suffers from insomnia

INSOMUCH *adverb* to such a degree

INSPECT *verb* **INSPECTS, INSPECTING, INSPECTED** to look at or examine closely, often to find faults or mistakes

INSPECTOR *noun* **INSPECTORS** someone whose job is to inspect something, especially officially

INSPIRE *verb* **INSPIRES, INSPIRING, INSPIRED** to stimulate someone into activity, especially into artistic or creative activity

INSPIRED *adj* so good, skilful, accurate, etc as to seem to be the result of inspiration, especially divine inspiration

INSPIRER *noun* **INSPIRERS** a person or thing that inspires

INSPIRING *adj* said of something or someone: providing inspiration; stimulating, encouraging, guiding, etc

INSTABLE *adj* unstable

INSTAL *verb* **INSTALS, INSTALING, INSTALED** to install

INSTALL *verb* **INSTALLS, INSTALLING, INSTALLED** to put (equipment, machinery, etc) in place and make it ready for use

INSTANCE *noun* **INSTANCES** an example, especially one of a particular condition or circumstance

INSTANT *adj* said of food and drink, etc: quickly and easily prepared, especially by reheating or the addition of boiling water □ *noun* **INSTANTS** a particular moment in time, especially the present

INSTANTLY *adverb* at once; immediately

INSTAR *noun* **INSTARS** the form of

an insect at any stage of its physical development between two successive moults, before it has become fully mature

INSTATE *verb* **INSTATES, INSTATING, INSTATED** to install someone (in an official position, etc)

INSTEAD *adverb* as a substitute or alternative; in place of something or someone

INSTEP *noun* **INSTEPS** the prominent arched middle section of the human foot, between the ankle and the toes

INSTIGATE *verb* **INSTIGATES, INSTIGATING, INSTIGATED** to urge someone on or incite them, especially to do something wrong or evil

INSTIL *verb* **INSTILS, INSTILLING, INSTILLED** to impress, fix or plant (ideas, feelings, etc) slowly or gradually in someone's mind

INSTILL *verb* **INSTILLS, INSTILLING, INSTILLED** to instil

INSTINCT *noun* **INSTINCTS** in animal behaviour: an inherited and usually fixed pattern of response to a particular stimulus, common to all members of a species, and not learned but based on a biological need, especially for survival or reproduction

INSTITUTE *noun* **INSTITUTES** a society or organization which promotes research, education or a particular cause □ *verb* **INSTITUTES, INSTITUTING, INSTITUTED** to set up, establish or organize something

INSTRUCT *verb* **INSTRUCTS, INSTRUCTING, INSTRUCTED** to teach or train someone in a subject or skill

INSULAR *adj* belonging or relating to an island, or to the inhabitants of an island

INSULATE *verb* **INSULATES, INSULATING, INSULATED** to surround (a body, device or space) with a material that prevents or slows down the flow of heat, electricity or sound

INSULATOR *noun* **INSULATORS** any material that is a poor conductor of heat or electricity, eg plastics, glass or ceramics

INSULIN *noun* **INSULINS** a hormone secreted by the islets of Langerhans in the pancreas, which controls the concentration of sugar in the blood

INSULT *verb* **INSULTS, INSULTING, INSULTED** to speak rudely or offensively to or about someone or something □ *noun* **INSULTS** a rude or offensive remark or action

INSULTING *adj* that insults or causes offence

INSURABLE *adj* capable of being insured

INSURANCE *noun* **INSURANCES** an agreement by which one party promises to pay another party money in the event of loss, theft or damage to property, personal injury or death, etc

INSURE *verb* **INSURES, INSURING, INSURED** to arrange for the payment of an amount of money in the event of the loss or theft of or damage to (property) or injury to or the death of (a person), etc by paying regular amounts of money to an insurance company

INSURED *adj* covered by insurance

INSURER *noun* **INSURERS** a person or company that provides insurance

INSURGENT *adj* opposed to and fighting against the government of the country; rebellious □ *noun* **INSURGENTS** a rebel

INTACT *adj* whole; not broken or damaged; untouched

INTAGLIO *noun* **INTAGLIOS** a stone or gem which has a design engraved in its surface

INTAKE *noun* **INTAKES** a thing or quantity taken in or accepted

INTARSIA *noun* **INTARSIAS** decorative wood inlay work

INTEGER *noun* **INTEGERS** in maths: any of the positive or negative whole numbers or zero, eg $0, 8, -12$

INTEGRAL *adj* being a necessary part of a whole □ *noun* **INTEGRALS** in maths: the result of integrating a function

INTEGRAND *noun* **INTEGRANDS** in maths: a function that is to be integrated

INTEGRATE *verb* **INTEGRATES, INTEGRATING, INTEGRATED** to fit (parts) together to form a whole

INTEGRITY *noun* **INTEGRITIES** strict adherence to moral values and principles; uprightness

INTELLECT *noun* **INTELLECTS** the part of the mind that uses both memory and intelligence in order to think, reason creatively and understand concepts

INTEND *verb* **INTENDS,**

INTENDING, INTENDED to plan or have in mind as one's purpose or aim

INTENDED *adj* meant; done on purpose or planned □ *noun* **INTENDEDS** someone's future husband or wife

INTENSE *adj* **INTENSER, INTENSEST** very great or extreme

INTENSELY *adverb* in an intense way

INTENSIFY *verb* **INTENSIFIES, INTENSIFYING, INTENSIFIED** to make or become intense or more intense

INTENSION *noun* **INTENSIONS** the set of qualities by which a general name is determined

INTENSITY *noun* **INTENSITIES** the quality or state of being intense

INTENSIVE *adj* using, done with or requiring considerable amounts of thought, effort, time, etc within a relatively short period □ *noun* **INTENSIVES** an intensifier, an adverb or adjective which adds emphasis to or intensifies the word or phrase which follows it, eg *very*

INTENT *noun* **INTENTS** something which is aimed at or intended; a purpose □ *adj* fixed with close attention; concentrating on a particular aim or purpose

INTENTION *noun* **INTENTIONS** something that someone plans or intends to do; an aim or purpose

INTENTLY *adverb* in an intent way

INTER *verb* **INTERS, INTERRING, INTERRED** to bury (a dead person, etc) in the earth or a tomb

INTERACT *verb* **INTERACTS, INTERACTING, INTERACTED** to act with or on one another

INTERCEDE *verb* **INTERCEDES, INTERCEDING, INTERCEDED** to act as a peacemaker between (two parties, countries, etc)

INTERCEPT *verb* **INTERCEPTS, INTERCEPTING, INTERCEPTED** to stop or catch (eg a person, missile, aircraft, etc) on their or its way from one place to another □ *noun* **INTERCEPTS** in maths: the part of a line or plane that is cut off by another line or plane crossing it, especially the distance from the origin to the point where a straight line or a curve crosses one of the axes of a coordinate system

INTERCITY *adj* said of rail transport: denoting an express service between major cities □ *noun* **INTERCITIES** an intercity train

INTERCOM noun **INTERCOMS** an internal system which allows communication within a building, aircraft, ship, etc

INTERCUT verb **INTERCUTS, INTERCUTTING, INTERCUT** to alternate (contrasting shots) within a sequence by cutting

INTERDICT noun **INTERDICTS** an official order forbidding someone to do something ▫ verb **INTERDICTS, INTERDICTING, INTERDICTED** to place under an interdict; to forbid or prohibit

INTEREST noun **INTERESTS** the desire to learn or know about someone or something; curiosity ▫ verb **INTERESTS, INTERESTING, INTERESTED** to attract the attention and curiosity of someone

INTERESTED adj showing or having a concern or interest

INTERESTING adj attracting interest; holding the attention

INTERFACE noun **INTERFACES** a surface forming a common boundary between two regions, things, etc which cannot be mixed, eg oil and water ▫ verb **INTERFACES, INTERFACING, INTERFACED** to connect (a piece of equipment, etc) with another so as to make them compatible

INTERFACING noun **INTERFACINGS** a piece of stiff fabric sewn between two layers of material to give shape and firmness

INTERFERE verb **INTERFERES, INTERFERING, INTERFERED** said of a person: to be involved in or meddle with something not considered their business

INTERFERING adj that interferes

INTERFUSE verb **INTERFUSES, INTERFUSING, INTERFUSED** to mix (with something)

INTERIM adj not intended to be final or to last; provisional, temporary

INTERIOR adj on, of, suitable for, happening or acting in, or coming from the inside; inner ▫ noun **INTERIORS** an internal or inner part; the inside

INTERJECT verb **INTERJECTS, INTERJECTING, INTERJECTED** to say or add abruptly; to interrupt with something

INTERLACE verb **INTERLACES, INTERLACING, INTERLACED** to join by lacing or by crossing over

INTERLARD verb **INTERLARDS,**

INTERLARDING, INTERLARDED to add foreign words, quotations, unusual phrases, etc to (a speech or piece of writing), especially to do so excessively

INTERLAY verb **INTERLAYS, INTERLAYING, INTERLAID** to lay (eg layers) between; to interpose

INTERLEAF noun **INTERLEAVES** a leaf of paper, usually a blank one, inserted between any two leaves of a book

INTERLINE verb **INTERLINES, INTERLINING, INTERLINED** to put an extra lining between the first lining and the fabric (of a garment), especially for stiffness

INTERLINING noun **INTERLININGS** a piece of material used as an extra lining

INTERLINK verb **INTERLINKS, INTERLINKING, INTERLINKED** to join or connect together

INTERLOCK verb **INTERLOCKS, INTERLOCKING, INTERLOCKED** to fit, fasten or connect together, especially by the means of teeth or parts which fit into each other ▫ noun **INTERLOCKS** a device or mechanism that connects and co-ordinates the functions of the parts or components of eg a machine ▫ adj said of a fabric or garment: knitted with closely locking stitches

INTERLOCKING adj that interlock

INTERLUDE noun **INTERLUDES** a short period of time between two events or a short period of a different activity; a brief distraction

INTERMENT noun **INTERMENTS** burial, especially with appropriate ceremony

INTERMIT verb **INTERMITS, INTERMITTING, INTERMITTED** to suspend or cause to suspend; to stop for a while

INTERN verb **INTERNS, INTERNING, INTERNED** to confine within a country, restricted area or prison, especially during a war ▫ noun **INTERNS** an advanced student or graduate who gains practical experience by working, especially in a hospital or medical centre

INTERNAL adj on, in, belonging to or suitable for the inside; inner

INTERNE noun **INTERNES** an intern

INTERNEE noun **INTERNEES** someone who is interned

INTERNIST noun **INTERNISTS** a specialist in internal diseases

INTERNODE noun **INTERNODES** the part of a plant stem that lies between two successive nodes

INTERPLAY noun **INTERPLAYS** the action and influence of two or more things on each other

INTERPOSE verb **INTERPOSES, INTERPOSING, INTERPOSED** to put something, or come, between two other things

INTERPRET verb **INTERPRETS, INTERPRETING, INTERPRETED** to explain the meaning of (a foreign word, dream, etc)

INTERRUPT verb **INTERRUPTS, INTERRUPTING, INTERRUPTED** to break into (a conversation or monologue) by asking a question or making a comment

INTERSECT verb **INTERSECTS, INTERSECTING, INTERSECTED** to divide (lines, an area, etc) by passing or cutting through or across

INTERSEX noun **INTERSEXES** an individual that has characteristics of both sexes

INTERVAL noun **INTERVALS** a period of time between two events

INTERVENE verb **INTERVENES, INTERVENING, INTERVENED** to involve oneself in something which is happening in order to affect the outcome

INTERVIEW noun **INTERVIEWS** a formal meeting and discussion with someone, especially one at which an employer meets and judges a prospective employee ▫ verb **INTERVIEWS, INTERVIEWING, INTERVIEWED** to hold an interview

INTESTACY noun **INTESTACIES** the state of someone dying without having made a valid will

INTESTATE adj said of a person: not having made a valid will before their death ▫ noun **INTESTATES** someone who dies without making a valid will

INTESTINE noun **INTESTINES** the muscular tube-like part of the alimentary canal leading from the stomach to the anus, divided into the large intestine and the small intestine

INTIMACY noun **INTIMACIES** warm close personal friendship

INTIMATE adj marked by or sharing a close and affectionate friendship ▫ noun **INTIMATES** a close friend □ verb **INTIMATES, INTIMATING, INTIMATED** to announce or make known

INTIMISM noun **INTIMISMS** a genre of French Impressionist painting characterized by the representation of everyday subjects, such as domestic interiors, portrayal of close family members and friends in their home

INTO prep to or towards the inside or middle of something

INTONATE verb **INTONATES, INTONATING, INTONATED** to intone

INTONE verb **INTONES, INTONING, INTONED** to recite (a prayer, etc) in a solemn monotonous voice or in singing tones

INTRENCH verb **INTRENCHES, INTRENCHING, INTRENCHED** to fix or establish something firmly, often too firmly

INTREPID adj bold and daring; fearless; brave

INTRICACY noun **INTRICACIES** complexity; the quality or state of being intricate

INTRICATE adj full of complicated, interrelating or tangled details or parts and therefore difficult to understand, analyse or sort out

INTRIGUE noun **INTRIGUES** secret plotting or underhand scheming □ verb **INTRIGUES, INTRIGUING, INTRIGUED** to arouse the curiosity or interest of someone; to fascinate

INTRIGUING adj that arouses curiosity or interest; fascinating

INTRINSIC adj belonging to something or someone as an inherent and essential part of their nature

INTRO noun **INTROS** an introduction, especially to a piece of music

INTRODUCE verb **INTRODUCES, INTRODUCING, INTRODUCED** formally to make known or acquainted; to bring in, establish

INTROIT noun **INTROITS** a hymn, psalm or anthem sung at the beginning of a service or, in the RC Church, as the priest approaches the altar to celebrate Mass

INTRON noun **INTRONS** any segment of DNA in a gene that does not carry coded instructions for the manufacture of a protein

INTROVERT noun **INTROVERTS** someone who is more concerned with their thoughts and inner feelings than with the outside world and social relationships □ adj concerned more with one's own thoughts and feelings than with other people and outside events □ verb **INTROVERTS, INTROVERTING, INTROVERTED** to turn (one's thoughts) inward to concentrate on oneself

INTRUDE verb **INTRUDES, INTRUDING, INTRUDED** to force or impose (oneself, one's presence or something) without welcome or invitation

INTRUDER noun **INTRUDERS** someone who enters premises secretly or by force, especially in order to commit a crime

INTRUSION noun **INTRUSIONS** an act or process of intruding, especially on someone else's property

INTRUSIVE adj tending to intrude

INTRUST verb **INTRUSTS, INTRUSTING, INTRUSTED** to entrust

INTUBATE verb **INTUBATES, INTUBATING, INTUBATED** to insert a tube into (a hollow body part such as the trachea to assist breathing during anaesthesia)

INTUIT verb **INTUITS, INTUITING, INTUITED** to know or become aware of something by intuition

INTUITION noun **INTUITIONS** the power of understanding or realizing something without conscious rational thought or analysis

INTUITIVE adj having, showing or based on intuition

INTUMESCE verb **INTUMESCES, INTUMESCING, INTUMESCED** to swell up

INULIN noun **INULINS** a water-soluble carbohydrate stored as a food reserve in the roots and tubers of certain plants, eg dahlia

INUNCTION noun **INUNCTIONS** the application of ointment or liniment to the skin by rubbing or smearing

INUNDATE verb **INUNDATES, INUNDATING, INUNDATED** to overwhelm with water

INURE verb **INURES, INURING, INURED** to accustom someone to something unpleasant or unwelcome

INUREMENT noun **INUREMENTS** the act of inuring; the state of being inured

INVADE verb **INVADES, INVADING,**

INVADED to enter (a country) by force with an army

INVADER noun **INVADERS** a person who invades

INVALID noun **INVALIDS** someone who is constantly ill or who is disabled □ adj suitable for or being an invalid □ verb **INVALIDS, INVALIDING, INVALIDED** to discharge (a soldier, etc) from service because of illness

INVALIDLY adverb in a way that is not valid; without validity

INVARIANT noun **INVARIANTS** a property of a mathematical equation, geometric figure, etc, that is unaltered by a particular procedure □ adj invariable

INVASION noun **INVASIONS** an act of invading or process of being invaded, eg by a hostile country

INVASIVE adj invading; aggressive; encroaching; infringing another's rights

INVECTIVE noun **INVECTIVES** severe or bitter accusation or denunciation, using sarcastic or abusive language □ adj characterized by such an attack

INVEIGH verb **INVEIGHS, INVEIGHING, INVEIGHED** to speak strongly or passionately against someone or something, especially in criticism or protest

INVEIGLE verb **INVEIGLES, INVEIGLING, INVEIGLED** to entice; to persuade by cajolery

INVENT verb **INVENTS, INVENTING, INVENTED** to be the first person to make or use (a machine, game, method, etc)

INVENTION noun **INVENTIONS** something invented, especially a device, machine, etc

INVENTIVE adj skilled at inventing; creative; resourceful

INVENTOR noun **INVENTORS** someone who invents, especially as an occupation

INVENTORY noun **INVENTORIES** a formal and complete list of the articles, goods, etc found in a particular place, eg of goods for sale in a shop, or of furniture and possessions in a house □ verb **INVENTORIES, INVENTORYING, INVENTORIES** to make an inventory of items; to list in an inventory

INVERSE adj opposite or reverse in order, sequence, direction, effect, etc □ noun **INVERSES** a direct opposite

INVERSELY adverb in an inverse way

INVERSION noun **INVERSIONS** the act of turning upside down or inside out, or otherwise inverting

INVERT verb **INVERTS, INVERTING, INVERTED** to turn upside down or inside out

INVERTASE noun **INVERTASES** an enzyme found in yeasts that breaks down sucrose to form glucose and fructose

INVEST verb **INVESTS, INVESTING, INVESTED** to put (money) into a company or business, eg by buying shares in it, in order to make a profit

INVESTOR noun **INVESTORS** a person who invests, especially money

INVIDIOUS adj likely to cause envy, resentment or indignation, especially by being or seeming to be unfair

INVIOLATE adj not broken, violated or injured

INVISIBLE adj not able to be seen ▫ noun **INVISIBLES** an invisible item of trade

INVISIBLY adverb in an invisible way; so that it cannot be seen

INVITE verb **INVITES, INVITING, INVITED** to request the presence of someone at one's house, at a party, etc, especially formally or politely ▫ noun **INVITES** an invitation

INVITING adj attractive or tempting

INVOICE noun **INVOICES** a list of goods supplied, delivered with the goods and giving details of price and quantity, usually treated as a request for payment ▫ verb **INVOICES, INVOICING, INVOICED** to send an invoice to (a customer)

INVOKE verb **INVOKES, INVOKING, INVOKED** to make an appeal to (God, some deity, a Muse, authority, etc) for help, support or inspiration

INVOLUCRE noun **INVOLUCRES** an enveloping membrane

INVOLUTE adj entangled; intricate ▫ noun **INVOLUTES** in geometry: the curve traced out by the different points on a piece of string unwinding from the curve ▫ verb **INVOLUTES, INVOLUTING, INVOLUTED** to become involute or undergo involution

INVOLVE verb **INVOLVES, INVOLVING, INVOLVED** to require as a necessary part

INVOLVED adj concerned; implicated; complicated

INWARD adj placed or being within ▫ adverb towards the inside or the centre

INWARDLY adverb on the inside; internally

INWARDS adverb inward

IO noun **IOS** a cry of joy, triumph or grief

IODIDE noun **IODIDES** a chemical compound containing iodine and another element or radical, eg potassium iodide, methyl iodide

IODINE noun **IODINES** a non-metallic element consisting of dark-violet crystals that sublime to a violet vapour when heated, and which is used as an antiseptic, in the production of dyes, and as a catalyst and chemical reagent

IODISE verb **IODISES, IODISING, IODISED** to iodize

IODIZE verb **IODIZES, IODIZING, IODIZED** to treat something with iodine, especially common salt so as to provide iodine as a nutritional supplement

ION noun **IONS** an atom or group of atoms that has acquired a net positive charge as a result of losing one or more electrons, or a net negative charge as a result of gaining one or more electrons

IONIC adj belonging or relating to or using ions

IONISE verb **IONISES, IONISING, IONISED** to ionize

IONISER noun **IONISERS** an ionizer

IONIZE verb **IONIZES, IONIZING, IONIZED** to produce or make something produce ions

IONIZER noun **IONIZERS** a device that produces negatively charged ions, considered to relieve headaches, fatigue and other symptoms which are said to be caused by the accumulation of positive ions in rooms and buildings where electrical machinery, computers, etc, are in frequent use

IONOMER noun **IONOMERS** a resilient and highly transparent thermoplastic which has both organic and inorganic components, and is used to make goggles, shields, bottles, refrigerator trays, toys and electrical parts

IOS plural of **io**

IOTA noun **IOTAS** the ninth letter of the Greek alphabet

IPECAC noun **IPECACS** a small Latin American shrub

IRASCIBLE adj easily made angry; irritable

IRASCIBLY adverb in an irascible way

IRATE adj **IRATER, IRATEST** very angry; enraged

IRATELY adverb in an irate way

IRE noun **IRES** anger

IREFUL adj full of ire or wrath; resentful

IRENIC adj tending to create peace

IRENICAL adj irenic

IRIDIUM noun **IRIDIUMS** a silvery metallic element that is resistant to corrosion, and is mainly used in hard alloys with platinum or osmium to make surgical instruments, pen nibs, bearings, electrical contacts and crucibles

IRIS noun **IRISES** a perennial plant that arises from a rhizome or a corm, and has flattened sword-shaped leaves and large brilliantly coloured flowers, consisting of equal numbers of upright and hanging petals

IRK verb **IRKS, IRKING, IRKED** to annoy or irritate, especially persistently

IRKSOME adj annoying, irritating or boring

IRKSOMELY adverb in an irksome way

IRON noun **IRONS** a strong hard silvery-white metallic element that is naturally magnetic, and is thought to be the main component of the Earth's core; a household tool used for smoothing out creases and pressing clothes ▫ adj made of iron ▫ verb **IRONS, IRONING, IRONED** to smooth the creases out of or press (eg clothes) with an iron

IRONIC adj containing, characterized by or expressing irony

IRONICAL adj ironic

IRONING noun **IRONINGS** clothes and household linen, etc which need to be or have just been ironed

IRONSTONE noun **IRONSTONES** a sedimentary rock, at least 15 per cent of which comprises iron minerals such as haematite and pyrite

IRONWARE noun **IRONWARES** things made of iron, especially household hardware

IRONWORK noun **IRONWORKS** articles made of iron, especially iron which has been specially shaped for decoration, such as gates and railings

IRONY[1] noun **IRONIES** a linguistic device or form of humour that takes its effect from stating or implying the opposite of what is the case or what is intended, eg saying 'You've made a really good job of that, haven't you', when someone has done something badly

IRONY[2] adj **IRONIER, IRONIEST** belonging or relating to, or containing, iron

IRRADIATE verb **IRRADIATES, IRRADIATING, IRRADIATED** to expose (a part of the body) to irradiation

IRREGULAR adj not happening or occurring at regular or equal intervals ◻ noun **IRREGULARS** an irregular soldier, one who does not belong to the regular army

IRRIGABLE adj capable of being irrigated

IRRIGATE verb **IRRIGATES, IRRIGATING, IRRIGATED** said of a river, etc: to provide (land) with a supply of water

IRRITABLE adj easily annoyed, angered or excited

IRRITABLY adverb in an irritable way

IRRITANT noun **IRRITANTS** any chemical, physical or biological agent that causes irritation of a tissue, especially inflammation of the skin or eyes ◻ adj irritating

IRRITATE verb **IRRITATES, IRRITATING, IRRITATED** to make someone angry or annoyed

IRRITATING adj that irritates

IRRUPT verb **IRRUPTS, IRRUPTING, IRRUPTED** to burst into or enter (a place, etc) suddenly with speed and violence

IRRUPTION noun **IRRUPTIONS** a breaking or bursting in; a sudden invasion or incursion

IRRUPTIVE adj rushing suddenly in

IS a form of **be**

ISAGOGIC adj introductory

ISAGOGICS singular noun introductory studies, especially in theology

ISCHAEMIA noun **ISCHAEMIAS** an inadequate flow of blood to a part of the body, caused by blockage or constriction of a blood vessel

ISCHEMIA noun **ISCHEMIAS** ischaemia

ISCHIUM noun **ISCHIA** a posterior bone in the pelvic girdle

ISH noun **ISHES** a Scottish legal word meaning *issue* or *expiry*

ISINGLASS noun **ISINGLASSES** the purest form of animal gelatine, made from the dried swim bladders of certain fish, eg sturgeon, which has strong adhesive properties, and is used in glues, cements and printing inks

ISLAND noun **ISLANDS** a piece of land, smaller than a continent, which is completely surrounded by water, eg Britain, Cyprus, Greenland, etc

ISLANDER noun **ISLANDERS** someone who lives on an island

ISLE noun **ISLES** an island, especially a small one

ISLET noun **ISLETS** a small island

ISM noun **ISMS** a distinctive and formal set of ideas, principles or beliefs

ISO noun **ISOS** short for isolated replay, a TV and film facility

ISOBAR noun **ISOBARS** a line drawn on a weather chart connecting points that have the same atmospheric pressure at a given time

ISOBARIC adj containing or relating to isobars

ISOBATH noun **ISOBATHS** a contour line connecting points of equal underwater depth

ISOBATHIC adj containing or relating to isobaths

ISOCLINAL adj in geology: folded with the same or nearly the same dip in each limb ◻ noun

ISOCLINALS a contour line which connects points on the surface of the earth which have the same magnetic dip

ISOCRACY noun **ISOCRACIES** equality of political power

ISOCRATIC adj of or relating to isocracy

ISOCYCLIC adj said of a compound: having a closed chain of similar atoms

ISOGLOSS noun **ISOGLOSSES** a line drawn on a map, which marks the boundaries of areas which manifest particular linguistic features

ISOHEL noun **ISOHELS** a line drawn on a weather map connecting places with equal periods of sunshine

ISOHYET noun **ISOHYETS** a line drawn on a weather map connecting places with equal amounts of rainfall

ISOLATE verb **ISOLATES, ISOLATING, ISOLATED** to separate from others; to cause to be alone ◻ noun **ISOLATES** someone or something that is isolated

ISOLATED adj placed or standing alone or apart

ISOLATION noun **ISOLATIONS** the action of isolating; the fact or condition of being isolated

ISOMER noun **ISOMERS** one of two or more chemical compounds that have the same chemical formula, ie the same molecular composition, but different three-dimensional structures

ISOMERIC adj identical in percentage composition and molecular weight but different in constitution or the mode in which the atoms are arranged

ISOMETRIC adj having equal size or measurements

ISOMETRICS singular or plural noun **ISOMETRICS** a system of physical exercises for strengthening and toning the body in which the muscles are pushed either together or against an immovable object and are not contracted, flexed or made to bend limbs

ISOMORPH noun **ISOMORPHS** any object that is similar or identical in structure or shape to another object

ISONOMY noun **ISONOMIES** equal law, rights or privileges

ISOPRENE noun **ISOPRENES** a colourless liquid hydrocarbon that is the basic unit of natural rubber, and can be polymerized to form synthetic rubber

ISOSCELES adj said of a triangle: having two sides of equal length

ISOSTASY noun **ISOSTASIES** a theoretical state of equilibrium in which the Earth's crust, which is considered to consist of relatively low density material, floats on the surface of the much denser semi-solid material of the Earth's mantle

ISOTHERE noun **ISOTHERES** a line on a weather map connecting places where the mean summer temperature is the same

For longer words, see *The Chambers Dictionary*

ISOTHERM *noun* **ISOTHERMS** a line on a weather map connecting places where the temperature is the same at a particular time or for a particular period of time

ISOTONIC *adj* a solution that has the same osmotic pressure as another solution with which it is being compared

ISOTOPE *noun* **ISOTOPES** one of two or more atoms of the same chemical element that contain the same number of protons but different numbers of neutrons in their nuclei and therefore have the same atomic number and chemical properties, but different mass numbers and physical properties

ISOTOPIC *adj* of or relating to an isotope

ISOTOPY *noun* **ISOTOPIES** the fact or condition of being isotopic

ISOTROPIC *adj* said of a substance, material, etc: having physical properties that are identical in all directions

ISOTROPY *noun* **ISOTROPIES** the condition or quality of being isotropic

ISSUE *noun* **ISSUES** the giving out, publishing or making available of something, eg stamps, a magazine, etc ◻ *verb* **ISSUES, ISSUING, ISSUED** to give or send out, distribute, publish or make available, especially officially or formally

ISTHMUS *noun* **ISTHMUSES** a narrow strip of land, bounded by water on both sides, that joins two larger areas of land

ISTLE *noun* **ISTLES** a valuable fibre obtained from various tropical

trees such as the agave and yucca and which is used for cords, carpets, etc

IT *pronoun* the thing, animal, small baby or group already mentioned ◻ *noun* **ITS** the person in a children's game who has to oppose all the others, eg by trying to catch them

ITA *noun* **ITAS** a type of palm

ITALIC *adj* said of a typeface: containing characters which slope upwards to the right ◻ *noun* **ITALICS** a typeface with characters which slope upwards to the right, usually used to show emphasis, foreign words, etc

ITALICISE *verb* **ITALICISES, ITALICISING, ITALICISED** to italicize

ITALICIZE *verb* **ITALICIZES, ITALICIZING, ITALICIZED** to print or write in italics; to change (characters, words, etc in normal typeface) to italics

ITCH *noun* **ITCHES** an unpleasant or ticklish irritation on the surface of the skin which makes one want to scratch ◻ *verb* **ITCHES, ITCHING, ITCHED** to have an itch and want to scratch

ITCHINESS *noun* **ITCHINESSES** the state of being itcy; an itchy area

ITCHY *adj* **ITCHIER, ITCHIEST** causing or affected with an itch or itching

ITEM *noun* **ITEMS** a separate object or unit, especially one on a list

ITEMISE *verb* **ITEMISES, ITEMISING, ITEMISED** to itemize

ITEMIZE *verb* **ITEMIZES, ITEMIZING, ITEMIZED** to list

(things) separately, eg on a bill

ITERATE *verb* **ITERATES, ITERATING, ITERATED** to say or do again; to repeat

ITERATION *noun* **ITERATIONS** repetition

ITERATIVE *adj* repeating

ITINERANT *adj* travelling from place to place, eg on business ◻ *noun* **ITINERANTS** an itinerant person, especially one whose work involves going from place to place or one who has no fixed address

ITINERARY *noun* **ITINERARIES** a planned route for a journey or trip, especially one that gives details of the expected stops, visits, etc ◻ *adj* belonging or relating to journeys

ITS *adj* belonging to it ◻ *pronoun* the one or ones belonging to it

ITSELF *pronoun* the reflexive form of *it*

IVORY *noun* **IVORIES** a hard white material that forms the tusks of the elephant, walrus, etc, formerly used to make ornaments, art objects and piano keys ◻ *adj* ivory-coloured, often with the implication of smoothness

IVY *noun* **IVIES** a woody evergreen climbing or trailing plant, with dark glossy leaves with five points and black berry-like fruits

IXIA *noun* **IXIAS** a plant of the iris family with large showy flowers, originally found in S Africa

IXTLE *noun* **IXTLES** a valuable fibre obtained from various tropical trees such as the agave and yucca and which is used for cords, carpets, etc

IZARD *noun* **IZARDS** the Pyrenean ibex

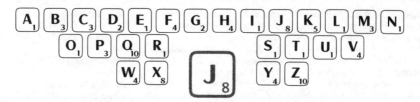

JAB verb **JABS, JABBING, JABBED** to poke or prod □ noun **JABS** a poke or prod

JABBER verb **JABBERS, JABBERING, JABBERED** to talk or utter rapidly and indistinctly □ noun **JABBERS** rapid indistinct speech

JABBERER noun **JABBERERS** someone who jabbers

JABBERING noun **JABBERINGS** the act of jabbering □ adj that jabbers

JABOT noun **JABOTS** a lace ruffle for a shirt front, especially one worn with full Highland dress

JACARANDA noun **JACARANDAS** a tropical tree with lilac-coloured flowers and fern-like leaves

JACINTH noun **JACINTHS** a blue gemstone, perhaps sapphire

JACK noun **JACKS** a device for raising a heavy weight, such as a car, off the ground □ verb **JACKS, JACKING, JACKED** to raise with a jack

JACKAL noun **JACKALS** a mainly nocturnal, carnivorous, scavenging mammal, closely related to the dog and wolf, that lives in deserts, grassland and woodland in Asia and Africa

JACKAROO noun **JACKAROOS** a newcomer, or novice, on a sheep- or cattle-station □ verb **JACKAROOS, JACKAROOING, JACKAROOED** to be a jackaroo

JACKASS noun **JACKASSES** a male ass or donkey

JACKBOOT noun **JACKBOOTS** a tall leather knee-high military boot

JACKDAW noun **JACKDAWS** a bird of the crow family with black plumage shot with blue on the back and head, and a reputation for stealing bright objects

JACKEROO noun **JACKEROOS** a jackaroo □ verb **JACKEROOS, JACKEROOING, JACKEROOED** to jackaroo

JACKET noun **JACKETS** a short coat, especially a long-sleeved, hip-length one

JACKKNIFE noun **JACKKNIVES** a large pocket knife with a folding blade □ verb **JACKKNIFES, JACKKNIFING, JACKKNIFED** said of an articulated vehicle: to go out of control in such a way that the trailer swings round against the cab

JACKPOT noun **JACKPOTS** the maximum win, to be made in a lottery, card game, etc, especially one consisting of the accumulated stakes

JACKS noun **JACKS** a game in which playing-pieces (originally small bones or pebbles) are tossed and caught on the back of the hand

JACONET noun **JACONETS** a type of cotton fabric, especially one with a waterproof backing and used for medical dressings

JACQUARD noun **JACQUARDS** a piece of equipment consisting of a set of coded perforated cards that can be fitted to a loom to produce a fabric with an intricate woven pattern

JACUZZI noun **JACUZZIS** a bathe in a Jacuzzi®, a large bath or pool with underwater jets that massage and invigorate the body

JADE noun **JADES** a very hard, green, white, brown or yellow semi-precious stone consisting of either jadeite or nephrite, used to make vases and carved ornaments

JADED adj fatigued; dull and bored

JADEITE noun **JADEITES** a tough fibrous mineral with a slightly greasy lustre, a translucent green form of which is the most highly prized form of jade

JAG noun **JAGS** a sharp projection □ verb **JAGS, JAGGING, JAGGED** to prick, sting or pierce something or someone

JAGGED adj having a rough or sharp uneven edge

JAGGEDLY adverb in a jagged way

JAGGERY noun **JAGGERIES** sugar obtained from the sap of certain species of palm trees

JAGGY adj **JAGGIER, JAGGIEST** having rough, untidy or uneven edges

JAGUAR noun **JAGUARS** the largest of the American big cats, with a deep yellow or tawny coat covered with black spots, and found mainly in tropical forests

JAIL noun **JAILS** prison □ verb **JAILS, JAILING, JAILED** to imprison

JAILER noun **JAILERS** a person in charge of a jail or of prisoners

JAILOR noun **JAILORS** a jailer

JAK noun **JAKS** an East Indian tree

JALAPEÑO noun **JALAPEÑOS** an especially hot type of capsicum pepper, used in Mexican cooking

JALOPPY noun **JALOPPIES** a jalopy

JALOPY noun **JALOPIES** a worn-out old car

JALOUSIE noun **JALOUSIES** an outside shutter with slats

JALOUSIED adj equipped with a jalousie

JAM noun **JAMS** a thick sticky food made from fruit boiled with sugar, used as a spread on bread, etc □ verb **JAMS, JAMMING, JAMMED** to stick or wedge something so as to make it immovable

JAMB noun **JAMBS** the vertical post at the side of a door, window or fireplace

JAMBALAYA noun **JAMBALAYAS** a Creole or Cajun dish made with rice mixed with seafood or chicken, seasonings, etc

JAMBOREE noun **JAMBOREES** a large rally of Scouts, Guides, etc

JAMMY adj **JAMMIER, JAMMIEST** covered or filled with jam

JAMPAN noun **JAMPANS** an Indian sedan chair

JAMPANEE noun **JAMPANEES** the bearer of a jampan

JAMPANI noun **JAMPANIS** a jampanee

JANGLE verb **JANGLES, JANGLING, JANGLED** to make or cause something to make an irritating, discordant ringing noise □ noun **JANGLES** an unpleasant dissonant ringing sound

JANGLING noun **JANGLINGS** a loud discordant ringing noise

JANGLY adj **JANGLIER, JANGLIEST** loud and discordant

JANISSARY noun **JANISSARIES** a soldier of the Turkish sultan's personal guard

JANITOR noun **JANITORS** a caretaker, especially of a school

JANKERS noun **JANKERS** punishment, detention, etc for defaulting

JAP verb **JAPS, JAPPING, JAPPED** a Scots word meaning to splash

JAPAN noun **JAPANS** a hard glossy black lacquer, originally from Japan, used to coat wood and metal ▫ verb **JAPANS, JAPANNING, JAPANNED** to lacquer something with japan

JAPE noun **JAPES** a trick, prank or joke ▫ verb **JAPES, JAPING, JAPED** to jest or joke

JAPER noun **JAPERS** someone who jests or jokes

JAPING noun **JAPINGS** jesting or joking

JAPONICA noun **JAPONICAS** an ornamental, scarlet- or pink-flowered deciduous shrub of the quince family, native to E Asia, which bears round green, white or yellow fruit

JAR ¹ noun **JARS** a wide-mouthed cylindrical container, usually made of glass

JAR ² verb **JARS, JARRING, JARRED** to have a harsh effect; to grate

JARFUL noun **JARFULS** the amount a jar can hold

JARGON noun **JARGONS** the specialized vocabulary of a particular trade, profession, group or activity

JARGONEER noun **JARGONEERS** someone who uses jargon

JARGONISE verb **JARGONISES, JARGONISING, JARGONISED** to jargonize

JARGONIST noun **JARGONISTS** someone who uses jargon

JARGONIZE verb **JARGONIZES, JARGONIZING, JARGONIZED** to express something in jargon

JARGOON noun **JARGOONS** a brilliant, colourless or pale zircon

JARL noun **JARLS** a Scandinavian noble or chief

JARRED past form of **jar**

JARRING ¹ noun **JARRINGS** harsh discordant sound

JARRING ² a form of **jar**

JARRINGLY adverb in a jarring way

JASMINE noun **JASMINES** a shrub or vine native to Asia, widely cultivated as an ornamental plant and whose fragrant flowers are used as a source of jasmine oil in perfumery and also to scent tea

JASPER noun **JASPERS** a red, yellow, brown or green semi-precious gemstone, an impure form of chalcedony, used to make jewellery and ornaments

JATAKA noun **JATAKAS** a nativity; the birth-story of Buddha

JATO noun **JATOS** in aeronautics: a jet-assisted take-off

JAUNDICE noun **JAUNDICES** a condition which turns the skin and the whites of the eyes a yellowish colour, resulting from an excess of bilirubin in the blood, and often a symptom of liver disease

JAUNDICED adj suffering from jaundice

JAUNT noun **JAUNTS** a short journey for pleasure ▫ verb **JAUNTS, JAUNTING, JAUNTED** to go for a jaunt

JAUNTILY adverb in a jaunty way

JAUNTY adj **JAUNTIER, JAUNTIEST** said of someone's manner or personality: breezy and exuberant

JAVELIN noun **JAVELINS** a light spear for throwing, either as a weapon or in sport

JAW noun **JAWS** in most vertebrates: either of the two bony structures that form the framework of the mouth and in which the teeth are set ▫ verb **JAWS, JAWING, JAWED** to chatter, gossip or talk

JAWBONE noun **JAWBONES** the upper or lower bone of the jaw

JAY noun **JAYS** a noisy bird of the crow family which has pinkish-brown plumage and blue, black and white bands on its wings

JAYWALK verb **JAYWALKS, JAYWALKING, JAYWALKED** to cross streets wherever one likes, regardless of traffic signals

JAYWALKER noun **JAYWALKERS** a careless pedestrian whom motorists are expected to avoid knocking down

JAYWALKING noun **JAYWALKINGS** the action of crossing streets wherever one likes, regardless of traffic signals

JAZZ noun **JAZZES** a type of popular music of Black American origin, with strong catchy rhythms, performed with much improvisation ▫ verb **JAZZES, JAZZING, JAZZED** to impart a jazz character to

JAZZILY adverb in a jazzy way

JAZZY adj **JAZZIER, JAZZIEST** in the style of, or like, jazz

JEALOUS adj envious of someone else, their possessions, success, talents, etc

JEALOUSLY adverb in a jealous way

JEALOUSY noun **JEALOUSIES** the emotion of envy or suspicious possessiveness

JEANS plural noun casual trousers made especially of denim, corduroy or other similar material

JEE verb **JEES, JEEING, JEED** to gee

JEEPERS exclamation expressing surprise

JEER verb **JEERS, JEERING, JEERED** to mock or deride (a speaker, performer, etc) ▫ noun **JEERS** a taunt, insult or hoot of derision

JEERER noun **JEERERS** someone who jeers

JEERING noun **JEERINGS** the action of mocking or deriding (a speaker, performer, etc) ▫ adj that jeers; mocking

JEERINGLY adverb in a jeering way

JEHAD noun **JEHADS** a jihad

JEJUNE adj said of writing, ideas, etc: dull, banal, unoriginal and empty of imagination

JEJUNELY adverb in a jejune way

JEJUNITY noun **JEJUNITIES** the state of being jejune

JEJUNUM noun **JEJUNA** in mammals: the part of the small intestine between the duodenum and the ileum, the main function of which is to absorb digested food

JELL verb **JELLS, JELLING, JELLED** to become firm; to set

JELLIED adj set in jelly

JELLIFY verb **JELLIFIES, JELLIFYING, JELLIFIED** to make something into jelly

JELLY noun **JELLIES** a wobbly, transparent, fruit-flavoured dessert set with gelatine

JELLYFISH noun **JELLYFISHES** any

of various marine coelenterates, usually having an umbrella-shaped body and tentacles containing stinging cells

JEMMY *noun* **JEMMIES** a small crowbar used by burglars for forcing open windows, etc □ *verb* **JEMMIES, JEMMYING, JEMMIED** to force something open with a jemmy or similar tool

JENNET *noun* **JENNETS** a small Spanish donkey

JENNY *noun* **JENNIES** a name given to the female of certain animals, especially the donkey, ass, owl and wren

JEOPARDY *noun* **JEOPARDIES** danger of harm, loss or destruction

JERBOA *noun* **JERBOAS** a small nocturnal burrowing rodent of N Africa and Asia, with long hind legs adapted for jumping, an extremely long tail and large ears

JEREMIAD *noun* **JEREMIADS** a lengthy and mournful tale of woe

JERK *noun* **JERKS** a quick tug or pull □ *verb* **JERKS, JERKING, JERKED** to pull or tug sharply

JERKIN *noun* **JERKINS** a sleeveless jacket, short coat or close-fitting waistcoat

JERKINESS *noun* **JERKINESSES** the state of being jerky; a jerky action

JERKY *adj* **JERKIER, JERKIEST** making sudden movements or jerks

JEROBOAM *noun* **JEROBOAMS** a large wine bottle holding the equivalent of four standard bottles

JERRY *noun* **JERRIES** hastily made using poor materials

JERSEY *noun* **JERSEYS** a knitted garment worn on the upper part of the body, pulled on over the head; a pullover

JESS *noun* **JESSES** a short leather strap attached to the leg of a hawk

JESSAMINE *noun* **JESSAMINES** jasmine

JESSED *adj* having jesses on

JESSIE *noun* **JESSIES** an effeminate, feeble or namby-pamby man or boy

JEST *noun* **JESTS** a joke or prank □ *verb* **JESTS, JESTING, JESTED** to make a jest; to joke

JESTER *noun* **JESTERS** a colourfully-dressed professional clown, employed by a king or noble to amuse the court

JESTFUL *adj* given to jesting

JESTING *noun* **JESTINGS** the action

of making a jest; joking □ *adj* that jests or jokes

JESTINGLY *adverb* in a jesting way

JET *noun* **JETS** a strong continuous stream of liquid gas, forced under pressure from a narrow opening □ *verb* **JETS, JETTING, JETTED** to travel or be transported by jet aircraft

JETFOIL *noun* **JETFOILS** an advanced form of hydrofoil propelled by water jets

JETON *noun* **JETONS** a jetton

JETSAM *noun* **JETSAMS** goods jettisoned from a ship and washed up on the shore

JETTISON *verb* **JETTISONS, JETTISONING, JETTISONED** to throw (cargo) overboard to lighten a ship, aircraft, etc in an emergency

JETTON *noun* **JETTONS** a counter or chip used in card games or other gambling games

JETTY *noun* **JETTIES** a stone or wooden landing-stage

JEU *noun* **JEUX** a French word for *game*

JEWEL *noun* **JEWELS** a precious stone □ *verb* **JEWELS, JEWELLING, JEWELLED** to adorn someone or something with jewels

JEWELLED *adj* adorned with jewels

JEWELLER *noun* **JEWELLERS** a person who deals in, makes or repairs jewellery, watches and objects of gold and silver

JEWELLERY *noun* **JEWELLERIES** articles worn for personal adornment, eg bracelets, necklaces, brooches and rings

JEWELRY *noun* **JEWELRIES** jewellery

JIB *noun* **JIBS** a small three-cornered sail in front of the mainsail of a yacht □ *verb* **JIBS, JIBBING, JIBBED** said of a horse: to refuse a jump, etc

JIBE *verb* **JIBES, JIBING, JIBED** to gybe □ *noun* **JIBES** a gybe

JIFF *noun* **JIFFS** a moment

JIFFY *noun* **JIFFIES** a moment

JIG *noun* **JIGS** a lively country dance or folk dance □ *verb* **JIGS, JIGGING, JIGGED** to dance a jig

JIGGER *noun* **JIGGERS** a chigger

JIGGERED *adj* exhausted

JIGGLE *verb* **JIGGLES, JIGGLING, JIGGLED** to jump or make something jump or jerk about □ *noun* **JIGGLES** a jiggling movement

JIGSAW *noun* **JIGSAWS** a picture, mounted on wood or cardboard and cut into interlocking irregularly shaped pieces, to be fitted together again □ *verb* **JIGSAWS, JIGSAWING, JIGSAWED** to cut something with a jigsaw (a fine-bladed saw for cutting intricate patterns)

JIHAD *noun* **JIHADS** a holy war, against infidels, fought by Muslims on behalf of Islam

JILLAROO *noun* **JILLAROOS** a female jackaroo □ *verb* **JILLAROOS, JILLAROOING, JILLAROOED** to work as a jillaroo

JILT *noun* **JILTS** a person, originally and especially a woman, who encourages and then rejects a lover □ *verb* **JILTS, JILTING, JILTED** to leave and abruptly discard a previously encouraged lover

JIMJAMS *plural noun* a state of nervous excitement

JINGLE *noun* **JINGLES** a light ringing or clinking sound, eg of small bells, coins, keys, etc □ *verb* **JINGLES, JINGLING, JINGLED** to make or cause something to make a ringing or clinking sound

JINGLER *noun* **JINGLERS** someone who writes jingles

JINGLY *adj* **JINGLIER, JINGLIEST** that jingles

JINGO *noun* **JINGOES** a ranting patriot

JINGOISM *noun* **JINGOISMS** over-enthusiastic or aggressive patriotism

JINGOIST *noun* **JINGOISTS** someone who takes part in jingoism

JINK *verb* **JINKS, JINKING, JINKED** to dodge □ *noun* **JINKS** a dodge; a jinking movement

JINNEE *noun* **JINN** jinni

JINNI *noun* **JINN** in Muslim folklore: a supernatural being able to adopt human or animal form

JINX *noun* **JINXES** an evil spell or influence, held responsible for misfortune □ *verb* **JINXES, JINXING, JINXED** to bring bad luck to, or put a jinx on, someone or something

JINXED *adj* beset with bad luck

JISM *noun* **JISMS** energy; force

JISSOM *noun* **JISSOMS** jism

JITTER *verb* **JITTERS, JITTERING, JITTERED** to shake with nerves; to behave in a flustered way □ *noun* **JITTERS** an attack of nervousness

JITTERBUG *noun* **JITTERBUGS** an

energetic dance like the jive, popular in the 1940s □ verb **JITTERBUGS, JITTERBUGGING, JITTERBUGGED** to dance the jitterbug

JITTERY adj **JITTERIER, JITTERIEST** nervous; flustered

JIVE noun **JIVES** a lively style of jazz music or swing, popular in the 1950s □ verb **JIVES, JIVING, JIVED** to play or dance jive

JIVER noun **JIVERS** someone who jives

JIZ noun **JIZZES** a Scots word for a wig

JIZZ noun **JIZZES** the characteristic features of a bird, animal or plant which distinguish it from other species that resemble it

JO noun **JOES** a Scots word for a loved one
ⓘ A useful two-letter word for using up a **J**.

JOB noun **JOBS** a person's regular paid employment □ verb **JOBS, JOBBING, JOBBED** to do casual jobs

JOBBER noun **JOBBERS** someone who, until 1986, engaged in trading on the stock exchange by selling securities to brokers rather than dealing directly with the public

JOBBERY noun **JOBBERIES** the abuse of public office for private gain

JOBCENTRE noun **JOBCENTRES** a government office displaying information on available jobs

JOBLESS adj having no paid employment; unemployed

JOBSWORTH noun **JOBSWORTHS** a minor official, especially one who sticks rigidly and unco-operatively to petty rules

JOCK noun **JOCKS** a male athlete

JOCKEY noun **JOCKEYS** a rider, especially a professional one, in horse races □ verb **JOCKEYS, JOCKEYING, JOCKEYED** to ride (a horse) in a race

JOCKEYISM noun **JOCKEYISMS** the practice of jockeys

JOCKSTRAP noun **JOCKSTRAPS** a garment for supporting the genitals, worn by male athletes

JOCOSE adj playful; humorous

JOCOSELY adverb in a jocose way

JOCOSITY noun **JOCOSITIES** the quality of being jocose

JOCULAR adj said of a person: given to joking; good-humoured

JOCULARLY adverb in a jocular way

JOCUND adj cheerful; merry; good-humoured

JOCUNDITY noun **JOCUNDITIES** the quality of being jocund

JOCUNDLY adverb in a jocund way

JODHPURS plural noun riding-breeches that are loose-fitting over the buttocks and thighs, and tight-fitting from knee to calf

JOE noun **JOES** a beloved person

JOEY noun **JOEYS** a young animal, especially a kangaroo

JOG verb **JOGS, JOGGING, JOGGED** to run at a slowish steady pace, especially for exercise □ noun **JOGS** a period or spell of jogging

JOGGER noun **JOGGERS** someone who jogs, especially on a regular basis for exercise

JOGGING noun **JOGGINGS** running at a slowish steady pace

JOGGLE verb **JOGGLES, JOGGLING, JOGGLED** to jolt, shake or wobble □ noun **JOGGLES** a shake or jolt

JOHN noun **JOHNS** a lavatory

JOHNNY noun **JOHNNIES** a chap; a fellow

JOIN verb **JOINS, JOINING, JOINED** to connect, attach, link or unite □ noun **JOINS** a seam or joint

JOINER noun **JOINERS** a craftsman who makes and fits wooden doors, window frames, stairs, shelves, etc

JOINERY noun **JOINERIES** the trade or work of a joiner

JOINT noun **JOINTS** the place where two or more pieces join □ verb **JOINTS, JOINTING, JOINTED** to connect to something by joints □ adj owned or done, etc in common; shared

JOINTED adj having joints

JOINTLY adverb in a joint manner; unitedly or in combination; together

JOINTNESS noun **JOINTNESSES** the state of being joint

JOINTURE noun **JOINTURES** property settled on a woman by her husband for her use after his death □ verb **JOINTURES, JOINTURING, JOINTURED** to provide (a woman) with a jointure

JOIST noun **JOISTS** any of the beams supporting a floor or ceiling □ verb **JOISTS, JOISTING, JOISTED** to fit something with joists

JOJOBA noun **JOJOBAS** a N American shrub whose edible seeds contain a waxy oil chemically similar to spermaceti, used in the manufacture of cosmetics and lubricants

JOKE noun **JOKES** a humorous story □ verb **JOKES, JOKING, JOKED** to make jokes

JOKER noun **JOKERS** an extra card in a pack, usually bearing a picture of a jester, used in certain games

JOKEY adj **JOKIER, JOKIEST** given to joking, good-humoured

JOKINGLY adverb as a joke

JOLLIFY verb **JOLLIFIES, JOLLIFYING, JOLLIFIED** to make something jolly

JOLLINESS noun **JOLLINESSES** the state or quality of being jolly

JOLLITY noun **JOLLITIES** merriment

JOLLY adj **JOLLIER, JOLLIEST** good-humoured; cheerful □ verb **JOLLIES, JOLLYING, JOLLIED** to put or keep in good humour; amuse

JOLLYBOAT noun **JOLLYBOATS** a small boat carried on a larger ship

JOLT verb **JOLTS, JOLTING, JOLTED** to move along jerkily □ noun **JOLTS** a jarring shake

JONQUIL noun **JONQUILS** a species of small daffodil native to Europe and Asia, widely cultivated for its fragrant white or yellow flowers

JOR noun **JORS** the second movement of a raga

JOSH verb **JOSHES, JOSHING, JOSHED** to tease □ noun **JOSHES** a bit of teasing; a joke

JOSHER noun **JOSHERS** someone who joshes

JOSTLE verb **JOSTLES, JOSTLING, JOSTLED** to push and shove

JOT noun **JOTS** the least bit □ verb **JOTS, JOTTING, JOTTED** to set down briefly; to make a memorandum of

JOTTER noun **JOTTERS** a school notebook for rough work and notes

JOTTING noun **JOTTINGS** something jotted down

JOUK verb **JOUKS, JOUKING, JOUKED** to duck; to dodge

JOULE noun **JOULES** in the SI system: a unit of work and energy, equal to the work done when a force of one newton moves through a distance of one metre in the direction of the force

JOURNAL *noun* **JOURNALS** a magazine or periodical, eg one dealing with a specialized subject ◻ *verb* **JOURNALS, JOURNALLING, JOURNALLED** to provide something with, or fix something as, a journal (part of an axle or rotating shaft)

JOURNEY *noun* **JOURNEYS** a process of travelling from one place to another ◻ *verb* **JOURNEYS, JOURNEYING, JOURNEYED** to make a journey

JOURNO *noun* **JOURNOS** a journalist

JOUST *noun* **JOUSTS** a contest between two knights on horseback armed with lances ◻ *verb* **JOUSTS, JOUSTING, JOUSTED** to take part in a joust

JOUSTER *noun* **JOUSTERS** someone who jousts

JOVIAL *adj* good-humoured; merry; cheerful

JOVIALITY *noun* **JOVIALITIES** the quality of being jovial

JOVIALLY *adverb* in a jovial way

JOW *verb* **JOWS, JOWING, JOWED** a Scots word meaning to toll ◻ *noun* **JOWS** a stroke of a bell

JOWL *noun* **JOWLS** the lower jaw

JOWLED *adj* having jowls of a specified kind

JOWLY *adj* **JOWLIER, JOWLIEST** with heavy or droopy jaws

JOY *noun* **JOYS** a feeling of happiness; intense gladness; delight ◻ *verb* **JOYS, JOYING, JOYED** an obsolete word meaning to rejoice

JOYFUL *adj* happy; full of joy

JOYFULLY *adverb* in a joyful way

JOYLESS *adj* without joy; not giving joy

JOYLESSLY *adverb* in a joyless way

JOYOUS *adj* filled with, causing or showing joy

JOYOUSLY *adverb* in a joyous way

JUBA *noun* **JUBAS** a type of rustic dance

JUBATE *adj* maned

JUBE *noun* **JUBES** shortened form of jujube

JUBILANT *adj* showing and expressing triumphant joy; rejoicing

JUBILEE *noun* **JUBILEES** a special

anniversary of a significant event, eg the succession of a monarch

JUD *noun* **JUDS** a mass of coal

JUDAS *noun* **JUDASES** a spy-hole in a door, etc

JUDDER *verb* **JUDDERS, JUDDERING, JUDDERED** said of machinery: to jolt, shake, shudder or vibrate ◻ *noun* **JUDDERS** a shuddering vibration, especially of machinery

JUDGE *noun* **JUDGES** a public officer who hears and decides cases in a law court ◻ *verb* **JUDGES, JUDGING, JUDGED** to try (a legal case) in a law court as a judge; to decide (questions of guiltiness, etc)

JUDGEMENT *noun* **JUDGEMENTS** the decision of a judge in a court of law

JUDGESHIP *noun* **JUDGESHIPS** the office or function of a judge

JUDGMENT *noun* **JUDGMENTS** judgement

JUDICIAL *adj* relating or referring to a court of law, judges or the decisions of judges

JUDICIARY *noun* **JUDICIARIES** the branch of government concerned with the legal system and the administration of justice

JUDICIOUS *adj* shrewd, sensible, wise or tactful

JUDO *noun* **JUDOS** a Japanese sport and physical discipline based on unarmed self-defence techniques, developed from ju-jitsu

JUDOGI *noun* **JUDOGIS** the costume (jacket and trousers) worn by a judoist

JUDOIST *noun* **JUDOISTS** a person who practises, or is expert in, judo

JUDOKA *noun* **JUDOKAS** a judoist

JUG *noun* **JUGS** a deep container for liquids, with a handle and a shaped lip for pouring ◻ *verb* **JUGS, JUGGING, JUGGED** to stew (meat, especially hare) in an earthenware container

JUGATE *adj* paired

JUGFUL *noun* **JUGFULS** the amount a jug can hold

JUGGINS *noun* **JUGGINSES** a simpleton

JUGGLE *verb* **JUGGLES, JUGGLING, JUGGLED** to keep several objects simultaneously in the air by skilful throwing and catching

JUGGLER *noun* **JUGGLERS**

someone who entertains people by keeping several objects simultaneously in the air by skilful throwing and catching

JUGGLING *noun* **JUGGLINGS** the action of keeping several objects simultaneously in the air by skilful throwing and catching ◻ *adj* that juggles; deceptive

JUGULAR *adj* relating to the neck or throat ◻ *noun* **JUGULARS** any of several veins that carry deoxygenated blood from the head to the heart in vertebrates

JUGULATE *verb* **JUGULATES, JUGULATING, JUGULATED** to cut the throat of (a person or animal)

JUICE *noun* **JUICES** the liquid or sap from fruit or vegetables ◻ *verb* **JUICES, JUICING, JUICED** to squeeze juice from (a fruit, etc)

JUICELESS *adj* lacking juice

JUICER *noun* **JUICERS** a device for extracting the juice from fruit and vegetables

JUICINESS *noun* **JUICINESSES** the quality of being juicy

JUICY *adj* **JUICIER, JUICIEST** full of juice; rich and succulent

JUJU *noun* **JUJUS** a charm or fetish used by W African tribes

JUJUBE *noun* **JUJUBES** a soft fruit-flavoured sweet made with gelatine

JULEP *noun* **JULEPS** a sweet drink, often a medicated one

JULIENNE *noun* **JULIENNES** a clear soup, with shredded vegetables ◻ *adj* said of vegetables: in thin strips; shredded

JUMBLE *verb* **JUMBLES, JUMBLING, JUMBLED** to mix or confuse things, physically or mentally ◻ *noun* **JUMBLES** a confused mass

JUMBO *adj* extra-large ◻ *noun* **JUMBOS** a jumbo jet

JUMBUCK *noun* **JUMBUCKS** a sheep

JUMP *verb* **JUMPS, JUMPING, JUMPED** to spring off the ground, pushing off with the feet ◻ *noun* **JUMPS** an act of jumping

JUMPER *noun* **JUMPERS** a knitted garment for the top half of the body

JUMPILY *adverb* in a jumpy way

JUMPINESS *noun* **JUMPINESSES** the state of being jumpy

JUMPY *adj* **JUMPIER, JUMPIEST** nervy; anxious

JUNCTION *noun* **JUNCTIONS** a place where roads or railway lines meet or cross; an intersection

JUNCTURE noun **JUNCTURES** a joining; a union

JUNGLE noun **JUNGLES** an area of dense vegetation in an open area of tropical rainforest, eg on the site of former tree clearings, along a river bank, or at the forest edge

JUNGLY adj **JUNGLIER, JUNGLIEST** resembling or characterized by jungle

JUNIOR adj low or lower in rank ◻ noun **JUNIORS** a person of low or lower rank in a profession, organization, etc

JUNIPER noun **JUNIPERS** an evergreen coniferous tree or shrub native to N temperate regions, with sharp greyish needles and purple berry-like cones, oils from which are used to flavour gin

JUNK noun **JUNKS** worthless or rejected material; rubbish ◻ verb **JUNKS, JUNKING, JUNKED** to treat something as junk

JUNKET noun **JUNKETS** a dessert made from sweetened and curdled milk ◻ verb **JUNKETS, JUNKETING, JUNKETED** to feast, celebrate or make merry

JUNKETEER noun **JUNKETEERS** someone who junkets

JUNKIE noun **JUNKIES** a drug addict or drug-pusher

JUNKY adj **JUNKIER, JUNKIEST** rubbishy; worthless

JUNTA noun **JUNTAS** a group, clique or faction, usually of army officers, in control of a country after a coup d'état

JURAT noun **JURATS** especially in France and the Channel Islands: a magistrate

JURIDIC adj relating or referring to the law or the administration of justice

JURIDICAL adj relating or referring to the law or the administration of justice

JURIST noun **JURISTS** an expert in the science of law, especially Roman or civil law

JURISTIC adj relating to jurists

JUROR noun **JURORS** a member of a jury in a court of law

JURY noun **JURIES** a body of people sworn to give an honest verdict on the evidence presented to a court of law on a particular case

JURYMAN noun **JURYMEN** a member of a jury; a juror

JURYWOMAN noun **JURYWOMEN** a member of a jury; a juror

JUS noun **JURA** a Latin word for a law or a legal right

JUST adj **JUSTER, JUSTEST** fair; impartial ◻ adverb exactly; precisely

JUSTICE noun **JUSTICES** the quality of being just; just treatment; fairness

JUSTIFIER noun **JUSTIFIERS** someone who defends or vindicates

JUSTIFY verb **JUSTIFIES, JUSTIFYING, JUSTIFIED** to prove or show something to be right, just or reasonable

JUSTLY adverb in a just manner; equitably; accurately; by right

JUSTNESS noun **JUSTNESSES** equity; fittingness; exactness

JUT verb **JUTS, JUTTING, JUTTED** to stick out; to project ◻ noun **JUTS** a projection

JUTE noun **JUTES** fibre from certain types of tropical bark, used for making sacking, ropes, etc

JUTTING adj projecting or protruding

JUVENILE adj young; youthful ◻ noun **JUVENILES** a young person

JUVENILIA plural noun the works produced by a writer or artist during their youth

JUXTAPOSE verb **JUXTAPOSES, JUXTAPOSING, JUXTAPOSED** to place things side by side

JYNX noun **JYNXES** a wryneck (a small bird related to the woodpecker)

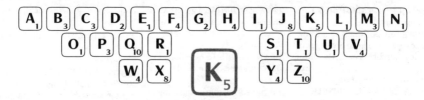

KA noun **KAS** the spirit or soul

KABALA noun **KABALAS** the cabbala

KABBALA noun **KABBALAS** the cabbala

KABUKI noun **KABUKIS** a popular traditional form of Japanese drama in which men play both male and female roles

KACCHA noun **KACCHAS** the short trousers traditionally worn by Sikhs

KADI noun **KADIS** a cadi

KAE verb **KAES, KAEING, KAED** to serve

KAFFIYEH noun **KAFFIYEHS** an Arab headdress of cloth folded and held by a cord around the head

KAFTAN noun **KAFTANS** a caftan

KAGOULE noun **KAGOULES** a cagoule

KAI noun **KAIS** in New Zealand, etc: food, a meal

KAIL noun **KAILS** kale

KAILYARD noun **KAILYARDS** a vegetable garden

KAINITE noun **KAINITES** hydrated magnesium sulphate with potassium chloride, found in salt deposits, used as a fertilizer

KAISER noun **KAISERS** an emperor, especially any of the emperors of Germany, Austria or the Holy Roman Empire

KAISERDOM noun **KAISERDOMS** the office or rule of a kaiser

KAKA noun **KAKAS** a green New Zealand parrot with a long bill

KAKAPO noun **KAKAPOS** a nocturnal flightless parrot, resembling an owl, found only in the rainforests of New Zealand

KAKEMONO noun **KAKEMONOS** a Japanese wall-picture or calligraphic inscription on a roller

KAKIEMON noun **KAKIEMONS** a type of Japanese porcelain first made in the 17c by Sakaida Kakiemon, recognizable from the characteristic use of iron-red

KALANCHOE noun **KALANCHOES** a succulent herb or shrub which bears flower clusters on long stems, native to tropical Africa and Madagascar

KALE noun **KALES** a variety of cabbage with loose wrinkled or curled leaves that do not form a head, widely cultivated in Europe as a vegetable and fodder crop

KALENDS plural noun calends

KALI noun **KALIS** the prickly saltwort or glasswort

KALIF noun **KALIFS** the caliph

KALMIA noun **KALMIAS** a N American evergreen shrub belonging to the heath family, notable for its clusters of flowers

KALONG noun **KALONGS** a large fruit bat

KAM adj a Shakespearean word meaning *awry*

KAME noun **KAMES** a long narrow steep-sided mound or ridge of gravel, sand, etc, deposited by water at the edge of a melting glacier

KAMEEZ noun **KAMEEZES** a loose tunic with tight sleeves worn by women in or from S Asia

KAMIK noun **KAMIKS** a knee-length sealskin boot

KAMIKAZE noun **KAMIKAZES** in World War II: a Japanese plane loaded with explosives that the pilot would deliberately crash into an enemy target □ adj relating or referring to such an attack or the pilot concerned

KAMPONG noun **KAMPONGS** a Malaysian village or settlement

KANGA noun **KANGAS** a piece of cotton cloth, usually brightly decorated, wound around the body as a woman's dress

KANGAROO noun **KANGAROOS** a herbivorous marsupial mammal with a thick muscular tail and large powerful hind legs adapted for leaping, native to Australia and New Guinea □ verb **KANGAROOS, KANGAROOING, KANGAROOED** said of a car: to move forward in jerks because of the driver's poor clutch control

KANGHA noun **KANGHAS** the comb traditionally worn by Sikhs in their hair

KANJI noun **KANJIS** a Japanese writing system using characters derived from Chinese ideographs

KAOLIN noun **KAOLINS** a soft white clay composed of kaolinite and other clay minerals, used for making fine porcelain, bricks and cement, as a filler in rubber, paper and paints, and medicinally to treat diarrhoea and vomiting

KAOLINE noun **KAOLINES** kaolin

KAOLINISE verb **KAOLINISES, KAOLINISING, KAOLINISED** to kaolinize

KAOLINITE noun **KAOLINITES** a white, grey or yellowish clay mineral consisting of hydrated aluminium silicate formed as a result of the alteration of feldspars by steam from underground sources or weathering

KAOLINIZE verb **KAOLINIZES, KAOLINIZING, KAOLINIZED** to turn into kaolin

KAON noun **KAONS** an elementary particle, which with the pion and psi particles, comprises mesons involved in the forces holding together protons and neutrons in the atomic nucleus

KAPOK noun **KAPOKS** the light waterproof silky fibres that surround the seeds of the kapok tree, used for padding and stuffing eg pillows

KAPPA noun **KAPPAS** the tenth letter of the Greek alphabet

KAPUT adj broken, from French *être capot* to hold no tricks in the card game piquet

KARA noun **KARAS** the steel bangle signifying the unity of God, traditionally worn by Sikhs

KARABINER noun **KARABINERS** a steel coupling link with a spring clip in one side

KARAKUL noun **KARAKULS** a breed of sheep, native to central Asia, which has coarse black, brown or grey wool

KARAOKE noun **KARAOKES** a

form of entertainment originally developed in Japan, in which amateur performers sing pop songs to the accompaniment of pre-recorded music

KARAT *noun* **KARATS** a carat

KARATE *noun* **KARATES** a system of unarmed self-defence, using blows and kicks, originally Japanese, now a popular combative sport

KARATEKA *noun* **KARATEKAS** a competitor or an expert in karate

KARMA *noun* **KARMAS** the sum of someone's lifetime's actions, seen as governing their fate in the next life

KARMIC *adj* of or relating to karma

KAROSS *noun* **KAROSSES** a S African sleeveless jacket made of animal skins with the hair left on

KARRI *noun* **KARRIS** a W Australian eucalyptus tree

KARSEY *noun* **KARSEYS** a kazi

KARST *noun* **KARSTS** any landscape characterized by gorges, caves, potholes, underground streams and other features produced by the action of water on limestone rock formations

KARSY *noun* **KARSIES** a kazi

KART *noun* **KARTS** a go-kart

KARTER *noun* **KARTERS** someone who takes part in go-kart racing

KARTING *noun* **KARTINGS** go-kart racing

KARYOLOGY *noun* **KARYOLOGIES** a former name for the study of cell nuclei, especially of chromosomes, which is now covered under molecular biology

KARYOTYPE *noun* **KARYOTYPES** the number, size and structure of the chromosomes in the nucleus of a cell, characteristic of all the diploid cells of a particular individual, strain or species □ *verb* **KARYOTYPES, KARYOTYPING, KARYOTYPED** to investigate or determine the karyotype of (a cell)

KARZY *noun* **KARZIES** a kazi

KAS plural of **ka**

KASBAH *noun* **KASBAHS** a castle or fortress in a N African town

KASHA *noun* **KASHAS** a porridge or gruel-like dish made from crushed cereal

KASHRUS *noun* **KASHRUSES** the kasrut

KASHRUT *noun* **KASHRUTS** the Jewish system of dietary laws

relating to the fitness and preparation of food

KASHRUTH *noun* **KASHRUTHS** the kashrut

KAT *noun* **KATS** a shrub of E Africa, Arabia, etc

KATA *noun* **KATAS** a formal sequence of practice movements and exercises that are performed in martial arts such as judo and karate

KATABATIC *adj* said of winds: blowing down a slope because of air density differences resulting from overnight cooling, etc

KATAKANA *noun* **KATAKANAS** one of the two syllabic writing systems in Japanese

KATYDID *noun* **KATYDIDS** any of various species of grasshopper, with antennae often much longer than its body

KAURI *noun* **KAURIS** a tall broad-leaved coniferous tree, native to SE Asia and Australasia, the source of valuable timber and an important resin

KAVA *noun* **KAVAS** an aromatic plant of the pepper family

KAW *noun* **KAWS** a caw □ *verb* **KAWS, KAWING, KAWED** to caw

KAY *noun* **KAYS** the letter 'K'

KAYAK *noun* **KAYAKS** a sealskin-covered canoe for one person used by the Inuit

KAYO *verb* **KAYOS, KAYOES, KAYOING, KAYOED** to knock someone out

KAYOING *noun* **KAYOINGS** the action of knocking someone out

KAZI *noun* **KAZIS** a lavatory

KAZOO *noun* **KAZOOS** a crude wind instrument consisting of a short metal tube with a strip of parchment or plastic etc, stretched across a hole in its upper surface which vibrates with a buzz when someone blows or hums into it

KEA *noun* **KEAS** an olive-coloured parrot with blue and red markings on its wings, found only on South Island, New Zealand

KEB *verb* **KEBS, KEBBING, KEBBED** a Scots word meaning to give birth to a premature or stillborn lamb □ *noun* **KEBS** a ewe giving birth to such a lamb

KEBAB *noun* **KEBABS** a dish of

small pieces of meat and vegetable grilled on a skewer □ *verb* **KEBABS, KEBABBING, KEBABBED** to skewer something

KECKS *singular noun* trousers

KED *noun* **KEDS** a wingless fly that infests sheep

KEDGE *verb* **KEDGES, KEDGING, KEDGED** to manoeuvre by means of a hawser attached to a light anchor □ *noun* **KEDGES** a light anchor used for kedging

KEDGEREE *noun* **KEDGEREES** a European, but especially British, dish, now usually a mixture of rice, fish and eggs

KEEK *noun* **KEEKS** a peep □ *verb* **KEEKS, KEEKING, KEEKED** to take a peep

KEEL *noun* **KEELS** the timber or metal strut extending from stem to stern along the base of a ship, from which the hull is built up □ *verb* **KEELS, KEELING, KEELED** to capsize

KEELBOAT *noun* **KEELBOATS** a type of yacht with a heavy external keel providing weight to offset that of the sails

KEELED *adj* keel-shaped

KEELHAUL *verb* **KEELHAULS, KEELHAULING, KEELHAULED** to drag someone under the keel of a ship from one side to the other, as a naval punishment

KEELMAN *noun* **KEELMEN** a man who works on a barge

KEELSON *noun* **KEELSONS** a kelson

KEEN [1] *adj* **KEENER, KEENEST** eager; willing

KEEN [2] *verb* **KEENS, KEENING, KEENED** especially in Ireland: to lament or mourn in a loud wailing voice □ *noun* **KEENS** a lament for the dead

KEENING *noun* **KEENINGS** wailing; lamentation

KEENLY *adverb* in a keen way; sharply; acutely

KEENNESS *noun* **KEENNESSES** the quality of being keen; sharpness; acuteness

KEEP *verb* **KEEPS, KEEPING, KEPT** to have; to possess □ *noun* **KEEPS** the cost of one's food and other daily expenses

KEEPER *noun* **KEEPERS** a person who looks after something, eg a collection in a museum

KEEPING *noun* **KEEPINGS** care or charge

KEEPNET *noun* **KEEPNETS** a cone-shaped net suspended in a river, etc, in which fish caught by anglers can be kept alive

KEEPSAKE *noun* **KEEPSAKES** something kept in memory of the giver, or of a particular event or place

KEF *noun* **KEFS** a state of dreamy euphoria

KEFFIYEH *noun* **KEFFIYEHS** a kaffiyeh

KEFUFFLE *noun* **KEFUFFLES** a carfuffle

KEG *noun* **KEGS** a small barrel, usually containing less than 10 gallons

KEISTER *noun* **KEISTERS** the buttocks

KEKS *singular noun* trousers

KELIM *noun* **KELIMS** a kilim

KELOID *noun* **KELOIDS** excessive hard smooth growth of harmless scar tissue at the site of a skin injury, common in dark-skinned people but unusual in fair-skinned people

KELOIDAL *adj* of the nature of keloid

KELP *noun* **KELPS** a common name for any large brown seaweed that grows below the low-tide mark

KELPER *noun* **KELPERS** the local name for a citizen or inhabitant of, or person born in, the Falkland Islands

KELPIE *noun* **KELPIES** a malignant water spirit in the form of a horse, usually associated with fords

KELPY *noun* **KELPIES** a kelpie

KELSON *noun* **KELSONS** a timber fixed along a ship's keel for strength

KELT *noun* **KELTS** a salmon that has just spawned

KELTER *noun* **KELTERS** kilter

KELVIN *noun* **KELVINS** in the SI system: a unit of thermodynamic or absolute temperature, equal to $\frac{1}{273.16}$ of the absolute temperature of the triple point of water, and equal in magnitude to one degree on the Celsius scale □ *adj* relating to the Kelvin scale of temperature

KEMPT *adj* said especially of hair: neatly combed or kept

KEN *verb* **KENS, KENNING, KENNED, KENT** to know **KEN** *noun* range of knowledge; perception

KENAF *noun* **KENAFS** a tropical Asian herbaceous plant, the fibres of which can be used as a substitute for wood pulp in making paper

KENDO *noun* **KENDOS** a Japanese art of fencing using bamboo staves or sometimes real swords, while observing strict ritual

KENNED a past form of **ken**

KENNEL *noun* **KENNELS** a small shelter for a dog □ *verb* **KENNELS, KENNELLING, KENNELLED** to put or keep (an animal) in a kennel

KENNING a form of **ken**

KENSPECK *adj* conspicuous; easily recognized

KENT a past form of **ken**

KEP *verb* **KEPS, KEPPING, KEPPIT** a dialect word meaning to catch □ *noun* **KEPS** a catch

KEPI *noun* **KEPIS** a French military cap with a flat circular crown and horizontal straight-edged peak

KEPT past form of **keep**

KERATIN *noun* **KERATINS** a tough fibrous protein produced by the epidermis in vertebrates, and forming the main component of hair, nails, claws, horns, feathers and the dead outer layers of skin cells

KERATITIS *noun* **KERATITISES** inflammation of the cornea

KERATOID *adj* resembling horn or keratin

KERATOSE *adj* said especially of certain sponges: having a horny skeleton

KERATOSIS *noun* **KERATOSES** a horny growth on or over the skin, eg a wart

KERB *noun* **KERBS** the row of stones or concrete edging forming the edge of a pavement □ *adj* said of a market or dealing, etc: unofficial; outside official trading hours

KERBSIDE *noun* **KERBSIDES** the edge of the pavement

KERBSTONE *noun* **KERBSTONES** one of the stones used to form a kerb

KERCHIEF *noun* **KERCHIEFS** a square of cloth or a scarf for wearing over the head or round the neck

KERF *noun* **KERFS** the cut, notch or groove, etc made by a saw

KERFUFFLE *noun* **KERFUFFLES** a carfuffle

KERMES *plural noun* the dried bodies of the female scale insect used as a red dyestuff

KERMESSE *noun* **KERMESSES** a cycle race held in an urban area

KERMIS *noun* **KERMISES** a fair or festival held to raise money for charity

KERNEL *noun* **KERNELS** the inner part of a seed, eg the edible part of a nut

KEROSENE *noun* **KEROSENES** kerosine

KEROSINE *noun* **KEROSINES** a combustible oily mixture of hydrocarbons obtained mainly by distillation of petroleum, used as a fuel for jet aircraft, domestic heating systems and lamps, and as a solvent

KERRIA *noun* **KERRIAS** a deciduous yellow-flowered shrub

KERSEY *noun* **KERSEYS** a coarse woollen cloth

KESH *noun* **KESHES** the uncut beard and hair traditionally worn by Sikhs

KESTREL *noun* **KESTRELS** a small falcon with a long tail and broad pointed wings, often seen hovering a few metres above ground while searching for prey

KET *noun* **KETS** a Scots word for *carrion*

KETA *noun* **KETAS** a Pacific salmon

KETAMINE *noun* **KETAMINES** a crystalline anaesthetic and analgesic substance often used in veterinary medicine and sometimes illicitly for its hallucinatory properties

KETCH *noun* **KETCHES** a small two-masted sailing boat, the foremast being the taller

KETCHUP *noun* **KETCHUPS** a thick sauce made from tomatoes, vinegar, spices, etc

KETONE *noun* **KETONES** any of a class of organic chemical compounds that are formed by the oxidation of secondary alcohols, eg acetone

KETONURIA *noun* **KETONURIAS** the presence of abnormally large numbers of ketone bodies in urine, a characteristic sign of diabetes, prolonged starvation, etc

KETOSIS *noun* **KETOSES** the excessive formation of acetone or ketone bodies in the body, due to incomplete oxidation of fats, which occurs in diabetes and is also an indicator of starvation

KETTLE *noun* **KETTLES** a container with a spout, lid and handle, for boiling water

KETTLEFUL noun **KETTLEFULS** the amount a kettle will hold

KEX noun **KEXES** a dry stalk ⓘ This word is worth 14 points and is useful for using up **X** and **K**.

KEY noun **KEYS** a device for opening or closing a lock, or for winding up, turning, tuning, tightening or loosening ▫ adj centrally important ▫ verb **KEYS, KEYING, KEYED** to enter (data) into a computer, calculator, etc by means of a keyboard; to keyboard

KEYBOARD noun **KEYBOARDS** the set of keys on a piano, etc ▫ verb **KEYBOARDS, KEYBOARDING, KEYBOARDED** to operate the keyboard of a computer

KEYED adj equipped with a key or keys

KEYHOLE noun **KEYHOLES** the hole through which a key is inserted into a lock

KEYLESS adj without a key or keys

KEYNOTE noun **KEYNOTES** the note on which a musical scale or key is based; the tonic ▫ adj said of a speech, etc: expounding central principles ▫ verb **KEYNOTES, KEYNOTING, KEYNOTED** to deliver a keynote speech

KEYPAD noun **KEYPADS** a small device with push-button controls, eg a TV remote control unit or a pocket calculator

KEYPUNCH noun **KEYPUNCHES** a device, operated by a keyboard, that transfers data on to cards by punching holes in them, formerly used when computer data was routinely stored on punched cards ▫ verb **KEYPUNCHES, KEYPUNCHING, KEYPUNCHED** to transfer (data) in this way

KEYSTONE noun **KEYSTONES** the central supporting stone at the high point of an arch

KEYSTROKE noun **KEYSTROKES** a single press of a key on a keyboard, etc

KEYWORD noun **KEYWORDS** a word that sums up or gives an indication of the nature of the passage in which it occurs

KHADDAR noun **KHADDARS** hand-spun, hand-woven cotton cloth, produced in India

KHADI noun **KHADIS** khaddar

KHAKI noun **KHAKIS** a dull brownish-yellow or brownish-green colour

KHALIF noun **KHALIFS** the caliph

KHAMSIN noun **KHAMSINS** a hot south or south-east wind in Egypt, which blows for about 50 days from mid-March

KHAN noun **KHANS** an Eastern inn, especially a caravanserai

KHANGA noun **KHANGAS** a kanga

KHAT noun **KHATS** a kat

KHEDIVA noun **KHEDIVAS** the wife of the viceroy of Egypt

KHEDIVAL adj of or relating to the khedive

KHEDIVATE noun **KHEDIVATES** the office of the khedive

KHEDIVE noun **KHEDIVES** the title of the viceroy of Egypt during Turkish rule from 1867–1914

KHOJA noun **KHOJAS** a Middle-Eastern title of respect

KHUTBAH noun **KHUTBAHS** a Muslim prayer and sermon delivered in the mosques on Fridays

KIANG noun **KIANGS** a variety of wild ass found in Tibet and neighbouring regions

KIBBLE 1 noun **KIBBLES** a bucket on a chain or rope used in a well, or one used in mining, etc

KIBBLE 2 verb **KIBBLES, KIBBLING, KIBBLED** to grind (cereal, etc) fairly coarsely

KIBBUTZ noun **KIBBUTZIM** in Israel: a communal farm or other concern owned and run jointly as a co-operative by its workers

KIBE noun **KIBES** a chilblain, especially one on the heel

KIBITZ verb **KIBITZES, KIBITZING, KIBITZED** to give unwanted advice; to comment out of turn

KIBITZER noun **KIBITZERS** an onlooker, eg at cards, etc, who gives unwanted advice

KIBLAH noun **KIBLAHS** the direction of Mecca, the point which Muslims turn towards in prayer

KIBOSH noun **KIBOSHES** rubbish; nonsense

KICK verb **KICKS, KICKING, KICKED** to hit with the foot ▫ noun **KICKS** a blow or fling with the foot

KICKBACK noun **KICKBACKS** part of a sum of money received that is paid to someone else for help or favours already received or to come, especially if this is illegally given

KICKDOWN noun **KICKDOWNS** a

method of changing gear in a car with automatic transmission, by pressing the accelerator pedal right down

KICKER noun **KICKERS** someone or something that kicks

KICKSHAW noun **KICKSHAWS** a trinket; a cheap article of no value

KICKSTAND noun **KICKSTANDS** a metal device attached to a bicycle or motorcycle, etc, which is kicked down into position to hold the vehicle upright when it is parked

KID 1 noun **KIDS** a child; a young person ▫ adj younger

KID 2 verb **KIDS, KIDDING, KIDDED** to fool or deceive someone, especially light-heartedly or in fun

KIDDER noun **KIDDERS** someone who kids

KIDDUSH noun **KIDDUSHES** a Jewish blessing pronounced over wine and bread by the head of the household to usher in the Sabbath and other holy days

KIDDY noun **KIDDIES** a small child

KIDDYWINK noun **KIDDYWINKS** a small child

KIDNAP verb **KIDNAPS, KIDNAPPING, KIDNAPPED** to seize and hold someone prisoner illegally, usually demanding a ransom for their release

KIDNAPPER noun **KIDNAPPERS** someone who kidnaps a person

KIDNEY noun **KIDNEYS** in vertebrates: either of a pair of organs at the back of the abdomen whose function is the removal of waste products from the blood, and the excretion of such compounds from the body, usually in the form of urine

KIDOLOGY noun **KIDOLOGIES** the art of deceiving or bluffing, sometimes used to gain a psychological advantage

KIF noun **KIFS** a kef

KILEY noun **KILEYS** a type of boomerang

KILIM noun **KILIMS** a woven rug without any pile, traditionally made in the Middle East

KILL verb **KILLS, KILLING, KILLED** to cause the death of (an animal or person); to put someone to death; to murder; to slaughter; to destroy someone or something ▫ noun **KILLS** an act of killing

KILLDEER noun **KILLDEERS** the largest N American ring-necked plover

KILLER *noun* **KILLERS** a person or creature that kills

KILLICK *noun* **KILLICKS** a small anchor, especially an improvised one made from a heavy stone

KILLIFISH *noun* **KILLIFISHES** any of various species of small fish, resembling a minnow, found in fresh and brackish waters

KILLING *noun* **KILLINGS** an act of slaying ❑ *adj* exhausting

KILLJOY *noun* **KILLJOYS** someone who spoils the pleasure of others

KILLOCK *noun* **KILLOCKS** a killick

KILN *noun* **KILNS** a heated oven or furnace used for drying timber, grain or hops, or for firing bricks, pottery, etc ❑ *verb* **KILNS, KILNING, KILNED** to dry or fire something in a kiln

KILO *noun* **KILOS** a kilogram; a kilometre

KILOBAR *noun* **KILOBARS** 1 000 bars

KILOBIT *noun* **KILOBITS** 1 024 bits

KILOBYTE *noun* **KILOBYTES** in computing: a unit of memory equal to 1 024 bytes

KILOCYCLE *noun* **KILOCYCLES** a kilohertz

KILOGRAM *noun* **KILOGRAMS** in the SI system: the basic unit of mass, equal to 1 000 grams (2.205 lb)

KILOGRAY *noun* **KILOGRAYS** 1 000 grays, an SI unit used to measure the absorbed dose of radiation, eg in food irradiation

KILOHERTZ *noun* **KILOHERTZES** an SI unit of frequency equal to 1 000 hertz or 1 000 cycles per second, used to measure the frequency of sound and radio waves

KILOJOULE *noun* **KILOJOULES** 1 000 joules, an SI unit used to measure energy, work and heat, replacing the metric unit kilocalorie (1 kj = 0.2388 kcal)

KILOMETRE *noun* **KILOMETRES** a metric unit of length equal to 1 000 metres (0.62 miles)

KILOTON *noun* **KILOTONS** a metric unit of explosive power equivalent to that of 1 000 tonnes of TNT

KILOVOLT *noun* **KILOVOLTS** SI unit: 1 000 volts

KILOWATT *noun* **KILOWATTS** an SI unit of electrical power equal to 1 000 watts or about 1.34 horsepower

KILT *noun* **KILTS** a pleated tartan knee-length wraparound skirt, traditionally worn by men as part of Scottish Highland dress ❑ *verb* **KILTS, KILTING, KILTED** to pleat something vertically

KILTED *adj* wearing a kilt

KILTER *noun* **KILTERS** good condition

KILTIE *noun* **KILTIES** a person wearing a kilt, especially a soldier in a Highland Regiment

KILTY *noun* **KILTIES** a kiltie

KIMCHI *noun* **KIMCHIS** a very spicy Korean dish made with a variety of raw vegetables

KIMONO *noun* **KIMONOS** a long, loose, wide-sleeved Japanese garment fastened by a sash at the waist

KIN *noun* **KINS** one's relatives ❑ *adj* related

KIND[1] *noun* **KINDS** a group, class, sort, race or type

KIND[2] *adj* **KINDER, KINDEST** friendly, helpful, well-meaning, generous, benevolent or considerate

KINDA *adverb* somewhat, sort of

KINDLE *verb* **KINDLES, KINDLING, KINDLED** to start or make something, etc start burning

KINDLER *noun* **KINDLERS** someone who kindles or starts something burning

KINDLING *noun* **KINDLINGS** materials for starting a fire, eg dry twigs or leaves, sticks, etc

KINDLY *adverb* in a kind manner ❑ *adj* **KINDLIER, KINDLIEST** kind, friendly, generous or good-natured

KINDNESS *noun* **KINDNESSES** the quality or fact of being kind; a kind act

KINDRED *noun* **KINDREDS** one's relatives; family ❑ *adj* related

KINDY *noun* **KINDIES** a kindergarten

KINE *plural noun* cattle

KINEMATIC *adj* of or relating to kinematics

KINEMATICS *singular noun* the branch of mechanics concerned with the motion of objects, without consideration of the forces acting on them

KINESICS *singular noun* body movements which convey information in the absence of speech, eg frowning, winking

KINESIS *noun* **KINESES** the movement of a living organism or cell in response to a simple stimulus (eg light or humidity), the rate of movement being dependent on the intensity as opposed to the direction of the stimulus

KINETIC *adj* relating to or producing motion

KINETICS *singular noun* the branch of mechanics concerned with the relationship between moving objects, their masses and the forces acting on them

KINFOLK *singular or plural noun* **KINFOLKS** kinsfolk

KING *noun* **KINGS** a male ruler of a nation, especially a hereditary monarch

KINGCUP *noun* **KINGCUPS** the common name for any of various plants with yellow flowers, especially the marsh marigold or the buttercup

KINGDOM *noun* **KINGDOMS** a region, state or people ruled, or previously ruled, by a king or queen

KINGFISH *noun* **KINGFISHES** any of various fish notable for their size or value

KINGLESS *adj* having no king

KINGLY *adj* **KINGLIER, KINGLIEST** belonging to, or suitable for, a king; royal; kinglike

KINGMAKER *noun* **KINGMAKERS** someone who has influence over the choice of people for high office

KINGSHIP *noun* **KINGSHIPS** the state, office or dignity of a king

KININ *noun* **KININS** any of a group of peptides, found in blood, that are associated with inflammation (eg as a result of insect stings), and cause contraction of smooth muscles, dilation of blood vessels, and an increase in the permeability of capillaries

KINK *noun* **KINKS** a bend or twist in hair or in a string, rope, wire, etc ❑ *verb* **KINKS, KINKING, KINKED** to develop, or cause something to develop, a kink

KINKAJOU *noun* **KINKAJOUS** a nocturnal fruit-eating mammal of Central and S America, which has a rounded head, slender body, yellowish-brown fur and a long prehensile tail

KINKY *adj* **KINKIER, KINKIEST** interested in or practising unusual or perverted sexual acts

KINO *noun* **KINOS** a resin exuded by various tropical trees, used as an astringent and in tanning

KINSFOLK *singular or plural noun* **KINSFOLKS** one's relations

KINSHIP *noun* **KINSHIPS** family relationship

KINSMAN *noun* **KINSMEN** a relative by blood or marriage

KINSWOMAN *noun* **KINSWOMEN** a relative by blood or marriage

KIOSK *noun* **KIOSKS** a small, roofed and sometimes movable booth or stall for the sale of sweets, newspapers, etc

KIP *noun* **KIPS** sleep or a sleep □ *verb* **KIPS, KIPPING, KIPPED** to sleep

KIPPER *noun* **KIPPERS** a fish, especially a herring, that has been split open, salted and smoked □ *verb* **KIPPERS, KIPPERING, KIPPERED** to cure (herring, etc) by salting and smoking

KIR *noun* **KIRS** a drink made from white wine and cassis

KIRBIGRIP *noun* **KIRBIGRIPS** a type of hairgrip with one straight side and the other bent into ridges to prevent slipping

KIRK *noun* **KIRKS** a church □ *verb* **KIRKS, KIRKING, KIRKED** to bring (a newly delivered mother, members of a newly appointed civic authority, etc) to church for special ceremonies

KIRKING *noun* **KIRKINGS** the first attendance at church of a couple after marriage, of a woman after giving birth, or of a magistrate after election

KIRMESS *noun* **KIRMESSES** a kermis

KIRPAN *noun* **KIRPANS** a small sword or dagger worn by Sikh men as a symbol of religious loyalty

KIRSCH *noun* **KIRSCHES** a clear liqueur distilled from black cherries

KISMET *noun* **KISMETS** the will of Allah

KISS *verb* **KISSES, KISSING, KISSED** to touch someone with the lips, or to press one's lips against them, as a greeting, sign of affection, etc □ *noun* **KISSES** an act of kissing

KISSABLE *adj* pleasant to kiss

KISSAGRAM *noun* **KISSAGRAMS** a kissogram

KISSER *noun* **KISSERS** a person who kisses in a specified way

KISSOGRAM *noun* **KISSOGRAMS** a fun greetings service that involves employing someone to deliver a kiss to someone else on a special occasion

KIT *noun* **KITS** a set of instruments, equipment, etc needed for a purpose, especially one kept in a container □ *verb* **KITS, KITTING, KITTED** to provide someone with the clothes and equipment necessary for a particular occupation, assignment, etc

KITCHEN *noun* **KITCHENS** a room or an area in a building where food is prepared and cooked

KITE *noun* **KITES** a bird of prey of the hawk family, noted for its long pointed wings, deeply forked tail, and soaring graceful flight □ *verb* **KITES, KITING, KITED** to write (a cheque) before one has sufficient funds in one's account to cover it

KITH *noun* **KITHS** friends

KITING *noun* **KITINGS** kite-flying

KITSCH *noun* **KITSCHES** sentimental, pretentious or vulgar tastelessness in art, design, writing, film-making, etc

KITSCHY *adj* **KITSCHIER, KITSCHIEST** sentimental, pretentious or vulgarly tasteless

KITTEN *noun* **KITTENS** a young cat □ *verb* **KITTENS, KITTENING, KITTENED** said of a cat: to give birth

KITTENISH *adj* like a kitten; playful

KITTIWAKE *noun* **KITTIWAKES** either of two species of gull found on open water far from shore, especially that found in Arctic and N Atlantic coastal regions, which has white plumage with dark-grey back and wings, a yellow bill and black legs

KITTY *noun* **KITTIES** a fund contributed to jointly, for communal use by a group of people

KIWI *noun* **KIWIS** a nocturnal flightless bird with hair-like brown or grey feathers, a long slender bill and no tail, found only in pine forests in New Zealand and used as its national emblem

KLAXON *noun* **KLAXONS** a loud horn used as a warning signal on ambulances, fire engines, etc

KLEZMER *noun* **KLEZMORIM** traditional E European Yiddish music, revived in the 1980s with a jazz influence

KLONDIKE *noun* **KLONDIKES** a very rich source of wealth □ *verb* **KLONDIKES, KLONDIKING, KLONDIKED** to export (fresh fish, especially herring) direct from Scotland to Europe, etc

KLONDIKER *noun* **KLONDIKERS** a factory ship

KLONDYKE *noun* **KLONDYKES** klondike □ *verb* **KLONDYKES, KLONDYKING, KLONDYKED** to klondike

KLONDYKER *noun* **KLONDYKERS** a klondiker

KLOOF *noun* **KLOOFS** a mountain ravine or pass

KLUDGE *noun* **KLUDGES** in computing: a botched or makeshift device or program which is unreliable or inadequate in function

KLUTZ *noun* **KLUTZES** an idiot; an awkward, stupid person

KLYSTRON *noun* **KLYSTRONS** an evacuated electron tube used to generate or amplify microwaves

KNACK *noun* **KNACKS** the ability to do something effectively and skilfully

KNACKER *noun* **KNACKERS** a buyer of worn-out old horses for slaughter □ *verb* **KNACKERS, KNACKERING, KNACKERED** to exhaust

KNAG *noun* **KNAGS** a knot in wood

KNAGGY *adj* **KNAGGIER, KNAGGIEST** knotty

KNAPSACK *noun* **KNAPSACKS** a hiker's or traveller's bag for food, clothes, etc, traditionally made of canvas or leather, carried on the back or over the shoulder

KNAPWEED *noun* **KNAPWEEDS** a perennial plant native to Europe, with tough stems, toothed basal leaves with shallow lobes, untoothed stem leaves, and hard knob-like reddish-purple flower heads

KNAR *noun* **KNARS** a knot on a tree

KNAVE *noun* **KNAVES** a mischievous young man; a scoundrel

KNAVERY *noun* **KNAVERIES** mischief; trickery

KNAVISH *adj* fraudulent; rascally

KNEAD *verb* **KNEADS, KNEADING, KNEADED** to work (dough) with one's fingers and knuckles into a uniform mass

KNEADER *noun* **KNEADERS** someone who kneads

KNEE *noun* **KNEES** in humans: the joint in the middle of the leg where the lower end of the femur articulates with the upper end of the tibia □ *verb* **KNEES, KNEEING, KNEED** to hit, nudge or shove

For longer words, see The Chambers Dictionary

someone or something with the knee

KNEECAP *noun* **KNEECAPS** a small plate of bone situated in front of and protecting the knee joint in humans and most other mammals □ *verb* **KNEECAPS, KNEECAPPING, KNEECAPPED** to shoot or otherwise damage someone's kneecaps as a form of revenge, torture or unofficial punishment

KNEECAPPING *noun* **KNEECAPPINGS** a form of torture or (terrorist) punishment in which the victim is shot or otherwise injured in the kneecap

KNEED *adj* said of trousers: baggy at the knees

KNEEHOLE *noun* **KNEEHOLES** the space beneath a desk, etc for one's knees

KNEEL *verb* **KNEELS, KNEELING, KNELT, KNEELED** to support one's weight on, or lower oneself onto, one's knees

KNEELER *noun* **KNEELERS** a cushion for kneeling on, especially in church

KNELL *noun* **KNELLS** the tolling of a bell announcing a death or funeral □ *verb* **KNELLS, KNELLING, KNELLED** to announce something or summon someone by, or as if by, a tolling bell

KNEW a past form of **know**

KNICKERS *plural noun* an undergarment for women and girls with two separate legs or legholes □ *exclamation* a mild expression of exasperation, etc

KNIFE *noun* **KNIVES** a cutting instrument, typically in the form of a blade fitted into a handle or into machinery, and sometimes also used for spreading □ *verb* **KNIFES, KNIFING, KNIFED** to cut

KNIFING *noun* **KNIFINGS** the act of attacking and injuring someone using a knife

KNIGHT *noun* **KNIGHTS** a man who has been awarded the highest or second highest class of distinction in any of the four British orders of chivalry, ie honours for service or merit awarded by the Queen or the Government □ *verb* **KNIGHTS, KNIGHTING, KNIGHTED** to confer a knighthood on someone

KNIGHTLY *adj* **KNIGHTLIER, KNIGHTLIEST** relating to, like or befitting a knight; chivalrous

KNIPHOFIA *noun* **KNIPHOFIAS** a

tall straight garden plant with long spikes of red or orange flowers, commonly known as the red-hot poker

KNISH *noun* **KNISHES** in Jewish cookery: dough with a filling of potato, meat, etc, baked or fried

KNIT *verb* **KNITS, KNITTING, KNIT, KNITTED** to produce a fabric composed of interlocking loops of yarn, using a pair of knitting needles or a knitting machine □ *adj* united in a specified way □ *noun* **KNITS** a fabric or a garment made by knitting

KNITTER *noun* **KNITTERS** someone who knits

KNITTING *noun* **KNITTINGS** a garment, etc that is in the process of being knitted

KNITWEAR *noun* **KNITWEARS** knitted clothing, especially sweaters and cardigans

KNIVES plural of **knife**

KNOB *noun* **KNOBS** a hard rounded projection

KNOBBLE *noun* **KNOBBLES** a little knob

KNOBBLY *adj* **KNOBBLIER, KNOBBLIEST** covered with or full of knobs; knotty

KNOBBY *adj* **KNOBBIER, KNOBBIEST** having, or full of, knobs

KNOCK *verb* **KNOCKS, KNOCKING, KNOCKED** to tap or rap with the knuckles or some object, especially on a door for admittance □ *noun* **KNOCKS** an act of knocking

KNOCKER *noun* **KNOCKERS** a heavy piece of metal, usually of a decorative shape, fixed to a door by a hinge and used for knocking

KNOCKING *noun* **KNOCKINGS** a rap or beating on a door, etc

KNOCKOUT *noun* **KNOCKOUTS** someone or something stunning □ *adj* said of a competition: in which the losers in each round are eliminated

KNOLL *noun* **KNOLLS** a small round, usually grassy hill

KNOT *noun* **KNOTS** a join or tie in string, etc made by looping the ends around each other and pulling tight □ *verb* **KNOTS, KNOTTING, KNOTTED** to tie something in a knot

KNOTGRASS *noun* **KNOTGRASSES** an annual plant which is widespread throughout most of Europe

KNOTLESS *adj* without a knot or knots

KNOTTED *adj* full of knots; having a knot or knots

KNOTTY *adj* **KNOTTIER, KNOTTIEST** full of knots

KNOTWEED *noun* **KNOTWEEDS** an annual plant which is widespread throughout most of Europe

KNOW *verb* **KNOWS, KNOWING, KNEW, KNOWN** to be informed or assured of; to be acquainted with

KNOWABLE *adj* capable of being known, discovered, or understood

KNOWING *adj* shrewd; canny; clever

KNOWINGLY *adverb* in a knowing way

KNOWLEDGE *noun* **KNOWLEDGES** the fact of knowing; awareness; understanding

KNOWN *adj* widely recognized

KNUCKLE *noun* **KNUCKLES** a joint of a finger, especially one that links a finger to the hand □ *verb* **KNUCKLES, KNUCKLING, KNUCKLED** to touch or press something with the knuckle or knuckles

KNUR *noun* **KNURS** a knot on a tree

KNURL *noun* **KNURLS** a ridge, especially one of a series □ *verb* **KNURLS, KNURLING, KNURLED** to make ridges in something

KNURLED *adj* covered with ridges

KNURLING *noun* **KNURLINGS** mouldings or other woodwork decorated along the edge with a series of ridges or beadings

KNURLY *adj* **KNURLIER, KNURLIEST** gnarled

KNURR *noun* **KNURRS** a knur

KO *noun* **KOS** a Maori digging stick

KOA *noun* **KOAS** an acacia native to Hawaii

KOALA *noun* **KOALAS** an Australian tree-climbing marsupial with thick grey fur and bushy ears

KOAN *noun* **KOANS** in Zen Buddhism: a nonsensical question given to students as a subject for meditation in order to demonstrate the uselessness of logical thinking

KOB *noun* **KOBS** an African waterbuck

KOBOLD *noun* KOBOLDS a spirit of the mines

KOFTA *noun* KOFTAS in Indian cookery: minced and seasoned meat or vegetables, shaped into balls and fried

KOHL *noun* KOHLS a cosmetic for darkening the eyelids

KOHLRABI *noun* KOHLRABIS a variety of cabbage with a short swollen green or purple edible stem

KOI *noun* KOI any one of various ornamental varieties of common carp

KOINE *noun* KOINES any dialect which has come to be used as the common language of a larger area

KOLA *noun* KOLAS an evergreen tree, native to Africa but cultivated in other tropical regions for its seeds called cola nuts

KOLINSKY *noun* KOLINSKIES any variety of the Siberian mink which has a brown coat even in winter

KOLKHOZ *noun* KOLKHOZES a large-scale collective farm in the former Soviet Union

KOMATIK *noun* KOMATIKS an Inuit sled with wooden runners and drawn by dogs

KOMBU *noun* KOMBUS an edible brown seaweed, used especially for making stock

KON *verb* KONS, KONNING, KOND a Spenserian word meaning to know

KOODOO *noun* KOODOOS a kudu

KOOK *noun* KOOKS a crazy or eccentric person

KOOKIE *adj* KOOKIER, KOOKIEST kooky

KOOKY *adj* KOOKIER, KOOKIEST with the qualities of a kook

KOORI *noun* KOORIS an Aborigine

KOP *noun* KOPS a hill

KOPECK *noun* KOPECKS a coin or unit of currency of Russia, and the former Soviet Union, worth one hundredth of a rouble

KOPJE *noun* KOPJES a koppie

KOPPIE *noun* KOPPIES a low hill

KORFBALL *noun* KORFBALLS a game similar to basketball, played by two teams, consisting each of six men and six women

KORMA *noun* KORMAS in Indian cookery: a mild-flavoured dish of meat or vegetables braised in stock, yoghurt or cream

KORUNA *noun* KORUNAS the standard unit of currency of the Czech Republic and Slovakia

KOS *noun* KOSES an Indian measure of distance

KOSHER *adj* in accordance with Jewish law □ *noun* KOSHERS kosher food

KOTO *noun* KOTOS a Japanese musical instrument consisting of a long box strung with 13 silk strings

KOUMISS *noun* KOUMISSES a kumiss

KOUPREY *noun* KOUPREYS an endangered species of wild cattle, native to the forests of SE Asia, with a large blackish-brown body, white legs, and cylindrical horns

KOW *noun* KOWS a Scots word for a bunch of twigs

KOWHAI *noun* KOWHAIS a small leguminous tree which bears clusters of golden flowers, found in New Zealand and Chile

KOWTOW *verb* KOWTOWS, KOWTOWING, KOWTOWED to touch the forehead to the ground as a gesture of deference □ *noun* KOWTOWS an act of kowtowing

KRAAL *noun* KRAALS a S African village of huts surrounded by a fence

KRAB *noun* KRABS a karabiner

KRAFT *noun* KRAFTS a type of strong brown wrapping paper

KRAIT *noun* KRAITS a venomous S Asian rock snake

KRAKEN *noun* KRAKENS a legendary gigantic sea monster

KRANS *noun* KRANSES a crown of rock on a mountain top

KRANTZ *noun* KRANTZES a krans

KRANZ *noun* KRANZES a krans

KREMLIN *noun* KREMLINS the citadel of a Russian town, especially the one in Moscow

KRILL *noun* KRILLS a shrimp-like crustacean that feeds on plankton and which lives in enormous swarms

KRIMMER *noun* KRIMMERS a tightly curled grey or black fur from a Crimean type of lamb

KRIS *noun* KRISES a Malay or Indonesian dagger with a wavy blade

KROMESKY *noun* KROMESKIES a croquette of minced beef or fish cooked with a binding sauce and allowed to cool

KRONA *noun* KRONOR the standard unit of currency of Sweden

KRÓNA *noun* KRÓNUR the standard unit of currency of Iceland

KRONE *noun* KRONER, KRONEN the standard unit of currency of Denmark and Norway

KRUMMHORN *noun* KRUMMHORNS an early double-reed wind instrument with a curved end

KRYPTON *noun* KRYPTONS a colourless odourless tasteless noble gas that is almost inert, used in lasers, fluorescent lamps and discharge tubes

KUDOS *noun* KUDOSES credit, honour or prestige

KUDU *noun* KUDUS either of two species of lightly striped African antelope, the male of which has long spiral horns

KUDZU *noun* KUDZUS an ornamental climbing plant with edible root tubers and a stem from which fibre can be obtained

KUFIYAH *noun* KUFIYAHS a kaffiyeh

KUKRI *noun* KUKRIS a heavy curved knife or short sword used by Gurkhas

KULAK *noun* KULAKS a wealthy, property-owning Russian peasant

KUMARA *noun* KUMARAS the sweet potato

KUMISS *noun* KUMISSES a drink made from fermented milk, especially mare's milk

KÜMMEL *noun* KÜMMELS a German liqueur flavoured with cumin and caraway seeds

KUMQUAT *noun* KUMQUATS a small spiny evergreen citrus shrub or tree, native to China

KURI *noun* KURIS a mongrel dog

KURRAJONG *noun* KURRAJONGS a name for various Australian trees and shrubs with tough fibrous bark

KURTOSIS *noun* KURTOSES in statistics: the relative sharpness of the peak on a frequency-distribution curve, which indicates the concentration of a distribution about its mean value

KVASS *noun* KVASSES an E European rye beer

KVETCH *verb* KVETCHES, KVETCHING, KVETCHED to complain or whine, especially incessantly □ *noun* KVETCHES a complainer; a fault-finder

KVETCHER *noun* KVETCHERS a kvetch

KWACHA *noun* **KWACHAS** the standard unit of currency of Zambia and Malawi

KWANZA *noun* **KWANZAS** the standard unit of currency in Angola

KY *plural noun* a Scots word for *cows*

KYANISE *verb* **KYANISES, KYANISING, KYANISED** to kyanize

KYANITE *noun* **KYANITES** a mineral, an aluminium silicate, generally sky-blue

KYANIZE *verb* **KYANIZES, KYANIZING, KYANIZED** to preserve (wood) from decay by injecting corrosive sublimate into its pores

KYBOSH *noun* **KYBOSHES** kibosh

KYE *plural noun* a Scots word for *cows*

KYLE *noun* **KYLES** a channel, strait or sound, a common element in placenames

KYLIE *noun* **KYLIES** an Australian boomerang

KYLIX *noun* **KYLICES** a shallow two-handled drinking cup

KYLOE *noun* **KYLOES** one of the small long-haired cattle of the Scottish Highlands and Hebrides

KYMOGRAM *noun* **KYMOGRAMS** a record made by kymograph

KYMOGRAPH *noun* **KYMOGRAPHS** originally an apparatus comprising a slowly rotating cylinder encircled with sooted paper such that physiological responses (especially muscle contraction) could be recorded continuously by a tracking stylus scraping the soot from the paper, but now exclusively an electronic apparatus based on the same principle

KYPHOSIS *noun* **KYPHOSES** excessive curvature of the spine causing a convex backwards arching of the back

KYU *noun* **KYUS** one of the six novice grades in judo (the least experienced being sixth kyu)

For longer words, see *The Chambers Dictionary*

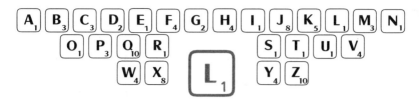

LA *noun* **LAS** in sol-fa notation: the sixth note of the major scale

LAB *noun* **LABS** contraction of *laboratory*

LABEL *noun* **LABELS** a note, tag or sticker that specifies details of something's contents, destination, ownership, etc ▫ *verb* **LABELS, LABELLING, LABELLED** to mark something in a specified way with a special tag, sticker, etc

LABIAL *adj* relating to or beside the lips ▫ *noun* **LABIALS** a sound that involves some active use of one of the lips in its production

LABIALLY *adverb* with a labial sound

LABIATE *noun* **LABIATES** any of a family of flowering plants, including mint and thyme, in which the stems are usually square, and the corolla of petals is divided into two lips ▫ *adj* referring or relating to the labiate family of plants

LABILE *adj* unstable

LABIUM *noun* **LABIA** a lip or lip-like structure

LABOR *noun* **LABORS** labour ▫ *verb* **LABORS, LABORING, LABORED** to labour

LABORED *adj* laboured

LABORIOUS *adj* said of a task, etc: requiring hard work or much effort, especially when the work involved is tedious and boring

LABOUR *noun* **LABOURS** strenuous and prolonged work, especially of the physical kind that is done for payment ▫ *verb* **LABOURS, LABOURING, LABOURED** to work hard or with difficulty

LABOURED *adj* showing signs of effort or difficulty

LABOURER *noun* **LABOURERS** someone who is employed to do heavy, usually unskilled, physical work

LABURNUM *noun* **LABURNUMS** a small tree of the pea family, all parts of which are poisonous, especially the seeds, and which has hanging clusters of bright yellow flowers

LABYRINTH *noun* **LABYRINTHS** a highly complex network of interconnected, sometimes underground, passages and chambers designed to be difficult to find one's way around

LAC *noun* **LACS** a resinous substance produced by certain tropical Asian insects and deposited on the twigs of various trees, used to make varnish, especially shellac, as well as sealing wax, abrasives and a red dye

LACCOLITH *noun* **LACCOLITHS** a lens-shaped mass of igneous rock, usually with a domed upper surface and a flat base, formed when magma bursts into the surrounding strata and then cools and solidifies

LACE *noun* **LACES** a delicate material made by knotting, looping or twisting thread into open intricate symmetrical patterns; a string or cord for fastening shoes ▫ *verb* **LACES, LACING, LACED** to fasten or be fastened with a lace or laces

LACED *adj* said of food, drink, etc: having alcohol, drugs, poison, etc added to it

LACERATE *verb* **LACERATES, LACERATING, LACERATED** to tear or cut (especially flesh) roughly ▫ *adj* having serrated or ragged edges

LACERATED *adj* rent or torn

LACEWING *noun* **LACEWINGS** an insect with long antennae, a slender body and two pairs of distinctly-veined gauzy wings

LACHES *noun* **LACHESES** negligence or excessive delay in carrying out some legal duty or in asserting a right

LACHRYMAL *adj* referring or relating to tears or the glands that secrete them

LACING *noun* **LACINGS** a reinforcing course of bricks, stones, etc incorporated in a wall, especially a wall that is constructed from flint, rubble, small stones, etc

LACINIATE *adj* said of a leaf, petal, the mouthparts of some insects, etc: deeply jagged

LACK *noun* **LACKS** something missing or in short supply; a deficiency or want ▫ *verb* **LACKS, LACKING, LACKED** to be without or to have too little of something

LACKEY *noun* **LACKEYS** someone who does menial work ▫ *verb* **LACKEYS, LACKEYING, LACKEYED** to do menial work, especially under the direction of someone else

LACKING *adj* deficient

LACONIC *adj* said of someone's speech or writing: using few words; neatly concise and to the point

LACQUER *noun* **LACQUERS** a substance that forms a hard shiny and usually transparent covering on wood and metal ▫ *verb* **LACQUERS, LACQUERING, LACQUERED** to cover with lacquer

LACQUERED *adj* covered with lacquer

LACRIMAL *adj* lachrymal

LACROSSE *noun* **LACROSSES** a team game where each player has a long stick with a netted pocket which is used for catching, carrying and throwing a small ball, the object being to put the ball into the opponents' goal-net

LACTARIAN *noun* **LACTARIANS** a vegetarian whose diet includes milk and other dairy products ▫ *adj* relating to a vegetarian whose diet includes milk and other dairy products

LACTATE *verb* **LACTATES, LACTATING, LACTATED** said of the mammary glands of mammals: to secrete milk

LACTATION *noun* **LACTATIONS** in mammals: the hormonally controlled secretion of milk by the mammary glands in order to feed a baby or young animal until it is weaned

LACTEAL *adj* referring or relating to, or consisting of, milk □ *noun* **LACTEALS** any small lymphatic vessel that absorbs the products of digestion of fats in the small intestine

LACTIC *adj* relating to, derived from or containing milk

LACTOSE *noun* **LACTOSES** a white crystalline disaccharide sugar which consists of a galactose molecule linked to a glucose molecule, found only in milk and used in the manufacture of baby milk, and as a laxative and diuretic

LACUNA *noun* **LACUNAE** a gap or a space where something is missing, especially in printed text

LACY *adj* **LACIER, LACIEST** like lace, especially when used to suggest the fine delicate nature of something

LAD *noun* **LADS** a boy or youth

LADDER *noun* **LADDERS** a piece of equipment which is used for climbing up or down, consisting of a set of parallel horizontal rungs or steps set at right angles between two long vertical supports; a long narrow flaw in tights or stockings □ *verb* **LADDERS, LADDERING, LADDERED** said of stockings, etc: to develop a ladder

LADDERED *adj* said of stockings, etc: having a ladder or ladders

LADDIE *noun* **LADDIES** a young boy or lad, often used as a familiar or endearing form of address

LADDISH *adj* said of some young males or their behaviour: characterized by loud swaggering arrogance, vulgarity and sometimes aggression, often brought on by excessive drinking

LADE *verb* **LADES, LADING, LADED** to load; to burden

LADEN *adj* said of a ship: loaded with cargo

LADING *noun* **LADINGS** the cargo or load that a ship, etc carries

LADLE *noun* **LADLES** a large spoon with a long handle and deep bowl, for serving or transferring liquid □ *verb* **LADLES, LADLING, LADLED** to serve or transfer with a ladle

LADLEFUL *noun* **LADLEFULS** the amount a ladle can hold

LADY *noun* **LADIES** a woman who is regarded as having good manners and elegant or refined behaviour

LADYBIRD *noun* **LADYBIRDS** a kind of small beetle whose oval body is usually bright red or yellow with black spots, and which feeds mainly on aphids and scale insects, playing an important part in the control of garden pests

LADYBUG *noun* **LADYBUGS** a ladybird

LADYLIKE *adj* showing attributes, such as social poise, good manners, elegance, etc, that are like or appropriate to those of a lady

LADYSHIP *noun* **LADYSHIPS** a title used to address peeresses (but not duchesses) and the wives and daughters of peers and knights

LAG *verb* **LAGS, LAGGING, LAGGED** to move or progress so slowly as to become separated or left behind □ *noun* **LAGS** a lagging behind; a delay

LAGER *noun* **LAGERS** a light beer available in bottles or on draught

LAGGARD *noun* **LAGGARDS** someone or something that lags behind

LAGGING *noun* **LAGGINGS** insulating cover for pipes, boilers, etc

LAGOMORPH *noun* **LAGOMORPHS** a mammal such as a rabbit or hare with upper front teeth specially adapted for gnawing

LAGOON *noun* **LAGOONS** a relatively shallow body of often brackish water that is separated from the open sea by a barrier such as a reef or a narrow bank of sand or shingle

LAH *noun* **LAHS** in sol-fa notation: the sixth note of the major scale

LAID past form of **lay**[1]

LAIN past form of **lie**[2]

LAIR *noun* **LAIRS** a wild animal's den

LAIRD *noun* **LAIRDS** someone who owns a large estate, especially one that is divided up amongst tenant farmers

LAITY *noun* **LAITIES** the people who are not members of a particular profession, especially those who are not part of the clergy

LAKE *noun* **LAKES** a large area of still fresh or salt water, surrounded by land and lying in a depression in the Earth's surface, which receives water from rivers, streams, springs, etc

LAKESIDE *adj* situated beside a lake

LAM *verb* **LAMS, LAMMING, LAMMED** to thrash □ *noun* **LAMS** an escape, especially from the police

LAMA *noun* **LAMAS** the title of a Buddhist priest or monk in Tibet and Mongolia

LAMAISTIC *adj* of or relating to the lamaists

LAMB *noun* **LAMBS** a young sheep □ *verb* **LAMBS, LAMBING, LAMBED** said of a ewe: to give birth to a lamb or lambs

LAMBADA *noun* **LAMBADAS** a Brazilian dance in which couples make fast erotic hip movements

LAMBAST *verb* **LAMBASTS, LAMBASTING, LAMBASTED** to lambaste

LAMBASTE *verb* **LAMBASTES, LAMBASTING, LAMBASTED** to thrash or beat severely

LAMBDA *noun* **LAMBDAS** the eleventh letter of the Greek alphabet

LAMBENCY *noun* **LAMBENCIES** the quality of being lambent; a flicker

LAMBENT *adj* said of a flame or light: flickering over a surface

LAMBENTLY *adverb* in a lambent way

LAMBERT *noun* **LAMBERTS** a former unit of brightness, equal to the luminance radiated into a hemisphere by one square centimetre of a uniformly diffusing surface

LAMBSKIN *noun* **LAMBSKINS** the skin of a lamb, usually with the wool left on it, used to make slippers, coats, etc

LAME *adj* not able to walk properly, especially due to an injury or defect of the leg, hip, etc □ *verb* **LAMES, LAMING, LAMED** to make lame

LAMÉ *noun* **LAMÉS** a fabric which has metallic threads, usually gold or silver, woven into it

LAMELLA *noun* **LAMELLAE** a thin sheet or plate of tissue, especially one of the many thin layers of which compact bone is formed

LAMELY *adverb* in a lame way

LAMENESS *noun* **LAMENESSES** the condition of being lame

LAMENT *verb* **LAMENTS, LAMENTING, LAMENTED** to feel or express regret or sadness □ *noun* **LAMENTS** an expression of sadness, grief, regret, etc

LAMENTED *adj* said of a dead person: sadly missed; mourned for

LAMINA noun **LAMINAE** a thin plate or layer of a material of uniform thickness, especially bone, rock or metal

LAMINATE verb **LAMINATES, LAMINATING, LAMINATED** to beat (a material, especially metal) into thin sheets □ noun **LAMINATES** a sheet of composite material formed by bonding or gluing together two or more thin sheets of that material □ adj laminated

LAMINATED adj covered with a thin layer of protective or strengthening material

LAMP noun **LAMPS** a piece of equipment designed to give out light, now especially one with an electricity supply, a means of holding a light-bulb and a shade

LAMPLIGHT noun **LAMPLIGHTS** the light given off by a lamp or lamps

LAMPOON noun **LAMPOONS** an attack, usually in the form of satirical prose or verse, on someone or on the style or content of their writing □ verb **LAMPOONS, LAMPOONING, LAMPOONED** to use a lampoon to attack or laugh at someone or their writing

LAMPOONER noun **LAMPOONERS** someone who lampoons

LAMPPOST noun **LAMPPOSTS** a tall post that supports a streetlamp

LAMPREY noun **LAMPREYS** any of about 30 species of primitive jawless fish resembling eels, which feed by clinging to other fishes with their sucker-like mouths and sucking the blood of their hosts

LAMPSHADE noun **LAMPSHADES** a shade placed over a lamp or light bulb to soften or direct the light coming from it

LANCE noun **LANCES** a long spear with a hard pointed head at one end and sometimes a small flag at the other, used as a weapon by charging horsemen □ verb **LANCES, LANCING, LANCED** to cut open (a boil, abscess, etc) with a lancet

LANCER noun **LANCERS** a cavalry soldier belonging to a regiment armed with lances

LANCERS singular noun a set of quadrilles, or the music for it

LANCET noun **LANCETS** a small pointed surgical knife which has both edges sharpened

LAND noun **LANDS** the solid part of the Earth's surface as opposed to the area covered by water; a country □ verb **LANDS, LANDING, LANDED** to come or bring to rest on the ground or water, or in a particular place, after flight through the air

LANDAU noun **LANDAUS** a four-wheeled horse-drawn carriage with a removable front cover and a back cover which folds down

LANDED adj owning land or estates

LANDFALL noun **LANDFALLS** the first land visible towards the end of a journey by sea or air

LANDFILL noun **LANDFILLS** a site where rubbish is disposed of by burying it under layers of earth

LANDING noun **LANDINGS** the act of coming or being put ashore or of returning to the ground

LANDLADY noun **LANDLADIES** a woman who rents property out to a tenant or tenants

LANDLORD noun **LANDLORDS** a man who rents property out to a tenant or tenants

LANDMARK noun **LANDMARKS** a distinctive feature on the land that is conspicuous or well-known, especially when it can be used by sailors or travellers as an indication of where they are

LANDMASS noun **LANDMASSES** a large area of land unbroken by seas

LANDOWNER noun **LANDOWNERS** someone who owns land

LANDSCAPE noun **LANDSCAPES** the area and features of land that can be seen in a broad view, especially when they form a particular type of scenery □ verb **LANDSCAPES, LANDSCAPING, LANDSCAPED** to improve the look of (a garden, park, the layout of a housing estate, etc) by enhancing the existing natural features or by artificially creating new ones

LANDSIDE noun **LANDSIDES** that part of an airport accessible to the general public

LANDSLIDE noun **LANDSLIDES** the sudden downward movement of a mass of soil and rock material, especially in mountainous areas, under the influence of gravity, usually as a result of heavy rain or snow, earthquakes, or blasting operations

LANDWARD adj lying or facing toward the land □ adverb towards land

LANE noun **LANES** a narrow road or street

LANGLAUF noun **LANGLAUFS** cross-country skiing

LANGOUSTE noun **LANGOUSTES** a salt-water crustacean similar to the lobster but rather smaller and with no claws

LANGUAGE noun **LANGUAGES** any formalized system of communication, especially one that uses sounds or written symbols which the majority of a particular community will readily understand

LANGUE noun **LANGUES** the entire language system of a particular speech community, theoretically available to every member of that community

LANGUID adj lacking in energy or vitality; listless

LANGUIDLY adverb in a languid way

LANGUISH verb **LANGUISHES, LANGUISHING, LANGUISHED** to spend time in hardship or discomfort

LANGUISHING adj expressive of languor, or merely sentimental emotion; lingering

LANGUOR noun **LANGUORS** a feeling of dullness or lack of energy

LANGUR noun **LANGURS** a long-tailed monkey, native to S and SE Asia

LANIARD noun **LANIARDS** a lanyard

LANK adj **LANKER, LANKEST** long and thin

LANKINESS noun **LANKINESSES** the state of being lanky

LANKNESS noun **LANKNESSES** the condition of being lank

LANKY adj **LANKIER, LANKIEST** said of a person or animal: thin and tall, especially in an awkward and ungainly way

LANNERET noun **LANNERETS** the male lanner falcon, a species of large falcon native to arid regions in Africa, SE Asia, etc

LANOLIN noun **LANOLINS** a yellowish viscous substance derived from the grease that occurs naturally in sheep's wool, used in cosmetics, ointments and soaps, and for treating leather

LANTERN noun **LANTERNS** a lamp or light contained in a transparent case, usually of glass, so that it can be held or carried

LANTHANUM noun **LANTHANUMS** a silvery-white metallic element (one of the lanthanide series) that ignites spontaneously in air, and is used in rocket propellants, electronic devices, alloys for lighter flints and as a catalyst for the cracking of petroleum

LANUGO noun **LANUGOS** the soft downy hairs that cover the body of the human fetus from about 20 weeks, which are shed in the ninth month of gestation and so are usually only seen on premature babies

LANX noun **LANCES** a platter

LANYARD noun **LANYARDS** a cord for hanging a knife, whistle, etc round the neck, especially as worn by sailors

LAP noun **LAPS** one circuit of a racecourse or other track □ verb **LAPS, LAPPING, LAPPED** to get ahead of (another competitor in a race) by one or more laps

LAPDOG noun **LAPDOGS** a small pet dog

LAPEL noun **LAPELS** the part of a collar on a coat or jacket that is folded out across the chest towards the shoulders

LAPIDARY noun **LAPIDARIES** someone whose job is to cut and polish gemstones □ adj relating to stones

LAPJE noun **LAPJES** a rag or piece of cloth

LAPPET noun **LAPPETS** a small flap or fold in material, a piece of clothing, etc

LAPSANG noun **LAPSANGS** a type of tea with a particularly smoky flavour

LAPSE noun **LAPSES** a slight mistake or failure □ verb **LAPSES, LAPSING, LAPSED** to fail to behave in what is perceived as a proper or morally acceptable way

LAPSED adj having fallen into bad habits or having resumed former bad habits

LAPTOP noun **LAPTOPS** a portable personal computer, small enough to be used on someone's lap

LAPWING noun **LAPWINGS** a subgroup of the plover family, the only nesting species in Europe, having greenish-black and white feathers and a crest

LAR noun **LARES** the Roman god of a house

LARCENOUS adj relating to larceny

LARCENY noun **LARCENIES** theft of personal property

LARCH noun **LARCHES** any of various deciduous coniferous trees, native to cold northern regions, with short linear needles arranged spirally in rosettes on woody terminal shoots, and egg-shaped cones

LARD noun **LARDS** a soft white preparation made from the purified fat of pigs, used in cooking and baking, ointments and perfumes □ verb **LARDS, LARDING, LARDED** to coat (meat, etc) in lard

LARDER noun **LARDERS** a cool room or cupboard for storing food, originally bacon

LARDON noun **LARDONS** a strip or cube of fatty bacon or pork used in larding and sometimes in French salads

LARDOON noun **LARDOONS** a lardon

LARGE adj **LARGER, LARGEST** occupying a comparatively big space □ adverb importantly; prominently

LARGELY adverb mainly or chiefly

LARGENESS noun **LARGENESSES** greatness in size, extent, amount, etc

LARGESS noun **LARGESSES** generosity

LARGESSE noun **LARGESSES** generosity

LARGISH adj somewhat large

LARGO adverb slowly and with dignity □ adj slow and dignified □ noun **LARGOS** a piece of music to be played slowly and with dignity

LARIAT noun **LARIATS** a lasso

LARK noun **LARKS** a joke or piece of fun □ verb **LARKS, LARKING, LARKED** to play or fool about frivolously

LARKSPUR noun **LARKSPURS** a plant with spur-like calyces and blue, white or pink flowers, related to the delphinium

LARRIGAN noun **LARRIGANS** a knee-high boot made of oiled leather and worn by lumberjacks, trappers, etc

LARRIKIN noun **LARRIKINS** a hooligan or lout

LARVA noun **LARVAE** the immature stage in the life cycle of many insects, amphibians and fish, in which it hatches from the fertilized egg and is capable of independent existence, eg the caterpillar of butterflies, the tadpole of frogs, etc

LARVAL adj of or relating to a larva

LARYNGEAL adj relating to the larynx

LARYNX noun **LARYNXES, LARYNGES** in mammals and other higher vertebrates: the expanded upper part of the trachea, which contains the vocal cords and is responsible for the production of vocal sounds

LASAGNA noun **LASAGNAS** lasagne

LASAGNE noun **LASAGNES** pasta in the form of thin flat sheets which can be flavoured with spinach, tomato, etc

LASER noun **LASERS** a device that produces a very powerful narrow beam of coherent light of a single wavelength by stimulating the emission of photons from atoms, molecules or ions

LASH noun **LASHES** a stroke or blow, usually one made with a whip and delivered as a form of punishment; the flexible part of a whip □ verb **LASHES, LASHING, LASHED** to hit or beat with a lash

LASHING noun **LASHINGS** a beating with a whip □ adj said of rain: falling heavily and persistently

LASS noun **LASSES** a girl or young woman

LASSIE noun **LASSIES** often used as a familiar or endearing form of address: a young girl

LASSITUDE noun **LASSITUDES** a feeling of physical or mental tiredness; a lack of energy and enthusiasm

LASSO noun **LASSOS** a long rope used for catching cattle, horses, etc with a sliding loop at one end so that, when the rope is pulled, the noose tightens around the animal's neck □ verb **LASSOS, LASSOES, LASSOING, LASSOED** to catch with a lasso

LAST [1] adj being, coming or occurring at the end of a series or after all others □ adverb most recently

LAST[2] *verb* **LASTS, LASTING, LASTED** to take a specified amount of time to complete, happen, come to an end, etc

LAST[3] *noun* **LASTS** a foot-shaped piece of wood or metal used in the making and repairing of shoes

LASTING *adj* existing or continuing for a long time or permanently

LASTLY *adverb* used to introduce the last item or items in a series or list: finally

LAT *noun* **LATS** short form of *latrine*

LATCH *noun* **LATCHES** a door catch consisting of a bar which is lowered or raised from its notch by a lever or string □ *verb* **LATCHES, LATCHING, LATCHED** to fasten or be fastened with a latch

LATCHKEY *noun* **LATCHKEYS** a key for a door, gate, etc that has a latch

LATE *adj* **LATER, LATEST** coming, arriving, etc after the expected or usual time □ *adverb* after the expected or usual time

LATEEN *adj* said of a ship: having a triangular sail on a long sloping yard

LATELY *adverb* in the recent past; not long ago

LATENCY *noun* **LATENCIES** the condition of being latent

LATENESS *noun* **LATENESSES** the condition of being late

LATENT *adj* said of a characteristic, tendency, etc: present or existing in an undeveloped or hidden form

LATENTLY *adverb* in a latent way

LATER *adj* more late □ *adverb* at some time after, or in the near future

LATERAL *adj* at, from or relating to a side or the side of something □ *noun* **LATERALS** something, eg a branch, shoot, side road, tributary, etc, that forks off from the main part

LATERALLY *adverb* sideways

LATERITE *noun* **LATERITES** a soft porous soil or hard dense rock, composed mainly of hydroxides of iron and aluminium, formed as a result of the weathering of igneous rocks in humid tropical climates, and often used as a building material

LATEST *adj* most recent

LATEX *noun* **LATEXES, LATICES** a thick milky juice that is produced

by some plants and used commercially, especially in the manufacture of rubber

LATH *noun* **LATHS** a thin narrow strip of wood, especially one of a series used to support plaster, tiles, slates, etc □ *verb* **LATHS, LATHING, LATHED** to prepare a ceiling, wall, roof, etc with laths before plastering, tiling, etc

LATHE *noun* **LATHES** a machine tool used to cut, drill or polish a piece of metal, wood or plastic that is rotated against the cutting edge of the lathe

LATHER *noun* **LATHERS** a foam made by mixing water and soap or detergent □ *verb* **LATHERS, LATHERING, LATHERED** to form a lather

LATHERY *adj* covered with lather

LATHI *noun* **LATHIS** a long heavy wooden or bamboo stick used as a weapon

LATICES a plural of **latex**

LATISH *adj* slightly late □ *adverb* slightly late

LATITUDE *noun* **LATITUDES** any of a series of imaginary circles drawn around the Earth parallel to the equator, representing the angular distance north or south of the equator, measured from 0 degrees at the equator to 90 degrees at the north and south poles

LATRINE *noun* **LATRINES** a lavatory, especially in a barracks or camp, etc

LATTER *adj* nearer the end than the beginning

LATTERLY *adverb* recently

LATTICE *noun* **LATTICES** an open frame made by crossing narrow strips of wood or metal over each other to form an ornamental pattern and used especially in gates and fences

LATTICED *adj* having a lattice or lattice-work

LAUD *verb* **LAUDS, LAUDING, LAUDED** to praise □ *noun* **LAUDS** praise

LAUDABLE *adj* worthy of praise; commendable

LAUDABLY *adverb* in a laudable way

LAUDANUM *noun* **LAUDANUMS** a solution of morphine in alcohol, prepared from raw opium, formerly often taken by mouth to relieve pain, aid sleep, etc

LAUDATORY *adj* containing or expressing praise

LAUDS *plural noun* the first of the canonical hours of the day

LAUGH *verb* **LAUGHS, LAUGHING, LAUGHED** to make spontaneous sounds associated with happiness, amusement, scorn, etc □ *noun* **LAUGHS** an act or sound of laughing

LAUGHABLE *adj* deserving to be laughed at

LAUGHABLY *adverb* in a laughable way

LAUGHING *noun* **LAUGHINGS** laughter

LAUGHTER *noun* **LAUGHTERS** the act or sound of laughing

LAUNCH *verb* **LAUNCHES, LAUNCHING, LAUNCHED** to send (a ship or boat, etc) into the water at the beginning of a voyage □ *noun* **LAUNCHES** the action or an instance of a ship, spacecraft, missile, etc being sent off into the water or into the air

LAUNCHER *noun* **LAUNCHERS** a device used for launching a spacecraft or missile, etc

LAUNDER *verb* **LAUNDERS, LAUNDERING, LAUNDERED** to wash and iron (clothes, linen, etc)

LAUNDRESS *noun* **LAUNDRESSES** a woman who washes and irons clothes, linen, etc, especially one who does this for a living

LAUNDRY *noun* **LAUNDRIES** a place where clothes, linen, etc are washed

LAUREATE *adj* honoured for artistic or intellectual distinction □ *noun* **LAUREATES** someone honoured for artistic or intellectual achievement, especially a poet laureate

LAUREL *noun* **LAURELS** a small evergreen tree with smooth dark shiny leaves that are used for flavouring in cooking and sometimes medicinally

LAV *noun* **LAVS** short form of *lavatory*

LAVA *noun* **LAVAS** magma that has erupted from a volcano or fissure and flowed on to the Earth's surface or the ocean floor

LAVATORY *noun* **LAVATORIES** a piece of equipment, usually bowl-shaped with a seat, where urine and faeces are deposited and then flushed away by water into a sewer

LAVENDER *noun* **LAVENDERS** a plant or shrub with sweet-smelling pale bluish-purple flowers

LAVER noun **LAVERS** any of various edible seaweeds, used to make laver bread

LAVISH adj **LAVISHER, LAVISHEST** spending or giving generously ▫ verb **LAVISHES, LAVISHING, LAVISHED** to spend (money) or give (praise, etc) freely or generously

LAVISHLY adverb in a lavish way

LAW noun **LAWS** a customary rule recognized as allowing or prohibiting certain actions ▫ verb **LAWS, LAWING, LAWED** an obsolete word meaning to take to court

LAWFUL adj allowed by or according to law

LAWFULLY adverb in a lawful way

LAWLESS adj ignoring or breaking the law, especially violently

LAWLESSLY adverb in a lawless way

LAWN noun **LAWNS** an area of smooth mown cultivated grass, especially as part of a garden or park

LAWNMOWER noun **LAWNMOWERS** an electric, petrol-driven or manually powered machine for cutting grass

LAWSUIT noun **LAWSUITS** an argument or disagreement taken to a court of law to be settled

LAWYER noun **LAWYERS** a person, especially a solicitor, whose job is to know about the law, and give legal advice and help

LAX¹ adj **LAXER, LAXEST** showing little care or concern over behaviour, morals, etc

LAX² noun **LAX, LAXES** a salmon, especially one caught in Norwegian or Swedish waters

LAXATIVE adj inducing movement of the bowels ▫ noun **LAXATIVES** a medicine or food that induces movement of the bowels

LAXITY noun **LAXITIES** the quality of being lax

LAXLY adverb in a lax manner

LAY¹ verb **LAYS, LAYING, LAID** to place something on a surface, especially in a lying or horizontal position

LAY² adj relating to or involving people who are not members of the clergy

LAY³ noun **LAYS** a short narrative or lyric poem, especially one that is meant to be sung

LAY⁴ a past form of **lie²**

LAYABOUT noun **LAYABOUTS** someone who is habitually lazy or idle

LAYER noun **LAYERS** a thickness or covering, especially one of several on top of each other ▫ verb **LAYERS, LAYERING, LAYERED** to arrange or cut in layers

LAYERED adj composed of layers

LAYETTE noun **LAYETTES** a complete set of clothes, blankets, etc for a new baby

LAYMAN noun **LAYMEN** someone who is not a member of the clergy

LAYOUT noun **LAYOUTS** an arrangement or plan of how land, buildings, pages of a book, etc are to be set out

LAYPERSON noun **LAYPERSONS** someone who is not a member of the clergy

LAYWOMAN noun **LAYWOMEN** someone who is not a member of the clergy

LAZAR noun **LAZARS** a leper

LAZE verb **LAZES, LAZING, LAZED** to be idle or lazy ▫ noun **LAZES** a period of time spent lazing

LAZILY adverb in a lazy way

LAZY adj **LAZIER, LAZIEST** disinclined to work or do anything requiring effort

LEA adj fallow ▫ noun **LEAS** arable land that has been left uncultivated

LEACH verb **LEACHES, LEACHING, LEACHED** to wash a soluble substance out of (a solid) by allowing a suitable liquid solvent to percolate through it

LEAD¹ verb **LEADS, LEADING, LED** to guide by going in front ▫ noun **LEADS** an instance of guidance given by leading

LEAD² noun **LEADS** a soft, heavy, bluish-grey, highly toxic metallic element that is resistant to corrosion, used in the building and roofing trades, as a protective shielding against radiation and as a component of high-quality glass and numerous alloys ▫ adj made of lead

LEADEN adj made of lead

LEADENLY adverb in a leaden way; heavily or slowly; dully

LEADER noun **LEADERS** someone or something that leads or guides others

LEADING adj acting as leader ▫ noun **LEADINGS** guidance; leadership

LEAF noun **LEAVES** an expanded outgrowth, usually green and flattened, from the stem of a plant, that contains the pigment chlorophyll and is the main site of photosynthesis in green plants ▫ verb **LEAFS, LEAVES, LEAFING, LEAFED** said of plants: to produce leaves

LEAFAGE noun **LEAFAGES** the leaves of plants

LEAFLESS adj without leaves

LEAFLET noun **LEAFLETS** a single sheet of paper, or several sheets of paper folded together, giving information, advertising products, etc, usually given away free ▫ verb **LEAFLETS, LEAFLETING, LEAFLETTING, LEAFLETED, LEAFLETTED** to distribute leaflets

LEAFY adj **LEAFIER, LEAFIEST** having or covered with leaves

LEAGUE noun **LEAGUES** a union of persons, nations, etc formed for the benefit of the members ▫ verb **LEAGUES, LEAGUING, LEAGUED** to form or be formed into a league

LEAK noun **LEAKS** an unwanted crack or hole in a container, pipe, etc where liquid or gas can pass in or out ▫ verb **LEAKS, LEAKING, LEAKED** said of liquid, gas, etc: to pass accidentally in or out of an unwanted crack or hole

LEAKAGE noun **LEAKAGES** an act or instance of leaking

LEAKINESS noun **LEAKINESSES** the state of being leaky

LEAKY adj **LEAKIER, LEAKIEST** having a leak or leaks

LEAN¹ verb **LEANS, LEANING, LEANT, LEANED** to slope or be placed in a sloping position ▫ noun **LEANS** an act or condition of leaning

LEAN² adj **LEANER, LEANEST** said of a person or animal: thin

LEANING noun **LEANINGS** a liking or preference; tendency

LEANNESS noun **LEANNESSES** the condition of being lean or thin

LEAP verb **LEAPS, LEAPING, LEAPT, LEAPED** to jump or spring suddenly or with force ▫ noun **LEAPS** an act of leaping or jumping

LEARN verb **LEARNS, LEARNING, LEARNT, LEARNED** to be or become informed or to hear of something

LEARNED adj having great knowledge or learning, especially through years of study

LEARNEDLY adverb in a learned way

LEARNER noun **LEARNERS** someone who is learning or being taught something

LEARNING noun **LEARNINGS** knowledge gained through study

LEASABLE adj that may be leased

LEASE noun **LEASES** a contract by which the owner of a house, land, etc agrees to let someone else use it for a stated period of time in return for payment ◻ verb **LEASES, LEASING, LEASED** said of an owner: to allow someone else to use (a house, land, etc) under the terms of a lease

LEASEBACK noun **LEASEBACKS** an arrangement whereby the seller of a property, land, etc then leases it from the buyer

LEASEHOLD noun **LEASEHOLDS** the holding of land or buildings by lease

LEASER noun **LEASERS** someone granted the use of property by lease

LEASH noun **LEASHES** a strip of leather or chain used for leading or holding a dog or other animal ◻ verb **LEASHES, LEASHING, LEASHED** to put a leash on

LEAST adj smallest; slightest; denoting the smallest number or amount ◻ adverb in the smallest or lowest degree ◻ pronoun the smallest amount

LEATHER noun **LEATHERS** the skin of an animal made smooth by tanning ◻ verb **LEATHERS, LEATHERING, LEATHERED** to cover or polish with leather

LEATHERING noun **LEATHERINGS** a severe beating

LEATHERN adj of or like leather

LEATHERY adj **LEATHERIER, LEATHERIEST** tough

LEAVE [1] verb **LEAVES, LEAVING, LEFT** to go away from someone or somewhere

LEAVE [2] noun **LEAVES** permission to do something

LEAVEN noun **LEAVENS** a substance, especially yeast, added to dough to make it rise ◻ verb **LEAVENS, LEAVENING, LEAVENED** to cause (dough) to rise with leaven

LEAVER noun **LEAVERS** someone who leaves

LEAVES plural of **leaf**

LEAVINGS plural noun things which are left over; rubbish

LECH noun **LECHES** someone who

acts lustfully ◻ verb **LECHES, LECHING, LECHED** to behave lustfully

LECHER noun **LECHERS** someone who acts lustfully ◻ verb **LECHERS, LECHERING, LECHERED** to behave in a lustful way

LECHEROUS adj having or showing great or excessive sexual desire, especially in ways which are offensive

LECHERY noun **LECHERIES** excessive sexual desire, especially in ways which are offensive

LECHWE noun **LECHWES** an African antelope, related to but smaller than the waterbuck, with a light brownish-yellow coat

LECITHIN noun **LECITHINS** an organic chemical compound that is a major component of cell membranes in higher animals and plants, and is also used in foods, pharmaceuticals, cosmetics and paints

LECTERN noun **LECTERNS** a stand with a sloping surface for holding a book, notes, etc for someone to read from, especially in a church or lecture-hall

LECTIN noun **LECTINS** any of numerous proteins, found mainly in plant seeds, some of which cause agglutination of the red blood cells in certain blood groups

LECTION noun **LECTIONS** a reading

LECTOR noun **LECTORS** a reader, especially in a college or university

LECTURE noun **LECTURES** a formal talk on a particular subject given to an audience ◻ verb **LECTURES, LECTURING, LECTURED** to give or read a lecture or lectures to (a group of people)

LECTURER noun **LECTURERS** someone who lectures, especially in a college or university

LED past form of **lead** [1]

LEDGE noun **LEDGES** a narrow horizontal shelf or shelf-like part

LEDGER noun **LEDGERS** the chief book of accounts of an office or shop, in which details of all transactions are recorded; a weighted line in fishing ◻ verb **LEDGERS, LEDGERING, LEDGERED** to fish with a weighted line

LEE [1] noun **LEES** shelter given by a neighbouring object ◻ adj relating to the sheltered side

LEE [2] verb **LEES, LEEING, LEED** a Scots word meaning to tell a lie

LEECH noun **LEECHES** any of various annelid worms with a cylindrical or flattened body bearing suckers at each end, especially a blood-sucking species which was formerly used for bloodletting as a treatment for many ailments ◻ verb **LEECHES, LEECHING, LEECHED** formerly, to treat (a patient) by applying leeches

LEEK noun **LEEKS** a long thin vegetable with broad flat dark green leaves and a white base, closely related to the onion

LEER noun **LEERS** a lecherous look or grin ◻ verb **LEERS, LEERING, LEERED** to look or grin lecherously

LEERING adj that looks or grins lecherously ◻ noun **LEERINGS** the action of looking or grinning lecherously

LEERINGLY adverb in a leering way

LEERY adj **LEERIER, LEERIEST** sly; cunning

LEES plural noun the sediment that settles at the bottom of liquids and alcoholic drinks, especially wine

LEET noun **LEETS** a list of candidates for some office or position; a shortlist

LEEWARD adj in or towards the direction in which the wind blows ◻ adverb in or towards the direction in which the wind blows ◻ noun **LEEWARDS** the sheltered side

LEEWAY noun **LEEWAYS** scope for freedom of movement or action

LEFT [1] adj referring, relating to, or indicating the side facing west from the point of view of someone or something facing north; in politics: inclined towards socialism ◻ adverb on or towards the left side ◻ noun **LEFTS** the left side, part, direction, etc

LEFT [2] a past form of **leave** [1]

LEFTISM noun **LEFTISMS** the principles and policies of the political left

LEFTIST noun **LEFTISTS** a supporter of the political left

LEFTY noun **LEFTIES** a left-winger

LEG noun **LEGS** one of the limbs on which animals, birds and people walk and stand ◻ verb **LEGS, LEGGING, LEGGED** to propel (a barge) through a canal tunnel by pushing with the feet on the walls or roof

LEGACY *noun* **LEGACIES** an amount of property or money left in a will

LEGAL *adj* lawful; allowed by the law

LEGALESE *noun* **LEGALESES** complicated legal jargon

LEGALISE *verb* **LEGALISES, LEGALISING, LEGALISED** to legalize

LEGALISM *noun* **LEGALISMS** strict adherence to the law

LEGALIST *noun* **LEGALISTS** someone who adheres strictly to the law

LEGALITY *noun* **LEGALITIES** the state of being legal; lawfulness

LEGALIZE *verb* **LEGALIZES, LEGALIZING, LEGALIZED** to make something that was once against the law legal or lawful

LEGALLY *adverb* in accordance with or as regards the law

LEGATE *noun* **LEGATES** an ambassador or representative, especially from the Pope

LEGATEE *noun* **LEGATEES** someone who is left a legacy by the terms of a will

LEGATION *noun* **LEGATIONS** a diplomatic mission or group of delegates

LEGATO *adverb* smoothly, with the notes running into each other □ *adj* smooth and flowing □ *noun* **LEGATOS** a piece of music to be played smoothly, with the notes running into each other

LEGEND *noun* **LEGENDS** a traditional story which has popularly come to be regarded as true, but has not been confirmed as such

LEGENDARY *adj* relating to or in the nature of legend □ *noun* **LEGENDARIES** a writer of legends

LEGGED *adj* having a specified number or type of legs

LEGGINGS *plural noun* close-fitting stretch coverings for the legs, worn by girls and women

LEGGY *adj* **LEGGIER, LEGGIEST** said especially of a woman: having attractively long slim legs

LEGHORN *noun* **LEGHORNS** fine straw plait made in Tuscany

LEGIBLE *adj* said especially of handwriting: clear enough to be read

LEGIBLY *adverb* in a legible way

LEGION *noun* **LEGIONS** a unit in the ancient Roman army, containing between three

thousand and six thousand soldiers □ *adj* great in number

LEGIONARY *noun* **LEGIONARIES** a soldier in an ancient Roman legion □ *adj* relating to legions

LEGISLATE *verb* **LEGISLATES, LEGISLATING, LEGISLATED** to make laws

LEGLESS *adj* very drunk

LEGROOM *noun* **LEGROOMS** the amount of space available for someone's legs, especially in a confined area such as a car, aeroplane, cinema, theatre, etc

LEGUME *noun* **LEGUMES** any of a family of flowering plants that produce a dry dehiscent fruit in the form of a pod, eg pea, bean, lentil

LEGWORK *noun* **LEGWORKS** work that involves a lot of research or travelling around

LEI ¹ *noun* **LEIS** a Polynesian garland of flowers, shells or feathers worn round the neck, often given as a symbol of welcome or affection

LEI ² plural of **leu**

LEISURE *noun* **LEISURES** time when one is free to relax and do as one wishes

LEISURED *adj* having ample leisure time

LEISURELY *adj* not hurried; relaxed □ *adverb* without hurrying; taking plenty of time

LEITMOTIF *noun* **LEITMOTIFS** a theme or image, etc which recurs throughout a piece of music, novel, etc

LEITMOTIV *noun* **LEITMOTIVS** a leitmotif

LEK *noun* **LEKS** a piece of ground where certain male game birds such as the black grouse and the capercailzie perform sexual displays to attract females □ *verb* **LEKS, LEKKING, LEKKED** to gather and display at a lek

LEKYTHOS *noun* **LEKYTHOI** a Greek flask or vase with a narrow neck

LEMMA *noun* **LEMMAS, LEMMATA** a preliminary proposition, or a premise taken for granted

LEMMATISE *verb* **LEMMATISES, LEMMATISING, LEMMATISED** to lemmatize

LEMMATIZE *verb* **LEMMATIZES, LEMMATIZING, LEMMATIZED** to organize (words in a text) so that

all inflected and variant forms of the same word are grouped together under one lemma or headword

LEMMING *noun* **LEMMINGS** a small burrowing rodent, native to northern regions of Europe, Asia and N America, which occasionally participates in huge migrations once popularly but erroneously believed to result in mass drownings at sea

LEMON *noun* **LEMONS** a small oval citrus fruit with pointed ends and a tough yellow rind enclosing sour-tasting juicy flesh rich in vitamin C □ *adj* pale yellow in colour

LEMONADE *noun* **LEMONADES** a fizzy or still drink flavoured with or made from lemons

LEMONY *adj* **LEMONIER, LEMONIEST** tasting of or flavoured with lemon

LEMPIRA *noun* **LEMPIRAS** the unit of currency of Honduras, equal to 100 centavos

LEMUR *noun* **LEMURS** a nocturnal tree-dwelling primate, now confined to Madagascar, with large eyes and a long bushy tail, many species of which are now endangered

LEND *verb* **LENDS, LENDING, LENT** to allow someone to use something on the understanding that it (or its equivalent) will be returned

LENDER *noun* **LENDERS** someone who lends something, especially money

LENES plural of **lenis**

LENGTH *noun* **LENGTHS** the distance from one end of an object to the other, normally the longest dimension

LENGTHEN *verb* **LENGTHENS, LENGTHENING, LENGTHENED** to make or become longer

LENGTHILY *adverb* at length

LENGTHY *adj* **LENGTHIER, LENGTHIEST** being of great, often excessive, length

LENIENCE *noun* **LENIENCES** lenient behaviour

LENIENCY *noun* **LENIENCIES** the quality of being lenient

LENIENT *adj* mild and tolerant, especially in punishing; not severe

LENIENTLY *adverb* in a lenient way

LENIS *adj* a term used in phonetics to refer to a sound articulated with relatively little muscular effort and pressure of breath □ noun **LENES** a consonant that is pronounced in this way

LENITY noun **LENITIES** mildness; mercifulness

LENS noun **LENSES** an optical device consisting of a piece of glass, clear plastic, etc curved on one or both sides, used for converging or diverging a beam of light

LENT past form of **lend**

LENTEN adj relating to or happening during Lent

LENTIC adj associated with standing water

LENTICLE noun **LENTICLES** a mass that is lens-shaped

LENTIL noun **LENTILS** a small orange, brown or green seed used as food

LENTO adverb slowly □ adj slow □ noun **LENTOS, LENTI** a piece of music to be performed slowly

LEONE noun **LEONES** the standard currency of Sierra Leone, equal to 100 Sierra Leone cents

LEONINE adj relating to or like a lion

LEOPARD noun **LEOPARDS** a large member of the cat family, native to Africa and Asia, which has tawny yellow fur covered with small black spots, and whitish underparts

LEOTARD noun **LEOTARDS** a stretchy one-piece tight-fitting garment worn for dancing and exercise, made in a variety of different styles from long-sleeved to sleeveless and with or without legs

LEP verb **LEPS, LEPPING, LEPPED, LEP, LEPT** a dialect word meaning to leap

LEPER noun **LEPERS** someone who has leprosy

LEPORINE adj relating to or resembling the hare

LEPROSY noun **LEPROSIES** an infectious disease of the skin, mucous membranes and nerves, mainly occurring in tropical regions, caused by a bacterium, formerly often leading to paralysis, disfigurement and deformity but now treatable with antibacterial drugs

LEPROUS adj suffering from leprosy

LEPTON noun **LEPTONS** any of various subatomic particles, including electrons, muons and tau particles, that only participate in weak interactions with other particles □ noun **LEPTA** a modern Greek coin worth $\frac{1}{100}$ of a drachma

LEPTONIC adj of or relating to leptons

LEPTOSOME noun **LEPTOSOMES** someone with a slender physical build

LESBIAN noun **LESBIANS** a woman who is sexually attracted to other women

LESION noun **LESIONS** an injury or wound

LESS adj smaller size, quantity, duration, etc □ adverb not so much; to a smaller extent □ pronoun a smaller amount or number □ prep without; minus

LESSEE noun **LESSEES** someone granted the use of property by lease

LESSEN verb **LESSENS, LESSENING, LESSENED** to make or become less

LESSER adj used in names, especially plant, animal and place names: smaller in size, quantity or importance

LESSON noun **LESSONS** an amount taught or learned at one time

LESSOR noun **LESSORS** someone who rents out property by lease

LEST conj in case

LET verb **LETS, LETTING, LET** to allow, permit, or cause to do something □ noun **LETS** the leasing of a property, etc

LETHAL adj causing or enough to cause death

LETHALLY adverb in a lethal way

LETHARGIC adj lacking in energy or vitality

LETHARGY noun **LETHARGIES** lack of energy and vitality

LETTABLE adj fit to be leased or capable of being leased

LETTER noun **LETTERS** a conventional written or printed mark, usually part of an alphabet, used to represent a speech sound or sounds □ verb **LETTERS, LETTERING, LETTERED** to write or mark letters on something

LETTERED adj well educated; literary

LETTERING noun **LETTERINGS** the act of forming letters; the way in which they are formed

LETTERS plural noun literature

LETTUCE noun **LETTUCES** a green plant with large edible leaves used in salads

LEU noun **LEI** the standard Romanian unit of currency, equal to 100 bani

LEUCIN noun **LEUCINS** leucine

LEUCINE noun **LEUCINES** an essential amino acid, found in proteins

LEUCOCYTE noun **LEUCOCYTES** a white blood cell or corpuscle

LEUCOMA noun **LEUCOMAS** an opaque white spot on the cornea of the eye, usually caused by scarring

LEUCOTOMY noun **LEUCOTOMIES** a lobotomy, an operation in which the nerve fibres connecting the frontal lobes with the rest of the brain are severed, in an attempt to treat certain severe mental disorders

LEUKAEMIA noun **LEUKAEMIAS** any of various malignant diseases which affect the bone marrow and other blood-forming organs, resulting in the overproduction of abnormal white blood cells, and extreme susceptibility to infection

LEUKEMIA noun **LEUKEMIAS** leukaemia

LEV noun **LEVA** the standard unit of Bulgarian currency, equal to 100 stotinki

LEVATOR noun **LEVATORS** any muscle contraction which raises a part of the body

LEVEE noun **LEVEES** especially on the Lower Mississippi: the natural embankment of silt and sand that is deposited along the banks of a river or stream during flooding

LEVEL noun **LEVELS** a horizontal plane or line □ adj **LEVELLER, LEVELLEST** having a flat smooth even surface □ verb **LEVELS, LEVELLING, LEVELLED** to make flat, smooth or horizontal

LEVELLER noun **LEVELLERS** someone or something that flattens or makes equal

LEVER noun **LEVERS** a simple device for lifting and moving heavy loads, consisting of a rigid bar supported by and pivoting about a fulcrum at some point along its length, so that an effort applied at one point can be used to move an object (the load) at another point □ verb **LEVERS, LEVERING, LEVERED** to move or open using a lever

LEVERAGE noun **LEVERAGES** the

mechanical power or advantage gained through using a lever

LEVERET *noun* **LEVERETS** a young hare, especially one less than a year old

LEVIATHAN *noun* **LEVIATHANS** a sea-monster

LEVIGATE *verb* **LEVIGATES, LEVIGATING, LEVIGATED** to smooth

LEVIS *plural noun* jeans with points of particular strain strengthened by copper rivets

LEVITATE *verb* **LEVITATES, LEVITATING, LEVITATED** to float or cause to float in the air, especially by invoking some supernatural power or through spiritualism

LEVITY *noun* **LEVITIES** a lack of seriousness; silliness

LEVY *verb* **LEVIES, LEVYING, LEVIED** to calculate and then collect (a tax, etc) ▫ *noun* **LEVIES** the collection of a tax, etc

LEW *adj* tepid

LEWD *adj* **LEWDER, LEWDEST** feeling, expressing or designed to stimulate crude sexual desire or lust

LEWDLY *adverb* in a lewd way

LEWDNESS *noun* **LEWDNESSES** obscene or indecent behaviour

LEWIS *noun* **LEWISES** a dovetail iron tenon for lifting large stone blocks, etc

LEWISIA *noun* **LEWISIAS** a perennial herb that has a rosette of leaves at ground level and pink or white flowers

LEWISITE *noun* **LEWISITES** a dark brown mineral

LEX *noun* **LEGES** Latin word for *law*

LEXEME *noun* **LEXEMES** a unit of language consisting of one or more written words, or occasionally just a part of a written word, that maintains a constant semantic element in its various forms. For example, the words *buys, buying* and *bought* are variant forms of the lexeme *buy*

LEXICAL *adj* referring or relating to the meanings of words in a language as opposed to their grammatical functions

LEXICALLY *adverb* with reference to vocabulary

LEXICON *noun* **LEXICONS** a dictionary, especially one for Arabic, Greek, Hebrew or Syriac

LEXIGRAM *noun* **LEXIGRAMS** a sign which represents a whole word

LEXIS *noun* **LEXISES, LEXES** the way a piece of writing is expressed in words

LEY *noun* **LEYS** a straight line, thought to be the route of a prehistoric road, that joins prominent features of the landscape, most commonly hilltops, and that is supposed to have had some kind of scientific or magical significance in the past

LI *noun* **LIS** a Chinese unit of distance

LIABILITY *noun* **LIABILITIES** the state of being legally liable or responsible for something

LIABLE *adj* legally bound or responsible

LIAISE *verb* **LIAISES, LIAISING, LIAISED** to communicate with or be in contact with someone, often in order to discuss something of mutual benefit

LIAISON *noun* **LIAISONS** communication or co-operation between individuals or groups

LIANA *noun* **LIANAS** any of various woody climbing plants found mainly in tropical rain forests

LIANE *noun* **LIANES** a liana

LIAR *noun* **LIARS** someone who tells lies, especially habitually

LIB *noun* **LIBS** used especially in the names of movements: short form of liberation

LIB *verb* **LIBS, LIBBING, LIBBED** a dialect word meaning to geld

LIBATION *noun* **LIBATIONS** the pouring out of wine, etc in honour of a god

LIBBER *noun* **LIBBERS** short form of liberationist

LIBEL *noun* **LIBELS** the publication of a statement in some permanent form (including broadcasting) which has the potential to damage someone's reputation and which is claimed to be false ▫ *verb* **LIBELS, LIBELLING, LIBELING, LIBELLED, LIBELED** to publish a libellous statement about someone

LIBELANT *noun* **LIBELANTS** a libellant

LIBELER *noun* **LIBELERS** a libeller

LIBELLANT *noun* **LIBELLANTS** someone who writes, broadcasts or publishes something libellous

LIBELLEE *noun* **LIBELLEES** someone who has something libellous written, broadcast or published against them

LIBELLER *noun* **LIBELLERS** someone who writes, broadcasts or publishes something libellous

LIBELLOUS *adj* containing or forming a libel; damaging to someone's reputation

LIBELOUS *adj* libellous

LIBERAL *adj* given or giving generously, freely or abundantly ▫ *noun* **LIBERALS** someone who has liberal views, either politically or in general

LIBERALLY *adverb* freely; generously

LIBERATE *verb* **LIBERATES, LIBERATING, LIBERATED** to set free

LIBERATED *adj* not bound by traditional ideas about sexuality, morality, the roles conventionally assigned to men and women, etc

LIBERATOR *noun* **LIBERATORS** someone who liberates, especially from oppression

LIBERO *noun* **LIBEROS** a sweeper, a football player covering the whole area behind a line of defenders

LIBERTINE *noun* **LIBERTINES** someone, especially a man, who is not bound by the generally accepted codes of morality ▫ *adj* unrestrained; dissolute; promiscuous

LIBERTY *noun* **LIBERTIES** freedom from captivity, slavery, restrictions, etc

LIBIDINAL *adj* referring to or related to libido

LIBIDO *noun* **LIBIDOS** sexual urge or desire

LIBRARIAN *noun* **LIBRARIANS** someone who works in a library or is in charge of a library

LIBRARY *noun* **LIBRARIES** a room, rooms or building where books, films, records, videos, etc are kept for study, reference, reading or for lending

LIBRETTO *noun* **LIBRETTOS, LIBRETTI** the words or text of an opera, oratorio, or musical

LICE *plural of* **louse**

LICENCE *noun* **LICENCES** an official document that allows someone to drive, sell alcohol, get married etc

LICENSE verb **LICENSES, LICENSING, LICENSED** to give a licence or permit for something such as the sale of alcohol

LICENSED adj said of a shop, hotel, etc: legally allowed to sell alcohol

LICENSEE noun **LICENSEES** someone who has been given a licence, especially to sell alcohol

LICHEE noun **LICHEES** a lychee

LICHEN noun **LICHENS** any of numerous primitive plants formed by the symbiotic association between a fungus and a green or blue-green alga, usually found on rocks, walls or tree trunks

LICHGATE noun **LICHGATES** a roofed gateway to a churchyard, originally used to shelter a coffin until a member of the clergy arrived to conduct the funeral

LICIT adj lawful; permitted

LICITLY adverb lawfully

LICK verb **LICKS, LICKING, LICKED** to pass the tongue over in order to moisten, taste or clean ▫ noun **LICKS** an act of licking with the tongue

LICKING noun **LICKINGS** a thrashing, both physical and figurative

LICORICE noun **LICORICES** liquorice

LICTOR noun **LICTORS** an officer who attended a magistrate, usually carrying the fasces, and who had various duties such as clearing a way for the magistrate through a crowd and seeing that sentences on offenders were carried out

LID noun **LIDS** a removable or hinged cover for a pot, box, etc

LIDDED adj having a lid

LIDLESS adj having no lid

LIDO noun **LIDOS** a fashionable beach

LIE[1] noun **LIES** a false statement made with the intention of deceiving ▫ verb **LIES, LYING, LIED** to say things that are not true with the intention of deceiving

LIE[2] verb **LIES, LYING, LAY, LAIN** to be in or take on a flat or more or less horizontal position on a supporting surface

LIED noun **LIEDER** a German song for solo voice and piano accompaniment as developed by Schubert and his successors during the Romantic period

LIEGE adj entitled to receive feudal service or homage from a vassal ▫ noun **LIEGES** a feudal superior, lord or sovereign

LIEN noun **LIENS** a right to keep someone's property until a debt has been paid

LIEU noun **LIEUS** place or stead

LIFE noun **LIVES** the quality or state which distinguishes living animals and plants from dead ones

LIFEBELT noun **LIFEBELTS** a ring or belt that floats in water and can be used to support someone who is in danger of drowning

LIFEBOAT noun **LIFEBOATS** a boat for rescuing people who are in trouble at sea

LIFEBUOY noun **LIFEBUOYS** a float for supporting someone in the water until they are rescued

LIFEGUARD noun **LIFEGUARDS** an expert swimmer employed at a swimming-pool or beach to rescue people in danger of drowning

LIFELESS adj dead

LIFELIKE adj said of a portrait, etc: very like the person or thing represented

LIFELINE noun **LIFELINES** a rope for support in dangerous operations or for saving lives

LIFELONG adj lasting the whole length of someone's life

LIFER noun **LIFERS** someone sent to prison for life

LIFESTYLE noun **LIFESTYLES** the way of living of a group or individual

LIFETIME noun **LIFETIMES** the duration of someone's life

LIFT verb **LIFTS, LIFTING, LIFTED** to raise or rise to a higher position ▫ noun **LIFTS** an act of lifting

LIG verb **LIGS, LIGGING, LIGGED** to lie about idly

LIGAMENT noun **LIGAMENTS** anything that binds

LIGAND noun **LIGANDS** an atom, molecule, radicle or ion that is attached to the central atom of certain types of compound

LIGASE noun **LIGASES** any of a class of enzymes that play an important part in the synthesis and repair of certain complex molecules, including DNA, in living cells

LIGATE verb **LIGATES, LIGATING, LIGATED** to tie up (a blood vessel or duct)

LIGATION noun **LIGATIONS** the act of binding, especially with a ligature

LIGATURE noun **LIGATURES**

anything that binds or ties ▫ verb **LIGATURES, LIGATURING, LIGATURED** to bind with a ligature

LIGER noun **LIGERS** the offspring of a lion and a female tiger

LIGGER noun **LIGGERS** a lower millstone

LIGHT[1] noun **LIGHTS** a form of electromagnetic radiation that travels freely through space, and can be absorbed and reflected, especially that part of the spectrum which can be seen with the human eye; a flame or spark for igniting ▫ verb **LIGHTS, LIGHTING, LIT, LIGHTED** to provide light for something

LIGHT[2] adj **LIGHTER, LIGHTEST** being of little weight; easy to lift or carry ▫ adverb in a light manner

LIGHTEN verb **LIGHTENS, LIGHTENING, LIGHTENED** to make or become less heavy

LIGHTENING noun **LIGHTENINGS** a making or becoming brighter or less dark

LIGHTER noun **LIGHTERS** a device for lighting cigarettes, etc

LIGHTING noun **LIGHTINGS** equipment for providing light

LIGHTISH adj somewhat light

LIGHTLY adverb in a light manner

LIGHTNESS noun **LIGHTNESSES** the quality of being light

LIGHTNING noun **LIGHTNINGS** a bright flash of light produced by the discharge of static electricity between or within clouds, or between a cloud and the Earth's surface, accompanied by thunder ▫ adj very quick and sudden

LIGHTS plural noun the lungs of an animal, used as food

LIGHTSHIP noun **LIGHTSHIPS** a ship with a beacon, that acts as a lighthouse

LIGNEOUS adj composed of or resembling wood; woody

LIGNIFY verb **LIGNIFIES, LIGNIFYING, LIGNIFIED** said of the walls of plant cells: to thicken and become woody as a result of the deposition of lignin

LIGNIN noun **LIGNINS** the complex polymer that cements together the fibres within the cell walls of plants, making them woody and rigid

LIGNITE noun **LIGNITES** a soft brown low-grade form of coal, intermediate between peat and bituminous coal, that burns with a smoky flame and give out little heat

LIGNUM noun **LIGNUMS** the woody outer surface of certain plants

LIKABLE adj likeable

LIKE ¹ adj similar; resembling ▫ prep in the same manner as; to the same extent as ▫ adverb approximately ▫ conj as if; as though

LIKE ² verb **LIKES, LIKING, LIKED** to be pleased with something ▫ noun **LIKES** a thing that someone has a preference for

LIKEABLE adj easy to like

LIKELY adj **LIKELIER, LIKELIEST** probable ▫ adverb probably

LIKEN verb **LIKENS, LIKENING, LIKENED** to see two things as being the same or similar

LIKENESS noun **LIKENESSES** a similarity

LIKEWISE adverb in the same or a similar manner

LIKING noun **LIKINGS** a fondness

LILAC noun **LILACS** a small European tree or shrub of the olive family, with white or pale pinkish-purple sweet-smelling flowers ▫ adj pale pinkish-purple in colour

LILO noun **LILOS** a type of inflatable mattress used in camping or on the beach, etc

LILT noun **LILTS** a light graceful swinging rhythm ▫ verb **LILTS, LILTING, LILTED** to speak, sing or move with a lilt

LILTING adj characterized by a light graceful swinging rhythm

LILY noun **LILIES** any of various perennial plants that have underground bulbs, narrow leaves, and white or brightly coloured flowers ▫ adj pale; white

LIMA noun **LIMA, LIMAS** a flat white edible bean from tropical America

LIMAX noun **LIMACES** a type of slug

LIMB noun **LIMBS** an arm, leg or wing

LIMBER adj flexible and supple ▫ verb **LIMBERS, LIMBERING, LIMBERED** to make flexible and supple

LIMBLESS adj having no limbs

LIMBO noun **LIMBOS** a West Indian dance in which the object is to lean backwards and shuffle under a rope or bar which is gradually lowered towards the floor, a highly skilled performer being able to do this with only a few inches clearance

LIME noun **LIMES** calcium oxide ▫ verb **LIMES, LIMING, LIMED** to cover with lime

LIMEKILN noun **LIMEKILNS** a kiln for heating limestone to produce lime

LIMELIGHT noun **LIMELIGHTS** formerly used in theatres: a bright white light produced by heating a block of lime in a flame ▫ verb **LIMELIGHTS, LIMELIGHTING, LIMELIGHTED** to subject someone or something to the glare of limelight

LIMERICK noun **LIMERICKS** a humorous poem with five lines that always have the same rhyme and metre patterns, lines one, two and five sharing the same rhyme and lines three and four rhyming with each other

LIMESTONE noun **LIMESTONES** any of various sedimentary rocks composed mainly of calcium carbonate, used as a building material and in iron smelting, cement manufacture, etc

LIMEWASH noun **LIMEWASHES** whitewash

LIMEWATER noun **LIMEWATERS** an alkaline solution of calcium hydroxide in water, sometimes used as an antacid

LIMEY noun **LIMEYS** a British person

LIMINESS noun **LIMINESSES** the state of being limy

LIMING noun **LIMINGS** in the preparation of leather, etc: the soaking of skins in limewater to remove the hair

LIMIT noun **LIMITS** a point, degree, amount or boundary, especially one which cannot or should not be passed ▫ verb **LIMITS, LIMITING, LIMITED** to be a limit or boundary to someone or something

LIMITABLE adj that may be limited

LIMITARY adj of a boundary; placed at the boundary

LIMITED adj having a limit or limits

LIMITEDLY adverb in a limited way

LIMITER noun **LIMITERS** a person, device or circumstance that limits or confines

LIMITLESS adj having no limit

LIMNOLOGY noun **LIMNOLOGIES** the scientific study of freshwater habitats, including chemical, physical and biological factors

LIMO noun **LIMOS** short form of limousine

LIMOUSINE noun **LIMOUSINES** a large, luxurious motor car, especially one with a screen separating the driver from the passengers

LIMP ¹ verb **LIMPS, LIMPING, LIMPED** to walk with an awkward or uneven step, often because one leg is weak or injured ▫ noun **LIMPS** the walk of someone who limps

LIMP ² adj **LIMPER, LIMPEST** not stiff or firm; hanging loosely

LIMPET noun **LIMPETS** any of various marine gastropod molluscs that have a ridged conical shell and cling firmly to rock surfaces by means of a muscular foot

LIMPID adj said of water, the air, eyes, etc: clear; transparent

LIMPIDITY noun **LIMPIDITIES** clearness; transparency

LIMPIDLY adverb in a limpid way

LIMPING noun **LIMPINGS** the act of walking with a limp ▫ adj involving a limp; halting

LIMPINGLY adverb in a limping way

LIMPKIN noun **LIMPKINS** an American wading bird similar to a rail

LIMPLY adverb in a limp way

LIMPNESS noun **LIMPNESSES** the condition of being limp

LIMY adj **LIMIER, LIMIEST** like or tasting of the citrus fruit lime

LIN ¹ noun **LINS** a waterfall

LIN ² verb **LINS, LINNING, LINNED** a Spenserian word meaning to cease

LINAGE noun **LINAGES** the number of lines in a piece of printed matter

LINCHPIN noun **LINCHPINS** a pin-shaped rod passed through an axle to keep a wheel in place

LINCTUS noun **LINCTUSES** a syrupy liquid medicine, taken by mouth to relieve coughs and sore throats

LINDEN noun **LINDENS** a tree or shrub with heart-shaped leaves and fragrant green, yellow or white flowers

LINE noun **LINES** a long narrow mark, streak or stripe ▫ verb **LINES, LINING, LINED** to cover or mark something with lines

LINEAGE noun **LINEAGES** ancestry, especially when it can be

traced from one particular
ancestor

LINEAL adj said of family descent:
in a direct line

LINEALLY adverb in a lineal way

LINEAMENT noun **LINEAMENTS** a
feature

LINEAR adj referring to, consisting
of or like a line or lines

LINEARITY noun **LINEARITIES** the
quality of being linear

LINEATION noun **LINEATIONS** the
act of marking something with
lines

LINED adj having lines

LINEN adj made of or like linen
□ noun **LINENS** cloth made from
flax

LINER noun **LINERS** something
used for lining

LINESMAN noun **LINESMEN** an
official at a boundary line in some
sports, eg football, whose job is to
indicate when the ball has gone out
of play

LING noun **LINGS** a fish which has
a long slender body, and is a
member of the cod family

LINGA noun **LINGAS** lingam

LINGAM noun **LINGAMS** the
Hindu phallus, a symbol of the god
Siva

LINGER verb **LINGERS,
LINGERING, LINGERED** said of
sensations: to remain for a long
time

LINGERER noun **LINGERERS**
someone who lingers

LINGERIE noun **LINGERIES**
women's underwear and
nightclothes

LINGERING adj said especially of a
sensation, a memory or a thought:
persisting □ noun **LINGERINGS** the
action of remaining for a long time

LINGO noun **LINGOES** a language,
especially one that is not highly
thought of or that is not
understood

LINGUAL adj pronounced using the
tongue

LINGUALLY adverb in a lingual way

LINGUINE plural noun linguini

LINGUINI plural noun flat ribbon-
like strips of pasta

LINGUIST noun **LINGUISTS**
someone who has an excellent
knowledge of languages

LINIMENT noun **LINIMENTS** a kind
of thin oily cream for rubbing into
the skin to ease muscle pain

LINING noun **LININGS** the material

used for covering the inside of
clothes, boxes, curtains, etc

LINK noun **LINKS** a ring of a chain,
or in chain-mail □ verb **LINKS,
LINKING, LINKED** to connect or
join

LINKAGE noun **LINKAGES** an act,
method or fact of linking

LINKS plural noun a stretch of more
or less flat ground along a shore
near the sea

LINN noun **LINNS** a waterfall

LINNET noun **LINNETS** a small
brown songbird of the finch family

LINO noun **LINOS** linoleum

LINOCUT noun **LINOCUTS** a design
cut in relief in linoleum

LINOLEUM noun **LINOLEUMS** a
smooth hard-wearing covering for
floors, made by impregnating a
fabric with a mixture of substances
such as linseed oil and cork

LINSEED noun **LINSEEDS** the seed
of the flax which contains linseed
oil

LINT noun **LINTS** linen or cotton
with a raised nap on one side, for
dressing wounds

LINTEL noun **LINTELS** a horizontal
wooden or stone beam placed over
a doorway or window

LION noun **LIONS** a large member
of the cat family, found mainly in
Africa, with a tawny coat, a tufted
tail, and, in the male, a long thick
tawny or black mane on the head,
neck and shoulders

LIONESS noun **LIONESSES** a
female lion

LIONISE verb **LIONISES,
LIONISING, LIONISED** to lionize

LIONIZE verb **LIONIZES,
LIONIZING, LIONIZED** to treat
someone as a celebrity or hero

LIP noun **LIPS** either of the two
fleshy parts which form the edge of
the mouth □ verb **LIPS, LIPPING,
LIPPED** to use or touch with the
lips

LIPID noun **LIPIDS** any of a group
of organic compounds, mainly oils
and fats, that occur naturally in
living organisms, and are generally
insoluble in water

LIPOGRAM noun **LIPOGRAMS** a
piece of writing, usually in verse
form, in which all the words
containing a certain letter are
omitted

LIPOSOME noun **LIPOSOMES** a
naturally-occurring lipid globule
in the cytoplasm of a cell

LIPPED adj said especially of a

container: having a lip or edge
extended to form a small spout

LIPPY adj **LIPPIER, LIPPIEST** cheeky

LIPSTICK noun **LIPSTICKS** a stick
of cosmetic colouring for the lips

LIQUEFIER noun **LIQUEFIERS** a
person or thing that liquefies

LIQUEFY verb **LIQUEFIES,
LIQUEFYING, LIQUEFIED** to make
or become liquid

LIQUEUR noun **LIQUEURS** a potent
alcoholic drink, sweetened and
highly flavoured, and usually
drunk at the end of a meal

LIQUID noun **LIQUIDS** a state of
matter between solid and gas,
where the volume remains
constant, but the shape depends
on that of its container □ adj said of
a substance: able to flow and
change shape

LIQUIDATE verb **LIQUIDATES,
LIQUIDATING, LIQUIDATED** to
bring to an end the trading of (an
individual or a company), and have
debts and assets calculated

LIQUIDISE verb **LIQUIDISES,
LIQUIDISING, LIQUIDISED** to
liquidize

LIQUIDIZE verb **LIQUIDIZES,
LIQUIDIZING, LIQUIDIZED** to make
liquid

LIQUOR noun **LIQUORS** strong
alcoholic drink, especially some
that has been distilled

LIQUORICE noun **LIQUORICES** a
Mediterranean plant with sweet
roots used to make confectionery
and also in medicine, mainly as a
laxative

LIRA noun **LIRAS** the standard unit
of currency in Italy and Turkey

LIS noun **LIS, LISSES** a fleur-de-
lis, a stylized lily or iris used as a
heraldic device

LISLE noun **LISLES** fine smooth
cotton thread used for making
gloves, stockings and underwear

LISP verb **LISPS, LISPING,
LISPED** to pronounce the sounds
of s and z in the same way as the th
sounds in thin and this respectively
□ noun the act or habit of lisping

LISPER noun **LISPERS** someone
who lisps

LISPING noun **LISPINGS** the
action of pronouncing words with
a lisp □ adj characterized by lisping

LISPINGLY adverb in a lisping way

LISSOM adj graceful and supple in
shape or movement

LISSOME adj lissom

LIST noun **LISTS** a series of names, numbers, prices, etc printed out, written down or said one after the other □ verb **LISTS, LISTING, LISTED** to make a list of something

LISTEN verb **LISTENS, LISTENING, LISTENED** to try to hear someone or something

LISTENER noun **LISTENERS** someone who listens

LISTERIA noun **LISTERIAS** a bacterium sometimes found in certain foods, eg chicken and soft cheese, which if not killed in cooking may cause serious food poisoning

LISTING noun **LISTINGS** a list

LISTLESS adj tired and lacking energy or interest

LISTS plural noun the barriers enclosing an area used for jousting and tournaments

LIT a past form of **light** [1]

LITANY noun **LITANIES** a series of prayers or supplications with a response which is repeated several times by the congregation

LITCHI noun **LITCHIS** a lychee

LITE adverb light □ adj light

LITER noun **LITERS** a litre

LITERACY noun **LITERACIES** the ability to read and write

LITERAL adj said of words or a text: following the exact meaning, without allegorical or metaphorical interpretation □ noun **LITERALS** a misprint of one letter

LITERALLY adverb word for word

LITERARY adj referring or relating to, or concerned with, literature or writing

LITERATE adj able to read and write □ noun **LITERATES** someone who is literate

LITERATI plural noun learned people

LITES plural noun the lungs of an animal, used as food

LITHARGE noun **LITHARGES** lead monoxide

LITHE adj **LITHER, LITHEST** supple and flexible

LITHELY adverb in a lithe way

LITHENESS noun **LITHENESSES** the state of being lithe

LITHIA noun **LITHIAS** lithium oxide, a white or colourless powder used in ceramics and in the manufacture of lithium salts

LITHIUM noun **LITHIUMS** a soft silvery reactive metal, the lightest solid element, used in batteries and certain alloys, compounds of which are used in lubricants, glass, ceramics and drugs for treating certain psychiatric disorders

LITHO noun **LITHOS** lithography, a method of printing using a stone or metal plate which is treated so that ink adheres only to the image or design to be printed; a lithograph

LITHOLOGY noun **LITHOLOGIES** the study and description of the gross physical characteristics that define a particular rock, including colour, texture, mineral composition, and grain size

LITHOTOMY noun **LITHOTOMIES** a surgical operation to remove a calculus from an organ of the body, especially from the bladder

LITIGANT noun **LITIGANTS** someone involved in a lawsuit

LITIGATE verb **LITIGATES, LITIGATING, LITIGATED** to be involved in a lawsuit

LITIGIOUS adj relating to litigation or lawsuits

LITMUS noun **LITMUSES** a dye obtained from certain lichens, widely used as an indicator to distinguish between acid solutions, in which it turns red, and alkaline ones, in which it turns blue

LITOTES noun **LITOTES** understatement used for effect, especially by negating the opposite, as in *not a little angry* meaning *furious*

LITRE noun **LITRES** in the metric system: the basic unit of volume, equal to one cubic decimetre (10 000 cubic centimetres) or about 1.76 pints

LITTER noun **LITTERS** discarded paper, rubbish, etc lying in a public place □ verb **LITTERS, LITTERING, LITTERED** to make something untidy by spreading litter or objects about

LITTLE adj **LITTLER, LITTLEST** small in size, extent or amount □ adverb not much or at all □ pronoun not much

LITTORAL adj on or near the shore of a sea or lake □ noun **LITTORALS** the shore or an area of land on a shore or coast

LITURGY noun **LITURGIES** the standard form of service in a church

LIVE [1] verb **LIVES, LIVING, LIVED** to have life; to be alive

LIVE [2] adj having life, not dead; said of a radio or TV broadcast: heard or seen as the event takes place and not from a recording □ adverb at, during, or as a live performance

LIVEABLE adj said of a house, etc: fit to live in

LIVELONG adj said of the day or night: complete, in all its pleasant or tedious length

LIVELY adj **LIVELIER, LIVELIEST** active and full of life, energy and high spirits

LIVEN verb **LIVENS, LIVENING, LIVENED** to make or become lively

LIVER noun **LIVERS** in vertebrates: a large dark red glandular organ situated just below the diaphragm, whose main function is to regulate the chemical composition of the blood □ adj dark reddish-brown in colour

LIVERIED adj clothed in livery

LIVERISH adj suffering from a disordered liver

LIVERWORT noun **LIVERWORTS** any of a class of small spore-bearing plants without a vascular system, closely related to mosses, typically growing in moist shady conditions

LIVERY noun **LIVERIES** a distinctive uniform worn by male servants belonging to a particular household or by the members of a particular trade guild

LIVERYMAN noun **LIVERYMEN** a freeman of the City of London entitled to certain privileges and to wear the livery of his company

LIVES plural noun of **life**

LIVESTOCK noun **LIVESTOCKS** domesticated animals, especially sheep, cattle, pigs and poultry, kept for the production of meat, milk, wool, etc, or for breeding purposes

LIVEWARE noun **LIVEWARES** the people who work with a computer system, as distinct from hardware and software

LIVID adj **LIVIDER, LIVIDEST** extremely angry

LIVIDITY noun **LIVIDITIES** the quality of being livid

LIVIDLY adverb in a livid way

LIVIDNESS noun **LIVIDNESSES** the state of being livid

LIVING adj having life; alive □ noun **LIVINGS** livelihood or means of subsisting

LIZARD noun **LIZARDS** any of numerous small reptiles, closely related to snakes, but with movable eyelids, much less flexible jaws and in most species four well-developed limbs and a tapering tail

LLAMA noun **LLAMAS** a domesticated hoofed S American mammal related to the camel, with a long shaggy white brown or black coat, a long neck and large ears, kept for its meat, milk and wool, and used as a beast of burden

LO noun **LOS** an exclamation of look! see!

LOACH noun **LOACHES** a small freshwater fish of the carp family, found throughout Europe and Asia, with a slender body and spines around its mouth, often kept as an aquarium fish

LOAD noun **LOADS** something that is carried or transported ◻ verb **LOADS, LOADING, LOADED** to put (cargo, passengers, etc) on (a ship, vehicle, plane, etc)

LOADED adj carrying a load; with a load in place

LOADER noun **LOADERS** said of a gun or machine, etc: loaded in a specified way

LOADSTAR noun **LOADSTARS** a lodestar

LOADSTONE noun **LOADSTONES** a lodestone

LOAF¹ noun **LOAVES** a shaped lump of dough, especially after it has risen and been baked

LOAF² verb **LOAFS, LOAFING, LOAFED** to loiter

LOAFER noun **LOAFERS** someone who loafs about

LOAM noun **LOAMS** a dark fertile easily worked soil composed of sand, silt, small amounts of clay and humus ◻ verb **LOAMS, LOAMING, LOAMED** to treat, cover or dress something with loam

LOAMINESS noun **LOAMINESSES** the state of being loamy

LOAMY adj **LOAMIER, LOAMIEST** of or relating to loam

LOAN noun **LOANS** anything lent, especially money lent at interest ◻ verb **LOANS, LOANING, LOANED** to lend (especially money)

LOATH adj **LOATHER, LOATHEST** unwilling; reluctant

LOATHE verb **LOATHES, LOATHING, LOATHED** to dislike intensely

LOATHING noun **LOATHINGS** intense dislike or disgust

LOATHSOME adj causing intense dislike or disgust

LOAVES plural of **loaf**

LOB noun **LOBS** a ball hit in a high overhead path ◻ verb **LOBS, LOBBING, LOBBED** to hit, kick or throw (a ball) in this way

LOBAR adj relating to or affecting a lobe, especially in the lungs

LOBATE adj having lobes

LOBBY noun **LOBBIES** a small entrance-hall, passage or waiting-room from which several rooms open ◻ verb **LOBBIES, LOBBYING, LOBBIED** to try to influence (the Government, politicians, legislators, etc) to favour a particular cause

LOBBYING noun **LOBBYINGS** the action of trying to influence the Government, politicians, legislators, etc to favour a particular cause

LOBBYIST noun **LOBBYISTS** someone who lobbies

LOBE noun **LOBES** the soft lower part of the outer ear

LOBECTOMY noun **LOBECTOMIES** the surgical removal of a lobe from an organ or gland of the body

LOBED adj having a lobe or lobes

LOBELIA noun **LOBELIAS** a garden plant with red, white, purple, blue or yellow flowers

LOBO noun **LOBOS** a timber wolf

LOBOTOMY noun **LOBOTOMIES** any operation that involves cutting into a lobe of an organ or gland

LOBSTER noun **LOBSTERS** any of various large decapod crustaceans, typically having four pairs of walking legs, a pair of large pincers and a hard bluish-black outer shell which turns bright red when cooked

LOBULE noun **LOBULES** a small lobe

LOBWORM noun **LOBWORMS** a lugworm

LOCAL adj referring or belonging to a particular place ◻ noun **LOCALS** someone who lives in a particular area

LOCALE noun **LOCALES** the scene of some event or occurrence

LOCALISE verb **LOCALISES, LOCALISING, LOCALISED** to localize

LOCALISED adj localized

LOCALITY noun **LOCALITIES** a district or neighbourhood

LOCALIZE verb **LOCALIZES,**

LOCALIZING, LOCALIZED to restrict something to a place or area

LOCALIZED adj restricted to a place or area

LOCALLY adverb within or in terms of a particular area or the people living in it

LOCATE verb **LOCATES, LOCATING, LOCATED** to set in a particular place or position

LOCATION noun **LOCATIONS** a position or situation

LOCATIVE adj indicating the case that suggests 'the place where' ◻ noun **LOCATIVES** the locative case

LOCH noun **LOCHS** a lake

LOCHAN noun **LOCHANS** a small loch

LOCHIAL adj of or relating to lochia, discharge from the uterus through the vagina after childbirth

LOCI plural of **locus**

LOCK noun **LOCKS** a mechanical device, usually consisting of a sliding bolt moved by turning a key, dial, etc, that provides security by fastening a door, lid, machine, item of movable property, etc ◻ verb **LOCKS, LOCKING, LOCKED** to fasten (a door, box, bag, etc) with a lock

LOCKABLE adj said especially of a room or building: able to be locked

LOCKAGE noun **LOCKAGES** a system of canal locks

LOCKER noun **LOCKERS** a small lockable cupboard for personal, temporary use, eg for luggage at a station, for clothes and sports equipment at a gym or sports hall

LOCKET noun **LOCKETS** a small decorated case for holding a photograph or memento, worn on a chain round the neck

LOCKJAW noun **LOCKJAWS** difficulty in opening the mouth, caused by spasm of the jaw muscles, usually a symptom of tetanus, or associated with hysteria or dental disease

LOCKOUT noun **LOCKOUTS** the shutting out of employees by the management from their place of work during an industrial dispute, as a means of imposing certain conditions

LOCKSMITH noun **LOCKSMITHS** someone who makes and mends locks

LOCO noun **LOCOS** a locomotive (railway engine)

LOCOMOTOR adj relating to

locomotion (the power, process or capacity of moving from one place to another)

LOCOWEED noun **LOCOWEEDS** a leguminous plant which causes loco disease (disordered vision and paralysis) in farm animals

LOCULAR adj having loculi

LOCULUS noun **LOCULI** a small compartment or chamber

LOCUM noun **LOCUMS** someone who temporarily stands in for someone else, especially in the medical and clerical professions

LOCUS noun **LOCI** an exact place or location, especially one where some incident has taken place

LOCUST noun **LOCUSTS** any of various large grasshoppers noted for their tendency to form dense swarms and migrate, eating all the vegetation in their path, including crops

LOCUTION noun **LOCUTIONS** a style of speech

LOD noun **LODS** in statistics, the logarithm of the odds

LODE noun **LODES** a thin band or strip of rock containing metallic ore

LODEN noun **LODENS** a thick waterproof, often dark-green, woollen cloth, with a short pile

LODESTAR noun **LODESTARS** a star used as a guide by sailors and astronomers, especially the Pole Star

LODESTONE noun **LODESTONES** a form of magnetite which exhibits polarity, behaving, when freely suspended, as a magnet

LODGE noun **LODGES** a cottage at the gateway to the grounds of a large house or mansion ◻ verb **LODGES, LODGING, LODGED** to live, usually temporarily, in rented accommodation, especially in someone else's home

LODGER noun **LODGERS** someone who rents accommodation in someone else's home, often temporarily

LODGING noun **LODGINGS** a room or rooms rented in someone else's home

LOESS noun **LOESSES** a fine-grained loose quartz-based wind-blown loam found mostly in river valleys in central US, N Europe, Russia, China and Argentina

LOFT noun **LOFTS** a room or space under a roof ◻ verb **LOFTS,**

LOFTING, LOFTED to strike, kick or throw (a ball, etc) high up in the air

LOFTED adj said of a ball that has been struck: lifted into the air

LOFTILY adverb imposingly; proudly; haughtily

LOFTINESS noun **LOFTINESSES** the state or condition of being lofty

LOFTY adj **LOFTIER, LOFTIEST** very tall; being of great or imposing height

LOG noun **LOGS** part of a tree trunk or branch that has been cut, especially for firewood ◻ verb **LOGS, LOGGING, LOGGED** to record (distances covered on a journey, events, etc) in a book or logbook

LOGARITHM noun **LOGARITHMS** the power to which a real number, called the base, must be raised in order to give another number or variable, eg the logarithm of 100 to the base 10 is 2 (written $\log_{10} 100 = 2$)

LOGBOOK noun **LOGBOOKS** a book containing an official record of the voyage of a ship, aircraft, etc, including details of crew and any incidents which occur

LOGGIA noun **LOGGIAS** a roofed gallery or arcade on the side of a building that usually opens onto a garden

LOGGING noun **LOGGINGS** the work of cutting trees and preparing timber

LOGIC noun **LOGICS** the exploration of the validity or otherwise of arguments and reasoning, where the aim is not to prove or disprove the legitimacy of statements or premisses, but rather to show that the underlying thinking behind what is being proposed is well-founded

LOGICAL adj relating or according to logic

LOGICALLY adverb in a logical way

LOGICIAN noun **LOGICIANS** someone who studies or writes about logic

LOGISTIC adj relating to reasoning, to calculation, or to logistics

LOGISTICS singular and plural noun the organizing of everything needed for any large-scale operation

LOGLOG noun **LOGLOGS** a logarithm of a logarithm

LOGO noun **LOGOS** any easily recognizable or significant badge

or emblem used by a company, organization, etc as a trademark or symbol

LOGOGRAM noun **LOGOGRAMS** a logograph

LOGOGRAPH noun **LOGOGRAPHS** a single symbol which consistently stands for a morpheme, word or phrase, such as & for and

LOGORRHEA noun **LOGORRHEAS** a condition associated with certain mental illnesses characterized by incoherent and very rapid talking, often using nonsense words

LOGOTYPE noun **LOGOTYPES** a section of type with more than one letter or character on it

LOIN noun **LOINS** the area of the back and side in humans and some animals, stretching from the bottom rib to the pelvis

LOINCLOTH noun **LOINCLOTHS** a piece of material worn round the hips, covering the genitals, especially by people in non-industrial societies

LOITER verb **LOITERS, LOITERING, LOITERED** to walk slowly; to dawdle

LOITERER noun **LOITERERS** someone who loiters

LOLL verb **LOLLS, LOLLING, LOLLED** to lie or sit about lazily; to lounge or sprawl

LOLLER noun **LOLLERS** someone who lolls

LOLLINGLY adverb lazily

LOLLIPOP noun **LOLLIPOPS** a sweet on a stick

LOLLOP verb **LOLLOPS, LOLLOPING, LOLLOPED** to bound around, especially with big ungainly strides

LOLLY noun **LOLLIES** short form of lollipop

LONE adj without a companion

LONELY adj **LONELIER, LONELIEST** said of a person: sad because they have no companions or friends

LONER noun **LONERS** someone who prefers to be alone and who avoids close relationships

LONESOME adj sad and lonely

LONG[1] adj **LONGER, LONGEST** measuring a great distance in space from one end to the other ◻ adverb for, during or by a long period of time ◻ noun **LONGS** a signal in Morse code that corresponds with the dash

LONG[2] verb **LONGS, LONGING, LONGED** to desire something or someone very much

LONGBOAT noun **LONGBOATS** the largest boat carried by a sailing ship, used for ferrying people and goods from ship to shore and vice versa, or in times of emergency

LONGBOW noun **LONGBOWS** a large bow, drawn by hand, used for hunting and as a weapon, especially in England in the Middle Ages

LONGEVITY noun **LONGEVITIES** great length of life

LONGHAND noun **LONGHANDS** ordinary handwriting as opposed to shorthand, typing or word-processing

LONGHORN noun **LONGHORNS** an animal belonging to a breed of cattle with long horns

LONGING noun **LONGINGS** an intense desire or yearning

LONGINGLY adverb yearningly

LONGISH adj quite long

LONGITUDE noun **LONGITUDES** any of a series of imaginary circles that pass around the Earth through both poles, representing the angular distance east or west of the prime meridian, measured from 0 degrees at this meridian to 180 degrees east or west of it

LONGSHIP noun **LONGSHIPS** a long narrow Viking warship with a large squarish sail, which could also be powered by banks of rowers

LONGSHORE adj found on or employed along the shore

LONGUEUR noun **LONGUEURS** any period of extreme tedium or boredom

LONGWAYS adj in the direction of a thing's length; lengthways □ adverb in the direction of a thing's length; lengthways

LOO ¹ noun **LOOS** a lavatory

LOO ² verb **LOOS, LOOING, LOOED** to subject to a forfeit at the card game loo

LOOFA noun **LOOFAS** a loofah

LOOFAH noun **LOOFAHS** the roughly cylindrical dried inner part of a tropical gourd-like fruit, used as a kind of rough sponge

LOOK verb **LOOKS, LOOKING, LOOKED** to direct one's sight □ noun **LOOKS** an act or the action of looking; a glance or view

LOOKER noun **LOOKERS** someone, usually a woman, who is considered attractive

LOOKOUT noun **LOOKOUTS** a careful watch

LOOM ¹ noun **LOOMS** a machine, either hand-powered or mechanical, that weaves thread into fabric

LOOM ² verb **LOOMS, LOOMING, LOOMED** to appear indistinctly and usually in some enlarged or threatening form

LOON noun **LOONS** any one of various diving birds, especially one of a type of large bird, native to northern waters of the N hemisphere

LOONY noun **LOONIES** someone who is mad □ adj **LOONIER, LOONIEST** crazy; mad

LOOP noun **LOOPS** a rounded or oval-shaped single coil in a piece of thread, string, rope, chain, etc, formed as it crosses over itself □ verb **LOOPS, LOOPING, LOOPED** to fasten with or enclose in a loop

LOOPER noun **LOOPERS** a caterpillar of the geometrid moth, which moves by forming its body into a loop and planting its hinder legs close behind its six true legs

LOOPHOLE noun **LOOPHOLES** an inherent flaw, gap or ambiguity in a law, rule, contract, agreement, etc, especially one that is advantageous to a particular person or party, or one that allows someone to evade a responsibility, duty, obligation, etc legitimately

LOOPY adj **LOOPIER, LOOPIEST** mad; crazy

LOOSE adj **LOOSER, LOOSEST** not or no longer tied up or attached to something else; free □ adverb in an unrestrained way □ verb **LOOSES, LOOSING, LOOSED** to release or set free

LOOSELY adverb not tightly; droopily; insecurely

LOOSEN verb **LOOSENS, LOOSENING, LOOSENED** to make or become loose or looser

LOOSENESS noun **LOOSENESSES** the state of being loose

LOOT verb **LOOTS, LOOTING, LOOTED** said especially of a mob: to steal from shops, warehouses, etc, often with attendant vandalism or violence during or following rioting □ noun **LOOTS** money, goods or supplies stolen from shops, warehouses, etc, especially when taken during or following rioting

LOOTER noun **LOOTERS** someone who steals from shops, warehouses, etc, often with attendant vandalism or violence during or following rioting

LOOTING noun the theft of money, goods or supplies, especially when they have been taken from an enemy during a war or from shops, warehouses, etc during rioting

LOP verb **LOPS, LOPPING, LOPPED** to cut off (especially the branches of a tree)

LOPE verb **LOPES, LOPING, LOPED** to run with long bounding steps □ noun **LOPES** a bounding leap

LOPSIDED adj with one side smaller, lower or lighter than the other

LOQUACITY noun **LOQUACITIES** talkativeness

LOQUAT noun **LOQUATS** a small evergreen tree with very hairy branches, originally found in China but now widely grown in S Europe

LOR exclamation a colloquial form of lord expressing surprise

LORAN noun **LORANS** a widely used long-range radio navigation system that works by measuring the time of arrival of signals from two fixed synchronized transmitters

LORD noun **LORDS** a master or ruler

LORDLESS adj without a lord

LORDLY adj **LORDLIER, LORDLIEST** having attributes that are popularly associated with lords, especially in being grand or haughty

LORDOSIS noun **LORDOSES** a medical condition characterized by excessive inward curvature of the lumbar region of the spine, which may be congenital, or caused by faulty posture, muscular weakness, or disorders of the spine or hip

LORDOTIC adj affected with or relating to lordosis

LORDSHIP noun **LORDSHIPS** a title used to address bishops, judges and all peers except dukes

LORE noun **LORES** the whole body of knowledge on a particular subject, especially the kind of knowledge that has been enhanced by legends, anecdotes, traditional beliefs, etc

For longer words, see The Chambers Dictionary

LORGNETTE noun **LORGNETTES** a pair of spectacles that are held up to the eyes using a long handle, as opposed to the kind that rest on the nose

LORIS noun **LORISES** a small primitive S Asian primate with a pale face and large eyes with dark rings around them

LORRY noun **LORRIES** a large road vehicle for transporting heavy loads

LOS noun **LOSES** praise, reputation

LOSE verb **LOSES, LOSING, LOST** to fail to keep or obtain something, especially because of a mistake, carelessness, etc

LOSER noun **LOSERS** someone or something that is defeated

LOSING adj failing; never likely to be successful

LOSS noun **LOSSES** the act or fact of losing or being lost

LOST [1] adj having gone astray

LOST [2] past form of lose

LOT [1] noun **LOTS** a large number or amount of something

LOT [2] verb **LOTS, LOTTING, LOTTED** to allot

LOTH adj **LOTHER, LOTHEST** loath

LOTION noun **LOTIONS** any liquid, used either as a medicine or a cosmetic, for healing or cleaning the skin

LOTTERY noun **LOTTERIES** a system for raising money which involves randomly drawing numbered tickets from a drum, etc and giving prizes to those who hold the tickets with the same numbers as the ones that have been picked out

LOTTO noun **LOTTOS** an earlier name for the game now usually called bingo

LOTUS noun **LOTUSES** a popular name for a variety of different plants many of which are cultivated for their ornamental value

LOUD adj **LOUDER, LOUDEST** making a relatively great sound; noisy □ adverb in a loud manner

LOUDISH adj somewhat loud

LOUDNESS noun the quality or condition of being loud

LOUGH noun **LOUGHS** a loch

LOUNGE verb **LOUNGES, LOUNGING, LOUNGED** to lie, sit, stand, recline etc in a relaxed and comfortable way □ noun **LOUNGES** a sitting-room in a private house

LOUNGER noun **LOUNGERS** someone who lounges

LOUPE noun **LOUPES** a small magnifying glass held in the eye socket and used by jewellers, watchmakers, etc for close, intricate work or for examining pieces to assess their value

LOUR verb **LOURS, LOURING, LOURED** said of the sky or elements: to darken or threaten rain or storms □ noun **LOURS** a scowl

LOURING adj of the sky, etc: threatening

LOUSE noun **LICE** a wingless parasitic insect with a flat body and short legs, which survives by sucking the blood of its host □ verb **LOUSES, LOUSING, LOUSED** to get rid of lice from (clothing, hair, etc)

LOUSILY adverb in a lousy way

LOUSINESS noun **LOUSINESSES** the condition of being lousy

LOUSY adj **LOUSIER, LOUSIEST** poor or second-rate

LOUT noun **LOUTS** someone, usually male, who has little or no education or who behaves in a rude or ill-mannered way

LOUTISH adj awkward, ill-mannered and coarse

LOUVER noun **LOUVERS** a louvre

LOUVRE noun **LOUVRES** any one of a set of horizontal sloping overlapping slats in a door, etc which let air in but keep rain and light out

LOUVRED adj equipped with louvres

LOVABLE adj worthy of or inspiring love or affection

LOVAGE noun **LOVAGES** a S European flowering plant used medicinally and for flavouring

LOVAT noun **LOVATS** a palish dusky green colour □ adj palish dusky green in colour

LOVE verb **LOVES, LOVING, LOVED** to feel great affection for (especially a close relative, friend, etc) □ noun **LOVES** a feeling of great affection

LOVEABLE adj lovable

LOVEBIRD noun **LOVEBIRDS** a small parrot found in Africa and Madagascar, sometimes kept as a cagebird

LOVELESS adj devoid of love

LOVELORN adj sad because the love one feels for someone else is not returned

LOVELY adj **LOVELIER, LOVELIEST** strikingly attractive; beautiful □ noun **LOVELIES** a pretty woman

LOVER noun **LOVERS** someone who is in love with someone else, especially in a romantic or sexual way

LOVESICK adj infatuated with someone

LOVING adj affectionate and caring

LOVINGLY adverb in a loving way

LOW [1] adj **LOWER, LOWEST** said of a building, hill, etc: measuring comparatively little from top to bottom □ adverb in or to a low position, state or manner □ noun **LOWS** a depth, position, level, etc which is low or lowest

LOW [2] □ verb **LOWS, LOWING, LOWED** said of cattle: to make a gentle mooing sound

LOWER adj not as high in position, status, height, value, etc □ adverb in or to a lower position □ verb **LOWERS, LOWERING, LOWERED** to lessen or become less in amount, value, status, sound, etc

LOWING noun **LOWINGS** the mooing sound made by cattle

LOWLAND noun **LOWLANDS** land which is comparatively low-lying and flat

LOWLANDER noun **LOWLANDERS** a native of lowlands, especially the Lowlands of Scotland

LOWLINESS noun **LOWLINESSES** humility; modesty

LOWLY adj **LOWLIER, LOWLIEST** humble in rank, status or behaviour

LOWNESS noun **LOWNESSES** the quality or condition of being low

LOX noun **LOXES** a type of smoked salmon

LOY noun **LOYS** in Ireland, a long, narrow spade

LOYAL adj **LOYALLER, LOYALLEST** faithful and true

LOYALIST noun **LOYALISTS** a loyal supporter, especially of a sovereign or an established government

LOYALLY adverb in a loyal way

LOYALTY noun **LOYALTIES** the state or quality of being loyal

LOZEN noun **LOZENS** a Scots word for window-pane

LOZENGE noun **LOZENGES** a small

sweet or tablet, especially one with some kind of medicinal property, which dissolves in the mouth

LUBBER noun **LUBBERS** someone who is big, awkward and clumsy, especially if they are also thought of as tending to be lazy

LUBBERLY adj awkward, clumsy and lazy □ adverb in a lubberly manner

LUBRICANT noun **LUBRICANTS** oil, grease, etc used to reduce friction □ adj lubricating

LUBRICATE verb **LUBRICATES, LUBRICATING, LUBRICATED** to coat (engine parts, etc) with oil, grease, etc in order to reduce friction

LUBRICATING adj that lubricates

LUBRICITY noun **LUBRICITIES** lewdness

LUCENT adj bright; shiny

LUCERNE noun **LUCERNES** alfalfa

LUCID adj **LUCIDER, LUCIDEST** said of a speech, piece of writing, argument, etc: clearly presented and easily understood

LUCIDITY noun **LUCIDITIES** transparency of expression

LUCIDLY adverb in a lucid way; clearly

LUCIDNESS noun **LUCIDNESSES** lucidity

LUCK noun **LUCKS** chance, especially as it is perceived as influencing someone's life at specific points in time

LUCKILY adverb in a lucky way; I'm glad to say, fortunately

LUCKLESS adj without good luck; unhappy

LUCKY adj **LUCKIER, LUCKIEST** having good fortune

LUCRATIVE adj affording financial gain; profitable

LUCRE noun **LUCRES** profit or financial gain, especially when it is obtained in a way that is considered dishonourable, greedy or exploitative

LUD noun **LUDS** a form of *lord* (sometimes used when addressing a judge)

LUDIC adj playful, especially spontaneously and aimlessly

LUDICROUS adj said of a situation, proposal, etc: completely ridiculous because of its incongruity, unsuitability, absurdity, etc

LUDO noun **LUDOS** a children's

board game where each player has four counters of the same colour which they move according to the number shown each time they throw the dice, the object being to get all one's counters 'home', after a complete circuit of the board, before anyone else

LUFF verb **LUFFS, LUFFING, LUFFED** to steer a ship towards the wind, especially with accompanying flapping of the sails □ noun **LUFFS** the forward edge of a fore-and-aft sail

LUFFA noun **LUFFAS** a loofah

LUG noun **LUGS** an ear □ verb **LUGS, LUGGING, LUGGED** to carry, pull or drag something with difficulty, especially something that is bulky or heavy

LUGE noun **LUGES** a toboggan for either one or two people who must lie back in an almost flat, optimally aerodynamic position, steering with the feet and a hand rope □ verb **LUGES, LUGING, LUGED** to travel across snow or ice on a luge

LUGGAGE noun **LUGGAGES** suitcases, bags, etc used when travelling

LUGGER noun **LUGGERS** a small vessel with square sails attached to yards, which hang obliquely to the masts

LUGHOLE noun **LUGHOLES** the ear

LUGWORM noun **LUGWORMS** a large marine worm which burrows in the sand and soft earth on seashores and river estuaries and which is often used as fishing bait

LUKEWARM adj said especially of liquids: moderately warm

LULL verb **LULLS, LULLING, LULLED** to soothe or induce a feeling of well-being in someone, especially by caressing them, quietly singing, etc □ noun **LULLS** a period of calm and quiet

LULLABY noun **LULLABIES** a soft soothing song, especially one meant to pacify babies and little children or to help send them to sleep

LUM noun **LUMS** a Scots word for *chimney*

LUMBAGO noun **LUMBAGOS** chronic pain in the lower region of the back, usually caused by a strained muscle or ligament, arthritis, a slipped disc or a trapped nerve

LUMBAR adj relating to the back between the lowest ribs and the pelvis

LUMBER [1] noun **LUMBERS** disused articles of furniture, odds and ends that are no longer used, etc which have been stored away

LUMBER [2] verb **LUMBERS, LUMBERING, LUMBERED** to move about heavily and clumsily

LUMBERING adj that moves about heavily and clumsily

LUMEN noun **LUMENS, LUMINA** in the SI system: a unit of luminous flux, defined as the amount of light emitted by a point source of intensity one candela within a solid angle of one

LUMINANCE noun **LUMINANCES** a measure of the brightness of a surface that is radiating or reflecting light, expressed in candelas per square metre

LUMINARY noun **LUMINARIES** someone who is considered an expert or authority in a particular field

LUMINOUS adj full of or giving out light

LUMMOX noun **LUMMOXES** someone who is very clumsy or stupid

LUMP noun **LUMPS** a small solid mass that has no definite shape □ verb **LUMPS, LUMPING, LUMPED** to form or collect into lumps

LUMPEN adj boorish and stupid; incapable of, or not interested in, self-improvement

LUMPFISH noun **LUMPFISHES** a fish widespread in cold northern seas, which has a heavy rounded body with rows of spiny plates and a large sucker on its underside, and which is eaten salted or smoked

LUMPILY adverb in a lumpy way

LUMPINESS noun **LUMPINESSES** the state of being lumpy

LUMPISH adj heavy, dull or awkward

LUMPISHLY adverb in a lumpish way

LUMPY adj **LUMPIER, LUMPIEST** full of lumps

LUNACY noun **LUNACIES** insanity

LUNAR adj resembling the Moon

LUNATE adj crescent-shaped

LUNATIC adj insane □ noun **LUNATICS** someone who is foolish or highly eccentric

LUNCH noun **LUNCHES** a light meal eaten in the middle of the day

❑ *verb* **LUNCHES, LUNCHING, LUNCHED** to eat lunch

LUNCHEON *noun* **LUNCHEONS** a formal meal served in the middle of the day

LUNETTE *noun* **LUNETTES** anything that is crescent-shaped

LUNG *noun* **LUNGS** in the chest cavity of air-breathing vertebrates: one of a pair of large spongy respiratory organs which remove carbon dioxide from the blood and replace it with oxygen

LUNGE *noun* **LUNGES** a sudden plunge forwards ❑ *verb* **LUNGES, LUNGEING, LUNGING, LUNGED** to make a sudden strong or thrusting movement forwards

LUNGWORT *noun* **LUNGWORTS** a perennial shade-loving plant with pale spotted leaves and clusters of pink or blue bell-shaped flowers

LUNULA *noun* **LUNULAE** the whitish crescent-shaped area at the bottom of the human fingernail

LUPIN *noun* **LUPINS** a garden plant with long spikes of brightly coloured flowers

LUPINE *adj* relating to or like a wolf

LUPUS *noun* **LUPUSES** any of a variety of skin diseases characterized by the formation of ulcers and lesions

LUR *noun* **LURS** a Bronze Age trumpet

LURCH *verb* **LURCHES, LURCHING, LURCHED** said of a person: to stagger unsteadily ❑ *noun* **LURCHES** an act of staggering

LURCHER *noun* **LURCHERS** a cross-bred hunting-dog, usually a cross between a greyhound and a collie, formerly kept by poachers for catching rabbits and hares

LURE *verb* **LURES, LURING, LURED** to tempt or entice, often by the offer of some reward ❑ *noun* **LURES** someone or something which tempts, attracts or entices

LURGY *noun* **LURGIES** a highly infectious non-specific disease

LURID *adj* **LURIDER, LURIDEST** glaringly bright, especially when the surroundings are dark

LURIDLY *adj* in a lurid way

LURIDNESS *noun* **LURIDNESSES** the state of being lurid

LURK *verb* **LURKS, LURKING, LURKED** to lie in wait, especially in ambush, with some sinister purpose in mind

LUSCIOUS *adj* said of a smell, taste, etc: richly sweet; delicious

LUSH *adj* **LUSHER, LUSHEST** said of grass, foliage, etc: green and growing abundantly

LUSHLY *adverb* in a lush way

LUSHNESS *noun* **LUSHNESSES** the quality of being lush

LUST *noun* **LUSTS** strong sexual desire ❑ *verb* **LUSTS, LUSTING, LUSTED** to have strong sexual desire

LUSTER *noun* **LUSTERS** lustre

LUSTFUL *adj* having or showing strong sexual desire; characterized by lust

LUSTFULLY *adverb* in a lustful way

LUSTILY *adverb* in a lusty way

LUSTRE *noun* **LUSTRES** the shiny appearance of something in reflected light

LUSTROUS *adj* having a lustre; bright and shining

LUSTY *adj* **LUSTIER, LUSTIEST** vigorous or loud

LUTANIST *noun* **LUTANISTS** a lutenist

LUTE *noun* **LUTES** a stringed instrument with a long neck and a body shaped like a half pear, which is played by plucking

LUTECIUM *noun* **LUTECIUMS** lutetium

LUTEIN *noun* **LUTEINS** any of various yellow carotenoid pigments found in the corpus luteum and in the egg yolk of animals, and in the leaves, flowers and fruits of certain plants

LUTENIST *noun* **LUTENISTS** someone who plays the lute

LUTETIUM *noun* **LUTETIUMS** a very rare soft silvery metallic element, usually obtained by the processing of other metals, and used as a catalyst and in nuclear technology

LUTIST *noun* **LUTISTS** a lutenist

LUTZ *noun* **LUTZES** in skating: a jump, including one or more rotations, from the back outer edge of one skate to the back outer edge of the other

LUV *noun* **LUVS** love, a term of endearment

LUVVIE *noun* **LUVVIES** someone, originally in the theatre, but now also generally, who speaks and behaves in an overly pretentious or camp manner

LUVVY *noun* **LUVVIES** a luvvie

LUX *noun* **LUX, LUXES, LUCES** in the SI system: a unit of illuminance, equal to one lumen per square metre

LUXE *noun* **LUXES** luxury

LUXURIANT *adj* said of plants, etc: growing abundantly; lush

LUXURIATE *verb* **LUXURIATES, LUXURIATING, LUXURIATED** to live in great comfort or luxury

LUXURIOUS *adj* expensive and opulent

LUXURY *noun* **LUXURIES** expensive, rich and extremely comfortable surroundings and possessions

LUZ *noun* **LUZZES** a supposedly indestructible bone

LYCEUM *noun* **LYCEUMS** a place or building devoted to teaching, especially literature and philosophy

LYCHEE *noun* **LYCHEES** a small fruit with sweet white juicy flesh enclosing a single seed, originally from China but now widely cultivated in many tropical regions

LYCHGATE *noun* **LYCHGATES** a lichgate

LYE *noun* **LYES** an alkaline solution made by leaching water through wood ash, etc

LYING a form of **lie** ¹, **lie** ²

LYM *noun* **LYMS** a Shakespearean word for a leash

LYMPH *noun* **LYMPHS** in animals: a colourless fluid that bathes all the tissues and drains into the vessels of the lymphatic system, and which contains lymphocytes and antibodies which prevent the spread of infection

LYMPHATIC *adj* relating to lymph; carrying or secreting lymph

LYMPHOID *adj* lymphatic

LYMPHOMA *noun* **LYMPHOMAS** any tumour of the lymphatic tissues, especially a malignant tumour of the lymph nodes

LYNCH *verb* **LYNCHES, LYNCHING, LYNCHED** said of a group of people: to decide without holding a legal trial that someone is guilty of some crime or misdemeanour, and subsequently to put them to death, usually by hanging

LYNX *noun* **LYNXES** any of various wild members of the cat family with yellowish-grey or reddish fur, a short, stubby tail with a black tip, tufted ears and a ruff of fur around its face, found mainly in northern pine forests

LYONNAISE *adj* in cookery: made with sautéed sliced potatoes and onions or potatoes in an onion sauce

LYOPHILIC *adj* denoting a substance that has an affinity for liquid solvents

LYOPHOBIC *adj* denoting a substance that tends to repel liquid solvents

LYRATE *adj* lyre-shaped

LYRE *noun* **LYRES** a small U-shaped instrument made from wood or tortoiseshell, with three to twelve strings which are plucked with the fingers or with a plectrum, used, especially in ancient Greece, to accompany songs and poetry

LYRIC *adj* expressing personal, private or individual emotions ◻ *noun* **LYRICS** a short poem or song, usually written in the first person and expressing a particular emotion

LYRICAL *adj* lyric; song-like

LYRICALLY *adverb* in a lyrical way

LYRICISM *noun* **LYRICISMS** the state or quality of being lyrical

LYRICIST *noun* **LYRICISTS** someone who writes the words to songs

LYSINE *noun* **LYSINES** an essential amino acid found in proteins

LYSIS *noun* **LYSES** any process that causes the destruction of a living cell by the disruption of the cell membrane and release of the cell contents

LYSOSOME *noun* **LYSOSOMES** a specialized membrane-bound structure, found mainly in animal cells, containing digestive enzymes which play an important role in the destruction of foreign particles and the breakdown of damaged or worn-out cells

LYSOZYME *noun* **LYSOZYMES** an enzyme that breaks down bacterial cell walls and is present in many body fluids and secretions, eg saliva, tears, mucus, etc

MA noun **MAS** a mother

MAA verb **MAAS, MAAING, MAAED** of a goat: to bleat

MAC noun **MACS** short form of macintosh

MACABRE adj connected, or to do with, death in some way

MACADAM noun a road-making material consisting of layers of compacted broken stones, usually bound with tar

MACADAMIA noun **MACADAMIAS** an evergreen tree belonging to a native Australian genus

MACAQUE noun **MACAQUES** a type of short-tailed or tailless monkey of Asia and Africa, with large cheek-pouches

MACARONI noun **MACARONIS, MACARONIES** pasta in the form of short narrow tubes

MACAROON noun **MACAROONS** a sweet cake or biscuit made with sugar, eggs and crushed almonds or sometimes coconut

MACAW noun **MACAWS** any of numerous large brilliantly-coloured parrots with long tails and strong beaks, found mainly in the tropical forests of Central and S America

MACE noun **MACES** a ceremonial staff carried by some public officials (eg the Speaker of the House of Commons) as a symbol of authority

MACERATE verb **MACERATES, MACERATING, MACERATED** to break up or make something break up or become soft by soaking it

MACERATOR noun **MACERATORS** a machine or person that macerates

MACHETE noun **MACHETES** a long heavy broad-bladed knife used as a weapon or cutting tool, especially in S America and the W Indies

MACHINATE verb **MACHINATES, MACHINATING, MACHINATED** to form a plot or scheme, especially one to do something wrong or wicked, or designed to cause harm

MACHINE noun **MACHINES** a device with moving parts, and usually powered, designed to perform a particular task ▢ verb **MACHINES, MACHINING, MACHINED** to make, shape or cut something with a machine

MACHINERY noun **MACHINERIES** machines in general

MACHINIST noun **MACHINISTS** someone who operates a machine

MACHISMO noun **MACHISMOS** exaggerated manliness; the expression of male virility or masculine pride

MACHO adj exaggeratedly or aggressively manly; virile in a very conspicuous or forced way ▢ noun **MACHOS** a macho man

MACINTOSH noun **MACINTOSHES** a waterproof raincoat

MACK noun **MACKS** a mac

MACKEREL noun **MACKERELS** an important food fish of the tuna family, with a streamlined body that is blue-green above and silvery below, found especially in the N Atlantic

MACRAMÉ noun **MACRAMÉS** the art or practice of knotting string or coarse thread into patterns

MACRO noun **MACROS** in computing: a single instruction that brings a set of instructions into operation

MACROCOSM noun **MACROCOSMS** the universe as a whole

MACRON noun **MACRONS** a straight horizontal bar (ˉ) placed over a letter to show that it is a long or stressed vowel

MACROPOD noun **MACROPODS** an animal that belongs to the marsupial family which comprises the kangaroos and wallabies

MACULA noun **MACULAE** a spot, discoloured mark or blemish, eg a freckle on the skin or a sunspot on the sun

MACULAR adj spotted; patchy

MAD [1] adj **MADDER, MADDEST** mentally disturbed; insane

MAD [2] verb **MADS, MADDING, MADDED** a Shakespearean word meaning to drive mad

MADAM noun **MADAMS** a polite form of address to any woman, especially a married or elderly woman or any female customer in a shop, etc, used instead of a name

MADAME noun **MESDAMES** used instead of *Mrs* as a title for a Frenchwoman or a French-speaking woman

MADCAP noun **MADCAPS** a foolishly impulsive person

MADDEN verb **MADDENS, MADDENING, MADDENED** to make (a person or animal) mad, especially to enrage them or it

MADDENING adj referring to something that drives one to madness or rage; extremely annoying

MADDER noun **MADDERS** a Eurasian herbaceous plant with yellow flowers and a red root

MADE adj artificially produced or formed

MADELEINE noun **MADELEINES** a type of small rich sponge cake, shaped like a shell

MADHOUSE noun **MADHOUSES** a place of great confusion and noise

MADLY adverb in a mad way

MADMAN noun **MADMEN** an insane person

MADNESS noun insanity

MADRAS noun **MADRASES** a large, usually brightly-coloured scarf, of a type formerly exported from Madras in SE India

MADREPORE noun **MADREPORES** any coral of the common, reef-building type, occurring especially in tropical seas

MADRIGAL noun **MADRIGALS** an unaccompanied part song, typically about love or nature, of a type that originated in 14c Italy and became popular in England in the 16c and 17c

MADWOMAN noun **MADWOMEN** an insane woman

MAE *adverb* Scots word for *more* □ *adj* Scots word for *more*

MAELSTROM *noun* **MAELSTROMS** a place or state of uncontrollable confusion or destructive forces, especially one to which someone or something is inevitably drawn

MAENAD *noun* **MAENADS** in mythology: a female participant in orgies and rites in honour of Bacchus or Dionysus, the god of wine

MAENADIC *adj* resembling or relating to a maenad; frenzied; furious

MAESTRO *noun* **MAESTROS, MAESTRI** someone who is regarded as being specially gifted in a specified art, especially a distinguished musical composer, conductor, performer or teacher

MAFIA *noun* **MAFIAS** any group considered to be like the Mafia, a secret international criminal organization, originating in Sicily, that controls numerous illegal activities worldwide

MAFIOSO *noun* **MAFIOSI** a member of the Mafia or a mafia

MAG [1] *noun* **MAGS** a magazine or periodical

MAG [2] *verb* **MAGS, MAGGING, MAGGED** a dialect word meaning to tease or to chatter

MAGAZINE *noun* **MAGAZINES** a paperback periodical publication, usually a heavily illustrated one, containing articles, stories, etc by various writers

MAGENTA *adj* dark, purplish-red in colour □ *noun* **MAGENTAS** a purplish-red colour

MAGGOT *noun* **MAGGOTS** the worm-like larva of various flies, especially that of the housefly

MAGGOTY *adj* **MAGGOTIER, MAGGOTIEST** full of or infected with maggots, or like maggots

MAGI plural of **magus**

MAGIC *noun* **MAGICS** the supposed art or practice of using the power of supernatural forces, spells, etc to affect people, objects and events □ *adj* belonging or relating to, used in, or done by, sorcery or conjuring □ *verb* **MAGICS, MAGICKING, MAGICKED** to produce something by using, or as if by using, sorcery or conjuring

MAGICAL *adj* relating to the art or practice of magic

MAGICALLY *adverb* in a magical way

MAGICIAN *noun* **MAGICIANS** an entertainer who performs conjuring tricks, illusions, etc

MAGILP *noun* **MAGILPS** megilp

MAGISTRAL *adj* said of a treatment or medicine: specially prescribed for a particular case

MAGLEV *noun* **MAGLEVS** a high-speed transport system in which magnetism is used to keep an electrically-powered train gliding above a track

MAGMA *noun* **MAGMAS** hot molten rock material generated deep within the earth's crust or mantle

MAGMATIC *adj* of or relating to magma

MAGNATE *noun* **MAGNATES** someone of high rank or great power, especially in industry

MAGNESIA *noun* **MAGNESIAS** the common name for magnesium oxide

MAGNESIAN *adj* belonging to, containing, or resembling magnesia

MAGNESIUM *noun* **MAGNESIUMS** a reactive silvery-grey metallic element that burns with a dazzling white flame, used in fireworks and in strong light alloys for aircraft components, etc

MAGNET *noun* **MAGNETS** a piece of metal, especially a piece of iron, with the power to attract and repel iron, and the tendency to point in an approximate north-south direction when freely suspended

MAGNETIC *adj* belonging to, having the powers of, or operated by a magnet or magnetism

MAGNETISE *verb* **MAGNETISES, MAGNETISING, MAGNETISED** to magnetize

MAGNETISM *noun* **MAGNETISMS** the properties of attraction possessed by magnets

MAGNETITE *noun* **MAGNETITES** a shiny, black, strongly magnetic mineral form of iron oxide, an important ore of iron

MAGNETIZE *verb* **MAGNETIZES, MAGNETIZING, MAGNETIZED** to make something magnetic

MAGNETO *noun* **MAGNETOS** a simple electric generator consisting of a rotating magnet that induces an alternating current

in a coil surrounding it, used to provide the spark in the ignition system of petrol engines without batteries, eg in lawnmowers, outboard motors, etc

MAGNETRON *noun* **MAGNETRONS** a device for generating microwaves, developed for use in radar transmitters, and now widely used in microwave ovens

MAGNIFIER *noun* **MAGNIFIERS** an instrument which magnifies

MAGNIFY *verb* **MAGNIFIES, MAGNIFYING, MAGNIFIED** to make something appear larger, eg by using a microscope or telescope

MAGNITUDE *noun* **MAGNITUDES** importance or extent

MAGNOLIA *noun* **MAGNOLIAS** a tree or shrub with large sweet-smelling usually white or pink flowers □ *adj* having a very pale, pinkish-white or beige colour

MAGNOX *noun* **MAGNOXES** a material consisting of an aluminium-based alloy containing a small amount of magnesium, from which certain nuclear reactor fuel containers are made

MAGNUM *noun* **MAGNUMS** a champagne or wine bottle that holds approximately 1.5 litres, ie twice the normal amount

MAGPIE *noun* **MAGPIES** a black-and-white bird of the crow family, known for its chattering call and its habit of collecting shiny objects

MAGUS *noun* **MAGI** the three wise men or astrologers from the east who brought gifts to the infant Jesus, guided by a star

MAHARAJA *noun* **MAHARAJAS** a maharajah

MAHARAJAH *noun* **MAHARAJAHS** an Indian prince, especially any of the former rulers of the states of India

MAHARANEE *noun* **MAHARANEES** a maharani

MAHARANI *noun* **MAHARANIS** the wife or widow of a maharajah

MAHARISHI *noun* **MAHARISHIS** a Hindu religious teacher or spiritual leader

MAHATMA *noun* **MAHATMAS** a wise and holy Hindu leader

MAHLSTICK *noun* **MAHLSTICKS** a maulstick

MAHOGANY *noun* **MAHOGANIES** any of various tall evergreen trees of tropical Africa and America, especially a species grown commercially for timber

MAHOUT noun **MAHOUTS** used especially in India: someone who drives, trains and looks after elephants

MAID noun **MAIDS** a female servant

MAIDEN noun **MAIDENS** a young, unmarried woman □ adj first ever

MAIDENISH adj like a maiden

MAIDENLY adj suiting, or suitable for, a maiden; gentle or modest

MAIL ¹ noun **MAILS** the postal system □ verb **MAILS, MAILING, MAILED** to send (a letter, parcel, etc) by post

MAIL ² noun **MAILS** flexible armour for the body, made of small linked metal rings

MAILBAG noun **MAILBAGS** a large strong bag in which letters, etc are carried

MAILBOX noun **MAILBOXES** a public or private letter box or postbox

MAILED adj covered in or protected by mail

MAILMAN noun **MAILMEN** a postman

MAILMERGE noun **MAILMERGES** the process of producing a series of letters addressed to individuals by merging a file of names and addresses with a file containing the text of the letter □ verb **MAILMERGES, MAILMERGING, MAILMERGED** to produce a series of letters by mailmerge

MAILSHOT noun **MAILSHOTS** an unrequested item sent by post, especially a piece of advertising material

MAIM verb **MAIMS, MAIMING, MAIMED** to wound (a person or animal) seriously, especially to disable, mutilate or cripple them

MAIMED adj disabled, mutilated or crippled

MAIMING noun **MAIMINGS** the action of wounding (a person or animal) seriously, especially disabling, mutilating or crippling them

MAIN adj most important; chief; leading □ noun **MAINS** the chief pipe, conduit or cable in a branching system

MAINBRACE noun **MAINBRACES** the rope or brace controlling the movement of a ship's mainsail

MAINFRAME noun **MAINFRAMES** a large powerful computer to which several smaller computers can be linked, that is capable of

handling very large amounts of data at high speed and can usually run several programs simultaneously

MAINLAND noun **MAINLANDS** a country's principal mass of land, as distinct from a nearby island or islands forming part of the same country

MAINLINE verb **MAINLINES, MAINLINING, MAINLINED** to inject (a drug) into a principal vein, so that it has the quickest possible effect

MAINLINER noun **MAINLINERS** someone who injects a drug into a principal vein

MAINLINING noun **MAINLININGS** the action of injecting a drug into a principal vein

MAINLY adverb chiefly; for the most part; largely

MAINMAST noun **MAINMASTS** the principal mast of a sailing ship, usually the second mast from the prow

MAINSAIL noun **MAINSAILS** the largest and lowest sail on a sailing ship, generally attached to the mainmast

MAINSHEET noun **MAINSHEETS** the rope or sheet attached to the lower corner of the mainsail, for adjusting its angle, etc

MAINSTAY noun **MAINSTAYS** a rope stretching forward and down from the top of the mainmast of a sailing ship

MAINTAIN verb **MAINTAINS, MAINTAINING, MAINTAINED** to continue; to keep something in existence

MAINTAINED adj said of a school, etc: financially supported, eg from public funds

MAIOLICA noun **MAIOLICAS** majolica

MAIZE noun **MAIZES** a tall cereal plant belonging to the grass family, widely grown for its edible yellow grain which grows in large spikes called corncobs

MAJESTIC adj having or showing majesty; stately, dignified or grand in manner, style, appearance, etc

MAJESTY noun **MAJESTIES** great and impressive dignity, sovereign power or authority, eg the supreme greatness and power of God

MAJOLICA noun **MAJOLICAS** colourfully glazed or enamelled earthenware, as produced in Italy from the 14c, and especially that of

the early 16c decorated with scenes in the Renaissance style

MAJOR adj great, or greater, in number, size, extent, value, importance, etc □ noun **MAJORS** an officer in the army □ verb **MAJORS, MAJORING, MAJORED** to specialize in (a particular subject of study)

MAJORETTE noun **MAJORETTES** a member of a group of girls who march in parades, wearing decorative military-style uniforms with short skirts and performing elaborate displays of baton-twirling, etc

MAJORITY noun **MAJORITIES** the greater number; the largest group; the bulk

MAJUSCULE noun **MAJUSCULES** an extra large letter □ adj said of a letter: extra large

MAK verb **MAKS, MAKING, MADE** a Scots word meaning to make

MAKABLE adj that can be made

MAKE verb **MAKES, MAKING, MADE** to form, create, manufacture or produce something by mixing, combining or shaping materials □ noun **MAKES** a manufacturer's brand

MAKEABLE adj makable

MAKEOVER noun **MAKEOVERS** a complete change in a person's style of dress, appearance, make-up, hair, etc

MAKER noun **MAKERS** a person who makes something

MAKESHIFT adj serving as a temporary and less adequate substitute for something

MAKING noun **MAKINGS** the act or process of producing or forming the specified thing

MAKO noun **MAKOS** a small evergreen tree of New Zealand with red berries that turn purple as they ripen

MAL noun **MALS** a French word for *pain, sickness*

MALACHITE noun **MALACHITES** a bright green copper mineral that is used as a gemstone and as a minor ore of copper

MALADROIT adj clumsy; tactless; unskilful

MALADY noun **MALADIES** an illness or disease

MALAISE noun **MALAISES** a

feeling of uneasiness, discontent, general depression or despondency

MALARIA *noun* **MALARIAS** an infectious disease that produces anaemia and recurring bouts of fever, caused by a parasitic protozoan which is transmitted to humans by the bite of the mosquito

MALARIAL *adj* infected with malaria

MALARIOUS *adj* malarial

MALARKEY *noun* **MALARKEYS** nonsense; rubbish; absurd behaviour or talk

MALARKY *noun* **MALARKIES** malarkey

MALE *adj* denoting the sex that produces sperm and fertilizes the egg cell (ovum) produced by the female □ *noun* **MALES** a male person, animal or plant

MALFORMED *adj* badly or wrongly formed

MALICE *noun* **MALICES** the desire or intention to harm or hurt another or others

MALICIOUS *adj* feeling, or motivated by, hatred or by a desire to cause harm

MALIGN *verb* **MALIGNS, MALIGNING, MALIGNED** to say or write bad or unpleasant things about someone, especially falsely or spitefully □ *adj* said of a person: evil in nature or influence; threatening; displaying ill-will

MALIGNANT *adj* said of a person: feeling or showing hatred or the desire to do harm to another or others; malicious or malevolent

MALIGNER *noun* **MALIGNERS** someone who says or writes bad or unpleasant things about someone else, especially falsely or spitefully

MALIGNITY *noun* **MALIGNITIES** the quality or state of being malign, evil or deadly

MALIGNLY *adverb* in a malign way

MALINGER *verb* **MALINGERS, MALINGERING, MALINGERED** to pretend to be ill, especially in order to avoid having to work

MALL *noun* **MALLS** a shopping centre, street or area, etc with shops, that is closed to vehicles

MALLARD *noun* **MALLARDS** a very common species of wild duck, the drake of which has a green head and neck while the female is simply brown

MALLEABLE *adj* said of certain metals and alloys, etc: able to be beaten into a different shape, hammered into thin sheets and bent, etc without breaking

MALLET *noun* **MALLETS** a hammer with a large head, usually made of wood

MALLEUS *noun* **MALLEUSES** a small hammer-shaped bone in the middle ear, which, together with the incus and stapes, transmits sound waves from the eardrum to the inner ear

MALLOW *noun* **MALLOWS** any of various European plants with pink, purple or white flowers, and fine hairs on the leaves and stem

MALM *noun* **MALMS** an artificial mixture of clay and chalk used in the manufacture of bricks

MALMSEY *noun* **MALMSEYS** a strong sweet wine originally from Greece but now usually from Spain, Madeira, etc

MALT *noun* **MALTS** a mixture, used in brewing, prepared from barley or wheat grains that have been soaked in water, allowed to sprout and then dried in a kiln □ *verb* **MALTS, MALTING, MALTED** to treat or combine (eg a liquor) with malt

MALTASE *noun* **MALTASES** an enzyme in animals and plants that breaks down maltose into glucose

MALTED *adj* containing, made or flavoured with malt

MALTING *noun* **MALTINGS** a building where malt is made

MALTOSE *noun* **MALTOSES** a hard white crystalline sugar that occurs in starch and glycogen, and is composed of two glucose molecules linked together

MALTREAT *verb* **MALTREATS, MALTREATING, MALTREATED** to treat someone or something roughly or cruelly

MALTY *adj* **MALTIER, MALTIEST** containing or resembling malt

MAM *noun* **MAMS** mother

MAMA *noun* **MAMAS** now used chiefly by young children: mother

MAMBA *noun* **MAMBAS** a large, poisonous, black or green African snake

MAMBO *noun* **MAMBOS** a rhythmic Latin American dance resembling the rumba □ *verb* **MAMBOS, MAMBOING, MAMBOED** to dance the mambo

MAMILLA *noun* **MAMILLAE** the nipple of the mammary gland

MAMILLARY *adj* relating to the breast

MAMMA [1] *noun* **MAMMAE** the milk gland or mammary gland; the breast, udder, etc in female mammals

MAMMA [2] *noun* **MAMMAS** mama

MAMMAL *noun* **MAMMALS** any warm-blooded, vertebrate animal characterized by the possession in the female of mammary glands which secrete milk to feed its young, eg a human, monkey, whale, etc

MAMMALIAN *adj* relating to or typical of mammals

MAMMARY *adj* belonging to, of the nature of, or relating to the breasts or other milk-producing glands

MAMMIES plural of **mammy**

MAMMILLA *noun* **MAMMILLAE** the mamilla

MAMMON *noun* **MAMMONS** wealth when considered as the source of evil and immorality

MAMMONISH *adj* devoted to gaining wealth

MAMMONISM *noun* **MAMMONISMS** devotion to gaining wealth

MAMMONIST *noun* **MAMMONISTS** a person devoted to riches

MAMMOTH *noun* **MAMMOTHS** any of various extinct shaggy-haired, prehistoric elephants, some of which had long curved tusks up to 4m long □ *adj* huge; giant-sized

MAMMY *noun* **MAMMIES** mama

MAMSELLE *noun* **MAMSELLES** short form of mademoiselle, a title equivalent to *Miss*, used of an unmarried French or French-speaking woman

MAN *noun* **MEN** an adult male human being □ *verb* **MANS, MANNING, MANNED** to provide (eg a ship, industrial plant, etc) with men, ie workers

MANACLE *noun* **MANACLES** a handcuff; a shackle for the hand or wrist □ *verb* **MANACLES, MANACLING, MANACLED** to handcuff someone; to restrain someone with manacles

MANAGE *verb* **MANAGES, MANAGING, MANAGED** to be in overall control or charge of, or the manager of, something or someone

MANAGER *noun* **MANAGERS** someone who manages, especially someone in overall charge or

control of a commercial enterprise, organization, project, etc
MANAGING adj having executive control; administering
MAÑANA noun **MAÑANAS** tomorrow; some unspecified time, or at some unspecified time, in the future; later
MANATEE noun **MANATEES** a large plant-eating marine mammal of the tropical waters of America, Africa and the W Indies
MANDALA noun **MANDALAS** a circular symbol representing the Universe, usually a circle enclosing images of deities or geometric designs, used as an aid to meditation
MANDAMUS noun **MANDAMUSES** a writ or court order issued by a high court to a lower court, or to a tribunal, public official, etc, instructing it or them to perform a duty, especially one which it should have performed
MANDARIN noun **MANDARINS** a small citrus fruit, similar to the tangerine, with deep orange skin that peels easily
MANDATE noun **MANDATES** a right or authorization given to a nation, person, etc to act on behalf of others □ verb **MANDATES, MANDATING, MANDATED** to give authority or power to someone or something
MANDATORY adj not allowing any choice; compulsory
MANDIBLE noun **MANDIBLES** the lower jaw of a vertebrate
MANDOLIN noun **MANDOLINS** a musical instrument like a small guitar
MANDOLINE noun **MANDOLINES** a mandolin
MANDRAKE noun **MANDRAKES** a Eurasian plant with purple flowers and a forked root, formerly thought to have magical powers
MANDREL noun **MANDRELS** the rotating shaft on a lathe that the object being worked on is fixed to
MANDRIL noun **MANDRILS** a mandrel
MANDRILL noun **MANDRILLS** a large W African baboon with distinctive red and blue striped markings on its muzzle and hindquarters
MANE noun **MANES** on a horse, lion or other animal: the long hair growing from and around the neck
MANED adj having a mane of a specified kind

MANÈGE noun **MANÈGES** the skill or practice of training or handling horses; horsemanship
MANELESS adj without a mane
MANEUVER noun **MANEUVERS** a manoeuvre □ verb **MANEUVERS, MANEUVERING, MANEUVERED** to manoeuvre
MANFUL adj brave and determined; manly
MANFULLY adverb in a manful way
MANGANESE noun **MANGANESES** a hard brittle pinkish-grey metallic element, an essential trace element for plants and animals which is also widely used to make alloys that are very hard and resistant to wear, eg in railways lines, etc
MANGE noun **MANGES** a skin disease due to mites, that affects hairy animals such as cats and dogs, causing itching and loss of hair
MANGEL noun **MANGELS** a variety of beet with a large yellow root, used as cattle food
MANGER noun **MANGERS** an open box or trough from which cattle or horses feed
MANGETOUT noun **MANGETOUTS** a variety of garden pea of which the whole pod, containing the peas, is eaten
MANGEY adj **MANGIER, MANGIEST** mangy
MANGINESS noun **MANGINESSES** the state of being mangy
MANGLE¹ verb **MANGLES, MANGLING, MANGLED** to damage or destroy something or someone by cutting, crushing, tearing, etc
MANGLE² noun **MANGLES** a device, usually hand-operated, that consists of two large heavy rotating rollers which have wet laundry fed between them in order to squeeze most of the water out
MANGLED adj mutilated or disfigured
MANGLER noun **MANGLERS** someone who uses a mangle
MANGO noun **MANGOES** a heavy oblong fruit with a central stone surrounded by sweet, soft juicy orange flesh and a thick, green, yellow or red skin
MANGROVE noun **MANGROVES** any of several tropical and subtropical evergreen trees that grow in salt marshes and on mudflats, along tropical coasts and

in tidal estuaries, producing aerial roots from their branches that form a dense tangled network
MANGY adj **MANGIER, MANGIEST** said of an animal: suffering from mange
MANHANDLE verb **MANHANDLES, MANHANDLING, MANHANDLED** to treat someone or something roughly; to push, shove or use force to move them or it
MANHOLE noun **MANHOLES** an opening large enough to allow a person through, especially one in a road that leads down into a sewer
MANHOOD noun **MANHOODS** the state of being an adult male
MANHUNT noun **MANHUNTS** an intensive and usually large-scale organized search for someone, especially a criminal or fugitive
MANIA noun **MANIAS** a mental disorder characterized by great excitement or euphoria, rapid and incoherent thought and speech, hyperactivity, grandiose delusions and domineering behaviour which may become violent
MANIAC noun **MANIACS** a person who behaves wildly □ adj affected by or relating to mania
MANICALLY adverb energetically; wildly
MANICURE noun **MANICURES** the care and cosmetic treatment of the hands, especially the fingernails, usually carried out by a trained professional or manicurist □ verb **MANICURES, MANICURING, MANICURED** to carry out a manicure on (a person or their hands)
MANIFEST verb **MANIFESTS, MANIFESTING, MANIFESTED** to show or display something clearly □ adj easily seen or perceived; obvious □ noun **MANIFESTS** a customs document that gives details of a ship or aircraft, its cargo and its destination
MANIFESTO noun **MANIFESTOS** a written public declaration of policies, intentions, opinions or motives, especially one produced by a political party or candidate
MANIFOLD adj many and various; of many different kinds □ noun **MANIFOLDS** a pipe with several inlets and outlets
MANIKIN noun **MANIKINS** a model of the human body, used in teaching art and anatomy, etc
MANILA noun **MANILAS** a type of

thick strong brown paper, originally made from Manila hemp, that is used especially for wrapping

MANILLA noun **MANILLAS** manila

MANIOC noun **MANIOCS** the cassava

MANKIND noun **MANKINDS** the human race as a whole; human beings collectively

MANKY adj **MANKIER, MANKIEST** dirty

MANLINESS noun **MANLINESSES** the quality of being manly

MANLY adj **MANLIER, MANLIEST** displaying qualities considered admirable in a man, such as strength, determination, courage, etc

MANNA noun **MANNAS** in Christianity: in the Old Testament, the food miraculously provided by God for the Israelites in the wilderness (Exodus 16.14–36)

MANNED past form of **man** ▫ adj said of a ship, machine, spacecraft, etc: provided with men, operators, crew, etc

MANNEQUIN noun **MANNEQUINS** a fashion model, especially a woman, employed to model clothes, etc

MANNER noun **MANNERS** way; fashion

MANNERED adj unnatural and artificial; affected

MANNERISM noun **MANNERISMS** especially in art or literature: noticeable or excessive use of an individual or mannered style

MANNERIST noun **MANNERISTS** a person inclined to mannerism

MANNERLY adj polite; showing good manners

MANNIKIN noun **MANNIKINS** a manikin

MANNING a form of **man**

MANNISH adj said of a woman or child: having an appearance or qualities regarded as more typical of a man

MANOEUVRE noun **MANOEUVRES** a movement requiring, or performed with, skill or intelligence, eg one carried out by the driver of a vehicle or pilot of an aircraft ▫ verb **MANOEUVRES, MANOEUVRING, MANOEUVRED** to move something accurately and with skill

MANOMETER noun **MANOMETERS** an instrument for measuring the difference in

pressure between two fluids (liquids or gases)

MANOMETRY noun **MANOMETRIES** the use of manometers

MANOR noun **MANORS** the principal residence on a country estate, often the former home of a medieval lord

MANORIAL adj relating to or resembling a manor

MANPOWER noun **MANPOWERS** the number of available employees or people fit and ready to work

MANQUÉ adj applied to a specified kind of person: having once had the ambition or potential to be that kind of person, without achieving it; unfulfilled

MANSARD noun **MANSARDS** a four-sided roof, each side of which is in two parts, the lower part sloping more steeply

MANSE noun **MANSES** especially in Scotland: the house of a religious minister

MANSION noun **MANSIONS** a large house, usually a grand or luxurious one

MANTA noun **MANTAS** a type of fish, a giant ray, that may exceed 9m (30ft) in width and 2 tonnes in weight, with a broad mouth situated across the front of the head

MANTEL noun **MANTELS** a mantelpiece or mantelshelf

MANTILLA noun **MANTILLAS** a lace or silk scarf worn by women as a covering for the hair and shoulders, especially in Spain and S America

MANTIS noun **MANTISES** any of numerous mainly tropical insect-eating insects that have long bodies, large eyes and a tendency to sit in wait for prey with their two spikey front legs raised

MANTISSA noun **MANTISSAS** the part of a logarithm comprising the decimal point and the figures following it

MANTLE noun **MANTLES** a cloak or loose outer garment ▫ verb **MANTLES, MANTLING, MANTLED** to cover, conceal or obscure something or someone

MANTRA noun **MANTRAS** a sacred phrase, word or sound chanted repeatedly as part of meditation and prayer, as an aid to concentration and the development of spiritual power

MANTRAP noun **MANTRAPS** a trap or snare for catching trespassers, poachers, etc

MANUAL adj belonging or relating to the hand or hands ▫ noun **MANUALS** a book of instructions, eg for repairing a car or operating a machine

MANUALLY adverb with or by means of the hands

MANUKA noun **MANUKAS** an Australian and New Zealand tree of the myrtle family with hard wood and aromatic leaves

MANUMIT verb **MANUMITS, MANUMITTING, MANUMITTED** to release (a person) from slavery; to set someone free

MANURE noun **MANURES** any substance, especially animal dung, used on soil as a fertilizer ▫ verb **MANURES, MANURING, MANURED** to apply manure to (land, soil, etc); to enrich (soil) with a fertilizing substance

MANURER noun **MANURERS** someone who applies manure to land, soil, etc

MANURING noun **MANURINGS** the action of applying manure to land, soil, etc

MANY adj **MORE, MOST** consisting of a large number; numerous ▫ pronoun a great number (of people or things)

MAP noun **MAPS** a diagram of any part of the earth's surface, showing geographical and other features, eg the position of towns and roads ▫ verb **MAPS, MAPPING, MAPPED** to make a map of something

MAPLE noun **MAPLES** any of various broad-leaved deciduous trees of northern regions whose seeds float by means of winglike growths

MAPPER noun **MAPPERS** someone or something that maps or makes maps

MAPPING noun **MAPPINGS** the determination of the positions and relative distances of genes on chromosomes by means of linkage

MAQUETTE noun **MAQUETTES** a small model of something to be made on a larger scale, especially a clay, wax or plaster model made by a sculptor as a preliminary study for a full-size work

MAQUI noun **MAQUIS** a Chilean evergreen shrub

MAQUIS noun **MAQUIS** a type of

thick, shrubby vegetation found in coastal areas of the Mediterranean

MAR verb **MARS, MARRING, MARRED, MARD** to spoil something

MARABOU noun **MARABOUS** a large black-and-white African stork

MARABOUT noun **MARABOUTS** a marabou

MARACA noun **MARACAS** originally and especially in Latin America: a hand-held percussion instrument, usually one of a pair, consisting of a gourd or similar hollow shell filled with dried beans, pebbles, etc which make a rattling noise when shaken

MARATHON noun **MARATHONS** a long-distance race on foot, usually 42.195km (26ml 385yd) □ adj belonging or relating to a marathon

MARAUD verb **MARAUDS, MARAUDING, MARAUDED** to wander in search of people to attack and property to steal or destroy

MARAUDER noun **MARAUDERS** someone who marauds

MARAUDING adj that marauds

MARBLE noun **MARBLES** a hard, metamorphic rock formed of recrystallized limestone or dolomite, white when pure but usually mottled or streaked □ verb **MARBLES, MARBLING, MARBLED** to stain, vein or paint something (especially paper) to resemble marble

MARBLED adj mottled, or having irregular streaks of different colours, like marble

MARBLES plural noun any of several children's games played with small balls of glass or marble

MARBLING noun **MARBLINGS** a marbled appearance or colouring, eg in meat with streaks of fat

MARBLY adj **MARBLIER, MARBLIEST** like marble

MARC noun **MARCS** the leftover skins and stems of grapes used in winemaking

MARCASITE noun **MARCASITES** a pale yellow mineral, a compound of iron, formerly used in jewellery and now mined for use in the manufacture of sulphuric acid

MARCATO adverb in an emphatic or strongly-accented manner □ adj emphatic; strongly accented

MARCH verb **MARCHES,**

MARCHING, MARCHED to walk in a stiff, upright, formal manner, usually at a brisk pace and in step with others □ noun **MARCHES** an act of marching

MARCHER noun **MARCHERS** someone who takes part in a march

MARE [1] noun **MARES** an adult female horse, ass, zebra, etc

MARE [2] noun **MARIA** any of numerous large, flat areas on the surface of the Moon or Mars, seen from Earth as dark patches and originally thought to be seas

MARG noun **MARGS** margarine

MARGARINE noun **MARGARINES** a food product, usually made from vegetable oils with water, flavourings, colourings, vitamins, etc, that is used as a substitute for butter

MARGARITA noun **MARGARITAS** a cocktail made with tequila, lemon or lime juice, and an orange-flavoured liqueur, often served with salt around the top of the glass

MARGE noun **MARGES** margarine

MARGIN noun **MARGINS** the blank space around a page of writing or print

MARGINAL adj small and unimportant or insignificant; said of a political constituency: whose current MP or other representative was elected by only a small majority of votes at the last election □ noun **MARGINALS** a marginal constituency or seat

MARGINATE adj having a well-marked border or margin

MARGINED adj provided with a margin; having a border

MARIA plural of **mare** [2]

MARIGOLD noun **MARIGOLDS** a garden plant with bright orange or yellow flowers and strongly-scented leaves

MARIHUANA noun **MARIHUANAS** cannabis

MARIJUANA noun **MARIJUANAS** cannabis

MARIMBA noun **MARIMBAS** a type of xylophone, originally from Africa, consisting of a set of hardwood strips which, when struck with hammers, vibrate metal plates underneath to produce a musical sound

MARINA noun **MARINAS** a harbour for berthing private pleasure boats, usually with associated facilities provided

MARINADE noun **MARINADES** any liquid mixture, especially a mixture of oil, herbs, spices, vinegar or wine, etc, in which food, especially meat or fish, is soaked before cooking to add flavour or to tenderize it □ verb **MARINADES, MARINADING, MARINADED** to soak (meat or fish, etc) in a marinade

MARINATE verb **MARINATES, MARINATING, MARINATED** to marinade something

MARINE adj belonging to or concerned with the sea □ noun **MARINES** a soldier trained to serve on land or at sea

MARINER noun **MARINERS** a seaman

MARINIÈRE adj said especially of mussels: cooked in white wine with onions and herbs

MARITAL adj belonging or relating to marriage

MARITALLY adverb as a married person

MARITIME adj belonging or relating to the sea or ships, sea-trade, etc

MARJORAM noun **MARJORAMS** a purple-flowered Mediterranean plant whose sweet-smelling leaves are used to season food

MARK noun **MARKS** a visible blemish, such as a scratch or stain □ verb **MARKS, MARKING, MARKED** to spoil something with, or become spoiled by, a mark

MARKED adj obvious or noticeable

MARKEDLY adverb noticeably

MARKER noun **MARKERS** a pen with a thick point, for writing signs, etc

MARKET noun **MARKETS** a gathering of people that takes place periodically, where stalls, etc are set up allowing them to buy and sell a variety of goods or a specified type of goods □ verb **MARKETS, MARKETING, MARKETED** to offer something for sale; to promote (goods, etc)

MARKETEER noun **MARKETEERS** someone who trades at a market

MARKETER noun **MARKETERS** someone who goes to, or trades at, a market

MARKETING noun **MARKETINGS** the techniques or processes by which a product or service is sold, including assessment of its sales potential and responsibility for its promotion, distribution and development

MARKING *noun* **MARKINGS** a distinctive pattern of colours on an animal or plant

MARKKA *noun* **MARKKAS, MARKKAA** the standard currency unit in Finland

MARKSMAN *noun* **MARKSMEN** someone who can shoot a gun or other weapon accurately, especially a trained soldier, police officer, etc

MARL *noun* **MARLS** a mixture of clay and limestone ▫ *verb* **MARLS, MARLING, MARLED** to apply marl to (sandy soil, etc)

MARLIN *noun* **MARLINS** a large fish found in warm and tropical seas which has a long spear-like upper jaw

MARLINE *noun* **MARLINES** a small rope for winding around a larger one, to keep it from wearing

MARLING *noun* **MARLINGS** the process of adding marl to light sandy soil to improve its texture and fertility and to increase its water-holding capacity

MARLY *adj* **MARLIER, MARLIEST** like marl; containing large amounts of marl

MARMALADE *noun* **MARMALADES** jam made from the pulp and rind of any citrus fruit, especially oranges ▫ *adj* said of a cat: with a coat marked with orange and brown streaks

MARMELISE *verb* **MARMELISES, MARMELISING, MARMELISED** to marmelize

MARMELIZE *verb* **MARMELIZES, MARMELIZING, MARMELIZED** to thrash or defeat someone heavily; to destroy them

MARMITE *noun* **MARMITES** a lidded cooking pot, typically one made of glazed earthenware, used especially for making stock or soup

MARMOREAL *adj* like marble; cold, smooth, white, etc

MARMOSET *noun* **MARMOSETS** a small S American monkey with a long bushy tail and tufts of hair around the head and ears

MARMOT *noun* **MARMOTS** a stout, coarse-haired, burrowing rodent of Europe, Asia and N America

MAROON [1] *adj* dark brownish-red or purplish-red in colour ▫ *noun* **MAROONS** a dark brownish-red or purplish-red colour

MAROON [2] *verb* **MAROONS, MAROONING, MAROONED** to leave someone in isolation in a deserted place, especially on a desert island

MARQUE *noun* **MARQUES** applied especially to cars: a brand or make

MARQUEE *noun* **MARQUEES** a very large tent used for circuses, parties, etc

MARQUESS *noun* **MARQUESSES** a member of the nobility

MARQUETRY *noun* **MARQUETRIES** the art or practice of making decorative arrangements or patterns out of pieces of different-coloured woods, ivory, etc, especially set into the surface of wooden furniture

MARQUIS *noun* **MARQUISES** in various European countries: a nobleman next in rank above a count

MARQUISE *noun* **MARQUISES** in various European countries: the wife or widow of a marquis

MARRAM *noun* **MARRAMS** a coarse grass that grows on sandy shores, often planted to stop sand erosion

MARRIAGE *noun* **MARRIAGES** the state or relationship of being husband and wife

MARRIED *adj* having a husband or wife

MARROW *noun* **MARROWS** the soft tissue that fills the internal cavities of bones

MARROWFAT *noun* **MARROWFATS** a variety of large, edible pea

MARROWY *adj* full of marrow; strong

MARRY *verb* **MARRIES, MARRYING, MARRIED** to take someone as one's husband or wife

MARRYING *adj* likely to marry or inclined towards marriage

MARSH *noun* **MARSHES** a poorly-drained, low-lying, frequently-flooded area of land, commonly found at the mouths of rivers and alongside ponds and lakes ▫ *adj* inhabiting or found in marshes

MARSHAL *noun* **MARSHALS** any of various high-ranking officers in the armed forces ▫ *verb* **MARSHALS, MARSHALLING, MARSHALLED** to arrange (troops, competitors, facts, etc) in order

MARSHLAND *noun* **MARSHLANDS** marshy country

MARSHY *adj* **MARSHIER, MARSHIEST** like, or of the nature of, a marsh

MARSUPIAL *noun* **MARSUPIALS** any of a group of mammals including the kangaroo, koala and wombat in which the female lacks a placenta and the young, which are tiny and very immature when born, are carried and suckled in an external pouch on the mother's body until they are mature enough to survive independently ▫ *adj* belonging to or like a marsupial

MART *noun* **MARTS** a trading place; a market or auction

MARTELLO *noun* **MARTELLOS** a small circular fortified tower used for coastal defence

MARTEN *noun* **MARTENS** any of various small, tree-dwelling, predatory mammals with a long thin body and a bushy tail

MARTIAL *adj* belonging or relating to, or suitable for, war or the military; warlike; militant

MARTIALLY *adverb* in a martial way

MARTIN *noun* **MARTINS** any of various small birds of the swallow family, with a square or slightly forked tail, eg the house martin or the sand martin

MARTINET *noun* **MARTINETS** someone who maintains strict discipline

MARTINI *noun* **MARTINIS** an Italian brand of vermouth

MARTYR *noun* **MARTYRS** someone who chooses to be put to death as an act of witness to their faith, rather than abandon their religious beliefs ▫ *verb* **MARTYRS, MARTYRING, MARTYRED** to put someone to death as a martyr

MARTYRDOM *noun* **MARTYRDOMS** the death or suffering of a martyr

MARVEL *verb* **MARVELS, MARVELLING, MARVELLED** to be filled with astonishment or wonder ▫ *noun* **MARVELS** an astonishing or wonderful person or thing; a wonder

MARZIPAN *noun* **MARZIPANS** a sweet paste made of ground almonds, sugar and egg whites, used to decorate cakes, make sweets, etc

MAS *noun* **MAS** a house or farm in the south of France

MASALA *noun* **MASALAS** a blend

of spices ground into a powder or paste used in Indian cookery

MASCARA *noun* **MASCARAS** a cosmetic for darkening, lengthening and thickening the eyelashes, applied with a brush

MASCOT *noun* **MASCOTS** a person, animal or thing thought to bring good luck and adopted for this purpose by a person, team, etc

MASCULINE *adj* belonging to, typical of, peculiar to or suitable for a man or the male sex; male ▫ *noun* **MASCULINES** the masculine gender

MASER *noun* **MASERS** in radar and radio astronomy: a device for increasing the strength of microwaves

MASH *verb* **MASHES, MASHING, MASHED** to beat or crush into a pulpy mass ▫ *noun* **MASHES** a boiled mixture of grain and water used to feed farm animals

MASHED *adj* beaten or crushed into a pulpy mass

MASHER *noun* **MASHERS** an instrument for mashing

MASK *noun* **MASKS** any covering for the face or for part of the face, worn for amusement, protection or as a disguise, which is often painted and decorated ▫ *verb* **MASKS, MASKING, MASKED** to put a mask on someone or something

MASKED *adj* wearing, concealed or protected by a mask

MASKER *noun* **MASKERS** someone who takes part in a masque

MASOCHISM *noun* **MASOCHISMS** the practice of deriving sexual pleasure from pain or humiliation inflicted by another person

MASOCHIST *noun* **MASOCHISTS** someone who derives sexual pleasure from pain or humiliation

MASON *noun* **MASONS** a skilled builder who works with bricks or stone

MASONIC *adj* belonging or relating to freemasons

MASONRY *noun* **MASONRIES** the part of a building built by a mason; stonework and brickwork

MASQUE *noun* **MASQUES** in English royal courts during the 16c and 17c: a kind of dramatic entertainment performed to music by masked actors

MASS *noun* **MASSES** a large usually shapeless quantity gathered together; a lump ▫ *verb* **MASSES, MASSING, MASSED** to gather or form in a large quantity or number

MASSACRE *noun* **MASSACRES** a cruel and indiscriminate killing of large numbers of people or animals ▫ *verb* **MASSACRES, MASSACRING, MASSACRED** to kill (people or animals) cruelly, indiscriminately and in large numbers

MASSAGE *noun* **MASSAGES** a technique of easing pain or stiffness in the body, especially the muscles, by rubbing, kneading and tapping with the hands ▫ *verb* **MASSAGES, MASSAGING, MASSAGED** to perform massage on someone

MASSÉ *noun* **MASSÉS** in billiards: a sharp stroke made with the cue held vertically, or nearly vertically

MASSEUR *noun* **MASSEURS** someone who is trained to carry out massage, especially as their profession

MASSEUSE *noun* **MASSEUSES** a woman who is trained to carry out massage, especially as her profession

MASSIF *noun* **MASSIFS** a mountainous plateau that differs from the surrounding lowland, usually composed of rocks that are older and harder

MASSIVE *adj* said of physical objects: very big, bulky, solid and heavy

MASSIVELY *adverb* in a massive way; to a massive degree

MAST *noun* **MASTS** any upright wooden or metal supporting pole, especially one carrying the sails of a ship, or a radio or television aerial

MASTABA *noun* **MASTABAS** an ancient Egyptian tomb built of brick or stone with sloping sides and a flat roof, having an outer area in which offerings were made, connected to a secret inner room from which a shaft led to an underground burial chamber

MASTED *adj* having the specified type or number of masts

MASTER *noun* **MASTERS** someone, especially a man, who commands or controls ▫ *adj* fully qualified; highly skilled; expert ▫ *verb* **MASTERS, MASTERING, MASTERED** to overcome or defeat (eg feelings or an opponent)

MASTERFUL *adj* showing the authority, skill or power of a master

MASTERLY *adj* showing the skill of a master

MASTERY *noun* **MASTERIES** supreme skill or knowledge

MASTHEAD *noun* **MASTHEADS** the top of a ship's mast

MASTIC *noun* **MASTICS** a gum obtained from a Mediterranean evergreen tree, used in making varnish

MASTICATE *verb* **MASTICATES, MASTICATING, MASTICATED** to chew (food)

MASTIFF *noun* **MASTIFFS** a large powerful short-haired breed of dog, formerly used in hunting

MASTITIS *noun* **MASTITISES** inflammation of a woman's breast or an animal's udder, usually caused by bacterial infection

MASTODON *noun* **MASTODONS** any of several, now extinct, mammals from which elephants are thought to have evolved, which had two pairs of tusks, a long flexible trunk and a hairy coat

MASTOID *adj* like a nipple or breast ▫ *noun* **MASTOIDS** the raised area of bone behind the ear

MAT *noun* **MATS** a flat piece of any carpet-like material, used as a decorative or protective floor-covering, for wiping shoes on to remove dirt, or absorbing impact on landing or falling in gymnastics, etc ▫ *verb* **MATS, MATTING, MATTED** to become, or make something become, tangled or interwoven into a dense untidy mass

MATADOR *noun* **MATADORS** the principal toreador who kills the bull in bullfighting

MATCH 1 *verb* **MATCHES, MATCHING, MATCHED** to combine well; to be well suited, compatible or exactly alike; to put (matching people, colours, things, etc) together

MATCH 2 *noun* **MATCHES** a short thin piece of wood or strip of card coated on the tip with a substance that ignites when rubbed against a rough surface, used to light fires, etc

MATCHABLE *adj* that can be matched

MATCHBOX *noun* **MATCHBOXES** a small cardboard box for holding matches

MATCHING *adj* similar; compatible; part of the same set

MATCHLESS *adj* having no equal; superior to all

MATCHWOOD *noun* **MATCHWOODS** wood suitable for making matches

MATE *noun* **MATES** an animal's breeding partner □ *verb* **MATES, MATING, MATED** said of animals: to copulate

MATÉ *noun* **MATÉS** a S American species of holly tree

MATER *noun* **MATERS** a mother

MATERIAL *noun* **MATERIALS** any substance out of which something is, or may be, made □ *adj* relating to or consisting of solid matter, physical objects, etc; not abstract or spiritual

MATÉRIEL *noun* **MATÉRIELS** materials and equipment, especially the munitions, supplies, etc of an army

MATERNAL *adj* belonging to, typical of or like a mother

MATERNITY *noun* **MATERNITIES** the state of being or becoming a mother; motherhood

MATESHIP *noun* **MATESHIPS** the bond between close friends or mates

MATEY *adj* **MATIER, MATIEST** friendly or familiar

MATEYNESS *noun* **MATEYNESSES** the condition of being matey

MATH *singular noun* mathematics

MATHS *singular noun* mathematics

MATILY *adverb* in a matey way

MATINAL *adj* belonging or relating to matins

MATINÉE *noun* **MATINÉES** an afternoon performance of a play or showing of a film

MATINESS *noun* **MATINESSES** friendliness

MATINS *singular and plural noun* the first of the canonical hours, originally at midnight, but often now taken together with lauds

MATRIARCH *noun* **MATRIARCHS** the female head of a family, community or tribe

MATRICIDE *noun* **MATRICIDES** the killing of a mother by her own child

MATRIMONY *noun* **MATRIMONIES** the state of being married

MATRIX *noun* **MATRIXES, MATRICES** a square or rectangular arrangement of symbols or numbers, in rows or columns, used to summarize relationships between different quantities, etc

MATRON *noun* **MATRONS** the former title of the head of the nursing staff in a hospital

MATRONLY *adj* said of a woman: dignified; authoritative

MATT *adj* said eg of paint: having a dull surface without gloss or shine

MATTE *noun* **MATTES** a kind of mask used to block out areas of an image in cinematography, so that a different image can be superimposed

MATTED past form of **mat** □ *adj* often said of hair: tangled

MATTER *noun* **MATTERS** the substance from which all physical things are made; material □ *verb* **MATTERS, MATTERING, MATTERED** to be important or significant

MATTING *noun* **MATTINGS** material of rough woven fibres used for making mats

MATTOCK *noun* **MATTOCKS** a kind of pickaxe with a blade flattened horizontally at one end, used for breaking up soil, etc

MATTRESS *noun* **MATTRESSES** a large flat fabric-covered pad, now often made of foam rubber or springs, used for sleeping on, by itself or on a supporting frame

MATURATE *verb* **MATURATES, MATURATING, MATURATED** to discharge or cause something to discharge pus

MATURE *adj* **MATURER, MATUREST** fully grown or developed □ *verb* **MATURES, MATURING, MATURED** to make or become fully developed or adult in outlook

MATURELY *adverb* in a mature way

MATURITY *noun* **MATURITIES** full development; ripeness

MATY *adj* **MATIER, MATIEST** matey

MATZO *noun* **MATZOS** unleavened bread

MAUDLIN *adj* said especially of a drunk person: foolishly sad or sentimental

MAUL *verb* **MAULS, MAULING, MAULED** to attack someone or something fiercely, usually tearing the flesh □ *noun* **MAULS** in rugby: a quickly-formed gathering of players from both teams around a player who is holding the ball

MAULSTICK *noun* **MAULSTICKS** a stick or rod with a pad on one end, used by painters to steady their painting hand while executing delicate brushwork, by resting the padded end on the canvas or its frame

MAUNDER *verb* **MAUNDERS, MAUNDERING, MAUNDERED** to talk in a rambling way; to drivel

MAUNDERING *adj* rambling; drivelling

MAUNDY *noun* **MAUNDIES** a religious ceremony in which the sovereign washed the feet of the poor, in commemoration of Christ's washing of the disciples' feet, and distributed food, clothing and money (a tradition that remains only in the form of the ceremonial distribution of Maundy money)

MAUSOLEUM *noun* **MAUSOLEUMS** a grand or monumental tomb

MAUVE *adj* **MAUVER, MAUVEST** having a pale purple colour □ *noun* **MAUVES** a pale purple colour

MAVEN *noun* **MAVENS** an expert or pundit

MAVERICK *noun* **MAVERICKS** an unbranded stray animal, especially a calf

MAVIN *noun* **MAVINS** a maven

MAVIS *noun* **MAVISES** another name for the song thrush

MAW *noun* **MAWS** the jaws, throat or stomach of a voracious animal

MAWKISH *adj* weakly sentimental, maudlin or insipid

MAWKISHLY *adv* in a mawkish way

MAX *noun* **MAXES** an obsolete word for *gin*

MAXI *adj* said of a skirt, coat, etc: extra long; full length □ *noun* **MAXIS** a maxi garment

MAXILLA *noun* **MAXILLAE** the upper jaw or jawbone in animals

MAXILLARY *adj* of or relating to a jaw or maxilla

MAXIM *noun* **MAXIMS** a saying that expresses a general truth

MAXIMAL *adj* belonging or relating to a maximum; having the greatest possible size, value, etc

MAXIMALLY *adverb* in the maximum degree

MAXIMIN *noun* **MAXIMINS** the highest value in a set of minimum values

MAXIMISE *verb* **MAXIMISES, MAXIMISING, MAXIMISED** to maximize

MAXIMIZE *verb* **MAXIMIZES, MAXIMIZING, MAXIMIZED** to make something as high or great, etc as possible

MAXIMUM *noun* **MAXIMA** the greatest or most; the greatest possible number, quantity, degree, etc

MAXWELL *noun* **MAXWELLS** the cgs unit of magnetic flux

MAY [1] *auxiliary verb* **MAYST, MAYEST, MIGHT** used to express permission

MAY [2] *noun* **MAYS** the blossom of the hawthorn tree □ *verb* **MAYS, MAYING, MAYED** to gather may blossom

MAYBE *adverb* it may be; it is possible; perhaps □ *noun* **MAYBES** a possibility

MAYDAY *noun* **MAYDAYS** the international radio distress signal sent out by ships and aircraft

MAYFLOWER *noun* **MAYFLOWERS** the blossom of the hawthorn tree

MAYFLY *noun* **MAYFLIES** a short-lived insect with transparent wings, which appears briefly in spring

MAYHEM *noun* **MAYHEMS** a state of great confusion and disorder; chaos

MAYOR *noun* **MAYORS** in England, Wales and N Ireland: the head of the local council in a city, town or borough

MAYORAL *adj* belonging or relating to a mayor

MAYORALTY *noun* **MAYORALTIES** the position, or period of office, of a mayor

MAYORESS *noun* **MAYORESSES** a mayor's wife

MAYPOLE *noun* **MAYPOLES** a tall, decorated pole traditionally set up for dancing round on May Day

MAYWEED *noun* **MAYWEEDS** a type of camomile

MAZE *noun* **MAZES** a confusing network of paths bordered by high walls or hedges, laid out in a garden as a puzzling diversion in which a person might become lost or disorientated

MAZURKA *noun* **MAZURKAS** a lively Polish dance in triple time, quite like the polka

MAZUT *noun* **MAZUTS** petroleum residue after distillation

MAZY *adj* **MAZIER, MAZIEST** winding or convoluted as a maze

ME [1] *pronoun* the object form of *I*, used by a speaker or writer to refer to himself or herself

ME [2] *noun* **MES** in sol-fa notation: the third note of the major scale

MEAD *noun* **MEADS** an alcoholic drink made by fermenting honey and water, usually with spices added

MEADOW *noun* **MEADOWS** a low-lying field of grass, used for grazing animals or making hay

MEADOWY *adj* resembling a meadow

MEAGRE *adj* **MEAGRER, MEAGREST** lacking in quality or quantity; inadequate; scanty

MEAGRELY *adverb* in a meagre way

MEAL *noun* **MEALS** an occasion on which food is eaten, eg lunch, supper, dinner, etc

MEALIE *noun* **MEALIES** an ear of maize

MEALINESS *noun* **MEALINESSES** the state of being mealy

MEALY *adj* **MEALIER, MEALIEST** dry and powdery, or granular

MEAN *verb* [1] **MEANS, MEANING, MEANT** to express or intend to express, show or indicate something

MEAN [2] *adj* **MEANER, MEANEST** not generous

MEAN [3] *noun* **MEANS** a midway position or course, etc between two extremes

MEANDER *verb* **MEANDERS, MEANDERING, MEANDERED** said of a river: to bend and curve □ *noun* **MEANDERS** a bend; a winding course

MEANIE *noun* **MEANIES** a selfish or ungenerous person

MEANING *noun* **MEANINGS** the sense in which a statement, action, word, etc is intended to be understood □ *adj* intended to express special significance

MEANLY *adverb* in a mean way; stingily

MEANNESS *noun* **MEANNESSES** stinginess

MEANS *singular and plural noun* the instrument or method used to achieve some object

MEANT past form of **mean** [1]

MEANTIME *noun* **MEANTIMES** the time or period in between; the intervening time □ *adverb* during the time in between

MEANWHILE *adverb* during the time in between

MEANY *noun* **MEANIES** a meanie

MEASLES *singular noun* a highly infectious viral disease characterized by fever, a sore throat and a blotchy red rash that starts on the face and neck, and spreads to the rest of the body

MEASLY *adj* **MEASLIER, MEASLIEST** said of an amount, value, etc: very small; miserable; paltry

MEASURE *noun* **MEASURES** size, volume, etc determined by comparison with something of known size, etc, usually an instrument graded in standard units □ *verb* **MEASURES, MEASURING, MEASURED** to determine the size, volume, etc of, usually with a specially made instrument or by comparing it to something else

MEASURED *adj* slow and steady

MEASURING *noun* **MEASURINGS** the action of taking measurements

MEAT *noun* **MEATS** the flesh of any animal used as food

MEATBALL *noun* **MEATBALLS** a small ball of minced meat mixed with breadcrumbs and seasonings

MEATILY *adverb* in a way that is full of interesting information or ideas

MEATINESS *noun* **MEATINESSES** the state of being meaty

MEATLESS *adj* not containing meat

MEATUS *noun* **MEATUSES** a passage between body parts or an opening, eg the passage that leads from the external surface of the ear to the eardrum

MEATY *adj* **MEATIER, MEATIEST** full of, or containing, animal flesh

MECHANIC *noun* **MECHANICS** a skilled worker who repairs, maintains or constructs machinery

MECHANICS *singular noun* the branch of physics that deals with the motion of bodies and the forces that act on them □ *plural noun* the system on which something works

MECHANISE *verb* **MECHANISES, MECHANISING, MECHANISED** to mechanize

MECHANISM *noun* **MECHANISMS** a working part of a machine or its system of working parts

MECHANIZE *verb* **MECHANIZES,**

MECHANIZING, MECHANIZED to change (the production of something, a procedure, etc) from a manual to a mechanical process

MECONIUM noun **MECONIUMS** the first faeces passed by a baby after birth, or occasionally just before birth, which are dark-greenish and sticky

MEDAL noun **MEDALS** a flat piece of metal decorated with a design or inscription and awarded, eg to a soldier, sportsperson, etc, for merit or bravery, or produced in celebration of a special occasion

MEDALLION noun **MEDALLIONS** a large medal-like piece of jewellery, usually worn on a chain

MEDALLIST noun **MEDALLISTS** someone who is awarded a medal, especially for excellence in sport

MEDDLE verb **MEDDLES, MEDDLING, MEDDLED** to interfere

MEDDLER noun **MEDDLERS** someone who meddles

MEDDLING noun **MEDDLINGS** the action of interfering ◻ adj that meddles

MEDIA singular and plural noun the means by which news and information, etc is communicated to the public, usually considered to be TV, radio and the press collectively

MEDIAEVAL adj medieval

MEDIAL adj belonging to or situated in the middle; intermediate

MEDIALLY adverb in a medial position

MEDIAN noun **MEDIANS** a middle point or part ◻ adj situated in or passing through the middle

MEDIANT noun **MEDIANTS** in music: the third degree of a major or minor scale, lying midway between the tonic and the dominant

MEDIATE verb **MEDIATES, MEDIATING, MEDIATED** to intervene in or settle a dispute by seeking to reconcile the two sides involved ◻ adj resulting from mediation

MEDIATION noun **MEDIATIONS** the act or process of mediating

MEDIATOR noun **MEDIATORS** a person who mediates between parties in dispute

MEDIC noun **MEDICS** a doctor or medical student

MEDICABLE adj said of a

condition, illness, etc: able to be healed or treated

MEDICAID noun **MEDICAIDS** in the USA: a state- or federal-funded scheme which provides assistance with medical expenses for people with low incomes

MEDICAL adj belonging or relating to doctors or the science or practice of medicine ◻ noun **MEDICALS** a medical examination to discover a person's physical health

MEDICALLY adverb in a medical way; with reference to the medical profession

MEDICARE noun **MEDICARES** in the USA: a scheme which provides medical insurance for people aged 65 and over, and for certain categories of disabled people

MEDICATE verb **MEDICATES, MEDICATING, MEDICATED** to treat someone with medicine

MEDICINAL adj having healing qualities; used as a medicine

MEDICINE noun **MEDICINES** any substance used to treat or prevent disease or illness, especially one taken internally

MEDICO noun **MEDICOS** a medic

MEDIEVAL adj belonging or relating to, or characteristic of, the Middle Ages

MEDIOCRE adj only ordinary or average; rather inferior

MEDITATE verb **MEDITATES, MEDITATING, MEDITATED** to spend time in deep religious or spiritual thought, often with the mind in a practised state of emptiness

MEDIUM noun **MEDIUMS, MEDIA** something by or through which an effect is produced ◻ adj intermediate; midway; average

MEDLAR noun **MEDLARS** a small brown apple-like fruit eaten only when already decaying

MEDLEY noun **MEDLEYS** a piece of music made up of pieces from other songs, tunes, etc

MEDULLA noun **MEDULLAS, MEDULLAE** the central part of an organ or tissue, when this differs in structure or function from the outer layer, eg the pith of a plant stem

MEDULLAR adj of or relating to the medulla

MEDULLARY adj consisting of, or resembling, marrow or pith

MEDUSA noun **MEDUSAE,**

MEDUSAS a free-swimming, disc-shaped or bell-shaped organism with marginal tentacles and a mouth in the centre of its underside, representing the sexually-reproducing stage in the life cycle of a jellyfish or other coelenterate

MEDUSOID adj like a medusa

MEEK adj **MEEKER, MEEKEST** having a mild and gentle temperament

MEEKLY adverb in a meek way

MEEKNESS noun **MEEKNESSES** the state or quality of being meek

MEERKAT noun **MEERKATS** any of several species of mongoose-like carnivores native to S Africa, that live in large social groups and nest in burrows

MEET [1] verb **MEETS, MEETING, MET** to be introduced to someone for the first time ◻ noun **MEETS** the assembly of hounds and huntsmen and huntswomen before a fox-hunt begins

MEET [2] adj **MEETER, MEETEST** proper, correct or suitable

MEETING noun **MEETINGS** an act of coming together

MEETLY adverb correctly; suitably

MEG noun **MEGS** an obsolete word for a halfpenny

MEGA adj excellent

MEGABUCK noun **MEGABUCKS** a million dollars

MEGABYTE noun **MEGABYTES** in computing: a unit of storage capacity equal to 2^{20} or 1048576 bytes

MEGADEATH noun **MEGADEATHS** death of a million people, used as a unit in estimating casualties in nuclear war

MEGAFLOP noun **MEGAFLOPS** a complete failure, especially one that involves huge commercial losses

MEGAHERTZ noun **MEGAHERTZES** a unit of frequency equal to one million hertz

MEGALITH noun **MEGALITHS** a very large stone, especially one that forms part of a prehistoric monument

MEGAPHONE noun **MEGAPHONES** a funnel-shaped device which, when someone speaks into it, amplifies the voice

MEGASTORE noun **MEGASTORES**

a very large shop, especially any of the large chain stores

MEGATON noun **MEGATONS** a unit of weight equal to one million tons

MEGILP noun **MEGILPS** in oil-painting: a medium consisting of linseed oil and mastic varnish

MEIOSIS noun **MEIOSES** a type of cell division in which four daughter nuclei are produced, each containing half the number of chromosomes of the parent nucleus and resulting in the formation of male and female gametes

MEIOTIC adj characterized by meiosis

MEISTER noun **MEISTERS** someone who's an expert

MEL noun **MELS** honey

MELAMINE noun **MELAMINES** a white crystalline organic compound used to form artificial resins that are resistant to heat, water and many chemicals

MELANGE noun **MELANGES** a mixture, especially a varied or confused one

MELANIN noun **MELANINS** the black or dark brown pigment found to varying degrees in the skin, hair and eyes of humans and animals

MELANOMA noun **MELANOMAS**, **MELANOMATA** a cancerous tumour, usually of the skin, that is composed of melanocytes and may spread to other parts of the body, such as the lymph nodes

MELATONIN noun **MELATONINS** in vertebrates: a hormone secreted by the pineal gland that is involved in the control of certain daily and seasonal changes, and changes in pigmentation

MELD verb **MELDS**, **MELDING**, **MELDED** to merge, blend or combine

MELEE noun **MELEES** a riotous brawl involving large numbers of people

MELIORATE verb **MELIORATES**, **MELIORATING**, **MELIORATED** to improve

MELLOW adj **MELLOWER**, **MELLOWEST** said of a person or their character: calm and relaxed with age or experience ◻ verb **MELLOWS**, **MELLOWING**, **MELLOWED** to make or become mellow

MELODEON noun **MELODEONS** a small reed-organ; a harmonium

MELODIC adj relating or belonging to melody

MELODION noun **MELODIONS** a melodeon

MELODIOUS adj pleasant to listen to; tuneful

MELODIST noun **MELODISTS** someone who composes melodies

MELODRAMA noun **MELODRAMAS** as a theatrical genre especially popular during the 19c: drama often including musical items and featuring simplified characters, sensational events and traditional justice, usually in the form of a happy ending

MELODY noun **MELODIES** the sequence of single notes forming the core of a tune, as opposed to the harmony

MELON noun **MELONS** any of several plants of the gourd family, cultivated for their fruits

MELT verb **MELTS**, **MELTING**, **MELTED** to make or become soft or liquid, especially through the action of heat; to dissolve (something solid) ◻ noun **MELTS** the act of melting

MELTDOWN noun **MELTDOWNS** the overheating of the core of a nuclear reactor, causing radioactivity to escape into the environment

MELTING noun **MELTINGS** the action of dissolving something solid ◻ adj deeply touching

MELTINGLY adverb in a melting way

MEMBER noun **MEMBERS** someone who belongs to a group or organization

MEMBERED adj having limbs

MEMBRANE noun **MEMBRANES** a thin sheet of tissue that lines a body cavity or surrounds a body part, organ, etc

MEMENTO noun **MEMENTOS**, **MEMENTOES** a thing that serves as a reminder of the past; a souvenir

MEMOIR noun **MEMOIRS** a written record of events in the past, especially one based on personal experience

MEMOIRIST noun **MEMOIRISTS** a writer of memoirs

MEMORABLE adj worth remembering; easily remembered; remarkable

MEMORABLY adverb in a memorable way

MEMORIAL noun **MEMORIALS** a

thing that honours or commemorates a person or an event, eg a statue or monument ◻ adj serving to preserve the memory of a person or an event

MEMORISE verb **MEMORISES**, **MEMORISING**, **MEMORISED** to memorize

MEMORIZE verb **MEMORIZES**, **MEMORIZING**, **MEMORIZED** to learn something thoroughly, so as to be able to reproduce it exactly from memory

MEMORY noun **MEMORIES** the ability of the mind to remember

MEN plural of **man**

MENACE noun **MENACES** a source of threatening danger ◻ verb **MENACES**, **MENACING**, **MENACED** to threaten; to show an intention to damage or harm someone

MENACER noun **MENACERS** someone who menaces or threatens

MENACING adj threatening

MÉNAGE noun **MÉNAGES** a group of people living together; a household

MENAGERIE noun **MENAGERIES** a collection of wild animals caged for exhibition

MENARCHE noun **MENARCHES** the first menstruation

MEND verb **MENDS**, **MENDING**, **MENDED** to repair something ◻ noun **MENDS** on a garment, etc: a repaired part or place

MENDACITY noun **MENDACITIES** untruthfulness; the tendency to lie

MENDICANT noun **MENDICANTS** a monk who is a member of an order that is not allowed to own property and is therefore entirely dependent on charity, eg a Dominican or Franciscan friar ◻ adj dependent on charity

MENDICITY noun **MENDICITIES** the state of being a mendicant

MENDING noun **MENDINGS** the act or process of repairing

MENEER noun **MENEERS** mynheer

MENFOLK noun **MENFOLKS** men collectively, especially the male members of a particular group

MENHIR noun **MENHIRS** a prehistoric monument in the form of a single upright standing stone

MENIAL adj said of work: unskilled, uninteresting and of low status ◻ noun **MENIALS** a domestic servant

MENINGEAL *adj* of or relating to the meninges

MENINGES *plural noun* the three membranes that cover the brain and spinal cord

MENISCUS *noun* **MENISCUSES**, **MENISCI** the curved upper surface of a liquid in a partly-filled narrow tube, caused by the effects of surface tension

MENOPAUSE *noun* **MENOPAUSES** the period in a woman's life, typically between the ages of 45 and 55, when menstruation ceases and pregnancy is no longer possible

MENORAH *noun* **MENORAHS** a candelabrum with seven branches used in Jewish worship and regarded as a symbol of Judaism

MENORRHEA *noun* **MENORRHEAS** normal flow of blood during menstruation

MENSES *plural noun* the fluids discharged from the womb during menstruation

MENSTRUAL *adj* relating to or involving menstruation

MENSWEAR *noun* **MENSWEARS** clothing for men

MENTAL *adj* belonging or relating to, or done by using, the mind or intelligence

MENTALITY *noun* **MENTALITIES** an outlook; a certain way of thinking

MENTALLY *adverb* in the mind; as regards the mind

MENTHOL *noun* **MENTHOLS** a sharp-smelling substance obtained from peppermint oil, used as a decongestant and a painkiller

MENTION *verb* **MENTIONS**, **MENTIONING, MENTIONED** to speak of or make reference to something or someone ◻ *noun* **MENTIONS** a remark, usually a brief reference

MENTOR *noun* **MENTORS** a trusted teacher or adviser

MENTORING *noun* **MENTORINGS** the practice of acting as a mentor or of appointing mentors

MENU *noun* **MENUS** the range of dishes available in a restaurant, etc

MEOW *verb* **MEOWS, MEOWING, MEOWED** to miaow ◻ *noun* **MEOWS** a miaow

MEPACRINE *noun* **MEPACRINES** the anti-malarial drug atebrin

MERCENARY *adj* excessively concerned with the desire for personal gain, especially money ◻ *noun* **MERCENARIES** a soldier available for hire by a country or group

MERCER *noun* **MERCERS** a dealer in textiles, especially expensive ones

MERCERISE *verb* **MERCERISES**, **MERCERISING, MERCERISED** to mercerize

MERCERISED *adj* mercerized

MERCERIZE *verb* **MERCERIZES**, **MERCERIZING, MERCERIZED** to treat a material, especially cotton, with a substance which strengthens it and gives it a silky appearance

MERCERIZED *adj* of a material: treated with a substance which strengthens it and gives it a silky appearance

MERCHANT *noun* **MERCHANTS** a trader, especially a wholesale trader ◻ *adj* used for trade; commercial ◻ *verb* **MERCHANTS**, **MERCHANTING, MERCHANTED** to trade; to deal in something

MERCIFUL *adj* showing or exercising mercy; forgiving

MERCILESS *adj* without mercy; cruel; pitiless

MERCURIAL *adj* relating to or containing mercury

MERCURIC *adj* containing or relating to divalent mercury

MERCUROUS *adj* containing or relating to monovalent mercury

MERCURY *noun* **MERCURIES** a dense, silvery-white metallic element, and the only metal that is liquid at room temperature

MERCY *noun* **MERCIES** kindness or forgiveness shown when punishment is possible or justified

MERE [1] *adj* **MERER, MEREST** nothing more than; no better, more important or useful than (a specified thing)

MERE [2] *noun* **MERES** often in English place names: a lake or pool

MERELY *adverb* simply; only

MERGANSER *noun* **MERGANSERS** a kind of large diving duck found in northern countries, with a long, hooked, serrated bill

MERGE *verb* **MERGES, MERGING**, **MERGED** to blend, combine or join with something else

MERGER *noun* **MERGERS** a joining together, especially of business firms

MERIDIAN *noun* **MERIDIANS** an imaginary line on the Earth's surface passing through the poles at right angles to the equator; a line of longitude

MERINGUE *noun* **MERINGUES** a crisp, cooked mixture of sugar and egg-whites

MERINO *noun* **MERINOS** a type of sheep bred for its long, fine wool

MERISTEM *noun* **MERISTEMS** in a plant: a region of actively-dividing cells, mainly at the tips of shoots and roots

MERIT *noun* **MERITS** worth, excellence or praiseworthiness ◻ *verb* **MERITS, MERITING**, **MERITED** to deserve; to be worthy of or entitled to something

MERLIN *noun* **MERLINS** a small, dark-coloured falcon of the N hemisphere, with a black-striped tail

MERLON *noun* **MERLONS** in a battlement: the projecting part of the parapet between two embrasures

MERMAID *noun* **MERMAIDS** a mythical sea creature with a woman's head and upper body and a fish's tail

MERMAN *noun* **MERMEN** the male equivalent of a mermaid

MERRILY *adverb* in a merry way

MERRIMENT *noun* **MERRIMENTS** gaiety with laughter and noise; hilarity

MERRINESS *noun* **MERRINESSES** the state of being merry

MERRY *adj* **MERRIER, MERRIEST** cheerful and lively

MESA *noun* **MESAS** an isolated, flat-topped hill with at least one steep side or cliff

MESCAL *noun* **MESCALS** a globe-shaped cactus of Mexico and the SW USA, with buttonlike tubercles on its stems which have an intoxicating and hallucinogenic effect when chewed or made into an infusion and drunk

MESCALIN *noun* **MESCALINS** a hallucinogenic drug obtained from the mescal cactus

MESCLUN *noun* **MESCLUNS** a mixed green salad of young leaves and shoots, eg of endive, rocket, chicory, fennel, etc, usually dressed in vinaigrette flavoured with herbs

MESDAMES *plural* of **madame**

MESENTERY *noun* **MESENTERIES** in humans and animals: the double layer of membrane on the inner surface of the body wall that

serves to hold the stomach, small intestine, spleen, etc in place
MESH *noun* **MESHES** netting, or a piece of netting made of wire or thread ▫ *verb* **MESHES, MESHING, MESHED** said of the teeth on gear wheels: to engage
MESIAL *adj* said of a body part, etc: situated in or belonging to the middle of the body
MESIALLY *adverb* in a mesial position
MESMERIC *adj* relating to or producing mesmerism
MESMERISE *verb* **MESMERISES, MESMERISING, MESMERISED** to mesmerize
MESMERISING *adj* mesmerizing
MESMERISM *noun* **MESMERISMS** a former term for hypnotism
MESMERIST *noun* **MESMERISTS** a hypnotist
MESMERIZE *verb* **MESMERIZES, MESMERIZING, MESMERIZED** to grip the attention of someone; to fascinate
MESMERIZING *adj* that mesmerizes
MESODERM *noun* **MESODERMS** in a multicellular animal with two or more layers of body tissue: the layer of cells in an embryo between the ectoderm and the endoderm, which develops into the circulatory system, muscles and reproductive organs, etc
MESOMORPH *noun* **MESOMORPHS** a person of muscular body build, associated with an aggressive and extroverted personality type
MESON *noun* **MESONS** any of a group of unstable, strongly-interacting, elementary particles, with a mass between that of an electron and a nucleon
MESOPHYLL *noun* **MESOPHYLLS** the internal tissue between the upper and lower epidermal surfaces of a plant leaf
MESS *noun* **MESSES** an untidy or dirty state ▫ *verb* **MESSES, MESSING, MESSED** to make dirty or messy
MESSAGE *noun* **MESSAGES** a spoken or written communication sent from one person to another ▫ *verb* **MESSAGES, MESSAGING, MESSAGED** to transmit something by signalling, etc; to send it as a message
MESSENGER *noun* **MESSENGERS** someone who carries communications between people; a courier
MESSIAH *noun* **MESSIAHS** a hoped-for deliverer or saviour
MESSIANIC *adj* inspired, or as though inspired by, a messiah
MESSIEURS plural of **monsieur**
MESSILY *adverb* in a messy way
MESSINESS *noun* **MESSINESSES** the state of being messy
MESSY *adj* **MESSIER, MESSIEST** involving or making dirt or mess
MESTIZA *noun* **MESTIZAS** a female of mixed Spanish-American and Native American parentage
MESTIZO *noun* **MESTIZOS** a male of mixed Spanish-American and Native American parentage
MET [1] past form of **meet** [1]

MET [2] *noun* **METS** short form of *meteorology*, the study of weather

METABOLIC *adj* relating to an organism's metabolism
METAL *noun* **METALS** any of a class of chemical elements with certain shared characteristic properties, most being shiny, malleable, ductile and good conductors of heat and electricity, and all (except mercury) being solid at room temperature ▫ *adj* made of, or mainly of, metal ▫ *verb* **METALS, METALLING, METALING, METALLED, METALED** to fit or cover something with metal
METALLIC *adj* made of metal
METALLISE *verb* **METALLISES, METALLISING, METALLISED** to metallize
METALLIZE *verb* **METALLIZES, METALLIZING, METALLIZED** to give a metallic appearance to something
METALLOID *noun* **METALLOIDS** a chemical element that has both metallic and non-metallic properties, eg silicon and arsenic
METALWORK *noun* **METALWORKS** the craft, process or practice of shaping metal and making items of metal
METAPHASE *noun* **METAPHASES** in mitosis and meiosis: the second phase during which the membrane surrounding the nucleus breaks down
METAPHOR *noun* **METAPHORS** an expression in which the person, action or thing referred to is described as if it really were what it merely resembles, eg a rejection described as 'a slap in the face', or a ferocious person as 'a tiger'
METAZOAN *noun* **METAZOANS** any multicellular animal that has specialized differentiated body tissues ▫ *adj* belonging or relating to the Metazoa (many-celled animals)
METE *verb* **METES, METING, METED** to measure; to apportion
METEOR *noun* **METEORS** the streak of light seen when a meteoroid enters into the Earth's atmosphere, where it burns up as a result of friction
METEORIC *adj* belonging or relating to meteors
METEORITE *noun* **METEORITES** the remains of a meteoroid which has survived burn-up in its passage through the Earth's atmosphere as a meteor
METEOROID *noun* **METEOROIDS** in interplanetary space: a small, moving, solid object or dust particle, which becomes visible as a meteorite or a meteor if it enters the Earth's atmosphere
METER *noun* **METERS** an instrument for measuring and recording, especially quantities of electricity, gas, water, etc used ▫ *verb* **METERS, METERING, METERED** to measure and record (eg electricity) using a meter
METHADONE *noun* **METHADONES** a drug similar to morphine, but less addictive, used as a painkiller and as a heroin substitute for drug-addicts
METHANAL *noun* **METHANALS** formaldehyde
METHANE *noun* **METHANES** a colourless odourless flammable gas, used in the manufacture of organic chemicals and hydrogen, and as a cooking and heating fuel (in the form of natural gas of which it is the main component), and which occurs naturally as marsh gas and as firedamp
METHANOL *noun* **METHANOLS** a colourless flammable toxic liquid used as a solvent and antifreeze, and which can be catalytically converted to petrol
METHINKS *verb* **METHOUGHT** it seems to me
METHOD *noun* **METHODS** a way of doing something, especially an ordered set of procedures or an orderly system

METHODIC adj efficient and orderly; done in an orderly way

METHS singular noun methylated spirits

METHYLATE verb **METHYLATES, METHYLATING, METHYLATED** to mix or impregnate something with methanol

MÉTIER noun **MÉTIERS** a person's business or line of work

METOL noun **METOLS** a water-soluble colourless substance, used especially as the basis of a photographic developer

METONYMIC adj relating to or involving metonymy

METONYMY noun **METONYMIES** the use of a word referring to an element or attribute of something to mean the thing itself, eg *the bottle* for 'the drinking of alcohol' or *the Crown* for 'the sovereign'

METOPE noun **METOPES** in the frieze of a Doric entablature: a slab or tablet of plain or sculptured marble between the triglyph

METRE noun **METRES** in the SI system: the principal unit of length, equal to 39.37in or 1.094yd

METRIC adj relating to or based on the metre or the metric system

METRICAL adj in or relating to verse as distinct from prose

METRICATE verb **METRICATES, METRICATING, METRICATED** to convert (a non-metric measurement, system, etc) to a metric one using units of the metric system

METRO noun **METROS** an urban railway system, usually one that is mostly underground

METRONOME noun **METRONOMES** a device that indicates musical tempo by means of a ticking pendulum that can be set to move at different speeds

METTLE noun **METTLES** courage, determination and endurance

MEU noun **MEUS** the plant spignel

MEUNIÈRE adj said of a method of cooking fish: prepared by lightly flouring the fish, frying it gently in butter and serving it with a small portion of butter, lemon juice and parsley

MEW verb **MEWS, MEWING, MEWED** to make the cry of a cat; to miaow ▭ noun **MEWS** a cat's cry

MEWL verb **MEWLS, MEWLING, MEWLED** said especially of a

child: to cry feebly; to make a whimpering noise

MEWS noun **MEWSES** a set of stables around a yard or square, especially one converted into residential accommodation or garages

MEZUZAH noun **MEZUZAHS** a cylindrical box containing a parchment inscribed with religious texts from Deuteronomy, that is attached to the doorposts of some Jewish houses as a declaration of faith

MEZZANINE noun **MEZZANINES** in a building: a small storey between two main floors, usually the ground and first floors

MEZZO adverb moderately, quite or rather, as in *mezzo-forte* rather loud, and *mezzo-piano* rather soft

MEZZOTINT noun **MEZZOTINTS** a method of engraving a metal plate, especially a copper plate, by polishing and scraping to produce areas of light and shade, rendered obsolete by photographic reproduction in the late 19c

MHO noun **MHOS** a former unit of electrical inductance

MI noun **MIS** me, the musical note

MIAOW verb **MIAOWS, MIAOWING, MIAOWED** to make the cry of a cat ▭ noun **MIAOWS** a cat's cry

MIASMA noun **MIASMAS, MIASMATA** a thick foul-smelling vapour, especially one given off by swamps, marshes, etc

MIASMAL adj containing miasma

MIASMATIC adj relating to or typical of miasma

MIASMIC adj miasmatic

MICA noun **MICAS** any of a group of silicate minerals that split easily into thin flexible sheets and are used as electrical insulators, dielectrics, etc because they are poor conductors of heat and electricity

MICE plural of **mouse**

MICKLE adj much or great ▭ adverb much ▭ noun **MICKLES** a great quantity

MICRO noun **MICROS** a microcomputer or microprocessor

MICROBE noun **MICROBES** any micro-organism, especially a bacterium that is capable of causing disease

MICROBIAL adj of or relating to microbes

MICROBIC adj microbial

MICROCHIP noun **MICROCHIPS** in computing: a very thin piece of silicon or other semiconductor material, only a few millimetres square, on which all the components of an integrated circuit are arranged

MICROCODE noun **MICROCODES** in computing: a sequence of microinstructions

MICROCOSM noun **MICROCOSMS** any structure or system which contains, in miniature, all the features of the larger structure or system that it is part of

MICRODOT noun **MICRODOTS** a photograph, eg one taken of secret documents, reduced to the size of a pinhead

MICROFILM noun **MICROFILMS** a length of thin photographic film on which printed material is stored in miniaturized form ▭ verb **MICROFILMS, MICROFILMING, MICROFILMED** to record something on microfilm

MICROMESH noun **MICROMESHES** a very fine kind of mesh used to make hosiery, etc

MICRON noun **MICRONS** the former name for the micrometre

MICROPYLE noun **MICROPYLES** in flowering plants: a small opening or pore at the tip of the ovule through which the pollen tube normally enters during pollination

MICROTOME noun **MICROTOMES** an instrument for cutting thin sections of objects for microscopic examination

MICROWAVE noun **MICROWAVES** a form of electromagnetic radiation used in radar, communications and cooking ▭ verb **MICROWAVES, MICROWAVING, MICROWAVED** to cook something in a microwave oven

MICTURATE verb **MICTURATES, MICTURATING, MICTURATED** to urinate

MID adj referring to the middle point or in the middle of something ▭ noun **MIDS** the middle

MIDBRAIN noun **MIDBRAINS** the part of the brain which connects the forebrain to the hindbrain

MIDDAY noun **MIDDAYS** the middle of the day; twelve o'clock

MIDDEN noun **MIDDENS** a rubbish heap; a pile of dung

For longer words, see *The Chambers Dictionary*

MIDDLE *adj* at, or being, a point or position between two others, usually two ends or extremes, and especially the same distance from each □ *noun* **MIDDLES** the middle point, part or position of something □ *verb* **MIDDLES, MIDDLING, MIDDLED** to place something in the middle

MIDDLEMAN *noun* **MIDDLEMEN** a dealer who buys goods from a producer or manufacturer and sells them to shopkeepers or to the public

MIDDLING *adj* average; moderate; mediocre □ *adverb* said especially of a person's health: fairly good; moderately

MIDDY *noun* **MIDDIES** a measure of beer, varying in amount from one place to another

MIDFIELD *noun* **MIDFIELDS** in football: the middle area of the pitch, not close to the goal of either team

MIDGE *noun* **MIDGES** any of various small insects that gather near water, especially one of the kinds that bite people

MIDGET *noun* **MIDGETS** an unusually small person whose limbs and features are of normal proportions

MIDI *noun* **MIDIS** a skirt or coat of medium length or medium size

MIDIRON *noun* **MIDIRONS** a heavy golf club used for long approach shots

MIDLAND *adj* belonging or relating to the central, inland part of a country

MIDMOST *adverb* in the very middle □ *adj* nearest the middle

MIDNIGHT *noun* **MIDNIGHTS** twelve o'clock at night

MIDRIB *noun* **MIDRIBS** the rib that runs along the centre of a leaf and forms an extension of the petiole

MIDRIFF *noun* **MIDRIFFS** the part of the body between the chest and the waist

MIDSHIPS *adverb* amidships

MIDST *noun* **MIDSTS** middle

MIDSTREAM *noun* **MIDSTREAMS** the area of water in the middle of a river or stream, away from its banks

MIDSUMMER *noun* **MIDSUMMERS** the period of time in the middle of summer, or near the summer solstice, ie around 21 June in the N hemisphere or 22 December in the S hemisphere

MIDTERM *noun* **MIDTERMS** the middle of an academic term or term of office, etc

MIDWAY *adverb* halfway between two points in distance or time

MIDWIFE *noun* **MIDWIVES** a nurse, especially a female one, trained to assist women in childbirth and to provide care and advice for women before and after childbirth

MIDWIFERY *noun* **MIDWIFERIES** the skills or practice of a midwife; obstetrics

MIEN *noun* **MIENS** an appearance, expression or manner, especially one that reflects a mood

MIFF *verb* **MIFFS, MIFFING, MIFFED** to offend someone □ *noun* **MIFFS** a quarrel

MIFFED *adj* offended, upset or annoyed

MIFFY *adj* **MIFFIER, MIFFIEST** easily offended; touchy

MIGHT [1] past form of **may** [1]

MIGHT [2] *noun* **MIGHTS** power or strength

MIGHTILY *adverb* powerfully; to a great extent

MIGHTY *adj* **MIGHTIER, MIGHTIEST** having great strength or power □ *adverb* very

MIGNON *adj* small and dainty

MIGRAINE *noun* **MIGRAINES** a type of severe and recurring throbbing headache that usually affects one side of the head and is often accompanied by nausea or vomiting

MIGRANT *noun* **MIGRANTS** a person or animal that migrates □ *adj* regularly moving from one place to another

MIGRATE *verb* **MIGRATES, MIGRATING, MIGRATED** said of animals, especially birds: to travel from one region to another at certain times of the year

MIGRATION *noun* **MIGRATIONS** the movement of animals from one location to another, generally involving travel over very long distances by well-defined routes, in response to seasonal changes

MIGRATOR *noun* **MIGRATORS** a person or bird that migrates

MIGRATORY *adj* said eg of birds: that migrate or are accustomed to migrating

MIHRAB *noun* **MIHRABS** a niche or slab in a mosque indicating the direction of Mecca

MIKADO *noun* **MIKADOS** a title formerly given by foreigners to an emperor of Japan

MIKE *noun* **MIKES** a microphone

MIL *noun* **MILS** a unit of length equal to one thousandth of an inch

MILADY *noun* **MILADIES** a term formerly used to address, or to refer to, a rich English woman, especially an aristocratic one

MILCH *adj* said of cattle: producing milk

MILD *adj* **MILDER, MILDEST** gentle in temperament or behaviour □ *noun* **MILDS** dark beer less flavoured with hops than bitter beer

MILDEW *noun* **MILDEWS** any of various parasitic fungi that produce a fine white powdery coating on the surface of infected plants, or white or grey patches on the surface of paper, leather or other materials made from plant or animal material and subsequently kept in damp conditions □ *verb* **MILDEWS, MILDEWING, MILDEWED** to affect or become affected by mildew

MILDEWED *adj* affected with mildew

MILDEWY *adj* mildewed

MILDLY *adverb* in a mild way

MILDNESS *noun* **MILDNESSES** the quality of being mild

MILE *noun* **MILES** in the imperial system: a unit of distance equal to 1760yd (1.61km)

MILEAGE *noun* **MILEAGES** the number of miles travelled or to be travelled

MILER *noun* **MILERS** an athlete or horse that runs races of one mile

MILES *adverb* at a great distance; very much

MILESTONE *noun* **MILESTONES** a very important event; a significant point or stage

MILIARIA *noun* **MILIARIAS** prickly heat, an itchy skin rash caused by blockage of the sweat ducts

MILIEU *noun* **MILIEUS, MILIEUX** a social environment or set of surroundings

MILITANCY *noun* **MILITANCIES** the condition of being militant

MILITANT *adj* taking, or ready to take, strong or violent action; aggressively active □ *noun* **MILITANTS** a militant person

MILITARIA *plural noun* weapons, uniforms, medals, badges and other items connected with the military, often in the form of a collection

MILITARY adj by, for, or belonging or relating to the armed forces or warfare ◻ noun **MILITARIES** the armed forces

MILITATE verb **MILITATES, MILITATING, MILITATED** said of facts, etc: to have a strong influence or effect

MILITIA noun **MILITIAS** a civilian fighting force used to supplement a regular army in emergencies, eg the Territorial Army

MILK noun **MILKS** a white or yellowish liquid consisting mainly of water, with protein, fats, carbohydrates, vitamins and minerals (especially calcium), that is secreted by the mammary glands of female mammals to provide their young with nourishment ◻ verb **MILKS, MILKING, MILKED** to take milk from (an animal)

MILKER noun **MILKERS** a cow that is kept for milking

MILKILY adverb in a way that resembles milk; mildly

MILKINESS noun **MILKINESSES** cloudiness; mildness

MILKING noun **MILKINGS** the act, skill or process of milking

MILKMAID noun **MILKMAIDS** a woman who milks cows, goats, etc

MILKMAN noun **MILKMEN** a man who delivers milk to people's houses

MILKY adj **MILKIER, MILKIEST** like milk, eg in colour, opacity, mildness of taste or effect, etc

MILL noun **MILLS** a large machine that grinds grain into flour ◻ verb **MILLS, MILLING, MILLED** to grind (grain, etc)

MILLENARY noun **MILLENARIES** a thousand, especially a period of a thousand years ◻ adj consisting of, or relating to, a millenary

MILLEPEDE noun **MILLEPEDES** a millipede

MILLER noun **MILLERS** someone who owns or operates a mill, especially a grain mill

MILLET noun **MILLETS** the common name for several cereal grasses, especially certain fast-growing varieties tolerant of drought and poor soil which are grown as an important food crop in the drier regions of Africa and Asia, especially India and China, and are widely used as animal fodder

MILLIARD noun **MILLIARDS** a thousand million

MILLIBAR noun **MILLIBARS** a unit of atmospheric pressure equal to 10^{-3} (one thousandth) of a bar

MILLINER noun **MILLINERS** someone who makes or sells women's hats

MILLINERY noun **MILLINERIES** the hats and trimmings made or sold by milliners

MILLING noun **MILLINGS** the grinding of cereal grain to produce flour for use in making bread and other foodstuffs

MILLION noun **MILLIONS** the number or quantity 10^6, a thousand thousands ◻ adj 1 000 000 in number

MILLIONTH adj a thousand thousandth

MILLIPEDE noun **MILLIPEDES** any of various small wormlike creatures with many-jointed bodies and numerous pairs of legs

MILLPOND noun **MILLPONDS** a pond containing water which is, or used to be, used for driving a mill

MILLRACE noun **MILLRACES** a current of water that turns a mill wheel, or the channel in which it runs

MILLSTONE noun **MILLSTONES** either of the large, heavy stones between which grain is ground in a mill

MILOMETER noun **MILOMETERS** in a motor vehicle: an instrument for recording the total number of miles travelled

MILORD noun **MILORDS** a term formerly used on the continent to address or refer to a rich English gentleman, especially an aristocrat

MILT noun **MILTS** the testis or sperm of a fish

MIM adj **MIMMER, MIMMEST** a Scots and dialect word meaning *prim*

MIME noun **MIMES** the theatrical art of conveying meaning without words through gesture, movement and facial expression ◻ verb **MIMES, MIMING, MIMED** to act or express (feelings, etc) without words through gesture, movement and facial expression

MIMER noun **MIMERS** an actor who mimes; a mimic

MIMESIS noun **MIMESES** in art or literature: imitative representation

MIMETIC adj consisting of, showing, or relating to imitation; imitative

MIMIC verb **MIMICS, MIMICKING, MIMICKED** to imitate someone or something, especially for comic effect ◻ noun **MIMICS** someone who is skilled at imitating other people, especially in a comic manner ◻ adj imitative

MIMICKER noun **MIMICKERS** a person or thing that mimics

MIMICRY noun **MIMICRIES** the skill or practice of mimicking

MIMOSA noun **MIMOSAS** any of various tropical shrubs or trees which have leaves that droop when touched, and clusters of flowers, typically yellow ones

MINA noun **MINAS** a myna

MINARET noun **MINARETS** a tower on or attached to a mosque, with a balcony from which the muezzin calls Muslims to prayer

MINATORY adj threatening

MINCE verb **MINCES, MINCING, MINCED** to cut or shred something (especially meat) into very small pieces ◻ noun **MINCES** minced meat, especially beef

MINCEMEAT noun **MINCEMEATS** a spiced mixture of dried fruits, apples, candied peel, etc and often suet, used as a filling for pies

MINCER noun **MINCERS** a machine for mincing meat, etc

MINCING adj said of a manner of walking or behaving: over-delicate and affected

MINCINGLY adverb in a mincing way

MIND noun **MINDS** the power of thinking and understanding; the intelligence ◻ verb **MINDS, MINDING, MINDED** to look after, care for or keep something or someone safe ◻ exclamation be careful; watch out!

MINDED adj having an intention or desire

MINDER noun **MINDERS** someone who takes care of or supervises someone or something

MINDFUL adj keeping something in mind; attentive to it

MINDFULLY adverb attentively; thoughtfully

MINDLESS adj senseless; done without a reason

MINDSET noun **MINDSETS** an attitude or habit of mind, especially a firmly fixed one

MINE[1] pronoun something or someone belonging to, or connected with, me; the thing or things, etc belonging to me

For longer words, see *The Chambers Dictionary*

MINE [2] *noun* **MINES** an opening or excavation in the ground, used to remove minerals, metal ores, coal, etc, from the Earth's crust; an explosive device ◻ *verb* **MINES, MINING, MINED** to dig for (minerals, etc)

MINEFIELD *noun* **MINEFIELDS** an area of land or water in which mines have been laid

MINER *noun* **MINERS** someone who mines or works in a mine, especially a coal mine

MINERAL *noun* **MINERALS** a naturally occurring substance that is inorganic, usually crystalline, and has characteristic physical and chemical properties by which it may be identified ◻ *adj* belonging or relating to the nature of a mineral; containing minerals

MINGINESS *noun* **MINGINESSES** the state of being mingy

MINGLE *verb* **MINGLES, MINGLING, MINGLED** to become or make something become blended or mixed

MINGLER *noun* **MINGLERS** someone who mingles

MINGLING *noun* **MINGLINGS** a blending or mixing

MINGY *adj* **MINGIER, MINGIEST** ungenerous; mean; meagre

MINI *noun* **MINIS** something small or short of its kind, especially a miniskirt, or a type of small car ◻ *adj* **MINIER, MINIEST** small or short of its kind; miniature

MINIATURE *noun* **MINIATURES** a small copy, model or breed of anything ◻ *adj* minute or small-scale; referring to the nature of a miniature

MINIBREAK *noun* **MINIBREAKS** a short holiday, usually a weekend or long weekend break

MINIBUS *noun* **MINIBUSES** a small bus, usually one with between 12 and 15 seats in it

MINICAB *noun* **MINICABS** a taxi that is ordered by telephone from a private company, not one that can be stopped in the street

MINICAM *noun* **MINICAMS** a miniature, portable, shoulder-held TV camera, as used in news reporting

MINIDISK *noun* **MINIDISKS** a very compact magnetic disk storage medium for microcomputers

MINIM *noun* **MINIMS** a note half the length of a semibreve

MINIMAL *adj* very little indeed; negligible

MINIMAX *noun* **MINIMAXES** the lowest value in a set of maximum values

MINIMISE *verb* **MINIMISES, MINIMISING, MINIMISED** to minimize

MINIMIZE *verb* **MINIMIZES, MINIMIZING, MINIMIZED** to reduce something to a minimum

MINIMUM *noun* **MINIMA** the lowest possible number, value, quantity or degree ◻ *adj* relating or referring to the nature of a minimum; lowest possible

MINING *noun* **MININGS** the act or process of extracting minerals, etc from the ground

MINION *noun* **MINIONS** an employee or follower, especially one who is fawning or subservient

MINIPILL *noun* **MINIPILLS** a low-dose oral contraceptive containing progesterone but no oestrogen

MINISKIRT *noun* **MINISKIRTS** a very short skirt, with a hemline well above the knee

MINISTER *noun* **MINISTERS** the political head of, or a senior politician with responsibilities in, a government department ◻ *verb* **MINISTERS, MINISTERING, MINISTERED** to give attentive service (to)

MINISTRY *noun* **MINISTRIES** a government department

MINIVER *noun* **MINIVERS** a type of fur used for lining ceremonial robes

MINK *noun* **MINKS** a semi-aquatic European or N American mammal with a slender body, webbed feet and thick fur, brown except for a white patch on the chin

MINNEOLA *noun* **MINNEOLAS** an orange-like citrus fruit which is a cross between a grapefruit and a tangerine

MINNOW *noun* **MINNOWS** any of several kinds of small freshwater fish of the carp family

MINOR *adj* not as great in importance or size; fairly or relatively small or insignificant ◻ *noun* **MINORS** someone who is below the age of legal majority ◻ *verb* **MINORS, MINORING, MINORED** to study a specified minor or subsidary subject at college or university

MINORITY *noun* **MINORITIES** a small number, or the smaller of two numbers, sections or groups

MINSTER *noun* **MINSTERS** a large church or cathedral, especially one that was originally attached to a monastery

MINSTREL *noun* **MINSTRELS** in the Middle Ages: a travelling singer, musician and reciter of poetry, etc

MINT *noun* **MINTS** a place where coins are produced under government authority ◻ *verb* **MINTS, MINTING, MINTED** to manufacture (coins)

MINTAGE *noun* **MINTAGES** coining; coinage

MINTY *adj* **MINTIER, MINTIEST** tasting or smelling of the herb mint

MINUEND *noun* **MINUENDS** the number that another number is to be subtracted from

MINUET *noun* **MINUETS** a slow formal dance with short steps in triple time, popular in the 17c and 18c

MINUS *prep* with the subtraction of (a specified number) ◻ *adj* negative or less than zero ◻ *noun* **MINUSES** a sign (–) indicating a negative quantity or that the quantity which follows it is to be subtracted

MINUSCULE *adj* extremely small ◻ *noun* **MINUSCULES** a lower-case letter

MINUTE [1] *noun* **MINUTES** a unit of time equal to $\frac{1}{60}$ of an hour; 60 seconds ◻ *verb* **MINUTES, MINUTING, MINUTED** to make an official written record of what is said in (eg a meeting); to take or record something in the minutes of (eg a meeting)

MINUTE [2] *adj* **MINUTER, MINUTEST** very small; tiny

MINUTELY *adverb* on a minute scale; with great precision

MINUTEMAN *noun* **MINUTEMEN** especially in the US War of Independence: a member of a group of militiamen, particularly in New England, who were prepared to take up arms at very short notice

MINUTIAE *plural noun* small and often unimportant details

MINX *noun* **MINXES** a cheeky, playful, sly or flirtatious young woman

MIR *noun* **MIRS, MIRI** a Russian peasant farming commune

MIRACLE *noun* **MIRACLES** an act or event that breaks the laws of nature, and is therefore thought to be caused by the intervention of God or another supernatural force

MIRAGE noun **MIRAGES** an optical illusion that usually resembles a pool of water on the horizon reflecting light from the sky, commonly experienced in deserts, and caused by the refraction of light by very hot air near to the ground

MIRE noun **MIRES** deep mud; a boggy area ◻ verb **MIRES, MIRING, MIRED** to sink, or to make something or someone sink, in a mire

MIRIN noun **MIRINS** a sweet rice wine used in Japanese cookery

MIRK noun **MIRKS** murk

MIRROR noun **MIRRORS** a smooth highly-polished surface, such as glass, coated with a thin layer of metal, such as silver, that reflects an image of what is in front of it ◻ verb **MIRRORS, MIRRORING, MIRRORED** to represent or depict something faithfully

MIRTH noun laughter; merriment

MIRTHFUL adj full of mirth; causing mirth

MIRTHLESS adj joyless; sad

MIRY adj **MIRIER, MIRIEST** consisting of mire; covered with mire

MIS verb **MISSES, MISSING, MISSED** a Spenserian word meaning to fail

MISADVISE verb **MISADVISES, MISADVISING, MISADVISED** to advise someone wrongly or badly

MISALIGN verb **MISALIGNS, MISALIGNING, MISALIGNED** to align something wrongly

MISALLY verb **MISALLIES, MISALLYING, MISALLIED** to ally (people, parties, etc) in an unsuitable way

MISAPPLY verb **MISAPPLIES, MISAPPLYING, MISAPPLIED** to apply something wrongly

MISBEHAVE verb **MISBEHAVES, MISBEHAVING, MISBEHAVED** to behave badly

MISCALL verb **MISCALLS, MISCALLING, MISCALLED** to call someone or something by the wrong name; to misname

MISCARRY verb **MISCARRIES, MISCARRYING, MISCARRIED** to go wrong or fail

MISCAST verb **MISCASTS,**

MISCASTING, MISCAST to give an unsuitable part to (an actor) or put an unsuitable actor in (a part)

MISCHANCE noun **MISCHANCES** bad luck

MISCHIEF noun **MISCHIEFS** behaviour that annoys or irritates people but does not mean or cause any serious harm

MISCOUNT verb **MISCOUNTS, MISCOUNTING, MISCOUNTED** to count something wrongly; to miscalculate ◻ noun **MISCOUNTS** an act or instance of counting wrongly

MISCREANT noun **MISCREANTS** a malicious person; a villain or scoundrel ◻ adj villainous or wicked

MISCUE noun **MISCUES** in billiards, snooker and pool: a stroke in which the cue does not hit the cue ball properly, slips off it or misses it ◻ verb **MISCUES, MISCUEING, MISCUED** in billiards, snooker and pool: to make a miscue

MISDATE verb **MISDATES, MISDATING, MISDATED** to date (eg a letter) wrongly ◻ noun **MISDATES** a wrong date

MISDEAL noun **MISDEALS** in cards, etc: an incorrect deal ◻ verb **MISDEALS, MISDEALING, MISDEALT** to deal or divide something (especially playing cards) wrongly

MISDEED noun **MISDEEDS** an example of bad or criminal behaviour; a wrongdoing

MISDIAL verb **MISDIALS, MISDIALLING, MISDIALLED** to dial (a telephone number) incorrectly

MISDIRECT verb **MISDIRECTS, MISDIRECTING, MISDIRECTED** to give wrong directions to someone; to direct, address or instruct something or someone wrongly

MISER noun **MISERS** someone who lives in bleak, uncomfortable, etc conditions in order to store up their wealth

MISERABLE adj said of a person: very unhappy

MISERABLY adverb in a miserable way

MISÈRE noun **MISÈRES** in cards: a call made by a player meaning that they undertake not to take any tricks

MISERLY adj characteristic of a miser; stingy

MISERY noun **MISERIES** great unhappiness or suffering

MISFIELD verb **MISFIELDS, MISFIELDING, MISFIELDED** in cricket: to field badly or ineffectively ◻ noun **MISFIELDS** a mistake or failure in fielding

MISFILE verb **MISFILES, MISFILING, MISFILED** to file (eg papers) wrongly

MISFIRE verb **MISFIRES, MISFIRING, MISFIRED** said of a gun, etc: to fail to fire, or to fail to fire properly ◻ noun **MISFIRES** an instance of misfiring

MISFIT noun **MISFITS** someone who is not suited to the situation, job, social environment, etc that they are in

MISGIVING noun **MISGIVINGS** a feeling of uneasiness, doubt or suspicion

MISGUIDED adj acting from or showing mistaken ideas or bad judgement

MISHANDLE verb **MISHANDLES, MISHANDLING, MISHANDLED** to deal with something or someone carelessly or without skill

MISHAP noun **MISHAPS** an unfortunate accident, especially a minor one; a piece of bad luck

MISHEAR verb **MISHEARS, MISHEARING, MISHEARD** to hear something or someone incorrectly

MISHIT verb **MISHITS, MISHITTING, MISHIT** to fail to hit (eg a ball) cleanly or accurately ◻ noun **MISHITS** an act of mishitting

MISHMASH noun **MISHMASHES** a jumbled assortment or mixture

MISINFORM verb **MISINFORMS, MISINFORMING, MISINFORMED** to give someone incorrect or misleading information

MISJUDGE verb **MISJUDGES, MISJUDGING, MISJUDGED** to judge something or someone wrongly, or to have an unfairly low opinion of them

MISKEY verb **MISKEYS, MISKEYING, MISKEYED** to key (especially data) incorrectly

MISLAY verb **MISLAYS, MISLAYING, MISLAID** to lose something, usually temporarily, especially by forgetting where it was put

MISLEAD verb **MISLEADS, MISLEADING, MISLED** to make someone take a wrong or undesirable course of action

MISLEADING *adj* likely to mislead; deceptive

MISMANAGE *verb* **MISMANAGES, MISMANAGING, MISMANAGED** to manage or handle something or someone badly or carelessly

MISMATCH *verb* **MISMATCHES, MISMATCHING, MISMATCHED** to match (things or people) unsuitably or incorrectly ▫ *noun* **MISMATCHES** an unsuitable or incorrect match

MISNAME *verb* **MISNAMES, MISNAMING, MISNAMED** to call something or someone by the wrong name

MISNOMER *noun* **MISNOMERS** a wrong or unsuitable name

MISO *noun* **MISOS** a soy bean paste that has been fermented in brine, used for flavouring food

MISOGAMY *noun* **MISOGAMIES** hatred of marriage

MISOGYNY *noun* **MISOGYNIES** hatred of women

MISPLACE *verb* **MISPLACES, MISPLACING, MISPLACED** to lose something, usually temporarily, especially by forgetting where it was put

MISPLAY *verb* **MISPLAYS, MISPLAYING, MISPLAYED** in sports or games: to play (eg a ball, card, etc) wrongly or badly ▫ *noun* **MISPLAYS** an instance of wrong or bad play

MISPRINT *noun* **MISPRINTS** a mistake in printing, eg an incorrect or damaged character ▫ *verb* **MISPRINTS, MISPRINTING, MISPRINTED** to print something wrongly

MISQUOTE *verb* **MISQUOTES, MISQUOTING, MISQUOTED** to quote something or someone inaccurately, sometimes with the intention of deceiving

MISREAD *verb* **MISREADS, MISREADING, MISREAD** to read something incorrectly

MISREPORT *verb* **MISREPORTS, MISREPORTING, MISREPORTED** to report (eg a story) incorrectly, falsely or misleadingly

MISRULE *verb* **MISRULES, MISRULING, MISRULED** to govern (eg a country) in a disorderly or unjust way ▫ *noun* **MISRULES** bad or unjust government

MISS *verb* **MISSES, MISSING, MISSED** to fail to hit or catch something ▫ *noun* **MISSES** a failure to hit or catch something, etc

MISSABLE *adj* that can be missed

MISSAL *noun* **MISSALS** a book containing all the texts used in the service of mass throughout the year

MISSHAPEN *adj* badly shaped; deformed

MISSILE *noun* **MISSILES** a self-propelled flying bomb, eg a guided missile or a ballistic missile

MISSING *adj* absent; lost; not able to be found

MISSION *noun* **MISSIONS** a purpose for which a person or group of people is sent

MISSIS *noun* **MISSISES** a wife

MISSIVE *noun* **MISSIVES** a letter, especially a long or official one

MISSPELL *verb* **MISSPELLS, MISPELLING, MISPELT, MISPELLED** to spell something incorrectly

MISSPELLING *noun* **MISSPELLINGS** a wrong spelling

MISSPEND *verb* **MISSPENDS, MISSPENDING, MISSPENT** to spend (money, time, etc) foolishly or wastefully

MISSUS *noun* **MISSUSES** a wife

MISSY *noun* **MISSIES** a term used to address a girl or young woman

MIST *noun* **MISTS** condensed water vapour in the air near the ground; thin fog or low cloud ▫ *verb* **MISTS, MISTING, MISTED** to cover or become covered with mist, or as if with mist

MISTAKE *noun* **MISTAKES** an error ▫ *verb* **MISTAKES, MISTAKING, MISTOOK, MISTAKEN** to misinterpret or misunderstand something

MISTAKEN *adj* understood, thought, named, etc wrongly; incorrect

MISTER *noun* **MISTERS** the full form of the abbreviation *Mr*

MISTILY *adverb* in a misty way

MISTIME *verb* **MISTIMES, MISTIMING, MISTIMED** to do or say something at a wrong or unsuitable time

MISTINESS *noun* **MISTINESSES** obscurity; dimness

MISTLETOE *noun* **MISTLETOES** an evergreen shrub that grows as a parasite on trees and produces clusters of white berries in winter

MISTOOK a past form of **mistake**

MISTREAT *verb* **MISTREATS, MISTREATING, MISTREATED** to treat someone or something cruelly or without care

MISTRESS *noun* **MISTRESSES** the female lover of a man married to another woman

MISTRIAL *noun* **MISTRIALS** a trial not conducted properly according to the law and declared invalid

MISTRUST *verb* **MISTRUSTS, MISTRUSTING, MISTRUSTED** to have no trust in, or to be suspicious of, someone or something ▫ *noun* **MISTRUSTS** a lack of trust

MISTY *adj* **MISTIER, MISTIEST** covered with, or obscured by, mist

MISUSE *noun* **MISUSES** improper or inappropriate use ▫ *verb* **MISUSES, MISUSING, MISUSED** to put something to improper or inappropriate use

MISUSER *noun* **MISUSERS** someone who misuses something

MITE *noun* **MITES** a small, often microscopic, animal with a simple rounded body and eight short legs, some species of which are pests, transmit diseases or cause human allergies

MITER *noun* **MITERS** a mitre ▫ *verb* **MITERS, MITERING, MITERED** to mitre

MITIGATE *verb* **MITIGATES, MITIGATING, MITIGATED** to partially excuse something or make it less serious

MITIGATING *adj* extenuating or alleviating

MITIGATOR *noun* **MITIGATORS** a person or thing that mitigates or alleviates

MITOSIS *noun* **MITOSES** a type of cell division that results in the production of two daughter cells with identical nuclei, each of which contains the same genes and the same number of chromosomes as the parent nucleus

MITOTIC *adj* relating to or characterized by mitosis

MITRE *noun* **MITRES** in joinery, etc: a corner joint between two lengths of wood, made by fitting together two 45 sloping surfaces cut into their ends ▫ *verb* **MITRES, MITRING, MITRED** to join (two lengths of wood, etc) with a mitre

MITT *noun* **MITTS** a hand

MITTEN *noun* **MITTENS** a glove with one covering for the thumb and a large covering for all the other fingers together

MITTIMUS *noun* **MITTIMUSES** in law: an official order for the imprisonment of someone

MIX verb **MIXES, MIXING, MIXED** to combine so that the parts of one thing, or the things of one sort, are diffused among those of another ▫ noun **MIXES** a collection of people or things mixed together **MIXABLE** adj that can be mixed **MIXED** adj consisting of different and often opposite kinds of things, elements, characters, etc **MIXER** noun **MIXERS** a machine used for mixing **MIXTURE** noun **MIXTURES** a blend of ingredients prepared for a particular purpose

MIZ noun **MIZZES** short form of misery ▫ adj short form of miserable

MNA noun **MNAS** a Greek unit of weight or money

MNEMONIC noun **MNEMONICS** a device or form of words, often a short verse, used as a memory-aid ▫ adj serving to help the memory **MO** adj an old word for more **MOA** noun **MOAS** a flightless ostrich-like bird of New Zealand that has been extinct since the end of the 18c **MOAN** noun **MOANS** a low prolonged sound expressing sadness, grief or pain ▫ verb **MOANS, MOANING, MOANED** to utter or produce a moan **MOANER** noun **MOANERS** someone who moans; a complainer **MOANFUL** adj expressing sorrow; lamentable **MOAT** noun **MOATS** a deep trench, often filled with water, dug round a castle or other fortified position to provide extra defence **MOATED** adj surrounded by a moat **MOB** noun **MOBS** a large, disorderly crowd ▫ verb **MOBS, MOBBING, MOBBED** to attack something or someone as a mob **MOBBED** adj densely crowded; packed with people **MOBILE** adj able to be moved easily; not fixed ▫ noun **MOBILES** a hanging decoration or sculpture, etc made up of parts that are moved around by air currents **MOBILISE** verb **MOBILISES, MOBILISING, MOBILISED** to mobilize **MOBILISER** noun **MOBILISERS** a mobilizer

MOBILITY noun **MOBILITIES** the ability to move **MOBILIZE** verb **MOBILIZES, MOBILIZING, MOBILIZED** to organize or prepare something or someone for use, action, etc **MOBILIZER** noun **MOBILIZERS** a person or thing that mobilizes **MOBSTER** noun **MOBSTERS** a member of a gang or an organized group of criminals, especially the Mafia **MOCCASIN** noun **MOCCASINS** a deerskin or other soft leather shoe with a continuous sole and heel, as worn by Native Americans **MOCHA** noun **MOCHAS** a flavouring made from coffee and chocolate **MOCK** verb **MOCKS, MOCKING, MOCKED** to speak or behave disparagingly, derisively, or contemptuously towards someone or something ▫ adj false; sham; serving as practice for the similar but real or true thing, event, etc which is to come later ▫ noun **MOCKS** in England and Wales: a mock examination **MOCKER** noun **MOCKERS** a person who speaks or behaves disparagingly, derisively, or contemptuously towards someone or something **MOCKERY** noun **MOCKERIES** an imitation, especially a contemptible or insulting one **MOCKING** adj that mocks or ridicules ▫ noun **MOCKINGS** the action of speaking or behaving disparagingly, derisively, or contemptuously towards someone or something **MOCKINGLY** adverb in a mocking way **MOD** noun **MODS** a Scottish Gaelic literary and musical festival, held annually **MODAL** adj belonging or relating to, or concerning, mood or a mood ▫ noun **MODALS** a verb used as the auxiliary of another verb to express grammatical mood such as condition, possibility and obligation **MODALITY** noun **MODALITIES** the quality or characteristic of music as determined by its mode **MODALLY** adverb with reference to mode **MODE** noun **MODES** a way of doing something, or of living, acting, happening, operating, etc; either

of the two main scale systems used in music **MODEL** noun **MODELS** a small-scale representation of something that serves as a guide in constructing the full-scale version ▫ verb **MODELS, MODELLING, MODELED** to display (clothes) by wearing them **MODELING** noun **MODELINGS** modelling **MODELLER** noun **MODELLERS** someone who makes models **MODELLING** noun **MODELLINGS** the act or activity of making a model or models **MODELLO** noun **MODELLOS** a small but complete and detailed painting or drawing made to present the artist's ideas for a full-size work **MODEM** noun **MODEMS** an electronic device that transmits information from one computer to another along a telephone line, converting digital data into audio signals and back again **MODERATE** adj not extreme; not strong or violent ▫ noun **MODERATES** someone who holds moderate views, especially on politics ▫ verb **MODERATES, MODERATING, MODERATED** to make or become less extreme, violent or intense **MODERATO** adj at a restrained and moderate tempo ▫ adverb at a restrained and moderate tempo ▫ noun **MODERATOS** a piece of music to be played at a restrained and moderate tempo **MODERATOR** noun **MODERATORS** in a Presbyterian church: a minister who presides over a court or assembly **MODERN** adj **MODERNER, MODERNEST** belonging to the present or to recent times; not old or ancient ▫ noun **MODERNS** a person living in modern times, especially someone who follows the latest trends **MODERNISE** verb **MODERNISES, MODERNISING, MODERNISED** to modernize **MODERNISM** noun **MODERNISMS** modern spirit or character **MODERNIST** noun **MODERNISTS** an admirer of modern ideas, ways, etc ▫ adj relating to or typical of modern ideas or modernism **MODERNITY** noun **MODERNITIES** the quality or condition of being modern

MODERNIZE verb **MODERNIZES, MODERNIZING, MODERNIZED** to bring something up to modern standards, or adapt it to modern style, conditions, etc

MODEST adj **MODESTER, MODESTEST** not having or showing pride; humble; not pretentious or showy

MODESTLY adverb in a modest way

MODESTY noun **MODESTIES** the quality or fact of being modest

MODICUM noun **MODICUMS** a small amount

MODIFIER noun **MODIFIERS** a word or phrase that modifies or identifies the meaning of another word, eg *in the green hat* in the phrase *the man in the green hat*, and *vaguely* in the phrase *He was vaguely embarrassed*

MODIFY verb **MODIFIES, MODIFYING, MODIFIED** to change the form or quality of something, usually only slightly

MODISH adj stylish; fashionable

MODISHLY adverb in a modish way

MODULAR adj consisting of modules

MODULATE verb **MODULATES, MODULATING, MODULATED** to alter the tone or volume of (a sound, or one's voice)

MODULATOR noun **MODULATORS** a person or device that modulates

MODULE noun **MODULES** a separate self-contained unit that combines with others to form a larger unit, structure or system

MODULUS noun **MODULI** the absolute value of a real number, whether positive or negative

MOE noun **MOES** an obsolete word meaning a wry face

MOG noun **MOGS** a moggy

MOGGIE noun **MOGGIES** a moggy

MOGGY noun **MOGGIES** a cat, especially an ordinary domestic cat of mixed breeding

MOGUL noun **MOGULS** an important, powerful, or influential person, especially in business or the film industry

MOGULED adj of a ski run: having moguls (mounds of hard snow created as obstacles)

MOHAIR noun **MOHAIRS** the long soft hair of the Angora goat

MOHEL noun **MOHELS** in Judaism: an official who performs circumcisions

MOI pronoun a French word meaning *me*, used facetiously in English

MOIETY noun **MOIETIES** a half; one of two parts or divisions

MOIRE noun **MOIRES** a fabric, especially silk, with a pattern of glossy irregular waves

MOIRÉ adj said of a fabric: having a pattern of glossy irregular waves; watered □ noun **MOIRÉS** this pattern on the surface of a fabric or metal

MOIST adj **MOISTER, MOISTEST** damp or humid; slightly wet or watery

MOISTEN verb **MOISTENS, MOISTENING, MOISTENED** to make something moist, or become moist

MOISTLY adverb in a moist way

MOISTNESS noun **MOISTNESSES** the quality or state of being moist

MOISTURE noun **MOISTURES** liquid in vapour or spray form, or condensed as droplets

MOJO noun **MOJOS, MOJOES** magic; a spell or charm

MOKE noun **MOKES** a donkey

MOLAL adj said of a solution: containing one mole (an SI unit of an amount of a substance) of dissolved substance per kilogram of solvent

MOLAR noun **MOLARS** any of the large back teeth in humans and other mammals, used for chewing and grinding □ adj belonging or relating to a molar

MOLARITY noun **MOLARITIES** the concentration of a solution

MOLASSES singular noun the thickest kind of treacle, left over at the very end of the process of refining raw sugar

MOLD noun **MOLDS** a mould □ verb **MOLDS, MOLDING, MOLDED** to mould

MOLE noun **MOLES** a small insectivorous burrowing mammal with velvety greyish-black fur, very small eyes and very broad feet adapted for digging

MOLECULAR adj belonging or relating to molecules

MOLECULE noun **MOLECULES** the smallest particle of an element or

compound that can exist independently and participate in a reaction, consisting of two or more atoms bonded together

MOLEHILL noun **MOLEHILLS** a little pile of earth thrown up by a burrowing mole

MOLESKIN noun **MOLESKINS** mole's fur

MOLEST verb **MOLESTS, MOLESTING, MOLESTED** to attack or interfere with someone sexually

MOLESTER noun **MOLESTERS** a person who molests someone

MOLL noun **MOLLS** a gangster's girlfriend

MOLLIFIER noun **MOLLIFIERS** a person or thing that mollifies

MOLLIFY verb **MOLLIFIES, MOLLIFYING, MOLLIFIED** to make someone calmer or less angry

MOLLUSC noun **MOLLUSCS** any of a large group of invertebrate animals, typically one with a soft unsegmented body with a large, flattened, muscular foot on the underside and a mantle covering its upper surface protected by a hard, chalky shell, eg the snail, mussel, etc

MOLT verb **MOLTS, MOLTING, MOLTED** to moult □ noun **MOLTS** moult

MOLTEN adj in a melted state; liquefied

MOLTO adverb very; much □ adj very; much

MOM noun **MOMS** mother

MOMENT noun **MOMENTS** a short while

MOMENTARY adj lasting for only a moment

MOMENTOUS adj describing something of great importance or significance

MOMENTUM noun **MOMENTUMS, MOMENTA** continuous speed of progress; impetus

MOMMA noun **MOMMAS** mother

MOMMY noun **MOMMIES** mother

MON noun **MON** a Japanese family badge or crest

MONAD noun **MONADS** any self-contained non-physical unit of being, eg God, or a soul

MONADIC adj composed of monads

MONANDRY noun **MONANDRIES** the state or condition of being monandrous, or having only one husband or male sexual partner at a time

MONARCH noun **MONARCHS** a king, queen or other non-elected sovereign with a hereditary right to rule

MONARCHIC adj having the characteristics of a monarchy

MONARCHY noun **MONARCHIES** a form of government in which the head of state is a monarch

MONASTERY noun **MONASTERIES** the home of a community of monks, or sometimes nuns

MONASTIC adj belonging or relating to monasteries, monks or nuns

MONAURAL adj having, using, or relating to, one ear only

MONETARY adj belonging or relating to, or consisting of, money

MONEY noun **MONEYS, MONIES** coins or banknotes used as a means of buying things

MONEYBAGS singular noun a very rich person

MONEYED adj having much money; wealthy

MONGOOSE noun **MONGOOSES** a small mammal of SE Asia, Africa and Madagascar that preys on snakes, etc, and has a long, slender body, pointed muzzle and a bushy tail

MONGREL noun **MONGRELS** an animal, especially a dog, of mixed breeding ◻ adj characterized by being of mixed breeding, origin or nature

MONGRELLY adj resembling a mongrel

MONIED adj having much money; wealthy

MONIES a plural of **money**

MONIKER noun **MONIKERS** a nickname

MONISM noun **MONISMS** the theory that reality exists in one form only, especially that there is no difference in substance between body and soul

MONIST noun **MONISTS** someone who follows a doctrine of monism

MONISTIC adj relating to or involving monism

MONITION noun **MONITIONS** a warning or telling-off; an act or instance of admonishing

MONITIVE adj conveying admonition

MONITOR noun **MONITORS** any instrument designed to check, record or control something on a regular basis ◻ verb **MONITORS,**

MONITORING, MONITORED to check, record, track or control something on a regular basis; to observe or act as a monitor of something

MONITORY adj serving as a warning or telling-off

MONK noun **MONKS** a member of a religious community of men living disciplined austere lives devoted primarily to worship, under vows of poverty, chastity and obedience

MONKEY noun **MONKEYS** any mammal belonging to the primates other than a human, ape, chimpanzee, gibbon, orang utan or lemur, with a hairy coat, nails instead of claws and usually tree-dwelling ◻ verb **MONKEYS, MONKEYING, MONKEYED** to play, fool, interfere, etc with something

MONKFISH noun **MONKFISHES** a large cartilaginous fish with a flattened head, lateral gill openings, broad pectoral fins and a slender tail

MONKISH adj relating to or like a monk

MONKSHOOD noun **MONKSHOODS** aconite

MONO adj short form of monophonic and monounsaturated ◻ noun **MONOS** monophonic sound reproduction, ie on one channel only, not split into two, as with stereophonic systems

MONOCARP noun **MONOCARPS** a plant that flowers and fruits only once in its life cycle

MONOCLE noun **MONOCLES** a lens for correcting the sight in one eye only, held in place between the bones of the cheek and brow

MONOCLED adj wearing a monocle

MONOCLINE noun **MONOCLINES** in rock strata: a fold with one side that dips steeply, after which the strata resume their original direction

MONOCOQUE noun **MONOCOQUES** in aeronautics: a fuselage or nacelle in which all the structural loads are carried by the skin

MONOCRACY noun **MONOCRACIES** government by one person only

MONOCRAT noun **MONOCRATS** a supporter of monocracy; someone who rules alone

MONOCULAR adj for the use of, or relating to, one eye only

MONOCYTE noun **MONOCYTES** the largest type of white blood cell, which has a single, oval or kidney-shaped nucleus and clear cytoplasm

MONODIC adj relating to monody

MONODIST noun **MONODISTS** a person who writes monodies

MONODY noun **MONODIES** especially in Greek tragedy: a mournful song or speech performed by a single actor

MONOGAMY noun **MONOGAMIES** the state or practice of having only one husband or wife at any one time

MONOGLOT noun **MONOGLOTS** a person who only knows and speaks one language ◻ adj referring or relating to a person who only knows and speaks one language

MONOGRAM noun **MONOGRAMS** a design composed from letters, usually a person's initials, interlaced or written into a single character, often used on personal belongings, clothing, etc ◻ verb **MONOGRAMS, MONOGRAMMING, MONOGRAMMED** to mark something with a monogram

MONOGRAPH noun **MONOGRAPHS** a book or essay dealing with one particular subject or a specific aspect of it ◻ verb **MONOGRAPHS, MONOGRAPHING, MONOGRAPHED** to write a monograph on (a subject)

MONOHULL noun **MONOHULLS** a sailing craft with one hull, as distinct from a catamaran or a trimaran

MONOLITH noun **MONOLITHS** a single, tall block of stone, especially one shaped like or into a column or pillar

MONOLOGUE noun **MONOLOGUES** a long speech by one actor in a film or play

MONOMANIA noun **MONOMANIAS** domination of the mind by a single subject or concern, to an excessive degree

MONOMARK noun **MONOMARKS** a particular combination of letters or figures used as an identification mark

MONOMER noun **MONOMERS** a simple molecule that can be joined

For longer words, see *The Chambers Dictionary*

to many others to form a much larger molecule known as a polymer

MONOMERIC *adj* in the form of a monomer

MONOMIAL *noun* **MONOMIALS** an algebraic expression that consists of one term only □ *adj* consisting of one term

MONOPLANE *noun* **MONOPLANES** an aeroplane with a single set of wings

MONOPOLY *noun* **MONOPOLIES** the right to be, or the fact of being, the only supplier of a specified commodity or service

MONORAIL *noun* **MONORAILS** a railway system in which the trains run on, or are suspended from, a single rail

MONOTINT *noun* **MONOTINTS** representation in, or a drawing, painting, etc using, shades of one colour only; monochrome

MONOTONE *noun* **MONOTONES** in speech or sound: a single unvarying tone □ *adj* lacking in variety; unchanging

MONOTONY *noun* **MONOTONIES** the quality of being monotonous

MONOTREME *noun* **MONOTREMES** an animal, such as the echidna or the duck-billed platypus, that differ from other mammals in having a single opening, the cloaca, that serves for the passing of both urine and faeces

MONOTYPE *noun* **MONOTYPES** a one-off print made by applying oil paint or ink on to a sheet of glass or metal plate, and pressing paper against the wet surface to create on it a reverse image of the original

MONOTYPIC *adj* said eg of a plant or animal species: consisting of only one type or example

MONOXIDE *noun* **MONOXIDES** a compound that contains one oxygen atom in each molecule

MONSIEUR *noun* **MESSIEURS** a title of courtesy in France, equal to *Mr*

MONSOON *noun* **MONSOONS** in India: the heavy rains which accompany the summer wind

MONSOONAL *adj* of or relating to a monsoon

MONSTER *noun* **MONSTERS** especially in fables and folklore: any large and frightening imaginary creature □ *adj* huge; gigantic

MONSTERA *noun* **MONSTERAS** a tall tropical American climbing plant, popular as a house plant, with large shiny heart-shaped leaves and tough aerial roots growing from the stem

MONSTROUS *adj* like a monster; huge and horrible

MONTAGE *noun* **MONTAGES** the process of creating a picture by assembling and piecing together elements from other pictures, photographs, etc, and mounting them on to canvas, etc

MONTH *noun* **MONTHS** any of the 12 named divisions of the year, which vary in length between 28 and 31 days

MONTHLY *adj* happening, published, performed, etc once a month □ *adverb* once a month □ *noun* **MONTHLIES** a monthly periodical

MONUMENT *noun* **MONUMENTS** something, eg a statue, built to preserve the memory of a person or event

MOO *noun* **MOOS** the long low sound made by a cow, ox, etc □ *verb* **MOOS, MOOING, MOOED** to make this sound

MOOCH *verb* **MOOCHES, MOOCHING, MOOCHED** to wander around aimlessly

MOOD *noun* **MOODS** a state of mind at a particular time

MOODILY *adverb* in a moody way

MOODINESS *noun* **MOODINESSES** sullenness

MOODY *adj* **MOODIER, MOODIEST** tending to change mood often

MOOLI *noun* **MOOLIS** a long white carrot-shaped root that tastes similar to a radish

MOON [1] *noun* **MOONS** the Earth's natural satellite, illuminated to varying degrees by the Sun depending on its position and often visible in the sky, especially at night

MOON [2] *verb* **MOONS, MOONING, MOONED** to wander around aimlessly; to spend time idly

MOONBEAM *noun* **MOONBEAMS** a ray of sunlight reflected from the moon

MOONER *noun* **MOONERS** a person who moons about

MOONFACE *noun* **MOONFACES** a full, round face

MOONLESS *adj* destitute of moonlight

MOONLIGHT *noun* **MOONLIGHTS**

sunlight reflected by the moon □ *verb* **MOONLIGHTS, MOONLIGHTING, MOONLIGHTED** to work at a second job outside the working hours of one's main job, often evading income tax on the extra earnings

MOONLIGHTING *noun* **MOONLIGHTINGS** the practice of working at a second job outside the working hours of one's main job, often evading income tax on the extra earnings

MOONLIT *adj* illuminated by moonlight

MOONSCAPE *noun* **MOONSCAPES** the appearance of the surface of the moon, or a representation of it

MOONSHINE *noun* **MOONSHINES** foolish talk; nonsense

MOONSHOT *noun* **MOONSHOTS** a launching of an object, craft, etc to orbit or land on the moon

MOONSTONE *noun* **MOONSTONES** a transparent or opalescent, silvery or bluish feldspar, used as a semi-precious gemstone

MOONY *adj* **MOONIER, MOONIEST** in a dreamy, distracted mood

MOOR [1] *noun* **MOORS** a large area of open, uncultivated upland with an acid peaty soil

MOOR [2] *verb* **MOORS, MOORING, MOORED** to fasten (a ship or boat) by a rope, cable or anchor

MOORAGE *noun* **MOORAGES** a fee paid for mooring; a place for mooring

MOORCOCK *noun* **MOORCOCKS** a male moorfowl

MOORFOWL *noun* **MOORFOWLS** a red or black grouse

MOORHEN *noun* **MOORHENS** a small black water bird of the rail family, with a red beak

MOORING *noun* **MOORINGS** a place where a boat is moored

MOORLAND *noun* **MOORLANDS** a stretch of moor

MOOSE *noun* **MOOSE** a large deer with flat, rounded antlers

MOOT *verb* **MOOTS, MOOTING, MOOTED** to suggest; to bring something up for discussion □ *adj* open to argument; debatable □ *noun* **MOOTS** in Anglo-Saxon England: a court or administrative assembly

MOP *noun* **MOPS** a tool for washing or wiping floors, consisting of a large sponge or a set of thick threads fixed on to the end of a long handle ❑ verb **MOPS, MOPPING, MOPPED** to wash or wipe (eg a floor) with a mop

MOPE verb **MOPES, MOPING, MOPED** to behave in a depressed, sulky or aimless way ❑ noun **MOPES** a habitually sulky or depressed person

MOPED noun **MOPEDS** a small-engined motorcycle (under 50cc), especially one that is started by using pedals

MOPER noun **MOPERS** someone who mopes

MOPEY adj **MOPIER, MOPIEST** mopy

MOPPER noun **MOPPERS** someone who washes (eg a floor) with a mop

MOPPET noun **MOPPETS** a term of affection used to a small child

MOPY adj **MOPIER, MOPIEST** inclined to mope; dull, listless or miserable

MOQUETTE noun **MOQUETTES** thick velvety material used to make carpets and upholstery

MOR noun **MORS** a layer of humus

MORAINAL adj of or relating to a moraine

MORAINE noun **MORAINES** an area covered by a jumbled accumulation of different-sized rock fragments that have been carried from their place of origin and deposited by a glacier or ice sheet

MORAINIC adj morainal

MORAL adj belonging or relating to the principles of good and evil, or right and wrong ❑ noun **MORALS** a principle or practical lesson that can be learned from a story or event

MORALE noun **MORALES** the level of confidence or optimism in a person or group; spirits

MORALISE verb **MORALISES, MORALISING, MORALISED** to moralize

MORALISER noun **MORALISERS** a moralizer

MORALISM noun **MORALISMS** a moral saying

MORALIST noun **MORALISTS** someone who lives according to strict moral principles

MORALITY noun **MORALITIES** the quality of being moral

MORALIZE verb **MORALIZES, MORALIZING, MORALIZED** to write or speak, especially critically, about moral standards

MORALIZER noun **MORALIZERS** someone who moralizes

MORALLY adverb in a moral manner; in respect of morals

MORASS noun **MORASSES** an area of marshy or swampy ground

MORAY noun **MORAYS** a sharp-toothed eel of warm coastal waters

MORBID adj **MORBIDER, MORBIDEST** displaying an unhealthy interest in unpleasant things, especially death

MORBIDITY noun **MORBIDITIES** a morbid state

MORBIDLY adverb in a morbid way

MORDANCY noun **MORDANCIES** the quality of being sharply sarcastic or critical

MORDANT adj sharply sarcastic or critical; biting ❑ noun **MORDANTS** a chemical compound, usually a metallic oxide or salt, that is used to fix colour on textiles, etc that cannot be dyed directly

MORDANTLY adverb in a mordant way

MORDENT noun **MORDENTS** a grace note in which the principal note and the note above or below it are played before the note itself

MORE adj greater; additional ❑ adverb used to form the comparative form of many adjectives and most adverbs, especially those of two or more syllables ❑ pronoun a greater, or additional, number or quantity of people or things

MOREISH adj said especially of a food: so tasty, delicious, etc that one wants to keep eating more of it

MOREL noun **MORELS** an edible fungus whose fruiting body has a pale stalk and a brownish egg-shaped head covered with a network of ridges

MORELLO noun **MORELLOS** a bitter-tasting, dark-red cherry

MORENDO adverb dying away, in speed and tone

MOREOVER adverb also; besides; and what is more important

MORES plural noun social customs that reflect the basic moral and social values of a particular society

MORGUE noun **MORGUES** a mortuary; any gloomy or depressing place

MORIBUND adj dying; near the end of existence

MORISH adj moreish

MORN noun **MORNS** morning

MORNAY adj in cookery: served in a cheese sauce

MORNING noun **MORNINGS** the part of the day from sunrise to midday, or from midnight to midday

MORNINGS adverb in the morning, especially on a regular basis

MOROCCO noun **MOROCCOS** a type of soft fine goatskin leather

MORON noun **MORONS** a very stupid person

MORONIC adj stupid; foolish

MOROSE adj **MOROSER, MOROSEST** silently gloomy or bad-tempered

MOROSELY adverb in a morose way

MORPHEME noun **MORPHEMES** any of the grammatically or lexically meaningful units forming or underlying a word, not divisible themselves into smaller meaningful units, eg the morphemes *out*, *go* and *ing* forming the word, or 'lexeme', *outgoing*, or the 'plural' morpheme seen in the inflections in *cars*, *buses*, *children*, etc

MORPHEMIC adj relating to morphemes

MORPHINE noun **MORPHINES** a highly-addictive, narcotic drug obtained from opium, used medicinally as an analgesic to relieve severe and persistent pain, and as a sedative to induce sleep

MORPHING noun **MORPHINGS** the use of computer graphics to blend one screen image into another, eg to transform or manipulate an actor's body

MORSEL noun **MORSELS** a small piece of something, especially of food

MORTAL adj said especially of human beings: certain to die at some future time ❑ noun **MORTALS** a mortal being, especially a human being

MORTALITY noun **MORTALITIES** the state of being mortal

MORTALLY adverb in such a way that death results

MORTAR noun **MORTARS** a mixture of sand, water and cement or lime, used to bond bricks or stones ❑ verb **MORTARS,**

MORTARING, MORTARED to fix something (especially bricks) in place with mortar

MORTGAGE noun **MORTGAGES** a legal agreement by which a building society or bank, etc grants a client a loan for the purpose of buying property, ownership of the property being held by the building society, bank, etc until the loan is repaid □ verb **MORTGAGES, MORTGAGING, MORTGAGED** to give ownership of (property) as security for a loan

MORTGAGEE noun **MORTGAGEES** a bank or building society, etc that grants a mortgage

MORTGAGER noun **MORTGAGERS** a mortgagor

MORTGAGOR noun **MORTGAGORS** someone who takes out a mortgage

MORTICE noun **MORTICES** a mortise □ verb **MORTICES, MORTICING, MORTICED** to mortise

MORTICIAN noun **MORTICIANS** an undertaker

MORTIFY verb **MORTIFIES, MORTIFYING, MORTIFIED** to make someone feel humiliated or ashamed

MORTIFYING adj humiliating; shaming □ noun **MORTIFYINGS** the action of making someone feel humiliated or ashamed

MORTISE noun **MORTISES** a hole cut in a piece of wood, into which a tenon on another piece of wood fits to form a mortise and tenon joint □ verb **MORTISES, MORTISING, MORTISED** to cut a mortise in (a piece of wood, etc)

MORTISER noun **MORTISERS** someone who cuts a mortise in a piece of wood, etc

MORTUARY noun **MORTUARIES** a building or room in which dead bodies are laid out for identification or kept until they are buried or cremated □ adj relating to or connected with death, or the burial of the dead

MOSAIC noun **MOSAICS** a design or piece of work formed by fitting together lots of small pieces of coloured stone, glass, etc

MOSAICIST noun **MOSAICISTS** someone who is skilled in mosaic work

MOSCHATEL noun **MOSCHATELS** a small plant with pale-green flowers and a musky smell

MOSEY verb **MOSEYS, MOSEYING, MOSEYED** to walk in a leisurely way; to saunter or amble

MOSHING noun **MOSHINGS** a style of energetic sinuous dancing done in a crowded space especially to heavy metal or thrash music

MOSQUE noun **MOSQUES** a Muslim place of worship

MOSQUITO noun **MOSQUITOS, MOSQUITOES** any of numerous species of small two-winged insects with thin, feathery antennae, long legs and slender bodies, the females of which have piercing mouthparts for sucking the blood of birds and mammals

MOSS noun **MOSSES** the common name for a type of small spore-bearing plant without a vascular system, typically found growing in dense, spreading clusters in moist shady habitats

MOSSIE noun **MOSSIES** a mosquito

MOSSINESS noun **MOSSINESSES** the state of being mossy

MOSSY adj **MOSSIER, MOSSIEST** consisting of, covered with or like, moss

MOST adj the greatest number, amount, etc □ adverb used to form the superlative of many adjectives and most adverbs, especially those of more than two syllables □ pronoun the greatest number or quantity, or the majority of people or things

MOSTLY adverb mainly; almost completely

MOT noun **MOTS** a pithy or witty saying

MOTE noun **MOTES** a speck, especially a speck of dust

MOTEL noun **MOTELS** a hotel with extensive parking facilities, situated near a main road and intended for overnight stops by motorists

MOTET noun **MOTETS** a short piece of sacred music for several voices

MOTH noun **MOTHS** the common name for one of many winged insects belonging to the same order as butterflies but generally duller in colour and night-flying, typically having a proboscis and four broad wings which fold down when resting

MOTHBALL noun **MOTHBALLS** a small ball of camphor or naphthalene that is hung in wardrobes, etc to keep away the clothes moth □ verb **MOTHBALLS, MOTHBALLING, MOTHBALLED** to postpone work on something (eg a project), or to lay it aside, especially for an indefinitely long time

MOTHER noun **MOTHERS** a female parent □ verb **MOTHERS, MOTHERING, MOTHERED** to give birth to or give rise to someone or something

MOTHERLY adj like or characteristic of a mother

MOTHPROOF adj said of cloth: treated with chemicals which resist attack by the clothes moth □ verb **MOTHPROOFS, MOTHPROOFING, MOTHPROOFED** to treat (fabric) in this way

MOTIF noun **MOTIFS** on clothing, etc: a single design or symbol

MOTILE adj said of a living organism, such as spermatozoa, or a structure: capable of independent spontaneous movement

MOTILITY noun **MOTILITIES** the ability to make independent spontaneous movement

MOTION noun **MOTIONS** the act, state, process or manner of moving; a gesture or action □ verb **MOTIONS, MOTIONING, MOTIONED** to give a signal or direction

MOTIVATE verb **MOTIVATES, MOTIVATING, MOTIVATED** to be the motive of something or someone

MOTIVE noun **MOTIVES** a reason for, or underlying cause of, action of a certain kind □ adj causing motion

MOTLEY adj **MOTLIER, MOTLEYER, MOTLIEST, MOTLEYEST** made up of many different kinds □ noun **MOTLEYS** a jester's multicoloured costume

MOTOCROSS noun **MOTOCROSSES** a form of motorcycle racing in which specially-adapted motorcycles compete across rough terrain

MOTOR noun **MOTORS** an engine, especially the internal-combustion engine of a vehicle or machine □ adj said of a nerve: transmitting impulses from the central nervous system to a muscle or gland □ verb **MOTORS, MOTORING, MOTORED** to travel by

For longer words, see *The Chambers Dictionary*

motor vehicle, especially by private car

MOTORBIKE noun **MOTORBIKES** a motorcycle

MOTORCADE noun **MOTORCADES** a procession of cars carrying VIPs, especially political figures

MOTORISE verb **MOTORISES, MOTORISING, MOTORISED** to motorize

MOTORIST noun **MOTORISTS** someone who drives a car

MOTORIZE verb **MOTORIZES, MOTORIZING, MOTORIZED** to fit a motor or motors to something

MOTORWAY noun **MOTORWAYS** a major road for fast-moving traffic, especially one with three lanes per carriageway and limited access and exit points

MOTTLE verb **MOTTLES, MOTTLING, MOTTLED** to give something a blotched, streaked or variegated appearance, surface, etc

MOTTLED adj with a pattern of different coloured blotches or streaks

MOTTLING noun **MOTTLINGS** a mottled appearance

MOTTO noun **MOTTOES** a phrase adopted by a person, family, etc as a principle of behaviour

MOTZA noun **MOTZAS** an Australian word meaning a large amount of money

MOU noun **MOUS** a Scots word for a mouth

MOUE noun **MOUES** a grimace or pout expressing discontentment

MOULD noun **MOULDS** a hollow, shaped container into which a liquid substance is poured so that it takes on the container's shape when it cools and sets □ verb **MOULDS, MOULDING, MOULDED** to shape something in or using a mould

MOULDABLE adverb that can be moulded

MOULDER verb **MOULDERS, MOULDERING, MOULDERED** to become gradually rotten with age; to decay

MOULDING noun **MOULDINGS** a shaped, decorative strip, especially one made of wood or plaster

MOULDY adj **MOULDIER, MOULDIEST** covered with mould (a woolly growth of fungi)

MOULT verb **MOULTS, MOULTING, MOULTED** said of an animal: to shed feathers, hair or skin to make way for a new growth □ noun **MOULTS** the act or process of moulting

MOUND noun **MOUNDS** any small hill, or bank of earth or rock, either natural or man-made □ verb **MOUNDS, MOUNDING, MOUNDED** to form or pile up into a mound

MOUNT verb **MOUNTS, MOUNTING, MOUNTED** to go up □ noun **MOUNTS** a support or backing on which something is placed for display or use, etc

MOUNTAIN noun **MOUNTAINS** a very high, steep hill, often one of bare rock

MOUNTED adj said of a person, etc: on horseback

MOURN verb **MOURNS, MOURNING, MOURNED** to be in mourning or wear mourning

MOURNER noun **MOURNERS** someone who mourns

MOURNFUL adj feeling or expressing grief

MOURNING noun **MOURNINGS** grief felt or shown over a death

MOUSE noun **MICE** any of various small rodents found worldwide, with a grey or brown coat, pointed muzzle, sharp teeth and a long naked tail □ verb **MOUSES, MOUSING, MOUSED** said of an animal, especially a cat: to hunt mice

MOUSER noun **MOUSERS** a cat that catches mice, or is kept especially for catching mice

MOUSEY adj **MOUSIER, MOUSIEST** mousy

MOUSING noun **MOUSINGS** the action of hunting mice

MOUSSAKA noun **MOUSSAKAS** a dish made with minced meat, aubergines, onions, tomatoes, etc, covered with a cheese sauce and baked, traditionally eaten in Greece, Turkey and the Balkans

MOUSSE noun **MOUSSES** a dessert made from a whipped mixture of cream, eggs and flavouring, eaten cold

MOUSTACHE noun **MOUSTACHES** unshaved hair growing across the top of the upper lip

MOUSY adj **MOUSIER, MOUSIEST** like a mouse, or belonging or relating to a mouse

MOUTH noun **MOUTHS** in humans, animals, etc: an opening in the head through which food is taken in and speech or sounds emitted, and containing the teeth, gums, tongue, etc □ verb **MOUTHS, MOUTHING, MOUTHED** to form (words) without actually speaking

MOUTHED adj using a specified kind of language; having a specified kind of mouth

MOUTHFUL noun **MOUTHFULS** as much food or drink as fills the mouth or is in one's mouth

MOUTHWASH noun **MOUTHWASHES** an antiseptic liquid used for gargling or for rinsing or freshening the mouth

MOVABLE adj not fixed in one place; portable

MOVE verb **MOVES, MOVING, MOVED** to change position or make something change position or go from one place to another □ noun **MOVES** an act of moving the body; a movement

MOVEABLE adj movable

MOVEMENT noun **MOVEMENTS** a process of changing position or going from one point to another

MOVER noun **MOVERS** someone or something that moves

MOVIE noun **MOVIES** a cinema film

MOVIEGOER noun **MOVIEGOERS** someone who regularly attends the cinema

MOVING adj having an effect on the emotions; touching; stirring

MOVINGLY adverb in a moving way

MOW verb **MOWS, MOWING, MOWED, MOWN** to cut (grass, a lawn, crop, etc) by hand or with a machine

MOWER noun **MOWERS** something or someone that mows, especially a machine with revolving blades for mowing grass

MOXA noun **MOXAS** a pithy material (eg sunflower pith or cotton wool), formed into a cone or stick and used for applying heat in oriental medicine, acupuncture, etc

MOY noun **MOYS** a Shakespearean word for a coin or a measure

MOZ noun **MOZZES** an Australian word meaning a type of curse

MOZZIE noun **MOZZIES** a mosquito

MU *noun* **MUS** the twelfth letter of the Greek alphabet

MUCH *adj* **MORE, MOST** a great quantity of □ *adverb* to a great extent

MUCHNESS *noun* **MUCHNESSES** greatness

MUCILAGE *noun* **MUCILAGES** a type of gum-like substance that becomes viscous and slimy when added to water, present in or secreted by various plants

MUCK *noun* **MUCKS** dirt, especially wet or clinging dirt □ *verb* **MUCKS, MUCKING, MUCKED** to treat (soil) with manure

MUCKER *noun* **MUCKERS** a best friend, mate or sidekick

MUCKHEAP *noun* **MUCKHEAPS** a pile of muck; a dunghill

MUCKLE *noun* **MUCKLES** a mickle

MUCKY *adj* **MUCKIER, MUCKIEST** very dirty

MUCOSA *noun* **MUCOSAE** the technical term for mucous membrane

MUCOSITY *noun* **MUCOSITIES** sliminess

MUCOUS *adj* consisting of, like or producing mucus

MUCUS *noun* **MUCUSES** the thick slimy substance that protects and lubricates the surface of mucous membranes and traps bacteria and dust particles

MUD *noun* **MUDS** soft, wet earth □ *verb* **MUDS, MUDDING, MUDDED** to bury or hide in mud

MUDBATH *noun* **MUDBATHS** a medical treatment in which the body is covered in mud, especially hot mud, rich in minerals

MUDDIED past form of **muddy**

MUDDIER see under **muddy**

MUDDIES a form of **muddy**

MUDDIEST see under **muddy**

MUDDILY *adverb* in a muddy way

MUDDINESS *noun* **MUDDINESSES** the state of being muddy

MUDDLE *verb* **MUDDLES, MUDDLING, MUDDLED** to confuse (different things) in the mind □ *noun* **MUDDLES** a state of disorder or mental confusion

MUDDLED *adj* confused; disordered

MUDDLER *noun* **MUDDLERS** someone who muddles

MUDDY *adj* **MUDDIER, MUDDIEST** covered with or containing mud □ *verb* **MUDDIES, MUDDYING, MUDDIED** to make something muddy

MUDFLAP *noun* **MUDFLAPS** a flap of rubber, etc fixed behind the wheel of a vehicle to prevent mud, etc being thrown up behind

MUDFLAT *noun* **MUDFLATS** a relatively flat area of land near an estuary, etc formed by accumulated silt or mud brought in by the tide, and which is covered by a shallow layer of water at high tide

MUDGUARD *noun* **MUDGUARDS** a curved, metal guard over the upper half of the wheel of a bicycle or motorcycle to keep rain or mud from splashing up

MUDPACK *noun* **MUDPACKS** a thick paste that is applied to the face as a skin cleanser and toner

MUDPUPPY *noun* **MUDPUPPIES** a brownish-grey N American amphibian with feathery gills, that spends its entire life in water

MUDSTONE *noun* **MUDSTONES** a fine-grained brittle sedimentary rock that is a hardened consolidated form of mud, formed of roughly equal amounts of clay and silt

MUESLI *noun* **MUESLIS** a mixture of crushed grain, nuts and dried fruit, eaten with milk, especially for breakfast

MUEZZIN *noun* **MUEZZINS** the Muslim official who calls worshippers to prayer, usually from a minaret

MUFF *verb* **MUFFS, MUFFING, MUFFED** in sport: to miss (a catch) □ *noun* **MUFFS** a failure or bungle, especially a failure to hold a catch

MUFFIN *noun* **MUFFINS** a small round flat breadlike cake, usually eaten toasted or hot with butter

MUFFLE *verb* **MUFFLES, MUFFLING, MUFFLED** to make something quieter; to suppress (sound)

MUFFLED *adj* of a sound: made quieter; suppressed

MUFFLER *noun* **MUFFLERS** a thick scarf

MUFTI *noun* **MUFTIS** civilian clothes when worn by people who usually wear a uniform

MUG *noun* **MUGS** a drinking-vessel with a handle, used without a saucer □ *verb* **MUGS, MUGGING, MUGGED** to attack and rob

someone violently or under threat of violence

MUGFUL *noun* **MUGFULS** the amount a mug will hold

MUGGER *noun* **MUGGERS** a person who attacks and robs someone violently or under threat of violence

MUGGINESS *noun* **MUGGINESSES** the state of being muggy

MUGGING *noun* **MUGGINGS** assault and robbery

MUGGINS *noun* **MUGGINSES** a foolish person, used especially to describe oneself when one has been taken advantage of by others

MUGGY *adj* **MUGGIER, MUGGIEST** said of the weather: unpleasantly warm and damp; close

MUGSHOT *noun* **MUGSHOTS** a photograph of a criminal's face, taken for police records

MUGWUMP *noun* **MUGWUMPS** someone who is politically aloof

MUJAHEDIN *plural noun* in Afghanistan, Iran and Pakistan: Muslim fundamentalist guerillas who united to wage a jihad to defeat the Soviet invaders of Afghanistan after the 1979 invasion

MULBERRY *noun* **MULBERRIES** a deciduous tree of temperate regions that produces small edible purple berries □ *adj* belonging or relating to the tree or its berries

MULCH *noun* **MULCHES** straw, compost, shredded bark, etc laid on the soil around plants to retain moisture and prevent the growth of weeds □ *verb* **MULCHES, MULCHING, MULCHED** to cover (soil, etc) with mulch

MULCT *noun* **MULCTS** a fine or penalty □ *verb* **MULCTS, MULCTING, MULCTED** to fine someone

MULE *noun* **MULES** the offspring of a male donkey and a female horse, used as a working animal in many countries

MULETEER *noun* **MULETEERS** someone whose job is to drive mules

MULISH *adj* stubborn; obstinate

MULISHLY *adverb* in a mulish way

MULL ¹ *verb* **MULLS, MULLING, MULLED** to spice, sweeten and warm (wine or beer)

MULL ² *noun* **MULLS** a headland or promontory

MULLAH *noun* **MULLAHS** a

Muslim scholar and adviser in Islamic religion and sacred law
MULLED *adj* of wine or beer: spiced, sweetened and warmed
MULLEIN *noun* **MULLEINS** any of several tall stiff yellow-flowered, woolly plants of the Mediterranean area, especially Aaron's rod
MULLET *noun* **MULLETS** any of a family of thick-bodied edible marine fish, eg the red mullet
MULLION *noun* **MULLIONS** a vertical bar or post separating the panes or casements of a window
MULLIONED *adj* said of a window: having mullions
MULLOCK *noun* **MULLOCKS** rubbish, especially mining refuse
MULTIFORM *adj* having many different forms or shapes
MULTIGYM *noun* **MULTIGYMS** an apparatus consisting of an arrangement of weights and levers, designed for exercising and toning up all the muscles of the body
MULTIPARA *noun* **MULTIPARAS** a woman who has given birth for the second or subsequent time, or is about to do so
MULTIPLE *adj* having, involving or affecting many parts ◻ *noun* **MULTIPLES** a number or expression for which a given number or expression is a factor, eg 24 is a multiple of 12
MULTIPLEX *noun* **MULTIPLEXES** a large cinema building divided into several smaller cinemas ◻ *adj* having very many parts; manifold; complex ◻ *verb* **MULTIPLEXES, MULTIPLEXING, MULTIPLEXED** to incorporate or transmit (two or more signals) in a multiplex telecommunications system
MULTIPLY *verb* **MULTIPLIES, MULTIPLYING, MULTIPLIED** to add (one number or amount) to itself a specified number of times; to add (one number or amount) to itself as many times as is indicated by a second number, using the sign ×
MULTITUDE *noun* **MULTITUDES** a great number
MUM [1] *noun* **MUMS** a mother
MUM [2] *adj* silent; not speaking ◻ *verb* **MUMS, MUMMING, MUMMED** to act in a mime
MUMBLE *verb* **MUMBLES, MUMBLING, MUMBLED** to speak or say something unclearly, especially with the mouth partly closed ◻ *noun* **MUMBLES** the

sound of unclear, muffled or hushed speech
MUMBLER *noun* **MUMBLERS** someone who mumbles
MUMBLING *noun* **MUMBLINGS** the action of speaking or saying something unclearly, especially with the mouth partly closed ◻ *adj* that mumbles
MUMMER *noun* **MUMMERS** an actor in a traditional mimed folk play, usually performed at Christmas
MUMMERY *noun* **MUMMERIES** a performance by a group of mummers
MUMMIFIED *adj* said of a body, tissue, etc: dried up; shrivelled
MUMMIFY *verb* **MUMMIFIES, MUMMIFYING, MUMMIFIED** to preserve (a corpse) as a mummy
MUMMING *noun* **MUMMINGS** the action of performing in a traditional mimed folk play, usually at Christmas
MUMMY [1] *noun* **MUMMIES** a child's word for mother
MUMMY [2] *noun* **MUMMIES** especially in ancient Egypt: a human or animal corpse (with the internal organs removed), preserved with embalming spices and bandaged, in preparation for burial
MUMPS *singular noun* an infectious viral disease, mainly affecting children, that causes fever, headache and painful swelling of the salivary glands on one or both sides of the cheeks and under the jaw, and in older males, swelling and inflammation of one or both testes
MUMSY *adj* **MUMSIER, MUMSIEST** homely; comfy

> **MUN** *auxiliary verb* a dialect word for *must*

MUNCH *verb* **MUNCHES, MUNCHING, MUNCHED** to chew with a steady movement of the jaws, especially noisily
MUNCHER *noun* **MUNCHERS** someone who munches
MUNDANE *adj* **MUNDANER, MUNDANEST** ordinary; dull; everyday
MUNDANELY *adverb* in a mundane way
MUNDANITY *noun* **MUNDANITIES** the state of being mundane
MUNICIPAL *adj* belonging or relating to, or controlled by, the

local government of a town or region
MUNIMENTS *plural noun* official papers that prove ownership, especially title deeds to property
MUNITIONS *plural noun* military equipment, especially ammunition and weapons
MUNTIN *noun* **MUNTINS** a vertical framing piece that separates the panels of a door
MUNTING *noun* **MUNTINGS** a muntin
MUNTJAC *noun* **MUNTJACS** a small deer native to India and SE Asia whose face has a V-shaped ridge with the arms of the 'V' continuing as projecting, bony columns, the ends of which bear short antlers in the male
MUNTJAK *noun* **MUNTJAKS** a muntjac
MUON *noun* **MUONS** an elementary particle that behaves like a heavy electron, but decays to form an electron and neutrino
MUONIC *adj* of or relating to a muon
MURAL *noun* **MURALS** a painting that is painted directly on to a wall ◻ *adj* belonging or relating to, on or attached to, a wall or walls
MURALIST *noun* **MURALISTS** someone who paints or designs murals
MURDER *noun* **MURDERS** the act of unlawfully and intentionally killing a person ◻ *verb* **MURDERS, MURDERING, MURDERED** to kill someone unlawfully and intentionally
MURDERER *noun* **MURDERERS** a person who murders, or is guilty of murder
MURDERESS *noun* **MURDERESSES** a female who murders, or is guilty of murder
MURDEROUS *adj* said of a person, weapon, etc: intending, intended for, or capable of, causing or committing murder
MURINE *adj* mouselike
MURK *noun* **MURKS** darkness; gloom
MURKILY *adverb* in a murky way
MURKINESS *noun* **MURKINESSES** the state of being murky
MURKY *adj* **MURKIER, MURKIEST** dark; gloomy
MURMUR *noun* **MURMURS** a quiet, continuous sound, eg of running water or low voices ◻ *verb* **MURMURS, MURMURING,**

MURMURED to speak (words) softly and indistinctly

MURMURING noun **MURMURINGS** the action of speaking words softly and indistinctly □ adj that murmurs

MURMUROUS adj characterized by murmuring

MURRAIN noun **MURRAINS** any infectious cattle disease, especially foot-and-mouth disease

MUS plural of **mu**

MUSCADEL noun **MUSCADELS** muscatel

MUSCAT noun **MUSCATS** muscatel

MUSCATEL noun **MUSCATELS** a rich sweet white wine made from muscat grapes

MUSCLE noun **MUSCLES** an animal tissue composed of bundles of fibres that are capable of contracting to produce movement of part of the body □ verb **MUSCLES, MUSCLING, MUSCLED** to force one's way, thrust

MUSCLEMAN noun **MUSCLEMEN** a man with very big muscles, especially one employed to intimidate people

MUSCLY adj **MUSCLIER, MUSCLIEST** muscular

MUSCOVADO noun **MUSCOVADOS** sugar in its unrefined state after evaporating sugar-cane juice and draining off the molasses

MUSCOVITE noun **MUSCOVITES** a colourless silvery-grey, or pale brown, heat-resistant mineral of the mica group, used as an electrical and heat insulator, as a filler in paint, in wallpaper manufacture and roofing materials, etc

MUSCULAR adj having well-developed muscles; strong; brawny

MUSE verb **MUSES, MUSING, MUSED** to reflect or ponder silently □ noun **MUSES** the act of musing

MUSEUM noun **MUSEUMS** a place where objects of artistic, scientific or historical interest are displayed to the public, preserved and studied

MUSH [1] noun **MUSHES** a soft half-liquid mass of anything

MUSH [2] exclamation used especially to a team of dogs: go on! go faster! □ verb **MUSHES,**

MUSHING, MUSHED to travel on a sledge pulled by dogs

MUSHROOM noun **MUSHROOMS** any of various fungi that produce a fast-growing fruiting body consisting of a short white stem supporting a pale fleshy umbrella-shaped cap with numerous brown or pinkish spore-bearing gills on the underside □ verb

MUSHROOMS, MUSHROOMING, MUSHROOMED to develop or increase with alarming speed

MUSHY adj **MUSHIER, MUSHIEST** in a soft half-liquid state; consisting of or like mush

MUSIC noun **MUSICS** the art of making sound in a rhythmically organized, harmonious form, either sung or produced with instruments, and usually communicating some idea or emotion

MUSICAL adj consisting of, involving, relating to or producing music □ noun **MUSICALS** a play or film that features singing and dancing

MUSICALLY adverb in a musical way

MUSICIAN noun **MUSICIANS** someone who is skilled in music, especially in performing or composing it

MUSING adj thoughtful; reflective

MUSINGLY adverb in a musing way

MUSK noun **MUSKS** a strong-smelling substance much used in perfumes, secreted by the glands of various animals, especially the male musk deer

MUSKET noun **MUSKETS** an early rifle-like gun that was loaded through the barrel and fired from the shoulder, used by soldiers between the 16c and 19c

MUSKETEER noun **MUSKETEERS** a soldier armed with a musket

MUSKETRY noun **MUSKETRIES** the use of, or skill in using, muskets

MUSKILY adverb in a musky way

MUSKINESS noun **MUSKINESSES** the state of being musky

MUSKRAT noun **MUSKRATS** a large, N American water rodent, which produces a musky smell

MUSKY adj **MUSKIER, MUSKIEST** containing, or like the smell of, musk

MUSLIN noun **MUSLINS** a fine cotton cloth with a gauze-like appearance

MUSO noun **MUSOS** a pop or rock musician who concentrates too much on technique

MUSQUASH noun **MUSQUASHES** a muskrat

MUSS verb **MUSSES, MUSSING, MUSSED** to make something (especially clothes or hair) untidy; to mess up or disarrange □ noun **MUSSES** disorder or confusion; mess

MUSSEL noun **MUSSELS** a marine bivalve mollusc, especially the common or edible mussel, that has a bluish-black shell and uses a mass of tough threads to anchor itself to rocks, etc

MUSSY adj **MUSSIER, MUSSIEST** disordered

MUST auxiliary verb used to express necessity □ noun **MUSTS** a necessity; something essential

MUSTACHE noun **MUSTACHES** a moustache

MUSTACHIO noun **MUSTACHIOS** an elaborately curled moustache

MUSTANG noun **MUSTANGS** a small wild or half-wild horse native to the plains of the western US

MUSTARD noun **MUSTARDS** an annual plant native to Europe and W Asia, with bright yellow flowers; a hot-tasting paste used as a condiment, made from powdered or crushed seeds of the mustard plant mixed with water or vinegar □ adj having a light yellow or brown colour

MUSTER verb **MUSTERS, MUSTERING, MUSTERED** said especially of soldiers: to gather together for duty or inspection, etc □ noun **MUSTERS** any assembly or gathering, especially of troops for duty or inspection

MUSTH noun **MUSTHS** a dangerous frenzied state in certain male animals, especially bull elephants in the breeding season

MUSTILY adverb in a musty way

MUSTINESS noun **MUSTINESSES** the state of being musty

MUSTY adj **MUSTIER, MUSTIEST** mouldy or damp

MUTABLE adj subject to or able to change; variable

MUTABLY adverb in a mutable way

MUTAGEN noun **MUTAGENS** a chemical or physical agent, such as X-ray or ultraviolet radiation, that induces or increases the frequency of mutations in living organisms, either by altering the DNA of the genes, or by damaging the chromosomes

MUTAGENIC adj causing mutation

MUTANT noun **MUTANTS** a living organism or cell that carries a specific mutation of a gene which usually causes it to differ from previous generations in one particular characteristic ❑ adj said of an organism or cell: carrying or resulting from a mutation

MUTATE verb **MUTATES, MUTATING, MUTATED** to undergo or cause to undergo mutation

MUTATION noun **MUTATIONS** in a living organism: a change in the structure of a single gene, the arrangement of genes on a chromosome or the number of chromosomes, which may result in a change in the appearance or behaviour of the organism

MUTE adj **MUTER, MUTEST** said of a person: physically or psychologically unable to speak; dumb ❑ noun **MUTES** someone who is physically unable to speak, eg as a result of deafness since birth or brain damage ❑ verb **MUTES, MUTING, MUTED** to soften or deaden the sound of (a musical instrument)

MUTED adj said of sound or colour: not loud or harsh; soft

MUTELY adverb in a mute way

MUTENESS noun **MUTENESSES** the state of being mute

MUTI noun **MUTIS** traditional medicine, especially that associated with witchcraft or witch doctors

MUTILATE verb **MUTILATES, MUTILATING, MUTILATED** to cause severe injury to (a person or animal), especially by removing a limb or organ

MUTILATOR noun **MUTILATORS** someone who mutilates

MUTINEER noun **MUTINEERS** a person who mutinies or takes part in a mutiny

MUTINOUS adj said of a person, soldier, crew, etc: having mutinied or likely to mutiny

MUTINY noun **MUTINIES** rebellion, or an act of rebellion, against established authority, especially in the armed services ❑ verb **MUTINIES, MUTINYING, MUTINIED** to engage in mutiny

MUTISM noun **MUTISMS** inability or refusal to speak

MUTT noun **MUTTS** a dog, especially a mongrel

MUTTER verb **MUTTERS, MUTTERING, MUTTERED** to utter (words) in a quiet, barely audible or indistinct voice ❑ noun **MUTTERS** a soft, barely audible or indistinct tone of voice

MUTTERER noun **MUTTERERS** someone who mutters

MUTTERING noun **MUTTERINGS** the action of uttering words in a quiet, barely audible or indistinct voice ❑ adj that mutters

MUTTON noun **MUTTONS** the flesh of an adult sheep, used as food

MUTUAL adj felt by each of two or more people about the other or others; reciprocal

MUTUALISM noun **MUTUALISMS** a relationship between two organisms of different species, that is beneficial to both of them

MUTUALITY noun **MUTUALITIES** the quality or condition of being mutual; reciprocity

MUTUALLY adverb reciprocally

MUX verb **MUXES, MUXING, MUXED** a US and dialect word meaning to spoil, botch ❑ noun **MUXES** a mess

MUZZILY adverb in a muzzy way

MUZZINESS noun **MUZZINESSES** the state of being muzzy

MUZZLE noun **MUZZLES** the projecting jaws and nose of an animal, eg a dog; an arrangement of straps fitted round an animal's jaws to prevent it biting ❑ verb **MUZZLES, MUZZLING, MUZZLED** to put a muzzle on (eg a dog)

MUZZY adj **MUZZIER, MUZZIEST** not thinking clearly; confused

MY adj belonging or relating to me ❑ exclamation expressing surprise or amazement

MYALGIA noun **MYALGIAS** pain in the muscles or a muscle

MYALGIC adj affected with myalgia

MYCELIAL adj characterized by mycelium

MYCELIUM noun **MYCELIA** in multicellular fungi: a mass or network of threadlike filaments or hyphae formed when the non-reproductive tissues are growing

MYCOLOGIC adj relating to mycology

MYCOLOGY noun **MYCOLOGIES** the study of fungi

MYCOSIS noun **MYCOSES** any

disease that is due to the growth of a fungus

MYCOTIC adj characterized by mycosis

MYCOTOXIN noun **MYCOTOXINS** any poisonous substance produced by a fungus

MYELIN noun **MYELINS** a soft white substance that forms a thin insulating sheath around the axons of the nerve cells of vertebrates

MYELITIS noun **MYELITISES** inflammation of the spinal cord, which results in paralysis of the body below the affected region

MYELOMA noun **MYELOMAS** a tumour of the bone marrow, caused by the proliferation of malignant plasma cells

MYLONITE noun **MYLONITES** a dark fine-grained hard metamorphic rock, often banded or streaked and with a glassy appearance

MYNA noun **MYNAS** any of various large, SE Asian birds of the starling family, some of which can be taught to imitate human speech

MYNAH noun **MYNAHS** a myna

MYNHEER noun **MYNHEERS** a South African form of address for a man, used in place of sir or, when preceding a name, Mr

MYOFIBRIL noun **MYOFIBRILS** any of the minute filaments which together make up a single muscle fibre

MYOGLOBIN noun **MYOGLOBINS** a protein that stores oxygen in the muscles of vertebrates

MYOPIA noun **MYOPIAS** short-sightedness, in which parallel rays of light entering the eye are brought to a focus in front of the retina rather than on it, so that distant objects appear blurred

MYOPIC adj short-sighted

MYRIAD noun **MYRIADS** an exceedingly great number ❑ adj numberless; innumerable

MYRIAPOD noun **MYRIAPODS** a crawling, many-legged arthropod, eg the centipede or millipede

MYRMIDON noun **MYRMIDONS** a hired thug; a henchman

MYRRH noun **MYRRHS** any of various African and Asian trees and shrubs that produce a bitter, brown, aromatic resin

MYRTLE noun **MYRTLES** a S European evergreen shrub with pink or white flowers and dark blue, aromatic berries

MYSELF *pronoun* the reflexive form of *I* (used instead of *me* when the speaker or writer is the object of an action he or she performs)
MYSTERY *noun* **MYSTERIES** an event or phenomenon that cannot be, or has not been, explained
MYSTIC *noun* **MYSTICS** someone whose life is devoted to meditation or prayer in an attempt to achieve direct communication with and knowledge of God, regarded as the ultimate reality ▫ *adj* mystical
MYSTICAL *adj* relating to or involving truths about the nature of God and reality revealed only to those people with a spiritually-enlightened mind; esoteric
MYSTICISM *noun* **MYSTICISMS** the practice of gaining direct communication with God through prayer and meditation
MYSTIFY *verb* **MYSTIFIES,**

MYSTIFYING, MYSTIFIED to puzzle or bewilder
MYSTIFYING *adj* that mystifies
MYSTIQUE *noun* **MYSTIQUES** a mysterious, distinctive or compelling quality possessed by a person or thing
MYTH *noun* **MYTHS** an ancient story that deals with gods and heroes, especially one used to explain some natural phenomenon
MYTHICAL *adj* relating to myth
MYTHICISE *verb* **MYTHICISES, MYTHICISING, MYTHICISED** to mythicize
MYTHICIST *noun* **MYTHICISTS** someone who mythicizes
MYTHICIZE *verb* **MYTHICIZES, MYTHICIZING, MYTHICIZED** to make something or someone into a myth, or to explain it or them as a myth

MYTHOLOGY *noun* **MYTHOLOGIES** myths in general
MYXEDEMA *noun* **MYXEDEMAS** myxoedema
MYXOEDEMA *noun* **MYXOEDEMAS** a disease characterized by increased thickness and dryness of the skin, weight gain, hair loss, and reduction in mental and metabolic activity, often resulting from hypothyroidism
MYXOMA *noun* **MYXOMATA** a tumour composed of jellylike or mucous material that usually forms just beneath the skin
MYXOVIRUS *noun* **MYXOVIRUSES** any of a group of related viruses that cause influenza, mumps, etc

MZEE *noun* **MZEES** (in East Africa) an old person

NA *adverb* a Scots word for *no*

NAAN *noun* **NAANS** a nan
NAARTJE *noun* **NAARTJES** a nartjie
NAB *verb* **NABS, NABBING, NABBED** to catch someone in the act of doing wrong

NAB *noun* **NABS** a hilltop

NABBER *noun* **NABBERS** a thief
NABLA *noun* **NABLAS** in Cartesian co-ordinates: an inverted capital delta, representing the vector operator
NABOB *noun* **NABOBS** a wealthy influential person
NACELLE *noun* **NACELLES** the basket or gondola of a balloon or airship, etc
NACHO *noun* **NACHOS** a Mexican dish of tortilla chips topped with chillis, melted cheese, etc
NACRE *noun* **NACRES** a shellfish that produces mother-of-pearl
NACREOUS *adj* consisting of nacre
NADIR *noun* **NADIRS** the point on the celestial sphere directly beneath the observer and opposite to the zenith

NAE *adverb* a Scots form of *no*

NAEVOID *adj* like or typical of a naevus
NAEVUS *noun* **NAEVI** a birthmark or mole on the skin
NAFF *adj* stupid; foolish
NAG *verb* **NAGS, NAGGING, NAGGED** to scold someone constantly; to keep finding fault with them □ *noun* **NAGS** someone who nags
NAGANA *noun* **NAGANAS** a disease of horses and domestic cattle of central and southern Africa, caused by a trypanosome transmitted by the tsetse
NAGARI *noun* **NAGARIS** the group of alphabets to which devanagari belongs
NAGGER *noun* **NAGGERS** a person or problem that nags or annoys
NAGGING *adj* said of a problem or

anxiety: constantly worrying or causing concern
NAIAD *noun* **NAIADS, NAIADES** a river- or spring-nymph
NAÏF *adj* **NAÏFER, NAÏFEST** naive
NAIL *noun* **NAILS** a metal spike hammered into something, eg to join two objects together or to serve as a hook □ *verb* **NAILS, NAILING, NAILED** to fasten something with, or as if with, a nail or nails
NAILER *noun* **NAILERS** a maker of nails
NAILERY *noun* **NAILERIES** a place where nails are made
NAINSOOK *noun* **NAINSOOKS** a type of muslin
NAIRA *noun* **NAIRAS** the standard unit of currency in Nigeria
NAIVE *adj* **NAIVER, NAIVEST** simple, innocent or unsophisticated
NAIVELY *adverb* in a naive way
NAÏVETÉ *noun* **NAIVETÉS** naivety
NAIVETY *noun* **NAIVETIES** excessive trust or innocence
NAKED *adj* **NAKEDER, NAKEDEST** wearing no clothes; artless, blatant
NAKEDLY *adverb* in a naked way
NAKEDNESS *noun* **NAKEDNESSES** the state or condition of being naked

NAM *noun* **NAMS** distraint

NAMABLE *adj* that can be named
NAME *noun* **NAMES** a word or words by which an individual person, place or thing is identified and referred to □ *verb* **NAMES, NAMING, NAMED** to give a name to someone or something
NAMEABLE *adj* namable
NAMED *adj* mentioned by name
NAMELESS *adj* having no name
NAMELY *adverb* used to introduce an expansion or explanation of what has just been mentioned
NAMESAKE *noun* **NAMESAKES** someone with the same name as another person; someone named after another
NAMETAPE *noun* **NAMETAPES** a

piece of tape attached to a garment, etc marked with the owner's name
NAN *noun* **NANS** a slightly leavened bread, traditionally cooked in India and Pakistan, baked in a large round or teardrop shape
NANA *noun* **NANAS** an idiot, a fool
NANKEEN *noun* **NANKEENS** a buff-coloured cotton cloth
NANNY *noun* **NANNIES** a children's nurse □ *adj* said of institutions or the state, etc: protective to an intrusive extent □ *verb* **NANNIES, NANNYING, NANNIED** to over-protect or over-supervise
NANNYISH *adj* overprotective
NAP *noun* **NAPS** a short sleep □ *verb* **NAPS, NAPPING, NAPPED** to have a nap
NAPA *noun* **NAPAS** a soft leather made by a special tawing process, from sheepskin or goatskin
NAPALM *noun* **NAPALMS** an aluminium soap consisting of a mixture of various fatty acids, used as an incendiary agent in bombs and flame-throwers □ *verb* **NAPALMS, NAPALMING, NAPALMED** to attack or destroy something with napalm
NAPE *noun* **NAPES** the back of the neck
NAPHTHA *noun* **NAPHTHAS** any of several flammable liquids distilled from coal or petroleum under standardized temperature limits, used as solvents
NAPKIN *noun* **NAPKINS** a piece of cloth or paper for wiping one's mouth and fingers at mealtimes, and used to protect one's clothing
NAPLESS *adj* not napped, threadbare
NAPOLEON *noun* **NAPOLEONS** a twenty-franc gold coin issued by Napoleon I of France
NAPPA *noun* **NAPPAS** a napa
NAPPE *noun* **NAPPES** a large arch-shaped geological fold structure
NAPPED [1] *adj* said of fabric: with a nap, a woolly surface on cloth raised by a finishing process

NAPPPED² a form of **nap**

NAPPING a form of **nap**

NAPPY¹ *noun* **NAPPIES** a pad of disposable material, or a folded piece of towelling or other soft cloth, secured round a baby's bottom to absorb urine and faeces

NAPPY² *adj* **NAPPIER, NAPPIEST** said of beer: with a head; frothy

NARC *noun* **NARCS** a narcotics agent

NARCISSUS *noun* **NARCISSUSES, NARCISSI** a plant similar to the daffodil, which grows from a bulb and has white or yellow flowers, often heavily scented

NARCO *noun* **NARCOS** a narc

NARCOSIS *noun* **NARCOSES** drowsiness, unconsciousness, or other effects to the central nervous system produced by a narcotic

NARCOTIC *noun* **NARCOTICS** a drug causing numbness and drowsiness, and eventually unconsciousness, which deadens pain and produces a temporary sense of well-being, but which can be addictive □ *adj* belonging or relating to narcotics or the users of narcotics

NARCOTISE *verb* **NARCOTISES, NARCOTISING, NARCOTISED** to narcotize

NARCOTISM *noun* **NARCOTISMS** the influence of narcotics

NARCOTIZE *verb* **NARCOTIZES, NARCOTIZING, NARCOTIZED** to subject to the influence of a narcotic drug

NARD *noun* **NARDS** an Indian plant of the valerian family, from which spikenard (an aromatic oil) is obtained

NARDOO *noun* **NARDOOS** an Australian cloverlike fern

NARES *plural noun* the paired openings of the nasal cavity

NARGHILE *noun* **NARGHILES** a hookah

NARGILE *noun* **NARGILES** a narghile

NARGILEH *noun* **NARGILEHS** a narghile

NARIAL *adj* relating to the nostrils

NARINE *adj* narial

NARK *noun* **NARKS** a spy or informer working for the police □ *verb* **NARKS, NARKING, NARKED** to annoy

NARKED *adj* annoyed

NARKY *adj* **NARKIER, NARKIEST** irritable

NARRATE *verb* **NARRATES, NARRATING, NARRATED** to tell (a story); to relate

NARRATION *noun* **NARRATIONS** the act or process of telling something

NARRATIVE *noun* **NARRATIVES** an account of events □ *adj* telling a story; recounting events

NARRATOR *noun* **NARRATORS** someone who tells a story or narrative

NARRATORY *adj* like narrative; consisting of narrative

NARROW *adj* **NARROWER, NARROWEST** having little breadth, especially in comparison with length □ *noun* **NARROWS** a narrow part or place □ *verb* **NARROWS, NARROWING, NARROWED** to make or become narrow

NARROWLY *adverb* only just; barely

NARTHEX *noun* **NARTHEXES** a western portico of an early church or a basilica to which women and catachumens were admitted

NARTJIE *noun* **NARTJIES** a small sweet orange like a mandarin

NARWHAL *noun* **NARWHALS** an arctic whale, the male of which has a long spiral tusk

NARY *adverb* never; not

NASAL *adj* belonging or relating to the nose; pronounced through, or partly through, the nose □ *noun* **NASALS** a sound uttered through the nose

NASALISE *verb* **NASALISES, NASALISING, NASALISED** to nasalize

NASALITY *noun* **NASALITIES** the quality of being nasal

NASALIZE *verb* **NASALIZES, NASALIZING, NASALIZED** to pronounce or speak (a sound or words, etc) nasally

NASALLY *adverb* in a nasal way

NASCENCY *noun* **NASCENCIES** being brought into being

NASCENT *adj* in the process of coming into being; in the early stages of development

NASTILY *adverb* in a nasty way

NASTINESS *noun* **NASTINESSES** something that is nasty

NASTY *adj* **NASTIER, NASTIEST** unpleasant; disgusting □ *noun* **NASTIES** someone or something unpleasant, disgusting or offensive

NAT *noun* **NATS** a nationalist

NATAL *adj* connected with birth

NATALITY *noun* **NATALITIES** birth; birth-rate

NATATION *noun* **NATATIONS** swimming

NATATORY *adj* relating to swimming

NATCH *adverb* of course

NATES *plural noun* the buttocks

NATION *noun* **NATIONS** the people living in, belonging to, and together forming, a single state

NATIONAL *adj* belonging to a particular nation □ *noun* **NATIONALS** a citizen of a particular nation

NATIVE *adj* being or belonging to the place of one's upbringing □ *noun* **NATIVES** someone born in a certain place

NATIVELY *adverb* naturally; originally

NATIVISM *noun* **NATIVISMS** the belief that the mind possesses some ideas or forms of thought that are inborn

NATIVIST *noun* **NATIVISTS** someone who holds the doctrine of nativism

NATIVITY *noun* **NATIVITIES** birth, advent or origin

NATTER *verb* **NATTERS, NATTERING, NATTERED** to chat busily □ *noun* **NATTERS** an intensive chat

NATTILY *adverb* in a neat and smart manner

NATTINESS *noun* **NATTINESSES** the state of being natty

NATTY *adj* **NATTIER, NATTIEST** said of clothes: flashily smart

NATURAL *adj* normal; unsurprising □ *noun* **NATURALS** someone with an inborn feel for something

NATURALLY *adverb* of course; not surprisingly

NATURE *noun* **NATURES** the physical world not made by man; the forces that have formed it and control it

NATURISM *noun* **NATURISMS** nudism, regarded as a natural instinct

NATURIST *noun* **NATURISTS** a nudist

NAUGHT *noun* **NAUGHTS** nothing

NAUGHTILY *adverb* in a naughty way

NAUGHTY *adj* **NAUGHTIER, NAUGHTIEST** mischievous; disobedient □ *noun* **NAUGHTIES** an act of sexual intercourse

NAUPLIUS noun **NAUPLII** the larval form of many crustaceans, with one eye and three pairs of limbs

NAUSEA noun **NAUSEAS** a sensation that one is about to vomit, either by a reflex (eg irritation of stomach nerves) or conditioned (eg smell) stimulus

NAUSEATE verb **NAUSEATES, NAUSEATING, NAUSEATED** to make someone feel nausea

NAUSEATING adj offensively unpleasant

NAUSEOUS adj sickening; disgusting

NAUTICAL adj relating to ships, sailors or navigation

NAUTILUS noun **NAUTILUSES, NAUTILI** a sea creature related to the squid and octopus

NAVAL adj relating to a navy or to ships generally

NAVARIN noun **NAVARINS** a stew of lamb or mutton with root vegetables

NAVE noun **NAVES** the main central part of a church, where the congregation sits

NAVEL noun **NAVELS** in mammals: the small hollow or scar at the point where the umbilical cord was attached to the fetus

NAVELWORT noun **NAVELWORTS** a name given to various plants with round leaves

NAVICULAR adj boat-shaped □ noun **NAVICULARS** a small boat-shaped bone in the wrist or ankle, or in the equivalent position in animals, eg horses

NAVIGABLE adj said of a river or channel, etc: able to be sailed along or through, etc

NAVIGABLY adverb in a navigable way

NAVIGATE verb **NAVIGATES, NAVIGATING, NAVIGATED** to direct the course of a ship, aircraft or other vehicle

NAVIGATOR noun **NAVIGATORS** someone who navigates, especially a ship or aircraft

NAVVY noun **NAVVIES** a labourer, especially one employed in road-building or canal-building, etc □ verb **NAVVIES, NAVVYING, NAVVIED** to work as or like a navvy

NAVY noun **NAVIES** the warships of a state, usually considered together with the officers and other personnel manning them □ adj having a navy blue colour

NAWAB noun **NAWABS** a Muslim ruler or landowner in India

NAY exclamation no □ noun **NAYS** the word 'no'

NAZE noun **NAZES** a headland or cape

NAZIR noun **NAZIRS** an official

NÉ adj used in giving the original name of a titled man: born

NEAP noun **NEAPS** a tide occurring at the first and last quarters of the Moon, when there is the least variation between high and low water

NEAR prep at a short distance from something □ adj **NEARER, NEAREST** being a short distance away; close □ adverb almost; nearly □ verb **NEARS, NEARING, NEARED** to approach

NEARLY adverb almost

NEARNESS noun **NEARNESSES** proximity in space

NEARSIDE noun **NEARSIDES** the side of a vehicle, horse or team of horses nearer the kerb, ie in the UK the left side, and in most other countries the right side

NEAT adj **NEATER, NEATEST** tidy; clean; orderly

NEATEN verb **NEATENS, NEATENING, NEATENED** to make something neat and tidy

NEATH prep beneath

NEATLY adverb in a neat way

NEATNESS noun **NEATNESSES** the quality or condition of being neat

NEB noun **NEBS** a beak or bill □ verb **NEBS, NEBBING, NEBBED** to look around in a nosy way with the hope of seeing something to gossip about

NEBBICH noun **NEBBICHS** an insignificant person; an incompetent person; a perpetual victim

NEBBISH noun **NEBBISHES** a nebbich

NEBISH noun **NEBISHES** a nebbich

NEBULA noun **NEBULAE, NEBULAS** a luminous or dark patch in space representing a mass of dust or particles

NEBULAR adj relating to nebulae; like or of the nature of a nebula

NEBULISER noun **NEBULISERS** a nebulizer

NEBULIZER noun **NEBULIZERS** a device with a mouthpiece or

facemask through which a drug is administered in the form of a fine mist

NEBULOUS adj vague; hazy; lacking distinct shape, form or nature

NECESSARY adj needed; essential; indispensable; that must be done □ noun **NECESSARIES** something that is necessary; an essential item

NECESSITY noun **NECESSITIES** something necessary or essential

NECK noun **NECKS** the part of the body between the head and the shoulders □ verb **NECKS, NECKING, NECKED** to hug and kiss amorously

NECKBAND noun **NECKBANDS** a band or strip of material sewn round the neck of a garment to finish it, or as the base for a collar

NECKCLOTH noun **NECKCLOTHS** a piece of cloth, usually white, or sometimes a piece of lace, folded and worn around the neck by men

NECKING noun **NECKINGS** kissing and embracing

NECKLACE noun **NECKLACES** a string of beads or jewels, etc, or a chain, worn round the neck as jewellery □ verb **NECKLACES, NECKLACING, NECKLACED** in S Africa: to kill someone by placing a tyre soaked in petrol around their neck or shoulders and setting it alight

NECKLET noun **NECKLETS** a simple necklace

NECKLINE noun **NECKLINES** the edge of a garment at the neck, or its shape

NECKTIE noun **NECKTIES** a man's tie

NECKWEAR noun **NECKWEARS** ties, scarves or other articles of clothing worn around the neck

NECROPSY noun **NECROPSIES** a post-mortem examination

NECROSIS noun **NECROSES** the death of living tissue or bone, especially where the blood supply has been interrupted

NECROTIC adj characterized by necrosis

NECTAR noun **NECTARS** a sugary substance produced in the flowers of plants to attract pollinating insects and which is collected by bees to make honey

NECTAREAN adj of or like nectar

NECTARINE noun **NECTARINES** a variety of peach with a shiny downless skin

NECTAROUS *adj* of or relating to nectar

NECTARY *noun* **NECTARIES** in flowering plants: a specialized gland, usually situated at the base of the flower, that secretes nectar

NED *noun* **NEDS** a young hooligan; a disruptive male adolescent

NEDDY *noun* **NEDDIES** a donkey

NÉE *adj* used in giving a married woman's maiden name: born

NEED *verb* **NEEDS, NEEDING, NEEDED** to lack; to require ▫ *noun* **NEEDS** something one requires

NEEDFUL *adj* necessary ▫ *noun* whatever action is necessary

NEEDFULLY *adverb* necessarily

NEEDIER see under **needy**

NEEDIEST see under **needy**

NEEDINESS *noun* **NEEDINESSES** the state or condition of being needy; poverty

NEEDLE *noun* **NEEDLES** a slender pointed steel sewing instrument with a hole for the thread ▫ *verb* **NEEDLES, NEEDLING, NEEDLED** to provoke or irritate someone, especially deliberately

NEEDLESS *adj* unnecessary

NEEDS *adverb* of necessity; inevitably ▫ *plural noun* what is required; necessities

NEEDY *adj* **NEEDIER, NEEDIEST** in severe need; poverty-stricken; destitute

NEEP *noun* **NEEPS** a turnip

NEEZE *verb* **NEEZES, NEEZING, NEEZED** to sneeze ▫ *noun* **NEEZES** a sneeze

NEF *noun* **NEFS** an obsolete word for a church nave

NEFARIOUS *adj* wicked; evil

NEGATE *verb* **NEGATES, NEGATING, NEGATED** to cancel or destroy the effect of something

NEGATION *noun* **NEGATIONS** the act of negating

NEGATIVE *adj* meaning or saying 'no'; expressing denial, refusal or prohibition ▫ *noun* **NEGATIVES** a word, statement or grammatical form expressing denial ▫ *verb* **NEGATIVES, NEGATIVING, NEGATIVED** to reject something; to veto it

NEGLECT *verb* **NEGLECTS, NEGLECTING, NEGLECTED** not to give proper care and attention to someone or something ▫ *noun* **NEGLECTS** lack of proper care

NÉGLIGÉE *noun* **NÉGLIGÉES** a woman's thin light dressing-gown

NEGLIGENT *adj* not giving proper care and attention

NEGOTIATE *verb* **NEGOTIATES, NEGOTIATING, NEGOTIATED** to confer; to bargain

NEIGH *noun* **NEIGHS** the characteristic cry of a horse ▫ *verb* **NEIGHS, NEIGHING, NEIGHED** to make the characteristic cry of a horse or a sound like it

NEIGHBOR *noun* **NEIGHBORS** a neighbour

NEIGHBOUR *noun* **NEIGHBOURS** someone near or next door to one

NEIGHBOURING *adj* nearby; adjoining

NEITHER *adj* not the one nor the other (thing or person) ▫ *pronoun* not the one nor the other (thing or person) ▫ *conj* not ▫ *adverb* nor; also not

NEK *noun* **NEKS** a South African word for *col*

NEKTON *noun* **NEKTONS** the actively swimming organisms that inhabit seas and lakes, etc, eg fish

NELLY *noun* **NELLIES** a large petrel

NELSON *noun* **NELSONS** in wrestling: a hold in which one passes one's arms under and over one's opponent's from behind, with the palms against the back of their neck

NEMATODE *noun* **NEMATODES** any of several long thin unsegmented cylindrical worms, occurring as parasites in plants and animals as well as in soil or sediment

NEMESIA *noun* **NEMESIAS** a plant of the figwort family, originally found in S Africa, grown for its brightly coloured flowers

NEMESIS *noun* **NEMESES** retribution or just punishment

NEODYMIUM *noun* **NEODYMIUMS** a silvery metallic element, one of the rare earth elements

NEOLOGISE *verb* **NEOLOGISES, NEOLOGISING, NEOLOGISED** to neologize

NEOLOGISM *noun* **NEOLOGISMS** a new word or expression

NEOLOGIST *noun* **NEOLOGISTS** someone who introduces new words

NEOLOGIZE *verb* **NEOLOGIZES, NEOLOGIZING, NEOLOGIZED** to introduce new words; to coin neologisms

NEOMYCIN *noun* **NEOMYCINS** an antibiotic used to treat skin and eye infections

NEON *noun* **NEONS** an element, a colourless gas that glows red when electricity is passed through it, used eg in illuminated signs and advertisements

NEONATAL *adj* relating to newly born children

NEONATE *noun* **NEONATES** a newly born child

NEOPHOBE *noun* **NEOPHOBES** someone who dreads or hates what is new

NEOPHOBIA *noun* **NEOPHOBIAS** a dread or hatred of novelty

NEOPHOBIC *adj* characterized by neophobia

NEOPHYTE *noun* **NEOPHYTES** a beginner

NEOPRENE *noun* **NEOPRENES** an oil-resisting and heat-resisting synthetic rubber made by polymerizing chloroprene

NEOTENY *noun* **NEOTENIES** retention of juvenile features in the adult form, an important mechanism in evolution

NEOTERIC *adj* modern; recent ▫ *noun* **NEOTERICS** a modern writer or philosopher

NEP *noun* **NEPS** a dialect word for *catmint*

NEPENTHE *noun* **NEPENTHES** a drug or drink that allows one to forget one's sorrows

NEPHEW *noun* **NEPHEWS** the son of one's brother or sister, or of the brother or sister of one's wife or husband

NEPHOLOGY *noun* **NEPHOLOGIES** the study of clouds

NEPHRITE *noun* **NEPHRITES** a hard glistening mineral that occurs in a wide range of colours including black, green and white

NEPHRITIC *adj* relating to the kidneys or nephritis

NEPHRITIS *noun* **NEPHRITISES** inflammation of a kidney

NEPHRON *noun* **NEPHRONS** one of over a million functional units in the vertebrate kidney, responsible for reabsorption of water and nutrients and for the filtration of waste products from the blood to form urine

NEPOTIC *adj* of or relating to nepotism

NEPOTISM *noun* **NEPOTISMS** the

practice of favouring one's relatives or friends, especially in making official appointments

NEPOTIST *noun* **NEPOTISTS** someone who practises nepotism

NEPTUNIUM *noun* **NEPTUNIUMS** a metallic element obtained artificially in nuclear reactors during the production of plutonium

NERD *noun* **NERDS** someone who is foolish or annoying, often because they are so wrapped up in something that isn't thought worthy of such interest

NERDY *adj* **NERDIER, NERDIEST** characteristic of a nerd

NEREID *noun* **NEREIDS, NEREIDES** a sea-nymph, daughter of the god Nereus

NERKA *noun* **NERKAS** the sockeye salmon

NEROLI *noun* **NEROLIS** an oil distilled from orange flowers

NERVE *noun* **NERVES** one of the cords, consisting of a bundle of fibres, that carry instructions for movement and information on sensation between the brain or spinal cord and other parts of the body ◻ *verb* **NERVES, NERVING, NERVED** to give strength, resolution, or courage to (oneself, etc)

NERVED *adj* supplied with nerves

NERVELESS *adj* lacking feeling or strength; inert

NERVILY *adverb* in a nervy way

NERVIER see under **nervy**

NERVIEST see under **nervy**

NERVINESS *noun* **NERVINESSES** the state of being nervy

NERVOUS *adj* timid; easily agitated

NERVOUSLY *adverb* in a nervous way

NERVURE *noun* **NERVURES** a leaf-vein

NERVY *adj* **NERVIER, NERVIEST** excitable

NESCIENCE *noun* **NESCIENCES** lack of knowledge; ignorance

NESCIENT *adj* ignorant

NESS *noun* **NESSES** a headland

NEST *noun* **NESTS** a structure built by birds or other creatures, eg rats and wasps, etc in which to lay eggs, or give birth to and look after young ◻ *verb* **NESTS, NESTING, NESTED** to build and occupy a nest

NESTLE *verb* **NESTLES, NESTLING, NESTLED** to lie or settle snugly

NESTLING *noun* **NESTLINGS** a young bird still unable to fly

NET [1] *noun* **NETS** an openwork material made of thread or cord, etc knotted, twisted or woven so as to form regularly shaped meshes ◻ *verb* **NETS, NETTING, NETTED** to catch something in a net

NET [2] *adj* said of profit: remaining after all expenses, etc have been paid

NETBALL *noun* **NETBALLS** a game played between teams of seven women or girls on a hard court, indoors or outdoors, the aim being to score points by throwing the ball through a net hanging from a ring at the top of a pole

NETHER *adj* lower or under

NETSUKE *noun* **NETSUKES** a small Japanese carved ornament, once used to fasten small objects (eg a purse, or a pouch for tobacco or medicines, etc) to a sash

NETTED *adj* made into a net

NETTING *noun* **NETTINGS** any material with meshes, made by knotting or twisting thread, cord or wire, etc

NETTLE *noun* **NETTLES** a plant covered with hairs that sting if touched ◻ *verb* **NETTLES, NETTLING, NETTLED** to offend or irritate someone

NETWORK *noun* **NETWORKS** any co-ordinated system involving a large number of people or branches ◻ *verb* **NETWORKS, NETWORKING, NETWORKED** to broadcast something on a network

NETWORKER *noun* **NETWORKERS** an employee who works from home on a personal computer linked to the computer network in his or her company's offices

NEUM *noun* **NEUMS** a neume

NEUME *noun* **NEUMES** in medieval music: a succession of notes sung to one syllable

NEURAL *adj* relating to the nerves or nervous system

NEURALGIA *noun* **NEURALGIAS** spasmodic pain originating along the course of a nerve

NEURALGIC *adj* characterized by or affected with neuralgia

NEURALLY *adverb* by the nerves or nervous system

NEURITIS *noun* **NEURITISES** inflammation of a nerve or nerves, in some cases with defective functioning of the affected part

NEUROGLIA *noun* **NEUROGLIAS** the glia

NEUROLOGY *noun* **NEUROLOGIES** the study of the structure, functions, diseases and disorders of the central nervous system, and the peripheral nerves

NEURON *noun* **NEURONS** a neurone

NEURONE *noun* **NEURONES** any of a large number of specialized cells that transmit nerve impulses from one part of the body to another

NEUROSIS *noun* **NEUROSES** a mental disorder that causes obsessive fears, depression and unreasonable behaviour

NEUROTIC *adj* relating to, or suffering from, a neurosis ◻ *noun* **NEUROTICS** someone suffering from a neurosis

NEUTER *adj* in many languages: belonging or referring to the gender to which nouns and pronouns that are neither masculine or feminine belong ◻ *noun* **NEUTERS** the neuter gender ◻ *verb* **NEUTERS, NEUTERING, NEUTERED** to castrate (an animal)

NEUTRAL *adj* not taking sides in a quarrel or war ◻ *noun* **NEUTRALS** a person or nation taking no part in a war or quarrel and not allied to any side

NEUTRALLY *adverb* in a neutral way

NEUTRINO *noun* **NEUTRINOS** a stable subatomic particle that has no electric charge, virtually no mass, and travels at or near the speed of light

NEUTRON *noun* **NEUTRONS** one of the electrically uncharged particles in the nucleus of an atom

NÉVÉ *noun* **NÉVÉS** the granular snow, not yet compacted into ice, that lies on the surface at the upper end of a glacier

NEVER *adverb* not ever; at no time

NEVERMORE *adverb* never again

NEVUS *noun* **NEVI** a naevus

NEW *adj* **NEWER, NEWEST** recently made, bought, built, opened, etc ◻ *adverb* only just; freshly ◻ *verb* **NEWS, NEWING, NEWED** an old word meaning to renew

NEWBORN *adj* just or very recently born

NEWCOMER *noun* **NEWCOMERS** someone recently arrived

NEWEL *noun* **NEWELS** the central

spindle round which a spiral stair winds

NEWELLED *adj* having a newel

NEWISH *adj* rather new or nearly new

NEWISHLY *adverb* in a newish way

NEWLY *adverb* only just; recently

NEWMARKET *noun* **NEWMARKETS** a game in which the stakes are won by those who succeed in playing out cards whose duplicates lie on the table

NEWNESS *noun* **NEWNESSES** the quality of being new

NEWS *singular noun* information about recent events, now especially as reported in newspapers, on radio or TV, or via the Internet

NEWSAGENT *noun* **NEWSAGENTS** a shop, or the proprietor of a shop, that sells newspapers and sometimes confectionery, etc

NEWSBOY *noun* **NEWSBOYS** a boy who sells or delivers newspapers

NEWSCAST *noun* **NEWSCASTS** a radio or TV broadcast of news items

NEWSFLASH *noun* **NEWSFLASHES** a brief announcement of important news that interrupts a radio or TV broadcast

NEWSGIRL *noun* **NEWSGIRLS** a girl who sells or delivers newspapers

NEWSHOUND *noun* **NEWSHOUNDS** a newspaper reporter

NEWSIER see under **newsy**

NEWSIEST see under **newsy**

NEWSINESS *noun* **NEWSINESSES** the state of being newsy

NEWSMAN *noun* **NEWSMEN** a male reporter for a newspaper or for a broadcast news programme

NEWSPAPER *noun* **NEWSPAPERS** a daily or weekly publication composed of folded sheets, containing news, advertisements, topical articles, correspondence, etc

NEWSPEAK *noun* **NEWSPEAKS** the ambiguous language, full of the latest distortions and euphemisms, used by politicians and other persuaders

NEWSPRINT *noun* **NEWSPRINTS** the paper on which newspapers are printed

NEWSREEL *noun* **NEWSREELS** a film of news events, once a regular cinema feature

NEWSROOM *noun* **NEWSROOMS** a room in a newspaper office or broadcasting station where news stories are received and edited for publication or broadcasting

NEWSY *adj* **NEWSIER, NEWSIEST** full of news, especially gossip

NEWT *noun* **NEWTS** a small amphibious animal with a long body and tail and short legs

NEWTON *noun* **NEWTONS** in the SI system: a unit of force equivalent to that which gives a one kilogram mass an acceleration of one second every second

NEXT *adj* following in time or order □ *noun* someone or something that is next □ *adverb* immediately after that or this

NEXUS *noun* **NEXUS** a connected series or group

NGAIO *noun* **NGAIOS** an evergreen New Zealand tree with white wood

NIACIN *noun* **NIACINS** vitamin B_7

NIB *noun* **NIBS** the writing-point of a pen, especially a metal one with a divided tip □ *verb* **NIBS, NIBBING, NIBBED** to provide with a pen-point or nib

NIBBLE *verb* **NIBBLES, NIBBLING, NIBBLED** to take very small bites of something; to eat a little at a time

NIBBLER *noun* **NIBBLERS** a person or animal that nibbles

NIBBLING *noun* **NIBBLINGS** the action of taking very small bites of something

NIBLICK *noun* **NIBLICKS** an old-fashioned golf club with a heavy head and wide face

NICAD *noun* **NICADS** nickel-cadmium, used to make batteries

NICCOLITE *noun* **NICCOLITES** a hexagonal mineral, nickel arsenide

NICE *adj* **NICER, NICEST** pleasant; agreeable; respectable

NICELY *adverb* in a nice or satisfactory way

NICENESS *noun* **NICENESSES** the quality of being nice

NICETY *noun* **NICETIES** precision

NICHE *noun* **NICHES** a shallow recess in a wall, suitable for a lamp, ornament or statue, etc □ *verb* **NICHES, NICHING, NICHED** to place something in a niche

NICHED *adj* placed in a niche

NICK *noun* **NICKS** a small cut; a notch □ *verb* **NICKS, NICKING, NICKED** to make a small cut in something; to cut something slightly; to snip it

NICKEL *noun* **NICKELS** one of the elements, a greyish-white metal used especially in alloys and for plating □ *verb* **NICKELS, NICKELLING, NICKELLED** to plate something with nickel

NICKELINE *noun* **NICKELINES** niccolite

NICKER *noun* **NICKERS** a pound sterling

NICKNAME *noun* **NICKNAMES** a name, usually additional to the real one, given to a person or place in fun, affection or contempt □ *verb* **NICKNAMES, NICKNAMING, NICKNAMED** to give a nickname to someone

NICOTIANA *noun* **NICOTIANAS** a plant related to tobacco, originally found in America and Australia, cultivated for its colourful flowers and scent

NICOTINE *noun* **NICOTINES** a poisonous alkaline substance contained in tobacco

NICTATE *verb* **NICTATES, NICTATING, NICTATED** to wink or blink

NICTATION *noun* **NICTATIONS** the action of winking or blinking

NICTITATE *verb* **NICTITATES, NICTITATING, NICTITATED** to nictate

NID *noun* **NIDS** a pheasant's nest or brood

NIDIFY *verb* **NIDIFIES, NIDIFYING, NIDIFIED** said of a bird: to make a nest or nests

NIE *adj* an obsolete spelling of *nigh*

NIECE *noun* **NIECES** the daughter of one's sister or brother, or the sister or brother of one's husband or wife

NIELLO *noun* **NIELLOS** a method of ornamenting metal by engraving, and then filling up the lines with a black compound; a piece of work produced in this way □ *verb* **NIELLOS, NIELLOING, NIELLOED** to decorate something with niello

NIFF *noun* **NIFFS** a bad smell □ *verb* **NIFFS, NIFFING, NIFFED** to smell bad

NIFFY *adj* **NIFFIER, NIFFIEST** smelly

NIFTILY *adverb* in a nifty way

NIFTINESS *noun* **NIFTINESSES** the state of being nifty

NIFTY *adj* **NIFTIER, NIFTIEST** clever; adroit; agile

NIGELLA *noun* **NIGELLAS** one of a group of plants with finely dissected leaves and whitish, blue or yellow flowers

NIGGARD *noun* **NIGGARDS** a stingy person

NIGGARDLY *adj* stingy; miserly

NIGGLE *verb* **NIGGLES, NIGGLING, NIGGLED** to complain about small or unimportant details □ *noun* **NIGGLES** a slight nagging worry

NIGGLER *noun* **NIGGLERS** someone who niggles

NIGGLING *adj* fussy; trivially troublesome or worrying

NIGH *adj* near

NIGHT *noun* **NIGHTS** the time of darkness between sunset and sunrise □ *adj* belonging to, occurring, or done in the night

NIGHTCAP *noun* **NIGHTCAPS** a drink, especially an alcoholic one, taken before going to bed

NIGHTCLUB *noun* **NIGHTCLUBS** a club open in the evening and running late into the night for drinking, dancing, entertainment, etc

NIGHTFALL *noun* **NIGHTFALLS** the end of the day and the beginning of night; dusk

NIGHTGOWN *noun* **NIGHTGOWNS** a loose garment for sleeping in

NIGHTIE *noun* **NIGHTIES** a loose garment for sleeping in, worn by women and girls

NIGHTJAR *noun* **NIGHTJARS** a nocturnal bird of the swift family that has a harsh discordant cry

NIGHTLIFE *noun* **NIGHTLIVES** entertainment available in a city or resort, etc, late into the night

NIGHTLONG *adj* throughout the night □ *adverb* throughout the night

NIGHTLY *adj* done or happening at night or every night □ *adverb* at night; every night

NIGHTMARE *noun* **NIGHTMARES** a frightening dream

NIGHTS *adverb* at night; most nights or every night

NIGHTY *noun* **NIGHTIES** a nightie

NIHILISM *noun* **NIHILISMS** the rejection of moral and religious principles

NIHILIST *noun* **NIHILISTS** someone who rejects moral and religious principles

NIHILITY *noun* **NIHILITIES** being nothing; nothingness

NIL *noun* **NILS** a score of nothing; zero

NILGAI *noun* **NILGAIS** a large Indian antelope, the male being a slaty-grey colour, and the female tawny

NILGAU *noun* **NILGAUS** a nilgai

NIM *verb* **NIMS, NIMMING, NIMMED, NAM** an obsolete word meaning to take or steal

NIMBLE *adj* **NIMBLER, NIMBLEST** quick and light in movement; agile

NIMBLY *adverb* in a nimble way

NIMBUS *noun* **NIMBUSES, NIMBI** a heavy dark type of cloud bringing rain or snow

NIMBYISM *noun* **NIMBYISMS** the attitude that it is acceptable to let something happen, eg the building of a new road, as long as it does not disrupt one's own locality

NINE *noun* **NINES** the cardinal number 9 □ *adj* totalling nine

NINEFOLD *adj* equal to nine times as much or many □ *adverb* by nine times as much

NINEPINS *singular noun* a game similar to skittles, using a wooden ball and nine skittles arranged in a triangle

NINETEEN *noun* **NINETEENS** the cardinal number 19 □ *adj* totalling nineteen

NINETIES *plural noun* the period of time between one's ninetieth and hundredth birthdays

NINETIETH *adj* in counting: next after eighty-ninth □ *noun* **NINETIETHS** one of ninety equal parts

NINETY *noun* **NINETIES** the cardinal number 90 □ *adj* totalling ninety

NINJA *noun* **NINJAS** especially in medieval Japan: one of a body of professional assassins trained in martial arts and stealth

NINJITSU *noun* **NINJITSUS** ninjutsu

NINJUTSU *noun* **NINJUTSUS** an armed Japanese martial art with strong emphasis on stealth and camouflage

NINNY *noun* **NINNIES** a foolish person

NINON *noun* **NINONS** a silk voile or other thin fabric

NINTH *adj* in counting: next after eighth □ *noun* **NINTHS** one of nine equal parts □ *adverb* ninthly

NINTHLY *adverb* used to introduce the ninth point in a list

NIOBIUM *noun* **NIOBIUMS** a relatively unreactive soft greyish-blue metallic element with a brilliant lustre, resistant to corrosion

NIP *verb* **NIPS, NIPPING, NIPPED** to pinch or squeeze something or someone sharply □ *noun* **NIPS** a pinch or squeeze

NIPPER *noun* **NIPPERS** the large claw of a crab or lobster, etc

NIPPINESS *noun* **NIPPINESSES** the state of being nippy

NIPPLE *noun* **NIPPLES** the deep-coloured pointed projection on a breast

NIPPY *adj* **NIPPIER, NIPPIEST** cold; chilly

NIRVANA *noun* **NIRVANAS** in Buddhism and Hinduism: the ultimate state of spiritual tranquillity attained through release from everyday concerns and extinction of individual passions

NIS *noun* **NISSES** in Scandinavian folklore: a brownie or goblin

NISEI *noun* **NISEIS** an American or Canadian born of Japanese immigrant parents

NISI *adj* said of a court order: to take effect on the date stated, unless in the meantime a reason is given why it should not

NIT *noun* **NITS** the egg or young of a louse, found eg in hair

NITRATE *noun* **NITRATES** a salt or ester of nitric acid □ *verb* **NITRATES, NITRATING, NITRATED** to treat something with nitric acid or a nitrate

NITRATION *noun* **NITRATIONS** the process of converting something into a nitrate

NITRE *noun* **NITRES** potassium nitrate; saltpetre

NITRIC *adj* belonging to or containing nitrogen

NITRIDE *noun* **NITRIDES** a compound of nitrogen with another, metallic, element

NITRIFY *verb* **NITRIFIES, NITRIFYING, NITRIFIED** usually said of ammonia: to convert or be converted into nitrates or nitrites, through the action of bacteria

NITRITE *noun* **NITRITES** a salt or ester of nitrous acid

NITROGEN *noun* **NITROGENS** an element which is the colourless, odourless and tasteless gas making up four-fifths of the air we breathe

NITROUS *adj* relating to or containing nitrogen in a low valency

NITTY *adj* **NITTIER, NITTIEST** full of nits

NITWIT *noun* **NITWITS** a stupid person

NIX *verb* **NIXES, NIXING, NIXED** to veto or cancel

NIZAM *noun* **NIZAMS** a Turkish soldier

NO [1] *exclamation* used as a negative reply, expressing denial, refusal or disagreement □ *adverb* not any □ *noun* **NOES, NOS** a negative reply or vote

NO [2] *adj* not any

NOB *noun* **NOBS** someone of wealth or high social rank

NOBBLE *verb* **NOBBLES, NOBBLING, NOBBLED** to drug or otherwise interfere with (a horse) to stop it winning

NOBELIUM *noun* **NOBELIUMS** a radioactive element produced artificially from the element curium

NOBILITY *noun* **NOBILITIES** the quality of being noble, in character, conduct or rank

NOBLE *adj* **NOBLER, NOBLEST** honourable □ *noun* **NOBLES** a person of noble rank

NOBLEMAN *noun* **NOBLEMEN** a member of the nobility

NOBLENESS *noun* **NOBLENESSES** nobility

NOBLY *adverb* with a noble manner; honourably

NOBODY *pronoun* no person; no one □ *noun* **NOBODIES** someone of no significance

NOCK *noun* **NOCKS** a notch, or a part carrying a notch, especially on an arrow or a bow □ *verb* **NOCKS, NOCKING, NOCKED** to notch

NOCTULE *noun* **NOCTULES** a large brown bat, the largest found in Britain

NOCTURNAL *adj* said of animals, etc: active at night

NOCTURNE *noun* **NOCTURNES** a dreamy piece of music, usually for the piano

NOD *noun* **NODS** a quick bending forward of the head; a slight bow; a movement of the head as a gesture of assent, greeting or command □ *verb* **NODS, NODDING, NODDED** to make such a movement

NODAL *adj* of or like a node or nodes

NODDLE *noun* **NODDLES** the head or brain

NODDY *noun* **NODDIES** any of several tropical birds of the tern family, so unafraid of humans as to seem stupid

NODE *noun* **NODES** a knob, lump, swelling or knotty mass

NODOSE *adj* having nodes, knots or swellings

NODOSITY *noun* **NODOSITIES** knottiness

NODULAR *adj* relating to a nodule or nodules

NODULATED *adj* having nodules

NODULE *noun* **NODULES** a small round lump

NODULOSE *adj* having small round lumps

NODULOUS *adj* nodular

NOEL *noun* **NOELS** a Christmas carol

NOES a plural of no [1]

NOESIS *noun* **NOESES** the activity of the intellect

NOETIC *adj* of or relating to the mind or intellect

NOG *noun* **NOGS** a wooden peg □ *verb* **NOGS, NOGGING, NOGGED** to fix with a nog

NOGGIN *noun* **NOGGINS** a small measure or quantity of alcoholic spirits

NOGGING *noun* **NOGGINGS** a brick or rough timber filling between timbers in a partition or wall

NOH *noun* **NOH** Japanese drama in the traditional style, developed from religious dance

NOHOW *adverb* in no way, not at all

NOISE *noun* **NOISES** a sound □ *verb* **NOISES, NOISING, NOISED** to make something generally known; to spread (a rumour, etc)

NOISELESS *adj* lacking noise; silent

NOISETTE *noun* **NOISETTES** a nut-like or nut-flavoured sweet □ *adj* flavoured with or containing hazelnuts

NOISILY *adverb* in a noisy way

NOISINESS *noun* **NOISINESSES** the quality of being noisy

NOISOME *adj* disgusting; offensive; stinking

NOISOMELY *adverb* in a noisome way

NOISY *adj* **NOISIER, NOISIEST** making a lot of noise

NOM *noun* **NOMS** a French word for *name*

NOMAD *noun* **NOMADS** a member of a people without a permanent home, who travel from place to place seeking food and pasture

NOMADIC *adj* said of a people: wandering from place to place; not settled

NOMADISE *verb* **NOMADISES, NOMADISING, NOMADISED** to nomadize

NOMADISM *noun* **NOMADISMS** the state of living a wandering life

NOMADIZE *verb* **NOMADIZES, NOMADIZING, NOMADIZED** to lead the life of a nomad or vagabond

NOMINAL *adj* in name only; so called, but actually not something specified □ *noun* **NOMINALS** a noun, or a phrase, etc standing as a noun

NOMINALLY *adverb* in name only; theoretically rather than actually

NOMINATE *verb* **NOMINATES, NOMINATING, NOMINATED** to propose formally for election, a job, etc

NOMINATOR *noun* **NOMINATORS** a person who nominates

NOMINEE *noun* **NOMINEES** someone who is nominated as a candidate for a job or position, etc

NOMOGRAM *noun* **NOMOGRAMS** a chart or diagram of scaled lines or curves used to help in mathematical calculations, comprising three scales in which a line joining values on two determines a third

NOMOGRAPH *noun* **NOMOGRAPHS** a nomogram

NON *adverb* a Latin word for *not*

NONAGE *noun* **NONAGES** the condition of being under age; one's minority or period of immaturity

NONAGON *noun* **NONAGONS** a nine-sided figure

NONARY *adj* said of a mathematical system: based on nine

NONCE *noun* **NONCES** a sexual offender, especially one who assaults children

NONE [1] *pronoun* not any

NONE ² *noun* NONES the fifth of the canonical hours

NONENTITY *noun* NONENTITIES someone of no significance, character or ability, etc

NONES *plural noun* in the Roman calendar: the seventh day of March, May, July and October, and the fifth day of other months

NONESUCH *noun* NONESUCHES a unique, unparalleled or extraordinary thing

NONET *noun* NONETS a composition for nine instruments or voices; a group of nine musicians or singers

NONG *noun* NONGS a fool or an idiot

NONILLION *noun* NONILLIONS in certain EC countries: the number shown as 10^{54}, a million raised to the ninth power

NONPAREIL *adj* having no equal; matchless ❑ *noun* NONPAREILS a person or thing without equal

NONPLUS *verb* NONPLUSES, NONPLUSING, NONPLUSED, NONPLUSSES, NONPLUSSING, NONPLUSSED to puzzle; to disconcert

NONSENSE *noun* NONSENSES words or ideas that do not make sense ❑ *exclamation* you're quite wrong

NONSUCH *noun* NONSUCHES nonesuch

NONSUIT *noun* NONSUITS the stopping of a suit in law either by the voluntary withdrawal of the plaintiff, or by the judge when the plaintiff has failed to make out cause of action, or to bring evidence ❑ *verb* NONSUITS, NONSUITING, NONSUITED to order that a suit be dismissed

NOODLE *noun* NOODLES a thin strip of pasta, often made with egg

NOOK *noun* NOOKS a secluded retreat

NOON *noun* NOONS midday; twelve o'clock

NOONDAY *noun* NOONDAYS midday ❑ *adj* belonging to or relating to midday

NOONTIDE *noun* NOONTIDES midday

NOOSE *noun* NOOSES a loop made in the end of a rope, etc, with a sliding knot, used eg for killing someone by hanging ❑ *verb* NOOSES, NOOSING, NOOSED to tie or snare someone or something in a noose

NOPE *exclamation* emphatic form of no

NOR *conj* used to introduce alternatives after neither ❑ *adverb* not either

NORI *noun* NORIS a seaweed used in Japanese cookery, either in dried sheets or as a paste

NORIA *noun* NORIAS an endless chain of buckets on a wheel, for raising water, eg from a stream into irrigation channels

NORM *noun* NORMS a typical pattern or situation

NORMAL *adj* usual; typical; not extraordinary ❑ *noun* NORMALS what is average or usual

NORMALCY *noun* NORMALCIES being normal; a normal state or quality

NORMALISE *verb* NORMALISES, NORMALISING, NORMALISED to normalize

NORMALITY *noun* NORMALITIES being normal; a normal state or quality

NORMALIZE *verb* NORMALIZES, NORMALIZING, NORMALIZED to make or become normal or regular

NORMALLY *adverb* in an ordinary or natural way

NORMATIVE *adj* establishing a guiding standard or rules

NORTH *noun* NORTHS the direction to one's left when one faces the rising Sun ❑ *adj* in the north; on the side that is on or nearest the north ❑ *adverb* towards the north

NORTHER *noun* NORTHERS a wind or storm from the north, especially a winter wind that blows from the north over Texas and the Gulf of Mexico

NORTHERLY *adj* said of a wind, etc: coming from the north ❑ *adverb* to or towards the north ❑ *noun* NORTHERLIES a northerly wind

NORTHERN *adj* belonging or relating to the north

NORTHING *noun* NORTHINGS motion, distance or tendency northward

NORTHWARD *adj* towards the north ❑ *adverb* towards the north ❑ *noun* NORTHWARDS the northward direction or sector, etc

NOSE *noun* NOSES the projecting organ above the mouth, with which one smells and breathes ❑ *verb* NOSES, NOSING, NOSED to move carefully forward

NOSEBAG *noun* NOSEBAGS a

food bag for a horse, hung over its head

NOSEBAND *noun* NOSEBANDS the part of a bridle that goes over the horse's nose

NOSEBLEED *noun* NOSEBLEEDS a flow of blood from the nose

NOSED *adj* having a nose of a specified type

NOSEDIVE *noun* NOSEDIVES a steep nose-downward plunge by an aircraft ❑ *verb* NOSEDIVES, NOSEDIVING, NOSEDIVED to plunge or fall suddenly

NOSEGAY *noun* NOSEGAYS a posy, traditionally made up of fragrant flowers

NOSELESS *adj* lacking a nose

NOSEY *adj* NOSIER, NOSIEST nosy ❑ *noun* NOSEYS a nosy

NOSH *noun* NOSHES food ❑ *verb* NOSHES, NOSHING, NOSHED to eat

NOSILY *adverb* in a nosy way

NOSINESS *noun* NOSINESSES a tendency to pry

NOSING *noun* NOSINGS the act of nuzzling something

NOSOLOGY *noun* NOSOLOGIES that branch of medicine which deals with the classification of diseases

NOSTALGIA *noun* NOSTALGIAS a yearning for the past

NOSTALGIC *adj* characterized by nostalgia

NOSTOC *noun* NOSTOCS a blue-green alga which is motile, forming a slime layer, and is found in soil, fresh water and the sea

NOSTRIL *noun* NOSTRILS either of the two external openings in the nose, through which one breathes and smells, etc

NOSTRUM *noun* NOSTRUMS a patent medicine; a panacea or cure-all

NOSY *adj* NOSIER, NOSIEST inquisitive; prying ❑ *noun* NOSIES a nickname for a prying person

NOT *adverb* used to make a negative statement, etc

NOTABLE *adj* worth noting; significant ❑ *noun* NOTABLES a notable person

NOTABLY *adverb* as something or someone notable, especially in a list or group

NOTAPHILY *noun* NOTAPHILIES the collecting of banknotes and cheques, etc as a hobby

NOTARIAL *adj* relating to notaries or their work

NOTARISE *verb* **NOTARISES, NOTARISING, NOTARISED** to notarize

NOTARIZE *verb* **NOTARIZES, NOTARIZING, NOTARIZED** to attest to something

NOTARY *noun* **NOTARIES** a public official with the legal power to draw up and witness official documents, and to administer oaths, etc

NOTATE *verb* **NOTATES, NOTATING, NOTATED** to write (music, etc) in notation

NOTATION *noun* **NOTATIONS** the representation of quantities, numbers, musical sounds or movements, etc by symbols

NOTCH *noun* **NOTCHES** a small V-shaped cut or indentation □ *verb* **NOTCHES, NOTCHING, NOTCHED** to cut a notch in something

NOTCHED *adj* nicked

NOTCHY *adj* **NOTCHIER, NOTCHIEST** having notches

NOTE *noun* **NOTES** a brief written record made for later reference □ *verb* **NOTES, NOTING, NOTED** to make a note of

NOTEBOOK *noun* **NOTEBOOKS** a small book in which to write notes, etc

NOTECASE *noun* **NOTECASES** a wallet

NOTED *adj* famous; eminent

NOTEDLY *adverb* especially; markedly

NOTELESS *adj* not attracting notice; unmusical

NOTELET *noun* **NOTELETS** a folded piece of notepaper, often a decorated one, for writing short letters or notes on

NOTEPAPER *noun* **NOTEPAPERS** paper for writing letters on

NOTHING *noun* **NOTHINGS** no thing; not anything □ *adverb* not at all

NOTICE *noun* **NOTICES** an announcement displayed or delivered publicly □ *verb* **NOTICES, NOTICING, NOTICED** to observe; to become aware of something

NOTIFY *verb* **NOTIFIES, NOTIFYING, NOTIFIED** to tell or to inform

NOTION *noun* **NOTIONS** an impression, conception or understanding

NOTIONAL *adj* existing in imagination only

NOTOCHORD *noun* **NOTOCHORDS** a flexible rod-like structure, which

strengthens and supports the body in the embryos and adults of more primitive animals

NOTORIETY *noun* **NOTORIETIES** fame or reputation, usually for something disreputable

NOTORIOUS *adj* famous, usually for something disreputable

NOUGAT *noun* **NOUGATS** a chewy sweet containing chopped nuts, cherries, etc

NOUGHT *noun* **NOUGHTS** the figure 0; zero

NOUN *noun* **NOUNS** a word used as the name of a person, animal, thing, place or quality

NOUNAL *adj* belonging to, being or relating to a noun

NOUNY *adj* **NOUNIER, NOUNIEST** having many nouns; nounlike

NOURISH *verb* **NOURISHES, NOURISHING, NOURISHED** to supply someone or something with food needed for survival and growth

NOURISHER *noun* **NOURISHERS** a person or thing that nourishes

NOURISHING *adj* providing nourishment or much nourishment

NOUS *noun* **NOUSES** common sense; gumption

NOVA *noun* **NOVAE, NOVAS** a normally faint star that suddenly flares into brightness and then fades again

NOVEL [1] *noun* **NOVELS** a book-length fictional story usually involving relationships between characters, their emotional crises and events concerning them

NOVEL [2] *adj* new; original; previously unheard-of

NOVELESE *noun* **NOVELESES** a hackneyed style of writing typical of poor novels

NOVELETTE *noun* **NOVELETTES** a short novel, especially one that is trite or sentimental

NOVELISH *adj* suggestive of a novel

NOVELIST *noun* **NOVELISTS** a writer of a novel or novels

NOVELLA *noun* **NOVELLAS, NOVELLAE** a short story or short novel

NOVELTY *noun* **NOVELTIES** the quality of being new and intriguing

NOVENA *noun* **NOVENAS** a series of special prayers and services held over a period of nine days

NOVICE *noun* **NOVICES** someone new in anything; a beginner

NOVICIATE *noun* **NOVICIATES** the period of being a novice, especially one in a religious community

NOVITIATE *noun* **NOVITIATES** a noviciate

NOW *adverb* at the present time or moment □ *noun* **NOWS** the present time □ *conj* because at last; because at this time

NOWADAYS *adverb* in these present times

NOWAY *adverb* in no way, manner or degree

NOWAYS *adverb* in no way, manner or degree

NOWHERE *adverb* in or to no place; not anywhere □ *noun* **NOWHERES** a non-existent place

NOWISE *adverb* in no way, manner or degree

NOWT *noun* **NOWTS** nothing

NOX *noun* **NOXES** nitrogen oxide

NOXAL *adj* relating to wrongful injury by an object or animal belonging to another

NOXIOUS *adj* harmful; poisonous

NOXIOUSLY *adverb* in a noxious way

NOY *verb* **NOYS, NOYING, NOYED** a Spenserian word meaning to hurt or annoy

NOZZLE *noun* **NOZZLES** an outlet tube or spout, especially as a fitting attached to the end of a hose, etc

NTH *adj* denoting an indefinite position in a sequence

NU *noun* **NUS** the thirteenth letter of the Greek alphabet

NUANCE *noun* **NUANCES** a subtle variation in colour, meaning or expression, etc

NUB *noun* **NUBS** the point or gist

NUBILE *adj* said of a young woman: sexually mature

NUBILITY *noun* **NUBILITIES** the state of being marriageable

NUCELLUS *noun* **NUCELLI** in seed-bearing plants: the greater part of the ovule, containing the embryo sac and nutritive tissue

NUCHA *noun* **NUCHAE** the nape of the neck

NUCHAL *adj* of or relating to the nape of the neck

NUCLEAR *adj* having the nature of, or like, a nucleus

NUCLEASE *noun* **NUCLEASES** any enzyme that catalyses the splitting of the chain of nucleotides comprising nucleic acids

NUCLEATE *verb* **NUCLEATES, NUCLEATING, NUCLEATED** to form, or form something into, a nucleus ▫ *adj* having a nucleus

NUCLEOLUS *noun* **NUCLEOLI** a spherical body in the nucleus of most plant and animal cells, comprising protein and nucleotides, and concerned with the production of protein

NUCLEON *noun* **NUCLEONS** a proton or neutron

NUCLEUS *noun* **NUCLEI** the positively charged tiny central part of an atom, consisting of neutrons and protons and surrounded by electrons

NUCLIDE *noun* **NUCLIDES** one of two or more atoms that contain the same number of protons and the same number of neutrons in their nuclei, and so have the same atomic number and mass number

NUDE *adj* **NUDER, NUDEST** bare; wearing no clothes; naked ▫ *noun* **NUDES** a representation of one or more naked figures in painting or sculpture, etc

NUDELY *adverb* nakedly; barely

NUDENESS *noun* **NUDENESSES** the state of being nude

NUDGE *verb* **NUDGES, NUDGING, NUDGED** to poke or push someone gently, especially with the elbow, to get attention, etc ▫ *noun* **NUDGES** a gentle prod

NUDIE *adj* said of films, shows and magazines, etc: featuring nudity ▫ *noun* **NUDIES** such a film, etc

NUDISM *noun* **NUDISMS** the practice of not wearing clothes, as a matter of principle

NUDIST *noun* **NUDISTS** someone who wears no clothes, as a matter of principle

NUDITY *noun* **NUDITIES** the state of being nude

NUGATORY *adj* worthless; trifling; valueless

NUGGET *noun* **NUGGETS** a lump, especially of gold

NUGGETY *adj* stocky, thickset

NUISANCE *noun* **NUISANCES** an annoying or troublesome person, thing or circumstance

NUKE *verb* **NUKES, NUKING, NUKED** to attack with nuclear weapons ▫ *noun* **NUKES** a nuclear weapon

NULL *adj* legally invalid

NULLIFIER *noun* **NULLIFIERS** someone who nullifies

NULLIFY *verb* **NULLIFIES, NULLIFYING, NULLIFIED** to cause or declare something to be legally invalid

NULLITY *noun* **NULLITIES** the state of being null or void

NULLNESS *noun* **NULLNESSES** the state of being null

NUMB *adj* **NUMBER, NUMBEST** deprived completely, or to some degree, of sensation ▫ *verb* **NUMBS, NUMBING, NUMBED** to make something numb

NUMBAT *noun* **NUMBATS** a small marsupial which feeds on termites

NUMBER *noun* **NUMBERS** the means or system by which groups or sets, etc of individual things, etc are counted; a quantity calculated in units ▫ *verb* **NUMBERS, NUMBERING, NUMBERED** to give a number to something; to mark it with a number

NUMBLY *adverb* in a numb way

NUMBNESS *noun* **NUMBNESSES** the state of being numb

NUMBSKULL *noun* **NUMBSKULLS** a numskull

NUMEN *noun* **NUMINA** a presiding deity

NUMERABLE *adj* that may be numbered or counted

NUMERABLY *adverb* in a numerable way

NUMERACY *noun* **NUMERACIES** the state of being numerate

NUMERAL *noun* **NUMERALS** an arithmetical symbol or group of symbols used to express a number ▫ *adj* relating to, consisting of, or expressing a number

NUMERATE *adj* able to perform arithmetical operations

NUMERATOR *noun* **NUMERATORS** the number above the line in a fraction

NUMERIC *adj* relating to, using, or consisting of, numbers

NUMERICAL *adj* numeric

NUMEROUS *adj* many

NUMINA plural of **numen**

NUMINOUS *adj* mysterious; awe-inspiring

NUMSKULL *noun* **NUMSKULLS** a stupid person

NUN *noun* **NUNS** a member of a female religious order living within a community, in obedience to certain vows

NUNCHAKU *noun* **NUNCHAKUS** a weapon that consists of two short thick sticks joined by a length of chain, used in certain martial arts

NUNCIO *noun* **NUNCIOS** an ambassador from the pope

NUNNERY *noun* **NUNNERIES** a house in which a group of nuns lives; a convent

NUNNISH *adj* like a nun

NUPTIAL *adj* relating to marriage ▫ *noun* **NUPTIALS** a marriage ceremony

NUR *noun* **NURS** a knur

NURD *noun* **NURDS** a nerd

NURL *noun* **NURLS** a knurl ▫ *verb* **NURLS, NURLING, NURLED** to knurl

NURSE *noun* **NURSES** someone trained to look after sick, injured or feeble people, especially in hospital ▫ *verb* **NURSES, NURSING, NURSED** to look after (sick or injured people) especially in a hospital

NURSELING *noun* **NURSELINGS** a nursling

NURSEMAID *noun* **NURSEMAIDS** a children's nurse in a household

NURSERY *noun* **NURSERIES** a place where children are looked after while their parents are at work, etc

NURSING *noun* **NURSINGS** the profession or practice of caring for the sick, feeble or injured ▫ *adj* that nurses

NURSLING *noun* **NURSLINGS** a young child or animal that is being nursed or fostered

NURTURAL *adj* caused by nurture

NURTURE *noun* **NURTURES** care, nourishment and encouragement given to a growing child, animal or plant ▫ *verb* **NURTURES, NURTURING, NURTURED** to nourish and tend (a growing child, animal or plant)

NURTURER *noun* **NURTURERS** someone who nurtures

NUS plural of **nu**

NUT *noun* **NUTS** a fruit consisting of a kernel contained in a hard shell, eg a hazelnut or walnut ▫ *verb* **NUTS, NUTTING, NUTTED** to look for and gather nuts

NUTANT *adj* nodding; pendulous

NUTATION *noun* **NUTATIONS** the act of nodding

NUTCASE *noun* **NUTCASES** a crazy person

NUTGALL *noun* **NUTGALLS** a gall shaped like a nut, produced by the gall wasp, chiefly on oak trees

NUTHATCH *noun* **NUTHATCHES** any of various birds that seek out and feed on insects in the bark of trees, and also eat nuts and seeds

NUTHOUSE *noun* **NUTHOUSES** a mental hospital

NUTMEG *noun* **NUTMEGS** the hard aromatic seed of the fruit of an E Indian tree, used ground or grated as a spice

NUTMEGGY *adj* tasting of nutmeg

NUTRIA *noun* **NUTRIAS** the coypu

NUTRIENT *noun* **NUTRIENTS** any nourishing substance ◻ *adj* nourishing

NUTRIMENT *noun* **NUTRIMENTS** nourishment; food

NUTRITION *noun* **NUTRITIONS** the act or process of nourishing

NUTRITIVE *adj* nourishing

NUTS *adj* insane; crazy

NUTSHELL *noun* **NUTSHELLS** the case containing the kernel of a nut

NUTTER *noun* **NUTTERS** a crazy person

NUTTINESS *noun* **NUTTINESSES** the state of being nutty

NUTTING *noun* **NUTTINGS** the gathering of nuts

NUTTY *adj* **NUTTIER, NUTTIEST** full of, or tasting of, nuts

NUZZLE *verb* **NUZZLES, NUZZLING, NUZZLED** to push or rub someone or something with the nose

NY *adj* an obsolete spelling of *nigh*

NYALA *noun* **NYALAS** a large southern African antelope with a spiral horn

NYE *adj* near

NYLON *noun* **NYLONS** any of numerous polymeric amides that can be formed into fibres, bristles or sheets, from which a wide variety of products are manufactured, including clothing, hosiery, ropes and brushes

NYMPH *noun* **NYMPHS** a goddess that inhabits mountains, water, trees, etc

NYMPHAL *adj* of or belonging to a nymph or nymphs

NYMPHEAN *adj* nymphal

NYMPHET *noun* **NYMPHETS** a sexually attractive and precocious girl in early adolescence

NYS a Spenserian word meaning is not

NYSTAGMIC *adj* of the nature of nystagmus

NYSTAGMUS *noun* **NYSTAGMUSES** a spasmodic involuntary movement of the eye

NYSTATIN *noun* **NYSTATINS** an antifungal and antibiotic agent

OAF *noun* **OAFS, OAVES** a stupid, awkward or loutish, usually male, person

OAFISH *adj* loutish; clumsy

OAK *noun* **OAKS** a tree which produces a fruit called an acorn; the wood of this tree □ *adj* made of oak wood

OAKEN *adj* made of oak

OAKUM *noun* **OAKUMS** pieces of old, usually tarred, rope untwisted and pulled apart, used to fill small holes and cracks in wooden boats and ships

OAR *noun* **OARS** a long pole with a broad flat blade at one end, used for rowing a boat □ *verb* **OARS, OARING, OARED** to row or propel (a boat, etc) with or as if with oars

OARED *adj* with an oar or oars, usually of a specified number

OARLESS *adj* having no oar or oars

OARSMAN *noun* **OARSMEN** a man skilled in rowing; a rower

OARSWOMAN *noun* **OARSWOMEN** a woman skilled in rowing; a rower

OASIS *noun* **OASES** a fertile area in a desert, where water is found and plants grow

OAST *noun* **OASTS** a kiln for drying hops or, formerly, malt

OAT *noun* **OATS** a cereal and type of grass, thought to be native to the Mediterranean region and now cultivated mainly in cool moist temperate regions as a food crop

OATCAKE *noun* **OATCAKES** a thin dry savoury biscuit made from oatmeal

OATEN *adj* made of oats or oatmeal

OATH *noun* **OATHS** a solemn promise to tell the truth or to be loyal, etc, usually naming God as a witness

OATMEAL *noun* **OATMEALS** meal ground from oats, used to make oatcakes, etc

OAVES a plural of **oaf**

OB *noun* **OBS** an objection

OBA *noun* **OBAS** in West Africa, a chief or ruler

OBBLIGATO *noun* **OBBLIGATOS, OBBLIGATI** an accompaniment that forms an essential part of a piece of music, especially one played by a single instrument accompanying a voice

OBCONIC *adj* said of a fruit: conical and attached by the apex

OBCONICAL *adj* obconic

OBCORDATE *adj* said eg of a leaf: inversely heart-shaped and attached by the point

OBDURACY *noun* **OBDURACIES** hard-heartedness

OBDURATE *adj* hard-hearted

OBEAH *noun* **OBEAHS** a kind of witchcraft practised in the W Indies and Guyana, etc

OBEDIENCE *noun* **OBEDIENCES** the act or practice of obeying

OBEDIENT *adj* obeying; willing to obey

OBEISANCE *noun* **OBEISANCES** a bow, act or other expression of obedience or respect

OBEISANT *adj* obedient; respectful

OBELISK *noun* **OBELISKS** a tall tapering, usually four-sided, stone pillar with a pyramidal top, erected as a landmark or for religious or commemorative purposes, etc

OBELUS *noun* **OBELI** a dagger-shaped mark (†) used especially for referring to footnotes

OBESE *adj* **OBESER, OBESEST** very or abnormally fat

OBESENESS *noun* **OBESENESSES** obesity

OBESITY *noun* **OBESITIES** the condition of someone who is overweight as a result of the accumulation of excess fat in the body

OBEY *verb* **OBEYS, OBEYING, OBEYED** to do what one is told to do by someone

OBFUSCATE *verb* **OBFUSCATES, OBFUSCATING, OBFUSCATED** to darken or obscure something

OBI *noun* **OBIS** a broad sash, tied in a large flat bow at the back, that is worn with a Japanese kimono

OBITUARY *noun* **OBITUARIES** a notice or announcement, especially in a newspaper, of a person's death, often with a short account of their life □ *adj* relating to or recording the death of a person or persons

OBJECT[1] *noun* **OBJECTS** a material thing that can be seen or touched

OBJECT[2] *verb* **OBJECTS, OBJECTING, OBJECTED** to be opposed, or to feel or express disapproval

OBJECTIFY *verb* **OBJECTIFIES, OBJECTIFYING, OBJECTIFIED** to make something into or present it as an object

OBJECTION *noun* **OBJECTIONS** the act of objecting

OBJECTIVE *adj* not depending on, or influenced by, personal opinions or prejudices □ *noun* **OBJECTIVES** a thing aimed at or wished for; a goal

OBJECTOR *noun* **OBJECTORS** someone who objects

OBJET *noun* **OBJETS** an object, usually one displayed as an ornament

OBJURGATE *verb* **OBJURGATES, OBJURGATING, OBJURGATED** to rebuke someone; to scold or chide

OBLAST *noun* **OBLASTS** in some republics of the former Soviet Union and earlier in Russia: an administrative district; a region

OBLATE[1] *adj* said of something approximately spherical: flattened at the poles, like the Earth

OBLATE[2] *noun* **OBLATES** someone dedicated to monastic life (but without having taken vows) or to a religious life

OBLATION *noun* **OBLATIONS** the offering of the bread and wine to God at a Eucharist

OBLATORY *adj* of or relating to an oblation

OBLIGATE *adj* said of an organism, especially a bacterium: limited to specific functions and by specific conditions □ *verb* **OBLIGATES, OBLIGATING, OBLIGATED** to bind or oblige someone by contract, duty or moral obligation

OBLIGATO noun **OBLIGATOS, OBLIGATI** an obbligato

OBLIGE verb **OBLIGES, OBLIGING, OBLIGED** to bind someone morally or legally; to compel

OBLIGING adj ready to help others; courteously helpful

OBLIQUE adj **OBLIQUER, OBLIQUEST** sloping; not vertical or horizontal ◻ noun **OBLIQUES** an oblique line; a solidus (/) ◻ verb **OBLIQUES, OBLIQUING, OBLIQUED** to advance obliquely

OBLIQUELY adverb in an oblique way

OBLIQUITY noun **OBLIQUITIES** the state of being oblique

OBLIVION noun **OBLIVIONS** the state or fact of having forgotten or of being unconscious

OBLIVIOUS adj forgetful; absent-mindedly unaware

OBLONG adj rectangular with adjacent sides of unequal length; with a greater breadth than height ◻ noun **OBLONGS** a rectangular figure

OBLOQUY noun **OBLOQUIES** abuse, blame or censure

OBNOXIOUS adj offensive; objectionable

OBO noun **OBOS** a vessel for carrying oil and bulk ore

OBOE noun **OBOES** a double-reed treble woodwind instrument with a penetrating tone

OBOIST noun **OBOISTS** a player on the oboe

OBOL noun **OBOLS** in ancient Greece: the sixth part of a drachma in weight or in money

OBS plural of **ob**

OBSCENE adj **OBSCENER, OBSCENEST** offensive to accepted standards of behaviour or morality, especially sexual morality

OBSCENELY adverb in an obscene way

OBSCENITY noun **OBSCENITIES** the state or quality of being obscene

OBSCURANT noun **OBSCURANTS** someone who tries to prevent enlightenment or reform

OBSCURE adj **OBSCURER, OBSCUREST** dark; dim ◻ verb **OBSCURES, OBSCURING, OBSCURED** to make something dark or dim

OBSCURELY adverb in an obscure way

OBSCURITY noun **OBSCURITIES** the state of being obscure

OBSEQUENT adj said of a stream or river: flowing in a contrary direction to the original slope of the land

OBSEQUIES plural noun funeral rites

OBSERVANT adj quick to notice; perceptive

OBSERVE verb **OBSERVES, OBSERVING, OBSERVED** to notice or become conscious of something

OBSERVER noun **OBSERVERS** a person who observes

OBSESS verb **OBSESSES, OBSESSING, OBSESSED** to occupy someone's thoughts or mind completely, persistently or constantly; to preoccupy or haunt

OBSESSION noun **OBSESSIONS** a persistent or dominating thought, idea, feeling, etc

OBSESSIVE adj relating to or resulting from obsession, an obsession or obsessions

OBSIDIAN noun **OBSIDIANS** the commonest type of volcanic glass, usually black, but sometimes red or brown in colour, formed by the rapid cooling and solidification of granite magma

OBSOLESCE verb **OBSOLESCES, OBSOLESCING, OBSOLESCED** to become obsolete; to be going out of use

OBSOLETE adj no longer in use or in practice

OBSTACLE noun **OBSTACLES** someone or something that obstructs, or hinders or prevents advance

OBSTETRIC adj relating to obstetrics

OBSTETRICS singular noun the branch of medicine and surgery that deals with pregnancy, childbirth and the care of the mother

OBSTINACY noun **OBSTINACIES** the quality or state of being obstinate; stubbornness

OBSTINATE adj refusing to change one's opinion or course of action; stubborn; inflexible

OBSTRUCT verb **OBSTRUCTS, OBSTRUCTING, OBSTRUCTED** to block or close (a passage or opening, etc)

OBTAIN verb **OBTAINS, OBTAINING, OBTAINED** to get

something; to become the owner, or come into possession, of something, often by effort or planning; to gain something

OBTAINER noun **OBTAINERS** someone who obtains or gains something

OBTRUDE verb **OBTRUDES, OBTRUDING, OBTRUDED** to be or become unpleasantly noticeable or prominent

OBTRUDER noun **OBTRUDERS** someone who obtrudes

OBTRUSION noun **OBTRUSIONS** an unwanted thrusting in, forward or upon

OBTRUSIVE adj unpleasantly noticeable or prominent

OBTUSE adj **OBTUSER, OBTUSEST** stupid and slow to understand; not very perceptive or sensitive

OBTUSELY adverb in an obtuse way; stupidly; dully

OBTUSITY noun **OBTUSITIES** the quality of being obtuse; stupidity; dullness

OBVERSE adj turned towards or facing the observer ◻ noun **OBVERSES** the side of a coin with the head or main design on it

OBVERSELY adverb in an obverse way

OBVERSION noun **OBVERSIONS** the act of turning a thing towards one

OBVIATE verb **OBVIATES, OBVIATING, OBVIATED** to prevent or remove (a potential difficulty or problem, etc) in advance; to forestall

OBVIATION noun **OBVIATIONS** the action of obviating; prevention

OBVIOUS adj easily seen or understood; clearly evident ◻ noun something which is obvious

OBVIOUSLY adverb evidently

OCA noun **OCAS** a South American wood-sorrel

OCARINA noun **OCARINAS** a small simple fluty-toned wind instrument that has an egg-shaped body with fingerholes and a projecting mouthpiece

OCCAM noun **OCCAMS** in computing: a software language

OCCASION noun **OCCASIONS** a particular event or happening, or the time at which it occurs ◻ verb **OCCASIONS, OCCASIONING, OCCASIONED** to cause something; to bring it about, especially incidentally

OCCIDENT noun **OCCIDENTS** the countries in the west, especially those in Europe and America regarded as culturally distinct from eastern countries (the Orient)

OCCIPITAL adj relating to or in the region of the back of the head □ noun **OCCIPITALS** the bone that forms the back of the skull and part of its base, and encircles the spinal column

OCCIPUT noun **OCCIPUTS** the back of the head or skull

OCCLUDE verb **OCCLUDES, OCCLUDING, OCCLUDED** to block up or cover (eg a pore or some other opening or orifice)

OCCLUDENT adj causing or resulting in occlusion □ noun **OCCLUDENTS** that which occludes

OCCLUDER noun **OCCLUDERS** a device used to occlude an eye

OCCLUSION noun **OCCLUSIONS** the closing of an orifice, etc

OCCLUSIVE adj serving to close

OCCULT adj involving, using or dealing with that which is magical, mystical or supernatural □ verb **OCCULTS, OCCULTING, OCCULTED** to hide or conceal something, or to be hidden or concealed

OCCULTISM noun **OCCULTISMS** the doctrine or study of the supernatural, and practices purporting to achieve communication with things hidden and mysterious

OCCULTIST noun **OCCULTISTS** someone who believes in occult things

OCCULTLY adverb in an occult way

OCCUPANCY noun **OCCUPANCIES** the act or condition of occupying (a house or flat, etc), or the fact of its being occupied

OCCUPANT noun **OCCUPANTS** someone who occupies, holds or resides in a property, or in a particular position, etc

OCCUPIER noun **OCCUPIERS** someone who lives in a building, either as a tenant or owner; an occupant

OCCUPY verb **OCCUPIES, OCCUPYING, OCCUPIED** to have possession of or live in (a house, etc)

OCCUR verb **OCCURS, OCCURRING, OCCURRED** to happen or take place

OCCURRENT adj happening or incidental

OCEAN noun **OCEANS** the continuous expanse of salt water that covers about 70% of the Earth's surface and surrounds the continental land masses

OCEANIC adj relating to the ocean

OCELLAR adj like or relating to an ocellus

OCELLATE adj having an eyelike spot or spots

OCELLATED adj ocellate

OCELLUS noun **OCELLI** in insects and other lower animals: a simple eye or eyespot, as distinct from a compound eye

OCELOT noun **OCELOTS** a medium-sized wild cat, found in the forests of Central and S America, that has dark-yellow fur marked with spots and stripes

OCH exclamation expressing surprise, impatience, disagreement, annoyance or regret, etc

OCHE noun **OCHES** the line, groove or ridge on the floor behind which a darts player must stand to throw

OCHER noun **OCHERS** ochre □ adj ochre □ verb **OCHERS, OCHERING, OCHERED** to ochre

OCHLOCRAT noun **OCHLOCRATS** someone who believes in mob rule

OCHONE exclamation ohone

OCHRE noun **OCHRES** any of various fine earths or clays that contain ferric oxide, silica or alumina, used as a red, yellow or brown pigment □ adj with the colour of ochre □ verb **OCHRES, OCHRING, OCHRED** to mark or colour something with ochre

OCHREA noun **OCHREAE** a sheath formed by two or more stipulate leaves joined round a stem

OCHREATE adj having or relating to an ochrea

OCHREOUS adj of or like ochre; yellowish

OCHROUS adj ochreous

OCHRY adj ochreous

OCKER noun **OCKERS** an oafish uncultured Australian man □ adj typical of an ocker; boorish; uncultured

OCREA noun **OCREAE** ochrea

OCTACHORD noun **OCTACHORDS** a diatonic series of eight notes

OCTAD noun **OCTADS** a group, series or set, etc of eight things

OCTADIC adj of or relating to an octad

OCTAGON noun **OCTAGONS** a flat figure with eight straight sides and eight angles

OCTAGONAL adj shaped like an octagon

OCTAL adj relating to or based on the number 8 □ noun **OCTALS** a numbering system using the base 8 and the digits 0 to 7, eg 9 (decimal) is 11 (octal)

OCTAMETER noun **OCTAMETERS** a line of eight metrical feet

OCTANE noun **OCTANES** a colourless liquid belonging to the alkane series of hydrocarbons

OCTANT noun **OCTANTS** one eighth of the circumference of a circle

OCTANTAL adj of or relating to an octant

OCTAROON noun **OCTAROONS** an octoroon

OCTAVE noun **OCTAVES** any group or series of eight

OCTAVO noun **OCTAVOS** a size of book or page

OCTENNIAL adj happening every eight years

OCTET noun **OCTETS** any group of eight people or things

OCTETTE noun **OCTETTES** an octet

OCTILLION noun **OCTILLIONS** in Britain and Germany: a million raised to the eighth power, 10^{48}; in North America and France: a thousand raised to the ninth power, 10^{27}

OCTOPUS noun **OCTOPUSES** any of about 150 species of marine mollusc, found mainly in tropical regions, with a soft rounded body, no external shell, and eight arms, each of which bears two rows of suckers

OCTOPUSH noun **OCTOPUSHES** an underwater game similar to hockey, played in a swimming pool by two teams of six players, who attempt to score goals with a lead puck

OCTOROON noun **OCTOROONS** a person having one black African or Caribbean great-grandparent; the offspring of a quadroon and person of European descent

OCTROI noun **OCTROIS** especially in some European countries: a duty levied on certain articles brought into a town

OCTUPLE adj eight times as large; eightfold □ verb **OCTUPLES, OCTUPLING, OCTUPLED** to multiply by eight; to become or make something eight times as many or as much, etc

OCTUPLET noun **OCTUPLETS** in music: a group of eight notes to be played in the time of six

OCULAR adj relating to or in the region of the eye □ noun **OCULARS** the eye

OCULARIST noun **OCULARISTS** a maker of artificial eyes

OCULARLY adverb in an ocular way

OCULATE adj with eyelike spots or markings

OCULATED adj oculate

OCULIST noun **OCULISTS** a specialist in diseases and defects of the eye; an optician or ophthalmologist

OCULUS noun **OCULI** a round window

OD noun **ODS** a hypothetical force

ODA noun **ODAS** a room in a harem

ODALISK noun **ODALISKS** an odalisque

ODALISQUE noun **ODALISQUES** a female slave or concubine in a harem, especially in the harem belonging to the Turkish Sultan

ODD adj **ODDER, ODDEST** unusual; strange □ noun **ODDS** a golf stroke that makes a player's total number of strokes for a particular hole one more than their opponent's

ODDBALL noun **ODDBALLS** a strange or eccentric person □ adj said of a thing, a plan or circumstances, etc: eccentric; peculiar

ODDISH adj rather odd

ODDITY noun **ODDITIES** a strange or odd person or thing

ODDLY adverb in an odd way

ODDMENT noun **ODDMENTS** something left over or remaining from a greater quantity

ODDNESS noun **ODDNESSES** the state or condition or quality, etc of being odd

ODDS plural noun the chance or possibility, expressed as a ratio, that something will or will not happen

ODE noun **ODES** a lyric poem, usually a fairly long one, with lines of different lengths and complex rhythms, addressed to a particular person or thing

ODIOUS adj hateful; repulsive; extremely unpleasant or offensive

ODIOUSLY adverb in an odious way

ODIUM noun **ODIUMS** hatred, strong dislike, or disapproval of a person or thing, especially when widespread

ODOMETER noun **ODOMETERS** a device for measuring and displaying the distance travelled by a wheeled vehicle or a person, eg the mileometer incorporated in the speedometer of a car

ODOMETRY noun **ODOMETRIES** the science of measuring, or the measurement of, distance

ODONTALGY noun **ODONTALGIES** toothache

ODONTOID noun **ODONTOIDS** a tooth-like structure

ODOR noun **ODORS** an odour

ODOROUS adj with or giving off an odour

ODOROUSLY adverb in an odorous way

ODOUR noun **ODOURS** a distinctive smell; scent

ODOURLESS adj having no odour

ODS plural of **od**

ODYSSEY noun **ODYSSEYS** a long and adventurous journey or series of wanderings

OE noun **OES** a Scots word for a grandchild

OEDEMA noun **OEDEMAS** an abnormal and excessive accumulation of fluid within body tissues or body cavities, causing generalized or local swelling

OENOLOGY noun **OENOLOGIES** the study or knowledge of wine

OENOPHILE noun **OENOPHILES** a lover or connoisseur of wine

OERLIKON noun **OERLIKONS** any of various guns and fittings, especially a type of anti-aircraft cannon

OERSTED noun **OERSTEDS** in the cgs unit system: a unit of magnetic field strength

OES plural of **oe**

OESTRAL adj of or relating to oestrus

OESTROGEN noun **OESTROGENS** any of a group of steroid hormones, produced mainly by the ovaries, that control the growth and functioning of the female sex

organs and the appearance of female secondary sexual characteristics, eg breast development, and that regulate the menstrual cycle

OESTROUS adj of or relating to oestrus

OESTRUS noun **OESTRUSES** a regularly occurring but restricted period of sexual receptivity that occurs in most female mammals apart from humans

OF prep belonging to

OFF adverb away; at or to a distance □ adj said of an electrical device: not functioning or operating; disconnected; not on □ prep from or away from something □ noun **OFFS** the start, eg of a race or journey □ verb **OFFS, OFFING, OFFED** to go off

OFFAL noun **OFFALS** the heart, brains, liver and kidneys, etc of an animal, used as food

OFFBEAT noun **OFFBEATS** any of the usually unaccented beats in a bar, eg the second or fourth in four-four time □ adj relating to offbeats; with a rhythm on the offbeats

OFFCUT noun **OFFCUTS** a small piece of eg wood or cloth, etc cut off or left over from a larger quantity, especially when making or shaping something

OFFENCE noun **OFFENCES** displeasure, annoyance or anger; the breaking of a rule or law, etc; a crime

OFFEND verb **OFFENDS, OFFENDING, OFFENDED** to make someone feel hurt or angry; to insult them; to commit a sin or crime

OFFENDER noun **OFFENDERS** someone who offends, especially criminally

OFFENDING adj causing offence

OFFENSE noun **OFFENSES** the breaking of a rule or law, etc

OFFENSIVE adj giving or likely to give offence; insulting □ noun **OFFENSIVES** an aggressive action or attitude

OFFER verb **OFFERS, OFFERING, OFFERED** to put forward (a gift, payment or suggestion, etc) for acceptance, refusal or consideration □ noun **OFFERS** an act of offering

OFFERER noun **OFFERERS** someone who offers something, especially shares for sale

OFFERING noun **OFFERINGS** the act of making an offer

OFFEROR noun **OFFERORS** an offerer

OFFERTORY noun **OFFERTORIES** the offering of bread and wine to God during a Eucharist

OFFHAND adj casual or careless, often with the result of being rude

OFFHANDED adj offhand

OFFICE noun **OFFICES** the room, set of rooms or building in which the business of a firm is done, or in which a particular kind of business, clerical work, etc is done

OFFICER noun **OFFICERS** someone in a position of authority and responsibility in the armed forces □ verb **OFFICERS, OFFICERING, OFFICERED** to provide officers for (the army or navy)

OFFICIAL adj relating or belonging to an office or position of authority □ noun **OFFICIALS** someone who holds office or who is in a position of authority

OFFICIANT noun **OFFICIANTS** someone who officiates at a religious ceremony

OFFICIATE verb **OFFICIATES, OFFICIATING, OFFICIATED** to act in an official capacity

OFFICINAL adj said of a drug, etc: sold as a medicine

OFFICIOUS adj too ready to offer help or advice, etc, especially when it is not wanted; interfering

OFFING noun **OFFINGS** the more distant part of the sea that is visible from the shore

OFFISH adj said of a person's manner, etc: aloof; distant

OFFLOAD verb **OFFLOADS, OFFLOADING, OFFLOADED** to unload

OFFPRINT noun **OFFPRINTS** a separately printed copy of an article that originally formed part of a larger magazine or periodical

OFFSET noun **OFFSETS** a start; the outset □ verb **OFFSETS, OFFSETTING, OFFSET** to counterbalance or compensate for something

OFFSHOOT noun **OFFSHOOTS** a shoot growing from a plant's main stem

OFFSHORE adj situated in, at, or on the sea, not far from the coast

OFFSIDE adj in eg football, rugby: in an illegal position between the ball and the opponents' goal

□ adverb in eg football, rugby: in an illegal position between the ball and the opponents' goal □ noun **OFFSIDES** the side of a vehicle or horse nearest the centre of the road, in the UK the right side

OFFSPRING noun **OFFSPRINGS** a person's child or children

OFT adverb often

OFTEN adj **OFTENER, OFTENEST** done, made or happening, etc many times; frequent □ adverb many times; frequently

OGAM noun **OGAMS** an ancient alphabet, consisting of 20 or 25 characters, used from the 4c BC in Celtic and Pictish inscriptions

OGAMIC adj of or relating to ogam

OGEE noun **OGEES** an S-shaped curve or line

OGGIN noun **OGGINS** the sea

OGHAM noun **OGHAMS** ogam

OGHAMIC adj ogamic

OGIVAL adj of or relating to an ogive

OGIVE noun **OGIVES** a diagonal rib of a vault

OGLE verb **OGLES, OGLING, OGLED** to cast flirtatious or amorous glances □ noun **OGLES** a flirtatious or lecherous look

OGRE noun **OGRES** in fairy stories: a frightening, cruel, ugly, man-eating giant

OGREISH adj resembling an ogre

OGRESS noun **OGRESSES** in fairy stories: a frightening, cruel, ugly, man-eating female giant

OGRISH adj of or like an ogre

OH exclamation expressing surprise, admiration, pleasure, anger or fear, etc

OHM noun **OHMS** in the SI and MKSA systems: a unit of electrical resistance, equal to the resistance of a circuit in which a potential difference of one volt is required to maintain a current of one ampere

OHMAGE noun **OHMAGES** electrical resistance measured in ohms

OHMMETER noun **OHMMETERS** a device for measuring electrical resistance

OHO noun **OHOS** an exclamation expressng surprise, triumphant satisfaction or derision

OHONE exclamation expressing lamentation or grief

OI exclamation used to attract attention

OIK noun **OIKS** someone thought of as inferior, especially because of being rude, ignorant, badly educated or lower class

OIL noun **OILS** any greasy, viscous and usually flammable substance, insoluble in water but soluble in organic compounds, that is derived from animals, plants or mineral deposits, or manufactured artificially, and used as a fuel, lubricant or food □ verb **OILS, OILING, OILED** to apply oil to something; to lubricate or treat something with oil

OILCLOTH noun **OILCLOTHS** cloth, often cotton, treated with oil to make it waterproof

OILED adj smeared, treated, lubricated or impregnated with oil

OILER noun **OILERS** a person or thing that oils

OILFIELD noun **OILFIELDS** an area of land that contains reserves of petroleum, especially one that is already being exploited

OILIER see under **oily**

OILIEST see under **oily**

OILILY adverb in an oily way

OILINESS noun **OILINESSES** the quality of being oily

OILMAN noun **OILMEN** a man who deals in oil

OILSKIN noun **OILSKINS** cloth treated with oil to make it waterproof

OILSTONE noun **OILSTONES** a whetstone used with oil

OILY adj **OILIER, OILIEST** like oil; greasy

OINK noun **OINKS** a representation of the characteristic grunting noise made by a pig □ verb **OINKS, OINKING, OINKED** to make the grunting noise characteristic of a pig

OINTMENT noun **OINTMENTS** any greasy or oily semi-solid preparation, usually medicated, that can be applied externally to the skin in order to heal, soothe or protect it

OJIME noun **OJIMES** a carved Japanese bead

OKAPI noun **OKAPIS** a ruminant animal from central Africa, the only living relative of the giraffe but with a shorter neck

OKAY adj all correct; all right; satisfactory □ adverb well; satisfactorily □ noun **OKAYS** approval, sanction or agreement □ verb **OKAYS, OKAYING, OKAYED**

to approve or pass something as satisfactory

OKE *noun* OKES a Turkish weight

OKRA *noun* OKRAS a tall annual plant native to tropical Africa that has red and yellow flowers

OLD *adj* OLDER, OLDEST advanced in age; that has existed for a long time; not young □ *noun* OLDS an earlier time

OLDEN *adj* former; past

OLDIE *noun* OLDIES an old person

OLDISH *adj* somewhat old

OLDSTER *noun* OLDSTERS an old or elderly person

OLÉ *exclamation* Spanish exclamation expressing approval or support

OLEACEOUS *adj* relating or belonging to a family of trees and shrubs that includes the olive, ash, jasmine and privet

OLEANDER *noun* OLEANDERS a poisonous shrub with leathery evergreen leaves and clusters of fragrant white, pink or purple flowers

OLEARIA *noun* OLEARIAS an Australasian evergreen shrub with white, yellow or mauve daisy-like flowers

OLEASTER *noun* OLEASTERS the true wild olive

OLEATE *noun* OLEATES a salt or ester of oleic acid

OLEFIN *noun* OLEFINS alkene

OLEIN *noun* OLEINS a glycerine ester of oleic acid

OLEO *noun* OLEOS short form of oleograph or oleomargarine

OLEOGRAPH *noun* OLEOGRAPHS a lithograph printed in oil colours to imitate an oil painting

OLEUM *noun* OLEUMS a solution of sulphur trioxide in sulphuric acid

OLFACTORY *adj* relating to the sense of smell □ *noun* OLFACTORIES an organ or nerve of smell

OLIBANUM *noun* OLIBANUMS an aromatic gum obtained from trees found especially in Somaliland and Arabia; a kind of frankincense

OLIGARCH *noun* OLIGARCHS a member of an oligarchy

OLIGARCHY *noun* OLIGARCHIES government by a small group of people

OLIGOPOLY *noun* OLIGOPOLIES a

situation in which there are few sellers of a particular product or service, and a small number of competitive firms control the market

OLIO *noun* OLIOS a highly spiced Spanish or Portuguese stew of different sorts of meat and vegetables

OLIVE *noun* OLIVES a small evergreen tree with a twisted gnarled trunk and narrow leathery silvery-green leaves, cultivated mainly in the Mediterranean region for its fruit and the oil obtained from the fruit □ *adj* dull yellowish-green in colour

OLIVINE *noun* OLIVINES any of a group of hard glassy rock-forming silicate minerals, typically olive-green, but sometimes yellowish or brown

OLLA *noun* OLLAS a jar or cooking pot

OLM *noun* OLMS a blind eel-like salamander, found in caves in Austria

OLOGY *noun* OLOGIES any science or branch of knowledge

OLOROSO *noun* OLOROSOS a golden-coloured medium-sweet sherry

OLYMPIAD *noun* OLYMPIADS an international contest

OM *noun* OMS a sacred syllable intoned in mantras and prayers, etc

OMASUM *noun* OMASA the third stomach of a ruminant

OMBRE *noun* OMBRES a card game popular in the 17th and 18th centuries

OMBRÉ *adj* said of fabric, etc: with colours gradually shading into each other □ *noun* OMBRÉS a fabric, etc, that has such shading

OMBUDSMAN *noun* OMBUDSMEN an official appointed to investigate complaints against public authorities, government departments or the people who work for them

OMEGA *noun* OMEGAS the 24th and last letter of the Greek alphabet, pronounced as a long open o

OMELET *noun* OMELETS an omelette

OMELETTE *noun* OMELETTES a dish made of beaten eggs fried in a pan, often folded round a savoury or sometimes sweet filling such as cheese or jam

OMEN *noun* OMENS a circumstance, phenomenon, etc that is regarded as a sign of a future event, either good or evil □ *verb* OMENS, OMENING, OMENED to portend

OMENED *adj* with omens of a specified kind

OMENTUM *noun* OMENTA abdominal lining linking the intestinal tract to other organs

OMERTÀ *noun* OMERTÀS the Mafia code of honour that requires silence about criminal activities and stresses the disgrace of informing

OMICRON *noun* OMICRONS the 15th letter of the Greek alphabet, pronounced as a short o

OMINOUS *adj* threatening; containing a warning of something evil or bad that will happen

OMINOUSLY *adverb* in an ominous way

OMISSIBLE *adj* referring to something that may be omitted

OMISSION *noun* OMISSIONS something that has been left out or neglected

OMISSIVE *adj* omitting, of the nature of omission

OMIT *verb* OMITS, OMITTING, OMITTED to leave something out, either by mistake or on purpose

OMMATEUM *noun* OMMATEA in insects: a compound eye, an eye made up of many separate units

OMNIBUS *noun* OMNIBUSES a book that contains reprints of a number of works by a single author, or several works on the same subject or of a similar type □ *adj* said especially of a legislative bill: relating to, dealing with or made up of several different items or parts

OMNIFIC *adj* all-creating

OMNIUM *noun* OMNIUMS the aggregate value of the different stocks in which a loan is funded

OMNIVORE *noun* OMNIVORES a person or animal that eats any type of food

OMNIVORY *noun* OMNIVORIES omnivorousness

ON *prep* touching, supported by, attached to, covering, or enclosing □ *adverb* said especially of clothes: in or into contact or a state of enclosing, covering, or being worn, etc □ *adj* working, broadcasting or performing □ *noun* ONS in cricket: the on side

ONAGER *noun* **ONAGERS** a variety of wild ass found in central Asia

ONANISM *noun* **ONANISMS** sexual intercourse in which the penis is withdrawn from the vagina before ejaculation; coitus interruptus

ONANIST *noun* **ONANISTS** someone who practises onanism

ONANISTIC *adj* relating to onanism

ONCE *adverb* a single time □ *conj* as soon as; when once or if once □ *noun* **ONCES** one time or occasion

ONCER *noun* **ONCERS** someone or something that does a particular thing only once

ONCOGENE *noun* **ONCOGENES** a gene that causes a normal cell to develop into a cancerous cell, or to multiply in an uncontrolled manner

ONCOGENIC *adj* causing tumours

ONCOLOGY *noun* **ONCOLOGIES** the branch of medicine that deals with the study of tumours, especially cancerous ones

ONCOMING *adj* approaching; advancing □ *noun* **ONCOMINGS** an approach

ONCOST *noun* **ONCOSTS** overhead expenses

ONE *noun* **ONES** the cardinal number 1 □ *adj* being a single unit, number or thing □ *pronoun* (often referring to a noun already mentioned or implied) an individual person, thing or instance

ONEIRIC *adj* belonging or relating to dreams or dreaming

ONENESS *noun* **ONENESSES** the state or quality of being one; singleness

ONEROUS *adj* heavy; difficult to do or bear; oppressive

ONEROUSLY *adverb* in an onerous way

ONESELF *pronoun* the reflexive form of one

ONFALL *noun* **ONFALLS** an attack; an onslaught

ONFLOW *verb* **ONFLOWS, ONFLOWING, ONFLOWED** to flow on □ *noun* **ONFLOWS** a flowing on

ONGOING *adj* in progress; going on □ *noun* **ONGOINGS** the action of going on

ONION *noun* **ONIONS** any of numerous varieties of a biennial plant belonging to the lily family, native to SW Asia

ONIONY *adj* **ONIONIER,**

ONIONIEST smelling or tasting of onions

ONIRIC *adj* belonging or relating to dreams or dreaming

ONLOOKER *noun* **ONLOOKERS** someone who watches and does not take part; an observer

ONLOOKING *adj* that looks on

ONLY *adj* without any others of the same type □ *adverb* not more than; just □ *conj* but; however

ONRUSH *noun* **ONRUSHES** a sudden and strong movement forward

ONSET *noun* **ONSETS** an attack; an assault

ONSHORE *adverb* towards, on, or on to the shore □ *adj* said of the wind: blowing or moving from the sea towards the shore

ONSIDE *adj* said of a player in rugby, football etc: in a position where the ball may legally be played; not offside □ *adverb* said of a player in rugby, football etc: in a position where the ball may legally be played; not offside

ONSLAUGHT *noun* **ONSLAUGHTS** a fierce attack; an onset

ONTO *prep* on to

ONTOGENIC *adj* relating to ontogeny

ONTOGENY *noun* **ONTOGENIES** the branch of science that deals with the history of the development of an individual living organism, from fertilization of the ovum to sexual maturity

ONTOLOGIC *adj* relating to ontology

ONTOLOGY *noun* **ONTOLOGIES** the branch of metaphysics that deals with the nature and essence of things or of existence

ONUS *noun* **ONUSES** a responsibility or burden

ONWARD *adj* moving forward in place or time; advancing □ *adverb* towards or at a place or time which is advanced or in front; ahead

ONYX *noun* **ONYXES** a very hard variety of agate with straight alternating bands of one or more colours, eg a form with black and white bands widely used to make jewellery and ornaments

OO *noun* **OOS** a Scots word for *wool*

OOCYTE *noun* **OOCYTES** a cell that gives rise to an ovum by two meiotic divisions

OODLES *plural noun* lots; a great quantity

OOF *noun* **OOFS** money

OOGAMOUS *adj* relating to or characterized by oogamy

OOGAMY *noun* **OOGAMIES** a form of sexual reproduction in which a large non-motile female gamete (the ovum or egg cell) is fertilized by a small motile male gamete

OOGENESIS *noun* **OOGENESES** the production and development of an ovum in the ovary of an animal

OOH *exclamation* expressing pleasure, surprise, excitement or pain □ *verb* **OOHS, OOHING, OOHED** to make an ooh sound to show surprise or excitement, etc

OOLITE *noun* **OOLITES** a sedimentary rock, usually a form of limestone, consisting of masses of small round particles that resemble fish eggs

OOLITIC *adj* of or relating to oolite

OOLOGIST *noun* **OOLOGISTS** someone who studies or collects birds' eggs

OOLOGY *noun* **OOLOGIES** the science or study of birds' eggs

OOLONG *noun* **OOLONGS** a variety of black China tea that is partly fermented before it is dried and has the flavour of green tea

OOM *noun* **OOMS** a South African word for *uncle*

OOMIAK *noun* **OOMIAKS** a large open boat made from a wooden frame covered with stretched skins, typically paddled by women

OOMPAH *noun* **OOMPAHS** a common way of representing the deep sound made by a large brass musical instrument, such as a tuba

OOMPH *noun* **OOMPHS** energy; enthusiasm

OON *noun* **OONS** a Scots word for *oven*

OOP *verb* **OOPS, OOPING, OOPED** to oup

OOPS *exclamation* expressing surprise or apology, eg when one makes a mistake or drops something, etc

OOR *adj* a Scots word for *our*

OORIAL *noun* **OORIALS** an urial

OOS *plural of* **oo**

OOSPORE noun **OOSPORES** a fertilized ovum

OOZE verb **OOZES, OOZING, OOZED** to flow or leak out gently or slowly ▫ noun **OOZES** anything which oozes

OOZILY adverb in an oozy way

OOZINESS noun the state of being oozy

OOZY adj **OOZIER, OOZIEST** like or containing ooze; slimy

OP noun **OPS** a surgical operation

OPACITY noun **OPACITIES** opaqueness

OPAH noun **OPAHS** a large brilliantly coloured sea-fish with a laterally flattened body

OPAL noun **OPALS** a milky-white, black or coloured form of silica, combined with variable amounts of water, usually with a characteristic internal 'play' of coloured flashes caused by light reflected from different layers within the stone

OPALINE noun **OPALINES** a whitish semi-translucent glass

OPAQUE adj **OPAQUER, OPAQUEST** not allowing light to pass through; not transparent or translucent ▫ noun **OPAQUES** something, eg a space or medium, that is opaque ▫ verb **OPAQUES, OPAQUING, OPAQUED** to make something opaque

OPAQUELY adverb in an opaque way

OPE verb **OPES, OPING, OPED** to open

OPEN adj **OPENER, OPENEST** said of a door or barrier, etc: not closed or locked ▫ verb **OPENS, OPENING, OPENED** to unfasten or move (eg a door or barrier) to allow access ▫ noun **OPENS** an area of open country; an area not obstructed by buildings, etc

OPENABLE adj that can be opened

OPENER noun **OPENERS** a device for opening something

OPENING noun **OPENINGS** the act of making or becoming open ▫ adj relating to or forming an opening; first

OPENLY adverb in an open way

OPENNESS noun **OPENNESSES** the condition of being open

OPENWORK noun **OPENWORKS** work in cloth, metal or wood, etc constructed so as to have gaps or holes in it, used especially for decoration

OPERA noun **OPERAS** a dramatic work set to music, in which the singers are usually accompanied by an orchestra

OPERABLE adj said of a disease or injury, etc: that can be treated by surgery

OPERAND noun **OPERANDS** a quantity on which a mathematical operation is performed

OPERANT adj operative; producing effects ▫ noun **OPERANTS** someone or something that operates; an operator

OPERATE verb **OPERATES, OPERATING, OPERATED** to function or work

OPERATIC adj relating to or like opera

OPERATION noun **OPERATIONS** an act, method or process of working or operating

OPERATIVE adj working; in action; having an effect ▫ noun **OPERATIVES** a worker, especially one with special skills

OPERATOR noun **OPERATORS** someone who operates a machine or apparatus

OPERCULAR adj belonging to the operculum

OPERCULUM noun **OPERCULA** in some gastropods: a horny plate that covers the opening of the shell

OPERETTA noun **OPERETTAS** a short light opera, with spoken dialogue and often dancing

OPHIDIAN adj belonging or relating to the suborder of reptiles that includes snakes ▫ noun **OPHIDIANS** a snake

OPHITE noun **OPHITES** igneous rock in which large silicate crystals completely enclose smaller feldspars

OPHITIC adj relating to ophite

OPIATE noun **OPIATES** any of a group of drugs containing or derived from opium, eg morphine, heroin or codeine, that depress the central nervous system, and can be used as steroid analgesics ▫ adj soporific; sleep-inducing ▫ verb **OPIATES, OPIATING, OPIATED** to treat or put someone to sleep with opium

OPINE verb **OPINES, OPINING, OPINED** to suppose or express something as an opinion

OPINION noun **OPINIONS** a belief or judgement which seems likely to be true, but which is not based on proof

OPIUM noun **OPIUMS** a highly addictive narcotic drug extracted from the opium poppy, used in medicine to bring sleep and relieve pain

OPOSSUM noun **OPOSSUMS** any of several small tree-dwelling marsupials with thick fur, an opposable thumb on each hindfoot and a hairless prehensile tail

OPPONENCY noun **OPPONENCIES** opposition; antagonism

OPPONENT noun **OPPONENTS** someone who belongs to the opposing side in an argument, contest or battle, etc ▫ adj opposed; contrary

OPPORTUNE adj said of an action: happening at a time which is suitable, proper or correct

OPPOSABLE adj said of a digit, especially the thumb: able to be placed in a position so that it faces and can touch the ends of the other digits of the same hand or foot

OPPOSE verb **OPPOSES, OPPOSING, OPPOSED** to resist or fight against someone or something by force or argument

OPPOSER noun **OPPOSERS** someone who opposes a person, argument, etc

OPPOSING adj that opposes or acts against

OPPOSITE adj placed or being on the other side of, or at the other end of, a real or imaginary line or space ▫ noun **OPPOSITES** an opposite person or thing ▫ adverb in or into an opposite position ▫ prep in a position across from and facing someone or something

OPPRESS verb **OPPRESSES, OPPRESSING, OPPRESSED** to govern with cruelty and injustice

OPPRESSOR noun **OPPRESSORS** someone who oppresses

OPPUGN verb **OPPUGNS, OPPUGNING, OPPUGNED** to call into question; to dispute

OPPUGNER noun **OPPUGNERS** someone who oppugns

OPS plural of **op**

OPT verb **OPTS, OPTING, OPTED** to decide between several possibilities; to choose

OPTATIVE adj characterized by desire or choice ▫ noun **OPTATIVES** the optative mood

OPTIC *adj* relating to the eye or vision ◻ *noun* the eye

OPTICAL *adj* relating to sight or to what one sees

OPTICALLY *adverb* in relation to sight or optics

OPTICIAN *noun* **OPTICIANS** someone who fits and sells glasses and contact lenses but is not qualified to prescribe them

OPTICS *singular noun* the study of light (especially visible light, but also ultraviolet and infra-red light)

OPTIMAL *adj* most favourable; optimum

OPTIMALLY *adverb* in the most favourable or advantageous way

OPTIMISE *verb* **OPTIMISES, OPTIMISING, OPTIMISED** to optimize

OPTIMISM *noun* **OPTIMISMS** the tendency to take a bright, hopeful view of things and expect the best possible outcome

OPTIMIST *noun* **OPTIMISTS** someone who has a bright and hopeful nature

OPTIMIZE *verb* **OPTIMIZES, OPTIMIZING, OPTIMIZED** to make the most or best of (a particular situation or opportunity, etc)

OPTIMUM *noun* **OPTIMA** the condition, situation, amount or level, etc that is the most favourable or gives the best results ◻ *adj* best or most favourable

OPTION *noun* **OPTIONS** that which is or which may be chosen ◻ *verb* **OPTIONS, OPTIONING, OPTIONED** to buy or sell something under option

OPTIONAL *adj* left to choice; not compulsory

OPTOMETER *noun* **OPTOMETERS** a device for testing vision

OPTOMETRY *noun* **OPTOMETRIES** the science of vision and eyecare

OPTOPHONE *noun* **OPTOPHONES** a device that, by translating printed characters into arbitrary sounds, enables a blind person to interpret printed type

OPULENCE *noun* **OPULENCES** conspicuous wealth; luxury

OPULENT *adj* rich; wealthy

OPULENTLY *adverb* in an opulent way

OPUNTIA *noun* **OPUNTIAS** a cactus of genus Opuntia, especially the prickly pear

OPUS *noun* **OPUSES, OPERA** an artistic work, especially a musical composition, often used with a number to show the order in which a composer's works were written or catalogued

OR[1] *conj* used to introduce alternatives

OR[2] *noun* **ORS** a gold colour

ORA plural of os [1]

ORACLE *noun* **ORACLES** in ancient Greece or Rome: a holy place where a god was believed to give advice and prophecy

ORACULAR *adj* relating to or like an oracle

ORACY *noun* **ORACIES** the ability to express oneself coherently and to communicate freely with others by word of mouth

ORAL *adj* spoken; not written ◻ *noun* **ORALS** a spoken test or examination

ORALLY *adverb* by word of mouth

ORANGE *noun* **ORANGES** a round citrus fruit with a tough reddish-yellow outer rind or peel enclosing segments filled with sweet or sharp-tasting juicy flesh that is rich in vitamin C ◻ *adj* **ORANGER, ORANGEST** orange-coloured

ORANGEADE *noun* **ORANGEADES** an orange-flavoured drink, usually fizzy

ORANGERY *noun* **ORANGERIES** a greenhouse in which orange trees can be grown in cool climates

ORANGEY *adj* **ORANGIER, ORANGIEST** somewhat orange in colour, flavour, etc

ORATE *verb* **ORATES, ORATING, ORATED** to make an oration

ORATION *noun* **ORATIONS** a formal or ceremonial public speech delivered in dignified language

ORATOR *noun* **ORATORS** someone who is skilled in persuading, moving or exciting people through public speech

ORATORIAL *adj* relating to or characteristic of an orator

ORATORIO *noun* **ORATORIOS** a musical composition, usually based on a Biblical or religious theme or story, sung by soloists and a chorus accompanied by an orchestra, but with no scenery, costumes or acting

ORATORY *noun* **ORATORIES** a chapel or small place set aside for private prayer

ORB *noun* **ORBS** a globe with a cross on top that is decorated with jewels and is carried as part of a monarch's regalia ◻ *verb* **ORBS, ORBING, ORBED** to form something into a circle or sphere

ORBICULAR *adj* approximately circular or spherical

ORBIT *noun* **ORBITS** in space: the elliptical path of one celestial body around another, eg the Earth's orbit around the Sun, or of an artificial satellite or spacecraft, etc around a celestial body ◻ *verb* **ORBITS, ORBITING, ORBITED** said of a celestial body, or a spacecraft, etc: to circle (the Earth or another planet, etc) in space

ORBITAL *noun* **ORBITALS** any region of space outside the nucleus of an atom or molecule where there is a high probability of finding an electron ◻ *adj* relating to or going round in an orbit

ORBITER *noun* **ORBITERS** a spacecraft or satellite that orbits the Earth or another planet but does not land on it

ORC *noun* **ORCS** any of various whales or ferocious sea creatures, eg the killer whale

ORCHARD *noun* **ORCHARDS** a garden or piece of land where fruit trees are grown

ORCHESTRA *noun* **ORCHESTRAS** a large group of instrumentalists who play together as an ensemble, led by a conductor, usually comprising four main sections, ie strings, woodwind, brass and percussion

ORCHID *noun* **ORCHIDS** a plant which is best known for its complex and exotic flowers

ORCHIL *noun* **ORCHILS** a red or violet dye made from various lichens

ORCHILLA *noun* **ORCHILLAS** orchil

ORD *noun* **ORDS** an obsolete word meaning a point, eg of a weapon

ORDAIN *verb* **ORDAINS, ORDAINING, ORDAINED** to appoint or admit someone as a priest or vicar, etc; to confer holy orders on them

ORDAINER *noun* **ORDAINERS** an ordaining minister or priest

ORDEAL *noun* **ORDEALS** a difficult, painful or testing experience

ORDER *noun* **ORDERS** a state in which everything is in its proper

place; tidiness □ verb **ORDERS,
ORDERING, ORDERED** to give a
command to someone
ORDERED adj placed in order
ORDERLY adj in good order; well
arranged □ noun **ORDERLIES** an
attendant, usually without
medical training, who does
various jobs in a hospital, such as
moving patients
ORDINAL noun **ORDINALS** a book
containing the services for the
ordination of ministers □ adj
denoting a position in a sequence
of numbers
ORDINANCE noun **ORDINANCES** a
law, order or ruling
ORDINAND noun **ORDINANDS**
someone who is training to
become a minister of the church; a
candidate for ordination
ORDINARY adj of the usual
everyday kind; unexceptional
□ noun **ORDINARIES** a judge of
ecclesiastical or other causes who
acts in his own right, such as a
bishop or his deputy
ORDINATE noun **ORDINATES** in
coordinate geometry: the second
of a pair of numbers (x and y),
known as the y coordinate
ORDNANCE noun **ORDNANCES**
heavy guns and military supplies
ORDURE noun **ORDURES** waste
matter from the bowels;
excrement
ORDUROUS adj dirty; filthy
ORE noun **ORES** a solid naturally
occurring mineral deposit from
which one or more economically
valuable substances, especially
metals, can be extracted, and for
which it is mined
OREGANO noun **OREGANOS** a
sweet-smelling Mediterranean
herb, a variety of wild marjoram

| **ORF** noun **ORFS** a viral infection of sheep |

ORGAN noun **ORGANS** a part of a
body or plant which has a special
function, eg a kidney, a leaf
ORGANDIE noun **ORGANDIES** a
very fine thin cotton fabric which
has been stiffened
ORGANELLE noun **ORGANELLES**
in the cell of a living organism: any
of various different types of
membrane-bound structure, each
of which has a specialized
function, eg mitochondria,
ribosomes and chloroplasts
ORGANIC adj relating to, derived

from, or with the characteristics of
a living organism
ORGANISE verb **ORGANISES,
ORGANISING, ORGANISED** to
organize
ORGANISER noun **ORGANISERS**
an organizer
ORGANISM noun **ORGANISMS**
any living structure, such as a
plant, animal, fungus or
bacterium, capable of growth and
reproduction
ORGANIST noun **ORGANISTS** a
person who plays the organ
ORGANIZE verb **ORGANIZES,
ORGANIZING, ORGANIZED** to give
an orderly structure to something;
to arrange, provide or prepare
ORGANIZER noun **ORGANIZERS**
someone or something that
organizes
ORGANZA noun **ORGANZAS** a
very fine stiff dress material made
of silk or synthetic fibres
ORGANZINE noun **ORGANZINES** a
silk yarn formed by twisting
together two or more threads
ORGASM noun **ORGASMS** the
climax of sexual excitement,
experienced as an intensely
pleasurable sensation caused by a
series of strong involuntary
contractions of the muscles of the
genital organs □ verb **ORGASMS,
ORGASMING, ORGASMED** to
experience an orgasm
ORGASMIC adj of or relating to
sexual orgasm
ORGIASTIC adj of the nature of an
orgy
ORGY noun **ORGIES** a wild party or
celebration involving
indiscriminate sexual activity and
excessive drinking
ORIBI noun **ORIBIS** a small fawn-
coloured antelope found in the
plains of southern and eastern
Africa
ORIEL noun **ORIELS** a small room
or recess with a polygonal bay
window, especially one supported
on brackets or corbels
ORIENT noun **ORIENTS** the part of
the sky where the sun rises □ verb
ORIENTS, ORIENTING, ORIENTED
to place something in a definite
position in relation to the points of
the compass or some other fixed
or known point
ORIENTAL adj from or relating to
the Orient; eastern □ noun
ORIENTALS a person born in the
Orient; an Asiatic

ORIENTATE verb **ORIENTATES,
ORIENTATING, ORIENTATED** to
orient
ORIENTED adj directed towards
something
ORIENTEER verb **ORIENTEERS,
ORIENTEERING, ORIENTEERED** to
take part in orienteering
ORIENTEERING noun
ORIENTEERINGS a sport in which
contestants race on foot and on
skis, etc over an unfamiliar cross-
country course, finding their way
to official check points using a
map and compass
ORIFICE noun **ORIFICES** a usually
small opening or mouthlike hole,
especially one in the body or a
body cavity
ORIFICIAL adj of or relating to an
orifice
ORIFLAMME noun **ORIFLAMMES**
a small banner of red silk split into
many points and carried on a gilt
staff, used as the ancient royal
standard of France
ORIGAMI noun **ORIGAMIS** the
originally Japanese art of folding
paper into decorative shapes and
figures
ORIGANUM noun **ORIGANUMS**
any of various aromatic herbs of
the marjoram genus of labiates or
other genus, used in cookery
ORIGIN noun **ORIGINS** a beginning
or starting-point; a source
ORIGINAL adj relating to an origin
or beginning □ noun **ORIGINALS**
the first example of something,
such as a document, photograph
or text, etc, which is copied,
reproduced or translated to
produce others, but which is not
itself copied or derived, etc from
something else
ORIGINATE verb **ORIGINATES,
ORIGINATING, ORIGINATED** to
bring or come into being; to start
ORIOLE noun **ORIOLES** any of a
family of brightly coloured
songbirds native to the forests of
Europe, Asia and Africa
ORISON noun **ORISONS** a prayer
ORLE noun **ORLES** a border within
a shield that follows the outline at a
short distance from the edge
ORLOP noun **ORLOPS** in a ship
with four or more decks: the lowest
deck, forming a covering for the
hold
ORMER noun **ORMERS** a marine
gastropod mollusc with an ear-
shaped shell, the inside of which is

bright and iridescent; a type of abalone

ORMOLU *noun* ORMOLUS gold or gold leaf prepared for gilding bronze or brass, etc

ORNAMENT *noun* ORNAMENTS something that decorates or adds grace or beauty to a person or thing ▫ *verb* ORNAMENTS, ORNAMENTING, ORNAMENTED to decorate something with ornaments or serve as an ornament to something; to adorn

ORNATE *adj* ORNATER, ORNATEST highly or excessively decorated

ORNATELY *adverb* in an ornate way

ORNERY *adj* stubborn or cantankerous

OROGEN *noun* OROGENS a usually elongated region of the Earth's crust which has undergone an orogeny

OROGENIC *adj* mountain-building

OROGENY *noun* OROGENIES the process of mountain-building, often lasting for hundreds of millions of years, involving deformation and the subsequent uplift of rocks within the mountains

OROGRAPHY *noun* OROGRAPHIES the branch of physical geography that deals with the description, formation, etc of mountains

OROIDE *noun* OROIDES an alloy of copper, nickel or tin, etc that imitates gold

OROLOGIST *noun* OROLOGISTS someone skilled in orology

OROLOGY *noun* OROLOGIES the scientific study of mountains

OROTUND *adj* said of the voice: full, loud and grand

ORPHAN *noun* ORPHANS a child who has lost both parents, or, more rarely, one parent ▫ *verb* ORPHANS, ORPHANING, ORPHANED to make (a child) an orphan

ORPHANAGE *noun* ORPHANAGES a home for orphans

ORPHREY *noun* ORPHREYS gold or other rich embroidery, especially that bordering an ecclesiastical vestment

ORPIMENT *noun* ORPIMENTS a yellow mineral, arsenic trisulphide, used as a pigment

ORPIN *noun* ORPINS an orpine

ORPINE *noun* ORPINES a purple-flowered broad-leafed stonecrop

ORRERY *noun* ORRERIES a clockwork model of the Sun and the planets which revolve around it

ORRIS *noun* ORRISES an iris, especially the Florentine iris which has white flowers and fragrant fleshy rhizomes

ORS plural of **or** [2]

ORT *noun* ORTS a dialect word for a leftover from a meal

ORTANIQUE *noun* ORTANIQUES a citrus fruit grown in the W Indies, produced by crossing an orange and a tangerine

ORTHODOX *adj* believing in, living according to, or conforming with established or generally accepted opinions, especially in religion or morals; conventional

ORTHODOXY *noun* ORTHODOXIES the state or quality of being orthodox

ORTHOEPY *noun* ORTHOEPIES accepted or usual pronunciation

ORTHOPTIC *adj* relating to normal vision

ORTHOPTICS *singular noun* the science or practice of correcting defective vision by non-surgical methods, especially the use of specific exercises to strengthen weak eye muscles

ORTHOSIS *noun* ORTHOSES an external device used to support, correct deformities in, or improve the movement of, the limbs or spine

ORTHOTIC *adj* of or relating to orthotics

ORTHOTICS *singular noun* the rehabilitation of injured or weakened joints or muscles by the use of orthoses

ORTHOTIST *noun* ORTHOTISTS someone skilled in orthotics

ORTOLAN *noun* ORTOLANS a small bunting, native to Europe, Asia and N Africa, eaten as a delicacy

ORYX *noun* ORYXES a large grazing antelope with very long slender horns

ORZO *noun* ORZOS pasta in the form of small pieces like rice or barley

OS [1] *noun* ORA a mouth or mouthlike opening, originally used only in Latin names of particular structures

OS [2] *noun* OSSA bone, used only in Latin names of particular bones

OSCILLATE *verb* OSCILLATES, OSCILLATING, OSCILLATED to swing or make something swing backwards and forwards like a pendulum

OSCILLATING *adj* swinging backwards and forwards like a pendulum

OSCINE *adj* belonging or relating to songbirds

OSCULAR *adj* relating to the mouth or to kissing

OSCULATE *verb* OSCULATES, OSCULATING, OSCULATED to kiss

OSCULUM *noun* OSCULA a mouthlike aperture, especially in a sponge

OSIER *noun* OSIERS any of various species of willow tree or shrub

OSMIUM *noun* OSMIUMS a very hard dense bluish-white metal, the densest known element, used as a catalyst, and as a hardening agent in alloys with platinum and iridium, eg in pen nibs

OSMOSE *verb* OSMOSES, OSMOSING, OSMOSED to undergo or cause something to undergo osmosis

OSMOSIS *noun* OSMOSES the spontaneous movement of a solvent, eg water, across a semi-permeable membrane from a more dilute solution to a more concentrated one, which stops when the concentrations of the two solutions are equal, or when an external pressure is applied to the more concentrated solution

OSMOTIC *adj* of or relating to osmosis

OSPREY *noun* OSPREYS a large fish-eating bird of prey found near water in most parts of the world, with a dark-brown body, white head and legs, and a characteristic dark line on the side of the head

OSSA plural of **os** [2]

OSSEOUS *adj* relating to, like, containing, or formed from bone; bony

OSSIA *conj* used in musical directions to indicate an alternative, usually easier, way of playing a particular passage: or; alternatively

OSSICLE *noun* OSSICLES a small bone, especially each of the three small bones of the middle ear

OSSIFRAGE *noun* OSSIFRAGES a rare type of vulture

OSSIFY *verb* OSSIFIES, OSSIFYING, OSSIFIED to turn into

or make something turn into bone or a bonelike substance

OSSUARY *noun* **OSSUARIES** any place, eg a vault or charnel house, or an urn or other container, in which the bones of the dead are kept

OSTEAL *adj* relating to, composed of, or resembling bone

OSTEITIS *noun* **OSTEITISES** inflammation of a bone

OSTENSIVE *adj* directly or manifestly demonstrative

OSTEOLOGY *noun* **OSTEOLOGIES** the branch of human anatomy that deals with the study of bones and the skeleton

OSTEOMA *noun* **OSTEOMAS** a benign tumour of bone or bonelike tissue

OSTEOPATH *noun* **OSTEOPATHS** a practitioner of osteopathy

OSTINATO *adj* frequently repeated □ *noun* **OSTINATOS** a melodic phrase that recurs throughout a piece

OSTLER *noun* **OSTLERS** someone who attends to horses at an inn

OSTRACISE *verb* **OSTRACISES, OSTRACISING, OSTRACISED** to ostracize

OSTRACISM *noun* **OSTRACISMS** exclusion from a group or society

OSTRACIZE *verb* **OSTRACIZES, OSTRACIZING, OSTRACIZED** to exclude someone from a group or society, etc; to refuse to associate with them

OSTRICH *noun* **OSTRICHES** the largest living bird, found on dry plains in E Africa, having an extremely long neck and legs, and only two toes on each foot, up to 2.5m in height and, although flightless, capable of running at speeds of up to 60km per hour (about 40mph)

OTALGIA *noun* **OTALGIAS** earache

OTARINE *adj* like a sea lion

OTHER *adj* remaining from a group of two or more when one or some have been specified already □ *pronoun* another person or thing □ *adverb* otherwise; differently □ *noun* **OTHERS** someone or something considered separate, different, additional to, apart from, etc the rest

OTHERNESS *noun* **OTHERNESSES** the fact or condition of being other or different

OTHERWISE *adverb* in other

respects □ *conj* or else; if not □ *adj* different

OTIC *adj* relating to the ear

OTIOSE *adj* futile

OTIOSITY *noun* **OTIOSITIES** ease, idleness

OTITIS *noun* **OTITISES** inflammation of the ear or of part of the ear

OTOLITH *noun* **OTOLITHS** any of the calcareous granules found in the inner ear of vertebrates, the movement of which helps the animal to maintain equilibrium

OTOLOGIST *noun* **OTOLOGISTS** someone skilled in otology

OTOLOGY *noun* **OTOLOGIES** the branch of medicine concerned with the ear

OTOSCOPE *noun* **OTOSCOPES** a device used for examining the external ear

OTTER *noun* **OTTERS** a solitary and rather elusive carnivorous semi-aquatic mammal, found in all parts of the world except Australasia and Antarctica, with a long body covered with short smooth fur, a broad flat head, short legs, a stout tail tapering towards the tip and large webbed hind feet

OTTOMAN *noun* **OTTOMANS** a low, stuffed seat without a back, sometimes in the form of a chest

> **OU** *exclamation* a Scots word expressing concession

OUBLIETTE *noun* **OUBLIETTES** a secret dungeon with a single, often concealed, opening at the top

OUCH *exclamation* expressing sudden sharp pain

> **OUD** *noun* **OUDS** an Arab stringed instrument

OUGHT *auxiliary verb* used to express duty or obligation

OUIJA *noun* **OUIJAS** a board with the letters of the alphabet printed round the edge, used at séances with a glass, pointer or other object to spell out messages supposed to be from the dead

> **OUK** *noun* **OUKS** a Scots word for *week*

OULONG *noun* **OULONGS** oolong

OUNCE *noun* **OUNCES** in the imperial system: a unit of weight equal to one sixteenth of a pound (28.35g)

> **OUP** *verb* **OUPS, OUPING, OUPED** a Scots word meaning to bind with thread or to join

OUR *adj* relating or belonging to, associated with, or done by us

OURS *pronoun* the one or ones belonging to us

OURSELF *pronoun* formerly used by monarchs: myself

OURSELVES *pronoun* reflexive form of *we*; us

OUSEL *noun* **OUSELS** an ouzel

OUST *verb* **OUSTS, OUSTING, OUSTED** to eject someone from a possession; to deprive them of an inheritance

OUSTER *noun* **OUSTERS** ejection; dispossession

OUT *adverb* away from the inside; not in or at a place □ *adj* external □ *prep* out of something □ *noun* **OUTS** a way out, a way of escape; an excuse □ *verb* **OUTS, OUTING, OUTED** to become publicly known

OUTAGE *noun* **OUTAGES** the amount of a commodity lost in transport or storage

OUTBACK *noun* **OUTBACKS** isolated remote areas of a country, especially in Australia

OUTBID *verb* **OUTBIDS, OUTBIDDING, OUTBID, OUTBIDDEN** to offer a higher price than someone else, especially at an auction

OUTBOARD *adj* said of a motor or engine: portable and designed to be attached to the outside of a boat's stern □ *adverb* nearer or towards the outside of a ship or aircraft □ *noun* **OUTBOARDS** an outboard motor or engine

OUTBOUND *adj* said of a vehicle, flight, carriageway, etc: going away from home or a station, etc; departing

OUTBREAK *noun* **OUTBREAKS** a sudden, usually violent beginning or occurrence, usually of something unpleasant, eg of disease or rioting, etc

OUTBURST *noun* **OUTBURSTS** a sudden violent expression of strong emotion, especially anger

OUTCAST *noun* **OUTCASTS** someone who has been rejected by their friends or by society □ *adj* rejected or cast out

OUTCASTE *noun* **OUTCASTES** a Hindu who has lost their caste

OUTCLASS *verb* **OUTCLASSES, OUTCLASSING, OUTCLASSED** to be or become of a much better quality or class than something else

OUTCOME *noun* **OUTCOMES** the result of some action or situation, etc; consequence

OUTCROP *noun* **OUTCROPS** a rock or group of rocks which sticks out above the surface of the ground ▫ *verb* **OUTCROPS, OUTCROPPING, OUTCROPPED** said of a rock or group of rocks: to stick out from the ground

OUTCRY *noun* **OUTCRIES** a widespread and public show of anger or disapproval

OUTDANCE *verb* **OUTDANCES, OUTDANCING, OUTDANCED** to dance more, or in a better way than someone else

OUTDATED *adj* no longer useful or in fashion; obsolete

OUTDO *verb* **OUTDOES, OUTDOING, OUTDID, OUTDONE** to do much better than someone or something else; to surpass them

OUTDOOR *adj* done, taking place, situated or for use, etc in the open air

OUTDOORS *adverb* in or into the open air; outside a building ▫ *singular noun* the open air; the world outside buildings

OUTEAT *verb* **OUTEATS, OUTEATING, OUTATE, OUTEATEN** to eat more than someone else

OUTER *adj* external; belonging to or for the outside ▫ *noun* **OUTERS** the outermost ring on a target

OUTERMOST *adj* nearest the edge; furthest from the centre; most remote

OUTERWEAR *noun* **OUTERWEARS** clothing to be worn on top of other garments or for outdoors

OUTFACE *verb* **OUTFACES, OUTFACING, OUTFACED** to stare at someone until they look away

OUTFALL *noun* **OUTFALLS** the mouth of a river or sewer, etc where it flows into the sea; an outlet

OUTFIELD *noun* **OUTFIELDS** the outlying land on a farm

OUTFIGHT *verb* **OUTFIGHTS, OUTFIGHTING, OUTFOUGHT** to fight more successfully than someone else

OUTFIT *noun* **OUTFITS** a set of clothes worn together, especially for a particular occasion ▫ *verb* **OUTFITS, OUTFITTING, OUTFITTED** to provide someone with an outfit, especially of clothes

OUTFITTER *noun* **OUTFITTERS** someone who provides outfits, especially one who sells men's clothes

OUTFLANK *verb* **OUTFLANKS, OUTFLANKING, OUTFLANKED** to go round the side or sides of an enemy's position and attack from behind

OUTFLOW *noun* **OUTFLOWS** a flowing out

OUTFLY *verb* **OUTFLIES, OUTFLYING, OUTFLEW, OUTFLOWN** to fly more successfully than someone else

OUTFOX *verb* **OUTFOXES, OUTFOXING, OUTFOXED** to get the better of someone by being more cunning; to outwit someone

OUTGO *noun* **OUTGOES** the fact of going out ▫ *verb* **OUTGOES, OUTGOING, OUTWENT, OUTGONE** to surpass; to outstrip

OUTGOING *adj* said of a person: friendly and sociable; extrovert ▫ *noun* **OUTGOINGS** the act of going out

OUTGOINGS *plural noun* money spent; expenditure

OUTGROW *verb* **OUTGROWS, OUTGROWING, OUTGROWN** to grow too large for (one's clothes)

OUTGROWTH *noun* **OUTGROWTHS** the act or process of growing out

OUTGUN *verb* **OUTGUNS, OUTGUNNING, OUTGUNNED** to defeat by means of superior weapons or force, etc

OUTGUSH *noun* **OUTGUSHES** a gushing out

OUTHIT *verb* **OUTHITS, OUTHITTING, OUTHIT** to hit (eg a ball) further or better than someone else

OUTHOUSE *noun* **OUTHOUSES** a building, usually a small one such as a shed, etc built close to a house

OUTING *noun* **OUTINGS** a short pleasure trip or excursion

OUTJOCKEY *verb* **OUTJOCKEYS, OUTJOCKEYING, OUTJOCKEYED** to outwit someone by trickery

OUTJUMP *verb* **OUTJUMPS, OUTJUMPING, OUTJUMPED** to surpass someone at jumping

OUTLAST *verb* **OUTLASTS, OUTLASTING, OUTLASTED** to last longer than someone or something else

OUTLAW *noun* **OUTLAWS** someone excluded from, and deprived of the protection of, the

law ▫ *verb* **OUTLAWS, OUTLAWING, OUTLAWED** to deprive someone of the benefit and protection of the law; to make them an outlaw

OUTLAWRY *noun* **OUTLAWRIES** the act of putting someone out of the protection of the law; the state of being an outlaw

OUTLAY *noun* **OUTLAYS** money, or occasionally time, spent on something; expenditure ▫ *verb* **OUTLAYS, OUTLAYING, OUTLAID** to spend (money, etc)

OUTLET *noun* **OUTLETS** a vent or way out, especially for water or steam

OUTLIER *noun* **OUTLIERS** a detached portion of anything lying some way off or out

OUTLINE *noun* **OUTLINES** a line that forms or marks the outer edge of an object ▫ *verb* **OUTLINES, OUTLINING, OUTLINED** to draw the outline of something

OUTLIVE *verb* **OUTLIVES, OUTLIVING, OUTLIVED** to live or survive longer than someone or something else

OUTLOOK *noun* **OUTLOOKS** a view from a particular place

OUTMATCH *verb* **OUTMATCHES, OUTMATCHING, OUTMATCHED** to be better than (an opponent, etc)

OUTMODED *adj* no longer in fashion; out of date

OUTMOST *adj* nearest the edge; furthest from the centre; most remote

OUTNUMBER *verb* **OUTNUMBERS, OUTNUMBERING, OUTNUMBERED** to exceed in number

OUTPACE *verb* **OUTPACES, OUTPACING, OUTPACED** to walk or go faster than

OUTPLAY *verb* **OUTPLAYS, OUTPLAYING, OUTPLAYED** to play better than

OUTPOST *noun* **OUTPOSTS** a group of soldiers stationed at a distance from the main body, especially to protect it from a surprise attack

OUTPOURING *noun* **OUTPOURINGS** a powerful or violent show of emotion

OUTPUT *noun* **OUTPUTS** the quantity or amount of something produced ▫ *verb* **OUTPUTS, OUTPUTTING, OUTPUT** to produce (information or power, etc) as output

For longer words, see *The Chambers Dictionary*

OUTRAGE *noun* **OUTRAGES** an act of great cruelty or violence ◻ *verb* **OUTRAGES, OUTRAGING, OUTRAGED** to insult, shock or anger someone greatly

OUTRANK *verb* **OUTRANKS, OUTRANKING, OUTRANKED** to have a higher rank than someone; to be superior to them

OUTRÉ *adj* not conventional; eccentric; shocking

OUTRIDE *verb* **OUTRIDES, OUTRIDING, OUTRODE, OUTRIDDEN** to ride faster than (another vehicle, horse, etc or someone else)

OUTRIDER *noun* **OUTRIDERS** an attendant or guard who rides a horse or motorcycle at the side or ahead of a carriage or car conveying an important person

OUTRIGGER *noun* **OUTRIGGERS** a beam or framework sticking out from the side of a boat to help balance the vessel and prevent it capsizing

OUTRIGHT *adverb* immediately; at once ◻ *adj* open; honest

OUTRIVAL *verb* **OUTRIVALS, OUTRIVALLING, OUTRIVALLED** to be better than or superior to someone or something else

OUTRUN *verb* **OUTRUNS, OUTRUNNING, OUTRAN** to run faster or further than

OUTSELL *verb* **OUTSELLS, OUTSELLING, OUTSOLD** to sell more than

OUTSET *noun* **OUTSETS** a beginning or start

OUTSHINE *verb* **OUTSHINES, OUTSHINING, OUTSHONE** to shine more brightly than

OUTSHOOT *verb* **OUTSHOOTS, OUTSHOOTING, OUTSHOT** to shoot better or more often than (someone else)

OUTSIDE *noun* **OUTSIDES** the outer surface; the external parts ◻ *adj* relating to, on or near the outside ◻ *adverb* on or to the outside; outdoors ◻ *prep* on or to the outside of something

OUTSIDER *noun* **OUTSIDERS** someone who is not part of a group, etc or who refuses to accept the general values of society

OUTSIT *verb* **OUTSITS, OUTSITTING, OUTSAT** to sit for longer than

OUTSIZE *adj* over normal or standard size ◻ *noun* **OUTSIZES**

anything, especially a garment, that is larger than standard size

OUTSKIRTS *plural noun* the outer parts or area, especially of a town or city

OUTSMART *verb* **OUTSMARTS, OUTSMARTING, OUTSMARTED** to get the better of someone or something by being cleverer or more cunning; to outwit

OUTSOURCE *verb* **OUTSOURCES, OUTSOURCING, OUTSOURCED** said of a business, company, etc: to subcontract (work) to another company; to contract (work) out

OUTSOURCING *noun* the act of subcontracting work to another company

OUTSPOKEN *adj* said of a person: saying exactly what they think; frank

OUTSPREAD *verb* **OUTSPREADS, OUTSPREADING, OUTSPREAD** to spread or stretch out; to extend ◻ *adj* said of the arms, etc: stretched or spread out widely or fully ◻ *noun* **OUTSPREADS** a spreading out; an expansion

OUTSTARE *verb* **OUTSTARES, OUTSTARING, OUTSTARED** to outdo someone in staring

OUTSTAY *verb* **OUTSTAYS, OUTSTAYING, OUTSTAYED** to stay longer than the length of (one's invitation, etc); to overstay

OUTSTRIP *verb* **OUTSTRIPS, OUTSTRIPPING, OUTSTRIPPED** to go faster than someone or something else

OUTSWIM *verb* **OUTSWIMS, OUTSWIMMING, OUTSWAM, OUTSWUM** to outdo someone at swimming

OUTSWING *noun* **OUTSWINGS** an outward swing or swerve

OUTTAKE *noun* **OUTTAKES** a section of film or tape removed from the final edited version of a motion picture or video

OUTTHINK *verb* **OUTTHINKS, OUTTHINKING, OUTTHOUGHT** to outdo someone in thinking

OUTTURN *noun* **OUTTURNS** output

OUTVOTE *verb* **OUTVOTES, OUTVOTING, OUTVOTED** to obtain more votes than someone or something else; to defeat them by a majority of votes

OUTWALK *verb* **OUTWALKS, OUTWALKING, OUTWALKED** to walk faster or further than

OUTWARD *adj* on or towards the outside ◻ *adverb* towards the outside; in an outward direction

OUTWARDLY *adverb* in appearance; on the outside; superficially

OUTWEAR *verb* **OUTWEARS, OUTWEARING, OUTWORE, OUTWORN** to destroy something by wearing; to wear it away

OUTWEIGH *verb* **OUTWEIGHS, OUTWEIGHING, OUTWEIGHED** to be greater than something in weight

OUTWIT *verb* **OUTWITS, OUTWITTING, OUTWITTED** to get the better of or defeat someone by being cleverer or more cunning than they are

OUTWITH *prep* outside; beyond

OUTWORK *noun* **OUTWORKS** a defence work that is outside the main line of fortifications

OUTWORKER *noun* **OUTWORKERS** an employee who works at home for a company, factory or shop, etc

OUTWORN *adj* said especially of an idea, belief or institution: no longer useful or in fashion; out of date; obsolete

OUZEL *noun* **OUZELS** a thrush, native to Europe, N Africa and SW Asia, with dark plumage, pale silvery wings and a characteristic broad white band across its throat

OUZO *noun* **OUZOS** a Greek alcoholic drink flavoured with aniseed and usually diluted with water

OVA *plural of* **ovum**

OVAL *adj* with the outline of an egg or shaped like an egg ◻ *noun* **OVALS** any egg-shaped figure or object

OVALLY *adverb* in the form of an oval

OVARIAN *adj* of or relating to the ovary

OVARITIS *noun* **OVARITISES** inflammation of the ovary

OVARY *noun* **OVARIES** in a female animal: the reproductive organ in which the ova are produced

OVATE *adj* egg-shaped ◻ *noun* **OVATES** an implement with an oval shape, especially a type of hand-axe from the lower Palaeolithic period

OVATION *noun* **OVATIONS** sustained applause or cheering to express approval or welcome, etc

OVEN *noun* **OVENS** a closed compartment or arched cavity in which substances may be heated, used especially for baking or roasting food, drying clay, etc

For longer words, see *The Chambers Dictionary*

OVENWARE noun **OVENWARES** heat-resistant or ovenproof dishes, bowls, etc

OVER adverb above and across ◻ prep in or to a position which is above or higher in place, importance, authority, value or number, etc ◻ adj upper; higher ◻ noun **OVERS** in cricket: a series of six balls bowled by the same bowler from the same end of the pitch

OVERACT verb **OVERACTS, OVERACTING, OVERACTED** to act (a part) with too much expression or emotion

OVERALL noun **OVERALLS** a loose-fitting coat-like garment worn over ordinary clothes to protect them ◻ adj including everything ◻ adverb as a whole; in general

OVERARCH verb **OVERARCHES, OVERARCHING, OVERARCHED** to form an arch over something **OVERARCHING** adj forming an arch over something

OVERARM adj said of a ball, especially in cricket: bowled or thrown with the hand and arm raised over and moving round the shoulder ◻ adverb said of a ball, especially in cricket: bowled or thrown with the hand and arm raised over and moving round the shoulder

OVERAWE verb **OVERAWES, OVERAWING, OVERAWED** to subdue or restrain someone by filling them with awe, fear or astonishment

OVERBLOWN adj overdone; excessive

OVERBOARD adverb over the side of a ship or boat into the water

OVERBOIL verb **OVERBOILS, OVERBOILING, OVERBOILED** to boil (liquid, etc) excessively

OVERBOLD adj excessively bold

OVERBOOK verb **OVERBOOKS, OVERBOOKING, OVERBOOKED** to make more reservations than the number of places (in a plane, hotel, etc) actually available

OVERCAST adj said of the sky or weather: cloudy

OVERCLAD adj excessively clad

OVERCLOUD verb **OVERCLOUDS, OVERCLOUDING, OVERCLOUDED** to cover something, or become covered, with clouds

OVERCOAT noun **OVERCOATS** a warm heavy coat worn especially in winter

OVERCOME verb **OVERCOMES, OVERCOMING, OVERCAME, OVERCOME** to defeat someone or something; to succeed in a struggle against them or it; to deal successfully with them or it

OVERCOOK verb **OVERCOOKS, OVERCOOKING, OVERCOOKED** to cook too much or for too long

OVERCROWD verb **OVERCROWDS, OVERCROWDING, OVERCROWDED** to crowd too many people, animals, etc into (a space or place)

OVERDO verb **OVERDOES, OVERDOING, OVERDID, OVERDONE** to do something too much; to exaggerate

OVERDOSE noun **OVERDOSES** an excessive dose of a drug, etc ◻ verb **OVERDOSES, OVERDOSING, OVERDOSED** to take an overdose or give an excessive dose to someone

OVERDRAFT noun **OVERDRAFTS** the excess of money taken from one's bank account over the sum that was in it

OVERDRAW verb **OVERDRAWS, OVERDRAWING, OVERDREW, OVERDRAWN** to draw more money from (one's bank account) than one has in it

OVERDRAWN adj with an overdraft at a bank

OVERDRESS verb **OVERDRESSES, OVERDRESSING, OVERDRESSED** to dress someone or oneself, or to be dressed, in clothes that are too formal, smart or expensive for the occasion ◻ noun **OVERDRESSES** a dress that may be worn over a blouse or jumper, etc

OVERDRIVE noun **OVERDRIVES** an additional very high gear in a motor vehicle's gearbox, which reduces wear on the engine and saves fuel when travelling at high speeds ◻ verb **OVERDRIVES, OVERDRIVING, OVERDROVE, OVERDRIVEN** to drive something too hard; to overwork it

OVERDUE adj said of bills or work, etc: not yet paid, done or delivered, etc, although the date for doing this has passed

OVEREAT verb **OVEREATS, OVEREATING, OVERATE, OVEREATEN** to eat too much

OVEREXERT verb **OVEREXERTS, OVEREXERTING, OVEREXERTED** to do too much strenuous activity

OVERFEED verb **OVERFEEDS, OVERFEEDING, OVERFED** to give too much food to

OVERFILL verb **OVERFILLS, OVERFILLING, OVERFILLED** to fill (a container) beyond its capacity

OVERFINE adj excessively fine

OVERFISH verb **OVERFISHES, OVERFISHING, OVERFISHED** to remove too many fish from (a sea or river, etc) thereby depleting the population of certain species by reducing the number available to breed

OVERFLOW verb **OVERFLOWS, OVERFLOWING, OVERFLOWED** to flow over (a brim) or go beyond (the limits or edge of something) ◻ noun **OVERFLOWS** that which overflows

OVERFOND adj too fond

OVERFULL adj too full

OVERGROWN adj said of a garden, etc: dense with plants that have grown too large and thick

OVERHAND adj thrown or performed, etc with the hand brought downwards from above the shoulder; overarm or with an overarm action ◻ adverb thrown or performed, etc with the hand brought downwards from above the shoulder; overarm or with an overarm action

OVERHANG verb **OVERHANGS, OVERHANGING, OVERHUNG** to project or hang out over something ◻ noun **OVERHANGS** a piece of rock or part of a roof, etc that overhangs

OVERHASTY adj excessively hasty

OVERHAUL verb **OVERHAULS, OVERHAULING, OVERHAULED** to examine carefully and repair something ◻ noun **OVERHAULS** a thorough examination and repair

OVERHEAD adj above; over one's head ◻ adverb above; over one's head ◻ noun **OVERHEADS** the regular costs of a business, such as rent, wages and electricity

OVERHEAR verb **OVERHEARS, OVERHEARING, OVERHEARD** to hear (a person or remark, etc) without the speaker knowing, either by accident or on purpose

OVERHEAT verb **OVERHEATS, OVERHEATING, OVERHEATED** to heat something excessively **OVERHEATED** adj said of an argument, discussion, etc: angry and excited; passionate

OVERISSUE verb **OVERISSUES, OVERISSUING, OVERISSUED** to issue in excess (eg banknotes)

OVERJOYED adj very glad; elated

OVERKILL noun **OVERKILLS** the capability to destroy an enemy using a larger force than is actually needed to win a victory □ verb **OVERKILLS, OVERKILLING, OVERKILLED** to practise overkill against, or subject someone or something to overkill

OVERKIND adj excessively kind

OVERLADEN adj overloaded

OVERLAND adverb said of a journey, etc: across land □ adj said of a journey, etc: across land

OVERLAP verb **OVERLAPS, OVERLAPPING, OVERLAPPED** said of part of an object: to partly cover (another object) □ noun **OVERLAPS** an overlapping part

OVERLAY verb **OVERLAYS, OVERLAYING, OVERLAID** to lay one thing on or over another □ noun **OVERLAYS** a covering; something that is laid over something else

OVERLEAF adverb on the other side of the page

OVERLIE verb **OVERLIES, OVERLYING, OVERLAY, OVERLAIN** to lie on

OVERLOAD verb **OVERLOADS, OVERLOADING, OVERLOADED** to load something too heavily □ noun **OVERLOADS** too great an electric current flowing through a circuit

OVERLONG adj excessively long

OVERLOOK verb **OVERLOOKS, OVERLOOKING, OVERLOOKED** to give a view of something from a higher position □ noun **OVERLOOKS** a failure to see or notice something; an oversight

OVERLORD noun **OVERLORDS** a lord or ruler with supreme power

OVERLY adverb too; excessively

OVERMAN verb **OVERMANS, OVERMANNING, OVERMANNED** to provide (eg a ship, industrial plant, etc) with too many workers

OVERMATCH verb **OVERMATCHES, OVERMATCHING, OVERMATCHED** to be more than a match for someone □ noun **OVERMATCHES** a superior opponent

OVERMUCH adj too much; very much □ adverb too much; very much

OVERNICE adj fussy; critical and hard to please

OVERNIGHT adverb during the night □ adj done or occurring in the night

OVERPASS noun **OVERPASSES** a flyover

OVERPAY verb **OVERPAYS, OVERPAYING, OVERPAID** to pay too much

OVERPLAY verb **OVERPLAYS, OVERPLAYING, OVERPLAYED** to exaggerate or overemphasize (the importance of something)

OVERPOWER verb **OVERPOWERS, OVERPOWERING, OVERPOWERED** to defeat or subdue by greater strength

OVERPRICE verb **OVERPRICES, OVERPRICING, OVERPRICED** to ask too high a price for

OVERPRINT verb **OVERPRINTS, OVERPRINTING, OVERPRINTED** to print over (something already printed, especially a postage stamp) □ noun **OVERPRINTS** the action of overprinting

OVERRATE verb **OVERRATES, OVERRATING, OVERRATED** to assess or think too highly of something or someone; to overestimate it or them

OVERRATED adj having been given too high a value; overestimated

OVERREACH verb **OVERREACHES, OVERREACHING, OVERREACHED** to defeat (oneself) by trying to do too much, or be too clever, etc

OVERREACT verb **OVERREACTS, OVERREACTING, OVERREACTED** to react excessively or too strongly

OVERRIDE verb **OVERRIDES, OVERRIDING, OVERRODE, OVERRIDDEN** to ride over; to cross (an area) by riding □ noun **OVERRIDES** the action or process of suspending an automatic control

OVERRIDER noun **OVERRIDERS** an attachment fitted to the bumper of a motor vehicle to prevent another bumper becoming interlocked with it

OVERRIDING adj dominant; most important

OVERRIPE adj too ripe

OVERRULE verb **OVERRULES, OVERRULING, OVERRULED** to rule against or cancel (especially a previous decision or judgement) by higher authority

OVERRUN verb **OVERRUNS, OVERRUNNING, OVERRAN, OVERRUN** to spread over or through something; to infest it □ noun **OVERRUNS** the act or an instance of overrunning

OVERSEAS adverb in or to a land beyond the sea; abroad □ adj across or from beyond the sea; foreign □ noun a foreign country or foreign countries in general

OVERSEE verb **OVERSEES, OVERSEEING, OVERSAW, OVERSEEN** to supervise

OVERSEER noun **OVERSEERS** someone who oversees workers; a supervisor

OVERSELL verb **OVERSELLS, OVERSELLING, OVERSOLD** to sell something at too high a price or in greater quantities than can be supplied □ noun **OVERSELLS** excessively aggressive or ambitious selling of commodities or goods, etc

OVERSEW verb **OVERSEWS, OVERSEWING, OVERSEWED, OVERSEWN** to sew (two edges) together with close stitches that pass over both edges

OVERSEXED adj with unusually strong sexual urges

OVERSHIRT noun **OVERSHIRTS** a shirt worn on top of other clothes

OVERSHOE noun **OVERSHOES** a shoe, usually made of rubber or plastic, worn over normal shoes to protect them in wet weather

OVERSHOOT verb **OVERSHOOTS, OVERSHOOTING, OVERSHOT** to shoot or go farther than (a target aimed at) □ noun **OVERSHOOTS** the action or an act of overshooting

OVERSHOT adj with the upper jaw protruding beyond the lower one

OVERSIGHT noun **OVERSIGHTS** a mistake or omission, especially one made through a failure to notice something

OVERSIZE adj very large; larger then normal □ noun **OVERSIZES** a size that is larger than normal

OVERSKIRT noun **OVERSKIRTS** a skirt worn on top of other clothes

OVERSLEEP verb **OVERSLEEPS, OVERSLEEPING, OVERSLEPT** to sleep longer than one intended

OVERSPEND verb **OVERSPENDS, OVERSPENDING, OVERSPENT** to exhaust something; to wear it out □ noun **OVERSPENDS** the action or an act of overspending

OVERSPILL noun **OVERSPILLS** the

people leaving an overcrowded or derelict town area to live elsewhere
OVERSTAFF verb **OVERSTAFFS, OVERSTAFFING, OVERSTAFFED** to provide too many people as staff for (eg a business)
OVERSTAIN verb **OVERSTAINS, OVERSTAINING, OVERSTAINED** to apply a stain over
OVERSTATE verb **OVERSTATES, OVERSTATING, OVERSTATED** to state something too strongly or with undue emphasis; to exaggerate
OVERSTAY verb **OVERSTAYS, OVERSTAYING, OVERSTAYED** to stay longer than the length of (one's invitation, etc)
OVERSTEER verb **OVERSTEERS, OVERSTEERING, OVERSTEERED** said of a vehicle: to turn more sharply than the driver intends; to exaggerate the degree of turn applied by the steering wheel
OVERSTEP verb **OVERSTEPS, OVERSTEPPING, OVERSTEPPED** to go beyond or exceed (a certain limit, or what is prudent or reasonable)
OVERSTOCK verb **OVERSTOCKS, OVERSTOCKING, OVERSTOCKED** to supply too much of something, or more than is demanded ▢ *noun* **OVERSTOCKS** a surplus supply or quantity of something due to overstocking
OVERSTUFF verb **OVERSTUFFS, OVERSTUFFING, OVERSTUFFED** to stuff something more than is necessary
OVERT adj not hidden or secret; open; public
OVERTAKE verb **OVERTAKES, OVERTAKING, OVERTOOK, OVERTAKEN** to catch up with and go past (a car or a person, etc) moving in the same direction
OVERTAX verb **OVERTAXES, OVERTAXING, OVERTAXED** to demand too much tax from someone
OVERTHROW verb **OVERTHROWS, OVERTHROWING, OVERTHREW, OVERTHROWN** to defeat completely (an established order or a government, etc) ▢ *noun* **OVERTHROWS** the act of overthrowing or state of being overthrown
OVERTIME *noun* **OVERTIMES** time spent working at one's job beyond one's regular hours ▢ *adverb*

during overtime; in addition to one's regular hours ▢ *verb*
OVERTIMES, OVERTIMING, OVERTIMED to go beyond the correct allowance of time for (a photographic exposure, etc)
OVERTIRE verb **OVERTIRES, OVERTIRING, OVERTIRED** to exhaust someone; to wear them out
OVERTLY adverb in an overt way
OVERTONE *noun* **OVERTONES** a subtle hint, quality or meaning; a nuance
OVERTRAIN verb **OVERTRAINS, OVERTRAINING, OVERTRAINED** to train so far as to harm
OVERTRUMP verb **OVERTRUMPS, OVERTRUMPING, OVERTRUMPED** in card games: to trump with a higher card than the trump already played
OVERTURE *noun* **OVERTURES** an orchestral introduction to an opera, oratorio or ballet
OVERTURN verb **OVERTURNS, OVERTURNING, OVERTURNED** to turn something or be turned over or upside down
OVERUSE verb **OVERUSES, OVERUSING, OVERUSED** to use something excessively ▢ *noun* **OVERUSES** excessive use
OVERVALUE verb **OVERVALUES, OVERVALUING, OVERVALUED** to set too high a value on
OVERVIEW *noun* **OVERVIEWS** a brief general account or description of a subject, etc; a summary
OVERWEARY adj excessively weary
OVERWHELM verb **OVERWHELMS, OVERWHELMING, OVERWHELMED** to crush mentally; to overpower (a person's emotions or thoughts, etc)
OVERWHELMING adj physically or mentally crushing; intensely powerful
OVERWIND verb **OVERWINDS, OVERWINDING, OVERWOUND** to wind (a watch, etc) too far
OVERWISE adj too wise; affectedly wise
OVERWORK verb **OVERWORKS, OVERWORKING, OVERWORKED** to work too hard ▢ *noun* **OVERWORKS** the act of working too hard; excessive work
OVERWRITE verb **OVERWRITES, OVERWRITING, OVERWROTE,**

OVERWRITTEN in computing: to write new information over (existing data), thereby destroying (it)
OVIDUCAL adj relating to an oviduct
OVIDUCT *noun* **OVIDUCTS** the tube that conveys ova from the ovary to another organ, such as the uterus, or to the outside of the body
OVIDUCTAL adj oviducal
OVIFORM adj egg-shaped
OVINE adj relating to or characteristic of a sheep or sheep; sheeplike
OVIPARITY *noun* **OVIPARITIES** the condition of being oviparous
OVIPAROUS adj said of many birds, reptiles, amphibians, bony fishes, etc: laying eggs that develop and hatch outside the mother's body
OVOID adj egg-shaped; oval ▢ *noun* **OVOIDS** an egg-shaped or oval form or object
OVOLO *noun* **OVOLI** a moulding with the rounded part composed of a quarter of a circle, or of an arc of an ellipse with the curve greatest at the top
OVULAR adj of or relating to an ovule
OVULATE verb **OVULATES, OVULATING, OVULATED** to release an ovum or egg cell from the ovary
OVULATION *noun* **OVULATIONS** the release of an ovum or egg cell from the ovary
OVULE *noun* **OVULES** in flowering plants characteristic of spermatophytes: the structure that develops into a seed after fertilization
OVUM *noun* **OVA** an unfertilized egg or egg cell produced by the ovary of an animal; a female gamete

OW *exclamation* expressing sudden, usually mild, pain

OWE verb **OWES, OWING, OWED** to be under an obligation to pay (money) to someone
OWING adj still to be paid; due
OWL *noun* **OWLS** a nocturnal bird of prey found in all parts of the world except Antarctica, with a large broad head, a flat face, large forward-facing eyes and a short hooked beak ▢ *verb* **OWLS, OWLING, OWLED** to behave like an owl

OWLET *noun* **OWLETS** a young or small owl
OWLISH *adj* relating to or like an owl
OWN *adj* often used for emphasis: belonging to or for oneself or itself □ *pronoun* one belonging (or something belonging) to oneself or itself □ *verb* **OWNS, OWNING, OWNED** to have something as a possession or property
OWNER *noun* **OWNERS** a possessor, proprietor
OWNERSHIP *noun* **OWNERSHIPS** possession

OWT *noun* **OWTS** a dialect word for *anything*

OX *noun* **OXEN** the general name for any bovine mammal, especially the male or female of common domestic cattle
OXALIS *noun* **OXALISES** any of various plants with delicate white, pink, red or yellow flowers and clover-like leaves that contain oxalic acid
OXBLOOD *noun* **OXBLOODS** a dark reddish-brown colour
OXER *noun* **OXERS** a show-jumping obstacle in the form of a fence with a rail, and a ditch
OXFORD *noun* **OXFORDS** a low-heeled shoe which laces up across the instep
OXIDANT *noun* **OXIDANTS** an oxidizing agent
OXIDASE *noun* **OXIDASES** any of a group of enzymes that catalyse oxidation in plant and animal cells
OXIDATION *noun* **OXIDATIONS** a chemical reaction that involves the addition of oxygen to or the removal of hydrogen from a substance which loses electrons, and which is always accompanied by reduction
OXIDE *noun* **OXIDES** any compound of oxygen and another

element, often formed by burning that element or one of its compounds in oxygen or air
OXIDISE *verb* **OXIDISES, OXIDISING, OXIDISED** to oxidize
OXIDISER *noun* **OXIDISERS** an oxidizer
OXIDIZE *verb* **OXIDIZES, OXIDIZING, OXIDIZED** to undergo, or cause (a substance) to undergo, a chemical reaction with oxygen
OXIDIZER *noun* **OXIDIZERS** an oxidizing agent
OXLIP *noun* **OXLIPS** a naturally occurring hybrid of the common primrose and the cowslip, with deep-yellow flowers
OXTAIL *noun* **OXTAILS** the tail of an ox, used especially in soups and stews
OXTER *noun* **OXTERS** the armpit
OXYGEN *noun* **OXYGENS** a colourless odourless tasteless gas, the atmospheric form of which is produced by photosynthesis, and which is an essential requirement of most forms of plant and animal life
OXYGENATE *verb* **OXYGENATES, OXYGENATING, OXYGENATED** to combine, treat, supply or enrich something (eg the blood) with oxygen
OXYGENISE *verb* **OXYGENISES, OXYGENISING, OXYGENISED** to oxygenate
OXYGENIZE *verb* **OXYGENIZES, OXYGENIZING, OXYGENIZED** to oxygenate
OXYGENOUS *adj* containing or consisting of oxygen
OXYMORON *noun* **OXYMORONS** a rhetorical figure of speech in which contradictory terms are used together, often for emphasis or effect
OXYTOCIC *adj* said of a drug: that stimulates uterine muscle contractions and therefore induces

or accelerates labour □ *noun* **OXYTOCICS** an oxytocic drug
OXYTOCIN *noun* **OXYTOCINS** a hormone, released by the pituitary gland, that induces contractions of the uterus during labour, and stimulates the flow of milk from the breasts during suckling
OXYTONE *adj* with an acute accent on the last syllable □ *noun* **OXYTONES** a word with an acute accent on the last syllable

OY *noun* **OYS** a Scots word for *grandchild*

OYES *exclamation* oyez
OYEZ *exclamation* a cry for silence and attention, usually shouted three times by an official before a public announcement or in a court of law

OYS plural of **oy**

OYSTER *noun* **OYSTERS** the common name for a family of marine bivalve molluscs with a soft fleshy body enclosed by a hinged shell, the fleshy part being a popular seafood
OZEKI *noun* **OZEKIS** a champion sumo wrestler
OZONE *noun* **OZONES** a toxic pungent unstable bluish gas that is an allotrope of oxygen, and at ground level may be a pollutant (photochemical smog)
OZONISE *verb* **OZONISES, OZONISING, OZONISED** to ozonize
OZONISER *noun* **OZONISERS** an ozonizer
OZONIZE *verb* **OZONIZES, OZONIZING, OZONIZED** to convert (oxygen) into ozone
OZONIZER *noun* **OZONIZERS** an apparatus for turning oxygen into ozone

PA *noun* **PAS** a familiar or childish word for father

PACA *noun* **PACAS** a large rat-like nocturnal rodent, native to Central and S America, with a brown or black coat marked with four rows of white spots, a very short tail, and large cheek pouches

PACE *noun* **PACES** a single step ◻ *verb* **PACES, PACING, PACED** to keep walking about, in a preoccupied or frustrated way

PACEMAKER *noun* **PACEMAKERS** a small mass of specialized muscle-cells in the heart which control the rate and the rhythm of the heartbeat

PACER *noun* **PACERS** someone who paces

PACEY *adj* **PACIER, PACIEST** fast

PACHINKO *noun* **PACHINKOS** a form of pinball popular in Japan

PACHISI *noun* **PACHISIS** an Indian board game resembling backgammon or ludo

PACHYDERM *noun* **PACHYDERMS** any animal belonging to a (now obsolete) category of large thick-skinned non-ruminant hoofed mammals, especially the elephant, rhinoceros or hippopotamus

PACIFIC *adj* tending to make peace or keep the peace; peaceful; peaceable

PACIFIER *noun* **PACIFIERS** a baby's dummy

PACIFISM *noun* **PACIFISMS** the beliefs and practices of pacifists

PACIFIST *noun* **PACIFISTS** someone who believes that violence is unjustified and who refuses to take part in making war

PACIFY *verb* **PACIFIES, PACIFYING, PACIFIED** to calm, soothe or appease someone

PACK *noun* **PACKS** a collection of things tied into a bundle for carrying ◻ *verb* **PACKS, PACKING, PACKED** to stow (goods, clothes, etc) compactly in cases, boxes, etc for transport or travel

PACKAGE *noun* **PACKAGES** something wrapped and secured with string, adhesive tape, etc; a parcel

PACKAGER *noun* **PACKAGERS** an independent company specializing in the packaging of something

PACKAGING *noun* **PACKAGINGS** the wrappers or containers in which goods are packed and presented for sale; the design and complete production of eg illustrated books, etc for sale to a publisher, etc

PACKER *noun* **PACKERS** someone who packs, especially goods ready for distribution

PACKET *noun* **PACKETS** a wrapper or container made of paper, cardboard or plastic, with its contents

PACKING *noun* **PACKINGS** materials used for padding or wrapping goods for transport, etc

PACT *noun* **PACTS** an agreement reached between two or more parties, states, etc for mutual advantage

PACY *adj* **PACIER, PACIEST** fast

PAD *noun* **PADS** a wad of material used to cushion, protect, shape or clean ◻ *verb* **PADS, PADDING, PADDED** to cover, fill, stuff, cushion or shape something with layers of soft material

PADDING *noun* **PADDINGS** material for cushioning, shaping or filling

PADDLE *noun* **PADDLES** a short light oar with a blade at one or both ends, used to propel and steer a canoe, kayak, etc ◻ *verb* **PADDLES, PADDLING, PADDLED** to propel (a canoe, kayak, etc) with paddles

PADDOCK *noun* **PADDOCKS** a small enclosed field for keeping a horse in

PADDY *noun* **PADDIES** a field filled with water in which rice is grown

PADLOCK *noun* **PADLOCKS** a detachable lock with a U-shaped bar that pivots at one side, so that it can be passed through a ring or chain and locked in position ◻ *verb* **PADLOCKS, PADLOCKING, PADLOCKED** to fasten (a door, cupboard, etc) with a padlock

PADRE *noun* **PADRES** a chaplain in any of the armed services

PADSAW *noun* **PADSAWS** a small saw-blade with a detachable handle, used for cutting curves and awkward angles

PAEAN *noun* **PAEANS** a song of triumph, praise or thanksgiving

PAEDERAST *noun* **PAEDERASTS** a pederast

PAEDOLOGY *noun* **PAEDOLOGIES** the scientific study of physiological and psychological aspects of childhood

PAELLA *noun* **PAELLAS** a Spanish rice dish of fish or chicken with vegetables and saffron

PAEONY *noun* **PAEONIES** a peony

PAGAN *adj* following any pre-Christian religion ◻ *noun* **PAGANS** a pagan person

PAGANISE *verb* **PAGANISES, PAGANISING, PAGANISED** to paganize

PAGANISM *noun* **PAGANISMS** the beliefs and practices of pagans

PAGANIZE *verb* **PAGANIZES, PAGANIZING, PAGANIZED** to convert someone to paganism

PAGE *noun* **PAGES** one side of a leaf in a book, etc ◻ *verb* **PAGES, PAGING, PAGED** to paginate (a text)

PAGEANT *noun* **PAGEANTS** a series of tableaux or dramatic scenes, usually depicting local historical events or other topical matters

PAGEANTRY *noun* **PAGEANTRIES** splendid display; pomp

PAGER *noun* **PAGERS** a small individually-worn radio receiver and transmitter that enables its user to receive a signal (typically a 'beep' or a short message) to which they can respond with a phone call, etc to the sender

PAGINATE *verb* **PAGINATES, PAGINATING, PAGINATED** to give consecutive numbers to the pages of (a text), carried out by a

command within a word-processing package, or as part of the printing process, etc
PAGING a form of **page**
PAGODA noun **PAGODAS** a Buddhist shrine or memorial-building in India, China and parts of SE Asia, especially in the form of a tall tower with many storeys, each one having its own projecting roof with upturned eaves

PAH noun **PAHS** a Maori fort or settlement

PAHOEHOE noun **PAHOEHOES** a hardened lava with a smooth undulating shiny surface
PAID past form of **pay**
PAIL noun **PAILS** a bucket
PAILFUL noun **PAILFULS** the amount a pail can hold
PAILLASSE noun **PAILLASSES** a palliasse
PAIN noun **PAINS** an uncomfortable, distressing or agonizing sensation caused by the stimulation of specialized nerve endings by heat, cold, pressure or other strong stimuli ◻ verb **PAINS, PAINING, PAINED** to cause distress to someone
PAINED adj said of an expression, tone of voice, etc: expressing distress or disapproval
PAINFUL adj **PAINFULLER, PAINFULLEST** causing pain
PAINFULLY adverb in a painful way; with great care; excessively
PAINLESS adj without pain
PAINT noun **PAINTS** colouring matter in the form of a liquid which is applied to a surface and dries forming a hard surface ◻ verb **PAINTS, PAINTING, PAINTED** to apply a coat of paint to (walls, woodwork, etc)
PAINTABLE adj suitable for painting
PAINTBALL noun **PAINTBALLS** a type of war game in which participants stalk each other and fight battles with paint fired from compressed-air guns
PAINTER noun **PAINTERS** someone who decorates houses internally or externally with paint
PAINTING noun **PAINTINGS** a painted picture
PAINTY adj **PAINTIER, PAINTIEST** said of a smell, texture, etc: like paint
PAIR noun **PAIRS** a set of two

identical or corresponding things, eg shoes or gloves, intended for use together ◻ verb **PAIRS, PAIRING, PAIRED** to divide into groups of two; to sort out in pairs
PAIRED adj arranged in pairs
PAIRS plural noun another name for the card game pelmanism
PAIRWISE adverb in pairs
PAISANO noun **PAISANOS** a person from the same area or town; a compatriot
PAISLEY noun **PAISLEYS** a fabric with a pattern resembling the paisley pattern
PAJAMAS plural noun pyjamas
PAKAPOO noun **PAKAPOOS** a Chinese version of lotto, in which betting tickets are filled in with Chinese characters
PAKORA noun **PAKORAS** an Indian dish of chopped spiced vegetables formed into balls, coated in batter and deep-fried, served with a spicy sauce
PAL noun **PALS** a friend; a mate ◻ verb **PALS, PALLING, PALLED** to associate as a pal
PALACE noun **PALACES** the official residence of a sovereign, bishop, archbishop or president
PALADIN noun **PALADINS** any of the 12 peers of Charlemagne's court
PALAMINO noun **PALAMINOS** a palomino
PALANKEEN noun **PALANKEENS** a palanquin
PALANQUIN noun **PALANQUINS** a light covered litter used in the Orient, suspended from poles carried on the shoulders of four or six bearers
PALATABLE adj having a pleasant taste; appetizing
PALATABLY adverb in a palatable way
PALATAL adj relating to the palate ◻ noun **PALATALS** a sound produced by bringing the tongue to or near the hard palate
PALATE noun **PALATES** the roof of the mouth, consisting of the hard palate in front and the soft palate behind
PALATIAL adj like a palace in magnificence, spaciousness, etc
PALATINE adj referring to the Palatine Hill in Rome, or the palace of Roman emperors on that hill
PALAVER noun **PALAVERS** a long, boring, complicated and

seemingly pointless exercise; an unnecessary fuss ◻ verb **PALAVERS, PALAVERING, PALAVERED** to chatter idly
PALAZZO noun **PALAZZI** an Italian palace, often one converted into a museum
PALE[1] adj **PALER, PALEST** said of a person, face, etc: having less colour than normal, eg from illness, fear, shock, etc ◻ verb **PALES, PALING, PALED** to become pale
PALE[2] noun **PALES** a wooden or metal post or stake used for making fences
PALEBUCK noun **PALEBUCKS** the oribi
PALEFACE noun **PALEFACES** the term supposed to have been used by Native Americans for the white settlers
PALELY adverb in a pale way
PALENESS noun **PALENESSES** the quality or condition of being pale
PALER see under **pale**[1]
PALEST see under **pale**[1]
PALETTE noun **PALETTES** a hand-held board with a thumb-hole, on which an artist mixes colours
PALIMONY noun **PALIMONIES** alimony or its equivalent demanded by one partner when the couple have been cohabiting without being married
PALING noun **PALINGS** a fence constructed of pales
PALISADE noun **PALISADES** a tall fence of pointed wooden stakes fixed edge to edge, for defence or protection
PALISH adj somewhat pale; quite pale
PALL[1] noun **PALLS** the cloth that covers a coffin at a funeral
PALL[2] verb **PALLS, PALLING, PALLED** to begin to bore or seem tedious
PALLADIUM noun **PALLADIUMS** a soft silvery-white metallic element used as a catalyst, and in gold dental alloys, jewellery, electrical components, and catalytic converters for car exhausts
PALLED past form of **pal, pall**[2]
PALLET noun **PALLETS** a small wooden platform on which goods can be stacked for lifting and transporting, especially by forklift truck
PALLIASSE noun **PALLIASSES** a straw-filled mattress
PALLIATE verb **PALLIATES,**

PALLIATING, PALLIATED to ease the symptoms of (a disease) without curing it

PALLID adj **PALLIDER, PALLIDEST** pale, especially unhealthily so

PALLING a form of **pal, pall**²

PALLIUM noun **PALLIA** a white woollen vestment shaped like a double Y, embroidered with six purple crosses signifying episcopal power and union with the Holy See of Rome, worn by the pope and conferred by him on archbishops

PALLOR noun **PALLORS** paleness, especially of complexion

PALLY adj **PALLIER, PALLIEST** friendly; companionable

PALM noun **PALMS** the inner surface of the hand between the wrist and the fingers ▫ verb **PALMS, PALMING, PALMED** to conceal something in the palm of the hand

PALMAR adj relating to the palm of the hand

PALMATE adj said of a leaf: divided into lobes that radiate from a central point, resembling an open hand

PALMATED adj palmate

PALMETTO noun **PALMETTOS, PALMETTOES** any of various small palm trees, mainly native to tropical regions, which have fan-shaped leaves

PALMHOUSE noun **PALMHOUSES** a glasshouse for palms and other tropical plants, usually found in botanical gardens in temperate climates where palms do not grow naturally

PALMIST noun **PALMISTS** someone who practises palmistry

PALMISTRY noun **PALMISTRIES** the art and practice of telling someone's fortune by reading the lines on the palm of their hand

PALMITATE noun **PALMITATES** a salt of palmitic acid

PALMTOP noun **PALMTOPS** a portable computer, smaller than a laptop, and usually small enough to be held in the hand

PALMY adj **PALMIER, PALMIEST** effortlessly successful and prosperous

PALMYRA noun **PALMYRAS** an African and Asiatic palm yielding toddy, jaggery and palmyra nuts

PALOLO noun **PALOLOS** an edible sea-worm that burrows in coral reefs, abundant in parts of the Pacific

PALOMINO noun **PALOMINOS** a golden or cream horse, largely of Arab blood, with a white or silver tail and mane

PALOOKA noun **PALOOKAS** a stupid or clumsy person, especially in sports

PALP noun **PALPS** a jointed sense-organ attached in pairs to the mouthparts of insects and crustaceans

PALPABLE adj easily detected; obvious

PALPABLY adverb in a palpable way

PALPAL adj relating to a palp

PALPATE verb **PALPATES, PALPATING, PALPATED** to examine (the body or a part of it) by touching or pressing, especially in order to diagnose medical disorders or diseases

PALPITATE verb **PALPITATES, PALPITATING, PALPITATED** said of the heart: to beat abnormally rapidly, eg as a result of physical exertion, fear, emotion or heart disease

PALPUS noun **PALPI** a palp

PALSY¹ noun **PALSIES** paralysis, or loss of control or feeling in a part of the body ▫ verb **PALSIES, PALSYING, PALSIED** to affect someone or something with palsy; to paralyse

PALSY² adj **PALSIER, PALSIEST** over-friendly; ingratiatingly intimate

PALTRILY adverb in a paltry way

PALTRY adj **PALTRIER, PALTRIEST** worthless; trivial; meagre; insignificant or insultingly inadequate

PALUDAL adj relating to marshes; marshy

PALY adj **PALIER, PALIEST** divided by vertical lines

PAM noun **PAMS** in a pack of playing cards: the knave of clubs

PAMPER verb **PAMPERS, PAMPERING, PAMPERED** to treat (a person or animal) over-indulgently and over-protectively; to cosset or spoil them

PAMPERER noun **PAMPERERS** someone who pampers

PAMPHLET noun **PAMPHLETS** a booklet or leaflet providing information or dealing with a current topic

PAN noun **PANS** a pot, usually made of metal, used for cooking ▫ verb **PANS, PANNING, PANNED** to wash (river gravel) in a shallow metal vessel in search for (eg gold)

PANACEA noun **PANACEAS** a universal remedy; a cure-all for any ill, problem, etc

PANACHE noun **PANACHES** flamboyant self-assurance; a grand manner

PANADA noun **PANADAS** a dish made by boiling bread to a pulp in water or milk and flavouring it

PANAMA noun **PANAMAS** a lightweight brimmed hat for men made from the plaited leaves of a palm-like Central American tree, made in Ecuador, not Panama

PANATELLA noun **PANATELLAS** a long slim cigar

PANAX noun **PANAXES** a type of tree or shrub

PANCAKE noun **PANCAKES** a thin cake made from a batter of eggs, flour and milk, cooked on both sides in a frying-pan or on a griddle, and traditional in many parts of the world

PANCHAX noun **PANCHAXES** any of several kinds of brightly coloured fish native to Africa and SE Asia

PANCREAS noun **PANCREASES** in vertebrates: a large carrot-shaped gland lying between the duodenum and the spleen, that secretes pancreatic juice serving hormonal and digestive functions

PANDA noun **PANDAS** a large bear-like mammal, native to Tibet and south-west China, which has thick white fur and black legs, shoulders, ears and patches round the eyes

PANDEMIC adj describing a widespread epidemic of a disease, one that affects a whole country, continent, etc

PANDER noun **PANDERS** someone who obtains a sexual partner for someone else ▫ verb **PANDERS, PANDERING, PANDERED** to play the pander for someone

PANDIT noun **PANDITS** a Hindu learned in Hindu culture, philosophy and law

PANE noun **PANES** a sheet of glass, especially one fitted into a window or door

PANEGYRIC noun **PANEGYRICS** a speech or piece of writing in praise of someone or something, especially an elaborate one; a eulogy □ adj of the nature of a panegyric

PANEL noun PANELS a rectangular wooden board forming a section, especially an ornamentally sunken or raised one, of a wall or door □ verb PANELS, PANELLING, PANELLED to fit (a wall or door) with wooden panels

PANELLING noun PANELLINGS panels covering a wall or part of a wall, usually as decoration

PANELLIST noun PANELLISTS a member of a panel or team of people, especially in a panel game on TV or radio

PANETTONE noun PANETTONI a kind of spiced cake, usually containing sultanas, traditionally eaten at Christmas in Italy

PANFUL noun PANFULS the amount a pan can hold

PANG noun PANGS a brief but painfully acute feeling of hunger, guilt, remorse, etc

PANGOLIN noun PANGOLINS a toothless mammal that is covered with large overlapping horny plates, has a pointed head and a long broad tail, and can curl into an armoured ball when threatened by a predator

PANGRAM noun PANGRAMS a sentence or verse containing all the letters of the alphabet

PANHANDLE noun PANHANDLES a narrow strip of territory stretching out from the main body into another territory, eg part of a state which stretches into another

PANIC noun PANICS a sudden overpowering fear that affects an individual, or especially one that grips a crowd or population □ verb PANICS, PANICKING, PANICKED to feel panic, or make someone feel panic

PANICKY adj PANICKIER, PANICKIEST inclined to or affected by panic

PANICLE noun PANICLES a branched flower-head, common in grasses, in which the youngest flowers are at the tip of the flower-stalk, and the oldest ones are near its base

PANICLED adj having, arranged in, or like, panicles

PANISLAM noun PANISLAMS the whole Muslim world

PANNE noun PANNES a fabric resembling velvet with a long nap

PANNED past form of pan

PANNIER noun PANNIERS one of a pair of baskets carried over the back of a donkey or other pack animal

PANNIKIN noun PANNIKINS a small metal cup

PANNING a form of pan

PANNOSE adj like felt

PANNUS noun PANNUSES a layer of new connective tissue that forms over the joints in rheumatoid arthritis

PANOCHA noun PANOCHAS a coarse brown Mexican sugar

PANOPLY noun PANOPLIES the full splendid assemblage got together for a ceremony, etc

PANOPTIC adj all-embracing; viewing all aspects

PANORAMA noun PANORAMAS an open and extensive or all-round view, eg of a landscape

PANORAMIC adj said of a view or prospect: like a panorama; open and extensive

PANSY noun PANSIES any of various species of violet, native to Europe, which have flat flowers with five rounded white, yellow or purple petals

PANT verb PANTS, PANTING, PANTED to breathe in and out with quick, shallow, short gasps as a result of physical exertion □ noun PANTS a gasping breath

PANTHEISM noun PANTHEISMS the belief that equates all the matter and forces in the Universe with God

PANTHEIST noun PANTHEISTS someone who holds the doctrine of pantheism

PANTHENOL noun PANTHENOLS a vitamin of the vitamin B complex

PANTHER noun PANTHERS a leopard, especially a black one, formerly believed to be a different species

PANTIES plural noun thin light knickers, mainly for women and children

PANTIHOSE plural noun women's tights

PANTILE noun PANTILES a roofing tile with an S-shaped cross section, laid so that the upward curve of one tile fits under the downward curve of the next

PANTILED adj covered with pantiles

PANTILING noun PANTILINGS the covering of a roof with pantiles

PANTING noun PANTINGS the action of breathing in and out with quick, shallow, short gasps as a result of physical exertion □ adj that pants

PANTINGLY adverb in a panting way

PANTO noun PANTOS short form of pantomime

PANTOMIME noun PANTOMIMES a Christmas entertainment usually based on a popular fairy tale, with songs, dancing, comedy acts, etc

PANTRY noun PANTRIES a small room or cupboard for storing food, cooking utensils, etc; a larder

PANTS plural noun an undergarment worn over the buttocks and genital area; underpants

PAP noun PAPS soft semi-liquid food for babies and sick people □ verb PAPS, PAPPING, PAPPED to feed with pap

PAPA noun PAPAS a child's word for father

PAPACY noun PAPACIES the position, power or period of office of a pope

PAPAIN noun PAPAINS a digestive enzyme in the juice of papaya fruits and leaves, used for tenderizing meat

PAPALISM noun PAPALISMS the situation of the pope as the head of the RC Church, his power and authority; the papal system

PAPALIST noun PAPALISTS a supporter of the pope and of the papal system

PAPARAZZO noun PAPARAZZI a newspaper photographer who follows famous people about in the hope of photographing them in unguarded moments

PAPAW noun PAPAWS a tree with purple flowers native to N America

PAPAYA noun PAPAYAS a papaw

PAPER noun PAPERS a material manufactured in thin sheets from pulped wood, rags, or other forms of cellulose, used for writing and printing on, wrapping things, etc □ adj consisting of or made of paper □ verb PAPERS, PAPERING, PAPERED to decorate (a wall, room, etc) with wallpaper

PAPERBACK noun PAPERBACKS a book with a thin flexible paper binding, as opposed to a hardback

❑ *verb* **PAPERBACKS, PAPERBACKING, PAPERBACKED** to publish (a book) in paperback form

PAPERER *noun* **PAPERERS** someone who decorates a wall, room, etc with wallpaper

PAPERING *noun* **PAPERINGS** the activity of covering something with paper, especially wallpaper

PAPERLESS *adj* using especially electronic means, rather than paper, for communicating, recording, etc

PAPERWORK *noun* **PAPERWORKS** routine written work, eg filling out forms, keeping files, writing letters and reports, etc, most of which is necessary to ensure the smooth running of a job, company, etc; clerical work

PAPERY *adj* **PAPERIER, PAPERIEST** like paper in texture

PAPILLA *noun* **PAPILLAE** a small nipple-like projection from the surface of a structure

PAPILLARY *adj* like or having papillae

PAPILLATE *adj* having papillae

PAPILLOMA *noun* **PAPILLOMAS** a benign tumour formed by the abnormal enlargement of a papilla or papillae, such as a wart

PAPILLON *noun* **PAPILLONS** a breed of toy dog which has a small body and a long fine coat that is thickest on the neck, chest and upper legs

PAPILLOTE *noun* **PAPILLOTES** a small decorative paper frill used to garnish the bone end of a lamb or veal chop

PAPOOSE *noun* **PAPOOSES** a Native American baby or young child

PAPPADOM *noun* **PAPPADOMS** a poppadum

PAPPUS *noun* **PAPPUSES** in composites and some other plants, eg dandelions and thistles: a ring or parachute of fine hair or down, which grows above the seed and helps in wind dispersal

PAPPY[1] *noun* **PAPPIES** father; papa

PAPPY[2] *adj* **PAPPIER, PAPPIEST** like pap in consistency; soft and wet

PAPRIKA *noun* **PAPRIKAS** a powdered hot spice made from red peppers

PAPULA *noun* **PAPULAE** a pimple; a papilla

PAPULAR *adj* relating to papulae or pimples

PAPULE *noun* **PAPULES** a papula

PAPYRUS *noun* **PAPYRI** a tall plant of the sedge family, common in ancient Egypt

PAR *noun* **PARS** a normal level or standard

PARA *noun* **PARAS** a paratrooper

PARABLE *noun* **PARABLES** a story which is realistic but usually made up, intended to convey a moral or religious lesson; an allegorical tale

PARABOLA *noun* **PARABOLAS** a conic section produced when a plane intersects a cone, and the plane is parallel to the cone's sloping side

PARABOLIC *adj* like or expressed in a parable

PARABRAKE *noun* **PARABRAKES** a parachute released behind an aircraft to help it slow down once it has landed

PARACHUTE *noun* **PARACHUTES** an umbrella-shaped apparatus consisting of light fabric, with a harness for attaching to, and slowing the fall of, a person or package dropped from an aircraft ❑ *verb* **PARACHUTES, PARACHUTING, PARACHUTED** to drop from the air by parachute

PARACLETE *noun* an advocate or legal helper, or intercessor; a pleader on behalf of another

PARADE *noun* **PARADES** a ceremonial procession of people, vehicles, etc ❑ *verb* **PARADES, PARADING, PARADED** to walk or make (a body of soldiers, etc) walk or march in procession, eg across a square, along a street, etc

PARADIGM *noun* **PARADIGMS** an example, model or pattern

PARADISAL *adj* relating to or resembling paradise

PARADISE *noun* **PARADISES** heaven

PARADOX *noun* **PARADOXES** a statement that seems to contradict itself, eg *More haste, less speed*

PARADOXY *noun* **PARADOXIES** the quality of being paradoxical

PARAFFIN *noun* **PARAFFINS** a fuel oil obtained from petroleum or coal and used in aircraft, domestic heaters, etc

PARAFFINY *adj* relating to or suggestive of paraffin

PARAGON *noun* **PARAGONS** someone who is a model of excellence or perfection

PARAGRAPH *noun* **PARAGRAPHS** a section of a piece of writing of variable length, starting on a fresh, often indented, line, and dealing with a distinct point or idea ❑ *verb* **PARAGRAPHS, PARAGRAPHING, PARAGRAPHED** to divide (text) into paragraphs

PARAKEET *noun* **PARAKEETS** any of various small brightly-coloured parrots with long pointed tails, native to tropical regions worldwide, which live in groups and usually roost in trees

PARALALIA *noun* **PARALALIAS** a form of speech disturbance, especially one in which a different sound or syllable is produced in place of the intended one

PARALLAX *noun* **PARALLAXES** the apparent change in the position of an object, relative to a distant background, when it is viewed from two different positions

PARALLEL *adj* said of lines, planes, etc: the same distance apart at every point; alongside and never meeting or intersecting ❑ *adverb* alongside and at an unvarying distance ❑ *noun* **PARALLELS** a line or plane parallel to another ❑ *verb* **PARALLELS, PARALLELING, PARALLELED** to equal

PARALYSE *verb* **PARALYSES, PARALYSING, PARALYSED** to affect (a person or bodily part) with paralysis

PARALYSER *noun* **PARALYSERS** something that paralyses

PARALYSIS *noun* **PARALYSES** a temporary or permanent loss of muscular function or sensation in any part of the body, usually caused by nerve damage, eg as a result of disease or injury

PARALYTIC *adj* relating to, caused by or suffering from paralysis ❑ *noun* **PARALYTICS** a person affected by paralysis

PARALYZE *verb* **PARALYZES, PARALYZING, PARALYZED** to paralyse

PARAMATTA *noun* **PARAMATTAS** a fabric like merino wool, made of worsted and cotton

PARAMEDIC *noun* **PARAMEDICS** a person, especially one trained in emergency medical procedures, whose work supplements and supports that of the medical profession

PARAMETER *noun* **PARAMETERS** a constant or variable that, when altered, affects the form of a mathematical expression in which it appears

PARAMOUNT *adj* foremost; supreme; of supreme importance

PARAMOUR *noun* **PARAMOURS** a male or female lover, usually the lover of someone who is married

PARANOIA *noun* **PARANOIAS** a rare mental disorder, characterized by delusions of persecution by others, especially if this is attributed to one's own importance or unique gifts

PARANOIAC *adj* paranoid ◻ *noun* **PARANOIACS** a paranoid

PARANOIC *adj* paranoid ◻ *noun* **PARANOICS** a paranoid

PARANOID *adj* relating to or affected by paranoia ◻ *noun* **PARANOIDS** a person affected by paranoia

PARANYM *noun* **PARANYMS** a word used to describe an event, etc which evades or conceals some important aspect of it, eg *liberation* used for *conquest*; a word which is nearly, but not exactly, a synonym

PARAPET *noun* **PARAPETS** a low wall along the edge of a bridge, balcony, roof, etc, sometimes with battlements and usually ornamental

PARAPH *noun* **PARAPHS** a mark or flourish under one's signature

PARASITE *noun* **PARASITES** a plant or animal that for all or part of its life obtains food and physical protection from a living organism of another species (the host) which is usually damaged by and never benefits from its presence

PARASITIC *adj* of, of the nature of, caused by or like a parasite

PARASOL *noun* **PARASOLS** a light umbrella used as a protection against the Sun; a sunshade

PARATHA *noun* **PARATHAS** a thin unleavened cake made of flour, water and clarified butter, originating in India

PARAVANE *noun* **PARAVANES** a torpedo-shaped device, with fins and vanes, towed from the bow of a vessel in order to deflect mines along a wire and to sever their moorings

PARAZOAN *noun* **PARAZOANS** any member of the group Parazoa, the sponges

PARBOIL *verb* **PARBOILS, PARBOILING, PARBOILED** to boil

something until it is partially cooked

PARCEL *noun* **PARCELS** something wrapped in paper, etc and secured with string or sticky tape; a package ◻ *verb* **PARCELS, PARCELLING, PARCELLED** to make up into parcels or a parcel

PARCH *verb* **PARCHES, PARCHING, PARCHED** to dry something up; to deprive (soil, plants, etc) of water

PARCHED *adj* very thirsty

PARCHMENT *noun* **PARCHMENTS** a material formerly used for bookbinding and for writing on, made from goatskin, calfskin or sheepskin

PARD *noun* **PARDS** friend or partner

PARDNER *noun* **PARDNERS** a pard

PARDON *verb* **PARDONS, PARDONING, PARDONED** to forgive or excuse someone for a fault or offence ◻ *noun* **PARDONS** forgiveness

PARDONER *noun* **PARDONERS** someone who pardons

PARE *verb* **PARES, PARING, PARED** to trim off (skin, etc) in layers

PAREGORIC *adj* soothing; lessening pain ◻ *noun* **PAREGORICS** a medicine that soothes pain, especially an alcoholic solution of opium, benzoic acid, camphor and oil of anise

PARENT *noun* **PARENTS** a father or mother ◻ *verb* **PARENTS, PARENTING, PARENTED** to be or act as a parent; to care for someone or something as a parent ◻ *adj* referring to an organization, etc that has established a branch or branches over which it retains some control

PARENTAGE *noun* **PARENTAGES** descent from parents

PARENTAL *adj* related to or concerning parents

PARENTING *noun* **PARENTINGS** the activities and duties of a parent

PAREO *noun* **PAREOS** a pareu

PARESIS *noun* **PARESES** a partial form of paralysis affecting muscle movements but not diminishing sensation

PARETIC *adj* of or relating to paresis

PAREU *noun* **PAREUS** a

wraparound skirt worn by women and men in Polynesia

PARFAIT *noun* **PARFAITS** a kind of frozen dessert containing whipped cream, fruit and eggs

PARGET *noun* **PARGETS** plaster spread over a surface ◻ *verb* **PARGETS, PARGETING, PARGETED** to plaster over something

PARHELIC *adj* relating to or resembling a parhelion

PARHELION *noun* **PARHELIA** a bright spot on the parhelic circle, a band of luminosity parallel to the horizon

PARIAH *noun* **PARIAHS** someone scorned and avoided by others; a social outcast

PARIETAL *adj* relating to, or forming, the wall of a bodily cavity, eg the skull

PARING a form of **pare**

PARISH *noun* **PARISHES** a district or area served by its own church and priest or minister, usually the established church of that particular area ◻ *adj* belonging or relating to a parish

PARISON *noun* **PARISONS** a lump of glass before it is moulded into its final shape

PARITY *noun* **PARITIES** equality in status, eg in pay

PARK *noun* **PARKS** an area in a town with grass and trees, reserved for public recreation ◻ *verb* **PARKS, PARKING, PARKED** to leave (a vehicle) temporarily at the side of the road or in a car park

PARKA *noun* **PARKAS** a hooded jacket made of skins, worn by the Inuit and Aleut people of the Arctic

PARKIE *noun* **PARKIES** a park keeper

PARKIN *noun* **PARKINS** a moist ginger-flavoured oatmeal cake made with treacle

PARKLAND *noun* **PARKLANDS** pasture and woodland forming part of a country estate

PARKWAY *noun* **PARKWAYS** a broad thoroughfare incorporating grassy areas and lined with trees, often connecting the parks of a town

PARKY *adj* **PARKIER, PARKIEST** said of the weather: somewhat cold; chilly

PARLANCE *noun* **PARLANCES** a particular style or way of using words

PARLANDO *adj* said of a passage of vocal music: that the singer should actually speak, or give the impression of speaking □ *adverb* in declamatory style

PARLEY *verb* **PARLEYS, PARLEYING, PARLEYED** to discuss peace terms, etc with an enemy, especially under truce □ *noun* **PARLEYS** a meeting with an enemy to discuss peace terms, etc

PARLOUR *noun* **PARLOURS** a shop or commercial premises providing specified goods or services

PARLOUS *adj* precarious; perilous; dire

PAROCHIAL *adj* said of tastes, attitudes, etc: concerned only with local affairs; narrow, limited or provincial in outlook

PARODIC *adj* of the nature of a parody

PARODICAL *adj* of or relating to parody

PARODIST *noun* **PARODISTS** the author of a parody

PARODY *noun* **PARODIES** a comic or satirical imitation of a work, or the style, of a particular writer, composer, etc □ *verb* **PARODIES, PARODYING, PARODIED** to ridicule something through parody; to mimic satirically

PAROLE *noun* **PAROLES** the release of a prisoner before the end of their sentence, on promise of good behaviour □ *verb* **PAROLES, PAROLING, PAROLED** to release or place (a prisoner) on parole

PAROLEE *noun* **PAROLEES** a prisoner who has been conditionally released

PARONYM *noun* **PARONYMS** a word from the same root, or having the same sound, as another; a cognate

PAROTID *adj* situated beside or near the ear □ *noun* **PAROTIDS** the parotid gland, a salivary gland in front of the ear

PAROUSIA *noun* **PAROUSIAS** the second coming of Christ which, in Christian thought, will be marked by a heavenly appearance, God's judgement of all humanity, and the resurrection of the dead

PAROXYSM *noun* **PAROXYSMS** a sudden emotional outburst, eg of rage or laughter

PARPEN *noun* **PARPENS** a stone forming part of a wall which can be seen from both sides

PARQUET *noun* **PARQUETS** flooring composed of small inlaid blocks of wood arranged in a geometric pattern

PARQUETRY *noun* **PARQUETRIES** inlaid work in wood arranged in a geometric pattern, used especially to cover floors or to decorate furniture, etc

PARR *noun* **PARRS** a young salmon aged up to two years, before it becomes a smolt

PARRAKEET *noun* **PARRAKEETS** a parakeet

PARRICIDE *noun* **PARRICIDES** the act of killing one's own parent or near relative

PARROT *noun* **PARROTS** any of numerous usually brightly-coloured birds, native to forests of warmer regions, with a large head, a strong hooked bill, and two of the four toes on each foot pointing backwards □ *verb* **PARROTS, PARROTING, PARROTED** to repeat or mimic (another's words, etc) unthinkingly

PARROTER *noun* **PARROTERS** someone who mechanically recites something learned by heart

PARRY *verb* **PARRIES, PARRYING, PARRIED** to fend off (a blow) □ *noun* **PARRIES** an act of parrying, especially in fencing

PARSE *verb* **PARSES, PARSING, PARSED** to analyse (a sentence) grammatically; to give the part of speech of and explain the grammatical role of (a word)

PARSEC *noun* **PARSECS** a unit of astronomical measurement equal to 3.26 light years or 3.09×10^{13} km

PARSER *noun* **PARSERS** a program which parses sentences

PARSIMONY *noun* **PARSIMONIES** reluctance or extreme care in spending money

PARSLEY *noun* **PARSLEYS** an annual or biennial plant with finely-divided bright green curly aromatic leaves, used fresh or dried as a culinary herb, and also used fresh as a garnish

PARSNIP *noun* **PARSNIPS** a biennial plant widely grown for its thick fleshy edible tap root

PARSON *noun* **PARSONS** a parish priest in the Church of England

PARSONAGE *noun* **PARSONAGES** the residence of a parson

PART *noun* **PARTS** a portion, piece or bit; some but not all □ *verb* **PARTS, PARTING, PARTED** to

divide; to separate □ *adj* in part; partial

PARTAKE *verb* **PARTAKES, PARTAKING, PARTOOK, PARTAKEN** to take or have a part or share

PARTED *adj* divided; separated

PARTERRE *noun* **PARTERRES** a formal ornamental flower-garden laid out with lawns and paths

PARTIAL *adj* incomplete; in part only □ *noun* **PARTIALS** one of the single-frequency tones which go together to form a sound actually heard

PARTIALLY *adverb* not completely or wholly; not yet to the point of completion

PARTIBLE *adj* said especially of inherited property: able to be divided up

PARTICLE *noun* **PARTICLES** a tiny piece; a minute piece of matter

PARTING *noun* **PARTINGS** the act of taking leave □ *adj* referring to, or at the time of, leaving; departing

PARTISAN *noun* **PARTISANS** an enthusiastic supporter of a party, person, cause, etc □ *adj* strongly loyal to one side, especially blindly so; biased

PARTITA *noun* **PARTITAS** referring especially to the 18c: a suite of instrumental dances, such as those by J S Bach

PARTITE *adj* divided into the specified number of parts

PARTITION *noun* **PARTITIONS** something which divides an object into a number of parts □ *verb* **PARTITIONS, PARTITIONING, PARTITIONED** to separate with a partition

PARTITIVE *adj* said of a word, form, etc: denoting a part of a whole of what is being described □ *noun* **PARTITIVES** a partitive word or form, eg some, any, most

PARTLY *adverb* in part, or in some parts; to a certain extent, not wholly

PARTNER *noun* **PARTNERS** one of two or more people who jointly own or run a business or other enterprise on an equal footing □ *verb* **PARTNERS, PARTNERING, PARTNERED** to join as a partner with someone; to be the partner of someone

PARTOOK past form of **partake**

PARTRIDGE *noun* **PARTRIDGES** any of various plump ground-dwelling gamebirds, usually with brown or grey plumage, unfeathered legs and feet, and a very short tail

PARTWORK noun **PARTWORKS** one of a series of publications, especially magazines, issued at regular intervals, eventually forming a complete course or book

PARTY noun **PARTIES** a social gathering, especially of invited guests, for enjoyment or celebration □ verb **PARTIES, PARTYING, PARTIED** to gather as a group to drink, chat, dance, etc for enjoyment; to have fun

PARVENU noun **PARVENUS** a man who has recently acquired substantial wealth but lacks the social refinement sometimes thought necessary to go with it

PARVIS noun **PARVISES** an enclosed space, or sometimes a portico, at the front of a church

PARVISE noun **PARVISES** a parvis

PAS noun **PAS** a step or dance, especially in ballet

PASCAL noun **PASCALS** in the SI system: a unit of pressure, equal to a force of one newton per square metre

PASCHAL adj relating to the Jewish festival of Passover

PASH noun **PASHES** short form of passion

PASHA noun **PASHAS** placed after the name in titles: a high-ranking Turkish official in the Ottoman Empire

PASHM noun **PASHMS** the fine underfleece of the goats of N India, used for making rugs, shawls, etc

PASS verb **PASSES, PASSING, PASSED** to come alongside and progress beyond something or someone □ noun **PASSES** a route through a gap in a mountain range

PASSABLE adj barely adequate

PASSABLY adverb fairly well; tolerably

PASSADE noun **PASSADES** the motion of a horse to and fro over the same ground in dressage exercises

PASSAGE¹ noun **PASSAGES** a route through; a corridor, narrow street, or channel

PASSAGE² verb **PASSAGES, PASSAGING, PASSAGED** to cause (a horse) to move at a passage (a slow sideways walk)

PASSATA noun **PASSATAS** an Italian sauce of puréed and sieved tomatoes

PASSÉ adj outmoded; old-fashioned; having faded out of popularity

PASSENGER noun **PASSENGERS** a traveller in a vehicle, boat, aeroplane, etc driven, sailed or piloted by someone else □ adj relating to, or for, passengers

PASSERINE adj belonging or relating to the largest order of birds, characterized by a perching habit and the possession of four toes, and which includes the songbirds □ noun **PASSERINES** any bird belonging to this order

PASSIBLE adj susceptible to or capable of suffering or feeling

PASSIM adverb said of a word, reference, etc: occurring frequently throughout the literary or academic work in question

PASSING adj lasting only briefly □ noun **PASSINGS** a place where one may pass

PASSION noun **PASSIONS** a violent emotion, eg hate, anger or envy

PASSIONAL adj referring or relating to the sufferings of a Christian martyr □ noun **PASSIONALS** a book of the sufferings of saints and martyrs

PASSIVE adj lacking positive or assertive qualities; submissive □ noun **PASSIVES** the form or forms that a passive verb takes

PASSIVELY adverb in a passive way

PASSIVITY noun **PASSIVITIES** submissiveness

PASSKEY noun **PASSKEYS** a key designed to open a varied set of locks; a master key

PASSPORT noun **PASSPORTS** an official document issued by the government, giving proof of the holder's identity and nationality, and permission to travel abroad with its protection

PASSWORD noun **PASSWORDS** a secret word allowing entry to a high-security area or past a checkpoint, etc

PAST adj referring to an earlier time; of long ago; bygone □ prep up to and beyond □ adverb so as to pass by □ noun **PASTS** the time before the present

PASTA noun **PASTAS** a dough made with flour, water and eggs,

shaped into a variety of forms such as spaghetti, macaroni, lasagne, etc

PASTE noun **PASTES** a stiff moist mixture made from a powder and water, and traditionally made from flour and water, used as an adhesive □ verb **PASTES, PASTING, PASTED** to stick something with paste

PASTEL noun **PASTELS** a chalk-like crayon made from ground pigment □ adj said of colours: delicately pale; soft, quiet

PASTERN noun **PASTERNS** the part of a horse's foot between the hoof and the fetlock

PASTICHE noun **PASTICHES** a musical, artistic or literary work in someone else's style, or in a mixture of styles

PASTIER see under **pasty**²

PASTIEST see under **pasty**²

PASTILLE noun **PASTILLES** a small fruit-flavoured sweet, sometimes medicated

PASTIME noun **PASTIMES** a spare-time pursuit; a hobby

PASTINESS noun **PASTINESSES** a pasty consistency or quality

PASTING noun **PASTINGS** a thrashing

PASTIS noun **PASTISES** an alcoholic drink flavoured with anise

PASTOR noun **PASTORS** a member of the clergy, especially in churches other than Anglican and Catholic, with responsibility for a congregation

PASTORAL adj relating to the countryside or country life □ noun **PASTORALS** a pastoral poem or painting

PASTORALE noun **PASTORALES** a musical work that evokes the countryside; a pastoral

PASTORATE noun **PASTORATES** the office, authority or residence of a pastor

PASTRAMI noun **PASTRAMIS** a smoked highly-seasoned cut of beef, especially a shoulder

PASTRY noun **PASTRIES** dough made with flour, fat and water, used for piecrusts

PASTURAGE noun **PASTURAGES** an area of land where livestock is allowed to graze

PASTURAL adj of pasture

PASTURE noun **PASTURES** an area of grassland suitable for used for the grazing of livestock □ verb

PASTURES, PASTURING, PASTURED to put (animals) in pasture to graze

PASTY¹ *noun* **PASTIES** a pie consisting of pastry folded round a savoury or sweet filling

PASTY² *adj* **PASTIER, PASTIEST** like a paste in texture or colour

PAT *verb* **PATS, PATTING, PATTED** to strike (a person or animal) lightly or affectionately with the palm of one's hand ❑ *noun* **PATS** a light blow, especially an affectionate one, with the palm of the hand ❑ *adverb* especially of things said: immediately and fluently, as if memorized ❑ *adj* said of answers, etc: quickly and easily supplied

PATCH *noun* **PATCHES** a piece of material sewn on or applied, eg to a garment or piece of fabric, etc, so as to cover a hole or reinforce a worn area ❑ *verb* **PATCHES, PATCHING, PATCHED** to mend (a hole or garment) by sewing a patch or patches on or over it

PATCHILY *adverb* in a patchy way; unevenly

PATCHOULI *noun* **PATCHOULIS** a shrubby perennial SE Asian plant that yields an aromatic essential oil used in perfumery

PATCHWORK *noun* **PATCHWORKS** needlework done by sewing together small pieces of contrastingly patterned fabric to make a larger piece of fabric

PATCHY *adj* **PATCHIER, PATCHIEST** forming, or occurring in, patches

PATE *noun* **PATES** the head or skull, especially when alluding to baldness or intelligence

PÂTÉ *noun* **PÂTÉS** a spread made from ground or chopped meat, fish or vegetables blended with herbs, spices, etc

PATELLA *noun* **PATELLAE, PATELLAS** the kneecap

PATEN *noun* **PATENS** a circular metal plate, often of silver or gold, on which the bread is placed in the celebration of the Eucharist

PATENT *noun* **PATENTS** an official licence from the government granting a person or business the sole right, for a certain period, to make and sell a particular article ❑ *verb* **PATENTS, PATENTING, PATENTED** to obtain a patent for (an invention, design, etc) ❑ *adj* very evident

PATENTEE *noun* **PATENTEES** the person obtaining or holding a patent

PATENTLY *adverb* openly; clearly

PATENTOR *noun* **PATENTORS** a person, organization, authority, etc that grants patents

PATER *noun* **PATERS** father

PATERNAL *adj* referring, relating, or appropriate to a father

PATERNITY *noun* **PATERNITIES** the quality or condition of being a father; fatherhood

PATH *noun* **PATHS** a track trodden by, or specially surfaced for, walking

PATHETIC *adj* moving one to pity; touching, heart-rending, poignant or pitiful

PATHOGEN *noun* **PATHOGENS** any micro-organism, especially a bacterium or virus, that causes disease in a living organism

PATHOGENY *noun* **PATHOGENIES** the development of a disease or disorder, mainly as observed at the biochemical or cellular level

PATHOLOGY *noun* **PATHOLOGIES** the branch of medicine concerned with the study of the nature of diseases

PATHOS *noun* **PATHOSES** a quality in a situation, etc, especially in literature, that moves one to pity

PATHWAY *noun* **PATHWAYS** a path

PATIENCE *noun* **PATIENCES** the ability to endure delay, trouble, pain or hardship in a calm and contained way

PATIENT *adj* **PATIENTER, PATIENTEST** having or showing patience ❑ *noun* **PATIENTS** a person who is being treated by, or is registered with, a doctor, dentist, etc

PATIENTLY *adverb* in a patient way; with patience

PATINA *noun* **PATINAS** a coating formed on a metal surface by oxidation, especially the greenish coating of verdigris on bronze or copper

PATINATED *adj* covered with a patina

PATIO *noun* **PATIOS** an open paved area beside a house

PATOIS *noun* **PATOIS** the local dialect of a region, used usually in informal everyday situations, as opposed to the language used in literature, education, etc

PATRIAL *noun* **PATRIALS** someone who, being a citizen of the UK, a British colony or the British Commonwealth, or the child or grandchild of someone born in the UK, has a legal right to live in the UK

PATRIARCH *noun* **PATRIARCHS** the male head of a family or tribe

PATRICIAN *noun* **PATRICIANS** a member of the aristocracy of ancient Rome ❑ *adj* belonging or relating to the aristocracy, especially that of ancient Rome

PATRICIDE *noun* **PATRICIDES** the act of killing one's own father

PATRIMONY *noun* **PATRIMONIES** property inherited from one's father or ancestors

PATRIOT *noun* **PATRIOTS** someone who loves and serves their fatherland or country devotedly

PATRIOTIC *adj* devoted to one's country

PATRISTIC *adj* referring or relating to the Fathers of the Christian Church

PATROL *verb* **PATROLS, PATROLLING, PATROLLED** to make a regular systematic tour of (an area) to maintain security or surveillance ❑ *noun* **PATROLS** the act of patrolling

PATROLLER *noun* **PATROLLERS** someone who is on patrol

PATROLMAN *noun* **PATROLMEN** the lowest-ranking police officer; a police officer on the beat

PATRON *noun* **PATRONS** someone who gives financial support and encouragement eg to an artist, the arts, a movement or charity

PATRONAGE *noun* **PATRONAGES** the support given by a patron

PATRONAL *adj* of or relating to a patron

PATRONESS *noun* **PATRONESSES** a female patron

PATRONISE *verb* **PATRONISES, PATRONISING, PATRONISED** to patronize

PATRONISING *adj* patronizing

PATRONIZE *verb* **PATRONIZES, PATRONIZING, PATRONIZED** to treat someone condescendingly, or with benevolent superiority, especially inappropriately

PATRONIZING *adj* that patronizes; condescending; superior

PATSY *noun* **PATSIES** an easy victim; a sucker; a scapegoat or fall guy

PATTEN *noun* **PATTENS** an overshoe with a wooden or metal mount to raise the wearer above mud or water

PATTER verb **PATTERS, PATTERING, PATTERED** said of rain, footsteps, etc: to make a light rapid tapping noise ◻ noun **PATTERS** the light rapid tapping of footsteps or rain

PATTERN noun **PATTERNS** a model, guide or set of instructions for making something ◻ verb **PATTERNS, PATTERNING, PATTERNED** to take as a pattern; to fashion after a pattern

PATTERNED adj said of a fabric, etc: having a decorative design; not plain

PATTY noun **PATTIES** a flat round cake of minced meat, vegetables, etc

PAUCITY noun **PAUCITIES** smallness of quantity; fewness; a scarcity or lack; dearth

PAUNCH noun **PAUNCHES** a protruding belly, especially in a man

PAUNCHY adj **PAUNCHIER, PAUNCHIEST** big-bellied

PAUPER noun **PAUPERS** a poverty-stricken person

PAUPERISE verb **PAUPERISES, PAUPERISING, PAUPERISED** to pauperize

PAUPERISM noun **PAUPERISMS** the condition of paupers

PAUPERIZE verb **PAUPERIZES, PAUPERIZING, PAUPERIZED** to make someone a pauper

PAUSE noun **PAUSES** a relatively short break in some activity, etc ◻ verb **PAUSES, PAUSING, PAUSED** to have a break; to stop briefly

PAUSELESS adj without a pause; uninterrupted

PAUSER noun **PAUSERS** someone who pauses

PAUSING noun **PAUSINGS** the action of stopping briefly ◻ adj that pauses

PAVAN noun **PAVANS** a slow and sombre stately 16c and 17c dance

PAVANE noun **PAVANES** a pavan

PAVE verb **PAVES, PAVING, PAVED** to surface (especially a footpath, but also a street, etc) with stone slabs, cobbles, etc

PAVED adj covered with stone slabs, cobbles, etc

PAVEMENT noun **PAVEMENTS** a raised footpath edging a road, etc, often but not always paved

PAVILION noun **PAVILIONS** a building in a sports ground in which players change their clothes, store equipment, etc

PAVING noun **PAVINGS** stones or slabs used to pave a surface

PAVLOVA noun **PAVLOVAS** a dessert consisting of meringue topped with fruit and whipped cream

PAW noun **PAWS** the foot, usually clawed, of a four-legged mammal ◻ verb **PAWS, PAWING, PAWED** to finger or handle something clumsily; to touch or caress someone with unwelcome familiarity

PAWKY adj **PAWKIER, PAWKIEST** drily witty

PAWL noun **PAWLS** a catch that engages with the teeth of a ratchet wheel to limit its movement to one direction only

PAWN [1] verb **PAWNS, PAWNING, PAWNED** to deposit (an article of value) with a pawnbroker as a pledge for a sum of money borrowed

PAWN [2] noun **PAWNS** a chess piece of lowest value

PAWNEE noun **PAWNEES** someone who lends money in exchange for pawned articles

PAWNER noun **PAWNERS** someone who deposits something in pawn, especially with a pawnbroker, as a security for money borrowed

PAWNSHOP noun **PAWNSHOPS** a pawnbroker's place of business

PAWPAW noun **PAWPAWS** a papaw

PAX noun **PAXES** the kiss of peace, usually uttered as a greeting during the Eucharist ◻ exclamation truce! let's call a truce!

PAY [1] verb **PAYS, PAYING, PAID** to give (money) to someone in exchange for goods, services, etc ◻ noun **PAYS** money given or received for work, etc; wages; salary

PAY [2] verb **PAYS, PAYING, PAYED** to smear (a wooden boat) with tar, etc as waterproofing

PAYABLE adj that can or must be paid

PAYEE noun **PAYEES** someone to whom money is paid or a cheque is made out

PAYER noun **PAYERS** someone who pays for something

PAYMASTER noun **PAYMASTERS** an official in charge of the payment of wages and salaries

PAYMENT noun **PAYMENTS** a sum of money paid

PAYOLA noun **PAYOLAS** a bribe for promoting a product, given to someone, eg a disc jockey, in a position to do this

PAYROLL noun **PAYROLLS** a register of employees that lists the wage or salary due to each

PAYSAGE noun **PAYSAGES** a landscape or landscape painting

PAYSAGIST noun **PAYSAGISTS** a landscape painter

PAZAZZ noun **PAZAZZES** pizazz

PEA noun **PEAS** an annual climbing plant of the pulse family, cultivated in cool temperate regions for its edible seeds, which are produced in long dehiscent pods

PEACE noun **PEACES** freedom from or absence of war

PEACEABLE adj peace-loving; mild; placid

PEACEABLY adverb in a peaceable way

PEACEFUL adj calm and quiet

PEACETIME noun **PEACETIMES** periods that are free of war

PEACH [1] noun **PEACHES** any of numerous varieties of a small deciduous tree, widely cultivated in warm temperate regions for its yellowish-pink edible fruit ◻ adj peach-coloured

PEACH [2] verb **PEACHES, PEACHING, PEACHED** to become an informer

PEACHY adj **PEACHIER, PEACHIEST** coloured like or tasting like a peach

PEACOCK noun **PEACOCKS** a large bird belonging to the pheasant family, the male of which has a train of green and gold eyespot feathers which it fans showily during courtship

PEAFOWL noun **PEAFOWLS** a male or female peacock, although peacock is usually used as the generic term

PEAK noun **PEAKS** a sharp pointed summit ◻ verb **PEAKS, PEAKING, PEAKED** to reach a maximum

PEAKED adj having a peak or peaks

PEAKY adj **PEAKIER, PEAKIEST** ill-looking; pallid

PEAL noun **PEALS** the ringing of a bell or set of bells ◻ verb **PEALS, PEALING, PEALED** to ring or resound

PEAN noun **PEANS** a paean

PEANUT noun **PEANUTS** a low-growing annual plant of the pulse family, native to tropical America, widely cultivated for its edible seeds which are produced under the ground in pods

PEAPOD noun **PEAPODS** the seedcase of a pea

PEAR noun **PEARS** a deciduous tree belonging to the rose family, widely cultivated in temperate regions for its edible fruit and ornamental flowers

PEARL noun **PEARLS** a bead of smooth hard lustrous material found inside the shell of certain molluscs, eg oysters, and used in jewellery as a gem □ adj like a pearl in colour or shape □ verb **PEARLS, PEARLING, PEARLED** to set something with, or as if with, pearls

PEARLED adj ornamented with pearls

PEARLER noun **PEARLERS** a pearl-fisher

PEARLIES plural noun pearl buttons

PEARLISED adj pearlized

PEARLITE noun **PEARLITES** perlite

PEARLITIC adj perlitic

PEARLIZED adj treated so as to give a pearly or lustrous surface

PEARLY adj **PEARLIER, PEARLIEST** like a pearl

PEARMAIN noun **PEARMAINS** a variety of apple

PEASANT noun **PEASANTS** in poor agricultural societies: a farm worker or small farmer

PEASANTRY noun **PEASANTRIES** the peasant class

PEASANTY adj in the style of a peasant

PEASE noun **PEASE, PEASON** a pea or pea-plant

PEAT noun **PEATS** a mass of dark-brown or black fibrous plant material, produced by the compression of partially decomposed vegetation, used in compost and manure, and in dried form as a fuel

PEATY adj **PEATIER, PEATIEST** like or consisting of peat

PEAVEY noun **PEAVEYS** a lumberjack's spiked and hooked lever

PEAVY noun **PEAVIES** a peavey

PEBBLE noun **PEBBLES** a small fragment of rock, especially one worn round and smooth by the action of water □ verb **PEBBLES, PEBBLING, PEBBLED** to cover with pebbles

PEBBLED adj covered with pebbles

PEBBLY adj **PEBBLIER, PEBBLIEST** full of or covered with pebbles

PEC noun **PECS** a pectoral muscle

PECAN noun **PECANS** a deciduous N American tree, widely cultivated for its edible nut

PECCABLE adj liable to sin

PECCARY noun **PECCARIES** a hoofed mammal, native to Central and S America, similar to but smaller than the Old World wild pig

PECK verb **PECKS, PECKING, PECKED** said of a bird: to strike, nip or pick at with the beak □ noun **PECKS** a tap or nip with the beak

PECKER noun **PECKERS** something that pecks; a beak

PECKISH adj quite hungry

PECTEN noun **PECTINES** a comb-like structure, eg in a bird's or reptile's eye

PECTIN noun **PECTINS** a complex carbohydrate that functions as a cement-like material within and between plant cell-walls

PECTINATE adj toothed like a comb; having narrow parallel segments or lobes

PECTORAL adj referring or relating to the breast or chest □ noun **PECTORALS** a pectoral muscle

PECTOSE noun **PECTOSES** a substance that yields pectin, contained in the fleshy pulp of unripe fruit

PECULATE verb **PECULATES, PECULATING, PECULATED** to appropriate something dishonestly for one's own use; to pilfer; to embezzle

PECULATOR noun **PECULATORS** an embezzler

PECULIAR adj strange; odd

PECUNIARY adj relating to, concerning or consisting of money

PED noun **PEDS** short for *pedestrian*, a person who travels on foot

PEDAGOGIC adj relating to or characteristic of a pedagogue

PEDAGOGUE noun **PEDAGOGUES** a teacher, especially a strict or pedantic one

PEDAGOGY noun **PEDAGOGIES** the science, principles or work of teaching

PEDAL noun **PEDALS** a lever operated by the foot, eg on a machine, vehicle or musical instrument □ verb **PEDALS, PEDALLING, PEDALLED** to move or operate by means of a pedal or pedals □ adj referring or relating to the foot or feet

PEDALO noun **PEDALOS, PEDALOES** a small pedal-operated boat, used especially on lakes for pleasure

PEDANT noun **PEDANTS** someone who is over-concerned with correctness of detail, especially in academic matters

PEDANTIC adj over-concerned with correctness

PEDANTRY noun **PEDANTRIES** excessive concern with correctness

PEDATE adj footed or foot-like; (of a plant) with the outer branches forked

PEDATELY adverb in a pedate way

PEDDLE verb **PEDDLES, PEDDLING, PEDDLED** to go from place to place selling (a selection of small goods)

PEDDLER noun **PEDDLERS** a pedlar

PEDERAST noun **PEDERASTS** an adult who practises pederasty

PEDERASTY noun **PEDERASTIES** sexual relations between adults and children

PEDESTAL noun **PEDESTALS** the base on which a vase, statue, column, etc is placed or mounted

PEDICAB noun **PEDICABS** a light vehicle consisting of a tricycle with a second seat attached, usually behind, covered by a half-hood for one or two passengers

PEDICEL noun **PEDICELS** the stalk of a single flower

PEDICLE noun **PEDICLES** a short stalk; a pedicel

PEDICURE noun **PEDICURES** a medical or cosmetic treatment of the feet and toenails

PEDIGREE noun **PEDIGREES** a person's or animal's line of descent, especially if long and distinguished, or proof of pure breeding □ adj said of an animal: pure-bred; descended from a long line of known ancestors of the same breed

PEDIGREED adj having a pedigree

PEDIMENT noun **PEDIMENTS** a wide triangular gable set over a classical portico or the face of a building

PEDLAR *noun* **PEDLARS** someone who peddles

PEDOLOGY *noun* **PEDOLOGIES** the scientific study of the origin, properties and uses of soil

PEDOMETER *noun* **PEDOMETERS** a device that measures distance walked by recording the number of steps taken

PEDUNCLE *noun* **PEDUNCLES** a short stalk, eg one carrying an inflorescence or a single flower-head

PEE *verb* **PEES, PEEING, PEED** to urinate ▫ *noun* **PEES** an act of urinating

PEEK *verb* **PEEKS, PEEKING, PEEKED** to glance briefly and surreptitiously; to peep ▫ *noun* **PEEKS** a brief furtive glance

PEEKABOO *noun* **PEEKABOOS** a child's game in which one person covers their face with their hands and suddenly uncovers it saying 'peekaboo', usually making a young child laugh

PEEL *noun* **PEELS** the skin or rind of vegetables or fruit, especially citrus fruit ▫ *verb* **PEELS, PEELING, PEELED** to strip the skin or rind off (a fruit or vegetable)

PEELER *noun* **PEELERS** a small knife or device for peeling fruit and vegetables

PEELINGS *plural noun* strips of peel removed from a fruit or vegetable

PEEN *noun* **PEENS** the end of a hammer-head opposite the hammering face ▫ *verb* **PEENS, PEENING, PEENED** to strike or work (metal) with a peen

PEEP *verb* **PEEPS, PEEPING, PEEPED** to look quickly and covertly, eg through a narrow opening or from a place of concealment; to peek ▫ *noun* **PEEPS** a quick covert look

PEEPERS *plural noun* the eyes

PEEPUL *noun* **PEEPULS** a pipal

PEER [1] *noun* **PEERS** a member of the nobility, such as, in Britain, a duke, marquess, earl, viscount or baron

PEER [2] *verb* **PEERS, PEERING, PEERED** to look narrowly or closely

PEERAGE *noun* **PEERAGES** the title or rank of a peer

PEERESS *noun* **PEERESSES** the wife or widow of a peer

PEERLESS *adj* without equal; excelling all; matchless

PEEVE *verb* **PEEVES, PEEVING, PEEVED** to irritate, annoy or offend ▫ *noun* **PEEVES** a cause of vexation or irritation

PEEVED *adj* annoyed

PEEVISH *adj* irritable; cantankerous; inclined to whine or complain

PEEVISHLY *adverb* in a peevish way

PEEWIT *noun* **PEEWITS** a lapwing

PEG *noun* **PEGS** a little shaft of wood, metal or plastic shaped for any of various fixing, fastening or marking uses ▫ *verb* **PEGS, PEGGING, PEGGED** to insert a peg into something

PEGMATITE *noun* **PEGMATITES** any of various coarse-grained igneous rocks, many of which are sources of economically important minerals such as mica, tourmaline and garnet

PEIGNOIR *noun* **PEIGNOIRS** a woman's light dressing-gown

PEIN *noun* **PEINS** a peen ▫ *verb* **PEINS, PEINING, PEINED** to peen

PEKAN *noun* **PEKANS** a large N American marten with dark brown fur

PEKE *noun* **PEKES** a Pekinese dog

PEKOE *noun* **PEKOES** a high-quality scented black China tea

PELAGE *noun* **PELAGES** an animal's coat of hair or wool

PELAGIC *adj* relating to, or carried out on, the deep open sea

PELF *noun* **PELFS** riches; money; lucre

PELHAM *noun* **PELHAMS** a type of bit on a horse's bridle, a combination of the curb and snaffle designs

PELICAN *noun* **PELICANS** a large aquatic bird that has an enormous beak with a pouch below it, and mainly white plumage

PELISSE *noun* **PELISSES** a long mantle of silk, velvet, etc, worn especially by women

PELITE *noun* **PELITES** any rock derived from clay or mud, such as shale

PELITIC *adj* of the nature of pelite

PELLAGRA *noun* **PELLAGRAS** a deficiency disease caused by lack of nicotinic acid or the amino acid tryptophan, characterized by scaly discoloration of the skin, diarrhoea, vomiting, and psychological disturbances

PELLAGRIN *noun* **PELLAGRINS** someone afflicted with pellagra

PELLET *noun* **PELLETS** a small rounded mass of compressed material, eg paper ▫ *verb* **PELLETS, PELLETING, PELLETED** to form (especially seeds) into pellets by coating it with a substance, eg to aid planting

PELLICLE *noun* **PELLICLES** a thin skin or film

PELLITORY *noun* **PELLITORIES** a plant of the nettle family, growing especially on walls

PELLUCID *adj* transparent

PELMANISM *noun* **PELMANISMS** a card game in which the cards are spread out face down and must be turned up in matching pairs

PELMET *noun* **PELMETS** a strip of fabric or a narrow board fitted along the top of a window to conceal the curtain rail

PELORUS *noun* **PELORUSES** a kind of compass from which bearings can be taken

PELOTA *noun* **PELOTAS** a court game of Basque origin, played in Spain, SW France and Latin America, in which the players use a basket-like device strapped to their wrists to catch and throw a ball against a specially marked wall

PELT [1] *noun* **PELTS** the skin of a dead animal, especially with the fur still on it

PELT [2] *verb* **PELTS, PELTING, PELTED** to bombard with missiles

PELTRY *noun* **PELTRIES** the skins of animals with the fur on them; furs collectively

PELVIC *adj* relating to or in the region of the pelvis

PELVIS *noun* **PELVISES** the basin-shaped cavity formed by the bones of the pelvic girdle

PEMICAN *noun* **PEMICANS** pemmican

PEMMICAN *noun* **PEMMICANS** a Native American food of dried meat beaten to a paste and mixed with fat

PEN [1] *noun* **PENS** a writing instrument that uses ink ▫ *verb* **PENS, PENNING, PENNED** to compose and write (a letter, poem, etc) with a pen

PEN [2] *verb* **PENS, PENNING, PENNED, PENT** to enclose or confine in a pen, a small enclosure

PENAL *adj* relating to punishment, especially by law

PENALISE *verb* **PENALISES, PENALISING, PENALISED** to penalize

PENALIZE verb **PENALIZES, PENALIZING, PENALIZED** to impose a penalty on someone, for wrongdoing, cheating, breaking a rule, committing a foul in sport, etc

PENALLY adverb in a penal manner

PENALTY noun **PENALTIES** a punishment, such as imprisonment, a fine, etc, imposed for wrongdoing, breaking a contract or rule, etc

PENANCE noun **PENANCES** repentance or atonement for an offence or wrongdoing, or an act of repentance

PENCE a plural of **penny**

PENCHANT noun **PENCHANTS** a taste, liking, inclination or tendency

PENCIL noun **PENCILS** a writing and drawing instrument consisting of a wooden shaft containing a stick of graphite or other material, which is sharpened for use, and makes more or less erasable marks □ verb **PENCILS, PENCILLING, PENCILLED** to write, draw or mark something with a pencil

PENCILLER noun **PENCILLERS** someone who writes, draws or marks using a pencil; a draughtsman

PENCILLING noun **PENCILLINGS** the art or act of painting, writing, sketching or marking with a pencil

PEND verb **PENDS, PENDING, PENDED** to hang, as in a balance; to impend

PENDANT noun **PENDANTS** an ornament suspended from a neck chain, necklace, bracelet, etc

PENDENT adj hanging; suspended; dangling

PENDENTLY adverb in a pendent way

PENDING adj remaining undecided; waiting to be decided or dealt with □ prep until; awaiting; during

PENDULAR adj relating to or like a pendulum

PENDULOUS adj hanging down loosely; drooping; swinging freely

PENDULUM noun **PENDULUMS** a weight, suspended from a fixed point, that swings freely back and forth through a small angle with simple harmonic motion

PENEPLAIN noun **PENEPLAINS** a land surface which is worn down

to such an extent by denudation as to be almost a plain

PENES a plural of **penis**

PENETRANT adj penetrating □ noun **PENETRANTS** a substance which increases the penetration of a liquid into a porous material or between contiguous surfaces, by lowering its surface tension

PENETRATE verb **PENETRATES, PENETRATING, PENETRATED** to find a way into; to enter, especially with difficulty

PENETRATING adj said of a voice, etc: all too loud and clear; strident; carrying

PENFOLD noun **PENFOLDS** a small enclosure to keep cattle or sheep in

PENGUIN noun **PENGUINS** any of various flightless sea birds with a stout body, small almost featherless wings, short legs, bluish-grey or black plumage, and a white belly

PENILE adj relating to or resembling the penis

PENILLION plural of **pennill**

PENINSULA noun **PENINSULAS** a piece of land projecting into water from a larger landmass and almost completely surrounded by water

PENIS noun **PENISES, PENES** in higher vertebrates: the male organ of copulation which is used to transfer sperm to the female reproductive tract and also contains the urethra through which urine is passed

PENITENCE noun **PENITENCES** regret for wrong one has done, and a desire to put it right; repentance

PENITENT adj regretful for wrong one has done, and feeling a desire to reform; repentant □ noun **PENITENTS** a repentant person, especially one doing penance on the instruction of a confessor

PENKNIFE noun **PENKNIVES** a pocket knife with blades that fold into the handle

PENNA noun **PENNAE** a feather, especially one of the large feathers of the wings or tail

PENNANT noun **PENNANTS** a dangling line from the masthead, etc, with a block for tackle, etc

PENNATE adj winged; feathered; shaped like a wing

PENNED a past form of **pen** [1], **pen** [2]

PENNILESS adj without money; poverty-stricken

PENNILL noun **PENILLION** a form of Welsh improvised verse

PENNING a form of **pen** [1], **pen** [2]

PENNON noun **PENNONS** a long narrow flag with a tapering divided tip, eg borne on his lance by a knight

PENNY noun **PENNIES, PENCE** in the UK: a hundredth part of £1, or a bronze coin having this value

PENOLOGY noun **PENOLOGIES** the study of crime and punishment

PENSILE adj hanging; suspended; overhanging

PENSILITY noun **PENSILITIES** the state of being pensile

PENSION noun **PENSIONS** a government allowance to a retired, disabled or widowed person □ verb **PENSIONS, PENSIONING, PENSIONED** to grant a pension to (a person)

PENSIONER noun **PENSIONERS** someone who is in receipt of a pension

PENSIVE adj preoccupied with one's thoughts; thoughtful

PENSIVELY adverb in a pensive way

PENSTEMON noun **PENSTEMONS** a N American plant with showy flowers which have five stamens, one of which is sterile

PENSTOCK noun **PENSTOCKS** a sluice

PENT past form of **pen** [2]

PENTACLE noun **PENTACLES** a pentagram or similar figure or amulet used as a defence against demons

PENTAD noun **PENTADS** a set of five things

PENTAGON noun **PENTAGONS** a plane figure with five sides and five angles

PENTAGRAM noun **PENTAGRAMS** a figure in the shape of a star with five points and consisting of five lines

PENTANE noun **PENTANES** a hydrocarbon, fifth member of the methane series

PENTANGLE noun **PENTANGLES** a pentacle

PENTHOUSE noun **PENTHOUSES** an apartment, especially a luxuriously appointed one, built on to the roof of a tall building

PENTOSE noun **PENTOSES** any monosaccharide with five carbon atoms

PENTOXIDE noun **PENTOXIDES** a

compound with five atoms of oxygen bonded to another element or radical

PENULT *noun* **PENULTS** the last but one syllable in a word

PENULTIMA *noun* **PENULTIMAS** the penult

PENUMBRA *noun* **PENUMBRAS** the lighter outer shadow that surrounds the dark central shadow produced by a large unfocused light-source shining on an opaque object

PENUMBRAL *adj* of or relating to a penumbra

PENURIOUS *adj* mean with money; miserly

PENURY *noun* **PENURIES** extreme poverty

PEON *noun* **PEONS** in India and Ceylon: an office messenger; an attendant

PEONAGE *noun* **PEONAGES** the state of being a peon

PEONISM *noun* **PEONISMS** peonage

PEONY *noun* **PEONIES** a shrub or herbaceous plant with large, showy red, pink, yellow or white globular flowers with five to ten petals and numerous stamens

PEOPLE *noun* **PEOPLES** a set or group of persons ◻ *verb* **PEOPLES, PEOPLING, PEOPLED** to fill or supply (a region, etc) with people; to populate

PEP *noun* **PEPS** energy; vitality; go ◻ *verb* **PEPS, PEPPING, PEPPED** to enliven or invigorate someone or something

PEPEROMIA *noun* **PEPEROMIAS** any one of a large genus of subtropical herbaceous plants, many of which are grown as house plants for their ornamental foliage

PEPERONI *noun* **PEPERONIS** pepperoni

PEPINO *noun* **PEPINOS** a purple-striped pale yellow fruit with sweet flesh and an elongated oval shape

PEPLUM *noun* **PEPLUMS** a short skirt-like section attached to the waistline of a dress, blouse or jacket

PEPO *noun* **PEPOS** a large many-seeded berry, usually with a hard epicarp

PEPPER *noun* **PEPPERS** a perennial climbing shrub, widely cultivated for its small red berries which are dried to form peppercorns ◻ *verb* **PEPPERS, PEPPERING, PEPPERED** to

bombard something or someone (with missiles)

PEPPERONI *noun* **PEPPERONIS** a hard, spicy beef and pork sausage

PEPPERY *adj* **PEPPERIER, PEPPERIEST** well seasoned with pepper; tasting of pepper; hot-tasting or pungent

PEPPY *adj* **PEPPIER, PEPPIEST** full of energy or vitality

PEPSIN *noun* **PEPSINS** in the stomach of vertebrates: a digestive enzyme produced by the gastric glands that catalyses the partial breakdown of dietary protein

PEPTIC *adj* referring or relating to digestion

PEPTIDE *noun* **PEPTIDES** a molecule that consists of a relatively short chain of amino acids

PER *prep* out of every

PERCEIVE *verb* **PERCEIVES, PERCEIVING, PERCEIVED** to observe, notice, or discern

PERCEPT *noun* **PERCEPTS** an object perceived by the senses

PERCH *noun* **PERCHES** a branch or other narrow support above ground for a bird to rest or roost on ◻ *verb* **PERCHES, PERCHING, PERCHED** said of a bird: to alight and rest on a perch

PERCHANCE *adverb* by chance

PERCOID *adj* referring or relating to, or resembling, perch (a type of fish)

PERCOLATE *verb* **PERCOLATES, PERCOLATING, PERCOLATED** to undergo or subject (a liquid) to the process of percolation; to ooze, trickle or filter

PERCUSS *verb* **PERCUSSES, PERCUSSING, PERCUSSED** to tap (a part of the body) with the fingertips or a plexor for purposes of diagnosis

PERCUSSOR *noun* **PERCUSSORS** a plexor

PERDITION *noun* **PERDITIONS** everlasting punishment after death; damnation; hell

PEREGRINE *noun* **PEREGRINES** a large falcon with greyish-blue plumage on its back and wings, striped with darker bars, and paler underparts, also barred

PEREIRA *noun* **PEREIRAS** a Brazilian tree, the bark of which is used in herbal medicine

PERENNIAL *adj* referring or relating to a plant that lives for several to many years, either growing continuously, as in the

case of woody trees and shrubs, or having stems that die back each autumn ◻ *noun* **PERENNIALS** a perennial plant

PERFECT *adj* complete in all essential elements ◻ *noun* **PERFECTS** the perfect tense, in English formed with the auxiliary verb *have* and the past participle ◻ *verb* **PERFECTS, PERFECTING, PERFECTED** to improve something to one's satisfaction

PERFECTA *noun* **PERFECTAS** a form of bet in which the punter has to select, and place in the correct order, the two horses, dogs, etc which will come first and second in a race

PERFECTLY *adverb* in a perfect way

PERFERVID *adj* extremely fervid; ardent; eager

PERFIDY *noun* **PERFIDIES** treachery

PERFORATE *verb* **PERFORATES, PERFORATING, PERFORATED** to make a hole or holes in something; to pierce

PERFORCE *adverb* necessarily; inevitably or unavoidably

PERFORM *verb* **PERFORMS, PERFORMING, PERFORMED** to carry out (a task, job, action, etc); to do or accomplish

PERFORMER *noun* **PERFORMERS** someone who takes part in a performance or performances; an entertainer

PERFORMING *adj* referring to something or someone that performs

PERFUME *noun* **PERFUMES** a sweet smell; a scent or fragrance ◻ *verb* **PERFUMES, PERFUMING, PERFUMED** to give a sweet smell to something; to apply perfume to something

PERFUMED *adj* scented; fragrant; sweet-smelling

PERFUMER *noun* **PERFUMERS** a maker or seller of perfumes

PERFUMERY *noun* **PERFUMERIES** a place where perfumes are made or sold

PERFUMY *adj* having a perfume; fragrant

PERFUSION *noun* **PERFUSIONS** the movement of a fluid through a tissue or organ

PERGOLA *noun* **PERGOLAS** a framework constructed from slender branches, for plants to climb up; a trellis

PERHAPS adverb possibly; maybe
PERIANTH noun **PERIANTHS** the outer part of a flower, usually consisting of a circle of petals within a circle of sepals
PERICARP noun **PERICARPS** in plants: the wall of a fruit, which develops from the ovary wall after fertilization
PERICLASE noun **PERICLASES** a magnesium oxide occurring naturally in isometric crystals
PERIDOT noun **PERIDOTS** a green olivine used in jewellery
PERIDOTIC adj relating to or containing peridot
PERIGEE noun **PERIGEES** the point in the orbit of the Moon or an artificial satellite around the Earth when it is closest to the Earth
PERIL noun **PERILS** grave danger
PERILOUS adj very dangerous
PERILUNE noun **PERILUNES** the point in a spacecraft's orbit round the Moon when it is closest to the Moon
PERIMETER noun **PERIMETERS** the boundary of an enclosed area
PERINATAL adj denoting or relating to the period extending from the 28th week of pregnancy to about one month after childbirth
PERINEAL adj of or relating to the perineum
PERINEUM noun **PERINEUMS** the region of the body between the genital organs and the anus
PERIOD noun **PERIODS** a portion of time ◻ adj dating from, or designed in the style of, the historical period in question
PERIODIC adj happening at intervals, especially regular intervals
PERIPETIA noun **PERIPETIAS** especially in drama: a sudden change of fortune
PERIPHERY noun **PERIPHERIES** the edge or boundary of something
PERIQUE noun **PERIQUES** a strongly-flavoured tobacco from Louisiana
PERISCOPE noun **PERISCOPES** a system of prisms or mirrors that enables the user to view objects that are above eye-level or obscured by a closer object, used in submarines, military tanks, etc
PERISH verb **PERISHES, PERISHING, PERISHED** to die; to be destroyed or ruined
PERISHED adj feeling the cold severely

PERISHER noun **PERISHERS** a mischievous child or other troublesome person
PERISHING adj said of weather, etc: very cold
PERISPERM noun **PERISPERMS** nutritive tissue in a seed derived from the nucellus
PERISTYLE noun **PERISTYLES** a colonnade round a courtyard or building
PERIWIG noun **PERIWIGS** a man's wig of the 17c and 18c
PERJURE verb **PERJURES, PERJURING, PERJURED** to forswear oneself in a court of law, ie lie while under oath; to commit perjury
PERJURER noun **PERJURERS** someone who commits perjury
PERJURY noun **PERJURIES** the crime of lying while under oath in a court of law
PERK [1] noun **PERKS** a benefit, additional to income, derived from employment, such as membership of a health club, the use of a company car, etc
PERK [2] verb **PERKS, PERKING, PERKED** to percolate (coffee)
PERKILY adverb in a perky way
PERKIN noun **PERKINS** a parkin
PERKINESS noun **PERKINESSES** the state of being perky
PERKY adj **PERKIER, PERKIEST** lively and cheerful
PERLITE noun **PERLITES** any volcanic glass with small concentric spheroidal or spiral cracks between rectilineal ones
PERLITIC adj showing small concentric spheroidal or spiral cracks between rectilineal ones
PERM noun **PERMS** a hair treatment using chemicals that give a long-lasting wave or curl ◻ verb **PERMS, PERMING, PERMED** to curl or wave (hair) with a perm
PERMALLOY noun **PERMALLOYS** any of various alloys of iron and nickel, which often contain other elements, such as copper, molybdenum and chromium, and which have high magnetic permeability
PERMANENT adj lasting, or intended to last, indefinitely; not temporary
PERMEABLE adj said of a porous material or membrane: allowing certain liquids or gases to pass through it

PERMEABLY adverb in a permeable way
PERMEANCE noun **PERMEANCES** the act of permeating
PERMEATE verb **PERMEATES, PERMEATING, PERMEATED** said of a liquid or gas: to pass, penetrate or diffuse through (a fine or porous material or a membrane)
PERMIT verb **PERMITS, PERMITTING, PERMITTED** to consent to or give permission for something ◻ noun **PERMITS** a document that authorizes something
PERMUTATE verb **PERMUTATES, PERMUTATING, PERMUTATED** to permute
PERMUTE verb **PERMUTES, PERMUTING, PERMUTED** to rearrange (a set of things) in different orders, especially in every possible order in succession; to go through the possible permutations of (a set of things)
PERONEAL adj referring or relating to the fibula
PERORATE verb **PERORATES, PERORATING, PERORATED** to make a long formal speech
PEROXIDE noun **PEROXIDES** any of various strong oxidizing agents that release hydrogen peroxide when treated with acid, used in rocket fuels, antiseptics, disinfectants and bleaches ◻ verb **PEROXIDES, PEROXIDING, PEROXIDED** to bleach (hair) with hydrogen peroxide
PERPEND noun **PERPENDS** a parpen
PERPETUAL adj everlasting; eternal; continuous; permanent
PERPLEX verb **PERPLEXES, PERPLEXING, PERPLEXED** to puzzle, confuse or baffle someone with intricacies or difficulties
PERPLEXED adj puzzled, confused or baffled
PERPLEXING adj puzzling, confusing or baffling
PERRON noun **PERRONS** a raised platform or terrace at an entrance door
PERRY noun **PERRIES** an alcoholic drink made from fermented pear juice
PERSE adj dark-blue; bluish-grey ◻ noun **PERSES** a dark blue colour
PERSECUTE verb **PERSECUTES, PERSECUTING, PERSECUTED** to ill-treat, oppress, torment or put to death (a person or people),

especially on the grounds of their religious or political beliefs

PERSEVERE *verb* **PERSEVERES, PERSEVERING, PERSEVERED** to keep on striving; to persist steadily

PERSEVERING *adj* that perseveres; persistent; steadfast

PERSIENNE *noun* **PERSIENNES** an Eastern cambric or muslin fabric with a coloured printed pattern

PERSIMMON *noun* **PERSIMMONS** any of various tall trees, native to warm temperate regions, widely cultivated for their hard wood and edible fruits

PERSIST *verb* **PERSISTS, PERSISTING, PERSISTED** to continue in spite of resistance, difficulty, discouragement, etc

PERSON *noun* **PERSONS** an individual human being

PERSONA *noun* **PERSONAE, PERSONAS** a character in fiction, especially in a play or novel

PERSONAGE *noun* **PERSONAGES** a well-known, important or distinguished person

PERSONAL *adj* said of a comment, opinion, etc: coming from someone as an individual, not from a group or organization

PERSONATE *verb* **PERSONATES, PERSONATING, PERSONATED** to play the part of (a character in a play, etc)

PERSONIFY *verb* **PERSONIFIES, PERSONIFYING, PERSONIFIED** in literature, etc: to represent (an abstract quality, etc) as a human being or as having human qualities

PERSONNEL *plural noun* the people employed in a business company, an armed service or other organization □ *singular noun* **PERSONNELS** a department within such an organization that deals with matters concerning employees

PERSPIRE *verb* **PERSPIRES, PERSPIRING, PERSPIRED** to secrete fluid from the sweat glands of the skin; to sweat

PERSUADE *verb* **PERSUADES, PERSUADING, PERSUADED** to urge successfully; to prevail on or induce someone

PERSUADER *noun* **PERSUADERS** someone or something that persuades

PERT *adj* **PERTER, PERTEST** impudent; cheeky

PERTAIN *verb* **PERTAINS,**

PERTAINING, PERTAINED to belong; to relate

PERTINENT *adj* relating to or concerned with someone or something; relevant

PERTLY *adverb* in a pert way

PERTNESS *noun* **PERTNESSES** the quality of being pert

PERTURB *verb* **PERTURBS, PERTURBING, PERTURBED** to make someone anxious, agitated, worried, etc

PERTURBED *adj* anxious, agitated or worried

PERTUSSAL *adj* of or relating to pertussis

PERTUSSIS *noun* **PERTUSSISES** whooping cough

PERUKE *noun* **PERUKES** a 17c and 18c style of wig, with side curls and a tail at the back

PERUSAL *noun* **PERUSALS** the act of perusing; careful examination

PERUSE *verb* **PERUSES, PERUSING, PERUSED** to read through (a book, magazine, etc) carefully

PERUSER *noun* **PERUSERS** someone who peruses

PERVADE *verb* **PERVADES, PERVADING, PERVADED** to spread or extend throughout something; to affect throughout something; to permeate

PERVASION *noun* **PERVASIONS** permeation; penetration

PERVASIVE *adj* tending to or having the power to spread everywhere

PERVERSE *adj* **PERVERSER, PERVERSEST** deliberately departing from what is normal and reasonable

PERVERT *verb* **PERVERTS, PERVERTING, PERVERTED** to divert something or someone illicitly from what is normal or right □ *noun* **PERVERTS** someone who is morally or sexually perverted

PESETA *noun* **PESETAS** the standard unit of currency of Spain

PESKILY *adverb* in a pesky way

PESKY *adj* **PESKIER, PESKIEST** troublesome or infuriating

PESO *noun* **PESOS** the standard unit of currency of many Central and S American countries and the Philippines

PESSARY *noun* **PESSARIES** a vaginal suppository

PESSIMISM *noun* **PESSIMISMS**

the tendency to emphasize the gloomiest aspects of anything, and to expect the worst to happen

PESSIMIST *noun* **PESSIMISTS** someone who has a sombre gloomy nature

PEST *noun* **PESTS** a living organism, such as an insect, fungus or weed, that has a damaging effect on animal livestock, crop plants or stored produce

PESTER *verb* **PESTERS, PESTERING, PESTERED** to annoy constantly

PESTERER *noun* **PESTERERS** someone who pesters

PESTERING *adj* that pesters

PESTICIDE *noun* **PESTICIDES** any of various chemical compounds, including insecticides, herbicides and fungicides, that are used to kill pests

PESTILENT *adj* deadly, harmful or destructive

PESTLE *noun* **PESTLES** a club-shaped utensil for pounding, crushing and mixing substances in a mortar □ *verb* **PESTLES, PESTLING, PESTLED** to pound or crush, etc something with a pestle

PESTO *noun* **PESTOS** an Italian sauce for pasta made by crushing and mixing together fresh basil leaves, pine kernels, olive oil, garlic and Parmesan cheese

PESTOLOGY *noun* **PESTOLOGIES** the study of agricultural pests and methods of combating them

PET *noun* **PETS** a tame animal or bird kept as a companion □ *adj* kept as a pet □ *verb* **PETS, PETTING, PETTED** to pat or stroke (an animal, etc); said of two people: to fondle and caress each other for erotic pleasure

PETAL *noun* **PETALS** in a flower: one of the modified leaves, often scented and brightly coloured, which in insect-pollinated plants serve to attract passing insects

PÉTANQUE *noun* **PÉTANQUES** the name given in S France to a game that originated in Provence, in which steel bowls are rolled or hurled towards a wooden marker ball

PETARD *noun* **PETARDS** a small bomb for blasting a hole in a wall, door, etc

PETECHIA *noun* **PETECHIAE** a small red or purple spot on the skin

PETECHIAL adj relating to or characterized by petechiae

PETER verb PETERS, PETERING, PETERED to dwindle away to nothing

PETERSHAM noun PETERSHAMS a stiff ribbed silk ribbon used for reinforcing waistbands, etc

PETHIDINE noun PETHIDINES a mildly sedative pain-relieving drug, widely used in childbirth

PETIOLE noun PETIOLES the stalk that attaches a leaf to the stem of a plant

PETITE adj said of a woman or girl: characterized by having a small and dainty build

PETITION noun PETITIONS a formal written request to an authority to take some action, signed by a large number of people ◻ verb PETITIONS, PETITIONING, PETITIONED to address a petition to someone for or against some cause; to make an appeal or request

PETREL noun PETRELS any of numerous small seabirds with a hooked bill and external tube-shaped nostrils, especially the storm petrel

PETRIFY verb PETRIFIES, PETRIFYING, PETRIFIED to terrify; to paralyse someone with fright

PETROL noun PETROLS a volatile flammable liquid mixture of hydrocarbons, used as a fuel in most internal combustion engines

PETROLEUM noun PETROLEUMS a naturally occurring oil consisting of a thick dark liquid mixture of hydrocarbons, distillation of which yields a wide range of petrochemicals, eg liquid and gas fuels, asphalt, and raw materials for the manufacture of plastics, solvents, drugs, etc

PETROLOGY noun PETROLOGIES the scientific study of the structure, origin, distribution and history of rocks

PETROUS adj stony; characterized by having a consistency like rocks

PETTED past form of pet

PETTICOAT noun PETTICOATS a woman's underskirt

PETTIFOG verb PETTIFOGS, PETTIFOGGING, PETTIFOGGED to act as a pettifogger, a lawyer who deals, often deceptively and quibblingly, with trivial cases

PETTIFOGGING noun

PETTIFOGGINGS paltry, trivial, cavilling behaviour ◻ adj paltry, trivial, cavilling

PETTILY adverb in a petty way

PETTINESS noun PETTINESSES the quality of being petty

PETTING a form of pet ◻ noun PETTINGS fondling and caressing for erotic pleasure

PETTISH adj peevish; sulky

PETTISHLY adverb in a pettish way

PETTY adj PETTIER, PETTIEST being of minor importance; trivial

PETULANCE noun PETULANCES ill-tempered or peevish behaviour

PETULANCY noun PETULANCIES petulance

PETULANT adj ill-tempered; peevish

PETUNIA noun PETUNIAS any of various annual plants with large funnel-shaped, often striped, flowers in a range of bright colours, including white, pink and purple

PEW noun PEWS one of the long benches with backs used as seating in a church

PEWIT noun PEWITS a lapwing

PEWTER noun PEWTERS a silvery alloy with a bluish tinge, composed of tin and lead, used to make tableware (eg tankards), jewellery and other decorative objects

PEWTERER noun PEWTERERS someone who makes or works in pewter

PEYOTE noun PEYOTES the mescal cactus, native to N Mexico and the south-west USA

PFENNIG noun PFENNIGS a German unit of currency worth a hundredth of a Deutschmark

PH noun PHS a measure of the relative acidity or alkalinity of a solution

PHACOID adj lentil-shaped

PHAETON noun PHAETONS an open four-wheeled carriage for one or two horses

PHAGE noun PHAGES short for bacteriophage

PHAGOCYTE noun PHAGOCYTES a cell, especially a white blood cell, that engulfs and usually destroys micro-organisms and other foreign particles

PHALANGE noun PHALANGES the Christian right-wing group in Lebanon, modelled on the Spanish Falange

PHALANGER noun PHALANGERS any of various nocturnal tree-dwelling marsupials, native to Australia and New Guinea, with thick fur, small fox-like ears and large forward-facing eyes

PHALANX noun PHALANXES in ancient Greece: a body of infantry in close-packed formation

PHALAROPE noun PHALAROPES any of various small aquatic birds of the sandpiper family, the female of which courts the male who then incubates the eggs and cares for the young

PHALLIC adj relating to or resembling a phallus

PHALLISM noun PHALLISMS worship of the generative power of nature

PHALLUS noun PHALLUSES, PHALLI a penis

PHANTASM noun PHANTASMS an illusion or fantasy

PHANTASY noun PHANTASIES an old spelling of fantasy

PHANTOM noun PHANTOMS a ghost or spectre ◻ adj referring to the nature of a phantom; spectral

PHARAONIC adj of or relating to the Pharaohs of ancient Egypt

PHARISAIC adj relating to or like the Pharisees; hypocritical

PHARMACY noun PHARMACIES the mixing and dispensing of drugs and medicines

PHARYNGAL adj relating to or in the region of the pharynx or throat

PHARYNX noun PHARYNXES, PHARYNGES in mammals: the part of the alimentary canal that links the mouth and nasal passages with the oesophagus and trachea

PHASE noun PHASES a stage or period in growth or development ◻ verb PHASES, PHASING, PHASED to organize or carry out (changes, etc) in stages

PHEASANT noun PHEASANTS any of various species of ground-dwelling bird, the males of which are usually brightly coloured and have long pointed tails

PHELLEM noun PHELLEMS the technical word for cork

PHENETIC adj of or relating to phenetics

PHENETICS singular noun a system of classification of organisms based on observable similarities and differences irrespective of whether or not the organisms are related

PHENOL *noun* **PHENOLS** a colourless crystalline toxic solid used in the manufacture of phenolic and epoxy resins, nylon, solvents, explosives, drugs, dyes and perfumes

PHENOLOGY *noun* **PHENOLOGIES** the study of organisms as affected by climate, especially dates of seasonal phenomena, such as the opening of flowers, arrival of migrant animals, etc

PHENOTYPE *noun* **PHENOTYPES** the observable characteristics of an organism, determined by the interaction between its genotype and environmental factors

PHENYL *noun* **PHENYLS** an organic radical found in benzene, phenol, etc

PHEROMONE *noun* **PHEROMONES** any chemical substance secreted in minute amounts by an animal, especially an insect or mammal, which has a specific effect on the behaviour of other members of the same species

PHEW *exclamation* used to express relief, astonishment or exhaustion

PHI *noun* **PHIS** the twenty-first letter of the Greek alphabet

PHIAL *noun* **PHIALS** a little medicine bottle

PHILANDER *verb* **PHILANDERS, PHILANDERING, PHILANDERED** said of men: to flirt or have casual love affairs with women; to womanize

PHILATELY *noun* **PHILATELIES** the study and collecting of postage stamps

PHILIBEG *noun* **PHILIBEGS** a kilt

PHILIPPIC *noun* **PHILIPPICS** a speech making a bitter attack on someone or something

PHILOLOGY *noun* **PHILOLOGIES** the study of language, its history and development; the comparative study of related languages; linguistics

PHILTRE *noun* **PHILTRES** a magic potion for arousing sexual desire

PHIMOSIS *noun* narrowness or constriction of the foreskin which prevents it being drawn back over the glans penis

PHIZ *noun* **PHIZZES** the face

PHIZOG *noun* **PHIZOGS** the face

PHLEBITIS *noun* inflammation of the wall of a vein, often resulting in

the formation of a blood clot at the affected site

PHLEGM *noun* **PHLEGMS** a thick yellowish substance produced by the mucous membrane that lines the air passages, brought up by coughing

PHLEGMY *adj* **PHLEGMIER, PHLEGMIEST** characterized by or containing phlegm

PHLOEM *noun* **PHLOEMS** the plant tissue that is responsible for the transport of sugars and other nutrients from the leaves to all other parts of the plant

PHLOMIS *noun* **PHLOMISES** a plant belonging to a genus of labiate herbs and shrubs with whorls of white, yellow or purple flowers and wrinkled, often woolly, leaves

PHLOX *noun* **PHLOXES** any of various mat-forming, trailing or erect plants with white, pink, red or purple tubular flowers borne in large dense terminal clusters

PHLYCTENA *noun* **PHLYCTENAE** a small blister or vesicle

PHO *noun* **PHOS** an exclamation expressing contempt or disgust

PHOBIA *noun* **PHOBIAS** an obsessive and persistent fear of a specific object or situation, eg spiders, open spaces, etc, representing a form of neurosis

PHOBIC *adj* relating to or involving a phobia

PHOEBE *noun* **PHOEBES** a N American flycatcher

PHOENIX *noun* **PHOENIXES** in Arabian legend: a bird which every 500 years sets itself on fire and is reborn from its ashes to live a further 500 years

PHON *noun* **PHONS** a unit of loudness, measured as the number of decibels above a pure tone with a frequency of 1000 hertz

PHONE *noun* **PHONES** a telephone □ *verb* **PHONES, PHONING, PHONED** to telephone someone

PHONECARD *noun* **PHONECARDS** a card that can be used to pay for phone calls from public telephones

PHONEME *noun* **PHONEMES** the smallest unit of sound in a language that has significance in distinguishing one word from another

PHONEMIC *adj* of or relating to phonemes

PHONEMICS *singular noun* the study and analysis of phonemes

PHONETIC *adj* referring or relating to the sounds of a spoken language

PHONETICS *singular noun* the branch of linguistics that deals with speech sounds, especially how they are produced and perceived

PHONETIST *noun* **PHONETISTS** a phonetician; an advocate or user of phonetic spelling

PHONEY *adj* **PHONIER, PHONIEST** not genuine; fake, sham, bogus or insincere □ *noun* **PHONEYS** someone or something bogus; a fake or humbug

PHONIC *adj* relating to sounds, especially vocal sounds

PHONICS *singular noun* a method used in the teaching of reading, based on recognition of the relationships between individual letters, or groups of letters, and sounds

PHONINESS *noun* **PHONINESSES** the state of being phoney

PHONOLITE *noun* **PHONOLITES** a fine-grained igneous rock that rings when struck by a hammer

PHONOLOGY *noun* **PHONOLOGIES** the study of speech sounds in general, or of those in any particular language

PHONY *adj* **PHONIER, PHONIEST** phoney □ *noun* **PHONIES** a phoney

PHOOEY *exclamation* an exclamation of scorn, contempt, disbelief, etc

PHOSGENE *noun* **PHOSGENES** a poisonous gas, carbonyl chloride, used in the manufacture of pesticides and dyes

PHOSPHATE *noun* **PHOSPHATES** any salt or ester of phosphoric acid, found in living organisms and in many minerals, and used in fertilizers, detergents, water softeners, etc

PHOSPHOR *noun* **PHOSPHORS** any substance that is capable of phosphorescence, used to coat the inner surface of television screens and fluorescent light tubes, and as a brightener in detergents

PHOT *noun* **PHOTS** in the cgs system: the unit of illumination equal to one lumen per square centimetre

PHOTIC *adj* referring to or concerned with light

PHOTO *noun* **PHOTOS** a photograph

PHOTOCELL *noun* **PHOTOCELLS** a light-sensitive device that converts light energy into electrical energy, used in light meters, burglar alarms, etc
PHOTOCOPY *noun* **PHOTOCOPIES** a photographic copy of a document, drawing, etc ◻ *verb* **PHOTOCOPIES, PHOTOCOPYING, PHOTOCOPIED** to make a photographic copy of (a document, etc)
PHOTOCOPYING *noun* **PHOTOCOPYINGS** the act of making a photocopy or photocopies
PHOTOFIT *noun* **PHOTOFITS** a system used by the police for building up a likeness of someone to fit a witness's description, similar to Identikit but using photographs rather than drawings of individual features
PHOTOGRAM *noun* **PHOTOGRAMS** a type of picture produced by placing an object on or near photographic paper which is then exposed to light
PHOTON *noun* **PHOTONS** a particle of electromagnetic radiation that travels at the speed of light, used to explain phenomena that require light to behave as particles rather than as waves
PHRASAL *adj* consisting of, or of the nature of, a phrase
PHRASE *noun* **PHRASES** a set of words expressing a single idea, forming part of a sentence though not constituting a clause ◻ *verb* **PHRASES, PHRASING, PHRASED** to express; to word something
PHRASING *noun* **PHRASINGS** the wording of a speech or passage
PHREAKING *noun* **PHREAKINGS** the practice of tampering electronically with a telephone to enable the user to make free calls
PHREATIC *adj* relating to underground water-supplying wells or springs, or to the soil or rocks containing them
PHRENETIC *adj* frenetic
PHRENIC *adj* relating to the diaphragm, and especially the associated nerve

PHS plural of **ph**

PHTHISIS *noun* **PHTHISES** any wasting disease, especially tuberculosis
PHUT *noun* **PHUTS** the noise of a small explosion

PHYCOLOGY *noun* **PHYCOLOGIES** the scientific study of algae
PHYLA plural of **phylum**
PHYLETIC *adj* relating to a phylum
PHYLLITE *noun* **PHYLLITES** any of various fine-grained metamorphic rocks intermediate between slate and schist
PHYLLO *noun* **PHYLLOS** filo
PHYLLODE *noun* **PHYLLODES** a petiole with the appearance and function of a leaf blade
PHYLOGENY *noun* **PHYLOGENIES** the sequence of changes that has occurred during the evolution of a particular species of living organism or a group of related organisms
PHYLUM *noun* **PHYLA** in taxonomy: any of the major groups, eg Chordata (the vertebrates), into which the animal kingdom is divided and which in turn is subdivided into one or more classes
PHYSIC *noun* **PHYSICS** the skill or art of healing ◻ *verb* **PHYSICS, PHYSICKING, PHYSICKED** to dose someone with medicine
PHYSICAL *adj* relating to the body rather than the mind; bodily
PHYSICIAN *noun* **PHYSICIANS** in the UK: a registered medical practitioner who specializes in medical as opposed to surgical treatment of diseases and disorders
PHYSICISM *noun* **PHYSICISMS** belief in the material and physical as opposed to the spiritual
PHYSICIST *noun* **PHYSICISTS** a scientist who specializes in physics
PHYSICS *singular noun* the scientific study of the properties and inter-relationships of matter, energy, force and motion
PHYSIO *noun* **PHYSIOS** a physiotherapist; physiotherapy
PHYSIQUE *noun* **PHYSIQUES** the structure of the body with regard to size, shape, proportions and muscular development; the build
PHYTOGENY *noun* **PHYTOGENIES** the branch of botany concerned with the evolution of plants

PI *noun* **PIS** the sixteenth letter of the Greek alphabet

PIA *noun* **PIAS** a tropical plant

PIACEVOLE *adverb* in a pleasant or playful manner ◻ *adj* pleasant or playful

PIAFFE *verb* **PIAFFES, PIAFFING, PIAFFED** to move at a piaffer
PIAFFER *noun* **PIAFFERS** a gait in which the horse's feet are lifted in the same succession as a trot, but more slowly
PIANIST *noun* **PIANISTS** someone who plays the piano
PIANO [1] *adj* soft ◻ *adverb* softly ◻ *noun* **PIANOS** a passage of music to be played or performed softly
PIANO [2] *noun* **PIANOS** a large musical instrument with a keyboard, the keys being pressed down to operate a set of hammers that strike tautened wires to produce the sound
PIANOLIST *noun* **PIANOLISTS** a person who operates a Pianola®, a type of mechanical piano
PIASSABA *noun* **PIASSABAS** piassava
PIASSAVA *noun* **PIASSAVAS** a coarse stiff fibre used for making brooms, etc, obtained from Brazilian palms
PIAZZA *noun* **PIAZZAS** a public square in an Italian town
PIBROCH *noun* **PIBROCHS** a series of variations on a martial theme or lament, played on the Scottish bagpipes
PIC *noun* **PICS, PIX** a photograph or picture
PICA *noun* **PICAS** an old type-size, giving about six lines to the inch, approximately 12-point and still used synonymously for that point size
PICADOR *noun* **PICADORS** a toreador who weakens the bull by wounding it with a lance
PICAROON *noun* **PICAROONS** a rogue, cheat or pirate
PICAYUNE *noun* **PICAYUNES** anything of little or no value ◻ *adj* petty; trifling
PICCOLO *noun* **PICCOLOS** a small transverse flute pitched one octave higher than the standard flute and with a range of about three octaves
PICCY *noun* **PICCIES** a photograph or picture
PICHURIM *noun* **PICHURIMS** a S American tree of the laurel family
PICK [1] *noun* **PICKS** a tool with a long metal head pointed at one or both ends, for breaking ground, rock, ice, etc
PICK [2] *verb* **PICKS, PICKING, PICKED** to choose or select
PICKABACK *noun* **PICKABACKS** a

piggyback ❑ adj piggyback ❑ adverb piggyback

PICKAXE noun PICKAXES a large pick, especially one with a point at one end of its head and a cutting edge at the other

PICKED adj selected or chosen

PICKER noun PICKERS a person who picks or gathers

PICKEREL noun PICKERELS a young pike

PICKET noun PICKETS a person or group of people stationed outside a place of work to persuade other employees not to go in during a strike ❑ verb PICKETS, PICKETING, PICKETED to station pickets or act as a picket at (a factory, etc)

PICKIER see under picky

PICKIEST see under picky

PICKINGS plural noun profits made easily or casually from something

PICKLE noun PICKLES a preserve of vegetables, eg onions, cucumber or cauliflower, in vinegar, salt water or a tart sauce ❑ verb PICKLES, PICKLING, PICKLED to preserve something in vinegar, salt water, etc

PICKLED adj preserved in vinegar, salt water, etc

PICKLER noun PICKLERS a container in which vegetables, etc are pickled

PICKLOCK noun PICKLOCKS an instrument for picking or opening locks

PICKY adj PICKIER, PICKIEST choosy or fussy, especially excessively so; difficult to please

PICNIC noun PICNICS an outing on which one takes food for eating in the open air ❑ verb PICNICS, PICNICKING, PICNICKED to have a picnic

PICNICKER noun PICNICKERS someone taking part in a picnic

PICOT noun PICOTS a loop in an ornamental edging

PICOTEE noun PICOTEES a variety of carnation, originally speckled, now edged with a colour

PICTOGRAM noun PICTOGRAMS a picture or symbol that represents a word, as in Chinese writing

PICTORIAL adj relating to, or consisting of, pictures ❑ noun PICTORIALS a periodical with a high proportion of pictures as opposed to text

PICTURE noun PICTURES a representation of someone or something on a flat surface; a drawing, painting or photograph ❑ verb PICTURES, PICTURING, PICTURED to imagine or visualize

PIDDLE verb PIDDLES, PIDDLING, PIDDLED to urinate ❑ noun PIDDLES urine

PIDDLER noun PIDDLERS a trifler

PIDDLING adj trivial; trifling

PIDGIN noun PIDGINS a type of simplified language used especially for trading purposes between speakers of different languages, consisting of a combination of the languages concerned

PIE¹ noun PIES a savoury or sweet dish, usually cooked in a container, consisting of a quantity of food with a covering of pastry, a base of pastry, or both

PIE² verb PIES, PIEING, PIED to reduce to confusion

PIEBALD adj having contrasting patches of colour, especially black and white ❑ noun PIEBALDS a horse with black and white markings

PIECE noun PIECES a portion of some material; a bit ❑ verb PIECES, PIECING, PIECED to enlarge by adding a piece; to patch; to combine

PIECEMEAL adverb a bit at a time

PIECRUST noun PIECRUSTS the dough or pastry covering or enclosing a pie

PIED adj said of a bird: having variegated plumage, especially black and white

PIER noun PIERS a structure built of stone, wood or iron, projecting into water for use as a landing-stage or breakwater

PIERCE verb PIERCES, PIERCING, PIERCED said of a sharp object or a person using one: to make a hole in or through; to puncture; to make (a hole) with something sharp

PIERCING adj referring to something that pierces ❑ noun PIERCINGS body piercing, the practice of piercing parts of the body other than the earlobes

PIERROT noun PIERROTS a clown dressed and made up like Pierrot, the traditional male character from French pantomime, with a whitened face, white frilled outfit and pointed hat

PIETÀ noun PIETÀS in painting and sculpture: a representation of the dead Christ mourned by angels, apostles or holy women

PIETISM noun PIETISMS pious feeling or an exaggerated show of piety

PIETIST noun PIETISTS someone marked by strong devotional feeling

PIETISTIC adj relating to pietists or pietism

PIETY noun PIETIES dutifulness; devoutness

PIFFLE noun PIFFLES nonsense; rubbish

PIFFLING adj trivial, trifling or petty

PIG noun PIGS a hoofed omnivorous mammal with a stout heavy bristle-covered body, a protruding flattened snout and a corkscrew-like tail, kept worldwide for its meat ❑ verb PIGS, PIGGING, PIGGED said of a pig: to produce young

PIGEON noun PIGEONS a medium-sized bird with a plump body, a rounded tail and dense soft grey, brown or pink plumage

PIGEONRY noun PIGEONRIES a place for keeping pigeons

PIGGERY noun PIGGERIES a place where pigs are bred

PIGGIE noun PIGGIES a piggy ❑ adj piggy

PIGGISH adj greedy, dirty, selfish, mean or ill-mannered

PIGGISHLY adverb in a piggish way

PIGGY noun PIGGIES a pig; a little pig ❑ adj PIGGIER, PIGGIEST pig-like

PIGGYBACK noun PIGGYBACKS a ride on someone's back, with the legs supported by the bearer's arms ❑ adj carried on the back of someone else ❑ adverb on the back of someone else

PIGHEADED adj stupidly obstinate

PIGLET noun PIGLETS a young pig

PIGMENT noun PIGMENTS any insoluble colouring matter that is used in suspension in water, oil or other liquids to give colour to paint, paper, etc ❑ verb PIGMENTS, PIGMENTING, PIGMENTED to colour something with pigment; to dye or stain

PIGMENTED adj coloured with pigment; dyed or stained

PIGMY noun PIGMIES a pygmy ❑ adj pygmy

PIGNUT noun PIGNUTS the earthnut

PIGSKIN noun **PIGSKINS** leather made from the skin of a pig

PIGSTY noun **PIGSTIES** a pen on a farm, etc for pigs; a sty

PIGSWILL noun **PIGSWILLS** kitchen or brewery waste for feeding to pigs

PIGTAIL noun **PIGTAILS** a plaited length of hair, especially one of a pair, worn hanging at the sides or back of the head

PIKA noun **PIKAS** a mammal, native to Asia and N America, that resembles a small rabbit and has short legs, short rounded ears and a minute tail

PIKE [1] noun **PIKES** any of various large predatory freshwater fish with a mottled yellowish-green body, a narrow pointed head and a small number of large teeth in the lower jaw

PIKE [2] adj said of a body position: bent sharply at the hips with the legs kept straight at the knees and toes pointed ◻ verb **PIKES, PIKING, PIKED** to move into a position in which the body is bent sharply at the hips while the legs are kept straight at the knees and the toes are pointed

PIKESTAFF noun **PIKESTAFFS** the shaft of a pike, a spear-like weapon

PILAFF noun **PILAFFS** pilau

PILASTER noun **PILASTERS** a rectangular column that stands out in relief from the façade of a building, as a decorative feature

PILAU noun **PILAUS** an oriental dish of spiced rice with, or to accompany, chicken, fish, etc

PILCHARD noun **PILCHARDS** a small edible marine fish of the herring family, bluish-green above and silvery below, covered with large scales

PILE noun **PILES** a number of things lying on top of each other; a quantity of something in a heap or mound ◻ verb **PILES, PILING, PILED** to accumulate into a pile

PILEATE adj cap-shaped; capped; crested

PILEATED adj pileate

PILES plural noun haemorrhoids

PILEUM noun **PILEA** the top of a bird's head

PILEUS noun **PILEI** the cap-shaped part of a mushroom, toadstool or other fungus

PILFER verb **PILFERS, PILFERING, PILFERED** to steal in small quantities

PILFERAGE noun **PILFERAGES** petty theft

PILFERER noun **PILFERERS** a petty thief

PILFERING noun **PILFERINGS** pilferage

PILGRIM noun **PILGRIMS** someone who makes a journey to a holy place as an act of reverence and religious faith

PILIFORM adj hairlike

PILL noun **PILLS** a small ball or tablet of medicine, for swallowing

PILLAGE verb **PILLAGES, PILLAGING, PILLAGED** to plunder or loot ◻ noun **PILLAGES** the act of pillaging

PILLAGER noun **PILLAGERS** someone who pillages

PILLAR noun **PILLARS** a vertical post of wood, stone, metal or concrete serving as a support to a main structure; a column

PILLHEAD noun **PILLHEADS** a regular taker of sedative or stimulant pills or both, particularly an addict of these

PILLION noun **PILLIONS** a seat for a passenger on a motorcycle or horse, behind the driver or rider ◻ adverb on a pillion

PILLOCK noun **PILLOCKS** a stupid or foolish person

PILLORY noun **PILLORIES** a wooden frame with holes for the hands and head, into which wrongdoers were locked as a punishment and publicly ridiculed ◻ verb **PILLORIES, PILLORYING, PILLORIED** to hold someone up to public ridicule

PILLOW noun **PILLOWS** a cushion for the head, especially a large rectangular one on a bed ◻ verb **PILLOWS, PILLOWING, PILLOWED** to rest (one's head) as though on a pillow

PILOSE adj said especially of plants: having hairs

PILOSITY noun **PILOSITIES** hairiness

PILOT noun **PILOTS** someone who flies an aircraft, hovercraft, spacecraft, etc ◻ verb **PILOTS, PILOTING, PILOTED** to act as pilot to someone

PILOTAGE noun **PILOTAGES** the act of piloting an aircraft, ship, etc

PILOTLESS adj without a pilot

PILSENER noun **PILSENERS** a light, strongly-flavoured lager beer

PILSNER noun **PILSNERS** pilsener

PILULAR adj of or relating to a pilule

PILULE noun **PILULES** a little pill

PIMENTO noun **PIMENTOS** a small tropical evergreen tree, cultivated mainly in Jamaica

PIMIENTO noun **PIMIENTOS** a variety of sweet pepper, native to tropical America, widely cultivated for its mild-flavoured red fruit

PIMP noun **PIMPS** a man who finds customers for a prostitute or a brothel and lives off the earnings ◻ verb **PIMPS, PIMPING, PIMPED** to act as a pimp

PIMPERNEL noun **PIMPERNELS** any of various small sprawling plants, especially the scarlet pimpernel

PIMPLE noun **PIMPLES** a small raised often pus-containing swelling on the skin; a spot

PIMPLED adj having pimples

PIMPLY adj **PIMPLIER, PIMPLIEST** having pimples

PIN noun **PINS** a short slender implement with a sharp point and small round head, usually made of stainless steel, for fastening, attaching, etc, and used especially in dressmaking ◻ verb **PINS, PINNING, PINNED** to fasten with a pin

PINAFORE noun **PINAFORES** an apron, especially one with a bib

PINBALL noun **PINBALLS** a game played on a slot machine, in which a small metal ball is propelled by flippers round a course, the score depending on what hazards it avoids and targets it hits; a form of bagatelle

PINCERS plural noun a hinged tool with two claw-like jaws joined by a pivot, used for gripping objects, pulling nails, etc

PINCH noun **PINCHES** an act of pinching; a nip or squeeze ◻ verb **PINCHES, PINCHING, PINCHED** to squeeze or nip the flesh of someone or something, between thumb and finger

PINCHBECK noun **PINCHBECKS** a copper-zinc alloy with the appearance of gold, used in cheap jewellery ◻ adj cheap, artificial, sham, counterfeit or imitation

PINCHED adj said of a person's appearance: pale and haggard from tiredness, cold or other discomfort

PINE [1] noun **PINES** any of numerous evergreen coniferous trees with narrow needle-like leaves, native to cool northern temperate regions

PINE² *verb* **PINES, PINING, PINED** to waste away, especially under pain or mental distress

PINEAPPLE *noun* **PINEAPPLES** a tropical S American plant with spiky sword-shaped leaves, widely cultivated for its large edible fruit

PINEWOOD *noun* **PINEWOODS** a wood of pine trees

PING *noun* **PINGS** a sharp ringing sound like that made by plucking a taut wire, lightly striking glass or metal, etc ▫ *verb* **PINGS, PINGING, PINGED** to make or cause something to make this sound

PINGER *noun* **PINGERS** a clockwork device used in the home, eg to time something that is being cooked, which can be set to give a warning signal such as a pinging sound, after a certain amount of time

PINGO *noun* **PINGOES** a large cone-shaped mound with a core of ice formed by the upward expansion of freezing water surrounded by permafrost

PINHEAD *noun* **PINHEADS** the little rounded or flattened head of a pin

PINHOLE *noun* **PINHOLES** a tiny hole made by, or as if by, a pin

PINIER see under **piny**

PINIEST see under **piny**

PINION¹ *verb* **PINIONS, PINIONING, PINIONED** to immobilize someone by holding or binding their arms; to hold or bind (someone's arms)

PINION² *noun* **PINIONS** a small cogwheel that engages with a larger wheel or rack

PINK¹ *noun* **PINKS** a light or pale-red colour, between red and white ▫ *adj* **PINKER, PINKEST** having, being or referring to the colour pink

PINK² *verb* **PINKS, PINKING, PINKED** to cut (cloth) with a notched or serrated edge that frays less readily than a straight edge

PINKIE *noun* **PINKIES** the little finger

PINKINESS *noun* **PINKINESSES** the state of being pinky

PINKISH *adj* somewhat pink

PINKNESS *noun* **PINKNESSES** the state of being pink

PINKO *noun* **PINKOS, PINKOES** a mild or half-hearted socialist

PINKY¹ *adj* **PINKIER, PINKIEST** slightly pink

PINKY² *noun* **PINKIES** the pinkie

PINNA *noun* **PINNAE** in mammals: the part of the outer ear that projects from the head and that in certain mammals can be moved independently in order to detect the direction of sounds

PINNACE *noun* **PINNACES** a small boat carried on a larger ship; a ship's boat

PINNACLE *noun* **PINNACLES** a slender spire crowning a buttress, gable, roof or tower ▫ *verb* **PINNACLES, PINNACLING, PINNACLED** to be the pinnacle or high point of something

PINNATE *adj* denoting a compound leaf that consists of pairs of leaflets arranged in two rows on either side of a central axis or midrib

PINNATELY *adverb* in a pinnate way

PINNED past form of **pin**

PINNING a form of **pin**

PINNULE *noun* **PINNULES** a lobe of a leaflet of a pinnate leaf

PINNY *noun* **PINNIES** a pinafore

PINOCHLE *noun* **PINOCHLES** a card game derived from bézique, in which two packs of 24 cards are shuffled together, with all cards of a lower value than nine discarded, the object of the game being to win tricks as in whist

PINOCLE *noun* **PINOCLES** pinochle

PINOLE *noun* **PINOLES** a fine flour made from parched Indian corn or other seeds, sweetened with sugar and eaten with milk, mainly in Mexico and SW states of the US

PINPOINT *verb* **PINPOINTS, PINPOINTING, PINPOINTED** to place, define or identify something precisely

PINT *noun* **PINTS** in the UK, in the imperial system: a unit of liquid measure equivalent to $\frac{1}{8}$ of a gallon or 20fl oz, equivalent to 0.568 litre (liquid or dry)

PINTA *noun* **PINTAS** a pint of milk

PINTAIL *noun* **PINTAILS** a species of duck with a long slender neck, and a pointed tail which is greatly elongated in the male

PINTLE *noun* **PINTLES** a bolt or pin, especially one which is turned by something

PINTO *adj* mottled; piebald ▫ *noun* **PINTOS** a piebald horse

PINY *adj* **PINIER, PINIEST** referring to, resembling or covered in pine trees

PION *noun* **PIONS** in physics: the source of the nuclear force holding protons and neutrons together

PIONEER *noun* **PIONEERS** an explorer of, or settler in, hitherto unknown or wild country ▫ *verb* **PIONEERS, PIONEERING, PIONEERED** to be a pioneer; to be innovative

PIOUS *adj* religiously devout

PIOUSLY *adverb* in a pious way

PIP¹ *noun* **PIPS** the small seed of a fruit such as an apple, pear, orange or grape

PIP² *verb* **PIPS, PIPPING, PIPPED** to defeat someone narrowly

PIPA *noun* **PIPAS** a S American toad, the female of which is noted for carrying her developing young on her back

PIPAL *noun* **PIPALS** the bo tree, a variety of Indian fig tree

PIPE *noun* **PIPES** a tubular conveyance for water, gas, oil, etc ▫ *verb* **PIPES, PIPING, PIPED** to convey (gas, water, oil, etc) through pipes

PIPECLAY *noun* **PIPECLAYS** fine white clay for making tobacco pipes and delicate crockery

PIPEFISH *noun* **PIPEFISHES** any of various fish of the seahorse family, a long thin fish covered with hard plates, its jaws forming a long tube

PIPEFUL *noun* **PIPEFULS** the amount a pipe can hold

PIPELESS *adj* without a pipe or pipes

PIPELINE *noun* **PIPELINES** a series of connected pipes laid underground to carry oil, natural gas, water, etc, across large distances

PIPER *noun* **PIPERS** a player of a pipe or the bagpipes

PIPERINE *noun* **PIPERINES** an alkaloid found in pepper

PIPESTONE *noun* **PIPESTONES** a red clayey stone used by Native American people for making tobacco pipes

PIPETTE *noun* **PIPETTES** a small laboratory device usually consisting of a narrow tube into which liquid can be sucked and from which it can subsequently be dispensed in known amounts ▫ *verb* **PIPETTES, PIPETTING, PIPETTED** to measure or transfer (a liquid) by means of a pipette

For longer words, see The Chambers Dictionary

PIPEWORK noun **PIPEWORKS** a vein of ore in the form of a pipe
PIPING noun **PIPINGS** a length of pipe, or a system or series of pipes conveying water, oil, etc □ adj said of a child's voice: small and shrill
PIPIT noun **PIPITS** any of various small ground-dwelling songbirds with a slender body, streaked brown plumage with paler underparts, a narrow beak and a long tail
PIPKIN noun **PIPKINS** a small pot, now only an earthenware one
PIPLESS adj having no pips
PIPPIN noun **PIPPINS** any of several varieties of eating apple with a green or rosy skin
PIPPY adj **PIPPIER, PIPPIEST** full of pips
PIPSQUEAK noun **PIPSQUEAKS** someone or something insignificant or contemptible
PIPUL noun **PIPULS** a pipal
PIQUANCY noun **PIQUANCIES** the state of being piquant
PIQUANT adj having a pleasantly spicy taste or tang
PIQUANTLY adverb in a piquant way
PIQUE noun **PIQUES** resentment; hurt pride □ verb **PIQUES, PIQUING, PIQUED** to hurt someone's pride; to offend or nettle them
PIQUÉ noun **PIQUÉS** a stiff corded fabric, especially of cotton
PIQUET noun **PIQUETS** a card game for two, played with 32 cards
PIR noun **PIRS** a Muslim title of honour given to a holy man or religious leader
PIRACY noun **PIRACIES** the activity of pirates, such as robbery on the high seas
PIRAÑA noun **PIRAÑAS** a piranha
PIRANHA noun **PIRANHAS** any of various extremely aggressive S American freshwater fishes, usually dark in colour, with strong jaws, sharp interlocking saw-edged teeth and a slender muscular tail with a broad tail-fin
PIRATE noun **PIRATES** someone who attacks and robs ships at sea □ verb **PIRATES, PIRATING, PIRATED** to publish, reproduce or use (someone else's literary or artistic work, or ideas) without legal permission
PIRATIC adj relating to a pirate; practising piracy
PIRATICAL adj piratic

PIROSHKI plural noun pirozhki
PIROUETTE noun **PIROUETTES** a spin or twirl executed on tiptoe in dancing □ verb **PIROUETTES, PIROUETTING, PIROUETTED** to execute a pirouette or a series of them
PIROZHKI plural noun small triangular pastries with meat, fish, cream cheese or vegetable fillings

PIS plural of **pi**

PISCATORY adj relating to fish or fishing
PISCINA noun **PISCINAS, PISCINAE** a stone basin with a drain, found in older churches, in which to empty water used for rinsing the sacred vessels, generally situated in a niche on the south side of the altar
PISCINE adj referring or relating to, or resembling, a fish or fishes
PISH exclamation an expression of impatience, contempt or disgust
PISSOIR noun **PISSOIRS** a public urinal enclosed by a screen or wall
PISTACHIO noun **PISTACHIOS** a small deciduous tree with greenish flowers borne in long loose heads, and reddish-brown nut-like fruits containing edible seeds
PISTE noun **PISTES** a ski slope or track of smooth compacted snow
PISTIL noun **PISTILS** in a flowering plant: the female reproductive structure, which may be a single carpel consisting of a stigma, style and ovary, or a group of fused carpels
PISTOL noun **PISTOLS** a small gun held in one hand when fired
PISTOLE noun **PISTOLES** an old gold coin, especially a Spanish one
PISTON noun **PISTONS** a cylindrical device that moves up and down in the cylinder of a petrol, diesel or steam engine
PIT noun **PITS** a big deep hole in the ground □ verb **PITS, PITTING, PITTED** to mark something with scars and holes
PITCH verb **PITCHES, PITCHING, PITCHED** to set up (a tent or camp) □ noun **PITCHES** the field or area of play in any of several sports
PITCHER noun **PITCHERS** a large earthenware jug with either one or two handles
PITCHFORK noun **PITCHFORKS** a long-handled fork with two or three sharp prongs, for tossing hay

PITCHPINE noun **PITCHPINES** a name for several N American pine trees that yield wood tar and timber
PITCHY adj **PITCHIER, PITCHIEST** smeared with or full of pitch (a thick black sticky substance obtained from coal tar)
PITEOUS adj arousing one's pity; moving, poignant, heartrending or pathetic
PITEOUSLY adverb in a piteous way
PITFALL noun **PITFALLS** a hidden danger, unsuspected hazard or unforeseen difficulty
PITH noun **PITHS** the soft white tissue that lies beneath the rind of many citrus fruits, eg orange □ verb **PITHS, PITHING, PITHED** to remove the pith from (a plant)
PITHEAD noun **PITHEADS** the entrance to a mineshaft and the machinery round it
PITHILY adverb in a pithy way
PITHINESS noun **PITHINESSES** sententiousness
PITHLESS adj having no pith
PITHY adj **PITHIER, PITHIEST** said of a saying, comment, etc: brief, forceful and to the point
PITIABLE adj arousing pity
PITIFUL adj arousing pity; wretched or pathetic
PITIFULLY adverb in a pitiful way
PITILESS adj showing no pity; merciless, cruel or relentless
PITON noun **PITONS** a metal peg or spike with an eye for passing a rope through, hammered into a rockface as an aid to climbers
PITTA noun **PITTAS** a Middle-Eastern slightly leavened bread, usually in a hollow oval shape that can be filled with other foods
PITTANCE noun **PITTANCES** a meagre allowance or wage
PITTED past form of **pit**
PITTING a form of **pit**
PITUITARY noun **PITUITARIES** short form of pituitary gland □ adj relating to this gland
PITY noun **PITIES** a feeling of sorrow for the troubles and sufferings of others; compassion □ verb **PITIES, PITYING, PITIED** to feel or show pity for someone or something
PITYING adj compassionate
PITYINGLY adverb in a pitying way

PIÙ adverb Italian word for *more*

PIUPIU noun **PIUPIUS** a skirt,

traditionally made from strips of flax, worn by Maori men and women for dances, celebrations and ceremonial occasions

PIVOT *noun* **PIVOTS** a central pin, spindle or pointed shaft round which something revolves, turns, balances or oscillates □ *verb* **PIVOTS, PIVOTING, PIVOTED** to turn, swivel or revolve

PIVOTAL *adj* constructed as or acting like a pivot; crucially important

PIVOTALLY *adverb* in a pivotal way

PIX *noun* **PIXES** a pyx

PIXEL *noun* **PIXELS** the smallest element of the image displayed on a computer or TV screen, consisting of a single dot which may be illuminated (ie on) or dark (off)

PIXIE *noun* **PIXIES** a kind of fairy, traditionally with mischievous tendencies

PIXILATED *adj* bemused or bewildered

PIXY *noun* **PIXIES** a pixie

PIZAZZ *noun* **PIZAZZES** a quality that is a combination of boldness, vigour, dash and flamboyance

PIZE *noun* **PIZES** pox; pest

PIZZA *noun* **PIZZAS** a circle of dough spread with cheese, tomatoes, etc and baked, made originally in Italy

PIZZERIA *noun* **PIZZERIAS** a restaurant that specializes in pizzas

PIZZICATO *adj* said of music for stringed instruments: played using the fingers to pluck the strings □ *adverb* said of music for stringed instruments: played using the fingers to pluck the strings □ *noun* **PIZZICATOS** a passage of music to be played in this way

PLACABLE *adj* easily appeased

PLACABLY *adverb* in a placable way

PLACARD *noun* **PLACARDS** a board or stiff card bearing a notice, advertisement, slogan, message of protest, etc, carried or displayed in public □ *verb* **PLACARDS, PLACARDING, PLACARDED** to put placards on (a wall, etc)

PLACATE *verb* **PLACATES, PLACATING, PLACATED** to pacify or appease (someone who is angry, etc)

PLACATION *noun* **PLACATIONS** an act of pacifying or appeasing (someone who is angry, etc)

PLACATORY *adj* conciliatory

PLACE *noun* **PLACES** a portion of the Earth's surface, particularly one considered as a unit, such as an area, region, district, locality, etc □ *verb* **PLACES, PLACING, PLACED** to put, position, etc in a particular place

PLACEBO *noun* **PLACEBOS** a substance that is administered as a drug but has no medicinal content, either given to a patient for its reassuring and therefore beneficial effect, or used in a clinical trial of a real drug as a control

PLACEMAN *noun* **PLACEMEN** someone appointed by a government, etc to a committee or organization and expected to represent the appointer's opinion

PLACEMENT *noun* **PLACEMENTS** the act or process of placing or positioning

PLACENTA *noun* **PLACENTAE** in mammals: a disc-shaped organ attached to the lining of the uterus during pregnancy and through which the embryo obtains nutrients and oxygen

PLACENTAL *adj* of or relating to the placenta

PLACER *noun* **PLACERS** in mining: a superficial deposit containing gold or other valuable minerals, which can be washed from the deposit

PLACET *noun* **PLACETS** a vote of assent in a governing body

PLACID *adj* **PLACIDER, PLACIDEST** calm; tranquil

PLACIDITY *noun* **PLACIDITIES** the state or condition or quality, etc of being placid

PLACIDLY *adverb* in a calm, tranquil way

PLACKET *noun* **PLACKETS** an opening in a skirt for a pocket or at the fastening

PLACODERM *noun* **PLACODERMS** a fossil fish covered with bony plates

PLACOID *adj* said of scales: plate-like

PLAFOND *noun* **PLAFONDS** a ceiling, especially a decorated one

PLAGUE *noun* **PLAGUES** any of several epidemic diseases with a high mortality rate, especially one transmitted by rats □ *verb* **PLAGUES, PLAGUING, PLAGUED** to afflict someone

PLAICE *noun* **PLAICES** a flatfish that has a brown upper surface covered with bright orange spots, and is an important food fish

PLAID *noun* **PLAIDS** tartan cloth

PLAIN *adj* **PLAINER, PLAINEST** all of one colour; unpatterned; undecorated □ *noun* **PLAINS** a large area of relatively smooth flat land without significant hills or valleys □ *adverb* utterly; quite

PLAINLY *adverb* in a plain, undecorated, unadorned way

PLAINNESS *noun* **PLAINNESSES** the state or condition or quality of being plain, unadorned or undecorated

PLAINSONG *noun* **PLAINSONGS** in the medieval Church, and still in the RC and some Anglican churches: music for unaccompanied voices, sung in unison

PLAINT *noun* **PLAINTS** an expression of woe; a lamentation

PLAINTIFF *noun* **PLAINTIFFS** someone who brings a case against another person in a court of law

PLAINTIVE *adj* mournful-sounding; sad; wistful

PLAIT *verb* **PLAITS, PLAITING, PLAITED** to arrange something (especially hair) by interweaving three or more lengths of it □ *noun* **PLAITS** a length of hair or other material interwoven in this way

PLAITER *noun* **PLAITERS** someone who plaits

PLAN *noun* **PLANS** a thought-out arrangement or method for doing something □ *verb* **PLANS, PLANNING, PLANNED** to devise a scheme for something

PLANAR *adj* of or relating to a flat surface

PLANARIAN *noun* **PLANARIANS** any of several kinds of aquatic flatworm

PLANCHET *noun* **PLANCHETS** a blank disk to be stamped as a coin

PLANE *noun* **PLANES** a carpenter's tool for producing a smooth surface □ *verb* **PLANES, PLANING, PLANED** to smooth (a surface, especially wood) with a plane

PLANER *noun* **PLANERS** someone who uses a carpenter's plane

PLANET *noun* **PLANETS** a celestial body, in orbit around the Sun or another star, which has too small a mass to become a star itself, and shines by reflecting light from the star around which it revolves

PLANETARY adj relating to or resembling a planet

PLANETOID noun **PLANETOIDS** a minor planet or asteroid

PLANGENCY noun **PLANGENCIES** the state or condition or quality of being plangent

PLANGENT adj said of a sound: deep, ringing and mournful

PLANING a form of **plane**

PLANISH verb **PLANISHES, PLANISHING, PLANISHED** to polish (metal, etc)

PLANISHER noun **PLANISHERS** a person or tool that planishes

PLANK noun **PLANKS** a long flat piece of timber thicker than a board ▫ verb **PLANKS, PLANKING, PLANKED** to fit or cover something with planks

PLANKING noun **PLANKINGS** planks, or a surface, etc constructed of them

PLANKTON noun **PLANKTONS** microscopic animals and plants that passively float or drift with the current in the surface waters of seas and lakes

PLANNED past form of **plan**

PLANNER noun **PLANNERS** someone who draws up plans or designs

PLANNING a form of **plan**

PLANT noun **PLANTS** any living organism, such as a shrub or herb, that is capable of manufacturing carbohydrates by the process of photosynthesis and that typically possesses cell walls containing cellulose ▫ verb **PLANTS, PLANTING, PLANTED** to put (seeds or plants) into the ground to grow

PLANTABLE adj that can be planted in the ground

PLANTAIN noun **PLANTAINS** a plant belonging to the banana family, widely cultivated in humid tropical regions for its edible fruit

PLANTAR adj belonging or relating to the sole of the foot

PLANTER noun **PLANTERS** the owner or manager of a plantation

PLANTSMAN noun **PLANTSMEN** someone who has extensive knowledge of and experience in gardening

PLAQUE noun **PLAQUES** a commemorative inscribed tablet fixed to or set into a wall

PLASM noun **PLASMS** protoplasm or plasma

PLASMA noun **PLASMAS** the colourless liquid component of blood or lymph, in which the blood cells are suspended

PLASMATIC adj referring to, or occurring in, plasma

PLASMID noun **PLASMIDS** a small circular loop of DNA that moves from one bacterium to another, transferring genetic information and often endowing its host with useful characteristics, eg resistance to antibiotics

PLASMIN noun **PLASMINS** an enzyme that breaks down the fibrous protein in blood clots

PLASTER noun **PLASTERS** a material consisting of lime, sand and water that is applied to walls when soft and dries to form a hard smooth surface ▫ verb **PLASTERS, PLASTERING, PLASTERED** to apply plaster to (walls, etc)

PLASTERER noun **PLASTERERS** someone whose job is to apply plaster to walls, ceilings, etc

PLASTERING noun **PLASTERINGS** an act of applying plaster to walls, ceilings, etc

PLASTERY adj like plaster

PLASTIC noun **PLASTICS** any of a large number of synthetic materials that can be moulded by heat and/or pressure into a rigid or semi-rigid shape, used to make bottles, bowls and other containers, fibres, film, packaging, toys, construction materials, etc ▫ adj made of plastic

PLASTID noun **PLASTIDS** any of various highly specialized membrane-bound structures found in plant cells

PLASTIQUE noun **PLASTIQUES** graceful poses and movements in dancing

PLASTRAL adj of or relating to a plastron

PLASTRON noun **PLASTRONS** a steel breastplate, part of a suit of armour

PLATAN noun **PLATANS** a platane

PLATANE noun **PLATANES** a type of tree with bur-like fruits

PLATE noun **PLATES** a shallow dish, especially one made of earthenware or porcelain, for serving food on ▫ verb **PLATES, PLATING, PLATED** to coat (a base metal) with a thin layer of a precious one

PLATEAU noun **PLATEAUX, PLATEAUS** an extensive area of relatively flat high land, usually bounded by steep sides ▫ verb

PLATEAUS, PLATEAUING, PLATEAUED to reach a level; to even out

PLATED adj covered with plates of metal

PLATEFUL noun **PLATEFULS** the amount a plate can hold

PLATELET noun **PLATELETS** in mammalian blood: any of the small disc-shaped cell fragments that are responsible for starting the formation of a blood clot when bleeding occurs

PLATEN noun **PLATENS** in some printing-presses: a plate that pushes the paper against the type

PLATER noun **PLATERS** a metal, etc that is used to plate something

PLATFORM noun **PLATFORMS** a raised floor for speakers, performers, etc

PLATING noun **PLATINGS** a thin coating of gold, silver or tin applied to a base metal

PLATINIC adj referring or relating to, or containing, platinum, especially in the tetravalent state

PLATINISE verb **PLATINISES, PLATINISING, PLATINISED** to platinize

PLATINIZE verb **PLATINIZES, PLATINIZING, PLATINIZED** to coat something with platinum

PLATINOUS adj referring or relating to, or containing bivalent platinum

PLATINUM noun **PLATINUMS** a silvery-white precious metallic element that does not tarnish or corrode, used to make jewellery, coins, electrical contacts, surgical instruments, etc

PLATITUDE noun **PLATITUDES** an empty, unoriginal or redundant comment, especially one made as though it were important

PLATONIC adj said of human love: not involving sexual relations

PLATOON noun **PLATOONS** in the army: a subdivision of a company

PLATTER noun **PLATTERS** a large flat dish

PLATYPUS noun **PLATYPUSES** an egg-laying amphibious mammal with dense brown fur, a long flattened toothless snout, webbed feet and a broad flat tail, found in Tasmania and E Australia

PLAUDIT noun **PLAUDITS** a commendation; an expression of praise

PLAUSIBLE *adj* said of an explanation, etc: credible, reasonable or likely

PLAUSIBLY *adverb* in a plausible way

PLAY *verb* **PLAYS, PLAYING, PLAYED** said especially of children: to spend time in recreation, eg dancing about, kicking a ball around, doing things in make-believe, generally having fun, etc □ *noun* **PLAYS** recreation; playing games for fun and amusement

PLAYA *noun* **PLAYAS** a basin which becomes a shallow lake after heavy rainfall and dries out again in hot weather

PLAYABLE *adj* said of a pitch, ground, etc: fit to be played on

PLAYBACK *noun* **PLAYBACKS** a playing back of a sound recording or film

PLAYBILL *noun* **PLAYBILLS** a poster that advertises a play or show

PLAYBOY *noun* **PLAYBOYS** a man of wealth, leisure and frivolous lifestyle

PLAYER *noun* **PLAYERS** someone who plays

PLAYFUL *adj* full of fun; frisky

PLAYFULLY *adverb* in a playful way

PLAYGROUP *noun* **PLAYGROUPS** an organized group of preschool children that meets for regular supervised play

PLAYHOUSE *noun* **PLAYHOUSES** a theatre

PLAYMATE *noun* **PLAYMATES** a companion to play with

PLAYPEN *noun* **PLAYPENS** a collapsible frame that when erected forms an enclosure inside which a baby may safely play

PLAYTHING *noun* **PLAYTHINGS** a toy, or a person or thing treated as if they were a toy

PLAYTIME *noun* **PLAYTIMES** a period for recreation, especially a set period for playing out of doors as part of a school timetable

PLAZA *noun* **PLAZAS** a large public square or market place, especially one in a Spanish town

PLEA *noun* **PLEAS** an earnest appeal

PLEAD *verb* **PLEADS, PLEADING, PLED, PLEADED** to appeal earnestly

PLEADABLE *adj* capable of being pleaded

PLEADER *noun* **PLEADERS** a person who pleads; an advocate

PLEADING *adj* appealing earnestly; imploring □ *noun*

PLEADINGS the act of putting forward or conducting a plea

PLEASANT *adj* **PLEASANTER, PLEASANTEST** giving pleasure; enjoyable; agreeable

PLEASE *verb* **PLEASES, PLEASING, PLEASED** to give satisfaction, pleasure or enjoyment; to be agreeable to someone □ *adverb* used politely to accompany a request, order, acceptance of an offer, protest, a call for attention, etc

PLEASED *adj* happy; satisfied; contented

PLEASING *adj* causing pleasure or satisfaction

PLEASURE *noun* **PLEASURES** a feeling of enjoyment or satisfaction □ *verb* **PLEASURES, PLEASURING, PLEASURED** to give pleasure to someone

PLEAT *noun* **PLEATS** a fold sewn or pressed into cloth, etc □ *verb* **PLEATS, PLEATING, PLEATED** to make pleats in (cloth, etc)

PLEB *noun* **PLEBS** someone who has coarse or vulgar tastes, manners or habits

PLEBBY *adj* **PLEBBIER, PLEBBIEST** vulgar; coarse

PLEBEIAN *noun* **PLEBEIANS** a member of the common people, especially of ancient Rome □ *adj* referring or belonging to the common people

PLECTRUM *noun* **PLECTRUMS, PLECTRA** a small flat implement of metal, plastic, horn, etc used for plucking the strings of a guitar

PLED a past form of **plead**

PLEDGE *noun* **PLEDGES** a solemn promise □ *verb* **PLEDGES, PLEDGING, PLEDGED** to promise (money, loyalty, etc) to someone

PLEDGEE *noun* **PLEDGEES** the person to whom a thing is pledged

PLEDGEOR *noun* **PLEDGEORS** a pledger

PLEDGER *noun* **PLEDGERS** the person who pledges something

PLEDGET *noun* **PLEDGETS** a wad of lint, cotton, etc used to cover a wound or sore

PLEDGOR *noun* **PLEDGORS** a pledger

PLENARILY *adverb* fully; completely

PLENARY *adj* full; complete; having full powers; attended by all members

PLENITUDE *noun* **PLENITUDES** abundance; profusion

PLENTEOUS *adj* plentiful; abundant

PLENTIFUL *adj* in good supply; copious; abundant

PLENTY *noun* a lot; a full supply □ *pronoun* enough, or more than enough □ *adverb* fully

PLENUM *noun* **PLENUMS** a meeting attended by all members

PLEONASM *noun* **PLEONASMS** the use of more words than are needed to express something

PLESSOR *noun* **PLESSORS** a plexor

PLETHORA *noun* **PLETHORAS** a large or excessive amount

PLEURA *noun* **PLEURAE** in mammals: the double membrane that covers the lungs and lines the chest cavity

PLEURAL *adj* of or relating to the pleura

PLEURISY *noun* **PLEURISIES** inflammation of the pleura

PLEURITIC *adj* of or relating to or suffering from pleurisy

PLEXOR *noun* **PLEXORS** a small hammer used in percussing

PLEXUS *noun* **PLEXUSES** a network of nerves or blood vessels, eg the solar plexus behind the stomach

PLIABLE *adj* easily bent; flexible

PLIABLY *adverb* flexibly

PLIANCY *noun* **PLIANCIES** the state or condition or quality of being easily bent or flexible

PLIANT *adj* bending easily; pliable, flexible or supple

PLIANTLY *adverb* in a pliant way

PLIÉ *noun* **PLIÉS** in ballet: a movement in which the knees are bent while the body remains upright

PLIED past form of **ply** [2]

PLIER *noun* **PLIERS** someone who continually supplies another person with something that they may or may not want

PLIERS *plural noun* a hinged tool with jaws for gripping small objects, bending or cutting wire, etc

PLIES plural of **ply** [1], a form of **ply** [2]

PLIGHT [1] *noun* **PLIGHTS** a danger, difficulty or situation of hardship that one finds oneself in; a predicament

PLIGHT [2] *verb* **PLIGHTS,**

PLIGHTING, PLIGHTED to promise something solemnly; to pledge

PLIMSOLE *noun* **PLIMSOLES** a plimsoll

PLIMSOLL *noun* **PLIMSOLLS** a light rubber-soled canvas shoe worn for gymnastics, etc

PLINTH *noun* **PLINTHS** a square block serving as the base of a column, pillar, etc

PLISSÉ *adj* said of a fabric: chemically treated to produce a shirred or wrinkled effect

PLOD *verb* **PLODS, PLODDING, PLODDED** to walk slowly with a heavy tread □ *noun* **PLODS** a heavy walk

PLODDER *noun* **PLODDERS** someone who plods on

PLODDING *adj* slow; laborious □ *noun* **PLODDINGS** an act of walking with a slow, heavy tread

PLOIDY *noun* **PLOIDIES** the number of complete chromosome sets present in a cell or living organism

PLONK [1] *noun* **PLONKS** cheap, undistinguished wine

PLONK [2] *verb* **PLONKS, PLONKING, PLONKED** to put or place something with a thud or with finality

PLONKER *noun* **PLONKERS** a stupid person; an idiot

PLOOK *noun* **PLOOKS** a plouk

PLOP *noun* **PLOPS** the sound of a small object dropping into water without a splash □ *verb* **PLOPS, PLOPPING, PLOPPED** to fall or drop with this sound □ *adverb* with a plop

PLOSIVE *noun* **PLOSIVES** a consonant made by the sudden release of breath after stoppage, such as the sound typically expressed by the letters *p*, *t* or *k*

PLOT *noun* **PLOTS** a secret plan, especially one laid jointly with others, for contriving something illegal or evil; a conspiracy □ *verb* **PLOTS, PLOTTING, PLOTTED** to plan something (especially something illegal or evil), usually with others

PLOTLESS *adj* without a plot

PLOTTER *noun* **PLOTTERS** someone who plots

PLOUGH *noun* **PLOUGHS** a bladed farm implement used to turn over the surface of the soil and bury stubble, weeds, etc, in preparation for the cultivation of a crop □ *verb* **PLOUGHS,**

PLOUGHING, PLOUGHED to till or turn over (soil, land, etc) with a plough

PLOUGHMAN *noun* **PLOUGHMEN** someone who steers a plough

PLOUK *noun* **PLOUKS** a spot or pimple

PLOVER *noun* **PLOVERS** any of various wading birds with boldly patterned plumage, large pointed wings, long legs and a short straight bill

PLOW *noun* **PLOWS** a plough □ *verb* **PLOWS, PLOWING, PLOWED** to plough

PLOY *noun* **PLOYS** a stratagem, dodge or manoeuvre to gain an advantage

PLUCK *verb* **PLUCKS, PLUCKING, PLUCKED** to pull the feathers off (a bird) before cooking it □ *noun* **PLUCKS** courage; guts

PLUCKILY *adverb* in a courageous or spirited way

PLUCKY *adj* **PLUCKIER, PLUCKIEST** courageous; spirited

PLUG *noun* **PLUGS** a piece of rubber, plastic, etc shaped to fit a hole as a stopper, eg in a bath or sink □ *verb* **PLUGS, PLUGGING, PLUGGED** to stop or block up (a hole, etc) with something

PLUGGER *noun* **PLUGGERS** a person or thing that plugs, especially a dentist's instrument

PLUM *noun* **PLUMS** a shrub or small tree, cultivated in temperate regions for its edible fruit; a deep dark-red colour □ *adj* plum-coloured

PLUMAGE *noun* **PLUMAGES** a bird's feathers, especially with regard to colour

PLUMB *noun* **PLUMBS** a lead weight, usually suspended from a line, used for measuring water depth or for testing a wall, etc for perpendicularity □ *adj* straight, vertical or perpendicular □ *verb* **PLUMBS, PLUMBING, PLUMBED** to measure the depth of (water), test (a structure) for verticality, or adjust something to the vertical, using a plumb

PLUMBAGO *noun* **PLUMBAGOS** another name for graphite

PLUMBER *noun* **PLUMBERS** someone who fits and repairs water pipes, and water- or gas-using appliances

PLUMBING *noun* **PLUMBINGS** the system of water and gas pipes in a building, etc

PLUMBISM *noun* **PLUMBISMS** lead poisoning

PLUME *noun* **PLUMES** a feather, especially a large showy one □ *verb* **PLUMES, PLUMING, PLUMED** said of a bird: to clean or preen (itself or its feathers)

PLUMMET *verb* **PLUMMETS, PLUMMETING, PLUMMETED** to fall or drop rapidly; to plunge or hurtle downwards □ *noun* **PLUMMETS** the weight on a plumbline or fishing-line

PLUMMY *adj* **PLUMMIER, PLUMMIEST** said of a job, etc: desirable; worth having; choice

PLUMP *adj* **PLUMPER, PLUMPEST** full, rounded or chubby □ *verb* **PLUMPS, PLUMPING, PLUMPED** to shake (cushions or pillows) to give them their full soft bulk

PLUMPLY *adverb* in a plump way

PLUMPNESS *noun* **PLUMPNESSES** the state or condition or quality of being plump

PLUMULE *noun* **PLUMULES** the embryonic shoot of a germinating seedling

PLUMY *adj* **PLUMIER, PLUMIEST** covered or adorned with down or plumes

PLUNDER *verb* **PLUNDERS, PLUNDERING, PLUNDERED** to steal (valuable goods) or loot (a place), especially with open force during a war; to rob or ransack □ *noun* **PLUNDERS** the goods plundered; loot; booty

PLUNDERER *noun* **PLUNDERERS** someone who plunders

PLUNGE *verb* **PLUNGES, PLUNGING, PLUNGED** to dive, throw oneself, fall or rush headlong in or into something □ *noun* **PLUNGES** an act of plunging; a dive

PLUNGER *noun* **PLUNGERS** a rubber suction cup at the end of a long handle, used to clear blocked drains, etc

PLUNK *verb* **PLUNKS, PLUNKING, PLUNKED** to pluck (the strings of a banjo, etc); to twang □ *noun* **PLUNKS** the act of plunking or the sound this makes

PLURAL *adj* denoting or referring to two or more people, things, etc as opposed to only one □ *noun* **PLURALS** a word or form of a word expressing the idea or involvement of two or more people, things, etc

PLURALISE *verb* **PLURALISES,**

PLURALISING, PLURALISED to pluralize

PLURALISM noun **PLURALISMS** the existence within a society of a variety of ethnic, cultural and religious groups

PLURALIST noun **PLURALISTS** someone who believes in pluralism

PLURALITY noun **PLURALITIES** the state or condition of being plural

PLURALIZE verb **PLURALIZES, PLURALIZING, PLURALIZED** to make or become plural

PLUS noun **PLUSES** the symbol '+', denoting addition or positive value

PLUSH noun **PLUSHES** a fabric with a long velvety pile □ adj **PLUSHER, PLUSHEST** made of plush

PLUSHY adj **PLUSHIER, PLUSHIEST** luxurious, opulent, stylish or costly

PLUTOCRAT noun **PLUTOCRATS** a member of a plutocracy, ie a state governed by the wealthy

PLUTONIC adj relating to coarse-grained igneous rocks that are formed by the slow crystallization of magma deep within the Earth's crust, eg granites and gabbros

PLUTONIUM noun **PLUTONIUMS** a dense highly poisonous silvery-grey radioactive metallic element

PLUVIAL noun **PLUVIALS** a period of prolonged rainfall

PLY [1] noun **PLIES** thickness of yarn, rope or wood, measured by the number of strands or layers that compose it

PLY [2] verb **PLIES, PLYING, PLIED** to keep supplying someone with something or making a repeated, often annoying, onslaught on them

PLYWOOD noun **PLYWOODS** wood which consists of thin layers glued together, widely used in the construction industry

PNEUMATIC adj relating to air or gases

PNEUMONIA noun **PNEUMONIAS** inflammation of one or more lobes of the lungs, usually as a result of bacterial or viral infection, which was formerly a major cause of death but is now treatable with antibiotics

PO noun **POS** a chamberpot

POA noun **POAS** any of various species of grass with green hairless leaves, often wrinkled or with a

purplish tinge, abundant in meadows and pastures

POACH verb **POACHES, POACHING, POACHED** to cook (an egg without its shell) in or over boiling water

POACHER noun **POACHERS** someone who catches game or fish illegally

POACHING noun **POACHINGS** cooking by gentle simmering

POCHARD noun **POCHARDS** any of various diving ducks found in Europe and N America, the common variety of which has a short neck, a steep sloping forehead and a large bill

POCHOIR noun **POCHOIRS** a form of colour stencilling, by hand, on to a printed illustration

POCK noun **POCKS** a small inflamed area on the skin, containing pus, especially one caused by smallpox

POCKET noun **POCKETS** an extra piece sewn into or on to a garment to form a pouch for carrying things in □ verb **POCKETS, POCKETING, POCKETED** to put in one's pocket

POCKETFUL noun **POCKETFULS** the amount a pocket can hold

POCKMARK noun **POCKMARKS** a small pit or hollow in the skin left by a pock, especially one caused by chickenpox or smallpox

POCO adj a little

POD noun **PODS** a seedcase produced by leguminous plants, eg peas and beans □ verb **PODS, PODDING, PODDED** to extract (peas, beans, etc) from their pods; to hull

PODAGRA noun gout of the feet

PODAGRAL adj of or relating to podagra

PODEX noun **PODEXES** the rump

PODGY adj **PODGIER, PODGIEST** plump or chubby; short and squat

PODIATRY noun **PODIATRIES** chiropody

PODIUM noun **PODIA** a small platform for a public speaker, orchestra conductor, etc

PODSOL noun **PODSOLS** any of a group of soils, found under heathland and coniferous forests in cold temperate regions

PODZOL noun **PODZOLS** a podsol

POEM noun **POEMS** a literary composition, typically, but not

necessarily, in verse, often with elevated and/or imaginatively expressed content

POENOLOGY noun **POENOLOGIES** the study of crime and punishment

POESY noun **POESIES** poetry

POET noun **POETS** a male or female writer of poems

POETESS noun **POETESSES** a female writer of poems

POETIC adj relating to poets or poetry

POETICAL adj poetic

POETRY noun **POETRIES** the art of composing poems

POGO verb **POGOS, POGOING, POGOED** to jump on a pogo stick, a spring-mounted pole with a handlebar and foot rests, on which to bounce □ noun **POGOS** an instance of jumping using a pogo stick

POGROM noun **POGROMS** an organized persecution or massacre of a particular group of people, originally that of Jews in 19c Russia

POH exclamation expressing impatient contempt

POI noun **POIS** a Hawaiian dish, fermented taro

POIGNANCY noun **POIGNANCIES** the state or condition or quality of being poignant

POIGNANT adj painful to the feelings

POINCIANA noun **POINCIANAS** a tropical tree with large red or orange flowers

POINT noun **POINTS** a sharp or tapering end or tip □ verb **POINTS, POINTING, POINTED** to aim something

POINTED adj having or ending in a point; of a remark: having a marked personal application

POINTEDLY adverb with a marked personal application

POINTER noun **POINTERS** a rod used by a speaker for indicating positions on a wall map, chart, etc

POINTING noun **POINTINGS** the cement or mortar filling the gaps between the bricks or stones of a wall

POINTLESS adj without a point

POISE noun **POISES** self-confidence, calm or composure □ verb **POISES, POISING, POISED** to balance or suspend

POISED *adj* said of behaviour, etc: calm and dignified

POISON *noun* **POISONS** any substance that damages tissues or causes death when injected, absorbed or swallowed by living organisms, eg arsenic and cyanide □ *verb* **POISONS, POISONING, POISONED** to harm or kill with poison

POISONER *noun* **POISONERS** someone who poisons another person

POISONOUS *adj* liable to cause injury or death if swallowed, inhaled or absorbed by the skin

POKE *verb* **POKES, POKING, POKED** to thrust; to prod or jab □ *noun* **POKES** a jab or prod

POKEBERRY *noun* **POKEBERRIES** pokeweed

POKER *noun* **POKERS** a metal rod for stirring a fire to make it burn better

POKEWEED *noun* **POKEWEEDS** a tall hardy American plant with pale yellow flowers and purple berries, used medicinally in a test for allergy

POKY *adj* **POKIER, POKIEST** said of a room, house, etc: small and confined or cramped

POLAR *adj* belonging or relating to the North or South Pole, or the regions round them

POLARISE *verb* **POLARISES, POLARISING, POLARISED** to polarize

POLARITY *noun* **POLARITIES** the state of having two opposite poles

POLARIZE *verb* **POLARIZES, POLARIZING, POLARIZED** to give magnetic or electrical polarity to something

POLDER *noun* **POLDERS** an area of low-lying land which has been reclaimed from the sea, a river or lake, especially in the Netherlands

POLE *noun* **POLES** either of two points representing the north and south ends of the axis about which the Earth rotates, known as the North Pole and South Pole respectively

POLECAT *noun* **POLECATS** a mammal resembling a large weasel, with coarse dark-brown fur, creamy yellow underfur and white patches on its face, that produces a foul-smelling discharge when alarmed or when marking territory

POLEMIC *noun* **POLEMICS** a controversial speech or piece of writing that fiercely attacks or defends an idea, opinion, etc □ *adj* relating to or involving polemics or controversy

POLEMICS *singular noun* the art of verbal dispute and debate

POLENTA *noun* **POLENTAS** an Italian dish of cooked ground maize

POLICE *plural noun* the body of men and women employed by the government of a country to keep order, enforce the law, prevent crime, etc □ *verb* **POLICES, POLICING, POLICED** to keep law and order in (an area) using the police, army, etc

POLICEMAN *noun* **POLICEMEN** a male member of a police force

POLICY *noun* **POLICIES** a plan of action, usually based on certain principles, decided on by a body or individual

POLIO *noun* **POLIOS** a viral disease of the brain and spinal cord, which in some cases can result in permanent paralysis

POLISH *verb* **POLISHES, POLISHING, POLISHED** to make or become smooth and glossy by rubbing □ *noun* **POLISHES** a substance used for polishing surfaces

POLITE *adj* **POLITER, POLITEST** said of a person or their actions, etc: well-mannered; considerate towards others; courteous

POLITELY *adverb* in a polite way

POLITIC *adj* said of a course of action: prudent; wise; shrewd

POLITICAL *adj* relating or belonging to government or public affairs

POLITICO *noun* **POLITICOS, POLITICOES** a politician or someone who is keen on politics

POLITICS *singular noun* the science or business of government

POLITY *noun* **POLITIES** a politically organized body such as a state, church or association

POLKA *noun* **POLKAS** a lively Bohemian dance usually performed with a partner, which has a pattern of three steps followed by a hop □ *verb* **POLKAS, POLKAING, POLKAED** to dance a polka

POLL *noun* **POLLS** a political election □ *verb* **POLLS, POLLING, POLLED** to win (a number of votes) in an election

POLLACK *noun* **POLLACKS** a marine fish belonging to the cod family, with a greenish-brown back, pale-yellow sides and a white belly

POLLAN *noun* **POLLANS** a type of whitefish found in the lakes of N Ireland

POLLARD *noun* **POLLARDS** a tree whose branches have been cut back, in order to produce a crown of shoots at the top of the trunk, so as to be out of reach of grazing animals, or for periodic harvesting for firewood or fencing, etc □ *verb* **POLLARDS, POLLARDING, POLLARDED** to make a pollard of a tree

POLLEN *noun* **POLLENS** the fine, usually yellow, dust-like powder produced by the anthers of flowering plants, and by the male cones of cone-bearing plants

POLLEX *noun* **POLLICES** the first digit on the forelimb of mammals, reptiles, amphibians and birds, eg the thumb in humans

POLLINATE *verb* **POLLINATES, POLLINATING, POLLINATED** in flowering and cone-bearing plants: to transfer pollen in order to achieve fertilization and subsequent development of seed

POLLOCK *noun* **POLLOCKS** a pollack

POLLSTER *noun* **POLLSTERS** someone who organizes and carries out opinion polls

POLLUTANT *noun* **POLLUTANTS** any substance or agent that pollutes

POLLUTE *verb* **POLLUTES, POLLUTING, POLLUTED** to contaminate something with harmful substances or impurities; to cause pollution in something

POLLUTION *noun* **POLLUTIONS** the adverse effect on the natural environment, including human, animal or plant life, of a harmful substance, eg industrial and radioactive waste

POLLYANNA *noun* **POLLYANNAS** someone who is unfailingly optimistic, often in a naive way

POLO *noun* **POLOS** a game, similar to hockey, played on horseback by two teams of four players, using long-handled mallets to propel the ball along the ground

POLONAISE *noun* **POLONAISES** a stately Polish marching dance

POLONIUM *noun* **POLONIUMS** a rare radioactive metallic element

POLONY *noun* **POLONIES** a dry sausage made of partly cooked meat

POLTROON *noun* **POLTROONS** a despicable coward

POLY *noun* **POLYS** a polytechnic, a college of higher education providing a wide range of subjects, especially of a technical or vocational kind

POLYAMIDE *noun* **POLYAMIDES** a polymer formed by the linking of the amino group of one molecule with the carboxyl group of the next, eg nylon

POLYANDRY *noun* **POLYANDRIES** the custom or practice of having more than one husband at the same time

POLYARCHY *noun* **POLYARCHIES** government of a state by many

POLYESTER *noun* **POLYESTERS** a synthetic resin used to form strong durable crease-resistant artificial fibres, widely used in textiles for clothing, etc

POLYGAMY *noun* **POLYGAMIES** the custom or practice of having more than one husband or wife at the same time

POLYGENE *noun* **POLYGENES** any of a group of genes that control quantitative characteristics, eg height, with their individual effects being too small to be noticed

POLYGLOT *noun* **POLYGLOTS** someone who speaks many languages

POLYGON *noun* **POLYGONS** a figure with a number of straight sides, usually more than three, eg a pentagon

POLYGONAL *adj* of or relating to a polygon; having the form of a polygon

POLYGRAPH *noun* **POLYGRAPHS** a device, sometimes used as a lie-detector, that monitors several body functions simultaneously, eg pulse, blood pressure and conductivity of the skin

POLYGYNY *noun* **POLYGYNIES** the condition or custom of having more than one wife at the same time

POLYMATH *noun* **POLYMATHS** someone who is well educated in a wide variety of subjects

POLYMATHY *noun* **POLYMATHIES** the state or condition or quality of being a polymath

POLYMER *noun* **POLYMERS** a very large molecule consisting of a long chain of monomers linked end to end to form a series of repeating units

POLYMERIC *adj* of or relating to polymers

POLYP *noun* **POLYPS, POLYPES** a small abnormal but usually benign growth projecting from a mucous membrane, especially inside the nose

POLYPHONE *noun* **POLYPHONES** a letter which can be pronounced or sounded in more than one way, eg the letter *g* in English

POLYPHONY *noun* **POLYPHONIES** a style of musical composition in which each part or voice has an independent melodic value

POLYPLOID *adj* having more than twice the haploid number of chromosomes □ *noun* **POLYPLOIDS** a polyploid organism

POLYPOUS *adj* of, relating to or like a polyp

POLYPTYCH *noun* **POLYPTYCHS** an altarpiece consisting of several panels with a separate picture in each, surrounded by an elaborate, usually gilded, frame

POLYSEMY *noun* **POLYSEMIES** the existence of more than one meaning for a single word, such as *table*

POLYSOME *noun* **POLYSOMES** a form of RNA that is being processed simultaneously by several ribosomes in the synthesis of proteins

POLYTHENE *noun* **POLYTHENES** a waxy translucent easily-moulded thermoplastic, used in the form of film or sheeting to package food products, clothing, etc, and to make pipes, moulded articles, etc

POM *noun* **POMS** a colloquial word for a Pomeranian dog

POMACE *noun* **POMACES** crushed apples for cider-making

POMADE *noun* **POMADES** a perfumed ointment for the hair and scalp □ *verb* **POMADES, POMADING, POMADED** to put pomade on (a person's hair, etc)

POMANDER *noun* **POMANDERS** a perfumed ball composed of various aromatic substances, originally carried as scent or to ward off infection

POME *noun* **POMES** a type of fruit in which a fleshy outer layer surrounds a central core that contains a number of seeds, eg the apple and the pear

POMELO *noun* **POMELOS** a tropical tree, native to SE Asia, cultivated for its edible citrus fruit

POMFRET *noun* **POMFRETS** a disc-shaped liquorice sweet

POMMEL *noun* **POMMELS** the raised forepart of a saddle □ *verb* **POMMELS, POMMELLING, POMMELLED** to pummel

POMP *noun* **POMPS** ceremonial grandeur

POMPADOUR *noun* **POMPADOURS** a fashion of dressing women's hair by rolling it back from the forehead over a small cushion or pad, to give extra height

POMPOM *noun* **POMPOMS** a ball made of cut wool or other yarn, used as a trimming on clothes, etc

POMPOSITY *noun* **POMPOSITIES** a pompous quality or manner

POMPOUS *adj* solemnly self-important

POMPOUSLY *adverb* in a pompous way

PONCHO *noun* **PONCHOS** an outer garment, originally S American, made of a large piece of cloth with a hole in the middle for the head to go through

POND *noun* **PONDS** a small area of still fresh water surrounded by land, either lying in a natural depression in the Earth's surface, or artificially constructed, eg in a garden

PONDER *verb* **PONDERS, PONDERING, PONDERED** to consider or contemplate something deeply

PONDEROUS *adj* said of speech, humour, etc: heavy-handed, laborious, over-solemn or pompous

PONDOK *noun* **PONDOKS** a crude dwelling hut; a shack

PONDOKKIE *noun* **PONDOKKIES** a pondok

PONE *noun* **PONES** a kind of maize bread

PONG *noun* **PONGS** a stink; a bad smell □ *verb* **PONGS, PONGING, PONGED** to smell bad

PONGEE *noun* **PONGEES** a soft unbleached silk made from the cocoons of a wild silkworm

PONGO *noun* **PONGOS** an anthropoid ape, originally a gorilla but now used of an orang-utan

PONGY *adj* **PONGIER, PONGIEST** stinking; smelly

PONIARD *noun* **PONIARDS** a slim-bladed dagger □ *verb* **PONIARDS, PONIARDING, PONIARDED** to stab someone or something with a poniard

PONS *noun* **PONTES** in the brain of mammals: the mass of nerve fibres that relays nerve impulses between different parts of the brain

PONTIFF *noun* **PONTIFFS** a title for the Pope

PONTOON *noun* **PONTOONS** any of a number of flat-bottomed craft, punts, barges, etc, anchored side by side across a river, to support a temporary bridge or platform, etc by providing buoyancy in the water

PONY *noun* **PONIES** any of several small hardy breeds of horse, usually less than 14.2 hands (1.5m) in height when fully grown, noted for their intelligence

PONYTAIL *noun* **PONYTAILS** a hairstyle in which a person's hair is drawn back and gathered by a band at the back of the head, so that it hangs free like a pony's tail

POO *noun* **POOS** faeces □ *verb* **POOS, POOING, POOED** to defecate

POOCH *noun* **POOCHES** a dog, especially a mongrel

POODLE *noun* **POODLES** a breed of lively pet dog of various sizes which has a narrow head with pendulous ears and a long curly black, white, grey or brown coat, often clipped into an elaborate style

POOH *exclamation* an exclamation of scorn or disgust, especially at an offensive smell

POOJA *noun* **POOJAS** puja

POOKA *noun* **POOKAS** in Irish folklore: a malevolent goblin or spirit which sometimes assumes the form of an animal, and is said to haunt bogs and marshes

POOL [1] *noun* **POOLS** a small area of still water

POOL [2] *verb* **POOLS, POOLING, POOLED** to put (money or other resources) into a common supply for general use

POOP [1] *noun* **POOPS** the raised enclosed part at the stern of old sailing ships

POOP [2] *verb* **POOPS, POOPING, POOPED** to become winded or exhausted

POOPED *adj* exhausted

POOR *adj* **POORER, POOREST** not having sufficient money or means to live comfortably

POORHOUSE *noun* **POORHOUSES** an institution maintained at public expense, for housing the poor; a workhouse

POORLY *adverb* not well; badly □ *adj* **POORLIER, POORLIEST** not well; ill

POORNESS *noun* **POORNESSES** the state or condition or quality of being poor

POP *noun* **POPS** a sharp explosive noise, like that of a cork coming out of a bottle □ *verb* **POPS, POPPING, POPPED** to make or cause something to make a pop

POPCORN *noun* **POPCORNS** maize grains that puff up and burst open when heated

POPE *noun* **POPES** the Bishop of Rome, the head of the Roman Catholic Church

POPEDOM *noun* **POPEDOMS** the office, dignity or jurisdiction of the pope; a pope's tenure of office

POPINJAY *noun* **POPINJAYS** a vain or conceited person; a dandy or fop

POPLAR *noun* **POPLARS** a tall slender deciduous tree found in northern temperate regions, with broad simple leaves which tremble in a slight breeze, often planted for ornament or shelter

POPLIN *noun* **POPLINS** a strong cotton cloth with a finely ribbed finish

POPLITEAL *adj* belonging or relating to the part of the leg behind the knee

POPPADUM *noun* **POPPADUMS** a paper-thin pancake, grilled or fried till crisp, served with Indian dishes

POPPER *noun* **POPPERS** someone or something that pops

POPPET *noun* **POPPETS** a term of endearment for someone lovable

POPPLE *verb* **POPPLES, POPPLING, POPPLED** said of boiling water or of sea water: to bubble or ripple □ *noun* **POPPLES** a poppling movement

POPPY *noun* **POPPIES** any of numerous northern temperate plants with large brightly-coloured bowl-shaped flowers

POPPYCOCK *noun* **POPPYCOCKS** nonsense

POPSY *noun* **POPSIES** a term of endearment for a young girl or woman

POPULACE *noun* **POPULACES** the body of ordinary citizens; the common people

POPULAR *adj* liked or enjoyed by most people

POPULARLY *adverb* in a popular way; by most people

POPULATE *verb* **POPULATES, POPULATING, POPULATED** said of people, animals or plants: to inhabit or live in (a certain area)

POPULISM *noun* **POPULISMS** political activity or notions that are thought to reflect the opinions and interests of ordinary people

POPULIST *noun* **POPULISTS** a person who believes in the right and ability of the common people to play a major part in government

POPULOUS *adj* densely inhabited

PORBEAGLE *noun* **PORBEAGLES** a large heavily-built shark with a broad deep tail

PORCELAIN *noun* **PORCELAINS** a fine white translucent earthenware, originally made in China

PORCH *noun* **PORCHES** a structure that forms a covered entrance to the doorway of a building

PORCINE *adj* relating to or resembling a pig

PORCUPINE *noun* **PORCUPINES** any of various large nocturnal rodents with long sharp black-and-white spikes or quills on the back and sides of the body

PORE [1] *noun* **PORES** a small, usually round opening in the surface of a living organism, eg in the skin, through which fluids, gases and other substances can pass

PORE [2] *verb* **PORES, PORING, PORED** to study (books, documents, etc) with intense concentration

PORGE *verb* **PORGES, PORGING, PORGED** in Judaism: to cleanse (a slaughtered animal) ceremonially by removing the forbidden fat, sinews, etc

PORIFERAN *adj* said of an animal: belonging to the Porifera phylum, the sponges

PORK *noun* **PORKS** the flesh of a pig used as food

PORKER *noun* **PORKERS** a pig that shows fast growth and reaches maturity at a relatively light weight,

reared for fresh meat as opposed to processed meats such as bacon
PORKY *adj* **PORKIER, PORKIEST** plump
PORN *noun* **PORNS** pornography
PORNO *noun* **PORNOS** a pornographic book, film or magazine
POROSITY *noun* **POROSITIES** said of a solid material: the property of being porous
POROUS *adj* referring or relating to a material that contains pores or cavities
PORPHYRY *noun* **PORPHYRIES** any igneous rock that contains large crystals surrounded by much smaller ones
PORPOISE *noun* **PORPOISES** a beakless whale, smaller than a dolphin, with a blunt snout, found in northern coastal waters and around the coasts of S America and SE Asia
PORRIDGE *noun* **PORRIDGES** a dish of oatmeal or some other cereal which is boiled in water or milk until it reaches a thick consistency
PORRINGER *noun* **PORRINGERS** a bowl, with a handle, for soup or porridge
PORT *noun* **PORTS** the left side of a ship or aircraft ◻ *verb* **PORTS, PORTING, PORTED** to turn or be turned to the left
PORTABLE *adj* easily carried or moved, and usually designed to be so ◻ *noun* **PORTABLES** a portable radio, television, typewriter, etc
PORTAGE *noun* **PORTAGES** an act of carrying ◻ *verb* **PORTAGES, PORTAGING, PORTAGED** to transport (ships, etc) overland
PORTAL *noun* **PORTALS** an entrance, gateway or doorway, especially an imposing or awesome one
PORTEND *verb* **PORTENDS, PORTENDING, PORTENDED** to warn of (usually something bad); to signify or foreshadow it
PORTENT *noun* **PORTENTS** a prophetic sign; an omen
PORTER *noun* **PORTERS** someone employed to carry luggage or parcels, eg at a railway station
PORTFOLIO *noun* **PORTFOLIOS** a flat case for carrying papers, drawings, photographs, etc
PORTHOLE *noun* **PORTHOLES** an opening, usually a round one, in a ship's side to admit light and air

PORTICO *noun* **PORTICOS, PORTICOES** a colonnade forming a porch or covered way alongside a building
PORTIÈRE *noun* **PORTIÈRES** a curtain hung over the door or doorway of a room
PORTION *noun* **PORTIONS** a piece or part of a whole ◻ *verb* **PORTIONS, PORTIONING, PORTIONED** to divide up; to share out
PORTLY *adj* **PORTLIER, PORTLIEST** said especially of a man: somewhat stout
PORTRAIT *noun* **PORTRAITS** a drawing, painting or photograph of a person, especially of the face only
PORTRAY *verb* **PORTRAYS, PORTRAYING, PORTRAYED** to make a portrait of someone or something
PORTRAYAL *noun* **PORTRAYALS** the act of portraying; a representation
PORTRAYER *noun* **PORTRAYERS** a person or thing that portrays something

POS plural of **po**

POSE *noun* **POSES** a position or attitude of the body ◻ *verb* **POSES, POSING, POSED** to take up a position oneself, or position (someone else), for a photograph, portrait, etc
POSER *noun* **POSERS** a puzzling or perplexing question
POSEUR *noun* **POSEURS** someone who behaves in an affected or insincere way, especially to impress others
POSH *adj* **POSHER, POSHEST** high-quality, expensive, smart or stylish ◻ *adverb* in a way associated with the upper class ◻ *verb* **POSHES, POSHING, POSHED** to smarten up
POSIT *verb* **POSITS, POSITING, POSITED** to lay down or assume something as a basis for discussion; to postulate ◻ *noun* **POSITS** a statement made on the assumption that it will be proved valid
POSITION *noun* **POSITIONS** a place where someone or something is ◻ *verb* **POSITIONS, POSITIONING, POSITIONED** to place; to put something or someone in position
POSITIVE *adj* sure; certain; convinced

POSITRON *noun* **POSITRONS** a type of particle that has the same mass as an electron, and an equal but opposite charge
POSOLOGY *noun* **POSOLOGIES** the branch of medicine that deals with the quantities in which drugs or medicines should be administered
POSSE *noun* **POSSES** a mounted troop of men at the service of a local sheriff
POSSESS *verb* **POSSESSES, POSSESSING, POSSESSED** to own
POSSESSED *adj* controlled or driven by demons, etc
POSSESSOR *noun* **POSSESSORS** a person or thing that owns something
POSSET *noun* **POSSETS** a drink of hot milk, curdled with eg wine, ale or vinegar, and flavoured with spices, formerly used as a remedy for colds, etc ◻ *verb* **POSSETS, POSSETING, POSSETED** said of a baby: to bring up some curdled milk
POSSIBLE *adj* achievable; able to be done ◻ *noun* **POSSIBLES** someone or something potentially selectable or attainable; a possibility
POSSIBLY *adverb* perhaps; maybe
POSSUM *noun* **POSSUMS** an opossum
POST *noun* **POSTS** the official system for the delivery of mail ◻ *verb* **POSTS, POSTING, POSTED** to send something by post
POSTAGE *noun* **POSTAGES** the charge for sending a letter, etc through the post
POSTAL *adj* relating or belonging to the post office or to delivery of mail
POSTBAG *noun* **POSTBAGS** a mailbag
POSTBUS *noun* **POSTBUSES, POSTBUSSES** a small bus, van or similar vehicle, used for delivering mail and carrying passengers, especially in rural areas
POSTCARD *noun* **POSTCARDS** a card for writing messages on, often with a picture on one side, designed for sending through the post without an envelope
POSTCODE *noun* **POSTCODES** a code used to identify a postal address, made up of a combination of letters and numerals
POSTDATE *verb* **POSTDATES,**

POSTDATING, POSTDATED to put a future date on (a cheque, etc)
POSTERnoun **POSTERS** a large notice or advertisement for public display
POSTERIORadj placed behind, after or at the back of something ◻ noun **POSTERIORS** the buttocks
POSTERITYnoun **POSTERITIES** future generations
POSTERNnoun **POSTERNS** a back door, back gate or private entrance
POSTHASTEadverb with the utmost speed
POSTHORSEnoun **POSTHORSES** a horse kept for conveying the mail
POSTHOUSEnoun **POSTHOUSES** an inn where posthorses were kept for the use of travellers wishing to change horses, etc
POSTICHEnoun **POSTICHES** anything that is falsely or superfluously added
POSTILIONnoun **POSTILIONS** a rider on the nearside horse of one of the pairs of posthorses drawing a carriage, who, in the absence of a coachman, guides the team
POSTMANnoun **POSTMEN** a person whose job is to deliver mail
POSTMARKnoun **POSTMARKS** a mark stamped on mail by the post office, cancelling the stamp and showing the date and place of posting ◻ verb **POSTMARKS, POSTMARKING, POSTMARKED** to mark (mail) in this way
POSTNASALadj situated or occurring at the back of the nose or nasal cavity
POSTNATALadj relating to or occurring during the period immediately after childbirth
POSTPONEverb **POSTPONES, POSTPONING, POSTPONED** to delay or put off something till later
POSTULANTnoun **POSTULANTS** someone who asks or petitions for something, especially a candidate for holy orders or admission to a religious community
POSTULATEverb **POSTULATES, POSTULATING, POSTULATED** to assume or suggest something as the basis for discussion; to take it for granted
POSTURALadj of or relating to posture
POSTUREnoun **POSTURES** the way one holds one's body while standing, sitting or walking ◻ verb **POSTURES, POSTURING,**

POSTURED to take up a particular bodily attitude
POSTURERnoun **POSTURERS** someone who strikes postures or attitudes
POSTWARadj relating or belonging to the period following a war
POSTWOMANnoun **POSTWOMEN** a woman whose job is to deliver mail
POSYnoun **POSIES** a small bunch of flowers
POTnoun **POTS** any of various domestic containers, usually deep round ones, used as cooking or serving utensils, or for storage ◻ verb **POTS, POTTING, POTTED** to plant something in a plant pot
POTABLEadj fit or suitable for drinking
POTAGEnoun **POTAGES** a thick soup
POTASHnoun **POTASHES** any of various compounds of potassium, especially potassium carbonate or potassium hydroxide
POTASSIUMnoun **POTASSIUMS** a soft silvery-white metallic element, compounds of which are used in fertilizers, explosives, laboratory reagents, soaps and some types of glass
POTATOnoun **POTATOES** a perennial plant that produces edible tubers and is a staple crop of temperate regions worldwide
POTEENnoun **POTEENS** illicitly distilled Irish whiskey
POTENCYnoun **POTENCIES** strength or effectiveness, eg of a drug
POTENTadj strong; effective; powerful
POTENTATEnoun **POTENTATES** a powerful ruler; a monarch
POTENTIALadj possible or likely, though as yet not tested or actual ◻ noun **POTENTIALS** the range of capabilities that someone or something has; powers or resources not yet developed or made use of
POTFULnoun **POTFULS** the amount a pot can hold
POTHERnoun **POTHERS** a fuss or commotion ◻ verb **POTHERS, POTHERING, POTHERED** to be, or make someone, flustered or upset
POTIONnoun **POTIONS** a draught of medicine, poison or some magic elixir
POTLATCHnoun **POTLATCHES** a

winter festival held by some Native American peoples, in which there is competitive and extravagant gift-giving, to demonstrate the status of the chief
POTOROOnoun **POTOROOS** a small marsupial related to the kangaroo, with a stocky body and long hindlegs
POTPOURRInoun **POTPOURRIS** a fragrant mixture of dried flowers, leaves, etc placed in containers and used to scent rooms
POTSHERDnoun **POTSHERDS** a fragment of pottery
POTTAGEnoun **POTTAGES** a thick soup
POTTEDadj abridged, especially in order to give a simplified version
POTTER[1]noun **POTTERS** someone who makes pottery
POTTER[2]verb **POTTERS, POTTERING, POTTERED** to busy oneself in a mild way with trifling tasks
POTTERERnoun **POTTERERS** someone who potters
POTTERYnoun **POTTERIES** containers, pots or other objects of baked clay
POTTINESSnoun **POTTINESSES** the state of being potty
POTTOnoun **POTTOS** a slow-moving lemur-like primate that lives in the equatorial forests of W Africa
POTTY[1]adj **POTTIER, POTTIEST** mad; crazy
POTTY[2]noun **POTTIES** a child's chamberpot
POUCHnoun **POUCHES** a purse or small bag ◻ verb **POUCHES, POUCHING, POUCHED** to form, or form into, a pouch
POUCHYadj **POUCHIER, POUCHIEST** of or like a pouch
POUFnoun **POUFS** a pouffe
POUFFEnoun **POUFFES** a firmly stuffed drum-shaped or cube-shaped cushion for use as a low seat
POULARDnoun **POULARDS** a female hen that has been spayed and fattened for eating
POULTnoun **POULTS** a young domestic fowl or game bird, eg a young chicken, turkey, pheasant, etc
POULTERERnoun **POULTERERS** a dealer in poultry and game
POULTICEnoun **POULTICES** a hot, semi-liquid mixture spread on a bandage and applied to the skin to

POULTRY *noun* **POULTRIES** domesticated birds kept for their eggs or meat, or both, eg chickens, ducks, turkeys, geese, etc

POUNCE *verb* **POUNCES, POUNCING, POUNCED** to leap or swoop suddenly in an attempt to attack or seize ◻ *noun* **POUNCES** an act of pouncing

POUND [1] *noun* **POUNDS** the standard unit of currency of the UK (symbol £); a measure of weight equal to 16 ounces

POUND [2] *verb* **POUNDS, POUNDING, POUNDED** to beat or bang something vigorously

POUNDAGE *noun* **POUNDAGES** a fee or commission charged per pound in weight or money

POUNDAL *noun* **POUNDALS** a unit of force that is equivalent to the force required to make a mass weighing one pound accelerate by one foot per second per second

POUR *verb* **POURS, POURING, POURED** to flow or cause something to flow in a downward stream

POURBOIRE *noun* **POURBOIRES** a tip or gratuity

POURER *noun* **POURERS** a person or thing that pours

POUSSIN *noun* **POUSSINS** a young chicken reared for eating at the age of four to six weeks

POUT *verb* **POUTS, POUTING, POUTED** to push the lower lip or both lips forward as an indication of sulkiness or seductiveness ◻ *noun* **POUTS** an act of pouting

POUTER *noun* **POUTERS** a person or thing that pouts

POUTINGLY *adverb* with a pout

POUTY *adj* **POUTIER, POUTIEST** inclined to pout; sulky

POVERTY *noun* **POVERTIES** the condition of being poor; want

POW *noun* **POWS** a Scots word for *head*

POWDER *noun* **POWDERS** any substance in the form of fine dust-like particles ◻ *verb* **POWDERS, POWDERING, POWDERED** to apply powder to (eg one's face); to sprinkle or cover something with powder

POWDERY *adj* **POWDERIER, POWDERIEST** having the consistency or nature of powder; powderlike

POWER *noun* **POWERS** control and influence exercised over others; any form of energy ◻ *verb* **POWERS, POWERING, POWERED** to supply something with power

POWERFUL *adj* having great power, strength or vigour

POWERLESS *adj* deprived of power or authority

POWWOW *noun* **POWWOWS** a meeting for discussion ◻ *verb* **POWWOWS, POWWOWING, POWWOWED** to hold a powwow

POX *noun* **POXES** any of various infectious viral diseases that cause a skin rash consisting of pimples containing pus ◻ *verb* **POXES, POXING, POXED** to infect with pox

POXY *adj* **POXIER, POXIEST** worthless, second-rate, trashy

POZ *adj* old short form of *positive*

PRACTICAL *adj* concerned with or involving action rather than theory ◻ *noun* **PRACTICALS** a practical lesson or examination, eg in a scientific subject

PRACTICE *noun* **PRACTICES** the process of carrying something out

PRACTISE *verb* **PRACTISES, PRACTISING, PRACTISED** to do exercises repeatedly in (an art or sport, etc) so as to improve one's performance

PRACTISED *adj* skilled; experienced

PRACTISING *adj* actively engaged in or currently pursuing or observing

PRAENOMEN *noun* **PRAENOMENS** in Roman history: someone's first or personal name, eg 'Gaius' in 'Gaius Julius Caesar'

PRAETOR *noun* **PRAETORS** in Roman history: one of the chief law officers of the state, elected annually, and second to the consul in importance

PRAGMATIC *adj* concerned with what is practicable, expedient and convenient, rather than with theories and ideals; matter-of-fact; realistic

PRAGMATICS *singular noun* the branch of linguistic study that deals with how language is used, especially the factors that influence people's choice of words

PRAHU *noun* **PRAHUS** a proa

PRAIRIE *noun* **PRAIRIES** in N America: a large expanse of flat or rolling natural grassland, usually without trees

PRAISE *verb* **PRAISES, PRAISING, PRAISED** to express admiration or approval of someone or something ◻ *noun* the expression of admiration or approval; commendation

PRALINE *noun* **PRALINES** a sweet consisting of nuts in caramelized sugar

PRAM *noun* **PRAMS** a wheeled baby carriage pushed by someone on foot

PRANA *noun* **PRANAS** breath as the essential life force

PRANCE *verb* **PRANCES, PRANCING, PRANCED** said especially of a horse: to walk with lively springing steps

PRANDIAL *adj* belonging or relating to dinner

PRANG *verb* **PRANGS, PRANGING, PRANGED** to crash (a vehicle) ◻ *noun* **PRANGS** a vehicle crash

PRANK *noun* **PRANKS** a playful trick; a practical joke

PRANKSTER *noun* **PRANKSTERS** someone who plays tricks and practical jokes

PRATE *verb* **PRATES, PRATING, PRATED** to talk or utter foolishly; to blab ◻ *noun* idle chatter

PRATFALL *noun* **PRATFALLS** a ridiculous tumble in which someone, especially a clown or comedian, lands on their bottom

PRATTLE *verb* **PRATTLES, PRATTLING, PRATTLED** to chatter or utter childishly or foolishly ◻ *noun* **PRATTLES** childish or foolish chatter

PRATTLER *noun* **PRATTLERS** someone who chatters childishly or foolishly

PRAU *noun* **PRAUS** a proa

PRAWN *noun* **PRAWNS** any of various small edible shrimp-like marine crustaceans with long tail fans, which are almost transparent when alive but pinkish-orange when cooked

PRAXIS *noun* **PRAXES** practice as opposed to theory

PRAY *verb* **PRAYS, PRAYING, PRAYED** to address one's god, making earnest requests or giving thanks

PRAYER *noun* **PRAYERS** an address to one's god, making a request or giving thanks

PRAYERFUL *adj* said of someone: devout; tending to pray a lot or often

PRE *prep* colloquial word meaning *before*

PREACH *verb* **PREACHES, PREACHING, PREACHED** to deliver (a sermon) as part of a religious service **PREACHER** *noun* **PREACHERS** someone who preaches, especially a minister of religion **PREACHY** *adj* **PREACHIER, PREACHIEST** said of someone, their attitude, speech, etc: tending to be moralistic **PREAMBLE** *noun* **PREAMBLES** an introduction or preface, eg to a speech or document; an opening statement **PREBEND** *noun* **PREBENDS** an allowance paid out of the revenues of a cathedral or collegiate church to its canons or chapter members **PREBENDAL** *adj* of or relating to a prebend **PRECAST** *adj* said of concrete, etc: made into blocks, before being put into position **PRECEDE** *verb* **PRECEDES, PRECEDING, PRECEDED** to go or be before someone or something, in time, order, position, rank or importance **PRECEDENT** *noun* **PRECEDENTS** a previous incident or legal case, etc that has something in common with the one under consideration, serving as a basis for a decision in the present one **PRECEDING** *adj* going before in time, position, etc; previous **PRECENTOR** *noun* **PRECENTORS** someone who leads the singing of a church congregation, or the prayers in a synagogue **PRECEPT** *noun* **PRECEPTS** a rule or principle, especially one of a moral kind, that is seen or used as a guide to behaviour **PRECEPTOR** *noun* **PRECEPTORS** a teacher or instructor **PRECINCT** *noun* **PRECINCTS** the enclosed grounds of a large building, etc **PRECIOUS** *adj* valuable **PRECIPICE** *noun* **PRECIPICES** a steep, vertical or overhanging cliff or rock face **PRÉCIS** *noun* **PRÉCIS** a summary of a piece of writing ❑ *verb* **PRÉCISES, PRÉCISING, PRÉCISED** to make a précis of something **PRECISE** *adj* exact; very

PRECISELY *adverb* in a precise manner **PRECISION** *noun* **PRECISIONS** accuracy **PRECLUDE** *verb* **PRECLUDES, PRECLUDING, PRECLUDED** to rule out or eliminate something or make it impossible **PRECOCIAL** *adj* said of the newly-hatched young of certain birds: covered with feathers and able to see, and so able to leave the nest relatively soon after hatching **PRECOCITY** *noun* **PRECOCITIES** the state or condition or quality of being advanced in mental development, or in speech or behaviour **PRECONISE** *verb* **PRECONISES, PRECONISING, PRECONISED** to preconize **PRECONIZE** *verb* **PRECONIZES, PRECONIZING, PRECONIZED** to proclaim something publicly **PRECURSOR** *noun* **PRECURSORS** something that precedes, and is a sign of, an approaching event **PREDATE** *verb* **PREDATES, PREDATING, PREDATED** to write an earlier date on (a document, cheque, etc) **PREDATION** *noun* **PREDATIONS** the killing and consuming of other animals for survival; the activity of preying **PREDATOR** *noun* **PREDATORS** any, animal that obtains food by catching, usually killing, and eating other animals **PREDATORY** *adj* said of an animal: obtaining food by catching and eating other animals **PREDELLA** *noun* **PREDELLAS** a small painting or panel enclosed in a compartment attached to the lower edge of an altarpiece, especially one that illustrates scenes from the life of the saint represented in the main panel **PREDICATE** *noun* **PREDICATES** the word or words in a sentence that make a statement about the subject, usually consisting of a verb and its complement, eg *ran* in *John ran* and *knew exactly what to do* in *The people in charge knew exactly what to do* ❑ *verb* **PREDICATES, PREDICATING, PREDICATED** to assert **PREDICT** *verb* **PREDICTS, PREDICTING, PREDICTED** to prophesy, foretell or forecast **PREDIGEST** *verb* **PREDIGESTS,**

PREDIGESTING, PREDIGESTED to digest (food) artificially before introducing it into the body **PREDIKANT** *noun* **PREDIKANTS** a minister in the Dutch Reformed Church, especially in S Africa **PREEN** *verb* **PREENS, PREENING, PREENED** said of a bird: to clean and smooth (feathers, etc) with its beak **PREFAB** *noun* **PREFABS** a prefabricated building, especially a domestic house **PREFACE** *noun* **PREFACES** an explanatory statement at the beginning of a book ❑ *verb* **PREFACES, PREFACING, PREFACED** to provide (a book, etc) with a preface **PREFATORY** *adj* relating to a preface **PREFECT** *noun* **PREFECTS** in a school: a senior pupil with minor disciplinary powers **PREFER** *verb* **PREFERS, PREFERRING, PREFERRED** to like someone or something better than another **PREFIGURE** *verb* **PREFIGURES, PREFIGURING, PREFIGURED** to be an advance sign or representation of something that is to come; to foreshadow **PREFIX** *noun* **PREFIXES** an element such as *un-, pre-, non-, de-*, etc which is added to the beginning of a word to create a new word ❑ *verb* **PREFIXES, PREFIXING, PREFIXED** to add something as an introduction **PREGGERS** *adj* pregnant **PREGNABLE** *adj* capable of being taken by force; vulnerable **PREGNANCY** *noun* **PREGNANCIES** in female mammals, including humans: the period between fertilization or conception and birth, during which a developing embryo is carried in the womb **PREGNANT** *adj* said of a female mammal, including humans: carrying a child or young in the womb **PREHEAT** *verb* **PREHEATS, PREHEATING, PREHEATED** to heat (an oven, furnace, etc) before use **PREJUDGE** *verb* **PREJUDGES, PREJUDGING, PREJUDGED** to form an opinion on (an issue, etc) without having all the relevant facts **PREJUDICE** *noun* **PREJUDICES** a biased opinion, based on

insufficient knowledge ❑ *verb*
PREJUDICES, PREJUDICING, PREJUDICED to make someone feel prejudice; to bias

PRELACY *noun* **PRELACIES** the office of a prelate

PRELATE *noun* **PRELATES** a bishop, abbot or other high-ranking ecclesiastic

PRELATIC *adj* of or relating to a prelate

PRELIM *noun* **PRELIMS** in Scotland: any one of a set of school examinations taken before the public ones

PRELUDE *noun* **PRELUDES** an introductory passage or first movement, eg of a fugue or suite ❑ *verb* **PRELUDES, PRELUDING, PRELUDED** to act as a prelude to something

PRELUSIVE *adj* of the nature of a prelude

PREMATURE *adj* said of human birth: occurring less than 37 weeks after conception

PREMED *noun* **PREMEDS** drugs given to sedate and prepare a patient, especially for the administration of a general anaesthetic before surgery

PREMIER *noun* **PREMIERS** a prime minister

PREMIÈRE *noun* **PREMIÈRES** the first public performance of a play or showing of a film ❑ *verb* **PREMIÈRES, PREMIÈRING, PREMIÈRED** to present a première of (a film, etc)

PREMISE *noun* **PREMISES** something assumed to be true as a basis for stating something further ❑ *verb* **PREMISES, PREMISING, PREMISED** to assume or state as a premise

PREMISES *plural noun* a building and its grounds, especially as a place of business

PREMIUM *noun* **PREMIUMS, PREMIA** an amount paid, usually annually, on an insurance agreement

PREMOLAR *noun* **PREMOLARS** any of the teeth between the canine teeth and the molars

PRENATAL *adj* before birth

PREOCCUPIED *adj* lost in thought

PREOCCUPY *verb* **PREOCCUPIES, PREOCCUPYING, PREOCCUPIED** to occupy the attention of someone wholly; to engross or obsess

PREORDAIN *verb* **PREORDAINS, PREORDAINING, PREORDAINED**

to decide or determine beforehand

PREP *verb* **PREPS, PREPPING, PREPPED** to get (a patient) ready for an operation, etc, especially by giving a sedative

PREPACK *verb* **PREPACKS, PREPACKING, PREPACKED** to pack (food, etc) before offering it for sale

PREPAID *adj* paid for in advance

PREPARE *verb* **PREPARES, PREPARING, PREPARED** to make or get ready

PREPARED *adj* said of a person: willing and able

PREPAY *verb* **PREPAYS, PREPAYING, PREPAID** to pay for something, especially postage, in advance

PREPENSE *adj* premeditated; intentional

PREPOTENT *adj* powerfully more influential than others

PREPPY *adj* **PREPPIER, PREPPIEST** said of dress sense, etc: neat and conservative ❑ *noun* **PREPPIES** someone who dresses in such a way

PREPUCE *noun* **PREPUCES** the fold of skin that covers the top of the penis

PREQUEL *noun* **PREQUELS** a book or film produced after one that has been a popular success, but with the story beginning prior to the start of the original story

PRERECORD *verb* **PRERECORDS, PRERECORDING, PRERECORDED** to record (a programme for radio or TV) in advance of its scheduled broadcasting time

PRESAGE *verb* **PRESAGES, PRESAGING, PRESAGED** to warn of or be a warning sign of something; to foreshadow, forebode or portend ❑ *noun* **PRESAGES** a portent, warning or omen

PRESAGER *noun* **PRESAGERS** a person or thing that is or gives a warning sign

PRESBYTER *noun* **PRESBYTERS** in the early Christian church: an administrative official with some teaching and priestly duties

PRESCHOOL *adj* denoting or relating to children before they are old enough to attend school

PRESCIENT *adj* having foresight

PRESCRIBE *verb* **PRESCRIBES, PRESCRIBING, PRESCRIBED** said especially of a doctor: to advise (a

medicine) as a remedy, especially by completing a prescription

PRESCRIPT *noun* **PRESCRIPTS** a law, rule, principle, etc that has been laid down

PRESENCE *noun* **PRESENCES** the state or circumstance of being present

PRESENT [1] *adj* being at the place or occasion in question

PRESENT [2] *noun* **PRESENTS** something given; a gift

PRESENT [3] *verb* **PRESENTS, PRESENTING, PRESENTED** to give or award something, especially formally or ceremonially

PRESENTER *noun* **PRESENTERS** someone who introduces a programme and provides a linking commentary between items

PRESENTLY *adverb* soon; shortly

PRESERVE *verb* **PRESERVES, PRESERVING, PRESERVED** to save something from loss, damage, decay or deterioration ❑ *noun* **PRESERVES** an area of work or activity that is restricted to certain people

PRESERVER *noun* **PRESERVERS** a person or thing that preserves

PRESET *verb* **PRESETS, PRESETTING, PRESET** to adjust (a piece of electronic equipment, etc) so that it will operate at the required time

PRESIDE *verb* **PRESIDES, PRESIDING, PRESIDED** to take the lead at (an event), the chair at (a meeting, etc); to be in charge

PRESIDENT *noun* **PRESIDENTS** the elected head of state in a republic

PRESIDIUM *noun* **PRESIDIUMS, PRESIDIA** in a Communist state: a standing executive committee

PRESS *verb* **PRESSES, PRESSING, PRESSED** to push steadily, especially with the finger; to flatten or squash ❑ *noun* **PRESSES** any apparatus for pressing, flattening, squeezing, etc

PRESSED *adj* said of a person: under pressure; in a hurry

PRESSIE *noun* **PRESSIES** a present or gift

PRESSING *noun* **PRESSINGS** in the music industry: a number of records produced from a single mould

PRESSMAN *noun* **PRESSMEN** a journalist or reporter

PRESSURE *noun* **PRESSURES** the force exerted on a surface divided by the area of the surface to which it is applied ◻ verb **PRESSURES, PRESSURING, PRESSURED** to try to persuade; to coerce, force or pressurize

PRESTIGEnoun **PRESTIGES** fame, distinction or reputation due to rank or success

PRESTO adverb in a very fast manner ◻ adj very fast ◻ noun **PRESTOS** a piece of music to be played in this way

PRESUMEverb **PRESUMES, PRESUMING, PRESUMED** to suppose (something to be the case) without proof; to take something for granted

PRETENCEnoun **PRETENCES** the act of pretending

PRETENDverb **PRETENDS, PRETENDING, PRETENDED** to make believe; to act as if, or give the impression that, something is the case when it is not

PRETENDERnoun **PRETENDERS** someone who pretends or pretended to something, especially the throne

PRETENSEnoun **PRETENSES** pretence

PRETERITEnoun **PRETERITES** a verb tense that expresses past action, eg *hit, moved, ran*

PRETERMadj born or occurring before the end of the normal length of a pregnancy

PRETEXTnoun **PRETEXTS** a false reason given for doing something in order to disguise the real one; an excuse

PRETTIFYverb **PRETTIFIES, PRETTIFYING, PRETTIFIED** to attempt to make something or someone prettier by superficial ornamentation

PRETTILYadverb in a pretty way

PRETTYadj **PRETTIER, PRETTIEST** usually said of a woman or girl: facially attractive, especially in a feminine way

PRETZELnoun **PRETZELS** a crisp salted biscuit in the shape of a knot

PREVAILverb **PREVAILS, PREVAILING, PREVAILED** to be victorious; to win through

PREVAILINGadj most common or frequent

PREVALENTadj common; widespread

PREVENTverb **PREVENTS, PREVENTING, PREVENTED** to stop someone from doing something, or something from happening; to hinder

PREVIEWnoun **PREVIEWS** an advance view ◻ verb **PREVIEWS, PREVIEWING, PREVIEWED** to show or view (a film, etc) in advance to a select audience

PREVIOUSadj earlier; former; prior

PREYsingular or plural noun **PREYS** an animal or animals hunted as food by another animal ◻ verb **PREYS, PREYING, PREYED** said of an animal: to hunt or catch (another animal) as food

PREZZIEnoun **PREZZIES** a pressie

PRIALnoun **PRIALS** a set of three cards of the same denomination, eg three queens, three sixes, etc

PRIAPISMnoun **PRIAPISMS** persistent abnormal erection of the penis, which may be a symptom of spinal injury, or of various diseases and disorders

PRICEnoun **PRICES** the amount, usually in money, for which a thing is sold or offered ◻ verb **PRICES, PRICING, PRICED** to fix a price for or mark a price on something

PRICELESSadj too valuable to have a price; inestimably precious

PRICEYadj **PRICIER, PRICIEST** expensive

PRICKverb **PRICKS, PRICKING, PRICKED** to pierce slightly with a fine point ◻ noun **PRICKS** an act of pricking or feeling of being pricked

PRICKLEnoun **PRICKLES** a hard pointed structure growing from the surface of a plant or animal ◻ verb **PRICKLES, PRICKLING, PRICKLED** to cause, affect something with or be affected with, a pricking sensation

PRICKLYadj **PRICKLIER, PRICKLIEST** covered with or full of prickles

PRICYadj **PRICIER, PRICIEST** pricey

PRIDEnoun **PRIDES** a feeling of pleasure and satisfaction at one's own or another's accomplishments, possessions, etc ◻ verb **PRIDES, PRIDING, PRIDED** to congratulate oneself on account of something

PRIED past form of **pry**

PRIES a form of **pry**

PRIESTnoun **PRIESTS** in the Roman Catholic and Orthodox churches: an ordained minister authorized to administer the sacraments

PRIESTESSnoun **PRIESTESSES**

in non-Christian religions: a female priest

PRIESTLYadj **PRIESTLIER, PRIESTLIEST** of or relating to a priest or the priesthood

PRIGnoun **PRIGS** someone who is self-righteously moralistic

PRIGGERYnoun **PRIGGERIES** the state or condition or quality of being a prig

PRIGGISHadj of or like a prig; self-righteous; moralistic

PRIMadj **PRIMMER, PRIMMEST** stiffly formal, over-modest or over-proper ◻ verb **PRIMS, PRIMMING, PRIMMED** to purse (the mouth, lips, etc) into an expression of primness

PRIMACYnoun **PRIMACIES** the condition of being first in rank, importance or order

PRIMAEVALadj primeval

PRIMALadj relating to the beginnings of life; original

PRIMARILYadverb chiefly; mainly

PRIMARYadj first or most important; principal ◻ noun **PRIMARIES** a school for pupils aged from 5 to 11

PRIMATEnoun **PRIMATES** any member of an order of mammalian vertebrates which have a large brain, forward-facing eyes, nails instead of claws, and hands with grasping thumbs facing the other digits, eg a human, ape, etc

PRIMEadj chief; fundamental ◻ noun **PRIMES** the best, most productive or active stage in the life of a person or thing ◻ verb **PRIMES, PRIMING, PRIMED** to prepare something (eg wood for painting) by applying a sealing coat of size, etc, (a gun or explosive device for firing or detonating) by inserting the igniting material, or (a pump for use) by filling it with water, etc

PRIMERnoun **PRIMERS** any material that is used to provide an initial coating for a surface before it is painted

PRIMEVALadj relating or belonging to the Earth's beginnings

PRIMIPARAnoun **PRIMIPARAS, PRIMIPARAE** a woman who has given birth for the first time or is about to do so

PRIMITIVEadj relating or belonging to earliest times or the earliest stages of development

❑ noun **PRIMITIVES** an unsophisticated person or thing

PRIMLY adverb in a prim way

PRIMMER see under **prim**

PRIMMEST see under **prim**

PRIMNESS noun **PRIMNESSES** the state or condition or quality of being prim

PRIMO noun **PRIMOS** the upper or right-hand part in a piano duet

PRIMP verb **PRIMPS, PRIMPING, PRIMPED** to groom, preen or titivate

PRIMROSE noun **PRIMROSES** a small perennial plant with a rosette of oval leaves, and long-stalked flowers with five pale yellow or (occasionally) pink petals

PRIMULA noun **PRIMULAS** any of various temperate plants with white, pink, purple or yellow flowers with five spreading petals, including the primrose

PRINCE noun **PRINCES** in the UK: the son of a sovereign

PRINCEDOM noun **PRINCEDOMS** the estate, jurisdiction, sovereignty or rank of a prince

PRINCELY adj **PRINCELIER, PRINCELIEST** characteristic of or suitable for a prince

PRINCESS noun **PRINCESSES** the wife or daughter of a prince

PRINCIPAL adj first in rank or importance; chief; main ❑ noun **PRINCIPALS** the head of an educational institution

PRINCIPLE noun **PRINCIPLES** a general truth or assumption from which to argue

PRINCIPLED adj holding, or proceeding from principles, especially high moral principles

PRINK verb **PRINKS, PRINKING, PRINKED** to dress (oneself) up; to smarten (oneself) up

PRINT verb **PRINTS, PRINTING, PRINTED** to reproduce (text or pictures) on paper with ink, using a printing-press or other mechanical means ❑ noun **PRINTS** a mark made on a surface by the pressure of something in contact with it

PRINTABLE adj capable of being printed

PRINTER noun **PRINTERS** a person or business engaged in printing books, newspapers, etc

PRINTING noun **PRINTINGS** the art or business of producing books, etc in print

PRINTOUT noun **PRINTOUTS** output from a computer system in the form of a printed paper copy

PRIOR [1] adj said of an engagement: already arranged for the time in question; previous

PRIOR [2] noun **PRIORS** the head of a community of certain orders of monks and friars

PRIORESS noun **PRIORESSES** the head of a priory of nuns

PRIORITY noun **PRIORITIES** the right to be or go first; precedence or preference

PRIORY noun **PRIORIES** a religious house under the supervision of a prior or prioress

PRISE verb **PRISES, PRISING, PRISED** to lever something open, off, out, etc, usually with some difficulty

PRISM noun **PRISMS** a solid figure in which the two ends are matching parallel polygons (eg triangles or squares) and all other surfaces are parallelograms

PRISMATIC adj produced by or relating to a prism

PRISON noun **PRISONS** a building for the confinement of convicted criminals and certain accused persons awaiting trial

PRISONER noun **PRISONERS** someone who is under arrest or confined in prison

PRISSY adj **PRISSIER, PRISSIEST** insipidly prim and prudish

PRISTINE adj fresh, clean, unused or untouched

PRIVACY noun **PRIVACIES** freedom from intrusion by the public, especially as a right

PRIVATE adj **PRIVATER, PRIVATEST** not open to, or available for the use of, the general public ❑ noun **PRIVATES** a soldier, not an officer or NCO

PRIVATEER noun **PRIVATEERS** a privately owned ship engaged by a government to seize and plunder an enemy's ships in wartime

PRIVATELY adverb in a private way; not in public

PRIVATION noun **PRIVATIONS** the condition of not having, or being deprived of, life's comforts or necessities

PRIVATISE verb **PRIVATISES, PRIVATISING, PRIVATISED** to privatize

PRIVATIVE adj lacking some quality that is usually, or expected to be, present

PRIVATIZE verb **PRIVATIZES, PRIVATIZING, PRIVATIZED** to transfer (a state-owned business) to private ownership

PRIVET noun **PRIVETS** any of various evergreen or deciduous shrubs with glossy lance-shaped dark-green leaves and strongly scented creamy-white flowers, used especially in garden hedges

PRIVILEGE noun **PRIVILEGES** a right granted to an individual or a select few, bestowing an advantage not enjoyed by others ❑ verb **PRIVILEGES, PRIVILEGING, PRIVILEGED** to grant a right, privilege or special favour to someone or something

PRIVILEGED adj enjoying the advantages of wealth and class

PRIVILY adverb privately; secretly

PRIVITY noun **PRIVITIES** a legally recognized relationship between two parties, eg in a contract, lease, etc

PRIVY noun **PRIVIES** a lavatory

PRIZE noun **PRIZES** something won in a competition, lottery, etc ❑ verb **PRIZES, PRIZING, PRIZED** to value or regard highly

PRO prep in favour of something ❑ noun **PROS** a reason, argument or choice in favour of something ❑ adverb in favour

PROA noun **PROAS** a Malay sailing- or rowing-boat, especially a fast one with a large triangular sail and an outrigger kept to the leeward side

PROACTIVE adj actively initiating change in anticipation of future developments, rather than merely reacting to events as they occur

PROB noun **PROBS** a problem

PROBABLE adj likely to happen ❑ noun **PROBABLES** someone or something likely to be selected

PROBABLY adverb almost certainly; in all likelihood

PROBAND noun **PROBANDS** someone who is regarded as the starting point for an investigation of the inheritance of a particular disease or disorder within a family

PROBANG noun **PROBANGS** an instrument consisting of a flexible rod with a piece of sponge at the end, which is inserted into the oesophagus so as to apply medication or remove an obstruction

PROBATE noun **PROBATES** the process of establishing that a will is valid

PROBATION noun **PROBATIONS** the system whereby offenders, especially young or first offenders, are allowed their freedom under supervision, on condition of good behaviour

PROBE noun **PROBES** a long, slender and usually metal instrument used by doctors to examine a wound, locate a bullet, etc ◻ verb **PROBES, PROBING, PROBED** to investigate something closely

PROBITY noun **PROBITIES** integrity; honesty

PROBLEM noun **PROBLEMS** a situation or matter that is difficult to understand or deal with

PROBOSCIS noun **PROBOSCISES, PROBOSCIDES** the flexible elongated snout of the elephant or tapir

PROCAINE noun **PROCAINES** a colourless crystalline substance used as a local anaesthetic

PROCEDURE noun **PROCEDURES** the method and order followed in doing something

PROCEED verb **PROCEEDS, PROCEEDING, PROCEEDED** to make one's way

PROCEEDING noun **PROCEEDINGS** an action; a piece of behaviour

PROCEEDS plural noun money made by an event, sale, transaction, etc

PROCESS noun **PROCESSES** a series of operations performed during manufacture, etc ◻ verb **PROCESSES, PROCESSING, PROCESSED** to put something through the required process; to deal with (eg an application) appropriately

PROCESSOR noun **PROCESSORS** a machine or person that processes something

PROCLAIM verb **PROCLAIMS, PROCLAIMING, PROCLAIMED** to announce something publicly

PROCLITIC adj said of a word: closely attached to the following word and forming a single sound unit with it

PROCONSUL noun **PROCONSULS** a governor or military commander in a province

PROCREANT noun **PROCREANTS** a person who produces offspring

PROCREATE verb **PROCREATES, PROCREATING, PROCREATED** to produce (offspring); to reproduce

PROCTOR noun **PROCTORS** in some English universities: an official whose functions include enforcement of discipline

PROCURACY noun **PROCURACIES** the office of procurator, an agent with power of attorney in a law court

PROCURE verb **PROCURES, PROCURING, PROCURED** to manage to obtain something or bring it about

PROCURER noun **PROCURERS** a person who provides prostitutes for clients

PROCURESS noun **PROCURESSES** a woman who provides prostitutes for clients

PROD verb **PRODS, PRODDING, PRODDED** to poke or jab something ◻ noun **PRODS** a poke, jab or nudge

PRODIGAL adj heedlessly extravagant or wasteful ◻ noun **PRODIGALS** a squanderer, wastrel or spendthrift

PRODIGY noun **PRODIGIES** something that causes astonishment; a wonder; an extraordinary phenomenon

PRODUCE verb **PRODUCES, PRODUCING, PRODUCED** to make or manufacture something ◻ noun **PRODUCES** foodstuffs derived from crops or animal livestock, eg fruit, vegetables, eggs and dairy products

PRODUCER noun **PRODUCERS** a person, organization or thing that produces

PRODUCT noun **PRODUCTS** something produced, eg through manufacture or agriculture

PROEM noun **PROEMS** an introduction, prelude or preface, especially at the beginning of a book

PROF noun **PROFS** a professor

PROFANE adj showing disrespect for sacred things; irreverent ◻ verb **PROFANES, PROFANING, PROFANED** to treat (something sacred) irreverently

PROFANELY adverb irreverently

PROFANITY noun **PROFANITIES** blasphemous language; a blasphemy, swear word, oath, etc

PROFESS verb **PROFESSES, PROFESSING, PROFESSED** to make an open declaration of (beliefs, etc)

PROFESSED adj self-acknowledged; self-confessed

PROFESSOR noun **PROFESSORS** a teacher of the highest rank in a university; the head of a university department

PROFFER verb **PROFFERS, PROFFERING, PROFFERED** to offer something for someone to accept; to tender ◻ noun **PROFFERS** the act of proffering; an offer

PROFILE noun **PROFILES** a side view of something, especially of a face or head ◻ verb **PROFILES, PROFILING, PROFILED** to represent in profile

PROFIT noun **PROFITS** the money gained from selling something for more than it originally cost ◻ verb **PROFITS, PROFITING, PROFITED** to benefit from something

PROFITEER noun **PROFITEERS** someone who takes advantage of a shortage or other emergency to make exorbitant profits ◻ verb **PROFITEERS, PROFITEEING, PROFITEERED** to make excessive profits in such a way

PROFOUND adj **PROFOUNDER, PROFOUNDEST** radical, extensive, far-reaching

PROFUSE adj overflowing; exaggerated; excessive

PROFUSELY adverb in a profuse way; liberally

PROFUSION noun **PROFUSIONS** the state or condition or quality of being profuse; a great amount or extravagance

PROGENY noun **PROGENIES** children; offspring; descendants

PROGESTIN noun **PROGESTINS** any of a range of hormones of the progesterone type

PROGNOSIS noun **PROGNOSES** an informed forecast of developments in any situation

PROGRAM noun **PROGRAMS** a programme ◻ verb **PROGRAMS, PROGRAMMING, PROGRAMMED** to programme

PROGRAMME noun **PROGRAMMES** the schedule of proceedings for, and list of participants in, a theatre performance, entertainment, ceremony, etc ◻ verb **PROGRAMMES, PROGRAMMING, PROGRAMMED** to include something in a programme; to schedule

PROGRESS noun **PROGRESSES** movement while travelling in any direction ◻ verb **PROGRESSES,**

PROGRESSING, PROGRESSED to move forwards or onwards; to proceed towards a goal

PROHIBIT verb **PROHIBITS, PROHIBITING, PROHIBITED** to forbid something, especially by law; to ban

PROJECT noun **PROJECTS** a plan, scheme or proposal □ verb **PROJECTS, PROJECTING, PROJECTED** to jut out; to protrude

PROJECTOR noun **PROJECTORS** an instrument containing a system of lenses that projects an enlarged version of an illuminated still or moving image on to a screen

PROLACTIN noun **PROLACTINS** a hormone, secreted by the pituitary gland, which initiates lactation in mammals, and stimulates the production of progesterone

PROLAPSE noun **PROLAPSES** the slipping out of place or falling down of an organ or other body part, especially the slipping of the uterus into the vagina □ verb **PROLAPSES, PROLAPSING, PROLAPSED** said of an organ: to slip out of place

PROLAPSUS noun **PROLAPSUSES** prolapse

PROLATE adj said of something approximately spherical: more pointed at the poles

PROLATELY adverb in a prolate way

PROLE noun **PROLES** proletarian

PROLEPSIS noun **PROLEPSES** a debating device that involves the speaker putting forward arguments or objections before they are raised by someone else in order to detract from their possible effects

PROLEPTIC adj of or relating to prolepsis

PROLIFIC adj abundant in growth; producing plentiful fruit or offspring

PROLINE noun **PROLINES** an amino acid that is found in proteins

PROLIX adj said of speech or writing: tediously long-winded; wordy; verbose

PROLIXITY noun **PROLIXITIES** the state or condition or quality of being prolix

PROLIXLY adverb in a prolix way

PROLOGUE noun **PROLOGUES** a speech addressed to the audience at the beginning of a play □ verb **PROLOGUES, PROLOGUING,**

PROLOGUED to introduce or preface something with a prologue

PROLONG verb **PROLONGS, PROLONGING, PROLONGED** to make something longer; to extend or protract

PROM noun **PROMS** a walkway or promenade

PROMENADE noun **PROMENADES** a broad paved walk, especially along a seafront □ verb **PROMENADES, PROMENADING, PROMENADED** to stroll in a stately fashion

PROMINENT adj jutting out; projecting; protruding; bulging

PROMISE verb **PROMISES, PROMISING, PROMISED** to give an undertaking (to do or not do something) □ noun **PROMISES** an assurance to give, do or not do something

PROMISEE noun **PROMISEES** the person to whom a promise is made

PROMISER noun **PROMISERS** the person who makes a promise

PROMISING adj showing promise; talented; apt

PROMISOR noun **PROMISORS** a person making a promise in law

PROMO noun **PROMOS** something which is used to publicize a product, especially a video for a pop single

PROMOTE verb **PROMOTES, PROMOTING, PROMOTED** to raise someone to a more senior position

PROMOTER noun **PROMOTERS** the organizer or financer of a sporting event or other undertaking

PROMOTION noun **PROMOTIONS** the state or condition or quality of being promoted to a more senior position

PROMPT adj **PROMPTER, PROMPTEST** immediate; quick; punctual □ adverb punctually □ noun **PROMPTS** something serving as a reminder □ verb **PROMPTS, PROMPTING, PROMPTED** to cause, lead or remind someone to do something

PROMPTER noun **PROMPTERS** someone positioned offstage to prompt actors if they forget their lines

PROMPTLY adverb immediately; quickly; punctually

PRONATOR noun **PRONATORS** a muscle in the forearm or forelimb that allows the hand or foot to face downwards

PRONE adj **PRONER, PRONEST** lying flat, especially face downwards; predisposed or liable to something

PRONELY adverb lying flat, especially face downwards

PRONENESS noun **PRONENESSES** the state or condition of lying flat, especially face downwards

PRONG noun **PRONGS** a point or spike, especially one of those making up the head of a fork □ verb **PRONGS, PRONGING, PRONGED** to stab or pierce something with or as with a prong

PRONGBUCK noun **PRONGBUCKS** a pronghorn

PRONGED adj said of a fork, etc: with a specified number of prongs or directions

PRONGHORN noun **PRONGHORNS** a N American antelope-like mammal with short horns in the female and prong-like backward curving horns in the male

PRONK verb **PRONKS, PRONKING, PRONKED** said of several hoofed mammals, eg the springbok: to leap repeatedly off the ground and land on all four legs simultaneously

PRONOUN noun **PRONOUNS** a word such as she, him, they, it, etc used in place of, and to refer to, a noun, phrase, clause, etc

PRONOUNCE verb **PRONOUNCES, PRONOUNCING, PRONOUNCED** to say or utter (words, sounds, letters, etc); to articulate or enunciate

PRONOUNCED adj noticeable; distinct

PRONTO adverb immediately

PROOF noun **PROOFS** evidence, especially conclusive evidence, that something is true or a fact □ verb **PROOFS, PROOFING, PROOFED** to make something resistant to or proof against a specified thing

PROP noun **PROPS** a rigid support, especially a vertical one, of any of various kinds □ verb **PROPS, PROPPING, PROPPED** to support or hold something upright with, or as if with, a prop

PROPAGATE verb **PROPAGATES, PROPAGATING, PROPAGATED** said of a plant: to multiply

PROPANE noun **PROPANES** a colourless odourless flammable gas, obtained from petroleum

PROPEL verb **PROPELS, PROPELLING, PROPELLED** to drive or push something forward
PROPELLER noun **PROPELLERS** a device consisting of a revolving hub with radiating blades that produce thrust or power, used to propel aircraft, ships, etc
PROPER adj **PROPERER, PROPEREST** real; genuine; able to be correctly described as (a specified thing)
PROPERLY adverb suitably; appropriately; correctly
PROPERTIED adj owning property, especially land
PROPERTY noun **PROPERTIES** something someone owns
PROPHASE noun **PROPHASES** in mitosis and meiosis: the first stage of cell division, during which the chromosomes coil, thicken and divide longitudinally to form chromatids, and the membrane surrounding the nucleus disintegrates
PROPHECY noun **PROPHECIES** the interpretation of divine will
PROPHESY verb **PROPHESIES, PROPHESYING, PROPHESIED** to foretell (future happenings); to predict
PROPHET noun **PROPHETS** someone who is able to express the will of God or a god
PROPHETIC adj foretelling the future
PROPONENT noun **PROPONENTS** a supporter or advocate of something; someone who argues in favour of their cause
PROPOSAL noun **PROPOSALS** the act of proposing something
PROPOSE verb **PROPOSES, PROPOSING, PROPOSED** to offer (a plan, etc) for consideration; to suggest
PROPOSER noun **PROPOSERS** someone who proposes or advocates something
PROPOUND verb **PROPOUNDS, PROPOUNDING, PROPOUNDED** to put forward (an idea or theory, etc) for consideration or discussion
PROPRIETY noun **PROPRIETIES** conformity to socially acceptable behaviour, especially between the sexes; modesty or decorum
PROPYL noun **PROPYLS** an alcohol radical
PROPYLON noun **PROPYLA** in classical architecture: a

monumental entrance gateway or vestibule, usually in front of a temple
PROROGUE verb **PROROGUES, PROROGUING, PROROGUED** to discontinue the meetings of (a legislative assembly) for a time, without dissolving it
PROSAIC adj unpoetic; unimaginative
PROSCRIBE verb **PROSCRIBES, PROSCRIBING, PROSCRIBED** to prohibit or condemn something (eg a practice)
PROSE noun **PROSES** the ordinary form of written or spoken language as distinct from verse or poetry
PROSECUTE verb **PROSECUTES, PROSECUTING, PROSECUTED** to bring a criminal action against someone
PROSELYTE noun **PROSELYTES** a convert, especially a Gentile turning to Judaism
PROSIER see under **prosy**
PROSIEST see under **prosy**
PROSIMIAN noun **PROSIMIANS** any of several primitive primates, eg the lemur, loris, tarsier, etc ◻ adj belonging or relating to these primates
PROSODIC adj of or relating to prosody
PROSODIST noun **PROSODISTS** someone skilled in prosody
PROSODY noun **PROSODIES** the study of verse-composition, especially poetic metre
PROSPECT noun **PROSPECTS** an expectation of something due or likely to happen ◻ verb **PROSPECTS, PROSPECTING, PROSPECTED** to search or explore (an area, region, etc) for gold or other minerals
PROSPER verb **PROSPERS, PROSPERING, PROSPERED** said of someone: to do well, especially financially
PROSTATE noun **PROSTATES** in male mammals: a muscular gland around the base of the bladder, controlled by sex hormones, which produces an alkaline fluid that activates sperm during ejaculation ◻ adj relating or belonging to the prostate gland
PROSTRATE adj lying face downwards in an attitude of abject submission, humility or adoration ◻ verb **PROSTRATES, PROSTRATING, PROSTRATED** to

throw (oneself) face down in submission or adoration
PROSTYLE noun **PROSTYLES** in classical architecture: a type of portico in front of a Greek temple, where the columns, never exceeding four in number, are set in front of the building
PROSY adj **PROSIER, PROSIEST** said of speech or writing: prose-like; dull and tedious
PROTASIS noun **PROTASES** the conditional clause of a conditional sentence, eg in *If Winter comes, can Spring be far behind?* the part before the comma is the protasis
PROTEA noun **PROTEAS** any of various evergreen shrubs and small trees which have large heads of flowers surrounded by colourful bracts
PROTEAN adj readily able to change shape or appearance; variable; changeable
PROTEASE noun **PROTEASES** any enzyme that catalyses the breakdown of proteins
PROTECT verb **PROTECTS, PROTECTING, PROTECTED** to shield someone or something from danger; to guard them or it against injury, destruction, etc; to keep safe
PROTECTOR noun **PROTECTORS** someone or something that protects
PROTÉGÉ noun **PROTÉGÉS** a person under the guidance, protection, tutelage, patronage, etc of someone wiser or more important
PROTÉGÉE noun **PROTÉGÉES** the feminine form of *protégé*
PROTEIN noun **PROTEINS** any of thousands of different organic compounds, characteristic of all living organisms, that have large molecules consisting of long chains of amino acids
PROTEST verb **PROTESTS, PROTESTING, PROTESTED** to express an objection, disapproval, opposition or disagreement ◻ noun **PROTESTS** a declaration of disapproval or dissent; an objection
PROTESTER noun **PROTESTERS** someone who protests against something
PROTESTOR noun **PROTESTORS** a protester
PROTHESIS noun **PROTHESES** the addition of a sound or syllable at

the beginning of a word, eg the Spanish 'escuela' meaning 'school' developed in this way from Latin 'schola'

PROTHETIC adj of or relating to prothesis

PROTIST noun **PROTISTS** any member of the kingdom of organisms Protista, including single-celled algae, bacteria, fungi, etc

PROTOCOL noun **PROTOCOLS** correct formal or diplomatic etiquette or procedure

PROTON noun **PROTONS** any of the positively charged subatomic particles that are found inside the nucleus at the centre of an atom

PROTOTYPE noun **PROTOTYPES** an original model from which later forms are copied, developed or derived

PROTOZOAL adj protozoan

PROTOZOAN noun **PROTOZOANS** a member of a phylum of single-celled organisms, the Protozoa, including both plant-like and animal-like forms, eg amoeba and disease-carrying parasites □ adj of or relating to protozoans

PROTRACT verb **PROTRACTS, PROTRACTING, PROTRACTED** to prolong; to cause something to last a long time

PROTRACTED adj lasting longer than usual or longer than expected

PROTRUDE verb **PROTRUDES, PROTRUDING, PROTRUDED** to project; to stick out

PROUD adj **PROUDER, PROUDEST** feeling satisfaction, delight, etc with one's own or another's accomplishments, possessions, etc

PROUDLY adverb in a proud way

PROUDNESS noun **PROUDNESSES** the state of being proud

PROVABLE adj able to be proved

PROVE verb **PROVES, PROVING, PROVED** to show something to be true, correct or a fact

PROVEABLE adj provable

PROVEN adj shown to be true, worthy, etc

PROVENDER noun **PROVENDERS** dry food for livestock, eg corn and hay

PROVERB noun **PROVERBS** any of a body of well-known neatly-expressed sayings that give advice or express a supposed truth

PROVIDE verb **PROVIDES, PROVIDING, PROVIDED** to supply

PROVIDED conj on the condition or understanding (that a specified thing happens, etc)

PROVIDENT adj having foresight and making provisions for the future

PROVIDER noun **PROVIDERS** someone who provides something

PROVIDING conj on the condition or understanding (that a specified thing happens, etc)

PROVINCE noun **PROVINCES** an administrative division of a country

PROVIRAL adj of or relating to proviruses

PROVIRUS noun **PROVIRUSES** the form of a virus when it is integrated into the DNA of a host cell

PROVISION noun **PROVISIONS** the act or process of providing □ verb **PROVISIONS, PROVISIONING, PROVISIONED** to supply (eg an army, country, boat) with food

PROVISO noun **PROVISOS, PROVISOES** a condition or stipulation

PROVISORY adj containing a proviso or condition; conditional

PROVOKE verb **PROVOKES, PROVOKING, PROVOKED** to annoy or infuriate someone, especially deliberately

PROVOKING adj annoying

PROVOST noun **PROVOSTS** the head of some university colleges

PROW noun **PROWS** the projecting front part of a ship; the bow

PROWESS noun **PROWESSES** skill; ability; expertise

PROWL verb **PROWLS, PROWLING, PROWLED** to go about stealthily, eg in search of prey □ noun **PROWLS** an act of prowling

PROWLER noun **PROWLERS** someone who prowls

PROXIMAL adj at the near, inner or attached end

PROXIMATE adj nearest

PROXIMITY noun **PROXIMITIES** nearness; closeness in space or time

PROXIMO adverb used mainly in formal correspondence: in or during the next month

PROXY noun **PROXIES** a person authorized to act or vote on another's behalf

PRUDE noun **PRUDES** someone who is, or affects to be, shocked by

improper behaviour, mention of sexual matters, etc; a prim or priggish person

PRUDENCE noun **PRUDENCES** careful or wise conduct or behaviour

PRUDENT adj wise or careful in conduct

PRUDENTLY adverb carefully; wisely

PRUDERY noun **PRUDERIES** the state or condition or quality of being prim or priggish

PRUDISH adj prim; priggish

PRUNE [1] verb **PRUNES, PRUNING, PRUNED** to cut off (branches, etc) from (a tree or shrub) in order to stimulate its growth, improve the production of fruit or flowers, etc

PRUNE [2] noun **PRUNES** a plum that has been preserved by drying, which gives it a black wrinkled appearance

PRUNELLA noun **PRUNELLAS** a strong silk or woollen material, formerly used for academic and clerical gowns and women's shoes

PRUNER noun **PRUNERS** someone who prunes shrubs, trees, etc

PRURIENCE noun **PRURIENCES** an unhealthy interest in sexual matters

PRURIENT adj unhealthily or excessively interested in sexual matters

PRURIGO noun **PRURIGOS** a skin disease characterized by red, slightly raised, intensely itchy patches

PRURITIC adj of or relating to pruritus

PRURITUS noun **PRURITUSES** itching

PRY verb **PRIES, PRYING, PRIED** to investigate, especially the personal affairs of others; to nose or snoop □ noun **PRIES** the act of prying

PSALM noun **PSALMS** a sacred song, especially one from the Book of Psalms in the Old Testament

PSALMIST noun **PSALMISTS** a composer of psalms

PSALMODY noun **PSALMODIES** the art of singing psalms

PSALTER noun **PSALTERS** the Psalms, often applied to a metrical version intended for singing

PSALTERY noun **PSALTERIES** a stringed instrument similar to a zither, played by plucking

PSEUD noun **PSEUDS** a

pretentious person; a bogus intellectual; a phoney
PSEUDO *adj* false; sham; phoney
PSEUDONYM *noun*
PSEUDONYMS a false or assumed name, especially one used by an author; a pen name or nom de plume

PSI *noun* **PSIS** the twenty-third letter of the Greek alphabet

PSORIASIS *noun* **PSORIASES** a common non-contagious skin disease of unknown cause, characterized by red patches covered with white scales, mainly on the elbows, knees, scalp and torso
PSST *exclamation* used to draw someone's attention quietly or surreptitiously
PST *exclamation* psst
PSYCH *verb* **PSYCHS, PSYCHING, PSYCHED** to psychoanalyse someone
PSYCHE *noun* **PSYCHES** the mind or spirit, especially with regard to the deep feelings and attitudes that account for someone's opinions and behaviour
PSYCHIC *adj* relating to mental processes or experiences that are not scientifically explainable, eg telepathy ◻ *noun* **PSYCHICS** someone who possesses psychic powers
PSYCHO *noun* **PSYCHOS** a psychopath ◻ *adj* psychopathic
PSYCHOSIS *noun* **PSYCHOSES** one of the two divisions of psychiatric disorders, characterized by a loss of contact with reality, in the form of delusions or hallucinations and belief that only one's own actions are rational
PSYCHOTIC *noun* **PSYCHOTICS** someone suffering from a psychosis
PTARMIGAN *noun* **PTARMIGANS** a mountain-dwelling game-bird with white winter plumage
PTEROSAUR *noun* **PTEROSAURS** any of the order of extinct flying reptiles previously known as pterodactyls, with narrow leathery wings, known from the late Triassic to the end of the Cretaceous period
PTOMAINE *noun* **PTOMAINES** any of a group of nitrogenous organic compounds, some of which are poisonous, produced during the

bacterial decomposition of dead animal and plant matter
PTYALIN *noun* **PTYALINS** in mammals: an enzyme present in the saliva that is responsible for the initial stages of the breakdown of starch
PUB *noun* **PUBS** a public house, an establishment licensed to sell alcohol for consumption on the premises
PUBERTY *noun* **PUBERTIES** in humans and other primates: the onset of sexual maturity, when the secondary sexual characteristics appear and the reproductive organs become functional
PUBES *noun* **PUBES** the pubic region of the lower abdomen; the groin
PUBESCENT *adj* of or relating to puberty
PUBIC *adj* belonging or relating to the pubis or pubes
PUBIS *noun* **PUBISES** in most vertebrates: one of the two bones forming the lower front part of each side of the pelvis
PUBLIC *adj* relating to or concerning all the people of a country or community ◻ *singular or plural noun* **PUBLICS** the people or community
PUBLICAN *noun* **PUBLICANS** the keeper of a public house
PUBLICISE *verb* **PUBLICISES, PUBLICISING, PUBLICISED** to publicize
PUBLICITY *noun* **PUBLICITIES** advertising or other activity designed to rouse public interest in something
PUBLICIZE *verb* **PUBLICIZES, PUBLICIZING, PUBLICIZED** to make something generally or widely known
PUBLISH *verb* **PUBLISHES, PUBLISHING, PUBLISHED** to prepare, produce and distribute (printed material, computer software, etc) for sale to the public
PUBLISHER *noun* **PUBLISHERS** a person or company engaged in the business of publishing books, newspapers, music, software, etc
PUCE *noun* **PUCES** a colour anywhere in the range between deep purplish-pink and purplish-brown ◻ *adj* **PUCER, PUCEST** puce-coloured
PUCK *noun* **PUCKS** a thick disc of hard rubber used in ice hockey instead of a ball

PUCKER *verb* **PUCKERS, PUCKERING, PUCKERED** to gather into creases, folds or wrinkles; to wrinkle ◻ *noun* **PUCKERS** a wrinkle, fold or crease
PUCKISH *adj* mischievous
PUD *noun* **PUDS** pudding
PUDDING *noun* **PUDDINGS** any of several sweet or savoury foods usually made with flour and eggs and cooked by steaming, boiling or baking
PUDDLE *noun* **PUDDLES** a small pool, especially one of rainwater; a non-porous watertight material ◻ *verb* **PUDDLES, PUDDLING, PUDDLED** to make something watertight by means of puddle
PUDDLING *noun* **PUDDLINGS** the original process for converting pig iron into wrought iron by melting it in a furnace and stirring to remove carbon
PUDENDUM *noun* **PUDENDA** the external sexual organs, especially those of a woman
PUDGY *adj* **PUDGIER, PUDGIEST** plump or chubby; short and squat
PUEBLO *noun* **PUEBLOS** in Spanish-speaking countries: a town or settlement
PUERILE *adj* childish; silly; immature
PUERILITY *noun* **PUERILITIES** childish, silly or immature behaviour
PUERPERAL *adj* referring or relating to childbirth
PUFF *noun* **PUFFS** a small rush, gust or blast of air or wind, etc ◻ *verb* **PUFFS, PUFFING, PUFFED** to blow or breathe in small blasts
PUFFBALL *noun* **PUFFBALLS** the spore-bearing structure of certain fungi, consisting of a hollow ball of white or beige fleshy tissue from which spores are released as puffs of fine dust through a hole in the top
PUFFER *noun* **PUFFERS** a small steam-boat used to carry cargo around the west coast and Western Isles of Scotland
PUFFILY *adverb* in a puffy way
PUFFIN *noun* **PUFFINS** a short stout black-and-white seabird of the auk family, which has a large triangular bill with red, yellow and blue stripes
PUFFINESS *noun* **PUFFINESSES** the state or condition or quality of being puffy or swollen
PUFFY *adj* **PUFFIER, PUFFIEST**

swollen as a result of injury or ill health

PUG [1] *noun* **PUGS** a small breed of dog with a compact body, a short coat, a flattened face with a wrinkled snout and a short curled tail

PUG [2] *verb* **PUGS, PUGGING, PUGGED** to mix (clay) with water so as to make it into a soft paste

PUGGING *noun* **PUGGINGS** clay, sawdust, plaster, etc put between floors to deaden sound

PUGILISM *noun* **PUGILISMS** the art or practice of boxing or prizefighting

PUGILIST *noun* **PUGILISTS** a boxer

PUGNACITY *noun* **PUGNACITIES** inclination or readiness to fight

PUH *exclamation* Shakespearean spelling of *pooh*

PUISNE *adj* said of a judge: junior; lesser in rank

PUISSANCE *noun* **PUISSANCES** a competition that tests the horse's ability to jump high fences

PUISSANT *adj* strong, mighty or powerful

PUJA *noun* **PUJAS** in Hinduism: (an act of) worship

PUKE *verb* **PUKES, PUKING, PUKED** to vomit □ *noun* **PUKES** vomit

PUKEKO *noun* **PUKEKOS** a New Zealand wading bird with bright plumage

PUKKA *adj* superior; high-quality

PULE *verb* **PULES, PULING, PULED** to whimper or whine

PULER *noun* **PULERS** someone who whimpers or whines

PULIER see under **puly**

PULIEST see under **puly**

PULING *adj* whimpering or whining

PULINGLY *adverb* in a whimpering or whining way

PULL *verb* **PULLS, PULLING, PULLED** to grip something or someone strongly and draw or force it or them towards oneself; to tug or drag □ *noun* **PULLS** an act of pulling

PULLET *noun* **PULLETS** a young female hen in its first laying year

PULLEY *noun* **PULLEYS** a simple mechanism for lifting and lowering weights, consisting of a wheel with a grooved rim over which a rope or belt runs

PULLOVER *noun* **PULLOVERS** a knitted garment pulled on over the head; a sweater or jumper

PULLULATE *verb* **PULLULATES, PULLULATING, PULLULATED** to teem or abound

PULMONARY *adj* belonging or relating to, or affecting, the lungs

PULP *noun* **PULPS** the flesh of a fruit or vegetable; a soft wet mass of mashed food or other material □ *verb* **PULPS, PULPING, PULPED** to reduce or be reduced to a pulp

PULPIT *noun* **PULPITS** a small enclosed platform in a church, from which the preacher delivers the sermon

PULPY *adj* **PULPIER, PULPIEST** softy and fleshy

PULQUE *noun* **PULQUES** an alcoholic drink made in Mexico from agave sap

PULSAR *noun* **PULSARS** in space: a source of electromagnetic radiation emitted in brief regular pulses, mainly at radio frequency, believed to be a rapidly revolving neutron star

PULSATE *verb* **PULSATES, PULSATING, PULSATED** to beat or throb

PULSATION *noun* **PULSATIONS** the state or condition of beating or throbbing

PULSE *noun* **PULSES** the rhythmic beat that can be detected in an artery, corresponding to the regular contraction of the left ventricle of the heart as it pumps blood around the body □ *verb* **PULSES, PULSING, PULSED** to throb or pulsate

PULVERISE *verb* **PULVERISES, PULVERISING, PULVERISED** to pulverize

PULVERIZE *verb* **PULVERIZES, PULVERIZING, PULVERIZED** to crush or crumble to dust or powder

PULY *adj* **PULIER, PULIEST** whining; sickly

PUMA *noun* **PUMAS** one of the large cats of America, with short yellowish-brown or reddish fur, found in mountain regions, forests, plains and deserts

PUMICE *noun* **PUMICES** a very light porous white or grey form of solidified lava, used as an abrasive and polishing agent □ *verb* **PUMICES, PUMICING, PUMICED** to polish or rub something with pumice

PUMMEL *verb* **PUMMELS,**

PUMMELLING, PUMMELLED to beat something repeatedly with the fists

PUMP *noun* **PUMPS** any of various piston-operated or other devices for forcing or driving liquids or gases into or out of something, etc □ *verb* **PUMPS, PUMPING, PUMPED** to raise, force or drive (a liquid or gas) out of or into something with a pump

PUMPKIN *noun* **PUMPKINS** a perennial trailing or climbing plant which produces yellow flowers and large round fruits at ground level

PUN *noun* **PUNS** a form of joke consisting of the use of a word or phrase that can be understood in two different ways, especially one where an association is created between words of similar sound but different meaning □ *verb* **PUNS, PUNNING, PUNNED** to make a pun

PUNCH *verb* **PUNCHES, PUNCHING, PUNCHED** to hit someone or something with the fist □ *noun* **PUNCHES** a blow with the fist

PUNCHY *adj* **PUNCHIER, PUNCHIEST** said of speech or writing: vigorous and effective; forcefully expressed

PUNCTUAL *adj* arriving or happening at the arranged time; not late

PUNCTUATE *verb* **PUNCTUATES, PUNCTUATING, PUNCTUATED** to put punctuation marks into (a piece of writing)

PUNCTURE *noun* **PUNCTURES** a small hole pierced in something with a sharp point □ *verb* **PUNCTURES, PUNCTURING, PUNCTURED** to make a puncture in something, or to be punctured

PUNDIT *noun* **PUNDITS** an authority or supposed authority on a particular subject, especially one who is regularly consulted

PUNGENCY *noun* **PUNGENCIES** the state or condition or quality of being strong and sharp

PUNGENT *adj* said of a taste or smell: sharp and strong

PUNGENTLY *adverb* in a pungent way

PUNIER see under **puny**

PUNIEST see under **puny**

PUNISH *verb* **PUNISHES, PUNISHING, PUNISHED** to cause (an offender) to suffer for an offence

PUNISHING *adj* harsh; severe

PUNITIVE *adj* relating to, inflicting or intended to inflict punishment

PUNK *noun* **PUNKS** a youth-orientated, anti-establishment movement, at its height in the mid-to late-70s, which was characterized by aggressive music and dress style and vividly coloured hair □ *adj* relating to or characteristic of punk music or the punk movement

PUNKA *noun* **PUNKAS** a fan made from leaf-palm

PUNKAH *noun* **PUNKAHS** a punka

PUNNED past form of **pun**

PUNNET *noun* **PUNNETS** a small basket or container, usually made of cardboard or plastic, for soft fruit

PUNNING a form of **pun**

PUNSTER *noun* **PUNSTERS** someone who makes puns, especially habitually

PUNT *noun* **PUNTS** a long, flat-bottomed open boat with square ends, propelled by a pole pushed against the bed of the river, etc □ *verb* **PUNTS, PUNTING, PUNTED** to travel by or operate a punt

PUNTER *noun* **PUNTERS** someone who bets on horses; a gambler

PUNY *adj* **PUNIER, PUNIEST** small, weak or undersized

PUP *noun* **PUPS** a young dog □ *verb* **PUPS, PUPPING, PUPPED** to give birth to pups

PUPA *noun* **PUPAE, PUPAS** in the life cycle of certain insects, eg butterflies and moths: the inactive stage during which a larva is transformed into a sexually mature adult while enclosed in a protective case

PUPAL *adj* of or relating to a pupa

PUPIL *noun* **PUPILS** someone who is being taught; a schoolchild or student

PUPPET *noun* **PUPPETS** a type of doll that can be moved in a number of ways, eg one operated by strings or sticks attached to its limbs, or one designed to fit over the hand and operated by the fingers and thumb

PUPPETEER *noun* **PUPPETEERS** someone skilled in manipulating puppets and giving puppet shows

PUPPETRY *noun* **PUPPETRIES** the art of making and manipulating puppets

PUPPY *noun* **PUPPIES** a young dog

PUR *verb* **PURS, PURRING, PURRED** an obsolete spelling of *purr*

PURBLIND *adj* nearly blind; dim-sighted

PURCHASE *verb* **PURCHASES, PURCHASING, PURCHASED** to obtain something in return for payment; to buy □ *noun* **PURCHASES** something that has been bought

PURCHASER *noun* **PURCHASERS** someone who buys something

PURDAH *noun* **PURDAHS** in some Muslim and Hindu societies: the seclusion of women from public view

PURE *adj* **PURER, PUREST** consisting of itself only; unmixed with anything else

PURÉE *noun* **PURÉES** a quantity of fruit, vegetables, meat, fish, game, etc reduced to a smooth pulp by liquidizing or rubbing through a sieve □ *verb* **PURÉES, PURÉEING, PURÉED** to reduce something to a purée

PURELY *adverb* in a pure way

PURENESS *noun* **PURENESSES** the state or condition or quality of being pure

PURFLE *noun* **PURFLES** a decorative border on clothing or furniture, etc □ *verb* **PURFLES, PURFLING, PURFLED** to ornament (the edge of something) with such a border

PURGATIVE *noun* **PURGATIVES** a medicine that causes the bowels to empty

PURGATORY *noun* **PURGATORIES** a place or state into which the soul passes after death, where it is cleansed of pardonable sins before going to heaven

PURGE *verb* **PURGES, PURGING, PURGED** to rid (eg the soul or body) of unwholesome thoughts or substances □ *noun* **PURGES** an act of purging

PURI *noun* **PURIS** a small cake of unleavened Indian bread, deep-fried and served hot

PURIFIER *noun* **PURIFIERS** a person or thing that purifies

PURIFY *verb* **PURIFIES, PURIFYING, PURIFIED** to make or become pure

PURIM *noun* **PURIMS** the Feast of Lots, held about 1 March, in which the Jews celebrate their deliverance from a plot to have them massacred

PURIN *noun* **PURINS** purine

PURINE *noun* **PURINES** a nitrogenous base with a double ring structure, the most important derivatives of which are major constituents of the nucleic acids DNA and RNA

PURISM *noun* **PURISMS** insistence on the traditional elements of the content and style of a particular subject, especially of language

PURIST *noun* **PURISTS** someone who insists on the traditional elements of the content and style of a particular subject, especially of language

PURITAN *noun* **PURITANS** in the 16c and 17c: a supporter of the Protestant movement in England and America that sought to rid church worship of ritual

PURITY *noun* **PURITIES** the state of being pure or unmixed

PURL *noun* **PURLS** a stitch in knitting □ *verb* **PURLS, PURLING, PURLED** to knit in purl

PURLIEU *noun* **PURLIEUS** the surroundings or immediate neighbourhood of a place

PURLIN *noun* **PURLINS** a roof timber stretching across the principal rafters or between the tops of walls, which supports the common or subsidiary rafters or the sheets of roof-covering material

PURLINE *noun* **PURLINES** purlin

PURLOIN *verb* **PURLOINS, PURLOINING, PURLOINED** to steal, filch or pilfer

PURPLE *noun* **PURPLES** a colour that is a mixture of blue and red □ *adj* **PURPLER, PURPLEST** purple-coloured

PURPORT *verb* **PURPORTS, PURPORTING, PURPORTED** said of a picture, piece of writing, document, etc: to profess by its appearance, etc (to be something) □ *noun* **PURPORTS** meaning, significance, point or gist

PURPOSE *noun* **PURPOSES** the object or aim in doing something □ *verb* **PURPOSES, PURPOSING, PURPOSED** to intend (to do something)

PURPOSELY *adj* intentionally

PURPOSIVE *adj* having a clear purpose

PURR *verb* **PURRS, PURRING, PURRED** said of a cat: to make a soft low vibrating sound

associated with contentment
□ *noun* **PURRS** a purring sound
PURSE *noun* **PURSES** a small
container carried in the pocket or
handbag, for keeping cash, etc in
□ *verb* **PURSES, PURSING,**
PURSED to draw (the lips) together
in disapproval or deep thought
PURSER *noun* **PURSERS** the ship's
officer responsible for keeping the
accounts and, on a passenger
ship, seeing to the welfare of
passengers
PURSUANCE *noun* **PURSUANCES**
the process of pursuing
PURSUE *verb* **PURSUES,**
PURSUING, PURSUED to follow
someone or something in order to
overtake, capture or attack them or
it, etc; to chase
PURSUER *noun* **PURSUERS**
someone who chases someone or
something
PURSUIT *noun* **PURSUITS** the act
of pursuing or chasing
PURULENCE *noun* **PURULENCES**
the state or condition or quality of
being full of pus
PURULENT *adj* belonging or
relating to, or full of, pus
PURVEY *verb* **PURVEYS,**
PURVEYING, PURVEYED to supply
(food or provisions, etc) as a
business
PURVEYOR *noun* **PURVEYORS**
someone whose business is to
provide food or meals
PURVIEW *noun* **PURVIEWS** scope
of responsibility or concern, eg of a
court of law
PUS *noun* **PUSES** the thick,
usually yellowish liquid that forms
in abscesses or infected wounds,
composed of dead white blood
cells, serum, bacteria and tissue
debris
PUSH *verb* **PUSHES, PUSHING,**
PUSHED to exert pressure to force
something away from one; to
press, thrust or shove it □ *noun*
PUSHES an act of pushing; a
thrust or shove
PUSHER *noun* **PUSHERS** someone
who sells illegal drugs
PUSHY *adj* **PUSHIER, PUSHIEST**
aggressively self-assertive or
ambitious
PUSS *noun* **PUSSES** a cat
PUSSY *noun* **PUSSIES** a cat
PUSSYFOOT *verb* **PUSSYFOOTS,**
PUSSYFOOTING, PUSSYFOOTED
to behave indecisively; to avoid
committing oneself

PUSTULAR *adj* of or relating to
pustules
PUSTULE *noun* **PUSTULES** a small
inflammation on the skin,
containing pus; a pimple
PUT *verb* **PUTS, PUTTING, PUT** to
place something or someone in or
convey them or it to a specified
position or situation
PUTATIVE *adj* supposed; assumed
PUTREFY *verb* **PUTREFIES,**
PUTREFYING, PUTREFIED said of
flesh or other organic matter: to go
bad, rot or decay, especially with a
foul smell
PUTRID *adj* **PUTRIDER,**
PUTRIDEST said of organic matter:
decayed; rotten
PUTSCH *noun* **PUTSCHES** a
secretly-planned sudden attempt
to remove a government from
power
PUTT *verb* **PUTTS, PUTTING,**
PUTTED in golf, etc: to send (the
ball) gently forward on the green
and into or nearer the hole □ *noun*
PUTTS a putting stroke
PUTTEE *noun* **PUTTEES** a long strip
of cloth worn by wrapping it
around the leg from the ankle to
the knee and used as protection or
support
PUTTER *noun* **PUTTERS** a club
used for putting
PUTTING *noun* **PUTTINGS** the act
of putting a ball towards a hole
PUTTO *noun* **PUTTI** in
Renaissance or Baroque art: an
idealized representation of a
naked young boy or cherub, often
with wings
PUTTY *noun* **PUTTIES** a paste of
ground chalk and linseed oil, used
for fixing glass in window frames,
filling holes in wood, etc □ *verb*
PUTTIES, PUTTYING, PUTTIED to
fix, coat or fill something with
putty

PUY *noun* **PUYS** a small volcanic
cone

PUZZLE *verb* **PUZZLES,**
PUZZLING, PUZZLED to perplex,
mystify, bewilder or baffle □ *noun*
PUZZLES a baffling problem
PUZZLER *noun* **PUZZLERS** a
challenging problem or question
PUZZLING *adj* challenging;
perplexing
PYAEMIA *noun* **PYAEMIAS** a form
of blood poisoning caused by the
release of pus-forming micro-
organisms, especially bacteria,

into the bloodstream from an
abscess or wound

PYE *verb* **PYES, PYING, PIED** to
reduce to confusion

PYELITIC *adj* of or relating to
pyelitis
PYELITIS *noun* **PYELITISES**
inflammation of part of the kidney
PYEMIA *noun* **PYEMIAS** pyaemia
PYGMAEAN *adj* of or relating to
pygmies
PYGMEAN *adj* pygmaean
PYGMY *noun* **PYGMIES** a member
of one of the unusually short
peoples of equatorial Africa
PYJAMAS *plural noun* a sleeping-
suit consisting of a loose jacket or
top, and trousers
PYKNIC *adj* said of a human type:
characterized by a short, stocky
stature, with a domed abdomen
and relatively short limbs and neck
PYLON *noun* **PYLONS** a tall steel
structure for supporting electric
power cables
PYLORIC *adj* of or relating to the
pylorus
PYLORUS *noun* **PYLORUSES** the
opening at the base of the stomach
that allows partially digested food
to pass into the duodenum
PYORRHOEA *noun* **PYORRHOEAS**
a discharge of pus, especially from
the gum or tooth sockets
PYRAMID *noun* **PYRAMIDS** any of
the huge ancient Egyptian royal
tombs built on a square base, with
four sloping triangular sides
meeting in a common apex
PYRAMIDAL *adj* of, relating to or
like a pyramid
PYRAMIDIC *adj* pyramidal
PYRE *noun* **PYRES** a pile of wood
on which a dead body is
ceremonially cremated
PYRETHRUM *noun* **PYRETHRUMS**
the name formerly used for any of
various perennial plants of the
Chrysanthemum genus, especially
a species with finely divided
silvery-grey leaves and solitary
large white, pink, red or purple
daisy-like flower-heads
PYRETIC *adj* relating to,
accompanied by or producing
fever
PYREXIA *noun* **PYREXIAS** fever
PYRIDINE *noun* **PYRIDINES** a
cancer-causing flammable
colourless liquid with a strong
unpleasant smell, used in the

manufacture of other chemicals, in paints and textile dyes and as a solvent

PYRITE *noun* **PYRITES** the commonest sulphide mineral, used as a source of sulphur, and in the production of sulphuric acid

PYRITES *noun* **PYRITES** any of a large class of mineral sulphides

PYROCLAST *noun* **PYROCLASTS** an individual fragment of lava that has been ejected into the atmosphere during a volcanic eruption

PYROGEN *noun* **PYROGENS** a substance which causes heat or fever

PYROGENIC *adj* produced by or producing heat or fever

PYROLYSIS *noun* **PYROLYSES** the chemical decomposition of a substance that occurs when it is heated to a high temperature in the absence of air

PYROMANIA *noun* **PYROMANIAS** an obsessive urge to set fire to things

PYROMETER *noun* **PYROMETERS** a type of thermometer used to measure high temperatures

PYROMETRY *noun* **PYROMETRIES** the measuring of high temperatures

PYROPE *noun* **PYROPES** a red magnesia-alumina garnet, used as a gemstone

PYROXENE *noun* **PYROXENES** any of a group of white, yellow, green, greenish-black or brown silicate minerals, including the most highly prized form of jade

PYRROLE *noun* **PYRROLES** a yellowish toxic oil used in the manufacture of drugs from which many naturally occurring compounds are derived

PYTHON *noun* **PYTHONS** any non-venomous egg-laying snake of the boa family that coils its body around its prey and squeezes it until it suffocates

PYTHONIC *adj* of, relating to or like a python

PYX [1] *verb* **PYXES, PYXING, PYXED** to test

PYX [2] *noun* **PYXES** a container in which the consecrated Communion bread is kept

PYXIS *noun* **PYXIDES** a little box or casket for jewels, etc

PZAZZ *noun* **PZAZZES** pizazz

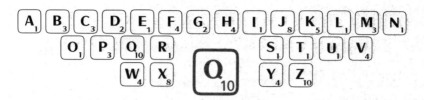

QADI *noun* **QADIS** in Muslim countries: a judge or magistrate

QAT *noun* **QATS** a shrub of E Africa, Arabia, etc
ⓘThis word is useful for using up **Q** when you do not have a **U** or there are none on the board.

QAWWAL *noun* **QAWWALS** a man who sings qawwali music
QAWWALI *noun* **QAWWALIS** a type of Sufi music

QI *noun* **QIS** the life force that is believed to flow along a network of meridians in a person's body and which is vital to their physical and spiritual health
ⓘThis word is very useful for using up **Q** when you do not have a **U** or there are none on the board.

QIBLA *noun* **QIBLAS** kiblah

QIS plural of **qi**

QUA *prep* in the capacity of something; considered as being something; in the role of something

QUACK ¹ *noun* **QUACKS** the noise that a duck makes □ *verb* **QUACKS, QUACKING, QUACKED** said of a duck: to make this noise

QUACK ² *noun* **QUACKS** someone who practises medicine or who claims to have medical knowledge, but who has no formal training in the subject

QUACKER *noun* **QUACKERS** an animal that quacks

QUACKERY *noun* **QUACKERIES** the practices, methods and activities, etc that are typical of a quack or charlatan

QUAD *noun* **QUADS** a quadruplet, one of four children or animals born at the same time to the same mother

QUADRANT *noun* **QUADRANTS** a quarter of the circumference of a circle

QUADRAT *noun* **QUADRATS** a random sample area of ground enclosed within a frame, often one metre square, which is studied in order to determine what plant and animal species it supports

QUADRATE *noun* **QUADRATES** a body part, eg a muscle or bone, that has a square or rectangular shape □ *verb* **QUADRATES, QUADRATING, QUADRATED** to make something square

QUADRATIC *noun* **QUADRATICS** an algebraic equation that involves the square, but no higher power, of an unknown quantity or variable

QUADRELLA *noun* **QUADRELLAS** a type of bet where the punter selects the winner in four races

QUADRIC *adj* in maths, said of function with more than two variables: being of the second degree □ *noun* **QUADRICS** a quadric curve, surface or function

QUADRIFID *adj* said of a plant part: divided into four or having four lobes

QUADRILLE *noun* **QUADRILLES** a square dance for four couples, in five or six movements

QUADROON *noun* **QUADROONS** someone who is genetically one quarter black

QUADRUPED *noun* **QUADRUPEDS** an animal, especially a mammal, that has its four limbs specially adapted for walking

QUADRUPLE *adj* four times as great, many or much □ *verb* **QUADRUPLES, QUADRUPLING, QUADRUPLED** to make or become four times as great, much or many □ *noun* **QUADRUPLES** an amount that is four times greater than the original or usual, etc amount

QUADRUPLY *adverb* in a fourfold manner

QUAFF *verb* **QUAFFS, QUAFFING, QUAFFED** to drink eagerly or deeply

QUAFFER *noun* **QUAFFERS** someone who quaffs

QUAG *noun* **QUAGS** a boggy or marshy place, especially one that has a layer of turf on it and which can be felt to shake or give way slightly underfoot

QUAGGA *noun* **QUAGGAS** an extinct member of the zebra family found in S Africa until the late 19c which had stripes only on the area around the head and shoulders, the rest of its body being a yellowish-brown colour

QUAGGY *adj* **QUAGGIER, QUAGGIEST** boggy; marshy

QUAGMIRE *noun* **QUAGMIRES** an area of soft marshy ground; a bog

QUAHAUG *noun* **QUAHAUGS** a quahog

QUAHOG *noun* **QUAHOGS** an edible round clam found off the Atlantic coast of N America

QUAICH *noun* **QUAICHS** a two-handled drinking cup

QUAIL ¹ *noun* **QUAILS** any of several small migratory game birds of the partridge family

QUAIL ² *verb* **QUAILS, QUAILING, QUAILED** to lose courage; to be apprehensive with fear; to flinch

QUAINT *adj* **QUAINTER, QUAINTEST** old-fashioned, strange or unusual especially in a charming, pretty or dainty, etc way

QUAINTLY *adverb* in a quaint way

QUAKE *verb* **QUAKES, QUAKING, QUAKED** said of people: to shake or tremble with fear, etc □ *noun* **QUAKES** an earthquake

QUAKINESS *noun* **QUAKINESSES** the state of being quaky

QUAKING *noun* **QUAKINGS** an act of shaking or trembling with fear, etc

QUAKINGLY *adverb* as if shaking or trembling with fear

QUAKY *adj* **QUAKIER, QUAKIEST** tending to quake

QUALIFIED *adj* having the necessary competency, ability or attributes, etc (to do something)

QUALIFIER *noun* **QUALIFIERS** someone who has qualified for eg the final stages of a race or competition

QUALIFY *verb* **QUALIFIES, QUALIFYING, QUALIFIED** to complete a training or pass an

examination, etc, especially in order to practise a specified profession, occupation, etc
QUALIFYINGnoun **QUALIFYINGS** the completion of training or passing of an examination, etc
QUALITYnoun **QUALITIES** the degree or extent of excellence of something
QUALMnoun **QUALMS** a sudden feeling of nervousness or apprehension
QUALMISHadj having qualms
QUANDANGnoun **QUANDANGS** a quandong
QUANDARYnoun **QUANDARIES** a state of indecision, uncertainty, doubt or perplexity
QUANDONGnoun **QUANDONGS** a name for either of two native Australian trees
QUANGOnoun **QUANGOS** a semi-public administrative body that functions outwith the civil service but which is government-funded and which has its senior appointments made by the government
QUANTnoun **QUANTS** a type of punting pole that has a prong at the lower end so that it can be pushed into the bed of a river or canal, etc to propel a barge along ❑ verb **QUANTS, QUANTING, QUANTED** to propel (a barge) along using a quant
QUANTA plural of **quantum**
QUANTICnoun **QUANTICS** in maths: a rational integral homogeneous function of two or more variables
QUANTICALadj of or relating to quantics
QUANTIFYverb **QUANTIFIES, QUANTIFYING, QUANTIFIED** to determine the quantity of something or to measure or express it as a quantity
QUANTISEverb **QUANTISES, QUANTISING, QUANTISED** to quantize
QUANTITYnoun **QUANTITIES** a specified number or amount
QUANTIZEverb **QUANTIZES, QUANTIZING, QUANTIZED** to form into quanta
QUANTONGnoun **QUANTONGS** a quandong
QUANTUMnoun **QUANTA** an amount or quantity, especially a specified one ❑ adj major, large or impressive but also sudden, unexpected or abrupt, etc

QUARKnoun **QUARKS** the smallest known bit of matter, being any of a group of subatomic particles which, in different combinations, are thought to make up all protons, neutrons and other hadrons
QUARRELnoun **QUARRELS** an angry disagreement or argument ❑ verb **QUARRELS, QUARRELLING, QUARRELLED** to argue or dispute angrily
QUARRELLINGnoun **QUARRELLINGS** an act of arguing angrily
QUARRYnoun **QUARRIES** an open excavation for the purpose of extracting stone or slate for building ❑ verb **QUARRIES, QUARRYING, QUARRIED** to extract (stone, etc) from a quarry
QUARRYMANnoun **QUARRYMEN** a man who works in a quarry
QUARTnoun **QUARTS** a liquid measure equivalent to one quarter of a gallon, two pints (1.136 litres) or 40 fluid ounces
QUARTANadj said of a fever, etc: recurring every third day
QUARTEnoun **QUARTES** in fencing: the fourth of the eight parrying or attacking positions that are taught
QUARTERnoun **QUARTERS** one of four equal parts that an object or quantity is or can be divided into ❑ verb **QUARTERS, QUARTERING, QUARTERED** to divide something into quarters
QUARTERINGnoun **QUARTERINGS** the coats of arms displayed on a shield to indicate family alliances
QUARTERLYadj produced, occurring, published, paid or due, etc once every quarter of a year ❑ adverb once every quarter ❑ noun **QUARTERLIES** a quarterly publication
QUARTETnoun **QUARTETS** an ensemble of four singers or instrumentalists
QUARTETTEnoun **QUARTETTES** a quartet
QUARTICadj in maths: involving the fourth degree ❑ noun **QUARTICS** an equation, etc of this kind
QUARTILEadj said of the aspect of two heavenly bodies: 90° apart ❑ noun **QUARTILES** a quartile aspect between two heavenly bodies

QUARTOnoun **QUARTOS** a size of paper produced by folding a sheet in half twice to give four leaves or eight pages
QUARTZnoun **QUARTZES** a common colourless mineral that is often tinged with impurities that give a wide variety of shades making it suitable as a gemstone, eg purple (amethyst), brown (cairngorm), pink (rose quartz), etc
QUARTZITEnoun **QUARTZITES** any of various pale or white highly durable rocks that are composed largely or entirely of quartz and which are used as a construction material in the building industry
QUASARnoun **QUASARS** a highly intense luminous star-like source of light and radio waves that exists thousands of millions of light years outside the Earth's galaxy
QUASHverb **QUASHES, QUASHING, QUASHED** to subdue, crush or suppress, etc (eg a rebellion or protest)
QUASIadverb as it were; so to speak
QUASSIAnoun **QUASSIAS** a S American tree whose bitter wood and bark are used as a tonic

QUATnoun **QUATS** a pimple

QUATORZEnoun **QUATORZES** in piquet: a set of four aces, kings, queens, jacks or tens in a hand which scores 14
QUATRAINnoun **QUATRAINS** a verse or poem of four lines which usually rhyme alternately
QUAVERverb **QUAVERS, QUAVERING, QUAVERED** said of a voice or a musical sound, etc: to be unsteady; to shake or tremble ❑ noun **QUAVERS** a note that lasts half as long as a crotchet and usually represented in notation by ♪
QUAVERERnoun **QUAVERERS** someone whose voice quavers
QUAVERINGadj quavery
QUAVERYadj **QUAVERIER, QUAVERIEST** trembling or shaking
QUAYnoun **QUAYS** an artificial structure that projects into the water for the loading and unloading of ships
QUAYAGEnoun **QUAYAGES** the amount that is levied for the use of a quay

QUAYDadj a Spenserian word meaning *daunted*

QUAYSIDE *noun* **QUAYSIDES** the area around a quay, especially the edge along the water

QUEASILY *adj* in a queasy way

QUEASY *adj* **QUEASIER, QUEASIEST** said of a person: feeling slightly sick

QUEBRACHO *noun* **QUEBRACHOS** either of two types of S American trees with a hard wood which is rich in tannin

QUEEN *noun* **QUEENS** a woman who rules a country, having inherited her position by birth; the most powerful piece on a chess board □ *verb* **QUEENS, QUEENING, QUEENED** in chess: to advance (a pawn) to the opponent's side of the board and convert it into a queen

QUEENDOM *noun* **QUEENDOMS** the realm of a queen

QUEENLY *adj* **QUEENLIER, QUEENLIEST** suitable for or appropriate to a queen

QUEENSHIP *noun* **QUEENSHIPS** the state or condition of being a queen

QUEER *adj* **QUEERER, QUEEREST** odd, strange or unusual □ *verb* **QUEERS, QUEERING, QUEERED** to spoil something

QUEERISH *adj* a bit odd, strange or unusual

QUEERLY *adverb* in an odd, strange or unusual way

QUEERNESS *noun* **QUEERNESSES** the state or condition or quality of being odd, strange or unusual

QUELL *verb* **QUELLS, QUELLING, QUELLED** to crush or subdue (riots, disturbances or opposition, etc)

QUELLER *noun* **QUELLERS** a person or thing that quells something

QUEME *verb* **QUEMES, QUEMING, QUEMED** a Spenserian word meaning to please, suit or fit

QUENCH *verb* **QUENCHES, QUENCHING, QUENCHED** to satisfy (thirst) by drinking

QUENCHER *noun* **QUENCHERS** a drink that quenches thirst

QUENCHING *noun* **QUENCHINGS** the act of satisfying eg thirst by drinking

QUENELLE *noun* **QUENELLES** an oval or sausage-shaped dumpling made from spiced meat-paste, eg

fish, chicken or veal, etc, which is bound together with fat and eggs and poached in water

QUERIST *noun* **QUERISTS** someone who asks a question or makes an inquiry

QUERN *noun* **QUERNS** a mill, usually consisting of two circular stones one on top of the other, used for grinding grain by hand

QUERULOUS *adj* said of someone or their disposition: inclined or ready to complain

QUERY *noun* **QUERIES** a question, especially one that raises a doubt or objection, etc □ *verb* **QUERIES, QUERYING, QUERIED** to raise a doubt about or an objection to something

QUERYING *noun* **QUERYINGS** an act of raising a doubt about something

QUEST *noun* **QUESTS** a search or hunt □ *verb* **QUESTS, QUESTING, QUESTED** to search about; to roam around in search of something

QUESTER *noun* **QUESTERS** someone who searches for something

QUESTING *noun* **QUESTINGS** an act of searching for something

QUESTION *noun* **QUESTIONS** a written or spoken sentence that is worded in such a way as to request information or an answer □ *verb* **QUESTIONS, QUESTIONING, QUESTIONED** to ask someone questions; to interrogate them

QUESTIONING *noun* **QUESTIONINGS** an act or the process of asking a question or questions □ *adj* characterized by doubt or uncertainty; mildly confused

QUESTOR *noun* **QUESTORS** a quester

QUETZAL *noun* **QUETZALS** a flamboyant bird of Central and S America, the male of which has bright coppery-green feathers on its upper parts and crimson ones below

QUEUE *noun* **QUEUES** a line or file of people or vehicles, etc, especially ones that are waiting for something □ *verb* **QUEUES, QUEUEING, QUEUED** to form a queue

QUIBBLE *verb* **QUIBBLES, QUIBBLING, QUIBBLED** to argue over trifles; to make petty objections □ *noun* **QUIBBLES** a trifling objection

QUIBBLER *noun* **QUIBBLERS** someone who quibbles about something

QUICHE *noun* **QUICHES** a type of open tart that is usually made with a filling of beaten eggs and cream with various savoury flavourings, and which can be served either hot or cold

QUICK *adj* **QUICKER, QUICKEST** taking little time □ *adverb* rapidly □ *noun* **QUICKS** an area of sensitive flesh, especially at the base of the fingernail or toenail

QUICKEN *verb* **QUICKENS, QUICKENING, QUICKENED** to make or become quicker; to accelerate

QUICKENER *noun* **QUICKENERS** that which quickens

QUICKIE *noun* **QUICKIES** something that is dealt with or done rapidly or in a short time

QUICKLIME *noun* **QUICKLIMES** a white chemical compound used in producing other calcium compounds, such as slaked lime, and in agriculture as an alkali to reduce acidity in soil

QUICKLY *adverb* in a short space of time; rapidly; speedily

QUICKNESS *noun* **QUICKNESSES** the state or condition or quality of being quick

QUICKSAND *noun* **QUICKSANDS** loose, wet sand that can suck down anything that lands or falls on it, often swallowing it up completely

QUICKSET *noun* **QUICKSETS** a living slip or cutting from a plant, especially from a hawthorn or other shrub, that is put into the ground with others where they will grow to form a hedge

QUICKSTEP *noun* **QUICKSTEPS** a fast modern ballroom dance in quadruple time □ *verb* **QUICKSTEPS, QUICKSTEPPING, QUICKSTEPPED** to dance the quickstep

QUID *noun* **QUIDS** a pound sterling

QUIDDITY *noun* **QUIDDITIES** the essence of something; the distinctive qualities, etc that make a thing what it is

QUIESCENT *adj* quiet, silent, at rest or in an inactive state, usually temporarily

QUIET *adj* **QUIETER, QUIETEST** making little or no noise □ *noun* **QUIETS** absence of, or freedom from, noise or commotion, etc □ *verb* **QUIETS, QUIETING,**

QUIETED to make something or become quiet or calm
QUIETEN *verb* **QUIETENS, QUIETENING, QUIETENED** to make or become quiet
QUIETISM *noun* **QUIETISMS** a state of calmness and passivity; the doctrine that religious perfection on earth consists in passive and uninterrupted contemplation of God
QUIETIST *noun* **QUIETISTS** someone who believes in the doctrine of quietism
QUIETLY *adverb* without making any or very much noise
QUIETNESS *noun* **QUIETNESSES** the state or condition or quality of being quiet
QUIETUDE *noun* **QUIETUDES** quietness; tranquillity
QUIETUS *noun* **QUIETUSES** release from life; death
QUIFF *noun* **QUIFFS** a tuft of hair at the front of the head that is brushed up into a crest and which is sometimes made to hang over the forehead ❑ *verb* **QUIFFS, QUIFFING, QUIFFED** to style (hair) into a quiff
QUILL *noun* **QUILLS** a large stiff feather from a bird's wing or tail ❑ *verb* **QUILLS, QUILLING, QUILLED** to form (material in a ruff) into tubular folds
QUILT *noun* **QUILTS** a type of bedcover that is made by sewing together two layers of fabric, usually with some kind of soft padding material, eg feathers or wadding, etc in between them ❑ *verb* **QUILTS, QUILTING, QUILTED** to sew (two layers of material, etc) together with a filling in between, usually by using stitching that produces regular or decorative patterns
QUILTER *noun* **QUILTERS** a person or machine that quilts
QUILTING *noun* **QUILTINGS** the act of making a quilt or quilted material
QUIN *noun* **QUINS** a quintuplet, one of five children or animals born to the same mother at the same time
QUINARY *adj* relating or referring to the number five ❑ *noun* **QUINARIES** a set or group of five
QUINATE *adj* said of a leaf: having five leaflets
QUINCE *noun* **QUINCES** a small Asian tree of the rose family; the acidic hard yellow fruit of this tree
QUINCUNX *noun* **QUINCUNXES** an arrangement in which each of the four corners of a square or rectangle and the point at its centre are all indicated by some object
QUINELLA *noun* **QUINELLAS** a type of bet where punters select two horses, dogs, etc, ie the one that comes second in a specified race as well as the race winner, although they do not have to specify which is which
QUINIDINE *noun* **QUINIDINES** a drug that is obtained from the bark of the cinchona and which is used for treating irregularities in heartbeat rates
QUININE *noun* **QUININES** an alkaloid that is found in the bark of the cinchona
QUINOL *noun* **QUINOLS** a reducing agent and photographic developer
QUINOLINE *noun* **QUINOLINES** a water-soluble aromatic nitrogen compound in the form of an oily colourless liquid, used in the manufacture of dyes and antiseptics and as a food preservative
QUINONE *noun* **QUINONES** a yellow crystalline compound that is made by oxidizing aniline, used in the manufacture of dyes
QUINSIED *adj* suffering from quinsy
QUINSY *noun* **QUINSIES** inflammation of the tonsils and the area of the throat round about them, accompanied by the formation of an abscess or abscesses on the tonsils
QUINT *noun* **QUINTS** in the game of piquet: a hand with a run of five cards of the same suit and which scores 15
QUINTA *noun* **QUINTAS** a country house, villa or estate in Spain and Portugal
QUINTAL *noun* **QUINTALS** a unit of weight that is equal to a hundredweight, 112 lbs in Britain or 100 lbs in the US
QUINTAN *adj* said of a fever, etc: flaring up every fourth day
QUINTE *noun* **QUINTES** in fencing: the fifth of the eight parrying or attacking positions that are taught
QUINTET *noun* **QUINTETS** a group of five singers or musicians
QUINTETTE *noun* **QUINTETTES** a quintet
QUINTUPLE *adj* five times as great, much or many ❑ *verb* **QUINTUPLES, QUINTUPLING, QUINTUPLED** to make or become five times as great, much or many ❑ *noun* **QUINTUPLES** an amount that is five times greater than the original or usual, etc amount
QUIP *noun* **QUIPS** a witty saying ❑ *verb* **QUIPS, QUIPPING, QUIPPED** to make a quip or quips
QUIPPISH *adj* of or like a quip; witty
QUIPSTER *noun* **QUIPSTERS** a person given to making clever remarks

> **QUIPU** *noun* **QUIPUS** a mnemonic device used by the ancient Peruvians

QUIRE *noun* **QUIRES** a measure for paper that is equivalent to 25 (formerly 24) sheets and one-twentieth of a ream
QUIRK *noun* **QUIRKS** an odd habit, mannerism or aspect of personality, etc
QUIRKISH *adj* quirky
QUIRKY *adj* **QUIRKIER, QUIRKIEST** having quirks; odd; tricky
QUIRT *noun* **QUIRTS** a short-handled riding whip with a braided leather lash, about 61cm (2ft) long ❑ *verb* **QUIRTS, QUIRTING, QUIRTED** to strike (the flank of a horse) with a quirt
QUISLING *noun* **QUISLINGS** a traitor
QUIT *verb* **QUITS, QUITTING, QUIT, QUITTED** to leave or depart from (a place, etc)
QUITCH *noun* **QUITCHES** another name for couch grass
QUITE *adverb* completely; entirely
QUITS *adj* on an equal footing
QUITTANCE *noun* **QUITTANCES** release from debt or other obligation
QUITTER *noun* **QUITTERS** someone who gives up too easily
QUIVER [1] *verb* **QUIVERS, QUIVERING, QUIVERED** to shake or tremble slightly because of something; to shiver
QUIVER [2] *noun* **QUIVERS** a long narrow case that is used for carrying arrows
QUIVERING *adj* shaking or trembling
QUIVERY *adj* **QUIVERIER, QUIVERIEST** shaky
QUIXOTIC *adj* absurdly generous or chivalrous
QUIXOTISM *noun* **QUIXOTISMS** an

instance of absurdly generous or chivalrous behaviour

QUIXOTRY *noun* **QUIXOTRIES** quixotism

QUIZ *noun* **QUIZZES** an entertainment, eg on radio or TV, in which the knowledge of a panel of contestants is tested through a series of questions □ *verb* **QUIZZES, QUIZZING, QUIZZED** to question or interrogate someone

QUIZZER *noun* **QUIZZERS** someone who questions or interrogates someone

QUIZZICAL *adj* said of a look or expression, etc: mildly amused or perplexed; mocking; questioning

QUOD *noun* **QUODS** prison □ *verb* **QUODS, QUODDING, QUODDED** to imprison someone

QUODLIBET *noun* **QUODLIBETS** in philosophy or theology: a question or argument that is put forward for discussion or debate

QUOIN *noun* **QUOINS** the external angle of a wall or building □ *verb* **QUOINS, QUOINING, QUOINED** to secure or raise something with a wedge

QUOIT *noun* **QUOITS** a ring made of metal, rubber or rope used in the game of quoits □ *verb* **QUOITS,**

QUOITING, QUOITED to throw something in a similar way to throwing a quoit

QUOITER *noun* **QUOITERS** someone who plays quoits

QUOITS *singular noun* a game in which a quoit is thrown at a peg, with the aim of encircling it or landing close to it

QUOKKA *noun* **QUOKKAS** a small short-tailed wallaby that is found in SW Australia

QUONK *noun* **QUONKS** an accidental noise made too close to a microphone □ *verb* **QUONKS, QUONKING, QUONKED** to make such a noise

QUORATE *adj* said of a meeting, etc: attended by or consisting of enough people to form a quorum

QUORUM *noun* **QUORUMS** the fixed minimum number of members of an organization or society, etc who must be present at a meeting for its business to be valid

QUOTA *noun* **QUOTAS** the proportional or allocated share or part that is, or that should be, done, paid or contributed, etc out of a total amount, sum, etc

QUOTABLE *adj* worthy of or suitable for quoting

QUOTATION *noun* **QUOTATIONS** a remark or a piece of writing, etc that is quoted

QUOTE *verb* **QUOTES, QUOTING, QUOTED** to cite or offer (someone else or the words or ideas, etc of someone else) to substantiate an argument □ *noun* **QUOTES** a quotation

QUOTH an old word meaning *said*

QUOTIDIAN *adj* everyday; common-place □ *noun* **QUOTIDIANS** a fever that flares up every day

QUOTIENT *noun* **QUOTIENTS** the result of a division sum, eg when 72 is divided by 12 the quotient is 6, or when 80 is divided by 12, the quotient is still 6 with a remainder of 8

QWERTY *adj* said of an English-language typewriter, word processor or other keyboard: having the standard arrangement of keys, ie with the letters *q w e r t y* appearing in that order at the top left of the letters section

RABBET *noun* **RABBETS** a groove cut along the edge of a piece of wood, etc, usually to join with a tongue or projection in a matching piece □ *verb* **RABBETS, RABBETING, RABBETED** to cut a rabbet in something

RABBI *noun* **RABBIS** a Jewish religious leader

RABBINATE *noun* **RABBINATES** the post or tenure of office of a rabbi

RABBINIC *adj* of or relating to rabbis, their opinions, learning or language

RABBIT *noun* **RABBITS** a small burrowing herbivorous mammal belonging to the same family as the hare □ *verb* **RABBITS, RABBITING, RABBITED** to hunt rabbits

RABBITER *noun* **RABBITERS** a person or animal that hunts rabbits

RABBITRY *noun* **RABBITRIES** a place where rabbits are kept

RABBITY *adj* of or like a rabbit, eg in appearance

RABBLE[1] *noun* **RABBLES** a noisy disorderly crowd or mob

RABBLE[2] *noun* **RABBLES** a device for stirring molten iron, etc in a furnace □ *verb* **RABBLES, RABBLING, RABBLED** to stir with a rabble

RABBLER *noun* **RABBLERS** someone who stirs molten iron with a rabble

RABI *noun* **RABIS** in India, Pakistan, etc: the spring grain harvest

RABID *adj* **RABIDER, RABIDEST** said of dogs, etc: suffering from rabies

RABIDITY *noun* **RABIDITIES** the state or condition of suffering from rabies

RABIDLY *adverb* suffering from, or as if suffering from, rabies

RABIDNESS *noun* **RABIDNESSES** the state of being rabid

RABIES *noun* **RABIES** a viral disease of the central nervous system, usually fatal and transmitted in saliva from the bite of an infected animal, which causes convulsions, paralysis and fear of water

RACCOON *noun* **RACCOONS** a smallish solitary nocturnal mammal, found in N and C America, which has dense greyish fur, characteristic black patches around the eyes and black rings on the tail

RACE[1] *noun* **RACES** a contest of speed between runners, horses, cars, etc □ *verb* **RACES, RACING, RACED** to take part in a race

RACE[2] *noun* **RACES** any of the major divisions of humankind distinguished by a particular set of physical characteristics, such as size, hair type or skin colour

RACECARD *noun* **RACECARDS** a programme or list of all the competitors and races at a race meeting

RACEGOER *noun* **RACEGOERS** someone who attends race meetings, especially regularly

RACEGOING *noun* **RACEGOINGS** an act of going to a race, especially a horse race

RACEHORSE *noun* **RACEHORSES** a horse bred and used for racing

RACEMATE *noun* **RACEMATES** a racemic mixture

RACEME *noun* **RACEMES** a flower-head consisting of individual flowers attached to a main unbranched stem by means of short stalks, the youngest flowers being at the tip of the stem and the oldest ones near its base, eg bluebell, lupin

RACEMED *adj* consisting of, or having, racemes

RACEMIC *adj* applied to an acid obtained from a certain kind of grape: an optically inactive form of tartaric acid

RACEMISE *verb* **RACEMISES, RACEMISING, RACEMISED** to racemize

RACEMISM *noun* **RACEMISMS** the quality of being racemic

RACEMIZE *verb* **RACEMIZES, RACEMIZING, RACEMIZED** to change into a racemic form

RACEMOSE *adj* like a raceme or racemes

RACER *noun* **RACERS** a person, animal or thing that races or is raced

RACETRACK *noun* **RACETRACKS** a course or track used for racing horses, cars, bicycles, runners, etc

RACEWAY *noun* **RACEWAYS** a millrace

RACHIS *noun* **RACHISES, RACHIDES** the spine

RACHITIC *adj* of or related to or suffering from rickets

RACHITIS *noun* **RACHITISES** rickets

RACIAL *adj* of or relating to race

RACIALIST *noun* **RACIALISTS** a racist

RACIALLY *adverb* in a racial way

RACIER see under **racy**

RACIEST see under **racy**

RACILY *adverb* in a lively or spirited way

RACINESS *noun* **RACINESSES** the state or condition or quality of being lively or spirited

RACING *noun* **RACINGS** the sport or practice of using animals (especially horses or dogs) or vehicles in contests of speed

RACISM *noun* **RACISMS** hatred, rivalry or bad feeling between races

RACIST *noun* **RACISTS** someone who believes that some races are superior to others □ *adj* believing that some races are superior to others

RACK *noun* **RACKS** a framework with rails, shelves, hooks, etc for holding or storing things □ *verb* **RACKS, RACKING, RACKED** to put something in a rack

RACKED *adj* tortured; tormented; distressed

RACKET *noun* **RACKETS** a bat with a handle ending in a roughly oval head, made of a frame of wood, metal or other material, with a network of strings (originally catgut, now usually a synthetic material), used for playing tennis, badminton, squash, etc

RACKETEER *noun* **RACKETEERS** someone who makes money in some illegal way, often by threats of violence ◻ *verb* **RACKETEERS, RACKETEERING, RACKETEERED** to make money as a racketeer

RACKETEERING *noun* **RACKETEERINGS** an act of making money in some illegal way, often by threats of violence

RACKETER *noun* **RACKETERS** a noisy person

RACKETY *adj* **RACKETIER, RACKETIEST** noisy; energetic and excitable

RACLETTE *noun* **RACLETTES** a dish of melted cheese and jacket potatoes, originally from the Valais region of Switzerland

RACON *noun* **RACONS** a radar beacon

RACONTEUR *noun* **RACONTEURS** someone who tells anecdotes in an amusing or entertaining way

RACOON *noun* **RACOONS** a raccoon

RACQUET *noun* **RACQUETS** a racket

RACY *adj* **RACIER, RACIEST** said of writing, a way of life, etc: lively or spirited; slightly indecent

RAD *noun* **RADS** the unit formerly used to measure the amount of ionizing radiation absorbed, equal to 0.01 joule per kilogram of absorbing material

RADAR *noun* **RADARS** a system for detecting the presence of distant objects, or determining one's own position, by transmitting short pulses of high-frequency radio waves from a rotating aerial, and detecting the signals reflected back from the surface of any object in their path

RADDLE *noun* **RADDLES** ruddle ◻ *verb* **RADDLES, RADDLING, RADDLED** to ruddle

RADDLED *adj* said of a person or a person's face: worn out and haggard-looking through debauchery

RADIAL *adj* said of lines: spreading out from the centre of a circle, like rays ◻ *noun* **RADIALS** a radiating part

RADIALLY *adverb* spreading out from the centre, like rays

RADIAN *noun* **RADIANS** the SI unit of plane angular measurement, approximately 57°, defined as the angle that is made at the centre of a circle by an arc (a segment of the circumference) whose length is equal to the radius of the circle

RADIANCE *noun* **RADIANCES** the state of being radiant

RADIANCY *noun* **RADIANCIES** radiance

RADIANT *adj* glowing or shining; beaming with love or happiness ◻ *noun* **RADIANTS** a point or object that emits electromagnetic radiation, eg light or heat

RADIANTLY *adverb* in a radiant way

RADIATE *verb* **RADIATES, RADIATING, RADIATED** to send out rays (of light, heat, electromagnetic radiation, etc)

RADIATION *noun* **RADIATIONS** energy (usually electromagnetic radiation, eg radio waves, microwaves, infrared, visible light, ultraviolet, X-rays) that is emitted from a source and travels in the form of waves or particles (photons) through a medium, eg air or a vacuum

RADIATOR *noun* **RADIATORS** an apparatus for heating, consisting of a series of pipes through which hot water or hot oil is circulated

RADICAL *adj* in favour of or tending to produce thoroughgoing or extreme political or social reforms ◻ *noun* **RADICALS** someone who is a member of a radical group, or who holds radical political views

RADICALLY *adverb* in an extreme or radical way

RADICCHIO *noun* **RADICCHIOS** a purple-leaved variety of chicory from Italy, used raw in salads

RADICES plural of **radix**

RADICLE *noun* **RADICLES** the part of a plant embryo which develops into the root

RADII plural of **radius**

RADIO *noun* **RADIOS** a wireless device that receives, and may also transmit, programmes, messages and computer data by means of electromagnetic waves ◻ *verb* **RADIOS, RADIOING, RADIOED** to send (a message) to someone by radio

RADIOGRAM *noun* **RADIOGRAMS** an image (such as an X-ray) of the inside of the body, used to help detect tumours, broken bones etc

RADIOLOGY *noun* **RADIOLOGIES** the branch of medicine concerned with the use of radiation (eg X-rays) and radioactive isotopes to diagnose and treat diseases

RADISH *noun* **RADISHES** a plant of the mustard family, with pungent-tasting red-skinned white roots, which are eaten raw in salads

RADIUM *noun* **RADIUMS** a silvery-white highly toxic radioactive metallic element obtained from uranium ores, especially pitchblende

RADIUS *noun* **RADII** a straight line running from the centre to any point on the circumference of a circle or the surface of a sphere

RADIX *noun* **RADICES** a source, root or basis

RADOME *noun* **RADOMES** a protective covering for microwave radar antennae which is transparent to radio waves

RADON *noun* **RADONS** a highly toxic, colourless, extremely dense, radioactive gas that is formed by the decay of radium

RADULA *noun* **RADULAE** a tongue-like organ of molluscs, comprising a toothed, horny strip which is used for rasping, boring or scraping off particles of food

RADULAR *adj* of, relating to or like radulae

RADULATE *adj* of, relating to or like radulae

RADWASTE *noun* **RADWASTES** radioactive waste

RAFALE *noun* **RAFALES** a burst of artillery in quick rounds

RAFFIA *noun* **RAFFIAS** ribbon-like fibre obtained from the leaves of the Raphia palm, used for weaving mats, baskets, etc

RAFFISH *adj* said of appearance, dress, behaviour, etc: slightly shady or disreputable, often attractively so; rakish

RAFFISHLY *adverb* in a raffish way

RAFFLE *noun* **RAFFLES** a lottery, often to raise money for charity, in which numbered tickets, which are drawn from a container holding all the numbers sold, win prizes for the holders of the tickets that match the numbers drawn ◻ *verb* **RAFFLES, RAFFLING, RAFFLED** to offer something as a prize in a raffle

RAFFLER *noun* **RAFFLERS** someone who runs a raffle

RAFT *noun* **RAFTS** a flat structure of logs, timber, etc, fastened together so as to float on water, used for transport or as a platform ◻ *verb* **RAFTS, RAFTING, RAFTED** to transport something by raft

RAFTER noun RAFTERS a sloping beam supporting a roof □ verb RAFTERS, RAFTERING, RAFTERED to equip with rafters RAFTERED adj said of a building or structure: having (especially visible) rafters

RAFTSMAN noun RAFTSMEN someone who works on a raft

RAG noun RAGS a worn, torn or waste scrap of cloth □ verb RAGS, RAGGING, RAGGED to tear to rags

RAGA noun RAGAS in Hindu classical music: a traditional pattern of notes around which melodies can be improvised

RAGBOLT noun RAGBOLTS a bolt with barb-like projections to prevent withdrawal once it is locked in position

RAGE noun RAGES madness; overpowering passion of any kind □ verb RAGES, RAGING, RAGED to be violently angry

RAGG noun RAGGS a rough hard stone of various kinds, especially one which naturally breaks into slabs

RAGGA noun RAGGAS a style of rap music influenced by dance rhythms

RAGGED ¹ adj RAGGEDER, RAGGEDEST said of clothes: old, worn and tattered

RAGGED ² past form of rag

RAGGEDLY adverb in a ragged way

RAGGEDY adj uneven in quality

RAGGING a form of rag

RAGGY adj RAGGIER, RAGGIEST rough, torn and ragged; like rags

RAGING adj overwhelmed by passion; angry; mad □ noun RAGINGS an act of madness or of overpowering passion

RAGINGLY adverb in a raging way

RAGLAN noun RAGLANS an overcoat with the sleeve in one piece with the shoulder

RAGOUT noun RAGOUTS a highly seasoned stew of meat and vegetables □ verb RAGOUTS, RAGOUTING, RAGOUTED to make a ragout of meat, etc

RAGSTONE noun RAGSTONES undressed masonry slabs

RAGTAG noun RAGTAGS the rabble; the common herd

RAGTIME noun RAGTIMES a type of jazz piano music with a highly syncopated rhythm, originated by Black American musicians in the 1890s

RAGWEED noun RAGWEEDS ragwort

RAGWORK noun RAGWORKS ragstone

RAGWORM noun RAGWORMS a pearly white burrowing marine worm, used as bait by fishermen

RAGWORT noun RAGWORTS a common plant which has yellow flowers with ragged petals

RAH verb RAHS, RAHING, RAHED to shout 'hurrah'

RAI noun RAIS a style of popular music from Algeria, blending traditional Arabic, Spanish flamenco and Western disco rhythms

RAID noun RAIDS a sudden unexpected attack □ verb RAIDS, RAIDING, RAIDED to make a raid on (a person, place, etc)

RAIDER noun RAIDERS someone who goes on raids

RAIL ¹ noun RAILS a bar, usually a horizontal one, supported by vertical posts, forming a fence or barrier

RAIL ² verb RAILS, RAILING, RAILED to complain or criticize something or someone abusively or bitterly

RAILCARD noun RAILCARDS a special card, eg for students, the elderly, etc, giving the holder the right to reduced train fares

RAILER noun RAILERS someone who complains or criticizes something or someone

RAILHEAD noun RAILHEADS a railway terminal

RAILING noun RAILINGS fencing, especially a barrier or ornamental fence

RAILINGLY adverb in a complaining or critical way

RAILLERY noun RAILLERIES good-humoured teasing

RAILROAD noun RAILROADS a railway □ verb RAILROADS, RAILROADING, RAILROADED to rush or force someone unfairly into doing something

RAILWAY noun RAILWAYS a track or set of tracks for trains to run on

RAIMENT noun RAIMENTS clothing

RAIN noun RAINS condensed moisture falling as separate water droplets from the atmosphere □ verb RAINS, RAINING, RAINED said of rain: to fall

RAINBOW noun RAINBOWS an arch of all the colours of the spectrum, ie red, orange, yellow, green, blue, indigo and violet, that can be seen in the sky when falling raindrops reflect and refract sunlight

RAINBOWY adj of or like a rainbow

RAINCOAT noun RAINCOATS a light waterproof coat worn to keep out the rain

RAINDROP noun RAINDROPS a drop of rain

RAINFALL noun RAINFALLS the amount of rain that falls in a certain place over a certain period, measured by depth of water

RAININESS noun RAININESSES the state of being rainy

RAINLESS adj without rain; dry

RAINPROOF adj more or less impervious to rain □ verb RAINPROOFS, RAINPROOFING, RAINPROOFED to make something rainproof □ noun RAINPROOFS a rainproof overcoat

RAINY adj RAINIER, RAINIEST said of a period of time: characterized by stretches of time when it is raining

RAISABLE adj able to be raised

RAISE verb RAISES, RAISING, RAISED to move or lift to a higher position or level □ noun RAISES an increase in salary

RAISEABLE adj raisable

RAISER noun RAISERS a person or thing that raises a building

RAISIN noun RAISINS a dried grape

RAISING noun RAISINGS an act of raising something

RAITA noun RAITAS an Indian dish of chopped vegetables, especially cucumber, in yoghurt

RAJ noun RAJES in India: rule, sovereignity; government

RAJA noun RAJAS an Indian king or prince

RAJAH noun RAJAHS a raja

RAJAHSHIP noun RAJAHSHIPS rajaship

RAJASHIP noun RAJASHIPS the state or condition of being a raja

RAKE noun RAKES a long-handled garden tool with a comb-like part at one end, used for smoothing or breaking up earth, gathering leaves together, etc □ verb RAKES, RAKING, RAKED to collect, gather or remove with, or as if with, a rake

RAKEE noun RAKEES raki

RAKERY noun **RAKERIES** dissoluteness

RAKI noun **RAKIS** an aromatic alcoholic liquor drunk in the Levant, Greece and Turkey

RAKISH adj dashing or jaunty, often with a suspicious or piratical appearance

RAKISHLY adverb in a rakish way

RAKU noun **RAKUS** a type of coarse-grained, lead-glazed pottery fired at low temperature, traditionally used in Japan to make tea bowls

RALE noun **RALES** an abnormal 'rattling' sound, caused by an accumulation of fluid, heard when listening to the lungs with a stethoscope

RALLIER noun **RALLIERS** someone who rallies

RALLY verb **RALLIES, RALLYING, RALLIED** to come or bring together again after being dispersed ◻ noun **RALLIES** a reassembling of forces to make a new effort

RALLYING noun **RALLYINGS** long distance motor racing over public roads

RALLYIST noun **RALLYISTS** someone who takes part in rallying

RAM noun **RAMS** an uncastrated male sheep ◻ verb **RAMS, RAMMING, RAMMED** to force something down or into position by pushing hard

RAMAKIN noun **RAMAKINS** a ramekin

RAMAL adj relating to a branch

RAMATE adj branched

RAMBLE verb **RAMBLES, RAMBLING, RAMBLED** to go where one pleases; to wander ◻ noun **RAMBLES** a walk, usually a longish one and especially in the countryside, for pleasure

RAMBLER noun **RAMBLERS** someone who takes long walks in the countryside for pleasure

RAMBLING adj wandering; nomadic

RAMBUTAN noun **RAMBUTANS** a tree of the same family as the lychee, found throughout SE Asia

RAMEKIN noun **RAMEKINS** a small round straight-sided baking dish or mould for a single serving of food

RAMEN noun **RAMENS** a Japanese dish of clear broth containing vegetables, noodles and often pieces of meat

RAMEQUIN noun **RAMEQUINS** a ramekin

RAMIE noun **RAMIES** a plant of the nettle family, cultivated in China

RAMIFORM adj having a branched shape

RAMIFY verb **RAMIFIES, RAMIFYING, RAMIFIED** to separate or cause to separate into branches or sections

RAMIN noun **RAMINS** a Malaysian tree that grows in swamps

RAMJET noun **RAMJETS** a type of jet engine consisting of forward air intake, combustion chamber and rear expansion nozzle, in which thrust is generated by compression due solely to forward motion

RAMMED past form of **ram**

RAMMER noun **RAMMERS** a person or thing that rams someone or something else

RAMMING a form of **ram**

RAMOSE adj branched

RAMOUS adj ramal

RAMP noun **RAMPS** a sloping surface between two different levels, especially one which can be used instead of steps ◻ verb **RAMPS, RAMPING, RAMPED** to provide with a ramp

RAMPAGE verb **RAMPAGES, RAMPAGING, RAMPAGED** to rush about wildly, angrily, violently or excitedly ◻ noun **RAMPAGES** storming about or behaving wildly and violently in anger, excitement, exuberance, etc

RAMPAGING noun **RAMPAGINGS** an act of rushing about wildly, angrily, violently or excitedly

RAMPANCY noun **RAMPANCIES** the state or condition of being uncontrolled or unrestrained

RAMPANT adj uncontrolled; unrestrained

RAMPANTLY adverb in a rampant way

RAMPART noun **RAMPARTS** a broad mound or wall for defence, usually with a wall or parapet on top ◻ verb **RAMPARTS, RAMPARTING, RAMPARTED** to fortify or surround with ramparts

RAMPER noun **RAMPERS** a person who rushes around, especially someone who makes a disturbance to cover the activities of others

RAMPING noun **RAMPINGS** the practice of causing large false increases in the prices of shares, etc by dishonest means

RAMPION noun **RAMPIONS** a bell-flower whose root is eaten as a salad vegetable

RAMROD noun **RAMRODS** a rod for ramming charge down into, or for cleaning, the barrel of a gun

RAMSONS singular noun a wild garlic, native to woodland of Europe and Asia

RAMUS noun **RAMI** a branch of anything, especially a nerve

RAN a past form of **run**

RANCH noun **RANCHES** an extensive grassland stock-farm where sheep, cattle or horses are raised ◻ verb **RANCHES, RANCHING, RANCHED** to own, manage or work on a ranch

RANCHER noun **RANCHERS** someone who owns, manages or works on a ranch

RANCID adj **RANCIDER, RANCIDEST** said of butter, oil, etc that is going bad: tasting or smelling rank or sour

RANCIDITY noun **RANCIDITIES** the state or condition or quality of being rancid

RANCOROUS adj bitter; spiteful

RANCOUR noun **RANCOURS** a long-lasting feeling of bitterness, dislike or hatred

RAND noun **RAND, RANDS** the standard monetary unit used in South Africa and some neighbouring countries

RANDEM noun **RANDEMS** a carriage or team of horses driven in tandem with three horses in a line, one in front of the other

RANDOM adj lacking a definite plan, system or order; haphazard; irregular

RANDOMISE verb **RANDOMISES, RANDOMISING, RANDOMISED** to randomize

RANDOMIZE verb **RANDOMIZES, RANDOMIZING, RANDOMIZED** to arrange or set up so as to occur in a random manner

RANDOMLY adverb in a random way

RANDY adj **RANDIER, RANDIEST** sexually excited; lustful

RANEE noun **RANEES** a rani

RANG a past form of **ring** [2]

RANGE noun **RANGES** an area between limits within which things may move, function, etc ◻ verb **RANGES, RANGING, RANGED** to put in a row or rows

RANGER noun **RANGERS**

someone who looks after a royal or national forest or park

RANGY *adj* **RANGIER, RANGIEST** said of a person: with long thin limbs and a slender body

RANI *noun* **RANIS** an Indian queen or princess

RANK [1] *noun* **RANKS** a line or row of people or things ❑ *verb* **RANKS, RANKING, RANKED** to arrange (people or things) in a row or line

RANK [2] *adj* **RANKER, RANKEST** said of eg plants: coarsely overgrown and untidy

RANKER *noun* **RANKERS** a soldier who serves or has served in the ranks, especially an officer who has been promoted up through the ranks

RANKLE *verb* **RANKLES, RANKLING, RANKLED** to continue to cause feelings of annoyance or bitterness

RANKLY *adverb* in a coarse, overgrown and untidy way

RANKNESS *noun* **RANKNESSES** the state or condition or quality of being coarse, overgrown and untidy

RANSACK *verb* **RANSACKS, RANSACKING, RANSACKED** to search (eg a house) thoroughly and often roughly

RANSACKER *noun* **RANSACKERS** someone who searches something thoroughly and roughly

RANSOM *noun* **RANSOMS** money demanded in return for the release of a kidnapped person, for the return of property, etc ❑ *verb* **RANSOMS, RANSOMING, RANSOMED** to pay, demand or accept a ransom for someone or something

RANT *verb* **RANTS, RANTING, RANTED** to talk in a loud, angry, pompous way ❑ *noun* **RANTS** loud, pompous, empty speech

RANTER *noun* **RANTERS** someone, especially a preacher, who rants

RANTING *noun* **RANTINGS** an act of speaking in a loud, pompous way

RANTINGLY *adverb* in a loud, pompous way

RAP *noun* **RAPS** a quick short tap or blow ❑ *verb* **RAPS, RAPPING, RAPPED** to strike sharply

RAPACIOUS *adj* greedy and grasping, especially for money

RAPACITY *noun* **RAPACITIES** the state or condition or quality of being greedy or grasping

RAPE *noun* **RAPES** the crime of forcing a person, especially a woman, to have sexual intercourse against their will ❑ *verb* **RAPES, RAPING, RAPED** to commit rape on someone

RAPHIA *noun* **RAPHIAS** raffia

RAPID *adj* **RAPIDER, RAPIDEST** moving, acting or happening quickly; fast ❑ *noun* **RAPIDS** a part of a river where the water flows quickly, usually over dangerous, sharply descending rocks

RAPIDITY *noun* **RAPIDITIES** the state or condition of being quick or fast

RAPIDLY *adverb* quickly

RAPIDNESS *noun* **RAPIDNESSES** rapidity

RAPIER *noun* **RAPIERS** a long thin sword for thrusting

RAPINE *noun* **RAPINES** the seizing of property, etc by force

RAPIST *noun* **RAPISTS** someone who commits the crime of rape

RAPPED past form of **rap**

RAPPER *noun* **RAPPERS** someone who performs songs with a fast rhythmic monologue to music with a pronounced beat

RAPPING a form of **rap**

RAPPORT *noun* **RAPPORTS** a feeling of sympathy and understanding; a close emotional bond

RAPT *adj* enraptured; entranced

RAPTLY *adverb* in a rapt way

RAPTOR *noun* **RAPTORS** any bird of prey, eg an owl or falcon

RAPTORIAL *adj* of or relating to raptors

RAPTURE *noun* **RAPTURES** great delight; ecstasy

RAPTUROUS *adj* delighted; ecstatic

RARE *adj* **RARER, RAREST** not done, found or occurring very often; unusual

RAREBIT *noun* **RAREBITS** a dish consisting of melted cheese, usually with butter, ale and seasoning mixed in, served on toast

RAREFIED *adj* said of the air, atmosphere, etc: thin; with a very low oxygen content

RAREFY *verb* **RAREFIES, RAREFYING, RAREFIED** to make or become rarer, or less dense or solid

RARELY *adverb* not very often

RARENESS *noun* **RARENESSES**

the state or condition of not happening or being found very often

RARING *adj* keen and enthusiastic; willing and very ready to do something

RARITY *noun* **RARITIES** uncommonness

RAS *noun* **RASES** an Ethiopian prince

RASCAL *noun* **RASCALS** a dishonest person; a rogue

RASCALLY *adj* **RASCALLIEST** dishonest; roguish

RASE *verb* **RASES, RASING, RASED** to raze

RASH [1] *adj* **RASHER, RASHEST** said of an action, etc: over-hasty; done without considering the consequences

RASH [2] *noun* **RASHES** an outbreak of red spots or patches on the skin, usually either a symptom of an infectious disease such as measles or chickenpox, or of a skin allergy

RASHER *noun* **RASHERS** a thin slice of bacon or ham

RASHLY *adverb* without considering the consequences

RASHNESS *noun* **RASHNESSES** the state or condition of being rash

RASING a form of **rase**

RASP *noun* **RASPS** a coarse, rough file ❑ *verb* **RASPS, RASPING, RASPED** to scrape roughly, especially with a rasp

RASPBERRY *noun* **RASPBERRIES** the cone-shaped berry made up of several usually reddish drupelets each of which contains a single seed

RASPING *adj* rough; grating

RASPINGLY *adverb* in a rasping way; roughly

RASPY *adj* **RASPIER, RASPIEST** rough; coarse

RASTER *noun* **RASTERS** in TV: a complete set of scanning lines appearing at the receiver as a rectangular patch of light on which the image is reproduced

RAT *noun* **RATS** any of various small rodents, similar to mice but larger, which are found worldwide in huge numbers, and are notorious pests and transmitters of disease ❑ *verb* **RATS, RATTING, RATTED** to hunt or chase rats

RATABLE *adj* rateable

RATAFIA *noun* **RATAFIAS** a

flavouring essence made with the essential oil of almonds

RATAN noun **RATANS** rattan

RATBAG noun **RATBAGS** a mean, despicable person

RATCHET noun **RATCHETS** a bar which fits into the notches of a toothed wheel so as to cause the wheel to turn in one direction only

RATE noun **RATES** the number of times something happens, etc within a given period of time; the amount of something considered in relation to, or measured according to, another amount □ verb **RATES, RATING, RATED** to give (a value) to something

RATEABLE adj said of property: able to have its value assessed for the purpose of payment of rates

RATEL noun **RATELS** a badger-like animal, found in Africa and India

RATEPAYER noun **RATEPAYERS** a person or institution that would have paid local rates

RATES plural noun in the UK until 1990: a tax payable by each household and collected by a local authority to pay for public services based on the assessed value of their property

RATFINK noun **RATFINKS** a mean, despicable or deceitful person

RATHER adverb more readily; more willingly; to a limited degree □ exclamation yes indeed; very much

RATIFY verb **RATIFIES, RATIFYING, RATIFIED** to give formal consent to (eg a treaty, agreement, etc), especially by signature

RATING noun **RATINGS** a classification according to order, rank or value

RATIO noun **RATIOS** the number or degree of one class of things in relation to another, or between one thing and another, expressed as a proportion

RATION noun **RATIONS** a fixed allowance of food, clothing, petrol, etc, during a time of war or shortage □ verb **RATIONS, RATIONING, RATIONED** to distribute or share something out (especially when it is in short supply), usually in fixed amounts

RATIONAL adj related to or based on reason or logic

RATIONALE noun **RATIONALES** the underlying principles or reasons on which a decision, belief, action, etc is based

RATPACK noun **RATPACKS** a rowdy gang of young people

RATTAN noun **RATTANS** a climbing palm with long thin tough stems

RATTED past form of **rat**

RATTER noun **RATTERS** a dog or other animal that catches and kills rats

RATTIER see under **ratty**

RATTIEST see under **ratty**

RATTING a form of **rat**

RATTLE verb **RATTLES, RATTLING, RATTLED** to make a series of short sharp hard sounds in quick succession □ noun **RATTLES** a series of short sharp sounds made in quick succession that gives the effect of a continuous sound

RATTLER noun **RATTLERS** a rattlesnake

RATTLING adj smart □ adverb smartly

RATTLY adj **RATTLIER, RATTLIEST** making a rattling noise; often rattling

RATTY adj **RATTIER, RATTIEST** relating to or like a rat; irritable

RAUCOUS adj said of a sound, especially a voice, shout, etc: hoarse; harsh

RAUCOUSLY adverb in a raucous way

RAUNCHILY adverb in a raunchy way

RAUNCHY adj **RAUNCHIER, RAUNCHIEST** coarsely or openly sexual; lewd or smutty

RAVAGE verb **RAVAGES, RAVAGING, RAVAGED** to cause extensive damage to a place; to destroy it □ noun **RAVAGES** damage or destruction

RAVE verb **RAVES, RAVING, RAVED** to talk wildly as if mad or delirious; to talk enthusiastically about □ noun **RAVES** extravagant praise

RAVEL verb **RAVELS, RAVELLING, RAVELLED** to tangle or become tangled up; to become untangled □ noun **RAVELS** a tangle or knot

RAVELIN noun **RAVELINS** in a fortification: a detached work with two embankments

RAVELLING noun **RAVELLINGS** a thread that has been untangled

RAVEN noun **RAVENS** a large blue-black bird of the crow family □ adj glossy blue-black in colour

RAVENING adj said especially of meat-eating animals: hungrily seeking food

RAVENOUS adj extremely hungry or greedy

RAVER noun **RAVERS** someone who leads a full, very lively and often wild social life

RAVINE noun **RAVINES** a deep narrow steep-sided gorge

RAVING adj frenzied; delirious □ noun **RAVINGS** wild, frenzied or delirious talk

RAVIOLI noun **RAVIOLIS** small square pasta cases with a savoury filling of meat, cheese, etc

RAVISH verb **RAVISHES, RAVISHING, RAVISHED** to overwhelm someone with joy, delight, etc; to enrapture

RAVISHING adj delightful; lovely; very attractive

RAW adj **RAWER, RAWEST** said of meat, vegetables, etc: not cooked □ noun **RAWS** a sore, inflamed or sensitive place

RAWBONED adj lean and gaunt

RAWHIDE noun **RAWHIDES** untanned leather

RAWNESS noun **RAWNESSES** the state or condition or quality of being raw

RAX verb **RAXES, RAXING, RAXED** a dialect word meaning to stretch □ noun **RAXES** a stretch

RAY noun **RAYS** a narrow beam of light or radioactive particles □ verb **RAYS, RAYING, RAYED** to radiate

RAYON noun **RAYONS** a strong, durable, easily dyed artificial fibre consisting of regenerated cellulose that has been spun into filaments

RAZE verb **RAZES, RAZING, RAZED** to destroy or demolish (buildings, a town, etc) completely

RAZOO noun **RAZOOS** an imaginary coin of insignificant value

RAZOR noun **RAZORS** a sharp-edged instrument used for shaving □ verb **RAZORS, RAZORING, RAZORED** to use a razor on something or someone

RAZZLE noun **RAZZLES** a lively spree, outing or party, especially involving a lot of drinking

RE noun **RES** in sol-fa notation: the second note of the major scale

REACH verb **REACHES, REACHING, REACHED** to arrive at or get as far as (a place, position, etc) □ noun **REACHES** the distance one can stretch one's arm, hand, etc

REACHABLE *adj* able to be reached

REACQUIRE *verb* **REAQUIRES, REACQUIRING, REACQUIRED** to acquire again

REACT *verb* **REACTS, REACTING, REACTED** to act in response to something said or done, or to another person

REACTANCE *noun* **REACTANCES** in an electric circuit carrying alternating current: the property of an inductor or capacitor that causes it to oppose the flow of current

REACTANT *noun* **REACTANTS** a substance which takes part in a chemical reaction

REACTION *noun* **REACTIONS** a response to stimulus

REACTIVE *adj* showing a reaction; liable to react; sensitive to stimuli

REACTOR *noun* **REACTORS** an apparatus for producing nuclear energy, eg to generate electricity

READ *verb* **READS, READING, READ** to look at and understand (printed or written words) ❑ *noun* **READS** a period or act of reading

READABLE *adj* legible; able to be read

READAPT *verb* **READAPTS, READAPTING, READAPTED** to adapt again, or again in a different way

READDRESS *verb* **READDRESSES, READDRESSING, READDRESSED** to address again differently

READER *noun* **READERS** someone who reads

READIER see under **ready**

READIEST see under **ready**

READILY *adverb* willingly; quickly and without difficulty

READINESS *noun* **READINESSES** the state or condition of being available for use or action

READING *noun* **READINGS** the action of someone who reads ❑ *adj* fond of or addicted to reading

READJUST *verb* **READJUSTS, READJUSTING, READJUSTED** to adjust again, or again in a different way

READMIT *verb* **READMITS, READMITTING, READMITTED** to admit again

READOPT *verb* **READOPTS, READOPTING, READOPTED** to adopt again

READVANCE *verb* **READVANCES, READVANCING, READVANCED** to advance again

READVISE *verb* **READVISES, READVISING, READVISED** to advise again, or again in a different way

READY *adj* **READIER, READIEST** prepared and available for use or action ❑ *noun* **READIES** money at hand, especially bank notes, for immediate use; cash ❑ *adverb* prepared or made beforehand ❑ *verb* **READIES, READYING, READIED** to make ready; to prepare

REAFFIRM *verb* **REAFFIRMS, REAFFIRMING, REAFFIRMED** to affirm again

REAGENCY *noun* **REAGENCIES** a chemical reaction

REAGENT *noun* **REAGENTS** any chemical compound that participates in a chemical reaction

REAL [1] *adj* **REALER, REALEST** actually or physically existing; not imaginary

REAL [2] *noun* **REALS** a small silver Spanish or Spanish-American coin

REALGAR *noun* **REALGARS** a bright red mineral, arsenic monosulphide

REALIGN *verb* **REALIGNS, REALIGNING, REALIGNED** to align again

REALISE *verb* **REALISES, REALISING, REALISED** to realize

REALISER *noun* **REALISERS** a realizer

REALISM *noun* **REALISMS** the tendency to consider, accept or deal with things as they really are

REALIST *noun* **REALISTS** someone who accepts or deals with things as they really are

REALISTIC *adj* showing awareness or acceptance of things as they really are

REALITY *noun* **REALITIES** the state or fact of being real

REALIZE *verb* **REALIZES, REALIZING, REALIZED** to become aware of something; to know or understand it

REALIZER *noun* **REALIZERS** someone who makes something real, makes it happen

REALLOT *verb* **REALLOTS, REALLOTTING, REALLOTTED** to allot again, or again in a different way

REALLY *adverb* actually; in fact

❑ *exclamation* expressing surprise, doubt or mild protest

REALM *noun* **REALMS** a kingdom

REALMLESS *adj* without a kingdom

REALNESS *noun* **REALNESSES** the state of being real

REALTOR *noun* **REALTORS** in N America: an estate agent

REALTY *noun* **REALTIES** real estate

REAM [1] *noun* **REAMS** a number of sheets of paper equivalent to 20 quires, formerly 480, now usually 500 or 516

REAM [2] *verb* **REAMS, REAMING, REAMED** to enlarge the bore of something

REAMER *noun* **REAMERS** a rotating instrument for enlarging, shaping or finishing a bore

REANIMATE *verb* **REANIMATES, REANIMATING, REANIMATED** to restore to life; to infuse new life into

REAP *verb* **REAPS, REAPING, REAPED** to cut or gather (grain, etc); to harvest

REAPER *noun* **REAPERS** someone who reaps

REAPPEAR *verb* **REAPPEARS, REAPPEARING, REAPPEARED** to appear again

REAPPLY *verb* **REAPPLIES, REAPPLYING, REAPPLIED** to apply again

REAPPOINT *verb* **REAPPOINTS, REAPPOINTING, REAPPOINTED** to appoint again

REAR [1] *noun* **REARS** the back part; the area at the back ❑ *adj* situated or positioned at the back

REAR [2] *verb* **REARS, REARING, REARED** to feed, care for and educate (children); to bring up (children)

REARGUARD *noun* **REARGUARDS** a group of soldiers who protect the rear of an army, especially in retreats

REARM *verb* **REARMS, REARMING, REARMED** to arm again; to arm with new or improved weapons

REARMOST *adj* last of all; nearest the back

REARRANGE *verb* **REARRANGES, REARRANGING, REARRANGED** to arrange again, or again in a different way

REARREST *verb* **REARRESTS, REARRESTING, REARRESTED** to arrest again

REARWARD *adj* positioned in or at the rear □ *adverb* towards the back

REARWARDS *adverb* rearward

REASON *noun* **REASONS** a justification or motive for an action, belief, etc □ *verb* **REASONS, REASONING, REASONED** to use one's mind to form opinions and judgements, reach logical conclusions, deduce, etc

REASONED *adj* well thought out or argued

REASONING *noun* **REASONINGS** the forming of judgements or opinions using reason or careful argument

REASSERT *verb* **REASSERTS, REASSERTING, REASSERTED** to assert again

REASSESS *verb* **REASSESSES, REASSESSING, REASSESSED** to assess again

REASSIGN *verb* **REASSIGNS, REASSIGNING, REASSIGNED** to assign again

REASSUME *verb* **REASSUMES, REASSUMING, REASSUMED** to assume again

REASSURE *verb* **REASSURES, REASSURING, REASSURED** to relieve someone of anxiety or worry

REASSURER *noun* **REASSURERS** someone who reassures someone else

REASSURING *adj* relieving from anxiety or worry; calming

REATTACH *verb* **REATTACHES, REATTACHING, REATTACHED** to attach again

REATTAIN *verb* **REATTAINS, REATTAINING, REATTAINED** to attain again

REATTEMPT *verb* **REATTEMPTS, REATTEMPTING, REATTEMPTED** to attempt again

REAWAKE *verb* **REAWAKES, REAWAKING, REAWOKE, REAWAKED, REAWOKEN** to awake again

REAWAKEN *verb* **REAWAKENS, REAWAKENING, REAWAKENED** to awaken again

REBAPTISE *verb* **REBAPTISES, REBAPTISING, REBAPTISED** to rebaptize

REBAPTISM *noun* **REBAPTISMS** an act or instance of baptizing again

REBAPTIZE *verb* **REBAPTIZES, REBAPTIZING, REBAPTIZED** to baptize again

REBATE *noun* **REBATES** a refund of part of a sum of money paid □ *verb* **REBATES, REBATING, REBATED** to refund part of a sum of money paid

REBEL *verb* **REBELS, REBELLING, REBELLED** to resist openly or fight against authority or oppressive conditions □ *noun* **REBELS** someone who rebels

REBELLION *noun* **REBELLIONS** an act of rebelling; a revolt

REBID *verb* **REBIDS, REBIDDING, REBID, REBIDDEN** to bid again

REBIND *verb* **REBINDS, REBINDING, REBOUND** to bind (especially a book) again

REBIRTH *noun* **REBIRTHS** a second or new birth

REBOOT *verb* **REBOOTS, REBOOTING, REBOOTED** to restart (a computer), either by pressing a specified combination of keys or switching it off and on again at the power source when the computer has crashed or hung

REBORE *verb* **REBORES, REBORING, REBORED** to renew or widen the bore of (a cylinder) in an internal combustion engine □ *noun* **REBORES** the process or result of reboring

REBORN *adj* born again

REBOUND *verb* **REBOUNDS, REBOUNDING, REBOUNDED** to bounce or spring back after an impact □ *noun* **REBOUNDS** an instance of rebounding; a recoil

REBUFF *noun* **REBUFFS** a sudden check, curb or setback □ *verb* **REBUFFS, REBUFFING, REBUFFED** to check or curb

REBUILD *verb* **REBUILDS, REBUILDING, REBUILT** to build again

REBUKABLE *adj* able to be rebuked

REBUKE *verb* **REBUKES, REBUKING, REBUKED** to speak severely to someone because they have done wrong; to reprimand □ *noun* **REBUKES** a stern reprimand or reproach

REBUKER *noun* **REBUKERS** someone who rebukes

REBURIAL *noun* **REBURIALS** an act or instance of reburying

REBURY *verb* **REBURIES, REBURYING, REBURIED** to bury again

REBUS *noun* **REBUSES** a sort of visual pun in which pictures, symbols or letters are used to represent words or syllables in

order to form a message or phrase

REBUT *verb* **REBUTS, REBUTTING, REBUTTED** to disprove or refute (a charge or claim), especially by offering opposing evidence

REBUTTAL *noun* **REBUTTALS** an act of rebutting a charge or claim

REBUTTER *noun* **REBUTTERS** a person or an argument that rebuts

REBUTTON *verb* **REBUTTONS, REBUTTONING, REBUTTONED** to button again

REC *noun* **RECS** a recreation ground; recreation

RECALESCE *verb* **RECALESCES, RECALESCING, RECALESCED** to display a state of glowing heat again

RECALL *verb* **RECALLS, RECALLING, RECALLED** to call back □ *noun* **RECALLS** an act of recalling

RECANT *verb* **RECANTS, RECANTING, RECANTED** to revoke a former declaration

RECANTER *noun* **RECANTERS** someone who recants

RECAP *verb* **RECAPS, RECAPPING, RECAPPED** to go over the chief points (of an argument, statement) again □ *noun* **RECAPS** an act or instance of summing up or recapping

RECAPTURE *verb* **RECAPTURES, RECAPTURING, RECAPTURED** to capture again □ *noun* **RECAPTURES** the act of recapturing or fact of being recaptured

RECAST *verb* **RECASTS, RECASTING, RECAST** to cast again, or again in a different way

RECCE *verb* **RECCES, RECCEING, RECCED, RECCEED** to examine or survey (land, enemy troops, etc) with a view to military operations etc

RECEDE *verb* **RECEDES, RECEDING, RECEDED** to go or move back or backwards

RECEDING *adj* going or moving backwards

RECEIPT *noun* **RECEIPTS** a printed or written note acknowledging that money, goods etc have been received □ *verb* **RECEIPTS, RECEIPTING, RECEIPTED** to mark (a bill) as paid

RECEIVE *verb* **RECEIVES, RECEIVING, RECEIVED** to get, be given or accept (something offered, sent, etc)

For longer words, see The Chambers Dictionary

RECEIVED adj generally accepted
RECEIVER noun **RECEIVERS** someone or something that receives
RECENSION noun **RECENSIONS** a critical revision of a text
RECENT adj **RECENTER**, **RECENTEST** happening, done, having appeared, etc not long ago
RECENTLY adverb not long ago
RECENTRE verb **RECENTRES**, **RECENTRING**, **RECENTRED** to centre again
RECEPTION noun **RECEPTIONS** the act of receiving or fact of being received
RECEPTIVE adj capable of receiving
RECEPTOR noun **RECEPTORS** an element of the nervous system adapted for reception of stimuli, eg a sense organ or sensory nerve-ending
RECESS noun **RECESSES** a space, such as a niche or alcove, set in a wall ◻ verb **RECESSES**, **RECESSING**, **RECESSED** to put something in a recess
RECESSION noun **RECESSIONS** the act of receding or state of being set back
RECESSIVE adj tending to recede
RECHARGE verb **RECHARGES**, **RECHARGING**, **RECHARGED** to charge (eg batteries) again
RÉCHAUFFÉ noun **RÉCHAUFFÉS** a warmed-up dish ◻ adj said of food: warmed-up; reheated
RECHECK verb **RECHECKS**, **RECHECKING**, **RECHECKED** to check again
RECHERCHÉ adj rare, exotic or particularly exquisite
RECIPE noun **RECIPES** directions for making something, especially for preparing and cooking food, usually consisting of a list of ingredients and instructions point-by-point
RECIPIENT noun **RECIPIENTS** a person or thing that receives something
RECISION noun **RECISIONS** the act of annulling or cancelling something; rescinding
RÉCIT noun **RÉCITS** in music: a solo part for the voice or an instrument
RECITAL noun **RECITALS** a public performance of music, usually by a soloist or a small group
RECITE verb **RECITES**, **RECITING**, **RECITED** to repeat aloud (eg a poem, etc) from memory, especially before an audience
RECITER noun **RECITERS** someone who recites eg a poem from memory
RECKLESS adj said of a person: very careless; rash
RECKON verb **RECKONS**, **RECKONING**, **RECKONED** to calculate, compute or estimate something
RECKONER noun **RECKONERS** someone or something that reckons
RECKONING noun **RECKONINGS** calculation; counting
RECLAIM verb **RECLAIMS**, **RECLAIMING**, **RECLAIMED** to seek to regain possession of something; to claim something back ◻ noun **RECLAIMS** the action of reclaiming something or someone, or the state of being reclaimed
RECLAIMER noun **RECLAIMERS** someone who reclaims something
RECLIMB verb **RECLIMBS**, **RECLIMBING**, **RECLIMBED** to climb again
RECLINATE adj said especially of the leaf or stem of a plant: curved or bent down or backwards
RECLINE verb **RECLINES**, **RECLINING**, **RECLINED** to lean or lie on one's back or side, especially when resting; to lie back
RECLINER noun **RECLINERS** someone or something that reclines, especially a type of easy chair with a back which can be adjusted to slope at different angles
RECLOTHE verb **RECLOTHES**, **RECLOTHING**, **RECLOTHED** to clothe again
RECLUSE noun **RECLUSES** someone who lives alone and has little contact with society
RECLUSION noun **RECLUSIONS** religious seclusion
RECLUSIVE adj of or living in seclusion
RECOGNISE verb **RECOGNISES**, **RECOGNISING**, **RECOGNISED** to recognize
RECOGNIZE verb **RECOGNIZES**, **RECOGNIZING**, **RECOGNIZED** to identify (a person or thing known or experienced before)
RECOIL verb **RECOILS**, **RECOILING**, **RECOILED** to spring back or rebound ◻ noun **RECOILS** the act of recoiling, especially the backwards movement of a gun when fired
RECOILER noun **RECOILERS** a person or thing that recoils
RECOLLECT verb **RECOLLECTS**, **RECOLLECTING**, **RECOLLECTED** to recall to memory
RECOMBINE verb **RECOMBINES**, **RECOMBINING**, **RECOMBINED** to combine again
RECOMMEND verb **RECOMMENDS**, **RECOMMENDING**, **RECOMMENDED** to suggest as being suitable to be accepted, chosen, etc; to commend
RECOMMIT verb **RECOMMITS**, **RECOMMITTING**, **RECOMMITTED** to commit again
RECONCILE verb **RECONCILES**, **RECONCILING**, **RECONCILED** to put two or more people on friendly terms again, especially after a quarrel
RECONDITE adj said of a subject or knowledge: difficult to understand; little known
RECONFIRM verb **RECONFIRMS**, **RECONFIRMING**, **RECONFIRMED** to confirm again
RECONNECT verb **RECONNECTS**, **RECONNECTING**, **RECONNECTED** to connect again
RECONQUER verb **RECONQUERS**, **RECONQUERING**, **RECONQUERED** to conquer again
RECONVENE verb **RECONVENES**, **RECONVENING**, **RECONVENED** to convene again
RECONVERT verb **RECONVERTS**, **RECONVERTING**, **RECONVERTED** to convert again to a former state, religion, etc
RECONVEY verb **RECONVEYS**, **RECONVEYING**, **RECONVEYED** (of an estate, etc) to transfer again to a former owner
RECORD noun **RECORDS** a formal written report or statement of facts, events or information ◻ verb **RECORDS**, **RECORDING**, **RECORDED** to set something down in writing or some other permanent form, especially for use in the future
RECORDER noun **RECORDERS** a wooden or plastic wind instrument with a tapering mouthpiece and holes which are covered by the player's fingers in various configurations to make the notes
RECORDING noun **RECORDINGS** the process of registering sounds or images on a record, tape, video, . etc

For longer words, see *The Chambers Dictionary*

RECOUNT verb **RECOUNTS, RECOUNTING, RECOUNTED** to narrate or tell (a story, etc) in detail
RECOUP verb **RECOUPS, RECOUPING, RECOUPED** to recover or get back (something lost, eg money)
RECOURSE noun **RECOURSES** the act of turning to someone, or resorting to a particular course of action, for help or protection, especially in an emergency or a case of extreme need
RECOVER verb **RECOVERS, RECOVERING, RECOVERED** to get or find something again
RECOVERY noun **RECOVERIES** an act, instance or process of recovering
RECREANT noun **RECREANTS** a cowardly or disloyal person
RECREATE verb **RECREATES, RECREATING, RECREATED** to create something again; to reproduce
RECROSS verb **RECROSSES, RECROSSING, RECROSSED** to cross again
RECRUIT noun **RECRUITS** a newly enlisted member of the army, air force, navy, etc ◻ verb **RECRUITS, RECRUITING, RECRUITED** to enlist (people) as recruits
RECRUITAL noun **RECRUITALS** renewed supply; restoration
RECRUITER noun **RECRUITERS** someone who recruits others
RECTA a plural of **rectum**
RECTAL adj of or relating to the rectum
RECTALLY adverb in a way that relates to the rectum
RECTANGLE noun **RECTANGLES** a four-sided figure with opposite sides of equal length and all its angles right angles
RECTI plural of **rectus**
RECTIFIER noun **RECTIFIERS** someone or something that rectifies
RECTIFY verb **RECTIFIES, RECTIFYING, RECTIFIED** to put (a mistake, etc) right or correct
RECTITUDE noun **RECTITUDES** rightness; correctness of behaviour or judgement
RECTO noun **RECTOS** the right-hand page of an open book
RECTOR noun **RECTORS** in the Church of England: a clergyman in charge of a parish who would, formerly, have been entitled to receive all the tithes of that parish

RECTORATE noun **RECTORATES** a rector's office or term of office
RECTORIAL adj of or relating to a rector
RECTORY noun **RECTORIES** the house or residence of a rector
RECTRIX noun **RECTRICES** a long stiff feather of a bird's tail, used to help control direction in flight
RECTUM noun **RECTUMS, RECTA** the lower part of the alimentary canal, ending at the anus
RECTUS noun **RECTI** a straight muscle
RECUMBENT adj lying down; reclining
RECUR verb **RECURS, RECURRING, RECURRED** to happen or come round again
RECURRENT adj happening often or regularly
RECURSION noun **RECURSIONS** a going back; a return
RECURSIVE adj of a mathematical definition: consisting of rules that allow values or meaning to be determined with certainty
RECUSANCE noun **RECUSANCES** a refusal to submit to authority
RECUSANCY noun **RECUSANCIES** recusance
RECUSANT noun **RECUSANTS** said especially of Roman Catholics: someone who refused to attend Church of England services when these were obligatory (between c.1570 and c.1790)
RECYCLE verb **RECYCLES, RECYCLING, RECYCLED** to process or treat waste material (eg paper, glass or plastic) so that it can be used again
RED¹ adj **REDDER, REDDEST** referring to the colour of blood, or a colour similar to it ◻ noun **REDS** the colour of blood, or a similar shade

RED² verb **REDS, REDDING, RED** a Scots word meaning to tidy

REDACT verb **REDACTS, REDACTING, REDACTED** to edit; to put (a text) into the appropriate literary form
REDACTION noun **REDACTIONS** an act of editing a text
REDACTOR noun **REDACTORS** someone who edits text
REDBACK noun **REDBACKS** a poisonous Australian spider the

female of which has a red stripe on its back
REDBREAST noun **REDBREASTS** any bird that has a red breast, especially a robin
REDBRICK adj said of a British university: established in the late 19c or early 20c, eg Leeds, Manchester and Birmingham universities, as opposed to the more traditional ones such as Oxford, Cambridge, Edinburgh, etc
REDCOAT noun **REDCOATS** a British soldier
REDDEN verb **REDDENS, REDDENING, REDDENED** to make red or redder
REDDER see under **red**
REDDEST see under **red**
REDDISH adj somewhat red
REDDLE noun **REDDLES** ruddle ◻ verb **REDDLES, REDDLING, REDDLED** to ruddle
REDDY adj **REDDIER, REDDIEST** somewhat red
REDEAL verb **REDEALS, REDEALING, REDEALT** to deal again ◻ noun **REDEALS** an act or instance of redealing
REDEEM verb **REDEEMS, REDEEMING, REDEEMED** to buy someone or something back
REDEEMER noun **REDEEMERS** someone who redeems
REDEEMING adj making up for faults or shortcomings
REDEFINE verb **REDEFINES, REDEFINING, REDEFINED** to define again, or again in a different way
REDEPLOY verb **REDEPLOYS, REDEPLOYING, REDEPLOYED** to transfer (soldiers, industrial workers, supplies, etc) to another place or job
REDESIGN verb **REDESIGNS, REDESIGNING, REDESIGNED** to design again, or again in a different way
REDEVELOP verb **REDEVELOPS, REDEVELOPING, REDEVELOPED** to develop again
REDHEAD noun **REDHEADS** a person, especially a woman, with red hair
REDIAL verb **REDIALS, REDIALLING, REDIALLED** to dial again
REDINGOTE noun **REDINGOTES** a long double-breasted overcoat, originally for a man, later for a woman

REDIRECT verb **REDIRECTS, REDIRECTING, REDIRECTED** to direct again, or again in a different way

REDNESS noun **REDNESSES** the state or condition or quality of being red

REDO verb **REDOES, REDOING, REDID, REDONE** to do something again or differently

REDOLENCE noun **REDOLENCES** the state or condition of being redolent

REDOLENCY noun **REDOLENCIES** redolence

REDOLENT adj fragrant; smelling strongly of; strongly suggestive of

REDOUBLE verb **REDOUBLES, REDOUBLING, REDOUBLED** to double; to repeat □ noun **REDOUBLES** the act of redoubling

REDOUBT noun **REDOUBTS** a fortification, especially a temporary one defending a pass or hilltop

REDOUND verb **REDOUNDS, REDOUNDING, REDOUNDED** to have a direct, usually beneficial, but also sometimes detrimental, effect on someone

REDRAW verb **REDRAWS, REDRAWING, REDREW, REDRAWN** to draw again

REDRESS verb **REDRESSES, REDRESSING, REDRESSED** to set right or compensate for (something wrong) □ noun **REDRESSES** the act of redressing or being redressed

REDRIVE verb **REDRIVES, REDRIVING, REDROVE, REDRIVEN** to drive again

REDSHANK noun **REDSHANKS** a wading bird of the sandpiper family which has a scarlet bill and legs, a white rump and a broad white wing bar visible in flight

REDSTART noun **REDSTARTS** a European bird with a conspicuous chestnut-coloured tail

REDUCE verb **REDUCES, REDUCING, REDUCED** to make or become less, smaller, etc

REDUCER noun **REDUCERS** someone or something that reduces

REDUCIBLE adj able to be reduced

REDUCTASE noun **REDUCTASES** an enzyme which brings about the reduction of organic compounds

REDUCTION noun **REDUCTIONS** an act, instance or process of reducing; the state of being reduced

REDUCTIVE adj reducing, narrowing, limiting

REDUNDANT adj not needed; superfluous

REDWING noun **REDWINGS** a type of thrush that has reddish sides below the wings

REDWOOD noun **REDWOODS** an extremely tall and long-lived sequoia, native to California that reaches heights of 120m

REE noun **REES** a Scots word for an enclosure (for sheep, etc)

REEBOK noun **REEBOKS** a S African antelope

REED noun **REEDS** any of a group of grasses that grow in shallow water by the margins of streams, lakes and ponds

REEDINESS noun **REEDINESSES** the state of being reedy

REEDMACE noun **REEDMACES** a reed-like plant that grows in marshy ground and which has a long tubular flowerhead made up of small, closely-packed brownish flowers

REEDY adj **REEDIER, REEDIEST** full of reeds

REEF [1] noun **REEFS** in shallow coastal water: a mass of rock, coral, sand, etc that either projects above the surface at low tide, or is permanently covered by shallow water

REEF [2] verb **REEFS, REEFING, REEFED** to reduce the area of (a sail) exposed to the wind by folding in a reef (a foldable part of the sail)

REEFER noun **REEFERS** a thick woollen double-breasted jacket

REEFING noun **REEFINGS** an act of reefing a sail

REEK noun **REEKS** a strong, unpleasant and often offensive smell □ verb **REEKS, REEKING, REEKED** to give off a strong, usually unpleasant smell

REEL noun **REELS** a round wheel-shaped or cylindrical object of plastic, metal, etc on which thread, film, fishing-lines, etc can be wound □ verb **REELS, REELING, REELED** to wind something on a reel

REEVE [1] noun **REEVES** the chief magistrate of a town or district

REEVE [2] verb **REEVES, REEVING, ROVE, REEVED** to pass (a rope, etc) through a hole, opening or ring

REF noun **REFS** a referee □ verb **REFS, REFFING, REFFED** to referee

REFASHION verb **REFASHIONS, REFASHIONING, REFASHIONED** to fashion again, or again in a different way

REFECTORY noun **REFECTORIES** a dining-hall, especially one in a monastery or university

REFER verb **REFERS, REFERRING, REFERRED** to direct a candidate to sit an examination again; to fail them

REFERABLE adj capable of being referred or assigned

REFEREE noun **REFEREES** a person to whom reference is made to settle a question, dispute, etc □ verb **REFEREES, REFEREEING, REFEREED** to act as a referee in a game, dispute, etc

REFERENCE noun **REFERENCES** a mention of something; an allusion to it □ verb **REFERENCES, REFERENCING, REFERENCED** to make a reference to something

REFERRAL noun **REFERRALS** the act of referring to someone else or being referred to someone else, especially the sending of a patient by a GP to a specialist for treatment

REFILL noun **REFILLS** a new filling for something which becomes empty through use; a container for this plus contents □ verb **REFILLS, REFILLING, REFILLED** to fill again

REFINE verb **REFINES, REFINING, REFINED** to make something pure by removing dirt, waste substances, etc

REFINED adj very polite; well-mannered

REFINEDLY adverb in a polite and well-mannered way

REFINER noun **REFINERS** a person or thing that refines

REFINERY noun **REFINERIES** a factory where raw materials such as sugar and oil are purified

REFINING noun **REFININGS** an act of making something pure by removing dirt, waste substances, etc

REFIT verb **REFITS, REFITTING, REFITTED** to repair or fit new parts to (especially a ship) □ noun **REFITS** the process of refitting or being refitted

REFITMENT noun **REFITMENTS** an act of refitting

REFLAG verb **REFLAGS, REFLAGGING, REFLAGGED** to change the country of registration of (a merchant ship), usually for some commercial advantage

REFLATE verb **REFLATES, REFLATING, REFLATED** to bring about reflation of (an economy)

REFLATION noun **REFLATIONS** an increase in economic activity and in the amount of money and credit available, designed to increase industrial production after a period of deflation

REFLECT verb **REFLECTS, REFLECTING, REFLECTED** said of a surface: to send back (light, heat, sound, etc)

REFLECTOR noun **REFLECTORS** a polished surface that reflects light, heat, etc

REFLET noun **REFLETS** an iridescent or metallic lustre, especially on ceramics

REFLEX noun **REFLEXES** a response to a sensory, physical or chemical stimulus ◻ adj denoting an angle that is greater than 180° but less than 360° ◻ verb **REFLEXES, REFLEXING, REFLEXED** to bend something back

REFLEXION noun **REFLEXIONS** the change in direction of a particle or wave, eg the turning back of a ray of light, either when it strikes a smooth surface that it does not penetrate, such as a mirror or polished metal, or when it reaches the boundary between two media

REFLEXIVE adj said of a pronoun: showing that the object of a verb is the same as the subject, eg in *He cut himself, himself* is a reflexive pronoun; said of a verb: used with a reflexive pronoun as object, eg *shave* as in *He shaved himself* ◻ noun **REFLEXIVES** a reflexive pronoun or verb

REFLOAT verb **REFLOATS, REFLOATING, REFLOATED** to float again

REFLOWER verb **REFLOWERS, REFLOWERING, REFLOWERED** to flower again

REFLUX noun **REFLUXES** the boiling of a liquid for long periods in a container attached to a condenser so that the vapour produced condenses and continuously flows back into the container ◻ verb **REFLUXES,**

REFLUXING, REFLUXED to boil or be boiled under reflux

REFOCUS verb **REFOCUSES, REFOCUSING, REFOCUSED** to focus again

REFORM verb **REFORMS, REFORMING, REFORMED** to improve or remove faults from (a person, behaviour, etc) ◻ noun **REFORMS** a correction or improvement, especially in some social or political system

REFORMAT verb **REFORMATS, REFORMATTING, REFORMATTED** to format again, or again in a different way

REFORMER noun **REFORMERS** someone who tries to reform others, society, a political system etc

REFORMISM noun **REFORMISMS** any doctrine or movement that advocates social and political change in a gradual manner within a democratic framework, rather than revolutionary change

REFORMIST noun **REFORMISTS** a reformer; an advocate of reform

REFRACT verb **REFRACTS, REFRACTING, REFRACTED** said of a medium, eg water, glass: to cause the direction of (a wave of light, sound, etc) to change when it crosses the boundary between this medium and another through which it travels at a different speed, eg between air and glass

REFRACTOR noun **REFRACTORS** a telescope in which light rays are collected by means of a lens of long focal length and magnified by a lens of short focal length

REFRAIN[1] noun **REFRAINS** a phrase or group of lines repeated at the end of each stanza or verse in a poem or song

REFRAIN[2] verb **REFRAINS, REFRAINING, REFRAINED** to keep oneself from acting in some way or doing something; to avoid it

REFRAME verb **REFRAMES, REFRAMING, REFRAMED** to put a new frame on a picture, etc

REFREEZE verb **REFREEZES, REFREEZING, REFROZEN** to freeze again

REFRESH verb **REFRESHES, REFRESHING, REFRESHED** to make fresh again

REFRESHER noun **REFRESHERS** anything that refreshes, eg a cold drink

REFRESHING adj giving new

strength, energy or enthusiasm; cooling

REFUEL verb **REFUELS, REFUELLING, REFUELLED** to supply (an aircraft, car, etc) with more fuel

REFUGE noun **REFUGES** shelter or protection from danger or trouble

REFUGEE noun **REFUGEES** someone who seeks refuge, especially from religious or political persecution, in another country

REFUGIUM noun **REFUGIA** a region that has retained earlier geographical, climatic, etc conditions, and therefore becomes a haven for older varieties of flora and fauna

REFULGENT adj shining brightly; radiant; beaming

REFUND verb **REFUNDS, REFUNDING, REFUNDED** to pay (money, etc) back to someone because the goods or service that they had purchased was faulty, not up to standard, etc; to repay ◻ noun **REFUNDS** the paying back of money, etc

REFUNDER noun **REFUNDERS** someone who pays money back

REFURBISH verb **REFURBISHES, REFURBISHING, REFURBISHED** to renovate

REFURNISH verb **REFURNISHES, REFURNISHING, REFURNISHED** to furnish again

REFUSABLE adj able to be refused or turned down

REFUSAL noun **REFUSALS** an act of refusing to accept something

REFUSE[1] verb **REFUSES, REFUSING, REFUSED** to declare oneself unwilling to do what one has been asked or told to do, etc; to say 'no'

REFUSE[2] noun **REFUSES** rubbish; waste

REFUSENIK noun **REFUSENIKS** in the former Sovet Union: someone, especially a Jew, who was refused permission to emigrate (usually to Israel)

REFUSNIK noun **REFUSNIKS** a refusenik

REFUTABLE adj that can be refuted

REFUTABLY adverb in a way that refutes

REFUTE verb **REFUTES, REFUTING, REFUTED** to prove that (a person, statement, theory, etc) is wrong

REFUTER noun **REFUTERS** someone who refutes something
REGAIN verb **REGAINS, REGAINING, REGAINED** to get back again or recover
REGAINER noun **REGAINERS** someone who regains something
REGAL adj relating to, like, or suitable for a king or queen
REGALE verb **REGALES, REGALING, REGALED** to amuse someone, eg with stories, etc
REGALIA plural noun the insignia of royalty, eg the crown and sceptre
REGALITY noun **REGALITIES** the state or condition of being regal
REGALLY adverb in a regal way
REGARD verb **REGARDS, REGARDING, REGARDED** to consider someone or something in a specified way ◻ noun **REGARDS** esteem
REGARDER noun **REGARDERS** a person who regards
REGARDFUL adj respectful
REGARDING prep about; concerning
REGATTA noun **REGATTAS** a yacht or boat race-meeting
REGELATE verb **REGELATES, REGELATING, REGELATED** to freeze together again
REGENCY noun **REGENCIES** government by regent ◻ adj said of art, furniture, etc: belonging to or in the style prevailing during the English or French Regency
REGENT noun **REGENTS** someone who governs a country during a monarch's childhood or illness ◻ adj acting as regent
REGGAE noun **REGGAES** popular music of W Indian origin which has a strong syncopated beat, usually with four beats to the bar and a characteristic strongly-accented upbeat
REGICIDAL adj of or relating to regicide
REGICIDE noun **REGICIDES** the killing of a king
REGIME noun **REGIMES** a system of government
REGIMEN noun **REGIMENS** a course of treatment, especially of diet and exercise, which is recommended for good health
REGIMENT noun **REGIMENTS** a body of soldiers, the largest permanent army unit, consisting of several companies and commanded by a colonel ◻ verb **REGIMENTS, REGIMENTING,**

REGIMENTED to organize or control (people, etc) strictly, usually too strictly
REGION noun **REGIONS** an area of the world or of a country, especially one with particular geographical, social, etc characteristics
REGIONAL adj of, relating to or found in a particular region
RÉGISSEUR noun **RÉGISSEURS** in a ballet company: a director
REGISTER noun **REGISTERS** a written list or record of names, events, etc ◻ verb **REGISTERS, REGISTERING, REGISTERED** to enter (an event, name, etc) in an official register
REGISTRAR noun **REGISTRARS** someone who keeps an official register, especially of births, deaths and marriages
REGISTRY noun **REGISTRIES** an office or place where registers are kept
REGLET noun **REGLETS** in architecture: a flat narrow moulding
REGNAL adj relating to a reign or to a monarch
REGNANT adj prevalent
REGORGE verb **REGORGES, REGORGING, REGORGED** to disgorge
REGRADE verb **REGRADES, REGRADING, REGRADED** to grade again
REGRESS verb **REGRESSES, REGRESSING, REGRESSED** to go back ◻ noun **REGRESSES** a going back
REGRET verb **REGRETS, REGRETTING, REGRETTED** to feel sorry, repentant, distressed, disappointed, etc about (something one has done or that has happened) ◻ noun **REGRETS** a feeling of sorrow, repentance, distress, disappointment, etc
REGRETFUL adj feeling sorry; repentant
REGRIND verb **REGRINDS, REGRINDING, REGROUND** to grind again
REGROUP verb **REGROUPS, REGROUPING, REGROUPED** to group again
REGROWTH noun **REGROWTHS** an act or instance of growing again
REGULAR adj usual; normal; customary ◻ noun **REGULARS** a soldier in a professional permanent army

REGULARLY adverb in a regular way; frequently; often
REGULATE verb **REGULATES, REGULATING, REGULATED** to control or adjust (the amount of available heat, sound, etc)
REGULATOR noun **REGULATORS** a person or thing that regulates, such as a controlling device that controls the speed of a clock or watch
REGULINE adj of or relating to a regulus
REGULUS noun **REGULUSES** an impure metal formed as an intermediate product in the smelting of ores

REH noun **REHS** a deposit of salts on soil in India, etc

REHASH verb **REHASHES, REHASHING, REHASHED** to rework or reuse (material which has been used before), but with no significant changes or improvements ◻ noun **REHASHES** a reworking or reuse of existing material with little or no change
REHEAR verb **REHEARS, REHEARING, REHEARD** to hear again
REHEARSAL noun **REHEARSALS** the act of rehearsing
REHEARSE verb **REHEARSES, REHEARSING, REHEARSED** to practise (a play, piece of music, etc) before performing it in front of an audience
REHEARSER noun **REHEARSERS** someone who rehearses
REHEARSING noun **REHEARSINGS** an act of practising before performing in front of an audience
REHEAT verb **REHEATS, REHEATING, REHEATED** to heat again ◻ noun **REHEATS** a device for injecting fuel into the hot exhaust gases of a turbojet in order to obtain increased thrust
REHEATER noun **REHEATERS** a person or apparatus that reheats
REHOBOAM noun **REHOBOAMS** a large liquor measure or vessel, especially for champagne, that holds six times the amount of a standard bottle
REHOUSE verb **REHOUSES, REHOUSING, REHOUSED** to provide with new and usually better accommodation or premises
REHOUSING noun **REHOUSINGS**

an act of providing with new accommodation or premises **REHYDRATE** verb **REHYDRATES, REHYDRATING, REHYDRATED** to absorb water again after dehydration

REIFY verb **REIFIES, REIFYING, REIFIED** to think of (something abstract) as a material thing; to materialize

REIGN noun **REIGNS** the period of time for which a king or queen rules □ verb **REIGNS, REIGNING, REIGNED** to be a ruling king or queen

REIMBURSE verb **REIMBURSES, REIMBURSING, REIMBURSED** to repay (money spent)

REIMPORT verb **REIMPORTS, REIMPORTING, REIMPORTED** to import again

REIN noun **REINS** the strap, or either of the two halves of the strap, attached to a bridle and used to guide and control a horse □ verb **REINS, REINING, REINED** to provide with reins

REINDEER noun **REINDEERS** a species of large deer, antlered in both sexes, that is found in arctic and subarctic regions of Europe and Asia and is closely related to the caribou

REINFORCE verb **REINFORCES, REINFORCING, REINFORCED** to strengthen or give additional support to something

REINFORM verb **REINFORMS, REINFORMING, REINFORMED** to inform anew; to give form to again

REINHABIT verb **REINHABITS, REINHABITING, REINHABITED** to inhabit again

REINSERT verb **REINSERTS, REINSERTED, REINSERTING** to insert again

REINSTATE verb **REINSTATES, REINSTATING, REINSTATED** to instate someone again

REINSURE verb **REINSURES, REINSURING, REINSURED** to insure something again

REINVEST verb **REINVESTS, REINVESTING, REINVESTED** to invest again

REISSUE verb **REISSUES, REISSUING, REISSUED** to issue again

REISTAFEL noun **REISTAFELS** rijstafel

REITERATE verb **REITERATES, REITERATING, REITERATED** to repeat

REJECT verb **REJECTS, REJECTING, REJECTED** to refuse to accept, agree to, admit, believe, etc; to throw away or discard □ noun **REJECTS** someone or something that is rejected

REJECTER noun **REJECTERS** a rejector

REJECTION noun **REJECTIONS** an act of rejecting

REJECTIVE adj tending to reject

REJECTOR noun **REJECTORS** someone who rejects

REJIG verb **REJIGS, REJIGGING, REJIGGED** to rearrange or reorganize something □ noun **REJIGS** the act of rejigging

REJIGGER verb **REJIGGERS, REJIGGERING, REJIGGERED** to rejig

REJOICE verb **REJOICES, REJOICING, REJOICED** to feel, show or express great happiness or joy

REJOICER noun **REJOICERS** someone who rejoices

REJOICING noun **REJOICINGS** an act of showing or expressing great happiness or joy

REJOIN verb **REJOINS, REJOINING, REJOINED** to say something in reply, especially abruptly or wittily

REJOINDER noun **REJOINDERS** an answer or remark, especially one made abruptly or wittily in reply to something; a retort

REJÓN noun **REJONES** in bullfighting: a lance with a wooden handle, usually thrust at a bull from horseback

REKINDLE verb **REKINDLES, REKINDLING, REKINDLED** to relight or revive something (eg a fire, emotions)

RELAPSE verb **RELAPSES, RELAPSING, RELAPSED** to sink or fall back into a former state or condition, especially one involving evil or bad habits □ noun **RELAPSES** the act or process of relapsing

RELAPSER noun **RELAPSERS** someone who relapses

RELATE verb **RELATES, RELATING, RELATED** to tell or narrate (a story, anecdote, etc)

RELATED adj belonging to the same family

RELATION noun **RELATIONS** an act of relating

RELATIVE noun **RELATIVES** a person who is related to someone

else by birth or marriage □ adj compared with something else; comparative

RELAX verb **RELAXES, RELAXING, RELAXED** to make (part of the body, muscles, one's grip, etc) less tense, stiff or rigid

RELAXANT adj relating to or causing someone or something to relax □ noun **RELAXANTS** a drug that makes a person feel less tense and helps them to relax, or one that relaxes the skeletal muscles

RELAXIN noun **RELAXINS** a hormone produced during pregnancy which has a relaxing effect on the pelvic muscles

RELAY noun **RELAYS** a set of workers, supply of materials, etc that replace others doing, or being used for, some task, etc □ verb **RELAYS, RELAYING, RELAYED** to receive and pass on (news, a message, a TV programme, etc)

RELEASE verb **RELEASES, RELEASING, RELEASED** to free (a prisoner, etc) from captivity □ noun **RELEASES** the act of releasing or state of being released, from captivity, duty, oppression, etc

RELEASER noun **RELEASERS** someone who releases eg a prisoner from captivity

RELEGABLE adj able to be relegated

RELEGATE verb **RELEGATES, RELEGATING, RELEGATED** to move someone down to a lower grade, position, status, etc

RELENT verb **RELENTS, RELENTING, RELENTED** to become less severe or unkind; to soften

RELENTING noun **RELENTINGS** an act of becoming less severe or unkind; a softening

RELET verb **RELETS, RELETTING, RELET** to let (eg a property) again

RELEVANCE noun **RELEVANCES** the state or condition of being relevant

RELEVANCY noun **RELEVANCIES** relevance

RELEVANT adj directly connected with or related to the matter in hand; pertinent

RELIABLE adj to be relied on; trustworthy

RELIABLY adverb in a reliable way

RELIANCE noun **RELIANCES** trust; that in which one trusts

RELIANT adj trusting in or depending on (something)

RELIC noun **RELICS** a fragment or part of an object left after the rest has decayed

RELICT noun **RELICTS** a species or organ occurring in circumstances different from those in which it originated

RELIED past form of **rely**

RELIEF noun **RELIEFS** the lessening or removal of pain, worry, oppression or distress

RELIES a form of **rely**

RELIEVE verb **RELIEVES, RELIEVING, RELIEVED** to lessen or stop (someone's pain, worry, boredom, etc)

RELIEVED adj freed from anxiety or concern, usually about a particular matter

RELIEVER noun **RELIEVERS** someone who relieves another's anxiety or concerns

RELIEVO noun **RELIEVOS** a method of sculpture in which figures project from a flat surface

RELIGHT verb **RELIGHTS, RELIGHTING, RELIT, RELIGHTED** to light again

RELIGIEUX noun **RELIGIEUX** a monk or friar

RELIGION noun **RELIGIONS** a belief in, or the worship of, a god or gods

RELIGIOSE adj morbidly or sentimentally religious

RELIGIOUS adj relating to religion ▫ noun **RELIGIOUS** a person bound by monastic vows, eg a monk or nun

RELINE verb **RELINES, RELINING, RELINED** to line again

RELIQUARY noun **RELIQUARIES** a container for holy relics

RELIQUIAE plural noun remains, especially fossil remains of plants or animals

RELISH verb **RELISHES, RELISHING, RELISHED** to enjoy something greatly or with discrimination ▫ noun **RELISHES** pleasure; enjoyment

RELIVE verb **RELIVES, RELIVING, RELIVED** to live again

RELOAD verb **RELOADS, RELOADING, RELOADED** to load again

RELOCATE verb **RELOCATES, RELOCATING, RELOCATED** to locate again

RELUCTANT adj unwilling or not wanting to do something

RELY verb **RELIES, RELYING, RELIED** to depend on or need someone or something

REM noun **REMS** a former unit of radiation dosage, replaced by the sievert (1 rem = 0.01 Sv)

REMAIN verb **REMAINS, REMAINING, REMAINED** to be left after others, or other parts of the whole, have been used up, taken away, lost, etc

REMAINDER noun **REMAINDERS** what is left after others, or other parts, have gone, been used up, taken away, etc; the rest ▫ verb **REMAINDERS, REMAINDERING, REMAINDERED** to sell (a copy or copies of a book) at a reduced price because its sales have fallen off

REMAINDERED adj said of a book, especially a specified edition: offered for sale at a reduced price

REMAINS plural noun what is left after part has been taken away, eaten, destroyed, etc

REMAKE verb **REMAKES, REMAKING, REMADE** to make something again or in a new way ▫ noun **REMAKES** something that is made again, especially a new version of an old film

REMAND verb **REMANDS, REMANDING, REMANDED** to send (a person accused of a crime) back into custody to await trial, especially to allow more evidence to be collected ▫ noun **REMANDS** the act or process of sending an accused person back into custody to await trial

REMANENCE noun **REMANENCES** something that remains, especially the magnetism that remains after the removal of a magnetizing field

REMANENCY noun **REMANENCIES** remanence

REMANENT adj remaining

REMARK verb **REMARKS, REMARKING, REMARKED** to notice and comment on something ▫ noun **REMARKS** a comment, often a casual one

REMARKED adj conspicuous

REMARKER noun **REMARKERS** someone who makes remarks

REMARQUE noun **REMARQUES** an indication on the edge of a plate that usually takes the form of a small sketch denoting the stage that the engraving has reached

REMARRY verb **REMARRIES, REMARRYING, REMARRIED** to marry again

REMATCH noun **REMATCHES** in sport: a second match or game between two people or teams

REMEASURE verb **REMEASURES, REMEASURING, REMEASURED** to measure again

REMEDIAL adj affording a remedy

REMEDY noun **REMEDIES** any drug or treatment which cures or controls a disease ▫ verb **REMEDIES, REMEDYING, REMEDIED** to cure or control (a disease, etc)

REMEMBER verb **REMEMBERS, REMEMBERING, REMEMBERED** to bring someone or something from the past to mind

REMEX noun **REMIGES** any of the large primary or secondary flight feathers of a bird's wing

REMIGIAL adj of or relating to a remex

REMIND verb **REMINDS, REMINDING, REMINDED** to cause someone to remember (something or to do something)

REMINDER noun **REMINDERS** something that reminds

REMINDFUL adj mindful; prompting memories

REMINISCE verb **REMINISCES, REMINISCING, REMINISCED** to think, talk or write about things remembered from the past

REMISE verb **REMISES, REMISING, REMISED** to give up or surrender (a right, claim, etc) ▫ noun **REMISES** the giving up or surrender of a right or claim

REMISS adj careless; failing to pay attention; negligent

REMISSION noun **REMISSIONS** a lessening in force or effect, especially in the symptoms of a disease such as cancer

REMISSIVE adj remitting; forgiving

REMISSLY adverb carelessly

REMIT verb **REMITS, REMITTING, REMITTED** to cancel or refrain from demanding (a debt, punishment, etc) ▫ noun **REMITS** the authority or terms of reference given to an official, committee, etc in dealing with a matter

REMITMENT noun **REMITMENTS** the sending of money, etc to a distance

REMITTAL noun **REMITTALS** in law: reference to another court

REMITTEE noun **REMITTEES** the person to whom money is sent in payment

REMITTENT adj said of a disease: becoming less severe at times

REMITTER noun **REMITTERS** someone who sends money to someone in payment

REMITTOR noun **REMITTORS** a remitter

REMIX verb **REMIXES, REMIXING, REMIXED** to mix again in a different way, especially to mix (a recording) again, changing the balance of the different parts, etc □ noun **REMIXES** a remixed recording

REMNANT noun **REMNANTS** a remaining small piece or amount of something larger, or a small number of things left from a larger quantity

REMODEL verb **REMODELS, REMODELLING, REMODELING, REMODELLED, REMODELED** to model again, or again in a different way

REMODIFY verb **REMODIFIES, REMODIFYING, REMODIFIED** to modify again

REMONTANT noun **REMONTANTS** a plant that blooms more than once in the same season, especially a rose or a strawberry plant

REMORA noun **REMORAS** any of several slender marine fish which attach themselves to rocks, other fish, etc by means of a large sucker on the top of the head

REMORSE noun **REMORSES** a deep feeling of guilt, regret and bitterness for something wrong or bad which one has done

REMOTE adj **REMOTER, REMOTEST** far away; distant in time or place □ noun **REMOTES** an outside broadcast

REMOTELY adverb from far away; from a distance

REMOULADE noun **REMOULADES** a sauce made by adding herbs, capers, mustard, etc to mayonnaise, and served with fish, salad, etc

REMOULD verb **REMOULDS, REMOULDING, REMOULDED** to mould again □ noun **REMOULDS** a tyre that has had new tread bonded onto it

REMOUNT verb **REMOUNTS, REMOUNTING, REMOUNTED** to get on or mount again (especially a horse, bicycle, etc) □ noun **REMOUNTS** a fresh horse

REMOVABLE adj able to be removed

REMOVAL noun **REMOVALS** an act of moving, especially to a new house

REMOVE verb **REMOVES, REMOVING, REMOVED** to move someone or something to a different place □ noun **REMOVES** a removal

REMOVER noun **REMOVERS** someone whose job is to move possessions, furniture, etc from one house to another

REMUAGE noun **REMUAGES** the process of turning or shaking wine bottles so that the sediment collects at the cork end for removal

REMUEUR noun **REMUEURS** in wine-making: the person who turns the bottles

REN verb **RENS, RENNING, RENNED** old spelling of run

RENAL adj relating to, or in the area of, the kidneys

RENAME verb **RENAMES, RENAMING, RENAMED** to name again, with a different name

RENASCENT adj being reborn; reviving

REND verb **RENDS, RENDING, RENT** to tear something apart, especially using force or violence; to split

RENDER verb **RENDERS, RENDERING, RENDERED** to cause something to be or become; to give or provide (a service etc) □ noun **RENDERS** a first coat of plaster or rendering applied to brick or stonework

RENDERER noun **RENDERERS** someone who renders

RENDERING noun **RENDERINGS** a coat of plaster

RENDITION noun **RENDITIONS** a performance or interpretation of a piece of music, a dramatic role, etc

RENDZINA noun **RENDZINAS** any of a group of dark fertile soils, typical of humid or semi-arid grassland and limestone regions, rich in humus and calcium carbonate, that have developed over limestone bedrock

RENEGADE noun **RENEGADES** someone who deserts the religious, political, etc group which they belong to, and joins an enemy or rival group

RENEGE verb **RENEGES, RENEGING, RENEGED** to go back on (a promise, agreement, deal, etc)

RENEGER noun **RENEGERS** someone who reneges

RENEGUE verb **RENEGUES, RENEGUING, RENEGUED** to renege

RENEGUER noun **RENEGUERS** a reneger

RENEW verb **RENEWS, RENEWING, RENEWED** to make something fresh or like new again

RENEWABLE adj able to be renewed

RENEWAL noun **RENEWALS** an act of renewing

RENEWER noun **RENEWERS** someone who renews something

RENEWING noun **RENEWINGS** an act of making something fresh or like new again

RENIFORM adj kidney-shaped

RENIN noun **RENINS** an enzyme, produced by the kidneys, that is secreted into the bloodstream and is involved in the formation of a hormone which raises the blood pressure by constricting the arteries

RENNET noun **RENNETS** a substance used for curdling milk, especially and originally an extract obtained from the stomachs of calves that contains the enzyme rennin

RENNIN noun **RENNINS** an enzyme found in gastric juice that causes milk to curdle

RENOUNCE verb **RENOUNCES, RENOUNCING, RENOUNCED** to give up (a claim, title, right, etc), especially formally and publicly □ noun **RENOUNCES** in card games: a failure to follow suit

RENOUNCER noun **RENOUNCERS** someone who renounces something

RENOVATE verb **RENOVATES, RENOVATING, RENOVATED** to renew or make new again

RENOVATOR noun **RENOVATORS** someone who renovates eg old buildings

RENOWN noun **RENOWNS** fame

RENOWNED adj famous; celebrated

RENT noun **RENTS** money paid periodically to the owner of a property by a tenant in return for the use or occupation of that property □ verb **RENTS, RENTING, RENTED** to pay rent for (a building, house, flat, etc)

For longer words, see *The Chambers Dictionary*

RENTABLE adj able to be rented

RENTAL noun **RENTALS** the act of renting; something rented or hired, such as a car

RENTER noun **RENTERS** a tenant who pays rent

RENUMBER verb **RENUMBERS, RENUMBERING, RENUMBERED** to number again

REOCCUPY verb **REOCCUPIES, REOCCUPYING, REOCCUPIED** to occupy again

REOFFEND verb **REOFFENDS, REOFFENDING, REOFFENDED** to offend again

REOPEN verb **REOPENS, REOPENING, REOPENED** to open again

REORDER verb **REORDERS, REORDERING, REORDERED** to order again

REORIENT verb **REORIENTS, REORIENTING, REORIENTED** to orient again

REP noun **REPS** a representative, especially a travelling salesperson ❑ verb **REPS, REPPING, REPPED** to work or act as a commercial representative

REPACK verb **REPACKS, REPACKING, REPACKED** to pack again, or again in a different way

REPAINT verb **REPAINTS, REPAINTING, REPAINTED** to paint over or again ❑ noun **REPAINTS** the act or process of repainting or fact of being repainted

REPAIR verb **REPAIRS, REPAIRING, REPAIRED** to restore (something damaged or broken) to good working condition ❑ noun **REPAIRS** an act or the process of repairing

REPAIRER noun **REPAIRERS** someone who repairs things

REPAND adj with slightly wavy edge or margin

REPAPER verb **REPAPERS, REPAPERING, REPAPERED** to paper over or again

REPARABLE adj capable of being repaired or made good

REPARABLY adverb in a reparable way

REPARTEE noun **REPARTEES** the practice or skill of making spontaneous witty replies

REPAST noun **REPASTS** a meal

REPAY verb **REPAYS, REPAYING, REPAID** to pay back or refund (money)

REPAYABLE adj able to be repaid

REPAYMENT noun **REPAYMENTS** an act of repaying eg money; an amount of money paid back

REPEAL verb **REPEALS, REPEALING, REPEALED** to make (a law, etc) no longer valid; to annul (a law, etc) ❑ noun **REPEALS** the act of repealing (a law, etc); annulment

REPEALER noun **REPEALERS** someone who repeals eg a law

REPEAT verb **REPEATS, REPEATING, REPEATED** to say, do, etc, again or several times ❑ noun **REPEATS** the act of repeating

REPEATER noun **REPEATERS** someone who repeats something

REPEATING noun **REPEATINGS** an act of repeating something

REPECHAGE noun **REPECHAGES** a supplementary heat in a competition that allows runners-up from earlier eliminating heats a second chance to go on to the final

REPEL verb **REPELS, REPELLING, REPELLED** to force or drive something or someone back or away

REPELLANT noun **REPELLANTS** a repellent ❑ adj repellent

REPELLENT noun **REPELLENTS** something that repels, especially that repels insects ❑ adj forcing or driving back or away; repelling

REPELLER noun **REPELLERS** a person or thing that repels

REPENT verb **REPENTS, REPENTING, REPENTED** to feel great sorrow or regret for something one has done

REPENTANT adj repenting

REPENTER noun **REPENTERS** someone who repents of an action

REPEOPLE verb **REPEOPLES, REPEOPLING, REPEOPLED** to people again

REPERTORY noun **REPERTORIES** a repertoire, especially the complete list of plays that a theatre company is able and ready to perform

REPETEND noun **REPETENDS** the figure or figures that repeat themselves in a recurring decimal number

REPHRASE verb **REPHRASES, REPHRASING, REPHRASED** to put or express something in different words, especially to make it more understandable, acceptable, etc

REPINE verb **REPINES, REPINING, REPINED** to fret

REPLACE verb **REPLACES, REPLACING, REPLACED** to put something back in its previous position

REPLACER noun **REPLACERS** a substitute

REPLAN verb **REPLANS, REPLANNING, REPLANNED** to plan again

REPLANT verb **REPLANTS, REPLANTING, REPLANTED** to plant again

REPLAY noun **REPLAYS** the playing of a game, football match, etc again, usually because there was no clear winner the first time ❑ verb **REPLAYS, REPLAYING, REPLAYED** to play (a tape, recording, football match, etc) again

REPLENISH verb **REPLENISHES, REPLENISHING, REPLENISHED** to fill up or make complete again, especially a supply of something which has been used up

REPLETE adj completely or well supplied with something

REPLETION noun **REPLETIONS** fullness; plethora

REPLICA noun **REPLICAS** an exact copy, especially of a work of art, sometimes by the original artist, and often on a smaller scale

REPLICATE verb **REPLICATES, REPLICATING, REPLICATED** to make a replica of something ❑ noun **REPLICATES** in music: a tone one or more octaves from a given tone

REPLIER noun **REPLIERS** someone who replies

REPLY verb **REPLIES, REPLYING, REPLIED** to answer or respond to something in words, writing or action ❑ noun **REPLIES** an answer; a response

REPO noun **REPOS** repossession

REPOINT verb **REPOINTS, REPOINTING, REPOINTED** to repair (stone or brickwork) by renewing the cement or mortar between the joins

REPORT noun **REPORTS** a detailed statement, description or account, especially one made after some form of investigation ❑ verb **REPORTS, REPORTING, REPORTED** to bring back (information, etc) as an answer, news or account

REPORTAGE noun **REPORTAGES** journalistic reporting

REPORTER noun **REPORTERS**

someone who reports on events, especially for a newspaper

REPOSE *noun* **REPOSES** a state of rest, calm or peacefulness □ *verb* **REPOSES, REPOSING, REPOSED** to rest

REPOSEDLY *adverb* in a restful, calm or peaceful way

REPOSEFUL *adj* resting, calm, peaceful

REPOSSESS *verb* **REPOSSESSES, REPOSSESSING, REPOSSESSED** said of a creditor: to regain possession of (property or goods), especially because the debtor has defaulted on payment

REPOT *verb* **REPOTS, REPOTTING, REPOTTED** to plant again

REPOUSSÉ *adj* said of metalwork: raised in relief by hammering from behind or within □ *noun* **REPOUSSÉS** a piece of metalwork made in this way

REPP *noun* **REPPS** a corded cloth, made of wool, silk, cotton or rayon, used as a furnishing fabric

REPREHEND *verb* **REPREHENDS, REPREHENDING, REPREHENDED** to find fault with something

REPRESENT *verb* **REPRESENTS, REPRESENTING, REPRESENTED** to serve as a symbol or sign for something

REPRESS *verb* **REPRESSES, REPRESSING, REPRESSED** to keep (an impulse, a desire to do something, etc) under control

REPRESSED *adj* controlled; restrained

REPRESSOR *noun* **REPRESSORS** someone who represses

REPRIEVE *verb* **REPRIEVES, REPRIEVING, REPRIEVED** to delay or cancel (someone's punishment, especially the execution of a prisoner condemned to death) □ *noun* **REPRIEVES** the act of delaying or cancelling criminal sentence, especially a death sentence

REPRIMAND *verb* **REPRIMANDS, REPRIMANDING, REPRIMANDED** to criticize or rebuke someone angrily or severely, especially publicly or formally □ *noun* **REPRIMANDS** angry or severe and usually formal criticism or rebuke

REPRINT *verb* **REPRINTS, REPRINTING, REPRINTED** to print something again □ *noun* **REPRINTS** the act of reprinting

REPRISAL *noun* **REPRISALS** revenge or retaliation

REPRISE *noun* **REPRISES** the repeating of a passage or theme □ *verb* **REPRISES, REPRISING, REPRISED** to repeat (an earlier passage or theme)

REPRO *noun* **REPROS** a copy or reproduction, eg of a work of art

REPROACH *verb* **REPROACHES, REPROACHING, REPROACHED** to express disapproval of, or disappointment with, someone for a fault or some wrong done □ *noun* **REPROACHES** an act of reproaching

REPROBACY *noun* **REPROBACIES** the state or condition of being immoral or unprincipled

REPROBATE *noun* **REPROBATES** an immoral unprincipled person □ *verb* **REPROBATES, REPROBATING, REPROBATED** to disapprove of someone

REPROCESS *verb* **REPROCESSES, REPROCESSING, REPROCESSED** to process something again, especially to make (something already used, eg spent nuclear fuel) into a new reuseable form

REPRODUCE *verb* **REPRODUCES, REPRODUCING, REPRODUCED** to make or produce something again

REPROOF[1] *noun* **REPROOFS** an act of reproving

REPROOF[2] *verb* **REPROOFS, REPROOFING, REPROOFED** to make (a coat, etc) waterproof again

REPROVE *verb* **REPROVES, REPROVING, REPROVED** to rebuke

REPROVER *noun* **REPROVERS** someone who reproves

REPTANT *adj* creeping

REPTILE *noun* **REPTILES** any cold-blooded scaly vertebrate animal, eg lizards, snakes, tortoises, turtles, crocodiles, alligators, and many extinct species, including dinosaurs and pterodactyls

REPTILIAN *adj* of, relating to or like a reptile

REPUBLIC *noun* **REPUBLICS** a form of government without a monarch and in which supreme power is held by the people or their elected representatives, especially one in which the head of state is an elected or nominated president

REPUBLISH *verb* **REPUBLISHES, REPUBLISHING, REPUBLISHED** to publish again

REPUDIATE *verb* **REPUDIATES,**

REPUDIATING, REPUDIATED to deny or reject something as unfounded

REPUGNANT *adj* distasteful; disgusting

REPULSE *verb* **REPULSES, REPULSING, REPULSED** to drive or force back (an enemy, attacking force, etc) □ *noun* **REPULSES** the act of repulsing or state of being repulsed

REPULSION *noun* **REPULSIONS** an act of repulsing

REPULSIVE *adj* provoking a feeling of disgust, horror or loathing

REPUTABLE *adj* respected; well thought of

REPUTABLY *adverb* in a reputable way

REPUTE *verb* **REPUTES, REPUTING, REPUTED** to consider someone or something to be as specified or to have some specified quality; to deem □ *noun* **REPUTES** general opinion or impression

REPUTED *adj* supposed; generally considered to be

REPUTEDLY *adverb* supposedly

REQUEST *noun* **REQUESTS** the act or an instance of asking for something □ *verb* **REQUESTS, REQUESTING, REQUESTED** to ask for something

REQUESTER *noun* **REQUESTERS** someone who makes a request

REQUIEM *noun* **REQUIEMS** a mass for the souls of the dead

REQUIRE *verb* **REQUIRES, REQUIRING, REQUIRED** to need something

REQUIRER *noun* **REQUIRERS** someone who requires something

REQUIRING *noun* **REQUIRINGS** an act of requiring something

REQUISITE *adj* required or necessary □ *noun* **REQUISITES** something that is required, necessary or indispensable for some purpose

REQUITAL *noun* **REQUITALS** an act of requiting; recompense

REQUITE *verb* **REQUITES, REQUITING, REQUITED** to make a suitable return in response to (someone's kindness or injury)

REQUITER *noun* **REQUITERS** someone who requites

REQUOTE *verb* **REQUOTES, REQUOTING, REQUOTED** to quote again

REREAD *verb* **REREADS, REREADING, REREAD** to read again

REREDOS *noun* **REREDOSES** a stone or wooden screen or partition wall, usually an ornamental one, behind an altar

REREVISE *verb* **REREVISES, REREVISING, REREVISED** to revise again

REROUTE *verb* **REROUTES, REROUTING, REROUTED** to direct (traffic, aircraft, etc) along an alternative route, usually because the usual route cannot be used because of an accident, heavy traffic, bad weather, etc; to redirect

RERUN *verb* **RERUNS, RERUNNING, RERAN, RERUN** to run (a race, etc) again because a result could not be determined from the first run □ *noun* **RERUNS** a race that is run again

RES *noun* **RESES** in N America: a reservation

RESALE *noun* **RESALES** the selling of an article again

RESAY *verb* **RESAYS, RESAYING, RESAID** to say again

RESCIND *verb* **RESCINDS, RESCINDING, RESCINDED** to cancel, annul or revoke (an order, law, custom, etc)

RESCORE *verb* **RESCORES, RESCORING, RESCORED** to rewrite (a musical score) for different instruments, voices, etc

RESCRIPT *noun* **RESCRIPTS** the official answer from a pope to a question, petition, etc

RESCUE *verb* **RESCUES, RESCUING, RESCUED** to free someone or something from danger, evil, trouble, captivity, etc; to save □ *noun* **RESCUES** the act or an instance of rescuing or being rescued

RESCUER *noun* **RESCUERS** someone who rescues others

RESEAL *verb* **RESEALS, RESEALING, RESEALED** to seal again

RESEARCH *noun* **RESEARCHES** detailed and careful investigation into some subject or area of study with the aim of discovering and applying new facts or information □ *verb* **RESEARCHES, RESEARCHING, RESEARCHED** to carry out a detailed and careful investigation into some subject

RESEAT *verb* **RESEATS, RESEATING, RESEATED** to seat someone in a different chair or place

RESECT *verb* **RESECTS, RESECTING, RESECTED** to cut away or remove (part of a bone, organ, etc)

RESECTION *noun* **RESECTIONS** the cutting away or removal of part of a bone, organ etc

RESELECT *verb* **RESELECTS, RESELECTING, RESELECTED** to select again

RESELL *verb* **RESELLS, RESELLING, RESOLD** to sell again

RESEMBLE *verb* **RESEMBLES, RESEMBLING, RESEMBLED** to be like or similar to someone or something else, especially in appearance

RESENT *verb* **RESENTS, RESENTING, RESENTED** to take or consider something as an insult or an affront

RESENTFUL *adj* resenting something

RESERPINE *noun* **RESERPINES** a drug obtained from a tropical tree or shrub, used to treat high blood pressure and as a tranquillizer

RESERVE *verb* **RESERVES, RESERVING, RESERVED** to keep something back or set it aside for future use, for the use of a particular person, or for some particular purpose □ *noun* **RESERVES** something kept back or set aside, epecially for future use or possible need

RESERVED *adj* kept back, set aside or destined for a particular use or for a particular person

RESERVIST *noun* **RESERVISTS** a member of a reserve force

RESERVOIR *noun* **RESERVOIRS** a large natural or man-made lake, or a tank, in which water is collected and stored for public use, irrigation, etc

RESET *verb* **RESETS, RESETTING, RESETTED** to set (eg a broken limb, the type of a book, a stone in a piece of jewellery, etc) again or differently □ *noun* **RESETS** the action of setting something again or differently

RESETTER *noun* **RESETTERS** someone who knowingly receives stolen goods

RESETTLE *verb* **RESETTLES, RESETTLING, RESETTLED** to settle again, or again in a new place

RESHAPE *verb* **RESHAPES, RESHAPING, RESHAPED** to shape again, or again in a different way

RESHUFFLE *verb* **RESHUFFLES,**

RESHUFFLING, RESHUFFLED to shuffle (cards) again or differently □ *noun* **RESHUFFLES** an act of reshuffling

RESIDE *verb* **RESIDES, RESIDING, RESIDED** to live or have one's home in a particular place, especially permanently

RESIDENCE *noun* **RESIDENCES** a house or dwelling, especially a large, impressive and imposing one

RESIDENCY *noun* **RESIDENCIES** a residence

RESIDENT *noun* **RESIDENTS** someone who lives permanently in a particular place □ *adj* living or dwelling in a particular place, especially permanently or for some length of time

RESIDER *noun* **RESIDERS** someone who resides in a particular place

RESIDUAL *noun* **RESIDUALS** something which remains or is left over as a residue

RESIDUARY *adj* relating to or constituting a residue

RESIDUE *noun* **RESIDUES** what remains of something, or is left over, when a part has been taken away, used up, etc; the remainder

RESIDUUM *noun* **RESIDUA** a residue

RESIGN *verb* **RESIGNS, RESIGNING, RESIGNED** to give up employment or an official position, etc

RESIGNED *adj* having or showing patient and calm acceptance of something, usually something unpleasant or unwelcome, that is considered inevitable

RESIGNER *noun* **RESIGNERS** someone who resigns

RESILE *verb* **RESILES, RESILING, RESILED** to draw back from a contract or agreement

RESILIENT *adj* said of a person: able to recover quickly from, or to deal readily with, illness, sudden, unexpected difficulties, hardship, etc

RESIN *noun* **RESINS** any of several substances obtained from the sap of various plants and trees, especially conifers, often aromatic and usually in the form of a brittle, translucent solid or a viscous liquid □ *verb* **RESINS, RESINING, RESINED** to treat something with resin

RESINATE *verb* **RESINATES,**

RESINATING, RESINATED to impregnate something with resin
RESINIFY verb **RESINIFIES, RESINIFYING, RESINIFIED** to make into, or become, a resin or resinous
RESINOUS adj of, like, relating to or containing resin
RESIST verb **RESISTS, RESISTING, RESISTED** to oppose or fight against someone or something; to refuse to give in or comply to it ◻ noun **RESISTS** a protective coating of a resistant substance, especially one applied to parts of a fabric that are not to be dyed or printed, or a light-sensitive coating on a silicon wafer
RESISTANT adj able to resist, withstand or remain unaffected or undamaged by something
RESISTOR noun **RESISTORS** a device which introduces a known value of resistance to electrical flow into a circuit
RESIT verb **RESITS, RESITTING, RESAT** to take (an examination) again, usually having failed it before, or in order to improve one's grade ◻ noun **RESITS** the action of taking an examination again
RESOLE verb **RESOLES, RESOLING, RESOLED** to fit (a shoe or boot) with a new sole
RESOLUBLE adj able to be resolved or analysed
RESOLUTE adj said of a person or their attitude, etc: with a fixed purpose or belief
RESOLVE verb **RESOLVES, RESOLVING, RESOLVED** to decide firmly or to determine to do something ◻ noun **RESOLVES** determination or firmness of purpose
RESOLVED adj said of a person: determined; firm in purpose
RESOLVENT noun **RESOLVENTS** a drug that reduces swelling or inflammation
RESOLVER noun **RESOLVERS** a person or thing that resolves
RESONANCE noun **RESONANCES** the quality or state of being resonant
RESONANT adj said of sounds: echoing; continuing to sound; resounding
RESONATE verb **RESONATES, RESONATING, RESONATED** to resound or make something resound or echo
RESONATOR noun **RESONATORS**

a resonating body or device, eg one for increasing sonority or analysing sound
RESORB verb **RESORBS, RESORBING, RESORBED** to absorb something again or absorb it back into itself
RESORBENT adj able to absorb something back again
RESORCIN noun **RESORCINS** a white crystalline phenol used in dyeing, photography and pharmaceuticals, and also to make resins and adhesives
RESORT verb **RESORTS, RESORTING, RESORTED** to turn to something or someone as a means of solving a problem, etc; to have recourse to something or someone ◻ noun **RESORTS** a place visited by many people, especially one, eg a seaside town, that provides accommodation and recreation for holidaymakers
RESORTER noun **RESORTERS** someone who resorts to someone or something
RESOUND verb **RESOUNDS, RESOUNDING, RESOUNDED** said of sounds: to ring or echo
RESOURCE noun **RESOURCES** someone or something that provides a source of help, support, etc when needed ◻ verb **RESOURCES, RESOURCING, RESOURCED** to provide support, usually financial, for someone or something
RESPECT noun **RESPECTS** admiration; good opinion ◻ verb **RESPECTS, RESPECTING, RESPECTED** to show or feel admiration or high regard for someone or something
RESPECTER noun **RESPECTERS** a person who respects eg other people
RESPECTING prep about; concerning; with regard to
RESPELL verb **RESPELLS, RESPELLING, RESPELT, RESPELLED** to spell again
RESPIRE verb **RESPIRES, RESPIRING, RESPIRED** to inhale and exhale (air, etc); to breathe
RESPITE noun **RESPITES** a period of rest or relief from, or a temporary stopping of, something unpleasant, difficult, etc ◻ verb **RESPITES, RESPITING, RESPITED** to grant a respite to someone; to reprieve
RESPOND verb **RESPONDS,**

RESPONDING, RESPONDED to answer or reply; to say something in reply ◻ noun **RESPONDS** a response to a versicle in liturgy
RESPONSE noun **RESPONSES** an act of responding, replying or reacting to something
RESPONSOR noun **RESPONSORS** in radar: a device that receives and processes signals
RESPRAY verb **RESPRAYS, RESPRAYING, RESPRAYED** to spray (especially the bodywork of a vehicle) again, either with the same colour (especially part of the vehicle), or with a different colour of paint ◻ noun **RESPRAYS** the action of respraying
REST noun **RESTS** a period of relaxation or freedom from work, activity, worry, etc ◻ verb **RESTS, RESTING, RESTED** to stop or make something stop working or moving
RESTAFF verb **RESTAFFS, RESTAFFING, RESTAFFED** to provide (an establishment) with new staff
RESTAGE verb **RESTAGES, RESTAGING, RESTAGED** to stage again, or again in a different way
RESTART verb **RESTARTS, RESTARTING, RESTARTED** to start again
RESTATE verb **RESTATES, RESTATING, RESTATED** to state again
RESTER noun **RESTERS** someone who rests
RESTFUL adj **RESTFULLER, RESTFULLEST** bringing or giving rest; tranquil
RESTFULLY adverb in a restful way
RESTIVE adj restless; nervous; uneasy
RESTIVELY adverb in a restive way; nervously
RESTLESS adj unable to stay quiet or still; unable to relax
RESTOCK verb **RESTOCKS, RESTOCKING, RESTOCKED** to stock again
RESTORE verb **RESTORES, RESTORING, RESTORED** to return (a building, painting, etc) to a former condition by repairing or cleaning it, etc
RESTORER noun **RESTORERS** a person who restores eg old buildings, works of art, etc
RESTRAIN verb **RESTRAINS, RESTRAINING, RESTRAINED** to prevent (someone, oneself, etc) from doing something

RESTRAINT *noun* **RESTRAINTS** the act of restraining or the state of being restrained

RESTRICT *verb* **RESTRICTS, RESTRICTING, RESTRICTED** to keep someone or something within certain limits

RESTRING *verb* **RESTRINGS, RESTRINGING, RESTRUNG** to fit or provide with a new string or strings

RESTYLE *verb* **RESTYLES, RESTYLING, RESTYLED** to style again, or again in a different way

RESUBMIT *verb* **RESUBMITS, RESUBMITTING, RESUBMITTED** to submit again

RESULT *noun* **RESULTS** an outcome or consequence of something □ *verb* **RESULTS, RESULTING, RESULTED** to be a consequence or outcome of some action, event, etc

RESULTANT *adj* resulting □ *noun* **RESULTANTS** in mathematics: a single force which is the equivalent of two or more forces acting on an object

RESUMABLE *adj* able to be resumed

RESUME *verb* **RESUMES, RESUMING, RESUMED** to return to something or begin it again after an interruption

RÉSUMÉ *noun* **RÉSUMÉS** a summary

RESURFACE *verb* **RESURFACES, RESURFACING, RESURFACED** to put a new surface on something, especially a road

RESURGENT *adj* returning to life or activity again

RESURRECT *verb* **RESURRECTS, RESURRECTING, RESURRECTED** to bring someone back to life from the dead

RESURVEY *verb* **RESURVEYS, RESURVEYING, RESURVEYED** to survey again

RET *verb* **RETS, RETTING, RETTED** to soften (flax, hemp, etc) by moistening or soaking

RETABLE *noun* **RETABLES** a shelf or ornamental setting for panels, etc above and behind an altar

RETAIL *noun* **RETAILS** the sale of goods, either individually or in small quantities, to customers who will not resell them but who buy them for their own use □ *adj* relating to, concerned with, or engaged in such sale of goods □ *verb* **RETAILS, RETAILING,**

RETAILED to sell (goods) in small quantities

RETAILER *noun* **RETAILERS** someone who sells goods, often a shop-owner

RETAIN *verb* **RETAINS, RETAINING, RETAINED** to keep or continue to have something

RETAINER *noun* **RETAINERS** someone or something that retains

RETAKE *verb* **RETAKES, RETAKING, RETOOK, RETAKEN** to take again □ *noun* **RETAKES** the action of retaking something, especially a second filming of a scene in a movie

RETAKER *noun* **RETAKERS** someone who takes something again

RETALIATE *verb* **RETALIATES, RETALIATING, RETALIATED** to repay an injury, wrong, etc in kind; to get revenge

RETARD *verb* **RETARDS, RETARDING, RETARDED** to slow down or delay something

RETARDANT *noun* **RETARDANTS** a substance that retards, especially one that has the effect of slowing down or delaying some specified reaction, process, etc

RETARDED *adj* slowed down or delayed

RETARDER *noun* **RETARDERS** a substance that is used to slow down the rate of some process, chemical change, etc, eg a substance used to delay or prevent the setting of cement

RETCH *verb* **RETCHES, RETCHING, RETCHED** to strain as if to vomit, but without actually doing so □ *noun* **RETCHES** an act of retching

RETE *noun* **RETES** a network of blood vessels or nerves

RETENTION *noun* **RETENTIONS** the act of retaining something or the state of being retained

RETENTIVE *adj* able to keep or retain, especially memories or information

RETEXTURE *verb* **RETEXTURES, RETEXTURING, RETEXTURED** to treat (a blanket, garment, etc) with chemicals which restore the original texture of the material

RETHINK *verb* **RETHINKS, RETHINKING, RETHOUGHT** to think about or consider (a plan, etc) again, usually with a view to changing one's mind about it or reaching a different conclusion

□ *noun* **RETHINKS** an act of rethinking

RETIAL *adj* of or relating to a rete

RETICENCE *noun* **RETICENCES** the state or condition of being quiet and reserved

RETICENT *adj* not saying very much; not willing to communicate

RETICLE *noun* **RETICLES** an attachment to an optical instrument, consisting of a network of lines of reference

RETICULAR *adj* netted; netlike

RETICULE *noun* **RETICULES** a woman's small pouch-like bag, often netted or beaded, and fastening with a drawstring

RETICULUM *noun* **RETICULUMS** a fine network, especially one of fibres, vessels, etc

RETIE *verb* **RETIES, RETYING, RETIED** to tie again

RETIFORM *adj* having the form of a net; netlike

RETILE *verb* **RETILES, RETILING, RETILED** to tile again

RETINA *noun* **RETINAS, RETINAE** the light-sensitive tissue that lines much of the back of the eyeball, in which nerve impulses are generated which are relayed to the brain and interpreted as vision

RETINAL *adj* of or relating to the retina

RETINITIS *noun* **RETINITISES** inflammation of the retina

RETINOL *noun* **RETINOLS** vitamin A

RETINUE *noun* **RETINUES** the servants, officials, aides, etc who travel with and attend an important person

RETIRAL *noun* **RETIRALS** an act of retiring, eg from work, or of going away from a place

RETIRE *verb* **RETIRES, RETIRING, RETIRED** to stop or make someone stop working permanently, usually on reaching an age at which a pension can be received

RETIRING *adj* shy and reserved; not liking to be noticed

RETITLE *verb* **RETITLES, RETITLING, RETITLED** to give a new title to (a book, film, etc)

RETOOK a past form of **retake**

RETORT *verb* **RETORTS, RETORTING, RETORTED** to make a quick and clever or angry reply □ *noun* **RETORTS** a quick and clever or angry reply

RETORTION noun **RETORTIONS** retorting; bending back

RETOUCH verb **RETOUCHES, RETOUCHING, RETOUCHED** to improve or repair (a photograph, negative, painting, etc) by adding extra touches or making small alterations ◻ noun **RETOUCHES** an act of improving, especially of making small repairs or adjustments to a photograph by pencil-work on the negative

RETOUCHER noun **RETOUCHERS** someone who retouches eg photographs

RETRACE verb **RETRACES, RETRACING, RETRACED** to go back over (a route, path, etc)

RETRACT verb **RETRACTS, RETRACTING, RETRACTED** to draw something in or back

RETRACTOR noun **RETRACTORS** an instrument for holding back tissue, skin, an organ, etc from the area being operated on

RETRAIN verb **RETRAINS, RETRAINING, RETRAINED** to teach (a person or animal) new skills

RETREAD[1] verb **RETREADS, RETREADING, RETROD, RETRODDEN** to tread (a path, one's steps, etc) again

RETREAD[2] verb **RETREADS, RETREADING, RETREADED** to bond new tread onto (an old or worn tyre) ◻ noun **RETREADS** a tyre that has had new tread bonded on to it

RETREAT verb **RETREATS, RETREATING, RETREATED** said of a military force, army, etc: to move back or away from the enemy or retire after defeat ◻ noun **RETREATS** the act of retreating, especially from battle, a military position, danger, etc

RETRENCH verb **RETRENCHES, RETRENCHING, RETRENCHED** to reduce or cut down (expenses, money spent, etc); to economize

RETRIAL noun **RETRIALS** a further judicial trial

RETRIEVAL noun **RETRIEVALS** an act of retrieving something

RETRIEVE verb **RETRIEVES, RETRIEVING, RETRIEVED** to get or bring something back again; to recover

RETRIEVER noun **RETRIEVERS** a large dog with a golden or black water-resistant coat, that can be trained to retrieve game

RETRO adj reminiscent of, reverting to, recreating or imitating a style, fashion, etc from the past ◻ noun **RETROS** a retro-rocket, a small rocket that is fired in the opposite direction from that in which a spacecraft or satellite is travelling, in order to slow it down

RETROACT verb **RETROACTS, RETROACTING, RETROACTED** to react

RETROCEDE verb **RETROCEDES, RETROCEDING, RETROCEDED** to move back; to recede

RETROD a past form of **retread**[1]

RETRODDEN a past form of **retread**[1]

RETROFIT verb **RETROFITS, RETROFITTING, RETROFITTED** to modify (a house, car, aircraft, etc) some time after construction or manufacture by equipping with new or more up-to-date parts, etc

RETROFLEX adj turned or bent backwards

RETRORSE adj said especially of parts of plants: turned or pointing backwards

RETROUSSÉ adj said especially of the nose: turned up at the end

RETROVERT verb **RETROVERTS, RETROVERTING, RETROVERTED** to turn back

RETROVERTED adj bent backwards

RETRY verb **RETRIES, RETRYING, RETRIED** to submit to further judicial trial

RETSINA noun **RETSINAS** a Greek white or rosé wine flavoured with pine resin

RETTED past form of **ret**

RETTING a form of **ret**

RETUNE verb **RETUNES, RETUNING, RETUNED** to tune (a musical instrument) again

RETURF verb **RETURFS, RETURFING, RETURFED** to turf again

RETURN verb **RETURNS, RETURNING, RETURNED** to come or go back again to a former place, state or owner ◻ noun **RETURNS** an act of coming back from a place, state, etc

RETUSE adj in botany: with the tip blunt and broadly notched

REUNIFY verb **REUNIFIES, REUNIFYING, REUNIFIED** to unify (a country, republic, etc that has been divided) again or anew

REUNION noun **REUNIONS** a meeting of people (eg relatives, friends, former colleagues, etc) who have not met for some time

REUNITE verb **REUNITES, REUNITING, REUNITED** to bring or come together again after being separated

REUSABLE adj said of a product, etc: designed to be used more than once

REUSE verb **REUSES, REUSING, REUSED** to use again, to use more than once

REV noun **REVS** one cycle of events or one revolution in an internal combustion engine, the number of revolutions often being used as an indication of engine speed ◻ verb **REVS, REVVING, REVVED** to increase the speed of revolution of (a car engine, etc)

REVALUE verb **REVALUES, REVALUING, REVALUED** to make a new valuation of something

REVAMP verb **REVAMPS, REVAMPING, REVAMPED** to revise, renovate or patch something up, usually with the aim of improving it ◻ noun **REVAMPS** the act of revamping

REVEAL verb **REVEALS, REVEALING, REVEALED** to make (a secret, etc) known; to disclose it

REVEALER noun **REVEALERS** a person or thing that reveals something

REVEILLE noun **REVEILLES** a signal given in the morning, usually by a drum or bugle call, to waken soldiers, etc

REVEL verb **REVELS, REVELLING, REVELLED** to enjoy oneself in a noisy lively way; to make merry ◻ noun **REVELS** an occasion of revelling; noisy lively enjoyment, festivities or merrymaking

REVELLER noun **REVELLERS** a person behaving in a noisy lively way, especially at a party

REVELRY noun **REVELRIES** the action of revelling; noisy lively merrymaking

REVENANT noun **REVENANTS** someone who returns after a long absence, especially supposedly from the dead

REVENGE noun **REVENGES** malicious injury, harm or wrong done in return for injury, harm or wrong received; retaliation; vengeance ◻ verb **REVENGES, REVENGING, REVENGED** to do similar injury, harm, etc in return for injury, harm, etc received

For longer words, see The Chambers Dictionary

REVENGER noun **REVENGERS** someone who seeks revenge
REVENUE noun **REVENUES** money which comes to a person, organization, etc from any source, eg property, shares, etc
REVERB noun **REVERBS** reverberation, or an echoing effect of sound, especially that produced by an amplifier or an electronic musical instrument
REVERE verb **REVERES, REVERING, REVERED** to feel or show great respect or reverence for someone or something; to venerate
REVERENCE noun **REVERENCES** great respect or veneration, especially that shown to something sacred or holy ◻ verb **REVERENCES, REVERENCING, REVERENCED** to regard someone or something with great reverence; to venerate
REVEREND noun **REVERENDS** a member of the clergy
REVERENT adj showing, feeling or characterized by great respect or reverence
REVERER noun **REVERERS** someone who feels great respect for someone or something
REVERIE noun **REVERIES** a state of pleasantly dreamy and absented-minded thought
REVERS noun **REVERS** any part of a garment that is turned back, especially a lapel
REVERSAL noun **REVERSALS** an act of reversing something, or the state of being reversed
REVERSE verb **REVERSES, REVERSING, REVERSED** to move or make something move backwards or in an opposite direction ◻ noun **REVERSES** the opposite or contrary of something ◻ adj opposite, contrary or turned round in order, position, direction, etc; inverted
REVERSELY adverb in or towards the reverse
REVERSER noun **REVERSERS** a person or thing that reverses
REVERSING noun **REVERSINGS** an act of moving or making something move backwards or in an opposite direction
REVERSION noun **REVERSIONS** a return to an earlier state, belief, etc
REVERT verb **REVERTS, REVERTING, REVERTED** to return to as a topic in thought or conversation

REVETMENT noun **REVETMENTS** a facing of masonry or other material that protects or supports a wall, rampart, etc; a retaining wall
REVICTUAL verb **REVICTUALS, REVICTUALLING, REVICTUALLED** to supply with new victuals
REVIEW noun **REVIEWS** an act of examining, reviewing or revising, or the state of being examined, reviewed or revised ◻ verb **REVIEWS, REVIEWING, REVIEWED** to see or view something again; to examine or go over something, especially critically or formally
REVIEWAL noun **REVIEWALS** reviewing
REVIEWER noun **REVIEWERS** someone who reviews, especially someone whose job is to write critical reviews of books, films, plays etc
REVILE verb **REVILES, REVILING, REVILED** to abuse or criticize someone or something bitterly or scornfully
REVILER noun **REVILERS** someone who reviles someone or something
REVISABLE adj liable to revision
REVISAL noun **REVISALS** the action of revising; a revision
REVISE verb **REVISES, REVISING, REVISED** to examine something again in order to identify and correct faults, improve it or to take new circumstances into account, etc; to study for an exam ◻ noun **REVISES** the action or result of revising; a revision
REVISER noun **REVISERS** someone who revises, especially for an exam
REVISION noun **REVISIONS** the action or result of revising, or process of being revised
REVISIT verb **REVISITS, REVISITING, REVISITED** to visit again
REVISORY adj relating to revision; having the power to revise
REVIVABLE adj able to be revived
REVIVABLY adverb in a revivable way
REVIVAL noun **REVIVALS** the act or process of reviving or state of being revived
REVIVE verb **REVIVES, REVIVING, REVIVED** to come or bring someone back to consciousness, strength, health, vitality, etc

REVIVER noun **REVIVERS** a person or thing that revives
REVIVIFY verb **REVIVIFIES, REVIVIFYING, REVIVIFIED** to put new life into someone or something; to revive
REVIVING noun **REVIVINGS** an act of coming or bringing someone back to consciousness, strength, health, vitality, etc
REVOCABLE adj capable of being revoked or recalled
REVOCABLY adverb in a revocable way
REVOKABLE adj revocable
REVOKE verb **REVOKES, REVOKING, REVOKED** to cancel or make (a will, agreement, etc) no longer valid; to annul
REVOLT verb **REVOLTS, REVOLTING, REVOLTED** to rebel or rise up against a government, authority, etc ◻ noun **REVOLTS** a rebellion or uprising against a government, authority, etc
REVOLTED adj disgusted; horrified
REVOLUTE adj said of the edges of a leaf: rolled backwards and usually downwards
REVOLVE verb **REVOLVES, REVOLVING, REVOLVED** to move or turn, or make something move or turn, in a circle around a central point; to rotate ◻ noun **REVOLVES** a section of a theatre stage that can be rotated, providing a means of scene-changing
REVOLVER noun **REVOLVERS** a pistol with a revolving cylinder that holds several bullets, which allows the pistol to be fired several times without reloading
REVUE noun **REVUES** a humorous theatrical show, that includes songs, sketches, etc which are often satirical
REVULSION noun **REVULSIONS** a feeling of complete disgust, distaste or repugnance
REVULSIVE adj causing feelings of disgust or revulsion
REVVED past form of **rev**
REVVING a form of **rev**

REW noun **REWS** a Spenserian spelling of *row*

REWARD noun **REWARDS** something given or received in return for work done, a service rendered, good behaviour, etc ◻ verb **REWARDS, REWARDING, REWARDED** to give something to someone to show gratitude or in recompense for work done, services rendered, help, good behaviour, etc

REWARDER *noun* **REWARDERS** someone who gives a reward

REWARDING *adj* giving personal pleasure or satisfaction; worthwhile

REWAREWA *noun* **REWAREWAS** a tall New Zealand forest tree

REWEIGH *verb* **REWEIGHS, REWEIGHING, REWEIGHED** to weigh again

REWIND *verb* **REWINDS, REWINDING, REWOUND** to wind (eg thread) again □ *noun* **REWINDS** the action of rewinding

REWIRE *verb* **REWIRES, REWIRING, REWIRED** to fit (a house, etc) with a new system of electrical wiring

REWORD *verb* **REWORDS, REWORDING, REWORDED** to express something in different words

REWORK *verb* **REWORKS, REWORKING, REWORKED** to work something again

REWRAP *verb* **REWRAPS, REWRAPPING, REWRAPPED** to wrap again

REWRITE *verb* **REWRITES, REWRITING, REWROTE, REWRITTEN** to write something again or in different words □ *noun* **REWRITES** the action of rewriting

REX *plural noun* obsolete word meaning tricks or pranks

REYNARD *noun* **REYNARDS** a name for a fox, especially in stories, fables, etc

REZ *noun* **REZZES** a res

RHACHIS *noun* **RHACHISES, RHACHIDES** the spine

RHAGADES *plural noun* cracks or fissures in the skin

RHAPSODIC *adj* of, like or relating to a rhapsody

RHAPSODY *noun* **RHAPSODIES** a piece of music, emotional in character and usually written to suggest a free form or improvisation

RHATANY *noun* **RHATANIES** either of two S American leguminous plants

RHEA *noun* **RHEAS** a S American flightless bird resembling the ostrich but smaller

RHENIUM *noun* **RHENIUMS** a rare silvery-white metallic element whose very high melting point (3180°C) makes it a useful ingredient in alloys

RHEOLOGY *noun* **RHEOLOGIES** the scientific study of the deformation and flow of matter subjected to force

RHEOSTAT *noun* **RHEOSTATS** a variable resistor that enables the resistance to a current in an electric circuit to be increased or decreased, thereby varying the current without interrupting the current flow, eg as when dimming a light bulb

RHESUS *noun* **RHESUSES** a macaque, a small N Indian monkey

RHETORIC *noun* **RHETORICS** the art of speaking and writing well, elegantly and effectively, especially in order to persuade or influence others

RHEUM *noun* **RHEUMS** a watery mucous discharge from the nose or eyes

RHEUMATIC *noun* **RHEUMATICS** someone who suffers from rheumatism

RHEUMED *adj* suffering from rheum

RHEUMY *adj* **RHEUMIER, RHEUMIEST** of the nose or eyes: with a mucous discharge

RHINAL *adj* relating to the nose

RHINITIS *noun* **RHINITISES** inflammation of the mucous membrane of the nasal passages, accompanied by the discharge of mucus, eg as a symptom of the common cold or of certain allergies

RHINO *noun* **RHINOS** a rhinoceros

RHINOLOGY *noun* **RHINOLOGIES** the branch of medicine that deals with the study of the nose

RHIZOCARP *noun* **RHIZOCARPS** a perennial herb

RHIZOID *noun* **RHIZOIDS** a small, often colourless, hairlike outgrowth that functions as a root in certain algae, and in mosses, liverworts and some ferns, absorbing water and mineral salts, and providing anchorage

RHIZOIDAL *adj* of or relating to rhizoids

RHIZOME *noun* **RHIZOMES** a thick horizontal underground stem which produces roots and leafy shoots

RHIZOPOD *noun* **RHIZOPODS** a protozoan with rootlike protrusions for movement and feeding

RHO *noun* **RHOS** the seventeenth letter of the Greek alphabet, corresponding to R

RHODAMINE *noun* **RHODAMINES** any of a group of synthetic dyestuffs, usually red or pink

RHODIE *noun* **RHODIES** a rhododendron bush

RHODIUM *noun* **RHODIUMS** a hard, silvery-white metallic element, used to make temperature-resistant platinum alloys for electrical components, to plate jewellery, and to coat reflectors on optical instruments

RHODOLITE *noun* **RHODOLITES** a pink or purple garnet, used as a gemstone

RHODONITE *noun* **RHODONITES** manganese silicate in crystalline form, often with some calcium, iron or magnesium, brownish in colour or rose-red when pure

RHODOPSIN *noun* **RHODOPSINS** the light-sensitive pigment found in rod cells in the retina of the vertebrate eye which, on exposure to light, is chemically converted to its components, opsin and retinal, which stimulate the production of a nerve impulse to allow vision, particularly in dim light (night vision)

RHODY *noun* **RHODIES** a rhododendron bush

RHOMB *noun* **RHOMBS** a rhombus

RHOMBIC *adj* of or relating to a rhombus

RHOMBOID *noun* **RHOMBOIDS** a four-sided shape, usually one that is neither a rhombus nor a rectangle, that has opposite sides and angles equal, two angles being greater and two smaller than a right angle, and two sides being longer than the other two □ *adj* shaped like a rhomboid or a rhombus

RHOMBUS *noun* **RHOMBUSES, RHOMBI** a four-sided shape with all four sides equal, two opposite angles being greater than a right angle and two smaller

RHONCHAL *adj* of or relating to a rhonchus

RHONCHIAL *adj* rhonchal

RHONCHUS *noun* **RHONCHI** a rasping or whistling, similar to the sound of snoring, produced when air passes through partly blocked or restricted bronchi

RHUBARB noun **RHUBARBS** a perennial plant, cultivated in N temperate regions, that has very large poisonous leaves with long fleshy edible stalks

RHUMB noun **RHUMBS** an imaginary line on the surface of the earth that intersects all meridians at the same angle, used in navigation to plot direction on a chart

RHUMBA noun **RHUMBAS** the rumba ◻ verb **RHUMBAS, RHUMBAING, RHUMBAED** to rumba

RHY noun **RHIES** a Spenserian spelling of *rye*

RHYME noun **RHYMES** a pattern of words which have the same final sounds at the ends of lines in a poem ◻ verb **RHYMES, RHYMING, RHYMED** said of words: to have the same final sounds and so form rhymes

RHYMELESS adj without rhyme

RHYMER noun **RHYMERS** a poet

RHYMESTER noun **RHYMESTERS** a would-be poet, especially one who is not very talented

RHYMIST noun **RHYMISTS** someone who writes verse

RHYOLITE noun **RHYOLITES** any of a group of fine-grained light-coloured igneous rocks, similar in chemical composition to granite, that often contain larger crystals of especially quartz or potassium feldspar

RHYOLITIC adj of or relating to rhyolite

RHYTHM noun **RHYTHMS** a regularly repeated pattern, movement, beat or sequence of events

RHYTHMIC adj with a regular rhythm

RHYTHMIST noun **RHYTHMISTS** someone who is knowledgeable about or skilled in rhythm

RIA noun **RIAS** a long narrow coastal inlet, differing from a fjord in that it gradually decreases in depth and width from its mouth inland, usually surrounded by hills, and formed by the flooding of river valleys

RIAL noun **RIALS** the standard unit of currency of Iran

RIB noun **RIBS** in vertebrates: any

one of the slightly flexible bones which curve round and forward from the spine, forming the chest wall and protecting the heart and lungs ◻ verb **RIBS, RIBBING, RIBBED** to provide, support or enclose (an object, structure, etc) with ribs

RIBALD adj said of language, a speaker, humour, etc: humorous in an obscene, vulgar or indecently disrespectful way ◻ noun **RIBALDS** someone who speaks, behaves, etc in such a way

RIBALDRY noun **RIBALDRIES** ribald language or behaviour

RIBAND noun **RIBANDS** a ribbon, now especially one awarded as a prize in sport, etc

RIBBAND noun **RIBBANDS** a riband

RIBBED adj with ribs or ridges, or riblike markings

RIBBING noun **RIBBINGS** an arrangement of ribs or a riblike structure

RIBBON noun **RIBBONS** fine, usually coloured, material such as silk, etc, formed into a long narrow strip or band ◻ verb **RIBBONS, RIBBONING, RIBBONED** to decorate or tie something with a ribbon or ribbons

RIBCAGE noun **RIBCAGES** the chest wall, formed by the ribs, which protects the heart and lungs

RIBLESS adj without ribs

RIBOSE noun **RIBOSES** a type of sugar that is an important component of ribonucleic acid and whose derivative deoxyribose is a constituent of DNA

RIBOSOMAL adj of or relating to ribosomes

RIBOSOME noun **RIBOSOMES** in the cytoplasm of a living cell: any of many small particles that are the site of protein manufacture, each consisting of two subunits of different sizes and composed of RNA and protein

RIBWORT noun **RIBWORTS** a common plant that has narrow pointed leaves with prominent ribs

RICE noun **RICES** an important cereal plant of the grass family, native to SE Asia and having branched flower-heads bearing numerous starchy grain-like seeds ◻ verb **RICES, RICING, RICED** to press soft food, especially cooked potatoes, through a coarse sieve to

form strands or to give it a roughly mashed consistency

RICER noun **RICERS** a kitchen utensil for ricing food

RICEY adj **RICIER, RICIEST** of or like rice

RICH adj **RICHER, RICHEST** having a lot of money, property or possessions; wealthy

RICHES plural noun wealth in general, or a particular form of abundance or wealth

RICHLY adverb in a rich or elaborate way

RICHNESS noun **RICHNESSES** the state or condition of being rich; wealth

RICK verb **RICKS, RICKING, RICKED** to sprain or wrench (one's neck, back, etc) ◻ noun **RICKS** a sprain or wrench

RICKER noun **RICKERS** a spar or pole made from a young tree trunk

RICKETS singular and plural noun a disease, especially of children, caused by vitamin D deficiency (either due to a poor diet or lack of sunlight), characterized by softness and imperfect formation of the bones, and often resulting in bow legs

RICKETY adj **RICKETIER, RICKETIEST** said of a construction, piece of furniture, etc: unsteady and likely to collapse; shaky or unstable

RICKSHA noun **RICKSHAS** a rickshaw

RICKSHAW noun **RICKSHAWS** a small two-wheeled hooded carriage, either drawn by a person on foot, or attached to a bicycle or motorcycle

RICOCHET noun **RICOCHETS** the action, especially of a bullet or other missile, of hitting a surface and then rebounding ◻ verb **RICOCHETS, RICOCHETING, RICOCHETTING, RICOCHETED, RICOCHETTED** said of an object, especially a bullet, projectile, etc: to hit or glance off a surface and rebound

RICOTTA noun **RICOTTAS** a soft white unsalted Italian curd cheese made from sheep's or cow's milk and often used in sauces for ravioli, lasagne, etc

RICTAL adj of or relating to a rictus

RICTUS noun **RICTUSES** the gape of an open mouth, especially of a bird's beak

RICY adj **RICIER, RICIEST** ricey

RID verb **RIDS, RIDDING, RID, RIDDED** to disencumber or free someone, something or oneself from something undesirable or unwanted

RIDDANCE noun **RIDDANCES** the act of freeing oneself from something undesirable or unwanted

RIDDLE noun **RIDDLES** a short and usually humorous puzzle, often in the form of a question, which describes something or someone in an obscure or misleading way, and which can only be solved or understood using ingenuity ◻ verb **RIDDLES, RIDDLING, RIDDLED** to speak in riddles; to speak enigmatically or obscurely

RIDDLER noun **RIDDLERS** someone who speaks in riddles

RIDE verb **RIDES, RIDING, RODE, RIDDEN** to sit, usually astride, on and control the movements of (especially a horse, bicycle, motorbike, etc) ◻ noun **RIDES** a journey or certain distance covered on horseback, on a bicycle or in a vehicle

RIDERLESS adj without a rider

RIDGE noun **RIDGES** a strip of ground raised either side of a ploughed furrow; any long narrow raised area on an otherwise flat surface ◻ verb **RIDGES, RIDGING, RIDGED** to form or make something into ridges

RIDGEWAY noun **RIDGEWAYS** a track along the crest or ridge of a hill, especially a long one

RIDGING noun **RIDGINGS** the forming of ridges

RIDICULE noun **RIDICULES** language, laughter, behaviour, etc intended to make someone or something appear foolish or humiliated; mockery or derision ◻ verb **RIDICULES, RIDICULING, RIDICULED** to laugh at someone or something; to make fun of them or mock them

RIDICULER noun **RIDICULERS** someone who ridicules other people

RIDING noun **RIDINGS** the art and practice of riding horses; a track for horseback riding

RIEL noun **RIELS** the standard unit of currency of Cambodia

RIFE adj **RIFER, RIFEST** usually said of something unfavourable: very common or frequently occurring

RIFENESS noun **RIFENESSES** the state of being rife

RIFF noun **RIFFS** a short passage of music played repeatedly, often over changing chords or harmonies, or as an accompaniment to a solo improvisation ◻ verb **RIFFS, RIFFING, RIFFED** to play riffs

RIFFLE verb **RIFFLES, RIFFLING, RIFFLED** to flick or leaf through (the pages of a book, a pile of papers, etc) rapidly, especially in a casual search for something ◻ noun **RIFFLES** the action of riffling, eg cards

RIFLE ¹ noun **RIFLES** a large gun that is fired from the shoulder and has a long barrel with a spiral groove on the inside, giving the gun greater accuracy over a long distance

RIFLE ² verb **RIFLES, RIFLING, RIFLED** to search through (eg a house, safe, etc) thoroughly, usually in order to steal something from it

RIFLEMAN noun **RIFLEMEN** a soldier armed with a rifle

RIFLER noun **RIFLERS** someone who rifles through eg a house or safe

RIFLING noun **RIFLINGS** the spiral grooving of a gun-bore

RIFT noun **RIFTS** a split or crack, especially one in the earth or in rock; a fissure ◻ verb **RIFTS, RIFTING, RIFTED** to tear or split something apart

RIFTLESS adj without rifts

RIG verb **RIGS, RIGGING, RIGGED** to fit (a ship, masts, etc) with ropes, sails and rigging ◻ noun **RIGS** the particular arrangement of sails, ropes and masts on a ship

RIGADOON noun **RIGADOONS** an old dance, of Provençal origin, in lively duple or quadruple time, for one couple

RIGGING noun **RIGGINGS** the system of ropes, wires etc which support and control a ship's masts and sails

RIGHT adj **RIGHTER, RIGHTEST** indicating, relating or referring to, or on, the side facing east from the point of view of someone or something facing north; correct, true ◻ adverb on or towards the right side ◻ noun **RIGHTS** a power, privilege, title, etc that someone may claim legally or that is morally due to them ◻ verb **RIGHTS,**

RIGHTING, RIGHTED to put or come back to the correct or normal, especially upright, position

RIGHTABLE adj capable of being righted

RIGHTEOUS adj said of a person: virtuous, free from sin or guilt

RIGHTFUL adj having a legally just claim

RIGHTIST noun **RIGHTISTS** a supporter of the political right; a conservative

RIGHTLY adverb correctly; justly

RIGHTNESS noun **RIGHTNESSES** the state or condition of being right or correct

RIGHTO noun **RIGHTOS** an expression of usually cheerful agreement or compliance

RIGHTWARD adj on or towards the right ◻ adverb on or towards the right

RIGHTWARDS adj rightward

RIGID adj **RIGIDER, RIGIDEST** completely stiff and inflexible

RIGIDIFY verb **RIGIDIFIES, RIGIDIFYING, RIGIDIFIED** to become or make something rigid

RIGIDITY noun **RIGIDITIES** the state or condition or quality of being rigid

RIGIDLY adverb without moving; in a rigid way

RIGIDNESS noun **RIGIDNESSES** the state of being rigid

RIGMAROLE noun **RIGMAROLES** an unnecessarily or absurdly long, and often pointless or boring, complicated series of actions, instructions or procedures

RIGOR noun **RIGORS** a sense of chilliness accompanied by shivering, a preliminary symptom of many diseases

RIGOROUS adj showing or having rigour; strict; harsh; severe

RIGOUR noun **RIGOURS** stiffness; hardness

RIJSTAFEL noun **RIJSTAFELS** an Indonesian food consisting of a number of rice dishes served with a variety of foods

RILE verb **RILES, RILING, RILED** to anger or annoy someone

RILIEVO noun relievo

RILL noun **RILLS** a small stream or brook

RILLE noun **RILLES** a long narrow trench or valley on the moon, formed by volcanic activity

RILLED *adj* characterized by small streams

RILLETTES *singular and plural noun* a French type of potted meat, made by cooking shreds of both lean and fat pork, etc in lard until crisp, then pounding them to form a paste

RIM *noun* **RIMS** a raised edge or border, especially of something curved or circular □ *verb* **RIMS, RIMMING, RIMMED** to form or provide an edge or rim to something; to edge

RIME *noun* **RIMES** thick white frost formed especially from frozen water droplets from cloud or fog □ *verb* **RIMES, RIMING, RIMED** to cover something with rime

RIMLESS *adj* without a rim

RIMU *noun* **RIMUS** a tall evergreen coniferous tree of New Zealand

RIMY *adj* **RIMIER, RIMIEST** frosty; covered with rime

RIN *verb* **RINS, RINNING, RAN** a Scots form of *run*

RIND *noun* **RINDS** a thick hard outer layer or covering on cheese or bacon □ *verb* **RINDS, RINDING, RINDED** to remove the rind from something

RINDLESS *adj* without a rind

RING [1] *noun* **RINGS** a small circle or band of gold, silver or some other metal or material, worn on the finger

RING [2] *verb* **RINGS, RINGING, RANG, RUNG** to sound (a bell) eg by striking it or by pulling a rope attached to it, often as a summons or to signal or announce something

RINGBONE *noun* **RINGBONES** a bony callus on a horse's pastern-bone

RINGED *adj* having or bearing rings

RINGER *noun* **RINGERS** someone or something that rings a bell, etc

RINGHALS *noun* **RINGHALSES** a venomous snake of southern Africa, that spits or sprays venom at its victims

RINGING *noun* **RINGINGS** an act of ringing a bell

RINGINGLY *adverb* with a ringing sound

RINGLET *noun* **RINGLETS** a long spiral curl of hair

RINGLETED *adj* having or formed into ringlets

RINGSIDE *noun* **RINGSIDES** the seating area immediately next to a boxing-, circus-ring, etc

RINGTAIL *noun* **RINGTAILS** the female, or young male, of the hen-harrier, so called because of the rust-coloured ring on its tail-feathers

RINGWORM *noun* **RINGWORMS** any of various highly contagious fungal infections, characterized by the formation of small red itchy circular patches on soft areas of skin such as the scalp or groin, or between the toes (athlete's foot)

RINK *noun* **RINKS** an area of ice prepared for skating, curling or ice-hockey

RINKHALS *noun* **RINKHALSES** a ringhals

RINSE *verb* **RINSES, RINSING, RINSED** to wash (soap, detergent, etc) out of (clothes, hair, dishes, etc) with clean water □ *noun* **RINSES** the action or an act of rinsing

RINSER *noun* **RINSERS** a board or rack for rinsing washed dishes

RINSING *noun* **RINSINGS** an act of washing something out with clean water

RIOT *noun* **RIOTS** a noisy public disturbance or disorder, usually by a large group of people □ *verb* **RIOTS, RIOTING, RIOTED** to take part in a riot

RIOTER *noun* **RIOTERS** someone taking part in a riot

RIOTING *noun* **RIOTINGS** an act of taking part in a riot

RIOTOUS *adj* participating in or likely to start a riot

RIOTOUSLY *adverb* noisily, wildly

RIP *verb* **RIPS, RIPPING, RIPPED, RIPT** to tear or come apart violently or roughly □ *noun* **RIPS** a violent or rough tear or split

RIPARIAL *adj* riparian

RIPARIAN *adj* relating to, occurring or living on a riverbank □ *noun* **RIPARIANS** an owner of land that borders a river

RIPE *adj* **RIPER, RIPEST** said of fruit, grain, etc: fully matured and ready to be picked or harvested and eaten

RIPELY *adverb* in a ripe way

RIPEN *verb* **RIPENS, RIPENING, RIPENED** to make or become ripe or riper

RIPENESS *noun* **RIPENESSES** the state or condition or quality of being ripe

RIPIENO *adj* in music: supplementary □ *noun* **RIPIENOS, RIPIENI** a supplementary instrument or player

RIPOSTE *noun* **RIPOSTES** a quick sharp reply; a retort □ *verb* **RIPOSTES, RIPOSTING, RIPOSTED** to answer with a riposte

RIPPED *adj* torn or rent

RIPPER *noun* **RIPPERS** someone who rips

RIPPING *adj* splendid; excellent

RIPPINGLY *adverb* in a ripping way

RIPPLE *noun* **RIPPLES** a slight wave or undulation, or a series of these, on the surface of water □ *verb* **RIPPLES, RIPPLING, RIPPLED** to ruffle or agitate the surface of (water, etc)

RIPPLER *noun* **RIPPLERS** a person or thing that removes the seeds from flax or hemp

RIPPLING *noun* **RIPPLINGS** an act of ruffling or agitating the surface of (water, etc)

RIPPLY *adj* **RIPPLIER, RIPPLIEST** having ripples

RIPTIDE *noun* **RIPTIDES** a strong surface current coming out at intervals from the shore

RISE *verb* **RISES, RISING, ROSE, RISEN** to get or stand up, especially from a sitting, kneeling or lying position □ *noun* **RISES** the act or action of rising

RISER *noun* **RISERS** someone who gets out of bed, usually at a specified time

RISIBLE *adj* causing laughter; laughable; ludicrous

RISK *noun* **RISKS** the chance or possibility of suffering loss, injury, damage, etc; danger □ *verb* **RISKS, RISKING, RISKED** to expose someone or something to loss, injury, danger, etc

RISKILY *adverb* in a risky way

RISKINESS *noun* **RISKINESSES** the state or condition of being risky

RISKY *adj* **RISKIER, RISKIEST** dangerous; likely to cause loss, damage, mishap, etc

RISOLUTO *adj* with emphasis; boldly

RISOTTO *noun* **RISOTTOS** an Italian dish of rice cooked in a meat or seafood stock with onions, tomatoes, cheese, etc

RISQUÉ *adj* said of a story, joke, etc: bordering on the rude or indecent

RISSOLE *noun* **RISSOLES** a small fried cake or ball of chopped meat coated in breadcrumbs

> **RIT** *verb* **RITS, RITTING, RITTED** a Scots word meaning to slit

RITE *noun* **RITES** a formal ceremony or observance, especially a religious one
RITELESS *adj* having no rites
RITENUTO *adj* in music: with a sudden slowing down of tempo; restrained ▫ *adverb* with a sudden slowing down of tempo; restrained ▫ *noun* **RITENUTOS** a ritenuto passage or phrase
RITUAL *noun* **RITUALS** the set order or words used in a religious ceremony; an often repeated procedure or series of actions ▫ *adj* relating to, like or used for religious, social or other rites or rituals
RITUALISE *verb* **RITUALISES, RITUALISING, RITUALISED** to ritualize
RITUALISM *noun* **RITUALISMS** excessive belief in the importance of, or excessive practice of, ritual, often without regard to its meaning or function
RITUALIST *noun* **RITUALISTS** someone who is skilled in the rituals of a particular religious ceremony
RITUALIZE *verb* **RITUALIZES, RITUALIZING, RITUALIZED** to practise or convert to ritualism
RITUALLY *adverb* in a ritual way; as part of a ritual
RITZY *adj* **RITZIER, RITZIEST** very smart and elegant
RIVAL *noun* **RIVALS** a person or group of people competing with another for the same objective or in the same field ▫ *adj* standing as a rival ▫ *verb* **RIVALS, RIVALLING, RIVALLED** to try to gain the same objective as someone or something else; to be in competition with them or it
RIVALLESS *adj* having no rival
RIVALRY *noun* **RIVALRIES** the state of being a rival or rivals
RIVE *verb* **RIVES, RIVING, RIVED** to tear something or tear it apart
RIVER *noun* **RIVERS** a large permanent stream of water, originating at a source and flowing along a fixed course, usually into a lake or the sea at its mouth
RIVERED *adj* watered by rivers
RIVERINE *adj* living or situated on or near a river; riparian
RIVERLESS *adj* without rivers
RIVERSIDE *noun* **RIVERSIDES** the bank of a river
RIVERY *adj* of or like a river
RIVET *noun* **RIVETS** a metal pin or bolt with a head at one end, used for joining pieces of metal, etc by passing it through a hole in each of the pieces, then hammering the protruding end flat ▫ *verb* **RIVETS, RIVETING, RIVETED** to fasten (pieces of metal, etc) with a rivet
RIVETER *noun* **RIVETERS** someone whose job is to rivet
RIVETING *noun* **RIVETINGS** the joining of pieces of metal, etc by means of a rivet or rivets ▫ *adj* fascinating; enthralling
RIVIERA *noun* **RIVIERAS** a coastal area that has a warm climate and is popular as a holiday resort
RIVIÈRE *noun* **RIVIÈRES** in needlework: a row of openwork
RIVULET *noun* **RIVULETS** a small river or stream
RIYAL *noun* **RIYALS** the standard unit of currency of Qatar

> **RIZ** US past form of **rise**

RIZA *noun* **RIZAS** an ornamental plate or plaque, usually of silver, that frames the face and other features of a Russian icon
ROACH *noun* **ROACHES** a silvery freshwater fish of the carp family
ROAD *noun* **ROADS** an open way, usually specially surfaced or paved, for people, vehicles or animals to travel on from one place to another
ROADBLOCK *noun* **ROADBLOCKS** a barrier put across a road, usually by the police or army, to stop and check vehicles and drivers before letting them pass on their way
ROADHOUSE *noun* **ROADHOUSES** a public house or inn at the side of a major road
ROADIE *noun* **ROADIES** a person who helps move and organize the instruments and equipment for a rock or pop group, especially on tour
ROADLESS *adj* having no roads
ROADMAN *noun* **ROADMEN** someone whose job is to make roads or keep them in good repair
ROADSIDE *noun* **ROADSIDES** the ground or land beside or along a road
ROADSTEAD *noun* **ROADSTEADS** a relatively sheltered area of water near the shore where ships may be anchored
ROADSTER *noun* **ROADSTERS** an open sports car for two people
ROADWAY *noun* **ROADWAYS** the part of a road or street used by cars
ROADWORKS *plural noun* the building or repairing of a road, or other work that involves digging up a road
ROAM *verb* **ROAMS, ROAMING, ROAMED** to ramble or wander, especially over a large area, with no fixed purpose or direction ▫ *noun* **ROAMS** the act of roaming
ROAN *adj* said of a horse's coat: black, bay or chestnut, thickly flecked with grey or white hairs ▫ *noun* **ROANS** a roan colour
ROAR *noun* **ROARS** a loud deep prolonged cry, such as that of a lion, a cheering crowd, a person in pain or anger, etc ▫ *verb* **ROARS, ROARING, ROARED** to give such a cry
ROARER *noun* **ROARERS** a person or animal that roars
ROARING *noun* **ROARINGS** any loud deep cry or sound
ROARINGLY *adverb* making or accompanied by roaring
ROAST *verb* **ROASTS, ROASTING, ROASTED** to cook (meat or other food) by exposure to dry heat, often with the addition of fat and especially in an oven ▫ *noun* **ROASTS** a piece of meat which has been roasted or is suitable for roasting
ROASTER *noun* **ROASTERS** an oven or dish for roasting food
ROASTING *noun* **ROASTINGS** a dose of severe criticism
ROB *verb* **ROBS, ROBBING, ROBBED** to steal something from (a person or place), especially by force or threats
ROBBER *noun* **ROBBERS** someone who robs; a thief
ROBBERY *noun* **ROBBERIES** the act or process, or an instance, of robbing, especially theft with threats, force or violence
ROBE *noun* **ROBES** a long loose flowing garment, especially the official vestment worn on ceremonial occasions by peers, judges, mayors, academics, the clergy, etc ▫ *verb* **ROBES, ROBING, ROBED** to clothe (oneself or someone else) in a robe or robes
ROBIN *noun* **ROBINS** a small

brown European thrush with a red breast and white abdomen

ROBINIA *noun* **ROBINIAS** any of various leguminous plants, especially the false acacia

ROBORANT *noun* **ROBORANTS** a strengthening drug or tonic

ROBOT *noun* **ROBOTS** especially in science-fiction: a machine that vaguely resembles a human being and which can be programmed to carry out tasks

ROBOTIC *adj* of or like a robot, especially moving like a robot

ROBOTICS *singular noun* the branch of engineering concerned with the design, construction, operation and use of industrial robots, and which incorporates many of the concepts used in artificial intelligence

ROBOTISE *verb* **ROBOTISES, ROBOTISING, ROBOTISED** to robotize

ROBOTIZE *verb* **ROBOTIZES, ROBOTIZING, ROBOTIZED** to automate (a job, etc)

ROBUST *adj* **ROBUSTER, ROBUSTEST** said of a person: strong and healthy; with a strong constitution

ROBUSTA *noun* **ROBUSTAS** a variety of coffee grown especially in E Africa, which is more disease-resistant than other arabicas but gives a coffee of an inferior quality

ROBUSTLY *adverb* in a robust way

> **ROC** *noun* **ROCS** in Arabian legends: an enormous bird that was strong enough to carry off an elephant

ROCAILLE *noun* **ROCAILLES** ornate ornamental rockwork or shellwork

ROCAMBOLE *noun* **ROCAMBOLES** a plant with a garlic-like bulb used for seasoning

ROCHET *noun* **ROCHETS** a full-length white linen robe similar to a surplice, worn by bishops, especially of the Anglican Communion, on ceremonial occasions

ROCK¹ *noun* **ROCKS** a large stone or boulder

ROCK² *verb* **ROCKS, ROCKING, ROCKED** to sway or make something sway gently backwards and forwards or from side to side

ROCKER *noun* **ROCKERS** one of usually two curved supports on which a chair, cradle, etc rocks

ROCKERY *noun* **ROCKERIES** a garden made with both rocks and earth, in which plants are grown

ROCKET *noun* **ROCKETS** a projectile or vehicle, especially a space vehicle, that obtains thrust from a backward jet of hot gases □ *verb* **ROCKETS, ROCKETING, ROCKETED** to move, especially upwards, extremely quickly, as if with the speed of a rocket

ROCKETEER *noun* **ROCKETEERS** a rocket technician or pilot

ROCKETRY *noun* **ROCKETRIES** the scientific study and use of rockets

ROCKFISH *noun* **ROCKFISHES** any of various types of fish that live among rocks

ROCKILY *adverb* shakily

ROCKINESS *noun* **ROCKINESSES** the state of being rocky

ROCKLING *noun* **ROCKLINGS** any of several small fish of the cod family with barbels on both jaws, found in the N Atlantic Ocean

ROCKY *adj* **ROCKIER, ROCKIEST** said of an object: with a tendency to rock; shaky; unstable

ROCOCO *noun* **ROCOCOS** a style of architecture, decoration and furniture-making originating in France in the early 18c, characterized by elaborate ornamentation and unsymmetrical and broken curves; a freer development of the baroque

ROD *noun* **RODS** a long slender stick or bar of wood, metal, etc □ *verb* **RODS, RODDING, RODDED** to push or force a rod through (a drain, etc) to clear it

RODE a past form of **ride**

RODENT *noun* **RODENTS** an animal belonging to the order of mostly nocturnal mammals that includes rats, mice, squirrels, beavers, etc

RODEO *noun* **RODEOS** a round-up of cattle, eg for purposes of counting or branding them

RODLESS *adj* without a rod

RODLIKE *adj* like a rod, eg in shape

ROE *noun* **ROES** a small deer, native to Europe and Asia, with a reddish-brown coat and white underparts in summer, turning greyish-fawn in winter, a white rump and virtually no tail

ROEBUCK *noun* **ROEBUCKS** the male roe deer

ROED *adj* containing fish eggs

ROENTGEN *noun* **ROENTGENS** a former unit for measurement of X-rays or gamma rays, defined in terms of the ionization produced in $1cm^3$ of air under specific conditions

ROGATION *noun* **ROGATIONS** solemn supplication, especially in ceremonial form

ROGER *exclamation* in radio communications and signalling, etc: message received and understood

ROGUE *noun* **ROGUES** a dishonest or unscrupulous person □ *verb* **ROGUES, ROGUING, ROGUED** to eliminate inferior plants from (a crop, etc)

ROGUERY *noun* **ROGUERIES** behaviour or an action that is typical of a rogue

ROGUISH *adj* characteristic of a rogue

ROGUISHLY *adverb* in a roguish way

ROIL *verb* **ROILS, ROILING, ROILED** to make (water or other liquid) cloudy by mixing up dregs or sediment

ROISTER *verb* **ROISTERS, ROISTERING, ROISTERED** to enjoy oneself noisily and boisterously

ROISTERER *noun* **ROISTERERS** someone who roisters

> **ROJI** *noun* **ROJIS** a form of Japanese garden design

> **ROK** *noun* **ROKS** a roc

ROLE *noun* **ROLES** an actor's part or character in a play, film, etc

ROLFING *noun* **ROLFINGS** a therapeutic technique for correcting postural faults and improving physical wellbeing through manipulation of the muscles and joints, so that the body is realigned symmetrically and the best use made of gravity in maintaining balance

ROLL *noun* **ROLLS** a small individually baked portion of bread □ *verb* **ROLLS, ROLLING, ROLLED** to move or make something move by turning over and over, as if on an axis, and often in a specified direction

ROLLER *noun* **ROLLERS** any cylindrical object or machine used

for flattening, crushing, spreading, printing, applying paint, etc
ROLLICK *verb* **ROLLICKS, ROLLICKING, ROLLICKED** to behave in a carefree, swaggering, boisterous or playful manner ▫ *noun* **ROLLICKS** a boisterous romp
ROLLICKING *adj* boisterous, noisy and carefree
ROLLING *adj* said of land, countryside, etc: with low, gentle hills and valleys, and without steep slopes and crags
ROLLMOP *noun* **ROLLMOPS** a fillet of raw herring rolled up usually round a slice of onion, and pickled in spiced vinegar
ROM *noun* **ROMA, ROMAS** a male Gypsy; a Romany
ROMAN *noun* **ROMANS** ordinary type commonly used in printing, or a letter in this type
ROMANCE *noun* **ROMANCES** a love affair ▫ *verb* **ROMANCES, ROMANCING, ROMANCED** to try to win someone's love
ROMANCER *noun* **ROMANCERS** someone who romances others
ROMANCING *noun* **ROMANCINGS** an act of trying to win someone's love
ROMANTIC *noun* **ROMANTICS** someone who has a romantic, idealized, impractical or sentimental view of love, etc
ROMNEYA *noun* **ROMNEYAS** either of two shrubby Californian plants with large white poppy-like flowers
ROMP *verb* **ROMPS, ROMPING, ROMPED** to play or run about in a lively boisterous way ▫ *noun* **ROMPS** an act of romping
ROMPER *noun* **ROMPERS** someone who romps
ROMPERS *plural noun* a baby's suit, usually one-piece, with short-legged trousers and either a short-sleeved top or a bib top
ROMPINGLY *adverb* in a romping way
RONDAVEL *noun* **RONDAVELS** a round hut or similar type of building, usually with a thatched roof
RONDEAU *noun* **RONDEAUX** a poem of 13 or sometimes 10 lines with only two rhymes, and with the first line used as a refrain after the eighth and thirteenth lines
RONDEL *noun* **RONDELS** a variation of the rondeau
RONDO *noun* **RONDOS** a piece of music, especially one forming the last movement of a sonata or a concerto, with a principal theme which recurs or is repeated as a refrain
RONE *noun* **RONES** a roof-gutter
RONGGENG *noun* **RONGGENGS** a Malaysian dancing-girl
RÖNTGEN *noun* **RÖNTGENS** a roentgen
ROO *noun* **ROOS** a short form of kangaroo
ROOD *noun* **ROODS** a cross or crucifix, especially a large one set on a beam or screen at the entrance to a church chancel
ROOF *noun* **ROOFS** the top outside covering of a building ▫ *verb* **ROOFS, ROOFING, ROOFED** to cover or provide something with a roof
ROOFED *adj* with a roof
ROOFER *noun* **ROOFERS** someone who makes or repairs roofs
ROOFING *noun* **ROOFINGS** materials for building a roof
ROOFLESS *adj* without a roof
ROOFLIKE *adj* like a roof
ROOFTOP *noun* **ROOFTOPS** the outside of a roof of a building
ROOK *noun* **ROOKS** a large, crow-like bird with lustrous black plumage ▫ *verb* **ROOKS, ROOKING, ROOKED** to cheat or defraud, especially at cards
ROOKERY *noun* **ROOKERIES** a colony of rooks
ROOKIE *noun* **ROOKIES** a new or raw recruit, especially in the police or the army
ROOKY *noun* **ROOKIES** a rookie
ROOM *noun* **ROOMS** an area within a building enclosed by a ceiling, floor and walls ▫ *verb* **ROOMS, ROOMING, ROOMED** to lodge; to occupy a room or rooms as a lodger
ROOMED *adj* having rooms of a specified kind or number
ROOMER *noun* **ROOMERS** a lodger, usually one who takes their meals elsewhere
ROOMETTE *noun* **ROOMETTES** a sleeping compartment on a train
ROOMFUL *noun* **ROOMFULS** as much or as many (people, objects, etc) as a room can hold
ROOMILY *adverb* in a roomy way
ROOMINESS *noun* **ROOMINESSES** the state or condition of being roomy
ROOMY *adj* **ROOMIER, ROOMIEST** with plenty of room; spacious
ROOST *noun* **ROOSTS** a branch, perch, etc on which birds, especially domestic fowl, rest at night ▫ *verb* **ROOSTS, ROOSTING, ROOSTED** said especially of birds: to settle on a roost, especially for sleep
ROOSTER *noun* **ROOSTERS** a farmyard cock
ROOT *noun* **ROOTS** a structure in a plant, usually beneath the soil surface, which anchors the plant in the soil and absorbs water and nutrients ▫ *verb* **ROOTS, ROOTING, ROOTED** to grow roots
ROOTED *adj* fixed by or as if by roots; firmly established
ROOTEDLY *adverb* in a rooted way
ROOTER *noun* **ROOTERS** a person or animal that rummages about
ROOTLESS *adj* having no roots
ROOTLET *noun* **ROOTLETS** a small root
ROOTLIKE *adj* like a root
ROOTSTOCK *noun* **ROOTSTOCKS** an underground plant stem that bears buds; a rhizome
ROOTSY *adj* **ROOTSIER, ROOTSIEST** said especially of music: influenced by, or incorporating, traditional ethnic or folk styles
ROPABLE *adj* ropeable
ROPE *noun* **ROPES** strong thick cord made by twisting fibres of hemp, wire or some other material together ▫ *verb* **ROPES, ROPING, ROPED** to tie, fasten or bind with rope or as if with rope
ROPEABLE *adj* able to be roped
ROPEWAY *noun* **ROPEWAYS** a cable railway
ROPEY *adj* **ROPIER, ROPIEST** ropy
ROPILY *adverb* in a ropey way; badly
ROPINESS *noun* **ROPINESSES** the state of being ropey
ROPY *adj* **ROPIER, ROPIEST** said of a substance or its texture: stringy; of poor quality

> **ROQUE** *noun* **ROQUES** a version of croquet played in N America

ROQUET *noun* **ROQUETS** in croquet: a stroke where a player strikes an opponent's ball with their own ▫ *verb* **ROQUETS, ROQUETING, ROQUETED** to play a roquet
RORQUAL *noun* **RORQUALS** any of

several baleen whales that have a longitudinally furrowed throat (allowing for expansion when feeding) and a small dorsal fin near the tail

RORT *noun* **RORTS** a trick or fraud □ *verb* **RORTS, RORTING, RORTED** to shout or protest loudly

RORTER *noun* **RORTERS** someone who rorts

RORTY *adj* **RORTIER, RORTIEST** lively and enjoyable

ROSACE *noun* **ROSACES** a rose-shaped ornament or decoration

ROSACEOUS *adj* denoting a plant that belongs to the family Rosaceae, including eg the rose, apple, strawberry, cherry and almond

ROSARIAN *noun* **ROSARIANS** someone who is keen on cultivating varieties of roses, either professionally or as a pastime

ROSARIUM *noun* **ROSARIUMS** a rose-garden

ROSARY *noun* **ROSARIES** a string of 165 beads divided into fifteen sets used to count prayers as they are recited

ROSE [1] *noun* **ROSES** an erect or climbing thorny shrub that produces large, often fragrant, flowers which may be red, pink, yellow, orange or white, or some combination of these colours, followed by bright-coloured fleshy fruits known as hips

ROSE [2] past form of **rise**

ROSÉ *noun* **ROSÉS** a light-pink wine properly made by removing the skins of red grapes after fermentation has begun

ROSEATE *adj* like a rose, especially in colour

ROSEBAY *noun* **ROSEBAYS** a common wild plant that has spikes of pale purple flowers and produces many fluffy seeds

ROSEBUD *noun* **ROSEBUDS** the bud of a rose

ROSEHIP *noun* **ROSEHIPS** the red berry-like fruit of the rose

ROSELESS *adj* without roses

ROSELIKE *adj* like a rose, eg in shape or colour

ROSELLA *noun* **ROSELLAS** any of various brightly coloured Australian parrots

ROSEMARY *noun* **ROSEMARIES** a fragrant evergreen shrub with stiff needle-like leaves, used in cookery and perfumery

ROSEOLA *noun* **ROSEOLAS** any rose-coloured rash

ROSERY *noun* **ROSERIES** a rosary

ROSETTE *noun* **ROSETTES** a badge or decoration made in coloured ribbon to resemble the form of a rose, often awarded as a prize or worn to show membership of some group, etc

ROSETTED *adj* having been awarded or wearing a rosette

ROSEWOOD *noun* **ROSEWOODS** the valuable dark red or purplish wood of any of various tropical trees used in making high quality furniture

ROSIER see under **rosy**

ROSIEST see under **rosy**

ROSILY *adverb* in a rosy way

ROSIN *noun* **ROSINS** a clear hard resin, produced by distilling turpentine □ *verb* **ROSINS, ROSINING, ROSINED** to rub rosin on (the bow of a violin, etc)

ROSINESS *noun* **ROSINESSES** the state or condition or quality of being rosy

ROSINY *adj* of or like rosin

ROSOGLIO *noun* **ROSOGLIOS** rosolio

ROSOLIO *noun* **ROSOLIOS** a sweet cordial, made especially in Italy, with raisins, alcohol, spices, etc

ROSTER *noun* **ROSTERS** a list or roll of people's names, especially one that shows the order in which they are to do various duties, go on leave, etc □ *verb* **ROSTERS, ROSTERING, ROSTERED** to put (someone's name) on a roster

ROSTERING *noun* **ROSTERINGS** an act of putting (someone's name) on a roster

ROSTRAL *adj* relating to or like a rostrum

ROSTRUM *noun* **ROSTRA, ROSTRUMS** a platform on which a public speaker stands

ROSY *adj* **ROSIER, ROSIEST** rose-coloured; pink

ROT *verb* **ROTS, ROTTING, ROTTED** to decay or cause to decay or become putrefied as a result of the activity of bacteria and/or fungi □ *noun* **ROTS** decay

ROTA *noun* **ROTAS** a list of duties that are to be done with the names and order of the people who are to take turns doing them

ROTARY *adj* turning on an axis like a wheel □ *noun* **ROTARIES** a rotary machine

ROTATABLE *adj* capable of being rotated

ROTATE *verb* **ROTATES, ROTATING, ROTATED** to turn or make something turn about an axis like a wheel; to revolve

ROTATION *noun* **ROTATIONS** the action of rotating or state of being rotated

ROTATOR *noun* **ROTATORS** a device that rotates or makes something else rotate

ROTAVATE *verb* **ROTAVATES, ROTAVATING, ROTAVATED** to break up (soil) with a rotavator

ROTAVATOR *noun* **ROTAVATORS** a machine with a rotating blade for breaking up the soil

ROTE *noun* **ROTES** mechanical use of the memory to repeat or perform something, without necessarily understanding what is memorized

ROTENONE *noun* **ROTENONES** a toxic crystalline substance made from derris and other plants, commonly used in ecological studies to paralyse fish and medicinally to control head lice

ROTGUT *noun* **ROTGUTS** cheap alcoholic drink, especially spirits, of inferior quality

ROTI *noun* **ROTIS** a cake of unleavened bread, traditionally made in parts of India and the Caribbean

ROTIFER *noun* **ROTIFERS** any of various microscopic aquatic invertebrate animals that have an unsegmented body and swim by means of a ring of beating hair-like structures that resembles a spinning wheel

ROTOR *noun* **ROTORS** a rotating part of a machine, especially in an internal combustion engine

ROTOVATE *verb* **ROTOVATES, ROTOVATING, ROTOVATED** to rotavate

ROTOVATOR *noun* **ROTOVATORS** a rotavator

ROTTED past form of **rot**

ROTTEN *adj* **ROTTENER, ROTTENEST** gone bad, decayed, rotted

ROTTENLY *adverb* in a rotten way

ROTTER *noun* **ROTTERS** a thoroughly depraved, worthless or despicable person

ROTTING a form of **rot**

ROTUND *adj* **ROTUNDER, ROTUNDEST** round or rounded in form; nearly spherical; plump

ROTUNDA noun **ROTUNDAS** a round, usually domed, building or hall

ROTUNDITY noun **ROTUNDITIES** the state or condition of being rotund

ROTUNDLY adverb in a rotund way

ROUBLE noun **ROUBLES** the standard unit of currency in Russia and some other states of the CIS

ROUCOU noun **ROUCOUS** annatto

ROUÉ noun **ROUÉS** a debauched, disreputable man

ROUGE noun **ROUGES** a pink or red cosmetic powder or cream used to colour the cheeks, originally a mixture of safflower and talc ◻ verb **ROUGES, ROUGING, ROUGED** to apply rouge to (the cheeks, etc)

ROUGH adj **ROUGHER, ROUGHEST** said of a surface or texture: not smooth, even or regular ◻ noun **ROUGHS** rough ground, especially the uncut grass at the side of a golf fairway ◻ adverb roughly ◻ verb **ROUGHS, ROUGHING, ROUGHED** to make something rough; to roughen

ROUGHAGE noun **ROUGHAGES** fibre in food

ROUGHCAST noun **ROUGHCASTS** a mixture of plaster and small stones used to cover the outside walls of buildings ◻ verb **ROUGHCASTS, ROUGHCASTING, ROUGHCASTED, ROUGHCAST** to cover (a wall) with roughcast

ROUGHEN verb **ROUGHENS, ROUGHENING, ROUGHENED** to make something rough or to become rough

ROUGHISH adj somewhat rough

ROUGHLY adverb in a rough way

ROUGHNECK noun **ROUGHNECKS** a worker on an oil rig, especially an unskilled labourer

ROUGHNESS noun **ROUGHNESSES** the state or condition of being rough; a rough place

ROUGHSHOD adj said of a horse: with horse-shoes that have projecting nails which prevent the horse from slipping in wet weather

ROULADE noun **ROULADES** melodic embellishment

ROULETTE noun **ROULETTES** a gambling game in which a ball is dropped into a revolving wheel, the players betting on which of its many small, numbered

compartments the ball will come to rest in

ROUND adj **ROUNDER, ROUNDEST** shaped like, or approximately like, a circle or a ball ◻ adverb in a circular direction or with a circular or revolving movement ◻ prep on all sides of so as to surround or enclose ◻ noun **ROUNDS** something round, and often flat, in shape ◻ verb **ROUNDS, ROUNDING, ROUNDED** to make something round

ROUNDED adj curved; not angular

ROUNDEL noun **ROUNDELS** a small circular window or design

ROUNDELAY noun **ROUNDELAYS** a simple song with a refrain

ROUNDERS singular noun a team game similar to baseball, in which each team sends players in to bat in turn while the other team bowls and fields

ROUNDHAND noun **ROUNDHANDS** a style of hand-writing in which the letters are well rounded and free

ROUNDISH adj slightly round in shape

ROUNDLY adverb frankly; bluntly

ROUNDNESS noun **ROUNDNESSES** the state or condition of being round

ROUNDWORM noun **ROUNDWORMS** an invertebrate, mostly parasitic, animal with a long slender unsegmented body

ROUP noun **ROUPS** a sale by auction ◻ verb **ROUPS, ROUPING, ROUPED** to sell something by auction

ROUSE verb **ROUSES, ROUSING, ROUSED** to arouse or awaken oneself or someone else from sleep, listlessness or lethargy

ROUSER noun **ROUSERS** a person or thing that rouses

ROUSING adj stirring; exciting

ROUSINGLY adverb in a rousing way; excitingly

ROUT verb **ROUTS, ROUTING, ROUTED** to defeat (an army, troops, a sporting team, etc) completely ◻ noun **ROUTS** a complete and overwhelming defeat

ROUTE noun **ROUTES** the way travelled on a regular journey ◻ verb **ROUTES, ROUTING, ROUTEING, ROUTED** to arrange a route for (a journey, etc)

ROUTEMAN noun **ROUTEMEN**

someone who delivers goods for a shop

ROUTINE noun **ROUTINES** a regular or unvarying series of actions or way of doing things ◻ adj unvarying

ROUTINELY adverb without varying; in a routine way

ROUTINISE verb **ROUTINISES, ROUTINISING, ROUTINISED** to routinize

ROUTINIZE verb **ROUTINIZES, ROUTINIZING, ROUTINIZED** to make something into a routine

ROUX noun **ROUX** a cooked mixture of flour and fat, usually butter, used to thicken sauces

ROVE [1] verb **ROVES, ROVING, ROVED** to roam about aimlessly ◻ noun **ROVES** the act of roving

ROVE [2] a past form of **reeve** [2]

ROVER noun **ROVERS** someone who roves; a wanderer

ROVING adj wandering; likely to ramble or stray

ROVINGLY adverb in a roving way

ROW [1] noun **ROWS** a number of people or things arranged in a line

ROW [2] verb **ROWS, ROWING, ROWED** to move (a boat) through the water using oars

ROWAN noun **ROWANS** a tree of the rose family, with small pinnate leaves

ROWBOAT noun **ROWBOATS** a rowing boat

ROWDILY adverb in a rowdy way

ROWDINESS noun **ROWDINESSES** the state or condition of being rowdy

ROWDY adj **ROWDIER, ROWDIEST** noisy and rough; disorderly; creating disturbance ◻ noun **ROWDIES** a noisy, rough, disorderly person

ROWDYISM noun **ROWDYISMS** rowdy behaviour

ROWEL noun **ROWELS** a small spiked wheel attached to a spur ◻ verb **ROWELS, ROWELLING, ROWELLED** to spur (a horse) with a rowel

ROWER noun **ROWERS** someone who rows a boat

ROWLOCK noun **ROWLOCKS** a device that holds an oar in place and acts as a fulcrum for it

ROYAL adj **ROYALLER, ROYALLEST** relating to or suitable for a king or queen ◻ noun **ROYALS** a member of a royal family

ROYALISM noun **ROYALISMS** support of the institution of monarchy

ROYALIST noun **ROYALISTS** a supporter of monarchy or of a specified monarchy

ROYALLY adverb in a royal way; richly

ROYALTY noun **ROYALTIES** the character, state, office or power of a king or queen

ROZZER noun **ROZZERS** a policeman

RUB verb **RUBS, RUBBING, RUBBED** to apply pressure and friction to something by moving one's hand or an object backwards and forwards over its surface □ noun **RUBS** the process or an act of rubbing

RUBAIYAT noun **RUBAIYATS** a Persian verse form consisting of four-line stanzas

RUBATO noun **RUBATOS, RUBATI** a modified or distorted tempo in which certain notes of a phrase, etc may be shortened (by a slight quickening of tempo) and others lengthened but the overall length of the phrase remains the same

RUBBER noun **RUBBERS** any of various natural or synthetic polymers characterized by their elasticity, strength and resilience, obtained from the latex of certain plants, especially the rubber tree, or manufactured artificially from petroleum and coal products

RUBBERISE verb **RUBBERISES, RUBBERISING, RUBBERISED** to rubberize

RUBBERIZE verb **RUBBERIZES, RUBBERIZING, RUBBERIZED** to coat or impregnate (a substance, especially a textile) with rubber

RUBBERY adj **RUBBERIER, RUBBERIEST** like rubber

RUBBING a form of **rub** □ noun **RUBBINGS** an impression or copy made by placing paper over a raised surface and rubbing the paper with crayon or chalk

RUBBISH noun **RUBBISHES** waste material; refuse; litter □ verb **RUBBISHES, RUBBISHING, RUBBISHED** to criticize or dismiss something as worthless

RUBBISHY adj worthless; trashy

RUBBLE noun **RUBBLES** pieces of broken stones, bricks, plaster, etc, usually from ruined or demolished buildings

RUBE noun **RUBES** a country

bumpkin; an uncouth or unsophisticated person

RUBELLA noun **RUBELLAS** a viral disease similar to measles that is highly contagious, especially in childhood, characterized by a reddish-pink rash and swelling of the lymph glands

RUBELLITE noun **RUBELLITES** a red variety of the mineral tourmaline, used as a gemstone

RUBEOLA noun **RUBEOLAS** measles

RUBICON noun **RUBICONS** a boundary which, once crossed, commits someone crossing it to an irrevocable course of action

RUBICUND adj said especially of the face or complexion: red or rosy; ruddy

RUBIDIUM noun **RUBIDIUMS** a silvery-white, highly reactive metallic element, used in photoelectric cells

RUBLE noun **RUBLES** the rouble

RUBRIC noun **RUBRICS** a heading, especially one in a book or manuscript, originally one written or underlined in red; in Christianity: a rule or direction for the conduct of divine service, added in red to the liturgy

RUBRICATE verb **RUBRICATES, RUBRICATING, RUBRICATED** to write or mark something in red

RUBRICIAN noun **RUBRICIANS** someone versed in liturgical rubrics

RUBY noun **RUBIES** a valuable gemstone, a red impure variety of the mineral corundum, containing traces of chromium oxide which imparts its colour

RUC noun **RUCS** a roc

RUCHE noun **RUCHES** a pleated or gathered frill of lace, ribbon, etc, used as a trimming □ verb **RUCHES, RUCHING, RUCHED** to trim (an item of clothing, etc) with a ruche or ruches

RUCHED adj trimmed with or gathered into a ruche or ruches

RUCHING noun **RUCHINGS** ruched trimming

RUCK noun **RUCKS** a heap or mass of indistinguishable people or things □ verb **RUCKS, RUCKING, RUCKED** to heap or pile up (hay, etc)

RUCKSACK noun **RUCKSACKS** a bag carried on the back with straps over the shoulders

RUCKUS noun **RUCKUSES** a disturbance; a commotion

RUCTION noun **RUCTIONS** a noisy disturbance; uproar

RUD verb **RUDS, RUDDING, RUDDED** a Spenserian word meaning to redden

RUDBECKIA noun **RUDBECKIAS** any of various N American composite plants of the daisy family

RUDD noun **RUDDS** a freshwater fish, widespread in European rivers and lakes, greenish-brown in colour on the back, with yellow sides and reddish fins

RUDDER noun **RUDDERS** a flat piece of wood, metal, etc fixed vertically to a ship's stern for steering

RUDDILY adverb in a ruddy way

RUDDINESS noun **RUDDINESSES** the state or condition or quality of being ruddy

RUDDLE noun **RUDDLES** red ochre, used especially to mark sheep □ verb **RUDDLES, RUDDLING, RUDDLED** to mark (sheep) with ruddle

RUDDY adj **RUDDIER, RUDDIEST** said of the face, complexion, etc: glowing; with a healthy rosy or pink colour

RUDE adj **RUDER, RUDEST** impolite; bad-mannered; discourteous

RUDELY adj in a rude way

RUDENESS noun **RUDENESSES** being rude; rude language or behaviour

RUDERAL noun **RUDERALS** a plant that grows in waste places or among rubbish

RUDERY noun **RUDERIES** rude language or behaviour

RUDIMENT noun **RUDIMENTS** the fundamental facts, rules or skills of a subject

RUE[1] verb **RUES, RUEING, RUING, RUED** to regret; to wish that something had not been or had not happened

RUE[2] noun **RUES** a strongly scented evergreen plant with bitter leaves which were formerly used in medicine

RUEFUL adj regretful

RUEFULLY adverb regretfully

RUFESCENT adj tending to redness

RUFF[1] noun **RUFFS** a circular pleated or frilled collar, worn in the late 16c and early 17c, or more recently by the members of some choirs

RUFF ² *verb* **RUFFS, RUFFING, RUFFED** in cards: to trump

RUFFE *noun* **RUFFES** a small freshwater fish of the perch family, which has one dorsal fin

RUFFED *adj* having a ruff

RUFFIAN *noun* **RUFFIANS** a coarse, violent, brutal or lawless person

RUFFIANLY *adj* in a coarse, violent way

RUFFLE *verb* **RUFFLES, RUFFLING, RUFFLED** said of a bird: to make its feathers erect, usually in anger □ *noun* **RUFFLES** a frill of lace, linen, etc worn either round the neck or wrists

RUFFLING *noun* **RUFFLINGS** an act of ruffling

RUFIYAA *noun* **RUFIYAAS** the standard monetary unit of the Maldives

RUFOUS *adj* said especially of a bird or animal: reddish or brownish-red in colour

RUG *noun* **RUGS** a thick heavy mat or small carpet for covering a floor

RUG *verb* **RUGS, RUGGING, RUGGED** a Scots word meaning to pull roughly

RUGBY *noun* **RUGBIES** a team game played with an oval ball which players may pick up and run with and may pass from hand to hand

RUGGED *adj* **RUGGEDER, RUGGEDEST** said of landscape, hills, ground, etc: with a rough, uneven surface; steep and rocky

RUGGEDLY *adverb* in a rugged way

RUGGER *noun* **RUGGERS** rugby

RUGOSE *adj* wrinkled; marked with folds or ridges

RUGOSELY *adverb* in a rugose way

RUGOSITY *noun* **RUGOSITIES** the state or condition of being rugose

RUIN *noun* **RUINS** a broken, destroyed, decayed or collapsed state □ *verb* **RUINS, RUINING, RUINED** to reduce or bring someone or something to ruin; to destroy them

RUINATION *noun* **RUINATIONS** an act of ruining; the state of being ruined

RUINER *noun* **RUINERS** a person or thing that causes ruin

RUING a form of **rue** ¹

RUINOUS *adj* likely to bring about ruin

RUINOUSLY *adverb* in a ruinous way

RULABLE *adj* capable of being ruled

RULE *noun* **RULES** a principle, regulation, order or direction which governs or controls some action, function, form, use, etc □ *verb* **RULES, RULING, RULED** to govern; to exercise authority over someone

RULELESS *adj* without rules or laws

RULER *noun* **RULERS** someone, eg a sovereign, who rules or governs

RULING *noun* **RULINGS** an official or authoritative decision

RUM ¹ *noun* **RUMS** a spirit distilled from fermented sugar-cane juice or from molasses

RUM ² *adj* **RUMMER, RUMMEST** strange; odd; bizarre

RUMBA *noun* **RUMBAS** a lively Afro-Cuban dance □ *verb* **RUMBAS, RUMBAING, RUMBAED** to dance the rumba

RUMBLE *verb* **RUMBLES, RUMBLING, RUMBLED** to make a deep low grumbling sound □ *noun* **RUMBLES** a deep low grumbling sound

RUMBLING *noun* **RUMBLINGS** an act or instance of making a rumble

RUMEN *noun* **RUMINA** in a ruminant animal such as a cow or sheep: the first and largest chamber of the complex stomach, in which food is stored and partly digested before being regurgitated

RUMINANT *noun* **RUMINANTS** an even-toed hoofed mammal, eg a cow, sheep or goat, that chews the cud and has a complex stomach with four chambers □ *adj* relating or belonging to this group of mammals

RUMINATE *verb* **RUMINATES, RUMINATING, RUMINATED** said of a ruminant: to chew the cud

RUMINATOR *noun* **RUMINATORS** an animal that ruminates

RUMLY *adverb* in a rum way; bizarrely

RUMMAGE *verb* **RUMMAGES, RUMMAGING, RUMMAGED** to search messily through (a collection of things, a cupboard, etc) □ *noun* **RUMMAGES** a search

RUMMAGER *noun* **RUMMAGERS** someone who rummages

RUMMER *noun* **RUMMERS** a large drinking-glass

RUMMY ¹ *noun* **RUMMIES** a card game in which each player tries to collect sets or sequences of three or more cards

RUMMY ² *adj* **RUMMIER, RUMMIEST** of, relating to or like rum

RUMNESS *noun* **RUMNESSES** the state of being rum or bizarre

RUMOR *noun* **RUMORS** a rumour □ *verb* **RUMORS, RUMORING, RUMORED** to rumour

RUMOUR *noun* **RUMOURS** a piece of news or information which is passed from person to person and which may or may not be true □ *verb* **RUMOURS, RUMOURING, RUMOURED** to report or spread (news, information, etc) by rumour

RUMP *noun* **RUMPS** the rear part of an animal's or bird's body; the area around the tail

RUMPLE *verb* **RUMPLES, RUMPLING, RUMPLED** to become or to make (hair, clothes, etc) untidy, creased or wrinkled □ *noun* **RUMPLES** a wrinkle or crease

RUMPUS *noun* **RUMPUSES** a noisy disturbance, fuss, brawl or uproar

RUN *verb* **RUNS, RUNNING, RAN, RUN** said of a person or an animal: to move at a pace quicker than walking and in such a way that both or all feet are off the ground together for an instant during part of each step □ *noun* **RUNS** an act of running

RUNABOUT *noun* **RUNABOUTS** a small light car, boat or aircraft

RUNAROUND *noun* **RUNAROUNDS** a runabout car

RUNAWAY *noun* **RUNAWAYS** a person or animal that has run away or fled □ *adj* in the process of running away; out of control

RUNE *noun* **RUNES** any of the letters of an early alphabet used by the Germanic peoples between about AD 200 and AD 600, used especially in inscriptions

RUNG ¹ *noun* **RUNGS** a step on a ladder

RUNG ² a past form of **ring** ²

RUNIC *adj* of or relating to runes

RUNNABLE *adj* said of a stag: fit for hunting

RUNNEL *noun* **RUNNELS** a small stream

RUNNER *noun* **RUNNERS** someone or something that runs

RUNNING *noun* **RUNNINGS** the act of moving quickly □ *adj* relating to or for running

RUNNY adj RUNNIER, RUNNIEST tending to run or flow with liquid

RUNT noun RUNTS the smallest animal in a litter

RUNWAY noun RUNWAYS a wide hard surface from which aircraft take off and on which they land

RUPEE noun RUPEES the standard unit of currency in India, Pakistan, Bhutan, Nepal, Sri Lanka, Mauritius and the Seychelles

RUPIAH noun RUPIAHS the standard unit of currency of Indonesia

RUPTURE noun RUPTURES a breach; a breaking or bursting □ verb RUPTURES, RUPTURING, RUPTURED to break, tear or burst something

RURAL adj relating to or suggestive of the country or countryside

RURALISE verb RURALISES, RURALISING, RURALISED to ruralize

RURALITY noun RURALITIES the state or condition of being rural

RURALIZE verb RURALIZES, RURALIZING, RURALIZED to make something rural

RURP noun RURPS a very small hook-like piton

RUSA noun RUSAS a large E Indian deer, especially the sambar

RUSE noun RUSES a clever strategem or plan intended to deceive or trick

RUSH [1] verb RUSHES, RUSHING, RUSHED to hurry; to move forward or go quickly

RUSH [2] noun RUSHES a densely tufted annual or evergreen perennial plant, typically found in cold wet regions of the northern hemisphere, usually on moors or marshy ground

RUSHES plural noun in cinematography: the first unedited prints of a scene or scenes

RUSHY adj RUSHIER, RUSHIEST of, relating to, like or characterized by rushes

RUSK noun RUSKS a piece of bread which has been rebaked, or a hard dry biscuit resembling this, given as food to babies

RUSSET noun RUSSETS a reddish-brown colour

RUSSETY adj reddish brown in colour

RUST noun RUSTS a reddish-brown coating that forms on the surface of iron or steel that has been exposed to air and moisture □ verb RUSTS, RUSTING, RUSTED to become rusty or coated with rust

RUSTIC adj relating to, characteristic of, or living in the country; rural □ noun RUSTICS a person from, or who lives in, the country, especially one who is thought of as being simple and unsophisticated; a peasant

RUSTICATE verb RUSTICATES, RUSTICATING, RUSTICATED to live or go to live in the country

RUSTICISM noun RUSTICISMS a rustic saying or custom

RUSTICITY noun RUSTICITIES rustic manner; simplicity

RUSTILY adverb in a rusty way

RUSTINESS noun RUSTINESSES the state or condition of being rusty

RUSTLE verb RUSTLES, RUSTLING, RUSTLED to make a soft whispering sound like that of dry leaves □ noun RUSTLES a quick succession of small soft dry crisp sounds like that of dry leaves; a rustling

RUSTLER noun RUSTLERS someone who steals cattle or horses

RUSTLING noun RUSTLINGS an act of making a soft whispering sound like that of dry leaves

RUSTY adj RUSTIER, RUSTIEST said of iron, steel or other metals: covered with rust; rusted; out of practice

RUT [1] noun RUTS a deep track or furrow in soft ground, especially one made by wheels

RUT [2] verb RUTS, RUTTING, RUTTED said of male animals: to be in a period of sexual excitement

RUTABAGA noun RUTABAGAS a swede

RUTHENIUM noun RUTHENIUMS a brittle, silvery-white metallic element that occurs in small amounts in some platinum ores

RUTHLESS adj without pity; merciless

RUTILE noun RUTILES a reddish-brown or black lustrous mineral form of titanium oxide, commonly found in igneous and metamorphic rocks, and in beach sand

RUTTING noun RUTTINGS the time of year when animals rut

RUTTY adj RUTTIER, RUTTIEST having a lot of ruts or deep furrows

RYA noun RYAS a type of Scandinavian knotted-pile rug with a distinctive colourful pattern

RYE noun RYES a cereal belonging to the grass family that resembles barley but has longer and narrower ears, cultivated mainly in central Europe and eastern Europe, eg Poland, Ukraine, Russia, etc □ adj of or relating to rye

RYOKAN noun RYOKANS a traditional Japanese inn

RYOT noun RYOTS in the Indian subcontinent: a peasant or tenant farmer

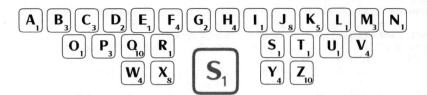

SAB *noun* **SABS** a saboteur

SABADILLA *noun* **SABADILLAS** a tropical plant of the lily genus
SABER *noun* **SABERS** a sabre ◻ *verb* **SABERS, SABERING, SABERED** to sabre
SABIN *noun* **SABINS** a unit of acoustic absorption
SABLE *noun* **SABLES** a small carnivorous mammal, native to Europe and Asia, that is a species of the marten and inhabits coniferous forests, usually near streams
SABOT *noun* **SABOTS** a wooden clog, or a shoe with a wooden sole, as formerly worn by the French peasantry
SABOTAGE *noun* **SABOTAGES** deliberate or underhand damage or destruction, especially carried out for military or political reasons ◻ *verb* **SABOTAGES, SABOTAGING, SABOTAGED** to deliberately destroy, damage or disrupt something
SABOTEUR *noun* **SABOTEURS** someone who sabotages
SABRA *noun* **SABRAS** a native-born Israeli, not an immigrant
SABRE *noun* **SABRES** a curved single-edged cavalry sword ◻ *verb* **SABRES, SABRING, SABRED** to wound or kill using a sabre
SAC *noun* **SACS** any bag-like part in a plant or animal
SACCADE *noun* **SACCADES** a short jerky movement of the eye as it switches from one point to another, and may be voluntary, as in reading, or involuntary
SACCADIC *adj* jerky; consisting of or relating to saccades
SACCATE *adj* enclosed in a sac; pouchlike
SACCHARIN *noun* **SACCHARINS** a white crystalline substance, about 550 times sweeter than sugar and with no energy value, used as an artificial sweetener, especially by diabetics and dieters
SACCULE *noun* **SACCULES** a small sac

SACCULUS *noun* **SACCULI** a saccule
SACHEM *noun* **SACHEMS** a political leader
SACHET *noun* **SACHETS** a small sealed packet, usually made of plastic, containing a liquid, cream or powder
SACK ¹ *noun* **SACKS** a large bag, especially one made of coarse cloth or paper
SACK ² *verb* **SACKS, SACKING, SACKED** to plunder, pillage and destroy a town
SACKBUT *noun* **SACKBUTS** an early wind instrument with a slide like a trombone
SACKCLOTH *noun* **SACKCLOTHS** coarse cloth used to make sacks; sacking
SACKFUL *noun* **SACKFULS** the amount a sack will hold
SACKING *noun* **SACKINGS** coarse cloth used to make sacks
SACRA plural of **sacrum**
SACRAL *adj* referring or relating to sacred rites
SACRAMENT *noun* **SACRAMENTS** in Christianity: any of various religious rites or ceremonies, eg baptism, regarded as a channel to and from God or as a sign of grace
SACRARIUM *noun* **SACRARIA** the area around the altar of a church; the sanctuary
SACRED *adj* devoted to a deity, therefore regarded with deep and solemn respect; consecrated
SACREDLY *adverb* in a sacred way
SACRIFICE *noun* **SACRIFICES** the offering of a slaughtered person or animal on an altar to God or a god ◻ *verb* **SACRIFICES, SACRIFICING, SACRIFICED** to offer someone or something as a sacrifice to God or a god
SACRILEGE *noun* **SACRILEGES** a profanation or extreme disrespect for something holy or greatly respected
SACRIST *noun* **SACRISTS** a sacristan
SACRISTAN *noun* **SACRISTANS** someone responsible for the safety

of the sacred vessels and other contents of a church
SACRISTY *noun* **SACRISTIES** a room in a church where sacred utensils and vestments are kept; a vestry
SACRUM *noun* **SACRA** a large triangular bone composed of fused vertebrae, forming the keystone of the pelvic arch in humans
SAD *adj* **SADDER, SADDEST** feeling unhappy or sorrowful
SADDEN *verb* **SADDENS, SADDENING, SADDENED** to make someone sad
SADDHU *noun* **SADDHUS** a sadhu
SADDLE *noun* **SADDLES** a leather seat for horse-riding, which fits on the horse's back and is secured under its belly ◻ *verb* **SADDLES, SADDLING, SADDLED** to put a saddle on (an animal)
SADDLEBAG *noun* **SADDLEBAGS** a small bag carried at or attached to the saddle of a horse
SADDLEBOW *noun* **SADDLEBOWS** the arched front of a saddle
SADDLER *noun* **SADDLERS** a person who makes or sells saddles, harness, and related equipment for horses
SADDLERY *noun* **SADDLERIES** the occupation or profession of a saddler
SADHU *noun* **SADHUS** a nomadic Hindu holy man, living an austere life and existing on charity
SADISM *noun* **SADISMS** the pleasure, especially sexual, gained by inflicting pain on others
SADIST *noun* **SADISTS** someone who indulges in sadism, or who gains pleasure from inflicting pain on others
SADISTIC *adj* relating to or involving sadism
SADLY *adverb* in a sad way; sorrowfully
SADNESS *noun* **SADNESSES** the state or condition of being sad; unhappiness

SADZA noun **SADZAS** a type of African porridge made from maize flour

SAE adverb a Scots form of so

SAFARI noun **SAFARIS** an expedition or tour to hunt or observe wild animals, especially in Africa

SAFE adj **SAFER, SAFEST** free from danger or harm ◻ noun **SAFES** a sturdily constructed cabinet, usually made of metal, in which money and valuables can be locked away

SAFEGUARD noun **SAFEGUARDS** a person, device or arrangement giving protection against danger or harm ◻ verb **SAFEGUARDS, SAFEGUARDING, SAFEGUARDED** to protect from harm; to ensure the safety of someone or something

SAFELY adverb in a safe way

SAFENESS noun **SAFENESSES** the quality or condition of being safe

SAFETY noun **SAFETIES** the quality or condition of being safe

SAFFIAN noun **SAFFIANS** leather tanned with sumac and dyed in bright colours

SAFFLOWER noun **SAFFLOWERS** a plant with large thistle-like heads of orange-red flowers that yield yellow and red dyes, and seeds that yield oil which is used in cooking, medicines, paints and varnishes

SAFFRON noun **SAFFRONS** an autumn-flowering species of crocus which has lilac flowers with large bright orange stigmas divided into three branches; the dried stigmas of this species, used to dye and flavour food

SAFFRONED adj of or like saffron

SAFFRONY adj of or like saffron, eg in colour, taste or smell

SAFRANIN noun **SAFRANINS** safranine

SAFRANINE noun **SAFRANINES** a coal-tar dye giving various different colours for fabrics

SAG verb **SAGS, SAGGING, SAGGED** to bend, sink, or hang down, especially in the middle, under or as if under weight ◻ noun **SAGS** a sagging state or condition

SAGA noun **SAGAS** a medieval prose tale of the deeds of legendary Icelandic or Norwegian heroes and events

SAGACIOUS adj having or showing intelligence and good judgement; wise or discerning

SAGACITY noun **SAGACITIES** the quality or condition of being sagacious

SAGAMORE noun **SAGAMORES** a Native N American chief

SAGE [1] noun **SAGES** a low-growing perennial shrub with wrinkled greyish-green aromatic leaves and bluish-lilac two-lipped flowers

SAGE [2] noun **SAGES** someone of great wisdom and knowledge, especially an ancient philosopher ◻ adj **SAGER, SAGEST** extremely wise and prudent

SAGEBRUSH noun **SAGEBRUSHES** any of various species of N American plant, especially an aromatic shrub with many branches, with wedge-shaped silvery leaves and small white flowers borne in large clusters

SAGELY adj wisely

SAGENESS noun **SAGENESSES** the state of being sage or wise

SAGGAR noun **SAGGARS** a large clay box in which pottery is packed for firing in a kiln

SAGGER noun **SAGGERS** a saggar

SAGGY adj **SAGGIER, SAGGIEST** tending to sag

SAGITTAL adj shaped like an arrow

SAGO noun **SAGOS** a starchy grain or powder obtained from the soft pith of the sago palm, a staple food in the tropics, and also widely used in desserts

SAGUARO noun **SAGUAROS** a giant cactus of up to 50ft (15m) in height, native to the south west US and Mexico, and with a tree-like trunk and edible red fruits

SAHIB noun **SAHIBS** in India: a term of respect used after a man's name, equivalent to Mr or Sir, and formerly used on its own to address or refer to a European man

SAI noun **SAIS** the capuchin monkey

SAID [1] adj previously or already mentioned

SAID [2] noun **SAIDS** a sayyid

SAIGA noun **SAIGAS** a type of antelope from W Asia, with a characteristic swollen snout

SAIL noun **SAILS** a sheet of canvas, or similar structure, spread to catch the wind as a means of propelling a ship ◻ verb **SAILS, SAILING, SAILED** to travel by boat or ship

SAILABLE adj navigable

SAILBOARD noun **SAILBOARDS** a windsurfing board, like a surfboard with a sail attached, controlled by a hand-held boom

SAILCLOTH noun **SAILCLOTHS** strong cloth, such as canvas, used to make sails

SAILED adj having sails

SAILER noun **SAILERS** a boat or ship that can sail in a specific manner

SAILFISH noun **SAILFISHES** a large agile fish, bluish-grey above and silvery beneath, named after its sail-like dorsal fin and highly prized as a sport fish

SAILING noun **SAILINGS** going by boat or ship

SAILLESS adj without sails

SAILOR noun **SAILORS** any member of a ship's crew, especially one who is not an officer

SAILPLANE noun **SAILPLANES** a lightweight glider that can rise with upward currents

SAINFOIN noun **SAINFOINS** a leguminous perennial plant, widely cultivated as a fodder crop, with pinnate leaves, spiked flower-heads and bright pink to red flowers veined with purple

SAINT noun **SAINTS** a person whose profound holiness is formally recognized after death, especially by a Christian church ◻ verb **SAINTS, SAINTING, SAINTED** to make a saint of someone

SAINTED adj formally declared a saint

SAINTHOOD noun **SAINTHOODS** the position or status of a saint

SAINTLIKE adj like a saint, especially in behaviour

SAINTLY adj **SAINTLIER, SAINTLIEST** similar to, characteristic of, or befitting a saint

SAITH an archaic form of say

SAITHE noun **SAITHES** the coley

SAKE noun **SAKES** benefit or advantage; behalf; account

SAKER noun **SAKERS** a species of falcon, especially the female, used in hawking

SAKERET noun **SAKERETS** a male saker

SAKI *noun* **SAKIS** a Japanese fermented alcoholic drink made from rice

SAL *noun* **SALS** a salt

SALAAM *noun* **SALAAMS** a Muslim greeting or show of respect in the form of a low bow with the palm of the right hand on the forehead □ *verb* **SALAAMS, SALAAMING, SALAAMED** to perform the salaam to someone

SALABLE *adj* saleable

SALACIOUS *adj* unnaturally preoccupied with sex; lecherous or lustful

SALACITY *noun* **SALACITIES** the state of being salacious

SALAD *noun* **SALADS** a cold dish of vegetables or herbs, either raw or pre-cooked, often served with a dressing, and eaten either on its own or as an accompaniment to a main meal

SALAMI *noun* **SALAMIS** a highly seasoned type of sausage, usually, served very thinly sliced

SALARIED *adj* having or receiving a salary

SALARY *noun* **SALARIES** a fixed regular payment, usually made monthly, for especially non-manual work □ *verb* **SALARIES, SALARYING, SALARIED** to pay a salary to someone

SALCHOW *noun* **SALCHOWS** in ice-skating: a jump where the skater takes off from the inside back edge of one skate, spins up to three times in the air, and lands on the outside back edge of the other skate

SALE *noun* **SALES** the act or practice of selling

SALEABLE *adj* suitable for selling

SALEROOM *noun* **SALEROOMS** a room where goods for sale, especially at a public auction, are displayed

SALESMAN *noun* **SALESMEN** a man who sells goods to customers, especially in a shop

SALESROOM *noun* **SALESROOMS** a room where goods for sale, especially at a public auction, are displayed

SALICIN *noun* **SALICINS** a bitter crystalline glucoside procured from willow-bark, used medicinally as an analgesic or painkiller

SALICINE *noun* **SALICINES** salicin

SALIENCE *noun* **SALIENCES** the quality or condition of being salient

SALIENCY *noun* **SALIENCIES** salience

SALIENT *adj* striking; outstanding or prominent □ *noun* **SALIENTS** a projecting angle, part or section, eg of a fortification or a defensive line of troops

SALIENTLY *adverb* in a salient way

SALINA *noun* **SALINAS** a salt lagoon, marsh, lake or spring

SALINE *adj* said of a substance: containing sodium chloride (common salt); salty □ *noun* **SALINES** a salina

SALINITY *noun* **SALINITIES** the quality or condition of being salty

SALIVA *noun* **SALIVAS** a clear alkaline liquid produced by the salivary glands of the mouth, that moistens and softens the food and begins the process of digestion

SALIVARY *adj* relating to, secreting or conveying saliva

SALIVATE *verb* **SALIVATES, SALIVATING, SALIVATED** said of the salivary glands: to produce a flow of saliva into the mouth in response to the thought or sight of food

SALLOW [1] *adj* **SALLOWER, SALLOWEST** said of a person's complexion: being a pale yellowish colour, often through poor health □ *verb* **SALLOWS, SALLOWING, SALLOWED** to make or become sallow

SALLOW [2] *noun* **SALLOWS** a willow, especially the broader-leaved type with brittle twigs

SALLOWISH *adj* somewhat sallow; pale

SALLOWY *adj* full of sallows

SALLY *noun* **SALLIES** a sudden rushing forward or advance of troops to attack besiegers □ *verb* **SALLIES, SALLYING, SALLIED** said of troops: to carry out a sally

SALMON *noun* **SALMONS** any of various medium-sized to large silvery streamlined fish that migrate to freshwater rivers and streams in order to spawn, highly prized as a food and game fish

SALON *noun* **SALONS** a reception room, especially in a large house

SALOON *noun* **SALOONS** a large public room for functions or some other specified purpose, such as billiards, dancing, hairdressing, etc

SALPINX *noun* **SALPINGES,**

SALPINXES the Eustachian tube, leading from the middle ear to the pharynx

SALSA *noun* **SALSAS** rhythmic music of Latin-American origin, containing elements of jazz and rock

SALSIFY *noun* **SALSIFIES** a biennial plant with a long white cylindrical tap root, grass-like leaves and large solitary heads of violet-purple flowers surrounded by bracts

SALT *noun* **SALTS** sodium chloride, especially as used to season and preserve food □ *adj* containing salt □ *verb* **SALTS, SALTING, SALTED** to season or preserve (food) with salt

SALTANT *adj* said of animals: leaping

SALTATION *noun* **SALTATIONS** a leaping or jumping

SALTATORY *adj* leaping or jumping

SALTBUSH *noun* **SALTBUSHES** any shrubby plant of the goosefoot family, growing in arid regions

SALTED *adj* cured or preserved in salt

SALTIER [1] *noun* **SALTIERS** a saltire

SALTIER [2] see under **salty**

SALTIEST see under **salty**

SALTINESS *noun* **SALTINESSES** the quality or state of being salty

SALTING *noun* **SALTINGS** the act of preserving, seasoning, etc (food) with salt

SALTIRE *noun* **SALTIRES** the flag of Scotland, a white St Andrew's cross on a blue background

SALTISH *adj* somewhat salty

SALTLESS *adj* without salt

SALTLY *adverb* in a salty way

SALTPETER *noun* **SALTPETERS** saltpetre

SALTPETRE *noun* **SALTPETRES** potassium nitrate

SALTUS *noun* **SALTUSES** a breach of continuity, especially a jump to a conclusion

SALTWORKS *singular noun* a building or site, etc where salt is produced

SALTWORT *noun* **SALTWORTS** a fleshy prickly plant of the goosefoot family, with green flowers, which inhabits sandy seashores and salt marshes

SALTY *adj* **SALTIER, SALTIEST** containing salt

SALUBRITY *noun* **SALUBRITIES** the state of being healthy or of promoting good health

SALUKI noun **SALUKIS** a breed of dog of Arabian origin, with a tall slender body and a silky fawn, cream or white coat, with longer hair on the ears, tail and backs of the legs

SALUTARY adj beneficial; bringing or containing a timely warning

SALUTE verb **SALUTES**, **SALUTING, SALUTED** to greet with friendly words or especially a gesture, such as a kiss ◻ noun **SALUTES** a greeting

SALUTER noun **SALUTERS** someone who salutes

SALVAGE noun **SALVAGES** the rescue of a ship or its cargo from the danger of destruction or loss ◻ verb **SALVAGES, SALVAGING, SALVAGED** to rescue (property or a ship) from potential destruction or loss, eg in a fire or shipwreck, or from disposal as waste

SALVATION noun **SALVATIONS** the act of saving someone or something from harm

SALVE noun **SALVES** ointment or remedy to heal or soothe ◻ verb **SALVES, SALVING, SALVED** to smear with salve

SALVER noun **SALVERS** a small ornamented tray, usually of silver, on which something is presented

SALVIA noun **SALVIAS** any of numerous herbaceous plants or small shrubs of the mint family, including ornamental species and culinary herbs, eg sage

SALVO noun **SALVOS, SALVOES** a burst of gunfire from several guns firing simultaneously, as a salute or in battle

SAM adverb a Spenserian word meaning *together*

SAMARA noun **SAMARAS** a dry, one-seeded fruit with a wing-like appendage allowing easier distribution on air currents

SAMARIUM noun **SAMARIUMS** a soft silvery metallic element, used in alloys with cobalt to make strong permanent magnets

SAMBA noun **SAMBAS** a lively Brazilian dance in duple time

SAMBAR noun **SAMBARS** a large Indian or Asian deer with three-pronged antlers

SAMBUR noun **SAMBURS** a sambar

SAME adj identical or very similar ◻ pronoun the same person or thing, or the one previously

referred to ◻ adverb similarly; likewise

SAMENESS noun **SAMENESSES** the quality or state of being the same

SAMEY adj **SAMIER, SAMIEST** boringly similar or unchanging; monotonous

SAMFOO noun **SAMFOOS** a suit worn by Chinese women, comprising a jacket and trousers

SAMFU noun **SAMFUS** a samfoo

SAMISEN noun **SAMISENS** a Japanese musical instrument, similar to a guitar, but with three strings, a long fingerboard and a rectangular soundbox

SAMIZDAT noun **SAMIZDATS** in the former Soviet Union: the secret printing and distribution of writings banned by the government

SAMOSA noun **SAMOSAS** a small deep-fried triangular pastry turnover, of Indian origin, filled with spicy meat or vegetables

SAMOVAR noun **SAMOVARS** a Russian water boiler, used for making tea, etc, often elaborately decorated, and traditionally heated by a central pipe filled with charcoal

SAMPAN noun **SAMPANS** a small Oriental boat with no engine, which is propelled by oars

SAMPHIRE noun **SAMPHIRES** a fleshy perennial plant with strongly aromatic bluish-green leaves, formerly popular as a pickled delicacy, and clusters of tiny yellowish-green flowers

SAMPLE noun **SAMPLES** a specimen; a small portion or part used to represent the quality and nature of others or of a whole ◻ adj used as or serving as a sample ◻ verb **SAMPLES, SAMPLING, SAMPLED** to take or try as a sample

SAMPLER noun **SAMPLERS** a collection of samples

SAMPLING noun **SAMPLINGS** the taking, testing, etc of a sample

SAMURAI noun **SAMURAI** an aristocratic caste or class of Japanese warriors, between the 11c and 19c

SAN noun **SANS** a Japanese form of address

SANATIVE noun **SANATIVES** a remedy or cure ◻ adj curing or healing

SANCTA a plural of **sanctum**

SANCTIFY verb **SANCTIFIES, SANCTIFYING, SANCTIFIED** to make, consider or show to be sacred or holy

SANCTION noun **SANCTIONS** official permission or authority ◻ verb **SANCTIONS, SANCTIONING, SANCTIONED** to authorize or confirm formally

SANCTITY noun **SANCTITIES** the quality of being holy or sacred

SANCTUARY noun **SANCTUARIES** a holy or sacred place, eg a church or temple

SANCTUM noun **SANCTA, SANCTUMS** a sacred place

SAND noun **SANDS** tiny rounded particles or grains of rock, especially quartz ◻ adj made of sand ◻ verb **SANDS, SANDING, SANDED** to smooth or polish a surface with sandpaper or a sander

SANDAL noun **SANDALS** a type of lightweight shoe consisting of a sole attached to the foot by straps

SANDALLED adj wearing sandals

SANDARAC noun **SANDARACS** a sandarach

SANDARACH noun **SANDARACHS** a tree native to Australia, NW Africa, and N America, with sturdy fragrant wood

SANDBAG noun **SANDBAGS** a sack filled with sand or earth, used with others to form a protective barrier against bomb blasts, gunfire or floods, or used as ballast ◻ verb **SANDBAGS, SANDBAGGING, SANDBAGGED** to barricade or weigh down with sandbags

SANDBANK noun **SANDBANKS** a bank of sand in a river, river mouth or sea, formed by currents and often above the water level at low tide

SANDBLAST noun **SANDBLASTS** a jet of sand forced from a tube by air or steam pressure, used for glass-engraving, cleaning and polishing metal and stone surfaces, etc ◻ verb **SANDBLASTS, SANDBLASTING, SANDBLASTED** to clean or engrave with a sandblast

SANDBOX noun **SANDBOXES** a box of sand, especially one for sprinkling on railway lines or roads

SANDBOY noun **SANDBOYS** a boy selling sand

SANDER noun **SANDERS** a power-driven tool fitted with sandpaper or an abrasive disc, used for sanding wood, etc

SANDFLY noun **SANDFLIES** a small bloodsucking midge

SANDIER see under **sandy**

SANDIEST see under **sandy**

SANDINESS noun **SANDINESSES** the state of being sandy

SANDPAPER noun **SANDPAPERS** abrasive paper with a coating originally of sand, now usually of crushed glass, glued to one side, used for smoothing and polishing surfaces ◻ verb **SANDPAPERS, SANDPAPERING, SANDPAPERED** to smooth or polish with sandpaper

SANDPIPER noun **SANDPIPERS** any of various ground-dwelling wading birds inhabiting shores in the N hemisphere, with long legs and bills, camouflaged plumage, and a high-pitched piping call

SANDPIT noun **SANDPITS** a shallow pit filled with sand for children to play in

SANDSHOE noun **SANDSHOES** a shoe with a canvas upper and rubber sole; a plimsoll

SANDSTONE noun **SANDSTONES** a hard or soft sedimentary rock consisting of compacted sand cemented together with clay, silica, etc, widely used in the construction of buildings

SANDSTORM noun **SANDSTORMS** a strong wind that sweeps clouds of sand through the air

SANDWICH noun **SANDWICHES** a snack consisting of two slices of bread or a roll with a filling of cheese, meat, etc ◻ verb **SANDWICHES, SANDWICHING, SANDWICHED** to place, especially with little or no gaps, between two layers

SANDY adj **SANDIER, SANDIEST** covered with or containing sand

SANE adj **SANER, SANEST** sound in mind; not mentally impaired

SANELY adverb in a sane way

SANENESS noun **SANENESSES** sanity

SANG a past form of **sing**

SANGFROID noun **SANGFROIDS** calmness or composure; cool-headedness

SANGRIA noun **SANGRIAS** a Spanish drink of red wine, fruit juice, sugar and spices

SANGUINE adj cheerful, confident and full of hope ◻ noun

SANGUINES a blood-red colour

SANIES noun **SANIES** a watery discharge from wounds and sores, containing serum, blood, and pus

SANIOUS adj of or relating to sanies

SANITARY adj concerned with and promoting hygiene, good health and the prevention of disease

SANITISE verb **SANITISES, SANITISING, SANITISED** to sanitize

SANITIZE verb **SANITIZES, SANITIZING, SANITIZED** to make hygienic or sanitary

SANITY noun **SANITIES** soundness of mind; rationality

SANK a past form of **sink**

SANPAN noun **SANPANS** a sampan

SANSERIF noun **SANSERIFS** a type in which the letters have no serifs

SANTONICA noun **SANTONICAS** the dried unopened flower-heads of a species of wormwood

SANTONIN noun **SANTONINS** a substance extracted from santonica, used as a drug to destroy or expel intestinal worms

SAP noun **SAPS** a vital liquid containing sugars and other nutrients that circulates in plants ◻ verb **SAPS, SAPPING, SAPPED** to drain or extract sap from something

SAPELE noun **SAPELES** a type of wood resembling mahogany, used to make furniture

SAPID adj said of food: having a decided taste or flavour, usually pleasant

SAPIDITY noun **SAPIDITIES** the quality or condition of being sapid

SAPIENCE noun **SAPIENCES** discernment or judgement; sagacity

SAPIENT adj having or showing good judgement; wise

SAPIENTLY adverb wisely

SAPLING noun **SAPLINGS** a young tree

SAPODILLA noun **SAPODILLAS** a large evergreen tree of tropical America

SAPONIFY verb **SAPONIFIES, SAPONIFYING, SAPONIFIED** to carry out a process where the hydrolysis of an ester by an alkali converts fats into soap

SAPONIN noun **SAPONINS** a glucoside extracted from plants, eg soapwort, which gives a soapy lather

SAPOR noun **SAPORS** taste; flavour

SAPOROUS adj of or relating to sapor

SAPPER noun **SAPPERS** a soldier, especially a private, in the Royal Engineers

SAPPHIC noun **SAPPHICS** the form of verse invented by Sappho, an ancient Greek poetess

SAPPHIRE noun **SAPPHIRES** any gem variety of the mineral corundum other than ruby, especially the hard transparent blue variety, prized as a gemstone, and also used in record player styluses, etc

SAPPHISM noun **SAPPHISMS** lesbianism

SAPPHIST noun **SAPPHISTS** a lesbian

SAPPINESS noun **SAPPINESSES** the state or condition of being full of sap

SAPPY adj **SAPPIER, SAPPIEST** said of plants: full of sap

SAPROLITE noun **SAPROLITES** a soft earthy red or brown deposit formed by chemical weathering of igneous or metamorphic rock, especially in humid climates

SAPROZOIC adj said of organisms: feeding on dead or decaying organic matter

SAPSUCKER noun **SAPSUCKERS** a N American woodpecker which feeds on the sap of trees

SAPWOOD noun **SAPWOODS** the soft wood between the inner bark and the heartwood

SAR verb **SARS, SARING, SARED** a Scots word meaning to savour

SARABAND noun **SARABANDS** a sarabande

SARABANDE noun **SARABANDES** a slow formal Spanish dance

SARCASM noun **SARCASMS** an often ironical expression of scorn or contempt

SARCASTIC adj containing sarcasm

SARCENET noun **SARCENETS** sarsenet ◻ adj sarsenet

SARCOCARP noun **SARCOCARPS** the fleshy pericarp of a stone fruit

SARCOMA noun **SARCOMATA, SARCOMAS** a cancerous tumour arising in connective tissue

SARCOUS *adj* referring or relating to flesh or muscle

SARD *noun* **SARDS** a deep-red variety of fine-grained quartz

SARDINE *noun* **SARDINES** a young pilchard, an important food fish, commonly tinned in oil

SARDIUS *noun* **SARDIUSES** sard

SARDONIC *adj* mocking or scornful; sneering

SARDONYX *noun* **SARDONYXES** a gem variety of quartz with alternating straight parallel bands of colour, usually white and reddish-brown

SAREE *noun* **SAREES** a sari

SARGASSO *noun* **SARGASSOS** a brown seaweed with branching ribbon-like fronds that floats freely in huge masses, especially on the waters of the Sargasso Sea, a calm stretch of the N Atlantic ocean, near the West Indies

SARGE *noun* **SARGES** especially as a form of address: sergeant

SARI *noun* **SARIS** a traditional garment of Hindu women, consisting of a single long piece of fabric wound round the waist and draped over one shoulder and sometimes the head

SARKING *noun* **SARKINGS** a lining for a roof, usually made of wood or felt

SARKY *adj* **SARKIER, SARKIEST** sarcastic

SARNIE *noun* **SARNIES** a sandwich

SAROD *noun* **SARODS** an Indian stringed instrument similar to a cello, played with a bow or by plucking the strings

SARONG *noun* **SARONGS** a Malay garment worn by both sexes, consisting of a long piece of fabric wrapped around the waist or chest

SAROS *noun* **SAROSES** a cycle of 6585 days and 8 hours, or 18 years and 11 days, after which the relative positions of the Sun and Moon recur, so eclipses repeat their cycle

SARSENET *noun* **SARSENETS** a thin tissue of extremely fine silk ◻ *adj* made of sarsenet

SARTORIAL *adj* referring or relating to a tailor, tailoring or clothes in general

SARTORIUS *noun* **SARTORII** a muscle in the thigh that crosses the leg, helping to flex the knee

SASH *noun* **SASHES** a broad band of cloth, worn round the waist or over the shoulder, originally as part of a uniform ◻ *verb* **SASHES, SASHING, SASHED** to dress or adorn with a sash

SASHAY *verb* **SASHAYS, SASHAYING, SASHAYED** to walk or move in a gliding or ostentatious way ◻ *noun* **SASHAYS** an excursion or trip

SASHIMI *noun* **SASHIMIS** a Japanese dish consisting of thinly sliced raw fish

SASQUATCH *noun* **SASQUATCHES** a large hairy manlike creature believed by some to inhabit parts of N America and W Canada

SASS *noun* **SASSES** impertinent talk or behaviour ◻ *verb* **SASSES, SASSING, SASSED** to speak or behave impertinently

SASSABY *noun* **SASSABIES** a large S African antelope

SASSAFRAS *noun* **SASSAFRASES** any of various deciduous N American trees with oval aromatic leaves and long clusters of greenish-yellow flowers

SASSY *adj* **SASSIER, SASSIEST** impertinent

SAT past form of **sit**

SATANIC *adj* referring or relating to Satan

SATANICAL *adj* satanic

SATANISM *noun* **SATANISMS** the worship of Satan

SATAY *noun* **SATAYS** a Malaysian dish of marinated meat barbecued on skewers

SATCHEL *noun* **SATCHELS** a small briefcase-like bag for schoolbooks, often leather, and usually with shoulder straps

SATE *verb* **SATES, SATING, SATED** to satisfy (a longing or appetite) to the full or to excess

SATEDNESS *noun* **SATEDNESSES** the state of being sated

SATEEN *noun* **SATEENS** a glossy cotton or woollen fabric, similar to satin

SATELLITE *noun* **SATELLITES** a celestial body that orbits a much larger celestial body, eg the Moon which orbits, and is a satellite of, the Earth

SATI *noun* **SATIS** suttee

SATIABLE *adj* able to be satisfied or satiated

SATIATE *verb* **SATIATES, SATIATING, SATIATED** to gratify fully; to satisfy to excess

SATIATION *noun* **SATIATIONS** satisfaction

SATIETY *noun* **SATIETIES** the state of being satiated; surfeit

SATIN *noun* **SATINS** silk or rayon closely woven to produce a shiny finish, showing much of the warp ◻ *adj* similar to or resembling satin

SATINET *noun* **SATINETS** a thin satin

SATINETTE *noun* **SATINETTES** satinet

SATINWOOD *noun* **SATINWOODS** a shiny light-coloured ornamental hardwood from E India, used for fine furniture

SATINY *adj* similar to or resembling satin

SATIRE *noun* **SATIRES** a literary composition, originally in verse, which holds up follies and vices for criticism, ridicule and scorn

SATIRIC *adj* satirical

SATIRICAL *adj* relating to or containing satire

SATIRISE *verb* **SATIRISES, SATIRISING, SATIRISED** to satirize

SATIRIST *noun* **SATIRISTS** a writer or performer of satires

SATIRIZE *verb* **SATIRIZES, SATIRIZING, SATIRIZED** to write satire

SATISFIED *adj* pleased or contented

SATISFY *verb* **SATISFIES, SATISFYING, SATISFIED** to fulfil the needs, desires or expectations of someone

SATORI *noun* **SATORIS** sudden enlightenment, sought in Zen Buddhism

SATRAP *noun* **SATRAPS** a viceroy or governor of an ancient Persian province

SATRAPAL *adj* of or relating to a satrap

SATRAPY *noun* **SATRAPIES** a satrap's province, office or period of office

SATSUMA *noun* **SATSUMAS** a thin-skinned easily peeled seedless type of mandarin orange

SATURABLE *adj* able to be saturated

SATURANT *adj* having a tendency to saturate ◻ *noun* **SATURANTS** a saturating substance; one that causes saturation

SATURATE *verb* **SATURATES, SATURATING, SATURATED** to soak ◻ *noun* **SATURATES** a saturated compound

SATURATED *adj* said of a solution: containing as much of a solute as can be dissolved at a particular temperature and pressure

SATURNISM *noun* **SATURNISMS** lead-poisoning

SATYR *noun* **SATYRS** in mythology: a lecherous woodland god, part man, part goat

SATYRIC *adj* of, relating to or like a satyr

SATYRICAL *adj* satyric

SATYRID *noun* **SATYRIDS** any of several kinds of butterfly that have brownish wings marked with circles which resemble eyes

SAUCE *noun* **SAUCES** any liquid, often thickened, cooked or served with food ◻ *verb* **SAUCES, SAUCING, SAUCED** to add sauce to (food)

SAUCEPAN *noun* **SAUCEPANS** a deep cooking pot with a long handle and usually a lid

SAUCER *noun* **SAUCERS** a small shallow round dish, especially one for placing under a tea or coffee cup

SAUCERFUL *noun* **SAUCERFULS** the amount a saucer will hold

SAUCILY *adverb* cheekily

SAUCINESS *noun* **SAUCINESSES** the quality or condition of being saucy

SAUCY *adj* **SAUCIER, SAUCIEST** cheeky; forward; pert

SAUNA *noun* **SAUNAS** a Finnish-style bath where the person is exposed to dry heat, with occasional short blasts of steam created by pouring water on hot coals, usually followed by a cold plunge

SAUNTER *verb* **SAUNTERS, SAUNTERING, SAUNTERED** to walk, often aimlessly, at a leisurely pace; to wander or stroll idly ◻ *noun* **SAUNTERS** a sauntering gait

SAUNTERER *noun* **SAUNTERERS** someone who saunters

SAUNTERING *noun* **SAUNTERINGS** an act of walking, often aimlessly, at a leisurely pace

SAURIAN *noun* **SAURIANS** a lizard

SAURY *noun* **SAURIES** a long sharp-nosed marine fish

SAUSAGE *noun* **SAUSAGES** a mass of chopped or minced seasoned meat, especially pork or beef, sometimes mixed with fat, cereal, vegetables, etc, and stuffed into a tube of gut

SAUTÉ *verb* **SAUTÉS, SAUTÉING, SAUTÉEING, SAUTÉED** to fry

lightly for a short time ◻ *noun* **SAUTÉS** a dish of sautéed food ◻ *adj* fried in this way

SAVABLE *adj* able to be saved

SAVAGE *adj* said of animals: untamed or undomesticated ◻ *noun* **SAVAGES** an uncultured or cruel person ◻ *verb* **SAVAGES, SAVAGING, SAVAGED** to attack ferociously, especially with the teeth, causing severe injury

SAVAGELY *adverb* ferociously

SAVAGERY *noun* **SAVAGERIES** cruelty, ferocity or barbarousness; an act of cruelty

SAVANNA *noun* **SAVANNAS** an expanse of level grassland, either treeless or dotted with trees and bushes, characteristic especially of tropical and subtropical Africa

SAVANNAH *noun* **SAVANNAHS** a savanna

SAVANT *noun* **SAVANTS** a wise and learned man

SAVATE *noun* **SAVATES** a form of boxing in which the feet as well as the fists are used

SAVE *noun* **SAVES** in sport: an act of saving a ball or shot, or of preventing a goal ◻ *verb* **SAVES, SAVING, SAVED** to rescue, protect or preserve someone or something from danger, evil, loss or failure

SAVELOY *noun* **SAVELOYS** a spicy smoked pork sausage, originally made from brains

SAVER *noun* **SAVERS** a person or thing that saves

SAVIN *noun* **SAVINS** a species of juniper with small leaves, native to Europe and Asia

SAVINE *noun* **SAVINES** savin

SAVING *adj* protecting or preserving ◻ *noun* **SAVINGS** something saved, especially an economy made

SAVINGLY *adverb* in a saving way

SAVIOUR *noun* **SAVIOURS** a person who saves someone or something else from danger or destruction

SAVOR *noun* **SAVORS** savour ◻ *verb* **SAVORS, SAVORING, SAVORED** to savour

SAVORY *adj* savoury ◻ *noun* **SAVORIES** a savoury

SAVOUR *noun* **SAVOURS** the characteristic taste or smell of something ◻ *verb* **SAVOURS, SAVOURING, SAVOURED** to taste or smell with relish

SAVOURILY *adverb* in a savoury way

SAVOURY *adj* having a salty, sharp or piquant taste or smell; not sweet ◻ *noun* **SAVOURIES** a savoury course or snack, especially served as an hors d'oeuvre

SAVOY *noun* **SAVOYS** a winter variety of cabbage which has a large compact head and wrinkled leaves

SAVVY *verb* **SAVVIES, SAVVYING, SAVVIED** to know or understand ◻ *noun* **SAVVIES** general ability or common sense; shrewdness

SAW [1] a past form of **see** [1]

SAW [2] *noun* **SAWS** any of various toothed cutting tools, either hand-operated or power-driven, used especially for cutting wood ◻ *verb* **SAWS, SAWING, SAWED, SAWN** to cut with, or as if with, a saw

SAWBONES *noun* **SAWBONES** a surgeon

SAWDUST *noun* **SAWDUSTS** dust or small particles of wood, made by sawing

SAWFISH *noun* **SAWFISHES** any of various large cartilaginous fishes, native to tropical and subtropical seas, with a long flattened sawlike snout bearing a row of sharp teeth on each side

SAWHORSE *noun* **SAWHORSES** a trestle for supporting wood that is being sawn

SAWMILL *noun* **SAWMILLS** a factory in which timber is cut into planks

SAWN past form of **saw**

SAWYER *noun* **SAWYERS** a person who saws timber, especially in a sawmill

SAX *noun* **SAXES** a saxophone

SAXHORN *noun* **SAXHORNS** a valved brass instrument, similar to a small tuba, with a long winding tube and a bell opening, which is made in seven sizes

SAXIFRAGE *noun* **SAXIFRAGES** any of numerous low-growing mainly alpine plants, often forming cushions or mats, with a basal rosette of fleshy leaves and small white, yellow, pink, red or purple flowers

SAXOPHONE *noun* **SAXOPHONES** a single-reeded wind instrument with a long S-shaped metal body, usually played in jazz and dance bands

SAY *verb* **SAYS, SAYING, SAID** to speak, utter or articulate ◻ *noun* **SAYS** a chance to express an opinion

SAYER noun **SAYERS** someone who utters or articulates statements of a particular kind
SAYID noun **SAYIDS** a sayyid
SAYING noun **SAYINGS** a proverb or maxim
SAYYID noun **SAYYIDS** a descendant of Muhammad's daughter, Fatima

SAZ noun **SAZES** a stringed instrument of Turkey, North Africa, etc

SCAB noun **SCABS** a crust of dried blood formed over a healing wound ◊ verb **SCABS, SCABBING, SCABBED** to become covered by a scab
SCABBARD noun **SCABBARDS** a sheath, especially for a sword or dagger
SCABBY adj **SCABBIER, SCABBIEST** covered with scabs
SCABIES noun **SCABIES** a contagious skin disease characterized by severe itching, caused by a secretion of the itch mite, which bores under the skin to lay its eggs
SCABIOUS noun **SCABIOUSES** any of various annual or perennial plants with pinnately lobed leaves and flat heads of small bluish-lilac flowers
SCABROUS adj said of skin, etc: rough and flaky or scaly; scurfy
SCAD noun **SCADS** a fish with an armoured and keeled lateral line, related to the mackerel
SCAFFIE noun **SCAFFIES** a refuse collector
SCAFFOLD noun **SCAFFOLDS** a temporary framework of metal poles and planks used as a platform from which building repairs or construction can be carried out ◊ verb **SCAFFOLDS, SCAFFOLDING, SCAFFOLDED** to supply with a scaffold
SCAFFOLDING noun **SCAFFOLDINGS** an arrangement of scaffolds
SCAG noun **SCAGS** heroin
SCALABLE adj able to be climbed or scaled
SCALAR adj denoting a quantity that has magnitude but not direction, such as distance, speed and mass ◊ noun **SCALARS** a scalar quantity
SCALAWAG noun **SCALAWAGS** a scallywag

SCALD verb **SCALDS, SCALDING, SCALDED** to injure with hot liquid or steam ◊ noun **SCALDS** an injury caused by scalding
SCALDER noun **SCALDERS** something that scalds
SCALDFISH noun **SCALDFISHES** a small European flatfish with large scales
SCALDING noun **SCALDINGS** an act of scalding, or instance of being scalded
SCALE[1] verb **SCALES, SCALING, SCALED** to climb
SCALE[2] noun **SCALES** any of the small thin plates that provide a protective covering on the skin of fish, reptiles and on the legs of birds
SCALELESS adj without scales
SCALELIKE adj like scales
SCALENE adj said of a triangle: having each side a different length
SCALER noun **SCALERS** a person who removes the scales from fish
SCALIER see under **scaly**
SCALIEST see under **scaly**
SCALINESS noun **SCALINESSES** the state of being scaly
SCALLAWAG noun **SCALLAWAGS** a scallywag
SCALLION noun **SCALLIONS** any of various onions with a small bulb and long edible leaves, eg the spring onion
SCALLOP noun **SCALLOPS** any of numerous species of marine bivalve molluscs with a strongly ribbed yellow, brown, pink or orange shell consisting of two valves with wavy edges that are almost circular in outline ◊ verb **SCALLOPS, SCALLOPING, SCALLOPED** to shape (an edge) into curves or a series of curves
SCALLOPED adj said eg of fabric: having the edge or border shaped into curves or a series of curves
SCALLYWAG noun **SCALLYWAGS** a rascal or scamp; a good-for-nothing
SCALP noun **SCALPS** the area of the head covered, or usually covered, by hair ◊ verb **SCALPS, SCALPING, SCALPED** to remove the scalp of someone or something
SCALPEL noun **SCALPELS** a small surgical knife with a thin blade
SCALPER noun **SCALPERS** someone who scalps
SCALPLESS adj without a scalp
SCALY adj **SCALIER, SCALIEST** covered with scales

SCAM noun **SCAMS** a trick or swindle
SCAMP noun **SCAMPS** a mischievous person, especially a child
SCAMPER verb **SCAMPERS, SCAMPERING, SCAMPERED** to run or skip about briskly, especially in play ◊ noun **SCAMPERS** an act of scampering
SCAMPI plural noun large prawns ◊ singular noun **SCAMPIS** a dish of these prawns, usually deep-fried in breadcrumbs
SCAMPISH adj mischievous; cheeky
SCAN verb **SCANS, SCANNING, SCANNED** to read through or examine something carefully or critically ◊ noun **SCANS** an act of scanning
SCANDAL noun **SCANDALS** widespread public outrage and loss of reputation
SCANDIUM noun **SCANDIUMS** a soft silvery-white metallic element with a pinkish tinge
SCANNER noun **SCANNERS** a person or device that scans or can scan
SCANSION noun **SCANSIONS** the division of a verse into metrical feet
SCANT adj **SCANTER, SCANTEST** in short supply; deficient ◊ verb **SCANTS, SCANTING, SCANTED** to limit, restrict or reduce something
SCANTILY adverb in a scanty way; hardly or barely
SCANTLY adverb barely
SCANTNESS noun **SCANTNESSES** the state of being scant
SCANTY adj **SCANTIER, SCANTIEST** small or lacking in size or amount; barely enough
SCAPEGOAT noun **SCAPEGOATS** someone made to take the blame or punishment for the errors and mistakes of others
SCAPHOID noun **SCAPHOIDS** a small boat-shaped bone in the wrist or ankle
SCAPULA noun **SCAPULAS** the broad flat triangular bone at the back of the shoulder
SCAPULAR noun **SCAPULARS** a monk's garment consisting of a broad strip of cloth with a hole for the head, hanging loosely over a habit in front and behind
SCAPULARY noun **SCAPULARIES** a scapular

SCAR *noun* **SCARS** a mark left on the skin after a sore or wound has healed ▫ *verb* **SCARS, SCARRING, SCARRED** to mark or become marked with a scar
SCARAB *noun* **SCARABS** any of various dung beetles that are renowned for their habit of rolling and burying balls of dung, and which were regarded as sacred by the ancient Egyptians
SCARCE *adj* **SCARCER, SCARCEST** not often found; rare ▫ *adverb* scarcely; hardly ever
SCARCELY *adverb* only just
SCARCITY *noun* **SCARCITIES** a short supply or lack
SCARE *verb* **SCARES, SCARING, SCARED** to make or become afraid ▫ *noun* **SCARES** a fright or panic
SCARECROW *noun* **SCARECROWS** a device, usually in the shape of a human figure, set up in fields to scare birds
SCARER *noun* **SCARERS** a person or thing that scares eg birds
SCARF[1] *noun* **SCARFS, SCARVES** a strip or square of often patterned fabric, worn around the neck, shoulders or head for warmth or decoration
SCARF[2] *verb* **SCARFS, SCARFING, SCARFED** to join (eg two pieces of wood) by cutting an overlapping joint
SCARIER see under **scary**
SCARIEST see under **scary**
SCARIFIER *noun* **SCARIFIERS** an implement used for breaking up or loosening the surface of soil or of a road
SCARIFY *verb* **SCARIFIES, SCARIFYING, SCARIFIED** to make a number of scratches, shallow cuts, or lacerations in (the skin, etc)
SCARLET *noun* **SCARLETS** a brilliant red colour
SCARP *noun* **SCARPS** the steep side of a hill or rock; an escarpment ▫ *verb* **SCARPS, SCARPING, SCARPED** to cut into a scarp or slope
SCARPER *verb* **SCARPERS, SCARPERING, SCARPERED** to run away or escape; to go away unnoticed
SCARVES a plural of **scarf**[1]
SCARY *adj* **SCARIER, SCARIEST** causing fear or anxiety; frightening
SCAT *noun* **SCATS** a form of jazz singing consisting of improvised sounds rather than words ▫ *verb* **SCATS, SCATTING, SCATTED** to sing jazz in this way
SCATHING *adj* scornfully critical; detrimental
SCATOLOGY *noun* **SCATOLOGIES** the scientific study of excrement, especially in medicine for the purpose of diagnosis
SCATTER *verb* **SCATTERS, SCATTERING, SCATTERED** to disperse ▫ *noun* **SCATTERS** an act of scattering
SCATTERER *noun* **SCATTERERS** a person or thing that scatters things
SCATTERING *noun* **SCATTERINGS** dispersion
SCATTY *adj* **SCATTIER, SCATTIEST** mentally disorganized
SCAUR *noun* **SCAURS** a steep rocky outcrop or crag on the side of a hill or mountain; a cliff
SCAVENGE *verb* **SCAVENGES, SCAVENGING, SCAVENGED** to behave or act as a scavenger
SCAVENGER *noun* **SCAVENGERS** a person who searches among waste for usable items
SCENA *noun* **SCENE** in opera: an elaborate and dramatic recitative followed by an aria
SCENARIO *noun* **SCENARIOS** a rough outline of a dramatic work, film, etc; a synopsis
SCENE *noun* **SCENES** a division of a play, indicated by the fall of the curtain, a change of place or the entry or exit of an important character
SCENERY *noun* **SCENERIES** a picturesque landscape, especially one that is attractively rural
SCENIC *adj* referring to, being or including attractive natural landscapes
SCENT *noun* **SCENTS** the distinctive smell of a person, animal or plant ▫ *verb* **SCENTS, SCENTING, SCENTED** to smell; to discover or discern by smell
SCENTED *adj* having a smell; fragrant or perfumed
SCEPTIC *noun* **SCEPTICS** someone with a tendency to doubt the validity or substance of other situations, people, etc
SCEPTICAL *adj* doubtful; inclined to be incredulous
SCEPTRE *noun* **SCEPTRES** a ceremonial staff or baton carried by a monarch as a symbol of sovereignty
SCEPTRED *adj* regal; bearing a sceptre
SCHEDULE *noun* **SCHEDULES** a list of events or activities planned to take place at certain times ▫ *verb* **SCHEDULES, SCHEDULING, SCHEDULED** to plan or arrange something to take place at a certain time
SCHEELITE *noun* **SCHEELITES** the mineral calcium tungstate, a major source of tungsten
SCHEMA *noun* **SCHEMATA** a scheme or plan
SCHEMATIC *adj* following or involving a particular plan or arrangement
SCHEME *noun* **SCHEMES** a plan of action ▫ *verb* **SCHEMES, SCHEMING, SCHEMED** to plan or act secretly and often maliciously
SCHEMER *noun* **SCHEMERS** someone who plots
SCHEMING *adj* tending to plot or scheme ▫ *noun* **SCHEMINGS** the act or process of making a plot or scheme
SCHERZO *noun* **SCHERZOS, SCHERZI** a lively piece of music, usually with a trio, generally the second or third part of a symphony, sonata, etc, replacing the minuet
SCHILLING *noun* **SCHILLINGS** the standard unit of currency of Austria
SCHISM *noun* **SCHISMS** a breach or separation from the main group, or into opposing groups
SCHIST *noun* **SCHISTS** any of a group of common coarse-grained metamorphic rocks that characteristically contain broad wavy bands of minerals that readily split into layers
SCHISTOSE *adj* of or relating to schist
SCHIZO *noun* **SCHIZOS** a schizophrenic person ▫ *adj* schizophrenic
SCHIZOID *adj* displaying some symptoms of schizophrenia, such as introversion or tendency to fantasy, but without a diagnosed mental disorder ▫ *noun* **SCHIZOIDS** a schizoid person
SCHLEP *verb* **SCHLEPS, SCHLEPPING, SCHLEPPED** to carry, pull or drag with difficulty ▫ *noun* **SCHLEPS** a clumsy, stupid or incompetent person
SCHLEPP *verb* **SCHLEPPS, SCHLEPPING, SCHLEPPED** to schlep ▫ *noun* a schlep
SCHLEPPY *adj* **SCHLEPPIER,**

SCHLEPPIEST clumsy, stupid or incompetent
SCHLOCK noun **SCHLOCKS** inferior quality; shoddy production
SCHLOCKY adj **SCHLOCKIER**, **SCHLOCKIEST** shoddy
SCHMALTZ noun **SCHMALTZES** extreme or excessive sentimentality, especially in music or other art
SCHMALTZY adj **SCHMALTZIER**, **SCHMALTZIEST** sentimental
SCHMOOZE verb **SCHMOOZES**, **SCHMOOZING, SCHMOOZED** to gossip or chat in a friendly or intimate manner ◻ noun **SCHMOOZES** such a chat, especially at a social gathering
SCHNAPPER noun **SCHNAPPERS** a snapper
SCHNAPPS noun **SCHNAPPSES** in N Europe: any strong dry alcoholic spirit, especially Dutch gin distilled from potatoes
SCHNAPS noun **SCHNAPSES** schnapps
SCHNAUZER noun **SCHNAUZERS** a type of German terrier with a thick wiry coat, marked eyebrows, moustache, beard and short pendulous ears
SCHNITZEL noun **SCHNITZELS** a veal cutlet
SCHNORKEL noun **SCHNORKELS** a snorkel
SCHNOZZLE noun **SCHNOZZLES** a nose
SCHOLAR noun **SCHOLARS** a learned person, especially an academic
SCHOLARLY adj learned; academic
SCHOLIAST noun **SCHOLIASTS** someone who writes explanatory notes and comments on literary works, especially an ancient grammarian writing on manuscripts
SCHOOL noun **SCHOOLS** a place or institution where education is received, especially primary or secondary education ◻ verb **SCHOOLS, SCHOOLING, SCHOOLED** to educate in a school
SCHOOLING noun **SCHOOLINGS** education or instruction, especially received at school
SCHOONER noun **SCHOONERS** a fast sailing-ship with two or more masts, and rigged fore-and-aft
SCHTOOK noun **SCHTOOKS** shtook

SCHTOOM adj shtoom
SCHUSS noun **SCHUSSES** in skiing: a straight slope on which it is possible to make a fast run ◻ verb **SCHUSSES, SCHUSSING, SCHUSSED** to make such a run
SCHWA noun **SCHWAS** the indistinct English vowel sound that occurs in unstressed syllables, as in the first and last syllables of *together* in normal speech, and in other words such as *to* and *the* in rapid speech
SCIATIC adj referring or relating to the hip region
SCIATICA noun **SCIATICAS** intense and intermittent pain in the lower back, buttocks and backs of the thighs caused by pressure on the sciatic nerve
SCIENCE noun **SCIENCES** the systematic observation and classification of natural phenomena in order to learn about them and bring them under general principles and laws
SCIENTIAL adj referring or relating to science; scientific
SCIENTISM noun **SCIENTISMS** the methods or attitudes of people of science
SCIENTIST noun **SCIENTISTS** a person trained in or engaged in some field of science
SCILICET adverb only in writing: namely; that is to say
SCILLA noun **SCILLAS** the squill genus of the lily family, having bright blue spring flowers
SCIMITAR noun **SCIMITARS** a sword with a short curved single-edged blade, broadest at the point end, used by Turks and Persians
SCINTILLA noun **SCINTILLAS** a hint or trace; an iota
SCIOLISM noun **SCIOLISMS** superficial pretensions to knowledge
SCIOLIST noun **SCIOLISTS** someone who pretends to know about eg science
SCIOLOUS adj with superficial pretensions to knowledge
SCION noun **SCIONS** the detached shoot of a plant inserted into a cut in the outer stem of another plant when making a graft
SCIROCCO noun **SCIROCCOS** a sirocco
SCIRRHOID adj of or relating to a scirrhus
SCIRRHOUS adj scirrhoid
SCIRRHUS noun **SCIRRHUSES** a

hard swelling, especially a hard cancer
SCISSOR verb **SCISSORS**, **SCISSORING, SCISSORED** to cut with scissors
SCISSORS plural noun a one-handed cutting device with two long blades pivoted in the middle so the cutting edges close and overlap
SCIURINE adj relating or belonging to a genus of rodents, including squirrels
SCLERA noun **SCLERAS** the outermost membrane of the eyeball
SCLEROMA noun **SCLEROMAS**, **SCLEROMATA** a hardening of tissue, especially of mucous membrane or skin, eg forming nodules in the nose
SCLEROSIS noun **SCLEROSES** abnormal hardening or thickening of an artery or other body part, especially as a result of inflammation or disease
SCLEROTIC noun **SCLEROTICS** in vertebrates: the white fibrous outer layer of the eyeball, which is modified at the front of the eye to form the transparent cornea ◻ adj hard or firm
SCLEROUS adj hardened or indurated
SCOFF verb **SCOFFS, SCOFFING, SCOFFED** to express scorn or contempt for someone; to jeer ◻ noun **SCOFFS** an expression of scorn; a jeer
SCOFFER noun **SCOFFERS** someone who scoffs
SCOFFING noun **SCOFFINGS** an act of expressing scorn or contempt for someone
SCOLD verb **SCOLDS, SCOLDING, SCOLDED** to reprimand or rebuke ◻ noun **SCOLDS** a nagging or quarrelsome person, especially a woman
SCOLDER noun **SCOLDERS** someone who scolds
SCOLDING noun **SCOLDINGS** a telling-off
SCOLIOSIS noun **SCOLIOSES** lateral curvature of the spine
SCOLIOTIC adj of or relating to scoliosis
SCOLLOP noun **SCOLLOPS** a scallop ◻ verb **SCOLLOPS**, **SCOLLOPING, SCOLLOPED** to scallop
SCONCE noun **SCONCES** a candlestick or lantern with a

handle, or one fixed by a bracket to a wall

SCONE *noun* **SCONES** a small flattish plain cake, baked with or without dried fruit, and usually eaten halved and spread with butter and jam, etc

SCOOP *verb* **SCOOPS, SCOOPING, SCOOPED** to lift, dig or remove something with a sweeping circular movement □ *noun* **SCOOPS** a spoonlike implement for handling or serving food

SCOOPER *noun* **SCOOPERS** a person or thing that scoops

SCOOPFUL *noun* **SCOOPFULS** the amount contained in a scoop

SCOOT *verb* **SCOOTS, SCOOTING, SCOOTED** to make off quickly or speedily □ *noun* **SCOOTS** the act of scooting

SCOOTER *noun* **SCOOTERS** a child's toy vehicle consisting of a board on a two-wheeled frame, with tall handlebars connected to the front wheel, propelled by pushing against the ground with one foot

SCOPE[1] *noun* **SCOPES** the size or range of a subject or topic covered

SCOPE[2] *verb* **SCOPES, SCOPING, SCOPED** to examine internal organs of the body using a viewing device

SCORBUTIC *adj* relating to or suffering from scurvy

SCORCH *verb* **SCORCHES, SCORCHING, SCORCHED** to burn or be burned slightly or superficially □ *noun* **SCORCHES** an act of scorching

SCORCHER *noun* **SCORCHERS** someone or something that scorches

SCORE *noun* **SCORES** a total number of points gained or achieved eg in a game □ *verb* **SCORES, SCORING, SCORED** to gain or achieve (a point) in a game

SCORECARD *noun* **SCORECARDS** a card for recording the score in a game

SCORER *noun* **SCORERS** a person who scores or who keeps the score during a match or game

SCORIA *noun* **SCORIAE** dross or slag produced from the smelting of metal from its ore

SCORIFY *verb* **SCORIFIES, SCORIFYING, SCORIFIED** to rid metals of impurities by forming scoria

SCORN *noun* **SCORNS** extreme or mocking contempt □ *verb* **SCORNS, SCORNING, SCORNED** to treat someone or something with scorn; to express scorn for

SCORNER *noun* **SCORNERS** someone who scorns others

SCORNFUL *adj* contemptuous

SCORPION *noun* **SCORPIONS** any of numerous species of invertebrate animal, found in hot regions, with eight legs, powerful claw-like pincers and a long thin segmented abdomen or 'tail', bearing a poisonous sting, that is carried arched over its back

SCOTCH *verb* **SCOTCHES, SCOTCHING, SCOTCHED** to ruin or hinder eg plans □ *noun* **SCOTCHES** a line marked on the ground, especially for hopscotch

SCOTOMA *noun* **SCOTOMAS, SCOTOMATA** a blind spot due to disease of the retina or optic nerve

SCOUNDREL *noun* **SCOUNDRELS** an unprincipled or villainous rogue

SCOUR *verb* **SCOURS, SCOURING, SCOURED** to clean, polish or remove by hard rubbing □ *noun* **SCOURS** an act of scouring

SCOURER *noun* **SCOURERS** an implement used for scouring

SCOURGE *noun* **SCOURGES** a cause of great suffering and affliction, especially to many people □ *verb* **SCOURGES, SCOURGING, SCOURGED** to cause suffering to; to afflict

SCOURGER *noun* **SCOURGERS** someone who scourges

SCOURING *noun* **SCOURINGS** an act of cleaning, polishing or removing by hard rubbing

SCOUT *noun* **SCOUTS** a person or group sent out to observe the enemy and bring back information □ *verb* **SCOUTS, SCOUTING, SCOUTED** to make a search

SCOUTER *noun* **SCOUTERS** an adult leader in the Scout Association

SCOW *noun* **SCOWS** a large flat-bottomed barge for freight

SCOWL *verb* **SCOWLS, SCOWLING, SCOWLED** to wrinkle the brow in a malevolent or angry look □ *noun* **SCOWLS** a scowling expression

SCRABBLE *verb* **SCRABBLES, SCRABBLING, SCRABBLED** to scratch, grope or struggle frantically □ *noun* **SCRABBLES** an act of scrabbling

SCRAG *noun* **SCRAGS** the thin part of a neck of mutton or veal, providing poor quality meat □ *verb* **SCRAGS, SCRAGGING, SCRAGGED** to wring the neck of (an animal); to throttle

SCRAGGY *adj* **SCRAGGIER, SCRAGGIEST** unhealthily thin; scrawny

SCRAM *verb* **SCRAMS, SCRAMMING, SCRAMMED** often as a command: to go away at once; to be off

SCRAMBLE *verb* **SCRAMBLES, SCRAMBLING, SCRAMBLED** to crawl or climb using hands and feet, especially hurriedly or frantically □ *noun* **SCRAMBLES** an act of scrambling

SCRAMBLER *noun* **SCRAMBLERS** an electronic device, used to transmit secret communications, etc that modifies radio or telephone signals so that they can only be made intelligible by means of a special decoding device

SCRAMBLING *noun* **SCRAMBLINGS** an act of crawling or climbing using hands and feet

SCRAMJET *noun* **SCRAMJETS** a ramjet engine that operates at supersonic speeds, the air required for combustion being compressed by the forward motion of the engine

SCRAP *noun* **SCRAPS** a small piece; a fragment □ *verb* **SCRAPS, SCRAPPING, SCRAPPED** to discard or cease to use; to abandon as unworkable

SCRAPBOOK *noun* **SCRAPBOOKS** a book with blank pages for pasting in cuttings, pictures, etc

SCRAPE *verb* **SCRAPES, SCRAPING, SCRAPED** to push or drag (especially a sharp object) along or over (a hard or rough surface) □ *noun* **SCRAPES** an instance, process or act of dragging or grazing

SCRAPER *noun* **SCRAPERS** an implement for scraping

SCRAPIE *noun* **SCRAPIES** an often fatal disease of sheep, often characterized by severe itching and a tendency to rub against trees and other objects for relief, resulting in wool loss

SCRAPPILY *adverb* in a scrappy way

SCRAPPY *adj* **SCRAPPIER, SCRAPPIEST** fragmentary or disjointed; not uniform or flowing

SCRATCH *verb* **SCRATCHES, SCRATCHING, SCRATCHED** to draw a sharp or pointed object across (a surface), causing damage or making marks ◻ *noun* **SCRATCHES** an act of scratching
SCRATCHER *noun* **SCRATCHERS** a person or thing that scratches
SCRATCHY *adj* **SCRATCHIER, SCRATCHIEST** making the marks or noises of scratching
SCRAWL *verb* **SCRAWLS, SCRAWLING, SCRAWLED** to write or draw illegibly, untidily or hurriedly ◻ *noun* **SCRAWLS** untidy or illegible handwriting
SCRAWLER *noun* **SCRAWLERS** a person that scrawls
SCRAWLY *adj* **SCRAWLIER, SCRAWLIEST** untidy
SCRAWNY *adj* **SCRAWNIER, SCRAWNIEST** unhealthily thin and bony
SCREAM *verb* **SCREAMS, SCREAMING, SCREAMED** to cry out in a loud high-pitched voice, as in fear, pain or anger ◻ *noun* **SCREAMS** a sudden loud piercing cry or noise
SCREAMER *noun* **SCREAMERS** someone or something that screams
SCREE *noun* **SCREES** a sloping mass of rock debris that piles up at the base of cliffs or on the side of a mountain
SCREECH *noun* **SCREECHES** a harsh, shrill and sudden cry, voice or noise ◻ *verb* **SCREECHES, SCREECHING, SCREECHED** to utter a screech or make a sound like a screech
SCREECHER *noun* **SCREECHERS** a person or thing that screeches
SCREECHY *adj* **SCREECHIER, SCREECHIEST** shrill and harsh, like a screech
SCREED *noun* **SCREEDS** a long and often tedious spoken or written passage
SCREEDER *noun* **SCREEDERS** a person whose job is to layer mortar on a floor to finish off the surface
SCREEN *noun* **SCREENS** a movable set of foldable hinged panels, used to partition off part of a room for privacy ◻ *verb* **SCREENS, SCREENING, SCREENED** to shelter or conceal
SCREENER *noun* **SCREENERS** a person or thing that screens
SCREENING *noun* **SCREENINGS** a showing of a film, etc

SCREENINGS *plural noun* material eliminated by sifting
SCREW *noun* **SCREWS** a small metal cylinder with a spiral ridge or thread down the shaft and a slot in its head, driven into position in wood, etc by rotation using a screwdriver, usually used as a fastening device ◻ *verb* **SCREWS, SCREWING, SCREWED** to twist (a screw) into place
SCREWBALL *noun* **SCREWBALLS** a crazy person; an eccentric
SCREWER *noun* **SCREWERS** a person or thing that screws
SCREWY *adj* **SCREWIER, SCREWIEST** crazy; eccentric
SCRIBAL *adj* of or relating to scribes
SCRIBBLE *verb* **SCRIBBLES, SCRIBBLING, SCRIBBLED** to write quickly or untidily; to scrawl ◻ *noun* **SCRIBBLES** untidy or illegible handwriting; scrawl
SCRIBBLY *adj* **SCRIBBLIER, SCRIBBLIEST** untidy
SCRIBE *noun* **SCRIBES** a person employed to make handwritten copies of documents before printing was invented; a tool with a pointed blade for scoring lines on wood or metal ◻ *verb* **SCRIBES, SCRIBING, SCRIBED** to mark or score lines with a scribe or anything similar
SCRIBER *noun* **SCRIBERS** a scribing tool
SCRIM *noun* **SCRIMS** a thin open cotton fabric used as lining in upholstery, in bookbinding, for curtains, etc
SCRIMMAGE *noun* **SCRIMMAGES** a noisy brawl or struggle ◻ *verb* **SCRIMMAGES, SCRIMMAGING, SCRIMMAGED** to take part in a scrimmage
SCRIMP *verb* **SCRIMPS, SCRIMPING, SCRIMPED** to live economically; to be frugal or sparing
SCRIMPY *adj* **SCRIMPIER, SCRIMPIEST** scanty
SCRIMSHAW *noun* **SCRIMSHAWS** handicrafts done by sailors in their spare time, such as engraving or carving designs on shells, ivory, bone, etc ◻ *verb* **SCRIMSHAWS, SCRIMSHAWING, SCRIMSHAWED** to work or decorate something in this way
SCRIP *noun* **SCRIPS** a scrap of paper, especially one with writing on it

SCRIPT *noun* **SCRIPTS** a piece of handwriting ◻ *verb* **SCRIPTS, SCRIPTING, SCRIPTED** to write the script of (a play, film or broadcast)
SCRIPTURE *noun* **SCRIPTURES** the sacred writings of a religion
SCRIVENER *noun* **SCRIVENERS** a person who drafts or writes out copies of legal or other official documents
SCROFULA *noun* **SCROFULAS** the former name for tuberculosis of the lymph nodes, especially of the neck
SCROLL *noun* **SCROLLS** a roll of paper or parchment usually containing an inscription, now only a ceremonial format, eg for academic degrees ◻ *verb* **SCROLLS, SCROLLING, SCROLLED** to roll into a scroll or scrolls
SCROTAL *adj* relating to or in the region of the scrotum
SCROTUM *noun* **SCROTA, SCROTUMS** the sac of skin that encloses the testicles
SCROUNGE *verb* **SCROUNGES, SCROUNGING, SCROUNGED** to get something by shamelessly asking or begging; to cadge or sponge
SCROUNGER *noun* **SCROUNGERS** someone who scrounges
SCROUNGING *noun* **SCROUNGINGS** an act of getting something by shamelessly asking or begging
SCRUB[1] *verb* **SCRUBS, SCRUBBING, SCRUBBED** to rub hard, especially with a stiff brush, in order to remove dirt ◻ *noun* **SCRUBS** an act of scrubbing
SCRUB[2] *noun* **SCRUBS** vegetation consisting of stunted trees and evergreen shrubs collectively
SCRUBBER *noun* **SCRUBBERS** someone who scrubs
SCRUBBY *adj* **SCRUBBIER, SCRUBBIEST** covered with scrub
SCRUFF *noun* **SCRUFFS** a dirty untidy person
SCRUFFY *adj* **SCRUFFIER, SCRUFFIEST** shabby and untidy
SCRUM *noun* **SCRUMS** in rugby: the restarting of play when the players from both teams hunch together and tightly interlock their arms and heads in readiness for the ball being thrown in
SCRUMMAGE *noun* **SCRUMMAGES** scrimmage ◻ *verb*

SCRUMMAGES, SCRUMMAGING, SCRUMMAGED to scrimmage
SCRUMMY adj **SCRUMMIER, SCRUMMIEST** delicious; scrumptious
SCRUMPY noun **SCRUMPIES** strong dry cider with a harsh taste made from small sweet apples, especially as brewed in the West Country
SCRUNCH verb **SCRUNCHES, SCRUNCHING, SCRUNCHED** to crunch or crush, especially with relation to the noise produced □ noun **SCRUNCHES** an act or the sound of scrunching
SCRUNCHY adj **SCRUNCHIER, SCRUNCHIEST** referring or relating to a scrunching sound □ noun **SCRUNCHIES** a tight ring of elastic covered in coloured fabric used to hold the hair in a ponytail
SCRUPLE noun **SCRUPLES** a sense of moral responsibility making one reluctant or unwilling to do wrong □ verb **SCRUPLES, SCRUPLING, SCRUPLED** to be reluctant or unwilling because of scruples
SCRUTINY noun **SCRUTINIES** a close, careful and thorough examination or inspection
SCUBA noun **SCUBAS** a device used by skin-divers, consisting of one or two cylinders of compressed air connected by a tube to a mouthpiece allowing underwater breathing
SCUD verb **SCUDS, SCUDDING, SCUDDED** said especially of clouds: to sweep quickly and easily across the sky □ noun **SCUDS** the act of scudding
SCUDDER noun **SCUDDERS** a thing that scuds
SCUFF verb **SCUFFS, SCUFFING, SCUFFED** to brush, graze or scrape (especially shoes or heels) while walking □ noun **SCUFFS** the act of scuffing
SCUFFLE noun **SCUFFLES** a confused fight or struggle □ verb **SCUFFLES, SCUFFLING, SCUFFLED** to take part in a scuffle
SCULL noun **SCULLS** either of a pair of short light oars used by one rower □ verb **SCULLS, SCULLING, SCULLED** to propel with a scull or sculls
SCULLER noun **SCULLERS** a person who sculls
SCULLERY noun **SCULLERIES** a room attached to the kitchen

where basic chores, such as the cleaning of kitchen utensils, are carried out
SCULLING noun **SCULLINGS** an act of rowing with sculls
SCULPT verb **SCULPTS, SCULPTING, SCULPTED** to carve or model
SCULPTOR noun **SCULPTORS** a person who practises the art of sculpture
SCULPTURE noun **SCULPTURES** the art or act of carving or modelling with clay, wood, stone, plaster, etc □ verb **SCULPTURES, SCULPTURING, SCULPTURED** to carve, mould or sculpt
SCUM noun **SCUMS** dirt or waste matter floating on the surface of a liquid, especially in the form of foam or froth □ verb **SCUMS, SCUMMING, SCUMMED** to remove the scum from (a liquid)
SCUMBLE verb **SCUMBLES, SCUMBLING, SCUMBLED** to soften the effect of a drawing or painting by a very thin coat of opaque or semi-opaque colour, by light rubbing or by applying paint with a dry brush □ noun **SCUMBLES** colour applied in this way
SCUMBLING noun **SCUMBLINGS** an act of applying scumble to a painting
SCUMMER noun **SCUMMERS** an instrument for removing scum
SCUMMY adj **SCUMMIER, SCUMMIEST** characterized by scum
SCUPPER verb **SCUPPERS, SCUPPERING, SCUPPERED** to ruin or put an end to (a plan, an idea, etc)
SCURF noun **SCURFS** small flakes of dead skin, especially dandruff
SCURFY adj **SCURFIER, SCURFIEST** having or characterized by scurf
SCURRY noun **SCURRIES** an act of or the sound of scurrying
SCURVILY adverb in a scurvy way; meanly
SCURVY noun **SCURVIES** a disease caused by dietary deficiency of vitamin C and characterized by swollen bleeding gums, amnesia, bruising and pain in the joints □ adj **SCURVIER, SCURVIEST** vile; contemptible
SCUT noun **SCUTS** a short tail, especially of a rabbit, hare or deer
SCUTAL adj of or relating to a scute
SCUTATE adj said of animals:

protected by hard bony plates or scutes
SCUTE noun **SCUTES** a hard bony plate forming part of the skin of animals such as armadillos, tortoises, etc
SCUTELLUM noun **SCUTELLA** in the seeds of certain flowering plants, eg maize: the tissue that surrounds, and serves as a food store for, the developing embryo
SCUTTER verb **SCUTTERS, SCUTTERING, SCUTTERED** to scurry or run hastily □ noun **SCUTTERS** a hasty run
SCUTTLE verb **SCUTTLES, SCUTTLING, SCUTTLED** to move quickly and with haste; to scurry □ noun **SCUTTLES** a scuttling pace or movement
SCUTUM noun **SCUTA** the second dorsal plate of an insect's thorax
SCUZZY adj **SCUZZIER, SCUZZIEST** filthy or scummy; sleazy
SCYTHE noun **SCYTHES** a tool with a wooden handle and a large curved blade, for cutting tall crops or grass by hand with a sweeping action □ verb **SCYTHES, SCYTHING, SCYTHED** to cut with a scythe
SEA noun **SEAS** the large expanse of salt water covering the greater part of the Earth's surface
SEABOARD noun **SEABOARDS** a coast; the boundary between land and sea
SEABORNE adj carried on or transported by the sea
SEAFARER noun **SEAFARERS** a person who travels by sea; a sailor
SEAFARING adj travelling by or working at sea
SEAFOOD noun **SEAFOODS** shellfish and other edible marine fish
SEAFRONT noun **SEAFRONTS** the side of the land, a town or a building facing the sea
SEAGULL noun **SEAGULLS** an omnivorous seabird with white and grey plumage, a hooked bill and webbed feet
SEAHORSE noun **SEAHORSES** any of various species of a small fish, native to warm coastal waters, that swims in an upright position, with its elongated head bent at right angles to its body
SEAL [1] verb **SEALS, SEALING, SEALED** to close, especially permanently or for a long time
SEAL [2] noun **SEALS** any of various

marine mammals with a smooth-skinned or furry streamlined body and limbs modified to form webbed flippers

SEALANT *noun* **SEALANTS** any material used for sealing a gap to prevent the leaking of water, etc

SEALER *noun* **SEALERS** a seal hunter

SEALSKIN *noun* **SEALSKINS** the prepared skin of a furry seal, or an imitation of it

SEAM *noun* **SEAMS** a join between edges, especially one that has been welded □ *verb* **SEAMS, SEAMING, SEAMED** to join edge to edge

SEAMAN *noun* **SEAMEN** a sailor below the rank of officer

SEAMANLY *adj* of, relating to or like a seaman

SEAMER *noun* **SEAMERS** in cricket: a ball delivered by seam bowling (using the seam of the ball to affect the ball's flight)

SEAMINESS *noun* **SEAMINESSES** the state of being seamy

SEAMLESS *adj* having no seams; made from a single piece of fabric

SEAMY *adj* **SEAMIER, SEAMIEST** sordid; disreputable

SÉANCE *noun* **SÉANCES** a meeting at which a person, especially a spiritualist, attempts to contact the spirits of dead people on behalf of other people present

SEAPLANE *noun* **SEAPLANES** an aeroplane designed to take off from and land on water

SEAPORT *noun* **SEAPORTS** a coastal town with a port for seagoing ships

SEAR *verb* **SEARS, SEARING, SEARED** to scorch □ *noun* **SEARS** a mark made by scorching

SEARCH *verb* **SEARCHES, SEARCHING, SEARCHED** to explore something thoroughly in order to try to find someone or something □ *noun* **SEARCHES** an act of searching

SEARCHING *adj* seeking to discover the truth by intensive examination or observation

SEARING *adj* burning or intense

SEASCAPE *noun* **SEASCAPES** a picture or photograph of a scene at sea

SEASHELL *noun* **SEASHELLS** the empty shell of a marine invertebrate, especially a mollusc

SEASHORE *noun* **SEASHORES** the land immediately adjacent to the sea

SEASICK *adj* **SEASICKER, SEASICKEST** nauseous owing to the rolling movement of a vessel at sea

SEASIDE *noun* **SEASIDES** a coastal area or town, especially a holiday resort

SEASON *noun* **SEASONS** any of the four major periods (spring, summer, autumn and winter) into which the year is divided according to changes in weather patterns □ *verb* **SEASONS, SEASONING, SEASONED** to flavour (food) by adding salt, pepper and/or other herbs and spices

SEASONAL *adj* available, taking place or occurring only at certain times of the year

SEASONED *adj* said of food: flavoured

SEASONER *noun* **SEASONERS** a person who seasons food

SEASONING *noun* **SEASONINGS** the process by which anything is seasoned

SEAT *noun* **SEATS** anything designed or intended for sitting on □ *verb* **SEATS, SEATING, SEATED** to place on a seat

SEATING *noun* **SEATINGS** the provision of seats

SEAWARD *adj* facing or moving toward the sea □ *adverb* towards the sea

SEAWEED *noun* **SEAWEEDS** the common name for any of numerous species of marine algae

SEAWORTHY *adj* said of a ship: fit for a voyage at sea

SEBACEOUS *adj* similar to, characteristic of or secreting sebum

SEBUM *noun* **SEBUMS** the oily substance secreted by the sebaceous glands that lubricates and waterproofs the hair and skin

SEC [1] *noun* **SECS** a second

SEC [2] *adj* said of wine: dry

SECANT *noun* **SECANTS** a straight line that cuts a curve at one or more places

SECATEURS *plural noun* small sharp shears for pruning bushes, etc

SECEDE *verb* **SECEDES, SECEDING, SECEDED** to withdraw formally, eg from a political or religious body or alliance

SECEDER *noun* **SECEDERS** a country, etc that secedes

SECESSION *noun* **SECESSIONS** the act of seceding

SECLUDE *verb* **SECLUDES, SECLUDING, SECLUDED** to keep away or isolate from other contacts, associations or influences

SECLUDED *adj* protected or away from people and noise; private and quiet

SECLUSION *noun* **SECLUSIONS** the state of being secluded or the act of secluding

SECOND [1] *adj* in counting: next after or below the first, in order of sequence or importance □ *verb* **SECONDS, SECONDING, SECONDED** to declare formal support for (a proposal, or the person making it) □ *adverb* secondly

SECOND [2] *noun* **SECONDS** a unit of time equal to one-sixtieth of a minute

SECONDARY *noun* **SECONDARIES** a school for pupils aged between 11 and 18 □ *adj* being of lesser importance than the principal or primary concern; subordinate

SECONDER *noun* **SECONDERS** a person who seconds a proposal or the person making it

SECONDLY *adverb* in the second place; as a second consideration

SECRECY *noun* **SECRECIES** the state or fact of being secret

SECRET *adj* kept hidden or away from the knowledge of others □ *noun* **SECRETS** something not disclosed, or not to be disclosed, to others

SECRETARY *noun* **SECRETARIES** a person employed to perform administrative or clerical tasks for a company or individual

SECRETE [1] *verb* **SECRETES, SECRETING, SECRETED** said of a gland or similar organ: to form and release (a substance)

SECRETE [2] *verb* **SECRETES, SECRETING, SECRETED** to hide away or conceal

SECRETION *noun* **SECRETIONS** the process whereby glands of the body discharge or release particular substances

SECRETIVE *adj* inclined to or fond of secrecy; reticent

SECRETLY *adverb* in secret

SECRETORY *adj* said of a gland, etc: referring or relating to or involved in the process of secretion

SECT *noun* **SECTS** a religious or

other group whose views and practices differ from those of an established body or from those of a body from which it has separated; used sometimes as an expression of disapproval by non-members
SECTARIAN *noun* **SECTARIANS** a member of a sect, especially a bigoted person
SECTARY *noun* **SECTARIES** a member of a sect
SECTION *noun* **SECTIONS** the act or process of cutting □ *verb* **SECTIONS, SECTIONING, SECTIONED** to divide something into sections
SECTIONAL *adj* made in sections
SECTOR *noun* **SECTORS** a part of an area divided up for military purposes
SECTORAL *adj* of or relating to a sector
SECTORIAL *adj* sectoral; relating to a sector
SECULAR *noun* **SECULARS** a clergyman (eg parish priest) not bound by monastic rules; a layman
SECULARLY *adverb* in a way not bound by monastic rules
SECUND *adj* said eg of leaves: turned to or positioned on the same side
SECURABLE *adj* able to be secured
SECURE *adj* **SECURER, SECUREST** free from danger; providing safety □ *verb* **SECURES, SECURING, SECURED** to fasten or attach firmly
SECURELY *adverb* in a secure way
SECURER *noun* **SECURERS** a person who secures or fastens
SECURITY *noun* **SECURITIES** the state of being secure

| **SED** a Miltonic spelling of *said* |

SEDAN *noun* **SEDANS** a large enclosed chair for one person, carried on two horizontal poles by two bearers
SEDATE *adj* **SEDATER, SEDATEST** calm and dignified in manner □ *verb* **SEDATES, SEDATING, SEDATED** to calm or quieten someone by means of a sedative
SEDATELY *adverb* calmly
SEDATION *noun* **SEDATIONS** the act of calming or the state of having been calmed, especially by means of sedatives
SEDATIVE *noun* **SEDATIVES** any agent, especially a drug, that has a

calming effect and is used to treat insomnia, pain, delirium, etc
SEDENTARY *adj* said of work: involving much sitting
SEDGE *noun* **SEDGES** any member of a family of plants resembling grasses or rushes, found in bogs, fens, marshes and other poorly drained areas, and characterized by solid stems which are triangular in cross-section
SEDGY *adj* **SEDGIER, SEDGIEST** of, relating to or like sedge
SEDIMENT *noun* **SEDIMENTS** insoluble solid particles that have settled at the bottom of a liquid in which they were previously suspended
SEDITION *noun* **SEDITIONS** public speech, writing or action encouraging public disorder, especially rebellion against the government
SEDITIOUS *adj* relating to or involving sedition
SEDUCE *verb* **SEDUCES, SEDUCING, SEDUCED** to lure or entice someone into having sexual intercourse
SEDUCER *noun* **SEDUCERS** someone who seduces another
SEDUCTION *noun* **SEDUCTIONS** the act or practice of seducing or the condition of being seduced
SEDUCTIVE *adj* tending or intended to seduce
SEDULITY *noun* **SEDULITIES** the state or condition of being sedulous
SEDULOUS *adj* assiduous and diligent; steadily hardworking
SEDUM *noun* **SEDUMS** any of various rock plants with thick fleshy leaves and clusters of white, yellow or pink flowers
SEE¹ *verb* **SEES, SEEING, SAW, SEEN** to perceive by the sense operated in the eyes
SEE² *noun* **SEES** the office of bishop of a particular diocese
SEED *noun* **SEEDS** in flowering and cone-bearing plants: the highly resistant structure that develops from the ovule after fertilization, and is capable of developing into a new plant □ *verb* **SEEDS, SEEDING, SEEDED** said of a plant: to produce seeds
SEEDBED *noun* **SEEDBEDS** a piece of ground prepared for the planting of seeds
SEEDCAKE *noun* **SEEDCAKES** a cake flavoured with caraway seeds

SEEDINESS *noun* **SEEDINESSES** the state or condition of being seedy
SEEDLESS *adj* having no seeds
SEEDLING *noun* **SEEDLINGS** a young plant grown from seed
SEEDY *adj* **SEEDIER, SEEDIEST** full of seeds; shabby, disreputable
SEEING *conj* given (that); since
SEEK *verb* **SEEKS, SEEKING, SOUGHT** to look for someone or something
SEEKER *noun* **SEEKERS** a person who is looking for someone or something
SEEM *verb* **SEEMS, SEEMING, SEEMED** to appear to the eye; to give the impression of (being)
SEEMING *adj* apparent; ostensible □ *noun* **SEEMINGS** appearance; a false appearance
SEEMINGLY *adverb* apparently
SEEMLY *adj* **SEEMLIER, SEEMLIEST** fitting or suitable; becoming
SEEN past form of **see**¹
SEEP *verb* **SEEPS, SEEPING, SEEPED** said of a liquid: to escape slowly or ooze through, or as if through, a narrow opening
SEEPAGE *noun* **SEEPAGES** an act of seeping
SEEPY *adj* **SEEPIER, SEEPIEST** seeping or oozing
SEER *noun* **SEERS** a person who predicts future events; a clairvoyant
SEESAW *noun* **SEESAWS** a plaything consisting of a plank balanced in the middle allowing people, especially children, when seated on the ends to propel each other up and down by pushing off the ground with the feet □ *verb* **SEESAWS, SEESAWING, SEESAWED** to move alternately up-and-down or back-and-forth
SEETHE *verb* **SEETHES, SEETHING, SEETHED** said of a liquid: to churn and foam as if boiling

| **SEG** *noun* **SEGS** a stud in the sole of a shoe |

SEGMENT *noun* **SEGMENTS** a part, section or portion □ *verb* **SEGMENTS, SEGMENTING, SEGMENTED** to divide into segments
SEGMENTAL *adj* forming or formed of segments
SEGREGATE *verb* **SEGREGATES,**

SEGREGATING, SEGREGATED to set apart or isolate
SEGUE *verb* **SEGUES, SEGUEING, SEGUED** to proceed or follow on to the next song, movement, etc without a pause ❑ *noun* **SEGUES** the term or direction to segue

SEI *noun* **SEIS** a whale, a kind of rorqual

SEIGNEUR *noun* **SEIGNEURS** a feudal lord, especially in France or French Canada
SEIGNIOR *noun* **SEIGNIORS** a seigneur
SEINE *noun* **SEINES** a large vertical fishing net held underwater by floats and weights, and whose ends are brought together and hauled ❑ *verb* **SEINES, SEINING, SEINED** to catch or fish with a seine
SEISMIC *adj* relating to or characteristic of earthquakes
SEIZABLE *adj* capable of being seized
SEIZE *verb* **SEIZES, SEIZING, SEIZED** to take or grab suddenly, eagerly or forcibly
SEIZURE *noun* **SEIZURES** the act of seizing

SEL *noun* **SELS** a Scots form of *self*

SELACHIAN *noun* **SELACHIANS** any fish of the subclass Selachii, including sharks, rays, skates and dogfish
SELDOM *adverb* rarely
SELECT *verb* **SELECTS, SELECTING, SELECTED** to choose from several by preference ❑ *adj* picked out or chosen in preference to others
SELECTION *noun* **SELECTIONS** the act or process of selecting or being selected
SELECTIVE *adj* exercising the right to select
SELECTOR *noun* **SELECTORS** a person who selects or chooses eg members of a sports team
SELENITE *noun* **SELENITES** a variety of gypsum occurring as clear colourless crystals
SELENIUM *noun* **SELENIUMS** a metalloid element that is a semiconductor, used in electronic devices, photoelectric cells and photographic exposure meters
SELF *noun* **SELVES** personality, or a particular aspect of it ❑ *pronoun* myself, yourself, himself or herself
SELFISH *adj* concerned only with one's personal welfare, with total disregard to that of others
SELFISHLY *adverb* in a selfish way
SELFLESS *adj* tending to consider the welfare of others before one's own; altruistic
SELL *verb* **SELLS, SELLING, SOLD** to give something to someone in exchange for money ❑ *noun* **SELLS** the act or process of selling
SELLABLE *adj* able to be sold
SELLER *noun* **SELLERS** a person selling something
SELLOTAPE *noun* **SELLOTAPES** a form of usually transparent adhesive tape, especially for use on paper ❑ *verb* **SELLOTAPES, SELLOTAPING, SELLOTAPED** to stick using sellotape
SELVA *noun* **SELVAS** a dense wet forest in the Amazonian basin
SELVAGE *noun* **SELVAGES** an edge of a length of fabric sewn or woven so as to prevent fraying
SELVAGED *adj* having a selvage
SELVEDGE *noun* **SELVEDGES** selvage
SELVES plural of **self**
SEMANTIC *adj* referring or relating to meaning, especially of words
SEMANTICS *singular noun* the branch of linguistics that deals with the meaning of words
SEMAPHORE *noun* **SEMAPHORES** a system of signalling in which flags, or simply the arms, are held in positions that represent individual letters and numbers; a device used for this ❑ *verb* **SEMAPHORES, SEMAPHORING, SEMAPHORED** to signal using semaphore or a semaphore
SEMATIC *adj* said of an animal's colouring: serving for recognition, attraction or warning
SEMBLANCE *noun* **SEMBLANCES** outer appearance, especially when superficial or deceptive
SEMEME *noun* **SEMEMES** a unit of meaning, specifically of the smallest linguistically analysable unit
SEMEN *noun* **SEMENS** a thick whitish liquid carrying spermatozoa, ejaculated by the penis
SEMESTER *noun* **SEMESTERS** in German and US, and now some UK, universities: an academic term lasting for half an academic year
SEMI *noun* **SEMIS** a semi-detached house
SEMIBREVE *noun* **SEMIBREVES** the longest note in common use, equal to half a breve, two minims or four crotchets
SEMICOLON *noun* **SEMICOLONS** a punctuation mark (;) indicating a pause stronger than that marked by a comma but weaker than that marked by a full stop
SEMIFINAL *noun* **SEMIFINALS** in competitions, sports tournaments, etc: either of two matches, the winners of which play each other in the final
SEMINAL *adj* referring or relating to seed, semen or reproduction in general
SEMINALLY *adverb* in a seminal way
SEMINAR *noun* **SEMINARS** a class in which a small group of students and a tutor discuss a particular topic
SEMINARY *noun* **SEMINARIES** a college for the training of priests, ministers and rabbis
SEMIOLOGY *noun* **SEMIOLOGIES** semiotics
SEMIOTIC *adj* of or relating to semiotics
SEMIOTICS *singular noun* the study of human communication, especially the relationship between words and the objects or concepts they represent
SEMITONE *noun* **SEMITONES** half a tone
SEMITONIC *adj* of or relating to a semitone
SEMIVOWEL *noun* **SEMIVOWELS** a speech sound having the qualities of both a vowel and a consonant
SEMOLINA *noun* **SEMOLINAS** the hard particles of wheat not ground into flour during milling, used for thickening soups, making puddings, etc

SEN *noun* **SEN, SENS** a monetary unit (in Japan, etc) of various values; a coin of these values

SENATE *noun* **SENATES** in ancient Rome: the chief legislative and administrative body
SENATOR *noun* **SENATORS** a member of a senate
SEND *verb* **SENDS, SENDING, SENT** to cause, direct or order to go or be conveyed

SENDER noun **SENDERS** a person who sends something

SENESCENT adj growing old; ageing

SENESCHAL noun **SENESCHALS** a steward in charge of the household or estate of a medieval lord or prince

SENILE adj displaying the feebleness and decay of mind or body brought on by old age

SENILITY noun **SENILITIES** the state or condition or quality of being senile

SENIOR noun **SENIORS** a person who is older or of a higher rank

SENIORITY noun **SENIORITIES** the state or fact of being senior

SENNA noun **SENNAS** any of various trees and shrubs, native to Africa and Arabia, with leaves divided into oval leaflets, and long clusters of yellow flowers

SENSATION noun **SENSATIONS** an awareness of an external or internal stimulus, eg heat, pain or emotions, as a result of its perception by the senses

SENSE noun **SENSES** any of the five main faculties used by an animal to obtain information about its external or internal environment, namely sight, hearing, smell, taste and touch ◻ verb **SENSES, SENSING, SENSED** to detect a stimulus by means of any of the five main senses

SENSELESS adj unconscious

SENSIBLE adj **SENSIBLER, SENSIBLEST** having or showing reasonableness or good judgement; wise

SENSIBLY adverb in a sensible way

SENSITISE verb **SENSITISES, SENSITISING, SENSITISED** to sensitize

SENSITIVE adj feeling or responding readily, strongly or painfully

SENSITIZE verb **SENSITIZES, SENSITIZING, SENSITIZED** to make sensitive

SENSOR noun **SENSORS** any of various devices that detect or measure a change in a physical quantity, usually by converting it into an electrical signal, eg burglar alarms, smoke detectors, etc

SENSORY adj referring or relating to the senses or sensation

SENSUAL adj relating to the senses and the body rather than the mind or the spirit

SENSUALLY adverb in a sensual way

SENSUOUS adj appealing to the senses aesthetically, with no suggestion of sexual pleasure

SENT past form of **send**

SENTENCE noun **SENTENCES** a sequence of words forming a meaningful grammatical structure that can stand alone as a complete utterance; a punishment pronounced by a court or judge ◻ verb **SENTENCES, SENTENCING, SENTENCED** to announce the judgement or sentence to be given to someone

SENTIENCE noun **SENTIENCES** the quality or condition of being sentient

SENTIENT adj capable of sensation or feeling; conscious or aware of something

SENTIMENT noun **SENTIMENTS** a thought or emotion, especially when expressed

SENTINEL noun **SENTINELS** someone posted on guard; a sentry ◻ verb **SENTINELS, SENTINELLING, SENTINELLED** to watch over as a sentinel

SENTRY noun **SENTRIES** a person, usually a soldier, posted on guard to control entry or passage

SENZA prep in music: without

SEPAL noun **SEPALS** in a flower: one of the modified leaves, usually green but sometimes brightly coloured, that together form the calyx which surrounds the petals

SEPARABLE adj able to be separated or disjoined

SEPARABLY adverb in a separable way

SEPARATE verb **SEPARATES, SEPARATING, SEPARATED** to take, force or keep apart (from others or each other) ◻ adj separated; divided ◻ noun **SEPARATES** an individual item which forms a unit with others and which is often purchased separately to mix and match, eg items of women's clothing eg blouse, skirt, etc forming separate parts of an outfit, rather than a suit

SEPARATOR noun **SEPARATORS** a person or thing that separates

SEPIA noun **SEPIAS** a rich reddish-brown pigment, obtained from a fluid secreted by the cuttlefish

SEPOY noun **SEPOYS** an Indian

soldier in service with a European (especially British) army

SEPPUKU noun **SEPPUKUS** ritual suicide by cutting one's belly open with a sword

SEPSIS noun **SEPSES** the presence of disease-causing micro-organisms, especially viruses or bacteria, and their toxins in the body tissues

SEPT noun **SEPTS** especially in Scotland or Ireland: a clan; a division of a tribe

SEPTET noun **SEPTETS** a group of seven musicians

SEPTETTE noun **SEPTETTES** a septet

SEPTIC adj said of a wound: contaminated with pathogenic bacteria

SEPTUM noun **SEPTA** any partition between cavities, eg nostrils, areas of soft tissue, etc

SEPTUPLE adj being seven times as much or as many; sevenfold ◻ verb **SEPTUPLES, SEPTUPLING, SEPTUPLED** to multiply or increase sevenfold

SEPTUPLET noun **SEPTUPLETS** any of seven children or animals born at one birth to the same mother

SEPULCHER noun **SEPULCHERS** a sepulchre ◻ verb **SEPULCHERS, SEPULCHERING, SEPULCHERED** to sepulchre

SEPULCHRE noun **SEPULCHRES** a tomb or burial vault ◻ verb **SEPULCHRES, SEPULCHRING, SEPULCHRED** to bury in a sepulchre; to entomb

SEPULTURE noun **SEPULTURES** the act of burial, especially in a sepulchre

SEQUEL noun **SEQUELS** a book, film or play that continues an earlier story

SEQUELA noun **SEQUELAE** any abnormal condition following or related to a previous disease

SEQUENCE noun **SEQUENCES** the state or fact of being sequent or consequent; a series of things following in order ◻ verb **SEQUENCES, SEQUENCING, SEQUENCED** to place in sequence

SEQUENCING noun **SEQUENCINGS** the process of determining the order of amino acids in a protein

SEQUENT noun **SEQUENTS** a thing or quantity that follows

SEQUESTER verb **SEQUESTERS,**

SEQUESTERING, SEQUESTERED to set aside or isolate

SEQUIN noun **SEQUINS** a small round shiny disc of foil or plastic, sewn on a garment for decoration

SEQUINED adj covered or decorated with sequins

SEQUINNED adj sequined

SEQUOIA noun **SEQUOIAS** either of two species of massive evergreen trees, native to N America, the Californian redwood (the tallest known tree) and the giant sequoia (the largest known tree)

SERAGLIO noun **SERAGLIOS** women's quarters in a Muslim house or palace; a harem

SERAPE noun **SERAPES** a Spanish-American woollen blanket or cape, usually brightly coloured, worn by men while riding

SERAPH noun **SERAPHS** in the traditional medieval hierarchy of nine ranks of angels: an angel of the highest rank

SERAPHIC adj of, relating to or like a seraph; angelic

SERENADE noun **SERENADES** a song or piece of music performed at night under a woman's window by her suitor ◻ verb **SERENADES, SERENADING, SERENADED** to entertain (a person) with a serenade

SERENADER noun **SERENADERS** someone who performs a serenade

SERENE adj **SERENER, SERENEST** said of a person: calm and composed; at peace

SERENELY adverb in a serene way

SERENITY noun **SERENITIES** the quality or condition of being serene

SERF noun **SERFS** in medieval Europe: a worker in modified slavery, bought and sold with the land on which they worked

SERFDOM noun **SERFDOMS** the condition of a serf

SERFHOOD noun **SERFHOODS** serfdom

SERGE noun **SERGES** a strong twilled fabric, especially of wool or worsted ◻ adj made of serge

SERGEANCY noun **SERGEANCIES** the office or rank of a sergeant

SERGEANT noun **SERGEANTS** in the armed forces: a non-commissioned officer of the rank next above corporal

SERIAL noun **SERIALS** a story,

television programme, etc published or broadcast in regular instalments

SERIALISE verb **SERIALISES, SERIALISING, SERIALISED** to serialize

SERIALISM noun **SERIALISMS** the technique of using a series or succession of related notes as the basis for a musical composition, the most common type being 12-note serialism

SERIALIZE verb **SERIALIZES, SERIALIZING, SERIALIZED** to publish or broadcast (a story, television programme, etc) in instalments

SERICEOUS adj silky

SERIES noun **SERIES** a number of similar, related or identical things arranged or produced in line or in succession, such as a set of similar books issued by the same publishing house

SERIF noun **SERIFS** a short decorative line or stroke on the end of a printed letter, as opposed to sanserif

SERIGRAPH noun **SERIGRAPHS** a print made by silk-screen process

SERIN noun **SERINS** any of a genus of small European finches, including the canary

SERINE noun **SERINES** an amino acid that is found in proteins

SERIOUS adj grave or solemn; not inclined to flippancy or lightness of mood

SERIOUSLY adverb in a serious way

SERJEANT noun **SERJEANTS** a sergeant

SERMON noun **SERMONS** a public speech or discourse, especially one forming part of a church service, about morals, religious duties or some aspect of religious doctrine

SERMONISE verb **SERMONISES, SERMONISING, SERMONISED** to sermonize

SERMONIZE verb **SERMONIZES, SERMONIZING, SERMONIZED** to compose and conduct sermons

SEROLOGY noun **SEROLOGIES** the study of blood serum and its constituents, especially antibodies and antigens

SEROTONIN noun **SEROTONINS** a hormone that transmits impulses between nerves in the central nervous system, and also causes narrowing of blood vessels by stimulating their contraction

SEROUS adj characteristic of, relating to or containing serum

SERPENT noun **SERPENTS** a snake

SERPIGO noun **SERPIGOES, SERPIGINES** any spreading skin disease, especially ringworm

SERRATE verb **SERRATES, SERRATING, SERRATED** to notch

SERRATION noun **SERRATIONS** the condition of being saw-like or serrated

SERRIED adj closely packed or grouped together

SERUM noun **SERA, SERUMS** the yellowish fluid component of blood, which contains specific antibodies and can therefore be used in a vaccine

SERVANT noun **SERVANTS** a person employed by another to do household or menial work for them

SERVE verb **SERVES, SERVING, SERVED** to work for someone as a domestic servant; to be in the service of someone ◻ noun **SERVES** in racket sports: an act of serving (putting the ball in play)

SERVER noun **SERVERS** a person who serves

SERVICE noun **SERVICES** the condition or occupation of being a servant or someone who serves ◻ verb **SERVICES, SERVICING, SERVICED** to subject (a vehicle, etc) to a periodic check

SERVIETTE noun **SERVIETTES** a table napkin

SERVILE adj slavishly respectful or obedient; fawning or submissive

SERVILELY adverb in a servile way

SERVILITY noun **SERVILITIES** the state or condition of being servile

SERVING noun **SERVINGS** a portion of food or drink served at one time; a helping

SERVITUDE noun **SERVITUDES** slavery; the state of being a slave

SERVO adj denoting a system in which the main mechanism is set in operation by a subsidiary mechanism and is able to develop a force greater than the force communicated to it

SESAME noun **SESAMES** an annual plant with opposite leaves below and alternate leaves above, and solitary white flowers, usually marked with purple or yellow

SESAMOID adj shaped like a sesame seed ◻ noun **SESAMOIDS** a small rounded bone or cartilage structure formed in the substance of a tendon, eg in the tendon of the big toe

SESSILE *adj* said of a flower or leaf: attached directly to the plant, rather than by a stalk

SESSION *noun* **SESSIONS** a meeting of a court, council or parliament, or the period during which such meetings are regularly held

SESSIONAL *adj* of or happening in sessions

SESTERCE *noun* **SESTERCES** a Roman coin

SESTET *noun* **SESTETS** a group of six people or things

SESTINA *noun* **SESTINAS** an old form of poetry consisting of six verses of six lines, where the end-words of the first verse are repeated in different orders in the last five verses

SET ¹ *verb* **SETS, SETTING, SET** to put, place or fix into a specified position or condition □ *adj* fixed or rigid; allowing no alterations or variations

SET ² *noun* **SETS** a group of related people or things

SETA *noun* **SETAE** a bristle; a bristle-like structure

SETACEOUS *adj* of or relating to setae

SETBACK *noun* **SETBACKS** a delay, check or reversal to progress

SETLINE *noun* **SETLINES** any of various kinds of fishing lines suspended between buoys, etc and having shorter baited lines attached to it

SETOSE *adj* bristle-like

SETSCREW *noun* **SETSCREWS** a screw that prevents relative motion by exerting pressure with its point

SETT *noun* **SETTS** a badger's burrow

SETTEE *noun* **SETTEES** a long indoor seat with a back and arms, usually able to hold two or more people; a sofa

SETTER *noun* **SETTERS** any of various large breeds of sporting dog with a long smooth coat (rich red in colour in the Irish setter and white with black, liver or tan markings in the English setter) and a feathered tail

SETTING *noun* **SETTINGS** a situation or background within or against which action takes place

SETTLE *verb* **SETTLES, SETTLING, SETTLED** to make or become securely, comfortably or

satisfactorily positioned or established

SETTLE ² *noun* **SETTLES** a wooden bench with arms and a solid high back, often with a storage chest fitted below the seat

SETTLER *noun* **SETTLERS** someone who settles in a country that is being newly populated

SEVEN *noun* **SEVENS** the cardinal number 7 □ *adj* totalling seven

SEVENFOLD *adj* equal to seven times as much or as many □ *adverb* by seven times as much or many

SEVENTEEN *noun* **SEVENTEENS** the cardinal number 17 □ *adj* totalling seventeen

SEVENTH *adj* in counting: next after sixth □ *noun* **SEVENTHS** one of seven equal parts □ *adverb* seventhly

SEVENTHLY *adverb* used to introduce the seventh point in a list

SEVENTIES *plural noun* the period of time between one's seventieth and eightieth birthdays

SEVENTY *noun* **SEVENTIES** the cardinal number 70 □ *adj* totalling seventy

SEVER *verb* **SEVERS, SEVERING, SEVERED** to cut off physically

SEVERABLE *adj* able to be severed

SEVERAL *adj* more than a few, but not a great number □ *pronoun* quite a few people or things

SEVERALLY *adj* separately or singly

SEVERANCE *noun* **SEVERANCES** the act or process of severing or being severed

SEVERE *adj* **SEVERER, SEVEREST** extreme and difficult to endure; marked by extreme conditions

SEVERELY *adverb* in a severe way

SEVERITY *noun* **SEVERITIES** the quality or condition of being severe; seriousness

SEW *verb* **SEWS, SEWING, SEWED, SEWN** to stitch, attach or repair (especially fabric) with thread, either by hand with a needle or by machine

SEWAGE *noun* **SEWAGES** any liquid-borne waste matter, especially human excrement, carried away in drains

SEWER *noun* **SEWERS** a large underground pipe or channel for carrying away sewage from drains and water from road surfaces □ *verb* **SEWERS, SEWERING, SEWERED** to provide with sewers

SEWERAGE *noun* **SEWERAGES** a system or network of sewers

SEWING *noun* **SEWINGS** the act of stitching with thread

SEX *noun* **SEXES** either of the two classes, male and female, into which animals and plants are divided according to their role in reproduction □ *verb* **SEXES, SEXING, SEXED** to identify or determine the sex of (an animal)

SEXED *adj* having sexual desires or urges as specified to engage in sexual activity

SEXINESS *noun* **SEXINESSES** the state of being attractive in a sexual way

SEXISM *noun* **SEXISMS** contempt shown for or discrimination against a particular sex, usually by men of women, based on prejudice or stereotype

SEXIST *noun* **SEXISTS** someone whose beliefs and actions are characterized by sexism □ *adj* relating to or characteristic of sexism

SEXLESS *adj* neither male nor female

SEXOLOGY *noun* **SEXOLOGIES** the study of human sexual behaviour, sexuality and relationships

SEXPERT *noun* **SEXPERTS** especially in the US: an expert in human sexual behaviour

SEXPOT *noun* **SEXPOTS** a person of obvious and very great physical attraction

SEXT *noun* **SEXTS** the fourth of the canonical hours

SEXTANT *noun* **SEXTANTS** a device consisting of a small telescope mounted on a graded metal arc, used in navigation and surveying for measuring angular distances

SEXTET *noun* **SEXTETS** a group of six singers or musicians

SEXTON *noun* **SEXTONS** someone responsible for the church buildings and churchyard, often also having bell-ringing, grave-digging and other duties

SEXTUPLE *noun* **SEXTUPLES** a value or quantity six times as much □ *verb* **SEXTUPLES, SEXTUPLING, SEXTUPLED** to multiply or increase sixfold

SEXTUPLET *noun* **SEXTUPLETS** any of six children or animals born at the same time to the same mother

SEXUAL *adj* concerned with or suggestive of sex

SEXUALITY noun **SEXUALITIES** a sexual state or condition
SEXUALLY adverb in a sexual way
SEXY adj **SEXIER, SEXIEST** said of a person: sexually attractive; stimulating or arousing sexual desire

SEY noun **SEYS** a Scots word for a part of a carcase of beef

SEZ a slang spelling of *says*

SFORZANDO adverb of music: played with sudden emphasis ▫ adj of music: played with sudden emphasis
SFORZATO adverb sforzando ▫ adj sforzando
SFUMATO noun **SFUMATOS** in painting and drawing: a misty indistinct effect obtained by gradually blending together areas of different colour or tone
SGRAFFITO noun **SGRAFFITI** a decorative technique in art in which one colour is laid over another and the top layer scratched away to form a design, by revealing the colour beneath

SH exclamation hush; be quiet

SHABBILY adverb in a shabby way
SHABBY adj **SHABBIER, SHABBIEST** said especially of clothes or furnishings: old and worn; threadbare or dingy
SHACK noun **SHACKS** a crudely built hut or shanty
SHACKLE noun **SHACKLES** a metal ring locked round the ankle or wrist of a prisoner or slave to limit movement, usually one of a pair joined by a chain ▫ verb **SHACKLES, SHACKLING, SHACKLED** to restrain with or as if with shackles
SHAD noun **SHADS** any of various marine fish resembling a large herring but with a deeper body
SHADBUSH noun **SHADBUSHES** a N American rosaceous shrub, flowering at shad spawning-time
SHADE noun **SHADES** the blocking or partial blocking out of sunlight, or the relative darkness caused by this ▫ verb **SHADES, SHADING, SHADED** to block or partially block out sunlight from someone or something
SHADELESS adj without shade
SHADILY adverb dishonestly; mysteriously

SHADINESS noun **SHADINESSES** the state or condition of being shady
SHADING noun **SHADINGS** in drawing and painting: the representation of areas of shade or shadows, eg by close parallel lines
SHADOOF noun **SHADOOFS** an irrigation device for lifting water from a river or watercourse and transferring it to the land, consisting of a bucket suspended from a counterpoised pivoted rod, used mainly for irrigation in the Nile flood plain
SHADOW noun **SHADOWS** a dark shape cast on a surface when an object stands between the surface and the source of light ▫ verb **SHADOWS, SHADOWING, SHADOWED** to put into darkness by blocking out light
SHADOWY adj **SHADOWIER, SHADOWIEST** dark and shady; not clearly visible
SHADUF noun **SHADUFS** a shadoof
SHADY adj **SHADIER, SHADIEST** sheltered or giving shelter from heat or sunlight
SHAFT noun **SHAFTS** the long straight handle of a tool or weapon ▫ verb **SHAFTS, SHAFTING, SHAFTED** to dupe, cheat or swindle
SHAG noun **SHAGS** a species of cormorant with glossy dark-green plumage, a long neck, webbed feet and an upright stance
SHAGGILY adverb in a shaggy way
SHAGGY adj **SHAGGIER, SHAGGIEST** said of hair, fur, wool, etc: long and coarse; rough and untidy in appearance
SHAGREEN noun **SHAGREENS** a coarse leather, often dyed green, made from the skin of animals, especially a horse or donkey
SHAH noun **SHAHS** a title of the former rulers of Iran and other Eastern countries
SHAKE verb **SHAKES, SHAKING, SHAKEN, SHOOK** to move with quick, often forceful to-and-fro or up-and-down movements ▫ noun **SHAKES** an act or the action of shaking
SHAKEABLE adj capable of being shaken
SHAKEDOWN noun **SHAKEDOWNS** a makeshift or temporary bed, originally made by shaking down straw

SHAKER noun **SHAKERS** someone or something that shakes
SHAKILY adverb in a shaky way
SHAKINESS noun **SHAKINESSES** the quality or condition of being shaky
SHAKO noun **SHAKOS, SHAKOES** a tall, and usually cylindrical, military cap with a plume
SHAKY adj **SHAKIER, SHAKIEST** trembling or inclined to tremble with, or as if with, weakness, fear or illness
SHALE noun **SHALES** a fine-grained black, grey, brown or red sedimentary rock, easily split into thin layers, formed as a result of the compression of clay, silt or sand by overlying rocks
SHALL auxiliary verb expressing: the future tense of other verbs, especially when the subject is *I* or *we*
SHALLOP noun **SHALLOPS** a dinghy; a small or light boat for use in shallow water
SHALLOT noun **SHALLOTS** a species of small onion, widely cultivated as a vegetable, that produces clusters of oval bulbs which are smaller and milder in flavour than the onion
SHALLOW adj **SHALLOWER, SHALLOWEST** having no great depth ▫ noun **SHALLOWS** a shallow place or part, especially in water ▫ verb **SHALLOWS, SHALLOWING, SHALLOWED** to make something shallow
SHALLOWLY adverb in a shallow way
SHALOT noun **SHALOTS** a shallot
SHALT used with *thou*: a form of **shall**
SHALY adj **SHALIER, SHALIEST** of, relating to or characterized by shale
SHAM adj false, counterfeit or pretended ▫ verb **SHAMS, SHAMMING, SHAMMED** to pretend or feign ▫ noun **SHAMS** anything not genuine
SHAMAN noun **SHAMANS** especially among certain N Asian and Native American peoples: a doctor-priest or medicine man or medicine woman using magic to cure illness, make contact with gods and spirits, predict the future, etc
SHAMANISM noun **SHAMANISMS** especially among certain N Asian and Native American peoples: a

religion dominated by shamans, based essentially on magic, spiritualism and sorcery

SHAMANIST *noun* **SHAMANISTS** someone who believes in or practises shamanism

SHAMATEUR *noun* **SHAMATEURS** in sport: someone rated as an amateur, but still making money from playing or competing

SHAMBLE *verb* **SHAMBLES, SHAMBLING, SHAMBLED** to walk with slow awkward tottering steps ◻ *noun* **SHAMBLES** a shambling walk or pace

SHAMBLES *singular noun* a confused mess or muddle; a state of total disorder

SHAMBLING *noun* **SHAMBLINGS** an act of shambling

SHAMBOLIC *adj* totally disorganized; chaotic

SHAME *noun* **SHAMES** the humiliating feeling of having appeared unfavourably in one's own eyes, or those of others, as a result of one's own offensive or disrespectful actions, or those of an associate ◻ *verb* **SHAMES, SHAMING, SHAMED** to make someone feel shame

SHAMEFUL *adj* bringing or deserving shame; disgraceful

SHAMELESS *adj* incapable of feeling shame; showing no shame

SHAMMY *noun* **SHAMMIES** a chamois leather

SHAMPOO *noun* **SHAMPOOS** a soapy liquid for washing the hair and scalp ◻ *verb* **SHAMPOOS, SHAMPOOING, SHAMPOOED** to wash or clean with shampoo

SHAMROCK *noun* **SHAMROCKS** any of various plants with leaves divided into three rounded leaflets, especially various species of clover, adopted as the national emblem of Ireland

SHANDY *noun* **SHANDIES** a mixture of beer or lager with lemonade or ginger beer

SHANGHAI *noun* **SHANGHAIS** a catapult ◻ *verb* **SHANGHAIS, SHANGHAIING, SHANGHAIED** to drug or make drunk and kidnap and send to sea as a sailor; to shoot using a shanghai

SHANK *noun* **SHANKS** the lower leg between the knee and the foot ◻ *verb* **SHANKS, SHANKING, SHANKED** of plants: to become affected with disease of the footstalk

SHANNY *noun* **SHANNIES** the smooth blenny, a small marine fish found in rock pools and coastal areas

SHANTUNG *noun* **SHANTUNGS** a plain and usually undyed fabric of wild silk with a rough finish

SHANTY *noun* **SHANTIES** a roughly built hut or cabin; a shack

SHAPE *noun* **SHAPES** the outline or form of anything ◻ *verb* **SHAPES, SHAPING, SHAPED** to form or fashion; to give a particular form to something

SHAPEABLE *adj* capable of being of shaped

SHAPELESS *adj* having an ill-defined or irregular shape

SHAPELY *adj* **SHAPELIER, SHAPELIEST** said especially of the human body: having an attractive, well-proportioned shape or figure

SHARD *noun* **SHARDS** a fragment of something brittle, usually pottery, especially when found on an archaeological site

SHARE *noun* **SHARES** a part allotted, contributed, or owned by each of several people or groups ◻ *verb* **SHARES, SHARING, SHARED** to have in common

SHARECROP *verb* **SHARECROPS, SHARECROPPING, SHARECROPPED** to pay for the rent of a farm by supplying a share of the crop in lieu of rent

SHARER *noun* **SHARERS** a person who shares something with others

SHAREWARE *noun* **SHAREWARES** software readily available for a nominal fee

SHARIA *noun* **SHARIAS** the body of Islamic religious law

SHARIAT *noun* **SHARIATS** sharia

SHARK *noun* **SHARKS** any of 400 species of large cartilaginous fishes which have remained virtually unchanged for millions of years, with a spindle-shaped body covered with tooth-like scales, and a tail fin with a long upper lobe and shorter lower lobe

SHARKSKIN *noun* **SHARKSKINS** leather made from a shark's skin

SHARP *adj* **SHARPER, SHARPEST** having a thin edge or point that cuts or pierces ◻ *noun* **SHARPS** in music: a note raised by a semitone, or the sign indicating this (♯) ◻ *adverb* punctually; on the dot

SHARPEN *verb* **SHARPENS, SHARPENING, SHARPENED** to make or become sharp

SHARPENER *noun* **SHARPENERS** an implement for sharpening, eg pencils

SHARPER *noun* **SHARPERS** a practised cheat

SHARPISH *adj* quite sharp ◻ *adverb* quickly; promptly

SHARPLY *adverb* in a sharp way

SHARPNESS *noun* **SHARPNESSES** the quality or condition of being sharp

SHATTER *verb* **SHATTERS, SHATTERING, SHATTERED** to break into tiny fragments, usually suddenly or with force

SHAVE *verb* **SHAVES, SHAVING, SHAVED** to cut off (hair) from (especially the face) with a razor or shaver ◻ *noun* **SHAVES** an act or the process of shaving one's facial hair

SHAVEN *adj* shaved; close-cut or smooth

SHAVER *noun* **SHAVERS** an electrical device with a moving blade or set of blades for shaving hair

SHAVING *noun* **SHAVINGS** the removal of hair with a razor

SHAWL *noun* **SHAWLS** a large single piece of fabric used to cover the head or shoulders or to wrap a baby

SHAWM *noun* **SHAWMS** an instrument, a predecessor of the oboe, with a double reed and a flat circular mouthpiece

SHE *pronoun* a female person or animal, or thing thought of as female (eg a ship), named before or understood from the context ◻ *noun* **SHES** a female person or animal ◻ *adj* female

SHEA *noun* **SHEAS** an African tree

SHEADING *noun* **SHEADINGS** any of the six divisions of the Isle of Man

SHEAF *noun* **SHEAVES** a bundle of things tied together, especially of reaped corn ◻ *verb* **SHEAFS, SHEAVES, SHEAFING, SHEAVING, SHEAFED, SHEAVED** to tie up in a bundle

SHEAR *verb* **SHEARS, SHEARING, SHEARED, SHORN** to clip or cut off something, especially with a large pair of clippers ◻ *noun* **SHEARS** the act of shearing

SHEARER *noun* **SHEARERS** someone who shears sheep

SHEARLING *noun* **SHEARLINGS** a young sheep that has been shorn for the first time

SHEATH noun **SHEATHS** a case or covering for the blade of a sword or knife
SHEATHE verb **SHEATHES, SHEATHING, SHEATHED** to put into or cover with a sheath or case
SHEATHING noun **SHEATHINGS** something which sheathes; casing
SHEAVE noun **SHEAVES** a grooved wheel, especially a pulley-wheel
SHEAVED adj tied up in a bundle
SHEBANG noun **SHEBANGS** an affair or matter; a situation
SHEBEEN noun **SHEBEENS** an illicit liquor-shop
SHED [1] noun **SHEDS** a wooden or metal outbuilding, usually small, sometimes open-fronted, for working in, for storage or for shelter
SHED [2] verb **SHEDS, SHEDDING, SHED** to release or make something flow
SHEDDER noun **SHEDDERS** a person who milks cows in a milking shed
SHEEN noun **SHEENS** shine, lustre or radiance; glossiness
SHEENY adj **SHEENIER, SHEENIEST** glossy
SHEEP noun **SHEEP** any of various wild or domesticated species of a herbivorous mammal with a stocky body covered with a thick woolly fleece, kept worldwide as a farm animal for its meat and wool
SHEEPCOTE noun **SHEEPCOTES** an enclosure for sheep
SHEEPDOG noun **SHEEPDOGS** any working dog that is used to guard sheep from wild animals or to assist in herding
SHEEPISH adj embarrassed through having done something wrong or foolish
SHEEPSKIN noun **SHEEPSKINS** the skin of a sheep, either with or without the fleece attached to it
SHEEPWALK noun **SHEEPWALKS** a range of pasture specifically for sheep
SHEER [1] adj **SHEERER, SHEEREST** complete; absolute or downright □ adverb completely
SHEER [2] noun **SHEERS** a deviation □ verb **SHEERS, SHEERING, SHEERED** to make something change course or deviate
SHEERLY adverb in a sheer way
SHEET noun **SHEETS** a large broad rectangular piece of fabric, especially for covering the mattress of a bed □ verb **SHEETS,**

SHEETING, SHEETED to wrap or cover with or as if with a sheet
SHEETING noun **SHEETINGS** fabric used for making sheets
SHEIK noun **SHEIKS** a sheikh
SHEIKH noun **SHEIKHS** the chief of an Arab tribe, village or family
SHEIKHDOM noun **SHEIKHDOMS** the territory of a sheikh
SHEILA noun **SHEILAS** a woman or girl
SHEKEL noun **SHEKELS** the standard unit of currency in Israel, divided into 100 agorot
SHELDRAKE noun **SHELDRAKES** a male shelduck
SHELDUCK noun **SHELDUCKS** a large goose-like duck which has white plumage with bold patterns of chestnut and black, a dark green head, a red bill and pink legs
SHELF noun **SHELVES** a usually narrow, flat board fixed to a wall or part of a cupboard, bookcase, etc, for storing or laying things on
SHELL noun **SHELLS** the hard protective structure covering the seed or fruit of some plants □ verb **SHELLS, SHELLING, SHELLED** to remove the shell from something
SHELLAC noun **SHELLACS** a yellow or orange resin produced by the lac insect □ verb **SHELLACS, SHELLACKING, SHELLACKED** to coat with shellac
SHELLFIRE noun **SHELLFIRES** bombardment with artillery shells or ammunition
SHELLFISH noun **SHELLFISHES** a shelled edible aquatic invertebrate, especially a mollusc or crustacean, eg prawn, crab, shrimp, lobster
SHELLING noun **SHELLINGS** removal of the shell or shells
SHELTER noun **SHELTERS** protection against weather or danger □ verb **SHELTERS, SHELTERING, SHELTERED** to protect someone or something from the effects of weather or danger
SHELTERED adj protected from the effects of weather
SHELTERER noun **SHELTERERS** a person or thing that provides shelter
SHELTIE noun **SHELTIES** a Shetland pony or Shetland sheepdog
SHELTY noun **SHELTIES** a sheltie
SHELVE verb **SHELVES, SHELVING, SHELVED** to place or store on a shelf

SHELVES plural of **shelf**
SHELVING noun **SHELVINGS** material used for making shelves
SHEMOZZLE noun **SHEMOZZLES** a rumpus or commotion
SHEPHERD noun **SHEPHERDS** someone who looks after, or herds, sheep □ verb **SHEPHERDS, SHEPHERDING, SHEPHERDED** to watch over or herd sheep
SHERBET noun **SHERBETS** a fruit-flavoured powder eaten as confectionery, or made into an effervescent drink
SHERD noun **SHERDS** a shard
SHEREEF noun **SHEREEFS** a sherif
SHERIF noun **SHERIFS** a descendant of Muhammad through his daughter Fatima
SHERIFF noun **SHERIFFS** in a US county: the chief elected police officer mainly responsible for maintaining peace and order, attending courts, serving processes and executing judgements
SHERPA noun **SHERPAS** a member of an E Tibetan people living high on the south side of the Himalayas
SHERRY noun **SHERRIES** a fortified wine ranging in colour from pale gold to dark brown
SHEWBREAD noun
SHEWBREADS in ancient Israel: the twelve loaves offered every Sabbath on the table beside the altar of incense in the sanctuary by Jewish priests
SHIATSU noun **SHIATSUS** a Japanese healing massage technique involving the application of pressure, mainly with the fingers and palms of hands, to parts of the body that are distant from the affected region
SHIATZU noun **SHIATZUS** shiatsu
SHIED past form of **shy**
SHIELD noun **SHIELDS** a piece of armour consisting of a broad plate, especially one with a straight top and tapering curved sides, carried to deflect weapons □ verb **SHIELDS, SHIELDING, SHIELDED** to protect from danger or harm
SHIES a form of **shy**
SHIFT verb **SHIFTS, SHIFTING, SHIFTED** to change the position or direction of something; to change position or direction □ noun **SHIFTS** a change, or change of position

SHIFTILY adverb in a shifty way; dishonestly

SHIFTLESS adj having no motivation or initiative

SHIFTY adj **SHIFTIER, SHIFTIEST** said of a person or behaviour: sly, shady or dubious; untrustworthy or dishonest

SHIGELLA noun **SHIGELLAS** a rod-shaped bacterium, especially one of a species that causes dysentery

SHILLING noun **SHILLINGS** in the UK: a monetary unit and coin, before the introduction of decimal currency in 1971, worth one twentieth of a pound or 12 old pence (12d)

SHIM noun **SHIMS** a thin washer or slip of metal, wood, plastic, etc used to adjust or fill a gap between machine parts, especially gears ◻ verb **SHIMS, SHIMMING, SHIMMED** to fill or adjust with a shim or shims

SHIMMER verb **SHIMMERS, SHIMMERING, SHIMMERED** to shine tremulously and quiveringly with reflected light; to glisten ◻ noun **SHIMMERS** a tremulous or quivering gleam of reflected light

SHIMMERY adj with a gleam; shimmering

SHIMMY noun **SHIMMIES** a vivacious body-shaking dance, particularly popular during the 1920s ◻ verb **SHIMMIES, SHIMMYING, SHIMMIED** to dance the shimmy, or to make similar movements

SHIN noun **SHINS** the bony front part of the leg below the knee ◻ verb **SHINS, SHINNING, SHINNED** to climb by gripping with the hands and legs

SHINBONE noun **SHINBONES** the tibia

SHINDIG noun **SHINDIGS** a lively party or celebration

SHINDY noun **SHINDIES** a row or rumpus; a commotion

SHINE verb **SHINES, SHINING, SHONE** to give out or reflect light; to beam with a steady radiance ◻ verb **SHINES, SHINING, SHINED** to make bright and gleaming by polishing ◻ noun **SHINES** shining quality; brightness or lustre

SHINER noun **SHINERS** someone or something that shines

SHINGLE [1] noun **SHINGLES** a thin rectangular tile, especially made of wood, laid with others in overlapping rows on a roof or wall ◻ verb **SHINGLES, SHINGLING, SHINGLED** to tile with shingles

SHINGLE [2] noun **SHINGLES** small pebbles that have been worn smooth by water, found especially in a series of parallel ridges on beaches

SHINGLES singular noun the disease herpes zoster, caused by the chickenpox virus, in which acute inflammation of spinal nerve ganglia produces pain and then a series of blisters along the path of the nerve

SHINGLY adj **SHINGLIER, SHINGLIEST** of, relating to or characterized by shingle

SHINTY noun **SHINTIES** a game, originally Scottish, similar to hockey, played by two teams of 12

SHINY adj **SHINIER, SHINIEST** reflecting light; polished to brightness

SHIP noun **SHIPS** a large engine-propelled vessel, intended for sea travel ◻ verb **SHIPS, SHIPPING, SHIPPED** to send or transport by ship

SHIPBOARD noun **SHIPBOARDS** the side of a ship

SHIPLOAD noun **SHIPLOADS** the actual or possible load or capacity of a ship

SHIPMATE noun **SHIPMATES** a fellow sailor

SHIPMENT noun **SHIPMENTS** the act or practice of shipping cargo

SHIPPING noun **SHIPPINGS** the commercial transportation of freight, especially by ship

SHIPSHAPE adj in good order; neat and tidy

SHIPWRECK noun **SHIPWRECKS** the accidental sinking or destruction of a ship ◻ verb **SHIPWRECKS, SHIPWRECKING, SHIPWRECKED** to be or make someone the victim of a ship's accidental sinking or destruction

SHIPYARD noun **SHIPYARDS** a place where ships are built and repaired

SHIRE noun **SHIRES** a county

SHIRK verb **SHIRKS, SHIRKING, SHIRKED** to evade (work, a duty, etc) ◻ noun **SHIRKS** someone who shirks

SHIRKER noun **SHIRKERS** a person who evades work, duty etc

SHIRT noun **SHIRTS** a man's loose-sleeved garment for the upper body, typically with buttons down the front, and fitted collar and cuffs

SHIRTY adj **SHIRTIER, SHIRTIEST** ill-tempered or irritable; annoyed

SHIVER verb **SHIVERS, SHIVERING, SHIVERED** to quiver or tremble, eg with fear or because of illness ◻ noun **SHIVERS** an act of shivering; a shivering movement or sensation

SHIVERY adj **SHIVERIER, SHIVERIEST** inclined to shiver

SHOAL noun **SHOALS** a multitude of fish swimming together ◻ verb **SHOALS, SHOALING, SHOALED** to gather or move in a shoal; to swarm

SHOCK noun **SHOCKS** a strong emotional disturbance, especially a feeling of extreme surprise, outrage or disgust ◻ verb **SHOCKS, SHOCKING, SHOCKED** to make someone feel extreme surprise, outrage or disgust

SHOCKER noun **SHOCKERS** a very sensational tale

SHOCKING adj giving a shock

SHODDILY adverb in a shoddy way

SHODDY adj **SHODDIER, SHODDIEST** of poor quality; carelessly done or made ◻ noun **SHODDIES** wool made from shredded rags

SHOE noun **SHOES** either of a pair of shaped outer coverings for the feet, especially ones made of leather or other stiff material, usually finishing below the ankle ◻ verb **SHOES, SHOEING, SHOED, SHOD** to provide with shoes

SHOEHORN noun **SHOEHORNS** a curved piece of metal, plastic or (originally) horn, used for levering the heel into a shoe ◻ verb **SHOEHORNS, SHOEHORNING, SHOEHORNED** to fit, squeeze or compress into a tight or insufficient space

SHOELACE noun **SHOELACES** a string or cord passed through eyelet holes to fasten a shoe

SHOEMAKER noun **SHOEMAKERS** someone who makes, though now more often only sells or repairs, shoes and boots

SHOESHINE noun **SHOESHINES** the act of polishing shoes

SHOGI noun **SHOGIS** a Japanese form of chess, played on a squared board, each player having 20 pieces

SHOGUN noun **SHOGUNS** any of

the hereditary military governors who were the effective rulers of Japan from the 12c until 1867 when the emperor regained power

SHOGUNAL *adj* of or relating to a shogun

SHOGUNATE *noun* **SHOGUNATES** the office, jurisdiction or state of a shogun

SHOJI *noun* **SHOJI, SHOJIS** a screen of paper on a wooden framework, forming a wall or partition in Japanese houses

SHONE past form of **shine**

SHOO *exclamation* an expression used to scare or chase away a person or animal □ *verb* **SHOOS, SHOOING, SHOOED** to cry 'Shoo!'

SHOOK past form of **shake**

SHOOT *verb* **SHOOTS, SHOOTING, SHOT** to fire a gun or other weapon □ *noun* **SHOOTS** an act of shooting

SHOOTER *noun* **SHOOTERS** someone or something that shoots

SHOOTIST *noun* **SHOOTISTS** someone who shoots

SHOP *noun* **SHOPS** a room or building where goods are sold or services are provided □ *verb* **SHOPS, SHOPPING, SHOPPED** to visit a shop or shops, especially in order to buy goods

SHOPPER *noun* **SHOPPERS** someone who shops

SHOPPING *noun* **SHOPPINGS** the act of visiting shops to look at or buy goods

SHORAN *noun* **SHORANS** a system of aircraft navigation using the measurement of the time taken for two dispatched radar signals to return from known locations

SHORE *noun* **SHORES** a narrow strip of land bordering on the sea, a lake or any other large body of water □ *verb* **SHORES, SHORING, SHORED** to set on shore

SHORELINE *noun* **SHORELINES** the line formed where land meets water

SHORING *noun* **SHORINGS** a set of props that support something

SHORN a past form of **shear**

SHORT *adj* **SHORTER, SHORTEST** having little physical length; not long □ *adverb* abruptly; briefly □ *noun* **SHORTS** something that is short □ *verb* **SHORTS, SHORTING, SHORTED** to short-circuit; to cause a short circuit in something

SHORTAGE *noun* **SHORTAGES** a lack or deficiency

SHORTCAKE *noun* **SHORTCAKES** shortbread or other crumbly cake

SHORTEN *verb* **SHORTENS, SHORTENING, SHORTENED** to make or become shorter

SHORTENING *noun* **SHORTENINGS** butter, lard or other fat used for making pastry more crumbly

SHORTFALL *noun* **SHORTFALLS** a failure to reach a desired or expected level or specification

SHORTHAND *noun* **SHORTHANDS** any of various systems of combined strokes and dots representing speech sounds and groups of sounds, used as a fast way of recording speech in writing

SHORTHORN *noun* **SHORTHORNS** any of various breeds of beef and dairy cattle with very short horns and usually with a red and white, roan or white coat

SHORTIE *noun* **SHORTIES** a shorty

SHORTLY *adverb* soon; within a short period of time

SHORTNESS *noun* **SHORTNESSES** the quality or condition of being short

SHORTS *plural noun* trousers, worn by males or females, extending from the waist to anywhere between the upper thigh and the knee

SHORTY *noun* **SHORTIES** a person or thing (eg a garment) that is shorter than average

SHOT[1] *noun* **SHOTS** an act of shooting or firing a gun □ *verb* **SHOTS, SHOTTING, SHOTTED** to load (a gun) with bullets or small pellets

SHOT[2] *adj* said of a fabric: woven with different-coloured threads in the warp and weft so that movement produces the effect of changing colours

SHOTGUN *noun* **SHOTGUNS** a gun with a long, wide, smooth barrel for firing small shot

SHOULD *auxiliary verb* expressing: obligation, duty or recommendation; ought to

SHOULDER *noun* **SHOULDERS** in humans and animals: the part on either side of the body, just below the neck, where the arm or forelimb joins the trunk □ *verb* **SHOULDERS, SHOULDERING, SHOULDERED** to bear (eg a responsibility)

SHOUT *noun* **SHOUTS** a loud cry or call □ *verb* **SHOUTS, SHOUTING, SHOUTED** to utter a loud cry or call

SHOUTER *noun* **SHOUTERS** a person who shouts

SHOVE *verb* **SHOVES, SHOVING, SHOVED** to push or thrust with force □ *noun* **SHOVES** a forceful push

SHOVEL *noun* **SHOVELS** a tool with a deep-sided spade-like blade and a handle, for lifting and carrying loose material □ *verb* **SHOVELS, SHOVELLING, SHOVELLED** to lift or carry with, or as if with, a shovel

SHOVELER *noun* **SHOVELERS** a shoveller

SHOVELFUL *noun* **SHOVELFULS** the amount a shovel can hold

SHOVELLER *noun* **SHOVELLERS** someone or something that shovels

SHOVER *noun* **SHOVERS** someone who shoves

SHOW *verb* **SHOWS, SHOWING, SHOWED, SHOWN** to make or become visible, known or noticeable □ *noun* **SHOWS** an act of showing

SHOWBIZ *noun* **SHOWBIZZES** show business

SHOWBOAT *noun* **SHOWBOATS** a river boat, usually a paddle-steamer, serving as a travelling theatre

SHOWBREAD *noun* **SHOWBREADS** shewbread

SHOWCASE *noun* **SHOWCASES** a glass case for displaying objects, especially in a museum or shop

SHOWDOWN *noun* **SHOWDOWNS** a confrontation or fight by which a long-term dispute may be finally settled

SHOWED a past form of **show**

SHOWER *noun* **SHOWERS** a sudden but short and usually light fall of rain, snow or hail □ *verb* **SHOWERS, SHOWERING, SHOWERED** to cover, bestow, fall or come abundantly

SHOWERY *adj* **SHOWERIER, SHOWERIEST** marked by showers

SHOWGIRL *noun* **SHOWGIRLS** a girl who performs in variety entertainments, usually as a dancer or singer

SHOWIER see under **showy**

SHOWIEST see under **showy**

SHOWILY *adverb* in a showy way

SHOWINESS *noun* **SHOWINESSES** the quality or condition of being showy

SHOWING noun **SHOWINGS** an act of exhibiting or displaying
SHOWMAN noun **SHOWMEN** someone who owns, exhibits or manages a circus, a stall at a fairground, or other entertainment
SHOWN a past form of **show**
SHOWPIECE noun **SHOWPIECES** an item on display; an exhibit
SHOWPLACE noun **SHOWPLACES** a place visited or shown as a sight
SHOWROOM noun **SHOWROOMS** a room where examples of goods for sale, especially large and expensive items, are displayed
SHOWY adj **SHOWIER, SHOWIEST** making an impressive or exciting display
SHOYU noun **SHOYUS** a rich soy sauce made from soya beans naturally fermented with wheat or barley, and used as a flavouring in Japanese cookery
SHRANK a past form of **shrink**
SHRAPNEL noun **SHRAPNELS** a shell, filled with pellets or metal fragments, which explodes shortly before impact
SHRED noun **SHREDS** a thin scrap or strip cut or ripped off □ verb **SHREDS, SHREDDING, SHREDDED** to cut, tear or scrape into shreds
SHREDDER noun **SHREDDERS** a device for shredding eg documents
SHREW noun **SHREWS** a small nocturnal mammal with velvety fur, small eyes and a pointed snout, that is extremely active and must feed almost continuously on worms, insects, etc in order to survive
SHREWD adj **SHREWDER, SHREWDEST** possessing or showing keen judgement gained from practical experience; astute
SHREWDLY adverb in a shrewd way
SHREWISH adj like a shrew
SHRIEK verb **SHRIEKS, SHRIEKING, SHRIEKED** to cry out with a piercing scream □ noun **SHRIEKS** such a piercing cry
SHRIEKER noun **SHRIEKERS** a person who shrieks
SHRIEVAL adj referring or relating to a sheriff
SHRIFT noun **SHRIFTS** absolution; confession
SHRIKE noun **SHRIKES** any of various small perching birds with a powerful slightly hooked beak, which feed on insects, small birds and rodents, often impaling their prey on thorns, twigs or barbed wire
SHRILL adj **SHRILLER, SHRILLEST** said of a voice, sound, etc: high-pitched and piercing □ verb **SHRILLS, SHRILLING, SHRILLED** to utter in such a high-pitched manner
SHRILLY adverb in a shrill way
SHRIMP noun **SHRIMPS** any of numerous small aquatic crustaceans with a cylindrical semi-transparent body and five pairs of jointed legs, including several economically important edible species □ verb **SHRIMPS, SHRIMPING, SHRIMPED** to fish for shrimps
SHRIMPING noun **SHRIMPINGS** an act of fishing for shrimps
SHRINE noun **SHRINES** a sacred place of worship □ verb **SHRINES, SHRINING, SHRINED** to enshrine
SHRINK verb **SHRINKS, SHRINKING, SHRANK, SHRUNK, SHRUNKEN** to make or become smaller in size or extent, especially through exposure to heat, cold or moisture □ noun **SHRINKS** an act of shrinking
SHRINKAGE noun **SHRINKAGES** the act of shrinking
SHRIVE verb **SHRIVES, SHRIVING, SHRIVED** to hear a confession from and give absolution to someone
SHRIVEL verb **SHRIVELS, SHRIVELLING, SHRIVELLED** to make or become shrunken and wrinkled, especially as a result of drying out
SHROUD noun **SHROUDS** a garment or cloth in which a corpse is wrapped □ verb **SHROUDS, SHROUDING, SHROUDED** to wrap in a shroud
SHRUB noun **SHRUBS** a woody plant or bush, without any main trunk, which branches into several main stems at or just below ground level
SHRUBBERY noun **SHRUBBERIES** a place, especially a part of a garden, where shrubs are grown
SHRUBBY adj **SHRUBBIER, SHRUBBIEST** having the character of or similar to a shrub
SHRUG verb **SHRUGS, SHRUGGING, SHRUGGED** to raise up and drop the shoulders briefly as an indication of doubt, indifference, etc □ noun **SHRUGS** an act of shrugging
SHRUNK a past form of **shrink**
SHRUNKEN adj having shrunk or having been shrunk
SHTOOK noun **SHTOOKS** trouble; bother
SHTOOM adj silent; quiet
SHTUM adj shtoom
SHTUMM adj shtoom
SHUCK noun **SHUCKS** a husk, pod or shell □ verb **SHUCKS, SHUCKING, SHUCKED** to remove the shuck from something
SHUDDER verb **SHUDDERS, SHUDDERING, SHUDDERED** to shiver or tremble, especially with fear, cold or disgust □ noun **SHUDDERS** such a trembling movement or feeling
SHUDDERY adj likely to shudder
SHUFFLE verb **SHUFFLES, SHUFFLING, SHUFFLED** to move or drag (one's feet) with short quick sliding steps; to walk in this fashion □ noun **SHUFFLES** an act or sound of shuffling
SHUFFLER noun **SHUFFLERS** someone who shuffles
SHUFTI noun **SHUFTIS** a look or glance
SHUFTY noun **SHUFTIES** a shufti
SHUN verb **SHUNS, SHUNNING, SHUNNED** to intentionally avoid or keep away from someone or something
SHUNT verb **SHUNTS, SHUNTING, SHUNTED** to move (a train or carriage) from one track to another □ noun **SHUNTS** an act of shunting or being shunted
SHUNTER noun **SHUNTERS** a person or thing that shunts eg trains
SHUSH exclamation be quiet! □ verb **SHUSHES, SHUSHING, SHUSHED** to make someone or something quiet by, or as if by, saying 'Shush!'
SHUT verb **SHUTS, SHUTTING, SHUT** to place or move so as to close an opening □ adj not open; closed
SHUTDOWN noun **SHUTDOWNS** a temporary closing of a factory or business
SHUTTER noun **SHUTTERS** someone or something that shuts; a movable internal or external cover for a window, especially one of a pair of hinged wooden or metal panels □ verb **SHUTTERS, SHUTTERING, SHUTTERED** to fit

or cover (a window) with a shutter or shutters

SHUTTLE *noun* **SHUTTLES** the device that carries the horizontal thread (the weft) backwards and forwards between the vertical threads (the warp) □ *verb* **SHUTTLES, SHUTTLING, SHUTTLED** to move or make someone or something move backwards and forwards

SHWA *noun* **SHWAS** a schwa

SHY *adj* **SHIER, SHYER, SHIEST, SHYEST** said of a person: embarrassed or unnerved by the company or attention of others □ *verb* **SHIES, SHYING, SHIED** said eg of a horse: to jump suddenly aside or back in fear; to be startled □ *noun* **SHIES** an act of shying

SHYLY *adverb* in a shy way

SHYNESS *noun* **SHYNESSES** the quality or condition of being shy

SHYSTER *noun* **SHYSTERS** an unscrupulous or disreputable lawyer

SI *noun* **SIS** an earlier form of *ti*, a musical note

SIAL *noun* **SIALS** the granite rocks, rich in silica and aluminium, that form the upper layer of the Earth's crust

SIAMANG *noun* **SIAMANGS** a large black gibbon, native to Sumatra and the Malay Peninsula

SIB *noun* **SIBS** a blood relation, a kinsman

SIBILANCE *noun* **SIBILANCES** the quality or condition of being sibilant

SIBILANCY *noun* **SIBILANCIES** sibilance

SIBILANT *adj* similar to, having or pronounced with a hissing sound □ *noun* **SIBILANTS** a consonant with such a sound, eg *s* and *z*

SIBILATE *verb* **SIBILATES, SIBILATING, SIBILATED** to produce or pronounce (words) with a hissing sound

SIBLING *noun* **SIBLINGS** a blood relation; a brother or sister

SIBYL *noun* **SIBYLS** any of several prophetesses of ancient Rome, Greece, Babylonia, Egypt, etc

SIC [1] *adverb* a term used in brackets after a word or phrase in a quotation to indicate that it is quoted accurately, even if it appears to be a mistake

SIC [2] *verb* **SICS, SICKING, SICKED** to incite (a dog to attack)

SICCATIVE *noun* **SICCATIVES** a drying agent

SICK *adj* **SICKER, SICKEST** vomiting; feeling the need to vomit □ *noun* **SICKS** vomit □ *verb* **SICKS, SICKING, SICKED** to vomit

SICKBED *noun* **SICKBEDS** a bed on which someone lies when sick

SICKEN *verb* **SICKENS, SICKENING, SICKENED** to make someone or something feel like vomiting

SICKENING *adj* causing nausea

SICKIE *noun* **SICKIES** a day's sick leave, often without the person actually being ill

SICKLE *noun* **SICKLES** a tool with a short handle and a curved blade for cutting grain crops with a horizontal sweeping action

SICKLY *adj* **SICKLIER, SICKLIEST** susceptible or prone to illness; ailing or feeble □ *adverb* to an extent that suggests illness

SICKNESS *noun* **SICKNESSES** the condition of being ill; an illness

SIDALCEA *noun* **SIDALCEAS** a herbaceous perennial plant of the mallow family with tall spikes of white, pink or purple flowers

SIDE *noun* **SIDES** any of the usually flat or flattish surfaces that form the outer extent of something; any of these surfaces other than the front, back, top or bottom □ *adj* located at the side □ *verb* **SIDES, SIDING, SIDED** to take on someone's position or point of view; to join forces with them

SIDEARM *noun* **SIDEARMS** a weapon worn at the side or in a belt

SIDEBAND *noun* **SIDEBANDS** in radio: a band of frequencies slightly above or below the carrier frequency, containing additional frequencies constituting the information to be conveyed, introduced by modulation

SIDEBOARD *noun* **SIDEBOARDS** a large piece of furniture, often consisting of shelves or cabinets mounted above drawers or cupboards, for holding plates, ornaments, etc

SIDECAR *noun* **SIDECARS** a small carriage for one or two passengers, attached to the side of a motorcycle

SIDED *adj* having a specified number of sides

SIDEKICK *noun* **SIDEKICKS** a close or special friend; a partner or deputy

SIDELIGHT *noun* **SIDELIGHTS** a small light fitted on the front and rear of a motor vehicle, used in fading daylight

SIDELINE *noun* **SIDELINES** a line marking either side boundary of a sports pitch □ *verb* **SIDELINES, SIDELINING, SIDELINED** to remove or suspend (a player) from a team

SIDELONG *adverb* from or to one side; not direct or directly

SIDEREAL *adj* referring or relating to, or determined by the stars

SIDERITE *noun* **SIDERITES** a meteorite consisting mainly of metallic iron

SIDEROSIS *noun* **SIDEROSES** a lung disease caused by breathing in iron or other metal fragments

SIDESHOW *noun* **SIDESHOWS** an exhibition or show subordinate to a larger one

SIDESLIP *noun* **SIDESLIPS** a skid, especially by a road vehicle

SIDESMAN *noun* **SIDESMEN** a deputy churchwarden

SIDESTEP *verb* **SIDESTEPS, SIDESTEPPING, SIDESTEPPED** to avoid by, or as if by, stepping aside □ *noun* **SIDESTEPS** a step taken to one side

SIDESWIPE *noun* **SIDESWIPES** a blow coming from the side, as opposed to head-on

SIDETRACK *verb* **SIDETRACKS, SIDETRACKING, SIDETRACKED** to divert the attention of away from the matter in hand

SIDEWALK *noun* **SIDEWALKS** a pavement

SIDEWALL *noun* **SIDEWALLS** the side section of a pneumatic tyre, between the tread and wheel rim

SIDEWAYS *adverb* from, to or towards one side □ *adj* from, to or towards one side

SIDING *noun* **SIDINGS** a short dead-end railway line onto which trains, wagons, etc can be shunted temporarily from the main line

SIDLE *verb* **SIDLES, SIDLING, SIDLED** to go or edge along sideways, especially in a cautious, furtive and ingratiating manner

SIEGE *noun* **SIEGES** the act or process of surrounding a fort or town with troops, cutting off its supplies and subjecting it to persistent attack with the intention of forcing its surrender

SIEMENS *noun* **SIEMENS** the SI unit of conductance, equal to the conductance at which a potential of one volt produces a current of one ampere

SIENNA *noun* **SIENNAS** a pigment obtained from a type of earth with a high clay and iron content

SIERRA *noun* **SIERRAS** especially in Spanish-speaking countries and the US: a mountain range, especially when jagged

SIESTA *noun* **SIESTAS** in hot countries: a sleep or rest after the midday meal

SIEVE *noun* **SIEVES** a utensil with a meshed or perforated bottom, used for straining solids from liquids or for sifting large particles from smaller ones □ *verb* **SIEVES, SIEVING, SIEVED** to strain or sift with a sieve

SIEVERT *noun* **SIEVERTS** the SI unit of radioaction dose equivalent, equal to the absorbed dose multiplied by its relative biological effectiveness, used in radiation safety measurements

SIFT *verb* **SIFTS, SIFTING, SIFTED** to pass through a sieve in order to separate out lumps or larger particles

SIFTER *noun* **SIFTERS** a person or thing that sifts

SIGH *verb* **SIGHS, SIGHING, SIGHED** to release a long deep audible breath, expressive of sadness, longing, tiredness or relief □ *noun* **SIGHS** an act or the sound of sighing

SIGHT *noun* **SIGHTS** the power or faculty of seeing; vision □ *verb* **SIGHTS, SIGHTING, SIGHTED** to get a look at or glimpse of someone or something

SIGHTED *adj* having the power of sight; not blind

SIGHTLESS *adj* blind

SIGHTLY *adj* **SIGHTLIER, SIGHTLIEST** pleasing to the eye; attractive or appealing

SIGHTSEE *verb* **SIGHTSEES, SIGHTSEEING, SIGHTSAW, SIGHTSEEN** to visit places of interest, especially as a tourist

SIGHTSEEING *noun* **SIGHTSEEINGS** an act of sightseeing

SIGHTSEER *noun* **SIGHTSEERS** someone who goes sightseeing

SIGLA *plural noun* abbreviations, symbols and signs, as used in manuscripts, seals, documents, etc

SIGMA *noun* **SIGMAS** the eighteenth letter of the Greek alphabet

SIGN *noun* **SIGNS** a printed mark with a meaning; a symbol □ *verb* **SIGNS, SIGNING, SIGNED** to give a signal or indication

SIGNAL *noun* **SIGNALS** a message in the form of a gesture, light, sound, etc, conveying information or indicating the time for action, often over a distance □ *verb* **SIGNALS, SIGNALLING, SIGNALING, SIGNALLED, SIGNALED** to transmit or convey (a message) using signals

SIGNALISE *verb* **SIGNALISES, SIGNALISING, SIGNALISED** to signalize

SIGNALIZE *verb* **SIGNALIZES, SIGNALIZING, SIGNALIZED** to mark or distinguish; to make notable

SIGNALLY *adverb* notably

SIGNALMAN *noun* **SIGNALMEN** a controller who works railway signals

SIGNATORY *noun* **SIGNATORIES** a person, organization or state that is a party to a contract, treaty or other document

SIGNATURE *noun* **SIGNATURES** one's name written by oneself, or a representative symbol, as a formal mark of authorization, etc

SIGNER *noun* **SIGNERS** someone who uses or makes signs, especially someone skilled in using sign language

SIGNET *noun* **SIGNETS** a small seal used for stamping documents, etc

SIGNIFY *verb* **SIGNIFIES, SIGNIFYING, SIGNIFIED** to be a sign for something or someone; to suggest or mean

SIGNOR *noun* **SIGNORS** a gentleman

SIGNORA *noun* **SIGNORE** a lady

SIGNORE *noun* **SIGNORI** a gentleman

SIGNORINA *noun* **SIGNORINE** a young lady

SIGNPOST *noun* **SIGNPOSTS** a post supporting a sign that gives information or directions to motorists or pedestrians □ *verb* **SIGNPOSTS, SIGNPOSTING, SIGNPOSTED** to mark (a route) with signposts

SIJO *noun* **SIJOS** a Korean verse form of three lines each of four groups of syllables

SIKA *noun* **SIKAS** a small deer that inhabits Japan and Eastern Asia, and develops a white spotted coat in the summer

SILAGE *noun* **SILAGES** animal fodder made from forage crops such as grass, maize, etc which are compressed and then preserved by controlled fermentation, eg in a silo

SILD *noun* **SILDS** a young herring

SILENCE *noun* **SILENCES** absence of sound or speech □ *verb* **SILENCES, SILENCING, SILENCED** to make someone or something stop speaking, making a noise, or giving away information

SILENCER *noun* **SILENCERS** someone or something that silences

SILENT *adj* **SILENTER, SILENTEST** free from noise; unaccompanied by sound □ *noun* **SILENTS** a silent film

SILENTLY *adverb* in a silent way; quietly

SILENUS *noun* **SILENI** in Greek mythology: a woodland god or elderly satyr

SILEX *noun* **SILEXES** a silica of quartz

SILICA *noun* **SILICAS** a hard white or colourless glassy solid that occurs naturally as quartz, sand and flint, and also as silicate compounds, and is used in the manufacture of glasses, glazes and enamels

SILICATE *noun* **SILICATES** any of various chemical compounds containing silicon, oxygen and one or more metals, including the main components of most rocks and many minerals, eg clay, mica, feldspar

SILICEOUS *adj* belonging or relating to, or containing, silica

SILICIC *adj* belonging or relating to, or containing, silicon or an acid containing silicon

SILICIFY *verb* **SILICIFIES, SILICIFYING, SILICIFIED** to transform or make something transform into silica

SILICIOUS *adj* siliceous

SILICON *noun* **SILICONS** a non-metallic element that occurs naturally as silicate minerals in clays and rocks, and as silica in sand and quartz, used as a semiconductor to make transistors and silicon chips

SILICONE *noun* **SILICONES** any of

numerous synthetic polymers, usually occurring in the form of oily liquids, waxes, plastics or rubbers, used in lubricants, electrical insulators, paints, water repellents, adhesives and surgical breast implants

SILICOSIS noun **SILICOSES** a lung disease caused by prolonged inhalation of dust containing silica

SILK noun **SILKS** a fine soft fibre produced by the larva of the silkworm

SILKEN adj made of silk

SILKWORM noun **SILKWORMS** the caterpillar of the silk moth, which spins a cocoon of unbroken silk thread, farmed in India, China and Japan to provide silk on a commercial basis

SILKY adj **SILKIER, SILKIEST** soft and shiny like silk

SILL noun **SILLS** the bottom part of the framework around the inside of a window or door

SILLABUB noun **SILLABUBS** a syllabub

SILLINESS noun **SILLINESSES** the state or condition of being silly

SILLY adj **SILLIER, SILLIEST** not sensible; foolish; trivial or frivolous ◻ noun **SILLIES** a foolish person

SILO noun **SILOS** a tall round airtight tower for storing green crops and converting them into silage

SILT noun **SILTS** sedimentary material, finer than sand and coarser than clay, consisting of very small rock fragments or mineral particles, deposited by or suspended in running or still water ◻ verb **SILTS, SILTING, SILTED** to become blocked up with silt

SILVAN adj sylvan

SILVER noun **SILVERS** an element, a soft white lustrous precious metal that is an excellent conductor of heat and electricity, and is used in jewellery, ornaments, mirrors, coins, electrical contacts and for electroplating tableware ◻ verb **SILVERS, SILVERING, SILVERED** to apply a thin coating of silver; to plate with silver

SILVERY adj **SILVERIER, SILVERIEST** having the colour or shiny quality of silver

SIM noun **SIMS** short for *Simeonite*, an evangelical

SIMA noun **SIMAS** the basaltic rocks rich in silica and magnesium that form the lower layer of the Earth's crust

SIMIAN noun **SIMIANS** a monkey or ape ◻ adj belonging or relating to, or resembling, a monkey or ape

SIMILAR adj having a close resemblance to something; being of the same kind, but not identical; alike

SIMILARLY adverb in a similar way

SIMILE noun **SIMILES** a figure of speech in which a thing is described by being likened to something, usually using *as* or *like*, as in *eyes sparkling like diamonds*

SIMMER verb **SIMMERS, SIMMERING, SIMMERED** to cook or make something cook gently at just below boiling point ◻ noun **SIMMERS** a simmering state

SIMNEL noun **SIMNELS** a sweet fruit cake covered with marzipan, traditionally baked at Easter or Mid-Lent

SIMONY noun **SIMONIES** the practice of buying or selling a religious post, benefice or other privilege

SIMOOM noun **SIMOOMS** a hot suffocating desert wind in Arabia and N Africa

SIMOON noun **SIMOONS** a simoom

SIMPATICO adj sympathetic; amiable, especially because of being kind-hearted

SIMPER verb **SIMPERS, SIMPERING, SIMPERED** to smile in a weak affected manner ◻ noun **SIMPERS** a simpering smile

SIMPLE adj **SIMPLER, SIMPLEST** easy; not difficult ◻ noun **SIMPLES** a medicine of one constituent

SIMPLETON noun **SIMPLETONS** a foolish or unintelligent person

SIMPLIFY verb **SIMPLIFIES, SIMPLIFYING, SIMPLIFIED** to make something less difficult or complicated; to make it easier to understand

SIMPLY adverb in a straightforward, uncomplicated manner

SIMULATE verb **SIMULATES, SIMULATING, SIMULATED** to convincingly re-create (a set of conditions or a real-life event), especially for the purposes of training

SIMULATED adj not genuine; imitation

SIMULATOR noun **SIMULATORS** a device that simulates a system, process or set of conditions, especially in order to test it, or for training purposes

SIMULCAST noun **SIMULCASTS** a programme broadcast simultaneously on radio and television

SIN noun **SINS** an act that breaches a moral and especially a religious law or teaching ◻ verb **SINS, SINNING, SINNED** to commit a sin

SINCE conj from the time that; seeing that ◻ prep during or throughout the period between now and some earlier stated time ◻ adverb from that time onwards

SINCERE adj **SINCERER, SINCEREST** genuine; not pretended or affected

SINCERELY adverb in a sincere way

SINCERITY noun **SINCERITIES** the quality or condition of being sincere

SINCIPUT noun **SINCIPUTS** the forepart of the head or skull

SINE noun **SINES** in a right-angled triangle: a function of any angle, defined as the length of the side opposite the angle divided by the length of the hypotenuse

SINECURE noun **SINECURES** a paid job involving little or no work

SINEW noun **SINEWS** a strong piece of fibrous tissue joining a muscle to a bone; a tendon

SINEWY adj **SINEWIER, SINEWIEST** of, like or characterized by sinew

SINFONIA noun **SINFONIAS** an orchestral piece; a symphony

SINFUL adj wicked; involving sin; morally wrong

SINFULLY adverb in a sinful way

SING verb **SINGS, SINGING, SANG, SUNG** to utter (words, sounds, etc) in a melodic rhythmic fashion, especially to the accompaniment of music

SINGALONG noun **SINGALONGS** a song in which an audience, etc can join in with the words

SINGE verb **SINGES, SINGEING, SINGED** to burn lightly on the surface; to scorch or become scorched ◻ noun **SINGES** a light surface burn

SINGER noun **SINGERS** a person or bird that sings

SINGLE adj comprising only one part; solitary ◻ noun **SINGLES** a record usually with only one track on each side, now also referring to a cassette single and those on compact disc ◻ *verb* **SINGLES, SINGLING, SINGLED** to pick someone or something from among others

SINGLES *plural noun* in tennis, etc: a match where one player competes against another

SINGLET *noun* **SINGLETS** a sleeveless vest or undershirt

SINGLETON *noun* **SINGLETONS** the only playing-card of a particular suit in a hand

SINGLY *adverb* one at a time; individually

SINGSONG *noun* **SINGSONGS** an informal gathering at which friends, etc sing together for pleasure ◻ *adj* said of a speaking voice, etc: having a fluctuating intonation and rhythm

SINGULAR *adj* single; unique ◻ *noun* **SINGULARS** a word or form of a word expressing the idea or involvement of one person, thing, etc as opposed to two or more

SINISTER *adj* suggesting or threatening evil or danger; malign

SINISTRAL *adj* positioned on or relating to the left side

SINK *verb* **SINKS, SINKING, SANK, SUNK, SUNKEN** to fall or cause to fall and remain below the surface of water, either partially or completely ◻ *noun* **SINKS** a basin, often mounted on a wall, with built-in water supply and drainage, for washing dishes, etc

SINKER *noun* **SINKERS** someone who sinks

SINNER *noun* **SINNERS** someone who sins or has sinned

SINTER *noun* **SINTERS** a siliceous deposit from hot springs ◻ *verb* **SINTERS, SINTERING, SINTERED** to heat a mixture of powdered metals, sometimes under pressure, to the melting-point of the metal in the mixture which has the lowest melting-point, which then binds together the harder particles

SINUATE *adj* having many curves or bends; meandering

SINUATED *adj* sinuate

SINUATION *noun* **SINUATIONS** the state of being sinuate

SINUOSITY *noun* **SINUOSITIES** the state or condition of being sinuous

SINUOUS *adj* wavy; winding; sinuate

SINUOUSLY *adverb* in a sinuous way

SINUS *noun* **SINUSES** a cavity or depression filled with air, especially in the bones of mammals

SINUSITIS *noun* **SINUSITISES** inflammation of the lining of the sinuses, especially the nasal ones

SINUSOID *noun* **SINUSOIDS** a small blood vessel in certain organs, such as the liver, heart, etc ◻ *adj* similar to or referring to a sinus

SIP *verb* **SIPS, SIPPING, SIPPED** to drink in very small mouthfuls ◻ *noun* **SIPS** an act of sipping

SIPHON *noun* **SIPHONS** a tube held in an inverted U-shape that can be used to transfer liquid from one container at a higher level into another at a lower level, used to empty car petrol tanks, etc ◻ *verb* **SIPHONS, SIPHONING, SIPHONED** to transfer (liquid) from one container to another using such a device

SIPPER *noun* **SIPPERS** someone who sips

SIPPET *noun* **SIPPETS** a morsel of bread or toast, especially with soup

SIR *noun* **SIRS** a polite and respectful address for a man ◻ *verb* **SIRS, SIRRING, SIRRED** to address as 'sir'

SIRE *noun* **SIRES** the father of a horse or other animal ◻ *verb* **SIRES, SIRING, SIRED** said of an animal: to father (young)

SIREN *noun* **SIRENS** a device that gives out a loud wailing noise, usually as a warning signal

SIRLOIN *noun* **SIRLOINS** a fine cut of beef from the loin or the upper part of the loin

SIROCCO *noun* **SIROCCOS** in S Europe: a dry hot dusty wind blowing from N Africa, and becoming more moist as it moves further north

SIS *noun* a sister

SISAL *noun* **SISALS** any of various perennial plants, native to Central America, which have a rosette of swollen stout sword-like leaves tipped with sharp spines

SISKIN *noun* **SISKINS** any of various small finches, the male of which usually has yellowish-green plumage with a black crown and chin, a bold yellow rump and a deeply forked black tail

SISSY *noun* **SISSIES** a feeble, cowardly or effeminate male ◻ *adj* **SISSIER, SISSIEST** having the characteristics of a sissy

SISTER *noun* **SISTERS** a female child of the same parents as another

SISTERLY *adj* said of a woman or her behaviour: like a sister, especially in being kind and affectionate

SIT *verb* **SITS, SITTING, SAT, SATE** to rest the body on the buttocks, with the upper body more or less vertical

SITAR *noun* **SITARS** a guitar-like instrument of Indian origin, with a long neck, rounded body and two sets of strings

SITCOM *noun* **SITCOMS** a situation comedy, a comedy with a series of episodes set in the same location and with a group of regularly appearing characters

SITE *noun* **SITES** the place where something was, is or is to be situated ◻ *verb* **SITES, SITING, SITED** to position or situate

SITTER *noun* **SITTERS** a person or animal that sits

SITTING *noun* **SITTINGS** the act or state of being seated ◻ *adj* currently holding office

SITUATE *verb* **SITUATES, SITUATING, SITUATED** to place in a certain position, context or set of circumstances

SITUATION *noun* **SITUATIONS** a set of circumstances or state of affairs

SIX *noun* **SIXES** the cardinal number 6 ◻ *adj* totalling six

SIXER *noun* **SIXERS** the Cub Scout or Brownie Guide leader of a team of six Cubs or Brownies

SIXFOLD *adj* equal to six times as much ◻ *adverb* by six times as much

SIXPENCE *noun* **SIXPENCES** in Britain: a former small silver coin worth six old pennies (6d), equivalent in value to 2½p

SIXPENNY *adj* worth or costing six old pennies

SIXTE *noun* **SIXTES** a type of parry in fencing

SIXTEEN *noun* **SIXTEENS** the cardinal number 16 ◻ *adj* totalling sixteen

SIXTEENTH *adj* in counting: next after fifteenth ◻ *noun* **SIXTEENTHS** one of sixteen equal parts

For longer words, see *The Chambers Dictionary*

SIXTH adj in counting: next after fifth ◻ noun **SIXTHS** one of six equal parts

SIXTHLY adverb used to introduce the sixth point in a list

SIXTIES plural noun the period of time between one's sixtieth and seventieth birthdays

SIXTIETH adj in counting: next after fifty-ninth ◻ noun **SIXTIETHS** one of sixty equal parts

SIXTY noun **SIXTIES** the cardinal number 60 ◻ adj totalling sixty

SIZABLE adj sizeable

SIZAR noun **SIZARS** at Cambridge University and Trinity College in Dublin: a student receiving an allowance from their college towards expenses

SIZARSHIP noun **SIZARSHIPS** the position of holding a sizar

SIZE noun **SIZES** length, breadth, height or volume, or a combination of these; the dimensions of something ◻ verb **SIZES, SIZING, SIZED** to measure something in order to determine size

SIZEABLE adj fairly large; being of a considerable size

SIZED adj having a particular size

SIZEISM noun **SIZEISMS** discrimination against overweight people

SIZEIST noun **SIZEISTS** someone who discriminates against overweight people

SIZER noun **SIZERS** a measurer or gauge

SIZISM noun **SIZISMS** sizeism

SIZZLE verb **SIZZLES, SIZZLING, SIZZLED** to make a hissing sound when, or as if when, frying in hot fat ◻ noun **SIZZLES** a sizzling sound

SIZZLER noun **SIZZLERS** a sizzling heat or day

SJAMBOK noun **SJAMBOKS** in S Africa: a whip made from dried rhinoceros or hippopotamus hide

SKA noun **SKAS** a style of Jamaican popular music similar to reggae, played on trumpet, saxophone, etc, in an unpolished style with fast blaring rhythms

SKAG noun **SKAGS** heroin

SKAT noun **SKATS** a three-handed card game using 32 cards

SKATE noun **SKATES** a boot with a device fitted to the sole for gliding smoothly over surfaces, either a steel blade for use on ice (ice skate) or a set of small wheels for use on wooden and other surfaces (roller skate) ◻ verb **SKATES, SKATING, SKATED** to move around on skates

SKATER noun **SKATERS** someone who skates

SKATING noun **SKATINGS** moving on skates

SKEDADDLE verb **SKEDADDLES, SKEDADDLING, SKEDADDLED** to run away or leave quickly ◻ noun **SKEDADDLES** a hurried departure

SKEET noun **SKEETS** a form of clay-pigeon shooting in which the targets are launched at various angles

SKEIN noun **SKEINS** a loosely tied coil of wool or thread

SKELETAL adj similar to or like a skeleton

SKELETON noun **SKELETONS** the framework of bones that supports and often protects the body of an animal, and to which the muscles are usually attached

SKEP noun **SKEPS** a large round wickerwork basket

SKEPFUL noun **SKEPFULS** the amount that a skep will hold

SKEPTIC noun **SKEPTICS** a sceptic

SKEPTICAL adj sceptical

SKERRICK noun **SKERRICKS** a minute quantity; a scrap

SKERRY noun **SKERRIES** a reef of rock or a small rocky island

SKETCH noun **SKETCHES** a rough drawing quickly done, especially one without much detail used as a study towards a more finished work ◻ verb **SKETCHES, SKETCHING, SKETCHED** to do a rough drawing or drawings of something

SKETCHER noun **SKETCHERS** someone who sketches

SKETCHILY adverb vaguely; in an incomplete way

SKETCHY adj **SKETCHIER, SKETCHIEST** like a sketch; incomplete; vague

SKEW adj **SKEWER, SKEWEST** slanted; oblique; askew ◻ verb **SKEWS, SKEWING, SKEWED** to slant or cause to slant ◻ noun **SKEWS** a slanting position; obliquity

SKEWBALD noun **SKEWBALDS** a horse marked with patches of white and another colour (other than black)

SKEWER noun **SKEWERS** a long wooden or metal pin pushed through chunks of meat or vegetables which are to be roasted ◻ verb **SKEWERS, SKEWERING, SKEWERED** to fasten or pierce with, or as if with, a skewer

SKEWNESS noun **SKEWNESSES** in maths: a measure of the degree of asymmetry about the central value of a distribution

SKI noun **SKIS, SKI** one of a pair of long narrow runners of wood, metal or plastic, upturned at the front and attached to each of a pair of boots or to a vehicle for gliding over snow ◻ verb **SKIS, SKIING, SKIED** to move on skis, especially as a sport or leisure activity

SKIABLE adj said of a surface: having conditions suitable for skiing

SKID verb **SKIDS, SKIDDING, SKIDDED** said of a wheel, etc: to slide along without revolving ◻ noun **SKIDS** an instance of skidding

SKIDOO noun **SKIDOOS** a motorized sledge, fitted with tracks at the rear and steerable skis at the front ◻ verb **SKIDOOS, SKIDOOING, SKIDOOED** to use a skidoo

SKIER noun **SKIERS** someone who skis

SKIES plural of sky

SKIFF noun **SKIFFS** a small light boat

SKIFFLE noun **SKIFFLES** a strongly accented type of folk music influenced by jazz and blues, played with guitars, drums, washboard and often other unconventional instruments

SKIING noun **SKIINGS** the art of propelling oneself along snow using skis, with the aid of poles

SKILFUL adj having or showing skill

SKILFULLY adverb in a skillful way

SKILL noun **SKILLS** expertness; dexterity

SKILLED adj said of people: possessing skills; trained or experienced

SKILLET noun **SKILLETS** a small long-handled saucepan

SKILLFUL adj skilful

SKILLY noun **SKILLIES** a thin gruel or soup made from oatmeal

SKIM verb **SKIMS, SKIMMING, SKIMMED** to remove floating matter from the surface of (a liquid) ◻ noun **SKIMS** the act or process of skimming

SKIMMER noun **SKIMMERS** someone or something that skims

SKIMMIA noun **SKIMMIAS** any of various Asiatic evergreen shrubs, cultivated for their holly-like leaves and red berries

SKIMP verb **SKIMPS, SKIMPING, SKIMPED** to spend, use or give too little or only just enough of something ◻ adj scanty

SKIMPILY adverb in a skimpy way

SKIMPY adj **SKIMPIER, SKIMPIEST** inadequate; barely enough

SKIN noun **SKINS** the tough flexible waterproof covering of the human or animal body ◻ verb **SKINS, SKINNING, SKINNED** to remove or strip the skin from something

SKINCARE noun **SKINCARES** care and protection of the skin by using specific cosmetic products

SKINFLINT noun **SKINFLINTS** a very ungenerous or stingy person

SKINFUL noun **SKINFULS** a large amount of alcohol, enough to make one thoroughly drunk

SKINHEAD noun **SKINHEADS** a person, especially a white youth and generally one of a gang, with closely cropped hair, tight jeans, heavy boots and anti-establishment attitudes

SKINK noun **SKINKS** a lizard found in tropical and temperate regions worldwide, usually with a long thin body, a broad rounded tongue, and short legs or none at all

SKINNED adj having had the skin removed

SKINNY adj **SKINNIER, SKINNIEST** thin, especially unattractively thin

SKINT adj **SKINTER, SKINTEST** without money; hard up; broke

SKIP [1] verb **SKIPS, SKIPPING, SKIPPED** to move along with light springing or hopping steps on alternate feet

SKIP [2] noun **SKIPS** a large metal container for rubbish from eg building work

SKIPJACK noun **SKIPJACKS** any of a number of different species of fish which are able to jump out of the water

SKIPPER noun **SKIPPERS** a ship's captain ◻ verb **SKIPPERS, SKIPPERING, SKIPPERED** to act as skipper

SKIPPET noun **SKIPPETS** a flat wooden box for protecting a seal on a document

SKIPPING noun **SKIPPINGS** the art or activity of skipping using a skipping-rope

SKIRL noun **SKIRLS** the high-pitched sound of bagpipes ◻ verb **SKIRLS, SKIRLING, SKIRLED** to make this sound

SKIRMISH noun **SKIRMISHES** a brief battle during a war, especially away from the main fighting ◻ verb **SKIRMISHES, SKIRMISHING, SKIRMISHED** to engage in a skirmish

SKIRT noun **SKIRTS** a garment that hangs from the waist, worn chiefly by women and girls ◻ verb **SKIRTS, SKIRTING, SKIRTED** to border something

SKIRTING noun **SKIRTINGS** fabric used for skirts

SKIT noun **SKITS** a short satirical piece of writing or drama

SKITE verb **SKITES, SKITING, SKITED** to boast ◻ noun **SKITES** boastful chatter

SKITTER verb **SKITTERS, SKITTERING, SKITTERED** to skim over the surface of water

SKITTISH adj lively and playful; spirited

SKITTLE noun **SKITTLES** each of the upright bottle-shaped wooden or plastic targets used in certain games

SKIVE verb **SKIVES, SKIVING, SKIVED** to evade eg work, duty or school, usually through laziness ◻ noun **SKIVES** the act or an instance of skiving

SKIVER noun **SKIVERS** split sheepskin leather

SKIVING noun **SKIVINGS** an act of evading work, duty or school

SKIVVY noun **SKIVVIES** a servant, especially a woman, who does unpleasant household jobs ◻ verb **SKIVVIES, SKIVVYING, SKIVVIED** to work as, or as if as, a skivvy

SKIVY adj **SKIVIER, SKIVIEST** of or like someone who evades eg work, duty or school through laziness

SKOAL exclamation skol

SKOL exclamation hail!; a loud friendly toast before drinking

SKUA noun **SKUAS** any of various large predatory gull-like seabirds, native to Arctic and Antarctic waters, usually with dark brown plumage and pale underparts

SKULK verb **SKULKS, SKULKING, SKULKED** to sneak off out of the way

SKULKER noun **SKULKERS** someone who skulks

SKULKING noun **SKULKINGS** an act of sneaking off out of the way

SKULL noun **SKULLS** in vertebrates: the hard cartilaginous or bony framework of the head, including the cranium (which encloses the brain), face and jaws

SKULLCAP noun **SKULLCAPS** a small brimless cap fitting closely on the head

SKUNK noun **SKUNKS** a small American mammal related to the weasel, best known for the foul-smelling liquid which it squirts from musk glands at the base of its tail in order to deter predators

SKY noun **SKIES** the apparent dome of space in which the Sun, Moon and stars can be seen ◻ verb **SKIES, SKYING, SKIED** in cricket: to mishit (a ball) high into the air

SKYER noun **SKYERS** in cricket: a hit high into the air

SKYJACK verb **SKYJACKS, SKYJACKING, SKYJACKED** to hijack (an aircraft)

SKYJACKER noun **SKYJACKERS** someone who hijacks an aircraft

SKYJACKING noun **SKYJACKINGS** an act of hijacking an aircraft

SKYLAB noun **SKYLABS** any orbiting experimental space station

SKYLARK noun **SKYLARKS** a small lark, native to Europe and Asia, which inhabits open country and is known for its loud clear warbling song, performed in flight ◻ verb **SKYLARKS, SKYLARKING, SKYLARKED** to lark about; to frolic

SKYLARKING noun **SKYLARKINGS** an act of larking about

SKYLIGHT noun **SKYLIGHTS** a (usually small) window in a roof or ceiling

SKYLINE noun **SKYLINES** the outline of buildings, hills and trees seen against the sky; the horizon

SKYROCKET noun **SKYROCKETS** a firework that explodes very high in the sky ◻ verb **SKYROCKETS, SKYROCKETING, SKYROCKETED** to rise high and fast

SKYWARD adj directed towards the sky ◻ adverb towards the sky

SKYWARDS adverb skyward

SKYWAY noun **SKYWAYS** a route used by aircraft

SLAB noun **SLABS** a thick flat rectangular piece of stone, etc

SLABS *verb* **SLABS, SLABBING, SLABBED** to cut or make into slabs

SLACK *adj* **SLACKER, SLACKEST** limp or loose; not pulled or stretched tight ◻ *adverb* in a slack manner; partially ◻ *noun* **SLACKS** a loosely hanging part, especially of a rope ◻ *verb* **SLACKS, SLACKING, SLACKED** to become slower; to slow one's working pace through tiredness or laziness

SLACKEN *verb* **SLACKENS, SLACKENING, SLACKENED** to slack

SLACKER *noun* **SLACKERS** an idle person; a shirker

SLACKS *plural noun* a type of loose casual trousers, worn by both males and females

SLAG *noun* **SLAGS** the layer of waste material that forms on the surface of molten metal ore during smelting and refining ◻ *verb* **SLAGS, SLAGGING, SLAGGED** said of molten metal ore: to throw up or form into a surface layer of slag

SLAIN a past form of **slay**

SLAKE *verb* **SLAKES, SLAKING, SLAKED** to satisfy or quench (thirst, desire or anger)

SLALOM *noun* **SLALOMS** a race, on skis or in canoes, in and out of obstacles on a winding course designed to test tactical skill

SLAM *verb* **SLAMS, SLAMMING, SLAMMED** to shut loudly and with violence ◻ *noun* **SLAMS** the act or sound of slamming

SLAMMER *noun* **SLAMMERS** prison

SLANDER *noun* **SLANDERS** damaging defamation by spoken words, or by looks or gestures ◻ *verb* **SLANDERS, SLANDERING, SLANDERED** to speak about someone in such a way

SLANDERER *noun* **SLANDERERS** someone who slanders others

SLANG *noun* **SLANGS** language not accepted for dignified or formal use ◻ *verb* **SLANGS, SLANGING, SLANGED** to speak abusively to someone using coarse language

SLANGING *noun* **SLANGINGS** an act of speaking abusively to someone

SLANGY *adj* **SLANGIER, SLANGIEST** of, relating to or like slang

SLANT *verb* **SLANTS, SLANTING, SLANTED** to be at an angle as opposed to horizontal or vertical; to slope ◻ *noun* **SLANTS** a sloping position, surface or line

SLANTWAYS *adverb* slantwise

SLANTWISE *adverb* at an angle; slanting

SLAP *noun* **SLAPS** a blow with the palm of the hand or anything flat ◻ *verb* **SLAPS, SLAPPING, SLAPPED** to strike with the open hand or anything flat

SLAPSTICK *noun* **SLAPSTICKS** comedy in which the humour is derived from boisterous antics of all kinds

SLASH *verb* **SLASHES, SLASHING, SLASHED** to make sweeping cuts or cutting strokes, especially repeatedly ◻ *noun* **SLASHES** a sweeping cutting stroke

SLASHER *noun* **SLASHERS** a person or thing that slashes

SLASHING *noun* **SLASHINGS** a slash or slashes

SLAT *noun* **SLATS** a thin strip, especially of wood or metal

SLATE *noun* **SLATES** a shiny dark grey metamorphic rock that is easily split into thin flat layers, formed by the compression of clays and shales, and used for roofing and flooring ◻ *verb* **SLATES, SLATING, SLATED** to cover (a roof) with slates ◻ *adj* made of slate

SLATING *noun* **SLATINGS** a covering of slates

SLATTED *adj* having, or made up of, slats

SLATTERN *noun* **SLATTERNS** a woman of dirty or untidy appearance or habits; a slut

SLATY *adj* **SLATIER, SLATIEST** of or like slate

SLAUGHTER *noun* **SLAUGHTERS** the killing of animals, especially for food ◻ *verb* **SLAUGHTERS, SLAUGHTERING, SLAUGHTERED** to subject to slaughter

SLAVE *noun* **SLAVES** someone owned by and acting as servant to another, with no personal freedom ◻ *verb* **SLAVES, SLAVING, SLAVED** to work like or as a slave; to work hard and ceaselessly

SLAVER [1] *noun* **SLAVERS** someone involved in the buying and selling of slaves

SLAVER [2] *verb* **SLAVERS, SLAVERING, SLAVERED** to let spittle run from the mouth; to dribble

SLAVERER *noun* **SLAVERERS** a person or animal that slavers

SLAVERY *noun* **SLAVERIES** the state of being a slave

SLAVISH *adj* rigid or unwavering in following rules or instructions

SLAVISHLY *adverb* in a slavish way

SLAW *noun* **SLAWS** cabbage salad; coleslaw

SLAY *verb* **SLAYS, SLAYING, SLEW, SLAIN** to kill

SLAYER *noun* **SLAYERS** a person who slays

SLEAZE *noun* **SLEAZES** the condition or state of being sleazy

SLEAZILY *adverb* in a sleazy way

SLEAZY *adj* **SLEAZIER, SLEAZIEST** dirty and neglected-looking

SLED *noun* **SLEDS** a structure without wheels used for conveying goods, especially on snow ◻ *verb* **SLEDS, SLEDDING, SLEDDED** to convey someone or something by sled

SLEDDING *noun* **SLEDDINGS** an act of conveying someone or something by sled

SLEDGE *noun* **SLEDGES** a vehicle with runners for travelling on snow ◻ *verb* **SLEDGES, SLEDGING, SLEDGED** to travel by sledge

SLEDGER *noun* **SLEDGERS** someone who travels by or plays on a sledge

SLEDGING *noun* **SLEDGINGS** an act of travelling by sledge

SLEEK *adj* **SLEEKER, SLEEKEST** said of hair, fur, etc: smooth, soft and glossy ◻ *verb* **SLEEKS, SLEEKING, SLEEKED** to smooth (especially hair)

SLEEKLY *adverb* in a sleek way

SLEEKNESS *noun* **SLEEKNESSES** the quality or condition of being sleek

SLEEP *noun* **SLEEPS** in humans and many animals: a readily reversible state of natural unconsciousness during which the body's functional powers are restored, and physical movements are minimal ◻ *verb* **SLEEPS, SLEEPING, SLEPT** to rest in a state of sleep

SLEEPER *noun* **SLEEPERS** someone who sleeps, especially in a specified way

SLEEPILY *adverb* in a sleepy way

SLEEPLESS *adj* characterized by an inability to sleep

SLEEPY adj **SLEEPIER, SLEEPIEST** feeling the desire or need to sleep; drowsy

SLEET noun **SLEETS** rain mixed with snow and/or hail ▫ verb **SLEETS, SLEETING, SLEETED** to rain and snow simultaneously

SLEETY adj **SLEETIER, SLEETIEST** of or like sleet

SLEEVE noun **SLEEVES** the part of a garment that covers the arm

SLEEVED adj having sleeves

SLEEVING noun **SLEEVINGS** a tubular flexible insulation for bare conductor wires

SLEIGH noun **SLEIGHS** a large horse-drawn sledge ▫ verb **SLEIGHS, SLEIGHING, SLEIGHED** to travel by sleigh

SLEIGHT noun **SLEIGHTS** dexterity

SLENDER adj **SLENDERER, SLENDEREST** attractively slim

SLENDERLY adverb in a slender way

SLEPT past form of **sleep**

SLEUTH noun **SLEUTHS** a detective ▫ verb **SLEUTHS, SLEUTHING, SLEUTHED** to work as a detective

SLEW [1] a past form of **slay**

SLEW [2] verb **SLEWS, SLEWING, SLEWED** to turn about the axis ▫ noun **SLEWS** an instance of slewing

SLICE noun **SLICES** a thin broad piece, wedge or segment that is cut off ▫ verb **SLICES, SLICING, SLICED** to cut up into slices

SLICER noun **SLICERS** a person or machine that slices

SLICING noun **SLICINGS** an act of slicing

SLICK adj **SLICKER, SLICKEST** dishonestly or slyly clever ▫ verb **SLICKS, SLICKING, SLICKED** to smooth (especially hair) ▫ noun **SLICKS** a wide layer of spilled oil floating on the surface of water, often as a result of damage to or discharge from an oil tanker or pipelines, etc

SLICKER noun **SLICKERS** a sophisticated city-dweller

SLICKLY adverb in a slick way

SLICKNESS noun **SLICKNESSES** the state or condition of being slick

SLIDE verb **SLIDES, SLIDING, SLID** to move or cause to move or run smoothly along a surface ▫ noun **SLIDES** an apparatus for children to play on, usually with a ladder to climb up and a narrow sloping part to slide down

SLIDER noun **SLIDERS** a person or thing that slides

SLIDING noun **SLIDINGS** an act of moving or causing to move or run smoothly along a surface

SLIGHT adj **SLIGHTER, SLIGHTEST** small in extent, significance or seriousness; negligible ▫ verb **SLIGHTS, SLIGHTING, SLIGHTED** to insult someone by ignoring or dismissing them abruptly; to snub them ▫ noun **SLIGHTS** an insult by snubbing or showing neglect

SLIGHTING adj scornful or disrespectful

SLIGHTLY adverb to a small extent; in a small way

SLILY adverb slyly

SLIM adj **SLIMMER, SLIMMEST** said of people: attractively thin; slender ▫ verb **SLIMS, SLIMMING, SLIMMED** to make oneself slimmer, especially by diet and/or exercise

SLIME noun **SLIMES** any thin, unpleasantly slippery or gluey, mud-like substance ▫ verb **SLIMES, SLIMING, SLIMED** to smear or cover with slime

SLIMILY adverb in a slimy way

SLIMINESS noun **SLIMINESSES** the quality or condition of being slimy

SLIMLY adverb in a slim way

SLIMMER noun **SLIMMERS** someone who is trying to lose weight

SLIMMING noun **SLIMMINGS** the act of trying to lose weight

SLIMNESS noun **SLIMNESSES** the state or condition of being slim

SLIMY adj **SLIMIER, SLIMIEST** similar to, covered with or consisting of slime; exaggeratedly obedient or attentive

SLING noun **SLINGS** a cloth hoop that hangs from the neck to support an injured arm ▫ verb **SLINGS, SLINGING, SLUNG** to throw, especially with force; to fling

SLINGBACK noun **SLINGBACKS** a shoe with no cover for the heel, just a strap fastening round it to hold the shoe on

SLINGSHOT noun **SLINGSHOTS** a catapult

SLINK verb **SLINKS, SLINKING, SLUNK** to go or move sneakingly or ashamedly ▫ noun **SLINKS** a slinking gait

SLINKY adj **SLINKIER, SLINKIEST** said of clothing: attractively close-fitting

SLIP [1] verb **SLIPS, SLIPPING, SLIPPED** to lose one's footing and slide accidentally

SLIP [2] noun **SLIPS** a small strip or piece of paper

SLIPCASE noun **SLIPCASES** a boxlike case for a book or set of books, open on one side and leaving the spine or spines visible

SLIPPAGE noun **SLIPPAGES** an act or instance of slipping

SLIPPER noun **SLIPPERS** a soft loose laceless indoor shoe ▫ verb **SLIPPERS, SLIPPERING, SLIPPERED** to beat with a slipper

SLIPPERED adj wearing a slipper or slippers

SLIPPERY adj **SLIPPERIER, SLIPPERIEST** so smooth, wet, etc as to cause or allow slipping

SLIPPY adj **SLIPPIER, SLIPPIEST** said of a thing: liable to slip; slippery

SLIPSHOD adj untidy and careless; carelessly done

SLIPWARE noun **SLIPWARES** pottery that has been decorated with slip (a creamy mixture of clay and water)

SLIPWAY noun **SLIPWAYS** a ramp in a dock or shipyard that slopes into water, for launching boats

SLIT noun **SLITS** a long narrow cut or opening ▫ verb **SLITS, SLITTING, SLIT** to cut a slit in something, especially lengthwise

SLITHER verb **SLITHERS, SLITHERING, SLITHERED** to slide or slip unsteadily while walking, especially on ice ▫ noun **SLITHERS** a slithering movement

SLITHERY adj **SLITHERIER, SLITHERIEST** slippery

SLITTER noun **SLITTERS** a person or thing that slits

SLIVER noun **SLIVERS** a long thin piece cut or broken off ▫ verb **SLIVERS, SLIVERING, SLIVERED** to break or cut into slivers

SLIVOVITZ noun **SLIVOVITZES** a dry colourless plum brandy from E Europe

SLOB noun **SLOBS** a lazy, untidy and slovenly person ▫ verb **SLOBS, SLOBBING, SLOBBED** to move or behave in a lazy, untidy or slovenly way

SLOBBER verb **SLOBBERS, SLOBBERING, SLOBBERED** to let saliva run from the mouth; to dribble or slaver ▫ noun **SLOBBERS** dribbled saliva

SLOBBERY adj **SLOBBERIER,**

For longer words, see *The Chambers Dictionary*

SLOBBERIEST of or characterized by slobber

SLOBBISH *adj* of or like a slob

SLOBBY *adj* **SLOBBIER, SLOBBIEST** of or like a slob

SLOE *noun* **SLOES** the fruit of the blackthorn bush

SLOG *verb* **SLOGS, SLOGGING, SLOGGED** to hit hard and wildly □ *noun* **SLOGS** a hard wild blow or stroke

SLOGAN *noun* **SLOGANS** a phrase used to identify a group or organization, or to advertise a product

SLOGGER *noun* **SLOGGERS** someone who slogs

SLOOP *noun* **SLOOPS** a single-masted sailing boat with fore-and-aft sails

SLOP *verb* **SLOPS, SLOPPING, SLOPPED** to splash or cause to splash or spill violently □ *noun* **SLOPS** spilled liquid; a puddle

SLOPE *noun* **SLOPES** a slanting surface; an incline □ *verb* **SLOPES, SLOPING, SLOPED** to rise or fall at an angle

SLOPPILY *adverb* in a sloppy way

SLOPPY *adj* **SLOPPIER, SLOPPIEST** wet or muddy

SLOSH *verb* **SLOSHES, SLOSHING, SLOSHED** to splash or cause to splash or spill noisily □ *noun* **SLOSHES** the sound of splashing or spilling

SLOSHED *adj* drunk; intoxicated

SLOT *noun* **SLOTS** a long narrow rectangular opening into which something is fitted or inserted □ *verb* **SLOTS, SLOTTING, SLOTTED** to make a slot in

SLOTH *noun* **SLOTHS** a herbivorous tree-dwelling mammal with long slender limbs and hook-like claws, noted for its very slow movements

SLOTHFUL *adj* lazy; inactive

SLOUCH *verb* **SLOUCHES, SLOUCHING, SLOUCHED** to sit, stand or walk with a tired, lazy or drooping posture □ *noun* **SLOUCHES** such a posture

SLOUCHER *noun* **SLOUCHERS** someone who slouches

SLOUGH *noun* **SLOUGHS** any outer part of an animal cast off or moulted, especially a snake's dead skin □ *verb* **SLOUGHS, SLOUGHING, SLOUGHED** to shed (eg a dead skin)

SLOVEN *noun* **SLOVENS** someone who is carelessly or untidily

dressed; a person of shoddy appearance

SLOVENLY *adj* **SLOVENLIER, SLOVENLIEST** careless, untidy or dirty in appearance

SLOW *adj* **SLOWER, SLOWEST** having little speed or pace; not moving fast or swiftly □ *adverb* in a slow manner □ *verb* **SLOWS, SLOWING, SLOWED** to reduce or make something reduce speed, pace or rate of progress

SLOWCOACH *noun* **SLOWCOACHES** someone who moves or works at a slow pace

SLOWLY *adverb* in a slow way; not quickly

SLOWNESS *noun* **SLOWNESSES** the state or condition of being slow

SLOWWORM *noun* **SLOWWORMS** a harmless species of legless lizard with a small mouth and a smooth shiny brownish-grey to coppery body

SLUB *verb* **SLUBS, SLUBBING, SLUBBED** to twist (fibre) after carding, so as to prepare for spinning □ *noun* **SLUBS** a piece of fibre twisted in this way

SLUBBER *noun* **SLUBBERS** a person or thing that slubs

SLUBBY *adj* **SLUBBIER, SLUBBIEST** lumpy or knobbly in texture

SLUDGE *noun* **SLUDGES** soft slimy mud or mire

SLUDGY *adj* **SLUDGIER, SLUDGIEST** of or like sludge

SLUE *verb* **SLUES, SLUEING, SLUED** to slew □ *noun* **SLUES** a slew

SLUG [1] *noun* **SLUGS** any of various terrestrial molluscs, including many garden pests, belonging to the same class as snails, but having a long fleshy body and little or no shell

SLUG [2] *verb* **SLUGS, SLUGGING, SLUGGED** to strike with a heavy blow

SLUGGARD *noun* **SLUGGARDS** a habitually lazy or inactive person

SLUGGER *noun* **SLUGGERS** someone who slugs another person

SLUGGISH *adj* unenergetic; habitually lazy or inactive

SLUICE *noun* **SLUICES** a channel or drain for water □ *verb* **SLUICES, SLUICING, SLUICED** to let out or drain by means of a sluice

SLUM *noun* **SLUMS** a run-down, dirty and usually overcrowded

house □ *verb* **SLUMS, SLUMMING, SLUMMED** to visit an area of slums

SLUMBER *noun* **SLUMBERS** sleep □ *verb* **SLUMBERS, SLUMBERING, SLUMBERED** to sleep, especially lightly

SLUMBERER *noun* **SLUMBERERS** someone who slumbers

SLUMBERING *noun* **SLUMBERINGS** an act of sleeping

SLUMBROUS *adj* inviting or causing sleep

SLUMMY *adj* **SLUMMIER, SLUMMIEST** like a slum; run-down or squalid

SLUMP *verb* **SLUMPS, SLUMPING, SLUMPED** to drop or sink suddenly and heavily, eg with tiredness □ *noun* **SLUMPS** an act or instance of slumping

SLUNG past form of **sling**

SLUNK past form of **slink**

SLUR *verb* **SLURS, SLURRING, SLURRED** to pronounce (words) indistinctly, eg through drunkenness □ *noun* **SLURS** a disparaging remark intended to damage a reputation

SLURP *verb* **SLURPS, SLURPING, SLURPED** to eat or drink noisily with a sucking action □ *noun* **SLURPS** a slurping sound

SLURRY *noun* **SLURRIES** a thin paste or semi-fluid mixture

SLUSH *noun* **SLUSHES** half-melted snow

SLUSHY *adj* **SLUSHIER, SLUSHIEST** like or consisting of slush

SLUT *noun* **SLUTS** a woman who regularly engages in casual sex

SLUTTISH *adj* of or like a slut

SLY *adj* **SLYER, SLYEST** said of people: clever; cunning or wily

SLYLY *adverb* in a sly way

SLYNESS *noun* **SLYNESSES** the quality or condition of being sly

SMA *adj* a Scots word for *small*

SMACK *verb* **SMACKS, SMACKING, SMACKED** to slap loudly and smartly, especially with the hand □ *noun* **SMACKS** an act, or the sound, of slapping loudly and smartly, especially with the hand

SMACKER *noun* **SMACKERS** a loud enthusiastic kiss

SMACKING *noun* **SMACKINGS** an act of slapping, especially with the hand

SMALL *adj* **SMALLER, SMALLEST**

little in size or quantity □ *noun*
SMALLS the narrow part,
especially of the back □ *adverb* on
a small scale

SMALLISH *adj* somewhat small

SMALLNESS *noun* the quality or
condition of being small

SMALLPOX *noun* **SMALLPOXES** a
highly contagious viral disease,
characterized by fever, vomiting,
backache and a rash that usually
leaves permanent pitted scars
(pocks) on the skin

SMARM *verb* **SMARMS,
SMARMING, SMARMED** to be
exaggeratedly and insincerely
flattering; to fawn ingratiatingly
□ *noun* **SMARMS** exaggerated or
insincere flattery

SMARMILY *adverb* in a smarmy
way

SMARMY *adj* **SMARMIER,
SMARMIEST** ingratiatingly
flattering or respectful

SMART *adj* **SMARTER, SMARTEST**
neat, trim and well-dressed □ *verb*
SMARTS, SMARTING, SMARTED
to feel or be the cause of a sharp
stinging pain □ *noun* **SMARTS** a
sharp stinging pain □ *adverb* in a
smart manner

SMARTEN *verb* **SMARTENS,
SMARTENING, SMARTENED** to
make or become smarter; to
brighten up

SMARTIE *noun* **SMARTIES** a smarty

SMARTLY *adverb* in a smart way;
neatly

SMARTNESS *noun*
SMARTNESSES the quality or
condition of being smart

SMARTY *noun* **SMARTIES** a know-
all

SMASH *verb* **SMASHES,
SMASHING, SMASHED** to break or
shatter violently into pieces; to
destroy or be destroyed in this way
□ *noun* **SMASHES** an act, or the
sound, of smashing □ *adverb* with
a smashing sound

SMASHED *adj* extremely drunk

SMASHER *noun* **SMASHERS**
someone or something very much
liked or admired

SMASHING *adj* excellent; splendid

SMATTER *noun* **SMATTERS** a
smattering □ *verb* **SMATTERS,
SMATTERING, SMATTERED** to
have a superficial knowledge; to
dabble

SMATTERING *noun*
SMATTERINGS a few scraps of
superficial knowledge

SMEAR *verb* **SMEARS,
SMEARING, SMEARED** to spread
(something sticky or oily) thickly
over (a surface) □ *noun* **SMEARS** a
greasy mark or patch

SMEARILY *adverb* greasily

SMEARY *adj* **SMEARIER,
SMEARIEST** sticky or greasy;
showing smears

SMECTIC *adj* said of liquid
crystals: having molecular layers
oriented in parallel planes

SMEGMA *noun* **SMEGMAS** a thick
white secretion that accumulates
underneath the foreskin of the
penis

SMELL *noun* **SMELLS** the sense
that allows different odours to be
recognized by specialized
receptors in the mucous
membranes of the nose □ *verb*
**SMELLS, SMELLING, SMELT,
SMELLED** to recognize (a
substance) by its odour

SMELLER *noun* **SMELLERS** a
person or animal that can
recognize substances by their
odour

SMELLY *adj* **SMELLIER,
SMELLIEST** having a strong or
unpleasant smell

SMELT[1] *verb* **SMELTS, SMELTING,
SMELTED** to process (an ore),
especially by melting it, in order to
separate out the crude metal

SMELT[2] *noun* **SMELTS, SMELT** any
of various small marine and
freshwater fish of the salmon
family, including several edible
species, with a slender silvery body
and a jutting lower jaw

SMELT[3] a past form of **smell**

SMELTER *noun* **SMELTERS** a
person whose work is smelting
metal

SMELTING *noun* **SMELTINGS** an
act or an instance of smelting ore

SMIDGEN *noun* **SMIDGENS** a very
small amount

SMIDGEON *noun* **SMIDGEONS** a
smidgen

SMIDGIN *noun* **SMIDGINS** a
smidgen

SMILAX *noun* **SMILAXES** a
climbing plant of the lily family,
with net-veined leaves

SMILE *verb* **SMILES, SMILING,
SMILED** to turn up the corners of
the mouth, often showing the
teeth, usually as an expression of
pleasure, favour or amusement,
but sometimes as an expression of
slight contempt or displeasure

□ *noun* **SMILES** an act or way of
smiling

SMILER *noun* **SMILERS** someone
who smiles

SMILEY *noun* **SMILEYS** in
computing: a symbol created from
a number of symbols on the
keyboard (eg :-/) intended to look
like a smiling face (sideways on),
used to indicate irony or pleasure

SMILING *noun* **SMILINGS** an act of
turning up the corners of the
mouth, often showing the teeth

SMILINGLY *adverb* in a smiling
way; with a smile

SMIRCH *verb* **SMIRCHES,
SMIRCHING, SMIRCHED** to make
dirty; to soil or stain □ *noun*
SMIRCHES a stain

SMIRK *verb* **SMIRKS, SMIRKING,
SMIRKED** to smile in a self-satisfied,
affected or foolish manner □ *noun*
SMIRKS such a smile

SMITE *verb* **SMITES, SMITING,
SMOTE, SMITTEN** to strike or beat
with a heavy blow or blows

SMITER *noun* **SMITERS** someone
who smites

SMITH *noun* **SMITHS** a person who
makes articles in metal

SMITHY *noun* **SMITHIES** a
blacksmith's workshop

SMITTEN *adj* in love; obsessed

SMOCK *noun* **SMOCKS** any loose
shirt-like garment, usually of
coarse cloth, worn over other
clothes for protection especially by
artists, etc

SMOCKING *noun* **SMOCKINGS**
honeycomb-patterned stitching
used on gathered or tucked
material for decoration

SMOG *noun* **SMOGS** a mixture of
smoke and fog, especially in urban
or industrial areas, produced by
the burning of coal or other fuels

SMOGGY *adj* **SMOGGIER,
SMOGGIEST** foggy and smoky

SMOKABLE *adj* fit or able to be
smoked

SMOKE *noun* **SMOKES** a visible
cloud given off by a burning
substance, and consisting of tiny
particles of carbon dispersed in a
gas or a mixture of gases, eg air
□ *verb* **SMOKES, SMOKING,
SMOKED** to give off smoke, visible
fumes or vapours

SMOKED *adj* cured or treated with
smoke

SMOKELESS *adj* said of a fuel:
giving off little or no smoke when
burned, eg coke

SMOKER noun **SMOKERS** someone who smokes tobacco products

SMOKILY adverb in a smoky way

SMOKINESS noun **SMOKINESSES** the state of being smoky

SMOKING noun **SMOKINGS** the practice of inhaling the fumes from burning cigarettes or other forms of tobacco, known to be a causative factor in the development of several diseases, especially lung cancer

SMOKY adj **SMOKIER, SMOKIEST** giving out much or excessive smoke

SMOLT noun **SMOLTS** a young salmon migrating from fresh water to the sea

SMOOCH verb **SMOOCHES, SMOOCHING, SMOOCHED** to kiss and cuddle ◻ noun **SMOOCHES** the act of smooching

SMOOTH adj **SMOOTHER, SMOOTHEST** having an even regular surface; not rough, coarse, bumpy or wavy ◻ verb **SMOOTHS, SMOOTHING, SMOOTHED** to make something smooth ◻ adverb smoothly ◻ noun **SMOOTHES** the act or process of smoothing

SMOOTHIE noun **SMOOTHIES** a person who is very elegant, charming or suave in dress or manner, especially one excessively or insincerely so

SMOOTHLY adverb in a smooth way; regularly; evenly

SMORZANDO adverb gradually fading away

SMOTE a past form of **smite**

SMOTHER verb **SMOTHERS, SMOTHERING, SMOTHERED** to kill with or die from lack of air, especially with an obstruction over the mouth and nose; to suffocate ◻ noun **SMOTHERS** thick floating dust

SMOTHERER noun **SMOTHERERS** a person or thing that smothers

SMOTHERY adj smothering

SMOULDER verb **SMOULDERS, SMOULDERING, SMOULDERED** to burn slowly or without flame; said of emotions: to linger on in a suppressed state ◻ noun **SMOULDERS** a smouldering fire or emotion

SMOULDERING noun **SMOULDERINGS** an act of burning slowly or without flame

SMUDGE noun **SMUDGES** a mark or blot caused or spread by rubbing ◻ verb **SMUDGES, SMUDGING, SMUDGED** to make a smudge on or of something

SMUDGER noun **SMUDGERS** someone who smudges something

SMUDGILY adverb in a smudgy way

SMUDGY adj **SMUDGIER, SMUDGIEST** marked, blotted or blurred

SMUG adj **SMUGGER, SMUGGEST** arrogantly self-complacent or self-satisfied

SMUGGLE verb **SMUGGLES, SMUGGLING, SMUGGLED** to take (goods) into or out of a country secretly and illegally, eg to avoid paying duty

SMUGGLER noun **SMUGGLERS** someone who smuggles goods, especially drugs, cigarettes or alchohol, into a state

SMUGGLING noun **SMUGGLINGS** an act of taking (goods) into or out of a country secretly and illegally

SMUGLY adverb arrogantly

SMUGNESS noun **SMUGNESSES** the quality or condition of being smug; arrogance

SMUT noun **SMUTS** soot ◻ verb **SMUTS, SMUTTING, SMUTTED** to dirty or affect with smut

SMUTTILY adverb in a smutty way; dirtily

SMUTTY adj **SMUTTIER, SMUTTIEST** dirtied by smut; mildly obscene

SNACK noun **SNACKS** a light meal often taken quickly, or a bite to eat between meals ◻ verb **SNACKS, SNACKING, SNACKED** to eat a snack

SNAFFLE noun **SNAFFLES** a simple bridle-bit for a horse ◻ verb **SNAFFLES, SNAFFLING, SNAFFLED** to fit (a horse) with a snaffle

SNAFU noun **SNAFUS** chaos

SNAG noun **SNAGS** a problem or drawback; a protruding sharp or jagged edge ◻ verb **SNAGS, SNAGGING, SNAGGED** to catch or tear on a snag

SNAGGY adj **SNAGGIER, SNAGGIEST** likely to snag

SNAIL noun **SNAILS** any of numerous marine, freshwater, and terrestrial molluscs belonging to the same class as slugs, but carrying a coiled or conical shell on their backs, into which the whole body can be withdrawn

SNAKE noun **SNAKES** any one of numerous species of a carnivorous reptile which has a long narrow body covered with scaly skin, and a forked tongue, and that differs from lizards in that it lacks limbs, moveable eyelids or visible ears ◻ verb **SNAKES, SNAKING, SNAKED** to move windingly or follow a winding course

SNAKEBIRD noun **SNAKEBIRDS** a wryneck

SNAKEBITE noun **SNAKEBITES** the wound or poisoned condition caused by the bite of a venomous snake

SNAKELIKE adj like a snake

SNAKILY adverb in a snaky way

SNAKINESS noun **SNAKINESSES** the state of being snaky

SNAKY adj **SNAKIER, SNAKIEST** like a snake, especially long, thin and flexible or winding

SNAP verb **SNAPS, SNAPPING, SNAPPED** to break suddenly and cleanly with a sharp cracking noise ◻ noun **SNAPS** the act or sound of snapping

SNAPPER noun **SNAPPERS** a kind of food fish found in tropical seas

SNAPPILY adverb in a snappy way

SNAPPING noun **SNAPPINGS** an act of breaking suddenly and cleanly with a sharp cracking noise

SNAPPY adj **SNAPPIER, SNAPPIEST** irritable; inclined to snap; lively

SNAPSHOT noun **SNAPSHOTS** a photograph, especially one taken spontaneously and with a hand-held camera

SNARE noun **SNARES** an animal trap, especially one with a string or wire noose to catch the animal's foot ◻ verb **SNARES, SNARING, SNARED** to catch, trap or entangle in, or as if in, a snare

SNARER noun **SNARERS** a person or thing that snares eg animals

SNARING noun **SNARINGS** an act of catching, trapping or entangling in, or as if in, a snare

SNARL verb **SNARLS, SNARLING, SNARLED** said of an animal: to growl angrily, showing the teeth ◻ noun **SNARLS** an act of snarling

SNARLER noun **SNARLERS** a person or animal that snarls

SNARLING noun **SNARLINGS** an act of growling angrily, showing the teeth

SNARLY adj **SNARLIER, SNARLIEST** likely to growl angrily

SNATCH verb **SNATCHES, SNATCHING, SNATCHED** to seize or grab suddenly ▫ noun **SNATCHES** an act of snatching

SNATCHER noun **SNATCHERS** someone who snatches

SNATCHILY adverb irregularly

SNATCHY adj **SNATCHIER, SNATCHIEST** irregular

SNAZZY adj **SNAZZIER, SNAZZIEST** fashionably and often flashily smart or elegant

SNEAK verb **SNEAKS, SNEAKING, SNUCK, SNEAKED** to move, go or depart quietly or unnoticed ▫ noun **SNEAKS** someone who sneaks; a tell-tale

SNEAKERS plural noun sports shoes; soft-soled, usually canvas, shoes

SNEAKILY adverb in a sneaky way

SNEAKING adj said of a feeling, etc: slight but not easily suppressed

SNEAKY adj **SNEAKIER, SNEAKIEST** done or operating with secretive unfairness or dishonesty; underhand

SNECK noun **SNECKS** a latch; a door-catch ▫ verb **SNECKS, SNECKING, SNECKED** to fasten with a sneck

SNEER verb **SNEERS, SNEERING, SNEERED** to show scorn or contempt, especially by drawing the top lip up at one side ▫ noun **SNEERS** an act of sneering

SNEERER noun **SNEERERS** someone who sneers

SNEERING noun **SNEERINGS** an act of showing scorn or contempt, especially by drawing the top lip up at one side

SNEEZE verb **SNEEZES, SNEEZING, SNEEZED** to blow air out through the nose suddenly, violently and involuntarily, especially because of irritation in the nostrils ▫ noun **SNEEZES** an act or the sound of sneezing

SNEEZER noun **SNEEZERS** someone who sneezes

SNEEZING noun **SNEEZINGS** an act of blowing air out through the nose suddenly, violently and involuntarily

SNEEZY adj **SNEEZIER, SNEEZIEST** liable to sneeze

SNIB noun **SNIBS** a small bolt or catch for a door or window-sash ▫ verb **SNIBS, SNIBBING, SNIBBED** to fasten with a snib

SNICK noun **SNICKS** a small cut; a nick ▫ verb **SNICKS, SNICKING,**

SNICKED to make a small cut in something

SNICKER verb **SNICKERS, SNICKERING, SNICKERED** to snigger ▫ noun **SNICKERS** a giggle

SNIDE adj **SNIDER, SNIDEST** expressing criticism or disapproval in an offensive, sly or malicious manner

SNIDELY adverb in a snide way

SNIDENESS noun **SNIDENESSES** the state of being snide

SNIFF verb **SNIFFS, SNIFFING, SNIFFED** to draw in air with the breath through the nose ▫ noun **SNIFFS** an act or the sound of sniffing

SNIFFER noun **SNIFFERS** a person or animal that sniffs

SNIFFILY adverb in a sniffy way; with a sniff

SNIFFING noun **SNIFFINGS** an act of drawing in air with the breath through the nose

SNIFFLE verb **SNIFFLES, SNIFFLING, SNIFFLED** to sniff repeatedly, eg because of having a cold ▫ noun **SNIFFLES** an act or the sound of sniffling

SNIFFLER noun **SNIFFLERS** someone who sniffles

SNIFFY adj **SNIFFIER, SNIFFIEST** contemptuous or disdainful

SNIFTER noun **SNIFTERS** a drink of alcohol, especially alcoholic spirit; a tipple or dram

SNIGGER verb **SNIGGERS, SNIGGERING, SNIGGERED** to laugh in a stifled or suppressed way, often derisively or mockingly ▫ noun **SNIGGERS** a stifled or suppressed laugh

SNIGGERER noun **SNIGGERERS** someone who sniggers

SNIGGERING noun **SNIGGERINGS** an act of laughing in a stifled or suppressed way

SNIP verb **SNIPS, SNIPPING, SNIPPED** to cut, especially with a single quick action or actions, with scissors ▫ noun **SNIPS** an act or the action of snipping

SNIPE noun **SNIPES** any of various wading birds with a long straight bill, relatively short legs and mottled and barred dark brown plumage ▫ verb **SNIPES, SNIPING, SNIPED** to shoot snipe for sport

SNIPER noun **SNIPERS** someone who shoots from a concealed position

SNIPING noun **SNIPINGS** an act of shooting snipe for sport

SNIPPER noun **SNIPPERS** someone who snips

SNIPPET noun **SNIPPETS** a scrap, eg of information, news, etc

SNIPPETY adj **SNIPPETIER, SNIPPETIEST** trivial; fragmentary

SNIPPING noun **SNIPPINGS** a piece snipped off from a larger item; a clipping

SNITCH noun **SNITCHES** the nose ▫ verb **SNITCHES, SNITCHING, SNITCHED** to betray others; to inform on them

SNITCHER noun **SNITCHERS** an informer

SNIVEL verb **SNIVELS, SNIVELLING, SNIVELLED** to whine or complain tearfully ▫ noun **SNIVELS** an act of snivelling

SNIVELLER noun **SNIVELLERS** someone who snivels

SNIVELLY adj liable to snivel

SNOB noun **SNOBS** someone who places too high a value on social status, treating those higher up the social ladder obsequiously, and those lower down the social ladder with condescension and contempt

SNOBBERY noun **SNOBBERIES** snobbishness

SNOBBISH adj characteristic of a snob

SNOBBISM noun **SNOBBISMS** snobbish behaviour or opinions

SNOBBY adj **SNOBBIER, SNOBBIEST** snobbish

SNOEK noun **SNOEKS** a snook

SNOG verb **SNOGS, SNOGGING, SNOGGED** to embrace, kiss and cuddle ▫ noun **SNOGS** a kiss and cuddle

SNOOD noun **SNOODS** a decorative pouch of netting or fabric worn by women on the back of the head, keeping the hair in a bundle

SNOOK noun **SNOOKS** any of several marine fishes

SNOOKER noun **SNOOKERS** a game played with cues, 15 red balls, one white cue ball and six balls of other colours, the object being to use the white cue ball to knock the non-white balls in a certain order into the pockets on the corners and sides of a large cloth-covered table, and to gain more points than the opponent ▫ verb **SNOOKERS, SNOOKERING, SNOOKERED** in snooker: to force (an opponent) to attempt to hit an obstructed target ball

SNOOP verb **SNOOPS,**

SNOOPING, SNOOPED to go about sneakingly and inquisitively; to pry ▢ *noun* **SNOOPS** an act of snooping

SNOOPER *noun* **SNOOPERS** a person who snoops

SNOOPY *adj* **SNOOPIER, SNOOPIEST** liable to snoop; prying

SNOOT *noun* **SNOOTS** the nose

SNOOTILY *adverb* haughtily

SNOOTY *adj* **SNOOTIER, SNOOTIEST** haughty; snobbish

SNOOZE *verb* **SNOOZES, SNOOZING, SNOOZED** to sleep lightly; to doze ▢ *noun* **SNOOZES** a brief period of light sleeping; a nap

SNOOZER *noun* **SNOOZERS** someone who snoozes

SNOOZY *adj* **SNOOZIER, SNOOZIEST** liable to snooze; sleepy

SNORE *verb* **SNORES, SNORING, SNORED** to breathe heavily and with a snorting sound while sleeping ▢ *noun* **SNORES** an act or the sound of snoring

SNORER *noun* **SNORERS** someone who snores

SNORKEL *noun* **SNORKELS** a rigid tube through which air from above the surface of water can be drawn into the mouth while one is swimming just below the surface

SNORT *verb* **SNORTS, SNORTING, SNORTED** said especially of animals: to force air violently and noisily out through the nostrils; to make a similar noise while taking air in ▢ *noun* **SNORTS** an act or the sound of snorting

SNORTER *noun* **SNORTERS** someone or something that snorts

SNORTING *noun* **SNORTINGS** an act of forcing air violently and noisily out through the nostrils

SNOT *noun* **SNOTS** mucus of the nose

SNOTTILY *adverb* in a snotty way

SNOTTY *adj* **SNOTTIER, SNOTTIEST** covered or messy with nasal mucus; haughty or stand-offish

SNOUT *noun* **SNOUTS** the projecting nose and mouth parts of certain animals, eg the pig

SNOUTED *adj* having a snout

SNOUTY *adj* **SNOUTIER, SNOUTIEST** resembling a snout

SNOW *noun* **SNOWS** precipitation in the form of aggregations of ice crystals falling to the ground in soft white flakes, or lying on the ground as a soft white mass ▢ *verb* **SNOWS, SNOWING, SNOWED** said of snow: to fall

SNOWBALL *noun* **SNOWBALLS** a small mass of snow pressed hard together, often used for fun as a missile ▢ *verb* **SNOWBALLS, SNOWBALLING, SNOWBALLED** to throw snowballs at someone or something

SNOWBERRY *noun* **SNOWBERRIES** any of various deciduous shrubs native to N America and W China, especially a N American species with simple leaves, small pinkish flowers and white spherical berry-like fruits

SNOWBOARD *noun* **SNOWBOARDS** a board resembling a skateboard without wheels, used on snow and guided with movements of the feet and body

SNOWBOUND *adj* shut in or prevented from travelling because of heavy falls of snow

SNOWCAP *noun* **SNOWCAPS** a cap of snow, as on the polar regions or a mountain-top

SNOWDRIFT *noun* **SNOWDRIFTS** a bank of snow blown together by the wind

SNOWDROP *noun* **SNOWDROPS** a bulbous early-flowering perennial plant with narrow strap-shaped bluish-green leaves and small solitary drooping white bell-shaped flowers

SNOWFALL *noun* **SNOWFALLS** a fall of snow

SNOWFIELD *noun* **SNOWFIELDS** a wide expanse of snow, especially one that is permanent

SNOWFLAKE *noun* **SNOWFLAKES** any of the single small feathery clumps of crystals of frozen water vapour that make up snow

SNOWILY *adverb* in a snowy way

SNOWINESS *noun* **SNOWINESSES** the state of being snowy

SNOWLINE *noun* **SNOWLINES** the level or height on a mountain or other upland area above which there is a permanent covering of snow, or where snow accumulates seasonally

SNOWMAN *noun* **SNOWMEN** a figure, resembling a person, made from packed snow

SNOWSHOE *noun* **SNOWSHOES** either of a pair of racket-like frameworks strapped to the feet for walking over deep snow

SNOWSTORM *noun* **SNOWSTORMS** a heavy fall of snow, especially accompanied by a strong gale

SNOWY *adj* **SNOWIER, SNOWIEST** abounding or covered with snow

SNUB *verb* **SNUBS, SNUBBING, SNUBBED** to insult by openly ignoring, rejecting or otherwise showing contempt ▢ *noun* **SNUBS** an act of snubbing ▢ *adj* **SNUBBER, SNUBBEST** short and flat; blunt

SNUBBING *noun* **SNUBBINGS** an act of insulting by openly ignoring, rejecting or otherwise showing contempt

SNUBBY *adj* **SNUBBIER, SNUBBIEST** inclined to snub or check

SNUCK a past form of **sneak**

SNUFF [1] *noun* **SNUFFS** powdered tobacco for inhaling through the nose

SNUFF [2] *verb* **SNUFFS, SNUFFING, SNUFFED** to snip off the burnt part of the wick of (a candle or lamp) ▢ *noun* **SNUFFS** the burnt part of the wick of a lamp or candle

SNUFFBOX *noun* **SNUFFBOXES** a small and often decorative lidded box, usually made of metal, for containing snuff

SNUFFER *noun* **SNUFFERS** a device with a cap-shaped part for extinguishing candles

SNUFFLE *verb* **SNUFFLES, SNUFFLING, SNUFFLED** to breathe, especially breathe in, through a partially blocked nose ▢ *noun* **SNUFFLES** an act or the sound of snuffling

SNUFFLER *noun* **SNUFFLERS** a person or animal that snuffles

SNUFFLING *noun* **SNUFFLINGS** an act of breathing, especially breathing in, through a partially blocked nose

SNUFFY *adj* **SNUFFIER, SNUFFIEST** similar to, smelling of or soiled with snuff

SNUG *adj* **SNUGGER, SNUGGEST** warm, cosy and comfortable ▢ *noun* **SNUGS** a snuggery

SNUGGERY *noun* **SNUGGERIES** a small comfortable room or compartment in a pub

SNUGGLE *verb* **SNUGGLES, SNUGGLING, SNUGGLED** to settle oneself into a position of warmth and comfort

SNUGLY *adverb* cosily

SNUGNESS *noun* **SNUGNESSES** the state of being snug

SNY *noun* **SNIES** a side channel of a river

SO [1] *adverb* to such an extent □ *conj* therefore; thereafter □ *adj* the case; true

SO [2] *noun* **SOS** soh

SOAK *verb* **SOAKS, SOAKING, SOAKED** to stand or leave to stand in a liquid for some time □ *noun* **SOAKS** an act of soaking

SOAKAGE *noun* **SOAKAGES** liquid that has percolated

SOAKAWAY *noun* **SOAKAWAYS** a depression in the ground into which water percolates

SOAKED *adj* drenched; very wet (eg because of rain)

SOAKER *noun* **SOAKERS** a person or thing that soaks

SOAKING *noun* **SOAKINGS** an act of standing or leaving to stand in a liquid for some time

SOAKINGLY *adverb* in a soaking way

SOAP *noun* **SOAPS** a sodium or potassium salt of a fatty acid that is soluble in water that is used for washing □ *verb* **SOAPS, SOAPING, SOAPED** to apply soap to something

SOAPBOX *noun* **SOAPBOXES** a crate for packing soap

SOAPILY *adverb* in a soapy way

SOAPINESS *noun* **SOAPINESSES** the state or condition of being soapy

SOAPSTONE *noun* **SOAPSTONES** a soft usually grey or brown variety of the mineral talc, widely used for ornamental carvings

SOAPSUDS *plural noun* soapy water, especially when frothy

SOAPWORT *noun* **SOAPWORTS** a tall herb, native to Europe, with pink or white flowers, and whose roots and leaves contain saponin

SOAPY *adj* **SOAPIER, SOAPIEST** like soap; covered with soap

SOAR *verb* **SOARS, SOARING, SOARED** to rise or fly high into the air

SOARING *noun* **SOARINGS** an act of soaring in the sky

SOARINGLY *adverb* in a soaring way

SOB *verb* **SOBS, SOBBING, SOBBED** to cry uncontrollably with intermittent gulps for breath □ *noun* **SOBS** a gulp for breath between bouts of crying

SOBBING *noun* **SOBBINGS** an act of crying uncontrollably with intermittent gulps for breath

SOBBINGLY *adverb* in a sobbing way; while sobbing

SOBER *adj* **SOBERER, SOBEREST** not at all drunk; serious, solemn or restrained □ *verb* **SOBERS, SOBERING, SOBERED** to become, or make someone, quieter, less excited, etc

SOBERING *adj* causing someone to become serious or thoughtful

SOBERLY *adverb* in a sober way

SOBRIETY *noun* **SOBRIETIES** the state of being sober, especially not drunk

SOBRIQUET *noun* **SOBRIQUETS** a nickname

SOC *noun* **SOCS** historically, the right of holding a local court

SOCA *noun* **SOCAS** a type of Caribbean calypso incorporating elements of American soul music

SOCCER *noun* **SOCCERS** the game of football

SOCIABLE *adj* fond of the company of others; friendly

SOCIABLY *adverb* in a sociable way

SOCIAL *adj* relating to or for people or society as a whole □ *noun* **SOCIALS** a social gathering, especially one organized by a club or other group

SOCIALISE *verb* **SOCIALISES, SOCIALISING, SOCIALISED** to socialize

SOCIALISM *noun* **SOCIALISMS** a political doctrine or system which aims to create a classless society by removing the nation's wealth (land, industries, transport systems, etc) out of private and into public hands

SOCIALIST *noun* **SOCIALISTS** a supporter of socialism □ *adj* relating to or characteristic of socialism

SOCIALITE *noun* **SOCIALITES** someone who mixes with people of high social status

SOCIALITY *noun* **SOCIALITIES** the fact or quality of being social

SOCIALIZE *verb* **SOCIALIZES, SOCIALIZING, SOCIALIZED** to meet with people on an informal, friendly basis

SOCIALLY *adverb* in a social way

SOCIETY *noun* **SOCIETIES** humankind as a whole, or a part of

it such as one nation, considered as a single community

SOCIOLOGY *noun* **SOCIOLOGIES** the scientific study of the nature, structure and workings of human society

SOCIOPATH *noun* **SOCIOPATHS** a person suffering from a personality disorder characterized by antisocial behaviour

SOCK [1] *noun* **SOCKS** a fabric covering for the foot and ankle, sometimes reaching to or over the knee, worn inside a shoe or boot

SOCK [2] *verb* **SOCKS, SOCKING, SOCKED** to hit with a powerful blow

SOCKET *noun* **SOCKETS** a specially shaped hole or set of holes into which something is inserted or fitted □ *verb* **SOCKETS, SOCKETING, SOCKETED** to provide with or place in a socket

SOCKEYE *noun* **SOCKEYES** the blueblack salmon which inhabits coastal waters from Japan to California

SOCLE *noun* **SOCLES** a plain projecting block or plinth at the base of a wall, column or pier

SOD *noun* **SODS** a slab of earth with grass growing on it; a turf □ *verb* **SODS, SODDING, SODDED** to cover with sods

SODA *noun* **SODAS** a common name given to any of various compounds of sodium in everyday use, eg sodium bicarbonate or bicarbonate of soda

SODALITY *noun* **SODALITIES** especially in the RC Church: a fellowship or fraternity

SODDEN *adj* heavy with moisture; saturated; thoroughly soaked

SODIUM *noun* **SODIUMS** a soft silvery-white metallic element used in alloys

SOEVER *adverb* generally used to extend or make indefinite the sense of something

SOFA *noun* **SOFAS** an upholstered seat with a back and arms, for two or more people

SOFFIT *noun* **SOFFITS** a term variously applied to the under surface of an arch, the underside of a stair, the underside of the top of a door or window opening, etc

SOFT *adj* **SOFTER, SOFTEST** easily yielding or changing shape when pressed; pliable or malleable □ *adverb* softly; gently

SOFTBACK noun **SOFTBACKS** a paperback

SOFTBALL noun **SOFTBALLS** a game similar to baseball, played with a larger, softer ball which is pitched underarm, as opposed to overarm in baseball

SOFTEN verb **SOFTENS, SOFTENING, SOFTENED** to make or become soft or softer

SOFTENER noun **SOFTENERS** a substance added to another to increase its softness, pliability, etc, such as fabric softener

SOFTENING noun **SOFTENINGS** an act of making or becoming softer

SOFTHEAD noun **SOFTHEADS** a simpleton

SOFTIE noun **SOFTIES** a softy

SOFTLY adverb in a soft way; quietly

SOFTNESS noun **SOFTNESSES** the quality or condition of being soft

SOFTWARE noun **SOFTWARES** the programs that are used in a computer system (eg operating systems, and applications programs such as word-processing or database programs), and the magnetic disks, tapes, etc, on which they are recorded

SOFTWOOD noun **SOFTWOODS** the wood of a coniferous tree, eg pine, including some woods that are in fact very hard and durable

SOFTY noun **SOFTIES** someone who is easily upset

SOG verb **SOGS, SOGGING, SOGGED** to soak

SOGGILY adverb in a soggy way

SOGGINESS noun **SOGGINESSES** the state of being soggy

SOGGY adj **SOGGIER, SOGGIEST** thoroughly soaked or wet; saturated

SOH noun **SOHS** in sol-fa notation: the fifth note of a major or minor scale

SOIGNÉ adj said of a man: well-groomed; smart

SOIGNÉE adj said of a woman: well-groomed; smart

SOIL [1] noun **SOILS** the mixture of fragmented rock, plant and animal debris that lies on the surface of the Earth, above the bedrock, containing water and air, as well as living organisms such as bacteria, fungi and invertebrates

SOIL [2] verb **SOILS, SOILING, SOILED** to stain or make dirty

SOIRÉE noun **SOIRÉES** a formal party held in the evening

SOJOURN noun **SOJOURNS** a short stay ◌ verb **SOJOURNS, SOJOURNING, SOJOURNED** to stay for a short while

SOJOURNER noun **SOJOURNERS** someone who sojourns

SOL noun **SOLS** soh

SOLACE noun **SOLACES** comfort in time of disappointment or sorrow ◌ verb **SOLACES, SOLACING, SOLACED** to provide with such comfort

SOLAR adj referring or relating to the Sun

SOLARIUM noun **SOLARIUMS, SOLARIA** a room or establishment equipped with sunbeds

SOLATIUM noun **SOLATIA** compensation for disappointment, inconvenience and disappointment

SOLD past form of **sell**

SOLDER noun **SOLDERS** any of several alloys with a low melting point, often containing tin and lead, applied when molten to the joint between two metals to form an airtight seal ◌ verb **SOLDERS, SOLDERING, SOLDERED** to join (two pieces of metal) without melting them, by applying a layer of molten alloy to the joint between them and allowing it to cool and solidify

SOLDERER noun **SOLDERERS** a person or thing that solders

SOLDERING noun **SOLDERINGS** an act of joining (two pieces of metal) without melting them, by applying a layer of molten alloy to the joint between them and allowing it to cool and solidify

SOLDIER noun **SOLDIERS** a member of a fighting force, especially a national army ◌ verb **SOLDIERS, SOLDIERING, SOLDIERED** to serve as a soldier

SOLDIERLY adj of or like a soldier

SOLE [1] noun **SOLES** the underside of the foot ◌ verb **SOLES, SOLING, SOLED** to fit (a shoe or boot) with a sole

SOLE [2] adj alone; only

SOLECISM noun **SOLECISMS** a mistake in the use of language; a breach of syntax, grammar, etc

SOLELY adverb alone; without others

SOLEMN adj **SOLEMNER,**

SOLEMNEST done, made or carried out in earnest and seriousness

SOLEMNISE verb **SOLEMNISES, SOLEMNISING, SOLEMNISED** to solemnize

SOLEMNITY noun **SOLEMNITIES** the state of being solemn

SOLEMNIZE verb **SOLEMNIZES, SOLEMNIZING, SOLEMNIZED** to celebrate (a religious event) with rites

SOLEMNLY adverb in a solemn way

SOLENOID noun **SOLENOIDS** a cylindrical coil of wire that produces a magnetic field when an electric current is passed through it, and often contains a movable iron or steel core that can be used to operate a switch, relay, circuit breaker, etc

SOLFATARA noun **SOLFATARAS** a volcanic vent emitting only gases, especially one emitting acid gases, such as hydrochloric acid and sulphur dioxide, and water vapour

SOLFEGGIO noun **SOLFEGGIOS** in music: an exercise in sol-fa syllables

SOLICIT verb **SOLICITS, SOLICITING, SOLICITED** to ask for something, or for something from someone

SOLICITING noun **SOLICITINGS** an act of asking for something, or for something from someone

SOLICITOR noun **SOLICITORS** in Britain: a lawyer who prepares legal documents, gives legal advice and, in the lower courts only, speaks on behalf of clients

SOLID adj **SOLIDER, SOLIDEST** in a form other than liquid or gas, and resisting changes in shape due to firmly cohering particles ◌ noun **SOLIDS** a solid substance or body

SOLIDIFY verb **SOLIDIFIES, SOLIDIFYING, SOLIDIFIED** to make or become solid

SOLIDITY noun **SOLIDITIES** the state or condition of being solid

SOLIDLY adverb in a solid way; without changing

SOLIDUS noun **SOLIDI** a printed line sloping from right to left, eg separating alternatives, as in and/ or; a stroke or slash mark

SOLILOQUY noun **SOLILOQUIES** an act of talking to oneself, especially a speech in a play, etc in which a character reveals thoughts or intentions to the audience by talking aloud

SOLIPSISM noun **SOLIPSISMS** the theory that one's own existence is the only certainty

SOLIPSIST noun **SOLIPSISTS** someone who believes in solipsism

SOLITAIRE noun **SOLITAIRES** any of several games for one player only, especially one whose object is to eliminate pegs or marbles from a board and leave only one

SOLITARY adj single; lone ▫ noun **SOLITARIES** someone who lives alone, especially a hermit

SOLITUDE noun **SOLITUDES** the state of being alone or secluded, especially pleasantly

SOLO noun **SOLOS** a piece of music, or a passage within it, for a single voice or instrument, with or without accompaniment ▫ verb **SOLOS, SOLOING, SOLOED** to play a solo

SOLOIST noun **SOLOISTS** someone who performs a solo or solos

SOLSTICE noun **SOLSTICES** either of the times when the Sun is furthest from the equator: the longest day (summer solstice) around June 21 in the N hemisphere and the shortest day (winter solstice) around December 21 in the N hemisphere

SOLUBLE adj of a substance: capable of being dissolved in a liquid

SOLUTE noun **SOLUTES** any substance that is dissolved in a solvent, eg water to form a solution

SOLUTION noun **SOLUTIONS** the process of finding an answer to a problem or puzzle; the answer sought or found; a mixture consisting of a solid or gas and the liquid in which it is completely dissolved

SOLVABLE adj capable of being solved

SOLVATION noun **SOLVATIONS** the interaction between the ions of a solute and the molecules of a solvent, which enables an ionic solid to dissolve in a solvent to form a solution, or to swell or form a gel in the presence of a solvent

SOLVE verb **SOLVES, SOLVING, SOLVED** to discover the answer to (a puzzle) or a way out of (a problem)

SOLVENCY noun **SOLVENCIES** the ability to pay one's debts

SOLVENT adj able to pay all one's debts ▫ noun **SOLVENTS** in a

solution: the liquid in which a solid or gas (the solute) is dissolved, eg water and organic chemicals such as ethanol (alcohol), ether, and acetone

SOLVER noun **SOLVERS** someone who solves eg problems

SOMA noun **SOMAS** the body of a plant or animal, excluding its germ-cells

SOMATIC adj referring or relating to the body, rather than the mind

SOMBRE adj **SOMBRER, SOMBREST** sad and serious; grave

SOMBRELY adverb in a sombre way

SOMBRERO noun **SOMBREROS** a wide-brimmed straw or felt hat, especially popular in Mexico

SOME adj signifying an unknown or unspecified amount or number of something ▫ adverb to an unspecified extent ▫ pronoun certain unspecified things or people

SOMEBODY pronoun an unknown or unspecified person; someone

SOMEDAY adverb at an unknown or unspecified time in the future

SOMEHOW adverb in some way not yet known

SOMEONE pronoun somebody

SOMETHING pronoun a thing not known or not stated

SOMETIME adverb at an unknown or unspecified time in the future or the past ▫ adj former; late

SOMETIMES adverb occasionally; now and then

SOMEWHAT adverb rather; a little

SOMEWHERE adverb in or to some place or degree, or at some point, not known or not specified

SOMNIFIC adj causing sleep

SOMNOLENT adj sleepy or drowsy; causing sleepiness or drowsiness

SON noun **SONS** a male child or offspring

SONANCE noun **SONANCES** a sounding

SONANT adj said of a sound: voiced; syllabic ▫ noun **SONANTS** a voiced or syllabic sound

SONAR noun **SONARS** a system that is used to determine the location of underwater objects, eg submarines, shoals of fish, especially by transmitting ultrasound signals from the bottom of a ship and measuring the time taken for their echoes to return when they strike an obstacle

SONATA noun **SONATAS** a piece of classical music written in three or more movements for a solo instrument, especially the piano

SONATINA noun **SONATINAS** a short sonata, usually one which is technically straightforward

SONDE noun **SONDES** one of various devices for obtaining information about atmospheric and weather conditions at high altitudes

SONG noun **SONGS** a set of words, short poem, etc to be sung, usually with accompanying music

SONGBIRD noun **SONGBIRDS** in the classification of the animal kingdom: any of a suborder of perching birds, most of which have a musical call, eg larks, thrushes, tits, etc

SONGBOOK noun **SONGBOOKS** a book containing songs together with their music

SONGSMITH noun **SONGSMITHS** a composer of songs

SONGSTER noun **SONGSTERS** a talented singer

SONIC adj relating to or using sound or sound waves

SONICS singular noun the study of the technological application of sounds, especially supersonic waves

SONNET noun **SONNETS** a short poem with 14 lines of 10 or 11 syllables each and a regular rhyming pattern according to the scheme: the Italian sonnet consists of an octave and a sestet, whereas the English sonnet consists of three quatrains and ends with a rhyming couplet

SONNY noun **SONNIES** a familiar and often condescending term of address used to a boy or man

SONOBUOY noun **SONOBUOYS** sonar equipment dropped to float on the sea, pick up underwater noise, eg from a submarine, and transmit bearings of the source to aircraft

SONOGRAM noun **SONOGRAMS** a visual representation of a sound, produced by a sonograph

SONOGRAPH noun **SONOGRAPHS** a device for scanning and recording sound and its component frequencies

SONORANT noun **SONORANTS** a frictionless consonant or nasal (l, r, m, n, ng) capable of fulfilling a consonantal or vocalic function

SONORITY noun **SONORITIES** the quality or state of being sonorous

SONOROUS adj sounding impressively loud and deep

SOOK noun **SOOKS** a soft, timid or cowardly person

SOON adverb **SOONER, SOONEST** in a short time from now or from a stated time

SOOT noun **SOOTS** a black powdery substance produced when coal or wood is imperfectly burned; smut □ verb **SOOTS, SOOTING, SOOTED** to cover, smear or dirty with soot

SOOTHE verb **SOOTHES, SOOTHING, SOOTHED** to bring relief from (a pain, etc); to allay

SOOTHER noun **SOOTHERS** a person or thing that soothes

SOOTHING noun **SOOTHINGS** an act of bringing relief from (a pain, etc)

SOOTHSAY verb **SOOTHSAYS, SOOTHSAYING, SOOTHSAID** to foretell or divine

SOOTILY adverb in a sooty way

SOOTINESS noun **SOOTINESSES** the state of being sooty

SOOTY adj **SOOTIER, SOOTIEST** covered with soot

SOP noun **SOPS** a piece of food, especially bread, dipped or soaked in a liquid, eg soup □ verb **SOPS, SOPPING, SOPPED** to soak or become soaked

SOPHISM noun **SOPHISMS** a convincing but false argument or explanation, especially one intended to deceive

SOPHIST noun **SOPHISTS** someone who argues with shrewd but intentionally fallacious reasoning

SOPHISTIC adj referring to or characteristic of a sophist or sophistry

SOPHISTRY noun **SOPHISTRIES** plausibly deceptive or fallacious reasoning, or an instance of this

SOPHOMORE noun **SOPHOMORES** a second-year student at a school or university

SOPOR noun **SOPORS** an unnaturally deep sleep

SOPORIFIC adj causing sleep or drowsiness □ noun **SOPORIFICS** a sleep-inducing drug

SOPPILY adverb in a soppy way

SOPPINESS noun **SOPPINESSES** the state or condition of being soppy

SOPPING adverb thoroughly wet; soaking

SOPPY adj **SOPPIER, SOPPIEST** weakly sentimental

SOPRANINO noun **SOPRANINOS, SOPRANINI** an instrument with a pitch higher than the corresponding soprano

SOPRANO noun **SOPRANOS** a singing voice of the highest pitch for a woman or a boy

SORB noun **SORBS** service tree (a European flowering tree with toothed leaves, bearing edible fruit)

SORBET noun **SORBETS** a water ice

SORBITOL noun **SORBITOLS** a water-soluble white crystalline carbohydrate, used as a food additive and sweetening agent

SORCERER noun **SORCERERS** someone who practises black magic

SORCERESS noun **SORCERESSES** a woman who practises black magic

SORCEROUS adj of or relating to sorcery

SORCERY noun **SORCERIES** the art or use of magic, especially black magic that is associated with the power of evil spirits, supernatural forces, etc

SORDID adj **SORDIDER, SORDIDEST** repulsively filthy; squalid

SORDIDLY adverb in a sordid way

SORDINO noun **SORDINI** a mute on a musical instrument that is used to soften or deaden the sound

SORE adj **SORER, SOREST** said of a wound, injury, part of the body, etc: painful or tender □ noun **SORES** a diseased or injured spot or area, especially an ulcer or boil

SORELY adverb acutely; very much

SORENESS noun **SORENESSES** the quality or condition of being sore

SOREX noun **SOREXES** any member of the common shrew genus

SORGHUM noun **SORGHUMS** any of several different varieties of grass that are related to the sugar cane and which are widely cultivated in Africa and parts of Asia as a cereal crop and a source of syrup

SORI plural of **sorus**

SORORAL adj characteristic, or relating or referring to a sister or sisters

SORORIAL adj sororal

SORORITY noun **SORORITIES** a women's club or society, especially one affiliated to a US university, college or church

SOROSIS noun **SOROSES** a fleshy fruit, such as the pineapple or mulberry, that is formed from a large collection of flowers that grow in the shape of a spike around a pulpy stem

SORREL [1] noun **SORRELS** any of various low-growing perennial plants, many of which have spear-shaped leaves which give an acid taste

SORREL [2] adj being reddish-brown or light chestnut in colour □ noun a horse or other animal of this colour

SORRILY adverb in a sorry way

SORRINESS noun **SORRINESSES** the state of being sorry

SORROW noun **SORROWS** a feeling of grief or deep sadness, especially one that arises from loss or disappointment □ verb **SORROWS, SORROWING, SORROWED** to have or express such feeling

SORROWER noun **SORROWERS** someone who is grieving

SORROWFUL adj sad

SORROWING adj sad □ noun **SORROWINGS** grief

SORRY adj **SORRIER, SORRIEST** distressed or full of regret or shame, especially over something that one has done or said, something one feels responsible for, something that has happened, etc

SORRYISH adj somewhat sorry

SORT noun **SORTS** a kind, type or class □ verb **SORTS, SORTING, SORTED** to arrange into different groups according to some specified criterion

SORTABLE adj capable of being sorted

SORTER noun **SORTERS** someone who sorts things

SORTIE noun **SORTIES** a sudden attack by besieged troops □ verb **SORTIES, SORTIEING, SORTIED** to make a sortie

SORTILEGE noun **SORTILEGES** the practice of predicting the future by drawing lots

SORTILEGY noun **SORTILEGIES** prediction by drawing lots

SORTING noun **SORTINGS** an act of arranging into different groups according to some specified criterion

SORUS noun **SORI** a cluster of sporangia on the under side of some fern leaves

SOS plural of **so** [2]

SOSTENUTO adverb in a steady and sustained manner □ adj steady and sustained

SOT noun **SOTS** someone who is drunk or who habitually drinks a lot of alcohol □ verb **SOTS, SOTTING, SOTTED** to act as a sot

SOTERIAL adj relating to salvation

SOTTISH adj foolish; stupid with drink

SOU noun **SOUS** a French coin of low value, which was later used to designate the five-centime piece

SOUBRETTE noun **SOUBRETTES** a minor female part in a play, opera, etc, especially the role of a pert, impudent, flirtatious or intriguing maid

SOUCHONG noun **SOUCHONGS** a type of fine black China tea

SOUFFLE noun **SOUFFLES** a soft murmuring noise that can be heard coming from various body organs, eg by using a stethoscope

SOUFFLÉ noun **SOUFFLÉS** a light fluffy sweet or savoury dish that is made by gently combining egg yolks and other ingredients with stiffly beaten egg-whites

SOUGH noun **SOUGHS** a sighing, rustling or murmuring sound that is made by the wind blowing through trees, etc □ verb **SOUGHS, SOUGHING, SOUGHED** said of the wind: to make this sound

SOUGHT past form of **seek**

SOUK noun **SOUKS** an open-air market or market-place in Muslim countries, especially in N Africa and the Middle East

SOUKOUS noun **SOUKOUSES** a central African style of dance music that originated in Zaire and which combines guitar, drumming and vocal melodies

SOUL noun **SOULS** the spiritual, non-physical part of someone or something which is often regarded as the source of individuality, personality, morality, will, emotions and intellect, and which is widely believed to survive in

some form after the death of the body

SOULFUL adj having, expressing, etc deep feelings, especially of sadness

SOULFULLY adverb in a soulful way

SOULLESS adj having, showing, etc no emotional sensitivity, morality, etc

SOUND [1] noun **SOUNDS** a noise □ verb **SOUNDS, SOUNDING, SOUNDED** to produce or cause to produce a sound

SOUND [2] adj **SOUNDER, SOUNDEST** not damaged or injured; in good condition; healthy

SOUNDBITE noun **SOUNDBITES** a short and succinct statement, especially one that has been deliberately extracted from a longer speech given by some public figure, and which is quoted on TV or radio or in the press because it can be used to epitomize a particular view

SOUNDCARD noun **SOUNDCARDS** a printed circuit board that can be added to a computer to provide or enhance sound effects

SOUNDING noun **SOUNDINGS** the act or process of measuring depth, especially of the sea, eg by using echo

SOUNDLY adverb in a sound way; safely

SOUNDNESS noun **SOUNDNESSES** the state or condition of being sound

SOUP noun **SOUPS** a liquid food that is made by boiling meat, vegetables, grains, etc together in a stock or in water □ verb **SOUPS, SOUPING, SOUPED** to make changes to a vehicle or its engine in order to increase its speed or power

SOUPÇON noun **SOUPÇONS** the slightest amount; a hint or dash

SOUPY adj **SOUPIER, SOUPIEST** of or like soup

SOUR adj **SOURER, SOUREST** having an acid taste or smell, similar to that of lemon juice or vinegar □ verb **SOURS, SOURING, SOURED** to make or become sour

SOURCE noun **SOURCES** the place, thing, person, circumstance, etc that something begins or develops from; the origin □ verb **SOURCES, SOURCING, SOURCED** to acknowledge or mention as a source

SOURCING noun **SOURCINGS** an act of finding a source

SOURDOUGH noun **SOURDOUGHS** a piece of fermenting dough that is kept back to be used as a leaven in the next batch of bread-making

SOURING noun **SOURINGS** an act of making sour

SOURISH adj somewhat sour

SOURISHLY adverb in a sour way

SOURLY adverb in a sour way

SOURNESS noun **SOURNESSES** the quality or condition of being sour

SOURPUSS noun **SOURPUSSES** a habitually sullen or miserable person

SOURSOP noun **SOURSOPS** an evergreen tree that is found in the W Indies

SOUSE verb **SOUSES, SOUSING, SOUSED** to steep or cook something in vinegar or white wine □ noun **SOUSES** an act of sousing

SOUSED adj drunk

SOUSING noun **SOUSINGS** an act of steeping or cooking something in vinegar or white wine

SOUSLIK noun **SOUSLIKS** a suslik

SOUTACHE noun **SOUTACHES** a narrow decorative braid or ribbon that is usually embroidered with flowers and sewn onto garments

SOUTANE noun **SOUTANES** a long plain robe or cassock that a priest wears

SOUTER noun **SOUTERS** someone whose job is to make or mend shoes; a cobbler or shoemaker

SOUTH noun **SOUTHS** one of the four main points of the compass which, if a person is facing the rising sun in the N hemisphere, is the direction that lies to their right □ adverb towards the south □ adj belonging, referring or relating to, facing or lying in the south; on the side or in the part that is nearest the south

SOUTHERLY adj said of a wind, etc: coming from the south □ adverb to or towards the south □ noun **SOUTHERLIES** a southerly wind

SOUTHERN adj belonging, relating or referring to, or in, the south

SOUTHPAW noun **SOUTHPAWS** someone whose left hand is more dominant than their right, especially a boxer □ adj left-handed

SOUTHWARD adj towards the south □ adverb towards the south

SOUTHWARDS adj southward ◻ adverb southward

SOUVENIR noun **SOUVENIRS** something that is bought, kept or given as a reminder of a place, person, occasion, etc; a memento ◻ verb **SOUVENIRS, SOUVENIRING, SOUVENIRED** to steal

SOV noun **SOVS** a pound sterling

SOVEREIGN noun **SOVEREIGNS** a supreme ruler or head, especially a monarch

SOVIET noun **SOVIETS** any of the councils that made up the local and national governments of the former Soviet Union

SOW [1] verb **SOWS, SOWING, SOWED, SOWN** to scatter or place (plant seeds, a crop, etc) on or in the earth, in a plant pot, etc

SOW [2] noun **SOWS** an adult female pig, especially one that has had a litter of piglets

SOWER noun **SOWERS** a person or implement that sows

SOX plural noun a colloquial or commercial plural of sock

SOY noun **SOYS** a salty dark brown sauce that is made from soya beans which ferment for around six months and which is used especially in oriental fish dishes

SOYA noun **SOYAS** any of numerous varieties of an annual plant of the pulse family, that are native to SW Asia but which are now more widely cultivated for their edible seeds

SOZZLED adj drunk

SPA noun **SPAS** a mineral water spring; a resort where such a spring is located ◻ verb **SPAS, SPAING, SPAED** to stay at a spa

SPACE noun **SPACES** the limitless three-dimensional expanse where all matter exists ◻ verb **SPACES, SPACING, SPACED** to set or place at intervals

SPACED adj being, acting, appearing to be, etc in a dazed, euphoric, stupefied or dreamlike state, especially one that is or seems to be induced by drugs

SPACELESS adj without space

SPACEMAN noun **SPACEMEN** someone who travels in space

SPACER noun **SPACERS** a person or thing that spaces

SPACIAL adj spatial

SPACING noun **SPACINGS** an act

of spacing; the space between two things

SPACIOUS adj having ample room or space; extending over a large area

SPADE noun **SPADES** a long-handled digging tool with a broad metal blade which is designed to be pushed into the ground with the foot ◻ verb **SPADES, SPADING, SPADED** to dig or turn over (ground) with a spade

SPADEFUL noun **SPADEFULS** the amount that can be carried on a spade

SPADELIKE adj like a spade, eg in shape

SPADER noun **SPADERS** someone who uses a spade; a digger

SPADEWORK noun **SPADEWORKS** hard or boring preparatory work

SPADIX noun **SPADICES** a spike-shaped structure that consists of numerous tiny flowers on a fleshy axis and which is usually enclosed by a spathe

SPAGHETTI noun **SPAGHETTIS** a type of pasta that is in the form of long thin solid string-like strands

SPAHI noun **SPAHIS** a member of the Turkish cavalry

SPAKE an old past form of **speak**

SPALL noun **SPALLS** a chip or splinter, especially one of rock or ore ◻ verb **SPALLS, SPALLING, SPALLED** to chip, splinter or split or make (rock or ore) to chip, splinter or split before sorting or treating

SPAM noun electronic junk mail ◻ verb **SPAMS, SPAMMING, SPAMMED** to send electronic junk mail

SPAN noun **SPANS** the distance, interval, length, etc between two points in space or time ◻ verb **SPANS, SPANNING, SPANNED** said of a bridge, pier, ceiling, rainbow, etc: to extend across or over, especially in an arched shape

SPANDEX noun **SPANDEXES** a synthetic elastic fibre made chiefly from polyurethane

SPANDREL noun **SPANDRELS** the triangular space between the curve of an arch and the enclosing mouldings, string-course, etc

SPANDRIL noun **SPANDRILS** a spandrel

SPANGLE noun **SPANGLES** a small piece of glittering material, especially a sequin ◻ verb

SPANGLES, SPANGLING, SPANGLED to decorate (eg a piece of clothing) with spangles

SPANGLING noun **SPANGLINGS** sparkling decoration

SPANGLY adj **SPANGLIER, SPANGLIEST** glittering, sparkling

SPANIEL noun **SPANIELS** any of various kinds of dog, such as the King Charles spaniel, cocker spaniel, springer spaniel, etc that have wavy coats and long silky dangly ears

SPANK verb **SPANKS, SPANKING, SPANKED** to smack, usually on the buttocks with the flat of the hand, a slipper, belt, etc, often several times ◻ noun **SPANKS** such a smack

SPANKER noun **SPANKERS** someone who spanks

SPANKING [1] noun **SPANKINGS** an act or instance or the process of delivering a series of smacks, eg as a punishment to a child

SPANKING [2] adverb absolutely; strikingly ◻ adj impressively fine; striking

SPANNER noun **SPANNERS** a metal hand tool that has an opening (sometimes an adjustable one) or various sizes of openings at one or both ends and which is used for gripping, tightening or loosening nuts, bolts, etc

SPAR [1] verb **SPARS, SPARRING, SPARRED** to box, especially in a way that deliberately avoids the exchange of heavy blows, eg for practice ◻ noun **SPARS** an act or instance of sparring

SPAR [2] noun **SPARS** a translucent non-metallic mineral, such as feldspar and fluorspar, that can be easily split into layers

SPARABLE noun **SPARABLES** a small headless nail that is used in the manufacture and mending of soles and heels of shoes and boots

SPARAXIS noun **SPARAXISES** any of several S African cormous plants that are related to the iris, that have jagged edges to their spathes and which are cultivated for their pretty star-shaped purple, red or orange flowers

SPARE adj **SPARER, SPAREST** kept for occasional use ◻ verb **SPARES, SPARING, SPARED** to afford to give, give away or do without ◻ noun **SPARES** a duplicate kept in reserve for use as a replacement

For longer words, see The Chambers Dictionary

SPARELY adverb frugally

SPARENESS noun the state of being spare

SPARGE verb **SPARGES, SPARGING, SPARGED** to sprinkle or moisten with water, especially in brewing

SPARING adj inclined to be economical or frugal, often to the point of inadequacy or meanness

SPARINGLY adverb in a sparing way; meanly

SPARK noun **SPARKS** a tiny red-hot glowing fiery particle that jumps out from some burning material ◻ verb **SPARKS, SPARKING, SPARKED** to emit sparks

SPARKLE verb **SPARKLES, SPARKLING, SPARKLED** to give off sparks ◻ noun **SPARKLES** a point of bright shiny light; an act of sparkling; sparkling appearance

SPARKLER noun **SPARKLERS** a type of small firework that produces gentle showers of silvery sparks and which can be held in the hand

SPARKLING adj said of wine, mineral water, etc: having a fizz that is produced by escaping carbon dioxide

SPARKLY adj **SPARKLIER, SPARKLIEST** liable to sparkle; bright

SPARKY adj **SPARKIER, SPARKIEST** liable to give off sparks

SPARRER noun **SPARRERS** someone who boxes

SPARRING noun **SPARRINGS** boxing

SPARROW noun **SPARROWS** any of various small grey or brown perching birds that have short conical beaks which are well adapted for cracking seeds

SPARRY adj **SPARRIER, SPARRIEST** of or like spar

SPARSE adj **SPARSER, SPARSEST** thinly scattered or dotted about; scanty

SPARSELY adverb in a sparse way

SPARSITY noun **SPARSITIES** the state or condition of being sparse

SPARTAN adj belonging, relating or referring to or characteristic of ancient Sparta, its inhabitants, customs, etc ◻ noun **SPARTANS** a citizen or inhabitant of ancient Sparta

SPASM noun **SPASMS** a sudden uncontrollable contraction of a muscle or muscles ◻ verb

SPASMS, SPASMING, SPASMED to twitch or go into a spasm

SPASMODIC adj being or occurring in, or consisting of, short periods; not constant or regular; intermittent

SPASTIC noun **SPASTICS** someone who suffers from cerebal palsy

SPAT [1] past form of **spit**

SPAT [2] noun **SPATS** a trivial or petty fight or quarrel ◻ verb

SPATS, SPATTING, SPATTED to engage in a trivial or petty fight or quarrel

SPATE noun **SPATES** a sudden rush or increased quantity; a burst

SPATHE noun **SPATHES** a large bract that surrounds and protects the inflorescence or spadix of certain plant families such as the arums and palms

SPATHED adj having a spathe

SPATHIC adj said of a mineral: having the qualities of a spar

SPATHOSE adj spathic

SPATIAL adj belonging, referring or relating to space

SPATIALLY adverb in a spatial way

SPATTER verb **SPATTERS, SPATTERING, SPATTERED** said of mud, etc: to spray, cover, shower or splash in scattered drops or patches ◻ noun **SPATTERS** a quantity spattered; a sprinkling

SPATULA noun **SPATULAS** an implement that has a broad blunt and often flexible blade and which can be used for a variety of purposes, such as stirring, spreading, mixing, turning foods during frying, etc

SPATULAR adj of or like a spatula

SPATULATE adj said of fingers, etc: having a broad flat tip

SPAVIN noun **SPAVINS** a condition in horses where there is swelling on the leg, in the region of either the shank bone or the hock bone

SPAWN noun **SPAWNS** the cohering jelly-like mass or stream of eggs that amphibians, fish, molluscs, crustaceans, etc lay in water ◻ verb **SPAWNS, SPAWNING, SPAWNED** said of amphibians, fish, etc: to lay eggs

SPAWNER noun **SPAWNERS** something that spawns

SPAWNING noun **SPAWNINGS** said of amphibians, fish, etc: an act of laying eggs

SPAY verb **SPAYS, SPAYING, SPAYED** to remove the ovaries

from (especially a domestic animal) in order to prevent it from breeding

SPEAK verb **SPEAKS, SPEAKING, SPOKE, SPAKE, SPOKEN** to utter words in an ordinary voice (as opposed to eg shouting, singing or screaming)

SPEAKABLE adj able to be spoken or expressed in speech

SPEAKEASY noun **SPEAKEASIES** a bar or other place where alcohol was sold illicitly, especially one that operated during the period when the US prohibition laws were in force

SPEAKER noun **SPEAKERS** someone who speaks, especially someone who gives a formal speech

SPEAKING adj able to produce speech ◻ noun **SPEAKINGS** an act, instance or the process of saying something

SPEAR noun **SPEARS** a weapon that consists of a long pole with a hard sharp point, usually a metal one, and which is thrown from the shoulder (eg at prey, fish or an enemy) ◻ verb **SPEARS, SPEARING, SPEARED** to pierce with a spear or something similar to a spear

SPEARFISH noun **SPEARFISHES** a marlin

SPEARHEAD noun **SPEARHEADS** the tip of a spear ◻ verb **SPEARHEADS, SPEARHEADING, SPEARHEADED** to lead (a movement, campaign, attack, etc)

SPEARMINT noun **SPEARMINTS** a herbaceous perennial plant of the mint family with lance-shaped aromatic leaves and spikes of purple flowers

SPEC noun **SPECS** specification

SPECIAL adj distinct from, and usually better than, others of the same or a similar kind; exceptional ◻ noun **SPECIALS** something that is special, eg an extra edition of a newspaper, etc, an extra train that is put on over and above the time-tabled ones, an item offered at a low price, a dish on a menu, etc

SPECIALLY adverb in a special way

SPECIALTY noun **SPECIALTIES** a deed that is a contractual document and which must be signed by its maker in the presence of a witness, or, if it is executed by a company, by a director and the secretary or by two directors, or executed by a seal if the company has one

SPECIE noun **SPECIES** money in the form of coins as opposed to notes

SPECIES noun **SPECIES** any group of plants or animals that share some common characteristics

SPECIFIC adj particular; exact; precisely identified ◻ noun **SPECIFICS** a specific detail, factor or feature, eg of a plan, scheme, etc

SPECIFY verb **SPECIFIES, SPECIFYING, SPECIFIED** to refer to, name or identify precisely

SPECIMEN noun **SPECIMENS** a sample or example of something, especially one that will be studied or put in a collection

SPECIOUS adj superficially or apparently convincing, sound or just, but really false, flawed or lacking in sincerity

SPECK noun **SPECKS** a small spot, stain or mark ◻ verb **SPECKS, SPECKING, SPECKED** to mark with specks

SPECKLE noun **SPECKLES** a little spot, especially one of several on a different-coloured background, eg on feathers, a bird's egg, etc ◻ verb **SPECKLES, SPECKLING, SPECKLED** to mark with speckles

SPECKLED adj said especially of certain fish and birds or birds' eggs: covered or marked with specks or speckles

SPECKLESS adj without a mark or blemish

SPECKY adj **SPECKIER, SPECKIEST** marked with spots

SPECS plural noun spectacles

SPECTACLE noun **SPECTACLES** something that can be seen; a sight, especially one that is impressive, wonderful, disturbing, ridiculous, etc

SPECTACLES plural noun a frame that sits on the nose, that has two legs that fit behind the ears, and that contains two lenses that are designed to correct defective eyesight

SPECTATE verb **SPECTATES, SPECTATING, SPECTATED** to be a spectator; to look on rather than participate

SPECTATOR noun **SPECTATORS** someone who watches an event or incident

SPECTER noun **SPECTERS** a spectre

SPECTRAL adj relating to or like a spectre or ghost

SPECTRE noun **SPECTRES** a ghost or an apparition

SPECTRUM noun **SPECTRA** the band of colours (red, orange, yellow, green, blue, indigo and violet) that is produced when white light is split into its constituent wavelengths by passing it through a prism

SPECULAR adj belonging or relating to a mirror

SPECULATE verb **SPECULATES, SPECULATING, SPECULATED** to consider the circumstances or possibilities regarding something, usually without any factual basis and without coming to a definite conclusion

SPECULUM noun **SPECULA** a mirror with a reflective surface usually of polished metal, especially one that forms part of a telescope

SPEECH noun **SPEECHES** the act or an instance of speaking; the ability to speak

SPEECHIFY verb **SPEECHIFIES, SPEECHIFYING, SPEECHIFIED** to make a speech or speeches, especially of a long and tedious nature

SPEED noun **SPEEDS** rate of movement or action, especially distance travelled per unit of time ◻ verb **SPEEDS, SPEEDING, SPED** to move quickly ◻ verb **SPEEDS, SPEEDING, SPEEDED** to drive at a speed higher than the legal limit

SPEEDBALL noun **SPEEDBALLS** a mixture of cocaine and morphine or of cocaine and heroin

SPEEDBOAT noun **SPEEDBOATS** a motor boat that has an engine designed to make it capable of high speeds

SPEEDER noun **SPEEDERS** a person or thing that speeds

SPEEDILY adverb quickly

SPEEDING noun **SPEEDINGS** an act, instance or the process of going fast ◻ adj moving, acting, etc fast

SPEEDO noun **SPEEDOS** a device that indicates the speed at which a vehicle is travelling

SPEEDWAY noun **SPEEDWAYS** a sport or pastime that involves racing round a cinder track on lightweight motorcycles

SPEEDWELL noun **SPEEDWELLS** any of various low-growing annual

or perennial plants with opposite lance-shaped or oval leaves and small bluish (or occasionally white) four-petalled flowers

SPEEDY adj **SPEEDIER, SPEEDIEST** fast; prompt; without delay

SPEISS noun **SPEISSES** the arsenides and antimonides that are produced during the smelting of cobalt and lead ores

SPELAEAN adj said of an animal, etc: tending to live in a cave

SPELEAN adj spelaean

SPELL [1] verb **SPELLS, SPELLING, SPELT, SPELLED** to write or name (the constituent letters of a word or words) in their correct order

SPELL [2] noun **SPELLS** a set of words which, especially when spoken, is believed to have magical power, often of an evil nature

SPELLABLE adj capable of being spelled correctly

SPELLBIND verb **SPELLBINDS, SPELLBINDING, SPELLBOUND** to captivate, enchant, entrance or fascinate

SPELLER noun **SPELLERS** someone who spells a word or words

SPELLICAN noun **SPELLICANS** a spillikin

SPELLING noun **SPELLINGS** the ability to spell

SPELT [1] a past form of **spell** [1]

SPELT [2] noun **SPELTS** a type of grain which was once widely cultivated throughout Europe, but which has now largely been superseded by wheat, which it is related to, although it is still grown in some mountainous regions of S Europe

SPELTER noun **SPELTERS** impure zinc that contains lead or other impurities

SPELUNKER noun **SPELUNKERS** someone who takes part in the sport or activity of exploring caves; a potholer

SPENCER noun **SPENCERS** a short close-fitting men's overcoat that was worn around the turn of the 19c

SPEND verb **SPENDS, SPENDING, SPENT** to pay out (money, etc) eg on buying something new, for a service, repair, etc ◻ noun **SPENDS** an act or the process of spending (especially money)

SPENDABLE adj capable of being spent

SPENDER noun **SPENDERS** someone who spends money
SPENDING noun **SPENDINGS** an act of spending money
SPENT adj used up; exhausted
SPERM noun **SPERMS** semen
SPERMATIC adj belonging, relating or referring to sperm
SPERMATID noun **SPERMATIDS** an immature male gamete
SPEW verb **SPEWS, SPEWING, SPEWED** to vomit □ noun **SPEWS** vomit
SPEWER noun **SPEWERS** a person or thing that vomits
SPHAGNUM noun **SPHAGNUMS** any of numerous species of moss that grow on temperate boggy or marshy ground, which have a spongy structure that retains water, making them suitable for use as a packing material, eg for potting plants, and which form peat when they decay
SPHERAL adj of or like a sphere
SPHERE noun **SPHERES** a round three-dimensional figure where all points on the surface are an equal distance from the centre
SPHERED adj like a sphere in shape
SPHERIC adj spherical
SPHERICAL adj having or being in the shape of a sphere
SPHEROID adj characterized by having, or being in, almost the shape of a sphere □ noun **SPHEROIDS** a figure or body of this shape
SPHERULAR adj of or like a spherule
SPHERULE noun **SPHERULES** a small sphere
SPHINCTER noun **SPHINCTERS** a ring of muscle that, when it contracts, closes the entrance to a cavity in the body
SPHINX noun **SPHINXES, SPHINGES** in mythology: a monster, with the head of a woman and the body of a lion, which strangled travellers who could not solve its riddle and which was dashed to pieces on the rocks when it leapt from its lair in rage after Oedipus did give the correct answer to the riddle
SPICA noun **SPICAS** a flower spike or other part that resembles a spike
SPICATE adj having, forming or in a spike; relating to a spike
SPICATED adj spicate

SPICCATO adj said of a style of staccato on stringed instruments: played with a kind of light controlled bouncing movement of the bow □ adverb said of a style of staccato on stringed instruments: played with a kind of light controlled bouncing movement of the bow □ noun **SPICCATOS** a piece of music or a series of notes played in this way
SPICE noun **SPICES** any of various aromatic or pungent substances, such as pepper, ginger, nutmeg, cloves, cinnamon, etc that are derived from plants and used for flavouring food, eg in sauces, curries, etc, and for drinks such as punch □ verb **SPICES, SPICING, SPICED** to flavour with spice
SPICEBUSH noun **SPICEBUSHES** an aromatic shrub that is native to America and which is related to the laurel family
SPICED adj flavoured with spices
SPICILY adverb in a spicy way
SPICINESS noun **SPICINESSES** the quality or condition of being spicy
SPICULE noun **SPICULES** something that is small, sharp, hard and pointed, such as a splinter, a shard of glass, crystal or bone, etc
SPICY adj **SPICIER, SPICIEST** flavoured with or tasting or smelling of spices; pungent; piquant
SPIDER noun **SPIDERS** any of thousands of species of invertebrate animals that are found in virtually all habitats, which have eight legs and two main body parts, and which, in most cases, can produce silk for spinning webs to trap their prey
SPIDERMAN noun **SPIDERMEN** someone whose job is to do building work on high structures such as scaffolding, steeples, etc
SPIDERY adj **SPIDERIER, SPIDERIEST** thin and straggly
SPIED past for of **spy**
SPIEL noun **SPIELS** a long rambling, often implausible, story, especially one that contains an excuse, one that the speaker hopes will divert attention from something else or one given as sales patter □ verb **SPIELS, SPIELING, SPIELED** to talk endlessly or glibly

SPIELER noun **SPIELERS** someone who spiels
SPIES plural of **spy**
SPIFFING adj excellent; splendid
SPIGOT noun **SPIGOTS** a peg or plug, especially one that is used for stopping the vent hole in a cask or barrel
SPIKE noun **SPIKES** any thin sharp point □ verb **SPIKES, SPIKING, SPIKED** to strike, pierce or impale with a pointed object
SPIKELET noun **SPIKELETS** a small spike such as those that form the inflorescences of many grasses, often enclosed by a pair of bracts
SPIKENARD noun **SPIKENARDS** an aromatic plant that is native to the Himalayas and which has rose-purple flowers and aromatic underground stems
SPIKILY adverb in a spiky way
SPIKINESS noun **SPIKINESSES** the state of being spiky
SPIKY adj **SPIKIER, SPIKIEST** having spikes or pointed ends
SPILIKIN noun **SPILIKINS** a spillikin
SPILL verb **SPILLS, SPILLING, SPILT, SPILLED** to run or flow or cause (a liquid, etc) to run or flow out from a container, especially accidentally □ noun **SPILLS** an act of spilling
SPILLAGE noun **SPILLAGES** the act or process of spilling
SPILLIKIN noun **SPILLIKINS** a small thin strip of wood, bone, etc
SPILLOVER noun **SPILLOVERS** an overflowing
SPILTH noun **SPILTHS** an act or the process of spilling
SPIN verb **SPINS, SPINNING, SPUN** to rotate or cause to rotate repeatedly, especially quickly □ noun **SPINS** an act or process of spinning or a spinning motion
SPINACH noun **SPINACHES** an annual plant that is native to Asia, but which is now widely cultivated in temperate regions for its edible leaves
SPINAL adj belonging, relating or referring to the spine
SPINDLE noun **SPINDLES** a rod with a notched or tapered end that is designed for twisting the thread in hand-spinning and which is the place where the spun thread is wound
SPINDLY adj **SPINDLIER, SPINDLIEST** long, thin and, often, frail-looking

SPINDRIFT *noun* **SPINDRIFTS** spray that is blown from the crests of waves

SPINE *noun* **SPINES** in vertebrates: the flexible bony structure, consisting of a column of vertebrae connected by cartilage discs, that surrounds and protects the spinal cord and articulates with the skull, ribs and pelvic girdle

SPINEL *noun* **SPINELS** any of a group of hard glassy crystalline minerals of various colours, that contain oxides of magnesium, aluminium, iron, zinc or manganese and which are used as gemstones

SPINELESS *adj* invertebrate

SPINET *noun* **SPINETS** a musical instrument like a small harpsichord

SPININESS *noun* **SPININESSES** the state of being spiny

SPINNAKER *noun* **SPINNAKERS** a large triangular sail set at the front of a yacht

SPINNER *noun* **SPINNERS** someone or something that spins

SPINNERET *noun* **SPINNERETS** in spiders, silkworms, etc: a small tubular organ that produces the silky thread which they use in making webs, cocoons, etc

SPINNEY *noun* **SPINNEYS** a small wood or thicket, especially one that has a prickly undergrowth

SPINNING *noun* **SPINNINGS** an act of rotating or causing to rotate repeatedly, especially quickly

SPINOSE *adj* said of a plant or animal, or of a specified body part: covered with spines; prickly

SPINOUS *adj* relating to or resembling a spine or thorn

SPINSTER *noun* **SPINSTERS** a woman, especially one who is middle-aged or older, who has never been married

SPINULE *noun* **SPINULES** a tiny spine or thorn

SPINULOSE *adj* characterized by spinules

SPINULOUS *adj* of or like a spinule

SPINY *adj* **SPINIER, SPINIEST** said of plants or animals: covered with spines; prickly

SPIRACLE *noun* **SPIRACLES** any of various paired openings along the side of an insect's body that are used for breathing, each of which represents the external opening of a trachea

SPIRAEA *noun* **SPIRAEAS** a

deciduous northern temperate shrub of the rose family which has clusters of small white or pink flowers

SPIRAL *noun* **SPIRALS** the pattern that is made by a line winding outwards from a central point in circles or near-circles of regularly increasing size □ *verb* **SPIRALS, SPIRALLING, SPIRALLED** to follow a spiral course or pattern

SPIRALITY *noun* **SPIRALITIES** the state or condition of being spiral

SPIRALLY *adverb* in the form of a spiral

SPIRATED *adj* spirally twisted

SPIRE *noun* **SPIRES** a tall thin structure tapering upwards to a point, especially the top of a tower on a church roof

SPIREA *noun* **SPIREAS** a spiraea

SPIRIT *noun* **SPIRITS** the animating or vitalizing essence or force that motivates, invigorates or energizes someone or something □ *verb* **SPIRITS, SPIRITING, SPIRITED** to carry or convey someone or something mysteriously or magically

SPIRITED *adj* full of courage or liveliness

SPIRITUAL *adj* belonging, referring or relating to the spirit or soul rather than to the body or to physical things □ *noun* **SPIRITUALS** a type of religious song that is characterized by voice harmonies

SPIROGYRA *noun* **SPIROGYRAS** a green alga which is found either floating or fixed to stones in ponds and streams and whose colour is due to its spiralling chloroplasts

SPIRT *verb* **SPIRTS, SPIRTING, SPIRTED** to spurt □ *noun* **SPIRTS** a spurt

SPIRTLE *noun* **SPIRTLES** a spurtle

SPIT *verb* **SPITS, SPITTING, SPAT** to expel (saliva or phlegm) from the mouth □ *noun* **SPITS** spittle; a blob of saliva or phlegm that has been spat from the mouth

SPITE *noun* **SPITES** the desire to intentionally and maliciously hurt or offend; ill-will □ *verb* **SPITES, SPITING, SPITED** chiefly used in the infinitive form: to annoy, offend, thwart, etc intentionally and maliciously

SPITEFUL *adj* **SPITEFULLER, SPITEFULLEST** motivated by spite; vengeful; malicious

SPITFIRE *noun* **SPITFIRES**

someone who has a quick or fiery temper, especially a woman or girl

SPITTER *noun* **SPITTERS** someone who spits

SPITTING *noun* **SPITTINGS** an act of expelling (saliva or phlegm) from the mouth

SPITTLE *noun* **SPITTLES** saliva, especially when it has been spat from the mouth; spit

SPITTOON *noun* **SPITTOONS** a container for spitting into, especially one that would formerly have been placed on the floor of a pub

SPITZ *noun* **SPITZES** a breed of dog with a thick coat, a pointed foxy face, pricked ears and a tail that curls up over its back

SPIV *noun* **SPIVS** a man who sells, deals in, or is otherwise involved in the trading of, illicit, blackmarket or stolen goods, and who is usually dressed in a very flashy way

SPIVVY *adj* **SPIVVIER, SPIVVIEST** of or like a spiv

SPLASH *verb* **SPLASHES, SPLASHING, SPLASHED** to make (a liquid or semi-liquid substance) to fly around or land in drops □ *noun* **SPLASHES** a sound of splashing

SPLASHING *noun* **SPLASHINGS** an act or the sound of making a liquid fly around or land in drops

SPLASHY *adj* **SPLASHIER, SPLASHIEST** splashing; with splashing

SPLAT *noun* **SPLATS** the sound made by a soft wet object striking a surface □ *verb* **SPLATS, SPLATTED, SPLATTED** to hit, fall, land, etc with a splat

SPLATTER *verb* **SPLATTERS, SPLATTERING, SPLATTERED** to make something dirty with lots of small scattered drops □ *noun* **SPLATTERS** a splashing sound, especially a repeated or continuous one

SPLAY *verb* **SPLAYS, SPLAYING, SPLAYED** to spread (eg the fingers) □ *noun* **SPLAYS** a sloping surface that is at an oblique angle to a wall, especially one that widens the aspect of a window, door, etc

SPLEEN *noun* **SPLEENS** a delicate organ which is involved in the production of lymphocytes, and also destroys red blood cells that are no longer functional and acts as a reservoir for blood

SPLENDID *adj* **SPLENDIDER,**

SPLENDIDEST very good; excellent

SPLENDOR noun **SPLENDORS** splendour

SPLENDOUR noun **SPLENDOURS** magnificence, opulence or grandeur

SPLENETIC adj belonging, referring or relating to the spleen

SPLENIAL adj of or relating to the splenii

SPLENIC adj splenetic

SPLENITIS noun **SPLENITISES** inflammation of the spleen

SPLENIUS noun **SPLENII, SPLENIUSES** either of the two large thick muscles in the back of the neck

SPLICE verb **SPLICES, SPLICING, SPLICED** to join (two pieces of rope) by weaving the strands of one into the other □ noun **SPLICES** a join eg in rope made in this way

SPLICER noun **SPLICERS** someone who splices ropes

SPLINE noun **SPLINES** any of a number of rectangular keys that fit into the grooves in the shaft of a wheel and which allow for longitudinal movement □ verb **SPLINES, SPLINING, SPLINED** to fit with splines

SPLINT noun **SPLINTS** a piece of rigid material that is strapped to a broken limb, etc to hold it in position while the bone heals □ verb **SPLINTS, SPLINTING, SPLINTED** to bind or hold (a broken limb, etc) in position using a splint

SPLINTER noun **SPLINTERS** a small thin sharp piece that has broken off a hard substance, eg wood or glass □ verb **SPLINTERS, SPLINTERING, SPLINTERED** to break into splinters

SPLINTERY adj **SPLINTERIER, SPLINTERIEST** liable to splinter

SPLIT verb **SPLITS, SPLITTING, SPLIT** to divide or break or cause to divide or break apart or into, usually two, pieces, especially lengthways □ noun **SPLITS** an act or the process of separating or dividing

SPLITTER noun **SPLITTERS** a person or thing that splits

SPLITTING adj said of a headache: very painful; severe

SPLODGE noun **SPLODGES** a large splash, stain or patch □ verb **SPLODGES, SPLODGING, SPLODGED** to mark with splodges

SPLODGILY adverb in a splodgy way

SPLODGY adj **SPLODGIER, SPLODGIEST** marked with splodges

SPLOSH verb **SPLOSHES, SPLOSHING, SPLOSHED** to splash

SPLOTCH noun **SPLOTCHES** a splodge □ verb **SPLOTCHES, SPLOTCHING, SPLOTCHED** to splodge

SPLURGE noun **SPLURGES** an ostentatious display □ verb **SPLURGES, SPLURGING, SPLURGED** to spend extravagantly or ostentatiously

SPLURGY adj **SPLURGIER, SPLURGIEST** of or like a splurge

SPLUTTER verb **SPLUTTERS, SPLUTTERING, SPLUTTERED** to put or throw out drops of liquid, bits of food, sparks, etc with spitting sounds □ noun **SPLUTTERS** the act or noise of spluttering

SPLUTTERING noun **SPLUTTERINGS** an act or the sound of putting or throwing out drops of liquid, etc with spitting sounds

SPLUTTERY adj liable to splutter; spluttering

SPODE noun **SPODES** a type of fine china or porcelain

SPOIL verb **SPOILS, SPOILING, SPOILT, SPOILED** to impair, ruin or make useless or valueless □ noun **SPOILS** possessions taken by force; plunder

SPOILAGE noun **SPOILAGES** an act or the process of spoiling

SPOILED adj said of a child, pet, etc: selfish, demanding, greedy, etc, especially because of having been over-indulged, pampered, etc

SPOILER noun **SPOILERS** a flap on an aircraft wing that is used for increasing drag and so assists in its descent by reducing the air speed

SPOILT adj spoiled

SPOKE ¹ a past form of **speak**

SPOKE ² noun **SPOKES** any of the radiating rods or bars that fan out from the hub of a wheel and attach it to the rim □ verb **SPOKES, SPOKING, SPOKED** to fit with a spoke or spokes

SPOKEN a past form of **speak** □ adj uttered or expressed in speech

SPOKESMAN noun **SPOKESMEN** someone who is appointed to speak on behalf of other people

SPOLIATE verb **SPOLIATES,**

SPOLIATING, SPOLIATED to plunder

SPOLIATOR noun **SPOLIATORS** someone who spoliates

SPONDAIC adj said of a verse or part of a verse: having spondees or being written predominantly in spondees

SPONDEE noun **SPONDEES** a metrical foot of two long syllables or two stressed syllables and which in English verse tends to suggest weariness, depression, slowness, etc

SPONGE noun **SPONGES** any of several hundred different species of aquatic, usually marine, invertebrate animals that consist of a large cluster of cells attached to a solid object such as a rock; a piece of the soft porous skeleton of this animal used in washing, bathing, etc □ verb **SPONGES, SPONGING, SPONGED** to wash or clean with a cloth or sponge and water

SPONGER noun **SPONGERS** someone who survives by habitually imposing on other people, expecting them to pay for things, etc

SPONGILY adverb in a spongy way

SPONGY adj **SPONGIER, SPONGIEST** soft and springy, and perhaps absorbent, like a sponge

SPONSION noun **SPONSIONS** the act of becoming surety for another

SPONSON noun **SPONSONS** a structure that juts out from the deck of a boat and which provides a platform for a gun

SPONSOR noun **SPONSORS** a person or organization that finances an event or broadcast in return for advertising □ verb **SPONSORS, SPONSORING, SPONSORED** to act as a sponsor for someone or something

SPONSORED adj having a sponsor or sponsors

SPOOF noun **SPOOFS** a satirical imitation; a parody □ verb **SPOOFS, SPOOFING, SPOOFED** to parody; to play a hoax

SPOOK noun **SPOOKS** a ghost □ verb **SPOOKS, SPOOKING, SPOOKED** to frighten or startle

SPOOKED adj frightened, startled or wary

SPOOKILY adverb in a spooky way

SPOOKISH adj somewhat spooky

SPOOKY adj **SPOOKIER, SPOOKIEST** uncanny; eerie

SPOOL noun **SPOOLS** a small

cylinder, usually with a hole down the centre and with extended rims at either end, on which thread, photographic film, tape, etc is wound; a reel

SPOON noun **SPOONS** a metal, wooden or plastic utensil that has a handle with a round or oval shallow bowl-like part at one end and which is used for eating, serving or stirring food □ verb **SPOONS, SPOONING, SPOONED** to lift or transfer (food) with a spoon

SPOONBILL noun **SPOONBILLS** any of several types of wading bird that are similar to the ibis, and which have a long flat broad bill with a spoon-shaped tip

SPOONFUL noun **SPOONFULS** the amount a spoon will hold

SPOOR noun **SPOORS** the track or scent left by an animal, especially an animal that is being hunted as game

SPORADIC adj occurring from time to time, at irregular intervals; intermittent

SPORE noun **SPORES** one of the tiny reproductive bodies that are produced in vast quantities by some micro-organisms and certain non-flowering plants, such as ferns and mosses, and which are capable of developing into new individuals

SPOROPHYL noun **SPOROPHYLS** in certain non-flowering plants, such as some mosses, ferns, etc: a leaf that bears sporangia and which, in many cases, has become so highly modified for this purpose that it no longer looks like a conventional leaf

SPORRAN noun **SPORRANS** a pouch for carrying money that is traditionally worn hanging from a belt in front of the kilt in Scottish Highland dress and which is usually made of leather or fur, sometimes with the face of an animal or tassels of animal fur on it

SPORT noun **SPORTS** an activity, pastime, competition, etc that usually involves a degree of physical exertion, eg football, tennis, squash, swimming, boxing, snooker, etc and which people take part in for exercise and/or pleasure □ verb **SPORTS, SPORTING, SPORTED** to wear or display, especially proudly

SPORTILY adj in a sporty way

SPORTING adj belonging, referring or relating to sport

SPORTIVE adj playful

SPORTSMAN noun **SPORTSMEN** a man who takes part in sport, especially at a professional level

SPORTY adj **SPORTIER, SPORTIEST** said of someone: habitually taking part in sport, or being especially fond of, good at, etc sport

SPORULAR adj of or relating to sporules

SPORULE noun **SPORULES** a small spore

SPOT noun **SPOTS** a small mark or stain □ verb **SPOTS, SPOTTING, SPOTTED** to mark with spots

SPOTLESS adj absolutely clean

SPOTLIGHT noun **SPOTLIGHTS** a concentrated circle of light that can be directed onto a small area, especially of a theatre stage □ verb **SPOTLIGHTS, SPOTLIGHTING, SPOTLIT, SPOTLIGHTED** to illuminate with a spotlight

SPOTTED adj patterned or covered with spots

SPOTTER noun **SPOTTERS** someone or something that keeps a vigilant watch

SPOTTING noun **SPOTTINGS** an act of spotting something

SPOTTY adj **SPOTTIER, SPOTTIEST** marked with a pattern of spots

SPOUSE noun **SPOUSES** a husband or wife

SPOUT noun **SPOUTS** a projecting tube or lip, eg on a kettle, teapot, jug, fountain, etc, that allows liquid to pass through or through which it can be poured □ verb **SPOUTS, SPOUTING, SPOUTED** to flow or make something flow out in a jet or stream

SPRAIN verb **SPRAINS, SPRAINING, SPRAINED** to injure (a joint) by the sudden overstretching or tearing of a ligament or ligaments □ noun **SPRAINS** such an injury, which can cause painful swelling that may take several months to heal

SPRANG a past form of **spring**

SPRAT noun **SPRATS** a small edible fish of the herring family

SPRAWL verb **SPRAWLS, SPRAWLING, SPRAWLED** to sit or lie lazily, especially with the arms and legs spread out wide □ noun **SPRAWLS** a sprawling position

SPRAY noun **SPRAYS** a fine mist of small flying drops of liquid □ verb

SPRAYS, SPRAYING, SPRAYED to squirt (a liquid) in the form of a mist

SPREAD verb **SPREADS, SPREADING, SPREAD** to apply, or be capable of being applied, in a smooth coating over a surface □ noun **SPREADS** the act, process or extent of spreading

SPREADER noun **SPREADERS** a machine for spreading bulk materials

SPREADING adj increasing in size, extent, etc

SPREE noun **SPREES** a period of fun, extravagance or excess, especially one that involves spending a lot of money or drinking a lot of alcohol □ verb **SPREES, SPREEING, SPREED** to go on a spree

SPRIG noun **SPRIGS** a small shoot or twig □ verb **SPRIGS, SPRIGGING, SPRIGGED** to embroider or decorate with sprigs

SPRIGHTLY adj **SPRIGHTLIER, SPRIGHTLIEST** said of someone: lively and quick-witted; vivacious

SPRING verb **SPRINGS, SPRINGING, SPRANG, SPRUNG** to leap with a sudden quick launching action □ noun **SPRINGS** a metal coil that can be stretched or compressed, and which will return to its original shape when the pull or pressure is released, especially one where this can be done at a controlled rate so that it can be used to turn a mechanism, eg in a clock, watch, etc

SPRINGBOK noun **SPRINGBOKS** a type of South African antelope that is renowned for its high springing leap when it runs

SPRINGE noun **SPRINGES** a sprung snare that is used for trapping small wild animals and birds □ verb **SPRINGES, SPRINGING, SPRINGED** to set this kind of snare

SPRINGILY adverb in a springy way

SPRINGY adj **SPRINGIER, SPRINGIEST** having the ability to readily spring back to the original shape when any pressure that has been exerted is released; bouncy; elastic; resilient

SPRINKLE verb **SPRINKLES, SPRINKLING, SPRINKLED** to scatter in, or cover with a scattering of, tiny drops or particles □ noun **SPRINKLES** an act of sprinkling

For longer words, see *The Chambers Dictionary*

SPRINKLER *noun* **SPRINKLERS** a person or device that sprinkles, especially one that sprinkles water over plants, a lawn, etc or one for extinguishing fires

SPRINKLING *noun* **SPRINKLINGS** a small amount of something, especially when it is thinly scattered

SPRINT *noun* **SPRINTS** a race at high speed over a short distance □ *verb* **SPRINTS, SPRINTING, SPRINTED** to run at full speed

SPRINTER *noun* **SPRINTERS** an athlete, cyclist, etc who sprints

SPRIT *noun* **SPRITS** a small diagonal spar used to spread a sail

SPRITE *noun* **SPRITES** a playful fairy; an elf or imp

SPRITSAIL *noun* **SPRITSAILS** a sail spread wide by a sprit

SPRITZ *verb* **SPRITZES, SPRITZING, SPRITZED** to spray or squirt something □ *noun* **SPRITZES** an act of spritzing

SPRITZER *noun* **SPRITZERS** a drink of white wine and soda water

SPRITZIG *noun* **SPRITZIGS** a slightly sparkling, usually German, wine

SPROCKET *noun* **SPROCKETS** any of a set of teeth on the rim of a driving wheel, eg fitting into the links of a chain or the holes on a strip of film

SPROG *noun* **SPROGS** a child

SPROUT *verb* **SPROUTS, SPROUTING, SPROUTED** to develop (a new growth, eg of leaves or hair) □ *noun* **SPROUTS** a new growth; a shoot or bud

SPRUCE ¹ *noun* **SPRUCES** any of several kinds of evergreen pyramid-shaped trees which have needle-like leaves and which can be distinguished from fir trees by the way their cones point downwards rather than up

SPRUCE ² *adj* **SPRUCER, SPRUCEST** neat and smart, especially in appearance and dress □ *verb* **SPRUCES, SPRUCING, SPRUCED** to make oneself, someone or something neat and tidy

SPRUCELY *adverb* neatly; smartly

SPRUE *noun* **SPRUES** a vertical channel that leads into a mould and through which molten plastic or metal can be poured

SPRUIK *verb* **SPRUIKS, SPRUIKING, SPRUIKED** said especially of showmen, salesmen, etc: to speak in public, especially at length and using ornate language

SPRUIKER *noun* **SPRUIKERS** someone who spruiks

SPRUNG a past form of **spring** □ *adj* fitted with a spring or springs

SPRY *adj* **SPRYER, SPRYEST** lively; active

SPRYLY *adverb* in a spry way

SPRYNESS *noun* **SPRYNESSES** the state of being spry

SPUD *noun* **SPUDS** a potato; a small narrow digging tool with a chisel-shaped blade □ *verb* **SPUDS, SPUDDING, SPUDDED** to pull up (weeds) using a spud

SPUMANTE *noun* **SPUMANTES** a sparkling, usually sweet Italian wine

SPUME *noun* **SPUMES** foam or froth, especially on the sea □ *verb* **SPUMES, SPUMING, SPUMED** to foam or froth

SPUMY *adj* **SPUMIER, SPUMIEST** foamy

SPUN *adj* formed or made by a spinning process

SPUNK *noun* **SPUNKS** courage; mettle

SPUNKY *adj* **SPUNKIER, SPUNKIEST** brave

SPUR *noun* **SPURS** a device with a spiky metal wheel, fitted to the heel of a horse-rider's boot, which is used for pressing into the horse's side to make it go faster □ *verb* **SPURS, SPURRING, SPURRED** to urge

SPURGE *noun* **SPURGES** any of various plants which produce a bitter, often poisonous, milky juice that was formerly used as a laxative

SPURIOUS *adj* false, counterfeit or untrue, especially when superficially seeming to be genuine

SPURLESS *adj* without spurs

SPURN *verb* **SPURNS, SPURNING, SPURNED** to reject (eg a person's love) scornfully □ *noun* **SPURNS** an act or instance of spurning

SPURNING *noun* **SPURNINGS** an act of rejecting (eg a person's love) scornfully

SPURREY *noun* **SPURREYS** any of several varieties of annual plants or weeds, related to the pearlworts, which have very slender stems and leaves and small delicate flowers

SPURRY *adj* **SPURRIER, SPURRIEST** like or having spurs

SPURT *verb* **SPURTS, SPURTING, SPURTED** to flow out or make something flow out in a sudden sharp jet □ *noun* **SPURTS** a jet of liquid that suddenly gushes out

SPURTLE *noun* **SPURTLES** a wooden stick used for stirring porridge, soup, etc

SPUTNIK *noun* **SPUTNIKS** an artificial satellite that orbits the Earth, especially one of those launched by the former Soviet Union between 1957 and 1961

SPUTTER *verb* **SPUTTERS, SPUTTERING, SPUTTERED** to speak or say haltingly or incoherently □ *noun* **SPUTTERS** disjointed, incomprehensible speech

SPUTTERER *noun* **SPUTTERERS** someone who sputters

SPUTTERY *adj* with a sputter; liable to sputter

SPUTUM *noun* **SPUTA** a mixture of saliva, mucus and/or pus that is coughed up from the bronchial passages, and is indicative of an inflammatory disorder, especially in smoking-related conditions and other pulmonary conditions such as bronchitis, etc

SPY *noun* **SPIES** someone who is employed by a government or organization to gather information about political enemies, competitors, etc □ *verb* **SPIES, SPYING, SPIED** to act or be employed as a spy

SPYGLASS *noun* **SPYGLASSES** a small hand-held telescope

SPYHOLE *noun* **SPYHOLES** a small glass hole in a door that enables someone to see who is there before deciding to open the door; a peephole

SQUAB *noun* **SQUABS** a young unfledged bird, especially a pigeon □ *adj* **SQUABBER, SQUABBEST** said of a bird: newly hatched and unfledged

SQUABBLE *verb* **SQUABBLES, SQUABBLING, SQUABBLED** to quarrel noisily, especially about something trivial □ *noun* **SQUABBLES** a noisy quarrel, especially a petty one

SQUABBLER *noun* **SQUABBLERS** someone who squabbles

SQUABBY *adj* **SQUABBIER, SQUABBIEST** squat

SQUACCO *noun* **SQUACCOS** a small crested heron found in S Europe

SQUAD noun **SQUADS** a small group of soldiers, often twelve, who do drill formation together or who work together

SQUADDIE noun **SQUADDIES** a squaddy

SQUADDY noun **SQUADDIES** an ordinary soldier; a private

SQUADRON noun **SQUADRONS** a group of between 10 and 18 military aircraft which form the principal unit of an air force ◻ verb **SQUADRONS, SQUADRONING, SQUADRONED** to form into squadrons

SQUADRONED adj formed into squadrons

SQUALID adj **SQUALIDER, SQUALIDEST** said especially of places to live: disgustingly filthy and neglected

SQUALIDLY adverb in a squalid way

SQUALL noun **SQUALLS** a sudden or short-lived violent gust of wind, usually accompanied by rain or sleet ◻ verb **SQUALLS, SQUALLING, SQUALLED** said of a wind: to blow in a squall

SQUALLER noun **SQUALLERS** someone who yells

SQUALLY adj **SQUALLIER, SQUALLIEST** disturbed with squalls or gusts of wind

SQUALOR noun **SQUALORS** the condition or quality of being disgustingly filthy

SQUAMA noun **SQUAMAE** a scale or scale-like structure

SQUAMOSE adj scaly

SQUAMOUS adj squamose

SQUANDER verb **SQUANDERS, SQUANDERING, SQUANDERED** to use up (money, time, etc) wastefully

SQUARE adj **SQUARER, SQUAREST** shaped like a square or, sometimes, like a cube ◻ noun **SQUARES** a two-dimensional figure with four sides of equal length and four right angles ◻ verb **SQUARES, SQUARING, SQUARED** to make square in shape, especially to make right-angled

SQUARELY adverb in a square way

SQUARER noun **SQUARERS** a person or thing that squares

SQUARIAL noun **SQUARIALS** a flat diamond-shaped (as opposed to round) aerial for receiving satellite television broadcasts

SQUARISH adj somewhat square

SQUARROSE adj rough; having scaly projections

SQUASH verb **SQUASHES, SQUASHING, SQUASHED** to crush or flatten by pressing or squeezing ◻ noun **SQUASHES** a concentrated fruit syrup, or a drink made by diluting this

SQUASHILY adverb in a squashy way

SQUASHY adj **SQUASHIER, SQUASHIEST** soft and easily squashed

SQUAT verb **SQUATS, SQUATTING, SQUATTED** to take up, or be sitting in, a low position with the knees fully bent and the weight on the soles of the feet ◻ noun **SQUATS** a squatting position ◻ adj

SQUATTER, SQUATTEST short and broad or fat

SQUATNESS noun **SQUATNESSES** the state of being squat

SQUATTER noun **SQUATTERS** someone who unlawfully occupies a building, usually an empty one

SQUAWK noun **SQUAWKS** a loud harsh screeching noise, especially one made by a bird, eg a parrot ◻ verb **SQUAWKS, SQUAWKING, SQUAWKED** to make a loud harsh screeching noise

SQUAWKER noun **SQUAWKERS** a person or animal that squawks

SQUAWKY adj **SQUAWKIER, SQUAWKIEST** loud and screeching

SQUEAK noun **SQUEAKS** a short high-pitched cry or sound, like that made by a mouse or a rusty gate ◻ verb **SQUEAKS, SQUEAKING, SQUEAKED** to utter a squeak or with a squeak

SQUEAKER noun **SQUEAKERS** a person or thing that squeaks

SQUEAKILY adverb in a squeaky way

SQUEAKY adj **SQUEAKIER, SQUEAKIEST** characterized by squeaks or tending to squeak

SQUEAL noun **SQUEALS** a long high-pitched noise, cry or yelp, like that of a pig, a child, etc ◻ verb **SQUEALS, SQUEALING, SQUEALED** to utter a squeal or with a squeal

SQUEALER noun **SQUEALERS** someone or something that squeals

SQUEAMISH adj slightly nauseous; easily made nauseous

SQUEEGEE noun **SQUEEGEES** a device with a rubber blade for scraping water off a surface, eg a window, windscreen, vinyl floor, etc ◻ verb **SQUEEGEES,**

SQUEEGEEING, SQUEEGEED to use a squeegee to remove water from (a window, photographic print, etc)

SQUEEZE verb **SQUEEZES, SQUEEZING, SQUEEZED** to grasp or embrace tightly ◻ noun **SQUEEZES** an act of squeezing

SQUEEZER noun **SQUEEZERS** a person, device, machine, etc that squeezes something (especially fruit)

SQUEEZY adj **SQUEEZIER, SQUEEZIEST** said of a bottle, container, etc: soft and flexible so that its contents can be squeezed out

SQUEG verb **SQUEGS, SQUEGGING, SQUEGGED** to oscillate intermittently or irregularly

SQUELCH noun **SQUELCHES** a loud gurgling or sucking sound made by contact with a thick sticky substance, eg wet mud ◻ verb **SQUELCHES, SQUELCHING, SQUELCHED** to walk through wet ground or with water in one's shoes and so make this sound

SQUELCHER noun **SQUELCHERS** a person or thing that squelches

SQUELCHY adj **SQUELCHIER, SQUELCHIEST** liable to squelch

SQUIB noun **SQUIBS** a small firework that jumps around on the ground before exploding

SQUID noun **SQUIDS** any of about 350 species of marine mollusc, related to the octopus and cuttlefish, which have a torpedo-shaped body supported by an internal horny plate, two well-developed eyes, eight sucker-bearing arms and two longer tentacles which they use to seize fish

SQUIDGE verb **SQUIDGES, SQUIDGING, SQUIDGED** to squash; to squeeze together; to squelch

SQUIDGY adj **SQUIDGIER, SQUIDGIEST** soft, pliant and sometimes soggy

SQUIFFY adj **SQUIFFIER, SQUIFFIEST** slightly drunk; tipsy

SQUIGGLE noun **SQUIGGLES** a wavy scribbled line ◻ verb **SQUIGGLES, SQUIGGLING, SQUIGGLED** to wriggle

SQUIGGLY adj **SQUIGGLIER, SQUIGGLIEST** wriggly

SQUILL noun **SQUILLS** any of

several perennial plants of the lily family that have small onion-like bulbs and white, blue or purply-blue flowers

SQUINCH noun **SQUINCHES** a small arch running diagonally across each corner of a square building or room, creating an octagonal base on which a tower or circular dome may be supported

SQUINT noun **SQUINTS** the condition of having one or both eyes set slightly off-centre, preventing parallel vision; a quick look □ verb **SQUINTS, SQUINTING, SQUINTED** to be affected by a squint □ adj **SQUINTER, SQUINTEST** not being properly straight

SQUINTER noun **SQUINTERS** someone who squints

SQUINTING noun **SQUINTINGS** a quick look

SQUIRE noun **SQUIRES** formerly, in England and Ireland: an owner of a large area of rural land, especially the chief landowner in a district

SQUIRM verb **SQUIRMS, SQUIRMING, SQUIRMED** to wriggle along □ noun **SQUIRMS** a writhing or wriggling movement

SQUIRMY adj **SQUIRMIER, SQUIRMIEST** squirming

SQUIRREL noun **SQUIRRELS** any of various medium-sized rodents that are found almost worldwide, which have a bushy tail, beady eyes and tufty ears, and which are noted for holding their food in their front paws as they feed □ verb **SQUIRRELS, SQUIRRELLING, SQUIRRELLED** to store or put away something for future use

SQUIRT verb **SQUIRTS, SQUIRTING, SQUIRTED** to shoot (a liquid, etc) out in a narrow jet □ noun **SQUIRTS** an act or instance of squirting

SQUIRTER noun **SQUIRTERS** a person or thing that squirts

SQUIRTING noun **SQUIRTINGS** an act of shooting (a liquid, etc) out in a narrow jet

SQUISH noun **SQUISHES** a gentle splashing or squelching sound □ verb **SQUISHES, SQUISHING, SQUISHED** to make this sound; to move with this sound

SQUISHY adj **SQUISHIER, SQUISHIEST** squelchy

SQUIT noun **SQUITS** an insignificant person

SQUIZ noun **SQUIZZES** an Australian slang term for a quick, close look

ST exclamation requesting silence

STAB verb **STABS, STABBING, STABBED** to wound or pierce with a sharp or pointed instrument or weapon □ noun **STABS** an act of stabbing

STABBER noun **STABBERS** someone who stabs

STABBING noun **STABBINGS** an act or the action or process of using a sharp implement to cut, wound, etc

STABILISE verb **STABILISES, STABILISING, STABILISED** to stabilize

STABILITY noun **STABILITIES** the state or quality of being stable

STABILIZE verb **STABILIZES, STABILIZING, STABILIZED** to make or become stable or more stable

STABLE[1] adj **STABLER, STABLEST** firmly balanced or fixed; not likely to wobble or fall over

STABLE[2] noun **STABLES** a building where horses are kept □ verb **STABLES, STABLING, STABLED** to put (a horse) into or back into its stable

STABLING noun **STABLINGS** a stable

STABLY adverb in a stable way; firmly

STACCATO adverb in a short, abrupt manner □ adj short and abrupt □ noun **STACCATOS** a piece of music or a series of notes to be played in this way

STACK noun **STACKS** a large pile □ verb **STACKS, STACKING, STACKED** to arrange in a stack or stacks

STACKED adj gathered into a pile

STACKER noun **STACKERS** a person who stacks, especially someone employed to fill supermarket shelves

STADIUM noun **STADIUMS, STADIA** a large sports arena in which the spectators' seats are arranged in rising tiers

STAFF noun **STAFFS** the total number of employees working in an establishment or organization □ verb **STAFFS, STAFFING, STAFFED** to provide (an establishment) with staff

STAFFER noun **STAFFERS** someone employed on a permanent basis, especially in journalism, as opposed to someone on a temporary contract or a freelance or casual worker

STAG noun **STAGS** an adult male deer, especially a red deer

STAGE noun **STAGES** a platform on which a performance takes place, especially one in a theatre □ verb **STAGES, STAGING, STAGED** to present a performance of (a play)

STAGER noun **STAGERS** someone who has had plenty of experience in a specified field

STAGEY adj **STAGIER, STAGIEST** stagy

STAGGER verb **STAGGERS, STAGGERING, STAGGERED** to walk or move unsteadily □ noun **STAGGERS** the action or an act of staggering

STAGGERED adj arranged in such a way that the beginning, ending, etc do not coincide; alternate

STAGGERING adj amazing; shockingly surprising

STAGGERS singular noun a disease of the brain in horses and cattle that causes them to stagger

STAGILY adverb in a stagy way

STAGINESS noun **STAGINESSES** the state of being stagy

STAGING noun **STAGINGS** scaffolding, especially the horizontal planks used for walking on; any temporary platform

STAGNANCY noun **STAGNANCIES** the state of being stagnant

STAGNANT adj said of water: not flowing; dirty and foul-smelling because of a lack of movement

STAGNATE verb **STAGNATES, STAGNATING, STAGNATED** to be or become stagnant

STAGY adj **STAGIER, STAGIEST** theatrical; artificial or affectedly pretentious

STAID adj **STAIDER, STAIDEST** serious or sober in character or manner, especially to the point of being dull

STAIDLY adverb in a staid way

STAIDNESS noun **STAIDNESSES** the state or condition of being staid

STAIN verb **STAINS, STAINING, STAINED** to make or become marked or discoloured, often permanently □ noun **STAINS** a mark or discoloration

For longer words, see *The Chambers Dictionary*

STAINER *noun* **STAINERS** someone who stains

STAINLESS *adj* without a stain

STAIR *noun* **STAIRS** any of a set of indoor steps connecting the floors of a building

STAIRCASE *noun* **STAIRCASES** a set of stairs, often including the stairwell

STAIRWAY *noun* **STAIRWAYS** a way into a building or part of a building that involves going up a staircase

STAIRWELL *noun* **STAIRWELLS** the vertical shaft containing a staircase

STAKE *noun* **STAKES** a stick or post, usually with one pointed end, that is knocked into the ground as a support, eg for a young tree or a fence ❑ *verb* **STAKES, STAKING, STAKED** to support or fasten to the ground with a stake

STALAG *noun* **STALAGS** during World War II: a prisoner-of-war camp set up by the Germans for non-commissioned officers and men

STALE[1] *adj* **STALER, STALEST** said of food: past its best because it has been kept too long; not fresh and, therefore, unpalatable

STALE[2] *verb* **STALES, STALING, STALED** said of horses and cattle: to urinate

STALELY *adverb* in a stale way

STALEMATE *noun* **STALEMATES** in chess: a position where either player cannot make a move without putting their king in check and which results in a draw

STALENESS *noun* **STALENESSES** the state or condition of being stale

STALK[1] *noun* **STALKS** the main stem of a plant

STALK[2] *verb* **STALKS, STALKING, STALKED** to hunt, follow, or approach stealthily

STALKER *noun* **STALKERS** someone who stalks, especially game

STALKING *noun* **STALKINGS** an act of hunting, following or approaching stealthily

STALKLESS *adj* without a stalk

STALL *noun* **STALLS** a compartment in a cowshed, stable, etc for housing a single animal ❑ *verb* **STALLS, STALLING, STALLED** said of a motor vehicle or its engine: to cut out or make it cut out unintentionally, especially by not using the clutch properly

STALLION *noun* **STALLIONS** an uncastrated adult male horse, especially one kept for breeding

STALWART *adj* strong and sturdy ❑ *noun* **STALWARTS** a long-standing and committed supporter, especially a political one

STAMEN *noun* **STAMENS, STAMINA** in flowering plants: the male reproductive structure, which consists of a stalk-like filament that supports a specialized double-celled chamber at its end where the pollen grains are produced

STAMINA *noun* **STAMINAS** energy and staying power, especially of the kind that is needed to tackle and withstand prolonged physical or mental exertion

STAMINATE *adj* said of certain flowering plants: having male reproductive parts, but no female ones

STAMMER *verb* **STAMMERS, STAMMERING, STAMMERED** to speak or say something in a faltering or hesitant way, often by repeating words or parts of words, usually because of indecision, heightened emotion or a pathological disorder that affects the speech organs or the nervous system ❑ *noun* **STAMMERS** a way of speaking that is characterized by this kind of faltering or hesitancy

STAMMERER *noun* **STAMMERERS** someone who stammers

STAMMERING *noun* **STAMMERINGS** an act of stammering; a stammered statement

STAMP *verb* **STAMPS, STAMPING, STAMPED** to bring (the foot) down with force ❑ *noun* **STAMPS** a small piece of gummed paper bearing an official mark and indicating that a tax or fee has been paid, especially a postage stamp

STAMPEDE *noun* **STAMPEDES** a sudden dash made by a group of startled animals, especially when they all go charging off in the same direction ❑ *verb* **STAMPEDES, STAMPEDING, STAMPEDED** to rush or make (people or animals) rush in a herd or crowd

STAMPER *noun* **STAMPERS** a person or thing that stamps

STAMPING *noun* **STAMPINGS** an act of bringing (the foot) down with force

STANCE *noun* **STANCES** point of view; a specified attitude towards something

STANCH *verb* **STANCHES, STANCHING, STANCHED** to staunch

STANCHION *noun* **STANCHIONS** an upright beam or pole that functions as a support, eg in a window, ship, mine, etc

STAND *verb* **STANDS, STANDING, STOOD** to be in, remain in or move into an upright position supported by the legs or a base ❑ *noun* **STANDS** a base on which something sits or is supported

STANDARD *noun* **STANDARDS** an established or accepted model ❑ *adj* having features that are generally accepted as normal or expected; typical; average; unexceptional

STANDING *noun* **STANDINGS** position, status, or reputation

STANDOUT *noun* **STANDOUTS** someone or something that is of high quality

STANDPIPE *noun* **STANDPIPES** a vertical pipe leading from a water supply, especially one that provides an emergency supply in the street when household water is cut off

STANHOPE *noun* **STANHOPES** a light open one-seater carriage originally with two wheels but later commonly with four

STANK a past form of **stink**

STANNARY *noun* **STANNARIES** a tin-mining district

STANNIC *adj* said of a compound: containing tin, especially in the tetravalent state

STANNITE *noun* **STANNITES** sulphur of copper, iron and tin which usually occurs in tin-bearing veins

STANNOUS *adj* said of a compound: containing tin, especially in the bivalent state

STANZA *noun* **STANZAS** a verse in poetry

STANZAIC *adj* of or relating to stanzas

STAPES *noun* **STAPES, STAPEDES** a small stirrup-shaped bone in the middle ear which, together with the malleus and incus, transmits sound waves from the eardrum to the inner ear

STAPLE *noun* **STAPLES** a squared-off U-shaped wire fastener for holding sheets of paper together and which is forced through the paper from a special device that has several of these loaded into it □ *verb* **STAPLES, STAPLING, STAPLED** to fasten or attach with a staple or staples

STAPLER *noun* **STAPLERS** a device for driving staples through paper

STAR *noun* **STARS** any celestial body that can be seen in a clear night sky as a twinkling white light, which consists of a sphere of gaseous material that is held together entirely by its own gravitational field □ *verb* **STARS, STARRING, STARRED** to feature someone as a principal performer or to appear in (a film, TV programme, theatre production, etc) as a principal performer

STARBOARD *noun* **STARBOARDS** the right side of a ship or aircraft as you look towards the front of it □ *adj* relating to, on or towards the right side □ *adverb* relating to, on or towards the right side

STARCH *noun* **STARCHES** a carbohydrate that occurs in all green plants, where it serves as an energy store, usually in the form of small white granules in seeds, tubers, etc □ *verb* **STARCHES, STARCHING, STARCHED** to stiffen (fabrics, paper, etc) with starch

STARCHER *noun* **STARCHERS** someone who starches

STARCHILY *adverb* in a stiff or formal way

STARCHY *adj* **STARCHIER, STARCHIEST** like or containing starch; stiff, formal

STARDOM *noun* **STARDOMS** the state of being a being or causing someone or something to be slightly shocked or surprised

STARDUST *noun* **STARDUSTS** an imaginary dust that blinds someone's eyes to reality and fills their thoughts with romantic illusions

STARE *verb* **STARES, STARING, STARED** said of someone or their eyes: to look with a fixed gaze □ *noun* **STARES** an act of staring

STARFISH *noun* **STARFISHES** the popular name for any of numerous types of marine invertebrate animals that have a number of arms (usually five) radiating outward from a flattened central disc-like body

STARGAZER *noun* **STARGAZERS** an astronomer; an astrologer

STARK *adj* **STARKER, STARKEST** barren or severely bare; harsh or simple □ *adverb* utterly; completely

STARKERS *adj* stark-naked

STARKLY *adverb* in a stark way

STARKNESS *noun* **STARKNESSES** the state of being stark

STARLESS *adj* without stars

STARLET *noun* **STARLETS** a young film actress, especially one who is thought to have the potential to become a star of the future

STARLIGHT *noun* **STARLIGHTS** the light from the stars

STARLIKE *adj* like a star, especially in twinkling

STARLING *noun* **STARLINGS** a small common gregarious songbird which has dark glossy speckled feathers and a short tail

STARLIT *adj* lit by the stars

STARRILY *adverb* in a starry way

STARRY *adj* **STARRIER, STARRIEST** relating to or like a star or the stars; filled or decorated with stars

START *verb* **STARTS, STARTING, STARTED** to begin; to bring or come into being □ *noun* **STARTS** the first or early part

STARTER *noun* **STARTERS** an official who gives the signal for a race to begin

STARTLE *verb* **STARTLES, STARTLING, STARTLED** to be or cause someone or something to be slightly shocked or surprised, often with an attendant jump or twitch □ *noun* **STARTLES** a slight shock or surprise

STARTLER *noun* **STARTLERS** someone who startles

STARTLING *noun* **STARTLINGS** an act of being or causing someone or something to be slightly shocked or surprised

STARVE *verb* **STARVES, STARVING, STARVED** to die or cause someone or something to die because of a long-term lack of food

STARVING *noun* **STARVINGS** an act of dying or causing someone or something to die through lack of food

STARWORT *noun* **STARWORTS** an aquatic plant with a star-shaped rosette of leaves

STASH *verb* **STASHES, STASHING, STASHED** to put into a hiding-place □ *noun* **STASHES** a hidden supply or store of something, or its hiding-place

STASIS *noun* **STASES** a condition where the normal circulation or flow of some body fluid, such as blood, urine, etc, has stopped

STATABLE *adj* capable of being stated

STATE *noun* **STATES** the condition, eg of health, appearance, emotions, etc that someone or something is in at a particular time □ *verb* **STATES, STATING, STATED** to express clearly, either in written or spoken form; to affirm or assert

STATEHOOD *noun* **STATEHOODS** the condition of being a state

STATELESS *adj* having no nationality or citizenship

STATELY *adj* **STATELIER, STATELIEST** noble, dignified and impressive in appearance or manner

STATEMENT *noun* **STATEMENTS** a thing stated, especially a formal written or spoken declaration

STATEROOM *noun* **STATEROOMS** a large room in a palace, etc that is used for ceremonial occasions

STATESIDE *adj* belonging, referring or relating to, or in, the USA □ *adverb* to or towards the USA

STATESMAN *noun* **STATESMEN** an experienced and distinguished male politician

STATIC *adj* not moving; stationary □ *noun* **STATICS** an accumulation of electric charges that remain at rest instead of moving to form a flow of current, eg electricity produced by friction between two materials such as hair and a plastic comb

STATICS *singular noun* the branch of mechanics that deals with the action of balanced forces on bodies such that they remain at rest or in unaccelerated motion

STATION *noun* **STATIONS** a place where trains or buses regularly stop so that people can get off and on, goods can be loaded and unloaded, refuelling can be done, tickets bought, etc □ *verb* **STATIONS, STATIONING, STATIONED** to assign or appoint to a post or place of duty

STATIONER *noun* **STATIONERS** a person or shop that sells stationery

STATISTIC *noun* **STATISTICS** a specified piece of information or data

STATISTICS *plural noun* items of related information that have been collected, collated, interpreted, analysed and presented to show particular trends ◻ *singular noun* the branch of mathematics concerned with drawing inferences from numerical data, based on probability theory, especially in so far as conclusions can be made on the basis of an appropriate sample from a population

STATIVE *adj* said of verbs: indicating a state as opposed to an action; *seem* and *like* would fall into this category, whereas *look* and *walk* would not ◻ *noun* **STATIVES** a verb of this kind

STATOR *noun* **STATORS** the part in an electric motor or generator that does not move

STATUARY *noun* **STATUARIES** statues collectively ◻ *adj* belonging or referring to statues or to the sculpting of them

STATUE *noun* **STATUES** a sculpted, moulded or cast figure, especially of a person or animal, usually life-size or larger, and often erected in a public place to commemorate someone famous

STATUETTE *noun* **STATUETTES** a small statue

STATURE *noun* **STATURES** the height of a person, animal, tree, etc

STATUS *noun* **STATUSES** rank or position in relation to others, within society, an organization, etc

STATUTE *noun* **STATUTES** a law made by the legislative assembly of a country and recorded in a formal document

STATUTORY *adj* required or prescribed by law or a rule

STAUNCH ¹ *adj* **STAUNCHER, STAUNCHEST** loyal; trusty; steadfast

STAUNCH ² *verb* **STAUNCHES, STAUNCHING, STAUNCHED** to stop the flow of (something, such as blood from a wound, information, gossip, etc)

STAUNCHLY *adverb* in a staunch way

STAVE *noun* **STAVES** any of the vertical wooden strips that are joined together to form a barrel, tub, boat hull, etc ◻ *verb* **STAVES, STAVING, STOVE, STAVED** to smash (a hole, etc in something)

STAY *verb* **STAYS, STAYING, STAYED** to remain in the same place or condition, without moving or changing ◻ *noun* **STAYS**

a period of temporary residence; a visit

STAYER *noun* **STAYERS** a person or animal who has great powers of endurance

STAYSAIL *noun* **STAYSAILS** an auxiliary sail that is usually triangular

STEAD *noun* **STEADS** the place of someone or something else

STEADFAST *adj* firm; resolute; determinedly unwavering

STEADILY *adverb* in a steady way

STEADING *noun* **STEADINGS** the outbuildings of a farm

STEADY *adj* **STEADIER, STEADIEST** firmly fixed or balanced; not tottering or wobbling ◻ *verb* **STEADIES, STEADYING, STEADIED** to make or become steady or steadier ◻ *adverb* in a steady manner

STEAK *noun* **STEAKS** fine quality beef for frying or grilling

STEAL *verb* **STEALS, STEALING, STOLE, STOLEN** to take away (another person's property) without permission or legal right, especially secretly ◻ *noun* **STEALS** a bargain; something that can be easily obtained

STEALTH *noun* **STEALTHS** softness and quietness of movement in order to avoid being noticed

STEALTHY *adj* **STEALTHIER, STEALTHIEST** acting or done with stealth; furtive

STEAM *noun* **STEAMS** the colourless gas formed by vaporizing water at $100°C$, which becomes visible in air due to suspended water droplets, and which can be used as a source of power or energy, eg in steam engines ◻ *verb* **STEAMS, STEAMING, STEAMED** to give off steam

STEAMBOAT *noun* **STEAMBOATS** a vessel that is driven by steam

STEAMER *noun* **STEAMERS** a ship whose engines are powered by steam

STEAMIE *noun* **STEAMIES** formerly, in Scotland: a public building, generally in densely populated areas, where people could do their washing

STEAMILY *adverb* in a steamy way

STEAMING *adj* said of a liquid: very hot ◻ *noun* **STEAMINGS** the act or process of cooking with steam

STEAMY *adj* **STEAMIER,**

STEAMIEST full of, clouded by, emitting, etc steam

STEARATE *noun* **STEARATES** any of the salts or esters of stearic acid

STEARIC *adj* derived from, containing, etc fat

STEARIN *noun* **STEARINS** any of the three glyceryl esters of stearic acid

STEARINE *adj* of or relating to stearin

STEATITE *noun* **STEATITES** soapstone

STEATITIC *adj* of or relating to steatite

STEED *noun* **STEEDS** a horse, especially one that is lively and bold

STEEL *noun* **STEELS** any of a number of iron alloys that contain small amounts of carbon and, in some cases, additional elements, eg chromium, nickel, manganese, silicon, molybdenum, and which are used in the manufacture of motor vehicles, ships, bridges, machinery, tools, etc ◻ *verb* **STEELS, STEELING, STEELED** to harden oneself or prepare oneself emotionally, especially for something unpleasant or unwelcome

STEELWORK *noun* **STEELWORKS** welded steel beams and columns that are constructed to form the frames in large building projects such as office blocks and warehouses

STEELWORKS *singular and plural noun* a factory where steel is manufactured

STEELY *adj* **STEELIER, STEELIEST** cold, hard and unyielding

STEELYARD *noun* **STEELYARDS** a type of weighing machine that has one short arm that the object to be weighed is put onto and another longer graduated arm which has a single weight on it which is pushed along the arm until the balance is established

STEENBOK *noun* **STEENBOKS** a small S African antelope

STEENBRAS *noun* **STEENBRASES** any of several kinds of marine fish found especially in the estuaries of S African rivers and used as food

STEEP ¹ *adj* **STEEPER, STEEPEST** sloping sharply

STEEP ² *verb* **STEEPS, STEEPING, STEEPED** to soak something thoroughly in liquid

STEEPEN verb **STEEPENS, STEEPENING, STEEPENED** to make or become steep or steeper

STEEPER noun **STEEPERS** a vessel for steeping things in

STEEPISH adj somewhat steep

STEEPLE noun **STEEPLES** a tower, especially one with a spire, that forms part of a church or temple

STEEPLED adj having a steeple

STEEPLY adverb in a steep way

STEEPNESS noun the state or condition of being steep

STEER[1] verb **STEERS, STEERING, STEERED** to guide or control the direction of (a vehicle or vessel) using a steering wheel, rudder, etc

STEER[2] noun **STEERS** a young castrated bull or male ox, especially one that is being reared for beef

STEERABLE adj capable of being steered

STEERAGE noun **STEERAGES** the cheapest accommodation on board a passenger ship, traditionally near the rudder

STEERER noun **STEERERS** someone who steers

STEERING noun **STEERINGS** an act or the process of guiding or controlling the direction of (a vehicle or vessel) using a steering wheel, rudder, etc

STEEVE noun **STEEVES** the angular elevation of a bowsprit, etc ▫ verb **STEEVES, STEEVING, STEEVED** to incline (a bowsprit, etc) upwards at an angle to the horizon

STEIN noun **STEINS** a large metal or earthenware beer mug, often with a hinged lid

STEINBOCK noun **STEINBOCKS** another name for the Alpine ibex

STELA noun **STELAE** the central cylinder in the stems and roots of vascular plants

STELAR adj of or relating to stelae

STELE noun **STELAE** an ancient stone pillar or upright slab, usually carved or engraved

STELLAR adj referring or relating to or resembling a star or stars

STELLATE adj shaped like a star

STELLATED adj stellate

STELLULAR adj shaped like a little star

STEM noun **STEMS** the central part of a plant that grows upward from its root ▫ verb **STEMS, STEMMING, STEMMED** to

originate or derive from something or someone

STEMLESS adj without a stem

STEMLET noun **STEMLETS** a small stem

STEMMA noun **STEMMATA** a family tree or a diagrammatic representation of one

STEMSON noun **STEMSONS** a curved timber that is fitted into the stem and keelson at the bow of a wooden vessel

STENCH noun **STENCHES** a strong and extremely unpleasant smell

STENCIL noun **STENCILS** a card or plate that has shapes cut out of it to form a pattern, letter, etc and which is put onto a surface, eg paper, a wall, etc, and ink or paint applied so that the cut-out design is transferred to the surface ▫ verb **STENCILS, STENCILLING, STENCILLED** to mark or decorate (a surface) using a stencil

STENCILLING noun **STENCILLINGS** an act of using a stencil

STENOSIS noun **STENOSES** the abnormal narrowing of a passageway, duct or canal

STENOTIC adj of or relating to stenosis

STEP noun **STEPS** a single complete action of lifting then placing down the foot in walking or running ▫ verb **STEPS, STEPPING, STEPPED** to move by lifting up each foot alternately and setting it down in a different place

STEPCHILD noun **STEPCHILDREN** a child of someone's spouse or partner who is the offspring of a previous relationship

STEPPE noun **STEPPES** an extensive dry grassy and usually treeless plain, especially one found in SE Europe and Asia extending east from the Ukraine through to the Manchurian plains of China

STEPPER noun **STEPPERS** someone who steps

STEPSON noun **STEPSONS** a child of someone's spouse or partner who is the offspring of a previous relationship

STERADIAN noun **STERADIANS** the SI unit that is used for measuring solid (three-dimensional) angles

STERE noun **STERES** a measurement used for timber and equal to a cubic metre (35.315 cubic feet)

STEREO noun **STEREOS** a cassette player, hi-fi system etc that gives stereophonic reproduction of sound

STERIC adj pertaining, referring or relating to the spacial arrangement of atoms in a molecule

STERILE adj biologically incapable of producing offspring, fruit or seeds

STERILISE verb **STERILISES, STERILISING, STERILISED** to sterilize

STERILITY noun **STERILITIES** the state or condition of being sterile

STERILIZE verb **STERILIZES, STERILIZING, STERILIZED** to make something germ-free

STERLING noun **STERLINGS** British money ▫ adj good quality; worthy; reliable

STERN[1] adj **STERNER, STERNEST** extremely strict; authoritarian

STERN[2] noun **STERNS** the rear of a ship or boat

STERNAL adj of or relating to the sternum

STERNLY adverb in a stern way

STERNMOST adj nearest the stern

STERNNESS noun **STERNNESSES** the state or condition of being stern

STERNPORT noun **STERNPORTS** an opening in the stern of a ship

STERNPOST noun **STERNPOSTS** an upright beam in the stern of a ship that supports the rudder

STERNUM noun **STERNUMS, STERNA** in humans: the broad vertical bone in the chest that the ribs and collarbone are attached to; the breastbone

STEROID noun **STEROIDS** any of a large group of fat-soluble organic compounds, such as sterols, some sex harmones, bile acids, etc that have a complex molecular structure (17-carbon-atom, four-linked ring system), and which are important both physiologically and pharmacologically

STEROL noun **STEROLS** any of a group of colourless waxy solid steroid alcohols that are found in plants, animals and fungi, eg cholesterol

STET noun **STETS** a conventionalized direction that is usually found in the margin of a manuscript or other text to indicate that something which has been changed or marked for deletion is to be retained in its original form after all □ *verb* **STETS, STETTING, STETTED** to put this kind of mark on a manuscript, etc

STEVEDORE *noun* **STEVEDORES** someone whose job is to load and unload ships; a docker □ *verb* **STEVEDORES, STEVEDORING, STEVEDORED** to load or unload (a ship or a ship's cargo)

STEW *verb* **STEWS, STEWING, STEWED** to cook (especially meat) by long simmering □ *noun* **STEWS** a dish of food, especially a mixture of meat and vegetables, that has been cooked by stewing

STEWARD *noun* **STEWARDS** someone whose job is to look after the needs of passengers on a ship or aircraft □ *verb* **STEWARDS, STEWARDING, STEWARDED** to serve as a steward of something

STEWED *adj* said of meat, vegetables, fruit, etc: cooked by stewing

STHENIC *adj* said of a disease or its symptoms: having excessive muscular strength or energy

STIBINE *noun* **STIBINES** a colourless poisonous gas that is slightly water-soluble

STIBNITE *noun* **STIBNITES** a grey mineral that is found in quartz veins and which is the chief ore of antimony

STICH *noun* **STICHS** a piece of poetry or prose of a designated length; a line or verse

STICHIC *adj* of or relating to stichs

STICK [1] *noun* **STICKS** a twig or thin branch of a tree □ *verb* **STICKS, STICKING, STICKED** to support (a plant) using a stick or sticks

STICK [2] *verb* **STICKS, STICKING, STUCK** to push or thrust (especially something long and thin or pointed)

STICKER *noun* **STICKERS** an adhesive label or small poster, card etc, especially one displaying a message or advertisement in a shop window, on a car, etc or that children swap and collect

STICKILY *adverb* in a sticky way

STICKLER *noun* **STICKLERS** someone who fastidiously insists on something

STICKY *adj* **STICKIER, STICKIEST** covered with something that is tacky or gluey □ *verb* **STICKIES, STICKYING, STICKIED** to make something sticky

STIES a plural of **sty**

STIFF *adj* **STIFFER, STIFFEST** not easily bent or folded; rigid □ *noun* **STIFFS** a corpse

STIFFEN *verb* **STIFFENS, STIFFENING, STIFFENED** to make or become stiff or stiffer

STIFFENER *noun* **STIFFENERS** a strong alcoholic drink

STIFFENING *noun* **STIFFENINGS** an act of making or becoming stiff or stiffer; material used to stiffen something

STIFFISH *adj* somewhat stiff

STIFFLY *adverb* in a stiff way

STIFFNESS *noun* **STIFFNESSES** the state or condition of being stiff

STIFFWARE *noun* **STIFFWARES** software that is difficult or impossible to modify because it has been customized or there is incomplete documentation, etc

STIFLE [1] *verb* **STIFLES, STIFLING, STIFLED** to suppress (a feeling or action)

STIFLE [2] *noun* **STIFLES** the joint in the hind leg of a horse, dog or other four-legged animal that is between the femur and the tibia and which corresponds to the human knee

STIFLER *noun* **STIFLERS** someone who stifles

STIFLING *adj* unpleasantly hot or airless

STIGMA *noun* **STIGMAS** shame or social disgrace

STIGMATA *plural noun* marks which are said to have appeared on the bodies of certain holy people and that are thought to resemble Christ's crucifixion wounds

STIGMATIC *noun* **STIGMATICS** someone marked by stigmata

STILB *noun* **STILBS** a unit of luminance that is equal to one candela per square centimetre

STILBENE *noun* **STILBENES** a crystalline hydrocarbon that is used in the manufacture of dyes

STILE *noun* **STILES** a step, or set of steps, that is incorporated into a fence or wall so that people can cross but animals cannot

STILETTO *noun* **STILETTOS** a high thin heel on a woman's shoe; a dagger with a narrow tapering blade □ *verb* **STILETTOS, STILETTOING, STILETTOED** to stab using a dagger of this kind

STILL [1] *adj* **STILLER, STILLEST** motionless; inactive; silent □ *adverb* continuing as before, now or at some future time □ *verb*

STILLS, STILLING, STILLED to make or become still, silent, etc

STILL [2] *noun* **STILLS** an apparatus for the distillation of alcoholic spirit

STILLAGE *noun* **STILLAGES** a frame, stand or stool for keeping things, eg casks, off the floor or ground

STILLBORN *adj* said of a baby or fetus: dead when born

STILLNESS *noun* **STILLNESSES** the state or condition of being still

STILT *noun* **STILTS** either of a pair of long poles that have supports for the feet part of the way up so that someone can walk around supported high above the ground □ *verb* **STILTS, STILTING, STILTED** to raise or place on stilts or as though on stilts

STILTED *adj* said of language: unnatural-sounding and over-formal

STILTEDLY *adverb* in a stilted way

STIMULANT *noun* **STIMULANTS** any substance, such as a drug, that produces an increase in the activity of a particular body organ or function, eg caffeine, nicotine, amphetamines

STIMULATE *verb* **STIMULATES, STIMULATING, STIMULATED** to cause physical activity, or increased activity, in (eg an organ of the body)

STIMULATING *adj* exciting; invigorating; arousing interest

STIMULUS *noun* **STIMULI** something that acts as an incentive, inspiration, provocation, etc

STING *noun* **STINGS** a defensive puncturing organ that is found in certain animals and plants, which can inject poison or venom, eg the spine of a sting-ray, the hairs of a stinging nettle, etc □ *verb* **STINGS, STINGING, STUNG** to pierce, poison or wound with a sting

STINGAREE *noun* **STINGAREES** a type of flatfish with a barbed dorsal spine on its tail

STINGED *adj* having a sting

STINGER *noun* **STINGERS** a person or thing that stings

STINGILY *adverb* in a stingy way

STINGLESS *adj* without a sting

STINGY *adj* **STINGIER, STINGIEST** ungenerous; mean; miserly

STINK *noun* **STINKS** a strong and very unpleasant smell □ *verb* **STINKS, STINKING, STANK,**

STUNK to give off an offensive smell

STINKER noun **STINKERS** a very difficult task, question, etc

STINKHORN noun **STINKHORNS** any of several kinds of fungus that are found in woodland and which have a cap that is covered with a pungent-smelling slime that attracts insects which eat the slime and disperse the spores

STINKING adj offensively smelly ◻ adverb extremely; disgustingly

STINKWOOD noun **STINKWOODS** the name given to several trees that emit an offensive smell

STINT verb **STINTS, STINTING, STINTED** to be mean or grudging in giving or supplying something ◻ noun **STINTS** an allotted amount of work or a fixed time for it

STINTED adj mean or grudging

STINTEDLY adverb in a stinted way

STINTER noun **STINTERS** someone who is mean or grudging

STIPE noun **STIPES** a stalk, especially one that supports a reproductive part such as a carpel or the cap of a fungus, or one that the leaflets of a fern or the fronds of seaweed are attached to

STIPEL noun **STIPELS** one of a pair of small stipule-like appendages at the base of a leaflet

STIPEND noun **STIPENDS** a salary or allowance, now especially one that is paid to a member of the clergy, but originally the pay of a soldier

STIPES noun **STIPITES** a stipe

STIPITATE adj of or relating to a stipe

STIPPLE verb **STIPPLES, STIPPLING, STIPPLED** to paint, engrave or draw something in dots or dabs as opposed to using lines or masses of colour ◻ noun **STIPPLES** a pattern produced by stippling

STIPPLER noun **STIPPLERS** a person or tool that stipples

STIPULAR adj of or relating to a stipule

STIPULATE verb **STIPULATES, STIPULATING, STIPULATED** in a contract, agreement, etc: to specify as a necessary condition

STIPULE noun **STIPULES** a small leaf-like structure, usually one of a pair, that is found at the base of some leaves or leaf stalks

STIPULED adj having stipules

STIR verb **STIRS, STIRRING,**

STIRRED to mix or agitate (a liquid or semi-liquid substance) by repeated circular strokes with a spoon or other utensil ◻ noun **STIRS** an act of stirring (a liquid, etc); a commotion

STIRLESS adj without stir

STIRRER noun **STIRRERS** someone or something that stirs

STIRRING noun **STIRRINGS** an act of mixing or agitating (a liquid etc) with eg a spoon

STIRRUP noun **STIRRUPS** either of a pair of leather or metal loops which are suspended from straps that are attached to a horse's saddle and which are used as footrests for the rider

STITCH noun **STITCHES** a single interlinking loop of thread or yarn in sewing or knitting ◻ verb **STITCHES, STITCHING, STITCHED** to join, close, decorate, etc with stitches

STITCHER noun **STITCHERS** a person or machine that stitches

STITCHERY noun **STITCHERIES** stitches; stitching

STITCHING noun **STITCHINGS** an act of joining, closing, decorating, etc with stitches

STOA noun **STOAE, STOAI, STOAS** a portico or roofed colonnade

STOAT noun **STOATS** a small flesh-eating mammal that is closely related to the weasel and which has a long slender body and reddish-brown fur with white underparts, although in northern regions the fur turns white in winter, during which time it is known as the ermine

STOCIOUS adj drunk

STOCK noun **STOCKS** goods or raw material that a shop, factory, warehouse, etc has on the premises at a given time ◻ verb **STOCKS, STOCKING, STOCKED** to keep a supply for sale

STOCKADE noun **STOCKADES** a defensive fence or enclosure that is built of upright tall heavy posts ◻ verb **STOCKADES, STOCKADING, STOCKADED** to protect or defend with a stockade

STOCKFISH noun **STOCKFISHES** fish, especially cod or haddock, that is cured by being split and left to dry in the open air

STOCKILY adverb in a stocky way

STOCKING noun **STOCKINGS** either of a pair of close-fitting coverings for women's legs which

are made of fine semi-transparent nylon or silk and which can be either self-supporting or supported by suspenders

STOCKIST noun **STOCKISTS** a person or shop that stocks a particular item or brand

STOCKMAN noun **STOCKMEN** someone whose job is keeping, rearing, etc farm animals, especially cattle

STOCKPILE noun **STOCKPILES** a reserve supply that has been accumulated ◻ verb **STOCKPILES, STOCKPILING, STOCKPILED** to accumulate a large reserve supply

STOCKROOM noun **STOCKROOMS** a storeroom, especially in a shop

STOCKTAKE verb **STOCKTAKES, STOCKTAKING, STOCKTAKEN, STOCKTOOK** to make an inventory and valuation of stock

STOCKTAKING noun **STOCKTAKINGS** the process of making a detailed inventory and valuation of all the goods, raw materials, etc that are held on the premises of a shop, factory, etc at a particular time

STOCKY adj **STOCKIER, STOCKIEST** said of a person or animal: broad, strong-looking and usually not very tall

STOCKYARD noun **STOCKYARDS** a large yard or enclosure that is usually sectioned off into pens, where livestock are kept temporarily, eg before being auctioned

STODGE noun **STODGES** food that is heavy, filling and, usually, fairly tasteless ◻ verb **STODGES, STODGING, STODGED** to stuff with food

STODGILY adverb in a stodgy way

STODGY adj **STODGIER, STODGIEST** said of food: heavy and filling but usually fairly tasteless and unappetizing

STOEP noun **STOEPS** a raised terraced verandah that runs along the front, and sometimes the sides, of a house

STOIC noun **STOICS** someone who can repress emotions and show patient resignation under difficult circumstances

STOICAL adj accepting suffering or misfortune uncomplainingly

STOICALLY adverb in a stoical way

STOICISM noun **STOICISMS** brave or patient acceptance of suffering and misfortune

STOKE *verb* **STOKES, STOKING, STOKED** to put coal or other fuel on (eg a fire, the furnace of a boiler)

STOKEHOLD *noun* **STOKEHOLDS** the boiler room on a steamship

STOKER *noun* **STOKERS** someone whose job is to stoke a furnace, especially on a steamship or steam train

STOLE [1] *noun* **STOLES** a woman's scarf-like garment, often made of fur, that is worn around the shoulders

STOLE [2] a past form of **steal**

STOLEN a past form of **steal**

STOLID *adj* **STOLIDER, STOLIDEST** showing little or no interest or emotion; impassive

STOLIDITY *noun* **STOLIDITIES** the quality or condition of being stolid

STOLIDLY *adverb* in a stolid way

STOLLEN *noun* **STOLLENS** a rich sweet fruit loaf that is traditionally served at Christmas and which contains dried fruit, glacé cherries, candied peel and often a layer of marzipan in the middle

STOLON *noun* **STOLONS** a stem that grows horizontally out of the base of certain plants and which has a node or nodes that can root and form new independent plants

STOMA *noun* **STOMATA** one of many tiny pores that are found on the stems and leaves of vascular plants, which are the sites where water loss from the plant and gaseous exchange between plant tissue and the atmosphere take place

STOMACH *noun* **STOMACHS** in the alimentary canal of vertebrates: a large sac-like organ, sometimes, eg in ruminants, one of several, where food is temporarily stored until gastric juices and the contractions of the muscular walls partially digest the food to a semiliquid mass ◻ *verb* **STOMACHS, STOMACHING, STOMACHED** to bear or put up with

STOMACHAL *adj* of or relating to the stomach

STOMACHER *noun* **STOMACHERS** an ornate covering for the chest and abdomen that was often decorated with jewels and which was worn by women underneath a laced bodice up until the end of the 19c

STOMACHIC *adj* stomachal

STOMACHY *adj* having a large belly

STOMATA plural of **stoma**

STOMATAL *adj* of or relating to a stoma

STOMATIC *adj* stomatal

STOMP *verb* **STOMPS, STOMPING, STOMPED** to stamp or tread heavily ◻ *noun* **STOMPS** a kind of lively jazz dance that involves stamping movements

STONE *noun* **STONES** the hard solid material that rocks are made of; a piece of this material ◻ *verb* **STONES, STONING, STONED** to pelt with stones as a punishment

STONECHAT *noun* **STONECHATS** a small brownish European bird whose call is like stones knocking together

STONECROP *noun* **STONECROPS** any of various species of succulent plant that are mostly native perennials of northern temperate regions and which have fleshy leaves and star-like yellow, white or red flowers

STONED *adj* in a state of drug-induced euphoria

STONEFISH *noun* **STONEFISHES** a poisonous tropical sea fish that resembles a rock on the seabed when it lies in wait for its prey

STONEFLY *noun* **STONEFLIES** an insect that is found near water and whose larvae live under stones in streams

STONELESS *adj* without stones

STONER *noun* **STONERS** a person who stones

STONEWALL *verb* **STONEWALLS, STONEWALLING, STONEWALLED** to hold up progress, especially in parliament, intentionally, eg by obstructing discussion, giving long irrelevant speeches, etc

STONEWARE *noun* **STONEWARES** a type of hard coarse pottery made from clay that has a high proportion of silica, sand or flint in it

STONEWORK *noun* **STONEWORKS** a structure or building part that has been made out of stone

STONILY *adverb* in a stony way

STONINESS *noun* **STONINESSES** the state or condition of being stony

STONK *noun* **STONKS** an intense artillery bombardment ◻ *verb* **STONKS, STONKING, STONKED** to bombard with intense artillery fire

STONKER *verb* **STONKERS,**

STONKERING, STONKERED to put out of action; to thwart; to kill

STONKERED *adj* drunk

STONKING *adj* excellent

STONY *adj* **STONIER, STONIEST** covered with stones

STOOD past form of **stand**

STOOGE *noun* **STOOGES** a performer whose function is to provide a comedian with opportunities for making jokes and who is often also the butt of the jokes ◻ *verb* **STOOGES, STOOGING, STOOGED** to act as a stooge for someone

STOOK *noun* **STOOKS** a group of sheaves that are propped upright together in a field ◻ *verb* **STOOKS, STOOKING, STOOKED** to prop up (grain) in sheaves in a field

STOOKER *noun* **STOOKERS** someone who sets up stooks

STOOL *noun* **STOOLS** a simple seat without a back, usually with three or four legs ◻ *verb* **STOOLS, STOOLING, STOOLED** said of a felled tree stump, etc: to send up shoots

STOOLBALL *noun* **STOOLBALLS** an old-fashioned 11-a-side bat-and-ball game similar to cricket and rounders

STOOP *verb* **STOOPS, STOOPING, STOOPED** to bend the upper body forward and down ◻ *noun* **STOOPS** a bent posture

STOOPED *adj* bent

STOOSHIE *noun* **STOOSHIES** a stushie

STOP *verb* **STOPS, STOPPING, STOPPED** to bring or come to rest, a standstill or an end; to cease or cause to cease moving, operating or progressing ◻ *noun* **STOPS** an act of stopping

STOPCOCK *noun* **STOPCOCKS** a valve that controls the flow of liquid, gas, steam, etc in a pipe and which is usually operated by an external lever or handle

STOPE *noun* **STOPES** a horizontal step or notch in the wall of a pit ◻ *verb* **STOPES, STOPING, STOPED** to mine in horizontal layers

STOPGAP *noun* **STOPGAPS** a temporary substitute

STOPING *noun* **STOPINGS** an act of mining in horizontal layers

STOPLESS *adj* without a stop

STOPPAGE *noun* **STOPPAGES** an act of stopping or the state of being stopped

STOPPED past form of **stop**

STOPPER noun **STOPPERS** a cork, plug or bung

STOPPING a form of **stop** ◻ noun **STOPPINGS** an act of bringing or coming to rest, a standstill or an end; an act of ceasing

STOPWATCH noun **STOPWATCHES** a watch that is used for accurately recording the elapsed time in races, etc

STORABLE adj capable of being stored

STORAGE noun **STORAGES** the act of storing or the state of being stored

STORAX noun **STORAXES** any of several tropical or subtropical trees which have clusters of white showy flowers

STORE noun **STORES** a supply, usually one that is kept in reserve for use in the future ◻ verb **STORES, STORING, STORED** to put aside for future use

STOREMAN noun **STOREMEN** a person whose job is to look after and monitor goods, etc that are kept in store

STOREROOM noun **STOREROOMS** a room that is used for keeping things in

STOREY noun **STOREYS** a level, floor or tier of a building

STOREYED adj having a specified number of floors

STORK noun **STORKS** any of various species of large wading bird that are mostly found near water in warm regions of the world, which have long legs, a long bill and neck, and usually loose black and white plumage and which is related to the heron and ibis

STORM noun **STORMS** an outbreak of violent weather, with severe winds and heavy falls of rain, hail or snow that is often accompanied by thunder and lightning ◻ verb **STORMS, STORMING, STORMED** to go or come loudly and angrily

STORMILY adverb in a stormy way

STORMING noun **STORMINGS** an act of going or coming loudly and angrily

STORMLESS adj without storms

STORMY adj **STORMIER, STORMIEST** affected by storms or high winds

STORY noun **STORIES** a written or spoken description of an event or series of events which can be real or imaginary ◻ verb **STORIES, STORYING, STORIED** to decorate (a pot, etc) with scenes that depict events from history, legend, etc

STORYBOOK noun **STORYBOOKS** a book that contains a tale or a collection of tales, especially one for children

STORYLINE noun **STORYLINES** the plot of a novel, play or film

STOT verb **STOTS, STOTTING, STOTTED** to bounce or cause (a ball, etc) to bounce

STOTINKA noun **STOTINKI** a Bulgarian unit of currency which is worth one-hundredth of a lev

STOTIOUS adj drunk

STOTTER noun **STOTTERS** something or someone, especially a woman, that meets with approval

STOTTING adj drunk

STOUP noun **STOUPS** a basin for holy water

STOUT adj **STOUTER, STOUTEST** said of someone: well-built; on the fat side ◻ noun **STOUTS** dark beer that has a strong malt flavour

STOUTISH adj somewhat stout

STOUTLY adverb in a stout way

STOUTNESS noun **STOUTNESSES** the state or condition of being stout

STOVE [1] noun **STOVES** a domestic cooker

STOVE [2] a past form of **stave**

STOVEPIPE noun **STOVEPIPES** a metal funnel that takes smoke away from a stove

STOVIES plural noun a traditional dish of seasoned potatoes and onion that sometimes has leftover meat added to it and which is cooked slowly on top of the cooker

STOW verb **STOWS, STOWING, STOWED** to pack or store something, especially out of sight

STOWAGE noun **STOWAGES** a place, charge, space, etc for stowing things

STOWAWAY noun **STOWAWAYS** someone who hides on a ship, aeroplane, etc in the hope of being able to get to the destination undetected and so avoid paying the fare

STOWER noun **STOWERS** someone who stows things away

STOWING noun **STOWINGS** an act of stowing things away

STRAD noun **STRADS** a violin made by Antonio Stradivari (1644–1737)

STRADDLE verb **STRADDLES, STRADDLING, STRADDLED** to have one leg or part on either side of something or someone ◻ noun **STRADDLES** an act of straddling

STRAFE verb **STRAFES, STRAFING, STRAFED** to attack someone or something with heavy machine-gun fire from a low-flying aircraft ◻ noun **STRAFES** an attack or punishment

STRAGGLE verb **STRAGGLES, STRAGGLING, STRAGGLED** to grow or spread untidily

STRAGGLER noun **STRAGGLERS** someone who trails along behind

STRAGGLING noun **STRAGGLINGS** variation of energy or range of particles in a beam passed through absorbing material, resulting from random interactions

STRAGGLY adj **STRAGGLIER, STRAGGLIEST** said of a plant, etc: having long dangling stems, especially ones that do not produce many leaves

STRAIGHT adj **STRAIGHTER, STRAIGHTEST** not curved, bent, curly or wavy, etc ◻ adverb in or into a level, upright, etc position or posture ◻ noun **STRAIGHTS** a straight line or part, eg of a race track

STRAIN verb **STRAINS, STRAINING, STRAINED** to injure or weaken (oneself or a part of one's body) through over-exertion ◻ noun **STRAINS** an injury caused by over-exertion, especially a wrenching of the muscles

STRAINED adj said of an action, way of talking, someone's manner, etc: not natural or easy; forced

STRAINER noun **STRAINERS** a small sieve or colander

STRAINING noun **STRAININGS** an act of injuring or weakening (oneself or a part of one's body) through over-exertion

STRAIT noun **STRAITS** a narrow strip of water that links two larger areas of ocean or sea

STRAITEN verb **STRAITENS, STRAITENING, STRAITENED** to distress, especially financially

STRAKE noun **STRAKES** a section of the rim of a cartwheel

STRAND verb **STRANDS, STRANDING, STRANDED** to run (a ship) aground ◻ noun **STRANDS** a shore or beach

STRANDED adj left without any money, means of transport, etc

STRANGE adj **STRANGER,
STRANGEST** not known or
experienced before; unfamiliar or
alien
STRANGELY adverb in a strange
way
STRANGER noun **STRANGERS**
someone that one does not know
STRANGLE verb **STRANGLES,
STRANGLING, STRANGLED** to kill
or attempt to kill by squeezing the
throat with the hands, a cord, etc
STRANGLER noun **STRANGLERS**
someone who strangles
STRANGLES singular noun a
contagious disease that affects
horses, which is characterized by
inflammation of the upper
respiratory tract
STRANGURY noun **STRANGURIES**
a condition that is characterized by
slow painful urination
STRAP noun **STRAPS** a narrow strip
of leather or fabric which can be
used for hanging something from,
carrying or fastening something, etc
◻ verb **STRAPS, STRAPPING,
STRAPPED** to fasten or bind
something with a strap or straps
STRAPLESS adj without straps
STRAPPED adj short of money
STRAPPER noun **STRAPPERS** a
tall strong-looking person
STRAPPING adj tall and strong-
looking
STRAPPY adj **STRAPPIER,
STRAPPIEST** said of shoes,
clothes, etc: distinguished by
having lots of straps
STRATA plural of **stratum**
STRATAGEM noun **STRATAGEMS**
a trick or plan, especially one for
deceiving an enemy or gaining an
advantage
STRATEGIC adj characteristic of or
relating to strategy or a strategy
STRATEGY noun **STRATEGIES** the
process of, or skill in, planning
and conducting a military
campaign
STRATH noun **STRATHS** a broad
flat valley with a river running
through it
STRATIFY verb **STRATIFIES,
STRATIFYING, STRATIFIED** to
deposit (rock) in layers or strata
STRATOSE adj of or relating to a
stratum
STRATUM noun **STRATA** a layer of
sedimentary rock
STRATUS noun **STRATI** a wide
horizontal sheet of low grey
layered cloud

STRAW noun **STRAWS** the parts of
cereal crops that remain after
threshing, which may be ploughed
back into the soil, burned as
stubble or used as litter or feedstuff
for animals, for thatching and
weaving into hats, baskets, etc
STRAWLIKE adj like straw
STRAWY adj **STRAWIER,
STRAWIEST** like straw
STRAY verb **STRAYS, STRAYING,
STRAYED** to wander away from the
right path or place, usually
unintentionally ◻ noun **STRAYS** a
homeless, ownerless, lost pet, farm
animal, child, etc
STRAYER noun **STRAYERS** a
person or animal that strays
STREAK noun **STREAKS** a long
irregular stripe or band ◻ verb
**STREAKS, STREAKING,
STREAKED** to mark with a streak
or streaks
STREAKER noun **STREAKERS**
someone who makes a naked dash
in public
STREAKILY adverb in a streaky
way
STREAKING noun **STREAKINGS**
an act of running naked through a
public place
STREAKY adj **STREAKIER,
STREAKIEST** marked with streaks
STREAM noun **STREAMS** a very
narrow river; a brook, burn or
rivulet ◻ verb **STREAMS,
STREAMING, STREAMED** to flow
or move continuously and in large
quantities or numbers
STREAMER noun **STREAMERS** a
long paper ribbon used to decorate
a room
STREAMING noun **STREAMINGS**
an act of flowing or moving
continuously and in large
quantities or numbers
STREAMY adj **STREAMIER,
STREAMIEST** said of an area:
having lots of streams
STREET noun **STREETS** a public
road with pavements and buildings
at the side or sides, especially one
in a town
STREETCAR noun **STREETCARS** a
tram
STRENGTH noun **STRENGTHS** the
quality or degree of being
physically or mentally strong
STRENUOUS adj characterized by
the need for or the use of great
effort or energy
STREP adj streptococcal
STRESS noun **STRESSES** physical

or mental overexertion ◻ verb
**STRESSES, STRESSING,
STRESSED** to emphasize or attach
importance to something
STRESSED adj said of a syllable:
given a more forceful
pronunciation than the other
syllable or syllables in the same
word
STRESSFUL adj causing stress
STRESSOR noun **STRESSORS** an
agent or factor that causes stress
STRETCH verb **STRETCHES,
STRETCHING, STRETCHED** to
make or become temporarily or
permanently longer or wider by
pulling or drawing out ◻ noun
STRETCHES an act of stretching,
especially (a part of) the body
STRETCHER noun **STRETCHERS** a
device that is used for carrying a
sick or wounded person in a lying
position ◻ verb **STRETCHERS,
STRETCHERING, STRETCHERED**
to carry someone on a stretcher
STRETCHY adj **STRETCHIER,
STRETCHIEST** said of materials,
clothes, etc: characterized by
having the ability or tendency to
stretch
STRETTA noun **STRETTE** in music:
a passage played in quicker time
STRETTO noun **STRETTI** in fugue:
the overlapping of a second or
subsequent voice with the one that
goes before it so that subject and
answer are brought more closely
together and the excitement of the
piece is increased
STREW verb **STREWS,
STREWING, STREWED, STREWN**
to scatter untidily
STREWER noun **STREWERS**
someone who strews
STREWTH exclamation an
expression of surprise or
annoyance
STRIA noun **STRIAE** any of a series
of parallel grooves in rock, or
furrows or streaks of colour in
plants and animals
STRIATED adj marked with striae;
striped
STRIATION noun **STRIATIONS** the
patterning of striae
STRICKEN adj deeply affected,
especially by grief, sorrow, panic,
etc
STRICKLE noun **STRICKLES** an
implement for levelling off a
measure of grain or for shaping the
surface of a mould
STRICT adj **STRICTER, STRICTEST**

demanding obedience or close observance of rules; severe
STRICTISH *adj* somewhat strict
STRICTLY *adverb* with or in a strict manner
STRICTURE *noun* **STRICTURES** a severe criticism
STRIDE *noun* **STRIDES** a single long step in walking ▫ *verb* **STRIDES, STRIDING, STRODE, STRIDDEN** to walk with long steps
STRIDENCE *noun* **STRIDENCES** the quality or condition of being strident
STRIDENCY *noun* **STRIDENCIES** stridence
STRIDENT *adj* said of a sound, especially a voice: loud and harsh
STRIDOR *noun* **STRIDORS** a harsh grating noise
STRIFE *noun* **STRIFES** bitter conflict or fighting
STRIGA *noun* **STRIGAE** in botany: a stiff bristle, usually one of many that are arranged in rows
STRIGIL *noun* **STRIGILS** in ancient Greece and Rome: a scraper used to clean the skin after bathing
STRIGOSE *adj* marked with streaks
STRIKE *verb* **STRIKES, STRIKING, STRUCK, STRICKEN** to hit someone or something; to give a blow to them ▫ *noun* **STRIKES** an act of hitting or dealing a blow
STRIKER *noun* **STRIKERS** someone who refuses to work in order to protest against an employer
STRIKING *adj* impressive; arresting; attractive, especially in an unconventional way
STRING *noun* **STRINGS** thin cord, or a piece of this; a stretched piece of wire, catgut, etc for a musical instrument ▫ *verb* **STRINGS, STRINGING, STRUNG** to fit or provide with a string or strings
STRINGED *adj* said of a musical instrument: having strings
STRINGENT *adj* said of rules, terms, etc: severe; rigorous; strictly enforced
STRINGER *noun* **STRINGERS** a horizontal beam in a framework
STRINGILY *adverb* in a stringy way
STRINGY *adj* **STRINGIER, STRINGIEST** like string, especially thin and thread-like
STRIP [1] *verb* **STRIPS, STRIPPING, STRIPPED** to remove (a covering, wallpaper, etc) by peeling or pulling it off
STRIP [2] *noun* **STRIPS** a long narrow, usually flat, piece of material, paper, land, etc
STRIPE *noun* **STRIPES** a band of colour ▫ *verb* **STRIPES, STRIPING, STRIPED** to mark with stripes
STRIPED *adj* having, or marked with, stripes
STRIPLING *noun* **STRIPLINGS** a boy or youth
STRIPPER *noun* **STRIPPERS** a striptease artiste
STRIPPING *noun* **STRIPPINGS** an act of removing (wallpaper, etc) by peeling or pulling it off
STRIPY *adj* **STRIPIER, STRIPIEST** marked with stripes; striped
STRIVE *verb* **STRIVES, STRIVING, STROVE, STRIVEN** to try extremely hard; to struggle
STROBE *noun* **STROBES** a powerful rapidly flashing light
STROBIC *adj* spinning or appearing to spin
STROBILA *noun* **STROBILAE** (in the lifecycle of jellyfishes) a chain of segments, cone within cone, that separate
STROBILE *noun* **STROBILES** a strobila
STROBILUS *noun* **STROBILI** a scaly spike of female flowers, such as the hop
STRODE a past form of **stride**
STROKE *noun* **STROKES** any act or way of striking ▫ *verb* **STROKES, STROKING, STROKED** to caress in kindness or affection, often repeatedly
STROKING *noun* **STROKINGS** the act of caressing in kindness or affection
STROLL *verb* **STROLLS, STROLLING, STROLLED** to walk in a slow leisurely way ▫ *noun* **STROLLS** a leisurely walk
STROLLER *noun* **STROLLERS** someone who strolls
STROMA *noun* **STROMATA** the supporting framework of a body part, organ, blood corpuscle or cell
STROMATIC *adj* of or relating to a stroma
STRONG *adj* **STRONGER, STRONGEST** exerting or capable of great force or power
STRONGARM *adj* aggressively forceful ▫ *verb* **STRONGARMS, STRONGARMING, STRONGARMED** to compel with aggressive forcefulness or threats of violence
STRONGBOX *noun* **STRONGBOXES** a safe, or other sturdy, usually lockable, box for storing money or valuables in
STRONGISH *adj* somewhat strong
STRONGLY *adverb* in a strong way
STRONTIUM *noun* **STRONTIUMS** a soft silvery-white highly reactive metallic element that is a good conductor of electricity
STROP *noun* **STROPS** a strip of coarse leather or other abrasive material that is used for sharpening razors ▫ *verb* **STROPS, STROPPING, STROPPED** to sharpen (a razor) on a strop
STROPHE *noun* **STROPHES** in a Greek play: the song sung by the chorus as it moved towards one side, answered by the antistrophe
STROPHIC *adj* of or relating to strophes
STROPPY *adj* **STROPPIER, STROPPIEST** quarrelsome, bad-tempered and awkward to deal with
STROVE a past form of **strive**
STRUCK a past form of **strike**
STRUCTURE *noun* **STRUCTURES** the way in which the parts of a thing are arranged or organized ▫ *verb* **STRUCTURES, STRUCTURING, STRUCTURED** to put into an organized form or arrangement
STRUDEL *noun* **STRUDELS** a baked roll of thin pastry with a filling of fruit, especially apple
STRUGGLE *verb* **STRUGGLES, STRUGGLING, STRUGGLED** to strive vigorously or make a strenuous effort under difficult conditions ▫ *noun* **STRUGGLES** an act of struggling
STRUGGLER *noun* **STRUGGLERS** someone who struggles
STRUGGLING *noun* **STRUGGLINGS** a struggle
STRUM *verb* **STRUMS, STRUMMING, STRUMMED** to play (a stringed musical instrument, such as a guitar, or a tune on it) with sweeps of the fingers or thumb rather than with precise plucking ▫ *noun* **STRUMS** an act or bout of strumming
STRUMA *noun* **STRUMAE** an abnormal swelling of the thyroid gland; a goitre
STRUMATIC *adj* of or relating to strumae
STRUMOSE *adj* strumatic
STRUMOUS *adj* strumatic

STRUMPET *noun* **STRUMPETS** a prostitute or a woman who engages in casual sex

STRUNG *adj* said of a musical instrument: fitted with strings

STRUT *verb* **STRUTS, STRUTTING, STRUTTED** to walk in a proud or self-important way ▫ *noun* **STRUTS** a strutting way of walking

STUB *noun* **STUBS** a short piece of something that remains when the rest of it has been used up, eg a cigarette, a pencil, etc ▫ *verb* **STUBS, STUBBING, STUBBED** to accidentally bump the end of (one's toe) against a hard surface

STUBBED *adj* cut, broken or worn down

STUBBLE *noun* **STUBBLES** a short early growth of beard

STUBBLED *adj* stubbly

STUBBLY *adj* **STUBBLIER, STUBBLIEST** like or covered with stubble

STUBBORN *adj* **STUBBORNER, STUBBORNEST** resolutely or unreasonably unwilling to change one's opinions, ways, plans, etc; obstinate

STUBBY *adj* **STUBBIER, STUBBIEST** short and broad or thick-set ▫ *noun* **STUBBIES** a small squat bottle of beer or the beer contained in such a bottle

STUCCO *noun* **STUCCOS** a fine plaster that is used for coating indoor walls and ceilings and for forming decorative cornices, mouldings, etc ▫ *verb* **STUCCOS, STUCCOING, STUCCOED** to coat with or mould out of stucco

STUCK *adj* unable to give an answer, reason, etc

STUD *noun* **STUDS** a rivet-like metal peg that is fitted on to a surface, eg of a garment, for decoration ▫ *verb* **STUDS, STUDDING, STUDDED** to fasten or decorate with a stud or studs

STUDDED *adj* having lots of studs

STUDENT *noun* **STUDENTS** someone who is following a formal course of study, especially in higher or further education, although the word is now often applied to secondary school pupils too

STUDIED *adj* said of an attitude, expression, etc: carefully practised or thought through and adopted or produced for effect; unspontaneous and affected

STUDIO *noun* **STUDIOS** the workroom of an artist or photographer

STUDIOUS *adj* characterized by a serious hard-working approach, especially to study

STUDY *verb* **STUDIES, STUDYING, STUDIED** to set one's mind to acquiring knowledge and understanding, especially by reading, research, etc ▫ *noun* **STUDIES** the act or process of studying

STUFF *noun* **STUFFS** any material or substance ▫ *verb* **STUFFS, STUFFING, STUFFED** to cram or thrust

STUFFED *adj* said of a food: having a filling

STUFFILY *adverb* in a stuffy way

STUFFING *noun* **STUFFINGS** any material that children's toys, cushions, animal skins, etc are filled with

STUFFY *adj* **STUFFIER, STUFFIEST** said of a room, atmosphere, etc: lacking fresh, cool air; badly ventilated

STULTIFY *verb* **STULTIFIES, STULTIFYING, STULTIFIED** to make someone or something appear absurd, foolish, contradictory, etc

STUM *noun* **STUMS** partly fermented grape juice ▫ *verb* **STUMS, STUMMING, STUMMED** to add stum to (a wine) and so restart the fermentation process

STUMBLE *verb* **STUMBLES, STUMBLING, STUMBLED** to lose one's balance and trip forwards after accidentally catching or misplacing one's foot ▫ *noun* **STUMBLES** an act of stumbling

STUMM *adj* shtoom

STUMP *noun* **STUMPS** the part of a felled or fallen tree that is left in the ground ▫ *verb* **STUMPS, STUMPING, STUMPED** to baffle or perplex

STUMPER *noun* **STUMPERS** a person or thing that stumps

STUMPILY *adverb* in a stumpy way

STUMPY *adj* **STUMPIER, STUMPIEST** short and thick

STUN *verb* **STUNS, STUNNING, STUNNED** to make someone unconscious, eg by a blow to the head ▫ *noun* **STUNS** the act of stunning or state of being stunned

STUNG past form of **sting**

STUNK a past form of **stink**

STUNNER *noun* **STUNNERS** someone or something that is extraordinarily beautiful, attractive, etc

STUNNING *adj* extraordinarily beautiful, attractive, etc

STUNSAIL *noun* **STUNSAILS** a light narrow sail that is set at the outer edges of a square sail when the wind is light

STUNT [1] *verb* **STUNTS, STUNTING, STUNTED** to curtail the growth or development of (a plant, animal, someone's mind, a business project, etc) to its full potential

STUNT [2] *noun* **STUNTS** a daring act or spectacular event that is intended to show off talent or attract publicity

STUNTMAN *noun* **STUNTMEN** someone who performs stunts, especially someone whose job is to act as a stand-in for a film actor

STUPA *noun* **STUPAS** a domed monument that is used for housing Buddhist relics

STUPE *noun* **STUPES** a piece of cloth that has been moistened with a medicinal substance and which is used for relieving pain, medicating wounds, etc ▫ *verb* **STUPES, STUPING, STUPED** to treat with a stupe

STUPEFIER *noun* **STUPEFIERS** a person or thing that stupefies

STUPEFY *verb* **STUPEFIES, STUPEFYING, STUPEFIED** to stun with amazement, fear, confusion or bewilderment

STUPID *adj* **STUPIDER, STUPIDEST** having or showing a lack of common sense, comprehension, perception, etc ▫ *noun* **STUPIDS** a stupid person

STUPIDITY *noun* **STUPIDITIES** a stupid state or condition; extreme foolishness

STUPIDLY *adverb* in a stupid way

STUPOR *noun* **STUPORS** a state of unconsciousness or near-unconsciousness, especially one caused by drugs, alcohol, etc

STUPOROUS *adj* unconscious

STURDILY *adverb* in a sturdy way

STURDY *adj* **STURDIER, STURDIEST** said of limbs, etc: thick and strong-looking

STURGEON *noun* **STURGEONS** a large long-snouted fish with rows of spines on its back that is common in the rivers and coastal waters of the N hemisphere and which is used as food and valued as the source of isinglass and true caviar

STURMER *noun* **STURMERS** a variety of crisp green-skinned eating apple that has creamy white flesh

STUSHIE *noun* **STUSHIES** a rumpus or row

STUTTER *verb* **STUTTERS, STUTTERING, STUTTERED** to speak or say something in a faltering or hesitant way, often by repeating parts of words, especially the first consonant, usually because of indecision, heightened emotion or some pathological disorder that affects the speech organs or the nervous system □ *noun* **STUTTERS** a way of speaking that is characterized by this kind of faltering or hesitancy

STUTTERER *noun* **STUTTERERS** someone who stutters

STUTTERING *noun* **STUTTERINGS** an act of speaking or saying something in a faltering or hesitant way, often by repeating parts of words

STY *noun* **STIES, STYES** a pen where pigs are kept □ *verb* **STYES, STIES, STYING, STIED, STYED** to put or keep (a pig, etc) in a sty

STYE *noun* **STYES** an inflamed swelling on the eyelid at the base of the lash

STYLE *noun* **STYLES** a manner or way of doing something, eg writing, speaking, painting, designing buildings, etc □ *verb* **STYLES, STYLING, STYLED** to design, shape, groom, etc something in a particular way

STYLISE *verb* **STYLISES, STYLISING, STYLISED** to stylize

STYLISED *adj* stylized

STYLISH *adj* elegant; fashionable

STYLISHLY *adverb* in a stylish way

STYLIST *noun* **STYLISTS** a trained hairdresser

STYLISTIC *adj* relating to artistic or literary style

STYLISTICS *singular noun* the systematic study of style, especially literary, ranging from features of language which can be identified with an individual (eg Shakespeare's style, Joyce's style), to those which identify major occupation groups (eg legal style, journalistic style), and those characteristic of speakers and writers in particular situations (eg parliamentary style)

STYLIZE *verb* **STYLIZES, STYLIZING, STYLIZED** to give a distinctive, conventionalized or elaborate style to something so that an impression of unnaturalness is created

STYLIZED *adj* conventionalized and unnaturalistic

STYLOBATE *noun* **STYLOBATES** a continuous platform of masonry that supports a row of columns

STYLUS *noun* **STYLUSES, STYLI** a hard pointed device, usually made from diamond or sapphire, at the tip of the needle-like part of the cartridge at the end of the arm of a record-player, which picks up the sound from the record's grooves

STYMIE *verb* **STYMIES, STYMIEING, STYMIED** to prevent, thwart, hinder or frustrate □ *noun* **STYMIES** any tricky or obstructed situation

STYMIED *adj* placed in an awkward situation; unable to take the kind of action required or desired

STYPTIC *adj* said of a drug or other substance: having the effect of stopping, slowing down or preventing bleeding, either by causing the blood vessels to contract or by accelerating the clotting of the blood □ *noun* **STYPTICS** a drug or other substance has this type of effect and which is used in the treatment of minor cuts, as well as bleeding disorders such as haemophilia

SUABILITY *noun* **SUABILITIES** the state or condition of being suable

SUABLE *adj* said of an offence, etc: able or liable to be pursued through the courts

SUAVE *adj* **SUAVER, SUAVEST** said of someone, especially a man, or their manner, attitude, etc: polite, charming and sophisticated, especially in an insincere way

SUAVELY *adverb* in a suave way

SUAVITY *noun* **SUAVITIES** suave behaviour

SUB *noun* **SUBS** in sport: a substitute player □ *verb* **SUBS, SUBBING, SUBBED** to act as a substitute

SUBAGENCY *noun* **SUBAGENCIES** a part of an agency

SUBALPINE *adj* belonging or relating to the region at the foot of the Alps

SUBALTERN *adj* inferior; lower in status, rank, etc □ *noun* **SUBALTERNS** any army officer below the rank of captain

SUBAQUA *adj* belonging, relating or referring to underwater activities

SUBARCTIC *adj* of or relating to the area bordering the Arctic

SUBARID *adj* denoting a region or climate characterized by little rainfall, but with less harsh conditions than an arid region

SUBATOMIC *adj* smaller than an atom

SUBBED past form of **sub**

SUBBING a form of **sub**

SUBBRANCH *noun* **SUBBRANCHES** a subsidiary branch

SUBBREED *noun* **SUBBREEDS** a subdivision of a breed

SUBCLASS *noun* **SUBCLASSES** a division in taxonomy

SUBCLAUSE *noun* **SUBCLAUSES** a subsidiary clause

SUBDEACON *noun* **SUBDEACONS** a member of the clergy who is immediately below a deacon in rank and whose duties include helping the deacon, especially by preparing the sacred vessels for the celebration of the eucharist

SUBDEAN *noun* **SUBDEANS** a person of the rank below dean

SUBDIVIDE *verb* **SUBDIVIDES, SUBDIVIDING, SUBDIVIDED** to divide (especially something that is already divided) into even smaller parts

SUBDUABLE *adj* capable of being subdued

SUBDUAL *noun* **SUBDUALS** an act of subduing

SUBDUE *verb* **SUBDUES, SUBDUING, SUBDUED** to overpower and bring under control

SUBDUED *adj* said of lighting, colour, noise, etc: not intense, bright, harsh, loud, etc; toned down

SUBDUEDLY *adverb* in a subdued way

SUBEDIT *verb* **SUBEDITS, SUBEDITING, SUBEDITED** to prepare (copy) for the ultimate sanction of the editor-in-chief, especially on a newspaper

SUBEDITOR *noun* **SUBEDITORS** someone whose job is to select and prepare material, eg articles, etc in a newspaper or magazine, for printing

SUBER *noun* **SUBERS** another term for cork or for the bark of the cork tree

SUBERATE *noun* **SUBERATES** a salt of suberic acid, derived from cork
SUBEREOUS *adj* of or relating to cork
SUBERIC *adj* subereous
SUBERIN *noun* **SUBERINS** the substance in cork which makes it water-repellant
SUBERISE *verb* **SUBERISES, SUBERISING, SUBERISED** to suberize
SUBERIZE *verb* **SUBERIZES, SUBERIZING, SUBERIZED** said of plant cell walls: to be impregnated with suberin and so become corky
SUBEROSE *adj* subereous
SUBFAMILY *noun* **SUBFAMILIES** in the taxonomy of plants, animals, languages, etc: a group within a family that consists of more than one genus
SUBFLOOR *noun* **SUBFLOORS** a rough floor that functions as the foundation for the finished floor
SUBFRAME *noun* **SUBFRAMES** the frame that supports the bodywork of a motor vehicle
SUBFUSC *noun* **SUBFUSCS** dark formal clothes that are worn for examinations and at certain formal occasions at Oxford and Cambridge universities
SUBGENUS *noun* **SUBGENUSES, SUBGENERA** in the taxonomy of plants and animals: a category below a genus but higher than a species
SUBGRADE *noun* **SUBGRADES** the layer that lies below the foundations of a road, pavement or railway and which can either occur naturally or be constructed
SUBGROUP *noun* **SUBGROUPS** a part or subdivision of a group
SUBHEAD *noun* **SUBHEADS** a subordinate title in a book, chapter, article, etc
SUBHUMAN *adj* relating or referring to animals that are just below *Homo sapiens* on the evolutionary scale
SUBITO *adverb* suddenly, quickly or immediately
SUBJACENT *adj* underlying
SUBJECT *noun* **SUBJECTS** a matter, topic, person, etc that is under discussion or consideration or that features as the major theme in a book, film, play, etc ▫ *verb* **SUBJECTS, SUBJECTING, SUBJECTED** to cause someone or something to undergo or experience something unwelcome, unpleasant, etc
SUBJECTED *adj* under the domination of another
SUBJOIN *verb* **SUBJOINS, SUBJOINING, SUBJOINED** to add at the end of something written or spoken
SUBJUGATE *verb* **SUBJUGATES, SUBJUGATING, SUBJUGATED** said especially of one country, people, nation, etc in regard to another: to dominate them; to bring them under control
SUBLEASE *verb* **SUBLEASES, SUBLEASING, SUBLEASED** to rent out (property one is renting from someone else) to another person ▫ *noun* **SUBLEASES** an agreement to rent out a property in this way
SUBLESSEE *noun* **SUBLESSEES** someone who holds a sublease on a property
SUBLESSOR *noun* **SUBLESSORS** someone who grants a sublease
SUBLET *verb* **SUBLETS, SUBLETTING, SUBLET** to rent out (property one is renting from someone else) to another person ▫ *noun* **SUBLETS** an agreement to rent out a property in this way
SUBLETTER *noun* **SUBLETTERS** someone who sublets property
SUBLETTING *noun* **SUBLETTINGS** an act of subletting property
SUBLIMATE *verb* **SUBLIMATES, SUBLIMATING, SUBLIMATED** to channel a morally or socially unacceptable impulse towards something more acceptable, especially something creative
SUBLIME *adj* **SUBLIMER, SUBLIMEST** said of someone: displaying the highest or noblest nature, especially in terms of their morality, intellectuality, spirituality, etc ▫ *noun* **SUBLIMES** the ultimate or ideal example or instance ▫ *verb* **SUBLIMES, SUBLIMING, SUBLIMED** to heat (a substance) and convert it from its solid state into a vapour or gas without an intermediate liquid stage, usually allowing it to resolidify
SUBLIMELY *adverb* in a sublime way
SUBLIMITY *noun* **SUBLIMITIES** the state of being sublime
SUBLUNAR *adj* sublunary
SUBLUNARY *adj* situated below the Moon
SUBMARINE *noun* **SUBMARINES** a vessel, especially a military one, that is designed for underwater travel
SUBMERGE *verb* **SUBMERGES, SUBMERGING, SUBMERGED** to plunge or sink or cause to plunge or sink under the surface of water or other liquid
SUBMERGED *adj* sunk
SUBMERSE *verb* **SUBMERSES, SUBMERSING, SUBMERSED** to submerge
SUBMERSED *adj* sunk
SUBMIT *verb* **SUBMITS, SUBMITTING, SUBMITTED** to surrender; to give in, especially to the wishes or control of another person; to stop resisting
SUBMITTER *noun* **SUBMITTERS** someone who submits
SUBMITTING *noun* **SUBMITTINGS** an act of surrendering; an act of giving in, especially to the wishes or control of another person
SUBMUCOSA *noun* **SUBMUCOSAE** the layer of tissue that lies below a mucus membrane
SUBMUCOUS *adj* of or relating to the submucosa
SUBNORMAL *adj* said especially of someone's level of intelligence with regard to possible academic achievement: lower than normal ▫ *noun* **SUBNORMALS** a subnormal person
SUBOFFICE *noun* **SUBOFFICES** a subordinate or secondary office
SUBORDER *noun* **SUBORDERS** a part or subdivision of an order
SUBORN *verb* **SUBORNS, SUBORNING, SUBORNED** to persuade someone to commit perjury, a crime or other wrongful act, eg by bribing them
SUBORNER *noun* **SUBORNERS** someone who suborns
SUBPHYLUM *noun* **SUBPHYLA** in the taxonomy of plants, animals, etc: a subdivision of a phylum
SUBPLOT *noun* **SUBPLOTS** a minor storyline that runs parallel to the main plot in a novel, film, play, opera, etc and which often serves to comment on, emphasize or contrast the issues, themes, etc raised by the main plot
SUBPOENA *noun* **SUBPOENAS** a legal document that orders someone to appear in a court of law at a specified time; a summons ▫ *verb* **SUBPOENAS, SUBPOENAING, SUBPOENAED** to serve with a subpoena

SUBREGION noun **SUBREGIONS** a subdivision of a region

SUBROGATE verb **SUBROGATES, SUBROGATING, SUBROGATED** to substitute (one party for another) as creditor with the attendant transfer of rights

SUBSCRIBE verb **SUBSCRIBES, SUBSCRIBING, SUBSCRIBED** to contribute or undertake to contribute (a sum of money), especially on a regular basis

SUBSCRIPT adj said of a character, especially one in chemistry and maths: set below the level of the line □ noun **SUBSCRIPTS** a character that is in this position

SUBSEA adj used especially in the North Sea oil industry: situated or occurring underwater; designed for use underwater

SUBSERIES noun **SUBSERIES** a subdivision of a series

SUBSERVE verb **SUBSERVES, SUBSERVING, SUBSERVED** to help in furthering (a purpose, action, etc)

SUBSET noun **SUBSETS** a set that forms one part of a larger set

SUBSIDE verb **SUBSIDES, SUBSIDING, SUBSIDED** said of land, buildings, etc: to sink to a lower level; to settle

SUBSIDISE verb **SUBSIDISES, SUBSIDISING, SUBSIDISED** to subsidize

SUBSIDIZE verb **SUBSIDIZES, SUBSIDIZING, SUBSIDIZED** to provide or support with a subsidy

SUBSIDY noun **SUBSIDIES** a sum of money given, eg by a government to an industry, to help with running costs or to keep product prices low

SUBSIST verb **SUBSISTS, SUBSISTING, SUBSISTED** to live or manage to stay alive by means of something

SUBSOIL noun **SUBSOILS** the layer of soil that lies beneath the topsoil and which contains clay minerals that have leached from the topsoil, but very little organic matter □ verb **SUBSOILS, SUBSOILING, SUBSOILED** to plough through the topsoil to an unusually deep level in order to loosen and turn over the subsoil

SUBSOLAR adj said of a point on the Earth's surface: directly below the Sun

SUBSONIC adj relating to, being or travelling at speeds below the speed of sound

SUBSTANCE noun **SUBSTANCES** the matter or material that a thing is made of

SUBSTRATE noun **SUBSTRATES** the material or medium (eg soil, rock, agar, etc) that a living organism, such as a plant, bacterium, lichen, crustacean, etc, grows on or is attached to, and which often provides it with nutrients and support

SUBSUME verb **SUBSUMES, SUBSUMING, SUBSUMED** to include (an example, instance, idea, etc) in or regard it as part of a larger, more general group, category, rule, principle, etc

SUBSYSTEM noun **SUBSYSTEMS** a subsidiary system

SUBTEEN noun **SUBTEENS** a child below the age of 13

SUBTENANT noun **SUBTENANTS** someone who rents or leases a property from someone who already holds a lease for that propery

SUBTEND verb **SUBTENDS, SUBTENDING, SUBTENDED** said of the line opposite a specified angle in a triangle or the chord of an arc in geometry: to be opposite and bounding

SUBTEXT noun **SUBTEXTS** the implied message that the author, director, painter, etc of a play, film, book, picture, etc creates, either consciously or subconsciously at a level below that of plot, character, language, image, etc and which can be discovered by the informed or attentive reader or viewer

SUBTILISE verb **SUBTILISES, SUBTILISING, SUBTILISED** to refine

SUBTILIZE verb **SUBTILIZES, SUBTILIZING, SUBTILIZED** to refine

SUBTITLE noun **SUBTITLES** a printed translation of the dialogue of a foreign film that appears bit by bit at the bottom of the frame □ verb **SUBTITLES, SUBTITLING, SUBTITLED** to give a subtitle to (a literary work, film, etc)

SUBTLE adj **SUBTLER, SUBTLEST** not straightforwardly or obviously stated or displayed

SUBTLETY noun **SUBTLETIES** the state or quality of being subtle

SUBTLY adverb in a subtle way

SUBTONIC noun **SUBTONICS** the seventh note of a musical scale above the tonic note

SUBTOPIA noun **SUBTOPIAS** an area of ugly suburban expansion into the rural landscape, especially when it swallows up traditional villages and so detracts from their character

SUBTOPIAN adj of or relating to subtopia

SUBTOTAL noun **SUBTOTALS** the amount that a column of figures adds up to and which forms part of a larger total □ verb **SUBTOTALS, SUBTOTALLING, SUBTOTALLED** to add up (a column of figures)

SUBTRACT verb **SUBTRACTS, SUBTRACTING, SUBTRACTED** to take (one number, quantity, etc) away from another; to deduct

SUBTROPIC adj of or relating to the subtropics

SUBTROPICS plural noun the areas of the world that lie between the tropics and the temperate zone, and that have a near-tropical climate or experience tropical conditions for part of the year

SUBULATE adj said especially of plant parts: narrow and tapering

SUBURB noun **SUBURBS** a residential district that lies on the edge of a town or city

SUBURBAN adj belonging or relating to or situated in a suburb or the suburbs

SUBURBIA noun **SUBURBIAS** the suburbs and its inhabitants and way of life thought of collectively, especially in terms of being characterized by conventional uniformity, provinciality, lacking sophistication, etc

SUBVERT verb **SUBVERTS, SUBVERTING, SUBVERTED** to undermine or overthrow (especially eg a government or other legally established body)

SUBVERTER noun **SUBVERTERS** someone who subverts

SUBVIRAL adj belonging or referring to or caused by a structural part of a virus

SUBWARDEN noun **SUBWARDENS** a person of the rank below warden

SUBWAY noun **SUBWAYS** an underground passage or tunnel that pedestrians or vehicles can use for crossing under a road, railway, river, etc

SUBZERO adj said especially of a temperature: below zero degrees

SUCCEED verb **SUCCEEDS,**

SUCCEEDING, SUCCEEDED to achieve an aim or purpose

SUCCESS noun **SUCCESSES** the quality of succeeding or the state of having succeeded

SUCCESSOR noun **SUCCESSORS** someone who follows another, especially someone who takes over another's job, position, title, etc

SUCCINATE noun **SUCCINATES** a salt of succinic acid

SUCCINCT adj **SUCCINCTER, SUCCINCTEST** said of someone or of the way they write or speak: brief, precise and to the point; concise

SUCCINIC adj belonging or relating to, or contained in or obtained from, amber

SUCCOTASH noun **SUCCOTASHES** a traditional Native American dish that consists of under-ripe maize and beans boiled together, and which sometimes has red and green peppers or pork added to it

SUCCOTH noun **SUCCOTHS** sukkoth

SUCCOUR noun **SUCCOURS** help or relief in time of distress or need □ verb **SUCCOURS, SUCCOURING, SUCCOURED** to give help or relief to someone or something

SUCCOURER noun **SUCCOURERS** someone who offers succour

SUCCUBA noun **SUCCUBAE, SUCCUBAS** a succubus

SUCCUBUS noun **SUCCUBUSES, SUCCUBI** in folklore: a female evil spirit which was believed to have sexual intercourse with sleeping men and so conceive demonic children

SUCCULENT adj full of juice; juicy; tender and tasty □ noun **SUCCULENTS** a plant that is specially adapted to living in arid conditions by having thick fleshy leaves or stems or both which allow it to store water

SUCCUMB verb **SUCCUMBS, SUCCUMBING, SUCCUMBED** to give in to (eg pressure, temptation, desire, etc)

SUCH adj of that kind, or of the same or a similar kind □ pronoun a person or thing, or people or things, like that or those which have just been mentioned; suchlike

SUCHLIKE pronoun things of the same kind □ adj of the same kind

SUCK verb **SUCKS, SUCKING, SUCKED** to draw (liquid) into the mouth □ noun **SUCKS** an act or bout of sucking

SUCKER noun **SUCKERS** someone who is gullible or who can be easily deceived or taken advantage of □ verb **SUCKERS, SUCKERING, SUCKERED** to deceive, cheat, trick or fool

SUCKLE verb **SUCKLES, SUCKLING, SUCKLED** to feed (a baby or young mammal) with milk from the nipple or udder

SUCKLER noun **SUCKLERS** someone who suckles eg young

SUCKLING noun **SUCKLINGS** a baby or young animal that is still being fed with its mother's milk

SUCROSE noun **SUCROSES** a white soluble crystalline sugar, found in most plants

SUCTION noun **SUCTIONS** an act, an instance or the process of sucking

SUCTORIAL adj said of an organ or other body part: specially adapted for sucking or adhering

SUD noun rare singular form of suds

SUDARIUM noun **SUDARIA** a cloth for mopping up sweat

SUDATORY adj relating to or producing sweat □ noun **SUDATORIES** a drug that has the effect of producing sweat

SUDDEN adj happening or done quickly, without warning or unexpectedly

SUDDENLY adverb in a sudden way; without warning

SUDORIFIC adj said of a drug: causing sweating □ noun **SUDORIFICS** a drug, remedy or substance that causes sweating

SUDS plural noun a mass of bubbles produced on water when soap or other detergent is dissolved

SUDSY adj **SUDSIER, SUDSIEST** characterized by or covered in suds

SUE verb **SUES, SUING, SUED** to take legal proceedings against (a person or company)

SUEDE noun **SUEDES** originally kidskin, but now any soft leather, where the flesh side is rubbed or brushed so that it has a velvety finish

SUER noun **SUERS** someone who sues

SUET noun **SUETS** hard fat from around the kidneys of sheep or cattle, used for making pastry, puddings, etc and in the manufacture of tallow

SUETY adj **SUETIER, SUETIEST** of or like suet

SUFFER verb **SUFFERS, SUFFERING, SUFFERED** to undergo or endure (physical or mental pain or other unpleasantness)

SUFFERER noun **SUFFERERS** someone who suffers

SUFFERING noun **SUFFERINGS** pain, distress, etc

SUFFICE verb **SUFFICES, SUFFICING, SUFFICED** to be adequate, sufficient, good enough, etc for a particular purpose

SUFFIX noun **SUFFIXES** a word-forming element that can be added to the end of a word or to the base form of a word, eg as a grammatical inflection such as -ed or -s in walked and monkeys or in the formation of derivatives, such as -less and -ly in helpless and lovely □ verb **SUFFIXES, SUFFIXING, SUFFIXED** to attach something as a suffix to a word

SUFFOCATE verb **SUFFOCATES, SUFFOCATING, SUFFOCATED** to kill or be killed by a lack of air, eg because the air passages are blocked or because of smoke inhalation, etc

SUFFRAGAN noun **SUFFRAGANS** a bishop who is appointed to assist a diocesan bishop in running the diocese

SUFFRAGE noun **SUFFRAGES** the right to vote in political elections

SUFFUSE verb **SUFFUSES, SUFFUSING, SUFFUSED** to be covered or spread over or throughout with (colour, light, liquid, etc)

SUFFUSION noun **SUFFUSIONS** an act of suffusing

SUFFUSIVE adj suffusing or likely to suffuse

SUGAR noun **SUGARS** any of a group of white crystalline carbohydrates that are soluble in water, typically have a sweet taste and which are widely used as sweeteners in confectionery, desserts, soft drinks, etc □ verb **SUGARS, SUGARING, SUGARED** to sweeten something with sugar

SUGARED adj sugar-coated; candied

SUGARING noun **SUGARINGS** sweetening with sugar

SUGARLESS adj without sugar

SUGARY adj **SUGARIER, SUGARIEST** like sugar in taste or appearance

SUGGEST *verb* **SUGGESTS,
SUGGESTING, SUGGESTED** to put
forward as a possibility or
recommendation

SUGGING *noun* **SUGGINGS** selling
under the guise of marketing

SUI Latin word meaning of
himself, herself or itself

SUICIDAL *adj* involving or
indicating suicide

SUICIDE *noun* **SUICIDES** the act or
an instance of killing oneself
deliberately

SUING a form of **sue**

SUIT *noun* **SUITS** a set of clothes
designed to be worn together,
usually made from the same or
contrasting material and which
consists of a jacket and either
trousers or a skirt and sometimes a
waistcoat □ *verb* **SUITS, SUITING,
SUITED** to be acceptable to or what
is required by someone

SUITABLE *adj* appropriate, fitting,
proper, agreeable, etc

SUITABLY *adverb* in a suitable way

SUITCASE *noun* **SUITCASES** a
stiffened portable travelling case
that is used for carrying clothes

SUITE *noun* **SUITES** a set of rooms
forming a self-contained unit
within a larger building

SUITED *adj* dressed in a suit

SUITING *noun* **SUITINGS** material
that is used for making suits of
clothes

SUITOR *noun* **SUITORS** a man who
woos a woman, especially with the
intention of asking her to marry
him

SUK *noun* **SUKS** a souk

SUKH *noun* **SUKHS** a souk

SUKIYAKI *noun* **SUKIYAKIS** a
traditional Japanese dish which
consists of vegetables, noodles and
very thin strips of meat, usually
beef, which are all sautéed together
at the table, after which a sweet soy
sauce is added

SUKKOTH *noun* **SUKKOTHS** a
Jewish harvest festival
commemorating the period when
the Israelites lived in tents in the
desert during the Exodus from
Egypt

SULCATE *adj* furrowed; grooved

SULCATED *adj* furrowed

SULCUS *noun* **SULCI** a
longitudinal furrow in a body part,
especially the brain

SULFA *noun* **SULFAS** sulpha

SULFATE *noun* **SULFATES** a
sulphate □ *verb* **SULFATE,
SULFATING, SULFATED** to sulphate

SULFIDE *noun* **SULFIDES** a
sulphide

SULFITE *noun* **SULFITES** a
sulphite

SULFONE *noun* **SULFONES** a
sulphone

SULFUR *noun* **SULFURS** sulphur
□ *verb* **SULFURS, SULFURING,
SULFURED** to sulphur

SULFURATE *verb* **SULFURATES,
SULFURATING, SULFURATED** to
combine, or cause to react, with
sulphur

SULK *verb* **SULKS, SULKING,
SULKED** to be silent, grumpy,
unsociable, etc, especially because
of some petty resentment, a feeling
of being hard done by, etc □ *noun*
SULKS a bout of sulking

SULKILY *adverb* in a sulky way

SULKINESS *noun* **SULKINESSES**
the state or condition of being
sulky

SULKY *adj* **SULKIER, SULKIEST**
inclined to moodiness, especially
when taking the form of grumpy
silence, resentful unsociability, etc
□ *noun* **SULKIES** a light two-
wheeled horse-drawn vehicle for
one person

SULLAGE *noun* **SULLAGES** refuse,
sewage or other waste

SULLEN *adj* **SULLENER,
SULLENEST** silently and
stubbornly angry, serious, morose,
moody or unsociable

SULLENLY *adverb* in a sullen way

SULLIED *adj* tarnished

SULLY *verb* **SULLIES, SULLYING,
SULLIED** to tarnish or mar (a
reputation, etc)

SULPHA *noun* **SULPHAS** any
synthetic drug that is derived from
sulphanilamide

SULPHATE *noun* **SULPHATES** a
salt or ester of sulphuric acid
□ *verb* **SULPHATES, SULPHATING,
SULPHATED** to form a deposit of
lead sulphate on something

SULPHIDE *noun* **SULPHIDES** a
compound that contains sulphur
and another more electropositive
element

SULPHITE *noun* **SULPHITES** a salt
or ester of sulphurous acid

SULPHONE *noun* **SULPHONES** any
substance that consists of two
organic radicals combined with
sulphur dioxide

SULPHUR *noun* **SULPHURS** a
yellow solid non-metallic element
that occurs naturally in volcanic
regions and areas around hot
springs □ *verb* **SULPHURS,
SULPHURING, SULPHURED** to
treat or fumigate using sulphur

SULPHURIC *adj* of or relating to
sulphur

SULPHURY *adj* like sulphur

SULTAN *noun* **SULTANS** the ruler of
any of various Muslim countries,
especially the former ruler of the
Ottoman empire

SULTANA *noun* **SULTANAS** a pale
seedless raisin that is used in
making cakes, puddings, etc

SULTANATE *noun* **SULTANATES**
the rank or office of a sultan

SULTANIC *adj* of or relating to a
sultan

SULTRILY *adverb* in a sultry way

SULTRY *adj* **SULTRIER, SULTRIEST**
said of the weather: hot and
humid; close

SUM *noun* **SUMS** the total that is
arrived at when two or more
numbers, quantities, ideas,
feelings, etc are added together
□ *verb* **SUMS, SUMMING,
SUMMED** to calculate the sum of
something

SUMAC *noun* **SUMACS** any of
several varieties of small trees or
shrubs that are common across S
Europe, Asia and NE America
and which have a resinous milky
sap, branches that have clusters of
small flowers at the ends and small
hairy single-seeded fruits

SUMACH *noun* **SUMACHS** sumac

SUMMARILY *adverb* in a summary
way

SUMMARISE *verb* **SUMMARISES,
SUMMARISING, SUMMARISED** to
summarize

SUMMARIST *noun* **SUMMARISTS**
someone who summarizes

SUMMARIZE *verb* **SUMMARIZES,
SUMMARIZING, SUMMARIZED** to
make, present or be a summary of
something; to state something
concisely

SUMMARY *noun* **SUMMARIES** a
short account that outlines or
picks out the main points

SUMMATION *noun* **SUMMATIONS**
the process of finding the sum;
addition

SUMMATIVE *adj* summing up

SUMMED past form of **sum**

SUMMING a form of **sum**

SUMMER *noun* **SUMMERS** the
warmest season of the year,

between spring and autumn,
extending from about June to
August in the N hemisphere and
from about December to February
in the S hemisphere ◻ *verb*
**SUMMERS, SUMMERING,
SUMMERED** to pass the summer
SUMMERY *adj* **SUMMERIER,
SUMMERIEST** of or relating to the
summer
SUMMIT *noun* **SUMMITS** the
highest point of a mountain
or hill
SUMMON *verb* **SUMMONS,
SUMMONING, SUMMONED** to
order someone to come or appear,
eg in a court of law as a witness,
defendant, etc
SUMMONER *noun* **SUMMONERS**
someone who summons
SUMMONS *noun* **SUMMONSES** a
written order that legally obliges
someone to attend a court of law at
a specified time ◻ *verb*
**SUMMONSES, SUMMONSING,
SUMMONSED** to serve someone
with a summons
SUMO *noun* **SUMOS** a style of
traditional Japanese wrestling
where contestants of great bulk try
to force an opponent out of the
unroped ring or to make them
touch the floor with any part of
their body other than the soles of
the feet
SUMOTORI *noun* **SUMOTORIS** a
sumo wrestler
SUMP *noun* **SUMPS** a small
depression inside a vehicle's
engine that acts as a reservoir so
that lubricating oil can drain into it
SUMPTUARY *adj* relating to or
regulating expense
SUMPTUOUS *adj* wildly expensive;
extravagantly luxurious
SUN *noun* **SUNS** the star that the
planets revolve around and which
gives out the heat and light energy
necessary to enable living
organisms to survive on Earth
◻ *verb* **SUNS, SUNNING, SUNNED**
to expose (something or oneself)
to the Sun's rays
SUNBATHE *verb* **SUNBATHES,
SUNBATHING, SUNBATHED** to
expose one's body to the Sun in
order to get a suntan
SUNBATHER *noun* **SUNBATHERS**
someone who sunbathes
SUNBATHING *noun*
SUNBATHINGS an act of exposing
one's body to the Sun in order to
get a suntan

SUNBEAM *noun* **SUNBEAMS** a ray
of sunlight
SUNBED *noun* **SUNBEDS** a device
that has sun-lamps fitted above
and often beneath a transparent
screen and which someone can lie
on in order to artificially tan the
whole body
SUNBELT *noun* **SUNBELTS** an area
that has a warm sunny climate and
which is therefore considered an
ideal place to live
SUNBIRD *noun* **SUNBIRDS** a small
brilliantly coloured tropical or
subtropical bird that is found in
Africa, Asia and Australia and
which resembles the humming-
bird
SUNBLIND *noun* **SUNBLINDS** an
awning over the outside of a
window that is designed to block
out the Sun's rays
SUNBLOCK *noun* **SUNBLOCKS** a
lotion, cream, etc that completely
or almost completely protects the
skin from the harmful effects of the
Sun's rays
SUNBOW *noun* **SUNBOWS** a
rainbow-like effect that is
produced especially when the Sun
shines on spraying water
SUNBURN *noun* **SUNBURNS**
soreness and reddening of the skin
caused by over-exposure to the
Sun's rays
SUNBURNED *adj* sunburnt
SUNBURNT *adj* suffering from
sunburn
SUNBURST *noun* **SUNBURSTS** a
sudden outbreak of strong
sunshine, eg when the Sun appears
from behind a cloud
SUNDAE *noun* **SUNDAES** a portion
of ice-cream topped with fruit,
nuts, syrup, etc
SUNDECK *noun* **SUNDECKS** an
upper open deck on a passenger
ship where people can sit in the sun
SUNDER *verb* **SUNDERS,
SUNDERING, SUNDERED** to sever
or separate
SUNDEW *noun* **SUNDEWS** an
insectivorous plant that grows in
bogs where nitrogen is scarce and
which has leaves that are covered
with long sticky hairs so that it can
trap and digest insects which act as
a nitrogen supplement
SUNDIAL *noun* **SUNDIALS** an
instrument that uses sunlight to
tell the time, by the changing
position of the shadow that a
vertical arm casts on a horizontal

plate with graded markings that
indicate the hours
SUNDOWN *noun* **SUNDOWNS**
sunset
SUNDOWNER *noun*
SUNDOWNERS a tramp,
originally one who arrives at a
sheep station too late in the day to
work but who still hopes to get
food and lodgings
SUNDRY *adj* various; assorted;
miscellaneous; several ◻ *noun*
SUNDRIES various small
unspecified items; oddments
SUNFAST *adj* said of a dye: not
liable to fade when exposed to
sunlight
SUNFISH *noun* **SUNFISHES** a
name applied to a variety of
different fish, most commonly to a
type of large rounded marine fish
that measures up to 3.5m (about
11½ft) and weighs around 20 tonnes
and which can be seen basking in
the Sun in tropical and temperate
seas
SUNFLOWER *noun* **SUNFLOWERS**
an annual plant that can grow to
around 3m (about 10ft) in height
and which produces large flattened
circular flowerheads of up to 50cm
(about 20in) diameter that have a
great many closely-packed seeds in
the middle and yellow petals
radiating outwards
SUNG a past form of **sing**
SUNGLASS *noun* **SUNGLASSES** a
burning-glass
SUNHAT *noun* **SUNHATS** a hat that
has a wide brim and which is worn
to shade the face from the rays of
the Sun
SUNK a past form of **sink**
SUNKEN *adj* situated or fitted at a
lower level than the surrounding
area
SUNLESS *adj* without Sun
SUNLIGHT *noun* **SUNLIGHTS** light
from the Sun
SUNLIKE *adj* like the Sun
SUNLIT *adj* lit by the Sun
SUNNILY *adverb* in a sunny way
SUNNINESS *noun* **SUNNINESSES**
the state or condition of being
sunny
SUNNY *adj* **SUNNIER, SUNNIEST**
said of a day, the weather, etc:
characterized by long spells of
sunshine or sunlight
SUNRISE *noun* **SUNRISES** the
Sun's appearance above the
horizon in the morning
SUNROOF *noun* **SUNROOFS** a

transparent panel in the roof of a car that lets sunlight in and that can usually open for ventilation

SUNSCREEN noun **SUNSCREENS** a preparation that protects the skin and minimizes the possibility of sunburn because it blocks out some or most of the Sun's harmful rays

SUNSET noun **SUNSETS** the Sun's disappearance below the horizon in the evening

SUNSHADE noun **SUNSHADES** a type of umbrella that is used as protection in strong sunshine; a parasol

SUNSHINE noun **SUNSHINES** the light or heat of the Sun

SUNSHINY adj bright with sunshine

SUNSPOT noun **SUNSPOTS** a relatively dark patch on the Sun's surface which indicates a transient cooler area that can measure anything from 100 to 100 000 miles in diameter and can last for a few hours or up to several months

SUNSTROKE noun **SUNSTROKES** a condition of collapse brought on by over-exposure to the Sun and sometimes accompanied by fever

SUNTAN noun **SUNTANS** a browning of the skin through exposure to the Sun or a sun-lamp

SUNTRAP noun **SUNTRAPS** a sheltered sunny place

SUNWARD adverb towards the Sun

SUNWARDS adverb sunward

SUNWISE adverb sunward

SUP verb **SUPS, SUPPING, SUPPED** to drink in small mouthfuls ◻ noun **SUPS** a small quantity, especially of something liquid; a sip

SUPER adj extremely good; excellent; wonderful ◻ noun **SUPERS** something of superior quality or grade, eg petrol

SUPERABLE adj said of a problem, difficulty, obstacle, etc: able to be overcome; surmountable

SUPERADD verb **SUPERADDS, SUPERADDING, SUPERADDED** to add something over and above

SUPERB adj **SUPERBER, SUPERBEST** outstandingly excellent

SUPERBLY adverb in a superb way

SUPERCOOL verb **SUPERCOOLS, SUPERCOOLING, SUPERCOOLED** to cool (a liquid) to a point below its usual freezing point without it becoming solid or crystallized

SUPEREGO noun **SUPEREGOS** in Freudian theory: that aspect of the psyche where someone's individual moral standards are internalized, especially parental and social ones that act as a censor on the ego

SUPERFINE noun **SUPERFINES** a commodity, especially cloth, that is of the highest quality

SUPERGLUE noun **SUPERGLUES** a type of quick-acting extra strong adhesive ◻ verb **SUPERGLUES, SUPERGLUING, SUPERGLUED** to bond something with superglue

SUPERHERO noun **SUPERHEROES** a character in a film, novel, cartoon, comic, etc that has extraordinary powers, especially for saving the world from disaster

SUPERIOR adj better in some way ◻ noun **SUPERIORS** someone who is of higher rank or position

SUPERMAN noun **SUPERMEN** in Nietzschean terms: an ideal man as he will have evolved in the future, especially in having extraordinary strength, power, ability, etc

SUPERNOVA noun **SUPERNOVAS, SUPERNOVAE** a vast stellar explosion which takes a few days to complete and which results in the star becoming temporarily millions of times brighter than it was

SUPERSEDE verb **SUPERSEDES, SUPERSEDING, SUPERSEDED** to take the place of (something, especially something outdated or no longer valid)

SUPERSTAR noun **SUPERSTARS** an internationally famous celebrity, especially from the world of film, popular music or sport

SUPERTAX noun **SUPERTAXES** a surtax

SUPERVENE verb **SUPERVENES, SUPERVENING, SUPERVENED** to occur as an interruption to some process, especially unexpectedly

SUPERVISE verb **SUPERVISES, SUPERVISING, SUPERVISED** to be in overall charge of (employees, etc)

SUPINATOR noun **SUPINATORS** a muscle in the forearm or foreleg that allows the hand or foot to turn and face upwards

SUPINE adj lying on one's back ◻ noun **SUPINES** said of a verbal noun in Latin: one of two forms

that denote either purpose or motion

SUPINELY adverb in a supine way

SUPPED past form of **sup**

SUPPER noun **SUPPERS** an evening meal, especially a light one

SUPPING a form of **sup**

SUPPLANT verb **SUPPLANTS, SUPPLANTING, SUPPLANTED** to take the place of someone, often by force or unfair means

SUPPLE adj **SUPPLER, SUPPLEST** said of a person, their joints, etc: bending easily; flexible

SUPPLELY adverb in a supple way

SUPPLIANT adj expressing or involving humble entreaty ◻ noun **SUPPLIANTS** someone who makes a humble entreaty

SUPPLIER noun **SUPPLIERS** someone who supplies something

SUPPLY verb **SUPPLIES, SUPPLYING, SUPPLIED** to provide or furnish (something believed to be necessary) ◻ noun **SUPPLIES** an act or instance of providing

SUPPORT verb **SUPPORTS, SUPPORTING, SUPPORTED** to keep something upright or in place ◻ noun **SUPPORTS** the act of supporting; the state of being supported

SUPPORTER noun **SUPPORTERS** someone who is in favour of a cause, proposal, etc

SUPPORTING noun **SUPPORTINGS** an act of keeping something upright or in place

SUPPOSE verb **SUPPOSES, SUPPOSING, SUPPOSED** to considering something likely, even when there is a lack of tangible evidence for it to be so

SUPPOSER noun **SUPPOSERS** someone who supposes something

SUPPOSING noun **SUPPOSINGS** an act of considering something likely, even when there is a lack of tangible evidence for it to be so

SUPPRESS verb **SUPPRESSES, SUPPRESSING, SUPPRESSED** to hold back or restrain (feelings, laughter, a yawn, etc)

SUPPURATE verb **SUPPURATES, SUPPURATING, SUPPURATED** said of a wound, boil, cyst, ulcer, etc: to gather and release pus; to fester; to come to a head

SUPREMACY noun **SUPREMACIES** supreme power or authority

SUPREME adj **SUPREMER,**

SUPREMEST highest in rank, power, importance, etc; greatest **SUPRÊME** noun **SUPRÊMES** the boneless breast of a chicken or game bird with the wing still attached
SUPREMELY adverb in a supreme way
SUPREMO noun **SUPREMOS** a supreme head or leader
SUQ noun **SUQS** a souk

SUR prep a French word for on, above

SURA noun **SURAS** any one of the 114 chapters of the Koran
SURAH noun **SURAHS** a soft twilled silk that is used in making dresses, blouses, scarves, etc
SURAL adj belonging or relating to the calf of the leg
SURBAHAR noun **SURBAHARS** an Indian stringed instrument that is similar to the sitar but larger
SURBASE noun **SURBASES** an upper series of mouldings on a pedestal, skirting board, etc
SURCHARGE noun **SURCHARGES** an extra charge, often as a penalty for late payment of a bill ◻ verb **SURCHARGES, SURCHARGING, SURCHARGED** to impose a surcharge on someone
SURCINGLE noun **SURCINGLES** a strap fastened round a horse's body to keep a blanket, pack, saddle, etc in place on its back
SURD adj said of a number: unable to be expressed in finite terms; irrational ◻ noun **SURDS** an irrational number that is a root of a rational number, so can never be determined exactly
SURE adj **SURER, SUREST** confident beyond doubt in one's belief or knowledge; convinced ◻ adverb certainly; of course
SURELY adverb without doubt; certainly
SURETY noun **SURETIES** someone who agrees to become legally responsible for another person's behaviour, debts, etc
SURF noun **SURFS** the sea as it breaks against the shore, a reef, etc ◻ verb **SURFS, SURFING, SURFED** to take part in a sport or recreation where the object is to stand or lie on a long narrow board, try to catch the crest of a wave and ride it to the shore
SURFACE noun **SURFACES** the upper or outer side of anything,

often with regard to texture or appearance ◻ verb **SURFACES, SURFACING, SURFACED** to rise to the surface of a liquid
SURFACER noun **SURFACERS** a person or thing that smooths or levels a surface
SURFACING noun **SURFACINGS** material used to form a surface layer
SURFBIRD noun **SURFBIRDS** a Pacific shore bird related to the sandpiper
SURFBOARD noun **SURFBOARDS** a long narrow shaped fibreglass board that a surfer stands or lies on ◻ verb **SURFBOARDS, SURFBOARDING, SURFBOARDED** to ride on a surfboard
SURFEIT noun **SURFEITS** an excess ◻ verb **SURFEITS, SURFEITING, SURFEITED** to indulge, especially in an excess of food or drink, until stuffed or disgusted
SURFER noun **SURFERS** someone who surfs
SURFING noun **SURFINGS** the sport of riding breaking waves on a surfboard
SURFY adj **SURFIER, SURFIEST** of or like surf
SURGE noun **SURGES** a sudden powerful mass movement of a crowd, especially forwards ◻ verb **SURGES, SURGING, SURGED** said of the sea, waves, etc: to move up and down or swell with force
SURGEON noun **SURGEONS** a person who is professionally qualified to practise surgery
SURGERY noun **SURGERIES** a doctor's, etc consulting-room; the branch of medicine that is concerned with treating disease, disorder or injury by cutting into the patient's body to operate directly on or remove the affected part
SURGICAL adj belonging or relating to, involving, caused by, used in, or by means of surgery
SURGING noun **SURGINGS** said of the sea, waves, etc: an act of moving up and down or swelling with force
SURICATE noun **SURICATES** a S African burrowing carnivore with a lemur-like face and four-toed feet
SURLILY adverb in a surly way
SURLINESS noun **SURLINESSES** the state or condition of being surly
SURLY adj **SURLIER, SURLIEST**

grumpily bad-tempered; abrupt and impolite in manner or speech
SURMISE verb **SURMISES, SURMISING, SURMISED** to conclude something from the information available, especially when the information is incomplete or insubstantial ◻ noun **SURMISES** a conclusion drawn from such information
SURMISER noun **SURMISERS** someone who surmises
SURMISING noun **SURMISINGS** an act of concluding something from the information available
SURMOUNT verb **SURMOUNTS, SURMOUNTING, SURMOUNTED** to overcome (problems, obstacles, etc)
SURMOUNTING noun **SURMOUNTINGS** an act of overcoming (problems, obstacles, etc)
SURMULLET noun **SURMULLETS** the red mullet
SURNAME noun **SURNAMES** a family name or last name, as opposed to a forename or Christian name ◻ verb **SURNAMES, SURNAMING, SURNAMED** to give a specified last name
SURPASS verb **SURPASSES, SURPASSING, SURPASSED** to go or be beyond in degree or extent; to exceed
SURPLICE noun **SURPLICES** a loose wide-sleeved white linen garment that is worn ceremonially by members of the clergy and choir singers over their robes
SURPLUS noun **SURPLUSES** an amount that exceeds the amount required or used; an amount that is left over after requirements have been met ◻ adj left over after needs have been met; extra
SURPRISE noun **SURPRISES** a sudden, unexpected, astounding, amazing, etc event, factor, gift, etc ◻ verb **SURPRISES, SURPRISING, SURPRISED** to cause someone to experience surprise by presenting them with or subjecting them to something unexpected, amazing, etc
SURPRISED adj taken unawares or off-guard
SURPRISER noun **SURPRISERS** someone who surprises
SURPRISING adj unexpected, shocking or amazing; causing surprise

SURRA noun **SURRAS** a tropical disease spread by horseflies, mainly affecting horses, but contractable by other domestic animals

SURREAL adj dreamlike; very odd or bizarre

SURRENDER verb **SURRENDERS, SURRENDERING, SURRENDERED** to accede or agree to an enemy's, the police's, etc demand for an end to resistance, hostilities, etc □ noun **SURRENDERS** an act, instance or the process of surrendering

SURREY noun **SURREYS** a type of four-wheeled horse-drawn carriage

SURROGACY noun **SURROGACIES** the state of being a surrogate

SURROGATE noun **SURROGATES** someone or something that takes the place of or is substituted for another

SURROUND verb **SURROUNDS, SURROUNDING, SURROUNDED** to extend all around; to encircle □ noun **SURROUNDS** a border or edge, or an ornamental structure fitted round this

SURROUNDINGS plural noun the places and/or things that are usually round about someone or something; environment

SURTAX noun **SURTAXES** an additional tax, especially one that is levied on incomes above a certain level □ verb **SURTAXES, SURTAXING, SURTAXED** to levy such a tax on someone or something

SURTITLE noun **SURTITLES** any of a sequence of captions that are projected onto a screen to the side of, or above, the stage during a foreign-language opera or play and which give a running translation of the libretto or dialogue as it is performed

SURVEY verb **SURVEYS, SURVEYING, SURVEYED** to look at or examine at length or in detail, in order to get a general view □ noun **SURVEYS** a detailed examination or investigation, eg to find out public opinion or customer preference

SURVEYING noun **SURVEYINGS** an act of looking or examining at length or in detail

SURVEYOR noun **SURVEYORS** a person who is professionally qualified to survey land, buildings, etc

SURVIVAL noun **SURVIVALS** said of an individual: the fact of continuing to live, especially after some risk that might have prevented this

SURVIVE verb **SURVIVES, SURVIVING, SURVIVED** to remain alive, especially despite (some risk that might prevent this)

SURVIVOR noun **SURVIVORS** someone or something that survives

SUS verb **SUSSES, SUSSING, SUSSED** to suss □ noun **SUSES, SUSSES** a suss

SUSHI noun **SUSHIS** a Japanese dish of small rolls or balls of cold boiled rice that has been flavoured with vinegar and topped with egg, raw fish or vegetables

SUSLIK noun **SUSLIKS** a ground squirrel that is found in S Europe and parts of Asia

SUSPECT verb **SUSPECTS, SUSPECTING, SUSPECTED** to consider or believe likely □ noun **SUSPECTS** someone who is suspected of committing a crime, etc □ adj thought to be possibly false, untrue or dangerous; dubious

SUSPEND verb **SUSPENDS, SUSPENDING, SUSPENDED** to hang or hang up something

SUSPENDER noun **SUSPENDERS** an elasticated strap that can be attached to the top of a stocking or sock to hold it in place

SUSPENSE noun **SUSPENSES** a state of nervous or excited tension or uncertainty

SUSPICION noun **SUSPICIONS** an act, instance or feeling of suspecting

SUSS verb **SUSSES, SUSSING, SUSSED** to discover, assess or establish something, especially by investigation or intuition □ noun **SUSSES** a suspect

SUSTAIN verb **SUSTAINS, SUSTAINING, SUSTAINED** to keep going

SUSTAINED adj kept up over a prolonged time, especially without wavering or flagging

SUSTAINER noun **SUSTAINERS** a person or thing that sustains

SUSTAINING noun **SUSTAININGS** an act of keeping something up over a long time

SUSURRUS noun **SUSURRUSES** a soft whispering or rustling sound

SUTRA noun **SUTRAS** in Sanskrit

literature: a set of aphorisms that relate to ritual, grammar, metre, philosophy, etc

SUTTEE noun **SUTTEES** a Hindu custom that was abolished by the British authorities in India in 1829, in which a widow would sacrifice herself by being burned alive on her dead husband's funeral pyre

SUTURE noun **SUTURES** a stitch that joins the edges of a wound, surgical incision, etc together □ verb **SUTURES, SUTURING, SUTURED** to sew up (a wound, surgical incision, etc)

SUZERAIN noun **SUZERAINS** a nation, state or ruler that exercises some control over another state but which allows it to retain its own ruler or government

SVELTE adj **SVELTER, SVELTEST** slim or slender, especially in a graceful or attractive way

SWAB noun **SWABS** a piece of cotton wool, gauze, etc that is used for cleaning wounds, applying antiseptics, taking a medical specimen, etc □ verb **SWABS, SWABBING, SWABBED** to use a swab or something like a swab for cleaning or mopping something (eg a wound, a ship's deck, etc); to clean or clean out with, or as if with, a swab

SWABBER noun **SWABBERS** a person who uses a swab

SWADDLE verb **SWADDLES, SWADDLING, SWADDLED** to bandage

SWAG noun **SWAGS** stolen goods □ verb **SWAGS, SWAGGING, SWAGGED** to sway or sag

SWAGE noun **SWAGES** a tool that is used in the working and shaping of cold metal □ verb **SWAGES, SWAGING, SWAGED** to work or shape (cold metal) using a swage

SWAGGER verb **SWAGGERS, SWAGGERING, SWAGGERED** to walk with an air of self-importance □ noun **SWAGGERS** a swaggering way of walking or behaving

SWAGGERER noun **SWAGGERERS** someone who swaggers

SWAGGERING noun **SWAGGERINGS** an act of walking with an air of self-importance

SWAGGIE noun **SWAGGIES** a swagman

SWAGMAN noun **SWAGMEN** someone, especially an itinerant workman, who travels about on foot and who carries their belongings in a traveller's pack or rolled bundle

SWAIN noun **SWAINS** a country youth

SWALLOW [1] verb **SWALLOWS, SWALLOWING, SWALLOWED** to perform a muscular movement to make (food or drink) go from the mouth, down the oesophagus and into the stomach

SWALLOW [2] noun **SWALLOWS** any of various small migratory fast-flying insect-eating birds that have long pointed wings and a long forked tail

SWALLOWER noun **SWALLOWERS** someone who swallows

SWAM a past form of **swim**

SWAMI noun **SWAMIS** an honorific title for a Hindu male religious teacher

SWAMP noun **SWAMPS** an area of land that is permanently waterlogged but which has a dense covering of vegetation, eg, in certain tropical regions, trees and shrubs, such as mangroves or, in the more temperate zones, willows or reeds ▫ verb **SWAMPS, SWAMPING, SWAMPED** to overwhelm or inundate

SWAMPY adj **SWAMPIER, SWAMPIEST** of or like a swamp

SWAN noun **SWANS** any of several species of a large graceful aquatic birds related to ducks and geese, which have a long slender elegant neck, powerful wings and webbed feet ▫ verb **SWANS, SWANNING, SWANNED** to spend time idly; to wander aimlessly or gracefully

SWANK verb **SWANKS, SWANKING, SWANKED** to boast or show off ▫ noun **SWANKS** flashiness, ostentation, etc; boastfulness ▫ adj **SWANKER, SWANKEST** swanky

SWANKER noun **SWANKERS** someone who shows off or boasts

SWANKY adj **SWANKIER, SWANKIEST** boastful

SWANLIKE adj like a swan, especially in being graceful

SWANNERY noun **SWANNERIES** a place where swans are kept or bred

SWAP verb **SWAPS, SWAPPING, SWAPPED** to exchange or trade (something or someone) for another ▫ noun **SWAPS** an exchange or trading

SWAPPER noun **SWAPPERS** someone who swaps

SWAPPING noun **SWAPPINGS** an act of exchanging or trading (something or someone) for another

SWARD noun **SWARDS** a large, usually grassy, area of land

SWARDED adj covered with turf

SWARF noun **SWARFS** the grindings, filings or strips of waste that are produced in machine tooling

SWARM noun **SWARMS** a large group of flying bees, led by a queen, that have left their hive in order to set up a new home ▫ verb **SWARMS, SWARMING, SWARMED** to gather, move, go, etc in a swarm

SWARMING noun **SWARMINGS** an act of gathering, moving, going etc in a swarm

SWARTHY adj **SWARTHIER, SWARTHIEST** having a dark complexion

SWASH verb **SWASHES, SWASHING, SWASHED** to move about in water making a splashing noise ▫ noun **SWASHES** a watery splashing noise

SWASTIKA noun **SWASTIKAS** a plain cross with arms of equal length which are bent at right angles, usually clockwise, at or close to their mid point

SWAT verb **SWATS, SWATTING, SWATTED** to hit (especially a fly) with a heavy slapping blow ▫ noun **SWATS** a heavy slap or blow

SWATCH noun **SWATCHES** a small sample, especially of fabric but also of wallpaper, carpet, etc

SWATH noun **SWATHS** a strip of grass, corn, etc cut by a scythe, mower or harvester

SWATHE verb **SWATHES, SWATHING, SWATHED** to bind or wrap someone or something in strips or bands of cloth or fabric, eg bandages ▫ noun **SWATHES** a wrapping, especially a strip of cloth or fabric; a bandage

SWATTER noun **SWATTERS** a device for swatting flies with, usually consisting of a long thin handle and a wide flat flexible head

SWAY verb **SWAYS, SWAYING, SWAYED** to swing, or make something swing, backwards and forwards or from side to side, especially slowly and smoothly ▫ noun **SWAYS** a swaying motion

SWAYING noun **SWAYINGS** an act

of swinging backwards and forwards or from side to side

SWEAR verb **SWEARS, SWEARING, SWORE, SWORN** to use indecent or blasphemous language ▫ noun **SWEARS** an act of swearing

SWEARER noun **SWEARERS** someone who swears

SWEARING noun **SWEARINGS** an act of using indecent or blasphemous language

SWEAT noun **SWEATS** the salty liquid produced actively by the sweat glands and given out through the pores of the skin, especially in response to great heat, physical exertion, nervousness or fear ▫ verb **SWEATS, SWEATING, SWEAT, SWEATED** to give out sweat through the pores of the skin

SWEATER noun **SWEATERS** a knitted jersey or pullover, originally of a kind often worn before and after hard exercise

SWEATSUIT noun **SWEATSUITS** a loose-fitting suit of sweatshirt and trousers, usually tight-fitting at the wrists and ankles, worn by athletes or as leisurewear

SWEATY adj **SWEATIER, SWEATIEST** causing sweat

SWEDE noun **SWEDES** an annual or biennial plant, widely cultivated in cool temperate regions for its edible root

SWEEP verb **SWEEPS, SWEEPING, SWEPT** to clean (a room, a floor, etc) with a brush or broom ▫ noun **SWEEPS** an act of sweeping

SWEEPBACK noun **SWEEPBACKS** the form or state of a wing of an aircraft or bird that is angled towards the back as opposed to standing at right angles to the body

SWEEPER noun **SWEEPERS** someone who sweeps

SWEEPING adj said of a search, change, etc: wide-ranging and thorough ▫ noun **SWEEPINGS** something swept up

SWEET adj **SWEETER, SWEETEST** tasting like sugar; not sour, salty or bitter ▫ noun **SWEETS** any small sugar-based confection that is sucked or chewed ▫ adverb sweetly

SWEETCORN noun **SWEETCORNS** kernels of a variety of maize eaten young while still sweet

SWEETEN verb **SWEETENS,**

SWEETENING, SWEETENED to make (food) sweet or sweeter

SWEETENER noun **SWEETENERS** a substance used for sweetening food, especially one other than sugar

SWEETENING noun **SWEETENINGS** a substance used to make food sweeter

SWEETIE noun **SWEETIES** a sweet for sucking or chewing

SWEETLY adverb in a sweet way

SWEETMEAL adj said of biscuits: made of sweetened wholemeal

SWEETMEAT noun **SWEETMEATS** any small sugar-based confection or cake

SWEETNESS noun **SWEETNESSES** the state, or degree, of being sweet

SWEETPEA noun **SWEETPEAS** a garden plant with bright-coloured fragrant flowers

SWEETSOP noun **SWEETSOPS** a tropical American evergreen shrub with a sweet edible pulpy fruit

SWEETY noun **SWEETIES** a sweetie

SWELL verb **SWELLS, SWELLING, SWELLED, SWOLLEN** to become, or make something, bigger or fatter through injury or infection, or by filling with liquid or air ◻ noun **SWELLS** a heaving of the sea without waves ◻ adj **SWELLER, SWELLEST** excellent

SWELLING noun **SWELLINGS** an area of the body that is temporarily swollen as a result of injury or infection

SWELTER verb **SWELTERS, SWELTERING, SWELTERED** to sweat heavily or feel extremely or oppressively hot ◻ noun **SWELTERS** a sweltering feeling or state; sweltering weather

SWELTERING adj said of the weather: extremely or oppressively hot

SWEPT past form of **sweep**

SWEPTBACK adj said of the wing of an aircraft: having sweepback

SWEPTWING adj said of an aircraft: having sweptback wings

SWERVE verb **SWERVES, SWERVING, SWERVED** to turn or move aside suddenly and sharply, eg to avoid a collision ◻ noun **SWERVES** an act of turning or moving aside suddenly and sharply; a swerving movement

SWERVER noun **SWERVERS** someone who swerves

SWERVING noun **SWERVINGS** a swerve

SWIFT adj **SWIFTER, SWIFTEST** fast-moving; able to move fast ◻ adverb swiftly ◻ noun **SWIFTS** any of various small fast-flying birds that have dark brown or grey plumage, long narrow pointed wings and a forked tail, and that feed, and sometimes mate, while in flight

SWIFTLET noun **SWIFTLETS** any member of a genus of small swifts, some species of which make nests from edible saliva-based gelatinous material, used in making a type of soup (bird's nest soup) greatly esteemed in parts of the Far East

SWIFTLY adverb quickly

SWIFTNESS noun **SWIFTNESSES** the quality or condition of being swift

SWIG verb **SWIGS, SWIGGING, SWIGGED** to drink in gulps, especially from a bottle ◻ noun **SWIGS** a large drink or gulp

SWILL verb **SWILLS, SWILLING, SWILLED** to rinse something by splashing water round or over it ◻ noun **SWILLS** any mushy mixture of scraps fed to pigs

SWIM verb **SWIMS, SWIMMING, SWAM, SWUM** to propel oneself through water by moving the arms and legs or (in fish) the tail and fins ◻ noun **SWIMS** a spell of swimming

SWIMMABLE adj capable of being swum

SWIMMER noun **SWIMMERS** someone who swims

SWIMMERET noun **SWIMMERETS** any of a number of leg-like abdominal appendages on the body of many crustaceans, used in swimming and for carrying eggs

SWIMMING noun **SWIMMINGS** the sport or recreation of propelling oneself through water by moving the arms and legs

SWIMSUIT noun **SWIMSUITS** a garment worn for swimming

SWINDLE verb **SWINDLES, SWINDLING, SWINDLED** to cheat or trick someone in order to obtain money from them; to obtain (money, etc) by cheating or trickery ◻ noun **SWINDLES** an act of swindling

SWINDLER noun **SWINDLERS** someone who swindles others

SWINE noun **SWINE** a pig

SWINEHERD noun **SWINEHERDS** someone who looks after pigs

SWING verb **SWINGS, SWINGING, SWUNG** to move in a curving motion, pivoting from a fixed point ◻ noun **SWINGS** a seat suspended from a frame or branch for a child (or sometimes an adult) to swing on

SWINGBOAT noun **SWINGBOATS** a boat-shaped swinging carriage in which rides are given at a fairground

SWINGEING adj hard to bear; severe, extensive

SWINGER noun **SWINGERS** someone who has a very active social life, especially with much dancing and drinking

SWINGING adj moving or turning with a swing

SWINISH adj like a swine

SWINISHLY adverb in a swinish way

SWIPE verb **SWIPES, SWIPING, SWIPED** to hit with a heavy sweeping blow ◻ noun **SWIPES** a heavy sweeping blow

SWIRL verb **SWIRLS, SWIRLING, SWIRLED** to flow or cause to flow or move with a whirling or circling motion ◻ noun **SWIRLS** a whirling or circling motion

SWISH [1] verb **SWISHES, SWISHING, SWISHED** to move with a brushing, rustling, rushing, hissing or whooshing sound ◻ noun **SWISHES** a brushing, rustling, rushing, hissing or whooshing sound, or movement causing such a sound

SWISH [2] adj **SWISHER, SWISHEST** smart and stylish

SWITCH noun **SWITCHES** a manually operated or automatic device that is used to open or close an electric circuit, eg a lever or button that makes or breaks a pair of contacts ◻ verb **SWITCHES, SWITCHING, SWITCHED** to exchange (one thing or person for another), especially quickly and without notice in order to deceive

SWITHER verb **SWITHERS, SWITHERING, SWITHERED** to hesitate; to be undecided; to consider possible alternatives ◻ noun **SWITHERS** hesitation; indecision

SWIVEL noun **SWIVELS** a joint between two parts enabling one part to turn or pivot freely and independently of the other ◻ verb

SWIVELS, SWIVELLING, SWIVELLED to turn or pivot on a swivel or as if on a swivel

SWIZZLE noun **SWIZZLES** a thing that, in reality, is disappointingly inferior to what was cheatingly promised ◻ verb **SWIZZLES, SWIZZLING, SWIZZLED** to cheat, let down, etc with a swizzle

SWOLLEN a past form of **swell**

SWOON verb **SWOONS, SWOONING, SWOONED** to faint, especially from over-excitement ◻ noun **SWOONS** an act of swooning

SWOOP verb **SWOOPS, SWOOPING, SWOOPED** to fly down with a fast sweeping movement ◻ noun **SWOOPS** an act of swooping

SWOOSH noun **SWOOSHES** the noise of a rush of air or water, or any noise resembling this ◻ verb **SWOOSHES, SWOOSHING, SWOOSHED** to make or move with such a noise

SWOP verb **SWOPS, SWOPPING, SWOPPED** to swap ◻ noun **SWOPS** a swap

SWORD noun **SWORDS** a weapon like a large long knife, with a blade sharpened on one or both edges and usually ending in a point

SWORDFISH noun **SWORDFISHES** a large fast-swimming marine fish, so called because its upper jaw is prolonged into a long flat sword-shaped snout

SWORDPLAY noun **SWORDPLAYS** the activity or art of fencing

SWORDSMAN noun **SWORDSMEN** a man skilled in fighting with a sword

SWORE a past form of **swear**

SWORN adj bound or confirmed by, or as if by, having taken an oath

SWOT verb **SWOTS, SWOTTING, SWOTTED** to study hard and seriously ◻ noun **SWOTS** someone who studies hard, especially single-mindedly or in order to impress a teacher

SWOTTING noun **SWOTTINGS** an act of revising or studying hard

SWUM a past form of **swim**

SWUNG past form of **swing**

SWY noun **SWIES** an Australian gambling game

SYBARITE noun **SYBARITES** someone devoted to a life of luxury and pleasure

SYBARITIC adj luxurious

SYCAMORE noun **SYCAMORES** a large fast-growing deciduous tree with dark green leaves divided into five toothed lobes, yellowish flowers borne in long pendulous spikes, and two-winged fruits

SYCOPHANT noun **SYCOPHANTS** someone who flatters in a servile way; a crawler

SYE verb **SYES, SYEING, SYED** to strain

SYLLABARY noun **SYLLABARIES** a writing system in which the symbols represent spoken syllables (although in fact some stand for single speech sounds)

SYLLABIC adj relating to syllables or the division of words into syllables

SYLLABIFY verb **SYLLABIFIES, SYLLABIFYING, SYLLABIFIED** to divide (a word) into syllables

SYLLABLE noun **SYLLABLES** a segment of a spoken word consisting of one sound or of two or more sounds said as a single unit of speech (*segment* and *spoken* each consist of two syllables; *consisting* has three syllables)

SYLLABUB noun **SYLLABUBS** a frothy dessert made by whipping a sweetened mixture of cream or milk and wine

SYLLABUS noun **SYLLABUSES, SYLLABI** a series of topics prescribed for a course of study

SYLLEPSIS noun **SYLLEPSES** a figure of speech in which one word in a sentence stands in the same grammatical relationship to two or more words or phrases but with different senses, as does *in* in *She left home in tears and a taxi*

SYLLEPTIC adj of or relating to a syllepsis

SYLLOGISE verb **SYLLOGISES, SYLLOGISING, SYLLOGISED** to syllogize

SYLLOGISM noun **SYLLOGISMS** an argument in which a conclusion, whether valid or invalid, is drawn from two independent statements using logic, as in *All dogs are animals, foxhounds are dogs, therefore foxhounds are animals*

SYLLOGIZE verb **SYLLOGIZES, SYLLOGIZING, SYLLOGIZED** to reason, argue or deduce by syllogisms

SYLPH noun **SYLPHS** in folklore: a spirit of the air

SYLVAN adj relating to woods or woodland; wooded

SYMBIONT noun **SYMBIONTS** either of two organisms living in a symbiotic relationship

SYMBIOSIS noun **SYMBIOSES** a close association between two organisms of different species, usually to the benefit of both partners, and often essential for mutual survival

SYMBIOTIC adj relating to or involving symbiosis

SYMBOL noun **SYMBOLS** a thing that represents or stands for another, usually something concrete or material representing an idea or emotion, eg the colour red representing danger

SYMBOLIC adj representing or standing for something

SYMBOLISE verb **SYMBOLISES, SYMBOLISING, SYMBOLISED** to symbolize

SYMBOLISM noun **SYMBOLISMS** the use of symbols, especially to express ideas or emotions in literature, cinema, etc

SYMBOLIST noun **SYMBOLISTS** an artist or writer who uses symbolism

SYMBOLIZE verb **SYMBOLIZES, SYMBOLIZING, SYMBOLIZED** to be a symbol of something; to stand for something

SYMBOLOGY noun **SYMBOLOGIES** the study or use of symbols

SYMMETRY noun **SYMMETRIES** exact similarity between two parts or halves, as if one were a mirror image of the other

SYMPATHY noun **SYMPATHIES** an understanding of and feeling for the sadness or suffering of others, often shown in expressions of sorrow or pity

SYMPHONIC adj said of music: suitable for performance by a symphony orchestra

SYMPHONY noun **SYMPHONIES** a long musical work divided into several movements, played by a full orchestra

SYMPOSIUM noun **SYMPOSIA** a conference held to discuss a particular subject, especially an academic subject

SYMPTOM noun **SYMPTOMS** an indication of the presence of a disease or disorder, especially

For longer words, see The Chambers Dictionary

something perceived by the patient and not outwardly visible, eg pain, nausea, dizziness

SYNAGOGUE *noun* **SYNAGOGUES** a Jewish place of worship and religious instruction

SYNAPSE *noun* **SYNAPSES** in the nervous system: a region where one neurone communicates with the next, consisting of a minute gap across which nerve impulses are transmitted by means of a chemical substance known as a neurotransmitter

SYNAPSIS *noun* **SYNAPSES** the pairing of chromosomes of paternal and maternal origin during meiosis

SYNAPTIC *adj* of or relating to synapsis

SYNC *noun* **SYNCS** synch ❑ *verb* **SYNCS, SYNCING, SYNCED** to synch

SYNCH *noun* **SYNCHS** synchronization, especially of sound and picture in film and television ❑ *verb* **SYNCHS, SYNCHING, SYNCHED** to synchronize

SYNCHRO *noun* **SYNCHROS** synchronized swimming

SYNCHRONY *noun* **SYNCHRONIES** the fact or state of being synchronous or synchronic; simultaneousness

SYNCLINE *noun* **SYNCLINES** a large generally U-shaped fold in the stratified rocks of the Earth's crust

SYNCOPATE *verb* **SYNCOPATES, SYNCOPATING, SYNCOPATED** to alter (the rhythm of music) by putting the stress on beats not usually stressed

SYNCOPE *noun* **SYNCOPES** a sudden temporary loss of consciousness; a faint

SYNDIC *noun* **SYNDICS** someone who represents a university, company or other body in business or legal matters

SYNDICATE *noun* **SYNDICATES** any association of people or groups working together on a single project ❑ *verb* **SYNDICATES, SYNDICATING, SYNDICATED** to form into a syndicate

SYNDROME *noun* **SYNDROMES** a group of signs or symptoms whose appearance together usually indicates the presence of a particular disease or disorder

SYNERGISM *noun* **SYNERGISMS** synergy

SYNERGY *noun* **SYNERGIES** the phenomenon in which the combined action of two or more compounds, especially drugs or hormones, is greater than the sum of the individual effects of each compound

SYNOD *noun* **SYNODS** a local or national council of members of the clergy

SYNONYM *noun* **SYNONYMS** a word having the same, or very nearly the same, meaning as another

SYNONYMY *noun* **SYNONYMIES** the state of being synonymous

SYNOPSIS *noun* **SYNOPSES** a brief outline, eg of the plot of a book; a summary

SYNOPTIC *adj* being or like a synopsis; giving or taking an overall view

SYNOVIA *noun* **SYNOVIAS** the transparent liquid, produced by the synovial membranes of a joint, which serves to lubricate that joint

SYNOVITIS *noun* **SYNOVITISES** inflammation of a synovial membrane

SYNROC *noun* **SYNROCS** any of various types of synthetic rock developed to fuse with radioactive waste and hold it in a stable condition buried deep underground

SYNTACTIC *adj* of or relating to syntax

SYNTAX *noun* **SYNTAXES** the positioning of words in a sentence and their relationship to each other

SYNTH *noun* **SYNTHS** a synthesizer

SYNTHESIS *noun* **SYNTHESES** the process of putting together separate parts to form a complex whole

SYNTHETIC *adj* referring or

relating to, or produced by, chemical synthesis; not naturally produced; man-made ❑ *noun* **SYNTHETICS** a synthetic substance

SYPHILIS *noun* **SYPHILISES** a sexually transmitted disease caused by bacterial infection and characterized by painless ulcers on the genitals, fever and a faint red rash, which if left untreated may eventually result in heart damage, blindness, paralysis and death

SYPHON *noun* **SYPHONS** a siphon ❑ *verb* **SYPHONS, SYPHONING, SYPHONED** to siphon

SYRINGA *noun* **SYRINGAS** the name commonly, but technically incorrectly, used to refer to the mock orange shrub

SYRINGE *noun* **SYRINGES** a medical instrument for injecting or drawing off liquid, consisting of a hollow cylinder with a plunger inside and a thin hollow needle attached ❑ *verb* **SYRINGES, SYRINGING, SYRINGED** to clean, spray or inject using a syringe

SYRINX *noun* **SYRINXES, SYRINGES** the vocal organ of birds

SYRUP *noun* **SYRUPS** a sweet, sticky, almost saturated solution of sugar, widely used in cooking, baking, etc, and obtained from various plants, eg sugar cane, maple, or manufactured commercially, eg golden syrup

SYRUPY *adj* **SYRUPIER, SYRUPIEST** of or like syrup, especially in being thick, runny and very sweet

SYSTALTIC *adj* said especially of the heart: alternately contracting and dilating

SYSTEM *noun* **SYSTEMS** a set of interconnected or interrelated parts forming a complex whole

SYSTEMIC *adj* referring or relating to a whole organism

SYSTOLE *noun* **SYSTOLES** contraction of the heart muscle, during which blood is pumped from the ventricle into the arteries

SYSTOLIC *adj* relating to systole

TA *exclamation* thank you

TAB *noun* **TABS** a small flap, tag, strip of material, etc attached to an article, for hanging it up, opening, holding or identifying it, etc □ *verb* **TABS, TABBING, TABBED** to fix a tab to something or someone

TABARD *noun* **TABARDS** a short loose sleeveless jacket or tunic, worn especially by a knight over his armour or, with the arms of the king or queen on the front, by a herald

TABARET *noun* **TABARETS** a type of silk fabric, used especially by upholsterers, with alternate stripes of watered and satin surface

TABBOULEH *noun* **TABBOULEHS** a Mediterranean salad made with cracked wheat which has been moistened with water, lemon juice and olive oil, and mixed with chopped vegetables, especially tomatoes, cucumber and garlic

TABBY *noun* **TABBIES** a usually grey or brown cat with darker stripes □ *adj* characterized by dark stripes or wavy markings

TABES *noun* **TABES** a wasting away of the body or parts of the body

TABLA *noun* **TABLAS** a pair of small drums played with the hands in Indian music

TABLATURE *noun* **TABLATURES** a system of musical notation indicating the keys, frets, etc to be used rather than the pitch to be sounded, which is still used for the guitar and other fretted instruments

TABLE *noun* **TABLES** a piece of furniture consisting of a flat horizontal surface supported by one or more legs □ *verb* **TABLES, TABLING, TABLED** to put something forward for discussion

TABLEAU *noun* **TABLEAUX** a picture or pictorial representation of a group or scene

TABLELAND *noun* **TABLELANDS** a broad high plain or a plateau, usually with steep sides and rising sharply from the surrounding lowland

TABLET *noun* **TABLETS** a small solid measured amount of a medicine or drug; a pill

TABLEWARE *noun* **TABLEWARES** dishes, plates and cutlery, etc collectively for use at table

TABLOID *noun* **TABLOIDS** a newspaper with relatively small pages (approximately 12 x 16in, 30 x 40cm), especially one written in an informal and often sensationalist style and with many photographs

TABOO *noun* **TABOOS** anything which is forbidden or disapproved of for religious reasons or by social custom □ *verb* **TABOOS, TABOOING, TABOOED** to forbid (a custom, or the use of a word, etc) as a taboo

TABOR *noun* **TABORS** a small single-headed drum, used especially in the Middle Ages, played with one hand while the same player plays a pipe or fife with the other

TABORET *noun* **TABORETS** a tabouret

TABOURET *noun* **TABOURETS** a low stool or seat

TABU *noun* **TABUS** a taboo □ *verb* **TABUS, TABUING, TABUED** to taboo

TABULAR *adj* arranged in systematic columns; in the form of or according to a table

TABULATE *verb* **TABULATES, TABULATING, TABULATED** to arrange (information) in tabular form

TABULATOR *noun* **TABULATORS** a machine which reads data from a computer storage device, especially punched cards, and prints it out on continuous sheets of paper

TACAMAHAC *noun* **TACAMAHACS** a gum-resin yielded by various tropical trees

TACET *verb* used as a direction on a score: be silent or pause

TACHE *noun* **TACHES** a moustache

TACHISM *noun* **TACHISMS** a term used, especially in France, to describe a movement in mid-20c abstract painting in which paint

was laid on in thick patches intended to be interesting in themselves, irrespective of whether a motif was represented

TACHISME *noun* **TACHISMES** tachism

TACHIST *noun* **TACHISTS** a follower of tachism

TACHISTE *noun* **TACHISTES** a tachist

TACIT *adj* silent; unspoken

TACITLY *adverb* in a tacit way

TACITNESS *noun* **TACITNESSES** the state of being tacit

TACITURN *adj* saying little; quiet and uncommunicative

TACK *noun* **TACKS** a short nail with a sharp point and a broad flat head □ *verb* **TACKS, TACKING, TACKED** to fasten or attach something with tacks

TACKILY *adverb* in a tacky way

TACKINESS *noun* **TACKINESSES** the quality or condition of being tacky

TACKLE *noun* **TACKLES** in sport: an act of trying to get the ball away from a player on the opposing team □ *verb* **TACKLES, TACKLING, TACKLED** to grasp or seize and struggle with something or someone, especially to try to restrain them

TACKLER *noun* **TACKLERS** someone who tackles

TACKY *adj* **TACKIER, TACKIEST** slightly sticky

TACO *noun* **TACOS** in Mexican cookery: a tortilla which is fried until crisp and stuffed with a filling, usually of meat

TACT *noun* **TACTS** an awareness of the best or most considerate way to deal with others so as to avoid offence, upset, antagonism or resentment

TACTFUL *adj* showing or demonstrating tact

TACTFULLY *adverb* in a tactful way

TACTIC *noun* **TACTICS** a tactical manoeuvre

TACTICAL *adj* relating to or forming tactics

TACTICIAN noun **TACTICIANS** a person who is good at tactics or successful planning

TACTICS singular and plural noun the art or science of employing and manoeuvring troops to win or gain an advantage over the enemy

TACTILE adj belonging or relating to, or having, a sense of touch

TACTLESS adj lacking tact

TAD noun **TADS** a small amount

TADPOLE noun **TADPOLES** the larval stage of many frogs and toads, which initially appears to consist of a small head and a tail

TAE noun **TAES** Scots form of toe

TAENIA noun **TAENIAE, TAENIAS** in anatomy: any ribbon-like structure

TAFFETA noun **TAFFETAS** a stiff shiny fabric woven from silk or some silk-like material, eg rayon

TAFFRAIL noun **TAFFRAILS** a rail round a ship's stern

TAG noun **TAGS** a piece of material, paper or leather, etc that carries information (eg washing instructions or price, etc) about the object to which it is attached □ verb **TAGS, TAGGING, TAGGED** to put a tag or tags on something or someone

TAHINI noun **TAHINIS** a thick paste made from ground sesame seeds

TAI noun **TAIS** a Japanese sea bream

TAIGA noun **TAIGAS** in northern parts of the N hemisphere: the large area of predominantly coniferous forest located south of the arctic and subarctic tundra regions

TAIL noun **TAILS** the part of an animal's body that projects from the lower or rear end of the back to form a flexible appendage □ verb **TAILS, TAILING, TAILED** to remove the stalks (from fruit or vegetables)

TAILBACK noun **TAILBACKS** a long queue of traffic stretching back from an accident or roadworks, etc blocking the road

TAILBOARD noun **TAILBOARDS** a hinged or removable flap at the rear of a lorry, cart or wagon

TAILGATE noun **TAILGATES** the rear door which opens upwards on a hatchback vehicle

TAILLESS adj without a tail

TAILOR noun **TAILORS** someone who makes suits, jackets, trousers and overcoats, etc to measure, especially for men □ verb **TAILORS, TAILORING, TAILORED** to make and style (garments) so that they fit well

TAILPIECE noun **TAILPIECES** a piece at the end or tail

TAILPLANE noun **TAILPLANES** a small horizontal wing at the rear of an aircraft

TAILSPIN noun **TAILSPINS** a spiral dive of an aeroplane

TAILSTOCK noun **TAILSTOCKS** a slidable casting mounted on a lathe, used to support the free end of the piece being worked on

TAINT verb **TAINTS, TAINTING, TAINTED** to affect or be affected by pollution, putrefaction or contamination □ noun **TAINTS** a spot, mark or trace of decay, contamination, infection or something bad or evil

TAIPAN noun **TAIPANS** a highly venomous snake native to NE Australia and New Guinea, which is brown in colour with a paler head and feeds mainly on small mammals

TAJ noun **TAJES** a crown

TAK verb **TAKS, TAKING** Scots form of take

TAKA noun **TAKAS** the standard unit of currency of Bangladesh

TAKE verb **TAKES, TAKING, TOOK, TAKEN** to reach out for and grasp, lift or pull, etc (something chosen or known); to grasp or enter, etc something for use □ noun **TAKES** a scene filmed or piece of music recorded during an uninterrupted period of filming or recording

TAKEAWAY noun **TAKEAWAYS** a cooked meal prepared and bought in a restaurant but taken away and eaten somewhere else, eg at home □ adj said of cooked food: prepared in a shop or restaurant for the customer to take away

TAKEOVER noun **TAKEOVERS** the act of taking control of something, especially of a company by buying the majority of its shares

TAKER noun **TAKERS** someone who takes or accepts something, especially a bet, offer or challenge

TAKING adj attractive; charming □ noun **TAKINGS** the amount of money taken at a concert or in a shop, etc; receipts

TALA noun **TALAS** a traditional rhythmic pattern in Indian music

TALAQ noun **TALAQS** under Islamic law: a form of divorce

TALC noun **TALCS** a white, green or grey mineral form of magnesium silicate, one of the softest minerals, used in eg talcum powder and other cosmetics

TALCUM noun **TALCUMS** talc

TALE noun **TALES** a story or narrative

TALENT noun **TALENTS** a special or innate skill, aptitude or ability, especially for art or music, etc

TALENTED adj skilled, especially in eg art or music

TALES noun **TALES** the filling up, from those who are present in court, of a vacancy in the number of jurors

TALIPES noun **TALIPES** club foot

TALISMAN noun **TALISMANS** a small object, such as a stone, supposed to have magic powers to protect its owner from evil, bring good luck or work magic; a charm or amulet

TALK verb **TALKS, TALKING, TALKED** to express one's ideas, feelings and thoughts by means of spoken words, or by sign language, etc; to have a conversation or discussion □ noun **TALKS** a conversation or discussion

TALKATIVE adj talking a lot; chatty

TALKER noun **TALKERS** someone who talks

TALKIE noun **TALKIES** a cinema film with sound, especially one of the first such films

TALL adj **TALLER, TALLEST** usually said of a person: above average height

TALLBOY noun **TALLBOYS** a tall chest of drawers, consisting of an upper and slightly smaller section standing on a larger lower one

TALLITH noun **TALLITHS, TALLITHIM** a shawl worn by Jewish men, especially for prayer

TALLNESS noun **TALLNESSES** the state or condition of being tall

TALLOW noun **TALLOWS** hard fat from sheep and cattle which is melted down and used to make candles and soap, etc □ verb **TALLOWS, TALLOWING, TALLOWED** to cover or grease something with tallow

TALLY noun **TALLIES** an account or

reckoning, eg of work done, debts, or the score in a game □ verb **TALLIES, TALLYING, TALLIED** to agree, correspond or match

TALLYMAN noun **TALLYMEN** someone who keeps a tally

TALMUD noun **TALMUDS** the body of Jewish civil and canon law

TALON noun **TALONS** a hooked claw, especially of a bird of prey

TALUS noun **TALI** the ankle bone

TAM noun **TAMS** a cap with a broad circular flat top

TAMABLE adj capable of being tamed

TAMARI noun **TAMARIS** a concentrated sauce made of soya beans and salt, used especially in Japanese cookery

TAMARILLO noun **TAMARILLOS** a shrub that bears a tomato-like fruit

TAMARIND noun **TAMARINDS** a tropical evergreen tree which bears yellow flowers and brown seedpods

TAMARISK noun **TAMARISKS** any of various evergreen shrubs and small trees native to the Mediterranean region and Asia, which have tiny scale-like leaves and dense cylindrical spikes of small pink or white flowers

TAMBOUR noun **TAMBOURS** a frame for embroidery □ verb **TAMBOURS, TAMBOURING, TAMBOURED** to embroider something on a tambour

TAME adj **TAMER, TAMEST** said of animals: used to living or working with people; not wild or dangerous □ verb **TAMES, TAMING, TAMED** to make (an animal) used to living or working with people

TAMEABLE adj capable of being tamed

TAMENESS noun **TAMENESSES** the state of being tame

TAMER noun **TAMERS** someone who tames eg wild animals

TAMMY noun **TAMMIES** a tam-o'-shanter

TAMOXIFEN noun **TAMOXIFENS** a drug that inhibits the effects of oestrogens, and is used in the treatment of specific advanced breast cancers and also to stimulate ovulation in the treatment of female infertility

TAMP verb **TAMPS, TAMPING, TAMPED** to fill up (a hole containing explosive) with earth or cement, etc before setting off the explosion

TAMPER [1] verb **TAMPERS, TAMPERING, TAMPERED** to interfere or meddle, especially in a harmful way

TAMPER [2] noun **TAMPERS** someone or something that tamps

TAMPERER noun **TAMPERERS** someone who tampers or meddles

TAMPERING noun **TAMPERINGS** an act of interfering or meddling, especially in a harmful way

TAMPION noun **TAMPIONS** a plug, especially a protective plug placed in the muzzle of a gun when it is not in use

TAMPON noun **TAMPONS** a plug of cotton wool or other soft absorbent material inserted into a cavity or wound to absorb blood and other secretions, especially one for use in the vagina during menstruation □ verb **TAMPONS, TAMPONING, TAMPONED** to insert a tampon in something

TAN noun **TANS** the brown colour of the skin after exposure to the Sun's ultraviolet rays; a suntan □ adj **TANNER, TANNEST** tawny-brown in colour □ verb **TANS, TANNING, TANNED** to make or become brown in the sun

TANAGER noun **TANAGERS** any member of a S American family of birds, closely allied to the finches, the males of which have brightly coloured plumage

TANDEM noun **TANDEMS** a type of long three-wheeled bicycle for two people, with two seats and two sets of pedals placed one behind the other

TANDOORI noun **TANDOORIS** an Indian method of cooking food on a spit over charcoal in a clay oven

TANG noun **TANGS** a strong or sharp taste, flavour or smell

TANGA noun **TANGAS** underpants for men or women which have no material at the sides other than the waistband

TANGELO noun **TANGELOS** a hybrid between a tangerine and a pomelo

TANGENT noun **TANGENTS** in geometry: a straight line that touches a curve at one point, and has the same gradient as the curve at the point of contact

TANGERINE noun **TANGERINES** any of several varieties of a tree, native to Asia but widely cultivated in warm regions for its fruit

TANGIBLE adj able to be felt by touch

TANGIBLY adverb in a tangible way

TANGLE noun **TANGLES** an untidy and confused or knotted state or mass, eg of hair or fibres □ verb **TANGLES, TANGLING, TANGLED** said especially of hair and fibres, etc: to become untidy, knotted and confused

TANGLY adj **TANGLIER, TANGLIEST** tangled

TANGO noun **TANGOS** a Latin-American dance with dramatic stylized body positions and long pauses □ verb **TANGOS, TANGOING, TANGOED** to perform this dance

TANGRAM noun **TANGRAMS** a Chinese puzzle consisting of a square cut into seven pieces that will fit in various forms

TANGY adj **TANGIER, TANGIEST** with a fresh sharp smell or flavour

TANH noun **TANHS** a conventional short form for hyperbolic tangent

TANK noun **TANKS** a large container for holding, storing or transporting liquids or gas □ verb **TANKS, TANKING, TANKED** to put or store something in a tank

TANKARD noun **TANKARDS** a large drinking-mug, usually made from silver, pewter or pottery, sometimes with a hinged lid, and used especially for drinking beer

TANKER noun **TANKERS** a ship or large lorry which transports liquid in bulk

TANKFUL noun **TANKFULS** the amount a tank can hold

TANNED adj having a suntan

TANNER noun **TANNERS** someone whose job is to produce leather from hide

TANNERY noun **TANNERIES** a place where hides are turned into leather

TANNIN noun **TANNINS** any of several substances obtained from certain tree barks and other plants, used in tanning leather, dyeing, ink-making and medicine (especially for treating burns), and which also occurs in, and gives a distinctive flavour to, red wine and tea

TANNING noun **TANNINGS** the art or practice of converting hides into leather

TANSY noun **TANSIES** a perennial plant, native to Europe, with tubular yellow flowers in flat-topped clusters, whose aromatic leaves are used in cooking and formerly in medicine

TANTALISE verb **TANTALISES,**

TANTALISING, TANTALISED to tantalize

TANTALIZE verb **TANTALIZES, TANTALIZING, TANTALIZED** to tease or torment someone by keeping something they want just out of reach

TANTALUM noun **TANTALUMS** a hard bluish-grey metallic element with a high melting point, that is resistant to corrosion and is used to make certain alloys

TANTALUS noun **TANTALUSES** a case for holding decanters of alcoholic drink so that they are visible but locked up

TANTARA noun **TANTARAS** a flourish or blast on a trumpet or horn

TANTRA noun **TANTRAS** any of a number of Hindu or Buddhist texts giving religious teaching and ritual instructions which may include descriptions of spells, magical formulas, mantras, meditative practices and rituals to be performed

TANTRIC adj of or relating to tantras

TANTRUM noun **TANTRUMS** an outburst of childish or petulant bad temper

TAOISEACH noun **TAOISEACHS** the prime minister of the Republic of Ireland

TAP [1] verb **TAPS, TAPPING, TAPPED** to strike or knock lightly

TAP [2] noun **TAPS** a device consisting of a valve, with a handle for opening and shutting it, attached to a pipe for controlling the flow of liquid or gas

TAPAS plural noun light savoury snacks or appetizers, especially those based on Spanish foods and cooking techniques and served with drinks

TAPE noun **TAPES** a narrow strip of woven cloth used for tying or fastening, etc □ verb **TAPES, TAPING, TAPED** to fasten, tie or seal with tape

TAPER noun **TAPERS** a long thin candle □ verb **TAPERS, TAPERING, TAPERED** to make or become gradually narrower towards one end

TAPESTRIED adj covered or decorated with tapestry

TAPESTRY noun **TAPESTRIES** a thick woven textile with an ornamental design (often a picture) on it, used for curtains, wall-hangings or chair coverings,

etc □ verb **TAPESTRIES, TAPESTRYING, TAPESTRIED** to hang with tapestry; to work or represent in tapestry

TAPEWORM noun **TAPEWORMS** any of a group of segmented flatworms that live as parasites in the intestines of humans and other vertebrates

TAPHONOMY noun **TAPHONOMIES** the study or science of how plants and animals die and become fossilized

TAPIOCA noun **TAPIOCAS** hard white grains of starch from the root of the cassava plant, often made into a pudding with sugar and milk

TAPIR noun **TAPIRS** a brown or black-and-white nocturnal hoofed mammal with a long flexible snout, found near water in tropical forests of Central and S America and SE Asia, where it browses on water plants and low-growing vegetation on land

TAPPED past form of **tap** [1]

TAPPET noun **TAPPETS** a lever or projection that transmits motion from one part of a machine to another, especially in an internal-combustion engine from the camshaft to the valves

TAPPING a form of **tap** [1]

TAPROOM noun **TAPROOMS** a bar that serves alcoholic drinks, especially beer direct from casks

TAPROOT noun **TAPROOTS** a long straight main nutrient-storing root derived from the radicle and characteristic of some plants (eg carrot), from which smaller lateral roots develop and which allows perennial growth

TAPS singular noun a bugle call for lights out in army camps, etc

TAR noun **TARS** a dark sticky pungent liquid obtained by distillation of coal or wood, or by petroleum-refining, which is used in road construction, as a wood preservative and also as a component of some antiseptics □ verb **TARS, TARRING, TARRED** to cover with tar

TARANTULA noun **TARANTULAS** a large European wolf spider

TARBOOSH noun **TARBOOSHES** a fez

TARDILY adverb in a tardy way

TARDINESS noun **TARDINESSES** the state or condition of being tardy

TARDY adj **TARDIER, TARDIEST**

slow to move, progress or grow; sluggish

TARE noun **TARES** in older translations of the Bible: a weed which grows in corn fields

TARGET noun **TARGETS** an object aimed at in shooting practice or competitions, especially a flat round board marked with concentric circles and with a bull's-eye in the centre □ verb **TARGETS, TARGETING, TARGETED** to direct or aim something

TARIFF noun **TARIFFS** eg in a hotel: a list of prices or charges □ verb **TARIFFS, TARIFFING, TARIFFED** to set a tariff on something or someone

TARLATAN noun **TARLATANS** an open transparent muslin, used for stiffening garments

TARMAC noun **TARMACS** a mixture of small stones bound together with tar, used for road surfaces

TARN noun **TARNS** a small, often circular, mountain lake, especially one formed in a cirque

TARNISH verb **TARNISHES, TARNISHING, TARNISHED** said of metal: to make or become dull and discoloured, especially through the action of air or dirt □ noun **TARNISHES** a loss of shine or lustre

TARO noun **TAROS** a plant of the arum family, widely cultivated in the Pacific islands for its edible rootstock

TAROT noun **TAROTS** a pack of 78 playing-cards consisting of four suits of 14 cards and a fifth suit of 22 trump cards, now used mainly in fortune-telling

TARPAULIN noun **TARPAULINS** heavy canvas which has been made waterproof, especially with tar

TARRAGON noun **TARRAGONS** a bushy perennial plant native to Europe, with narrow lance-shaped leaves and small greenish-white flowers borne in globular heads arranged in groups

TARRIER noun **TARRIERS** someone who lingers in a place

TARRINESS noun the state of being tarry

TARRY [1] verb **TARRIES, TARRYING, TARRIED** to linger or stay in a place

TARRY [2] adj **TARRIER, TARRIEST** like tar or covered with tar

TARSAL adj relating to the bones of

the tarsus ◻ *noun* **TARSALS** in terrestrial vertebrates: any of the bones that form the tarsus

TARSUS *noun* **TARSI** the seven bones forming the upper part of the foot and ankle

TART [1] *adj* **TARTER, TARTEST** sharp or sour in taste

TART [2] *noun* **TARTS** a pastry case, especially one without a top, with a sweet or savoury filling ◻ *verb* **TARTS, TARTING, TARTED** to decorate or embellish someone or something, especially in a showy or tasteless way

TARTAN *noun* **TARTANS** a distinctive checked pattern which can be produced with checks of different widths and different colours, especially one of the many designs which are each associated with a different Scottish clan

TARTAR *noun* **TARTARS** a violent or fierce person

TARTLY *adverb* sharply; sourly

TARTNESS *noun* **TARTNESSES** the quality or condition of being sharp or sour

TARTRATE *noun* **TARTRATES** argol

TARTY *adj* **TARTIER, TARTIEST** said of a woman or women's clothing: blatantly sexual or promiscuous

TASH *noun* **TASHES** a moustache

TASK *noun* **TASKS** a piece of work that is required to be done

TASSEL *noun* **TASSELS** a decoration (eg on a curtain or cushion) consisting of a hanging bunch of threads held firmly by a knot at one end and loose at the other ◻ *verb* **TASSELS, TASSELLING, TASSELING, TASSELLED, TASSELED** to adorn something with tassels

TASTABLE *adj* capable of being tasted

TASTE *verb* **TASTES, TASTING, TASTED** to perceive the flavour of (food, drink or some other substance) by means of the sensation produced on the surface of the tongue ◻ *noun* **TASTES** the particular sensation produced when food, drink or other substances are placed on the tongue

TASTEFUL *adj* showing good judgement or taste

TASTELESS *adj* lacking flavour

TASTER *noun* **TASTERS** someone whose job is to taste and judge the quality of food or drink

TASTILY *adverb* in a tasty way

TASTINESS *noun* **TASTINESSES** the quality or condition of being tasty

TASTING *noun* **TASTINGS** a social event at which wine or some other food or drink is sampled

TASTY *adj* **TASTIER, TASTIEST** having a good, especially savoury, flavour

TAT [1] *noun* **TATS** rubbish or junk

TAT [2] *verb* **TATS, TATTING, TATTED** to make something by tatting

TATTER *noun* **TATTERS** a torn ragged shred of cloth, especially of clothing

TATTERED *adj* ragged or torn

TATTIE *noun* **TATTIES** a potato

TATTILY *adverb* in a tatty way

TATTINESS *noun* **TATTINESSES** the state of being tatty

TATTING *noun* **TATTINGS** delicate knotted lace trimming made from sewing-thread and worked by hand with a small shuttle

TATTLE *noun* **TATTLES** idle chatter or gossip ◻ *verb* **TATTLES, TATTLING, TATTLED** to chat or gossip idly

TATTLER *noun* **TATTLERS** a gossip

TATTOO [1] *verb* **TATTOOS, TATTOOING, TATTOOED** to mark (coloured designs or pictures) on (a person or part of the body) by pricking the skin and putting in indelible dyes ◻ *noun* **TATTOOS** a design tattooed on the skin

TATTOO [2] *noun* **TATTOOS** a signal by drum or bugle calling soldiers to quarters, especially in the evening

TATTOOER *noun* **TATTOOERS** someone who tattoos

TATTOOIST *noun* **TATTOOISTS** a tattoo artist

TATTY *adj* **TATTIER, TATTIEST** shabby and untidy

TAU *noun* **TAUS** the nineteenth letter of the Greek alphabet

TAUGHT past form of **teach**

TAUNT *verb* **TAUNTS, TAUNTING, TAUNTED** to tease, say unpleasant things to or jeer at someone in a cruel and hurtful way ◻ *noun* **TAUNTS** a cruel, unpleasant and often hurtful or provoking remark

TAUNTING *noun* **TAUNTINGS** an act of teasing someone

TAUPE *noun* **TAUPES** a brownish-grey colour

TAUREAN *adj* of or relating to a bull

TAUT *adj* **TAUTER, TAUTEST** pulled or stretched tight

TAUTEN *verb* **TAUTENS,**

TAUTENING, TAUTENED to make or become taut

TAUTOLOGY *noun* **TAUTOLOGIES** the use of words which repeat the meaning found in other words already used, as in *I myself personally am a vegetarian*

TAVERN *noun* **TAVERNS** an inn or public house

TAVERNA *noun* **TAVERNAS** in Greece: a type of guesthouse with a bar, popular as holiday accommodation

TAW [1] *verb* **TAWS, TAWING, TAWED** to prepare and dress (skins) to make leather, using an alum and salt solution rather than tannin

TAW [2] *noun* **TAWS** a large or choice marble

TAWDRILY *adverb* in a tawdry way

TAWDRY *adj* **TAWDRIER, TAWDRIEST** cheap and showy and of poor quality

TAWER *noun* **TAWERS** someone who prepares and dresses skins to make leather

TAWNY *noun* **TAWNIES** a yellowish-brown colour ◻ *adj* **TAWNIER, TAWNIEST** yellowish-brown

TAWS *noun* **TAWSES** a leather strap divided into strips at one end, formerly used for corporal punishment in schools

TAWSE *noun* **TAWSES** a taws

TAX *noun* **TAXES** a compulsory contribution towards a country's expenses raised by the government from people's salaries, property and from the sale of goods and services ◻ *verb* **TAXES, TAXING, TAXED** to impose a tax on (a person or goods, etc) or take tax from (a salary)

TAXATION *noun* **TAXATIONS** the act or system of imposing taxes

TAXI *noun* **TAXIS** a car which may be hired together with its driver to carry passengers on usually short journeys, and which is usually fitted with a taximeter for calculating the fare ◻ *verb* **TAXIS, TAXIES, TAXYING, TAXIING, TAXIED** said of an aircraft: to move slowly along the ground before take-off or after landing

TAXIDERMY *noun* **TAXIDERMIES** the art of preparing, stuffing and mounting animal skins and birds so that they present a lifelike appearance

TAXIMETER *noun* **TAXIMETERS** a

meter fitted to a taxi which monitors the time taken and the distance travelled, and displays the fare due for the journey

TAXING *adj* requiring a lot of mental or physical effort; demanding

TAXIS *noun* **TAXES** the movement of a single cell in response to an external stimulus from a specific direction (eg light)

TAXOL *noun* **TAXOLS** a drug obtained from the bark of the Pacific yew

TAXONOMIC *adj* of or relating to taxonomy

TAXONOMY *noun* **TAXONOMIES** the theory and techniques of describing, naming and classifying living and extinct organisms on the basis of the similarity of their anatomical and morphological features and structures, etc

TAY *noun* **TAYS** a dialect, especially Irish, word for *tea*

TE *noun* **TES** in sol-fa notation: the seventh note of the major scale

TEA *noun* **TEAS** a beverage prepared by infusing the dried leaves of the tea plant, often served with either milk or lemon, and sometimes with sugar □ *verb* **TEAS, TEAING, TEAED** to provide tea for

TEACH *verb* **TEACHES, TEACHING, TAUGHT** to give knowledge to someone; to instruct someone in a skill or help them to learn

TEACHABLE *adj* capable of being taught

TEACHER *noun* **TEACHERS** someone whose job is to teach, especially in a school

TEACHING *noun* **TEACHINGS** the work or profession of a teacher

TEACUP *noun* **TEACUPS** a medium-sized cup used especially for drinking tea

TEACUPFUL *noun* **TEACUPFULS** the amount a teacup can hold

TEAK *noun* **TEAKS** a large evergreen tree, native to S India and SE Asia which is cultivated for its high-quality timber

TEAL *noun* **TEALS** any of several kinds of small freshwater duck closely related to the mallard, native to Europe, Asia and N America

TEAM *noun* **TEAMS** a group of people who form one side in a game □ *verb* **TEAMS, TEAMING, TEAMED** to form a team for some common action

TEAMSTER *noun* **TEAMSTERS** a driver of a team of animals

TEAMWORK *noun* **TEAMWORKS** co-operation between those who are working together on a task

TEAPOT *noun* **TEAPOTS** a pot with a spout and handle used for making and pouring tea

TEAR *verb* **TEARS, TEARING, TORE, TORN** to pull or rip something apart by force □ *noun* **TEARS** a hole or other damage caused by tearing

TEARAWAY *noun* **TEARAWAYS** an undisciplined and reckless young person

TEARFUL *adj* inclined to cry or weep

TEARFULLY *adverb* in a tearful way

TEARING *adj* furious; overwhelming

TEASE *verb* **TEASES, TEASING, TEASED** to annoy or irritate someone deliberately or unkindly □ *noun* **TEASES** someone or something that teases

TEASEL *noun* **TEASELS** any of various biennial plants with white or mauve flower-heads surrounded by curved prickly bracts

TEASER *noun* **TEASERS** a puzzle or tricky problem

TEASING *noun* **TEASINGS** the act or practice of annoying or irritating someone deliberately or unkindly □ *adj* taunting; tantalizing

TEASINGLY *adverb* in a teasing way

TEASPOON *noun* **TEASPOONS** a small spoon for use with a teacup

TEAT *noun* **TEATS** the nipple of a breast or udder

TEAZEL *noun* **TEAZELS** a teasel

TEAZLE *noun* **TEAZLES** a teasel

TECH *noun* **TECHS** a technical college

TECHNICAL *adj* possessing knowledge of, specializing in or relating to a practical skill or applied science, especially those sciences which are useful to industry

TECHNICS *singular and plural noun* the practical use of scientific knowledge in industry and everyday life; technical details

TECHNIQUE *noun* **TECHNIQUES** proficiency or skill in the practical or formal aspects of an art, especially painting, music and sport, etc

TECHNO *noun* **TECHNOS** a style of dance music that makes use of electronic effects over a frenzied rhythm, and produces fast but often unmelodic sounds

TECTONICS *singular noun* the study of structures which form the Earth's crust and the forces which change it

TECTORIAL *adj* forming a covering

TECTRIX *noun* **TECTRICES** a feather covering the quill bases on a bird's wing and tail

TED *verb* **TEDS, TEDDING, TEDDED** to spread out (newly-mown grass) for drying

TEDDER *noun* **TEDDERS** an implement for tedding

TEDDY *noun* **TEDDIES** a child's stuffed toy bear

TEDIOUS *adj* tiresomely long-winded or dull; monotonous

TEDIOUSLY *adverb* in a tedious way

TEDIUM *noun* **TEDIUMS** tediousness; boredom

TEE *noun* **TEES** in golf: a small peg with a concave top, or a small pile of sand, used to support a ball when the first shot is taken at the beginning of a hole □ *verb* **TEES, TEEING, TEED** to place a golf ball on a tee ready to be played

TEEM *verb* **TEEMS, TEEMING, TEEMED** to be full of people or things, or to abound in them

TEEN *noun* **TEENS** a person aged between 13 and 19 □ *adj* for or relating to teenagers

TEENAGE *adj* in one's teens

TEENAGER *noun* **TEENAGERS** a person aged between 13 and 19

TEENSY *adj* **TEENSIER, TEENSIEST** tiny

TEENY *adj* **TEENIER, TEENIEST** tiny

TEEPEE *noun* **TEEPEES** a tepee

TEETER *verb* **TEETERS, TEETERING, TEETERED** to stand or move unsteadily; to wobble

TEETH plural of **tooth**

TEETHE *verb* **TEETHES, TEETHING, TEETHED** said of a baby: to develop or cut milk teeth

TEETHING *noun* **TEETHINGS** the condition of cutting or developing teeth

TEETOTAL *adj* abstaining completely from alcoholic drink

TEETOTUM *noun* **TEETOTUMS** a

small spinning top with four sides, each of which is inscribed with a letter, to determine whether the person spinning it has lost or won

TEF noun **TEFS** an Ethiopian cereal grass

TEFILLIN plural noun certain passages from Scripture, worn in a box on the left arm or forehead by Jews

TEG noun **TEGS** a sheep in its second year

TEGMEN noun **TEGMINA** the inner coat of a seed covering

TEGUMENT noun **TEGUMENTS** the skin or other natural covering of an animal or plant

TEKTITE noun **TEKTITES** a type of small glassy stone found in several areas around the world, thought to be a result of meteoric impacts

TEL noun **TELS** a tell

TELECAST verb **TELECASTS, TELECASTING, TELECASTED** to broadcast by TV ◻ noun **TELECASTS** a TV broadcast

TELEGRAM noun **TELEGRAMS** a message sent by telegraph and delivered in printed form, now used (in the UK) only for messages sent abroad and replaced by Telemessage for inland messages

TELEGRAPH noun **TELEGRAPHS** a system of or instrument for sending messages or information to a distance, especially by sending electrical impulses along a wire ◻ verb **TELEGRAPHS, TELEGRAPHING, TELEGRAPHED** to send (a message) to someone by telegraph

TELEMETER noun **TELEMETERS** an instrument that is used to take measurements, eg of meteorological data, and send the readings obtained, usually by means of electrical or radio signals, to a location remote from the site of measurement ◻ verb **TELEMETERS, TELEMETERING, TELEMETERED** to record and signal (data) in this way

TELEMETRY noun **TELEMETRIES** the practice of obtaining and sending data using a telemeter

TELEOLOGY noun **TELEOLOGIES** the doctrine that the universe, all phenomena and natural processes are directed towards a goal or are designed according to some purpose

TELEPATHY noun **TELEPATHIES**

the apparent communication of thoughts directly from one person's mind to another's without using any of the five known senses

TELEPHONE noun **TELEPHONES** an instrument with a mouthpiece and an earpiece mounted on a handset, for transmitting human speech in the form of electrical signals or radio waves, enabling people to communicate with each other over a distance ◻ verb **TELEPHONES, TELEPHONING, TELEPHONED** to seek or establish contact and speak to someone by telephone

TELEPHONY noun **TELEPHONIES** the use or system of communication by means of the telephone

TELESCOPE noun **TELESCOPES** an optical instrument containing a powerful magnifying lens or mirror that makes distant objects appear larger ◻ verb **TELESCOPES, TELESCOPING, TELESCOPED** to be in the form of several cylinders which slide out of or into each other for opening and closing, like the sections of a folding telescope

TELETEXT noun **TELETEXTS** a non-interactive news and information service that is produced and regularly updated by a TV company, and that can be viewed on TV sets

TELETHON noun **TELETHONS** a TV programme, usually a day-long one, broadcast to raise money for charity

TELEVISE verb **TELEVISES, TELEVISING, TELEVISED** to broadcast something by television

TELEX noun **TELEXES** an international telecommunications network that uses radio and satellite links to enable subscribers to the network to send and receive messages ◻ verb **TELEXES, TELEXING, TELEXED** to send a message to someone via such a network

TELL [1] verb **TELLS, TELLING, TOLD** to inform or give information to someone in speech or writing

TELL [2] noun **TELLS** especially in the Middle East: an artificial mound or hill formed from the accumulated remains of former settlements

TELLER noun **TELLERS** someone who tells, especially someone who tells stories

TELLING adj producing a great or marked effect

TELLINGLY adverb in a telling way

TELLTALE noun **TELLTALES** someone who spreads gossip and rumours, especially about another person's private affairs or misdeeds ◻ adj revealing or indicating something secret or hidden

TELLURIAN adj belonging or relating to, or living on, the Earth ◻ noun **TELLURIANS** especially in science fiction: an inhabitant of the Earth

TELLURIC adj belonging or relating to, or coming from, the Earth

TELLURIUM noun **TELLURIUMS** a brittle silvery-white element obtained from gold, silver and copper ores, which is added to alloys of lead or steel to increase their hardness

TELLY noun **TELLIES** television

TELOPHASE noun **TELOPHASES** the final stage of cell division

TELSON noun **TELSONS** the hindmost segment on the abdomen of a crustacean or arachnid

TEMAZEPAM noun **TEMAZEPAMS** a drug used to treat insomnia, and as a sedative before operations

TEMERITY noun **TEMERITIES** rashness or boldness; an unreasonable lack of fear

TEMP noun **TEMPS** an employee, especially a secretary, typist or other office worker, employed on a temporary basis ◻ verb **TEMPS, TEMPING, TEMPED** to work as a temp

TEMPER noun **TEMPERS** a characteristic state of mind; mood or humour ◻ verb **TEMPERS, TEMPERING, TEMPERED** to soften something or make it less severe

TEMPERA noun **TEMPERAS** a method of painting in which powdered pigment is mixed with an emulsion made usually of egg yolks and water

TEMPERATE adj moderate and self-restrained, especially in appetite, consumption of alcoholic drink, and behaviour

TEMPEST noun **TEMPESTS** a violent storm with very strong winds

TEMPI a plural of **tempo**

TEMPLATE noun **TEMPLATES** a piece of metal, plastic or wood cut in a particular shape and used as a pattern when cutting out material or drawing, etc

TEMPLE *noun* **TEMPLES** a building in which people worship, especially in ancient and non-Christian religions, and in some Christian sects such as the Mormons

TEMPLET *noun* **TEMPLETS** a template

TEMPO *noun* **TEMPOS, TEMPI** the speed at which a piece of music should be or is played

TEMPORAL *adj* belonging or relating to time, often in being relatively short

TEMPORARY *adj* lasting, acting or used, etc for a limited period of time only □ *noun* **TEMPORARIES** a worker employed temporarily; a temp

TEMPORISE *verb* **TEMPORISES, TEMPORISING, TEMPORISED** to temporize

TEMPORIZE *verb* **TEMPORIZES, TEMPORIZING, TEMPORIZED** to avoid taking a decision or committing oneself to some course of action, in order to gain time and perhaps win a compromise

TEMPT *verb* **TEMPTS, TEMPTING, TEMPTED** to seek to attract and persuade someone to do something, especially something wrong or foolish

TEMPTER *noun* **TEMPTERS** someone who tempts

TEMPTING *adj* attractive; inviting; enticing

TEMPTRESS *noun* **TEMPTRESSES** a female tempter; an enticing woman

TEMPURA *noun* **TEMPURAS** a Japanese dish of seafood or vegetables deep-fried in batter

TEN *noun* **TENS** the cardinal number 10 □ *adj* totalling ten

TENABLE *adj* able to be believed, upheld or maintained

TENACIOUS *adj* holding or sticking firmly

TENACULUM *noun* **TENACULA** a surgical hook, used for picking up blood vessels, etc

TENANCY *noun* **TENANCIES** the temporary renting of property or land by a tenant

TENANT *noun* **TENANTS** someone who pays rent to another for the use of property or land □ *verb* **TENANTS, TENANTING, TENANTED** to occupy (land, etc) as a tenant

TENANTRY *noun* **TENANTRIES** tenants collectively

TENCH *noun* **TENCHES** a European freshwater fish belonging to the carp family, with a green or brownish body

TEND *verb* **TENDS, TENDING, TENDED** to take care of or look after someone or something; to wait on or serve them

TENDENCY *noun* **TENDENCIES** a likelihood of acting or thinking, or an inclination to act or think, in a particular way

TENDER [1] *adj* **TENDERER, TENDEREST** soft and delicate; fragile

TENDER [2] *verb* **TENDERS, TENDERING, TENDERED** to offer or present (an apology or resignation, etc) □ *noun* **TENDERS** a formal offer, usually in writing, to do work or supply goods for a stated amount of money and within a stated period of time

TENDERISE *verb* **TENDERISES, TENDERISING, TENDERISED** to tenderize

TENDERIZE *verb* **TENDERIZES, TENDERIZING, TENDERIZED** to make (meat) tender by pounding it or by adding an acidic substance

TENDERLY *adverb* in a tender way

TENDON *noun* **TENDONS** a cord of strong fibrous tissue that joins a muscle to a bone or some other structure

TENDRIL *noun* **TENDRILS** a long, often spirally twisted, thread-like extension of a stem or leaf, by means of which many climbing plants attach themselves to solid objects for support

TENEBRISM *noun* **TENEBRISMS** a 17c Italian and Spanish school of painting, characterized by large expanses of shadow

TENEBROUS *adj* dark; gloomy

TENEMENT *noun* **TENEMENTS** a large building divided into several self-contained flats or apartments

TENESMUS *noun* **TENESMUSES** a painful and ineffectual straining to relieve the bowel and bladder

TENET *noun* **TENETS** a belief, opinion or doctrine

TENFOLD *adj* equal to ten times as much □ *adverb* by ten times as much

TENNER *noun* **TENNERS** a £10 note

TENNIS *noun* **TENNISES** a game in which two players or two pairs of players use rackets to hit a small

light ball across a net on a rectangular grass, clay or cement court

TENON *noun* **TENONS** a projection at the end of a piece of wood, etc, formed to fit into a socket or mortise in another piece □ *verb* **TENONS, TENONING, TENONED** to fix with a tenon

TENOR *noun* **TENORS** a singing voice of the highest normal range for an adult man

TENSE [1] *noun* **TENSES** a form or set of forms of a verb showing the time of its action in relation to the time of speaking and whether that action is completed or not, eg past tense, present tense, future tense

TENSE [2] *adj* **TENSER, TENSEST** feeling, showing or marked by emotional, nervous or mental strain □ *verb* **TENSES, TENSING, TENSED** to make or become tense

TENSELY *adverb* in a tense way

TENSENESS *noun* **TENSENESSES** the quality or condition of being tense

TENSILE *adj* able to be stretched

TENSILITY *noun* **TENSILITIES** the quality or condition of being tensile

TENSION *noun* **TENSIONS** an act of stretching, the state of being stretched or the degree to which something is stretched □ *verb* **TENSIONS, TENSIONING, TENSIONED** to give the required tightness or tension to something

TENT *noun* **TENTS** a shelter made of canvas or other material supported by poles or a frame and fastened to the ground with ropes and pegs, that can be taken down and carried from place to place □ *verb* **TENTS, TENTING, TENTED** to camp in a tent

TENTACLE *noun* **TENTACLES** any of the long thin flexible appendages growing on the head or near the mouth of many invertebrate animals, eg the sea anemone and octopus, etc, used as sense organs or for defence, for grasping prey or for attachment to surfaces

TENTACLED *adj* having tentacles

TENTATIVE *adj* not finalized or completed; provisional

TENTER *noun* **TENTERS** a frame on which cloth is stretched, especially so that it dries without losing its shape □ *verb* **TENTERS, TENTERING, TENTERED** to stretch (cloth) on a tenter

TENTH *adj* in counting: next after ninth ▫ *noun* **TENTHS** one of ten equal parts ▫ *adverb* tenthly
TENTHLY *adverb* used to introduce the tenth point in a list
TENUOUS *adj* slight; with little strength or substance
TENUOUSLY *adverb* in a tenuous way
TENURE *noun* **TENURES** the holding of an office, position or property; conditions on which property or a position is held
TENURED *adj* having tenure
TENURIAL *adj* of or relating to tenure
TENUTO *adverb* in a sustained manner ▫ *adj* sustained ▫ *noun* **TENUTOS** a sustained note or chord
TEPEE *noun* **TEPEES** a conical tent formed by skins stretched over a frame of poles, used by some Native Americans
TEPHILLIN *plural noun* a tefillin
TEPHRA *noun* **TEPHRAS** ash and debris ejected by a volcano during an eruption
TEPID *adj* **TEPIDER, TEPIDEST** slightly or only just warm; lukewarm
TEPIDITY *noun* **TEPIDITIES** the quality or condition of being tepid
TEPIDLY *adverb* in a tepid way
TEQUILA *noun* **TEQUILAS** a Mexican spirit obtained from the agave plant, used as the basis for many alcoholic drinks
TERATOGEN *noun* **TERATOGENS** a substance or procedure, eg a drug, disease or radiation, etc that interferes with the normal development of the fetus and leads to the development of physical abnormalities
TERATOID *adj* monstrous; resembling a monster
TERATOMA *noun* **TERATOMATA** a tumour consisting of tissue that is foreign to the place of growth
TERBIUM *noun* **TERBIUMS** a silvery metallic element that is used in semiconductor devices and phosphors
TERCE *noun* **TERCES** the third of the canonical hours
TERCEL *noun* **TERCELS** a male hawk
TERCET *noun* **TERCETS** a set of three lines in a poem which rhyme or which are connected by rhyme to a preceding or following group of three lines
TEREBINTH *noun* **TEREBINTHS** a small Mediterranean tree that yields a resin that can be distilled to give turpentine
TEREDO *noun* **TEREDOS, TEREDINES** any of several bivalve molluscs which bore into wooden ships
TERM *noun* **TERMS** a word or expression, especially one used with a precise meaning in a specialized field ▫ *verb* **TERMS, TERMING, TERMED** to name or call
TERMAGANT *noun* **TERMAGANTS** a scolding, brawling and overbearing woman
TERMINAL *adj* said of an illness: causing death; fatal ▫ *noun* **TERMINALS** an arrival and departure building at an airport
TERMINATE *verb* **TERMINATES, TERMINATING, TERMINATED** to bring or come to an end
TERMINUS *noun* **TERMINI, TERMINUSES** the end of a railway line or bus route, usually with a station
TERMITE *noun* **TERMITES** an ant-like social insect which lives in highly organized colonies, mainly in tropical areas, some of which feed on wood, causing damage to trees and buildings, etc
TERMLY *adj* happening every school, academic or legal session
TERN *noun* **TERNS** any of several sea-birds related to the gulls, with grey and white plumage and a long forked tail
TERNARY *adj* containing three parts
TERPENE *noun* **TERPENES** any of three classes of unsaturated hydrocarbons present in plant resins
TERRACE *noun* **TERRACES** each one of a series of raised level banks of earth, like large steps on the side of a hill, used for cultivation ▫ *verb* **TERRACES, TERRACING, TERRACED** to form something into a terrace or terraces
TERRAIN *noun* **TERRAINS** a stretch of land, especially with regard to its physical features or as a battle area
TERRAPIN *noun* **TERRAPINS** in the UK: any small freshwater turtle
TERRARIUM *noun* **TERRARIUMS, TERRARIA** an enclosed area or container in which small land animals are kept
TERRAZZO *noun* **TERRAZZOS** a mosaic covering for concrete floors consisting of marble or other chips set in cement and then polished
TERRIBLE *adj* very bad
TERRIBLY *adverb* very; extremely
TERRIER *noun* **TERRIERS** any of several mostly small breeds of dog originally bred to hunt animals in burrows
TERRIFIC *adj* marvellous; excellent
TERRIFY *verb* **TERRIFIES, TERRIFYING, TERRIFIED** to make very frightened; to fill with terror
TERRINE *noun* **TERRINES** an oval or round earthenware dish in which food may be cooked and served
TERRITORY *noun* **TERRITORIES** a stretch of land; a region
TERROR *noun* **TERRORS** very great fear or dread
TERRORISE *verb* **TERRORISES, TERRORISING, TERRORISED** to terrorize
TERRORISM *noun* **TERRORISMS** the systematic and organized use of violence and intimidation to force a government or community, etc to act in a certain way or accept certain demands
TERRORIST *noun* **TERRORISTS** someone who uses violence and intimidation to force a government or community to act in a certain way
TERRORIZE *verb* **TERRORIZES, TERRORIZING, TERRORIZED** to frighten greatly
TERRY *noun* **TERRIES** an absorbent fabric with uncut loops on one side used especially for towels
TERSE *adj* **TERSER, TERSEST** said of language: brief and concise; succinct
TERSELY *adverb* in a terse way
TERSENESS *noun* **TERSENESSES** the quality or condition of being terse
TERTIARY *adj* third in order, degree, importance, etc ▫ *noun* **TERTIARIES** a lay person who is affiliated to a monastic order and who follows a slightly modified form of that order's rule

TES plural of **te**

TESLA *noun* **TESLAS** in the SI system: a unit of magnetic flux density, defined as a magnetic flux of one weber per square metre

TESSERA noun **TESSERAE** a square piece of stone or glass, etc used in mosaics

TESSITURA noun **TESSITURAS** the natural range of the pitch or compass of a particular voice, or of a vocal or instrumental part in a particular piece

TEST noun **TESTS** a critical examination or trial of a person's or thing's qualities or abilities, etc □ verb **TESTS, TESTING, TESTED** to examine someone or something especially by trial

TESTA noun **TESTAE** the hard outer covering of a seed

TESTABLE adj capable of being tested

TESTAMENT noun **TESTAMENTS** a written statement of someone's wishes, especially of what they want to be done with their property after death

TESTATE adj having made and left a valid will

TESTATOR noun **TESTATORS** someone who leaves a will at death

TESTATRIX noun **TESTATRICES** a female testator

TESTEE noun **TESTEES** someone who is tested or examined in some way

TESTER noun **TESTERS** someone who tests

TESTES plural of **testis**

TESTICLE noun **TESTICLES** a testis

TESTIFY verb **TESTIFIES, TESTIFYING, TESTIFIED** to give evidence in court

TESTILY adverb irritably

TESTIMONY noun **TESTIMONIES** a statement made under oath, especially in a law court

TESTINESS noun **TESTINESSES** the state of being testy

TESTING noun **TESTINGS** the assessment of an individual level of knowledge or skill, etc by a variety of methods

TESTIS noun **TESTES** in male animals: either of the two reproductive glands that produce sperm and are either internally or externally positioned, enclosed in the scrotum

TESTY adj **TESTIER, TESTIEST** irritable; bad-tempered; touchy

TETANUS noun **TETANUSES** an infectious and potentially fatal disease, caused by the release of toxins from a bacterium, the spores of which are found in soil

TETCHILY adverb in a tetchy way

TETCHY adj **TETCHIER, TETCHIEST** irritable; peevish

TETHER noun **TETHERS** a rope or chain for tying an animal to a post or confining it to a particular spot □ verb **TETHERS, TETHERING, TETHERED** to tie or restrain with a tether

TETRA noun **TETRAS** any of many small colourful freshwater fish from S and Central America, which are often kept in aquariums

TETRAD noun **TETRADS** a group of four

TETRAGON noun **TETRAGONS** a plane figure with four angles and four sides

TETRALOGY noun **TETRALOGIES** a group of four dramas, usually three tragic and one satiric

TETRAPOD noun **TETRAPODS** any animal with four limbs or derived from four-legged ancestors, including amphibians, reptiles, birds and mammals

TEW verb **TEWS, TEWING, TEWED** to hustle

TEXT noun **TEXTS** the main body of printed words in a book as opposed to the notes and illustrations, etc

TEXTBOOK noun **TEXTBOOKS** a book that contains the standard principles and information of a subject

TEXTILE noun **TEXTILES** any cloth or fabric made by weaving or knitting

TEXTUAL adj belonging or relating to, found in, or based on, a text or texts

TEXTUALLY adverb in a textual way

TEXTURAL adj of or relating to texture

TEXTURE noun **TEXTURES** the way the surface of a material or substance feels when touched □ verb **TEXTURES, TEXTURING, TEXTURED** to give a particular texture to (eg food or fabric)

TEXTURISE verb **TEXTURISES, TEXTURISING, TEXTURISED** to texturize

TEXTURIZE verb **TEXTURIZES, TEXTURIZING, TEXTURIZED** to give a particular texture to (eg food or fabric)

THALAMUS noun **THALAMI** in the forebrain of vertebrates: either of two egg-shaped masses of grey matter that lie within the cerebral hemispheres, relaying sensory nerve impulses to the cerebral cortex

THALLIUM noun **THALLIUMS** a soft bluish-white metallic element that is used in electronic equipment, experimental alloys and optical glass

THALLOID adj of or relating to a thallus

THALLUS noun **THALLUSES, THALLI** in fungi, lichens and seaweeds, etc: a flattened and sometimes branched structure that is not differentiated into stems, leaves and roots

THAN conj used to introduce the second part of a comparison, or that part which is taken as the basis of a comparison □ prep in comparison with

THANE noun **THANES** in Anglo-Saxon England: a man holding land from the king or some other superior in exchange for military service

THANK verb **THANKS, THANKING, THANKED** to express gratitude to someone □ noun **THANKS** gratitude or an expression of gratitude

THANKFUL adj grateful; relieved and happy

THANKLESS adj bringing no thanks, pleasure or profit

THANKYOU noun **THANKYOUS** an utterance of 'thank you'

THAT adj indicating the thing, person or idea already mentioned, specified or understood □ pronoun the person, thing or idea just mentioned, already spoken of or understood □ conj used to introduce a noun clause, or a clause showing reason, purpose, consequence or a result or expressing a wish or desire □ adverb to the degree or extent shown or understood

THATCH noun **THATCHES** a roof covering of straw or reeds, etc □ verb **THATCHES, THATCHING, THATCHED** to cover (a roof or building) with thatch

THATCHER noun **THATCHERS** someone who thatches roofs

THAW verb **THAWS, THAWING, THAWED** said of snow or ice: to melt □ noun **THAWS** an act or the process of thawing

THE definite article used to refer to a particular person or thing, or group of people or things, already mentioned, implied or known

THEARCHY noun **THEARCHIES** government by a god or gods

THEATER noun **THEATERS** a theatre

THEATRE noun **THEATRES** a building or area outside specially designed for the performance of plays and operas, etc

THEBAINE noun **THEBAINES** a poisonous alkaloid obtained from opium

THECA noun **THECAE** an enclosing sheath, case or sac

THEE pronoun the objective form of *thou*

THEFT noun **THEFTS** stealing; an act of stealing someone else's property, with the intention of permanently depriving them of it

THEINE noun **THEINES** caffeine

THEIR adj belonging or relating to them

THEIRS pronoun a person or thing that belongs to them

THEISM noun **THEISMS** the belief in the existence of God or a god, especially one revealed supernaturally to humans

THEIST noun **THEISTS** a follower of theism

THEISTIC adj of or relating to theism

THEM pronoun people or things already mentioned or spoken about, or understood from the context

THEMATIC adj of or relating to a theme

THEME noun **THEMES** the subject of a discussion, speech or piece of writing, etc

THEN adverb at that time ▫ noun **THENS** that time ▫ adj being or acting at that time

THENAR noun **THENARS** the ball of muscle at the base of the thumb

THENCE adverb from that place or time

THEOCRACY noun **THEOCRACIES** government by a deity or by priests representing a deity

THEOCRAT noun **THEOCRATS** a supporter of theocracy

THEOLOGY noun **THEOLOGIES** the study of God, religion, religious belief and revelation

THEORBO noun **THEORBOS** a type of large lute widely used in the 17c

THEOREM noun **THEOREMS** a scientific or mathematical statement which makes certain assumptions in order to explain

observed phenomena, and which has been proved to be correct

THEORETIC adj concerned with or based on theory rather than practical knowledge or experience

THEORISE verb **THEORISES, THEORISING, THEORISED** to theorize

THEORIST noun **THEORISTS** someone who speculates or invents theories

THEORIZE verb **THEORIZES, THEORIZING, THEORIZED** to devise theories; to speculate

THEORY noun **THEORIES** a series of ideas and general principles which seek to explain some aspect of the world

THEOSOPHY noun **THEOSOPHIES** a religious philosophy based on the belief that a knowledge of God can be achieved through intuition, mysticism and divine inspiration

THERAPIST noun **THERAPISTS** a person who practises therapy of a particular kind

THERAPY noun **THERAPIES** the treatment of physical, social or mental diseases and disorders by means other than surgery or drugs

THERE adverb at, in or to a place or position ▫ noun **THERES** that place or point

THEREBY adverb by that means

THEREFORE adverb for that reason; as a consequence

THEREIN adverb in or into that or it

THEREOF adverb belonging or relating to, or from, that or it

THEREON adverb on or on to that or it

THERETO adverb to that or it; in addition

THEREUPON adverb on that matter or point

THERM noun **THERMS** a unit of heat equal to 100 000 British thermal units, used to measure the amount of gas supplied

THERMAL adj belonging or relating to, caused by, or producing heat ▫ noun **THERMALS** a rising current of warm air, used by birds, gliders to move upwards

THERMALLY adverb in a thermal way

THERMION noun **THERMIONS** an electrically charged particle emitted by an extremely hot or incandescent substance

THESAURUS noun **THESAURUSES, THESAURI** a book

which lists words and their synonyms according to sense

THESE pronoun the people, animals, things or ideas already mentioned, about to be mentioned, specified or understood from the context ▫ adj indicating the people, animals or things which are nearby, especially closer than someone or something else

THESIS noun **THESES** a long written dissertation or report, especially one based on original research and presented for an advanced university degree such as the MSc, MLitt or PhD

THESPIAN noun **THESPIANS** an actor or actress

THETA noun **THETAS** the eighth letter of the Greek alphabet

THEURGY noun **THEURGIES** magic by the agency of good spirits

THEW noun **THEWS, THEWES** moral quality or strength

THEY pronoun the people, animals or things already spoken about, being indicated, or known from the context

THIAMIN noun **THIAMINS** thiamine

THIAMINE noun **THIAMINES** vitamin B_1

THICK adj **THICKER, THICKEST** having a relatively large distance between opposite sides ▫ adverb thickly ▫ noun **THICKS** the busiest, most active or most intense part

THICKEN verb **THICKENS, THICKENING, THICKENED** to make or become thick or thicker

THICKENING noun **THICKENINGS** something used to thicken liquid

THICKET noun **THICKETS** a dense mass of bushes and trees

THICKHEAD noun **THICKHEADS** a stupid person

THICKLY adverb in a thick way; densely

THICKNESS noun **THICKNESSES** the state, quality or degree of being thick

THICKSET adj heavily built; having a thick, short body

THIEF noun **THIEVES** a person who steals, especially secretly and usually without violence

THIEVE verb **THIEVES, THIEVING, THIEVED** to steal

THIEVING noun **THIEVINGS** an act of stealing

THIEVISH adj of or like a thief; likely to steal

THIGH noun **THIGHS** the fleshy part of the leg between the knee and hip in humans, or the corresponding part in animals

THIMBLE noun **THIMBLES** a small metal, ceramic or plastic cap worn on the finger to protect it and push the needle when sewing

THIN adj **THINNER, THINNEST** said of people, animals: not fat; lean □ adverb thinly □ verb **THINS, THINNING, THINNED** to make or become thin, thinner, sparser or less dense

THINE pronoun something which belongs to thee

THING noun **THINGS** any object, especially one that is inanimate

THINGAMY noun **THINGAMIES** thingummy

THINGUMMY noun **THINGUMMIES** someone or something whose name is unknown, forgotten or deliberately not used

THINK verb **THINKS, THINKING, THOUGHT** to have or form ideas in the mind □ noun **THINKS** an act of thinking

THINKER noun **THINKERS** someone who thinks, especially deeply and constructively or in a specified way

THINKING noun **THINKINGS** the act of using one's mind to produce thoughts □ adj said of people: using or able to use the mind intelligently and constructively

THINLY adverb in a thin way

THINNER [1] noun **THINNERS** a liquid such as turpentine that is added to paint or varnish to dilute it

THINNER [2] see under **thin**

THINNESS noun **THINNESSES** the state or condition of being thin

THINNEST see under **thin**

THIRD adj in counting: next after second □ noun **THIRDS** one of three equal parts □ adverb used to introduce the third point in a list

THIRDLY adverb used to introduce the third point in a list

THIRST noun **THIRSTS** the need to drink, or the feeling of dryness in the mouth that this causes □ verb **THIRSTS, THIRSTING, THIRSTED** to have a great desire or long for something

THIRSTILY adverb in a thirsty way

THIRSTY adj **THIRSTIER, THIRSTIEST** needing or wanting to drink

THIRTEEN noun **THIRTEENS** the cardinal number 13 □ adj totalling thirteen

THIRTIES plural noun the period of time between one's thirtieth and fortieth birthdays

THIRTIETH adj in counting: next after twenty-ninth □ noun

THIRTIETHS one of thirty equal parts

THIRTY noun **THIRTIES** the cardinal number 30 □ adj totalling thirty

THIS pronoun a person, animal, thing or idea already mentioned, about to be mentioned, indicated or otherwise understood from the context □ adj being the person, animal, thing or idea which is nearby, especially closer than someone or something else □ adverb to this (extreme) degree or extent

THISTLE noun **THISTLES** any of various annual or perennial plants with deeply indented prickly leaves and usually with globular purple, red or white flowerheads

THITHER adverb to or towards that place

THO adj a Spenserian word for those

THOLE [1] noun **THOLES** either one of a pair of pins in the side of a boat to keep an oar in place

THOLE [2] verb **THOLES, THOLING, THOLED** to endure or tolerate

THONG noun **THONGS** a narrow strip of leather used eg to fasten something, or as the lash of a whip

THORACIC adj belonging or relating to, or in the region of, the thorax

THORAX noun **THORAXES, THORACES** in humans and other vertebrates: the part of the body between the head and abdomen; the chest

THORIUM noun **THORIUMS** a silvery-grey radioactive metallic element used in X-ray tubes

THORN noun **THORNS** a hard sharp point sticking out from the stem or branch of certain plants

THORNY adj **THORNIER, THORNIEST** full of or covered with thorns

THOROUGH adj **THOROUGHER, THOROUGHEST** said of a person: extremely careful and attending to every detail

THORP noun **THORPS** mainly in place names: a village; a hamlet

THORPE noun **THORPES** a thorp

THOSE adj indicating the things, people or ideas already mentioned, specified or understood from the context □ pronoun the things, people or ideas already mentioned, etc

THOU [1] pronoun you (singular)

THOU [2] noun **THOUS** a thousand

THOUGH conj despite the fact that □ adverb however; nevertheless

THOUGHT noun **THOUGHTS** an idea, concept or opinion

THOUSAND noun **THOUSANDS** the number 1000 □ adj numbering 1000

THRALL noun **THRALLS** someone who is in the power of another person or thing; a slave

THRASH verb **THRASHES, THRASHING, THRASHED** to beat soundly, especially with blows or a whip □ noun **THRASHES** an act of thrashing

THRASHER noun **THRASHERS** any of various N American birds of the mockingbird family

THRASHING noun **THRASHINGS** a beating

THRAWN adj twisted; misshapen

THREAD noun **THREADS** a very thin strand of silk, cotton or wool, especially when several such strands are twisted together for sewing □ verb **THREADS, THREADING, THREADED** to pass a thread through (eg the eye of a needle)

THREADY adj **THREADIER, THREADIEST** resembling a thread; thread-like

THREAT noun **THREATS** a warning that one is going to or might hurt or punish someone

THREATEN verb **THREATENS, THREATENING, THREATENED** to make or be a threat to someone or something

THREE noun **THREES** the cardinal number 3 □ adj totalling three

THREEFOLD adj equal to three times as much □ adverb by three times as much

THREESOME noun **THREESOMES** a group of three

THRENODE noun **THRENODES** a threnody

THRENODY noun **THRENODIES** a song or ode of lamentation, especially for a person's death

THREONINE noun **THREONINES** an amino acid essential for bodily growth and health

THRESH verb **THRESHES, THRESHING, THRESHED** to separate the grain or seeds from the stalks of cereal plants by beating

THRESHER noun **THRESHERS** a machine or person that threshes corn, etc

THRESHOLD noun **THRESHOLDS** a piece of wood or stone forming the bottom of a doorway

THREW a past form of **throw**

THRICE adverb three times

THRIFT noun **THRIFTS** careful spending, use or management of resources, especially money

THRIFTILY adverb in a thrifty way

THRIFTY adj **THRIFTIER, THRIFTIEST** showing thrift; economical; frugal

THRILL verb **THRILLS, THRILLING, THRILLED** to feel or make someone feel a sudden strong glowing, tingling or throbbing sensation, especially of excitement, emotion or pleasure ◻ noun **THRILLS** a sudden tingling feeling of excitement, happiness or pleasure

THRILLED adj excited; delighted

THRILLER noun **THRILLERS** an exciting novel, play or film, usually one involving crime, espionage or adventure

THRIPS noun **THRIPSES** any of various minute black insects, which feed by sucking sap from plants and thereby often cause damage to crops

THRIVE verb **THRIVES, THRIVING, THRIVED, THROVE, THRIVEN** to grow strong and healthy

THRIVING adj prosperous; successful

THRO adj through

THROAT noun **THROATS** the top part of the windpipe

THROATILY adverb in a throaty way

THROATY adj **THROATIER, THROATIEST** said of a voice: deep and hoarse; husky

THROB verb **THROBS, THROBBING, THROBBED** to beat, especially with unusual force, in response to excitement, emotion, exercise or pain ◻ noun **THROBS** a regular beat; pulse

THROE noun **THROES** a violent pang or spasm, especially during childbirth or before death

THROMBIN noun **THROMBINS** an enzyme that causes the blood to clot

THROMBUS noun **THROMBI** a

blood clot which forms in an artery or vein, blocking blood circulation to surrounding tissues which may die or dislodge causing a stroke

THRONE noun **THRONES** the ceremonial chair of a monarch or bishop, used on official occasions ◻ verb **THRONES, THRONING, THRONED** to place someone on a throne; to enthrone

THRONG noun **THRONGS** a crowd of people or things, especially in a small space; a multitude ◻ verb **THRONGS, THRONGING, THRONGED** to crowd or fill

THROSTLE noun **THROSTLES** a machine for drawing, twisting and winding wool or cotton fibres

THROTTLE noun **THROTTLES** a valve which regulates the amount of fuel or steam, etc supplied to an engine ◻ verb **THROTTLES, THROTTLING, THROTTLED** to injure or kill by choking or strangling

THROUGH prep going from one side or end of something to the other ◻ adverb into and out of; from one side or end to the other ◻ adj said of a journey, route, train or ticket, etc: going or allowing one to go all the way to one's destination without requiring a change of line or train, etc or a new ticket

THROVE a past form of **thrive**

THROW verb **THROWS, THROWING, THREW, THROWN** to propel or hurl through the air with force, especially with a rapid forward movement of the hand and arm ◻ noun **THROWS** an act of throwing or instance of being thrown

THROWAWAY adj meant to be thrown away after use

THROWBACK noun **THROWBACKS** someone or something that reverts back to earlier or ancestral characteristics

THRU prep through ◻ adverb through ◻ adj through

THRUM verb **THRUMS, THRUMMING, THRUMMED** to strum idly on (a stringed instrument) ◻ noun **THRUMS** repetitive strumming, or the sound of this

THRUSH noun **THRUSHES** any of several common small or medium-sized songbirds, typically having brown feathers and a spotted chest

THRUST verb **THRUSTS, THRUSTING, THRUST** to push suddenly and violently ◻ noun **THRUSTS** a sudden or violent movement forward; a push or lunge

THUD noun **THUDS** a dull sound like that of something heavy falling to the ground ◻ verb **THUDS, THUDDING, THUDDED** to move or fall with a thud

THUG noun **THUGS** a violent or brutal person

THUGGERY noun **THUGGERIES** brutal, violent behaviour

THUJA noun **THUJAS** an evergreen tree with small, scalelike leaves

THULIUM noun **THULIUMS** a soft silvery-white metallic element that is used as a source of X-rays and gamma rays

THUMB noun **THUMBS** in humans: the two-boned digit on the inner side of the hand, set lower than and at a different angle to the other four digits ◻ verb **THUMBS, THUMBING, THUMBED** to turn over the pages of (a book or magazine, etc) to glance at the contents

THUMBTACK noun **THUMBTACKS** a drawing-pin

THUMP noun **THUMPS** a heavy blow, or the dull sound of a blow ◻ verb **THUMPS, THUMPING, THUMPED** to beat or strike with dull-sounding heavy blows

THUMPING adj very big

THUNDER noun **THUNDERS** a deep rumbling or loud cracking sound heard after a flash of lightning, due to the lightning causing gases in the atmosphere to expand suddenly ◻ verb **THUNDERS, THUNDERING, THUNDERED** said of thunder: to sound or rumble

THUNDERING adj very great ◻ adverb in a thundering way

THUNDERY adj **THUNDERIER, THUNDERIEST** said of the weather: liable to have thunder

THURIBLE noun **THURIBLES** a censer

THUS adverb in the way or manner shown or mentioned; in this manner

THWACK noun **THWACKS** a blow with something flat ◻ verb **THWACKS, THWACKING, THWACKED** to strike someone or something with such a noise

THWART verb **THWARTS,**

THWARTING, THWARTED to prevent or hinder someone or something □ noun **THWARTS** a seat for a rower that lies across a boat

THY adj belonging or relating to thee

THYLACINE noun **THYLACINES** a carnivorous marsupial, perhaps still existing in some remote mountainous regions of Tasmania, with a light-brown coat with many dark vertical stripes across the hindquarters

THYME noun **THYMES** any of various herbs and shrubs, especially those whose aromatic-smelling leaves are used to season food

THYMINE noun **THYMINES** one of the four bases found in DNA

THYMOL noun **THYMOLS** a white crystalline compound obtained from thyme and used as an antiseptic

THYMUS noun **THYMI** in vertebrates: a gland just above the heart, which plays an important role in the development of the immune response to invasion of the body by pathogens

THYROID noun **THYROIDS** in vertebrates: a shield-shaped gland situated in the neck, in front of the trachea, which secretes several hormones which control growth, development and metabolic rate □ adj belonging or relating to the thyroid gland

THYROXIN noun **THYROXINS** thyroxine

THYROXINE noun **THYROXINES** the principal hormone secreted by the thyroid gland

THYSELF pronoun the reflexive form of thy

TI noun **TIS** te

TIARA noun **TIARAS** a jewelled head-ornament similar to a crown, worn by women

TIBIA noun **TIBIAS, TIBIAE** in the human skeleton: the inner and usually larger of the two bones between the knee and ankle; the shinbone

TIBIAL adj of or relating to the tibia

TIC noun **TICS** a habitual nervous involuntary movement or twitch of a muscle, especially of the face

TICH noun **TICHES** a titch

TICK noun **TICKS** a regular tapping or clicking sound, such as that made by a watch or clock □ verb

TICKS, TICKING, TICKED said eg of a clock: to make a tick or ticks

TICKER noun **TICKERS** anything that ticks, eg a watch or heart

TICKET noun **TICKETS** a printed piece of paper or card which shows that the holder has paid a fare, eg for travel on a bus or train, or for admission, eg to a theatre or cinema, or has the right to use certain services, eg a library □ verb **TICKETS, TICKETING, TICKETED** to give or attach a ticket or label to someone or something

TICKING noun **TICKINGS** a strong coarse, usually striped, cotton fabric used to make mattresses, pillows and bolsters, etc

TICKLE verb **TICKLES, TICKLING, TICKLED** to touch (a person or part of the body) lightly and so as to provoke a tingling or light prickling sensation or laughter □ noun **TICKLES** an act of tickling

TICKLISH adj sensitive to tickling

TID noun **TIDS** a Scots word meaning mood, a temporary state of mind

TIDAL adj belonging or relating to, or affected by, tides

TIDBIT noun **TIDBITS** a titbit

TIDDLER noun **TIDDLERS** a small fish, especially a stickleback or a minnow

TIDDLY adj **TIDDLIER, TIDDLIEST** small; little

TIDE noun **TIDES** the twice-daily rise and fall of the water level in the oceans and seas, caused by the gravitational pull of the Sun and especially the Moon □ verb **TIDES, TIDING, TIDED** to drift with or be carried on the tide

TIDEMARK noun **TIDEMARKS** a mark showing the highest level that the tide has reached or usually reaches

TIDEWATER noun **TIDEWATERS** water brought in by the tides

TIDEWAY noun **TIDEWAYS** a channel in which a tide runs, especially that part of a river which has a tide

TIDILY adverb neatly

TIDINESS noun **TIDINESSES** the state or condition of being tidy

TIDINGS plural noun news

TIDY adj **TIDIER, TIDIEST** neat and in good order □ noun **TIDIES** a receptacle for odds and ends, especially one in a kitchen unit for waste scraps or on a desk for pens,

paper-clips, etc □ verb **TIDIES, TIDYING, TIDIED** to make something neat; to put things away or arrange them neatly

TIE verb **TIES, TYING, TIED** to fasten with a string, ribbon or rope, etc □ noun **TIES** a narrow strip of material worn, especially by men, round the neck under a shirt collar and tied in a knot or bow at the front

TIER noun **TIERS** any series of levels, ranks or grades, etc placed one above the other, eg of seats in a theatre □ verb **TIERS, TIERING, TIERED** to place in tiers

TIERCE noun **TIERCES** terce

TIERCEL noun **TIERCELS** a tercel

TIFF noun **TIFFS** a slight petty quarrel □ verb **TIFFS, TIFFING, TIFFED** to have a tiff; to squabble

TIFFANY noun **TIFFANIES** a sheer silk-like gauze

TIFFIN noun **TIFFINS** a light midday meal, especially as taken by members of the British Raj in India

TIG noun **TIGS** a children's game in which one child chases the others and tries to catch or touch one of them, who then becomes the chaser □ verb **TIGS, TIGGING, TIGGED** to catch or touch someone in, or as if in, the game of tig

TIGER noun **TIGERS** a carnivorous animal, the largest member of the cat family, native to Asia and typically having a fawn or reddish coat, with black or brownish-black transverse stripes

TIGERISH adj of or like a tiger

TIGHT adj **TIGHTER, TIGHTEST** fitting very or too closely

TIGHTEN verb **TIGHTENS, TIGHTENING, TIGHTENED** to make or become tight or tighter

TIGHTLY adverb in a tight way

TIGHTNESS noun **TIGHTNESSES** the quality or condition of being tight

TIGHTROPE noun **TIGHTROPES** a tightly stretched rope or wire on which acrobats balance

TIGHTS plural noun a close-fitting, usually nylon or woollen, garment which covers the feet, legs and body up to the waist, and is worn usually by women, as well as dancers and acrobats, etc

TIGHTWAD noun **TIGHTWADS** a skinflint; a miser

TIGLON noun **TIGLONS** a tigon

TIGON noun TIGONS the offspring of a tiger and lioness

TIGRESS noun TIGRESSES a female tiger

TIKE noun TIKES a tyke

TIKKA noun TIKKAS in Indian cookery: meat that is marinated in yoghurt and spices and cooked in a clay oven

TIL noun TILS sesame

TILDE noun TILDES a mark (~) placed over *n* in Spanish to show that it is pronounced *ny* and over *a* and *o* in Portuguese to show they are nasalized

TILE noun TILES a flat thin slab of fired clay, or a similar one of cork or linoleum, used to cover roofs, floors and walls, etc ◻ verb TILES, TILING, TILED to cover something with tiles

TILER noun TILERS someone who lays tiles

TILING noun TILINGS an area covered with tiles

TILL ¹ noun TILLS a container or drawer in which money taken from customers is put, now usually part of a cash register

TILL ² verb TILLS, TILLING, TILLED to prepare and cultivate (land) for the growing of crops

TILLABLE adj arable

TILLAGE noun TILLAGES the preparing and cultivating of land for crops

TILLER noun TILLERS the lever used to turn the rudder of a boat

TILT verb TILTS, TILTING, TILTED to slope or make something slope; to be or put in a slanting position ◻ noun TILTS a slant; a sloping position or angle

TILTER noun TILTERS a person or thing that tilts

TILTH noun TILTHS the act or process of cultivation

TIMBAL noun TIMBALS a type of drum

TIMBALE noun TIMBALES a dish of meat or fish, etc cooked in a cup-shaped mould or shell

TIMBER noun TIMBERS wood, especially wood prepared for building or carpentry ◻ verb TIMBERS, TIMBERING, TIMBERED to provide with timber or beams

TIMBERED adj built completely or partly of wood

TIMBERING noun TIMBERINGS timber collectively

TIMBRE noun TIMBRES the distinctive quality of the tone produced by a musical instrument or voice, as opposed to pitch and loudness

TIMBREL noun TIMBRELS a small tambourine

TIME noun TIMES the continuous passing and succession of minutes, days and years, etc ◻ verb TIMES, TIMING, TIMED to measure the time taken by (an event or journey, etc)

TIMELESS adj not belonging to or typical of any particular time or date

TIMELY adj TIMELIER, TIMELIEST coming at the right or a suitable moment; opportune

TIMEPIECE noun TIMEPIECES an instrument for keeping time, such as a watch or clock

TIMER noun TIMERS a device like a clock which switches an appliance on or off at pre-set times, or which makes a sound when a set amount of time has passed

TIMESCALE noun TIMESCALES the time envisaged for the completion of a particular project or stage of a project

TIMETABLE noun TIMETABLES a list of the departure and arrival times of trains, coaches or buses, etc ◻ verb TIMETABLES, TIMETABLING, TIMETABLED to arrange or include something in a timetable; to schedule or plan

TIMID adj TIMIDER, TIMIDEST easily frightened or alarmed; nervous; shy

TIMIDITY noun TIMIDITIES the quality or state of being timid

TIMIDLY adj in a timid way

TIMING noun TIMINGS the regulating and co-ordinating of actions and events to achieve the best possible effect, especially the regulating of the speed of dialogue, action and interaction between characters in a play or film, etc

TIMOCRACY noun TIMOCRACIES a form of government in which ownership of property is a qualification for office

TIMOROUS adj very timid; frightened

TIMPANI plural noun a set of two or three kettledrums

TIMPANIST noun TIMPANISTS someone who plays the timpani

TIN noun TINS a soft silvery-white metallic element used as a thin protective coating for steel, eg in

'tin' cans ◻ adj made of tin ◻ verb TINS, TINNING, TINNED to pack (food) in tins; to can

TINCTURE noun TINCTURES a slight flavour, trace or addition ◻ verb TINCTURES, TINCTURING, TINCTURED to give a trace of a colour or flavour, etc to something

TINDER noun TINDERS dry material, especially wood, which is easily set alight and can be used as kindling

TINDERBOX noun TINDERBOXES a box containing tinder, a flint and steel for striking a spark to light a fire

TINE noun TINES a slender prong or tooth, eg of a comb, fork or antler

TINEA noun TINEAS ringworm

TINFOIL noun TINFOILS tin, aluminium or other metal in the form of very thin, paper-like sheets, used especially for wrapping food

TINFUL noun TINFULS the amount a tin can hold

TING noun TINGS a high metallic tinkling sound such as that made by a small bell ◻ verb TINGS, TINGING, TINGED to produce or make something produce this sound

TINGE noun TINGES a trace or slight amount of colour ◻ verb TINGES, TINGING, TINGED to give a slight colour to something or someone

TINGLE verb TINGLES, TINGLING, TINGLED to feel or make someone or something feel a prickling or slightly stinging sensation, as with cold or embarrassment ◻ noun TINGLES a prickling or slightly stinging sensation

TINHORN noun TINHORNS a cheap pretentious second-rate person ◻ adj cheap and pretentious

TINIER see under tiny

TINIEST see under tiny

TININESS noun TININESSES the state or condition of being tiny

TINKER noun TINKERS a travelling mender of pots, pans and other household utensils ◻ verb TINKERS, TINKERING, TINKERED to work in an unskilled way, meddle or fiddle with machinery, etc, especially to try to improve it

TINKLE verb TINKLES, TINKLING, TINKLED to make, or cause something to make, a sound of or like the jingling of small bells

▫ *noun* **TINKLES** a ringing or jingling sound

TINKLY *adj* **TINKLIER, TINKLIEST** making a ringing sound

TINNED *adj* coated or plated with tin

TINNITUS *noun* **TINNITUSES** any noise (ringing, buzzing or whistling, etc) in the ears not caused by external sounds

TINNY *adj* **TINNIER, TINNIEST** belonging to or resembling tin, especially in appearance or taste ▫ *noun* **TINNIES** a can of beer

TINPOT *adj* cheap or poor quality; paltry or contemptible

TINSEL *noun* **TINSELS** a long strip of glittering coloured metal threads used as a decoration, especially at Christmas ▫ *verb* **TINSELS, TINSELLING, TINSELING, TINSELLED, TINSELED** to adorn with, or as if with, tinsel

TINSELLY *adj* like tinsel; gaudy, showy

TINSMITH *noun* **TINSMITHS** a worker in tin and tin plate

TINT *noun* **TINTS** a variety or (usually slightly) different shade of a colour ▫ *verb* **TINTS, TINTING, TINTED** to give a tint to (eg hair); to colour slightly

TINY *adj* **TINIER, TINIEST** very small

TIP *noun* **TIPS** the usually small pointed end of something ▫ *verb* **TIPS, TIPPING, TIPPED** to lean or make something lean or slant

TIPPET *noun* **TIPPETS** a shoulder-cape made from fur or cloth

TIPPLE *verb* **TIPPLES, TIPPLING, TIPPLED** to drink alcohol regularly, especially in relatively small amounts ▫ *noun* **TIPPLES** alcoholic drink

TIPPLER *noun* **TIPPLERS** someone who tipples

TIPSILY *adverb* in a tipsy way

TIPSINESS *noun* **TIPSINESSES** the state or condition of being tipsy

TIPSTAFF *noun* **TIPSTAFFS** a metal-tipped staff used as a symbol of office

TIPSTER *noun* **TIPSTERS** someone who gives tips, especially as to which horses to bet on

TIPSY *adj* **TIPSIER, TIPSIEST** slightly drunk; tiddly

TIPTOE *verb* **TIPTOES, TIPTOEING, TIPTOED** to walk quietly or stealthily on the tips of the toes ▫ *noun* **TIPTOES** the tips of the toes

TIPTOP *adj* excellent; first-class

▫ *noun* **TIPTOPS** the very best; the height of excellence

TIRADE *noun* **TIRADES** a long angry speech, harangue or denunciation

TIRE [1] *verb* **TIRES, TIRING, TIRED** to make or become physically or mentally weary and in need of rest

TIRE [2] *noun* **TIRES** a tyre

TIREDLY *adverb* in a tired way

TIREDNESS *noun* **TIREDNESSES** the state or condition of being tired

TIRELESS *adj* never becoming weary or exhausted

TIRESOME *adj* troublesome and irritating; annoying; tedious

TIRO *noun* **TIROS** a tyro

TISANE *noun* **TISANES** a medicinal infusion of herbs, etc

TISSUE *noun* **TISSUES** a piece of thin, soft disposable paper used as a handkerchief

TIT [1] *noun* **TITS** any of several small agile songbirds

TIT [2] *verb* **TITS, TITTING, TITTED** to tug

TITAN *noun* **TITANS** someone or something of very great strength, size, intellect or importance

TITANIC *adj* having great strength or size; colossal; gigantic

TITANIUM *noun* **TITANIUMS** a silvery-white metallic element used to make strong light corrosion-resistant alloys for components of aircraft and missiles, etc

TITBIT *noun* **TITBITS** a choice or small tasty morsel of something, eg food or gossip

TITCH *noun* **TITCHES** a very small person

TITCHY *adj* **TITCHIER, TITCHIEST** very small

TITER *noun* **TITERS** titre

TITFER *noun* **TITFERS** a hat

TITHABLE *adj* subject to the payment of tithes

TITHE *noun* **TITHES** a tenth part of someone's annual income or produce, paid as a tax to support the church or clergy in a parish ▫ *verb* **TITHES, TITHING, TITHED** to demand a tithe or tithes from someone or something

TITIAN *noun* **TITIANS** a bright reddish-gold colour

TITILLATE *verb* **TITILLATES, TITILLATING, TITILLATED** to excite someone or something gently, especially in a sexual way

TITIVATE *verb* **TITIVATES, TITIVATING, TITIVATED** to smarten up or put the finishing touches to something or someone

TITLARK *noun* **TITLARKS** any bird belonging to the pipit family

TITLE *noun* **TITLES** the distinguishing name of a book, play, work of art, piece of music, etc ▫ *verb* **TITLES, TITLING, TITLED** to give a title to something or someone

TITLED *adj* having a title, especially one that shows noble rank

TITMOUSE *noun* **TITMICE** a tit

TITRATE *verb* **TITRATES, TITRATING, TITRATED** to determine the concentration of (a chemical substance in a solution) by titration

TITRATION *noun* **TITRATIONS** a method of chemical analysis in which the concentration of a particular solution is determined by adding measured amounts of another solution of known concentration until the reaction between the two reaches its end-point

TITRE *noun* **TITRES** the concentration of a solution as determined by titration with a solution of known concentration

TITTER *verb* **TITTERS, TITTERING, TITTERED** to giggle or snigger in a stifled way ▫ *noun* **TITTERS** a stifled giggle or snigger

TITTIVATE *verb* **TITTIVATES, TITTIVATING, TITTIVATED** to titivate

TITTLE *noun* **TITTLES** a small written or printed sign, mark or dot

TITULAR *adj* having the title of an office or position but none of the authority or duties ▫ *noun* **TITULARS** someone invested with a title

TITULARLY *adj* in a titular way

TIZZ *noun* **TIZZES** a tizzy

TIZZY *noun* **TIZZIES** a nervous highly excited or confused state

TO *prep* towards; in the direction of, or with the destination of somewhere or something ▫ *adverb* in or into a nearly closed position

TOAD *noun* **TOADS** a tailless amphibian, with a short squat head and body, and moist skin which may contain poison glands which help to deter predators

TOADFLAX *noun* **TOADFLAXES** any of various perennial plants typically having narrow leaves resembling flax and spurred bright-yellow flowers

TOADSTOOL noun **TOADSTOOLS** any of various fungi, most of which are poisonous or inedible, that produce a fruiting body consisting of an umbrella-shaped cap with spore-bearing gills on the underside

TOADY noun **TOADIES** someone who flatters someone else, does everything they want and hangs on their every word; a sycophant ▫ verb **TOADIES, TOADYING, TOADIED** to flatter someone and behave obsequiously towards them

TOADYISH adj obsequious

TOADYISM noun **TOADYISMS** the behaviour of a toady

TOAST verb **TOASTS, TOASTING, TOASTED** to make something (especially bread) brown by exposing it to direct heat, eg under a grill ▫ noun **TOASTS** bread which has been browned by being exposed to direct heat, eg under a grill

TOASTER noun **TOASTERS** an electric machine for toasting bread

TOASTIE noun **TOASTIES** a toasted sandwich

TOBACCO noun **TOBACCOS, TOBACCOES** any of various plants, with large leaves which, in certain species, contain nicotine

TOBOGGAN noun **TOBOGGANS** a long light sledge which curves up at the front, used for riding over snow and ice ▫ verb **TOBOGGANS, TOBOGGANING, TOBOGGANED** to ride on a toboggan

---

TOC noun **TOCS** the telecommunications code for signalling the letter 'T'

TOCCATA noun **TOCCATAS** a piece of music for a keyboard instrument intended to show off the performer's skill and touch in a series of runs and chords before breaking into a fugue

TOCSIN noun **TOCSINS** an alarm bell or warning signal

TOD [1] noun **TODS** a fox

TOD [2] verb **TODS, TODDING, TODDED** to yield a tod, an old wool weight

---

TODAY noun **TODAYS** this day ▫ adverb on or during this day

TODDLE verb **TODDLES, TODDLING, TODDLED** to walk with

unsteady steps, as or like a young child ▫ noun **TODDLES** a toddling walk

TODDLER noun **TODDLERS** a very young child who is just beginning or has just learnt to walk

TODDY noun **TODDIES** a drink made of spirits, sugar, hot water, lemon juice and sometimes spices

TOE noun **TOES** in humans: any of the five digits at the end of each foot, whose main function is to assist balance and walking ▫ verb **TOES, TOEING, TOED** to kick, strike or touch with the toes

TOECAP noun **TOECAPS** a piece of reinforced metal or leather covering the toe of a boot or shoe

TOEHOLD noun **TOEHOLDS** a place where one's toes can grip, eg when climbing

TOENAIL noun **TOENAILS** a nail covering a toe ▫ verb **TOENAILS, TOENAILING, TOENAILED** in carpentry: to fasten by driving a nail obliquely

TOERAG noun **TOERAGS** a rascal

TOFF noun **TOFFS** an upper-class and usually smartly dressed person

TOFFEE noun **TOFFEES** a type of sticky sweet which can be chewy or hard, made by boiling sugar and butter

TOFU noun **TOFUS** a curd made from soya beans, with a creamy colour and bland flavour, used especially in Japanese cooking

TOG [1] noun **TOGS** a unit for measuring the warmth of fabrics, clothes and quilts, etc

TOG [2] verb **TOGS, TOGGING, TOGGED** to dress in one's best or warmest clothes

TOGA noun **TOGAS** a loose outer garment, consisting of a large piece of cloth draped round the body, worn by a citizen of ancient Rome

TOGAED adj wearing a toga

TOGETHER adverb with someone or something else; in company ▫ adj well organized; competent

TOGGLE noun **TOGGLES** a fastening, eg for garments, consisting of a small bar of wood or plastic, etc which will pass one way only through a loop of material or rope, etc ▫ verb **TOGGLES, TOGGLING, TOGGLED** to provide or fasten something with a toggle

TOIL verb **TOILS, TOILING, TOILED**

to work long and hard; to labour ▫ noun **TOILS** long hard work

TOILE noun **TOILES** a thin cotton or linen material used to make clothes

TOILET noun **TOILETS** a lavatory

TOILETRY noun **TOILETRIES** an article or cosmetic used when washing, arranging the hair, making up, etc

TOILSOME adj involving long hard work

TOKAMAK noun **TOKAMAKS** a toroidal apparatus for containing plasma by means of two magnetic fields

TOKE noun **TOKES** a draw on a cigarette, especially one containing marijuana ▫ verb **TOKES, TOKING, TOKED** to take a draw on such a cigarette

TOKEN noun **TOKENS** a mark, sign or distinctive feature

TOKENISM noun **TOKENISMS** the principle or practice of doing no more than the minimum in a particular area, in pretence that one is committed to it, eg employing one black person in a company to avoid charges of racism

TOLBOOTH noun **TOLBOOTHS** an office where tolls are or were collected

TOLD past form of **tell** [1]

TOLERABLE adj able to be borne or endured; fairly good

TOLERABLY adverb in a tolerable way

TOLERANCE noun **TOLERANCES** the ability to be fair towards and accepting of other people's religious, political, etc beliefs or opinions

TOLERANT adj tolerating the beliefs and opinions of others

TOLERATE verb **TOLERATES, TOLERATING, TOLERATED** to bear or endure someone or something; to put up with it

TOLL [1] verb **TOLLS, TOLLING, TOLLED** to ring (a bell) with slow measured strokes

TOLL [2] noun **TOLLS** a fee or tax paid for the use of some bridges and roads

TOLLBOOTH noun **TOLLBOOTHS** a tolbooth

TOLU noun **TOLUS** a sweet-smelling balsam obtained from a S American tree, used in the manufacture of medicine and perfume

---

For longer words, see The Chambers Dictionary

TOLUENE *noun* **TOLUENES** a toxic organic compound, a colourless flammable liquid derived from benzene and used as an industrial solvent

TOM *noun* **TOMS** a male of various animals, especially a male cat

TOMAHAWK *noun* **TOMAHAWKS** a small axe used as a weapon by Native Americans

TOMATO *noun* **TOMATOES** any of various annual plants cultivated worldwide for their fleshy fruit

TOMB *noun* **TOMBS** a chamber or vault for a dead body, especially one below the ground, and often one that serves as a monument; a grave

TOMBAC *noun* **TOMBACS** an alloy of copper with a little zinc, used to make cheap jewellery

TOMBOLA *noun* **TOMBOLAS** a lottery in which winning tickets are drawn from a revolving drum

TOMBOY *noun* **TOMBOYS** a girl who dresses in a boyish way and who likes boisterous and adventurous activities supposedly more suited to boys

TOMBOYISH *adj* of or like a tomboy

TOMBSTONE *noun* **TOMBSTONES** an ornamental stone placed over a grave, on which the dead person's name and dates, etc are engraved

TOMCAT *noun* **TOMCATS** a male cat

TOME *noun* **TOMES** a large, heavy and usually learned book

TOMENTUM *noun* **TOMENTA** a matted down found on leaves, etc

TOMFOOL *noun* **TOMFOOLS** an absolute fool

TOMMY *noun* **TOMMIES** a private in the British army

TOMORROW *noun* **TOMORROWS** the day after today □ *adverb* on the day after today

TOMPION *noun* **TOMPIONS** a tampion

TOMTIT *noun* **TOMTITS** a tit, especially a bluetit

TON *noun* **TONS** a unit of weight equal to 2 240lb (approximately 1 016.06kg)

TONAL *adj* belonging or relating to tone or tonality

TONALITY *noun* **TONALITIES** the organization of all of the notes and chords of a piece of music in relation to a single tonic

TONDO *noun* **TONDOS, TONDI** a circular painting or circular carving in relief

TONE *noun* **TONES** a musical or vocal sound with reference to its quality and pitch □ *verb* **TONES, TONING, TONED** to fit in well; to harmonize

TONELESS *adj* without a tone

TONEME *noun* **TONEMES** one of two or more tones which serve to distinguish different words in a language

TONEMIC *adj* of or relating to tonemes

TONEPAD *noun* **TONEPADS** an electronic device similar to a remote control for a TV, etc, which allows data to be input into a central computer from a distance, usually via a telephone link

TONG *noun* **TONGS** a Chinese guild or secret society, especially one responsible for organized crime

TONGS *plural noun* a tool consisting of two arms joined by a hinge or pivot, for holding and lifting objects

TONGUE *noun* **TONGUES** in certain animals: the fleshy muscular organ attached to the floor of the mouth, used for tasting, licking and swallowing, and in humans as the main organ of speech □ *verb* **TONGUES, TONGUING, TONGUED** to touch or lick something with the tongue

TONGUING *noun* **TONGUINGS** a way of playing a wind instrument which allows individual notes to be articulated separately by the tongue opening and blocking the passage of air

TONIC *noun* **TONICS** a medicine that increases strength, energy and the general wellbeing of the body □ *adj* increasing strength, energy and wellbeing

TONIGHT *noun* **TONIGHTS** the night of this present day □ *adverb* on or during the night of the present day

TONNAGE *noun* **TONNAGES** the space available in a ship for carrying cargo, measured in tons

TONNE *noun* **TONNES** the metric ton, a unit of weight equal to 1 000kg (approximately 2 204.6lb)

TONSIL *noun* **TONSILS** either of two almond-shaped lumps of tissue at the back of the mouth

TONSILLAR *adj* of or relating to tonsils

TONSORIAL *adj* belonging or relating to barbers or hairdressing

TONSURE *noun* **TONSURES** in the RC church, until 1973: a shaved patch on the crown of a monk's or priest's head □ *verb* **TONSURES, TONSURING, TONSURED** to shave the head of someone

TONTINE *noun* **TONTINES** an annuity scheme in which several subscribers share a common fund, with their individual benefits increasing as members die until only one member is left alive and receives everything, or until a specified date at which the proceeds will be shared amongst the survivors

TOO *adverb* to a greater extent or more than is required, desirable or suitable

TOOK a past form of **take**

TOOL *noun* **TOOLS** an implement, especially one used by hand, for cutting or digging, etc, such as a spade or hammer, etc □ *verb* **TOOLS, TOOLING, TOOLED** to work or engrave (eg stone or leather) with tools

TOOLBAG *noun* **TOOLBAGS** a bag for carrying and storing tools

TOOLBOX *noun* **TOOLBOXES** a box for carrying and storing tools

TOOLKIT *noun* **TOOLKITS** a set of tools, especially those required for a particular trade or purpose

TOOLMAKER *noun* **TOOLMAKERS** someone who makes or repairs machine tools

TOOT *noun* **TOOTS** a quick sharp blast of a trumpet, whistle or horn, etc □ *verb* **TOOTS, TOOTING, TOOTED** to sound or make (a trumpet or horn, etc) sound with a quick sharp blast

TOOTH *noun* **TEETH** in vertebrates: any of the hard structures, usually embedded in the upper and lower jaw bones, that are used for biting and chewing food □ *verb* **TOOTHS, TOOTHING, TOOTHED** to provide something with teeth

TOOTHACHE *noun* **TOOTHACHES** an ache or pain in a tooth, usually as a result of tooth decay

TOOTHILY *adverb* in a toothy way

TOOTHLESS *adj* without teeth

TOOTHPICK *noun* **TOOTHPICKS** a small sharp piece of wood or plastic, etc for removing food stuck between the teeth

TOOTHSOME *adj* appetizing; delicious; attractive

TOOTHY *adj* **TOOTHIER, TOOTHIEST** showing or having a lot of teeth, especially large prominent ones

TOOTLE verb **TOOTLES, TOOTLING, TOOTLED** to toot gently or continuously □ noun **TOOTLES** a tootling sound

TOOTSIE noun **TOOTSIES** a foot

TOOTSY noun **TOOTSIES** a foot

TOP noun **TOPS** the highest part, point or level of anything □ verb **TOPS, TOPPING, TOPPED** to cover or form the top of something, especially as a finishing or decorative touch

TOPAZ noun **TOPAZES** an aluminium silicate mineral, sometimes formed as enormous hard crystals, the pale yellow variety of which is most highly prized as a semi-precious gemstone

TOPCOAT noun **TOPCOATS** an overcoat

TOPE verb **TOPES, TOPING, TOPED** to drink alcohol to excess □ noun **TOPES** a small shark, native to temperate and tropical seas, with a slender white and dark-grey body

TOPEE noun **TOPEES** a topi

TOPER noun **TOPERS** a drunkard

TOPI noun **TOPIS** a lightweight hat, shaped like a helmet, worn in hot countries as protection against the sun

TOPIARIAN adj of or relating to topiary

TOPIARIST noun **TOPIARISTS** someone who practises topiary

TOPIARY noun **TOPIARIES** the art of cutting trees, bushes and hedges into ornamental shapes

TOPIC noun **TOPICS** a subject or theme for a book, film or discussion, etc

TOPICAL adj relating to matters of interest at the present time; dealing with current affairs

TOPICALLY adverb in a topical way

TOPKNOT noun **TOPKNOTS** a knot of ribbons, etc worn on the top of the head as decoration

TOPLESS adj having no top

TOPMAST noun **TOPMASTS** the second mast, usually directly above the lower mast

TOPMOST adj the very highest of all

TOPOLOGY noun **TOPOLOGIES** the branch of geometry concerned with those properties of a geometrical figure that remain unchanged even when the figure is deformed by bending, stretching or twisting, etc

TOPONYM noun **TOPONYMS** a place name

TOPONYMIC adj of or relating to place names

TOPONYMY noun **TOPONYMIES** the study of place names

TOPPER noun **TOPPERS** a top hat

TOPPING noun **TOPPINGS** something that forms a covering or garnish for food

TOPPLE verb **TOPPLES, TOPPLING, TOPPLED** to fall, or make someone or something fall, by overbalancing

TOPSAIL noun **TOPSAILS** a square sail set across the topmast

TOPSIDE noun **TOPSIDES** a lean cut of beef from the rump □ adverb on deck

TOPSOIL noun **TOPSOILS** the uppermost layer of soil, rich in organic matter, where most plant roots develop

TOPSPIN noun **TOPSPINS** a spin given to a ball by hitting it sharply on the upper half with a forward and upward stroke to make it travel higher, further or faster

TOQUE noun **TOQUES** a small close-fitting brimless hat worn by women

TOR noun **TORS** a tower-like block of unweathered rock formed by erosion of surrounding weathered rock

TORC noun **TORCS** a torque

TORCH noun **TORCHES** a small portable light powered by electric batteries □ verb **TORCHES, TORCHING, TORCHED** to set fire to something deliberately

TORE a past form of **tear**

TOREADOR noun **TOREADORS** a bullfighter, especially one on horseback

TORERO noun **TOREROS** a bullfighter, especially one on foot

TORI plural of **torus**

TORIC adj of or having the form of a torus

TORMENT noun **TORMENTS** very great pain, suffering or anxiety □ verb **TORMENTS, TORMENTING, TORMENTED** to cause great pain, suffering or anxiety to someone or something

TORMENTIL noun **TORMENTILS** a perennial plant with clusters of bright-yellow flowers and an astringent woody root, which is used in herbal medicine

TORMENTOR noun **TORMENTORS** someone who torments

TORN a past form of **tear**

TORNADO noun **TORNADOS, TORNADOES** a violently destructive storm characterized by a funnel-shaped rotating column of air which can be seen extending downward from thunder clouds to the ground, tracing a narrow path across the land

TOROID noun **TOROIDS** a figure shaped like a torus

TOROIDAL adj of or relating to a toroid

TORPEDO noun **TORPEDOES, TORPEDOS** a long self-propelling underwater missile which explodes on impact with its target (usually a ship) and can be fired from submarines, ships and aircraft □ verb **TORPEDOES, TORPEDOING, TORPEDOED** to attack with torpedoes

TORPID adj sluggish and dull; unenergetic

TORPIDITY noun **TORPIDITIES** the quality or condition of being torpid

TORPIDLY adverb in a torpid way

TORPOR noun **TORPORS** the state of being torpid

TORQUE noun **TORQUES** a necklace made of metal twisted into a band, worn by the ancient Britons and Gauls

TORR noun **TORRS** a unit of pressure equal to 133.32 pascals, used to measure very low pressures, eg in high-vacuum technology

TORREFY verb **TORREFIES, TORREFYING, TORREFIED** to dry or parch (ores or drugs, etc) by heat

TORRENT noun **TORRENTS** a great rushing stream or downpour of water or lava, etc

TORRID adj **TORRIDER, TORRIDEST** said of the weather: so hot and dry as to scorch the land

TORSION noun **TORSIONS** the act or process of twisting something by applying force to one end while the other is held firm or twisted in the opposite direction

TORSIONAL adj of or relating to torsion

TORSO noun **TORSOS** the main part of the human body, without the limbs and head; the trunk

TORT noun **TORTS** any wrongful act, other than breach of contract, for which an action for damages or compensation may be brought

TORTE *noun* **TORTES** a rich sweet cake or pastry, often garnished or filled with fruit, nuts, cream or chocolate, etc
TORTILLA *noun* **TORTILLAS** a thin round Mexican maize cake cooked on a griddle and usually eaten hot, with a filling or topping of meat or cheese
TORTOISE *noun* **TORTOISES** any of various slow-moving, toothless reptiles with a high domed shell into which the head, short scaly legs and tail can be withdrawn for safety
TORTUOUS *adj* full of twists and turns
TORTURE *noun* **TORTURES** the infliction of severe pain or mental suffering, especially as a punishment or as a means of persuading someone to give information ▫ *verb* **TORTURES, TORTURING, TORTURED** to subject someone to torture
TORTUROUS *adj* causing torture or violent distortion
TORUS *noun* **TORI** a solid curved surface with a hole in it, resembling a doughnut
TOSH *noun* **TOSHES** twaddle; nonsense
TOSS *verb* **TOSSES, TOSSING, TOSSED** to throw something up into the air ▫ *noun* **TOSSES** an act or an instance of tossing
TOT[1] *noun* **TOTS** a small child; a toddler
TOT[2] *verb* **TOTS, TOTTING, TOTTED** to add something together
TOTAL *noun* **TOTALS** the whole or complete amount, eg of various things added together ▫ *verb* **TOTALS, TOTALLING, TOTALLED** to amount to a specified sum
TOTALISER *noun* **TOTALISERS** a totalizer
TOTALITY *noun* **TOTALITIES** completeness
TOTALIZER *noun* **TOTALIZERS** a system of betting in which the total amount staked, minus tax, etc, is paid out to the winners in proportion to the size of their stake
TOTALLY *adverb* completely
TOTE *verb* **TOTES, TOTING, TOTED** to carry, drag or wear something, especially something heavy
TOTEM *noun* **TOTEMS** in Native American culture: a natural object, especially an animal, used as the badge or sign of a tribe or an individual
TOTEMIC *adj* of or relating to a totem
TOTEMISM *noun* **TOTEMISMS** the use of totems as the foundation of a social system of obligation and restriction
TOTEMIST *noun* **TOTEMISTS** an individual or group designated by a totem
TOTHER *pronoun* the other
TOTTED past form of **tot**[2]
TOTTER *verb* **TOTTERS, TOTTERING, TOTTERED** to walk or move unsteadily, shakily or weakly ▫ *noun* **TOTTERS** a weak and unsteady movement or gait
TOTTERER *noun* **TOTTERERS** someone who totters
TOTTERY *adj* liable to totter; unsteady
TOTTING a form of **tot**[2]
TOUCAN *noun* **TOUCANS** a tropical American fruit-eating bird with a huge beak and brightly coloured feathers
TOUCH *verb* **TOUCHES, TOUCHING, TOUCHED** to bring something, such as a hand, into contact, usually lightly, with something else ▫ *noun* **TOUCHES** an act of touching or the sensation of being touched
TOUCHDOWN *noun* **TOUCHDOWNS** the act, an instance or the process of an aircraft or spacecraft making contact with the ground when landing
TOUCHÉ *exclamation* in fencing: expressing that a hit is acknowledged
TOUCHED *adj* having a feeling of pity, sympathy, quiet pleasure, etc
TOUCHILY *adverb* in a touchy way
TOUCHING *adj* causing feelings of pity or sympathy; moving
TOUCHLINE *noun* **TOUCHLINES** either of the two lines that mark the side boundaries of the pitch
TOUCHWOOD *noun* **TOUCHWOODS** dry or decayed wood which has been softened by fungi, making it particularly suitable for kindling fires
TOUCHY *adj* **TOUCHIER, TOUCHIEST** easily annoyed or offended
TOUGH *adj* **TOUGHER, TOUGHEST** strong and durable; not easily cut, broken, torn or worn out ▫ *noun* **TOUGHS** a rough violent person, especially a bully or criminal ▫ *adverb* aggressively; in a macho way
TOUGHEN *verb* **TOUGHENS, TOUGHENING, TOUGHENED** to become, or make someone, tough or tougher
TOUGHENER *noun* **TOUGHENERS** a person or thing that toughens
TOUGHENING *noun* **TOUGHENINGS** an act of becoming, or making someone, tough or tougher
TOUGHIE *noun* **TOUGHIES** someone who is quite aggressive, violent, etc
TOUGHISH *adj* somewhat tough
TOUGHLY *adverb* in a tough way
TOUGHNESS *noun* **TOUGHNESSES** the quality or condition of being tough
TOUPEE *noun* **TOUPEES** a small wig or hair-piece worn usually by men to cover a bald patch
TOUR *noun* **TOURS** an extended journey round an area, country, etc with stops at various places of interest along the route and which usually returns to the starting-point at the end ▫ *verb* **TOURS, TOURING, TOURED** to travel round (a place)
TOURACO *noun* **TOURACOS** a turaco
TOURING *noun* **TOURINGS** an act of travelling round (a place)
TOURISM *noun* **TOURISMS** the practice of travelling to and visiting places for pleasure and relaxation
TOURIST *noun* **TOURISTS** someone who travels for pleasure and relaxation; a holiday-maker
TOURISTIC *adj* of or relating to tourists
TOURISTY *adj* designed for, appealing to, frequented by or full of tourists
TOURNEDOS *noun* **TOURNEDOS** a small round thick cut of beef fillet that is usually grilled or sautéed and served with a rich sauce, often on a crouton bed with pâté
TOURNEY *noun* **TOURNEYS** a medieval tournament ▫ *verb* **TOURNEYS, TOURNEYING, TOURNEYED** to take part in a medieval tournament
TOUSLE *verb* **TOUSLES, TOUSLING, TOUSLED** to make (especially hair) untidy ▫ *noun* **TOUSLES** a tousled mass
TOUT *verb* **TOUTS, TOUTING, TOUTED** to persistently try to persuade people to buy something, give their support, etc ▫ *noun*

TOUTS someone who buys up large numbers of tickets for a popular sporting event, concert, etc and sells them at inflated prices to members of the public

TOUTER noun **TOUTERS** someone who touts tickets

TOUZLE verb **TOUZLES, TOUZLING, TOUZLED** to tousle □ noun **TOUZLES** a tousle

TOVARICH noun **TOVARICHES** a tovarisch

TOVARISCH noun **TOVARISCHES** in the former USSR: a comrade, often used as a form of address

TOVARISH noun **TOVARISHES** a tovarisch

TOW verb **TOWS, TOWING, TOWED** to pull (a ship, barge, caravan, trailer, etc) behind the vehicle one is driving □ noun **TOWS** an act or the process of towing; the state of being towed

TOWABLE adj capable of being towed

TOWAGE noun **TOWAGES** an act or the process of towing

TOWARD prep in the direction of

TOWARDS prep in the direction of

TOWEL noun **TOWELS** a piece of absorbent cloth that is used for drying oneself, another person, etc □ verb **TOWELS, TOWELLING, TOWELING, TOWELLED, TOWELED** to rub, wipe or dry someone or something with a towel

TOWELLING noun **TOWELLINGS** a type of material that is formed with many tiny loops of, usually cotton, thread which makes it highly absorbent and therefore an ideal fabric for towels, bathrobes, etc

TOWER noun **TOWERS** a tall narrow structure, usually circular or square in shape, that often forms part of a larger lower building such as a church or castle □ verb **TOWERS, TOWERING, TOWERED** to reach a great height, or rise high above something or someone

TOWING noun **TOWINGS** an act of pulling (a ship, barge, caravan, etc) behind the vehicle one is driving

TOWLINE noun **TOWLINES** a rope used to attach a vehicle or vessel that is on tow

TOWN noun **TOWNS** an urban area with relatively defined boundaries and a name, smaller than a city but larger than a village

TOWNEE noun **TOWNEES**

someone who lives in a town, especially as opposed to a member of a town's university or someone who lives in the countryside

TOWNIE noun **TOWNIES** a townee

TOWNSCAPE noun **TOWNSCAPES** the general appearance of, or visual impression created by, a town

TOWNSFOLK singular or plural noun **TOWNSFOLKS** the people who live in a particular town or city

TOWNSHIP noun **TOWNSHIPS** an urban area that was formerly set aside for non-white citizens to live in

TOWNSMAN noun **TOWNSMEN** a man who lives in a town or city

TOWPATH noun **TOWPATHS** a path that runs alongside a canal or river where a horse can walk while towing a barge

TOXAEMIA noun **TOXAEMIAS** a condition in which there are toxic substances present in the bloodstream, eg of the kind released from a local site of bacterial infection such as an abscess or that result from kidney failure

TOXAEMIC adj of or relating to toxaemia

TOXEMIA noun **TOXEMIAS** toxaemia

TOXIC adj poisonous

TOXICALLY adverb in a toxic way

TOXICANT noun **TOXICANTS** a substance that can produce poisonous or toxic effects

TOXICITY noun **TOXICITIES** the degree of strength of a poison

TOXIN noun **TOXINS** any poison that is produced by a micro-organism, especially one that is present in an animal or human and which stimulates the body to produce antibodies to fight the infection that results from its presence

TOXOCARA noun **TOXOCARAS** any of various worms which parasitically infest the intestines of dogs and cats

TOXOID noun **TOXOIDS** a toxin that has been treated so as to remove its toxic properties without destroying its ability to stimulate the production of antibodies, eg chemically treated preparations of diphtheria and tetanus toxins used as vaccines

TOY noun **TOYS** an object that is made, especially for a child, to play

with □ verb **TOYS, TOYING, TOYED** to flirt or amuse oneself with someone or their feelings, etc

TOYER noun **TOYERS** someone who toys with something or someone

TOYING noun **TOYINGS** an act of flirting or amusing oneself with someone or something

TOZE verb **TOZES, TOZING, TOZED** to tease or comb out

TRABECULA noun **TRABECULAE** in anatomy: any beam-like structure, especially a supporting one that goes across a cavity or one that divides an organ, such as the heart, into chambers

TRACE noun **TRACES** a mark or sign that some person, animal or thing has been in a particular place □ verb **TRACES, TRACING, TRACED** to track and discover by or as if by following clues, a trail, etc

TRACEABLE adj capable of being traced

TRACEABLY adverb in a traceable way

TRACELESS adj without leaving traces

TRACER noun **TRACERS** someone whose job is to trace, eg architectural, civil engineering, etc drawings

TRACERIED adj decorated with tracery

TRACERY noun **TRACERIES** ornamental open stonework used to form a decorative pattern, especially in the top part of a Gothic window

TRACHEA noun **TRACHEAE** an air tube, usually stiffened by rings of cartilage, that extends from the larynx to the bronchus of each lung

TRACHEAL adj of or relating to the trachea

TRACHOMA noun **TRACHOMAS** a contagious eye disease, causing inflammation, redness and pain, common in the Third World

TRACHYTE noun **TRACHYTES** any of several kinds of light-coloured rough volcanic rock

TRACHYTIC adj of or relating to trachyte

TRACING noun **TRACINGS** a copy of a drawing, etc that is made on semi-transparent paper

TRACK noun **TRACKS** a mark or series of marks that something leaves behind □ verb **TRACKS, TRACKING, TRACKED** to follow the marks, footprints, etc left by (a person or animal)

TRACKBALL noun **TRACKBALLS** a ball mounted in a small box that is linked to a computer terminal and which can be rotated with the palm to move a cursor correspondingly on a screen

TRACKING noun **TRACKINGS** the act or process of following someone or something

TRACT noun **TRACTS** an area of land, usually of indefinite extent

TRACTABLE adj said especially of a child, animal, etc or their disposition: easily managed, controlled, etc; docile

TRACTABLY adverb in a tractable way

TRACTATE noun **TRACTATES** a treatise

TRACTION noun **TRACTIONS** the action or process of pulling

TRACTIVE adj of or relating to traction

TRACTOR noun **TRACTORS** a slow-moving motor vehicle that has two large rear wheels and a high seat, and which is used especially for pulling farm machinery, heavy loads, etc

TRAD noun **TRADS** traditional jazz, a style of jazz that follows on from the kind of music first played in the early 20c in New Orleans

TRADE noun **TRADES** the act, an instance or the process of buying and selling □ verb **TRADES, TRADING, TRADED** to buy and sell; to engage in trading

TRADEMARK noun **TRADEMARKS** a name, word or symbol, especially one that is officially registered and protected by law, which a company or individual uses as identification on all the goods made or sold by them

TRADENAME noun **TRADENAMES** a name that is given to an article or product, or a group of these, by the trade which produces them

TRADER noun **TRADERS** someone who trades, often one who owns or runs a shop or market stall, or who trades in a particular group of goods

TRADESMAN noun **TRADESMEN** a man who is engaged in trading, eg a shopkeeper

TRADING noun **TRADINGS** an act of buying and selling

TRADITION noun **TRADITIONS** something, such as a doctrine, belief, custom, story, etc, that is passed on from generation to generation, especially orally or by example

TRADUCE verb **TRADUCES, TRADUCING, TRADUCED** to say or write unpleasant things about someone or something; to malign or misrepresent them

TRADUCER noun **TRADUCERS** someone who traduces others

TRAFFIC noun **TRAFFICS** the vehicles that are moving along a route □ verb **TRAFFICS, TRAFFICKING, TRAFFICKED** to deal or trade in something, especially illegally or dishonestly

TRAFFICKING noun **TRAFFICKINGS** an act of trading illegally, eg in drugs

TRAGEDIAN noun **TRAGEDIANS** an actor who specializes in acting tragic roles

TRAGEDY noun **TRAGEDIES** a serious catastrophe, accident, natural disaster, etc

TRAGIC adj said especially of a death, disaster, accident, etc: very sad; intensely distressing

TRAGICAL adj tragic

TRAGOPAN noun **TRAGOPANS** any of several types of Asian pheasant that have erect fleshy horns on their heads

TRAIL verb **TRAILS, TRAILING, TRAILED** to drag or be dragged loosely along the ground or other surface □ noun **TRAILS** a track, series of marks, footprints, etc left by a passing person, animal or thing, especially one followed in hunting

TRAILER noun **TRAILERS** a preview or foretaste, in the form of a brief excerpt or series of excerpts, from a film, TV or radio programme, etc, that serves as advance publicity before its release or showing □ verb **TRAILERS, TRAILERING, TRAILERED** to advertise (a film, programme, etc) with a trailer

TRAIN noun **TRAINS** a string of railway carriages or wagons with a locomotive □ verb **TRAINS, TRAINING, TRAINED** to teach or prepare (a person or animal) for something through instruction, practice, exercises, etc

TRAINABLE adj capable of being trained

TRAINED adj said of a person, animal, etc: having received training

TRAINEE noun **TRAINEES** someone who is in the process of being trained for a particular job

TRAINER noun **TRAINERS** someone who trains racehorses, athletes, etc

TRAINING noun **TRAININGS** the act or process of being prepared for something, of being taught or learning a particular skill and practising it until the required standard is reached

TRAIPSE verb **TRAIPSES, TRAIPSING, TRAIPSED** to walk or trudge along idly or wearily □ noun **TRAIPSES** a long tiring walk

TRAIT noun **TRAITS** an identifying feature or quality, especially one that distinguishes someone's character

TRAITOR noun **TRAITORS** someone who betrays their country, sovereign, government, etc

TRAITRESS noun **TRAITRESSES** a female traitor

TRAM noun **TRAMS** an electrically-powered passenger vehicle that runs on rails laid in the streets

TRAMLINE noun **TRAMLINES** either of a pair of rails that form the track for trams to run on

TRAMMEL noun **TRAMMELS** anything that hinders or prevents free action or movement □ verb **TRAMMELS, TRAMMELLING, TRAMMELLED** to hinder, restrain or prevent free movement

TRAMP verb **TRAMPS, TRAMPING, TRAMPED** to walk with firm heavy footsteps □ noun **TRAMPS** someone who has no fixed home or job and who often travels from place to place on foot doing odd jobs or begging

TRAMPET noun **TRAMPETS** a small trampoline

TRAMPETTE noun **TRAMPETTES** a trampet

TRAMPLE verb **TRAMPLES, TRAMPLING, TRAMPLED** to tread on something heavily or roughly □ noun **TRAMPLES** an act of trampling or the sound made by trampling

TRAMPLER noun **TRAMPLERS** someone who tramples

TRAMWAY noun **TRAMWAYS** a system of tracks for trams

TRANCE noun **TRANCES** a sleep-like or half-conscious state in which the ability to react to stimuli such as pain, etc is temporarily lost

TRANCHE noun **TRANCHES** a part, piece or division of something

TRANNIE noun **TRANNIES** a transistor radio

TRANNY noun **TRANNIES** a trannie

TRANQUIL adj **TRANQUILLER, TRANQUILLEST** serenely quiet or peaceful; undisturbed

TRANSACT verb **TRANSACTS, TRANSACTING, TRANSACTED** to conduct or carry out (business)

TRANSCEND verb **TRANSCENDS, TRANSCENDING, TRANSCENDED** to be beyond the limits, scope, range, etc of something

TRANSEPT noun **TRANSEPTS** in a cross-shaped building, especially a church: either of the two arms (the north and south transepts) that are at right angles to the nave

TRANSFER verb **TRANSFERS, TRANSFERRING, TRANSFERRED** to move from one place, person, group, etc to another ◻ noun **TRANSFERS** an act, instance or the process of transferring or being transferred

TRANSFIX verb **TRANSFIXES, TRANSFIXING, TRANSFIXED** to immobilize through surprise, fear, horror, etc

TRANSFORM verb **TRANSFORMS, TRANSFORMING, TRANSFORMED** to change in appearance, nature, function, etc, often completely and dramatically

TRANSFORMING noun **TRANSFORMINGS** an act of changing in appearance, etc

TRANSFUSE verb **TRANSFUSES, TRANSFUSING, TRANSFUSED** to transfer (blood or plasma) from one person or animal into the blood vessels of another

TRANSHIP verb **TRANSHIPS, TRANSHIPPING, TRANSHIPPED** to transfer from one ship or form of transport to another

TRANSHIPPING noun **TRANSHIPPINGS** an act of transferring from one ship to another

TRANSIENT adj lasting, staying, visiting, etc for only a short time; passing quickly ◻ noun **TRANSIENTS** a temporary resident, worker, etc

TRANSIT noun **TRANSITS** the act or process of carrying or moving goods, passengers, etc from one place to another ◻ verb **TRANSITS, TRANSITING, TRANSITED** to pass across or through

TRANSLATE verb **TRANSLATES, TRANSLATING, TRANSLATED** to express (a word, speech, written text, etc) in another language, closely preserving the meaning of the original

TRANSMIT verb **TRANSMITS, TRANSMITTING, TRANSMITTED** to pass or hand on (especially a message, a genetic characteristic, an inheritance, or an infection or disease)

TRANSMUTE verb **TRANSMUTES, TRANSMUTING, TRANSMUTED** to change the form, substance or nature of

TRANSOM noun **TRANSOMS** a horizontal bar of wood or stone that divides a window

TRANSPIRE verb **TRANSPIRES, TRANSPIRING, TRANSPIRED** said especially of something secret: to become known; to come to light

TRANSPORT verb **TRANSPORTS, TRANSPORTING, TRANSPORTED** to carry (goods, passengers, etc) from one place to another ◻ noun **TRANSPORTS** a means of getting or being transported from place to place

TRANSPOSE verb **TRANSPOSES, TRANSPOSING, TRANSPOSED** to make (two or more things, letters, words, etc) change places

TRANSPOSING noun **TRANSPOSINGS** an act of making two or more things change places

TRANSSHIP verb **TRANSSHIPS, TRANSSHIPPING, TRANSSHIPPED** to transfer from one ship or form of transport to another

TRANSUDE verb **TRANSUDES, TRANSUDING, TRANSUDED** said of a fluid, especially a bodily fluid such as sweat: to ooze out, through pores or some permeable membrane

TRAP noun **TRAPS** a device or hole, usually baited, for catching animals, sometimes killing them in the process ◻ verb **TRAPS, TRAPPING, TRAPPED** to catch (an animal) in a trap

TRAPDOOR noun **TRAPDOORS** a small door or opening in a floor, ceiling, theatre stage, etc that is usually set flush with its surface

TRAPES verb **TRAPESES, TRAPESING, TRAPESED** to traipse ◻ noun **TRAPESES** a traipse

TRAPEZE noun **TRAPEZES** a swing-like apparatus that consists of a short horizontal bar hanging on two ropes and is used by gymnasts and acrobats in their routines

TRAPEZIAL adj of or like a trapezium

TRAPEZIUM noun **TRAPEZIUMS, TRAPEZIA** a four-sided geometric figure that has one pair of its opposite sides parallel

TRAPEZIUS noun **TRAPEZIUSES, TRAPEZII** either of a pair of large flat triangular muscles that extend over the back of the neck and the shoulders

TRAPEZOID noun **TRAPEZOIDS** a four-sided geometric figure that has no sides parallel

TRAPPED past form of **trap**

TRAPPER noun **TRAPPERS** someone who traps wild animals, usually with the intention of selling their fur

TRAPPING a form of **trap**

TRAPPINGS plural noun clothes or ornaments suitable for or indicative of a particular occasion, ceremony, status, office or person

TRAPS plural noun personal luggage

TRASH noun **TRASHES** rubbish; waste material or objects ◻ verb **TRASHES, TRASHING, TRASHED** to wreck

TRASHCAN noun **TRASHCANS** a dustbin

TRASHILY adverb in a trashy way

TRASHY adj **TRASHIER, TRASHIEST** worthless; of poor quality

TRATTORIA noun **TRATTORIAS, TRATTORIE** a restaurant, especially an informal one that serves Italian food

TRAUMA noun **TRAUMAS, TRAUMATA** a physical injury or wound

TRAUMATIC adj relating to, resulting from or causing physical wounds

TRAVAIL noun **TRAVAILS** painful or extremely hard work or labour ◻ verb **TRAVAILS, TRAVAILING, TRAVAILED** to work hard or with pain

TRAVEL verb **TRAVELS, TRAVELLING, TRAVELING, TRAVELLED, TRAVELED** to go from place to place; to journey, especially abroad or far from home; to journey through, across or over (a region, country, etc) ◻ noun **TRAVELS** an act or process of travelling

TRAVELLED adj having made many journeys, especially abroad
TRAVELLER noun **TRAVELLERS** someone who travels
TRAVERSAL noun **TRAVERSALS** the action of traversing
TRAVERSE verb **TRAVERSES, TRAVERSING, TRAVERSED** to go across or through something □ noun **TRAVERSES** an act or the process of crossing or traversing
TRAVERSER noun **TRAVERSERS** a person who traverses
TRAVERSING noun **TRAVERSINGS** an act of going across or through something
TRAVESTY noun **TRAVESTIES** a ridiculous or crude distortion; a mockery or caricature □ verb **TRAVESTIES, TRAVESTYING, TRAVESTIED** to make a travesty of
TRAWL noun **TRAWLS** a large bag-shaped net with a wide mouth, used for catching fish at sea □ verb **TRAWLS, TRAWLING, TRAWLED** to fish (the sea, an area of sea, etc) using a trawl-net
TRAWLER noun **TRAWLERS** a fishing-boat used in trawling
TRAWLING noun **TRAWLINGS** an act of fishing using a trawl-net
TRAY noun **TRAYS** a flat piece of wood, metal, plastic, etc, usually with a small raised edge, used for carrying dishes, crockery, etc
TRAYFUL noun **TRAYFULS** the amount a tray can hold
TREACHERY noun **TREACHERIES** deceit, betrayal, cheating or treason
TREACLE noun **TREACLES** the thick dark sticky liquid that remains after the crystallization and removal of sugar from extracts of sugar-cane or sugar-beet
TREACLY adj **TREACLIER, TREACLIEST** of or like treacle
TREAD verb **TREADS, TREADING, TROD, TRODDEN** to put a foot or feet on something; to walk or step on something □ noun **TREADS** a manner, style or sound of walking
TREADER noun **TREADERS** someone who treads
TREADING noun **TREADINGS** an act of putting a foot or feet on something; an act of walking or stepping on something
TREADLE noun **TREADLES** a foot pedal that can be pushed back and forward in a rhythmic motion and so produce the momentum to drive a machine, such as a sewing-machine or loom □ verb **TREADLES, TREADLING, TREADLED** to work a treadle
TREADMILL noun **TREADMILLS** a monotonous and dreary routine
TREASON noun **TREASONS** disloyalty to or betrayal of one's country, sovereign or government
TREASURE noun **TREASURES** wealth and riches, especially in the form of gold, silver, precious stones and jewels, etc which have been accumulated over a period of time and which can be hoarded □ verb **TREASURES, TREASURING, TREASURED** to value greatly or think of as very precious
TREASURER noun **TREASURERS** the person in a club, society, etc who is in charge of the money and accounts
TREASURY noun **TREASURIES** the income or funds of a state, government, organization, society, etc
TREAT verb **TREATS, TREATING, TREATED** to care for or deal with (a person, illness, injury) medically □ noun **TREATS** a gift, such as an outing, meal, present, etc, that one person gives to another
TREATABLE adj capable of being treated
TREATER noun **TREATERS** someone who treats others
TREATING noun **TREATINGS** an act of caring for or dealing with (a person, injury, etc) medically
TREATISE noun **TREATISES** a formal piece of writing that deals with a subject systematically and in depth
TREATMENT noun **TREATMENTS** the medical or surgical care that a patient is given to cure an illness or injury
TREATY noun **TREATIES** a formal agreement between states or governments, especially one that ratifies a peace or trade agreement
TREBLE noun **TREBLES** anything that is three times as much or as many □ adj three times as much or as many; threefold; triple □ adverb with a soprano voice □ verb **TREBLES, TREBLING, TREBLED** to make or become three times as much or as many
TREBLY adverb three times
TREBUCHET noun **TREBUCHETS** a large sling-like machine used during sieges in the Middle Ages
TRECENTO noun **TRECENTOS** the fourteenth century, especially as thought of in terms of the style of Italian art and literature of that period
TREE noun **TREES** a tall woody perennial plant that typically has one main stem or trunk and which, unlike a shrub, usually only begins to branch at some distance from the ground □ verb **TREES, TREEING, TREED** to drive or chase up a tree
TREELESS adj without trees
TREEN adj wooden; made from trees
TREENAIL noun **TREENAILS** a long cylindrical wooden pin used for fastening timbers together, eg in shipbuilding
TREETOP noun **TREETOPS** the upper leaves and branches of a tree
TREF adj trefa
TREFA adj in Judaism, said of the flesh of an animal: not fit for human consumption because it has not been slaughtered in the prescribed way
TREFOIL noun **TREFOILS** a leaf which is divided into three sections
TREK verb **TREKS, TREKKING, TREKKED** to make a long hard journey □ noun **TREKS** a long hard journey
TREKKER noun **TREKKERS** someone who undertakes a trek
TRELLIS noun **TRELLISES** an open lattice framework of narrow interwoven strips of metal, wood, etc that is usually fixed to a wall and which is designed to support or train climbing plants, fruit trees, etc □ verb **TRELLISES, TRELLISING, TRELLISED** to provide or support with a trellis
TREMATODE noun **TREMATODES** any of several kinds of parasitic flatworm that have hooks or suckers and which live in the alimentary canals of animals and humans
TREMATOID adj of or relating to trematodes
TREMBLE verb **TREMBLES, TREMBLING, TREMBLED** to shake or shudder involuntarily, eg with cold, fear, weakness, etc □ noun **TREMBLES** a trembling movement; a shudder or tremor
TREMBLER noun **TREMBLERS** a person or thing that shakes
TREMBLING noun **TREMBLINGS** an act of shaking or shuddering involuntarily

TREMBLY adj **TREMBLIER, TREMBLIEST** shaky

TREMOLO noun **TREMOLOS** a trembling effect achieved by rapidly repeating a note or notes, or by quickly alternating notes, eg on a stringed instrument, organ, etc

TREMOR noun **TREMORS** a shaking or quivering ▫ verb **TREMORS, TREMORING, TREMORED** to shake

TREMULOUS adj said of someone, their limbs, voice, etc: quivering, especially with fear, worry, nervousness, excitement, etc

TRENAIL noun **TRENAILS** a treenail

TRENCH noun **TRENCHES** a long narrow ditch in the ground ▫ verb **TRENCHES, TRENCHING, TRENCHED** to dig a trench or trenches

TRENCHANT adj incisive; penetrating

TRENCHER noun **TRENCHERS** a wooden platter or board that is used for cutting or serving food

TREND noun **TRENDS** a general direction or tendency ▫ verb **TRENDS, TRENDING, TRENDED** to turn or have a tendency to turn in a specified direction

TRENDY adj **TRENDIER, TRENDIEST** said of someone: following the latest fashions ▫ noun **TRENDIES** someone who is, or who tries to be, at the forefront of fashion

TREPAN noun **TREPANS** a type of small cylindrical saw that was formerly used for removing part of a bone, especially part of the skull ▫ verb **TREPANS, TREPANNING, TREPANNED** to remove (a piece of bone) with a trepan

TREPANG noun **TREPANGS** any of several types of large sea cucumber especially prized by the Chinese for their dried body walls which are used as food

TREPANNER noun **TREPANNERS** someone who trepans the skulls of others

TREPANNING noun **TREPANNINGS** an act of removing (a piece of bone) with a trepan

TREPHINE noun **TREPHINES** an improved version of the trepan ▫ verb **TREPHINES, TREPHINING, TREPHINED** to remove (a circular piece of bone) with a trephine

TREPHINER noun **TREPHINERS**

someone who trephines the skulls of others

TRESPASS verb **TRESPASSES, TRESPASSING, TRESPASSED** to enter (someone else's property) without the right or permission to do so ▫ noun **TRESPASSES** the act or process of entering someone else's property without the right or permission to do so

TRESS noun **TRESSES** a long lock or plait of hair ▫ verb **TRESSES, TRESSING, TRESSED** to arrange (hair) in tresses

TRESSY adj **TRESSIER, TRESSIEST** having or like tresses

TRESTLE noun **TRESTLES** a type of supporting framework that has a horizontal beam, the end of which rests on a pair of legs which slope outwards, eg the kind that a board can be put onto to form a table

TREVALLY noun **TREVALLIES** a name for several Australasian marine fish, especially the horse mackerels, that are used as food

TREWS plural noun trousers, especially ones that are close-fitting and made from tartan cloth

TREY noun **TREYS** the three in cards or on a dice

TRIABLE adj capable of or liable to being tried in a court of law

TRIACID adj having three replaceable hydrogen atoms

TRIAD noun **TRIADS** any group of three people or things

TRIADIC adj of or relating to a triad

TRIAL noun **TRIALS** a legal process in which someone who stands accused of a crime or misdemeanour is judged in a court of law ▫ verb **TRIALS, TRIALLING, TRIALLED** to put (a new product, etc) to the test

TRIALIST noun **TRIALISTS** a person taking part in a trial or test

TRIALLIST noun **TRIALLISTS** a trialist

TRIANGLE noun **TRIANGLES** a two-dimensional figure that has three sides and three internal angles which always total 180°

TRIATHLON noun **TRIATHLONS** an athletic contest that consists of three events, usually swimming, running and cycling

TRIATOMIC adj having three atoms in the molecule

TRIBAL adj of, relating or belonging to a tribe

TRIBALISM noun **TRIBALISMS** the

system of tribes as a way of organizing society

TRIBALLY adverb in a tribal way

TRIBE noun **TRIBES** a group of people, families, clans or communities who share social, economic, political, etc ties and often a common ancestor and who usually have a common culture, dialect and leader

TRIBESMAN noun **TRIBESMEN** a man who belongs to a tribe

TRIBOLOGY noun **TRIBOLOGIES** the branch of science and technology that deals with the study of friction, wear, lubrication, etc

TRIBRACH noun **TRIBRACHS** a type of metrical foot that consists of three unstressed or short syllables

TRIBUNAL noun **TRIBUNALS** a court of justice

TRIBUNATE noun **TRIBUNATES** the office of tribune

TRIBUNE noun **TRIBUNES** a high official who was elected by the ordinary people of ancient Rome to represent them and defend their rights, etc, especially against the interests of the wealthier patricians

TRIBUTARY noun **TRIBUTARIES** a stream or river that flows into a larger river or a lake

TRIBUTE noun **TRIBUTES** something, eg a speech, gift, etc, that is said or given as an expression of praise, thanks, admiration, affection, etc

TRICEPS noun **TRICEPSES** any muscle that is attached in three places, especially the large muscle at the back of the upper arm which allows the elbow to bend and straighten

TRICHINA noun **TRICHINAS, TRICHINAE** a type of tiny parasitic nematode worm that infests the gut of humans and other mammals

TRICHOME noun **TRICHOMES** any outgrowth, such as a prickle, hair or scale, from the epidermis of a plant

TRICHOSIS noun **TRICHOSES** any disorder or disease of the hair

TRICHROIC adj said especially of crystals: having or showing three different colours

TRICK noun **TRICKS** something which is done or said to cheat, deceive, fool or humiliate someone

◻ *verb* **TRICKS, TRICKING, TRICKED** to cheat, deceive or defraud

TRICKERY *noun* **TRICKERIES** an act, instance, or the practice, of deceiving or cheating

TRICKILY *adverb* in a tricky way

TRICKLE *verb* **TRICKLES, TRICKLING, TRICKLED** to flow or make something flow in a thin slow stream or drops ◻ *noun* **TRICKLES** a thin slow stream, flow or movement

TRICKSTER *noun* **TRICKSTERS** someone who deceives, cheats or plays tricks

TRICKY *adj* **TRICKIER, TRICKIEST** difficult to handle or do; needing skill and care

TRICLINIC *adj* said of crystalline forms: having three unequal axes that are obliquely inclined

TRICOLOR *noun* **TRICOLORS** a tricolour ◻ *adj* tricolour

TRICOLOUR *noun* **TRICOLOURS** a three-coloured flag, especially one with three equal stripes of different colours, such as the French and Irish flags ◻ *adj* having or being of three different colours

TRICORN *adj* tricorne ◻ *noun* **TRICORNS** a tricorne

TRICORNE *adj* having three horns or corners ◻ *noun* **TRICORNES** a type of three-cornered cocked hat that has the brim turned back on three sides

TRICOT *noun* **TRICOTS** a hand-knitted woollen fabric

TRICUSPID *adj* having three points or cusps ◻ *noun* **TRICUSPIDS** something, such as a tooth, leaf, etc, that has three points or cusps

TRICYCLE *noun* **TRICYCLES** a pedal-driven vehicle with two wheels at the back and one at the front ◻ *verb* **TRICYCLES, TRICYCLING, TRICYCLED** to ride a tricycle

TRIDENT *noun* **TRIDENTS** a spear with three prongs

TRIDENTAL *adj* three-pronged

TRIECIOUS *adj* said of a plant: occurring in three different sexual forms, ie male, female and hermaphrodite

TRIED past form of **try** ◻ *adj* tested and proved to be good, efficient, etc

TRIENNIAL *noun* **TRIENNIALS** a period of three years

TRIER *noun* **TRIERS** someone who perseveres at something, especially something they have

little talent or aptitude for

TRIES a form of **try**

TRIFECTA *noun* **TRIFECTAS** a betting system requiring that the horses which finish first, second and third in a race are selected in the correct order

TRIFID *adj* split or divided into three parts or lobes

TRIFLE *noun* **TRIFLES** anything that has little or no value ◻ *verb* **TRIFLES, TRIFLING, TRIFLED** to treat (someone, their feelings, etc) frivolously, insensitively or with a lack of seriousness or respect

TRIFLER *noun* **TRIFLERS** someone who trifles

TRIFLING *adj* unimportant; trivial

TRIFOCAL *noun* **TRIFOCALS** spectacles that have lenses with three different focal lengths

TRIFORIUM *noun* **TRIFORIA** a gallery or arcade that runs along the top of the arches at the sides of the nave, choir and sometimes the transepts in some large churches and cathedrals

TRIFORM *adj* having or consisting of three different parts

TRIFORMED *adj* having or consisting of three different parts

TRIG *adj* **TRIGGER, TRIGGEST** said of a person or place: smart or tidy in appearance ◻ *verb* **TRIGS, TRIGGING, TRIGGED** to smarten or tidy up

TRIGGER *noun* **TRIGGERS** a small lever which can be squeezed and released in order to set a mechanism going, especially one that fires a gun ◻ *verb* **TRIGGERS, TRIGGERING, TRIGGERED** to set (a train of events, actions, reactions, etc) in motion

TRIGLYPH *noun* **TRIGLYPHS** in the frieze of a Doric entablature: a block or tablet that has three parallel vertical grooves and which usually alternates with a metope

TRIGON *noun* **TRIGONS** a triangle

TRIGONAL *adj* belonging or relating to a trigon

TRIGRAM *noun* **TRIGRAMS** a trigraph

TRIGRAPH *noun* **TRIGRAPHS** a combination of three letters or characters that represents a single sound

TRIKE *noun* **TRIKES** a tricycle

TRILBY *noun* **TRILBIES** a soft felt hat with an indented crown and narrow brim

TRILL *noun* **TRILLS** a sound that is

produced by repeatedly playing or singing a note and a note above in rapid succession ◻ *verb* **TRILLS, TRILLING, TRILLED** to play, sing, pronounce, etc something with a trill

TRILLION *noun* **TRILLIONS** a million million

TRILLIUM *noun* **TRILLIUMS** any of several beautiful low-growing perennial spring-flowering wild plants of the lily family, native to N America, with three leaves, three green sepals and three showy petals

TRILOBATE *adj* said especially of a leaf: having or consisting of three lobes

TRILOBITE *noun* **TRILOBITES** any of several types of extinct marine arthropod which had a flat oval body with an exoskeleton that was divided lengthwise into three lobes

TRILOGY *noun* **TRILOGIES** a group of three plays, novels, poems, operas, etc that are usually related in some way, eg by theme, by having a particular character or characters in all three, etc

TRIM *verb* **TRIMS, TRIMMING, TRIMMED** to make something neat and tidy, especially by clipping ◻ *noun* **TRIMS** a haircut that is intended to neaten up an existing hairstyle rather than radically change the style ◻ *adj* **TRIMMER, TRIMMEST** in good order; neat and tidy

TRIMARAN *noun* **TRIMARANS** a boat that has three hulls side by side

TRIMER *noun* **TRIMERS** a substance whose molecules are formed from three molecules of a monomer

TRIMERIC *adj* of or relating to trimers

TRIMEROUS *adj* said of a flower, leaf, etc: having three parts or being in a group of three

TRIMESTER *noun* **TRIMESTERS** a period of three months, eg one of the three such periods of human gestation

TRIMETER *noun* **TRIMETERS** a line of verse that has three metrical feet

TRIMMED past form of **trim**

TRIMMER *noun* **TRIMMERS** someone or something that trims

TRIMMING a form of **trim** ◻ *noun* **TRIMMINGS** ribbon, lace, etc that is attached to clothes, furniture, etc for a decorative effect

For longer words, see *The Chambers Dictionary*

TRINAL *adj* of or relating to a trine

TRINARY *adj* triple; threefold

TRINE *adj* said of two heavenly bodies: separated by one third of the zodiac, and so thought to be having a favourable influence ◦ *noun* **TRINES** in astrology: a trine aspect

TRINITY *noun* **TRINITIES** the state of being three; a group of three

TRINKET *noun* **TRINKETS** a small ornament or piece of jewellery, especially one that is of little value

TRINKETRY *noun* **TRINKETRIES** trinkets collectively

TRINOMIAL *noun* **TRINOMIALS** a scientific or mathematical expression that has three parts to it, eg, in taxonomy, the genus, species and subspecies of an organism

TRIO *noun* **TRIOS** a group or set of three

TRIODE *noun* **TRIODES** a thermionic valve that has three electrodes

TRIOLET *noun* **TRIOLETS** a verse of eight lines that rhyme *abaaabab* in which the first line is repeated as the fourth and seventh lines and the second line is repeated as the eighth

TRIOXIDE *noun* **TRIOXIDES** an oxide that contains three atoms of oxygen

TRIP *verb* **TRIPS, TRIPPING, TRIPPED** to stumble or make someone stumble ◦ *noun* **TRIPS** a short journey or excursion, especially for pleasure and usually to a place and back again

TRIPE *noun* **TRIPES** parts of the stomach of a cow or sheep, used as food

TRIPLE *adj* three times as great, as much or as many ◦ *verb* **TRIPLES, TRIPLING, TRIPLED** to make or become three times as great, as much or as many ◦ *noun* **TRIPLES** an amount that is three times greater than the original, usual, etc amount

TRIPLET *noun* **TRIPLETS** one of three children or animals born to the same mother at one birth

TRIPLOID *adj* said of an organism or cell: having three times the haploid number of chromosomes ◦ *noun* **TRIPLOIDS** an organism or cell of this kind

TRIPLY *adverb* three times

TRIPOD *noun* **TRIPODS** a type of stand that has three legs and which is designed for supporting something, eg a camera, compass, etc

TRIPODAL *adj* of or relating to a tripod

TRIPOS *noun* **TRIPOSES** the final honours examination in the BA degree at Cambridge University

TRIPPED past form of **trip**

TRIPPER *noun* **TRIPPERS** someone who goes on a journey for pleasure; a tourist

TRIPPING a form of **trip**

TRIPPY *adj* **TRIPPIER, TRIPPIEST** said of music, film camerawork, etc: producing psychedelic effects that are similar to those experienced after taking a drug such as LSD

TRIPTANE *noun* **TRIPTANES** a type of powerful hydrocarbon used in high-octane aviation fuel

TRIPTYCH *noun* **TRIPTYCHS** a picture or carving that covers three panels joined together by hinges to form a single work of art, often used as an altarpiece

TRIPTYQUE *noun* **TRIPTYQUES** a type of international pass for a motor vehicle that allows it to go through customs

TRIREME *noun* **TRIREMES** a type of ancient galley, originally Greek but later also adopted by the Romans, that had three banks of rowers on each side and which was principally used as a warship

TRISECT *verb* **TRISECTS, TRISECTING, TRISECTED** to divide something into three parts, usually of equal size

TRISECTOR *noun* **TRISECTORS** a person who trisects

TRISHAW *noun* **TRISHAWS** a type of three-wheeled vehicle driven by pedals, commonly used in Asian cities as a taxi

TRISKELE *noun* **TRISKELES** a symbol that has three bent limbs or lines radiating from a common centre, eg the emblem of the Isle of Man

TRISMUS *noun* **TRISMUSES** lockjaw

TRISOMIC *adj* designating an otherwise normal diploid organism in which one chromosome type is represented three times instead of twice

TRISOMY *noun* **TRISOMIES** a condition in which there is an extra copy of a chromosome in the cell nuclei

TRISTESSE *noun* **TRISTESSES** sadness

TRITE *adj* **TRITER, TRITEST** said of a remark, phrase, etc: having no meaning or effectiveness because it has been repeated or used so often; hackneyed

TRITELY *adverb* in a trite way

TRITENESS *noun* **TRITENESSES** the state or condition of being trite

TRITHEISM *noun* **TRITHEISMS** belief in three gods, especially the belief that the Trinity is composed of three distinct gods

TRITHEIST *noun* **TRITHEISTS** someone who believes in tritheism

TRITIATE *verb* **TRITIATES, TRITIATING, TRITIATED** to introduce tritium to (a substance) and replace an ordinary atom of hydrogen with it

TRITIUM *noun* **TRITIUMS** a radioactive isotope of hydrogen that has two neutrons as well as one proton in its nucleus and which is used in fusion reactors

TRITON *noun* **TRITONS** a nucleus of a tritium atom which is composed of one proton and two neutrons

TRITONE *noun* **TRITONES** in music: an augmented fourth interval, which is comprised of three tones

TRITURATE *verb* **TRITURATES, TRITURATING, TRITURATED** to grind or rub to a powder

TRIUMPH *noun* **TRIUMPHS** a great or notable victory, success, achievement, etc ◦ *verb* **TRIUMPHS, TRIUMPHING, TRIUMPHED** to win a victory or be successful; to prevail

TRIUMPHAL *adj* of or like a triumph

TRIUMPHER *noun* **TRIUMPHERS** someone who triumphs

TRIUMPHING *noun* **TRIUMPHINGS** an act of winning a victory or being successful

TRIUMVIR *noun* **TRIUMVIRS, TRIUMVIRI** someone who shares an official position, power, authority, etc equally with two other people

TRIUNE *adj* said of a godhead, especially the Trinity: three in one

TRIVALENT *adj* having a valency of three

TRIVET *noun* **TRIVETS** a three-legged stand or bracket that can be hooked on to a grate and which is used as a support for cooking vessels over a fire

TRIVIA *plural noun* unimportant or petty matters or details

For longer words, see *The Chambers Dictionary*

TRIVIAL *adj* having or being of very little importance or value

TRIVIALLY *adverb* in a trivial way

TRIVIUM *noun* **TRIVIUMS** the three liberal arts, ie grammar, rhetoric and logic, that formed part of a medieval university course

TROCAR *noun* **TROCARS** an instrument that has a perforator enclosed in a tube, used for drawing off fluid from a body cavity, etc, eg in conditions such as oedema

TROCHAIC *adj* said of a verse, rhythm, etc: consisting mainly of trochees

TROCHAL *adj* resembling or shaped like a wheel

TROCHE *noun* **TROCHES** a flat round medicinal tablet that is usually dissolved on the tongue

TROCHEE *noun* **TROCHEES** a metrical foot of one long or stressed syllable followed by one short or unstressed one

TROCHLEA *noun* **TROCHLEAS** any bony or cartilaginous structure that functions or looks like a pulley and which has a tendon or bone articulating with it or sliding over it, eg the one at the elbow end of the humerus

TROCHLEAR *adj* of or relating to the trochlea

TROCHOID *noun* **TROCHOIDS** the curve that a fixed point on the radius, but not on the circumference, of a circle describes as the circle rolls along a straight line or along another circle

TROD a past form of **tread**

TRODDEN a past form of **tread**

TROGON *noun* **TROGONS** any of several different kinds of tropical birds that have brightly coloured plumage and long tails

TROIKA *noun* **TROIKAS** a type of Russian vehicle drawn by three horses abreast

TROLL [1] *noun* **TROLLS** an ugly, evil-tempered, human-like creature that can take the form of either a dwarf or a giant

TROLL [2] *verb* **TROLLS, TROLLING, TROLLED** to fish by trailing bait on a line through water

TROLLEY *noun* **TROLLEYS** a small cart or basket on wheels that is used for conveying luggage, shopping, etc

TROLLOP *noun* **TROLLOPS** a promiscuous or disreputable girl or woman

TROLLOPY *adj* of or like a trollop

TROMBONE *noun* **TROMBONES** a type of brass musical wind instrument that has tubes that can slide in and out of each other to alter the pitch of notes

TROMMEL *noun* **TROMMELS** a rotating cylindrical sieve used for cleaning or sizing ore

TROMP *noun* **TROMPS** a trompe

TROMPE *noun* **TROMPES** a device in a furnace that produces a blast of air by using a column of water to force air into a receiver where it is compressed before going into the blast-pipe

TROOP *noun* **TROOPS** armed forces; soldiers ◻ *verb* **TROOPS, TROOPING, TROOPED** to move as a group

TROOPER *noun* **TROOPERS** a private soldier, especially one in a cavalry or armoured unit

TROPE *noun* **TROPES** a word or expression that is used in a figurative way, eg a metaphor

TROPHY *noun* **TROPHIES** a cup, medal, plate, etc awarded as a prize for victory or success in some contest, especially in sport

TROPIC *noun* **TROPICS** either of two lines of latitude that encircle the earth (the tropic of Cancer and the tropic of Capricorn)

TROPICAL *adj* relating to, found in or originating from the tropics

TROPISM *noun* **TROPISMS** the change of direction of an organism, especially a plant or plant part, in response to an external stimulus such as gravity, light or heat

TROT *verb* **TROTS, TROTTING, TROTTED** said of a horse: to move at a steady, fairly fast pace, moving each diagonally opposite pair of legs together in a bouncy kind of walk ◻ *noun* the pace at which a horse, rider, etc moves when trotting

TROTH *noun* **TROTHS** faith or fidelity

TROTTER *noun* **TROTTERS** a pig's foot

TROUBLE *noun* **TROUBLES** distress, worry or concern ◻ *verb* **TROUBLES, TROUBLING, TROUBLED** to cause distress, worry, concern, anger, sadness, etc to

TROUBLED *adj* agitated, disturbed, etc or reflecting, showing, having experienced, etc some kind of trouble

TROUBLOUS *adj* full of troubles; disturbed

TROUGH *noun* **TROUGHS** a long narrow open container that animal feed or water is put into

TROUNCE *verb* **TROUNCES, TROUNCING, TROUNCED** to beat or defeat completely; to thrash

TROUNCING *noun* **TROUNCINGS** an act of beating or defeating completely

TROUPE *noun* **TROUPES** a group or company of performers

TROUPER *noun* **TROUPERS** a member of a troupe

TROUSERS *plural noun* an outer garment for the lower part of the body, reaching from the waist and covering each leg separately, usually down to the ankle

TROUSSEAU *noun* **TROUSSEAUS, TROUSSEAUX** a set of new clothes, linen, etc that is traditionally bought by a woman who is engaged to be married and which she keeps for her wedding and married life

TROUT *noun* **TROUTS** any of several freshwater fish of the salmon family that are highly valued as food and by anglers

TROWEL *noun* **TROWELS** a small hand-held tool with a flat blade that is used for applying and spreading mortar, plaster, etc ◻ *verb* **TROWELS, TROWELLING, TROWELLED** to use a trowel, eg to apply, spread, etc (plaster, etc)

TROY *noun* **TROYS** a system of weights used for precious metals and gemstones in which there are 12 ounces or 5 760 grains to the pound

TRUANCY *noun* **TRUANCIES** an instance of being truant, eg from school

TRUANT *noun* **TRUANTS** someone who stays away from school or work without good reason or without permission ◻ *verb* **TRUANTS, TRUANTING, TRUANTED** to be a truant

TRUCE *noun* **TRUCES** an agreement to stop fighting, usually temporarily

TRUCK *noun* **TRUCKS** an open railway wagon for carrying goods ◻ *verb* **TRUCKS, TRUCKING, TRUCKED** to put on or into a truck

TRUCKER *noun* **TRUCKERS** someone whose job is to drive a lorry, especially over long distances

TRUCKING *noun* **TRUCKINGS** the

process of transporting (goods, etc) by trucks

TRUCKLE *noun* **TRUCKLES** a low bed, usually on wheels, that can be stored away when not in use under a larger bed ◻ *verb* **TRUCKLES, TRUCKLING, TRUCKLED** to submit or give in passively or weakly

TRUCULENT *adj* aggressively defiant, quarrelsome or discourteous

TRUDGE *verb* **TRUDGES, TRUDGING, TRUDGED** to walk with slow and weary steps ◻ *noun* **TRUDGES** a long and tiring walk

TRUE *adj* **TRUER, TRUEST** agreeing with fact or reality; not false or wrong ◻ *adverb* truthfully ◻ *verb* **TRUES, TRUEING, TRUING, TRUED** to bring or restore (eg machinery) into an accurate or required position

TRUFFLE *noun* **TRUFFLES** any of several dark round fungi that grow underground and which are considered a delicacy

TRUG *noun* **TRUGS** a shallow rectangular basket with a handle, used for carrying flowers, fruit, vegetables, small garden tools, etc

TRUISM *noun* **TRUISMS** a statement that is so obviously true that it requires no discussion; a platitude

TRUISTIC *adj* of or relating to a truism

TRULY *adverb* really

TRUMEAU *noun* **TRUMEAUX** a stone pillar or a section of wall that divides a doorway, etc

TRUMP *noun* **TRUMPS** the suit of cards that is declared to be of a higher value than any other suit ◻ *verb* **TRUMPS, TRUMPING, TRUMPED** to defeat (an ordinary card, a trick with no trumps or an opponent) by playing a trump

TRUMPERY *noun* **TRUMPERIES** showy but worthless articles

TRUMPET *noun* **TRUMPETS** a brass musical wind instrument with a narrow tube and flared bell and a set of valves ◻ *verb* **TRUMPETS, TRUMPETING, TRUMPETED** said of an elephant: to make a loud cry

TRUMPETER *noun* **TRUMPETERS** someone who plays a trumpet

TRUMPETING *noun* **TRUMPETINGS** an act of making a loud cry like that of an elephant

TRUNCATE *verb* **TRUNCATES, TRUNCATING, TRUNCATED** to cut something, eg a tree, word, piece of writing, etc, so as to shorten it

TRUNCHEON *noun* **TRUNCHEONS** a short thick heavy stick that police officers carry and which is used in self-defence or for subduing the unruly, eg in riots, difficult arrest situations, etc

TRUNDLE *verb* **TRUNDLES, TRUNDLING, TRUNDLED** to move or roll, or make something move or roll, heavily and clumsily ◻ *noun* **TRUNDLES** an act or the process of trundling

TRUNK *noun* **TRUNKS** the main stem of a tree without the branches and roots

TRUSS *noun* **TRUSSES** a framework, eg of wooden or metal beams, that supports a roof, bridge, etc ◻ *verb* **TRUSSES, TRUSSING, TRUSSED** to tie up or bind tightly

TRUSSER *noun* **TRUSSERS** someone who trusses something

TRUSSING *noun* **TRUSSINGS** an act of tying up or binding tightly

TRUST *noun* **TRUSTS** belief or confidence in, or reliance on, the truth, goodness, character, power, ability, etc of someone or something ◻ *verb* **TRUSTS, TRUSTING, TRUSTED** to have confidence or faith in someone or something; to depend or rely on someone or something

TRUSTEE *noun* **TRUSTEES** someone who manages money or property for someone else

TRUSTER *noun* **TRUSTERS** someone who trusts something or someone

TRUSTFUL *adj* having confidence or trust in others

TRUSTILY *adverb* in a trusting way

TRUSTING *adj* showing trust or having a trustful nature

TRUSTY *adj* **TRUSTIER, TRUSTIEST** able to be trusted or depended on ◻ *noun* **TRUSTIES** a trusted person, especially a convict who is granted special privileges for good behaviour

TRUTH *noun* **TRUTHS** the quality or state of being true, genuine or factual

TRUTHFUL *adj* said of a person: telling the truth

TRY *verb* **TRIES, TRYING, TRIED** to attempt or make an effort; to seek to attain or achieve ◻ *noun* **TRIES** an attempt or effort

TRYING *adj* causing strain or anxiety; stretching one's patience to the limit

TRYPSIN *noun* **TRYPSINS** a digestive enzyme secreted by the pancreas and which converts proteins into peptones

TRYPTIC *adj* of or relating to trypsin

TRYSAIL *noun* **TRYSAILS** a small strong fore-and-aft sail used in stormy weather

TRYST *noun* **TRYSTS** an arrangement to meet someone, especially a lover ◻ *verb* **TRYSTS, TRYSTING, TRYSTED** to arrange a meeting, especially a secret one

TSAR *noun* **TSARS** the title of the former emperors of Russia

TSARDOM *noun* **TSARDOMS** the office or condition of being a tsar

TSAREVNA *noun* **TSAREVNAS** the daughter of a tsar

TSARINA *noun* **TSARINAS** the title of a former Russian empress

TSARISM *noun* **TSARISMS** the government of the Russian tsars

TSARIST *noun* **TSARISTS** an upholder of tsarism

TSETSE *noun* **TSETSES** any of several kinds of African fly which feed on human and animal blood and which transmit several dangerous diseases including sleeping sickness

TSUNAMI *noun* **TSUNAMIS** a type of fast-moving and often very destructive high wave caused by some form of movement in the Earth's surface, eg a volcanic eruption, landslide, etc

TUATARA *noun* **TUATARAS** a type of rare lizard-like reptile once native throughout New Zealand but now found only on certain islands off the mainland

TUB *noun* **TUBS** any of various large, low, round, wooden, metal or plastic containers, usually for holding water ◻ *verb* **TUBS, TUBBING, TUBBED** to soak, bathe, wash, etc in a tub

TUBA *noun* **TUBAS** a type of bass brass musical wind instrument that has three to five valves, a mouthpiece set at right angles, a conical bore and a wide bell that points upward

TUBAL *adj* tubular

TUBBINESS *noun* **TUBBINESSES** the state of being tubby

TUBBY *adj* **TUBBIER, TUBBIEST** said of a person: plump; podgy

TUBE *noun* **TUBES** a long hollow cylinder which can be flexible or rigid and which is designed for holding or conveying air, liquids, etc ◻ verb **TUBES, TUBING, TUBED** to fit with a tube or tubes

TUBECTOMY noun **TUBECTOMIES** the removal of a Fallopian tube

TUBELESS adj without a tube or tubes

TUBELIKE adj like a tube, eg in shape

TUBER noun **TUBERS** a swollen rounded underground stem or rhizome, such as that of the potato, where food is stored allowing the plant to survive from one growing season to the next

TUBERCLE noun **TUBERCLES** a small round swelling or lump, eg on a bone

TUBERCLED adj having tubercles

TUBEROSE noun **TUBEROSES** a plant that has large creamy-white funnel-shaped flowers and a tuberous root and which is valued for its strong sweet perfume

TUBEROUS adj having tubers

TUBFUL noun **TUBFULS** the amount a tub can hold

TUBIFORM adj shaped like a tube

TUBING noun **TUBINGS** a length of tube or a system of tubes

TUBULAR adj made or consisting of tubes or tube-shaped pieces

TUBULE noun **TUBULES** a small tube in the body of an animal or plant

TUCK verb **TUCKS, TUCKING, TUCKED** to push or fold something into a specified position ◻ noun **TUCKS** a flat pleat or fold sewn into a garment or piece of material, especially one that shortens it, makes it tighter or has a decorative effect

TUCKER¹ noun **TUCKERS** someone or something that tucks

TUCKER² verb **TUCKERS, TUCKERING, TUCKERED** to tire

TUCKERBAG noun **TUCKERBAGS** a bag used for carrying food

TUCKERBOX noun **TUCKERBOXES** a box used for carrying food

TUFA noun **TUFAS** a type of white spongy porous rock that forms in a calcium carbonate incrustation in areas around springs, streams, etc that are rich in lime

TUFACEOUS adj of or relating to tufa

TUFF noun **TUFFS** rock that is largely composed of fine volcanic fragments and dust

TUFFET noun **TUFFETS** a small grassy mound

TUFT noun **TUFTS** a small bunch or clump of grass, hair, feathers, wool, etc attached or growing together at the base ◻ verb **TUFTS, TUFTING, TUFTED** to grow or form in a tuft or tufts

TUFTED adj having, forming or growing in a tuft or tufts

TUFTING noun **TUFTINGS** a tuft

TUFTY adj **TUFTIER, TUFTIEST** having tufts

TUG verb **TUGS, TUGGING, TUGGED** to pull sharply or strongly ◻ noun **TUGS** a strong sharp pull

TUGGER noun **TUGGERS** someone who tugs

TUGGING noun **TUGGINGS** an act of pulling sharply or strongly

TUGRIK noun **TUGRIKS** the standard unit of currency of Mongolia

TUI noun **TUIS** a type of New Zealand honey-eater that has glossy black feathers with a distinctive tuft of white ones at its throat, renowned as a mimic of human voices and of other songbirds

TUITION noun **TUITIONS** teaching or instruction, especially when paid for, or in a college or university

TUITIONAL adj of or relating to tuition

TULAREMIA noun **TULAREMIAS** a type of infectious disease that affects rodents and rabbits and which can be transmitted to humans by infected insects or by handling infected animals or their flesh

TULIP noun **TULIPS** any of several spring-flowering perennial plants which each have an underground bulb and produce a single cup-shaped flower on a long stem

TULLE noun **TULLES** a delicate thin netted cloth made of silk or rayon that was popularly used, especially in the 19c, for making veils, dresses, hats, etc

TUM noun **TUMS** the stomach

TUMBLE verb **TUMBLES, TUMBLING, TUMBLED** to fall or make someone or something fall headlong, especially suddenly or clumsily ◻ noun **TUMBLES** an act of tumbling

TUMBLER noun **TUMBLERS** a flat-bottomed drinking cup without a stem or handle, usually of glass or plastic

TUMBLING noun **TUMBLINGS** an

act of falling or making someone or something fall headlong

TUMBREL noun **TUMBRELS** a two-wheeled cart that can be tipped over backwards to empty its load

TUMBRIL noun **TUMBRILS** a tumbrel

TUMEFY verb **TUMEFIES, TUMEFYING, TUMEFIED** to swell or puff up

TUMESCENT adj swollen or becoming swollen, especially with blood as a response to sexual stimulation

TUMID adj said of an organ or body part: swollen, enlarged or bulging, especially abnormally so

TUMIDITY noun **TUMIDITIES** the quality or condition of being swollen

TUMIDLY adverb in a tumid way

TUMIDNESS noun **TUMIDNESSES** the state of being tumid

TUMMY noun **TUMMIES** a name for the stomach

TUMOR noun **TUMORS** a tumour

TUMOROUS adj having or like a tumour

TUMOUR noun **TUMOURS** an abnormal growth of benign or malignant cells that develops in, or on the surface of, normal body tissue

TUMULAR adj of or like a tumulus

TUMULT noun **TUMULTS** a great or confused noise, eg as made by a crowd; an uproar

TUMULUS noun **TUMULI** an ancient burial mound or barrow

TUN noun **TUNS** a large cask for holding liquid, eg ale, beer or wine ◻ verb **TUNS, TUNNING, TUNNED** to put or store (liquid, eg ale, beer or wine) in a tun

TUNA noun **TUNAS** any of several large marine fish that live in warm and tropical seas and are related to the mackerel

TUNABLE adj capable of being tuned

TUNDRA noun **TUNDRAS** any of the vast relatively flat treeless zones that lie to the south of the polar ice cap in America and Eurasia where the subsoil is permanently frozen

TUNE noun **TUNES** a pleasing succession of musical notes; a melody ◻ verb **TUNES, TUNING, TUNED** to adjust (a musical instrument or instruments, their keys or strings, etc) to the correct or a standard pitch

TUNEFUL adj having a good, clear, pleasant, etc tune; melodious
TUNEFULLY adverb in a tuneful way
TUNELESS adj lacking a good, pleasant, etc tune; not melodious
TUNER noun **TUNERS** someone whose job is tuning instruments, especially pianos
TUNGSTEN noun **TUNGSTENS** a very hard silvery-white metallic element that occurs naturally in scheelite and is notable for its very high melting point
TUNIC noun **TUNICS** a close-fitting, usually belted jacket which forms part of the uniform of the military, police, security services, etc
TUNICKED adj wearing a tunic
TUNICLE noun **TUNICLES** a garment similar to the dalmatic that a subdeacon wears over the alb
TUNING noun **TUNINGS** an act of correcting the pitch of eg a piano
TUNNED past form of **tun**
TUNNEL noun **TUNNELS** a constructed underground passage through or under some obstruction, eg a hill, river, road, etc, allowing access for pedestrians, vehicles, trains, etc ◻ verb **TUNNELS, TUNNELLING, TUNNELING, TUNNELLED, TUNNELED** to make a tunnel through, under, etc (a hill, river, road, etc)
TUNNELLER noun **TUNNELLERS** a person, animal or implement that tunnels
TUNNELLING noun **TUNNELLINGS** an act of making a tunnel through, under, etc
TUNNING a form of **tun**
TUNNY noun **TUNNIES** tuna
TUP noun **TUPS** a ram ◻ verb **TUPS, TUPPING, TUPPED** said of a ram: to copulate with (a ewe)
TUPELO noun **TUPELOS** any of several large deciduous N American trees, eg the American gum tree, that grow in the swamps and on the river banks in the southern states
TUPIK noun **TUPIKS** a type of traditional seal or caribou skin tent or hut that Inuits in the Canadian Arctic use for shelter during the summer
TUPPENCE noun **TUPPENCES** twopence
TUPPENNY adj twopenny

TUQUE noun **TUQUES** a type of Canadian tubular cap that is closed at both ends and which is worn by tucking one end inside itself to form the part where the head goes while the other end is left free
TURACO noun **TURACOS** any of several varieties of large African fruit-eating birds that are noted for the vivid scarlets, blues and greens of their feathers and their prominent crests
TURBAN noun **TURBANS** a type of headdress formed by wrapping a long cloth sash around the head or a cap and which is worn especially by Muslim and Sikh men
TURBANED adj wearing a turban
TURBARY noun **TURBARIES** an area of land that has been designated as a place where peat may be dug
TURBID adj said of liquid, etc: cloudy; not clear
TURBIDITY noun **TURBIDITIES** the quality or state of being turbid
TURBIDLY adverb in a turbid way
TURBINAL noun **TURBINALS** a scroll-like bone of the nose
TURBINATE adj like a spinning top
TURBINE noun **TURBINES** any of several types of power-generating machine that have a rotating wheel driven by water, steam, gas, etc
TURBIT noun **TURBITS** a fancy variety of domestic pigeon that has a squat body, a short beak and a frill around its neck and breast
TURBO noun **TURBOS** a turbocharger
TURBOFAN noun **TURBOFANS** a jet engine driven by a gas turbine in which part of the power developed is used to drive a fan which blows air out of the exhaust and so increases thrust
TURBOJET noun **TURBOJETS** a type of gas turbine that uses exhaust gases to provide the propulsive thrust in an aircraft
TURBOPROP noun **TURBOPROPS** a jet engine in which the turbine drives a propeller
TURBOT noun **TURBOTS** a large flatfish that has bony tubercles instead of scales and eyes on the left side of its head and which is highly valued as food
TURBULENT adj violently disturbed; wild; unruly

TUREEN noun **TUREENS** a large deep dish with a cover that food, especially soup or vegetables, is served from at table
TURF noun **TURFS, TURVES** the surface of an area of grassland that consists of a layer of grass, weeds, matted roots, etc plus the surrounding earth ◻ verb **TURFS, TURFING, TURFED** to cover (an area of land, garden, etc) with turf
TURFINESS noun **TURFINESSES** the state of being turfy
TURFY adj **TURFIER, TURFIEST** resembling, covered in, associated with or consisting of turf
TURGID adj **TURGIDER, TURGIDEST** swollen; inflated or distended
TURGIDITY noun **TURGIDITIES** the state or condition of being turgid
TURGIDLY adverb in a turgid way
TURGOR noun **TURGORS** the rigidity of a plant's cells
TURION noun **TURIONS** an underground bud that gives rise to a new shoot
TURKEY noun **TURKEYS** a large gamebird, now farmed in most parts of the world, with dark plumage with a greenish sheen and a bald blue or red head with red wattles
TURMERIC noun **TURMERICS** an E Indian plant of the ginger family
TURMOIL noun **TURMOILS** wild confusion, agitation or disorder; upheaval
TURN verb **TURNS, TURNING, TURNED** to move or go round in a circle or with a circular movement ◻ noun **TURNS** an act, instance or the process of turning; a complete or partial rotation
TURNABOUT noun **TURNABOUTS** an act of turning to face the opposite way
TURNCOAT noun **TURNCOATS** someone who turns against or leaves his or her party, principles, etc and joins the opposing side
TURNER noun **TURNERS** someone or something that turns
TURNING noun **TURNINGS** a place where one road branches off from another
TURNIP noun **TURNIPS** a plant of the cabbage family which has a large round white or yellowish root
TURNKEY noun **TURNKEYS** someone who keeps the keys in a prison; a gaoler
TURNOVER noun **TURNOVERS** the

total value of sales in a business during a certain time

TURNPIKE *noun* **TURNPIKES** a gate or barrier that goes across a road or bridge and which is lifted only after travellers have paid the toll

TURNSTILE *noun* **TURNSTILES** a gate that has revolving metal arms which allow only one person to pass through at a time, especially one for controlling admissions, eg to a football ground, etc

TURNTABLE *noun* **TURNTABLES** the revolving platform on a record-player where records are placed

TURPETH *noun* **TURPETHS** an E Indian plant of the morning glory family

TURPITUDE *noun* **TURPITUDES** vileness; depravity

TURQUOISE *noun* **TURQUOISES** an opaque semi-precious stone that comes in varying shades of light blue or greenish blue and which consists of hydrated copper aluminium phosphate

TURRET *noun* **TURRETS** a small tower, usually rounded in shape and projecting from a wall of a castle or other building

TURRETED *adj* having turrets

TURTLE *noun* **TURTLES** any of several marine and freshwater reptiles with bodies enclosed in a bony shell similar to that of the tortoises, but which have flippers or webbed toes, making them excellent swimmers

TURVES a plural of **turf**

TUSCHE *noun* **TUSCHES** a greasy black water-repellent liquid used for drawing the design in lithography and as the blocking medium in silk-screen printing

TUSH *noun* **TUSHES** a horse's canine tooth

TUSK *noun* **TUSKS** one of a pair of long, curved, pointed teeth which project from the mouth area of certain animals, eg the elephant, walrus, narwhal and wild boar

TUSKED *adj* having tusks

TUSKER *noun* **TUSKERS** an elephant, walrus, wild boar, etc that has especially well-developed tusks

TUSKLESS *adj* without tusks

TUSSER *noun* **TUSSERS** a type of coarse brownish silk

TUSSIVE *adj* relating or referring to, or caused by, a cough

TUSSLE *noun* **TUSSLES** a verbal or physical struggle or fight □ *verb*

TUSSLES, TUSSLING, TUSSLED to engage in a tussle

TUSSOCK *noun* **TUSSOCKS** a clump of grass or other vegetation

TUSSOCKY *adj* having tussocks

TUSSORE *noun* **TUSSORES** tusser

TUT *verb* **TUTS, TUTTING, TUTTED** to express mild disapproval, annoyance or rebuke by saying 'tut' or 'tut-tut' □ *noun* **TUTS** an act of saying 'tut' or 'tut-tut'

TUTEE *noun* **TUTEES** someone who is tutored

TUTELAGE *noun* **TUTELAGES** the state or office of being a guardian

TUTELAR *adj* tutelary

TUTELARY *adj* having the power or role of a guardian

TUTOR *noun* **TUTORS** a university or college teacher who teaches undergraduate students individually or in small groups, or who is responsible for the general welfare and progress of a certain number of students □ *verb* **TUTORS, TUTORING, TUTORED** to act or work as a tutor to someone

TUTORAGE *noun* **TUTORAGES** tutorship

TUTORIAL *noun* **TUTORIALS** a period of instruction when a university or college tutor and an individual student or small group of students meet, usually to discuss an assignment, lectures, etc

TUTORING *noun* **TUTORINGS** an act of working as a tutor to someone

TUTORSHIP *noun* **TUTORSHIPS** tutoring; charge for tutoring

TUTSAN *noun* **TUTSANS** a plant of the St John's wort family, formerly used in healing wounds, etc

TUTTI *adverb* with all the instruments and singers together □ *noun* **TUTTIS** a passage to be played or sung by all the instruments and singers together

TUTTY *noun* **TUTTIES** impure zinc oxide that collects in the flues of zinc-smelting furnaces and which is used in powder form as a polish

TUTU *noun* **TUTUS** a very short protruding skirt that consists of layers of stiffened frills of net, etc and is worn by female ballet dancers

TUX *noun* **TUXES** short for *tuxedo*

TUXEDO *noun* **TUXEDOS, TUXEDOES** an evening suit with a dinner-jacket

TUYÈRE *noun* **TUYÈRES** a nozzle that the blast of air is forced through in a forge or furnace

TWA *noun* **TWAS** Scots form of *two* □ *adj* Scots form of *two*

TWADDLE *noun* **TWADDLES** nonsense; senseless or silly writing or talk □ *verb* **TWADDLES, TWADDLING, TWADDLED** to speak or write nonsense

TWADDLER *noun* **TWADDLERS** someone who twaddles

TWADDLING *noun* **TWADDLINGS** an act of speaking or writing nonsense

TWADDLY *adj* **TWADDLIER, TWADDLIEST** of or like twaddle; tedious; meaningless

TWAIN *adj* two □ *noun* **TWAINS** a couple or pair

TWANG *noun* **TWANGS** a sharp ringing sound like that produced by plucking a tightly-stretched string or wire □ *verb* **TWANGS, TWANGING, TWANGED** to make or cause to make a twang

TWANGING *noun* **TWANGINGS** an act of making or causing to make a twang

TWANGY *adj* **TWANGIER, TWANGIEST** twanging

TWEAK *verb* **TWEAKS, TWEAKING, TWEAKED** to get hold of and pull or twist something with a sudden jerk □ *noun* **TWEAKS** an act or instance, or the process, of tweaking

TWEE *adj* **TWEER, TWEEST** affectedly or pretentiously pretty, sweet, cute, quaint, sentimental, etc

TWEED *noun* **TWEEDS** a thick roughish woollen cloth, usually with coloured flecks, used for making suits, jackets, skirts, etc and often identified with the town, area, etc where it is produced

TWEEDY *adj* **TWEEDIER, TWEEDIEST** relating to or like tweed

TWEELY *adverb* in a twee way

TWEENESS *noun* **TWEENESSES** the state of being twee; something that is twee

TWEET *noun* **TWEETS** a melodious chirping sound made by a small bird □ *verb* **TWEETS, TWEETING, TWEETED** to chirp melodiously

TWEETER *noun* **TWEETERS** a loudspeaker that is designed to reproduce high-frequency sounds

TWEEZERS *plural noun* a small

pair of pincers for pulling out individual hairs, holding small objects, etc
TWELFTH adj in counting: next after eleventh ❑ noun **TWELFTHS** one of twelve equal parts ❑ adverb used to introduce the twelfth point in a list
TWELFTHLY adverb twelfth
TWELVE noun **TWELVES** the cardinal number 12 ❑ adj totalling 12
TWELVEMO noun **TWELVEMOS** in printing and publishing: a book formed of sheets folded so as to make twelve leaves
TWENTIES plural noun the period of time between one's 20th and 30th birthdays
TWENTIETH adj in counting: next after nineteenth ❑ noun **TWENTIETHS** one of twenty equal parts
TWENTY noun **TWENTIES** the cardinal number 20 ❑ adj totalling 20
TWENTYISH adj about twenty
TWERP noun **TWERPS** a silly or contemptible person
TWIBILL noun **TWIBILLS** a battle-axe that has a double blade
TWICE adverb two times
TWIDDLE verb **TWIDDLES, TWIDDLING, TWIDDLED** to twist something round and round ❑ noun **TWIDDLES** an act of twiddling
TWIDDLER noun **TWIDDLERS** someone who twiddles
TWIDDLING noun **TWIDDLINGS** an act of twisting something round and round
TWIDDLY adj **TWIDDLIER, TWIDDLIEST** fiddly; twisted
TWIG [1] noun **TWIGS** a small shoot or branch of a tree, bush, etc
TWIG [2] verb **TWIGS, TWIGGING, TWIGGED** to understand (a joke, situation, etc), especially suddenly
TWIGGY adj **TWIGGIER, TWIGGIEST** of or like a twig, especially in being thin
TWILIGHT noun **TWILIGHTS** the faint diffused light in the sky when the sun is just below the horizon, especially the kind that can be seen just after sunset, but also the kind that can be seen just before sunrise ❑ adj belonging, relating or referring to, or occurring at, twilight ❑ verb **TWILIGHTS, TWILIGHTING, TWILIT, TWILIGHTED** to illuminate faintly

TWILIGHTED adj twilit
TWILIT adj lit by or as if by twilight
TWILL noun **TWILLS** a strong fabric woven in such a way that it has a surface pattern of parallel diagonal ridges ❑ verb **TWILLS, TWILLING, TWILLED** to weave (fabric) with a twill
TWIN noun **TWINS** either of two people or animals that are born at the same time and have the same mother ❑ adj being one of a pair or consisting of very similar or closely connected parts ❑ verb **TWINS, TWINNING, TWINNED** to bring or come together closely or intimately
TWINE noun **TWINES** strong string or cord made from two or more threads of cotton, hemp, etc twisted together ❑ verb **TWINES, TWINING, TWINED** to twist together; to interweave
TWINGE noun **TWINGES** a sudden sharp stabbing or shooting pain ❑ verb **TWINGES, TWINGING, TWINGED** to feel or make someone feel a sharp pain or pang
TWINING noun **TWININGS** an act of twisting together
TWININGLY adverb in a twining or twisting way
TWINKLE verb **TWINKLES, TWINKLING, TWINKLED** said of a star, etc: to shine with a bright, flickering light ❑ noun **TWINKLES** a gleam or sparkle in the eyes
TWINKLER noun **TWINKLERS** a person or thing that twinkles
TWINKLING noun **TWINKLINGS** an act of shining with a bright, flickering light
TWINNING noun **TWINNINGS** an act of bringing or coming together closely or intimately
TWINSET noun **TWINSETS** a woman's matching sweater and cardigan
TWINY adj **TWINIER, TWINIEST** of or like twine
TWIRL verb **TWIRLS, TWIRLING, TWIRLED** to turn, spin or twist round ❑ noun **TWIRLS** an act of twirling
TWIRLER noun **TWIRLERS** someone who twirls
TWIRLY adj **TWIRLIER, TWIRLIEST** curly; spinning
TWIRP noun **TWIRPS** a twerp
TWIST verb **TWISTS, TWISTING, TWISTED** to wind or turn round, especially by moving only a single part or by moving different parts in opposite directions ❑ noun

TWISTS an act or the process of twisting
TWISTABLE adj capable of being twisted
TWISTED adj full of twists; coiled or distorted
TWISTER noun **TWISTERS** a dishonest or deceiving person; a swindler
TWISTY adj **TWISTIER, TWISTIEST** full of twists or turns
TWIT [1] noun **TWITS** a fool or idiot
TWIT [2] verb **TWITS, TWITTING, TWITTED** to tease, reproach or criticize, usually with good humour or affection
TWITCH verb **TWITCHES, TWITCHING, TWITCHED** said of a muscle, limb, etc: to move involuntarily with a spasm ❑ noun **TWITCHES** a sudden involuntary spasm of a muscle, limb, etc
TWITCHER noun **TWITCHERS** someone or something that twitches
TWITCHING noun **TWITCHINGS** an act of moving involuntarily with a spasm
TWITCHY adj **TWITCHIER, TWITCHIEST** nervous, anxious or restless
TWITE noun **TWITES** a small brown moorland bird of the linnet family that lives in N Britain and Scandinavia, migrating south in large flocks in the summer
TWITTER noun **TWITTERS** a light repeated chirping sound made by especially small birds ❑ verb **TWITTERS, TWITTERING, TWITTERED** said especially of a bird: to make a light repeated chirping sound or similar high-pitched trembling sounds
TWITTERER noun **TWITTERERS** someone or something that twitters
TWITTERING noun **TWITTERINGS** an act of making a light repeated chirping sound
TWITTERY adj twittering
TWIZZLE verb **TWIZZLES, TWIZZLING, TWIZZLED** to spin round rapidly ❑ noun **TWIZZLES** a twist or turn
TWO noun **TWOS** the cardinal number 2 ❑ adj totalling two
TWOFOLD adj twice as much or as many ❑ adverb by twice as much
TWOPENCE noun **TWOPENCES** the sum of two pence, especially before the introduction of decimal coinage

TWOPENNY adj worth or costing twopence

TWOSOME noun **TWOSOMES** a game, dance, etc for two people

TWP adj a Welsh word for dim-witted, stupid

TWYER noun **TWYERS** a tuyère

TYCOON noun **TYCOONS** someone who has power and influence, eg in business, industry, politics, etc; a magnate

TYE noun **TYES** a trough for washing ore □ verb **TYES, TYEING, TYED** to wash in a tye

TYG noun **TYGS** an old drinking-cup with two or more handles

TYING a form of **tie**

TYKE noun **TYKES** a dog, especially a mongrel

TYKISH adj of or like a tyke

TYLOPOD noun **TYLOPODS** any ruminant mammal, such as the camel or llama, that has pads on its feet rather than hoofs

TYMBAL noun **TYMBALS** a timbal

TYMPAN noun **TYMPANS** a device in a printing press that fits between the platen and the sheet that is to be printed, so as to soften and equalize the pressure

TYMPANI plural noun timpani

TYMPANIC adj belonging or relating to, or in the region of, the eardrum

TYMPANIST noun **TYMPANIST** a timpanist

TYMPANUM noun **TYMPANA** the cavity of the middle ear

TYPE noun **TYPES** a class or group of people, animals or things which share similar characteristics; a kind or variety □ verb **TYPES, TYPING, TYPED** to write (words, text, etc) using a typewriter or word processor

TYPECAST verb **TYPECASTS, TYPECASTING, TYPECAST** to put (an actor or actress) regularly in the same kind of part, usually because they have had previous box-office success in similar roles or because they fit the physical requirements of the role □ adj said of an actor or actress: regularly cast in the same kind of part

TYPESET verb **TYPESETS, TYPESETTING, TYPESET** to arrange (type) or set (a page, etc) in type ready for printing

TYPEWRITE verb **TYPEWRITES, TYPEWRITING, TYPEWROTE, TYPEWRITTEN** to print or copy with a typewriter

TYPEWRITING noun **TYPEWRITINGS** text written with a typewriter

TYPEWRITTEN adj said of a document, etc: produced using a typewriter

TYPHLITIC adj of or relating to typhlitis

TYPHLITIS noun **TYPHLITISES** inflammation of the caecum

TYPHOID noun **TYPHOIDS** a serious and sometimes fatal infection of the digestive system, caught by eating or drinking contaminated food and drinking water

TYPHOIDAL adj of or relating to typhoid

TYPHONIC adj of or relating to a typhoon

TYPHOON noun **TYPHOONS** a cyclonic tropical storm that occurs over the W Pacific Ocean, the South China Sea and the surrounding areas, usually during the period from July to October

TYPHOUS adj of or relating to typhus

TYPHUS noun **TYPHUSES** any of a group of infectious diseases that are transmitted to humans by lice carried by rodents

TYPICAL adj having or showing the usual features, traits, etc, or being a characteristic or representative example

TYPICALLY adverb in a typical way

TYPIFIER noun **TYPIFIERS** a symbol of something

TYPIFY verb **TYPIFIES, TYPIFYING, TYPIFIED** to be an excellent or characteristic example of something

TYPING noun **TYPINGS** the act or process of using a typewriter

TYPIST noun **TYPISTS** someone whose job is to type

TYPO noun **TYPOS** an error made in the typesetting of a text, such as the use of one letter in place of another

TYRANNIC adj belonging or relating to, or like, a tyrant

TYRANNISE verb **TYRANNISES, TYRANNISING, TYRANNISED** to tyrannize

TYRANNIZE verb **TYRANNIZES, TYRANNIZING, TYRANNIZED** to rule or treat in a cruel, unjust and oppressive way

TYRANNOUS adj tyrannic

TYRANNY noun **TYRANNIES** the use of cruelty, injustice, oppression, etc to enforce authority or power

TYRANT noun **TYRANTS** a cruel, unjust and oppressive ruler with absolute power

TYRE noun **TYRES** a rubber ring that fits around the outside edge of the wheel of a vehicle such as a bicycle, pram, wheelbarrow, etc to give traction and help minimize the effect of bumps and hollows in road surfaces

TYRO noun **TYROES, TYROS** a novice or beginner

TYROSINE noun **TYROSINES** an amino acid found in proteins and which is the precursor of certain hormones

TZAR noun **TZARS** a tsar

TZATZIKI noun **TZATZIKIS** a Greek dip made of yoghurt and chopped cucumber, flavoured with mint and garlic

UBIETY *noun* **UBIETIES** the state or condition of being in a definite place; location

UBIQUE *adverb* Latin word for *everywhere*

UBIQUITY *noun* **UBIQUITIES** existence everywhere at the same time; omnipresence

UDDER *noun* **UDDERS** in certain mammals, eg cows, goats, etc: the bag-like structure, with two or more teats, containing the mammary glands that secrete milk

UDO *noun* **UDOS** a Japanese ivy

UDOMETER *noun* **UDOMETERS** a rain-gauge

UDS *exclamation* an old exclamation meaning *God's* or *God save*

UEY *noun* **UEYS** a U-turn

UFO *noun* **UFOS** an unidentified flying object

UFOLOGIST *noun* **UFOLOGISTS** someone who studies ufos

UFOLOGY *noun* **UFOLOGIES** the study of ufos

UG *verb* **UGS, UGGING, UGGED** to loath

UGH *exclamation* expressing dislike or disgust ◻ *noun* **UGHS** used to represent the sound of a cough or grunt

UGLIFY *verb* **UGLIFIES, UGLIFYING, UGLIFIED** to make something ugly; to disfigure it

UGLILY *adverb* in an ugly way

UGLINESS *noun* **UGLINESSES** the quality or state of being ugly

UGLY *adj* **UGLIER, UGLIEST** unpleasant to look at; extremely unattractive

UGS a form of **ug**

UHLAN *noun* **UHLANS** in certain European armies, especially the Polish or, later, German armies: a light cavalryman or lancer

UHURU *noun* **UHURUS** freedom, eg from slavery

UITLANDER *noun* **UITLANDERS** a foreigner, originally a British person who went to the Transvaal or Orange Free State before the Boer War of 1899–1902

UKASE *noun* **UKASES** a command issued by a supreme ruler, especially the Tsar in Imperial Russia

UKE *noun* **UKES** a ukulele

UKELELE *noun* **UKELELES** a ukulele

UKULELE *noun* **UKULELES** a small guitar, usually with four strings, that developed in Hawaii from an earlier Portuguese instrument

ULCER *noun* **ULCERS** a persistent open sore, often accompanied by inflammation, on the surface of the skin or of the mucous membranes lining a body cavity

ULCERATE *verb* **ULCERATES, ULCERATING, ULCERATED** to form or cause an ulcer on or in a part of the body

ULCERED *adj* having ulcers

ULCEROUS *adj* characterized by ulcers

ULE *noun* **ULES** a Central American rubber tree

ULEMA *noun* **ULEMAS** in a Muslim country or society: the body of professional theologians who are regarded as the authority on religious law

ULEX *noun* **ULEXES** a plant of the gorse genus

ULLAGE *noun* **ULLAGES** the amount of wine, etc by which a container falls short of being full

ULNA *noun* **ULNAE** the thinner and longer of the two bones of the human forearm

ULNAR *adj* of or relating to the ulna

ULSTER *noun* **ULSTERS** a man's loose heavy double-breasted overcoat, often worn with a belt

ULTERIOR *adj* said of motives, etc: beyond or other than what is apparent or admitted

ULTIMA *noun* **ULTIMAS** the last syllable of a word

ULTIMATE *adj* last or final in a series or process ◻ *noun* **ULTIMATES** the final point; the end or conclusion

ULTIMATUM *noun* **ULTIMATA** in a dispute, negotiations, etc: a final statement from one of the parties involved to another, declaring an intention to take hostile action unless specified conditions are fulfilled

ULTIMO *adj* used mainly in formal correspondence: of or during last month

ULTRA *noun* **ULTRAS** someone who holds extreme opinions, especially in political or religious matters

ULTRAISM *noun* **ULTRAISMS** extreme principle, opinion or measure

ULTRAIST *noun* **ULTRAISTS** someone with extreme principles or opinions

ULULANT *adj* ululating

ULULATE *verb* **ULULATES, ULULATING, ULULATED** to howl, wail or screech

ULZIE *noun* **ULZIES** an obsolete Scots form of *oil*

UM *exclamation* expressing hesitation, uncertainty, etc

UMBEL *noun* **UMBELS** a flower-head in which a cluster of flowers with stalks of the same length arise from the same point on the main stem, such as cow parsley and hogweed

UMBELLAR *adj* of, relating to or like an umbel

UMBELLATE *adj* having umbels

UMBER *noun* **UMBERS** a dark yellowish-brown earthy mineral containing oxides of iron and manganese, used to make pigments

UMBILICAL *adj* relating to the umbilicus or the umbilical cord

UMBILICUS *noun* **UMBILICUSES** the navel

UMBLES *plural noun* the entrails (the liver, heart, lungs, etc) of an animal, especially a deer

UMBO *noun* **UMBOS, UMBONES** the central boss of a shield

UMBONAL *adj* of or relating to an umbo

UMBONATE *adj* in the form of an umbo; having umbos

UMBRA *noun* **UMBRAS** the central and darkest part of a shadow

UMBRAGE *noun* **UMBRAGES** annoyance; offence

UMBRAL *adj* of or relating to an umbra

UMBRELLA *noun* **UMBRELLAS** a device carried to give shelter from rain, etc, consisting of a rounded fabric canopy supported on a lightweight, usually metal, collapsible framework of ribs fitted around a central stick or handle

UMIAK *noun* **UMIAKS** a large open boat made from a wooden frame covered with stretched skins, typically paddled by women

UMLAUT *noun* **UMLAUTS** in Germanic languages: a mark consisting of two dots placed above a vowel

UMPIRE *noun* **UMPIRES** an impartial person who supervises play in various sports, eg cricket and tennis, enforcing the rules and deciding disputes □ *verb* **UMPIRES, UMPIRING, UMPIRED** to act as umpire in a match, dispute, etc

UMPTEEN *adj* very many; innumerable

UMPTEENTH *adj* latest or last of very many

UN *noun* **UNS** one

UNABASHED *adj* not abashed

UNABATED *adj* not abated

UNABLE *adj* not able; not having sufficient strength, skill or authority (to do something)

UNACTABLE *adj* unable to be acted; not suitable for theatrical performance

UNACTED *adj* not acted

UNADAPTED *adj* not adapted

UNADOPTED *adj* not adopted

UNADORNED *adj* not adorned

UNADVISED *adj* not advised; without advice

UNAFRAID *adj* not afraid

UNAIDED *adj* without help

UNAIMED *adj* not aimed

UNAIRED *adj* not aired

UNALIGNED *adj* not aligned

UNALIKE *adj* not alike

UNALLAYED *adj* no less intense

UNALLIED *adj* not allied

UNALLOYED *adj* not alloyed; pure

UNALTERED *adj* not altered

UNAMAZED *adj* not amazed

UNAMENDED *adj* not amended

UNAMIABLE *adj* not amiable, not friendly

UNAMUSED *adj* not amused

UNAMUSING *adj* not amusing

UNANIMITY *noun* **UNANIMITIES** the state of being unanimous; unanimous agreement

UNANIMOUS *adj* all in complete agreement; of one mind

UNAPPLIED *adj* not applied

UNAPT *adj* not fitted for something; unsuitable

UNAPTLY *adverb* in an unapt way

UNAPTNESS *noun* **UNAPTNESSES** the state of being unapt

UNARMED *adj* not armed; without weapons

UNASHAMED *adj* not ashamed

UNASKED *adj* without having been asked

UNATONED *adj* not atoned

UNAU *noun* **UNAUS** the two-toed sloth

UNAVOWED *adj* not avowed

UNAWARE *adj* with no knowledge (of something); not aware or conscious (of it)

UNAWARES *adverb* unexpectedly; by surprise

UNAWED *adj* not awed

UNBACKED *adj* said eg of a chair: without a back

UNBALANCE *verb* **UNBALANCES, UNBALANCING, UNBALANCED** to throw someone or something off balance □ *noun* **UNBALANCES** lack of balance or (mental) stability

UNBALANCED *adj* not in a state of physical balance

UNBANKED *adj* not banked

UNBAR *verb* **UNBARS, UNBARRING, UNBARRED** to remove a bar or bars from (a door, gate, etc)

UNBEATEN *adj* not beaten, especially not defeated or surpassed

UNBEKNOWN *adverb* unknown to someone; without their knowledge

UNBELIEF *noun* **UNBELIEFS** disbelief; lack of belief, especially of religious belief

UNBELIEVE *verb* **UNBELIEVES, UNBELIEVING, UNBELIEVED** to disbelieve; to refrain from believing

UNBELIEVING *adj* not believing, especially in a particular religion; without belief

UNBELOVED *adj* not beloved

UNBELT *verb* **UNBELTS, UNBELTING, UNBELTED** to undo or remove the belt of

UNBELTED *adj* with the belt undone or removed

UNBEND *verb* **UNBENDS, UNBENDING, UNBENDED** to release the tension from or unstring (a bow)

UNBENDING *adj* not bending; unyielding or inflexible

UNBENT *adj* not bent or bowed

UNBIASED *adj* not biased; unprejudiced or impartial

UNBIASSED *adj* unbiased

UNBIDDEN *adj* not commanded or ordered; spontaneous or voluntary

UNBIND *verb* **UNBINDS, UNBINDING, UNBOUND** to release or free someone from a bond or restraint

UNBINDING *noun* **UNBINDINGS** the action of releasing from a bond or restraint □ *adj* not binding

UNBLAMED *adj* not blamed

UNBLENDED *adj* not blended

UNBLESSED *adj* not blessed

UNBLOCK *verb* **UNBLOCKS, UNBLOCKING, UNBLOCKED** to remove a blockage in something

UNBLOODED *adj* said of an animal: not having pure blood

UNBLOWN *adj* not blown

UNBLUNTED *adj* not blunted

UNBOLT *verb* **UNBOLTS, UNBOLTING, UNBOLTED** to unfasten or open (a door, etc) by undoing or drawing back a bolt

UNBOOKISH *adj* not bookish

UNBORN *adj* said of a baby: not yet born; still in the womb

UNBOSOM *verb* **UNBOSOMS, UNBOSOMING, UNBOSOMED** to reveal or confess something

UNBOUND past form of **unbind** □ *adj* not bound or restrained

UNBOUNDED *adj* without bounds or limits

UNBOWED *adj* not bowed or bent

UNBOX verb **UNBOXES, UNBOXING, UNBOXED** to remove from a box or crate

UNBRACE verb **UNBRACES, UNBRACING, UNBRACED** to remove a brace or braces from

UNBRIDGED adj not spanned by a bridge

UNBRIDLED adj said of a horse: not wearing a bridle

UNBROKEN adj not broken; intact

UNBRUISED adj not bruised or damaged

UNBUCKLE verb **UNBUCKLES, UNBUCKLING, UNBUCKLED** to undo the buckle of (eg a belt)

UNBUILT adj not built

UNBUNDLE verb **UNBUNDLES, UNBUNDLING, UNBUNDLED** to remove something from a bundle; to unpack it

UNBUNDLER noun **UNBUNDLERS** someone who unbundles or unpacks something

UNBURDEN verb **UNBURDENS, UNBURDENING, UNBURDENED** to remove a load or burden from someone or something

UNBURIED adj not buried

UNBURNED adj not burned

UNBURNT adj not burned

UNBUTTON verb **UNBUTTONS, UNBUTTONING, UNBUTTONED** to undo the button or buttons on (a garment)

UNCAGED adj released from a cage

UNCANDID adj not candid

UNCANNILY adverb in an uncanny way

UNCANNY adj **UNCANNIER, UNCANNIEST** weird, strange or mysterious, especially in an unsettling or uneasy way

UNCAP verb **UNCAPS, UNCAPPING, UNCAPPED** to remove a cap from (the head or another person)

UNCAPPED adj never having played for a national team

UNCARING adj without anxiety, concern or caution

UNCASHED adj said of a cheque: not cashed in

UNCAUGHT adj not yet caught

UNCEASING adj not ceasing; never-ending

UNCERTAIN adj not sure, certain or confident

UNCHAIN verb **UNCHAINS, UNCHAINING, UNCHAINED** to release something from a chain or chains; to set free

UNCHANGED adj not changed, remaining the same

UNCHARGED adj not charged

UNCHARTED adj said of territory, etc: not fully explored or mapped in detail

UNCHASTE adj not chaste; not pure

UNCHECKED adj not restrained

UNCHEERED adj not cheered; not made happy

UNCHEWED adj said of food: not chewed

UNCHOSEN adj not chosen

UNCHURCH verb **UNCHURCHES, UNCHURCHING, UNCHURCHED** to remove or exclude someone from a church; to excommunicate them

UNCIAL adj said of a form of writing: in large rounded letters with flowing strokes, of a kind used in ancient manuscripts ◻ noun **UNCIALS** an uncial letter or form of writing

UNCIVIL adj discourteous; rude or impolite

UNCIVILLY adverb in an uncivil way

UNCLAD adj not clad; undressed

UNCLAIMED adj said of a prize etc: not claimed by anyone

UNCLASP verb **UNCLASPS, UNCLASPING, UNCLASPED** to unfasten the clasp or clasps on something

UNCLE noun **UNCLES** the brother or brother-in-law of a father or mother

UNCLEAN adj **UNCLEANER, UNCLEANEST** morally or spiritually impure

UNCLEANLY adverb in an unclean manner ◻ adj unclean; characterized by a lack of cleanliness

UNCLEAR adj **UNCLEARER, UNCLEAREST** not clear; hazy or uncertain

UNCLEARED adj not cleared

UNCLEARLY adverb not clearly; in a hazy or uncertain way

UNCLENCH verb **UNCLENCHES, UNCLENCHING, UNCLENCHED** to release clenched teeth or fists

UNCLOG verb **UNCLOGS, UNCLOGGING, UNCLOGGED** to free something from an obstruction; to unblock it

UNCLOSE verb **UNCLOSES, UNCLOSING, UNCLOSED** to open

UNCLOTHE verb **UNCLOTHES, UNCLOTHING, UNCLOTHED** to remove the clothes from someone

UNCLOUDED adj not clouded; clear

UNCO adj strange; weird; unusual ◻ noun **UNCOS** something strange or new

UNCOIL verb **UNCOILS, UNCOILING, UNCOILED** to untwist or unwind something, or to become untwisted

UNCOMBED adj said of hair: not combed; messy

UNCOMMON adj **UNCOMMONER, UNCOMMENEST** rare or unusual

UNCONCERN noun **UNCONCERNS** lack of concern or interest; indifference

UNCONFINED adj free

UNCOOKED adj said of food: raw

UNCOOL adj unsophisticated; not smart or fashionable

UNCORK verb **UNCORKS, UNCORKING, UNCORKED** to remove the cork from (a bottle, etc)

UNCOUNTED adj not counted

UNCOUPLE verb **UNCOUPLES, UNCOUPLING, UNCOUPLED** to undo the coupling of, or between (two or more things); to disconnect or release

UNCOUTH adj **UNCOUTHER, UNCOUTHEST** coarse or awkward in behaviour, manners or language; uncultured or lacking refinement

UNCOUTHLY adverb in an uncouth way

UNCOVER verb **UNCOVERS, UNCOVERING, UNCOVERED** to remove the cover or top from something

UNCOVERED adj not covered; bare; revealed or exposed

UNCROPPED adj not cropped

UNCROSS verb **UNCROSSES, UNCROSSING, UNCROSSED** to change or move something from a crossed position

UNCROSSED adj not crossed

UNCROWDED adj not crowded; with room to move

UNCROWNED adj said of a monarch: not yet crowned

UNCRUMPLE verb **UNCRUMPLES, UNCRUMPLING, UNCRUMPLED** to remove the crumples from something, to flatten it

UNCTION noun **UNCTIONS** the act of ceremonially anointing a person with oil

UNCTUOUS adj insincerely and excessively charming

UNCURBED adj not curbed; not restrained

UNCURED *adj* said of food, especially meat and fish: not dried, salted or smoked

UNCURL *verb* **UNCURLS, UNCURLING, UNCURLED** to take or come out of a curl, twist or roll

UNCUT *adj* not cut

UNDAMAGED *adj* not damaged

UNDAMNED *adj* not damned

UNDAMPED *adj* said of a person, hopes, etc: not discouraged or subdued

UNDATED *adj* with no date marked or assigned

UNDAUNTED *adj* not daunted; not discouraged or put off

UNDEAD *adj* said eg of a vampire, zombie, etc: supposedly dead but still able to move around, etc

UNDECEIVE *verb* **UNDECEIVES, UNDECEIVING, UNDECEIVED** to free someone from a mistaken belief; to reveal the truth to them

UNDECIDED *adj* said of a problem, question, etc: not (yet) decided; not settled

UNDEFILED *adj* not defiled; pure and clean

UNDEFINED *adj* not defined; indefinite

UNDER *prep* below or beneath something but not in contact with it ◻ *adj* lower ◻ *adverb* in or to a lower place, position or rank

UNDERACT *verb* **UNDERACTS, UNDERACTING, UNDERACTED** to play (a part) with insufficient emphasis

UNDERARM *adj* said of a style of bowling in sports, especially cricket, or of a service in tennis, etc: performed with the arm kept below the level of the shoulder

UNDERBID *verb* **UNDERBIDS, UNDERBIDDING, UNDERBID, UNDERBIDDEN** to make an offer that is too low ◻ *noun* **UNDERBIDS** a bid too low to be valid

UNDERBRED *adj* said of an animal: not pure bred

UNDERBUY *verb* **UNDERBUYS, UNDERBUYING, UNDERBOUGHT** to buy less of something than required

UNDERCARD *noun* **UNDERCARDS** in boxing: a programme of matches supporting the main event

UNDERCART *noun* **UNDERCARTS** the landing gear of an aircraft, including wheels; undercarriage

UNDERCOAT *noun* **UNDERCOATS** a layer of paint applied as preparation for the top or finishing coat

UNDERCOOK *verb* **UNDERCOOKS, UNDERCOOKING, UNDERCOOKED** to cook (food) insufficiently or for too short a time

UNDERCUT *verb* **UNDERCUTS, UNDERCUTTING, UNDERCUT** to offer goods or services at a lower price than (a competitor) ◻ *noun* **UNDERCUTS** the action or an act of cutting underneath something

UNDERDO *verb* **UNDERDOES, UNDERDOING, UNDERDID, UNDERDONE** to do something incompletely or inadequately, especially to cook (food) insufficiently or (too) lightly

UNDERDOG *noun* **UNDERDOGS** the person who is losing or who is defeated in a fight, contest, etc

UNDERFEED *verb* **UNDERFEEDS, UNDERFEEDING, UNDERFED** to give (a person or animal) too little food

UNDERFELT *noun* **UNDERFELTS** an old type of underlay, made of felt

UNDERFOOT *adverb* beneath the foot or feet; on the ground

UNDERFUND *verb* **UNDERFUNDS, UNDERFUNDING, UNDERFUNDED** to provide (an organization, public service, etc) with insufficient funding to carry out all the planned activities

UNDERFUR *noun* **UNDERFURS** a layer of short dense fur that grows under the longer outer layer of an animal's fur or coat

UNDERGO *verb* **UNDERGOES, UNDERGOING, UNDERWENT, UNDERGONE** to endure, experience or be subjected to something

UNDERGRAD *noun* **UNDERGRADS** someone studying for a first degree in a higher education establishment

UNDERHAND *adj* secretively deceitful or dishonest; sly ◻ *noun* **UNDERHANDS** in sport: an underarm ball

UNDERHUNG *adj* said of a lower jaw: protruding beyond the upper jaw

UNDERLAY *verb* **UNDERLAYS, UNDERLAYING, UNDERLAID** to lay underneath something, or support or provide with something laid underneath ◻ *noun* **UNDERLAYS** a thing laid underneath another, especially felt or rubber matting laid under a carpet for protection

UNDERLIE *verb* **UNDERLIES, UNDERLYING, UNDERLAY, UNDERLAIN** to lie underneath something

UNDERLINE *verb* **UNDERLINES, UNDERLINING, UNDERLINED** to draw a line under (eg a word or piece of text)

UNDERLING *noun* **UNDERLINGS** a subordinate

UNDERLYING *adj* lying under or beneath

UNDERMINE *verb* **UNDERMINES, UNDERMINING, UNDERMINED** to weaken or destroy something, especially gradually and imperceptibly

UNDERMOST *adj* lowest ◻ *adverb* in or to the lowest position; underneath

UNDERNOTE *noun* **UNDERNOTES** an undertone

UNDERPAID *adj* not paid sufficiently; paid less than is due

UNDERPART *noun* **UNDERPARTS** the lower side, especially the underside, or part of the underside, of an animal, bird, etc

UNDERPASS *noun* **UNDERPASSES** a tunnel for pedestrians under a road or railway; a subway

UNDERPAY *verb* **UNDERPAYS, UNDERPAYING, UNDERPAID** to pay less than is required or deserved

UNDERPIN *verb* **UNDERPINS, UNDERPINNING, UNDERPINNED** to support (a structure) from beneath, usually temporarily, with brickwork or a prop

UNDERPLAY *verb* **UNDERPLAYS, UNDERPLAYING, UNDERPLAYED** to lead or follow suit with a lower card while holding a higher one

UNDERRATE *verb* **UNDERRATES, UNDERRATING, UNDERRATED** to rate or assess something at a lower worth or value than it deserves; to have too low an opinion of something

UNDERSEA *adj* situated or lying below the surface of the sea ◻ *adverb* below the sea or the surface of the sea

UNDERSEAL *noun* **UNDERSEALS** an anti-rusting substance painted on to the underside of a motor vehicle ◻ *verb* **UNDERSEALS, UNDERSEALING, UNDERSEALED** to apply such a substance to (a vehicle) in order to seal the metal for protection

UNDERSELL *verb* **UNDERSELLS, UNDERSELLING, UNDERSOLD** to sell goods or services at a lower price than (a competitor)

UNDERSHOT *adj* said of a water wheel: driven by the weight of a flow of water that passes under rather than over the wheel

UNDERSIDE *noun* **UNDERSIDES** the downward-facing side or surface

UNDERTAKE *verb* **UNDERTAKES, UNDERTAKING, UNDERTOOK, UNDERTAKEN** to accept (a duty, responsibility or task)

UNDERTAKING *noun* **UNDERTAKINGS** a duty, responsibility or task undertaken

UNDERTONE *noun* **UNDERTONES** a quiet tone of voice

UNDERTOW *noun* **UNDERTOWS** the strong current that flows away from the shore underneath a breaking wave

UNDERUSE *noun* **UNDERUSES** insufficient use of resources, a facility, etc □ *verb* **UNDERUSES, UNDERUSING, UNDERUSED** to make insufficient use of (resources, a facility, etc)

UNDERVEST *noun* **UNDERVESTS** an undergarment worn on the upper part of the body; a vest

UNDERWEAR *noun* **UNDERWEARS** clothes, eg bras, pants, etc, worn under shirts, trousers, dresses and skirts, etc, and usually next to the skin

UNDERWENT a past form of **undergo**

UNDERWING *noun* **UNDERWINGS** the hindwing of an insect

UNDERWOOD *noun* **UNDERWOODS** undergrowth

UNDESIRED *adj* not desired or wanted

UNDIES *plural noun* items of underwear, especially women's bras, pants, etc

UNDILUTED *adj* not diluted

UNDIMMED *adj* not dimmed

UNDINE *noun* **UNDINES** a nymph; a female water spirit

UNDIVIDED *adj* said of one's attention to something: wholly concentrated, not distracted

UNDO *verb* **UNDOES, UNDOING, UNDID, UNDONE** to open, unfasten or untie (something)

UNDOCK *verb* **UNDOCKS, UNDOCKING, UNDOCKED** said eg

of a space shuttle, etc: to separate from another craft in space

UNDOING *noun* **UNDOINGS** the act or action of unfastening, untying, opening etc

UNDONE *adj* unfastened, untied, etc

UNDOUBTED *adj* beyond doubt or question; clear; evident

UNDRAINED *adj* not drained

UNDRAPED *adj* not covered by draping

UNDREAMED *adj* not even imagined or dreamed of, especially thought never to be likely or possible

UNDREAMT *adj* undreamed

UNDRESS *verb* **UNDRESSES, UNDRESSING, UNDRESSED** to take the clothes off oneself (or another person) □ *noun* nakedness, or near-nakedness

UNDRESSED *adj* said of hair: not styled, combed, etc

UNDUBBED *adj* not dubbed

UNDUE *adj* unjustifiable; improper

UNDULANT *adj* rising and falling like waves

UNDULATE *verb* **UNDULATES, UNDULATING, UNDULATED** to move or to make something move in or like waves

UNDULY *adverb* excessively; unreasonably

UNDYED *adj* not dyed

UNDYING *adj* referring to something that does not die; everlasting; eternal

UNDYINGLY *adverb* in an undying way

UNEARNED *adj* not deserved or merited

UNEARTH *verb* **UNEARTHS, UNEARTHING, UNEARTHED** to dig something up out of the ground

UNEARTHLY *adj* **UNEARTHLIER, UNEARTHLIEST** not of this Earth; heavenly or sublime

UNEASE *noun* **UNEASES** lack of ease; discomfort or apprehension

UNEASILY *adverb* in an uneasy way

UNEASY *adj* **UNEASIER, UNEASIEST** nervous, anxious or unsettled; ill at ease

UNEATABLE *adj* not eatable

UNEATEN *adj* not eaten

UNEDITED *adj* said of a text, etc: not edited; never before published

UNELECTED *adj* not elected

UNEMPTIED *adj* not emptied

UNENDING *adj* endless; everlasting

UNENDOWED *adj* not endowed

UNENGAGED *adj* not engaged; not occupied

UNENTERED *adj* not entered

UNENVIED *adj* not envied

UNEQUAL *adj* not equal in quantity, value, rank, size, etc

UNEQUALLY *adverb* in an unequal way

UNERRING *adj* not missing the mark or target; sure or certain

UNETHICAL *adj* not ethical; going against ethics

UNEVEN *adj* **UNEVENER, UNEVENEST** said of a surface, etc: not smooth or flat; bumpy

UNEVENLY *adverb* in an uneven way

UNEXCITED *adj* not excited

UNEXPIRED *adj* said of an agreement, ticket, etc: still valid; having not yet expired

UNEXPOSED *adj* not exposed

UNFADED *adj* not faded

UNFADING *adj* not fading

UNFAILING *adj* remaining constant; never weakening or failing

UNFAIR *adj* **UNFAIRER, UNFAIREST** not fair or just; inequitable

UNFAIRLY *adverb* in an unfair way

UNFASTEN *verb* **UNFASTENS, UNFASTENING, UNFASTENED** to undo or release something from a fastening

UNFAZED *adj* not fazed; not disconcerted or perturbed

UNFEELING *adj* without physical feeling or sensation

UNFEIGNED *adj* not feigned, real

UNFENCED *adj* said of a piece of land, etc: not surrounded by a fence

UNFETTER *verb* **UNFETTERS, UNFETTERING, UNFETTERED** to free from fetters; to release from chains

UNFETTERED *adj* not controlled or restrained

UNFILIAL *adj* not becoming of a son or daughter

UNFILLED *adj* not filled

UNFIRED *adj* said of a gun: not yet fired

UNFISHED *adj* said eg of a stretch of river: not fished

UNFIT *adj* **UNFITTER, UNFITTEST** said of a person: not suitably qualified for something; not good enough; incompetent

UNFITLY *adverb* in an unfit way

UNFITNESS noun **UNFITNESSES** the state or condition of being unfit or unsuitable

UNFITTED adj not adapted or suited (for, to or to do something)

UNFITTING adj not suitable; unbecoming

UNFIX verb **UNFIXES, UNFIXING, UNFIXED** to loosen or release something; to detach it

UNFIXED adj unfastened; not settled

UNFLEDGED adj said of a bird: not yet fledged; not yet having developed adult flight feathers

UNFOCUSED adj not focused

UNFOLD verb **UNFOLDS, UNFOLDING, UNFOLDED** to open out the folds of something; to spread something out

UNFOLDER noun **UNFOLDERS** someone who unfolds something

UNFORCED adj not compelled

UNFORMED adj not formed; undeveloped

UNFOUNDED adj said of allegations, ideas, rumours, etc: not based on fact; without foundation; groundless

UNFRAMED adj said of a picture: not set in a frame

UNFRANKED adj said of a stamp: not franked

UNFREE adj not free: in servitude

UNFREEZE verb **UNFREEZES, UNFREEZING, UNFROZE, UNFROZEN** to thaw or cause something to thaw

UNFROCK verb **UNFROCKS, UNFROCKING, UNFROCKED** to defrock; to deprive (someone in holy orders) of ecclesiastical office or function

UNFROZEN adj not frozen

UNFUNDED adj said of a public debt, etc: not funded, floating, in the form of exchequer bills and bonds, to be paid up at certain dates

UNFUNNY adj not funny

UNFURL verb **UNFURLS, UNFURLING, UNFURLED** to open, spread out or unroll something from a rolled-up or tied-up state

UNGAINLY adj **UNGAINLIER, UNGAINLIEST** awkward and ungraceful in movement; clumsy

UNGALLANT adj said of a man's behaviour: not gallant

UNGAUGED adj not gauged; not measured

UNGENIAL adj not sympathetically cheerful

UNGENTLE adj not gentle

UNGIFTED adj said of a person: not gifted

UNGIRD verb **UNGIRDS, UNGIRDING, UNGIRDED** to free from a girdle or band

UNGLAZED adj not having windows

UNGLOSSED adj said of a text: without an explanatory gloss

UNGLOVED adj not wearing gloves

UNGODLY adj **UNGODLIER, UNGODLIEST** wicked or sinful; irreligious

UNGRADED adj not classified in grades

UNGRAZED adj said of land: not grazed by livestock

UNGUAL adj relating to, like or affecting the fingernails or toenails

UNGUARDED adj without guard; unprotected

UNGUENT noun **UNGUENTS** ointment or salve

UNGUIDED adj not guided

UNGUIS noun **UNGUES** a nail or claw

UNGULATE adj with the form of a hoof; hoof-shaped ▫ noun **UNGULATES** a hoofed mammal

UNGUMMED adj not gummed; freed from gum or gumming

UNHAND verb **UNHANDS, UNHANDING, UNHANDED** to let go of someone; to release them from one's grasp or take one's hands off them

UNHANDY adj awkward; difficult to handle or manage

UNHAPPILY adverb in an unhappy way

UNHAPPY adj **UNHAPPIER, UNHAPPIEST** sad; in low spirits; miserable

UNHARMED adj not harmed

UNHARMFUL adj not harmful

UNHARNESS verb **UNHARNESSES, UNHARNESSING, UNHARNESSED** to take the harness or the armour off (a person or animal)

UNHATCHED adj not out of the egg

UNHAUNTED adj not haunted

UNHEALTHY adj **UNHEALTHIER, UNHEALTHIEST** not conducive to health; harmful

UNHEARD adj not heard; not perceived with the ear

UNHEATED adj not heated

UNHEEDED adj not heeded; not listened to

UNHEEDFUL adj not heedful; not listening to

UNHEEDING adj not heeding; not listening to

UNHELPED adj without help of any kind

UNHELPFUL adj not helpful

UNHEROIC adj not heroic

UNHEWN adj said of rock, etc: not cut

UNHINGE verb **UNHINGES, UNHINGING, UNHINGED** to remove (a door, etc) from its hinges

UNHIP adj not hip; not trendy or fashionable

UNHITCH verb **UNHITCHES, UNHITCHING, UNHITCHED** to undo or unfasten something which has been tied up

UNHOLY adj **UNHOLIER, UNHOLIEST** not holy or sacred

UNHOOK verb **UNHOOKS, UNHOOKING, UNHOOKED** to remove or free something from a hook or hooks

UNHOPEFUL adj not hopeful

UNHORSE verb **UNHORSES, UNHORSING, UNHORSED** to throw or force (a rider) off a horse

UNHOUSED adj houseless; deprived of a place to live

UNHUMAN adj not human

UNHUNG adj not hung; without hangings

UNHURRIED adj not hurried; relaxed

UNHURT adj not hurt

UNI noun **UNIS** a university

UNIAXIAL adj said of plants: with one main unbranched axis

UNICORN noun **UNICORNS** a mythical animal in the form of a horse (usually a white one) with a long straight spiralled horn growing from its forehead

UNICYCLE noun **UNICYCLES** a cycle consisting of a single wheel with a seat and pedals attached, used especially by acrobats in circus performances, etc

UNIFIABLE adj capable of being unified

UNIFIER noun **UNIFIERS** someone who unifies, eg two opposing groups

UNIFORM noun **UNIFORMS** distinctive clothing, always of the same colour, cut, etc, worn by all members of a particular organization or profession, eg by schoolchildren or soldiers ▫ adj unchanging or unvarying in form, nature or appearance; always the same, regardless of changes in circumstances, etc ◻ *verb* **UNIFORMS, UNIFORMING, UNIFORMED** to make (several people or things) uniform or alike **UNIFORMED** *adj* wearing a uniform

UNIFORMLY *adverb* in a uniform way

UNIFY *verb* **UNIFIES, UNIFYING, UNIFIED** to bring (two or more things) together to form a single unit or whole; to unite

UNIMPEDED *adj* not impeded; not hindered

UNINDEXED *adj* not index-linked

UNINJURED *adj* not injured

UNINSURED *adj* not insured

UNINVITED *adj* not invited; unwelcome

UNION *noun* **UNIONS** the action or an act of uniting two or more things

UNIONISE *verb* **UNIONISES, UNIONISING, UNIONISED** to unionize

UNIONISM *noun* **UNIONISMS** advocacy of combination into one body for the purposes of social or political organization

UNIONIST *noun* **UNIONISTS** an advocate or supporter of unionism, especially as a system of social or political organization

UNIONIZE *verb* **UNIONIZES, UNIONIZING, UNIONIZED** to organize (a workforce) into a trade union or trade unions

UNIPAROUS *adj* relating to or characterized by producing only one offspring at any one birth

UNIPED *noun* **UNIPEDS** a person or creature with only one foot or leg

UNIPOD *noun* **UNIPODS** a one-legged stand or support for a camera

UNIPOLAR *adj* with, relating to, or using one magnetic or electronic pole only

UNIQUE *adj* **UNIQUER, UNIQUEST** sole or solitary; of which there is only one ◻ *noun* **UNIQUES** anything, especially formerly a coin or medal, of which there is only one example or copy

UNIQUELY *adverb* in a unique way

UNIRONED *adj* said of clothes, etc: not ironed; wrinkly

UNISEX *adj* suited to, for use by, or wearable by, both men and women

UNISEXUAL *adj* relating to or restricted to one sex only

UNISON *noun* **UNISONS** the interval between two notes of the same pitch, or which are one or more octaves apart

UNISONAL *adj* of or relating to a unison

UNISONANT *adj* in unison

UNISONOUS *adj* unisonant

UNIT *noun* **UNITS** a single item or element regarded as the smallest subdivision of a whole; a single person or thing

UNITARD *noun* **UNITARDS** a close-fitting one-piece garment of stretchable fabric that covers the body from the neck to the feet, worn especially by gymnasts, dancers, etc

UNITARY *adj* relating to, characterized by or based on unity

UNITE *verb* **UNITES, UNITING, UNITED** to make or become a single unit or whole

UNITED *adj* referring to something that is or has been united; joined together or combined

UNITEDLY *adverb* in a united way

UNITER *noun* **UNITERS** someone who unites people or things

UNITING *noun* **UNITINGS** an act of joining together

UNITISE *verb* **UNITISES, UNITISING, UNITISED** to unitize

UNITIVE *adj* with the quality of uniting spiritually to God

UNITIZE *verb* **UNITIZES, UNITIZING, UNITIZED** to form something into a unit; to unite or make one

UNITY *noun* **UNITIES** the state or quality of being one; oneness

UNIVALENT *adj* said of a chromosome during meiosis: not paired with its homologue

UNIVALVE *adj* with one valve or shell ◻ *noun* **UNIVALVES** an undivided shell

UNIVERSAL *adj* relating to the universe ◻ *noun* **UNIVERSALS** something that is universal

UNIVERSE *noun* **UNIVERSES** all existing space, energy and matter, ie the whole of space and all the galaxies, stars, planets, moons, asteroids and other bodies contained within it; the cosmos

UNIVOCAL *adj* said of a word or term: with one meaning only; unambiguous ◻ *noun* **UNIVOCALS** a univocal word or term

UNJOINT *verb* **UNJOINTS, UNJOINTING, UNJOINTED** to disjoint; to dislocate

UNJUST *adj* not just; unfair

UNJUSTLY *adverb* in an unjust way

UNKEMPT *adj* said of hair: uncombed; messy

UNKEPT *adj* not kept; untended

UNKIND *adj* **UNKINDER, UNKINDEST** unsympathetic, cruel or harsh

UNKINDLY *adverb* in an unkind way

UNKISSED *adj* not yet kissed

UNKNIT *verb* **UNKNITS, UNKNITTING, UNKNITTED** to untie

UNKNOT *verb* **UNKNOTS, UNKNOTTING, UNKNOTTED** to free from knots

UNKNOWING *adj* not knowing; ignorant

UNKNOWN *adj* not known; unfamiliar ◻ *noun* **UNKNOWNS** an unknown person or thing

UNLACE *verb* **UNLACES, UNLACING, UNLACED** to undo or loosen the lace or laces of (shoes, etc)

UNLADEN *adj* not laden; without a load

UNLAID *adj* not laid

UNLATCH *verb* **UNLATCH, UNLATCHING, UNLATCHED** to lift the latch of (eg a door)

UNLAWFUL *adj* forbidden by law

UNLAY *verb* **UNLAYS, UNLAYING, UNLAID** to untwist (a rope, cable, etc) into its separate strands

UNLEADED *adj* said of petrol: free from lead additives

UNLEARN *verb* **UNLEARNS, UNLEARNING, UNLEARNED** to try actively to forget something learned; to rid the memory of it

UNLEARNED *adj* not well educated; uneducated

UNLEARNT *adj* said of a lesson, etc: not learnt

UNLEASED *adj* said of a property, etc: not leased

UNLEASH *verb* **UNLEASHES, UNLEASHING, UNLEASHED** to release (eg a dog) from a leash

UNLESS *conj* if not; except when; except if

UNLET *adj* said of a property, etc: not let

UNLIGHTED *adj* not lighted

UNLIKABLE *adj* not easy to like

UNLIKE *prep* different from ◻ *adj* not like or alike; different; dissimilar

UNLIKELY adj **UNLIKELIER,**
UNLIKELIEST not expected or
likely to happen
UNLIMBER verb **UNLIMBERS,**
UNLIMBERING, UNLIMBERED to
remove (a gun) from its limber in
preparation for use
UNLIMITED adj not limited or
restricted
UNLINED adj free from or not
marked with lines
UNLISTED adj not entered on a list
UNLIT adj not lit; without lights or
lighting
UNLIVABLE adj said of a house,
conditions, etc: not fit to live in
UNLOAD verb **UNLOADS,**
UNLOADING, UNLOADED to
remove (a load or cargo) from (a
vehicle, ship, etc)
UNLOADER noun **UNLOADERS**
someone whose job is to unload
goods or cargo
UNLOCK verb **UNLOCKS,**
UNLOCKING, UNLOCKED to undo
the lock of (a door, etc)
UNLOOSE verb **UNLOOSES,**
UNLOOSING, UNLOOSED to make
something less tight; to loosen it
UNLOOSEN verb **UNLOOSENS,**
UNLOOSENING, UNLOOSENED to
unloose
UNLOSABLE adj not able to be lost
UNLOVABLE adj not able to be
loved
UNLOVED adj not loved
UNLOVELY adj **UNLOVELIER,**
UNLOVELIEST unattractive;
unpleasant or ugly
UNLOVING adj not loving
UNLUCKILY adverb in an unlucky
way
UNLUCKY adj **UNLUCKIER,**
UNLUCKIEST bringing, resulting
from or constituting bad luck
UNMADE adj not yet made
UNMAKE verb **UNMAKES,**
UNMAKING, UNMADE to cancel or
destroy the (especially beneficial)
effect of something
UNMAN verb **UNMANS,**
UNMANNING, UNMANNED to
cause someone to lose self-control,
especially to overcome with
emotion
UNMANAGED adj not managed
UNMANLY adj **UNMANLIER,**
UNMANLIEST not manly; not
virile or masculine
UNMANNED adj said especially of a
vehicle or spacecraft: without
personnel or a crew, especially

controlled remotely or
automatically; not manned
UNMARKED adj bearing no mark;
not noticed
UNMARRED adj not marred
UNMARRIED adj not married,
usually never having been married
UNMASK verb **UNMASKS,**
UNMASKING, UNMASKED to
remove a mask or disguise from
(oneself or someone else)
UNMASKER noun **UNMASKERS**
someone who unmasks others
UNMATCHED adj matchless;
without equal
UNMATURED adj said of cheese,
etc: not matured; not aged
UNMEANING adj without any aim
or purpose
UNMEANT adj not meant
UNMELTED adj not melted
UNMERITED adj not merited; not
deserved
UNMET adj said of a target, quota,
etc: not achieved
UNMINDED adj unheeded;
unregarded
UNMINDFUL adj not mindful of
something; careless or heedless of
something
UNMISSED adj not missed
UNMIXED adj not mixed
UNMOOR verb **UNMOORS,**
UNMOORING, UNMOORED to
release or free (a vessel) from
moorings
UNMORAL adj not moral; with no
relation to morality; amoral
UNMOUNTED adj not mounted
UNMOVABLE adj not movable
UNMOVED adj still in the same
place
UNMOVING adj still; stationary
UNMOWN adj said of a lawn, etc:
not mown
UNMUSICAL adj not musical
UNMUZZLE verb **UNMUZZLES,**
UNMUZZLING, UNMUZZLED to
remove the muzzle from (a dog,
etc)
UNNAMABLE adj impossible to
name
UNNAMED adj not named
UNNATURAL adj contrary to the
way things usually happen in
nature
UNNEEDED adj not needed
UNNEEDFUL adj having no need
UNNERVE verb **UNNERVES,**
UNNERVING, UNNERVED to
deprive of strength; to weaken
UNNOTED adj not noted

UNNOTICED adj not noticed
UNOILED adj not oiled
UNOPENED adj not opened
UNOPPOSED adj not opposed
UNORDERED adj not arranged
UNOWNED adj ownerless
UNPACK verb **UNPACKS,**
UNPACKING, UNPACKED to take
something out of a packed state
UNPAGED adj said of a book: with
no page numbers
UNPAID adj said of work, etc: not
paid
UNPAINTED adj not painted
UNPAIRED adj not paired; not
forming one of a pair
UNPAPERED adj not papered
UNPAVED adj without pavement
UNPAYABLE adj not able to be paid
UNPEG verb **UNPEGS,**
UNPEGGING, UNPEGGED to
unfasten something by removing a
peg or pegs from it
UNPEOPLE verb **UNPEOPLES,**
UNPEOPLING, UNPEOPLED to
empty (an area, etc) of people; to
depopulate
UNPERSON noun **UNPERSONS**
someone whose existence is
officially denied or ignored and
who is deemed not to have existed,
often to the extent that their name
is removed from official records
◻ verb **UNPERSONS,**
UNPERSONING, UNPERSONED to
make someone into an unperson
UNPICK verb **UNPICKS,**
UNPICKING, UNPICKED to undo
(stitches)
UNPICKED adj not gathered; not
selected
UNPIERCED adj not pierced
UNPIN verb **UNPINS, UNPINNING,**
UNPINNED to remove a pin or pins
from something
UNPITIED adj not pitied
UNPITYING adj showing no pity
UNPLACED adj said eg of a
racehorse, greyhound, athlete, etc:
not one of the first three, or
sometimes four, to finish a race
UNPLANNED adj not planned or
scheduled
UNPLANTED adj not planted
UNPLIABLE adj not pliable; rigid
UNPLUG verb **UNPLUGS,**
UNPLUGGING, UNPLUGGED to
unblock or unstop (something that
is plugged or blocked)
UNPLUMBED adj said of a
building, etc: without plumbing
UNPOETIC adj not poetic

UNPOINTED adj not sharp or drawn to a point or points
UNPOISED adj not poised
UNPOLICED adj not policed
UNPOLISHED adj not polished
UNPOLITIC adj unwise; not to be advised
UNPOLLED adj not having voted at an election
UNPOPULAR adj not popular; not liked by an individual or by people in general
UNPOSED adj not posed; natural
UNPOSTED adj not posted
UNPRESSED adj not pressed
UNPRICED adj having no fixed or stated price
UNPRIMED adj not primed; unprepared
UNPRINTED adj not printed
UNPROVED adj not proved
UNPROVEN adj not proven
UNPURGED adj not purged
UNQUALIFIED adj not having any formal qualifications; lacking the formal qualifications required for a particular job, etc
UNQUELLED adj not quelled
UNQUIET adj anxious; ill at ease; restless ◻ noun **UNQUIETS** disquiet; disturbance or unrest
UNQUIETLY adverb in an unquiet way
UNQUOTE verb **UNQUOTES, UNQUOTING, UNQUOTED** to indicate (in speech) the end of something that was said by someone else
UNQUOTED adj said of a company: not quoted on the Stock Exchange
UNRATED adj not rated
UNRAVEL verb **UNRAVELS, UNRAVELLING, UNRAVELLED** to separate out the strands of (a knitted or woven fabric)
UNREACHED adj not reached
UNREAD adj said of a book, etc: not having been read
UNREADY adj **UNREADIER, UNREADIEST** not ready
UNREAL adj not real; illusory or imaginary
UNREALITY noun **UNREALITIES** the state or condition of not being real
UNREALLY adverb in an unreal way
UNREASON noun **UNREASONS** lack of reason or reasonableness
UNREDUCED adj not reduced
UNREEL verb **UNREELS, UNREELING, UNREELED** to unwind something from a reel

UNREFINED adj not refined
UNRELATED adj not related
UNRELAXED adj not relaxed; uptight
UNRENEWED adj not renewed
UNRESERVE noun **UNRESERVES** absence of reserve
UNREST noun **UNRESTS** a state of (especially public) discontent bordering on riotousness
UNREVISED adj not revised
UNREVOKED adj not revoked
UNRHYMED adj not rhymed
UNRIDABLE adj not ridable
UNRIDDEN adj never ridden
UNRIDDLE verb **UNRIDDLES, UNRIDDLING, UNRIDDLED** to solve or explain (a riddle, mystery, etc)
UNRIDDLER noun **UNRIDDLERS** someone who solves or explains riddles
UNRIFLED adj not rifled
UNRIG verb **UNRIGS, UNRIGGING, UNRIGGED** to remove all the rigging from (a ship)
UNRIP verb **UNRIPS, UNRIPPING, UNRIPPED** to rip open
UNRIPE adj **UNRIPER, UNRIPEST** not (yet) fully developed; not matured
UNRIPENED adj not (yet) fully ripe
UNRISEN adj not risen
UNROLL verb **UNROLLS, UNROLLING, UNROLLED** to open something out from a rolled state
UNROUNDED adj not rounded
UNRUFFLED adj said of a surface: smooth or still
UNRULED adj not governed; without ruled lines
UNRULY adj **UNRULIER, UNRULIEST** disobedient or disorderly, especially habitually
UNRUMPLED adj not rumpled

UNS plural of **un**

UNSADDLE verb **UNSADDLES, UNSADDLING, UNSADDLED** to take the saddle off (a horse)
UNSAFE adj **UNSAFER, UNSAFEST** not safe or secure; dangerous
UNSAID adj not said, expressed, spoken, etc, especially when it might have been or should have been
UNSALTED adj with no added salt
UNSAVED adj not saved
UNSAVOURY adj unpleasant or distasteful

UNSAY verb **UNSAYS, UNSAYING, UNSAID** to take back or withdraw (something said, eg a statement, etc)
UNSAYABLE adj that cannot be said
UNSCALED adj never climbed
UNSCARRED adj not scarred
UNSCATHED adj not harmed or injured
UNSCENTED adj with no added scent
UNSCREW verb **UNSCREWS, UNSCREWING, UNSCREWED** to remove or loosen something by taking out a screw or screws, or with a twisting or screwing action
UNSEAL verb **UNSEALS, UNSEALING, UNSEALED** to remove or break open the seal of (a letter, container, etc)
UNSEALED adj not sealed; not closed, marked, etc with a seal
UNSEAT verb **UNSEATS, UNSEATING, UNSEATED** said of a horse: to throw or knock (its rider) off
UNSECURED adj not secured
UNSEEDED adj not placed among the top players in the preliminary rounds of a tournament
UNSEEING adj not seeing; unobservant
UNSEEMLY adj **UNSEEMLIER, UNSEEMLIEST** not seemly; not becoming or fitting, especially because of being indecent
UNSEEN adj not seen or noticed ◻ noun **UNSEENS** an unseen text for translation in an examination
UNSELFISH adj having or showing concern for others
UNSET verb **UNSETS, UNSETTING, UNSET** to undo the setting of
UNSETTLE verb **UNSETTLES, UNSETTLING, UNSETTLED** to make someone ill at ease; to disturb, discompose, confuse or disconcert them
UNSETTLED adj lacking stability
UNSEWN adj not sewn
UNSEX verb **UNSEXES, UNSEXING, UNSEXED** to deprive someone of their gender, sexuality or the typical attributes of their gender
UNSHACKLE verb **UNSHACKLES, UNSHACKLING, UNSHACKLED** to release someone from a shackle or shackles; to remove a shackle from them
UNSHAKEN adj not shaken

UNSHAPED *adj* not shaped
UNSHAPELY *adj* **UNSHAPELIER,**
UNSHAPELIEST not shapely
UNSHARED *adj* not shared
UNSHAVED *adj* not shaved
UNSHAVEN *adj* not shaven
UNSHEATHE *verb* **UNSHEATHES,**
UNSHEATHING, UNSHEATHED to
draw (especially a sword, knife,
etc) from a sheathe
UNSHED *adj* not shed
UNSHELL *verb* **UNSHELLS,**
UNSHELLING, UNSHELLED to shell,
remove the shell from (eg peas)
UNSHIP *verb* **UNSHIPS,**
UNSHIPPING, UNSHIPPED to
unload or disembark from a ship
UNSHOCKED *adj* not shocked
UNSHOD *adj* shoeless; with shoe or
shoes removed
UNSIGHTED *adj* said of a gun:
without sights
UNSIGHTLY *adj* **UNSIGHTLIER,**
UNSIGHTLIEST not pleasant to
look at; ugly
UNSIGNED *adj* not signed
UNSIZED *adj* not fitted, adjusted or
sorted in respect of size
UNSKILFUL *adj* not skilful
UNSKILLED *adj* lacking skill;
inexpert
UNSKIMMED *adj* not skimmed
UNSLICED *adj* not sliced
UNSLING *verb* **UNSLINGS,**
UNSLINGING, UNSLUNG to
remove something from a sling or
from a slung position
UNSMILING *adj* not smiling
UNSNAP *verb* **UNSNAPS,**
UNSNAPPING, UNSNAPPED to
undo or unfasten the snap or snaps
of something
UNSNARL *verb* **UNSNARLS,**
UNSNARLING, UNSNARLED to
untangle or free something from
snarls
UNSOCIAL *adj* annoying, or likely
to annoy, other people; antisocial
UNSOILED *adj* not soiled; clean
UNSOLD *adj* not yet sold
UNSOLID *adj* not solid
UNSOLVED *adj* not solved
UNSORTED *adj* not sorted or
arranged
UNSOUGHT *adj* not sought or
solicited
UNSOUND *adj* **UNSOUNDER,**
UNSOUNDEST not reliable; not
based on sound reasoning
UNSOUNDED *adj* not uttered
UNSOUNDLY *adverb* in an
unsound way

UNSOWN *adj* not sown
UNSPARING *adj* giving generously
or liberally
UNSPENT *adj* not spent
UNSPILLED *adj* not spilled
UNSPILT *adj* not spilt
UNSPOILED *adj* not spoiled
UNSPOILT *adj* not spoilt
UNSPOKEN *adj* not spoken
UNSPOTTED *adj* not spotted; clean
UNSPRUNG *adj* without springs
UNSTABLE *adj* not stable
UNSTAINED *adj* not stained
UNSTAMPED *adj* not stamped
UNSTATED *adj* not stated or
declared
UNSTEADY *adj* **UNSTEADIER,**
UNSTEADIEST not secure or firm
UNSTERILE *adj* not sterile
UNSTICK *verb* **UNSTICKS,**
UNSTICKING, UNSTUCK to free or
separate something that is stuck to
something else
UNSTIFLED *adj* not stifled
UNSTINTED *adj* not stinted
UNSTIRRED *adj* not stirred
UNSTITCH *verb* **UNSTITCHES,**
UNSTITCHING, UNSTITCHED to
take out the stitches of
UNSTOP *verb* **UNSTOPS,**
UNSTOPPING, UNSTOPPED to free
something from being stopped or
blocked
UNSTOPPER *verb* **UNSTOPPERS,**
UNSTOPPERING, UNSTOPPED to
take the stoppper from
UNSTRAP *verb* **UNSTRAPS,**
UNSTRAPPING, UNSTRAPPED to
undo the straps of
UNSTRING *verb* **UNSTRINGS,**
UNSTRINGING, UNSTRINGED to
relax or remove the string or
strings of (a bow, a musical
instrument, etc)
UNSTRIPED *adj* not striped
UNSTRUNG *adj* said of a stringed
instrument: with strings removed
UNSTUCK *adj* loosened or released
from a stuck state
UNSTUDIED *adj* not affected;
natural and spontaneous
UNSTUFFED *adj* not stuffed
UNSUBDUED *adj* not subdued
UNSUBTLE *adj* not subtle
UNSUITED *adj* not suited or
adapted
UNSULLIED *adj* not sullied
UNSUNG *adj* said of someone, an
achievement, etc: not praised or
recognized
UNSURE *adj* uncertain; doubtful

UNSWAYED *adj* not persuaded
UNSWEPT *adj* not swept
UNSWORN *adj* not confirmed, or
not bound, by oath
UNTACK *verb* **UNTACKS,**
UNTACKING, UNTACKED to
unharness
UNTAINTED *adj* not tainted;
umblemished
UNTAMABLE *adj* that cannot be
tamed
UNTAMED *adj* not tamed; wild
UNTANGLE *verb* **UNTANGLES,**
UNTANGLING, UNTANGLED to
disentangle something; to free
something from a tangled state
UNTANNED *adj* not tanned
UNTAPPED *adj* not tapped
UNTASTED *adj* not tasted
UNTAUGHT *adj* without education
or instruction; ignorant
UNTAXED *adj* not taxed
UNTEMPTED *adj* not tempted
UNTENABLE *adj* said of an
opinion, theory, argument, etc:
not able to be maintained,
defended or justified
UNTENDED *adj* not tended
UNTESTED *adj* not tested
UNTETHER *verb* **UNTETHERS,**
UNTETHERING, UNTETHERED to
release from a tether
UNTHANKED *adj* not thanked
UNTHINKING *adj* inconsiderate;
thoughtless
UNTHREAD *verb* **UNTHREADS,**
UNTHREADING, UNTHREADED to
take the thread out of (a needle,
etc)
UNTHRIFTY *adj* not thrifty;
wasteful
UNTIDILY *adverb* in an untidy way
UNTIDY *adj* **UNTIDIER, UNTIDIEST**
not tidy; messy or disordered
▫ *verb* **UNTIDIES, UNTIDYING,**
UNTIDIED to make untidy
UNTIE *verb* **UNTIES, UNTYING,**
UNTIED to undo (a knot, parcel,
etc) from a tied state
UNTIL *prep* up to the time of ▫ *conj*
up to the time that
UNTILLED *adj* of land: not tilled
UNTIMELY *adj* **UNTIMELIER,**
UNTIMELIEST happening before
the proper or expected time
UNTINGED *adj* not tinged
UNTIRING *adj* not tiring
UNTITLED *adj* having no title
UNTO *prep* to
UNTOLD *adj* not told
UNTOUCHED *adj* not touched;
intact

For longer words, see The Chambers Dictionary

UNTOWARD adj inconvenient; unfortunate

UNTRACED adj not traced or found

UNTRAINED adj not trained

UNTREATED adj not treated

UNTRIED adj not tried, tested or attempted

UNTRIMMED adj not trimmed

UNTRODDEN adj not trodden upon; unfrequented

UNTRUE adj **UNTRUER, UNTRUEST** not true

UNTRULY adverb in an untrue way

UNTRUSS verb **UNTRUSSES, UNTRUSSING, UNTRUSSED** to unfasten or release something from, or as if from, a truss

UNTRUTH noun **UNTRUTHS** the fact or quality of being untrue

UNTUCK verb **UNTUCKS, UNTUCKING, UNTUCKED** to free (a person, bedclothes, etc) from being tucked in

UNTUCKED adj not tucked up or in

UNTUNED adj not tuned

UNTUNEFUL adj not tuneful

UNTUTORED adj uneducated; untaught

UNTWINE verb **UNTWINES, UNTWINING, UNTWINED** to untwist; to separate by untwisting

UNTWIST verb **UNTWISTS, UNTWISTING, UNTWISTED** to twist backwards so as to open out

UNTWISTED adj not twisted

UNTYPABLE adj unable to be assigned to a particular type

UNTYPICAL adj not typical

UNUSABLE adj not usable

UNUSED adj brand new; never used

UNUSUAL adj not usual; uncommon; rare

UNUSUALLY adverb in an unusual way

UNUTTERED adj not uttered; unsaid

UNVALUED adj not prized or highly esteemed

UNVARIED adj not varied

UNVARYING adj not varying

UNVEIL verb **UNVEILS, UNVEILING, UNVEILED** to remove a veil from (one's own or someone else's face)

UNVEILING noun **UNVEILINGS** an act of unveiling

UNVERSED adj not experienced in something

UNVIABLE adj not viable

UNVIEWED adj not viewed

UNVISITED adj not visited

UNVOICED adj not spoken

UNWAGED adj said of work: unpaid

UNWALLED adj without a wall

UNWANTED adj not wanted; not desired

UNWARILY adverb in an unwary way

UNWARLIKE adj not warlike

UNWARMED adj not warmed

UNWARNED adj not warned

UNWARPED adj not warped

UNWARY adj **UNWARIER, UNWARIEST** not wary; careless or incautious; not aware of possible danger

UNWASHED adj not washed; not clean

UNWATCHED adj not watched

UNWEARIED adj not wearied; not tired

UNWEARY adj not weary; not tired

UNWEBBED adj not webbed

UNWED adj not married

UNWEDDED adj unwed

UNWEEDED adj said of eg a garden: not weeded

UNWEIGHED adj said of goods, quantities, etc: not weighed

UNWELCOME adj not welcome

UNWELL adj not well; ill

UNWEPT adj said of a person: not wept for; unlamented

UNWHIPPED adj not whipped

UNWIELDY adj **UNWIELDIER, UNWIELDIEST** said of an object: large and awkward to carry or manage; cumbersome

UNWILLING adj reluctant; loath

UNWIND verb **UNWINDS, UNWINDING, UNWOUND** to undo, slacken, untwist, etc something that has been wound or coiled up

UNWINGED adj not winged

UNWINKING adj not winking

UNWIPED adj not wiped

UNWISE adj **UNWISER, UNWISEST** not prudent; ill-advised; foolish

UNWISELY adverb in an unwise way

UNWISHED adj unwelcome; uninvited

UNWITTING adj not realizing or being aware

UNWOMANLY adj **UNWOMANLIER, UNWOMANLIEST** not befitting a woman

UNWONTED adj not usual or habitual

UNWOODED adj not wooded

UNWORLDLY adj **UNWORLDLIER, UNWORLDLIEST** not relating or belonging to this world; otherworldly

UNWORN adj not worn

UNWORRIED adj not worried; relaxed

UNWORTHY adj **UNWORTHIER, UNWORTHIEST** not deserving or worthy of something

UNWOUND past form of **unwind**

UNWOUNDED adj not wounded

UNWRAP verb **UNWRAPS, UNWRAPPING, UNWRAPPED** to remove the covering from something; to open something by removing its wrapping

UNWRITTEN adj not recorded in writing or print

UNWROUGHT adj not done or worked; not fashioned

UNYOKE verb **UNYOKES, UNYOKING, UNYOKED** to release (an animal) from a yoke or harness

UNZIP verb **UNZIPS, UNZIPPING, UNZIPPED** to unfasten or open (a garment, etc) by undoing a zip

UP prep at or to a higher position on, or a position further along □ adverb at or to a higher position or level □ adj placed in, or moving or directed to, a higher position □ verb **UPS, UPPING, UPPED** to raise or increase something □ noun **UPS** a success or advantage

UPBEAT adj cheerful; optimistic

UPBRAID verb **UPBRAIDS, UPBRAIDING, UPBRAIDED** to scold or reproach someone

UPBRAIDING noun **UPBRAIDINGS** an act of scolding or reproaching someone

UPBRINGING noun **UPBRINGINGS** the all-round instruction and education of a child, which influences their character and values

UPCHUCK verb **UPCHUCKS, UPCHUCKING, UPCHUCKED** to vomit

UPCOMING adj forthcoming; approaching

UPDATE verb **UPDATES, UPDATING, UPDATED** to make or bring something or someone up to date □ noun **UPDATES** an act of updating

UPFRONT adj candid; open

UPGRADE verb **UPGRADES, UPGRADING, UPGRADED** to promote someone □ noun **UPGRADES** an act or the process of upgrading someone

UPHEAVAL noun **UPHEAVALS** a change or disturbance that brings about great disruption

UPHEAVE verb **UPHEAVES, UPHEAVING, UPHEAVED** to heave or lift something up, especially forcibly

UPHILL adj sloping upwards; ascending □ noun **UPHILLS** an upward slope; an ascent or incline

UPHOLD verb **UPHOLDS, UPHOLDING, UPHELD** to support (an action), defend (a right) or maintain (the law), especially against opposition

UPHOLDER noun **UPHOLDERS** someone who upholds or supports a particular position

UPHOLSTER verb **UPHOLSTERS, UPHOLSTERING, UPHOLSTERED** to fit (chairs, sofas, etc) with upholstery

UPJET verb **UPJETS, UPJETTING, UPJETTED** to spout up

UPKEEP noun **UPKEEPS** the task or process of keeping something in good order or condition; maintenance

UPLAND noun **UPLANDS** a high or hilly region □ adj relating to or situated in such a region

UPLIFT verb **UPLIFTS, UPLIFTING, UPLIFTED** to lift something up; to raise it □ noun **UPLIFTS** the action or result of lifting up

UPLIFTING adj cheering; inspiring with hope

UPLIGHTER noun **UPLIGHTERS** a type of lamp or wall light placed or designed so as to throw light upwards

UPLOAD verb **UPLOADS, UPLOADING, UPLOADED** to send (data, files, etc) from one computer to another, eg by means of a telephone line and modem

UPMOST adj uppermost

UPON prep on or on to

UPPED past form of **up**

UPPER adj higher; situated above □ noun **UPPERS** the part of a shoe above the sole

UPPERCUT noun **UPPERCUTS** a forceful upward blow with the fist, usually under the chin

UPPERMOST adj at, in or into the highest or most prominent position

UPPING a form of **up**

UPPISH adj arrogant or snobbish

UPPISHLY adverb in an uppish way

UPPITY adj self-important; arrogant; uppish

UPRAISE verb **UPRAISES, UPRAISING, UPRAISED** to raise or lift something up; to elevate it

UPRATE verb **UPRATES, UPRATING, UPRATED** to upgrade something; to increase its rate, value, performance, etc

UPRIGHT adj standing straight up; erect or vertical □ noun **UPRIGHTS** a vertical (usually supporting) post or pole

UPRIGHTLY adverb in an upright way

UPRISE verb **UPRISES, UPRISING, UPROSE, UPRISEN** to rise up □ noun **UPRISES** the action of rising to a higher level or position

UPRISING noun **UPRISINGS** a rebellion or revolt

UPROAR noun **UPROARS** an outbreak of noisy and boisterous behaviour, especially angry protest

UPROOT verb **UPROOTS, UPROOTING, UPROOTED** to displace (a person or people) from their usual surroundings or home

UPRUSH verb **UPRUSHES, UPRUSHING, UPRUSHED** to rush up □ noun **UPRUSHES** a sudden upward rush or flow, eg of emotion, ideas, etc

UPSCALE adj pertaining to or designed to appeal to the wealthier in society; up-market

UPSET verb **UPSETS, UPSETTING, UPSET** to disturb or distress someone emotionally □ noun **UPSETS** a disturbance or disorder, eg of plans, the digestion, etc

UPSETTER noun **UPSETTERS** a person who upsets someone or something

UPSHOT noun **UPSHOTS** the final outcome or ultimate effect; the result or consequence, often of a particular course of action or series of events

UPSIDE noun **UPSIDES** the upper part or side of anything

UPSIDES adverb on a par; beside

UPSILON noun **UPSILONS** the twentieth letter of the Greek alphabet

UPSTAGE noun **UPSTAGES** the back of a theatre stage, the part furthest from the audience □ verb **UPSTAGES, UPSTAGING, UPSTAGED** said of an actor: to move upstage and force (another actor) to turn their back to the audience

UPSTAIRS singular and plural noun an upper floor or the upper floors of a building, especially the part of a house above the ground floor

UPSTART noun **UPSTARTS** someone who has suddenly acquired wealth or risen to a position of power or importance, especially one who is considered arrogant, or not to have the appropriate qualifications for such a position

UPSTATE adverb in, to or towards the part of a state remotest from, and usually to the north of, the principal city of the state

UPSTREAM adj situated towards the source of a river or stream □ adverb towards the source of a river or stream

UPSTROKE noun **UPSTROKES** an upward stroke or movement, especially of a pen or brush

UPSURGE noun **UPSURGES** a sudden sharp rise or increase; a surging up

UPSWEEP noun **UPSWEEPS** a sweep or curve upwards; a raising up

UPSWEPT adj made clear or thrown up by sweeping

UPSWING noun **UPSWINGS** a recovery in the trade cycle or a period during which this occurs

UPTAKE noun **UPTAKES** a pipe or flue with upward current

UPTHROW noun **UPTHROWS** an uplift; a raising up

UPTHRUST noun **UPTHRUSTS** an upward thrust or push

UPTIGHT adj **UPTIGHTER, UPTIGHTEST** nervous; anxious; tense

UPTOWN adverb in, into or towards the part of a town or city that is away from the centre, usually the more business or residential area □ adj situated in, relating, or belonging to or characteristic of this part of a town or city □ noun **UPTOWNS** the uptown part of a town or city

UPTOWNER noun **UPTOWNERS** someone who lives in a prosperous residential area of a city

UPTURN noun **UPTURNS** an upheaval □ verb **UPTURNS, UPTURNING, UPTURNED** to turn something over, up or upside-down

UPWARD adj moving or directed upwards, to a higher position, etc

UPWARDLY adverb in an upward way

UPWIND adverb against the direction of the wind; into the wind □ adj going against or exposed to the wind

UR exclamation expressing hesitation

URACIL noun **URACILS** one of the bases, derived from pyrimidine, that is present in the nucleic acid RNA

URAEMIA noun **URAEMIAS** the presence of excessive amounts of urea and other waste matter in the blood

URAEMIC adj of, relating to or suffering from uraemia

URANIC adj of or relating to uranium

URANINITE noun **URANINITES** a hard, slightly greasy, black, brown, grey or greenish mineral form of uranium oxide that is the principal ore of uranium and is highly radioactive

URANIUM noun **URANIUMS** a dense silvery-white radioactive metallic element, originally discovered in pitchblende in 1789

URATE noun **URATES** any salt or ester of uric acid

URBAN adj relating or belonging to, constituting, or characteristic of a city or town

URBANE adj **URBANER**, **URBANEST** with refined manners; suave; courteous

URBANELY adverb in an urbane way

URBANISE verb **URBANISES**, **URBANISING**, **URBANISED** to urbanize

URBANITY noun **URBANITIES** the quality of being urbane; refinement or elegance of manner, etc

URBANIZE verb **URBANIZES**, **URBANIZING**, **URBANIZED** to make (an area) less rural and more town-like

URCEOLATE adj shaped like a pitcher or urn

URCHIN noun **URCHINS** a mischievous child

URD noun **URDS** an Indian bean

URE noun **URES** an extinct wild ox

UREA noun **UREAS** a compound, white and crystalline when purified, formed during amino-acid breakdown in the liver of mammals, and excreted in the urine

UREAL adj of or relating to urea

UREIC adj of or relating to urea

UREIDE noun **UREIDES** any of various acyl derivatives of urea

UREMIA noun **UREMIAS** uraemia

URETER noun **URETERS** one of the two tubes through which urine is carried from the kidneys to the bladder

URETERAL adj of or relating to the ureter

URETERIC adj ureteral

URETHANE noun **URETHANES** a crystalline amide used eg in pesticides and formerly as an anaesthetic

URETHRA noun **URETHRAS**, **URETHRAE** the tube through which urine passes from the bladder out of the body and which, in males, also conveys semen

URETHRAL adj of or relating to the urethra

URGE verb **URGES**, **URGING**, **URGED** to persuade someone forcefully or incite them (to do something) □ noun **URGES** a strong impulse, desire or motivation (to do something)

URGENCY noun **URGENCIES** the state or condition of being urgent

URGENT adj requiring or demanding immediate attention, action, etc; pressing

URGENTLY adverb in an urgent way

URGER noun **URGERS** a person who urges someone to do something

URIAL noun **URIALS** a Himalyan wild sheep with long curved horns and reddish wool

URIC adj relating to, present in, or derived from, urine

URIDINE noun **URIDINES** a pyrimidine nucleoside based on uracil and ribose, obtained from RNA

URINAL noun **URINALS** any receptacle or sanitary fitting, especially one attached to a wall, designed for men to urinate into

URINARY noun **URINARIES** a reservoir for urine

URINATE verb **URINATES**, **URINATING**, **URINATED** to discharge urine

URINATION noun **URINATIONS** an act of urinating

URINE noun **URINES** the yellowish slightly acidic liquid consisting mainly of water and containing urea, uric acid, and other nitrogenous waste products filtered from the blood by the kidneys

URINOUS adj of or relating to urine

URN noun **URNS** a vase or vessel with a rounded body, usually a small narrow neck and a base or foot □ verb **URNS**, **URNING**, **URNED** to put in an urn

URNFIELD noun **URNFIELDS** a late Bronze Age cemetery of individual graves with urns containing ashes

URODELE noun **URODELES** any amphibian of the order Urodela, eg a newt or salamander, which is characterized by having a tail in the adult stage

UROGRAPHY noun **UROGRAPHIES** radiological examination of the urinary tract

UROLOGIC adj of or relating to urology

UROLOGIST noun **UROLOGISTS** someone who studies urology

UROLOGY noun **UROLOGIES** the branch of medicine that deals with the study and treatment of diseases and disorders of the male and female urinary tracts, and of the male genital tract

UROPYGIUM noun **UROPYGIUMS**, **UROPYGIA** the rump of a bird, that supports the tail feathers

UROSTYLE noun **UROSTYLES** in certain of the lower vertebrates: a prolongation of the last vertebra in frogs, toads and certain other amphibians

URSINE adj belonging, relating or referring to a bear or bears

URTICA noun **URTICAS** any plant of the nettle genus; a stinging nettle

URTICARIA noun **URTICARIAS** an allergic skin reaction with raised red or white itchy patches

URTICATE verb **URTICATES**, **URTICATING**, **URTICATED** to sting

URUS noun **URUSES** an aurochs

US pronoun the speaker or writer together with another person or other people; the object form of we

USABILITY noun **USABILITIES** the state or condition of being usable

USABLE adj able to be used

USAGE noun **USAGES** the act or way of using, or fact of being used; use; employment

USANCE noun **USANCES** the time

For longer words, see *The Chambers Dictionary*

allowed for the payment of bills of exchange, especially foreign ones
USE verb **USES, USING, USED** to put to a particular purpose □ noun **USES** the act of using
USED adj not new; second-hand
USEFUL adj able to be used advantageously; serving a helpful purpose; able to be put to various purposes
USEFULLY adverb in a useful way
USELESS adj serving no practical purpose
USELESSLY adverb in a useless way
USER noun **USERS** someone who uses a specified facility such as a leisure centre, a computer network, etc
USHER noun **USHERS** someone whose job is to show people to their seats, eg in a theatre, cinema, etc □ verb **USHERS, USHERING, USHERED** to conduct or escort someone, eg into or out of a building, room, etc
USHERETTE noun **USHERETTES** a woman who shows people to their seats in a theatre or cinema
USUAL adj done, happening, etc most often; customary □ noun **USUALS** something which is usual, customary, etc
USUALLY adverb ordinarily; normally
USUALNESS noun **USUALNESSES** the state of being usual
USUFRUCT noun **USUFRUCTS** the right to use and profit from another's property, as long as the property is not damaged or diminished in any way □ verb **USUFRUCTS, USUFRUCTING, USUFRUCTED** to hold (property) in usufruct
USURER noun **USURERS** someone who lends money, especially one who charges exorbitant rates of interest
USURIOUS adj relating to or involving usury

USURP verb **USURPS, USURPING, USURPED** to take possession of (eg land) or assume (eg power, authority, a title, etc) by force, without right or unjustly
USURPER noun **USURPERS** someone who usurps
USURY noun **USURIES** the practice of lending money at an unfairly or illegally high rate of interest

UT noun **UTS** the syllable (now called *doh*) once generally used for the first note of a musical scale and for the note C

UTE noun **UTES** a utility truck or utility vehicle
UTENSIL noun **UTENSILS** an implement or tool, especially one for everyday or domestic use
UTERINE adj relating to, in the region of or affecting the uterus
UTERUS noun **UTERI** the womb
UTILISE verb **UTILISES, UTILISING, UTILISED** to utilize
UTILISER noun **UTILISERS** a utilizer
UTILITY noun **UTILITIES** usefulness; practicality □ adj designed for usefulness or practicality, rather than beauty
UTILIZE verb **UTILIZES, UTILIZING, UTILIZED** to make practical use of something; to use it
UTILIZER noun **UTILIZERS** someone who utilizes something
UTMOST adj greatest possible in degree, number or amount □ noun **UTMOSTS** the greatest possible amount, degree or extent
UTOPIA noun **UTOPIAS** any imaginary place, state or society of idealized perfection
UTOPIAN noun **UTOPIANS** an inhabitant of utopia
UTRICLE noun **UTRICLES** a small cell, bag or bladder-like structure, especially the larger of the two parts of the membranous labyrinth of the inner ear

UTRICULAR adj of or relating to an utricle

UTS plural of **ut**

UTTER [1] verb **UTTERS, UTTERING, UTTERED** to give audible vocal expression to (an emotion, etc); to emit (a sound) with the voice
UTTER [2] adj **UTTERER, UTTEREST** complete; total; absolute
UTTERABLE adj capable of being uttered
UTTERANCE noun **UTTERANCES** the act of uttering or expressing something with the voice
UTTERER noun **UTTERERS** someone who utters
UTTERLY adverb completely; totally
UTTERMOST adj utmost □ noun **UTTERMOSTS** utmost
UTTERNESS noun **UTTERNESSES** the state of being total, complete or absolute

UTU noun **UTUS** a Maori word for the settlement of a debt

UVA noun **UVAS, UVAE** a grape or grape-like berry

UVAROVITE noun **UVAROVITES** an emerald-green variety of garnet, found in deposits of chromium
UVULA noun **UVULAS, UVULAE** the small fleshy part of the soft palate that hangs over the back of the tongue at the entrance to the throat
UVULAR adj of or relating to the uvula
UXORIAL adj relating or pertaining to a wife or wives
UXORICIDE noun **UXORICIDES** a man who kills his wife
UXORIOUS adj excessively or submissively fond of one's wife

VAC [1] *noun* **VACS** a vacation, especially between terms at a university or college

VAC [2] *verb* **VACS, VACKING, VACKED** to clean with a vacuum cleaner

VACANCY *noun* **VACANCIES** the state of being vacant; emptiness

VACANT *adj* empty or unoccupied

VACANTLY *adverb* in a vacant way

VACATE *verb* **VACATES, VACATING, VACATED** to make something empty; to empty something out

VACATION *noun* **VACATIONS** a holiday □ *verb* **VACATIONS, VACATIONING, VACATIONED** to take a holiday

VACCINAL *adj* of or relating to a vaccine

VACCINATE *verb* **VACCINATES, VACCINATING, VACCINATED** to administer to a person or an animal a vaccine that gives immunity from a disease; to inoculate

VACCINE *noun* **VACCINES** a preparation containing killed or weakened (attenuated) bacteria or viruses, or serum containing specific antibodies, used in vaccination to confer temporary or permanent immunity to a bacterial or viral disease by stimulating the body to produce antibodies to a specific bacterium or virus

VACCINIA *noun* **VACCINIAS** cowpox

VACHERIN *noun* **VACHERINS** a dessert made of a ring of meringue or almond paste filled with ice cream or whipped cream

VACILLATE *verb* **VACILLATES, VACILLATING, VACILLATED** to change opinions or decisions frequently; to waver

VACUA a plural of **vacuum**

VACUITY *noun* **VACUITIES** the state or quality of being vacuous

VACUOLAR *adj* of or relating to a vacuole

VACUOLE *noun* **VACUOLES** a space within the cytoplasm of a living cell that is filled with air or liquid and, in plant cells only, is surrounded by a membrane that controls the movement of substances into and out of that space

VACUOUS *adj* unintelligent; stupid; inane

VACUOUSLY *adverb* in a vacuous way

VACUUM *noun* **VACUUMS, VACUA** a space from which all matter has been removed □ *verb* **VACUUMS, VACUUMING, VACUUMED** to clean with a vacuum cleaner

VAE *noun* **VAES** a voe

VAGABOND *noun* **VAGABONDS** someone with no fixed home who lives an unsettled wandering life, especially someone regarded as lazy or worthless □ *adj* wandering; roving

VAGAL *adj* of or relating to the vagus

VAGARY *noun* **VAGARIES** an unpredictable and erratic act or turn of events

VAGI plural of **vagus**

VAGINA *noun* **VAGINAS, VAGINAE** in the reproductive system of most female mammals: the muscular canal that leads from the cervix of the uterus to the exterior of the body

VAGINAL *adj* of or relating to the vagina

VAGINITIS *noun* **VAGINITISES** inflammation of the vagina

VAGRANCY *noun* **VAGRANCIES** the state or condition of being a vagrant

VAGRANT *noun* **VAGRANTS** someone who has no permanent home or place of work

VAGUE *adj* **VAGUER, VAGUEST** indistinct or imprecise

VAGUELY *adverb* in a vague way

VAGUENESS *noun* **VAGUENESSES** the state or condition of being vague

VAGUS *noun* **VAGI** the tenth cranial nerve, concerned in regulating the heart, rhythm of breathing etc

VAIN *adj* **VAINER, VAINEST** having too much pride in one's appearance, achievements or possessions; conceited

VAINGLORY *noun* **VAINGLORIES** extreme boastfulness; excessive pride in oneself

VAINLY *adverb* in a vain way

VAINNESS *noun* **VAINNESSES** the state of being vain

VALANCE *noun* **VALANCES** a decorative strip of fabric hung over a curtain rail or round the frame of a bed

VALANCED *adj* trimmed with a valance

VALE *noun* **VALES** a valley

VALENCE *noun* **VALENCES** a positive or negative whole number that denotes the combining power of an atom of a particular element

VALENCY *noun* **VALENCIES** valence

VALENTINE *noun* **VALENTINES** a card or other message given, often anonymously, as a token of love or affection on St Valentine's Day

VALERIAN *noun* **VALERIANS** any of a family of small flowering plants of Europe and Asia with pinnate leaves, toothed leaflets, pink tubular flowers borne in dense terminal heads, and rhizome roots

VALET *noun* **VALETS** a man's personal servant, who attends to his clothes, dressing, etc □ *verb* **VALETS, VALETING, VALETED** to work as a valet

VALETA *noun* **VALETAS** a veleta

VALIANT *adj* outstandingly brave and heroic

VALIANTLY *adverb* in a valiant way

VALID *adj* **VALIDER, VALIDEST** based on truth or sound reasoning; legally acceptable for use

VALIDATE *verb* **VALIDATES, VALIDATING, VALIDATED** to make (a document, a ticket, etc) valid, eg by marking it with an official stamp

VALIDITY *noun* **VALIDITIES** the state or condition of being valid

VALIDLY adverb in a valid way

VALINE noun **VALINES** an amino acid

VALISE noun **VALISES** a small overnight case or bag

VALLEY noun **VALLEYS** a long flat area of land, usually containing a river or stream, flanked on both sides by higher land, eg hills or mountains

VALLUM noun **VALLUMS** a rampart or earth-work

VALONIA noun **VALONIAS** a tanning material consisting of the acorns of an oak, especially of the Levantine oak

VALOR noun **VALORS** valour

VALORISE verb **VALORISES, VALORISING, VALORISED** to valorize

VALORIZE verb **VALORIZES, VALORIZING, VALORIZED** to fix or stabilize the price of (a commodity, etc), especially by a policy imposed by a government or other controlling body

VALOROUS adj courageous, brave

VALOUR noun **VALOURS** courage or bravery, especially in battle

VALUABLE adj having considerable value or usefulness ▫ noun **VALUABLES** a personal possession of high financial or other value

VALUABLY adverb in a valuable way

VALUATION noun **VALUATIONS** an assessment of the monetary value of something, especially from an expert or authority

VALUE noun **VALUES** worth in monetary terms ▫ verb **VALUES, VALUING, VALUED** to consider something to be of a certain value, especially a high value; to esteem

VALUED adj considered valuable or precious; highly prized

VALUELESS adj without value

VALUER noun **VALUERS** someone who puts a value on eg property

VALUTA noun **VALUTAS** the comparative value of one currency with respect to another

VALVATE adj with a valve or valves

VALVE noun **VALVES** any device that regulates the flow of a liquid or gas through a pipe by opening or closing an aperture

VALVED adj having a valve or valves

VALVULAR adj of or having a valve or valves

VAMOOSE verb **VAMOOSES, VAMOOSING, VAMOOSED** to depart hurriedly; to clear off

VAMP noun **VAMPS** a woman who flaunts her sexual charm, especially in order to exploit men ▫ verb **VAMPS, VAMPING, VAMPED** to seduce (a man) with intent to exploit him

VAMPIRE noun **VAMPIRES** in folklore: a dead person who supposedly rises from the grave at night to suck the blood of the living

VAMPIRIC adj of or relating to vampires or vampirism

VAMPIRISM noun **VAMPIRISMS** belief in human vampires; the actions of a vampire

VAN noun **VANS** a commercial road vehicle with luggage space at the rear, lighter than a lorry or truck ▫ verb **VANS, VANNING, VANNED** to go or send in a van

VANADIUM noun **VANADIUMS** a soft silvery-grey metallic element that is used to increase the toughness and shock resistance of steel alloys, eg for components of cars

VANDAL noun **VANDALS** someone who wantonly damages or destroys personal and public property

VANDALISE verb **VANDALISES, VANDALISING, VANDALISED** to vandalize

VANDALISM noun **VANDALISMS** the actions of a vandal

VANDALIZE verb **VANDALIZES, VANDALIZING, VANDALIZED** to inflict wilful and senseless damage on (property, etc)

VANDYKE noun **VANDYKES** a broad collar with the edge cut into deep points

VANE noun **VANES** each of the blades of a windmill, propeller or revolving fan

VANED adj having vanes

VANELESS adj without vanes

VANGUARD noun **VANGUARDS** the part of a military force that advances first

VANILLA noun **VANILLAS** a Mexican climbing orchid having large fragrant white or yellow flowers followed by pod-like fruits; the fruit of this plant

VANILLIN noun **VANILLINS** the aromatic principle of vanilla, used in eg perfumes

VANISH verb **VANISHES, VANISHING, VANISHED** to disappear suddenly

VANITAS noun **VANITASES** a type of still-life picture, produced mainly by 17c Dutch artists, in which symbolic motifs such as skulls, hourglasses and old books feature as reminders of the vanity of earthly pleasures and the transience of human life and aspirations

VANITY noun **VANITIES** the quality of being vain or conceited; a thing one is conceited about

VANNED past form of **van**

VANNING a form of **van**

VANQUISH verb **VANQUISHES, VANQUISHING, VANQUISHED** to defeat or overcome someone

VANTAGE noun **VANTAGES** advantage

VAPID adj **VAPIDER, VAPIDEST** dull; uninteresting; insipid

VAPIDITY noun **VAPIDITIES** the quality or state of being vapid

VAPIDLY adverb in a vapid way

VAPIDNESS noun **VAPIDNESSES** the state of being vapid

VAPOR noun **VAPORS** a vapour ▫ verb **VAPORS, VAPORING, VAPORED** to vapour

VAPORETTO noun **VAPORETTI, VAPORETTOS** a small ship (originally steam, now motor) that plies the canals in Venice

VAPORISE verb **VAPORISES, VAPORISING, VAPORISED** to vaporize

VAPORISER noun **VAPORISERS** a vaporizer

VAPORIZE verb **VAPORIZES, VAPORIZING, VAPORIZED** to convert something into vapour

VAPORIZER noun **VAPORIZERS** something that vaporizes

VAPOROUS adj of, relating to, like or in the form of vapour

VAPOUR noun **VAPOURS** a substance in the form of a mist, fume or smoke, especially one coming off from a solid or liquid ▫ verb **VAPOURS, VAPOURING, VAPOURED** to rise as vapour; to evaporate

VAPOURISH adj vapoury

VAPOURY adj full of vapour

VARACTOR noun **VARACTORS** a two-electrode semiconductor device in which capacitance varies with voltage

VARIABLE adj referring to something that varies or tends to vary; not steady or regular; changeable ▫ noun **VARIABLES** a thing that can vary unpredictably in nature or degree

ARIABLY *adverb* in a variable way
ARIANCE *noun* **VARIANCES** the
ate of being different or
consistent
ARIANT *noun* **VARIANTS** a form
f a thing that varies from another
rm, eg the ending of a story or
ne of several permissible
ellings of a word
ARIATE *noun* **VARIATES** the
ariable quantity which is being
udied
ARIATION *noun* **VARIATIONS** the
ct or process of varying or
anging
ARICELLA *noun* **VARICELLAS**
ickenpox
ARICES plural of **varix**
ARICOSE *adj* said of a superficial
ein: abnormally swollen and
visted so that it produces a raised
nd often painful knot on the skin
rface, usually of the legs
ARIED past form of **vary** □ *adj*
aving variety; diverse
ARIEGATE *verb* **VARIEGATES,**
ARIEGATING, VARIEGATED to
lter the appearance of something,
pecially with patches of colours
ARIEGATED *adj* said of leaves or
owers: marked with patches of
vo or more colours
ARIES a form of **vary**
ARIETY *noun* **VARIETIES** any of
arious types of the same thing; a
ind or sort; diversity
ARIFOCAL *adj* said of lenses:
aving variable focal lengths
ARIFOCALS *plural noun* a pair of
lasses with varifocal lenses
ARIFORM *adj* referring to
mething whose shape or form
ay vary
ARIOLA *noun* **VARIOLAS**
nallpox
ARIOLAR *adj* of or relating to
ariola
ARIORUM *adj* said of an edition of
text: including the notes of earlier
ommentators or editors or
cluding variant meanings □ *noun*
ARIORUMS a variorum edition
ARIOUS *adj* several different;
iverse
ARIOUSLY *adverb* in different
ays; diversely
ARISTOR *noun* **VARISTORS** a
vo-electrode semi-conductor
sed to short-circuit transient high
ltages in delicate electronic
evices
ARIX *noun* **VARICES** an

abnormally dilated, lengthened
and tortuous vein, artery or
lymphatic vessel
VARLET *noun* **VARLETS** a menial
servant
VARMINT *noun* **VARMINTS** a
troublesome animal or person
VARNISH *noun* **VARNISHES** an oil-
based liquid containing resin,
painted on a surface such as wood
to give a hard transparent and
often glossy finish □ *verb*
VARNISHES, VARNISHING,
VARNISHED to apply varnish to
something
VARNISHER *noun* **VARNISHERS**
someone who varnishes eg
furniture
VARNISHING *noun* **VARNISHINGS**
an act of applying varnish to
something
VARSITY *noun* **VARSITIES** a
university, especially with
reference to sport
VARUS *adj* said of a foot or hand:
displaced from normal alignment
so as to deviate towards the
midline of the body
VARVE *noun* **VARVES** a seasonal
deposit of clay in still water, used
to determine Ice Age chronology
VARY *verb* **VARIES, VARYING,**
VARIED to change, or be of
different kinds, especially
according to different
circumstances
VARYING *noun* **VARYINGS** an act
of changing things
VAS *noun* **VASA** a vessel, tube or
duct carrying liquid
VASAL *adj* of or relating to a vas
VASCULAR *adj* relating to the
blood vessels of animals or the
sap-conducting tissues of plants
VASE *noun* **VASES** an ornamental
glass or pottery container,
especially one for holding cut
flowers
VASECTOMY *noun* **VASECTOMIES**
a surgical operation involving the
tying and cutting of the *vas
deferens* in the male reproduction
system, as a means of sterilization
VASSAL *noun* **VASSALS** someone
acting as a servant to, and fighting
on behalf of, a medieval lord in
return for land or protection or
both
VASSALAGE *noun* **VASSALAGES**
the state of being a vassal
VAST *adj* **VASTER, VASTEST**
extremely great in size, extent or
amount □ *noun* **VASTS** an

immense tract; a boundless or
empty expanse of space or time
VASTLY *adverb* in a vast way; to a
great extent
VASTNESS *noun* **VASTNESSES** the
state or condition of being vast
VAT *noun* **VATS** a large barrel or
tank for storing or holding liquids,
often used for fermentation,
dyeing or tanning □ *verb* **VATS,**
VATTING, VATTED to put something
into, or treat it in, a vat
VATMAN *noun* **VATMEN** an
employee of the Customs and
Excise Board responsible for
administering, assessing and
collecting VAT (value added tax)

VAU *noun* **VAUS** an obsolete
letter in the Greek alphabet

VAULT[1] *noun* **VAULTS** an arched
roof or ceiling, especially in a
church
VAULT[2] *verb* **VAULTS, VAULTING,**
VAULTED to spring or leap over
something, especially assisted by
the hands or a pole
VAULTING *noun* **VAULTINGS** a
series of vaults, eg in a church,
considered collectively
VAUNT *verb* **VAUNTS, VAUNTING,**
VAUNTED to boast or behave
boastfully about something □ *noun*
VAUNTS a boast
VAUNTER *noun* **VAUNTERS**
someone who boasts about
something
VAUNTING *noun* **VAUNTINGS** an
act of boasting or behaving
boastfully about something
VAVASOUR *noun* **VAVASOURS** a
knight, noble, etc with vassals
under him who is himself the
vassal of a greater noble
VEAL *noun* **VEALS** the flesh of a
calf, used as food
VECTOR *noun* **VECTORS** a quantity
which has both magnitude and
direction, eg force, velocity,
acceleration, often represented by
an arrow pointing in an
appropriate direction, whose
length is proportional to its
magnitude □ *verb* **VECTORS,**
VECTORING, VECTORED to direct
(an aircraft in flight) to the
required destination, especially
when the directions are given from
the ground
VEDALIA *noun* **VEDALIAS** an
Australian ladybird used as a
means of biological control
VEDUTA *noun* **VEDUTE** a painting

depicting a panoramic view of a place, usually a city, in a topographically accurate and decorative manner, popular especially in the 18c

VEE noun **VEES** a representation of the twenty-second letter of the English alphabet, 'V'

VEER verb **VEERS, VEERING, VEERED** to move abruptly in a different direction ▫ noun **VEERS** a change of direction

VEG ¹ noun **VEG, VEGES** a vegetable or vegetables

VEG ² verb **VEGGES, VEGGING, VEGGED** to be inactive or engage in mindless activity, especially after a period of over-exertion

VEGAN noun **VEGANS** someone who does not eat meat, fish, dairy products or any foods containing animal fats or extracts, such as eggs, cheese and honey, often also avoiding using wool, leather and other animal-based substances ▫ adj referring to or for vegans

VEGANISM noun **VEGANISMS** the practice of not eating meat, fish or dairy products

VEGETABLE noun **VEGETABLES** a plant or any of its parts, other than fruits and seeds, that is used for food, eg roots, tubers, stems or leaves

VEGETAL adj consisting of or relating to vegetables or to plant life in general

VEGETATE verb **VEGETATES, VEGETATING, VEGETATED** said of a person: to live a dull inactive life

VEGGED past form of **veg** ²

VEGGES a form of **veg** ²

VEGGIE noun **VEGGIES** a vegetarian

VEGGING a form of **veg** ²

VEGIE noun **VEGIES** a vegetarian

VEHEMENCE noun **VEHEMENCES** strong and forceful feeling

VEHEMENT adj expressed with strong feeling or firm conviction; forceful; emphatic

VEHICLE noun **VEHICLES** a conveyance for transporting people or things, especially a self-powered one

VEHICULAR adj relating to or for the use of vehicles

VEIL noun **VEILS** a fabric covering for a woman's head or face, forming part of traditional dress in some societies ▫ verb **VEILS, VEILING, VEILED** to cover something, or cover the face of someone, with a veil

VEILING noun **VEILINGS** material for making veils

VEIN noun **VEINS** a blood vessel that carries deoxygenated blood back towards the heart ▫ verb **VEINS, VEINING, VEINED** to form veins or the appearance of veins in something

VEINLET noun **VEINLETS** a small vein

VEINY adj **VEINIER, VEINIEST** having veins

VELA plural of **velum**

VELAMEN noun **VELAMINA** a multi-layered covering of dead cells on some aerial roots

VELAR adj referring to or attached to the velum ▫ noun **VELARS** a sound produced by the back of the tongue brought close to, or in contact with, the velum, such as k and g

VELARISE verb **VELARISES, VELARISING, VELARISED** to velarize

VELARIZE verb **VELARIZES, VELARIZING, VELARIZED** to pronounce (a sound that is usually non-velar) with the back of the tongue brought close to the soft palate

VELD noun **VELDS** a wide grassy plane with few or no trees, especially in S Africa

VELDT noun **VELDTS** a veld

VELETA noun **VELETAS** a ballroom dance or dance tune with a fast waltz-like rhythm

VELLUM noun **VELLUMS** a fine kind of parchment, originally made from calfskin

VELOCE adverb in music: with great rapidity

VELOCITY noun **VELOCITIES** rate of motion, ie distance per unit of time, in a particular direction, being a vector quantity

VELODROME noun **VELODROMES** a building containing a cycle-racing track

VELOUR noun **VELOURS** any fabric with a velvet-like pile, used especially for upholstery

VELOUTÉ noun **VELOUTÉS** a smooth white sauce made with stock

VELUM noun **VELA** the soft palate

VELVET noun **VELVETS** a fabric, usually cotton, nylon or silk, with a very short soft closely woven pile on one side

VELVETEEN noun **VELVETEENS** cotton fabric with a velvet-like pile

VELVETY adj **VELVETIER, VELVETIEST** of or like velvet

VENA noun **VENAE** a vein

VENAL adj said of a person: willing to be persuaded by corrupt means especially bribery

VENALITY noun **VENALITIES** the state or condition of being venal

VENALLY adverb in a venal way

VENATION noun **VENATIONS** the arrangement of veins in the wing of an insect

VEND verb **VENDS, VENDING, VENDED** to sell or offer (especially small wares) for sale

VENDACE noun **VENDACES** a freshwater white fish found in lochs in SW Scotland

VENDEE noun **VENDEES** a buyer, especially of property

VENDER noun **VENDERS** a vendor

VENDETTA noun **VENDETTAS** a bitter feud in which the family of a murdered person takes revenge by killing the murderer or one of their relatives

VENDIBLE noun **VENDIBLES** something that is for sale

VENDOR noun **VENDORS** a seller, especially of property

VENEER noun **VENEERS** a thin layer of a fine material, especially wood, fixed to the surface of an inferior material to give an attractive finish ▫ verb **VENEERS, VENEERING, VENEERED** to put a veneer on something

VENEERER noun **VENEERERS** someone who applies veneer

VENEERING noun **VENEERINGS** an act of applying veneer

VENERABLE adj deserving to be greatly respected or revered, especially on account of age or religious association

VENERABLY adverb in a venerable way

VENERATE verb **VENERATES, VENERATING, VENERATED** to regard someone or something with deep respect or awe; to revere someone or something

VENEREAL adj said of a disease or infection: transmitted by sexual intercourse

VENGEANCE noun **VENGEANCES** punishment inflicted as a revenge; retribution

VENGEFUL adj eager for revenge

VENISON noun **VENISONS** the flesh of a deer, used as food

VENITE noun **VENITES** the 95th

Psalm, beginning *Venite exultemus* O come, let us rejoice

VENOM *noun* **VENOMS** a poisonous liquid that some creatures, including scorpions and certain snakes, inject in a bite or sting

VENOMED *adj* venomous

VENOMOUS *adj* said of snake, etc: poisonous

VENOSE *adj* with very marked veins; veiny

VENOSITY *noun* **VENOSITIES** the state or condition of being venose

VENOUS *adj* relating to or contained in veins

VENT *noun* **VENTS** an opening that allows air, gas or liquid into or out of a confined space □ *verb* **VENTS, VENTING, VENTED** to make a vent in something

VENTER *noun* **VENTERS** the abdomen

VENTIL *noun* **VENTILS** a valve in a wind instrument

VENTILATE *verb* **VENTILATES, VENTILATING, VENTILATED** to allow fresh air to circulate throughout (a room, building, etc)

VENTRAL *adj* denoting the lower surface of an animal that walks on four legs, of any invertebrate, or of a structure such as a leaf or wing

VENTRALLY *adverb* in a ventral way

VENTRICLE *noun* **VENTRICLES** in mammals: either of the two lower chambers of the heart which have thick muscular walls

VENTURE *noun* **VENTURES** an exercise or operation involving danger or uncertainty □ *verb* **VENTURES, VENTURING, VENTURED** to be so bold as to; to dare

VENTURER *noun* **VENTURERS** someone who takes part in a venture or enterprise

VENTURI *noun* **VENTURIS** a tube or duct which is narrow in the middle and wider at both ends, used in measuring the flow rate of fluids, as a means of accelerating air flow, or to alter pressure

VENUE *noun* **VENUES** the chosen location for a sports event, a concert or other entertainment

VENULE *noun* **VENULES** a branch of a vein in an insect's wing

VERACIOUS *adj* truthful

VERACITY *noun* **VERACITIES** truthfulness

VERANDA *noun* **VERANDAS** a sheltered terrace attached to a house or other building

VERANDAH *noun* **VERANDAHS** a veranda

VERATRINE *noun* **VERATRINES** a toxic compound obtained from sabadilla seeds, formerly used as a counter-irritant in the treatment of neuralgia and rheumatism

VERB *noun* **VERBS** a word or group of words that belongs to a grammatical class denoting an action, experience, occurrence or state, eg *feel*, *happen*, *love*

VERBAL *adj* relating to or consisting of words; oral; spoken □ *noun* **VERBALS** a word, especially a noun, derived from a verb

VERBALISE *verb* **VERBALISES, VERBALISING, VERBALISED** to verbalize

VERBALISM *noun* **VERBALISMS** excessive attention paid to words used, rather than to ideas expressed, especially in literary criticism; literalism

VERBALIST *noun* **VERBALISTS** a person skilled in the use of words

VERBALIZE *verb* **VERBALIZES, VERBALIZING, VERBALIZED** to express (ideas, thoughts, etc) in words

VERBALLY *adverb* in a verbal way; orally

VERBATIM *adverb* using exactly the same words; word-for-word

VERBENA *noun* **VERBENAS** any of a group of plants of mild and tropical climates with clusters of fragrant white, pink, red or purplish tubular flowers, used in herbal medicine and cosmetics

VERBIAGE *noun* **VERBIAGES** the use of language that is wordy or needlessly complicated, and often meaningless

VERBOSE *adj* **VERBOSER, VERBOSEST** using or containing too many words; boringly or irritatingly long-winded

VERBOSELY *adverb* in a verbose way

VERBOSITY *noun* **VERBOSITIES** the state or condition of being verbose

VERBOTEN *adj* forbidden; not allowed

VERDANCY *noun* **VERDANCIES** the quality or state of being verdant

VERDANT *adj* covered with lush green grass or vegetation

VERDANTLY *adverb* in a verdant way

VERDELHO *noun* **VERDELHOS** a white Madeira wine, or the grape from which it is made

VERDICT *noun* **VERDICTS** a decision arrived at by a jury in a court of law

VERDIGRIS *noun* **VERDIGRISES** a blueish-green coating of basic copper salts, especially copper carbonate, that forms as a result of corrosion when copper, brass or bronze surfaces are exposed to air and moisture for long periods

VERDURE *noun* **VERDURES** lush green vegetation

VERDUROUS *adj* of, relating to or like verdure

VERGE *noun* **VERGES** a limit, boundary or border □ *verb* **VERGES, VERGING, VERGED** to serve as the border or boundary of something

VERGER *noun* **VERGERS** a church official who assists the minister and acts as caretaker

VERGLAS *noun* **VERGLASES** a thin transparent coating of ice on eg rock

VERIDICAL *adj* coinciding with fact

VERIER see under **very**

VERIEST see under **very**

VERIFIER *noun* **VERIFIERS** someone who verifies something

VERIFY *verb* **VERIFIES, VERIFYING, VERIFIED** to check or confirm the truth or accuracy of something

VERILY *adverb* truly; really

VERISM *noun* **VERISMS** use of everyday contemporary material, including what is ugly or sordid, in art and literature

VERISMO *noun* **VERISMOS** a style of opera drawing on themes from everyday life, especially of certain Italian operas of the early 20c

VERIST *noun* **VERISTS** a follower of verism

VERISTIC *adj* of or relating to verism

VERITABLE *adj* accurately described as such; real

VERITABLY *adverb* in a veritable way; truly

VERITY *noun* **VERITIES** a true statement, especially one of fundamental wisdom or importance; a maxim

VERJUICE *noun* **VERJUICES** the acidic juice of unripe fruit

VERLIGTE *adj* referring to liberal,

politically enlightened attitudes, especially with regard to apartheid and particularly those of an Afrikaner nationalist ▫ *noun* **VERLIGTES** someone with such attitudes

VERMEIL *noun* **VERMEILS** gilt bronze or silver gilt

VERMES plural of **vermis**

VERMIAN *adj* of or relating to the vermis

VERMICIDE *noun* **VERMICIDES** a worm-killing agent

VERMIFORM *adj* like a worm; worm-shaped

VERMILION *noun* **VERMILIONS** a bright scarlet colour

VERMIN *singular or plural noun* **VERMINS** a collective name for wild animals that spread disease or generally cause a nuisance, especially rats and other rodents

VERMINOUS *adj* of or relating to vermin

VERMIS *noun* **VERMES** a wormlike structure, such as the *vermis cerebelli*, the central lobe of the cerebellum

VERMOUTH *noun* **VERMOUTHS** an alcoholic drink consisting of wine flavoured with aromatic herbs, originally wormwood

VERNAL *adj* relating to or appropriate to spring; happening or appearing in spring

VERNALLY *adverb* in a vernal way

VERNATION *noun* **VERNATIONS** the arrangement of the leaves in a bud

VERNICLE *noun* **VERNICLES** a cloth bearing the face of Christ

VERNIER *noun* **VERNIERS** a small sliding device on some measuring instruments, eg barometers and theodolites, used to measure fractions of units

VERONICA *noun* **VERONICAS** a plant of the foxglove family, native to temperate and cold regions, with small blue, pink or white flowers, including the speedwell

VERRUCA *noun* **VERRUCAS, VERRUCAE** a wart, especially one on the sole of the foot

VERRUCOSE *adj* of, like or having verrucas; warty

VERRUCOUS *adj* verrucose

VERSANT *noun* **VERSANTS** the general slope of land

VERSATILE *adj* adapting easily to different tasks

VERSE *noun* **VERSES** a division of a poem; a stanza

VERSED *adj* familiar with or skilled in eg a subject

VERSICLE *noun* **VERSICLES** in liturgy: a verse said or sung by a minister and responded to by the congregation

VERSIFIER *noun* **VERSIFIERS** someone who writes poetry

VERSIFY *verb* **VERSIFIES, VERSIFYING, VERSIFIED** to write poetry

VERSIN *noun* **VERSINS** in maths: versed sine, a trigonometrical function of an angle equal to one minus the cosine

VERSINE *noun* **VERSINES** a versin

VERSION *noun* **VERSIONS** any of several types or forms in which a thing exists or is available, eg a particular edition or translation of a book, or one person's account of an incident

VERSIONAL *adj* of or relating to a version

VERSO *noun* **VERSOS** the back of a loose sheet of printed paper

VERSUS *prep* in a contest or lawsuit: against

VERTEBRA *noun* **VERTEBRAE** in vertebrates: any of the small bones or cartilaginous segments that form the backbone, each vertebra containing a central canal through which the spinal cord passes

VERTEBRAL *adj* of or relating to the vertebrae

VERTEX *noun* **VERTICES, VERTEXES** the highest point; the peak or summit

VERTICAL *adj* perpendicular to the horizon; upright ▫ *noun* **VERTICALS** a vertical line or direction

VERTICIL *noun* **VERTICILS** a set of parts arranged in a circle around an axis

VERTIGO *noun* **VERTIGOS, VERTIGOES** a whirling sensation felt when the sense of balance is disturbed; dizziness; giddiness

VERTU *noun* **VERTUS** a virtu

VERVAIN *noun* **VERVAINS** a wild verbena native to Europe, Asia and N Africa having small white, lilac or purple flowers borne in long slender spikes

VERVE *noun* **VERVES** great liveliness or enthusiasm, especially that which animates a poet or artist

VERVET *noun* **VERVETS** an African guenon monkey

VERY *adverb* to a high degree or extent ▫ *adj* **VERIER, VERIEST** (used for emphasis) absolute, precise, exact

VESICA *noun* **VESICAE** a bladder or sac, especially the urinary bladder

VESICAL *adj* of or relating to a vesica

VESICANT *noun* **VESICANTS** anything that causes blisters

VESICATE *verb* **VESICATES, VESICATING, VESICATED** to raise blisters on (the skin, etc), or become blistered

VESICLE *noun* **VESICLES** any small sac or cavity, especially one filled with fluid, within the cytoplasm of a living cell

VESPERS *singular noun* the sixth of the canonical hours, taking place towards evening

VESSEL *noun* **VESSELS** a ship or large boat

VEST *noun* **VESTS** an undergarment for the top half of the body ▫ *verb* **VESTS, VESTING, VESTED** to put on ecclesiastical robes

VESTAL *noun* **VESTALS** a chaste woman, especially a nun

VESTED *adj* usually said of property or money held in trust: recognized as belonging to a person, although not perhaps available to them until some future date

VESTIBULE *noun* **VESTIBULES** an entrance hall

VESTIGE *noun* **VESTIGES** a slight amount; a hint or shred

VESTMENT *noun* **VESTMENTS** any of various garments worn ceremonially by members of the clergy and church choir

VESTRAL *adj* of or relating to a vestry

VESTRY *noun* **VESTRIES** a room in a church where the vestments are kept, often also used for meetings, Sunday school classes, etc

VESTURE *noun* **VESTURES** clothing; garments

VET *noun* **VETS** a person qualified to treat diseases of animals ▫ *verb* **VETS, VETTING, VETTED** to examine or investigate (especially a person) thoroughly; to check someone for suitability or reliability for a particular activity, especially a job which requires a high degree of loyalty or trust

VETCH *noun* **VETCHES** any of various climbing plants of the pea family native to northern temperate regions and S America, with blue or purple flowers

VETCHLING noun **VETCHLINGS** any plant of the sweetpea genus, related to the vetch

VETERAN noun **VETERANS** someone with many years of experience in a particular activity

VETO noun **VETOES** the right to formally reject a proposal or forbid an action, eg in a law-making assembly ◻ verb **VETOES, VETOING, VETOED** to formally and authoritatively reject or forbid

VEX verb **VEXES, VEXING, VEXED** to annoy or irritate someone

VEXATION noun **VEXATIONS** the state or feeling of being vexed

VEXATIOUS adj vexing; annoying; troublesome

VEXED adj annoyed; angry; troubled

VEXILLUM noun **VEXILLA** the series of barbs on the sides of the shaft of a feather

VEXING adj annoying

VIA [1] prep by way of or by means of; through

VIA [2] noun **VIAS, VIAE** Latin word for way or road

VIABILITY noun **VIABILITIES** the state or condition of being viable

VIABLE adj said of a plan, etc: having a chance of success; feasible; practicable

VIADUCT noun **VIADUCTS** a bridge-like structure of stone arches supporting a road or railway across a valley, etc

VIAL noun **VIALS** a phial

VIANDS plural noun items of food; provisions

VIATICUM noun **VIATICUMS, VIATICA** in the RC Church: the Eucharist given to a dying person

VIBES singular noun feelings, sensations or an atmosphere experienced or communicated

VIBEX noun **VIBICES** a streak under the skin due to the leakage of blood

VIBRANCY noun **VIBRANCIES** the state or condition of being vibrant

VIBRANT adj extremely lively or exciting; made strikingly animated or energetic

VIBRANTLY adverb in a vibrant way

VIBRATE verb **VIBRATES, VIBRATING, VIBRATED** to move a short distance back and forth very rapidly

VIBRATION noun **VIBRATIONS** a vibrating motion

VIBRATO noun **VIBRATOS** a faint trembling effect in singing or the playing of string and wind instruments, achieved by vibrating the throat muscles or the fingers

VIBRATOR noun **VIBRATORS** any device that produces a vibrating motion, eg for massage

VIBRISSA noun **VIBRISSAE** a tactile bristle, such as a cat's whisker

VICAR noun **VICARS** the minister of a parish

VICARAGE noun **VICARAGES** a vicar's residence or benefice

VICARIAL adj referring to or serving as a vicar

VICARIATE noun **VICARIATES** the office, authority, time of office or sphere of a vicar

VICARIOUS adj experienced not directly but through witnessing the experience of another person

VICARSHIP noun **VICARSHIPS** the office of vicar

VICE noun **VICES** a tool with heavy movable metal jaws, usually fixed to a bench, for gripping an object being worked on

VICENNIAL adj lasting, or coming at the end of, twenty years

VICEREINE noun **VICEREINES** a viceroy's wife

VICEROY noun **VICEROYS** a male governor of a province or colony ruling in the name of, and with the authority of, a monarch or national government

VICESIMAL adj based on the number twenty

VICINITY noun **VICINITIES** a neighbourhood

VICIOUS adj violent or ferocious

VICIOUSLY adverb in a vicious way

VICTIM noun **VICTIMS** a person or animal subjected to death, suffering, ill-treatment or trickery

VICTIMISE verb **VICTIMISES, VICTIMISING, VICTIMISED** to victimize

VICTIMIZE verb **VICTIMIZES, VICTIMIZING, VICTIMIZED** to single someone or something out for hostile, unfair or vindictive treatment

VICTOR noun **VICTORS** the winner or winning side in a war or contest

VICTORIA noun **VICTORIAS** a large oval red and yellow variety of plum with a sweet flavour

VICTORY noun **VICTORIES** success against an opponent in a war or contest

VICTUAL verb **VICTUALS, VICTUALLING, VICTUALLED** to supply with victuals

VICTUALS plural noun food; provisions

VICUÑA noun **VICUÑAS** a ruminant mammal belonging to the camel family native to high grassland in the Andes Mountains of S America, resembling a llama but smaller and slenderer with a light-brown coat and a yellowish-red bib

VID noun **VIDS** video

VIDE verb used as an instruction in a text: refer to or see, eg a particular page-number or section

VIDELICET adverb used especially in writing: namely; that is

VIDEO noun **VIDEOS** a video cassette ◻ verb **VIDEOS, VIDEOING, VIDEOED** to make a video cassette recording of (a TV programme, a film, etc)

VIDEOFIT noun **VIDEOFITS** a type of identikit picture put together using a database of electronic images manipulated on a computer screen

VIDEOTAPE noun **VIDEOTAPES** magnetic tape on which visual images and sound can be recorded

VIDEOTEXT noun **VIDEOTEXTS** any system in which computerized information is displayed on a TV screen, eg teletext or viewdata

VIDIMUS noun **VIDIMUSES** an attested copy; an inspection, eg of accounts, etc

VIE verb **VIES, VYING, VIED** to compete or struggle with someone for some gain or advantage

VIEW noun **VIEWS** an act or opportunity of seeing without obstruction ◻ verb **VIEWS, VIEWING, VIEWED** to see or look at something

VIEWABLE adj able to be seen

VIEWDATA noun **VIEWDATAS** a system by which computerized information can be displayed on a TV screen by means of a telephone link with a computer source

VIEWER noun **VIEWERS** any device used for viewing something, especially a photographic slide

VIEWING noun **VIEWINGS** an act or opportunity of seeing or inspecting something, eg an exhibition or a house for sale

VIEWPOINT *noun* **VIEWPOINTS** an interpretation of facts received

VIGESIMAL *adj* based on the number twenty

VIGIL *noun* **VIGILS** a period of staying awake, usually to guard or watch over a person or thing

VIGILANCE *noun* **VIGILANCES** the state of being watchful or observant

VIGILANT *adj* ready for possible trouble or danger; alert; watchful

VIGILANTE *noun* **VIGILANTES** a member of an organization looking after the interests of a group threatened in some way, especially a self-appointed and unofficial policeman

VIGNETTE *noun* **VIGNETTES** a photographic portrait with the background deliberately faded □ *verb* **VIGNETTES, VIGNETTING, VIGNETTED** to make a vignette of something or someone

VIGOR *noun* **VIGORS** vigour

VIGORISH *noun* **VIGORISHES** a percentage of a gambler's winnings taken by the bookmaker, organizers of a game, etc

VIGORO *noun* **VIGOROS** a 12-a-side game with similarities to cricket and baseball

VIGOROUS *adj* strong and active

VIGOUR *noun* **VIGOURS** great strength and energy of body or mind

VIHARA *noun* **VIHARAS** a Buddist or Jain temple, monastery or nunnery

VIKING *noun* **VIKINGS** any of the Scandinavian seafaring peoples who raided and settled in much of NW Europe between the 8c and 11c

VILE *adj* **VILER, VILEST** morally evil or wicked; repulsive; disgusting

VILELY *adverb* in a vile way

VILENESS *noun* **VILENESSES** the state or condition of being vile

VILIFIER *noun* **VILIFIERS** someone who vilifies others

VILIFY *verb* **VILIFIES, VILIFYING, VILIFIED** to say insulting or abusive things about someone or something; to malign or defame someone

VILLA *noun* **VILLAS** in ancient Rome: a large country house or mansion

VILLAGE *noun* **VILLAGES** a group of houses, shops and other buildings, smaller than a town and larger than a hamlet, especially in or near the countryside

VILLAGER *noun* **VILLAGERS** someone who lives in a village

VILLAIN *noun* **VILLAINS** the principal wicked character in a story

VILLAINY *noun* **VILLAINIES** wicked or vile behaviour

VILLEIN *noun* **VILLEINS** a peasant worker bound to a lord and showing allegiance to him

VILLIFORM *adj* like a villus in shape

VILLOUS *adj* of or relating to a villus

VILLUS *noun* **VILLI** any of many tiny fingerlike projections that line the inside of the small intestine and absorb the products of digestion

VIM *noun* **VIMS** energy; liveliness

VIMANA *noun* **VIMANAS** the central shrine of an Indian temple with a pyramidal roof

VIN *noun* **VINS** a French word for *wine*

VINA *noun* **VINAS** an Indian stringed instrument with a fretted fingerboard over two gourds

VINCIBLE *adj* able to be overcome or defeated

VINCULUM *noun* **VINCULA** a horizontal line placed above part of an equation as an alternative to brackets

VINDALOO *noun* **VINDALOOS** a hot Indian curry, usually made with meat, poultry or fish

VINDICATE *verb* **VINDICATES, VINDICATING, VINDICATED** to clear someone of blame or criticism

VINE *noun* **VINES** any of various woody climbing plants that produce grapes

VINEGAR *noun* **VINEGARS** a sour liquid consisting of a dilute solution of acetic acid, which is produced by the bacterial fermentation of alcoholic beverages such as cider or wine and is used as a condiment and preservative

VINEGARY *adj* of or like vinegar; especially in taste

VINEYARD *noun* **VINEYARDS** a plantation of grape-bearing vines, especially for wine-making

VINO *noun* **VINOS** wine, especially of poor quality

VINOSITY *noun* **VINOSITIES** the state or condition of being vinous

VINOUS *adj* belonging or relating to, or resembling, wine

VINTAGE *noun* **VINTAGES** the grape-harvest of a particular year □ *adj* said of wine: good quality and from a specified year

VINTNER *noun* **VINTNERS** a wine-merchant

VINY *adj* **VINIER, VINIEST** of, relating to or like a vine

VINYL *noun* **VINYLS** any of a group of tough plastics manufactured in various forms, eg paint additives and carpet fibres

VIOL *noun* **VIOLS** any of a family of Renaissance stringed musical instruments played with a bow

VIOLA *noun* **VIOLAS** a musical instrument of the violin family, larger than the violin and lower in pitch

VIOLABLE *adj* capable of being violated

VIOLATE *verb* **VIOLATES, VIOLATING, VIOLATED** to disregard or break (a law, agreement or oath)

VIOLATION *noun* **VIOLATIONS** an act of breaking a law, agreement or oath

VIOLATOR *noun* **VIOLATORS** someone who breaks a law, agreement or oath

VIOLENCE *noun* **VIOLENCES** the state or quality of being violent

VIOLENT *adj* marked by or using extreme physical force

VIOLENTLY *adverb* in a violent way

VIOLET *noun* **VIOLETS** any of various flowering perennial plants, native to temperate regions, with large purple, blue or white petals

VIOLIN *noun* **VIOLINS** a four-stringed musical instrument with a shaped body, which is usually held with one end under the chin and played with a bow

VIOLINIST *noun* **VIOLINISTS** someone who plays the violin

VIOLIST *noun* **VIOLISTS** someone who plays the viol or viola

VIPER *noun* **VIPERS** any of a large family of poisonous snakes found in Europe, Asia and Africa with long tubular fangs through which venom is injected into the prey

VIPERISH *adj* spiteful

VIPEROUS *adj* of or like a viper; venomous

VIRAGO *noun* **VIRAGOS,**

VIRAGOES a loudly fierce or abusive woman
VIRAL *adj* belonging or relating to or caused by a virus
VIREMENT *noun* **VIREMENTS** in finance: the authorized transference of funds from one account to another
VIRES plural of **vis**
VIRGA *singular or plural noun* **VIRGAS** trails of water drops or ice particles coming from a cloud, which evaporate before reaching the ground
VIRGIN *noun* **VIRGINS** a person, especially a woman, who has never had sexual intercourse
VIRGINAL *noun* **VIRGINALS** a keyboard instrument, used in the 16c and 17c, like a small harpsichord but with strings set at right angles to the keys
VIRGINITY *noun* **VIRGINITIES** the state of being a virgin
VIRGULE *noun* **VIRGULES** a solidus
VIRILE *adj* said of a man: having a high level of sexual desire
VIRILITY *noun* **VIRILITIES** manhood; energy; vigour
VIROLOGY *noun* **VIROLOGIES** the branch of microbiology concerned with the study of viruses and viral diseases
VIRTU *noun* **VIRTUS** a love of works of fine art or curiosities
VIRTUAL *adj* being so in effect or in practice, but not in name
VIRTUALLY *adverb* in practice, though not strictly speaking
VIRTUE *noun* **VIRTUES** a quality regarded as morally good
VIRTUOSO *noun* **VIRTUOSOS, VIRTUOSI** someone with remarkable artistic skill, especially a brilliant musical performer
VIRTUOUS *adj* possessing or showing virtue; morally sound
VIRULENCE *noun* **VIRULENCES** the state or condition of being virulent
VIRULENT *adj* said of a disease: having a rapidly harmful effect
VIRUS *noun* **VIRUSES** an infectious particle, consisting of a core of DNA or RNA enclosed in a protein shell, that invades the cells of animals, plants and bacteria
VIS *noun* **VIRES** force; power
VISA *noun* **VISAS** a permit stamped into a passport, or a similar document, allowing the holder to enter or leave the country which issues it ❑ *verb* **VISAS, VISAING, VISAED** to stamp (a passport, etc) with a visa
VISAGE *noun* **VISAGES** the face
VISCACHA *noun* **VISCACHAS** a burrowing rodent native to S America, that resembles a chinchilla but is slightly larger
VISCERA *plural noun* the internal organs of the body, especially those found in the abdominal cavity
VISCERAL *adj* belonging or relating to the viscera
VISCID *adj* glutinous; sticky
VISCIDITY *noun* **VISCIDITIES** the state or condition of being viscid
VISCOSE *noun* **VISCOSES** cellulose in a viscous state, able to be made into thread
VISCOSITY *noun* **VISCOSITIES** a measure of the resistance of a fluid to flow
VISCOUNT *noun* **VISCOUNTS** a member of the British nobility ranked below an earl and above a baron
VISCOUNTY *noun* **VISCOUNTIES** the rank or dignity of a viscount
VISCOUS *adj* with a thick semi-liquid consistency; not flowing easily
VISCUS *noun* **VISCERA** any one of the body's large internal organs
VISE *noun* **VISES** a vice
VISIBLE *adj* able to be seen
VISIBLY *adverb* in a visible way
VISION *noun* **VISIONS** the ability or faculty of perceiving with the eye; sight
VISIONAL *adj* of or relating to vision
VISIONARY *adj* showing or marked by great foresight or imagination ❑ *noun* **VISIONARIES** a visionary person
VISIT *verb* **VISITS, VISITING, VISITED** to go or come to see (a person or place) socially or professionally ❑ *noun* **VISITS** an act of visiting; a social or professional call
VISITABLE *adj* capable of being visited
VISITANT *noun* **VISITANTS** a person appearing in a supernatural vision; an apparition
VISITOR *noun* **VISITORS** someone who visits a person or place
VISOR *noun* **VISORS** the movable part of a helmet, covering the face
VISTA *noun* **VISTAS** a view into the distance, especially one bounded narrowly on both sides, eg by rows of trees
VISUAL *adj* relating to or received through sight or vision ❑ *noun* **VISUALS** a rough sketch of the layout of an advertisement
VISUALISE *verb* **VISUALISES, VISUALISING, VISUALISED** to visualize
VISUALIZE *verb* **VISUALIZES, VISUALIZING, VISUALIZED** to form a clear mental image of someone or something
VISUALLY *adverb* in a visual way
VITAL *adj* relating to or essential for life ❑ *noun* **VITALS** the vital organs, including the brain, heart and lungs
VITALISE *verb* **VITALISES, VITALISING, VITALISED** to vitalize
VITALITY *noun* **VITALITIES** liveliness and energy
VITALIZE *verb* **VITALIZES, VITALIZING, VITALIZED** to fill someone with life or energy
VITALLY *adverb* in a vital way; essentially
VITAMIN *noun* **VITAMINS** any of various organic compounds that occur in small amounts in many foods, are also manufactured synthetically and are essential in small amounts for the normal growth and functioning of the body
VITIATE *verb* **VITIATES, VITIATING, VITIATED** to impair the quality or effectiveness of (eg an argument); to make something faulty or defective
VITIATION *noun* **VITIATIONS** an act of vitiating
VITIATOR *noun* **VITIATORS** someone who vitiates
VITILIGO *noun* **VITILIGOS** a condition in which irregular patches of the skin lose colour and turn white
VITREOUS *adj* relating to or consisting of glass
VITRIFORM *adj* resembling glass in form or appearance
VITRIFY *verb* **VITRIFIES, VITRIFYING, VITRIFIED** to make into or become glass or something like glass, especially by heating
VITRIOL *noun* **VITRIOLS** concentrated sulphuric acid
VITRIOLIC *adj* extremely bitter or hateful, especially with reference to speech or criticism
VITTA *noun* **VITTAE** a thin elongated

cavity containing oil found in the pericarps of some fruits

VIVA verb **VIVAS, VIVAING, VIVAED** to examine someone orally

VIVACE adverb in music: in a lively manner

VIVACIOUS adj attractively lively and animated, especially with reference to a person

VIVACITY noun **VIVACITIES** the state or condition of being vivacious

VIVARIUM noun **VIVARIA, VIVARIUMS** any place or enclosure in which live animals are kept, especially in conditions resembling their natural habitat

VIVID adj **VIVIDER, VIVIDEST** said of a colour: strong and bright

VIVIDLY adverb in a vivid way

VIVIDNESS noun **VIVIDNESSES** the state or condition of being vivid

VIVIFY verb **VIVIFIES, VIVIFYING, VIVIFIED** to endue something with life

VIVISECT verb **VIVISECTS, VIVISECTING, VIVISECTED** to dissect living animals for experimental purposes

VIXEN noun **VIXENS** a female fox

VIXENISH adj bad-tempered

VIXENLY adj vixenish

VIZCACHA noun **VIZCACHAS** a viscacha

VIZIER noun **VIZIERS** a high-ranking government official in certain Muslim countries, especially in Turkey during the Ottoman Empire

VIZIERATE noun **VIZIERATES** the office of a vizier

VIZIERIAL adj of or relating to a vizier

VIZOR noun **VIZORS** a visor

VIZSLA noun **VIZSLAS** a breed of Hungarian hunting dog with a smooth red or rust-coloured coat

VLY noun **VLIES** low-lying wet ground, a swamp

VOCAB noun **VOCABS** vocabulary

VOCABLE noun **VOCABLES** a spoken word or single sound in a word

VOCAL adj expressing opinions or criticism freely and forcefully ▫ noun **VOCALS** the parts of a musical composition that are sung, as distinct from the instrumental accompaniment

VOCALIC adj belonging or relating to, or containing, a vowel or vowels

VOCALISE verb **VOCALISES, VOCALISING, VOCALISED** to vocalize

VOCALISM noun **VOCALISMS** the use of the voice as in singing or speaking

VOCALIST noun **VOCALISTS** a singer, especially in a pop group or jazz band

VOCALIZE verb **VOCALIZES, VOCALIZING, VOCALIZED** to utter or produce something with the voice

VOCALLY adverb in a vocal way

VOCATION noun **VOCATIONS** a particular occupation or profession, especially one regarded as needing dedication and skill

VOCATIVE noun **VOCATIVES** in some languages, eg Greek and Latin: the form of a noun, pronoun or adjective used when a person or thing is addressed directly

VOCODER noun **VOCODERS** a type of synthesizer used to impose human speech patterns onto the sound of musical instruments

VODKA noun **VODKAS** a clear alcoholic spirit of Russian origin, traditionally made from rye, but sometimes from potatoes

VOE noun **VOES** in Orkney and Shetland: a bay; a creek

VOGUE noun **VOGUES** the current fashion or trend in any sphere

VOGUISH adj fashionable

VOICE noun **VOICES** a sound produced by the vocal organs and uttered through the mouth, especially by humans in speech or song ▫ verb **VOICES, VOICING, VOICED** to express something in speech

VOICED adj expressed in speech

VOICELESS adj without a voice

VOID adj not valid or legally binding ▫ noun **VOIDS** an empty space ▫ verb **VOIDS, VOIDING, VOIDED** to make empty or clear

VOIDABLE adj capable of being voided

VOIDANCE noun **VOIDANCES** a vacancy in a benefice

VOIDNESS noun **VOIDNESSES** the state or condition of being void

VOILE noun **VOILES** any very thin semi-transparent fabric

VOL noun **VOLS** in heraldry, two wings displayed and conjoined

VOLANT adj belonging or relating to flight

VOLATILE adj changing quickly from a solid or liquid into a vapour; explosive ▫ noun **VOLATILES** a volatile substance

VOLCANIC adj relating to or produced by a volcano or volcanoes

VOLCANO noun **VOLCANOES** any of various vents in the Earth's crust through which magma is or has previously been forced out onto the surface, forming various structures, usually a conical hill

VOLE noun **VOLES** a small rodent related to the lemming, with a small tail, blunt snout and smaller eyes and ears, found in Europe, Asia, N Africa and N America

VOLITION noun **VOLITIONS** the act of willing or choosing; the exercising of one's will

VOLITIVE adj belonging or relating to the will

VOLLEY noun **VOLLEYS** a firing of several guns or other weapons simultaneously ▫ verb **VOLLEYS, VOLLEYING, VOLLEYED** to fire (weapons) in a volley

VOLLEYER noun **VOLLEYERS** someone who volleys

VOLT noun **VOLTS** in the SI system: a unit of electric potential, the difference in potential that will carry a current of one ampere across a resistance of one ohm

VOLTAGE noun **VOLTAGES** potential difference expressed as a number of volts

VOLTE noun **VOLTES** in fencing: a sudden movement or leap to avoid a thrust

VOLTMETER noun **VOLTMETERS** an instrument that measures electromotive force in volts

VOLUBLE adj speaking or spoken insistently, uninterruptedly or with ease

VOLUBLY adverb in a voluble way

VOLUME noun **VOLUMES** the amount of three-dimensional space occupied by an object, gas or liquid

VOLUNTARY adj done or acting by free choice, not by compulsion ▫ noun **VOLUNTARIES** a piece of music, usually for an organ, played before, during or after a church service

VOLUNTEER verb **VOLUNTEERS, VOLUNTEERING, VOLUNTEERED** to offer one's help or services freely, without being persuaded or forced □ *noun* **VOLUNTEERS** someone who volunteers

VOLUTE *noun* **VOLUTES** a spiral

VOMIT *verb* **VOMITS, VOMITING, VOMITED** to eject the contents of the stomach forcefully through the mouth through a reflex action; to be sick □ *noun* **VOMITS** the contents of the stomach ejected during the process of vomiting

VOODOO *noun* **VOODOOS** witchcraft of a type originally practised by the Black peoples of the West Indies and southern US □ *verb* **VOODOOS, VOODOOING, VOODOOED** to bewitch someone or something using, or as if using, voodoo methods

> **VOR** *verb* **VORS, VORRING, VORRED** a Shakespearean word meaning to warn

VORACIOUS *adj* eating or craving food in large quantities

VORACITY *noun* **VORACITIES** the state or condition of being voracious

VORTEX *noun* **VORTEXES, VORTICES** a whirlpool or whirlwind; any whirling mass or motion

VORTICAL *adj* of or relating to a vortex

VORTICISM *noun* **VORTICISMS** a British movement in painting developed from futurism, which blended cubism and expressionism, and emphasized the complications of machinery that characterize modern life

VORTICIST *noun* **VORTICISTS** a follower of vorticism

VOTARIST *noun* **VOTARISTS** a votary

VOTARY *noun* **VOTARIES** someone bound by solemn vows to a religious life

VOTE *noun* **VOTES** a formal indication of choice or opinion, eg in an election or debate □ *verb* **VOTES, VOTING, VOTED** to cast a vote in an election

VOTER *noun* **VOTERS** someone who votes in an election

VOTIVE *adj* done or given in thanks to a deity, or to fulfil a vow or promise

VOUCH *verb* **VOUCHES, VOUCHING, VOUCHED** to give a firm assurance or guarantee of

someone or something's authenticity, trustworthiness, etc

VOUCHER *noun* **VOUCHERS** a ticket or paper serving as proof, eg of the purchase or receipt of goods

VOUCHSAFE *verb* **VOUCHSAFES, VOUCHSAFING, VOUCHSAFED** to agree or condescend to do, give, grant or allow

VOUSSOIR *noun* **VOUSSOIRS** one of the wedge-shaped stones that form part of the centre line of an arch □ *verb* **VOUSSOIRS, VOUSSOIRING, VOUSSOIRED** to form (an arch) with voussoirs

VOW *noun* **VOWS** a solemn and binding promise, especially one made to or in the name of a deity □ *verb* **VOWS, VOWING, VOWED** to promise or declare solemnly, or threaten emphatically; to swear

VOWEL *noun* **VOWELS** any speech-sound made with an open mouth and no contact between mouth, lips, teeth or tongue

VOWELISE *verb* **VOWELISES, VOWELISING, VOWELISED** to vowelize

VOWELIZE *verb* **VOWELIZES, VOWELIZING, VOWELIZED** to mark the vowel points in (a shorthand, Hebrew, etc text)

> **VOX** *noun* **VOCES** voice

> **VOXEL** *noun* **VOXELS** a point in a three-dimensional computer image

VOYAGE *noun* **VOYAGES** a long journey to a distant place, especially by air or sea □ *verb* **VOYAGES, VOYAGING, VOYAGED** to go on a voyage; to travel

VOYAGER *noun* **VOYAGERS** someone who goes on a voyage

VOYEUR *noun* **VOYEURS** someone who derives gratification from furtively watching the sexual attributes or activities of others

VOYEURISM *noun* **VOYEURISMS** the behaviour of voyeurs

> **VOZHD** *noun* **VOZHDS** a supreme leader in Russia

VROOM *noun* **VROOMS** power, drive and energy □ *verb* **VROOMS, VROOMING, VROOMED** to travel at speed

> **VUG** *noun* **VUGS** a Cornish word for a cavity in a rock

VULCANISE *verb* **VULCANISES, VULCANISING, VULCANISED** to vulcanize

VULCANITE *noun* **VULCANITES** hard black vulcanized rubber

VULCANIZE *verb* **VULCANIZES, VULCANIZING, VULCANIZED** to treat natural or artificial rubber with various concentrations of sulphur or sulphur compounds at high temperatures for specific times, so as to harden it and increase its elasticity

VULGAR *adj* **VULGARER, VULGAREST** marked by a lack of politeness or social or cultural refinement; coarse

VULGARIAN *noun* **VULGARIANS** a vulgar person, especially one who is rich

VULGARISE *verb* **VULGARISES, VULGARISING, VULGARISED** to vulgarize

VULGARISM *noun* **VULGARISMS** a vulgar expression in speech

VULGARITY *noun* **VULGARITIES** coarseness in speech or behaviour

VULGARIZE *verb* **VULGARIZES, VULGARIZING, VULGARIZED** to make something vulgar

VULGARLY *adverb* in a vulgar way

VULGATE *noun* **VULGATES** commonly used or accepted speech

VULNERARY *noun* **VULNERARIES** a drug or medicine useful for healing wounds

VULPINE *adj* belonging or relating to, or resembling, a fox

VULTURE *noun* **VULTURES** any of various large carnivorous birds with brown or black plumage, long broad wings, a bare head and a strongly curved beak, which feed on carrion

VULVA *noun* **VULVAS** the two pairs of labia surrounding the opening to the vagina; the external female genitals

VULVAL *adj* of or relating to the vulva

VULVAR *adj* vulval

> **VUM** *verb* **VUMS, VUMMING, VUMMED** a US word meaning to vow

VYING a form of **vie**

WACKILY adv in a wacky way

WACKINESS noun
WACKINESSES the state of being wacky; wacky behaviour

WACKO adj mad or crazy; eccentric

WACKY adj **WACKIER, WACKIEST** mad or crazy; eccentric

WAD noun **WADS** a compressed mass of soft material used for packing, padding or stuffing, etc □ verb **WADS, WADDING, WADDED** to roll or form something into a wad

WADDING noun **WADDINGS** material used as padding or stuffing

WADDLE verb **WADDLES, WADDLING, WADDLED** said of a duck: to sway from side to side in walking □ noun **WADDLES** the act of waddling

WADDLER noun **WADDLERS** a person or animal that waddles

WADDY noun **WADDIES** a wooden club used in warfare by Australian Aboriginals □ verb **WADDIES, WADDYING, WADDIED** to strike someone using a waddy

WADE verb **WADES, WADING, WADED** to walk through something, especially deep water, which does not allow easy movement of the feet; to cross (a river, etc) by wading □ noun **WADES** the act of wading

WADER noun **WADERS** someone or something that wades

WADI noun **WADIS** a rocky river bed in N Africa and Arabia, dry except during the rains

WADY noun **WADIES** a wadi

WAE noun **WAES** a Scots word for *woe*

WAFER noun **WAFERS** a thin light finely layered kind of biscuit, served eg with ice cream; a thin disc of adhesive material used instead of a seal on documents, etc □ verb **WAFERS, WAFERING, WAFERED** to close, fasten or stick with a wafer

WAFERY adj of or like a wafer, especially in being thin or finely layered

WAFFLE [1] noun **WAFFLES** a light-textured cake made of batter, with a distinctive grid-like surface pattern formed by the hinged iron mould in which it is baked

WAFFLE [2] verb **WAFFLES, WAFFLING, WAFFLED** to talk or write at length but to little purpose

WAFFLER noun **WAFFLERS** someone who waffles

WAFT verb **WAFTS, WAFTING, WAFTED** to float or make something float or drift gently, especially through the air □ noun **WAFTS** the action of wafting

WAG verb **WAGS, WAGGING, WAGGED** to wave to and fro vigorously □ noun **WAGS** a wagging movement

WAGE verb **WAGES, WAGING, WAGED** to engage in or fight (a war or battle) □ noun **WAGES** a regular, especially daily or weekly rather than monthly, payment from an employer to an employee, especially an unskilled or semi-skilled one

WAGER noun **WAGERS** a bet on the outcome or result of something □ verb **WAGERS, WAGERING, WAGERED** to bet; to stake something in a bet

WAGERER noun **WAGERERS** someone who wagers

WAGGED past form of **wag**

WAGGING a form of **wag**

WAGGISH adj amusing; mischievous

WAGGLE verb **WAGGLES, WAGGLING, WAGGLED** to move or make something move to and fro □ noun **WAGGLES** a wobble or wobbling motion

WAGGLY adj **WAGGLIER, WAGGLIEST** wagging

WAGGON noun **WAGGONS** a wagon

WAGON noun **WAGONS** a four-wheeled vehicle, often horse-drawn, used especially for carrying loads; a cart

WAGONER noun **WAGONERS** the driver of a wagon

WAGONETTE noun **WAGONETTES** a kind of horse-drawn carriage with one or two seats positioned crosswise in the front, and two back seats positioned lengthwise and facing each other

WAGONLOAD noun **WAGONLOADS** the load carried by a wagon

WAGTAIL noun **WAGTAILS** any of various birds so called because of the constant wagging motion of their long tails

WAHINE noun **WAHINES** a Maori woman

WAHOO noun **WAHOOS** a large fast-moving marine food and game fish, related to the mackerel

WAIF noun **WAIFS** an orphaned, abandoned or homeless child

WAIL noun **WAILS** a prolonged and high-pitched mournful or complaining cry □ verb **WAILS, WAILING, WAILED** to make, or utter something with, such a cry

WAILER noun **WAILERS** someone who wails

WAILING noun **WAILINGS** an act of making or uttering a wail

WAILINGLY adverb with a wail

WAIN noun **WAINS** an open wagon, especially for hay or other agricultural produce

WAINSCOT noun **WAINSCOTS** wooden panelling or boarding covering the lower part of the walls of a room

WAINSCOTING noun
WAINSCOTINGS the wainscot

WAINSCOTTING noun
WAINSCOTTINGS the wainscot

WAIST noun **WAISTS** the narrow part of the human body between the ribs and hips

WAISTBAND noun **WAISTBANDS** the reinforced strip of cloth on a skirt or trousers, etc that fits round the waist

WAISTCOAT noun **WAISTCOATS** a close-fitting sleeveless garment, usually waist-length, worn especially by men under a jacket

WAISTED adj having a waist, often of a specified kind

WAISTLINE noun **WAISTLINES** the line marking the waist

WAIT verb **WAITS, WAITING, WAITED** said of a task, etc: to remain temporarily undealt with

WAITER noun **WAITERS** a man who serves people with food at a hotel or restaurant, etc

WAITRESS noun **WAITRESSES** a woman who serves people with food at a hotel or restaurant, etc

WAIVE verb **WAIVES, WAIVING, WAIVED** to refrain from insisting upon something; to voluntarily give up (a claim or right, etc)

WAIVER noun **WAIVERS** a written statement voluntarily giving up one's claim or right

WAKE[1] verb **WAKES, WAKING, WOKE, WAKED, WOKEN** to rouse or be roused from sleep

WAKE[2] noun **WAKES** a trail of disturbed water left by a ship, or of disturbed air left by an aircraft

WAKEFUL adj not asleep or unable to sleep

WAKEFULLY adverb in a wakeful way

WAKEN verb **WAKENS, WAKENING, WAKENED** to rouse or be roused from sleep

WAKING noun **WAKINGS** an act of rousing or being roused from sleep

WALE noun **WALES** a raised mark on the skin ◻ verb **WALES, WALING, WALED** to create wales by striking

WALK verb **WALKS, WALKING, WALKED** to move along in some direction on foot, moving one's feet alternately and always having one or other foot on the ground ◻ noun **WALKS** the motion, or pace of walking

WALKABOUT noun **WALKABOUTS** a casual stroll through a crowd of ordinary people by a celebrity, especially a member of the royal family or a politician, etc

WALKATHON noun **WALKATHONS** a long-distance walk, either as a race or in aid of charity

WALKER noun **WALKERS** someone who walks, especially for pleasure

WALKWAY noun **WALKWAYS** a paved path or passage for pedestrians

WALL noun **WALLS** a solid vertical

brick or stone construction serving eg as a barrier, territorial division or protection ◻ verb **WALLS, WALLING, WALLED** to surround something with, or as if with, a wall

WALLA noun **WALLAS** a wallah

WALLABY noun **WALLABIES** any of several species of a plant-eating marsupial, belonging to the same family as the kangaroo, and native to Australia

WALLAH noun **WALLAHS** a person who performs a specified task

WALLAROO noun **WALLAROOS** a large kind of kangaroo

WALLET noun **WALLETS** a flat folding case, often made of leather, for holding banknotes, etc and carried in the pocket or handbag

WALLIES plural of **wally**

WALLOP verb **WALLOPS, WALLOPING, WALLOPED** to hit or strike someone or something vigorously ◻ noun **WALLOPS** a hit or a thrashing

WALLOPER noun **WALLOPERS** someone who wallops something

WALLOPING noun **WALLOPINGS** a thrashing

WALLOW verb **WALLOWS, WALLOWING, WALLOWED** to lie or roll about (in water or mud, etc) ◻ noun **WALLOWS** the act of wallowing

WALLOWER noun **WALLOWERS** a person or thing that wallows

WALLOWING noun **WALLOWINGS** an act of lying or rolling about (in water or mud, etc)

WALLPAPER noun **WALLPAPERS** paper, often coloured or patterned, used to decorate the interior walls and ceilings of houses, etc

WALLY noun **WALLIES** an ineffectual, stupid or foolish person

WALNUT noun **WALNUTS** any of various deciduous trees found in N temperate regions, with large compound leaves, cultivated for their timber and edible nut

WALRUS noun **WALRUSES** a large carnivorous marine mammal related to the seal, with thick wrinkled skin, webbed flippers and two long tusks, which is found in the northern waters of the Atlantic and Pacific oceans

WALTZ noun **WALTZES** a slow or fast ballroom dance in triple time, in which the dancers spin round

the room ◻ verb **WALTZES, WALTZING, WALTZED** to dance a waltz

WALTZER noun **WALTZERS** someone who waltzes

WAMPUM noun **WAMPUMS** shells strung together for use as money among the Native Americans

WAN adj **WANNER, WANNEST** pale and pinched-looking, especially from illness, exhaustion or grief ◻ verb **WANS, WANNING, WANNED** to make or become wan

WAND noun **WANDS** a slender rod used by magicians, conjurors and fairies, etc for performing magic

WANDER verb **WANDERS, WANDERING, WANDERED** to walk, move or travel about, with no particular destination; to ramble ◻ noun **WANDERS** a ramble or stroll

WANDERER noun **WANDERERS** someone who wanders

WANDERING noun **WANDERINGS** an act of walking, moving or travelling about, with no particular destination

WANDEROO noun **WANDEROOS** a langur from Sri Lanka

WANDOO noun **WANDOOS** a W Australian eucalyptus with white bark and durable wood

WANE verb **WANES, WANING, WANED** said of the Moon: to appear to grow narrower as the Sun illuminates less of its surface ◻ noun **WANES** the process of waning or declining

WANEY adj **WANIER, WANIEST** waning

WANGLE verb **WANGLES, WANGLING, WANGLED** to contrive or obtain something by persuasiveness ◻ noun **WANGLES** an act of wangling

WANGLER noun **WANGLERS** someone who wangles something

WANLY adverb in a wan way

WANNABE noun **WANNABES** someone who admires and imitates the appearance, mannerisms and habits, etc of another person

WANNABEE noun **WANNABEES** a wannabe

WANNED past form of **wan**

WANNER see under **wan**

WANNESS noun **WANNESSES** the quality or condition of being wan

WANNEST see under **wan**

WANNING a form of **wan**

WANT verb **WANTS, WANTING, WANTED** to feel a need or desire for something □ noun **WANTS** a need or requirement

WANTED adj needed or desired

WANTER noun **WANTERS** someone who wants something

WANTING adj missing; lacking

WANTON adj **WANTONER, WANTONEST** thoughtlessly and needlessly cruel □ noun **WANTONS** an immoral woman

WANTONLY adverb in a wanton way

WANY adj **WANIER, WANIEST** waning

WAP verb **WAPS, WAPPING, WAPPED** to throw or pull quickly

WAPITI noun **WAPITIS** a type of large N American deer, reddish in colour with a light patch on its rump, and with large branched antlers

WAQF noun **WAQFS** in Islam: the donation of land, property or money for charitable or pious purposes

WAR noun **WARS** an open state of armed conflict, especially between nations □ verb **WARS, WARRING, WARRED** to fight wars

WARATAH noun **WARATAHS** any of a genus of Australian shrubs with flamboyant scarlet flowers

WARBLE verb **WARBLES, WARBLING, WARBLED** said of a bird: to sing melodiously □ noun **WARBLES** the act of warbling

WARBLER noun **WARBLERS** someone or something that warbles

WARD noun **WARDS** a room in a hospital with beds for patients □ verb **WARDS, WARDING, WARDED** to fend off, turn aside, or parry (a blow)

WARDEN noun **WARDENS** someone in charge of a hostel, student residence or old people's home, etc

WARDER noun **WARDERS** a male prison officer

WARDRESS noun **WARDRESSES** a female prison officer

WARDROBE noun **WARDROBES** a tall cupboard in which clothes are kept

WARDROOM noun **WARDROOMS** the officers' quarters on board a warship

WARE noun **WARES** manufactured goods of a specified material or for a specified range of use

WAREHOUSE noun **WAREHOUSES** a large building or room for storing goods □ verb **WAREHOUSES, WAREHOUSING, WAREHOUSED** to deposit or store in a warehouse

WAREHOUSING noun **WAREHOUSINGS** the act of depositing goods in a warehouse

WARFARE noun **WARFARES** the activity or process of waging or engaging in war

WARFARIN noun **WARFARINS** a crystalline substance used in medicine as an anticoagulant, either to prevent the clotting of blood or to break up existing clots, and otherwise as a poison for rats, etc

WARHEAD noun **WARHEADS** the front part of a missile or torpedo etc that contains the explosives

WARHORSE noun **WARHORSES** formerly, a powerful horse on which a knight rode into battle

WARIER see under **wary**

WARIEST see under **wary**

WARILY adverb in a wary way

WARINESS noun **WARINESSES** the state or condition of being wary

WARLIKE adj fond of fighting; aggressive or belligerent

WARLOCK noun **WARLOCKS** a wizard, male magician or sorcerer

WARLORD noun **WARLORDS** a powerful military leader

WARM adj **WARMER, WARMEST** moderately, comfortably or pleasantly hot □ verb **WARMS, WARMING, WARMED** to make or become warm or warmer

WARMLY adverb in a warm way

WARMONGER noun **WARMONGERS** someone who tries to precipitate war, or who generates enthusiasm for it

WARMTH noun **WARMTHS** the condition of being warm

WARN verb **WARNS, WARNING, WARNED** to make someone aware of (possible or approaching danger or difficulty)

WARNER noun **WARNERS** a person or thing that gives a warning

WARNING noun **WARNINGS** a caution against eg danger

WARP verb **WARPS, WARPING,**

WARPED said of wood and other hard materials: to become, or make it become, twisted out of shape through the shrinking and expanding effects of damp or heat, etc □ noun **WARPS** the state or fact of being warped

WARPATH noun **WARPATHS** the march to war; battle; conflict

WARPER noun **WARPERS** a person or thing that warps

WARPLANE noun **WARPLANES** any aircraft designed or intended for use in warfare

WARRAGAL noun **WARRAGALS** the warrigal □ adj warrigal

WARRANT noun **WARRANTS** a written legal authorization for doing something, eg arresting someone, or searching property □ verb **WARRANTS, WARRANTING, WARRANTED** to justify something

WARRANTEE noun **WARRANTEES** someone to whom a warranty is given

WARRANTER noun **WARRANTERS** a warrantor

WARRANTOR noun **WARRANTORS** someone who gives a warrant or warranty

WARRANTY noun **WARRANTIES** an assurance of the quality of goods being sold, usually with an acceptance of responsibility for repairs during an initial period of use

WARRED past form of **war**

WARREN noun **WARRENS** an underground labyrinth of interconnecting rabbit burrows

WARRIGAL noun **WARRIGALS** the wild dog or dingo □ adj wild; savage

WARRING a form of **war**

WARRIOR noun **WARRIORS** a skilled fighting man, especially one belonging to earlier times

WARSHIP noun **WARSHIPS** a ship armed with guns, etc for use in naval battles

WART noun **WARTS** a small and usually hard benign growth with a horny surface, transmitted by a virus, and found on the skin, especially of the fingers, hands and face

WARTHOG noun **WARTHOGS** a large wild pig, native to Africa south of the Sahara, with a greyish-brown skin, wart-like lumps on its face, sparse shaggy hair, a bristly mane and two pairs of backward-curving tusks

WARTIME noun **WARTIMES** a period during which a war is going on

WARTY adj **WARTIER, WARTIEST** of, like or covered with warts

WARY adj **WARIER, WARIEST** alert, vigilant or cautious; on one's guard

WAS a past form of **be**

WASH verb **WASHES, WASHING, WASHED** to cleanse someone or something with water or other liquid, and usually soap or detergent ◻ noun **WASHES** the process of washing or being washed

WASHABLE adj said especially of clothes: able to be washed without damage

WASHBASIN noun **WASHBASINS** a shallow sink in which to wash one's face and hands

WASHBOARD noun **WASHBOARDS** a corrugated board for rubbing clothes on while washing them

WASHCLOTH noun **WASHCLOTHS** a cloth for washing the face and body

WASHDAY noun **WASHDAYS** a day, often the same day each week, on which one's washing is done

WASHER noun **WASHERS** someone who washes

WASHERMAN noun **WASHERMEN** a man paid to wash clothes

WASHHOUSE noun **WASHHOUSES** an outhouse or basement room for washing clothes

WASHIER see under **washy**

WASHIEST see under **washy**

WASHING noun **WASHINGS** the act of cleansing, wetting or coating with liquid

WASHOUT noun **WASHOUTS** a flop or failure

WASHRAG noun **WASHRAGS** a washcloth

WASHROOM noun **WASHROOMS** a lavatory

WASHSTAND noun **WASHSTANDS** a small table in a bedroom for holding a jug and basin for washing one's hands and face

WASHY adj **WASHIER, WASHIEST** said of a drink: watery or weak, usually excessively so

WASP noun **WASPS** any of numerous social or solitary stinging insects which have slender black-and-yellow striped bodies and narrow waists, belonging to the same order as bees and ants, and found worldwide

WASPISH adj sharp-tongued; caustic or venomous

WASPISHLY adverb in a waspish way

WASPY adj **WASPIER, WASPIEST** waspish

WASSAIL noun **WASSAILS** a festive bout of drinking ◻ verb **WASSAILS, WASSAILING, WASSAILED** to hold a wassail

WASSAILER noun **WASSAILERS** someone who wassails

WASTAGE noun **WASTAGES** the process of wasting; loss through wasting

WASTE verb **WASTES, WASTING, WASTED** to use or spend something purposelessly or extravagantly; to squander ◻ adj rejected as useless, unneeded or excess to requirements ◻ noun **WASTES** the act or an instance of wasting, or the condition of being wasted

WASTED adj not exploited; squandered

WASTEFUL adj causing waste; extravagant

WASTELAND noun **WASTELANDS** a desolate and barren region

WASTER noun **WASTERS** an idler, good-for-nothing or wastrel

WASTREL noun **WASTRELS** an idle spendthrift; a good-for-nothing

WAT noun **WATS** a Thai Buddhist temple or monastery

WATCH verb **WATCHES, WATCHING, WATCHED** to look at or focus one's attention on someone or something that is moving or doing something, etc ◻ noun **WATCHES** a small timepiece, usually worn strapped to the wrist or on a chain in the waistcoat pocket or attached to clothing

WATCHABLE adj able to be watched; enjoyable

WATCHCASE noun **WATCHCASES** an outer protective case for a watch

WATCHDOG noun **WATCHDOGS** a dog kept to guard premises, etc

WATCHFUL adj alert, vigilant and wary

WATCHMAN noun **WATCHMEN** a man employed to guard premises at night

WATCHWORD noun **WATCHWORDS** a catchphrase or slogan that encapsulates the principles of a party, group or profession, etc

WATER noun **WATERS** a colourless odourless tasteless liquid that freezes to form ice at 0°C and boils to form steam at 100°C, at normal atmospheric pressure ◻ verb **WATERS, WATERING, WATERED** to wet, soak or sprinkle something with water

WATERER noun **WATERERS** a person or thing that waters

WATERFALL noun **WATERFALLS** a sudden interruption in the course of a river or stream where water falls more or less vertically, in some cases for a considerable distance, eg over the edge of a plateau or where overhanging softer rock has been eroded away

WATERFOWL noun **WATERFOWLS** a bird that lives on or near water, especially a swimming bird such as a duck or swan, typically having webbed feet, short legs, narrow pointed wings and a broad flattened bill

WATERLESS adj without water

WATERLINE noun **WATERLINES** the level reached by the water on the hull of a floating vessel when under different conditions of loading

WATERLOGGED adj saturated with water

WATERMAN noun **WATERMEN** a man who plies a boat for hire; a boatman

WATERMARK noun **WATERMARKS** the limit reached by the sea at high or low tide; a waterline ◻ verb **WATERMARKS, WATERMARKING, WATERMARKED** to impress (paper) with a watermark

WATERSHED noun **WATERSHEDS** the line that separates two river basins

WATERSIDE noun **WATERSIDES** the edge of a river, lake or sea

WATERWAY noun **WATERWAYS** a navigable channel, eg a canal or river, used by ships or smaller boats either for travel or for conveying goods

WATERWORKS noun **WATERWORKS** an installation where water is purified and stored for distribution to an area

WATERY adj **WATERIER, WATERIEST** relating to, consisting of or containing water

WATT noun **WATTS** in the SI system: a unit of power, defined as the power that gives rise to the production of energy at the rate of one joule per second

WATTAGE noun **WATTAGES** an amount of electrical power expressed in watts

WATTLE noun **WATTLES** rods or branches, etc forming eg a framework for a wall, fences or roofs, especially when interwoven □ verb **WATTLES, WATTLING, WATTLED** to bind something with wattle or twigs

WATTMETER noun **WATTMETERS** an instrument for measuring the power consumption (usually in watt-hours or units) in an alternating-current electric circuit

WAUL verb **WAULS, WAULING, WAULED** to cry in the manner of a cat or newborn baby □ noun **WAULS** such a cry

WAVE verb **WAVES, WAVING, WAVED** to move (one's hand) to and fro in greeting, farewell or as a signal □ noun **WAVES** any of a series of moving ridges on the surface of the sea or some other body of water

WAVEBAND noun **WAVEBANDS** a range of frequencies in the electromagnetic spectrum occupied by radio or TV broadcasting transmission

WAVEFORM noun **WAVEFORMS** a graph that shows the variation of amplitude of an electrical signal, or other wave, against time

WAVER verb **WAVERS, WAVERING, WAVERED** to move to and fro

WAVERER noun **WAVERERS** someone who wavers

WAVESHAPE noun **WAVESHAPES** a waveform

WAVILY adverb in a wavy way

WAVINESS noun **WAVINESSES** the state or condition of being wavy

WAVY adj **WAVIER, WAVIEST** said of hair: full of loose, soft curls

WAW noun **WAWS** a Spenserian word meaning a wave

WAWL verb **WAWLS, WAWLING, WAWLED** to waul □ noun **WAWLS** a waul

WAX noun **WAXES** any of a wide variety of solid or semi-solid lipids, either natural or synthetic, that are typically shiny, have a low melting point, are easily moulded when warm, and are insoluble in water □ verb **WAXES, WAXING, WAXED** to use or apply a natural or mineral wax on something, eg prior to polishing

WAXBERRY noun **WAXBERRIES** the wax myrtle; the waxy-surfaced fruit from this plant

WAXBILL noun **WAXBILLS** any of various small seed-eating birds with coloured bills resembling sealing-wax in colour

WAXCLOTH noun **WAXCLOTHS** an oilcloth

WAXEN adj made of or covered with wax

WAXILY adverb in a waxy way

WAXINESS noun **WAXINESSES** the state of being waxy

WAXWING noun **WAXWINGS** a songbird of the N hemisphere, which has a crested head, greyish-brown plumage with a black tail, and red wax-like marks on the tips of its wings

WAXWORK noun **WAXWORKS** a lifelike model, especially of a famous person or a celebrity, made of wax

WAXY adj **WAXIER, WAXIEST** similar to or resembling wax in appearance or feel

WAY ¹ noun **WAYS** a route, entrance or exit, etc that provides passage or access somewhere □ adverb far; a long way

WAY ² verb **WAYS, WAYING, WAYED** a Spenserian word meaning to journey

WAYBILL noun **WAYBILLS** a list that gives details of goods or passengers being carried by a public vehicle

WAYFARER noun **WAYFARERS** a traveller, especially on foot

WAYFARING noun **WAYFARINGS** travel

WAYLAY verb **WAYLAYS, WAYLAYING, WAYLAID** to lie in wait for and ambush someone

WAYLAYER noun **WAYLAYERS** someone who waylays others

WAYLEAVE noun **WAYLEAVES** permission given to pass over another's ground or property, usually on payment of a fee

WAYMARK noun **WAYMARKS** a signpost; something that serves as a guide for a traveller

WAYSIDE noun **WAYSIDES** the edge of a road, or the area to the side of it □ adj growing, situated or lying near the edge of roads

WAYWARD adj undisciplined or self-willed; headstrong, wilful or rebellious

WAYWARDLY adverb in a wayward way

WAZIR noun **WAZIRS** a vizier

WE pronoun used as the subject of a verb: to refer to oneself in company with another or others

WEAK adj **WEAKER, WEAKEST** lacking physical strength

WEAKEN verb **WEAKENS, WEAKENING, WEAKENED** to make or become weaker

WEAKENER noun **WEAKENERS** someone who weakens something

WEAKLING noun **WEAKLINGS** a sickly or physically weak person or animal

WEAKLY adj sickly; not strong or robust

WEAKNESS noun **WEAKNESSES** the condition of being weak

WEAL noun **WEALS** a long raised reddened mark on the skin caused eg by a slash with a whip or sword

WEALD noun **WEALDS** an area of open or forested country

WEALTH noun **WEALTHS** riches, valuables and property, or the possession of them

WEALTHILY adverb in a wealthy way

WEALTHY adj **WEALTHIER, WEALTHIEST** possessing riches and property; rich or prosperous

WEAN verb **WEANS, WEANING, WEANED** to accustom (a baby or young mammal) to taking food other than its mother's milk

WEANER noun **WEANERS** a young animal, especially a pig, that has recently been weaned

WEAPON noun **WEAPONS** an instrument or device used to kill or injure people, usually in a war or fight

WEAPONED adj armed; having weapons

WEAPONRY noun **WEAPONRIES** weapons collectively; armament

WEAR verb **WEARS, WEARING, WORE, WORN** to be dressed in something, or have it on one's body □ noun **WEARS** the act of wearing or state of being worn

WEARABLE *adj* capable of being worn; good for wearing
WEARER *noun* **WEARERS** someone wearing something
WEARILY *adverb* in a weary way
WEARINESS *noun*
WEARINESSES the state or condition of being weary
WEARING *adj* exhausting or tiring
WEARISOME *adj* tiring, tedious or frustrating
WEARY *adj* **WEARIER, WEARIEST** tired out; exhausted □ *verb* **WEARIES, WEARYING, WEARIED** to make or become weary
WEASEL *noun* **WEASELS** a small nocturnal carnivorous mammal, closely related to the stoat and found in most N temperate regions, with a slender body, short legs and reddish-brown fur with white underparts □ *verb* **WEASELS, WEASELLING, WEASELING, WEASELLED, WEASELED** to equivocate
WEASELLY *adj* of or like a weasel, especially in appearance
WEATHER *noun* **WEATHERS** the atmospheric conditions in any area at any time, with regard to Sun, cloud, temperature, wind and rain, etc □ *verb* **WEATHERS, WEATHERING, WEATHERED** to expose or be exposed to the effects of wind, Sun and rain, etc; to alter or be altered in colour, texture and shape, etc through such exposure
WEATHERING *noun*
WEATHERINGS the physical disintegration and chemical decomposition of rocks on or just beneath the Earth's surface, which occurs as a result of exposure to wind, rain, humidity, extremes of temperature (eg frost), etc
WEAVE *verb* **WEAVES, WEAVING, WOVE, WOVEN** to make (cloth or tapestry) in a loom, passing threads under and over the threads of a fixed warp; to interlace (threads) in this way □ *noun* **WEAVES** the pattern, compactness or texture of the weaving in a fabric
WEAVER *noun* **WEAVERS** someone who weaves
WEB *noun* **WEBS** a network of slender threads constructed by a spider to trap insects □ *verb* **WEBS, WEBBING, WEBBED** to make or weave a web
WEBBED *adj* said of fingers and toes: partially joined together by a membrane of skin

WEBBING *noun* **WEBBINGS** strong jute or nylon fabric woven into strips for use as belts, straps and supporting bands in upholstery
WEBER *noun* **WEBERS** in the SI system: a unit of magnetic flux
WEBFOOT *noun* **WEBFEET** a foot the toes of which are joined together by a membrane of skin
WED *verb* **WEDS, WEDDING, WEDDED, WED** to marry
WEDDING *noun* **WEDDINGS** a marriage ceremony, or the ceremony together with the associated celebrations
WEDGE *noun* **WEDGES** a piece of solid wood, metal or other material, tapering to a thin edge, that is driven into eg wood to split it, pushed into a narrow gap between moving parts to immobilize them, or used to hold a door open, etc □ *verb* **WEDGES, WEDGING, WEDGED** to fix or immobilize something in position with, or as if with, a wedge
WEDGY *adj* **WEDGIER, WEDGIEST** like a wedge
WEDLOCK *noun* **WEDLOCKS** the condition of being married; marriage
WEE [1] *adj* **WEER, WEEST** small; tiny
WEE [2] *verb* **WEES, WEEING, WEED** to urinate □ *noun* **WEES** an act of urinating
WEED *noun* **WEEDS** any plant that grows wild and has no specific use or aesthetic value □ *verb* **WEEDS, WEEDING, WEEDED** to uproot weeds from (a garden or flowerbed, etc)
WEEDER *noun* **WEEDERS** someone who weeds
WEEDINESS *noun* **WEEDINESSES** the state of being weedy
WEEDING *noun* **WEEDINGS** the task of uprooting weeds
WEEDLESS *adj* without weeds
WEEDS *plural noun* the black mourning clothes worn by a widow
WEEDY *adj* **WEEDIER, WEEDIEST** overrun with weeds
WEEK *noun* **WEEKS** a sequence of seven consecutive days, usually beginning on Sunday
WEEKDAY *noun* **WEEKDAYS** any day except Sunday, or except Saturday and Sunday
WEEKEND *noun* **WEEKENDS** the period from Friday evening to Sunday night

WEEKENDER *noun*
WEEKENDERS someone who goes away from home at weekends
WEEKLY *adj* occurring, produced or issued every week, or once a week □ *noun* **WEEKLIES** a magazine or newspaper published once a week
WEEKNIGHT *noun* **WEEKNIGHTS** the evening or night of a weekday
WEEN *verb* **WEENS, WEENING, WEENED** to think or believe
WEENY *adj* **WEENIER, WEENIEST** used especially by a child: very small; tiny
WEEP *verb* **WEEPS, WEEPING, WEPT** to shed tears as an expression of grief or other emotion □ *noun* **WEEPS** a bout of weeping
WEEPER *noun* **WEEPERS** someone who weeps
WEEPIE *adj* weepy □ *noun*
WEEPIES a weepy
WEEPING *adj* said of a tree variety: having low-drooping branches
WEEPY *adj* **WEEPIER, WEEPIEST** tearful □ *noun* **WEEPIES** a sentimental film or novel
WEER see under **wee** [1]
WEEST see under **wee** [1]
WEEVER *noun* **WEEVERS** a fish with sharp poisonous spines in the area of the dorsal fin and gills
WEEVIL *noun* **WEEVILS** any of several beetles with an elongated proboscis, which both as adult and larva can damage fruit, grain, nuts and trees
WEEVILY *adj* of or having weevils
WEFT *noun* **WEFTS** the threads that are passed over and under the fixed threads of the warp in a loom
WEIGELA *noun* **WEIGELAS** an Asian deciduous shrub with large showy pink, purplish or white flowers
WEIGH *verb* **WEIGHS, WEIGHING, WEIGHED** to measure the weight of something
WEIGHABLE *adj* capable of being weighed
WEIGHER *noun* **WEIGHERS** an official who weighs articles or tests weights
WEIGHT *noun* **WEIGHTS** the heaviness of something; the amount that it weighs □ *verb* **WEIGHTS, WEIGHTING, WEIGHTED** to add weight to something, eg to restrict movement
WEIGHTILY *adverb* in a weighty way

For longer words, see *The Chambers Dictionary*

WEIGHTING noun **WEIGHTINGS** a supplement to a salary, usually to compensate for high living costs

WEIGHTY adj **WEIGHTIER**, **WEIGHTIEST** heavy; grave

WEIR noun **WEIRS** a shallow dam constructed across a river to control its flow

WEIRD adj **WEIRDER**, **WEIRDEST** eerie or supernatural; uncanny

WEIRDIE noun **WEIRDIES** a weirdo

WEIRDLY adverb in a weird way

WEIRDNESS noun **WEIRDNESSES** the state or condition of being weird

WEIRDO noun **WEIRDOS** someone who behaves or dresses bizarrely or oddly

WELCH verb **WELCHES**, **WELCHING**, **WELCHED** to welsh

WELCHER noun **WELCHERS** a welsher

WELCOME verb **WELCOMES**, **WELCOMING**, **WELCOMED** to receive (a guest or visitor, etc) with a warm greeting or kind hospitality ◻ noun **WELCOMES** the act of welcoming ◻ adj warmly received

WELD verb **WELDS**, **WELDING**, **WELDED** to join (two pieces of metal) by heating them to melting point and fusing them together, or by applying pressure alone, producing a stronger joint than soldering ◻ noun **WELDS** a joint between two metals formed by welding

WELDABLE adj capable of being welded

WELDER noun **WELDERS** a person or device that welds

WELDOR noun **WELDORS** a welder

WELFARE noun **WELFARES** the health, comfort, happiness and general wellbeing of a person or group, etc

WELL [1] adverb competently; skilfully ◻ adj **BETTER**, **BEST** healthy

WELL [2] noun **WELLS** a lined shaft that is sunk from ground level to a considerable depth below ground in order to obtain a supply of water, oil or gas, etc ◻ verb **WELLS**, **WELLING**, **WELLED** said of a liquid: to spring, flow or flood to the surface

WELLBEING noun **WELLBEINGS** the state of being healthy and contented, etc; welfare

WELLHEAD noun **WELLHEADS** the source of a stream; a spring

WELLIE noun **WELLIES** a welly

WELLY noun **WELLIES** a waterproof plastic or rubber boot loosely covering the foot and lower half of the leg

WELSH verb **WELSHES**, **WELSHING**, **WELSHED** to fail to pay one's debts or fulfil one's obligations

WELSHER noun **WELSHERS** someone who welshes

WELT noun **WELTS** a reinforcing band or border fastened to an edge, eg the ribbing at the waist of a knitted garment ◻ verb **WELTS**, **WELTING**, **WELTED** to fit a welt

WELTER noun **WELTERS** a state of turmoil or confusion ◻ verb **WELTERS**, **WELTERING**, **WELTERED** to lie, roll or wallow

WEM noun **WEMS** an old word for the womb or belly

WEN noun **WENS** a sebaceous cyst on the skin, usually of the scalp

WENCH noun **WENCHES** a girl; a woman ◻ verb **WENCHES**, **WENCHING**, **WENCHED** to associate with prostitutes

WEND verb **WENDS**, **WENDING**, **WENDED** to go or direct (one's course)

WENT a past form of **go** [1]

WEPT past form of **weep**

WERE a past form of **be**

WEREWOLF noun **WEREWOLVES** someone who is changed, or changes at free will, into a wolf, usually at full moon

WEST noun **WESTS** the quarter of the sky in which the Sun sets ◻ adj in the west; on the side that is on or nearer the west

WESTBOUND adj going or leading towards the west

WESTERING adj said especially of the Sun: sinking towards the west

WESTERLY adj said of a wind: coming from the west ◻ noun **WESTERLIES** a wind blowing from the west

WESTERN adj situated in the west ◻ noun **WESTERNS** a film or novel featuring cowboys in the west of the USA, especially during the 19c

WESTERNER noun **WESTERNERS** someone who lives in or comes from the west of anywhere, especially the western part of the USA

WESTWARD adj towards the west

WESTWARDS adj westward

WET adj **WETTER**, **WETTEST** covered or soaked in water, rain, perspiration, or other liquid ◻ noun **WETS** moisture ◻ verb **WETS**, **WETTING**, **WET**, **WETTED** to make someone or something wet; to splash or soak them or it

WETHER noun **WETHERS** a castrated ram

WETLAND noun **WETLANDS** a region of marshy land

WETLY adverb in a wet way

WETNESS noun **WETNESSES** the state or condition of being wet

WEX verb **WEXES**, **WEXING**, **WEXED** an obsolete form of *wax*

WEY noun **WEYS** a measure for dry goods

WHA pronoun a Scots form of *who*

WHACK verb **WHACKS**, **WHACKING**, **WHACKED** to hit something or someone sharply and resoundingly ◻ noun **WHACKS** a sharp resounding blow

WHACKED adj exhausted; worn out

WHACKER noun **WHACKERS** something big of its kind, especially a blatant lie

WHACKING noun **WHACKINGS** a beating ◻ adj enormous; huge ◻ adverb extremely

WHACKO adj wacko

WHACKY adj **WHACKIER**, **WHACKIEST** wacky

WHALE noun **WHALES** any of various large marine mammals which have a torpedo-shaped body, two flippers, flat horizontal tail blades, and a blowhole on the top of the head for breathing ◻ verb **WHALES**, **WHALING**, **WHALED** to hunt whales

WHALEBOAT noun **WHALEBOATS** a long narrow boat, sharp at both ends, originally used in pursuit of whales

WHALEBONE noun **WHALEBONES** the light flexible horny substance consisting of the baleen plates of toothless whales, used especially formerly for stiffening corsets, etc

WHALER noun **WHALERS** a person or ship engaged in hunting and killing whales

WHALING noun **WHALINGS** the hunting and killing of whales

WHAM noun **WHAMS** a resounding noise made by a hard blow ▫ verb **WHAMS, WHAMMING, WHAMMED** to hit or make something hit with a wham

WHAMMY noun **WHAMMIES** an unfortunate or malevolent influence

WHANG noun **WHANGS** a resounding noise ▫ verb **WHANGS, WHANGING, WHANGED** to make, or hit with, a whang

WHANGEE noun **WHANGEES** any of several grasses related to bamboo, native to China and Japan

WHARF noun **WHARFS, WHARVES** a landing-stage built along a waterfront for loading and unloading vessels

WHARFAGE noun **WHARFAGES** dues paid for the use of a wharf

WHAT pronoun used in questions, indirect questions and statements, identifying, or seeking to identify or classify, a thing or person ▫ adverb used in questions, indirect questions and statements: to how great an extent or degree?

WHATEVER pronoun used as an emphatic form of *what*

WHATNOT noun **WHATNOTS** a stand with shelves for ornaments, etc

WHATSIT noun **WHATSITS** used as a substitute for an unknown or forgotten name for a person or thing

WHAUP noun **WHAUPS** a curlew

WHEAT noun **WHEATS** a cereal grass which is the most important cereal crop in terms of harvested area, native to the Middle East but now cultivated in temperate regions worldwide

WHEATEAR noun **WHEATEARS** any of various small migratory songbirds of the thrush family, native to Europe, W Asia, Africa and N America, which have light grey plumage with a conspicuous white rump, and black and white wings and tail

WHEATEN adj made of wheat flour or grain

WHEATMEAL noun **WHEATMEALS** wheat flour containing most of the powdered whole grain (bran and germ)

WHEE exclamation expressing excitement or delight

WHEEDLE verb **WHEEDLES,**

WHEEDLING, WHEEDLED to coax or cajole someone; to persuade them by flattery

WHEEDLER noun **WHEEDLERS** someone who wheedles

WHEEL noun **WHEELS** a circular object or frame rotating on an axle, used eg for moving a vehicle along the ground ▫ verb **WHEELS, WHEELING, WHEELED** to fit something with a wheel or wheels

WHEELBASE noun **WHEELBASES** the distance between the front and rear axles of a vehicle

WHEELIE noun **WHEELIES** a trick performed on a motorbike or bicycle in which the front wheel is lifted off the ground, either while stationary or in motion

WHEESHT verb **WHEESHTS, WHEESHTING, WHEESHTED** to whisht ▫ noun **WHEESHTS** whisht

WHEEZE verb **WHEEZES, WHEEZING, WHEEZED** to breathe in a laboured way with a gasping or rasping noise, when suffering from a lung infection, etc ▫ noun **WHEEZES** a wheezing breath or sound

WHEEZILY adverb in a wheezy way

WHEEZY adj **WHEEZIER, WHEEZIEST** wheezing

WHELK noun **WHELKS** any of various large predatory marine snails with a pointed spirally-coiled shell, especially the common whelk, native to the coasts of Europe and N America

WHELP noun **WHELPS** the young of a dog or wolf; a puppy ▫ verb **WHELPS, WHELPING, WHELPED** to give birth to puppies or cubs

WHEN adverb used in questions, indirect questions and statements: at what time?; during what period?; at which time ▫ pronoun what or which time

WHENCE adverb used in questions, indirect questions and statements: from what place?; from which place

WHENEVER conj at any or every time that ▫ adverb an emphatic form of *when*

WHERE adverb used in questions, indirect questions and statements: in, at or to which place; in what direction ▫ pronoun what place?

WHEREAS conj when in fact

WHEREAT adverb at which; at what?

WHEREBY pronoun by means of which

WHEREFORE adverb for what reason? why? ▫ noun **WHEREFORES** a reason

WHEREIN adverb in what place?; in what respect? ▫ pronoun in which place or thing

WHEREOF pronoun of which; of what?

WHEREON pronoun on which; on what?

WHEREUPON conj at which point; in consequence of which

WHEREVER pronoun any or every place that ▫ adverb an emphatic form of *where*

WHEREWITH pronoun with which

WHERRY noun **WHERRIES** a long light rowing boat, especially for transporting passengers

WHET verb **WHETS, WHETTING, WHETTED** to sharpen (the blade of a tool) by rubbing it against stone, etc ▫ noun **WHETS** the act of whetting

WHETHER conj used to introduce an indirect question

WHETSTONE noun **WHETSTONES** a stone for sharpening bladed tools

WHETTER noun **WHETTERS** someone who whets the blades of tools

WHEW exclamation expressing relief or amazement

WHEY noun **WHEYS** the watery content of milk, separated from the curd in making cheese and junket, etc

WHICH adj used in questions, indirect questions and statements: to identify or specify a thing or person, usually from a known set or group ▫ pronoun used in questions, indirect questions and statements: to identify or specify a thing or person, usually from a known set or group

WHICHEVER pronoun the one or ones that; any that ▫ adj the one or ones that; any that

WHICKER verb **WHICKERS, WHICKERING, WHICKERED** said of a horse: to neigh or whinny ▫ noun **WHICKERS** a neigh or whinny

WHIDAH noun **WHIDAHS** a whydah

WHIFF noun **WHIFFS** a puff or slight rush of air or smoke, etc ▫ verb **WHIFFS, WHIFFING, WHIFFED** to puff or blow something in whiffs

WHIFFLE verb **WHIFFLES, WHIFFLING, WHIFFLED** to blow in puffs or light wafts, especially like the wind

WHIFFLING *noun* **WHIFFLINGS** an act of blowing in puffs or light wafts

WHIFFY *adj* **WHIFFIER, WHIFFIEST** smelly

WHILE *adverb* at or during which ▫ *noun* **WHILES** a space or lapse of time ▫ *verb* **WHILES, WHILING, WHILED** to pass (time or hours, etc) in a leisurely or undemanding way

WHILST *conj* while

WHIM *noun* **WHIMS** a sudden fanciful idea; a caprice

WHIMBREL *noun* **WHIMBRELS** a species of small curlew

WHIMPER *verb* **WHIMPERS, WHIMPERING, WHIMPERED** to cry feebly or plaintively ▫ *noun* **WHIMPERS** a feebly plaintive cry

WHIMPERER *noun* **WHIMPERERS** a person or animal that whimpers

WHIMPERING *noun* **WHIMPERINGS** an act of crying feebly or plaintively

WHIMSEY *noun* **WHIMSEYS** whimsy

WHIMSICAL *adj* delicately fanciful or playful

WHIMSILY *adverb* in a whimsical way

WHIMSY *noun* **WHIMSIES** quaint or fanciful humour

WHIN *noun* **WHINS** gorse

WHINE *verb* **WHINES, WHINING, WHINED** to complain peevishly or querulously ▫ *noun* **WHINES** a continuous shrill or high-pitched noise

WHINER *noun* **WHINERS** someone who whines

WHINGE *verb* **WHINGES, WHINGEING, WHINGED** to complain irritably; to whine ▫ *noun* **WHINGES** a peevish complaint

WHINGEING *noun* **WHINGEINGS** an act of complaining irritably; whining

WHINGER *noun* **WHINGERS** someone who whinges

WHINING *noun* **WHININGS** an act of complaining peevishly or querulously

WHININGLY *adverb* with a whine

WHINNY *verb* **WHINNIES, WHINNYING, WHINNIED** said of a horse: to neigh softly ▫ *noun* **WHINNIES** a gentle neigh

WHINSTONE *noun* **WHINSTONES**

quartz-dolerite or quartz-basalt igneous rock

WHINY *adj* **WHINIER, WHINIEST** whining; moaning

WHIP *noun* **WHIPS** a lash with a handle for driving animals or punishing people ▫ *verb* **WHIPS, WHIPPING, WHIPPED** to strike or thrash with a whip

WHIPBIRD *noun* **WHIPBIRDS** either of two types of Australian songbird that make a sound like the crack of a whip

WHIPCORD *noun* **WHIPCORDS** strong fine tightly twisted cord, as used for making whips

WHIPLASH *noun* **WHIPLASHES** the springy end of a whip

WHIPPER *noun* **WHIPPERS** someone who whips

WHIPPET *noun* **WHIPPETS** a small slender breed of dog, resembling a greyhound but with a slightly deeper body, developed in northern England and probably produced by cross-breeding small greyhounds with terriers

WHIPPING *noun* **WHIPPINGS** an act of striking or thrashing with a whip

WHIPPY *adj* **WHIPPIER, WHIPPIEST** said of a stick or cane: springy; flexible

WHIPSAW *noun* **WHIPSAWS** a narrow saw used for dividing timber lengthways, usually set in a frame and worked by two people, one at each end ▫ *verb* **WHIPSAWS, WHIPSAWING, WHIPSAWED** to cut something with a whipsaw

WHIPSTOCK *noun* **WHIPSTOCKS** the rod or handle of a whip

WHIR *noun* **WHIRS** a whirr ▫ *verb* **WHIRS, WHIRRING, WHIRRED** to whirr

WHIRL *verb* **WHIRLS, WHIRLING, WHIRLED** to spin or revolve rapidly ▫ *noun* **WHIRLS** a circling or spiralling movement or pattern

WHIRLER *noun* **WHIRLERS** someone who whirls

WHIRLIGIG *noun* **WHIRLIGIGS** a spinning toy, especially a top

WHIRLING *noun* **WHIRLINGS** an act of spinning or revolving rapidly

WHIRLPOOL *noun* **WHIRLPOOLS** a violent circular eddy of water that occurs in a river or sea at a point where several strong opposing currents converge

WHIRLWIND *noun* **WHIRLWINDS** a violently spiralling column of air

over land or sea, sometimes extending upwards to a height of several hundred feet ▫ *adj* referring or relating to anything that developed rapidly or violently

WHIRR *noun* **WHIRRS** a rapid drawn-out whirling, humming or vibratory sound ▫ *verb* **WHIRRS, WHIRRING, WHIRRED** to turn or spin with a whirring noise

WHISHT *verb* **WHISHTS, WHISHTING, WHISHTED** to be quiet; to keep silent ▫ *noun* **WHISHTS** hush or silence; a whisper

WHISK *verb* **WHISKS, WHISKING, WHISKED** to transport someone or something rapidly; to move something with a brisk waving motion ▫ *noun* **WHISKS** a whisking movement or action

WHISKER *noun* **WHISKERS** any of the long coarse hairs that grow round the mouth of a cat or mouse, etc

WHISKERED *adj* having whiskers

WHISKERY *adj* whiskered

WHISKEY *noun* **WHISKEYS** whisky

WHISKY *noun* **WHISKIES** an alcoholic spirit distilled from a fermented mash of cereal grains, eg barley, wheat or rye

WHISPER *verb* **WHISPERS, WHISPERING, WHISPERED** to speak or say something quietly, breathing rather than voicing the words ▫ *noun* **WHISPERS** a whispered level of speech

WHISPERER *noun* **WHISPERERS** someone who whispers

WHISPERING *noun* **WHISPERINGS** a whisper

WHIST [1] *noun* **WHISTS** a card game, usually for two pairs of players, in which the object is to take a majority of 13 tricks, each trick over six scoring one point

WHIST [2] *verb* **WHIST, WHISTING, WHISTED** to whisht ▫ *noun* whisht

WHISTLE *noun* **WHISTLES** a shrill sound produced through pursed lips or through the teeth, used to signal or to express surprise, etc ▫ *verb* **WHISTLES, WHISTLING, WHISTLED** to produce a whistle through pursed lips or teeth; to perform (a tune), signal or communicate with this sound

WHISTLER *noun* **WHISTLERS** someone or something that whistles

WHIT *noun* **WHITS** the least bit; the smallest particle imaginable

WHITE *adj* **WHITER, WHITEST** having the colour of snow, the colour that reflects all light □ *noun* **WHITES** the colour of snow

WHITEBAIT *noun* **WHITEBAITS** the young of any of various silvery fishes, especially herrings and sprats, abundant in shallow coastal waters and estuaries, and which are often fried and eaten whole

WHITEBEAM *noun* **WHITEBEAMS** a small tree whose leaves are white and downy on the underside

WHITEFLY *noun* **WHITEFLIES** a small sap-sucking bug, whose body and wings are covered with a white waxy powder

WHITEHEAD *noun* **WHITEHEADS** a pimple or pustule with a white top

WHITEN *verb* **WHITENS, WHITENING, WHITENED** to make or become white or whiter; to bleach

WHITENER *noun* **WHITENERS** someone or something that whitens

WHITENESS *noun* **WHITENESSES** the state or condition of being white

WHITENING *noun* **WHITENINGS** a substance used to make things white

WHITEWASH *noun* **WHITEWASHES** a mixture of lime and water, used to give a white coating to walls, especially outside walls □ *verb* **WHITEWASHES, WHITEWASHING, WHITEWASHED** to coat something with whitewash

WHITEWOOD *noun* **WHITEWOODS** any of various trees with a light-coloured timber, eg the tulip tree

WHITHER *adverb* to what place? □ *pronoun* to the, or any, place that; towards which

WHITING *noun* **WHITINGS** ground and washed white chalk, used in putty, whitewash and silver-cleaner

WHITISH *adj* somewhat white; nearly white

WHITLOW *noun* **WHITLOWS** an inflammation of the finger or toe, especially near the nail

WHITTLE *verb* **WHITTLES, WHITTLING, WHITTLED** to cut, carve or pare (a stick or piece of wood, etc) with a knife

WHITTLER *noun* **WHITTLERS** someone who whittles

WHIZ *verb* **WHIZZES, WHIZZING, WHIZZED** to whizz □ *noun* **WHIZZES** a whizz

WHIZZ *verb* **WHIZZES, WHIZZING, WHIZZED** to fly through the air, especially with a whistling or hissing noise □ *noun* **WHIZZES** a whistling or hissing sound

WHO *pronoun* used in questions, indirect questions and statements: which or what person; which or what people

WHOA *exclamation* a command to stop, especially to a horse

WHODUNNIT *noun* **WHODUNNITS** a detective novel or play, etc; a mystery

WHOEVER *pronoun* used in questions, indirect questions and statements as an emphatic form of *who* or *whom*

WHOLE *noun* **WHOLES** all the constituents or components of something □ *adj* comprising all of something; no less than the whole; entire

WHOLEFOOD *noun* **WHOLEFOODS** food which is processed or treated as little as possible, and produced without the use of any fertilizers or pesticides, etc

WHOLEMEAL *adj* said of flour: made from the entire wheat grain

WHOLENESS *noun* **WHOLENESSES** the state or condition of being whole

WHOLESALE *noun* **WHOLESALES** the sale of goods in large quantities to a retailer □ *adj* buying and selling, or concerned with buying and selling in this way

WHOLESOME *adj* **WHOLESOMER, WHOLESOMEST** attractively healthy

WHOLLY *adverb* completely; altogether

WHOM *pronoun* used as the object of a verb or preposition (but often replaced by *who*, especially in less formal usage): in seeking to identify which or what person

WHOMEVER *pronoun* used as the object of a verb or preposition to mean 'any person or people that'

WHOOP *noun* **WHOOPS** a loud cry of delight, joy or triumph, etc □ *verb* **WHOOPS, WHOOPING, WHOOPED** to utter or say something with a whoop

WHOOPEE *noun* **WHOOPEES** exuberant delight or excitement

WHOOPER *noun* **WHOOPERS** a swan, common in N Europe and Asia, that is easily distinguished by its straight neck and yellow-and-black bill

WHOOPS *exclamation* expressing surprise or concern, eg when one has a slight accident, makes an error, etc or sees someone else do so

WHOOSH *noun* **WHOOSHES** the sound of, or like that made by, something passing rapidly through the air □ *verb* **WHOOSHES, WHOOSHING, WHOOSHED** to move with or make such a sound

WHOP *verb* **WHOPS, WHOPPING, WHOPPED** to hit or thrash someone □ *noun* **WHOPS** a blow or bump; the sound made by either of these

WHOPPER *noun* **WHOPPERS** anything very large of its kind

WHOPPING *adj* huge; enormous; unusually large □ *noun* **WHOPPINGS** a thrashing

WHORL *noun* **WHORLS** one complete coil in the spiral shell of a mollusc, the number of which indicates the shell's age

WHORLED *adj* having whorls

WHOSE *pronoun* used in questions, indirect questions and statements: belonging to which person or people □ *adj* used in questions, indirect questions and statements: belonging to which person or people

WHOSOEVER *pronoun* used in statements: whoever

WHY *adverb* used in questions, indirect questions and statements: for what reason □ *conj* for, or because of, which □ *exclamation* expressing surprise, indignation, impatience or recognition, etc □ *noun* **WHYS** a reason

WHYDAH *noun* **WHYDAHS** any of various African weaverbirds, with mostly black plumage, and very long tail feathers

WICK *noun* **WICKS** the twisted string running up through a candle or lamp and projecting at the top, that burns when lit and draws up the wax or inflammable liquid into the flame

WICKED *adj* **WICKEDER, WICKEDEST** evil or sinful; immoral

WICKEDLY *adverb* in a wicked way

WICKER *noun* **WICKERS** a small pliant twig, cane, etc

WICKET noun **WICKETS** in cricket: a row of three small wooden posts stuck upright in the ground behind either crease

WIDE adj **WIDER, WIDEST** large in extent from side to side □ noun **WIDES** in cricket: a ball bowled out of the batsman's reach

WIDELY adverb over a wide area or range

WIDEN verb **WIDENS, WIDENING, WIDENED** to make, or become, wide or wider

WIDENER noun **WIDENERS** a person or thing that widens

WIDENESS noun **WIDENESSES** the state or condition of being wide

WIDGEON noun **WIDGEONS** a wigeon

WIDGET noun **WIDGETS** a device attached to the bottom of cans of draught beer so that when it is poured it has a proper head and resembles a glass of beer as poured from a tap in a pub

WIDISH adj somewhat wide

WIDOW noun **WIDOWS** a woman whose husband is dead and who has not remarried □ verb **WIDOWS, WIDOWING, WIDOWED** to leave or make someone a widow or widower

WIDOWER noun **WIDOWERS** a man whose wife is dead, and who has not remarried

WIDOWHOOD noun **WIDOWHOODS** the state of being a widow

WIDTH noun **WIDTHS** extent from side to side; breadth

WIDTHWAYS adj across the width

WIDTHWISE adj widthways

WIELD verb **WIELDS, WIELDING, WIELDED** to brandish or use (a tool or weapon, etc)

WIELDER noun **WIELDERS** someone who wields a weapon or tool

WIELDY adj **WIELDIER, WIELDIEST** easy to wield; manageable

WIFE noun **WIVES** the woman to whom a man is married; a married woman

WIFEHOOD noun **WIFEHOODS** the state of being a wife

WIFELY adj of or like a wife

WIG [1] noun **WIGS** an artificial covering of natural or synthetic hair for the head to conceal baldness or as a fashion accessory, a disguise, as period costume or as part of a specific uniform, as for a judge or barrister

WIG [2] verb **WIGS, WIGGING, WIGGED** to scold someone severely

WIGEON noun **WIGEONS** any of various freshwater dabbling ducks, native to Europe, Asia, N Africa and the New World, having long pointed wings and a wedge-shaped tail

WIGGING noun **WIGGINGS** a scolding

WIGGLE verb **WIGGLES, WIGGLING, WIGGLED** to move or cause something to move, especially jerkily, from side to side or up and down □ noun **WIGGLES** an act of wiggling

WIGGLER noun **WIGGLERS** someone who wiggles

WIGGLY adj **WIGGLIER, WIGGLIEST** wriggly

WIGLESS adj without a wig

WIGWAG verb **WIGWAGS, WIGWAGGING, WIGWAGGED** to twist about □ noun **WIGWAGS** an act of wigwagging

WIGWAM noun **WIGWAMS** a domed Native American dwelling made of a framework of arched poles covered with skins, bark or mats

WILD adj **WILDER, WILDEST** said of animals: untamed or undomesticated; not dependent on humans □ noun **WILDS** a wild animal's or plant's natural environment or life in it

WILDCAT noun **WILDCATS** an undomesticated cat of Europe and Asia, which has a longer stouter body and longer legs than the domestic cat, and a thick bushy tail □ adj said of an industrial strike: not called or approved by a trade union

WILDFIRE noun **WILDFIRES** a highly flammable liquid originally used in warfare

WILDFOWL singular or plural noun **WILDFOWLS** a game bird or game birds, especially waterfowl

WILDING noun **WILDINGS** a wild crab apple

WILDISH adj somewhat wild

WILDLIFE noun **WILDLIVES** wild animals, birds and plants in general

WILDLY adverb in a wild way

WILDNESS noun the state or condition of being wild

WILDWOOD noun **WILDWOODS** wild, uncultivated or unfrequented woodland

WILE noun **WILES** charming personal ways □ verb **WILES, WILING, WILED** to lure or entice someone

WILFUL adj deliberate; intentional

WILFULLY adverb in a wilful way

WILIER see under **wily**

WILIEST see under **wily**

WILINESS noun **WILINESSES** the quality or state of being wily

WILJA noun **WILJAS** in Australia: an Aboriginal shelter or hut

WILL [1] auxiliary verb expressing or indicating: the future tense of other verbs; intention or determination

WILL [2] noun **WILLS** the power of conscious decision and deliberate choice of action □ verb **WILLS, WILLING, WILLED** to try to compel someone by, or as if by, exerting one's will

WILLED adj having a will

WILLET noun **WILLETS** a large N American bird of the snipe family

WILLFUL adj wilful

WILLIE noun **WILLIES** a penis

WILLING adj ready, glad or not disinclined to do something

WILLINGLY adverb in a willing way

WILLOW noun **WILLOWS** a deciduous tree or shrub found mainly in the N hemisphere, generally growing near water, and having slender flexible branches, narrow leaves, and spikes or catkins of male and female flowers

WILLOWY adj **WILLOWIER, WILLOWIEST** said of a person, especially a woman: slender and graceful

WILLPOWER noun **WILLPOWERS** the determination, persistence and self-discipline needed to accomplish something

WILLY noun **WILLIES** a penis

WILT verb **WILTS, WILTING, WILTED** said of a plant organ or tissue: to droop or become limp because there is insufficient water to maintain the individual cells in a turgid state □ noun **WILTS** the act or process of wilting

WILY adj **WILIER, WILIEST** cunning; crafty or devious

WIMP noun **WIMPS** a feeble person

WIMPISH adj weak, feeble

WIMPISHLY adverb weakly
WIMPLE noun **WIMPLES** a veil folded around the head, neck and cheeks, originally a women's fashion and still worn as part of a nun's dress □ verb **WIMPLES, WIMPLING, WIMPLED** to wrap in or hide (eg a head) with a wimple
WIN verb **WINS, WINNING, WON** to be victorious or come first in (a contest, race or bet, etc) □ noun **WINS** a victory or success
WINCE verb **WINCES, WINCING, WINCED** to shrink back, start or grimace, eg in pain or anticipation of something; to flinch □ noun **WINCES** a start or grimace in reaction to pain, etc
WINCER noun **WINCERS** someone who winces
WINCH noun **WINCHES** a reel or roller round which a rope or chain is wound for hoisting or hauling heavy loads; a windlass □ verb **WINCHES, WINCHING, WINCHED** to hoist or haul something with a winch
WIND [1] noun **WINDS** the movement of air, especially horizontally, across the Earth's surface as a result of differences in atmospheric pressure between one location and another
WIND [2] verb **WINDS, WINDING, WOUND** to wrap or coil, or be wrapped or coiled
WINDAGE noun **WINDAGES** the deflection of a missile, eg a bullet, caused by wind
WINDBAG noun **WINDBAGS** an excessively talkative person who communicates little of any value
WINDBORNE adj said of pollen, seeds, etc: carried by the wind
WINDBOUND adj said of a ship, etc: prevented from sailing by contrary winds
WINDBREAK noun **WINDBREAKS** a barrier, eg in the form of a screen, fence or line of trees, that provides protection from the wind
WINDBURN noun **WINDBURNS** inflammation and soreness of the skin caused by overexposure to the wind
WINDER noun **WINDERS** someone or something that winds
WINDFALL noun **WINDFALLS** a fruit, especially an apple, blown down from its tree
WINDIER see under **windy**
WINDIEST see under **windy**
WINDILY adverb in a windy way

WINDINESS noun **WINDINESSES** the state of being windy
WINDLASS noun **WINDLASSES** a drum-shaped axle round which a rope or chain is wound for hauling or hoisting weights □ verb **WINDLASSES, WINDLASSING, WINDLASSED** to haul or hoist something using a windlass
WINDMILL noun **WINDMILLS** a mechanical device operated by wind-driven sails or vanes that revolve about a fixed shaft, formerly used in W Europe to mill flour, now used in many developing countries to pump water (eg for land drainage) and to generate electricity □ verb **WINDMILLS, WINDMILLING, WINDMILLED** to move, or make something move, like the vanes of a windmill
WINDOW noun **WINDOWS** an opening in a wall to look through, or let in light and air, consisting of a wooden or metal frame fitted with panes of glass; a pane
WINDPIPE noun **WINDPIPES** the trachea
WINDSOCK noun **WINDSOCKS** an open-ended cone of fabric flying from a mast, eg at an airport, which shows the direction and speed of the wind
WINDSTORM noun **WINDSTORMS** a storm consisting of very strong winds
WINDSURF verb **WINDSURFS, WINDSURFING, WINDSURFED** to go windsurfing
WINDSURFING noun **WINDSURFINGS** the sport of riding the waves on a sailboard; sailboarding
WINDSWEPT adj exposed to strong winds
WINDWARD noun **WINDWARDS** the side of a boat, etc facing the wind □ adj on this side
WINDY adj **WINDIER, WINDIEST** exposed to, or characterized by, strong wind
WINE noun **WINES** an alcoholic drink made from the fermented juice of grapes □ verb **WINES, WINING, WINED** to entertain someone with wine
WINEPRESS noun **WINEPRESSES** in the manufacture of wine: a machine in which grapes are pressed to extract the juice
WINERY noun **WINERIES** a place where wine is prepared and stored

WINESKIN noun **WINESKINS** the skin of a goat or sheep sewn up and used for holding wine
WING noun **WINGS** one of the two modified forelimbs of a bird or bat that are adapted for flight □ verb **WINGS, WINGING, WINGED** to make one's way by flying, or with speed
WINGBEAT noun **WINGBEATS** the beat or flap of a bird's or insect's wings
WINGDING noun **WINGDINGS** a wild or boisterous party
WINGER noun **WINGERS** in football and hockey, etc: a player at either extreme of the forward line
WINGLESS adj without wings
WINGSPAN noun **WINGSPANS** the distance from tip to tip of the wings of an aircraft, or of a bird's wings when outstretched
WINIER see under **winy**
WINIEST see under **winy**
WINK verb **WINKS, WINKING, WINKED** to shut an eye briefly as an informal or cheeky gesture or greeting □ noun **WINKS** an act of winking
WINKER noun **WINKERS** someone or something that winks
WINKING noun **WINKINGS** an act of shutting an eye briefly
WINKINGLY adverb with a wink
WINKLE noun **WINKLES** a small edible snail-shaped shellfish; a periwinkle □ verb **WINKLES, WINKLING, WINKLED** to force or prise something out
WINNABLE adj capable of being won
WINNER noun **WINNERS** a person, animal or vehicle, etc that wins a contest or race
WINNING adj attractive or charming; persuasive □ noun **WINNINGS** the achieving of victory
WINNINGLY adverb in a winning way
WINNOW verb **WINNOWS, WINNOWING, WINNOWED** to separate chaff from (grain) by blowing a current of air through it or fanning it
WINNOWER noun **WINNOWERS** someone who winnows grain
WINO noun **WINOS** someone, especially a down-and-out, addicted to cheap wine; an alcoholic
WINSOME adj **WINSOMER, WINSOMEST** charming; captivating

WINSOMELY adverb in a winsome way

WINTER noun **WINTERS** the coldest season of the year, coming between autumn and spring, in the N hemisphere from November or December to February or March □ verb **WINTERS, WINTERING, WINTERED** to spend the winter in a specified place, usually other than one's normal home

WINTERISE verb **WINTERISES, WINTERISING, WINTERISED** to winterize

WINTERIZE verb **WINTERIZES, WINTERIZING, WINTERIZED** to make (a car, etc) suitable for use in wintry conditions

WINTERY adj **WINTERIER, WINTERIEST** wintry

WINTRY adj **WINTRIER, WINTRIEST** said of weather, etc: like or characteristic of winter

WINY adj **WINIER, WINIEST** having a wine-like flavour

WIPE verb **WIPES, WIPING, WIPED** to clean or dry something with a cloth, etc □ noun **WIPES** the act of cleaning something by rubbing

WIPEOUT noun **WIPEOUTS** a fall from a surfboard or skis, etc

WIPER noun **WIPERS** someone or something that wipes

WIRE noun **WIRES** metal drawn out into a narrow flexible strand □ verb **WIRES, WIRING, WIRED** to send a telegram to someone

WIRED adj highly-strung; stressed-out

WIREDRAW verb **WIREDRAWS, WIREDRAWING, WIREDREW, WIREDRAWN** to draw (metal) into wire by pulling it through successively smaller holes in a series of hard steel dies

WIREDRAWING noun **WIREDRAWINGS** an act of drawing (metal) into wire

WIRELESS noun **WIRELESSES** a radio

WIRER noun **WIRERS** someone who uses wire, eg to snare animals

WIRETAP verb **WIRETAPS, WIRETAPPING, WIRETAPPED** to tap (a telephone) or the telephone of (a person)

WIREWORM noun **WIREWORMS** the hard-bodied worm-like larva of the click beetle, which lives in soil where it is extremely destructive to plant roots

WIRILY adverb in a wiry way

WIRINESS noun **WIRINESSES** the state of being wiry

WIRING noun **WIRINGS** the arrangement of wires that connects the individual components of electric circuits into an operating system, eg the mains wiring of a house

WIRY adj **WIRIER, WIRIEST** said of a person: of slight build, but strong and agile

WIS verb **WISSES, WISSING, WISSED** a sham archaic word meaning to know

WISDOM noun **WISDOMS** the quality of being wise

WISE adj **WISER, WISEST** having or showing wisdom; prudent; sensible

WISEACRE noun **WISEACRES** someone who assumes an air of superior wisdom

WISECRACK noun **WISECRACKS** a smart, clever or knowing remark □ verb **WISECRACKS, WISECRACKING, WISECRACKED** to make a wisecrack

WISELY adverb in a wise way

WISH verb **WISHES, WISHING, WISHED** to want; to have a desire □ noun **WISHES** a desire

WISHBONE noun **WISHBONES** a V-shaped bone in the breast of poultry, formed by fused clavicles

WISHER noun **WISHERS** someone who wishes

WISHFUL adj having a desire or wish

WISHFULLY adverb in a wishful way

WISP noun **WISPS** a strand; a thin fine tuft or shred

WISPY adj **WISPIER, WISPIEST** wisp-like; light, fine and insubstantial in texture

WIST past form of **wit²**

WISTARIA noun **WISTARIAS** wisteria

WISTERIA noun **WISTERIAS** a deciduous climbing shrub, native to E Asia and N America, which has leaves divided into leaflets, and lilac, violet or white flowers borne in long pendulous clusters

WISTFUL adj sadly or vainly yearning

WISTFULLY adverb in a wistful way

WIT¹ noun **WITS** the ability to express oneself amusingly; humour

WIT² verb **WOT, WITTING, WIST** to know how; to discern

WITCH noun **WITCHES** someone,

especially a woman, supposed to have magical powers used usually, but not always, malevolently □ verb **WITCHES, WITCHING, WITCHED** to bewitch

WITCHERY noun **WITCHERIES** the activities of witches

WITCHETTY noun **WITCHETTIES** any of the large grubs of species of certain moths, eaten by the Aboriginals

WITCHLIKE adj like a witch

WITH prep in the company of someone

WITHAL adverb as well; into the bargain

WITHDRAW verb **WITHDRAWS, WITHDRAWING, WITHDREW, WITHDRAWN** to move somewhere else, especially more private

WITHDRAWN adj said of a person or their manner, etc: unresponsive, shy or reserved

WITHE noun **WITHES** a pliable branch or twig, especially one from the willow tree □ verb **WITHES, WITHING, WITHED** to bind with a withe or withes

WITHER verb **WITHERS, WITHERING, WITHERED** said of plants: to fade or make them fade, dry up and die

WITHERS plural noun the ridge between the shoulder blades of a horse

WITHHOLD verb **WITHHOLDS, WITHHOLDING, WITHHELD** to refuse to give or grant something

WITHIN prep inside; enclosed by something □ adverb in the mind, soul or heart, etc

WITHOUT prep not having the company of someone; not having something; lacking something

WITHSTAND verb **WITHSTANDS, WITHSTANDING, WITHSTOOD** to maintain one's position or stance against someone or something

WITHY noun **WITHIES** any type of willow

WITLESS adj stupid or brainless; lacking wit, sense or wisdom

WITLESSLY adverb in a witless way

WITNESS noun **WITNESSES** someone who sees, and can therefore give a direct account of, an event or occurrence, etc □ verb **WITNESSES, WITNESSING, WITNESSED** to be present as an observer at (an event or occurrence, etc)

WITNESSER noun **WITNESSERS** a witness

For longer words, see The Chambers Dictionary

WITTER verb **WITTERS, WITTERING, WITTERED** to talk or mutter ceaselessly and ineffectually

WITTICISM noun **WITTICISMS** a witty remark or comment

WITTILY adverb in a witty way

WITTINESS noun the quality or condition of being witty

WITTING adj conscious; deliberate

WITTINGLY adverb in a witting way

WITTY adj **WITTIER, WITTIEST** able to express oneself cleverly and amusingly

WIVERN noun **WIVERNS** a wyvern

WIVES plural of **wife**

WIZARD noun **WIZARDS** someone, especially a man, supposed to have magic powers; a magician or sorcerer

WIZARDRY noun **WIZARDRIES** sorcery

WIZEN verb **WIZENS, WIZENING, WIZENED** to make or become dry and shrivelled ◻ adj wizened

WIZENED adj shrivelled or wrinkled, especially with age

WO noun **WOS** an older variant of woe

WOAD noun **WOADS** a cruciferous plant from whose leaves a blue dye is obtained

WOBBEGONG noun **WOBBEGONGS** an Australian brown shark with a patterned back

WOBBLE verb **WOBBLES, WOBBLING, WOBBLED** to rock or make something rock, sway or shake unsteadily ◻ noun **WOBBLES** a wobbling, rocking or swaying motion

WOBBLER noun **WOBBLERS** a person or thing that wobbles

WOBBLY adj **WOBBLIER, WOBBLIEST** unsteady; shaky; inclined to wobble ◻ noun **WOBBLIES** a fit of anger; a tantrum

WODGE noun **WODGES** a large lump, wad or chunk

WOE noun **WOES** grief; misery

WOEBEGONE adj dismal-looking; showing sorrow

WOEFUL adj **WOEFULLER, WOEFULLEST** mournful; sorrowful

WOEFULLY adverb in a woeful way

WOGGLE noun **WOGGLES** a ring, usually of leather or plastic, through which Cubs, Scouts and Guides, etc thread their neckerchiefs

WOK noun **WOKS** an almost hemispherical pan used in Chinese cookery

WOKE a past form of wake [1]

WOKEN a past form of wake [1]

WOLD noun **WOLDS** a tract of open rolling upland

WOLF noun **WOLVES** a species of carnivorous mammal belonging to the dog family which hunts in packs, and has erect ears, a long muzzle and a long bushy tail ◻ verb **WOLFS, WOLFING, WOLFED** to gobble food quickly and greedily

WOLFHOUND noun **WOLFHOUNDS** any of several large breeds of domestic dog, such as the Irish wolfhound, formerly used for hunting wolves

WOLFISH adj like a wolf

WOLFISHLY adverb in a wolfish way

WOLFRAM noun **WOLFRAMS** tungsten

WOLFSBANE noun **WOLFSBANES** aconite

WOLVERENE noun **WOLVERENES** a wolverine

WOLVERINE noun **WOLVERINES** a large carnivorous animal of the weasel family, which inhabits forests in N America and Eurasia

WOLVES plural of **wolf**

WOMAN noun **WOMEN** an adult human female

WOMANHOOD noun **WOMANHOODS** the state of being a woman

WOMANISE verb **WOMANISES, WOMANISING, WOMANISED** to womanize

WOMANISER noun **WOMANISERS** a womanizer

WOMANISH adj associated with women

WOMANIZE verb **WOMANIZES, WOMANIZING, WOMANIZED** said of a man: to pursue and have casual affairs with women

WOMANIZER noun **WOMANIZERS** a man who womanizes

WOMANKIND noun **WOMANKINDS** women generally; the female sex

WOMANLIKE adj like a woman

WOMANLY adj **WOMANLIER, WOMANLIEST** having characteristics specific to a woman; feminine

WOMB noun **WOMBS** the organ in female mammals in which the young develop after conception and remain till birth

WOMBAT noun **WOMBATS** a nocturnal marsupial of Australia, well adapted for burrowing, with a compact body, short legs, a large flat head and no tail

WOMEN plural of **woman**

WOMENFOLK noun **WOMENFOLKS** women generally

WOMERA noun **WOMERAS** a woomera

WON [1] noun **WONS** the standard monetary unit of currency in both N and S Korea

WON [2] past form of **win**

WONDER noun **WONDERS** the state of mind produced by something extraordinary, new or unexpected; amazement or awe ◻ verb **WONDERS, WONDERING, WONDERED** to be curious

WONDERER noun **WONDERERS** someone who wonders

WONDERFUL adj arousing wonder; extraordinary

WONDERING adj full of wonder

WONDROUS adj wonderful, strange or awesome

WONGA noun **WONGAS** money

WONKY adj **WONKIER, WONKIEST** unsound, unsteady or wobbly

WONT noun **WONTS** a habit that one has ◻ verb **WONTS, WONTING, WONTED** to become, or make someone become, accustomed

WOO verb **WOOS, WOOING, WOOED** said of a man: to try to win the love and affection of (a woman) especially in the hope of marrying her

WOOD noun **WOODS** the hard tissue beneath the bark, that forms the bulk of woody trees and shrubs ◻ verb **WOODS, WOODING, WOODED** to cover (land, etc) with trees

WOODBINE noun **WOODBINES** honeysuckle

WOODBLOCK noun **WOODBLOCKS** a woodcut

WOODCHIP noun **WOODCHIPS** a chip of wood

WOODCHUCK noun **WOODCHUCKS** a N American marmot

WOODCOCK noun **WOODCOCKS** a long-billed game bird related to the snipe, but with a bulkier body and shorter, stronger legs

For longer words, see *The Chambers Dictionary*

WOODCUT noun **WOODCUTS** a design cut into a wooden block

WOODED adj said of land: covered with trees

WOODEN adj **WOODENER, WOODENEST** made of or like wood

WOODENLY adverb in a wooden way

WOODINESS noun **WOODINESSES** the state of being woody

WOODLAND noun **WOODLANDS** an area of land planted with relatively short trees that are more widely spaced than those in a forest

WOODLARK noun **WOODLARKS** a species of lark that habitually perches in trees, and tends to sing in flight

WOODLOUSE noun **WOODLICE** a crustacean with a grey oval plated body, found in damp places, under stones and bark

WOODMAN noun **WOODMEN** a woodcutter (someone who fells trees and chops wood)

WOODPILE noun **WOODPILES** a pile of wood, especially that intended to be used as firewood

WOODRUFF noun **WOODRUFFS** a sweet-smelling plant with small white flowers and whorled leaves

WOODSCREW noun **WOODSCREWS** a tapered screw for fastening together pieces of wood, or wood and metal, etc

WOODSHED noun **WOODSHEDS** a shed for storing wood and tools, etc

WOODSMAN noun **WOODSMEN** a woodman

WOODWIND noun **WOODWINDS** orchestral wind instruments made, or formerly made, of wood, including the flute, oboe, clarinet and bassoon

WOODWORK noun **WOODWORKS** the art of making things out of wood; carpentry

WOODWORM noun **WOODWORMS** the larva of any of several beetles, that bores into wood

WOODY adj **WOODIER, WOODIEST** said of countryside: wooded; covered in trees

WOOER noun **WOOERS** someone who woos

WOOF noun **WOOFS** the sound of, or an imitation of, a dog's bark □ verb **WOOFS, WOOFING, WOOFED** said of a dog: to give a bark

WOOFER noun **WOOFERS** a large loudspeaker for reproducing low-frequency sounds

WOOING noun **WOOINGS** an act of trying to win the love and affection of someone

WOOINGLY adverb in a wooing way

WOOL noun **WOOLS** the soft wavy hair of sheep and certain other animals

WOOLEN adj woollen □ noun **WOOLENS** a woollen

WOOLLEN adj made of or relating to wool □ noun **WOOLLENS** a woollen, especially knitted, garment

WOOLLY adj **WOOLLIER, WOOLLIEST** made of, similar to, or covered with wool or wool-like fibres, etc; fluffy and soft □ noun **WOOLLIES** a woollen, usually knitted garment

WOOLSACK noun **WOOLSACKS** the seat of the Lord Chancellor in the House of Lords, which is a large square wool-stuffed sack covered with scarlet

WOOLSHED noun **WOOLSHEDS** a large shed for shearing sheep and baling wool

WOOMERA noun **WOOMERAS** a notched stick used by the Aboriginals to launch a dart or spear with greater force

WOOSH noun **WOOSHES** a whoosh □ verb **WOOSHES, WOOSHING, WOOSHED** to whoosh

WOOTZ noun **WOOTZES** steel made in India from ancient times

WOOZILY adverb in a woozy way

WOOZINESS noun **WOOZINESSES** the state of being woozy

WOOZY adj **WOOZIER, WOOZIEST** dazed or stupefied; having blurred senses, due to drink or drugs, etc

WOP verb **WOPS, WOPPING, WOPPED** to whop

WORD noun **WORDS** the smallest unit of spoken or written language that can be used independently, usually separated off by spaces in writing and printing □ verb **WORDS, WORDING, WORDED** to express something in carefully chosen words

WORDAGE noun **WORDAGES** words generally, especially text as opposed to pictures

WORDBOOK noun **WORDBOOKS** a book containing lists of words; a dictionary or vocabulary

WORDGAME noun **WORDGAMES** any game or puzzle in which words are constructed or deciphered, etc

WORDILY adverb in a wordy way

WORDINESS noun **WORDINESSES** the state or condition of being wordy

WORDING noun **WORDINGS** the choice and arrangement of words used to express something

WORDSMITH noun **WORDSMITHS** an articulate user of words

WORDY adj **WORDIER, WORDIEST** using or containing too many words; long-winded, especially pompously so

WORE past form of **wear**

WORK noun **WORKS** physical or mental effort made in order to achieve or make something, eg labour, study, research, etc □ verb **WORKS, WORKING, WORKED** to do work; to exert oneself mentally or physically; to toil, labour or study

WORKABLE adj said of a scheme, etc: able to be carried out; practicable

WORKADAY adj ordinary or mundane; commonplace

WORKBAG noun **WORKBAGS** a bag for holding sewing materials and implements

WORKBENCH noun **WORKBENCHES** a table, usually a purpose-built one, at which a mechanic or craftsman, etc works

WORKBOOK noun **WORKBOOKS** a book of exercises, often with spaces included for the answers

WORKBOX noun **WORKBOXES** a box for holding sewing materials and implements

WORKDAY noun **WORKDAYS** a day on which people go to work as usual

WORKED adj having been treated or fashioned in some way, especially embroidered or ornamented

WORKER noun **WORKERS** someone who works

WORKFARE noun **WORKFARES** an unemployment benefit scheme under which the payment recipients are required to do work of some kind, usually some form of public service

WORKFORCE *noun* **WORKFORCES** the number of workers engaged in a particular industry, factory, etc; the total number of workers potentially available
WORKHORSE *noun* **WORKHORSES** a horse used for labouring purposes rather than for recreation or racing, etc
WORKHOUSE *noun* **WORKHOUSES** a house where any work or manufacture is carried out
WORKING *noun* **WORKINGS** the act or process of shaping, making, effecting or solving, etc ❑ *adj* said of a period of time: devoted to work, or denoting that part that is devoted to work
WORKLESS *adj* without work
WORKLOAD *noun* **WORKLOADS** the amount of work to be done by a person or machine, especially in a specified time
WORKMAN *noun* **WORKMEN** a man employed to do manual work
WORKMATE *noun* **WORKMATES** someone who works with another or others in their place of work; a fellow-worker or colleague
WORKPIECE *noun* **WORKPIECES** an object that is being or has been worked on with a machine or tool
WORKPLACE *noun* **WORKPLACES** an office, factory, etc
WORKROOM *noun* **WORKROOMS** a room in which work, usually of a specific kind, is done
WORKSHEET *noun* **WORKSHEETS** a paper or form detailing work being planned or already in operation
WORKSHOP *noun* **WORKSHOPS** a room or building where construction and repairs are carried out
WORKSHY *adj* lazy; inclined to avoid work
WORKTOP *noun* **WORKTOPS** a flat surface constructed along the top of kitchen installations such as fridge and cupboards, on which to prepare food, etc
WORKWEAR *noun* **WORKWEARS** clothing worn specifically for work, especially overalls, issued to factory workers, etc
WORKWEEK *noun* **WORKWEEKS** the period in the week during which work is normally done
WORLD *noun* **WORLDS** the Earth
WORLDLING *noun* **WORLDLINGS** someone who is devoted to worldly pursuits and possessions; a worldly person
WORLDLY *adj* **WORLDLIER, WORLDLIEST** relating to this world; material, as opposed to spiritual or eternal
WORLDWIDE *adj* extending or known throughout the world ❑ *adverb* extending or known throughout the world
WORM *noun* **WORMS** any member of several unrelated groups of small soft-bodied limbless invertebrates that are characteristically long and slender, either cylindrical and segmented (eg the earthworm) or flat (eg the tapeworm) ❑ *verb* **WORMS, WORMING, WORMED** to move or crawl like a worm
WORMCAST *noun* **WORMCASTS** a coiled heap of sand or earth excreted by a burrowing earthworm or lugworm
WORMHOLE *noun* **WORMHOLES** a hole left by a burrowing grub, in eg furniture, books or fruit
WORMHOLED *adj* having wormholes
WORMWOOD *noun* **WORMWOODS** a bitter-tasting herb from which the flavouring for absinthe is obtained
WORMY *adj* **WORMIER, WORMIEST** similar to or full of worms
WORN past form of **wear** ❑ *adj* haggard with weariness
WORRIED *adj* anxious; troubled
WORRIEDLY *adverb* in a worried way
WORRIER *noun* **WORRIERS** someone who worries
WORRIMENT *noun* **WORRIMENTS** worry; anxiety
WORRISOME *adj* causing worry; perturbing or vexing
WORRY *verb* **WORRIES, WORRYING, WORRIED** to be anxious; to fret ❑ *noun* **WORRIES** a state of anxiety
WORRYGUTS *singular noun* someone who worries unnecessarily and excessively
WORRYING *noun* **WORRYINGS** an act of being anxious; fretting ❑ *adj* causing worry
WORRYWART *noun* **WORRYWARTS** a worryguts
WORSE *adj* more bad ❑ *adverb* less well; more badly
WORSEN *verb* **WORSENS, WORSENING, WORSENED** to make or become worse
WORSHIP *verb* **WORSHIPS, WORSHIPPING, WORSHIPPED** to honour (God or a god) with praise, prayer, hymns, etc ❑ *noun* **WORSHIPS** the activity of worshipping
WORST *adj* most bad, awful, or unpleasant, etc ❑ *noun* **WORSTS** the worst thing, part or possibility ❑ *adverb* most severely; most badly ❑ *verb* **WORSTS, WORSTING, WORSTED** to defeat someone; to get the better of them
WORSTED *noun* **WORSTEDS** a fine strong twisted yarn spun out from long combed wool
WORT *noun* **WORTS** a plant
WORTH *noun* **WORTHS** value, importance or usefulness ❑ *adj* having a value of a specified amount
WORTHILY *adverb* in a worthy way
WORTHLESS *adj* having no value or significance
WORTHY *adj* **WORTHIER, WORTHIEST** admirable, excellent or deserving ❑ *noun* **WORTHIES** an esteemed person; a dignitary

WOS plural of **wo**

WOT a form of **wit** ²
WOTCHER *exclamation* a greeting
WOULD *auxiliary verb* used in reported speech as the past tense of *will*
WOUND ¹ *noun* **WOUNDS** any local injury to living tissue of a human, animal or plant, caused by an external physical means such as cutting, piercing, crushing or tearing ❑ *verb* **WOUNDS, WOUNDING, WOUNDED** to inflict a wound on (a person, creature or limb, etc)
WOUND ² past form of **wind** ²
WOUNDING *noun* **WOUNDINGS** an act of inflicting a wound on
WOUNDWORT *noun* **WOUNDWORTS** any of several plants of the mint family, popularly believed to have wound-healing properties
WOVE a past form of **weave**
WOVEN a past form of **weave**
WOW *noun* **WOWS** a huge success ❑ *verb* **WOWS, WOWING, WOWED** to impress or amaze hugely
WOWSER *noun* **WOWSERS** a puritanical person who tries to

interfere with the pleasures of others; a spoilsport

WOX an obsolete past form of **wax**

WRACK noun **WRACKS** a type of seaweed, especially one of the large brown varieties, floating, cast-up or growing on the beach **WRACKED** adj tortured; tormented; distressed
WRAITH noun **WRAITHS** a ghost; a spectre
WRANGLE verb **WRANGLES, WRANGLING, WRANGLED** to quarrel, argue or debate noisily or bitterly □ noun **WRANGLES** the act of disputing noisily
WRANGLER noun **WRANGLERS** someone who disputes, especially angrily and noisily
WRANGLING noun **WRANGLINGS** an act of quarrelling, arguing or debating noisily or bitterly
WRAP verb **WRAPS, WRAPPING, WRAPPED** to fold or wind something round someone or something □ noun **WRAPS** a warm garment, especially a shawl or stole for the shoulders
WRAPPER noun **WRAPPERS** someone or something that wraps
WRAPPING noun **WRAPPINGS** any of various types of cover, wrapper or packing material
WRAPROUND adj said of clothing, eg a skirt or blouse: designed to wrap round with one edge overlapping the other and usually tied □ noun **WRAPROUNDS** a skirt or blouse designed to wrap round with one edge overlapping the other and usually tied
WRASSE noun **WRASSES** a brightly coloured bony sea fish with thick lips and powerful teeth
WRATH noun **WRATHS** violent anger; resentment or indignation
WRATHFUL adj angry
WREAK verb **WREAKS, WREAKING, WREAKED** to cause (damage or chaos, etc) on a disastrous scale
WREATH noun **WREATHS** a ring-shaped garland of flowers and foliage placed on a grave or memorial as a tribute
WREATHE verb **WREATHES, WREATHING, WREATHED** to coil, twine or intertwine
WRECK noun **WRECKS** the destruction, especially accidental, of a ship at sea □ verb **WRECKS,**

WRECKING, WRECKED to break or destroy something
WRECKAGE noun **WRECKAGES** the act of wrecking
WRECKER noun **WRECKERS** someone or something that wrecks
WRECKFISH noun **WRECKFISHES** a large sea fish of the perch family that has spiny fins and which is found in the Mediterranean and the Atlantic
WRECKING noun **WRECKINGS** an act of breaking or destroying something
WREN noun **WRENS** a very small songbird with short wings and a short erect tail
WRENCH verb **WRENCHES, WRENCHING, WRENCHED** to pull or twist something violently □ noun **WRENCHES** an act or instance of wrenching
WREST verb **WRESTS, WRESTING, WRESTED** to turn or twist something □ noun **WRESTS** the act of wresting
WRESTER noun **WRESTERS** someone who wrests
WRESTLE verb **WRESTLES, WRESTLING, WRESTLED** to fight by trying to grip, throw and pinion one's opponent □ noun **WRESTLES** a spell of wrestling
WRESTLER noun **WRESTLERS** someone who wrestles, especially for sport
WRESTLING noun **WRESTLINGS** the sport or exercise, governed by certain fixed rules, in which two people wrestle
WRETCH noun **WRETCHES** a miserable, unfortunate and pitiful person
WRETCHED adj **WRETCHEDER, WRETCHEDEST** pitiable
WRICK verb **WRICKS, WRICKING, WRICKED** to rick □ noun **WRICKS** a rick
WRIGGLE verb **WRIGGLES, WRIGGLING, WRIGGLED** to twist to and fro □ noun **WRIGGLES** a wriggling action or motion
WRIGGLER noun **WRIGGLERS** someone who wriggles
WRIGGLING noun **WRIGGLINGS** an act of twisting to and fro
WRIGGLY adj **WRIGGLIER, WRIGGLIEST** wriggling
WRIGHT noun **WRIGHTS** a maker, creator or repairer, usually of a specified thing
WRING verb **WRINGS, WRINGING, WRUNG** to force liquid from

something by twisting or squeezing
WRINGER noun **WRINGERS** a machine with two rollers for squeezing water out of wet clothes
WRINKLE noun **WRINKLES** a crease or line in the skin, especially of the face, appearing with advancing age □ verb **WRINKLES, WRINKLING, WRINKLED** to develop or make something develop wrinkles
WRINKLY adj **WRINKLIER, WRINKLIEST** having or full of wrinkles □ noun **WRINKLIES** an elderly person
WRIST noun **WRISTS** in terrestrial vertebrates: the joint formed by the radius and three of the small bones of the hand
WRISTBAND noun **WRISTBANDS** a band or part of the sleeve that covers the wrist
WRISTLET noun **WRISTLETS** a decorative or supporting band for the wrist, a bracelet
WRISTY adj **WRISTIER, WRISTIEST** said of a shot in golf, tennis, etc: made with extensive use of the wrist or wrists
WRIT noun **WRITS** a legal document issued by a court in the name of a sovereign, by which someone is summoned, or required to do or refrain from doing something
WRITE verb **WRITES, WRITING, WROTE, WRITTEN** to mark or produce (letters, symbols, numbers, words, sentences, etc) on a surface, especially paper, usually using a pen or pencil
WRITER noun **WRITERS** someone who writes, especially as a living; an author
WRITHE verb **WRITHES, WRITHING, WRITHED** to twist violently, especially in pain or discomfort; to squirm □ noun **WRITHES** the action of writhing; a twist or contortion
WRITHING noun **WRITHINGS** an act of twisting violently, especially in pain or discomfort
WRITING noun **WRITINGS** written or printed words
WRITTEN adj expressed in writing, and so undeniable
WRONG adj **WRONGER, WRONGEST** not correct □ noun **WRONGS** whatever is not right or just □ verb **WRONGS, WRONGING,**

WRONGED to treat someone unjustly; to do wrong to someone
WRONGDOER *noun*
WRONGDOERS someone guilty of an evil, immoral or illegal act
WRONGER *noun* **WRONGERS** a person who wrongs another
WRONGFUL *adj* unlawful; unjust
WRONGLY *adverb* in the wrong direction or way
WRONGNESS *noun*
WRONGNESSES the state or condition of being wrong
WROTE a past form of **write**
WROTH *adj* angry; full of wrath
WROUGHT *adj* made, formed or shaped; fashioned
WRUNG past form of **wring**
WRY ¹ *adj* **WRYER, WRYEST** said eg of a smile: slightly mocking or bitter; ironic

> **WRY** ² *verb* **WRIES, WRYING, WRIED** to give a twist to

WRYBILL *noun* **WRYBILLS** a New Zealand bird related to the plover,
with a bill that bends sideways which it uses to obtain food from under stones
WRYLY *adverb* in a wry way
WRYNECK *noun* **WRYNECKS** a small woodpecker, native to Europe, Asia and N Africa, with a mottled greyish-brown plumage, a short bill and a long tail, and which twists its head to look backwards over its shoulder when alarmed
WRYNESS *noun* **WRYNESSES** the state of being wry

> **WUD** *noun* **WUDS** a Scots form of *wood*

WURST *noun* **WURSTS** any of various types of large German or Austrian sausage

> **WUS** *noun* **WUSES** a term used in Wales when addressing a companion

WUSS *noun* **WUSSES** a weakling; a feeble person

WUTHERING *adj* said of wind: to blow strongly and with a roaring sound
WYANDOTTE *noun* **WYANDOTTES** a member of a Native American tribe

> **WYE** *noun* **WYES** the letter 'Y', or anything shaped like it

WYN *noun* **WYNS** a rune with the value of modern English *w*
WYND *noun* **WYNDS** a narrow lane or alley leading off a main street in a town
WYNN *noun* **WYNNS** wyn
WYSIWYG *adj* said of type or characters appearing on a computer screen: appearing exactly as they will look on the printed page
WYVERN *noun* **WYVERNS** a fictitious monster with wings, two legs and a barbed tail, that combines the characteristics of a dragon and griffin

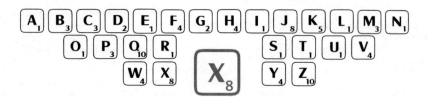

XANTHENE *noun* **XANTHENES** a white or yellowish crystalline compound, used as a fungicide and as a source of various dyes

XANTHOMA *noun* **XANTHOMAS, XANTHOMATA** a small yellowish lump or swelling in the skin, often on the eyelid, formed by deposits of fat, and usually a symptom of high blood cholesterol levels

XEBEC *noun* **XEBECS** a small three-masted ship

XENIUM *noun* **XENIA** a present made to a guest or an ambassador

XENOLITH *noun* **XENOLITHS** a piece of foreign material that occurs within a body of igneous rock

XENON *noun* **XENONS** an element, a colourless odourless inert gas, one of the noble gases, used in fluorescent lamps, photographic flash tubes, and lasers

XENOPHOBE *noun* **XENOPHOBES** a person who fears or hates foreigners and foreign things

XERAFIN *noun* **XERAFINS** a former silver coin of Goa

XERAPHIN *noun* **XERAPHINS** a xerafin

XERIC *adj* dry, lacking in moisture

XEROPHYTE *noun* **XEROPHYTES** a plant that is adapted to grow under conditions where water is very scarce and that often shows structural modifications, eg swollen stems or leaves reduced to spines

XI *noun* **XIS** the fourteenth letter of the Greek alphabet
ⓘ This is a useful two-letter word if you are having trouble using up your **X** or if there are very few scoring opportunities on the board.

XU *noun* **XU** a Vietnamese coin
ⓘ This is a useful two-letter word if you are having trouble using up your **X** or if there are very few scoring opportunities on the board.

XYLEM *noun* **XYLEMS** the woody tissue that transports water and mineral nutrients from the roots to all other parts of a plant, and also provides structural support

XYLENE *noun* **XYLENES** a colourless liquid hydrocarbon obtained from coal tar, etc, and used as a solvent

XYLOL *noun* **XYLOLS** xylene

XYLOPHONE *noun* **XYLOPHONES** a musical instrument consisting of a series of wooden or sometimes metal bars of different lengths, played by being struck by wooden hammers

YACHT *noun* **YACHTS** a boat or small ship, usually with sails and often with an engine, built for racing or cruising
YACHTING *noun* **YACHTINGS** sailing in yachts, especially as a sport
YACHTSMAN *noun* **YACHTSMEN** a person who sails a yacht
YACK *verb* **YACKS, YACKING, YACKED** to talk at length and often foolishly or annoyingly □ *noun* **YACKS** persistent, foolish or annoying chatter

YAH *noun* **YAHS** yea

YAHOO *noun* **YAHOOS** a lout or ruffian
YAK ¹ *noun* **YAKS** a large ox-like Tibetan mammal with a stocky body, a thick shaggy black coat, humped shoulders, a white muzzle and large upward-curving horns
YAK ² *verb* **YAKS, YAKKING, YAKKED** to yack
YAKITORI *noun* **YAKITORIS** a Japanese dish of boneless pieces of chicken grilled on skewers and basted with a thick sweet sauce of rice wine, mirin and soy sauce
YAM *noun* **YAMS** any of various perennial climbing plants cultivated in tropical and subtropical regions for their thick edible tubers
YAMMER *verb* **YAMMERS, YAMMERING, YAMMERED** to complain whiningly; to grumble □ *noun* **YAMMERS** the act or sound of yammering
YANG *noun* **YANGS** in traditional Chinese philosophy, religion, medicine, etc: one of the two opposing and complementary principles, being the positive, masculine, light, warm and active element or force
YANK *noun* **YANKS** a sudden sharp pull □ *verb* **YANKS, YANKING, YANKED** to pull suddenly and sharply
YAP *verb* **YAPS, YAPPING, YAPPED** said of a puppy or small dog: to give a high-pitched bark □ *noun*

YAPS a short high-pitched bark
YAPPER *noun* **YAPPERS** a person or animal that yaps
YAPPY *adj* **YAPPIER, YAPPIEST** said of a dog: inclined to yap
YARD *noun* **YARDS** in the imperial system: a unit of measurement equal to 3 feet (0.9144m)
YARDAGE *noun* **YARDAGES** the length of something, measured in yards
YARDSTICK *noun* **YARDSTICKS** a standard for comparison
YARMULKA *noun* **YARMULKAS** a skullcap worn by Jewish men on ceremonial or ritual occasions, and at all times by the orthodox
YARMULKE *noun* **YARMULKES** a yarmulka
YARN *noun* **YARNS** thread spun from wool, cotton, etc
YARROW *noun* **YARROWS** a creeping perennial plant, formerly used widely in herbal medicine, with finely divided aromatic leaves and white or pink flower-heads in dense flat-topped clusters
YASHMAK *noun* **YASHMAKS** a veil worn by Muslim women that covers the face below the eyes
YAW *verb* **YAWS, YAWING, YAWED** said of a ship: to move temporarily from, or fail to keep to, the direct line of its course □ *noun* **YAWS** an act of yawing
YAWL *noun* **YAWLS** a type of small fishing- or sailing-boat, especially one with two masts
YAWN *verb* **YAWNS, YAWNING, YAWNED** to open one's mouth wide and take a deep involuntary breath when tired or bored □ *noun* **YAWNS** an act or an instance of yawning
YAWS *singular noun* an infectious skin disease of tropical countries, characterized by red ulcerating sores
YE *pronoun* you (plural)
YEA *exclamation* yes □ *noun* **YEAS** a yes
YEAH *exclamation* yes
YEAR *noun* **YEARS** the period of time the Earth takes to go once round the Sun, about 365¼ days

YEARBOOK *noun* **YEARBOOKS** a book of information updated and published every year, especially one that records the events, etc of the previous year
YEARLING *noun* **YEARLINGS** an animal which is a year old
YEARLONG *adj* lasting all year
YEARLY *adj* happening, etc every year □ *adverb* every year
YEARN *verb* **YEARNS, YEARNING, YEARNED** to feel a great desire for something; to long for it
YEARNER *noun* **YEARNERS** someone who yearns
YEARNING *noun* **YEARNINGS** a desire
YEARS *plural noun* a very long time
YEAS *plural of* **yea**
YEAST *noun* **YEASTS** any of various single-celled fungi that are capable of fermenting carbohydrates, widely used in the brewing and baking industries, and in genetic and biochemical research
YEASTY *adj* **YEASTIER, YEASTIEST** consisting, tasting or smelling of yeast
YELL *noun* **YELLS** a loud shout or cry □ *verb* **YELLS, YELLING, YELLED** to shout or cry out
YELLOW *adj* **YELLOWER, YELLOWEST** of the colour of gold, butter, egg-yolk, a lemon, etc □ *noun* **YELLOWS** any shade of the colour of gold, butter, egg-yolk, etc □ *verb* **YELLOWS, YELLOWING, YELLOWED** to make or become yellow
YELLOWISH *adj* somewhat yellow
YELLOWY *adj* **YELLOWIER, YELLOWIEST** yellowish
YELP *verb* **YELPS, YELPING, YELPED** said of a dog, etc: to give a sharp sudden cry □ *noun* **YELPS** such a cry
YELPER *noun* **YELPERS** a person or animal that yelps
YEN *noun* **YENS** a desire □ *verb* **YENS, YENNING, YENNED** to feel a longing or craving for something
YEOMAN *noun* **YEOMEN** a farmer who owned and worked his own

land, often serving as a foot-soldier when required

YEOMANRY noun **YEOMANRIES** the class of land-owning farmers

YEP exclamation yes □ noun **YEPS** a yes

YERBA noun **YERBAS** maté

YES exclamation used to express agreement or consent □ noun **YESES, YESSES** an expression of agreement or consent

YESHIVA noun **YESHIVAS** in Judaism: a school for the study of the Talmud

YESTERDAY noun **YESTERDAYS** the day before today □ adverb on the day before today

YESTREEN adverb yesterday evening

YET adverb up till now or then; by now or by that time □ conj nevertheless

YETI noun **YETIS** an ape-like creature supposed to live in the Himalayas

YEW noun **YEWS** any of various cone-bearing evergreen trees or shrubs with reddish-brown flaky bark and narrow flattened dark-green leaves

YEX verb **YEXES, YEXING, YEXED** a Scots word meaning to hiccup

YGO a Spenserian past form of **go**

YIELD verb **YIELDS, YIELDING, YIELDED** to produce (an animal product such as meat or milk, or a crop) □ noun **YIELDS** the amount produced

YIKES exclamation expressing alarm or astonishment

YIKKER verb **YIKKERS, YIKKERING, YIKKERED** said of a bird or animal: to utter sharp little cries

YIN noun **YINS** in traditional Chinese philosophy, religion, medicine, etc: one of the two opposing and complementary principles, being the negative, feminine, dark, cold and passive element or force

YIP verb **YIPS, YIPPING, YIPPED** to give a short, sudden cry □ noun **YIPS** such a cry

YIPPEE exclamation expressing excitement, delight, etc

YLEM noun **YLEMS** in the big bang

theory: the original substance from which the elements developed

YO noun **YOS** a sound used to call someone's attention

YOB noun **YOBS** a bad-mannered aggressive young person (usually male); a lout or hooligan

YOBBISH adj bad-mannered, aggressive behaviour

YOBBO noun **YOBBOS, YOBBOES** a yob

YODEL verb **YODELS, YODELLING, YODELLED** to sing (a melody, etc), changing frequently from a normal to a falsetto voice and back again □ noun **YODELS** an act of yodelling

YODELLER noun **YODELLERS** someone who yodels

YOGA noun **YOGAS** a system of Hindu philosophy showing how to free the soul from reincarnation and reunite it with God

YOGH noun **YOGHS** a letter, used in writing Middle English, representing either a consonantal y or a gh sound

YOGHOURT noun **YOGHOURTS** yoghurt

YOGHURT noun **YOGHURTS** a type of semi-liquid food made from fermented milk, now often flavoured with fruit

YOGI noun **YOGIS** a person who practises yoga and the physical and mental disciplines associated with it

YOGIC adj of or relating to yoga or yogis

YOGIN noun **YOGINS** a yogi

YOGINI noun **YOGINIS** a female yogi

YOGURT noun **YOGURTS** yoghurt

YOICKS exclamation in fox-hunting: used to urge on the hounds

YOK verb **YOKS, YOKKING, YOKKED** to laugh □ noun **YOKS** a laugh

YOKE noun **YOKES** a wooden frame placed over the necks of oxen to hold them together when they are pulling a plough, cart, etc □ verb **YOKES, YOKING, YOKED** to join things under or with a yoke

YOKEL noun **YOKELS** an unsophisticated person from the country, usually a male

YOLK noun **YOLKS** in the eggs of birds and some reptiles: the yellow

spherical mass of nutritive material

YON adj that or those

YONDER adj situated over there

YONI noun **YONIS** a representation of the female genitals, the symbol under which the Hindu goddess Sakti is worshipped

YONKS plural noun ages; a long time

YORE noun **YORES** times past or long ago

YORKER noun **YORKERS** in cricket: a ball pitched to a point directly under the bat

YORKIE noun **YORKIES** a Yorkshire terrier

YOS plural of **yo**

YOU pronoun the person or people, etc spoken or written to, with or without others; any or every person

YOUNG adj **YOUNGER, YOUNGEST** in the first part of life, growth, development, etc; not old

YOUNGISH adj somewhat young

YOUNGSTER noun **YOUNGSTERS** a young person

YOUR adj belonging to you

YOURS pronoun something belonging to you

YOURSELF pronoun the reflexive form of you

YOUTH noun **YOUTHS** a young person, especially a young man or boy

YOUTHFUL adj young, especially in manner or appearance

YOW noun **YOWS** a ewe

YOWL verb **YOWLS, YOWLING, YOWLED** said especially of an animal: to howl or cry sadly □ noun **YOWLS** such a howl

YOWLING noun **YOWLINGS** an act of howling

YTTERBIUM noun **YTTERBIUMS** a soft silvery lustrous metallic element, used in lasers, and for making steel and other alloys

YTTRIOUS adj like or containing yttrium

YTTRIUM noun **YTTRIUMS** a silvery-grey metallic element used in alloys to make superconductors and strong permanent magnets

YU noun **YUS** precious jade

YUAN noun **YUAN** the standard

unit of currency of the People's Republic of China

YUCCA *noun* **YUCCAS** any of various tropical and subtropical American plants with a short thick trunk, stiff narrow sword-shaped leaves and waxy white bell-shaped flowers in large pyramidal clusters

YUCK *noun* **YUCKS** a disgusting mess; filth

YUCKY *adj* **YUCKIER, YUCKIEST** messy; disgusting

YUG *noun* **YUGS** one of the four Hindu ages of the world

YUK *noun* **YUKS** a yuck

YUKKY *adj* **YUKKIER, YUKKIEST** yucky

YUKO *noun* **YUKOS** in judo: an award of five points

YULAN *noun* #**YULANS** a Chinese magnolia

YULE *noun* **YULES** Christmas

YUMMY *adj* **YUMMIER, YUMMIEST** delicious

YUNX *noun* **YUNXES** a wryneck

YUP *exclamation* yes ▫ *noun* **YUPS** a yes

YUPPIE *noun* **YUPPIES** an

ambitious young professional person working in a city job

YUPPIEDOM *noun* **YUPPIEDOMS** the state of being a yuppie

YUPPIFY *verb* **YUPPIFIES, YUPPIFYING, YUPPIFIED** to alter (usually a place) so as to conform to yuppie taste

YUPPY *noun* **YUPPIES** a yuppie

YURT *noun* **YURTS** a light circular tent of skins or felt on a framework of poles, used by nomads in Central Asia and Siberia

YUS plural of **yu**

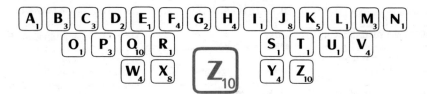

ZAG noun **ZAGS** either of the alternative directions on a zigzag course, or the change to either of them □ verb **ZAGS, ZAGGING, ZAGGED** to veer sharply in either of the alternative directions on a zigzag course

ZAIRE noun **ZAIRE** the standard unit of currency of Zaire

ZAKAT noun **ZAKATS** the tax of 2½ per cent payable as alms by all Muslims, levied annually on income and capital

ZANINESS noun **ZANINESSES** the state or condition of being zany; zany behaviour

ZANY adj **ZANIER, ZANIEST** amusingly crazy

ZAP verb **ZAPS, ZAPPING, ZAPPED** to hit, destroy or shoot something, especially suddenly

ZAPPER noun **ZAPPERS** a remote control device that operates a TV or video recorder

ZARF noun **ZARFS** an ornamental holder for a hot coffee-cup

ZARZUELA noun **ZARZUELAS** a type of popular Spanish opera, either comic or serious, with spoken dialogue

ZAX noun **ZAXES** a zex

ZEA noun **ZEAS** part of a cereal plant, once used as a diuretic

ZEAL noun **ZEALS** great, and sometimes excessive, enthusiasm or keenness

ZEALOT noun **ZEALOTS** a single-minded and determined supporter of a political cause, religion, etc

ZEALOTRY noun **ZEALOTRIES** single-minded, determined support of a political cause, religion, etc

ZEALOUS adj enthusiastic; keen

ZEALOUSLY adverb in a zealous way

ZEBRA noun **ZEBRAS** a stocky black-and-white striped African mammal with a stubby mane, related to the horse and ass

ZEBROID noun **ZEBROIDS** a cross between a horse and a zebra □ adj resembling a zebra

ZEBU noun **ZEBUS** a species of domestic cattle, native to S Asia, with a light-coloured coat, large upturned horns, long pendulous ears and a prominent hump on its shoulders, used as a draught animal

ZED noun **ZEDS** a name for the letter 'Z'

ZEDOARY noun **ZEDOARIES** a plant of the ginger family, native to parts of Asia, with aromatic bitter rootstocks which are used as a drug, as a condiment and in making perfume

ZEE noun **ZEES** a name for the letter 'Z'

ZEITGEIST noun **ZEITGEISTS** the spirit of the age; the attitudes or viewpoint of a specific period

ZEK noun **ZEKS** an inmate of a USSR prison or labour camp

ZEL noun **ZELS** an Oriental cymbal

ZENANA noun **ZENANAS** in India, Iran, etc: a part of a house in which women and girls are secluded

ZENITH noun **ZENITHS** the point on the celestial sphere diametrically opposite the nadir and directly above the observer

ZEOLITE noun **ZEOLITES** any of numerous hydrated aluminosilicate minerals, usually containing sodium, potassium, or calcium, widely used as 'molecular sieves' for separating substances, and as water softeners

ZEOLITIC adj of or relating to zeolite

ZEPHYR noun **ZEPHYRS** a light gentle breeze

ZEPPELIN noun **ZEPPELINS** a cigar-shaped airship of the type originally designed by the German Count Zeppelin in 1900

ZERO noun **ZEROS** the number, figure or symbol 0 □ verb **ZEROS, ZEROING, ZEROED** to set or adjust something to zero

ZEROTH adj in a series: coming before what would normally be regarded as the first term

ZEST noun **ZESTS** keen enjoyment; enthusiasm

ZESTFUL adj keen; enthusiastic

ZESTFULLY adverb in a zestful way

ZESTY adj **ZESTIER, ZESTIEST** piquant; agreeably sharp-tasting

ZETA noun **ZETAS** the sixth letter of the Greek alphabet

ZEUGMA noun **ZEUGMAS** a figure of speech in which a word, usually an adjective or verb, is applied to two nouns although strictly it is appropriate to only one of them, or it has a different sense with each, as in *weeping eyes and hearts*

ZEX noun **ZEXES** a chopper for trimming slates
ⓘ This word is worth 19 points and is an extremely valuable word to remember for using up X and Z.

ZHO noun **ZHOS** a zo

ZIFF noun **ZIFFS** a beard

ZIG noun **ZIGS** either of the alternative directions on a zigzag course, or the change to either of them □ verb **ZIGS, ZIGGING, ZIGGED** to veer sharply in either of the alternative directions on a zigzag course

ZIGGURAT noun **ZIGGURATS** in ancient Mesopotamia: a pyramid-like temple, consisting of many storeys each of which is smaller than the one below

ZIGZAG noun **ZIGZAGS** two or more sharp bends to alternate sides in a path, etc □ verb **ZIGZAGS, ZIGZAGGING, ZIGZAGGED** to move in a zigzag direction

ZILCH noun **ZILCHES** nothing

ZILLION noun **ZILLIONS** a very large but unspecified number

ZIMMER noun **ZIMMERS** a tubular metal frame, used as a support for walking by the disabled or infirm

ZINC noun **ZINCS** a brittle bluish-